Living Literature

To the memory of Virginia Lieson Brereton, 1944–2004

My inspiration

Living Literature

AN INTRODUCTION TO FICTION, POETRY, AND DRAMA

John C. Brereton

PEARSON

Longman

New York San Francisco Boston
London Toronto Sydney Tokyo Singapore Madrid
Mexico City Munich Paris Cape Town Hong Kong Montreal

Editor-in-Chief: Joseph Terry
Development Director: Mary Ellen Curley
Senior Development Editor: Mikola De Roo
Senior Supplements Editor: Donna Campion
Media Supplements Editor: Jenna Egan
Executive Marketing Manager: Ann Stypuloski
Production Manager: Eric Jorgensen
Project Coordination, Text Design, and Electronic Page Makeup: Electronic Publishing
Services Inc., NYC
Cover Design Manager: Wendy Ann Fredericks
Cover Designer: Base Art Co., Ltd.
Cover Photos: *travelers:* © Liquid Library; *Ray Charles:* © Derick A. Thomas, Dat's
Jazz/Corbis; *Gwendolyn Brooks:* © Bettmann/Corbis; *guitar player:* © IStock Photo.com;
Frank O'Hara: © John Jonas Gruen/Hulton Archive/Getty Images, Inc.; *Lorraine
Hansberry:* © Bettmann/Corbis; *Charles Baxter:* © Bassouls Sophie/Corbis SYGMA;
Bono: © Kieran Doherty/Reuters/Corbis; *Kenneth Branagh portraying Hamlet in 1993 for
The Royal Shakespeare Theatre:* © RSC Royal Shakespeare Theatre; *woman with digital
music player:* © Istock Photo.com; *poetry reading at Café:* © Kevin Fleming/Corbis;
Robert Altman: © Nicolas Guerin/Azimuts Production/Corbis; *Flannery O'Connor:*
AP/Wide World Photos; and *A Streetcar Named Desire:* Library of Congress
Photo Researcher: Linda Sykes
Senior Manufacturing Buyer: Dennis J. Para
Printer and Binder: Quebecor World Taunton
Cover Printer: Coral Graphics

For permission to use copyrighted material, grateful acknowledgment is made to the
copyright holders on pp. 2068–2082, which are hereby made part of this copyright page.

Library of Congress Cataloging-in-Publication Data
Living literature: an introduction to fiction, poetry, and drama / [compiled by] John C.
Brereton.
    p. cm.
  Includes bibliographical references and indexes.
  ISBN 0-321-08899-9 (pbk.)
  ISBN-13 9780321088994
  1. College readers. 2. English language—Rhetoric—Problems, exercises, etc.
3. Reading (Higher education)—Problems, exercises, etc. 4. Academic writing—
Problems, exercises, etc. 5. American literature. 6. English literature. I. Brereton,
John C. II. Title.
PE1417.L647 2006
808—dc22

2008006716

Please visit us at www.ablongman.com

ISBN 0-321-08899-9
ISBN-13 9780321088994

1 2 3 4 5 6 7 8 9 10—QWT—10 09 08 07

Brief Contents

Detailed Contents

2. Stories: Point of View, Theme, Symbol, Tone, Performance   48

3. Writing about Stories   111

A MOMENT IN FICTION

A MOMENT IN FICTION

PART II   Poetry   717

10. Poems: Tone, Image, Language   719

Shaping Experience 719

Tone 724

For Further Reading: Tone 729

12. Writing about Poetry   795

14. A Poet in Depth: Emily Dickinson   879

15. A Poet in Depth: Gwendolyn Brooks   904

Gwendolyn Brooks Timeline   909
Poems by Gwendolyn Brooks   910

A MOMENT IN POETRY

16. Passionate Verse: Love Poetry of the English Renaissance   924

English Renaissance Timeline   925
Reading English Renaissance Love Poems   928

A MOMENT IN POETRY

17. Writing Out Loud: Popular Victorian Narratives 962

18. Poems for Further Reading   1004

PART III Drama   1157

24. Drama Becomes Modern   1560

A MOMENT IN DRAMA

25. Sweet Home Chicago: From Chicago Renaissance to *A Raisin in the Sun*   1742

Preface

The central goal of *Living Literature* is to introduce students to the diverse and vibrant study of literature and to give them the tools they need to move toward informed, analytical readings and interpretations of the literary works they read, both in discussion as well as in their own critical essays. Toward this end, *Living Literature* presents a diverse collection of excellent, thought-provoking stories, poems, and plays—a balance of old and new classics—and provides beginning literature students with concrete examples of specific literary elements and techniques most experienced readers and critics examine for a close analysis of a text.

Living Literature is divided into four parts. The first three sections concentrate on each of the three major literary forms: stories, poetry, and drama. In each of these sections, a full chapter—"Writing about Stories," "Writing about Poetry," and "Writing about Plays"—serves as a guide to writing about the specific literary genre. The fourth section, "Literary Research," offers a comprehensive primer on the research process and the literary research paper, from finding a topic, developing a thesis, and finding and evaluating legitimate sources, to writing the final research essay.

What makes *Living Literature* distinct is its focus on examining literature as one part of a living, fluid conversation across cultures and time periods. In our media-saturated twenty-first century, one of the biggest challenges in any literature classroom is engaging students and showing them how literature and the cultural conversation about it are relevant to their lives. We all know that sometimes consciously, sometimes unconsciously, poets take their cues from musicians, playwrights from painters, fiction writers from other fiction writers—and vice versa—and many of us have attempted to make those connections in the classroom. Most introductory texts, though, either ignore the important role that artistic and critical dialogue plays in the creative process, or they only scratch the surface of those links between the cultural present and past. *Living Literature* is my attempt to address the common student complaint that literature is boring, nothing more than a march of monuments. It is my call for active participation.

The vibrant works gathered in this collection have complex, interesting connections to the world. The more ways students can relate to these works, the more they can understand them, enjoy them, and write about them thoughtfully. From the beginning, *Living Literature* was designed to help students make those connections, to show them that literature, and indeed all art, is not created in a vacuum. The book's features emphasize that literature is very much connected to and in dialogue with other artistic works and critical responses, including many of the cultural icons with which students are so familiar—from celebrity pop and hip-hop stars to modern movie plots to well-known cartoons. By supplementing the literature itself with extensive, relevant contextual information and thought-provoking apparatus,

Living Literature gives students a more thorough understanding of the big picture, of the literary landscape—a way to appreciate literature as individual works unto themselves and as part of a larger, evolving culture.

This holistic approach not only excites students by linking the literature to the modern world they live in, but it enables them to read, think, discuss, and write critically about literary works with a more astute and analytical eye. Moreover, it shows them how the ongoing cultural conversation in thinking, speaking, and writing about literature is a powerful means of participating in the world around us, of playing our roles as community and world citizens.

FEATURES

Breadth and flexibility—a wide range of exciting literary selections and authors

The 68 stories, 344 poems, and 17 plays in *Living Literature* represent a diverse range of perspectives, styles, themes, voices, and cultures—giving students a sense of the broad scope of literary history and giving instructors a text that is flexible enough to accommodate a wide range of teaching styles. The selections are a balance of canonical works by classic writers such as Ernest Hemingway, Flannery O'Connor, John Keats, W. B. Yeats, Henrik Ibsen, and Arthur Miller with fresh, contemporary voices such as Jhumpa Lahiri, Louise Glück, Gary Soto, Anna Deavere Smith, and Philip Kan Gotanda. Every selection has been chosen with the classroom in mind, both for its ability to draw students in as well as its usefulness as an example of particular literary elements and techniques.

A brief note about the inclusion of nonfiction in Chapter 9: "Stories for Further Reading" offers two dozen selections. Most are fiction, and everything collected here is a story, but four nonfiction stories—by James Thurber, E. B. White, Jonathan Swift, and George Orwell—have also been included. These stories are in fact memoir or, in Swift's case, argument, but they all read like fiction and make ample use of the techniques that characterize fiction. Their inclusion here is simply one more indication of how story is a category that can include fiction and nonfiction alike.

Five "Moments" chapters gather literary works from one particular time, place, or cultural perspective, and frame and closely examine the connections between them.

- **Chapter 7, "More than Magnolias: Southern Women Storytellers,"** shows how the fiction of Alice Walker, Lee Smith, Mary Hood, and Dorothy Allison can be seen as both a response to and an extension of the writing of Eudora Welty, Flannery O'Connor, and Zora Neale Hurston.
- **Chapter 8, "Passage to America: New Immigrants Tell Their Stories,"** gathers together a diverse array of contemporary voices—Pat Mora, Julia Alvarez, Jhumpa Lahiri, Gish Jen, Esmeralda Santiago, Junot Díaz, and Anjana Appachana—who touch upon the immigrant experience in the United States. Their works explore a range of immigrant-related themes and experi-

ences, such as ethnic and cultural duality, assimilation, clashes between cultures, and conflicts between the new generation of Americans versus the old.

- **Chapter 16, "Passionate Verse: Love Poetry of the English Renaissance,"** presents a rich variety of love poems by major authors of the period, including William Shakespeare, John Donne, Christopher Marlowe, Walter Raleigh, Andrew Marvell, Ben Jonson, Robert Herrick, Lady Mary Wroth, and Katherine Philips.

- **Chapter 17, "Writing Out Loud: Popular Victorian Narratives,"** examines poetry's oral and performative history through Victorian-era works by such poets as Felicia Hemans, Edgar Allan Poe, Henry Wadsworth Longfellow, but also includes examples of popular "parlor poetry," such as "Casey at the Bat" and "A Visit from St. Nicholas."

- **Chapter 25, "Sweet Home Chicago: From Chicago Renaissance to *A Raisin in the Sun*,"** traces the artistic flowering that followed the African American migration from the South to the cities of the North during the early twentieth century, as seen in works by such poets as Gwendolyn Brooks, Margaret Danner, and Frank Marshall Davis; the musicians Willie Dixon, Muddy Waters, and Thomas A. Dorsey; fiction writer Richard Wright; and playwright Lorraine Hansberry.

Writers-in-depth chapters in each genre section offer a focused treatment of two or more major figures. Here, *Living Literature* presents works by Nathaniel Hawthorne, Willa Cather, and Charles Baxter; a range of poems by Walt Whitman, Emily Dickinson, and Gwendolyn Brooks, and two plays apiece by Sophocles and Shakespeare.

A consistent emphasis on cultural and historical context

"Inspiration" sections in every chapter focus on artists and works that ignited or drew their creative spark from a writer or work in the book: for example, how a Bruce Springsteen song takes its cues from Flannery O'Connor; how poetry slams, hip-hop, and Russell Simmons's *Def Poetry Jam* all echo the older performative tradition of Victorian poetry; and how Sophocles' Oedipus has been influential again and again in modern films.

"Locales" in every chapter prompt students to seek out additional contextual resources that will enrich their understanding of a particular text. *Literary Locales* identify and describe real-life places with relevant literary associations, such as Edgar Allan Poe's house and Shakespeare's Globe Theater. *Virtual Locales* refer students to related online resources for additional background information and research. *Audio* and *Video Locales* direct students to pertinent recordings, performances, filmed versions, or other adaptations linked to a selection.

Commentaries present students with accessible critical responses to literary works—from Willa Cather on *Hamlet* to Freud on *Oedipus* to Marge Piercy on Whitman—as well as essays, articles, reviews, letters, interviews, and journals that bring to life the dialogue surrounding literary texts.

Full-color Image Galleries accompany the chapters on Southern women writers, Victorian narrative poetry, and the Chicago Renaissance, presenting images linked historically or thematically to the writers and literary selections in each of these chapters. Each color section opens with an introductory headnote, and each image is followed by two question sets, **"Reading the Image"** and **"Linking Image to Text,"** which call for students to respond to and analyze the images as well as the corresponding literary texts.

Biographical headnotes with author photos and timelines complement the literature in the book.

Particular attention to the oral and the performed

Reading is framed for students not just as a passive act of translation or "decoding" but as an active way of interpreting.

An analysis of the role performance plays in fiction, poetry, and drama is included in the core introductory chapters for each literary genre.

Discussion questions in the book stress the impact of performance, asking how a character might inflect a line of dialogue in a story, how a particular poem should be or could be recited, or how an actor might deliver a particular line from a play.

Many of the **Inspirations** and **Locales** encourage students to go online, to the library, or to the video or music store to take in the performed versions of the literature.

Numerous questions for reading, discussion, and writing

Thought-provoking discussion questions and writing assignments for every selection—"Talking about the Text," "Writing about the Text," and "Linking the Text to Other Texts"—prompt student participation in reading, discussion, and writing. The apparatus also maintains a focus on analyzing the language and techniques being employed as a means to understanding what is happening in a particular text and why.

"Reading the Image" and **"Linking Image to Text"** questions hone students' ability to analyze visual texts and make connections between those images and their meaning to related literary texts.

Comprehensive, practical advice on critical reading, writing (including argument), and research

"Starting Points for Further Research" in every chapter direct students to a reputable modern edition of an author's work, a standard biography, an interview, an accessible article or scholarly work, or all of the above.

Five comprehensive chapters on reading and writing about literature:

- **The introduction for students, "Reading with or without a Theory,"** explains what critical reading means, why it matters, and how to approach reading literature with a critical eye. It also gives students a basic guide to using *Living Literature* and its features to aid and enhance their reading and writing about the selections in the book.

- **Three full chapters, "Writing about Stories" (3), "Writing about Poetry" (12), and "Writing about Plays" (21),** focus on genre-specific approaches to writing about literary works. Each chapter contains concrete advice on annotating, summarizing, note-taking, and journaling as students read; "Questions to Develop Ideas" for writing about that particular genre; examples of professional reviews, popular criticism, and scholarly criticism; examples and models of student writing, from developing a topic and thesis to a final essay; a section on "Formats for Writing" about the genre; and extensive coverage of the kinds of essays students are likely to be assigned in introductory courses (e.g., response papers, explication, and analysis).

- **Part IV, "Literary Research,"** offers a comprehensive primer on the research process and the literary research paper, from finding a topic, developing a thesis, and finding and evaluating legitimate sources, to writing the final research essay. "The Literary Research Project" (27) is a comprehensive guide to the choices and opportunities students face when they embark on a research project, with a literary research essay as the final result presenting their findings. The chapter includes practical advice (and student examples) on finding a topic and developing a research question; finding, evaluating, and incorporating print and online sources; avoiding plagiarism; using quotations; and current MLA documentation guidelines. Particular attention is given to developing a thesis and to presenting different types of literary research projects—among them, expository reports, comparison-contrast, and argumentative essays. The chapter concludes with a sample student literary research project, from the initial assignment to the finished paper.

Literary terms important to the study of literature appear in boldface in the text and are defined in lucid, thorough language and supplemented by useful examples from literary texts. These same terms and definitions appear in a complete glossary at the end of the book for easy reference.

RESOURCES FOR STUDENTS AND INSTRUCTORS

MyLiteratureLab MyLiteratureLab (www.myliteraturelab.com) is a Web-based state-of-the-art interactive learning system designed to enhance the study of literature. Of special note are the Longman Lectures—evocative, richly illustrated audio readings, along with advice on how to read, interpret, and write about literary works from our roster of Longman authors, including a lecture by John Brereton. This powerful program also features Diagnostic Tests, Interactive Readings with clickable prompts, sample student papers, critical essays, Literature Timelines, Avoiding Plagiarism and Research Navigator research tools, and Exchange, an electronic instructor/peer feedback tool. *MyLiteratureLab.com* can be delivered within Course Compass, Web CT, or Blackboard course management systems, enabling instructors to administer their entire course online. Contact your sales representative for more details: www.ablongman.com/replocater.

Instructor's Manual to Accompany Living Literature (Instructor/ISBN 0-321-41489-6) This comprehensive manual offers commentary, teaching ideas, and support on every literary selection in the book, with a wealth of resources for both seasoned and new instructors, including additional discussion questions; references to useful critical pieces, interviews, and useful contextual information; suggestions for incorporating the Inspiration sections and the images in the full-color inserts in engaging ways in classroom discussion.

Responding to Literature: A Writer's Journal, by Daniel Kline (ISBN 0-321-09542-1) This beautiful spiral-bound journal provides students with their own personal space for recording their reactions to the literature they read. Guided writing prompts, suggested writing assignments, and overviews of literary terms provide students with the tools—and ideas—they need for responding to fiction, poetry, and drama. Available at no additional cost when value-packed with *Living Literature*.

Evaluating a Performance, by Michael Greenwald (ISBN 0-321-09541-3) Designed to look like a playbill, this supplement is the perfect tool for students assigned to review and respond to local productions or readings, offering a convenient place to record notes and reactions. Useful tips and suggestions of elements to consider when evaluating a performance are included. Available at no additional cost when value-packed with *Living Literature*.

Evaluating Plays on Film and Video, by Anne Marie Welsh and Martin Morawski (ISBN 0-321-18794-6) This guide steps students through the process of analyzing and writing about plays on film, whether in a short review or a longer essay. Four appendices include writing and editing tips and a glossary of film terms. Worksheets aid students in organizing their notes and thoughts before they begin writing. Available at no additional cost when value-packed with *Living Literature*.

Penguin Putnam Novel Discount Program In cooperation with Penguin Putnam, Inc., our sibling company, Longman is proud to offer a variety of Penguin paperbacks—by a broad range of authors, from Mary Shelley and Shakespeare to Toni Morrison and Julia Alvarez—at a significant discount when packaged with any Longman title. Ask your Longman sales representative for a special package ISBN to take advantage of this offer: www.ablongman.com/replocater. To review a complete list of available titles and discounted prices of individual Penguin novels, visit the Longman-Penguin-Putnam Web site at www.ablongman.com/penguin.

Video Program For qualified adopters, an impressive selection of videotapes is available to enrich students' experience of literature. Contact your sales representative—see www.ablongman.com/replocater—for more details.

Teaching Literature Online, Second Edition, by Dan Kline (Instructor/ISBN 0-321-10618-0) Concise and practical, *Teaching Literature Online* gives instructors strategies and advice for integrating elements of computer technology into the literature classroom. Offering a range of information and examples, this manual provides ideas and activities for enhancing literature course with the help of technology tools. Available at no additional cost when value-packed with *Living Literature*.

What Every Student Should Know about Researching Online, by David Munger and Shireen Campbell (ISBN 0-321-44531-7) This guide teaches students how to conduct research in the first place they will look: the Web. They'll learn how to use search engines and databases and judge what they find, how to document the materials they borrow, and how to avoid online plagiarism. Annotated screen shots of Web pages show students where to locate the information they need to create a proper citation. Numerous examples of properly cited online and electronic sources are also provided.

What Every Student Should Know about Avoiding Plagiarism (ISBN 0-321-44689-5) This guide teaches students to take plagiarism seriously and understand its consequences. Here, source usage methods—summary, paraphrase, and quotation—are explained, with examples. The most common types of plagiarism are discussed, from simple mistakes such as forgetting to use quotation marks when using someone else's exact words, or failing to acknowledge another's thoughts and ideas, to wholesale fraudulence, such as purchasing student papers from online sites and claiming them as one's own work. A brief essential guide to citing sources using both MLA and APA documentation styles is also included.

What Every Student Should Know about Citing Sources (with MLA Documentation), by Michael Greer (ISBN 0-321-44737-9) This guide provides specific instructions on writing and referencing in the Modern Language Association (MLA) style. It offers a comprehensive listing of in-text and works cited models for a wide variety of print, electronic, and online sources. Included too are frequently asked questions about MLA style and guidelines for formatting research papers.

The Longman Printed Testbank for Literature, by Heidi L.M. Jacobs (Instructor/ISBN 0-321-14312-4); **The Longman Electronic Testbank for Literature, by Heidi L.M. Jacobs** (Instructor/CD ISBN 0-321-14314-0) This testbank features various objective questions on the major works of fiction, short fiction, poetry, and drama. A versatile and handy resource, this easy-to-use testbank can be used for all quizzing and testing needs. The user-friendly CD-ROM allows instructors to choose questions from the electronic testbank and then print out the completed test for distribution. Available at no additional cost when value-packed with *Living Literature*.

Glossary of Literary and Critical Terms, by Heidi L.M. Jacobs (ISBN 0-321-12691-2) *The Glossary of Literary and Critical Terms* is a quick, reliable, and portable resource for students of literature and creative writing. This easy-to-use glossary includes definitions, explanations, and examples for over 100 literary and critical terms which students commonly encounter in their readings or hear in their lectures and class discussions. In addition to basic terms related to form and genre, the glossary also includes terms and explanations related to literary history, criticism, and theory. Available at no additional cost when value-packed with *Living Literature*.

The New American Webster Handy College Dictionary (ISBN 0-451-18166-2) This superior paperback reference text contains more than 100,000 entries, including clear and concise definitions, selected etymologies, current phrases, slang, abbreviations, and scientific terms. Available at no additional cost when value-packed with *Living Literature*.

Sourcebooks Shakespeare Longman Publishers, in conjunction with Sourcebooks, Inc., proudly offers *The Sourcebooks Shakespeare*—a revolutionary new book and CD format that brings the Bard's plays to life. For the first time, text, audio, and illustration come together to create a remarkable new way of experiencing Shakespeare's timeless works. Package one *Sourcebooks Shakespeare* title with *Living Literature* at no additional cost. Contact your representative for a special package ISBN. Now available: *Romeo and Juliet*, *Othello*, *A Midsummer Night's Dream*, *Julius Caesar*, *Macbeth*, *Hamlet*, and *Much Ado about Nothing*. Visit the Sourcebooks Web site: www.ablongman.com/sourcebooks.

ACKNOWLEDGMENTS

I am grateful to the following individuals at Longman for their hard work and dedication to this project: Joe Terry, for believing in the vision for this book and for his help in making that vision a reality; Mary Ellen Curley, Ann Stypuloski, and Laura Coaty for their support and tireless efforts in implementing the book's marketing campaign; senior development editor Mika De Roo for her editorial acumen and diligence in guiding the project from the early stages of development to the final book; Patti Brecht and Eric Jorgensen for overseeing production of a complex book on an extremely challenging schedule, working with Lake Lloyd and the fantastic team at EPS; Christine Halsey and Tansal Arnas for coordinating reviews and handling administrative tasks, large and small, to ready the manuscript for production; Abby Lindquist and Whitney Baer for additional support with reviews; and Robert Ravas and Cheryl Besenjak for their guidance on permissions. I would also like to thank Ann Bailey for her vigorous efforts on text permissions and Linda Sykes for researching the extensive art program. A debt of gratitude is owed to Joanna Imm for her help on the Inspirations and Locales, for her thorough fact-checking of disputable dates for accuracy and consistency, and for her excellent work on the *Instructor's Manual*, with the support of Jeremy Frey at the University of Arizona on the manual's poetry section.

This book also benefited immensely from the comments, corrections, and suggestions of astute reviewers whose close reading of the manuscript at every stage produced thoughtful feedback from the proposal stage to the finished book: Jennifer Dawes Adkinson, Idaho State University; Dan Albergotti, Elon University; Laura Albritton, University of Miami; B. J. Alexander, Tarleton State University; Paul Almonte, Salt Lake City Community College; Joe Antinarella, Tidewater Community College; Sara Atwood, Columbus State University; Dr. Lee Baginski, Trident Technical College; Mary McAleer Balkun, Seton Hall University; John Beard, Coastal Carolina University; Mojgan Behmand, George Mason University; Velma Brown Blackmon, Elizabeth City State University; Jacqueline A. Blackwell, Thomas Nelson Community College; Karen Blomain, Kutztown University; Nancy E. Bowden, University of the Cumberlands; Allen Braden, Tacoma Community College; Gaylord Brewer, Middle Tennessee State University; Dawn Brickey, Charleston Southern University; Mechel Camp,

Jackson State Community College; Susan Carlson, Pittsburg State University; Seamus Cooney, Western Michigan University; David Cope, Grand Rapids Community College; Bene Scanlon Cox, Middle Tennessee State University; Matilda W. Cox, Old Dominion University; Michel de Benedictis, Miami Dade College; Chard deNiord, Providence College; Marcia Denius, Florida Institute of Technology; Michael Edward Dimmick, Virginia Polytechnic Institute; Peter Dorman, Central Virginia Community College; Marianne Dzik, Illinois Valley Community College; Mark Ende, Onondaga Community College; Daniel J. Ennis, Coastal Carolina University; Nancy Enright, Seton Hall University; Judith P. Fabisch, Cornerstone University; Miriam Fankhauser, Tiffin University; Darren Felty, Trident Technical College; Adam Fischer, Bowie State University; Joseph Francavilla, Columbus State University; William Franklin, North Central Texas College; Jennifer C. Garlen, University of Alabama–Huntsville; Keith Geekie, Johnson County Community College; Noelle Geiger, Valencia Community College; Simone M. Gers, Pima Community College; Judith Goleman, University of Massachusetts–Boston; Karen B. Golightly, University of Memphis; Andrew Green, University of Miami; Allen W. Grove, Alfred State University; Keith Hale, South Texas College; Barbara Hanna, East Mississippi Community College; Ann Hawkins, Austen Peay State University; Audrey A. Herbrich, Blinn College–Schulenburg Campus; Darlene S. Hollon, Northern Kentucky University; Carolina Hospital, Miami-Dade Community College; Dr. Mary Lee Stephenson Huffer, Lake Sumter Community College; Ann Jagoe, North Central Texas College; Doris O. Jellig, Tidewater Community College; Ruth Y. Jenkins, California State University–Fresno; Virginia F. Joczik, Trident Technical College; Alan G. Johnson, Idaho State University; Andrew Kelley, Jackson State Community College; Lola A. King, Trinity Valley Community College; Mary Kramer, University of Massachusetts–Lowell; Dr. Anne M. Kuhta, Northern Virginia Community College; Chikako D. Kumamoto, College of DuPage; Ellen A. Laird, Hudson Valley Community College; Catherine Lally, Brevard Community College; Thomas Lawrence Long, Thomas Nelson Community College; Veronica Makowsky, University of Connecticut; Stephen March, Elizabeth City State University; Jeff McCarthy, Westminster College; Barbara McCauley, North Florida Community College; Miles McCrimmon, J. Sergeant Reynolds Community College; Alan Merickel, Tallahassee Community College; Jeffrey N. Nelson, University of Alabama–Huntsville; Melissa Nicolas, University of Louisiana–Lafayette; Dr. Anita Obermeier, University of New Mexico; Erin O'Brien, Valencia Community College; Cyrus Patell, New York University; Della Paul, Valencia Community College; Michelle Paulsen, Victoria College; Michael Raleigh, Truman College; Lou Ethel Roliston, Bergen Community College; Charles G. Rooney, Northwest State Community College; Kelly Rogers Rupp, Redlands Community College; Valerie Russell, Valencia Community College; Georgeanna Sellers, High Point University; Margaret Senatore, University of Southwestern Colorado; Angelia Sharp, University of Alabama–Huntsville; Debra Shein, Idaho State University; Kristi Siegel, Mount Saint Mary College; Donald L. Skinner, Indian River Community College; Beverly J. Slaughter, Brevard Community College; Tom Smith, Sinclair Community College; Carolyn Sturgeon, West Virginia State University; Kevin Sweeney, Southern Maine

Community College; Terry Thaxton, University of Central Florida; Kathleen Thornton, University of Albany; Joseph Trimmer, Ball State University; April Van Camp, Indian River Community College; Robert Vettese, Southern Maine Community College; Linda S. Weeks, Dyersburg State Community College; Roger West, Trident Technical College; Clyde V. Williams, Mississippi State University; Jim Wilson, University of Florida; Lloyd Worley, University of Northern Colorado; Scott D. Yarbrough, Charleston Southern University; and Sam Zahran, Fayetteville Technical Community College.

Working on such a large project as this took a great deal of time and energy. I would never have begun it without the help and encouragement of my late wife, Virginia Lieson Brereton, of the Tufts University English Department. She was a tireless reader as well as a brilliant teacher. Her suggestions about what to include are evident everywhere throughout the text. Working on compiling the book always included conversations with her about the selections, the introductions, and the questions. She was my best reader and shrewdest critic. I'm sorry she didn't live to see the book completed, but I've acknowledged her very special contributions in the dedication.

I want to thank my former colleagues in the English Department of the University of Massachusetts–Boston, for providing me with examples of excellent, dedicated teaching. Among them I wish to single out Ann E. Berthoff, Judith Goleman, Neal Bruss, Louise Smith, Eleanor Kutz, Bob Crossley, Dick Cluster, and Jack Tobin, all of whom contributed in one way or another to this book, either through inspiration or direct example. I also want to thank my former colleagues in the Department of English and American Literature at Brandeis University for their suggestions and for setting an excellent example. Among them Olga Broumas, John Burt, Michael Gilmore, Caren Irr, and William Flesch served as models of superb teaching and scholarship. I wish particularly to thank two Brandeis graduate research assistants, Sari Edelstein and Emily Bernhard Jackson, who provided so much help in compiling the biographies of the authors. And I also want to thank my students at Harvard University for their warm reception of my latest thinking about literature as well as their willingness to engage fruitfully with my writing assignments. At the Boston Athenaeum Jenny Desai provided key support and encouragement. Finally, I want to thank Carol Hollar-Zwick, editor extraordinaire, whose early work on this text made it stronger and more readable.

John C. Brereton

Living Literature

Introduction

Reading with
or without a Theory

"How shall I read it?" asked Alice.
　　"Begin at the beginning, read it through to the end, then
stop," said the King.

Lewis Carroll, Alice in Wonderland

Yes, reading a text straight through, pausing at nothing, getting everything "right," is one good, and familiar, way to read. Many people read this way all the time. Others, however, have devised different ways or alternative strategies. Some people insist on looking at the last page of a novel first, to spare themselves the suspense. Others cannot imagine anything so silly. (In the 1967 movie *Bedazzled*, the Devil goes around bookstores tearing out the last page of mystery novels, in the certainty that readers will react by committing the sin of anger.) You are in good company if you enjoy reading by doing just what you want: reading a story here, a whole book there, then part of a poem, a single act of a play, then a book chapter, then dipping into the beginning of one book or reading the first page of a story. The contemporary French novelist Daniel Pennac, an experienced teacher of literature, once listed ten "inalienable" rights every reader possesses:

1. The right not to read.
2. The right to skip pages.
3. The right to not finish.
4. The right to reread.

1

5. The right to read anything.
6. The right to escapism.
7. The right to read anywhere.
8. The right to browse.
9. The right to read out loud.
10. The right to not defend your tastes.

So reading for pleasure, to pass the time, or to be taken out of ourselves on an adventure, a love affair, or a detective story are all excellent and legitimate ways to enjoy stories, plays, and poems. The verb "read," Pennac says, doesn't really permit the imperative: you can say to someone, "Read!" but it has just as much effect as if you were to say "Love!" or "Dream!" Real reading has to come from within, from one's will or inclinations, from desire.

But we all do other kinds of reading, beyond reading for pleasure. We read to accumulate information, for example. Such reading may be fast and cursory or slow and pondering, depending on the nature of the information, the degree of understanding needed, and how high the stakes. Sometimes you need only skim a text in order to orient yourself, asking: What is the text about? How long will it take to read? Does it have relevance for me? Will I be interested in it? Where might the potential difficulties lie? At other times the reading precedes a test about it, so you must understand and commit to memory the concepts and terms, at least until test day.

Sometimes we do a more careful, attentive reading that can succeed with all kinds of material but usually corresponds best with writing that is richer, denser, and more complex than informational texts or the usual best-sellers or page-turners. Sometimes such reading can overlap with the light reading done for escape or pleasure: the first time through a short story you may read fairly fast because you are caught up in the plot or an interesting character and you want to know how the story comes out. But then you may follow an impulse to read—and reread—more slowly and carefully. You may want to understand better how the story "worked," perhaps confirming some guesses, or you may look more carefully at the language, puzzle out a part that was hard to interpret, or just savor a particularly lush or funny image. Maybe you anticipate a conversation or discussion—formal or informal—that will benefit from a more thoughtful reading. Maybe you have an essay to write on the text; such a task will definitely require a more considered reading. The fact that you need to talk or write about a story helps to produce a reading that is richer and more careful.

This more careful reading can be helped immeasurably with more knowledge and more understanding of the ways in which stories and poems and plays work, and of what you yourself are like as a reader. For example, on a business trip a traveler stops at an airport newsstand and buys a paperback, a romance aimed at women readers, set in the days of pirates. Reading the book on the plane passes the time, carrying her to an imaginary world far away from the cramped, claustrophobic airliner. Let us call this an *innocent reading*. But imagine another traveler buying the same book, one who has given a good deal of thought to how romance novels work. She might have read a great many romances, as well as some studies of romance novels in popular culture—say Janice Radway's excellent, pathbreaking book, *Reading the Romance*. She will still read romance novels and enjoy them, but her reading will be different. As she reads the book, she will be more aware of how the novel follows clearly defined formulas, of how it inscribes and reinforces patterns of male domination or patriarchy, of how the genre has changed over time, and of how romance novels can be reflections of their particular culture. This knowledge provides a richer, more nuanced reading, one that is no longer innocent but consciously *informed* by a richer understanding. That does not mean she will enjoy the romance novel less. In fact, understanding the book in its context provides a richer, more powerful, more enjoyable experience, much more in tune with the complexities of an educated imagination.

In truth, it is unlikely that someone could read a story or poem or play in total innocence. Everyone comes to the act of reading with certain preconceptions, experiences, and tendencies. A sixty-year-old African American grandmother will bring different things to her reading than a nineteen-year-old gay white man; their readings will never be precisely the same. Inevitably, we all read poems and plays and stories (as well as the world) through the lens formed by our culture, by who we are. Every reader is what critics call *situated*. Because we each have our own place in the world, different people find different things in literature. And we are also situated by our particular time and location. It is impossible for us to become like the first readers of Ernest Hemingway in the 1920s or of Harriet Beecher Stowe in the 1850s or of John Donne in the 1600s. How could we be? In an informed reading of Hemingway or Stowe or Donne, we cannot help but be aware of how events have changed since those times, and be aware too of how expectations for stories and novels and poems have changed as well. We read the past through eyes formed in the present, and though we can try to imagine ourselves as the first readers of Hemingway, Stowe, or Donne, we can never leave our situated-ness fully behind.

The more we become aware of ourselves as situated readers, as people who are reading works that were written by situated writers, the better we can understand the act of reading. Similarly, the more we understand how literature works, the more we can understand and enjoy what we are reading now, choose what we want to read next, and get more out of what we select. We recognize this process with other arts. Some people can look at a painting and immediately see details and relationships lost on the rest of us. Or some can hear a musical performance and instantly pick out the inner voices and underlying bass lines. These people often seem to have innately greater insight or some kind of built-in perception, but in reality what they have are trained eyes and ears. Learning about how literature works is analogous to cultivating a trained eye as a viewer of art or a trained ear as a listener to music. You notice more.

What kind of training does one need to be a reader with greater insight? What type of training will produce informed readings? What kind of information or attitude makes for a successful reading? To guide and encourage the reader toward an informed reading—without violating Pennac's bill of rights for readers—is the purpose of this book. It provides the technical terms most experienced readers use; a collection of interesting stories, poems, and plays to provide both diverse experiences and some contexts for reading; and exercises and assignments to focus your reading on answering particular questions, since writing about a work can focus your attention on it and on the terms you will use to discuss it.

Here is one important caution that connects back to Pennac's bill of rights. Every reading is partial, incomplete, provisional. No matter how careful and informed your reading, you will never absorb and remember all parts of the text equally. If you are like most readers, you will forget some parts of what you have read—some immediately, some after a few days. It is impossible to notice and retain everything, even from a brief and plainly written one-act play, short story, or poem. But the provisional, incomplete nature of reading has a positive dimension to it: forgetting (or on the other hand remembering vividly) tells you a lot about how you (and probably others as well) have responded to a text—maybe about what scene you did not want to deal with, or what part was least effectively written. As you read and reread, try to become more aware of what "gets" to you most, as well as what gives you the most difficulty. Remember: you will never read a literary text primarily for its "information" content, simply in order to know "what happened next." Your course instructor will no doubt expect you to know the major events of the plot or story but will treat them as the starting point for analysis and reaction, never the goal of your reading.

Everyone who talks and writes about literature inevitably employs a model of the reading process, whether that model is expressed or implicit, conscious or unconscious. Readers who want their fiction to be entertaining, for instance, think of stories in different ways from someone who regards stories as providing insight into the state of culture or the intricacies of a human personality. And both of these kinds of readers think about stories differently from readers who look mainly at a writer's style, or the art that goes into forming the sentences and paragraphs. Still different are readers who see stories as expressions of universal human consciousness, of psychological states, of myths, or as analysis of vast social transformations. All these models and approaches and theories of reading can be valid; all have been used profitably to produce successful readings. Each model provides a set of spectacles that concentrates readers' attention on one part or aspect of a work and inevitably produces a particular kind of reading. And of course many works lend themselves to any number of different readings. Here are a few reasons and ways to read that will be particularly important in this book:

First, one can read any kind of literature to broaden and deepen and confirm the way one sees the world—to receive affirmation and clarification for our thoughts and feelings from an eloquent writer full of insight.

Second, one can read any writing, but particularly classic literature, to understand one's own culture and traditions and to connect with people who have come before. Classic texts provide a link between ourselves and other eras, and a knowledge of such texts helps constitute a community of readers who have shared similar experiences. When used in an exclusionary way, classics can serve as a private, members-only club. Taught with a welcoming attitude, the classics can include new types of readers and new, original readings from new perspectives.

Third, we can read to "defamiliarize" our ordinary lives, to see the familiar in a different way. Literature often forces us to experience the everyday world from a new and even bizarre point of view—for instance, that of a fly on the wall, or of a visitor from a different time or culture or moral universe. As novelist Charles Baxter (see Chapter 6) remarks: "as one gets older, the story of Hansel and Gretel becomes more interesting only when told from the point of view of the witch." He goes on to say, "defamiliarization is finally more about the way in which we recognize ourselves in an action and simultaneously see someone we don't recognize."

Fourth, we may read about completely different attitudes and beliefs and moralities, thus informing ourselves about others in an increasingly close global community—and also (to return to defamiliarization) giving ourselves a new viewpoint on our own lives and commitments. Sometimes this new perspective can be intoxicating, sometimes a little scary or irritating or puzzling—sometimes both pleasant and unpleasant at the same time. But habit and routine can get boring, and we as individuals can enhance the intensity of our experiences through seeing other people and cultures.

Finally, literature can broaden our public lives as well as our personal experiences. When we are able to place ourselves in relation to the ideas and feelings of others, or if we are disposed to recognize that our way of seeing the world is not the only legitimate way, then we become more likely to tolerate others' perspectives and listen to what they say in a political or public forum. Communicating and working with other people in venues like clubs, voluntary organizations, or teams, in school or the workplace, requires us to connect with "the other," to recognize and accept difference. In this way the cultural conversation involved in thinking, speaking, and writing about literature is a powerful means of participating in the world around us—of playing our parts as community and world citizens.

* * *

Some of the readings in this book will be a delight the first time through; some selections will seem like hard work. Perhaps a difficult text is so different in viewpoint or time period or language use that at first it makes little sense. The questions and commentary that follow selections are designed to help you figure out the language and begin to appreciate the work as a whole. Class discussions and writing assignments—essential parts of the conversation—will also help. The gratification may be delayed, but with rereading and rethinking, it will likely arrive eventually. Or perhaps you will find a grudging admiration for some works. You do not have to like a text to get something out of it, and you do not have to get something out of everything you read.

A word about the book's principle of selection is in order, since big as it is, it nonetheless contains only a small fraction of what might have been included. This is especially true today, when the notion of what is "literature" has vastly expanded. At one time, the "canon"—the list of approved or accepted works— was mostly Greek and Roman writers. College students in 1850 could not take a class on Shakespeare; he was too "easy," too familiar. Only in the late nineteenth century did the canon evolve to include classic writers in English such as William Shakespeare, Edmund Spenser, and John Milton. And only in the twentieth century did it expand to include American writers. Most of these approved and accepted writers were, of course, white males. Gradually, students of literature began to pay careful attention to women writers and to writers from the nineteenth-century waves of immigration: Jews, Italians, and Irish. More recently, literary studies broadened to include the work of Chinese Americans, Japanese Americans, Indian Americans, Chicanos and Chicanas, Cubans and Dominicans, and on and on. African American writers are assuredly part of the canon these days, as are Native Americans and gays, but they certainly were not widely read in school and college as recently as 1950. And more and more—though not enough yet—readers have access to translated works from all over the world. In fact, a great deal of world literature is written in English—thanks to the increasing importance of English in places like Africa and India—and publishers are bringing more and more of Anglophone world literature to us. Most of the works in this book were originally written in English, on the principle that translation of poetry is a very difficult task, and that there are sufficient works written in English to provide a good introduction to literature. But let us be clear: this book contains only a very small slice of interesting work, and a whole world awaits readers, with works written in Spanish, Urdu, Farsi, Arabic, Mandarin, and a host of languages other than English.

One question always arises: what qualifies as "literature"? From one point of view almost everything does, including film (which obviously has a close connection to drama), letters, publicity, and transcripts of interviews. You will see that *Living Literature* takes a generous attitude toward this question, bringing a good many untraditional works into the conversation. Each major section includes nonfiction texts, valuable in themselves and also in light of the others in that section. You will also see a great deal of literature surrounded by the cultural artifacts of its time: clothing, music, visual arts, and illustrations of theatrical performances. Literature has rarely been just words on a page, to be read and interpreted in silence. It has often been performed, out loud, in a particular context, and this collection attempts to provide some of the rich surroundings that accompanied a work at the time of its creation and original appearance. One way this anthology follows traditional practice is that it divides its contents basically into story, poetry, and drama, but here *story* means narrative, which includes mostly fiction but some nonfiction as well.

As you address the highlighted sections, questions, and activities accompanying the selections in the book, you might notice some special emphases:

- **You will note an emphasis throughout on connections between the literary works contained here and real-life places, other artistic works, or related outside resources.** These brief contextual sections will enrich your understanding of a particular text or author and will also serve as a reminder that literature can grow out of a particular place and time. **Literary Locales** identify and describe real-life places with relevant literary associations, such as Edgar Allan Poe's house, Shakespeare's Globe Theatre, and Robert Frost's farm. **Virtual Locales** refer you to related online resources for additional background information and research. **Audio and Video Locales** direct you to pertinent recordings, performances, filmed versions, or other adaptations linked to a selection. (You may even find that you already know of some of these literary places and alternate versions of literary texts from your own traveling, viewing, and listening.) Similarly, **Inspiration** sections in nearly every chapter show how the work of a specific writer, or in many instances, a particular story, poem, or play, has given rise to artistic works in other genres (e.g., films or musical performances), which react or respond to the presence of the initial work. Or, conversely, sometimes a literary text has drawn its own creative spark from another artist or artistic work, such as a painting or a piece of music. For example, you will be able to explore how a Flannery O'Connor short story inspired a famous song by Bruce Springsteen or discover how a Björk pop song is related to an E. E. Cummings poem. These Locales and Inspiration sections help illuminate the idea that the literature here is more than simply pages in a book. The works in *Living Literature* have complex, interesting connections to the world, and the more ways you can relate to them, the more you can understand and enjoy them.

- **You will see a particular attention to the oral and the performed**. Thus, some of the questions in the book ask, "How would you say this poem?" or "How would you deliver this particular line in this play?" You are also encouraged to go online, to the library, or to the video or music store to take in the performed versions of the literature—especially, but not only, drama and song. Poems spring into life when we hear the rhythms and tones of voice of a good reader; a story read aloud takes on new dimensions of meaning. Reading is, of course, not just a passive act of translation or "decoding" but an active way of interpreting. As you read, think about how certain words and lines should "go." Feel free to backtrack to give a different emphasis. That is part of your right as a reader.

- **The questions, activities, and writing assignments following the selections—*Talking about the Text, Writing about the Text,* and *Linking the Text to Other Texts*—are designed to make you think hard about what you are reading**. What is happening in a particular text, and why? How do you as reader respond to each text? What in your own experience or in the experience of your friends and family might connect to and comment upon that text? Does the text have a moral or ethical dimension? Does the writer seem to have designs on you, hoping to alter your perception of the world? How does your view of the work change as you compare it to another work of literature or popular culture? If the questions are successful, they will push you more deeply into the complexities of the text and of life itself. The reading you give will be your own, governed by your understanding both of the world and of how texts work. You will rarely perform a passive reading, simply taking a text in; instead, you will be asked to respond actively to whatever you read. This is a kind of "talking back" to the texts, part of a rich tradition of literary response.

- **You will also have ample opportunity to talk about the texts in the book**. The talking sometimes starts with an oral reading, which of course requires some interpretation (and even rehearsal) if you are to produce a satisfactory performance of a story, poem, or part of a drama. That oral reading will be followed by plenty of discussion, in which you and other members of the class talk about your reactions, what you noticed, and how it connects with other readings and with your lives. Literature often leads to conversation, and good conversation often leads right back to rereading the text that started the whole process.

■ **What you have to say about texts will often take the form of writing**. Think of the writing you do as entering into a conversation both with the text itself and with others who have taken time to read and think about the text. The initial reader of your writing, of course, is you, particularly as you are in the act of composing. Surely you will not write everything at the last minute. You will be shrewd enough to save a little time for the cooking and creative doodling that encourage productive thinking. And you will be sure to build in time for revising, since revising produces the best writing. Even as you compose your drafts, you will loop back to the text and reread passages, and then write some more. Reading and writing are reciprocal, a kind of shuttling back and forth between page and text. The writing you do about literature will help you to become not only a better reader, but also a better thinker and a more confident writer.

Apart from yourself, your instructor is a primary reader of your writing. You will be "publishing" what you write for an audience of one and possibly for others in class. Sometimes this publishing will take the form of workshopping (an approach often used with great success in creative writing courses), giving you opportunities for feedback and ideas for revisions and mid-course corrections before the writing is due. As part of a workshop group, you need to be a helpful member of the conversation, giving useful, focused feedback to classmates. Finally, some of your writing—particularly any research project you do—may also assume the form of an oral presentation, done aloud, and then revised for submission as a research paper or project report. That is often a demanding task, but one that pays off in excellent training in clear thinking and building confidence. To help guide you toward useful, reliable sources on research-related projects, *Starting Points for Further Research* sections direct you to a reputable modern edition of an author's work, a standard biography, a recent article with bibliography, an interview, or an accessible article.

A course in reading is inevitably an insight into other minds: how significant writers and thinkers of the past and the present have told stories, dramatized events, or constructed poems. In another sense, though, a course in reading is about you as reader and talker and thinker, providing you with interesting, demanding texts, the information and terms you need to begin to interpret them, and the opportunities to talk and write about them. Ultimately, the course is more about how critical thinking and writing develop in the context of a wide range of literary forms and the writers who mastered them. It sounds like a formidable intellectual project. And it is. But be sure to leave room for fun, for pure enjoyment, as Pennac so wisely suggests.

PART
I

Fiction

1

Stories

Plot, Character, Setting

Narration, or telling stories, draws on something deeply and characteristically human. No matter how times change and with them people's interests and beliefs, stories retain their power and importance. True or invented, based on fact or on myth, stories help people give shape and meaning to their experience. Every religion has its creation stories; every nation has its heroes whose deeds merit retelling to younger generations. In our own lives, the stories we tell about what happens to us help us sort out what matters most from what is less important. In fact, many times the incidents that happen to us are just isolated events; they do not make sense until we can shape them into a story. Similarly, the scattered incidents of the lives of others often come into focus when we are able to endow them with the contours of a story. We ask, is this chance encounter the beginning of a love story? Is it the start of a mystery? Or will it end in a twist of fate? The story patterns are already there, awaiting the turn of events and the shape we decide to give them.

Interestingly, this shaping and sorting function of stories works whether the stories are true or invented. Truth and fiction often take on the same forms, and the terms we use for stories that really happened are often the same ones we use for stories describing the fantastic and the fictional. It is no accident that in many languages, including English, the word for "story" and the word for "history" are closely related. We acknowledge the same relatedness when we turn to a "news story" for fact and a "short story" for fiction. Much as we may prize the

11

distinction between truth and fiction, their shapes in stories can be remarkably similar.

Story with a Lesson

Here is a famous and familiar story, "The Hare and the Tortoise," from Aesop's *Fables*, a well-known book of moral tales from antiquity, originally written in Greek.

For many readers, this story is familiar in form and content. "The Hare and the Tortoise" is one of Aesop's fables, seemingly simple tales, with an explicit **moral** or concise lesson or principle contained within a story. It is a type familiar to readers and listeners for thousands of years. As adults and children we all learn some of the most important things about life through narratives like these.

The Hare and the Tortoise

TRANSLATED BY JOSEPH JACOBS

The Hare was once boasting of his speed before the other animals. "I have never yet been beaten," said he, "when I put forth my full speed. I challenge any one here to race with me."

The Tortoise said quietly, "I accept your challenge."

"That is a good joke," said the Hare; "I could dance round you all the way."

"Keep your boasting till you've beaten," answered the Tortoise. "Shall we race?"

So a course was fixed and a start was made. The Hare darted almost out of sight at once, but soon stopped and, to show his contempt for the Tortoise, lay down to have a nap. The Tortoise plodded on and plodded on, and when the Hare awoke from his nap, he saw the Tortoise just near the winning-post and could not run up in time to save the race. Then said the Tortoise:

"Plodding wins the race."

The story of the Hare and the Tortoise carries with it the elements that all stories possess. First and foremost, it relies on narration, the recounting of the sequence of events. It also uses **exposition**, which consists of the details and background we need in order to understand the characters and their circumstances in the story. Here the exposition is minimal: the Hare was boasting about his speed and issued a challenge. The Tortoise, the story's **protagonist**, or central character, took him up, much to the scorn of the hare, the story's **antagonist**, the character whose role is to oppose or contrast with the protagonist. This is all the exposition we are given, but we need no more: we have a pair of opposed contestants, with two distinct types of approach to a race: speedy and boasting, or slow and quiet. They confront each other in **dialogue**, or verbal interplay, providing us with the key **conflict** or struggle between ideas, characters, or groups that are essential to narrative, in this case over the best way to win the contest. The conflict is presented as a kind of **prologue**, an introduction to the central **action**, the primary event or occurrence in a work. In this instance, the main action is the race itself: the

☀ INSPIRATION Animation and *The Tortoise and the Hare*

From Disney 1935 animated film directed by Wilfred Jackson.

This ancient, very familiar story has been the source of four superb Hollywood cartoons: Walt Disney's *The Tortoise and the Hare* (1935), directed by Wilfred Jackson, which won an Oscar for Best Cartoon, and three by Warner Brothers: *Tortoise Beats Hare* by Fred "Tex" Avery (1941), *Tortoise Wins by a Hare* by Bob Clampett (1943), and *Rabbit Transit* by Friz Freleng (1947). In the Warner Brothers cartoons, quick-witted Bugs Bunny is outwitted every time by Cecil the Tortoise, some of the few occasions in which Bugs does not get the best of his adversary.

Fables became a natural subject for cartoonists, since they involved animals, were aimed at an audience that included many children, and seemed quite moral. It was this later quality that provided the Bugs Bunny cartoons with their source of the most fun, since the witty, rascally Bugs enjoyed nothing more than mocking the dull maxims of his earnest, bumbling adversaries.

Tortoise starts out by moving steadily, while the Hare runs ahead and then, to display his contempt, ostentatiously takes a nap. The actual race to the finish line, though full of dramatic possibilities, is barely described. We get no close-up of the action, no storytelling about how hard each is laboring to reach the goal. In dramatic terms, the major action essentially occurs **offstage**, where we cannot see what happens.

Books of morality central to a civilization, like Aesop's *Fables*, the Hebrew scriptures, or the Christian gospels, make plentiful use of stories like this one to teach lessons to young and old alike. Aesop's tales were **fables**, brief animal stories told to illustrate a moral. Readers and listeners were comfortable with the type; they all regarded such familiar tales as illustrations of a key moral point, and just in case they didn't get it, the fables ended with a brief restatement of the moral. In this case, "Plodding wins the race." In the Christian scriptures, when Jesus told **parables** or brief moral stories like the story of the Prodigal Son, he addressed a listening audience, sometimes just of a few disciples, sometimes a large crowd, reminding us that some of the most influential and powerful stories began as explicit oral performances, done out loud in order to reach the assembled listeners, many of whom were illiterate and could not be reached any other way. Only afterwards were the parables written down, to be read silently or aloud. Similarly, in the Hebrew scriptures the Cain and Abel story was heard by many more people than could actually read it. Like Aesop's *Fables*, those other stories started out as part of an oral tradition and were eventually written down so that others could read what had been said aloud.

A story from the oral tradition like "The Hare and the Tortoise" needs to have a clear moral point, and it also needs to frame the issue starkly, without a great deal of exposition or unnecessary detail. And though Aesop's *Fables* are great examples of how some stories have helped shape thousands of years of human moral consciousness, they do not always explain everything very easily. What motivated the hare to make such a boast? Why did the tortoise take up his challenge? What does the race stand for? Is it a **symbol**, a word or object that stands for something else, or does it just refer to particular kinds of contests requiring steady work? Does the moral truly make sense? Does "plodding" actually "win the race"? In what ways could this be said to be true? Is Aesop expecting this moral to apply to all of life or just certain contests? Sometimes, as in this particular story, what seems at first to be a simple moral can give rise to as many questions as it answers, and that is a fascinating part of stories as well. They require **interpretation**, an active engagement with them as we ponder what they seem to be getting at. A good reading produces another kind of dialogue, between writer and reader, in which we ask ourselves questions about what seems to be going on, both in the story and in us, as we react to it.

Talking about the Text

1. In this story where few details are provided, those that do appear can really matter. Explain why the Hare's jibes matter.
2. Is the Tortoise admirable? Does he pursue a course of action you would recommend? Under which circumstances?

Writing about the Text

1. Summarize the story of the Tortoise and the Hare in two or three sentences, including as much material as you can without allowing the sentences to get out of control.
2. Write a modern version of the Tortoise and the Hare story, placing the actions in the twenty-first century.

Linking the Text to Other Texts

1. Examine similar fables from Aesop or from a folk tradition you know. Examples might include "The Ant and the Grasshopper" or "The Fox and Crow." What do such fables all have in common?
2. Discuss other stories in which animals are models of different types of human behavior. Some examples might include Garfield, Calvin and Hobbes, or certain Disney movies.

 **VIDEO LOCALE**

Bugs Bunny Cartoons of *The Tortoise and the Hare*. All three Warner Brothers cartoon versions of *The Tortoise and the Hare*, cited above, can be found on the extensive DVD collections *Looney Tunes Premiere Collection*, Vols. 1 and 2 (2003, 2004). These three films are also available on the video collection *Bugs Bunny's Zaniest Toons* (Warner Bros., 1991).

PLOT

Most of us know someone who can tell a story really well. A universal characteristic of a good storyteller is the ability to give a story an artful shape by imposing order on the events. This ordering of events is what gives a story its plot, which is not quite the same as story. **Story** has been described as the whole arc of what happened, every detail from beginning to end. **Plot** includes what happens, but it also deals with how and why events unfold the way they do. For the audience of Homer's great epic poem *The Iliad*, every part of the story was familiar: the Trojan War, beginning with Paris stealing Helen of Troy, the Greeks departing for Troy, the actual battles that preceded the fall of Troy, the fall itself, and then the aftermath. But Homer chose not to tell it that way. As an artist, he devised his own original plot—which can be defined as the particular way he shaped and told the story—and decided to begin in the middle, among the Greeks camped on the plains in front of Troy, many years after the action began. Thus, story includes everything that happened; plot is how the story gets told by the storyteller's artful shaping. In other words, in any given story, the combination of specific conflicts, causations, reactions, oppositions, and interactions is what creates a plot out of a series of actions. Consequently, the same basic story, whether it is the fall of Troy or Cinderella, can give rise to many different plots.

Ordering the Plot

Some elements of a plot are familiar to everyone. The order can be **chronological**, beginning at the beginning and going straight through to the end, as in "The Hare and the Tortoise." One way of complicating the straight chronological order is to use a **flashback**, an intentional break in chronological sequence in which the narration switches to past events ("I suddenly remembered when . . . "). Another alternative is the slightly more complex **flash forward**, also a deliberate break in chronological order, but one in which the narration switches to future events ("Later I would relive these moments . . . "). Another technique is **foreshadowing**, which warns or suggests to readers what lies ahead, sometimes through **symbolism**, in which something has more than its **literal**, everyday meaning but also stands for something else ("The evening shadows lengthened as he stepped into the dark forest, and from dense undergrowth he heard an animal cry of warning . . . "). Sometimes we pick up on foreshadowing right away on a first reading, though often we might not notice it until we reread the story. Finally, a **narrator**, the one who tells the story, can begin as Homer did, **in medias res**, in the middle of the action, with Achilles sulking in his tent in front of the walls of Troy, and rely on **retrospective narration**, a later retelling that fills in the earlier parts of the story. In medias res is a very common technique in modern fiction as well, since we are all living our lives in the middle of things, and often it is only in retrospect that we realize we have done or experienced something that we could make into a story.

These terms are no doubt fairly familiar, since they refer to many different types of story, from religious parables to complex action films. Recent theoretical and critical approaches by literary scholars have added layers of interesting complexity to the issue of plot, but the main thing is to think of plot as the particular order an author imposes on the material. The plot of a story is a key part of its art.

Kate Chopin's "The Story of an Hour" is an excellent example of a story that revolves around a **twist** or clever surprise in its plot, with a narrator who consciously shapes the material to keep us in suspense. Chopin set many of her stories in a world she knew well, late-nineteenth-century New Orleans, and was highly influenced by popular stories that depended on odd twists of plot. In addition to highly shaped plots, Chopin's stories had an explicitly feminist point of view, and today she is viewed as an early southern rebel against the sexual repression of women.

KATE CHOPIN   (1851–1904)

Of Irish-Creole descent, Kate Chopin grew up in well-to-do circumstances in St. Louis, Missouri. After marriage to businessman Oscar Chopin, she moved to New Orleans, but she only began her literary career after his death and her return to St. Louis, with her six children. Her early novels, mostly set in Louisiana, revealed her talent for portraying Creole culture. Her most famous novel, The Awakening *(1899), generated intense controversy for its sympathetic depiction of female sexuality. Chopin's work fell out of favor for many years, but since the 1970s* The Awakening *has been reprinted many times and praised for its early feminist insights.*

The Story of an Hour   (1894)

Knowing that Mrs. Mallard was afflicted with a heart trouble, great care was taken to break to her as gently as possible the news of her husband's death.

It was her sister Josephine who told her, in broken sentences, veiled hints that revealed in half concealing. Her husband's friend Richards was there, too, near her. It was he who had been in the newspaper office when intelligence of the railroad disaster was received, with Brently Mallard's name leading the list of "killed." He had only taken the time to assure himself of its truth by a second telegram, and had hastened to forestall any less careful, less tender friend in bearing the sad message.

She did not hear the story as many women have heard the same, with a paralyzed inability to accept its significance. She wept at once, with sudden, wild abandonment, in her sister's arms. When the storm of grief had spent itself she went away to her room alone. She would have no one follow her.

There stood, facing the open window, a comfortable, roomy armchair. Into this she sank, pressed down by a physical exhaustion that haunted her body and seemed to reach into her soul.

She could see in the open square before her house the tops of trees that were   5 all aquiver with the new spring life. The delicious breath of rain was in the air. In the street below a peddler was crying his wares. The notes of a distant song which some one was singing reached her faintly, and countless sparrows were twittering in the eaves.

There were patches of blue sky showing here and there through the clouds that had met and piled one above the other in the west facing her window.

She sat with her head thrown back upon the cushion of the chair, quite motionless, except when a sob came up into her throat and shook her, as a child who has cried itself to sleep continues to sob in its dreams.

She was young, with a fair, calm face, whose lines bespoke repression and even a certain strength. But now there was a dull stare in her eyes, whose gaze was fixed away off yonder on one of those patches of blue sky. It was not a glance of reflection, but rather indicated a suspension of intelligent thought.

There was something coming to her and she was waiting for it, fearfully. What was it? She did not know; it was too subtle and elusive to name. But she felt it, creeping out of the sky, reaching toward her through the sounds, the scents, the color that filled the air.

Now her bosom rose and fell tumultuously. She was beginning to recognize   10 this thing that was approaching to possess her, and she was striving to beat it back with her will—as powerless as her two white slender hands would have been.

When she abandoned herself a little whispered word escaped her slightly parted lips. She said it over and over under her breath: "Free, free, free!" The vacant stare and the look of terror that had followed it went from her eyes. They stayed keen and bright. Her pulses beat fast, and the coursing blood warmed and relaxed every inch of her body.

She did not stop to ask if it were or were not a monstrous joy that held her. A clear and exalted perception enabled her to dismiss the suggestion as trivial.

She knew that she would weep again when she saw the kind, tender hands folded in death; the face that had never looked save with love upon her, fixed and gray and dead. But she saw beyond that bitter moment a long procession of years to come that would belong to her absolutely. And she opened and spread her arms out to them in welcome.

There would be no one to live for during those coming years; she would live for herself. There would be no powerful will bending hers in that blind persistence with which men and women believe they have a right to impose a private will upon a fellow-creature. A kind intention or a cruel intention made the act seem no less a crime as she looked upon it in that brief moment of illumination.

And yet she had loved him—sometimes. Often she had not. What did it   15
matter! What could love, the unsolved mystery, count for in face of this possession of self-assertion which she suddenly recognized as the strongest impulse of
her being!

"Free! Body and soul free!" she kept whispering.

Josephine was kneeling before the closed door with her lips to the keyhole,
imploring for admission. "Louise, open the door! I beg, open the door—you will
make yourself ill. What are you doing, Louise? For heaven's sake open the door."

"Go away. I am not making myself ill." No; she was drinking in a very elixir
of life through that open window.

Her fancy was running riot along those days ahead of her. Spring days, and
summer days, and all sorts of days that would be her own. She breathed a quick
prayer that life might be long. It was only yesterday she had thought with a shudder that life might be long.

She arose at length and opened the door to her sister's importunities. There   20
was a feverish triumph in her eyes, and she carried herself unwittingly like a goddess of Victory. She clasped her sister's waist, and together they descended the
stairs. Richards stood waiting for them at the bottom.

Some one was opening the front door with a latchkey. It was Brently Mallard who entered, a little travel-stained, composedly carrying his grip-sack and
umbrella. He had been far from the scene of accident, and did not even know
there had been one. He stood amazed at Josephine's piercing cry; at Richards'
quick motion to screen him from the view of his wife.

But Richards was too late.

When the doctors came they said she had died of heart disease—of joy that
kills.

Chopin's short tale lets us see the clear difference between story and plot.
Imagine this story as told from the beginning of the journey, with Brently Mallard
leaving the house and his wife Louise thinking how glad she was he was going. Or
imagine it beginning with a scene in which Richards gets the news and then confers in hushed tones with Josephine. Or imagine it beginning with a scene giving
their exact words when they tell Louise the awful news. No, Chopin has chosen
to compress all that and to begin with a half-sentence of exposition about Louise's
weak heart (a piece of foreshadowing, of course) followed by three sentences of
exposition about how they heard the awful news and checked to make sure it was
accurate. This is a consciously contrived plot, designed to keep readers in suspense. A newspaper story about what happened would obviously lead with what
happens at the end: "A New Orleans wife died of heart failure [or "of joy"] just as
her husband, believed killed in a train wreck, unexpectedly returned home."
Chopin provides us with a different picture, because her tight plot allows her to
focus on the changing reactions inside Mrs. Mallard's mind as the news sinks in.
Chopin's way of shaping the plot gives her time to concentrate on both the story,
and on her **theme**, the subject or idea dramatized in the story, of a woman's anticipated freedom from male domination, no matter how benign.

Talking about the Text

1. What changes does Louise Mallard experience in this story? How might they explain her death?
2. When in the story do we get an account of what is happening inside Louise Mallard's mind? When do we not get such information?

Writing about the Text

1. Write a brief essay on how we, as attentive readers of this story, "know" more than the characters who surround Louise Mallard. For example, they misinterpret her reaction as well as the cause of her death; even Louise herself doesn't fully understand the situation.
2. Some readers feel manipulated by the plot of this story. Argue for or against this feeling of manipulation. Is it too neat and contrived? Or is its contrived quality an integral part of its effect?

Linking the Text to Other Texts

1. Compare Louise Mallard's situation here with that of Mrs. Wright in Susan Glaspell's play *Trifles*, p. 1166. How do men misunderstand each of them? How do they respond to their husband's influence over their lives?
2. Look at Marge Piercy's poems "Barbie Doll" (pp. 790–791) and list the similarities between the women in her poem and Mrs. Brently Mallard.

Starting Points for Further Research: Kate Chopin

- **Edition:** Kate Chopin. *Complete Novels and Stories.* New York: Library of America, 2002.
- **Biography:** Emily Toth. *Unveiling Kate Chopin.* Jackson: University Press of Mississippi, 1999.
- **Critical Essay:** Maria Mikolchak. "Kate Chopin's *The Awakening* as Part of the Nineteenth-Century American Literary Tradition." *Interdisciplinary Literary Studies: A Journal of Criticism and Theory* 5:2 (Spring 2004): 29–49.

For Further Reading: Plot

Mississippi-born Richard Ford has written many stories and novels based on close observation of human behavior. His story "Under the Radar" involves a tense modern couple and includes a nicely shaped plot that has some qualities in common with "The Story of an Hour."

RICHARD FORD   (B. 1944)

Born in Jackson, Mississippi, Richard Ford grew up in the same town as author Eudora Welty. Known for his spare prose style, Ford made an auspicious debut with his novel The Sportswriter *(1986). Its sequel,* Independence Day *(1995), earned him the Pulitzer Prize. Ford's other novels include* A Piece of My Heart *(1976),* The Ultimate Good Luck *(1981), and* Wildlife *(1990). In addition to many short stories, Ford has also written essays, a play, and a screenplay. He has lived in New Orleans and now makes his home in Montana.*

Under the Radar   (2001)

On the drive over to the Nicholsons' for dinner—their first in some time—
Marjorie Reeves told her husband, Steven Reeves, that she had had an affair with
George Nicholson (their host) a year ago, but that it was all over with now and
she hoped he—Steven—would not be mad about it and could go on with life.

At this point they were driving along Quaker Bridge Road where it leaves
the Perkins Great Woods Road and begins to border the Shenipsit Reservoir,
dark and shadowy and calmly mirrored in the late spring twilight. On the right
was dense young timber, beech and alder saplings in pale leaf, the ground damp
and cakey. Peepers were calling out from the watery lows. Their turn onto Apple
Orchard Lane was still a mile on.

Steven, on hearing this news, began gradually and very carefully to steer
their car—a tan Mercedes wagon with hooded yellow headlights—off of Quaker
Bridge Road and onto the damp grassy shoulder so he could organize this information properly before going on.

They were extremely young. Steven Reeves was twenty-eight. Marjorie
Reeves a year younger. They weren't rich, but they'd been lucky. Steven's job at
Packard-Wells was to stay on top of a small segment of a larger segment of a
rather small prefabrication intersection that serviced the automobile industry,
and where any sudden alteration, or even the rumor of an alteration in certain
polymer-bonding formulas could tip crucial down-the-line demand patterns, and
in that way affect the betting lines and comfort zones of a good many meaningful
client positions. His job meant poring over dense and esoteric petrochemical-in-
dustry journals, attending technical seminars, flying to vendor conventions, then
writing up detailed status reports and all the while keeping an eye on the market
for the benefit of his higher-ups. He'd been a scholarship boy at Bates, studied
chemistry, was the only son of a hard-put but upright lobstering family in Pe-
maquid, Maine, and had done well. His bosses at Packard-Wells liked him, saw
themselves in him, and also in him saw character qualities they'd never quite
owned—blond and slender callowness tending to gullibility, but backed by caution, ingenuity and a thoroughgoing, compact toughness. He was sharp. It was
his seventh year with the company—his first job. He and Marjorie had been
married two years. They had no children. The car had been his bonus two
Christmases ago.

When the station wagon eased to a stop, Steven sat for a minute with the   5
motor running, the salmon-colored dash lights illuminating his face. The radio
had been playing softly—the last of the news, then an interlude for French
horns. Responding to no particular signal, he pressed off the radio and in the
same movement switched off the ignition, which left the headlights shining on
the empty, countrified road. The windows were down to attract the fresh spring
air, and when the engine noise ceased the evening's ambient sounds were waiting. The peepers. A sound of thrush wings fluttering in the brush only a few
yards away. The noise of something falling from a small distance and hitting an
invisible water surface. Beyond the stand of saplings was the west, and through
the darkened trunks, the sky was still pale yellow with the day's light, though
here on Quaker Bridge Road it was nearly dark.

When Marjorie said what she had just said, she'd been looking straight
ahead to where the headlights made a bright path in the dark. Perhaps she'd

looked at Steven once, but having said what she'd said, she kept her hands in her lap and continued looking ahead. She was a pretty, blond, convictionless girl with small demure features—small nose, small ears, small chin, though with a surprisingly full-lipped smile which she practiced on everyone. She was fond of getting a little tipsy at parties and lowering her voice and sitting on a flowered ottoman or a burl table top with a glass of something and showing too much of her legs or inappropriate amounts of her small breasts. She had grown up in Indiana, studied art at Purdue. Steven had met her in New York at a party while she was working for a firm that did child-focused advertising for a large toymaker. He'd liked her bobbed hair, her fragile, wispy features, translucent skin and the slightly husky voice that made her seem more sophisticated than she was, but somehow convinced her she was, too. In their community, east of Hartford, the women who knew Marjorie Reeves thought of her as a bimbo who would not stay married to sweet Steven Reeves for very long. His second wife would be the right wife for him. Marjorie was just a starter.

Marjorie, however, did not think of herself that way, only that she liked men and felt happy and confident around them and assumed Steven thought this was fine and that in the long run it would help his career to have a pretty, spirited wife no one could pigeonhole. To set herself apart and to take an interest in the community she'd gone to work as a volunteer at a grieving-children's center in Hartford, which meant all black. And it was in Hartford that she'd had the chance to encounter George Nicholson and fuck him at a Red Roof Inn until they'd both gotten tired of it. It would never happen again, was her view, since in a year it hadn't happened again.

For the two or possibly five minutes now that they had sat on the side of Quaker Bridge Road in the still airish evening, with the noises of spring floating in and out of the open window, Marjorie had said nothing and Steven had also said nothing, though he realized that he was saying nothing because he was at a loss for words. A loss for words, he realized, meant that nothing that comes to mind seems very interesting to say as a next thing to what has just been said. He knew he was a callow man—a boy in some ways, still—but he was not stupid. At Bates, he had taken Dr. Sudofsky's class on *Ulysses*, and come away with a sense of irony and humor and the assurance that true knowledge was a spiritual process, a quest, not a storage of dry facts—a thing like freedom, which you only fully experienced in practice. He'd also played hockey, and knew that knowledge and aggressiveness were a subtle and surprising and uncommon combination. He had sought to practice both at Packard-Wells.

But for a brief and terrifying instant in the cool padded semi-darkness, just when he began experiencing his loss for words, he entered or at least nearly slipped into a softened fuguelike state in which he began to fear that he perhaps *could* not say another word; that something (work fatigue, shock, disappointment over what Marjorie had admitted) was at that moment causing him to detach from reality and to slide away from the present, and in fact to begin to lose his mind and go crazy to the extent that he was in jeopardy of beginning to gibber like a chimp, or just to slowly slump sideways against the upholstered door and not speak for a long, long time—months—and then only with the aid of drugs be able merely to speak in simple utterances that would seem cryptic, so that eventually he would have to be looked after by his mother's family in Damariscotta. A terrible thought.

And so to avoid that—to save his life and sanity—he abruptly just said a   10
word, any word that he could say into the perfumed twilight inhabiting the car,
where his wife was obviously anticipating his reply to her unhappy confession.

And for some reason the word—phrase, really—that he uttered was "ground
clutter." Something he'd heard on the TV weather report as they were dressing
for dinner.

"Hm?" Marjorie said. "What was it?" She turned her pretty, small-featured
face toward him so that her pearl earrings caught light from some unknown
source. She was wearing a tiny green cocktail dress and green satin shoes that
showed off her incredibly thin ankles and slender, bare brown calves. She had
two tiny matching green bows in her hair. She smelled sweet. "I know this wasn't
what you wanted to hear, Steven," she said, "but I felt I should tell you before we
got to George's. The Nicholsons', I mean. It's all over. It'll never happen again. I
promise you. No one will ever mention it. I just lost my bearings last year with
the move. I'm sorry." She had made a little steeple of her fingertips, as if she'd
been concentrating very hard as she spoke these words. But now she put her
hands again calmly in her minty green lap. She had bought her dress especially
for this night at the Nicholsons'. She'd thought George would like it and
Steven, too. She turned her face away and exhaled a small but detectable sigh in
the car. It was then that the headlights went off automatically.

George Nicholson was a big squash-playing, thick-chested, hairy-armed Yale
lawyer who sailed his own Hinckley 61 out of Essex and had started backing off
from his high-priced Hartford plaintiffs' practice at fifty to devote more time to
competitive racket sports and senior skiing. George was a college roommate of
one of Steven's firm's senior partners and had "adopted" the Reeveses when they
moved into the community following their wedding. Marjorie had volunteered
Saturdays with George's wife, Patsy, at the Episcopal Thrift Shop during their
first six months in Connecticut. To Steven, George Nicholson had recounted a
memorable, seasoning summer spent hauling deep-water lobster traps with some
tough old sea dogs out of Matinicus, Maine. Later, he'd been a Marine, and
sported a faded anchor, ball and chain tattooed on his forearm. Later yet he'd
fucked Steven's wife.

Having said something, even something that made no sense, Steven felt a
sense of glum and deflated relief as he sat in the silent car beside Marjorie, who
was still facing forward. Two thoughts had begun to compete in his reviving
awareness. One was clearly occasioned by his conception of George Nicholson.
He thought of George Nicholson as a gasbag, but also a forceful man who'd made
his pile by letting very little stand in his way. When he thought about George he
always remembered the story about Matinicus, which then put into his mind a
mental picture of his own father and himself hauling traps somewhere out toward Monhegan. The reek of the bait, the toss of the ocean in late spring, the
consoling monotony of the solid, tree-lined shore barely visible through the
mists. Thinking through that circuitry always made him vaguely admire George
Nicholson and, oddly, made him think he liked George even now, in spite of
everything.

The other competing thought was that part of Marjorie's character had al-   15
ways been to confess upsetting things that turned out, he believed, not to be
true: being a hooker for a summer up in Saugatuck; topless dancing while she
was an undergraduate; heroin experimentation; taking part in armed robberies

with her high-school boyfriend in Goshen, Indiana, where she was from. When she told these far-fetched stories she would grow distracted and shake her head, as though they were true. And now, while he didn't particularly think any of these stories was a bit truer, he did realize that he didn't really know his wife at all; and that in fact the entire conception of knowing another person—of trust, of closeness, of marriage itself—while not exactly a lie since it existed *someplace* if only as an idea (in his parents' life, at least marginally) was still completely out-of-date, defunct, was something typifying another era, now unfortunately gone. Meeting a girl, falling in love, marrying her, moving to Connecticut, buying a fucking house, starting a life with her and thinking you really knew anything about her—the last part was a complete fiction, which made all the rest a joke. Marjorie might as well have *been* a hooker or held up 7-Elevens and shot people, for all he really knew about her. And what was more, if he'd said any of this to her, sitting next to him thinking he would never know what, she either would not have understood a word of it or simply would've said, "Well, okay, that's fine." When people talked about the bottom line, Steven Reeves thought, they weren't talking about money, they were talking about what *this* meant, *this* kind of fatal ignorance. Money—losing it, gaining it, spending it, hoarding it— all that was only an emblem, though a good one, of what was happening here right now.

At this moment a pair of car lights rounded a curve somewhere out ahead of where the two of them sat in their station wagon. The lights found both their white faces staring forward in silence. The lights also found a raccoon just crossing the road from the reservoir shore, headed for the woods that were beside them. The car was going faster than might've been evident. The raccoon paused to peer up into the approaching beams, then continued on into the safe, opposite lane. But only then did it look up and notice Steven and Marjorie's car stopped on the verge of the road, silent in the murky evening. And because of that notice it must've decided that where it had been was much better than where it was going, and so turned to scamper back across Quaker Bridge Road toward the cool waters of the reservoir, which was what caused the car—actually it was a beat-up Ford pickup—to rumble over it, pitching and spinning it off to the side and then motionlessness near the opposite shoulder. "Yaaaa-haaaa-yipeeee!" a man's shrill voice shouted from inside the dark cab of the pickup, followed by another man's laughter.

And then it became very silent again. The raccoon lay on the road twenty yards in front of the Reeveses' car. It didn't struggle. It was merely there.

"Gross," Marjorie said.

Steven said nothing, though he felt less at a loss for words now. His eyes, indeed, felt relieved to fix on the still corpse of the raccoon.

"Do we do something?" Marjorie said. She had leaned forward a few inches as if to study the raccoon through the windshield. Light was dying away behind the slender young beech trees to the west of them.

"No," Steven said. These were his first words—except for the words he took no responsibility for—since Marjorie had said what she'd importantly said and their car was still moving toward dinner.

It was then that he hit her. He hit her before he knew he'd hit her, but not before he knew he wanted to. He hit her with the back of his open hand without even looking at her, hit her straight in the front of her face, straight in the nose.

And hard. In a way, it was more a gesture than a blow, though it was, he understood, a blow. He felt the soft tip of her nose, and then the knuckly cartilage against the hard bones of the backs of his fingers. He had never hit a woman before, and he had never even thought of hitting Marjorie, always imagining he *couldn't* hit her when he'd read newspaper accounts of such things happening in the sad lives of others. He'd hit other people, been hit by other people, plenty of times—tough Maine boys on the ice rinks. Girls were out, though. His father always made that clear. His mother, too.

"Oh, my goodness" was all that Marjorie said when she received the blow. She put her hand over her nose immediately, but then sat silently in the car while neither of them said anything. His heart was not beating hard. The back of his hand hurt a little. This was all new ground. Steven had a small rosy birthmark just where his left sideburn ended and his shaved face began. It resembled the shape of the state of West Virginia. He thought he could feel this birthmark now. His skin tingled there.

And the truth was he felt even more relieved, and didn't feel at all sorry for Marjorie, sitting there stoically, making a little tent of her hand to cover her nose and staring ahead as if nothing had happened. He thought she would cry, certainly. She was a girl who cried—when she was unhappy, when he said something insensitive, when she was approaching her period. Crying was natural. Clearly, though, it was a new experience for her to be hit. And so it called upon something new, and if not new then some strength, resilience, self-mastery normally reserved for other experiences.

"I can't go to the Nicholsons' now," Marjorie said almost patiently. She removed her hand and viewed her palm as if her palm had her nose in it. Of course it was blood she was thinking about. He heard her breathe in through what sounded like a congested nose, then the breath was completed out through her mouth. She was not crying yet. And for that moment he felt not even sure he *had* smacked her—if it hadn't just been a thought he'd entertained, a gesture somehow uncommissioned.

What he wanted to do, however, was skip to the most important things now, not get mired down in wrong, extraneous details. Because he didn't give a shit about George Nicholson or the particulars of what they'd done in some shitty motel. Marjorie would never leave him for George Nicholson or anyone like George Nicholson, and George Nicholson and men like him—high rollers with Hinckleys—didn't throw it all away for unimportant little women like Marjorie. He thought of her nose, red, swollen, smeared with sticky blood dripping onto her green dress. He didn't suppose it could be broken. Noses held up. And, of course, there was a phone in the car. He could simply make a call to the party. He pictured the Nicholsons' great rambling white-shingled house brightly lit beyond the curving drive, the original elms exorbitantly preserved, the footlights, the low-lit clay court where they'd all played, the heated pool, the Henry Moore out on the darkened lawn where you just stumbled onto it. He imagined saying to someone—not George Nicholson—that Marjorie was ill, had thrown up on the side of the road.

The *right* details, though. The right details to ascertain from her were: *Are you sorry?* (he'd forgotten Marjorie had already said she was sorry) and *What does this mean for the future?* These were the details that mattered.

Surprisingly, the raccoon that had been cartwheeled by the pickup and then lain motionless, a blob in the near-darkness, had come back to life and was now trying to drag itself and its useless hinder parts off of Quaker Bridge Road and onto the grassy verge and into the underbrush that bordered the reservoir.

"Oh, for God's sake," Marjorie said, and put her hand over her damaged nose again. She could see the raccoon's struggle and turned her head away.

"Aren't you even sorry?" Steven said.

"Yes," Marjorie said, her nose still covered as if she wasn't thinking about the fact that she was covering it. Probably, he thought, the pain had gone away some. It hadn't been so bad. "I mean no," she said.

He wanted to hit her again then—this time in the ear—but he didn't. He wasn't sure why not. No one would ever know. "Well, which is it?" he said, and felt for the first time completely furious. The thing that made him furious—all his life, the very maddest—was to be put into a situation in which everything he did was wrong, when right was no longer an option. Now felt like one of those situations. "Which is it?" he said again angrily. "Really." He should just take her to the Nicholsons', he thought, swollen nose, bloody lips, all stoppered up, and let her deal with it. Or let her sit out in the car, or else start walking the 11.6 miles home. Maybe George could come out and drive her in his Rover. These were only thoughts, of course. "Which is it?" he said for the third time. He was stuck on these words, on this bit of barren curiosity.

"I was sorry when I told you," Marjorie said, very composed. She lowered her hand from her nose to her lap. One of the little green bows that had been in her hair was now resting on her bare shoulder. "Though not very sorry," she said. "Only sorry because I had to tell you. And now that I've told you and you've hit me in my face and probably broken my nose, I'm not sorry about anything—except that. Though I'm sorry about being married to you, which I'll remedy as soon as I can." She was still not crying. "So *now*, will you as a gesture of whatever good there is in you, get out and go over and do something to help that poor injured creature that those motherfucking rednecks maimed with their motherfucking pickup truck and then because they're pieces of shit and low forms of degraded humanity, laughed about? Can you do that, Steven? Is that in your range?" She sniffed back hard through her nose, then expelled a short, deep and defeated moan. Her voice seemed more nasal, more mid-western even, now that her nose was congested.

"I'm sorry I hit you," Steven Reeves said, and opened the car door onto the silent road.

"I know," Marjorie said in an emotionless voice. "And you'll be sorrier."

When he had walked down the empty macadam road in his tan suit to where the raccoon had been struck then bounced over onto the road's edge, there was nothing now there. Only a small circle of dark blood he could just make out on the nubbly road surface and that might've been an oil smudge. No raccoon. The raccoon with its last reserves of savage, unthinking will had found the strength to pull itself off into the bushes to die. Steven peered down into the dark, stalky confinement of scrubs and bramble that separated the road from the reservoir. It was very still there. He thought he heard a rustling in the low brush where a creature might be, getting itself settled into the soft grass and damp earth to go to sleep forever. Someplace out on the lake he heard a young girl's voice, very distinctly laughing. Then a car door closed farther away. Then another sort of door, a screen door, slapped shut. And then a man's voice saying "Oh no, oh-ho-ho-ho-ho, no." A small white light came on farther back in the trees beyond the reservoir, where he hadn't imagined there was a house. He wondered about how long it would be before his angry feelings stopped mattering to him. He considered briefly why Marjorie would admit this to him now. It seemed so odd.

Then he heard his own car start. The muffled-metal diesel racket of the Mercedes. The headlights came smartly on and disclosed him. Music was instantly loud inside. He turned just in time to see Marjorie's pretty face illuminated, as his own had been, by the salmon dashboard light. He saw the tips of her fingers atop the arc of the steering wheel, heard the surge of the engine. In the woods he noticed a strange glow coming through the trees, something yellow, something out of the low wet earth, a mist, a vapor, something that might be magical. The air smelled sweet now. The peepers stopped peeping. And then that was all.

Starting Point for Further Research: Richard Ford

- **Interview:** Jennifer Levasseur. "Invitation to the Story: An Interview with Richard Ford." *Kenyon Review* 23:3–4 (Summer–Fall 2001): 123–43.

CHARACTER

The novelist and short story master Henry James pointed to the tight link between plot and character when he wrote, "What is character but the determination of an incident? What is incident but the illustration of character?" James forces us to note that the terms are both really abstractions, since one would barely exist without the other. Characters are developed through plot; and part of why plot exists is to depict character.

Some stories, like "The Story of an Hour" and "Under the Radar," seem at first highly **plot-driven**: they recount a startling or stunning or powerful action, often with an unexpected twist at the end. In such a story, the characters do not seem nearly as important as the actions themselves, the plot. Often there is an absence of rich **characterization**—that is, description of character through gesture, actions, dialogue—and few subtleties about motivation or feeling. Everyone has read romance or action-adventure books in which the characters seem stock (as if taken off the shelf) or cardboard, the dialogue stiff, the narration wooden, but in which the action moves the story along. (When the stock characters come from standardized portrayals of particular ethnic, professional, social, or personality types, they are often called **stereotypes**—because they create oversimplified, often prejudicial, pictures of those characters and groups.) Such action-driven books—some call them page-turners or **formula fiction**, since they follow a pretty common design—seem perfect reading for a trip, but they usually do not repay rereading, unless they are exceptionally well written.

Other stories are not so obviously about exterior action but interior feeling. James Joyce's "Araby" (later in this chapter, p. 34) makes a dramatic story out of a young boy's desire simply to get to a sleepy provincial circus. People seeing the events or listening to a plain description of them would not think much happened, but Joyce's narrator is transformed by the experience. In such a story the outward actions of the characters seem unimportant or trivial, while their inward actions are all-powerful. The drama comes only because Joyce has created a character who is someone we recognize and care about. On the other hand, Tim O'Brien's "Stockings," a brief short story from his Vietnam book *The Things They Carried* (1990), presents us with a simple character who seems to represent all Americans.

TIM O'BRIEN   (B. 1946)

Tim O'Brien was born and raised in rural Minnesota and graduated from Macalester College in St. Paul. After graduation he was drafted into the Army, served honorably in Vietnam, where he earned a Purple Heart, and continued to be firmly against that war. He turned his Vietnam experience into the powerful, highly successful story collection The Things They Carried *(1990), which includes "Stockings." O'Brien's work includes* Northern Lights *(1975),* Going after Cacciato *(1978), and his war memoir* If I Die in a Combat Zone, Box Me Up and Ship Me Home *(1973). O'Brien lives in Austin, Texas.*

Stockings   (1990)

Henry Dobbins was a good man, and a superb soldier, but sophistication was not his strong suit. The ironies went beyond him. In many ways he was like America itself, big and strong, full of good intentions, a roll of fat jiggling at his belly, slow of foot but always plodding along, always there when you needed him, a believer in the virtues of simplicity and directness and hard labor. Like his country, too, Dobbins was drawn toward sentimentality.

Even now, twenty years later, I can see him wrapping his girlfriend's pantyhose around his neck before heading out on ambush.

It was his one eccentricity. The pantyhose, he said, had the properties of a good-luck charm. He liked putting his nose into the nylon and breathing in the scent of his girlfriend's body; he liked the memories this inspired; he sometimes slept with the stockings up against his face, the way an infant sleeps with a flannel blanket, secure and peaceful. More than anything, though, the stockings were a talisman for him. They kept him safe. They gave access to a spiritual world, where things were soft and intimate, a place where he might someday take his girlfriend to live. Like many of us in Vietnam, Dobbins felt the pull of superstition, and he believed firmly and absolutely in the protective power of the stockings. They were like body armor, he thought. Whenever we saddled up for a late-night ambush, putting on our helmets and flak jackets, Henry Dobbins would make a ritual out of arranging the nylons around his neck, carefully tying a knot, draping the two leg sections over his left shoulder. There were some jokes, of course, but we came to appreciate the mystery of it all. Dobbins was invulnerable. Never wounded, never a scratch. In August, he tripped a Bouncing Betty, which failed to detonate. And a week later he got caught in the open during a fierce little firefight, no cover at all, but he just slipped the pantyhose over his nose and breathed deep and let the magic do its work.

It turned us into a platoon of believers. You don't dispute facts.

But then, near the end of October, his girlfriend dumped him. It was a hard   5
blow. Dobbins went quiet for a while, staring down at her letter, then after a time he took out the stockings and tied them around his neck as a comforter.

"No sweat," he said. "The magic doesn't go away."

Talking about the Text

1. How do you regard the comparison of Dobbins's character with America? Favorable? Unfavorable? Wildly inaccurate? On target? What general characteristics of the comparison seem to be most apt?
2. Do you or does anyone you know carry any kind of odd "talisman" comparable to the pantyhose Dobbins carries? How does that connect to what you think of that person's character?

Writing about the Text

1. List Dobbins's character traits, using what the narrator tells us directly in the first paragraph as well as what you can glean from the second and third paragraphs.
2. Describe in a paragraph or two some person or character, real or fictional, who also can be seen as standing for something, as Dobbins does for America.

Linking the Text to Other Texts

1. "Talismanic" objects are common in films and stories. Compare one you know of from your experience to the one in "Stockings."
2. Compare Dobbins's naiveté in "Stockings" with the narrator's naiveté in "Araby" (p. 34). How does the naiveté help make them endearing characters?

Starting Points for Further Research: Tim O'Brien

- **Critical Essay:** Alex Vernon. "Salvation, Storytelling, and Pilgrimage in Tim O'Brien's *The Things They Carried.*" *Mosaic: A Journal for the Interdisciplinary Study of Literature* 36:4 (December 2003): 171–88.
- **Interview:** "Interview with Tim O'Brien." *Readers Read.* 2003. http://www.readersread.com/features/timobrien.htm.

Types of Characters

Characters come in many forms, from complex, finely drawn ones to more general "types," deliberately simplified, one-dimensional characters, like Richards in "The Story of an Hour," who are only sketched in and who seem to stand for something else, in his case for "the family friend." Good short stories do not always provide rich character descriptions; instead we see characters at a single moment in their lives, or made vivid by a single action. The more leisurely world of a 300-page novel provides opportunities for richer, more complex characterization than a ten- or twenty-page story that concentrates on a single event or action. Short story characters by necessity come distilled, sketched in.

For novels, critics have traditionally made a distinction between **round characters**, whose attributes we know well from the detailed descriptions the narrator provides, and **flat characters**, who seem to have only one attribute, or who are there for the sake of the plot. We meet round characters in many different situations and settings, and unlike flat characters, they develop over time. This distinction—first made by novelist E. M. Forster—is less important for short stories, where few characters get rich novelistic description or are visualized in many different situations. Instead, short stories rely more on **compression**, focusing on a single salient detail to reveal character, as with Dobbins and the pantyhose in "Stockings." In "The Story of an Hour" we recognize quickly that Mrs. Mallard is more developed than anyone else, and that she changes over time, first when she hears the news of her husband's death, and then when she finds out the truth. In fact, the story concentrates on those moments when, alone in her room, she moves quickly from grief to newfound joy at her freedom. In a very few pages we see her almost complete transformation, though we never learn what she looked like or her exact age or background. The other characters are all flat, existing only to further the plot. The story revolves entirely around the inner drama of Mrs. Mallard's thoughts and perceptions.

For Further Reading: Character

In the short story "Prue," Canadian writer Alice Munro uses a very ordinary situation and very little plot to depict the oddities of her main character. Munro is famous for her ability to suggest complexity of character with just a few deft strokes, an important component of the short story writer's art.

ALICE MUNRO   (B. 1931)

Born on an Ontario farm, Alice Munro attended the University of Western Ontario but had to leave when her scholarship money ran out. She married and moved to Vancouver, where she began writing stories and publishing them occasionally. Her first collection, Dance of the Happy Shades, *appeared in 1968, when it won the Governor General's Award. Munro is now Canada's most acclaimed contemporary short story writer. Her stories treat powerful themes of sexuality and feminism in lucid, elegant prose. Her story collections include* Something I've Been Meaning to Tell You *(1974),* The Beggar Maid *(1979),* The Progress of Love *(1986),* Friend of My Youth *(1990),* The Love of a Good Woman *(1998),* Hateship, Friendship, Courtship, Loveship, Marriage *(2001), and* Runaway *(2004). Munro also has written one novel,* Lives of Girls and Women *(1971).*

Prue   (1982)

Prue used to live with Gordon. This was after Gordon had left his wife and before he went back to her—a year and four months in all. Some time later, he and his wife were divorced. After that came a period of indecision, of living together off and on; then the wife went away to New Zealand, most likely for good.

Prue did not go back to Vancouver Island, where Gordon had met her when she was working as a dining-room hostess in a resort hotel. She got a job in Toronto, working in a plant shop. She had many friends in Toronto by that time, most of them Gordon's friends and his wife's friends. They liked Prue and were ready to feel sorry for her, but she laughed them out of it. She is very likable. She has what eastern Canadians call an English accent, though she was born in Canada—in Duncan, on Vancouver Island. This accent helps her to say the most cynical things in a winning and lighthearted way. She presents her life in anecdotes, and though it is the point of most of her anecdotes that hopes are dashed, dreams ridiculed, things never turn out as expected, everything is altered in a bizarre way and there is no explanation ever, people always feel cheered up after listening to her; they say of her that it is a relief to meet somebody who doesn't take herself too seriously, who is so unintense, and civilized, and never makes any real demands or complaints.

The only thing she complains about readily is her name. Prue is a schoolgirl, she says, and Prudence is an old virgin; the parents who gave her that name must have been too shortsighted even to take account of puberty. What if she had grown a great bosom, she says, or developed a sultry look? Or was the name itself a guarantee that she wouldn't? In her late forties now, slight and fair, attending to customers with a dutiful vivacity, giving pleasure to dinner guests, she might not be far from what those parents had in mind: bright and thoughtful, a cheerful spectator. It is hard to grant her maturity, maternity, real troubles.

Her grownup children, the products of an early Vancouver Island marriage she calls a cosmic disaster, come to see her, and instead of wanting money, like other people's children, they bring presents, try to do her accounts, arrange to have her house insulated. She is delighted with their presents, listens to their advice, and, like a flighty daughter, neglects to answer their letters.

Her children hope she is not staying on in Toronto because of Gordon.   5
Everybody hopes that. She would laugh at the idea. She gives parties and goes to parties: she goes out sometimes with other men. Her attitude toward sex is very comforting to those of her friends who get into terrible states of passion and jealousy, and feel cut loose from their moorings. She seems to regard sex as a wholesome, slightly silly indulgence, like dancing and nice dinners—something that shouldn't interfere with people's being kind and cheerful to each other.

Now that his wife is gone for good. Gordon comes to see Prue occasionally, and sometimes asks her out for dinner. They may not go to a restaurant; they may go to his house. Gordon is a good cook. When Prue or his wife lived with him he couldn't cook at all, but as soon as he put his mind to it he became—he says truthfully—better than either of them.

Recently he and Prue were having dinner at his house. He had made Chicken Kiev, and crème brûlée for dessert. Like most new, serious cooks, he talked about food.

Gordon is rich, by Prue's—and most people's—standards. He is a neurologist. His house is new, built on a hillside north of the city, where there used to be picturesque, unprofitable farms. Now there are one-of-a-kind, architect-designed, very expensive houses on half-acre lots. Prue, describing Gordon's house, will say, "Do you know there are four bathrooms? So that if four people want to have baths at the same time there's no problem. It seems a bit much, but it's very nice, really, and you'd never have to go through the hall."

Gordon's house has a raised dining area—a sort of platform, surrounded by a conversation pit, a music pit, and a bank of heavy greenery under sloping glass. You can't see the entrance area from the dining area, but there are no intervening walls, so that from one area you can hear something of what is going on in the other.

During dinner the doorbell rang. Gordon excused himself and went down   10
the steps. Prue heard a female voice. The person it belonged to was still outside, so she could not hear the words. She heard Gordon's voice, pitched low, cautioning. The door didn't close—it seemed the person had not been invited in—but the voices went on, muted and angry. Suddenly there was a cry from Gordon, and he appeared halfway up the steps, waving his arms.

"The crème brûlée," he said. "Could you?" He ran back down as Prue got up and went into the kitchen to save the dessert. When she returned he was climbing the stairs more slowly, looking both agitated and tired.

"A friend," he said gloomily. "Was it all right?"

Prue realized he was speaking of the crème brûlée, and she said yes, it was perfect, she had got it just in time. He thanked her but did not cheer up. It seemed it was not the dessert he was troubled over but whatever had happened at the door. To take his mind off it, Prue started asking him professional questions about the plants.

"I don't know a thing about them," he said. "You know that."

"I thought you might have picked it up. Like the cooking."   15

"She takes care of them."

"Mrs. Carr?" said Prue, naming his housekeeper.

"Who did you think?"

Prue blushed. She hated to be thought suspicious.

"The problem is that I think I would like to marry you," said Gordon, with   20
no noticeable lightening of his spirits. Gordon is a large man, with heavy features. He likes to wear thick clothing, bulky sweaters. His blue eyes are often bloodshot, and their expression indicates that there is a helpless, baffled soul squirming around inside this doughty fortress.

"What a problem," said Prue lightly, though she knew Gordon well enough to know that it was.

The doorbell rang again, rang twice, three times, before Gordon could get to it. This time there was a crash, as of something flung and landing hard. The door slammed and Gordon was immediately back in view. He staggered on the steps and held his hand to his head, meanwhile making a gesture with the other hand to signify that nothing serious had happened, Prue was to sit down.

"Bloody overnight bag," he said. "She threw it at me."

"Did it hit you?"

"Glancing."   25

"It made a hard sound for an overnight bag. Were there rocks in it?"

"Probably cans. Her deodorant and so forth."

"Oh."

Prue watched him pour himself a drink. "I'd like some coffee, if I might," she said. She went to the kitchen to put the water on, and Gordon followed her.

"I think I'm in love with this person," he said.   30

"Who is she?"

"You don't know her. She's quite young."

"Oh."

"But I do think I want to marry you, in a few years' time."

"After you get over being in love?"

"Yes."

"Well. I guess nobody knows what can happen in a few years' time."

When Prue tells about this, she says, "I think he was afraid I was going to laugh. He doesn't know why people laugh or throw their overnight bags at him, but he's noticed they do. He's such a proper person, really. The lovely dinner. Then she comes and throws her overnight bag. And it's quite reasonable to think of marrying me in a few years' time, when he gets over being in love. I think he first thought of telling me to sort of put my mind at rest."

She doesn't mention that the next morning she picked up one of Gordon's cufflinks from his dresser. The cufflinks are made of amber and he bought them in Russia, on the holiday he and wife took when they got back together again. They look like squares of candy, golden, translucent, and this one warms quickly in her hand. She drops it into the pocket of her jacket. Taking one is not a real theft. It could be a reminder, an intimate prank, a piece of nonsense.

She is alone in Gordon's house; he has gone off early, as he always does. The housekeeper does not come till nine. Prue doesn't have to be at the shop until ten; she could make herself breakfast, stay and have coffee with the housekeeper, who is her friend from olden times. But once she has the cufflink in her pocket she doesn't linger. The house seems too bleak a place to spend an extra moment in. It was Prue, actually, who helped choose the building lot. But she's not responsible for approving the plans—the wife was back by that time.

When she gets home she puts the cufflink in an old tobacco tin. The children bought this tobacco tin in a junk shop years ago, and gave it to her for a present. She used to smoke, in those days, and the children were worried about her, so they gave her this tin full of toffees, jelly beans, and gumdrops, with a note saying, "Please get fat instead." That was for her birthday. Now the tin has in it several things besides the cufflink—all small things, not of great value but not worthless, either. A little enameled dish, a sterling-silver spoon for salt, a crystal fish. These are not sentimental keepsakes. She never looks at them, and often forgets what she has there. They are not booty, they don't have ritualistic significance. She does not take something every time she goes to Gordon's house, or every time she stays over, or to mark what she might call memorable visits. She doesn't do it in a daze and she doesn't seem to be under a compulsion. She just takes something, every now and then, and puts it away in the dark of the old tobacco tin, and more or less forgets about it.

Starting Point for Further Research: Alice Munro

- **Critical Essay:** Robert McGill. "Where Do You Think You Are?': Alice Munro's Open Houses." *Mosaic: A Journal for the Interdisciplinary Study of Literature* 35:3 (December 2002): 103–19.

SETTING

The **setting**, the time and place where the story happens, can have a powerful influence on how we understand it. We have already seen that some stories supply practically no setting: "The Hare and the Tortoise" has none, for instance. "Stockings" is set in Vietnam, but that is all we know; we are told nothing about the jungle, the crowded cities, or the famously beautiful landscape. Another story in this book, Anjana Appachana's "Her Mother" (p. 491), simply describes a mother at her table in India writing to her daughter who has moved to America. We are given no description at all of the mother's house, no details to help us "place" her. The single, overriding fact of a mother in India and a daughter in America provides all the setting Appachana thinks we need. Such minimal settings nonetheless carry their own message: the events are being played out in a timeless, practically nameless place: "the world" of "The Hare and the Tortoise," a country at war in "Stockings," and India, far from America, in "Her Mother."

But more often, short story writers provide us with vivid, memorable settings. The gritty South Side Chicago streets of Cyrus Colter's "Mary's Convert" (p. 40) or the poor Dublin neighborhood of James Joyce's "Araby," below, speak volumes: the characters operate in grim, oppressive settings they struggle against, captured by the hope of a religion or the dreams of a circus. Ultimately, in these stories the settings win out, and the characters end up dominated by them, as with Richard Wright's "The Man Who Lived Underground" (p. 582), where the setting literally shapes the story's outcome and defines the possibilities. When the characters are poor, usually it's a good bet that the setting will help explain their situation as well as limit their possibilities for change. What seem like literal settings—a table in India, a Chicago slum, a run-down Dublin carnival—carry huge symbolic values to every reader: the distance between mother and daughter, the grind of poverty, the illusions conveyed by a circus with the glittering name "Araby." We all recognize the suggestive power of even the most realistically rendered setting.

In "Araby," James Joyce depicts the grim world of provincial Dublin, creating characters who yearn for escape but who are dragged down by an oppression and poverty that are both physical and spiritual. Although the story's title, "Araby," suggests the exotic lands of Arabia, sun drenched, and adventure filled, the reality of the setting is quite different.

JAMES JOYCE (1882–1941)

1922 portrait of James Joyce by Man Ray.

Born in Dublin, the oldest of ten children, James Joyce attended Catholic schools and then University College, Dublin. Ireland plays a powerful role in all his fiction, though he was unappreciated at home and chose to live a life of exile in Trieste, Paris, and Zurich. His short story collection, Dubliners *(1914), which contains "Araby," portrays a provincial city in moral as well as physical decline. His first novel,* A Portrait of the Artist as a Young Man *(1916), is a semi-autobiographical account of its young hero, Stephen Dedalus. Joyce's masterpiece is* Ulysses *(1922), a long book with a narrative based on Homer's Odyssey; it is full of humor, with a small cast of unforgettable characters and a tragic sense of Ireland's decay. Joyce's last work,* Finnegans Wake *(1939), carries his prose experiments too far for many readers, but it is regarded by others as the culmination of his style.*

Araby (WRITTEN C. 1904–1905; PUBLISHED 1914)

North Richmond Street, being blind, was a quiet street except at the hour when the Christian Brothers' School set the boys free. An uninhabited house of two stories stood at the blind end, detached from its neighbors in a square ground. The other houses of the street, conscious of decent lives within them, gazed at one another with brown imperturbable faces.

The former tenant of our house, a priest, had died in the back drawing-room. Air, musty from having long been enclosed, hung in all the rooms, and the waste room behind the kitchen was littered with old useless papers. Among these I found a few papercovered books, the pages of which were curled and damp: *The Abbot*, by Walter Scott, *The Devout Communicant* and *The Memoirs of Vidocq*. I liked the last best because its leaves were yellow. The wild garden behind the house contained a central apple-tree and a few straggling bushes under one of which I found the late tenant's rusty bicycle-pump. He had been a very charitable priest; in his will he had left all his money to institutions and the furniture of his house to his sister.

When the short days of winter came dusk fell before we had well eaten our dinners. When we met in the street the houses had grown sombre. The space of sky above us was the colour of everchanging violet and towards it the lamps of the street lifted their feeble lanterns. The cold air stung us and we played till our bodies glowed. Our shouts echoed in the silent street. The career of our play brought us through the dark muddy lanes behind the houses where we ran the gauntlet of the rough tribes from the cottages, to the back doors of the dark dripping gardens where odours arose from the ashpits, to the dark odorous stables where a coachman smoothed and combed the horse or shook music from the buckled harness. When we returned to the street light from the kitchen windows had filled the areas. If my uncle was seen turning the corner we hid in the shadow until we had seen him safely housed. Or if Mangan's sister came out on the doorstep to call her brother in to his tea we watched her from our shadow peer up and down the street. We waited to see whether she would remain or go in and, if she remained, we left our shadow and walked up to Mangan's steps resignedly. She was waiting for us, her figure defined by the light from the half-opened door. Her brother always teased her before he obeyed and I stood by the railings looking at her. Her dress swung as she moved her body and the soft rope of her hair tossed from side to side.

Every morning I lay on the floor in the front parlour watching her door. The blind was pulled down to within an inch of the sash so that I could not be seen. When she came out on the doorstep my heart leaped. I ran to the hall, seized my books and followed her. I kept her brown figure always in my eye and, when we came near the point at which our ways diverged, I quickened my pace and passed her. This happened morning after morning. I had never spoken to her, except for a few casual words, and yet her name was like a summons to all my foolish blood.

Her image accompanied me even in places the most hostile to romance. On Saturday evenings when my aunt went marketing I had to go to carry some of the parcels. We walked through the flaring streets, jostled by drunken men and bargaining women, amid the curses of labourers, the shrill litanies of shop-boys who stood on guard by the barrels of pigs' cheeks, the nasal chanting of street-singers, who sang a *come-all-you* about O'Donovan Rossa, or a ballad about the

5

troubles in our native land. These noises converged in a single sensation of life for me: I imagined that I bore my chalice safely through a throng of foes. Her name sprang to my lips at moments in strange prayers and praises which I myself did not understand. My eyes were often full of tears (I could not tell why) and at times a flood from my heart seemed to pour itself out into my bosom. I thought little of the future. I did not know whether I would ever speak to her or not or, if I spoke to her, how I could tell her of my confused adoration. But my body was like a harp and her words and gestures were like fingers running upon the wires.

One evening I went into the back drawing-room in which the priest had died. It was a dark rainy evening and there was no sound in the house. Through one of the broken panes I heard the rain impinge upon the earth, the fine incessant needles of water playing in the sodden beds. Some distant lamp or lighted window gleamed below me. I was thankful that I could see so little. All my senses seemed to desire to veil themselves and, feeling that I was about to slip from them, I pressed the palms of my hands together until they trembled, murmuring: O love! O love! many times.

At last she spoke to me. When she addressed the first words to me I was so confused that I did not know what to answer. She asked me was I going to Araby.

I forget whether I answered yes or no. It would be a splendid bazaar, she said; she would love to go.

—And why can't you? I asked.

While she spoke she turned a silver bracelet round and round her wrist. She   10
could not go, she said, because there would be a retreat that week in her convent. Her brother and two other boys were fighting for their caps and I was alone at the railings. She held one of the spikes, bowing her head towards me. The light from the lamp opposite our door caught the white curve of her neck, lit up her hair that rested there and, falling, lit up the hand upon the railing. It fell over one side of her dress and caught the white border of a petticoat, just visible as she stood at ease.

—It's well for you, she said.

—If I go, I said, I will bring you something.

What innumerable follies laid waste my waking and sleeping thoughts after that evening! I wished to annihilate the tedious intervening days. I chafed against the work of school. At night in my bedroom and by day in the classroom her image came between me and the page I strove to read. The syllables of the word *Araby* were called to me through the silence in which my soul luxuriated and cast an Eastern enchantment over me. I asked for leave to go to the bazaar on Saturday night. My aunt was surprised and hoped it was not some Freemason[1] affair. I answered a few questions in class, I watched my master's face pass from amiability to sternness; he hoped I was not beginning to idle. I could not call my wandering thoughts together. I had hardly any patience with the serious work of life which, now that it stood between me and my desire, seemed to me child's play, ugly monotonous child's play.

On Saturday morning I reminded my uncle that I wished to go to the bazaar in the evening. He was fussing at the hallstand, looking for the hatbrush, and answered me curtly: 15

—Yes, boy, I know.

---

[1]Catholics did not approve of Masons, who were Protestant.

As he was in the hall I could not go into the front parlour and lie at the window. I left the house in bad humour and walked slowly towards the school. The air was pitilessly raw and already my heart misgave me.

When I came home to dinner my uncle had not yet been home. Still it was early. I sat staring at the clock for some time and, when its ticking began to irritate me, I left the room. I mounted the staircase and gained the upper part of the house. The high cold empty gloomy rooms liberated me and I went from room to room singing. From the front window I saw my companions playing below in the street. Their cries reached me weakened and indistinct and, leaning my forehead against the cool glass, I looked over at the dark house where she lived. I may have stood there for an hour, seeing nothing but the brown clad figure cast by my imagination, touched discreetly by the lamplight at the curved neck, at the hand upon the railings and at the border below the dress.

When I came downstairs again I found Mrs. Mercer sitting at the fire. She was an old garrulous woman, a pawnbroker's widow, who collected used stamps for some pious purpose. I had to endure the gossip of the teatable. The meal was prolonged beyond an hour and still my uncle did not come. Mrs. Mercer stood up to go: she was sorry she couldn't wait any longer, but it was after eight o'clock and she did not like to be out late, as the night air was bad for her. When she had gone I began to walk up and down the room, clenching my fists. My aunt said:

—I'm afraid you may put off your bazaar for this night of Our Lord.

At nine o'clock I heard my uncle's latchkey in the halldoor. I heard him talking to himself and heard the hallstand rocking when it had received the weight of his overcoat. I could interpret these signs. When he was midway through his dinner I asked him to give me the money to go to the bazaar. He had forgotten.

—The people are in bed and after their first sleep now, he said.

I did not smile. My aunt said to him energetically:

—Can't you give him the money and let him go? You've kept him late enough as it is.

My uncle said he was very sorry he had forgotten. He said he believed in the old saying: *All work and no play makes Jack a dull boy.* He asked me where I was going and, when I had told him a second time he asked me did I know *The Arab's Farewell to His Steed.*[2] When I left the kitchen he was about to recite the opening lines of the piece to my aunt.

I held a florin tightly in my hand as I strode down Buckingham Street towards the station. The sight of the streets thronged with buyers and glaring with gas recalled to me the purpose of my journey. I took my seat in a third-class carriage of a deserted train. After an intolerable delay the train moved out of the station slowly. It crept onward among ruinous houses and over the twinkling river. At Westland Row Station a crowd of people pressed to the carriage doors; but the porters moved them back, saying that it was a special train for the bazaar. I remained alone in the bare carriage. In a few minutes the train drew up beside an improvised wooden platform. I passed out on to the road and saw by the

20

25

---

[2]Popular poem by Caroline Norton (1808–1877).

lighted dial of a clock that it was ten minutes to ten. In front of me was a large building which displayed the magical name.

I could not find any sixpenny entrance and, fearing that the bazaar would be closed, I passed in quickly through a turnstile, handing a shilling to a weary-looking man. I found myself in a big hall girdled at half its height by a gallery. Nearly all the stalls were closed and the greater part of the hall was in darkness. I recognised a silence like that which pervades a church after a service. I walked into the center of the bazaar timidly. A few people were gathered about the stalls which were still open. Before a curtain, over which the words *Café Chantant* were written in coloured lamps, two men were counting money on a salver. I listened to the fall of the coins.

Remembering with difficulty why I had come I went over to one of the stalls and examined porcelain vases and flowered tea-sets. At the door of the stall a young lady was talking and laughing with two young gentlemen. I remarked their English accents and listened vaguely to their conversation.

—O, I never said such a thing!

—O, but you did!

—O, but I didn't!

—Didn't she say that?

—Yes! I heard her.

—O, there's a . . . fib!

Observing me the young lady came over and asked me did I wish to buy anything. The tone of her voice was not encouraging; she seemed to have spoken to me out of a sense of duty. I looked humbly at the great jars that stood like eastern guards at either side of the dark entrance to the stall and murmured:

—No, thank you.

The young lady changed the position of one of the vases and went back to the two young men. They began to talk of the same subject. Once or twice the young lady glanced at me over her shoulder.

I lingered before her stall, though I knew my stay was useless, to make my interest in her wares seem the more real. Then I turned away slowly and walked down the middle of the bazaar. I allowed the two pennies to fall against the sixpence in my pocket. I heard a voice call from one end of the gallery that the light was out. The upper part of the hall was now completely dark.

Gazing up into the darkness I saw myself as a creature driven and derided by vanity; and my eyes burned with anguish and anger.

Talking about the Text

1. Explore the story's setting by listing the items present in the yard.
2. How does the way Joyce describes the weather connect to the overall feeling at the opening? In other words, explain how weather is part of the setting.

Writing about the Text

1. Describe a physical space, true or fictional, carefully selecting the details in order to provide an overall sense of the significance you want to give to it. (It does not have to be gloomy, as the yard in "Araby.")
2. Recount a time when the reality of a particular place failed to live up to your expectations, basing your account on the way Joyce shaped "Araby."

Linking the Text to Other Texts

1. Compare "Araby" with another story in which there is a gap between the narrator's hopes and the reality of the setting. Describe the elements that story and "Araby" share.

2. Compare the "workers" in "Araby" to the "workers" in Updike's "A & P" (p. 58). In what ways do these characters connect to their setting?

Starting Points for Further Research: James Joyce

- **Editions:** James Joyce. *Dubliners*. New York: Penguin, 1996.
  ———. *A Portrait of the Artist as a Young Man*. New York: Penguin, 1991.
  ———. *Ulysses*. Ed. Hans Walter Gabler. New York: Vintage, 1986.
- **Biography:** Richard Ellman. *James Joyce*. New York: Oxford University Press, 1984.
- **Critical Essay:** James Buzard. " 'Culture' and the Critics of *Dubliners*." *James Joyce Quarterly* 37 (1999–2000): 43–61.

L I T E R A R Y   L O C A L E

James Joyce and Davy Byrnes Pub. Censors delayed the publication of *Dubliners* for years, but now his native city loves to celebrate James Joyce. A bar he favored and wrote about—in passing in *Dubliners* and more extensively in *Ulysses*—is Davy Byrnes, 21 Duke Street, in Dublin, Ireland, which displays Joyce memorabilia. In conjunction with the annual Bloomsday activities on June 16th—in which the events of protagonist Leopold Bloom's day in *Ulysses* are reenacted by participants and his itinerary in the book is followed all across Dublin—the pub is the traditional stopping place to grab a gorgonzola sandwich and a glass of burgundy, just as Bloom did.

Symbolic Setting

The setting of a story can be *explicitly* symbolic. For instance, in "The Story of an Hour," Louise sits in her chair and watches the spring sunshine breaking through the clouds as she slowly realizes that with her husband dead she is free, with the rest of her life in front of her. The narrator tells us that Louise notices that "the trees were all aquiver with the new spring life." Surely we are entitled to regard the spring sunshine as symbolic, whether we note it at first reading or not. Similar symbolic settings will operate in other stories in this book. The dark New England forest of Nathaniel Hawthorne's "Young Goodman Brown" (p. 147) is imagined as filled with lurking Indians (or at least the threat of Indians, for we never see any) and evil apparitions. Is this the real New England, or simply Brown's mental landscape? Hawthorne's narrator refuses to tell us, allowing us to decide the question ourselves. Yet in the compressed world of a short story, when the narrator devotes precious space and time to describing the setting, there's usually something to be gained by examining it closely. The achingly hot rural Spanish train station in Hemingway's "Hills Like White Elephants" (p. 537) suggests something of the oppression the two characters feel, just as the woman's suggestion that the hills look like white elephants connects to her ability to go beyond the facts of the situation she finds herself in, as her male companion cannot. In a story where almost everything is unsaid, the woman's leap of imagination about the setting (highlighted by making it the title) concentrates our attention.

For Further Reading: Setting

Set against the background of the grim streets of the South Side of Chicago that he knew well, where intense dramas of life and death take place every day, Cyrus Colter's "Mary's Convert" presents an intriguing tale of deception, dominated at first by the setting.

 L I T E R A R Y   L O C A L E

Colter's Chicago: The South Side and the El. The South Side of Chicago— long known for its grittiness, its working-class communities of mostly immigrants and blacks, its energy, its poverty, and the ever-present rumblings of the Chicago El (the city's public elevated train system)—has served as the setting and inspiration

The Chicago El.

(continued)

not only for Cyrus Colter but for numerous other authors spanning several generations, including Nelson Algren, Richard Wright, Gwendolyn Brooks (see Chapter
15, "A Poet in Depth: Gwendolyn Brooks"), and in more recent years Stuart Dybek (see Chapters 2 and 9 for two of Dybek's short stories). Algren might have
taken his cues from the same Chicago depicted in Colter's "Mary's Convert" when
he wrote in his prose poem "Chicago: City on the Make": "By nights when the yellow salamanders of the El bend all one way and the cold rain runs with the red-lit
rain. / By the way the city's million wires are burdened only by lightest snow; /
When chairs are stacked and glasses are turned and arc-lamps all are dimmed. / By
days when the wind bangs alley gates ajar and the sun goes by on the wind. / By
nights when the moon is an only child above the measured thunder of the cars,
you may know Chicago's heart at last." The Green Line of Chicago's El of Colter's
story still stops at East 43rd St. and South Calumet, on the South Side. The location is north of the University of Chicago and south of U.S. Cellular Field (formerly known as Comiskey Park), where the White Sox play.

CYRUS COLTER (1910–2002)

*Born in Noblesville, Indiana, Cyrus Colter spent his life in the Mid-
west. He was a lawyer who only began writing after he discovered
Russian literature as an adult, and he only published his first story
when he was sixty. His short story collection* The Beach Umbrella
*(1970) was warmly greeted, and in following years Colter published
many stories and poems as well as six novels, including* The Rivers of
Eros *(1972),* The Hippodrome *(1973),* A Chocolate Soldier
(1988), and City of Light *(1993).*

Mary's Convert (1965)

Forty-third Street, near the "el," the street of rib joints and taverns, was more
cluttered and overrun than usual. It was the heat. It lay on the sidewalk like an
electric blanket and scores of restless people were in motion. Driven from their
baking kitchenettes, they looked uprooted and a little dazed, as some stood at
the curb and moped, or turned in at a corner door for beer.

Jerome stood wiry tall and casual at the newsstand, inspecting the headlines
and the cover girls; he looked young even for a teen-ager, and wore skin-tight,
hep cat pants.

"Whutaaya want, boy?—a comic book?" the dirty man selling newspapers
said.

Jerome made no reply, but watched as an old Cadillac with a roasting radiator crept by, and two clowning loafers shouted obscenities across the street at
each other. Then he resumed with the headlines.

"These here papers are for *sale*," the newsman insisted, joking. "This ain't no   5
library."

Jerome paused and gave him an unruffled look. Finally he said, "Okay,
gim'me a comic book."

The newsman's black horny hand reached up for a book. Jerome's shirt was open at the throat but despite the heat, the long sleeves were buttoned at the wrists. He extracted a tightly folded dollar bill from his pants watch pocket.

"Ten," the newsman said, taking the dollar bill and handing over the comic book. He gave back ninety cents change, and Jerome checked the two quarters and four dimes in his palm before sticking them in his watch pocket. Then he hesitated, his young, brown face expressionless, and viewed the newsman. "Seen the Red Lion 'round here this afternoon?" he asked.

The grimy newsman stiffened. He stood staring at Jerome. "Whut'd you say?" he scowled.

"Seen the Red Lion 'round?" Jerome repeated.   10

"You git outa my face," the newsman whispered. "—you little bastard, you. You ain't sixteen!"

"What's it to you?" Jerome's face was all flat nose, so spreading flat that there were only slits for nostrils. He watched the newsman with a level gaze. "You know Tommy," he said, " . . . you take care o' him all right."

"I ain't even talkin' to you." The newsman turned his sweaty back. "Go on, *beat it!*"

Jerome studied him. "Okay . . . ole *Red Lion*," he said. Then he sauntered off, leaving the newsman glowering.

Along 43rd Street, the few people still left in the hot, mangy, brick and   15
stone kitchenette buildings were hanging out of their windows in hope of a breath of air. They were mostly frowzy women, of all shapes and colors, who would often yell down at their children or passing friends on the sidewalk where the pigeons were liberal with droppings and floss. Jerome was in no hurry as he walked. The hell with the Lion . . . who was he trying to kid; not him. He'd wait and see Tommy that evening; no problem. Tommy'd go to the Lion for him; Tommy was great people; swell, big-hearted—had given him his first fix. That was last spring, almost five months now. It seemed longer. They'd had many a one together since then. But Tommy always said any guy with sense could kick the habit, whenever he wanted to—and that a guy with sense always knew when he'd better *start* kicking too. Tommy was smart; never got puff-headed about anything—more like a brother, a big brother. And religious too—real religious; belonged to the Church of God in Christ.

Jerome opened the comic book as he walked and, casually turning the pages, scanned the cartoons. He hadn't meant to buy it—had let the Red Lion rush him, and still hadn't done any business with him; only got chased away. He approached the corner of 43rd and Calumet. Then he saw her. She was a young, brown-skinned woman—and wore flowing white robes. She was passing out leaflets and darted from one passer-by to the next, gesticulating, exhorting, thrusting her literature at them. Her head was draped to the shoulders in the same heavy, white fabric of her robes and despite the 95-degree heat no part of her body was visible except occasionally her feet, in high-heeled shoes, and her hands and face. But what Jerome could see of her face attracted him. There were gaudy rhinestone rings on her fingers and when she turned to face him he could see huge golden earrings dangling back up under her white head covering.

She jumped at him, shooting out a leaflet. "Young man, have you talked with Jesus today?" She blocked his path.

He said nothing and tried to step around her.

"Young man! Have you talked with Him?—just once today?" She pushed the leaflet at his chest.

Jerome was cowed. "No'm," he said.   20

"Then read this! Read it." She shook the leaflet at him.

Slow anger gathered in his face. "I don't want it, lady." He side-stepped toward the curb.

Suddenly she snatched the comic book from his hand and, breathing in his face, dropped it to the sidewalk.

His first impulse was to swing at her. But he stood motionless.

Then someone behind him gripped his arm. As he spun around, a squinty-   25
eyed black man, his face deeply pitted, grinned and pointed at the woman. "Don't pay her no mind," he sniggered. "That's Sanctified Mary." He turned to her. "Whut's th' matter, Mary? You off the stuff again? Kicked it, eh?—fuh a week or two—an' took up Jesus." He laughed.

Mary was sullen, silent.

"She's savin' souls *now*," the man said to Jerome, "but jus' ask her t'pull up that Kluxer sheet an' show you her arm. Go on—ask her."

Jerome looked at him, and then at Mary, but said nothing.

Suddenly the man leapt forward and seized her by the wrist, and yanked her to him.

She went raving wild. "You son of a bitch, you!" she screamed, fighting and   30
clawing him. "Take you filthy hands offa me, Jug Smith!" Her leaflets scattered to the sidewalk.

The man struggled and tugged her around in front of Jerome and with his free hand slid her robe sleeve up her arm to the shoulder. "Look!" he breathed. "Look here! Whut's Jesus gotta say 'bout *that*?" Near the elbow on the inside of her arm were a dozen purple-dotted needle scars. "Y'see?" Jug panted. "She's a mainliner. Y'*see*? Now you git t'hell outa here," he grinned at her, "an' leave this kid alone." He turned her loose.

She was incoherent. "*I'll kill you!*" she finally shrieked, lunging at him. Still grinning, he grabbed both her arms and held her off.

Someone yelled from across the street. "You-all better cut out all that 'who struck John' over there, Jug! See that squad car?—up in fronta the drug store."

Jug looked up toward the drug store and laughed. But he turned Mary loose again and trotted across the street.

She was ready to cry. Jerome stood by, helpless. Soon he stooped down and   35
picked up a few of the scattered leaflets, glancing at one. There was much fine print, but the caption in bold type read: KEEP LOOKING UP—JESUS NEVER FAILS. He offered her the leaflets, which she finally took grudgingly, still whispering curses to herself at Jug Smith.

"Don't worry 'bout that guy," Jerome said. "He ain't nothing but a hoodlum."

She still fought tears. "He made me forget m'self—and say all those bad words!" she whimpered, "and I been tryin' so hard . . . to do what Jesus wants. So hard."

Jerome began inching away. The heat from the pavement was coming through the soles of his shoes and his shirt was sticky.

Mary came alive. "Young man!"—she shoved a wrinkled leaflet at him— "put this in your pocket an' read it when you get home! An' keep on reading it. HE never fails."

Jerome took the leaflet and stuffed it in his shirt pocket, and then continued 40
down the street, leaving his comic book lying on the sidewalk.

About an hour later he was home, climbing the creaking stairs of the apartment building where he lived with his uncle and aunt. He was bored. He'd kill some time till Tommy got off from work at 5:30 . . . but he couldn't get Sanctified Mary off his mind; imagine *her* a hop-head; some nut; a real screw-ball; not a bad looking chick, though; if she just didn't wear all that mad get-up—robes! Jug Smith had identified them with the Klan. Kluxer sheets he called them; she wasn't a day over twenty-three or four; how could she put on all that hot crap in August and go out in the boiling sun and pass out leaflets about Jesus? He didn't get it; it didn't make *any* kind of sense; he'd tell Tommy. Tommy was religious.

He took out his key and let himself in. The blinds were all the way down, and he stumbled against a chair as he groped for the light switch. No one was home and the place was suffocating, with the windows shut tight and the sun outside on the west wall. But he knew not to open a window—his Aunt Bertha would raise hell for him "acting like a fool and letting in all that street heat." He went into the kitchen, opened the refrigerator and took out a cold bottle of milk. He uncapped the bottle, upped it and swilled almost half before he slumped in a kitchen chair, still holding the bottle, and sat staring at the sooty vacant wall, thinking of old fine Mary wearing her sharp high heels under the robes! and all that fake jewelry on both hands! that didn't look very religious to *him*; maybe she'd just forget to take the rings off whenever she'd switch over from sinning; and she could sin a while too, he bet—once you got her in a groovey mood; and a mainliner!—she was all mixed up; needed help; Tommy should see her; *she* hadn't kicked it; it *wasn't* all that easy, probably; she sure looked sexy, though—even in the funky robes.

He got up and put the milk back in the refrigerator. He stretched and yawned. His face rippled like rubber around his pancake-flat nose—and his boredom deepened. Then he remembered the leaflet in his shirt pocket and took it out to examine it. Soon he was sprawled in the chair again, reading:

KEEP LOOKING UP—JESUS NEVER FAILS

Elder Griffin, the great preacher and spiritual leader, asks: Have you talked with Jesus today? If you have not, or without success, then come to the Temple at 4178 Calumet, and pray with me. Only a small silver offering is asked. Open 8 AM to 10 PM, daily and Sundays.

The Elder says: Come to me if you are troubled and almost beat down to the ground. Are you sick, unhappy, disgusted with life? Does bad luck seem to follow you wherever you go? Then come to the Temple. I am here to help you see the mysteries of God's work—His mercy, and your salvation. I can do these things only through His will. I am nothing—Jesus is all. But to receive His Comfort and blessings, you must get right with God.

May I ask you the most important question in your whole life? It is this: Are you prepared to meet God? Your joy or your sorrow for all eternity depends upon this one question. If you are not, then you must make a start now. You must prepare! The Word of God tells us that because we are sinners we are condemned to die. "For the wages of sin is death." Romans 6:23. "Sin bringeth forth death." James 1:15. What does it mean to be a sinner condemned to die? It means separation from God, the Father, for all eternity. As you read this, won't you hear the voice of Jesus as He beckons you to come? "Ho, everyone that thirsteth, come ye to the waters." Isa. 55:1. "Incline your ear and come unto Me. Hear, and your soul shall live." Isa. 55:3.

Jerome read to the end and sat deep in thought. Finally he gave the leaflet a   45
methodical fold and put it back in his shirt pocket. Soon he got up and wandered into the living room. That stuff sounded like Aunt Bertha; she was nutty
on religion too, but she was older. It was okay for older people to be so religious if
they wanted to, but Mary . . . what could she see in an old bastard like Griffin? . . . *Elder* Griffin! . . . Ah, but maybe he wasn't so old; maybe he was a young
stud; hip to the tip—with a line for all the chicks; he'd love to see the Elder
once; a real weird deal, this was; he'd talk to Tommy about it. Finally he strolled
out the front door of the apartment and down into the hot street again. Maybe if
he went back down on 43rd, he'd run into Mary again.

When he reached 43rd and Calumet, Mary was nowhere to be seen. He
stood in the doorway of a sweltering fish shack and listened to the juke box
pouring out the blues—"Just a dre-e-e-am ah had on mah mind!. . . ." Finally he went in and sat at the counter and bought a grape pop. Maybe Mary
was up on King Drive with her handbills by now, he thought, swigging the pop;
or else she'd gone on home—to get out of those steamy robes; and take a bath;
she'd probably had enough of Jesus and Elder Griffin for one day—in all that
heat; she was just climbing in the tub now, maybe—buck naked. He wondered
if she knew the Red Lion—when she had been sinning, that is; all the main-
liners at one time or another knew the Lion; couldn't she get mad easy!—
flipped her lid on the street there when Jug got after her . . . and made her
backslide; Aunt Bertha always said there was nothing in the world worse than
a backslider—because they never had any religion in the first place; but she
didn't know Mary; that was okay too; she'd hate Mary; Aunt Bertha was always
talking about how she didn't want anything to do with any "low-down people"—whiskey-heads, and bad women, and all that; and hop-heads! Lord!—
she'd skin him alive if she knew about him and Tommy and all the fixes they'd
had together; maybe he ought to put Tommy down—and kick the habit; he
could kick it if he wanted to; maybe Tommy couldn't though, no matter what
he said; Mary hadn't. He sat at the counter with the sweating bottle of pop in
his hand, wishing he knew Mary better, wishing he knew where to find her;
she probably wouldn't have any time for somebody sixteen years old, though.
But before very long he finished the pop, got up, and sauntered out of the fish
shack into the street again.

It was quarter to five when he stood in the vestibule of a run-down apartment building on 48th Street bending forward to scan the stacks of penciled
names over the mail boxes. He had just come from the Temple, a large bare room
with a few folding chairs over a pool hall, where a woman, also in white robes,
had given him Mary's ("Sister Mary Bivens's") address. Looking now at the
names over one of the mail boxes, he saw that Mary lived, apparently with many
relatives, on the third floor. There was no doorbell to ring, so he went up. When
he reached the third floor, right side, he knocked. Inside he could hear noisy
children. Soon the door was opened by a little black girl, with a tooth out in
front. She appraised him.

"Miss Mary home?" he asked. He was shy.

The child viewed him with misgiving, and called back into the apartment.
"Mama! A man wants to see Aunt Mary!" Now three more children came galloping to the door.

Finally a woman wearing worn-out bedroom slippers appeared. She was 50 sweating. "My sister's 'sleep," she said. "Whatayou want?"

"Oh, I just wanted to see her." Jerome was offhand. "I was talkin' with her today—down on 43rd Street—and just thought I'd drop by. I can see her some other time."

"Are you from Elder Griffin's?" Her curtness softened some.

"I just came over from the Temple—yes'm." Jerome was quick.

"Are you one of Mary's converts?"

". . . Yes'm. . . ." 55

The woman studied him. ". . . Okay," she finally said, "come on in. I'll see if she'll come out." She stepped aside to let him in. "She's awful tired," she said, shuffling from the room.

Jerome stood in the middle of the bare floor. The children had lost interest in him now and were romping again. A pair of large oval portraits under glass hung on the wall over the sofa. They were apparently of grandparents, and were enlarged and touched-up in a blurry pastel-tint; the old man had a grey kinky beard, and wore a shirt fastened at the neck with a brass collar button but no collar or tie; the woman looked like a New Orleans creole, with her hair severely parted in the middle and her dress padded and built-up at the shoulders. But nothing in the room reminded him of Mary. Wouldn't she be surprised to see *him!*—she'd remember him all right. But she might be mad at him for seeing her disgraced right there on the street in front of him.

Mary's sister came back in the room. "Come on—in here," she summoned. He followed her into Mary's humid bedroom. Mary sat barefooted on the side of the bed in a dressing gown. She did look tired. On a chair in front of her was a tiny, whirring electric fan. As they entered, she quickly pulled the sheet around her and let it drape down to hide her feet. She still wore the rhinestone rings on her fingers.

"Well. . . ." She gave him a weary smile.

"Hello, Miss Mary." His voice was weak and bashful. 60

"Uh-huh, I knew it." She spoke with conviction. "You been thinking about what I told you—I can see it. You been talkin' to Jesus, like I told you." She smiled. "Ain't that right?"

"Yes'm." Jerome grinned and looked at the floor.

"Let me talk to him, Dillie." She was abrupt with her sister who stood in the doorway. Dillie left the room with a long face.

"What's your name, son?" Mary said.

"Jerome." 65

"Jerome what?"

"Jerome Williams."

"Uh-huh, and why'd you come here, Jerome?"

He hesitated—stumped. Then he thought of the leaflet. He fumbled in his shirt pocket, pulled it out, and stood holding it, saying nothing.

"My sister said you just come over from the Temple," Mary said. Then she 70 saw the leaflet—"What's that you got there?"

"It's what you was passing out today," Jerome said.

"Well, bless your heart! Ain't that nice. Do you understand what Elder Griffin was gettin' at?" She pulled up the bed sheet to swing her legs around onto the bed, as Jerome coolly glimpsed her bare knees before she could cover them. His quiet breath came faster. "That's why you came," she said, "you don't understand it all, do you?" She pointed at the leaflet in his hand. "Sit down there," she nodded toward a straight-back chair at the side of the dresser.

Reluctantly he backed away from the bed and sat down. The window was up and the sharp cries of playing children reached up from the sidewalks below.

"Jerome . . . y'know what?"

"No'm."   75

"I want you to go out tomorrow—with me—and pass out literature."

He looked at her. " . . . okay," he finally said. "You been getting the message all right . . . or you wouldn't be here. I told you—Jesus never fails."

Jerome shifted his feet.

"Now, what is there about it you don't seem to understand?" Unconsciously she wiggled her toes under the peak of the sheet.

He was too distracted to answer.   80

"Here, gim'me that," she said, and stretched from the bed toward him, took the leaflet, and then lay back again. She began to read: "What does it mean to be a sinner, condemned to die? It means separation from God, the Father, for all eternity." She stopped and looked at him. "Jerome, that's terrible . . . but it's true. D'you see the Elder's message there?"

Jerome hesitated. "I think so."

She took another passage. "The Word of God tells us that because we are sinners we are condemned to die. For the wages of sin is death. Romans 6:23. Sin bringeth forth death. James 1:15." She raised herself up now and stared out the window into space. " . . . Ah, we all understand *that*," she mused aloud.

Her dressing gown had fallen away from one shoulder, revealing an untidy brassiere strap. He sensed she hadn't bathed yet. But her face looked clean, and free of make-up. He recognized the break in the line of one eyebrow as scar tissue, put there by men's fists. She held the leaflet in her lap, still gazing off in space. Suddenly he noticed that the left sleeve of her dressing gown had worked up, exposing her forearm, and again he saw the needle scars.

She quickly caught him staring. "What's th' matter with you, Jerome? What   85
you looking at?"

His eyes swept up to her face.

"You were lookin' at my *arms!*" she suddenly cried, thrusting both arms out straight. The dark purple dots glared. Jerome, flustered, shook his head no. "Yes, you were too!" Her eyes blazed. "Is that what you come here for?—outa curiosity—to make fun of me?" She hurled back the bed sheet and sprang out of bed, the dressing gown parting and showing her thighs.

"Aw, no, Miss Mary!" He cringed in his chair as she stood over him. "I didn't come here for that, Miss Mary!"

"You damned little liar, you!" She began shaking him. "An' coming in her with my literature stuck in your pocket! Now, what'd you come here for? *Tell me!*" She gave him a savage shaking.

Jerome trying to fend off her hands could smell the sweaty perfume on her   90
body and underwear. "I come here to see *you*, Miss Mary."

She stepped back from him. "Don't lie to me, boy! Don't you lie, now!—Did Jug Smith tell you t'come here!—to pester me some more, to make it harder for me?—because I won't have nothing to do with dogs like him no more! *Did he?*"

"No'm! I *told* you!" Jerome pleaded.

She seemed not to hear him. "Nobody don't know, or care, about what I'm goin' through! Nobody!"

"You're wrong about me, Miss Mary."

"No, I ain't, either!" She stood over him again and glared.   95

Then slowly he began unbuttoning the left sleeve of his shirt. He turned the inside of his arm up and pushed the sleeve above the elbow. There sat a welter of purple-dotted needle scars.

" . . . Oh!" Mary gasped, and turned her back. She would not look at him and sank on the bed. "You poor boy, you! You poor boy!" Soon she was crying.

Jerome sat and watched her.

"I'm so sorry!" she moaned, crying in the bed sheet she held to her eyes. "I'm *so* sorry!"

Jerome was confident now. Tommy should see him, he thought. He got up   100
boldly and went to the bed and sat down beside her. The shouts of the children in the street below overcame the faint whirr of the little electric fan, as it fluttered the bed sheet against her leg. He put his arm around her waist. "I didn't mean to make you cry, Miss Mary."

"You came here for help," she looked at him through tearwet lashes, "and I acted awful . . . cussed you out. . . . Oh, forgive me, baby—you're only a baby."

He held her tighter now. Soon he pressed his lips hard against the side of her face. They sat silently. She seemed to relax.

She looked at him again. " . . . You're only a baby," she repeated, softly like a mother, and stroked his forehead, and then his flat nose, with her sensitive fingers. He could smell the musky-sweetish perfume and was racked with impatience. Suddenly he seized her and, moaning softly, crushed her mouth open with his lips.

Then she viewed him sadly. " . . . And you've started your bad ways so young," she said. "You shouldn't be like me—weak. I'm weak—*so* weak."

He felt the tornado inside him. But he kept his arm around her waist and waited.

Finally she gazed in his vacant face. "Go close the door, Jerome," she said,   105
" . . . and throw the lock."

He sprang at the door, eased it shut, and threw the lock. Hanging on the nail was her long white robe.

Starting Points for Further Research: Cyrus Colter

- **Editions:** Cyrus Colter. *The Amoralist and Other Tales.* St. Paul: Thunder's Mouth Press, 1988.
  ———. *The Beach Umbrella.* Iowa City: University of Iowa Press, 1970.
- **Critical Essay:** Leela Kapai. "Cyrus Colter." *Contemporary African American Novelists: A Bio-Bibliographical Critical Sourcebook.* Ed. Emmanuel Nelson. Westport: Greenwood, 1999. 102–107.
- **Interview:** Gilton Cross. "Fought for It and Paid Taxes Too: Four Interviews with Cyrus Colter." *Callaloo: A Journal of African-American and African Arts and Letters* (Fall 1991): 855–97.

CHAPTER

2

Stories

Point of View, Theme, Symbol, Tone, and Performance

The familiar trinity of plot, character, and setting provides a useful starting place to think about how stories work, but readers will gain a richer understanding when they think about three more elements: **point of view**, which is the perspective from which a story is told, the **theme**, which is the idea informing the story, and **symbolism**, which involves signs writers often employ to represent ideas or states of mind. Additionally, **tone**, the particular human voice behind the words, and **performance**, the way a story gets read or enacted aloud, can lead to an entirely new way of appreciating it.

POINT OF VIEW

The term **point of view** refers to perspective, position, or the vantage point from which a story is told. As readers, we need to ask not just what happens, which is a function of the plot, but who is telling us this story. Often the teller can matter as much as the tale itself, since there is always a relationship between the events in the story and the actual way they are presented. One simple way of figuring out the point of view is through noticing the type of narration, **first** or **third person**. These two categories are taken from traditional grammar: the first person is

"I," "me," "we," or "us"; the second person is "you"; the third person is "he," "she," "it," or "they." Is the narrator an "I" who is present as a character, or an invisible voice not present in the story?

First-Person Narration

When the **narrator**, the person who tells the story, is a character who witnesses or is involved in the action and uses "I," the narration is **first person**, as in Tim O'Brien's "Stockings" (p. 27) or in Edgar Allan Poe's "The Tell-Tale Heart" (p. 510). **Third-person** narrators never make an appearance in the story; there is no "I" present as a significant character.

First-person narration initially seems simple enough: the narrator tells the story about something that happened to him or her; the narrator is a witness, a character. We see everything in the story through the narrator's eyes, and so we rely on the narrator's perceptions. But naturally, there are complexities, which usually stem from how much the first-person narrator knows. For instance, in some first-person narratives (such as John Updike's "A & P," p. 58), we quickly realize that we do not share all the narrator's attitudes, beliefs, or understanding of what is going on. We know more than the narrator, and sense that we are in the presence of an **unreliable first-person narrator**, a character who tells the story but who demands interpretation as much as any other character in the story. Often first-person narrators are attractive but flawed characters, created to serve as our eyes and ears throughout the story, but as readers we can sometimes see more than they do.

Here is a famous example of an unreliable first-person narrator from the opening of a book everyone has heard of, *Gulliver's Travels*, by Jonathan Swift. Gulliver is introducing himself to his readers, and as you read, ask yourself what he thinks it is important for readers to know. What details does he concentrate on? What does he omit or gloss over?

> My father had a small estate in Nottinghamshire: I was the third of five sons. He sent me to Emanuel College in Cambridge, at fourteen years old, where I resided three years, and applied myself close to my studies: but the charge of maintaining me (although I had a very scanty allowance) being too great for a narrow fortune, I was bound apprentice to Mr. James Bates, an eminent surgeon in London, with whom I continued four years; and my father now and then sending me small sums of money, I laid them out in learning navigation, and other parts of the mathematics, useful to those who intend to travel, as I always believed it would be some time or other my fortune to do. When I left Mr. Bates, I went down to my father; where, by the assistance of him and my uncle John, and some other relations, I got forty pounds, and a promise of thirty pounds a year to maintain me at Leyden[1]: there I studied physic[2] two years and seven months, knowing it would be useful in long voyages.
>
> Soon after my return from Leyden, I was recommended by my good master Mr. Bates, to be surgeon to the *Swallow*, Captain Abraham Pannel commander;

---

[1] Dutch university famous for its medical school.
[2] Medicine.

with whom I continued three years and a half, making a voyage or two into the Levant,[3] and some other parts. When I came back, I resolved to settle in London, to which Mr. Bates, my master, encouraged me; and by him I was recommended to several patients. I took part of a small house in the Old Jewry; and being advised to alter my condition, I married Mrs.[4] Mary Burton, second daughter to Mr. Edmund Burton, hosier, in Newgate-street, with whom I received four hundred pounds for a portion.[5]

As a reader, what do you think this narrator might emphasize in the tale he tells? What might he overlook? That is part of the enjoyment of a book like *Gulliver's Travels*: the story in not just in the events that occur, but also in the narrator's "take" on them.

Third-Person Narration

Third-person narration—the most common type of all—has three separate variants, each defined by how much the narrator is able to tell the reader:

- A narrator who seems to know everything, including what every character is thinking, is called **omniscient** (Om ni′ scient: from the two Latin words *omni*, "universal," and *scient*, "knowing"). The narrator in "The Story of an Hour" (p. 16), who knows everything that Mrs. Mallard and all the other characters are thinking, is a good example of an omniscient narrator.
- A narrator who takes only a single character's perspective and does not claim to know the thoughts of other characters has a **limited point of view**. The narrator in "Mary's Convert" (p. 40) knows Jerome's thoughts, but not those of the other characters.
- A narrator who reports only on the outward action of the story and does not know what any characters are thinking is called an **objective** or **fly-on-the-wall narrator**. Alice Munro's "Prue" (p. 29) is an example of objective narration.

Subjective vs. Objective Narration

The effects of different points of view are significant. Stories that employ **subjective narration** are told strictly from the characters' internal thoughts and perspectives. Early twentieth-century writers such as James Joyce, Marcel Proust, and Virginia Woolf experimented with a highly subjective type of narration called **stream of consciousness**, with ideas and sensations coming into their characters' heads as they do in real life, seemingly unmediated by a narrator's shaping. As characters conceived ideas or made plans, these took the form of **interior monologue**, a kind of unspoken soliloquy, with the abrupt twists and turns characteristic of inner speech, and entirely lacking the carefully polished language we find in drama. Stream of consciousness narration was a clever, exciting illusion, of course, but it gave readers the feel of actually entering a charac-

[3]The eastern Mediterranean.
[4]"Mrs." was pronounced "mistress" and was used in reference to any woman, unmarried or married.
[5]Dowry.

ter's consciousness.

The opposite approach, **objective narration**, presents us with nothing but the outward actions, forcing us to infer a character's motivation entirely from behavior, just as in life. The objective approach has grown more and more common in contemporary fiction. While nineteenth- and early twentieth-century narrators described more of what their characters were experiencing and thinking, contemporary narrators tend to present matters dramatically, without insights into characters' minds, and sometimes without even a narrator who introduces characters by telling us about their age or appearance or background.

The story that follows, "Girl," was the first published piece of fiction by Caribbean-born Jamaica Kincaid; it first appeared in the *New Yorker*. This very brief story is presented mostly as a **dramatic monologue**, a long speech by one character, here with only a few words in response from another character. Kincaid chose simply to present the voice of a West Indian mother as she imperiously tells her young daughter how to behave.

JAMAICA KINCAID (B. 1949)

Born Elaine Potter Richardson in Antigua, Jamaica Kincaid immigrated to the United States as an au pair at seventeen. In 1976, with little formal training but an already developed distinctive writing style, she became a New Yorker *staff writer. Known at first for her stories of Caribbean life, Kincaid later began dealing with a wider range of personal themes. Her novels include* Lucy *(1990),* The Autobiography of My Mother *(1996), and* Mr. Potter *(2002). Kincaid has also written nonfiction, notably* A Small Place *(1988), about her home island of Antigua, and* My Brother *(1997), a powerful memoir of her brother's death from AIDS. She lives in Vermont, where in addition to writing she also tends a notable garden.*

Girl (1978)

Wash the white clothes on Monday and put them on the stone heap; wash the color clothes on Tuesday and put them on the clothesline to dry; don't walk barehead in the hot sun; cook pumpkin fritters in very hot sweet oil; soak your little cloths right after you take them off; when buying cotton to make yourself a nice blouse, be sure that it doesn't have gum on it, because that way it won't hold up well after a wash; soak salt fish overnight before you cook it; is it true that you sing benna[1] in Sunday school?; always eat your food in such a way that it won't turn someone else's stomach; on Sundays try to walk like a lady and not like the slut you are so bent on becoming; don't sing benna in Sunday school; you mustn't speak to wharf-rat boys, not even to give directions; don't eat fruits on the street—flies will follow you; *but I don't sing benna on Sundays at all and never in Sunday school*; this is how to sew on a button; this is how to make a button-hole for the button you have just sewed on; this is how to hem a dress when you see the hem coming down and so to prevent yourself from looking like the slut I know

---

[1]Calypso music.

you are so bent on becoming; this is how you iron your father's khaki shirt so that it doesn't have a crease; this is how you iron your father's khaki pants so that they don't have a crease; this is how you grow okra—far from the house, because okra tree harbors red ants; when you are growing dasheen, make sure it gets plenty of water or else it makes your throat itch when you are eating it; this is how you sweep a corner; this is how you sweep a whole house; this is how you sweep a yard; this is how you smile to someone you don't like too much; this is how you smile to someone you don't like at all; this is how you smile to someone you like completely; this is how you set a table for tea; this is how you set a table for dinner; this is how you set a table for dinner with an important guest; this is how you set a table for lunch; this is how you set a table for breakfast; this is how to behave in the presence of men who don't know you very well, and this way they won't recognize immediately the slut I have warned you against becoming; be sure to wash every day, even if it is with your own spit; don't squat down to play marbles—you are not a boy, you know; don't pick people's flowers—you might catch something; don't throw stones at blackbirds, because it might not be a blackbird at all; this is how to make a bread pudding; this is how to make doukona;[2] this is how to make pepper pot; this is how to make a good medicine for a cold; this is how to make a good medicine to throw away a child before it even becomes a child; this is how to catch a fish; this is how to throw back a fish you don't like, and that way something bad won't fall on you; this is how to bully a man; this is how a man bullies you; this is how to love a man, and if this doesn't work there are other ways, and if they don't work don't feel too bad about giving up; this is how to spit up in the air if you feel like it, and this is how to move quick so that it doesn't fall on you; this is how to make ends meet; always squeeze bread to make sure it's fresh; *but what if the baker won't let me feel the bread?*; you mean to say that after all you are really going to be the kind of woman who the baker won't let near the bread?

Talking about the Text

1. What is it like to read "Girl" for the first time? Describe the experience of reading a story without a narrator's voice to guide you.
2. Where is the conflict in "Girl"? Who is the protagonist, and who is the antagonist? What do the words in italics suggest is happening?

Writing about the Text

1. Create your own monologue, such as "Son" or "Daughter" or "Young Man" or "Young Lady." Or write the daughter's response to "Girl"; call it "Mother."
2. Rewrite part of "Girl," adding a narrator with your own directions about tone ("She said, bitterly . . ." or "In a rough tone, she growled . . .").

Linking the Text to Other Texts

1. Compare "Girl" with the advice Polonius gives to his son in *Hamlet*, Act 1, Scene 3, lines 63–88 (pp. 1469–1470). What kinds of connections do you see, both in tone and in content?

---

[2]Pudding.

2. Give some occasions (from your own experience or from a fictional character) when you have heard advice about behavior being delivered in such a manner. How do you think adults should "educate" young people about important matters?

Starting Points for Further Research: Jamaica Kincaid

- **Critical Essay:** Rhonda D. Frederick. "What If You're an 'Incredibly Unattractive, Fat, Pastrylike-Fleshed Man'? Teaching Jamaica Kincaid's *A Small Place*." *College Literature* 30:3 (Summer 2003): 1–18.
- **Interviews:** Moira Ferguson. "A Lot of Memory: An Interview with Jamaica Kincaid." *Kenyon Review* 16:1 (Winter 1994): 163–88.
  Pamela Buchanan Muirhead. "An Interview with Jamaica Kincaid." *Clockwatch Review: A Journal of the Arts* 9:1–2 (1994–1995): 39–48.

Point of View in "Girl"

Kincaid's demanding story is not "placed" for us. In fact, it does not even look like a story. It seems as if we get no plot, no setting, no narrator, nothing particular about point of view except that it is almost overheard, not told. Yet there is an incredible richness here; we do not feel the lack of anything. We almost have too much information, as when we confront a larger-than-life character on the stage. For instance, what can we say about the person who is speaking here? We can make a list of her beliefs: she is overwhelming; she takes a very traditional view of women's work and of male-female relationships; she thinks her daughter is up to no good, with her "sluttish" ways; she thinks she knows exactly how to live life; she believes that it is very important to regard the opinions of other people, including everyone from future husbands to bakers who will let you squeeze the bread.

The Narrator's Role

The teller of any story, the narrator, may be our only link to the story's events, but we need to understand that the narrator's role is always capable of interpretation. In some stories the narrator has a clear-cut, very obvious role, as when a first-person narrator plays a central part in the story's action. In other stories, a third-person narrator can appear to take a back seat and simply tell the tale, seeming to let the characters do the work. But that is not always the case, since what is revealed and what is withheld are always in the hands of the narrator. For instance, a famous scene in Hawthorne's "Young Goodman Brown" (p. 147) has Brown meeting an elderly man in the woods. The seemingly objective third-person narrator describes this man's "remarkable" looking staff, "which bore the likeness of a great black snake, so curiously wrought that it might almost be seen to twist and wriggle itself like a living serpent. This, of course, must have been an ocular deception, assisted by the uncertain light" (p. 149). We are mistaken if we take this description at face value. Our narrator has just presented us with a half-realistic, half-fantastic picture. What kind of person carries such a staff? Is it wriggling? "Almost"? Or is it truly, as the narrator concludes, "an ocular deception"? Hawthorne's narrator is playing an active role here, dramatizing a point about human consciousness as well as displaying his inability to account for such phenomena. The placid-seeming third-person narrator plays a very large part in this story, even though he is not a character. If we read "Young Goodman Brown" or any other story simply for the plot, for what happens, we are in danger of missing out on the interesting interplay between the events of the story and the narrator's recounting of them.

For Further Reading: Point of View

The stories of Canadian-born Margaret Atwood often involve manipulation of the narrator's role as well as perspectives that seem overt and very strongly felt. We are never in doubt about Atwood's general attitude in "Happy Endings," though she leaves us room to mull over the implications.

MARGARET ATWOOD   (B. 1939)

A Canadian, Margaret Atwood studied at the University of Toronto and at Harvard. Her first poem was published at age nineteen, and she has written essays, short stories, and novels, including The Edible Woman *(1969),* Surfacing *(1972),* The Handmaid's Tale *(1985), and* The Blind Assassin *(2000), which won the Booker Prize. Her most recent novel,* Oryx and Crake, *appeared in 2003.*

Happy Endings   (1983)

John and Mary meet.
What happens next?
If you want a happy ending, try A.

A

John and Mary fall in love and get married. They both have worthwhile and re- munerative jobs which they find stimulating and challenging. They buy a charming house. Real estate values go up. Eventually, when they can afford live- in help, they have two children, to whom they are devoted. The children turn out well. John and Mary have a stimulating and challenging sex life and worth- while friends. They go on fun vacations together. They retire. They both have hobbies which they find stimulating and challenging. Eventually they die. This is the end of the story.

B

Mary falls in love with John but John doesn't fall in love with Mary. He merely uses her body for selfish pleasure and ego gratification of a tepid kind. He comes to her apartment twice a week and she cooks him dinner, you'll notice that he doesn't even consider her worth the price of a dinner out, and after he's eaten the dinner he fucks her and after that he falls asleep, while she does the dishes so he won't think she's untidy, having all those dirty dishes lying around, and puts on fresh lipstick so she'll look good when he wakes up, but when he wakes up he doesn't even notice, he puts on his socks and his shorts and his pants and his shirt and his tie and his shoes, the reverse order from the one in which he took

5

them off. He doesn't take off Mary's clothes, she takes them off herself, she acts as if she's dying for it every time, not because she likes sex exactly, she doesn't, but she wants John to think she does because if they do it often enough surely he'll get used to her, he'll come to depend on her and they will get married, but John goes out the door with hardly so much as a good-night and three days later he turns up at six o'clock and they do the whole thing over again.

Mary gets run-down. Crying is bad for your face, everyone knows that and so does Mary but she can't stop. People at work notice. Her friends tell her John is a rat, a pig, a dog, he isn't good enough for her, but she can't believe it. Inside John, she thinks, is another John, who is much nicer. This other John will emerge like a butterfly from a cocoon, a Jack from a box, a pit from a prune, if the first John is only squeezed enough.

One evening John complains about the food. He has never complained about the food before. Mary is hurt.

Her friends tell her they've seen him in a restaurant with another woman, whose name is Madge. It's not even Madge that finally gets to Mary: it's the restaurant. John has never taken Mary to a restaurant. Mary collects all the sleeping pills and aspirins she can find, and takes them and a half a bottle of sherry. You can see what kind of a woman she is by the fact that it's not even whiskey. She leaves a note for John. She hopes he'll discover her and get her to the hospital in time and repent and then they can get married, but this fails to happen and she dies.

John marries Madge and everything continues as in A.

C

John, who is an older man, falls in love with Mary, and Mary, who is only   10
twenty-two, feels sorry for him because he's worried about his hair falling out. She sleeps with him even though she's not in love with him. She met him at work. She's in love with someone called James, who is twenty-two also and not yet ready to settle down.

John on the contrary settled down long ago: this is what is bothering him. John has a steady, respectable job and is getting ahead in his field, but Mary isn't impressed by him, she's impressed by James, who has a motorcycle and a fabulous record collection. But James is often away on his motorcycle, being free. Freedom isn't the same for girls, so in the meantime Mary spends Thursday evenings with John. Thursdays are the only days John can get away.

John is married to a woman called Madge and they have two children, a charming house which they bought just before the real estate values went up, and hobbies which they find stimulating and challenging, when they have the time. John tells Mary how important she is to him, but of course he can't leave his wife because a commitment is a commitment. He goes on about this more than is necessary and Mary finds it boring, but older men can keep it up longer so on the whole she has a fairly good time.

One day James breezes in on his motorcycle with some top-grade California hybrid and James and Mary get higher than you'd believe possible and they climb into bed. Everything becomes very underwater, but along comes John, who has a key to Mary's apartment. He finds them stoned and entwined. He's hardly in any position to be jealous, considering Madge, but nevertheless he's overcome with despair. Finally he's middle-aged, in two years he'll be bald as an egg and he can't stand it. He purchases a handgun, saying he needs it for target practice—this is the thin part of the plot, but it can be dealt with later—and shoots the two of them and himself.

Madge, after a suitable period of mourning, marries an understanding man called Fred and everything continues as in A, but under different names.

D

Fred and Madge have no problems. They get along exceptionally well and are   15 good at working out any little difficulties that may arise. But their charming house is by the seashore and one day a giant tidal wave approaches. Real estate values go down. The rest of the story is about what caused the tidal wave and how they escape from it. They do, though thousands drown, but Fred and Madge are virtuous and lucky. Finally on high ground they clasp each other, wet and dripping and grateful, and continue as in A.

E

Yes, but Fred has a bad heart. The rest of the story is about how kind and understanding they both are until Fred dies. Then Madge devotes herself to charity work until the end of A. If you like, it can be "Madge," "cancer," "guilty and confused," and "bird watching."

F

If you think this is all too bourgeois, make John a revolutionary and Mary a counterespionage agent and see how far that gets you. Remember, this is Canada. You'll still end up with A, though in between you may get a lustful brawling saga of passionate involvement, a chronicle of our times, sort of.

* * * *

You'll have to face it, the endings are the same however you slice it. Don't be deluded by any other endings, they're all fake, either deliberately fake, with malicious intent to deceive, or just motivated by excessive optimism if not by downright sentimentality.

The only authentic ending is the one provided here:

John and Mary die. John and Mary die. John and Mary die.   20

* * *

So much for endings. Beginnings are always more fun. True connoisseurs, however, are known to favor the stretch in between, since it's the hardest to do anything with.

That's about all that can be said for plots, which anyway are just one thing after another, a what and a what and a what.

Now try How and Why.

Starting Points for Further Research: Margaret Atwood

- **Article:** Brian Bethune. "Atwood Apocalyptic." *Maclean's*, April 28, 2003, 44–48.
- **Interview:** Earl G. Ingersoll, ed. *Margaret Atwood: Conversations.* Princeton, N.J.: Ontario Review Press, 1990.

THEME

What is it that writers dramatize? We call that idea or notion the **theme**, a loose term that relates to the central idea or issue that the writer contemplates or explores in the story. A theme is an abstraction we can point to, and a good story can have more than one. In "The Story of an Hour," what seems like a romance plot of freedom being delivered by a lucky accident turns into a shocking discovery that the husband still lives. What might we say are possible themes in Chopin's story? One theme is that women's "happy" marriages hide strong desires for freedom. Another theme might be that a woman cannot depend on chance to deliver her from the bonds of marriage. Still another theme might be that what friends and family interpret as happiness is in fact a deadness to the world.

Similarly, "The Hare and the Tortoise" has a host of simple themes we can readily see and understand: that boasters can be challenged; that initial speed matters less than steadiness; that overconfidence can lead to defeat. It is a tale about persistence being rewarded.

Likewise, we all know many of William Shakespeare's themes that have become part of our culture. For instance, everyone recognizes themes in *Romeo and Juliet*, even without having read the play: the passion of young love, and the fatal interference of opposing families. In *Macbeth* a theme is the overriding power of ambition; in *Hamlet* one theme is the necessity for revenge, even if it means one's own death. Those at least are the large, broad themes Shakespeare took on, and that the popular imagination instantly recognizes.

For writers like Kate Chopin and Shakespeare, theme is a way of holding everything together, to help give shape and meaning to the material. For readers, a theme sets up an expectation that familiar patterns will or will not be fulfilled. In "Stockings," for instance, what seems like a foolish talisman actually turns out to work, or at least something does, and Dobbins, however improbably, survives his time in Vietnam, protected only by the pantyhose of a young woman who dumped him. One theme in "Stockings" obviously connects to the crazy twists of fate that operate in wartime, and to the need for belief in something substantial, some reminder of home and love and passion, to keep one alive.

Different readers will discover different themes in the same story, and part of a good reading is coming to terms with what we regard as the story's theme. At the same time, we must be careful not to reduce a complex story's theme to a too easy lesson or moral. Writers may have strong convictions and powerful moral imaginations. But most writers want to do more than Aesop. They are first and foremost writers who tell stories, not moralists who set out to give their readers lessons. They rarely sit down and say "I want to write a story about the theme of _____."

"A & P," by John Updike, is told by a first-person narrator, perhaps a version of Updike himself, who in his youth lived north of Boston and might have worked at the kind of supermarket depicted here (though now A & P supermarkets, once very widespread, are found only in New York and New Jersey). Updike's story has powerful themes: how a young man asserts himself against the narrow rigidity of a large corporation's regulations; how attractive and unapproachable rich summer girls can be to a poor local boy; how a futile gesture that goes unnoticed is still worth making.

JOHN UPDIKE   (B. 1932)

 *Born in Pennsylvania, John Updike attended Harvard, where he was repeatedly turned down for admittance in poet Archibald MacLeish's creative writing classes. Upon graduation, Updike was hired as a staff writer at* The New Yorker, *where he published several memorable pieces, but after two years he left to write full-time. His most popular fiction deals with middle-class suburban life, with particular attention to aging males' frustrations with marriage.* Rabbit Run *(1960), the first of four "Rabbit" novels, established his reputation. In addition to his fiction, Updike has written extensively on art and religion and has been a prolific book reviewer.*

A & P   (1961)

In walks these three girls in nothing but bathing suits. I'm in the third checkout slot, with my back to the door, so I don't see them until they're over by the bread. The one that caught my eye first was the one in the plaid green two-piece. She was a chunky kid, with a good tan and a sweet broad soft-looking can with those two crescents of white just under it, where the sun never seems to hit, at the top of the backs of her legs. I stood there with my hand on a box of HiHo crackers trying to remember if I rang it up or not. I ring it up again and the customer starts giving me hell. She's one of these cash-register-watchers, a witch about fifty with rouge on her cheekbones and no eyebrows, and I know it made her day to trip me up. She'd been watching cash registers for fifty years and probably never seen a mistake before.

By the time I got her feathers smoothed and her goodies into a bag—she gives me a little snort in passing, if she'd been born at the right time they would have burned her over in Salem—by the time I get her on her way the girls had circled around the bread and were coming back, without a pushcart, back my way along the counters, in the aisle between the checkouts and the Special bins. They didn't even have shoes on. There was this chunky one, with the two-piece—it was bright green and the seams on the bra were still sharp and her belly was still pretty pale so I guessed she just got it (the suit)—there was this one, with one of those chubby berry-faces, the lips all bunched together under her nose, this one, and a tall one, with black hair that hadn't quite frizzed right, and one of these sunburns right across under the eyes, and a chin that was too long—you know, the kind of girl other girls think is very "striking" and "attractive" but never quite makes it, as they very well know, which is why they like her so much—and then the third one, that wasn't quite so tall. She was the queen. She kind of led them, the other two peeking around and making their shoulders round. She didn't look around, not this queen, she just walked straight on slowly, on these long white prima-donna legs. She came down a little hard on her heels, as if she didn't walk in her bare feet that much, putting down her heels and then letting the weight move along to her toes as if she was testing the floor with every step, putting a little deliberate extra action into it. You never know for sure how girls' minds work (do they really think it's a mind in there or just a little buzz like a bee in a glass jar?) but you got the idea she had talked the other two into coming in here with her, and now she was showing them how to do it, walk slow and hold yourself straight.

She had on a kind of dirty pink—beige maybe, I don't know—bathing suit with a little nubble all over it and, what got me, the straps were down. They were off her shoulders looped loose around the cool tops of her arms, and I guess as a result the suit had slipped on her, so all around the top of the cloth there was this shining rim. If it hadn't been there you wouldn't have known there could have been anything whiter than those shoulders. With the straps pushed off, there was nothing between the top of the suit and the top of her head except just *her*, this clean bare plane of the top of her chest down from the shoulder bones like a dented sheet of metal tilted in the light. I mean, it was more than pretty.

She had sort of oaky hair that the sun and salt had bleached, done up in a bun that was unravelling, and a kind of prim face. Walking into the A & P with your straps down, I suppose it's the only kind of face you *can* have. She held her head so high her neck, coming up out of those white shoulders, looked kind of stretched, but I didn't mind. The longer her neck was, the more of her there was.

She must have felt in the corner of her eye me and over my shoulder Stokesie in the second slot watching, but she didn't tip. Not this queen. She kept her eyes moving across the racks, and stopped, and turned so slow it made my stomach rub the inside of my apron, and buzzed to the other two, who kind of huddled against her for relief, and then they all three of them went up the cat and dog food-break- fast cereal-macaroni-rice-raisins-seasonings-spreads-spaghetti-soft drinks-crack- ers-and-cookies aisle. From the third slot I look straight up this aisle to the meat counter, and I watched them all the way. The fat one with the tan sort of fumbled with the cookies, but on second thought she put the package back. The sheep pushing their carts down the aisle—the girls were walking against the usual traffic (not that we have one-way signs or anything)—were pretty hilarious. You could see them, when Queenie's white shoulders dawned on them, kind of jerk, or hop, or hiccup, but their eyes snapped back to their own baskets and on they pushed. I bet you could set off dynamite in the A & P and the people would by and large keep reaching and checking oatmeal off their lists and muttering "Let me see, there was a third thing, began with A, asparagus, no, ah, yes, applesauce!" or whatever it is they do mutter. But there was no doubt, this jiggled them. A few house slaves in pin curlers even look around after pushing their carts past to make sure what they had seen was correct.

You know, it's one thing to have a girl in a bathing suit down on the beach, where what with the glare nobody can look at each other much anyway, and an- other thing in the cool of the A & P, under the fluorescent lights, against all those stacked packages, with her feet paddling along naked over our checker- board green-and-cream rubber-tile floor.

"Oh, Daddy," Stokesie said beside me. "I feel so faint."

"Darling," I said. "Hold me tight." Stokesie's married, with two babies chalked up on his fuselage already, but as far as I can tell that's the only differ- ence. He's twenty-two, and I was nineteen this April.

"Is it done?" he asks, the responsible married man finding his voice. I forgot to say he thinks he's going to be a manager some sunny day, maybe in 1990 when it's called the Great Alexandrov and Petrooshki Tea Company or something.

What he meant was, our town is five miles from a beach, with a big summer   10
colony out on the Point, but we're right in the middle of town, and the women
generally put on a shirt or shorts or something before they get out of the car into
the street. And anyway these are usually women with six children and varicose
veins mapping their legs and nobody, including them, could care less. As I say,
we're right in the middle of town, and if you stand at our front doors you can see
two banks and the Congregational church and the newspaper store and three
real estate offices and about twenty-seven old freeloaders tearing up Central
Street because the sewer broke again. It's not as if we're on the Cape; we're north
of Boston and there's people in this town haven't seen the ocean for twenty
years.

The girls had reached the meat counter and were asking McMahon something. He pointed, they pointed, and they shuffled out of sight behind a pyramid
of Diet Delight peaches. All that was left for us to see was old McMahon patting
his mouth and looking after them sizing up their joints. Poor kids, I began to feel
sorry for them, they couldn't help it.

Now here comes the sad part of the story, at least my family says it's sad, but
I don't think it's so sad myself. The store's pretty empty, it being Thursday afternoon, so there was nothing much to do except lean on the register and wait for
the girls to show up again. The whole store was like a pinball machine and I
didn't know which tunnel they'd come out of. After a while they come around
out of the far aisle, around the light bulbs, records at discount of the Caribbean
Six or Tony Martin Sings or some such gunk you wonder they waste the wax on,
six-packs of candy bars, and plastic toys done up in cellophane that fall apart
when a kid looks at them anyway. Around they come, Queenie still leading the
way, and holding a little gray jar in her hand. Slots Three through Seven are
unmanned and I could see her wondering between Stokes and me, but Stokesie
with his usual luck draws an old party in baggy gray pants who stumbles up with
four giant cans of pineapple juice (what do these bums *do* with all that pineapple juice? I've often asked myself) so the girls come to me. Queenie puts down
the jar and I take it into my fingers icy cold. Kingfish Fancy Herring Snacks in
Pure Sour Cream: 49¢. Now her hands are empty, not a ring or a bracelet, bare
as God made them, and I wonder where the money's coming from. Still with
the prim look she lifts a folded dollar bill out of the hollow at the center of her
nubbled pink top. The jar went heavy in my hand. Really, I thought that was so
cute.

Then everybody's luck begins to run out. Lengel comes in from haggling
with a truck full of cabbages on the lot and is about to scuttle into the door
marked manager behind which he hides all day when the girls touch his eye.
Lengel's pretty dreary, teaches Sunday school and the rest, but he doesn't miss
that much. He comes over and says, "Girls, this isn't the beach."

Queenie blushes, though maybe it's just a brush of sunburn I was noticing
for the first time, now that she was so close. "My mother asked me to pick up a
jar of herring snacks." Her voice kind of startled me, the way voices do when you
see the people first, coming out so flat and dumb yet kind of tony, too, the way it
ticked over "pick up" and "snacks." All of a sudden I slid right down her voice
into her living room. Her father and the other men were standing around in ice-
cream coats and bow ties and the women were in sandals picking up herring
snacks on toothpicks off a big glass plate and they were all holding drinks the

color of water with olives and sprigs of mint in them. When my parents have somebody over they get lemonade and if it's a real racy affair Schlitz in tall glasses with "They'll Do It Every Time" cartoons stencilled on.

"That's all right," Lengel said. "But this isn't the beach." His repeating this struck me as funny, as if it had just occurred to him, and he had been thinking all these years the A & P was a great big dune and he was the head lifeguard. He didn't like my smiling—as I say he doesn't miss much—but he concentrates on giving the girls that sad Sunday-school-superintendent stare.

Queenie's blush is no sunburn now, and the plump one in plaid, that I liked better from the back—a really sweet can—pipes up, "We weren't doing any shopping. We just came in for the one thing."

"That makes no difference," Lengel tells her, and I could see from the way his eyes went that he hadn't noticed she was wearing a two-piece before. "We want you decently dressed when you come in here."

"We are decent," Queenie says suddenly, her lower lip pushing, getting sore now that she remembers her place, a place from which the crowd that runs the A & P must look pretty crummy. Fancy Herring Snacks flashed in her very blue eyes.

"Girls, I don't want to argue with you. After this come in here with your shoulders covered. It's our policy." He turns his back. That's policy for you. Policy is what the kingpins want. What the others want is juvenile delinquency.

All this while, the customers had been showing up with their carts but, you know, sheep, seeing a scene, they had all bunched up on Stokesie, who shook open a paper bag as gently as peeling a peach, not wanting to miss a word. I could feel in the silence everybody getting nervous, most of all Lengel, who asks me, "Sammy, have you rung up this purchase?"

I thought and said "No" but it wasn't about that I was thinking. I go through the punches, 4, 9, GROC, TOT—it's more complicated than you think and after you do it often enough, it begins to make a little song, that you hear words to, in my case "Hello (*bing*) there, you (*gung*) hap-py *peepul* (*splat*)!"—the *splat* being the drawer flying out. I uncrease the bill, tenderly as you may imagine, it just having come from between the two smoothest scoops of vanilla I had ever known were there, and pass a half and a penny into her narrow pink palm and nestle the herrings in a bag and twist its neck and hand it over, all the time thinking.

The girls, and who'd blame them, are in a hurry to get out, so I say "I quit" to Lengel quick enough for them to hear, hoping they'll stop and watch me, their unsuspected hero. They keep right on going, into the electric eye; the door flies open and they flicker across the lot to their car, Queenie and Plaid and Big Tall Goony-Goony (not that as raw material she was so bad), leaving me with Lengel and a kink in his eyebrow.

"Did you say something, Sammy?"

"I said I quit."

"I thought you did."

"You didn't have to embarrass them."

"It was they who were embarrassing us."

I started to say something that came out "Fiddle-de-doo." It's a saying of my grandmother's, and I know she would have been pleased.

"I don't think you know what you're saying," Lengel said.

15

20

25

"I know you don't," I said. "But I do." I pull the bow at the back of my apron   30
and start shrugging it off my shoulders. A couple customers that had been heading for my slot begin to knock against each other, like scared pigs in a chute.

Lengel sighs and begins to look very patient and old and gray. He's been a
friend of my parents for years. "Sammy, you don't want to do this to your Mom
and Dad," he tells me. It's true, I don't. But it seems to me that once you begin a
gesture it's fatal not to go through with it. I fold the apron, "Sammy" stitched in
red on the pocket, and put it on the counter, and drop the bow tie on top of it.
The bow tie is theirs, if you've ever wondered. "You'll feel this for the rest of your
life," Lengel says, and I know that's true, too, but remembering how he made
that pretty girl blush makes me so scrunchy inside I punch the No Sale tab and
the machine whirs "pee-pul" and the drawer slats out. One advantage to this
scene taking place in summer, I can follow this up with a clean exit, there's no
fumbling around getting your coat and galoshes, I just saunter into the electric
eye in my white shirt that my mother ironed the night before, and the door
heaves itself open, and outside the sunshine is skating around on the asphalt.

I look around for my girls, but they're gone, of course. There wasn't anybody
but some young married screaming with her children about some candy they did-
n't get by the door of a powder-blue Falcon station wagon. Looking back in the
big windows, over the bags of peat moss and aluminum lawn furniture stacked on
the pavement, I could see Lengel in my place in the slot, checking the sheep
through. His face was dark gray and his back stiff, as if he'd just had an injection
of iron, and my stomach kind of fell as I felt how hard the world was going to be
to me hereafter.

Talking about the Text

1. Sammy's opening words, "In walks these three girls . . . ," are not quite grammatical. What is wrong with them? Would it have been better for Updike to have
   opened with a perfectly grammatical phrase? Is such an opening familiar to you
   from the way some people talk? How does this characterization foreshadow the
   story's major themes?
2. Sammy has a somewhat dim view of supermarket customers, at one point calling
   them "sheep" (paragraph 5). How does his attitude convey the story's theme?

Writing about the Text

1. Describe Sammy's attitude toward women. Then discuss how, even if we don't approve of his attitude, we can still find things about him to like. What are some?
2. Make a list of the terms Sammy uses to describe the three girls, and compare these
   terms to the ones he uses for older women.

Linking the Text to Other Texts

1. If you have ever worked in a retail setting, what specific resemblances are there between Sammy's outlook and your own?
2. Connect this "awakening" story to "Araby" (p. 34) which also ends with a revelation and a young person's new sense of understanding.

Starting Points for Further Research: John Updike

■ **Autobiography:** John Updike. *Self-consciousness: Memoirs.* New York: Knopf,
   1989.

- **Critical Essay:** "John Updike." *Eureka Studies in Teaching Short Fiction* 4:2 (Spring 2004): 6–70.
- **Interview:** James Plath. *Conversations with John Updike.* Jackson: University Press of Mississippi, 1994.

Theme in "A & P"

If theme is to be a useful tool for thinking about fiction, it needs to provide us with ways of generating helpful and interesting ideas about the stories. It also has to remain close enough to the stories to be an accurate reflection of what is in them and what other readers might see in them. And stories can link a number of themes together. Think of theme as a way into stories, not a final conclusion about them. Once you have noted a theme in a story, you are off to a good start, but you are closer to the beginning, not the end of your discussion. Here are three possible themes in "A & P":

- "A & P" dramatizes a *gesture*, one done at some personal cost. It is an occasion in which a young man with some disagreeable characteristics stands up for what he thinks is right.
- "A & P" concerns the value of empty gestures; a young man first thinks he will impress the three girls by sticking up for them, but they don't notice him. Ultimately, he acts out of self-respect.
- A working-class boy initially believes he can somehow bridge the distance between himself and the well-to-do "Queenie."

All these themes might be shown to be present in "A & P." In truth, such themes have a familiar ring to experienced readers of literature, where one person often faces a moment of truth and is called upon to do the right thing. All these themes are also generalizations about the story which need to be accurate as to facts and details, and which also need to be worth arguing or defending in a conversation or as the basis for a paper. For instance, one obvious theme in "A & P" has to do with the way supermarkets are dehumanizing places, with "slots," "sheep," and constricting rules. Is that the main theme of the story? No one would say so. Is it a theme running throughout the story? Yes, particularly if we associate it with Sammy's perspective, for he is the one who tells us everything.

Theme, Meaning, and Intention

Stories inevitably embody the ideas, perceptions, feelings, and worldview of their writers. And all authors write with a purpose: to change the world, because they love writing, because they write for a living, because they like being part of the literary life, to seek fame, to show readers what really matters. For many writers, their purpose is something as general as "to communicate," to make readers see things their way. At the same time, we should not confuse everything that happens in a story with the author's intentions. If stories embody ideas, those ideas are not necessarily easy to separate out of the stories themselves. First of all, as with drama, we must take the elementary precaution not to attribute a character's words and thoughts to the author. Shakespeare wrote the famous line from *Hamlet*: "Neither a borrower nor a lender be." Did he believe it? Remember that

Shakespeare put those words in the mouth of Polonius, a garrulous, foolish old man. The same is true for the evil Macbeth's agonized reflection on life: "It is a tale told by an idiot, full of sound and fury, signifying nothing." Shakespeare certainly wrote those words. Did he believe them? We will never prove it from the words in a play, though we can say that he had an amazing ability to imagine and depict other minds in brilliantly appropriate language. But Shakespeare's characters are not Shakespeare.

Similarly, we cannot equate what some of the characters say in "A & P" directly with John Updike, even though he had obvious intentions and points in mind when he wrote the story. Short story writers are full of ideas and beliefs, but like playwrights, they usually dramatize them through their characters. If they wanted to address these ideas and beliefs directly, they would be doing a different kind of writing, say an essay or philosophy or religion. As writer Flannery O'Connor memorably put it, "Some people have the notion that you can read the story and then climb out of it into the meaning, but for the fiction writer himself the whole story is the meaning." O'Connor does not suggest that stories don't have meanings, but she makes it clear that the meanings are not neat little messages to be abstracted or drawn from the stories.

For Further Reading: Theme

Anita Desai draws on powerful themes as she writes of her native India.

ANITA DESAI   (B. 1937)

Anita Desai was born in Mussoorie, a small mountain town north of Delhi in India. She started to write in English at seven, and at nine she published her first story. Desai's first novel, Cry, the Peacock, *appeared in 1963. She turned to Calcutta for the setting of her next novel,* Voices of the City *(1965). Desai's subject matter is the decline of Indian traditions in a changing world. She has lived in New Delhi, Calcutta, Bombay, and other Indian cities, and was for many years a professor of writing at MIT.*

Games at Twilight   (1978)

It was still too hot to play outdoors. They had had their tea, they had been washed and had their hair brushed, and after the long day of confinement in the house that was not cool but at least a protection from the sun, the children strained to get out. Their faces were red and bloated with the effort, but their mother would not open the door, everything was still curtained and shuttered in a way that stifled the children, made them feel that their lungs were stuffed with cotton wool and their noses with dust and if they didn't burst out into the light and see the sun and feel the air, they would choke.

'Please, ma, please,' they begged. 'We'll play in the veranda and porch—we won't go a step out of the porch.'

'You will, I know you will, and then—'

'No—we won't, we won't,' they wailed so horrendously that she actually let down the bolt of the front door so that they burst out like seeds from a crackling, over-ripe pod into the veranda, with such wild, maniacal yells that she retreated to her bath and the shower of talcum powder and the fresh sari that were to help her face the summer evening.

* * *

They faced the afternoon. It was too hot. Too bright. The white walls of the ve-   5
randa glared stridently in the sun. The bougainvillea hung about it, purple and magenta, in livid balloons. The garden outside was like a tray made of beaten brass, flattened out on the red gravel and the stony soil in all shades of metal—aluminium, tin, copper and brass. No life stirred at this arid time of day—the birds still drooped, like dead fruit, in the papery tents of the trees; some squirrels lay limp on the wet earth under the garden tap. The outdoor dog lay stretched as if dead on the veranda mat, his paws and ears and tail all reaching out like dying travellers in search of water. He rolled his eyes at the children—two white marbles rolling in the purple sockets, begging for sympathy—and attempted to lift his tail in a wag but could not. It only twitched and lay still.

Then, perhaps roused by the shrieks of the children, a band of parrots suddenly fell out of the eucalyptus tree, tumbled frantically in the still, sizzling air, then sorted themselves out into battle formation and streaked away across the white sky.

The children, too, felt released. They too began tumbling, shoving, pushing against each other, frantic to start. Start what? Start their business. The business of the children's day which is—play.

'Let's play hide-and-seek.'

'Who'll be It?'

'You be It.'

'Why should I? You be—'   10

'You're the eldest—'

'That doesn't mean—'

The shoves became harder. Some kicked out. The motherly Mira intervened. She pulled the boys roughly apart. There was a tearing sound of cloth but it was lost in the heavy panting and angry grumbling and no one paid attention to the small sleeve hanging loosely off a shoulder.

'Make a circle, make a circle!' she shouted, firmly pulling and pushing till a   15
kind of vague circle was formed. 'Now clap!' she roared and, clapping, they all chanted in melancholy unison: 'Dip, dip, dip—my blue ship—' and every now and then one or the other saw he was safe by the way his hands fell at the crucial moment—palm on palm, or back of hand on palm—and dropped out of the circle with a yell and a jump of relief and jubilation.

Raghu was It. He started to protest, to cry 'You cheated—Mira cheated—Anu cheated—' but it was too late, the others had all already streaked away. There was no one to hear when he called out, 'Only in the veranda—the porch—Ma said—Ma *said* to stay in the porch!' No one had stopped to listen, all he saw were their brown legs flashing through the dusty shrubs, scrambling up brick walls, leaping over compost heaps and hedges, and then the porch stood empty in the purple shade of the bougainvillea and the garden was as empty as before; even the limp squirrels had whisked away, leaving everything gleaming, brassy and bare.

Only small Manu suddenly reappeared, as if he had dropped out of an invisible cloud or from a bird's claws, and stood for a moment in the centre of the yellow lawn, chewing his finger and near to tears as he heard Raghu shouting, with his head pressed against the veranda wall, 'Eighty-three, eighty-five, eighty-nine, ninety . . .' and then made off in a panic, half of him wanting to fly north, the other half counselling south. Raghu turned just in time to see the flash of his white shorts and the uncertain skittering of his red sandals, and charged after him with such a blood-curdling yell that Manu stumbled over the hosepipe, fell into its rubber coils and lay there weeping, 'I won't be It—you have to find them all—all—All!'

'I know I have to, idiot,' Raghu said, superciliously kicking him with his toe. 'You're dead,' he said with satisfaction, licking the beads of perspiration off his upper lip, and then stalked off in search of worthier prey, whistling spiritedly so that the hiders should hear and tremble.

* * *

Ravi heard the whistling and picked his nose in a panic, trying to find comfort by burrowing the finger deep-deep into that soft tunnel. He felt himself too exposed, sitting on an upturned flower pot behind the garage. Where could he burrow? He could run around the garage if he heard Raghu come—around and around and around—but he hadn't much faith in his short legs when matched against Raghu's long, hefty, hairy footballer legs. Ravi had a frightening glimpse of them as Raghu combed the hedge of crotons and hibiscus, trampling delicate ferns underfoot as he did so. Ravi looked about him desperately, swallowing a small ball of snot in his fear.

The garage was locked with a great heavy lock to which the driver had the 20 key in his room, hanging from a nail on the wall under his work-shirt. Ravi had peeped in and seen him still sprawling on his string-cot in his vest and striped underpants, the hair on his chest and the hair in his nose shaking with the vibrations of his phlegm-obstructed snores. Ravi had wished he were tall enough, big enough to reach the key on the nail, but it was impossible, beyond his reach for years to come. He had sidled away and sat dejectedly on the flower pot. That at least was cut to his own size.

But next to the garage was another shed with a big green door. Also locked. No one even knew who had the key to the lock. That shed wasn't opened more than once a year when Ma turned out all the old broken bits of furniture and rolls of matting and leaking buckets, and the white ant hills were broken and swept away and Flit sprayed into the spider webs and rat holes so that the whole operation was like the looting of a poor, ruined and conquered city. The green leaves of the door sagged. They were nearly off their rusty hinges. The hinges were large and made a small gap between the door and the walls—only just large enough for rats, dogs and, possibly, Ravi to slip through.

Ravi had never cared to enter such a dark and depressing mortuary of defunct household goods seething with such unspeakable and alarming animal life but, as Raghu's whistling grew angrier and sharper and his crashing and storming in the hedge wilder, Ravi suddenly slipped off the flower pot and through the crack and was gone. He chuckled aloud with astonishment at his own temerity so that Raghu came out of the hedge, stood silent with his hands on his hips, listening, and finally shouted 'I heard you! I'm coming! *Got* you—' and came charging round the garage only to find the upturned flower pot, the yellow dust, the crawling of white ants in a mud-hill against the closed shed door—nothing. Snarling, he bent to pick up a stick and went off, whacking it against the garage and shed walls as if to beat out his prey.

* * *

Ravi shook, then shivered with delight, with self-congratulation. Also with fear. It was dark, spooky in the shed. It had a muffled smell, as of graves. Ravi had once got locked into the linen cupboard and sat there weeping for half an hour before he was rescued. But at least that had been a familiar place, and even smelt pleasantly of starch, laundry and, reassuringly, of his mother. But the shed smelt of rats, ant hills, dust and spider webs. Also of less definable, less recognizable horrors. And it was dark. Except for the white-hot cracks along the door, there was no light. The roof was very low. Although Ravi was small, he felt as if he could reach up and touch it with his finger tips. But he didn't stretch. He hunched himself into a ball so as not to bump into anything, touch or feel anything. What might there not be to touch him and feel him as he stood there, trying to see in the dark? Something cold, or slimy—like a snake. Snakes! He leapt up as Raghu whacked the wall with his stick—then, quickly realizing what it was, felt almost relieved to hear Raghu, hear his stick. It made him feel protected.

But Raghu soon moved away. There wasn't a sound once his footsteps had gone around the garage and disappeared. Ravi stood frozen inside the shed. Then he shivered all over. Something had tickled the back of his neck. It took him a while to pick up the courage to lift his hand and explore. It was an insect—perhaps a spider—exploring *him*. He squashed it and wondered how many more creatures were watching him, waiting to reach out and touch him, the stranger.

There was nothing now. After standing in that position—his hand still on his neck, feeling the wet splodge of the squashed spider gradually dry—for minutes, hours, his legs began to tremble with the effort, the inaction. By now he could see enough in the dark to make out the large solid shapes of old wardrobes, broken buckets and bedsteads piled on top of each other around him. He recognized an old bathtub—patches of enamel glimmered at him and at last he lowered himself onto its edge.

He contemplated slipping out of the shed and into the fray. He wondered if it would not be better to be captured by Raghu and be returned to the milling crowd as long as he could be in the sun, the light, the free spaces of the garden and the familiarity of his brothers, sisters and cousins. It would be evening soon. Their games would become legitimate. The parents would sit out on the lawn on cane basket chairs and watch them as they tore around the garden or gathered in knots to share a loot of mulberries or black, teeth-splitting *jamun* from the garden trees. The gardener would fix the hosepipe to the water tap and water would fall lavishly through the air to the ground, soaking the dry yellow grass and the red gravel and arousing the sweet, the intoxicating scent of water on dry earth—that loveliest scent in the world. Ravi sniffed for a whiff of it. He half-rose from the bathtub, then heard the despairing scream of one of the girls as Raghu bore down upon her. There was the sound of a crash, and of rolling about in the bushes, the shrubs, then screams and accusing sobs of, 'I touched the den—' 'You did not—' 'I did—' 'You liar, you did *not*' and then a fading away and silence again.

Ravi sat back on the harsh edge of the tub, deciding to hold out a bit longer. What fun if they were all found and caught—he alone left unconquered! He had never known that sensation. Nothing more wonderful had ever happened to him than being taken out by an uncle and bought a whole slab of chocolate all to himself, or being flung into the soda-man's pony cart and driven up to the gate by the friendly driver with the red beard and pointed ears. To defeat Raghu— that hirsute, hoarse-voiced football champion—and to be the winner in a circle of older, bigger, luckier children—that would be thrilling beyond imagination. He hugged his knees together and smiled to himself almost shyly at the thought of so much victory, such laurels.

* * *

There he sat smiling, knocking his heels against the bathtub, now and then getting up and going to the door to put his ear to the broad crack and listening for sounds of the game, the pursuer and the pursued, and then returning to his seat with the dogged determination of the true winner, a breaker of records, a champion.

It grew darker in the shed as the light at the door grew softer, fuzzier, turned to a kind of crumbling yellow pollen that turned to yellow fur, blue fur, grey fur. Evening. Twilight. The sound of water gushing, falling. The scent of earth receiving water, slaking its thirst in great gulps and releasing that green scent of freshness, coolness. Through the crack Ravi saw the long purple shadows of the shed and the garage lying still across the yard. Beyond that, the white walls of the house. The bougainvillea had lost its lividity, hung in dark bundles that quaked and twittered and seethed with masses of homing sparrows. The lawn was shut off from his view. Could he hear the children's voices? It seemed to him that he could. It seemed to him that he could hear them chanting, singing, laughing. But what about the game? What had happened? Could it be over? How could it when he was still not found?

It then occurred to him that he could have slipped out long ago, dashed 30 across the yard to the veranda and touched the 'den.' It was necessary to do that to win. He had forgotten. He had only remembered the part of hiding and trying to elude the seeker. He had done that so successfully, his success had occupied him so wholly that he had quite forgotten that success had to be clinched by that final dash to victory and the ringing cry of 'Den!'

With a whimper he burst through the crack, fell on his knees, got up and stumbled on stiff, benumbed legs across the shadowy yard, crying heartily by the time he reached the veranda so that when he flung himself at the white pillar and bawled, 'Den! Den! Den!' his voice broke with rage and pity at the disgrace of it all and he felt himself flooded with tears and misery.

Out on the lawn, the children stopped chanting. They all turned to stare at him in amazement. Their faces were pale and triangular in the dusk. The trees and bushes around them stood inky and sepulchral, spilling long shadows across them. They stared, wondering at his reappearance, his passion, his wild animal howling. Their mother rose from her basket chair and came towards him, worried, annoyed, saying, 'Stop it, stop it, Ravi. Don't be a baby. Have you hurt yourself?' Seeing him attended to, the children went back to clasping their hands and chanting 'The grass is green, the rose is red. . . .'

But Ravi would not let them. He tore himself out of his mother's grasp and pounded across the lawn into their midst, charging at them with his head lowered so that they scattered in surprise. 'I won, I won, I won,' he bawled, shaking his head so that the big tears flew. 'Raghu didn't find me. I won, I won—'

It took them a minute to grasp what he was saying, even who he was. They had quite forgotten him. Raghu had found all the others long ago. There had been a fight about who was to be It next. It had been so fierce that their mother had emerged from her bath and made them change to another game. Then they had played another and another. Broken mulberries from the tree and eaten them. Helped the driver wash the car when their father returned from work. Helped the gardener water the beds till he roared at them and swore he would complain to their parents. The parents had come out, taken up their positions on the cane chairs. They had begun to play again, sing and chant. All this time no one had remembered Ravi. Having disappeared from the scene, he had disappeared from their minds. Clean.

'Don't be a fool,' Raghu said roughly, pushing him aside, and even Mira said, 'Stop howling, Ravi. If you want to play, you can stand at the end of the line,' and she put him there very firmly.   35

The game proceeded. Two pairs of arms reached up and met in an arc. The children trooped under it again and again in a lugubrious circle, ducking their heads and intoning

'The grass is green,
The rose is red;
Remember me
When I am dead, dead, dead, dead . . .'

And the arc of thin arms trembled in the twilight, and the heads were bowed so sadly, and their feet tramped to that melancholy refrain so mournfully, so helplessly, that Ravi could not bear it. He would not follow them, he would not be included in this funeral game. He had wanted victory and triumph—not a funeral. But he had been forgotten, left out and he would not join them now. The ignominy of being forgotten—how could he face it? He felt his heart go heavy and ache inside him unbearably. He lay down full length on the damp grass, crushing his face into it, no longer crying, silenced by a terrible sense of his insignificance.

Starting Points for Further Research: Anita Desai

- **Critical Essay:** Lee Kyungsoon. "The Discourse of Nationalism and Gendered Subjectivity: Anita Desai's Clear Light of Day." *Studies in Modern Fiction* 8 (Winter 2001): 137–60.
- **Interview:** Magda Costa. "Interview with Anita Desai." January 30, 2001. http://www.sawnet.org/books/writing/desai_interview.html.

SYMBOL

In everyday life we easily distinguish between a **literal meaning**, where a word means just what it says, and another, more **symbolic meaning**, where some word or object stands for something else. When sunshine suggests nothing more than a pleasant day and perhaps the need for a hat and shades, we are being literal. When the sun coming from behind the clouds suggests the end of a gloomy time in one's life, we are using sun symbolically. People talk of retirement age symbolically as "sunset years," or emergency money put aside as a "rainy day fund." Yes, clouds are just clouds, as we all know, but they can also carry with them the notion of gloom, even of despair, while rainbows suggest much more than a simple effect of the sun's rays through water droplets. Just as we do every day, writers employ words symbolically, as a means of enriching their stories.

Writers are always aware of a human tendency to regard natural phenomena as more than what their surface, literal meanings seem to state. Consequently, when a writer spends some of the precious space of a tightly written story on the weather, readers should be alert to the possibilities of its symbolic significance. In a story where every word counts, you can suspect that clouds and rainbows, snowstorms and hurricanes, are often performing double duty, setting the literal as well as the symbolic scene. Similarly, when writers call our attention to certain colors (white, black, red, gold), the symbolism may help create a certain mood or feeling. We all know the bad cowboys are the ones in the black hats, while white can suggest both purity (wedding dress) or cold expanses of emptiness (ice fields). Still, we must be careful here: if white can symbolize *both* purity and emptiness, we cannot make a simple equation between color and meaning. For instance, black can certainly suggest evil or death, but in economics or accounting, being "in the black" means achieving financial health. Symbolic significance is therefore subject to interpretation, even a source of interesting disagreements, rather than a code or a simple kind of one-to-one correspondence to be solved like a puzzle.

Besides the everyday significance that we all recognize with **allusions**—brief references to people, places, events, literary works, or other elements that a reader is assumed to recognize—to the weather or time of year, symbolic language can become more complex and much less easy to resolve. The talismanic object Dobbins carried in "Stockings" (p. 27), for instance, does not have such an obvious significance as does winter suggesting death or spring signifying rebirth. And in fact, most writers who create symbols do not expect readers to form a simple one-to-one equivalence between symbol and thing symbolized. Unfortunately, too many readers have been eager to jump to conclusions about what everything "means." Such an attitude frustrated Flannery O'Connor, who consistently employed symbols in her stories but who always resisted linking each symbol to an easily identifiable "hidden meaning," and turning the reading process into a symbol hunt. In one of her letters to a friend, O'Connor revealed her exasperation over responding to questions in an English class about her story "A Good Man Is Hard to Find" (p. 374):

Week before last I went to Wesleyan and read "AGMIHTF." After it I went to one of the classes where I was asked questions. There were a couple of young teachers there and one of them, an earnest type, started asking me questions. "Miss O'Connor," he said, "why was the Misfit's hat black?" I said most countrymen in Georgia wore black hats. He looked pretty disappointed. Then he said, "Miss O'Connor, the Misfit represents Christ, does he not?" "He does not," I said. He looked crushed. "Well, Miss O'Connor," he said, "what is the significance of the Misfit's hat?" I said it was to cover his head; and after that he left me alone. Anyway, that what's happening to the teaching of literature.

At the same time, O'Connor's story really *is* full of symbolism, which her readers quite rightly picked up on. But her point is that symbolism is just not there in an obvious way, with a simple "this equals that" equation.

In Stuart Dybek's "The Palatski Man," symbols expand in our consciousness and set or shape our mood, frequently shimmering just out of our reach, obvious in one sense, but hard to fully comprehend in another. The story first appeared in the *Magazine of Fantasy and Science Fiction*.

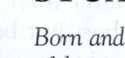

STUART DYBEK (B. 1942)

Born and raised on the South Side of Chicago, Stuart Dybek sets most of his stories in his native city. His first collection of short stories, Childhood and Other Neighborhoods (1980), depicts how grim urban streets influence the lives of their inhabitants. Dybek is particularly known for his portrayals of Chicago's struggling ethnic neighborhoods. His most recent book is I Sailed with Magellan (2003). Dybek is a professor of English at Western Michigan University in Kalamazoo.

The Palatski Man (1971)

He reappeared in spring, some Sunday morning, perhaps Easter, when the twigs of the catalpa trees budded and lawns smelled of mud and breaking seeds. Or Palm Sunday, returning from mass with handfuls of blessed, bending palms to be cut into crosses and pinned on your Sunday dress and the year-old palms removed by her brother, John, from behind the pictures of Jesus with his burning heart and the Virgin with her sad eyes, to be placed dusty and crumbling in an old coffee can and burned in the backyard. And once, walking back from church, Leon Sisca said these are what they lashed Jesus with. And she said no they aren't, they used whips. They used these, he insisted. What do you know, she said. And he told her she was a dumb girl and lashed her across her bare legs with his blessed palms. They stung her; she started to cry, that anyone could do such a thing, and he caught her running down Twenty-fifth Street with her skirt flying and got her against a fence, and grabbing her by the hair, he stuck his scratchy palms in her face, and suddenly he was lifted off the ground and flung to the sidewalk, and she saw John standing over him very red in the face; and when Leon Sisca tried to run away, John blocked him, and Leon tried to dodge around him as if they were playing football; and as he cut past, John slapped him across the face; Leon's head snapped back and his nose started to bleed. John didn't chase him and he ran halfway down the block, turned around and yelled through his tears with blood dripping on his white shirt: I hate you goddamn you I hate you! All the dressed-up people coming back from church saw it happen and shook their heads. John said c'mon Mary let's go home.

No, it wasn't that day, but it was in that season on a Sunday that he reappeared, and then every Sunday after that through the summer and into the fall, when school would resume and the green catalpa leaves fall like withered fans into the birdbaths, turning the water brown, the Palatski Man would come.

He was an old man who pushed a white cart through the neighborhood streets ringing a little golden bell. He would stop at each corner, and the children would come with their money to inspect the taffy apples sprinkled with chopped nuts, or the red candy apples on pointed sticks, or the *palatski* displayed under the glass of the white cart. She had seen taffy apples in the candy stores and even the red apples sold by clowns at circuses, but she had never seen *palatski* sold anywhere else. It was two crisp wafers stuck together with honey. The taste might have reminded you of an ice-cream cone spread with honey, but it reminded Mary of Holy Communion. It felt like the Eucharist in her mouth, the way it tasted walking back from the communion rail after waiting for Father Mike to stand before her wearing his rustling silk vestments with the organ playing and him saying the Latin prayer over and over faster than she could ever hope to pray and making a sign of the cross with the host just before placing it on someone's tongue. She knelt at the communion rail close enough to the altar to see the silk curtains drawn inside the open tabernacle and the beeswax candles flickering and to smell the flowers. Father Mike was moving down the line of communicants, holding the chalice, with the altar boy, an eighth-grader, sometimes even John, standing beside him in a lace surplice, holding the paten under each chin; and she would close her eyes and open her mouth, sticking her tongue out, and hear the prayer and feel the host placed gently on her tongue. Sometimes Father's hand brushed her bottom lip, and she would feel a spark from his finger, which Sister said was static electricity, not the Holy Spirit.

Then she would walk down the aisle between the lines of communicants, searching through half-shut eyes for her pew, her mind praying Jesus help me find it. And when she found her pew, she would kneel down and shut her eyes and bury her face in her hands praying over and over thank you Jesus for coming to me, feeling the host stuck to the roof of her mouth, melting against her tongue like a warm, wheaty snowflake; and she would turn the tip of her tongue inward and lick the host off the ridges of her mouth till it was loosened by saliva and swallowed into her soul.

Who was the Palatski Man? No one knew or even seemed to care. He was   5 an old man with an unremembered face, perhaps a never-seen face, a head hidden by a cloth-visored cap, and eyes concealed behind dark glasses with green, smoked lenses. His smile revealed only a gold crown and a missing tooth. His only voice was the ringing bell, and his hands were rough and red as if scrubbed with sandpaper and their skin very hard when you opened your hand for your change and his fingers brushed yours. His clothes were always the same— white—not starched and dazzling, but the soft white of many washings and wringings.

No one cared and he was left alone. The boys didn't torment him as they did the peddlers during the week. There was constant war between the boys and the peddlers, the umbrella menders, the knife sharpeners, anyone whose business carried him down the side streets or through the alleys. The peddlers came every day, spring, summer, and autumn, through the alleys behind the backyard fences crying, "Rags ol irn, rags ol irn!" Riding their ancient, rickety wagons with huge wooden-spoked wheels, heaped high with scraps of metal, frames of furniture, coal-black cobwebbed lumber, bundles of rags and filthy newspapers. The boys called them the Ragmen. They were all old, hunched men, bearded and bald, who bargained in a stammered foreign English and dressed in clothes extracted from the bundles of rags in their weather-beaten wagons.

Their horses seemed even more ancient than their masters, and Mary was always sorry for them as she watched their slow, arthritic gait up and down the alleys. Most of them were white horses, a dirty white as if their original colors had turned white with age, like the hair on an old man's head. They had enormous hooves with iron shoes that clacked down the alleys over the broken glass, which squealed against the concrete when the rusty, metal-rimmed wheels of the wagon ground over it. Their muzzles were pink without hair, and their tongues lolled out gray; their teeth were huge and yellow. Over their eyes were black blinders, around their shoulders a heavy black harness that looked always ready to slip off, leather straps hung all about their bodies. They ate from black, worn leather sacks tied over their faces, and as they ate, the flies flew up from their droppings and climbed all over their thick bodies and the horses swished at them with stringy tails.

The Ragmen drove down the crooked, interconnecting alleys crying, "Rags ol irn, rags ol irn," and the boys waited for a wagon to pass, hiding behind fences or garbage cans; and as soon as it passed they would follow, running half bent over so that they couldn't be seen if the Ragman turned around over the piles heaped on his wagon. They would run to the tailgate and grab on to it, swinging up, the taller ones, like John, stretching their legs onto the rear axle, the shorter ones just hanging as the wagon rolled along. Sometimes one of the bolder boys would try to climb up on the wagon itself and throw off some of the junk. The Ragman would see him and pull the reins, stopping the wagon. He would begin gesturing and yelling at the boys, who jumped from the wagon and stood back laughing and hollering, "Rags ol irn, rags ol irn!" Sometimes he'd grab a makeshift whip, a piece of clothesline tied to a stick, and stagger after them as they scattered laughing before him, disappearing over fences and down gangways only to reappear again around the corner of some other alley; or, lying flattened on a garage roof, they'd suddenly jump up and shower the wagon with garbage as it passed beneath.

Mary could never fully understand why her brother participated. He wasn't a bully like Leon Sisca and certainly not cruel like Denny Zmiga, who tortured cats. She sensed the boys vaguely condemned the Ragmen for the sad condition of their horses. But that was only a small part of it, for often the horses as well as their masters were harassed. She thought it was a venial sin and wondered if John confessed it the Thursday before each First Friday, when they would go together to confession in the afternoon: Bless me Father for I have sinned, I threw garbage on a Ragman five times this month. For your penance say five Our Fathers and five Hail Marys, go in peace. She never mentioned this to him, feeling that whatever made him do it was a part of what made him generally unafraid, a part of what the boys felt when they elected him captain of the St. Roman

Grammar School baseball team. She couldn't bear it if he thought she was a dumb girl. She never snitched on him. If she approached him when he was surrounded by his friends, he would loudly announce, "All right, nobody swear while Mary's here."

At home he often took her into his confidence. This was what she liked the most, when, after supper, while her parents watched TV in the parlor, he would come into her room, where she was doing her homework, and lie down on her bed and start talking, telling her who among his friends was a good first sacker, or which one of the girls in his class tried to get him to dance with her at the school party, just talking and sometimes even asking her opinion on something like if she thought he should let his hair grow long like that idiot Peter Noskin, who couldn't even make the team as a right fielder. What did she think of guys like that? She tried to tell him things back. How Sister Mary Valentine had caught Leon Sisca in the girls' washroom yesterday. And then one night he told her about Raymond Cruz, which she knew was a secret because their father had warned John not to hang around with him even if he was the best pitcher on the team. He told her how after school he and Raymond Cruz had followed a Ragman to Hobotown, which was far away, past Western Avenue, on the other side of the river, down by the river and the railroad tracks, and that they had a regular town there without any streets. They lived among huge heaps of junk, rubbled lots tangled with smashed, rusting cars and bathtubs, rotting mounds of rags and paper, woodpiles infested with river rats. Their wagons were all lined up and the horses kept in a deserted factory with broken windows. They lived in shacks that were falling apart, some of them made out of old boxcars, and there was a blacksmith with a burning forge working in a ruined shed made of bricks and timbers with a roof of canvas.

He told her how they had snuck around down the riverbank in the high weeds and watched the Ragmen come in from all parts of the city, pulled by their tired horses, hundreds of Ragmen arriving in silence, and how they assembled in front of a great fire burning in the middle of all the shacks, where something was cooking in a huge, charred pot.

Their scroungy dogs scratched and circled around the fire while the Ragmen stood about and seemed to be trading among one another: bales of worn clothing for baskets of tomatoes, bushels of fruit for twisted metals, cases of dust-filled bottles for scorched couches and lamps with frazzled wires. They knelt, peering out of the weeds and watching them, and then Ray whispered let's sneak around to the building where the horses are kept and look at them.

So they crouched through the weeds and ran from shack to shack until they came to the back of the old factory. They could smell the horses and hay inside and hear the horses sneezing. They snuck in through a busted window. The factory was dark and full of spiderwebs, and they felt their way through a passage that entered into a high-ceilinged hall where the horses were stabled. It was dim; rays of sun sifted down through the dust from the broken roof. The horses didn't look the same in the dimness without their harnesses. They looked huge and beautiful, and when you reached to pat them, their muscles quivered so that you flinched with fright.

"Wait'll the guys hear about this," John said.

And Ray whispered, "Let's steal one! We can take him to the river and ride him."

John didn't know what to say. Ray was fourteen. His parents were divorced. He had failed a year in school and often hung around with high-school guys. Everybody knew that he had been caught in a stolen car but that the police let him go because he was so much younger than the other guys. He was part Mexican and knew a lot about horses. John didn't like the idea of stealing.

"We couldn't get one out of here," he said.

"Sure we could," Ray said. "We could get on one and gallop out with him before they knew what was going on."

"Suppose we get caught," John said.

"Who'd believe the Ragmen anyway?" Ray asked him. "They can't even speak English. You chicken?"   20

So they picked out a huge white horse to ride, who stood still and uninterested when John boosted Ray up on his back and then Ray reached down and pulled him up. Ray held his mane and John held on to Ray's waist. Ray nudged his heels into the horse's flanks and he began to move, slowly swaying toward the light of the doorway.

"As soon as we get outside," Ray whispered, "hold on. I'm gonna goose him."

John's palms were sweating by this time because being on this horse felt like straddling a blimp as it rose over the roofs. When they got to the door, Ray hollered, "Heya!" and kicked his heels hard, and the horse bolted out, and before he knew what had happened, John felt himself sliding, dropping a long way, and then felt the sudden hard smack of the hay-strewn floor. He looked up and realized he had never made it out of the barn, and then he heard the shouting and barking of the dogs and, looking out, saw Ray half riding, half hanging from the horse, which reared again and again, surrounded by the shouting Ragmen, and he saw the look on Ray's face as he was bucked from the horse into their arms. There was a paralyzed second when they all glanced toward him standing in the doorway of the barn, and then he whirled around and stumbled past the now-pitching bulks of horses whinnying all about him and found the passage, struggling through it, bumping into walls, spiderwebs sticking to his face, with the shouts and barks gaining on him, and then he was out the window and running up a hill of weeds, crushed coal slipping under his feet, skidding up and down two more hills, down railroad tracks, not turning around, just running until he could no longer breathe, and above him he saw a bridge and clawed up the grassy embankment till he reached it.

It was rush hour and the bridge was crowded with people going home, factory workers carrying lunch pails and businessmen with attaché cases. The street was packed with traffic, and he didn't know where he was or what he should do about Ray. He decided to go home and see what would happen. He'd call Ray that night, and if he wasn't home, then he'd tell them about the Ragmen. But he couldn't find his way back. Finally he had to ask a cop where he was, and the cop put him on a trolley car that got him home.

He called Ray about eight o'clock, and his mother answered the phone and   25 told him Ray had just got in and went right to bed, and John asked her if he could speak to him, and she said she'd go see, and he heard her set down the receiver and her footsteps walk away. He realized his own heartbeat was no longer deafening and felt the knots in his stomach loosen. Then he heard Ray's mother say that she was sorry but that Ray didn't want to talk to him.

The next day, at school, he saw Ray and asked him what happened, if he was angry that he had run out on him, and Ray said, no, nothing happened, to forget it. He kept asking Ray how he got away, but Ray wouldn't say anything until John mentioned telling the other guys about it. Ray said if he told anybody he'd deny it ever happened, that there was such a place. John thought he was just kidding, but when he told the guys, Ray told them John made the whole thing up, and they almost got into a fight, pushing each other back and forth, nobody taking the first swing, until the guys stepped between them and broke it up. John lost his temper and said he'd take any of the guys who wanted to go next Saturday to see for themselves. They could go on their bikes and hide them in the weeds by the river and sneak up on the Ragmen. Ray said go on.

So on Saturday John and six guys met at his place and peddled toward the river and railroad tracks, down the busy trucking streets, where the semis passed you so fast your bike seemed about to be sucked away by the draft. They got to Western Avenue and the river, and it looked the same and didn't look the same. They left the street and pumped their bikes down a dirt road left through the weeds by bulldozers, passing rusty barges moored to the banks, seemingly abandoned in the oily river. They passed a shack or two, but they were empty. John kept looking for the three mounds of black cinders as a landmark but couldn't find them. They rode their bikes down the railroad tracks, and it wasn't like being in the center of the city at all, with the smell of milkweeds and the noise of birds and crickets all about them and the spring sun glinting down the railroad tracks. No one was around. It was like being far out in the country. They rode until they could see the skyline of downtown, skyscrapers rising up through the smoke of chimneys like a horizon of jagged mountains in the mist. By now everyone was kidding him about the Ragmen, and finally he had to admit he couldn't find them, and they gave up. They all peddled back, kidding him, and he bought everybody Cokes, and they admitted they had had a pretty good time anyway, even though he sure as hell was some storyteller.

And he figured something must have happened to Ray. It hit him Sunday night, lying in bed trying to sleep, and he knew he'd have to talk to him about it Monday when he saw him at school, but on Monday Ray was absent and was absent on Tuesday, and on Wednesday they found out that Ray had run away from home and no one could find him.

*   *   *

No one ever found him, and he wasn't there in June when John and his classmates filed down the aisle, their maroon robes flowing and white tassels swinging almost in time to the organ, to receive their diplomas and shake hands with Father Mike. And the next week it was summer, and she was permitted to go to the beach with her girlfriends. Her girlfriends came over and giggled whenever John came into the room.

On Sundays they went to late mass. She wore her flowered-print dress   30 and a white mantilla in church when she sat beside John among the adults. After mass they'd stop at the corner of Twenty-fifth Street on their way home and buy *palatski* and walk home eating it with its crispness melting and the sweet honey crust becoming chewy. She remembered how she used to pretend it was manna they'd been rewarded with for keeping the Sabbath. It tasted extra good because she had skipped breakfast. She fasted before receiving Communion.

Then it began to darken earlier, and the kids played tag and rolivio in the dusk and hid from each other behind trees and in doorways, and the girls laughed and blushed when the boys chased and tagged them. She had her own secret hiding place down the block, in a garden under a lilac bush, where no one could find her; and she would lie there listening to her name called in the darkness, Mary Mary free free free, by so many voices.

She shopped downtown with her mother at night for new school clothes, skirts, not dresses, green ribbons for her dark hair, and shoes without buckles, like slippers a ballerina wears. And that night she tried them on for John, dancing in her nightgown, and he said you're growing up. And later her mother came into her room—only the little bed lamp was burning—and explained to her what growing up was like. And after her mother left, she picked up a little rag doll that was kept as an ornament on her dresser and tried to imagine having a child, really having a child, it coming out of her body, and she looked at herself in the mirror and stood close to it and looked at the colors of her eyes: brown around the edges and then turning a milky gray that seemed to be smoking behind crystal and toward the center the gray turning green, getting greener till it was almost violet near her pupils. And in the black mirror of her pupils she saw herself looking at herself.

The next day, school started again and she was a sixth-grader. John was in high school, and Leon Sisca, who had grown much bigger over the summer and smoked, sneered at her and said, "Who'll protect you now?" She made a visit to the church at lunchtime and dropped a dime in the metal box by the ruby vigil lights and lit a candle high up on the rack with a long wax wick and said a prayer to the Blessed Virgin.

And it was late in October, and leaves wafted from the catalpa trees on their way to church on Sunday and fell like withered fans into the birdbaths, turning the water brown. They were walking back from mass, and she was thinking how little she saw John anymore, how he no longer came to her room to talk, and she said, "Let's do something together."

"What?" he asked.

"Let's follow the Palatski Man."

"Why would you want to do that?"

"I don't know," she said. "We could find out where he lives, where he makes his stuff. He won't come around pretty soon. Maybe we could go to his house in the winter and buy things from him."

John looked at her. Her hair, like his, was blowing about in the wind. "All right," he said.

So they waited at a corner where a man was raking leaves into a pile to burn, but each time he built the pile and turned to scrape a few more leaves from his small lawn, the wind blew and the leaves whirled off from the pile and sprayed out as if alive over their heads, and then the wind suddenly died, and they floated back about the raking man into the grass softly, looking like wrinkled snow. And in a rush of leaves they closed their eyes against, the Palatski Man pushed by.

They let him go down the block. He wasn't hard to follow, he went so slow, stopping at corners for customers. They didn't have to sneak behind him because

he never turned around. They followed him down the streets, and one street became another until they were out of their neighborhood, and the clothes the
people wore became poorer and brighter. They went through the next parish,
and there was less stopping because it was a poorer parish where more Mexicans
lived, and the children yelled in Spanish, and they felt odd in their new Sunday
clothes.

"Let's go back," John said.

But Mary thought there was something in his voice that wasn't sure, and she
took his arm and mock-pleaded, "No-o-o-o, this is fun, let's see where he goes."

The Palatski Man went up the streets, past the trucking lots full of semis
without cabs, where the wind blew more grit and dirty papers than leaves, where
he stopped hardly at all. Then past blocks of mesh-windowed factories shut
down for Sunday and the streets empty and the pavements powdered with brown
glass from broken beer bottles. They walked hand in hand a block behind the
white, bent figure of the Palatski Man pushing his cart over the fissured sidewalk.
When he crossed streets and looked from side to side for traffic, they jumped into
doorways, afraid he might turn around.

He crossed Western Avenue, which was a big street and so looked emptier   45
than any of the others without traffic on it. They followed him down Western
Avenue and over the rivet-studded, aluminum-girdered bridge that spanned the
river, watching the pigeons flitting through the cables. Just past the bridge he
turned into a pitted asphalt road that trucks used for hauling their cargoes to
freight trains. It wound into the acres of endless lots and railroad yards behind
the factories along the river.

John stopped. "We can't go any further," he said.

"Why?" she asked. "It's getting interesting."

"I've been here before," he said.

"When?"

"I don't remember, but I feel like I've been here before."   50

"C'mon, silly," she said, and tugged his arm with all her might and opened
her eyes very wide, and John let himself be tugged along, and they both started
laughing. But by now the Palatski Man had disappeared around a curve in the
road, and they had to run to catch up. When they turned the bend, they just
caught sight of him going over a hill, and the asphalt road they had to run up
had turned to cinder. At the top of the hill Mary cried, "Look!" and pointed off
to the left, along the river. They saw a wheat field in the center of the city, with
the wheat blowing and waving, and the Palatski Man, half man and half willowy
grain, was pushing his cart through the field past a scarecrow with straw arms
outstretched and huge black crows perched on them.

"It looks like he's hanging on a cross," Mary said.

"Let's go," John said, and she thought he meant turn back home and was
ready to agree because his voice sounded so determined, but he moved forward
instead to follow the Palatski Man.

"Where can he be going?" Mary said.

But John just looked at her and put his finger to his lips. They followed sin-   55
gle file down a trail trod smooth and twisting through the wheat field. When
they passed the scarecrow, the crows flapped off in great iridescent flutters, cawing at them while the scarecrow hung as if guarding a field of wings. Then, at the
edge of the field, the cinder path resumed sloping downhill toward the river.

John pointed and said, "The mounds of coal."

And she saw three black mounds rising up in the distance and sparkling in the sun.

"C'mon," John said, "we have to get off the path."

He led her down the slope and into the weeds that blended with the river grasses, rushes, and cattails. They sneaked through the weeds, which pulled at her dress and scratched her legs. John led the way; he seemed to know where he was going. He got down on his hands and knees and motioned for her to do the same, and they crawled forward without making a sound. Then John lay flat on his stomach, and she crawled beside him and flattened out. He parted the weeds, and she looked out and saw a group of men standing around a kettle on a fire and dressed in a strange assortment of ill-fitting suits, either too small or too large and baggy. None of the suit pieces matched, trousers blue and the suitcoat brown, striped pants and checked coats, countless combinations of colors. They wore crushed hats of all varieties: bowlers, straws, stetsons, derbies, homburgs. Their ties were the strangest of all, misshapen and dangling to their knees in wild designs of flowers, swirls, and polka dots.

"Who are they?" she whispered.

"The Ragmen. They must be dressed for Sunday," John hissed.

And then she noticed the shacks behind the men, with the empty wagons parked in front and the stacks of junk from uprooted basements and strewn attics, even the gutted factory just the way John had described it. She saw the dogs suddenly jump up barking and whining, and all the men by the fire turn around as the Palatski Man wheeled his cart into their midst.

He gestured to them, and they all parted as he walked to the fire, where he stood staring into the huge black pot. He turned and said something to one of them, and the man began to stir whatever was in the pot, and then the Palatski Man dipped a small ladle into it and raised it up, letting its contents pour back into the pot, and Mary felt herself get dizzy and gasp as she saw the bright red fluid in the sun and heard John exclaim, "Blood!" And she didn't want to see any more, how the men came to the pot and dipped their fingers in it and licked them off, nodding and smiling. She saw the horses filing out of their barn, looking ponderous and naked without their harnesses. She hid her face in her arms and wouldn't look, and then she heard the slow, sorrowful chanting and off-key wheezing behind it. And she looked up and realized all the Ragmen, like a choir of bums, had removed their crushed hats and stood bareheaded in the wind, singing. Among them someone worked a dilapidated accordion, squeezing out a mournful, foreign melody. In the center stood the Palatski Man, leading them with his arms like a conductor and sometimes intoning a word that all would echo in a chant. Their songs rose and fell but always rose again, sometimes nasal, then shifting into a rich baritone, building always louder and louder, more sorrowful, until the Palatski Man rang his bell and suddenly everything was silent. Not men or dogs or accordion or birds or crickets or wind made a sound. Only her breathing and a far-off throb that she seemed to feel more than hear, as if all the church bells in the city were tolling an hour. The sun was in the center of the sky. Directly below it stood the Palatski Man raising a *palatski*.

The Ragmen had all knelt. They rose and started a procession leading to where she and John hid in the grass. Then John was up and yelling, "Run!" and she scrambled to her feet, John dragging her by the arm. She tried to run but her legs wouldn't obey her. They felt so rubbery pumping through the weeds and John pulling her faster than she could go with the weeds tripping her and the vines clutching like fingers around her ankles.

Ragmen rose up in front of them and they stopped and ran the other way   65
but Ragmen were there too. Ragmen were everywhere in an embracing circle, so they stopped and stood still, holding hands.

"Don't be afraid," John told her.

And she wasn't. Her legs wouldn't move and she didn't care. She just didn't want to run anymore, choking at the acrid smell of the polluted river. Through her numbness she heard John's small voice lost over and over in the open daylight repeating, "We weren't doin' anything."

The Ragmen took them back to where the Palatski Man stood before the fire and the bubbling pot. John started to say something but stopped when the Palatski Man raised his finger to his lips. One of the Ragmen brought a bushel of shiny apples and another a handful of pointed little sticks. The Palatski Man took an apple and inserted the stick and dipped it into the pot and took it out coated with red. The red crystallized and turned hard, and suddenly she realized it was a red candy apple that he was handing her. She took it from his hand and held it dumbly while he made another for John and a third for himself. He bit into his and motioned for them to do the same. She looked up at John standing beside her, flushed and sweaty, and she bit into her apple. It was sweeter than anything she'd ever tasted, with the red candy crunching in her mouth, melting, mingling with apple juice.

And then from his cart he took a giant *palatski*, ten times bigger than any she had ever seen, and broke it again and again, handing the tiny bits to the circle of Ragmen, where they were passed from mouth to mouth. When there was only a small piece left, he broke it three ways and offered one to John. She saw it disappear in John's hand and watched him raise his hand to his mouth and at the same time felt him squeeze her hand very hard. The Palatski Man handed her a part. Honey stretched into threads from its torn edges. She put it in her mouth, expecting the crisp wafer and honey taste, but it was so bitter it brought tears to her eyes. She fought them back and swallowed, trying not to screw up her face, not knowing whether he had tricked her or given her a gift she didn't understand. He spoke quietly to one of the Ragmen in a language she couldn't follow and pointed to an enormous pile of rags beside a nearby shack. The man trudged to the pile and began sorting through it and returned with a white ribbon of immaculate, shining silk. The Palatski Man gave it to her, then turned and walked away, disappearing into the shack. As soon as he was gone, the circle of Ragmen broke and they trudged away, leaving the children standing dazed before the fire.

"Let's get out of here," John said. They turned and began walking slowly,   70
afraid the Ragmen would regroup at any second, but no one paid any attention to them. They walked away. Back through the wheat field, past silently perched crows, over the hill, down the cinder path that curved and became the pitted asphalt road. They walked over the Western Avenue bridge, which shook as a green trolley, empty with Sunday, clattered across it. They stopped in the middle of the bridge, and John opened his hand, and she saw the piece of *palatski* crushed into a little sour ball, dirty and pasty with sweat.

"Did you eat yours?" he asked.

"Yes," she said.

"I tried to stop you," he said. "Didn't you feel me squeezing your hand? It might have been poisoned."

"No," she lied, so he wouldn't worry, "it tasted fine."

"Nobody believed me," John said.

"I believed you."

"They'll see now."

And then he gently took the ribbon that she still unconsciously held in her hand—she had an impulse to clench her fist but didn't—and before she could say anything, he threw it over the railing into the river. They watched it, caught in the drafts of wind under the bridge, dipping and gliding among the wheeling pigeons, finally touching the green water and floating away.

"You don't want the folks to see that," John said. "They'd get all excited and nothing happened. I mean nothing really happened, we're both all right."

"Yes," she said. They looked at each other. Sunlight flashing through latticed girders made them squint; it reflected from the slits of eyes and off the river when their gaze dropped. Wind swooped over the railing and tangled their hair.

"You're the best girl I ever knew," John told her.

They both began to laugh, so hard they almost cried, and John stammered out, "We're late for dinner—I bet we're gonna really get it," and they hurried home.

They were sent to bed early that night without being permitted to watch TV. She undressed and put on her nightgown and climbed under her covers, feeling the sad, hollow Sunday-night feeling when the next morning will be Monday and the weekend is dying. The feeling always reminded her of all the past Sunday nights she'd had it, and she thought of all the future Sunday nights when it would come again. She wished John could come into her room so they could talk. She lay in bed tossing and seeking the cool places under her pillow with her arms and in the nooks of her blanket with her toes. She listened to the whole house go to sleep: the TV shut off after the late news, the voices of her parents discussing whether the doors had been locked for the night. She felt herself drifting to sleep and tried to think her nightly prayer, the Hail Mary before she slept, but it turned into a half dream that she woke out of with a faint recollection of Gabriel's wings, and she lay staring at the familiar shapes of furniture in her dark room. She heard the wind outside like a low whinny answered by cats. At last she climbed out of her bed and looked out the lace-curtained window. Across her backyard, over the catalpa tree, the moon hung low in the cold sky. It looked like a giant *palatski* snagged in the twigs. And then she heard the faint tinkle of the bell.

He stood below, staring up, the moon, like silver eyeballs, shining in the centers of his dark glasses. His horse, a windy white stallion, stamped and snorted behind him, and a gust of leaves funneled along the ground and swirled through the streetlight, and some of them stuck in the horse's tangled mane while its hooves kicked sparks in the dark alley. He offered her a *palatski*.

She ran from the window to the mirror and looked at herself in the dark, feeling her teeth growing and hair pushing through her skin in the tender parts of her body that had been bare and her breasts swelling like apples from her flat chest and her blood burning, and then in a lapse of wind, when the leaves fell back to earth, she heard his gold bell jangle again as if silver and knew that it was time to go.

Talking about the Text

1. Whatever else the *palatski* and the Palatski Man may represent, they are explicitly religious symbols, at least in Mary's mind. Trace the religious meanings as they appear in the story. What "objective" facts confirm Mary's religious interpretation of what she sees (and tastes)?
2. What difference does it make that the events in this story are seen through the eyes of a girl in sixth grade, just on the edge of young womanhood? What would happen to the symbolism if we had another person's point of view (perhaps John's, or even the Palatski Man's)?

Writing about the Text

1. In a brief essay, describe the complex brother-sister relationship between John and Mary. Why are they so close (even though Mary senses that the closeness is threatened as they grow older)? On what basis does Mary excuse John for joining the group of boys tormenting the Ragmen? How does the shared experience of their trip to the Ragmen's homes deepen or change their relationship?
2. Write about the last section of the story, where the sense of exactly what happens seems difficult to discern. Even the meaning of the last few words—"it was time to go"—is less than obvious. As you write, ask how our perceptions of the last section might be colored by what has gone before in the story.

Linking the Text to Other Texts

1. Does the symbol of the *palatski* and the Palatski Man require readers to know about the sacrament of Communion in the Catholic mass, which the symbol seems to invoke?
2. Compare the religious symbolism in Dybek's story with the religious symbolism in Raymond Carver's "Cathedral" (p. 89).

Starting Point for Further Research: Stuart Dybek

- **Interview:** Mike Nickel. "An Interview with Stuart Dybek." *Chicago Review* 43 (1997): 87–101.

For Further Reading: Symbol

García Márquez makes use of a particular style associated with Latin American storytelling, magic realism, which deliberately mixes the realistic and the fantastic.

GABRIEL GARCÍA MÁRQUEZ   (B. 1928)

Gabriel García Márquez was born in Colombia and raised by grandparents. His work, which is rooted in the history and social issues of his native Colombia, has reached a worldwide audience. He is best known for One Hundred Years of Solitude *(1967) and* Love in the Time of Cholera *(1985), both of which chronicle distant historical eras but focus on the implications for the present. His nonfiction* News of a Kidnapping *(1996) confronts the violence of his native country, specifically the drug-related abductions that characterize so much of the contemporary Colombian scene. García Márquez won the Nobel Prize for Literature in 1982.*

The Handsomest Drowned Man in the World: A Tale for Children

(1968)

TRANSLATED BY GREGORY RABASSA AND J. S. BERNSTEIN

The first children who saw the dark and slinky bulge approaching through the sea let themselves think it was an enemy ship. Then they saw it had no flags or masts and they thought it was a whale. But when it was washed up on the beach, they removed the clumps of seaweed, the jellyfish tentacles, and the remains of fish and flotsam, and only then did they see that it was a drowned man.

They had been playing with him all afternoon, burying him in the sand and digging him up again, when someone chanced to see them and spread the alarm in the village. The men who carried him to the nearest house noticed that he weighed more than any dead man they had ever known, almost as much as a horse, and they said to each other that maybe he'd been floating too long and the water had got into his bones. When they laid him on the floor they said he'd been taller than all other men because there was barely enough room for him in the house, but they thought that maybe the ability to keep on growing after death was part of the nature of certain drowned men. He had the smell of the sea about him and only his shape gave one to suppose that it was the corpse of a human being, because the skin was covered with a crust of mud and scales.

They did not even have to clean off his face to know that the dead man was a stranger. The village was made up of only twenty-odd wooden houses that had stone courtyards with no flowers and which were spread about on the end of a desertlike cape. There was so little land that mothers always went about with the fear that the wind would carry off their children and the few dead that the years had caused among them had to be thrown off the cliffs. But the sea was calm and bountiful and all the men fit into seven boats. So when they found the drowned man they simply had to look at one another to see that they were all there.

That night they did not go out to work at sea. While the men went to find out if anyone was missing in neighboring villages, the women stayed behind to care for the drowned man. They took the mud off with grass swabs, they removed the underwater stones entangled in his hair, and they scraped the crust off with tools used for scaling fish. As they were doing that they noticed that the vegetation on him came from faraway oceans and deep water and that his clothes were in tatters, as if he had sailed through labyrinths of coral. They noticed too that he bore his death with pride, for he did not have the lonely look of other drowned men who came out of the sea or that haggard, needy look of men who drowned in rivers. But only when they finished cleaning him off did they become aware of the kind of man he was and it left them breathless. Not only was he the tallest, strongest, most virile, and best built man they had ever seen, but even though they were looking at him there was no room for him in their imagination.

They could not find a bed in the village large enough to lay him on nor was there a table solid enough to use for his wake. The tallest men's holiday pants would not fit him, nor the fattest ones' Sunday shirts, nor the shoes of the one with the biggest feet. Fascinated by his huge size and his beauty, the women then decided to make him some pants from a large piece of sail and a shirt from some bridal brabant linen so that he could continue through his death with dignity. As they sewed, sitting in a circle and gazing at the corpse between stitches, it

5

seemed to them that the wind had never been so steady nor the sea so restless as on that night and they supposed that the change had something to do with the dead man. They thought that if that magnificent man had lived in the village, his house would have had the widest doors, the highest ceiling, and the strongest floor, his bedstead would have been made from a midship frame held together by iron bolts, and his wife would have been the happiest woman. They thought that he would have had so much authority that he could have drawn fish out of the sea simply by calling their names and that he would have put so much work into his land that spring would have burst forth from among the rocks so that he would have been able to plant flowers on the cliffs. They secretly compared him to their own men, thinking that for all their lives theirs were incapable of doing what he could do in one night, and they ended up dismissing them deep in their hearts as the weakest, meanest, and most useless creatures on earth. They were wandering through that maze of fantasy when the oldest woman, who as the old-est had looked upon the drowned man with more compassion than passion, sighed:

"He has the face of someone called Esteban."

It was true. Most of them had only to take another look at him to see that he could not have any other name. The more stubborn among them, who were the youngest, still lived for a few hours with the illusion that when they put his clothes on and he lay among the flowers in patent leather shoes his name might be Lautaro. But it was a vain illusion. There had not been enough canvas, the poorly cut and worse sewn pants were too tight, and the hidden strength of his heart popped the buttons on his shirt. After midnight the whistling of the wind died down and the sea fell into its Wednesday drowsiness. The silence put an end to any last doubts: he was Esteban. The women who had dressed him, who had combed his hair, had cut his nails and shaved him were unable to hold back a shudder of pity when they had to resign themselves to his being dragged along the ground. It was then that they understood how unhappy he must have been with that huge body since it bothered him even after death. They could see him in life, condemned to going through doors sideways, cracking his head on cross-beams, remaining on his feet during visits, not knowing what to do with his soft, pink, sea lion hands while the lady of the house looked for her most resistant chair and begged him, frightened to death, sit here, Esteban, please, and he, leaning against the wall, smiling, don't bother, ma'am, I'm fine where I am, his heels raw and his back roasted from having done the same thing so many times whenever he paid a visit, don't bother, ma'am, I'm fine where I am, just to avoid the embarrassment of breaking up the chair, and never knowing perhaps the ones who said don't go, Esteban, at least wait till the coffee's ready, were the ones who later on would whisper the big boob finally left, how nice, the handsome fool has gone. That was what the women were thinking beside the body a little before dawn. Later, when they covered his face with a handkerchief so that the light would not bother him, he looked so forever dead, so defenseless, so much like their men that the first furrows of tears opened in their hearts. It was one of the younger ones who began the weeping. The others, coming to, went from sighs to wails, and the more they sobbed the more they felt like weeping, because the drowned man was becoming all the more Esteban for them, and so they wept so much, for he was the most destitute, most peaceful, and most obliging man on earth, poor Esteban. So when the men returned with the news that the drowned man was not from the neighboring villages either, the women felt an opening of jubilation in the midst of their tears.

"Praise the Lord," they sighed, "he's ours!"

The men thought the fuss was only womanish frivolity. Fatigued because of the difficult nighttime inquiries, all they wanted was to get rid of the bother of the newcomer once and for all before the sun grew strong on that arid, windless day. They improvised a litter with the remains of foremasts and gaffs, tying it together with rigging so that it would bear the weight of the body until they reached the cliffs. They wanted to tie the anchor from a cargo ship to him so that he would sink easily into the deepest waves, where fish are blind and divers die of nostalgia, and bad currents would not bring him back to shore, as had happened with other bodies. But the more they hurried, the more the women thought of ways to waste time. They walked about like startled hens, pecking with the sea charms on their breasts, some interfering on one side to put a scapular of the good wind on the drowned man, some on the other side to put a wrist compass on him, and after a great deal of *get away from there, woman, stay out of the way, look, you almost made me fall on top of the dead man*, the men began to feel mistrust in their livers and started grumbling about why so many main-altar decorations for a stranger, because no matter how many nails and holy-water jars he had on him, the sharks would chew him all the same, but the women kept piling on their junk relics, running back and forth, stumbling, while they released in sighs what they did not in tears, so that the men finally exploded with *since when has there ever been such a fuss over a drifting corpse, a drowned nobody, a piece of cold Wednesday meat*. One of the women, mortified by so much lack of care, then removed the handkerchief from the dead man's face and the men were left breathless too.

He was Esteban. It was not necessary to repeat it for them to recognize him. 10 If they had been told Sir Walter Raleigh, even they might have been impressed with his gringo accent, the macaw on his shoulder, his cannibal-killing blunderbuss, but there could be only one Esteban in the world and there he was, stretched out like a sperm whale, shoeless, wearing the pants of an undersized child, and with those stony nails that had to be cut with a knife. They only had to take the handkerchief off his face to see that he was ashamed, that it was not his fault that he was so big or so heavy or so handsome, and if he had known that this was going to happen, he would have looked for a more discreet place to drown in, seriously, I even would have tied the anchor off a galleon around my neck and staggered off a cliff like someone who doesn't like things in order not to be upsetting people now with this Wednesday dead body, as you people say, in order not to be bothering anyone with this filthy piece of cold meat that doesn't have anything to do with me. There was so much truth in his manner that even the most mistrustful men, the ones who felt the bitterness of endless nights at sea fearing that their women would tire of dreaming about them and begin to dream of drowned men, even they and others who were harder still shuddered in the marrow of their bones at Esteban's sincerity.

That was how they came to hold the most splendid funeral they could conceive of for an abandoned drowned man. Some women who had gone to get flowers in the neighboring villages returned with other women who could not believe what they had been told, and those women went back for more flowers when they saw the dead man, and they brought more and more until there were so many flowers and so many people that it was hard to walk about. At the final moment it pained them to return him to the waters as an orphan and they chose a father and mother from among the best people, and aunts and uncles and cousins, so that through him all the inhabitants of the village became kinsmen. Some sailors who heard the weeping from a distance went off course and people heard of one who had himself tied to the mainmast, remembering ancient fables about sirens. While they fought for the privilege of carrying him on their shoulders along the steep escarpment by the cliffs, men and women became aware for the first time of the desolation of their streets, the dryness of their courtyards, the narrowness of their dreams as they faced the splendor and beauty of their drowned man. They let him go without an anchor so that he could come back if he wished and whenever he wished, and they all held their breath for the fraction of centuries the body took to fall into the abyss. They did not need to look at one another to realize that they were no longer all present, that they would never be. But they also knew that everything would be different from then on, that their houses would have wider doors, higher ceilings, and stronger floors so that Esteban's memory could go everywhere without bumping into beams and so that no one in the future would dare whisper the big boob finally died, too bad, the handsome fool has finally died, because they were going to paint their house fronts gay colors to make Esteban's memory eternal and they were going to break their backs digging for springs among the stones and planting flowers on the cliffs so that in future years at dawn the passengers on great liners would awaken, suffocated by the smell of gardens on the high seas, and the captain would have to come down from the bridge in his dress uniform, with his astrolabe, his pole star, and his row of war medals and, pointing to the promontory of roses on the horizon, he would say in fourteen languages, look there, where the wind is so peaceful now that it's gone to sleep beneath the beds, over there, where the sun's so bright that the sunflowers don't know which way to turn, yes, over there, that's Esteban's village.

Starting Points for Further Research: Gabriel García Márquez

- **Autobiography:** Gabriel García Márquez. *Living to Tell the Tale.* New York: Knopf, 2003.
- **Interview:** Carlos Orlando Pardo. "Interview with Gabriel García Márquez." *Readerly/Writerly Texts: Essays on Literature, Literary/Textual Criticism, and Pedagogy* 4:1 (Fall–Winter 1996): 219–33.

TONE

Tone is the way the writer suggests a particular human voice behind the words, the illusion of a person narrating or speaking the lines. An **ironic** tone, for example, would suggest that the narrator means the opposite of what he or she is literally saying. The ironic meaning might be expressed through the narrator's sarcasm, understatement, or exaggeration. Some writers have created garrulous narrators in vivid life-or-death situations, like the guilty murderer in Edgar Allan Poe's "The Tell-Tale Heart" (p. 510). Other writers, like Raymond Carver (see p. 89), have become famous almost entirely through their highly individualistic tone, not for

Tone   **87**

INSPIRATION   CARVER TO ALTMAN: FROM FICTION TO FILM

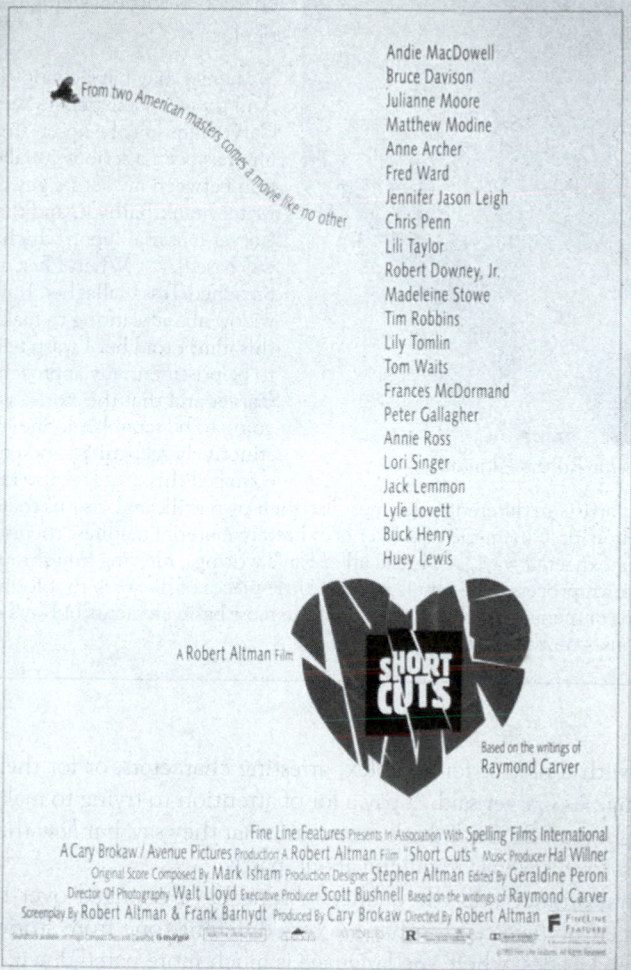

In 1992, four years after Raymond Carver's death, acclaimed filmmaker Robert Altman (director of *M*A*S*H*, *Nashville*, *The Player*, and more recently *Gosford Park*) put together an all-star ensemble cast to film *Short Cuts*, a series of loosely linked vignettes based on nine of Carver's short stories, "Neighbors," "So Much Water So Close to Home," and "A Small, Good Thing" among them. (The stories, which came from several different Carver collections, have been recollected in one volume in *Short Cuts*, published in 1993.) Rather than keeping each story self-contained, Altman took a kaleidoscopic approach to his

(continued on next page)

CARVER TO ALTMAN: FROM FICTION TO FILM

Director Robert Altman.

adaptation, with the intention of remaining true to the spirit of Carver's characters without being tied to particulars:

. . . names may have changed. And though some purists and Carver fans may be upset, this film has been a serious collaboration between my actors, my cowriter Frank Barhydt, and the Carver material [upon which it was based]. . . . When I first approached Tess Gallagher, Ray's widow about wanting to make this film, I told her I wasn't going to be pristine in my approach to Carver and that the stories were going to be scrambled. She instinctively recognized and encouraged this. . . . She also knew that artists in different fields must use their own skills and visions to do their work. Cinematic equivalents of literary material manifest themselves in unexpected ways. . . . I read all of Ray's writings, filtering him through my own process. The film is made of little pieces of his work that form sections of scenes and characters out of the most basic elements of Ray's creations—new but *not* new.

their way with a plot or for complex, arresting characters, or for their focus on a vivid setting. As Carver said, "I pay a lot of attention to trying to make the people talk the right way. By this I don't mean just *what* they say, but *how* they say it, and why. I guess *tone* is what I'm talking about, partly."

The importance and the quality of tone have changed over time. Stories written a century ago tend to have a very different tone from stories written in the last few decades, where the language is much more pared down, and the dialogue matters a great deal more than the third-person narrator's authorial voice. The difference is plain when one looks at a story by Hawthorne (p. 147) and then turns to the minimalist fiction of a Raymond Carver or an Alice Munro, where so little is explained and so much is implied. Since tone tends to play a bigger role nowadays, writers spend much of their time, as Carver did, working on "how" their characters talk.

"Cathedral," by Raymond Carver, reveals a writer who became famous for an understated tone that seems to capture the voice of his lower-middle-class and working-class characters, presenting them with a vividness that readers immediately notice. Carver soon became one of America's most influential short story writers of the late twentieth century. Many talented young writers aimed to study with him, and imitators sprang up everywhere. "Cathedral" also connects well to many of the terms in this chapter, since it has more than one central, significant symbol, an unmistakable tone, and an interestingly unreliable first-person narrator.

RAYMOND CARVER   (1938–1988)

Raymond Carver was raised in the Pacific Northwest, where many of his short stories are set. He was late to develop as a writer and only began publishing after taking creative writing courses from the novelist John Gardner. Carver developed a distinctive, minimal narrative style that proved highly influential in the 1980s and 1990s. His story collections include Will You Please Be Quiet, Please? *(1976),* What We Talk About When We Talk About Love *(1981),* Cathedral *(1983),* Where I'm Calling From *(1988), and* Call If You Need Me *(published posthumously in 2001).*

Cathedral   (1981)

This blind man, an old friend of my wife's, he was on his way to spend the night. His wife had died. So he was visiting the dead wife's relatives in Connecticut. He called my wife from his in-laws'. Arrangements were made. He would come by train, a five-hour trip, and my wife would meet him at the station. She hadn't seen him since she worked for him one summer in Seattle ten years ago. But she and the blind man had kept in touch. They made tapes and mailed them back and forth. I wasn't enthusiastic about his visit. He was no one I knew. And his being blind bothered me. My idea of blindness came from the movies. In the movies, the blind moved slowly and never laughed. Sometimes they were led by seeing-eye dogs. A blind man in my house was not something I looked forward to.

That summer in Seattle she had needed a job. She didn't have any money. The man she was going to marry at the end of the summer was in officers' training school. He didn't have any money, either. But she was in love with the guy, and he was in love with her, etc. She'd seen something in the paper: HELP WANTED—*Reading to Blind Man*, and a telephone number. She phoned and went over, was hired on the spot. She'd worked with this blind man all summer. She read stuff to him, case studies, reports, that sort of thing. She helped him organize his little office in the county social-service department. They'd become good friends, my wife and the blind man. How do I know these things? She told me. And she told me something else. On her last day in the office, the blind man asked if he could touch her face. She agreed to this. She told me he touched his fingers to every part of her face, her nose—even her neck! She never forgot it. She even tried to write a poem about it. She was always trying to write a poem. She wrote a poem or two every year, usually after something really important had happened to her.

When we first started going out together, she showed me the poem. In the poem, she recalled his fingers and the way they had moved around over her face. In the poem, she talked about what she had felt at the time, about what went through her mind when the blind man touched her nose and lips. I can remember I didn't think much of the poem. Of course, I didn't tell her that. Maybe I just don't understand poetry. I admit it's not the first thing I reach for when I pick up something to read.

Anyway, this man who'd first enjoyed her favors, the officer-to-be, he'd been her childhood sweetheart. So okay. I'm saying that at the end of the summer she let the blind man run his hands over her face, said goodbye to him, married her childhood etc., who was now a commissioned officer, and she moved away from Seattle. But they'd kept in touch, she and the blind man. She made the first contact after a year or so. She called him up one night from an Air Force base in Alabama. She wanted to talk. They talked. He asked her to send him a tape and tell him about her life. She did this. She sent the tape. On the tape, she told the blind man about her husband and about their life together in the military. She told the blind man she loved her husband but she didn't like it where they lived and she didn't like it that he was a part of the military-industrial thing. She told the blind man she'd written a poem and he was in it. She told him that she was writing a poem about what it was like to be an Air Force officer's wife. The poem wasn't finished yet. She was still writing it. The blind man made a tape. He sent her the tape. She made a tape. This went on for years. My wife's officer was posted to one base and then another. She sent tapes from Moody AFB, McGuire, McConnell, and finally Travis, near Sacramento, where one night she got to feeling lonely and cut off from people she kept losing in that moving-around life. She got to feeling she couldn't go it another step. She went in and swallowed all the pills and capsules in the medicine chest and washed them down with a bottle of gin. Then she got into a hot bath and passed out.

But instead of dying, she got sick. She threw up. Her officer—why should he   5
have a name? he was the childhood sweetheart, and what more does he want?—came home from somewhere, found her, and called the ambulance. In time, she put it all on a tape and sent the tape to the blind man. Over the years, she put all kinds of stuff on tapes and sent the tapes off lickety-split. Next to writing a poem every year, I think it was her chief means of recreation. On one tape, she told the blind man she'd decided to live away from her officer for a time. On another tape, she told him about her divorce. She and I began going out, and of course she told her blind man about it. She told him everything, or so it seemed to me. Once she asked me if I'd like to hear the latest tape from the blind man. This was a year ago. I was on the tape, she said. So I said okay, I'd listen to it. I got us drinks and we settled down in the living room. We made ready to listen. First she inserted the tape into the player and adjusted a couple of dials. Then she pushed a lever. The tape squeaked and someone began to talk in this loud voice. She lowered the volume. After a few minutes of harmless chitchat, I heard my own name in the mouth of this stranger, this blind man I didn't even know! And then this: "From all you've said about him, I can only conclude—" But we were interrupted, a knock at the door, something, and we didn't ever get back to the tape. Maybe it was just as well. I'd heard all I wanted to.

Now this same blind man was coming to sleep in my house.

"Maybe I could take him bowling," I said to my wife. She was at the draining board doing scalloped potatoes. She put down the knife she was using and turned around.

"If you love me," she said, "you can do this for me. If you don't love me, okay. But if you had a friend, any friend, and the friend came to visit, I'd make him feel comfortable." She wiped her hands with the dish towel.

"I don't have any blind friends," I said.

"You don't have *any* friends," she said. "Period. Besides," she said, "goddamn it, his wife's just died! Don't you understand that? The man's lost his wife!"

I didn't answer. She'd told me a little about the blind man's wife. Her name was Beulah. Beulah! That's a name for a colored woman.

"Was his wife Negro?" I asked.

"Are you crazy?" my wife said. "Have you just flipped or something?" She picked up a potato. I saw it hit the floor, then roll under the stove. "What's wrong with you?" she said. "Are you drunk?"

"I'm just asking," I said.

Right then my wife filled me in with more detail than I cared to know. I made a drink and sat at the kitchen table to listen. Pieces of the story began to fall into place.

Beulah had gone to work for the blind man the summer after my wife had stopped working for him. Pretty soon Beulah and the blind man had themselves a church wedding. It was a little wedding—who'd want to go to such a wedding in the first place?—just the two of them, plus the minister and the minister's wife. But it was a church wedding just the same. It was what Beulah had wanted, he'd said. But even then Beulah must have been carrying the cancer in her glands. After they had been inseparable for eight years—my wife's word, *inseparable*—Beulah's health went into a rapid decline. She died in a Seattle hospital room, the blind man sitting beside the bed and holding on to her hand. They'd married, lived and worked together, slept together—had sex, sure—and then the blind man had to bury her. All this without his having ever seen what the goddamned woman looked like. It was beyond my understanding. Hearing this, I felt sorry for the blind man for a little bit. And then I found myself thinking what a pitiful life this woman must have led. Imagine a woman who could never see herself as she was seen in the eyes of her loved one. A woman who could go on day after day and never receive the smallest compliment from her beloved. A woman whose husband could never read the expression on her face, be it misery or something better. Someone who could wear makeup or not—what difference to him? She could, if she wanted, wear green eye-shadow around one eye, a straight pin in her nostril, yellow slacks and purple shoes, no matter. And then to slip off into death, the blind man's hand on her hand, his blind eyes streaming tears—I'm imagining now—her last thought maybe this: that he never even knew what she looked like, and she on an express to the grave. Robert was left with a small insurance policy and half of a twenty-peso Mexican coin. The other half of the coin went into the box with her. Pathetic.

So when the time rolled around, my wife went to the depot to pick him up. With nothing to do but wait—sure, I blamed him for that—I was having a drink and watching the TV when I heard the car pull into the drive. I got up from the sofa with my drink and went to the window to have a look.

I saw my wife laughing as she parked the car. I saw her get out of the car and shut the door. She was still wearing a smile. Just amazing. She went around to the other side of the car to where the blind man was already starting to get out. This blind man, feature this, he was wearing a full beard! A beard on a blind man! Too much, I say. The blind man reached into the back seat and dragged out a suitcase. My wife took his arm, shut the car door, and, talking all the way, moved him down the drive and then up the steps to the front porch. I turned off the TV. I finished my drink, rinsed the glass, dried my hands. Then I went to the door.

My wife said, "I want you to meet Robert. Robert, this is my husband. I've told you all about him." She was beaming. She had this blind man by his coat sleeve.

The blind man let go of his suitcase and up came his hand.   20

I took it. He squeezed hard, held my hand, and then he let it go.

"I feel like we've already met," he boomed.

"Likewise," I said. I didn't know what else to say. Then I said, "Welcome. I've heard a lot about you." We began to move then, a little group, from the porch into the living room, my wife guiding him by the arm. The blind man was carrying his suitcase in his other hand. My wife said things like, "To your left here, Robert. That's right. Now watch it, there's a chair. That's it. Sit down right here. This is the sofa. We just bought this sofa two weeks ago."

I started to say something about the old sofa. I'd liked that old sofa. But I didn't say anything. Then I wanted to say something else, small-talk, about the scenic ride along the Hudson. How going *to* New York, you should sit on the right-hand side of the train, and coming *from* New York, the left-hand side.

"Did you have a good train ride?" I said. "Which side of the train did you sit   25
on, by the way?"

"What a question, which side!" my wife said. "What's it matter which side?" she said.

"I just asked," I said.

"Right side," the blind man said. "I hadn't been on a train in nearly forty years. Not since I was a kid. With my folks. That's been a long time. I'd nearly forgotten the sensation. I have winter in my beard now," he said. "So I've been told, anyway. Do I look distinguished, my dear?" the blind man said to my wife.

"You look distinguished, Robert," she said. "Robert," she said. "Robert, it's just so good to see you."

My wife finally took her eyes off the blind man and looked at me. I had the   30
feeling she didn't like what she saw. I shrugged.

I've never met, or personally known, anyone who was blind. This blind man was late forties, a heavy-set, balding man with stooped shoulders, as if he carried a great weight there. He wore brown slacks, brown shoes, a light-brown shirt, a tie, a sports coat. Spiffy. He also had this full beard. But he didn't use a cane and he didn't wear dark glasses. I'd always thought dark glasses were a must for the blind. Fact was, I wished he had a pair. At first glance, his eyes looked like anyone else's eyes. But if you look close, there was something different about them. Too much white in the iris, for one thing, and the pupils seemed to move around in the sockets without his knowing it or being able to stop it. Creepy. As I stared at his face, I saw the left pupil turn in toward his nose while the other made an effort to keep in one place. But it was only an effort, for that eye was on the roam without his knowing it or wanting it to be.

I said, "Let me get you a drink. What's your pleasure? We have a little of everything. It's one of our pastimes."

"Bub, I'm a Scotch man myself," he said fast enough in this big voice.

"Right," I said. Bub! "Sure you are, I knew it."

He let his fingers touch his suitcase, which was sitting alongside the sofa. He   35
was taking his bearings. I didn't blame him for that.

"I'll move that up to your room," my wife said.

"No, that's fine," the blind man said loudly. "It can go up when I go up."

"A little water with the Scotch?" I said.

"Very little," he said.

"I knew it," I said.

He said, "Just a tad. The Irish actor, Barry Fitzgerald? I'm like that fellow. When I drink water, Fitzgerald said, I drink water. When I drink whiskey, I drink whiskey." My wife laughed. The blind man brought his hand up under his beard. He lifted his beard slowly and let it drop.

I did the drinks, three big glasses of Scotch with a splash of water in each. Then we made ourselves comfortable and talked about Robert's travels. First the long flight from the West Coast to Connecticut, we covered that. Then from Connecticut up here by train. We had another drink concerning that leg of the trip.

I remembered having read somewhere that the blind didn't smoke because, as speculation had it, they couldn't see the smoke they exhaled. I thought I knew that much and that much only about blind people. But this blind man smoked his cigarette down to the nubbin and then lit another one. This blind man filled his ashtray and my wife emptied it.

When we sat down at the table for dinner, we had another drink. My wife heaped Robert's plate with cube steak, scalloped potatoes, green beans. I buttered him up two slices of bread. I said, "Here's bread and butter for you." I swallowed some of my drink. "Now let us pray," I said, and the blind man lowered his head. My wife looked at me, her mouth agape. "Pray the phone won't ring and the food doesn't get cold," I said.

We dug in. We ate everything there was to eat on the table. We ate like there was no tomorrow. We didn't talk. We ate. We scarfed. We grazed that table. We were into serious eating. The blind man had right away located his foods, he knew just where everything was on his plate. I watched with admiration as he used his knife and fork on the meat. He'd cut two pieces of meat, fork the meat into his mouth, and then go all out for the scalloped potatoes, the beans next, and then he'd tear off a hunk of buttered bread and eat that. He'd follow this up with a big drink of milk. It didn't seem to bother him to use his fingers once in a while, either.

We finished everything, including half a strawberry pie. For a few moments, we sat as if stunned. Sweat beaded on our faces. Finally, we got up from the table and left the dirty plates. We didn't look back. We took ourselves into the living room and sank into our places again. Robert and my wife sat on the sofa. I took the big chair. We had us two or three more drinks while they talked about the major things that had come to pass for them in the past ten years. For the most part, I just listened. Now and then I joined in. I didn't want him to think I'd left the room, and I didn't want her to think I was feeling left out. They talked of things that had happened to them—to them!—these past ten years. I waited in vain to hear my name on my wife's sweet lips: "And then my dear husband came into my life"—something like that. But I heard nothing of the sort. More talk of Robert. Robert had done a little of everything, it seemed, a regular blind jack-of-all-trades. But most recently he and his wife had had an Amway distributorship, from which, I gathered, they'd earned their living, such as it was. The blind man was also a ham radio operator. He talked in his loud voice about conversations

40

45

he'd had with fellow operators in Guam, in the Philippines, in Alaska, and even in Tahiti. He said he'd have a lot of friends there if he ever wanted to go visit those places. From time to time, he'd turn his blind face toward me, put his hand under his beard, ask me something. How long had I been in my present position? (Three years.) Did I like my work? (I didn't.) Was I going to stay with it? (What were the options?) Finally, when I thought he was beginning to run down, I got up and turned on the TV.

My wife looked at me with irritation. She was heading toward a boil. Then she looked at the blind man and said, "Robert, do you have a TV?"

The blind man said, "My dear, I have two TVs. I have a color set and a black-and-white thing, an old relic. It's funny, but if I turn the TV on, and I'm always turning it on, I turn on the color set. It's funny, don't you think?"

I didn't know what to say to that. I had absolutely nothing to say to that. No opinions. So I watched the news program and tried to listen to what the announcer was saying.

"This is a color TV," the blind man said. "Don't ask me how, but I can tell."   50

"We traded up a while ago," I said.

The blind man had another taste of his drink. He lifted his beard, sniffed it, and let it fall. He leaned forward on the sofa. He positioned his ashtray on the coffee table, then put the lighter to his cigarette. He leaned back on the sofa and crossed his legs at the ankles.

My wife covered her mouth, and then she yawned. She stretched. She said, "I think I'll go upstairs and put on my robe. I think I'll change into something else. Robert, you make yourself comfortable," she said.

"I'm comfortable," the blind man said.

"I want you to feel comfortable in this house," she said.   55

"I am comfortable," the blind man said.

After she'd left the room, he and I listened to the weather report and then to the sports roundup. By that time, she'd been gone so long I didn't know if she was going to come back. I thought she might have gone to bed. I wished she'd come back downstairs. I didn't want to be left alone with a blind man. I asked him if he wanted another drink, and he said sure. Then I asked if he wanted to smoke some dope with me. I said I'd just rolled a number. I hadn't, but I planned to do so in about two shakes.

"I'll try some with you," he said.

"Damn right," I said. "That's the stuff."

I got our drinks and sat down on the sofa with him. Then I rolled us two fat   60
numbers. I lit one and passed it. I brought it to his fingers. He took it and inhaled.

"Hold it as long as you can," I said. I could tell he didn't know the first thing.

My wife came back downstairs wearing her pink robe and her pink slippers.

"What do I smell?" she said.

"We thought we'd have us some cannabis," I said.

My wife gave me a savage look. Then she looked at the blind man and said,   65
"Robert, I didn't know you smoked."

He said, "I do now, my dear. There's a first time for everything. But I don't feel anything yet."

"This stuff is pretty mellow," I said. "This stuff is mild. It's dope you can reason with," I said. "It doesn't mess you up."

"Not much it doesn't, bub," he said, and laughed.

My wife sat on the sofa between the blind man and me. I passed her the number. She took it and toked and then passed it back to me. "Which way is this going?" she said. Then she said, "I shouldn't be smoking this. I can hardly keep my eyes open as it is. That dinner did me in. I shouldn't have eaten so much."

"It was the strawberry pie," the blind man said. "That's what did it," he said, 70 and he laughed his big laugh. Then he shook his head.

"There's more strawberry pie," I said.

"Do you want some more, Robert?" my wife said.

"Maybe in a little while," he said.

We gave our attention to the TV. My wife yawned again. She said, "Your bed is made up when you feel like going to bed, Robert. I know you must have had a long day. When you're ready to go to bed, say so." She pulled his arm. "Robert?"

He came to and said, "I've had a real nice time. This beats tapes, doesn't 75 it?"

I said, "Coming at you," and I put the number between his fingers. He inhaled, held the smoke, and then let it go. It was like he'd been doing it since he was nine years old.

"Thanks, bub," he said. "But I think this is all for me. I think I'm beginning to feel it," he said. He held the burning roach out for my wife.

"Same here," she said. "Ditto. Me, too." She took the roach and passed it to me. "I may just sit here for a while between you two guys with my eyes closed. But don't let me bother you, okay? Either one of you. If it bothers you, say so. Otherwise, I may just sit here with my eyes closed until you're ready to go to bed," she said. "Your bed's made up, Robert, when you're ready. It's right next to our room at the top of the stairs. We'll show you up when you're ready. You wake me up now, you guys, if I fall asleep." She said that and then she closed her eyes and went to sleep.

The news program ended. I got up and changed the channel. I sat back down on the sofa. I wished my wife hadn't pooped out. Her head lay across the back of the sofa, her mouth open. She'd turned so that her robe had slipped away from her legs, exposing a juicy thigh. I reached to draw her robe back over her, and it was then that I glanced at the blind man. What the hell! I flipped the robe open again.

"You say when you want some strawberry pie," I said. 80

"I will," he said.

I said, "Are you tired? Do you want me to take you up to your bed? Are you ready to hit the hay?"

"Not yet," he said. "No, I'll stay up with you, bub. If that's all right. I'll stay up until you're ready to turn in. We haven't had a chance to talk. Know what I mean? I feel like me and her monopolized the evening." He lifted his beard and he let it fall. He picked up his cigarettes and his lighter.

"That's all right," I said. Then I said, "I'm glad for the company."

And I guess I was. Every night I smoked dope and stayed up as long as I 85 could before I fell asleep. My wife and I hardly ever went to bed at the same time. When I did go to sleep, I had these dreams. Sometimes I'd wake up from one of them, my heart going crazy.

Something about the church and the Middle Ages was on the TV. Not your run-of-the-mill TV fare. I wanted to watch something else. I turned to the other channels. But there was nothing on them, either. So I turned back to the first channel and apologized.

"Bub, it's all right," the blind man said. "It's fine with me. Whatever you want to watch is okay. I'm always learning something. Learning never ends. It won't hurt me to learn something tonight. I got ears," he said.

We didn't say anything for a time. He was leaning forward with his head turned at me, his right ear aimed in the direction of the set. Very disconcerting. Now and then his eyelids drooped and then they snapped open again. Now and then he put his fingers into his beard and tugged, like he was thinking about something he was hearing on the television.

On the screen, a group of men wearing cowls was being set upon and tormented by men dressed in skeleton costumes and men dressed as devils. The men dressed as devils wore devil masks, horns, and long tails. This pageant was part of a procession. The Englishman who was narrating the thing said it took place in Spain once a year. I tried to explain to the blind man what was happening.

"Skeletons," he said. "I know about skeletons," he said, and he nodded.   90

The TV showed this one cathedral. Then there was a long, slow look at another one. Finally, the picture switched to the famous one in Paris, with its flying buttresses and its spires reaching up to the clouds. The camera pulled away to show the whole of the cathedral rising above the skyline.

There were times when the Englishman who was telling the thing would shut up, would simply let the camera move around over the cathedrals. Or else the camera would tour the countryside, men in fields walking behind oxen. I waited as long as I could. Then I felt I had to say something. I said, "They're showing the outside of this cathedral now. Gargoyles. Little statues carved to look like monsters. Now I guess they're in Italy. Yeah, they're in Italy. There's paintings on the walls of this one church."

"Are those fresco paintings, bub?" he asked, and he sipped from his drink.

I reached for my glass. But it was empty. I tried to remember what I could remember. "You're asking me are those frescoes?" I said. "That's a good question. I don't know."

The camera moved to a cathedral outside Lisbon. The differences in the   95
Portuguese cathedral compared with the French and Italian were not that great. But they were there. Mostly the interior stuff. Then something occurred to me, and I said, "Something has occurred to me. Do you have any idea what a cathedral is? What they look like, that is? Do you follow me? If somebody says cathedral to you, do you have any notion what they're talking about? Do you know the difference between that and a Baptist church, say?"

He let the smoke dribble from his mouth. "I know they took hundreds of workers fifty or a hundred years to build," he said. "I just heard the man say that, of course. I know generations of the same families worked on a cathedral. I heard him say that too. The men who began their life's work on them, they never lived to see the completion of their work. In that wise, bub, they're no different from the rest of us, right?" He laughed. Then his eyelids drooped again. His head nodded. He seemed to be snoozing. Maybe he was imagining himself in Portugal. The TV was showing another cathedral now. This one was in Germany. The Englishman's voice droned on. "Cathedrals," the blind man said. He sat up and rolled his head back and forth. "If you want the truth, bub, that's about all I know. What I just said. What I heard him say. But maybe you could describe one to me? I wish you'd do it. I'd like that. If you want to know, I really don't have a good idea."

I stared hard at the shot of the cathedral on the TV. How could I even begin to describe it? But say my life depended on it. Say my life was being threatened by an insane guy who said I had to do it or else.

I stared some more at the cathedral before the picture flipped off into the countryside. There was no use. I turned to the blind man and said. "To begin with, they're very tall." I was looking around the room for clues. "They reach way up. Up and up. Toward the sky. They're so big, some of them, they have to have these supports. To help hold them up, so to speak. These supports are called buttresses. They remind me of viaducts, for some reason. But maybe you don't know viaducts, either? Sometimes the cathedrals have devils and such carved into the front. Sometimes lords and ladies. Don't ask me why this is," I said.

He was nodding. The whole upper part of his body seemed to be moving back and forth.

"I'm not doing so good, am I?" I said.   100

He stopped nodding and leaned forward on the edge of the sofa. As he listened to me, he was running his fingers through his beard. I wasn't getting through to him, I could see that. But he waited for me to go on just the same. He nodded, like he was trying to encourage me. I tried to think what else to say. "They're really big," I said. "They're massive. They're built of stone. Marble, too, sometimes. In those olden days, when they built cathedrals, men wanted to be close to God. In those olden days, God was an important part of everyone's life. You could tell this from their cathedral-building. I'm sorry," I said, "but it looks like that's the best I can do for you. I'm just no good at it."

"That's all right, bub," the blind man said. "Hey, listen. I hope you don't mind my asking you. Can I ask you something? Let me ask you a simple question, yes or no. I'm just curious and there's no offense. You're my host. But let me ask if you are in any way religious? You don't mind my asking?"

I shook my head. He couldn't see that, though. A wink is the same as a nod to a blind man. "I guess I don't believe in it. In anything. Sometimes it's hard. You know what I'm saying?"

"Sure I do," he said.

"Right," I said.   105

The Englishman was still holding forth. My wife sighed in her sleep. She drew a long breath and went on with her sleeping.

"You'll have to forgive me." I said. "But I can't tell you what a cathedral looks like. It just isn't in me to do it. I can't do any more than I've done."

The blind man sat very still, his head down, as he listened to me.

I said, "The truth is, cathedrals don't mean anything special to me. Nothing. Cathedrals. They're something to look at on late-night TV. That's all they are."

It was then that the blind man cleared his throat. He brought something up.   110
He took a handkerchief from his back pocket. Then he said, "I get it, bub. It's okay. It happens. Don't worry about it," he said. "Hey, listen to me. Will you do

me a favor? I got an idea. Why don't you find us some heavy paper? And a pen. We'll do something. We'll draw one together. Get us a pen and some heavy paper. Go on, bub, get the stuff," he said.

So I went upstairs. My legs felt like they didn't have any strength in them. They felt like they did after I'd done some running. In my wife's room, I looked around. I found some ballpoints in a little basket on her table. And then I tried to think where to look for the kind of paper he was talking about.

Downstairs, in the kitchen, I found a shopping bag with onion skins in the bottom of the bag. I emptied the bag and shook it. I brought it into the living room and sat down with it near his legs. I moved some things, smoothed the wrinkles from the bag, spread it out on the coffee table.

The blind man got down from the sofa and sat next to me on the carpet.

He ran his fingers over the paper. He went up and down the sides of the paper. The edges, even the edges. He fingered the corners.

"All right," he said. "All right, let's do her."   115

He found my hand, the hand with the pen. He closed his hand over my hand. "Go ahead, bub, draw," he said. "Draw. You'll see. I'll follow along with you. It'll be okay. Just begin now like I'm telling you. You'll see. Draw," the blind man said.

So I began. First I drew a box that looked like a house. It could have been the house I lived in. Then I put a roof on it. At either end of the roof, I drew spires. Crazy.

"Swell," he said. "Terrific. You're doing fine," he said.

"Never thought anything like this could happen in your lifetime, did you, bub? Well, it's a strange life, we all know that. Go on now. Keep it up."

I put in windows with arches. I drew flying buttresses. I hung great doors. I   120 couldn't stop. The TV station went off the air. I put down the pen and closed and opened my fingers. The blind man felt round over the paper. He moved the tips of his fingers over the paper, all over what I had drawn, and he nodded.

"Doing fine," the blind man said.

I took up the pen again, and he found my hand. I kept at it. I'm no artist. But I kept drawing just the same.

My wife opened up her eyes and gazed at us. She sat up on the sofa, her robe hanging open. She said, "What are you doing? Tell me, I want to know."

I didn't answer her.

The blind man said, "We're drawing a cathedral. Me and him are working   125 on it. Press hard," he said to me. "That's right. That's good," he said. "Sure. You got it, bub. I can tell. You didn't think you could. But you can, can't you? You're cooking with gas now. You know what I'm saying? We're going to really have us something here in a minute. How's the old arm?" he said. "Put some people in there now. What's a cathedral without people?"

My wife said, "What's going on? Robert, what are you doing? What's going on?"

"It's all right," he said to her. "Close your eyes now," the blind man said to me.

I did it. I closed them just like he said.

"Are they closed?" he said. "Don't fudge."

"They're closed," I said.   130

"Keep them that way," he said. He said, "Don't stop now. Draw."

So we kept on with it. His fingers rode my fingers as my hand went over the paper. It was like nothing else in my life up to now.

Then he said, "I think that's it. I think you got it," he said. "Take a look. What do you think?"

But I had my eyes closed. I thought I'd keep them that way for a little longer. I thought it was something I ought to do.

"Well?" he said." Are you looking?"

My eyes were still closed. I was in my house. I knew that. But I didn't feel like I was inside anything.

"It's really something," I said.

Talking about the Text

1. What are three characteristics of the narrator's voice?
2. Speculate on what the symbolic significance of the cathedrals in the story might be.

Writing about the Text

1. In a short paper, compare the narrator's language and that of "the blind man." What differences do you see in the way Carver presents their talk?
2. Draw up a list of possible things "the blind man" might represent, then write one paragraph on each of three possibilities.

Linking the Text to Other Texts

1. Compare "the blind man" in "Cathedral" to the very different man who meets up with Young Goodman Brown (p. 149) in the forest in Hawthorne's story.
2. The unreliable narrator in John Updike's "A & P" shares some characteristics with the narrator here. Make a list of the most significant ones.

Starting Points for Further Research: Raymond Carver

- **Editions:** Raymond Carver. *Short Cuts: Selected Stories.* New York: Vintage Books, 1993.
  ———. *Where I'm Calling From: New and Selected Stories.* New York: Atlantic Monthly Press, 1988.
  ———. *Fires: Essays, Poems, Stories.* New York: Vintage Books, 1985.
- **Biography:** Sam Halpert. *Raymond Carver: An Oral Biography.* Iowa City: University of Iowa Press, 1995.
- **Critical Essay:** Charles E. May. "'Do You See What I'm Saying?': The Inadequacy of Explanation and the Uses of Story in the Short Fiction of Raymond Carver." *Yearbook of English Studies* (2001): 39–49.

For Further Reading: Tone

ANA CASTILLO (B. 1953)

Ana Castillo was born in Evanston, Illinois. Before turning to writing, she was a teacher of English and of Latin American studies. Most of her stories deal with the experience of Chicanas in America. Among her novels are the prize-winning The Mixquiahuala Letters *(1986) and* Peel My Love Like an Onion *(1999). Castillo has also published poetry, including* Women Are Not Roses *(1984) and* My Father Was a Toltec *(1988). She lives in Chicago.*

Loverboys   (1993)

Two boys are making out in the booth across from me. I ain't got nothing else to do, so I watch them. I drink the not-so-aged house brandy and I watch two boys make out. It's more like they're in the throes of passion, as they say. And they're not boys, really. I think I've seen them around before, somewhere on campus maybe. Not making out though.

One gets up, to get them each another drink I guess, and he and I check each other out briefly as he passes me up on his way to the bar. He's a white boy wearing a T-shirt with a graphic of Malcolm X on it.

This is the way my life is these days or maybe it's a sign of the nineties: a white boy with a picture of Malcolm X on his T-shirt and me, sitting here in a gay bar trying to forget a man.

Well, okay. He must not have been just any man and I'm sure not just any woman. Before him there were only women. Puras mujeres (¡sino mujeres puras)! A cast of thousands. Women's music festivals, feminist symposiums, women of color retreats and camp-outs, women's healing rituals under a full moon, ceremonies of union and not-so-ceremonious reunions, women-only panels and caucuses at conferences, en fin, women ad infinitum.

And then one day a boy—not much older than either of these two loving it   5
up in front of me, nor the half-dozen other clientele here on a dead Monday night for that matter—comes into my store asking for a copy of *The Rebel*. I point in the direction of Albert—whom once I was so fond of we were on a first-name basis—and he, the boy in my store, kind of casually goes over to check out what we got on the shelf. We're always stocked up on the existentialists, so I didn't bother to offer assistance.

My partner—who used to be my partner in all senses of the word and whom I bought out a year ago—and I opened up the store about ten years ago. We thought about making it a woman's bookstore, a lesbian bookstore, a gay and lesbian bookstore, a "Third World" bookstore, or even an exclusively Latina bookstore. Heaven knows, any town could use at least one of each of those kind of bookshops—stocked up on alternative-press publications that inform you about what's going on with the majority of the population when you sure don't hear it from the mass media. You know? But no, spirituality won out—since all roads eventually lead to one place, we reasoned.

So along with Camus, Sartre, and Kierkegaard, we . . . I carry almost anything you can imagine that comes out of the East and Native imaginations and ancient practices.

I sat back and picked up the book I was reading. I let the boy browse. I saw him leafing through some other things and, finally, he came over with a copy of *The Stranger*.

"Didn't you see *The Rebel* up on the shelf?" I asked, not really looking at him, just taking the book and ringing it up.

"Yeah. But I don't think I'm ready for it," he answered. "I read this in high   10
school. I think I'll read it again . . . I really like this translation anyway," he said, referring to the edition he had chosen.

I rang it up. But he didn't pick up his package right away. Just kept looking at me. I looked back and smiled, a little cockily. I'm a mirror that way. You look at me a certain way and I respond in kind. Just like with this white guy here who just passed me by again with two Coronas. He looks. He doesn't smile. He just looks like I don't belong here. *I* don't belong here? I helped start this joint about twelve years ago when you couldn't find a gay bar within ten miles of this town.

Me and Rosie and her compadre, who's over there tending bar—the big guy with the Pancho Villa charm and beer belly. He looks like someone's father, right? Not the kind of bartender you would expect to find in a gay bar. Well, just for the record, he *is* somebody's father. His oldest son enlisted in the air force— overcompensating for his dad's dubious machismo or patriotism, if you ask me. He just got shipped off to the Middle East last week. His daughter, Belinda, Rosie's godchild, got married last summer.

That's the way it goes.

Yeah. His wife knows he owns this bar. And she knows all the rest, too. But she's pretty religious and would never have thought to divorce him. Besides, Rosie told me that his wife really doesn't find the men in her husband's life a threat to her marriage. He's got it pretty good, huh?

Anyway, I say to this young man with Indian smooth skin like glazed clay, and the offhanded manner of a chile alegre if I ever saw one, after he's been staring at me for a good minute or so without saying anything, "Is there anything else I can help you with?"

His dark face got darker when he blushed, and he laughed a little, "Naw, naw . . . ," he said, shaking his head. "Actually, I *did* wanna get that one of his, too, but I can't afford it till payday," he admitted, referring to *The Rebel*.

Liking his white, uneven teeth, although I'm not very good with quotes, except to massacre them usually, I said, " 'I was placed halfway between poverty and the sun.' " With that he got this expression like I had just done a wondrous thing by quoting Albert spontaneously. I was ready to part the sea if I could continue to elicit that gaze of a devotee from those obsidian eyes, so I dared to continue quoting: "'Poverty kept me from thinking all was well under the sun and in history; the sun taught me that history was not everything . . .' "

He laughed out loud. He laughed like he had just discovered he was in the presence of Camus himself and he slapped his thigh, as if to say, "What a kick!" He stared at me some more and then he left, still laughing.

After that it was all out of our hands. He came back a few more times that week and finally one evening just before I closed. He wasn't buying anything, just browsing and talking with me when I had a minute between customers. By this time we were old chums—talking about all kinds of things, literature mostly. He likes poetry. He writes poetry. Well, at least he says he does. He never showed me anything. But who am I to question or to judge?

So we went to get a taco down the street at my favorite taco joint. I'm really a creature of habit, no doubt about it. There's only one place where I go for tacos and only one place where I go to get loaded. And there's my store. In between is home and sleep.

Anyway, then we came here, as you might have guessed, to have a drink. I used to come just on weekends but since about the time when we stopped hanging out I am here just about every night of the week, it seems.

That night we got pretty "hammered," his favorite word for what we used to do very well together—besides make love. We made love anytime, anyplace, as often as we could—like a happy pair of rabbits—with the one big difference that I don't reproduce—never did when I could and now I never will.

He's really gonna hate me for telling you all this (and I don't doubt that he'll find out someday that I have, since it was the very fact that I'm kind of a public person that scared him off), but little by little, his PMS started to get the better of him. You know, his "Pure Macho Shit." Maybe it's not fair to call what he started to feel towards me that, but I don't know what else it was. I can't explain none of it. I don't know why he's gone, why I'm here worrying about it . . . why *you're* here, for that matter . . .

Except to drink. And we know how far that will get you. It's just like that Mexican joke with the two drunks just barely hanging on to their bar stools. "Well, why do you drink?" one asks the other. "I drink to forget," the other guy replies. "And what's it you're trying to forget?" the first guy asks. The other looks up, kind of thinking for a bit, then says, "I dunno. I forgot."

Well, it's a lot funnier in Spanish. Or maybe you have to be Mexican. But   25
for sure, you have to be a drunk to get it . . . or maybe just drunk.

I went over to the pay phone when I first got here and tried to call him. Although I promised myself never to look for him again, I broke down finally—because between books and drinks, there's only him in my head, like one of those melodies where you only know half the words. I called him without thinking about it, like I had done so many times before, and him always on the other end, and pretty soon, he would be with me.

I called the gas station where he *used* to work 'cause I can't call his house, but apparently he's not gigging there anymore. The guy that answered couldn't tell me anything. High turnover in those places is all the consolation he could give me.

Where do you think my boy went? Fired, most likely. Left town, maybe? I doubt it. He's not ready for that kind of wandering, the kind of wandering his soul takes when he's alone and the kind of wandering loving me gave his imagination. Unless I really underestimated him.

Well, see, in the beginning he seemed very cool about my life. The fact that I had not been with a man since college, just women . . . one woman mostly. Considering himself a sensitive progressive politically conscious self-defined young male of color—*of course* he was cool about my life, he said. How could he not be, he insisted.

But that didn't stop him from jumping on top of me the first night we were   30
alone, did it?—when he came over to my place with the excuse to drop off a copy of Neruda's *Veinte poemas de amor y una canción desesperada* that he bought in Mexico where he lived for a semester as an exchange student.

A bright young man, he was. Is. A bright splendid ray in my life. But like Picasso said, "When you come right down to it, all you have is your self. Your self is a sun with a thousand rays in your belly. The rest is nothing." But for a while, he was all mine. Mio. Mio. Mio.

Then his brothers started ragging him about running around with a lesbian—or worse, a bisexual, nothing more shady or untrustworthy (except for a liberal)—who plays soccer and who knows how to do her own tune-ups and oil change. And his mother, about me being a woman with a past. And his father, about me being an independent businesswoman, and what could he teach an older woman?

As if my loverboy were not tormenting himself well enough on his own day and night over all this as it was. Once he was reading a book by a male psychologist that talked about the history of goddess worship and said that in early times the pig and cow represented the female and were considered powerful deities. So one night we were sleeping and his body gave a great jerk and we both woke up. He told me, "I was dreaming that I was at home in the kitchen and I was telling my brothers that a pig was after me . . . and suddenly this huge pig leaped right through the window at me . . . and I jumped!"

Well, of course it didn't take a genius to figure out who the pig was but I was pretty impressed by his metaphorical interpretation of what I was in his life. He was cool about us for a while, as I said, although he did spend the first months doing some hard drinking over it. Then he sobered up so that he could sort it all out with a clear head, he said.

And then he left.

I went on with my business without missing a beat. You know, I got the store to run. And I spoke at a pro-choice rally last weekend. I started dating a woman I met some time back who had asked me to go out with her before, but I was too busy being in love with an existentialist Catholic pseudo-poet manito fifteen years younger than me to have noticed even Queen Nefertiti herself gliding by on the shoulders of two eunuchs. ¡Jijola! Was I cruisin' for a bruisin'—¿o qué?

I stopped drinking too. You know? For about a week. I couldn't take the hangovers, I told my new friend, who was already frowning pretty seriously on the extent of my alcohol consumption. "You drink too much," she told me at the end of our first date as she walked me to my door. Then she turned around and left me standing there feeling bare-assed with my drunkenness showing and my broken heart, which I would not admit to no matter what. Like everybody, she comes from a dysfunctional family and all that brings up too much stuff for her, she said.

But the funny thing was that when I stopped drinking, I didn't feel any better about him, but I did feel worse about *her*. I just took a good, hard, sober look at her one day and thought, who wants someone around who's gonna be telling you about yourself all the time? Especially when you haven't asked her for her opinion in the first place.

So I told her last Sunday that we were gonna have to be just friends and we talked about it for a while on the phone (I didn't have it in me to tell her to her face) and she said, "Fine, I understand."

Yeah, yeah, yeah. After we hung up I went out. I came here, naturally, and around closing time I made it back home, seeing cross-eyed and hardly able to find the keyhole to get my key in the door when I jumped back and would have screamed like a banshee except that nothing came out of my mouth I was so scared by something moving suddenly out of the darkness coming right at me. And there she was. She had been sitting on the front porch all night waiting for me.

Now, I ask you: Is there justice to this life at all? Or maybe the question should be: Is life even supposed to make sense? Or maybe we shouldn't bother trying to figure it out, just go about our business tripping over it like that crack in the sidewalk that sends you flying in an embarrassing way and when you look back to see what tripped you, and everybody's looking at you, there's nothing there.

I mean, I have been half out of my mind since I said goodbye to my loverboy and I ain't heard nor seen hide nor hair of him since and meanwhile this woman,

35

40

whom I forgot the moment I hung up the phone saying goodbye, is convinced that God has put her on this planet for the sole purpose of rescuing me from myself!

Yeah, you heard right just now. I know I said earlier that he left me. But it was me who suggested we not see each other anymore. I mean, it was just a suggestion, right? A damn good one I thought at the time, driven by my self-respect as I am, since he had just told me that he was gonna take a trip and travel around South America with a college friend of his, and didn't know exactly when we'd see each other again. So I decided to give him a head start on feeling what it was to not see me anymore and said I was gonna be pretty busy myself and as of that moment didn't know when *I* could see *him.*

Well, let me tell you how it was with us. We had done all the hokey things people in love do. We stayed up in bed for hours after making love, just talking, confessing all our childhood traumas to each other; we cried together about a lot of things. We went to the zoo, the movies; we took walks and had picnics. We even kissed in the rain, making out in the downpour like nobody's business.

Which of course, it wasn't. He said to me once, "You are the kind of woman   45
who deserves to be kissed in front of everybody."

We had only one fight in all those months. I don't remember what stupid thing started it, but the next thing I know I threw a cushion at him that must've been tearing already because it hardly had an impact and there was fluff all over the place like it was snowing in the room. Well then, he throws a cushion at me. And before you know it, we're laughing and pounding each other with almo-hadas destripas, a flurry of feathers and fluff all over the room.

That's the way it was with us. A lot of laughs. A lot of good times. It's real hard to find someone to laugh with, you know?

Like, you see those two guys still sitting there in the dark? Now they're not smooching anymore. In fact, it looks like they're a little pissed off at each other. Who knows why? I was sitting here since before they came in and never once did those two laugh with each other. They came in, sat down without a word, and as soon as the one got the other a drink, they started making out. Now, they're mad at each other.

But those two will probaby grow old together because they really know how to be mad at each other, while me and my loverboy who didn't have a bad moment together have already gone up in smoke—with the force of burning copal and all the professed tragedy of La Noche Triste—succumbing to our destiny. Between the sun and poverty there was us for a little while.

Well, someone had to take my lunch away. I don't mind admitting it. I hurt   50
Rosie pretty bad after being with her all our adult lives, practically. I just fell out of love with her and even out of like, since we fought so much toward the end. Actually, I know by then that she was seeing that woman who she ran off to Las Cruces with. But she would never admit to that. I couldn't prove it, but I knew it in my heart—the little emaciated excuse for a heart I had left when she took off. But I can't say I blame her for leaving since it wasn't happening with us anymore.

Anyway, I don't really know why I'm telling you about Rosie. That's all over with. But it's like the one who matters is too hard to talk about. I can't talk about it without thinking I look ridiculous—like the classic jilted older woman. Of course it wasn't going to work out. *I* knew that. *He* knew that. And his family didn't help it any either. But even so. Somewhere in the middle of all its fatality, *we*, me, him, even his mother, who was busy having Masses said for her son's salvation—and I'm not putting down his mother either, in case you ever run into him and tell him any of this—*she* knew that what we had was indelible.

I'm gonna stop drinking. This time not because someone is shaming me out of it. And not because I can stand to go to bed at night thinking of him or waking up alone remembering waking up with him. But because it doesn't help anymore.

I'm gonna stop torturing myself in all the ways that I've been doing; I'll even stop playing all those Agustín Lara records he brought over—for us to make love to. And we did, over and over again.

I saw Agustín Lara perform in Mexico City when I was a kid. Did you know that? He was gaunt and very elegant. My mother was swooning. I was just a little kid, so I was just there. But when I mentioned it to my loverboy, he gave me the sign of la bendición—implying that I was among the blessed to have laid eyes on the late, great, inimitable saint of Mexican music:

Santa, santa mía, mujer que brilla en mi existencia . . . His saint he called   55
me, his saint and his treasure. His first and only love.

I've been thinking about renting the storefront next to my bookstore and extending my business to include a café. You know, café latte, avocado-and-sprout croissant sandwiches, and natural fruit drinks. I think this town is ready for a place like that. Maybe I'll exhibit local artists there, not that there are too many good ones around. But there are a few who are going places—I'll get them to show in my establishment before they do . . .

I think he already split town with his friend; he's probably somewhere in Veracruz at Carnival at this very moment—having a great old time. Well, at least for his sake, I hope so.

You think that maybe he misses me a little bit?

Probably the saddest boy in Mexico right now, you say?

I hope so.   60

Let me tell el compadre over there to send those two unhappy lovers a couple of beers, on me. There's something insupportable about being pissed with the one person on this planet that sends your adrenaline flowing to remind you that you're alive. It's almost like we're mad because we've been shocked out of our usual comatose state of being by feeling something for someone, for ourselves, for just a moment.

He made me feel alive, cliché or not. Drunk or sober. If he ever finds out I told you all this, he'll really be furious. I guess he felt like he was living in a glass bowl with me. Not that I'm not discreet, but everyone in town seems to know me, or at least think that they do. But I like my privacy, too, you know? Mis cosas son mis cosas. I just had to talk to somebody about it. Been carrying it around inside me like a sin, a crime, like that guy in *Crime and Punishment*. And it wasn't like that at all—far from it.

Anyway, I haven't used any names, in case you didn't notice, not even yours—even though people'll figure it out soon enough. And everybody already knows who I am. I run the only bookstore in town that deals with the question of the soul. All roads sooner or later will lead you there.

Starting Point for Further Research: Ana Castillo

- **Interview:** Renee H. Shea. "No Silence for this Dreamer." *Poets & Writers* (March/April 2000): 32–39.

STORY AND PERFORMANCE

A well-known biblical parable such as "The Prodigal Son" was spoken by Jesus, delivered out loud, and only later transcribed. Such parables are still read aloud in many Christian churches, every year at the appropriate time. And of course they are read silently as well, by millions who read the Bible. The same is true of the stories of Abraham and Isaac and Cain and Abel, which appear in the Hebrew scriptures as well as the Christian Bible. Biblical stories, which are profound religious tales meant in part for reading aloud, and stories like John Updike's "A & P," delivered with such a strongly marked voice, help us think about how stories should *sound*, what role the human voice should play in reading. It has become too easy to believe that the kind of reading most of us now do, silently, is the only kind there is. Far removed from the time when the oral performance of tales and poems was common, we are used to taking in literature through the eye, not the ear.

Yet we do not need to return to biblical times to find a rich oral tradition of telling meaningful stories. There was a time, not so very long ago, when plenty of fiction reading was done out loud, for the benefit of listeners. A century ago, in millions of homes, people gathered together as someone read aloud to the group. Reading aloud within a family is still repeated nightly in millions of homes, as parents tell bedtime stories to their young children. In fact, for almost all of us, our first experience of story was listening to it, as an adult created it on the spot or read it aloud to us from a book. From that powerful early experience of a live reader, we all have learned that good readers are performers. They do not read or tell stories straight through, in a monotone; they add sound effects or they change tone of voice or they alter their voice to indicate new characters or to heighten suspense. In children's stories we are directly confronted with a characteristic that once defined a great deal of literature: it was written to be performed aloud.

Children's stories are hardly the only survival of the performative tradition. Alberto Manguel's *A History of Reading* recounts how cigar makers in Havana or Tampa—too busy at work to read on their own yet eager to improve themselves—would pay to have someone read to them as they rolled the tobacco in their factories. Today, many people listen to stories as they drive, thanks to books on tape or CD. Everything from literary classics to thrillers or romances to current best-sellers is available, most of it read by trained professionals, some by very aptly chosen actors. Many blind readers, of course, have long made use of audiobooks; now many more of us take in books by the ear rather than the eye.

And what happens when a writer comes to visit a town? She or he frequently gives a reading of a story or a chapter to an assembled audience. This reading is often quite revealing, since the way a writer chooses to read gives us another entry into a story or book, a chance to hear how the writer emphasizes particular words or phrases or presents certain characters. But the benefit of these readings doesn't all accrue to the listeners; the practice of the "reading" has proved extremely valuable to writers themselves. Knowing they will be called upon to read their work has helped some writers become aware of voice, of the way something needs to sound, even if it is on the page. Shrewd writers admit they have grown when they have read aloud. In a 1955 letter to a reader who later became a close friend, Flannery O'Connor comments on the topic of how she learned by reading her work aloud as follows:

> I am glad you read the stories aloud as I like to do it myself and I think most of them gain in the reading. I do it every time I go to Nashville or anytime anybody asks me, which is not often. Usually it works very well; however, the funnier the story, the straighter the face it should be read with and I am the kind who laughs heartily at my own jokes. This weekend I read the first story in the book and disgraced myself in this fashion.

Similarly, in her essay "Reading Blind," writer Margaret Atwood discusses the value of reading aloud:

> I've spoken of "the voice of the story," which has become a sort of catchall phrase; but by it I intend something more specific: a speaking voice, like the singing voice in music, that moves not across space, across the page, but through time. Surely every written story is, in the final analysis, a score for voice. Those little black marks on the page mean nothing without their retranslation into sound. Even when we read silently, we read with the ear, unless we are reading bank statements.
>
> Perhaps, by abolishing the Victorian practice of family reading and removing from our school curricula those old standbys, the set memory piece and the recitation, we've deprived both writers and readers of something essential to stories. We've led them to believe that prose comes in visual blocks, not in rhythms and cadences; that its texture should be flat because a page is flat; that written emotion should not be immediate, like a drumbeat, but more remote, like a painted landscape: something to be contemplated. But understatement can be overdone, plainsong can get too plain. When I asked a group of young writers, earlier this year, how many of them ever read their own work aloud, not one of them said she did.
>
> I'm not arguing for the abolition of the eye, merely for the reinstatement of the voice, and for an appreciation of the way it carries the listener along with it at the page of the story.

In the following nonfiction piece, "A Note on Technique," Wallace Stegner, one of America's best-known creative writing teachers and a formidable writer of fiction, describes how short stories must be dramatized.

WALLACE STEGNER (1909–1993)

A Note on Technique (2002; PUBLISHED POSTHUMOUSLY)

To make a novel, Dumas said, you need a passion and four walls. He might have added that to make a passion you need people in a bind, a situation full of love, hate, ambition, longing, some tension that cries to be resolved. A beginning writer may have trouble finding his real situation—he may have only clues, characters, a place, an atmosphere, the haunting association of ideas in his mind. In a novel he may even be able to grope for the situation through his first chapters (though one formula for the novel proposed by the late Bernard De-Voto was to throw away the first five chapters and start with number six), but in a short story the situation must be located at once, for even more than a novel, a short story must start off running, must begin on a rolling slope, as near the end as possible.

Because no situation can exist apart from what brought it about and what it leads to—apart, that is, from its antecedents and its consequences—the writer will be led both forward and backward from his germinal knot of tension. He must deal at least a little with the past, which in fictional technique is called *summary* or *exposition*; and he must deal with the dramatic present, which is called *scene*. Summary and scene are all there is to fiction, but neither is simple.

To make a scene is to put your characters onstage and let them act out their own story. The point of view may not be strictly objective—there may be some equivalent of the Stage Manager of *Our Town* lounging around somewhere—but any scene is essentially dramatic; it follows George M. Cohan's celebrated advice, "Don't tell 'em—show 'em." A scene must persuade us in all its aspects, which means that the characters must be credible and consistent; that the dialog must approximate real talk without being cluttered by real talk's monotony, fatuousness, and repetition; that the action must move in a direct line, without wanderings or irrelevancies, and that an internal logic must hold the scene together, beginning and middle and end; and that the setting must be sensuously realized and then never permitted to drop away and be forgotten. If any object is important enough to be mentioned, it should be put to some use. As Chekhov says, if you hang a gun on the wall at the beginning, it has to go off before the end. If there is a fireplace in a scene, characters should warm themselves by it, or lean on its mantel, as part of their stage business, their real-seeming.

One does not learn to do a job such as this by the old classroom method of practicing whole paragraphs of description, whole chunks of setting or characterization. The elements interweave; there are many balls to be kept in the air at once; a single paragraph may contain a fragment of action, a bit of dialog which by its content or its manner and tone characterizes the speaker, a sensuous perception of some detail of setting, a glance backward in memory, dialog, or external comment to pick up a meaningful bit of the past. Any page of fiction will have descriptive, narrative, dramatic, and expository writing all entangled. To make it all the more complicated, in modern fiction even the summary is likely to be worked into the scene.

There is reason why it should be, for by its very nature summary is inert. It has already happened, and so can have none of the excitement of what is dramatically happening now. Badly handled, it gives itself away by its lumbering use of the past perfect tense and by the weight of its blocks of dead stoppage while the past is gathered up. Well handled, summary can even achieve a kind of suspense, for suspense is gained primarily by keeping back essential information, by refusing to answer questions that arise in the reader's mind, and if a writer will remember never to explain too much, and when he does explain, to explain in-

5

directly and a little at a time, he is not likely to bring his story to a grinding halt while the past perfect goes by in the other direction. Bring the summary in by the side door; keep her masked; she is an ugly girl with three left feet, and she will not do to dance with, but she can cook and keep house, and if you treat her well she will stay out of sight.

* * *

Now for a few rules of thumb; some of them repetitions:

1. Start in the middle of things; begin in motion.
2. Stay in motion by not letting the summary intrude; keep the summary feeding into the scene in hints and driblets, by what Ibsen called the "uncovering" technique.
3. Never explain too much; a reader is offended if he cannot participate and use his mind and imagination, and a story loses much of its suspense the moment everything is explained.
4. Stay out of your story; pick a point of view and (especially in the short story) stay with it. Nobody has less right in your story than yourself.
5. Don't show off in your style. The writing should match the characters and the situation, not you. This applies as well to obscenity and profanity as to other matters. Where character and situation call for them, they belong; elsewhere they may be a sign that the author is trying to catch someone's attention.
6. Nothing is to be gained, except a breaking of the dramatic illusion, by attempts to find substitutes for the word "said" in dialog tags. "Said" is a colorless word that disappears; elegant variations show up.
7. Stopping a story is as hard as saying goodnight. Learn to do it cleanly, without leftovers or repetitions.

Story and Performance in "A Note on Technique"

Short stories are obviously different from plays; everyone agrees. But Stegner's insider emphasis on dramatizing makes us understand that the heart of successful stories is action, a dramatized moment when something changes, when someone discovers something or affects someone. The heart of fiction is like the heart of drama: action.

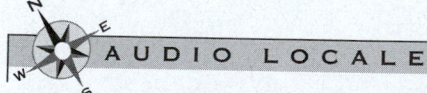

AUDIO LOCALE

Updike's "A & P" in Performance. An audio recording of Updike reading his short story can be found on the audio cassette set *American Masters: The Short Stories of Raymond Carver, John Cheever, and John Updike*. Another audio version of the story, read by actor Edward Herrmann, is part of the 6-hour, 5-CD set *The John Updike Audio Collection*. A video version of the 1996 film production of "A & P," along with an interview with Updike by journalist Donald M. Murray, is available from Films for the Humanities and Sciences.

Talking about the Text

1. Read the following three passages from John Updike's "A & P" aloud on your own, then listen to someone else reading them aloud: paragraph 1 (p. 58); paragraph 22 (p. 61); paragraph 32 (p. 62).
2. Based on your experience with these readings, what did you learn from hearing someone else read that you did not already know?
3. What specific things changed in your understanding when you heard someone else read?
4. If you heard the Updike recording, did he read it the way you would? What was different? What surprised you?

Writing about the Text

1. Listen to two classmates reading the same paragraph and write a brief paper describing the differences you hear. Then explain which works better and why.
2. Imagine you are directing readers in the right way to read one of these passages. Write down your directions.

Linking the Text to Other Texts

1. Make a recording of the way you think one of the passages in Updike's story should be read. Then, in a brief paper, compare Updike's recording to yours. What effect do the differences have on how listeners interpret the story?
2. Compare the way Chicago actor Scott Parkinson reads Charles Baxter's "Gryphon" (see the Audio Locale on p. 262 for information on this audio performance) with the way John Updike or actor Edward Hermann reads from "A&P" (see the Audio Locale on p. 109 for information on these audio performances).

CHAPTER

3

Writing about Stories

If you have ever browsed in a large bookstore or the book review section of a major newspaper or magazine, you have no doubt noticed the intense attention fiction receives in contemporary America. From mysteries, thrillers, and short stories to historical, mainstream, and romance novels, fiction seems to be everywhere. Yet the hardcover and paperback books featured in a newspaper's ads or on the bookstore shelves are only the beginning.

Novels and stories are accompanied by an enormous amount of writing *about* fiction, in many different forms, including reviews, commentary, and analysis of new and classic stories and novels. Many of the chapters in *Living Literature* are concerned with stories themselves; this chapter focuses on the writing done *about* stories, and particularly on how to relate your own writing about stories to the talk and the writing about fiction taking place every day throughout the country.

Writing about stories includes three distinct and familiar types: reviews, which serve as important guides to prospective readers; criticism, which is conducted by and for readers interested in fiction as a significant part of our culture; and school assignments, where writing about stories forms a key part of education, both to increase literary awareness and to promote critical thinking. Along with the literature itself, this writing about stories makes up an important part of the ongoing cultural and literary conversation.

THE CULTURAL CONVERSATION

To help us understand the notion of the critical discussion of literature that is always taking place in talk and in print, the critic Kenneth Burke suggested that we think of a parlor with an ongoing conversation, a discussion that has been taking place among thoughtful people for quite a while, long before you entered. People join the conversation with their own ideas and opinions, and share them with others who have thought about the same issues. They sometimes agree, sometimes disagree, but always have something to contribute to the discussion.

You and people you know participate in similar conversations when you talk about the movies, music, and books you like. When you tell friends or family about a film you have just seen, describing what you liked best about it and comparing it to another film you have all seen, you are taking part in the cultural conversation. Friends who have not seen the movie may want to know what it is like. Others will chime in, asking questions, or if they have seen it, agreeing or disagreeing, or pointing out their own favorite parts. In a similar way, literature provokes the same conversation, in talk and in print.

This conversation is taking place all the time, among many writers, readers, viewers, and listeners, just as it takes place among you and your friends, at home or at lunch or at school. This dialogue has even occurred on a wider scale with the huge resurgence of book clubs via national television shows, beginning with Oprah's Book Club, and more recently with the reading clubs linked to other national talk shows such as *Today* and *Good Morning America*. Aside from giving viewers a common list of books to read, these clubs invite the participants, now all reading the same thing, to take part in the cultural conversation.

Entering the written conversation about fiction, however, is not always as easy as talking with friends about what you do or do not like, be it about a novel, movie, or story. Casual opinion still counts, but now your informed and considered opinion counts for even more. You need to write with more care, more knowledge, and more awareness of what successful writing about fiction looks like. How do you learn to do such writing? One traditional way to learn is by reading good examples of writing about literature and trying out some assignments of your own. This chapter introduces you to some of the writing about fiction that is done by professional reviewers and critics. The chapter also gives you opportunities to employ some of the most common critical forms and styles, so that you can take part in the ongoing conversation about fiction.

REVIEWS

To start, you will need to become familiar with the venues in which the written cultural conversation appears. There are plenty of discussions in critical and scholarly books, certainly, but livelier points of entry are the reviews of new books that appear each week in magazines and newspapers. Magazines such as *Time*, the *New Yorker*, *Newsweek*, *Business Week*, *Vanity Fair*, and *Vogue* contain reviews of newly issued books of fiction that are likely to appeal to their readers.

Major newspapers, such as the *New York Times*, the *Los Angeles Times*, and the *Washington Post*, publish a separate, free-standing book review section each week. Other major newspapers cover books in their "culture" sections, reviewing five to ten new books each week. The reviews in these magazines and newspapers are timed to coincide with the publication of new books and aim to give the very large reading public an informed judgment of their quality. Thus, reviews help sort out the books that will sell well from those that do not, and so play a huge role in the whole process of writing, buying, and selling books.

Reviews in the popular press usually take two forms: the short, capsule review that just gives the key points and the reviewer's overall reaction to the book, or the full review that goes into much more detail. Here are two reviews of the first Harry Potter book, the beginning of a series that went on to worldwide acclaim and made the author, J. K. Rowling, a billionaire.

Short Review

Review of Harry Potter and the Sorcerer's Stone *by J. K. Rowling*

Publisher's Weekly   July 1998

Readers are in for a delightful romp with this award-winning debut from England that dances in the footsteps of P. L. Travers and Roald Dahl. The story opens with mysterious goings-on ruffling the self-satisfied suburban world of the Dursleys, which culminate in Dumbledore the sorcerer leaving their infant nephew Harry in a basket on their doorstep. Harry endures 11 years of abuse and neglect at the hands of the Dursleys and their swinish son Dudley, when suddenly he receives a letter and another and another, until a giant named Hagrid shows up. Then Harry learns that his parents were a wizard and a witch, and that he is to start Hogwarts witchcraft school. Most surprising of all, he is a legend in the witch world for having survived the attack by evil sorcerer Voldemort that killed his parents and left him with a lightning-shaped scar on his forehead. And so the fun begins, with Harry going off to boarding school like a typical English kid, only his supplies include a message-carrying owl and a magic wand. There is enchantment, suspense and danger galore (as well as enough goblins and other creepy creatures to satisfy the most bogey-loving readers) as Harry and his friends Ron and Hermione plumb the secrets of the forbidden corridor at Hogwarts and unravel the mystery behind Harry's scar. Rowling leaves the door wide open for a sequel; bedazzled readers will surely clamor for one. All ages.

Notice how the writer of this unsigned brief review begins by "placing" the book within a tradition of familiar books by P. L. Travers and Roald Dahl, much better-known writers in 1998, when this review was published, and when J. K. Rowling was unknown. Key words here are "delightful romp," describing the book's headlong quality, and "award-winning," suggesting that many other critics have read it and thought it worthy of very high praise.

A full review, usually 500 to 800 words, has more room for plot summary, but it too can situate a book by comparing it to similar books in its genre or to other books by the same author.

Full Review

Review of Harry Potter and the Sorcerer's Stone by J. K. Rowling

Michael Winerip, New York Times Book Review
FEBRUARY 1999

So many of the beloved heroes and heroines of children's literature—from Cinderella and Snow White to Oliver Twist and the Little Princess to Matilda, Maniac Magee and the great Gilly Hopkins—begin their lives being raised by monstrously wicked, clueless adults, too stupid to see what we the readers know practically from page 1: This is a terrific person we'd love to have for a best friend.

And so it is with Harry Potter, the star of *Harry Potter and the Sorcerer's Stone*, by J. K. Rowling, a wonderful first novel from England that won major literary awards and has been at the top of the adult best-seller lists there, and is having the same kind of success here too. Poor Harry Potter is orphaned as a baby and is sent to live with his odious aunt and uncle, Petunia and Vernon Dursley, and their fat son, Dudley. While Fat Dudley Dursley has two bedrooms (one just for his surplus toys, like the television set he put his foot through when his favorite show was canceled), Harry is forced to sleep in a crawl space under the stairs, has never had a birthday party in his 11 years and must wear his cousin's way baggy hand-me-down clothes.

But Harry is destined for greatness, as we know from the lightning-shaped scar on his forehead, and one day he mysteriously receives a notice in the mail announcing that he has been chosen to attend Hogwarts, the nation's elite school for training wizards and witches, the Harvard of sorcery. Before he is done, Harry Potter will meet a dragon, make friends with a melancholy centaur and do battle with a three-headed dog; he will learn how to fly a broom and how to use a cloak that makes him invisible. Though all this hocus-pocus is delightful, the magic in the book is not the real magic of the book. Much like Roald Dahl, J. K. Rowling has a gift for keeping the emotions, fears and triumphs of her characters on a human scale, even while the supernatural is popping out all over.

We feel Harry's fear when for the first time he is traveling to a faraway place, an 11-year-old boy arriving alone at the King's Cross train station with a trunk bigger than he is, and no idea how to find Platform 9. This is a world where some people know from birth that they are wizards, and are raised by their sorcerer parents to attend fair old Hogwarts, while others, like Harry—raised in human or what Rowling calls "Muggle" families—don't find out that they have special powers until they receive their acceptance letters. As Harry worries that first day about whether he can compete with the privileged children of Hogwarts alums, I found myself thinking back 30 years to my first days at Harvard, wondering how, coming from a blue-collar shipyard town and a public high school, I could ever compete with preppies from Exeter and Andover.

"I bet I'm the worst in the class," says Harry.

"You won't be," says a friend. "There's loads of people who come from Muggle families and they learn quick enough."

The book is full of wonderful, sly humor. Exam period at Hogwarts means not just essay tests, but practical exams too. "Professor Flitwick called them one by one into his class to see if they could make a pineapple tap-dance across a desk. Professor McGonagall watched them turn a mouse into a snuffbox—points were given for how pretty the snuffbox was, but taken away if it had whiskers."

Throughout most of the book, the characters are impressively three-dimensional (occasionally four-dimensional!) and move along seamlessly through the narrative. However, a few times in the last four chapters, the storytelling begins to sputter, and there are twists I found irritating and contrived. To serve the plot, characters begin behaving out of character. Most noticeably, Hagrid, the gentle giant of a groundskeeper who has selflessly protected Harry over and over, suddenly turns so selfish he is willing to let Harry be punished for something that is Hagrid's fault. That's not the Hagrid I'd come to know.

These are minor criticisms. On the whole, *Harry Potter and the Sorcerer's Stone* is as funny, moving and impressive as the story behind its writing. J. K. Rowling, a teacher by training, was a 30-year-old single mother living on welfare in a cold one-bedroom flat in Edinburgh when she began writing it in longhand during her baby daughter's nap times. But like Harry Potter, she had wizardry inside, and has soared beyond her modest Muggle surroundings to achieve something quite special.

Both these highly positive reviews take the book very seriously, as they ought. Reviewers who turn thumbs down on a book that becomes a classic are never allowed to forget it. Still, sometimes reviewers can be delightfully nasty or smart-alecky, as in this well-known quotation from a review by the poet and critic Dorothy Parker: "This is not a novel to be tossed aside lightly. It should be thrown with great force."

BEYOND REVIEWS: CRITICISM

The written conversation about fiction found in magazines and newspapers extends beyond reviews of the latest books. Publications that take fiction writing seriously also publish articles on up and coming writers, on writers whose work is becoming more widely known, on books that are becoming classics, on topics that are hot, and on cultural trends that are being treated in fiction. This focus on larger issues starts a different conversation from the one simply aimed at evaluating the latest books. It looks toward larger questions of culture, education, and the mindset of the reading public. This conversation has many names, but one of them is criticism.

Criticism can seem like a distinct world unto itself, populated by a large number of people—journalists, scholars, and readers—who take books very seriously. Some see themselves as professional critics. That is, they have a steady book-reviewing job at a journal, or they are university professors who write a great deal of criticism for weekly, monthly, or quarterly journals. Some may even write full-length books on literature: biographies, critical analyses, or textbooks. Criticism here can move into scholarship—especially when writers base their studies on research—or into pedagogy, when writers explain matters for students.

The difference between critical or scholarly writing is not always distinct; it usually has to do with the level of documentation as well as the audience it is written for. For example, in addition to weekly reviews of new books, magazines such as *Time* or *Newsweek* run regular feature articles on new authors, new types of books, or new trends in fiction, what might be called news pieces that incorporate critical writing. On the other hand, a small-circulation quarterly such as *Critical Inquiry* or the *Hudson Review* publishes up-to-date critical and scholarly studies for small groups of influential readers, the ones who set tastes, create trends, and decide what should be taught in universities. In between are journals like the *New York Review of Books*, a biweekly that publishes long review essays and articles by a mix of scholars and critics. All of these journals publish what we would call criticism, though of course in many different forms and for many different audiences.

An example of popular criticism is reproduced below from the July 17, 2000, *Newsweek*, which put Harry Potter on its cover and devoted a full story to an account of the Potter books and the publishing phenomenon they have become.

Popular Criticism

Why Harry's Hot

Newsweek   JULY 17, 2000

J. K. Rowling swears she never saw it coming. In her wildest dreams, she didn't think her Harry Potter books would appeal to more than a handful of readers. "I never expected a lot of people to like them," she insisted in a recent interview with Newsweek. "Well, it turned out I was very wrong, obviously. It strikes a chord with an enormous number of people." That's putting it mildly. With 35 million copies in print, in 35 languages, the first three Harry Potter books have earned a conservatively estimated $480 million in three years. And that was just the warm-up. With a first printing of 5.3 million copies and advance orders topping 1.8 million, "Harry Potter and the Goblet of Fire," the fourth installment of the series, promises to break every bookselling record in the book. Jack Morrissey, 12, of Wellesley, Mass., plainly speaks for a generation of readers when he says, "The Harry Potter books are like life, but better."

Red-eyed and rumpled, I cast my vote with Jack. The highest compliment I can pay "Harry Potter and the Goblet of Fire" is to say that from beginning to end, it made me want to stay up all night—or as long as it took to finish it. Rowling has gotten better with every book, and this time things move so smoothly that the story doesn't seem written so much as it seems to unfold on its own. Each of the books in the projected seven-volume series follows Harry through an academic year at Hogwarts School of Witchcraft and Wizardry. But this time Rowling has tossed in so many new elements that you never stop to hear the formula's gears grinding away behind the scenes. After a splendid set piece near the beginning when Rowling sends everyone off to the Quidditch World Cup . . . , the real plot kicks in with the Triwizard Tournament, to be held among three schools of wizardry, including Hogwarts. Meanwhile, Lord Voldemort, an evil wizard who killed Harry's parents when Harry was a baby, is once again on the prowl.

Amazingly, Rowling keeps her several plotlines clear of each other until the end, when she deftly brings everything together in a cataclysmic conclusion. For pure narrative power, this is the best Potter book yet.

When the book finally went on sale at 12:01 a.m. Saturday, thousands of children in Britain and North America rushed to claim their copies. Bookstores hosted pajama parties, hired magicians and served cookies and punch, but nobody needed to lift the spirits of these crowds. At The Book Stall in Winnetka, Ill., customers made such a big, happy noise that neighbors called the cops. At a Borders in Charlotte, N.C., Erin Rankin, 12, quickly thumbed to the back as soon as she got her copy. "I heard that a major character dies, and I really want to find out who," she said. But minutes later she gave up. "I just can't do it. I can't read the end first."

All in all, a pretty impressive level of excitement for a mere book. But at the same time it seemed somehow so anticlimactic, because months of planning by Rowling's publishers had laid the groundwork for this moment. In a campaign carried out with a level of secrecy sufficient to make Operation Overlord's commanders envious, the publishers succeeded in keeping the contents of the fourth book almost entirely under wraps. Even the title was closely guarded until just before publication. Printers and binders were sworn to secrecy. Booksellers had to promise not to open the boxes containing the new novel, which came stamped Harry Potter IV, not to be sold before July 8, 2000. . . .

* * *

The only sour notes in all the songs of joy over this phenomenon have come from parents and conservative religious leaders who say Rowling advocates witchcraft. Reading of the books has been challenged in 25 school districts in at least 17 states, and the books have been banned in schools in Kansas and Colorado. But that's nothing new, says Michael Patrick Hearn, a children's book scholar and editor of "The Annotated Wizard of Oz." "Any kind of magic is considered evil by some people," he says. " 'The Wizard of Oz' was attacked by fundamentalists in the mid-'80s."

But perhaps the most curious thing about the Potter phenomenon, especially given that it is all about books, is that almost no one has taken the time to say how good—or bad—these books are. The other day my 11-year-old daughter asked me if I thought Harry Potter was a classic. I gave her, I'm afraid, one of those very adult-sounding answers when I said, "Time will tell." This was not an outright lie. There's no telling which books will survive from one generation to the next. But the fact is, I was hedging. What my daughter really wanted to know was how well J. K. Rowling stacks up against the likes of Robert Louis Stevenson or Madeleine L'Engle.

I could have told her that I thought they were beautifully crafted works of entertainment, the literary equivalent of Steven Spielberg. I could also have told her I thought the Potter books were derivative. They share so many elements with so many children's classics that sometimes it seems as though Rowling had assembled her novels from a kit. However, these novels amount to much more than just the sum of their parts. The crucial aspect of their appeal is that they can be read by children and adults with equal pleasure. Only the best authors—and they can be as different as Dr. Seuss and Philip Pullman and, yes, J. K. Rowling—can pull that off. . . .

* * *

The Harry Potter books aren't perfect. What I miss most in these novels is the presence of a great villain. And by great villain I mean an interesting villain. Long John Silver is doubly frightening because he is both evil and charming. If he were just all bad, he wouldn't frighten us half as much. Voldemort is resistible precisely because he is just bad to the bone. That said, I should add that in the new book Rowling outdoes herself with a bad guy so seductive you'll never see him coming. And he is scary.

That quibble aside, Rowling's novels are probably the best books children have ever encountered that haven't been thrust upon them by an adult. I envy kids reading these books, because there was nothing this good when I was a boy—nothing this good, I mean, that we found on our own, the way kids are finding Harry. We affectionately remember the Hardy Boys and Nancy Drew, but try rereading them and their charm burns off pretty quickly. Rowling may not be as magisterial as Tolkien or as quirky as Dahl, but her books introduce fledgling readers to a very high standard of entertainment. With three books left to go in the series, it's too early to pass final judgment. But considering what we've seen so far, especially in the latest volume, Harry Potter has all the earmarks of a classic.

This *Newsweek* piece illustrates the difference between reviews—found as a regular feature and keyed to the initial appearance of single books—and an article on an author or on large-scale trends in fiction. This article is quite different from a review in both approach and purpose. It treats books as interesting and necessary components of our culture, and aims to bring readers up-to-date information and background material so they have an informed understanding of a particular writer or genre. The *Newsweek* article, one of many about the Harry Potter publishing phenomenon, explains the books' attraction as a sign that some young readers remain fascinated with a story well told, despite the lures of TV and video games. It is one part—a widely read one—of the cultural conversation.

Newsweek is not alone in treating fiction as newsworthy; many popular magazines do the same. For instance, over the more than eighty years since its founding, *Time* has put many fiction writers on its cover, including Toni Morrison, James Baldwin, William Faulkner (twice), Ernest Hemingway (twice), Willa Cather, Virginia Woolf, James Joyce (twice), Vladimir Nabokov, Stephen King (twice), and Gertrude Stein. The presence of these authors on the covers always signaled a long essay inside on fiction, usually a think piece about trends rather than a simple review of the latest novel or story collection by the featured writer.

Scholarly Articles

Another form of criticism is the scholarly article. One major difference between a critical piece in a popular magazine, such as the one in *Newsweek*, and a scholarly article lies in the level of research and documentation. The more popularly oriented critical piece contains no footnotes or endnotes and no list of works cited, and it usually aims to explain matters in general language for an educated general audience. A scholarly article, written by an expert in the field, usually presents an original claim or interpretation about a book or story, based on wide reading and research, and containing extensive documentation in support of the claims. Scholars generally aim their articles at other specialists—or at least well-informed readers—and use the particular language of the discipline. Of course, many scholars also write articles and reviews for wider audiences, and when they do they maintain their scholarly authority but employ less extensive documentation and considerably less specialized language.

The April 2001 issue of *The Lion and the Unicorn: A Critical Journal of Children's Literature* included a nearly twenty-page piece of academic literary criticism by Roni Natov, professor of English at Brooklyn College. This scholarly article focuses on issues of identity, selfhood, fantasy and realism, and point of view in the Harry Potter series. The short excerpt below focuses specifically on *Harry Potter and the Sorcerer's Stone*, and the sources cited in the excerpt appear at the end of the article in the "Works Cited" section. The numbers in parentheses indicate page numbers in the Harry Potter book or one of the other sources that Natov quotes from.

From *Harry Potter and the Extraordinariness of the Ordinary*
Roni Natov, *The Lion and the Unicorn* 25.2 (2001): 310–327

The Harry Potter series opens with the infiltration of the ordinary world by the luminous and magical as "a large, tawny owl flutters past the window" unobserved by the blunted Dursleys. Mr. Dursley "noticed the first sign of something peculiar—a cat reading a map," but assumed that "[i]t must have been a trick of the light . . . and put the cat out of his mind" (*Sorcerer's Stone* 2–3). He was aware of "a lot of strangely dressed people . . . in cloaks. Mr. Dursley couldn't bear people who dressed in funny clothes . . . [and] was enraged to see that a couple of them weren't young at all," dismissed them as "people [who] *were* obviously collecting for something [and put] his mind back on drills" (3). He was oblivious to "the owls swooping past in broad daylight, though people down in the street . . . pointed and gazed open-mouthed as owl after owl sped overhead" (4). With this startling image of the nocturnal in bright light, Rowling establishes three groups defined by their response to the magic of the world. The Dursleys represent those who are hostile to anything imaginative, new, unpredictable. The Muggles, who notice the owls but are remote from their magical aura, represent a kind of conventional center. Professor Dumbledore, Head of Hogwarts School of Witchcraft and Wizardry, an old man, whose silver hair and beard "were both long enough to tuck into his belt . . . [who wore] long robes, a purple cloak that swept the ground, and high-heeled, buckled boots" (8), and

Professor McGonagall, who has shape-shifted from cat to woman, indicated by her glasses with "exactly the shape of the markings the cat had had around its eyes" (9), embody the childhood world of magic and awe.

In most popular children's fantasies, the magical world is entirely separate from daily life. In C. S. Lewis's *The Lion, the Witch, and the Wardrobe*, for example, entry into the supernatural takes place through a wardrobe at the back of a strange house during the bombings of World War II and represents the child-heroes' escape into a reimagined and revitalized Christian realm. In Madeline L'Engle's *A Wrinkle in Time* and its successors, *A Wind in the Door* and *A Swiftly Tilting Planet*, the magical world is celestial, in keeping with science fiction and L'Engle's strong religious allegorical allusions. J. R. R. Tolkien's *The Hobbit* and *Lord of the Rings* trilogy take place entirely in a magical world and represent a refuge, an alternative to the real world.

Rowling noted the genius of Lewis and Tolkien, those predecessors with whom she has been frequently compared, but she claimed in the NPR radio interview that she was "doing something slightly different."[1] Though her stories contain the usual global battle between the forces of good and evil, Rowling, I believe, is essentially a novelist, strongest when writing about the real world. Harry has a psychology; his problems need resolution in the real world. Insofar as he is a real child, with little relief at home, at Hogwarts School of Witchcraft and Wizardry, where the supernatural reigns, he is freer to discover his own powers. In Rowling's stories, the interpenetration of the two worlds suggests the way in which we live, not only in childhood, though especially so—on more than one plane, with the life of the imagination and daily life moving in and out of our consciousness. The two realms, characterized in literature as the genres of romance and realism, are located in the imagination, which is, always, created by and rooted in the details of everyday life. In fantasy, always we are grounded; the unconscious invents nothing, or as Freud put it, "In the psychic life, there is nothing arbitrary, nothing undetermined" (qtd. in Todorov 161). The realm of the fantastic, based on the unconscious, is firmly and inevitably a reconfiguration of everyday reality, transformed and disguised though it may be. . . .

* * *

As Harry embodies both the ordinary and the extraordinary, his narratives contain realistic and romantic elements. Like other questing heroes, Harry must prove himself through a series of tests, each increasingly more difficult. Joseph Campbell noted how the hero's cycle corresponded to the dynamic movement through life stages, particularly the development of consciousness and the discovery of identity. Even the simplest of hero stories, the fairy tales, dramatize the complexity of the life struggles of Everyman/woman/child. For example, both Perrault's and the Grimms' most virtuous, Christianized, and domesticated girl-hero, Cinderella, must revolt against the wishes of the good fairy godmother (without the consciousness that she is doing so, of course). She must forget to leave the ball by midnight, in order that the prince find her and that her rightful

---

[1]Rowling herself mentions E. Nesbit's *The Story of the Treasure Seekers* as particularly influential in her conception of the Harry Potter series. [Roni Natov's original footnote]

place be restored. This tale acknowledges the hero's paradoxical struggle to maintain tradition and to subvert it for evolution to occur. Some taboo must be broken, some boundary crossed—this is at the heart of the hero's quest. Harry, who is, as Alison Lurie points out, a kind of Cinderlad himself, must break the very rules at Hogwarts needed to maintain order and its basic values.

Works Cited

Nesbit, E. *The Story of the Treasure Seekers*. 1899. London: Penguin, 1994.
Rowling, J. K. *Harry Potter and the Sorcerer's Stone*. New York: Scholastic P, 1997.
Todorov, Tzvetan. *The Fantastic: A Structural Approach to a Literary Genre*. Trans. Richard Howard. Cleveland: Case Western Reserve UP, 1973.

As you enter the ongoing conversation about fiction, and as you begin to write on your own, you will draw on each of the sources we have discussed—reviews, critical pieces, and particularly with research papers (see Chapter 27), scholarly articles.

HOW TO ENTER THE CONVERSATION

What part can first- or second-year college students take in discussions about fiction? How, for instance, can they write within this community? After all, most students will not become professional reviewers or writers about cultural trends. Where in this flood of writing is there room for students to get in a word? What equipment and experience does today's student need in order to talk and, especially, to write about fiction? How can a student make an intelligent contribution while lacking the experienced and confident tone of the scholar or the professional critic? Every one of these good questions has an answer. Students really can participate in the ongoing conversation; it's simply a matter of what level they enter. For instance, almost every college supports the publication of student writing about literary matters, either in a separate, free-standing literary magazine or in a "cultural" section of the college newspaper, or both.

One way to start is to tune in to the critical conversation that takes place in the sort of reviews discussed earlier in this chapter. There is no better preparation for entering the conversation than looking closely at reviews of books in a field that interests you. As you browse reviews, ask yourself about the tone, the frame of reference employed, the way judgments are handed down. We all know people who explain a movie they have seen by obscure references to other movies they know and we don't. It can be the same among music lovers with a new band, and it certainly can be the same among some book reviewers, who often seem to write for a closed circle of initiates. Other reviewers leave more room for the newcomer or explain matters thoughtfully for the most general public.

Another way to enter the conversation is to read critical pieces that discuss trends in fiction, such as the revival of certain kinds of stories, emerging fiction writers, books that are becoming classics, and topics or cultural issues that are hot. This focus on larger issues begins to move the conversation away from the latest books and best-selling authors and toward larger questions of the culture, education, and the mindset of the educated, aware public.

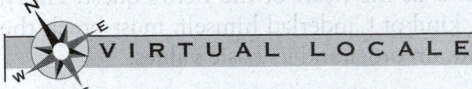

VIRTUAL LOCALE

Blogging about Stories. Personal reactions to stories are now the material for blogs, the weblogs of obsessed readers who have started virtual parlors of their own and invite like-minded readers to see what they have written. Sometimes they encourage readers to respond, and a genuine conversation begins. Clearly the quality is highly variable; the Web has made it possible to "publish" your side of a conversation almost immediately, without careful consideration, second thoughts, or even editing. That in fact is part of a blog's attraction, the immediacy that comes from unmediated reactions. Try looking at a few bloggers' sites for vivid illustrations of conversation in action, sometimes one-sided, sometimes self-indulgent, sometimes insightful, but often full of life and passion. Here are some guides to the crazy, delightful conversation available on the Web:

- Yahoo Listing of Literature Weblogs: <http://dir.yahoo.com/> Computers_and_Internet/Internet/World_Wide_Web/Weblogs/Literature/
- Bookslut: <www.bookslut.com/blog/>
- The Complete Review Quarterly's Overview of Literary Weblogs: <www.complete-review.com/quarterly/vol3/issue3/litblogs.htm>
- David Harris' Science and Literature Blog: <http://blogs.salon.com/ 0001092/2004/01/27.html>

Yet another way to tune into the world of fiction is to reflect on any of the classic novels you have read, such as *Jane Eyre, Huckleberry Finn,* or *The Great Gatsby.* Classic fiction is constantly the subject of written conjecture, speculation, and analysis. Characters from novels and stories play a large role in cultural discussions in print, whether or not people have actually read the books the characters appeared in. Fictional characters such as Anna Karenina and Emma Bovary are oft-cited examples of women who pay a heavy price in a search for love outside marriage, while Huck Finn is practically a universal embodiment of the dream of leaving it all behind and "lighting out for the territory." Holden Caulfield, in J. D. Salinger's famous 1951 novel *The Catcher in the Rye,* represents an adolescent boy's desire to escape the conformist life plotted for him by society. Such fictional characters seem more real than people who have actually lived. We know more about what they are thinking than we know about some of our family members. These characters who populate our literary consciousness form an enduring part of the continuing cultural conversation.

Contemporary writers, who are inevitably regarded and assessed in light of their predecessors, help create the conversation as well, and continue it with present-day concerns. The women in short stories by Alice Munro (p. 29) form part of many readers' consciousness, as do the men and women in Raymond Carver's short stories (p. 89). Writers like Munro and Carver depict characters who have struck a chord about modern life, raising troubling or funny or powerful notions about who we are. These writers—and their younger contemporaries—may not be known to everyone, but they are part of the landscape, and people with an interest in fiction talk and write about them. Those who care about literature are always in search of new voices, writers who have a fresh vision or a different take on the world around them, or who can invent characters or situations that engross us and make us think. Harry Potter is a perfect example of a brand-new character entering the scene and becoming an important part of the cultural landscape in just a few short years.

Colleges sponsor their own conversation about books in their newspapers and, on larger campuses, through literary magazines, where budding writers, artists, and critics can get published. Much more common is the critical conversation that takes place in literature classes, which aims to sharpen students' reading, thinking, analytical, and writing skills. Writing about fiction in this academic sense aims to develop students' skills through close reading and a variety of carefully framed writing assignments. The fact is, you learn more about something when you write about it, and nowhere is this more true than with literature. The close reading and rereading you have to do in order to write gives you precious insight, especially when you know what to look for and how to proceed.

QUESTIONS TO DEVELOP IDEAS ABOUT A STORY

This section and the one that follows provide you with two key approaches: ways to develop useful questions about a work of fiction, and helpful formats to use when you sit down to do the writing. Don't think of these two approaches as completely separate, since in fact they are intertwined. The questions to ask and the types of writing go together. The questions and formats are not abstract categories but instead living examples of how to enter into the cultural conversation through writing.

As you read a story or reread it, connect with it through questions like the ones that follow. The answers to these questions, often in the form of lists of specific examples, will provide you with material for writing about fiction in a wide variety of formats.

Point of View

1. What kind of person is telling us the story? Does the narrator seem to care about the characters in the story, or is the narrator totally removed and impersonal?
2. Is the narration first or third person?
3. How reliable does the narrator seem?
4. Is the narrator omniscient, or is the perspective limited to only one character?
5. Does the narrator comment on what happens? How?

Language

1. What is the level of the language? Formal? Informal?
2. Does the language seem contemporary, old-fashioned, or in between? Can you pin this answer down with examples?
3. Did you notice any specialized type of vocabulary? Any words you needed to look up? Any non-English words or phrases?
4. Was the language particularly colorful, or did it not draw attention to itself?
5. Did you note examples of irony? Symbolism? Any notable qualities of tone?

Setting

1. When and where did the story take place?
2. Did the setting seem an important part of the story?
3. Was the setting symbolic in any way?
4. What details of the setting receive the most attention from the narrator?

Character

1. Is it clear who the protagonist is? If not, why is it hard to tell? Who is the antagonist?
2. What is the main character's motivation?
3. Are the characters sharply delineated, with individual characteristics, or do they seem more like types?
4. Do you regard the characters as realistically portrayed?
5. What changes take place in characters over the story?
6. Did you find yourself identifying with any of the characters?

Plot

1. Can you state the story's main action in a sentence?
2. How does the plot unfold? Are the events presented chronologically? Are there flashbacks? Any foreshadowing?
3. Did you feel manipulated or were you willingly pulled along by the plot? Was there a surprise ending? Any tricks?
4. What kind of resolution occurs at the end?
5. Does the plot reach some inevitable conclusion, or are matters left open-ended?
6. Can you imagine other ways to tell the story?

Links to Other Texts or Performance

1. Did this story (or parts of it, including character or setting) seem like any others you know about, or any play or film?
2. Were there any passages you would like to hear read by a professional?
3. Can you imagine this story as a play or film? Who would play the roles?
4. What kind of performance-oriented reading would work with this story? What words or phrases would get special emphasis in reading aloud?
5. Which elements of the story would you like to see expanded or lengthened? Which can you imagine as shortened? What would be the gains and losses?

Response

1. Was one character especially attractive or repellent to you?
2. Did a particular sentence or phrase or situation catch your fancy?
3. What "got" to you in the story? A person? An incident? Something someone said?
4. Was there anything in the story that touches on what you have experienced in your own life, or in the life of someone you know?

These are only the beginning, of course, but they are exactly the questions any professional reviewer or critic asks of a story. The questions focus attention on the text itself. They represent ways of "interrogating" the story, of conducting a genuine dialogue with the text, forcing you to be an active rather than a passive reader. Answering the questions will pay off in three ways:

- You will develop a much more well-informed reading of a story.
- You will reflect on how you make meaning of your own life.
- You will assemble rich materials for the writing you will do in different formats.

Beginning students confronted with a writing assignment often ask, "Where do I start?" The answer is, "Start with these questions."

FORMATS FOR WRITING ABOUT STORIES

Reading a story with the preceding questions in mind produces a much richer encounter with the text. The answers to the questions can be shaped in many different ways, according to the writing format you choose or have assigned to you. These formats are listed below in the order of their length. They are presented as separate operations, though in reality many writers mix a good many of these formats in the same writing task.

- **Annotation:** marginal notes and underlinings for personal understanding (to guide your rereading; to prepare for discussion or a paper).
- **Summary:** a short "boiling down" of a story or passage.
- **Journal or notebook:** a collection of lines, phrases, and situations worth writing down. A double-entry notebook includes noteworthy lines, phrases, and summaries in one column, with reflections and reactions about them in a parallel column.
- **Response paper:** your thoughts or feelings as you read the text, connections to other texts you've read, and the story of your reading: "When I read the opening I expected. . . ."
- **Intervention:** altering or playing with or talking back to the text. One common form is a **parody,** an imitation that exaggerates some prominent characteristics for humorous effects. Another form is an extension, which involves adding material such as a new character or scene, or creating a different version.

- **Explication:** a close-up, critical look at every word or sentence of a passage.
- **Analysis paper:** concentrating on or explaining an interesting feature of the text such as language, characters, point of view, or setting, or how the story is put together. Usually an analysis paper (also called a **critical analysis**) makes a claim about something you have noted about the story.
- **Research project:** a scholarly work based on wider reading and research, and containing documentation in support of the claims. (For more information, see Chapter 27.)

You may want to think of these activities as a hierarchy, with the first six—annotation, summary, journal, response, intervention, and explication—as more personal responses to a text, perhaps steps in the process of writing a more formal paper about a text. In these, your conversation is largely with the text itself. The last two—analysis and research—also begin with your own responses, but they deal more with your understanding of the text and your examination of outside sources. With these two, you enter the larger conversation about literature. You can also think about the hierarchy in these terms: the first six activities encourage you to explore a text and your reading of it, while the last two use that exploration to present a claim or argument about the story to the "public," in this case to your class and your instructor. These last two are less about you and the story and more about the story itself and how it connects with its literary and cultural context. Analysis and research are where you learn how to construct a well-reasoned argument, one of the major features of a liberal education. Research writing, in fact, is so distinct that this book devotes a whole chapter to it, Chapter 27, since it has so many special requirements, even though it grows out of the formats presented here in this chapter.

Annotating a Story

An **annotation** gives you notes for a fuller, richer understanding of anything you read and is frequently a first step in any writing assignment. No doubt you have written annotations in the margins or your textbooks or marked important passages in stories. It is best to annotate a story actively, raising questions or noting interesting words, passages, or situations. Note the difference between this kind of active annotation and the kind of annotation you do for other coursework. In biology or psychology, for example, you frequently have to know the *content* in the textbook, so you annotate for *remembering*. You might annotate a story to help you remember certain points in the action, but the main purpose of annotating a literary work is to encourage *understanding* and *interpretation*. For example, you might be asked "What is the effect of the story's setting?" or "What are some of the key characteristics of the narrator's language." Responses to these questions will be based not on the plot or on pure information, but on how you responded to the text as you read it, what you think after having finished the text—and how you react afterwards to your own comments in the margins. You will use what you saw in the text as examples and evidence for your responses to such questions, so your annotations will be crucial for amassing evidence as well as retrieving it.

Annotations for a Page of Chopin's "The Story of an Hour"

These lines are so positive, full of life—and she's implicated(!) by the beginning.

She could see in the open square before her house the tops of trees that were all aquiver with the new spring life. The delicious breath of rain was in the air. In the street below a peddler was crying his wares. The notes of a distant song which some one was singing reached her faintly, and countless sparrows were twittering in the eaves.

Suggests that something in the distance is calling—from the west, no less.

That she's looking out the window seems important.

Is the "twittering" overdoing the joy?

The storm's clearing. The "sob" sounds sort of left over, like the clouds will soon be.

The sorrow is from a different consciousness, even a different life?

There were patches of blue sky showing here and there through the clouds that had met and piled one above the other in the west facing her window. She sat with her head thrown back upon the cushion of the chair, quite motionless, except when a sob came up into her throat and shook her, as a child who has cried itself to sleep continues to sob in its dreams.

We'd expect her head to be buried in her pillow. Sounds like she's got it made!

"Funny word, given what we seem to be working up to? "Fearfully" too is a funny word if her mind is suspended.

I react a little negatively to this word. What makes thought "intelligent"? She might not be quite where the top paragraph is, but we know she's getting there—sure as the blue sky is spreading.

She was young, with a fair, calm face, whose lines bespoke repression and even a certain strength. But now there was a dull stare in her eyes, whose gaze was fixed away off yonder on one of those patches of blue sky. It was not a glance of reflection, but rather indicated a suspension of intelligent thought. There was something coming to her and she was waiting for it, fearfully. What was it? She did not know; it was too subtle and elusive to name. But she felt it, creeping out of the sky, reaching toward her through the sounds, the scents, the color that filled the air.

Pretty satisfying—it feels as if this is where the section has been headed.

Writing about the Text

1. Annotate a passage from one of the stories in Chapter 1 or 2.
2. Using the annotations you created for #1 (above), describe what those annotations tend to cover. Are they equally attentive to all aspects of the passage, or do they have a particular focus?
3. If you have ever worked in a retail store or supermarket, use your knowledge to annotate "A & P" (p. 58), paying particular attention to Sammy's characterization of the store's operation.

Summarizing a Story

A **summary** is a concise restatement in your own language of the main idea of a literary work. Summaries are of varying lengths but are often very short: a 50,000-word novel can be summarized in a paragraph. A 20-page short story can be summarized in a few sentences. Writing single-sentence summaries is a demanding intellectual exercise: extraneous notions, characters, and details must be cut, and key themes and events highlighted. Summaries are usually written in what is called the **literary present tense**: "She notes the birds' singing outside her window." Literary present tense is traditionally used whenever writers discuss poems, short stories, and even speeches.

Summaries have many uses, from filling in readers about the overall plot or texture of a piece to linking the discussion of a small part of a story to its overall theme or structure. Reviews almost always include a summary, but here the writer must be careful not to give away too much of the plot, since many readers like to read for suspense.

For a college writing assignment, summaries can fill in background or cover a large amount of plot in a few lines, leaving you free to analyze and interpret. Still, use summaries sparingly. A sure sign of a writer's having too little to say is lapsing into plot summary when the purpose of the writing is supposed to be interpretation or analysis. When summarizing, be explicit, telling readers exactly what you are doing. For example, you could introduce a summary with a short sentence, as shown below.

Summaries of "The Story of an Hour"

```
    The plot of "The Story of an Hour" is simple.
Hearing a false report of her husband's death, a young,
frail, wealthy woman secretly exults in her newfound
freedom, but when he surprises her by returning
unharmed, she drops dead from shock and grief, which her
friends wrongly interpret as an excess of joy.
```

Here is another, somewhat longer summary of "The Story of an Hour," introduced the same way.

```
    The plot of "The Story of an Hour" is simple. Upon
hearing news that her husband was killed in a train
wreck, young Mrs. Mallard's friends try to break the
tragic news gently, for they believe she is frail and
prone to shock. In a daze at the news, she sits alone in
her room upstairs, windows open to the sounds of spring,
silently exulting at having regained her freedom. But
the report was false, and her husband soon returns,
completely unaware of the false report. Upon seeing him,
Mrs. Mallard falls dead from the shock. Her doctors and
friends ironically conclude that the death was from "an
excess of joy."
```

Summaries are usually part of a larger writing task. You provide readers with a summary in order to have something to base your explanation or analysis upon. Thus very few academic papers are all summary, but summarizing is a key skill often used in academic writing.

Writing about the Text

1. Summarize a short section of a story in chapter 1 or 2 as if you were describing it to someone who had never read it.
2. Write a one- or two-sentence summary of "Prue" (p. 29) or "Araby" (p. 34) or "Stockings" (p. 27).

Keeping a Personal Journal

Some writing assignments ask for your personal reaction to a story. Here what matters most is what you think and feel as you read, or what you think just after. A good tool for this kind of assignment is a reader's journal, or a notebook, which you write in as you do your reading. A personal reaction is similar to an annotation, but unlike an annotation it goes beyond the page and into your notebook. It can include not just your thoughts but also a collection of lines, phrases, or situations you think are worth writing down. (Readers used to do this all the time; collections of memorable passages and poems, copied out by readers, were called "commonplace books.")

The more structured and more powerful version of this reader's journal is the double-entry notebook approach pioneered by Ann E. Berthoff. In it, a reader collects noteworthy lines, phrases, and situation summaries in one column, and writes reflections and reactions in a parallel column. The whole point of such a notebook is to get readers to write down important or interesting things they have noticed, and then briefly to reflect about them in writing.

Double-Entry Reaction Journal on a Paragraph of "The Story of an Hour"

Paragraph 19 from Kate Chopin's "The Story of an Hour":

> Her fancy was running riot along those days ahead of her. Spring days, and summer days, and all sorts of days that would be her own. She breathed a quick prayer that life might be long. It was only yesterday she had thought with a shudder that life might be long.

Sentence two—not a grammatical sentence—abruptly states what raced through her mind, repeating the word "days."	The "days . . . days . . . days" and the form they're in suggest the "running riot" of the first sentence.
Sentences three and four are opposites: shuddering yesterday at the prospect of a long life, praying today for the same thing. Yet they both end the same way: " . . . that life might be long."	Louise is of course a more interesting character because she recognizes the irony of the turn of events—and also the two sentences suggest she enjoys the word play in "that life might be long."

Writing about the Text

1. Do a "commonplace book" type of journal (as described under "Keeping a Personal Journal," above) about a story in Chapter 1 or 2, copying lines you particularly like.
2. Take the journal you compiled in #1 and do your commentary on the entries in the form of a double-entry notebook.

Writing a Response Paper

Unlike a series of annotations or a quick personal reaction, the **response paper** usually takes the form of a short paper describing what happened as you read the work, or how the story made you think or feel. Here are three different types of responses such a paper can describe:

a. What you thought or felt as your read the story, or thought afterwards.
b. How the story connects in your mind with other things you've read.
c. The story of your reading: "When I read the opening I expected . . . ."

While a good response paper will have a main point, it does not have to involve an argument. There is no need for you to make a complex claim about the work; you are only stating what the work invoked in you. Naturally, a good response paper will concentrate both on the response and the particular details that produced the response.

From a Response Paper to "The Story of an Hour"

The twist of the plot at the end of "The Story of an Hour" seemed too neat for me, and I couldn't read it as a realistic tale, no matter how effective the details. Everything seemed a bit too carefully plotted, too schematic. For instance, just as Louise sits in her room to absorb the news, the birds outside start chirping away in the sunshine. Symbolic? Sure. But it seems a bit overdone now that I think about it. Or, and here's the key, it seems overdone if we are to take this story seriously as a realistic piece of fiction. Suppose we are not? Suppose we are to take this as a kind of allegory of the "secret life" of a woman? She's treated well, she is assumed by all around her to be in love with her husband, and yet she leads a genuine secret life in her mind, longing to be free from her husband's gentle and loving domination. Yet when she actually is free, she hides her exultation, because it will not do to be glad at the death of one's spouse.

Note that this writer concentrates on a single point, the "too neat" twist of plot at the end, and allows herself to speculate that "The Story of an Hour" is not meant to be taken as a realistic portrayal. The response paper starts with the personal, but the paper moves on to an interesting and provocative insight about Kate Chopin's intentions.

Writing about the Text

1. Write a response paper to "A & P" (p. 58), asking yourself whether Sammy seems right about the gesture he makes.

2. Respond to the behavior of Alice Munro's "Prue" (p. 29). How does she strike you? Are you shocked? Amused? Unimpressed? Scornful?

Writing an Intervention

The term **intervention**, employed by critic and writer Rob Pope, describes the practice of altering, playing with, or talking back to a text. A common type of intervention is the **parody**, which is an imitation with a humorous twist and takes aim at the style or the characteristics of an author.

Imagine what you could do to parody "The Story of an Hour." One parody might start with imagining what Louise would do now that she is free: become a trapeze artist in the circus? Leave her proper New Orleans neighborhood and open a saloon? Take up with beach boys on the Gulf Coast?

More unusual than the parody is the "expansion," which adds new material—a new character, another scene, or a different version. Such an intervention to "The Story of an Hour" might include the story as told by Mrs. Mallard's sister Josephine, by a good friend who was not present, or by her husband:

```
    When Josephine met her friend Alice, she was full of
the awful news of Louise's death from joy. "Alice," she
said, "you wouldn't believe how well Louise took the
awful news. She just nodded her head and went upstairs.
No tears, no lamentations, no crying out. She took it
like the good wife she was, calmly and graciously."
```

This kind of intervention reinforces the story itself; it is told in the same kind of voice, while Josephine does not differ from the sister we met in the original. In this expansion, she remains "in character." Doing an expansion can be an enjoyable exercise that also helps you concentrate on the style and tone of the original.

Writing about the Text

1. Write one of the interventions suggested about "The Story of an Hour" (p. 16) or pick a new one of your own. (Possibilities include a news story or a letter from a neighbor explaining matters to a distant friend.)
2. Add a section of your own to the end of "Araby" (p. 34) or "A & P" (p. 58) in which the young man returns home. What gets said? How does he act?

Writing an Explication

An **explication** is a close-up, careful, slow-paced examination of a single passage in a story. (It is also used for poetry; see p. 819.) There is no room for your own personal reaction or for biography or historical background. Explications are pure analysis, sentence by sentence or even word by word. They are powerful exercises, forcing you to focus simply on the words on the page rather than your own reaction or the complex historical, cultural, or social background. Think of explication as a necessary skill in writing about fiction.

The order of an explication is simple: you must follow the order of the passage, sentence by sentence, sticking quite closely to individual words and phrases. Pay particular attention to the word choice, the tone, and how individual parts of the passage connect to larger issues like the plot or the theme. Remember, your job in an explication is to supply a **close reading**, a word for word, sentence by sentence look at the passage, not an overall judgment or analysis. Since looking closely takes a good bit of time and energy, choose a short passage, no more than a page, and usually far less.

Explication of the Opening of "The Story of an Hour"

When the story opens, readers see Mrs. Mallard as a completely passive subject who is not allowed to speak for herself. Her faceless protectors treat her as an invalid, perhaps a child or a doll. The passive verb ("was afflicted by"), plus the allusion to her undefined "heart trouble," make her sound more acted upon than an actor in her own right. She is curiously kept at a distance as we first see her; she is introduced by the formal "Mrs. Mallard," while her sister first enters the scene as "Josephine." Josephine, presumably, is a "Miss" or "Mrs."; why Mrs. Mallard?

The hint of condescension in the first couple of lines is deepened in the second paragraph. Though a weak heart is hardly the same thing as a weak mind, the sister and the friend proceed as if they think a damaged heart is equivalent to a damaged personality or will. The sister is described, in effect, as bumbling: how could she expect to break such news gently? Obviously she wouldn't divulge any gory details if she happened to know them, nor would she break the news and then abruptly disappear to her own home. Who would? But what else could she say other than, in effect, "Louise, your husband has died in a train accident"? Of course, she could tell her nothing——and keep others at bay who might tell her——but that would just postpone the inevitable. (One irony is that such a plan might have had the effect of keeping Louise alive!)

Meanwhile, Richards seems smug and presumptuous in assuming that he is more "careful" and "tender" than other friends. How does he know? Rather, one would

expect him to be dreading his task and seeking
desperately for words of comfort.

   Given the implied passivity and fragility of
Louise——and the way any sense of intimacy with her is
discouraged by the attitude of the would be
"consolers"——it is surprising that she reacts with an
apparently robust crying spell, though the episode is
curiously described. Does she weep for a minute, five
minutes, twenty minutes? Is it a performance or a true
demonstration of grief, or somewhere in between?
Moreover, the narrator makes a point of saying that she
reacts differently from other wives in her situation.
In fact, is a "sudden, wild abandonment" of weeping so
atypical of a spouse who hears about her husband's
sudden and violent death? And is the wish to be alone
after an interval so unexpected? Is there indeed any
predictable set of responses to such news?

   By the end of the third paragraph, Louise has
become the reader's focus, but her behavior, as well
that of her comforters, is puzzling and confusing. It
is difficult to tell where the narrator locates
him/herself in regard to Louise's behavior. Thus, we
readers await some more information as we anticipate
witnessing the widow alone in her room.

Writing about the Text

1. Explicate the opening page of "Prue" (p. 29) or "Mary's Convert" (p. 40).
2. Do an explication of the last three paragraphs of "A & P" (p. 58), looking particularly at how much we can assume Sammy knows about his future.

Writing an Analytical Essay

When you write an analysis, you are making a claim or an argument about something you note about a story. You are explaining how one or more elements of the story operate. Here are some possible topics for an analytical essay about "The Story of an Hour":

a. Show that every character in "The Story of an Hour" misunderstands the true situation.
b. What is artificial about "The Story of an Hour"?
c. What would you say is the theme of "The Story of an Hour"?

An **analytical essay** (also sometimes called a critical analysis) calls for you to develop a central claim, or **thesis**, which you then support with examples or evidence from the story itself. An analytic essay cannot concentrate on everything in the story, only the claim you make about one or more elements. Nevertheless, analytic assignments require time to find a topic, to gather evidence, and to organize, draft, revise, and edit your paper. Be sure to give yourself time for each step of the process.

Developing a Thesis

The hardest part of an analytic assignment is often coming up with a claim or thesis that you can sustain for an entire essay. But if you have read and reread the story with the "Questions to Develop Ideas" (p. 123) in mind, you have made an excellent start. Similarly, you have an advantage if you have made annotations or journal entries, since you can build on them to develop a thesis. The following sections show three ways to develop a thesis for an analytic essay.

Build on Annotations, Journals, and Responses   Build on your annotations, journal entries, or response papers to develop a claim or argument substantial enough to be explored in the context of a longer paper. One student's annotations to "The Story of an Hour" revealed that every character is operating with incorrect information: Josephine and Richards, Louise, Brently, the doctors, and finally we the readers. A claim or thesis based on such an observation would show how misinformation about the train wreck, Louise's health, Brently's death, and the cause of Louise's death dominate the story and prepare us for the fact that Louise ultimately misunderstands the possibilities available to a woman, even one whose husband has just died. So the student was able to respond to the first assignment given above:

Question: Can "The Story of an Hour" be called artificial?

Here is her thesis:

Thesis: "The Story of an Hour" is clearly very artificial, and readers are likely to overreact to its artificial qualities.

The rest of this student's analytical essay (see the the complete essay on p. 136) demonstrates the accuracy of this claim or thesis by providing evidence from individual sentences and paragraphs.

Enter the Conversation   Enter the conversation explicitly by demonstrating, for example, whether "The Story of an Hour" fits in with a critic's claim about Kate Chopin or nineteenth-century American women writers. Your thesis will be "Critic X is right (or wrong) to argue thesis Y." Whom can you quote? Your best sources are critical books and articles, or reviews if you can find them. Don't feel as though you need to claim that someone is totally right or totally wrong; you can phrase an arguable claim in the form of "X overlooks a complication" or "X does not go far enough." As long as you can support *your* claim with convincing evidence, you can write a strong paper. The language of argument and claim, just like a good intellectual conversation, allows for complications and nuances as well as flat-out contradiction.

Here is how one student developed a thesis using someone else's claim about the story:

Question: What would you say is the theme of "The Story of an Hour"?

Source: Critic Jane Edwards: "Kate Chopin's 'The Story of an Hour' emphasizes how women in nineteenth-century America could be put on a pedestal and imagined as weak, frail creatures totally dependent upon husbands and family."

> **Thesis:** Edwards is right about the way Louise is treated
> in Kate Chopin's "The Story of an Hour." Everyone in the
> short story conspires to protect her from confronting
> life, accepting the notion that some women are too
> emotionally "fragile" to face reality.

The rest of the paper will develop this thesis, demonstrating that the critic Jane Edwards is right to draw attention to the context of Chopin's story in late-nineteenth-century American life.

From Topic to Thesis   When an analytic paper is assigned, your instructor will usually provide the general details: length, due date, opportunities for revision, and sometimes a few sample topics. You may do one of those topics, or you will often be permitted to develop a topic of your own. Note that when your instructor assigns a topic, the wording of the assignment helps dictate the kind of paper you are likely to write. For instance, if the assignment asks you to "explain," you will have to provide a satisfactory reason. If the assignment asks you to "describe," then you will have to go into some detail about the issue in question, providing satisfactory coverage and description, but not necessarily a motive. Use the form of the instructor's question as a guide for your paper's overall plan, but remember that it is your task to develop your own claim or thesis. Here is how two students turned general topics into theses that make clear claims:

Topic: Explain how the setting operates in "The Story of an Hour."

> **Thesis:** The setting in "The Story of an Hour" serves to
> underscore the story's action, with spare, unelaborated
> description at the beginning to the clear symbolism of
> the birds and sunshine in the crucial scene in Louise's
> bedroom.

Topic: Describe how characters in "The Story of an Hour" operate on incomplete understanding.

> **Thesis:** Every single character in "The Story of an Hour"
> thinks he or she understands the situation, yet everyone
> is wrong. There is no family death from the train wreck,

no freedom from Brently, no bottomless grief in Louise, and no death from an excess of joy at the end.

An analytic paper is your own contribution to the cultural conversation. You read a story many others have read, you annotate it or write a response paper, you speak to others in class about your progress, and perhaps you seek out a critical study. Then you commit yourself to a claim about the story and write a draft of your paper. Perhaps you discuss that draft in class, or with your classmates or instructor. Then you revise and submit it. That's your own contribution to the ongoing discussion, in the "parlor" of your own community, the classroom. Some of those papers may go beyond this community, either by being submitted for a prize or by being published in a class or college journal. The knowledge and experience you gain from this process will make you more confident and the next writing task simpler.

Student Analytical Essay of "The Story of an Hour"

O'Brien 1

Amanda O'Brien
Professor Gayle
English 112-5
March 20, 2006

The Story of an Artificial Hour

Kate Chopin's "The Story of an Hour" is clearly very artificial, and readers are likely to overreact to its artificial qualities. Calling a story artificial is not normally flattering. But perhaps the more interesting question is why and how the story has impact and power in spite of its artificiality.

The story is an easy target for critics who dislike the artificial. Though the story seems at first to be a psychological portrait of a wife under intense stress, the central protagonist Louise manages a series of emotional states——and her own demise—all inside of an hour. This progression of her feelings may be credible, but not in that time frame. Readers are also likely to wonder about the situation before the opening of the story. Has she really been so docile and compliant in the past? Certainly we readily accept that the suppression of her feelings has had bad effects on her heart, but can we believe in her complete ability to suppress her feelings and apparently avoid any friction with a domineering husband? Nor does the

husband ever become a real person: how exactly does he
manage to be both loving, with "kind, tender hands"
(17), and also domineering and insensitive at the same
time? It can happen, but the reader lacks any real
picture of what has made Louise's life so miserable.

Of course, artificiality adheres to the plot. How
likely is it that a man is reported dead in two
separate telegrams, then arrives unhurt and completely
unaware at his front door. A temporary uncertainty
about his fate is more believable, yet we are told that
"Richards had only taken time to assure himself" of the
death by means of "a second telegram" (17). Can two
telegrams be wrong? Likewise, it seems incredible that
Louise survives the shock of Mallard's death and then
does not survive the shock of his reappearance. Again,
it is unlikely that she has really had time to accustom
herself to his demise and to her sudden prospective
freedom. She moves too quickly from the sadness she
first feels to her "fancy . . . running riot" (18) as she
imagines the life of freedom that awaits her.

So how/why does the story work for us on some level?
Ultimately, there are several reasons. First, the story
works because the tale of women's oppression in the home,
followed by her liberation and the emergence of her true,
independent self has become so much a story of our time
that we enjoy this reenactment in spite of any qualms we
might have about its realism as Chopin depicts it. It
becomes almost a ritual acting out of an old freedom
story. On that level, who cares if Louise's
transformation takes only an hour? Who protests if Nora
slams the door in Ibsen's A Doll House in the span of five
acts? I am not at all sure "The Story of an Hour" was
intended to have that sort of ritual impact in 1894. The
cruelty of Louise's death due to "joy that kills" (18)
may have packed more of a wallop, more of a "message"
than it does now. It may have been in part an instrument
to incite rebellion, transformation in female readers.

There are other notes the story may strike in
readers: the ambiguity of our feelings about

O'Brien 3

relationships. We welcome and need them, but they are
also confining and full of obligations and routine;
sometimes it is even desirable that they be terminated.
The death of a partner spurs those ambiguities into
play. And then there is the inevitable drama of death(s)
and life. We know that irony is a close and frequent
companion of those forces. Chopin has poured it on
strong, but we know the essential fact of irony she
portrays is true enough.

O'Brien 3

Works Cited

Chopin, Kate. <u>Living Literature: An Introduction to
     Fiction, Poetry, and Drama</u>. Ed. John C. Brereton.
     New York: Longman, 2007. 16-18.

Writing about the Text

1. Write an analytical essay about one of these two topics:
   a. Show that every character in "The Story of an Hour" misunderstands the true situation.
   b. What would you say is the theme of "The Story of an Hour"?
2. Examine this chapter's three examples of critical writing aimed at nonspecialists—review (p. 114), short review (p. 113), critical essay (p. 119)—and analyze the language they use in evaluating the Harry Potter story. What characteristics of language do these forms have in common?

Researching the Text

1. After listening to the conversation that takes place in college classes and in talk with others about books, TV, and films, try to capture the precise evaluative terms people use. Make a brief list and decide what the terms have in common. Are they all personal? How much is insider's talk? What is the range of reference? Do people usually include much evidence?
2. Annotate the opening page of "Araby" (p. 34), concentrating on symbolic setting, and then compare what you noted with a well-known, commonly available critical or scholarly study of this opening. Examples would be Hugh Kenner, *Dublin's Joyce*; A. Walton Litz, *Dubliners*; William Y. Tindall, *A Reader's Guide to James Joyce*. Then write on the differences between your own annotations and what the critics and scholars are seeing in that opening.
3. Consulting magazines and newspapers, examine three reviews of books that interest you. You can use three reviews of the same book or reviews of different books. Report on the frame of reference in each review: was the review meant for insiders or outsiders? Explain the words or terms that led you to this conclusion.

CHAPTER
4

Nathaniel Hawthorne

Portrait of Nathaniel Hawthorne by Charles Osgood, 1840.

Anyone who studies American literature quickly comes to Nathaniel Hawthorne (1804–1864), one of the classic American writers practically everyone gets exposed to in school. Among the poets and fiction writers we now consider as icons of the nineteenth century—Hawthorne, Emily Dickinson, Edgar Allan Poe, Mark Twain, Walt Whitman, Herman Melville—Hawthorne is the only one who achieved classic status in his own era and has kept it ever since. Other classic writers of Hawthorne's time, such as Henry Wadsworth Longfellow and Washington Irving, have lost their exalted status, while some we now regard as icons were hardly thought so in the nineteenth century: Dickinson was unknown and practically unpublished in her lifetime, Whitman was considered far too dangerous by many, and Melville spent the last thirty years of his life in obscurity, unread and unloved.

Hawthorne's unique status as both an instant and an enduring classic is unusual, since he has few rabid enthusiasts. Scholars and readers all acknowledge that Hawthorne is admired and respected more than he is loved. He is serious, reserved, somewhat gloomy, without sparkling humor or delightful plots. Instead, what brings readers again and again to his writings is their psychological complexity and insight into human character. His somewhat ponderous style—which today seems decidedly old-fashioned—hardly makes him many friends these days, though it did in his lifetime. No, to account for Hawthorne's fame we need to look at his obsession with the darker, more intense sides of human nature. There we find that his peculiar, distinctive notion of human character sets him apart from other writers.

Hawthorne wrote most of his famous stories in the 1830s but set many of them when the Massachusetts Puritans of the 1600s dominated New England towns and their small, prosperous city of Boston. The Puritan brand of Protestantism combined a high intellectualism with a theology that insisted on humans' essentially depraved nature, marked by tendencies toward sin, evil, and wickedness. There was nothing humans could do to assure their salvation; they could be saved only by the radical intervention of God's will. Many of Hawthorne's most compelling stories dramatize the Puritan dilemma of striving to live a good life while repressing the personal demons that seemed to dwell everywhere, within people's minds as well as without, in the larger society.

Hawthorne's Puritan forebears had played a significant role in New England's history. One earned a reputation for his persecutions of Quakers. The Puritans had sailed to America to seek religious freedom for themselves but were unwilling to grant it to others; they rooted out dissenters from their colony,

Mary Dyer led to execution on Boston Common, June 1, 1660.

executing the Quaker Mary Dyer and driving the religious dissenter Anne Hutchinson out of Boston. Another Hawthorne ancestor served as a judge during the Salem witch trials in the 1690s, when panic seized the small community and twenty-nine innocent women were tortured and executed. Hawthorne, a Salem native, had a complex love-hate relationship with his ancestral town, drawing upon it for inspiration yet moving away as soon as he had the opportunity.

This troubled family history seems to have influenced Hawthorne's character, for his greatest stories have to do with hidden human failings in the young, intensely religious Puritan men who are his heroes, and the effect these failings have on those around them, particularly the strong and loyal women trapped in a patriarchal society. Many of Hawthorne's tales are set in a distant New England past in which Puritans feared that hostile Indians lurked behind every tree, and a narrow religious orthodoxy was strictly enforced. But their psychological complexity still speaks to us, keeping Hawthorne in the foreground of American writers who plumbed the human psyche.

Besides a family history tying him to religious persecutions, Hawthorne's biography is unusual both for the literary connections he made throughout his life and for the way so much of his most famous writing was concentrated into just a few short, spectacularly productive years, as if he had been saving up his work for when readers were ready to accept it.

His father, a Salem, Massachusetts, ship captain, died when Hawthorne was four, an early death that influenced him greatly. He was raised by his mother with the help of well-to-do Salem relatives, then spent an uneventful four years at Bowdoin College, where he graduated in the middle rank of his small class and made significant lifelong friends, including Franklin Pierce, later to be elected U.S. president, and Henry Wadsworth Longfellow, later to be America's most celebrated poet. After college Hawthorne determined to become a writer and moved back home, spending the next twelve years reading and writing, immersing himself in classical and English literature. When he published his first novel, *Fanshawe*, anonymously in 1828, it received no acclaim whatsoever. Later Hawthorne was ashamed of it and tried to buy up every existing copy.

While living at home during the 1830s, Hawthorne wrote and published short stories, or "tales" as he called them. At that time the short story was a relatively new form; Hawthorne, along with Washington Irving (who wrote "Rip Van Winkle") and Edgar Allan Poe (see p. 510), was one of the writers who made it popular in America. Many of Hawthorne's most famous tales, like the three collected here, share two significant characteristics: they were historical, usually taking place in the 1600s, well over a century before they were written, and they were "romances," not quite meant to be taken as realistic stories. In fact, the tales are also what are called **allegories**, meaning their significance lay partly in what the characters stood for and in the abstract ideas the stories represented. Thus in "Young Goodman Brown," the main character's name is meant literally: he is young and a "good man." His wife is named "Faith," and Hawthorne meant us to take that name to signify that she believed in the truths of her religion. These stories are not full of richly described characters: we know much more about their inward thoughts and feelings than their outward

Etching of Hawthorne's wife, Sophia Amelia Peabody Hawthorne, at age thirty-six, c. 1845, attributed to S. A. Schoff.

appearance. Hawthorne's allegories are moral tales, meant to provoke thought about the way people live their lives. The allegorical quality makes them a little old-fashioned seeming, yet it also helps account for their continued success. Once you have read a Hawthorne story, you can never forget it.

Many of Hawthorne's stories were well liked by reviewers (including Poe, who favorably reviewed *Twice-Told Tales* in 1842), but writing was barely able to bring in enough money to raise a family. When he married in 1842, he moved into the old parsonage in Concord, Massachusetts, a town then practically the center of American literature, since his neighbors were Ralph Waldo Emerson, Henry David Thoreau, Margaret Fuller, and Bronson Alcott, the father of Louisa May Alcott, who would write *Little Women*. Hawthorne soon was accepted into this community of writers, who became his friends during his lifetime and his influential supporters after his death. Four years after the move to Concord, however, Hawthorne had to seek work to support his family (he and his wife would have three children). He ended up back in Salem, working unhappily for three years in the seaport's Custom House, which he made famous in the Introduction to *The Scarlet Letter*.

Published in 1850, Hawthorne's breakthrough novel, *The Scarlet Letter*, established his literary reputation. Set in Puritan Salem, the novel employs the same allegory and romance elements that characterize so many of Hawthorne's great stories. The appearance of *The Scarlet Letter* began one of the most remarkable spurts of publication in American literature. As the

Hawthorne's three children, Una, Julian, and Rose, c. 1862.

Undated illustration of Hawthorne reading to his family.

Actress Lillian Gish as Hester Prynne in the 1926 film adaptation of The Scarlet Letter.

timeline on p. 147 shows, the next two years saw an enormous output: *The House of the Seven Gables*, a novel about his Salem ancestors; a second edition of *Twice-Told Tales*; *The Snow Image and Other Twice-Told Tales*; *The Blithedale Romance*, a novel; *A Wonder Book for Girls and Boys*; a campaign biography of his friend, *The Life of Franklin Pierce*.

The 1852 campaign biography Hawthorne wrote for his old college friend paid off when Franklin Pierce won the presidency and appointed Hawthorne U.S. consul in Liverpool, England. This enabled Hawthorne to write and travel through Europe, although his output was diminished compared with 1850–1852. Hawthorne's last novel, *The Marble Faun* (1860), was based on his experiences in Europe. After living in Rome and Florence, Hawthorne returned to America, moving back to Concord. He died suddenly in Plymouth, New Hampshire, in 1864, while traveling with his old friend, Pierce.

LITERARY LOCALE

Hawthorne's Massachusetts—Concord and Salem. Three sites in Massachusetts are closely associated with Hawthorne. Built by the family of transcendentalist writer, Ralph Waldo Emerson, the "Old Manse" is the house in Concord that Hawthorne rented and lived in following his marriage, from 1842 until 1846; it is also where he wrote many of the stories collected in *Mosses from an Old Manse.* The house is open to tourists, and among its furnishings is Hawthorne's writing desk. The property also displays a recreation (based on the journals of Hawthorne and George Bradford) of the vegetable garden that writer Henry David Thoreau planted for the Hawthornes before they arrived. In 1846,

The Old Manse, Concord, Massachusetts, frontispiece of Mosses from an Old Manse, *from Hawthorne's Works, vol. 2.*

(continued)

Custom House, Salem, Massachusetts, illustration from Twice-Told Tales, the "Salem Edition," 1893.

House of Seven Gables, c. 1900.

the Hawthornes moved to Salem, the coastal town some thirty miles east of Concord. The Salem Custom House building where Hawthorne once worked still stands, now a National Historical Landmark, located across from Derby Wharf. The structure, now part of the Salem Maritime National Historic Site, is open to the public, and on a visit, you can see exactly where Hawthorne worked while thinking about writing his most famous novel, *The Scarlet Letter*. Down the street from the Custom House is the home once owned by Hawthorne's relatives, the House of Seven Gables, which lent its name as the title of another Hawthorne novel.

The stories collected here represent a small part of Hawthorne's output, and they by no means represent all the types that he wrote, or even what his contemporaries valued most in his tales. Instead these are starkly moral tales with an emphasis on the darker side of human character. "Young Goodman Brown" focuses on a quintessential Hawthorne situation: a young, intense New England man in Puritan times comes face to face with what he regards as his own depravity. Parallel to the discovery of inner demons is the way Hawthorne describes the setting, from sunshine and promise at the opening to gloom and resignation by the end. "Lady Eleanore's Mantle" is a fable set among the non-Puritan English ruling classes who later came to dominate Boston. "The Maypole of Merry Mount" dramatizes the encounter between the strict Puritans and the looser living non-Puritan English. All three pieces are allegorical rather than realistic: some of the figures depicted might be based on genuinely historical people or events, but even more, they stand for parts of human nature.

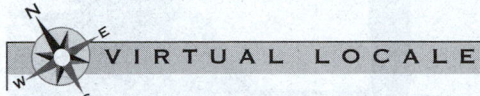

VIRTUAL LOCALE

Hawthorne in Salem. The Hawthorne in Salem website at http://www.hawthorneinsalem.org/ offers a full range of resources for further research on Hawthorne and his connections to Salem, Massachusetts. The site includes biographical information; historical and contextual resources on Hawthorne's writing; timelines; information on the Salem buildings and houses

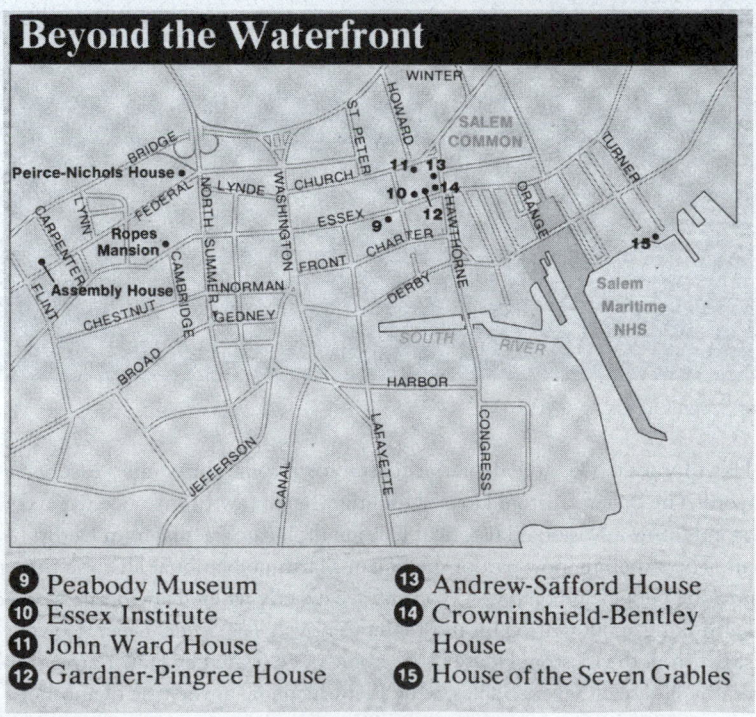

Map of Salem Harbor.

(continued)

important to Hawthorne's life and work (including photos and audio and virtual tours); photographs, fine art, maps, and historical documents; and a scholars' forum featuring complete papers, articles, and lectures on Hawthorne and his world by Hawthorne scholars.

NATHANIEL HAWTHORNE TIMELINE

1804	Nathaniel Hawthorne born July 4 into a prosperous Salem, Massachusetts, family.
1808	Hawthorne's father dies in British Guiana, in South America.
1825	Graduates from Bowdoin College. Classmates include Henry Wadsworth Longfellow and Franklin Pierce (future U.S. president).
1828	Publishes *Fanshawe*, an unsuccessful first novel he later tries to destroy.
1837	Publishes *Twice-Told Tales*, containing stories written and published over the previous seven years.
1842–1846	Marries and moves to Concord, Massachusetts.
1846	Publishes *Mosses from an Old Manse* (stories).
1846–1849	Works in Salem Custom House.
1850	Publishes *The Scarlet Letter*, set in Puritan Boston. Meets Herman Melville.
1851	Publishes *The House of the Seven Gables* (a novel); a new edition of *Twice-Told Tales*; *The Snow Image and Other Twice-Told Tales*; and *A Wonder Book for Girls and Boys*.
1852	Publishes *The Blithedale Romance* (a novel) and *The Life of Franklin Pierce* (campaign biography).
1853–1857	Appointed U.S. consul in Liverpool, England.
1857–1859	Lives in Italy.
1860	Returns to Concord; publishes *The Marble Faun* (a novel).
1864	Dies in Plymouth, New Hampshire, on a trip with Franklin Pierce.

STORIES BY NATHANIEL HAWTHORNE

Young Goodman Brown   (1835)

Young Goodman[1] Brown came forth, at sunset, into the street at Salem village; but put his head back, after crossing the threshold, to exchange a parting kiss with his young wife. And Faith, as the wife was aptly named, thrust her pretty head into the street, letting the wind play with the pink ribbons of her cap while she called to Goodman Brown.

---

[1]*Goodman* = a man of humble standing.

"Dearest heart," whispered she, softly and rather sadly, when her lips were close to his ear, "prithee put off your journey until sunrise and sleep in your own bed to-night. A lone woman is troubled with such dreams and such thoughts that she's afeared of herself sometimes. Pray tarry with me this night, dear husband, of all nights in the year."

"My love and my Faith," replied young Goodman Brown, "of all nights in the year, this one night must I tarry away from thee. My journey, as thou callest it, forth and back again, must needs be done 'twixt now and sunrise. What, my sweet, pretty wife, dost thou doubt me already, and we but three months married?"

"Then God bless you!" said Faith, with the pink ribbons; "and may you find all well when you come back."

"Amen!" cried Goodman Brown. "Say thy prayers, dear Faith, and go to bed at dusk, and no harm will come to thee."   5

So they parted; and the young man pursued his way until, being about to turn the corner by the meeting-house, he looked back and saw the head of Faith still peeping after him with a melancholy air, in spite of her pink ribbons.

"Poor little Faith!" thought he, for his heart smote him. "What a wretch am I to leave her on such an errand! She talks of dreams, too. Methought as she spoke there was trouble in her face, as if a dream had warned her what work is to be done to-night. But no, no; 'twould kill her to think it. Well, she's a blessed angel on earth, and after this one night, I'll cling to her skirts and follow her to heaven."

With this excellent resolve for the future, Goodman Brown felt himself justified in making more haste on his present evil purpose. He had taken a dreary road, darkened by all the gloomiest trees of the forest, which barely stood aside to let the narrow path creep through, and closed immediately behind. It was all as lonely as could be; and there is this peculiarity in such a solitude, that the traveller knows not who may be concealed by the innumerable trunks and the thick boughs overhead; so that with lonely footsteps he may yet be passing through an unseen multitude.

"There may be a devilish Indian behind every tree," said Goodman Brown, to himself and he glanced fearfully behind him as he added, "What if the devil himself should be at my very elbow!"

His head being turned back, he passed a crook of the road, and, looking forward again, beheld the figure of a man, in grave and decent attire, seated at the foot of an old tree. He arose at Goodman Brown's approach and walked onward side by side with him.   10

"You are late, Goodman Brown," said he. "The clock of the Old South was striking as I came through Boston, and that is full fifteen minutes agone."

"Faith kept me back a while," replied the young man, with a tremor in his voice, caused by the sudden appearance of his companion, though not wholly unexpected.

It was now deep dusk in the forest, and deepest in that part of it where these two were journeying. As nearly as could be discerned, the second traveller was about fifty years old, apparently in the same rank of life as Goodman Brown, and bearing a considerable resemblance to him, though perhaps more in expression than features. Still they might have been taken for father and son. And yet, though the elder person was as simply clad as the younger, and as simple in manner, too, he had an indescribable air of one who knew the world, and who would not have felt abashed at the governor's dinner table, or in King William's court, were it possible that his affairs should call him thither. But the only thing about him that could be fixed upon as remarkable was his staff, which bore the likeness of a great black snake, so curiously wrought that it might almost be seen to twist and wriggle itself like a living serpent. This, of course, must have been an ocular deception, assisted by the uncertain light.

"Come, Goodman Brown," cried his fellow-traveller, "this is a dull pace for the beginning of a journey. Take my staff, if you are so soon weary."

"Friend," said the other, exchanging his slow pace for a full stop, "having kept covenant by meeting thee here, it is my purpose now to return whence I came. I have scruples touching the matter thou wot'st[2] of." 15

"Sayest thou so?" replied he of the serpent, smiling apart. "Let us walk on, nevertheless, reasoning as we go; and if I convince thee not thou shalt turn back. We are but a little way in the forest yet."

"Too far! too far!" exclaimed the goodman unconsciously resuming his walk. "My father never went into the woods on such an errand, nor his father before him. We have been a race of honest men and good Christians since the days of the martyrs; and shall I be the first of the name of Brown that ever took this path and kept—"

"Such company, thou wouldst say," observed the elder person, interpreting his pause. "Well said, Goodman Brown! I have been as well acquainted with your family as with ever a one among the Puritans; and that's no trifle to say. I helped your grandfather, the constable, when he lashed the Quaker woman so smartly through the streets of Salem; and it was I that brought your father a pitch-pine knot, kindled at my own hearth, to set fire to an Indian village, in King Philip's war.[3] They were my good friends, both; and many a pleasant walk have we had along this path, and returned merrily after midnight. I would fain be friends with you for their sake."

"If it be as thou sayest," replied Goodman Brown, "I marvel they never spoke of these matters, or, verily, I marvel not, seeing that the least rumor of the sort would have driven them from New England. We are a people of prayer, and good works to boot, and abide no such wickedness."

"Wickedness or not," said the traveller with the twisted staff, "I have a very general acquaintance here in New England. The deacons of many a church have drunk the communion wine with me; the selectmen of divers towns make me their chairman; and a majority of the Great and General Court are firm supporters of my interest. The governor and I, too—But these are state secrets." 20

"Can this be so!" cried Goodman Brown, with a stare of amazement at his undisturbed companion. "Howbeit, I have nothing to do with the governor and council; they have their own ways, and are no rule for a simple husbandman like me. But, were I to go on with thee, how should I meet the eye of that good old man, our minister, at Salem village? Oh, his voice would make me tremble both Sabbath day and lecture day!"

---

[2]*wot'st* = know.
[3]War against the Wampanoag Indian leader known as "King Philip."

Thus far the elder traveller had listened with due gravity; but now burst into a fit of irrepressible mirth, shaking himself so violently that his snake-like staff actually seemed to wriggle in sympathy.

"Ha! ha! ha!" shouted he again and again; then composing himself, "Well, go on, Goodman Brown, go on; but, prithee, don't kill me with laughing."

"Well, then, to end the matter at once," said Goodman Brown, considerably nettled, "there is my wife, Faith. It would break her dear little heart; and I'd rather break my own."

"Nay, if that be the case," answered the other, "e'en go thy ways, Goodman   25
Brown. I would not for twenty old women like the one hobbling before us that Faith should come to any harm."

As he spoke he pointed his staff at a female figure on the path, in whom Goodman Brown recognized a very pious and exemplary dame, who had taught him his catechism in youth, and was still his moral and spiritual adviser, jointly with the minister and Deacon Gookin.

"A marvel, truly, that Goody[4] Cloyse should be so far in the wilderness at night fall," said he. "But with your leave, friend, I shall take a cut through the woods until we have left this Christian woman behind. Being a stranger to you, she might ask whom I was consorting with and whither I was going."

"Be it so," said his fellow-traveller. "Betake you the woods, and let me keep the path."

Accordingly the young man turned aside, but took care to watch his companion, who advanced softly along the road until he had come within a staff's length of the old dame. She, meanwhile, was making the best of her way, with singular speed for so aged a woman, and mumbling some indistinct words—a prayer, doubtless—as she went. The traveller put forth his staff and touched her withered neck with what seemed the serpent's tail.

"The devil!" screamed the pious old lady.   30

"Then Goody Cloyse knows her old friend?" observed the traveller, confronting her and leaning on his writhing stick.

"Ah, forsooth, and is it your worship indeed?" cried the good dame. "Yea, truly is it, and in the very image of my old gossip, Goodman Brown, the grandfather of the silly fellow that now is. But—would your worship believe it?—my broomstick hath strangely disappeared, stolen, as I suspect, by that unhanged witch, Goody Cory, and that, too, when I was all anointed with the juice of smallage and cinquefoil and wolf's bane—"

"Mingled with fine wheat and the fat of a new-born babe," said the shape of old Goodman Brown.

"Ah, your worship knows the recipe," cried the old lady, cackling aloud. "So, as I was saying, being all ready for the meeting, and no horse to ride on, I made up my mind to foot it; for they tell me there is a nice young man to be taken into communion to-night. But now your good worship will lend me your arm, and we shall be there in a twinkling."

"That can hardly be," answered her friend. "I may not spare you my arm,   35
Goody Cloyse; but here is my staff, if you will."

So saying, he threw it down at her feet, where, perhaps, it assumed life, being one of the rods which its owner had formerly lent to the Egyptian magi. Of

---

[4]*Goody* = contraction of Goodwife.

this fact, however, Goodman Brown could not take cognizance. He had cast up his eyes in astonishment, and, looking down again, beheld neither Goody Cloyse nor the serpentine staff but his fellow-traveller alone, who waited for him as calmly as if nothing had happened.

"That old woman taught me my catechism," said the young man; and there was a world of meaning in this simple comment.

They continued to walk onward, while the elder traveller exhorted his companion to make good speed and persevere in the path, discoursing so aptly that his arguments seemed rather to spring up in the bosom of his auditor than to be suggested by himself. As they went, he plucked a branch of maple to serve for a walking-stick, and began to strip it of the twigs and little boughs, which were wet with evening dew. The moment his fingers touched them they became strangely withered and dried up as with a week's sunshine. Thus the pair proceeded, at a good free pace, until suddenly, in a gloomy hollow of the road, Goodman Brown sat himself down on the stump of a tree and refused to go any farther.

"Friend," said he, stubbornly, "my mind is made up. Not another step will I budge on this errand. What if a wretched old woman do choose to go to the devil when I thought she was going to heaven: is that any reason why I should quit my dear Faith and go after her?"

"You will think better of this by and by," said his acquaintance, composedly. 40 "Sit here and rest yourself a while; and when you feel like moving again, there is my staff to help you along."

Without more words, he threw his companion the maple stick, and was as speedily out of sight as if he had vanished into the deepening gloom. The young man sat a few moments by the roadside, applauding himself greatly, and thinking with how clear a conscience he should meet the minister in his morning walk, nor shrink from the eye of good old Deacon Gookin. And what calm sleep would be his that very night, which was to have been spent so wickedly, but so purely and sweetly now, in the arms of Faith! Amidst these pleasant and praiseworthy meditations, Goodman Brown heard the tramp of horses along the road, and deemed it advisable to conceal himself within the verge of the forest, conscious of the guilty purpose that had brought him thither, though now so happily turned from it.

On came the hoof-tramps and the voices of the riders, two grave old voices, conversing soberly as they drew near. These mingled sounds appeared to pass along the road, within a few yards of the young man's hiding-place; but, owing doubtless to the depth of the gloom at that particular spot, neither the travellers nor their steeds were visible. Though their figures brushed the small boughs by the wayside, it could not be seen that they intercepted, even for a moment, the faint gleam from the strip of bright sky athwart which they must have passed. Goodman Brown alternately crouched and stood on tiptoe, pulling aside the branches and thrusting forth his head as far as he durst without discerning so much as a shadow. It vexed him the more, because he could have sworn, were such a thing possible, that he recognized the voices of the minister and Deacon Gookin, jogging along quietly, as they were wont to do, when bound to some ordination or ecclesiastical council. While yet within hearing, one of the riders stopped to pluck a switch.

"Of the two, reverend sir," said the voice like the deacon's, "I had rather miss an ordination dinner than to-night's meeting. They tell me that some of our community are to be here from Falmouth and beyond, and others from Connecticut and Rhode Island, besides several of the Indian powwows, who, after their fashion, know almost as much deviltry as the best of us. Moreover, there is a goodly young woman to be taken into communion."

"Mighty well, Deacon Gookin!" replied the solemn old tones of the minister. "Spur up, or we shall be late. Nothing can be done, you know, until I get on the ground."

The hoofs clattered again; and the voices, talking so strangely in the empty air, passed on through the forest, where no church had ever been gathered or solitary Christian prayed. Whither, then, could these holy men be journeying so deep into the heathen wilderness? Young Goodman Brown caught hold of a tree for support, being ready to sink down on the ground, faint and overburdened with the heavy sickness of his heart. He looked up to the sky, doubting whether there really was a heaven above him. Yet, there was the blue arch, and the stars brightening in it.

"With heaven above, and Faith below, I will yet stand firm against the devil!" cried Goodman Brown.

While he still gazed upward into the deep arch of the firmament and had lifted his hands to pray, a cloud, though no wind was stirring, hurried across the zenith and hid the brightening stars. The blue sky was still visible, except directly overhead, where this black mass of cloud was sweeping swiftly northward. Aloft in the air, as if from the depths of the cloud, came a confused and doubtful sound of voices. Once the listener fancied that he could distinguish the accents of towns-people of his own, men and women, both pious and ungodly, many of whom he had met at the communion table, and had seen others rioting at the tavern. The next moment, so indistinct were the sounds, he doubted whether he had heard aught but the murmur of the old forest, whispering without a wind. Then came a stronger swell of those familiar tones, heard daily in the sunshine at Salem village, but never until now from a cloud of night. There was one voice, of a young woman, uttering lamentations, yet with an uncertain sorrow, and entreating for some favor, which, perhaps, it would grieve her to obtain; and all the unseen multitude, both saints and sinners, seemed to encourage her onward.

"Faith!" shouted Goodman Brown, in a voice of agony and desperation; and the echoes of the forest mocked him, crying, "Faith! Faith!" as if bewildered wretches were seeking her all through the wilderness.

The cry of grief, rage, and terror was yet piercing the night, when the unhappy husband held his breath for a response. There was a scream, drowned immediately in a louder murmur of voices, fading into far-off laughter, as the dark cloud swept away, leaving the clear and silent sky above Goodman Brown. But something fluttered lightly down through the air and caught on the branch of a tree. The young man seized it, and beheld a pink ribbon.

"My Faith is gone!" cried he, after one stupefied moment. "There is no good on earth; and sin is but a name. Come, devil, for to thee is this world given."

And, maddened with despair, so that he laughed loud and long, did Goodman Brown grasp his staff and set forth again, at such a rate that he seemed to fly along the forest path, rather than to walk or run. The road grew wilder and drearier and more faintly traced, and vanished at length, leaving him in the heart of the dark wilderness, still rushing onward with the instinct that guides mortal man to evil. The whole forest was peopled with frightful sounds—the creaking of the trees, the howling of wild beasts, and the yell of Indians; while sometimes the wind tolled like a distant church bell, and sometimes gave a broad roar around the traveller, as if all Nature were laughing him to scorn. But he was himself the chief horror of the scene, and shrank not from its other horrors.

"Ha! ha! ha!" roared Goodman Brown when the wind laughed at him. "Let us hear which will laugh loudest! Think not to frighten me with your deviltry! Come witch, come lizard, come Indian powwow, come devil himself, and here comes Goodman Brown. You may as well fear him as he fear you!"

In truth, all through the haunted forest there could be nothing more frightful than the figure of Goodman Brown. On he flew among the black pines, brandishing his staff with frenzied gestures, now giving vent to an inspiration of horrid blasphemy, and now shouting forth such laughter as set all the echoes of the forest laughing like demons around him. The fiend in his own shape is less hideous than when he rages in the breast of man. Thus sped the demoniac on his course, until, quivering among the trees, he saw a red light before him, as when the felled trunks and branches of a clearing have been set on fire, and throw up their lurid blaze against the sky, at the hour of midnight. He paused, in a lull of the tempest that had driven him onward, and heard the swell of what seemed a hymn, rolling solemnly from a distance with the weight of many voices. He knew the tune; it was a familiar one in the choir of the village meeting-house. The verse died heavily away, and was lengthened by a chorus, not of human voices, but of all the sounds of the benighted wilderness pealing in awful harmony together. Goodman Brown cried out; and his cry was lost to his own ear by its unison with the cry of the desert.

In the interval of silence he stole forward until the light glared full upon his eyes. At one extremity of an open space, hemmed in by the dark wall of the forest, arose a rock, bearing some rude, natural resemblance either to an altar or a pulpit, and surrounded by four blazing pines, their tops aflame, their stems untouched, like candles at an evening meeting. The mass of foliage that had overgrown the summit of the rock was all on fire, blazing high into the night and fitfully illuminating the whole field. Each pendent twig and leafy festoon was in a blaze. As the red light arose and fell, a numerous congregation alternately shone forth, then disappeared in shadow, and again grew, as it were, out of the darkness, peopling the heart of the solitary woods at once.

"A grave and dark-clad company," quoth Goodman Brown.

55

In truth, they were such. Among them, quivering to-and-fro between gloom and splendor, appeared faces that would be seen next day at the council board of the province, and others which, Sabbath after Sabbath, looked devoutly heavenward, and benignantly over the crowded pews, from the holiest pulpits in the land. Some affirm that the lady of the governor was there. At least there were high dames well known to her, and wives of honored husbands, and widows, a great multitude, and ancient maidens, all of excellent repute, and fair young girls, who trembled lest their mothers should espy them. Either the sudden gleams of light flashing over the obscure field bedazzled Goodman Brown, or he recognized a score of the church-members of Salem village famous for their especial sanctity. Good old Deacon Gookin had arrived, and waited at the skirts of that venerable saint, his revered pastor. But, irreverently consorting with these grave, reputable, and pious people, these elders of the church, these chaste dames and dewy virgins, there were men of dissolute lives and women of spotted fame, wretches given over to all mean and filthy vice, and suspected even of horrid crimes. It was strange to see, that the good shrank not from the wicked, nor were the sinners abashed by the saints. Scattered also among their pale-faced enemies were the Indian priests, or powwows, who had often scared their native forest with more hideous incantations than any known to English witchcraft.

"But, where is Faith?" thought Goodman Brown; and, as hope came into his heart, he trembled.

Another verse of the hymn arose, a slow and mournful strain, such as the pious love, but joined to words which expressed all that our nature can conceive of sin, and darkly hinted at far more. Unfathomable to mere mortals is the lore of fiends. Verse after verse was sung: and still the chorus of the desert swelled between, like the deepest tone of a mighty organ; and with the final peal of that dreadful anthem there came a sound, as if the roaring wind, the rushing streams, the howling beasts, and every other voice of the unconcerted wilderness were mingling and according with the voice of guilty man in homage to the prince of all. The four blazing pines threw up a loftier flame, and obscurely discovered shapes and visages of horror on the smoke wreaths above the impious assembly. At the same moment the fire on the rock shot redly forth and formed a glowing arch above its base, where now appeared a figure. With reverence be it spoken, the figure bore no slight similitude, both in garb and manner, to some grave divine of the New England churches.

"Bring forth the converts!" cried a voice that echoed through the field and rolled into the forest.

At the word, Goodman Brown stepped forth from the shadow of the trees and approached the congregation, with whom he felt a loathful brotherhood by the sympathy of all that was wicked in his heart. He could have well nigh sworn that the shape of his own dead father beckoned him to advance, looking downward from a smoke wreath, while a woman, with dim features of despair, threw out her hand to warn him back. Was it his mother? But he had no power to retreat one step, nor to resist, even in thought, when the minister and good old Deacon Gookin seized his arms and led him to the blazing rock. Thither came also the slender form of a veiled female, led between Goody Cloyse, that pious teacher of the catechism, and Martha Carrier, who had received the devil's promise to be queen of hell. A rampant hag was she. And there stood the proselytes beneath the canopy of fire. 60

"Welcome, my children," said the dark figure, "to the communion of your race. Ye have found thus young your nature and your destiny. My children, look behind you!"

They turned; and flashing forth, as it were, in a sheet of flame, the fiend worshippers were seen; the smile of welcome gleamed darkly on every visage.

"There," resumed the sable form, "are all whom ye have reverenced from youth. Ye deemed them holier than yourselves, and shrank from your own sin, contrasting it with their lives of righteousness and prayerful aspirations heavenward. Yet here are they all in my worshipping assembly. This night it shall be granted you to know their secret deeds: how hoary-bearded elders of the church have whispered wanton words to the young maids of their households; how many a woman, eager for widow's weeds, has given her husband a drink at bedtime, and let him sleep his last sleep in her bosom; how beardless youths have made haste to inherit their fathers' wealth; and how fair damsels—blush not, sweet ones—have dug little graves in the garden, and bidden me, the sole guest, to an infant's funeral. By the sympathy of your human hearts for sin ye shall scent out all the places—whether in church, bedchamber, street, field, or forest—where crime has been committed, and shall exult to behold the whole earth one stain of guilt, one mighty blood spot. Far more than this. It shall be yours to penetrate, in every bosom, the deep mystery of sin, the fountain of all wicked arts, and which inexhaustibly supplies more evil impulses than human power—than my power at its utmost—can make manifest in deeds. And now, my children, look upon each other."

They did so; and, by the blaze of the hell-kindled torches, the wretched man beheld his Faith, and the wife her husband, trembling before that unhallowed altar.

"Lo, there ye stand, my children," said the figure, in a deep and solemn tone, almost sad with its despairing awfulness, as if his once angelic nature could yet mourn for our miserable race. "Depending upon one another's hearts, ye had still hoped that virtue were not all a dream. Now are ye undeceived. Evil is the nature of mankind. Evil must be your only happiness. Welcome, again, my children, to the communion of your race." 65

"Welcome," repeated the fiend worshippers, in one cry of despair and triumph.

And there they stood, the only pair, as it seemed, who were yet hesitating on the verge of wickedness in this dark world. A basin was hollowed, naturally, in the rock. Did it contain water, reddened by the lurid light? or was it blood? or, perchance, a liquid flame? Herein did the shape of evil dip his hand and prepare to lay the mark of baptism upon their foreheads, that they might be partakers of the mystery of sin, more conscious of the secret guilt of others, both in deed and thought, than they could now be of their own. The husband cast one look at his pale wife, and Faith at him. What polluted wretches would the next glance show them to each other, shuddering alike at what they disclosed and what they saw!

"Faith! Faith!" cried the husband, "look up to heaven, and resist the wicked one."

Whether Faith obeyed he knew not. Hardly had he spoken when he found himself amid calm night and solitude, listening to a roar of the wind which died heavily away through the forest. He staggered against the rock, and felt it chill and damp; while a hanging twig, that had been all on fire, besprinkled his cheek with the coldest dew.

The next morning young Goodman Brown came slowly into the street of Salem village, staring around him like a bewildered man. The good old minister was taking a walk along the graveyard to get an appetite for breakfast and meditate his sermon, and bestowed a blessing, as he passed, on Goodman Brown. He shrank from the venerable saint as if to avoid an anathema. Old Deacon Gookin was at domestic worship, and the holy words of his prayer were heard through the open wind. "What God doth the wizard pray to?" quoth Goodman Brown. Goody Cloyse, that excellent old Christian, stood in the early sunshine at her own lattice, catechizing a little girl who had brought her a pint of morning's milk. Goodman Brown snatched away the child as from the grasp of the fiend himself. Turning the corner by the meeting-house, he spied the head of Faith, with the pink ribbons, gazing anxiously forth, and bursting into such joy at sight of him that she skipped along the street and almost kissed her husband before 70 the whole village. But Goodman Brown looked sternly and sadly into her face, and passed on without a greeting.

Had Goodman Brown fallen asleep in the forest and only dreamed a wild dream of a witch-meeting?

Be it so, if you will; but, alas! it was a dream of evil omen for young Goodman Brown. A stern, a sad, a darkly meditative, a distrustful, if not a desperate man did he become from the night of that fearful dream. On the Sabbath day, when the congregation were singing a holy psalm, he could not listen because an anthem of sin rushed loudly upon his ear and drowned all the blessed strain. When the minister spoke from the pulpit with power and fervid eloquence, and, with his hand on the open Bible, of the sacred truths of our religion, and of saint-like lives and triumphant deaths, and of future bliss or misery unutterable, then did Goodman Brown turn pale, dreading lest the roof should thunder down upon the gray blasphemer and his hearers. Often, awakening suddenly at midnight, he shrank from the bosom of Faith; and at morning or eventide, when the family knelt down at prayer, he scowled and muttered to himself, and gazed sternly at his wife, and turned away. And when he had lived long, and was borne to his grave a hoary corpse, followed by Faith, an aged woman, and children and grandchildren, a goodly procession, besides neighbors, not a few, they carved no hopeful verse upon his tombstone, for his dying hour was gloom.

Talking about the Text

1. Characterize as carefully as you can the old man Brown meets in the forest.
2. The forest is treated as frightening and evil. How much of this might be allegory and how much might be based on genuine concerns of the Puritans at that time? (Consider, for example, that the Puritans were also recent colonialists.)
3. What do you make of the pink ribbons on Faith's bonnet?

Writing about the Text

1. Describe *how* you read the story, paying particular attention to when you started to realize that the events depicted here might be interior, in Brown's mind.
2. Imagine you are a psychologist. Write a letter to a colleague describing and discussing your new patient, Mr. Brown.
3. Retell part of "Young Goodman Brown" in the first person, from Brown's point of view.

Linking the Text to Other Texts

1. Compare the role of the narrator in "Young Goodman Brown" and "The Story of an Hour" (p. 16). Concentrate on how much the narrator keeps hidden from us as the story opens, and at what points the narrator reveals the most important information. To what extent can we say that the narrator is deceiving the readers?
2. Contrast the description of the forest with Welty's description of a southern forest in "A Worn Path" (p. 338). How are the two similar, both in what they seem like physically and in what they represent?

Lady Eleanore's Mantle   (1838)

Mine excellent friend, the landlord of the Province House, was pleased, the other evening, to invite Mr. Tiffany and myself to an oyster supper. This slight mark of respect and gratitude, as he handsomely observed, was far less than the ingenious tale-teller, and I, the humble note-taker of his narratives, had fairly earned, by the public notice which our joint lucubrations had attracted to his establishment. Many a cigar had been smoked within his premises—many a glass of wine, or more potent aqua vitæ, had been quaffed—many a dinner had been eaten by curious strangers, who, save for the fortunate conjunction of Mr. Tiffany and me, would never have ventured through that darksome avenue which gives access to the historic precincts of the Province House. In short, if any credit be due to the courteous assurances of Mr. Thomas Waite, we had brought his forgotten mansion almost as effectually into public view as if we had thrown down the vulgar range of shoe shops and dry goods stores, which hides its aristocratic front from Washington Street. It may be unadvisable, however, to speak too loudly of the increased custom of the house, lest Mr. Waite should find it difficult to renew the lease on so favorable terms as heretofore.

Being thus welcomed as benefactors, neither Mr. Tiffany nor myself felt any scruple in doing full justice to the good things that were set before us. If the feast were less magnificent than those same panelled walls had witnessed in a by-gone century,—if mine host presided with somewhat less of state than might have befitted a successor of the royal Governors,—if the guests made a less imposing show than the bewigged and powdered and embroidered dignitaries, who erst banqueted at the gubernatorial table, and now sleep, within their armorial tombs on Copp's Hill, or round King's Chapel,—yet never, I may boldly say, did a more comfortable little party assemble in the Province House, from Queen Anne's days to the Revolution. The occasion was rendered more interesting by the presence of a venerable personage, whose own actual reminiscences went back to the epoch of Gage and Howe, and even supplied him with a doubtful anecdote or two of Hutchinson. He was one of that small, and now all but extinguished, class, whose attachment to royalty, and to the colonial institutions and customs that were connected with it, had never yielded to the democratic heresies of after times. The young queen of Britain has not a more loyal subject in her realm—perhaps not one who would kneel before her throne with such reverential love—as this old grandsire, whose head has whitened beneath the mild sway of the Republic, which still, in his mellower moments, he terms a usurpation. Yet prejudices so obstinate have not made him an ungentle or impracticable companion. If the truth must be told, the life of the aged loyalist has been of such a scrambling and unsettled character,—he has had so little choice of friends and been so often destitute of any,—that I doubt whether he would refuse a cup of kindness with either Oliver Cromwell or John Hancock,—to say nothing of any democrat now upon the stage. In another paper of this series I may perhaps give the reader a closer glimpse of his portrait.

Our host, in due season, uncorked a bottle of Madeira, of such exquisite perfume and admirable flavor that he surely must have discovered it in an ancient bin, down deep beneath the deepest cellar, where some jolly old butler stored away the Governor's choicest wine, and forgot to reveal the secret on his deathbed. Peace to his red-nosed ghost, and a libation to his memory! This precious liquor was imbibed by Mr. Tiffany with peculiar zest; and after sipping the third glass, it was his pleasure to give us one of the oddest legends which he had yet raked from the storehouse where he keeps such matters. With some suitable adornments from my own fancy, it ran pretty much as follows.

Not long after Colonel Shute had assumed the government of Massachusetts Bay, now nearly a hundred and twenty years ago, a young lady of rank and fortune arrived from England, to claim his protection as her guardian. He was her distant relative, but the nearest who had survived the gradual extinction of her family; so that no more eligible shelter could be found for the rich and high-born Lady Eleanore Rochcliffe than within the Province House of a transatlantic colony. The consort of Governor Shute, moreover, had been as a mother to her childhood, and was now anxious to receive her, in the hope that a beautiful young woman would be exposed to infinitely less peril from the primitive society of New England than amid the artifices and corruptions of a court. If either the Governor or his lady had especially consulted their own comfort, they would probably have sought to devolve the responsibility on other hands; since, with some noble and splendid traits of character, Lady Eleanore was remarkable for a harsh, unyielding pride, a haughty consciousness of her hereditary and personal advantages, which made her almost incapable of control. Judging from many traditionary anecdotes, this peculiar temper was hardly less than a monomania; or, if the acts which it inspired were those of a sane person, it seemed due from Providence that pride so sinful should be followed by as severe a retribution. That tinge of the marvellous, which is thrown over so many of these half-forgotten legends, has probably imparted an additional wildness to the strange story of Lady Eleanore Rochcliffe.

The ship in which she came passenger had arrived at Newport, whence   5
Lady Eleanore was conveyed to Boston in the Governor's coach, attended by a small escort of gentlemen on horseback. The ponderous equipage, with its four black horses, attracted much notice as it rumbled through Cornhill, surrounded by the prancing steeds of half a dozen cavaliers, with swords dangling to their stirrups and pistols at their holsters. Through the large glass windows of the coach, as it rolled along, the people could discern the figure of Lady Eleanore, strangely combining an almost queenly stateliness with the grace and beauty of a maiden in her teens. A singular tale had gone abroad among the ladies of the province, that their fair rival was indebted for much of the irresistible charm of her appearance to a certain article of dress—an embroidered mantle—which had been wrought by the most skilful artist in London, and possessed even magical properties of adornment. On the present occasion, however, she owed nothing to the witchery of dress, being clad in a riding habit of velvet, which would have appeared stiff and ungraceful on any other form.

The coachman reined in his four black steeds, and the whole cavalcade came to a pause in front of the contorted iron balustrade that fenced the Province House from the public street. It was an awkward coincidence that the bell of the Old South was just then tolling for a funeral; so that, instead of a gladsome peal with which it was customary to announce the arrival of distinguished strangers, Lady Eleanore Rochcliffe was ushered by a doleful clang, as if calamity had come embodied in her beautiful person.

"A very great disrespect!" exclaimed Captain Langford, an English officer, who had recently brought dispatches to Governor Shute. "The funeral should have been deferred, lest Lady Eleanore's spirits be affected by such a dismal welcome."

"With your pardon, sir," replied Doctor Clarke, a physician, and a famous champion of the popular party, "whatever the heralds may pretend, a dead beggar must have precedence of a living queen. King Death confers high privileges."

These remarks were interchanged while the speakers waited a passage through the crowd, which had gathered on each side of the gateway, leaving an open avenue to the portal of the Province House. A black slave in livery now leaped from behind the coach, and threw open the door; while at the same moment Governor Shute descended the flight of steps from his mansion, to assist Lady Eleanore in alighting. But the Governor's stately approach was anticipated in a manner that excited general astonishment. A pale young man, with his black hair all in disorder, rushed from the throng, and prostrated himself beside the coach, thus offering his person as a footstool for Lady Eleanore Rochcliffe to tread upon. She held back an instant, yet with an expression as if doubting whether the young man were worthy to bear the weight of her footstep, rather than dissatisfied to receive such awful reverence from a fellow-mortal.

"Up, sir," said the Governor, sternly, at the same time lifting his cane over the intruder. "What means the Bedlamite by this freak?" 10

"Nay," answered Lady Eleanore playfully, but with more scorn than pity in her tone, "your Excellency shall not strike him. When men seek only to be trampled upon, it were a pity to deny them a favor so easily granted—and so well deserved!"

Then, though as lightly as a sunbeam on a cloud, she placed her foot upon the cowering form, and extended her hand to meet that of the Governor. There was a brief interval, during which Lady Eleanore retained this attitude; and never, surely, was there an apter emblem of aristocracy and hereditary pride trampling on human sympathies and the kindred of nature, than these two figures presented at that moment. Yet the spectators were so smitten with her beauty, and so essential did pride seem to the existence of such a creature, that they gave a simultaneous acclamation of applause.

"Who is this insolent young fellow?" inquired Captain Langford, who still remained beside Doctor Clarke.

Frank T. Merrill, "A Pale Young Man . . . *prostrated himself beside the Coach*"—*illustration for "Lady Eleanore's Mantle,"* c. 1906.

"If he be in his senses, his impertinence demands the bastinado. If mad, Lady Eleanore should be secured from further inconvenience, by his confinement."

"His name is Jervase Helwyse," answered the Doctor; "a youth of no birth or fortune, or other advantages, save the mind and soul that nature gave him; and being secretary to our colonial agent in London, it was his misfortune to meet this Lady Eleanore Rochcliffe. He loved her—and her scorn has driven him mad."

"He was mad so to aspire," observed the English officer.   15

"It may be so," said Doctor Clarke, frowning as he spoke. "But I tell you, sir, I could well-nigh doubt the justice of the Heaven above us if no signal humiliation overtake this lady, who now treads so haughtily into yonder mansion. She seeks to place herself above the sympathies of our common nature, which envelops all human souls. See, if that nature do not assert its claim over her in some mode that shall bring her level with the lowest!"

"Never!" cried Captain Langford indignantly—"neither in life, nor when they lay her with her ancestors."

Not many days afterwards the Governor gave a ball in honor of Lady Eleanore Rochcliffe. The principal gentry of the colony received invitations, which were distributed to their residences, far and near, by messengers on horseback, bearing missives sealed with all the formality of official dispatches. In obedience to the summons, there was a general gathering of rank, wealth, and beauty; and the wide door of the Province House had seldom given admittance to more numerous and honorable guests than on the evening of Lady Eleanore's ball. Without much extravagance of eulogy, the spectacle might even be termed splendid; for, according to the fashion of the times, the ladies shone in rich silks and satins, outspread over wide-projecting hoops; and the gentlemen glittered in gold embroidery, laid unsparingly upon the purple, or scarlet, or sky-blue velvet, which was the material of their coats and waistcoats. The latter article of dress was of great importance, since it enveloped the wearer's body nearly to the knees, and was perhaps bedizened with the amount of his whole year's income, in golden flowers and foliage. The altered taste of the present day—a taste symbolic of a deep change in the whole system of society—would look upon almost any of those gorgeous figures as ridiculous; although that evening the guests sought their reflections in the pier-glasses, and rejoiced to catch their own glitter amid the glittering crowd. What a pity that one of the stately mirrors has not preserved a picture of the scene, which, by the very traits that were so transitory, might have taught us much that would be worth knowing and remembering!

Would, at least, that either painter or mirror could convey to us some faint idea of a garment, already noticed in this legend,—the Lady Eleanore's embroidered mantle,—which the gossips whispered was invested with magic properties, so as to lend a new and untried grace to her figure each time that she put it on! Idle fancy as it is, this mysterious mantle has thrown an awe around my image of her, partly from its fabled virtues, and partly because it was the handiwork of a dying woman, and, perchance, owed the fantastic grace of its conception to the delirium of approaching death.

After the ceremonial greetings had been paid, Lady Eleanore Rochcliffe   20
stood apart from the mob of guests, insulating herself within a small and distinguished circle, to whom she accorded a more cordial favor than to the general throng. The waxen torches threw their radiance vividly over the scene, bringing

out its brilliant points in strong relief; but she gazed carelessly, and with now and then an expression of weariness or scorn, tempered with such feminine grace that her auditors scarcely perceived the moral deformity of which it was the ut-terance. She beheld the spectacle not with vulgar ridicule, as disdaining to be pleased with the provincial mockery of a court festival, but with the deeper scorn of one whose spirit held itself too high to participate in the enjoyment of other human souls. Whether or no the recollections of those who saw her that evening were influenced by the strange events with which she was subsequently con-nected, so it was that her figure ever after recurred to them as marked by some-thing wild and unnatural,—although, at the time, the general whisper was of her exceeding beauty, and of the indescribable charm which her mantle threw around her. Some close observers, indeed, detected a feverish flush and alternate paleness of countenance, with corresponding flow and revulsion of spirits, and once or twice a painful and helpless betrayal of lassitude, as if she were on the point of sinking to the ground. Then, with a nervous shudder, she seemed to arouse her energies and threw some bright and playful yet half-wicked sarcasm into the conversation. There was so strange a characteristic in her manners and sentiments that it astonished every right-minded listener; till looking in her face, a lurking and incomprehensible glance and smile perplexed them with doubts both as to her seriousness and sanity. Gradually, Lady Eleanore Rochcliffe's circle grew smaller, till only four gentlemen remained in it. These were Captain Langford, the English officer before mentioned; a Virginian planter, who had come to Massachusetts on some political errand; a young Epis-copal clergyman, the grandson of a British earl; and, lastly, the private secretary of Governor Shute, whose obsequiousness had won a sort of tolerance from Lady Eleanore.

At different periods of the evening the liveried servants of the Province House passed among the guests, bearing huge trays of refreshments and French and Spanish wines. Lady Eleanore Rochcliffe, who refused to wet her beautiful lips even with a bubble of Champagne, had sunk back into a large damask chair, apparently overwearied either with the excitement of the scene or its tedium, and while, for an instant, she was unconscious of voices, laughter and music, a young man stole forward, and knelt down at her feet. He bore a salver in his hand, on which was a chased silver goblet, filled to the brim with wine, which he offered as reverentially as to a crowned queen, or rather with the awful devotion of a priest doing sacrifice to his idol. Conscious that some one touched her robe, Lady Eleanore started, and unclosed her eyes upon the pale, wild features and di-shevelled hair of Jervase Helwyse.

"Why do you haunt me thus?" said she, in a languid tone, but with a kindlier feeling than she ordinarily permitted herself to express. "They tell me that I have done you harm."

"Heaven knows if that be so," replied the young man solemnly. "But, Lady Eleanore, in requital of that harm, if such there be, and for your own earthly and heavenly welfare, I pray you to take one sip of this holy wine, and then to pass the goblet round among the guests. And this shall be a symbol that you have not sought to withdraw yourself from the chain of human sympathies—which whoso would shake off must keep company with fallen angels."

"Where has this mad fellow stolen that sacramental vessel?" exclaimed the Episcopal clergyman.

This question drew the notice of the guests to the silver cup, which was rec-   25
ognized as appertaining to the communion plate of the Old South Church; and,
for aught that could be known, it was brimming over with the consecrated wine.

"Perhaps it is poisoned," half whispered the Governor's secretary.

"Pour it down the villain's throat!" cried the Virginian fiercely.

"Turn him out of the house!" cried Captain Langford, seizing Jervase Helwyse so roughly by the shoulder that the sacramental cup was overturned, and its
contents sprinkled upon Lady Eleanore's mantle. "Whether knave, fool, or Bedlamite, it is intolerable that the fellow should go at large."

"Pray, gentlemen, do my poor admirer no harm," said Lady Eleanore, with a
faint and weary smile. "Take him out of my sight, if such be your pleasure; for I
can find in my heart to do nothing but laugh at him; whereas, in all decency and
conscience, it would become me to weep for the mischief I have wrought!"

But while the by-standers were attempting to lead away the unfortunate   30
young man, he broke from them, and with a wild, impassioned earnestness, offered a new and equally strange petition to Lady Eleanore. It was no other than
that she should throw off the mantle, which, while he pressed the silver cup of
wine upon her, she had drawn more closely around her form, so as almost to
shroud herself within it.

"Cast it from you!" exclaimed Jervase Helwyse, clasping his hands in an
agony of entreaty. "It may not yet be too late! Give the accursed garment to the
flames!"

But Lady Eleanore, with a laugh of scorn, drew the rich folds of the embroidered mantle over her head, in such a fashion as to give a completely new aspect
to her beautiful face, which—half hidden, half revealed—seemed to belong to
some being of mysterious character and purposes.

"Farewell, Jervase Helwyse!" said she. "Keep my image in your remembrance, as you behold it now."

"Alas, lady!" he replied, in a tone no longer wild, but sad as a funeral bell.
"We must meet shortly, when your face may wear another aspect—and that shall
be the image that must abide within me."

He made no more resistance to the violent efforts of the gentlemen and ser-   35
vants, who almost dragged him out of the apartment, and dismissed him roughly
from the iron gate of the Province House. Captain Langford, who had been very
active in this affair, was returning to the presence of Lady Eleanore Rochcliffe,
when he encountered the physician, Doctor Clarke, with whom he had held
some casual talk on the day of her arrival. The Doctor stood apart, separated
from Lady Eleanore by the width of the room, but eying her with such keen
sagacity that Captain Langford involuntarily gave him credit for the discovery of
some deep secret.

"You appear to be smitten, after all, with the charms of this queenly
maiden," said he, hoping thus to draw forth the physician's hidden knowledge.

"God forbid!" answered Doctor Clarke, with a grave smile; "and if you be
wise you will put up the same prayer for yourself. Woe to those who shall be smitten by this beautiful Lady Eleanore! But yonder stands the Governor—and I
have a word or two for his private ear. Good night!"

He accordingly advanced to Governor Shute, and addressed him in so low a
tone that none of the by-standers could catch a word of what he said, although
the sudden change of his Excellency's hitherto cheerful visage betokened that

the communication could be of no agreeable import. A very few moments afterwards it was announced to the guests that an unforeseen circumstance rendered it necessary to put a premature close to the festival.

The ball at the Province House supplied a topic of conversation for the colonial metropolis for some days after its occurrence, and might still longer have been the general theme, only that a subject of all-engrossing interest thrust it, for a time, from the public recollection. This was the appearance of a dreadful epidemic, which, in that age and long before and afterwards, was wont to slay its hundreds and thousands on both sides of the Atlantic. On the occasion of which we speak, it was distinguished by a peculiar virulence, insomuch that it has left its traces—its pit-marks, to use an appropriate figure—on the history of the country, the affairs of which were thrown into confusion by its ravages. At first, unlike its ordinary course, the disease seemed to confine itself to the higher circles of society, selecting its victims from among the proud, the well-born, and the wealthy, entering unabashed into stately chambers, and lying down with the slumberers in silken beds. Some of the most distinguished guests of the Province House—even those whom the haughty Lady Eleanore Rochcliffe had deemed not unworthy of her favor—were stricken by this fatal scourge. It was noticed, with an ungenerous bitterness of feeling, that the four gentlemen—the Virginian, the British officer, the young clergyman, and the Governor's secretary—who had been her most devoted attendants on the evening of the ball, were the foremost on whom the plague stroke fell. But the disease, pursuing its onward progress, soon ceased to be exclusively a prerogative of aristocracy. Its red brand was no longer conferred like a noble's star, or an order of knighthood. It threaded its way through the narrow and crooked streets, and entered the low, mean, darksome dwellings, and laid its hand of death upon the artisans and laboring classes of the town. It compelled rich and poor to feel themselves brethren then; and stalking to and fro across the Three Hills, with a fierceness which made it almost a new pestilence, there was that mighty conqueror—that scourge and horror of our forefathers—the Small-Pox!

We cannot estimate the affright which this plague inspired of yore, by contemplating it as the fangless monster of the present day. We must remember, rather, with what awe we watched the gigantic footsteps of the Asiatic cholera, striding from shore to shore of the Atlantic, and marching like destiny upon cities far remote which flight had already half depopulated. There is no other fear so horrible and unhumanizing as that which makes man dread to breathe heaven's vital air lest it be poison, or to grasp the hand of a brother or friend lest the gripe of the pestilence should clutch him. Such was the dismay that now followed in the track of the disease, or ran before it throughout the town. Graves were hastily dug, and the pestilential relics as hastily covered, because the dead were enemies of the living, and strove to draw them headlong, as it were, into their own dismal pit. The public councils were suspended, as if mortal wisdom might relinquish its devices, now that an unearthly usurper had found his way into the ruler's mansion. Had an enemy's fleet been hovering on the coast, or his armies trampling on our soil, the people would probably have committed their defence to that same direful conqueror who had wrought their own calamity, and would permit no interference with his sway. This conqueror had a symbol of his triumphs. It was a blood-red flag, that fluttered in the tainted air, over the door of every dwelling into which the Small-Pox had entered.

40

Such a banner was long since waving over the portal of the Province House; for thence, as was proved by tracking its footsteps back, had all this dreadful mischief issued. It had been traced back to a lady's luxurious chamber—to the proudest of the proud—to her that was so delicate, and hardly owned herself of earthly mould—to the haughty one, who took her stand above human sympathies—to Lady Eleanore! There remained no room for doubt that the contagion had lurked in that gorgeous mantle, which threw so strange a grace around her at the festival. Its fantastic splendor had been conceived in the delirious brain of a woman on her death-bed, and was the last toil of her stiffening fingers, which had interwoven fate and misery with its golden threads. This dark tale, whispered at first, was now bruited far and wide. The people raved against the Lady Eleanore, and cried out that her pride and scorn had evoked a fiend, and that, between them both, this monstrous evil had been born. At times, their rage and despair took the semblance of grinning mirth; and whenever the red flag of the pestilence was hoisted over another and yet another door, they clapped their hands and shouted through the streets, in bitter mockery: "Behold a new triumph for the Lady Eleanore!"

One day, in the midst of these dismal times, a wild figure approached the portal of the Province House, and folding his arms, stood contemplating the scarlet banner which a passing breeze shook fitfully, as if to fling abroad the contagion that it typified. At length, climbing one of the pillars by means of the iron balustrade, he took down the flag and entered the mansion, waving it above his head. At the foot of the staircase he met the Governor, booted and spurred, with his cloak drawn around him, evidently on the point of setting forth upon a journey.

"Wretched lunatic, what do you seek here?" exclaimed Shute, extending his cane to guard himself from contact. "There is nothing here but Death. Back—or you will meet him!"

"Death will not touch me, the banner-bearer of the pestilence!" cried Jervase Helwyse, shaking the red flag aloft. "Death, and the Pestilence, who wears the aspect of the Lady Eleanore, will walk through the streets to-night, and I must march before them with this banner!"

"Why do I waste words on the fellow?" muttered the Governor, drawing his cloak across his mouth. "What matters his miserable life, when none of us are sure of twelve hours' breath? On, fool, to your own destruction!" 45

He made way for Jervase Helwyse, who immediately ascended the staircase, but, on the first landing place, was arrested by the firm grasp of a hand upon his shoulder. Looking fiercely up, with a madman's impulse to struggle with and rend asunder his opponent, he found himself powerless beneath a calm, stern eye, which possessed the mysterious property of quelling frenzy at its height. The person whom he had now encountered was the physician, Doctor Clarke, the duties of whose sad profession had led him to the Province House, where he was an infrequent guest in more prosperous times.

"Young man, what is your purpose?" demanded he.

"I seek the Lady Eleanore," answered Jervase Helwyse, submissively.

"All have fled from her," said the physician. "Why do you seek her now? I tell you, youth, her nurse fell death-stricken on the threshold of that fatal chamber. Know ye not, that never came such a curse to our shores as this lovely Lady Eleanore?—that her breath has filled the air with poison?—that she has shaken pestilence and death upon the land, from the folds of her accursed mantle?"

"Let me look upon her!" rejoined the mad youth, more wildly. "Let me be- 50
hold her, in her awful beauty, clad in the regal garments of the pestilence! She
and Death sit on a throne together. Let me kneel down before them!"

"Poor youth!" said Doctor Clarke; and, moved by a deep sense of human
weakness, a smile of caustic humor curled his lip even then. "Wilt thou still worship the destroyer and surround her image with fantasies the more magnificent,
the more evil she has wrought? Thus man doth ever to his tyrants. Approach,
then! Madness, as I have noted, has that good efficacy, that it will guard you
from contagion—and perchance its own cure may be found in yonder chamber."

Ascending another flight of stairs, he threw open a door and signed to Jervase Helwyse that he should enter. The poor lunatic, it seems probable, had
cherished a delusion that his haughty mistress sat in state, unharmed herself by
the pestilential influence, which, as by enchantment, she scattered round about
her. He dreamed, no doubt, that her beauty was not dimmed, but brightened
into superhuman splendor. With such anticipations, he stole reverentially to the
door at which the physician stood, but paused upon the threshold, gazing fearfully into the gloom of the darkened chamber.

"Where is the Lady Eleanore?" whispered he.

"Call her," replied the physician.

"Lady Eleanore!—Princess!—Queen of Death!" cried Jervase Helwyse, ad- 55
vancing three steps into the chamber. "She is not here! There, on yonder table, I
behold the sparkle of a diamond which once she wore upon her bosom.
There"—and he shuddered—"there hangs her mantle, on which a dead woman
embroidered a spell of dreadful potency. But where is the Lady Eleanore?"

Something stirred within the silken curtains of a canopied bed; and a low
moan was uttered, which, listening intently, Jervase Helwyse began to distinguish as a woman's voice, complaining dolefully of thirst. He fancied, even, that
he recognized its tones.

"My throat!—my throat is scorched," murmured the voice. "A drop of water!"

"What thing art thou?" said the brain-stricken youth, drawing near the bed
and tearing asunder its curtains. "Whose voice hast thou stolen for thy murmurs
and miserable petitions, as if Lady Eleanore could be conscious of mortal infirmity? Fie! Heap of diseased mortality, why lurkest thou in my lady's chamber?"

"O Jervase Helwyse," said the voice—and as it spoke the figure contorted itself, struggling to hide its blasted face—"look not now on the woman you once
loved! The curse of Heaven hath stricken me, because I would not call man my
brother, nor woman sister. I wrapped myself in PRIDE as in a MANTLE, and scorned
the sympathies of nature; and therefore has nature made this wretched body the
medium of a dreadful sympathy. You are avenged—they are all avenged—Nature
is avenged—for I am Eleanore Rochcliffe!"

The malice of his mental disease, the bitterness lurking at the bottom of his 60
heart, mad as he was, for a blighted and ruined life, and love that had been paid
with cruel scorn, awoke within the breast of Jervase Helwyse. He shook his finger at the wretched girl, and the chamber echoed, the curtains of the bed were
shaken, with his outburst of insane merriment.

"Another triumph for the Lady Eleanore!" he cried. "All have been her victims! Who so worthy to be the final victim as herself?"

Impelled by some new fantasy of his crazed intellect, he snatched the fatal
mantle and rushed from the chamber and the house. That night a procession

passed, by torchlight, through the streets, bearing in the midst the figure of a woman, enveloped with a richly embroidered mantle; while in advance stalked Jervase Helwyse, waving the red flag of the pestilence. Arriving opposite the Province House, the mob burned the effigy, and a strong wind came and swept away the ashes. It was said that, from that very hour, the pestilence abated, as if its sway had some mysterious connection, from the first plague stroke to the last, with Lady Eleanore's Mantle. A remarkable uncertainty broods over that unhappy lady's fate. There is a belief, however, that in a certain chamber of this mansion a female form may sometimes be duskily discerned, shrinking into the darkest corner and muffling her face within an embroidered mantle. Supposing the legend true, can this be other than the once proud Lady Eleanore?

* * *

Mine host and the old loyalist and I bestowed no little warmth of applause upon this narrative, in which we had all been deeply interested; for the reader can scarcely conceive how unspeakably the effect of such a tale is heightened when, as in the present case, we may repose perfect confidence in the veracity of him who tells it. For my own part, knowing how scrupulous is Mr. Tiffany to settle the foundation of his facts, I could not have believed him one whit the more faithfully had he professed himself an eye-witness of the doings and sufferings of poor Lady Eleanore. Some sceptics, it is true, might demand documentary evidence, or even require him to produce the embroidered mantle, forgetting that—Heaven be praised—it was consumed to ashes. But now the old loyalist, whose blood was warmed by the good cheer, began to talk, in his turn, about the traditions of the

Frank T. Merrill, "That Night a Procession passed by Torchlight"—illustration for "Lady Eleanore's Mantle," c. 1906.

Province House, and hinted that he, if it were agreeable, might add a few reminiscences to our legendary stock. Mr. Tiffany, having no cause to dread a rival, immediately besought him to favor us with a specimen; my own entreaties, of course, were urged to the same effect; and our venerable guest, well pleased to find willing auditors, awaited only the return of Mr. Thomas Waite, who had been summoned forth to provide accommodations for several new arrivals. Perchance the public—but be this as its own caprice and ours shall settle the matter—may read the result in another Tale of the Province House.

Talking about the Text

1. How soon do you suspect something is going to go wrong for the Governor? What leads you to this conclusion?
2. We find out very little about the doctor, yet he appears at very significant moments. What role does he play in the story?
3. What might be allegorical about the mantle itself?

Writing about the Text

1. In a one- to two-page essay, explain what similar methods are used by the narrator to describe the mantle in "Lady Eleanore's Mantle" and the walking stick in "Young Goodman Brown."
2. Describe the characteristics of Hawthorne's style in the first twenty lines of "Lady Eleanore's Mantle," looking carefully at sentence length, vocabulary, and figurative language (metaphor, exaggeration, etc.).
3. Write a concluding paragraph or two by Lady Eleanore herself. What would she say?

Linking the Text to Other Texts

1. Compare the doctor with the old man in "Young Goodman Brown" (p. 147), two very different characters who seem to have some interesting things in common. How does Hawthorne depict these two important "role-players" in these stories? Look for both physical and mental characteristics.
2. What characteristics do the high-society Bostonians share with the merrymakers in "The Maypole of Merry Mount" (below)? It may be best to think of the way both sets of people are contrasted with the Puritans who also inhabit both stories.

The Maypole of Merry Mount

(1836)

There is an admirable foundation for a philosophic romance in the curious history of the early settlement of Mount Wollaston, or Merry Mount. In the slight sketch here attempted, the facts, recorded on the grave pages of our New England annalists, have wrought themselves, almost spontaneously, into a sort of allegory. The masques, mummeries, and festive customs, described in the text, are in accordance with the manners of the age. Authority on these points may be found in Strutt's Book of English Sports and Pastimes.

Bright were the days at Merry Mount, when the Maypole was the banner staff of that gay colony! They who reared it, should their banner be triumphant, were to pour sunshine over New England's rugged hills, and scatter flower seeds

Illustration for "The Maypole of Merry Mount," from Hawthorne's Works, *vol. 1.*

throughout the soil. Jollity and gloom were contending for an empire. Midsummer eve had come, bringing deep verdure to the forest, and roses in her lap, of a more vivid hue than the tender buds of spring. But May, or her mirthful spirit, dwelt all the year round at Merry Mount, sporting with the Summer months, and revelling with Autumn, and basking in the glow of Winter's fireside. Through a world of toil and care she flitted with a dreamlike smile, and came hither to find a home among the lightsome hearts of Merry Mount.

Never had the Maypole been so gayly decked as at sunset on midsummer eve. This venerated emblem was a pine-tree, which had preserved the slender grace of youth, while it equalled the loftiest height of the old wood monarchs. From its top streamed a silken banner, colored like the rainbow. Down nearly to the ground the pole was dressed with birchen boughs, and others of the liveliest green, and some with silvery leaves, fastened by ribbons that fluttered in fantastic knots of twenty different colors, but no sad ones. Garden flowers, and blossoms of the wilderness, laughed gladly forth amid the verdure, so fresh and dewy that they must have grown by magic on that happy pine-tree. Where this green and flowery splendor terminated, the shaft of the Maypole was stained with the seven brilliant hues of the banner at its top. On the lowest green bough hung an abundant wreath of roses, some that had been gathered in the sunniest spots of the forest, and others, of still richer blush, which the colonists had reared from English seed. Oh, people of the Golden Age, the chief of your husbandry was to raise flowers!

But what was the wild throng that stood hand in hand about the Maypole? It could not be that the fauns and nymphs, when driven from their classic groves and homes of ancient fable, had sought refuge, as all the persecuted did, in the fresh woods of the West. These were Gothic monsters, though perhaps of Grecian ancestry. On the shoulders of a comely youth uprose the head and branching antlers of a stag; a second, human in all other points, had the grim visage of a wolf; a third, still with the trunk and limbs of a mortal man, showed the beard and horns of a venerable he-goat. There was the likeness of a bear erect, brute in all but his hind legs, which were adorned with pink silk stockings. And here again, almost as wondrous, stood a real bear of the dark forest, lending each of his fore paws to the grasp of a human hand, and as ready for the dance as any in that circle. His inferior nature rose half way, to meet his companions as they stooped. Other faces wore the similitude of man or woman, but distorted or extravagant, with red noses pendulous before their mouths, which seemed of awful depth, and stretched from ear to ear in an eternal fit of laughter. Here might be seen the Savage Man, well known in heraldry, hairy as a baboon, and girdled with green leaves. By his side, a noble figure, but still a counterfelt, appeared an Indian hunter, with feathery crest and wampum belt. Many of this strange company wore foolscaps, and had little bells appended to their garments, tinkling with a silvery sound, responsive to the inaudible music of their gleesome spirits. Some youths and maidens were of soberer garb, yet well maintained their places in the irregular throng by the expression of wild revelry upon their features. Such were the colonists of Merry Mount, as they stood in the broad smile of sunset round their venerated Maypole.

Had a wanderer, bewildered in the melancholy forest, heard their mirth, and stolen a half-affrighted glance, he might have fancied them the crew of Comus,[1] some already transformed to brutes, some midway between man and beast, and the others rioting in the flow of tipsy jollity that foreran the change. But a band of Puritans, who watched the scene, invisible themselves, compared the masques to those devils and ruined souls with whom their superstition peopled the black wilderness.

Within the ring of monsters appeared the two airiest forms that had ever trodden on any more solid footing than a purple and golden cloud. One was a youth in glistening apparel, with a scarf of the rainbow pattern crosswise on his breast. His right hand held a gilded staff, the ensign of high dignity among the revellers, and his left grasped the slender fingers of a fair maiden, not less gayly decorated than himself. Bright roses glowed in contrast with the dark and glossy curls of each, and were scattered round their feet, or had sprung up spontaneously there. Behind this lightsome couple, so close to the Maypole that its boughs shaded his jovial face, stood the figure of an English priest, canonically dressed, yet decked with flowers, in heathen fashion, and wearing a chaplet of the native vine leaves. By the riot of his rolling eye, and the pagan decorations of his holy garb, he seemed the wildest monster there, and the very Comus of the crew.

"Votaries of the Maypole," cried the flower-decked priest, "merrily, all day long, have the woods echoed to your mirth. But be this your merriest hour, my hearts! Lo, here stand the Lord and Lady of the May, whom I, a clerk of Oxford, and high priest of Merry Mount, am presently to join in holy matrimony. Up with your nimble spirits, ye morris-dancers, green men, and glee maidens, bears and wolves, and horned gentlemen! Come; a chorus now, rich with the old

---

[1]God of revelry.

mirth of Merry England, and the wilder glee of this fresh forest: and then a dance, to show the youthful pair what life is made of, and how airily they should go through it! All ye that love the Maypole, lend your voices to the nuptial song of the Lord and Lady of the May!"

This wedlock was more serious than most affairs of Merry Mount, where jest and delusion, trick and fantasy, kept up a continual carnival. The Lord and Lady of the May, though their titles must be laid down at sunset, were really and truly to be partners for the dance of life, beginning the measure that same bright eve. The wreath of roses, that hung from the lowest green bough of the Maypole, had been twined for them, and would be thrown over both their heads, in symbol of their flowery union. When the priest had spoken, therefore, a riotous uproar burst from the rout of monstrous figures.

"Begin you the stave,[2] reverend Sir," cried they all; "and never did the woods ring to such a merry peal as we of the Maypole shall send up!"

Immediately a prelude of pipe, cithern, and viol, touched with practised minstrelsy, began to play from a neighboring thicket, in such a mirthful cadence that the boughs of the Maypole quivered to the sound. But the May Lord, he of the gilded staff, chancing to look into his Lady's eyes, was wonder struck at the almost pensive glance that met his own.

"Edith, sweet Lady of the May," whispered he reproachfully, "is yon wreath of roses a garland to hang above our graves, that you look so sad? O, Edith, this is our golden time! Tarnish it not by any pensive shadow of the mind; for it may be that nothing of futurity will be brighter than the mere remembrance of what is now passing."   10

"That was the very thought that saddened me! How came it in your mind too?" said Edith, in a still lower tone than he, for it was high treason to be sad at Merry Mount. "Therefore do I sigh amid this festive music. And besides, dear Edgar, I struggle as with a dream, and fancy that these shapes of our jovial friends are visionary, and their mirth unreal, and that we are no true Lord and Lady of the May. What is the mystery in my heart?"

Just then, as if a spell had loosened them, down came a little shower of withering rose leaves from the Maypole. Alas, for the young lovers! No sooner had their hearts glowed with real passion than they were sensible of something vague and unsubstantial in their former pleasures, and felt a dreary presentiment of inevitable change. From the moment that they truly loved, they had subjected themselves to earth's doom of care and sorrow, and troubled joy, and had no more a home at Merry Mount. That was Edith's mystery. Now leave we the priest to marry them, and the masquers to sport round the Maypole, till the last sunbeam be withdrawn from its summit, and the shadows of the forest mingle gloomily in the dance. Meanwhile, we may discover who these gay people were.

Two hundred years ago, and more, the old world and its inhabitants became mutually weary of each other. Men voyaged by thousands to the West: some to barter glass beads, and such like jewels, for the furs of the Indian hunter; some to conquer virgin empires; and one stern band to pray. But none of these motives had much weight with the colonists of Merry Mount. Their leaders were men who had sported so long with life, that when Thought and Wisdom came, even these unwelcome guests were led astray by the crowd of vanities which they

---

[2]*stave*=stanza.

should have put to flight. Erring Thought and perverted Wisdom were made to put on masques, and play the fool. The men of whom we speak, after losing the heart's fresh gayety, imagined a wild philosophy of pleasure, and came hither to act out their latest day-dream. They gathered followers from all that giddy tribe whose whole life is like the festal days of soberer men. In their train were minstrels, not unknown in London streets; wandering players, whose theatres had been the halls of noblemen; mummers, rope-dancers, and mountebanks, who would long be missed at wakes, church ales, and fairs; in a word, mirth makers of every sort, such as abounded in that age, but now began to be discountenanced by the rapid growth of Puritanism. Light had their footsteps been on land, and as lightly they came across the sea. Many had been maddened by their previous troubles into a gay despair; others were as madly gay in the flush of youth, like the May Lord and his Lady; but whatever might be the quality of their mirth, old and young were gay at Merry Mount. The young deemed themselves happy. The elder spirits, if they knew that mirth was but the counterfeit of happiness, yet followed the false shadow wilfully, because at least her garments glittered brightest. Sworn triflers of a lifetime, they would not venture among the sober truths of life not even to be truly blest.

All the hereditary pastimes of Old England were transplanted hither. The King of Christmas was duly crowned, and the Lord of Misrule bore potent sway. On the Eve of St. John, they felled whole acres of the forest to make bonfires, and danced by the blaze all night, crowned with garlands, and throwing flowers into the flame. At harvest time, though their crop was of the smallest, they made an image with the sheaves of Indian corn, and wreathed it with autumnal garlands, and bore it home triumphantly. But what chiefly characterized the colonists of Merry Mount was their veneration for the Maypole. It has made their true history a poet's tale. Spring decked the hallowed emblem with young blossoms and fresh green boughs; Summer brought roses of the deepest blush, and the perfected foliage of the forest; Autumn enriched it with that red and yellow gorgeousness which converts each wildwood leaf into a painted flower; and Winter silvered it with sleet, and hung it round with icicles, till it flashed in the cold sunshine, itself a frozen sunbeam. Thus each alternate season did homage to the Maypole, and paid it a tribute of its own richest splendor. Its votaries danced round it, once, at least, in every month; sometimes they called it their religion, or their altar; but always, it was the banner staff of Merry Mount.

Unfortunately, there were men in the new world of a sterner faith than those Maypole worshippers. Not far from Merry Mount was a settlement of Puritans, most dismal wretches, who said their prayers before daylight, and then wrought in the forest or the cornfield till evening made it prayer time again. Their weapons were always at hand to shoot down the straggling savage. When they met in conclave, it was never to keep up the old English mirth, but to hear sermons three hours long, or to proclaim bounties on the heads of wolves and the scalps of Indians. Their festivals were fast days, and their chief pastime the singing of psalms. Woe to the youth or maiden who did but dream of a dance! The selectman nodded to the constable; and there sat the light-heeled reprobate in the stocks; or if he danced, it was round the whipping-post, which might be termed the Puritan Maypole.

A party of these grim Puritans, toiling through the difficult woods, each with a horseload of iron armor to burden his footsteps, would sometimes draw near the sunny precincts of Merry Mount. There were the silken colonists, sporting round their Maypole, perhaps teaching a bear to dance, or striving to communicate their mirth to the grave Indian; or masquerading in the skins of deer and wolves, which they had hunted for that especial purpose. Often, the whole colony were playing at blindman's buff, magistrates and all, with their eyes bandaged, except a single scapegoat, whom the blinded sinners pursued by the tinkling of the bells at his garments. Once, it is said, they were seen following a flower-decked corpse, with merriment and festive music, to his grave. But did the dead man laugh? In their quietest times, they sang ballads and told tales, for the edification of their pious visitors; or perplexed them with juggling tricks; or grinned at them through horse collars; and when sport itself grew wearisome, they made game of their own stupidity, and began a yawning match. At the very least of these enormities, the men of iron shook their heads and frowned so darkly that the revellers looked up imagining that a momentary cloud had overcast the sunshine, which was to be perpetual there. On the other hand, the Puritans affirmed that, when a psalm was pealing from their place of worship, the echo which the forest sent them back seemed often like the chorus of a jolly catch, closing with a roar of laughter. Who but the fiend, and his bond slaves, the crew of Merry Mount, had thus disturbed them? In due time, a feud arose, stern and bitter on one side, and as serious on the other as anything could be among such light spirits as had sworn allegiance to the Maypole. The future complexion of New England was involved in this important quarrel. Should the grizzly saints establish their jurisdiction over the gay sinners, then would their spirits darken all the clime, and make it a land of clouded visages, of hard toil, of sermon and psalm forever. But should the banner staff of Merry Mount be fortunate, sunshine would break upon the hills, and flowers would beautify the forest, and late posterity do homage to the Maypole.

After these authentic passages from history, we return to the nuptials of the Lord and Lady of the May. Alas! we have delayed too long, and must darken our tale too suddenly. As we glance again at the Maypole, a solitary sunbeam is fading from the summit, and leaves only a faint, golden tinge blended with the hues of the rainbow banner. Even that dim light is now withdrawn, relinquishing the whole domain of Merry Mount to the evening gloom, which has rushed so instantaneously from the black surrounding woods. But some of these black shadows have rushed forth in human shape.

Yes, with the setting sun, the last day of mirth had passed from Merry Mount. The ring of gay masquers was disordered and broken; the stag lowered his antlers in dismay; the wolf grew weaker than a lamb; the bells of the morris-dancers tinkled with tremulous affright. The Puritans had played a characteristic part in the Maypole mummeries. Their darksome figures were intermixed with the wild shapes of their foes, and made the scene a picture of the moment, when waking thoughts start up amid the scattered fantasies of a dream. The leader of the hostile party stood in the centre of the circle, while the route of monsters cowered around him, like evil spirits in the presence of a dread magician. No fantastic foolery could look him in the face. So stern was the energy of his aspect, that the whole man, visage, frame, and soul, seemed wrought of iron, gifted with life and thought, yet all of one substance with his headpiece and breastplate. It was the Puritan of Puritans; it was Endicott[3] himself!

---

[3]John Endicott (1589–1665), governor of the colony.

"Stand off, priest of Baal!" said he, with a grim frown and laying no reverent hand upon the surplice. "I know thee, Blackstone.[4] Thou art the man who couldst not abide the rule even of thine own corrupted church, and hast come hither to preach inequity, and to give example of it in thy life. But now shall it be seen that the Lord hath sanctified this wilderness for his peculiar people. Woe unto them that would defile it! And first, for this flower-decked abomination, the altar of thy worship!"

And with his keen sword Endicott assaulted the hallowed Maypole. Nor   20
long did it resist his arm. It groaned with a dismal sound; it showered leaves and rosebuds upon the remorseless enthusiast; and finally, with all its green boughs and ribbons and flowers, symbolic of departed pleasures, down fell the banner staff of Merry Mount. As it sank, tradition says, the evening sky grew darker, and the woods threw forth a more sombre shadow.

"There," cried Endicott, looking triumphantly on his work, "there lies the only Maypole in New England! The thought is strong within me that, by its fall, is shadowed forth the fate of light and idle mirth makers, amongst us and our posterity. Amen, saith John Endicott."

"Amen!" echoed his followers.

But the votaries of the Maypole gave one groan for their idol. At the sound, the Puritan leader glanced at the crew of Comus, each a figure of broad mirth, yet, at this moment, strangely expressive of sorrow and dismay.

"Valiant captain," quoth Peter Palfrey, the Ancient of the band, "what order shall be taken with the prisoners!"

"I thought not to repent me of cutting down a Maypole," replied Endicott,   25
"yet now I could find in my heart to plant it again, and give each of these bestial pagans one other dance round their idol. It would have served rarely for a whipping-post!"

"But there are pine-trees enow," suggested the lieutenant.

"True, good Ancient," said the leader. "Wherefore, bind the heathen crew, and bestow on them a small matter of stripes apiece, as earnest of our future justice. Set some of the rogues in the stocks to rest themselves, so soon as Providence shall bring us to one of our own well-ordered settlements where such accommodations may be found. Further penalties, such as branding and cropping of ears, shall be thought of hereafter."

"How many stripes for the priest?" inquired Ancient Palfrey.

"None as yet," answered Endicott, bending his iron frown upon the culprit. "It must be for the Great and General Court to determine, whether stripes and long imprisonment, and other grievous penalty, may atone for his transgressions. Let him look to himself! For such as violate our civil order, it may be permitted us to show mercy. But woe to the wretch that troubleth our religion."

"And this dancing bear," resumed the officer. "Must he share the stripes of   30
his fellows?"

"Shoot him through the head!" said the energetic Puritan. "I suspect witchcraft in the beast."

"Here be a couple of shining ones," continued Peter Palfrey, pointing his weapon at the Lord and Lady of the May. "They seem to be of high station

---

[4]Hawthorne's note: "Did Governor Endicott speak less positively, we should suspect a mistake here. The Rev. Mr. Blackstone, though an eccentric, is not known to have been an immoral man. We rather doubt his identity with the priest of Merry Mount."

among these misdoers. Methinks their dignity will not be fitted with less than a double share of stripes."

Endicott rested on his sword, and closely surveyed the dress and aspect of the hapless pair. There they stood, pale, downcast, and apprehensive. Yet there was an air of mutual support and of pure affection, seeking aid and giving it, that showed them to be man and wife, with the sanction of a priest upon their love. The youth, in the peril of the moment, had dropped his gilded staff, and thrown his arm about the Lady of the May, who leaned against his breast, too lightly to burden him, but with weight enough to express that their destinies were linked together, for good or evil. They looked first at each other, and then into the grim captain's face. There they stood, in the first hour of wedlock, while the idle pleasures, of which their companions were the emblems, had given place to the sternest cares of life, personified by the dark Puritans. But never had their youthful beauty seemed so pure and high as when its glow was chastened by adversity.

"Youth," said Endicott, "ye stand in an evil case thou and thy maiden wife. Make ready presently, for I am minded that ye shall both have a token to re-member your wedding day!"

"Stern man," cried the May Lord, "how can I move thee? Were the means at   35
hand, I would resist to the death. Being powerless, I entreat! Do with me as thou wilt, but let Edith go untouched!"

"Not so," replied the immitigable zealot. "We are not wont to show an idle courtesy to that sex, which requireth the stricter discipline. What sayest thou, maid? Shall thy silken bridegroom suffer thy share of the penalty, besides his own?"

"Be it death," said Edith, "and lay it all on me!"

Truly, as Endicott had said, the poor lovers stood in a woful case. Their foes were triumphant, their friends captive and abased, their home desolate, the be-nighted wilderness around them, and a rigorous destiny, in the shape of the Puri-tan leader, their only guide. Yet the deepening twilight could not altogether con-ceal that the iron man was softened; he smiled at the fair spectacle of early love; he almost sighed for the inevitable blight of early hopes.

"The troubles of life have come hastily on this young couple," observed En-dicott. "We will see how they comport themselves under their present trials ere we burden them with greater. If, among the spoil, there be any garments of a more decent fashion, let them be put upon this May Lord and his Lady, instead of their glistening vanities. Look to it, some of you."

"And shall not the youth's hair be cut?" asked Peter Palfrey, looking with ab-   40
horrence at the lovelock and long glossy curls of the young man.

"Crop it forthwith, and that in the true pumpkin-shell fashion," answered the captain. "Then bring them along with us, but more gently than their fellows. There be qualities in the youth, which may make him valiant to fight, and sober to toil, and pious to pray; and in the maiden, that may fit her to become a mother in our Israel, bringing up babes in better nurture than her own hath been. Nor think ye, young ones, that they are the happiest, even in our lifetime of a moment, who misspend it in dancing round a Maypole!"

And Endicott, the severest Puritan of all who laid the rock foundation of New England, lifted the wreath of roses from the ruin of the Maypole, and threw it, with his gauntleted hand, over the heads of the Lord and Lady of the May. It was a deed of prophecy. As the moral gloom of the world overpowers all systematic gayety, even was their home of wild mirth made desolate amid the sad forest. They returned to it no more. But as their flowery garland was wreathed of the brightest roses that had grown there, so, in the tie that united them, were intertwined all the purest and best of their early joys. They went heavenward, supporting each other along the difficult path which it was their lot to tread, and never wasted one regretful thought on the vanities of Merry Mount.

Talking about the Text

1. What parts of this story seem most realistic, and which the least?
2. Explain the last three lines of the story.
3. Can you make a good, convincing case for shutting down the maypole? What kinds of community standards and agreements would you need to justify such a drastic measure?

Writing about the Text

1. Explain what you think the narrator's attitude is toward the dancers. How did you reach your conclusion?
2. Looking at all three Hawthorne stories, write about the struggle between the natural and the supernatural, both of which can seem to be good as well as evil.
3. Assume the narrator's voice and write the brief dialogue he would have with the dancers.

Linking the Text to Other Texts

1. Examine Robert Herrick's poem on Julia's clothes (p. 935) for a revealing contemporary comparison of "loose" dress. Then compare the characteristic clothing styles of the Puritans with those of their contemporary adversaries, the English Royalists. Why would Puritans (or any strict religious group) be unhappy about such clothing?
2. Why can't the Puritans allow dances like the one in "The Maypole of Merry Mount"? Examine some sources on Puritanism's attitude toward dancing for your answer.
3. What would be a contemporary equivalent of shutting down the maypole celebration? What rationale would the "authorities" give nowadays?

✑ COMMENTARY

Nathaniel Hawthorne on His Art and His Life

On his stories, from the preface to the 2nd edition of Twice-Told Tales (1851)

Instead of passion there is sentiment; and, even in what purport to be pictures of actual life, we have allegory, not always warmly dressed in its habiliments of flesh and blood as to be taken into the reader's mind without a shiver.

On what his Puritan ancestors might have thought of him, from the introduction to The Scarlet Letter (1850)

No aim, that I have ever cherished, would they recognize as laudable; no success of mine . . . would they deem otherwise than worthless, if not positively disgraceful. "What is he?" murmurs one gray shadow of my forefathers to the other. "A writer of story-books! What kind of business in life,—what mode of glorifying God, or being serviceable to mankind in his day and generation,—may that be? Why, the degenerate fellow might as well have been a fiddler!" Such are the compliments bandied between my great-grandsires and myself, across the gulf of time! And yet, let them scorn me as they will, strong traits of their nature have intertwined themselves with mine.

On comparing the romance to the novel, from the preface to The House of the Seven Gables (1852)

The latter form of composition [i.e., the novel] is presumed to aim at a very minute fidelity, not merely to the possible, but to the probable and ordinary course of man's experience. The former [i.e., romance]—while, as a work of art, it must rigidly subject itself to laws, and while it sins unpardonably so far as it may swerve aside from the truth of the human heart—has fairly a right to present the truth under circumstances, to a great extent, of the writer's own choosing or creation.

On his anger after The Scarlet Letter's Custom House introductory chapter was attacked by newspapers, politicians, and clergymen

From Hawthorne's April 13, 1850 letter to his friend Horatio Bridge:

I feel an infinite contempt for them [his Salem neighbors]—and probably have expressed more of it than I intended—for my preliminary chapter has caused the greatest uproar that ever happened here since witch times. If I escape from town without being tarred and feathered, I shall consider it good-luck. I wish they would tar and feather me; it would be such an entirely novel kind of distinction for a literary man. And, from such judges as my fellow-citizens, I should look upon it as a higher honor than a laurel crown.

On women writers

From Hawthorne's 1855 letter to his publisher William D. Ticknor, in frustration, since women writers like Harriet Beecher Stowe (Uncle Tom's Cabin, 1852) were outselling him:

America is now wholly given over to a d****d mob of scribbling women, and I should have no chance of success while the public taste is occupied with their trash—and should be ashamed of myself if I did succeed. What is the mystery of these innumerable editions of *The Lamplighter* [by Maria Susanna Cummins], and other books neither better nor worse? Worse they could not be, and better they need not be, when they sell by the hundred thousand.

INSPIRATION HAWTHORNE AND MELVILLE: A LITERARY FRIENDSHIP

Herman Melville, c. 1860s.

Thomas Phillibrown engraving of Nathaniel Hawthorne, c. 1851.

Nathaniel Hawthorne and Herman Melville met in the summer of 1850 in the Berkshires of western Massachusetts. A fast friendship developed and flourished as the two men continued to discover similar interests and worldviews through periodic visits and written correspondence. Some mystery surrounds the nature of the cooling of their friendship in 1852; the intimate tone of the surviving letters from Melville to Hawthorne suggests that Melville may have had some romantic attachments to his much older mentor, even though both men were married. But during the time in which they remained close, each was a strong influence on the writing and literary pursuits of the other. It is said to be Hawthorne who pressed Melville to transform what would soon become his masterpiece *Moby-Dick* from an adventure story about whaling into an allegorical novel—and indeed the novel is dedicated to Hawthorne. Melville's admiration for Hawthorne's work is clear, as illustrated by his praise in his two-part review of Hawthorne's *Mosses from an Old Manse*, which appeared in the *Literary World* shortly after they met, excerpted below.

> Certain it is, however, that this great *power of blackness* in him derives its force from its appeals to that Calvinistic sense of *Innate Depravity and Original Sin*, from whose visitations, in some shape or other, no deeply thinking mind is always and wholly free. For, in certain moods, no man can weigh this world, without throwing in something, somehow like Original Sin, to strike the uneven balance. At all events, perhaps no writer has ever wielded this terrific thought with greater terror than this same

(continued on next page)

harmless Hawthorne. Still more: this black conceit pervades him, through and through. You may be witched by his sunlight,—transported by the bright gildings in the skies he builds over you;—but there is the *blackness of darkness* beyond.

Starting Points for Further Research: Nathaniel Hawthorne

- **Edition:** Nathaniel Hawthorne. *Collected Novels.* Ed. Millicent Bell. New York: Library of America, 1983.
- **Biography:** Brenda Wineapple. *Hawthorne: A Life.* New York: Random House, 2003.
- **Critical Essay:** Denis Donoghue. "Hawthorne and Sin." *Christianity and Literature* 52 (2003): 215–32.

CHAPTER
5

A FICTION WRITER IN DEPTH

Willa Cather

Willa Cather, c. 1902.

Willa Cather (1873–1947) is a paradoxical writer, full of puzzles and contradictions. Is she eastern or western? Committed or aloof? Socially aware or artistically indifferent? Gay or straight? A good case can be made for either side of any of these questions, so besides being enjoyable to read, Cather is very interesting to discuss.

Born in Virginia's Shenandoah Valley, Cather moved with her family at age nine to the plains of Nebraska, where she spent her formative years. After college at the University of Nebraska, Cather relocated east, living first in Pittsburgh and finally in New York City. But the years she spent in a small Nebraska prairie town gave Cather the material she drew on for inspiration the rest of her long life. Twenty years after leaving home, from her apartments in New York's Greenwich Village and Park Avenue, Cather would write movingly of the Nebraska plains she remembered well. Her books of the plains, written in Manhattan, made her famous.

Willa Cather lived through two world wars and an era of tumultuous political upheavals and revolutions, yet she rarely mentioned those events in her work. She witnessed at first hand the great movement for women's suffrage yet

Willa Cather Memorial Prairie. Part of the Willa Cather Thematic District in Red Cloud and Webster counties, Nebraska, this is part of over 600 acres of prairie land near Red Cloud and is characteristic of the flat, rural landscape Cather encountered when her family moved to Nebraska in 1883.

hardly spoke out on feminist issues. She shared her life in loving relationships with close female companions yet never came close to writing about lesbian themes. And while living comfortably in New York's Greenwich Village, she treasured the people of the American West who struggled against poverty and hostile conditions. This woman formed by the hardscrabble work of the plains took as her great subject artistic independence of the highest, most exalted kind. And though her short stories helped make her famous and are among her best work, she wanted to be judged by her novels, so she allowed only one short story ("Paul's Case," p. 187) to be reprinted in her lifetime.

Many of Cather's writings are rooted in place, particularly the Nebraska plains where she grew up (the novels *My Ántonia, O Pioneers!*) and the country around Santa Fe, Taos, and the desert Southwest she loved to visit (the novels *The Professor's House, Shadows on the Rock, Death Comes for the Archbishop*). Her themes often involve a struggle, usually over questions of art and the artist's calling. The four stories printed here display themes typical of Cather's work: an interest in the ordinary people of the western plains (especially Nebraska), an exaltation of the artist as almost a divine being, and a strong sympathy for potential artists who are destroyed by circumstances and the small-minded people around them. Not coincidentally, she is preoccupied with beauty, both natural and created, and the way we respond to it.

Cather grew up and sought her subject on the Nebraska plains, but she drew her artistic inspiration from the European classics, and she aimed her writing at the most refined audiences. She studied Latin carefully, taught Latin in school, and tried to model her style on the purity of the Latin masters, all the time writing of New Mexico, Manhattan, and Nebraska.

LITERARY LOCALE

Willa Cather's Red Cloud, Nebraska.

> As we drove further and further out into the country, I felt a good deal as if we had come to the end of everything—it was a kind of erasure of personality.
>
> *—Willa Cather in a 1913 interview, recalling her family's move to Nebraska*

> I had the feeling that the world was left behind, that we had got over the edge of it, and were outside man's jurisdiction. . . . The wagon jolted on, carrying me I knew not whither. I don't think I was homesick. If we never arrived anywhere, it did not matter. Between that earth and that sky I felt erased, blotted out. I did not say my prayers that night: here, I felt, what would be would be.
>
> *—from "The Shimerdas" section of Cather's novel* My Ántonia

> There is something frank and joyous and young in the open face of the country. It gives itself ungrudgingly to the moods of the season, holding nothing back. Like the plains of Lombardy, it seems to rise a little to meet the sun.
>
> *—from the "Neighboring Fields" chapter of Cather's novel* O Pioneers!

Although Cather was born in Virginia, her family moved to Red Cloud when she was a child. In a 1921 interview, Cather recalled that transition as the beginning of her lifelong, complex, and intimate relationship with the Nebraska landscape: "I was little and homesick and lonely. . . . So the country and I had it out together and by the end of the first autumn that shaggy grass country had gripped me with a passion that I have never been able to shake. It has been the happiness and curse of my life." Cather would go on to travel to and live in other, very different places throughout her life, including New York City, Taos, New Mexico, and at the base of Mt. Monadnock in Jaffrey, New Hampshire (where she is buried), but the flat, rural landscape of Nebraska—both the unforgiving quality of the harsh Nebraska plains as well as their beauty and openness—would continue to provide the backdrop for many of her novels as well as countless stories, including "Peter," (p. 185). Likewise, her contradictory feelings

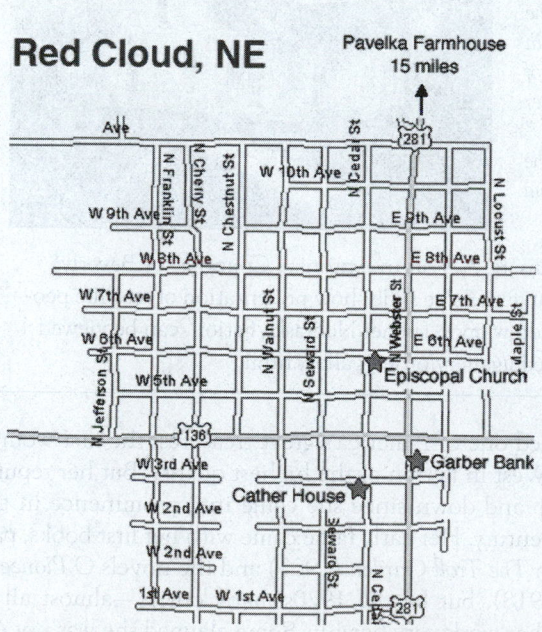

Street map of Red Cloud, Nebraska, and Cather-related historical sites.

(continued)

Willa Cather childhood home, Red Cloud, Nebraska. Cather lived here from 1884 to 1890, and this house is featured in The Song of the Lark, The Best Years, *and* Old Mrs. Harris. *It is now open to the public.*

about the land would show up in her varied accounts of the countryside, both in her fiction and in her interviews, as the range of quotations above suggests.

The Willa Cather Pioneer Memorial and Educational Foundation (WCPM), located in Red Cloud, offers guided tours of significant Cather-related buildings and sites in Red Cloud and the surrounding area, including Cather's childhood home, the 1885 Opera House, Garber Grove (the setting for *A Lost Lady*), the farmstead of her uncle, George Cather (the setting for *One of Ours*), and the Pavelka Farmstead (the setting for *My Ántonia*). Details about the available tours can be found online at http://www.willacather.org/visitorsguide.htm.

The Pavelka Farmstead. *Located northwest of Red Cloud, this farm is famous for being the inspiration for the setting in Book V (*"Cuzak's Boys"*) of* My Ántonia *as well as her short story* "Neighbor Rosicky." *Anna Pavelka also served as the basis for the character Ántonia in the novel.*

"More Dawns than Sunsets: A Visit to Ántonia's Country," by Beverly Cooper and James Goble, an extensive slide show presentation of real-life people and places that Cather drew upon for her Nebraska fiction, can be viewed online at http://cather.unl.edu/gallery/other_gallery.html.

Cather is now considered one of America's great treasures, the first woman to represent the American West in fiction of the highest quality. But her reputation as a writer has gone up and down since she came into prominence in the early part of the twentieth century. Her early fame came with her first books, particularly the story collection *The Troll Garden* (1905) and the novels *O Pioneers!* (1913) and *My Ántonia* (1918), but by the 1920s many critics—almost all of them male—began to treat her work very harshly. Some claimed she was not experimental enough—in the manner of Virginia Woolf or James Joyce, for instance—while others claimed that she was not social minded or politically astute enough, especially during the 1930s, when so many writers and critics embraced Marxism. She was also found wanting in the 1930s because she explicitly resisted many currents of modernism, such as Freudianism and urbanism, and was interested in taking religious faith seriously (most particularly in her novels *Death Comes for the Archbishop* and *Shadows on the Rock*). Some critics were perhaps especially severe because her books sold well and she continued to win prizes and readers, even though she followed no critical or political line. More recently, Cather has been dismissed by a few feminists for appearing to denigrate women in her nonfiction writings, and for failing to portray the women in her novels as strong, intelligent artists in their own right. Except for Thea Kronborg in *The Song of the Lark*, few of Cather's female protagonists succeed as artists, even though Cather was of course an accomplished creative artist herself. And even in *The Song of the Lark*, Thea Kronborg must give up most of the usual pleasures to succeed at her life's work, singing opera.

In many ways, then, Willa Cather was out of step with the major literary and social currents of her time. Though an independent and talented woman who survived and prospered entirely through her writing, she was far from being a militant feminist. She was probably a lesbian, but if so she hid her sexual identity from friends and the public alike. Despising many of the changes that engaged the modern world, she was most at home in the insulated and isolated

Cather, with a boyish haircut, c. mid to late 1880s.

ivory tower of the artist, or on the prairies of pioneer Nebraska. Today many writers eagerly celebrate technology and "the modern world," and tend not to privilege the artist's exalted "calling" as much as Cather did. Thus, Cather can seem a little old-fashioned, wedded as she was to an unattainable goal of artistic purity. She was well aware of this, of course, and often spoke of her difficulties with the modern temper. But Cather knew her strengths as well. She invokes perennial themes: the struggle for the beautiful in life as well as art; what is (or seems) permanent and unchanging in human experience; and most of all, the experience of the artist, who in Cather speaks for all of us.

WILLA CATHER TIMELINE

1873	Willa Sibert Cather born December 7 in Back Creek Valley, Virginia.
1883	Cather family moves to Webster County, Nebraska.
1884	Cather family moves to Red Cloud, Nebraska.

1890	Graduates from Red Cloud High School and enrolls at University of Nebraska.
1892	Publishes her short story "Peter" in a Boston magazine.
1893–1895	Works as drama critic and columnist for Lincoln and University of Nebraska newspapers.
1895	Graduates from University of Nebraska.
1896	Moves to Pittsburgh to edit *Home Monthly* magazine.
1901–1906	Teaches Latin and English in Pittsburgh schools.
1905	Publishes *The Troll Garden* (stories).
1906	Moves to New York to write for *McClure's*, a major magazine.
1908–1911	Editor of *McClure's*.
1912	Visits Southwest.
1913	Publishes *O Pioneers!*, the novel that establishes her literary reputation.
1915	Publishes *The Song of the Lark* (novel).
1918	Publishes *My Ántonia*, her most famous novel.
1923	Wins Pulitzer Prize for *One of Ours*; publishes *A Lost Lady* (novel).
1925	Publishes *The Professor's House* (novel).
1927	Publishes *Death Comes for the Archbishop* (novel).
1931	Publishes *Shadows on the Rock* (novel).
1935	Publishes *Lucy Gayheart* (novel).
1936	Publishes *Not Under Forty* (essays).
1940	Publishes *Sapphira and the Slave Girl* (novel).
1947	Dies and is buried in Jaffrey, New Hampshire.

Cather, c. 1893–1895, working at the Nebraska State Journal *in Lincoln, where she was a columnist and theater reviewer while still a student at the university.*

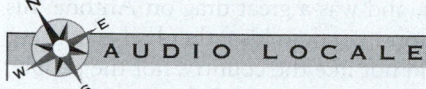

AUDIO LOCALE

Cather's 1933 Radio Speech. Cather won the Pulitzer Prize in 1923 for her novel *One of Ours*. In 1933, she attended the Pulitzer awards ceremony in New York City; past winners had been asked to speak briefly about the category for which they had won, and Cather was there to represent the Novel category. A transcript and an online audio file of her ten-minute speech are available as part of the Willa Cather Archive site at cather.unl.edu/multimedia/index.html. Because it includes reminiscences of Cather, also available is the shorter speech given by General John J. Pershing, a previous Pulitzer winner who was at the ceremony representing the History category and who had been a military instructor at the University of Nebraska during Cather's time there.

STORIES BY WILLA CATHER

Peter
(1892)

"No, Antone, I have told thee many times, no, thou shalt not sell it until I am gone."

"But I need money; what good is that old fiddle to thee? The very crows laugh at thee when thou art trying to play. Thy hand trembles so thou canst scarce hold the bow. Thou shalt go with me to the Blue to cut wood to-morrow. See to it thou art up early."

"What, on the Sabbath, Antone, when it is so cold? I get so very cold, my son, let us not go to-morrow."

"Yes, to-morrow, thou lazy old man. Do not I cut wood upon the Sabbath? Care I how cold it is? Wood thou shalt cut, and haul it too, and as for the fiddle, I tell thee I will sell it yet." Antone pulled his ragged cap down over his low heavy brow, and went out. The old man drew his stool up nearer the fire, and sat stroking his violin with trembling fingers and muttering, "Not while I live, not while I live."

Five years ago they had come here, Peter Sadelack, and his wife, and oldest son Antone, and countless smaller Sadelacks, here to the dreariest part of southwestern Nebraska, and had taken up a homestead. Antone was the acknowledged master of the premises, and people said he was a likely youth, and would do well. That he was mean and untrustworthy every one knew, but that made little difference. His corn was better tended than any in the county, and his wheat always yielded more than other men's.

Of Peter no one knew much, nor had any one a good word to say for him. He drank whenever he could get out of Antone's sight long enough to pawn his hat or coat for whiskey. Indeed there were but two things he would not pawn, his pipe and his violin. He was a lazy, absent minded old fellow, who liked to fiddle better than to plow, though Antone surely got work enough out of them all, for that matter. In the house of which Antone was master there was no one, from the little boy three years old, to the old man of sixty, who did not earn his bread.

Still people said that Peter was worthless, and was a great drag on Antone, his son, who never drank, and was a much better man than his father had ever been. Peter did not care what people said. He did not like the country, nor the people, least of all he liked the plowing. He was very homesick for Bohemia. Long ago, only eight years ago by the calendar, but it seemed eight centuries to Peter, he had been a second violinist in the great theatre at Prague. He had gone into the theatre very young, and had been there all his life, until he had a stroke of paralysis, which made his arm so weak that his bowing was uncertain. Then they told him he could go. Those were great days at the theatre. He had plenty to drink then, and wore a dress coat every evening, and there were always parties after the play. He could play in those days, ay, that he could! He could never read the notes well, so he did not play first; but his touch, he had a touch indeed, so Herr Mikilsdoff, who led the orchestra, had said. Sometimes now Peter thought he could plow better if he could only bow as he used to. He had seen all the lovely women in the world there, all the great singers and the great players. He was in the orchestra when Rachel played, and he heard Liszt play when the Countess d'Agoult sat in the stage box and threw the master white lilies. Once, a French woman came and played for weeks, he did not remember her name now. He did not remember her face very well either, for it changed so, it was never twice the same. But the beauty of it, and the great hunger men felt at the sight of it, that he remembered. Most of all he remembered her voice. He did not know French, and could not understand a word she said, but it seemed to him that she must be talking the music of Chopin. And her voice, he thought he should know that in the other world. The last night she played a play in which a man touched her arm, and she stabbed him. As Peter sat among the smoking gas jets down below the footlights with his fiddle on his knee, and looked up at her, he thought he would like to die too, if he could touch her arm once, and have her stab him so. Peter went home to his wife very drunk that night. Even in those days he was a foolish fellow, who cared for nothing but music and pretty faces.

It was all different now. He had nothing to drink and little to eat, and here, there was nothing but sun, and grass, and sky. He had forgotten almost everything, but some things he remembered well enough. He loved his violin and the holy Mary, and above all else he feared the Evil One, and his son Antone.

The fire was low, and it grew cold. Still Peter sat by the fire remembering. He dared not throw more cobs on the fire; Antone would be angry. He did not want to cut wood tomorrow, it would be Sunday, and he wanted to go to mass. Antone might let him do that. He held his violin under his wrinkled chin, his white hair fell over it, and he began to play "Ave Maria." His hand shook more than ever before, and at last refused to work the bow at all. He sat stupefied for a while, then arose, and taking his violin with him, stole out into the old sod stable. He took Antone's shot-gun down from its peg, and loaded it by the moonlight which streamed in through the door. He sat down on the dirt floor, and leaned back against the dirt wall. He heard the wolves howling in the distance, and the night wind screaming as it swept over the snow. Near him he heard the regular breathing of the horses in the dark. He put his crucifix above his heart, and folding his hands said brokenly all the Latin he had ever known, "*Pater noster, qui in cælum est.*" Then he raised his head and sighed, "Not one kreutzer will Antone pay them to pray for my soul, not one kreutzer, he is so careful of his money, is Antone, he does not waste it in drink, he is a better man than I, but hard sometimes. He works the girls too hard, women were not made to work so. But he shall not sell thee, my fiddle, I can play thee no more, but they shall not part us. We have seen it all together, and we will forget it together, the French woman and all." He held his fiddle under his chin a moment, where it had lain so often, then put it across his knee and broke it through the middle. He pulled off his old boot, held the gun between his knees with the muzzle against his forehead, and pressed the trigger with his toe.

In the morning Antone found him stiff, frozen fast in a pool of blood. They could not straighten him out enough to fit a coffin, so they buried him in a pine box. Before the funeral Antone carried to town the fiddle-bow which Peter had forgotten to break. Antone was very thrifty, and a better man than his father had been.

Talking about the Text

1. The narrator in "Peter" seems to side with Antone, Peter's successful son. Note the places in the story where the criticism of Peter is particularly strong. Yet in the end we feel sympathy and admiration for Peter. Why?
2. Using "Peter" as evidence, what can you say about the struggles between artists and "practical" people on the frontier?

Writing about the Text

1. In brief paragraphs, list three or four common "truths" or stereotypes about American culture that the narrator seems to rely on in "Peter."
2. In an essay using "Peter" and other Cather stories, explain which characters seem to be presented as the truest artists or appreciators of art. What are the marks of the genuine artists? What are their strengths and weaknesses? What do they gain and lose? What particular obstacles do they face?

Linking the Text to Other Texts

1. Compare Cather's portrayal of the rural midwestern landscape of Nebraska to Charles Baxter's more contemporary depiction of the Midwest and midwestern life, particularly his portrayal of small-town Michigan in "Saul and Patsy Are Pregnant" (p. 263).
2. Compare Cather's "portrait of the artist" Peter with any artist you might know of (either in person or by repute or through reading or film or television).

Paul's Case (1905)

It was Paul's afternoon to appear before the faculty of the Pittsburgh High School to account for his various misdemeanours. He had been suspended a week ago, and his father had called at the Principal's office and confessed his perplexity about his son. Paul entered the faculty room suave and smiling. His clothes were a trifle out-grown, and the tan velvet on the collar of his open overcoat was frayed and worn; but for all that there was something of the dandy about him, and he wore an opal pin in his nearly knotted black four-in-hand, and a red carnation in his button-hole. This latter adornment the faculty somehow felt was not properly significant of the contrite spirit befitting a boy under the ban of suspension.

Paul was tall for his age and very thin, with high, cramped shoulders and a narrow chest. His eyes were remarkable for a certain hysterical brilliancy, and he continually used them in a conscious, theatrical sort of way, peculiarly offensive in a boy. The pupils were abnormally large, as though he were addicted to belladonna, but there was a glassy glitter about them which that drug does not produce.

When questioned by the Principal as to why he was there, Paul stated, politely enough, that he wanted to come back to school. This was a lie, but Paul was quite accustomed to lying; found it, indeed, indispensable for overcoming friction. His teachers were asked to state their respective charges against him, which they did with such a rancour and aggrievedness as evinced that this was not a usual case. Disorder and impertinence were among the offences named, yet each of his instructors felt that it was scarcely possible to put into words the real cause of the trouble, which lay in a sort of hysterically defiant manner of the boy's; in the contempt which they all knew he felt for them, and which he seemingly made not the least effort to conceal. Once, when he had been making a synopsis of a paragraph at the blackboard, his English teacher had stepped to his side and attempted to guide his hand. Paul had started back with a shudder and thrust his hands violently behind him. The astonished woman could scarcely have been more hurt and embarrassed had he struck at her. The insult was so involuntary and definitely personal as to be unforgettable. In one way and another, he had made all his teachers, men and women alike, conscious of the same feeling of physical aversion. In one class he habitually sat with his hand shading his eyes; in another he always looked out of the window during the recitation; in another he made a running commentary on the lecture, with humorous intent.

His teachers felt this afternoon that his whole attitude was symbolized by his shrug and his flippantly red carnation flower, and they fell upon him without mercy, his English teacher leading the pack. He stood through it smiling, his pale lips parted over his white teeth. (His lips were continually twitching, and he had a habit of raising his eyebrows that was contemptuous and irritating to the last degree.) Older boys than Paul had broken down and shed tears under that ordeal, but his set smile did not once desert him, and his only sign of discomfort was the nervous trembling of the fingers that toyed with the buttons of his overcoat, and an occasional jerking of the other hand which held his hat. Paul was always smiling, always glancing about him, seeming to feel that people might be watching him and trying to detect something. This conscious expression, since it was as far as possible from boyish mirthfulness, was usually attributed to insolence or "smartness."

As the inquisition proceeded, one of his instructors repeated an impertinent remark of the boy's, and the Principal asked him whether he thought that a courteous speech to make to a woman. Paul shrugged his shoulders slightly and his eyebrows twitched. 5

"I don't know," he replied. "I didn't mean to be polite or impolite, either. I guess it's a sort of way I have, of saying things regardless."

The Principal asked him whether he didn't think that a way it would be well to get rid of. Paul grinned and said he guessed so. When he was told that he could go, he bowed gracefully and went out. His bow was like a repetition of the scandalous red carnation.

His teachers were in despair, and his drawing master voiced the feeling of them all when he declared there was something about the boy which none of them understood. He added: "I don't really believe that smile of his comes altogether from insolence; there's something sort of haunted about it. The boy is not strong, for one thing. There is something wrong about the fellow."

The drawing master had come to realize that, in looking at Paul, one saw only his white teeth and the forced animation of his eyes. One warm afternoon the boy had gone to sleep at his drawing-board, and his master had noted with amazement what a white, blue-veined face it was; drawn and wrinkled like an old man's about the eyes, the lips twitching even in his sleep.

His teachers left the building dissatisfied and unhappy; humiliated to have   10
felt so vindictive toward a mere boy, to have uttered this feeling in cutting terms, and to have set each other on, as it were, in the grewsome game of intemperate reproach. One of them remembered having seen a miserable street cat set at bay by a ring of tormentors.

As for Paul, he ran down the hill whistling the Soldiers' Chorus from *Faust*, looking wildly behind him now and then to see whether some of his teachers were not there to witness his light-heartedness. As it was now late in the afternoon and Paul was on duty that evening as usher at Carnegie Hall, he decided that he would not go home to supper.

When he reached the concert hall the doors were not yet open. It was chilly outside, and he decided to go up into the picture gallery—always deserted at this hour—where there were some of Raffelli's gay studies of Paris streets and an airy blue Venetian scene or two that always exhilarated him. He was delighted to find no one in the gallery but the old guard, who sat in the corner, a newspaper on his knee, a black patch over one eye and the other closed. Paul possessed himself of the place and walked confidently up and down, whistling under his breath. After a while he sat down before a blue Rico and lost himself. When he bethought him to look at his watch, it was after seven o'clock, and he rose with a start and ran downstairs, making a face at Augustus Cæsar, peering out from the cast-room, and an evil gesture at the Venus of Milo as he passed her on the stairway.

When Paul reached the ushers' dressing-room half-a-dozen boys were there already, and he began excitedly to tumble into his uniform. It was one of the few that at all approached fitting, and Paul thought it very becoming—though he knew the tight, straight coat accentuated his narrow chest, about which he was exceedingly sensitive. He was always excited while he dressed, twanging all over to the tuning of the strings and the preliminary flourishes of the horns in the music-room; but tonight he seemed quite beside himself, and he teased and plagued the boys until, telling him that he was crazy, they put him down on the floor and sat on him.

Somewhat calmed by his suppression, Paul dashed out to the front of the house to seat the early comers. He was a model usher. Gracious and smiling he ran up and down the aisles. Nothing was too much trouble for him; he carried messages and brought programs as though it were his greatest pleasure in life, and all the people in his section thought him a charming boy, feeling that he remembered and admired them. As the house filled, he grew more and more vivacious and animated, and the colour came to his cheeks and lips. It was very much as though this were a great reception and Paul were the host. Just as the musicians came out to take their places, his English teacher arrived with checks for the seats which a prominent manufacturer had taken for the season. She betrayed some embarrassment when she handed Paul the tickets, and a *hauteur* which subsequently made her feel very foolish. Paul was startled for a moment, and had the feeling of wanting to put her out; what business had she here among all these fine people and gay colours? He looked her over and decided that she was not appropriately dressed and must be a fool to sit downstairs in such togs. The tickets had probably been sent her out of kindness, he reflected, as he put down a seat for her, and she had about as much right to sit there as he had.

When the symphony began Paul sank into one of the rear seats with a long   15
sigh of relief, and lost himself as he had done before the Rico. It was not that symphonies, as such, meant anything in particular to Paul, but the first sigh of the instruments seemed to free some hilarious spirit within him; something that struggled there like the Genius in the bottle found by the Arab fisherman. He felt a sudden zest of life; the lights danced before his eyes and the concert hall blazed into unimaginable splendour. When the soprano soloist came on, Paul forgot even the nastiness of his teacher's being there, and gave himself up to the peculiar intoxication such personages always had for him. The soloist chanced to be a German woman, by no means in her first youth, and the mother of many children; but she wore a satin gown and a tiara, and she had that indefinable air of achievement, that world shine upon her, which always blinded Paul to any possible defects.

After a concert was over, Paul was often irritable and wretched until he got to sleep,—and tonight he was even more than usually restless. He had the feeling of not being able to let down; of its being impossible to give up this delicious excitement which was the only thing that could be called living at all. During the last number he withdrew and, after hastily changing his clothes in the dressing-room, slipped out to the side door where the singer's carriage stood. Here he began pacing rapidly up and down the walk, waiting to see her come out.

Over yonder the Schenley, in its vacant stretch, loomed big and square through the fine rain, the windows of its twelve stories glowing like those of a lighted card-board house under a Christmas tree. All the actors and singers of any importance stayed there when they were in the city, and a number of the big manufacturers of the place lived there in the winter. Paul had often hung about the hotel, watching the people go in and out, longing to enter and leave schoolmasters and dull care behind him for ever.

At last the singer came out, accompanied by the conductor, who helped her into her carriage and closed the door with a cordial *auf wiedersehen*,—which set Paul to wondering whether she were not an old sweetheart of his. Paul followed the carriage over to the hotel, walking so rapidly as not to be far from the entrance when the singer alighted and disappeared behind the swinging glass doors which were opened by a negro in a tall hat and a long coat. In the moment that the door was ajar, it seemed to Paul that he, too, entered. He seemed to feel himself go after her up the steps, into the warm, lighted building, into an exotic, a tropical world of shiny, glistening surfaces and basking ease. He reflected upon the mysterious dishes that were brought into the dining-room, the green bottles in buckets of ice, as he had seen them in the supper party pictures of the Sunday supplement. A quick gust of wind brought the rain down with sudden vehemence, and Paul was startled to find that he was still outside in the slush of the gravel driveway; that his boots were letting in the water and his scanty overcoat was clinging wet about him; that the lights in front of the concert hall were out, and that the rain was driving in sheets between him and the orange glow of the windows above him. There it was, what he wanted—tangibly before him, like the fairy world of a Christmas pantomime; as the rain beat in his face, Paul wondered whether he were destined always to shiver in the black night outside, looking up at it.

He turned and walked reluctantly toward the car tracks. The end had to come sometime; his father in his night-clothes at the top of the stairs, explanations that did not explain, hastily improvised fictions that were forever tripping him up, his upstairs room and its horrible yellow wall-paper, the creaking bureau with the greasy plush collar-box, and over his painted wooden bed the pictures of George Washington and John Calvin, and the framed motto, "Feed my Lambs," which had been worked in red worsted by his mother, whom Paul could not remember.

Half an hour later, Paul alighted from the Negley Avenue car and went   20
slowly down one of the side streets off the main thoroughfare. It was a highly repectable street, where all the houses were exactly alike, and where business men of moderate means begot and reared large families of children, all of whom went to Sabbath-school and learned the shorter catechism, and were interested in arithmetic; all of whom were as exactly alike as their homes, and of a piece with the monotony in which they lived. Paul never went up Cordelia Street without a shudder of loathing. His home was next the house of the Cumberland minister. He approached it tonight with the nerveless sense of defeat, the hopeless feeling of sinking back forever into ugliness and commonness that he had always had when he came home. The moment he turned into Cordelia Street he felt the waters close above his head. After each of these orgies of living, he experienced all the physical depression which follows a debauch; the loathing of respectable beds, of common food, of a house permeated by kitchen odours; a shuddering repulsion for the flavourless, colourless mass of every-day existence; a morbid desire for cool things and soft lights and fresh flowers.

The nearer he approached the house, the more absolutely unequal Paul felt to the sight of it all; his ugly sleeping chamber; the cold bath-room with the grimy zinc tub, the cracked mirror, the dripping spiggots; his father, at the top of the stairs, his hairy legs sticking out from his nightshirt, his feet thrust into carpet slippers. He was so much later than usual that there would certainly be inquiries and reproaches. Paul stopped short before the door. He felt that he could not be accosted by his father tonight; that he could not toss again on that miserable bed. He would not go in. He would tell his father that he had no car fare, and it was raining so hard he had gone home with one of the boys and stayed all night.

Meanwhile, he was wet and cold. He went around to the back of the house and tried one of the basement windows, found it open, raised it cautiously, and scrambled down the cellar wall to the floor. There he stood, holding his breath, terrified by the noise he had made; but the floor above him was silent, and there was no creak on the stairs. He found a soap-box, and carried it over to the soft ring of light that streamed from the furnace door, and sat down. He was horribly afraid of rats, so he did not try to sleep, but sat looking distrustfully at the dark, still terrified lest he might have awakened his father. In such reactions, after one of the experiences which made days and nights out of the dreary blanks of the calendar, when his senses were deadened, Paul's head was always singularly clear.

Suppose his father had heard him getting in at the window and had come down and shot him for a burglar? Then, again, suppose his father had come down, pistol in hand, and he had cried out in time to save himself, and his father had been horrified to think how nearly he had killed him? Then, again, suppose a day should come when his father would remember that night, and wish there had been no warning cry to stay his hand? With this last supposition Paul entertained himself until daybreak.

The following Sunday was fine; the sodden November chill was broken by the last flash of autumnal summer. In the morning Paul had to go to church and Sabbath-school, as always. On seasonable Sunday afternoons the burghers of Cordelia Street usually sat out on their front "stoops," and walked to their neighbours on the next stoop, or called to those across the street in neighbourly fashion. The men sat placidly on gay cushions placed upon the steps that led down to the sidewalk, while the women, in their Sunday "waists," sat in rockers on the cramped porches, pretending to be greatly at their ease. The children played in the streets; there were so many of them that the place resembled the recreation grounds of a kindergarten. The men on the steps—all in their shirt sleeves, their vests unbuttoned—sat with their legs well apart, their stomachs comfortably protruding, and talked of the prices of things, or told anecdotes of the sagacity of their various chiefs and overlords. They occasionally looked over the multitude of squabbling children, listened affectionately to their high-pitched, nasal voices, smiling to see their own proclivities reproduced in their offspring, and interspersed their legends of the iron kings with remarks about their sons' progress at school, their grades in arithmetic, and the amounts they had saved in their toy banks.

On this last Sunday of November, Paul sat all the afternoon on the lowest step of his "stoop," staring into the street, while his sisters, in their rockers, were talking to the minister's daughters next door about how many shirt-waists they had made in the last week, and how many waffles some one had eaten at the last church supper. When the weather was warm, and his father was in a particularly jovial frame of mind, the girls made lemonade, which was always brought out in a red-glass pitcher, ornamented with forget-me-nots in blue enamel. This the girls thought very fine, and the neighbours joked about the suspicious colour of the pitcher.

Today Paul's father, on the top step, was talking to a young man who shifted 25
a restless baby from knee to knee. He happened to be the young man who was daily held up to Paul as a model, and after whom it was his father's dearest hope that he would pattern. This young man was of a ruddy complexion, with a compressed, red mouth, and faded, near-sighted eyes, over which he wore thick spectacles, with gold bows that curved about his ears. He was clerk to one of the magnates of a great steel corporation, and was looked upon in Cordelia Street as a young man with a future. There was a story that, some five years ago—he was now barely twenty-six—he had been a trifle "dissipated," but in order to curb his appetites and save the loss of time and strength that a sowing of wild oats might have entailed, he had taken his chief's advice, oft reiterated to his employés, and at twenty-one had married the first woman whom he could persuade to share his fortunes. She happened to be an angular school-mistress, much older than he, who also wore thick glasses, and who had now borne him four children, all nearsighted, like herself.

The young man was relating how his chief, now cruising in the Mediterranean, kept in touch with all the details of the business, arranging his office hours on his yacht just as though he were at home, and "knocking off work enough to keep two stenographers busy." His father told, in turn, the plan his corporation was considering, of putting in an electric railway plant at Cairo. Paul snapped his teeth; he had an awful apprehension that they might spoil it all before he got there. Yet he rather liked to hear these legends of the iron kings, that were told and retold on Sundays and holidays; these stories of palaces in Venice, yachts on the Mediterranean, and high play at Monte Carlo appealed to his fancy, and he was interested in the triumphs of cash boys who had become famous, though he had no mind for the cash-boy stage.

After supper was over, and he had helped to dry the dishes, Paul nervously asked his father whether he could go to George's to get some help in his geometry, and still more nervously asked for car fare. This latter request he had to repeat, as his father, on principle, did not like to hear requests for money, whether much or little. He asked Paul whether he could not go to some boy who lived nearer, and told him that he ought not to leave his school work until Sunday; but he gave him the dime. He was not a poor man, but he had a worthy ambition to come up in the world. His only reason for allowing Paul to usher was that he thought a boy ought to be earning a little.

Paul bounded upstairs, scrubbed the greasy odour of the dish-water from his hands with the ill-smelling soap he hated, and then shook over his fingers a few drops of violet water from the bottle he kept hidden in his drawer. He left the house with his geometry conspicuously under his arm, and the moment he got out of Cordelia Street and boarded a downtown car, he shook off the lethargy of two deadening days, and began to live again.

The leading juvenile of the permanent stock company which played at one of the downtown theatres was an acquaintance of Paul's, and the boy had been invited to drop in at the Sunday-night rehearsals whenever he could. For more than a year Paul had spent every available moment loitering about Charley Edwards's dressing-room. He had won a place among Edwards's following not only because the young actor, who could not afford to employ a dresser, often found him useful, but because he recognized in Paul something akin to what churchmen term "vocation."

It was at the theatre and at Carnegie Hall that Paul really lived; the rest was 30 but a sleep and a forgetting. This was Paul's fairy tale, and it had for him all the allurement of a secret love. The moment he inhaled the gassy, painty, dusty odour behind the scenes, he breathed like a prisoner set free, and felt within him the possibility of doing or saying splendid, brilliant things. The moment the cracked orchestra beat out the overture from *Martha*, or jerked at the serenade from *Rigoletto*, all stupid and ugly things slid from him, and his senses were deliciously, yet delicately fired.

Perhaps it was because, in Paul's world, the natural nearly always wore the guise of ugliness, that a certain element of aritificiality seemed to him necessary in beauty. Perhaps it was because his experience of life elsewhere was so full of Sabbath-school picnics, petty economies, wholesome advice as to how to succeed in life, and the unescapable odours of cooking, that he found this existence so alluring, these smartly-clad men and women so attractive, that he was so moved by these starry apple orchards that bloomed perennially under the lime-light.

It would be difficult to put it strongly enough how convincingly the stage entrance of that theatre was for Paul the actual portal of Romance. Certainly none of the company ever suspected it, least of all Charley Edwards. It was very like the old stories that used to float about London of fabulously rich Jews, who had subterranean halls, with palms, and fountains, and soft lamps and richly apparelled women who never saw the disenchanting light of London day. So, in the midst of that smoke-palled city, enamoured of figures and grimy toil, Paul had his secret temple, his wishing-carpet, his bit of blue-and-white Mediterranean shore bathed in perpetual sunshine.

Several of Paul's teachers had a theory that his imagination had been perverted by garish fiction; but the truth was, he scarcely ever read at all. The books at home were not such as would either tempt or corrupt a youthful mind, and as for reading the novels that some of his friends urged upon him—well, he got what he wanted much more quickly from music; any sort of music, from an orchestra to a barrel organ. He needed only the spark, the indescribable thrill that made his imagination master of his senses, and he could make plots and pictures enough of his own. It was equally true that he was not stage-struck—not, at any rate, in the usual acceptation of that expression. He had no desire to become an actor, any more than he had to become a musician. He felt no necessity to do any of these things; what he wanted was to see, to be in the atmosphere, float on the wave of it, to be carried out, blue league after blue league, away from everything.

After a night behind the scenes, Paul found the school-room more than ever repulsive, the bare floors and naked walls; the prosy men who never wore frock coats, or violets in their buttonholes; the women with their dull gowns, shrill voices, and pitiful seriousness about prepositions that govern the dative. He could not bear to have the other pupils think, for a moment, that he took these people seriously; he must convey to them that he considered it all trivial, and was there only by way of a joke, anyway. He had autograph pictures of all the members of the stock company which he showed his classmates, telling them the most incredible stories of his familiarity with these people, of his acquaintance with the soloists who came to Carnegie Hall, his suppers with them and the flowers he sent them. When these stories lost their effect, and his audience grew listless, he would bid all the boys good-bye, announcing that he was going to travel for awhile; going to Naples, to California, to Egypt. Then, next Monday, he would slip back, conscious and nervously smiling; his sister was ill, and he would have to defer his voyage until spring.

Matters went steadily worse with Paul at school. In the itch to let his instructors know how heartily he despised them, and how thoroughly he was appreciated elsewhere, he mentioned once or twice that he had no time to fool with theorems; adding—with a twitch of the eyebrows and a touch of that nervous bravado which so perplexed them—that he was helping the people down at the stock company; they were old friends of his.

The upshot of the matter was, that the Principal went to Paul's father, and Paul was taken out of school and put to work. The manager at Carnegie Hall was told to get another usher in his stead; the doorkeeper at the theatre was warned not to admit him to the house; and Charley Edwards remorsefully promised the boy's father not to see him again.

The members of the stock company were vastly amused when some of Paul's stories reached them—especially the women. They were hard-working women, most of them supporting indolent husbands or brothers, and they laughed rather bitterly at having stirred the boy to such fervid and florid inventions. They agreed with the faculty and with his father, that Paul's was a bad case.

* * *

The east-bound train was ploughing through a January snow-storm; the dull dawn was beginning to show grey when the engine whistled a mile out of Newark. Paul started up from the seat where he had lain curled in uneasy slumber, rubbed the breath-misted window glass with his hand, and peered out. The snow was whirling in curling eddies above the white bottom lands, and the drifts lay already deep in the fields and along the fences, while here and there the long dead grass and dried weed stalks protruded black above it. Lights shone from the scattered houses, and a gang of labourers who stood beside the track waved their lanterns.

Paul had slept very little, and he felt grimy and uncomfortable. He had made the all-night journey in a day coach because he was afraid if he took a Pullman he might be seen by some Pittsburgh business man who had noticed him in Denny & Carson's office. When the whistle woke him, he clutched quickly at his breast pocket, glancing about him with an uncertain smile. But the little, clay-bespattered Italians were still sleeping, the slatternly women across the aisle were in open mouthed oblivion, and even the crumby, crying babies were for the nonce stilled. Paul settled back to struggle with his impatience as best he could.

When he arrived at the Jersey City station, he hurried through his breakfast, manifestly ill at ease and keeping a sharp eye about him. After he reached the Twenty-third Street station, he consulted a cabman, and had himself driven to a men's furnishing establishment which was just opening for the day. He spent upward of two hours there, buying with endless reconsidering and great care. His new street suit he put on in the fitting-room; the frock coat and dress clothes he had bundled into the cab with his new shirts. Then he drove to a hatter's and a shoe house. His next errand was at Tiffany's, where he selected silver mounted brushes and a scarf-pin. He would not wait to have his silver marked, he said. Lastly, he stopped at a trunk shop on Broadway, and had his purchases packed into various travelling bags.

It was a little after one o'clock when he drove up to the Waldorf, and, after settling with the cabman, went into the office. He registered from Washington; said his mother and father had been abroad, and that he had come down to await the arrival of their steamer. He told his story plausibly and had no trouble, since he offered to pay for them in advance, in engaging his rooms; a sleeping room, sitting-room and bath.

Not once, but a hundred times Paul had planned this entry into New York. He had gone over every detail of it with Charley Edwards, and in his scrap book at home there were pages of description about New York hotels, cut from the Sunday papers.

When he was shown to his sitting-room on the eighth floor, he saw at a glance that everything was as it should be; there was but one detail in his mental picture that the place did not realize, so he rang for the bell boy and sent him

40

down for flowers. He moved about nervously until the boy returned, putting away his new linen and fingering it delightedly as he did so. When the flowers came, he put them hastily into water, and then tumbled into a hot bath. Presently he came out of his white bath-room, resplendent in his new silk underwear, and playing with the tassels of his red robe. The snow was whirling so fiercely outside his windows that he could scarcely see across the street; but within, the air was deliciously soft and fragrant. He put the violets and jonquils on the tabouret beside the couch, and threw himself down with a long sigh, covering himself with a Roman blanket. He was thoroughly tired; he had been in such haste, he had stood up to such a strain, covered so much ground in the last twenty-four hours, that he wanted to think how it had all come about. Lulled by the sound of the wind, the warm air, and the cool fragrance of the flowers, he sank into deep, drowsy retrospection.

It had been wonderfully simple; when they had shut him out of the theatre and concert hall, when they had taken away his bone, the whole thing was virtually determined. The rest was a mere matter of opportunity. The only thing that at all surprised him was his own courage—for he realized well enough that he had always been tormented by fear, a sort of apprehensive dread that, of late years, as the meshes of the lies he had told closed about him, had been pulling the muscles of his body tighter and tighter. Until now, he could not remember a time when he had not been dreading something. Even when he was a little boy, it was always there—behind him, or before, or on either side. There had always been the shadowed corner, the dark place into which he dared not look, but from which something seemed always to be watching him—and Paul had done things that were not pretty to watch, he knew.

But now he had a curious sense of relief, as though he had at last thrown down the gauntlet to the thing in the corner.   45

Yet it was but a day since he had been sulking in the traces; but yesterday afternoon that he had been sent to the bank with Denny & Carson's deposit, as usual—but this time he was instructed to leave the book to be balanced. There was above two thousand dollars in checks, and nearly a thousand in the bank notes which he had taken from the book and quietly transferred to his pocket. At the bank he had made out a new deposit slip. His nerves had been steady enough to permit of his returning to the office, where he had finished his work and asked for a full day's holiday tomorrow, Saturday, giving a perfectly reasonable pretext. The bank book, he knew, would not be returned before Monday or Tuesday, and his father would be out of town for the next week. From the time he slipped the bank notes into his pocket until he boarded the night train for New York, he had not known a moment's hesitation.

How astonishingly easy it had all been; here he was, the thing done; and this time there would be no awakening, no figure at the top of the stairs. He watched the snow flakes whirling by his window until he fell asleep.

When he awoke, it was four o'clock in the afternoon. He bounded up with a start; one of his precious days gone already! He spent nearly an hour in dressing, watching every stage of his toilet carefully in the mirror. Everything was quite perfect; he was exactly the kind of boy he had always wanted to be.

When he went downstairs, Paul took a carriage and drove up Fifth avenue toward the Park. The snow had somewhat abated; carriages and tradesmen's wagons were hurrying soundlessly to and fro in the winter twilight; boys in woollen mufflers were shovelling off the doorsteps; the avenue stages made fine spots of colour against the white street. Here and there on the corners whole flower gardens blooming behind glass windows, against which the snow flakes stuck and melted; violets, roses, carnations, lilies of the valley—somehow vastly more lovely and alluring that they blossomed thus unnaturally in the snow. The Park itself was a wonderful stage winter-piece.

When he returned, the pause of the twilight had ceased, and the tune of the streets had changed. The snow was falling faster, lights streamed from the hotels that reared their many stories fearlessly up into the storm, defying the raging Atlantic winds. A long, black stream of carriages poured down the avenue, intersected here and there by other streams, tending horizontally. There were a score of cabs about the entrance of his hotel, and his driver had to wait. Boys in livery were running in and out of the awning stretched across the sidewalk, up and down the red velvet carpet laid from the door to the street. Above, about, within it all, was the rumble and roar, the hurry and toss of thousands of human beings as hot for pleasure as himself, and on every side of him towered the glaring affirmation of the omnipotence of wealth.

The boy set his teeth and drew his shoulders together in a spasm of realization; the plot of all dramas, the text of all romances, the nerve-stuff of all sensations was whirling about him like the snow flakes. He burnt like a faggot in a tempest.

When Paul came down to dinner, the music of the orchestra floated up the elevator shaft to greet him. As he stepped into the thronged corridor, he sank back into one of the chairs against the wall to get his breath. The lights, the chatter, the perfumes, the bewildering medley of colour—he had, for a moment, the feeling of not being able to stand it. But only for a moment; these were his own people, he told himself. He went slowly about the corridors, through the writing-rooms, smoking-rooms, reception-rooms, as though he were exploring the chambers of an enchanted palace, built and peopled for him alone.

When he reached the dining-room he sat down at a table near a window. The flowers, the white linen, the many-coloured wine glasses, the gay toilettes of the women, the low popping of corks, the undulating repetitions of the *Blue Danube* from the orchestra, all flooded Paul's dream with bewildering radiance. When the roseate tinge of his champagne was added—that cold, precious, bubbling stuff that creamed and foamed in his glass—Paul wondered that there were honest men in the world at all. This was what all the world was fighting for, he reflected; this was what all the struggle was about. He doubted the reality of his past. Had he ever known a place called Cordelia Street, a place where fagged looking business men boarded the early car? Mere rivets in a machine they seemed to Paul,—sickening men, with combings of children's hair always hanging to their coats, and the smell of cooking in their clothes. Cordelia Street—Ah, that belonged to another time and country! Had he not always been thus, had he not sat here night after night, from as far back as he could remember, looking pensively over just such shimmering textures, and slowly twirling the stem of a glass like this one between his thumb and middle finger? He rather thought he had.

He was not in the least abashed or lonely. He had no especial desire to meet or to know any of these people; all he demanded was the right to look on and conjecture, to watch the pageant. The mere stage properties were all he contended for. Nor was he lonely later in the evening, in his loge at the Opera. He was entirely rid of his nervous misgivings, of his forced aggressiveness, of the imperative desire to show himself different from his surroundings. He felt now that his surroundings explained him. Nobody questioned the purple; he had only to wear it passively. He had only to glance down at his dress coat to reassure himself that here it would be impossible for anyone to humiliate him.

He found it hard to leave his beautiful sitting-room to go to bed that night,   55 and sat long watching the raging storm from his turret window. When he went to sleep, it was with the lights turned on in his bedroom; partly because of his old timidity, and partly so that, if he should wake in the night, there would be no wretched moment of doubt, no horrible suspicion of yellow wall-paper, or of Washington and Calvin above his bed.

On Sunday morning the city was practically snow-bound. Paul breakfasted late, and in the afternoon he fell in with a wild San Francisco boy, a freshman at Yale, who said he had run down for a "little flyer" over Sunday. The young man offered to show Paul the night side of the town, and the two boys went off together after dinner, not returning to the hotel until seven o'clock the next morning. They had started out in the confiding warmth of a champagne friendship, but their parting in the elevator was singularly cool. The freshman pulled himself together to make his train, and Paul went to bed. He awoke at two o'clock in the afternoon, very thirsty and dizzy, and rang for ice-water, coffee, and the Pittsburgh papers.

On the part of the hotel management, Paul excited no suspicion. There was this to be said for him, that he wore his spoils with dignity and in no way made himself conspicuous. His chief greediness lay in his ears and eyes, and his excesses were not offensive ones. His dearest pleasures were the grey winter twilights in his sitting-room; his quiet enjoyment of his flowers, his clothes, his wide divan, his cigarette and his sense of power. He could not remember a time when he had felt so at peace with himself. The mere release from the necessity of petty lying, lying every day and every day, restored his self-respect. He had never lied for pleasure, even at school; but to make himself noticed and admired, to assert his difference from other Cordelia Street boys; and he felt a good deal more manly, more honest, even, now that he had no need for boastful pretensions, now that he could, as his actor friends used to say, "dress the part." It was characteristic that remorse did not occur to him. His golden days went by without a shadow, and he made each as perfect as he could.

On the eighth day after his arrival in New York, he found the whole affair exploited in the Pittsburgh papers, exploited with a wealth of detail which indicated that local news of a sensational nature was at a low ebb. The firm of Denny & Carson announced that the boy's father had refunded the full amount of his theft, and that they had no intention of prosecuting. The Cumberland minister had been interviewed, and expressed his hope of yet reclaiming the motherless lad, and Paul's Sabbath-school teacher declared that she would spare no effort to that end. The rumour had reached Pittsburgh that the boy had been seen in a New York hotel, and his father had gone East to find him and bring him home.

Paul had just come in to dress for dinner; he sank into a chair, weak in the knees, and clasped his head in his hands. It was to be worse than jail, even; the tepid waters of Cordelia Street were to close over him finally and forever. The grey monotony stretched before him in hopeless, unrelieved years; Sabbath-school, Young People's Meeting, the yellow-papered room, the damp dish-towels; it all rushed back upon him with sickening vividness. He had the old feeling that the orchestra had suddenly stopped, the sinking sensation that the play was over. The sweat broke out on his face, and he sprang to his feet, looked about him with his white, conscious smile, and winked at himself in the mirror. With something of the childish belief in miracles with which he had so often gone to class, all his lessons unlearned, Paul dressed and dashed whistling down the corridor to the elevator.

He had no sooner entered the dining-room and caught the measure of the 60 music, than his remembrance was lightened by his old elastic power of claiming the moment, mounting with it, and finding it all sufficient. The glare and glitter about him, the mere scenic accessories had again, and for the last time, their old potency. He would show himself that he was game, he would finish the thing splendidly. He doubted, more than ever, the existence of Cordelia Street, and for the first time he drank his wine recklessly. Was he not, after all, one of these fortunate beings? Was he not still himself, and in his own place? He drummed a nervous accompaniment to the music and looked about him, telling himself over and over that it had paid.

He reflected drowsily, to the swell of the violin and the chill sweetness of his wine, that he might have done it more wisely. He might have caught an outbound steamer and been well out of their clutches before now. But the other side of the world had seemed too far away and too uncertain then; he could not have waited for it; his need had been too sharp. If he had to choose over again, he would do the same thing tomorrow. He looked affectionately about the dining-room, now gilded with a soft mist. Ah, it had paid indeed!

Paul was awakened next morning by a painful throbbing in his head and feet. He had thrown himself across the bed without undressing, and had slept with his shoes on. His limbs and hands were lead heavy, and his tongue and throat were parched. There came upon him one of those fateful attacks of clear-headedness that never occurred except when he was physically exhausted and his nerves hung loose. He lay still and closed his eyes and let the tide of realities wash over him.

His father was in New York; "stopping at some joint or other," he told himself. The memory of successive summers on the front stoop fell upon him like a weight of black water. He had not a hundred dollars left; and he knew now, more than ever, that money was everything, the wall that stood between all he loathed and all he wanted. The thing was winding itself up; he had thought of that on his first glorious day in New York, and had even provided a way to snap the thread. It lay on his dressing-table now; he had got it out last night when he came blindly up from dinner,—but the shiny metal hurt his eyes, and he disliked the look of it, anyway.

He rose and moved about with a painful effort, succumbing now and again to attacks of nausea. It was the old depression exaggerated; all the world had become Cordelia Street. Yet somehow he was not afraid of anything, was absolutely calm; perhaps because he had looked into the dark corner at last, and knew. It was bad enough, what he saw there; but somehow not so bad as his long fear of it had been. He saw everything clearly now. He had a feeling that he had made the best of it, that he had lived the sort of life he was meant to live, and for half an hour he sat staring at the revolver. But he told himself that was not the way, so he went downstairs and took a cab to the ferry.

When Paul arrived at Newark, he got off the train and took another cab,   65
directing the driver to follow the Pennsylvania tracks out of the town. The snow
lay heavy on the roadways and had drifted deep in the open fields. Only here and
there the dead grass or dried weed stalks projected, singularly black, above it.
Once well into the country, Paul dismissed the carriage and walked, floundering
along the tracks, his mind a medley of irrelevant things. He seemed to hold in
his brain an actual picture of everything he had seen that morning. He remembered every feature of both his drivers, the toothless old woman from whom he
had bought the red flowers in his coat, the agent from whom he had got his
ticket, and all of his fellow-passengers on the ferry. His mind, unable to cope
with vital matters near at hand, worked feverishly and deftly at sorting and
grouping these images. They made for him a part of the ugliness of the world, of
the ache in his head, and the bitter burning on his tongue. He stooped and put a
handful of snow into his mouth as he walked, but that, too, seemed hot. When
he reached a little hillside, where the tracks ran through a cut some twenty feet
below him, he stopped and sat down.

The carnations in his coat were drooping with the cold, he noticed; all their
red glory over. It occurred to him that all the flowers he had seen in the show
windows that first night must have gone the same way, long before this. It was
only one splendid breath they had, in spite of their brave mockery at the winter
outside the glass. It was a losing game in the end, it seemed, this revolt against
the homilies by which the world is run. Paul took one of the blossoms carefully
from his coat and scooped a little hole in the snow, where he covered it up. Then
he dozed a while, from his weak condition, seeming insensible to the cold.

The sound of an approaching train woke him, and he started to his feet, remembering only his resolution, and afraid lest he should be too late. He stood
watching the approaching locomotive, his teeth chattering, his lips drawn away
from them in a frightened smile; once or twice he glanced nervously sidewise, as
though he were being watched. When the right moment came, he jumped. As
he fell, the folly of his haste occurred to him with merciless clearness, the vastness of what he had left undone. There flashed through his brain, clearer than
ever before, the blue of Adriatic water, the yellow of Algerian sands.

He felt something strike his chest,—his body was being thrown swiftly through
the air, on and on, immeasurably far and fast, while his limbs gently relaxed. Then,
because the picture making mechanism was crushed, the disturbing visions flashed
into black, and Paul dropped back into the immense design of things.

Talking about the Text

1. Where does our sympathy in "Paul's Case" lie? How does our sympathy seem to
   change over the course of the story?
2. What is the role of art and the artist in Paul's thinking? What does art mean to
   him?

Writing about the Text

1. Write a "biography" of Paul, filling in the missing parts in ways that are in keeping
   with the rest of the story.
2. Explain how Paul's trip to New York might represent a kind of success or fulfillment for him.

Linking the Text to Other Texts

1. What do you make of the title, especially the word "case"? What other categories of writing does it connect to?
2. Connect the significance of travel to New York in "Paul's Case" to some other instances of what the big city signifies. Draw your examples from a wide range of films or literature.

A Wagner Matinée (1904)

I received one morning a letter, written in pale ink on glassy, blue-lined note-paper, and bearing the postmark of a little Nebraska village. This communication, worn and rubbed, looking as if it had been carried for some days in a coat pocket that was none too clean, was from my uncle Howard, and informed me that his wife had been left a small legacy by a bachelor relative, and that it would be necessary for her to go to Boston to attend to the settling of the estate. He requested me to meet her at the station and render her whatever services might be necessary. On examining the date indicated as that of her arrival, I found it to be no later than tomorrow. He had characteristically delayed writing until, had I been away from home for a day, I must have missed my aunt altogether.

The name of my Aunt Georgiana opened before me a gulf of recollection so wide and deep that, as the letter dropped from my hand, I felt suddenly a stranger to all the present conditions of my existence, wholly ill at ease and out of place amid the familiar surroundings of my study. I became, in short, the gangling farmer-boy my aunt had known, scourged with chilblains and bashfulness, my hands cracked and sore from the corn husking. I sat again before her parlour organ, fumbling the scales with my stiff, red fingers, while she, beside me, made canvas mittens for the huskers.

The next morning, after preparing my landlady for a visitor, I set out for the station. When the train arrived I had some difficulty in finding my aunt. She was the last of the passengers to alight, and it was not until I got her into the carriage that she seemed really to recognize me. She had come all the way in a day coach; her linen duster had become black with soot and her black bonnet grey with dust during the journey. When we arrived at my boarding-house the landlady put her to bed at once and I did not see her again until the next morning.

Whatever shock Mrs. Springer experienced at my aunt's appearance, she considerably concealed. As for myself, I saw my aunt's battered figure with that feeling of awe and respect with which we behold explorers who have left their ears and fingers north of Franz-Joseph-Land, or their health somewhere along the Upper Congo. My Aunt Georgiana had been a music teacher at the Boston Conservatory, somewhere back in the latter sixties. One summer, while visiting in the little village among the Green Mountains where her ancestors had dwelt for generations, she had kindled the callow fancy of my uncle, Howard Carpenter, then an idle, shiftless boy of twenty-one. When she returned to her duties in Boston, Howard followed her, and the upshot of this infatuation was that she eloped with him, eluding the reproaches of her family and the criticism of her friends by going with him to the Nebraska frontier. Carpenter, who, of course, had no money, took up a homestead in Red Willow County, fifty miles from the railroad. There they had measured off their land themselves, driving across the prairie in a wagon, to the wheel of which they had tied a red cotton handker-chief, and counting its revolutions. They built a dug-out in the red hillside, one of those cave dwellings whose inmates so often reverted to primitive conditions. Their water they got from the lagoons where the buffalo drank, and their slender stock of provisions was always at the mercy of bands of roving Indians. For thirty years my aunt had not been farther than fifty miles from the homestead.

I owed to this woman most of the good that ever came my way in my boy-hood, and had a reverential affection for her. During the years when I was riding herd for my uncle, my aunt, after cooking the three meals—the first of which was ready at six o'clock in the morning—and putting the six children to bed, would often stand until midnight at her ironing-board, with me at the kitchen table beside her, hearing me recite Latin declensions and conjugations, gently shaking me when my drowsy head sank down over a page of irregular verbs. It was to her, at her ironing or mending, that I read my first Shakspere, and her old text-book on mythology was the first that ever came into my empty hands. She taught me my scales and exercises on the little parlour organ which her husband had bought her after fifteen years during which she had not so much as seen a musical instrument. She would sit beside me by the hour, darning and counting, while I struggled with the "Joyous Farmer." She seldom talked to me about mu-sic, and I understood why. Once when I had been doggedly beating out some easy passages from an old score of *Euryanthe* I had found among her music books, she came up to me and, putting her hands over my eyes, gently drew my head back upon her shoulder, saying tremulously, "Don't love it so well, Clark, or it may be taken from you."

When my aunt appeared on the morning after her arrival in Boston, she was still in a semi-somnambulant state. She seemed not to realize that she was in the city where she had spent her youth, the place longed for hungrily half a lifetime. She had been so wretchedly train-sick throughout the journey that she had no recollection of anything but her discomfort, and, to all intents and purposes, there were but a few hours of nightmare between the farm in Red Willow County and my study on Newbury Street. I had planned a little pleasure for her that afternoon, to repay her for some of the glorious moments she had given me when we used to milk together in the straw-thatched cowshed and she, because I was more than usually tired, or because her husband had spoken sharply to me, would tell me of the splendid performance of the *Huguenots* she had seen in Paris, in her youth.

At two o'clock the Symphony Orchestra was to give a Wagner program, and I intended to take my aunt; though, as I conversed with her, I grew doubtful about her enjoyment of it. I suggested our visiting the Conservatory and the Common before lunch, but she seemed altogether too timid to wish to venture out. She questioned me absently about various changes in the city, but she was chiefly concerned that she had forgotten to leave instructions about feeding half-skimmed milk to a certain weakling calf, "old Maggie's calf, you know, Clark," she explained, evidently having forgotten how long I had been away. She was further troubled because she had neglected to tell her daughter about the freshly-opened kit of mackerel in the cellar, which would spoil if it were not used directly.

I asked her whether she had ever heard any of the Wagnerian operas, and found that she had not, though she was perfectly familiar with their respective

5

situations, and had once possessed the piano score of *The Flying Dutchman*. I began to think it would be best to get her back to Red Willow County without waking her, and regretted having suggested the concert.

From the time we entered the concert hall, however, she was a trifle less passive and inert, and for the first time seemed to perceive her surroundings. I had felt some trepidation lest she might become aware of her queer, country clothes, or might experience some painful embarrassment at stepping suddenly into the world to which she had been dead for a quarter of a century. But, again, I found how superficially I had judged her. She sat looking about her with eyes as impersonal, almost as stony, as those with which the granite Rameses in a museum watches the froth and fret that ebbs and flows about his pedestal. I have seen this same aloofness in old miners who drift into the Brown hotel at Denver, their pockets full of bullion, their linen soiled, their haggard faces unshaven; standing in the thronged corridors as solitary as though they were still in a frozen camp on the Yukon.

The matinée audience was made up chiefly of women. One lost the contour   10
of faces and figures, indeed any effect of line whatever, and there was only the colour of bodices past counting, the shimmer of fabrics soft and firm, silky and sheer; red, mauve, pink, blue, lilac, purple, écru, rose, yellow, cream, and white, all the colours that an impressionist finds in a sunlit landscape, with here and there the dead shadow of a frock coat. My Aunt Georgiana regarded them as though they had been so many daubs of tube-paint on a palette.

When the musicians came out and took their places, she gave a little stir of anticipation, and looked with quickening interest down over the rail at that invariable grouping, perhaps the first wholly familiar thing that had greeted her eye since she had left old Maggie and her weakling calf. I could feel how all those details sank into her soul, for I had not forgotten how they had sunk into mine when I came fresh from ploughing forever and forever between green aisles of corn, where, as in a treadmill, one might walk from daybreak to dusk without perceiving a shadow of change. The clean profiles of the musicians, the gloss of their linen, the dull black of their coats, the beloved shapes of the instruments, the patches of yellow light on the smooth, varnished bellies of the cellos and the bass viols in the rear, the restless, wind-tossed forest of fiddle necks and bows—I recalled how, in the first orchestra I ever heard, those long bow-strokes seemed to draw the heart out of me, as a conjurer's stick reels out yards of paper ribbon from a hat.

The first number was the *Tannhauser* overture. When the horns drew out the first strain of the Pilgrim's chorus, Aunt Georgiana clutched my coat sleeve. Then it was I first realized that for her this broke a silence of thirty years. With the battle between the two motives, with the frenzy of the Venusberg theme and its ripping of strings, there came to me an overwhelming sense of the waste and wear we are so powerless to combat; and I saw again the tall, naked house on the prairie, black and grim as a wooden fortress; the black pond where I had learned to swim, its margin pitted with sun-dried cattle tracks; the rain gullied clay banks about the naked house, the four dwarf ash seedlings where the dish-cloths were always hung to dry before the kitchen door. The world there was the flat world of the ancients; to the east, a cornfield that stretched to daybreak; to the west, a corral that reached to sunset; between, the conquests of peace, dearer-bought than those of war.

The overture closed, my aunt released my coat sleeve, but she said nothing. She sat staring dully at the orchestra. What, I wondered, did she get from it? She had been a good pianist in her day, I knew, and her musical education had been broader than that of most music teachers of a quarter of a century ago. She had often told me of Mozart's operas and Meyerbeer's, and I could remember hearing her sing, years ago, certain melodies of Verdi. When I had fallen ill with a fever in her house she used to sit by my cot in the evening—when the cool, night wind blew in through the faded mosquito netting tacked over the window and I lay watching a certain bright star that burned red above the cornfield—and sing "Home to our mountains, O, let us return!" in a way fit to break the heart of a Vermont boy near dead of homesickness already.

I watched her closely through the prelude to *Tristan and Isolde*, trying vainly to conjecture what that seething turmoil of strings and winds might mean to her, but she sat mutely staring at the violin bows that drove obliquely downward, like the pelting streaks of rain in a summer shower. Had this music any message for her? Had she enough left to at all comprehend this power which had kindled the world since she had left it? I was in a fever of curiosity, but Aunt Georgiana sat silent upon her peak in Darien. She preserved this utter immobility throughout the number from *The Flying Dutchman*, though her fingers worked mechanically upon her black dress, as if, of themselves, they were recalling the piano score they had once played. Poor hands! They had been stretched and twisted into mere tentacles to hold and lift and knead with;—on one of them a thin, worn band that had once been a wedding ring. As I pressed and gently quieted one of those groping hands, I remembered with quivering eyelids their services for me in other days.

Soon after the tenor began the "Prize Song," I heard a quick drawn breath   15 and turned to my aunt. Her eyes were closed, but the tears were glistening on her cheeks, and I think, in a moment more, they were in my eyes as well. It never really died, then—the soul which can suffer so excruciatingly and so interminably; it withers to the outward eye only; like that strange moss which can lie on a dusty shelf half a century and yet, if placed in water, grows green again. She wept so throughout the development and elaboration of the melody.

During the intermission before the second half, I questioned my aunt and found that the "Prize Song" was not new to her. Some years before there had drifted to the farm in Red Willow County a young German, a tramp cow-puncher, who had sung in the chorus at Bayreuth when he was a boy, along with the other peasant boys and girls. Of a Sunday morning he used to sit on his gingham-sheeted bed in the hands' bedroom which opened off the kitchen, cleaning the leather of his boots and saddle, singing the "Prize Song," while my aunt went about her work in the kitchen. She had hovered over him until she had prevailed upon him to join the country church, though his sole fitness for this step, in so far as I could gather, lay in his boyish face and his possession of this divine melody. Shortly afterward, he had gone to town on the Fourth of July, been drunk for several days, lost his money at a faro table, ridden a sad-dled Texas steer on a bet, and disappeared with a fractured collar-bone. All this my aunt told me huskily, wanderingly, as though she were talking in the weak lapses of illness.

"Well, we have come to better things than the old *Trovatore* at any rate, Aunt Georgie?" I queried, with a well meant effort at jocularity.

Her lip quivered and she hastily put her handkerchief up to her mouth. From behind it she murmured, "And you have been hearing this ever since you left me, Clark?" Her question was the gentlest and saddest of reproaches.

The second half of the program consisted of four numbers from the *Ring*, and closed with Siegfried's funeral march. My aunt wept quietly, but almost continuously, as a shallow vessel overflows in a rain-storm. From time to time her dim eyes looked up at the lights, burning softly under their dull glass globes.

The deluge of sound poured on and on; I never knew what she found in the 20
shining current of it; I never knew how far it bore her, or past what happy islands. From the trembling of her face I could well believe that before the last number she had been carried out where the myriad graves are, into the grey, nameless burying grounds of the sea; or into some world of death vaster yet, where, from the beginning of the world, hope has lain down with hope and dream with dream and, renouncing, slept.

The concert was over; the people filed out of the hall chattering and laughing, glad to relax and find the living level again, but my kinswoman made no effort to rise. The harpist slipped the green felt cover over his instrument; the flute-players shook the water from their mouthpieces; the men of the orchestra went out one by one, leaving the stage to the chairs and music stands, empty as a winter cornfield.

I spoke to my aunt. She burst into tears and sobbed pleadingly. "I don't want to go, Clark, I don't want to go!"

I understood. For her, just outside the concert hall, lay the black pond with the cattle-tracked bluffs; the tall, unpainted house, with weather-curled boards, naked as a tower; the crook-backed ash seedlings where the dish-cloths hung to dry; the gaunt, moulting turkeys picking up refuse about the kitchen door.

Talking about the Text

1. Do you think Aunt Georgiana has led a futile, pointless life? Why or why not? Do you pity or admire her (or both)? Does she receive any compensation from living on a farm in Nebraska? Is she an artist still?
2. Note the economy of the writing. We readers don't know the circumstances of Clark's staying with Aunt Georgiana (he is said to be from Vermont), what job he holds in Boston, or much else about his life. And we don't know much about Aunt Georgiana's husband, Howard Carpenter. What assumptions do you make about this "missing" information. How does the economy add or detract from the story?

Writing about the Text

1. Write your own story, describing what happens the next day, after the matinee is over.
2. Write about the notion of "beauty" in this story. What is it? What does it involve?

Linking the Text to Other Texts

1. Connect the notion of beauty in "A Wagner Matinée" with beauty in another Cather story. What does it do for people? Does Cather seem to suggest that her characters have any special responsibilities toward beauty?
2. Research the American reputation of Wagner in 1900, around the time this story was set. What did Wagner's music stand for in American cultural life?

INSPIRATION   "A WAGNER MATINÉE" IN PERFORMANCE: CATHER FROM PAGE TO RADIO STAGE

Scribbling Women, a project of the Public Media Foundation, dramatizes stories by American women writers for national radio broadcast. The plays are distributed nationwide by National Public Radio. Among the works adapted for an audio dramatic format is Cather's "A Wagner Matinée," dramatized into a thirty-minute radio play by Sara Baker and directed by Martin Jenkins. One question to consider when comparing the story to the radio play is what elements must the playwrights have needed to weigh in adapting "A Wagner Matinée" from the fictional page to not only a dramatic, dialogue-based format, but one that is limited to expressing its gestures, emotions, and ideas exclusively through sound.

AUDIO LOCALE

Scribbling Women Recording: "A Wagner Matinée" Radio Play. The Scribbling Women website at http://www.scribblingwomen.org includes links to the online audio files of the project's radio plays, background information on the writers whose works they have adapted, relevant contextual information, related curriculum and lesson plans for teachers, and discussion questions. (Visitors need to register to gain full access to the site's resources, but there is no fee; log-in is free of charge.)

The Old Beauty   (WRITTEN 1936; PUBLISHED 1948)

I

One brilliant September morning in 1922 a slender, fair-skinned man with white moustaches, waxed and turned up at the ends, stepped hurriedly out of the Hôtel Splendide at Aix-les-Bains and stood uncertainly at the edge of the driveway. He stood there for some moments, holding, or rather clutching, his gloves in one hand, a light cane in the other. The pavement was wet, glassy with water. The boys were still sprinkling the walk farther down the hill, and the fuchsias and dahlias in the beds sparkled with water drops. The clear air had the freshness of early morning and the smell of autumn foliage.

Two closed litters, carried by porters, came out of a side door and went joggling down the hill toward the baths. The gentleman standing on the kerb followed these eagerly with his eyes, as if about to dash after them; indeed, his mind seemed to accompany them to the turn in the walk where they disappeared, then to come back to him where he stood and at once to dart off in still another direction.

The gentleman was Mr. Henry Seabury, aged fifty-five, American-born, educated in England, and lately returned from a long business career in China. His evident nervousness was due to a shock: an old acquaintance, who had been one of the brilliant figures in the world of the 1890's, had died a few hours ago in this hotel.

As he stood there he was thinking that he ought to send telegrams . . . but to whom? The lady had no immediate family, and the distinguished men of her time who had cherished the slightest attention from her were all dead. No, there was one (perhaps the most variously gifted of that group) who was still living: living in seclusion down on the Riviera, in a great white mansion set in miles of park and garden. A cloud had come over this man in the midst of a triumphant public life. His opponents had ruined his career by a whispering campaign. They had set going a rumour which would have killed any public man in England at that time. Mr. Seabury began composing his telegram to Lord H—. Lord H— would recognize that this death was more than the death of an individual. To him her name would recall a society whose manners, dress, conventions, loyalties, codes of honour, were different from anything existing in the world today.

And there were certainly old acquaintances like himself, men not of her intimate circle, scattered about over the world; in the States, in China, India. But how to reach them?

Three young men came up the hill to resolve his perplexity; three newspaper correspondents, English, French, American. The American spoke to his companions. "There's the man I've seen about with her so much. He's the one we want."

The three approached Mr. Seabury, and the American addressed him. "Mr. Seabury, I believe? Excuse my stopping you, but we have just learned through the British Consulate that the former Lady Longstreet died in this hotel last night. We are newspaper men, and must send dispatches to our papers." He paused to introduce his companions by their names and the names of their journals. "We thought you might be good enough to tell us something about Lady Longstreet, Madame de Couçy, as she was known here."

"Nothing but what all the world knows." This intrusion had steadied Mr. Seabury, brought his scattered faculties to a focus.

"But we must jog the world's memory a little. A great many things have happened since Lady Longstreet was known everywhere."

"Certainly. You have only to cable your papers that Madame de Couçy, formerly Lady Longstreet, died here last night. They have in their files more than I could tell you if I stood here all morning."

"But the circumstances of her death?"

"You can get that from the management. Her life was interesting, but she died like anyone else—just as you will, some day."

"Her old friends, everywhere, would of course like to learn something about her life here this summer. No one knew her except as Madame de Couçy, so no one observed her very closely. You were with her a great deal, and the simple story of her life here would be—"

"I understand, but it is quite impossible. Good morning, gentlemen." Mr. Seabury went to his room to write his telegram to Lord H—.

II

Two months ago Henry Seabury had come here almost directly from China. His   15
hurried trip across America and his few weeks in London scarcely counted. He
was hunting for something, some spot that was still more or less as it used to be.
Here, at Aix-les-Bains, he found the place unchanged,—and in the hotels many
people very like those who used to come there.

The first night after he had settled himself at the Splendide he became interested in two old English ladies who dined at a table not far from his own.
They had been coming here for many years, he felt sure. They had the old manner. They were at ease and reserved. Their dress was conservative. They were
neither painted not plucked, their nails were neither red nor green. One was
plump, distinctly plump, indeed, but as she entered the dining-room he had noticed that she was quick in her movements and light on her feet. She was radiantly cheerful and talkative. But it was the other lady who interested him. She
had an air of distinction, that unmistakable thing, which told him she had been
a personage. She was tall, had a fine figure and carriage, but either she was much
older than her friend, or life had used her more harshly. Something about her
eyes and brow teased his memory. Had he once known her, or did she merely recall a type of woman he used to know? No, he felt that he must have met her, at
least, long ago, when she was not a stern, gaunt-cheeked old woman with a yellowing complexion. The hotel management informed him that the lady was
Madame de Couçy. He had never known anyone of that name.

The next afternoon when he was sitting under the plane trees in the *Place*,
he saw the two ladies coming down the hill; the tall one moving with a peculiar
drifting ease, looking into the distance as if the unlevel walk beneath her would
naturally accommodate itself to her footing. She kept a white fur well up about
her cheeks, though the day was hot. The short one tripped along beside her.
They crossed the Square, sat down under the trees, and had tea brought out from
the confectioner's. Then the muffled lady let her fur fall back a little and glanced
about her. He was careful not to stare, but once, when he suddenly lifted his
eyes, she was looking directly at him. He thought he saw a spark of curiosity, perhaps recognition.

The two ladies had tea in the *Place* every afternoon unless it rained; when
they did not come Seabury felt disappointed. Sometimes the taller one would
pause before she sat down and suggest going farther, to the Casino. Once he was
near enough to hear the rosy one exclaiming: "Oh, no! It's much nicer here, really. You are always dissatisfied when we go to the Casino. There are more of the
kind you hate there."

The older one with a shrug and a mournful smile sat down resignedly in
front of the pastry shop. When she had finished her tea she drew her wrap up
about her chin as if about to leave, but her companion began to coax: "Let us
wait for the newspaper woman. It's almost time for her, and I do like to get the
home papers."

The other reminded her that there would be plenty of papers at the hotel.   20

"Yes, yes, I know. But I like to get them from her. I'm sure she's glad of our
pennies."

When they left their table they usually walked about the Square for a time,
keeping to the less frequented end toward the Park. They bought roses at the

flower booths, and cyclamen from an old country woman who tramped about with a basketful of them. Then they went slowly up the hill toward the hotel.

III

Seabury's first enlightenment about these solitary women came from a most unlikely source.

Going up to the summit of Mont Revard in the little railway train one morning, he made the acquaintance of an English family (father, mother, and two grown daughters) whom he liked very much. He spent the day on the mountain in their company, and after that he saw a great deal of them. They were from Devonshire, home-staying people, not tourists. (The daughters had never been on the Continent before.) They had come over to visit the son's grave in one of the war cemeteries in the north of France. The father brought them down to Aix to cheer them up a little. (He and his wife had come there on their honeymoon, long ago.) As the Thompsons were stopping at a cramped, rather mean little hotel down in the town, they spent most of the day out of doors. Usually the mother and one of the daughters sat the whole morning in the *Place*, while the other girl went off tramping with the father. The mother knitted, and the girl read aloud to her. Whichever daughter it happened to be kept watchful eye on Mrs. Thompson. If her face grew too pensive, the girl would close the book and say:

"Now, Mother, do let us have some chocolate and croissants. The breakfast at that hotel is horrid, and I'm famished." 25

Mr. Seabury often joined them in the morning. He found it very pleasant to be near that kind of family feeling. They felt his friendliness, the mother especially, and were pleased to have him join them at their chocolate, or to go with him to afternoon concerts at the Grand-Cercle.

One afternoon when the mother and both daughters were having tea with him near the Roman Arch, the two English ladies from his hotel crossed the Square and sat down at a table not far away. He noticed that Mrs. Thompson glanced often in their direction. Seabury kept his guests a long while at tea,— the afternoon was hot, and he knew their hotel was stuffy. He was telling the girls something about China, when the two unknown English ladies left their table and got into a taxi. Mrs. Thompson turned to Seabury and said in a low, agitated voice:

"Do you know, I believe the tall one of those two was Lady Longstreet."

Mr. Seabury started. "Oh, no! Could it be possible?"

"I am afraid it is. Yes, she is greatly changed. It's very sad. Six years ago she 30 stayed at a country place near us, in Devonshire, and I used often to see her out on her horse. She still rode then. I don't think I can be mistaken."

In a flash everything came back to Seabury. "You're right, I'm sure of it, Mrs. Thompson. The lady lives at my hotel, and I've been puzzling about her. I knew Lady Longstreet slightly many years ago. Now that you tell me, I can see it. But ... as you say, she is greatly changed. At the hotel she is known as Madame de Couçy."

"Yes, she married during the war; a Frenchman. But it must have been after she had lost her beauty. I had never heard of the marriage until he was killed,— in '17, I think. Then some of the English papers mentioned that he was the husband of Gabrielle Longstreet. It's very sad when those beautiful ones have to grow old, isn't it? We never have too many of them, at best."

The younger daughter threw her arms about Mrs. Thompson. "Oh, Mother, I wish you hadn't told us! I'm afraid Mr. Seabury does, too. It's such a shock."

He protested. "Yes, it is a shock, certainly. But I'm grateful to Mrs. Thompson. I must be very stupid not to have seen it. I'm glad to know. The two ladies seem very much alone, and the older one looks ill. I might be of some service, if she remembers me. It's all very strange: but one might be useful, perhaps, Mrs. Thompson?"

"That's the way to look at it, Mr. Seabury." Mrs. Thompson spoke gently. "I   35
think she does remember you. When you were talking to Dorothy, turned away from them, she glanced at you often. The lady with her is a friend, don't you think, not a paid companion?"

He said he was sure of it, and she gave him a warm, grateful glance as if he and she could understand how much that meant, then turned to her daughters: "Why, there is Father, come to look for us!" She made a little signal to the stout, flushed man who was tramping across the Square in climbing boots.

IV

Mr. Seabury did not go back to his hotel for dinner. He dined at a little place with tables in the garden, and returned late to the Splendide. He felt rather knocked up by what Mrs. Thompson had told him,—felt that in this world people have to pay an extortionate price for any exceptional gift whatever. Once in his own room, he lay for a long while in a chaise longue before an open window, watching the stars and the fireflies, recalling the whole romantic story,—all he had ever known of Lady Longstreet. And in this hotel, full of people, she was unknown—she!

Gabrielle Longstreet was a name known all over the globe,—even in China, when he went there twenty-seven years ago. Yet she was not an actress or an adventuress. She had come into the European world in a perfectly regular, if somewhat unusual, way.

Sir Wilfred Longstreet, a lover of yachting and adventure on the high seas, had been driven into Martinique by a tropical hurricane. Strolling about the harbour town, he saw a young girl coming out of a church with her mother, the girl was nineteen, the mother perhaps forty. They were the two most beautiful women he had ever seen. The hurricane passed and was forgotten, but Sir Wilfred Longstreet's yacht still lay in the harbour of Fort de France. He sought out the girl's father, an English colonial from Barbados, who was easily convinced. The mother not so easily: she was a person of character as well as severe beauty. Longstreet had sworn that he would never take his yacht out to sea unless he carried Gabrielle aboard her. The *Sea Nymph* might lie and rot there.

In time the mother was reassured by letters and documents from England.   40
She wished to do well for her daughter, and what very brilliant opportunities were there in Martinique? As for the girl, she wanted to see the world; she had never been off the island. Longstreet made a settlement upon Madame the mother, and submitted to the two services, civil and religious. He took his bride directly back to England. He had not advised his friends of his marriage; he was a young man who kept his affairs to himself.

He kept his wife in the country for some months. When he opened his town house and took her to London, things went as he could not possibly have foreseen. In six weeks she was the fashion of the town; the object of admiration among his friends, and his father's friends. Gabrielle was not socially ambitious, made no effort to please. She was not witty or especially clever,—had no accomplishments beyond speaking French as naturally as English. She said nothing memorable in either language. She was beautiful, that was all. And she was fresh. She came into that society of old London like a quiet country dawn.

She showed no great zest for this life so different from anything she had ever known; a quiet wonderment rather, faintly tinged with pleasure. There was no glitter about her, no sparkle. She never dressed in the mode: refused to wear crinoline in a world that billowed and swelled with it. Into drawing-rooms full of ladies enriched by marvels of hairdressing (switches, ringlets, puffs, pompadours, waves starred with gems), she came with her brown hair parted in the middle and coiled in a small knot at the back of her head. Hair-dressers protested, as one client after another adopted the 'mode Gabrielle.' (The knot at the nape of the neck! Charwomen had always worn it; it was as old as mops and pails.)

The English liked high colour, but Lady Longstreet had no red roses in her checks. Her skin had the soft glow of orient pearls,—the jewel to which she was most often compared. She was not spirited, she was not witty, but no one ever heard her say a stupid thing. She was often called cold. She seemed unawakened, as if she were still an island girl with reserved island good manners. No woman had been so much discussed and argued about for a long stretch of years. It was to the older men that she was (unconsciously, as it seemed) more gracious. She liked them to tell her about events and personages already in the past; things she had come too late to see.

Longstreet, her husband, was none too pleased by the flutter she caused. It was no great credit to him to have discovered a rare creature; since everyone else discovered her the moment they had a glimpse of her. Men much his superiors in rank and importance looked over his head at his wife, passed him with a nod on their way to her. He began to feel annoyance, and waited for this flurry to pass over. But pass it did not. With her second and third seasons in town her circle grew. Statesmen and officers twenty years Longstreet's senior seemed to find in Gabrielle an escape from long boredom. He was jealous without having the common pretexts for jealousy. He began to spend more and more time on his yacht in distant waters. He left his wife in his town house with his spinster cousin as chaperone. Gabrielle's mother came on from Martinique for a season, and was almost as much admired as her daughter. Sir Wilfred found that the Martiniquaises had considerably overshadowed him. He was no longer the interesting 'original' he had once been. His unexpected appearances and disappearances were mere incidents in the house and the life which his wife and his cousin had so well organized. He bore this for six years and then, unexpectedly, demanded divorce. He established the statutory grounds, she petitioning for the decree. He made her a generous settlement.

This brought about a great change in Gabrielle Longstreet's life. She remained in London, and bought a small house near St. James's Park. Longstreet's old cousin, to his great annoyance, stayed on with Gabrielle,—the only one of his family who had not treated her like a poor relation. The loyalty of this spinster, a woman of spirit, Scotch on the father's side, did a good deal to ease

45

Gabrielle's fall in the world. For fall it was, of course. She had her circle, but it was smaller and more intimate. Fewer women invited her now, fewer of the women she used to know. She did not go afield for those who affected art and advanced ideas; they would gladly have championed her cause. She replied to their overtures that she no longer went into society. Her men friends never flinched in their loyalty. Those unembarrassed by wives, the bachelors and widowers, were more assiduous than ever. At that dinner table where Gabrielle and "the Honourable MacPhairson," as the old cousin was called, were sometimes the only women, one met promising young men, not yet settled in their careers, and much older men, so solidly and successfully settled that their presence in a company established its propriety.

Nobody could ever say exactly why Gabrielle's house was so attractive. The men who had the entree there were not skilful at defining such a thing as 'charm' in words: that was not at all their line. And they would have been reluctant to admit that a negligible thing like temperature had anything to do with the pleasant relaxation they enjoyed there. The chill of London houses had been one of the cruellest trials the young Martiniquaise had to bear. When she took a house of her own, she (secretly, as if it were a disgraceful thing to do) had a hot-air furnace put in her cellar, and she kept coal fires burning in the grates at either end of the drawing-room. In colour, however, the rooms were not warm, but rather cool and spring-like. Always flowers, and not too many. There was something more flower-like than the flowers,—something in Gabrielle herself (now more herself than ever she had been as Lady Longstreet); the soft pleasure that came into her face when she put out her hand to greet a hero of perhaps seventy years, the look of admiration in her calm grey eyes. A century earlier her French grandmothers may have greeted the dignitaries of the Church with such a look,—deep feeling, without eagerness of any kind. To a badgered Minister, who came in out of committee meetings and dirty weather, the warm house, the charming companionship which had no request lurking behind it, must have been grateful. The lingering touch of a white hand on his black sleeve can do a great deal for an elderly man who has left a busy and fruitless day behind him and who is worn down by the unreasonable demands of his own party. Nothing said in that room got out into the world. Gabrielle never repeated one man to another,—and as for the Honourable MacPhairson, she never gave anything away, not even a good story!

In time there came about a succession of Great Protectors, and Gabrielle Longstreet was more talked about than in the days of her sensational debut. Whether any of them were ever her lovers, no one could say. They were all men much older than she, and only one of them was known for light behaviour with women. Young men were sometimes asked to her house, but they were made to feel it was by special kindness. Henry Seabury himself had been taken there by young Hardwick, when he was still an undergraduate. Seabury had not known her well, however, until she leased a house in New York and spent two winters there. A jealous woman, and a very clever one, had made things unpleasant for her in London, and Gabrielle had quitted England for a time.

* * *

Sitting alone that night, recalling all he had heard of Lady Longstreet, Seabury tried to remember her face just as it was in the days when he used to know her;

the beautiful contour of the cheeks, the low, straight brow, the lovely line from the chin to the base of the throat. Perhaps it was her eyes he remembered best; no glint in them, no sparkle, no drive. When she was moved by admiration, they did not glow, but became more soft, more grave; a kind of twilight shadow deepened in them. That look, with her calm white shoulders, her unconsciousness of her body and whatever clothed it, gave her the air of having come from afar off.

And now it was all gone. There was something tense, a little defiant in the shoulders now. The hands that used to lie on her dress forgotten, as a bunch of white violets might lie there . . . Well, it was all gone.

Plain women, he reflected, when they grow old are—simply plain women. 50 Often they improve. But a beautiful woman may become a ruin. The more delicate her beauty, the more it owes to some exquisite harmony in modelling and line, the more completely it is destroyed. Gabrielle Longstreet's face was now unrecognizable. She gave it no assistance, certainly. She was the only woman in the dining-room who used no make-up. She met the winter barefaced. Cheap counterfeits meant nothing to a woman who had had the real thing for so long. She must have been close upon forty when he knew her in New York,—and where was there such a creature in the world today? Certainly in his hurried trip across America and England he had not been gladdened by the sight of one. He had seen only cinema stars, and women curled and plucked and painted to look like them. Perhaps the few very beautiful women he remembered in the past had been illusions, had benefited by a romantic tradition which played upon them like a kindly light . . . and by an attitude in men which no longer existed.

V

When Mr. Seabury awoke the next day it was clear to him that any approach to Madame de Couçy must be made through the amiable-seeming friend, Madame Allison as she was called at the hotel, who always accompanied her. He had noticed that this lady usually went down into the town alone in the morning. After breakfasting he walked down the hill and loitered about the little streets. Presently he saw Madame Allison come out of the English bank, with several small parcels tucked under her arm. He stepped beside her.

"Pardon me, Madame, but I am stopping at your hotel, and I have noticed that you are a friend of Madame de Couçy, whom I think I used to know as Gabrielle Longstreet. It was many years ago, and naturally she does not recognize me. Would it displease her if I sent up my name, do you think?"

Mrs. Allison answered brightly. "Oh, she did recognize you, if you are Mr. Seabury. Shall we sit down in the shade for a moment? I find it very warm here, even for August."

When they were seated under the plane trees she turned to him with a friendly smile and frank curiosity. "She is here for a complete rest and isn't seeing people, but I think she would be glad to see an old friend. She remembers you very well. At first she was not sure about your name, but I asked the porter. She recalled it at once and said she met you with Hardwick, General Hardwick, who was killed in the war. Yes, I'm sure she would be glad to see an old friend."

He explained that he was scarcely an old friend, merely one of many admir- 55 ers; but he used to go to her house when she lived in New York.

"She said you did. She thought you did not recognize her. But we have all changed, haven't we?"

"And have you and I met before, Madame Allison?"

"Oh, drop the Madame, please! We both speak English, and I am Mrs. Allison. No, we never met. You may have seen me, if you went to the Alhambra. I was Cherry Beamish in those days."

"Then I last saw you in an Eton jacket, with your hair cropped. I never had the pleasure of seeing you out of your character parts, which accounts for my not recognizing—"

She cut him short with a jolly laugh. "Oh, thirty years and two stone would   60
account, would account perfectly! I always did boy parts, you remember. They wouldn't have me in skirts. So I had to keep my weight down. Such a comfort not to fuss about it now. One has a right to a little of one's life, don't you think?"

He agreed. "But I saw you in America also. You had great success there."

She nodded. "Yes, three seasons, grand engagements. I laid by a pretty penny. I was married over there, and divorced over there, quite in the American style! He was a Scotch boy, stranded in Philadelphia. We parted with no hard feelings, but he was too expensive to keep." Seeing the hotel bus, Mrs. Allison hailed it. "I *shall* be glad if Gabrielle feels up to seeing you. She is frightfully dull here and not very well."

VI

The following evening, as Seabury went into the dining-room and bowed to Mrs. Allison, she beckoned him to Madame de Couçy's table. That lady put out her jewelled hand and spoke abruptly.

"Chetty tells me we are old acquaintances, Mr. Seabury. Will you come up to us for coffee after dinner? This is the number of our apartment." As she gave him her card he saw that her hand trembled slightly. Her voice was much deeper than it used to be, and cold. It had always been cool, but soft, like a cool fragrance,—like her eyes and her white arms.

When he rang at Madame de Couçy's suite an hour later, her maid admitted   65
him. The two ladies were seated before an open window, the coffee table near them and the percolator bubbling. Mrs. Allison was the first to greet him. In a moment she retired, leaving him alone with Madame de Couçy.

"It is very pleasant to meet you again, after so many years, Seabury. How did you happen to come?"

Because he had liked the place long ago, he told her.

"And I, for the same reason. I live in Paris now. Mrs. Allison tells me you have been out in China all this while. And how are things there?"

"Not so good now, Lady Longstreet, may I still call you? China is rather falling to pieces."

"Just as here, eh? No, call me as I am known in this hotel, please. When we   70
are alone, you may use my first name; that has survived time and change. As to change, we have got used to it. But you, coming back upon it, this Europe, suddenly . . . it must give you rather a shock."

It was she herself who had given him the greatest shock of all, and in one quick, penetrating glance she seemed to read that fact. She shrugged: there was nothing to be done about it. "Chetty, where are you?" she called.

Mrs. Allison came quickly from another room and poured the coffee. Her presence warmed the atmosphere considerably. She seemed unperturbed by the grimness of her friend's manner; and she herself was a most comfortable little person. Even her too evident plumpness was comfortable, since she didn't seem to mind it. She didn't like living in Paris very well, she said; something rather stiff and chilly about it. But she often ran away and went home to see her nieces and nephews, and they were a jolly lot. Yes, she found it very pleasant here at Aix. And now that an old friend of Gabrielle's had obligingly turned up, they would have someone to talk to, and that would be a blessing.

Madame de Couçy gave a low, mirthless laugh. "She seems to take a good deal for granted, doesn't she?"

"Not where I am concerned, if you mean that. I should be deeply grateful for someone to talk to. Between the three of us we may find a great deal."

"Be sure we shall," said Mrs. Allison. "We have the past, and the present— which is really very interesting, if only you will let yourself think so. Some of the people here are very novel and amusing, and others are quite like people we used to know. Don't you find it so, Mr. Seabury?"

He agreed with her and turned to Madame de Couçy. "May I smoke?"

"What a question to ask in these days! Yes, you and Chetty may smoke. I will take a liqueur."

Mrs. Allison rose. "Gabrielle has a cognac so old and precious that we keep it locked in a cabinet behind the piano." In opening the cabinet she overturned a framed photograph which fell to the floor. "There goes the General again! No, he didn't break, dear. We carry so many photographs about with us, Mr. Seabury."

Madame de Couçy turned to Seabury. "Do you recognize some of my old friends? There are some of yours, too, perhaps. I think I was never sentimental when I was young, but now I travel with my photographs. My friends mean more to me now than when they were alive. I was too ignorant then to realize what remarkable men they were. I supposed the world was always full of great men."

She left her chair and walked with him about the salon and the long entrance hall, stopping before one and another; uniforms, military and naval, caps and gowns; photographs, drawings, engravings. As she spoke of them the character of her voice changed altogether,—became, indeed, the voice Seabury remembered. The hard, dry tone was a form of disguise, he conjectured; a protection behind which she addressed people from whom she expected neither recognition nor consideration.

"What an astonishing lot they are, seeing them together like this," he exclaimed with feeling. "How can a world manage to get on without them?"

"It hasn't managed very well, has it? You may remember that I was a rather ungrateful young woman. I took what came. A great man's time, his consideration, his affection, were mine in the natural course of things, I supposed. But it's not so now. I bow down to them in admiration . . . gratitude. They are dearer to me than when they were my living friends,—because I understand them better."

Seabury remarked that the men whose pictures looked down at them were too wise to expect youth and deep discernment in the same person.

"I'm not speaking of discernment; that I had, in a way. I mean ignorance. I simply didn't know all that lay behind them. I am better informed now. I read everything they wrote, and everything that has been written about them. That is my chief pleasure."

Seabury smiled indulgently and shook his head. "It wasn't for what you knew about them that they loved you."

She put her hand quickly on his arm. "Ah, you said that before you had time to think! You believe, then, that I did mean something to them?" For the first time she fixed on him the low, level, wondering look that he remembered of old: the woman he used to know seemed breathing beside him. When she turned away from him suddenly, he knew it was to hide the tears in her eyes. He had seen her cry once, a long time ago. He had not forgotten.

He took up a photograph and talked, to bridge over a silence in which she could not trust her voice. "What a fine likeness of X—! He was my hero, among the whole group. Perhaps his contradictions fascinated me. I could never see how one side of him managed to live with the other. Yet I know that both sides were perfectly genuine. He was a mystery. And his end was mysterious. No one will ever know where or how. A secret departure on a critical mission, and never an arrival anywhere. It was like him."

Madame de Couçy turned, with a glow in her eyes such as he had never seen there in her youth. "The evening his disappearance was announced . . . Shall I ever forget it! I was in London. The newsboys were crying it in the street. I did not go to bed that night. I sat up in the drawing-room until day-light; hoping, saying the old prayers I used to say with my mother. It was all one could do. . . . Young Harney was with him, you remember. I have always been glad of that. Whatever fate was in store for his chief, Harney would have chosen to share it."

Seabury stayed much longer with Madame de Couçy than he had intended. The ice once broken, he felt he might never find her so much herself again. They sat talking about people who were no longer in this world. She knew much more about them than he. Knew so much that her talk brought back not only the men, but their period; its security, the solid exterior, the exotic contradictions behind the screen; the deep, claret-coloured closing years of Victoria's reign. Nobody ever recognizes a period until it has gone by, he reflected: until it lies behind one it is merely everyday life.

VII

The next evening the Thompsons, all four of them, were to dine with Mr. Seabury at the Maison des Fleurs. Their holiday was over, and they would be leaving on the following afternoon. They would stop once more at that spot in the north, to place fresh wreaths, before they took the Channel boat.   90

When Seabury and his guests were seated and the dinner had been ordered, he was aware that the mother was looking at him rather wistfully. He felt he owed her some confidence, since it was she, really, who had enlightened him. He told her that he had called upon Gabrielle Longstreet last evening.

"And how is she, dear Mr. Seabury? Is she less—less forbidding than when we see her in the Square?"

"She was on her guard at first, but that soon passed. I stayed later than I should have done, but I had a delightful evening. I gather that she is a little antagonistic to the present order,—indifferent, at least. But when she talks about her old friends she is quite herself."

Mrs. Thompson listened eagerly. She hesitated and then asked: "Does she find life pleasant at all, do you think?"

Seabury told her how the lady was surrounded by the photographs and memoirs of her old friends; how she never travelled without them. It had struck   95 him that she was living her life over again,—more understandingly than she lived it the first time.

Mrs. Thompson breathed a little sigh. "Then I know that all is well with her. You have done so much to make our stay here pleasant, Mr. Seabury, but your telling us this is the best of all. Even Father will be interested to know that."

The stout man, who wore an ancient tail coat made for him when he was much thinner, came out indignantly. "Even Father! I like that! One of the great beauties of our time, and very popular before the divorce."

His daughter laughed and patted his sleeve. Seabury went on to tell Mrs. Thompson that she had been quite right in surmising the companion to be a friend, not a paid attendant. "And a very charming person, too. She was one of your cleverest music-hall stars. Cherry Beamish."

Here Father dropped his spoon into his soup. "What's that? Cherry Beamish? But we haven't had such another since! Remember her in that coster song, Mother? It went round the world, that did. We were all crazy about her, the boys called her Cherish Beamy. No monkeyshines for her, never got herself mixed up in anything shady."

"Such a womanly woman in private life," Mrs. Thompson murmured. "My 100 Dorothy went to school with two of her nieces. An excellent school, and quite dear. Their Aunt Chetty does everything for them. And now she is with Lady Longstreet! One wouldn't have supposed they'd ever meet, those two. But then things *are* strange now."

There was no lull in conversation at that dinner. After the father had enjoyed several glasses of champagne he delighted his daughters with an account of how Cherry Beamish used to do the tipsy schoolboy coming in at four in the morning and meeting his tutor in the garden.

VIII

Mr. Seabury sat waiting before the hotel in a comfortable car which he now hired by the week. Gabrielle and Chetty drove out with him every day. This afternoon they were to go to Annecy by the wild road along the Echelles. Presently Mrs. Allison came down alone. Gabrielle was staying in bed, she said. Last night Seabury had dined with them in their apartment, and Gabrielle had talked too much, she was afraid. "She didn't sleep afterward, but I think she will make it up today if she is quite alone."

Seabury handed her into the car. In a few minutes they were running past the lake of Bourget.

"This gives me an opportunity, Mrs. Allison, to ask you how it came about that you've become Lady Longstreet's protector. It's a beautiful friendship."

She laughed. "And an amazing one? But I think you must call me Chetty, as 105 she does, if we are to be confidential. Yes, I suppose it must seem to you the queerest partnership that war and desolation have made. But you see, she was so strangely left. When I first began to look after her a little, two years ago, she was ill in an hotel in Paris (we have taken a flat since), and there was no one, positively no one but the hotel people, the French doctor, and an English nurse who had chanced to be within call. It was the nurse, really, who gave me my cure. I had sent flowers, with no name, of course. (What would a bygone music-hall name mean to Gabrielle Longstreet?) And I called often to inquire. One morning I met Nurse Ames just as she was going out into the Champs-Élysées for her exercise, and she asked me to accompany her. She was an experienced woman, not young. She remembered when Gabrielle Longstreet's name and photographs were known all over the Continent, and when people at home were keen enough upon meeting her. And here she was, dangerously ill in a foreign hotel, and there was no one, simply no one. To be sure, she was registered under the name of her second husband."

Seabury interrupted. "And who was he, this de Couçy? I have heard nothing about him."

"I know very little myself, I never met him. They had been friends a long while, I believe. He was killed in action—less than a year after they were married. His name was a disguise for her, even then. She came from Martinique, you remember, and she had no relatives in England. Longstreet's people had never liked her. So, you see, she was quite alone."

Seabury took her plump little hand. "And that was where you came in, Chetty?"

She gave his fingers a squeeze. "Thank you! That's nice. It was Nurse Ames who did it. The war made a lot of wise nurses. After Gabrielle was well enough to see people, there was no one for her to see! The same thing that had happened to her friends in England had happened over here. The old men had paid the debt of nature, and the young ones were killed or disabled or had lost touch with her. She once had many friends in Paris. Nurse Ames told me that an old French officer, blinded in the war, sometimes came to see her, guided by his little granddaughter. She said her patient had expressed curiosity about the English woman who had sent so many flowers. I wrote a note, asking whether I could be of any service, and signed my professional name. She might recognize it, she might not. We had been on a committee together during the war. She told the nurse to admit me, and that's how it began."

Seabury took her hand again. "Now I want you to be frank with me. Had she   110 then, or has she now, money worries at all?"

Cherry Beamish chuckled. "Not she, you may believe! But I have had a few for her. On the whole, she's behaved very well. She sold her place in Devonshire to advantage, before the war. Her capital is in British bonds. She seems to you harassed?"

"Sometimes."

Mrs. Allison looked grave and was silent for a little. "Yes," with a sigh, "she gets very low at times. She suffers from strange regrets. She broods on the things she might have done for her friends and didn't,—thinks she was cold to them. Was she, in those days, so indifferent as she makes herself believe?"

Seabury reflected. "Not exactly indifferent. She wouldn't have been so attractive if she'd been that. She didn't take things very hard, perhaps. She used to strike me as . . . well, we might call it unawakened."

"But wasn't she the most beautiful creature then! I used to see her at the   115 races, and at charity bazaars, in my early professional days. After the war broke out and everybody was all mixed up, I was put on an entertainment committee with her. She wasn't quite the Lady Longstreet of my youth, but she still had that grand style. It was the illness in Paris that broke her. She's changed very fast ever since. You see she thought, once the war was over, the world would be just as it used to be. Of course it isn't."

By this time the car had reached Annecy, and they stopped for tea. The shore of the lake was crowded with young people taking their last dip for the day; sun-browned backs and shoulders, naked arms and legs. As Mrs. Allison was having her tea on the terrace, she watched the bathers. Presently she twinkled a sly smile at her host. "Do you know, I'm rather glad we didn't bring Gabrielle! It puts her out terribly to see young people bathing naked. She makes comments that are indecent, really! If only she had a swarm of young nieces and nephews, as I have, she'd see things quite differently, and she'd be much happier. Legs were never wicked to us stage people, and now all the young things know they are not wicked."

IX

When Madame de Couçy went out with Seabury alone, he missed the companionship of Cherry Beamish. With Cherry the old beauty always softened a little; seemed amused by the other's interest in whatever the day produced: the countryside, the weather, the number of cakes she permitted herself for tea. The imagination which made this strange friendship possible was certainly on the side of Cherry Beamish. For her, he could see, there was something in it; to be the anchor, the refuge, indeed, of one so out of her natural orbit,—selected by her long ago as an object of special admiration.

One afternoon when he called, the maid, answering his ring, said that Madame would not go out this afternoon, but hoped he would stay and have tea with her in her salon. He told the lift boy to dismiss the car and went in to Madame de Couçy. She received him with unusual warmth.

"Chetty is out for the afternoon, with some friends from home. Oh, she still has a great many! She is much younger than I, in every sense. Today I particularly wanted to see you alone. It's curious how the world runs away from one, slips by without one's realizing it."

He reminded her that the circumstances had been unusual. "We have lived 120 through a storm to which the French Revolution, which used to be our standard of horrors, was merely a breeze. A rather gentlemanly affair, as one looks back on it. . . . As for me, I am grateful to be alive, sitting here with you in a comfortable hotel (I might be in a prison full of rats), in a France still undestroyed."

The old lady looked into his eyes with the calm, level gaze so rare with her now. "Are you grateful? I am not. I think one should go out with one's time. I particularly wished to see you alone this afternoon. I want to thank you for your tact and gentleness with me one hideous evening long ago; in my house in New York. You were a darling boy to me that night. If you hadn't come along, I don't know how I would have got over it—out of it, even. One can't call the servants."

"But, Gabrielle, why recall a disagreeable incident when you have so many agreeable ones to remember?"

She seemed not to hear him, but went on, speaking deliberately, as if she were reflecting aloud. "It was strange, your coming in just when you did: that night it seemed to me like a miracle. Afterward, I remembered you had been expected at eight. But I had forgotten all that, forgotten everything. Never before or since have I been so frightened. It was something worse than fear."

There was a knock at the door. Madame de Couçy called: "*Entrez!*" without turning round. While the tea was brought she sat looking out of the window, frowning. When the waiter had gone she turned abruptly to Seabury:

"After that night I never saw you again until you walked into the dining-   125
room of this hotel a few weeks ago. I had gone into the country somewhere, hiding with friends, and when I came back to New York, you were already on your
way to China. I never had a chance to explain."

"There was certainly no need for that."

"Not for you, perhaps. But for me. You may have thought such scenes were
frequent in my life. Hear me out, please," as he protested. "That man had come
to my house at seven o'clock that evening and sent up a message begging me to
see him about some business matters. (I had been stupid enough to let him make
investments for me.) I finished dressing and hurried down to the drawing-room."
Here she stopped and slowly drank a cup of tea. "Do you know, after you came in
I did not see you at all, not for some time, I think. I was mired down in something . . . *the power of the dog*, the English Prayer Book calls it. But the moment I
heard your voice, I knew that I was safe . . . I felt the leech drop off. I have never
forgot the sound of your voice that night; so calm, with all a man's strength behind it,—and you were only a boy. You merely asked if you had come too early. I
felt the leech drop off. After that I remember nothing. I didn't see you, with my
eyes, until you gave me your handkerchief. You stayed with me and looked after
me all evening.

"You see, I had let the beast come to my house, oh, a number of times! I had
asked his advice and allowed him to make investments for me. I had done the
same thing at home with men who knew about such matters; they were men like
yourself and Hardwick. In a strange country one goes astray in one's reckonings.
I had met that man again and again at the houses of my friends,—your friends!
Of course his personality was repulsive to me. One knew at once that under his
smoothness he was a vulgar person. I supposed that was not unusual in great
bankers in the States."

"You simply chose the wrong banker, Gabrielle. The man's accent must
have told you that he belonged to a country you did not admire."

"But I tell you I met him at the houses of decent people."   130

Seabury shook his head. "Yes, I am afraid you must blame us for that. Americans, even those whom you call the decent ones, do ask people to their houses
who shouldn't be there. They are often asked *because* they are outrageous,—and
therefore considered amusing. Besides, that fellow had a very clever way of pushing himself. If a man is generous in his contributions to good causes, and is useful
on committees and commissions, he is asked to the houses of the people who
have these good causes at heart."

"And perhaps I, too, was asked because I was considered notorious? A divor-
cée, known to have more friends among men than among women at home? I
think I see what you mean. There are not many shades in your society. I left the
States soon after you sailed for China. I gave up my New York house at a loss to
be rid of it. The instant I recognized you in the dining-room downstairs, that
miserable evening came back to me. In so far as our acquaintance was concerned, all that had happened only the night before."

"Then I am reaping a reward I didn't deserve, some thirty years afterward! If
I had not happened to call that evening when you were so—so unpleasantly surprised, you would never have remembered me at all! We shouldn't be sitting together at this moment. Now may I ring for some fresh tea, dear? Let us be

comfortable. This afternoon has brought us closer together. And this little spot in Savoie is a nice place to renew old friendships, don't you think?"

X

Some hours later, when Mr. Seabury was dressing for dinner, he was thinking of that strange evening in Gabrielle Longstreet's house on Fifty-third Street, New York.

He was then twenty-four years old. She had been very gracious to him all 135 the winter.

On that particular evening he was to take her to dine at Delmonico's. Her cook and butler were excused to attend a wedding. The maid who answered his ring asked him to go up to the drawing-room on the second floor, where Madame was awaiting him. She followed him as far as the turn of the stairway, then, hearing another ring at the door, she excused herself.

He went on alone. As he approached the wide doorway leading into the drawing-room, he was conscious of something unusual; a sound, or perhaps an unnatural stillness. From the doorway he beheld something quite terrible. At the far end of the room Gabrielle Longstreet was seated on a little French sofa—not seated, but silently struggling. Behind the sofa stood a stout, dark man leaning over her. His left arm, about her waist, pinioned her against the flowered silk upholstery. His right hand was thrust deep into the low-cut bodice of her dinner gown. In her struggle she had turned a little on her side; her right arm was in the grip of his left hand, and she was trying to free the other, which was held down by the pressure of his elbow. Neither of those two made a sound. Her face was averted, half hidden against the blue silk back of the sofa. Young Seabury stood still just long enough to see what the situation really was. Then he stepped across the threshold and said with such coolness as he could command: "Am I too early, Madame Longstreet?"

The man behind her started from his crouching position, darted away from the sofa, and disappeared down the stairway. To reach the stairs he passed Seabury, without lifting his eyes, but his face was glistening wet.

The lady lay without stirring, her face now completely hidden. She looked so crushed and helpless, he thought she must be hurt physically. He spoke to her softly: "Madame Longstreet, shall I call—"

"Oh, don't call! Don't call anyone," She began shuddering violently, her 140 face still turned away. "Some brandy, please. Downstairs, in the dining-room."

He ran down the stairs, had to tell the solicitous maid that Madame wished to be alone for the present. When he came back Gabrielle had caught up the shoulder straps of her gown. Her right arm bore red finger marks. She was shivering and sobbing. He slipped his handkerchief into her hand, and she held it over her mouth. She took a little brandy. Then another fit of weeping came on. He begged her to come nearer to the fire. She put her hand on his arm, but seemed unable to rise. He lifted her from that seat of humiliation and took her, wavering between his supporting hands, to a low chair beside the coal grate. She sank into it, and he put a cushion under her feet. He persuaded her to drink the rest of the brandy. She stopped crying and leaned back, her eyes closed, her hands lying nerveless on the arms of the chair. Seabury thought he had never seen her when she was more beautiful . . . probably that was because she was helpless and he was young.

"Perhaps you would like me to go now?" he asked her.

She opened her eyes. "Oh, no! Don't leave me, please. I am so much safer with you here." She put her hand, still cold, on his for a moment, then closed her eyes and went back into that languor of exhaustion.

Perhaps half an hour went by. She did not stir, but he knew she was not asleep: an occasional trembling of the eyelids, tears stealing out from under her black lashes and glistening unregarded on her cheeks; like pearls he thought they were, transparent shimmers on velvet cheeks gone very white.

When suddenly she sat up, she spoke in her natural voice.   145

"But, my dear boy, you have gone dinnerless all this while! Won't you stay with me and have just a bit of something up here? Do ring for Hopkins, please."

The young man caught at the suggestion. If once he could get her mind on the duties of caring for a guest, that might lead to something. He must try to be very hungry.

The kitchen maid was in and, under Hopkins's direction, got together a creditable supper and brought it up to the drawing-room. Gabrielle took nothing but the hot soup and a little sherry. Young Seabury, once he tasted food, found he had no difficulty in doing away with cold pheasant and salad.

Gabrielle had quite recovered her self-control. She talked very little, but that was not unusual with her. He told her about Hardwick's approaching marriage. For him, the evening went by very pleasantly. He felt with her a closer intimacy than ever before.

When at midnight he rose to take his leave, she detained him beside her   150
chair, holding his hand. "At some other time I shall explain what you saw here tonight. How could such a thing happen in one's own house, in an English-speaking city . . . ?"

"But that was not an English-speaking man who went out from here. He is an immigrant who has made a lot of money. He does not belong."

"Yes, that is true. I wish you weren't going out to China. Not for long, I hope. It's a bad thing to be away from one's own people." Her voice broke, and tears came again. He kissed her hand softly, devotedly, and went downstairs.

He had not seen her again until his arrival at this hotel some weeks ago, when he did not recognize her.

XI

One evening when Mrs. Allison and Madame de Couçy had been dining with Seabury at the Maison des Fleurs, they went into the tea room to have their coffee and watch the dancing. It was now September, and almost everyone would be leaving next week. The floor was full of young people, English, American, French, moving monotonously to monotonous rhythms,—some of them scarcely moving at all. Gabrielle watched them through her lorgnette, with a look of resigned boredom.

Mrs. Allison frowned at her playfully. "Of course it's all very different," she   155
observed, "but then, so is everything." She turned to Seabury: "You know we used to have to put so much drive into a dance act, or it didn't go at all. Lottie Collins was the only lazy dancer who could get anything over. But the truth was, the dear thing couldn't dance at all; got on by swinging her foot! There must be something in all this new manner, if only one could get it. That couple down by

the bar now, the girl with the *very* low back: they are doing it beautifully; she dips and rises like a bird in the air . . . a tired bird, though. That's the disconcerting thing. It all seems so tired."

Seabury agreed with her cheerfully that it was charming, though tired. He felt a gathering chill in the lady on his right. Presently she said impatiently: "Haven't you had enough of this, Chetty?"

Mrs. Allison sighed. "You never see anything in it, do you, dear?"

"I see wriggling. They look to me like lizards dancing—or reptiles coupling."

"Oh, no, dear! No! They are such sweet young things. But they are dancing in a dream. I want to go and wake them up. They are missing so much fun. Dancing ought to be open and free, with the lungs full; not mysterious and breathless. I wish I could see a *spirited* waltz again."

Gabrielle shrugged and gave a dry laugh. "I wish I could dance one! I think I should try, if by any chance I should ever hear a waltz played again." 160

Seabury rose from his chair. "May I take you up on that? Will you?"

She seemed amused and incredulous, but nodded.

"Excuse me for a moment." He strolled toward the orchestra. When the tango was over he spoke to the conductor, handing him something from his vest pocket. The conductor smiled and bowed, then spoke to his men, who smiled in turn. The saxophone put down his instrument and grinned. The strings sat up in their chairs, pulled themselves up, as it were, tuned for a moment, and sat at attention. At the lift of the leader's hand they began the "Blue Danube."

Gabrielle took Mr. Seabury's arm. They passed a dozen couples who were making a sleepy effort and swung into the open square where the line of tables stopped. Seabury had never danced with Gabrielle Longstreet, and he was astonished. She had attack and style, the grand style, slightly military, quite right for her tall, straight figure. He held her hand very high, accordingly. The conductor caught the idea; smartened the tempo slightly, made the accents sharper. One by one the young couples dropped out and sat down to smoke. The two old waltzers were left alone on the floor. There was a stir of curiosity about the room; who were those two, and why were they doing it? Cherry Beamish heard remarks from the adjoining tables.

"She's rather stunning, the old dear!" 165

"Aren't they funny?"

"It's so quaint and theatrical. Quite effective in its way."

Seabury had not danced for some time. He thought the musicians drew the middle part out interminably; rather suspected they were playing a joke on him. But his partner lost none of her brilliance and verve. He tried to live up to her. He was grateful when those fiddlers snapped out the last phrase. As he took Gabrielle to her seat, a little breeze of applause broke out from the girls about the room.

"Dear young things!" murmured Chetty, who was flushed with pleasure and excitement. A group of older men who had come in from the dining-room were applauding.

"Let us go now, Seabury. I am afraid we have been making rather an exhibi- 170 tion," murmured Madame de Couçy. As they got into the car awaiting them outside, she laughed good-humouredly. "Do you know, Chetty, I quite enjoyed it!"

XII

The next morning Mrs. Allison telephoned Seabury that Gabrielle had slept well after an amusing evening: felt so fit that she thought they might seize upon this glorious morning for a drive to the Grande-Chartreuse. The drive, by the route they preferred, was a long one, and hitherto she had not felt quite equal to it. Accordingly, the three left the hotel at eleven o'clock with Seabury's trusty young Savoyard driver, and were soon in the mountains.

It was one of those high-heavenly days that often come among the mountains of Savoie in autumn. In the valleys the hillsides were pink with autumn crocuses thrusting up out of the short sunburned grass. The beech trees still held their satiny green. As the road wound higher and higher toward the heights, Seabury and his companions grew more and more silent. The lightness and purity of the air gave one a sense of detachment from everything one had left behind "down there, back yonder." Mere breathing was a delicate physical pleasure. One had the feeling that life would go on thus forever in high places, among naked peaks cut sharp against a stainless sky.

Ever afterward Seabury remembered that drive as strangely impersonal. He and the two ladies were each lost in a companionship much closer than any they could share with one another. The clean-cut mountain boy who drove them seemed lost in thoughts of his own. His eyes were on the road: he never spoke. Once, when the gold tones of an alpine horn floated down from some hidden pasture far overhead, he stopped the car of his own accord and shut off the engine. He threw a smiling glance back at Seabury and then sat still, while the simple, melancholy song floated down through the blue air. When it ceased, he waited a little, looking up. As the horn did not sing again, he drove on without comment.

At last, beyond a sharp turn in the road, the monastery came into view; acres of slate roof, of many heights and pitches, turrets and steep slopes. The terrifying white mountain crags overhung it from behind, and the green beech wood lay all about its walls. The sunlight blazing down upon that mothering roof showed ruined patches: the Government could not afford to keep such a wilderness of leading in repair.

The monastery, superb and solitary among the lonely mountains, was after 175 all a destination: brought Seabury's party down into man's world again, though it was the world of the past. They began to chatter foolishly, after hours of silent reflection. Mrs. Allison wished to see the kitchen of the Carthusians, and the chapel, but she thought Gabrielle should stay in the car. Madame de Couçy insisted that she was not tired: she would walk about the stone courtyard while the other two went into the monastery.

Except for a one-armed guard in uniform, the great court was empty. Herbs and little creeping plants grew between the cobblestones. The three walked toward the great open well and leaned against the stone wall that encircled it, looking down into its wide mouth. The hewn blocks of the coping were moss-grown, and there was water at the bottom. Madame de Couçy slipped a little mirror from her handbag and threw a sunbeam down into the stone-lined well. That yellow ray seemed to waken the black water at the bottom: little ripples stirred over the surface. She said nothing, but she smiled as she threw the gold plaque over the water and the wet moss of the lower coping. Chetty and Seabury left her there. When he glanced back, just before they disappeared into the labyrinth of buildings, she was still looking down into the well and playing with her little reflector, a faintly contemptuous smile on her lips.

After nearly two hours at the monastery the party started homeward. Seabury told the driver to regulate his speed so that they would see the last light on the mountains before they reached the hotel.

The return trip was ill-starred: they narrowly escaped a serious accident. As they rounded one of those sharp curves, with a steep wall on their right and an open gulf on the left, the chauffeur was confronted by a small car with two women, crossing the road just in front of him. To avoid throwing them over the precipice he ran sharply to the right, grazing the rock wall until he could bring his car to a stop. His passengers were thrown violently forward over the driver's seat. The light car had been on the wrong side of the road, and had attempted to cross on hearing the Savoyard's horn. His nerve and quickness had brought every one off alive, at least.

Immediately the two women from the other car sprang out and ran up to Seabury with shrill protestations; they were very careful drivers, had run this car twelve thousand miles and never had an accident, etc. They were Americans; bobbed, hatless, clad in dirty white knickers and sweaters. They addressed each other as "Marge" and "Jim." Seabury's forehead was bleeding: they repeatedly offered to plaster it up for him.

The Savoyard was in the road, working with his mudguard and his front wheel. Madame de Couçy was lying back in her seat, pale, her eyes closed, something very wrong with her breathing. Mrs. Allison was fanning her with Seabury's hat. The two girls who had caused all the trouble had lit cigarettes and were swaggering about with their hands in their trousers pockets, giving advice to the driver about his wheel. The Savoyard never lifted his eyes. He had not spoken since he ran his car into the wall. The sharp voices, knowingly ordering him to "*regardez, attendez,*" did not pierce his silence or his contempt. Seabury paid no attention to them because he was alarmed about Madame de Couçy, who looked desperately ill. She ought to lie down, he felt sure, but there was no place to put her—the road was cut along the face of a cliff for a long way back. Chetty had aromatic ammonia in her handbag; she persuaded Gabrielle to take it from the bottle, as they had no cup. While Seabury was leaning over her she opened her eyes and said distinctly:

"I think I am not hurt . . . faintness, a little palpitation. If you could get those creatures away . . . "

He sprang off the running-board and drew the two intruders aside. He addressed them; first politely, then forcibly. Their reply was impertinent, but they got into their dirty little car and went. The Savoyard was left in peace; the situation was simplified. Three elderly people had been badly shaken up and bruised, but the brief submersion in frightfulness was over. At last the driver said he could get his car home safely.

During the rest of the drive Madame de Couçy seemed quite restored. Her colour was not good, but her self-control was admirable.

"You must let me give that boy something on my own account, Seabury. Oh, I know you will be generous with him! But I feel a personal interest. He took a risk, and he took the right one. He couldn't run the chance of knocking two women over a precipice. They happened to be worth nobody's consideration, but that doesn't alter the code."

"Such an afternoon to put you through!" Seabury groaned.

"It was natural, wasn't it, after such a morning? After one has been *exaltée*, there usually comes a shock. Oh, I don't mean the bruises we got! I mean the white breeches." Gabrielle laughed, her good laugh, with no malice in it. She put her hand on his shoulder. "How ever did you manage to dispose of them so quickly?"

When the car stopped before the hotel, Madame de Couçy put a tiny card case into the driver's hand with a smile and a word. But when she tried to rise from the seat, she sank back. Seabury and the Savoyard lifted her out, carried her into the hotel and up the lift, into her own chamber. As they placed her on the bed, Seabury said he would call a doctor. Madame de Couçy opened her eyes and spoke firmly:

"That is not necessary. Chetty knows what to do for me. I shall be myself to-morrow. Thank you both, thank you."

Outside the chamber door Seabury asked Mrs. Allison whether he should telephone for Doctor Françon.

"I think not. A new person would only disturb her. I have all the remedies 190 her own doctor gave me for these attacks. Quiet is the most important thing, really."

* * *

The next morning Seabury was awakened very early, something before six o'-clock, by the buzz of his telephone. Mrs. Allison spoke, asking in a low voice if he would come to their apartment as soon as possible. He dressed rapidly. The lift was not yet running, so he went up two flights of stairs and rang at their door. Cherry Beamish, in her dressing-gown, admitted him. From her face he knew, at once,—though her smile was almost radiant as she took his hand.

"Yes, it is over for her, poor dear," she said softly. "It must have happened in her sleep. I was with her until after midnight. When I went in again, a little after five, I found her just as I want you to see her now; before her maid comes, before anyone has been informed."

She led him on tiptoe into Gabrielle's chamber. The first shafts of the morning sunlight slanted through the Venetian blinds. A blue dressing-gown hung on a tall chair beside the bed, blue slippers beneath it. Gabrielle lay on her back, her eyes closed. The face that had outfaced so many changes of fortune had no longer need to muffle itself in furs, to shrink away from curious eyes, or harden itself into scorn. It lay on the pillow regal, calm, victorious,—like an open confession.

Seabury stood for a moment looking down at her. Then he went to the window and peered out through the open slats at the sun, come at last over the mountains into a sky that had long been blue: the same mountains they were driving among yesterday.

Presently Cherry Beamish spoke to him. She pointed to the hand that lay 195 on the turned-back sheet. "See how changed her hands are, like those of a young woman. She forgot to take off her rings last night, or she was too tired. Yes, dear, you needed a long rest. And now you are with your own kind."

"I feel that, too, Chetty. She is with them. All is well. Thank you for letting me come." He stooped for a moment over the hand that had been gracious to his youth. They went out into the salon, carefully closing the door behind them.

"Now, my dear, stay here, with her. I will go to the management, and I will arrange all that must be done."

Some hours later, after he had gone through the formalities required by French law, Seabury encountered the three journalists in front of the hotel.

* * *

Next morning the great man from the Riviera to whom Seabury had telegraphed came in person, his car laden with flowers from his conservatories. He stood on the platform at the railway station, his white head uncovered, all the while that the box containing Gabrielle Longstreet's coffin was being carried across and put on the express. Then he shook Seabury's hand in farewell, and bent gallantly over Chetty's. Seabury and Chetty were going to Paris on that same express.

After her illness two years ago Gabrielle de Couçy had bought a lot *à perpé-* 200 *tuité* in Père-Lachaise. That was rather a fashion then: Adelina Patti, Sarah Bernhardt, and other ladies who had once held a place in the world made the same choice.

Talking about the Text

1. Of what did Gabrielle's beauty consist in her heyday? Is she still beautiful during the time of her stay at the Hotel Splendide?
2. How do we react to the old beauty's low estimate of the post–World War I era?

Writing about the Text

1. Write about the main character in "The Old Beauty." In particular, describe how you as a reader respond to her, as she is depicted.
2. The world represented in "The Old Beauty" is of the distant past. Write a description of a place or setting you know that contains echoes and memories of the recent or distant past.

Linking the Text to Other Texts

1. In a March 29, 1931, interview in the *San Francisco Chronicle*, Cather said: "I like my stories to be read because people like them. I didn't want to be 'assigned reading' for university classes, a duty, a target for information vampires." Compare her comments on university classes with those by Flannery O'Connor (p. 389). What do they seem to dislike the most? Write about a course you had in high school or college in which Cather's and O'Connor's criticisms make sense.
2. Using a number of Cather stories, explain what particular obstacles women face in relation to physical appearances.

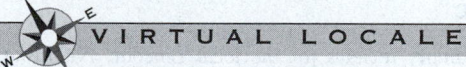
VIRTUAL LOCALE

The Willa Cather Archive. The online component of the Cather Project, http://www.cather.unl.edu, created by the Department of English at the University of Nebraska–Lincoln, is devoted to research and teaching that focuses on Cather's life and work. The site offers a vast array of resources for additional research on Cather, including transcripts of interviews from 1897 to 1940, online texts of Cather's writing (scholarly editions, first editions, short fiction, nonfiction, journalism, speeches, and letters), photos, biographical information, recent scholarship on Cather, and teaching resources.

✦ COMMENTARY

Willa Cather on Writing

The excerpts below come from the various Cather-related materials compiled in Willa Cather in Person: Interviews, Speeches, and Letters, *selected and edited by L. Brent Bohlke (Lincoln: University of Nebraska Press, 1986).*

On the craft of writing, from an interview in New York World, *April 19, 1925 (reprinted in* Nebraska State Journal, *April 25, 1925)*

I like horses better than automobiles, and I think fewer and better books would be a great improvement. I think it a great misfortune for every one to have the chance to write—to have a chance to read, for that matter. A little culture makes lazy handiwork, and handiwork is a beautiful education in itself, and something real. Good carpentry, good weaving, all the handicrafts were much sounder forms of education than what the people are getting now.

One sad feature of modern education is that the hand is so little trained among the people who have to earn their daily bread, and the head so superficially and poorly educated. . . . I am afraid we are only going to become more and more mechanical.

Death Comes for the Archbishop *from a March 29, 1931, interview in the* San Francisco Chronicle

I hope the readers of that story have enjoyed reading it as much as I enjoyed writing it. I like my stories to be read because people like them. I didn't want to be "assigned reading" for university classes, a duty, a target for information vampires. Why should anyone try to teach contemporary literature anyway? Stories are to be read. "Sincerity" again. The sincerity of feeling that is possible between a writer and a reader is one of the finest things I know.

✦ COMMENTARY

Willa Cather the Critic

During her college years, Cather wrote many reviews for the local Lincoln, Nebraska, newspaper and for her college newspaper as well. What follows is part of an essay about Hamlet *that she wrote for a University of Nebraska English class. Her professor liked it so much he sent it to be published. Cather was not yet eighteen when it appeared, her first published writing.*

From "Shakespeare and Hamlet*"* (1891)

The cause for the various current opinions upon the character of Hamlet, and the root of many of the dissensions and controversies is that many of the best

A 1936 portrait of Cather by American writer and photographer Carl Van Vechten, well-known for promoting notable figures of the Harlem Renaissance, including Langston Hughes.

scholars and critics try to make of Hamlet a much grander, more learned and more intellectual personage than the author of the play ever intended him to be. I don't think Shakespeare had any definite purpose even in writing *Hamlet*. It was not like him to plan a play which should be a puzzle for all time to come. He probably read the legend and felt sorry for the young prince, and as an expression of his sympathy wrote about him. He probably had no intention of giving the drama any more of himself than he gave to any other of his plays. The Danish prince had nothing in common with him except that both were misunderstood, and both suffered. He gradually grew into the play as he wrote it, without any special reason. Perhaps outside matters bore more heavily upon him than usual. It may be his feeling and individuality were wrought up intensely, and crept out into the play which he happened to be writing.

Hamlet was certainly not the philosopher, the intellectual monstrosity which he is often represented to be. He was not even the strong, broad-minded, world-worn statesman which Edwin Booth makes him. In years, Hamlet was but a boy who pounded at Virgil down at the old university at Wittenberg, and wrote love letters and bad verses to Ophelia. He was galloping about the court yard on Yorick's back only a few years ago. We are given no glimpse of his personal character before his great sorrow came upon him, but even through it some of his old boyish habits cling to him. His illustration of this is very prominent in the unsophisticated way in which, after his first meeting with the ghost, he pulls out his note book to note the fact that, "one may smile and smile and be a villain." Had Hamlet known the world a little better, or had he been a few years older, he would not have thought it necessary to make a note of that fact every time he was brought to a realization of it, or all Denmark could not have furnished him tablets enough. One can almost imagine the contents of that note book. Notes on the old classics, made at Wittenberg, raptures on everything in nature from the moon to roses, and vague effusions respecting his passion for Ophelia.

In the first act, his soliloquy is one of the most simple, touching passages in literature. His cry, "Frailty, thy name is woman!" is no cynical observation on the daughter of Eve. A cynic would have couched the thought in very different language, and would have somewhat enjoyed saying it. This is a boy's first glimpse of a thing that he shudders at. It is no light matter to him that women are fickle: his mother is a woman, and Ophelia is one. His, "Oh Soul! a beast that wants discourse of reason would have mourned longer," is no rhetorical flourish; it is positively piteous. During the first act, Hamlet learned many bitter lessons from experience, his best, perhaps his only teacher. But his experience also drove him mad and killed him. Suffering, though it embittered Hamlet's nature, could not poison it. In the second and third acts, his replies to fawning, scraping Rosencrantz and Guildenstern are certainly cynical. It is the tenderest, deepest feeling that, when once it is embittered, becomes most acrid. That man who has never hoped, never dreamed, never loved, never suffered, is never a cynic. But in the scene with the queen, Hamlet forgets his cynicism and becomes Gertrude's son again.

Hamlet had not the first element of the intellectual or of the philosophical in him. He was never able for a moment to lay aside that intense personality of him and view himself as one individual of a great species, a type of a race. He could not see Gertrude merely as a woman, committing an error common to women of her day, but always as "My mother." That the prince should have done much logical reasoning during that period of his life which the play covers, is improbable. Throughout the entire play he was under an intense nervous strain; his feelings were wrought up to the highest possible pitch. Logical reasoning and intense feeling are directly antagonistic. The Egyptian priests knew this when they demanded of a candidate that he first sacrifice his passions and his affections. A man who would be born unto knowledge must indeed become dead to the world. None of his great soliloquies are premeditated; all are perfectly spontaneous. The famous "to be, or not to be," does not look toward a universal affirmation; it is merely a chance remark. It is not very likely that at that particular time Hamlet would undertake a discussion of human destiny. He had at length determined upon a course by which to touch the king's conscience; but as he reflected upon the consequence, the confusion, the turmoil, the exposure of his mother's guilt, the dishonor to the state, he was almost tempted to take the easy way out of it, and—rest. Then the question came to him, as it has come to many another. If it is applicable to anyone else, I suppose Hamlet would not object; but at that particular moment he was thinking entirely too much about my Lord Hamlet to be devoting very much attention to humanity in general.

He is a poor philosopher, for he never reasons, he only suffers. He has premises, hundreds of them, and he jumps from major to minor, and from minor back to major, but he stops there; [the] syllogism ends with his premise; he never draws a conclusion. From the first act to the last, he makes but one absolute statement, one assertion of whose truth he is absolutely sure. That he makes when leaping into the grave of his loved Ophelia throwing his arms above his head, at Laertes, his white face glaring, he cries, "This is I, Hamlet the Dane!" In the last act, he even doubts his identity; he doubts everything. His dying words, "the rest is silence," are wonderfully in keeping with his character.

If we refuse to recognize intellect as the cause of that wonderful strength of Hamlet's, and lay it aside, we must substitute something, for we must acknowledge with Polonius, "Though this be madness, yet there is method in't." The keynote of Hamlet's character is merely this: He was very sensitive, he felt intensely, and he suffered more than other people, that was all. The intellectual school insist upon putting props under Hamlet because they do not understand him; for the first instinct of the intellect is to analyze, and you can only sympathize with Hamlet. They attempt to see in his every word a "means" to produce certain "dramatic effects," to account for his every act, when in reality they cannot account for them any more than Hamlet could. Goethe, more aspiring than the rest, but with better sense than most of them, brings his great German capacity to bear upon the subject, and in *Wilhelm Meister* mildly suggests that to rectify this shocking lack of art the whole plot be changed, the whole play be revolutionized, so that every cause may have its perceptible effect and every effect its perceptible cause. He advises, in short, that *Hamlet* be made dramatic! The intellectual school realize the importance of the play, but they never quite like it; they always prefer *Macbeth*, claiming that there is more art in it. This may be so; in *Hamlet* certainly we have "more matter with less art." Sometimes I wonder if Shakespeare would have quite known what was meant, if art, or the art purposes in his plays, had been mentioned to him. The emotional and intentional plane of life is infinitely higher than the intellectual. It is the source of every great purpose, of every exalted aim. It is not attained by study; it is not seen through a telescope, nor reached by mastering the pages of a Latin grammar. This upper world is only trodden by those who have reached it through suffering. Some men are born in it, and we call them geniuses. Some attain, but they must travel the old path to paradise, which leads down through hell. What is conceived and written in this rare atmosphere can be appreciated, estimated or judged only by men who breathe the same air.

Hamlet has been accorded the place of the greatest masterpiece of the greatest master, not by literary critics, but by popular taste. The critics themselves, preferring other of Shakespeare's plays, would spend little enough time on it were it not for the constant demand of the public. On the boards it has been presented oftener, and more successfully than any other Shakespearean drama. In the schools and colleges it is now indispensable, and by the great "unpopular public" it is more read than any other play in the English language. You will find a worn, marked copy in the office of almost every country doctor, lawyer or tradesman. Among the everyday men of the everyday world *Hamlet*, by a broad sort of metonymy, has come to mean Shakespeare. The play is a living, vital force in a living age, part of the spiritual life of the nineteenth century. The critics have been forced to study it. This they do from a wholly intellectual standpoint, and so see in it only the intellectual. The light streaming in through the stained glass of a cathedral window turns even the marble virgin's face to the color of blood. The critics have no other light than the intellectual, for they have declared that the emotions and intentions are not to be trusted. The altar lights they have called *ignis fatui*, and have put them out. They analyze the play in a scientific manner, and do it most skilfully. They take a microscope and see all the beauty of the cell organization, a field which men of the emotional school never enter. They say, "This caused life," or "This resulted from life," but life they never find. They think they have all, and indeed they have much; the massive framework, the delicate nerve structure, and all the perfectly formed organism upon which the eye of the anatomist loves to dwell. But they never feel the hot blood riot in the pulses, nor hear the great heartbeat. That is the one great joy which belongs exclusively to those of us who are unlearned, unlettered, to those of us who have nothing else. The critics laugh at us and say, of course there is emotion in *Hamlet*, but it is merely one of the primary elements of the play, that we have never advanced far enough to appreciate the more finished art. So be it. We can answer them only as an Indian prince answered an English astronomer when reproved for sun worshiping. The old prince patiently heard the man of science through and then lifted his eyes toward the murky London skies, dull and dark with the smoke of traffic and of commerce, and said: "Oh, my Lord, if you could but see the sun."

So much for the critic and for the intellectual students of literature. To a young author with his first book under his arm, who has had a great truth to tell, and has told it ill, they seem very strong and very terrible, these scribes and pharisees, who are so spotless in the observance of literary law, and the forms of their religions. Still, they are not so strong as they appear. They did their worst to Keats, and they only killed his body. They tried to change him, to polish him, to conventionalize him, and when he repulsed them and went his own way, they hated him as the Thracian maiden hated Orpheus. But their darts were powerless so long as the world stood spellbound at his music. So they raised a great cry through the *Edinburgh Review*, and drowned the music's voice with their clamor. Drunken with the brutal rites of their god, they rushed upon him and tore him limb from limb, and stained with his blood the rocks that were moved and melted by his music. But the lyre by chance fell into a great river, and it floated on past the old cities and the vineyards and the olive-crowned hills, silencing the nightingales and waking the soft Italian night with its music. And the children playing under the myrtle trees listened and wondered, and ceased playing, and were children no more. And the women who had trodden the wine press all day heard wearily, and their life seemed not so hard and they were less ashamed, and the red upon their feet seemed not so much like blood as it had seemed yesterday. Yet they murmured, "We will tread the press no more, we will be better tomorrow." And the shepherds far away on the hills, keeping their flocks by night, heard it, and they arose and their hearts grew strong and they whispered, "It is the annunciation; a new Christ comes." Then the lyre floated on, until Zeus, the son of Kronos, took it and placed it among the stars, where it lies,

> borne darkly, fearfully, afar;
> Whilst shining through the utmost veil of heaven[1]
> The soul of Adonais like a star
> Beacons from the abode where the Eternal are!

And the Thracians say, "We, put it there." So it is with all literature which reaches the hearts of the people, where it finds its noblest, surest immortality. The critics may kill the author, they may attack his productions and rend their structure to pieces, and declare the style imperfect; but the soul they never touch, for they have never reached it; the soul they never kill, for they have never seen it.

The position in which Hamlet was placed would not have been so terrible to anyone else. It would have been a very simple matter to Laertes indeed when

---

[1] The line is actually: "Whilst burning through the inmost veil of heaven" (*Adonais*, l. 439). [Cather's note]

Polonius was killed, and Ophelia driven mad. Laertes was not much burdened by a sense of filial or of fraternal obligation. He tried to throttle Hamlet, and then went through the duel more as a matter of form than anything else. It is not often that a northern country produces such a character as Hamlet. He would have been more natural, perhaps, as a lad of Venice or of Verona. To him it seemed that he was born for one end, to avenge his father. Foreign and repugnant as the touch [task?] was to his nature, he took it upon him as a sacred mission, a call from God, and broke his great heart upon it. He says himself,

> The time is out of joint; O cursed spite
> That I was ever ever born to set it right.[2]

Starting Points for Further Research: Willa Cather

- **Edition:** Willa Cather. *Novels and Stories, 1905–1918*. East Rutherford: Penguin Putnam, 1999.
- **Biography:** Sharon O'Brien. *Willa Cather: The Emerging Voice*. Cambridge: Harvard University Press, 1997.
- **Critical Essay:** Melissa Ryan. "The Enclosure of America: Civilization and Confinement in Willa Cather's *O Pioneers!*" *American Literature: A Journal of Literary History, Criticism, and Bibliography* (2003): 275–303.

[2]Correctly: "That ever I was born to set it right" (I. v. 189–190). [Cather's note]

CHAPTER

6

Charles Baxter

Charles Baxter, 1997.

Charles Baxter (b. 1947) identifies himself as a midwestern writer, and this strong regional identity is one characteristic that helps make his work special. His stories are almost always set in the Midwest, most often Michigan, with his most frequent setting the fictional small town of Five Oaks, though the real Ann Arbor and Detroit also appear. Saul Bernstein of "Saul and Patsy Are Pregnant," having chosen to relocate from Baltimore to Five Oaks, seems engaged in a love-hate relationship with the small-town Midwest; love or hate, he is constantly calling attention to his surroundings and interacting with them. Another part of Baxter's midwestern identity is the strong connection he feels with some of the best-known midwestern writers of the past—Sherwood Anderson, F. Scott Fitzgerald, and Willa Cather. Baxter is engaged with the expressive possibilities of midwesterners, people who (with the exception of outsiders like Saul) are not normally known for their expressiveness. For Baxter, such characters reveal unsuspected depths of feeling, the capacity for surprising actions, and an appreciation for the sudden strangeness of life. (For Baxter's comments on being a midwestern

234

writer, see "Literary Locale: Baxter's Michigan and the Mystery of the Mid-west" on p. 236.)

Baxter's midwestern identity comes naturally. He was born in Minneapolis and graduated from Macalester College in St. Paul, where he was editor of the literary magazine. He earned a Ph.D. in English at the State University of New York at Buffalo in 1974. He has taught at Wayne State University in Detroit and at the University of Michigan in Ann Arbor, where he has also headed the Master of Fine Arts program. He recently moved back to Minneapolis, his home-town, to teach creative writing at the University of Minnesota.

Baxter began his writing career as a poet, publishing two volumes by the time he finished his Ph.D. After struggling fruitlessly for three years to continue with his poetry, he turned his energy to fiction, spending a long apprenticeship cultivating his skills. Over the next six years he produced three failed novels, which he called "terrible," but he was able to cull some of the material for short stories. Since then, he has published four volumes of stories and three novels; the second, *Feast of Love*, was a National Book Award finalist in 2000. In 1997 he published a collection of essays, *Burning Down the House: Essays on Fiction*.

In Baxter's fiction, the ordinary world gets "defamiliarized," made unordinary in one way or other. With defamiliarization, characters see the same old world with new eyes. This can happen when the protagonist encounters a stranger, finds himself or herself in a new situation, or is simply endowed with an inquiring, un-conventional, "anxiety-prone" turn of mind. Additionally, in many stories Baxter plays with the boundaries of conventional reality. Thus in one story, "Gryphon," a key moment occurs when a character produces Tarot cards and begins telling fortunes. A mysterious albino deer shows up at the end of "Saul and Patsy Are Pregnant." Baxter says he likes to entertain the idea, cautiously, that nonhuman things—in nature and elsewhere in our world—have a life and sometimes an intelligence of their own; they can be seen as "half-sentient."

In an interview, Baxter speaks of his stories as "character-driven." He expands on this by saying writers need to create situations where their characters "will get into interesting trouble, where they will make interesting mistakes that they try to take responsibility for." The Baxter characters who get into this kind of trouble are often, but not always, men who complicate their lives by sudden impulse or strange decisions. Unlike Baxter's men, who seem like restless searchers, his women tend to be sensible, naturally content and uncomplicated, generally optimistic, somehow wiser about living than their male counterparts, though there are exceptions. To be sure, the men have their own virtues—with inquiring souls, for instance, they sometimes have a feel for the deeper, darker aspects of life. Sometimes it seems as if the men and women marvelously complement each other.

Like many successful writers, Baxter has regular work habits, writing from eight to twelve every morning. He values regularity in his life, saying, "I think if you are somewhat compulsive or habitual in your ordinary life, it gives you some latitude to be wild in your creative work." Baxter claims his favorite volume among his short stories is *A Relative Stranger*, the source of two of the four stories in this chapter.

CHARLES BAXTER TIMELINE

1947	Charles Baxter born in St. Paul, Minnesota.
1969	Graduates from Macalester College, St. Paul; teaches fourth grade, Pinconning, Michigan.
1974	Awarded Ph.D. in English, State University of New York at Buffalo.
1974	Starts teaching at Wayne State University, Detroit.
1976	Marries Martha Ann Hauser.
1984	Publishes *Harmony of the World* (short stories).
1985	Publishes *Through the Safety Net* (short stories).
1987	Publishes *First Light* (novel).
1988	Begins teaching at University of Michigan.
1989	Publishes *Imaginary Paintings* (poetry).
1990	Publishes *A Relative Stranger* (short stories).
1993	Publishes *Shadow Play* (novel).
1997	Publishes *Believers* (novella and short stories).
1997	Publishes *Burning Down the House* (essays on fiction).
1997	Receives Academy Award in Literature, American Academy of Arts and Letters.
2000	Publishes *The Feast of Love* (novel); finalist for National Book Award in Fiction.
2003	Assumes Edelstein-Keller Distinguished Chair in Creative Writing, University of Minnesota.
2003	Publishes *Saul and Patsy* (novel).

 L I T E R A R Y   L O C A L E

Baxter's Michigan and the Mystery of the Midwest. Born and raised in the St. Paul-Minneapolis area, Charles Baxter spent most of his adult life in Michigan, teaching first at Wayne State University in Detroit and then later at the University of Michigan in Ann Arbor. He recently moved back to Minneapolis and now teaches at the University of Minnesota. Given his familiarity with the Midwest, it

Midwestern United States.

comes as no surprise that much of his writing is set there, mostly in his fictional town of Five Oaks, Michigan. As he himself put it in a 1999 *Ploughshares* magazine profile, "There's something about the restriction, the glamour of the finality here, that fascinates me." He has often been called a "midwestern writer," both by himself and by journalists and critics, although more often than not, when other people use the term, what it means

(continued)

is left vague. Consequently, the label is technically accurate but can also bring to mind a range of stereotypical, unflattering connotations—that the flat plains of the midwestern landscape are boring and oppressive in their vastness and quietness, that the region is always politically conservative, and that in turn, the people living there are simple or bland and perhaps not worthy of story-telling. Baxter is well aware of these common, limited conceptions, and in his interviews, he has enjoyed dispelling the assumptions underlying them by explaining why and how the Midwest continues to intrigue him and inform his writing. In an August 7, 1997, *Atlantic Monthly* interview, Baxter explained his fascination in this way:

> Here I am, a Midwestern writer in a postmodern age. That's supposed to be impossible. We're all supposed to be citizens of a global village. So what if I say that it still matters if you live in Minnesota or Michigan or North Dakota? If we really lived in a global village, people would be moving uncomplainingly to the Dakotas. But we don't live in any such village, and people haven't been moving to North Dakota in great numbers. They don't have the discipline for it. Where you live shapes you. Midwesterners are a curious breed: laconic but talkative, forcibly modest. If it occurs to them, people apologize for living here. The lack of variety in the landscape here is our koan. You don't have the infinities of the oceans or the majesty of the Rockies or the historical mania and talkiness of the South or the beauties and pathologies of New England or the energies of the great cities, except in Chicago. You just have rolling fields and nondescript cities. Still, it's all lovable and mysterious. Alice Munro has her little parcel of Ontario. I have Michigan.

In the same interview, Baxter goes to say that there is a particularity to the mysteriousness of the Midwest that makes it unique: "Mystery can be found anywhere, but there is a quality in the Midwest having to do both with the blandness of the landscape and the ways in which people here don't always talk about what's on their minds. The combination of those two things creates an interesting field of vision for writers. It's simply not an area that gives up its secrets easily. I would put Midwestern writers such as Sherwood Anderson, F. Scott Fitzgerald, and Willa Cather against those of almost any area—except maybe the South—for the depth of their writing. If you write about the Midwest, you have to dig in order to find what motivates the characters you're writing about, the people you observe."

STORIES BY CHARLES BAXTER

Shelter
(1989)

Cooper had stopped at a red light on his way to work and was adjusting the dial on his radio when he looked up and saw a man in a filthy brown corduroy suit and a three-day growth of beard staring in through the front windshield and picking with his fingernails at Cooper's windshield wiper. Whenever Cooper had seen this man before, on various Ann Arbor street corners, he had felt a wave of uneasiness and unpleasant compassion. Rolling down the window and leaning out, Cooper said, "Wait a minute there. Just wait a minute. If you get out of this intersection and over to that sidewalk, I'll be with you in a minute"—the man stared at him—"*I'll have something for you.*"

Cooper parked his car at a meter two blocks up, and when he returned, the man in the corduroy suit was standing under a silver maple tree, rubbing his back against the bark.

"Didn't think you'd come back," the man said, glancing at Cooper. His hair fell over the top of his head in every direction.

"How do you do?" Cooper held his hand out, but the man—who seemed rather old, close up—didn't take it. "I'm Cooper." The man smelled of everything, a bit like a municipal dump. Cooper tried not to notice it.

"It doesn't matter who I am," the man said, standing unsteadily. "I don't care   5
who I am. It's not worth anybody thinking about it." He looked up at the sky and began to pick at his coat sleeve.

"What's your name?" Cooper asked softly. "Tell me your name, please."

The old man's expression changed. He stared at the blue sky, perfectly empty of clouds, and after a moment said, "My mother used to call me James."

"Good. Well, then, how do you do, James?" The man looked dubiously at his own hand, then reached over and shook. "Would you like something to eat?"

"I like sandwiches," the man said.

"Well, then," Cooper said, "that's what we'll get you."   10

As they went down the sidewalk, the man stumbled into the side of a bench at a bus stop and almost tripped over a fire hydrant. He had a splay-footed walk, as if one of his legs had once been broken. Cooper began to pilot him by touching him on his back.

"Would you like to hear a bit of the Gospels?" the man asked.

"All right. Sure."

He stopped and held on to a light pole. "This is the fourth book of the Gospels. Jesus is speaking. He says, 'I will not leave you desolate; I will come to you. Yet a little while, and the world will see me no more, but you will see me; because I live, you will live also.' That's from John," the man said. They were outside the Ann Arbor Diner, a neon-and-chrome Art Deco hamburger joint three blocks down from the university campus. "There's more," the old man said, "but I don't remember it."

"Wait here," Cooper said. "I'm going to get you a sandwich."   15

The man was looking uncertainly at his lapel, fingering a funguslike spot.

"James!" Cooper said loudly. "Promise me you won't go away!"

The man nodded.

When Cooper came out again with a bag of french fries, a carton of milk, and a hamburger, the man had moved down the street and was leaning against the plate-glass window of a seafood restaurant with his hands covering his face. "James!" Cooper said. "Here's your meal." He held out the bag.

"Thank you." When the man removed his hands from his face, Cooper saw   20
in his eyes a moment of complete lucidity and sanity, a glance that took in the street and himself, made a judgment about them all, and quickly withdrew from any engagement with them. He took the hamburger out of its wrapping, studied it for a moment, and then bit into it. As he ate, he gazed toward the horizon.

"I have to go to work now," Cooper said.

The man glanced at him, nodded again, and turned his face away.

* * *

"What are we going to do?" Cooper said to his wife. They were lying in bed at sunrise, when they liked to talk. His hand was on her thigh and was caressing it absently and familiarly. "What are we going to do about these characters? They're on the street corners. Every month there are more of them. Kids, men, women, everybody. It's a horde. They're sleeping in the arcade, and they're pushing those terrible grocery carts around with all their worldly belongings, and it makes me nuts to watch them. I don't know what I'm going to do, Christine, but whatever it is, I have to do it." With his other hand, he rubbed his eyes. "I dream about them."

"You're such a good person," she said sleepily. Her hand brushed over him. "I've noticed that about you."

"No, that's wrong," Cooper said. "This has nothing to do with good. Virtue   25 doesn't interest me. What this is about is not feeling crazy when I see those people."

"So what's your plan?"

He rose halfway out of bed and looked out the back window at the treehouse he had started for Alexander, their seven-year-old. Dawn was breaking, and the light came in through the slats of the blinds and fell in strips over him.

When he didn't say anything, she said, "I was just thinking. When I first met you, before you dropped out of law school, you always used to have your shirts laundered, with starch, and I remember the neat creases in your trouser legs, from somebody ironing them. You smelled of after-shave in those days. Sexually, you were ambitious. You took notes slowly. Fastidious penmanship. I like you better now."

"I remember," he said. "It was a lecture on proximate cause."

"No," she said. "It was contribution and indemnification."   30

"Whatever."

He took her hand and led her to the bathroom. Every morning Cooper and his wife showered together. He called it soul-showering. He had picked up the phrase from a previous girlfriend, though he had never told Christine that. Cooper had told his wife that by the time they were thirty they would probably not want to do this anymore, but they were both now twenty-eight, and she still seemed to like it.

Under the sputter of the water, Christine brushed some soap out of her eyes and said, "Cooper, were you ever a street person?"

"No."

"Smoke a lot of dope in high school?"   35

"No."

"I bet you drank a lot once." She was an assistant prosecutor in the district attorney's office and sometimes brought her professional habits home. "You tapped kegs and lay out on the lawns and howled at the sorority girls."

"Sometimes I did that," he said. He was soaping her back. She had wide flaring shoulders from all the swimming she had done, and the soap and water flowed down toward her waist in a pattern of V's. "I did all those things," he said, "but I never became that kind of person. What's your point?"

She turned around and faced him, the full display of her smile. "I think you're a latent vagrant," she said.

"But I'm not," he said. "I'm here. I have a job. *This* is where I am. I'm a fa-   40 ther. How can you say that?"

"Do I love you?" she asked, water pouring over her face. "Stay with me."   40
"Well, sure," he said. "That's my plan."

* * *

The second one he decided to do something about was standing out of the hot summer sun in the shade of a large catalpa tree near a corner newsstand. This one was holding what seemed to be a laundry sack with the words AMERICAN LINEN SUPPLY stenciled on it. She was wearing light summer clothes—a Hawaiian shirt showing a palm tree against a bloody splash of sunset, and a pair of light cotton trousers, and red Converse tennis shoes—and she stood reading a paper-back, beads of sweat falling off her face onto the pages.

This time Cooper went first to a fast-food restaurant, bought the hamburger, french fries, and milk, and then came back.

"I brought something for you," Cooper said, walking to the reading woman.   45
"I brought you some lunch." He held out a bag. "I've seen you out here on the streets many times."

"Thank you," the woman said, taking the bag. She opened it, looked inside, and sniffed appreciatively.

"Are you homeless?" Cooper asked.

"They have a place where you can go," the woman said. She put down the bag and looked at Cooper. "My name's Estelle," she said. "But we don't have to talk."

"Oh, that's all right. If you want. Where's this shelter?"

"Over there." The woman gestured with a french fry she had picked out.   50
She lifted the bag and began to eat. Cooper looked down at the book and saw that it was in a foreign language. The cover had fallen off. He asked her about it.

"Oh, that?" she said. She spoke with her mouth full of food, and Cooper felt a moment of superiority about her bad manners. "It's about women—what happens to women in this world. It's in French. I used to be Canadian. My mother taught me French."

Cooper stood uncomfortably. He took a key ring out of his pocket and twirled it around his index finger. "So what happens to women in this world?"

"What *doesn't?*" the woman said. "Everything happens. It's terrible but sometimes it's all right, and, besides, you get used to it."

"You seem so normal," Cooper said. "How come you're out here?"

The woman straightened up and looked at him. "My mind's not quite right,"   55
she said, scratching an eyelid. "Mostly it is but sometimes it isn't. They messed up my medication and one thing led to another and here I am. I'm not com-plaining. I don't have a bad life."

Cooper wanted to say that she *did* have a bad life, but stopped himself.

"If you want to help people," the woman said, "you should go to the shelter. They need volunteers. People to clean up. You could get rid of your guilt over there, mopping the floors."

"What guilt?" he asked.

"All men are guilty," she said. She was chewing but had put her bag of food on the ground and was staring hard and directly into Cooper's face. He turned toward the street. When he looked at the cars, everyone heading somewhere with a kind of fierce intentionality, braking hard at red lights and peeling rubber at the green, he felt as though he had been pushed out of his own life.

"You're still here," the woman said. "What do you want?"   60

"I was about to leave." He was surprised by how rude she was.

"I don't think you've ever seen the Rocky Mountains or even the Swiss Alps, for that matter," the woman said, bending down to inspect something close to the sidewalk.

"No, you're right. I haven't traveled much."

"We're not going to kiss, if that's what you think," the woman said, still bent over. Now she straightened up again, glanced at him, and looked away.

"No," Cooper said. "I just wanted to give you a meal."   65

"Yes, thank you," the woman said. "And now you have to go."

"I was . . . I *was* going to go."

"I don't want to talk to you anymore," the woman said. "It's nothing against you personally, but talking to men just tires me out terribly and drains me of all my strength. Thank you very much, and goodbye." She sat down again and opened up her paperback. She took some more french fries out of the sack and began to eat as she read.

* * *

"They're polite," Cooper said, lying next to his wife. "They're polite, but they aren't nice."

"Nice? Nice? Jesus, Cooper, I prosecute rapists! Why should they be nice?   70
They'd be crazy to be nice. Who cares about nice except you? This is the 1980s, Cooper. Get real."

He rolled over in bed and put his hand on her hip. "All right," he said.

They lay together for a while, listening to Alexander snoring in his bedroom across the hall.

"I can't sleep, Cooper," she said. "Tell me a story."

"Which one tonight?" Cooper was a good improviser of stories to help his wife relax and doze off. "Hannah, the snoopy cleaning woman?"

"No," Christine said. "I'm tired of Hannah."   75

"The adventures of Roderick, insurance adjuster?"

"I'm sick of him, too."

"How about another boring day in Paradise?"

"Yeah. Do that."

For the next twenty minutes, Cooper described the beauty and tedium of   80
Paradise—the perfect rainfalls, the parks with roped-off grassy areas, the sideshows and hot-air balloon rides, the soufflés that never fell—and in twenty minutes, Christine was asleep, her fingers touching him. He was aroused. "Christine?" he whispered. But she was sleeping.

* * *

The next morning, as Cooper worked at his baker's bench, rolling chocolate-almond croissants, he decided that he would check out the shelter in the afternoon to see if they needed any help. He looked up from his hands, with a trace of dough and sugar under the fingernails, over toward his boss, Gilbert, who was brewing coffee and humming along to some Coltrane coming out of his old radio perched on top of the mixer. Cooper loved the bakery where he worked. He loved the smell and everything they made there. He had noticed that bread made people unusually happy. Customers closed their eyes when they ate Cooper's doughnuts and croissants and danishes. He looked up toward the sky-light and saw that the sky had turned from pale blue to dark blue, what the 64 Crayola box called blue-indigo. He could tell from the tint of the sky that it was seven o'clock, time to unlock the front doors to let in the first of the customers. After Gilbert turned the key and the Firestone mechanics from down the street shuffled in to get their morning doughnuts and coffee in Styrofoam cups, Cooper stood behind the counter in his whites and watched their faces, the slow private smiles that always registered when they first caught the scent of the baked dough and the sugared fruit.

* * *

The shelter was in a downtown furniture store that had gone out of business during the recession of '79. To provide some privacy, the first volunteers had covered over the front plate-glass window with long strips of paper from giant rolls, with the result that during the daytime the light inside was colored an unusual tint, somewhere between orange and off-white. As soon as he volunteered, he was asked to do odd jobs. He first went to work in the evening ladling out food—stew, usually, with ice-cream-scoop mounds of mashed potatoes.

The director of the shelter was a brisk and slightly overweight woman named Marilyn Adams, who, though tough and efficient, seemed vaguely annoyed about everything. Cooper liked her officious irritability. He didn't want any baths of feeling in this place.

Around five o'clock on a Thursday afternoon—the bakery closed at four—Cooper was making beds near the front window when he heard a voice from behind him. "Hey," the voice said. "I want to get in here."

Cooper turned around. He saw the reddest person he had ever laid eyes on: the young man's hair was red, his face flamed with sunburn and freckles, and, as if to accentuate his skin and hair tone, he was wearing a bright pink Roxy Music T-shirt. He was standing near the window, with the light behind him, and all Cooper could see of him was a still, flat expression and deeply watchful eyes. When he turned, he had the concentrated otherworldliness of figures in religious paintings.

Cooper told the young man about the shelter's regulations and told him which bed he could have. The young man—he seemed almost a boy—stood listening, his right foot thumping against the floor and his right hand shaking in the air as if he were trying to get water off it. When the young man nodded, his head went up and down too fast, and Cooper thought he was being ironic. "Who are you?" he finally asked. "My name's Cooper."

"Billy Bell," the young man said. "That's a real weird name, isn't it?" He shook his head but didn't look at Cooper or wait for him to agree or disagree. "My mother threw me out last week. Why shouldn't she? I'm twenty-three. She thought I was doing drugs. I wasn't doing drugs. Drugs are so boring. Look at those awful capitalist lizards using them and you'll know what I mean. But I *was* a problem. She was right. She had to get on my case. She decided to throw me away for a while. Trash trash. So I've been sleeping in alleys and benches and I slept for a couple of nights in the Arboretum, but there are too many mosquitoes this time of year for that and I've got bites. I was living with a girl but all my desires left me. You live here, Cooper? You homeless yourself, or what?"

"I'm a volunteer," he said. "I just work here. I've got a home."

"I don't," Billy Bell said. "People should have homes. I don't work now. I lost my job. I'm full of energy but I'm apathetic. Very little appeals to me. I guess I'm going to start some of those greasy minimum-wage things if I can stand them. I'm smart. I'm not a loser. I'm definitely not one of these messed-up ghouls who call this place home."

Cooper stood up and walked toward the kitchen, knowing that the young   90
man would follow him. "They aren't ghouls," he said. "Look around. They're more normal than you are, probably. They're down on their luck."

"Of course they are, of course they are," Billy said, his voice floating a few inches behind Cooper's head. Cooper began to wipe off the kitchen counter, as the young man watched him. Then Billy began waving his right hand again. "My problem, Cooper, my problem is the problem of the month, which is point-lessness and the point of doing anything, which I can't see most of the time. I want to heal people but I can't do that. I'm stalled. What happened was, about a year ago, there was this day. I remember it was sunny, I mean the sun was out, and I heard these wings flapping over my head because I was out in the park with my girlfriend feeding Cheerios to the pigeons. Then this noise: *flap flap flap.* Wings, Cooper, *big* wings, taking my soul away. I didn't want to look behind me because I was afraid they'd taken my shadow, too. It could happen, Cooper, it could happen to anybody. Anyhow, after that, what I knew was, I didn't want what everybody else did, I mean I don't have any desires for anything, and at some times of day I *don't* cast a shadow. My desires just went away like that— poof, poor desires. I'm a saint now but I'm not enjoying it one bit. I can bless people but not heal them. Anybody could lose his soul the way I did. Now all I got is that sad robot feeling. You know, that five-o'clock feeling? But all day, with me."

"You mentioned your mother," Cooper said. He dropped some cleanser into the sink and began to scour. "What about your father?"

"Let me do that." Billy nudged Cooper aside and started to clean the sink with agitated, almost frantic hand motions. "I've done a *lot* of this. My father died last year. I did a lot of housecleaning. I'm a man-maid. My father was in the hospital, but we took him out, and I was trying to be, I don't know, a sophomore in college, which is a pretty dumb thing to aspire to, if you think about it. But I was also sitting by my father's bed and taking care of him—he had pancreatic cancer—and I was reading *Popular Mechanics* to him, the home-improvement section, and feeding him when he could eat, and then when he died, the wings flew over me, though that was later, and there wasn't much I wanted to do. What a sink."

As he talked, Billy's hand accelerated in its motions around the drain.

"Come on," Cooper said. "I'm going to take you somewhere."   95

* * *

His idea was to lift the young man's spirits, but he didn't know quite how to proceed. He took him to his car and drove him down the river road to a park, where

Billy got out of the car, took his shoes off, and waded into the water. He bent down, and, as Cooper watched, cupped his hands in the river before splashing it over his face. Cooper thought his face had a strange expression, something between ecstasy and despair. He couldn't think of a word in English for this expression but thought there might be a word in another language for it. German, for example. When Billy was finished washing his face, he looked up into the sky. Pigeons and killdeer were flying overhead. After he had settled back into the front seat of Cooper's car, drops of water from his face dripping onto the seat, Billy said, "That's a good feeling, Cooper. You should try it. You wash your face in the flowing water and then you hear the cries of the birds. I'd like to think it makes me a new man but I know it doesn't. How old are you, Cooper?"

"I'm twenty-eight."

"Five years older than me. And what did you say you did?"

"I'll show you."

He drove Billy to the bakery and parked in the back alley. It was getting close to twilight. After Cooper had unlocked the back door, Billy walked into the dark bakery kitchen and began to sniff. "I like this place," he said. "I like it very much." He shook some invisible water off his hand, then ran his finger along the bench. "What's this made of?"

"Hardrock maple. It's like the wood they use in bowling alleys. Hardest wood there is. You can't dent it or break it. Look up."

Billy twisted backwards. "A skylight," he said. "Cooper, your life is on the very top of the eggshell. You have grain from the earth and you have the sky overhead. Ever been broken into?"

"No."

Cooper looked at Billy and saw, returning to him, a steady gaze made out of the watchful and flat expression he had first seen on the young man's face when he had met him a few hours before. "No," he repeated, "never have." He felt, suddenly, that he had embarked all at once on a series of misjudgments. "What did your father do, Billy?"

"He was a surgeon," Billy said. "He did surgery on people."

They stood and studied each other in the dark bakery for a moment.

"We'll go one more place," Cooper said. "I'll get you a beer. Then I have to take you back to the shelter."

* * *

Cooper's dog, Hugo, came out through the backyard and jumped up on him as he got out of his car. A load of wash, mostly Alexander's shirts, flapped on the clothesline in the evening breeze. Cooper heard children calling from down the street.

"Here we are," Cooper said. "We'll go in through this door."

Inside the house, Christine was sitting at the dining-room table with two legal pads set up in front of her and a briefcase down by the floor. Behind her, in the living room, Alexander was lying on the floor in front of the TV set, his chin cupped in his hands. He was watching a Detroit Tigers game. They both looked up when Cooper knocked on the kitchen doorframe and came into the hallway, followed by Billy, whose hands were in his pockets and who nodded as he walked.

"Christine," Cooper said. "This is Billy. I met him at the shelter." Billy walked quickly around the table and shook Christine's hand. "I brought him here for a beer."

Christine did not change her posture. Behind a smile, she gave Billy a hard look. "Hello," she said. "And welcome, I guess."

"Thank you," Billy said. Cooper went out to the kitchen, opened a beer, and brought it back to him. Billy looked at the bottle, then took a long swig from it. After wiping his mouth, he said, "Well, my goodness. I certainly never expected to be here in your home tonight."

"Well, we didn't expect you either, Mr.—?"

"Bell," Billy said. "Billy Bell."   115

"We didn't expect you either, Mr. Bell. You're lucky. My husband never does this." She looked now at Cooper. "He never *never* does this."

Cooper pointed toward the living room. "Billy, that's Alexander over there. He's in the Alan Trammell fan club. I guess you can tell."

Alexander turned around, looked at Billy, and said, "Hi," waving quickly. Billy returned the greeting, but Alexander had already returned to the TV set, now showing a commercial for shaving cream.

"So, Mr. Bell," Christine said. "What brings you to Ann Arbor?"

"Oh, I've always lived here," Billy said. "Graduated from Pioneer High and   120
everything." He began a little jumping motion, then quelled it. "How about you?"

"Oh, not me," Christine said. "I'm from Dayton, Ohio. I came here to law school. That's where I met Cooper."

"I thought he was a baker."

"He is now. He dropped out of law school."

"You didn't drop out?" Billy glanced at Christine's legal pads. "You became a lawyer?"

"I became a prosecutor, yes, that's right. In the district attorney's office.   125
That's what I do."

"Do you like it?" Cooper thought Billy was about to explode in some way; he was getting redder and redder.

"Oh yes," Christine said. "I like it very much."

"Why?"

"Why?" She touched her face and her smile faded. "I came from a family of bullies, Mr. Bell. Three brothers. They tied me up and played tricks on me, and they did this for years. Little boy criminals. Every promise they made to me, they broke. Then I discovered the law, when I grew up. It's about limits and enforced regulation and binding agreements. It's a net of words, Mr. Bell. Legal formulas for proscribing behavior. That's what the law is. Now I have a career of putting promise-breakers behind bars. That makes me happy. What makes you happy, Mr. Bell?"

Billy hopped once, then leaned against the counter. "I didn't have any   130
dreams until today," Billy said, "but now I do, seeing your cute house and your cute family. Here's what I'd like to do. I want to be *just like all of you*. I'd put on a chef's hat and stand outside in my apron like one of those assholes you see in the Sunday magazine section with a spatula in his hand, and, like, I'll be flipping hamburgers and telling my kids to keep their hands out of the chive dip and go run in the sprinkler or do some shit like that. I'll belong to do-good groups like

Save the Rainforests, and I'll ask my wife how she likes her meat, rare or well-done, and she'll say well-done with that pretty smile she has, and that's how I'll do it. A wonderful fucking barbecue, this is, with folding aluminum chairs and paper plates and ketchup all over the goddamn place. Oceans of vodka and floods of beer. Oh, and we've sprayed the yard with that big spray that kills anything that moves, and all the flies and mosquitoes and bunnies are dead at our feet. Talk about the good life. That has got to be it."

Alexander had turned around and was staring at Billy, and Christine's face had become masklike and rigid. "Finish your beer, Mr. Bell," she said. "I think you absolutely have to go now. Don't let's waste another minute. Finish the beer and back you go."

"Yes," he said, nodding and grinning.

"I suppose you think what you just said was funny," Cooper said, from where he was standing in the back of the kitchen.

"No," Billy said. "I can't be funny. I've tried often. It doesn't work. No gift for that."

"Have you been in prison, Mr. Bell?" Christine asked, looking down at her 135 legal pad and writing something there.

"No," Billy said. "I have not."

"Oh good," Christine said. "I was afraid maybe you had been."

"Do you think that's what will become of me?" Billy asked. His voice had lowered from its previous manic delivery and become soft.

"Oh, who knows?" Christine said, running her hand through her hair. "It could happen, or maybe not."

"Because I think my life is out of my hands," Billy said. "I just don't think I 140 have control over it any longer."

"Back you go," Christine said. "Goodbye. Fare thee well."

"Thank you," Billy said. "That was a nice blessing. And thank you for the beer. Goodbye, Alexander. It was nice meeting you."

"Nice to meet you," the boy said from the floor.

"Let's go," Cooper said, picking at Billy's elbow.

"Back I go," Billy said. "Fare thee well, Billy, goodbye and Godspeed. So 145 long, Mr. Human Garbage. Okay, all right, yes, now I'm gone." He did a quick walk through the kitchen and let the screen door slam behind him. Christine gave Cooper a look, which he knew meant that she was preparing a speech for him, and then he followed Billy out to the car.

* * *

On the way to the shelter, Billy slouched down on the passenger side. He said nothing for five minutes. Then he said, "I noticed something about your house, Cooper. I noticed that in the kitchen there were all these glasses and cups and jars out on the counter, and the jars weren't labeled, not the way they usually label them, and so I looked inside one of them, one of those jars, and you know what I saw? I suppose you must know, because it's your kitchen."

"What?" Cooper asked.

"Pain," Billy said, looking straight ahead and nodding. "That jar was full of pain. I had to close the lid over it immediately. Now tell me something, because I don't have the answer to it. Why does a man like you, a baker, have a jar full of pain in his kitchen? Can you explain that?"

Out through the front windows, Cooper saw the reassuring lights of the city, the lamplights shining out through the front windows, and the street-lights beginning to go on. A few children were playing on the sidewalks, hop-scotch and tag, and in the sky a vapor trail from a jet was beginning to dis-solve into orange wisps. What was the price one paid for loving one's own life? He felt a tenderness toward existence and toward his own life, and felt guilty for that.

At the shelter, he let Billy out without saying good night. He watched the 150 young man do his hop-and-skip walk toward the front door; then he put the car into gear and drove home. As he expected, Christine was waiting up for him and gave him a lecture, in bed, about guilty liberalism and bringing the slime element into your own home.

"That's an exaggeration," Cooper said. He was lying on his side of the bed, his hip touching hers. "That's not what he was. I'm not wrong. I'm not." He felt her lips descending over him and remembered how she always thought that his failures in judgment made him sensual.

* * *

Two days later he arrived at work before dawn and found Gilbert standing mo-tionless in front of Cooper's own baker's bench. Cooper closed the door behind him and said, "Hey, Gilbert."

"It's all right," Gilbert said. "I already called the cops."

"What?"

Gilbert pointed. On the wood table were hundreds of pieces of broken glass 155 from the scattered skylight in a slice-of-pie pattern, and, over the glass, a circle of dried blood the width of a teacup. Smaller dots of blood, like afterthoughts, were scattered around the bench and led across the floor to the cash register, which had been jimmied open. Cooper felt himself looking up. A bird of a type he couldn't identify was perched on the broken skylight.

"Two hundred dollars," Gilbert said, overpronouncing the words. "Some-where somebody's all cut up for a lousy two hundred dollars. I'd give the son of a bitch a hundred not to break in, if he'd asked. But you know what I really mind?"

"The blood," Cooper said.

"Bingo." Gilbert nodded, as he coughed. "I hate the idea of this guy's blood in my kitchen, on the floor, on the table and over there in the mixing pans. I re-ally hate it. A bakery. What a fucking stupid place to break into."

* * *

"I told you so," Christine said, washing Cooper's face. Then she turned him around and ran the soapy washcloth down his back and over his buttocks.

August. Three days before Christine's birthday. Cooper and his son were 160 walking down Main Street toward a store called the Peaceable Kingdom to get Christine a present, a small stuffed pheasant that Alexander had had his eye on for many months. Alexander's hand was in Cooper's as they crossed at the cor-ner, after waiting for the WALK sign to go on. Alexander had been asking Cooper for an exact definition of trolls, and how they differ from ghouls. And what, he wanted to know, *what exactly* is a goblin, and how are they born? In forests? Can they be born anywhere, like trolls?

Up ahead, squatting against the window of a sporting-goods store, was the man perpetually dressed in the filthy brown corduroy suit: James. His hands were woven together at his forehead, thumbs at temples, to shade his eyes against the sun. As Cooper and his son passed by, James spoke up. He did not ask for money. He said, "Hello, Cooper."

"Hello, James," Cooper said.

"Is this your boy?" He pulled his hands apart and pointed at Alexander.

"Yes."

"Daddy," Alexander said, tugging at his father's hand.   165

"A fine boy," James said, squinting. "Looks a bit like you." The old man smelled as he had before: like a city dump, like everything.

"Thank you," Cooper said, beaming. "He's a handsome boy, isn't he?"

"Indeed," James said. "Would you like to hear a bit of the Gospels?"

"No, thank you, James," Cooper said. "We're on our way to get this young man's mother a birthday present."

"Well, I won't keep you," the old man said.   170

As Cooper reached for his wallet, Alexander suddenly spoke: "Daddy, don't."

"What?"

"Don't give him any money," the boy said.

"Why not?"

Alexander couldn't say. He began to shake his head, looking at James, then   175
at his father. He backed away, down the sidewalk, his lower lip beginning to stick out and his eyes starting to grow wet.

"Here, James," Cooper said, watching his son, who had retreated down the block and was hiding in the doorway of a hardware store. He handed the old man five dollars.

"Bless you," James said. "And bless Jesus." He put the money in his pocket, then placed his hands together in front of his chest, lowered himself to his knees, and began to pray.

"Goodbye, James," Cooper said. With his eyes closed, James nodded. Cooper ran down the block to catch up with his son.

After Alexander had finished crying, he told his father that he was afraid— afraid that he was going to bring that dirty man home, the way he did with the red-haired guy, and let him stay, maybe in the basement, in the extra room.

"I wouldn't do that," Cooper said. "Really. I wouldn't do that."   180

* * *

"Wouldn't you?" his wife asked, that night, in bed. "Wouldn't you? I think you might."

"No. Not home. Not again."

But he had been accused, and he rose up and walked down the hall to his son's room. The house was theirs, no one else's; his footsteps were the only audible ones. In Alexander's room, in the dim illumination spread by the Swiss-chalet nightlight, Cooper saw his son's model airplanes and the posters of his baseball heroes, but in looking around the room, he felt that something was missing. He glanced again at his son's dresser. The piggy bank, stuffed with pennies, was gone.

He's frightened of my charity, Cooper thought, looking under the bed and seeing the piggy bank there, next to Alexander's favorite softball.

Cooper returned to bed. "He's hidden his money from me," he said.   185

"They do that, you know," Christine said. "And they go on doing that."

"You can't sleep," Cooper said, touching his wife."

"No," she said. "But it's all right."

"I can't tell you about Paradise," Cooper told her. "I gave you all the stories I knew."

"Well, what *do* you want?" she asked.   190

He put his hands over hers. "Shelter me," he said.

"Oh, Cooper," she said. "Which way this time? Which way?"

To answer her, he rolled over, and, as quietly as he could, so as not to wake their son in the next room, he took her into his arms and held her there.

Talking about the Text

1. How does the word "shelter" work as a title and as a need in the story?
2. What do you make of the relationship between the characters? Do Cooper and his wife love each other? Think about Christine's remarks "You're such a good person, I've noticed that about you," "I think you're a latent vagrant," and "Do I love you? . . . Stay with me." Also, pay attention to their dialogue that ends the story.
3. Who is being judged in the story? More than one person or group? What kind of verdict is delivered?

Writing about the Text

1. Explain what can one do, besides being indifferent, to help people like James, Estelle, and Billy Bell. You can start to explore what it means to help others by talking with some of the people who provide this help.
2. Did Cooper behave admirably, up to a point? Do you think Cooper has done any serious damage to his son's psyche? Have Cooper and his son Alexander changed places in some respects? Explain. What has Cooper learned about his son?
3. Reread the speech Billy Bell gives when he is in Cooper's house (pp. 245–246). In a short (1–2 page) paper, write how you think readers should take it. Is the speech entirely the utterance of a madman, or might readers think it carries some truth?

Linking the Text to Other Texts

1. It's pretty clear that Cooper's impulses lead to some "misjudgments" (Cooper's own word). Have you ever made any analogous misjudgments in helping others?
2. In the film *Down and Out in Beverly Hills* (1986), which was based on a great 1932 French movie, *Boudu Saved from Drowning*, a rich Hollywood couple (Richard Dreyfuss and Bette Midler) take pity on a bum (Nick Nolte) and invite him in to live with them, with predictable comic results. See that film and connect it to "Shelter." Or, instead of watching the movie, connect "Shelter" to people's experiences with guests who are very hard to get rid of.

INSPIRATION   "Gryphon" in Performance: Chicago Public Radio's *Stories on Stage*

Gryphon Greiff

A gryphon, a mythical animal with the head and wings of an eagle and the body, hind legs, and tail of a lion.

Stories on Stage, an ongoing series that airs on Chicago Public Radio, presents dramatic readings of renowned literature performed by critically acclaimed Chicago actors. The performances are done live in front of a studio audience and then broadcast during the second half of the year. Authors whose works have been performed on the show include Eudora Welty, James Thurber, John Updike, Tim O'Brien, Lorrie Moore, and Stuart Dybek. Charles Baxter's "Gryphon" was performed by actor Scott Parkinson and directed by Abigail Desser in November 2002.

Gryphon   (1985)

On Wednesday afternoon, between the geography lesson on ancient Egypt's hand-operated irrigation system and an art project that involved drawing a model city next to a mountain, our fourth-grade teacher, Mr. Hibler, developed a cough. This cough began with a series of muffled throat-clearings and progressed to propulsive noises contained within Mr. Hibler's closed mouth. "Listen to him," Carol Peterson whispered to me. "He's gonna blow up." Mr. Hibler's laughter—dazed and infrequent—sounded a bit like his cough, but as we worked on our model cities we would look up, thinking he was enjoying a joke, and see Mr. Hibler's face turning red, his cheeks puffed out. This was not laughter. Twice he bent over, and his loose tie, like a plumb line, hung down straight from his neck as he exploded himself into a Kleenex. He would excuse himself, then go on coughing. "I'll bet you a dime," Carol Peterson whispered, "we get a substitute tomorrow."

Carol sat at the desk in front of mine and was a bad person—when she thought no one was looking she would blow her nose on notebook paper, then crumple it up and throw it into the wastebasket—but at times of crisis she spoke the truth. I knew I'd lose the dime.

"No deal," I said.

When Mr. Hibler stood us in formation at the door just prior to the final bell, he was almost incapable of speech. "I'm sorry, boys and girls," he said. "I seem to be coming down with something."

"I hope you feel better tomorrow. Mr. Hibler," Bobby Kryzanowicz, the fault- 5
less brown-noser, said, and I heard Carol Peterson's evil giggle. Then Mr. Hibler
opened the door and we walked out to the buses, a clique of us starting noisily to
hawk and laugh as soon as we thought we were a few feet beyond Mr. Hibler's
earshot.

* * *

Since Five Oaks was a rural community, and in Michigan, the supply of substitute teachers was limited to the town's unemployed community college graduates, a pool of about four mothers. These ladies fluttered, provided easeful class
days, and nervously covered material we had mastered weeks earlier. Therefore it
was a surprise when a woman we had never seen came into the class the next
day, carrying a purple purse, a checkerboard lunchbox, and a few books. She put
the books on one side of Mr. Hibler's desk and the lunchbox on the other, next
to the Voice of Music phonograph. Three of us in the back of the room were
playing with Heever, the chameleon that lived in a terrarium and on one of the
plastic drapes, when she walked in.

She clapped her hands at us. "Little boys," she said, "why are you bent over
together like that?" She didn't wait for us to answer. "Are you tormenting an animal? Put it back. Please sit down at your desks. I want no cabals this time of the
day." We just stared at her. "Boys," she repeated, "I asked you to sit down."

I put the chameleon in his terrarium and felt my way to my desk, never taking my eyes off the woman. With white and green chalk, she had started to draw
a tree on the left side of the blackboard. She didn't look usual. Furthermore, her
tree was outsized, disproportionate, for some reason.

"This room needs a tree," she said, with one line drawing the suggestion of a
leaf. "A large, leafy, shady, deciduous . . . oak."

Her fine, light hair had been done up in what I would learn years later was 10
called a chignon, and she wore gold-rimmed glasses whose lenses seemed to have
the faintest blue tint. Harold Knardahl, who sat across from me, whispered,
"Mars," and I nodded slowly, savoring the imminent weirdness of the day. The
substitute drew another branch with an extravagant arm gesture, then turned
around and said, "Good morning. I don't believe I said good morning to all of
you yet."

Facing us, she was no special age—an adult is an adult—but her face had
two prominent lines, descending vertically from the sides of her mouth to her
chin. I knew where I had seen those lines before: *Pinocchio*. They were marionette lines. "You may stare at me," she said to us, as a few more kids from the
last bus came into the room, their eyes fixed on her, "for a few more seconds, until the bell rings. Then I will permit no more staring. Looking I will permit. Staring, no. It is impolite to stare, and a sign of bad breeding. You cannot make a social effort while staring."

Harold Knardahl did not glance at me, or nudge, but I heard him whisper
"Mars" again, trying to get more mileage out of his single joke with the kids who
had just come in.

When everyone was seated, the substitute teacher finished her tree, put
down her chalk fastidiously on the phonograph, brushed her hands, and faced us.
"Good morning," she said. "I am Miss Ferenczi, your teacher for the day. I am

fairly new to your community, and I don't believe any of you know me. I will therefore start by telling you a story about myself."

While we settled back, she launched into her tale. She said her grandfather had been a Hungarian prince; her mother had been born in some place called Flanders, had been a pianist, and had played concerts for people Miss Ferenczi referred to as "crowned heads." She gave us a knowing look. "Grieg," she said, "the Norwegian master, wrote a concerto for piano that was . . ."—she paused— "my mother's triumph at her debut concert in London." Her eyes searched the ceiling. Our eyes followed. Nothing up there but ceiling tile. "For reasons that I shall not go into, my family's fortunes took us to Detroit, then north to dreadful Saginaw, and now here I am in Five Oaks, as your substitute teacher, for today, Thursday, October the eleventh. I believe it will be a good day: all the forecasts coincide. We shall start with your reading lesson. Take out your reading book. I believe it is called *Broad Horizons*, or something along those lines."

Jeannie Vermeesch raised her hand. Miss Ferenczi nodded at her. "Mr. Hibler always starts the day with the Pledge of Allegiance," Jeannie whined.   15

"Oh, does he? In that case," Miss Ferenczi said, "you must know it *very* well by now, and we certainly need not spend our time on it. No, no allegiance pledging on the premises today, by my reckoning. Not with so much sunlight coming into the room. A pledge does not suit my mood." She glanced at her watch. "Time *is* flying. Take out *Broad Horizons*."

* * *

She disappointed us by giving us an ordinary lesson, complete with vocabulary and drills, comprehension questions, and recitation. She didn't seem to care for the material, however. She sighed every few minutes and rubbed her glasses with a frilly handkerchief that she withdrew, magician-style, from her left sleeve.

After reading we moved on to arithmetic. It was my favorite time of the morning, when the lazy autumn sunlight dazzled its way through ribbons of clouds past the windows on the east side of the classroom and crept across the linoleum floor. On the playground the first group of children, the kindergartners, were running on the quack grass just beyond the monkey bars. We were doing multiplication tables. Miss Ferenczi had made John Wazny stand up at his desk in the front row. He was supposed to go through the tables of six. From where I was sitting, I could smell the Vitalis soaked into John's plastered hair. He was doing fine until he came to six times eleven and six times twelve. "Six times eleven," he said, "is sixty-eight. Six times twelve is . . ." He put his fingers to his head, quickly and secretly sniffed his fingertips, and said, ". . . seventy-two." Then he sat down.

"Fine," Miss Ferenczi said. "Well now. That was very good."

"Miss Ferenczi!" One of the Eddy twins was waving her hand desperately in the air. "Miss Ferenczi! Miss Ferenczi!"   20

"Yes?"

"John said that six times eleven is sixty-eight and you said he was right!"

"*Did I?*" She gazed at the class with a jolly look breaking across her marionette's face. "Did I say that? Well, what *is* six times eleven?"

"It's sixty-six!"

She nodded. "Yes. So it is. But, and I know some people will not entirely   25
agree with me, at some times it is sixty-eight."

"When? When is it sixty-eight?"

We were all waiting.

"In higher mathematics, which you children do not yet understand, six times eleven can be considered to be sixty-eight." She laughed through her nose. "In higher mathematics numbers are . . . more fluid. The only thing a number does is contain a certain amount of something. Think of water. A cup is not the only way to measure a certain amount of water, is it?" We were staring, shaking our heads. "You could use saucepans or thimbles. In either case, the water *would be the same*. Perhaps," she started again, "it would be better for you to think that six times eleven is sixty-eight only when I am in the room."

"Why is it sixty-eight," Mark Poole asked, "when you're in the room?"

"Because it's more interesting that way," she said, smiling very rapidly be- 30
hind her blue-tinted glasses. "Besides, I'm your substitute teacher, am I not?" We all nodded. "Well, then, think of six times eleven equals sixty-eight as a substitute fact."

"A substitute fact?"

"Yes." Then she looked at us carefully. "Do you think," she asked, "that anyone is going to be hurt by a substitute fact?"

We looked back at her.

"Will the plants on the windowsill be hurt?" We glanced at them. There were sensitive plants thriving in a green plastic tray, and several wilted ferns in small clay pots. "Your dogs and cats, or your moms and dads?" She waited. "So," she concluded, "what's the problem?"

"But it's wrong," Janice Weber said, "isn't it?" 35

"What's your name, young lady?"

"Janice Weber."

"And you think it's wrong, Janice?"

"I was just asking."

"Well, all right. You were just asking. I think we've spent enough time on 40
this matter by now, don't you, class? You are free to think what you like. When your teacher, Mr. Hibler, returns, six times eleven will be sixty-six again, you can rest assured. And it will be that for the rest of your lives in Five Oaks. Too bad, eh?" She raised her eyebrows and glinted herself at us. "But for now, it wasn't. So much for that. Let us go on to your assigned problems for today, as painstakingly outlined, I see, in Mr. Hibler's lesson plan. Take out a sheet of paper and write your names on the upper left-hand corner."

For the next half hour we did the rest of our arithmetic problems. We handed them in and then went on to spelling, my worst subject. Spelling always came before lunch. We were taking spelling dictation and looking at the clock. "Thorough," Miss Ferenczi said. "Boundary." She walked in the aisles between the desks, holding the spelling book open and looking down at our papers. "Balcony." I clutched my pencil. Somehow, the way she said those words, they seemed foreign, mis-voweled and mis-consonanted. I stared down at what I had spelled. *Balconie.* I turned the pencil upside down and erased my mistake. *Balconey.* That looked better, but still incorrect. I cursed the world of spelling and tried erasing it again and saw the paper beginning to wear away. *Balkony.* Suddenly I felt a hand on my shoulder.

"I don't like that word either," Miss Ferenczi whispered, bent over, her mouth near my ear. "It's ugly. My feeling is, if you don't like a word, you don't have to use it." She straightened up, leaving behind a slight odor of Clorets.

At lunchtime we went out to get our trays of sloppy joes, peaches in heavy syrup, coconut cookies, and milk, and brought them back to the classroom, where Miss Ferenczi was sitting at the desk, eating a brown sticky thing she had unwrapped from tightly rubber-banded waxed paper. "Miss Ferenczi," I said, raising my hand. "You don't have to eat with us. You can eat with the other teachers. There's a teacher's lounge," I ended up, "next to the principal's office."

"No, thank you," she said. "I prefer it here."

"We've got a room monitor," I said. "Mrs. Eddy." I pointed to where Mrs.   45
Eddy, Joyce and Judy's mother, sat silently at the back of the room, doing her knitting.

"That's fine," Miss Ferenczi said. "But I shall continue to eat here, with you children. I prefer it," she repeated.

"How come?" Wayne Razmer asked without raising his hand.

"I talked to the other teachers before class this morning," Miss Ferenczi said, biting into her brown food. "There was a great rattling of the words for the fewness of the ideas. I didn't care for their brand of hilarity. I don't like ditto-machine jokes."

"Oh," Wayne said.

"What's that you're eating?" Maxine Sylvester asked, twitching her nose. "Is   50
it food?"

"It most certainly is food. It's a stuffed fig. I had to drive almost down to Detroit to get it. I also brought some smoked sturgeon. And this," she said, lifting some green leaves out of her lunchbox, "is raw spinach, cleaned this morning."

"Why're you eating raw spinach?" Maxine asked.

"It's good for you," Miss Ferenczi said. "More stimulating than soda pop or smelling salts." I bit into my sloppy joe and stared blankly out the window. An almost invisible moon was faintly silvered in the daytime autumn sky. "As far as food is concerned," Miss Ferenczi was saying, "you have to shuffle the pack. Mix it up. Too many people eat . . . well, never mind."

"Miss Ferenczi," Carol Peterson said, "what are we going to do this afternoon?"

"Well," she said, looking down at Mr. Hibler's lesson plan, "I see that your   55
teacher, Mr. Hibler, has you scheduled for a unit on the Egyptians." Carol groaned. "Yessss," Miss Ferenczi continued, "that is what we will do: the Egyptians. A remarkable people. Almost as remarkable as the Americans. But not quite." She lowered her head, did her quick smile, and went back to eating her spinach.

*   *   *

After noon recess we came back into the classroom and saw that Miss Ferenczi had drawn a pyramid on the blackboard close to her oak tree. Some of us who had been playing baseball were messing around in the back of the room, dropping the bats and gloves into the playground box, and Ray Schontzeler had just slugged me when I heard Miss Ferenczi's high-pitched voice, quavering with emotions. "Boys," she said, "come to order right this minute and take your seats.

I do not wish to waste a minute of class time. Take out your geography books."
We trudged to our desks and, still sweating, pulled out *Distant Lands and Their People*. "Turn to page forty-two." She waited for thirty seconds, then looked over at Kelly Munger. "Young man," she said, "why are you still fossicking in your desk?"

Kelly looked as if his foot had been stepped on. "Why am I what?"

"Why are you . . . burrowing in your desk like that?"

"I'm lookin' for the book, Miss Ferenczi."

Bobby Kryzanowicz, the faultless brown-noser who sat in the first row by   60
choice, softly said, "His name is Kelly Munger. He can't ever find his stuff. He always does that."

"I don't care what his name is, especially after lunch," Miss Ferenczi said. *"Where is your book?"*

"I just found it." Kelly was peering into his desk and with both hands pulled at the book, shoveling along in front of it several pencils and crayons, which fell into his lap and then to the floor.

"I hate a mess," Miss Ferenczi said. "I hate a mess in a desk or a mind. It's . . . unsanitary. You wouldn't want your house at home to look like your desk at school, now, would you?" She didn't wait for an answer. "I should think not. A house at home should be as neat as human hands can make it. What were we talking about? Egypt. Page forty-two. I note from Mr. Hibler's lesson plan that you have been discussing the modes of Egyptian irrigation. Interesting, in my view, but not so interesting as what we are about to cover. The pyramids, and Egyptian slave labor. A plus on one side, a minus on the other." We had our books open to page forty-two, where there was a picture of a pyramid, but Miss Ferenczi wasn't looking at the book. Instead, she was staring at some object just outside the window.

"Pyramids," Miss Ferenczi said, still looking past the window. "I want you to think about pyramids. And what was inside. The bodies of the pharaohs, of course, and their attendant treasures. Scrolls. Perhaps," Miss Ferenczi said, her face gleeful but unsmiling, "these scrolls were novels for the pharaohs, helping them to pass the time in their long voyage through the centuries. But then, I am joking." I was looking at the lines on Miss Ferenczi's skin. "Pyramids," Miss Ferenczi went on, "were the repositories of special cosmic powers. The nature of a pyramid is to guide cosmic energy forces into a concentrated point. The Egyptians knew that; we have generally forgotten it. Did you know," she asked, walking to the side of the room so that she was standing by the coat closet, "that George Washington had Egyptian blood, from his grandmother? Certain features of the Constitution of the United States are notable for their Egyptian ideas."

Without glancing down at the book, she began to talk about the movement   65
of souls in Egyptian religion. She said that when people die, their souls return to Earth in the form of carpenter ants or walnut trees, depending on how they behaved—"well or ill"—in life. She said that the Egyptians believed that people act the way they do because of magnetism produced by tidal forces in the solar system, forces produced by the sun and by its "planetary ally," Jupiter. Jupiter, she said, was a planet, as we had been told, but had "certain properties of stars." She was speaking very fast. She said that the Egyptians were great explorers and conquerors. She said that the greatest of all the conquerors, Genghis Khan, had had forty horses and forty young women killed on the site of his grave. We listened.

No one tried to stop her. "I myself have been in Egypt," she said, "and have witnessed much dust and many brutalities." She said that an old man in Egypt who worked for a circus had personally shown her an animal in a cage, a monster, half bird and half lion. She said that this monster was called a gryphon and that she had heard about them but never seen them until she traveled to the outskirts of Cairo. She wrote the word out on the blackboard in large capital letters: GRYPHON. She said that Egyptian astronomers had discovered the planet Saturn but had not seen its rings. She said that the Egyptians were the first to discover that dogs, when they are ill, will not drink from rivers, but wait for rain, and hold their jaws open to catch it.

* * *

"She lies."

We were on the school bus home. I was sitting next to Carl Whiteside, who had bad breath and a huge collection of marbles. We were arguing. Carl thought she was lying. I said she wasn't, probably.

"I didn't believe that stuff about the bird," Carl said, "and what she told us about the pyramids? I didn't believe that, either. She didn't know what she was talking about."

"Oh yeah?" I had liked her. She was strange. I thought I could nail him. "If she was lying." I said, "what'd she say that was a lie?"

"Six times eleven isn't sixty-eight. It isn't ever. It's sixty-six, I know for a   70 fact."

"She said so. She admitted it. What else did she lie about?"

"I don't know," he said. "Stuff."

"What stuff?"

"Well." He swung his legs back and forth. "You ever see an animal that was half lion and half bird?" He crossed his arms. "It sounded real fakey to me."

"It could happen," I said. I had to improvise, to outrage him. "I read in this   75 newspaper my mom bought in the IGA about this scientist, this mad scientist in the Swiss Alps, and he's been putting genes and chromosomes and stuff together in test tubes, and he combined a human being and a hamster." I waited, for effect. "It's called a humster."

"You never." Carl was staring at me, his mouth open, his terrible bad breath making its way toward me. "What newspaper was it?"

"*The National Enquirer*," I said, "that they sell next to the cash registers." When I saw his look of recognition, I knew I had him. "And this mad scientist," I said, "his name was, um, Dr. Frankenbush." I realized belatedly that this name was a mistake and waited for Carl to notice its resemblance to the name of the other famous mad master of permutations, but he only sat there.

"A man and a hamster?" He was staring at me, squinting, his mouth opening in distaste. "Jeez. What'd it look like?"

* * *

When the bus reached my stop, I took off down our dirt road and ran up through the backyard, kicking the tire swing for good luck. I dropped my books on the back steps so I could hug and kiss our dog, Mr. Selby. Then I hurried inside. I could smell brussels sprouts cooking, my unfavorite vegetable. My mother was

washing other vegetables in the kitchen sink, and my baby brother was hollering
in his yellow playpen on the kitchen floor.

"Hi, Mom," I said, hopping around the playpen to kiss her. "Guess what?" 80

"I have no idea."

"We had this substitute today, Miss Ferenczi, and I'd never seen her before,
and she had all these stories and ideas and stuff."

"Well. That's good." My mother looked out the window in front of the sink,
her eyes on the pine woods west of our house. That time of the afternoon her
skin always looked so white to me. Strangers always said my mother looked like
Betty Crocker, framed by the giant spoon on the side of the Bisquick box. "Listen, Tommy," she said. "Would you please go upstairs and pick your clothes off
the floor in the bathroom, and then go outside to the shed and put the shovel
and ax away that your father left outside this morning?"

"She said that six times eleven was sometimes sixty-eight!" I said. "And she
said she once saw a monster that was half lion and half bird." I waited. "In
Egypt."

"Did you hear me?" my mother asked, raising her arm to wipe her forehead 85
with the back of her hand. "You have chores to do."

"I know," I said. "I was just telling you about the substitute."

"It's very interesting," my mother said, quickly glancing down at me, "and
we can talk about it later when your father gets home. But right now you have
some work to do."

"Okay, Mom." I took a cookie out of the jar on the counter and was about to
go outside when I had a thought. I ran into the living room, pulled out a dictionary next to the TV stand, and opened it to the Gs. After five minutes I found it.
Gryphon: variant of griffin. *Griffin:* "a *fabulous* beast with the head and wings of
an eagle and the body of a lion." Fabulous was right. I shouted with triumph and
ran outside to put my father's tools in their proper places.

*   *   *

Miss Ferenczi was back the next day, slightly altered. She had pulled her hair
down and twisted it into pigtails, with red rubber bands holding them tight one
inch from the ends. She was wearing a green blouse and pink scarf, making her
difficult to look at for a full class day. This time there was no pretense of doing a
reading lesson or moving on to arithmetic. As soon as the bell rang, she simply
began to talk.

She talked for forty minutes straight. There seemed to be less connection 90
between her ideas, but the ideas themselves were, as the dictionary would say,
fabulous. She said she had heard of a huge jewel, in what she called the an-
tipodes, that was so brilliant that when light shone into it at a certain angle it
would blind whoever was looking at its center. She said the biggest diamond in
the world was cursed and had killed everyone who owned it, and that by a trick
of fate it was called the Hope Diamond. Diamonds are magic, she said, and this is
why women wear them on their fingers, as a sign of the magic of womanhood.
Men have strength, Miss Ferenczi said, but no true magic. That is why men fall
in love with women but women do not fall in love with men: they just love being loved. George Washington had died because of a mistake he made about a
diamond. Washington was not the first *true* President, but she didn't say who

was. In some places in the world, she said, men and women still live in the trees and eat monkeys for breakfast. Their doctors are magicians. At the bottom of the sea are creatures thin as pancakes who have never been studied by scientists because when you take them up to air, the fish explode.

There was not a sound in the classroom, except for Miss Ferenczi's voice, and Donna DeShano's coughing. No one even went to the bathroom.

Beethoven, she said, had not been deaf; it was a trick to make himself famous, and it worked. As she talked, Miss Ferenczi's pigtails swung back and forth. There are trees in the world, she said, that eat meat: their leaves are sticky and close up on bugs like hands. She lifted her hands and brought them together, palm to palm. Venus, which most people think is the next closest planet to the sun, is not always closer, and, besides, it is the planet of greatest mystery because of its thick cloud cover. "I know what lies underneath those clouds," Miss Ferenczi said, and waited. After the silence, she said, "Angels. Angels live under those clouds." She said that angels were not invisible to everyone and were in fact smarter than most people. They did not dress in robes as was often claimed but instead wore formal evening clothes, as if they were about to attend a concert. Often angels *do* attend concerts and sit in the aisles, where, she said, most people pay no attention to them. She said the most terrible angel had the shape of the Sphinx. "There is no running away from that one," she said. She said that unquenchable fires burn just under the surface of the earth in Ohio, and that the baby Mozart fainted dead away in his cradle when he first heard the sound of a trumpet. She said that someone named Narzim al Harrardim was the greatest writer who ever lived. She said that planets control behavior, and anyone conceived during a solar eclipse would be born with webbed feet.

"I know you children like to hear these things," she said, "these secrets, and that is why I am telling you all this." We nodded. It was better than doing comprehension questions for the readings in *Broad Horizons*.

"I will tell you one more story," she said, "and then we will have to do arithmetic." She leaned over, and her voice grew soft. "There is no death," she said. "You must never be afraid. Never. That which is, cannot die. It will change into different earthly and unearthly elements, but I know this as sure as I stand here in front of you, and I swear it: you must not be afraid. I have seen this truth with these eyes. I know it because in a dream God kissed me. Here." And she pointed with her right index finger to the side of her head, below the mouth where the vertical lines were carved into her skin.

*   *   *

Absentmindedly we all did our arithmetic problems. At recess the class was out   95
on the playground, but no one was playing. We were all standing in small groups, talking about Miss Ferenczi. We didn't know if she was crazy, or what. I looked out beyond the playground, at the rusted cars piled in a small heap behind a clump of sumac, and I wanted to see shapes there, approaching me.

*   *   *

On the way home, Carl sat next to me again. He didn't say much, and I didn't either. At last he turned to me. "You know what she said about the leaves that close up on bugs?"

"Huh?"

"The leaves," Carl insisted. "The meat-eating plants. I know it's true. I saw it on television. The leaves have this icky glue that the plants have got smeared all over them and the insects can't get off 'cause they're stuck. I saw it." He seemed demoralized. "She's tellin' the truth."

"Yeah."

"You think she's seen all those angels?"   100

I shrugged.

"I don't think she has," Carl informed me. "I think she made that part up."

"There's a tree," I suddenly said. I was looking out the window at the farms along County Road H. I knew every barn, every broken windmill, every fence, every anhydrous ammonia tank, by heart. "There's a tree that's . . . that I've seen . . ."

"Don't you try to do it," Carl said. "You'll just sound like a jerk."

* * *

I kissed my mother. She was standing in front of the stove. "How was your day?"   105
she asked.

"Fine."

"Did you have Miss Ferenczi again?"

"Yeah."

"Well?"

"She was fine. Mom," I asked, "can I go to my room?"   110

"No," she said, "not until you've gone out to the vegetable garden and picked me a few tomatoes." She glanced at the sky. "I think it's going to rain. Skedaddle and do it now. Then you come back inside and watch your brother for a few minutes while I go upstairs. I need to clean up before dinner." She looked down at me. "You're looking a little pale, Tommy." She touched the back of her hand to my forehead and I felt her diamond ring against my skin. "Do you feel all right?"

"I'm fine," I said, and went out to pick the tomatoes.

* * *

Coughing mutedly, Mr. Hibler was back the next day, slipping lozenges into his mouth when his back was turned at forty-five-minute intervals and asking us how much of his prepared lesson plan Miss Ferenczi had followed. Edith Atwater took the responsibility for the class of explaining to Mr. Hibler that the substitute hadn't always done exactly what he, Mr. Hibler, would have done, but we had worked hard even though she talked a lot. About what? he asked. All kinds of things, Edith said. I sort of forgot. To our relief, Mr. Hibler seemed not at all interested in what Miss Ferenczi had said to fill the day. He probably thought it was woman's talk: unserious and not suited for school. It was enough that he had a pile of arithmetic problems from us to correct.

For the next month, the sumac turned a distracting red in the field, and the sun traveled toward the southern sky, so that its rays reached Mr. Hibler's Halloween display on the bulletin board in the back of the room, fading the pumpkin head scarecrow from orange to tan. Every three days I measured how much farther the sun had moved toward the southern horizon by making small marks with my black Crayola on the north wall, ant-sized marks only I knew were there.

And then in early December, four days after the first permanent snowfall, she appeared again in our classroom. The minute she came in the door, I felt my heart begin to pound. Once again, she was different: this time, her hair hung straight down and seemed hardly to have been combed. She hadn't brought her lunchbox with her, but she was carrying what seemed to be a small box. She greeted all of us and talked about the weather. Donna DeShano had to remind her to take her overcoat off.

When the bell to start the day finally rang, Miss Ferenczi looked out at all of us and said, "Children, I have enjoyed your company in the past, and today I am going to reward you." She held up the small box. "Do you know what this is?" She waited. "Of course you don't. It is a Tarot pack."

Edith Atwater raised her hand. "What's a Tarot pack, Miss Ferenczi?"

"It is used to tell fortunes," she said. "And that is what I shall do this morning. I shall tell your fortunes, as I have been taught to do."

"What's fortune?" Bobby Kryzanowicz asked.

"The future, young man. I shall tell you what your future will be. I can't do your whole future, of course. I shall have to limit myself to the five-card system, the wands, cups, swords, pentacles, and the higher arcanes. Now who wants to be first?"

There was a long silence. Then Carol Peterson raised her hand.

"All right," Miss Ferenczi said. She divided the pack into five smaller packs and walked back to Carol's desk, in front of mine. "Pick one card from each one of these packs," she said. I saw that Carol had a four of cups and a six of swords, but I couldn't see the other cards. Miss Ferenczi studied the cards on Carol's desk for a minute. "Not bad," she said. "I do not see much higher education. Probably an early marriage. Many children. There's something bleak and dreary here, but I can't tell what. Perhaps just the tasks of a housewife life. I think you'll do very well, for the most part." She smiled at Carol, a smile with a certain lack of interest. "Who wants to be next?"

Carl Whiteside raised his hand slowly.

"Yes," Miss Ferenczi said, "let's do a boy." She walked over to where Carl sat. After he picked his five cards, she gazed at them for a long time. "Travel," she said. "Much distant travel. You might go into the army. Not too much romantic interest here. A late marriage, if at all. But the Sun in your major arcana, that's a very good card." She giggled. "You'll have a happy life."

Next I raised my hand. She told me my future. She did the same with Bobby Kryzanowicz, Kelly Munger, Edith Atwater, and Kim Foor. Then she came to Wayne Razmer. He picked his five cards, and I could see that the Death card was one of them.

"What's your name?" Miss Ferenczi asked.

"Wayne."

"Well, Wayne," she said, "you will undergo a great metamorphosis, a change, before you become an adult. Your earthly element will no doubt leap higher, because you seem to be a sweet boy. This card, this nine of swords, tells me of suffering and desolation. And this ten of wands, well, that's a heavy load."

"What about this one?" Wayne pointed at the Death card.

"It means, my sweet, that you will die soon." She gathered up the cards. We 130
were all looking at Wayne. "But do not fear," she said. "It is not really death. Just
change. Out of your earthly shape." She put the cards on Mr. Hibler's desk. "And
now, let's do some arithmetic."

* * *

At lunchtime Wayne went to Mr. Faegre, the principal, and informed him of
what Miss Ferenczi had done. During the noon recess, we saw Miss Ferenczi
drive out of the parking lot in her rusting green Rambler American. I stood under the slide, listening to the other kids coasting down and landing in the little
depressive bowls at the bottom. I was kicking stones and tugging at my hair right
up to the moment when I saw Wayne come out to the playground. He smiled,
the dead fool, and with the fingers of his right hand he was showing everyone
how he had told on Miss Ferenczi.

I made my way toward Wayne, pushing myself past two girls from another
class. He was watching me with his little pinhead eyes.

"You told," I shouted at him. "She was just kidding."

"She shouldn't have," he shouted back. "We were supposed to be doing
arithmetic."

"She just scared you," I said. "You're a chicken. You're a chicken, Wayne. 135
You are. Scared of a little card," I sing-songed.

Wayne fell at me, his two fists hammering down on my nose. I gave him a
good one in the stomach and then I tried for his head. Aiming my fist, I saw that
he was crying. I slugged him.

"She was right," I yelled. "She was always right! She told the truth!" Other
kids were whooping. "You were just scared, that's all!"

And then large hands pulled at us, and it was my turn to speak to Mr.
Faegre.

* * *

In the afternoon Miss Ferenczi was gone, and my nose was stuffed with cotton
clotted with blood, and my lip had swelled, and our class had been combined
with Mrs. Mantei's sixth-grade class for a crowded afternoon science unit on insect life in ditches and swamps. I knew where Mrs. Mantei lived: she had a new
house trailer just down the road from us, at the Clearwater Park. She was no
mystery. Somehow she and Mr. Bodine, the other fourth-grade teacher, had
managed to fit forty-five desks into the room. Kelly Munger asked if Miss Ferenczi had been arrested, and Mrs. Mantei said no, of course not. All that afternoon, until the buses came to pick us up, we learned about field crickets and
two-striped grasshoppers, water bugs, cicadas, mosquitoes, flies, and moths. We
learned about insects' hard outer shell, the exoskeleton, and the usual parts of
the mouth, including the labrum, mandible, maxilla, and glossa. We learned
about compound eyes, and the four-stage metamorphosis from egg to larva to
pupa to adult. We learned something, but not much, about mating. Mrs. Mantei
drew, very skillfully, the internal anatomy of the grasshopper on the blackboard.
We learned about the dance of the honeybee, directing other bees in the hive to
pollen. We found out about which insects were pests to man, and which were

not. On lined white pieces of paper we made lists of insects we might actually see, then a list of insects too small to be clearly visible, such as fleas; Mrs. Mantei said that our assignment would be to memorize these lists for the next day, when Mr. Hibler would certainly return and test us on our knowledge.

Talking about the Text

1. Why the title "Gryphon"? Look up the word, if you don't know it, to think it through.
2. What do some of the kids like about Miss Ferenczi? How would the point of view of a parent, principal, or another teacher differ from the narrator's? At what point would they disapprove of Miss Ferenczi's words and actions? Do you approve or disapprove of Miss Ferenczi's behavior? (It's okay to be somewhat divided on the issue.)
3. What difference does it make that Miss Ferenczi is female? Could Baxter have cast her as a male substitute teacher? If you've read different stories by Charles Baxter, think about some of his other female characters. Do any of them have personality characteristics like Miss Ferenczi's?

Writing about the Text

1. Baxter once told an interviewer that when just out of college he taught fourth grade for a year. "Once, unprepared for class," reports the interviewer, "he winged it, making up facts on the spot about Egypt and irrigation." What sounds "winged" (improvised) in Baxter's "Gryphon"?
2. The narrator in "Gryphon" witnessed the events as a fourth-grader. Does he sound like a boy of nine or ten? What events sound as if they are being recollected many years later? Does it matter to the story?
3. Does the concluding paragraph show what the narrator thinks school is usually like? What do you think?

Linking the Text to Other Texts

1. Write a scene about something one of your grade school teachers did. Or make up a scene similar to one of the incidents in Baxter's story.
2. Does Miss Ferenczi remind you of any of your past teachers? How did you get along with him or her? What was your reaction? What were your interactions like, and how did they make you feel?

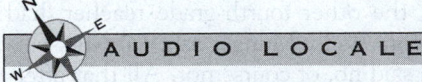

AUDIO LOCALE

Stories on Stage: "Gryphon" Dramatic Reading. The *Stories on Stage* website, part of the larger Chicago Public Radio site, at http://www.chicagopublicradio.org/programs/specials/sos/stories.asp includes an online audio library of the show's dramatic readings. The performance listings are organized by season starting in 2001 through the present day. The audio file for Baxter's story "Gryphon" can be found under the September 4 and 12 listing for the 2004 season at http://www.chicagopublicradio.org/audio_library/sos_04audio.asp, as well as under the 2002 season, when it was first broadcast.

Saul and Patsy Are Pregnant (1990)

A smell of spilled gasoline: when Saul opened his eyes, he was still strapped in behind his lap-and-shoulder belt, but the car he sat in was upside down and in a field of some sort. The Chevy's headlights illuminated a sky of dirt, and, in the distance, a tree growing downward from that same sky. Perhaps he had awakened out of sleep into another dream. "Patsy?" he said, turning with difficulty toward his wife, strapped in on the passenger side, her hair hanging down from her scalp, but, from Saul's perspective, standing up. She was still sleeping; she was always a sound sleeper; she could sleep upside down and was doing so now. The car's radio was playing Ray Charles's "Unchain My Heart," and Saul said, "You know, I've always liked that song." His voice was thick from beer and cigarettes, and he knew from the smell of the beer that this was no dream because he had never been able to imagine concrete details like that. No: he had fallen asleep at the wheel, driven off the road, and rolled the car. Here he was now. A thought passed through him, in an unpleasant slow-motion way, that the car was tilted and that the ignition was still on; he switched it off and felt intelligent for three seconds, until the lap belt began to hurt him and he felt stupid again. No ignition, no Ray Charles. His mind, often anxiety-prone, was moving slowly down a dark narrow alleyway cluttered with alcohol, fatigue, and the first onset of shock. Probably the car would blow up, and the only satisfaction his mother would receive from this accident would come years from now, when she would tell people, when they were all through reminiscing about Saul, "I *told* him not to drink. I told him about drinking and driving. But he never listened to me. Never."

"Patsy." He reached out and gave her a little shake.

"What?"

"Wake up. I rolled the car. Patsy, we've got to get out of here."

"Why?" 5

"Because we have to. Patsy, we're not at home. We're in the car. And we're upside down. Come on, honey, wake up. Please. This is serious."

"I am awake." She blinked, twisted her head, then looked calm. Her opal earring glittered in the light of the dashboard. The earring made Saul think of stability and a possible future life, if only he would normalize himself. Patsy smiled. Saul thought that this smile had something to do with guardian angels who, judging from the evidence, flew invisibly around her head, beaming down benevolence. "Well," she said, turning to look at him carefully, "are you all right?"

"Yes, yes. I'm not hurt at all."

"Good. Well. Neither am I." She reached up for the ceiling. "This isn't fun. Did *you* do this, Saul?"

"Yes, I did. How do we get out of here?" 10

"Let's see," she said, speaking calmly, in her usual tone. "What I think you do is, you release your seat belt, stick your arms straight up, then lower yourself slowly so you don't break your neck. Then you crawl out the window, the higher one. That would be yours."

"Okay." He held his arm up, then unfastened the clasp and felt himself dropping onto the car's ceiling. He pulled himself toward the side window. When he was outside, he leaned over, back in, and extended his hand to Patsy to help her out.

As she was emerging through the window, she was smiling. "Haven't you ever rolled a car before, Saul? I have. Or one of my boyfriends did, years ago." She was breathing rapidly. She dragged herself out, dusted her jeans, and strolled a few feet beyond the car's tire tracks in the mud, as if nothing much had happened. "Beautiful night," she said. "Look at those stars."

"Jeez, Patsy," Saul said, jumping down close to where she stood, "this is no time for being cosmic." Then he gazed up. She was right: the sky was pillowed with stars. She took his hand.

"Are you really okay?" she asked. "My God, feel that. You're shaking like a   15 leaf. You must be in shock." She wrapped her arms around him and held him for half a minute. "There," she said, "now that's better."

"We could have died," Saul said, his mouth dry.

"But we didn't."

"We *could* have."

"All right. Yes. I know. You can die in your sleep. You can die watching television." She watched him in the dark. "I wish I had been driving. It's so warm, a spring night, I think I would have been singing along to the radio. 'Unchain My Heart'—I would have been singing along to Ray Charles and we'd be home by now." She leaned over. "Smell the soil? It's loamy. You know, Saul, you should turn the car's headlights off."

"Patsy, the car is *wrecked!* Look at it."   20

"Don't be silly." She studied the car with equanimity, one hand raised to her face, the other hand cradling her elbow. Patsy's equanimity was otherworldly and constant. The combination of her beauty and her persistent unexplainable interest in Saul was the cause of his love for her; he loved her desperately and addictively. He had loved her this way before they were married, and it was still the same now. "Saul, that car is fine. We might be driving it tomorrow. The roof will have a dent, that's all. The car turned over slowly and softly. It's hardly hurt. What we have to do now is get to a house and call someone to help us. We could walk across this field, or we could just take the road back to Mad Dog's." Mad Dog was the host of the party they had come from. He was a high school gym teacher whose real name was Howard Bettermine. He looked, in fact, like a dog, but not a mad dog, as he thought, but a healthy and sober golden retriever.

"Patsy, I can't think. My brain has seized up."

"Well," she said, taking his hand, "I happen to like these stars, and that looks like a nice field, and I'd rather stay away from Highway 14 this time of night, what with the drunks on the road, and all." She gave him a tug on his sleeve, and he almost fell. "There you are," she said. "Come on."

* * *

As Saul walked across the field, hearing the slurp of his shoes in the spring mud, he saw the red blinking light of a radio tower in the distance, the only remotely friendly sight anywhere beneath the horizon. The fact that he was here at all was a sign, he thought, that his life was disordered, abandoned to chaos among Midwesterners, connoisseurs of violence and piety. He smelled manure, and somewhere behind him he thought he heard the predatory wingbeat of a bat or an owl.

Sick of cities, Saul had come to the Midwest two years before from Balti-   25 more as a high school history teacher, believing that he was a missionary of some new kind, bringing education and the higher enlightenments to rural, benighted adolescents, but somehow the conversion had gone the other way, and now he was acting like them: getting drunk, falling asleep, rolling his car. It was the sort of accident Christians had. He felt obscurely that he had given up personal complexity and become simple. He was like those girls who worked in the drugstore arranging greeting cards. They were so straightforward that two seconds before they did anything, like give change, you could see every gesture coming. He was becoming like that. As a personality, Saul had once prided himself on being interesting, almost Byzantine, a challenge to any therapist. But he had lately joined the school bowling league and couldn't seem to concentrate on Schopenhauer on those days when, at odds and ashamed with himself, he took the battered Signet Classic down from the shelf and glowered at the incomprehensible lines he had highlighted with yellow magic marker in college. When he did understand, the philosopher no longer seemed profound, but merely a disappointed idealist with a bad prose style.

"Saul?"

"What?"

"I've been talking to you. Didn't you hear me?"

"Guess not. I was lost in thought." He stumbled against a bush. He couldn't see much, and he reached out for Patsy's hand. "I was thinking about girls in drugstores and Schopenhauer and the reasons why we ever came to this place."

"Oh. That. If you had been listening to me, you wouldn't have stumbled   30
into that bush. That's what I was warning you about."

"Thanks. Where are we?"

"We're going down into this little gully, and when we get up on the other side, we'll be right near that farmhouse. What's the matter?"

He turned around and saw, across the field, the headlights of his car shining on the upturned dirt; he saw the Chevy's four tires facing the air; and he thought of his new jovial recklessness and of how he had almost killed himself and his wife. He said nothing because he was beginning to feel soul-sick, a state of spiritual dizziness. He was possessed by disequilibrium; he felt the urge to giggle, and was horrified by himself. He had a sudden marionette feeling.

"Saul! You're drifting off again. What is it this time?"

"Puppets."

"Puppets?"   35

"Yeah. You know: the way they don't have a center of gravity. The way they look . . ."

"Watch out for that stump."

He saw it in time to avoid it. "Patsy, how do you live in the world? This is a serious question."

"Stop it, Saul. You've been to a party. You're tired. Don't get metaphysical.   40
It's two in the morning. You live in the world by knocking on the door of that farmhouse, that's what you do. You ring the doorbell."

They walked up past a shed whose flaking red door was hanging open, and they crossed the pitted driveway onto a small front yard with an evenly mowed lawn. A tire swing, pendulating slowly, hung down from a tree branch. Saul couldn't see much of the house in the dark, but as they crossed the driveway, kicking a few stones, they heard the bark of a dog from inside the house, a low bark from a big dog: a farm dog.

"Anti-Semites," Saul said.

"Just ring the bell."

After a moment, the porch light went on, yellow, probably a bug light, Saul thought; and then under the oddly colored glare a very young woman appeared, pale blond hair and skin, very pretty, but under the effect of the bulb, looking a bit jaundiced. With her fists she was rubbing her eyes with sleepiness. She wore a bathrobe decorated with huge blue flowers. Saul and Patsy explained themselves and their predicament—Saul was sure he had seen this young woman before—and she invited them in to use the phone. When they entered, the dog—old, with a gray muzzle—growled from under a living-room table but did not bother to get up. After Patsy and the woman, whose name was Anne, began talking, it developed that they had met before in the insurance office where Patsy worked as a secretary. They leaned toward each other. Their voices quickly rose in the transfiguration of friendliness as they disappeared into the kitchen. They seemed suddenly chipper and cheery to Saul, as if a new party had started. He had the impression that women enjoyed being friendly, whereas for men it was an effort; at least it was an effort for *him*. He heard Patsy dialing a number on a rotary phone, laughing and whispering as she did so.

He was left alone in the living room. Having nothing else to do, he looked   45
around: high ceilings and elaborate wainscoting, lamps, table, rug, dog, calendar, the usual crucifix on the wall above the TV. There was something about the room that bothered him, and it took a moment before he knew what it was. It felt like a museum of earlier American feelings. Not a single ironic sentence had ever been spoken here. Everything in the room was sincere, everything except himself. In the midst of all this Midwestern earnestness, he was the one thing wrong. What was he doing here? What was he doing anywhere? He was accustomed to asking himself such questions.

"Mr. Bernstein?"

Saul turned around and saw the man of the house, who at first glance still seemed to be a boy, standing at the bottom of the stairs. He had his arms crossed, and he wore a sleepy but alert look on his face. He had on boxer shorts and a T-shirt, and Saul recognized, underneath the brown hair and the beard, a student from last year, Emory . . . something. Emory McPhee. That was it. A good-looking, solid kid. He had married this woman, Anne, last year, both of them barely eighteen years old, and moved out here. That was it. That was who they were. He had heard that Emory had become a housepainter.

"Emory," Saul said. The boy was stocky—he had played varsity football starting in his sophomore year—and he looked at Saul now with pleased curiosity. "Emory, my wife and I have had an accident, over there, on the other side of your field."

"What kind of accident, Mr. Bernstein?"

"We drove off the road." Saul waited, his hands in his pockets. Then he said   50
the rest of it. "The car turned over on us."

"Wow," Emory said. "You're lucky you weren't hurt. That's amazing. Good thing it wasn't worse."

"Well, yes, but the car was going slow." Saul always sounded stupid to himself late at night. The boy's bland blue-eyed gaze stayed on him now, not moving, genial but inquisitorial, and Saul thought of all the people who had hated school, never liked even a minute of it, and had had a low-level suspicion of teachers for the rest of their lives. They voted down school bond issues. They didn't even like to buy pencils.

"How did you go off the road?"

"I fell asleep, Emory. We'd been to a party and I fell asleep at the wheel. Never happened to me before."

"Wow," Emory said again, but slowly this time, with no real surprise in his voice. He shrugged his shoulders, then bent down as if he were doing calisthenics. Saul knew that his own breath smelled of beer, so there was no point in going into that. "Do you want a cup of coffee? I'd offer you a beer, but we don't have it." 55

Saul tried to smile, an effort. "I don't think so, Emory, not tonight." He looked down at the floor, at his socks—he had taken off his muddy shoes—and saw an ashtray filled with cigarette butts. "But I would like a cigarette, if you could spare one."

"Sure." The boy reached down and offered the pack in Saul's direction. "Didn't know you smoked. Didn't know you had any vices at all."

They exchanged a look. "I'm like everybody else," Saul said. "Sometimes the right thing just gets loose from me and I don't do it." He picked up a book of matches. He would have to watch his sentences: that one hadn't made any sense. On the outside of the matchbook was an advertisement.

SECRETS
OF THE
UNIVERSE
*** see inside ***

Saul put the matchbook into his pocket, after lighting up.

"Were you drunk?" the boy said suddenly.

"No, I don't think so."

"Teachers shouldn't drink," Emory said. "That's my belief." 60

"Well, maybe not."

Saul inhaled from the cigarette, and Emory came closer toward him and sat down on the floor. He gave off the smell of turpentine; he had flecks of white paint in his hair. He rubbed at his beard again. "Do you remember me from school?"

Saul leaned back. He tried to think. "Sure, of course I do. You sat in the back and you played with a ballpoint pen. You used to sketch the other kids in the class. Once when we were doing the First World War, you said it didn't make any sense no matter how much you read about it. I remember your report on the League of Nations. You stared out the window a lot. You sat near Anne in my class and you passed notes to her."

"I didn't think you'd remember that much." Emory whistled toward the dog, who thumped his tail and waddled over toward Emory's lap. "I wasn't very good. I thought it was a waste of time, no offense. I wanted to get married, that's all. I wanted to get married to Anne, and I wanted to be outside, not stuck inside, doing something, making a living, earning money. The thing is, I'm different now." He stood up, as if he were about to demonstrate how different he had become or had thought of something important to say. 65

"How are you different?"

"I'm real happy," Emory said, looking toward the kitchen. "I bet you don't believe that. I bet you think: here's this kid and his wife, out here, ignorant as a couple of plain pigs, and how could they be happy? But it's weird. You can't tell about anything." He was looking away from Saul. "Schools tell you that people like me aren't supposed to be happy or . . . what's that word you used in class all the time? 'Fulfilled'? We're not supposed to be that. But we're doing okay. But then I'm not trying to tell you anything."

"I know, Emory. I know that." Saul raised his hand to his scalp and touched his bald spot.

"Hell," Emory said, apparently building up steam, "you could work all your life to be as happy as Anne and me, and you might not do it. People . . . they try to be happy. They work at it. But it doesn't always take." He laughed. "I shouldn't be talking to you this way, Mr. Bernstein, and I wouldn't be, except it's the middle of the night, and I'm saying stuff. You know, I respected you. But now here you are, smelling of beer, and I remember the grades you gave me, all those D's, like you thought I'd never do anything in life except fail. But you can't hurt me now because I'm not in school anymore. So I apologize. See, I apologize for messing up in school and I forgive you for flunking me out."

Emory held out his hand, and Saul stood up and took it, thinking that he   70 might be making a mistake.

"You shouldn't flunk people out of school," Emory said, "if you're going to get drunk and roll cars."

Saul held on to Emory's hand and tried to grip hard and diligently in return. "I didn't get drunk, Emory. I fell asleep. And you didn't flunk out. You dropped out."

Emory released his hand. "Well, I don't care," he said. "I was sleeping when you came to our door. I don't go to parties anymore because I have to get up and work. I sleep because I'm married and working. I can't see anything outside that."

Saul suddenly wanted Patsy back in this room, so that they could go. Who the hell did this boy think he was, anyway?

"Well, none of this is nothing," Emory said at last. "I don't blame you for   75 anything at all. Maybe you did me a favor. I had to do something in my life, so I got my mom and dad to buy us this farm, which we're paying them back for every month, every dollar and cent, even though we aren't farming it. But we might. I'm reading up on horticulture." He pronounced the word carefully and proudly. "You want to sleep on the floor, you can, or on the sofa there. And there's a spare bed upstairs, you want it."

"Sorry about the bother," Saul said.

"No trouble."

"I appreciate this."

"Forget it." Emory patted the dog.

"But thanks."   80

"Sure."

The two men looked at each other for a moment, and Saul had one of his momentary envy-shocks: he looked at this man, this boy—he couldn't decide which he was—his hair standing up, and he thought: whatever else he is, this kid is real. Emory was living in the real; Saul felt himself floating up out of the unreal and rapidly sinking back into it, the lagoon of self-consciousness and irony.

In a kind of desperation, Saul looked up at the wall, where someone had hung a picture of a horse with a woman beside it, drawn in pencil, and framed in a cheap dime-store frame. The woman was probably Anne. She looked approximately like her. "Nice picture."

"I drew it."

"You have real talent, Emory," Saul said, insincerely examining the details. "You could be an artist."

"I *am* an artist," Emory said, staring at his old teacher. He picked at a scab on his calf. He turned his back to Saul. "I could draw from when I was a kid." A baby's cry came from upstairs. Emory looked at the ceiling, then exhaled.

"What kind of horse is that?" Saul asked, in what he vowed silently would be his final effort at politeness this evening. "Is that any kind of horse in particular?"

Emory was going back up the stairs. Then he faced Saul. "Every horse is some horse in particular, Mr. Bernstein. There aren't any horses in general. You can sleep there on the sofa if you want to. Good night."

"Good night."

Whatever happened to the God of the Old Testament, Saul wondered, looking at Emory's crucifix, the God that had chosen Israel above the other nations? Why had He allowed this scene to take place and why had He allowed Emory McPhee, this dropout, to make him feel like a putz? The Red Sea had not parted for Saul in a long time, in any sense; he felt he had about as much clout with God as, perhaps, a sparrow did. The whole evening was a joke at Saul's expense. He heard God laughing, a sound like surf on rocks.

When Patsy and Anne came out of the kitchen, announcing that an all-night towing service was on its way and would probably have the car turned over and running in about half an hour, Saul smiled as if everything would be as fine as they claimed. Anne and Patsy were laughing. The flowers on Anne's bathrobe were laughing. God was, even now, laughing and enjoying the joke. Feeling like a zombie, and not laughing himself, but wearing the smile of the classically undead, Saul hooked his hand into Patsy's and went back outside. Some nights, he knew, had a way of not ending. This was one.

"How was Emory?" Patsy asked.

"Emory? Oh, Emory was fine," Saul told her.

* * *

On the days following, Saul began to be obsessed with happiness, an unhealthy obsession, but he couldn't get rid of it. His feelings had always been the city of dreadful night. He was ball-and-chained to his emotions. On some days the obsession weighed him down so heavily that he could not get out of bed to go to work without groaning and reaching for his hair, as if to drag himself up bodily for the working day.

Prior to his accident and his meeting with Emory McPhee, Saul had managed to forget about happiness, a state that had once bothered him for its general inaccessibility. He loved Patsy; that he knew. Now he believed that compared to others he was actually and truly unhappy, especially since his mind insisted on thinking about the problem, poring over it, ragging him on and on. It was like the discontent of adolescence, the discontent with situations, but this was larger, the discontent with being itself, a psychic itch with nowhere to scratch. This was like Schopenhauer arriving at the door with a big suitcase, settling down for a long stay in the brain.

Patsy wasn't ordinary for many reasons but also because she loved Saul. Nevertheless, she was happy. Early in the summer he stole glances at her as she turned the pansies over in their pots, tamping them out, and planting them in the flower beds near the front walk. Blue sky, aggressive sun. She was barefoot, because she liked to go barefoot in the summer—her tomboy side—and she was squatting down in her shorts, wearing one of Saul's old flannel shirts flecked with dirt, and the sleeves rolled up to the elbows. Her brown hair fell backward down her shoulders. From the front window he watched her and studied her hands, those slender fingers doing their work. Helplessly, his eyes took in the clothed outlines of his wife. He was hers. That was that. She liked being a woman. She liked it in a way that, Saul now knew, he himself did not like being a man. There was the guilt, for one thing, for the manly hobbies of war and the thoroughgoing destruction of the earth. Patriarchy, carnage, rape, pleasurable bloodletting and bloodsport: Saul would admit a gender responsibility for all these, if anyone asked him, though no one ever did.

Patsy wiped her forehead with the back of her hand, saw Saul, and waved at him, turning her head slightly, tilting it, as she did whenever she caught sight of him. She smiled, a smile he had gladly given his life away for, a look of radiant intelligence. She was into the real, too; she didn't ponder it, she just planted flowers, if that was what she wanted to do. Beyond her was the driveway, and their Chevrolet with its bashed-in roof.

Saul turned from the window—it was Saturday morning—and tried to think for a moment of what he wanted to do. Taking a Detroit Tigers cap off the front-hall hat rack, he went outside and with great care put it, from behind and unannounced, on Patsy's head. "Save you from sunburn," he said, when she turned around and looked at him. "Save you from heatstroke."

"I want a motorcycle," Patsy said. "I've been thinking about it. We don't need another car, but I want a motorcycle. I always have. Women *can* ride motorcycles, Saul, don't deny it. Oh. And another thing." She dropped one hand into the dirt and balanced herself on it. "This morning I was trying to think of where the Cayuse Indians lived, and I couldn't remember, and we don't have an encyclopedia to check. We need that." She put her hand over her eyes, to shade them. "Saul, why are you looking like that? Are you in a state?"

"No, I'm not in a state."   100

"A motorcycle would do wonders for *both* of us, Saul. A small one, not one of those hogs. Do you like my petunias? Should I have some purple over there? Maybe this is too much red and white. What would you think of some dianthus right there?" She pointed with her trowel. "Or maybe some sweet william?"

"Sure, sure." He didn't know what either variety looked like. Flowers seemed so irrelevant to everything. He looked down at her bare feet.

"Where *did* the Cayuse Indians live, Saul?"

"Oregon, I think."

"What do you think about a motorcycle? For little trips into town."   105

"Sounds okay. They aren't exactly safe, you know. People get killed on motorcycles."

"Those people aren't careful. I'll be careful. I'll wear a helmet. I just want to do it. Imagine a girl—me—on one of those machines. Makes you feel good, doesn't it? A motorcycle girl in Michigan. The car's silly for small trips. Besides, I want to visit my friends in town."

It was true: Patsy already had many friends around Five Oaks. She belonged here, but she always seemed to belong anywhere. Now she stood up, dropping her trowel, and put her feet on Saul's shoes and leaned herself into him. The visor of her cap bumped into his forehead. But she embraced him for only a moment. "Want to help, Saul? Give me a hand putting the rest of these flowers in? And what do you say to some dianthus over there?"

"Not right now, Patsy. I don't think so."

"What's the matter?"

"I don't know."   110

"You *are* in a state."

"I guess I might be."

"What is it this time? Our recent brush with death? The McPhees?"

"What about the McPhees?" he asked. She had probably guessed.   115

"Well, they were so cute, the two of them. So sweet. And so young, too. And I know you, Saul, and I know what you thought. You thought: what have these two got that I don't have?"

She *had* guessed. She usually did. He stepped backward. "Yes," he said, "you're right. What *do* they have? And why don't I have it? I'm happy with *you*, but I—"

"You can't be like them because you can't, Saul. You fret. That's your hobby. It's how you stay occupied. You've heard about spots? About how a person can't change them? Well, I *like* your spots. I like how you're a professional worrier. And you always know about things like the Cayuse Indians. I'm not like that. And I don't want to be married to somebody like me. I'd put myself to sleep. But you're perfect. You're an early-warning system. You bark and growl at life. You're my dog. You do see that, don't you?"

"Yes." He nodded.

After he had kissed her, and returned to the house, he took the matchbook   120
he had pocketed at the McPhees' up to his study. At his desk, with a pair of scissors, he cut off the flap of the matches, filled in his name and address, and wrote a check for six dollars to the Wisdom Foundation, located at post office box number in Cincinnati, Ohio. Just to make sure, he enclosed a letter.

Dear Sirs,
     Enclosed please find a check for six dollars for your SECRETS OF THE UNIVERSE. Also included is my name and address, written on the back of this book of matches. You will also find them typed at the bottom of this letter. Thank you. I look forward, very much, to reading the secrets.
     Sincerely,
     Saul Bernstein

He examined the letter, wondering if the last sentence might not be too ironic, too . . . something. But he decided to leave it there. He took the letter, carefully stamped—he put commemorative stamps on all his important mail— out to the mailbox, and lifted the little red flag.

He thought: I am no longer a serious person. My grandfather read the Torah, my father read Spinoza and Heine and books on immunology, and here I am, writing off for this.

* * *

On his trips into town, Saul began to take the long route, past the McPhees' house, slowing down when he was close to their yard. Each time that he found himself within a mile of their farm, he felt his stomach knotting up in anxiety and sick curiosity. He felt himself twisting in the coils of something like envy, but not envy, not exactly. Driving past, at evening, he occasionally saw them out in the yard, Emory mowing or clipping, their baby strapped to his back, Anne up on a ladder doing something to the windows, or out in the garden like Patsy, planting. They could have been anybody, except that, for Saul, they gave off a disturbing aura of unreflective happiness.

The road was far enough away from their house and the flaking shed so that they wouldn't see him; his car was just another car. But on a particular Friday, in early June, after work, he drove past their property and saw Emory in the front yard, in the gold twilight, pushing his wife, who was sitting in the swing. Emory, the ex-football player, had on his face (through Saul's binoculars) a solemnly contented expression. The baby was in a stroller close by. His wife was in a white T-shirt and jeans, and Emory himself was wearing jeans but no shirt. She was probably proud of her breasts and he was probably proud of his shoulders. Anne held on to the ropes of the swing. Her hair flew up as she rose, and Saul, who took this all in in a few seconds, could hear her cries of delight from his car. Taking his surreptitious glances, he almost drove off the road again. Of course they were children, he knew that, and that wasn't it. They gave off a terrible glow. They had the blank glow of angels.

They lived smack in the middle of reality and never gave it a minute's thought. They'd never felt like actors. They'd never been sick with irony. The long tunnel of their thoughts had never swallowed them. They'd never had restless sleepless nights, the urgent wordless unexplainable wrestling matches with the shadowy bands of soul-thieves.

God damn it, Saul thought. Everybody gets to be happy except me. Saul heard Anne's cries. The sun was sweating all over his forehead. He felt faint, and Jewish, as usual. He turned on the radio. It happened to be tuned to a religious station and some choir was singing "When Jesus Wept."

* * *

"It's your play, Saul."

"I know, I know."

"What's the matter? You got some bad letters?"

"The worst. The worst letters I've ever had."

"You always say that. You whine and complain. You're such a whiner, Saul, you even whine in bed. You were complaining that time just before you spelled out 'axiom' over that triple word score and got all those points last winter. You do this act when we play Scrabble and then you always beat me." Patsy was sitting cross-legged in her chair, as she liked to do, with a root beer bottle positioned against her instep, as she arranged and rearranged the letters on her slate.

Saul examined the board. The only word he could think of spelling out was "paint," but the word made him think of Emory McPhee. The hand of fate again, playing tricks on him. Glancing down at the words on the board, he thought he saw that same hand at work, spelling out some invisible story.

```
                    DEER
                    O
                    U
     MOONBEAM
       U        T        I
ROAR                    LUST
    KEY                  D
    Y
```

Saul always treated Scrabble boards as if they were fortune-telling equipment, with the order creating a narrative. Patsy had started with "moon," and he had added "beam" onto it. When she hung a "mild" from the moonbeam, he spiced it up with "lust," but she had replied to his interest in sex with "murky," hanging the word from that same moonbeam. "Mild" and "murky" came close to how he felt. His mother, Delia, had said so on the phone yesterday. "Saul, darling," she said, "you're sounding rather *dark* and *mysterious* lately. What's gotten into you?" He had not told her about the accident. She would have been alarmed and would have stayed alarmed for several months. She was a fierce mother, always had been. "I'm okay, Ma," he had said. "I'm just working some things through."

"You're leaving Five Oaks?" she asked hopefully.

"No, Ma," he had said. "This town suits me."

"All that mud, Saulie," she had said, dubious as always about the soil. "All   135
those farms," she added vaguely. "You didn't have a *seder* this year, did you?"

"No, Ma. I told you we didn't."

"You didn't open the door for Elijah? When you were a little boy you loved to do that. When it came time in the service, you always ran for the front door and held it open and you—"

"Saul," Patsy said. "Wake up." She shook him. "You're wool-gathering."

"Just thinking about my mother," he said. He looked up at Patsy. "What are all those deer doing on our Scrabble board?" he asked. "Give me a swig of your root beer."

She handed it to him. He appreciated the golden color of the fine hairs on   140
her arm in the lamplight. "I think I saw some, as a matter of fact," she said. "I thought I saw, what would you call it, a herd of deer, far in back, beyond our property line, a few nights ago. If you ever go back up to the roof, honey, give a look around. You might see them."

"Right, right." He couldn't put all five of his letters for "paint" on the Scrabble board. He removed the *t*. Pain. He held the four letters for pain in his hand, and he added them to the final *t* in "lust."

"Funny how 'pain' and 'lust' give you 'paint,' " Patsy said. "Sort of makes me think of the McPhees and the heady smell of turpentine."

They glanced at each other, and he tried to smile. A fly was buzzing around the bulb in the lamp. He was thinking of Patsy's new blue motorcycle out back, shiny and powerful and dangerous to ride. The salesman had said it could go from zero to fifty in less than six seconds. The hand of fate was ready to give him a good slapping around. It had announced itself. Saul felt a groan coming on. He looked at Patsy with helpless love.

"Oh, Saul," she said. She clambered into his lap. "You always get this way during these games. You always do." He saw her smiling in the reflection of his love for her. "You're so cute," she said, then kissed him a long time.

* * *

At ten minutes past three o'clock, he rose out of bed, half to get a glass of water and half to look out the back window. When he did, he saw them: just about where Patsy said they would be, far in the distance, beyond their property line, a herd of deer, silently passing. He ran downstairs in his underwear and went out through the unlocked back door as quietly as he could. He stood in the yard in the June night, the crickets sounding, the moon dimly outlined behind a thin cloud in the shape of a scimitar. In this gauzy light, the deer, about eight of them, distant animal forms, walked across his neighbor's field into a stand of woods. He found himself transfixed with the mystery and beauty of it. Hunting animals suddenly made no sense to him. He went back to bed. "I saw the deer," he said. He didn't know if Patsy was asleep. During the summer she wore Saul's T-shirts to bed, and that was all; her arms were crossed on her chest like a Crusader. "I saw the deer," he said again, and, awake or asleep, she nodded.

* * *

Two days later, the letter containing the secrets of the universe came from the Wisdom Foundation in Cincinnati. Saul sat down on the front stoop and tore the letter open. It was six pages long and had been printed out by a computer, with Saul's name inserted here and there.

Dear **Mr. Bernstein,**
   Nothing is settled. Everything is still possible. Your thoughts are both yours and someone else's. Sometimes we say hello to the world and then goodbye, but that is not the end and we say hello again. God is love, **Mr. Bernstein**, denying it only makes us unhappy. Riches are mere appearances. **Our thoughts are more real than hammers and nails.** We can make others believe us, **Mr. Bernstein**, if the truth is in us. Buddha and Jesus the Christ and Mohammed agreed about just about everything. Causing pain to others only prolongs our own pain. A free and open heart is the best thing. Live simply. Don't pretend to know something you don't have a clue about. You may feel as if you are headed toward some terrible fate, **Mr. Bernstein**, but that may not come to pass. You can avoid it. **Throw your bad thoughts into the mental wastebasket.** There is a right way and a wrong way to dispose of bad thoughts. Everything about the universe worth knowing is known. What is not known about the universe is not worth knowing. Follow these steps. Remember that trees will always be with us, mice will always be with us, mosquitoes will always be with us. Therefore, avoid mental cleanliness. Never start a sentence with the words 'What if everybody . . .'

It went on for several more pages. Saul liked the letter. It sounded like his other grandfather, Isaac, the pious atheist, an exuberant man much given to laughter at appropriate and inappropriate moments, who offered advice as he passed out candy bars and halvah to his grandchildren. This letter, from the Wisdom Foundation, was signed by someone named Giovanni d'Amato.
   Saul looked up. For a moment the terrifying banality of the landscape seemed to dissolve into geometrical patterns of color and light. Taken by

surprise, he felt the habitual weight on his heart lifting, as if by pulleys, or, better yet, birds of the spirit sent by direct mail from Giovanni d'Amato. He decided to test this happiness and got into the dented car.

He drove toward the McPhees'. The dust on the dirt road whirled up behind him. He thought he would be able to stand their middle-American happiness. Besides, Emory was probably working. No: it was Saturday. They would both be home. He would just drive by and that would be that. So what if they were happy, these dropouts from school? He was happy, too. He would test his temporary happiness against theirs.

The trees rushed past the car in a kind of chaotic blur.   150

He pressed down on the accelerator. A solitary cloud—wandering and thick with moisture—straying overhead but not blocking the sun, let down a minute's worth of vagrant rainbowed shower on Saul's car. The water droplets, growing larger, actually bounced on the car's hood. He turned on the wipers, causing the dust to streak in perfect protractor curves. The rain made Saul's car smell like a nursery of newborn vegetation. He felt the car drive over something. He hoped it wasn't an animal, one of those anonymous rodents like mice and chipmunks that squealed and died and disappeared.

Ahead and to the left was the McPhees'.

As usual, it looked like something out of an American genre painting, the kind of second-rate canvas hidden in the back of most museums near the elevators. Happiness lived in such houses, where people like Saul had never been permitted. In the bright standing sunshine its Midwestern Gothic acute angles pointed up straight toward heaven, a place where there had been a land rush for centuries and all the stakes had been claimed. Standing there in the bright theatrical sun—the rain had gone off on its way—the house seemed to know something, to be an answer ending with an exclamation point.

Saul crept past the front driveway. His window was open, and, except for the engine, there was no sound: no dog barking. And no sign, either, of Anne or Emory or their baby, at least out here. Nothing on the front porch, nothing in the yard. He *could* stop and say hello. That was permitted. He could thank them for their help two weeks ago. He hadn't done that. Emory's pickup was in the driveway, so they were at home; happy people don't go much of anywhere anyway, Saul thought, backing his car up and parking halfway in on the driveway.

When he reached the backyard, Saul saw a flash of white, on legs, bounding   155 at the far distances of the McPhees' field into the woods. From this distance it looked like nothing he knew, a trick of the eye. Turning, he saw Anne McPhee sitting in a lawn chair, reading the morning paper, a glass of lemonade nearby, their baby in the crib in the shade of the house, and Emory, some distance away, in a hammock, reading the sports section. Both of them held up their newspapers so that their view of him was blocked.

Quietly he crossed their back lawn, then stood in the middle, between them. Emory turned the pages of his paper, then put it down and closed his eyes. Anne went on reading. Saul stood quietly. Only the baby saw him. Saul reached down and picked out of the lawn a sprig of grass. Anna McPhee coughed. The baby was rattling one of its crib toys.

He waited for a minute, then walked back to his car. Anne and Emory had not seen him, and he felt like a prowler, a spy from God. He felt literally now what he had once felt metaphorically: that he was invisible.

When he was almost home, he remembered, or thought he remembered, that Anne McPhee had been sunning herself and had not been wearing a blouse or a bra. Or was he now imagining this? He couldn't be sure.

* * *

Patsy nudged him in the middle of the night. "I know what it is," she said.

"What?"

"What's bothering you."

He waited. "What? What is it?"

"You're like men. You're a man and you're like them. You want to be everything. You want to have endless endless potential. But then you grow up. And you're one thing. Your body is, anyway. It's trapped in *this* life. You have to say goodbye to the dreams of everything."

"Dreams of everything."

"Yes." She rolled over and made designs on his chest with her fingers. "Don't pretend that you don't understand. You want to be an astronaut and a Don Juan and Elvis and Einstein."

"No. I want to be Magic Johnson."

"Whatever. But you want to be all those people. You want to be a whole roomful of people, Saul. That's kid stuff." She let her head drop so that her hair brushed against him.

"What about you?"

"Me? I don't want to be anything else," she said sleepily, beginning to rub his back. "I don't have to be a great person. I just want to do a little of this and a little of that."

"What's wrong with ambitions?" he asked. "You could be great at something."

Her hand moved into his hair, tickling him. "Being great is too tiring, Saul, and it's boring. Look at the great ambition people. They're wrecking the earth, aren't they. They're leaving it in bits and scraps." She concentrated on him in the dark. "Saul," she said.

"Your diaphragm's not on."

"I know."

"But."

"So?"

"Well, what if?"

"What if? You'd be a father, that's what if." She had turned him so that she was right up against him, her breasts pressing him, challenging him.

"No," he said. He drew back. "Not yet. Let me figure this out on my own. There'd be no future."

"For the baby?"

"No. For me." He waited, trying to figure out how to say this. "I'd have to be one person forever. Does that make sense?"

"From you, it does." She pulled herself slightly away from him. They rearranged themselves.

* * *

The following Saturday he drove into Five Oaks for a haircut. When his hair was so long that it made the back of his neck itch, he went to Harold, the barber, and had it trimmed back. Harold was a pale, slightly bland-looking Lutheran, a terrible barber with a nice disposition who was in the same bowling league with Saul and who sometimes practiced basketball at the same times that Saul did. Many of the men in Five Oaks looked slightly peculiar and asymmetrical, thanks to Harold. The last time Saul had come in, Harold had been deep in a conversation with a woman who was accusing him of things; Saul couldn't tell exactly what Harold was being accused of, but it sounded like a lovers' quarrel, and Saul liked that. Anyone else's troubles diminished his.

By coincidence, the same woman was back again in the barbershop with her son, whose hair Harold was cutting when Saul rang the bell over the door as he entered. To pass the time and achieve a moment's invisibility, he picked up a newspaper from the next chair over and read the morning's headlines.

SHOTS FIRED AT HOLBEIN REACTOR
Iranian Terrorists Suspected

Shielded by his paper, Saul heard the woman whispering directions to Harold, and Harold's faint, exasperated "Louise, I can do this." Saul pretended to read the article; the shots, as it turned out, had been harmless. Even though there had been no damage, some sort of investigation was going on. Saul thought Iranians could do better than this.

There was more whispering, which Saul tried not to hear. After the woman had paid for her son's haircut and left, Saul sat himself down in Harold's chair.

"Hey, Saul," Harold said, covering him with the white cloth. "You always 185 come in when she does. How do you do that?"

"Beats me. Her name Louise?"

"That's right. The usual trim, Saul?"

"The usual. Harold, this time try to keep it the same length on both sides, okay?"

"I try, Saul. It's just that your hair's so curly."

"Right, right." Saul saw his reflection in the mirror and closed his eyes. He 190 felt like asking Harold, the Lutheran, a moral question. "Harold," he said, "do you ever wonder where your thoughts come from? I mean, do we own our thoughts, or do they come from somewhere else, or what? For example, you can't always control your thoughts or your impulses, can you? So, whose thoughts are those, anyway, the ones you can't control? And another thing. Are you happy? Be honest."

The scissors stopped clipping. "Gosh, Saul, are you okay? What drugs have you been taking lately?"

"No drugs. Just tell me: are your thoughts always yours? That's what I need to know."

The barber looked into the mirror opposite them. Saul saw Harold's plain features. "All right," Harold said. "I'll answer your question." Then, with what Saul took to be great sadness, the barber said, "I don't have many thoughts. And when I do, they're all mine."

"Okay," Saul said. "I'm sorry. I was just asking." He tried to slump down in his chair, but the barber said, "Sit up straight, Saul." Saul did.

* * *

Days later, Saul is asleep. He knows this. He knows he is asleep next to Patsy. He 195 knows it is night, that cradle of dreams, but the earth's mad companion, the moon, is shining stainless-steel beams across the bed, and Saul is dreaming of being in a car that cannot stop rolling over, an endless flip of metal, and this time Patsy is not belted in, and something horrible must be happening to her, judging from the blur of her head. She is being hurt terribly thanks to the way he has driven the car, the mad way, the un-American way, and now she is walking across a bridge made of moonlight, and she falls. The door, Saul's door, is being kept open for Elijah, but Elijah does not come in. How will we recognize him? Saul's mind is not in Saul's head; it is above him, above his yarmulke, above his prayer shawl, his tallith. Patsy is hurt, she lies in a ditch. Deer and doubt mix with the murky roar of mild lust on the Scrabble board. And here, behind the barber chair, is Giovanni d'Amato, sage of Cincinnati, saying, "You shouldn't flunk people out of school if you're going to get drunk and roll cars." Saul, the child, is speaking to Saul the grown-up: "You'll never figure it out," and when Saul the adult asks, "What?" the child says, "Adulthood. Any of it." And then he says, "Saul, you're pregnant."

* * * * *

Saul woke and looked over at Patsy, still sleeping. He groaned audibly with relief that she hadn't been hurt. What an annoying dream. He had never even owned a tallith. After putting on his shirt, jeans, and boots, he went downstairs, and, taking the keys off the kitchen table, stepped outside.

The motorcycle felt quiet and powerful underneath him as he accelerated down Whitefeather Road. He had driven a motorcycle briefly in college—until a small embarrassing accident—and the process all came back to him now. This one, Patsy's new machine, painted pink and blue, 250 cc's, was easy to shift, and the machine gave him the impression that he was floating, or better yet, was flowing down the archways of dark stunted Michigan trees. His eyes watered, and bugs hit him in the face as he speeded up. He felt the rear wheel slip on the dirt. He didn't know what he was doing out here and he didn't care.

He turned left onto Highway 14, and then County Road H, also dirt, and he downshifted, feeling the tight, close gears meshing, and he let the clutch out, slowing him down. On the road the cycle's headlight was like a cone, leading him forward, away from himself, toward something more inviting and dangerous. In the grip of spiritual longing, a person goes anywhere, traveling over the speed limit. The night was warm, but none of the summer stars was visible. Behind the clouds the stars were even now rushing away in the infinity of expanding space. Saul felt like an astral body himself. He too would rush away into emptiness. In the green light of the speedometer he saw that he was doing a respectable fifty. Up ahead the wintry white eyes of a possum glanced toward him before the animal scurried into the high grass near the road. Saul wanted to be lost but knew he could not be. He knew exactly where he was: fields, forest, fields. He knew each one, and he knew whom they belonged to, he had been here that long.

And of course he knew where he was going: he was headed toward the McPhees', that house of happiness, that castle of light, where everyone, man woman and child, would be sleeping soundly, the sleep of the happy and just and thoughtless. Saul felt blank, gripped by obsession, simultaneously vacant and full of shame.

He looked at his watch. It was past midnight. Their house would be dark.   200

But it was not. On the road beyond their driveway, Saul slowed down and then shut off the engine, holding on tightly to the handlebars as he stared, like the prowler he was, toward the second-floor windows, from which sounds emerged. From where he was spying, Saul could see Anne sitting in a rocking chair by the window with their baby. The baby was crying, screaming; Saul could hear it from the road. And, in the background, back and forth, Saul could see Emory McPhee pacing, the all-night walk of the helpless father. An infant with colic, a rocking mother, a pacing father, screams of infant misery, and now the two of them, Anne and Emory, beginning to shout at each other over what to do.

Saul turned his motorcycle around, pushed it down the road, then started the engine. He felt better. He could have gone to their front door and welcomed them as the official greeter of ordinary disharmony. I was always just as real as they were, Saul thought. I always was.

On the left the broken fences bordering the farmland quavered up and down and seemed to start bouncing, visually, as he accelerated. The lines on the telephone poles jumped nervously as he passed them until they had the rapid and nervous movements of pens on graph paper marking an erratic heartbeat. Rain—he hadn't known it was going to rain, no one had told him—began falling, getting into his eyes and falling with cold precision on the backs of his hands. He felt the cloth of his shirt getting soaked and sticking to his shoulders. The rain was persistent and serious. He felt the tires of Patsy's motorcycle slipping on the mud, nudging the rear end of the bike off, slightly, thoughtfully, toward the left side. Then the road joined up with the highway, where the traction improved, but the rain was falling more heavily now, soaking him so he could hardly see. He came to a bridge, slowed the bike, and huddled in its shelter for a moment, until the rain seemed to let up, and he set out again. Accelerate, clutch, shift. He wanted to get home to Patsy. He wanted to dry his hair and get into bed next to her. He couldn't think of anything else he wanted.

A few hundred feet from his own driveway, he looked through the rain, only a drizzle now, and he saw, looking back at him, their eyes lit by his headlamp, the deer he had seen before, closer now, crossing his yard. They stood there, on his property. But this time, there was another, a last deer, one he hadn't seen before, behind the others, slightly smaller, as if reduced somehow. It was an albino. In the darkness and rain it moved in a haze of whiteness. Seeing it, Saul thought: oh my God, I'm about to die. The deer had stopped, momentarily frozen in the light. The albino's eyes—it was a doe—were pink, and its fur was as white as linen. The animal flicked its tail, nervously hypnotized. Its terrible pink eyes, blank as neutron stars at the center, stared at him. Saul turned off the engine and the headlight. Now, in the dark, two brown deer bounded toward the west, but the albino stood still, staring in Saul's direction, a purposeful stare. He gripped the handlebars so hard that his forearms began to knot into a cramp. The animal was a sign of some kind, he was sure—only a fool would think otherwise—and he felt a moment of dread pass through his body as the deer now turned her eyes away from his and began to walk off into the night. He saw her disappear behind a maple tree in his backyard, but he couldn't follow her beyond that. He was trembling now. Shivering spasms began at his wet shoulders and passed down his chest toward his legs. The dread he had felt before was turning rapidly into pure spiritual fright, alternating waves of chill and heat rushing up and down his body. He remembered to get off the road. He pushed the motorcycle into the garage, kicking down its stand. He crossed the yard and reached the back door. The rain picked up again and sprayed into him as the wind carried it. In his mind's eye he saw the deer looking back at him. He had been judged, and the judgment was that he, Saul, was only and always himself, now and onward into infinity. His boots were wet. They stank of wet leather. Outside the back door, on the lawn, he took the boots off, then his wet shirt and his jeans. It occurred to him to stand there naked. With no clothes on he stood in the rain and the dark, and he fell to his knees. He wasn't praying. He didn't know what he was doing. Something was filling him up. It felt like the spirit, but the spirit of what, he didn't know. He lay down on the grass. One sob tore through him, and then it was over.

He felt like getting up and running out into the field in back of the house, 205 but he knew he couldn't break through his self-consciousness enough to do that. In the rain, which no longer felt cold, he sensed that he was entering a condition that had nothing to do with happiness because it was so far beyond it. All he was sure about was that he was empty before and now was filled, filled with both fullness and emptiness. These emotions didn't quite make sense, but he didn't care. The emptiness was sweet; he could live with it. He hurried into the house and dried off his hair in the dark downstairs bathroom. Quickly he toweled himself down and then rushed up the stairs. There was a secret, after all. In fact there were probably a lot of secrets, but there was one he now knew.

He entered their bedroom. Rain fingernailed against the window glass. Patsy lay in bed in almost complete darkness, wearing one of Saul's T-shirts. Her arms were up above her head. He could see that she was watching him.

"Where were you?"

"I went out for a ride on your motorcycle. I couldn't sleep."

"Saul, it's raining. Why are you naked?"

"It's raining now. Not when I started."   210

"Why are you standing there? You don't have any clothes on."

"I saw something. I can't tell you. I think I'm not supposed to tell you what I saw. It was an animal. It was a private animal. Patsy, I took off my clothes and lay down on the lawn in the rain, and it didn't feel weird, it felt like just what I should do."

"Saul, what is this about?"

"I'm not sure."

"Try. Try to say."   215

"I think I'm pregnant."

"What does that mean?"

"I think it means that whoever I am, I'm not alone with myself."

"I don't understand that."

"I know."   220

"Come to bed, Saul. Get in under the sheet."

He climbed in and put his leg over hers.

"I can't quite get used to you," she said. "You're quite a mess of metaphors, Saul, you know that."

"Yes."

"A man being pregnant." She put her hand familiarly on his thigh. "I wonder what that means." 225

"It's a feeling, Patsy. It's a secret. Men have secrets, too."

"I never said they didn't. They love secrets. They have lodges and secret societies and stuff—the Fraternal Order of Moose."

"Can we make love now, right this minute? Because I love you. I love you like crazy."

"I love you, too, Saul. What if you make *me* pregnant? It could happen. What if I get knocked up? Is it all right now?"

"Yeah. What's the problem?" 230

"What will we say, for example?"

"We'll say, 'Saul and Patsy are pregnant.'"

"Oh sure we will."

"Okay, we won't say it." He had thrown the sheet back and was kissing the backs of her knees.

"Are you crying? Your face is wet." 235

"Yes."

"But you're being so jokey."

"That's how I handle it."

"Why are you crying?"

"Because . . ." He wanted to get this right. "Because there are signs and won- 240 ders. What can I tell you? It's all a feeling. In the morning, I'll deny I said this."

She was kissing him now, but she stopped, as if thinking about his recent sentences. "You *want* to make me pregnant, too, don't you?"

"Yes."

"So you're not alone in this."

"That's right."

"One more little ambassador from the present to the future. That's what you 245 want."

"Sort of." He moved up and took her fingers one by one into his mouth and bit them tenderly. Patsy had started to hum. She was humming "Unchain My Heart." Then she opened her mouth and sang quietly, "Unchain my heart, and set me free."

"I'll try, Patsy."

"Yes." They often talked while they made love. A moment later, she said, "This won't solve anything. There'll be tears. People—babies—you know how they cry."

"Yes." And even now Saul felt as though he heard someone wailing softly in the next room. Still he continued. Then he had a thought. "Patsy," he said, "the window. We should stand by the window."

"Why?" 250

"To try it." He disentangled himself from her, stood, and brought her over to the window. He opened it so that droplets of rain blew in over them. "Now," he said. There was a bit of lightning, and he lifted her to him. She held on, her arms clasped behind his neck. He felt as though a thousand eyes, but not human eyes, were looking in on them with tender indifference. They were and were not interested. They would and would not care. They would and would not love them. Finally they would turn away, as they tended to turn away from all human things, in time. Saul felt Patsy begin to tremble, a slight shivering along her back, a rising in tension before release. More rain came in, warm June rain on his arm. He felt Patsy's mouth on his curls, the ones recently cut by Harold; she was panting, and so was he, and for a split second, he understood it all. He understood everything, the secret of the universe. After an instant, he lost it. Having lost the secret, forgotten it, he felt the usual onset of the ordinary, of everything else, with Patsy around him, the two of them in their own familiar rhythms. He would not admit to anyone that he had known the secret of the universe for a split second. That part of his life was hidden away and would always be: the part that makes a person draw in the breath quickly, in surprise, and stare at the curtains in the morning, upon awakening.

Talking about the Text

1. What effect does the title of the story have on you, before and after you read the story? Is it an effective and true title for the story?
2. Something significant happens to Saul during the course of this story, though it is not clear to him or to us exactly what. How do you interpret what goes on within him? What exactly sets off his anxiety? Is it the accident or the "judgment" by Emory, or both equally? You can leave some matters in the form of questions and speculation.
3. A great deal is made of "happiness" in the story. Is Saul ever able to define it? Does Emory McPhee know what it is? Does Patsy? What does it mean to you?

Writing about the Text

1. What is the narrator's point of view toward Saul? What about Saul and his world does the narrator find humorous? Judging from what Patsy says, what would her point of view on Saul be, do you think?
2. The story is told from Saul's point of view, but not *by* Saul. Does it seem as if there's any difference between Saul's point of view and the narrator's?
3. Describe Patsy. In what ways does she seem a good spouse for Saul? What do you make of the narrator's comment that she is a woman and behaves like a woman? Why is Saul not apparently envious of her happiness?

Linking the Text to Other Texts

1. Comment on the role of Ray Charles's song "Unchain My Heart" in the story. (Recording information for this song can be found in the Audio Locale feature at the end of the chapter, on p. 309.)
2. Write about the undercurrent of the spiritual or metaphysical here, spurred by the fact that Saul has been interested in the gloomy German philosopher Schopenhauer. To help you get started, think of how some of the words and phrases connect, however simply, to the metaphysical. For Saul, Emory McPhee and Patsy are "into the real." What does he mean? Saul also wonders whether we are free and make our own decisions, or whether we're pretty much subject to fate. There's also an attention to the "spiritual," which you might want to bring into this connection.

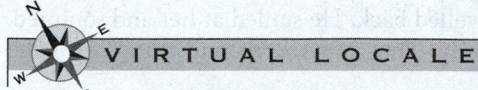

VIRTUAL LOCALE

Charles Baxter's Website. Charles Baxter's official website, at http://www. charlesbaxter.com, offers a range of information on Baxter's writing career, including biographical information; a complete list of his works, published and unpublished; a curriculum vitae; additional links for research, including recent interviews, profiles in magazines, and online audio clips from a September 2002 reading he gave at Michigan State University; and an itinerary of planned future readings. Using the "Question & Answer" form on the site, readers can e-mail Baxter about his work.

Kiss Away (1995)

The house had an upstairs sleeping porch, and she first saw the young man from up there, limping through the alley and carrying a torn orange and yellow Chinese kite. He had a dog with him, and both the dog and the man had an air of scruffy unseriousness. From the look of it, no project these two got involved with could last longer than ten minutes. That was the first thing she liked about them.

Mid-morning, midweek, midsummer: even teenagers were working, and in this flat July heat no one with any sense was trying to fly kites. No one but a fool would fly a kite in this weather.

The young man threw the ball of string and the ripped cloth into the alley's trash bin while the dog watched him. Then the dog sat down and with an expression of pained concentration scratched violently behind its ear. It looked around for something else to be interested in, barked at a cat on a window ledge, then gave up the effort and scratched its ear again.

From the upstairs sleeping porch, the young man looked exactly like the fool in the tarot pack—shaggy and loose-limbed, a songster at the edge of cliffs— and the dog was the image of the fool's dog, a frisky yellow mutt. Dogs tended to like fools. They had an affinity. Fools always gave dogs plenty to do. Considering this, the woman near the window felt her heart pound twice. Her heart was precise. It was like a doorbell.

She was unemployed. She had been out of college for a year, hadn't been able to find a job she could tolerate for more than a few days, and with the last of her savings had rented the second floor of this house in Minneapolis, which included an old-fashioned sleeping porch facing east. She slept out here, and then in the mornings she sat in a hard-backed chair reading books from the library, drinking coffee, and listening to classical music on the public radio station. Right now they were playing the *Goyescas* of Enrique Granados. She was running out of money and trying to stay calm about it, and the music helped her. The music seemed to say that she could sit like this all morning, and no one would punish her. It was very Spanish.

She put on her shoes and threw her keys into the pocket of her jeans. She raised the slatted blinds. "Hey!" she yelled down into the alley.

5

"Hey, yourself," the young man yelled back. He smiled at her and squinted. Apparently he couldn't see her clearly. That was the second thing she liked about him.

"You can't throw that kite in there," she said. "That dumpster's only for people who live in this building." She shaded her eyes against the sun to see him better. The guy's dog was now standing and wagging its tail.

"Okay," he said. "I'll take it out," and when she told him not to and that she'd be down in a second and he should just wait there, she knew he would do what she asked. What she hadn't expected was that he would smile enormously at her and, when she appeared, give her a hug—they were strangers after all—right out of the blue. She pushed him away but could not manage to get angry at him. Then she felt the dog's tongue slurping on her fingers, as if she'd spilled sauce on them and needed some cleaning.

* * *

He offered to buy her coffee, and he explained himself as they walked. He had once had good prospects, he said, and a future about which he could boast. He had been accepted into the Wayne State University Medical School eighteen months ago but had come down with a combination of mononucleosis and bacterial pneumonia, and after recuperating, he had lost all his interest in great plans. The two illnesses—one virus and one bacteria—had taken the starch out of him, he said. He actually used expressions like that. He had a handsome face when you saw him up close, but as soon as you walked a few feet away something went wrong with his appearance; it degenerated somehow.

His name was Walton Tyner Ross, but he liked to be called Glaze because of his taste for doughnuts and for his habitual faraway expression. She didn't think someone whose nickname was Glaze was ever going to become a successful practitioner of medicine, but in a certain light in the morning he was the finest thing she had seen in some time, especially when viewed from a few inches away, as they walked down Hennepin Avenue for breakfast.

Stopping under a tree that gave them both a moment of shade, he told her that if she wanted him to, he would show up regularly in the morning from now on. He needed motivation. Maybe she did too. They would project themselves into the world, he said. She agreed, and on the next few mornings he appeared in the alley with his dog, Einstein, a few feet behind him. He called up to her, and the dog barked in chorus. She didn't think it was very gallant, his yelling up at her like that, but she had had her phone disconnected, and his passion for her company pleased and moved her.

They would walk down Hennepin Avenue past what he called the Church of the Holy Oil Can—because of its unbecoming disproportionate spire—to one of several greasy smoky restaurants with plate-glass front windows and red and white checkered cafe curtains and front counters with stools. They always sat at the stools because Walton liked to watch the grill. The first time he bought Jodie a breakfast of scrambled eggs and a biscuit and orange juice. As the breakfast went on, he became more assertive. Outside, Einstein sat near a lamppost and watched the passing pedestrians.

Walton Tyner Ross—looking very much like a fool as he spilled his breakfast on his shirt—was a Roman candle of theories and ideas. Jodie admired his

10

idea that unemployment was like a virus. This virus was spreading and was contagious. The middle class was developing a positive taste for sloth. One person's unemployment could infect anyone else. "Take you," he said. "Take us." He wolfed down his toast slathered with jam. "We shouldn't feel guilty over not working. It's like a flu we've both got. We're infected with indifference. We didn't ask to get it. We inhaled it, or someone sneezed it on us."

"I don't know," she said. In front of her, the fry cook, a skinny African-American kid with half-steamed glasses, was sweating and wiping his brow on his shirtsleeve. The restaurant had the smell of morning ambition and resolution: coffee and cigarette smoke and maple syrup and cheap aftershave and hair spray. "Maybe you're right," she said. "But maybe we're both just kind of lazy. My sister says I'm lazy. I think it's more complicated than that. I once had plans, too," Jodie said, indicating with a flick of her wrist the small importance of these plans. 15

"Like what? What sort of plans?"

She was watching the fry cook and could hardly remember. "Oh," she said. "What I wanted was an office job. Keeping accounts and books. Something modest, a job that would leave the rest of my life alone and not eat up my resources." She waited a moment and touched her cheek with her finger. "In those days—I mean, a few months ago—my big project was love. I always wanted big love. Like that game, *Careers*, where you decide what you want out of life? I wanted a small job and huge love, like a big *event*. An event so big you couldn't say when it would ever stop."

He nodded. "But so far all the love you've gotten has been small."

She looked at him and shrugged. "Maybe it's the times. Maybe I'm not pretty enough."

He leaned back and grinned at her to dispute this. 20

"No, I mean it," she said. "I can say all this to you because we don't know each other. Anyway, I was once almost engaged. The guy was nice, and I guess he meant well, and my parents liked him. They didn't mind that he was kind of ragged, but almost as soon as he became serious about me, he was taking everything for granted. It's hard to explain," she said, pushing her scrambled eggs around on the plate and eyeing the ketchup bottle. "It wasn't his fault, exactly. He couldn't do it. He couldn't play me." She gave up and poured some ketchup on her eggs. "You don't have to play me all the time, but if you're going to get married, you should be played *sometimes*. You should play him, he should play you. With him, there was no tune coming out of me. Just prose. You know, Walton," she said suddenly, "you sometimes look like the fool illustration on the tarot pack. No offense. You just do."

"Sure, I do," he said, and when he turned, she could see that his ears were pierced, two crease incisions on each lobe. "Okay, look. Here's what's going to happen. You and me, we're going to go out together in the morning and look for work. Then in the afternoon we'll drive around, I don't know, a treasure hunt, something that doesn't cost anything. Then I don't know what we're going to do in the evening. You can decide that." He explained that good fortune had put them together but that maybe they should at least try to fight the virus of sloth.

She noticed a fat balding man on Walton's other side, with hideous yellow-green eyes, staring at her. "Okay," she said. "I'll think about it."

*   *   *

The next morning, he was there in the hot dusty alley with his morning paper and his dog and his limp, and she came down to him without his having to call up to her. She wasn't totally presentable—she was wearing the same jeans as the day before, and a hand-me-down shirt from her sister—but she had put on a silver bracelet for him. As they walked to the restaurant he complimented her on her pleasant sexiness. He told her that in the moments that she had descended the back steps, his heart had been stirred. "Your heart. Yeah, right," she said.

Walking with her toward the café, Einstein trotting behind them and snap-   25
ping at flies, he said that today they would scan the want ads and would calculate their prospects. In the late morning they would go to his apartment—he had a phone—and make a few calls. They would be active and brisk and aggressive. They would pretend that adulthood—getting a job—made sense. Matching his stride, enjoying his optimism, Jodie felt a passing impulse to take Walton's arm: he was gazing straight ahead, not glazed at all, and his shirtsleeves were rolled up, and she briefly admired his arms and the light on his skin.

In the restaurant, at the counter spotted with dried jam and brown gravy, where the waitress said, "Hiya, Glaze," and poured him his coffee without being asked, Jodie felt a pleasant shiver of jealousy. So many people seemed to know and to like this unremarkable but handsome guy; he, or something about him, was infectious. The thought occurred to her that he might change her life. By the time her Belgian waffle arrived, Jodie had circled six want ads for temp secretaries with extensive computer experience. She knew and understood computers backwards and forwards and hated them all, but they were like family members and she could work with them if she had to. She didn't really want the jobs—she wanted to sit on the sleeping porch with her feet up on the windowsill and listen to the piano music of Granados and watch things go by in the alley—but the atmosphere of early morning ambition in the café was beginning to move her to action. She had even brought along a pen.

She felt a nudge in her ribs.

She turned to her left and saw sitting next to her the same fat balding man with horrible yellow-green eyes whom she had seen the day before. His breath smelled of gin and graham crackers. He was smiling at her unpleasantly. He was quite a package. " 'Scuse me, Miss," he said. "Hate to bother you. I'm short bus fare. You got seventy-five cents?" His speech wore the clothes of an obscure untraceable Eastern European accent.

"Sure," she said without thinking. She fished out three quarters from her pocket and gave the money to him. "Here." She turned back to the want ads.

"Oboy," he said, scooping it up. "Are you lucky."   30

"Am I?" she asked.

"You got that right," he said. He rose unsteadily and his yellow-green eyes leered at her, and for a moment Jodie thought that he might topple over, like a collapsed circus tent, covering her underneath his untucked shirt and soiled beltless trousers. "I," he announced to the restaurant, although no one was paying any attention to him, "am the Genie of the Magic Lamp."

No one even looked up.

The fat man bent down toward her. "Come back tomorrow," he said in a ghoulish whisper. Now he smelled of fireplace ash. "You get your prize." After a moment, he staggered out of the restaurant in a series of forward-and-sideways lurching motions, almost knocking over on the way a stainless-steel coat rack. The waitress behind the counter watched him leave with an expression on her face of irritated indifference made more explicit by her hand on her hip and a pink bubble almost the color of blood expanding from her lips. Bubble gum was shockingly effective at expressing contempt, Jodie thought. All the great waitresses chewed gum.

"Who was that?" she asked Walton.   35

He shook his head like a spring-loaded toy on the back shelf of a car. As usual, he smiled before answering. "I don't know," he said. "Some guy. Tad or Tadeusz or like that. He always asks people for money. Usually people ignore him. Nobody's given him any money in a long time. Come on. We're going to my place to make some phone calls. Then we'll go on a treasure hunt."

When they came out to the sidewalk, Einstein cried and shivered with happiness to see them, barking twice as a greeting. Walton loosened her from a bicycle stand to which she had been tethered, while Jodie breathed in the hot summer air and said, "By the way, Walton, where did you get that thing in your walk? Is it, like, arthritis?"

He turned and smiled at her. Her heart started thumping again. She couldn't imagine why men didn't smile more often than they did. It was the most effective action they knew how to take, but they were always amateurs at it. Jodie thought that maybe she hadn't been smiled upon that much in her life. Perhaps that was it.

"Fascists," Walton said, getting up. "My dog and I fought the fascists."

* * *

Walton's apartment was upstairs from an ice cream parlor, and it smelled of fudge   40
and heavy cream. Although the apartment had a small study area with bookshelves and a desk, and a bedroom where the bed was neatly made and where even the dog's rubber squeak toys were kept in the corner, the effect of neatness was offset by a quality of gloom characteristic of places where sunlight had never penetrated. It was like Bluebeard's castle. The only unobstructed windows faced north. All the other windows faced brick or stone walls so that, no matter what time of day it was, the lamps had to be kept on.

They went through the circled want ads, made some telephone calls, and arranged for two interviews, one for Jodie as a receptionist at a discount brokerage house and one for Walton as a shipping clerk.

Having finished that task, Jodie dropped herself onto one of the floor pillows and examined a photograph on the wall over the desk showing a young couple, both smiling. Wearing a flowery summer dress, the woman sat on a swing, and the man stood behind her, about to give her a push.

"That's my father," Walton said, standing behind Jodie.

"It's your mother, too."

"I know it. I know it's my mother, too. But it's mostly my father. He always   45
liked to meet my girlfriends."

"I'm not your girlfriend, Walton," she said. "I hardly know you."

He was quiet for a moment. "Want a beer?" he asked. "For lunch?"

* * *

He said unemployed people should always seek out castoffs and that was what they would do during the afternoon, but just as they were about to go out to his car, he fell asleep in his chair, his dog at his feet, her front paws crossed.

Jodie sat where she was for a moment, painfully resisting the impulse to go rummaging through Walton's medicine cabinet and desk and dresser drawers. Instead, she brought a chair over next to him, sat down in it, and studied his face. Although it wasn't an unusual face, at this distance certain features about it were certainly noteworthy. The line where the beard began on his cheek—he was cleanshaven—was so straight that it seemed to have been implanted there with a ruler. He had two tiny, almost microscopic, pieces of dandruff in his eyebrows. His lashes were rather long, for a man. His lower lip was also rather full, but his upper lip was so small and flat at the bottom that you might not notice it unless you looked carefully. When he exhaled, his breath came in two puffs: It sounded like *burr burr*. He had a thin nose, and his left cheek appeared to have the remnant of an acne scar, a little blossom of reddening just beneath the skin like a truffle. With his head leaning forward, his hair in back fell halfway to his shoulders; these shoulders seemed to her to be about average width for a man of his height and weight. Even in sleep, his forehead was creased as if in thought. His hair had a wavy back and forth directionality, and it reminded Jodie of corrugated tin roofing. She found wavy hair mysterious; her own was quite straight. She reached up to touch his hair, being careful not to touch his scalp. That would wake him. She liked the feeling of his hair in her fingers. It was like managing a small profit after two quarters of losses.

She was sitting again on the floor pillow when he woke up five minutes   50
later. He shook his head and rubbed his face with his hands. He looked over to where Jodie was sitting. "Hi," he said.

"Here's 'hi' comin' back at you," she said. She waved all the fingers of her right hand at him.

* * *

That evening she went to a pay telephone and called her older sister, the married and employed success story. Her older sister told Jodie to take her time, to buy some nice clothes, to be careful not to lend him her credit card, and to watch and wait to see what would happen. Be careful; he might be a psychopath. Sit tight, she said. Jodie thought the advice was ironic because that kind of sitting was the only sort her sister knew how to do. She told Jodie to have her phone reconnected; it wouldn't cost that much, and after all, telephones were a necessity for a working girl in whom a man was taking an interest. She asked if Jodie needed a loan, and Jodie said no.

Her best friend gave Jodie the same advice, except with more happy laughter and enthusiasm. Wait and see, go for it, she said. What's the difference? It'll be fun either way. Come over. Let's talk.

Soon, Jodie said. We'll see each other soon.

* * *

Her dreams that night were packs of lies, lies piled on lies, an exhibit of lies.   55
Mayhem, penises on parade, angels in seersucker suits, that sort of thing. She

woke up on the sleeping porch ashamed of her unconscious life. She hated the vulgarity and silliness of her own dreams, their subtle unstated untruths.

Her job interview was scheduled for eleven o'clock the following morning, and after Walton had called up to her and taken her to the café, she stared down into her third cup of coffee and considered how she might make the best impression on her potential employers. She had worn a rather formal white ruffled blouse with the palm tree pin and a dark blue skirt, and she had a semi-matching blue purse, at the sight of which Walton had announced that Jodie had "starchy ideas of elegance," a phrase he didn't care to explain. He told her that at the interview she should be eager and honest and self-possessed. "It's a brokerage house," he said. "They like possession in places like that, especially self-possession. Be polite. Don't call them motherfuckers. They don't like that. But be honest. If you're straightforward, they'll notice and take to you right away. Just be yourself, you know, whatever that is."

But she wasn't convinced. At the moment, the idea of drifting like a broken twig on the surface of a muddy river was much more appealing. All through college she had worked at a clothing store as a checkout clerk, and the experience had filled her with bitter wisdom about the compromises of tedium and the hard bloody edge of necessity. She had had a gun pointed at her during a holdup her fourth day on the job. On two other occasions, the assistant manager had propositioned her in the stockroom. When she turned him down, she expected to be fired, but for some reason she had been kept on.

"There you are." A voice: her left ear: a phlegm rumble.

Jodie turned on her stool and saw the fat man with yellow-green eyes staring at her. "Yes," she said.

"I hadda get things in order," he said, grinning and snorting. He pulled out a handkerchief speckled with excretions and blew his nose into it. "I hadda get my ducks in a row. So. Here we are again. What's your three wishes?" 60

"Excuse me?"

"Just ignore the guy," Walton said, pouring some cream into his coffee. "Just ignore the guy."

"If I was you," the fat man said, "I'd ignore *him*. They don't call him Glaze for nothing. So what's your three wishes? I am the Genie of the Magic Lamp, like I said. You did me a favor, I do you a favor." Jodie noticed that the fat man's voice was hollow, as if it had emerged out of an echo chamber. Also, she had the momentary perception that the fat man's limbs were attached to the rest of his body with safety pins.

"I don't have three wishes," Jodie said, studying her coffee cup.

"Everybody's got three wishes," the fat man said. "Don't bullshit the Genie. 65 There's nobody on Earth that doesn't have three wishes. The three wishes," he proclaimed, "are universal."

"Listen, Tad," Walton said, turning himself toward the fat man and spreading himself a bit wider at the shoulders. He was beginning, Jodie noticed, a slow threatening male dancelike sway back and forth, the formal prelude to a fight. "Leave the lady alone."

"All I'm asking her for is three wishes," the fat man said. "That's not much." He ran his dirty fingers through his thinning hair. "You can whisper them if you want," he said. "There's some people that prefer that."

"All right, all right," Jodie said. She leaned toward him and lowered her voice toward the Genie of the Magic Lamp so that only he could hear. She just wanted to be left alone with Walton. She wanted to finish her coffee. Her needs were small. "I want a job," she said softly, "and I'd like that guy sitting next to me to love me, and I'd like a better radio when I listen to music in the morning."

"*That's it?*" The fat man stood up, a look of storybook outrage on his face. "I give you three wishes and you kiss them away like that? What's the matter with you? Give an American three wishes, and what do they do? Kiss them away! That's the trouble with this country. *No imagination when it comes to wishes!* All right, my pretty, you got it." And he dropped his dirty handkerchief in her lap. When she picked it up to remove it, she felt something travel up her arm—the electricity of disgust. The fat man rose and waddled out of the restaurant. She let go of the handkerchief and it drifted toward the floor.

"What was that?" Jodie asked. "What just happened?" She was shaking.   70

"That," Walton told her, "was a typical incident at Clara's Country Kitchen Café. The last time Tad gave someone three wishes, it was because the guy'd bought him a cup of coffee, and a tornado hit the guy's garage a couple of weeks later. Fat guys have really funny delusions, have you noticed that?" He waited. "You're shaking," he said, and put his hand on her shoulder. "What'd you ask for, Jodie?"

She turned to look out the front window and saw Walton's dog gazing straight back at her in an eerie manner.

"I asked for a job, and a better radio, and a million dollars."

"Then what was all that stuff about 'kiss away'?"

"Oh, I don't know. Walton, can we go, please? Can we pay our bill and   75 leave?"

"I just remembered," Walton said. "It's that Rolling Stones tune. It's on one of those antique albums. 'Gimme Shelter,' I think." He raised his head to sing.

Love, sister, is just a kiss away,
Kiss away, kiss away, kiss away.

"I don't think that's what he meant," Jodie said.

Walton leaned forward and gave her a little harmless peck on the cheek. "Who knows?" he said. "Maybe it was. Anyhow, just think of him as an overweight placebo-person. He doesn't grant you the wish because, after all, he's just a fat psycho, but he *could* put you in the right frame of mind. We've got to think positively here."

"I like how you defended me," Jodie said. "Getting all male and everything."

"No problem," Walton said, holding up his fist for inspection. "I like fights."   80

* * *

She thought that she had interviewed well, but she wasn't offered the job she had applied for that day. They called her a week later—she had finally had a phone installed—and told her that they had given the position to someone else but that they had been impressed by her qualities and might call her again soon if another position opened up.

She and Walton continued their job-and-castoffs hunt, and it was Walton who found a job first, at the loading dock of a retailer in the suburbs, a twenty-four-hour discount store known internationally for shoddy merchandise. The job went from midnight to 8 a.m.

She thought he wasn't quite physically robust enough for such work, but he claimed that he was stronger than he appeared. "It's all down here," he said, pointing to his lower back. "This is where you need it."

She didn't ask him what he was referring to—the muscles or the vertebrae or the cartilage. She had never seen his lower back. However, she was beginning to want to. On the passenger side of his car, she considered the swinging fuzzy dice and the intricately woven twigs of a bird's nest tossed on the top of the dashboard as he drove her to her various job interviews. His conversation was sprinkled with references to local geology and puzzles in medicine and biology. He was interested in most observable phenomena, and the pileup of souvenirs in the car reflected him. She liked this car. She had become accustomed to its ratty disarray and to the happy panting of Einstein, who always sat in the backseat, monitoring other dogs in other cars at intersections.

At one job interview, in a glass building so sterile she thought she should   85 wear surgery room snoods over her shoes, she was asked about her computer skills; at another, about what hobbies she liked to fill her spare time. She didn't think that the personnel director had any business asking her such questions. These days she filled her spare time daydreaming about sex with Walton. She didn't say so and didn't get the job. But at a wholesale supplier of office furniture and stationery, she was offered a position on the spot by a man whose suit was so wrinkled that it was prideful and emblematic. He was a gaudy slob. He owned the business. She was being asked to help them work on a program for inventory control. She would have other tasks. She sighed—those fucking computers were in her future again, they were unavoidable—but she took what they offered her. If she hadn't met Walton, if Walton and Einstein hadn't escorted her to the interview, she wouldn't have.

To celebrate, she and Walton decided to escape the August heat by hiking down Minnehaha Creek to its mouth at the Mississippi River across from Saint Paul. He didn't have to be at work for another four hours. Walton had brought his fishing pole and tackle box, and while he cast his line into the water, his dog sat behind him in the shade of a gnarled cottonwood and Jodie walked downriver, looking, but not looking for anything, exactly, just looking without a goal, for which she felt she had a talent. She found a bowling ball in usable condition and one bruised and broken point-and-shoot camera that she left under a bush.

She walked back along the river to Walton, carrying the bowling ball. On her face she had constructed an expression of delight. She was feeling hot and extremely beautiful.

"See what I've found?" She hoisted the ball.

"Hey, great," he said, casting her a smile. "See what I've caught?" He held up an imaginary line of invisible fish.

"Good for you," she said. His eyes were steady on her. He had been gazing at   90 her for the last few days in a prolonged way; she'd been watching him do it. She could feel his presence now in her stomach and her knees. She heard the double blast of a boat horn. Another boat passed, pulling a water-skier with a strangely unhappy look on her face. The clock stopped; the moment paused: when he said he wanted to make love to her, that he almost couldn't wait, that he had lost his appetite lately just thinking about her and couldn't sleep, she didn't quite hear him saying it, she was so happy. She threw the bowling ball out as far as she could into the river. She didn't notice whether it splashed. She took her time getting into his arms, and when he kissed her, first at the base of her neck and then, lifting her up, all over her exposed skin, she put her hands in his hair. Suddenly she liked kissing in public. She wanted people to see them together. "Walton," she said, "make love to me. Right here."

"Let's go to your place," he said. "Let's go there, okay?"

"Happy days," she said in agreement, putting her fingers down inside his loose beltless jeans.

* * *

He was a slow-motion lover. She had made him some iced tea, but instead of drinking from it, he raised the cold glass to her forehead. Einstein had found a corner where she was panting with her eyes closed.

She had taken him by the hand and had led him out to the sleeping porch. You couldn't have known it from the way he looked in his street clothes, but his body was lean and muscular, and he made love shyly at first and didn't really become easy and wild over her until he saw how she was responding to him. She was embarrassed by how quickly and how effortlessly he made her come. She put her arms up above her head and just gave in. Women were supposed to take longer than this. Her swift ecstasy made her feel cheap. Maybe it was his slow fire burning away down on her. When she came the first time, a window shade flew up in her mind, and she could see all of her feelings waiting to be touched and moved, like passengers in a bus station. When she called out, she discovered it was Walton's name she was calling. She kissed all of his scars. She kissed his knuckles.

Maybe fools made the best lovers. They were devotees of passing pleasures, connoisseurs of them, and this, being the best of the passing pleasures, was the one at which they were most adept. His fire didn't burn away. He wasn't ashamed of any impulse he had, so he kept having them. He couldn't stop bringing himself into her. "Look at me," she said, as she was about to come again, and he looked at her with a slow grin on his face, pleased with himself and pleased with her. When she looked back at him, she let him see into her soul, all the way down, where she'd never allowed anyone to own her nakedness before.

* * *

"So. Happy ever after?"

Walton was asleep after a night's work, and Jodie had gone down to Clara's Country Kitchen Café by herself. This morning the fat man with yellow-green eyes was full of mirthless merriment, and he seemed to be spilling over the counter stool on all sides. If anything, he was twice as big as before. He was like a balloon filled with gravy. Jodie had been in the middle of her second cup of coffee and her scrambled eggs with ketchup when he sat down next to her. It was hard to imagine someone who could be more deliberately disgusting than this gentleman. He had a rare talent, Jodie thought, for inspiring revulsion. The possible images of the Family of Humankind did not somehow include him. He sat there shoveling an omelet and sausages into his mouth. Only occasionally did he chew.

"Happy enough," she said.

He nodded and snorted. " 'Happy enough,' " he quoted back to her. Sounds of swallowing and digestion erupted from him. "I give you a wish and you ask for a radio. There you have it." His accent was even more obscure and curious this morning.

"Where are you from?" Jodie asked. She had to angle her left leg away from 100
his because his took up so much space under the counter. "You're not from here."

"No," he said. "I'm not really from anywhere. I was imported from Venice. A beautiful city, Venice. You ever been there?"

"Yes," she said, although she had not been. But she did love to read histories. "Lagoons, the Bridge of Sighs, and typhoid. Yeah, I've been there." She put her money down on the counter, and when she stood up, she felt a faint throbbing, almost a soreness but not quite that, Walton's desire, its trace, still inside her. "I have to go."

He resumed eating. "You didn't even thank me," the fat man said. "You smell of love and you didn't even thank me."

"All right. Thank you." She was hurrying out.

When she saw him in the mirror behind the cash register, he tipped an 105
imaginary hat. She had seen something in his eyes: malice, she thought. As soon as she was out on the sidewalk, under the café's faded orange awning, her thoughts returned to Walton. She wanted to see him immediately and touch him. She headed for the crosswalk, all thoughts of the fat man dispersing and vanishing like smoke.

* * *

On the way back, she saw a thimble in the gutter. She deposited it in her purse. A fountain pen on the brick ledge of a storefront income tax service gleamed at her in the cottony hazy heat, and she took that, too. Walton had given her the habit of appreciating foundlings. When she walked onto the sleeping porch, she took off her shoes. She still felt ceremonial with him. She showed him the thimble and the fountain pen. Then they were making love, their bodies slippery with sweat, and this time she stopped him for a moment and said, "I saw that fat man again," but he covered her mouth, and she sucked on his fingers. Afterward, she showered and dressed and caught the bus to work. Einstein groaned in her sleep as Jodie passed her in the hallway. The dog, Jodie thought, was probably jealous.

On the bus, Jodie hummed and smiled privately. She hadn't known about all these resources of pleasure in the world. It was a great secret. She looked at the other passengers with politeness but no special interest. Her love was a power that could attract and charm. She was radiantly burning with it. Everyone could see it.

Through the window she spotted a flock of geese in a V-pattern flying east and then veering south.

* * *

From time to time, at work—where she was bringing people rapidly into her orbit thanks to her aura of good fortune—she would think of her happiness and try to hide it. She remembered not to speak of it, good luck having a tendency to turn to its opposite when mentioned.

She called her sister and her mother, both of whom wanted to meet Walton   110
as soon as possible. Jodie tried to be dryly objective about him, but she couldn't
keep it up for long; with her sister, she began giggling and weeping with happiness. Her best friend, Marge, came over one stormy afternoon in a visit of
planned spontaneity and was so impressed by Walton that she took off her
glasses and sang for him, thunder and lightning crashing outside and the electric
lights flickering. She'd once been the vocalist in a band called Leaping Salmon,
which had failed because of the insipid legato prettiness of their songs; when
they changed their name to Toxic Waste and went for a grunge sound, the other
band members had ousted her. Singing in Leaping Salmon had been her only
life-adventure, and she always mentioned it in conversations to people she had
just met and wanted to impress, but while she was singing in her high honeyed
soprano, Walton walked over to Jodie, sat down next to her, and put his hand on
the inside of her thigh. So that was that.

I have a lover, Jodie thought. Most people have lovers without paying any attention to what they have. They think pleasure is a birthright. They don't even
know what luck they have when they have it.

At the end of the day she couldn't wait to see him. Every time she came into
the room, his face seemed alert, relaxed, and sensual. Sometimes, thinking about
him, she could feel a tightening, a prickling, all over her body. She was so in love
and her skin so sensitive that she had to wear soft fabrics, cottons repeatedly
washed. Her bras began to feel confining and priggish; on some days, she would-
n't wear them. The whole enterprise of love was old-fashioned and retrograde,
she knew, but so what? Sometimes she thought, *What's happening to me?* She felt
a certain evangelical enthusiasm and piety about sex, and pity for those who
were unlucky in love.

Her soul became absentminded.

On some nights when Walton didn't have to go to the loading dock, she lay
awake, with him draped around her. After lovemaking, his breath smelled of almonds. She would detach herself from him limb by limb and tiptoe into the
kitchen. There, naked under the overhead light, she would remove her tarot
pack from the coupon drawer and lay out the cards on the table.

Using the Celtic method of divination in the book of instructions, she   115
would set down the cards.

This covers me.

This crosses me.

This crowns me, this is beneath me, this is behind me, this is before me, this
is myself.

These are my hopes and fears.

The cards kept turning up in a peculiar manner. Instead of the cards promis-   120
ing blessings and fruitfulness, she found herself staring at the autumn and winter
cards, the coins and the swords. This is before me: the nine of swords, whose illustration is that of a woman waking at night with her face in her hands.

She had also been unnerved by the repeated appearance of the Chariot in
reverse, a sign described in the guidebooks as "failure in carrying out a project,
riot, litigation."

* * *

Propped up in her living room chair, she had been dozing after dinner when the phone rang. She answered it in a stupor. She barely managed a whispered "hello."

She could make out the voice, but it seemed to come from the tomb, it was so faint. It belonged to a woman and it had some business to transact, but Jodie couldn't make out what the business was. "What?" she asked. "What did you say?"

"I said we should talk," the woman told her in a voice barely above a whisper, but still rich in wounded private authority. "We could meet. I know I shouldn't intrude like this, but I feel that I could tell you things. About Glaze. I know that you know him."

"Who are you? Are you seeing him?"

125

"Oh no no no," the woman said. "It isn't that." Then she said her name was Glynnis or Glenna—something odd and possibly resistant to spelling. "You don't know anything about him, do you?" The woman waited a moment. "His past, I mean."

"I guess I don't know that much," Jodie admitted. "Who are you?"

"I can fill you in. Look," she said, "I hate to do this, I hate sounding like this and I hate being like this, but I just think there are some facts you should know. These are facts I have. I'm just . . . I don't know what I am. Maybe I'm just trying to help."

"All right," Jodie said. She uncrossed her legs and put her feet on the floor and tried to clear her mind. "I get off work at five. The office is near downtown." She named a bar where her friends sometimes went in the late afternoons.

"Oh, there?" the woman asked, her voice rising with disappointment. "Do

130

you really like that place?" When Jodie didn't respond, the woman said, "The *smoke* in there makes me *cough*. I have allergies. Quite a few allergies." She suggested another restaurant, an expensive Italian place with lazily stylish wrought-iron furniture on the terrace and its name above the door in leaded glass. Jodie remembered the decor—she hadn't liked it. However, she didn't want to prolong these negotiations for another minute. "And *don't* tell Glaze I called," the woman said. Her speech was full of italics.

When Jodie hung up, she began to chew her thumbnail. She glanced up and saw her reflection in a window. She pulled her thumb away quickly; then she tried to smile at herself.

* * *

She was seated in what she considered a good spot near a window in the non-smoking section when the woman entered the restaurant and was directed by the headwaiter to Jodie's table. The woman was twelve minutes late. Jodie leaned back and arranged her face into a temporary pleasantness. The stranger was pregnant and was walking with a slightly prideful sway, as if she herself were the china shop. Although she was sporting an attractive watercolor-hued peacock blue maternity blouse, she was also wearing shorts and sandals, apparently to show off her legs, which were deeply tanned. The ensemble didn't quite fit together, but it compelled attention. Her hair was carefully messed up, as if she had just come from an assignation, and she wore two opal earrings that went with the blouse. She was pretty enough, but it was the sort of prettiness that Jodie distrusted because there was nothing friendly about it, nothing settled or calm. She was the sort of woman whom other women instinctively didn't like. She looked like an aging groupie, a veteran of many beds, and she had the deadest eyes Jodie had ever seen, pale gray and icy.

"You must be Jodie," the woman said, putting one hand over her stomach and thrusting the other hand out. "I'm Gleinya Roberts." She laughed twice, as if her name itself was witty. When she stopped laughing, her mouth stayed open and her face froze momentarily, as more soundless laughter continued to emerge from her. Jodie found everything about her disconcerting, though she couldn't say why. "May I sit down?" the woman asked.

Feeling that she had been indeliberately rude, Jodie nodded and waved her hand toward the chair with the good view. The question had struck her as either preposterous or injured, and because she felt off-balance, she didn't remember to introduce herself until the right moment had passed. "I'm Jodie Sklar," she said.

"Well, I know *that*," Gleinya Roberts said, settling herself delicately into her   135
chair. "You must be wondering if this baby is Glaze's. Don't worry. I can assure you that it's not," she said with a frozen half-grin, a grin that seemed preserved in ice. The thought of the baby's father hadn't occurred to Jodie until that moment. "I'm in my *fifth* month," the woman continued, "and the Little Furnace is certainly heating me up these days. Bad timing! It's much better to be pregnant in Minnesota in the winter. You can keep yourself warm that way. You don't have any children yourself, Jodie, do you?"

Jodie was so taken aback by the woman's prying and familiarity that she just smiled and shook her head. All the same, she felt it was time to establish some boundaries. "No, not yet," she said, after a moment. "Maybe someday." She paused for a second to take a breath and then said, "You know, I'm pleased to meet you and everything, but you must know that I'm . . . well, I'm really curious about why you're here. Why'd you call me?"

"Oh, don't let's rush it. In a minute, in a minute," Gleinya Roberts said, tipping her head and staring with her dead eyes at Jodie's hair. "I just want to establish a friendly basis." She opened her mouth and her face froze again as soundless laughter rattled its way in Jodie's direction. "Jodie, I just can't take my eyes off your hair. You have such beautiful black hair. Men must love it. Where do you get it from?"

"From? Where do I get it from? Well, my father had dark hair. It was quite glossy. It shone sometimes."

"Oh," the woman said. "I don't think women get their hair from their fathers. I don't think that's where that gene comes from. It's the mother, I believe. I'm a zoologist, an ornithologist, actually, so I'm not up on hair. But I do know you don't get much from your father except trouble. Sklar. What kind of name is that? Do Sklars have beautiful black hair?"

Before Jodie could answer, the waitress appeared and asked for their order.   140
Gleinya Roberts reached for the menu, and while Jodie ordered a beer, the woman—Jodie was having trouble thinking of her as "Gleinya"—scanned the bill of fare with eyes slitted with skepticism and one eyebrow partially raised. "I'd *like* wine," Gleinya Roberts said, and just as the waitress was about to ask what kind, she continued, "but I can't have any because of the baby. What I *would* like is sparkling water but with no flavoring, no ice, and no sliced lemon or lime,

please." The waitress wrote this down. "Are you ordering anything to eat?" Gleinya Roberts asked Jodie. "I am. Perhaps a salad. Do your salads have croutons?" The waitress said that they did. "Well, *please* take them out for me. I can't eat them. They're treated." She asked for the Caesar salad, explaining that she positively lived on Caesar salad these days. "But no additives of any kind, please," she said, after the waitress had already turned to leave. Apparently the waitress hadn't heard, because she didn't stop or turn around. If Jodie had been that waitress, she believed that she wouldn't have turned around, either. "I'm afraid I'm terribly picky," Gleinya Roberts announced. "You have to be, these days. It's the Age of Additives."

"I eat anything," Jodie said, rather aggressively. "I've always eaten anything." Gleinya Roberts patted her stomach and smiled sadly at Jodie but said nothing. "Now, Gleinya," she pressed on, "perhaps you can tell me why we're here."

Gleinya held her left hand out with the fingers straight and examined her wedding ring. It was a quick mean-spirited gesture, but it was not lost on Jodie. "It's about Glaze, of course," she said. "Maybe you can guess that I used to be with him. It ended two years ago, but we still talk from time to time." She took a long sip of her water, and while she did, Jodie allowed herself to wonder who called whom. And when: probably late at night. "Anyway," she went on, "that's how I know about you." She put down her water glass and smiled unpleasantly. "That's how I know about your *sleeping* porch. He's been spending some nights there. He's terribly in love with you," she said. "You're just *all* he talks about."

Jodie moved back in her chair, sat up straight, and said, "He's a wonderful guy."

"Yes," the other woman said, rather slowly, to affirm that Jodie had said what she had in fact said but not to agree to it. Suddenly, and quite unexpectedly, Gleinya Roberts half stood up, then sat down again and settled herself, flinging her elbows out, and before Jodie could ask why she had done so, though at this point the inquiry did seem rather pointless, Gleinya Roberts said, "It's so hard to get comfortable in your second term. All those little infant kicks." She patted her stomach again.

"They don't seem to have hurt you, exactly," Jodie said.

145

"No, but you have to be careful." She touched the base of her neck with the third finger of her right hand, tapping the skin thoughtfully. "You have to try to keep your looks up. You have to try to keep *yourself* up. Men get fickle. Of course, my husband, Jerry, says I'm still pretty, 'prettier than ever,' he says, a sweet lie, though I don't mind hearing it. He only says that to please me. It's just a love-lie. Still, I try to believe him when he says those things."

I bet you do, Jodie thought. I bet it's no effort at all. "You were going to tell me about Walton."

"Yes, I was," she said. The waitress reappeared, placed Jodie's glass of beer, gowned in frost, in front of her, and Jodie took a long comforting gulp. All at once Gleinya Roberts' voice changed, going up half an octave. She had leaned forward, and her face was infected with old grudges and hatreds. "Jodie," she said, "I have to warn you. I have to do this, woman to woman. I want you to protect yourself. I know how suspicious this seems, coming from an old girlfriend, and I know that it must sound like sour grapes, but I have to tell you that what I'm saying is true, and I wouldn't say it unless I was worried for your safety. He likes fights. He likes fighting. You've seen how he favors his right foot, haven't you? That old injury?"

Jodie swallowed but could not bring herself to nod.

"He got it in a bar fight. Somebody kicked him in the ankle and shattered   150
the bone. I mean, that's all right, men get into fights, but what you have to know is that he used to beat *me* up, and the girl before me, he beat her up, too. He'd get drunk and coked up and start in on me. Sometimes he did it carefully so it wouldn't show—"

"—He doesn't drink," Jodie said, her mouth instantly dry. "He doesn't do drugs."

"Maybe not *now*, he doesn't," Gleinya Roberts said, smiling for a micro-second and patting the tablecloth with little grace-note gestures. "But he has and probably will again. His sweet side is so sweet that it's hard to figure out the other side. He just explodes. He's such a good lover that you don't want to notice it. He's quite the dick artist. But then he just turns, and it's like a nightmare. He waits until you're really, really happy, and then he blows up. Once, months and months and months ago, I told him that someday I wanted to go out to the West Coast and sit on the banks of the Pacific Ocean and go whale watching. You know, see the whales go spouting by, on their migrations. We both had a vaca-tion around the same time—"

"I don't think it's the 'banks' of the Pacific Ocean. That's for rivers. I think you mean 'shore,' " Jodie said.

Gleinya Roberts shrugged. "All *right*. 'Shore.' Anyway, we both had a vaca-tion around the same time, and we drove out there . . . no, we flew . . . and then we rented a car. . . ."

She put her hand over her mouth, appearing to remember, but instead her   155
eyes began to fill with dramatic, restaurant-scene tears; and at that moment Jodie felt a conviction that this woman was lying and was still probably in love with Walton.

"We rented a car," she was saying, "and we drove up from San Francisco to-ward Arcata, along there, along that coast. There are redwood forests a few miles back from the coastline, those big old trees. We'd stay in motels, and I'd make a picnic in the morning, and we'd go out, and Glaze would start drinking after breakfast, and by mid-afternoon he'd be silent and surly—he'd stop speaking to me—and by the time we got back to our motel, he'd be muttering, and I'd try to talk about what we had seen that day. I mean, usually when you go whale watch-ing *there aren't any whales*. But there *are* always seals. You can hear the seals bark-ing, down there on those rocks. I'd ask him if he didn't think the cliffs were beautiful or the wildflowers or the birds or whatever I had pointed out to him. But I always said something wrong. Something that was like a lighted match, and he'd blow up. And he'd start in on me. You ever been hit in the face?"

Jodie had turned so that she could see the sidewalk through the window. She was getting herself ready. It wasn't going to take much more.

"I didn't think so. It comes out of nowhere," Gleinya Roberts was saying, "and you're not ready for it, and then, boom, he lands the second one on you. The first time he beats you up, it's an initiation, and then he makes love to you to make up for it, but it makes the second one easier to do, because he's already done it. You don't expect it. Why *should* you? Why do you think he got thrown out of medical school? He hurt somebody there. He broke two of my ribs. I had a shoulder separation from him. He got very practiced in the ways of apology and remorse. He has a genius for remorse. And then of course he's a demon under the sheets. The man can fuck, I'll give him that, but, I don't know, after a while great sex is sort of a *gimmick*. It's like a 3-D movie, and you get tired of it. Well, maybe you're not tired of it yet."

Jodie said nothing.

"I don't blame you. I wouldn't say anything either. I thought he was Prince   160 Charming, too. I've been there. And believe me, I had to kiss a lot of frogs before I found the right guy. I had to kiss them in every damn place they had. But he won't tell you. *He* won't tell you about himself," she repeated. "Ask his father, though. His father will tell you. Well, maybe he'll tell you. You haven't met his father yet, have you?"

She speared a piece of her Caesar salad, chewed thoughtfully, then put down her fork.

"A woman has to tell another woman," she said, "in the case of a man like this. I wanted to help you. I wouldn't want you to be on daytime TV, one of those *afternoon* talk shows, in a body cast on stage, warning other women about men like this. Jodie, you can look in my eyes and see that what I'm telling you is true."

Jodie looked. The eyes she saw were gray and blank, and for a moment they reminded her of the blankness of the surface of the ocean, and then the waters parted, and she saw a seemingly endless landscape of rancor, a desert of gray rocks and black ashy flowers. Demons lived there. Then, just as quickly as it had appeared, the desert was covered over again, and Jodie knew that she had been right not to believe her.

"You're lying to me," Jodie said. She hadn't meant to say it, only to think it, but it had come out, and there it was.

Gleinya Roberts nodded, acknowledging her own implausibility. "You're just   165 denying. You're gaga over him. Just as I was. Taking a cruise on his pleasure ship. But Jodie, trust me, *that* cruise is going to end. Don't play the fool."

"What?"

"I said, 'Don't play the fool.' "

"I thought that was what you said."

Jodie, her head buzzing, and most of her cells on fire, found herself standing up. "You come in here," she said, "with your trophy wedding ring, and your trophy pregnancy, and your husband who says you're still pretty, and you tell me *this*, about Walton, spoiling the first happiness I've had in I don't know how long? Who the hell *are* you? *What* are you? You don't even look especially human." Gleinya Roberts tilted her head, considering this statement. Her face was unaccountably radiant. "I don't have to listen to you," Jodie said. "I don't have to listen to this nonsensical bullshit."

Her hands shaking, she reached into her purse for some money for the beer,   170 and she heard Gleinya Roberts say, "Oh, I'll pay for it," while Jodie found a ten-dollar bill and flung it on the table. She saw that Gleinya Roberts' face was paralyzed into that attitude of soundless laughter—maybe it was just strain—and Jodie was stricken to see that the woman's teeth were perfect and white and symmetrical, and her tongue—her tongue!—was dark red and sensual as it licked her upper lip. Jodie leaned forward to tip over her beer in Gleinya Roberts' direction, careful to give the action the clear appearance of accident.

What was left of the beer made its dull way over to the other side of the table and dribbled halfheartedly downward.

"He's beautiful," Jodie said quietly, as the other woman gathered up the cloth napkins to sop up the beer, "and he makes sense to me, and I don't have to listen to you now."

"No, you don't," she said. "You go live with Glaze. You do that. But just remember: that man is like the kea. Ever heard of it? I didn't think so. It's a beautiful bright green New Zealand bird. It's known for its playfulness. But it's a sheep killer. It picks out their eyes. Just remember the kea. And take this." From somewhere underneath the table she grasped for and then handed Jodie an audio cassette. "It's a predator tape. Used for attracting hawks and coyotes. It used to be his favorite listening. Just fascinated the hell out of him. It'll surprise you. *Women don't know about men.* Men don't let them."

Jodie had taken the tape, but she was now halfway out of the restaurant. Still, she heard behind her that voice coming after her. "Men don't want us to know. Jodie, they don't!"

* * *

In a purely distanced and distracted state, she took a bus over to Minnehaha 175
Creek and walked down the path alongside the flowing waters to the bank of the Mississippi River. The air smelled rotten and dreary. Underneath a bush she found two bottle caps and a tuna fish can. She left them there.

* * *

Sitting on the bus toward home, she tried to lean into the love she felt for Walton, and the love he said he felt for her, but instead of solid ground and rock just underneath the soil, and rock cliffs that comprised a wall where a human being could prop herself and stand, there was nothing: stone gave way to sand, and sand gave way to water, and the water drained away into darkness and emptiness. Into this emptiness, violence, like an ever-flowing stream, was poured—the violence of the kea, Walton's violence, Gleinya Roberts' violence, and finally her own. She traced every inch of her consciousness for a place on which she might set her foot against doubt, and she could not find it. Inside her was the impulse, as clear as blue sky on a fine summer morning, to acquire a pistol and shoot Gleinya Roberts through the heart. Her mind raced through the maze, back and forth, trying to find an exit.

Gleinya Roberts had lied to her. She was sure of that.

But it didn't matter. She was in fear of being struck. Although she had never been beaten by anyone, ever, in her life, the prospect frightened her so deeply that she felt parts of her psyche and her soul turning to stone. Other women might not be frightened. Other women would fight back, or were beaten and survived. But she was not them. She was herself, a woman mortally afraid of being violated.

* * *

Three blocks away from her apartment, she bought, in a drugstore, a radio with a cassette player in it, and she took it with her upstairs; and in the living room she placed it on the coffee table, next to Walton's latest found treasures: a pleasantly shaped rock with streaks of red, probably jasper; a squirt gun; and a little ring through which was placed a ballpoint pen.

She dropped the predator tape Gleinya Roberts had given her into the machine, and she pushed the *play* button. 180

From the speaker came the scream of a rabbit. Whoever had made this tape had probably snapped the serrated metal jaws of a trap on the rabbit's leg and then turned on the recorder. It wasn't a tape loop: the rabbit's screams were varied, no two alike. Although the screams had a certain sameness, the clarifying monotony of terror, there existed, as in a row of corn, a range of distinctive external variety. Terror gave way to pain, pain made room for terror. The soul of the animal was audibly ripped apart, and out of its mouth came this shrieking. Jodie felt herself getting sick and dizzy. The screams continued. They went on and on. In the forests of the night these screams rose with predictable regularity once darkness fell. Though wordless, they had supreme eloquence and a huge claim upon truth. Jodie was weeping now, the heels of her hands dug into her cheekbones. The screams did not cease. They rose in frequency and intensity. The tape almost academically laid out at disarming length the necessity of terror. All things innocent and forsaken had their moment of expression, as the strong, following their nature, crushed themselves into their prey. Still it went on, this bloody fluting. Apparently it was not to be stopped.

Jodie reached out and pressed the *pause* button. She was shaking now, shivering. She felt herself falling into shock, and when she looked up, she saw Walton standing near the door—he had a key by now—with Einstein wagging her tail next to him, and he was carrying his daily gift, this time a birdhouse, and he said, "She found you, didn't she? That miserable, crazy woman."

* * *

He puts down the birdhouse and squats near her. From this position, he drops to his knees. Kneeling thus before her, he tries to smile, and his eyes have that pleasant fool quality they have always had. This man may never make a fortune. He may never amount to much. That would be fine. His dog pants behind him, like a backup singer emphasizing the vocal line and giving it a harmony. Walton's hands start at her hair and then slowly descend to her shoulders and arms. Before she can stop him, he has taken her into his embrace.

He is murmuring. Yes, he knew Gleinya Roberts, and, yes, they did own a predator tape *she* had found somewhere, but, no, he did not listen to it more than once. Yes, he had lived with her for a while, but she was insane (his father had been dead for a year; she had lied about that, too), and she was insanely jealous, hysterical, actually, and given to lies and lying, habitual lies, crazy bedeviling lies, and casual lies: lies about whether the milk was spoiled, lies about how many stamps were still in the drawer, lies about trivial matters and large ones, a cornucopia of lies, a feast of untruth. Gleinya Roberts was not married, for starters. He could prove that.

I'm just what I seem, he says. A modest man who loves you, who will love 185
you forever. Did Gleinya tell you that I beat her up? Do you really think I am what that woman says I am? I used to get into barroom fights, but that's different. I never denied that. She's deluded. If what she said was true, would this dog be here with me?

Jodie looks at Walton and at his dog. Then she says, Raise your hand, fast, above Einstein's head. Look at her and raise your hand.

When he does what he is asked to do, Einstein neither cringes nor cowers. She watches Walton with her usual impassive interest, her tail still wagging. She has what seems to be a dog smile on her face. She approaches him, panting. She wants to play. She sits down next to where he kneels. She is the fool's dog. She looks at Walton—there is no mistaking this look—with straightforward dog love.

Jodie believes this dog. She believes this dog more than the woman.

Let me explain something, Walton is saying. You're beautiful. I started with that the first time I saw you. He does a little inventory: you lick your fingers after opening tin cans, you wear hats at a jaunty angle, you have a quick laugh like a bark, you move like a dancer, you're funny, you're great in bed, you love my dog, you're thoughtful, you have opinions. It's the whole package. How can I not love you?

And if I *ever* do to you what that woman says I did, you can just walk.   190

*   *   *

One day he will present her with an engagement ring, pretending that he found it in an ashtray at Clara's Country Kitchen Café. The ring will fit her finger, and it will be a seemingly perfect ring, with two tiny sapphires and one tiny diamond, probably all flawed, but flawless to the naked eye. They will be walking under a bridge on the south end of Lake of the Isles, and when they are halfway under the bridge, he will show her the ring and ask her to marry him.

Then she will sit for a few more days on the sleeping porch, considering this man. She won't be able to help it that when he moves suddenly, she will flinch. She will be distracted, but with the new radio on, she will from time to time do her best to read some of the books she never got around to reading before. Literature, however, will not help her in this instance. She will take out her tarot cards and place them in their proper order on the table.

This covers him.

This crosses him.

This crowns him.   195

This is beneath him.

This is behind him.

But the future will not unveil itself. The newspapers of the future are all blank. She will in exasperation throw all the tarot cards into the dumpster. She will buy a copy of the Rolling Stones' album *Let It Bleed*. She will listen to "Gimme Shelter," the song Walton had quoted, but now she hears two lines slurred hysterically and almost inaudibly in the background—lines she had never heard before.

Rape, murder, are just a kiss away,
Kiss away, kiss away, kiss away.

She will throw away the album, also, into the dumpster.

Once upon a time, happily ever after. She will look occasionally for the   200 hideous fat man at the breakfast counter on Hennepin Avenue, but of course he will have vanished. When you are awarded a wish, you must specify the conditions under which it is granted. Everyone knows that. The fat man could have told her this simple truth, but he did not. Women are supposed to know such things. They are supposed to arm themselves against the infidelities of the future.

She will feel herself getting ready to leap, to say *yes*.

And just before she does, just before she agrees to marry him, she will buy a recording of Granados' piano suite *Goyescas*. Again and again she will listen to the fourth of the pieces, "Quejas ó la Maja y el ruiseñor," the story in music of a maiden singing to her nightingale. Every question the maiden sings, the bird sings back.

One Sunday night around one o'clock she will hear the distant sound of gunshots, or perhaps a car backfiring. She will then hear voices raised in anger and agitation. Sirens, glass breaking, the clatter of a garbage can rolled on pavement: city sounds. But she will fall back to sleep easily, her hands tucked under her pillow, drowsy and calm.

Talking about the Text

1. The theme of truth and lies plays a central role in the text. How does Jodie come to trust Walton? What seals her decision in the end to stay with him? What does the ending scene suggest about her decision?

2. In what sense are Jodie's three wishes from Tad granted? Does she get what she asked for?

3. What feeling are you left with by the end of the story? Do you trust Walton? Do you think Jodie does? Examine in particular the last paragraph: what is the meaning of the many sounds Jodie hears?

Writing about the Text

1. Discuss the way that the term "kiss away" evolves throughout the story, starting with Tad's words to Jodie in the diner.

2. Examine the role of the fool in the story. Why does Walton strike Jodie as a fool? What does it mean to "play the fool"? Who, in the end, do you think might best be described as the fool? (You also might want to research what the Fool represents in tarot readings.)

3. What does Jodie base her judgment of Walton on in the end? What conflicting information about him is she given and how does she deal with it? Examine in particular the last section of the story, which is written in future tense.

Linking the Text to Other Texts

1. Comment on the role of the Rolling Stones' song "Gimme Shelter" in the story. (Recording information for this song can be found in the Audio Locale feature at the end of the chapter, on p. 309.)

2. In both "Shelter" and "Kiss Away," the main characters must confront the risk in trusting relative strangers/others. What is at stake for Cooper in "Shelter" when he trusts Billy, and what does he risk? In "Kiss Away," what does Jodie have a chance to gain in trusting Walton? What does she risk? What do these two stories suggest about what we might gain and lose by trusting others?

❧ COMMENTARY

Charles Baxter on Fiction and the Writer's Role

Charles Baxter has been interviewed at various stages of his career. As an articulate thinker about fiction, a teacher of writing, and an interested observer of his own writing processes, Baxter brings good insights to a conversation about his own work. Here are some excerpts from interviews Baxter has given over the past decade.

From a 1997 interview with Ron Hogan in the online journal Beatrice, *http://www.beatrice.com*

Q: How does a short story start for you? With an image, a scene. . . ?

Baxter: There's actually no rule. I've started sometimes with titles. In this book [*The Believers*], there were two titles that I had before I had the story, "Kiss Away" and "The Next Building I Plan to Bomb." Most of the time, though, they begin with dramatic imagery, a set of images that feel productively unstable. Something's going to come out of them that will be interesting because there will be something strange in the midst of the familiar, or familiar in the midst of the strange.

Another way of putting this is "one thing wrong in the midst of everything else right." And then I begin to act as a sort of matchmaker, putting this character next to this character in the hopes that something will emerge or explode. If I can't get those two to create something interesting amongst themselves, I'll introduce a third character to triangulate the relationship. My stories are almost always character-driven.

Q: The compactness of short stories: You mentioned the one thing wrong amidst everything right, and in some stories the way that one wrong thing drops into place, leaving you to deal with the emotional impact . . .

Baxter: I have a habit as a writer, and I think many short story writers do, of pulling the rug out from under my characters midway through a story, doing something that turns their lives upside down. Stories begin when things start to go wrong. You have to visit trouble upon characters one way or another to get some definitive action from them, to get them to engage in the sort of impulsive behavior that I think is often the core of short stories. Novels are about the plans people make, and the decisions that they make that can lead to good or bad outcomes. Short stories as a rule depend much less on the history of a character. What I do in stories is get characters you don't need to know too much about and get them to act out on the page.

Q: Had you always planned to go back and forth between short stories and novels?

Baxter: I started being serious about being a writer by writing novels. They were all terrible and I realized that I was not learning how to write by writing novels. I wasn't getting any better at writing. So I turned to short stories because I thought I would learn how to write more acutely by practicing that form. I fell in love with the form and still love it. I prefer it to the novel, I think I'm better at it than the novel, but the commercial pressures are such that you are encouraged, to put it in the mildest form, to write novels, so I have. But my novels tend to look at times like a short story writer's novels.

From an interview in the Atlantic Monthly, "Desire Rules," August 7, 1997

Q: A great deal of your writing is invested with a distinct, wry humor. Is humor an involuntary characteristic of your writing voice or is it something you employ deliberately?

Baxter: Humorists probably work very hard on the comic touch that they use. I have never known how to do that without making my writing seem somewhat willful. At the same time I do think that when you are working at bringing strangers together—as I like to do often in my fiction—you get a kind of incongruity in the story that often gives rise to humor in one form or another. It's partly situational and partly your voice.

Q: In your essay "Against Epiphanies" you argue that a "character's experiences in a story [don't] have to be validated by a conclusive insight or brilliant visionary stop-time moment" and go on to assert that "radiance, after a while, gets routine." Yet the characters in your short stories often do experience moments of startling revelation—and, in fact, many critics identify your graceful use of epiphanies as one of your unique talents. How do you reconcile the thoughts expressed in your essay with instances of revelation in your fiction?

Baxter: I can't reconcile them. Or maybe I'm like Huck Finn's father, who has perfected his denunciation of alcohol during the day and his back-alley binges at night. I disapprove of epiphanies and their phony auras but I am besotted by them—can't get enough of them in life or elsewhere. So sue me. Seriously though, as a person who was brought up with religious faith and then got out of it, I'm always looking for secular manifestations of the sacred. At the same time I know that when these moments are arranged—particularly at the end of short stories—they acquire an absolutely formulaic quality. I noticed it particularly a few years ago when I was reading an edition of Best American Short Stories and, just out of curiosity, I started skipping to the endings of all the short stories. It was an unsettling experience because in that edition I kept coming upon final pages in which there was a moment when a character stopped and looked off into the distance, and then a sentence the equivalent of "Suddenly she realized . . ." appeared.

Q: You're quite involved in the Writers' Harvest/Share Our Strength program in which writers band together to raise money to fight world hunger. What has this experience been like for you?

Baxter: Writing is such a private occupation that I like doing what I can to make some difference in the public realm. The readings we do to benefit local hunger-relief agencies are a small gesture to reduce a big problem. I think it's a good idea for writers to get involved in such things—it can reconnect them to a larger social world, if they need it. My work for SOS has been exhilarating, and I'm proud to have done it.

From Michigan Today, Spring 1997

Q: Spiritual, magical, religious themes occur in subtle ways throughout your work. Do you have particular spiritual or religious beliefs?

Baxter: Not very many, but some. I think of it more as a subject that at this point in our history, this time in our cultural life, is important for stories. And the reason I think so is that when you consider the way stories often work, there's usually a moment when a character is compelled to believe something. Many people out there are making their way in the world by telling other people things that aren't true. And so I started to think that belief was really one of those matters that made a majority of stories work as stories. And I thought: I can start this at the bottom with characters who are either liars or truth-tellers and make it a serious matter in the opening story, "Kiss Away," with a young woman who gets involved with a guy who may or may not be abusive. He hasn't been abusive to her, but somebody has told her that he has been at one time. Whom does she believe? Finally she believes the guy's dog.

✄ COMMENTARY

Charles Baxter, Critical Writing on Fiction

From "Dysfunctional Narratives, or: 'Mistakes Were Made,' " in Burning Down the House, 1997

Sometimes—if we are writers—we have to talk to our characters. We have to try to persuade them to do what they've only imagined doing. We have to nudge but not force them toward situations where they will get into interesting trouble, where they will make interesting mistakes that they try to take responsibility for. When we allow our characters to make mistakes, we release them from the grip of our own authorial narcissism. That's wonderful for them, it's wonderful for us, but it's best of all for the story.

From "Counterpointed Characterization," in Burning Down the House, 1997

It's often fictionally interesting to get strangers together in America and start them talking, just to see what gets flung over the wall of our habitual cheerfulness and isolation. Americans are fascinated when some hole opens up in the wall. It's a pause in the midst of consumerism and self-imposed isolation. It's a zoo story. It's the movement, through counterpointed characterization, toward some latent, blasted, vestigial, phantom-limb feeling for community.

✄ COMMENTARY

Critics on the Work of Charles Baxter

From Matthew Gilbert, "Even-Tempered, Unflashy Stories of America's Heartland," review of Believers by Charles Baxter, Boston Globe, March 23, 1997

Charles Baxter is a master of deceptive simplicity. Just when you're thinking a Baxter story amounts to simply a collection of handsomely rendered details, it reveals itself as a rich intersection of thought-provoking themes. There is a gift of significance in the closing moments, a flash that's not so much an epiphany as a charged accumulation of image and character. It is the gathering of the inner resources of the story. Baxter, who has just published his fourth collection of short fiction, *Believers*, might cringe at that perception. Along with *Believers*, he has just published a book of essays on fiction called *Burning Down the House*, in which he writes persuasively "against epiphanies" and the convenient insights writers often force at the ends of stories. But rather than offering facile or fashionably quirky bits of take-out wisdom, Baxter's endings heighten the questions central to the story, lifting the story into the realm of quandary. His endings are pleasingly inconclusive.

From Robert Taylor, review of A Relative Stranger *by Charles Baxter,* Boston Globe, *September 3, 1990*

Charles Baxter's short stories have perfect pitch. Like the protagonist of his title story, who can tell an F-sharp when he hears one, Baxter reveals an unerring ear for the harmonics of his medium.

Consider his openings. Many writers of short stories, conscious of the storyteller's mandate to procure the reader's attention, begin with a big bowwow effect. But the narrative hook in a short story is not identical with a journalist's "lead." The opening of a story is influenced by the subsequent material, which reflects back on the opening despite the story's forward momentum.

Thus "Fenstad's Mother" starts with the declarative, "On Sunday morning after communion Fenstad drove across town to visit his mother." The tale begins with characterization like the story called "Snow" ("Twelve years old, and I was so bored I was combing my hair just for the hell of it"), and raises by implication the element of suspense. (Is Fenstad's mother a churchgoer?) Baxter understands exactly the weight and size of that most elusive of qualities, tone.

Communication looms large, usually within marriage as it does in "Shelter," in which the baker-hero's compulsive charity is counterbalanced by his more practical wife, an attorney. . . . Fenstad's elderly mother can communicate with dispossessed people while her logical son, who thinks in terms of abstract theory, can only admire her warmth and openness.

With the insights of the longer and felicitous final story, "Saul and Patsy Are Pregnant," Baxter is back on home ground. The narrative deftly accommodates several themes, notably the epiphanies Saul experiences when he breaks through his self-consciousness to an acceptance of the world his serene wife already exemplifies. Notable too is the way in which the author works into the pattern a scene from an earlier story, "Scissors." Harold, the barber of that story, realizes that he is cutting the hair of his natural son. "Saul and Patsy" incorporates a variation of that episode, which takes on fresh significance through its new context. Later, Saul discovers "whoever I am, I'm not alone with myself."

The characters of Charles Baxter may or may not acquire spiritual illumination. All the same, they face universal questions, the consequences of their human predicaments. In these stories not only is his technique on pitch, but his sense of a universe tuned to ultimate mystery.

INSPIRATION　MUSIC IN THE FICTION OF CHARLES BAXTER

Poster for a Rolling Stones concert, c. 1969.

Charles Baxter's short stories often find their source or inspiration in popular music. His story "Kiss Away" (p. 283), from his 1997 collection *Believers*, concerns itself largely with the protagonist's looming doubts about the true nature of her new boyfriend's character. The haunting lyrics from the Rolling Stones' "Gimme Shelter" appear as a recurrent element within the story; the story's title is also derived from those lyrics. Likewise, in "Saul and Patsy Are Pregnant," (p. 263), from Baxter's 1990 collection *A Relative Stranger*, the Ray Charles song "Unchain My Heart" appears in the dramatic opening scene and takes on a thematic role. The complete lyrics to "Gimme Shelter" can be found online via the official Rolling Stones Web site at http://www.rollingstones.com, under the "Music" link. The lyrics to "Unchain My Heart" appear below.

Commenting on the musical references in his work in a November 2003 interview in *The Morning News* with Robert Birnbaum, Baxter observed, "I used to bestrew my fiction with them. I've been trying to put myself on a diet of that. There used to be [multitudes of musical allusions] in the stories. My first book of stories, *Harmony of the World*, is loaded down with them. There are musicians all through that book. And the title itself is a reference to an opera by Paul Hindemith on the life of Johannes Kepler. It must be that I've been thinking about music so long that the references start appearing automatically." When asked whether he has a feeling in mind that he is interjecting in the story when he alludes to a piece of music, Baxter replied, "I do. I do. I think those pieces must have been playing in my head while I was writing. I have no executive abilities at music at all. If you put me in front of a keyboard, I can do nothing. In fact, one of my recurring dreams is that I am off-stage, dressed in a tuxedo, with a conductor. And we are about to go on, and I am trying to explain to him that I can't play the piano, even though I am there as the pianist for a concerto. He says, 'Charlie'—this is in the dream—'You're so modest.' I say, 'No, I really can't play the piano.' He taps his watch and says, 'It's time to go on.' Anyway, yes, I *am* like a musician in

(continued on next page)

Ray Charles, 1960.

MUSIC IN THE FICTION OF CHARLES BAXTER

the sense that there is always music going through my head. Particularly when I am writing. Those references often appear because that's the music I am hearing."

As you examine the lyrics to the song below, consider what a writer has to gain from building in a reference to popular music. Does your knowledge of the song help you understand the stories better? Do you feel you are missing something when you don't know the words and music of a song Baxter refers to?

Teddy Powell/Bobby Sharp
Unchain My Heart

Unchain my heart, baby let me be
Unchain my heart 'cause you don't care about me
You've got me sewed up like a pillow case
but you let my love go to waste so
Unchain my heart oh! Please, please set me free

Unchain my heart, baby let me go
Unchain my heart, 'cause you don't love me no more
Ev'ry time I call you on the phone
Some fella tells me that you're not at home so
Unchain my heart oh! Please, please, set me free
I'm under you spell like a man in a trance
But I know darn well that I don't stand a chance so

Unchain my heart, let me go my way
Unchain my heart, you worry me night and day
Why lead me through a life of misery
when you don't care a bag of beans for me
So unchain my heart oh! Please please set me free.

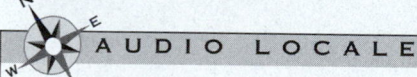

AUDIO LOCALE

"Gimme Shelter" and "Unchain My Heart." "Gimme Shelter" by the Rolling Stones was originally released on their 1969 album *Let It Bleed*. It also

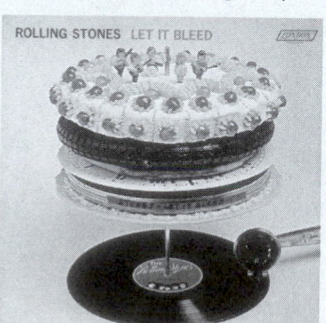

can be found on the CD *Live Licks* (Virgin Records, 2004). Ray Charles's recording of "Unchain My Heart" can be found on numerous greatest hits albums and Ray Charles compilations, including *Rhythm & Blues: Ray Charles—1954–1966* (Time-Life, 1991) and *The Very Best of Ray Charles* (Rhino, 2000).

Original 1969 album cover by graphic designer Robert Brownjohn of the Rolling Stones' Let It Bleed.

Starting Points for Further Research: Charles Baxter

- **Critical Essays:** Charles Baxter. "Dysfunctional Narratives, or: 'Mistakes Were Made.'" *Burning Down the House.* St. Paul, Minn.: Graywolf Press, 1997. 1–25.
  ———. "Against Epiphanies." *Burning Down the House.* St. Paul, Minn.: Graywolf Press, 1997. 51–77.
- **Interview:** Jennifer Lavasseur and Kevin Rabelais. "Interview." *Tin House Magazine* 7. http://www.tinhouse.com/Issues/Issue_7/baxter.html.

CHAPTER
7

More than Magnolias
Southern Women Storytellers

A commonly accepted assumption of American cultural life, encouraged by the memory of the Civil War, the legacy of slavery, and recent American politics, is that the southern United States is a separate and distinct place. Such a notion of the South's separateness and uniqueness is, of course, at least a partial fiction. For one thing, the South is big. The region includes the Mississippi Delta, the piney woods of Georgia, the bayous of Louisiana, the beaches of Florida, the hills of Appalachia, and large cities everywhere. There is the white South and the black South, the urban and the rural South, the lower-class and the middle-class South, to say nothing of the historical South and the modern South. For another thing, the rest of the United States has been somewhat "southernized." Through its migrants, its preachers, its politicians, and especially through its music and literature, the South has had a powerful influence on the rest of the nation. Thus, the notion in this chapter of the purely "southern writer" and even the purely "southern woman writer" is part truth and part fiction, something that writers and readers have agreed to ascribe to the South. It has something of a pleasing truth in it, though, and continues to influence the way emerging writers from the South think about their art.

So, with this disclaimer, how do we recognize or define a southern woman writer? First, southern women's short story writing is a distinct **subgenre**, a recognizable part of the larger category of American fiction. It is a phenomenon associated mostly with women born around the beginning of the twentieth century, plus another generation born about mid-century who have been highly conscious of writing in a tradition set by the earlier writers. To be sure, there were southern women writers in the mid and late nineteenth century, but the short story writers we call "southern" come from generations born in the early to mid twentieth century.

Second, southern writers are people who regard themselves as storytellers first and foremost. Georgia-born Mary Hood, in her brief 1986 essay "On Being a Southern Writer," captures this trait well:

> Suppose a man is walking across a field. To the question, "Who is that?" a Southerner would reply by saying something like "Wasn't his granddaddy the one whose dog and him got struck by lightning on the steel bridge? Mama's third cousin—dead before my time—found his railroad watch in that eight-pound catfish's stomach the next summer just above the dam. Big as Eunice's arm. The way he married for that new blue Cadillac automobile, reckon how come he's walking like he has on Sunday shoes, if that's who it is, and for sure it is." A Northerner would reply to the same question (only if directly asked, though never volunteering), "That's Joe Smith." To which the Southerner might think (but be too polite to say aloud), "They didn't ask his name, they asked who he is!"

Southern storytelling, then, operates by indirection, by encouraging the reader to read between the lines. It uses a special language, one laden with biblical allusions and quotes, with Protestant evangelicalism, with Shakespeare, with southern dialects, and with an attention to southern folklore. And this language pays attention to the specific details of everyday life: southern fauna and flora (e.g., catfish, redeye gravy), human ways and habits, specific place names.

Southern storytelling has recurrent themes: alcohol and violence, often at the point of a gun; the weight of the past; the pervasiveness of music (the blues, black and white gospel, jazz, bluegrass); a brand of moral blindness or hypocrisy stemming in part from the white South's self-righteous defense of slavery and the later Jim Crow laws; a focus on black-white relationships; a buried but explosive sexuality; and a love-hate attitude toward the eccentrics, the human oddities, the grotesques—those people who don't fit in. The setting of southern literature is mostly the rural or small-town South. And despite the seriousness of many of their themes, southern writers love humor and often tell side-splitting stories.

William Faulkner (1897–1962) is generally regarded as *the* giant of southern literature, but other names from his approximate era are also prominent: Erskine Caldwell, Robert Penn Warren, Katherine Anne Porter, Zora Neale Hurston, and Richard Wright, all writers who first made a name for themselves in the late 1920s or early 1930s. Following them are writers who became prominent in the late 1930s to the 1950s: Walker Percy, Flannery O'Connor, Eudora Welty,

Lillian Hellman, Tennessee Williams, Truman Capote, and Carson McCullers. Writers who have become well known since the 1970s and 1980s include Alice Walker, Mary Hood, Lee Smith, and Dorothy Allison, along with many others who represent a whole new generation of southern writers. Will they be as famous as their predecessors? It's too soon to tell.

What about the "women" aspect of this grouping, those whose names appear so prominently above? One might suppose that the southern tendency to shelter, subordinate, infantilize, and romanticize women, to see them as carriers of the faith and of morality, would leave women with no tales to tell, or at least not much freedom or encouragement to tell them. South Carolina writer Dorothy Allison (p. 416) portrays many of her female relatives as mute and long suffering. Trapped in their narrow, rural, familial settings, what would they have to say? But such lower-class southern women usually failed to qualify as "ladies," and therefore potentially had the freedom to speak. A more important point is that southern women of all classes were paradoxically widely conceived to be strong, enduring survivors. Not infrequently they were stubborn and rebellious. These traits are often ascribed to the circumstance that the white women had to run farms and households during the Civil War, sometimes with the enemy right at hand. Even when southern women remained mostly sheltered, they managed a rich inner life. As Eudora Welty says at the end of her memoir, *One Writer's Beginnings* (1984), "I am a writer who came of a sheltered life. A sheltered life can be a daring life as well. For all serious daring starts from within."

This chapter combines breakthrough writers and their self-proclaimed followers, and it takes its shape from the times in which these writers first published their work. Eudora Welty in the late 1930s and Flannery O'Connor in the mid-1940s helped establish the tradition of southern women writers. Mary Hood, Lee Smith, and Dorothy Allison, starting in the 1960s, did not quite imitate them but were working the same territory and showing many signs of their influence. Bracketing these five white women writers are two black women writers: Zora Neale Hurston, a pioneer from the 1920s, and Alice Walker, who revived interest in Hurston and consciously followed her lead, starting in the 1970s.

Did these two African American writers see themselves working in the same tradition as white writers? Not quite, since Hurston and Walker located themselves in the tradition of both African American writers and southerners. As W. E. B. Du Bois said in 1900, black Americans had a "double consciousness," first of being black, and second of being American. This double consciousness, appearing most prominently in Walker, meant that their experience of the South was inevitably different from that of their white counterparts. Nevertheless, there is no doubt that these two brilliant black writers very deliberately and proudly took the South as their base. Hurston in 1936, just as the fiction in this chapter was emerging, wrote: "But I do believe that we are seeing the birth of a new Southern tradition of writing." And when in 1973 Walker had a tombstone inscribed for Hurston's previously unmarked grave, she selected a telling accolade by the black poet Jean Toomer: "Genius of the South."

LITERARY LOCALE

The Gravesite of Zora Neale Hurston, Fort Pierce, Florida. Zora Neale
Hurston died in poverty in Fort Pierce, Florida, on January 28, 1960. Friends had
to raise $600 for her funeral, which was held at the Peek Funeral Chapel. She
was buried in an unmarked grave in a segregated cemetery called Genesee
Memorial Gardens. Alice Walker found the gravesite in the early 1970s as part of
a pilgrimage to uncover more about Hurston's life and work. With the publication of her essay "In Search of Zora Neale Hurston" in the March 1975 issue of
Ms. Magazine (later incorporated as "Looking for Zora" in her book *In Search of
Our Mothers' Gardens*), Walker is largely credited with bringing Hurston's body
of work, much of which was either out of print or forgotten, back into the literary canon and the public eye. Walker ordered the headstone that now marks
Hurston's final resting place with the epitaph "Genius of the South." The grave
can be visited at what is now the Garden of Heavenly Rest Cemetery, Avenue S
and 17th Street, Fort Pierce, Florida 34950. The site is part of the Zora Neale
Hurston Dust Tracks Heritage Trail, which offers a tour created in Hurston's
honor of more than half a dozen important Hurston-related sites in Fort Pierce.
A virtual tour of Fort Pierce can be viewed at the Zora Neale Hurston Dust
Tracks Heritage Trail website, *http://www.st-lucie.lib.fl.us/zora/index.htm.*

How did these writers emerge when they did? Hurston published first, in the
1920s, when she was associated with the Harlem Renaissance. Then came Welty, in
Jackson, Mississippi, benefiting from the early example of Texas-born Katherine
Anne Porter's 1930 collection, *Flowering Judas and Other Stories.* (See p. 542 for
Porter's short story, "The Jilting of Granny Weatherall.") In the late 1930s, Welty
and Porter were explicitly promoted by the *Southern Review,* Louisiana State

*Portrait of Katherine Anne Porter
at Yaddo (artists' colony), Saratoga
Springs, New York, 1940, by Eudora Welty.*

University's newly established literary magazine that dedicated itself to furthering the literature of the South. Like Welty, Flannery O'Connor would publish much of her early work in little magazines, with small circulations but influential readers. A promising story in a literary magazine could bring about the interest of a literary agent and even a contract with a New York publisher, which happened to both Welty and O'Connor early in their careers. After their early success in small magazines, neither had much trouble getting stories and novels published.

Another question is why this group of women emerged. They no doubt benefited from the publishing success of a whole group of promising southern writers, new voices in American letters: certainly Faulkner, though even his great novels did not sell well, but even more, best-sellers of the 1930s like Thomas Wolfe (*You Can't Go Home Again, The Web and the Rock, Of Time and the River*), Margaret Mitchell (*Gone with the Wind*), and Erskine Caldwell (*God's Little Acre, Tobacco Road*), all demonstrating that interesting, powerful voices from the South could attract readers. Talent scouts from New York publishing houses began to seek out new southern voices, and among them were Welty and O'Connor, who quickly earned reputations as writers with something distinctive to say.

Welty and O'Connor are now regarded as the two giants of the southern short story, certainly by southern writers but also by anyone who aspires to write short fiction. They dominated the 1950s and 1960s, and they spawned a host of male and female admirers. Some women, empowered by their example, set out to explore the same territory, the rural South, but with an updated perspective. Thus this chapter contains the work of successful southern women writers—Lee Smith, Mary Hood, Dorothy Allison, and Alice Walker—who consciously see themselves as influenced by Welty and O'Connor, though of course their themes and perceptions are very much their own. This is one way literary traditions get established: first the work of a few hardy pioneers, then the full flowering of talent, then the work of followers who build on the work of the greats. That is precisely what happened with the work of these southern women in the closing decades of the twentieth century.

Of course times change. The twenty-first-century South is a very different place from the South that Hurston, Welty, and O'Connor grew up in. And though most people would agree that today's South has become more "mainstream," there remains a strong sense of literary regionalism among black and white writers alike. Since 1994, a Southern Women Writers Conference has met periodically and has included a wide variety of younger fiction writers and poets. Time will tell whether such conferences will keep alive and nourish the rich strain of southern writing that characterized the late twentieth century or whether they will take southern writing in entirely new directions.

SOUTHERN WOMEN WRITERS TIMELINE

1890	Katherine Anne Porter born in Texas.
c. 1891	Zora Neale Hurston born in Florida.
1897	William Faulkner born in Mississippi.
1903	Erskine Caldwell born in Georgia.

1908	Richard Wright born in Mississippi.
1909	Eudora Welty born in Mississippi.
1911	Tennessee Williams born in Mississippi.
1916	Walker Percy born in Alabama.
1917	Carson McCullers born in Georgia.
1925	Flannery O'Connor born in Georgia.
1929	Faulkner publishes *The Sound and the Fury* (novel).
1930	Porter publishes *Flowering Judas and Other Stories*; Faulkner publishes "A Rose for Emily" (p. 549).
1932	Faulkner publishes *Light in August* (novel); Caldwell publishes *Tobacco Road* (novel).
1936	Faulkner publishes *Absalom, Absalom!* (novel); McCullers publishes "Wunderkind."
1937	Hurston publishes *Their Eyes Were Watching God* (novel).
1939	Porter publishes *Pale Horse, Pale Rider and Other Stories*.
1940	McCullers publishes *The Heart Is a Lonely Hunter* (novel).
1942	Hurston publishes *Dust Tracks on the Road* (autobiography).
1943	Welty publishes *The Wide Net* (short stories).
1944	Alice Walker born in Georgia; Lee Smith born in Virginia.
1946	Mary Hood born in Georgia; McCullers publishes *The Member of the Wedding* (novel).
1949	Welty publishes *The Golden Apples* (short stories); Dorothy Allison born in South Carolina; Faulkner wins the Nobel Prize for Literature.
1950	Faulkner publishes *Collected Stories*.
1952	O'Connor publishes *Wise Blood* (novel).
1955	O'Connor publishes *A Good Man Is Hard to Find* (short stories).
1960	Hurston dies in Florida.
1961	Percy publishes *The Moviegoer* (novel).
1962	Faulkner dies in Mississippi.
1964	O'Connor dies in Georgia.
1965	O'Connor's *Everything That Rises Must Converge* (short stories) is published posthumously.
1967	McCullers dies in New York.
1968	Smith publishes *The Last Day the Dogbushes Bloomed* (novel).
1971	O'Connor's *The Complete Stories* is published posthumously.
1973	Welty wins the Pulitzer Prize for *The Optimist's Daughter* (1972); Walker publishes *In Love and Trouble* (short stories).
1980	Welty publishes *Collected Stories*; Porter dies in Maryland.
1981	Smith publishes *Cakewalk* (short stories).
1983	Walker publishes *In Search of Our Mothers' Gardens* (essays) and wins the Pulitzer Prize for *The Color Purple* (1982); Tennessee Williams dies in New York.
1984	Hood publishes *How Far She Went* (short stories); Welty publishes *One Writer's Beginnings* (autobiography).
1986	Hood publishes *And Venus Is Blue* (short stories).
1988	Allison publishes *Trash* (short stories).

1990   Percy dies in Louisiana; Smith publishes *Me and My Baby View the Eclipse* (stories).

1992   Walker publishes *Possessing the Secret of Joy* (novel); Allison publishes *Bastard Out of Carolina* (novel).

1995   Hood publishes *Familiar Heat* (novel).

1998   Allison publishes *Cavedweller* (novel).

2001   Welty dies in Mississippi.

ZORA NEALE HURSTON   (C. 1891–1960)

Zora Neale Hurston is commonly claimed as both a southern writer and an important member of the Harlem Renaissance of the 1920s because her works show both her roots in the South and her engagement with intellectual life "up North." She grew up in the all-black town of Eatonville, Florida, and attended Howard University in Washington, D.C., and Barnard College in New York City, where she studied with and was much influenced by the great anthropologist Franz Boas. Through this exposure, she brought an anthropologist's perspective to African American life in the South, and also to her travels in Haiti and Jamaica. In keeping with her anthropological training, Hurston collected African American folktales from the rural South in Mules and Men *(1935) and* Tell My Horse *(1938).*

Hurston also wrote four novels, the best known of which is Their Eyes Were Watching God *(1937), and an autobiography,* Dust Tracks on a Road *(1942). Her plays include the comedy* Mule Bone *(1931), which was written in collaboration with her friend Langston Hughes but, due to a falling out between the two, was not produced until 1991. More recently, ten more of Hurston's plays—most unpublished and unproduced—were rediscovered. They had been deposited in the U.S. Copyright Office between 1925 and 1944 and remained in obscurity for more than half a century, until they were found again in the Copyright Deposit Drama Collection in 1997. Today, the manuscripts are housed in the Manuscript, Music, and Rare Books and Special Collections Division of the Library of Congress. Never a full member of any well-defined political movement, Hurston charted her own determined way, but she outlived her early fame. By the time of her death in 1960, her reputation was in eclipse and she died in poverty, buried in an unmarked grave. Her work languished in obscurity until the 1970s, when, with the help of Alice Walker, it was revived because of renewed interest in black literary history. Now Hurston is recognized as one of America's most individual authors and one of the most important voices in African American writing.*

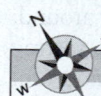 **LITERARY LOCALE**

The Zora Neale Hurston Festival, Eatonville, Florida. Since 1989, the annual Zora Neale Hurston Festival of the Arts and Humanities in Eatonville, Florida, just north of Orlando, has brought together arts and culture enthusiasts with renowned writers, scholars, and entertainment figures to participate in lectures, panel discussions, workshops, and entertainment events. Conceived of as a multicultural, multimedia celebration that honors not only the life and work of Zora Neale Hurston but also the town of Eatonville and the entire central

(continued)

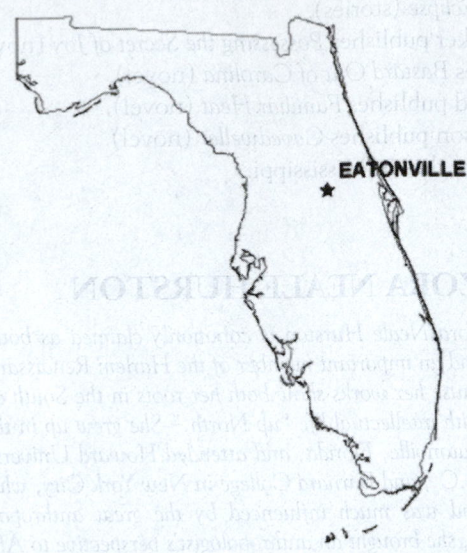

Florida area, the festival attracts over 50,000 guests each year and has included such participants as authors Alice Walker, Maya Angelou, Amiri Baraka, Nikki Giovanni, and Ntozake Shange; actors Ossie Davis, Ruby Dee, Danny Glover, Cicely Tyson, and Richard Roundtree; musicians Isaac Hayes and Celia Cruz; and historian John Hope Franklin. Further information about the festival can be found online at *http://www.zoranealehurston.cc/.*

Sweat   (1926)

I

It was eleven o'clock of a Spring night in Florida. It was Sunday. Any other night, Delia Jones would have been in bed for two hours by this time. But she was a washwoman, and Monday morning meant a great deal to her. So she collected the soiled clothes on Saturday when she returned the clean things. Sunday night after church, she sorted and put the white things to soak. It saved her almost a half-day's start. A great hamper in the bedroom held the clothes that she brought home. It was so much neater than a number of bundles lying around.

She squatted on the kitchen floor beside the great pile of clothes, sorting them into small heaps according to color, and humming a song in a mournful key, but wondering through it all where Sykes, her husband, had gone with her horse and buckboard.

Just then something long, round, limp, and black fell upon her shoulders and slithered to the floor beside her. A great terror took hold of her. It softened her knees and dried her mouth so that it was a full minute before she could cry out or move. Then she saw that it was the big bull whip her husband liked to carry when he drove.

She lifted her eyes to the door and saw him standing there bent over with laughter at her fright. She screamed at him.

"Sykes, what you throw dat whip on me like dat? You know it would skeer   5
me—looks just like a snake, an' you knows how skeered Ah is of snakes."

"Course Ah knowed it! That's how come Ah done it." He slapped his leg with his hand and almost rolled on the ground in his mirth. "If you such a big fool dat you got to have a fit over a earth worm or a string, Ah don't keer how bad Ah skeer you."

"You ain't got no business doing it. Gawd knows it's a sin. Some day Ah'm gointuh drop dead from some of yo' foolishness. 'Nother thing, where you been wid mah rig? Ah feeds dat pony. He ain't fuh you to be drivin' wid no bull whip."

"You sho' is one aggravatin' nigger woman!" he declared and stepped into the room. She resumed her work and did not answer him at once. "Ah done tole you time and again to keep them white folks' clothes outa dis house."

He picked up the whip and glared at her. Delia went on with her work. She went out into the yard and returned with a galvanized tub and set it on the wash-bench. She saw that Sykes had kicked all of the clothes together again, and now stood in her way truculently, his whole manner hoping, *praying*, for an argument. But she walked calmly around him and commenced to re-sort the things.

"Next time, Ah'm gointer kick 'em outdoors," he threatened as he struck a   10
match along the leg of his corduroy breeches.

Delia never looked up from her work, and her thin, stooped shoulders sagged further.

"Ah ain't for no fuss t'night, Sykes. Ah just come from taking sacrament at the church house."

He snorted scornfully. "Yeah, you just come from de church house on a Sunday night, but heah you is gone to work on them clothes. You ain't nothing but a hypocrite. One of them amen-corner Christians—sing, whoop, and shout, then come home and wash white folks' clothes on the Sabbath."

He stepped roughly upon the whitest pile of things, kicking them helter-skelter as he crossed the room. His wife gave a little scream of dismay, and quickly gathered them together again.

"Sykes, you quit grindin' dirt into these clothes! How can Ah git through by   15
Sat'day if Ah don't start on Sunday?"

"Ah don't keer if you never git through. Anyhow, Ah done promised Gawd and a couple of other men, Ah ain't gointer have it in mah house. Don't gimme no lip neither, else Ah'll throw 'em out and put mah fist up side yo' head to boot."

Delia's habitual meekness seemed to slip from her shoulders like a blown scarf. She was on her feet; her poor little body, her bare knuckly hands bravely defying the strapping hulk before her.

"Looka heah, Sykes, you done gone too fur. Ah been married to you fur fifteen years, and Ah been takin' in washin' fur fifteen years. Sweat, sweat, sweat! Work and sweat, cry and sweat, pray and sweat!"

"What's that got to do with me?" he asked brutally.

"What's it got to do with you, Sykes? Mah tub of suds is filled yo' belly with   20
vittles more times than yo' hands is filled it. Mah sweat is done paid for this house and Ah reckon Ah kin keep on sweatin' in it."

She seized the iron skillet from the stove and struck a defensive pose, which act surprised him greatly, coming from her. It cowed him and he did not strike her as he usually did.

"Naw you won't," she panted, "that ole snaggle-toothed black woman you runnin' with ain't comin' heah to pile up on *mah* sweat and blood. You ain't paid for nothin' on this place, and Ah'm gointer stay right heah till Ah'm toted out foot foremost."

"Well, you better quit gittin' me riled up, else they'll be totin' you out sooner than you expect. Ah'm so tired of you Ah don't know whut to do. Gawd! How Ah hates skinny wimmen!"

A little awed by this new Delia, he sidled out of the door and slammed the back gate after him. He did not say where he had gone, but she knew too well. She knew very well that he would not return until nearly daybreak also. Her work over, she went on to bed but not to sleep at once. Things had come to a pretty pass!

She lay awake, gazing upon the debris that cluttered their matrimonial trail.   25
Not an image left standing along the way. Anything like flowers had long ago been drowned in the salty stream that had been pressed from her heart. Her tears, her sweat, her blood. She had brought love to the union and he had brought a longing after the flesh. Two months after the wedding, he had given her the first brutal beating. She had the memory of his numerous trips to Orlando with all of his wages when he had returned to her penniless, even before the first year had passed. She was young and soft then, but now she thought of her knotty, muscled limbs, her harsh knuckly hands, and drew herself up into an unhappy little ball in the middle of the big feather bed. Too late now to hope for love, even if it were not Bertha it would be someone else. This case differed from the others only in that she was bolder than the others. Too late for everything except her little home. She had built it for her old days, and planted one by one the trees and flowers there. It was lovely to her, lovely.

Somehow, before sleep came, she found herself saying aloud: "Oh well, whatever goes over the Devil's back, is got to come under his belly. Sometime or ruther, Sykes, like everybody else, is gointer reap his sowing." After that she was able to build a spiritual earthworks against her husband. His shells could no longer reach her. AMEN. She went to sleep and slept until he announced his presence in bed by kicking her feet and rudely snatching the covers away.

"Gimme some kivah heah, an' git yo' damn foots over on yo' own side! Ah oughter mash you in yo' mouf fuh drawing dat skillet on me."

Delia went clear to the rail without answering him. A triumphant indifference to all that he was or did.

II

The week was full of work for Delia as all other weeks, and Saturday found her behind her little pony, collecting and delivering clothes.

It was a hot, hot day near the end of July. The village men on Joe Clarke's   30
porch even chewed cane listlessly. They did not hurl the cane-knots as usual. They let them dribble over the edge of the porch. Even conversation had collapsed under the heat.

"Heah come Delia Jones," Jim Merchant said, as the shaggy pony came 'round the bend of the road toward them. The rusty buckboard was heaped with baskets of crisp, clean laundry.

"Yep," Joe Lindsay agreed. "Hot or col', rain or shine, jes'ez reg'lar ez de weeks roll roun' Delia carries 'em an' fetches 'em on Sat'day."

"She better if she wanter eat," said Moss. "Syke Jones ain't wuth de shot an' powder hit would tek tuh kill 'em. Not to *huh* he ain't."

"He sho' ain't," Walter Thomas chimed in. "It's too bad, too, cause she wuz a right pretty li'l trick when he got huh. Ah'd uh mah'ied huh mahself if he hadnter beat me to it."

Delia nodded briefly at the men as she drove past.

"Too much knockin' will ruin *any* 'oman. He done beat huh 'nough tuh kill three women, let 'lone change they looks," said Elijah Moseley. "How Syke kin stommuck dat big black greasy Mogul he's layin' roun' wid, gits me. Ah swear dat eight-rock couldn't kiss a sardine can Ah done thowed out de back do' 'way las' yeah."

"Aw, she's fat, thass how come. He's allus been crazy 'bout fat women," put in Merchant. "He'd a' been tied up wid one long time ago if he could a' found one tuh have him. Did Ah tell yuh 'bout him come sidlin' roun' *mah* wife—bringin' her a basket uh peecans outa his yard fuh a present? Yessir, mah wife! She tol' him tuh take 'em right straight back home, 'cause Delia works so hard ovah dat washtub she reckon everything on de place taste lak sweat an' soapsuds. Ah jus' wisht Ah'd a' caught 'im 'roun' dere! Ah'd a' made his hips ketch on fiah down dat shell road."

"Ah know he done it, too. Ah sees 'im grinnin' at every 'oman dat passes," Walter Thomas said. "But even so, he useter eat some mighty big hunks uh humble pie tuh git dat li'l 'oman he got. She wuz ez pretty ez a speckled pup! Dat wuz fifteen years ago. He useter be so skeered uh losin' huh, she could make him do some parts of a husband's duty. Dey never wuz de same in de mind."

"There oughter be a law about him," said Lindsay. "He ain't fit tuh carry guts tuh a bear."

Clarke spoke for the first time. "Tain't no law on earth dat kin make a man be decent if it ain't in 'im. There's plenty men dat takes a wife lak dey do a joint uh sugar-cane. It's round, juicy, an' sweet when dey gits it. But dey squeeze an' grind, squeeze an' grind an' wring tell dey wring every drop uh pleasure dat's in 'em out. When dey's satisfied dat dey is wrung dry, dey treats 'em jes' lak dey do a cane-chew. Dey thows 'em away. Dey knows whut dey is doin' while dey is at it, an' hates theirselves fuh it but they keeps on hangin' after huh tell she's empty. Den dey hates huh fuh bein' a cane-chew an' in de way."

"We oughter take Syke an' dat stray 'oman uh his'n down in Lake Howell swamp an' lay on de rawhide till they cain't say Lawd a' mussy. He allus wuz uh ovahbearin niggah, but since dat white 'oman from up north done teached 'im how to run a automobile, he done got too beggety to live—an' we oughter kill 'im," Old Man Anderson advised.

A grunt of approval went around the porch. But the heat was melting their civic virtue and Elijah Moseley began to bait Joe Clarke.

"Come on, Joe, git a melon outa dere an' slice it up for yo' customers. We'se all sufferin' wid de heat. De bear's done got *me!*"

"Thass right, Joe, a watermelon is jes' whut Ah needs tuh cure de eppizudicks," Walter Thomas joined forces with Moseley. "Come on dere, Joe. We all is steady customers an' you ain't set us up in a long time. Ah chooses dat long, bowlegged Floridy favorite."

"A god, an' be dough. You all gimme twenty cents and slice away," Clarke   45
retorted. "Ah needs a col' slice m'self. Heah, everybody chip in. Ah'll lend y'all
mah meat knife."

The money was all quickly subscribed and the huge melon brought forth. At
that moment, Sykes and Bertha arrived. A determined silence fell on the porch
and the melon was put away again.

Merchant snapped down the blade of his jacknife and moved toward the
store door.

"Come on in, Joe, an' gimme a slab uh sow belly an' uh pound uh coffee—
almost fuhgot 'twas Sat'day. Got to git on home." Most of the men left also.

Just then Delia drove past on her way home, as Sykes was ordering magnifi-
cently for Bertha. It pleased him for Delia to see.

"Git whutsoever yo' heart desires, Honey. Wait a minute, Joe. Give huh two   50
bottles uh strawberry soda-water, uh quart parched ground-peas, an' a block uh
chewin' gum."

With all this they left the store, with Sykes reminding Bertha that this was
his town and she could have it if she wanted it.

The men returned soon after they left, and held their watermelon feast.

"Where did Syke Jones git da 'oman from nohow?" Lindsay asked.

"Ovah Apopka. Guess dey musta been cleanin' out de town when she lef'.
She don't look lak a thing but a hunk uh liver wid hair on it."

"Well, she sho' kin squall," Dave Carter contributed. "When she gits ready   55
tuh laff, she jes' opens huh mouf an' latches it back tuh de las' notch. No ole
granpa alligator down in Lake Bell ain't got nothin' on huh."

III

Bertha had been in town three months now. Sykes was still paying her room-rent
at Della Lewis'—the only house in town that would have taken her in. Sykes
took her frequently to Winter Park to "stomps." He still assured her that he was
the swellest man in the state.

"Sho' you kin have dat li'l ole house soon's Ah git dat 'oman outa dere.
Everything b'longs tuh me an' you sho' kin have it. Ah sho' 'bominates uh
skinny 'oman. Lawdy, you sho' is got one portly shape on you! You kin git
anything you wants. Dis is *mah* town an' you sho' kin have it."

Delia's work-worn knees crawled over the earth in Gethsemane[1] and up
the rocks of Calvary many, many times during these months. She avoided the
villagers and meeting places in her efforts to be blind and deaf. But Bertha
nullified this to a degree, by coming to Delia's house to call Sykes out to her
at the gate.

Delia and Sykes fought all the time now with no peaceful interludes. They
slept and ate in silence. Two or three times Delia had attempted a timid friendliness, but she was repulsed each time. It was plain that the breaches must remain
agape.

The sun had burned July to August. The heat streamed down like a mil-   60
lion hot arrows, smiting all things living upon the earth. Grass withered,
leaves browned, snakes went blind in shedding, and men and dogs went mad.
Dog days!

---

[1]A reference to the garden where Jesus was betrayed (in the Gospels) before being tried and crucified
on Calvary or Golgotha, the "hill of skulls."

Delia came home one day and found Sykes there before her. She wondered, but started to go on into the house without speaking, even though he was standing in the kitchen door and she must either stoop under his arm or ask him to move. He made no room for her. She noticed a soap box beside the steps, but paid no particular attention to it, knowing that he must have brought it there. As she was stooping to pass under his outstretched arm, he suddenly pushed her backward, laughingly.

"Look in de box dere Delia, Ah done brung yuh somethin'!"

She nearly fell upon the box in her stumbling, and when she saw what it held, she all but fainted outright.

"Syke! Syke, mah Gawd! You take dat rattlesnake 'way from heah! You *gottuh.* Oh, Jesus, have mussy!"

"Ah ain't got tuh do nuthin' uh de kin'—fact is Ah ain't got tuh do nothin' but die. Taint no use uh you puttin' on airs makin' out lak you skeered uh dat snake—he's gointer stay right heah tell he die. He wouldn't bite me cause Ah knows how tuh handle 'im. Nohow he wouldn't risk breakin' out his fangs 'gin yo skinny laigs." 65

"Naw, now Syke, don't keep dat thing 'round tryin' tuh skeer me tuh death. You knows Ah'm even feared uh earth worms. Thass de biggest snake Ah evah did se. Kill 'im Syke, please."

"Doan ast me tuh do nothin' fuh yuh. Goin' 'round tryin' tuh be so damn asterperious. Naw, Ah ain't gonna kill it. Ah think uh damn sight mo' uh him dan you! Dat's a nice snake an' anybody doan lak 'im kin jes' hit de grit."

The village soon heard that Sykes had the snake, and came to see and ask questions.

"How de hen-fire did you ketch dat six-foot rattler, Syke?" Thomas asked.

"He's full uh frogs so he cain't hardly move, thass how Ah eased up on 'm. But Ah'm a snake charmer an' knows how tuh handle 'em. Shux, dat ain't nothin'. Ah could ketch one eve'y day if Ah so wanted tuh." 70

"Whut he needs is a heavy hick'ry club leaned real heavy on his head. Dat's de bes' way tuh charm a rattlesnake."

"Naw, Walt, y' all jes' don't understand dese diamon' backs lak Ah do," said Sykes in a superior tone of voice.

The village agreed with Walter, but the snake stayed on. His box remained by the kitchen door with its screen wire covering. Two or three days later it had digested its meal of frogs and literally came to life. It rattled at every movement in the kitchen or the yard. One day as Delia came down the kitchen steps she saw his chalky-white fangs curved like scimitars hung in the wire meshes. This time she did not run away with averted eyes as usual. She stood for a long time in the doorway in a red fury that grew bloodier for every second that she regarded the creature that was her torment.

That night she broached the subject as soon as Sykes sat down to the table.

"Syke, Ah wants you tuh take dat snake 'way fum heah. You done starved me an' Ah put up widcher, you done beat me an Ah took dat, but you don kilt all mah insides bringin' dat varmint heah." 75

Sykes poured out a saucer full of coffee and drank it deliberately before he answered her.

"A whole lot Ah keer 'bout how you feels inside uh out. Dat snake ain't goin' no damn wheah till Ah gits ready fuh 'im tuh go. So fur as beatin' is concerned, yuh ain't took near all dat you gointer take ef yuh stay 'round *me.*"

Delia pushed back her plate and got up from the table. "Ah hates you, Sykes," she said calmly. "Ah hates you tuh de same degree dat Ah useter love yuh. Ah done took an' took till mah belly is full up tuh mah neck. Dat's de reason Ah got mah letter fum de church an' moved mah membership tuh Woodbridge—so Ah don't haftuh take no sacrament wid yuh. Ah don't wantuh see yuh 'round me atall. Lay 'round wid dat 'oman all yuh wants tuh, but gwan 'way from me an' mah house. Ah hates yuh lak uh suck-egg dog."

Sykes almost let the huge wad of corn bread and collard greens he was chewing fall out of his mouth in amazement. He had a hard time whipping himself up to the proper fury to try to answer Delia.

"Well, Ah'm glad you does hate me. Ah'm sho' tiahed uh you hangin' ontuh   80
me. Ah don't want yuh. Look at yuh stringey ole neck! Yo' rawbony laigs an' arms is enough tuh cut uh man tuh death. You looks jes' lak de devvul's doll-baby tuh *me*. You cain't hate me no worse dan Ah hates you. Ah been hatin' *you* fuh years."

"Yo' ole black hide don't look lak nothin' tuh me, but uh passle uh wrinkled up rubber, wid yo' big ole yeahs flappin' on each side lak uh paih uh buzzard wings. Don't think Ah'm gointuh be run 'way fum mah house neither. Ah'm goin' tuh de white folks 'bout *you*, mah young man, de very nex' time you lay yo' han's on me. Mah cup is done run ovah." Delia said this with no signs of fear and Sykes departed from the house, threatening her, but made not the slightest move to carry out any of them.

That night he did not return at all, and the next day being Sunday, Delia was glad she did not have to quarrel before she hitched up her pony and drove the four miles to Woodbridge.

She stayed to the night service—"love feast"—which was very warm and full of spirit. In the emotional winds her domestic trials were borne far and wide so that she sang as she drove homeward,

Jurden water, black an' col
Chills de body, not de soul
An' Ah wantah cross Jurden in uh calm time.

She came from the barn to the kitchen door and stopped.

"Whut's de mattah, ol' Satan, you ain't kicken' up yo' racket?" She addressed the snake's box. Complete silence. She went on into the house with a new hope in its birth struggles. Perhaps her threat to go to the white folks had frightened Sykes! Perhaps he was sorry! Fifteen years of misery and suppression had brought Delia to the place where she would hope *anything* that looked towards a way over or through her wall of inhibitions.

She felt in the match-safe behind the stove at once for a match. There was   85
only one there.

"Dat niggah wouldn't fetch nothin' heah tuh save his rotten neck, but he kin run thew whut Ah brings quick enough. Now he done toted off nigh on tuh haff uh box uh matches. He done had dat 'oman heah in mah house, too."

Nobody but a woman could tell how she knew this even before she struck the match. But she did and it put her into a new fury.

Presently she brought in the tubs to put the white things to soak. This time she decided she need not bring the hamper out of the bedroom; she would go in there and do the sorting. She picked up the pot-bellied lamp and went in. The room was small and the hamper stood hard by the foot of the white iron bed. She could sit and reach through the bedposts—resting as she worked.

"*Ah wantah cross Jurden in uh calm time.*" She was singing again. The mood of the "love feast" had returned. She threw back the lid of the basket almost gaily. Then, moved by both horror and terror, she sprang back toward the door. *There lay the snake in the basket!* He moved sluggishly at first, but even as she turned round and round, jumped up and down in an insanity of fear, he began to stir vigorously. She saw him pouring his awful beauty from the basket upon the bed, then she seized the lamp and ran as fast as she could to the kitchen. The wind from the open door blew out the light and the darkness added to her terror. She sped to the darkness of the yard, slamming the door after her before she thought to set down the lamp. She did not feel safe even on the ground, so she climbed up in the hay barn.

There for an hour or more she lay sprawled upon the hay a gibbering wreck. 90

Finally she grew quiet, and after that came coherent thought. With this stalked through her a cold, bloody rage. Hours of this. A period of introspection, a space of retrospection, then a mixture of both. Out of this an awful calm.

"Well, Ah done de bes' Ah could. If things ain't right, Gawd knows tain't mah fault."

She went to sleep—a twitch sleep—and woke up to a faint gray sky. There was a loud hollow sound below. She peered out. Sykes was at the woodpile, demolishing a wire-covered box.

He hurried to the kitchen door, but hung outside there some minutes before he entered, and stood some minutes more inside before he closed it after him.

The gray in the sky was spreading. Delia descended without fear now, and 95 crouched beneath the low bedroom window. The drawn shade shut out the dawn, shut in the night. But the thin walls held back no sound.

"Dat ol' scratch is woke up now!" She mused at the tremendous whirr inside, which every woodsman knows is one of the sound illusions. The rattler is a ventriloquist. His whirr sounds to the right, to the left, straight ahead, behind, close under foot—everywhere but where it is. Woe to him who guesses wrong unless he is prepared to hold up his end of the argument! Sometimes he strikes without rattling at all.

Inside, Sykes heard nothing until he knocked a pot lid off the stove while trying to reach the match-safe in the dark. He had emptied his pockets at Bertha's.

The snake seemed to wake up under the stove and Sykes made a quick leap into the bedroom. In spite of the gin he had had, his head was clearing now.

"Mah Gawd!" he chattered, "ef Ah could on'y strack uh light!"

The rattling ceased for a moment as he stood paralyzed. He waited. It 100 seemed that the snake waited also.

"Oh, fuh de light! Ah thought he'd be too sick"—Sykes was muttering to himself when the whirr began again, closer, right underfoot this time. Long before this, Sykes' ability to think had been flattened down to primitive instinct and he leaped—onto the bed.

Outside Delia heard a cry that might have come from a maddened chimpanzee, a stricken gorilla. All the terror, all the horror, all the rage that man possibly could express, without a recognizable human sound.

A tremendous stir inside there, another series of animal screams, the intermittent whirr of the reptile. The shade torn violently down from the window, letting in the red dawn, a huge brown hand seizing the window stick, great dull blows upon the wooden floor punctuating the gibberish of sound long after the rattle of the snake had abruptly subsided. All this Delia could see and hear from her place beneath the window, and it made her ill. She crept over to the four o'-clocks and stretched herself on the cool earth to recover.

She lay there. "Delia, Delia!" She could hear Sykes calling in a most despairing tone as one who expected no answer. The sun crept on up, and he called. Delia could not move—her legs had gone flabby. She never moved, he called, and the sun kept rising.

"Mah Gawd!" She heard him moan, "Mah Gawd fum Heben!" She heard   105
him stumbling about and got up from her flower-bed. The sun was growing warm. As she approached the door she heard him call out hopefully, "Delia, is dat you Ah heah?"

She saw him on his hands and knees as soon as she reached the door. He crept an inch or two toward her—all that he was able, and she saw his horribly swollen neck and his one open eye shining with hope. A surge of pity too strong to support bore her away from that eye that must, could not, fail to see the tubs. He would see the lamp. Orlando with its doctors was too far. She could scarcely reach the chinaberry tree, where she waited in the growing heat while inside she knew the cold river was creeping up and up to extinguish that eye which must know by now that she knew.

Talking about the Text

1. Does Sykes have any redeeming features? To what extent does he meet the "right" fate?
2. Were you surprised by the way the story ends? If so, why? If not, what made you expect it to end that way?
3. If Delia were faced with such a man today, how would she react?

Writing about the Text

1. Describe the rural southern setting Hurston provides for "Sweat," grouping the detailed descriptions she provides in order to make your own generalizations about the town and its surrounding countryside.
2. "Translate" the dialogue from paragraphs 5–8 into edited standard English, the kind Hurston's narrator uses. Then describe what difference the original black dialect makes to the story.

Linking the Text to Other Texts

1. Compare the way Hurston and Alice Walker (p. 423) depict the woman's role in the rural South in their fiction.
2. How is "Sweat" like "A Worn Path" (p. 338) and/or "A Shower of Gold" (p. 345)? Look both to the settings and the motivations of the characters.

Starting Points for Further Research: Zora Neale Hurston

- **Edition:** Zora Neale Hurston. *Novels and Stories.* New York: Library of America, 1995.

- **Biography:** Valerie Boyd. *Wrapped in Rainbows: The Life of Zora Neale Hurston.* New York: Scribner, 2004.
- **Critical Essay:** John Laudun. "Reading Hurston Writing." *African American Review* 38 (2004): 45–60.

INSPIRATION   "SWEAT" IN PERFORMANCE: HURSTON FROM PAGE TO RADIO STAGE

Scribbling Women, a project of the Public Media Foundation, dramatizes stories by American women writers for national radio broadcast. The plays are distributed nationwide by National Public Radio. Among the works adapted for an audio dramatic format is Hurston's "Sweat," dramatized into a thirty-minute radio play by Kia Corthron and directed by Martin Jenkins. What elements must the playwright have needed to weigh in adapting "Sweat" from the fictional page to not only a dramatic, dialogue-based format, but one that is limited to expressing its gestures, emotions, and ideas exclusively through sound?

Zora Neale Hurston, 1937.

AUDIO LOCALE

Scribbling Women Recording: "Sweat" Radio Play. The Scribbling Women website at *http://www.scribblingwomen.org* includes links to the online audio files of the project's radio plays, background information on the writers whose works they have adapted, relevant contextual information, related curriculum and lesson plans for teachers, and discussion questions. Visitors need to register to gain full access to the site's resources, but there is no fee.

EUDORA WELTY   (1909–2001)

One of the most important and best-loved twentieth-century American writers, Eudora Welty typically wrote about the inhabitants of rural Mississippi, including her home city of Jackson. She was born in Jackson and returned there after attending the Mississippi State College for Women, the University of Wisconsin, and the Columbia University School of Business. Based in Jackson in the 1930s, Welty worked for the Federal Works Progress Administration, reporting and taking re-markable photographs of Jackson and rural Mississippi (for Welty's photographs, see the accompanying color image gallery for this chapter, "Visual Literacy and Southern Women Writers.") For the rest of her long life, she was ensconced in her family home except for occasional lecture travels, leading a very quiet life and very reluctant to speak about personal matters other than her literary work. Like Flannery O'Connor, she was a very close observer of the life around her, as is evident from the short stories and from her brief autobiography, One Writer's Beginnings *(1984). Her characters are comic, eccentric, often grotesque, but nonetheless charming. A "writer's writer," Welty earned her reputation from the way she depicted her characters' dialect and speech intonations. Among her collections of short stories are* A Curtain of Green *(1941),* The Wide Net *(1943), and* The Bride of Innisfallen *(1955). Welty's novels include* Delta Wedding *(1946),* The Ponder Heart *(1954),* Losing Battles *(1970), and* The Optimist's Daughter *(1972). Her collected stories were published in 1980, the same year she was awarded the Presidential Medal of Freedom.*

LITERARY LOCALE

The Homes and Archives of Eudora Welty—Jackson, Mississippi. The frame house at 741 North Congress Street in Jackson, Mississippi, located just a few blocks from the state capitol, is the site of Eudora Welty's birth in 1909; it is also the site of many of the events in Welty's memoir *One Writer's Beginnings*. During her last two years of high school, her parents built a new home at 1119 Pinehurst Street in Jackson; this home is where Welty lived for more than seventy-five years until her death in 2001, and it is where she wrote almost all of her fiction and essays. During the 1950s, Welty began donating her manuscripts, letters, and other papers, as well as her photographs and negatives, to the Mississippi Department of Archives and History (MDAH). MDAH's Eudora Welty

Welty's birthplace and childhood home at North Congress Street in Jackson, Mississippi.

Collection is housed in downtown Jackson at the William F. Winter Archives and History Building and is utilized by researchers, scholars, and students worldwide. Information on visiting the collection for research purposes is available at the MDAH website at *http://mdah.state.ms.us/arlib/arlib_index.html*.

In 1986, Welty decided that the house at Pinehurst Street would be donated to the state of Mississippi as well. Now called the Eudora Welty House, the structure was declared a National Historic Landmark in 2004; it was under restoration for several years and opened to the public as a literary museum in the spring of 2006. (The garden is also open for tours by reservation.) The house is a significant landmark not only because of the time Welty spent there, but also because it is one of the most well-preserved, authentic historic sites of its kind: the external and interior structure and aesthetic, as well as the furnishings, remain more or less as they were

Welty's house at Pinehurst Street in Jackson, Mississippi.

when Welty lived there, including much of the original furniture, paintings and photographs, rugs, and books still in their original places. According to the Eudora Welty House Museum website at *http://www.mdah.state.ms.us/welty/*, which offers visiting and other information, "With virtually every wall lined with books, this house of a reader, a family of readers, shows how intensely family members valued the written word." An extensive virtual tour of the house is available at *http://www.mdah.state.ms.us/welty/house1.html*. Additional information can be found at the Eudora Welty Foundation website at *http://www.eudorawelty.org/*. Both sites include extensive information on Welty's life and work, and links to additional resources for research.

Why I Live at the P.O. (1941)

I was getting along fine with Mama, Papa-Daddy, and Uncle Rondo until my sister Stella-Rondo just separated from her husband and came back home again. Mr. Whitaker! Of course I went with Mr. Whitaker first, when he first appeared here in China Grove, taking "Pose Yourself" photos, and Stella-Rondo broke us up. Told him I was one-sided. Bigger on one side than the other, which is a deliberate, calculated falsehood: I'm the same. Stella-Rondo is exactly twelve months to the day younger than I am and for that reason she's spoiled.

She's always had anything in the world she wanted and then she'd throw it away. Papa-Daddy gave her this gorgeous Add-a-Pearl necklace when she was eight years old and she threw it away playing baseball when she was nine, with only two pearls.

So as soon as she got married and moved away from home the first thing she did was separate! From Mr. Whitaker! This photographer with the popeyes she said she trusted. Came home from one of those towns up in Illinois and to our complete surprise brought this child of two.

Mama said she like to make her drop dead for a second. "Here you had this marvelous blonde child and never so much as wrote your mother a word about it," says Mama. "I'm thoroughly ashamed of you." But of course she wasn't.

Stella-Rondo just calmly takes off this *hat.* I wish you could see it. She says, 5 "Why, Mama, Shirley-T.'s adopted, I can prove it."

"How?" says Mama, but all I says was, "H'm!" There I was over the hot stove, trying to stretch two chickens over five people and a completely unexpected child into the bargain, without one moment's notice.

"What do you mean—'H'm!'?" says Stella-Rondo, and Mama says, "I heard that, Sister."

I said that oh, I didn't mean a thing, only that whoever Shirley-T. was, she was the spit-image of Papa-Daddy if he'd cut off his beard, which of course he'd never do in the world. Papa-Daddy's Mama's papa and sulks.

Stella-Rondo got furious! She said, "Sister, I don't need to tell you you got a lot of nerve and always did have and I'll thank you to make no future reference to my adopted child whatsoever."

"Very well," I said. "Very well, very well. Of course I noticed at once she 10 looks like Mr. Whitaker's side too. That frown. She looks like a cross between Mr. Whitaker and Papa-Daddy."

"Well, all I can say is she isn't."

"She looks exactly like Shirley Temple to me," says Mama, but Shirley-T. just ran away from her.

So the first thing Stella-Rondo did at the table was turn Papa-Daddy against me.

"Papa-Daddy," she says. He was trying to cut up his meat. "Papa-Daddy!" I was taken completely by surprise. Papa-Daddy is about a million years old and's got this long-long beard. "Papa-Daddy, Sister says she fails to understand why you don't cut off your beard."

So Papa Daddy l-a-y-s down his knife and fork! He's real rich. Mama 15 says he is, he says he isn't. So he says, "Have I heard correctly? You don't understand why I don't cut off my beard?"

"Why," I says, "Papa-Daddy, of course I understand, I did not say any such of a thing, the idea!"

He says, "Hussy!"

I says, "Papa-Daddy, you know I wouldn't any more want you to cut off your beard than the man in the moon. It was the farthest thing from my mind! Stella-Rondo sat there and made that up while she was eating breast of chicken."

But he says, "So the postmistress fails to understand why I don't cut off my beard. Which job I got you through my influence with the government. 'Bird's nest'—is that what you call it?"

Not that it isn't the next to smallest P.O. in the entire state of Mississippi.   20

I says, "Oh, Papa-Daddy," I says, "I didn't say any such of a thing, I never dreamed it was a bird's nest, I have always been grateful though this is the next to smallest P.O. in the state of Mississippi, and I do not enjoy being referred to as a hussy by my own grandfather."

But Stella-Rondo says, "Yes, you did say it too. Anybody in the world could of heard you, that had ears."

"Stop right there," says Mama, looking at *me*.

So I pulled my napkin straight back through the napkin ring and left the table.

As soon as I was out of the room Mama says, "Call her back, or she'll starve   25
to death," but Papa-Daddy says, "This is the beard I started growing on the Coast when I was fifteen years old." He would of gone on till nightfall if Shirley-T. hadn't lost the Milky Way she ate in Cairo.

So Papa-Daddy says, "I am going out and lie in the hammock, and you can all sit here and remember my words: I'll never cut off my beard as long as I live, even one inch, and I don't appreciate it in you at all." Passed right by me in the hall and went straight out and got in the hammock.

It would be a holiday. It wasn't five minutes before Uncle Rondo suddenly appeared in the hall in one of Stella-Rondo's flesh-colored kimonos, all cut on the bias, like something Mr. Whitaker probably thought was gorgeous.

"Uncle Rondo!" I says. "I didn't know who that was! Where are you going?"

"Sister," he says, "get out of my way, I'm poisoned."

"If you're poisoned stay away from Papa-Daddy," I says. "Keep out of the   30
hammock. Papa-Daddy will certainly beat you on the head if you come within forty miles of him. He thinks I deliberately said he ought to cut off his beard after he got me the P.O., and I've told him and told him and told him, and he acts like he just don't hear me. Papa-Daddy must of gone stone deaf."

"He picked a fine day to do it then," says Uncle Rondo, and before you could say "Jack Robinson" flew out in the yard.

What he'd really done, he'd drunk another bottle of that prescription. He does it every single Fourth of July as sure as shooting, and it's horribly expensive. Then he falls over in the hammock and snores. So he insisted on zigzagging right on out to the hammock, looking like a half-wit.

Papa-Daddy woke up with this horrible yell and right there without moving an inch he tried to turn Uncle Rondo against me. I heard every word he said. Oh, he told Uncle Rondo I didn't learn to read till I was eight years old and he didn't see how in the world I ever got the mail put up at the P.O., much less read it all, and he said if Uncle Rondo could only fathom the lengths he had gone to get me that job! And he said on the other hand he thought Stella-Rondo had a brilliant mind and deserved credit for getting out of town. All the time he was just lying there swinging as pretty as you please and looping out his beard, and poor Uncle Rondo was *pleading* with him to slow down the hammock, it was making him as dizzy as a witch to watch it. But that's what Papa-Daddy likes about a hammock. So Uncle Rondo was too dizzy to get turned against me for the time being. He's Mama's only brother and is a good case of a one-track mind. Ask anybody. A certified pharmacist.

Just then I heard Stella-Rondo raising the upstairs window. While she was married she got this peculiar idea that it's cooler with the windows shut and locked. So she has to raise the window before she can make a soul hear her outdoors.

So she raises the window and says, "*Oh!*" You would have thought she was   35
mortally wounded.

Uncle Rondo and Papa-Daddy didn't even look up, but kept right on with what they were doing. I had to laugh.

I flew up the stairs and threw the door open! I says, "What in the wide world's the matter, Stella-Rondo? You mortally wounded?"

"No," she says, "I am not mortally wounded but I wish you would do me the favor of looking out that window there and telling me what you see."

So I shade my eyes and look out the window.

"I see the front yard," I says.   40

"Don't you see any human beings?" she says.

"I see Uncle Rondo trying to run Papa-Daddy out of the hammock," I says. "Nothing more. Naturally, it's so suffocating-hot in the house, with all the windows shut and locked, everybody who cares to stay in their right mind will have to go out and get in the hammock before the Fourth of July is over."

"Don't you notice anything different about Uncle Rondo?" asks Stella-Rondo.

"Why, no, except he's got on some terrible-looking flesh-colored contraption I wouldn't be found dead in, is all I can see," I says.

"Never mind, you won't be found dead in it, because it happens to be part of   45
my trousseau, and Mr. Whitaker took several dozen photographs of me in it," says Stella-Rondo. "What on earth could Uncle Rondo *mean* by wearing part of my trousseau out in the broad open daylight without saying so much as 'Kiss my foot,' *knowing* I only got home this morning after my separation and hung my negligee up on the bathroom door, just as nervous as I could be?"

"I'm sure I don't know, and what do you expect me to do about it?" I says. "Jump out the window?"

"No, I expect nothing of the kind. I simply declare that Uncle Rondo looks like a fool in it, that's all," she says. "It makes me sick to my stomach."

"Well, he looks as good as he can," I says. "As good as anybody in reason could." I stood up for Uncle Rondo, please remember. And I said to Stella-Rondo, "I think I would do well not to criticize so freely if I were you and came home with a two-year-old child I had never said a word about, and no explanation whatever about my separation."

"I asked you the instant I entered this house not to refer one more time to my adopted child, and you gave me your word of honor you would not," was all Stella-Rondo would say, and started pulling out every one of her eyebrows with some cheap Kress tweezers.

So I merely slammed the door behind me and went down and made some   50
green-tomato pickle. Somebody had to do it. Of course Mama had turned both

the niggers loose; she always said no earthly power could hold one anyway on the Fourth of July, so she wouldn't even try. It turned out that Jaypan fell in the lake and came within a very narrow limit of drowning.

So Mama trots in. Lifts up the lid and says, "H'm! Not very good for your Uncle Rondo in his precarious condition, I must say. Or poor little adopted Shirley-T. Shame on you!"

That made me tired. I says, "Well, Stella-Rondo had better thank her lucky stars it was her instead of me came trotting in with that very peculiar-looking child. Now if it had been me that trotted in from Illinois and brought a peculiar-looking child of two, I shudder to think of the reception I'd of got, much less controlled the diet of an entire family."

"But you must remember, Sister, that you were never married to Mr. Whitaker in the first place and didn't go up to Illinois to live," says Mama, shaking a spoon in my face. If you had I would have been just as overjoyed to see you and your little adopted girl as I was to see Stella-Rondo, when you wound up with your separation and came on back home."

"You would not," I says.

"Don't contradict me, I would," says Mama.   55

But I said she couldn't convince me though she talked till she was blue in the face. Then I said, "Besides, you know as well as I do that that child is not adopted."

"She most certainly is adopted," says Mama, stiff as a poker.

I says, "Why, Mama, Stella-Rondo had her just as sure as anything in this world, and just too stuck up to admit it."

"Why Sister," said Mama. "Here I thought we were going to have a pleasant Fourth of July, and you start right out not believing a word your own baby sister tells you!"

"Just like Cousin Annie Flo. Went to her grave denying the facts of life," I   60
remind Mama.

"I told you if you ever mentioned Annie Flo's name I'd slap your face," says Mama, and slaps my face.

"All right, you wait and see," I says.

"I," says Mama, "*I* prefer to take my children's word for anything when it's humanly possible." You ought to see Mama, she weighs two hundred pounds and has real tiny feet.

Just then something perfectly horrible occurred to me.

"Mama," I says, "can that child talk?" I simply had to whisper! "Mama, I   65
wonder if that child can be—you know—in any way? Do you realize," I says, "that she hasn't spoken one single, solitary word to a human being up to this minute? This is the way she looks," I says, and I looked like this.

Well, Mama and I just stood there and stared at each other. It was horrible!

"I remember well that Joe Whitaker frequently drank like a fish," says Mama. "I believed to my soul he drank *chemicals*." And without another word she marches to the foot of the stairs and calls Stella-Rondo.

"Stella-Rondo? O-o-o-o-o! Stella-Rondo!"

"What?" says Stella-Rondo from upstairs. Not even the grace to get up off the bed.

"Can that child of yours talk?" asks Mama.   70

Stella-Rondo yells back, "Can she what?"

"Talk! Talk!" says Mama. "Burdyburdyburdyburdy!"

So Stella-Rondo yells back, "Who says she can't talk?"

"Sister says so," says Mama.

"You didn't have to tell me, I know whose word of honor don't mean a thing   75
in this house," says Stella-Rondo.

And in a minute the loudest Yankee voice I ever heard in my life yells out,
"OE'm Pop-OE the Sailor-r-r-r Ma-a-an!" and then somebody jumps up and
down in the upstairs hall. In another second the house would of fallen down.

"Not only talks, she can tap-dance!" calls Stella-Rondo. "Which is more
than some people I won't name can do."

"Why, the little precious darling thing!" Mama says, so surprised. "Just as
smart as she can be!" Starts talking baby talk right there. Then she turns on me.
"Sister, you ought to be thoroughly ashamed! Run upstairs this instant and apologize to Stella-Rondo and Shirley-T."

"Apologize for what?" I says. "I merely wondered if the child was normal,
that's all. Now that she's proved she is, why, I have nothing further to say."

But Mama just turned on her heel and flew out, furious. She ran right up-   80
stairs and hugged the baby. She believed it was adopted. Stella-Rondo hadn't
done a thing but turn her against me from upstairs while I stood there helpless
over the hot stove. So that made Mama, Papa-Daddy, and the baby all on Stella-
Rondo's side.

Next, Uncle Rondo.

I must say that Uncle Rondo has been marvelous to me at various times in
the past and I was completely unprepared to be made to jump out of my skin, the
way it turned out. Once Stella-Rondo did something perfectly horrible to him—
broke a chain letter from Flanders Field[1]—and he took the radio back he had
given her and gave it to me. Stella-Rondo was furious! For six months we all had
to call her Stella instead of Stella-Rondo, or she wouldn't answer. I always
thought Uncle Rondo had all the brains of the entire family. Another time he
sent me to Mammoth Cave,[2] with all expenses paid.

But this would be the day he was drinking that prescription, the Fourth of
July.

So at supper Stella-Rondo speaks up and says she thinks Uncle Rondo ought
to try to eat a little something. So finally Uncle Rondo said he would try a little
cold biscuits and ketchup, but that was all. So *she* brought it to him.

"Do you think it is wise to disport with ketchup in Stella-Rondo's flesh-col-   85
ored kimono?" I says. Trying to be considerate! If Stella-Rondo couldn't watch
out for her trousseau, somebody had to.

"Any objections?" asks Uncle Rondo, just about to pour out all the ketchup.

"Don't mind what she says, Uncle Rondo," says Stella-Rondo. "Sister has
been devoting this solid afternoon to sneering out my bedroom window at the
way you look."

"What's that?" says Uncle Rondo. Uncle Rondo has got the most terrible
temper in the world. Anything is liable to make him tear the house down if it
comes at the wrong time.

---

[1]*Flanders Field:* an Allied military cemetery in Belgium for World War I soldiers made famous by a
John McCrae poem.

[2]*Mammoth Cave:* natural underground cavern in Kentucky.

So Stella-Rondo says, "Sister says, 'Uncle Rondo certainly does look like a fool in that pink kimono!'"

Do you remember who it was really said that?

Uncle Rondo spills out all the ketchup and jumps out of his chair and tears off the kimono and throws it down on the dirty floor and puts his foot on it. It had to be sent all the way to Jackson to the cleaners and re-pleated.

"So that's your opinion of your Uncle Rondo, is it?" he says. "I look like a fool, do I? Well, that's the last straw. A whole day in this house with nothing to do, and then to hear you come out with a remark like that behind my back!"

"I didn't say any such of a thing, Uncle Rondo," I says, "and I'm not saying who did, either. Why, I think you look all right. Just try to take care of yourself and not talk and eat at the same time," I says. "I think you better go lie down."

"Lie down my foot," says Uncle Rondo. I ought to of known by that he was fixing to do something perfectly horrible.

So he didn't do anything that night in the precarious state he was in—just played Casino with Mama and Stella-Rondo and Shirley-T. and gave Shirley-T. a nickel with a head on both sides. It tickled her nearly to death, and she called him "Papa." But at 6:30 A.M. the next morning, he threw a whole five-cent package of some unsold one-inch firecrackers from the store as hard as he could into my bedroom and they every one went off. Not one bad one in the string. Anybody else, there'd be one that wouldn't go off.

Well, I'm just terribly susceptible to noise of any kind, the doctor has always told me I was the most sensitive person he had ever seen in his whole life, and I was simply prostrated. I couldn't eat! People tell me they heard it as far as the cemetery, and old Aunt Jep Patterson, that had been holding her own so good, thought it was Judgment Day and she was going to meet her whole family. It's usually so quiet here.

And I'll tell you it didn't take me any longer than a minute to make up my mind what to do. There I was with the whole entire house on Stella-Rondo's side and turned against me. If I have anything at all I have pride.

So I just decided I'd go straight down to the P.O. There's plenty of room there in the back, I says to myself.

Well! I made no bones about letting the family catch on to what I was up to. I didn't try to conceal it.

The first thing they knew, I marched in where they were all playing Old Maid and pulled the electric oscillating fan out by the plug, and everything got real hot. Next I snatched the pillow I'd done the needlepoint on right off the davenport from behind Papa-Daddy. He went "Ugh!" I beat Stella-Rondo up the stairs and finally found my charm bracelet in her bureau drawer under a picture of Nelson Eddy.[3]

"So that's the way the land lies," says Uncle Rondo. There he was, piecing on the ham. "Well, Sister, I'll be glad to donate my army cot if you got any place to set it up, providing you'll leave right this minute and let me get some peace." Uncle Rondo was in France.

"Thank you kindly for the cot and 'peace' is hardly the word I would select if I had to resort to firecrackers at 6:30 A.M. in a young girl's bedroom," I says back

_____

[3]*Nelson Eddy:* a Depression-era popular singer (1901–1967).

to him. "And as to where I intend to go, you seem to forget my position as post-mistress of China Grove, Mississippi," I says. "I've always got the P.O."

Well, that made them all sit up and take notice.

I went out front and started digging up some four-o'clocks to plant around the P.O.

"Ah-ah-ah!" says Mama, raising the window. "Those happen to be my four- 105 o'clocks. Everything planted in that star is mine. I've never known you to make anything grow in your life."

"Very well," I says. "But I take the fern. Even you, Mama, can't stand there and deny that I'm the one watered that fern. And I happen to know where I can send in a box top and get a packet of one thousand mixed seeds, no two the same kind, free."

"Oh, where?" Mama wants to know.

But I says, "Too late. You 'tend to your house, and I'll 'tend to mine. You hear things like that all the time if you know how to listen to the radio. Perfectly marvelous offers. Get anything you want free."

So I hope to tell you I marched in and got that radio, and they could of all bit a nail in two, especially Stella-Rondo, that it used to belong to, and she well knew she couldn't get it back, I'd sue for it like a shot. And I very politely took the sewing-machine motor I helped pay the most on to give Mama for Christmas back in 1929, and a good big calendar, with the first-aid remedies on it. The thermometer and the Hawaiian ukulele certainly were rightfully mine, and I stood on the step-ladder and got all my watermelon-rind preserves and every fruit and vegetable I'd put up, every jar. Then I began to pull the tacks out of the bluebird wall vases on the archway to the dining room.

"Who told you you could have those, Miss Priss?" says Mama, fanning as 110 hard as she could.

"I bought 'em and I'll keep track of 'em," I says. "I'll tack 'em up one on each side the post-office window, and you can see 'em when you come to ask me for your mail, if you're so dead to see 'em."

"Not I! I'll never darken the door to that post office again if I live to be a hundred," Mama says. "Ungrateful child! After all the money we spent on you at the Normal."[4]

"Me either," says Stella-Rondo. "You can just let my mail lie there and *rot*, for all I care. I'll never come and relieve you of a single, solitary piece."

"I should worry," I says. "And who you think's going to sit down and write you all those big fat letters and postcards, by the way? Mr. Whitaker? Just be-cause he was the only man ever dropped down in China Grove and you got him—unfairly—is he going to sit down and write you a lengthy correspondence after you come home giving no rhyme nor reason whatsoever for your separation and no explanation for the presence of that child? I may not have your brilliant mind, but I fail to see it."

So Mama says, "Sister, I've told you a thousand times that Stella-Rondo 115 simply got homesick, and this child is far too big to be hers," and she says, "Now, why don't you just sit down and play Casino?"

Then Shirley-T. sticks out her tongue at me in this perfectly horrible way. She has no more manners than the man in the moon. I told her she was going to cross her eyes like that some day and they'd stick.

---

[4]*Normal:* a two-year college for the training of elementary school teachers.

"It's too late to stop me now," I says. "You should have tried that yesterday. I'm going to the P.O. and the only way you can possibly see me is to visit me there."

So Papa-Daddy says, "You'll never catch me setting foot in that post office, even if I should take a notion into my head to write a letter some place." He says, "I won't have you reachin' out of that little old window with a pair of shears and cuttin' off any beard of mine. I'm too smart for you!"

"We all are," says Stella-Rondo.

But I said, "If you're so smart, where's Mr. Whitaker?"   120

So then Uncle Rondo says, "I'll thank you from now on to stop reading all the orders I get on postcards and telling everybody in China Grove what you think is the matter with them," but I says, "I draw my own conclusions and will continue in the future to draw them." I says, "If people want to write their inmost secrets on penny postcards, there's nothing in the wide world you can do about it, Uncle Rondo."

"And if you think we'll ever *write* another postcard you're sadly mistaken," says Mama.

"Cutting off your nose to spite your face then," I says. "But if you're all determined to have no more to do with the U.S. mail, think of this: What will Stella-Rondo do now, if she wants to tell Mr. Whitaker to come after her?"

"Wah!" says Stella-Rondo. I knew she'd cry. She had a conniption fit right there in the kitchen.

"It will be interesting to see how long she holds out," I says. "And now—I   125
am leaving."

"Good-bye," says Uncle Rondo.

"Oh, I declare," says Mama, "to think that a family of mine should quarrel on the Fourth of July, or the day after, over Stella-Rondo leaving old Mr. Whitaker and having the sweetest little adopted child! It looks like we'd all be glad!"

"Wah!" says Stella-Rondo, and has a fresh conniption fit.

"*He* left *her*—you mark my words," I says. "That's Mr. Whitaker. I know Mr. Whitaker. After all, I knew him first. I said from the beginning he'd up and leave her. I foretold every single thing that's happened."

"Where did he go?" asks Mama.   130

"Probably to the North Pole, if he knows what's good for him," I says.

But Stella-Rondo just bawled and wouldn't say another word. She flew to her room and slammed the door.

"Now look what you've gone and done, Sister," says Mama. "You go apologize."

"I haven't got time, I'm leaving," I says.

"Well, what are you waiting around for?" asks Uncle Rondo.   135

So I just picked up the kitchen clock and marched off, without saying "Kiss my foot," or anything, and never did tell Stella-Rondo good-bye.

There was a nigger girl going along on a little wagon right in front.

"Nigger girl," I says, "come help me haul these things down the hill, I'm going to live in the post office."

Took her nine trips in her express wagon. Uncle Rondo came out on the porch and threw her a nickel.

And that's the last I've laid eyes on any of my family or my family laid eyes   140
on me for five solid days and nights. Stella-Rondo may be telling the most horrible tales in the world about Mr. Whitaker, but I haven't heard them. As I tell everybody, I draw my own conclusions.

But oh, I like it here. It's ideal, as I've been saying. You see, I've got every-thing cater-cornered, the way I like it. Hear the radio? All the war news. Radio, sewing machine, book ends, ironing board and that great big piano lamp—peace, that's what I like. Butter-bean vines planted all along the front where the strings are.

Of course, there's not much mail. My family are naturally the main people in China Grove, and if they prefer to vanish from the face of the earth, for all the mail they get or the mail they write, why, I'm not going to open my mouth. Some of the folks here in town are taking up for me and some turned against me. I know which is which. There are always people who will quit buying stamps just to get on the right side of Papa-Daddy.

But here I am, and here I'll stay. I want the world to know I'm happy.

And if Stella-Rondo should come to me this minute, on bended knees, and *attempt* to explain the incidents of her life with Mr. Whitaker, I'd simply put my fingers in both my ears and refuse to listen.

Talking about the Text

1. Make a list of the events that take place in the story.
2. Characterize the narrator's tone of voice. Include references to what you believe is specifically southern about her.
3. How close does the narrator assume she is to you as reader? What position does she put you in?

Writing about the Text

1. Write some additional dialogue between the narrator and her sister Stella-Rondo.
2. Write about the events of the story in the voice of another of the characters, par-ticularly the mother or Stella-Rondo.
3. In an essay, analyze "Why I Live at the P.O." as an example of regional fiction, paying particular attention to those details that characterize it as from rural Mississippi.

Linking the Text to Other Texts

1. Compare this story to Lee Smith's "Cakewalk" (p. 391), which was influenced by it. What alterations has Smith made to the rivalry between the two sisters?
2. In "Why I Live at the P.O." we are in the presence of an unreliable narrator. Ex-amine the narrator's voice here in light of other unreliable narrators collected here, notably Swift's narrator in "A Modest Proposal" (p. 504), Joyce's narrator in "Araby" (p. 34), or Updike's narrator in "A & P" (p. 58). How soon does the reader realize that the narrator cannot be trusted?
3. This story is full of fantastic events and situations that the narrator treats as com-monplace. Compare it to another story you know of where a similar thing hap-pens: "A Shower of Gold" (p. 345), or "Young Goodman Brown" (p. 147) are likely starting points.

A Worn Path
(1941)

It was December—a bright frozen day in the early morning. Far out in the coun-try there was an old Negro woman with her head tied in a red rag, coming along a path through the pinewoods. Her name was Phoenix Jackson. She was very old and small and she walked slowly in the dark pine shadows, moving a little from side to side in her steps, with the balanced heaviness and lightness of a pendulum in a grandfather clock. She carried a thin, small cane made from an umbrella, and with this she kept tapping the frozen earth in front of her. This made a grave and persistent noise in the still air, that seemed meditative like the chirping of a solitary little bird.

She wore a dark striped dress reaching down to her shoe tops, and an equally long apron of bleached sugar sacks, with a full pocket: all neat and tidy, but every time she took a step she might have fallen over her shoelaces, which dragged from her unlaced shoes. She looked straight ahead. Her eyes were blue with age. Her skin had a pattern all its own of numberless branching wrinkles and as though a whole little tree stood in the middle of her forehead, but a golden color ran underneath, and the two knobs of her cheeks were illuminated by a yellow burning under the dark. Under the red rag her hair came down on her neck in the frailest of ringlets, still black, and with an odor like copper.

Now and then there was a quivering in the thicket. Old Phoenix said, "Out of my way, all you foxes, owls, beetles, jack rabbits, coons, and wild animals! . . . Keep out from under these feet, little bob-whites. . . .Keep the big wild hogs out of my path. Don't let none of those come running my direction. I got a long way." Under her small black-freckled hand her cane, limber as a buggy whip, would switch at the brush as if to rouse up any hiding things.

On she went. The woods were deep and still. The sun made the pine needles almost too bright to look at, up where the wind rocked. The cones dropped as light as feathers. Down in the hollow was the mourning dove—it was not too late for him.

The path ran up a hill. "Seem like there is chains about my feet, time I get this far," she said, in the voice of argument old people keep to use with themselves. "Something always take a hold of me on this hill—pleads I should stay." 5

After she got to the top she turned and gave a full, severe look behind her were she had come. "Up through pines," she said at length. "Now down through oaks."

Her eyes opened their widest, and she started down gently. But before she got to the bottom of the hill a bush caught her dress.

Her fingers were busy and intent, but her skirts were full and long, so that before she could pull them free in one place they were caught in another. It was not possible to allow the dress to tear. "I in the thorny bush," she said. "Thorns, you doing your appointed work. Never want to let folks pass—no sir. Old eyes thought you was a pretty little *green* bush."

Finally, trembling all over, she stood free, and after a moment dared to stoop for her cane.

"Sun so high!" she cried, leaning back and looking, while the thick tears went over her eyes. "The time getting all gone here." 10

At the foot of this hill was a place where a log was laid across the creek.

"Now comes the trial," said Phoenix.

Putting her right foot out, she mounted the log and shut her eyes. Lifting her skirt, levelling her cane fiercely before her, like a festival figure in some parade, she began to march across. Then she opened her eyes and she was safe on the other side.

"I wasn't as old as I thought," she said.

But she sat down to rest. She spread her skirts on the bank around her and folded her hands over her knees. Up above her was a tree in a pearly cloud of mistletoe. She did not dare to close her eyes, and when a little boy brought her a little plate with a slice of marble-cake on it she spoke to him. "That would be acceptable," she said. But when she went to take it there was just her own hand in the air.

So she left that tree, and had to go through a barbed-wire fence. There she had to creep and crawl, spreading her knees and stretching her fingers like a baby trying to climb the steps. But she talked loudly to herself: she could not let her dress be torn now, so late in the day, and she could not pay for having her arm or leg sawed off if she got caught fast where she was.

At last she was safe through the fence and risen up out in the clearing. Big dead trees, like black men with one arm, were standing in the purple stalks of the withered cotton field. There sat a buzzard.

"Who you watching?"

In the furrow she made her way along.

"Glad this not the season for bulls," she said, looking sideways, "and the good Lord made his snakes to curl up and sleep in the winter. A pleasure I don't see no two-headed snake coming around that tree, where it come once. It took a while to get by him, back in the summer."

She passed through the old cotton and went into a field of dead corn. It whispered and shook and was taller than her head. "Through the maze now," she said, for there was no path.

Then there was something tall, black, and skinny there, moving before her.

*   *   *

At first she took it for a man. It could have been a man dancing in the field. But she stood still and listened, and it did not make a sound. It was as silent as a ghost.

"Ghost," she said sharply, "who be you the ghost of? For I have heard of nary death close by."

But there was no answer—only the ragged dancing in the wind.

She shut her eyes, reached out her hand, and touched a sleeve. She found a coat and inside that an emptiness, cold as ice.

"You scarecrow," she said. Her face lighted. "I ought to be shut up for good," she said with laughter. "My senses is gone, I too old. I the oldest people I ever know. Dance, old scarecrow," she said, "while I dancing with you."

She kicked her foot over the furrow, and with mouth drawn down, shook her head once or twice in a little strutting way. Some husks blew down and whirled in streamers about her skirts.

Then she went on, parting her way from side to side with the cane, through the whispering field. At last she came to the end, to a wagon track where the silver grass blew between the red ruts. The quail were walking around like pullets, seeming all dainty and unseen.

"Walk pretty," she said. "This the easy place. This the easy going."

She followed the track, swaying through the quiet bare fields, through the little strings of trees silver in their dead leaves, past cabins silver from weather, with the doors and windows boarded shut, all like old women under a spell sitting there. "I walking in their sleep," she said, nodding her head vigorously.

(*Text continues after color insert*)

Visual Literacy and Southern Women Writers

By virtue of its distinct culture and history, the American South has long been regarded—by its residents as well as outsiders—as a region with a particular "separateness and uniqueness" in the U.S. landscape. The Civil War, the legacy of slavery, racial and class tensions, and the importance of religion, music, and food have all played a part in influencing our reflections about the South. Those same elements have also shaped the themes in the rich and complex fiction from the region. The images presented here were chosen with an eye toward examining core American beliefs, attitudes, and myths about the South. As you examine them, see how they compare to the written depictions by the southern women writers in Chapter 7.

Album cover for Bruce Springsteen's *Nebraska* (1982)

Bruce Springsteen's Nebraska *album was based on the story of a real-life serial killer, Charlie Starkweather, who murdered nearly a dozen people in Nebraska during the 1950s. Although the story is set in a midwestern state, Springsteen drew on the work of a southern writer, Flannery O'Connor, for both tone and characterization, in particular the Misfit character in "A Good Man Is Hard to Find" (see p. 374).*

READING THE IMAGE. What about the album cover first captures your attention and why? What dominant tone does the photo evoke, and how is this effect achieved? How does it compare to the tone of O'Connor's story "A Good Man Is Hard to Find"?

LINKING IMAGE TO TEXT. Compare the lyrics of two O'Connor-inspired Springsteen songs, "Nebraska" and "A Good Man Is Hard to Find" (see pp. 385–388), with O'Connor's Misfit. How are these characters similar? How are they different? How do O'Connor and Springsteen each convey the shared qualities of these characters?

Eudora Welty (1909–2001)

Below: A Woman of the Thirties/Hinds County, Mississippi (1935)

Next page, top and bottom:
Saturday Off/Jackson, Mississippi (1930s)
Tomato-Packers' Recess/Copiah County, Mississippi (1936)

During the 1930s, beloved American fiction writer and Mississippi native Eudora Welty worked as a publicist for the Works Progress Administration (WPA), a federal program created to provide jobs during the Great Depression. Welty's job gave her the chance to travel all over Mississippi; along the way she took "snapshots," as she preferred calling them, on her own. They were eventually collected in One Time, One Place *(1971) and* Photographs *(1989).*

READING THE IMAGES.
What can you tell about life in Mississippi based on the photos Welty took? Based on what you see, what kind of lives do you think the people being photographed led?

LINKING IMAGES TO TEXT. In a 1989 interview, Welty was asked what an "outsider" viewing her Depression-era photos of black Southerners collected together might think. Welty replied, "They might or might not know that poverty in Mississippi, white and black, really didn't have too much to do with the Depression. It was ongoing. Mississippi was long since poor, long devastated. I took pictures of our poverty because that was reality, and I was recording it. The photographs speak for themselves. The same thing is true of my stories; I didn't announce my view editorially. I tried to *show* it." Evaluate this statement, based on the photos presented here and at least one of the Welty short stories in Chapter 7.

Richard Sexton (1954–)
Staircase, Ashland/Belle Helene Plantation (1997)

Richard Sexton was born in Atlanta, Georgia, and lives in New Orleans, Louisiana. The image below comes from his photo essay Vestiges of Grandeur: The Plantations of Louisiana's River Road *(1999), which focuses on the historic plantation architecture of the River Road between New Orleans and Baton Rouge.*

READING THE IMAGE. Reviewer Allen Freeman described Sexton's southern landscapes as "melancholy, contradictory, overripe, haunting, and scary." Do you agree with this assessment? Why or why not? Does the photo's title, which reveals its real-life setting, affect your reactions to it, and if so, how?

LINKING IMAGE TO TEXT. How does Sexton's depiction of the South compare with any of the fictional depictions in Chapter 7? What can Sexton convey about the South visually that could not be described verbally? What parts of the story you chose give an impression about the southern setting, and could those ideas have been presented in visual form instead of in words?

Richard Sexton (1954–)
Top: Temptation Can Never Be Too Lurid (1994)
Bottom: Reservations Are Required (1994)

In 1992 Richard Sexton began shooting highway road signs in the Florida panhandle and southwest Georgia. The images, along with an accompanying narrative, were published in his photo essay The Highway of Temptation and Redemption: A Gothic Travelogue in Two Dimensions *(2004). For more on Sexton, see the previous page.*

READING THE IMAGES.
What do you think Sexton is trying to convey through the signs he chooses? How do the photograph titles affect your interpretation of the messages in the road signs?

LINKING IMAGES TO TEXT.
Sexton and Flannery O'Connor both use a gothic and religious style to stress themes of temptation, redemption, grace, and mortality. How is Sexton's take on these themes different from O'Connor's? How does each artist use humor, and what function does that humor serve?

Peter Menzel/Charles Mann
The Skeen Family, 6:30 a.m., August 4, 1993, Pearland, Texas, U.S.A. (1993)

The image below comes from Material World, a collaboration between photographer Peter Menzel and journalist Charles Mann that shows "statistically average" families from thirty nations posed in front of their homes and surrounded by all their material possessions. Each photo is paired with a list of the objects pictured. The Skeen family was chosen to represent the United States.

READING THE IMAGES. What makes the family portrayed below look "American"? What, if anything, makes them seem distinctly "southern"? What does it mean that they were chosen as a "statistically average" family? How do they embody these labels? How do they defy these same labels?

LINKING IMAGES TO TEXT. Compare the Skeen Family to the family Alice Walker portrays in "Everyday Use" (see p. 424). How is Walker's portrait of a modern black southern family similar to and different from the white southern family shown below? What do the material objects presented in the photo and in the story say about each respective family? (Alternatively, you might compare the Skeen family to the characters depicted in Dorothy Allison's "I'm Working on My Charm.")

Objects in photo:Key to Big Picture: 1. Rick Skeen, father, 36   2. Pattie Skeen, mother, 34   3. Julie Skeen, daughter, 10   4. Michael Skeen, son, 7

- (foreground) family Bible (held by mother)
- (left to right) dog (Lucky, tied to real fire hydrant—souvenir of father's years as fireman)
- Sewing machine (antique, treadle-style)
- easy chair
- photo lights for shooting Big Picture
- (scattered throughout scene) end table with lamp
- living room couch
- coffee table
- marble-topped with books)
- storage cabinet
- television (on cabinet)
- 2nd easy chair
- stereo (on matching marble-topped table)
- speakers (4, on either side of secretary)
- dining table, chairs (6), place settings, bowl of fruit
- curio cabinet (with china)
- secretary (behind cabinet)
- bicycles (behind secretary)
- bookshelf (visible through window behind bicycles)
- computer and computer storage unit (obscured by father's head)
- motor vehicles (3, Ford F350 pickup, Ford Aerostar minivan, dune buggy)
- storage shelving (in garage)
- stuffed deer heads (2, above garage door)
- U.S. flag (between heads)
- dressers (2)
- dollhouse (on file cabinet)
- cane-backed chair, second end table, toys, U.S. map, globe
- refrigerator
- desk (with chair, toy train)
- 2nd TV (on table)
- washer, range, dryer (with food processor, mixer, coffee maker, pots, etc.)
- microwave (atop dishwasher)
- beds (3, with parents' guitar)
- ironing board and iron
- piano and piano bench
- 2nd sewing machine (electric with table chair)
- family portraits

Romare Bearden (1911–1988)
Mississippi Monday (date unknown)

Romare Bearden was born in North Carolina but raised in New York and then Pitts-burgh during the height of the Harlem Renaissance. All three locales and the images of African American life there served as inspirations for his art. Bearden also drew on the works of Western master painters and sculptors, jazz, literature, African American his-tory, and religion for his subject matter and his recurrent themes. Although he left the South as a child, he returned often through the mid-1920s to visit his paternal great-grandparents in Charlotte, and the region figured prominently in his art throughout his career. He experimented with different media and styles—oils and watercolor among them—but is best known for his collages. His collage The Piano Lesson inspired Au-gust Wilson's play of the same name (see p. 1916). For more on Bearden, see the Im-age Gallery accompanying Chapter 25, "Sweet Home Chicago."

READING THE IMAGE. What can you tell about life in Mississippi based on the image Bearden created? What might have attracted Bearden to depict these two women in the manner he did?

LINKING IMAGE TO TEXT. How does Bearden's picture of southern life above compare with the one portrayed by Zora Neale Hurston in her story "Sweat" (see p. 318)? Consider how the theme of hard, physical, everyday labor functions in both Bearden's image and Hurston's text.

In a ravine she went where a spring was silently flowing through a hollow log. Old Phoenix bent and drank. "Sweet-gum makes the water sweet," she said, and drank more. "Nobody know who made this well, for it was here when I was born."

The track crossed a swampy part where the moss hung as white as lace from every limb. "Sleep on, alligators, and blow your bubbles." Then the track went into the road.

Deep, deep the road went down between the high green-colored banks. Overhead the live-oaks met, and it was as dark as a cave.

A black dog with a lolling tongue came up out of the weeds by the ditch.   35
She was meditating, and not ready, and when he came at her she only hit him a little with her cane. Over she went in the ditch, like a little puff of milk-weed.

Down there, her senses drifted away. A dream visited her, and she reached her hand up, but nothing reached down and gave her a pull. So she lay there and presently went to talking. "Old woman," she said to herself, "that black dog come up out of the weeds to stall you off, and now there he sitting on his fine tail, smiling at you."

A white man finally came along and found her—a hunter, a young man, with his dog on a chain.

"Well, Granny!" he laughed. "what are you doing there?"

"Lying on my back like a June-bug waiting to be turned over, mister," she said, reaching up her hand.

He lifted her up, gave her a swing in the air, and set her down. "Anything   40
broken, Granny?"

"No sir, them old dead weeds is springy enough," said Phoenix, when she had got her breath. "I thank you for your trouble."

"Where do you live, Granny?" he asked, while the two dogs were growling at each other.

"Away back yonder, sir, behind the ridge. You can't even see it from here."

"On your way home?"

"No, sir, I going to town."   45

"Why, that's too far! That's as far as I walk when I come out myself, and I get something for my trouble." He patted the stuffed bag he carried, and there hung down a little closed claw. It was one of the bob-whites, with its beak hooked bitterly to show it was dead. "Now you go on home, Granny!"

"I bound to go to town, mister," said Phoenix. "The time come around."

He gave another laugh, filling the whole landscape. "I know you old colored people! Wouldn't miss going to town to see Santa Claus!"

But something held Old Phoenix very still. The deep lines in her face went into a fierce and different radiation. Without warning, she had seen with her own eyes a flashing nickel fall out of the man's pocket onto the ground.

"How old are you, Granny?" he was saying.   50

"There is no telling, mister," she said, "no telling."

Then she gave a little cry and clapped her hands and said, "Git on away from here, dog! Look! Look at that dog!" She laughed as if in admiration. "He ain't scared of nobody. He a big black dog." She whispered, "Sic him!"

"Watch me get rid of that cur," said the man. "Sic him, Pete! Sic him!"

Phoenix heard the dogs fighting, and heard the man running and throwing sticks. She even heard a gunshot. But she was slowly bending forward by that time, further and further forward, the lids stretched down over her eyes, as if she were doing this in her sleep. Her chin was lowered almost to her knees. The yellow palm of her hand came out from the fold of her apron. Her fingers slid down and along the ground under the piece of money with the grace and care they would have in lifting an egg from under a sitting hen. Then she slowly straightened up, she stood erect, and the nickel was in her apron pocket. A bird flew by. Her lips moved. "God watching me the whole time. I come to stealing."

The man came back, and his own dog panted about them. "Well, I scared   55 him off that time," he said, and then he laughed and lifted his gun and pointed it at Phoenix.

She stood straight and faced him.

"Doesn't the gun scare you?" he said, still pointing it.

"No, sir, I seen plenty go off closer by, in my day, and for less than what I done," she said, holding utterly still.

He smiled, and shouldered the gun. "Well, Granny," he said, "you must be a hundred years old, and scared of nothing. I'd give you a dime if I had any money with me. But you take my advice and stay home, and nothing will happen to you."

"I bound to go on my way, mister," said Phoenix. She inclined her head in   60 the red rag. Then they went in different directions, but she could hear the gun shooting again and again over the hill.

She walked on. The shadows hung from the oak trees to the road like curtains. Then she smelled wood-smoke, and smelled the river, and she saw a steeple and the cabins on their steep steps. Dozens of little black children whirled around her. There ahead was Natchez shining. Bells were ringing. She walked on.

In the paved city it was Christmas time. There were red and green electric lights strung and crisscrossed everywhere, and all turned on in the daytime. Old Phoenix would have been lost if she had not distrusted her eyesight and depended on her feet to know where to take her.

She paused quietly on the sidewalk where people were passing by. A lady came along in the crowd, carrying an armful of red-, green-, and silver-wrapped presents; she gave off perfume like the red roses in hot summer, and Phoenix stopped her.

"Please, missy, will you lace up my shoe?" She held up her foot.

"What do you want, Grandma?"   65

"See my shoe," said Phoenix. "Do all right for out in the country, but wouldn't look right to go in a big building."

"Stand still then, Grandma," said the lady. She put her packages down on the sidewalk beside her and laced and tied both shoes tightly.

"Can't lace 'em with a cane," said Phoenix. "Thank you, missy. I doesn't mind asking a nice lady to tie up my shoe, when I gets out on the street."

Moving slowly and from side to side, she went into the big building and into a tower of steps, where she walked up and around and around until her feet knew to stop.

She entered a door, and there she saw nailed up on the wall the document   70 that had been stamped with the gold seal and framed in the gold frame, which matched the dream that was hung up in her head.

"Here I be," she said. There was a fixed and ceremonial stiffness over her body.

"A charity case, I suppose," said an attendant who sat at the desk before her.

But Phoenix only looked above her head. There was sweat on her face, the wrinkles in her skin shone like a bright net.

"Speak up, Grandma," the woman said. "What's your name? We must have your history, you know. Have you been here before? What seems to be the trouble with you?"

Old Phoenix only gave a twitch to her face as if a fly were bothering her.   75

"Are you deaf?" cried the attendant.

But then the nurse came in.

"Oh, that's just old Aunt Phoenix," she said. "She doesn't come for herself—she has a little grandson. She makes these trips just as regular as clockwork. She lives away back off the old Natchez Trace." She bent down. "Well, Aunt Phoenix, why don't you just take a seat? We won't keep you standing after your long trip." She pointed.

The old woman sat down, bolt upright in the chair.

"Now, how is the boy?" asked the nurse.

Old Phoenix did not speak.   80

"I said, how is the boy?"

But Phoenix only waited and stared straight ahead, her face very solemn and withdrawn into rigidity.

"Is his throat any better?" asked the nurse. "Aunt Phoenix, don't you hear me? Is your grandson's throat any better since the last time you came for the medicine?"

With her hands on her knees, the old woman waited, silent, erect and motionless, just as if she were in armor.   85

"You mustn't take up our time this way, Aunt Phoenix," the nurse said. "Tell us quickly about your grandson, and get it over. He isn't dead, is he?"

At last there came a flicker and then a flame of comprehension across her face, and she spoke.

"My grandson. It was my memory had left me. There I sat and forgot why I made my long trip."

"Forgot?" The nurse frowned. "After you came so far?"

Then Phoenix was like an old woman begging a dignified forgiveness for   90
waking up frightened in the night. "I never did go to school, I was too old at the Surrender," she said in a soft voice. "I'm an old woman without an education. It was my memory fail me. My little grandson, he is just the same, and I forgot it in the coming."

"Throat never heals, does it?" said the nurse, speaking in a loud, sure voice to Old Phoenix. By now she had a card with something written on it, a little list. "Yes. Swallowed lye. When was it—January—two-three years ago—"

Phoenix spoke unasked now. "No, missy, he not dead, he just the same. Every little while his throat begin to close up again, and he not able to swallow. He not get his breath. He not able to help himself. So the time come around, and I go on another trip for the soothing medicine."

"All right. The doctor said as long as you came to get it, you could have it," said the nurse. "But it's an obstinate case."

"My little grandson, he sit up there in the house all wrapped up, waiting by himself," Phoenix went on. "We is the only two left in the world. He suffer and it don't seem to put him back at all. He got a sweet look. He going to last. He wear a little patch quilt and peep out holding his mouth open like a little bird. I remembers so plain now. I not going to forget him again, no, the whole enduring time. I could tell him from all the others in creation."

"All right." The nurse was trying to hush her now. She brought her a bottle   95
of medicine. "Charity," she said, making a check mark in a book.

Old Phoenix held the bottle close to her eyes and then carefully put it into her pocket.

"I thank you," she said.

"It's Christmas time, Grandma," said the attendant. "Could I give you a few pennies out of my purse?"

"Five pennies is a nickel," said Phoenix stiffly.

"Here's a nickel," said the attendant.   100

Phoenix rose carefully and held out her hand. She received the nickel and then fished the other nickel out of her pocket and laid it beside the new one. She stared at her palm closely, with her head on one side.

Then she gave a tap with her cane on the floor.

"This is what come to me to do," she said. "I going to the store and buy my child a little windmill they sells, made out of paper. He going to find it hard to believe there such a thing in the world. I'll march myself back where he waiting, holding it straight up in his hand."

She lifted her free hand, gave a little nod, turned round, and walked out of the doctor's office. Then her slow step began on the stairs, going down.

Talking about the Text

1. Give a brief summary of "A Worn Path," noting places where you are unsure of exactly what is happening.
2. What is the role of the path in the story? Why do you suppose it is in the title?

Writing about the Text

1. What do the people Phoenix encounters on her journey—and her interactions with them—suggest about race relations in the South in the 1940s?
2. Eudora Welty wrote in her memoir *One Writer's Beginnings*, "I am a writer who came of a sheltered life. A sheltered life can be a daring life as well. For all serious daring starts from within." In a brief essay, explain how the life of the main character in "A Worn Path" mixes "shelter" and "daring."
3. Describe and analyze the functions the setting of "A Worn Path" serves in the story, concentrating on both the locale of the path itself and the weather the characters encounter.

Linking the Text to Other Texts

1. Examine some of Welty's photographs. See the accompanying "Visual Literacy and Southern Women Writers" image gallery. Additional Welty photos can be found online at *http://www.artsandartists.org/exhpages/welty/images.html*. Can you connect the person who wrote the stories and the one who took the photos? What do these two aspects of Welty have in common?
2. Both "A Worn Path" and "How Far She Went" (p. 410) have what we might call a limited or "challenged" woman as the main character. In an essay, tell what these

characters have going for them, despite their limitations. Show how they triumph (or win limited victories) in the end.

A Shower of Gold (1949)

That was Miss Snowdie MacLain.

She comes after her butter, won't let me run over with it from just across the road. Her husband walked out of the house one day and left his hat on the banks of the Big Black River.—That could have started something, too.

We might have had a little run on doing that in Morgana, if it had been so willed. What King did, the copy-cats always might do. Well, King MacLain left a new straw hat on the banks of the Big Black and there are people that consider he headed West.

Snowdie grieved for him, but the decent way you'd grieve for the dead, more like, and nobody wanted to think, around her, that he treated her that way. But how long can you humor the humored? Well, always. But I could almost bring myself to talk about it—to a passer-by, that will never see her again, or me either. Sure I can churn and talk. My name's Mrs. Rainey.

You seen she wasn't ugly—and the little blinky lines to her eyelids comes from trying to see. She's an albino but nobody would ever try to call her ugly around here—with that tender, tender skin like a baby. Some said King figured out that if the babies started coming, he had a chance for a nestful of little albinos, and that swayed him. No, I don't say it. I say he was just willful. *He* wouldn't think ahead. 5

Willful and outrageous, to some several. Well: he married Snowdie.

Lots of worse men wouldn't have: no better sense. Them Hudsons had more than MacLains, but none of 'em had enough to count or worry over. Not by then. Hudson money built that house, and built it for *Snowdie* . . . they prayed over that. But take King: marrying must have been some of his showing off—like man never married at all till *he* flung in, then had to show the others how he could go right on acting. And like, "Look, everybody, this is what I think of Morgana and MacLain Courthouse and all the way between"—further, for all I know—"marrying a girl with pink eyes." "I swan!" we all say. Just like he wants us to, scoundrel. And Snowdie as sweet and gentle as you find them. Of course gentle people aren't the ones you lead best, he had that to find out, so know-all. No, sir, she'll beat him yet, balking. In the meantime children of his growing up in the County Orphans', so say several, and children known and unknown, scattered-like. When he does come, he's just as nice as he can be to Snowdie. Just as courteous. Was from the start.

Haven't you noticed it prevail, in the world in general? Beware of a man with manners. He never raised his voice to her, but then one day he walked out of the house. Oh, I don't mean once!

He went away for a good spell before he come back that time. She had a little story about him needing the waters. Next time it was more than a year, it was two—oh, it was three. I had two children myself, enduring his being gone, and one to die. Yes, and that time he sent her word ahead: "Meet me in the woods." No, he more invited her than told her to come—"Suppose you meet me in the woods." And it was nighttime he supposed to her. And Snowdie met him without asking "What for?" which I would want to know of Fate Rainey. After all, they were married—they had a right to sit inside and talk in the light and comfort, or lie down easy on a good goosefeather bed, either. I would even consider he might not be there when I came. Well, if Snowdie went without a question, then I can tell it without a question as long as I love Snowdie. Her version is that in the woods they met and both decided on what would be best.

Best for him, of course. We could see the writing on the wall.   10

"The woods" was Morgan's Woods. We would any of us know the place he meant, without trying—I could have streaked like an arrow to the very oak tree, one there to itself and all spready: a real shady place by *day*, is all I know. Can't you just see King MacLain leaning his length against that tree by the light of the moon as you come walking through Morgan's Woods and you hadn't seen him in three years? "Suppose you meet me in the woods." My foot. Oh, I don't know how poor Snowdie stood it, crossing the distance.

Then, twins.

That was where I come in, I could help when things got to there. I took her a little churning of butter with her milk and we took up. I hadn't been married long myself, and Mr. Rainey's health was already a little delicate so he'd thought best to quit heavy work. We was both hard workers fairly early.

I always thought twins might be nice. And might have been for them, by just the sound of it. The MacLains first come to Morgana bride and groom from MacLain and went into that new house. He was educated off, to practice law—well needed here. Snowdie was Miss Lollie Hudson's daughter, well known. Her father was Mr. Eugene Hudson, a storekeeper down at Crossroads past the Courthouse, but he was a lovely man. Snowdie was their only daughter, and they give her a nice education. And I guess people more or less expected her to teach school: not marry. She couldn't see all that well, was the only thing in the way, but Mr. Comus Stark here and the supervisors overlooked that, knowing the family and Snowdie's real good way with Sunday School children. Then before the school year even got a good start, she got took up by King MacLain all of a sudden. I think it was when jack-o'-lanterns was pasted on her window I used to see his buggy roll up right to the schoolhouse steps and wait on her. He courted her in Morgana and MacLain too, both ends, didn't skip a day.

It was no different—no quicker and no slower—than the like happens every   15 whipstitch, so I don't need to tell you they got married in the MacLain Presbyterian Church before you could shake a stick at it, no matter how surprised people were going to be. And once they dressed Snowdie all in white, you know she was whiter than your dreams.

So—he'd been educated in the law and he traveled for somebody, that was the first thing he did—I'll tell you in a minute what he sold, and she stayed home and cooked and kept house. I forget if she had a Negro, she didn't know how to tell one what to do if she had. And she put her eyes straight out, almost, going to work and making curtains for every room and all like that. So busy. At first it didn't look like they would have any children.

So it went the way I told you, slipped into it real easy, people took it for granted mighty early—him leaving and him being welcomed home, him leaving and him sending word, "Meet me in the woods," and him gone again, at last leaving the hat. I told my husband I was going to quit keeping count of King's comings and goings, and it wasn't long after that he did leave the hat. I don't know yet whether he meant it kind or cruel. Kind, I incline to believe. Or maybe she was winning. Why do I try to figure? Maybe because Fate Rainey ain't got a surprise in him, and proud of it. So Fate said, "Well now, let's have the women to settle down and pay attention to homefolks a while." That was all he could say about it.

So, you wouldn't have had to wait long. Here comes Snowdie across the road to bring the news. I seen her coming across my pasture in a different walk, it was the way somebody comes down an aisle. Her sunbonnet ribbons was jumping around her: springtime. Did you notice her little dainty waist she has still? I declare it's a mystery to think about her having the strength once. Look at me.

I was in the barn milking, and she come and took a stand there at the head of the little Jersey, Lady May. She had a quiet, picked-out way to tell news. She said, "I'm going to have a baby too, Miss Katie. Congratulate me."

Me and Lady May both had to just stop and look at her. She looked like   20
more than only the news had come over her. It was like a shower of something had struck her, like she'd been caught out in something bright. It was more than the day. There with her eyes all crinkled up with always fighting the light, yet she was looking out bold as a lion that day under her brim, and gazing into my bucket and into my stall like a visiting somebody. Poor Snowdie. I remember it was Easter time and how the pasture was all spotty there behind her little blue skirt, in sweet clover. He sold tea and spices, that's what it was.

It was sure enough nine months to the day the twins come after he went sallying out through those woods and fields and laid his hat down on the bank of the river with "King MacLain" on it.

I wish I'd seen him! I don't guess *I'd* have stopped him. I can't tell you why, but I wish I'd seen him! But nobody did.

For Snowdie's sake—here they come bringing the hat, and a hullaballoo raised—they drug the Big Black for nine miles down, or was it only eight, and sent word to Bovina and on, clear to Vicksburg, to watch out for anything to wash up or to catch in the trees in the river. Sure, there never was anything—just the hat. They found everybody else that ever honestly drowned along the Big Black in this neighborhood. Mr. Sissum at the store, he drowned later on and they found him. I think with the hat he ought to have laid his watch down, if he wanted to give it a better look.

Snowdie kept just as bright and brave, she didn't seem to give in. She must have had her thoughts and they must have been one of two things. One that he was dead—then why did her face have the glow? It had a glow—and the other that he left her and meant it. And like people said, if she smiled *then*, she was clear out of reach. I didn't know if I liked the glow. Why didn't she rage and storm a little—to me, anyway, just Mrs. Rainey? The Hudsons all hold themselves in. But it didn't seem to me, running in and out the way I was, that Snowdie had ever got a real good look at life, maybe. Maybe from the beginning. Maybe she just doesn't know the *extent*. Not the kind of look I got, and away back when I was twelve year old or so. Like something was put to my eye.

She just went on keeping house, and getting fairly big with what I told you   25
already was twins, and she seemed to settle into her content. Like a little white kitty in a basket, making you wonder if she just mightn't put up her paw and scratch, if anything was, after all, to come near. At her house it was like Sunday even in the mornings, every day, in that cleaned-up way. She was taking a joy in her fresh untracked rooms and that dark, quiet, real quiet hall that runs through her house. And I love Snowdie. I love her.

Except none of us felt very *close* to her all the while. I'll tell you what it was, what made her different. It was the not waiting any more, except where the babies waited, and that's not but one story. We were mad at her and protecting her all at once, when we couldn't be close to her.

And she come out in her pretty clean shirtwaists to water the ferns, and she had remarkable flowers—she had her mother's way with flowers, of course. And give just as many away, except it wasn't like I or you give. She was by her own self. Oh, her mother was dead by then, and Mr. Hudson fourteen miles down the road away, crippled up, running his store in a cane chair. We was every bit she had. Everybody tried to stay with her as much as they could spare, not let a day go by without one of us to run in and speak to her and say a word about an ordinary thing. Miss Lizzie Stark let her be in charge of raising money for the poor country people at Christmas that year, and like that. Of course we made all her little things for her, stitches like that was way beyond her. It was a good thing she got such a big stack.

The twins come the first day of January. Miss Lizzie Stark—she hates all men, and is real important: across yonder's her chimney—made Mr. Comus Stark, her husband, hitch up and drive to Vicksburg to bring back a Vicksburg doctor in her own buggy the night before, instead of using Dr. Loomis here, and stuck him in a cold room to sleep at her house; she said trust any doctor's buggy to break down on those bridges. Mrs. Stark stayed right by Snowdie, and of course several, and I, stayed too, but Mrs. Stark was not budging and took charge when pains commenced. Snowdie had the two little boys and neither one albino. They were both King all over again, if you want to know it. Mrs. Stark had so hoped for a girl, or two *girls*. Snowdie clapped the names on them of Lucius Randall and Eugene Hudson, after her own father and her mother's father.

It was the only sign she ever give Morgana that maybe she didn't think the name King MacLain had stayed beautiful. But not much of a sign; some women don't name after their husbands, until they get down to nothing else left. I don't think with Snowdie even *two* other names meant she had changed yet, not towards King, that scoundrel.

Time goes like a dream no matter how hard you run, and all the time we heard things from out in the world that we listened to but that still didn't mean we believed them. You know the kind of things. Somebody's cousin saw King MacLain. Mr. Comus Stark, the one the cotton and timber belongs to, he goes a little, and he claimed three or four times he saw his back, and once saw him getting a haircut in Texas. Those things you will hear forever when people go off, to keep up a few shots in the woods. They might mean something—might not.

Till the most outrageous was the time my husband went up to Jackson. He saw a man that was the spit-image of King in the parade, my husband told me in his good time, the inauguration of Governor Vardaman. He was right up with the big ones and astride a fine animal. Several from here went but as Mrs. Spights said, why wouldn't they be looking at the Governor? Or the New Capitol? But King MacLain could steal anyone's glory, so he thought.

When I asked the way he looked, I couldn't get a thing out of my husband, except he lifted his feet across the kitchen floor like a horse and man in one, and I went after him with my broom. I knew, though. If it was King, he looked like, "Hasn't everybody been wondering, though, been out of their minds to know, where I've been keeping myself!" I told my husband it reasoned to me like it was

30

up to Governor Vardaman to get hold of King and bring something out of him, but my husband said why pick on one man, and besides a parade was going on and what all. Men! I said if I'd been Governor Vardaman and spied King MacLain from Morgana marching in my parade as big as I was and no call for it, I'd have had the whole thing brought to a halt and called him to accounts. "Well, what good would it have done you?" my husband said. "A plenty," I said. I was excited at the time it happened. "That was just as good a spot as any to show him forth, right in front of the New Capitol in Jackson with the band going, and just as good a man to do it."

Well, sure, men like that need to be shown up before the world, I guess—not that any of us would be surprised. "Did you go and find him after the Governor got inaugurated to suit you then?" I asked my husband. But he said no, and reminded me. He went for me a new bucket; and brought me the wrong size. Just like the ones at Holifield's. But he said he saw King or his twin. What twin!

Well, through the years, we'd hear of him here or there—maybe two places at once, New Orleans and Mobile. That's people's careless way of using their eyes.

I believe he's been to California. Don't ask me why. But I picture him there. 35 I see King in the West, out where it's gold and all that. Everybody to their own visioning.

II

Well, what happened turned out to happen on Hallowe'en. Only last week—and seems already like something that couldn't happen at all.

My baby girl, Virgie, swallowed a button that same day—later on—and that *happened*, it seems like still, but not this. And not a word's been spoke out loud, for Snowdie's sake, so I trust the rest of the world will be as careful.

You can talk about a baby swallowing a button off a shirt and having to be up-ended and her behind pounded, and it sounds reasonable if you can just see the baby—there she runs—but get to talking about something that's only a kind of *near* thing—and hold your horses.

Well, Hallowe'en, about three o'clock, I was over at Snowdie's helping her cut out patterns—she's kept on sewing for those boys. Me, I have a little girl to sew for—she was right there, asleep on the bed in the next room—and it hurts my conscience being that lucky over Snowdie too. And the twins wouldn't play out in the yard that day but had hold of the scraps and the scissors and the paper of pins and all, and there underfoot they were dressing up and playing ghosts and boogers. Uppermost in their little minds was Hallowe'en.

They had on their masks, of course, tied on over their Buster Brown bobs 40 and pressing a rim around the back. I was used to how they looked by then—but I don't like masks. They both come from Spights' store and cost a nickel. One was the Chinese kind, all yellow and mean with slant eyes and a dreadful thin mustache of black horsy hair. The other one was a lady, with an almost scary-sweet smile on her lips. I never did take to that smile, with all day for it. Eugene Hudson wanted to be the Chinaman and so Lucius Randall had to be the lady.

So they were making tails and do-lollies and all kinds of foolishness, and sticking them on to their little middles and behinds, snatching every scrap from the shirts and flannels me and Snowdie was cutting out on the dining room table. Sometimes we could grab a little boy and baste something up on him whether or no, but we didn't really pay them much mind, we was talking about the prices of things for winter, and the funeral of an old maid.

So we never heard the step creak or the porch give, at all. That was a blessing. And if it wasn't for something that come from outside us all to tell about it, I wouldn't have the faith I have that it came about.

But happening along our road—like he does every day—was a real trustworthy nigger. He's one of Mrs. Stark's mother's niggers, Old Plez Morgan everybody calls him. Lives down beyond me. The real old kind, that knows everybody since time was. He knows more folks than I do, who they are, and all the *fine* people. If you wanted anybody in Morgana that wouldn't be likely to make a mistake in who a person is, you would ask for Old Plez.

So he was making his way down the road, by stages. He still has to do a few people's yards won't let him go, like Mrs. Stark, because he don't pull up things. He's no telling how old and starts early and takes his time coming home in the evening—always stopping to speak to people to ask after their health and tell them good evening all the way. Only that day, he said he didn't see a soul *else*— besides you'll hear who in a minute—on the way, not on porches or in the yards. I can't tell you why, unless it was those little gusts of north wind that had started blowing. Nobody likes that.

But yonder ahead of him was walking a man. Plez said it was a white man's   45
walk and a walk he knew—but it struck him it was from away in another year, another time. It wasn't just the walk of anybody supposed to be going along the road to MacLain right at that *time*—and yet it was too—and if it was, he still couldn't think what business that somebody would be up to. That was the careful way Plez was putting it to his mind.

If you saw Plez, you'd know it was him. He had some roses stuck in his hat that day, I saw him right after it happened. Some of Miss Lizzie's fall roses, big as a man's fist and red as blood—they were nodding side-to-side out of the band of his old black hat, and some other little scraps out of the garden laid around the brim, throwed away by Mrs. Stark; he'd been cleaning out her beds that day, it was fixing to rain.

He said later he wasn't in any great hurry, or he would have maybe caught up and passed the man. Up yonder ahead he went, going the same way Plez was going, and not much more interested in a race. And a real familiar stranger.

So Plez says presently the familiar stranger paused. It was in front of the MacLains'—and sunk his weight on one leg and just stood there, posey as statues, hand on his hip. Ha! Old Plez says, according, he just leaned himself against the Presbyterian Church gate and waited a while.

Next thing, the stranger—oh, it was King! By then Plez was calling him Mr. King to himself—went up through the yard and then didn't go right in like anybody else. First he looked around. He took in the yard and summerhouse and skimmed from cedar to cedar along the edge of where he lived, and under the fig tree at the back and under the wash (if he'd counted it!) and come close to the front again, sniffy like, and Plez said though he couldn't swear to seeing from the Presbyterian Church exactly what Mr. King was doing, he knows as good as seeing it that he looked through the blinds. He would have looked in the dining room—have mercy. We shut the West out of Snowdie's eyes of course.

At last he come full front again, around the flowers under the front bed-   50
room. Then he settled himself nice and started up the front steps.

The middle step sings when it's stepped on, but we didn't hear it. Plez said, well, he had on fine tennis shoes. So he got across the front porch and what do you think he's fixing to do but knock on that door? Why wasn't he satisfied with outdoors?

On his own front door. He makes a little shadow knock, like trying to see how it would look, and then puts his present behind his coat. Of course he had something there in a box for her. You know he constitutionally brought home the kind of presents that break your heart. He stands there with one leg out pretty, to surprise them. And I bet a nice smile on his face. Oh, don't ask me to go on!

Suppose Snowdie'd took a notion to glance down the hall—the dining room's at the end of it, and the folding-doors pushed back—and seen him, all "Come-kiss-me" like that. I don't know if she could have seen that good—but *I* could. I was a fool and didn't look.

It was the twins seen him. Through those little bitty mask holes, those eagle eyes! There ain't going to be no stopping those twins. And he didn't get to knock on the door, but he had his hand raised the second time and his knuckles sticking up, and out come the children on him, hollering "Boo!" and waving their arms up and down the way it would scare you to death, or it ought to, if you wasn't ready for them.

We heard them charge out, but we thought it was just a nigger that was go-ing by for them to scare, if we thought anything. 55

Plez says—allowing for all human mistakes—he seen on one side of King come rolling out Lucius Randall all dressed up, and on the other side, Eugene Hudson all dressed up. Could I have forgotten to speak of their being on skates? Oh, that was all afternoon. They're real good skaters, the little fellows, not to have a sidewalk. They sailed out the door and circled around their father, flying their arms and making their fingers go scary, and those little Buster Brown bobs going in a circle.

Lucius Randall, Plez said, had on something pink, and he did, the basted flannelette teddy-bears we had tried on on top of his clothes and he got away. And said Eugene was a Chinaman, and that was what he was. It would be hard to tell which would come at you the more outrageous of the two, but to me it would be Lucius Randall with the girl's face and the big white cotton gloves falling off his fingers, and oh! he had on *my hat.* This one I milk in.

And they made a tremendous uproar with their skates, Plez said, and that was no mistake, because I remember what a hard time Snowdie and me had hearing what each other had to say all afternoon.

Plez said King stood it a minute—he got to turning around too. They were skating around him and saying in high birdie voices, "How do you do, Mister Booger?" You know if children *can* be monkeys, they're going to be them. (With-out the masks, though, those two children would have been more polite about it—there's enough Hudson in them.) Skating around and around their papa, and just as ignorant! Poor little fellows. After all, they'd had nobody to scare all day for Hallowe'en, except one or two niggers that went by, and the Y. & M. V. train whistling through at two-fifteen, they scared that.

But monkeys—! Skating around their papa. Plez said if those children had 60 been black, he wouldn't hesitate to say they would remind a soul of little nigger cannibals in the jungle. When they got their papa in their ring-around-a-rosy

and he couldn't get out, Plez said it was enough to make an onlooker a little uneasy, and he called once or twice on the Lord. And after they went around high,
they crouched down and went around low, about his knees.

The minute come, when King just couldn't get out quick enough. Only he
had a hard time, and took him more than one try. He gathered himself together
and King is a man of six foot height and weighs like a horse, but he was confused,
I take it. But he got aloose and up and out like the Devil was after him—or in
him—finally. Right up over the bannister and the ferns, and down the yard and
over the ditch and gone. He plowed into the rough toward the Big Black, and
the willows waved behind him, and where he run then, Plez don't know and I
don't and don't nobody.

Plez said King passed right by him, that time, but didn't seem to know him,
and the opportunity had gone by then to speak. And where he run then, nobody
knows.

He should have wrote another note, instead of coming.

Well then, the children, I reckon, just held openmouth behind him, and
then something got to mounting up after it was all over, and scared them. They
come back in the dining room. There were innocent ladies visiting with each
other. The little boys had to scowl and frown and drag their skates over the carpet and follow us around the table where we was cutting out Eugene Hudson's
underbody, and pull on our skirts till we saw.

"Well, speak," said their mother, and they told her a booger had come up on   65
the front porch and when they went out to see him he said, "I'm going. You
stay," so they chased him down the steps and run him off. "But he looked back
like this!" Lucius Randall said, lifting off his mask and showing us on his little
naked face with the round blue eyes. And Eugene Hudson said the booger took a
handful of pecans before he got through the gate.

And Snowdie dropped her scissors on the mahogany, and her hand just
stayed in the air as still, and she looked at me, a look a minute long. And first she
caught her apron to her and then started shedding it in the hall while she run to
the door—so as not to be caught in it, I suppose, if anybody was still there. She
run and the little glass prisms shook in the parlor—I don't remember another
time, from *her*. She didn't stop at the door but run on through it and out on the
porch, and she looked both ways and was running down the steps. And she run
out in the yard and stood there holding to the tree, looking towards the country,
but I could tell by the way her head held there wasn't nobody.

When I got to the steps—I didn't like to follow right away—there was nobody at all but old Plez, who was coming by raising his hat.

"Plez, did you see a gentleman come up on my porch just now?" I heard
Snowdie call, and there was Plez, just ambling by with his hat raised, like he was
just that minute passing, like we thought. And Plez, of course, he said, "No'm,
Mistis, I don't recollect one soul pass me, whole way from town."

The little fellows held on to me, I could feel them tugging. And my little girl
slept through it all, inside, and then woke up to swallow that button.

Outdoors the leaves was rustling, different from when I'd went in. It was   70
coming on a rain. The day had a two-way look, like a day will at change of the
year—clouds dark and the gold air still in the road, and the trees lighter than the
sky was. And the oak leaves scuttling and scattering, blowing against Old Plez
and brushing on him, the old man.

"You're real positive, I guess, Plez?" asks Snowdie, and he answers comfort-ing-like to her, "*You* wasn't looking for nobody to come today, was you?"

It was later on that Mrs. Stark got hold of Plez and got the truth out of him, and I heard it after a while, through her church. But of course he wasn't going to let Miss Snowdie MacLain get hurt now, after we'd all watched her so long. So he fabricated.

After he'd gone by, Snowdie just stood there in the cool without a coat, with her face turned towards the country and her fingers pulling at little threads on her skirt and turning them loose in the wind, making little kind deeds of it, till I went and got her. She didn't cry.

* * *

"Course, could have been a ghost," Plez told Mrs. Stark, "but a ghost—I be-lieve—if he had come to see the lady of the house, would have waited to have word with her."

And he said he had nary doubt in his mind, that it was Mr. King MacLain, [75] starting home once more and thinking better of it. Miss Lizzie said to the church ladies, "I, for one, trust the Negro. I trust him the way you trust me, old Plez's mind has remained clear as a bell. I trust his story implicitly," she says, "because that's just what *I know* King MacLain'd do—run." And that's one time I feel in agreement about something with Miss Lizzie Stark, though she don't know about it, I guess.

And I live and hope *he* hit a stone and fell down running, before he got far off from here, and took the skin off his handsome nose, the devil.

And so that's why Snowdie comes to get her butter now, and won't let me bring it to her any longer. I think she kind of holds it against me, because I was there that day when he come; and she don't like my baby any more.

And you know, Fate says maybe King did know it was Hallowe'en. Do you think he'd go that far for a prank? And his own come back to him? Fate's usually more down to earth than that.

With men like King, your thoughts are bottomless. He was going like the wind, Plez swore to Miss Lizzie Stark; though he couldn't swear to the direc-tion—so he changed and said.

But I bet my little Jersey calf King tarried long enough to get him a child [80] somewhere.

What makes me say a thing like that? I wouldn't say it to my husband, you mind you forget it.

Talking about the Text

1. List the articles of clothing you noticed in your reading of "A Shower of Gold."
2. What might have been the outcome of the Hallowe'en visit? Speculate on what might happen to the characters if there were to be a follow-up story employing them again.

Writing about the Text

1. In the opening pages of her memoir *One Writer's Beginnings*, Welty wrote: "I devel-oped a strong meteorological sensibility. In years ahead when I wrote stories, at-mosphere took its influential role from the start. Commotion in the weather and

the inner feelings aroused by such a hovering disturbance emerged connected in dramatic form." Describe this connection between weather and motivation in "A Shower of Gold."

2. In a brief paper, describe your reading of "A Shower of Gold," telling what you expected at different points and whether those expectations were fulfilled.

Linking the Text to Other Texts

1. "A Shower of Gold" and "Cakewalk" (p. 391) concentrate mostly on women; the men frequently are absent or harmful, threatening characters. What do these stories suggest it has meant to be a woman in the South? Be specific about the relationships these women have with men and with other women.

2. Look up the story of Danaë in a dictionary of mythology, and describe what connections you see between that myth and this story.

✎ COMMENTARY

Eudora Welty on the Craft of Writing

From the time she became famous in the 1940s, Eudora Welty wrote essays and reviews, and was a constant subject of interviews. Here are some of her comments on writing, excerpted from interviews collected in two books, Conversations with Eudora Welty *(1984) and* More Conversations with Eudora Welty *(1996), both edited by Peggy Prenshaw as part of the "Conversations with" series published by the University Press of Mississippi.*

On the South

From "Eudora Welty in Type and Person," by Reynolds Price, in the May 7, 1978, New York Times Book Review:

I think of writing stories as going south and writing essays as going north. . . . I can't work on them simultaneously.

Eudora Welty signing books, 1984.

From a July 29, 1977, interview by Jean Todd Freeman:

A lot of conversation in the South, as you know, is of a narrative and dramatic structure and so when you listen to it, you're following a story. You're listening for how something is going to come out and that, also, I think, has something to do with the desire to write later. We would listen to talk forever. When you go up North, they don't want to hear it, you know. They want to hear in the starting-at-the-beginning-going-all-the-way-through style. They just want to hear the results.

* * *

[Place] seems very important to me. I think Southerners have such an intimate sense of place. We grew up in the fact that we live here with people about whom we know almost everything that can be known as a citizen of the same neighborhood or town. We learn significant things that way: we know what the place has made of these people; what they've made of the place through generations. We have a sense of continuity and that, I think, comes from place. It helps to give the meaning—another meaning to a human life that such life has been there all the time and will go on. Now that people are on the move a lot more, some of that sense of continuity is gone, but I feel . . . I believe it will always be in our roots, as Southerners, don't you? A sense of the place. Even if you move around, you know where you have your base. And I just think it's terribly important.

From Patricia Wheatley's 1986 interview for the BBC series documentary, Eudora Welty: A Writer's Beginnings:

I think it [Southern storytelling] comes from the remoteness of the South and the family feeling of the South and how many families live with almost nobody living anywhere near them. They depend on the family for their entertainment and their well being and knowledge and so on.

   My mother had five brothers and they used to tell all kind of tales about life in West Virginia, and when they'd come down here or up there they would sit around for ages telling stories. One of the features of it is that everybody already knows the stories, of course. They just want to hear them repeated the way you like to see an old Charlie Chaplin movie. The familiarity is part of the charm— and the presence of the family itself is part of its pride, you know.

On Writing as a Woman

From a January 24, 1972, interview by Charles T. Bunting, which appeared in The Southern Review *(October 1972):*

I am a woman. In writing fiction, I think imagination comes ahead of sex. A writer's got to be able to live inside all characters: male, female, old, young. To live inside any other person is the jump. Whether the other persons are male or female is subordinate.

On Short Stories

From the January 24, 1972, interview by Charles T. Bunting:

A short story to me, and I think most writers, is a different kind of entity from a novel. Each form has its own organization. But a short story is more a single thing, more one sustained effort, which has a beginning, a rise, and a fall. And, of course, a novel has so much wider scope, greater looseness of texture, and so much more room to expand. Many rises and falls are possible, and even necessary. A novel's different from the very first sentence. It's as if you were going to run a race. If you just had to go two hundred yards, you would rely on a different takeoff and drive and intention, a different wind, than if you were going to run three miles. (This is someone who never does run, so I don't know why I choose that.) But it is a sort of different girding up that you have to do. It's a different pace, a different timing.

In the case of the short story, you can't ever let the tautness of the line relax. It has to be all strung very tight upon its single thread usually, and everything is subordinated to the theme of the story: characters and mood and place and time; and none of those things are as important as the development itself. Whereas in a novel you have time to shade a character, allow him his growth, in a short story a character hardly changes from beginning to end. He's in there for the purpose of that story only, and any other modification is ruled out.

In a novel you have time for subordinate characters, gradations of mood, subsidiary plots, other things that complement the story or oppose it. The difference is much more than a matter of length—it's a matter of organization and intention and in final effect.

On Technique

From the January 24, 1972, interview by Charles T. Bunting:

[Symbols] occur naturally; they are organic. If they're a part of the story, they come readily to hand when you want them, and as often as you want them, and you use them with a proper sense of proportion, and with as light a touch as possible. There's a story that goes around—I'm sure it's true—about some students saying, "I've finished my story. All I have to do now is to back and put the symbols in." That isn't knowing what a symbol is. A book, a novel itself is a big symbol, and a word is a symbol. Color is a symbol. Anything can be a symbol if the way it's used refers us to the imagination. It's a vocabulary, and it's part of your equipment. But it does not exist for its own sake. Something dragged in with a big, red "S" on it. That way, of course, it would have no effect.

From an interview by Linda Kuehl, in The Paris Review *(Fall 1972):*

My natural temperament is one of positive feelings, and I really do work for resolution in a story. I don't think we often see life resolving itself, not in any sort of perfect way, but I like the fiction writer's feeling of being able to confront an experience and resolve it as art, however imperfectly and briefly—to give it a form and try to embody—to hold it and express it in a story's terms. You have more chance to try it in a novel. A short story is confined to one mood, to which everything in the story pertains. Characters, setting, time, events, are all subject to the mood. And you can try more ephemeral, more fleeting things in a story—you can work more by suggestion—than in a novel. Less is resolved, more is suggested, perhaps.

On Characters

From a July 29, 1977, interview by Jean Todd Freeman:

Asked about putting a person she has met "exactly as he is, on the printed page":

It would be impossible. You never know enough for that, to begin with. But also, you have to invent the character to suit the purpose of the story that you are trying to tell. That is his circumference and his point and his reason for being. I mean the character of a short story, not a novel.

From a 1973 interview by Alice Walker, which appeared in the Winter 1973 Harvard Advocate:

I never write about real people. You know, human beings are incapable of being made into characters, as is. They are so much more fluid, and so opaque in places where they need to be transparent and so transparent in places where they need to be opaque. But I think that what I put into a short story in the form of characters might be called certain *qualities* of people in certain situations—no, pin it down more—some quality that makes them unique. I try to dramatize something like this in a way that can show it better than life shows it. Better picked out.

From an interview with Bill Ferris, Summer 1975 and 1976:

I do not think you can transfer anything, as it's spoken, onto the page and have it come out at all convincingly. As you know from much of your work with the tape recorder, what comes out as a sound is not really at all what the speaker thinks he said, or really what he did say in context. It has to be absolutely rewritten on the page from the way it happens, but if you didn't know how it happened you couldn't start. It's a matter of condensation and getting the . . . oh, I don't want to say "universal" about the character, but getting his whole character into a speech about a little thing, perhaps. It's a shorthand. It's like action. It is a form of action in story. And people don't talk that way. You've got to make it seem that they talk that way. I'm sure that you, of all people, will agree, because you've had so much experience with interviews.

On "A Shower of Gold"

From a 1978 interview with Jeanne Rolfe Nostrandt, which appeared in the New Orleans Review *(1979):*

Asked why King McLain runs away from the twins on Halloween day:

He's somebody who comes and goes at will, and I think almost anything could have driven him off. But the sight of those little boys on roller skates with masks on must have been rather scary. . . . He was pretty easy to run off; he's just passing through. I think he came out of curiosity to see what had come of this. I don't think he was even prepared for twins.

On Myths and Legends in Her Work

From the 1978 interview by Jeanne Rolfe Nostrandt:

I didn't know what it means in the sense that people ask. You know, this is supposed to be this and this is supposed to be that, and the old black woman with the chicken means, as if everything has an equivalent. I just say that the whole thing was supposed to be a mesh of suggestions and insinuations that just sort of showed the whole mysteriousness of experience. I didn't want anything explicit.

Starting Points for Further Research: Eudora Welty

- **Editions:** Eudora Welty. *Complete Novels.* New York: Library of America, 1998.
  ———. *Stories, Essays, and Memoir.* New York: Library of America, 1998.
- **Critical Essay:** Peter Schmidt. "A New Study of Eudora Welty's Life and Writing." *Contemporary Literature* 44 (2003): 353–61.
- **Interview:** Dannye Romine Powell. "An Interview with Eudora Welty." *Mississippi Review* 20 (1991): 76–82.

INSPIRATION LEE SMITH ON FLANNERY O'CONNOR AND EUDORA WELTY

Flannery O'Connor, next to a self-portrait with one of her beloved peacocks.

(continued on next page)

In spite of the highly different writing styles and perspectives on the southern worlds depicted in their writing, Flannery O'Connor and Eudora Welty both served as inspirational literary ancestors to Virginian writer Lee Smith (p. 391).

Reading them both growing up, Smith found that it was Eudora Welty's approach to character and the oral tradition her stories spring from that drew her attention, but that O'Connor's appeal was the humor and darkness in her writing. In a 1990 interview with Irv Broughton, she observed, "Mainly I got [from Welty] an idea that it was okay to write about the kind of people that I would ultimately write about. Before that I thought that literature had to happen on some sort of high plane. Literally! I thought I had to write about glamorous people, stewardesses or something. Rich people, or people that I didn't know anything about. . . . It was a long time, maybe a year or so after I was in college, that I realized that you didn't have to have huge Biblical plots. It was all right to write about people like Miss Welty wrote about, people that may have even lived in Grundy [the town in Virginia where Smith grew up]. . . ." That said, Smith is quick to point out how nuánced and mythical Welty's stories are; in a 1994 interview in *Southern Quarterly*, she commented, ["Why I Live at the P.O."] is a very subtle story and my students . . . have problems with it. The ones that are really tuned into language get it, but the average freshman class at NC State, where I get so many brilliant kids in technology, they just don't get it . . . that Welty story is very much an oral story, a spoken story. That interests me too, writing that is supposed to be spoken and the different varieties of the first person speaker, whether it is a spoken story or whether it is written. . . ." Ultimately, Smith has found different models of inspiration and influence in Welty and O'Connor; comparing the two in a 1998 interview in *Mississippi Quarterly*, she said, "From Miss Welty—I think [I got inspired by] the element of myth, particularly in *The Golden Apples*, that she has. The sense of characters as being larger than life. And the sense that—I don't know, this enormous *grace*, in the telling of very simple things. And then with Flannery O'Connor—I *do* take a darker view than Miss Welty. And I'm real comfortable with Flannery O'Connor's points of view."

FLANNERY O'CONNOR   (1925–1964)

Born in Savannah, Georgia, Flannery O'Connor grew up an only child. Her family moved to Milledgeville, Georgia, in 1938, and O'Connor eventually attended the Georgia College for Women. In 1945, she won a scholarship to the State University of Iowa's prestigious Writers Workshop, where she received a Master of Fine Arts degree two years later. For the next four years, O'Connor's residence shifted around the country, from Iowa to Yaddo (an art colony near Saratoga Springs, New York) to New York City to Connecticut. Her first published work was the novel Wise Blood *(1952); she followed it with her renowned short story collection* A Good Man Is Hard to Find *(1955), which won her acclaim. Although she is now identified as the perfect example of the southern woman writer, in her lifetime O'Connor was an anomaly: a devout, intellectual Catholic in the largely Protestant South. In her work, she*

As a student at the Georgia State College for Women (now Georgia College and State University), O'Connor was editor of Corinthian, the literary magazine, for which she created block-print cartoons that poked fun at various aspects of campus life. The original caption for the block print depicted here read: "I don't enjoy looking at these old pictures either, but it doesn't hurt my reputation for people to think I'm a lover of fine arts."

stressed the themes of mystery, salvation, redemption, and grace (and, inevitably, sin and evil). Her distinctive stories are particularly known for their mix of the grotesque and a quest for spiritual redemption. O'Connor thought of her art as "incarnational," taking in the world through the senses rather than through abstractions. She wrote, "there's a certain grain of stupidity that the writer of fiction can hardly do without, and this is the quality of having to stare, of not getting the point at once. The longer you look at one object, the more of the world you see in it. . . ." Given what O'Connor has to say about staring and looking, it is not surprising that she was an amateur painter.

Another circumstance thrust O'Connor into the role of observer: in her mid-twenties, she suffered her first attack of the progressively crippling disease lupus—the disease that had killed her father and would eventually kill her at age thirty-nine—and consequently, she returned to Milledgeville, this time to live with her mother at the family farm, Andalusia, where they raised peacocks. Although she traveled to readings and lectures remarkably frequently, she was confined for long hours in bed and in a chair. She regularly wrote to her circle of friends, frequently sharing her rich and funny comments on the craft of writing and on the craziness of readers' interpretations of her work. Her witty, acerbic letters to a wide group of friends are collected by Sally Fitzgerald in The Habit of Being (1979). Gradually weakened by the degenerative disease, she was able to write another novel, The Violent Bear It Away (1960), and one more story collection, Everything That Rises Must Converge (posthumously published in 1965), before her death.

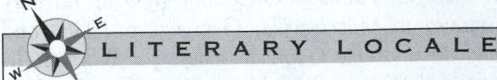

■ LITERARY LOCALE

The Georgia Homes of Flannery O'Connor: Savannah and Milledgeville.
Flannery O'Connor's childhood home in Savannah, Georgia, and the Andalusia farm in Milledgeville, Georgia, where she spent most of her adulthood are open to the public for tours. The Savannah house is located at 207 East Charlton Street and is open to the public on weekends, free of charge. Maintained by the Flannery O'Connor Childhood Home Foundation, the house functions as a historical site

(continued)

about O'Connor as well as a Savannah literary center where literary events are held throughout the year. Visitor information can be found at *http://www.llp.armstrong.edu/flannery/foundation.html*. The website also includes a history of the house, photos, biographical information, a select bibliography, and additional research links and book sources.

Following her diagnosis of lupus in 1950—a diagnosis she was not informed of for over one year—O'Connor returned to Milledgeville to live on her family's farm, Andalusia. Although she traveled periodically for speaking engagements, most of her writing was generated during her adult years at Andalusia, her primary residence until her death in 1964. Andalusia and the surrounding area also provided the backdrop against which most of her fiction was set. Her routine was to write every morning until noon *Flannery O'Connor's Andalusia Farm.*

and spend the rest of the day on the farm, tending to her birds or spending time with visitors. For additional information on tours, biographical information, a history of the farm, a photo gallery and virtual tour, and links to additional resources for research, go to *http://www.andalusiafarm.org*.

Parker's Back

(1965)

Parker's wife was sitting on the front porch floor, snapping beans. Parker was sitting on the step, some distance away, watching her sullenly. She was plain, plain. The skin on her face was thin and drawn as tight as the skin on an onion and her eyes were gray and sharp like the points of two icepicks. Parker understood why he had married her—he couldn't have got her any other way—but he couldn't understand why he stayed with her now. She was pregnant and pregnant women were not his favorite kind. Nevertheless, he stayed as if she had him conjured. He was puzzled and ashamed of himself.

The house they rented sat alone save for a single tall pecan tree on a high embankment overlooking a highway. At intervals a car would shoot past below and his wife's eyes would swerve suspiciously after the sound of it and then come back to rest on the newspaper full of beans in her lap. One of the things she did not approve of was automobiles. In addition to her other bad qualities, she was forever sniffing up sin. She did not smoke or dip, drink whiskey, use bad language or paint her face, and God knew some paint would have improved it, Parker thought. Her being against color, it was the more remarkable she had married him. Sometimes he supposed that she had married him because she meant to save him. At other times he had a suspicion that she actually liked everything she said she didn't. He could account for her one way or another; it was himself he could not understand.

She turned her head in his direction and said, "It's no reason you can't work for a man. It don't have to be a woman."

"Aw shut your mouth for a change," Parker muttered.

If he had been certain she was jealous of the woman he worked for he would have been pleased but more likely she was concerned with the sin that would result if he and the woman took a liking to each other. He had told her that the woman was a hefty young blonde; in fact she was nearly seventy years old and too dried up to have an interest in anything except getting as much work out of him as she could. Not that an old woman didn't sometimes get an interest in a young man, particularly if he was as attractive as Parker felt he was, but this old woman looked at him the same way she looked at her old tractor—as if she had to put up with it because it was all she had. The tractor had broken down the second day Parker was on it and she had set him at once to cutting bushes, saying out of the side of her mouth to the nigger, "Everything he touches, he breaks." She also asked him to wear his shirt when he worked; Parker had removed it even though the day was not sultry; he put it back on reluctantly.

This ugly woman Parker married was his first wife. He had had other women but he had planned never to get himself tied up legally. He had first seen her one morning when his truck broke down on the highway. He had managed to pull it off the road into a neatly swept yard on which sat a peeling two-room house. He got out and opened the hood of the truck and began to study the motor. Parker had an extra sense that told him when there was a woman nearby watching him. After he had leaned over the motor a few minutes, his neck began to prickle. He cast his eye over the empty yard and porch of the house. A woman he could not see was either nearby beyond a clump of honeysuckle or in the house, watching him out the window.

Suddenly Parker began to jump up and down and fling his hand about as if he had mashed it in the machinery. He doubled over and held his hand close to his chest. "God dammit!" he hollered, "Jesus Christ in hell! Jesus God Almighty damm! God dammit to hell!" he went on, flinging out the same few oaths over and over as loud as he could.

Without warning a terrible bristly claw slammed the side of his face and he fell backwards on the hood of the truck. "You don't talk no filth here!" a voice close to him shrilled.

Parker's vision was so blurred that for an instant he thought he had been attacked by some creature from above, a giant hawk-eyed angel wielding a hoary weapon. As his sight cleared, he saw before him a tall raw-boned girl with a broom.

"I hurt my hand," he said. "I HURT my hand." He was so incensed that he forgot that he hadn't hurt his hand. "My hand may be broke," he growled although his voice was still unsteady.

"Lemme see it," the girl demanded.

Parker stuck out his hand and she came closer and looked at it. There was no mark on the palm and she took the hand and turned it over. Her own hand was dry and hot and rough and Parker felt himself jolted back to life by her touch. He looked more closely at her. I don't want nothing to do with this one, he thought.

The girl's sharp eyes peered at the back of the stubby reddish hand she held. There emblazoned in red and blue was a tattooed eagle perched on a cannon. Parker's sleeve was rolled to the elbow. Above the eagle a serpent was coiled about a shield and in the spaces between the eagle and the serpent there were hearts, some with arrows through them. Above the serpent there was a spread hand of cards. Every space on the skin of Parker's arm, from wrist to elbow, was covered in some loud design. The girl gazed at this with an almost stupefied smile of shock, as if she had accidentally grasped a poisonous snake; she dropped the hand.

"I got most of my other ones in foreign parts," Parker said. "These here I mostly got in the United States. I got my first one when I was only fifteen year old."

"Don't tell me," the girl said, "I don't like it. I ain't got any use for it."   15

"You ought to see the ones you can't see," Parker said and winked.

Two circles of red appeared like apples on the girl's cheeks and softened her appearance. Parker was intrigued. He did not for a minute think that she didn't like the tattoos. He had never yet met a woman who was not attracted to them.

Parker was fourteen when he saw a man in a fair, tattooed from head to foot. Except for his loins which were girded with a panther hide, the man's skin was patterned in what seemed from Parker's distance—he was near the back of the tent, standing on a bench—a single intricate design of brilliant color. The man, who was small and sturdy, moved about on the platform, flexing his muscles so that the arabesque of men and beasts and flowers on his skin appeared to have a subtle motion of its own. Parker was filled with emotion, lifted up as some people are when the flag passes. He was a boy whose mouth habitually hung open. He was heavy and earnest, as ordinary as a loaf of bread. When the show was over, he had remained standing on the bench, staring where the tattooed man had been, until the tent was almost empty.

Parker had never before felt the least motion of wonder in himself. Until he saw the man at the fair, it did not enter his head that there was anything out of the ordinary about the fact that he existed. Even then it did not enter his head, but a peculiar unease settled in him. It was as if a blind boy had been turned so gently in a different direction that he did not know his destination had been changed.

He had his first tattoo some time after—the eagle perched on the cannon. It   20 was done by a local artist. It hurt very little, just enough to make it appear to Parker to be worth doing. This was peculiar too for before he had thought that only what did not hurt was worth doing. The next year he quit school because he was sixteen and could. He went to the trade school for a while, then he quit the trade school and worked for six months in a garage. The only reason he worked at all was to pay for more tattoos. His mother worked in a laundry and could support him, but she would not pay for any tattoo except her name on a heart, which he had put on, grumbling. However, her name was Betty Jean and nobody had to know it was his mother. He found out that the tattoos were attractive to the kind of girls he liked but who had never liked him before. He began to drink beer and get in fights. His mother wept over what was becoming of him. One night she dragged him off to a revival with her, not telling him where they were going. When he saw the big lighted church, he jerked out of her grasp and ran. The next day he lied about his age and joined the navy.

Parker was large for the tight sailor's pants but the silly white cap, sitting low on his forehead, made his face by contrast look thoughtful and almost intense. After a month or two in the navy, his mouth ceased to hang open. His features hardened into the features of a man. He stayed in the navy five years and seemed a natural part of the gray mechanical ship, except for his eyes, which were the same pale slate-color as the ocean and reflected the immense spaces around him as if they were a microcosm of the mysterious sea. In port Parker wandered about comparing the run-down places he was in to Birmingham, Alabama. Everywhere he went he picked up more tattoos.

He had stopped having lifeless ones like anchors and crossed rifles. He had a tiger and a panther on each shoulder, a cobra coiled about a torch on his chest, hawks on his thighs, Elizabeth II and Philip over where his stomach and liver were respectively. He did not care much what the subject was so long as it was colorful; on his abdomen he had a few obscenities but only because that seemed the proper place for them. Parker would be satisfied with each tattoo about a month, then something about it that had attracted him would wear off. Whenever a decent-sized mirror was available, he would get in front of it and study his overall look. The effect was not of one intricate arabesque of colors but of something haphazard and botched. A huge dissatisfaction would come over him and he would go off and find another tattooist and have another space filled up. The front of Parker was almost completely covered but there were no tattoos on his back. He had no desire for one anywhere he could not readily see it himself. As the space on the front of him for tattoos decreased, his dissatisfaction grew and became general.

After one of his furloughs, he didn't go back to the navy but remained away without official leave, drunk, in a rooming house in a city he did not know. His dissatisfaction, from being chronic and latent, had suddenly become acute and raged in him. It was as if the panther and the lion and the serpents and the eagles and the hawks had penetrated his skin and lived inside him in a raging warfare. The navy caught up with him, put him in the brig for nine months and then gave him a dishonorable discharge.

After that Parker decided that country air was the only kind fit to breathe. He rented the shack on the embankment and bought the old truck and took various jobs which he kept as long as it suited him. At the time he met his future wife, he was buying apples by the bushel and selling them for the same price by the pound to isolated homesteaders on back country roads.

"All that there," the woman said, pointing to his arm, "is no better than   25 what a fool Indian would do. It's a heap of vanity." She seemed to have found the word she wanted. "Vanity of vanities," she said.

Well what the hell do I care what she thinks of it? Parker asked himself, but he was plainly bewildered. "I reckon you like one of these better than another anyway," he said, dallying until he thought of something that would impress her. He thrust the arm back at her. "Which you like best?"

"None of them," she said, "but the chicken is not as bad as the rest."

"What chicken?" Parker almost yelled.

She pointed to the eagle.

"That's an eagle," Parker said. "What fool would waste their time having a   30 chicken put on themselves?"

"What fool would have any of it?" the girl said and turned away. She went slowly back to the house and left him there to get going. Parker remained for almost five minutes, looking agape at the dark door she had entered.

The next day he returned with a bushel of apples. He was not one to be outdone by anything that looked like her. He liked women with meat on them, so you didn't feel their muscles, much less their old bones. When he arrived, she was sitting on the top step and the yard was full of children, all as thin and poor as herself; Parker remembered it was Saturday. He hated to be making up to a woman when there were children around, but it was fortunate he had brought the bushel of apples off the truck. As the children approached him to see what he carried, he gave each child an apple and told it to get lost; in that way he cleared out the whole crowd.

The girl did nothing to acknowledge his presence. He might have been a stray pig or goat that had wandered into the yard and she too tired to take up the broom and send it off. He set the bushel of apples down next to her on the step. He sat down on a lower step.

"Hep yourself," he said, nodding at the basket; then he lapsed into silence.

She took an apple quickly as if the basket might disappear if she didn't make haste. Hungry people made Parker nervous. He had always had plenty to eat himself. He grew very uncomfortable. He reasoned he had nothing to say so why should he say it? He could not think now why he had come or why he didn't go before he wasted another bushel of apples on the crowd of children. He supposed they were her brothers and sisters.

She chewed the apple slowly but with a kind of relish of concentration, bent slightly but looking out ahead. The view from the porch stretched off across a long incline studded with iron weed and across the highway to a vast vista of hills and one small mountain. Long views depressed Parker. You look out into space like that and you begin to feel as if someone were after you, the navy or the government or religion.

"Who them children belong to, you?" he said at length.

"I ain't married yet," she said. "They belong to momma." She said it as if it were only a matter of time before she would be married.

Who in God's name would marry her? Parker thought.

A large barefooted woman with a wide gap-toothed face appeared in the door behind Parker. She had apparently been there for several minutes.

"Good evening," Parker said.

The woman crossed the porch and picked up what was left of the bushel of apples. "We thank you," she said and returned with it into the house.

"That your old woman?" Parker muttered.

The girl nodded. Parker knew a lot of sharp things he could have said like "You got my sympathy," but he was gloomily silent. He just sat there, looking at the view. He thought he must be coming down with something.

"If I pick up some peaches tomorrow I'll bring you some," he said.

"I'll be much obliged to you," the girl said.

Parker had no intention of taking any basket of peaches back there but the next day he found himself doing it. He and the girl had almost nothing to say to each other. One thing he did say was, "I ain't got any tattoo on my back."

"What you got on it?" the girl said.

"My shirt," Parker said. "Haw."

"Haw, haw," the girl said politely.

Parker thought he was losing his mind. He could not believe for a minute that he was attracted to a woman like this. She showed not the least interest in anything but what he brought until he appeared the third time with two cantaloups. "What's your name?" she asked.

"O. E. Parker," he said.

"What does the O. E. stand for?"

"You can just call me O. E.," Parker said. "Or Parker. Don't nobody call me by my name."

"What's it stand for?" she persisted.

"Never mind," Parker said. "What's yours?"

"I'll tell you when you tell me what them letters are the short of," she said. There was just a hint of flirtatiousness in her tone and it went rapidly to Parker's head. He had never revealed the name to any man or woman, only to the files of the navy and the government, and it was on his baptismal record which he got at the age of a month; his mother was a Methodist. When the name leaked out of the navy files, Parker narrowly missed killing the man who used it.

"You'll go blab it around," he said.

"I'll swear I'll never tell nobody," she said. "On God's holy word I swear it."

Parker sat for a few minutes in silence. Then he reached for the girl's neck, 60 drew her ear close to his mouth and revealed the name in low voice.

"Obadiah," she whispered. Her face slowly brightened as if the name came as a sign to her. "Obadiah," she said.

The name still stank in Parker's estimation.

"Obadiah Elihue," she said in a reverent voice.

"If you call me that aloud, I'll bust your head open," Parker said. "What's yours?"

"Sarah Ruth Cates," she said.   65

"Glad to meet you, Sarah Ruth," Parker said.

Sarah Ruth's father was a Straight Gospel preacher but he was away, spreading it in Florida. Her mother did not seem to mind his attention to the girl so long as he brought a basket of something with him when he came. As for Sarah Ruth herself, it was plain to Parker after he had visited three times that she was crazy about him. She liked him even though she insisted that pictures on the skin were vanity of vanities and even after hearing him curse, and even after she had asked him if he was saved and he had replied that he didn't see it was anything in particular to save him from. After that, inspired, Parker had said, "I'd be saved enough if you was to kiss me."

She scowled. "That ain't being saved," she said.

Not long after that she agreed to take a ride in his truck. Parker parked it on a deserted road and suggested to her that they lie down together in the back of it.

"Not until after we're married," she said—just like that.   70

"Oh that ain't necessary," Parker said and as he reached for her, she thrust him away with such force that the door of the truck came off and he found himself flat on his back on the ground. He made up his mind then and there to have nothing further to do with her.

They were married in the County Ordinary's office because Sarah Ruth thought churches were idolatrous. Parker had no opinion about that one way or the other. The Ordinary's office was lined with cardboard file boxes and record books with dusty yellow slips of paper hanging on out of them. The Ordinary was an old woman with red hair who had held office for forty years and looked as dusty as her books. She married them from behind the iron-grill of a stand-up desk and when she finished, she said with a flourish, "Three dollars and fifty cents and till death do you part!" and yanked some forms out of a machine.

Marriage did not change Sarah Ruth a jot and it made Parker gloomier than ever. Every morning he decided he had had enough and would not return that night; every night he returned. Whenever Parker couldn't stand the way he felt, he would have another tattoo, but the only surface left on him now was his back. To see a tattoo on his own back he would have to get two mirrors and stand between them in just the correct position and this seemed to Parker a good way to make an idiot of himself. Sarah Ruth who, if she had had better sense, could have enjoyed a tattoo on his back, would not even look at the ones he had elsewhere. When he attempted to point out especial details of them, she would shut her eyes tight and turn her back as well. Except in total darkness, she preferred Parker dressed and with his sleeves rolled down.

"At the judgement seat of God, Jesus is going to say to you, 'What you been doing all your life besides have pictures drawn all over you?'" she said.

"You don't fool me none," Parker said, "you're just afraid that hefty girl I work   75
for'll like me so much she'll say, 'Come on, Mr. Parker, let's you and me . . . .'"

"You're tempting sin," she said, "and at the judgement seat of God you'll have to answer for that too. You ought to go back to selling the fruits of the earth."

Parker did nothing much when he was at home but listen to what the judgement seat of God would be like for him if he didn't change his ways. When he could, he broke in with tales of the hefty girl he worked for. "'Mr. Parker,'" he said she said, "'I hired you for your brains.'" (She had added, "So why don't you use them?")

"And you should have seen her face the first time she saw me without my shirt," he said. "'Mr. Parker,' she said, 'you're a walking panner-rammer!'" This had, in fact, been her remark but it had been delivered out of one side of her mouth.

Dissatisfaction began to grow so great in Parker that there was no containing it outside of a tattoo. It had to be his back. There was no help for it. A dim half-formed inspiration began to work in his mind. He visualized having a tattoo put there that Sarah Ruth would not be able to resist—a religious subject. He thought of an open book with HOLY BIBLE tattooed under it and an actual verse printed on the page. This seemed just the thing for a while; then he began to hear her say, "Ain't I already got a real Bible? What you think I want to read the same verse over and over for when I can read it all?" He needed something better even than the Bible! He thought about it so much that he began to lose sleep. He was already losing flesh—Sarah Ruth just threw food in the pot and let it boil. Not knowing for certain why he continued to stay with a woman who was both ugly and pregnant and no cook made him generally nervous and irritable, and he developed a little tic in the side of his face.

Once or twice he found himself turning around abruptly as if someone were   80
trailing him. He had had a granddaddy who had ended in the state mental hospital, although not until he was seventy-five, but as urgent as it might be for him to get a tattoo, it was just as urgent that he get exactly the right one to bring Sarah Ruth to heel. As he continued to worry over it, his eyes took on a hollow preoccupied expression. The old woman he worked for told him that if he couldn't keep his mind on what he was doing, she knew where she could find a fourteen-year-old colored boy who could. Parker was too preoccupied even to be offended. At any time previous, he would have left her then and there, saying drily, "Well, you go ahead on and get him then."

Two or three mornings later he was baling hay with the old woman's sorry baler and her broken down tractor in a large field, cleared save for one enormous old tree standing in the middle of it. The old woman was the kind who would not cut down a large old tree because it was a large old tree. She had pointed it out to Parker as if he didn't have eyes and told him to be careful not to hit it as the machine picked up hay near it. Parker began at the outside of the field and made circles inward toward it. He had to get off the tractor every now and then and untangle the baling cord or kick a rock out of the way. The old woman had told him to carry the rocks to the edge of the field, which he did when she was there watching. When he thought he could make it, he ran over them. As he circled the field his mind was on a suitable design for his back. The sun, the size of a golf ball, began to switch regularly from in front to behind him, but he appeared to see it both places as if he had eyes in the back of his head. All at once he saw the tree reaching out to grasp him. A ferocious thud propelled him into the air, and he heard himself yelling in an unbelievably loud voice, "GOD ABOVE!"

He landed on his back while the tractor crashed upside down into the tree and burst into flame. The first thing Parker saw were his shoes, quickly being eaten by the fire; one was caught under the tractor, the other was some distance away, burning by itself. He was not in them. He could feel the hot breath of the burning tree on his face. He scrambled backwards, still sitting, his eyes cavernous, and if he had known how to cross himself he would have done it.

His truck was on a dirt road at the edge of the field. He moved toward it, still sitting, still backwards, but faster and faster; half-way to it he got up and began a kind of forward-bent run from which he collapsed on his knees twice. His legs felt like two old rusted rain gutters. He reached the truck finally and took off in it, zigzagging up the road. He drove past his house on the embankment and straight for the city, fifty miles distant.

Parker did not allow himself to think on the way to the city. He only knew that there had been a great change in his life, a leap forward into a worse unknown, and that there was nothing he could do about it. It was for all intents accomplished.

The artist had two large cluttered rooms over a chiropodist's office on a back   85
street. Parker, still barefooted, burst silently in on him at a little after three in the afternoon. The artist, who was about Parker's own age—twenty-eight—but thin and bald, was behind a small drawing table, tracing a design in green ink. He looked up with an annoyed glance and did not seem to recognize Parker in the hollow-eyed creature before him.

"Let me see the book you got with all the pictures of God in it," Parker said breathlessly. "The religious one."

The artist continued to look at him with his intellectual, superior stare. "I don't put tattoos on drunks," he said.

"You know me!" Parker cried indignantly. "I'm O. E. Parker! You done work for me before and I always paid!"

The artist looked at him another moment as if he were not altogether sure. "You've fallen off some," he said. "You must have been in jail."

"Married," Parker said.   90

"Oh," said the artist. With the aid of mirrors the artist had tattooed on the top of his head a miniature owl, perfect in every detail. It was about the size of a half-dollar and served him as a show piece. There were cheaper artists in town but Parker had never wanted anything but the best. The artist went over to a cabinet at the back of the room and began to look over some art books. "Who are you interested in?" he said, "saints, angels, Christs or what?"

"God," Parker said.

"Father, Son or Spirit?"

"Just God," Parker said impatiently. "Christ. I don't care. Just so it's God."

The artist returned with a book. He moved some papers off another table   95
and put the book down on it and told Parker to sit down and see what he liked. "The up-to-date ones are in the back," he said.

Parker sat down with the book and wet his thumb. He began to go through it, beginning at the back where the up-to-date pictures were. Some of them he recognized—The Good Shepherd, Forbid Them Not, The Smiling Jesus, Jesus the Physician's Friend, but he kept turning rapidly backwards and the pictures became less and less reassuring. One showed a gaunt green dead face streaked with blood. One was yellow with sagging purple eyes. Parker's heart began to beat faster and faster until it appeared to be roaring inside him like a great generator. He flipped the pages quickly, feeling that when he reached the one ordained, a sign would come. He continued to flip through until he had almost reached the front of the book. On one of the pages a pair of eyes glanced at him swiftly. Parker sped on, then stopped. His heart too appeared to cut off; there was absolute silence. It said as plainly as if silence were a language itself, GO BACK.

Parker returned to the picture—the haloed head of a flat stern Byzantine Christ with all-demanding eyes. He sat there trembling; his heart began slowly to beat again as if it were being brought to life by a subtle power.

"You found what you want?" the artist asked.

Parker's throat was too dry to speak. He got up and thrust the book at the artist, opened at the picture.

"That'll cost you plenty," the artist said. "You don't want all those little 100 blocks though, just the outline and some better features."

"Just like it is," Parker said, "just like it is or nothing."

"It's your funeral," the artist said, "but I don't do that kind of work for nothing."

"How much?" Parker asked.

"It'll take maybe two days work."

"How much?" Parker said. 105

"On time or cash?" the artist asked. Parker's other jobs had been on time, but he had paid.

"Ten down and ten for every day it takes," the artist said.

Parker drew ten dollar bills out of his wallet; he had three left in.

"You come back in the morning," the artist said, putting the money in his own pocket. "First I'll have to trace that out of the book."

"No no!" Parker said. "Trace it now or gimme my money back," and his eyes 110 blared as if he were ready for a fight.

The artist agreed. Any one stupid enough to want a Christ on his back, he reasoned, would be just as likely as not to change his mind the next minute, but once the work was begun he could hardly do so.

While he worked on the tracing, he told Parker to go wash his back at the sink with the special soap he used there. Parker did it and returned to pace back and forth across the room, nervously flexing his shoulders. He wanted to go look at the picture again but at the same time he did not want to. The artist got up finally and had Parker lie down on the table. He swabbed his back with ethyl chloride and then began to outline the head on it with his iodine pencil. Another hour passed before he took up his electric instrument. Parker felt no particular pain. In Japan he had had a tattoo of the Buddha done on his upper arm with ivory needles; in Burma, a little brown root of a man had made a peacock on each of his knees using thin pointed sticks, two feet long; amateurs had worked on him with pins and soot. Parker was usually so relaxed and easy under the hand of the artist that he often went to sleep, but this time he remained awake, every muscle taut.

At midnight the artist said he was ready to quit. He propped one mirror, four feet square, on a table by the wall and took a smaller mirror off the lavatory wall and put it in Parker's hands. Parker stood with his back to the one on the table and moved the other until he saw a flashing burst of color reflected from his back. It was almost completely covered with little red and blue and ivory and saffron squares; from them he made out the lineaments of the face—a mouth, the beginning of heavy brows, a straight nose, but the face was empty; the eyes had not yet been put in. The impression for the moment was almost as if the artist had tricked him and done the Physician's Friend.

"It don't have eyes," Parker cried out.

"That'll come," the artist said, "in due time. We have another day to go on 115 it yet."

Parker spent the night on a cot at the Haven of Light Christian Mission. He found these the best places to stay in the city because they were free and included a meal of sorts. He got the last available cot and because he was still barefooted, he accepted a pair of second-hand shoes which, in his confusion, he put on to go to bed; he was still shocked from all that had happened to him. All night he lay awake in the long dormitory of cots with lumpy figures on them. The only light was from a phosphorescent cross glowing at the end of the room. The tree reached out to grasp him again, then burst into flame; the shoe burned quietly by itself; the eyes in the book said to him distinctly GO BACK and at the same time did not utter a sound. He wished that he were not in this city, not in this Haven of Light Mission, not in a bed by himself. He longed miserably for Sarah Ruth. Her sharp tongue and icepick eyes were the only comfort he could bring to mind. He decided he was losing it. Her eyes appeared soft and dilatory compared with the eyes in the book, for even though he could not summon up the exact look of those eyes, he could still feel their penetration. He felt as though, under their gaze, he was as transparent as the wing of a fly.

The tattooist had told him not to come until ten in the morning, but when he arrived at that hour, Parker was sitting in the dark hallway on the floor, waiting for him. He had decided upon getting up that, once the tattoo was on him, he would not look at it, that all his sensations of the day and night before were those of a crazy man and that he would return to doing things according to his own sound judgement.

The artist began where he left off. "One thing I want to know," he said presently as he worked over Parker's back, "why do you want this on you? Have you gone and got religion? Are you saved?" he asked in a mocking voice.

Parker's throat felt salty and dry. "Naw," he said, "I ain't got no use for none of that. A man can't save his self from whatever it is he don't deserve none of my sympathy." These words seemed to leave his mouth like wraiths and to evaporate at once as if he had never uttered them.

"Then why . . ."   120

"I married this woman that's saved," Parker said. "I never should have done it. I ought to leave her. She's done gone and got pregnant."

"That's too bad," the artist said. "Then it's her making you have this tattoo."

"Naw," Parker said, "she don't know nothing about it. It's a surprise for her."

"You think she'll like it and lay off you a while?"

"She can't hep herself," Parker said. "She can't say she don't like the looks of 125 God." He decided he had told the artist enough of his business. Artists were all right in their place but he didn't like them poking their noses into the affairs of regular people. "I didn't get no sleep last night," he said. "I think I'll get some now."

That closed the mouth of the artist but it did not bring him any sleep. He lay there, imagining how Sarah Ruth would be struck speechless by the face on his back and every now and then this would be interrupted by a vision of the tree of fire and his empty shoe burning beneath it.

The artist worked steadily until nearly four o'clock, not stopping to have lunch, hardly pausing with the electric instrument except to wipe the dripping dye off Parker's back as he went along. Finally he finished. "You can get up and look at it now," he said.

Parker sat up but he remained on the edge of the table.

The artist was pleased with his work and wanted Parker to look at it at once. Instead Parker continued to sit on the edge of the table, bent forward slightly but with a vacant look. "What ails you?" the artist said. "Go look at it."

"Ain't nothing ail me," Parker said in a sudden belligerent voice. "That tat- 130 too ain't going nowhere. It'll be there when I get there." He reached for his shirt and began gingerly to put it on.

The artist took him roughly by the arm and propelled him between the two mirrors. "Now *look*," he said, angry at having his work ignored.

Parker looked, turned white and moved away. The eyes in the reflected face continued to look at him—still, straight, all-demanding, enclosed in silence.

"It was your idea, remember," the artist said. "I would have advised something else."

Parker said nothing. He put on his shirt and went out the door while the artist shouted, "I'll expect all of my money!"

Parker headed toward a package shop on the corner. He bought a pint of 135 whiskey and took it into a nearby alley and drank it all in five minutes. Then he moved on to a pool hall nearby which he frequented when he came to the city. It was a well-lighted barnlike place with a bar up one side and gambling machines on the other and pool tables in the back. As soon as Parker entered, a large man in a red and black checkered shirt hailed him by slapping him on the back and yelling, "Yeyyyyyy boy! O. E. Parker!"

Parker was not yet ready to be struck on the back. "Lay off," he said, "I got a fresh tattoo there."

"What you got this time?" the man asked and then yelled to a few at the machines. "O.E.'s got him another tattoo."

"Nothing special this time," Parker said and slunk over to a machine that was not being used.

"Come on," the big man said, "let's have a look at O.E.'s tattoo," and while Parker squirmed in their hands, they pulled up his shirt. Parker felt all the hands drop away instantly and his shirt fell again like a veil over the face. There was a silence in the pool room which seemed to Parker to grow from the circle around him until it extended to the foundations under the building and upward through the beams in the roof.

Finally some one said, "Christ!" Then they all broke into noise at once. 140 Parker turned around, an uncertain grin on his face.

"Leave it to O.E.!" the man in the checkered shirt said. "That boy's a real card!"

"Maybe he's gone and got religion," some one yelled.

"Not on your life," Parker said.

"O.E.'s got religion and is witnessing for Jesus, ain't you, O.E.?" a little man with a piece of cigar in his mouth said wryly, "An o-riginal way to do it if I ever saw one."

"Leave it to Parker to think of a new one!" the fat man said.   145

"Yyeeeeeeyyyyyyy boy!" someone yelled and they all began to whistle and curse in compliment until Parker said, "Aaa shut up."

"What'd you do it for?" somebody asked.

"For laughs," Parker said. "What's it to you?"

"Why ain't you laughing then?" somebody yelled. Parker lunged into the midst of them and like a whirlwind on a summer's day there began a fight that raged amid overturned tables and swinging fists until two of them grabbed him and ran to the door with him and threw him out. Then a calm descended on the pool hall as nerve shattering as if the long barnlike room were the ship from which Jonah had been cast into the sea.

Parker sat for a long time on the ground in the alley behind the pool hall,   150
examining his soul. He saw it as a spider web of facts and lies that was not at all important to him but which appeared to be necessary in spite of his opinion. The eyes that were now forever on his back were eyes to be obeyed. He was as certain of it as he had ever been of anything. Throughout his life, grumbling and sometimes cursing, often afraid, once in rapture, Parker had obeyed whatever instinct of this kind had come to him—in rapture when his spirit had lifted at the sight of the tattooed man at the fair, afraid when he had joined the navy, grumbling when he had married Sarah Ruth.

The thought of her brought him slowly to his feet. She would know what he had to do. She would clear up the rest of it, and she would at least be pleased. It seemed to him that, all along, that was what he wanted, to please her. His truck was still parked in front of the building where the artist had his place, but it was not far away. He got in it and drove out of the city and into the country night. His head was almost clear of liquor and he observed that his dissatisfaction was gone, but he felt not quite like himself. It was as if he were himself but a stranger to himself, driving into a new country though everything he saw was familiar to him, even at night.

He arrived finally at the house on the embankment, pulled the truck under the pecan tree and got out. He made as much noise as possible to assert that he was still in charge here, that his leaving her for a night without word meant nothing except it was the way he did things. He slammed the car door, stamped up the two steps and across the porch and rattled the door knob. It did not respond to his touch. "Sarah Ruth!" he yelled, "let me in."

There was no lock on the door and she had evidently placed the back of a chair against the knob. He began to beat on the door and rattle the knob at the same time.

He heard the bed springs screak and bent down and put his head to the keyhole, but it was stopped up with paper. "Let me in!" he hollered, bamming on the door again. "What you got me locked out for?"

A sharp voice close to the door said, "Who's there?"   155

"Me," Parker said, "O.E."

He waited a moment.

"Me," he said impatiently, "O.E."

Still no sound from inside.

He tried once more. "O.E.," he said, bamming the door two or three more 160 times. "O. E. Parker. You know me."

There was a silence. Then the voice said slowly, "I don't know no O.E."

"Quit fooling," Parker pleaded. "You ain't got any business doing me this way. It's me, old O.E., I'm back. You ain't afraid of me."

"Who's there?" the same unfeeling voice said.

Parker turned his head as if he expected someone behind him to give him the answer. The sky had lightened slightly and there were two or three streaks of yellow floating above the horizon. Then as he stood there, a tree of light burst over the skyline.

Parker fell back against the door as if he had been pinned there by a lance. 165

"Who's there?" the voice from inside said and there was a quality about it now that seemed final. The knob rattled and the voice said peremptorily, "Who's there, I ast you?"

Parker bent down and put his mouth near the stuffed keyhole. "Obadiah," he whispered and all at once he felt the light pouring through him, turning his spider web soul into a perfect arabesque of colors, a garden of trees and birds and beasts.

"Obadiah Elihue!" he whispered.

The door opened and he stumbled in. Sarah Ruth loomed there, hands on her hips. She began at once, "That was no hefty blonde woman you was working for and you'll have to pay her every penny on her tractor you busted up. She don't keep insurance on it. She came here and her and me had us a long talk and I . . ."

Trembling, Parker set about lighting the kerosene lamp. 170

"What's the matter with you, wasting that kerosene this near daylight?" she demanded. "I ain't got to look at you."

A yellow glow enveloped them. Parker put the match down and began to unbutton his shirt.

"And you ain't going to have none of me this near morning," she said.

"Shut your mouth," he said quietly. "Look at this and then I don't want to hear no more out of you." He removed the shirt and turned his back to her.

"Another picture," Sarah Ruth growled. "I might have known you was off 175 after putting some more trash on yourself."

Parker's knees went hollow under him. He wheeled around and cried, "Look at it! Don't just say that! *Look* at it!"

"I done looked," she said.

"Don't you know who it is?" he cried in anguish.

"No, who is it?" Sarah Ruth said. "It ain't anybody I know."

"It's him," Parker said. 180

"Him who?"

"God!" Parker cried.

"God? God don't look like that!"

"What do you know how he looks?" Parker moaned. "You ain't seen him."

"He don't *look*." Sarah Ruth said. "He's a spirit. No man shall see his face." 185

"Aw listen," Parker groaned, "this is just a picture of him."

"Idolatry!" Sarah Ruth screamed. "Idolatry! Enflaming yourself with idols under every green tree! I can put up with lies and vanity but I don't want no idolator in this house!" and she grabbed up the broom and began to thrash him across the shoulders with it.

Parker was too stunned to resist. He sat there and let her beat him until she had nearly knocked him senseless and large welts had formed on the face of the tattooed Christ. Then he staggered up and made for the door.

She stamped the broom two or three times on the floor and went to the window and shook it out to get the taint of him off it. Still gripping it, she looked toward the pecan tree and her eyes hardened still more. There he was—who called himself Obadiah Elihue—leaning against the tree, crying like a baby.

Talking about the Text

1. How do you respond to each of the main characters, Parker and Sarah Ruth? Which do you tend to side more with, and why?
2. Connect the very religious Sarah Ruth's refusal to get married in a church ("Sarah Ruth thought churches were idolatrous" p. 366, paragraph 72) with her outrage at Parker's tattoo. What thread runs between the two?

Writing about the Text

1. Describe three grotesque incidents, actions, or articles in the story, then speculate on what effect they seem to have on the story as a whole.
2. In an essay examining at least four incidents in the story, demonstrate that Parker and Sarah Ruth have completely different attitudes toward life, and especially the supernatural.

Linking the Text to Other Texts

1. Getting a tattoo in the 1950s, when "Parker's Back" was written, was a much more unusual action than it is today, when tattoos are far more common, among women as well as men. If you know any people with a tattoo, ask them three questions: how and why they got the tattoo, what they intended to convey by the tattoo, and what the reaction of friends and family was.
2. Describe the role of sudden violence in "Parker's Back" and "A Good Man Is Hard to Find." Did you expect the violence in each case? What differences did you note in the way violence is depicted in the two O'Connor stories?

A Good Man Is Hard to Find   (1955)

The grandmother didn't want to go to Florida. She wanted to visit some of her connections in east Tennessee and she was seizing every chance to change Bailey's mind. Bailey was the son she lived with, her only boy. He was sitting on the edge of his chair at the table, bent over the orange sports section of the *Journal*. "Now look here, Bailey," she said, "see here, read this," and she stood with one hand on her thin hip and the other rattling the newspaper at his bald head. "Here this fellow that calls himself The Misfit is aloose from the Federal Pen and headed toward Florida and you read here what it says he did to these people. Just you read it. I wouldn't take my children in any direction with a criminal like that aloose in it. I couldn't answer to my conscience if I did."

Bailey didn't look up from his reading so she wheeled around then and faced the children's mother, a young woman in slacks, whose face was as broad and innocent as a cabbage and was tied around with a green headkerchief that had two points on the top like rabbit's ears. She was sitting on the sofa, feeding the baby his apricots out of a jar. "The children have been to Florida before," the old lady said. "You all ought to take them somewhere else for a change so they would see different parts of the world and be broad. They never have been to east Tennessee."

The children's mother didn't seem to hear her, but the eight-year-old boy, John Wesley, a stocky child with glasses, said, "If you don't want to go to Florida, why dontcha stay at home?" He and the little girl, June Star, were reading the funny papers on the floor.

"She wouldn't stay at home to be queen for a day," June Star said without raising her yellow head.

"Yes, and what would you do if this fellow, The Misfit, caught you?" the   5
grandmother said.

"I'd smack his face," John Wesley said.

"She wouldn't stay at home for a million bucks," June Star said. "Afraid she'd miss something. She has to go everywhere we go."

"All right, Miss," the grandmother said. "Just remember that the next time you want me to curl your hair."

June Star said her hair was naturally curly.

The next morning the grandmother was the first one in the car, ready to go.   10
She had her big black valise that looked like the head of a hippopotamus in one corner, and underneath it she was hiding a basket with Pitty Sing, the cat, in it. She didn't intend for the cat to be left alone in the house for three days because he would miss her too much and she was afraid he might brush against one of the gas burners and accidentally asphyxiate himself. Her son, Bailey, didn't like to arrive at a motel with a cat.

She sat in the middle of the back seat with John Wesley and June Star on either side of her. Bailey and the children's mother and the baby sat in front and they left Atlanta at eight forty-five with the mileage on the car at 55890. The grandmother wrote this down because she thought it would be interesting to say how many miles they had been when they got back. It took them twenty minutes to reach the outskirts of the city.

The old lady settled herself comfortably, removing her white cotton gloves and putting them up with her purse on the shelf in front of the back window. The children's mother still had on slacks and still had her head tied up in a green kerchief, but the grandmother had on a navy blue straw sailor hat with a bunch of white violets on the brim and a navy blue dress with a small white dot in the print. Her collars and cuffs were white organdy trimmed with lace and at her neckline she had pinned a purple spray of cloth violets containing a sachet. In case of an accident, anyone seeing her dead on the highway would know at once that she was a lady.

She said she thought it was going to be a good day for driving, neither too hot nor too cold, and she cautioned Bailey that the speed limit was fifty-five miles an hour and that the patrolmen hid themselves behind bill-boards and small clumps of trees and sped out after you before you had a chance to slow down. She pointed out interesting details of the scenery: Stone Mountain; the blue granite that in some places came up to both sides of the highway; the brilliant red clay banks slightly streaked with purple; and the various crops that made rows of green lace-work on the ground. The trees were full of silver-white sunlight and the meanest of them sparkled. The children were reading comic magazines and their mother had gone back to sleep.

"Let's go through Georgia fast so we won't have to look at it much," John Wesley said.

"If I were a little boy," said the grandmother, "I wouldn't talk about my native state that way. Tennessee has the mountains and Georgia has the hills." 15

"Tennessee is just a hillbilly dumping ground," John Wesley said, "and Georgia is a lousy state too."

"You said it," June Star said.

"In my time," said the grandmother, folding her thin veined fingers, "children were more respectful of their native states and their parents and everything else. People did right then. Oh look at the cute little pickaninny!" she said and pointed to a Negro child standing in the door of a shack. "Wouldn't that make a picture, now?" she asked and they all turned and looked at the little Negro out of the back window. He waved.

"He didn't have any britches on," June Star said.

"He probably didn't have any," the grandmother explained. "Little niggers 20 in the country don't have things like we do. If I could paint, I'd paint that picture," she said.

The children exchanged comic books.

The grandmother offered to hold the baby and the children's mother passed him over the front seat to her. She set him on her knee and bounced him and told him about the things they were passing. She rolled her eyes and screwed up her mouth and stuck her leathery thin face into his smooth bland one. Occasionally he gave her a faraway smile. They passed a large cotton field with five or six graves fenced in the middle of it, like a small island. "Look at the graveyard!" the grandmother said, pointing it out. "That was the old family burying ground. That belonged to the plantation."

"Where's the plantation?" John Wesley asked.

"Gone With the Wind," said the grandmother. "Ha. Ha."

When the children finished all the comic books they had brought, they 25 opened the lunch and ate it. The grandmother ate a peanut butter sandwich and an olive and would not let the children throw the box and the paper napkins out the window. When there was nothing else to do they played a game by choosing a cloud and making the other two guess what shape it suggested. John Wesley took one the shape of a cow and June Star guessed a cow and John Wesley said, no, an automobile, and June Star said he didn't play fair, and they began to slap each other over the grandmother.

The grandmother said she would tell them a story if they would keep quite. When she told a story, she rolled her eyes and waved her head and was very dramatic. She said once when she was a maiden lady she had been courted by a Mr. Edgar Atkins Teagarden from Jasper, Georgia. She said he was a very good-looking man and a gentleman and that he brought her a watermelon every Saturday afternoon with his initials cut in it, E.A.T. Well, one Saturday, she said, Mr. Teagarden brought the watermelon and there was nobody at home and he left it on the front porch and returned in his buggy to Jasper, but she never got the watermelon, she said, because a nigger boy ate it when he saw the initials, E.A.T.! This story tickled John Wesley's funny bone and he giggled and giggled but June

Star didn't think it was any good. She said she wouldn't marry a man that just brought her a watermelon on Saturday. The grandmother said she would have done well to marry Mr. Teagarden because he was a gentleman and had bought Coca-Cola stock when it first came out and that he had died only a few years ago, a very wealthy man.

They stopped at The Tower for barbecued sandwiches. The Tower was a part-stucco and part-wood filling station and dance hall set in a clearing outside of Timothy. A fat man named Red Sammy Butts ran it and there were signs stuck here and there on the building and for miles up and down the highway saying, TRY RED SAMMY'S FAMOUS BARBECUE, NONE LIKE FAMOUS RED SAMMY'S! RED SAM! THE FAT BOY WITH THE HAPPY LAUGH. A VETERAN! RED SAMMY'S YOUR MAN!

Red Sammy was laying on the bare ground outside The Tower with his head under a truck while a gray monkey about a foot high, chained to a small chinaberry tree, chattered nearby. The monkey sprang back into the tree and got on the highest limb as soon as he saw the children jump out of the car and run toward him.

Inside, The Tower was a long dark room with a counter at one end and tables at the other and dancing space in the middle. They all sat down at a broad table next to the nickelodeon and Red Sam's wife, a tall burnt-brown woman with hair and eyes lighter than her skin, came and took their order. The children's mother put a dime in the machine and played "The Tennessee Waltz," and the grandmother said that tune always made her want to dance. She asked Bailey if he would like to dance but he only glared at her. He didn't have a naturally sunny disposition like she did and trips made him nervous. The grandmother's brown eyes were very bright. She swayed her head from side to side and pretended she was dancing in her chair. June Star said play something she could tap to so the children's mother put in another dime and played a fast number and June Star stepped out onto the dance floor and did her tap routine.

"Ain't she cute?" Red Sam's wife said, leaning over the counter. "Would you   30
like to come be my little girl?"

"No, I certainly wouldn't," June Star said. "I wouldn't live in a broken-down place like this for a million bucks!" and she ran back to the table.

"Ain't she cute?" the woman repeated, stretching her mouth politely.

"Aren't you ashamed?" hissed the grandmother.

Red Sam came in and told his wife to quit lounging on the counter and hurry with these people's order. His khaki trousers reached just to his hip bones and his stomach hung over them like a sack of meal swaying under his shirt. He came over and sat down at a table nearby and let out a combination sigh and yodel. "You can't win," he said, "You can't win," and he wiped his sweating red face off with a gray handkerchief. "These days you don't know who to trust," he said. "Ain't that the truth?"

"People are certainly not nice like they used to be," said the grandmother.   35

"Two fellers come in here last week," Red Sammy said, "driving a Chrysler. It was an old beat-up car but it was a good one and these boys looked all right to me. Said they worked at the mill and you know I let them fellers charge the gas they bought? Now why did I do that?"

"Because you're a good man!" the grandmother said at once.

"Yes'm, I suppose so," Red Sam said as if he were struck with this answer.

His wife brought the orders, carrying the five plates all at once without a tray, two in each hand and one balanced on her arm. "It isn't a soul in this green world of God's that you can trust," she said. "And I don't count nobody out of that, not nobody," she repeated, looking at Red Sammy.

"Did you read about that criminal, The Misfit, that's escaped?" asked the   40
grandmother.

"I wouldn't be a bit surprised if he didn't attack this place right here," said the woman. "If he hears about it being here, I wouldn't be none surprised to see him. If he hears it's two cent in the cash register, I wouldn't be a tall surprised if he . . ."

"That'll do," Red Sam said. "Go bring these people their Co'Colas," and the woman went off to get the rest of the order.

"A good man is hard to find," Red Sammy said. "Everything is getting terrible. I remember the day you could go off and leave your screen door unlatched. Not no more."

He and the grandmother discussed better times. The old lady said that in her opinion Europe was entirely to blame for the way things were now. She said the way Europe acted you would think we were made of money and Red Sam said it was no use talking about it, she was exactly right. The children ran outside into the white sunlight and looked at the monkey in the lacy chinaberry tree. He was busy catching fleas on himself and biting each one carefully between his teeth as if it were a delicacy.

They drove off again into the hot afternoon. The grandmother took cat   45
naps and woke up every five minutes with her own snoring. Outside of Toombsboro she woke up and recalled an old plantation that she had visited in this neighborhood once when she was a young lady. She said the house had six white columns across the front and that there was an avenue of oaks leading up to it and two little wooden trellis arbors on either side in front where you sat down with your suitor after a stroll in the garden. She recalled exactly which road to turn off to get to it. She knew that Bailey would not be willing to lose any time looking at an old house, but the more she talked about it, the more she wanted to see it once again and find out if the little twin arbors were still standing. "There was a secret panel in this house," she said craftily, not telling the truth but wishing that she were, "and the story went that all the family silver was hidden in it when Sherman came through but it was never found . . ."

"Hey!" John Wesley said. "Let's go see it! We'll find it! We'll poke all the woodwork and find it! Who lives there? Where do you turn off at? Hey, Pop, can't we turn off there?"

"We never have seen a house with a secret panel!" June Star shrieked. "Let's go to the house with the secret panel! Hey, Pop, can't we go see the house with the secret panel!"

"It's not far from here, I know," the grandmother said. "It wouldn't take over twenty minutes."

Bailey was looking straight ahead. His jaw was as rigid as a horsehoe. "No," he said.

The children began to yell and scream that they wanted to see the house   50
with the secret panel. John Wesley kicked the back of the front seat and June Star hung over her mother's shoulder and whined desperately into her ear that they never had any fun even on their vacation, that they could never do what

THEY wanted to do. The baby began to scream and John Wesley kicked the back of the seat so hard that his father could feel the blows in his kidney.

"All right!" he shouted and drew the car to a stop at the side of the road. "Will you all shut up? Will you all just shut up for one second? If you don't shut up, we won't go anywhere."

"It would be very educational for them," the grandmother murmured.

"All right," Bailey said, "but get this. This is the only time we're going to stop for anything like this. This is the one and only time."

"The dirt road that you have to turn down is about a mile back," the grandmother directed. "I marked it when we passed."

"A dirt road," Bailey groaned.   55

After they had turned around and were headed toward the dirt road, the grandmother recalled other points about the house, the beautiful glass over the front doorway and the candle lamp in the hall. John Welsey said that the secret panel was probably in the fireplace.

"You can't go inside this house," Bailey said. "You don't know who lives there."

"While you all talk to the people in front, I'll run around behind and get in a window," John Wesley suggested.

"We'll all stay in the car," his mother said.

They turned onto the dirt road and the car raced roughly along in a swirl of   60
pink dust. The grandmother recalled the times when there were no paved roads and thirty miles was a day's journey. The dirt road was hilly and there were sudden washes in it and sharp curves on dangerous embankments. All at once they would be on a hill, looking down over the blue tops of trees for miles around, then the next minute, they would be in a red depression with the dust-coated trees looking down on them.

"This place had better turn up in a minute," Bailey said, "or I'm going to turn around."

The road looked as if no one had traveled on it in months.

"It's not much farther," the grandmother said and just as she said it, a horrible thought came to her. The thought was so embarrassing that she turned red in the face and her eyes dilated and her feet jumped up, upsetting her valise in the corner. The instant the valise moved, the newspaper top she had over the basket under it rose with a snarl and Pitty Sing, the cat, spring onto Bailey's shoulder.

The children were thrown to the floor and their mother, clutching the baby, was thrown out the door onto the ground; the old lady was thrown into the front seat. The car turned over once and landed right-side-up in a gulch on the side of the road. Bailey remained in the driver's seat with the cat—gray-striped with a broad white face and an orange nose—clinging to his neck like a caterpillar.

As soon as the children saw they could move their arms and legs, they   65
scrambled out of the car, shouting, "We've had an ACCIDENT!" The grandmother was curled up under the dashboard, hoping she was injured so that Bailey's wrath would not come down on her all at once. The horrible thought she had had before the accident was that the house she had remembered so vividly was not in Georgia but in Tennessee.

Bailey removed the cat from his neck with both hands and flung it out the window against the side of a pine tree. Then he got out of the car and started looking for the children's mother. She was sitting against the side of the red gutted ditch, holding the screaming baby, but she only had a cut down her face and a broken shoulder. "We've had an ACCIDENT!" the children screamed in a frenzy of delight.

"But nobody's killed," June Star said with disappointment as the grandmother limped out of the car, her hat still pinned to her head but the broken front brim standing up at a jaunty angle and the violet spray hanging off the side. They all sat down in the ditch, except the children, to recover from the shock. They were all shaking.

"Maybe a car will come along," said the children's mother hoarsely.

"I believe I have injured an organ," said the grandmother, pressing her side, but no one answered her. Bailey's teeth were chattering. He had on a yellow sport shirt with bright blue parrots designed in it and his face was as yellow as the shirt. The grandmother decided that she would not mention that the house was in Tennessee.

The road was about ten feet above and they could see only the tops of the 70
trees on the other side of it. Behind the ditch they were sitting in there were more woods, tall and dark and deep. In a few minutes they saw a car some distance away on the top of a hill, coming slowly as if the occupants were watching them. The grandmother stood up and waved both arms dramatically to attract their attention. The car continued to come on slowly, disappeared around a bend and appeared again, moving even slower on top of the hill they had gone over. It was a big black battered hearselike automobile. There were three men in it.

It came to a stop just over them and for some minutes, the driver looked down with a steady expressionless gaze to where they were sitting, and didn't speak. Then he turned his head and muttered something to the other two and they got out. One was a fat boy in black trousers and a red sweat shirt with a silver stallion embossed on the front of it. He moved around on the right side of them and stood staring, his mouth partly open in a kind of loose grin. The other had on khaki pants and a blue striped coat and a gray hat pulled down very low, hiding most of his face. He came around slowly on the left side. Neither spoke.

The driver got out of the car and stood by the side of it, looking down at them. He was an older man than the other two. His hair was just beginning to gray and he wore silver-rimmed spectacles that gave him a scholarly look. He had a long creased face and didn't have on any shirt or undershirt. He had on blue jeans that were too tight for him and was holding a black hat and a gun. The two boys also had guns.

"We've had an ACCIDENT!" the children screamed.

The grandmother had the peculiar feeling that the bespectacled man was someone she knew. His face was as familiar to her as if she had known him all her life but she could not recall who he was. He moved away from the car and began to come down the embankment, placing his feet carefully so that he wouldn't slip. He had on tan and white shoes and no socks, and his ankles were red and thin. "Good afternoon," he said. "I see you all had you a little spill."

"We turned over twice!" said the grandmother. 75

"Oncet," he corrected. "We seen it happen. Try their car and see will it run, Hiram," he said quietly to the boy with the gray hat.

"What you got that gun for?" John Wesley asked. "Whatcha gonna do with that gun?"

"Lady," the man said to the children's mother, "would you mind calling them children to sit down by you? Children make me nervous. I want all you to sit down together there where you're at."

"What are you telling us what to do for?" June Star asked.

Behind them the line of woods gaped like a dark open mouth. "Come here," said their mother.

"Look here now," Bailey began suddenly, "we're in a predicament! We're in . . ."

The grandmother shrieked. She scrambled to her feet and stood staring. "You're The Misfit!" she said. "I recognized you at once!"

"Yes'm," the man said, smiling slightly as if he were pleased in spite of himself to be known, "but it would have been better for all of you, lady, if you hadn't of reckernized me."

Bailey turned his head sharply and said something to his mother that shocked even the children. The old lady began to cry and The Misfit reddened.

"Lady," he said, "don't get upset. Sometimes a man says things he don't mean. I don't reckon he meant to talk to you thataway."

"You wouldn't shoot a lady, would you?" the grandmother said and removed a clean handkerchief from her cuff and began to slap at her eyes with it.

The Misfit pointed the toe of his shoe into the ground and made a little hole and then covered it up again. "I would hate to have to," he said.

"Listen," the grandmother almost screamed, "I know you're a good man. You don't look a bit like you have common blood. I know you must come from nice people!"

"Yes, ma'am," he said, "finest people in the world." When he smiled he showed a row of strong white teeth. "God never made a finer woman than my mother and my daddy's heart was pure gold," he said. The boy with the red sweat shirt had come around behind them and was standing with his gun at his hip. The Misfit squatted down on the ground. "Watch them children, Bobby Lee," he said. "You know they make me nervous." He looked at the six of them huddled together in front of him and he seemed to be embarrassed as if he couldn't think of anything to say. "Ain't a cloud in the sky," he remarked, looking up at it. "Don't see no sun but don't see no cloud neither."

"Yes, it's a beautiful day," said the grandmother. "Listen," she said, "you shouldn't call yourself The Misfit because I know you're a good man at heart. I can just look at you and tell."

"Hush!" Bailey yelled, "Hush! Everybody shut up and let me handle this!" He was squatting in the position of a runner about to spring forward but he didn't move.

"I pre-chate that, lady," The Misfit said and drew a little circle in the ground with the butt of his gun.

"It'll take a half a hour to fix this here car," Hiram called, looking over the raised hood of it.

"Well, first you and Bobby Lee get him and that little boy to step over yonder with you," The Misfit said, pointing to Bailey and John Wesley. "The boys want to ask you something," he said to Bailey. "Would you mind stepping back in them woods there with them?"

"Listen," Bailey began, "we're in a terrible predicament! Nobody realizes what this is," and his voice cracked. His eyes were as blue and intense as the parrots in his shirt and he remained perfectly still.

The grandmother reached up to adjust her hat brim as if she were going to the woods with him but it came off in her hand. She stood staring at it and after a second she let it fall on the ground. Hiram pulled Bailey up by the arm as if he were assisting an old man. John Wesley caught hold of his father's hand and Bobby Lee followed. They went off toward the woods and just as they reached the dark edge, Bailey turned and supporting himself against a gray naked pine trunk, he shouted, "I'll be back in a minute, Mamma, wait on me!"

"Come back this instant!" his mother shrilled but they all disappeared into the woods.

"Bailey Boy!" the grandmother called in a tragic voice but she found she was looking at The Misfit squatting on the ground in front of her. "I just know you're a good man," she said desperately. "You're not a bit common!"

"Nome, I ain't a good man," The Misfit said after a second as if he had considered her statements carefully, "but I ain't the worst in the world either. My daddy said I was a different breed of dog from my brothers and sisters. 'You know,' Daddy said, 'It's some that can live their whole life without asking about it and it's others has to know why it is, and this boy is one of the latters. He's going to be into everything!'" He put on his black hat and looked up suddenly and then away deep into the woods as if he were embarrassed again. "I'm sorry I don't have on a shirt before you ladies," he said, hunching his shoulders slightly. "We buried our clothes that we had on when we escaped and we're just making do until we can get better. We borrowed these from some folks we met," he explained.

"That's perfectly all right," the grandmother said. "Maybe Bailey has an ex-   100
tra shirt in his suitcase."

"I'll look and see terrectly," The Misfit said.

"Where are they taking him?" the children's mother screamed.

"Daddy was a card himself," The Misfit said. "You couldn't put anything over on him. He never got in trouble with the Authorities though. Just had the knack of handling them."

"You could be honest too if you'd only try," said the grandmother. "Think how wonderful it would be to settle down and live a comfortable life and not have to think about somebody chasing you all the time."

The Misfit kept scratching in the ground with the butt of his gun as if he   105
were thinking about it. "Yes'm, somebody is always after you," he murmured.

The grandmother noticed how thin his shoulder blades were just behind his hat because she was standing up looking down on him. "Do you ever pray?" she asked.

He shook his head. All she saw was the black hat wiggled between his shoulder blades. "Nome," he said.

There was a pistol shot from the woods, followed closely by another. Then silence. The old lady's head jerked around. She could hear the wind move through the tree tops like a long satisfied insuck of breath. "Bailey Boy!" she called.

"I was a gospel singer for a while," The Misfit said. "I been most everything. Been in the arm service, both land and sea, at home and abroad, been twict married, been an undertaker, been with the railroads, plowed Mother Earth, been in a tornado, seen a man burnt alive oncet," and he looked up at the children's mother and the little girl who were sitting close together, their faces white and their eyes glassy; "I even seen a woman flogged," he said.

"Pray, pray," the grandmother began, "pray, pray. . . ."   110

"I never was a bad boy that I remember of," The Misfit said in an almost dreamy voice, "but somewheres along the line I done something wrong and got sent to the penitentiary. I was buried alive," and he looked up and held her attention to him by a steady stare.

"That's when you should have started to pray," she said. "What did you do to get sent up to the penitentiary that first time?"

"Turn to the right, it was a wall," The Misfit said, looking up again at the cloudless sky. "Turn to the left, it was a wall. Look up it was a ceiling, look down it was a floor. I forget what I done, lady. I set there and set there, trying to remember what it was I done and I ain't recalled it to this day. Oncet in a while, I would think it was coming to me, but it never come."

"Maybe they put you in by mistake," the old lady said vaguely.

"Nome," he said. "It wasn't no mistake. They had the papers on me."   115

"You must have stolen something," she said.

The Misfit sneered slightly. "Nobody had nothing I wanted," he said. "It was a head-doctor at the penitentiary said what I had done was kill my daddy but I known that for a lie. My daddy died in nineteen ought nineteen of the epidemic flu and I never had a thing to do with it. He was buried in the Mount Hopewell Baptist churchyard and you can go there and see for yourself."

"If you would pray," the old lady said, "Jesus would help you."

"That's right," The Misfit said.

"Well then, why don't you pray?" she asked trembling with delight suddenly. 120

"I don't want no hep," he said. "I'm doing all right by myself."

Bobby Lee and Hiram came ambling back from the woods. Bobby Lee was dragging a yellow shirt with bright blue parrots in it.

"Throw me that shirt, Bobby Lee," The Misfit said. The shirt came flying at him and landed on his shoulder and he put it on. The grandmother couldn't name what the shirt reminded her of. "No, lady," The Misfit said while he was buttoning it up, "I found out the crime don't matter. You can do one thing or you can do another, kill a man or take a tire off his car, because sooner or later you're going to forget what it was you done and just be punished for it."

The children's mother had begun to make heaving noises as if she couldn't get her breath. "Lady," he asked, "would you and that little girl like to step off yonder with Bobby Lee and Hiram and join your husband?"

"Yes, thank you," the mother said faintly. Her left arm dangled helplessly   125
and she was holding the baby, who had gone to sleep, in the other. "Hep that lady up, Hiram," The Misfit said as she struggled to climb out of the ditch, "and Bobby Lee, you hold onto that little girl's hand."

"I don't want to hold hands with him," June Star said. "He reminds me of a pig."

The fat boy blushed and laughed and caught her by the arm and pulled her off into the woods after Hiram and her mother.

Alone with The Misfit, the grandmother found that she had lost her voice. There was not a cloud in the sky nor any sun. There was nothing around her but woods. She wanted to tell him that he must pray. She opened and closed her mouth several times before anything came out. Finally, she found herself saying, "Jesus, Jesus," meaning, Jesus will help you, but the way she was saying it, it sounded as if she might be cursing.

"Yes'm," The Misfit said as if he agreed. "Jesus thown everything off balance. It was the same case with Him as with me except He hadn't committed any crime and they could prove I had committed one because they had the papers on me. Of course," he said, "they never shown me my papers. That's why I sign myself now. I said long ago, you get you a signature and sign everything you do and keep a copy of it. Then you'll know what you done and you can hold up the crime to the punishment and see do they match and in the end you'll have something to prove you ain't been treated right. I call myself The Misfit," he said "because I can't make what all I done wrong fit what all I gone through in punishment."

There was a piercing scream from the woods, followed closely by a pistol re- 130
port. "Does it seem right to you, lady, that one is punished a heap and another ain't punished at all?"

"Jesus!" the old lady cried. "You've got good blood! I know you wouldn't shoot a lady! I know you come from nice people! Pray! Jesus, you ought not to shoot a lady. I'll give you all the money I've got!"

"Lady," The Misfit said, looking beyond her far into the woods, "there never was a body that gave the undertaker a tip."

There were two more pistol reports and the grandmother raised her head like a parched old turkey hen crying for water and called, "Bailey Boy, Bailey Boy!" as if her heart would break.

"Jesus was the only One that ever raised the dead," The Misfit continued, "and He shouldn't have done it. He thrown everything off balance. If He did what He said, then it's nothing for you to do but thow away everything and follow Him, and if He didn't, then it's nothing for you to do but enjoy the few minutes you got left the best way you can—by killing somebody or burning down his house or doing some other meanness to him. No pleasure but meanness," he said and his voice had become almost a snarl.

"Maybe He didn't raise the dead," the old lady mumbled, not knowing what 135
she was saying and feeling so dizzy that she sank down in the ditch with her legs twisted under her.

"I wasn't there so I can't say He didn't," The Misfit said. "I wisht I had of been there," he said, hitting the ground with his fist. "It ain't right I wasn't there because if I had of been there I would of known. Listen lady," he said in a high voice, "if I had of been there I would of known and I wouldn't be like I am now." His voice seemed to crack and the grandmother's head cleared for an instant. She saw the man's face twisted close to her own as if he were going to cry and she murmured, "Why you're one of my babies. You're one of my own children!" She reached out and touched him on the shoulder. The Misfit sprang back as if a snake had bitten him and shot her three times through the chest. Then he put his gun down on the ground and took off his glasses and began to clean them.

Hiram and Bobby Lee returned from the woods and stood over the ditch, looking down at the grandmother who half sat and half lay in a puddle of blood with her legs cross under her like a child's and her face smiling up at the cloudless sky.

Without his glasses, The Misfit's eyes were red-rimmed and pale and defenseless-looking. "Take her off and thow her where you thown the others," he said, picking up the cat that was rubbing itself against his leg.

"She was a talker, wasn't she?" Bobby Lee said, sliding down the ditch with a yodel.

"She would of been a good woman," The Misfit said, "if it had been some- 140
body there to shoot her every minute of her life."

"Some fun!" Bobby Lee said.

"Shut up, Bobby Lee," The Misfit said. "It's no real pleasure in life."

Talking about the Text

1. Just who is the Misfit? Who do the other characters think he is? What kind of clues does the text give us about his identity? Is the Misfit redeemable? Under what circumstances

2. What kind of person is the grandmother? Does O'Connor's depiction of her change during the course of the story, and if so, how?

3. Do you think there's any chance that the Misfit would have spared the grandmother's life had events (or remarks) gone differently?

Writing about the Text

1. In a 1955 letter, O'Connor said: "there is nothing harder or less sentimental than Christian realism." Write about "A Good Man Is Hard to Find" as a "hard" and "unsentimental" story.

2. Writing of "A Good Man Is Hard to Find" in a 1960 letter to John Hawkes, O'Connor said: "The Misfit is touched by the Grace that comes through the old lady when she recognizes him as her child, as she has been touched by the Grace— that comes through him in his particular suffering. His shooting her is a recoil, a horror at her humanness." In an essay, explain how you understood the shooting when you read the story, how you respond now to O'Connor's "explanation," and how you regard such extra information from the author about her intentions.

Linking the Text to Other Texts

1. In a 1963 lecture she gave at Hollins College called "A Reasonable Use of the Unreasonable," O'Connor stated the following about "A Good Man Is Hard to Find": "The heroine of the story, the Grandmother, is in the most significant position life offers the Christian. She is facing death." Compare the story with another, less obviously religious story in which a character is facing a violent end. Suggestions: "Under the Radar" (p. 20) and "The Man Who Lived Underground" (p. 582).

2. O'Connor said she was a good reader of "A Good Man Is Hard to Find" because she sounded like the old lady. Choose a character you'd like to sound like and join with others to act out a comic section of the story, dramatizing the exchanges as if you were doing them for TV or a film.

 **INSPIRATION** **FLANNERY O'CONNOR AND BRUCE SPRINGSTEEN'S *NEBRASKA***

Bruce Springsteen's classic 1982 album *Nebraska* was considered a turning point for the musician, marking a departure into spare, melancholy instrumentation; darker, more pessimistic narratives and emotional landscapes; and

(continued on next page)

FLANNERY O'CONNOR AND BRUCE SPRINGSTEEN'S *NEBRASKA*

Bruce Springsteen.

more detailed portraits of desperate characters. The title track, "Nebraska," is loosely based on the story of real-life serial killer Charlie Starkweather, whose 1950s murder spree in Nebraska resulted in the deaths of nearly a dozen people. He was accompanied by his fourteen-year-old girlfriend, Caril Ann Fugate, despite the fact that three of his victims were her parents and sister. The story of their violent trek across Nebraska ended with their eventual capture and Starkweather's execution.

While the Starkweather story may have been a catalyst, Springsteen also drew upon literary influences to strike the right tone for his album. The male characters he creates in "Nebraska," as well as in the song "A Good Man Is Hard to Find" (clearly inspired by O'Connor's story of the same title), bear a strong resemblance to O'Connor's Misfit. As he explains in his 1998 book *Songs*, "At home, just before recording *Nebraska*, I was reading Flannery O'Connor. Her stories reminded me about the unknowability of God and contained a dark spirituality that resonated with my own feelings at the time." In a 1998 interview with Will Percy (nephew of Southern novelist Walker Percy) in *DoubleTake Magazine*, he elaborated on literature as a growing influence on his song writing and why O'Connor's stories specifically had the impact they did:

> I go through periods where I read, and I get a lot out of what I read, and that reading has affected my work since the late seventies. Films and novels and books, more so than music, are what have really been driving me since then. Your uncle [Walker Percy] once wrote that "American novels are about everything," and I was interested in writing about "everything" in some fashion in my music: how it felt to be alive now, a citizen of this country in this particular place and time and what that meant and what your possibilities were if you were born and alive now, what you could do, what you were capable of doing. Those were ideas that interested me.

The really important reading that I did began in my late twenties, with authors like Flannery O'Connor. There was something in those stories of hers that I felt captured a certain part of the American character that I was interested in writing about. They were a big, big revelation. She got to the heart of some part of meanness that she never spelled out, because if she spelled it out you wouldn't be getting it. It was always at the core of every one of her stories—the way that she'd left that hole there, that hole that's inside of everybody. There was some dark thing—a component of spirituality—that I sensed in her stories, and that set me off exploring characters of my own. She knew original sin—knew how to give it the flesh of a story. She had talent and she had ideas, and the one served the other.

I think I'd come out of a period of my own writing where I'd been writing big, sometimes operatic, and occasionally rhetorical things. I was interested in finding another way to write about those subjects, about people, another way to address what was going on around me and in the country—a more scaled-down, more personal, more restrained way of getting some of my ideas across. So right prior to the record *Nebraska*, I was deep into O'Connor.

The lyrics to "Nebraska" and "A Good Man Is Hard to Find" appear below. Lyrics to other songs on the *Nebraska* album can be found on Springsteen's website at *http://www.brucespringsteen.net/albums/nebraska.html*.

Bruce Springsteen
Nebraska

I saw her standin' on her front lawn just twirlin' her baton
Me and her went for a ride sir and ten innocent people died

From the town of Lincoln Nebraska with a sawed off .410 on my lap
Through to the badlands of Wyoming I killed everything in my path

I can't say that I'm sorry for the things that we done
At least for a little while sir me and her we had us some fun

The jury brought in a guilty verdict and the judge he sentenced me to death
Midnight in a prison storeroom with leather straps across my chest

Sheriff when the man pulls that switch sir and snaps my poor head back
You make sure my pretty baby is sittin' right there on my lap

They declared me unfit to live said into that great void my soul'd be hurled
They wanted to know why I did what I did
Well sir I guess there's just a meanness in this world

(continued on next page)

FLANNERY O'CONNOR AND BRUCE SPRINGSTEEN'S *NEBRASKA*

A Good Man Is Hard to Find (Pittsburgh)

It's cloudy out in Pittsburgh
It's raining in Saigon
Snow's fallin' all across the Michigan line
Well she sits by the lights of the Christmas tree
With the radio softly on
Thinkin' how a good man is so hard to find

Well once she had a fella
Once she was somebody's girl
And she gave all she had that one last time
Now there's a little girl asleep in the back room
She's gonna have to tell about the meanness in this world
And how a good man is so hard to find

Well there's pictures on the table by her bed
Him in his dress greens and her in her wedding white
She remembers how the world was the day he left
And now how that world is dead
And a good man is so hard to find

She got no time now for Casanovas
Yeah those days are gone
She don't want that anymore, she's made up her mind
Just somebody to hold her
As the nights get on
When a good man is so hard to find

Well she shuts off the TV
And without a word
Into bed she climbs
Well she thinks how it was all so wasted
And how expendable their dreams all were
When a good man was so hard to find
Well it's cloudy out in Pittsburgh

🐛 COMMENTARY

Flannery O'Connor on Her Craft

Like Eudora Welty, O'Connor was highly conscious of her art and provided a steady stream of insights through her letters and occasional essays. In her introduction to The Habit of Being: Letters of Flannery O'Connor (1979; revised edition published in 1988), from which the selections below have been excerpted, editor Sally Fitzgerald observes: "Almost all her close friendships were sustained through the post. . . . There is

much discussion of books in Flannery's letters, not just her own but all kinds of books. Understandably, reading was one of the great pleasures and interests in her life. She exchanged books with friends, and commentaries in turn."

On the South

From a letter to Andrew Lytle, September 15, 1955:

To my way of thinking, the only thing that keeps me from being a regional writer is being a Catholic and the only thing that keeps me from being a Catholic writer (in the narrow sense) is being a Southerner.

From a letter to John Hawkes, April 14, 1960:

It is interesting to me that your students naturally work their way to the idea that the Grandmother in "A Good Man" is not pure evil and may be a medium for Grace. If they were Southern students they would say this was because they all had grandmothers like her at home. These old ladies exactly reflect the banalities of the society and the effect is of the comical rather than the seriously evil. But Andrew [Lytle, one of her correspondents] insists that she is a witch, even down to the cat. These children, yr. students, know their grandmothers aren't witches.

From a letter to Marion Montgomery, July 9, 1961:

The Southern writer can outwrite anybody in the country because he has the Bible and a little history.

On the Short Story

From a letter to Catharine Carver, July 28, 1955:

I have been asked to talk on The Significance of the Short Story (UGH) at a wholesale gathering of the AAUW [American Association of University Women] in Lansing, Michigan—next April. It will take me from now until next April to find out what the significance of the short story is. Have you any idea? I think I will just tell them that this is no concern of the short-story writer.

From a letter to Robie Macauley, September 11, 1955:

Fancy me in this role. The lady called me up and asked me if I would talk on "The Significance of the Short Story." I don't have the foggiest notion what the significance of the short story is but I accepted at once as I like to make trips by plane, etc., and I figured I had ten months to find out . . . I think I'll tell them something very grand, such as that the short story restores the contemplative mentality, but I don't know exactly how I'll work it up.

On "A Good Man Is Hard to Find"

From a letter to "A.,"[1] July 20, 1955:

I am mighty tired of reading reviews that call A Good Man brutal and sarcastic. The stories are hard but they are hard because there is nothing harder or less sentimental than Christian realism. I believe that there are many rough beasts now slouching toward Bethlehem to be born and that I have reported the progress of a few of them, and when I see these stories described as horror stories I am always amused because the reviewer always has hold of the wrong horror.

From a letter to John Hawkes, December 26, 1959:

In general the Devil can always be a subject for my kind of comedy one way or another. I suppose this is because he is always accomplishing ends other than his own. More than in the Devil I am interested in the indication of Grace, the moment when you know that Grace has been offered and accepted—such as the moment when the Grandmother realizes the Misfit is one of her own children. These moments are prepared for (by me anyway) by the intensity of the evil circumstances.

From a letter to Andrew Lytle, February 4, 1960:

There is a moment of grace in most of the stories, or a moment where it is offered, and is usually rejected. Like when the Grandmother recognizes the Misfit as one of her own children and reaches out to touch him. It's the moment of grace for her anyway—a silly old woman—but it leads him to shoot her. This moment of grace excites the devil to frenzy.

From a letter to "A.," March 5, 1960:

You say there is love between man and God in the stories, but never between people—yet the Grandmother is not in the least concerned with God but reaches out to touch the Misfit.

From a letter to John Hawkes, April 14, 1960:

Perhaps it is a difference in theology, or rather the difference that ingrained theology makes in the sensibility. Grace, to the Catholic way of thinking, can and does use as its medium the imperfect, purely human, and even hypocritical. Cutting yourself off from Grace is a very decided matter, requiring a real choice, act of will, and affecting the very ground of the soul. The Misfit is touched by the Grace that comes through the old lady when she recognizes him as her child, as she has been touched by the Grace—that comes through him in his particular suffering. His shooting her is a recoil, a horror at her humanness, but after he has done it and cleaned his glasses, the Grace has worked in him and he pronounces his judgment: she would have been a good woman if he had been there every moment of her life. True enough. In the Protestant view, I think Grace and nature don't have much to do with each other. The old lady, because of her

---

[1] "A." was Betty Hester, who began writing to O'Connor in the summer of 1955, developing a steady friendship with her through their correspondence. In *The Habit of Being: Letters of Flannery O'Connor*, O'Connor's letters to her were labeled "To 'A.' " (short for anonymous) to protect Hester's privacy.

hypocrisy and humanness and banality couldn't be a medium for Grace. In the sense that I see things the other way, I'm a Catholic writer.

Starting Points for Further Research: Flannery O'Connor

- **Edition:** Flannery O'Connor. *Collected Works*. New York: Viking, 1988.
- **Biography:** Jean W. Cash. *Flannery O'Connor: A Life*. Knoxville: University of Tennessee Press, 2004.
- **Critical Essay:** Nicholas Crawford. "An Africanist Impasse: Race, Return, and Revelation in the Short Fiction of Flannery O'Connor." *South Atlantic Review* 68 (Spring 2003): 1–25.

LEE SMITH   (B. 1944)

Lee Smith grew up in rural Virginia, and during her senior year in high school she won a fellowship by submitting a draft of a novel to the Book-of-the-Month Club. That novel, The Last Day the Dog Bushes Bloomed (1968), became Smith's first published work. Smith identifies herself as an Appalachian writer as well as a southern writer, because she was born and brought up in a small mountain town, Grundy, in the extreme western corner of Virginia. She points out that her concerns are different from the non-mountain writers, since the population in her corner of the South historically has been largely white and poor. All the same, she feels closely connected to Welty and O'Connor, especially O'Connor's humor and often dark mood, and to Welty's proclivity to write about very humble, "ordinary" characters. Smith's protagonists are most often women, typically those with concerns and viewpoints that are undermined as they are being expressed. Certainly that is the case with Stella in "Cakewalk," whose seriousness about social propriety and social rank is sabotaged by what she says about her sister Florrie. Smith is often drawn to the woman "artist"—in this case Florrie and her decorative cakes—who sometimes operates a little outside the conventional female boundaries set for southern women. Smith's other women artists include country musicians, beauticians (who are also healers in their role as listeners), and writers of columns for small-town newspapers.

Like Welty and O'Connor, Smith's favorite literary form is the short story, and she has published two collections, Cakewalk (1981) and Me and My Baby View the Eclipse (1990). She specializes in the long short story and has also published nine novels, including Oral History (1983), Fair and Tender Ladies (1988), The Devil's Dream (1991), and Saving Grace (1995). She currently resides in North Carolina with her husband. As is characteristic of Smith's generation of southern writers, she has had a professional home in a southern academic setting, teaching writing at North Carolina State University in Raleigh.

Cakewalk   (1981)

They call Florrie the "cake lady" now and don't think Stella doesn't know it, even though of course no one has dared to say it to her face. Stella's face is smooth, strong, and handsome still—you'd have to say she's a handsome woman, instead of a pretty one—but her face is proud and stand-offish, too, sealed up tight with Estée Lauder makeup, ear to ear. Stella has run the cosmetics department at Belk's for twenty years and looks like it. Florrie, on the other hand, doesn't care what she looks like or what anybody thinks about it, either, and never has. Florrie wears running shoes, at her age, and wooly white athletic socks that fall in crinkles down around her ankles, and whatever else her eye lights on when she wakes up. At least that's what she looks like. Sometimes she'll have on one of those old flowered dresses that button all the way up the front, or sometimes she'll have on turquoise toreador pants or a felt skirt with a poodle on it— stuff she must have kept around for years and years, since she never throws anything at all away, stuff Stella wouldn't be caught dead in, as Stella frequently remarks to her husband, Claude, but whatever Florrie puts on, you can be sure she'll have white smudges all over it, at the skirt or on the sleeve, like she's been out in her own private snowfall. That's flour. She's always making those cakes. And then you can see her going through town carrying them so careful, her tired plump little face all crackled up and smiling, those Adidas just skimming the ground. She never wears a coat.

Oh Stella knows what they say! Just like Florrie is some poor soul on the order of Red Marcus' son who used to ride his blue bike around and around the Baptist Church until he either had a fit or somebody stopped him, or Martin Quesenberry's wife, Eloise, who is hooked on arthritis dope and has not come out of her nice Colonial frame house for eleven years, Stella knows the type and you do, too: a town character. It breaks Stella's heart. Because they were not raised to be town characters, the Ludington girls, they were brought up in considerable refinement thanks entirely to their sweet mother, Miss Bett, and not a day went by that she did not impress upon them in some subtle or some not-so-subtle way their obligations in this town as the crème de la crème, which is what she called them, which is what they were. Miss Bett learned this expression, and others, when she resided for one solid year in a treelined street in Europe in her youth. "Resided"—that's what she said.

Florrie and Stella resided in the big gray house on the corner of Lambert and Pine, the house with the gazebo, the handcarved banisters and heart pine floors, the same house that Florrie has made a shambles of and lives in, to this day, in the most perverse manner Stella can think of. But in those days it was the loveliest house in town and the Ludington family had always lived there, "aloft," as Stella told Claude, "on the top rung of the social crust."

So Stella was born with a natural gift for elegance, and this is why she loves Belk's. She goes in to work twenty minutes early every day with her own key on a special key ring by itself, a shiny brass key ring that spells out STELLA. After she lets herself in, she goes straight to the cosmetics department where everything is elegant, gleaming glass counters cleaned the night before by the hired help, all the shiny little bottles and tubes and perfume displays arranged just so, and she pours the tea from her thermos into a china cup and puts the thermos out of sight under the counter and settles herself on her high pink tufted stool and slowly sips her tea; she uses a saucer, too. The cosmetics department rises like an island on a rose pink carpet in the center of the store, close to the accessories but not too close, a long way from the bedspreads. After Stella has been there for about ten minutes or so, everybody else comes trickling in, too, and she speaks to them pleasantly one by one and pities their makeup and the way they look so thrown together, some of them, with their slips showing and sleep at the edges of their eyes. Then, five minutes before Mr. Thomas slides open the huge glass door to the rest of the mall, just when she has reached the hand-painted violet at the bottom of the china cup, then comes the moment she has been waiting for, the reason she gets up one whole hour before she has to and does her makeup by artificial light, which is not the way to do it, anybody can tell you that, and leaves the house in the pitch black frosty morning with Claude still sleeping humped up in the bed: this is it, the moment when Mr. Thomas flicks that master switch and her chandelier comes on. Of course, the cosmetics department is the only section in the store that has a chandelier, and it's a real beauty, hundreds and hundreds and maybe thousands of glass teardrops glowing like a million little stars, and all those shiny tubes and bottles winking back the light. The chandelier is as big as a Volkswagen, hanging right down over Stella, dead center at the soul of Belk's. It's just beautiful; Stella sighs when it comes on.

She checks her merchandise, then, and maybe she'll add something new or   5 drape a bright silk scarf around a mirror. Stella carries Erno Laszlo, Estée Lauder, Revlon, Clinique—all the most exclusive lines, and she sells to the very best people in town. Nobody else can afford these cosmetics, and Stella keeps it that way. The ladies she helps are the crème de la crème, so she never rushes them, and they will linger for hours sometimes in the sweet-smelling pink air of the cosmetics department, trying teal eyeliner or fuchsia blush, in the soft glow of the chandelier. Stella is calm, aloof, and refined, and it's a pleasure, in this day and age, to deal with someone like that. She doesn't seem to care if anybody buys anything or not, so the ladies buy and buy, just to *show* her. Stella makes a mint, her salary plus commissions, and whatever you read about in *Vogue*, she's already got it, she ordered it last month. If Pearls-in-Your-Bath are in, for instance, Stella has some pearls thrown out on black velvet in a tasteful little way to catch your eye, and the product set up in a pyramid at the side. Stella says she keeps one foot on the pulse of the future, and it's true. Stella has always stayed up with the times.

Florrie doesn't, though. If she made any real money from all those cakes, that would be different. But the way Stella figures it, Florrie just barely covers expenses. She won't use a mix, for one thing. And the way she gets herself up looking so awful, and the people she deals with—why, Florrie will make a cake for anybody, any class of person, and that's the plain truth, awful as it is. Stella shudders, thinking of it on this mid-October day, this cool nippy day with a jerky wind that whistles and whistles around the corner of Belk's although not one teardrop of the chandelier above Stella's cosmetics counter ever moves. Stella shudders, because today is the day she has circled in her mind to go over there (since she gets off early on Thursdays anyway) and try to talk some sense into Florrie for the umpteenth time.

She's got it all worked out in her head: if Florrie will quit making those embarrassing cakes and running around town like a mental person, Stella is prepared to be generous and let bygones be bygones, to let Florrie move in with her and Claude where she can do the cooking, since she likes to cook so much, and then they can sell Mama's house for a pretty penny. And all of this might be good for Claude, too, who has acted so funny since he retired from the electric company two years ago. Claude just bats around the house these days with his pajama top on over his slacks, leaving coffee cups any old place, which makes rings on all the furniture, smoking his pipe and smelling up the house, or taking that boat of his up to Kerr Lake and driving it around in the water all day by himself. It would be one thing if he were fishing, but he's not. He's just driving around in the water and looking back at the wake. Stella has colitis—that's why she's switched to tea instead of coffee—and the very thought of Claude out in that boat goes straight to her bowels. Well. At least she can go over and talk some sense into Florrie, something she's been trying to do ever since she can remember.

She can't remember a time when Florrie didn't need it, either, but she *can* remember, or thinks she can, when Florrie started making those cakes. In fact Stella can recall precisely, because she's got such a good head for business, several cakes in particular, and she narrows her frosty green eyelids and totally ignores the tacky woman on the other side of the counter asking if they carry Cover Girl, which of course they do *not*, and recalls these cakes one by one.

*   *   *

To understand the circumstances of Florrie's first cake, which she made practically over her mama's dead body when she was in the eighth grade—it was the dessert for a Methodist Youth Fellowship Progressive Dinner—you have to understand the way they used to live then, in that fine old house on the corner of Lambert and Pine. The house was number one on the House Tour every year, and you couldn't find a speck of dust in it, either, or one thing out of place. That Miss Bett kept her house this way was a triumph of mind over matter, because she was not a well woman, ever, and it wore her out to keep things so straight. But she did it anyway, and held her head up high in the face of her husband's failings, and even the towels were ironed. So you can see why the idea of fifteen teenagers tromping in for dessert would have run her right up the wall.

"But Mama," Florrie said, "they're *coming*. It's all settled. We're going to   10
have the first course at Rhonda's house, and the main course at Sue and Joey's, and then I invited them here for dessert. After that we'll go back to the church for the meeting."

"I never heard of such a thing," Miss Bett said. Miss Bett was a tall frail woman with jet black hair in a bun on the top of her head, and big dark eyes that could flash fire, as they did right then at Florrie. Miss Bett held famous dinner parties every year or so, which involved several weeks of preparations, all the silver polished and the china out, dinner parties that were so lovely that she had to go to bed for a day or two afterward to recover. "A Progressive Dinner!" she snorted. "The very idea!"

"Well, they're coming," Florrie said sweetly. That was her way—she never argued with her mother, or cried, just acted so sweet and did whatever she wanted to do. Stella wasn't fooled by this and neither was Miss Bett, but Florrie had everybody else in town eating out of the palm of her hand, including, of course, her daddy.

"Come on, Bett," Oliver Ludington said, standing in the kitchen doorway. "Don't embarrass her."

"I would talk about embarrassment if I were you," Miss Bett said. She stared at him until he said something under his breath and started to turn away, and then she looked back at her two daughters just in time to see Florrie give him a wink. That wink was the last straw.

"All right." She bit off the words. "Since Florrie has invited fifteen perfect   15
strangers into our home, we will entertain them properly. Stella," she directed, "go out and cut some glads and some of those snapdragons next to the lily pond."

Florrie giggled. "We don't have to have *flowers*," she said.

"*Stella!*" said Miss Bett, and Stella went out, furious because she was three years older and had never joined the MYF in the first place, even though she was more religious than Florrie, and now she had to cut the flowers.

Miss Bett began removing vases from the sideboard, considering them one by one.

"I'll just make a cake," Florrie suggested. She knew it would take her mother hours to arrange the flowers.

"You've never made a cake in your life," said Miss Bett. "You don't know the first thing about it." 20

"I won't make a mess," Florrie said.

"Florrie—" their mother began.

But Oliver Ludington, from the parlor, said, "That's all right, honey, Bessie can clean it up."

"Bessie doesn't come until *Monday*," Miss Bett reminded everybody, and of course it was only Sunday afternoon.

"I think I'll make a yellow cake with white icing," Florrie said. She had 25 taken all the cookbooks out of their drawer and piled them on the table in a heap, and now she was flipping through them in her disorganized way. "Where's that big flat cake pan?"

A sound that could have been a laugh, or maybe a cough, came from the parlor as Miss Bett found the pan and slammed it out on the table for Florrie.

"Stella, don't put the flowers right down on the counter like that, honey, put them on *newspaper*, they could have anything on them, and then please take sixteen salad forks out of the silver chest and polish them."

"*Mama*," Stella said, but after one look at Miss Bett, she did it.

By the time the members of the MYF arrived three hours later, the dining room looked just like a picture, silver forks and pink linen on the table and flowers in a cut-glass vase from Europe in the center. Stella was fit to be tied and refused to have dessert with the group, even though Florrie begged her, and Miss Bett had taken to her bed with a sick headache after one look at Florrie's cake. The cake would have been fine if Florrie had not gotten into the food coloring, which was never used in that house except at Christmas when Miss Bett made cookies for the help. But Florrie had found it, and she had tinted some of the white icing yellow and had made a great big wobbly cross in the center of the cake. Then she tinted the rest of the icing dark blue and wrote MYF on the cross, and put a little blue border all around its sides.

"Oh!" Miss Bett shrieked, and her hand fluttered up to her high pale fore- 30 head, and she turned without a word and climbed the steps, clutching the handsome banister all the way.

Florrie had cleaned up the kitchen the best she could, not really knowing how to do it, but she couldn't get the blue food coloring off her fingers so they stayed that way for the Progressive Dinner, even though she looked very nice otherwise, with her curly blond hair pinned back out of her eyes by silver barrettes, and wearing her pleated skirt. Oliver Ludington went upstairs and took a bath, singing "Bicycle Built for Two" as loud as he could, and then he appeared at the door in a sparkling white shirt, a red bow tie, and his best seersucker suit, just in time to welcome the whole Progressive Dinner to his house. "Come right in!" He bowed. "Glad to have you," he said, and Florrie smiled her full happy smile at him, showing her dimples, and giggled "Oh Daddy!" as she came through the hall trailed by the whole MYF in which all the boys had a crush on her, even then, and even then she knew how to flirt back, and laugh, and shake her blond curls, but that's *all* she did in those days—it was later, in high school, that boys became a problem.

* * *

Oliver Ludington died when Florrie was sixteen and Stella was off at college. He died of cirrhosis of the liver, as everyone knew he would, and it was a funny thing how many people showed up for his funeral, filling up the whole Methodist Church and then spilling out to fill up all that space between the church and the street. It was awful how Florrie took on. Miss Bett and Stella cried too, into their handkerchiefs, but to tell the truth everybody expected Miss Bett to be *relieved*, after it was all over, since Oliver Ludington drank so and since she had never been happy with the way he had refused to practice law and taught at the high school instead. But Miss Bett was not relieved, or at least she didn't seem to be. After Oliver died, all that fine dark fire went right out of her, and she crept around like a pastel ghost of herself for the rest of her life. It was like she had used herself completely up in her long constant struggle with Oliver, and lacking anybody to fight with or try to raise up by their bootstraps, she paled and died back like one of the flowers in her own garden, going to seed. She let the house go, too, even though Bessie still came in. The house seemed to sag at all its corners, the gazebo started to peel, worn places in the upholstery were left unrepaired, and a loose shutter flapped in the wind. She didn't even try to control Florrie, who went out with any boy who asked her, and when Stella tried to talk some sense into her, she didn't seem to hear.

"Mama," said Stella, just home from business school where she had a straight A average, "you have got to do something about Florrie. She's getting a *reputation*." Stella paused significantly, but her mother's dark eyes were looking beyond her face. "I might as well come right out and say it, Mother, I think she's fast. And Daddy used to think she was so smart, but look at her grades now! They're terrible, and she'll never make it to college at the rate she's going. Besides, I don't like the crowd she hangs around with, for instance that Barbara Whitley. Those people are common."

Miss Bett's fingers trembled on her lap, like she was brushing some insect, or some speck, off the flowered voile. "You haven't asked me how my stomach is," she said to Stella.

Stella sat straight up in her chair. "Well, how *is* it?" she said.

"I have my good days and I have my bad days," Miss Bett told her. "I just eat like a bird. Sometimes I have a little rice or a breast of chicken"—but just then Florrie came in from the kitchen with her lipstick on crooked, bringing her mama some tea, and Miss Bett sighed like she was dying and then drank it up in one gulp.

"Come on and go to the sidewalk carnival," Florrie said to Stella. "It's for the Fire Department, and they've got a band."

"I think somebody should stay here with Mama," Stella said.

"I think I could stand another cup of tea with a little more lemon in it," Miss Bett said, and then Stella decided to go after all, and she changed her dress while Florrie fixed Miss Bett's tea.

Florrie had made a cake for the carnival, a white sheet cake with yellow ic- 40
ing and a fire engine outlined on it in red, the engine's wheels made out of
chocolate nonpareils. The sisters walked downtown along the new sidewalk and
Stella thought how the town was growing since the aluminum company had
come, and how many new faces she saw. Everybody spoke to Florrie, though, and
stopped to admire her cake, and Florrie introduced them all, complete strangers,
to Stella. "She's away at school," Florrie would say.

"I wish you wouldn't do that," Stella told her finally, because she could tell
after twenty minutes or so that there was no one she wanted to meet.

The square had been roped off for the carnival, and Florrie took her cake
carefully up to the table in the center of it, a long table draped with red, white,
and blue, and put it right down in the middle. Everybody went "ooh, ah," and
Stella turned away and went to sit on the steps of the North Carolina National
Bank where to her surprise she fell into a conversation with Claude Lambeth, a
boy she hadn't seen since high school, a tall serious-looking boy who was studying electrical engineering at State. Now Stella was a beauty at that time. She
had Miss Bett's looks and her own way of walking so straight and inclining her
head. Stella and Claude Lambeth sat on the high steps of the bank, back from
the action, and watched the crowd mill around and watched the kids dancing in
front of the fountain to the band. They had a lot in common, Stella learned, as
they talked and talked and watched the dancing. Florrie was like a little whirlwind out there. First she went with one and then another, and even Stella had to
admit she was pretty, or would have been if her hair didn't fly out so much on the
turns and she didn't look quite so messy in general.

"That's your sister, isn't it?" Claude Lambeth said to Stella, and Stella said
yes it was. Claude Lambeth just shook his head, and then later, at the cakewalk,
he shook it again when the music stopped and five or six boys jumped on the
painted red dot for Florrie's cake and the right to walk her home. The boy who
ended up on the bottom was Harliss Reeves, who was generally up to no good,
and when the whole cakewalk was over, Claude Lambeth told Harliss Reeves
thanks anyway, he had promised their mother that he would drive Florrie and
Stella home in his car. And he did, leaving Harliss on the sidewalk with his cake
in both hands and his mouth wide open, Florrie mouthing apologies at him
through the closed glass window of Claude Lambeth's car. "What'd you do *that*
for?" she screamed at Claude, jerking her arm away from Stella, but Stella was
taken with Claude and approved his action with all her heart.

* * *

Which was broken when Claude Lambeth failed to write to her and dated her
little sister instead, all that spring and summer while Stella graduated and then
worked so hard in her first job as a teller trainee in Charlotte. Stella was so mad
she wouldn't come home at all, not even to try to talk some sense into Florrie
when her mama wrote that Florrie refused to go to college and was selling toys in
the five-and-dime, but then her mama wrote that Florrie and that nice Claude
Lambeth were unfortunately no longer seeing each other, and Stella knew he
had seen the light. She came home for a visit and married him on the spot, and
Florrie made them a three-tiered Lady Baltimore wedding cake.

"You ought to charge," Stella told her, eyeing the cake at her wedding recep- 45
tion. "You'll never get anywhere at the five-and-dime," she said, and Florrie

stopped playing with all their squealing little girl cousins long enough to say maybe she would.

* * *

Florrie never had a wedding cake of her own, poor thing, or a wedding reception either—she ran off in a snowstorm two years later with Earl Mingo, a drifter from northern Florida, and married him in a J.P.'s office in the middle of the night in Spartanburg, South Carolina, under a bare hanging light bulb. Now Earl Mingo was good looking, you would have to say that—but who knows what else she saw in him? Because Florrie could have had her pick in this town, and she didn't, she ran off with Earl Mingo instead, a man with Indian blood in him who had never made a decent living for himself or anybody else. He painted houses, or so he said, but if it was too cold, or too hot, or he didn't like the color of paint you had picked out, forget it. Earl Mingo kept guns and he went hunting a lot, out in the river woods or up on the mountain, and sometimes when you were trying to hire him he'd stare right past you, to where the road went off in the trees. Everybody knew who he was. He had men friends, hunting buddies, but they never asked him over for dinner, and neither did anyone else.

Stella didn't speak to Florrie for months after she did it, and Miss Bett had to be hospitalized it was such a shock. After her mother got out of the hospital, Stella used to drive over there to pick up Miss Bett and take her to church—of course Florrie and Earl didn't attend—and then she would drop her off again, but finally when Miss Bett told Stella that Florrie was pregnant, she decided to walk back in that house, meet Earl Mingo face to face, and make peace. Because Stella had had a baby herself by then, little Dawn Elizabeth, and this had softened her heart.

So finally, on this particular Sunday after church, Stella parked the car and walked her mother right up to the door in the pale March sunlight, her hand under Miss Bett's arm, and she couldn't help but notice now nobody had ever fixed that shutter, and how dirty the carpet was in the front hall. While her mother went upstairs to lie down, Stella stood at the last step, holding on to the banister, and hollered for Florrie.

Nobody answered.

But Stella smelled coffee and so she pressed her black patent leather purse up tight against her bosom and put her lips in one thin line and headed back toward the kitchen without another word. Forgive and forget, she thought. The swinging kitchen door was closed. When Stella pushed it open, the first thing she noticed was the *color*, of course, which her mother had never said the first word about and which was a big surprise as you can imagine, her mama's nice white kitchen painted bright blue like the sky. Now if it had been a kitchen color that would be one thing, such as pale blue or beige or yellow, but whoever heard of a sky blue kitchen? Even the cabinets were blue. Stella was too surprised to say a word, so she kept her mouth shut and blinked, and then she saw what she would have seen right away if that color hadn't been such a shock: Earl Mingo seated big as life at the kitchen table with Florrie on his lap, both their faces hidden by Florrie's tumbling yellow hair. Florrie was laughing and Earl Mingo was saying something too low for Stella to hear. Earl Mingo didn't even have a shirt on, and the kitchen table was cluttered with dishes that no one had bothered to wash.

When Stella said "Good morning!" though, Florrie jumped up giggling and pulled the tie of her pink chenille robe around her and tied it as fast as she could, but not before Stella could see she was naked as a jaybird underneath. This was in the *afternoon*, close to one o'clock.

"Stella, this is Earl," Florrie said exactly as if people ran around in nothing but pink chenille robes all day long.

"I'm pleased to meet you." Earl stood up in his bare chest and stuck out his hand to Stella, who seized it in her confusion and pumped it up and down too long. Later, she hoped Earl Mingo didn't think she meant anything by that because she could see in one glance that he was the kind of man who thinks a woman is only good for one thing, and Stella was not that kind of woman by a long shot.

Earl Mingo stood over six feet tall, with black hair, too long, brushed straight back from his high dark forehead and black eyes that looked right through you. He had a big nose, straight thick eyebrows, a hard chin and a thin crooked mouth that turned up at the corners, sometimes, in the wildest grin. When Earl Mingo grinned, he showed the prettiest, whitest teeth you can imagine on a man. He grinned at Stella like he was just delighted to meet her after all. "Have a cup of coffee," he said.

"Why don't you take off your hat and sit down," Florrie said, which is what she and Earl proceeded to do themselves, only this time Florrie sat in a separate chair. "That's a pretty hat," Florrie said. "I like that little veil."

"I'd just love to stay but I can't." Stella was lying through her teeth. "Claude is watching Dawn Elizabeth and I have to get right back. I just wanted to run in and say I'm real happy about the baby, Florrie, and I never have said congratulations either, so congratulations." Stella's eyes filled up with tears then—she had been having those crying spells ever since Dawn Elizabeth was born—and Florrie jumped right up and hugged her on the spot. Stella remembered holding her little sister by the hand when she started first grade, walking Florrie to school.

"Well, I've got to go," Stella said finally, and then for no reason at all she said, backing out that bright blue kitchen door, "You all be careful, now," and Earl Mingo threw back his head and laughed.

* * *

There comes a time in a woman's life when the children take over, and what you do is what you have to, and it seems like the days go by so slow then while you're home with them, and nothing ever really gets done around the house before you have to go off and do something else that doesn't ever get done either, and it can take you all day long to hem a skirt. Every day lasts a long, long time. But then before you know it, it's all over, those days gone like a fog on the mountain, and the kids are all in school and there you are with this awful light empty feeling in your stomach like the beginning of cramps, when you sit in the chair where you used to nurse the baby and listen to the radio news.

Not that Stella ever nursed Dawn Elizabeth or Robert either one, but Florrie had two babies in a row and nursed them all over town. Anyway, with Robert in school at last, Stella had her hair frosted, bought some new shoes, took a part-time job in the accounting department at Belk's, and started working her way up into her present job in the cosmetics department. It was like she just woke up from a long, long sleep. She had done her duty and stayed home with those

55

babies, and then she went back to the real world where she belonged. Not that
Stella ever neglected those kids while she worked: she had them organized like
the army, the whole family. Everybody had a chore, and she and Claude gave
them every advantage in the world—piano lessons, dancing lessons, braces, you
name it. Claude advanced steadily in his job at the electric company, a promotion every six years, and they built a nice brick ranch-style house with wall-to-
wall carpeting and a flagstone patio. Claude was elected president of the Kiwanis
Club, and Stella went on buying trips to New York City, where she stayed in hotels by herself.

And Florrie? Florrie never could seem to understand that those baby days   60
were over. She had Earlene—six months after she got married—and then she
had Earl Junior and then she had Paul who was born too soon and died, and anybody else would have left it at that. But nine years later, along came Bobby Joe,
and then Floyd, and Florrie seemed tickled pink. She raised her children in the
scatterbrained way she did everything else, and they ran loose like wild Indians
and stayed up as late as they pleased on a school night, and spent all their money
on gum. Then when they got to be older, they used to have all the other kids in
town over there in that big house, too, dancing to the radio in the parlor and
who knows what all, smoking cigarettes out in the yard. Florrie was always right
there in the middle of it, making a cake as often as not.

Because her business had grown and grown—she never gave it up even
when she had two of them in diapers at one time. And she never switched to
cake mixes either, although she would have saved herself hours if she had. Florrie still made plenty of birthday cakes with roses on them, and happy anniversary
cakes with bells, and seasonal cakes such as a green tree cake for Christmas with
candy ornaments on it, or a chocolate Yule log, or an orange pumpkin cake for
Halloween, and she had four different sizes of heart molds she used for Valentine's Day. But the town was growing and changing all the time, and you could
tell it by Florrie's cakes. After the new country club opened up, she made a cake
for Dolph Tillotson's birthday that was just like a nine-hole golf course, a huge
green sheet cake with hills and valleys and little dime store mirrors for the water
hazards, flags on all the greens, and a tiny sugar golf ball near the cup on the seventh hole. When the country club team won the state swim meet, they ordered
an Olympic pool cake with a chocolate board and twelve different lap lanes.
Once she worked for two solid days on a retirement cake for the head of the sec-
retarial pool out at the aluminum plant. This cake involved a lot of oblong layers
assembled just so to form a giant typewriter with Necco wafers as keys. The sheet
of paper in the blue typewriter was smooth white icing, and on it Florrie had put
"We'll Miss You, Miss Hugh" in black letters that looked like typing. When the
new Chevrolet agency opened, she filled an order for a chocolate convertible;
and after the community college started up, she made cakes and cakes for the
students, featuring anything they told her to write, such as "Give 'Em Hell,
Michelle" on a spice cake for a roommate's birthday.

The cake business and the children kept Florrie happy then, or seemed to, a
good thing since Earl Mingo did not amount to a hill of beans, which surprised
nobody. He painted houses for a while, and then he put in insulation, and then
he went away working on a pipeline. In between jobs he would go off hunting by
himself, or so he said, and stay gone for as long as a month. Then he'd show up
again, broke and grinning, and Florrie would be so happy to see him and all the

children would be too, and things would go on like that for a while before Earl Mingo went off again.

It was a marriage that caused a lot of talk in the beginning, talk that started up again every time Earl Mingo went away and then died back every time he came home, but since he kept doing it, the talk slacked off and finally stopped altogether and everybody just accepted the way it was with them, the way he came and went. Since it didn't seem to bother Florrie, it stopped bothering everybody else too—except Stella, who felt that Florrie had stepped off the upper crust straight into scum. Into *lowlife*, which is where in her opinion Florrie had been heading all along.

* * *

For years Miss Bett had her own rooms upstairs, with her pressed flowers and her pictures from Europe in silver frames, her little brocade settee and her Oriental rug and her gold-tasseled bed. So many of the other fine things in the rest of the house had been broken by Florrie's children. Which wasn't their *fault*, exactly, since nobody ever taught them any better or ever told them "no" in all their lives.

"It's just a madhouse over here!" Stella said, not for the first time, one day after work when she was sitting with her mama in what used to be called the east parlor, looking out on the front yard where Earl Junior and a whole gang of boys were playing football in spite of the boxwood hedges on either side of the walk. Stella and Miss Bett watched through the wavy French doors as Earl Junior and his friends caught the ball, and ran, and fell down in a pile and then got up. They watched as Earl Junior and his friends waved their arms frantically and shouted at one another, the breath of their words hanging white in the cold fall air. Sometimes they had a fight, but nobody stepped in to stop it, and after a while they would get tired of fighting it seemed, and roll over on their backs and start laughing. Stella was glad that her own son, Robert, was not out in that pile of boys. In the west parlor, Earlene was playing the piano—practically the only stick of furniture in that room that was left in one piece—practicing for a talent show at school. Her fingers ran over the same thing again and again, a tinkly little melody that got on Stella's nerves. Floyd and Bobby Joe were wrestling in the hall. Every now and then they rolled past the east parlor door, for all the world like two little monkeys. Back in the kitchen the TV set was on, Florrie watching her stories and smoking cigarettes, no doubt, while she cooked. Earl Mingo was gone.

Cold sunlight came in through those high French doors and fell across the worn blue carpet, pale fine golden sunlight that reminded Stella suddenly of their childhood in such a way that it caused her to suck in her breath so hard it hurt her chest, and blurt out something she didn't even know she'd been thinking about until she said it out loud.

"Mama," she said, "you don't have to stay here, you know. You could come to live with Claude and me, we'd be glad to have you."

Miss Bett looked so pitiful and small, her eyes like puddles in her little white face. She's *shrunk!* Stella noticed. She's shrinking up like a little old blow-up doll, and no one has noticed but me. "*Mama*," Stella said. "We could build you a little apartment over the garage."

"I had a bad day yesterday," Miss Bett said, looking past Stella out the French doors where Earl Junior was catching a pass. "Everything went through me like a sieve."

"Wouldn't you like to have your own apartment, Mama?" Stella went on.   70
"Wouldn't you like to have some peace?"

"I'd like a little peace." Miss Bett said this like she was in a dream.

"Well then!" Stella stood up. "I'll just talk to Florrie about it, and we'll—"

"No!" Miss Bett got all excited suddenly and twisted her hands around and around in her lap. She said it with such force that Stella stopped, halfway out the door.

"We'd love to have you," Stella said.

"I—" Miss Bett said. "I—" She moved her little blue hand in a circle   75
through the sunlight, then let it drop back in her lap. She looked straight at Stella. "I'll try to stand it a little longer," she said.

"We'll buy you a new TV."

Miss Bett lifted her head the way she used to, and touched a white wisp of her hair.

"I'll just have to bear it," she said.

But Stella sailed right past her into the kitchen where, sure enough, Florrie was sitting at the kitchen table reading a magazine and smoking a cigarette. The table was half covered up with newspapers and Popsicle sticks and glue.

"What's all that?" Stella pointed at the mess.   80

"Earl Junior is making this little old theater, like Shakespeare had, for school. It's the cutest thing," Florrie said.

"Listen." Stella sat down and started right in. "Listen here, I'm worried about Mother."

"*Mother?*" Florrie said it like she was surprised.

"I think she needs a change." Stella was going to be tactful, but then she just burst into tears. "Poor little thing. She's *shrinking*, Florrie. I swear she's just shrinking away."

Florrie put her cigarette out and giggled. "She's not shrinking, Stella," she   85
said.

"But what do you think about her *health*, Florrie? Now really—I wouldn't be surprised if it turned out to be all mental myself, if you want to know. I hope you won't take this wrong, but I just don't think it's good for her to live under such a strain. I don't think there's a thing wrong with her stomach, if you want to know what I think. I think if she could get a little peace and quiet, and if she had some *hobbies* or something—"

Florrie threw back her head and laughed. "I can just see Mama with a hobby!" she said. "Lord! Mama's already got a hobby, if you ask me."

"No, *really*, Florrie," Stella said. "Wouldn't it be a whole lot easier for you and Earl if she came and lived over our garage?" Floyd came in the kitchen crying then, and Florrie got him a Coke, and Stella went on. "Just think about it. Think about how much easier your life would be. What do you think about her health, anyway? I've been meaning to ask you."

Florrie looked at Stella. "Well, she has her good days and she has her bad days," Florrie said. "Sometimes everything goes through her like a sieve."

"*Oh!*" Stella was furious. "I can't talk to you. You're as bad as she is!" Stella   90
picked up her pocketbook and flounced out of there, right past Earlene playing the piano and Floyd and Bobby wrestling in the hall and her mother all shrunk up to nothing in the sunlight on the sofa in the east parlor; Stella sailed straight out the front door just as Earl Junior hollered "Hike!"

* * *

So Miss Bett lived with Florrie and Earl until she died of heart failure, and when she did, it was all Stella could do to persuade Florrie to let them bury her mama decently. Florrie wanted Miss Bett put in a pine box, of all things, where the worms could get in. Then Florrie revealed that in fact this was the way she and Earl Mingo had buried Paul, the baby who had died so long ago. Stella and Florrie had a big argument about all of this in front of everybody, right there in the funeral home, but since Earl Mingo was out of town and Earlene had gone off to college, Florrie had no one to take her side and finally Claude just gave Mr. Morrow a check and that settled it, or seemed to, since Florrie did not mention the pine box or the worms again though she cried for three solid weeks, despite the fact that Miss Bett had left her the whole house out of pity.

Lord knows where Florrie got such ideas in the first place, although you can be sure she passed them along to Earlene, who turned into a hippie beatnik and won a full scholarship to the North Carolina School of Arts while she was still in high school and went there, too, came home for vacations wearing purple tights and turtleneck sweaters and necklaces made out of string. Turned into a vegetarian and went away to college up North, where she majored in drama. Now that was Earlene.

Earl Junior was a horse of a different color. No brains to speak of, a big grin like his daddy, always wrecking a car or getting a girl in trouble. Earl Junior got a football scholarship to N.C. State where he played second string until his knee gave out, and then he quit school and got a job as some kind of salesman, nothing you would be proud of. But Earl Junior liked to travel, just like Earl. You would have thought Earl Junior owned all of North Carolina, South Carolina, Virginia, and Tennessee, the way he called it his "territory."

Bobby Joe and Floyd were boys that anybody would be proud of, though, in the Boy Scouts and on the Junior High basketball team for instance, boys with brushed-back sandy hair and steady gray eyes, who mowed everybody's grass on Saturdays. Stella was glad to see that those two were turning out so well in spite of the way they were raised with no advantages to speak of, and as years drew into years and it became perfectly clear who had succeeded and who had not, she pitied Florrie, and tried to be extra nice to her sometimes—bringing them a country ham just before Christmas, for instance, or having oranges sent—things that Florrie often failed to notice, scatterbrained as she was. Because there is a kind of flyaway manner that might be fetching in a young girl, but goes sour when the years mount up, and Florrie was pushing forty. She should have known how to say "thank you" by then. Bobby Joe and Floyd were almost through with high school the year that the worst thing that *could* happen, *did*.

Earlene had always been Florrie's favorite, in a way, her being the only girl, and this made it that much worse all the way around: Earlene was the *last* one, the very last person you would pick to be the agent of her mother's doom. But you know how Earlene changed when she went off to school, so you can imagine what her friends would be like: tall skinny girls with wild curly hair or long drooping hair and big eyes, like those pictures of foreign children you see in the drugstore, and of course Earlene was exactly like the rest of Florrie's children— sooner or later, she brought every one of them home.

Elizabeth Blackwell was the daughter of two Duke professors, Dr. Blackwell and Dr. Blackwell, of the History Department. You would never have guessed what was going to happen if you had ever seen her or heard her name, which sounded so well-bred and nice. But Elizabeth Blackwell wore blue jeans day in and day out when she was visiting Earlene, and she had light red hair so long she could sit on it if it hadn't been braided in one long thick plait down the back of her lumberjack shirt. Whenever Elizabeth came to visit Earlene, all she wanted to do was go hiking up on the mountain with Earlene and Floyd and Bobby Joe, and sometimes Earl went too, if he was home. Elizabeth Blackwell wore big square boots from the army-navy store, boots exactly like a man's, and no makeup at all on her pale freckled face, which would have been pretty if she had known what to do with it, especially those big eyes that were such an unusual color, no color really, something in between green and gray. She was not feminine at all, so when she and Earl Mingo ran away together it was the biggest shock in the world to everybody.

Except Earlene, who urged everybody not to feel harsh toward her friend because, she said, Elizabeth Blackwell was pregnant, and furthermore it was Earl Mingo's child. Earl Mingo must have been almost fifty by then, and Elizabeth Blackwell was nineteen years old. Now who can understand a thing like that? Not Bobby Joe, who shot out the new streetlight on the corner of Lambert and Pine with his daddy's Remington pump shotgun and then threw the shotgun itself in the river; not Floyd, who got a twitch in one eye, clammed up in all his classes at the high school, and started studying so hard he beat out Louise Watson for valedictorian of the class; not even Earlene, who took a week off from college to come home and cry and tell everybody it was all her fault. Nobody could understand it except possibly Florrie herself, who of course had known Earl Mingo better than anyone else and did not seem all that surprised. It made you wonder what else had gone on through all those years, and exactly what other crosses Florrie had had to bear.

"I would just die if it was Claude," Stella said several days after it happened, one night when she had come over to commiserate with her sister and find out more details if she could. "But of course Claude would never do anything like that," Stella added. "It would never enter Claude's mind."

Florrie stood back from the wedding cake she was working on and looked at Stella. "You never know what's going to happen in this world," she said. Florrie sounded like she knew a secret, which made her sister mad.

"Well, I know! Claude and I have been married for twenty-six years, and I guess I ought to know by now."

Florrie smiled. Her smile was still as pretty as ever, like there might be a giggle coming right along behind it, but she had aged a lot around the eyes, and that night her eyes were all red. Her hair had a lot of gray mixed in with the blond by that time, and she wore it chopped off just any old way. Florrie had six different-sized layers of white cake already baked, and she was building them up, pink icing between each layer. Floyd sat in the corner in his daddy's chair, reading a library book.

"Who's that cake for?" Stella asked.

"Jennifer Alley and Mark Priest," Florrie said. "Look here what they got in Raleigh for me to put on the top." She showed Stella the bride and groom in cellophane wrapping, a little couple so lifelike they might have been real, the bride in a satin dress.

"Lord, I wish you'd look at that," Stella said. "Look at that little old veil."

Florrie smiled. "Real seed pearls," she said.   105

"But Florrie—" Stella looked at her watch. "Isn't the wedding tomorrow?" Stella *knew* it was, actually, because she and Claude had been invited, but of course Florrie had not.

"Noon," Florrie said. She rubbed her hand across her forehead, leaving a white streak of flour.

"Are you going to get it done in time?" Stella asked as Florrie spread the smooth white icing over the whole thing and then mixed up more pink and put it in her pastry tube.

"Sure," Florrie said.

"If I were you, I'd just go to bed and get up in the morning and finish it," 110 Stella said.

"I like to make my wedding cakes at night," Florrie said. "You know I always do it this way."

"That's going to take you all night, though."

"Well." Florrie started on the tiny top layer, making pink bows all around the edge. "Light me a cigarette, honey, will you?" she said to Floyd, who did.

Stella sat up straight in the kitchen chair and put her mouth together in a line, but she kept it shut until Bobby Joe came in the kitchen for a Coke and told her hello, and then she said, "Listen, that's another reason I came over here tonight. Claude said for me to tell you that if you want to go off to school next year, Bobby Joe, you just let us know and we'll take care of it." Stella had been against this when Claude first brought it up, but now she was glad she had it to say, since everything was so pathetic over here at Florrie's. Floyd had a scholarship, of course, already. Floyd was a brain. "If you want to go to college, that is," Stella said for emphasis, since Bobby Joe was just standing there in the middle of the kitchen like he hadn't heard her right.

Bobby Joe stared at his aunt and then he popped off his pop top real loud. 115 "Thanks but no thanks," he said.

Well! Bobby Joe took a long drink out of the can and Stella stood up. "If that's how you feel about it," she said, "*all right.*"

Florrie was crying again without seeming to notice it, the tears leaking out as slow as Christmas, her blue eyes filling while she shaped three little red roses about each pink bow on the cake, crying right in front of her sons without a bit of shame.

Stella, who knew when she wasn't wanted, left. But the next day at Jennifer and Mark Priest's wedding reception, Stella couldn't eat *one bite* of that cake; it stuck fast in her throat, and thinking about Florrie gave her indigestion anyway, Florrie bent hunchbacked over that great huge cake the night before, making those tiny red roses.

*   *   *

And Lord knows whatever happened to Earl Mingo, or to Elizabeth Blackwell, or to that baby she either did or did not have. Nobody ever saw or heard from them again except for four postcards that Earl sent back over the next couple of years, from Disney World, from Mammoth Cave, from Death Valley, from Las Vegas—like that. He didn't write a thing on any of them except "Love, Earl Mingo." Florrie kept each one around for a while and then she threw it away, and kept on with her business, living hand-to-mouth some way, nobody knew quite how except that she had made some money when she sold off most of the backyard to Allstate Insurance, which tore up the gazebo and the fish pond and built a three-story brick office building on it right jam-up against that fine old house, and then Claude dropped by and did little odd jobs around the house that needed doing, and that was a savings, too. Other people came by all the time to see her. It seemed like there was always somebody in that kitchen having coffee with Florrie if it was winter, or Coke if it was summer, but then of course she had Earlene's children, Dolly and Bill, to take care of too, while Earlene was having a nervous breakdown after her divorce. Florrie took them in without a word and they lived with her for three years, which is how long it took Earlene to get her feet back on the ground, give up art, and get her license in real estate. Floyd is gone for good: he teaches at the college in Greensboro. Bobby Joe has never amounted to much, like Earl Junior who runs a Midget Golf in Myrtle Beach now. Bobby Joe is still in town. He lives in an apartment near the country club and works in a men's store at the mall, all dressed up like a swinging single in open-neck shirts and gold neck chains, still coming over to see his mama every day or so, breezing in through the screen porch door. Earl Junior's ex-wife, Johnnie Sue, came to visit about two years ago and brought their little boy, Chip, and she has stayed with Florrie ever since, leaving Chip with his grandmother while she teaches tap dancing at Arthur Murray's studio in Raleigh.

Johnnie Sue is not even related to Florrie, so who ever heard of such an 120 arrangement? Stella shakes her head, thinking about it, and smokes a Silva Thin in the car as she drives across town from Belk's to Florrie's house through the fine October day, the leaves all red and golden, swirling down with the wind against the windshield of Stella's new car. Florrie's house is almost the only one left standing on Lambert Street since it has been zoned commercial, and it looks so funny now with the Allstate Building rising up behind it and the Rexall Drugstore next door.

"It's real convenient," Florrie says when Stella mentions the Rexall, again, as tactfully as possible. "I just send Chip right over whenever there's something we need."

Stella sighs. This will be harder than she thought. She had hoped to find Florrie by herself, for one thing, but Chip is home with a cold and she can hear him upstairs right now, banging things around and singing in his high, thin voice. Chip is a hyperactive child who has to take pills every day of his life. Not a thing like Stella's own well-behaved grandchildren, who unfortunately live so far away. Well. At least nobody else is here, even though the table is littered with coffee cups and there's a strong smell of smoke, like pipe smoke, in the air. Florrie, who doesn't keep up with a thing, probably doesn't even know about room deodorizer sprays. Or no-wax wax, obviously, since the floor has clearly not been touched in ages. Stella sighs, taking a kitchen chair, at the memory of how this floor used to shine and how the sun coming in that kitchen window through the starched white curtains just gleamed on the white windowsill. Now the windowsill is blue and you can't even see it for the mess of African violets up there, and the windows have no curtains at all. It gives Stella a start. It's funny how you can be in a place for years and stop really noticing anything, and then one day suddenly you see it all, plain as day, before your face: things you haven't thought to see for years. She looks around Florrie's kitchen and notices Chip's Lego blocks all piled up in the corner, a pile of laundry in Earl's chair, the sink full of dirty dishes, a crack in the pane of the door—and then Stella's eyes travel back to the kitchen table and she sees what she must have seen when she first came in, or what she saw and didn't notice: smack in the middle of the table, on an ironstone platter, sits Florrie's weirdest cake yet.

This cake is shaped like a giant autumn leaf and it looks like a real leaf exactly, with icing that starts off red in the center and changes from flame to orange, to yellow, to gold. It's hard to tell where one color leaves off and turns into another, the way they flow together in the icing, and the icing itself seems to crinkle up, like a real leaf does, at all the edges of the cake.

"Mercy!" Stella says.

"I just made that this morning," Florrie remarks. She pushes the ironstone platter across the table so Stella can get a better look, but Stella scoots farther back in her chair. She can hear Chip coming down the stairs now, making a terrible racket, dragging something along behind him on his way.

"You want to know how I did it?" Florrie says. "I just thought it up today. What I did was, I made one big square cake, that's the middle of the leaf only you can't tell under all the icing, and a couple of little square cakes, and then I cut those all up to get the angles, see, for all the points of the leaves. Come here, honey," she says to Chip. "Let me blow your nose in this napkin. Now blow."

Stella looks away from them but there is no place for her to look in this kitchen, nothing her eye can light on without pain.

"Pretty!" Chip points at the cake. Chip is skinny, too small for his age, with thin light brown hair that sticks up on his head like straw.

"You should have seen what I made for his class," Florrie says to Stella. "It was back when they were doing their science projects about volcanos, and I made them a cake like Mount St. Helen's and took it over there and you should have seen them, they got the biggest kick out of it! Didn't you, Chip?"

"Va-ROOM!" Chip acts like a volcano. Then he falls down on the floor.

Florrie smiles down at him, then up at Stella. "Aren't you off early?" she asks.

"Well, yes, I am," Stella begins. "I certainly am. But as a matter of-fact I came over here for a special reason, Florrie, there's something I wanted to talk to you about. If you could maybe—" Stella raises her eyebrows and looks hard at Chip.

"Why don't you go over there and play some Legos?" Florrie asks him, pointing.

"No," Chip says. He starts singing again in his high little voice.

"I bet you could make a submarine," Florrie says, "like you were telling me about."

"No," Chip says, kicking the floor, but then he looks up and says he might like to go outside.

"I thought he had a cold," Stella says.

"He does. But I guess one little bike ride wouldn't make it any worse than it is already. OK," Florrie tells Chip. "Go on. But I want you back here in fifteen minutes."

Chip gives a whoop and runs out the door without a jacket; it will be a wonder if he lives to grow up at all.

"Now then." Florrie folds her hands in her lap and yawns and looks at Stella. "What is it?"

"Well, I've been thinking," Stella says, "about you living over here in this big old house with not even any real relatives to speak of, living with strangers, and how this property is zoned commercial now and we could make a pretty penny if we went ahead and sold it while the real estate market is so high—"

"This is my house," Florrie interrupts.

"Well, I know it is," Stella says, "but it's just so much for you to try to keep up, and if you sold it and moved in with Claude and me, why we could pool all our resources so to speak and none of us would ever have to worry about a thing."

"*Moved in with Claude and you?*" For some reason Florrie is grinning and then she's laughing out loud. It gives Stella a chill to see her; she knows that her suspicions are all true and Florrie's gone mental at last.

"*Moved in with Claude and you?*" Florrie keeps saying this over and over, and   145
laughing.

"Now this is serious," Stella tells her. "I don't see anything funny here at all. When I think of you over here with strangers—"

"They're not strangers," Florrie says. "Chip is my very own grandson as you very well know, and Johnnie Sue is Earl Junior's ex-wife."

"You might as well be running a boardinghouse!"

"Now there's an idea," Florrie says, and it's hard to tell from her face whether she's serious or not, the way her eyes are shining so blue and crinkling up like that at the corners. "I hadn't thought of a boardinghouse." She smiles.

"Oh Florrie!" Stella bursts out. "Don't you see? If you came to live with us   150
you wouldn't have to make these ridiculous cakes and drag them all over town."

"I like making cakes," Florrie says.

"Well, I know you do, but that's neither here nor there. The fact is, Florrie, and I might as well just tell you, the fact is you are going around here acting like a crazy old woman, whether you know it or not, and it's just real embarrassing for everybody in this family, and I'm telling you how you can stop. We can sell this house, you can come live with us. You're just a spectacle of yourself, Florrie, whether you know it or not."

"Does Claude know you came over here to tell me this?"

"Claude!" Stella bristles. "What does Claude have to do with anything?" Then Stella squints through her frosted eyelids, and drums her long red nails on the kitchen table. "Oh! I get it!" she said. "You're still jealous, aren't you? And I came over here prepared to let bygones be bygones."

"What bygones?" Florrie's eyes are bright, bright blue, and she has a deep   155
spot of color, like rouge, on each cheek. "What bygones?" she repeats.

"Well," Stella says, "I guess the dog is out of the bag now! I mean I know exactly how you feel. Don't you think for one minute I don't know. I know you are jealous of me and always have been. You are jealous of my position at Belk's and my house and you resent our place in the community, mine and Claude's, and don't try to deny it. You always have. Don't try to tell me. I know you resent how Robert and Dawn Elizabeth have turned out so well, and all of that, but mainly I know that you're still mad that you never got Claude in the first place, that Claude picked me over you."

"What?" Florrie says. "That Claude what?"

"You know what," Stella says.

Florrie sits looking at Stella for one long minute as the wind picks up again outside and rattles the kitchen window. Florrie looks at Stella with her mouth open, and then her mouth curves up and she's laughing, laughing to beat the band. "Lord, Stella!" Florrie is wiping her eyes.

Stella stands up and puts on her coat. "If that's how you feel about it," she   160
says.

"I can't move over there," Florrie finally manages to say. "It would never work out, Stella, believe me." Then she's laughing again—it's clear just how mental she is.

Some people are beyond help. So Stella says, "Well," almost to herself. "Nobody can say I didn't try." This ought to give her some satisfaction, but it does not. She stands on one side of the table and Florrie stands on the other, with that crazy cake between them.

"Who'd you make *that* for, anyway?" Stella asks, jerking her head toward it.

"Why, nobody," Florrie tells her. "Just nobody at all."

Stella shakes her head.   165

"But you can have it if you want it," Florrie says. "Go on, take it, you and Claude can have it for dinner."

"What kind is it?"

"Carrot cake." Florrie picks up the ironstone platter like she's fixing to wrap it up.

"You know I can't touch roughage." Stella sighs, leaving, but Florrie follows her out to the car still holding that cake while Chip rides by on a bike that used to be Floyd's, trailing his high wordless song out behind him in the wind, and real leaves fall all around them. Stella doesn't doubt for one minute that if Johnny Sue and Chip don't cut a piece of that cake within the next few hours, Florrie will go right out in the street and give it to the very next person who happens along. Chip puts his feet up on the handlebars, and waves both hands in the air. Stella turns her collar up against the wind: the first signs of a woman's age may be found around her eyes, on her hands, and at her throat.

Stella gets in her car and decides to drive back over to Belk's for a little   170
while, to put her new Venetian Court Colors display beneath the twinkling lights of her beautiful chandelier; while Claude, out driving his boat around and around in big slow circles at Kerr Lake, doesn't even pretend to fish but stares back at the long smooth trail of the wake on the cold blue water, with a little smile on his face as he thinks of Florrie; and Florrie stands out in the patchy grass of her front yard with the leaf cake still cradled in her bare arms, admiring the way the sunlight shines off the icing, thinking about Earl Mingo and thinking too about Earl's child off someplace in this world, that child related to her by more than blood it seems to Florrie, that child maybe squinting out at the sky right now like Earl did, through God knows what color of eyes.

Talking about the Text

1. Explore the "voice" of Stella in "Cakewalk." What are the characteristic phrases she uses? What doubts, if any, does she reveal about her perspective on life?

2. What were the advantages for Smith in using Stella's instead of Florrie's point of view?

Writing about the Text

1. Write three paragraphs from Florrie's point of view instead of Stella's, noting what adjustments you found it necessary to make.

2. In a brief essay, describe the importance Stella places on her job, and contrast her attitude with the attitude you as a reader have toward that job. How do your perceptions of Stella affect your reaction to the story?

Linking the Text to Other Texts

1. Is Florrie an artist of the everyday? Decide whether her "creativity" is comparable to the quilting in Alice Walker's "Everyday Use" (p. 424). Why or why not?
2. Being "proper" is important to Stella. Whose norms does she adopt? Can you describe a person or character you know of who is "proper" in some of the same ways as Stella? What do we think of that person or character?

Starting Point for Further Research: Lee Smith

- **Critical Essay:** Nancy Parrish. "Lee Smith." *The History of Southern Women's Literature*. Ed. Carol Perry and Mary Louise Weaks. Baton Rouge: Louisiana State University Press, 2002: 575–78.

MARY HOOD   (B. 1946)

A native of Brunswick, Georgia, Mary Hood pursued her writing while supporting herself through part-time work. Her short story collections How Far She Went *(1984) and* And Venus Is Blue *(1986) have earned her a fine reputation and prestigious awards. Familiar Heat, her first novel, was published in 1996. Hood has expressed surprise at finding herself identified and identifying as a southern writer. In her essay "On Being a Southern Writer," Hood describes how her father, a native New Yorker, and her surroundings infused her with a northern as well as southern sensibility: "My parentage has given me a duty toward both no-nonsense brevity and encompassing concatenations: the Northern preference for sifting out why in twenty-five words or less, the Southern for interminable savoring how, cherishing the chaff of irrelevancy around the essential kernel." The southerner won out, but not entirely: "When I began to write fiction, I made a conscious decision to try to sound like the Southern talkers I had heard tell such wonderful things, but every word I wrote had to pass the sternest censorship from that Northern conscience in me." In addition to writing, Hood spends much of her time teaching, having become a successful creative writing instructor at a number of colleges throughout the South. When not serving as a writer in residence, Hood lives in Jackson County, Georgia.*

How Far She Went   (1984)

They had quarreled all morning, squalled all summer about the incidentals: how tight the girl's cut-off jeans were, the "Every Inch a Woman" T-shirt, her choice of music and how loud she played it, her practiced inattention, her sullen look. Her granny wrung out the last boiled dishcloth, pinched it to the line, giving the basin a sling and a slap, the water flying out in a scalding arc onto the Queen Anne's lace by the path, never mind if it bloomed, that didn't make it worth anything except to chiggers, but the girl would cut it by the everlasting armload and cherish it in the old churn, going to that much trouble for a weed but not bending once—unbegged—to pick the nearest bean; she was sulking now. Bored. Displaced.

"And what do you think happens to a chigger if nobody ever walks by his weed?" her granny asked, heading for the house with that sidelong uneager unanswered glance, hoping for what? The surprise gift of a smile? Nothing. The woman shook her head and said it. "Nothing." The door slammed behind her. Let it.

"I hate it here!" the girl yelled then. She picked up a stick and broke it and threw the pieces—one from each hand—at the laundry drying in the noon. Missed. Missed.

Then she turned on her bare, haughty heel and set off high-shouldered into the heat, quick but not far, not far enough—no road was *that* long—only as far as she dared. At the gate, a rusty chain swinging between two lichened posts, she stopped, then backed up the raw drive to make a run at the barrier, lofting, clearing it clean, her long hair wild in the sun. Triumphant, she looked back at the house where she caught at the dark window her granny's face in its perpetual eclipse of disappointment, old at fifty. She stepped back, but the girl saw her.

"You don't know me!" the girl shouted, chin high, and ran till her ribs ached.   5

*   *   *

As she rested in the rattling shade of the willows, the little dog found her. He could be counted on. He barked all the way, and squealed when she pulled the burr from his ear. They started back to the house for lunch. By then the mailman had long come and gone in the old ruts, leaving the one letter folded now to fit the woman's apron pocket.

If bad news darkened her granny's face, the girl ignored it. Didn't talk at all, another of her distancings, her defiances. So it was as they ate that the woman summarized, "Your daddy wants you to cash in the plane ticket and buy you something. School clothes. For here."

Pale, the girl stared, defenseless only an instant before blurting out, "You're lying."

The woman had to stretch across the table to leave her handprint on that blank cheek. She said, not caring if it stung or not, "He's been planning it since he sent you here."

"I could turn this whole house over, dump it! Leave you slobbering over that   10
stinking jealous dog in the dust!" The girl trembled with the vision, with the strength it gave her. It made her laugh. "Scatter the Holy Bible like confetti and ravel the crochet into miles of stupid string! I could! I will! I won't stay here!" But she didn't move, not until her tears rose to meet her color, and then to escape the shame of minding so much she fled. Just headed away, blind. It didn't matter, this time, how far she went.

*   *   *

The woman set her thoughts against fretting over their bickering, just went on unalarmed with chores, clearing off after the uneaten meal, bringing in the laundry, scattering corn for the chickens, ladling manure tea onto the porch flowers. She listened though. She always had been a listener. It gave her a cocked look. She forgot why she had gone into the girl's empty room, that ungirlish, tenuous lodging place with its bleak order, its ready suitcases never unpacked, the narrow bed, the contested radio on the windowsill. The woman drew the cracked shade down between the radio and the August sun. There wasn't anything else to do.

It was after six when she tied on her rough oxfords and walked down the drive and dropped the gate chain and headed back to the creosoted shed where she kept her tools. She took a hoe for snakes, a rake, shears to trim the grass where it grew, and seed in her pocket to scatter where it never had grown at all. She put the tools and her gloves and the bucket in the trunk of the old Chevy, its prime and rust like an Appaloosa's spots through the chalky white finish. She left the trunk open and the tool handles sticking out. She wasn't going far.

The heat of the day had broken, but the air was thick, sultry, weighted with honeysuckle in second bloom and the Nu-Grape scent of kudzu. The maple and poplar leaves turned over, quaking, silver. There wouldn't be any rain. She told the dog to stay, but he knew a trick. He stowed away when she turned her back, leaped right into the trunk with the tools, then gave himself away with exultant barks. Hearing him, her court jester, she stopped the car and welcomed him into the front seat beside her. Then they went on. Not a mile from her gate she turned onto the blue gravel of the cemetery lane, hauled the gearshift into reverse to whoa them, and got out to take the idle walk down to her buried hopes, bending all along to rout out a handful of weeds from between the markers of old acquaintance. She stood there and read, slow. The dog whined at her hem; she picked him up and rested her chin on his head, then he wriggled and whined to run free, contrary and restless as a child.

The crows called strong and bold MOM! MOM! A trick of the ear to hear it like that. She knew it was the crows, but still she looked around. No one called her that now. She was done with that. And what was it worth anyway? It all came to this: solitary weeding. The sinful fumble of flesh, the fear, the listening for a return that never came, the shamed waiting, the unanswered prayers, the perjury on the certificate—hadn't she lain there weary of the whole lie and it only beginning? and a voice telling her, "Here's your baby, here's your girl," and the swaddled package meaning no more to her than an extra anything, something store-bought, something she could take back for a refund.

"Tie her to the fence and give her a bale of hay," she had murmured, drugged,   15
and they teased her, excused her for such a welcoming, blaming the anesthesia, but it went deeper than that; *she* knew, and the *baby* knew: there was no love in the begetting. That was the secret, unforgivable, that not another good thing could ever make up for, where all the bad had come from, like a visitation, a punishment. She knew that was why Sylvie had been wild, had gone to earth so early, and before dying had made this child in sudden wedlock, a child who would be just like her, would carry the hurting on into another generation. A matter of time. No use raising her hand. But she *had* raised her hand. Still wore on its palm the memory of the sting of the collision with the girl's cheek; had she broken her jaw? Her heart? Of course not. She said it aloud: "Takes more than that."

She went to work then, doing what she could with her old tools. She pecked the clay on Sylvie's grave, new-looking, unhealed after years. She tried again, scattering seeds from her pocket, every last possible one of them. Off in the west she could hear the pulpwood cutters sawing through another acre across the lake. Nearer, there was the racket of motorcycles laboring cross-country, insect-like, distracting.

She took her bucket to the well and hung it on the pump. She had half filled it when the bikers roared up, right down the blue gravel, straight at her. She let the bucket overflow, staring. On the back of one of the machines was the girl.

Sylvie's girl! Her bare arms wrapped around the shirtless man riding between her thighs. They were first. The second biker rode alone. She studied their strangers' faces as they circled her. They were the enemy, all of them. Laughing. The girl was laughing too, laughing like her mama did. Out in the middle of nowhere the girl had found these two men, some moth-musk about her drawing them (too soon!) to what? She shouted it: "What in God's—" They roared off without answering her, and the bucket of water tipped over, spilling its stain blood-dark on the red dust.

The dog went wild barking, leaping after them, snapping at the tires, and there was no calling him down. The bikers made a wide circuit of the church-yard, then roared straight across the graves, leaping the ditch and landing up-right on the road again, heading off toward the reservoir.

Furious, she ran to her car, past the barking dog, this time leaving him be-hind, driving after them, horn blowing nonstop, to get back what was not theirs. She drove after them knowing what they did not know, that all the roads beyond that point dead-ended. She surprised them, swinging the Impala across their path, cutting them off; let them hit it! They stopped. She got out, breathing hard, and said, when she could, "She's underage." Just that. And put out her claiming hand with an authority that made the girl's arms drop from the man's insolent waist and her legs tremble.

"I was just riding," the girl said, not looking up.   20

Behind them the sun was heading on toward down. The long shadows of the pines drifted back and forth in the same breeze that puffed the distant sails on the lake. Dead limbs creaked and clashed overhead like the antlers of locked and furious beasts.

"Sheeeut," the lone rider said. "I told you." He braced with his muddy boot and leaned out from his machine to spit. The man the girl had been riding with had the invading sort of eyes the woman had spent her lifetime bolting doors against. She met him now, face to face.

"Right there, missy," her granny said, pointing behind her to the car.

The girl slid off the motorcycle and stood halfway between her choices. She started slightly at the poosh! as he popped another top and chugged the beer in one uptilting of his head. His eyes never left the woman's. When he was through, he tossed the can high, flipping it end over end. Before it hit the ground he had his pistol out and, firing once, winged it into the lake.

"Freaking lucky shot," the other one grudged.   25

"I don't need luck," he said. He sighted down the barrel of the gun at the woman's head. "POW!" he yelled, and when she recoiled, he laughed. He swung around to the girl: he kept aiming the gun, here, there, high, low, all around. "Y'all settle it," he said, with a shrug.

The girl had to understand him then, had to know him, had to know better. But still she hesitated. He kept looking at her, then away.

"She's fifteen," her granny said. "You can go to jail."

"You can go to hell," he said.

"Probably will," her granny told him. "I'll save you a seat by the fire." She   30
took the girl by the arm and drew her to the car; she backed up, swung around, and headed out the road toward the churchyard for her tools and dog. The whole way the girl said nothing, just hunched against the far door, staring hard-eyed out at the pines going past.

The woman finished watering the seed in, and collected her tools. As she worked, she muttered, "It's your own kin buried here, you might have the decency to glance this way one time . . ." The girl was finger-tweezing her eyebrows in the side mirror. She didn't look around as the dog and the woman got in. Her granny shifted hard, sending the tools clattering in the trunk.

When they came to the main road, there were the men. Watching for them. Waiting for them. They kicked their machines into life and followed, close, bumping them, slapping the old fenders, yelling. The girl gave a wild glance around at the one by her door and said, "Gran'ma?" and as he drew his pistol, "Gran'ma!" just as the gun nosed into the open window. She frantically cranked the glass up between her and the weapon, and her granny, seeing, spat, "Fool!" She never had been one to pray for peace or rain. She stamped the accelerator right to the floor.

The motorcycles caught up. Now she braked, hard, and swerved off the road into an alley between the pines, not even wide enough for the school bus, just a fire scrape that came out a quarter mile from her own house, if she could get that far. She slewed on the pine straw, then righted, tearing along the dark tunnel through the woods. She had for the time being bested them; they were left behind. She was winning. Then she hit the wallow where the tadpoles were already five weeks old. The Chevy plowed in and stalled. When she got it cranked again, they were stuck. The tires spattered mud three feet up the near trunks as she tried to spin them out, to rock them out. Useless. "Get out and run!" she cried, but the trees were too close on the passenger side. The girl couldn't open her door. She wasted precious time having to crawl out under the steering wheel. The woman waited but the dog ran on.

They struggled through the dusky woods, their pace slowed by the thick straw and vines. Overhead, in the last light, the martins were reeling free and sure after their prey.

"Why? Why?" the girl gasped, as they lunged down the old deer trail. Behind them they could hear shots, and glass breaking as the men came to the bogged car. The woman kept on running, swatting their way clear through the shoulder-high weeds. They could see the Greer cottage, and made for it. But it was ivied-over, padlocked, the woodpile dry-rotting under its tarp, the electric meterbox empty on the pole. No help there.

The dog, excited, trotted on, yelping, his lips white-flecked. He scented the lake and headed that way, urging them on with thirsty yips. On the clay shore, treeless, deserted, at the utter limit of land, they stood defenseless, listening to the men coming on, between them and home. The woman pressed her hands to her mouth, stifling her cough. She was exhausted. She couldn't think.

"We can get under!" the girl cried suddenly, and pointed toward the Greers' dock, gap-planked, its walkway grounded on the mud. They splashed out to it, wading in, the woman grabbing up the telltale, tattletale dog in her arms. They waded out to the far end and ducked under. There was room between the foam floats for them to crouch neck-deep.

The dog wouldn't hush, even then; never had yet, and there wasn't time to teach him. When the woman realized that, she did what she had to do. She grabbed him whimpering; held him; held him under till the struggle ceased and the bubbles rose silver from his fur. They crouched there then, the two of them, submerged to the shoulders, feet unsteady on the slimed lake bed. They listened.

35

The sky went from rose to ocher to violet in the cracks over their heads. The motorcycles had stopped now. In the silence there was the glissando of locusts, the dry crunch of boots on the flinty beach, their low man-talk drifting as they prowled back and forth. One of them struck a match.

"—they in these woods we could burn 'em out."

The wind carried their voices away into the pines. Some few words eddied   40 back.

"—lippy old smartass do a little work on her knees besides praying—"

Laughter. It echoed off the deserted house. They were getting closer.

One of them strode directly out to the dock, walked on the planks over their heads. They could look up and see his boot soles. He was the one with the gun. He slapped a mosquito on his bare back and cursed. The carp, roused by the troubling of the waters, came nosing around the dock, guzzling and snorting. The girl and her granny held still, so still. The man fired his pistol into the shadows, and a wounded fish thrashed, dying. The man knelt and reached for it, chuffing out his beery breath. He belched. He pawed the lake for the dead fish, cursing as it floated out of reach. He shot it again, firing at it till it sank and the gun was empty. Cursed that too. He stood then and unzipped and relieved himself of some of the beer. They had to listen to that. To know that about him. To endure that, unprotesting.

Back and forth on shore the other one ranged, restless. He lit another cigarette. He coughed. He called. "Hey! They got away, man, that's all. Don't get your shorts in a wad. Let's go."

"Yeah." He finished. He zipped. He stumped back across the planks and   45 leaped to shore, leaving the dock tilting amid widening ripples. Underneath, they waited.

The bike cranked. The other ratcheted, ratcheted, then coughed, caught, roared. They circled, cut deep ruts, slung gravel, and went. Their roaring died away and away. Crickets resumed and a near frog bic-bic-bicked.

Under the dock, they waited a little longer to be sure. Then they ducked below the water, scraped out from under the pontoon, and came up into free air, slogging toward shore. It had seemed warm enough in the water. Now they shivered. It was almost night. One streak of light still stood reflected on the darkening lake, drew itself thinner, narrowing into a final cancellation of day. A plane winked its way west.

The girl was trembling. She ran her hands down her arms and legs, shedding water like a garment. She sighed, almost a sob. The woman held the dog in her arms; she dropped to her knees upon the random stones and murmured, private, haggard, "Oh, honey," three times, maybe all three times for the dog, maybe once for each of them. The girl waited, watching. Her granny rocked the dog like a baby, like a dead child, rocked slower and slower and was still.

"I'm sorry," the girl said then, avoiding the dog's inert, empty eye.

"It was him or you," her granny said, finally, looking up. Looking her over.   50 "Did they mess with you? With your britches? Did they?"

"No!" Then, quieter, "No, ma'am."

When the woman tried to stand up she staggered, lightheaded, clumsy with the freight of the dog. "No, ma'am," she echoed, fending off the girl's "Let me." And she said again, "It was him or you. I know that. I'm not going to rub your face in it." They saw each other as well as they could in that failing light, in any light.

The woman started toward home, saying, "Around here, we bear our own burdens." She led the way along the weedy shortcuts. The twilight bleached the dead limbs of the pines to bone. Insects sang in the thickets, silencing at their oncoming.

"We'll see about the car in the morning," the woman said. She bore her armful toward her own moth-ridden dusk-to-dawn security light with that country grace she had always had when the earth was reliably progressing underfoot. The girl walked close behind her, exactly where *she* walked, matching her pace, matching her stride, close enough to put her hand forth (if the need arose) and touch her granny's back where the faded voile was clinging damp, the merest gauze between their wounds.

Talking about the Text

1. What does the grandmother mean (p. 416, paragraph 53) when she says "we bear our own burdens"?
2. Speculate on the meaning of the story's title. Who went? The grandmother? The granddaughter?

Writing about the Text

1. Write a 1–2 page explanation of the role of setting in "How Far She Went."
2. Hood depicts the two men on motorcycles as evil characters. Determine for yourself whether they are or are not stereotypes, and write a brief essay supporting your conclusion.

Linking the Text to Other Texts

1. In "How Far She Went," there is a great deal of resignation and calm acceptance of difficulties. Examine whether there is similar resignation and bearing of burdens in two or more additional stories from this chapter. A good place to start is "A Worn Path" (p. 338), "A Shower of Gold" (p. 345), and "Sweat" (p. 318).
2. Hood is an avowed disciple of Flannery O'Connor. Describe what you see as similarities between Hood's story and one of O'Connor's (p. 359).

Starting Point for Further Research: Mary Hood

- **Critical Essay:** Joy A. Farmer. "Mary Hood and the Speed of Grace: Catching Up with Flannery O'Connor." *Studies in Short Fiction* 33 (Winter 1996): 91–99.

DOROTHY ALLISON (B. 1949)

Born in Greenville, South Carolina, to a fifteen-year-old unwed mother, Dorothy Allison grew up in great poverty and refers to her family as "redneck" or "white trash." She was sexually and physically abused by a stepfather, and observed other women and girls in her large extended family harried and abused in one way or another by their men. Her first book of poetry, The Women Who Hate Me *(1983), reflects a great deal of her personal pain. She struggled out of this milieu and now lives in California, but the South with its charms and its horrors remains very much the subject of her short story collection* Trash *(1988) and her two novels, the autobiographical* Bastard Out of Carolina *(1992) and* Cavedweller *(1998).* Bastard Out of Carolina *was her breakthrough to national fame and became a controversial television movie.*

✺ INSPIRATION WRITERS WHO INSPIRED DOROTHY ALLISON

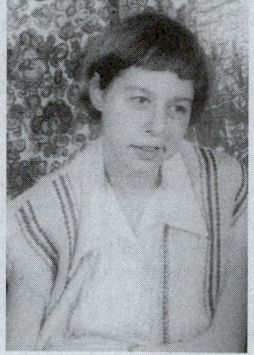

Tennessee Williams, 1955.   *Carson McCullers, 1959.*   *Toni Morrison.*

Regarding literary foremothers, Dorothy Allison particularly speaks of Toni Morrison, specifically of Morrison's first novel, *The Bluest Eye* (1970), the story of an eleven-year-old black girl whose central prayer in life is for her eyes to turn blue. Morrison's novel, Allison said in a 1995 interview, "gave me the idea that telling dangerous stories was the thing I needed to do. . . . With that base I went to the Southern classics—Flannery O'Connor, Carson McCullers, Tennessee Williams." Like O'Connor, Allison often expresses anger—at poverty, at men, at mothers who fail to protect their children, and at northerners who stereotype southerners. As Allison puts it, "I basically write about the working class in the way, I think, Flannery O'Connor wrote about the middle class." Allison is also an outspoken feminist and lesbian who frequently pays tribute to the women's movement.

I'm Working on My Charm   (1988)

I'm working on my charm.

It was one of those parties where everyone pretends to know everyone else. My borrowed silk blouse kept pulling out of my skirt, so I tried to stay with my back to the buffet and ignore the bartender who had a clear view of my problem. The woman who brushed my arm was a friend of the director of the organization where I worked, a woman who was known for her wardrobe and sudden acts of well-publicized generosity. She tossed her hair back when she saw me and laughed like an old familiar friend. "Southerners are so charming, I always say, giving their children such clever names."

She had a wine glass in one hand and a cherry tomato in the other, and she gestured with that tomato—a wide, witty, "charmed" gesture I do not remember ever seeing in the South. "I just love yours. There was a girl at school had a name like yours, two names said as one actually. Barbara-Jean, I think, or Ruth-Anne. I can't remember anymore, but she was the sweetest, most soft-spoken girl. I just loved her."

She smiled again, her eyes looking over my head at someone else. She leaned in close to me, "It's so wonderful that you can be with us, you know. Some of the people who have worked here, well . . . you know, well, we have so much to learn from you—gentility, you know, courtesy, manners, charm, all of that."

For a moment I was dizzy, overcome with the curious sensation of floating out of the top of my head. It was as if I looked down on all the other people in that crowded room, all of them sipping their wine and half of them eating cherry tomatoes. I watched the woman beside me click her teeth against the beveled edge of her wine glass and heard the sound of my mother's voice hissing in my left ear, *Yankeeeeeees!* It was all I could do not to nod.

When I was sixteen I worked counter with my mama back of a Moses Drugstore planted in the middle of a Highway 50 shopping mall. I was trying to save money to go to college, and ritually, every night, I'd pour my tips into a can on the back of my dresser. Sometimes my mama'd throw in a share of hers to encourage me, but mostly hers was spent even before we got home—at the Winn Dixie at the far end of the mall or the Maryland Fried Chicken right next to it.

Mama taught me the real skills of being a waitress—how to get an order right, get the drinks there first and the food as fast as possible so it would still be hot, and to do it all with an expression of relaxed good humor. "You don't have to smile," she explained, "but it does help." "Of course," she had to add, "don't go 'round like a grinning fool. Just smile like you know what you're doing, and never *look* like you're in a hurry." I found it difficult to keep from looking like I was in a hurry, especially when I got out of breath running from steam table to counter. Worse, moving at the speed I did, I tended to sway a little and occasionally lost control of a plate.

"Never," my mama told me, "serve food someone has seen fall to the floor. It's not only bad manners, it'll get us all in trouble. Take it in the back, clean it off, and return it to the steam table." After awhile I decided I could just run to the back, count to ten, and take it back out to the customer with an apology. Since I usually just dropped biscuits, cornbread, and baked potatoes—the kind of stuff that would roll on a plate—I figured brushing it off was sufficient. But once, in a real rush to an impatient customer, I watched a ten-ounce T-bone slip right off the plate, flip in the air, and smack the rubber floor mat. The customer's mouth flew open, and I saw my mama's eyes shoot fire. Hurriedly I picked it up by the bone and ran to the back with it. I was running water on it when Mama came in the back room.

"All right," she snapped, "you are not to run, you are not even to walk fast. And," she added, taking the meat out of my fingers and dropping it into the open waste can, "you are not, not ever to drop anything as expensive as that again." I watched smoky frost from the leaky cooler float up toward her blonde curls, and I promised her tearfully that I wouldn't.

* * *

The greater skills Mama taught me were less tangible than rules about speed and smiling. What I needed most from her had a lot to do with being as young as I was, as naive, and quick to believe the stories put across the counter by all those travelers heading North. Mama always said I was the smartest of her daughters and the most foolish. I believed everything I read in books, and most of the stuff I heard on the TV, and all of Mama's carefully framed warnings never seemed to quite slow down my capacity to take people as who they wanted me to think they were. I tried hard to be like my mama but, as she kept complaining, I was just too quick to trust—badly in need of a little practical experience.

My practical education began the day I started work. The first comment by the manager was cryptic but to the point. "Well, sixteen." Harriet smiled, looking me up and down, "At least you'll up the ante." Mama's friend, Mabel, came over and squeezed my arm. "Don't get nervous, young one. We'll keep moving you around. You'll never be left alone."

* * *

Mabel's voice was reassuring even if her words weren't, and I worked her station first. A family of four children, parents, and a grandmother took her biggest table. She took their order with a wide smile, but as she passed me going down to the ice drawer, her teeth were point on point. "Fifty cents," she snapped, and went on. Helping her clean the table thirty-five minutes later I watched her pick up two lone quarters and repeat "fifty cents," this time in a mournfully conclusive tone.

It was a game all the waitresses played. There was a butter bowl on the back counter where the difference was kept, the difference between what you guessed and what you got. No one had to play, but most of the women did. The rules were simple. You had to make your guess at the tip *before* the order was taken. Some of the women would cheat a little, bringing the menus with the water glasses and saying, "I want ya'll to just look this over carefully. We're serving one fine lunch today." Two lines of conversation and most of them could walk away with a guess within five cents.

However much the guess was off went into the bowl. If you said fifty cents and got seventy-five cents, then twenty-five cents went to the bowl. Even if you said seventy-five cents and got fifty cents instead, you had to throw in that quarter—guessing high was as bad as guessing short. "We used to just count the short guesses," Mabel explained, "but this makes it more interesting."

Once Mabel was sure she'd get a dollar and got stiffed instead. She was so 15 mad she counted out that dollar in nickels and pennies, and poured it into the bowl from a foot in the air. It made a very satisfying angry noise, and when those people came back a few weeks later no one wanted to serve them. Mama stood back by the pharmacy sign smoking her Pall Mall cigarette and whispered in my direction, "Yankees." I was sure I knew just what she meant.

At the end of each week, the women playing split the butter bowl evenly.

* * *

Mama said I wasn't that good a waitress, but I made up for it in eagerness. Mabel said I made up for it in "tail." "Those salesmen sure do like how you run back to that steam table," she said with a laugh, but she didn't say it where Mama could hear. Mama said it was how I smiled.

"You got a heartbreaker's smile," she told me. "You make them think of when they were young." Behind her back, Mabel gave me her own smile, and a long slow shake of her head.

Whatever it was, by the end of the first week I'd earned four dollars more in tips than my mama. It was almost embarrassing. But then they turned over the butter bowl and divided it evenly between everyone but me. I stared and Mama explained. "Another week and you can start adding to the pot. Then you'll get a share. For now just write down two dollars on Mr. Aubrey's form."

"But I made a lot more than that," I told her.   20

"Honey, the tax people don't need to know that." Her voice was patient. "Then when you're in the pot, just report your share. That way we all report the same amount. They expect that."

"Yeah, they don't know nothing about initiative," Mabel added, rolling her hips in illustration of her point. It made her heavy bosom move dramatically, and I remembered times I'd seen her do that at the counter. It made me feel even more embarrassed and angry.

When we were alone I asked Mama if she didn't think Mr. Aubrey knew that everyone's reports on their tips were faked.

"He doesn't say what he knows," she replied, "and I don't imagine he's got a reason to care."

I dropped the subject and started the next week guessing on my tips.   25

Salesmen and truckers were always a high guess. Women who came with a group were low, while women alone were usually a fair twenty-five cents on a light lunch—if you were polite and brought them their coffee first. It was 1966, after all, and a hamburger cost sixty-five cents. Tourists were more difficult. I learned that noisy kids meant a small tip, which seemed the highest injustice. Maybe it was a kind of defensive arrogance that made the parents of those kids leave so little, as if they were saying, "Just because little Kevin gave you a headache and poured ketchup on the floor doesn't mean I owe you anything."

Early morning tourists who asked first for tomato juice, lemon, and coffee were a bonus. They were almost surely leaving the Jamaica Inn just up the road, which had a terrible restaurant but served the strongest drinks in the county. If you talked softly you never got less than a dollar, and sometimes for nothing more than juice, coffee, and aspirin.

*   *   *

I picked it up. In three weeks I started to really catch on and started making sucker bets like the old man who ordered egg salad. Before I even carried the water glass over, I snapped out my counter rag, turned all the way around, and said, "five." Then as I turned to the stove and the rack of menus, I mouthed, "dollars."

Mama frowned while Mabel rolled her shoulders and said, "An't we growing up fast!"

I just smiled my heartbreaker's smile and got the man his sandwich. When   30 he left I snapped that five dollar bill loudly five times before I put it in my apron pocket. "My mama didn't raise no fool," I told the other women, who laughed and slapped my behind like they were glad to see me cutting up.

But Mama took me with her on her break. We walked up toward the Winn Dixie where she could get her cigarettes cheaper than in the drugstore.

"How'd you know?" she asked.

" 'Cause that's what he always leaves," I told her.

"What do you mean *always?*"

"Every Thursday evening when I close up." I said it knowing she was going   35 to be angry.

"He leaves you a five dollar bill every Thursday night!" Her voice sounded strange, not angry exactly but not at all pleased either.

"Always," I said, and I added, "and he pretty much always has egg salad."

Mama stopped to light her last cigarette. Then she just stood there for a moment, breathing deeply around the Pall Mall and watching me while my face got redder and redder.

"You think you can get along without it?" she asked finally.

"Why?" I asked her. "I don't think he's going to stop."

40

"Because," she said, dropping the cigarette and walking on, "you're not working any more Thursday nights."

* * *

On Sundays the counter didn't open until after church at one o'clock. But at one sharp, we started serving those big gravy lunches and went right on till four. People would come in prepared to sit and eat big—coffee, salad, country fried steak with potatoes and gravy, or ham with red-eye gravy and carrots and peas. You'd also get a side of hog's head biscuits and a choice of three pies for dessert.

Tips were as choice as the pies, but Sunday had its trials. Too often, some tight-browed couple would come in at two o'clock and order breakfast—fried eggs and hash browns. When you told them we didn't serve breakfast on Sundays, they'd get angry.

"Look girl," they might say, "just bring me some of that ham you're serving those people, only bring me eggs with it. You can do that," and the contempt in their voices clearly added, "even you."

It would make me mad as sin. "Sir, we don't cook on the grill on Sundays. 45 We only have what's on the Sunday menu. When you make up your mind, let me know."

"Tourists," I'd mutter to Mama.

"No, *Yankees*," she'd say, and Mabel would nod.

Then she might go over with an offer of boiled eggs, that ham, and a biscuit. She'd talk nice, drawling like she never did with me or friends, while she moved slower than you'd think a wide-awake person could. "Uh huh," she'd say, and "shore-nuf," and offer them honey for their biscuits or tell them how red-eye gravy is made, or talk about how sorry it is that we don't serve grits on Sunday. That couple would grin wide and start slowing their words down, while the regulars would choke on their coffee. Mama never bet on the tip, just put it all into the pot, and it was usually enough to provoke a round of applause after the couple was safely out the door.

Mama said nothing about it except the first time when she told me, "Yankees eat boiled eggs for breakfast," which may not sound like much, but had the force of a powerful insult. It was a fact that the only people we knew who ate boiled eggs in the morning were those stray tourists and people on the TV set who we therefore assumed had to be Yankees.

Yankees ate boiled eggs, laughed at grits but ate them in big helpings, and 50 had plenty of money to leave outrageous tips but might leave nothing for no reason that I could figure out. It wasn't the accent that marked Yankees. They talked different, but all kinds of different. There seemed to be a great many varieties of them, not just Northerners, but Westerners, Canadians, Black people who talked oddly enough to show they were foreign, and occasionally strangers who didn't even speak English. Some were friendly, some deliberately nasty. All of them were Yankees, strangers, unpredictable people with an enraging attitude of superiority who would say the rudest things as if they didn't know what an insult was.

"They're the ones the world was made for," Harriet told me late one night. "You and me, your mama, all of us, we just hold a place in the landscape for them. Far as they're concerned, once we're out of sight we just disappear."

Mabel plain hated them. Yankees didn't even look when she rolled her soft wide hips. "Son of a bitch," she'd say when some fish-eyed, clipped-tongue stranger would look right through her and leave her less than fifteen cents. "He must think we get fat on the honey of his smile." Which was even funnier when you'd seen that the man hadn't smiled at all.

"But give me an inch of edge and I can handle them," she'd tell me. "Sweets, you just stretch that drawl. Talk like you're from Mississippi, and they'll eat it up. For some reason, Yankees got strange sentimental notions about Mississippi."

"They're strange about other things too," Mama would throw in. "They think they can ask you personal questions just 'cause you served them a cup of coffee." Some salesman once asked her where she got her hose with the black thread sewed up the back and Mama hadn't forgiven him yet.

But the thing everyone told me and told me again was that you just couldn't   55
trust yourself with them. Nobody bet on Yankee tips, they might leave anything. Once someone even left a New York City subway token. Mama thought it a curiosity but not the equivalent of real money. Another one ordered one cup of coffee to go and twenty packs of sugar.

"They made 'road-liquor' out of it," Mabel said. "Just add an ounce of vodka and set it down by the engine exhaust for a month or so. It'll cook up into a bitter poison that'll knock you cross-eyed."

It sounded dangerous to me, but Mabel didn't think so. "Not that I would drink it," she'd say, "but I wouldn't fault a man who did."

They stole napkins, not one or two but a boxful at a time. Before we switched to sugar packets, they'd come in, unfold two or three napkins, open them like diapers, and fill them up with sugar before they left. Then they might take the knife and spoon to go with it. Once I watched a man take out a stack of napkins I was sure he was going to walk off with. But instead he sat there for thirty minutes making notes on them, then balled them all up and threw them away when he left.

My mama was scandalized by that. "And right over there on the shelf is a notebook selling for ten cents. What's wrong with these people!"

"They're living in the movies," Mabel whispered, looking back toward the   60
counter.

"Yeah, Bette Davis movies," I added.

"I don't know about the movies." Harriet put her hand on Mama's shoulder. "But they don't live in the real world with the rest of us."

"No," Mama said, "they don't."

* * *

I take a bite of cherry tomato and hear Mama's voice again. *No*, she says.

"No," I say. I tuck my blouse into my skirt and shift in my shoes. If I close my   65
eyes, I can see Mabel's brightly rouged cheekbones, Harriet's pitted skin, and my

mama's shadowed brown eyes. When I go home tonight I'll write her about this party and imagine how she'll laugh about it all. The woman who was talking to me has gone off across the room to the other bar. People are giving up nibbling and going on to more serious eating. One of the men I work with every day comes over with a full plate and a wide grin.

"Boy," he drawls around a bite of the cornbread I contributed to the buffet, "I bet you sure can cook."

"Bet on it," I say, with my Mississippi accent. I swallow the rest of a cherry tomato and give him my heartbreaker's smile.

Talking about the Text

1. How true does this story seem to workplaces you know about, either from personal experience or from TV, film, or stories? What similarities and differences did you note?
2. What do you think of the morality of the narrator's behavior? Ask others if they agree with you.

Writing about the Text

1. Create a dialogue in which the narrator of Allison's story attempts to "charm" one more customer.
2. Describe the power dynamics at work between the waitresses in Allison's story.

Linking the Text to Other Texts

1. Describe situations similar to the one in "I'm Working on My Charm" in which a server attempts to manipulate customers for additional money. How does it work? What does the server feel?
2. Connect "I'm Working on My Charm" to John Updike's "A & P" (p. 58), examining the attitude toward the public and the degree of the narrator's self-knowledge.

Starting Points for Further Research: Dorothy Allison

- **Interview:** Laura Miller. "The *Salon* Interview: Dorothy Allison." March 31, 1988. *Salon.com*. http://www.salon.com/books/int/1998/03/cov_si_31intb.html.
- **Article:** David L. Ulin. "Dorothy Allison's Past Still Shapes Her Novels." *Los Angeles Times*, April 24, 1988, E1.

ALICE WALKER   (B. 1944)

The youngest of eight children, Alice Walker was born to sharecroppers in Eatonton, Georgia. She attended Sarah Lawrence College and became an activist in racial and gender causes. As a young writer in training, Walker very much admired the work of Flannery O'Connor and Eudora Welty. It was only later, in Margaret Walker's class on African American writers at Jackson State College in Mississippi, that Walker came to know the work of Zora Neale Hurston. Since that time she has become a leading advocate of Hurston's writings. Much of Walker's own work builds on her travels in Africa and her experiences in the American civil rights movement.

Walker first became well known for the novel The Color Purple *(1982), which won the Pulitzer Prize and was made into a movie by Steven Spielberg. Her other novels include* Meridian *(1976),* The Temple of My Familiar *(1989),* By the Light of My Father's Smile *(1998), and* Now Is the Time to Open Your Heart *(2004). She has published collections of short stories and books of essays, including* In Search of Our Mothers' Gardens *(1983), in which she introduced the term "womanist prose," which she defined as the writing of African American feminists. Additional essay collections include* Living by the Word *(1988) and* Anything We Love Can Be Saved *(1997). Southern by birth and sensibility, Walker now lives in California but continues to write about herself as an African American southern woman.*

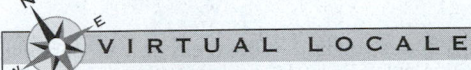

VIRTUAL LOCALE

Mississippi writer Margaret Walker.

Alice Walker and Other "Voices of Mississippi."
As a Mississippi writer, Alice Walker follows a tradition of great Mississippi writers such as William Faulkner, Walker Percy, Tennessee Williams, and especially Margaret Walker and Eudora Welty, two writers who have directly inspired her. The PBS website "Voices of Mississippi," part of a larger site on the work and life of Eudora Welty, offers an interactive state map locating the home of Mississippi's greatest writers, with their comments on being southern writers and excerpts from their work. You can locate this interactive project at *http://www.pbs.org/wgbh/masterpiece/americancollection/ponder/voices.html.*

Everyday Use   (1973)

for your grandmama

I will wait for her in the yard that Maggie and I made so clean and wavy yesterday afternoon. A yard like this is more comfortable than most people know. It is not just a yard. It is like an extended living room. When the hard clay is swept clean as a floor and the fine sand around the edges lined with tiny, irregular grooves, anyone can come and sit and look up into the elm tree and wait for the breezes that never come inside the house.

Maggie will be nervous until after her sister goes: she will stand hopelessly in corners, homely and ashamed of the burn scars down her arms and legs, eying her sister with a mixture of envy and awe. She thinks her sister has held life always in the palm of one hand, that "no" is a word the world never learned to say to her.

* * *

You've no doubt seen those TV shows where the child who has "made it" is confronted, as a surprise, by her own mother and father, tottering in weakly from backstage. (A pleasant surprise, of course: What would they do if parent and child came on the show only to curse out and insult each other?) On TV mother and child embrace and smile into each other's faces. Sometimes the mother and father weep, the child wraps them in her arms and leans across the table to tell how she would not have made it without their help. I have seen these programs.

Sometimes I dream a dream in which Dee and I are suddenly brought together on a TV program of this sort. Out of a dark and soft-seated limousine I am ushered into a bright room filled with many people. There I meet a smiling, gray, sporty man like Johnny Carson who shakes my hand and tells me what a fine girl I have. Then we are on the stage and Dee is embracing me with tears in her eyes. She pins on my dress a large orchid, even though she has told me once that she thinks orchids are tacky flowers.

In real life I am a large, big-boned woman with rough, man-working hands. 5 In the winter I wear flannel nightgowns to bed and overalls during the day. I can kill and clean a hog as mercilessly as a man. My fat keeps me hot in zero weather. I can work outside all day, breaking ice to get water for washing; I can eat pork liver cooked over the open fire minutes after it comes steaming from the hog. One winter I knocked a bull calf straight in the brain between the eyes with a sledge hammer and had the meat hung up to chill before nightfall. But of course all this does not show on television. I am the way my daughter would want me to be: a hundred pounds lighter, my skin like an uncooked barley pancake. My hair glistens in the hot bright lights. Johnny Carson has much to do to keep up with my quick and witty tongue.

But that is a mistake. I know even before I wake up. Who ever knew a Johnson with a quick tongue? Who can even imagine me looking a strange white man in the eye? It seems to me I have talked to them always with one foot raised in flight, with my head turned in whichever way is farthest from them. Dee, though. She would always look anyone in the eye. Hesitation was no part of her nature.

* * *

"How do I look, Mama?" Maggie says, showing just enough of her thin body enveloped in pink skirt and red blouse for me to know she's there, almost hidden by the door.

"Come out into the yard," I say.

Have you ever seen a lame animal, perhaps a dog run over by some careless person rich enough to own a car, sidle up to someone who is ignorant enough to be kind to him? That is the way my Maggie walks. She has been like this, chin on chest, eyes on ground, feet in shuffle, ever since the fire that burned the other house to the ground.

Dee is lighter than Maggie, with nicer hair and a fuller figure. She's a woman 10 now, though sometimes I forget. How long ago was it that the other house burned? Ten, twelve years? Sometimes I can still hear the flames and feel Maggie's arms sticking to me, her hair smoking and her dress falling off her in little black papery flakes. Her eyes seemed stretched open, blazed open by the flames reflected in them. And Dee. I see her standing off under the sweet gum tree she used to dig gum out of; a look of concentration on her face as she watched the last dingy gray board of the house fall in toward the red-hot brick chimney. Why don't you do a dance around the ashes? I'd wanted to ask her. She had hated the house that much.

I used to think she hated Maggie, too. But that was before we raised the money, the church and me, to send her to Augusta to school. She used to read to us without pity; forcing words, lies, other folks' habits, whole lives upon us two, sitting trapped and ignorant underneath her voice. She washed us in a river of make-believe, burned us with a lot of knowledge we didn't necessarily need to know. Pressed us to her with the serious way she read, to shove us away at just the moment, like dimwits, we seemed about to understand.

Dee wanted nice things. A yellow organdy dress to wear to her graduation from high school; black pumps to match a green suit she'd made from an old suit somebody gave me. She was determined to stare down any disaster in her efforts. Her eyelids would not flicker for minutes at a time. Often I fought off the temptation to shake her. At sixteen she had a style of her own: and knew what style was.

* * *

I never had an education myself. After second grade the school was closed down. Don't ask me why: in 1927 colored asked fewer questions than they do now. Sometimes Maggie reads to me. She stumbles along good-naturedly but can't see well. She knows she is not bright. Like good looks and money, quickness passed her by. She will marry John Thomas (who has mossy teeth in an earnest face) and then I'll be free to sit here and I guess just sing church songs to myself. Although I never was a good singer. Never could carry a tune. I was always better at a man's job. I used to love to milk till I was hooked in the side in '49. Cows are soothing and slow and don't bother you, unless you try to milk them the wrong way.

I have deliberately turned my back on the house. It is three rooms, just like the one that burned, except the roof is tin; they don't make shingle roofs any more. There are no real windows, just some holes cut in the sides, like the portholes in a ship, but not round and not square, with rawhide holding the shutters up on the outside. This house is in a pasture, too, like the other one. No doubt when Dee sees it she will want to tear it down. She wrote me once that no matter where we "choose" to live, she will manage to come see us. But she will never bring her friends. Maggie and I thought about this and Maggie asked me, "Mama, when did Dee ever *have* any friends?"

She had a few. Furtive boys in pink shirts hanging about on washday after 15
school. Nervous girls who never laughed. Impressed with her they worshiped the well-turned phrase, the cute shape, the scalding humor that erupted like bubbles in lye. She read to them.

When she was courting Jimmy T she didn't have much time to pay to us, but turned all her faultfinding power on him. He *flew* to marry a cheap city girl from a family of ignorant flashy people. She hardly had time to recompose herself.

* * *

When she comes I will meet—but there they are!

Maggie attempts to make a dash for the house, in her shuffling way, but I stay her with my hand. "Come back here," I say. And she stops and tries to dig a well in the sand with her toe.

It is hard to see them clearly through the strong sun. But even the first glimpse of leg out of the car tells me it is Dee. Her feet were always neat-looking, as if God himself had shaped them with a certain style. From the other side of the car comes a short, stocky man. Hair is all over his head a foot long and hanging from his chin like a kinky mule tail. I hear Maggie suck in her breath. "Uhnnnh," is what it sounds like. Like when you see the wriggling end of a snake just in front of your foot on the road. "Uhnnnh."

Dee next. A dress down to the ground, in this hot weather. A dress so loud it   20
hurts my eyes. There are yellows and oranges enough to throw back the light of the sun. I feel my whole face warming from the heat waves it throws out. Earrings gold, too, and hanging down to her shoulders. Bracelets dangling and making noises when she moves her arm up to shake the folds of the dress out of her armpits. The dress is loose and flows, and as she walks closer, I like it. I hear Maggie go "Uhnnnh" again. It is her sister's hair. It stands straight up like the wool on a sheep. It is black as night and around the edges are two long pigtails that rope about like small lizards disappearing behind her ears.

"Wa-su-zo-Tean-o!" she says, coming on in that gliding way the dress makes her move. The short stocky fellow with the hair to his navel is all grinning and he follows up with "Asalamalakim, my mother and sister!" He moves to hug Maggie but she falls back, right up against the back of my chair. I feel her trembling there and when I look up I see the perspiration falling off her chin.

"Don't get up," says Dee. Since I am stout it takes something of a push. You can see me trying to move a second or two before I make it. She turns, showing white heels through her sandals, and goes back to the car. Out she peeks next with a Polaroid. She stoops down quickly and lines up picture after picture of me sitting there in front of the house with Maggie cowering behind me. She never takes a shot without making sure the house is included. When a cow comes nibbling around the edge of the yard she snaps it and me and Maggie *and* the house. Then she puts the Polaroid in the back seat of the car, and comes up and kisses me on the forehead.

Meanwhile Asalamalakim is going through motions with Maggie's hand. Maggie's hand is as limp as a fish, and probably as cold, despite the sweat, and she keeps trying to pull it back. It looks like Asalamalakim wants to shake hands but wants to do it fancy. Or maybe he don't know how people shake hands. Anyhow, he soon gives up on Maggie.

"Well," I say. "Dee."

"No, Mama," she says. "Not 'Dee,' Wangero Leewanika Kemanjo!"   25

"What happened to 'Dee'?" I wanted to know.

"She's dead," Wangero said. "I couldn't bear it any longer, being named after the people who oppress me."

"You know as well as me you was named after your aunt Dicie," I said. Dicie is my sister. She named Dee. We called her "Big Dee" after Dee was born.

"But who was *she* named after?" asked Wangero.

"I guess after Grandma Dee," I said.   30

"And who was she named after?" asked Wangero.

"Her mother," I said, and saw Wangero was getting tired. "That's about as far back as I can trace it," I said. Though, in fact, I probably could have carried it back beyond the Civil War through the branches.

"Well," said Asalamalakim, "there you are."

"Uhnnnh," I heard Maggie say.

"There I was not," I said, "before 'Dicie' cropped up in our family, so why   35
should I try to trace it that far back?"

He just stood there grinning, looking down on me like somebody inspecting a Model A car. Every once in a while he and Wangero sent eye signals over my head.

"How do you pronounce this name?" I asked.

"You don't have to call me by it if you don't want to," said Wangero.

"Why shouldn't I?" I asked. "If that's what you want us to call you, we'll call you."

"I know it might sound awkward at first," said Wangero.   40

"I'll get used to it," I said. "Ream it out again."

Well, soon we got the name out of the way. Asalamalakim had a name twice as long and three times as hard. After I tripped over it two or three times he told me to just call him Hakim-a-barber. I wanted to ask him was he a barber, but I didn't really think he was, so I didn't ask.

"You must belong to those beef-cattle peoples down the road," I said. They said "Asalamalakim" when they met you, too, but they didn't shake hands. Always too busy: feeding the cattle, fixing the fences, putting up salt-lick shelters, throwing down hay. When the white folks poisoned some of the herd the men stayed all night with rifles in their hands. I walked a mile and a half just to see the sight.

Hakim-a-barber said, "I accept some of their doctrines, but farming and raising cattle is not my style." (They didn't tell me, and I didn't ask, whether Wangero (Dee) had really gone and married him.)

We sat down to eat and right away he said he didn't eat collards and pork was unclean. Wangero, though, went on through the chitlins and corn bread, the greens and everything else. She talked a blue streak over the sweet potatoes. Everything delighted her. Even the fact that we still used the benches her daddy made for the table when we couldn't afford to buy chairs.   45

"Oh, Mama!" she cried. Then turned to Hakim-a-barber. "I never knew how lovely these benches are. You can feel the rump prints," she said, running her hands underneath her and along the bench. Then she gave a sigh and her hand closed over Grandma Dee's butter dish. "That's it!" she said. "I knew there was something I wanted to ask you if I could have." She jumped up from the table and went over in the corner where the churn stood, the milk in it clabber by now. She looked at the churn and looked at it.

"This churn top is what I need," she said. "Didn't Uncle Buddy whittle it out of a tree you all used to have?"

"Yes," I said.

"Uh huh," she said happily. "And I want the dasher, too."

"Uncle Buddy whittle that, too?" asked the barber.   50

Dee (Wangero) looked up at me.

"Aunt Dee's first husband whittled the dash," said Maggie so low you almost couldn't hear her. "His name was Henry, but they called him Stash."

"Maggie's brain is like an elephant's," Wangero said, laughing. "I can use the churn top as a centerpiece for the alcove table," she said, sliding a plate over the churn, "and I'll think of something artistic to do with the dasher."

When she finished wrapping the dasher the handle stuck out. I took it for a moment in my hands. You didn't even have to look close to see where hands pushing the dasher up and down to make butter had left a kind of sink in the wood. In fact, there were a lot of small sinks; you could see where thumbs and fingers had sunk into the wood. It was beautiful light yellow wood, from a tree that grew in the yard where Big Dee and Stash had lived.

After dinner Dee (Wangero) went to the trunk at the foot of my bed and started rifling through it. Maggie hung back in the kitchen over the dishpan. Out came Wangero with two quilts. They had been pieced by Grandma Dee and then Big Dee and me had hung them on the quilt frames on the front porch and quilted them. One was in the Lone Star pattern. The other was Walk Around the Mountain. In both of them were scraps of dresses Grandma Dee had worn fifty and more years ago. Bits and pieces of Grandpa Jarrell's Paisley shirts. And one teeny faded blue piece, about the size of a penny matchbox, that was from Great Grandpa Ezra's uniform that he wore in the Civil War.

"Mama," Wangero said sweet as a bird. "Can I have these old quilts?"

I heard something fall in the kitchen, and a minute later the kitchen door slammed.

"Why don't you take one or two of the others?" I asked. "These old things was just done by me and Big Dee from some tops your grandma pieced before she died."

"No," said Wangero. "I don't want those. They are stitched around the borders by machine."

"That'll make them last better," I said.

"That's not the point," said Wangero. "These are all pieces of dresses Grandma used to wear. She did all this stitching by hand. Imagine!" She held the quilts securely in her arms, stroking them.

"Some of the pieces, like those lavender ones, come from old clothes her mother handed down to her," I said, moving up to touch the quilts. Dee (Wangero) moved back just enough so that I couldn't reach the quilts. They already belonged to her.

"Imagine!" she breathed again, clutching them closely to her bosom.

"The truth is," I said, "I promised to give them quilts to Maggie, for when she marries John Thomas."

She gasped like a bee had stung her.

"Maggie can't appreciate these quilts!" she said. "She'd probably be backward enough to put them to everyday use."

"I reckon she would," I said. "God knows I been saving 'em for long enough with nobody using 'em. I hope she will!" I didn't want to bring up how I had offered Dee (Wangero) a quilt when she went away to college. Then she had told me they were old-fashioned, out of style.

"But they're *priceless*!" she was saying now, furiously; for she has a temper. "Maggie would put them on the bed and in five years they'd be in rags. Less than that!"

"She can always make some more," I said. "Maggie knows how to quilt."

Dee (Wangero) looked at me with hatred. "You just will not understand. The point is these quilts, *these* quilts!"

"Well," I said, stumped. "What would *you* do with them?"

"Hang them," she said. As if that was the only thing you *could* do with quilts.

Maggie by now was standing in the door. I could almost hear the sound her feet made as they scraped over each other.

"She can have them, Mama," she said, like somebody used to never winning anything, or having anything reserved for her. "I can 'member Grandma Dee without the quilts."

I looked at her hard. She had filled her bottom lip with checkerberry snuff   75 and it gave her face a kind of dopey, hangdog look. It was Grandma Dee and Big Dee who taught her how to quilt herself. She stood there with her scarred hands hidden in the folds of her skirt. She looked at her sister with something like fear but she wasn't mad at her. This was Maggie's portion. This was the way she knew God to work.

When I looked at her like that something hit me in the top of my head and ran down to the soles of my feet. Just like when I'm in church and the spirit of God touches me and I get happy and shout. I did something I never had done before: hugged Maggie to me, then dragged her on into the room, snatched the quilts out of Miss Wangero's hands and dumped them into Maggie's lap. Maggie just sat there on my bed with her mouth open.

"Take one or two of the others," I said to Dee.

But she turned without a word and went out to Hakim-a-barber.

"You just don't understand," she said, as Maggie and I came out to the car.

"What don't I understand?" I wanted to know.   80

"Your heritage," she said. And then she turned to Maggie, kissed her, and said, "You ought to try to make something of yourself, too, Maggie. It's really a new day for us. But from the way you and Mama still live you'd never know it."

She put on some sunglasses that hid everything above the tip of her nose and her chin.

Maggie smiled; maybe at the sunglasses. But a real smile, not scared. After we watched the car dust settle I asked Maggie to bring me a dip of snuff. And then the two of us sat there just enjoying, until it was time to go in the house and go to bed.

Talking about the Text

1. The narrator moves back and forth between talking about herself and telling about Maggie and Dee. How does this affect the story?
2. What do you think Walker means by the dedication, "for your grandmamma"? Why do you think she phrases it that way?

Writing about the Text

1. In a brief essay, describe the ways in which Walker's narrator is reliable or unreliable, supporting your conclusions with details from the text.
2. Write about an activity or artifact that, like quilts, may seem ephemeral or unimportant or unstylish to many but is very valuable—and revealing—to those with the right kind of attitude or knowledge.
3. Describe and analyze the symbolic meaning of the quilts to each of the family members. In other words, how do Dee, Maggie, and Mama differ in their respective views and valuation of the quilts?

Linking the Text to Other Texts

1. "Everyday Use" revolves in part around the question of who is entitled to the "heirlooms" of the family, and in a larger way, who "owns" the African American heritage. In a somewhat different form, this is the issue in *A Raisin in the Sun* (p.

1791) and *The Piano Lesson* (p. 1918). Compare the "answers" to this ownership issue, using "Everyday Use" and one or both plays.

2. Research how Alice Walker "discovered" Zora Neale Hurston and put her back in the mainstream of American writers. What did it take? How did she go about it? (A good place to start is "Looking for Zora," an essay in Walker's *In Search of Our Mothers' Gardens*.)

Starting Points for Further Research: Alice Walker

- **Critical Essay:** Jae-Hyuk Yeo. "Alice Walker: Community, Quilting, and Sewing." *Studies in Modern Fiction* 8 (2002): 11–35.
- **Interview:** Howard Zinn. "Howard Zinn Talks to Alice Walker." *Brick* 53 (1996): 14–21.

✂ COMMENTARY

Contemporary Southern Women Writers Speak

On the South

Lee Smith, from a 1993 interview in Southwest Review:

My husband . . . is fascinated that Southerners read Southern novels so much and he can't quite figure it out because you don't have people in California wanting to read about people in California, you know—or Midwesterners wanting to read all about the Midwest. It's a Southern phenomenon and I think it has to do with a kind of self-canonization that Southerners are into anyway. They love to recognize themselves in their work. They love to get *Southern Living* magazine and see other people like themselves out there having hors d'oeuvres in their green pants on their patio. They love to see themselves depicted. John Shelton Reed has called them South-Americans, like Polish Americans, or Italian Americans, a real ethnic sub-group. One of the things is they have institutions that perpetuate their myth . . . .

I think a lot of people in the Northeast and elsewhere in this country just simply don't want to read Southern writing because so much of it is cliché and is about the same, you know, "dead mules" and "Mommy"—and so they have a notion that it's not something they read. I mean it's very interesting, . . . for instance, the difference in the way Eudora Welty is viewed in all Southern universities and then you go to, say, Toronto, and nobody's heard of Eudora Welty. Southern writing is still kind of a regional phenomenon and these books are just not treated nearly as seriously, I think, outside the South.

Lee Smith, from Jeanne McDonald's 1997 article "Lee Smith at Home in Appalachia" in Poets and Writers Magazine:

"The way Southerners tell a story is really specific to the South," Smith says. "It's a whole narrative strategy, it's an approach. Every kind of information is imparted in the form of a story." Ask for direction in the South? She laughs. "It's not just *turn left*, It's *I remember the time my cousin went up there and got bit by a mad dog*. It's a whole different approach to interactions between people and to transmitting information."

On Race and Feminism

Alice Walker, explaining her use of the term "womanist" (from a New York Times *interview, January 8, 1984):*

I just like to have words that describe things correctly. Now to me, 'black feminist' does not do that. I need a word that is organic, that really comes out of the culture, that really expresses the spirit that we see in black women. And it's just . . . womanish. You know, the posture with the hand on the hip, 'Honey, don't you get in my way.' . . . one of the problems with white feminism is that it is not a tradition that teaches white women that they are capable. Whereas my tradition assumes I'm capable. I have a tradition of people not letting me get the skills, but I have cleared fields, I have lifted whatever, I have done it. It ain't not a tradition of wondering whether or not I could do it because I'm a woman. . . . Part of our tradition as black women is that we are universalists. Black children, yellow children, red children, brown children, that is the black woman's normal, day-to-day relationship. In my family alone, we are about four different colors. When a black woman looks at the world, it is so different . . . when I look at the people in Iran they look like kinfolk. When I look at the people in Cuba, they look like my uncles and nieces.

On the Short Story

Lee Smith, from a 1985 interview, published in Southern Quarterly, *1990:*

The short story is my favorite form. I love it. It's very hard to get any of them published, and if you do you only make $30.00.

Lee Smith, from a 1987 interview with William J. Walsh:

I like the short stories better than anything else, but it's just really hard to write short stories. For one thing, you have to put as much energy into them as you do a novel. I like writing short stories better than anything else, but they're hard to place, they're hard to sell. Mine are particularly hard to sell, because they're not really arty, they're not really literary and there's nowhere they can go. I like to write about domestic things, like parents and children and families, and so that makes them not literary enough for many places. But, yet, they're not pabulum, so they can't be published in the *Ladies' Home Journal* or other places that publish schlock. They're not sophisticated enough for *The New Yorker*, so they fall in between. I like to write short stories, but if I can get an advance on a novel, I'll write one. The stories are very iffy.

On Women as Writers

Dorothy Allison, from a 1995 interview:

A lot of women are storytellers, but we never make the transition to becoming a writer. It is easy to be an entertainer as a woman. It is easy to tell stories to charm people. But mostly we believe our stories aren't worth anything, that our stories aren't important, and that if they are important, they're dangerous, and therefore too dangerous to tell anyone. The only way I ever began to write was because there was a woman's movement. If there had not been a women's liberation movement in the early 70's, I would not only have not started writing. I would not be alive. Because the women's movement was the place that told me my life was not small. That I was not contemptible. That women's lives are not contemptible. That I was in fact important. There had not been anything like that before.

Alice Walker on discovering Zora Neale Hurston's work while doing research (from The Progressive, *July 1, 1995):*

When I found Zora Neale Hurston, it was like getting kicked in the butt. It was a voice—the weird thing was that it was a voice that I heard in my head. That I was familiar with. The speech, the rhythms of my family, the kind of language that I grew up with resounded for me in the books written by those women. It didn't read to me black. It read to me working class.

VIDEO LOCALE

Welty and O'Connor Stories on Video. Eudora Welty's "A Worn Path" and Flannery O'Connor's "A Good Man Is Hard to Find" both exist in video versions. *A Worn Path* (1994) is available from Films for the Humanities, and *A Good Man Is Hard to Find* (1992) was produced by Mary Magdalene Films and distributed by MWF Video.

QUESTIONS FOR WRITING AND RESEARCH

1. Many of the stories in this chapter are about mothers and daughters, or grandmothers and granddaughters. Pick two of these cross-generational pairs and discuss the ways the authors treat these familial roles.

2. In their comments on what makes southern writing distinct, Welty (p. 328), Hood (p. 410), and Smith (p. 391) focus on talk, particularly narrative. Write a "southern" style narrative of about 150 words in which the emphasis is on the enjoyment of telling. Then write it in a "northern" style for contrast. (It's useful to ask yourself how much of these different styles depends on stereotypes.)

3. The sense of place—the setting—figures prominently in these stories. Write your own 1–2 page "southern" description of a place, lingering over the details the way these writers do.

4. The South is often referred to as the "Bible Belt" and these stories contain frequent references to and quotations of the Bible, especially the King James Version. What effects do the biblical language and allusions have on you as a reader? (If, like many students nowadays, you don't recognize the biblical references and quotations, do you feel left out, or as if these writers are writing for someone else? How strong is this feeling?)

5. Choose three stories in this chapter with similar examples of violence and threatened violence. Who or what does the violence come from? Why? What "use" does the violence have in the story? Explain how in some cases it might have positive aspects.

6. "A Worn Path" and "A Good Man Is Hard to Find" exist in video versions. (See the Video Locale feature above.) Choose one of these two treatments and describe precisely how much was added or removed from the original story. What do you think of the changes? What surprised you?

7. Examine the secondary source material (biographies, critical works) on the education that Welty or Hurston or O'Connor received. To what extent can any feature of the writing of one of these figures be traced to her education?

8. Research the origins of the *Southern Review* with particular reference to its two key editors, Cleanth Brooks and Robert Penn Warren, asking what they saw in the writing of Eudora Welty and Katherine Anne Porter (p. 542).

9. Research the kind of support received by the more recently published writers in this chapter, such as grants, fellowships, and prizes. How adequate is such support to nourish a career in writing?

CHAPTER
8

Passage to America
New Immigrants Tell Their Stories

The United States is a land of immigrants, so "coming to America" stories have always been part of the literary landscape, with each nationality accumulating its particular canon of characteristic tales. These narratives can trace their ancestry to the accounts of early settlements in New England or even the original Pilgrims; those early accounts have been succeeded by stories of settlement and adjustment to a new and unfamiliar land. More than four centuries of immigration have given Americans a rich cultural mix, as well as thousands of stories of arrival and settlement.

Recent decades, roughly from 1980 on, have witnessed a flood of exciting drama, poetry, memoir, and fiction depicting the arrival and uncertain progress of a new generation of immigrants to America's shores. A young, well-educated group of newly arrived Americans has begun to transform the literary landscape so that it's now hard to find a magazine specializing in fiction or a book-length collection of short stories without a good many of these new, distinctive voices, insistent on being heard. The familiar "Passage to

America" theme is still with us, but the immigrants and the stories they tell
have changed.

A major source for this dramatic change is rooted in federal law, the 1965
Immigration and Nationality Act, which did away with the old immigration
controls and instituted sweeping changes. The old rules, which limited immigration through rigid national quotas, had been set up to favor northern Europeans
and explicitly discriminated against immigrants from Asia, Africa, and Latin
America. The 1965 rules give priority to educated and skilled workers, and to
uniting families. The result has been large numbers of new residents from the
Caribbean, Central America, South America, China, India, Korea, and other
Asian nations. The chart below illustrates the changed patterns in immigration
over a fifty-year period.

This change in the source of immigrants has been accompanied by a corresponding change in the accomplishments of these new Americans, since many
were admitted because they possessed specific skills in medicine, business, science, or education. For instance, the chart shows that Asian immigration increased by 500 percent between 1951 and 2000, opening America to a wave of
new middle-class immigrants, including nurses from the Philippines, doctors
from China, and computer programmers from India. In addition, immigrants
from Cuba and Vietnam have had special treatment as refugees, and these immigrants also tended to be entrepreneurial and educated.

The new, upwardly mobile immigrants have worked hard to see their sons
and daughters get a good college education. They have also wanted their children to retain their ethnic heritage, but the children grow up as Americans, often eager to reject the culture of their parents' immigrant generation. The

U.S. Immigration by Region and Selected Country of Last Residence 1951–2000

(percentage of total from each source)

Region of Origin	1951–1960	1961–1970	1971–1980	1981–1990	1991–2000
Europe	52.7	33.8	17.8	10.4	14.9
Asia	6.1	12.9	35.3	37.3	30.7
Americas	39.6	51.7	44.1	49.3	49.3
Canada	15	12.4	3.8	2.1	2.1
Mexico	11.9	13.7	14.2	22.6	24.7
Caribbean[a]	4.9	14.2	16.5	11.9	10.8
Central America	1.8	3.1	3	6.4	5.8
South America	3.6	7.8	6.6	6.3	5.9
Africa	0.6	0.9	1.8	2.4	3.9
Other	1	0.7	1	0.6	1.2

[a] Cuba, Dominican Republic, Haiti, Jamaica, and other Caribbean countries.
Source: 2003 Statistical Yearbook of the Immigration and Naturalization Service,
http://uscis.gov/graphics/shared/aboutus/statistics/Immigs.htm.

resulting clash of cultures—new vs. old; secular, brash America vs. the rules and traditions of the "old" country—is perfect material for literature, since these dramatic conflicts can be variously wrenching, comic, or poignant. Usually written by the younger generation, the stories, poems, memoirs, and plays have found a ready audience among other children of immigrants. But they are also attractive to the wider American audience as well. Most Americans, no matter how long settled, are part of two communities: the living nation of the present, with its opportunities and challenges, the place where they are living their lives; and the country of their ancestry, part of it in collective memory, part in imagination. Almost all Americans can be claimed as part of a diaspora, a community that has left the homeland but is still in some ways connected, sometimes loosely, sometimes strongly.

A second source of the new wave of immigrant writing comes from south of America's very porous southern border, where for centuries much of the population has continually moved back and forth, no matter what the immigration laws say is legal. The border itself has changed, as the United States acquired new land beginning in the nineteenth century, which disrupted centuries-old patterns of migration and seasonal movement. By the year 2000, southern California, Arizona, New Mexico, and Texas all possessed huge Mexican American populations, many long-established, many very new. Not all these immigrants had entered the United States legally, but most wanted to get ahead, working in a country that provided jobs if not a warm welcome. Mexicans in the United States have been producing literature for generations, both in English and in Spanish, but they have become much more visible in the past twenty years, as education levels have risen and many younger people have become totally fluent in English, the major language for the literary marketplace. Not surprisingly, many of these Chicano and Chicana writers have some of the same conflicts to dramatize as other immigrants, along with many issues of their own.

Puerto Ricans, another large group of Spanish-speaking Americans, are a strong presence on the east coast, and they travel freely back and forth between the United States and the island of Puerto Rico. Puerto Rico has been part of the United States since it was acquired after the Spanish-American War in 1898, and since 1917 its residents have been recognized as U.S. citizens, free from immigration restrictions, but not always free from prejudice. Caught between two worlds, Puerto Ricans writing in English have frequently dramatized their situation, and many have made a significant impact on literature. Cubans, since the Castro revolution of 1959, have been granted special entry to America, and have settled in large numbers in New York and particularly in Miami. Similarly, Dominican immigration increased sharply after thirty years of restrictions came to a sudden end in 1961, following the assassination of dictator Rafael Trujillo.

As in the past, American society is adjusting to the changes in its population: racially, culturally, politically, linguistically, religiously. One recent development is the increased emphasis on teaching Spanish in school and college curriculums, with a consequent decline in French, German, and Italian. America is only beginning to absorb the implications of its increased number of Muslims, and one day Muslim writers may make their mark on American literature as writers like Salman Rushdie have on British literature.

The themes of the new writing, deriving from so many cultures, are inevitably complex and varied. But certain motifs stand out. A recurring theme is America as a land of freedom and opportunity (in Korea, for instance, the country is referred to as "beautiful land"). But another theme is America as a disappointment: because of discrimination and hard economic times, or because the transition from one culture to another is heartbreaking. There is also the shock of encountering sharp cultural differences or prejudice—not just from Americans of European backgrounds but from African Americans, Latinos, Native Americans, and others. Often the latest to arrive must elbow their way into a society that officially welcomes newcomers but in reality seems reluctant to accept them.

Children of immigrants have special dilemmas. Some must endure substandard schools and never master English, thus becoming effectively barred from much decent employment. The street is a temptation for them, as it has been for generations of new Americans in the past. The more fortunate children of middle-class families often find that their parents aim them toward a very practical, economically rewarding education, particularly in business or the professions, and away from literature, music, or other arts. Also, the parents, while welcoming their children's adjustment to American culture, still expect them to retain much of the old culture, and preferably to date and marry within that culture, often very narrowly defined. For instance, it is not enough for a Gujarati to marry someone from India; often only another Gujarati from a "good" family will do. But children inevitably have different ideas about such matters. Even when the children desire to hold on to their parents' culture and to speak their parents' language, they typically encounter a rude shock when they travel to the "old" country and are dismissed as thoroughly "American," though in America they have been defined as "Korean," "Chinese," "Puerto Rican," or "Indian."

This is rich material for stories, and writers and publishers have been eager to exploit it. Quite naturally, though, there are costs. While the literary marketplace has welcomed many of their stories and novels, writers sometimes resent feeling pigeonholed as Latin or Asian American, as if ethnic themes are the only ones they can be expected to deal with. A mindless multiculturalism can be a trap: Indian American writers don't want to be *forced* into treating arranged marriages or runaway brides, no matter how rich and powerful such material is. Chicanos want to write about more than the mean streets or Spanish/English language issues, important as they are. At the same time, they realize that their labels help them stand out from the crowd of writers wanting publication. A host of talented young writers from all backgrounds are clamoring for audiences, and if multicultural issues give ethnic writers an edge, they are tempted to exploit their situation. Such issues have been faced before, most notably by African Americans and Jewish Americans in the twentieth century, and they still resonate. To what extent should writers honor old traditions or cling to their ethnic heritage? Can they strike out on their own with a new subject? What does it take to become fully American?

The matter of language has proven particularly important for this generation of writers. They of course write in English, but they often insert words, phrases, and whole sentences from their parents' language, raising the question of whether readers need a glossary of Hindi or Japanese terms. For some writers, this becomes a political issue: the Dominican writer Junot Díaz (p. 479), for instance, refused to add a Spanish glossary to his short story collection *Drown*, because he claimed readers who don't know Spanish should experience—at least in some small way—the impenetrability of a language foreign to them as well as recognize that Spanish is an important language in twenty-first-century America.

Naturally, these young, well-educated writers have plenty to say about their craft, and particularly about their situation as part of a new generation. Most selections in this chapter conclude with comments from the writer on his or her situation. Most feel full of promise, looking back on the world of their parents, but confidently moving into the mainstream of both American society and American literature.

PASSAGE TO AMERICA TIMELINE

1790	The Naturalization Law of 1790 denies naturalized citizenship to non-whites until the 1940s.
1850s	Chinese laborers immigrate to U.S. West to work as miners.
1865–1869	Ten to twelve thousand Chinese American laborers help build the Central Pacific lines of the Transcontinental Railroad across the western United States.
1882	The Chinese Exclusion Act of 1882 bans Chinese workers from immigrating and denies citizenship to those already here.
1898	United States acquires Puerto Rico following the Spanish-American War.
1916–1924	United States occupies the Dominican Republic in response to popular democratic uprisings.
1917	Congress passes the Jones Act to extend U.S. citizenship to Puerto Ricans; Immigration Act of 1917 bars immigrants from Pacific countries, including China, Japan, India, Thailand.
1920	Alien Land Law of 1920 prevents Asian immigrants from owning U.S. land.
1930	Puerto Rican population in the U.S. climbs to 52,000 (from only 1,500 in 1910), most settling in New York City.
1942	Forced relocation to internment camps begins for thousands of Japanese Americans during World War II; Pat Mora born in El Paso, Texas.
1943	The Zoot Suit Riots in California are instigated by xenophobia against Hispanics.
1946	The Immigration Act of 1946 officially includes Indians in the Act and makes them eligible for naturalization.
1948	Esmeralda Santiago is born in Puerto Rico.
1950	Julia Alvarez is born in New York City.
1952	The United States grants Puerto Rico status as a commonwealth.
1956	Gish Jen born in Queens, New York, as Lillian Jen.

1957	Anjana Appachana is born in India.
1960s	The Chicano Renaissance brings a rise in activism for Chicanos in politics, education, labor, and art; the Chicano movement establishes bilingual presses, periodicals, art exhibitions, and university organizations for Mexican Americans.
1961	Assassination of Dominican Republic's dictator, Rafael Trujillo, leads to removal of emigration restrictions in place for thirty years.
1965	U.S. sends troops to the Dominican Republic in response to people's revolution for democracy; Immigration Act of 1965 repeals Pacific-zone restrictions and abolishes national quotas for immigration.
1967	Jhumpa Lahiri born in London, England.
1968	Junot Díaz is born in the Dominican Republic.
1969	Responding to student protests, Asian American studies programs are founded at U.S. universities and Japanese American history is taught for the first time.
1976	Maxine Hong Kingston, Chinese American author, publishes *The Woman Warrior*.
1980s	U.S. media name the 1980s "the Decade of the Hispanics."
1984	Pat Mora publishes her first book of poetry, *Chants*.
1985	Casa Dominica, an organization supporting Dominican literature and arts, is established in New York with the support of the Dominican government.
1990s	Indian population in United States grows to almost 800,000, up from 380,000 only a decade earlier.
1990	Amendments to Immigration Act give preference to immigrants with outstanding qualifications in science, art, business, or athletics; secondary preference given to those with advanced degrees, and third to laborers; Cuban American Oscar Hijuelos becomes first Hispanic American to win the Pulitzer Prize for fiction, for his novel *The Mambo Kings Play Songs of Love*.
1997	Pat Mora establishes national day for childhood and bilingual literacy called El Dia de los Ninos/El Dia de los Libros, part of National Poetry Month.
2000	U.S. Census names the Hispanic population the largest ethnic minority in North America; Jhumpa Lahiri wins the Pulitzer Prize for *Interpreter of Maladies*.

VIRTUAL LOCALE

The "Writers on America" Project: What It Means to Be an American Writer. Julia Alvarez's essay "I, Too, Sing América" (p. 443) was commissioned as one of fifteen essays by the U.S. Department of State's Bureau of International Information Programs. The essay collection, called Writers on America, can be viewed online at *http://usinfo.state.gov/products/pubs/writers/homepage.htm.* To put together the collection, the State Department solicited essays from

(continued)

fifteen respected and well-known American writers, the group in its entirety a reflection of the country's diverse population as well as the diversity of contemporary American literature. The assigned subject was the question, "In what sense do you see yourself as an American writer?" Visitors to the Writers on America website will find a huge range of American views on writing and, inevitably, the immigrant experience as well, from novelist Bharati Mukherjee's thoughts on "the weight of tradition" to poet Naomi Shihab Nye's discussion of cultural exclusion.

PAT MORA   (B. 1942)

Pat Mora grew up in a bilingual home in El Paso and graduated from the University of Texas at El Paso. Her sense of her own mixed Anglo-Chicana heritage, as well as a highly developed consciousness about immigration, emerges in much of her work. Her well-known poem "Immigrants" is full of the traditional kinds of loving expectations the older generation bestows on the younger. Some readers may regard it as full of an uncomplicated, positive attitude toward the immigrants' new land, while others might find echoes of a contradictory, less positive attitude. Mora's recent books include My Own True Name: New and Selected Poems for Young Adults, 1984–1999 *(2000),* Aunt Carmen's Book of Practical Saints *(1997), and* Agua Santa: Holy Water *(1995). In addition to her books of poetry, Mora is the author of many books for children, including* A Birthday Basket for Tía *(1992) and a memoir,* House of Houses *(1997). She lives in Santa Fe, New Mexico.*

Immigrants   (1986)

wrap their babies in the American flag,
feed them mashed hot dogs and apple pie,
name them Bill and Daisy,
buy them blonde dolls that blink blue
eyes or a football and tiny cleats   5
before the baby can even walk,
speak to them in thick English, hallo, babee, hallo.
whisper in Spanish or Polish
when the babies sleep, whisper
in a dark parent bed, that dark   10
parent fear, "Will they like
our boy, our girl, our fine american
boy, our fine american girl?"

Starting Point for Further Research: Pat Mora

- **Critical Essay:** Patrick D. Murphy. "Conserving Natural and Cultural Diversity: The Prose and Poetry of Pat Mora." *MELUS: The Journal of the Society for the Study of the Multi-Ethnic Literature of the United States* 21 (Spring 1996): 59–69.

INSPIRATION "I, TOO, SING AMÉRICA": ALL-AMERICAN WRITERS, FROM WHITMAN TO HUGHES TO ALVAREZ

Walt Whitman, in an 1895 print of an 1854 daguerrotype.

In her essay "I, Too, Sing América," Julia Alvarez recalls her immigration experience in all its dualities and complexities, the good and the bad, and frames it in terms of how that experience informed her larger identity and sense of self, including her decision to become a writer.

As a child in America, lonely and longing for the Dominican Republic, out of a yearning for connection, she became an avid reader. Shaped and inspired by the words of writers like Walt Whitman and Langston Hughes, writers considered "all-American," she "soon discovered that the world of the imagination was a portable homeland where everybody belonged." Between her recollections and

Langston Hughes, 1942.

contemplations on what it really means to be an American and specifically an American writer, Alvarez weaves in excerpts from Walt Whitman's "I Hear America Singing" (1900) and the entire text of the Hughes poem that was inspired by Whitman, "I, Too, Sing America" (1925). The essay concludes with Alvarez's own poetic response to Whitman and Hughes, "I, Too, Sing América."

For the full text of Whitman's "I Hear America Singing," see p. 870. For additional works by Walt Whitman, Langston Hughes, and Julia Alvarez, see Chapters 11, 13, 17, 18, and 25.

Julia Alvarez.

JULIA ALVAREZ   (B. 1950)

Julia Alvarez was born in New York City in 1950, but her family returned to the Dominican Republic when she was only three months old, so she spent the first ten years of her childhood there. In 1960, her family moved back to the United States, just a year before the Dominican Republic's dictator, Rafael Trujillo, was assassinated. Her first novel, How the García Girls Lost Their Accents *(1992), became a best-seller and is now considered by teachers, librarians, critics, and students to be a classic.*

I, Too, Sing América

I would never have become a writer unless my family had emigrated to the United States when I was ten years old.

I grew up in the '50s in a dictatorship on the little Caribbean half-island of the Dominican Republic. Although it was a highly oral culture rich in story-telling, it was not a literary culture. I grew up among people who thought of reading as an antisocial activity that could ruin your health and definitely take the fun out of life.

Reading/studying was not an activity that was encouraged in my family, especially for us girls. My grandmother, who only went up to fourth grade, used to tell the story that she only picked up a book when she heard the teacher's donkey braying as it climbed up the hill to her house.

Boys had to make the *sacrificio* and get an education in order to earn a living—but in moderation. My cousin was considered strange because he not only loved to read but as a teenager began to write poetry. "*Se va a enfermar,*" my aunt would say, shaking her head every time she found Juan sitting in a chair, reading a book. "He's going to get sick."

I was also growing up in a repressive and dangerous dictatorship. In a social studies class, a student wrote an essay in which he praised Trujillo, the dictator, as the true father of our country. The teacher commented that certainly Trujillo was one of the fathers of our country, but there were others. The boy, the son of a general, must have gone home and told his father. That night the teacher, his wife, and his two young children disappeared. Intellectuals, people who read and questioned, were suspect. A book in your hands might as well have been contraband.

In 1960, my father's underground activities against Trujillo were discovered, and we were forced to escape the country in a hurry. The minute we landed on American soil we became "spics" who spoke our English with heavy accents, immigrants with no money or prospects. Overnight, we had lost everything, our country, our home, our extended family structure, our language, for Spanish was the language of home, of *la familia*, of self understanding. We arrived in the United States at a time in history that was not very welcoming to people who were different, whose skins were a different color, whose language didn't sound like English. For the first time in my life I experienced prejudice and playground cruelty. I struggled with a language and a culture I didn't understand. I was homesick and heartbroken.

My sisters and I, being young, soon rallied to the challenge. We learned the new language, the new music, the new ways to dress and behave ourselves. But our success on these fronts soon created another kind of problem in our family. My parents wanted desperately to keep us to the old standards, and yet they also wanted us to succeed in this new culture. How could we study hard and earn all A's and get ahead but be sweet and submissive and let Papi make all the decisions? How could we remember our Spanish when we were forced to speak only English outside the home? How could we keep our mouths shut out of *respeto* for our parents when in school we were being taught to speak up and debate, if need be, with our teachers? How could we get along with our friends and yet never go over to their houses for parties and sleepovers because they might have older brothers or parents who allowed things my parents did not allow?

My sisters and I were caught between worlds, value systems, languages, customs. And this was our challenge, which is the challenge for many of us who are immigrants into a new world that is different from the old one of childhood: how to maintain a connection to our traditions, our roots, *and* also to grow and flourish in our new country? How to find creative ways to combine our different worlds, values, conflicting and sometimes warring parts of our selves so that we can become more expansive, not more diminished human beings?

But the problem was that no one was thinking like that back in those days. This was the United States of the early '60s, still locked in the civil rights struggles, pre-women's movement, pre-Equal Rights Amendment movement, pre-multicultural studies, pre-anything but the melting pot, that old assimilationist, mainstreaming model. Those were the days when the model for immigration was that you came to America, you assimilated, you cut off your ties to the past and the old ways, and that was the price you paid for the privilege of being an American citizen.

But sometimes it is these painful moments that can become opportunities   10
for expansion and self-creation. I had become a hybrid—as all of us who travel beyond an original self or hometown or homeland are bound to become. I was not a mainstream American girl and I wasn't a totally Dominican girl anymore. And yet I wanted desperately to belong somewhere. It was this intense loneliness and desire to connect with others that led me to books. Homesick and lonely in the USA, I soon discovered that the world of the imagination was a portable homeland where everybody belonged. I began to dream that maybe I, too, could create worlds where no one would be barred.

And so, it was through the wide open doors of its literature that I truly entered this country. Reading Mr. Walt Whitman, I heard America's promise and I fell in love with my new country. "I hear America singing, its varied carols I hear." As for melting all our variety into one mainstream model, Mr. Whitman disagreed: "I am large, I contain multitudes." This country was a nation of nations, a congregation of races. "I resist anything better than my own diversity."

Was this *allowed*? I wondered, looking over my shoulder. Wasn't this subversive? But Mr. Whitman's poems were printed in my English textbook where he was described as "the poet of America." He was saying what this country was really all about. Although America seemed to have forgotten its promises, its writers remembered and reminded us.

Slowly and not without struggle, America began to listen. As the 1960s progressed into the '70s, the country around me began to change. Under pressure from its own marginalized populations and from its growing number of immigrants, the nation was being forced to acknowledge its own diversity and become more inclusive. Citizens were challenging America to be true to its promises. The first time I attended a march in support of the Equal Rights Amendment to the Constitution and was not hauled off to be tortured in a dark prison chamber by the secret police, I understood that a free country was not one that was free of problems or inequalities or even hypocrisies. Such failures came with the territory of being a human being. Freedom was the opportunity to shape a country, to contribute to the ongoing experiment, never tried before, of making out of the many, one nation, indivisible with liberty and justice for all. The words were not just rhetoric. It was our right and responsibility to make the words come true, for ourselves and for others.

As the nation changed, our literature began to reflect these changes as well. Not only was there a Mr. Whitman, I discovered, but a Mr. Langston Hughes.

I, too, sing America.
I am the darker brother.
They send me to eat in the kitchen
When company comes,
But I laugh
And eat well,
And grow strong.

Tomorrow,
I'll be at the table
When company comes.
Nobody'll dare
Say to me,
"Eat in the kitchen,"
Then.
Besides,
They'll see how beautiful I am
And be ashamed—

I, too, am America.

Oh, that was music to my ears! I understood what Mr. Hughes was saying: 15
he was claiming his place in the chorus of American song. This was an important voice for a young girl of another culture and language and background to hear.

But the publishing world dragged its feet. In the early '80s, when I started sending out my manuscripts, the major publishers and mainstream market were reluctant to take a chance on new voices. Until they noticed that Afro-American literature had become a serious component of many college curriculums. That readers were buying up copies of Alice Walker, Toni Morrison, Oscar Hijuelos, Sandra Cisneros, Maxine Hong Kingston, Amy Tan, Gish Jen. The complexion of literary Americans had changed.

In 1991 when I was 41 years old, after over 25 years of struggling, my first novel, *How the García Girls Lost Their Accents*, was published by a small publisher willing to take a chance on a new voice. Eleven years later the book has been adopted as a text in many high schools and colleges. I, too, am now singing America.

I tell this story of my struggle to become an American writer because it was a struggle I shared with a country that was also struggling to become a more inclusive and representative nation. I feel lucky and privileged to have been part of this historical process. America gave me the gift of helping me discover and cultivate my talents. I would not have become a writer had I not come to this country as a young girl in 1960.

But as President Kennedy said, a few months after our arrival in this country, "Ask not what your country can do for you, ask what you can do for your country." My debt to my country is to pass on that opportunity to others. "The function of freedom," Toni Morrison has said, "is to free someone else." My work as well as my vote contribute to the richness and diversity of the whole. By our

active and committed presence as citizens of different ethnicities, races, traditions, and linguistic backgrounds, we challenge America to expand its understanding and compassion and thus grow stronger as a nation. We infuse its literature with new energy. We sing new rhythms, inflections, stories, traditions into
the whole.

But my responsibility does not stop within the American borders. Unlike   20
the old model of immigration, many of us immigrants continue to go back to
where we originally came from. With the vast migrations and mobility of the
second half of this passing century, most of us no longer fit the tight definitions of identity we were born into. Last year in California I met an Afro-Do-
minican-American who had married a Japanese woman and had a little baby.
Their son is an Afro-Dominican-Japanese-American. My Dominicana sister is
married to a Danish man; her kids know Danish, English, and Spanish, and
you know what they love to eat, *arroz con habichuelas* with pickled herrings.
We are becoming a planet of racial and cultural hybrids. We need an open
mind and a big heart and a compassionate imagination to allow for all the
combinations we are becoming as a nation and as a human family. Mr. Whitman's words remind us: "The United States themselves are essentially the
greatest poem . . . Here is not merely a nation but a teeming nation of nations
. . . and the American bard shall be kosmos . . . glad to pass any thing to any
one."

To create this kind of nation is to present a model of a world where we all
belong. But this America can only be achieved if each person is free to be the
rich and complex person he or she is. The dangers to be reductive are tempting,
to hole down in our racial and ethnic bunkers and forget that out of the *pluribus*
we have to make *unum*, one human family.

I would go even further and say that to embrace our selves in all our complexity and richness and also to embrace the multiplicity of selves out there—
that is our challenge not just as Americans but as human beings. Robert
Desnos, the French poet who died in a concentration camp, once said: "The
challenge of being a human being is not only to be oneself, but to become
each one." Terrence, the Roman slave who freed himself with his writing, put
it another way, "I am a human being," he said. "Nothing human is alien to
me." By becoming all we can individually be and by never forgetting our responsibility of helping each other achieve that same goal, we can create a nation and a world where everyone belongs and where each and every one of us
has our song.

In this spirit, I see myself more and more as an American writer, not just in
the national but in the hemispheric sense. With my roots in the southern part of
the Americas (my stories, my history, my traditions, my Spanish and Caribbean
rhythms) and my training and experience and flowering in the northern part of
the hemisphere, I am truly an all-American writer:

I, Too, Sing América.

I know it's been said before
but not in this voice
of the *plátano*
and the mango,

marimba y bongó,
not in this *sancocho*
of *inglés*
con *español*.

Ay sí,
it's my turn
to oh say
what I see,
I'm going to sing America!
with all América
inside me:
from the soles
of Tierra del Fuego
to the thin waist
of Chiriquí
up the spine of the Mississippi
through the heartland
of the Yanquis
to the great plain face of Canada—
all of us
singing America,
the whole hemispheric
familia
belting our *canción*,
singing our brown skin
into that white
and red and blue song—
the big song
that sings
all America,
el canto
que cuenta
con toda América:
un new song!

Ya llegó el momento,
our moment
under the sun—
ese sol that shines
on everyone.

So, hit it maestro!
give us that Latin beat,
¡*Uno-dos-tres!*
One-two-three!
Ay sí,
(*y bilingually*):
Yo también soy América
I, too, am America

Los Angeles's Latino Museum of History, Art, and Culture. Like El Museo del Barrio in New York, the Latino Museum of History, Art, and Culture in Los Angeles, California, focuses on the presentation, preservation, and advancement of Latino heritage and culture. Located at 112 South Main Street, the museum opened in 1995 and organizes exhibitions of Latino art as well as related educational programs.

JHUMPA LAHIRI   (B. 1967)

Jhumpa Lahiri was born to a Bengali family in London in 1967. The family moved to Rhode Island, where Lahiri grew up. Because her parents were born and raised in India, however, Lahiri has often visited Calcutta and India plays a central role in her writing. She attended Barnard College in New York and did graduate work in creative writing and literature at Boston University, earning a Ph.D. in Renaissance literature. "The Third and Final Continent" appeared in her first book, the short story collection Interpreter of Maladies, *which earned her the 2000 Pulitzer Prize for fiction, the PEN/Hemingway Award for fiction, and the O. Henry Award for the Best American Short Story for the title story. In 2003, Lahiri published her first novel,* The Namesake, *about a Bengali family who move to America; like many of her stories, it deals with issues of identity, ethnicity, and home.*

The Third and Final Continent   (1999)

I left India in 1964 with a certificate in commerce and the equivalent, in those days, of ten dollars to my name. For three weeks I sailed on the SS *Roma*, an Italian cargo vessel, in a cabin next to the ship's engine, across the Arabian Sea, the Red Sea, the Mediterranean, and finally to England. I lived in north London, in Finsbury Park, in a house occupied entirely by penniless Bengali bachelors like myself, at least a dozen and sometimes more, all struggling to educate and establish ourselves abroad.

I attended lectures at LSE and worked at the university library to get by. We lived three or four to a room, shared a single, icy toilet, and took turns cooking pots of egg curry, which we ate with our hands on a table covered with newspapers. Apart from our jobs we had few responsibilities. On weekends we lounged barefoot in drawstring pajamas, drinking tea and smoking Rothmans, or set out to watch cricket at Lord's. Some weekends the house was crammed with still more Bengalis, to whom we had introduced ourselves at the greengrocer, or on the Tube, and we made yet more egg curry, and played Mukesh on a Grundig reel-to-reel, and soaked our dirty dishes in the bathtub. Every now and then someone in the house moved out, to live with a woman whom his family back in Calcutta had determined he was to wed. In 1969, when I was thirty-six years old, my own marriage was arranged. Around the same time I was offered a full-time job in America, in the processing department of a library at MIT. The salary was generous enough to support a wife, and I was honored to be hired by a world-famous university, and so I obtained a sixth-preference green card, and prepared to travel farther still.

By now I had enough money to go by plane. I flew first to Calcutta, to attend my wedding, and a week later I flew to Boston, to begin my new job. During the flight I read *The Student Guide to North America*, a paperback volume that I'd bought before leaving London, for seven shillings six pence on Tottenham Court Road, for although I was no longer a student I was on a budget all the same. I learned that Americans drove on the right side of the road, not the left, and that they called a lift an elevator and an engaged phone busy. "The pace of life in North America is different from Britain as you will soon discover," the guidebook informed me. "Everybody feels he must get to the top. Don't expect an English cup of tea." As the plane began its descent over Boston Harbor, the pilot announced the weather and time, and that President Nixon had declared a national holiday: two American men had landed on the moon. Several passengers cheered. "God bless America!" one of them hollered. Across the aisle, I saw a woman praying.

I spent my first night at the YMCA in Central Square, Cambridge, an inexpensive accommodation recommended by my guidebook. It was walking distance from MIT, and steps from the post office and a supermarket called Purity Supreme. The room contained a cot, a desk, and a small wooden cross on one wall. A sign on the door said cooking was strictly forbidden. A bare window overlooked Massachusetts Avenue, a major thoroughfare with traffic in both directions. Car horns, shrill and prolonged, blared one after another. Flashing sirens heralded endless emergencies, and a fleet of buses rumbled past, their doors opening and closing with a powerful hiss, throughout the night. The noise was constantly distracting, at times suffocating. I felt it deep in my ribs, just as I had felt the furious drone of the engine on the SS *Roma*. But there was no ship's deck to escape to, no glittering ocean to thrill my soul, no breeze to cool my face, no one to talk to. I was too tired to pace the gloomy corridors of the YMCA in my drawstring pajamas. Instead I sat at the desk and stared out the window, at the city hall of Cambridge and a row of small shops. In the morning I reported to my job at the Dewey Library, a beige fortlike building by Memorial Drive. I also opened a bank account, rented a post office box, and bought a plastic bowl and a spoon at Woolworth's, a store whose name I recognized from London. I went to Purity Supreme, wandering up and down the aisles, converting ounces to grams and comparing prices to things in England. In the end I bought a small carton of milk and a box of cornflakes. This was my first meal in America. I ate it at my desk. I preferred it to hamburgers or hot dogs, the only alternative I could afford in the coffee shops on Massachusetts Avenue, and, besides, at the time I had yet to consume any beef. Even the simple chore of buying milk was new to me; in London we'd had bottles delivered each morning to our door.

* * *

In a week I had adjusted, more or less. I ate cornflakes and milk, morning and night, and bought some bananas for variety, slicing them into the bowl with the edge of my spoon. In addition I bought tea bags and a flask, which the salesman in Woolworth's referred to as a thermos (a flask, he informed me, was used to store whiskey, another thing I had never consumed). For the price of one cup of tea at a coffee shop, I filled the flask with boiling water on my way to work each morning, and brewed the four cups I drank in the course of a day. I bought a larger carton of milk, and learned to leave it on the shaded part of the windowsill, as I had seen another resident at the YMCA do. To pass the time in the evenings I read the *Boston Globe* downstairs, in a spacious room with stained-glass windows. I read every article and advertisement, so that I would grow familiar with things, and when my eyes grew tired I slept. Only I did not sleep well. Each night I had to keep the window wide open; it was the only source of air in the stifling room, and the noise was intolerable. I would lie on the cot with my fingers pressed into my ears, but when I drifted off to sleep my hands fell away, and the noise of the traffic would wake me up again. Pigeon feathers drifted onto the windowsill, and one evening, when I poured milk over my cornflakes, I saw that it had soured. Nevertheless I resolved to stay at the YMCA for six weeks, until my wife's passport and green card were ready. Once she arrived I would have to rent a proper apartment, and from time to time I studied the classified section of the newspaper, or stopped in at the housing office at MIT during my lunch break, to see what was available in my price range. It was in this manner that I discovered a room for immediate occupancy, in a house on a quiet street, the listing said, for eight dollars per week. I copied the number into my guidebook and dialed from a pay telephone, sorting through the coins with which I was still unfamiliar, smaller and lighter than shillings, heavier and brighter than *paisas*.

"Who is speaking?" a woman demanded. Her voice was bold and clamorous.

"Yes, good afternoon, madame. I am calling about the room for rent."

"Harvard or Tech?"

"I beg your pardon?"

"Are you from Harvard or Tech?"   10

Gathering that Tech referred to the Massachusetts Institute of Technology, I replied, "I work at Dewey Library," adding tentatively, "at Tech."

"I only rent rooms to boys from Harvard or Tech!"

"Yes, madame."

I was given an address and an appointment for seven o'clock that evening. Thirty minutes before the hour I set out, my guidebook in my pocket, my breath fresh with Listerine. I turned down a street shaded with trees, perpendicular to Massachusetts Avenue. Stray blades of grass poked between the cracks of the footpath. In spite of the heat I wore a coat and a tie, regarding the event as I would any other interview; I had never lived in the home of a person who was not Indian. The house, surrounded by a chain-link fence, was off-white with dark brown trim. Unlike the stucco row house I'd lived in in London, this house, fully detached, was covered with wooden shingles, with a tangle of forsythia bushes plastered against the front and sides. When I pressed the calling bell, the woman with whom I had spoken on the phone hollered from what seemed to be just the other side of the door, "One minute, please!"

Several minutes later the door was opened by a tiny, extremely old woman.   15 A mass of snowy hair was arranged like a small sack on top of her head. As I stepped into the house she sat down on a wooden bench positioned at the bottom of a narrow carpeted staircase. Once she was settled on the bench, in a small pool of light, she peered up at me with undivided attention. She wore a long black skirt that spread like a stiff tent to the floor, and a starched white shirt edged with ruffles at the throat and cuffs. Her hands, folded together in her lap, had long pallid fingers, with swollen knuckles and tough yellow nails. Age had battered her features so that she almost resembled a man, with sharp, shrunken eyes and prominent creases on either side of her nose. Her lips, chapped and faded, had nearly disappeared, and her eyebrows were missing altogether. Nevertheless she looked fierce.

"Lock up!" she commanded. She shouted even though I stood only a few feet away. "Fasten the chain and firmly press that button on the knob! This is the first thing you shall do when you enter, is that clear?"

I locked the door as directed and examined the house. Next to the bench on which the woman sat was a small round table, its legs fully concealed, much like the woman's, by a skirt of lace. The table held a lamp, a transistor radio, a leather change purse with a silver clasp, and a telephone. A thick wooden cane coated with a layer of dust was propped against one side. There was a parlor to my right, lined with bookcases and filled with shabby claw-footed furniture. In the corner of the parlor I saw a grand piano with its top down, piled with papers. The piano's bench was missing; it seemed to be the one on which the woman was sitting. Somewhere in the house a clock chimed seven times.

"You're punctual!" the woman proclaimed. "I expect you shall be so with the rent!"

"I have a letter, madame." In my jacket pocket was a letter confirming my employment from MIT, which I had brought along to prove that I was indeed from Tech.

She stared at the letter, then handed it back to me carefully, gripping it with   20
her fingers as if it were a dinner plate heaped with food instead of a sheet of paper. She did not wear glasses, and I wondered if she'd read a word of it. "The last boy was always late! Still owes me eight dollars! Harvard boys aren't what they used to be! Only Harvard and Tech in this house! How's Tech, boy?"

"It is very well."

"You checked the lock?"

"Yes, madame."

She slapped the space beside her on the bench with one hand, and told me to sit down. For a moment she was silent. Then she intoned, as if she alone possessed this knowledge:

"There is an American flag on the moon!"

"Yes, madame." Until then I had not thought very much about the moon   25
shot. It was in the newspaper, of course, article upon article. The astronauts had landed on the shores of the Sea of Tranquillity, I had read, traveling farther than anyone in the history of civilization. For a few hours they explored the moon's surface. They gathered rocks in their pockets, described their surroundings (a magnificent desolation, according to one astronaut), spoke by phone to the president, and planted a flag in lunar soil. The voyage was hailed as man's most awesome achievement. I had seen full-page photographs in the *Globe*, of the astronauts in their inflated costumes, and read about what certain people in Boston had been doing at the exact moment the astronauts landed, on a Sunday afternoon. A man said that he was operating a swan boat with a radio pressed to his ear; a woman had been baking rolls for her grandchildren.

The woman bellowed, "A flag on the moon, boy! I heard it on the radio! Isn't that splendid?"

"Yes, madame."

But she was not satisfied with my reply. Instead she commanded, "Say 'splendid'!"

I was both baffled and somewhat insulted by the request. It reminded me of   30
the way I was taught multiplication tables as a child, repeating after the master, sitting cross-legged, without shoes or pencils, on the floor of my one-room Tolly-gunge school. It also reminded me of my wedding, when I had repeated endless Sanskrit verses after the priest, verses I barely understood, which joined me to my wife. I said nothing.

"Say 'splendid'!" the woman bellowed once again.

"Splendid," I murmured. I had to repeat the word a second time at the top of my lungs, so she could hear. I am soft-spoken by nature and was especially reluctant to raise my voice to an elderly woman whom I had met only moments ago, but she did not appear to be offended. If anything the reply pleased her because her next command was:

"Go see the room!"

I rose from the bench and mounted the narrow carpeted staircase. There were five doors, two on either side of an equally narrow hallway, and one at the opposite end. Only one door was partly open. The room contained a twin bed under a sloping ceiling, a brown oval rug, a basin with an exposed pipe, and a chest of drawers. One door, painted white, led to a closet, another to a toilet and a tub. The walls were covered with gray and ivory striped paper. The window was open; net curtains stirred in the breeze. I lifted them away and inspected the view: a small back yard, with a few fruit trees and an empty clothesline. I was satisfied. From the bottom of the stairs I heard the woman demand, "What is your decision?"

When I returned to the foyer and told her, she picked up the leather change   35
purse on the table, opened the clasp, fished about with her fingers, and produced a key on a thin wire hoop. She informed me that there was a kitchen at the back of the house, accessible through the parlor. I was welcome to use the stove as long as I left it as I found it. Sheets and towels were provided, but keeping them clean was my own responsibility. The rent was due Friday mornings on the ledge above the piano keys. "And no lady visitors!"

"I am a married man, madame." It was the first time I had announced this fact to anyone.

But she had not heard. "No lady visitors!" she insisted. She introduced herself as Mrs. Croft.

* * *

My wife's name was Mala. The marriage had been arranged by my older brother and his wife. I regarded the proposition with neither objection nor enthusiasm. It was a duty expected of me, as it was expected of every man. She was the daughter of a schoolteacher in Beleghata. I was told that she could cook, knit, embroider, sketch landscapes, and recite poems by Tagore, but these talents could not make up for the fact that she did not possess a fair complexion, and so a string of men had rejected her to her face. She was twenty-seven, an age when her parents had begun to fear that she would never marry, and so they were willing to ship their only child halfway across the world in order to save her from spinsterhood.

For five nights we shared a bed. Each of those nights, after applying cold cream and braiding her hair, which she tied up at the end with a black cotton string, she turned from me and wept; she missed her parents. Although I would be leaving the country in a few days, custom dictated that she was now a part of my household, and for the next six weeks she was to live with my brother and his wife, cooking, cleaning, serving tea and sweets to guests. I did nothing to console her. I lay on my own side of the bed, reading my guidebook by flashlight and anticipating my journey. At times I thought of the tiny room on the other side of the wall which had belonged to my mother. Now the room was practically empty; the wooden pallet on which she'd once slept was piled with trunks and old bedding. Nearly six years ago, before leaving for London, I had watched her die on that bed, had found her playing with her excrement in her final days. Before we cremated her I had cleaned each of her fingernails with a hairpin, and then, because my brother could not bear it, I had assumed the role of eldest son, and had touched the flame to her temple, to release her tormented soul to heaven.

* * *

The next morning I moved into the room in Mrs. Croft's house. When I un-   40
locked the door I saw that she was sitting on the piano bench, on the same side as the previous evening. She wore the same black skirt, the same starched white blouse, and had her hands folded together the same way in her lap. She looked so much the same that I wondered if she'd spent the whole night on the bench. I put my suitcase upstairs, filled my flask with boiling water in the kitchen, and headed off to work. That evening when I came home from the university, she was still there.

"Sit down, boy!" She slapped the space beside her.

I perched beside her on the bench. I had a bag of groceries with me—more milk, more cornflakes, and more bananas, for my inspection of the kitchen earlier in the day had revealed no spare pots, pans, or cooking utensils. There were only two saucepans in the refrigerator, both containing some orange broth, and a copper kettle on the stove.

"Good evening, madame."

She asked me if I had checked the lock. I told her I had.

For a moment she was silent. Then suddenly she declared, with the equal   45
measures of disbelief and delight as the night before, "There's an American flag on the moon, boy!"

"Yes, madame."

"A flag on the moon! Isn't that splendid?"

I nodded, dreading what I knew was coming. "Yes, madame."

"Say 'splendid'!"

This time I paused, looking to either side in case anyone were there to over-   50
hear me, though I knew perfectly well that the house was empty. I felt like an idiot. But it was a small enough thing to ask. "Splendid!" I cried out.

Within days it became our routine. In the mornings when I left for the library Mrs. Croft was either hidden away in her bedroom, on the other side of the staircase, or she was sitting on the bench, oblivious to my presence, listening to the news or classical music on the radio. But each evening when I returned the same thing happened: she slapped the bench, ordered me to sit down, declared that there was a flag on the moon, and declared that it was splendid. I said it was splendid, too, and then we sat in silence. As awkward as it was, and as endless as it felt to me then, the nightly encounter lasted only about ten minutes; inevitably she would drift off to sleep, her head falling abruptly toward her chest, leaving me free to retire to my room. By then, of course, there was no flag standing on the moon. The astronauts, I had read in the paper, had seen it fall before they flew back to Earth. But I did not have the heart to tell her.

* * *

Friday morning, when my first week's rent was due, I went to the piano in the parlor to place my money on the ledge. The piano keys were dull and discolored. When I pressed one, it made no sound at all. I had put eight one-dollar bills in an envelope and written Mrs. Croft's name on the front of it. I was not in the habit of leaving money unmarked and unattended. From where I stood I could see the profile of her tent-shaped skirt. She was sitting on the bench, listening to the radio. It seemed unnecessary to make her get up and walk all the way to the piano. I never saw her walking about, and assumed, from the cane always propped against the round table at her side, that she did so with difficulty. When I approached the bench she peered up at me and demanded:

"What is your business?"

"The rent, madame."

"On the ledge above the piano keys!"   55

"I have it here." I extended the envelope toward her, but her fingers, folded together in her lap, did not budge. I bowed slightly and lowered the envelope, so that it hovered just above her hands. After a moment she accepted, and nodded her head.

That night when I came home, she did not slap the bench, but out of habit I sat beside her as usual. She asked me if I had checked the lock, but she mentioned nothing about the flag on the moon. Instead she said:

"It was very kind of you!"

"I beg your pardon, madame?"

"Very kind of you!"   60

She was still holding the envelope in her hands.

* * *

On Sunday there was a knock on my door. An elderly woman introduced herself: she was Mrs. Croft's daughter, Helen. She walked into the room and looked at each of the walls as if for signs of change, glancing at the shirts that hung in the closet, the neckties draped over the doorknob, the box of cornflakes on the chest of drawers, the dirty bowl and spoon in the basin. She was short and thick-waisted, with cropped silver hair and bright pink lipstick. She wore a sleeveless summer dress, a row of white plastic beads, and spectacles on a chain that hung like a swing against her chest. The backs of her legs were mapped with dark blue veins, and her upper arms sagged like the flesh of a roasted eggplant. She told me she lived in Arlington, a town farther up Massachusetts Avenue. "I come once a week to bring Mother groceries. Has she sent you packing yet?"

"It is very well, madame."

"Some of the boys run screaming. But I think she likes you. You're the first boarder she's ever referred to as a gentleman."

"Not at all, madame."

She looked at me, noticing my bare feet (I still felt strange wearing shoes indoors, and always removed them before entering my room). "Are you new to Boston?"

"New to America, madame."

"From?" She raised her eyebrows.

"I am from Calcutta, India."

"Is that right? We had a Brazilian fellow, about a year ago. You'll find Cambridge a very international city."

I nodded, and began to wonder how long our conversation would last. But at that moment we heard Mrs. Croft's electrifying voice rising up the stairs. When we stepped into the hallway we heard her hollering:

"You are to come downstairs immediately!"

"What is it?" Helen hollered back.

"Immediately!"

I put on my shoes at once. Helen sighed.

We walked down the staircase. It was too narrow for us to descend side by side, so I followed Helen, who seemed to be in no hurry, and complained at one point that she had a bad knee. "Have you been walking without your cane?" Helen called out. "You know you're not supposed to walk without that cane." She paused, resting her hand on the banister, and looked back at me. "She slips sometimes."

For the first time Mrs. Croft seemed vulnerable. I pictured her on the floor in front of the bench, flat on her back, staring at the ceiling, her feet pointing in opposite directions. But when we reached the bottom of the staircase she was sitting there as usual, her hands folded together in her lap. Two grocery bags were at her feet. When we stood before her she did not slap the bench, or ask us to sit down. She glared.

"What is it, Mother?"

"It's improper!"

"What's improper?"

"It is improper for a lady and gentleman who are not married to one another to hold a private conversation without a chaperone!"

Helen said she was sixty-eight years old, old enough to be my mother, but Mrs. Croft insisted that Helen and I speak to each other downstairs, in the parlor. She added that it was also improper for a lady of Helen's station to reveal her age, and to wear a dress so high above the ankle.

"For your information, Mother, it's 1969. What would you do if you actually left the house one day and saw a girl in a miniskirt?"

Mrs. Croft sniffed. "I'd have her arrested."

Helen shook her head and picked up one of the grocery bags. I picked up the other one, and followed her through the parlor and into the kitchen. The bags were filled with cans of soup, which Helen opened up one by one with a few cranks of a can opener. She tossed the old soup in the saucepans into the sink, rinsed the pans under the tap, filled them with soup from the newly opened cans, and put them back in the refrigerator. "A few years ago she could still open the cans herself," Helen said. "She hates that I do it for her now. But the piano killed her hands." She put on her spectacles, glanced at the cupboards, and spotted my tea bags. "Shall we have a cup?"

I filled the kettle on the stove. "I beg your pardon, madame. The piano?"

"She used to give lessons. For forty years. It was how she raised us after my father died." Helen put her hands on her hips, staring at the open refrigerator. She reached into the back, pulled out a wrapped stick of butter, frowned, and tossed it into the garbage. "That ought to do it," she said, and put the unopened cans of soup in the cupboard. I sat at the table and watched as Helen washed the dirty dishes, tied up the garbage bag, watered a spider plant over the sink, and poured boiling water into two cups. She handed one to me without milk, the string of the tea bag trailing over the side, and sat down at the table.

"Excuse me, madame, but is it enough?"

Helen took a sip of her tea. Her lipstick left a smiling pink stain on the inside rim of the cup. "Is what enough?"

"The soup in the pans. Is it enough food for Mrs. Croft?"   90

"She won't eat anything else. She stopped eating solids after she turned one hundred. That was, let's see, three years ago."

I was mortified. I had assumed Mrs. Croft was in her eighties, perhaps as old as ninety. I had never known a person who had lived for over a century. That this person was a widow who lived alone mortified me further still. It was widowhood that had driven my own mother insane. My father, who worked as a clerk at the General Post Office of Calcutta, died of encephalitis when I was sixteen. My mother refused to adjust to life without him; instead she sank deeper into a world of darkness from which neither I, nor my brother, nor concerned relatives, nor psychiatric clinics on Rash Behari Avenue could save her. What pained me most was to see her so unguarded, to hear her burp after meals or expel gas in front of company without the slightest embarrassment. After my father's death my brother abandoned his schooling and began to work in the jute mill he would eventually manage, in order to keep the household running. And so it was my job to sit by my mother's feet and study for my exams as she counted and recounted the bracelets on her arm as if they were the beads of an abacus. We tried to keep an eye on her. Once she had wandered half naked to the tram depot before we were able to bring her inside again.

"I am happy to warm Mrs. Croft's soup in the evenings," I suggested, removing the tea bag from my cup and squeezing out the liquor. "It is no trouble."

Helen looked at her watch, stood up, and poured the rest of her tea into the sink. "I wouldn't if I were you. That's the sort of thing that would kill her altogether."

* * *

That evening, when Helen had gone back to Arlington and Mrs. Croft and I   95 were alone again, I began to worry. Now that I knew how very old she was, I worried that something would happen to her in the middle of the night, or when I was out during the day. As vigorous as her voice was, and imperious as she seemed, I knew that even a scratch or a cough could kill a person that old; each day she lived, I knew, was something of a miracle. Although Helen had seemed friendly enough, a small part of me worried that she might accuse me of negligence if anything were to happen. Helen didn't seem worried. She came and went, bringing soup for Mrs. Croft, one Sunday after the next.

In this manner the six weeks of that summer passed. I came home each evening, after my hours at the library, and spent a few minutes on the piano bench with Mrs. Croft. I gave her a bit of my company, and assured her that I had checked the lock, and told her that the flag on the moon was splendid. Some evenings I sat beside her long after she had drifted off to sleep, still in awe of how many years she had spent on this earth. At times I tried to picture the world she had been born into, in 1866—a world, I imagined, filled with women in long black skirts, and chaste conversations in the parlor. Now, when I looked at her hands with their swollen knuckles folded together in her lap, I imagined them smooth and slim, striking the piano keys. At times I came downstairs before going to sleep, to make sure she was sitting upright on the bench, or was safe in her bedroom. On Fridays I made sure to put the rent in her hands. There was nothing I could do for her beyond these simple gestures. I was not her son, and apart from those eight dollars, I owed her nothing.

* * *

At the end of August, Mala's passport and green card were ready. I received a telegram with her flight information; my brother's house in Calcutta had no telephone. Around that time I also received a letter from her, written only a few days after we had parted. There was no salutation; addressing me by name would have assumed an intimacy we had not yet discovered. It contained only a few lines. "I write in English in preparation for the journey. Here I am very much lonely. Is it very cold there. Is there snow. Yours, Mala."

I was not touched by her words. We had spent only a handful of days in each other's company. And yet we were bound together; for six weeks she had worn an iron bangle on her wrist, and applied vermilion powder to the part in her hair, to signify to the world that she was a bride. In those six weeks I regarded her arrival as I would the arrival of a coming month, or season—something inevitable, but meaningless at the time. So little did I know her that, while details of her face sometimes rose to my memory, I could not conjure up the whole of it.

A few days after receiving the letter, as I was walking to work in the morning, I saw an Indian woman on the other side of Massachusetts Avenue, wearing a sari with its free end nearly dragging on the footpath, and pushing a child in a stroller. An American woman with a small black dog on a leash was walking to one side of her. Suddenly the dog began barking. From the other side of the street I watched as the Indian woman, startled, stopped in her path, at which point the dog leapt up and seized the end of the sari between its teeth. The American woman scolded the dog, appeared to apologize, and walked quickly away, leaving the Indian woman to fix her sari in the middle of the footpath, and quiet her crying child. She did not see me standing there, and eventually she continued on her way. Such a mishap, I realized that morning, would soon be my concern. It was my duty to take care of Mala, to welcome her and protect her. I would have to buy her her first pair of snow boots, her first winter coat. I would have to tell her which streets to avoid, which way the traffic came, tell her to wear her sari so that the free end did not drag on the footpath. A five-mile separation from her parents, I recalled with some irritation, had caused her to weep.

Unlike Mala, I was used to it all by then: used to cornflakes and milk, used to Helen's visits, used to sitting on the bench with Mrs. Croft. The only thing I was not used to was Mala. Nevertheless I did what I had to do. I went to the

100

housing office at MIT and found a furnished apartment a few blocks away, with a double bed and a private kitchen and bath, for forty dollars a week. One last Friday I handed Mrs. Croft eight one-dollar bills in an envelope, brought my suitcase downstairs, and informed her that I was moving. She put my key into her change purse. The last thing she asked me to do was hand her the cane propped against the table, so that she could walk to the door and lock it behind me. "Good-bye, then," she said, and retreated back into the house. I did not expect any display of emotion, but I was disappointed all the same. I was only a boarder, a man who paid her a bit of money and passed in and out of her home for six weeks. Compared to a century, it was no time at all.

*   *   *

At the airport I recognized Mala immediately. The free end of her sari did not drag on the floor, but was draped in a sign of bridal modesty over her head, just as it had draped my mother until the day my father died. Her thin brown arms were stacked with gold bracelets, a small red circle was painted on her forehead, and the edges of her feet were tinted with a decorative red dye. I did not embrace her, or kiss her, or take her hand. Instead I asked her, speaking Bengali for the first time in America, if she was hungry.

She hesitated, then nodded yes.

I told her I had prepared some egg curry at home. "What did they give you to eat on the plane?"

"I didn't eat."

"All the way from Calcutta?"   105

"The menu said oxtail soup."

"But surely there were other items."

"The thought of eating an ox's tail made me lose my appetite."

When we arrived home, Mala opened up one of her suitcases, and presented me with two pullover sweaters, both made with bright blue wool, which she had knitted in the course of our separation, one with a V neck, the other covered with cables. I tried them on; both were tight under the arms. She had also brought me two new pairs of drawstring pajamas, a letter from my brother, and a packet of loose Darjeeling tea. I had no present for her apart from the egg curry. We sat at a bare table, each of us staring at our plates. We ate with our hands, another thing I had not yet done in America.

"The house is nice," she said. "Also the egg curry." With her left hand she   110
held the end of her sari to her chest, so it would not slip off her head.

"I don't know many recipes."

She nodded, peeling the skin off each of her potatoes before eating them. At one point the sari slipped to her shoulders. She readjusted it at once.

"There is no need to cover your head," I said. "I don't mind. It doesn't matter here."

She kept it covered anyway.

I waited to get used to her, to her presence at my side, at my table and in my   115
bed, but a week later we were still strangers. I still was not used to coming home to an apartment that smelled of steamed rice, and finding that the basin in the bathroom was always wiped clean, our two toothbrushes lying side by side, a cake of Pears soap from India resting in the soap dish. I was not used to the fragrance of the coconut oil she rubbed every other night into her scalp, or the delicate

sound her bracelets made as she moved about the apartment. In the mornings she was always awake before I was. The first morning when I came into the kitchen she had heated up the leftovers and set a plate with a spoonful of salt on its edge on the table, assuming I would eat rice for breakfast, as most Bengali husbands did. I told her cereal would do, and the next morning when I came into the kitchen she had already poured the cornflakes into my bowl. One morning she walked with me down Massachusetts Avenue to MIT, where I gave her a short tour of the campus. On the way we stopped at a hardware store and I made a copy of the key, so that she could let herself into the apartment. The next morning before I left for work she asked me for a few dollars. I parted with them reluctantly, but I knew that this, too, was now normal. When I came home from work there was a potato peeler in the kitchen drawer, and a tablecloth on the table, and chicken curry made with fresh garlic and ginger on the stove. We did not have a television in those days. After dinner I read the newspaper, while Mala sat at the kitchen table, working on a cardigan for herself with more of the bright blue wool, or writing letters home.

At the end of our first week, on Friday, I suggested going out. Mala set down her knitting and disappeared into the bathroom. When she emerged I regretted the suggestion; she had put on a clean silk sari and extra bracelets, and coiled her hair with a flattering side part on top of her head. She was prepared as if for a party, or at the very least for the cinema, but I had no such destination in mind. The evening air was balmy. We walked several blocks down Massachusetts Avenue, looking into the windows of restaurants and shops. Then, without thinking, I led her down the quiet street where for so many nights I had walked alone.

"This is where I lived before you came," I said, stopping at Mrs. Croft's chain-link fence.

"In such a big house?"

"I had a small room upstairs. At the back."

"Who else lives there?" 120

"A very old woman."

"With her family?"

"Alone."

"But who takes care of her?"

I opened the gate. "For the most part she takes care of herself." 125

I wondered if Mrs. Croft would remember me; I wondered if she had a new boarder to sit with her on the bench each evening. When I pressed the bell I expected the same long wait as that day of our first meeting, when I did not have a key. But this time the door was opened almost immediately, by Helen. Mrs. Croft was not sitting on the bench. The bench was gone.

"Hello there," Helen said, smiling with her bright pink lips at Mala. "Mother's in the parlor. Will you be visiting awhile?"

"As you wish, madame."

"Then I think I'll run to the store, if you don't mind. She had a little accident. We can't leave her alone these days, not even for a minute."

I locked the door after Helen and walked into the parlor. Mrs. Croft was ly- 130 ing flat on her back, her head on a peach-colored cushion, a thin white quilt spread over her body. Her hands were folded together on top of her chest. When she saw me she pointed at the sofa, and told me to sit down. I took my place as directed, but Mala wandered over to the piano and sat on the bench, which was now positioned where it belonged.

"I broke my hip!" Mrs. Croft announced, as if no time had passed.

"Oh dear, madame."

"I fell off the bench!"

"I am so sorry, madame."

"It was the middle of the night! Do you know what I did, boy?"   135

I shook my head.

"I called the police!"

She stared up at the ceiling and grinned sedately, exposing a crowded row of long gray teeth. Not one was missing. "What do you say to that, boy?"

As stunned as I was, I knew what I had to say. With no hesitation at all, I cried out, "Splendid!"

Mala laughed then. Her voice was full of kindness, her eyes bright with   140 amusement. I had never heard her laugh before, and it was loud enough so that Mrs. Croft had heard, too. She turned to Mala and glared.

"Who is she, boy?"

"She is my wife, madame."

Mrs. Croft pressed her head at an angle against the cushion to get a better look. "Can you play the piano?"

"No, madame," Mala replied.

"Then stand up!"   145

Mala rose to her feet, adjusting the end of her sari over her head and holding it to her chest, and, for the first time since her arrival, I felt sympathy. I remembered my first days in London, learning how to take the Tube to Russell Square, riding an escalator for the first time, being unable to understand that when the man cried "piper" it meant "paper," being unable to decipher, for a whole year, that the conductor said "mind the gap" as the train pulled away from each station. Like me, Mala had traveled far from home, not knowing where she was going, or what she would find, for no reason other than to be my wife. As strange as it seemed, I knew in my heart that one day her death would affect me, and stranger still, that mine would affect her. I wanted somehow to explain this to Mrs. Croft, who was still scrutinizing Mala from top to toe with what seemed to be placid disdain. I wondered if Mrs. Croft had ever seen a woman in a sari, with a dot painted on her forehead and bracelets stacked on her wrists. I wondered what she would object to. I wondered if she could see the red dye still vivid on Mala's feet, all but obscured by the bottom edge of her sari. At last Mrs. Croft declared, with the equal measures of disbelief and delight I knew well:

"She is a perfect lady!"

Now it was I who laughed. I did so quietly, and Mrs. Croft did not hear me. But Mala had heard, and, for the first time, we looked at each other and smiled.

* * *

I like to think of that moment in Mrs. Croft's parlor as the moment when the distance between Mala and me began to lessen. Although we were not yet fully in love, I like to think of the months that followed as a honeymoon of sorts. Together we explored the city and met other Bengalis, some of whom are still friends today. We discovered that a man named Bill sold fresh fish on Prospect

Street, and that a shop in Harvard Square called Cardullo's sold bay leaves and cloves. In the evenings we walked to the Charles River to watch sailboats drift across the water, or had ice cream cones in Harvard Yard. We bought an Instamatic camera with which to document our life together, and I took pictures of her posing in front of the Prudential building, so that she could send them to her parents. At night we kissed, shy at first but quickly bold, and discovered pleasure and solace in each other's arms. I told her about my voyage on the SS *Roma*, and about Finsbury Park and the YMCA, and my evenings on the bench with Mrs. Croft. When I told her stories about my mother, she wept. It was Mala who consoled me when, reading the *Globe* one evening, I came across Mrs. Croft's obituary. I had not thought of her in several months—by then those six weeks of the summer were already a remote interlude in my past—but when I learned of her death I was stricken, so much so that when Mala looked up from her knitting she found me staring at the wall, the newspaper neglected in my lap, unable to speak. Mrs. Croft's was the first death I mourned in America, for hers was the first life I had admired; she had left this world at last, ancient and alone, never to return.

As for me, I have not strayed much farther. Mala and I live in a town about 150 twenty miles from Boston, on a tree-lined street much like Mrs. Croft's, in a house we own, with a garden that saves us from buying tomatoes in summer, and room for guests. We are American citizens now, so that we can collect social security when it is time. Though we visit Calcutta every few years, and bring back more drawstring pajamas and Darjeeling tea, we have decided to grow old here. I work in a small college library. We have a son who attends Harvard University. Mala no longer drapes the end of her sari over her head, or weeps at night for her parents, but occasionally she weeps for our son. So we drive to Cambridge to visit him, or bring him home for a weekend, so that he can eat rice with us with his hands, and speak in Bengali, things we sometimes worry he will no longer do after we die.

Whenever we make that drive, I always make it a point to take Massachusetts Avenue, in spite of the traffic. I barely recognize the buildings now, but each time I am there I return instantly to those six weeks as if they were only the other day, and I slow down and point to Mrs. Croft's street, saying to my son, here was my first home in America, where I lived with a woman who was 103. "Remember?" Mala says, and smiles, amazed, as I am, that there was ever a time that we were strangers. My son always expresses his astonishment, not at Mrs. Croft's age, but at how little I paid in rent, a fact nearly as inconceivable to him as a flag on the moon was to a woman born in 1866. In my son's eyes I see the ambition that had first hurled me across the world. In a few years he will graduate and pave his way, alone and unprotected. But I remind myself that he has a father who is still living, a mother who is happy and strong. Whenever he is discouraged, I tell him that if I can survive on three continents, then there is no obstacle he cannot conquer. While the astronauts, heroes forever, spent mere hours on the moon. I have remained in this new world for nearly thirty years. I know that my achievement is quite ordinary. I am not the only man to seek his fortune far from home, and certainly I am not the first. Still, there are times I am bewildered by each mile I have traveled, each meal I have eaten, each person I have known, each room in which I have slept. As ordinary as it all appears, there are times when it is beyond my imagination.

Talking about the Text

1. What reasons can you imagine for Lahiri's choosing the title "The Third and Final Continent"?
2. One theme of the story is a friendship—a friendship of few words between two strangers separated by differences of gender, age, ethnicity, religion. Why and how does this friendship between the narrator and Mrs. Croft work?

Writing about the Text

1. Mrs. Croft appears two ways in this story: as a nice person, and as difficult. Write two different descriptions of an elderly person, one to make her seem nice, one to make her seem difficult.
2. What Mrs. Croft commands the narrator to do is in a very real sense terribly offensive, especially when we recall that he comes from India, which only two decades before had been a colony of Great Britain. Is she aware of those connotations? Is the narrator? Explain why he doesn't just walk out when she starts acting so outrageously?

Linking the Text to Other Texts

1. Why and how does the connection between the narrator and Mrs. Croft make possible the husband and wife relation between the narrator and Mala? Compare this story with another in which a couple's relationship is affected by a third person.
2. Could this story have taken place anywhere in America, or is it rooted in a particular place? Choose one other story from this chapter and answer the same question about it.

✍ COMMENTARY

Jhumpa Lahiri on the Short Story

From an interview in Pif Magazine, July 28, 1999

Q: You've read from [*Interpreter of Maladies*] to Indians, to Asian American groups, and to general audiences in bookstores. Have their reactions differed?

Lahiri: The reactions haven't differed; the concerns have been different. When I read for a predominantly Indian audience, there are more questions that are based on issues of identity and representation. That also happened in England last week. Some Indians will come up and say that a story reminded them of something very specific to their experience. Which may or may not be the case for non-Indians. But I've also been receiving incredibly touching letters from people who are not Indian, not women, but (I'm assuming) older American men commenting on the story ["The Third and Final Continent"] in *The New Yorker*'s recent fiction issue about a young man's odyssey in the United States, and connecting to it in a way that I find quite remarkable.

Q: Would you advise a beginning short story writer to send his or her first submission to *The New Yorker* or to less known publications or simultaneously to all?

Lahiri: I would not send a first story anywhere. I would give myself time to write a number of stories.

   I started writing, and then I bought a book on where to send stories. I would send them out, they all came back, then I would write something else, this went on for years. Sometimes I got a nice note, and that gives you a little bit of inspiration for the next time you sit down to write. It's a combination of being attuned to that whole world out there, the editor, the publisher, blah, blah, blah, but also knowing that really is not the goal. If it happens, it happens; if it doesn't happen for a long time, that's okay too.

Starting Point for Further Research: Jhumpa Lahiri

- **Interview:** Arun Aguiar. "One on One with Jhumpa Lahiri." Pifmagazine.com. July 28, 1999. http://www.pifmagazine.com/vol28/i_agui.shtml.

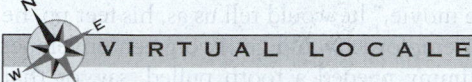

VIRTUAL LOCALE

The South Asian Women's Network's Online Bookshelf. An online forum for and about women from South Asia—Bangladesh, Bhutan, India, Maldives, Nepal, Pakistan, and Sri Lanka—the South Asian Women's Network (SAWNET) includes a page called SAWNET Bookshelf at *www.sawnet.org/ books/*, a lengthy section of resources and links on writing from all genres by South Asian women writers. While the site includes information about writers native to and still living in South Asia, it also covers the lives and works of South Asian writers who write predominantly in English and make their homes in English-speaking countries, the United Kingdom and the United States being the most common ones.

GISH JEN   (B. 1956)

Gish Jen was born in 1956 to an immigrant Chinese American family living in Queens, New York, and grew up in Scarsdale, a well-to-do New York suburb. She majored in English at Harvard and enrolled in the MBA program at Stanford, but she dropped out to write stories and went on to attend the University of Iowa's Writers Workshop. Jen has won many awards and honors for her humorous, sympathetic stories about Chinese American life. Her first novel, Typical American, *appeared in 1991 and was followed by* Mona in the Promised Land *(1996), the short story collection* Who's Irish? *(1999), and* The Love Wife *(2004), all of which treat Chinese families in the process of adapting to America. She lives in Cambridge, Massachusetts.*

In the American Society   (1986)

I. His Own Society

When my father took over the pancake house, it was to send my little sister Mona and me to college. We were only in junior high at the time, but my father believed in getting a jump on things. "Those Americans always saying it," he told us. "Smart guys thinking in advance." My mother elaborated, explaining that businesses took bringing up, like children. They could take years to get going, she said, years.

In this case, though, we got rich right away. At two months we were breaking even, and at four, those same hotcakes that could barely withstand the weight of butter and syrup were supporting our family with ease. My mother bought a station wagon with air conditioning, my father an oversized, red vinyl recliner for the back room; and as time went on and the business continued to thrive, my father started to talk about his grandfather and the village he had reigned over in China—things my father had never talked about when he worked for other people. He told us about the bags of rice his family would give out to the poor at New Year's, and about the people who came to beg, on their hands and knees, for his grandfather to intercede for the more wayward of their relatives. "Like that Godfather in the movie," he would tell us as, his feet up, he distributed paychecks. Sometimes an employee would get two green envelopes instead of one, which meant that Jimmy needed a tooth pulled, say, or that Tiffany's husband was in the clinker again.

"It's nothing, nothing," he would insist, sinking back into his chair. "Who else is going to take care of you people?"

My mother would mostly just sigh about it. "Your father thinks this is China," she would say, and then she would go back to her mending. Once in a while, though, when my father had given away a particularly large sum, she would exclaim, outraged, "But this here is the U—S—of—A!" this apparently having been what she used to tell immigrant stock boys when they came in late.

She didn't work at the supermarket anymore; but she had made it to the   5
rank of manager before she left, and this had given her not only new words and phrases, but new ideas about herself, and about America, and about what was what in general. She had opinions, now, on how downtown should be zoned; she could pump her own gas and check her own oil; and for all she used to chide Mona and me for being "copycats," she herself was now interested in espadrilles, and wallpaper, and most recently, the town country club.

"So join already," said Mona, flicking a fly off her knee.

My mother enumerated the problems as she sliced up a quarter round of watermelon: There was the cost. There was the waiting list. There was the fact that no one in our family played either tennis or golf.

"So what?" said Mona.

"It would be waste," said my mother.

"Me and Callie can swim in the pool."   10

"Plus you need that recommendation letter from a member."

"Come *on*," said Mona. "Annie's mom'd write you a letter in a *sec*."

My mother's knife glinted in the early summer sun. I spread some more newspaper on the picnic table.

"*Plus* you have to eat there twice a month. You know what that means." My mother cut another enormous slice of fruit.

"No, I *don't* know what that means," said Mona.   15

"It means Dad would have to wear a jacket, dummy," I said.

"Oh! Oh! Oh!" said Mona, clasping her hand to her breast. "Oh! Oh! Oh! Oh! Oh!"

We all laughed: my father had no use for nice clothes, and would wear only ten-year-old shirts, with grease-spotted pants, to show how little he cared what anyone thought.

"Your father doesn't believe in joining the American society," said my mother. "He wants to have his own society."

"So go to dinner without him." Mona shot her seeds out in long arcs over 20
the lawn. "Who cares what he thinks?"

But of course we all did care, and knew my mother could not simply up and do as she pleased. For in my father's mind, a family owed its head a degree of loyalty that left no room for dissent. To embrace what he embraced was to love; and to embrace something else was to betray him.

He demanded a similar sort of loyalty of his workers, whom he treated more like servants than employees. Not in the beginning, of course. In the beginning all he wanted was for them to keep on doing what they used to do, and to that end he concentrated mostly on leaving them alone. As the months passed, though, he expected more and more of them, with the result that for all his largesse, he began to have trouble keeping help. The cooks and busboys complained that he asked them to fix radiators and trim hedges, not only at the restaurant, but at our house; the waitresses that he sent them on errands and made them chauffeur him around. Our head waitress, Gertrude, claimed that he once even asked her to scratch his back.

"It's not just the blacks don't believe in slavery," she said when she quit.

My father never quite registered her complaint, though, nor those of the others who left. Even after Eleanor quit, then Tiffany, then Gerald, and Jimmy, and even his best cook, Eureka Andy, for whom he had bought new glasses, he remained mostly convinced that the fault lay with them.

"All they understand is that assembly line," he lamented. "Robots, they are. 25
They want to be robots."

There *were* occasions when the clear running truth seemed to eddy, when he would pinch the vinyl of his chair up into little peaks and wonder if he was doing things right. But with time he would always smooth the peaks back down; and when business started to slide in the spring, he kept on like a horse in his ways.

By the summer our dishboy was overwhelmed with scraping. It was no longer just the hashbrowns that people were leaving for trash, and the service was as bad as the food. The waitresses served up French pancakes instead of German, apple juice instead of orange, spilt things on laps, on coats. On the Fourth of July some greenhorn sent an entire side of fries slaloming down a lady's *massif centrale*. Meanwhile in the back room, my father labored through articles on the economy.

"What is housing starts?" he puzzled. "What is GNP?"

Mona and I did what we could, filling in as busgirls and bookkeepers and, one afternoon, stuffing the comments box that hung by the cashier's desk. That was Mona's idea. We rustled up a variety of pens and pencils, checked boxes for an hour, smeared the cards up with coffee and grease, and waited. It took a few days for my father to notice that the box was full, and he didn't say anything about it for a few days more. Finally, though, he started to complain of fatigue, and then he began to complain that the staff was not what it could be. We encouraged him in this—pointing out, for instance, how many dishes got chipped—but in the end all that happened was that, for the first time since we took over the restaurant, my father got it into his head to fire someone. Skip, a skinny busboy who was saving up for a sportscar, said nothing as my father mumbled on about the price of dishes. My father's hands shook as he wrote out the severance check; and he spent the rest of the day napping in his chair once it was over.

As it was going on midsummer, Skip wasn't easy to replace. We hung a sign   30
in the window and advertised in the paper, but no one called the first week, and the person who called the second didn't show up for his interview. The third week, my father phoned Skip to see if he would come back, but a friend of his had already sold him a Corvette for cheap.

Finally a Chinese guy named Booker turned up. He couldn't have been more than thirty, and was wearing a lighthearted seersucker suit, but he looked as though life had him pinned: his eyes were bloodshot and his chest sunken, and the muscles of his neck seemed to strain with the effort of holding his head up. In a single dry breath he told us that he had never bussed tables but was willing to learn, and that he was on the lam from the deportation authorities.

"I do not want to lie to you," he kept saying. He had come to the United States on a student visa, had run out of money, and was now in a bind. He was loath to go back to Taiwan, as it happened—he looked up at this point, to be sure my father wasn't pro-KMT[1]—but all he had was a phony social security card and a willingness to absorb all blame, should anything untoward come to pass.

"I do not think, anyway, that it is against law to hire me, only to be me," he said, smiling faintly.

Anyone else would have examined him on this, but my father conceived of laws as speed bumps rather than curbs. He wiped the counter with his sleeve, and told Booker to report the next morning.

"I will be good worker," said Booker.   35

"Good," said my father.

"Anything you want me to do, I will do."

My father nodded.

Booker seemed to sink into himself for a moment. "Thank you," he said finally. "I am appreciate your help. I am very, very appreciate for everything." He reached out to shake my father's hand.

My father looked at him. "Did you eat today?" he asked in Mandarin.   40

Booker pulled at the hem of his jacket.

"Sit down," said my father. "Please, have a seat."

* * *

My father didn't tell my mother about Booker, and my mother didn't tell my father about the country club. She would never have applied, except that Mona, while over at Annie's, had let it drop that our mother wanted to join. Mrs. Lardner came by the very next day.

"Why, I'd be honored and delighted to write you people a letter," she said. Her skirt billowed around her.

"Thank you so much," said my mother. "But it's too much trouble for you,   45
and also my husband is . . ."

---

[1]Pro-Kuomintang; that is, a supporter of China's anticommunist Nationalist Party, which took over the island of Taiwan in 1949.

"Oh, it's no trouble at all, no trouble at all. I tell you." She leaned forward so that her chest freckles showed. "I know just how it is. It's a secret of course, but you know, my natural father was Jewish. Can you see it? Just took at my skin."

"My husband," said my mother.

"I'd be honored and delighted," said Mrs. Lardner with a little wave of her hands. "Just honored and delighted."

Mona was triumphant. "See, Mom," she said, waltzing around the kitchen when Mrs. Lardner left. "What did I tell you? 'I'm just honored and delighted, just honored and delighted.'" She waved her hands in the air.

"You know, the Chinese have a saying," said my mother. "To do nothing is   50
better than to overdo. You mean well, but you tell me now what will happen."

"I'll talk Dad into it," said Mona, still waltzing. "Or I bet Callie can. He'll do anything Callie says."

"I can try, anyway," I said.

"Did you hear what I said?" said my mother. Mona bumped into the broom closet door. "You're not going to talk anything; you've already made enough trouble." She started on the dishes with a clatter.

Mona poked diffidently at a mop.

I sponged off the counter. "Anyway," I ventured, "I bet our name'll never   55
even come up."

"That's if we're lucky," said my mother.

"There's all these people waiting," I said.

"Good," she said. She started on a pot.

I looked over at Mona, who was still cowering in the broom closet. "In fact, there's some black family's been waiting so long, they're going to sue," I said.

My mother turned off the water. "Where'd you hear that?"   60

"Patty told me."

She turned the water back on, started to wash a dish, then put it back down and shut the faucet.

"I'm sorry," said Mona.

"Forget it" said my mother. "Just forget It."

* * *

Booker turned out to be a model worker, whose boundless gratitude translated   65
into a willingness to do anything. As he also learned quickly, he soon knew not only how to bus, but how to cook, and how to wait table, and how to keep the books. He fixed the walk-in door so that it stayed shut, reupholstered the torn seats in the dining room, and devised a system for tracking inventory. The only stone in the rice was that he tended to be sickly; but, reliable even in illness, he would always send a friend to take his place. In this way we got to know Ronald, Lynn, Dirk, and Cedric, all of whom, like Booker, had problems with their legal status and were anxious to please. They weren't all as capable as Booker, though, with the exception of Cedric, whom my father often hired even when Booker was well. A round wag of a man who called Mona and me *shou hou*—skinny monkeys—he was a professed nonsmoker who was nevertheless always begging drags off of other people's cigarettes. This last habit drove our head cook, Fernando, crazy, especially since, when refused a hit, Cedric would occasionally snitch one. Winking impishly at Mona and me, he would steal up to an ashtray, take a quick puff, and then break out laughing so that the smoke came rolling

out of his mouth in a great incriminatory cloud. Fernando accused him of stealing fresh cigarettes too, even whole packs.

"Why else do you think he's weaseling around in the back of the store all the time," he said. His face was blotchy with anger. "The man is a frigging thief."

Other members of the staff supported him in this contention and joined in on an "Operation Identification," which involved numbering and initialing their cigarettes—even though what they seemed to fear for wasn't so much their cigarettes as their jobs. Then one of the cooks quit; and rather than promote someone, my father hired Cedric for the position. Rumors flew that he was taking only half the normal salary, that Alex had been pressured to resign, and that my father was looking for a position with which to placate Booker, who had been bypassed because of his health.

The result was that Fernando categorically refused to work with Cedric.

"The only way I'll cook with that piece of slime," he said, shaking his huge tattooed fist, "is if it's his ass frying on the grill."

My father cajoled and cajoled, to no avail, and in the end was simply forced   70
to put them on different schedules.

The next week Fernando got caught stealing a carton of minute steaks. My father would not tell even Mona and me how he knew to be standing by the back door when Fernando was on his way out, but everyone suspected Booker. Everyone but Fernando, that is, who was sure Cedric had been the tip-off. My father held a staff meeting in which he tried to reassure everyone that Alex had left on his own, and that he had no intention of firing anyone. But though he was careful not to mention Fernando, everyone was so amazed that he was being allowed to stay that Fernando was incensed nonetheless.

"Don't you all be putting your bug eyes on me," he said. "*He's* the frigging crook." He grabbed Cedric by the collar.

Cedric raised an eyebrow. "Cook, you mean," he said.

At this Fernando punched Cedric in the mouth; and the words he had just uttered notwithstanding, my father fired him on the spot.

* * *

With everything that was happening, Mona and I were ready to be getting out of   75
the restaurant. It was almost time: the days were still stuffy with summer, but our window shade had started flapping in the evening as if gearing up to go out. That year the breezes were full of salt, as they sometimes were when they came in from the East, and they blew anchors and docks through my mind like so many tumbleweeds, filling my dreams with wherries and lobsters and grainy-faced men who squinted, day in and day out, at the sky.

It was time for a change, you could feel it; and yet the pancake house was the same as ever. The day before school started my father came home with bad news.

"Fernando called police," he said, wiping his hand on his pant leg.

My mother naturally wanted to know what police; and so with much coughing and hawing, the long story began, the latest installment of which had the police calling immigration, and immigration sending an investigator. My mother sat stiff as whalebone as my father described how the man summarily refused lunch on the house and how my father had admitted, under pressure, that he knew there were "things" about his workers.

"So now what happens?"

My father didn't know. "Booker and Cedric went with him to the jail," he said. "But me, here I am." He laughed uncomfortably.

The next day my father posted bail for "his boys" and waited apprehensively for something to happen. The day after that he waited again, and the day after that he called our neighbor's law student son, who suggested my father call the immigration department under an alias. My father took his advice; and it was thus that he discovered that Booker was right: it was illegal for aliens to work, but it wasn't to hire them.

In the happy interval that ensued, my father apologized to my mother, who in turn confessed about the country club, for which my father had no choice but to forgive her. Then he turned his attention back to "his boys."

My mother didn't see that there was anything to do.

"I like to talking to the judge," said my father.

"This is not China," said my mother.

"I'm only talking to him. I'm not give him money unless he wants it."

"You're going to land up in jail."

"So what else I should do?" My father threw up his hands. "Those are my boys."

"Your boys!" exploded my mother. "What about your family? What about your wife?"

My father took a long sip of tea. "You know," he said finally, "in the war my father sent our cook to the soldiers to use. He always said it—the province comes before the town, the town comes before the family."

"A restaurant is not a town," said my mother.

My father sipped at his tea again. "You know, when I first come to the United States, I also had to hide-and-seek with those deportation guys. If people did not help me, I'm not here today."

My mother scrutinized her hem.

After a minute I volunteered that before seeing a judge, he might try a lawyer.

He turned. "Since when did you become so afraid like your mother?"

I started to say that it wasn't a matter of fear, but he cut me off.

"What I need today," he said, "is a son."

My father and I spent the better part of the next day standing in lines at the immigration office. He did not get to speak to a judge, but with much persistence he managed to speak to a judge's clerk, who tried to persuade him that it was not her place to extend him advice. My father, though, shamelessly plied her with compliments and offers of free pancakes until she finally conceded that she personally doubted anything would happen to either Cedric or Booker.

"Especially if they're 'needed workers,' " she said, rubbing at the red marks her glasses left on her nose. She yawned. "Have you thought about sponsoring them to become permanent residents?"

Could he do that? My father was overjoyed. And what if he saw to it right away? Would she perhaps put in a good word with the judge?

She yawned again, her nostrils flaring. "Don't worry," she said. "They'll get a fair hearing."

My father returned jubilant. Booker and Cedric hailed him as their savior, their Buddha incarnate. He was like a father to them, they said; and laughing and clapping, they made him tell the story over and over, sorting over the details like jewels. And how old was the assistant judge? And what did she say?

That evening my father tipped the paperboy a dollar and bought a pot of mums for my mother, who suffered them to be placed on the dining room table. The next night he took us all out to dinner. Then on Saturday, Mona found a letter on my father's chair at the restaurant.

> Dear Mr. Chang,
>
> You are the grat boss. But, we do not like to trial, so will runing away now. Plese to excus us. People saying the law in America is fears like dragon. Here is only $140. We hope some day we can pay back the rest bale. You will getting intrest, as you diserving, so grat a boss you are. Thank you for every thing. In next life you will be burn in rich family, with no more pancaks.
>
> Yours truley,
> Booker + Cedric

In the weeks that followed my father went to the pancake house for crises, but otherwise hung around our house, fiddling idly with the sump pump and boiler in an effort, he said, to get ready for winter. It was as though he had gone into retirement, except that instead of moving South, he had moved to the basement. He even took to showering my mother with little attentions, and to calling her "old girl," and when we finally heard that the club had entertained all the applications it could for the year, he was so sympathetic that he seemed more disappointed than my mother.

II. In the American Society

Mrs. Lardner tempered the bad news with an invitation to a bon voyage "bash" 105 she was throwing for a friend of hers who was going to Greece for six months.

"Do come," she urged. "You'll meet everyone, and then, you know, if things open up in the spring . . ." She waved her hands.

My mother wondered if it would be appropriate to show up at a party for someone they didn't know, but "the honest truth" was that this was an annual affair. "If it's not Greece, it's Antibes," sighed Mrs. Lardner. "We really just do it because his wife left him and his daughter doesn't speak to him, and poor Jeremy just feels so *unloved*."

She also invited Mona and me to the goings on, as "*demi-guests*" to keep Annie out of the champagne. I wasn't too keen on the idea, but before I could say anything, she had already thanked us for so generously agreeing to honor her with our presence.

"A pair of little princesses, you are!" she told us. "A pair of princesses!"

The party was that Sunday. On Saturday, my mother took my father out 110 shopping for a suit. As it was the end of September, she insisted that he buy a worsted rather than a seersucker, even though it was only ten, rather than fifty percent off. My father protested that it was as hot out as ever, which was true—a thick Indian summer had cozied murderously up to us—but to no avail. Summer clothes, said my mother, were not properly worn after Labor Day.

The suit was unfortunately as extravagant in length as it was in price, which posed an additional quandary, since the tailor wouldn't be in until Monday. The salesgirl, though, found a way of tacking it up temporarily.

"Maybe this suit not fit me," fretted my father.

"Just don't take your jacket off," said the salesgirl.

He gave her a tip before they left, but when he got home refused to remove the price tag.

"I like to asking the tailor about the size," he insisted. 115

"You mean you're going to *wear* it and then return it?" Mona rolled her eyes.

"I didn't say I'm return it," said my father stiffly. "I like to asking the tailor, that's all."

* * *

The party started off swimmingly, except that most people were wearing bermudas or wrap skirts. Still, my parents carried on, sharing with great feeling the complaints about the heat. Of course my father tried to eat a cracker full of shallots and burnt himself in an attempt to help Mr. Lardner turn the coals of the barbecue; but on the whole he seemed to be doing all right. Not nearly so well as my mother, though, who had accepted an entire cupful of Mrs. Lardner's magic punch, and seemed indeed to be under some spell. As Mona and Annie skirmished over whether some boy in their class inhaled when he smoked, I watched my mother take off her shoes, laughing and laughing as a man with a beard regaled her with navy stories by the pool. Apparently he had been stationed in the Orient and remembered a few words of Chinese, which made my mother laugh still more. My father excused himself to go to the men's room, then drifted back and "dropped" anchor at the hors d'oeuvre table, while my mother sailed on to a group of women, who tinkled at length over the clarity of her complexion. I dug out a book I had brought.

Just when I'd cracked the spine, though, Mrs. Lardner came by to bewail her shortage of servers. Her caterers were criminals, I agreed; and the next thing I knew I was handing out bits of marine life, making the rounds as amicably as I could.

"Here you go, Dad," I said when I got to the hors d'oeuvre table. 120

"Everything is fine," he said.

I hesitated to leave him alone; but then the man with the beard zeroed in on him, and though he talked of nothing but my mother, I thought it would be okay to get back to work. Just that moment, though, Jeremy Brothers lurched our way, an empty, albeit corked, wine bottle in hand. He was a slim, well-proportioned man, with a Roman nose and small eyes and a nice manly jaw that he allowed to hang agape.

"Hello," he said drunkenly. "Pleased to meet you."

"Pleased to meeting you," said my father.

"Right," said Jeremy. "Right. Listen. I have this bottle here, this most recal- 125 citrant bottle. You see that it refuses to do my bidding. I bid it open sesame, please, and it does nothing." He pulled the cork out with his teeth, then turned the bottle upside down.

My father nodded.

"Would you have a word with it please?" said Jeremy. The man with the beard excused himself. "Would you please have a goddamned word with it?"

My father laughed uncomfortably.

"Ah!" Jeremy bowed a little. "Excuse me, excuse me, excuse me. You are not my man, not my man at all." He bowed again and started to leave, but then circled back. "Viticulture is not your forte, yes I can see that, see that plainly. But may I trouble you on another matter? Forget the damned bottle." He threw it into the pool, and winked at the people he splashed. "I have another matter. Do you speak Chinese?"

My father said he did not, but Jeremy pulled out a handkerchief with some   130 characters on it anyway, saying that his daughter had sent it from Hong Kong and that he thought the characters might be some secret message.

"Long life," said my father.

"But you haven't looked at it yet."

"I know what it says without looking." My father winked at me.

"You do?"

"Yes, I do."   135

"You're making fun of me, aren't you?"

"No, no, no," said my father, winking again.

"Who are you anyway?" said Jeremy.

His smile fading, my father shrugged.

"Who are you?"   140

My father shrugged again.

Jeremy began to roar. "This is my party, *my party*, and I've never seen you before in my life." My father backed up as Jeremy came toward him. "*Who are you? WHO ARE YOU?*"

Just as my father was going to step back into the pool, Mrs. Lardner came running up. Jeremy informed her that there was a man crashing his party.

"Nonsense," said Mrs. Lardner. "This is Ralph Chang, who I invited extra especially so he could meet you." She straightened the collar of Jeremy's peach-colored polo shirt for him.

"Yes, well we've had a chance to chat," said Jeremy.   145

She whispered in his ear; he mumbled something; she whispered something more.

"I do apologize," he said finally.

My father didn't say anything.

"I do." Jeremy seemed genuinely contrite. "Doubtless you've seen drunks before, haven't you? You must have them in China."

"Okay," said my father.   150

As Mrs. Lardner glided off, Jeremy clapped his arm over my father's shoulders. "You know, I really am quite sorry, quite sorry."

My father nodded.

"What can I do, how can I make it up to you?"

"No thank you."

"No, tell me, tell me," wheedled Jeremy. "Tickets to Casino night?" My fa-   155 ther shook his head. "You don't gamble. Dinner at Bartholomew's?" My father shook his head again. "You don't eat." Jeremy scratched his chin. "You know, my wife was like you. Old Annabelle could never let me make things up—never, never, never, never, never."

My father wriggled out from under his arm.

"How about sport clothes? You are rather overdressed, you know, excuse me for saying so. But here." He took off his polo shirt and folded it up. "You can have this with my most profound apologies." He ruffled his chest hairs with his free hand.

"No thank you," said my father.

"No, take it, take it. Accept my apologies." He thrust the shirt into my father's arms. "I'm so very sorry, so very sorry. Please, try it on."

Helplessly holding the shirt, my father searched the crowd for my mother.   160

"Here, I'll help you off with your coat."

My father froze.

Jeremy reached over and took his jacket off. "Milton's, one hundred twenty-five dollars reduced to one hundred twelve-fifty," he read. "What a bargain, what a bargain!"

"Please give it back," pleaded my father. "Please."

"Now for your shirt," ordered Jeremy.   165

Heads began to turn.

"Take off your shirt."

"I do not take orders like a servant," announced my father.

"Take off your shirt, or I'm going to throw this jacket right into the pool, just right into this little pool here." Jeremy held it over the water.

"Go ahead."   170

"One hundred twelve-fifty," taunted Jeremy. "One hundred twelve . . ."

My father flung the polo shirt into the water with such force that part of it bounced back up into the air like a fluorescent fountain. Then it settled into a soft heap on top of the water. My mother hurried up.

"You're a sport!" said Jeremy, suddenly breaking into a smile and slapping my father on the back. "You're a sport! I like that. A man with spirit, that's what you are. A man with panache. Allow me to return to you your jacket." He handed it back to my father. "Good value you got on that, good value."

My father hurled the coat into the pool too. "We're leaving," he said grimly. "Leaving!"

"Now, Ralphie," said Mrs. Lardner, bustling up; but my father was already   175
stomping off.

"Get your sister," he told me. To my mother: "Get your shoes."

* * *

"That was *great*, Dad," said Mona as we walked down to the car.

"You were *stupendous*."

"Way to show 'em," I said.

"What?" said my father offhandedly.   180

Although it was only just dusk, we were in a gulch, which made it hard to see anything except the gleam of his white shirt moving up the hill ahead of us.

"It was all my fault," began my mother.

"Forget it," said my father grandly. Then he said, "The only trouble is I left those keys in my jacket pocket."

"Oh *no*," said Mona.

"Oh no is right," said my mother.   185

"So we'll walk home," I said.

"But how're we going to get into the *house*," said Mona.

The noise of the party churned through the silence.

"Someone has to going back," said my father.

"Let's go to the pancake house first," suggested my mother. "We can wait   190
there until the party is finished, and then call Mrs. Lardner."

Having all agreed that that was a good plan, we started walking again.

"God, just think," said Mona. "We're going to have to *dive* for them."

My father stopped a moment. We waited.

"You girls are good swimmers," he said finally. "Not like me."

Then his shirt started moving again, and we trooped up the hill after it, into   195
the dark.

Talking about the Text

1. This is of course a very funny story. How does the humor work? How much does it depend on different cultural understandings? On linguistic differences?
2. What does Callie's mother mean when she says, "Your father thinks he is in China." Do you agree? Does Callie?

Writing about the Text

1. Jen's story focuses on the narrator's father and mother, but it's the father's behavior that gets the most attention. Write a description of the mother and examine her role and its effect on the story.
2. Can you imagine this story from the point of view of a son? Write what might be different.

Linking the Text to Other Texts

1. What does "joining the American society" mean to Callie's mother? To Callie? To us as readers? To the characters in other stories in this chapter?
2. Why does Mona respond to her father's gesture of throwing the new jacket into the pool by saying "That was *great*, Dad. You were *stupendous*." Do we readers agree? Does Mona's mother agree, do you think? What difference does it make that his keys were in the pocket? How does this family compare with families in other stories in the chapter?

✍ COMMENTARY

Gish Jen on Writing and on Being Asian American

From a 1996 interview with Ron Hogan in the online journal Beatrice, *http://www.beatrice.com*

Q: I want to explore the connections between your identity as a writer and your identity as an Asian-American.

Jen: The funny thing about it is that I was one of the earliest of this wave of Asian-American writers, but I can't say that being a writer is an extension of my being an Asian-American. Quite the contrary. My life as a fiction writer is directly related to my assimilation, particularly to the Jewish community in Scarsdale where I grew up, which is very much like the Scarshill in the book. That was a community that greatly esteemed fiction writing, which is how I first got interested in finding my voice and expressing myself. In my Chinese heritage, scholarship is greatly esteemed, but fiction writing is not considered scholarship. So as an "Asian-American" writer, the "Asian" is linked to the "writer" part by being an "American."

Q: Yet there's a shorthand in literary criticism, particularly at more mainstream levels, where a writer can get identified early on as "(fill-in-the-blank) American."

Jen: Of course you hope that the identification doesn't end up becoming a pigeonhole. I have to say that that hasn't been my experience, though I did bristle early on at being labeled an "Asian-American writer," because I think every writer likes to be seen as a universal writer. But today, I look at how many of my writer friends are greatly talented and hugely unknown, it occurs to me that we live in a culture where if you're not labeled you disappear. So as much as I hope I'm not limited by that moniker, and that people will use it as a starting point to think about my work rather than an ending point, I now see that I'm lucky to have the label, ironic as it may seem. I'm probably pigeonholed with respect to the press, but among general readers and universities I seem to have gotten out of that small cubicle.

Starting Points for Further Research: Gish Jen

- **Critical Essay:** Jonathan Freedman. " 'Who's Jewish?': Some Asian-American Writers and the Jewish-American Literary Canon." *Michigan Quarterly Review* 42 (2003): 230–54.
- **Interview:** Yuko Matsukawa. "MELUS Interview." *MELUS: The Journal of the Society for the Study of the Multi-Ethnic Literature of the United States* (Winter 1993). http://www.findarticles.com/p/articles/mi_m2278/is_n4_v18/ai_14878616.

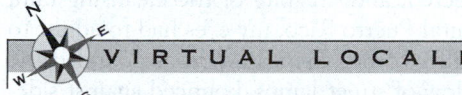

VIRTUAL LOCALE

Gish Jen on "Becoming American: Personal Journeys." Gish Jen is one of five prominent Chinese Americans interviewed by journalist Bill Moyers in "Becoming American: Personal Journeys," a three-part series that aired on Public Affairs Television. The five interviewees collectively represent the fields of literature, science, business, medicine, and the arts. A full transcript of Jen's thirty-minute interview with Moyers can be found online at *www.pbs.org/ becomingamerican/ap_pjourneys_transcript1.html*. Video versions are also available for sale on the PBS website.

ESMERALDA SANTIAGO   (B. 1948)

The oldest child in a family of eleven brothers and sisters, Esmeralda Santiago was born in San Juan, Puerto Rico, and moved to New York when she was thirteen. After high school, Santiago studied part-time for eight years in community colleges before winning a full scholarship to Harvard, where she graduated in 1976. Santiago collaborates on documentary films with her husband, the filmmaker Frank Cantor. Her publications include the memoir When I Was Puerto Rican *(1993), the novel* America's Dream *(1996), and the memoir* Almost a Woman *(1998), from which "Something Could Happen to You" is excerpted here. She lives in Westchester County, New York.*

Something Could Happen to You   (1998)

We came to Brooklyn in 1961, in search of medical care for my youngest brother, Raymond, whose toes were nearly severed by a bicycle chain when he was four. In Puerto Rico, doctors wanted to amputate the often red and swollen foot, because it wouldn't heal. In New York, Mami hoped, doctors could save it.

The day we arrived, a hot, humid afternoon had splintered into thunderstorms as the last rays of the sun dipped into the rest of the United States. I was thirteen and superstitious enough to believe thunder and lightning held significance beyond the meteorological. I stored the sights and sounds of that dreary night into memory as if their meaning would someday be revealed in a flash of insight to transform my life forever. When the insight came, nothing changed, for it wasn't the weather in Brooklyn that was important, but the fact that I was there to notice it.

One hand tightly grasped by Mami, the other by six-year-old Edna, we squeezed and pushed our way through the crowd of travelers. Five-year-old Raymond clung to Mami's other hand, his unbalanced gait drawing sympathetic smiles from people who moved aside to let us walk ahead of them.

At the end of the tunnel waited Tata, Mami's mother, in black lace and high heels, a pronged rhinestone pin on her left shoulder. When she hugged me, the pin pricked my cheek, pierced subtle flower-shaped indentations that I rubbed rhythmically as our taxi hurtled through drenched streets banked by high, angular buildings.

New York was darker than I expected, and, in spite of the cleansing rain,   5
dirtier. Used to the sensual curves of rural Puerto Rico, my eyes had to adjust to the regular, aggressive two-dimensionality of Brooklyn. Raindrops pounded the hard streets, captured the dim silver glow of street lamps, bounced against sidewalks in glistening sparks, then disappeared, like tiny ephemeral jewels, into the darkness. Mami and Tata teased that I was disillusioned because the streets were not paved with gold. But I had no such vision of New York. I was disappointed by the darkness and fixed my hopes on the promise of light deep within the sparkling raindrops.

* * *

Two days later, I leaned against the wall of our apartment building on McKibbin Street wondering where New York ended and the rest of the world began. It was hard to tell. There was no horizon in Brooklyn. Everywhere I looked, my eyes met a vertical maze of gray and brown straight-edged buildings with sharp corners and deep shadows. Every few blocks there was a cement playground surrounded by chain-link fence. And in between, weedy lots mounded with garbage and rusting cars.

A girl came out of the building next door, a jump rope in her hand. She appraised me shyly; I pretended to ignore her. She stepped on the rope, stretched the ends overhead as if to measure their length, and then began to skip, slowly, grunting each time she came down on the sidewalk. Swish splat grunt swish, she turned her back to me; swish splat grunt swish, she faced me again and smiled. I smiled back, and she hopped over.

"*¿Tú eres hispana?*" she asked, as she whirled the rope in lazy arcs.

"No, I'm Puerto Rican."

"Same thing. Puerto Rican, Hispanic. That's what we are here." She skipped   10
a tight circle, stopped abruptly, and shoved the rope in my direction. "Want a
turn?"

"Sure." I hopped on one leg, then the other. "So, if you're Puerto Rican,
they call you Hispanic?"

"Yeah. Anybody who speaks Spanish."

I jumped a circle, as she had done, but faster. "You mean, if you speak Spanish, you're Hispanic?"

"Well, yeah. No . . . I mean your parents have to be Puerto Rican or Cuban
or something."

I whirled the rope to the right, then the left, like a boxer. "Okay, your par-   15
ents are Cuban, let's say, and you're born here, but you don't speak Spanish. Are
you Hispanic?"

She bit her lower lip. "I guess so," she finally said. "It has to do with being
from a Spanish country. I mean, you or your parents, like, even if you don't speak
Spanish, you're Hispanic, you know?" She looked at me uncertainly. I nodded
and returned her rope.

But I didn't know. I'd always been Puerto Rican, and it hadn't occurred to
me that in Brooklyn I'd be someone else.

Later, I asked. "Are we Hispanics, Mami?"

"Yes, because we speak Spanish."

"But a girl said you don't have to speak the language to be Hispanic."   20
She scrunched her eyes. "What girl? Where did you meet a girl?"

"Outside. She lives in the next building."

"Who said you could go out to the sidewalk? This isn't Puerto Rico. *Algo te
puede suceder.*"

"Something could happen to you" was a variety of dangers outside the
locked doors of our apartment. I could be mugged. I could be dragged into any of
the dark, abandoned buildings on the way to or from school and be raped and
murdered. I could be accosted by gang members into whose turf I strayed. I could
be seduced by men who preyed on unchaperoned girls too willing to talk to
strangers. I listened to Mami's lecture with downcast eyes and the necessary, respectful expression of humility. But inside, I quaked. Two days in New York, and
I'd already become someone else. It wasn't hard to imagine that greater dangers
lay ahead.

Talking about the Text

1. Santiago's piece is nonfiction, a memoir. List the techniques and characteristics
   that it shares with short stories.
2. What seems to be the impulse behind Santiago's telling us this experience? For instance, is she interested in the rich store of stories in her life, or does she see herself as a model for others in her situation?

Writing about the Text

1. Write of a revealing incident in your own life, remaining true to "the facts" but
   shaping it like fiction, using a storyteller's techniques.
2. "Answer" Santiago with a piece in her mother's voice.

Linking the Text to Other Texts

1. In what ways is the Pat Mora poem that opens this chapter (p. 441) an accurate depiction of Santiago's situation?
2. Enumerate some situations and attitudes that Santiago shares with one other writer in this chapter.

✍ COMMENTARY

Esmeralda Santiago on Cultural Identity

From "A Note to the Reader" on her publisher's website, http://www.randomhouse.com/vintage/read/puerto/santiago.html

When I began writing [*When I Was Puerto Rican*], I had no idea it would result in a dialogue about cultural identity. But as I've traveled around the country talking about it, people tell me that, while the culture I'm describing may not be the same as the one they grew up in, the feelings and experiences are familiar, and some of the events could have been taken from their own lives. It has been particularly poignant to speak to immigrants who have returned to their countries, only to discover how much they have changed by immersion in North American culture. They accept and understand the irony of the past tense in the title, the feeling that, while at one time they could not identify themselves as anything but the nationality to which they were born, once they've lived in the U.S. their "cultural purity" has been compromised, and they no longer fit as well in their native countries, nor do they feel one hundred percent comfortable as Americans.

When I returned to Puerto Rico after living in New York for seven years, I was told I was no longer Puerto Rican because my Spanish was rusty, my gaze too direct, my personality too assertive for a Puerto Rican woman, and I refused to eat some of the traditional foods like morcilla and tripe stew. I felt as Puerto Rican as when I left the island, but to those who had never left, I was contaminated by Americanisms, and therefore, had become less than Puerto Rican. Yet, in the United States, my darkness, my accented speech, my frequent lapses into the confused silence between English and Spanish identified me as foreign, non-American. In writing the book I wanted to get back to that feeling of Puertoricanness I had before I came here. Its title reflects who I was then, and asks, who am I today?

Starting Points for Further Research: Esmeralda Santiago

- **Critical Essay:** Colleen A. Ruggieri. "Appreciating Ethnic Diversity with *When I Was Puerto Rican*." *English Journal* 91:5 (May 2002): 56–62.
- **Website:** http://www.esmeraldasantiago.com.

VIDEO LOCALE

Santiago in Performance: *Almost a Woman*. *Almost a Woman* is Esmeralda Santiago's 1998 sequel to her first memoir, *When I Was Puerto Rican*. While her first memoir focused on her years living in Puerto Rico, *Almost a Woman* charts Santiago's journey from the tenements of Brooklyn, New York, to her successful adult career as a writer. Santiago adapted *Almost a Woman* for

(continued)

a 2002 Masterpiece Theatre film. A video version of the film is available via the PBS website at *http://www.pbs.org* or through your local library. The PBS site for *Almost a Woman, www.pbs.org/wgbh/masterpiece/americancollection/ woman/*, offers extensive background on how Santiago adapted her memoir for the visual medium of film. It also includes essays and interview, a historical timeline on Puerto Rico, biographical information and a bibliography for Santiago, a teacher's guide, and links for further research.

JUNOT DÍAZ (B. 1968)

Junot Díaz was born in Santo Domingo, Dominican Republic, and when he was seven moved with his family to the low-income community of Parlin, New Jersey, home to many immigrants. He grew up very poor and right after high school worked in a local factory until he decided to attend college. After graduating from Rutgers University in 1992, Díaz applied to the MFA program in creative writing at Cornell, sending them the only story he had written. He was accepted and earned his MFA in creative writing in 1995. His first short story was published in 1996 and Díaz became an overnight sensation. Drown (1996), his first book, in which "Fiesta, 1980" appeared, shows his characters struggling to define themselves against the powerful influences of both Latin America and New York. He went on to teach creative writing at Syracuse University and now teaches writing at MIT.

Fiesta, 1980 (1996)

Mami's youngest sister—my tía Yrma—finally made it to the United States that year. She and tío Miguel got themselves an apartment in the Bronx, off the Grand Concourse and everybody decided that we should have a party. Actually, my pops decided, but everybody—meaning Mami, tía Yrma, tío Miguel and their neighbors—thought it a dope idea. On the afternoon of the party Papi came back from work around six. Right on time. We were all dressed by then, which was a smart move on our part. If Papi had walked in and caught us lounging around in our underwear, he would have kicked our asses something serious.

He didn't say nothing to nobody, not even my moms. He just pushed past her, held up his hand when she tried to talk to him and headed right into the shower. Rafa gave me the look and I gave it back to him; we both knew Papi had been with that Puerto Rican woman he was seeing and wanted to wash off the evidence quick.

Mami looked really nice that day. The United States had finally put some meat on her; she was no longer the same flaca who had arrived here three years before. She had cut her hair short and was wearing tons of cheap-ass jewelry which on her didn't look too lousy. She smelled like herself, like the wind through a tree. She always waited until the last possible minute to put on her perfume because she said it was a waste to spray it on early and then have to spray it on again once you got to the party.

We—meaning me, my brother, my little sister and Mami—waited for Papi to finish his shower. Mami seemed anxious, in her usual dispassionate way. Her hands adjusted the buckle of her belt over and over again. That morning, when she had gotten us up for school, Mami told us that she wanted to have a good time at the party. I want to dance, she said, but now, with the sun sliding out of the sky like spit off a wall, she seemed ready just to get this over with.

Rafa didn't much want to go to no party either, and me, I never wanted to go anywhere with my family. There was a baseball game in the parking lot outside and we could hear our friends, yelling, Hey, and, Cabrón, to one another. We heard the pop of a ball as it sailed over the cars, the clatter of an aluminum bat dropping to the concrete. Not that me or Rafa loved baseball; we just liked playing with the local kids, thrashing them at anything they were doing. By the sounds of the shouting, we both knew the game was close, either of us could have made a difference. Rafa frowned and when I frowned back, he put up his fist. Don't you mirror me, he said.

Don't you mirror me, I said.

He punched me—I would have hit him back but Papi marched into the living room with his towel around his waist, looking a lot smaller than he did when he was dressed. He had a few strands of hair around his nipples and a surly closed mouth expression, like maybe he'd scalded his tongue or something.

Have they eaten? he asked Mami.

She nodded. I made you something.

You didn't let him eat, did you?

Ay, Dios mío, she said, letting her arms fall to her side.

Ay, Dios mío is right, Papi said.

I was never supposed to eat before our car trips, but earlier, when she had put out our dinner of rice, beans and sweet platanos, guess who had been the first one to clean his plate? You couldn't blame Mami really, she had been busy—cooking, getting ready, dressing my sister Madai. I should have reminded her not to feed me but I wasn't that sort of son.

Papi turned to me. Coño, muchacho, why did you eat?

Rafa had already started inching away from me. I'd once told him I considered him a low-down chickenshit for moving out of the way every time Papi was going to smack me.

Collateral damage, Rafa had said. Ever heard of it?

No.

Look it up.

Chickenshit or not, I didn't dare glance at him. Papi was old-fashioned; he expected your undivided attention when you were getting your ass whupped. You couldn't look him in the eye either—that wasn't allowed. Better to stare at his belly button, which was perfectly round and immaculate. Papi pulled me to my feet by my ear.

If you throw up—

I won't, I cried, tears in my eyes, more out of reflex than pain.

Ya, Ramón, ya. It's not his fault, Mami said.

They've known about this party forever. How did they think we were going to get there? Fly?

He finally let go of my ear and I sat back down. Madai was too scared to open her eyes. Being around Papi all her life had turned her into a major-league

5

10

15

20

wuss. Anytime Papi raised his voice her lip would start trembling, like some specialized tuning fork. Rafa pretended that he had knuckles to crack and when I shoved him, he gave me a *Don't start* look. But even that little bit of recognition made me feel better.

I was the one who was always in trouble with my dad. It was like my God-given duty to piss him off, to do everything the way he hated. Our fights didn't bother me too much. I still wanted him to love me, something that never seemed strange or contradictory until years later, when he was out of our lives.

By the time my ear stopped stinging Papi was dressed and Mami was crossing each one of us, solemnly, like we were heading off to war. We said, in turn, Bendición, Mami, and she poked us in our five cardinal spots while saying, Que Dios te bendiga.

This was how all our trips began, the words that followed me every time I left the house.

None of us spoke until we were inside Papi's Volkswagen van. Brand-new, lime-green and bought to impress. Oh, we were impressed, but me, every time I was in that VW and Papi went above twenty miles an hour, I vomited. I'd never had trouble with cars before—that van was like my curse. Mami suspected it was the upholstery. In her mind, American things—appliances, mouthwash, funny-looking upholstery—all seemed to have an intrinsic badness about them. Papi was careful about taking me anywhere in the VW, but when he had to, I rode up front in Mami's usual seat so I could throw up out a window.

¿Cómo te sientes? Mami asked over my shoulder when Papi pulled onto the turnpike. She had her hand on the base of my neck. One thing about Mami, her palms never sweated.

I'm OK, I said, keeping my eyes straight ahead. I definitely didn't want to trade glances with Papi. He had this one look, furious and sharp, that always left me feeling bruised.

Toma. Mami handed me four mentas. She had thrown three out her window at the beginning of our trip, an offering to Eshú; the rest were for me.

I took one and sucked it slowly, my tongue knocking it up against my teeth. We passed Newark Airport without any incident. If Madai had been awake she would have cried because the planes flew so close to the cars.

How's he feeling? Papi asked.

Fine, I said. I glanced back at Rafa and he pretended like he didn't see me. That was the way he was, at school and at home. When I was in trouble, he didn't know me. Madai was solidly asleep, but even with her face all wrinkled up and drooling she looked cute, her hair all separated into twists.

I turned around and concentrated on the candy. Papi even started to joke that we might not have to scrub the van out tonight. He was beginning to loosen up, not checking his watch too much. Maybe he was thinking about that Puerto Rican woman or maybe he was just happy that we were all together. I could never tell. At the toll, he was feeling positive enough to actually get out of the van and search around under the basket for dropped coins. It was something he had once done to amuse Madai, but now it was habit. Cars behind us honked their horns and I slid down in my seat. Rafa didn't care; he grinned back at the other cars and waved. His actual job was to make sure no cops were coming. Mami shook Madai awake and as soon as she saw Papi stooping for a couple of quarters she let out this screech of delight that almost took off the top of my head.

That was the end of the good times. Just outside the Washington Bridge, I started feeling woozy. The smell of the upholstery got all up inside my head and I found myself with a mouthful of saliva. Mami's hand tensed on my shoulder and when I caught Papi's eye, he was like, No way. Don't do it.

The first time I got sick in the van Papi was taking me to the library. Rafa was with us and he couldn't believe I threw up. I was famous for my steel-lined stomach. A third-world childhood could give you that. Papi was worried enough that just as quick as Rafa could drop off the books we were on our way home. Mami fixed me one of her honey-and-onion concoctions and that made my stomach feel better. A week later we tried the library again and on this go-around I couldn't get the window open in time. When Papi got me home, he went and cleaned out the van himself, an expression of askho on his face. This was a big deal, since Papi almost never cleaned anything himself. He came back inside and found me sitting on the couch feeling like hell.

It's the car, he said to Mami. It's making him sick.

* * *

This time the damage was pretty minimal, nothing Papi couldn't wash off the door with a blast of the hose. He was pissed, though; he jammed his finger into my cheek, a nice solid thrust. That was the way he was with his punishments: imaginative. Earlier that year I'd written an essay in school called "My Father the Torturer," but the teacher made me write a new one. She thought I was kidding.

We drove the rest of the way to the Bronx in silence. We only stopped once,   40
so I could brush my teeth. Mami had brought along my toothbrush and a tube of toothpaste and while every car known to man sped by us she stood outside with me so I wouldn't feel alone.

* * *

Tío Miguel was about seven feet tall and had his hair combed up and out, into a demi-fro. He gave me and Rafa big spleen-crushing hugs and then kissed Mami and finally ended up with Madai on his shoulder. The last time I'd seen Tío was at the airport, his first day in the United States. I remembered how he hadn't seemed all that troubled to be in another country.

He looked down at me. Carajo, Yunior, you look horrible!

He threw up, my brother explained.

I pushed Rafa. Thanks a lot, ass-face.

Hey, he said. Tío asked.   45

Tío clapped a bricklayer's hand on my shoulder. Everybody gets sick some-times, he said. You should have seen me on the plane over here. Dios mio! He rolled his Asian-looking eyes for emphasis. I thought we were all going to die.

Everybody could tell he was lying. I smiled like he was making me feel better.

Do you want me to get you a drink? Tío asked. We got beer and rum.

Miguel, Mami said. He's young.

Young? Back in Santo Domingo, he'd be getting laid by now.   50

Mami thinned her lips, which took some doing.

Well, it's true, Tío said.

So, Mami, I said. When do I get to go visit the D.R.?

That's enough, Yunior.

It's the only pussy you'll ever get, Rafa said to me in English.   55

Not counting your girlfriend, of course.

Rafa smiled. He had to give me that one.

Papi came in from parking the van. He and Miguel gave each other the sort of handshakes that would have turned my fingers into Wonder bread.

Coño, compa'i, ¿cómo va todo? they said to each other.

Tía came out then, with an apron on and maybe the longest Lee Press-On   60 Nails I've ever seen in my life. There was this one guru mother-fucker in the *Guinness Book of World Records* who had longer nails, but I tell you, it was close. She gave everybody kisses, told me and Rafa how guapo we were—Rafa, of course, believed her—told Madai how bella she was, but when she got to Papi, she froze a little, like maybe she'd seen a wasp on the tip of his nose, but then kissed him all the same.

Mami told us to join the other kids in the living room. Tío said, Wait a minute, I want to show you the apartment. I was glad Tía said, Hold on, because from what I'd seen so far, the place had been furnished in Contemporary Dominican Tacky. The less I saw, the better. I mean, I liked plastic sofa covers but damn, Tío and Tía had taken it to another level. They had a disco ball hanging in the living room and the type of stucco ceilings that looked like stalactite heaven. The sofas all had golden tassels dangling from their edges. Tía came out of the kitchen with some people I didn't know and by the time she got done introducing everybody, only Papi and Mami were given the guided tour of the four-room third-floor apartment. Me and Rafa joined the kids in the living room. They'd already started eating. We were hungry, one of the girls explained, a pastelito in hand. The boy was about three years younger than me but the girl who'd spoken, Leti, was my age. She and another girl were on the sofa together and they were cute as hell.

Leti introduced them: the boy was her brother Wilquins and the other girl was her neighbor Mari. Leti had some serious tetas and I could tell that my brother was going to gun for her. His taste in girls was predictable. He sat down right between Leti and Mari and by the way they were smiling at him I knew he'd do fine. Neither of the girls gave me more than a cursory one-two, which didn't bother me. Sure, I liked girls but I was always too terrified to speak to them unless we were arguing or I was calling them stupidos, which was one of my favorite words that year. I turned to Wilquins and asked him what there was to do around here. Mari, who had the lowest voice I'd ever heard, said, He can't speak.

What does that mean?

He's mute.

I looked at Wilquins incredulously. He smiled and nodded, as if he'd won a   65 prize or something.

Does he understand? I asked.

Of course he understands, Rafa said. He's not dumb.

I could tell Rafa had said that just to score points with the girls. Both of them nodded. Low-voice Mari said, He's the best student in his grade.

I thought, Not bad for a mute. I sat next to Wilquins. After about two seconds of TV Wilquins whipped out a bag of dominos and motioned to me. Did I want to play? Sure. Me and him played Rafa and Leti and we whupped their collective asses twice, which put Rafa in a real bad mood. He looked at me like maybe he wanted to take a swing, just one to make him feel better. Leti kept whispering into Rafa's ear, telling him it was OK.

In the kitchen I could hear my parents slipping into their usual modes.   70 Papi's voice was loud and argumentative; you didn't have to be anywhere near him to catch his drift. And Mami, you had to put cups to your ears to hear hers. I went into the kitchen a few times—once so the tíos could show off how much bullshit I'd been able to cram in my head the last few years; another time for a bucket-sized cup of soda. Mami and Tía were frying tostones and the last of the pastelitos. She appeared happier now and the way her hands worked on our dinner you would think she had a life somewhere else making rare and precious things. She nudged Tía every now and then, shit they must have been doing all their lives. As soon as Mami saw me though, she gave me the eye. Don't stay long, that eye said. Don't piss your old man off.

Papi was too busy arguing about Elvis to notice me. Then somebody mentioned María Montez and Papi barked, María Montez? Let me tell you about María Montez, compa'i.

Maybe I was used to him. His voice—louder than most adults'—didn't bother me none, though the other kids shifted uneasily in their seats. Wilquins was about to raise the volume on the TV, but Rafa said, I wouldn't do that. Muteboy had balls, though. He did it anyway and then sat down. Wilquins's pop came into the living room a second later, a bottle of Presidente in hand. That dude must have had Spider-senses or something. Did you raise that? he asked Wilquins and Wilquins nodded.

Is this your house? his pops asked. He looked ready to beat Wilquins silly but he lowered the volume instead.

See, Rafa said. You nearly got your ass *kicked*.

* * *

I met the Puerto Rican woman right after Papi had gotten the van. He was tak-   75 ing me on short trips, trying to cure me of my vomiting. It wasn't really working but I looked forward to our trips, even though at the end of each one I'd be sick. These were the only times me and Papi did anything together. When we were alone he treated me much better, like maybe I was his son or something.

Before each drive Mami would cross me.

Bendición, Mami, I'd say.

She'd kiss my forehead. Que Dios te bendiga. And then she would give me a handful of mentas because she wanted me to be OK. Mami didn't think these excursions would cure anything, but the one time she had brought it up to Papi he had told her to shut up, what did she know about anything anyway?

Me and Papi didn't talk much. We just drove around our neighborhood. Occasionally he'd ask, How is it?

And I'd nod, no matter how I felt.   80

One day I was sick outside of Perth Amboy. Instead of taking me home he went the other way on Industrial Avenue, stopping a few minutes later in front of a light blue house I didn't recognize. It reminded me of the Easter eggs we colored at school, the ones we threw out the bus windows at other cars.

The Puerto Rican woman was there and she helped me clean up. She had dry papery hands and when she rubbed the towel on my chest, she did it hard, like I was a bumper she was waxing. She was very thin and had a cloud of brown hair rising above her narrow face and the sharpest blackest eyes you've ever seen.

He's cute, she said to Papi.

Not when he's throwing up, Papi said.

What's your name? she asked me. Are you Rafa?   85

I shook my head.

Then it's Yunior, right?

I nodded.

You're the smart one, she said, suddenly happy with herself. Maybe you want to see my books?

They weren't hers. I recognized them as ones my father must have left in her   90
house. Papi was a voracious reader, couldn't even go cheating without a paperback in his pocket.

Why don't you go watch TV? Papi suggested. He was looking at her like she was the last piece of chicken on earth.

We got plenty of channels, she said. Use the remote if you want.

The two of them went upstairs and I was too scared of what was happening to poke around. I just sat there, ashamed, expecting something big and fiery to crash down on our heads. I watched a whole hour of the news before Papi came downstairs and said, Let's go.

* * *

About two hours later the women laid out the food and like always nobody but the kids thanked them. It must be some Dominican tradition or something. There was everything I liked—chicharrones, fried chicken, tostones, sancocho, rice, fried cheese, yuca, avocado, potato salad, a meteor-sized hunk of pernil, even a tossed salad which I could do without—but when I joined the other kids around the serving table, Papi said, Oh no you don't, and took the paper plate out of my hand. His fingers weren't gentle.

What's wrong now? Tía asked, handing me another plate.   95

He ain't eating, Papi said. Mami pretended to help Rafa with the pernil.

Why can't he eat?

Because I said so.

The adults who didn't know us made like they hadn't heard a thing and Tío just smiled sheepishly and told everybody to go ahead and eat. All the kids—about ten of them now—trooped back into the living room with their plates a-heaping and all the adults ducked into the kitchen and the dining room, where the radio was playing loud-ass bachatas. I was the only one without a plate. Papi stopped me before I could get away from him. He kept his voice nice and low so nobody else could hear him.

If you eat anything, I'm going to beat you. ¿Entiendes?   100

I nodded.

And if your brother gives you any food, I'll beat him too. Right here in front of everybody. ¿Entiendes?

I nodded again. I wanted to kill him and he must have sensed it because he gave my head a little shove.

All the kids watched me come in and sit down in front of the TV.

What's wrong with your dad? Leti asked.   105

He's a dick, I said.

Rafa shook his head. Don't say that shit in front of people.

Easy for you to be nice when you're eating, I said.

Hey, if I was a pukey little baby, I wouldn't get no food either.

I almost said something back but I concentrated on the TV. I wasn't going   110
to start it. No fucking way. So I watched Bruce Lee beat Chuck Norris into the
floor of the Colosseum and tried to pretend that there was no food anywhere in
the house. It was Tía who finally saved me. She came into the living room and
said, Since you ain't eating, Yunior, you can at least help me get some ice.

I didn't want to, but she mistook my reluctance for something else.

I already asked your father.

She held my hand while we walked; Tía didn't have any kids but I could tell
she wanted them. She was the sort of relative who always remembered your
birthday but who you only went to visit because you had to. We didn't get past
the first-floor landing before she opened her pocketbook and handed me the first
of three pastelitos she had smuggled out of the apartment.

Go ahead, she said. And as soon as you get inside make sure you brush your
teeth.

Thanks a lot, Tía, I said.   115

Those pastelitos didn't stand a chance.

She sat next to me on the stairs and smoked her cigarette. All the way down
on the first floor and we could still hear the music and the adults and the television. Tía looked a ton like Mami; the two of them were both short and light-
skinned. Tía smiled a lot and that was what set them apart the most.

How is it at home, Yunior?

What do you mean?

How's it going in the apartment? Are you kids OK?   120

I knew an interrogation when I heard one, no matter how sugar-coated it
was. I didn't say anything. Don't get me wrong, I loved my tía, but something
told me to keep my mouth shut. Maybe it was family loyalty, maybe I just wanted
to protect Mami or I was afraid that Papi would find out—it could have been
anything really.

Is your mom all right?

I shrugged.

Have there been lots of fights?

None, I said. Too many shrugs would have been just as bad as an answer.   125
Papi's at work too much.

Work, Tía said, like it was somebody's name she didn't like.

* * *

Me and Rafa, we didn't talk much about the Puerto Rican woman. When we ate
dinner at her house, the few times Papi had taken us over there, we still acted
like nothing was out of the ordinary. Pass the ketchup, man. No sweat, bro. The
affair was like a hole in our living room floor, one we'd gotten so used to circum-
navigating that we sometimes forgot it was there.

* * *

By midnight all the adults were crazy dancing. I was sitting outside Tía's bedroom—where Madai was sleeping—trying not to attract attention. Rafa had me
guarding the door; he and Leti were in there too, with some of the other kids,

getting busy no doubt. Wilquins had gone across the hall to bed so I had me and the roaches to mess around with.

Whenever I peered into the main room I saw about twenty moms and dads dancing and drinking beers. Every now and then somebody yelled, ¡Quisqueya! And then everybody else would yell and stomp their feet. From what I could see my parents seemed to be enjoying themselves.

Mami and Tía spent a lot of time side by side, whispering, and I kept expecting something to come of this, a brawl maybe. I'd never once been out with my family when it hadn't turned to shit. We weren't even theatrical or straight crazy like other families. We fought like sixth-graders, without any real dignity. I guess the whole night I'd been waiting for a blowup, something between Papi and Mami. This was how I always figured Papi would be exposed, out in public, where everybody would know.

You're a cheater!

But everything was calmer than usual. And Mami didn't look like she was about to say anything to Papi. The two of them danced every now and then but they never lasted more than a song before Mami joined Tía again in whatever conversation they were having.

I tried to imagine Mami before Papi. Maybe I was tired, or just sad, thinking about the way my family was. Maybe I already knew how it would all end up in a few years, Mami without Papi, and that was why I did it. Picturing her alone wasn't easy. It seemed like Papi had always been with her, even when we were waiting in Santo Domingo for him to send for us.

The only photograph our family had of Mami as a young woman, before she married Papi, was the one that somebody took of her at an election party that I found one day while rummaging for money to go to the arcade. Mami had it tucked into her immigration papers. In the photo, she's surrounded by laughing cousins I will never meet, who are all shiny from dancing, whose clothes are rumpled and loose. You can tell it's night and hot and that the mosquitos have been biting. She sits straight and even in a crowd she stands out, smiling quietly like maybe she's the one everybody's celebrating. You can't see her hands but I imagined they're knotting a straw or a bit of thread. This was the woman my father met a year later on the Malecón, the woman Mami thought she'd always be.

Mami must have caught me studying her because she stopped what she was doing and gave me a smile, maybe her first one of the night. Suddenly I wanted to go over and hug her, for no other reason than I loved her, but there were about eleven fat jiggling bodies between us. So I sat down on the tiled floor and waited.

I must have fallen asleep because the next thing I knew Rafa was kicking me and saying, Let's go. He looked like he'd been hitting those girls off; he was all smiles. I got to my feet in time to kiss Tía and Tío good-bye. Mami was holding the serving dish she had brought with her.

Where's Papi? I asked.

He's downstairs, bringing the van around. Mami leaned down to kiss me.

You were good today, she said.

And then Papi burst in and told us to get the hell downstairs before some pendejo cop gave him a ticket. More kisses, more handshakes and then we were gone.

*   *   *

I don't remember being out of sorts after I met the Puerto Rican woman, but I must have been because Mami only asked me questions when she thought something was wrong in my life. It took her about ten passes but finally she cornered me one afternoon when we were alone in the apartment. Our upstairs neighbors were beating the crap out of their kids, and me and her had been listening to it all afternoon. She put her hand on mine and said, Is everything OK, Yunior? Have you been fighting with your brother?

Me and Rafa had already talked. We'd been in the basement, where our parents couldn't hear us. He told me that yeah, he knew about her.

Papi's taken me there twice now, he said.

Why didn't you tell me? I asked.

What the hell was I going to say? *Hey, Yunior, guess what happened yesterday? 145
I met Papi's sucia!*

I didn't say anything to Mami either. She watched me, very very closely. Later I would think, maybe if I had told her, she would have confronted him, would have done something, but who can know these things? I said I'd been having trouble in school and like that everything was back to normal between us. She put her hand on my shoulder and squeezed and that was that.

We were on the turnpike, just past Exit 11, when I started feeling it again. I sat up from leaning against Rafa. His fingers smelled and he'd gone to sleep almost as soon as he got into the van. Madai was out too but at least she wasn't snoring.

In the darkness, I saw that Papi had a hand on Mami's knee and that the two of them were quiet and still. They weren't slumped back or anything; they were both wide awake, bolted into their seats. I couldn't see either of their faces and no matter how hard I tried I could not imagine their expressions. Neither of them moved. Every now and then the van was filled with the bright rush of somebody else's headlights. Finally I said, Mami, and they both looked back, already knowing what was happening.

Talking about the Text

1. The narrative style in this story is determinedly "unliterary," at least in the usual sense, and rarely do the characters really say what they're feeling and thinking. How do you know those thoughts and feelings anyway?

2. How does the narrator feel about Papi? How do we readers seem to feel about him? Be as detailed as you can.

Writing about the Text

1. In a short (1–2 page) paper, first explain how the narrator feels about his mother, being sure to include details of how you know what his feelings are. Then write an account of how you as a reader react to the character of his mother.

2. Explain whether you believe the narrator will ultimately leave the neighborhood. Tell why or why not.

Linking the Text to Other Texts

1. Why the title "Fiesta, 1980"? In comparison with other titles in this chapter, is it more or less descriptive of the story?

2. What's your reaction to the Spanish words, some of them quite important?

🐛 **COMMENTARY**

Junot Díaz on Fiction

From an interview with the Cornell University Latino Alumni Association

Q: There is sort of a misconception about Latino children that because of language barriers or because of the lack of books at the home or that reading is not stressed, Latino children don't take to literature, they don't take to writing. Were you an unusual child because you had an interest in writing?

Díaz: Yeah. There is no doubt that when I came to the United States, I was not meant to be good at language. I remember coming up and having a very distinct sense that we were not supposed to, like, be interested in books. We were supposed to be the dumb students. There was expectations. I was supposed to be in the worst classes, I was not supposed to be interested in the library. So what was interesting though was how few of the "good, white-American kids" had no interest, or, I mean, few of them had any interest, in books either. So I was thought to be a freak growing up in that sense because I loved language. I loved speaking it and I loved reading it. I read very quickly when I came to the United States.

Q: Where did you get that from, your love of reading? Did your parents give it to you or did you pick it up somehow?

Díaz: Part of it was books were an easy language for me to control. Because when you read something, then you don't have to pronounce it correctly, you just have to know what it means. And so reading was easy for me. It was a place where a could show mastery because speaking was so awful—I was so terrible in speaking. I had a speech impediment, I had a lot of difficulties, I had a speech coach. It was a total escape. . . .

Q: In terms of your writing style, it seems as if you pretty much are open about your personal life. It's almost semi-autobiographical. When I read it it's almost like, man, I know a lot about Junot that I maybe didn't want to know at times. You seem to be very comfortable with that.

Díaz: Well, I'm writing fiction. It's just fiction. But as a writer, I feel very comfortable with being honest so when I'm a writer, almost all of the stories that I tend to tell, they are being told by a narrator to someone they trust. So the narrator is as if you have gathered around a group of your closest friends and you don't have to speak low. Don't need to hide s—t. So I often end up writing really blunt, honest, just like awful—like the truth, what we are thinking. And that is where I am comfortable. Most people are not used to that.

Q: Where do you see yourself in this—as well as with Chicano writers—this world of Latino literature other than being like supposedly the first Dominican-American in a sea of Chicano and Nuyorican writers?

Díaz: I feel myself as a part of an old tradition—it's a triple-tradition in a way. First, it's a tradition of the African Diaspora, which I believe strongly I fit into—I strongly believe that I strongly fit into it. Then the second tradition of Latino tradition writers, this huge tradition that combines Cubans, blah, blah, blah. And then there is a third, and for me an important but smaller tradition, which is a Dominican tradition. It's music, the few books that are out there, the short stories and just dealing with intellectual work. A lot of times I was unable to find novels by Dominicans but I found articles that would be helpful. So I just don't feel like anything new. I feel like I have come from a long line of people and I'm just trying to do this idea that like, yo, we young people have insights. I'm not that young anymore but like it takes a while to get a book done. When you're a new young writer, you need to say, yo, this is the way the world is and hope to God that, in a few years, another young writer modifies it and says this is the way the world is.

Starting Points for Further Research: Junot Díaz

- **Edition:** Junot Díaz. *Drown.* New York: Riverhead Books, 1996.
- **Interview:** Diogenes Cespedes. "Fiction Is the Poor Man's Cinema: An Interview with Junot Díaz." *Callaloo: A Journal of African-American and African Arts and Letters* (Summer 2000): 892–907.

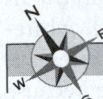 **LITERARY LOCALE**

New York's El Museo del Barrio. El Museo del Barrio was founded in 1969 by Puerto Rican educators, artists, and activists in the Spanish-speaking "el barrio" of East Harlem, a New York City neighborhood extending from 96th Street north to the Harlem River and from Fifth Avenue to the East River in Manhattan. Their aim was to create a cultural and educational institution that would present and preserve the art and culture of Puerto Ricans and all Latin Americans in the United States. Initially housed in a public school classroom and then a series of storefronts, since 1977 the museum's permanent home has been in the Heckscher Building at 1230 Fifth Avenue between 104th and 105th streets, in New York's Upper East Side. With extensive collections, exhibitions, publications, bilingual public programs, school activities, and special events, El Museo shares the richness of Caribbean and Latin American art and culture with the general public. Special events often include forays into nonvisual arts, concerts, and literary readings by Latino and Latina writers.

The virtual information center for El Museo del Barrio, *http://www.elmuseo. org*, offers information on the history of the museum and its mission, an overview of their permanent collection, educational resources for teachers, a list of current and past exhibitions, a calendar of special programming events, and visitor information.

ANJANA APPACHANA   (B. 1957)

Anjana Appachana was born in India and attended college there, receiving an M.A. in sociology from Jawaharlal Nehru University. After graduation she wrote and published short stories while working full-time in industry. She moved to the United States in 1984 and continued her studies at Penn State, receiving an MFA in Creative Writing in 1988. Her first book, Incantations and Other Stories *(published first in England in 1991 and in America in 1992), is a short story collection that examines middle-class Indian life, especially among families who cross international boundaries. Her novel* Listening Now *was published in 1998. She teaches writing at Arizona State University.*

Her Mother

(1989)

When she got her daughter's first letter from America, the mother had a good cry. Everything was fine, the daughter said. The plane journey was fine, her professor who met her at the airport was nice, her university was very nice, the house she shared with two American girls (nice girls) was fine, her classes were okay and her teaching was surprisingly fine. She ended the letter saying she was fine and hoping her mother and father were too. The mother let out a moan she could barely control and wept in an agony of longing and pain and frustration. Who would have dreamt that her daughter was doing a PhD in Comparative Literature, she thought, wiping her eyes with her saree palla, when all the words at her command were 'fine', 'nice', and 'okay'. Who would have imagined that she was a gold medallist from Delhi University? Who would know from the blandness of her letter, its vapidity, the monotony of its tone and the indifference of its adjectives that it came from a girl so intense and articulate? Her daughter had written promptly, as she had said she would, the mother thought, cleaning her smudged spectacles and beginning to re-read the letter. It had taken only ten days to arrive. She examined her daughter's handwriting. There seemed to be no trace of loneliness there, or discomfort, or insecurity—the writing was firm, rounded and clear. She hadn't mentioned if that over-friendly man at the airport had sat next to her on the plane. The mother hoped not. Once Indian men boarded the plane for a new country, the anonymity drove them crazy. They got drunk and made life hell for the air-hostesses and everyone else nearby, but of course, they thought they were flirting with finesse. Her daughter, for all her arguments with her parents, didn't know how to deal with such men. Most men. Her brows furrowed, the mother took out a letter-writing pad from her folder on the dining-table and began to write. Eat properly, she wrote. Have plenty of milk, cheese and cereal. Eating badly makes you age fast. That's why western women look so haggard. They might be pencil slim, but look at the lines on their faces. At thirty they start looking faded. So don't start these stupid, western dieting fads. Oil your hair every week and avoid shampoos. Chemicals ruin the hair. (You can get almond oil easily if coconut oil isn't available.) With all the hundreds of shampoos in America, American women's hair isn't a patch on Indian women's. Your grandmother had thick, black hair till the day she died.

One day, two months earlier, her daughter had cut off her long thick hair, just like that. The abruptness and sacrilege of this act still haunted the mother. That evening, when she opened the door for her daughter, her hair reached just below her ears. The daughter stood there, not looking at either her mother or father, but almost, it seemed, beyond them, her face a strange mixture of relief and defiance and anger, as her father, his face twisted, said, why, why? I like it short, she said. Fifteen years of growing it below her knees, of oiling it every week, and washing it so lovingly, the mother thought as she touched her daughter's cheek and said, you are angry with us . . . is this your revenge? Her daughter had brushed away her hand and moved past her parents, past her brother-in-law who was behind them and into her room. For the father it was as though a limb had been amputated. For days he brooded in his chair in the corner of the sitting-room, almost in mourning, avoiding even looking at her, while the mother murmured, you have perfected the art of hurting us.

Your brother-in-law has finally been allotted his three-bedroomed house, she wrote, and he moved into it last week. I think he was quite relieved to, after living with us these few months. So there he is, living all alone in that big house with two servants while your sister continues working in Bombay. Your sister says that commuting marriages are inevitable, and like you, is not interested in hearing her mother's opinion on the subject. I suppose they will go on like this for years, postponing having children, postponing being together, until one day when they're as old as your father and me, they'll have nothing to look forward to. Tell me, where would we have been without you both? Of course, you will only support your sister and your brother-in-law and their strange, selfish marriage. Perhaps that is your dream too. Nobody seems to have normal dreams any more. The mother had once dreamt of love and a large home, silk sarees and sapphires. The love she had got, but as her husband struggled in his job and the children came and as they took loans to marry off her husband's sisters, the rest she did not. In the next fifteen years she had collected a nice selection of silk sarees and jewellery for her daughters, but by that time, they showed no inclination for either. The older daughter and her husband had had a registered marriage, refused to have even a reception and did not accept so much as a handkerchief from their respective parents. And the younger one had said quite firmly before she left, that she wasn't even thinking of marriage.

The mother looked at her husband's back in the veranda. That's all he did after he came back from the office—sit in the veranda and think of his precious daughter, while she cooked and cleaned, attended to visitors and wrote to all her sisters and his sisters. Solitude to think—what a luxury! She had never thought in solitude. Her thoughts jumped to and fro and up and down and in and out as she dusted, cooked, cleaned, rearranged cupboards, polished the brass, put buttons on shirts and falls on sarees, as she sympathised with her neighbour's problems and scolded the dhobi for not putting enough starch on the sarees, as she reprimanded the milkman for watering down the milk and lit the kerosene stove because the gas had finished, as she took the dry clothes from the clothes-line and couldn't press them because the electricity had failed and realised that the cake in the oven would now never rise. The daughter was like her father, the mother thought—she too had wanted the escape of solitude, which meant, of course, that in the process she neither made her bed nor tidied up her room.

How will you look after yourself, my Rani Beti, she wrote. You have always   5
had your mother to look after your comforts. I'm your mother and I don't mind doing all this, but some day you'll have to do it for the man you marry and how will you, when you can't even thread a needle?

But of course, her daughter didn't want marriage. She had been saying so, vehemently, the last few months. The father blamed the mother. The mother had not taught her how to cook or sew and had only encouraged her and her sister to think and act with an independence quite uncalled for in daughters. How then, he asked her, could she expect her daughters to be suddenly amenable? How could she complain that she had no grandchildren and lose herself in self-pity when it was all her doing? Sometimes the mother fought with the father when he said such things, at other times she cried or brooded. But she was not much of a brooder, and losing her temper or crying helped her cope better.

The mother lay aside her pen. She had vowed not to lecture her daughter, 10
and there she was, filling pages of rubbish when all she wanted to do was cry out,
why did you leave us in such anger? What did we not do for you? Why, why? No,
she would not ask. She wasn't one to get after the poor child like that.

How far away you are, my pet, she wrote. How could you go away like that,
so angry with the world? Why, my love, why? Your father says that I taught you
to be so independent that all you hankered for was to get away from us. He says
it's all my fault. I have heard that refrain enough in my married life. After all
that I did for you, tutoring you, disciplining you, indulging you, caring for you,
he says he understands you better because you are like him. And I can't even
deny that because it's true. I must say it's very unfair, considering that all he did
for you and your sister was give you chocolates and books. When her daughter
was six, the mother recalled, the teacher had asked the class to make a sentence
with the word 'good'. She had written, my father is a good man. The mother
sighed as she recalled asking her, isn't your mother a good woman? And the
daughter's reply, Daddy is gooder. The mother wrote, no, I don't understand—
you talk like him, look like him, are as obstinate and as stupidly honest. It is as
though he conceived you and gave birth to you entirely on his own. She was an
ayah, the mother thought, putting her pen aside, that was all she was; she did all
the dirty work and her husband got all the love.

The next day, after her husband had left for the office, the mother continued her letter. She wrote in a tinier handwriting now, squeezing as much as possible into the thin air-mail sheet. Write a longer letter to me, next time, my
Rani, she wrote. Try and write as though you were talking to me. Describe the
trees, the buildings, the people. Try not to be your usual perfunctory self. Let
your mother experience America through your eyes. Also, before I forget, you
must bathe every day, regardless of how cold it gets. People there can be quite
dirty. But no, if I recall correctly, it is the English and other Europeans who hate
to bathe. Your Naina Aunty, after her trip to Europe, said that they smelled all
the time. Americans are almost as clean as Indians. And don't get into the dirty
habit of using toilet paper, all right?

The mother blew her nose and wiped her cheek. Two years, she wrote, or
even more for you to come back. I can't even begin to count the days for two
years. How we worry, how we worry. Had you gone abroad with a husband, we
would have been at peace, but now? If you fall ill who will look after you? You
can't even make dal. You can't live on bread and cheese forever, but knowing
you, you will. You will lose your complexion, your health, your hair. But why
should I concern myself with your hair? You cut it off, just like that.

The mother lay her cheek on her hand and gazed at the door where her
daughter had stood with her cropped hair, while she, her husband and her son-
in-law stood like three figures in a tableau. The short hair made her face look
even thinner. Suddenly she looked ordinary, like all the thousands of short-
haired, western-looking Delhi girls one saw, all ordinarily attractive like the others, all the same. Her husband saying, why, why? his hands up in the air, then
slowly, falling down at his sides, her son-in-law, his lazy grin suddenly wiped off
his face; she recalled it all, like a film in slow motion.

I always thought I understood you, she wrote, your dreams, your problems,
but suddenly it seems there is nothing that I understand. No, nothing, she
thought, the tiredness weighing down her eyes. She was ranting—the child

could do without it. But how, how could she not think of this daughter of hers, who in the last few months had rushed from her usual, settled quietness to such unsettled stillness that it seemed the very house would begin to balloon outwards, unable to contain her straining?

Enough, she wrote. Let me give you the news before I make you angry with my grief. The day after you left, Mrs Gupta from next door dropped in to comfort me, bless her. She said she had full faith you would come back, that only boys didn't. She says a daughter will always regard her parents' home as her only home, unlike sons who attach themselves to their wives. As you know, she has four sons, all married, and all, she says, under their wives' thumbs. But it was true, the mother thought. Her own husband fell to pieces every time she visited her parents without him. When he accompanied her there he needed so much looking after that she couldn't talk to her mother, so she preferred to go without him. With her parents she felt indulged and irresponsible. Who indulged her now? And when she came back from her parents the ayah would complain that her husband could never find his clothes, slept on the bedcover, constantly misplaced his spectacles, didn't know how to get himself a glass of water and kept waiting for the postman.

With all your talk about women's rights, she wrote, you refuse to see that your father has given me none. And on top of that he says that I am a nag. If I am a nag, it is because he's made me one. And talking of women's rights, some women take it too far. Mrs Parekh is having, as the books say, a torrid affair with a married man. This man's wife is presently with her parents and when Mrs Parekh's husband is on tour, she spends the night with him, and comes back early in the morning to get her children ready for school. Everyone has seen her car parked outside his flat in the middle of the night. Today our ayah said, memsahib, people like us do it for money. Why do memsahibs like her do it? But of course, you will launch into a tirade of how this is none of my business and sum it up with your famous phrase, each to her own. But my child, they're both married. Surely you won't defend it? Sometimes I don't understand how your strong principles co-exist with such strange values for what society says is wrong. Each to her own, you have often told me angrily, never seeming to realise that it is never one's own when one takes such a reckless step, that entire families disintegrate, that children bear scars forever. Each to her own indeed.

Yes, she was a straightforward girl, the mother thought, and so loyal to those she loved. When the older daughter had got married five years ago, and this one was only seventeen, how staunchly she had supported her sister and brother-in-law's decision to do without all the frills of an Indian wedding. How she had later defended her sister's decision to continue with her job in Bombay, when her husband came on a transfer to Delhi. She had lost her temper with her parents for writing reproachful letters to the older daughter, and scolded them when they expressed their worry to the son-in-law, saying that as long as he was living with them, they should say nothing.

The mother was fond of her son-in-law in her own way. But deep inside she felt that he was irresponsible, uncaring and lazy. Yes, he had infinite charm, but he didn't write regularly to his wife, didn't save a paisa of his salary (he didn't even have a life insurance policy and no thoughts at all of buying a house) and instead of spending his evenings in the house as befitted a married man, went on a binge of plays and other cultural programmes, often taking her daughter with him, spending huge amounts on petrol and eating out. His wife was too practical, he told the mother, especially about money. She believed in saving, he believed in spending. She wanted security, he wanted fun. He laughed as he said this, and gave her a huge box of the most expensive barfis. The mother had to smile. She wanted him to pine for her daughter. Instead, he joked about her passion for her work and how he was waiting for the day when she would be earning twice as much as him, so that he could resign from his job and live luxuriously off her, reading, trekking and sleeping. At such times the mother couldn't even force a smile. But her younger daughter would laugh and say that his priorities were clear. And the older daughter would write and urge the mother not to hound her sister about marriage, to let her pursue her interests. The sisters supported each other, the mother thought, irritated but happy.

Yesterday, the mother wrote, we got a letter from Naina Aunty. Her friend's son, a boy of twenty-six, is doing his PhD in Stanford. He is tall, fair and very handsome. He is also supposed to be very intellectual, so don't get on your high horse. His family background is very cultured. Both his parents are lawyers. They are looking for a suitable match for him and Naina Aunty who loves you so much, immediately thought of you and mentioned to them that you are also in the States. Now, before losing your temper with me, listen properly. This is just a suggestion. We are *not* forcing you into a marriage you don't want. But you must keep an open mind. At least meet him. Rather, *he* will come to the university to meet you. Talk, go out together, see how much you like each other. *Just* meet him and try and look pleasant and smile for a change. Give your father and me the pleasure of saying, there is someone who will look after our child. If something happens to us who will look after you? I know what a romantic you are, but believe me, arranged marriages work very well. Firstly, the bride is readily accepted by the family. Now look at me. Ours was a love marriage and his parents disliked me and disapproved of our marriage because my sister had married out of the community. They thought I was fast because in those days I played tennis with other men, wore lipstick and bras. I wonder why I bore it. I should have been cold and as distant as them. But I was ingratiating and accommodating. Then your father and I had to marry off his sisters. Now in an arranged marriage you can choose not to have such liabilities. I am not materialistic, but I am not a fool either. I know you want to be economically independent, and you must be that, but it will also help if your husband isn't burdened with debts. I am not blaming your father. Responsibilities are responsibilities. But if you can help it, why begin married life with them? Now don't write back and say you're sick of my nagging. You think I am a nag because it is I who wields the stick and your father who gives those wonderful, idealistic lectures. Perhaps when you marry you will realise that fathers and husbands are two very different things. In an arranged marriage you will not be disillusioned because you will not have any illusions to begin with. That is why arranged marriages work. Of course, we will not put any pressure on you. Let us know if it is all right for the boy to meet you and I will write to Naina Aunty accordingly. Each day I pray that you will not marry an American. That would be very hard on us. Now, look at your father and me. Whatever your father's faults, infidelity isn't one of them. Now these Americans, they will divorce you at the drop of a hat. They don't know the meaning of the phrase, 'sanctity of marriage'. My love, if you marry an American and he divorces you and we are no longer in this world, what will you do?

When the milkman came early this morning, he enquired about you. I told him how far away you are. He sighed and said that it was indeed very far. I think he feels for us because he hasn't watered down the milk since you left. I'm making the most of it and setting aside lots of thick malai for butter. When the postman came, he said, how is baby? I replied, now only you will bear her news for us. He immediately asked for baksheesh. I said, nothing doing, what do you mean, baksheesh, it isn't Diwali. He replied, when I got you baby's first letter, wasn't it like Diwali? So I tipped him. Our bai has had a fight with her husband because he got drunk again and spent his entire salary gambling it away. She is in a fury and has left the house saying she won't go back to him unless he swears in the temple that he will never drink again. Your father says, hats off to her. Your father is always enraptured by other women who stand up for themselves. If I stood up for myself he would think he was betrayed.

Betrayal, betrayal, the mother mulled. His job had betrayed him, his strict father had, by a lack of tenderness betrayed him. India herself had betrayed him after Independence, and this betrayal he raved against every evening, every night. He told her that sometimes he felt glad that his daughter had left a country where brides were burnt for dowry, where everyone was corrupt, where people killed each other in the name of religion and where so many still discriminated against Harijans. At least, he said, his daughter was in a more civilised country. At this the mother got very angry. She said, in America fathers molested their own children. Wives were abused and beaten up, just like the servant classes in India. Friends raped other friends. No one looked after the old. In India, the mother said, every woman got equal pay for equal work. In America they were still fighting for it. Could America ever have a woman president? Never. Could it ever have a Black president? Never. Americans were as foolish about religion as Indians, willing to give millions to charlatans who said that the Lord had asked for the money. She was also well read, the mother told her husband, and she knew that no Indian would part with his money so easily. As for discrimination against untouchables in India—it only happened among the uneducated, whereas discrimination against Blacks was rampant even among educated Americans. Blacks were the American untouchables. The mother was now in her element. She too had read *Time* and *Newsweek*, she told her husband, and she knew that in India there had never been any question of having segregation in buses where Harijans were concerned, as was the case in America, not so long ago.

Don't rant, her husband told her, and lower your voice, I can hear you without   20
your shrieking. The mother got into a terrible fury and the father left the room.

The mother wrote, you better give us your views about that country—you can give us a more balanced picture. Your father thinks I'm the proverbial frog in the well. Well, perhaps that is true, but he is another frog in another well and Americans are all frogs in one large, rich well. Imagine, when your Aunt was in America, several educated Americans asked her whether India had roads and if people lived in trees. They thought your Aunt had learnt all the English she knew in America.

The mother made herself a cup of tea and sipped it slowly. Her son-in-law hadn't even been at home the night her daughter had left. It upset the mother deeply. He could have offered to drive them to the airport at least, comforted them in their sorrow. But he had gone off for one of his plays and arrived a few minutes after they returned from the airport, his hair tousled, his eyes bright. He stopped briefly in the living-room where the mother and father sat quietly, at opposite ends, opened his mouth to say something, then shrugged slightly and went to his room.

Selfish, the mother thought. Thoughtless. The daughter hadn't even enquired about him when she left. Had she recognised that her fun-loving brother-in-law had not an ounce of consideration in him?

The two months before her daughter had left had been the worst. Not only had she stopped talking to her parents, but to him. It frightened the mother. One can say and do what one likes with parents, she told her silent child once, parents will take anything. Don't cold shoulder him too. If he takes a dislike to you and your moods, then you will be alienated even from your sister. Remember, marriage bonds are ultimately stronger than ties between sisters. The daughter had continued reading her book. And soon after, she had cut off her hair. Rapunzel, her brother-in-law had said once, as he watched her dry her hair in the courtyard and it fell like black silk below her knees. Rapunzel, he said again, as the mother smiled and watched her child comb it with her fingers, Rapunzel, Rapunzel, let down your hair. Oh, she won't do that, the mother had said, proud that she understood, she is too quiet and withdrawn, and her daughter had gone back to the room and the next day she had cut if off, just like that.

The mother finished her tea and continued her letter. Let me end with some advice, she wrote, and don't groan now. Firstly, keep your distance from American men. You are innocent and have no idea what men are like. Men have more physical feelings than women. I'm sure you understand. Platonic friendships between the two sexes does not exist. In America they do not even pretend that it does. There kissing is as casual as holding hands. And after that you know what happens. One thing can lead to another and the next thing we know you will bring us an American son-in-law. You know we will accept even that if we have to, but it will make us most unhappy. 25

Secondly, if there is an Indian association in your University, please join it. You might meet some nice Indian men there with the same interests that you have. For get-togethers there, always wear a saree and try to look pleasant. Your father doesn't believe in joining such associations, but I feel it is a must.

The mother was tired of giving advice. What changed you so much the last few months before you left, she wanted to cry, why was going abroad no longer an adventure but an escape? At the airport, when the mother hugged the daughter, she had felt with a mother's instinct that the daughter would not return.

There had been a brief period when her child had seemed suddenly happy, which was strange, considering her final exams were drawing closer. She would work late into the night and the mother would sometimes awaken at night to hear the sounds of her making coffee in the kitchen. Once, on the way to the bathroom she heard sounds of laughter in the kitchen and stepped in to see her daughter and son-in-law cooking a monstrous omelette. He had just returned from one of his late night jaunts. An omelette at 1 a.m., the mother grunted sleepily and the two laughed even more as the toast emerged burnt and the omelette stuck to the pan. Silly children, the mother said and went back to bed.

And then, a few weeks later, that peculiar, turbulent stillness as her daughter continued studying for her exams and stopped talking to all of them, her face pale and shadows under her eyes, emanating a tension that gripped the mother like tentacles and left the father hurt and confused. She snapped at them when they questioned her, so they stopped. I'll talk to her after her exams, the mother told herself. She even stopped having dinner with them, eating either before they all sat at the table, or much later, and then only in her room.

And that pinched look on her face . . . the mother jerked up. It was pain, not anger. Her daughter had been in pain, in pain. She was hiding something. Twelve years ago, when the child was ten, her mother had seen the same pinched, strained look on her face. The child bore her secret for three days, avoiding her parents and her sister, spending long hours in the bathroom and moving almost furtively around the house. The mother noticed that two rolls of cotton had disappeared from her dressing-table drawer and that an old bedsheet she had left in the cupboard to cut up and use as dusters, had also disappeared. On the third day she saw her daughter go to the bathroom with a suspicious lump in her shirt. She stopped her, her hands on the trembling child's arms, put her fingers into her shirt and took out a large roll of cotton. She guided the child to the bathroom, raised her skirt and pulled down her panties. The daughter watched her mother's face, her eyes filled with terror, waiting for the same terror to reflect on her face, as her mother saw the blood flowing from this unmentionable part of her body and recognised her daughter's imminent death. The mother said, my love, why didn't you tell me, and the child, seeing only compassion, knew she would live, and wept.

The omniscience of motherhood could last only so long, the mother thought, and she could no longer guess her daughter's secrets. Twelve years ago there had been the disappearing cotton and sheet, but now? The mother closed her eyes and her daughter's face swam before her, her eyes dark, that delicate nose and long plaited hair—no, no, it was gone now and she could never picture her with her new face. After her daughter had cut her hair, the mother temporarily lost her vivacity. And the daughter became uncharacteristically tidy—her room spick and span, her desk always in order, every corner dusted, even her cupboard neatly arranged. The mother's daily scoldings to her, which were equally her daily declarations of love, ceased, and she thought she would burst with sadness. So one day, when the mother saw her daughter standing in her room, looking out of the window, a large white handkerchief held to her face, the mother said, don't cry, my love, don't cry, and then, don't you know it's unhygienic to use someone else's hanky, does nothing I tell you register, my Rani? And her daughter, her face flushed, saying, it's clean, and the mother taking it out of her hand and smelling it and snorting, clean, what rubbish, and it isn't even your father's, it's your brother-in-law's, it smells of him, and it did, of cigarettes and aftershave and God knows what else and the mother had put it for a wash.

The mother's face jerked up. Her fingers' grip on the pen loosened and her eyes dilated. Her daughter had not been crying. Her eyes, as they turned to her mother, had that pinched look, but they were clear as she removed the handkerchief from her nose. It had smelled of him as she held it there and she wasn't wiping her tears.

The mother moaned. If God was omniscient, it hadn't seemed to hurt him. Why hadn't He denied the omniscience of motherhood? Oh, my love, the mother thought. She held her hand to her aching throat. The tears weren't flowing now. She began to write. Sometimes when one is troubled, she wrote, and there is no solution for the trouble, prayer helps. It gives you the strength to carry on. I know you don't believe in rituals, but all I'm asking you to do is to light the lamp in the morning, light an agarbatti, fold your hands, close your eyes and think of truth and correct actions. That's all. Keep these items and the silver idol of Ganesh which I put into your suitcase, in a corner in your cupboard or on your desk. For the mother, who had prayed all her life, prayer was like bathing or brushing her teeth or chopping onions. She had found some strength in the patterns these created, and sometimes, some peace. Once, when her husband reprimanded her for cooking only eight dishes for a dinner party, she had wanted to break all the crockery in the kitchen, but after five minutes in her corner with the Gods, she didn't break them. She couldn't explain this to her child. She couldn't say, it's all right, it happens; or say, you'll forget, knowing her daughter wouldn't. If you don't come back next year, she wrote, knowing her daughter wouldn't, I'll come and get you. She would pretend to have a heart attack, the mother said to herself, her heart beating very fast, her tears now falling very rapidly, holding her head in her hands, she would phone her daughter and say, I have to see you before I die, and then her daughter would come home, yes, she would come home, and she would grow her hair again.

Talking about the Text

1. We never hear Rani's thoughts, only her mother's, and she isn't particularly subtle. How complete a portrait of Rani do we get?
2. What is the proportion between the mother's actual letter to Rani and her other thoughts about what has happened in the past? Is it an effective proportion? How well does this method of storytelling work? How does it compare with having Rani as narrator, for example, or with our having the mother's thoughts without her actual words to her daughter?

Writing about the Text

1. Write a letter from Rani to her mother in which she confesses her love for her brother-in-law.
2. Decide whether the mother would have any more control or influence over the daughter if she were actually present in the United States, and then write your reasons for your conclusion.

Linking the Text to Other Texts

1. Why has it taken the mother so long to realize what has gone on between Rani and her brother-in-law? How is this mother and daughter relationship similar to and different from the one in Gish Jen's "In the American Society" (p. 463)?
2. Many of Rani's reasons for leaving India for school lie implicit in what the mother says about her own marriage and relations with her in-laws. Connect this story with other stories about interfering parents in this chapter, especially "Fiesta, 1980" (p. 479).

COMMENTARY

Anjana Appachana on Writing

On the Writing Process and Characterization

From http://www.arizonaarts.org:

Reading and writing all my life has taught me to write. Everything that I write has been rewritten countless times; each book that I wrote had twice as many pages that I threw away. I write a story not because I know it, but because of the need to discover it. . . . As I write I find myself exploring uncharted territory—an exhilarating and deeply satisfying journey. The wonder of writing lies in discovering truths that are otherwise often elusive. My characters invariably take me by surprise, for they refuse to be restrained by my expectations of them. They create my story by developing a life of their own and their lives enrich and feed mine.

Starting Point for Further Research: Anjana Appachana

- **Critical Essay:** Radhika Mohanram. "The Problems of Reading: Mother-Daughter Relationship and Indian Postcoloniality." *Women of Color: Mother-Daughter Relationships in 20th Century Literature.* Austin: University of Texas Press, 1996. 20–37.

QUESTIONS FOR WRITING AND RESEARCH

1. Write about what in some of these stories seems true to Pat Mora's vision in "Immigrants," and what seems more complex or separate.
2. Can you find examples in these stories of members of the older generation who seem to have integrity and good sense? Write an essay demonstrating that the parents are basically right, even though the children don't always think so. (You won't be able to use all of the stories, of course.)
3. Using the way the younger generation shows respect to the older generation, demonstrate that these stories are full of "old world" values.
4. Write about the world of romantic love in some of these stories.
5. If you have experience of the generation split and the arrival in a new land, write your own "coming to America story," true or fictional.
6. What kinds of patterns do these stories exhibit? Are there any common approaches to narration, point of view, characterization, or setting?
7. Conduct research on the writers who have influenced two of the generation of writers reflected in this chapter. These influences may be American or from a different culture. Start with interviews, but examine material in reviews as well.
8. Examine articles and book reviews to determine what kind of reception the writers in this chapter received from the older generation of writers in America, writers whose work first appeared in the 1950s and 1960s, some of whom may have been considered ethnic writers in their youth.
9. Choose a longer work (or two additional works) by one of the writers in this chapter, and describe the kind of reception that work received from critics.

View of lower New York City, showing Ellis Island, 1936.

Ellis Island: Gateway for Early U.S. Immigrants. The literary works in this chapter focus mostly on a recent period of the U.S. immigrant experience. A larger sense of the earlier waves of immigration may serve as a useful contextual backdrop to the stories included here. Located near the Statue of Liberty in New York Harbor, Ellis Island served as a port of entry for over 12 million immigrants arriving in the United States between 1892 and 1954. Before the commercialization of the airplane, New York was the most frequent destination for steamships crossing the Atlantic, so most immigrants entered the country through New York Harbor. Thus, for many years, the Ellis Island facility served as the central immigrant processing center, where newcomers underwent a sometimes grueling medical and legal inspection before being allowed onto the American mainland.

When U.S. embassies spread worldwide after World War I, the immigration process—applying for visas, doing the paperwork, and passing a medical exam—shifted to American consulates in the immigrants' countries of origin. After 1924, only problematic candidates, war refugees, and displaced persons were detained at Ellis Island. In the years that followed, the island continued to serve a variety of military functions until its closing in 1954.

Ellis Island was open to the public on a limited basis between 1976 and 1984. In 1984, the facility underwent the largest historic restoration in U.S. history. The Main Building was reopened in 1990 as the Ellis Island Immigration

(continued)

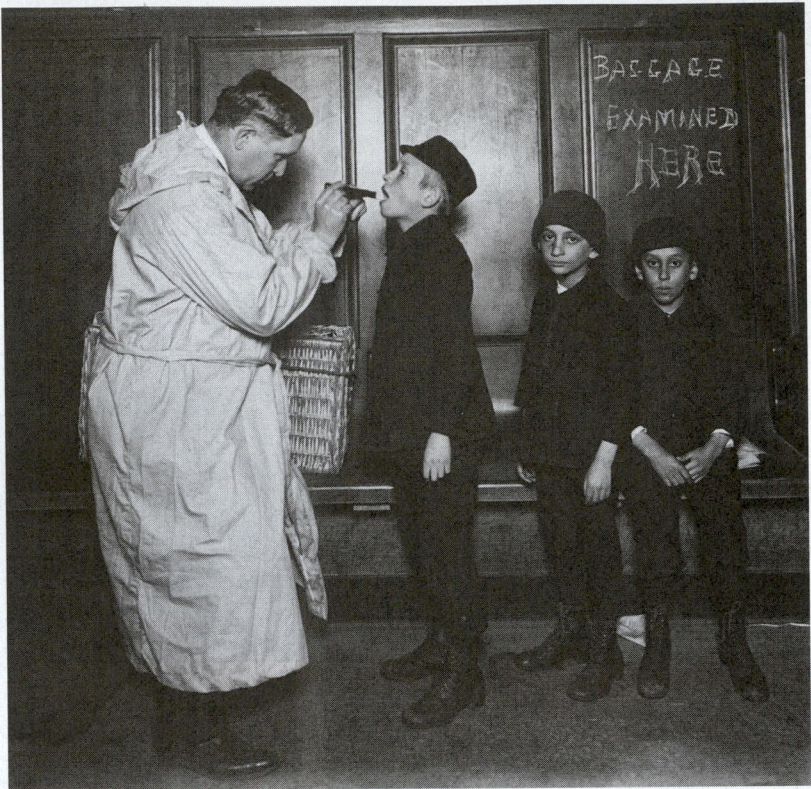

Medical exam of male immigrants, 1907.

Museum, an educational institution created to tell the tales of the immigrants who entered the United States through the gateway of Ellis Island. Highlights include an exhibit of photographs and artifacts; the American Family Immigration History Center, where visitors can access the passenger records of the ships that carried roughly 22 million immigrants to American shores; and screenings of the award-winning documentary *Island of Hope, Island of Tears.*

The website of the Ellis Island Immigration Museum, *http://ellisisland.org,* offers an abundant array of resources on U.S. immigration history. In addition to a detailed Ellis Island timeline, the site offers historical information, photographs, a "Passenger Search" section where visitors can search a database of passenger arrival records for their ancestors, and a genealogy section on how to research family history.

CHAPTER
9

Stories for Further Reading

Every piece included in this chapter reads like a story, but not all are classified as fiction. The works by James Thurber, E. B. White, and George Orwell all read like fiction and make ample use of the techniques of fiction, but they are in fact memoir, and Swift's piece is an argument in the form of a satirical essay. Each one of these writers was a master of fiction as well as nonfiction, so it is no accident that these nonfiction pieces use many of the same techniques and attitudes that characterize their fiction. The inclusion of these pieces here demonstrates how the elements that go into writing a story can be used for what is now frequently called "creative nonfiction."

The selections in this chapter have been arranged in chronological order to highlight the development of various elements of fiction—plot structure, characterization, setting, point of view, theme, symbol, tone, and so forth—that has taken place over time in English prose.

JONATHAN SWIFT   (1667–1745)

Jonathan Swift was born in Ireland, a member of the Protestant ruling class, and attended Trinity College in Dublin. He entered the ministry, and after a spell of tutoring in aristocratic households he became actively engaged in the London literary and political scene. When his allies and patrons fell from power, he returned to Ireland and received the post of dean of St. Patrick's Cathedral, one of the chief Protestant churches in Ireland. There he continued to write books, including Gulliver's Travels, *but gradually focused more and more on the plight of Ireland's poor, as he does in his famously satiric "A Modest Proposal."*

A Modest Proposal   (1729)

For Preventing the Children of Poor People in Ireland from Being a Burden to Their Parents or Country, and for Making Them Beneficial to the Public

It is a melancholy object to those who walk through this great town or travel in the country, when they see the streets, the roads, and cabin doors, crowded with beggars of the female-sex, followed by three, four, or six children, all in rags and importuning every passenger for an alms. These mothers, instead of being able to work for their honest livelihood, are forced to employ all their time in strolling to beg sustenance for their helpless infants, who, as they grow up, either turn thieves for want of work, or leave their dear native country to fight for the Pretender in Spain, or sell themselves to the Barbadoes.

I think it is agreed by all parties that this prodigious number of children in the arms, or on the backs, or at the heels of their mothers, and frequently of their fathers, is in the present deplorable state of the kingdom a very great additional grievance; and therefore whoever could find out a fair, cheap, and easy method of making these children sound, useful members of the commonwealth would deserve so well of the public as to have his statue set up for a preserver of the nation.

But my intention is very far from being confined to provide only for the children of professed beggars; it is of a much greater extent, and shall take in the whole number of infants at a certain age who are born of parents in effect as little able to support them as those who demand our charity in the streets.

As to my own part, having turned my thoughts for many years upon this important subject, and maturely weighed the several schemes of other projectors, I have always found them grossly mistaken in their computation. It is true, a child just dropped from its dam may be supported by her milk for a solar year, with little other nourishment; at most not above the value of two shillings, which the mother may certainly get, or the value in scraps, by her lawful occupation of begging; and it is exactly at one year old that I propose to provide for them in such a manner as instead of being a charge upon their parents or the parish, or wanting food and raiment for the rest of their lives, they shall on the contrary contribute to the feeding, and partly to the clothing, of many thousands.

There is likewise another great advantage in my scheme, that it will prevent those voluntary abortions, and that horrid practice of women murdering their bastard children, alas, too frequent among us, sacrificing the poor innocent

5

babes, I doubt, more to avoid the expense than the shame, which would move tears and pity in the most savage and inhuman breast.

The number of souls in this kingdom being usually reckoned one million and a half, of these I calculate there may be about two hundred thousand couple whose wives are breeders; from which number I subtract thirty thousand couples who are able to maintain their own children, although I apprehend there cannot be so many under the present distresses of the kingdom; but this being granted, there will remain an hundred and seventy thousand breeders. I again subtract fifty thousand for those women who miscarry, or whose children die by accident or disease within the year. There only remain an hundred and twenty thousand children of poor parents annually born. The question therefore is, how this number shall be reared and provided for, which, as I have already said, under the present situation of affairs, is utterly impossible by all the methods hitherto proposed. For we can neither employ them in handicraft or agriculture; we neither build houses (I mean in the country) nor cultivate land. They can very seldom pick up a livelihood by stealing till they arrive at six years old, except where they are of towardly parts,[2] although I confess they learn the rudiments much earlier, during which time they can however be looked upon only as probationers, as I have been informed by a principal gentleman in the county of Cavan, who protested to me that he never knew above one or two instances under the age of six, even in a part of the kingdom so renowned for the quickest proficiency in that art.

I am assured by our merchants that a boy or a girl before twelve years old is no salable commodity; and even when they come to this age they will not yield above three pounds, or three pounds and half a crown at most on the Exchange; which cannot turn to account either to the parents or the kingdom, the charge of nutriment and rags having been at least four times that value.

I shall now therefore humbly propose my own thoughts, which I hope will not be liable to the least objection.

I have been assured by a very knowing American of my acquaintance in London, that a young healthy child well nursed is at a year old a most delicious, nourishing, and wholesome food, whether stewed, roasted, baked, or boiled; and I make no doubt that it will equally serve in a fricassee or a ragout.

I do therefore humbly offer it to public consideration that of the hundred and twenty thousand children, already computed, twenty thousand may be reserved for breed, whereof only one fourth part to be males, which is more than we allow to sheep, black cattle, or swine; and my reason is that these children are seldom the fruits of marriage, a circumstance not much regarded by our savages, therefore one male will be sufficient to serve four females. That the remaining hundred thousand may at a year old be offered in sale to the persons of quality and fortune through the kingdom, always advising the mother to let them suck plentifully in the last month, so as to render them plump and fat for a good table. A child will make two dishes at an entertainment for friends; and when the family dines alone, the fore or hind quarter will make a reasonable dish, and seasoned with a little pepper or salt will be very good boiled on the fourth day, especially in winter.

10

---

[2]Promising abilities.

I have reckoned upon a medium that a child just born will weigh twelve pounds, and in a solar year if tolerably nursed increaseth to twenty-eight pounds.

I grant this food will be somewhat dear, and therefore very proper for landlords, who, as they have already devoured most of the parents, seem to have the best title to the children.

Infant's flesh will be in season throughout the year, but more plentiful in March, and a little before and after. For we are told by a grave author, an eminent French physician,[3] that fish being a prolific diet, there are more children born in Roman Catholic countries about nine months after Lent than at any other season; therefore, reckoning a year after Lent, the markets will be more glutted than usual, because the number of popish infants is at least three to one in this kingdom; and therefore it will have one other collateral advantage, by lessening the number of Papists among us.[4]

I have already computed the charge of nursing a beggar's child (in which list I reckon all cottagers, laborers, and four fifths of the farmers) to be about two shillings per annum, rags included; and I believe no gentleman would repine to give ten shillings for the carcass of a good fat child, which, as I have said, will make four dishes of excellent nutritive meat, when he hath only some particular friend or his own family to dine with him. Thus the squire will learn to be a good landlord, and grow popular among the tenants; the mother will have eight shillings net profit, and be fit for work till she produces another child.

Those who are more thrifty (as I must confess the times require) may flay the carcass; the skin of which artificially[5] dressed will make admirable gloves for ladies, and summer boots for fine gentlemen.

As to our city of Dublin, shambles[6] may be appointed for this purpose in the most convenient parts of it, and butchers we may be assured will not be wanting; although I rather recommend buying the children alive, and dressing them hot from the knife as we do roasting pigs.

A very worthy person, a true lover of his country, and whose virtues I highly esteem, was lately pleased in discoursing on this matter to offer a refinement upon my scheme. He said that many gentlemen of this kingdom, having of late destroyed their deer, he conceived that the want of venison might be well supplied by the bodies of young lads and maidens, not exceeding fourteen years of age nor under twelve, so great a number of both sexes in every county being now ready to starve for want of work and service; and these to be disposed of by their parents, if alive, or otherwise by their nearest relations. But with due deference to so excellent a friend and so deserving a patriot. I cannot be altogether in his sentiments; for as to the males, my American acquaintance assured me from frequent experience that their flesh was generally tough and lean, like that of our schoolboys, by continual exercise, and their taste disagreeable; and to fatten them would not answer the charge. Then as to the females, it would, I think with humble submission, be a loss to the public, because they soon would become breeders themselves: and besides, it is not improbable that some scrupulous people might be apt to censure such a practice (although indeed very unjustly)

15

---

[3]The comic writer François Rabelais (1483–1553).
[4]The speaker is addressing Protestant Anglo-Irish, who were the chief landowners.
[5]Artfully.
[6]Slaughterhouses.

as a little bordering upon cruelty; which, I confess, hath always been with me the strongest objection against any project, how well soever intended.

But in order to justify my friend, he confessed that this expedient was put into his head by the famous Psalmanazar, a native of the island Formosa,[7] who came from thence to London above twenty years ago, and in conversation told my friend that in his country when any young person happened to be put to death, the executioner sold the carcass to persons of quality as a prime dainty; and that in his time the body of a plump girl of fifteen, who was crucified for an attempt to poison the emperor, was sold to his Imperial Majesty's prime minister of state, and other great mandarins of the court, in joints from the gibbet, at four hundred crowns. Neither indeed can I deny that if the same use were made of several plump young girls in this town, who without one single groat to their fortunes cannot stir abroad without a chair, and appear at the playhouse and assemblies in foreign fineries which they never will pay for, the kingdom would not be the worse.

Some persons of a desponding spirit are in great concern about that vast number of poor people who are aged, diseased, or maimed, and I have been desired to employ my thoughts what course may be taken to ease the nation of so grievous an encumbrance. But I am not in the least pain upon that matter, because it is very well known that they are every day dying and rotting by cold and famine, and filth and vermin, as fast as can be reasonably expected. And as to the younger laborers, they are now in almost as hopeful a condition. They cannot get work, and consequently pine away for want of nourishment to a degree that if at any time they are accidentally hired to common labor, they have not strength to perform it; and thus the country and themselves are happily delivered from the evils to come.

I have too long digressed, and therefore shall return to my subject. I think the advantages by the proposal which I have made are obvious and many, as well as of the highest importance. 20

For first, as I have already observed, it would greatly lessen the number of Papists, with whom we are yearly overrun, being the principal breeders of the nation as well as our most dangerous enemies; and who stay at home on purpose to deliver the kingdom to the Pretender, hoping to take their advantage by the absence of so many good Protestants, who have chosen rather to leave their country than to stay at home and pay tithes against their conscience to an Episcopal curate.

Secondly, the poorer tenants will have something valuable of their own, which by law may be made liable to distress,[8] and help to pay their landlord's rent, their corn and cattle being already seized and money a thing unknown.

Thirdly, whereas the maintenance of an hundred thousand children, from two years old and upwards, cannot be computed at less than ten shillings a piece per annum, the nation's stock will be thereby increased fifty thousand pounds per annum, besides the profit of a new dish introduced to the tables of all gentlemen of fortune in the kingdom who have any refinement in taste. And the money will circulate among ourselves, the goods being entirely of our own growth and manufacture.

---

[7]George Psalmanazar had passed himself off as from Formosa.
[8]Seizure for nonpayment of debt.

Fourthly, the constant breeders, besides the gain of eight shillings sterling per annum by the sale of their children, will be rid of the charge of maintaining them after the first year.

Fifthly, this food would likewise bring great custom to taverns, where the   25 vintners will certainly be so prudent as to procure the best receipts for dressing it to perfection, and consequently have their houses frequented by all the fine gentlemen, who justly value themselves upon their knowledge in good eating; and a skillful cook, who understands how to oblige his guests, will contrive to make it as expensive as they please.

Sixthly, this would be a great inducement to marriage, which all wise nations have either encouraged by rewards or enforced by laws and penalties. It would increase the care and tenderness of mothers toward their children, when they were sure of a settlement for life to the poor babes, provided in some sort by the public, to their annual profit instead of expense. We should see an honest emulation among the married women, which of them could bring the fattest child to the market. Men would become as fond of their wives during the time of their pregnancy as they are now of their mares in foal, their cows in calf, or sows when they are ready to farrow; nor offer to beat or kick them (as is too frequent a practice) for fear of a miscarriage.

Many other advantages might be enumerated. For instance, the addition of some thousand carcasses in our exportation of barreled beef, the propagation of swine's flesh, and improvement in the art of making good bacon, so much wanted among us by the great destruction of pigs, too frequent at our tables, which are no way comparable in taste or magnificence to a well-grown, fat, yearling child, which roasted whole will make a considerable figure at a lord mayor's feast or any other public entertainment. But this and many others I omit, being studious of brevity.

Supposing that one thousand families in this city would be constant customers for infants' flesh, besides others who might have it at merry meetings, particularly weddings and christenings, I compute that Dublin would take off annually about twenty thousand carcasses, and the rest of the kingdom (where probably they will be sold somewhat cheaper) the remaining eighty thousand.

I can think of no one objection that will possibly be raised against this proposal, unless it should be urged that the number of people will be thereby much lessened in the kingdom. This I freely own, and it was indeed one principal design in offering it to the world. I desire the reader will observe, that I calculate my remedy for this one individual kingdom of Ireland and for no other that ever was, is, or I think ever can be upon earth. Therefore let no man talk to me of other expedients: of taxing our absentees at five shillings a pound: of using neither clothes nor household furniture except what is of our own growth and manufacture: of utterly rejecting the materials and instruments that promote foreign luxury: of curing the expensiveness of pride, vanity, idleness, and gaming in our women: of introducing a vein of parsimony, prudence, and temperance: of learning to love our country, in the want of which we differ even from Laplanders and the inhabitants of Topinamboo: of quitting our animosities and factions, nor acting any longer like the Jews, who were murdering one another at the very moment their city was taken: of being a little cautious not to sell our country and conscience for nothing: of teaching landlords to have at least one degree of mercy toward their tenants: lastly, of putting a spirit of honesty, industry, and skill into our shopkeepers; who, if a resolution could now be taken to buy only our native goods, would immediately unite to cheat and exact upon us in the price, the measure, and the goodness, nor could ever yet be brought to make one fair proposal of just dealing, though often and earnestly invited to it.

Therefore I repeat, let no man talk to me of these and the like expedients, till he hath at least some glimpse of hope that there will ever be some hearty and sincere attempt to put them in practice.

But as to myself, having been wearied out for many years with offering vain, idle, visionary thoughts, and at length utterly despairing of success, I fortunately fell upon this proposal, which, as it is wholly new, so it hath something solid and real, of no expense and little trouble, full in our own power, and whereby we can incur no danger in disobliging England. For this kind of commodity will not bear exportation, the flesh being of too tender a consistence to admit a long continuance in salt, although perhaps I could name a country which would be glad to eat up our whole nation without it.

After all, I am not so violently bent upon my own opinion as to reject any offer proposed by wise men, which shall be found equally innocent, cheap, easy, and effectual. But before something of that kind shall be advanced in contradiction to my scheme, and offering a better, I desire the author or authors will be pleased maturely to consider two points. First, as things now stand, how they will be able to find food and raiment for an hundred thousand useless mouths and backs. And secondly, there being a round million of creatures in human figure throughout this kingdom, whose sole subsistence put into a common stock would leave them in debt two millions of pounds sterling, adding those who are beggars by profession to the bulk of farmers, cottagers, and laborers, with their wives and children who are beggars in effect; I desire those politicians who dislike my overture, and may perhaps be so bold to attempt an answer, that they will first ask the parents of these mortals whether they would not at this day think it a great happiness to have been sold for food at a year old in the manner I prescribe, and thereby have avoided such a perpetual scene of misfortunes as they have since gone through by the oppression of landlords, the impossibility of paying rent without money or trade, the want of common sustenance, with neither house nor clothes to cover them from the inclemencies of the weather, and the most inevitable prospect of entailing the like or greater miseries upon their breed forever.

I profess, in the sincerity of my heart, that I have not the least personal interest in endeavoring to promote this necessary work, having no other motive than the public good of my country, by advancing our trade, providing for infants, relieving the poor, and giving some pleasure to the rich. I have no children by which I can propose to get a single penny; the youngest being nine years old, and my wife past childbearing.

Starting Points for Further Research: Jonathan Swift

- **Editions:** Jonathan Swift. *Gulliver's Travels*. Ed. Albert J. Rivero. New York: W. W. Norton, 2002.
  ———. *Writings of Jonathan Swift*. Ed. Robert A. Greenberg and William Piper. New York: W. W. Norton, 1973.
- **Biography:** Victoria Glendinning. *Jonathan Swift: A Portrait*. New York: Henry Holt, 1999.
- **Critical Essay:** John Richardson. "Swift, A Modest Proposal and Slavery." *Essays in Criticism: A Quarterly Journal of Literary Criticism* 51 (2001): 404–23.

EDGAR ALLAN POE (1809–1849)

Edgar Allan Poe was born in Boston, lost both of his parents at an early age, and was raised by his godfather, John Allan, a Richmond merchant. He attended the University of Virginia briefly, then West Point, which expelled him for attendance problems. He published a first volume of poems in 1827 and a second in 1829. In 1836 Poe married his cousin Virginia Clemm, then only thirteen, and in 1837 they went to New York City, where he published The Narrative of Arthur Gordon Pym *(1838). During the next decade, while earning a meager living writing magazine reviews, Poe published some of his own original stories, including "The Tell-Tale Heart," which he collected as* Tales of the Grotesque and Arabesque *(1840). From 1844 to 1847, Poe resided in New York, where he worked as an editor, critic, and writer; for a brief time he even owned and ran his own literary magazine,* The Broadway Journal, *though the journal failed after a few months. Although his work was widely admired, he never achieved much by way of financial success. For example, with the release of his famous poem "The Raven," he gained international recognition but reportedly only received $9 for its publication. Troubled by alcohol and the 1847 death of his wife to tuberculosis, he died in 1849 at the age of forty while visiting Baltimore, after a mysterious disappearance. Today Poe is acknowledged as one of the most brilliant and original writers in American literature.*

The Tell-Tale Heart (1843)

True!—nervous—very, very dreadfully nervous I had been and am; but why *will* you say that I am mad? The disease had sharpened my senses—not destroyed—not dulled them. Above all was the sense of hearing acute. I heard all things in the heaven and in the earth. I heard many things in hell. How, then, am I mad? Hearken! and observe how healthily—how calmly I can tell you the whole story.

It is impossible to say how first the idea entered my brain; but once conceived, it haunted me day and night. Object there was none. Passion there was none. I loved the old man. He had never wronged me. He had never given me insult. For his gold I had no desire. I think it was his eye! yes, it was this! One of his eyes resembled that of a vulture—a pale blue eye, with a film over it. Whenever it fell upon me, my blood ran cold; and so by degrees—very gradually—I made up my mind to take the life of the old man, and thus rid myself of the eye for ever.

Now this is the point. You fancy me mad. Madmen know nothing. But you should have seen *me*. You should have seen how wisely I proceeded—with what caution—with what foresight—with what dissimulation I went to work! I was never kinder to the old man than during the whole week before I killed him. And every night, about midnight, I turned the latch of his door and opened it—oh, so gently! And then, when I had made an opening sufficient for my head, I put in a dark lantern, all closed, closed, so that no light shone out, and then I thrust in my head. Oh, you would have laughed to see how cunningly I thrust it in! I moved it slowly—very, very slowly, so that I might not disturb the old man's sleep. It took me an hour to place my whole head within the opening so far that I could see him as he lay upon his bed. Ha—would a madman have been so wise as this? And then, when my head was well in the room, I undid the lantern cautiously—oh, so cautiously—cautiously (for the hinges creaked)—I undid it just so much that a single thin ray fell upon the vulture eye. And this I did for seven long nights—every night just after midnight—but I found the eye always closed;

and so it was impossible to do the work; for it was not the old man who vexed me, but his Evil Eye. And every morning, when the day broke, I went boldly into the chamber, and spoke courageously to him, calling him by name in a hearty tone, and inquiring how he had passed the night. So you see he would have been a very profound old man, indeed, to suspect that every night, just at twelve, I looked in upon him while he slept.

Upon the eighth night I was more than usually cautious in opening the door. A watch's minute hand moves more quickly than did mine. Never before that night had I *felt* the extent of my own powers—of my sagacity. I could scarcely contain my feelings of triumph. To think that there I was, opening the door, little by little, and he not even to dream of my secret deeds or thoughts. I fairly chuckled at the idea; and perhaps he heard me; for he moved on the bed suddenly, as if startled. Now you may think that I drew back—but no. His room was as black as pitch with the thick darkness (for the shutters were close fastened, through fear of robbers), and so I knew that he could not see the opening of the door, and I kept pushing it on steadily, steadily.

I had my head in, and was about to open the lantern, when my thumb 5 slipped upon the tin fastening, and the old man sprang up in the bed, crying out—"Who's there?"

I kept quite still and said nothing. For a whole hour I did not move a muscle, and in the meantime I did not hear him lie down. He was still sitting up in the bed listening;—just as I have done, night after night, hearkening to the death watches in the wall.

Presently I heard a slight groan, and I knew it was the groan of mortal terror. It was not a groan of pain or of grief—oh, no!—it was the low stifled sound that arises from the bottom of the soul when overcharged with awe. I knew the sound well. Many a night, just at midnight, when all the world slept, it has welled up from my own bosom, deepening with its dreadful echo, the terrors that distracted me. I say I knew it well. I knew what the old man felt, and pitied him, although I chuckled at heart. I knew that he had been lying awake ever since the first slight noise, when he had turned in the bed. His fears had been ever since growing upon him. He had been trying to fancy them causeless, but could not. He had been saying to himself—"It is nothing but the wind in the chimney—it is only a mouse crossing the floor," or "it is merely a cricket which has made a single chirp." Yes, he has been trying to comfort himself with these suppositions; but he had found all in vain. *All in vain;* because Death, in approaching him, had stalked with his black shadow before him, and enveloped the victim. And it was the mournful influence of the unperceived shadow that caused him to feel—although he neither saw nor heard—to *feel* the presence of my head within the room.

When I had waited a long time, very patiently, without hearing him lie down, I resolved to open a little—a very, very little crevice in the lantern. So I opened it—you cannot imagine how stealthily, stealthily—until, at length, a single dim ray, like the thread of the spider, shot from out the crevice and full upon the vulture eye.

It was open—wide, wide open—and I grew furious as I gazed upon it. I saw it with perfect distinctness—all a dull blue, with a hideous veil over it that chilled the very marrow in my bones, but I could see nothing else of the old man's face or person: for I had directed the ray as if by instinct, precisely upon the damned spot.

And now have I not told you that what you mistake for madness is but over- 10 acuteness of the senses?—now, I say, there came to my ears a low, dull, quick sound, such as a watch makes when enveloped in cotton. I knew *that* sound well too. It was the beating of the old man's heart. It increased my fury, as the beating of a drum stimulates the soldier into courage.

But even yet I refrained and kept still. I scarcely breathed. I held the lantern motionless. I tried how steadily I could maintain the ray upon the eye. Meantime the hellish tattoo of the heart increased. It grew quicker and quicker, and louder and louder every instant. The old man's terror *must* have been extreme! It grew louder, I say, louder every moment!—do you mark me well? I have told you that I am nervous: so I am. And now at the dead hour of the night, amid the dreadful silence of that old house, so strange a noise as this excited me to uncontrollable terror. Yet, for some minutes longer I refrained and stood still. But the beating grew louder, louder! I thought the heart must burst. And now a new anxiety seized me—the sound would be heard by a neighbor! The old man's hour had come! With a loud yell, I threw open the lantern and leaped into the room. He shrieked once—once only. In an instant I dragged him to the floor, and pulled the heavy bed over him. I then smiled gaily, to find the deed so far done. But, for many minutes, the heart beat on with a muffled sound. This, however, did not vex me; it would not be heard through the wall. At length it ceased. The old man was dead. I removed the bed and examined the corpse. Yes, he was stone, stone dead. I placed my hand upon the heart and held it there many minutes. There was no pulsation. He was stone dead. His eye would trouble me no more.

If still you think me mad, you will think so no longer when I describe the wise precautions I took for the concealment of the body. The night waned, and I worked hastily, but in silence. First of all I dismembered the corpse. I cut off the head and the arms and the legs.

I then took up three planks from the flooring of the chamber, and deposited all between the scantlings. I then replaced the boards so cleverly, so cunningly, that no human eye—not even *his*—could have detected anything wrong. There was nothing to wash out—no stain of any kind—no blood-spot whatever. I had been too wary for that. A tub had caught all—ha! ha!

When I had made an end of these labors, it was four o'clock—still dark as midnight. As the bell sounded the hour, there came a knocking at the street door. I went down to open it with a light heart—for what had I *now* to fear? There entered three men, who introduced themselves, with perfect suavity, as officers of the police. A shriek had been heard by a neighbor during the night; suspicion of foul play had been aroused; information had been lodged at the police office, and they (the officers) had been deputed to search the premises.

I smiled—for *what* had I to fear? I bade the gentlemen welcome. The shriek, 15
I said, was my own in a dream. The old man, I mentioned, was absent in the country. I took my visitors all over the house. I bade them search—search *well*. I led them, at length, to *his* chamber. I showed them his treasures, secure, undisturbed. In the enthusiasm of my confidence, I brought chairs into the room, and desired them *here* to rest from their fatigues, while I myself, in the wild audacity of my perfect triumph, placed my own seat upon the very spot beneath which reposed the corpse of the victim.

The officers were satisfied. My *manner* had convinced them. I was singularly at ease. They sat, and while I answered cheerily, they chatted familiar things. But, ere long, I felt myself getting pale and wished them gone. My head ached, and I fancied a ringing in my ears; but still they sat and still they chatted. The ringing became more distinct:—it continued and became more distinct: I talked more freely to get rid of the feeling: but it continued and gained definitiveness—until, at length, I found that the noise was *not* within my ears.

No doubt I now grew *very* pale;—but I talked more fluently, and with a heightened voice. Yet the sound increased—and what could I do? It was *a low, dull, quick sound—much such a sound as a watch makes when enveloped in cotton.* I gasped for breath—and yet the officers heard it not. I talked more quickly—more vehemently; but the noise steadily increased. I arose and argued about trifles, in a high key and with violent gesticulations, but the noise steadily increased. Why *would* they not be gone? I paced the floor to and fro with heavy strides, as if excited to fury by the observation of the men—but the noise steadily increased. Oh God! what *could* I do? I foamed—I raved—I swore! I swung the chair upon which I had been sitting, and grated it upon the boards, but the noise arose over all and continually increased. It grew louder—louder—*louder!* And still the men chatted pleasantly, and smiled. Was it possible they heard not? Almighty God!— no, no! They heard!—they suspected!—they *knew!*—they were making a mockery of my horror!—this I thought, and this I think. But any thing was better than this agony! Any thing was more tolerable than this derision! I could bear those hypocritical smiles no longer! I felt that I must scream or die!—and now— again!—hark! louder! louder! louder! *louder!*—

"Villains!" I shrieked, "dissemble no more! I admit the deed!—tear up the planks!—here, here!—it is the beating of his hideous heart!"

LITERARY LOCALE

Cover of Graham's Magazine, where Poe worked as an editor for a year and a half, during his years residing in Philadelphia.

Edgar Allan Poe: The Philadelphia Years. Edgar Allan Poe lived in Philadelphia for six years, from 1838 until 1844. His home near the Spring Garden neighborhood of the city, one of several rented homes in which Poe resided with his family, is the only one of his Philadelphia residences that has survived. It was in Philadephia that Poe lived his most productive years as a writer, and he achieved some of his greatest successes during this period, creating and publishing roughly sixty critical reviews in *Burton's Gentleman's Magazine* and *Graham's Magazine*, as well as such classic tales as "The Fall of the House of Usher," "The Pit and the Pendulum," "The Tell-Tale Heart," and "The Black Cat." It is also purportedly where he began working on his most famous poem, "The Raven," which was published in 1845. The house, located at 530–532 North Seventh St., was declared a National Historic Site in 1980 to commemorate Poe and his work. For visitor information, as well as extensive additional information on Poe's life and work, go to *http://www.nps.gov/edal/*, part of the National Park Service website.

Starting Points for Further Research: Edgar Allan Poe

- **Edition:** Edgar Allan Poe. *The Complete Tales and Poems of Edgar Allan Poe.* New York: Vintage, 1975.
- **Biography:** Arthur H. Quinn. *Edgar Allan Poe: A Critical Biography.* Baltimore: Johns Hopkins University Press, 1998.
- **Critical Essay:** Heyward Ehrlich. "Poe in Cyberspace: Electronic Guides to Printed and Online Research." *Edgar Allan Poe Review* 4 (Fall 2003): 93–97.

ANTON CHEKHOV   (1860–1904)

During his youth in a small Russian town, Anton Chekhov began writing as a means of supporting himself and his family. After earning his medical degree at the University of Moscow, Chekhov continued to write both short stories and plays. His first large collection, Motley Stories *(1886), earned critical respect, and it was followed by the collections* At Twilight *(1887) and* Stories *(1888). In his stories and plays, he created complex characters often shadowed by tragedy and loneliness. His plays were produced by Konstantin Stanislavsky, the director at the Moscow Art Theater, and consequently Chekhov's reputation as a dramatic genius was solidified. His dramatic masterpieces include* Uncle Vanya *(1899),* The Three Sisters *(1901), and* The Cherry Orchard *(1904).*

The Lady with the Pet Dog   (1899)

Translated by Avrahm Yarmolinsky   (1947)

I

A new person, it was said, had appeared on the esplanade: a lady with a pet dog. Dmitry Dmitrich Gurov, who had spent a fortnight at Yalta and had got used to the place, had also begun to take an interest in new arrivals. As he sat in Vernet's confectionery shop, he saw, walking on the esplanade, a fair-haired young woman of medium height, wearing a beret; a white Pomeranian was trotting behind her.

And afterwards he met her in the public garden and in the square several times a day. She walked alone, always wearing the same beret and always with the white dog; no one knew who she was and everyone called her simply "the lady with the pet dog."

"If she is here alone without husband or friends," Gurov reflected, "it wouldn't be a bad thing to make her acquaintance."

He was under forty, but he already had a daughter twelve years old, and two sons at school. They had found a wife for him when he was very young, a student in his second year, and by now she seemed half as old again as he. She was a tall, erect woman with dark eyebrows, stately and dignified and, as she said of herself, intellectual. She read a great deal, used simplified spelling in her letters, called her husband, not Dmitry, but Dimitry, while he privately considered her of limited intelligence, narrow-minded, dowdy, was afraid of her, and did not like to be at home. He had begun being unfaithful to her long ago—had been unfaithful to her often and, probably for that reason, almost always spoke ill of women, and when they were talked of in his presence used to call them "the inferior race."

It seemed to him that he had been sufficiently tutored by bitter experience to call them what he pleased, and yet he could not have lived without "the inferior race" for two days together. In the company of men he was bored and ill at ease, he was chilly and uncommunicative with them; but when he was among women he felt free, and knew what to speak to them about and how to comport himself; and even to be silent with them was no strain on him. In his appearance, in his character, in his whole makeup there was something attractive and elusive that disposed women in his favor and allured them. He knew that, and some force seemed to draw him to them, too.

Oft-repeated and really bitter experience had taught him long ago that with decent people—particularly Moscow people—who are irresolute and slow to move, every affair which at first seems a light and charming adventure inevitably grows into a whole problem of extreme complexity, and in the end a painful situation is created. But at every new meeting with an interesting woman this lesson of experience seemed to slip from his memory, and he was eager for life, and everything seemed so simple and diverting.

One evening while he was dining in the public garden the lady in the beret walked up without haste to take the next table. Her expression, her gait, her dress, and the way she did her hair told him that she belonged to the upper class, that she was married, that she was in Yalta for the first time and alone, and that she was bored there. The stories told of the immorality in Yalta are to a great extent untrue; he despised them, and knew that such stories were made up for the most part by persons who would have been glad to sin themselves if they had had the chance; but when the lady sat down at the next table three paces from him, he recalled these stories of easy conquests, of trips to the mountains, and the tempting thought of swift, fleeting liaison, a romance with an unknown woman of whose very name he was ignorant suddenly took hold of him.

He beckoned invitingly to the Pomeranian, and when the dog approached him, shook his finger at it. The Pomeranian growled; Gurov threatened it again.

The lady glanced at him and at once dropped her eyes.

"He doesn't bite," she said and blushed.

"May I give him a bone?" he asked; and when she nodded he inquired affably, "Have you been in Yalta long?"

"About five days."

"And I am dragging out the second week here."

There was a short silence.

"Time passes quickly, and yet it is so dull here!" she said, not looking at him.

"It's only the fashion to say it's dull here. A provincial will live in Belyov or Zhizdra and not be bored, but when he comes here it's 'Oh, the dullness! Oh, the dust!' One would think he came from Granada."

She laughed. Then both continued eating in silence, like strangers, but after dinner they walked together and there sprang up between them the light banter of people who are free and contented, to whom it does not matter where they go or what they talk about. They walked and talked of the strange light on the sea: the water was a soft, warm, lilac color, and there was a golden band of moonlight upon it. They talked of how sultry it was after a hot day. Gurov told her that he was a native of Moscow, that he had studied languages and literature at the university, but had a post in a bank; that at one time he had trained to become an opera singer but had given it up, that he owned two houses in Moscow. And he learned from her that she had grown up in Petersburg, but had lived in S— since her marriage two years previously, that she was going to stay in Yalta for about another month, and that her husband, who needed a rest, too, might perhaps come to fetch her. She was not certain whether her husband was a member of a Government Board or served on a Zemstvo Council,[1] and this amused her. And Gurov learned too that her name was Anna Sergeyevna.

Afterwards in his room at the hotel he thought about her—and was certain that he would meet her the next day. It was bound to happen. Getting into bed he recalled that she had been a schoolgirl only recently, doing lessons like his own daughter; he thought how much timidity and angularity there was still in her laugh and her manner of talking with a stranger. It must have been the first time in her life that she was alone in a setting in which she was followed, looked at, and spoken to for one secret purpose alone, which she could hardly fail to guess. He thought of her slim, delicate throat, her lovely gray eyes.

"There's something pathetic about her, though," he thought, and dropped off.

II

A week had passed since they had struck up an acquaintance. It was a holiday. It   20
was close indoors, while in the street the wind whirled the dust about and blew people's hats off. One was thirsty all day, and Gurov often went into the restaurant and offered Anna Sergeyevna a soft drink or ice cream. One did not know what to do with oneself.

In the evening when the wind had abated they went out on the pier to watch the steamer come in. There were a great many people walking about the dock; they had come to welcome someone and they were carrying bunches of flowers. And two peculiarities of a festive Yalta crowd stood out: the elderly ladies were dressed like young ones and there were many generals.

Owing to the choppy sea, the steamer arrived late, after sunset, and it was a long time tacking about before it put in at the pier. Anna Sergeyevna peered at the steamer and the passengers through her lorgnette as though looking for acquaintances, and whenever she turned to Gurov her eyes were shining. She talked a great deal and asked questions jerkily, forgetting the next moment what she had asked; then she lost her lorgnette in the crush.

The festive crowd began to disperse; it was now too dark to see people's faces; there was no wind any more, but Gurov and Anna Sergeyevna still stood as though waiting to see someone else come off the steamer. Anna Sergeyevna was silent now, and sniffed her flowers without looking at Gurov.

"The weather has improved this evening," he said. "Where shall we go now? Shall we drive somewhere?"

She did not reply.   25

Then he looked at her intently, and suddenly embraced her and kissed her on the lips, and the moist fragrance of her flowers enveloped him; and at once he looked round him anxiously, wondering if anyone had seen them.

"Let us go to your place," he said softly. And they walked off together rapidly.

---

[1]*Zemstvo Council:* a district council.

The air in her room was close and there was the smell of the perfume she had bought at the Japanese shop. Looking at her, Gurov thought: "What encounters life offers!" From the past he preserved the memory of carefree, good-natured women whom love made gay and who were grateful to him for the happiness he gave them, however brief it might be; and of women like his wife who loved without sincerity, with too many words, affectedly, hysterically, with an expression that it was not love or passion that engaged them but something more significant; and of two or three others, very beautiful, frigid women, across whose faces would suddenly flit a rapacious expression—an obstinate desire to take from life more than it could give, and these were women no longer young, capricious, unreflecting, domineering, unintelligent, and when Gurov grew cold to them their beauty aroused his hatred, and the lace on their lingerie seemed to him to resemble scales.

But here there was the timidity, the angularity of inexperienced youth, a feeling of awkwardness; and there was a sense of embarrassment, as though someone had suddenly knocked at the door. Anna Sergeyevna, "the lady with the pet dog," treated what had happened in a peculiar way, very seriously, as though it were her fall—so it seemed, and this was odd and inappropriate. Her features drooped and faded, and her long hair hung down sadly on either side of her face; she grew pensive and her dejected pose was that of a Magdalene in a picture by an old master.

"It's not right," she said. "You don't respect me now, you first of all."   30

There was a watermelon on the table. Gurov cut himself a slice and began eating it without haste. They were silent for at least half an hour.

There was something touching about Anna Sergeyevna; she had the purity of a well-bred, naive woman who has seen little of life. The single candle burning on the table barely illumined her face, yet it was clear that she was unhappy.

"Why should I stop respecting you, darling?" asked Gurov. "You don't know what you're saying."

"God forgive me," she said, and her eyes filled with tears. "It's terrible."

"It's as though you were trying to exonerate yourself."   35

"How can I exonerate myself? No. I am a bad, low woman; I despise myself and I have no thought of exonerating myself. It's not my husband but myself I have deceived. And not only just now; I have been deceiving myself for a long time. My husband may be a good, honest man, but he is a flunkey! I don't know what he does, what his work is, but I know he is a flunkey! I was twenty when I married him. I was tormented by curiosity; I wanted something better. 'There must be a different sort of life,' I said to myself. I wanted to live! To live, to live! Curiosity kept eating at me—you don't understand it, but I swear to God I could no longer control myself; something was going on in me: I could not be held back. I told my husband I was ill, and came here. And here I have been walking about as though in a daze, as though I were mad; and now I have become a vulgar, vile woman whom anyone may despise."

Gurov was already bored with her; he was irritated by her naive tone, by her repentance, so unexpected and so out of place; but for the tears in her eyes he might have thought she was joking or play-acting.

"I don't understand, my dear," he said softly. "What do you want?"

She hid her face on his breast and pressed close to him.

"Believe me, believe me, I beg you," she said, "I love honesty and purity, and   40
sin is loathsome to me; I don't know what I'm doing. Simple people say, 'The
Evil One has led me astray.' And I may say of myself now that the Evil One has
led me astray."

"Quiet, quiet," he murmured.

He looked into her fixed, frightened eyes, kissed her, spoke to her softly and
affectionately, and by degrees she calmed down, and her gaiety returned; both
began laughing.

Afterwards when they went out there was not a soul on the esplanade. The
town with its cypresses looked quite dead, but the sea was still sounding as it
broke upon the beach; a single launch was rocking on the waves and on it a
lantern was blinking sleepily.

They found a cab and drove to Oreanda.

"I found out your surname in the hall just now: it was written on the   45
board—von Dideritz," said Gurov. "Is your husband German?"

"No; I believe his grandfather was German, but he is Greek Orthodox
himself."

At Oreanda they sat on a bench not far from the church, looked down at
the sea, and were silent. Yalta was barely visible through the morning mist; white
clouds rested motionlessly on the mountaintops. The leaves did not stir on the
trees, cicadas twanged, and the monotonous muffled sound of the sea that rose
from below spoke of the peace, the eternal sleep awaiting us. So it rumbled below when there was no Yalta, no Oreanda here; so it rumbles now, and it will
rumble as indifferently and as hollowly when we are no more. And in this con-
stancy, in this complete indifference to the life and death of each of us, there
lies, perhaps, a pledge of our eternal salvation, of the unceasing advance of life
upon earth, of unceasing movement towards perfection. Sitting beside a young
woman who in the dawn seemed so lovely, Gurov, soothed and spellbound by
these magical surroundings—the sea, the mountains, the clouds, the wide sky—
thought how everything is really beautiful in this world when one reflects: everything except what we think or do ourselves when we forget the higher aims of
life and our own human dignity.

A man strolled up to them—probably a guard—looked at them and walked
away. And this detail, too, seemed so mysterious and beautiful. They saw a
steamer arrive from Feodosia, its lights extinguished in the glow of dawn.

"There is dew on the grass," said Anna Sergeyevna, after a silence.

"Yes, it's time to go home."   50

They returned to the city.

Then they met every day at twelve o'clock on the esplanade, lunched and
dined together, took walks, admired the sea. She complained that she slept
badly, that she had palpitations, asked the same questions, troubled now by jealousy and now by the fear that he did not respect her sufficiently. And often in
the square or the public garden, when there was no one near them, he suddenly
drew her to him and kissed her passionately. Complete idleness, these kisses in
broad daylight exchanged furtively in dread of someone's seeing them, the heat,
the smell of the sea, and the continual flitting before his eyes of idle, well-
dressed, well-fed people, worked a complete change in him; he kept telling Anna
Sergeyevna how beautiful she was, how seductive, was urgently passionate; he
would not move a step away from her, while she was often pensive and

continually pressed him to confess that he did not respect her, did not love her in the least, and saw in her nothing but a common woman. Almost every evening rather late they drove somewhere out of town, to Oreanda or to the waterfall; and the excursion was always a success, the scenery invariably impressed them as beautiful and magnificent.

They were expecting her husband, but a letter came from him saying that he had eye-trouble, and begging his wife to return home as soon as possible. Anna Sergeyevna made haste to go.

"It's a good thing I am leaving," she said to Gurov. "It's the hand of Fate!"

She took a carriage to the railway station, and he went with her. They were driving the whole day. When she had taken her place in the express, and when the second bell had rung, she said, "Let me look at you once more—let me look at you again. Like this."

She was not crying but was so sad that she seemed ill, and her face was quivering.

"I shall be thinking of you—remembering you," she said. "God bless you; be happy. Don't remember evil against me. We are parting forever—it has to be, for we ought never to have met. Well, God bless you."

The train moved off rapidly, its lights soon vanished, and a minute later there was no sound of it, as though everything had conspired to end as quickly as possible that sweet trance, that madness. Left alone on the platform, and gazing into the dark distance, Gurov listened to the twang of the grasshoppers and the hum of the telegraph wires, feeling as though he had just waked up. And he reflected, musing, that there had now been another episode or adventure in his life, and it, too, was at an end, and nothing was left of it but a memory. He was moved, sad, and slightly remorseful: this young woman whom he would never meet again had not been happy with him; he had been warm and affectionate with her, but yet in his manner, his tone, and his caresses there had been a shade of light irony, the slightly coarse arrogance of a happy male who was, besides, almost twice her age. She had constantly called him kind, exceptional, high-minded; obviously he had seemed to her different from what he really was, so he had involuntarily deceived her.

Here at the station there was already a scent of autumn in the air, it was a chilly evening.

"It is time for me to go north, too," thought Gurov as he left the platform. "High time!"

III

At home in Moscow the winter routine was already established: the stoves were heated, and in the morning it was still dark when the children were having breakfast and getting ready for school, and the nurse would light the lamp for a short time. There were frosts already. When the first snow falls, on the first day the sleighs are out, it is pleasant to see the white earth, the white roofs; one draws easy, delicious breaths, and the season brings back the days of one's youth. The old limes and birches, white with hoar-frost, have a good-natured look; they are closer to one's heart than cypresses and palms, and near them one no longer wants to think of mountains and the sea.

Gurov, a native of Moscow, arrived there on a fine frosty day, and when he put on his fur coat and warm gloves and took a walk along Petrovka, and when

55

60

on Saturday night he heard the bells ringing, his recent trip and the places he had visited lost all charm for him. Little by little he became immersed in Moscow life, greedily read three newspapers a day, and declared that he did not read the Moscow papers on principle. He already felt a longing for restaurants, clubs, formal dinners, anniversary celebrations, and it flattered him to entertain distinguished lawyers and actors, and to play cards with a professor at the physicians' club. He could eat a whole portion of meat stewed with pickled cabbage and served in a pan, Moscow style.

A month or so would pass and the image of Anna Sergeyevna, it seemed to him, would become misty in his memory, and only from time to time he would dream of her with her touching smile as he dreamed of others. But more than a month went by, winter came into its own, and everything was still clear in his memory as though he had parted from Anna Sergeyevna only yesterday. And his memories glowed more and more vividly. When in the evening stillness the voices of his children preparing their lessons reached his study, or when he listened to a song or to an organ playing in a restaurant, or when the storm howled in the chimney, suddenly everything would rise up in his memory: what had happened on the pier and the early morning with the mist on the mountains, and the steamer coming from Feodosia, and the kisses. He would pace about his room a long time, remembering and smiling; then his memories passed into reveries, and in his imagination the past would mingle with what was to come. He did not dream of Anna Sergeyevna, but she followed him about everywhere and watched him. When he shut his eyes he saw her before him as though she were there in the flesh; and she seemed to him lovelier, younger, tenderer than she had been; and he imagined himself a finer man than he had been in Yalta. Of evenings she peered out at him from the bookcase, from the fireplace, from the corner—he heard her breathing, the caressing rustle of her clothes. In the street he followed the women with his eyes, looking for someone who resembled her.

Already he was tormented by a strong desire to share his memories with someone. But in his home it was impossible to talk of his love, and he had no one to talk to outside; certainly he could not confide in his tenants or in anyone at the bank. And what was there to talk about? He hadn't loved her then, had he? Had there been anything beautiful, poetical, edifying, or simply interesting in his relations with Anna Sergeyevna? And he was forced to talk vaguely of love, of women, and no one guessed what he meant; only his wife would twitch her black eyebrows and say, "The part of a philanderer does not suit you at all, Dimitry."

One evening, coming out of the physicians' club with an official with whom   65
he had been playing cards, he could not resist saying:

"If you only knew what a fascinating woman I became acquainted with at Yalta!"

The official got into his sledge and was driving away, but turned suddenly and shouted: "Dmitry Dmitrich!"

"What is it?"

"You were right this evening: the sturgeon was a bit high."

These words, so commonplace, for some reason moved Gurov to indigna-   70
tion, and struck him as degrading and unclean. What savage manners, what mugs! What stupid nights, what dull, humdrum days! Frenzied gambling, gluttony, drunkenness, continual talk always about the same things! Futile pursuits

and conversations always about the same topics take up the better part of one's time, the better part of one's strength, and in the end there is left a life clipped and wingless, an absurd mess, and there is no escaping or getting away from it—just as though one were in a madhouse or a prison.

Gurov, boiling with indignation, did not sleep all night. And he had a headache all the next day. And the following nights too he slept badly; he sat up in bed, thinking, or paced up and down his room. He was fed up with his children, fed up with the bank; he had no desire to go anywhere or to talk of anything.

In December during the holidays he prepared to take a trip and told his wife he was going to Petersburg to do what he could for a young friend—and he set off for S——. What for? He did not know, himself. He wanted to see Anna Sergeyevna and talk with her, to arrange a rendezvous if possible.

He arrived at S—— in the morning, and at the hotel took the best room, in which the floor was covered with gray army cloth, and on the table there was an inkstand, gray with dust and topped by a figure on horseback, its hat in its raised hand and its head broken off. The porter gave him the necessary information: von Dideritz lived in a house of his own on Staro-Goncharnaya Street, not far from the hotel: he was rich and lived well and kept his own horses; everyone in the town knew him. The porter pronounced the name: "Dridiritz."

Without haste Gurov made his way to Staro-Goncharnaya Street and found the house. Directly opposite the house stretched a long gray fence studded with nails.

"A fence like that would make one run away," thought Gurov, looking now 75
at the fence, now at the windows of the house.

He reflected: this was a holiday, and the husband was apt to be at home. And in any case, it would be tactless to go into the house and disturb her. If he were to send her a note, it might fall into her husband's hands, and that might spoil everything. The best thing was to rely on chance. And he kept walking up and down the street and along the fence, waiting for the chance. He saw a beggar go in at the gate and heard the dogs attack him; then an hour later he heard a piano, and the sound came to him faintly and indistinctly. Probably it was Anna Sergeyevna playing. The front door opened suddenly, and an old woman came out, followed by the familiar white Pomeranian. Gurov was on the point of calling to the dog, but his heart began beating violently, and in his excitement he could not remember the Pomeranian's name.

He kept walking up and down, and hated the gray fence more and more, and by now he thought irritably that Anna Sergeyevna had forgotten him, and was perhaps already diverting herself with another man, and that that was very natural in a young woman who from morning till night had to look at that damn fence. He went back to his hotel room and sat on the couch for a long while, not knowing what to do, then he had dinner and a long nap.

"How stupid and annoying all this is!" he thought when he woke and looked at the dark windows: it was already evening. "Here I've had a good sleep for some reason. What am I going to do at night?"

He sat on the bed, which was covered with a cheap gray blanket of the kind seen in hospitals, and he twitted himself in his vexation:

"So there's your lady with the pet dog. There's your adventure. A nice place 80
to cool your heels in."

That morning at the station a playbill in large letters had caught his eye. *The Geisha* was to be given for the first time. He thought of this and drove to the theater.

"It's quite possible that she goes to first nights," he thought.

The theater was full. As in all provincial theaters, there was a haze above the chandelier, the gallery was noisy and restless; in the front row, before the beginning of the performance the local dandies were standing with their hands clasped behind their backs; in the Governor's box the Governor's daughter, wearing a boa, occupied the front seat, while the Governor himself hid modestly behind the portiere and only his hands were visible; the curtain swayed; the orchestra was a long time tuning up. While the audience were coming in and taking their seats, Gurov scanned the faces eagerly.

Anna Sergeyevna, too, came in. She sat down in the third row, and when Gurov looked at her his heart contracted, and he understood clearly that in the whole world there was no human being so near, so precious, and so important to him; she, this little, undistinguished woman, lost in a provincial crowd, with a vulgar lorgnette in her hand, filled his whole life now, was his sorrow and his joy, the only happiness that he now desired for himself, and to the sounds of the bad orchestra, of the miserable local violins, he thought how lovely she was. He thought and dreamed.

A young man with small side-whiskers, very tall and stooped, came in with   85
Anna Sergeyevna and sat down beside her; he nodded his head at every step and seemed to be bowing continually. Probably this was the husband whom at Yalta, in an excess of bitter feeling, she had called a flunkey. And there really was in his lanky figure, his side-whiskers, his small bald patch, something of a flunkey's retiring manner; his smile was mawkish, and in his buttonhole there was an academic badge like a waiter's number.

During the first intermission the husband went out to have a smoke; she remained in her seat. Gurov, who was also sitting in the orchestra, went up to her and said in a shaky voice, with a forced smile:

"Good evening!"

She glanced at him and turned pale, then looked at him again in horror, unable to believe her eyes, and gripped the fan and the lorgnette tightly together in her hands, evidently trying to keep herself from fainting. Both were silent. She was sitting, he was standing, frightened by her distress and not daring to take a seat beside her. The violins and the flute that were being tuned up sang out. He suddenly felt frightened: it seemed as if all the people in the boxes were looking at them. She got up and went hurriedly to the exit; he followed her, and both of them walked blindly along the corridors and up and down stairs, and figures in the uniforms prescribed for magistrates, teachers, and officials of the Department of Crown Lands, all wearing badges, flitted before their eyes, as did also ladies, and fur coats on hangers; they were conscious of drafts and the smell of stale tobacco. And Gurov, whose heart was beating violently, thought:

"Oh, Lord! Why are these people here and this orchestra!"

And at that instant he suddenly recalled how when he had seen Anna   90
Sergeyevna off at the station he had said to himself that all was over between them and that they would never meet again. But how distant the end still was!

On the narrow, gloomy staircase over which it said "To the Amphitheatre," she stopped.

"How you frightened me!" she said, breathing hard, still pale and stunned. "Oh, how you frightened me! I am barely alive. Why did you come? Why?"

"But do understand, Anna, do understand—" he said hurriedly, under his breath. "I implore you, do understand—"

She looked at him with fear, with entreaty, with love; she looked at him intently, to keep his features more distinctly in her memory.

"I suffer so," she went on, not listening to him. "All this time I have been   95
thinking of nothing but you; I live only by the thought of you. And I wanted to forget, to forget; but why, oh, why have you come?"

On the landing above them two high school boys were looking down and smoking, but it was all the same to Gurov; he drew Anna Sergeyevna to him and began kissing her face and her hands.

"What are you doing, what are you doing!" she was saying in horror, pushing him away. "We have lost our senses. Go away today; go away at once—I conjure you by all that is sacred, I implore you—People are coming this way!"

Someone was walking up the stairs.

"You must leave," Anna Sergeyevna went on in a whisper. "Do you hear, Dmitry Dmitrich? I will come and see you in Moscow. I have never been happy; I am unhappy now, and I never, never shall be happy, never! So don't make me suffer still more! I swear I'll come to Moscow. But now let us part. My dear, good, precious one, let us part!"

She pressed his hand and walked rapidly downstairs, turning to look round   100
at him, and from her eyes he could see that she really was unhappy. Gurov stood for a while, listening, then when all grew quiet, he found his coat and left the theater.

IV

And Anna Sergeyevna began coming to see him in Moscow. Once every two or three months she left S—, telling her husband that she was going to consult a doctor about a woman's ailment from which she was suffering—and her husband did and did not believe her. When she arrived in Moscow she would stop at the Slavyansky Bazar Hotel, and at once send a man in a red cap to Gurov. Gurov came to see her, and no one in Moscow knew of it.

Once he was going to see her in this way on a winter morning (the messenger had come the evening before and not found him in). With him walked his daughter, whom he wanted to take to school: it was on the way. Snow was coming down in big wet flakes.

"It's three degrees above zero,[2]" and yet it's snowing," Gurov was saying to his daughter. "But this temperature prevails only on the surface of the earth; in the upper layers of the atmosphere there is quite a different temperature."

"And why doesn't it thunder in winter, papa?"

He explained that, too. He talked, thinking all the while that he was on his   105
way to a rendezvous, and no living soul knew of it, and probably no one would ever know. He had two lives: an open one, seen and known by all who needed to know it, full of conventional truth and conventional falsehood, exactly like the lives of his friends and acquaintances; and another life that went on in secret. And through some strange, perhaps accidental, combination of circumstances,

_____

[2]three degrees above zero: on the Celsius scale; about thirty-eight degrees Fahrenheit.

everything that was of interest and importance to him, everything that was essential to him, everything about which he felt sincerely and did not deceive himself, everything that constituted the core of his life, was going on concealed from others; while all that was false, the shell in which he hid to cover the truth—his work at the bank, for instance, his discussions at the club, his references to the "inferior race," his appearances at anniversary celebrations with his wife—all that went on in the open. Judging others by himself, he did not believe what he saw, and always fancied that every man led his real, most interesting life under cover of secrecy as under cover of night. The personal life of every individual is based on secrecy, and perhaps it is partly for that reason that civilized man is so nervously anxious that personal privacy should be respected.

Having taken his daughter to school, Gurov went on to the Slavyansky Bazar Hotel. He took off his fur coat in the lobby, went upstairs, and knocked gently at the door. Anna Sergeyevna, wearing his favorite gray dress, exhausted by the journey and by waiting, had been expecting him since the previous evening. She was pale, and looked at him without a smile, and he had hardly entered when she flung herself on his breast. Their kiss was a long, lingering one, as though they had not seen one another for two years.

"Well, darling, how are you getting on there?" he asked. "What news?"

"Wait; I'll tell you in a moment—I can't speak."

She could not speak; she was crying. She turned away from him, and pressed her handkerchief to her eyes.

"Let her have her cry; meanwhile I'll sit down," he thought, and he seated   110
himself in an armchair.

Then he rang and ordered tea, and while he was having his tea she remained standing at the window with her back to him. She was crying out of sheer agitation, in the sorrowful consciousness that their life was so sad; that they could only see each other in secret and had to hide from people like thieves! Was it not a broken life?

"Come, stop now, dear!" he said.

It was plain to him that this love of theirs would not be over soon, that the end of it was not in sight. Anna Sergeyevna was growing more and more attached to him. She adored him, and it was unthinkable to tell her that their love was bound to come to an end some day; besides, she would not have believed it!

He went up to her and took her by the shoulders, to fondle her and say something diverting, and at that moment he caught sight of himself in the mirror.

His hair was already beginning to turn gray. And it seemed odd to him   115
that he had grown so much older in the last few years, and lost his looks. The shoulders on which his hands rested were warm and heaving. He felt compassion for this life, still so warm and lovely, but probably already about to begin to fade and wither like his own. Why did she love him so much? He always seemed to women different from what he was, and they loved in him not himself, but the man whom their imagination created and whom they had been eagerly seeking all their lives; and afterwards, when they saw their mistake, they loved him nevertheless. And not one of them had been happy with him. In the past he had met women, come together with them, parted from them, but he had never once loved; it was anything you please, but not love. And only now when his head was gray he had fallen in love, really, truly—for the first time in his life.

Anna Sergeyevna and he loved each other as people do who are very close and intimate, like man and wife, like tender friends; it seemed to them that Fate itself had meant them for one another, and they could not understand why he had a wife and she a husband; and it was as though they were a pair of migratory birds, male and female, caught and forced to live in different cages. They forgave each other what they were ashamed of in their past, they forgave everything in the present, and felt that this love of theirs had altered them both.

Formerly in moments of sadness he had soothed himself with whatever logical arguments came into his head, but now he no longer cared for logic; he felt profound compassion, he wanted to be sincere and tender.

"Give it up now, my darling," he said. "You've had your cry; that's enough. Let us have a talk now, we'll think up something."

Then they spent a long time taking counsel together, they talked of how to avoid the necessity for secrecy, for deception, for living in different cities, and not seeing one another for long stretches of time. How could they free themselves from these intolerable fetters?

"How? How?" he asked, clurching his head. "How?"

And it seemed as though in a little while the solution would be found, and then a new and glorious life would begin; and it was clear to both of them that the end was still far off, and that what was to be most complicated and difficult for them was only just beginning.

120

Starting Points for Further Research: Anton Chekhov

- **Edition:** Anton Chekhov. *Short Stories*. Ed. Cathy Popkin. New York: W. W. Norton, 2005.
- **Biography:** Donald Rayfield. *Anton Chekhov: A Life*. Evanston: Northwestern University Press, 1998.
- **Critical Essay:** Virginia Llewellyn. *Anton Chekov and the Lady with a Dog*. London: Oxford University Press, 1973.

D. H. LAWRENCE

(1885–1930)

The son of a Nottingham coal miner and a schoolteacher, D. H. Lawrence grew up as a sickly child, and through his mother's pressure he trained as a teacher. He first published some poems in 1909 in the English Review, *edited by Ford Maddox Ford, who encouraged publication of Lawrence's first novel,* The White Peacock *(1911). Lawrence's three most well-regarded novels,* Sons and Lovers *(1913),* The Rainbow *(1915), and* Women in Love *(1921), concentrate on establishing individual identity against the pressures of the world, especially against domination by others. Lawrence became notorious for his novel* Lady Chatterley's Lover *(1928), about an English noblewoman who seeks sexual fulfillment with her husband's working-class gamekeeper.*

Edward Weston's portrait of D. H. Lawrence, c. 1924.

The Horse Dealer's Daughter

(1922)

"Well, Mabel, and what are you going to do with yourself?" asked Joe, with foolish flippancy. He felt quite safe himself. Without listening for an answer, he turned aside, worked a grain of tobacco to the tip of his tongue, and spat it out. He did not care about anything, since he felt safe himself.

The three brothers and the sister sat round the desolate breakfast-table, attempting some sort of desultory consultation. The morning's post had given the final tap to the family fortunes, and all was over. The dreary dining-room itself, with its heavy mahogany furniture, looked as if it were waiting to be done away with.

But the consultation amounted to nothing. There was a strange air of ineffectuality about the three men, as they sprawled at table, smoking and reflecting vaguely on their own condition. The girl was alone, a rather short, sullen-looking young woman of twenty-seven. She did not share the same life as her brothers. She would have been good-looking, save for the impressive fixity of her face, "bull-dog," as her brothers called it.

There was a confused tramping of horses' feet outside. The three men all sprawled round in their chairs to watch. Beyond the dark holly bushes that separated the strip of lawn from the high-road, they could see a cavalcade of shire horses swinging out of their own yard, being taken for exercise. This was the last time. These were the last horses that would go through their hands. The young men watched with critical, callous looks. They were all frightened at the collapse of their lives, and the sense of disaster in which they were involved left them no inner freedom.

Yet they were three fine, well-set fellows enough. Joe, the eldest, was a man 5
of thirty-three, broad and handsome in a hot, flushed way. His face was red, he twisted his black mustache over a thick finger, his eyes were shallow and restless. He had a sensual way of uncovering his teeth when he laughed, and his bearing was stupid. Now he watched the horses with a glazed look of helplessness in his eyes, a certain stupor of downfall.

The great draft-horses swung past. They were tied head to tail, four of them, and they heaved along to where a lane branched off from the high-road, planting their great hoofs floutingly in the fine black mud, swinging their great rounded haunches sumptuously, and trotting a few sudden steps as they were led into the lane, round the corner. Every movement showed a massive, slumbrous strength, and a stupidity which held them in subjection. The groom at the head looked back, jerking the leading rope. And the cavalcade moved out of sight up the lane, the tail of the last horse, bobbed up tight and stiff, held out taut from the swinging great haunches as they rocked behind the hedges in a motionlike sleep.

Joe watched with glazed hopeless eyes. The horses were almost like his own body to him. He felt he was done for now. Luckily he was engaged to a woman as old as himself, and therefore her father, who was steward of a neighboring estate, would provide him with a job. He would marry and go into harness. His life was over, he would be a subject animal now.

He turned uneasily aside, the retreating steps of the horses echoing in his ears. Then, with foolish restlessness, he reached for the scraps of bacon-rind from the plates, and making a faint whistling sound, flung them to the terrier that lay against the fender. He watched the dog swallow them, and waited till the creature looked into his eyes. Then a faint grin came on his face, and in a high, foolish voice he said:

"You won't get much more bacon, shall you, you little b——?"

The dog faintly and dismally wagged its tail, then lowered its haunches, cir- 10
cled round, and lay down again.

There was another helpless silence at the table. Joe sprawled uneasily in his seat, not willing to go till the family conclave was dissolved. Fred Henry, the second brother, was erect, clean-limbed, alert. He had watched the passing of the horses with more *sang-froid*. If he was an animal, like Joe, he was an animal which controls, not one which is controlled. He was master of any horse, and he carried himself with a well-tempered air of mastery. But he was not master of the situations of life. He pushed his coarse brown mustache upwards, off his lip, and glanced irritably at his sister, who sat impassive and inscrutable.

"You'll go and stop with Lucy for a bit, shan't you?" he asked. The girl did not answer.

"I don't see what else you can do," persisted Fred Henry.

"Go as a skivvy,"[1] Joe interpolated laconically.

The girl did not move a muscle.   15

"If I was her, I should go in for training for a nurse," said Malcolm, the youngest of them all. He was the baby of the family, a young man of twenty-two, with a fresh, jaunty *museau*.[2]

But Mabel did not take any notice of him. They had talked at her and round her for so many years, that she hardly heard them at all.

The marble clock on the mantelpiece softly chimed the half-hour, the dog rose uneasily from the hearth-rug and looked at the party at the breakfast-table. But still they sat on in ineffectual conclave.

"Oh, all right," said Joe suddenly, apropos of nothing. "I'll get a move on."

He pushed back his chair, straddled his knees with a downward jerk, to get   20
them free, in horsey fashion, and went to the fire. Still he did not go out of the room; he was curious to know what the others would do or say. He began to charge his pipe, looking down at the dog and saying in a high, affected voice:

"Going wi' me? Going wi' me are ter? Tha'rt goin' further than tha counts on just now, dost hear?"

The dog faintly wagged its tail, the man stuck out his jaw and covered his pipe with his hands, and puffed intently, losing himself in the tobacco, looking down all the while at the dog with an absent brown eye. The dog looked up at him in mournful distrust. Joe stood with his knees stuck out, in real horsey fashion.

"Have you had a letter from Lucy?" Fred Henry asked of his sister.

"Last week," came the neutral reply.

"And what does she say?"   25

There was no answer.

"Does she *ask* you to go and stop there?" persisted Fred Henry.

"She says I can if I like."

"Well, then, you'd better. Tell her you'll come on Monday."

This was received in silence.   30

"That's what you'll do then, is it?" said Fred Henry, in some exasperation.

But she made no answer. There was a silence of futility and irritation in the room. Malcolm grinned fatuously.

"You'll have to make up your mind between now and next Wednesday," said Joe loudly, "or else find yourself lodgings on the curbstone."

---

[1]*skivvy*: Domestic worker.
[2]*museau*: Slang for face.

The face of the young woman darkened, but she sat on immutable.

"Here's Jack Fergusson!" exclaimed Malcolm, who was looking aimlessly out   35
of the window.

"Where?" exclaimed Joe loudly.

"Just gone past."

"Coming in?"

Malcolm craned his neck to see the gate.

"Yes," he said.   40

There was a silence. Mabel sat on like one condemned, at the head of the
table. Then a whistle was heard from the kitchen. The dog got up and barked
sharply. Joe opened the door and shouted:

"Come on."

After a moment a young man entered. He was muffled up in overcoat and a
purple woolen scarf, and his tweed cap, which he did not remove, was pulled
down on his head. He was of medium height, his face was rather long and pale,
his eyes looked tired.

"Hello, Jack! Well, Jack!" exclaimed Malcolm and Joe. Fred Henry merely
said: "Jack."

"What's doing?" asked the newcomer, evidently addressing Fred Henry.   45

"Same. We've got to be out by Wednesday. Got a cold?"

"I have—got it bad, too."

"Why don't you stop in?"

"*Me* stop in? When I can't stand on my legs, perhaps I shall have a chance,"
the young man spoke huskily. He had a slight Scotch accent.

"It's a knock-out, isn't it," said Joe, boisterously, "if a doctor goes round   50
croaking with a cold. Looks bad for the patients, doesn't it?"

The young doctor looked at him slowly.

"Anything the matter with *you*, then?" he asked sarcastically.

"Not as I know of. Damn your eyes, hope not. Why?"

"I thought you were very concerned about the patients, wondered if you
might be one yourself."

"Damn it, no, I've never been patient to no flaming doctor, and hope I   55
never shall be," returned Joe.

At this point Mabel rose from the table, and they all seemed to become
aware of her existence. She began putting the dishes together. The young doctor
looked at her, but did not address her. He had not greeted her. She went out of
the room with the tray, her face impassive and unchanged.

"When are you off then, all of you?" asked the doctor.

"I'm catching the eleven-forty," replied Malcolm. "Are you goin' down wi'
th' trap,[3] Joe?"

"Yes, I've told you I'm going down wi' th' trap, haven't I?"

"We'd better be getting her in then. So long, Jack, if I don't see you before I   60
go," said Malcolm, shaking hands.

He went out, followed by Joe, who seemed to have his tail between his legs.

"Well, this is the devil's own," exclaimed the doctor, when he was left alone
with Fred Henry. "Going before Wednesday, are you?"

"That's the orders," replied the other.

---

[3]*trap:* a two-wheeled carriage.

"Where, to Northampton?"

"That's it."   65

"The devil!" exclaimed Fergusson, with quiet chagrin.

And there was silence between the two.

"All settled up, are you?" asked Fergusson.

"About."

There was another pause.   70

"Well, I shall miss yer, Freddy, boy," said the young doctor.

"And I shall miss thee, Jack," returned the other.

"Miss you like hell," mused the doctor.

Fred Henry turned aside. There was nothing to say. Mabel came in again to finish clearing the table.

"What are *you* going to do, then, Miss Pervin?" asked Fergusson. "Going to   75
your sister's, are you?"

Mabel looked at him with her steady, dangerous eyes, that always made him uncomfortable, unsettling his superficial ease.

"No," she said.

"Well, what in the name of fortune *are* you going to do? Say what you mean to do," cried Fred Henry, with futile intensity.

But she only averted her head, and continued her work. She folded the white table-cloth, and put on the chenille cloth.

"The sulkiest bitch that ever trod!" muttered her brother.   80

But she finished her task with perfectly impassive face, the young doctor watching her interestedly all the while. Then she went out.

Fred Henry stared after her, clenching his lips, his blue eyes fixing in sharp antagonism, as he made a grimace of sour exasperation.

"You could bray her into bits, and that's all you'd get out of her," he said, in a small, narrowed tone.

The doctor smiled faintly.

"What's she *going* to do, then?" he asked.   85

"Strike me if *I* know!" returned the other.

There was a pause. Then the doctor stirred.

"I'll be seeing you tonight, shall I?" he said to his friend.

"Ay—where's it to be? Are we going over to Jessdale?"

"I don't know. I've got such a cold on me. I'll come round to the 'Moon and   90
Stars,' anyway."

"Let Lizzie and May miss their night for once, eh?"

"That's it—if I feel as I do now."

"All's one—"

The two young men went through the passage and down to the back door together. The house was large, but it was servantless now, and desolate. At the back was a small bricked houseyard and beyond that a big square, graveled fine and red, and having stables on two sides. Sloping, dank, winter-dark fields stretched away on the open sides.

But the stables were empty. Joseph Pervin, the father of the family, had been   95
a man of no education, who had become a fairly large horse dealer. The stables had been full of horses, there was a great turmoil and come-and-go of horses and of dealers and grooms. Then the kitchen was full of servants. But of late things had declined. The old man had married a second time, to retrieve his fortunes.

Now he was dead and everything was gone to the dogs, there was nothing but debt and threatening.

For months, Mabel had been servantless in the big house, keeping the home together in penury for her ineffectual brothers. She had kept house for ten years. But previously it was with unstinted means. Then, however brutal and coarse everything was, the sense of money had kept her proud, confident. The men might be foul-mouthed, the women in the kitchen might have bad reputations, her brothers might have illegitimate children. But so long as there was money, the girl felt herself established, and brutally proud, reserved.

No company came to the house, save dealers and coarse men. Mabel had no associates of her own sex, after her sister went away. But she did not mind. She went regularly to church, she attended to her father. And she lived in the memory of her mother, who had died when she was fourteen, and whom she had loved. She had loved her father, too, in a different way, depending upon him, and feeling secure in him, until at the age of fifty-four he married again. And then she had set hard against him. Now he had died and left them all hopelessly in debt.

She had suffered badly during the period of poverty. Nothing, however, could shake the curious, sullen, animal pride that dominated each member of the family. Now, for Mabel, the end had come. Still she would not cast about her. She would follow her own way just the same. She would always hold the keys of her own situation. Mindless and persistent, she endured from day to day. Why should she think? Why should she answer anybody? It was enough that this was the end, and there was no way out. She need not pass any more darkly along the main street of the small town, avoiding every eye. She need not demean herself any more, going into the shops and buying the cheapest food. This was at an end. She thought of nobody, not even of herself. Mindless and persistent, she seemed in a sort of ecstasy to be coming nearer to her fulfillment, her own glorification, approaching her dead mother, who was glorified.

In the afternoon she took a little bag, with shears and sponge and a small scrubbing-brush, and went out. It was a gray, wintry day, with saddened, dark green fields and an atmosphere blackened by the smoke of foundries not far off. She went quickly, darkly along the causeway, heeding nobody, through the town to the churchyard.

There she always felt secure, as if no one could see her, although as a matter 100 of fact she was exposed to the stare of everyone who passed along under the churchyard wall. Nevertheless, once under the shadow of the great looming church, among the graves, she felt immune from the world, reserved within the thick churchyard wall as in another country.

Carefully she clipped the grass from the grave, and arranged the pinky white, small chrysanthemums in the tin cross. When this was done, she took an empty jar from a neighboring grave, brought water, and carefully, most scrupulously sponged the marble headstone and the coping-stone.

It gave her sincere satisfaction to do this. She felt in immediate contact with the world of her mother. She took minute pains, went through the park in a state bordering on pure happiness, as if in performing this task she came into a subtle, intimate connection with her mother. For the life she followed here in the world was far less real than the world of death she inherited from her mother.

The doctor's house was just by the church. Fergusson, being a mere hired assistant, was slave to the countryside. As he hurried now to attend to the out-patients in the surgery, glancing across the graveyard with his quick eye, he saw the girl at her task at the grave. She seemed so intent and remote, it was like looking into another world. Some mystical element was touched in him. He slowed down as he walked, watching her as if spellbound.

She lifted her eyes, feeling him looking. Their eyes met. And each looked again at once, each feeling, in some way, found out by the other. He lifted his cap and passed on down the road. There remained distinct in his consciousness, like a vision, the memory of her face, lifted from the tombstone in the churchyard, and looking at him with slow, large, portentous eyes. It *was* portentous, her face. It seemed to mesmerize him. There was a heavy power in her eyes which laid hold of his whole being, as if he had drunk some powerful drug. He had been feeling weak and done before. Now the life came back into him, he felt delivered from his own fretted, daily self.

He finished his duties at the surgery as quickly as might be, hastily filling up 105
the bottles of the waiting people with cheap drugs. Then, in perpetual haste, he set off again to visit several cases in another part of his round, before teatime. At all times he preferred to walk if he could, but particularly when he was not well. He fancied the motion restored him.

The afternoon was falling. It was gray, deadened, and wintry, with a slow, moist, heavy coldness sinking in and deadening all the faculties. But why should he think or notice? He hastily climbed the hill and turned across the dark green fields, following the black cinder-track. In the distance, across a shallow dip in the country, the small town was clustered like smoldering ash, a tower, a spire, a heap of low, raw, extinct houses. And on the nearest fringe of the town, sloping into the dip, was Oldmeadow, the Pervins' house. He could see the stables and the outbuildings distinctly, as they lay towards him on the slope. Well, he would not go there many more times! Another resource would be lost to him, another place gone: the only company he cared for in the alien, ugly little town he was losing. Nothing but work, drudgery, constant hastening from dwelling to dwelling among the colliers and the iron-workers. It wore him out, but at the same time he had a craving for it. It was a stimulant to him to be in the homes of the working people, moving, as it were, through the innermost body of their life. His nerves were excited and gratified. He could come so near, into the very lives of the rough, inarticulate, powerful emotional men and women: He grumbled, he said he hated the hellish hole. But as a matter of fact it excited him, the contact with the rough, strongly-feeling people was a stimulant applied direct to his nerves.

Below Oldmeadow, in the green, shallow, soddened hollow of fields, lay a square, deep pond. Roving across the landscape, the doctor's quick eye detected a figure in black passing through the gate of the field, down towards the pond. He looked again. It would be Mabel Pervin. His mind suddenly became alive and attentive.

Why was she going down there? He pulled up on the path on the slope above, and stood staring. He could just make sure of the small black figure moving in the hollow of the failing day. He seemed to see her in the midst of such obscurity, that he was like a clairvoyant, seeing rather with the mind's eye than with ordinary sight. Yet he could see her positively enough, whilst he kept his eye attentive. He felt, if he looked away from her, in the thick, ugly falling dusk, he would lose her altogether.

He followed her minutely as she moved, direct and intent, like something transmitted rather than stirring in voluntary activity, straight down from the field towards the pond. There she stood on the bank for a moment. She never raised her head. Then she waded slowly into the water.

He stood motionless as the small black figure walked slowly and deliberately 110 towards the center of the pond, very slowly, gradually moving deeper into the motionless water, and still moving forward as the water got up to her breast. Then he could see her no more in the dusk of the dead afternoon.

"There!" he exclaimed. "Would you believe it?"

And he hastened straight down, running over the wet, soddened fields, pushing through the hedges, down into the depression of callous wintry obscurity. It took him several minutes to come to the pond. He stood on the bank, breathing heavily. He could see nothing. His eyes seemed to penetrate the dead water. Yes, perhaps that was the dark shadow of her black clothing beneath the surface of the water.

He slowly ventured into the pond. The bottom was deep, soft clay, he sank in, and the water clasped dead cold round his legs. As he stirred he could smell the cold, rotten clay that fouled up into the water. It was objectionable in his lungs. Still, repelled and yet not heeding, he moved deeper into the pond. The cold water rose over his things, over his loins, upon his abdomen. The lower part of his body was all sunk in the hideous cold element. And the bottom was so deeply soft and uncertain, he was afraid of pitching with his mouth underneath. He could not swim, and was afraid.

He crouched a little, spreading his hands under the water and moving them round, trying to feel for her. The dead cold pond swayed upon his chest. He moved again, a little deeper, and again, with his hands underneath, he felt all around under the water. And he touched her clothing. But it evaded his fingers. He made a desperate effort to grasp it.

And so doing he lost his balance and went under, horribly, suffocating in the 115 foul earthy water, struggling madly for a few moments. At last, after what seemed an eternity, he got his footing, rose again into the air, and looked around. He gasped, and knew he was in the world. Then he looked at the water. She had risen near him. He grasped her clothing, and drawing her nearer, turned to make his way to land again.

He went very slowly, carefully, absorbed in the slow progress. He rose higher, climbing out of the pond. The water was now only about his legs, he was thankful, full of relief to be out of the clutches of the pond. He lifted her and staggered on to the bank, out of the horror of wet, gray clay.

He laid her down on the bank. She was quite unconscious and running with water. He made the water come from her mouth, he worked to restore her. He did not have to work very long before he could feel the breathing begin again in her; she was breathing naturally. He worked a little longer. He could feel her live beneath his hands; she was coming back. He wiped her face, wrapped her in his overcoat, looked round into the dim, dark gray world, then lifted her and staggered down the bank and across the fields.

It seemed an unthinkably long way, and his burden so heavy he felt he would never get to the house. But at last he was in the stable-yard, and then in the house-yard. He opened the door and went into the house. In the kitchen he laid her down on the hearth-rug and called. The house was empty. But the fire was burning in the grate.

Then again he kneeled to attend to her. She was breathing regularly, her eyes were wide open and as if conscious, but there seemed something missing in her look. She was conscious in herself, but unconscious of her surroundings.

He ran upstairs, took blankets from a bed, and put them before the fire to 120 warm. Then he removed her saturated, earthy-smelling clothing, rubbed her dry with a towel, and wrapped her naked in the blankets. Then he went into the dining-room, to look for spirits. There was a little whiskey. He drank a gulp himself, and put some into her mouth.

The effect was instantaneous. She looked full into his face, as if she had been seeing him for some time, and yet had only just become conscious of him.

"Dr. Fergusson?" she said.

"What?" he answered.

He was divesting himself of his coat, intending to find some dry clothing upstairs. He could not bear the smell of the dead, clayey water, and he was mortally afraid for his own health.

"What did I do?" she asked. 125

"Walked into the pond," he replied. He had begun to shudder like one sick, and could hardly attend to her. Her eyes remained full on him, he seemed to be going dark in his mind, looking back at her helplessly. The shuddering became quieter in him, his life came back to him, dark and unknowing, but strong again.

"Was I out of my mind?" she asked, while her eyes were fixed on him all the time.

"Maybe, for the moment," he replied. He felt quiet, because his strength had come back. The strange fretful strain had left him.

"Am I out of my mind now?" she asked.

"Are you?" he reflected a moment. "No," he answered truthfully. "I don't see 130 that you are." He turned his face aside. He was afraid now, because he felt lazed, and felt dimly that her power was stronger than his, in this issue. And she continued to look at him fixedly all the time. "Can you tell me where I shall find some dry things to put on?" he asked.

"Did you dive into the pond for me?" she asked.

"No," he answered. "I walked in. But I went in overhead as well."

There was silence for a moment. He hesitated. He very much wanted to go upstairs to get into dry clothing. But there was another desire in him. And she seemed to hold him. His will seemed to have gone to sleep, and left him, standing there slack before her. But he felt warm inside himself. He did not shudder at all, though his clothes were sodden on him.

"Why did you?" she asked.

"Because I didn't want you to do such a foolish thing," he said. 135

"It wasn't foolish," she said, still gazing at him as she lay on the floor, with a sofa cushion under her head. "It was the right thing to do. *I* knew best, then."

"I'll go and shift these wet things," he said. But still he had not the power to move out of her presence, until she sent him. It was as if she had the life of his body in her hands, and he could not extricate himself. Or perhaps he did not want to.

Suddenly she sat up. Then she became aware of her own immediate condition. She felt the blankets about her, she knew her own limbs. For a moment it seemed as if her reason were going. She looked round, with wild eyes, as if seeking something. He stood still with fear. She saw her clothing lying scattered.

"Who undressed me?" she asked, her eyes resting full and inevitable on his face.

"I did," he replied, "to bring you round."   140

For some moments she sat and gazed at him, awfully, her lips parted.

"Do you love me, then?" she asked.

He only stood and stared at her, fascinated. His soul seemed to melt.

She shuffled forward on her knees, and put her arms round him, round his legs, as he stood there, pressing her breasts against his knees and thighs, clutching him with strange, convulsive certainty, pressing his thighs against her, drawing him to her face, her throat, as she looked up at him with flaring, humble eyes of transfiguration, triumphant in first possession.

"You love me," she murmured, in strange transport, yearning and tri-   145
umphant and confident. "You love me. I know you love me, I know."

And she was passionately kissing his knees, through the wet clothing passionately and indiscriminately kissing his knees, his legs, as if unaware of everything.

He looked down at the tangled wet hair, the wild, bare, animal shoulders. He was amazed, bewildered, and afraid. He had never thought of loving her. He had never wanted to love her. When he rescued her and restored her, he was a doctor, and she was a patient. He had had no single personal thought of her. Nay, this introduction of the personal element was very distasteful to him, a violation of his professional honor. It was horrible to have her there embracing his knees. It was horrible. He revolted from it, violently. And yet—and yet—he had not the power to break away.

She looked at him again, with the same supplication of powerful love, and that same transcendent, frightening light of triumph. In view of the delicate flame which seemed to come from her face like a light, he was powerless. And yet he had never intended to love her. He had never intended. And something stubborn in him could not give way.

"You love me," she repeated, in a murmur of deep, rhapsodic assurance "You love me."

Her hands were drawing him, drawing him down to her. He was afraid even   150
a little horrified. For he had, really, no intention of loving her. Yet her hands were drawing him towards her. He put out his hand quickly to steady himself, and grasped her bare shoulder. A flame seemed to burn the hand that grasped her soft shoulder. He had no intention of loving her: his whole will was against his yielding. It was horrible. And yet wonderful was the touch of her shoulders, beautiful the shining of her face. Was she perhaps mad? He had a horror of yielding to her. Yet something in him ached also.

He had been staring away at the door, away from her. But his hand remained on her shoulder. She had gone suddenly very still. He looked down at her. Her eyes were now wide with fear, with doubt, the light was dying from her face, a shadow of terrible grayness was returning. He could not bear the touch of her eyes' question upon him, and the look of death behind the question.

With an inward groan he gave way, and let his heart yield towards her. A sudden gentle smile came on his face. And her eyes, which never left his face, slowly, slowly filled with tears. He watched the strange water rise in her eyes like some slow fountain coming up. And his heart seemed to burn and melt away in his breast.

He could not bear to look at her any more. He dropped on his knees and caught her head with his arms and pressed her face against his throat. She was very still. His heart, which seemed to have broken, was burning with a kind of agony in his breast. And he felt her slow, hot tears wetting his throat. But he could not move.

He felt the hot tears wet his neck and the hollows of his neck, and he remained motionless, suspended through one of man's eternities. Only now it had become indispensable to him to have her face pressed close to him; he could never let her go again. He could never let her head go away from the close clutch of his arm. He wanted to remain like that for ever, with his heart hurting him in a pain that was also life to him. Without knowing, he was looking down on her damp, soft brown hair.

Then, as it were suddenly, he smelt the horrid stagnant smell of that water. 155 And at the same moment she drew away from him and looked at him. Her eyes were wistful and unfathomable. He was afraid of them, and he fell to kissing her, not knowing what he was doing. He wanted her eyes not to have that terrible, wistful, unfathomable look.

When she turned her face to him again, a faint delicate flush was glowing, and there was again dawning that terrible shining of joy in her eyes, which really terrified him, and yet which he now wanted to see, because he feared the look of doubt still more.

"You love me?" she said, rather faltering.

"Yes." The word cost him a painful effort. Not because it wasn't true. But because it was too newly true, the *saying* seemed to tear open again his newly-born heart. And he hardly wanted it to be true, even now.

She lifted her face to him, and he bent forward and kissed her on the mouth, gently, with the one kiss that is an eternal pledge. And as he kissed her his heart strained again in his breast. He never intended to love her. But now it was over. He had crossed over the gulf to her, and all that he had left behind had shriveled and become void.

After the kiss, her eyes again slowly filled with tears. She sat still, away from 160 him, with her face drooped aside, and her hands folded in her lap. The tears fell very slowly. There was complete silence. He too sat there motionless and silent on the hearth-rug. The strange pain of his heart that was broken seemed to consume him. That he should love her? That this was love! That he should be ripped open in this way! Him, a doctor! How they would all jeer if they knew! It was agony to him to think they might know.

In the curious naked pain of the thought he looked again to her. She was still sitting there drooped into a muse. He saw a tear fall, and his heart flared hot. He saw for the first time that one of her shoulders was quite uncovered, one arm bare, he could see one of her small breasts; dimly, because it had become almost dark in the room.

"Why are you crying?" he asked, in an altered voice.

She looked up at him, and behind her tears the consciousness of her situation for the first time brought a dark look of shame to her eyes.

"I'm not crying, really," she said, watching him, half frightened.

He reached his hand, and softly closed it on her bare arm. 165

"I love you! I love you!" he said in a soft, low vibrating voice, unlike himself.

She shrank, and dropped her head. The soft, penetrating grip of his hand on her arm distressed her. She looked up at him.

"I want to go," she said. "I want to go and get you some dry things."

"Why?" he said. "I'm all right."

"But I want to go," she said. "And I want you to change your things."   170

He released her arm, and she wrapped herself in the blanket, looking at him rather frightened. And still she did not rise.

"Kiss me," she said wistfully.

He kissed her, but briefly, half in anger.

Then, after a second, she rose nervously, all mixed up in the blanket. He watched her in her confusion as she tried to extricate herself and wrap herself up so that she could walk. He watched her relentlessly, as she knew. And as she went, the blanket trailing, and as he saw a glimpse of her feet and her white leg, he tried to remember her as she was when he had wrapped her in the blanket. But then he didn't want to remember, because she had been nothing to him then, and his nature revolted from remembering her as she was when she was nothing to him.

A tumbling, muffled noise from within the dark house startled him. Then he   175
heard her voice: "There are clothes." He rose and went to the foot of the stairs, and gathered up the garments she had thrown down. Then he came back to the fire, to rub himself down and dress. He grinned at his own appearance when he had finished.

The fire was sinking, so he put on coal. The house was now quite dark, save for the light of a street-lamp that shone in faintly from beyond the holly trees. He lit the gas with matches he found on the mantelpiece. Then he emptied the pockets of his own clothes, and threw all his wet things in a heap into the scullery. After which he gathered up her sodden clothes, gently, and put them in a separate heap on the copper-top in the scullery.

It was six o'clock on the clock. His own watch had stopped. He ought to go back to the surgery. He waited, and still she did not come down. So he went to the foot of the stairs and called:

"I shall have to go."

Almost immediately he heard her coming down. She had on her best dress of black voile, and her hair was tidy, but still damp. She looked at him—and in spite of herself, smiled.

"I don't like you in those clothes," she said.   180

"Do I look a sight?" he answered.

They were shy of one another.

"I'll make you some tea," she said.

"No, I must go."

"Must you?" And she looked at him again with the wide, strained, doubtful   185
eyes. And again, from the pain of his breast, he knew how he loved her. He went and bent to kiss her, gently, passionately, with his heart's painful kiss.

"And my hair smells so horrible," she murmured in distraction. "And I'm so awful, I'm so awful! Oh, no, I'm too awful." And she broke into bitter, heartbroken sobbing. "You can't want to love me, I'm horrible."

"Don't be silly, don't be silly," he said, trying to comfort her, kissing her, holding her in his arms. "I want you, I want to marry you, we're going to be married, quickly, quickly—tomorrow if I can."

But she only sobbed terribly, and cried:

"I feel awful. I feel awful. I feel I'm horrible to you."

"No, I want you, I want you," was all he answered, blindly, with that terrible   190
intonation which frightened her almost more than her horror lest he should *not* want her.

Starting Points for Further Research: D. H. Lawrence

- **Editions:** D. H. Lawrence. *The Complete Short Novels.* New York: Penguin, 2000.

  ———. *Complete Short Stories.* New York: Penguin, 1976–1977.
- **Biography:** Keith M. Sagar. *The Life of D. H. Lawrence.* Albuquerque: University of New Mexico Press, 1989.
- **Critical Essay:** Howard J. Booth. "D. H. Lawrence and Male Homosexual Desire." *Review of English Studies* 53 (2002): 86–107.

ERNEST HEMINGWAY · (1899–1961)

Ernest Hemingway grew up in the Chicago suburb of Oak Park, Illinois, and after high school worked as a reporter in Kansas City. During World War I, Hemingway was wounded while serving as an ambulance driver in northern Italy. He moved to Paris after the war, devoting himself to writing stories with a new, spare style that came to be his trademark. In Paris he was part of a circle of American expatriates, including Gertrude Stein and F. Scott Fitzgerald, who were part of what Stein called "the Lost Generation." Hemingway published a very successful novel, The Sun Also Rises, *in 1926 and later served as a newspaper correspondent in the Spanish Civil War and in World War II. He lived in Cuba for a time, and later settled in Idaho, continuing to maintain a macho lifestyle. Physical limitations and depression led him to commit suicide in 1961.*

Hills like White Elephants · (1927)

The hills across the valley of the Ebro were long and white. On this side there was no shade and no trees and the station was between two lines of rails in the sun. Close against the side of the station there was the warm shadow of the building and a curtain, made of strings of bamboo beads, hung across the open door into the bar, to keep out flies. The American and the girl with him sat at a table in the shade, outside the building. It was very hot and the express from Barcelona would come in forty minutes. It stopped at this junction for two minutes and went on to Madrid.

"What should we drink?" the girl asked. She had taken off her hat and put it on the table.

"It's pretty hot," the man said.

"Let's drink beer."

"Dos cervezas," the man said into the curtain.

"Big ones?" a woman asked from the doorway.   5

"Yes. Two big ones."

The woman brought two glasses of beer and two felt pads. She put the felt pads and the beer glasses on the table and looked at the man and the girl. The girl was looking off at the line of hills. They were white in the sun and the country was brown and dry.

"They look like white elephants," she said.

"I've never seen one," the man drank his beer.   10

"No, you wouldn't have."

"I might have," the man said. "Just because you say I wouldn't have doesn't prove anything."

The girl looked at the bead curtain. "They've painted something on it," she said. "What does it say?"

"Anis del Toro. It's a drink."

"Could we try it?"   15

The man called "Listen" through the curtain. The woman came out from the bar.

"Four reales."[1]

"We want two Anis del Toro."

"With water?"

"Do you want it with water?"   20

"I don't know," the girl said. "Is it good with water?"

"It's all right."

"You want them with water?" asked the woman.

"Yes, with water."

"It tastes like licorice," the girl said and put the glass down.   25

"That's the way with everything."

"Yes," said the girl. "Everything tastes of licorice. Especially all the things you've waited so long for, like absinthe."

"Oh, cut it out."

"You started it," the girl said. "I was being amused. I was having a fine time."

"Well, let's try and have a fine time."   30

"All right. I was trying. I said the mountains looked like white elephants. Wasn't that bright?"

"That was bright."

"I wanted to try this new drink. That's all we do, isn't it—look at things and try new drinks?"

"I guess so."

The girl looked across at the hills.   35

"They're lovely hills," she said. "They don't really look like white elephants. I just meant the coloring of their skin through the trees."

"Should we have another drink?"

"All right."

The warm wind blew the bead curtain against the table.

"The beer's nice and cool," the man said.   40

"It's lovely," the girl said.

"It's really an awfully simple operation, Jig," the man said. "It's not really an operation at all."

---

[1]Spanish money.

The girl looked at the ground the table legs rested on.

"I know you wouldn't mind it, Jig. It's really not anything. It's just to let the air in."

The girl did not say anything.   45

"I'll go with you and I'll stay with you all the time. They just let the air in and then it's all perfectly natural."

"Then what will we do afterward?"

"We'll be fine afterward. Just like we were before."

"What makes you think so?"

"That's the only thing that bothers us. It's the only thing that's made us un-   50
happy."

The girl looked at the bead curtain, put her hand out and took hold of two of the strings of beads.

"And you think then we'll be all right and be happy."

"I know we will. You don't have to be afraid. I've known lots of people that have done it."

"So have I," said the girl. "And afterward they were all so happy."

"Well," the man said, "if you don't want to you don't have to. I wouldn't   55
have you do it if you didn't want to. But I know it's perfectly simple."

"And you really want to?"

"I think it's the best thing to do. But I don't want you to do it if you don't really want to."

"And if I do it you'll be happy and things will be like they were and you'll love me?"

"I love you now. You know I love you."

"I know. But if I do it, then it will be nice again if I say things are like white   60
elephants, and you'll like it?"

"I'll love it. I love it now but I just can't think about it. You know how I get when I worry."

"If I do it you won't ever worry?"

"I won't worry about that because it's perfectly simple."

"Then I'll do it. Because I don't care about me."

"What do you mean?"   65

"I don't care about me."

"Well, I care about you."

"Oh, yes. But I don't care about me. And I'll do it and then everything will be fine."

"I don't want you to do it if you feel that way."

The girl stood up and walked to the end of the station. Across, on the other   70
side, were fields of grain and trees along the banks of the Ebro. Far away, beyond the river, were mountains. The shadow of a cloud moved across the field of grain and she saw the river through the trees.

"And we could have all this," she said. "And we could have everything and every day we make it more impossible."

"What did you say?"

"I said we could have everything."

"We can have everything."

"No, we can't."   75

"We can have the whole world."

"No, we can't."

"We can go everywhere."

"No, we can't. It isn't ours any more."

"It's ours."

"No, it isn't. And once they take it away, you never get it back."

"But they haven't taken it away."

"We'll wait and see."

"Come on back in the shade," he said. "You mustn't feel that way."

"I don't feel any way," the girl said. "I just know things."

"I don't want you to do anything that you don't want to do—"

"Nor that isn't good for me," she said. "I know. Could we have another beer?"

"All right. But you've got to realize—"

"I realize," the girl said. "Can't we maybe stop talking?"

They sat down at the table and the girl looked across at the hills on the dry side of the valley and the man looked at her and at the table.

"You've got to realize," he said, "that I don't want you to do it if you don't want to. I'm perfectly willing to go through with it if it means anything to you."

"Doesn't it mean anything to you? We could get along."

"Of course it does. But I don't want anybody but you. I don't want any one else. And I know it's perfectly simple."

"Yes, you know it's perfectly simple."

"It's all right for you to say that, but I do know it."

"Would you do something for me now?"

"I'd do anything for you."

"Would you please please please please please please please stop talking?"

He did not say anything but looked at the bags against the wall of the station. There were labels on them from all the hotels where they had spent nights.

"But I don't want you to," he said, "I don't care anything about it."

"I'll scream," the girl said.

The woman came out through the curtains with two glasses of beer and put them down on the damp felt pads. "The train comes in five minutes," she said.

"What did she say?" asked the girl.

"That the train is coming in five minutes."

The girl smiled brightly at the woman, to thank her.

"I'd better take the bags over to the other side of the station," the man said. She smiled at him.

"All right. Then come back and we'll finish the beer."

He picked up the two heavy bags and carried them around the station to the other tracks. He looked up the tracks but could not see the train. Coming back, he walked through the barroom, where people waiting for the train were drinking. He drank an Anis at the bar and looked at the people. They were all waiting reasonably for the train. He went out through the bead curtain. She was sitting at the table and smiled at him.

"Do you feel better?" he asked.

"I feel fine," she said. "There's nothing wrong with me. I feel fine."

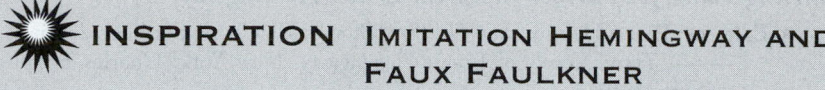

INSPIRATION IMITATION HEMINGWAY AND FAUX FAULKNER

Ralph Barton's Ernest Hemingway, *published in* Vanity Fair.

Every year, *Hemispheres Magazine* sponsors an Imitation Hemingway contest, requiring one-page parodies of his actual prose style. The 2002 winning entry, by editor Kathryn Bold, was "The Old Man and the Flea." First runner up was Nigel Ravenhill's "Harry Potter and the Gimlet of Fire." *Hemispheres* sponsors a Faux Faulkner contest as well.

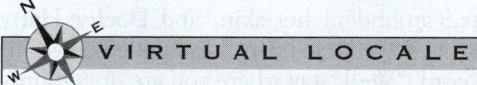

VIRTUAL LOCALE

Hemispheres Magazine. *Hemispheres Magazine* can be found online at *http://www.hemispheresmagazine.com/home.htm.* The site includes archives of the winning stories of the Imitation Hemingway and Faux Faulkner contests from 2000 to 2005, as well as information on how to enter the contests.

Starting Points for Further Research: Ernest Hemingway

- **Editions:** Ernest Hemingway. *The Short Stories*. New York: Scribner, 2003.
    ———. *Three Novels of Ernest Hemingway*. New York: Charles Scribner's Sons, 1962.
- **Biography:** Kenneth S. Lynn. *Hemingway*. Cambridge, Mass.: Harvard University Press, 1987.
- **Article:** Robert Fantina. "Hemingway's Masochism, Sodomy, and the Dominant Woman." *Hemingway Review* 23 (2003): 84–105.

KATHERINE ANNE PORTER   (1890–1980)

Katherine Anne Porter was born in rural Texas and raised by her grandmother. Married at sixteen, she worked as an actress and later a journalist, moving to Mexico in 1918. She lived in Paris in the 1920s and published her first short story in 1922. Though she never moved back to Mexico or Texas, they provided the settings for many of her stories, and no matter where she lived she thought of herself as a Texan. Her first book of short stories, Flowering Judas, *was published in 1930; a revised edition appeared in 1935. Her next book of stories,* Pale Horse, Pale Rider *(1939), won her acclaim.* The Leaning Tower and Other Stories *appeared in 1944, and her* Collected Stories *was awarded the Pulitzer Prize and the National Book Award in 1966. Her only novel,* Ship of Fools, *was published in 1962.*

The Jilting of Granny Weatherall   (1930)

She flicked her wrist neatly out of Doctor Harry's pudgy careful fingers and pulled the sheet up to her chin. The brat ought to be in knee breeches. Doctoring around the country with spectacles on his nose! "Get along now, take your schoolbooks and go. There's nothing wrong with me."

Doctor Harry spread a warm paw like a cushion on her forehead where the forked green vein danced and made her eyelids twitch. "Now, now, be a good girl, and we'll have you up in no time."

"That's no way to speak to a woman nearly eighty years old just because she's down. I'd have you respect your elders, young man."

"Well, Missy, excuse me." Doctor Harry patted her cheek. "But I've got to warn you, haven't I? You're a marvel, but you must be careful or you're going to be good and sorry."

"Don't tell me what I'm going to be. I'm on my feet now, morally speaking. It's Cornelia. I had to go to bed to get rid of her." 5

Her bones felt loose, and floated around in her skin, and Doctor Harry floated like a balloon around the foot of the bed. He floated and pulled down his waistcoat and swung his glasses on a cord. "Well, stay where you are, it certainly can't hurt you."

"Get along and doctor your sick," said Granny Weatherall. "Leave a well woman alone. I'll call for you when I want you. . . . Where were you forty years ago when I pulled through milk leg and double pneumonia? You weren't even born. Don't let Cornelia lead you on," she shouted, because Doctor Harry appeared to float up to the ceiling and out. "I pay my own bills, and I don't throw my money away on nonsense!"

She meant to wave good-by, but it was too much trouble. Her eyes closed of themselves, it was like a dark curtain drawn around the bed. The pillow rose and floated under her, pleasant as a hammock in a light wind. She listened to the leaves rustling outside the window. No, somebody was swishing newspapers: no, Cornelia and Doctor Harry were whispering together. She leaped broad awake, thinking they whispered in her ear.

"She was never like this, *never* like this!" "Well, what can we expect?" "Yes, eighty years old. . . ."

Well, and what if she was? She still had ears. It was like Cornelia to whisper   10 around doors. She always kept things secret in such a public way. She was always being tactful and kind. Cornelia was dutiful; that was the trouble with her. Dutiful and good: "So good and dutiful," said Granny, "that I'd like to spank her." She saw herself spanking Cornelia and making a fine job of it.

"What'd you say, Mother?"

Granny felt her face tying up in hard knots.

"Can't a body think, I'd like to know?"

"I thought you might want something."

"I do. I want a lot of things. First off, go away and don't whisper."   15

She lay and drowsed, hoping in her sleep that the children would keep out and let her rest a minute. It had been a long day. Not that she was tired. It was always pleasant to snatch a minute now and then. There was always so much to be done, let me see: tomorrow.

Tomorrow was far away and there was nothing to trouble about. Things were finished somehow when the time came; thank God there was always a little margin over for peace: then a person could spread out the plan of life and tuck in the edges orderly. It was good to have everything clean and folded away, with the hair brushes and tonic bottles sitting straight on the white embroidered linen: the day started without fuss and the pantry shelves laid out with rows of jelly glasses and brown jugs and white stone-china jars with blue whirligigs and words painted on them: coffee, tea, sugar, ginger, cinnamon, allspice: and the bronze clock with the lion on top nicely dusted off. The dust that lion could collect in twenty-four hours! The box in the attic with all those letters tied up, well, she'd have to go through that tomorrow. All those letters—George's letters and John's letters and her letters to them both—lying around for the children to find afterwards made her uneasy. Yes, that would be tomorrow's business. No use to let them know how silly she had been once.

While she was rummaging around she found death in her mind and it felt clammy and unfamiliar. She had spent so much time preparing for death there was no need for bringing it up again. Let it take care of itself now. When she was sixty she had felt very old, finished, and went around making farewell trips to see her children and grandchildren, with a secret in her mind: This is the very last of your mother, children! Then she made her will and came down with a long fever. That was all just a notion like a lot of other things, but it was lucky too, for she had once and for all got over the idea of dying for a long time. Now she couldn't be worried. She hoped she had better sense now. Her father had lived to be one hundred and two years old and had drunk a noggin of strong hot toddy on his last birthday. He told the reporters it was his daily habit, and he owed his long life to that. He had made quite a scandal and was very pleased about it. She believed she'd just plague Cornelia a little.

"Cornelia! Cornelia!" No footsteps, but a sudden hand on her cheek. "Bless you, where have you been?"

"Here, Mother."   20

"Well, Cornelia, I want a noggin of hot toddy."

"Are you cold, darling?"

"I'm chilly, Cornelia. Lying in bed stops the circulation. I must have told you that a thousand times."

Well, she could just hear Cornelia telling her husband that Mother was getting a little childish and they'd have to humor her. The thing that most annoyed her was that Cornelia thought she was deaf, dumb, and blind. Little hasty glances and tiny gestures tossed around her and over her head saying, "Don't cross her, let her have her way, she's eighty years old," and she sitting there as if she lived in a thin glass cage. Sometimes Granny almost made up her mind to pack up and move back to her own house where nobody could remind her every minute that she was old. Wait, wait, Cornelia, till your own children whisper behind your back!

In her day she had kept a better house and had got more work done. She   25
wasn't too old yet for Lydia to be driving eighty miles for advice when one of the children jumped the track, and Jimmy still dropped in and talked things over: "Now, Mammy, you've a good business head, I want to know what you think of this? . . ." Old. Cornelia couldn't change the furniture around without asking. Little things, little things! They had been so sweet when they were little. Granny wished the old days were back again with the children young and everything to be done over. It had been a hard pull, but not too much for her. When she thought of all the food she had cooked, and all the clothes she had cut and sewed, and all the gardens she had made—well, the children showed it. There they were, made out of her, and they couldn't get away from that. Sometimes she wanted to see John again and point to them and say, Well, I didn't do so badly, did I? But that would have to wait. That was for tomorrow. She used to think of him as a man, but now all the children were older than their father, and he would be a child beside her if she saw him now. It seemed strange and there was something wrong in the idea. Why, he couldn't possibly recognize her. She had fenced in a hundred acres once, digging the post holes herself and clamping the wires with just a negro boy to help. That changed a woman. John would be looking for a young woman with the peaked Spanish comb in her hair and the painted fan. Digging post holes changed a woman. Riding country roads in the winter when women had their babies was another thing: sitting up nights with sick horses and sick negroes and sick children and hardly ever losing one. John, I hardly ever lost one of them! John would see that in a minute, that would be something he could understand, she wouldn't have to explain anything!

It made her feel like rolling up her sleeves and putting the whole place to rights again. No matter if Cornelia was determined to be everywhere at once, there were a great many things left undone on this place. She would start tomorrow and do them. It was good to be strong enough for everything, even if all you made melted and changed and slipped under your hands, so that by the time you finished you almost forgot what you were working for. What was it I set out to do? she asked herself intently, but she could not remember. A fog rose over the valley, she saw it marching across the creek swallowing the trees and moving up the hill like an army of ghosts. Soon it would be at the near edge of the orchard, and then it was time to go in and light the lamps. Come in, children, don't stay out in the night air.

Lighting the lamps had been beautiful. The children huddled up to her and breathed like little calves waiting at the bars in the twilight. Their eyes followed the match and watched the flame rise and settle in a blue curve, then they moved away from her. The lamp was lit, they didn't have to be scared and hang on to mother any more. Never, never, never more. God, for all my life I thank Thee. Without Thee, my God, I could never have done it. Hail, Mary, full of grace.

I want you to pick all the fruit this year and see that nothing is wasted. There's always someone who can use it. Don't let good things rot for want of using. You waste life when you waste good food. Don't let things get lost. It's bitter to lose things. Now, don't let me get to thinking, not when I am tired and taking a little nap before supper. . . .

The pillow rose about her shoulders and pressed against her heart and the memory was being squeezed out of it: oh, push down the pillow, somebody: it would smother her if she tried to hold it. Such a fresh breeze blowing and such a green day with no threats in it. But he had not come, just the same. What does a woman do when she has put on the white veil and set out the white cake for a man and he doesn't come? She tried to remember. No, I swear he never harmed me but in that. He never harmed me but in that . . . and what if he did? There was the day, the day, but a whirl of dark smoke rose and covered it, crept up and over into the bright field where everything was planted so carefully in orderly rows. That was hell, she knew hell when she saw it. For sixty years she had prayed against remembering him and against losing her soul in the deep pit of hell, and now the two things were mingled in one and the thought of him was a smoky cloud from hell that moved and crept in her head when she had just got rid of Doctor Harry and was trying to rest a minute. Wounded vanity, Ellen, said a sharp voice in the top of her mind. Don't let your wounded vanity get the upper hand of you. Plenty of girls get jilted. You were jilted, weren't you? Then stand up to it. Her eyelids wavered and let in streamers of blue-gray light like tissue paper over her eyes. She must get up and pull the shades down or she'd never sleep. She was in bed again and the shades were not down. How could that happen? Better turn over, hide from the light, sleeping in the light gave you nightmares. "Mother, how do you feel now?" and a stinging wetness on her forehead. But I don't like having my face washed in cold water!

Hapsy? George? Lydia? Jimmy? No, Cornelia, and her features were swollen and full of little puddles. "They're coming, darling, they'll all be here soon." Go wash your face, child, you look funny.

Instead of obeying, Cornelia knelt down and put her head on the pillow. She seemed to be talking but there was no sound. "Well, are you tongue-tied? Whose birthday is it? Are you going to give a party?"

Cornelia's mouth moved urgently in strange shapes. "Don't do that, you bother me, daughter."

"O, no, Mother. Oh, no. . . ."

Nonsense. It was strange about children. They disputed your every word. "No what, Cornelia?"

"Here's Doctor Harry."

"I won't see that boy again. He just left five minutes ago."

"That was this morning, Mother. It's night now. Here's the nurse."

"This is Doctor Harry, Mrs. Weatherall. I never saw you look so young and happy!"

"Ah, I'll never be young again—but I'd be happy if they'd let me lie in peace and get rested."

She thought she spoke up loudly, but no one answered. A warm weight on   40
her forehead, a warm bracelet on her wrist, and a breeze went on whispering, trying to tell her something. A shuffle of leaves in the everlasting hand of God. He blew on them and they danced and rattled. "Mother, don't mind, we're going to give you a little hypodermic." "Look here, daughter, how do ants get in this bed? I saw sugar ants yesterday." Did you send for Hapsy too?

It was Hapsy she really wanted. She had to go a long way back through a great many rooms to find Hapsy standing with a baby on her arm. She seemed to herself to be Hapsy also, and the baby on Hapsy's arm was Hapsy and himself and herself, all at once, and there was no surprise in the meeting. Then Hapsy melted from within and turned flimsy as gray gauze and the baby was a gauzy shadow, and Hapsy came up close and said, "I thought you'd never come," and looked at her very searchingly and said, "You haven't changed a bit!" They leaned forward to kiss, when Cornelia began whispering from a long way off, "Oh, is there anything you want to tell me? Is there anything I can do for you?"

Yes, she had changed her mind after sixty years and she would like to see George. I want you to find George. Find him and be sure to tell him I forgot him. I want him to know I had my husband just the same and my children and my house like any other woman. A good house too and a good husband that I loved and fine children out of him. Better than I hoped for even. Tell him I was given back everything he took away and more. Oh, no, oh, God, no, there was something else besides the house and the man and the children. Oh, surely they were not all? What was it? Something not given back. . . . Her breath crowded down under her ribs and grew into a monstrous frightening shape with cutting edges; it bored up into her head, and the agony was unbelievable: Yes, John, get the Doctor now, no more talk, my time has come.

When this one was born it should be the last. The last. It should have been born first, for it was the one she had truly wanted. Everything came in good time. Nothing left out, left over. She was strong, in three days she would be as well as ever. Better. A woman needed milk in her to have her full health.

"Mother, do you hear me?"

"I've been telling you—"   45

"Mother, Father Connolly's here."

"I went to Holy Communion last week. Tell him I'm not so sinful as all that."

"Father just wants to speak to you."

He could speak as much as he pleased. It was like him to drop in and inquire about her soul as if it were a teething baby, and then stay on for a cup of tea and a round of cards and gossip. He always had a funny story of some sort, usually about an Irishman who made his little mistakes and confessed them, and the point lay in some absurd thing he would blurt out in the confessional showing his struggles between native piety and original sin. Granny felt easy about her soul. Cornelia, where are your manners? Give Father Connolly a chair. She had her secret comfortable understanding with a few favorite saints who cleared a straight road to God for her. All as surely signed and sealed as the papers for the new Forty Acres. Forever . . . heirs and assigns forever. Since the day the wedding cake was not cut, but thrown out and wasted. The whole bottom dropped out of the world, and there she was blind and sweating with nothing under her feet and the walls falling away. His hand had caught her under the breast, she had not fallen, there was the freshly polished floor with the green rug on it, just as before. He had cursed like a sailor's parrot and said, "I'll kill him for you." Don't lay a hand on him, for my sake leave something to God. "Now, Ellen, you must believe what I tell you. . . ."

So there was nothing, nothing to worry about any more, except sometimes   50
in the night one of the children screamed in a nightmare, and they both hustled out shaking and hunting for the matches and calling, "There, wait a minute, here we are!" John, get the doctor now, Hapsy's time has come. But there was Hapsy standing by the bed in a white cap. "Cornelia, tell Hapsy to take off her cap. I can't see her plain."

Her eyes opened very wide and the room stood out like a picture she had seen somewhere. Dark colors with the shadows rising towards the ceiling in long angles. The tall black dresser gleamed with nothing on it but John's picture, enlarged from a little one, with John's eyes very black when they should have been blue. You never saw him, so how do you know how he looked? But the man insisted the copy was perfect, it was very rich and handsome. For a picture, yes, but it's not my husband. The table by the bed had a linen cover and a candle and a crucifix. The light was blue from Cornelia's silk lampshades. No sort of light at all, just frippery. You had to live forty years with kerosene lamps to appreciate honest electricity. She felt very strong and she saw Doctor Harry with a rosy nimbus around him.

"You look like a saint, Doctor Harry, and I vow that's as near as you'll ever come to it."

"She's saying something."

"I heard you, Cornelia. What's all this carrying-on?"

"Father Connolly's saying—"   55

Cornelia's voice staggered and bumped like a cart in a bad road. It rounded corners and turned back again and arrived nowhere. Granny stepped up in the cart very lightly and reached for the reins, but a man sat beside her and she knew him by his hands, driving the cart. She did not look in his face, for she knew without seeing, but looked instead down the road where the trees leaned over and bowed to each other and a thousand birds were singing a Mass. She felt like singing too, but she put her hand in the bosom of her dress and pulled out a rosary, and Father Connolly murmured Latin in a very solemn voice and tickled her feet. My God, will you stop that nonsense? I'm a married woman. What if he did run away and leave me to face the priest by myself? I found another a whole world better. I wouldn't have exchanged my husband for anybody except St. Michael himself, and you may tell him that for me with a thank you in the bargain.

Light flashed on her closed eyelids, and a deep roaring shook her. Cornelia, is that lightning? I hear thunder. There's going to be a storm. Close all the windows. Call the children in. . . . "Mother, here we are, all of us." "Is that you, Hapsy?" "Oh, no, I'm Lydia. We drove as fast as we could." Their faces drifted above her, drifted away. The rosary fell out of her hands and Lydia put it back.

Jimmy tried to help, their hands fumbled together, and Granny closed two fingers around Jimmy's thumb. Beads wouldn't do, it must be something alive. She was so amazed her thoughts ran round and round. So, my dear Lord, this is my death and I wasn't even thinking about it. My children have come to see me die. But I can't, it's not time. Oh, I always hated surprises. I wanted to give Cornelia the amethyst set—Cornelia, you're to have the amethyst set, but Hapsy's to wear it when she wants, and, Doctor Harry, do shut up. Nobody sent for you. Oh, my dear Lord, do wait a minute. I meant to do something about the Forty Acres. Jimmy doesn't need it and Lydia will later on, with that worthless husband of hers. I meant to finish the altar cloth and send six bottles of wine to Sister Borgia for her dyspepsia. I want to send six bottles of wine to Sister Borgia, Father Connolly, now don't let me forget.

Cornelia's voice made short turns and tilted over and crashed. "Oh, Mother, oh, Mother, oh, Mother. . . ."

"I'm not going, Cornelia. I'm taken by surprise. I can't go."

You'll see Hapsy again. What about her? "I thought you'd never come." 60 Granny made a long journey outward, looking for Hapsy. What if I don't find her? What then? Her heart sank down and down, there was no bottom to death, she couldn't come to the end of it. The blue light from Cornelia's lampshade drew into a tiny point in the center of her brain, it flickered and winked like an eye, quietly it fluttered and dwindled. Granny lay curled down within herself, amazed and watchful, staring at the point of light that was herself; her body was now only a deeper mass of shadow in an endless darkness and this darkness would curl around the light and swallow it up. God, give a sign!

For the second time there was no sign. Again no bridegroom and the priest in the house. She could not remember any other sorrow because this grief wiped them all away. Oh, no, there's nothing more cruel than this—I'll never forgive it. She stretched herself with a deep breath and blew out the light.

Starting Points for Further Research: Katherine Anne Porter

- **Biography:** Janis P. Stout. *Katherine Anne Porter: A Sense of the Times.* Charlottesville: University of Virginia Press, 1995.
- **Critical Essay:** Virginia Spencer Carr, ed. *"Flowering Judas": A Casebook.* New Brunswick: Rutgers University Press, 1993.

WILLIAM FAULKNER   (1897–1962)

William Faulkner was born in Oxford, Mississippi, and attended the University of Mississippi before leaving for France as a pilot in World War I. He returned to his family home and tried to make a living as a writer. Most of his novels are set in Yoknapatawpha County, a fictional region he invented to examine the post–Civil War American South. He is known for his difficult, stream-of-consciousness prose style. The Sound and the Fury (1929), As I Lay Dying (1930), Light in August (1932), and Absalom, Absalom! (1936) are among his most famous novels, but they did not sell well when first published, and for a time Faulkner had to resort to writing screenplays for Hollywood studios. His reputation revived in the late 1940s and he received the Nobel Prize for Literature in 1950.

A Rose for Emily (1931)

I

When Miss Emily Grierson died, our whole town went to her funeral: the men through a sort of respectful affection for a fallen monument, the women mostly out of curiosity to see the inside of her house, which no one save an old manservant—a combined gardener and cook—had seen in at least ten years.

It was a big, squarish frame house that had once been white, decorated with cupolas and spires and scrolled balconies in the heavily lightsome style of the seventies, set on what had once been our most select street. But garages and cotton gins had encroached and obliterated even the august names of that neighborhood; only Miss Emily's house was left, lifting its stubborn and coquettish decay above the cotton wagons and the gasoline pumps—an eyesore among eyesores. And now Miss Emily had gone to join the representatives of those august names where they lay in the cedar-bemused cemetery among the ranked and anonymous graves of Union and Confederate soldiers who fell at the battle of Jefferson.

Alive, Miss Emily had been a tradition, a duty, and a care; a sort of hereditary obligation upon the town, dating from that day in 1894 when Colonel Sartoris, the mayor—he who fathered the edict that no Negro woman should appear on the streets without an apron—remitted her taxes, the dispensation dating from the death of her father on into perpetuity. Not that Miss Emily would have accepted charity. Colonel Sartoris invented an involved tale to the effect that Miss Emily's father had loaned money to the town, which the town, as a matter of business, preferred this way of repaying. Only a man of Colonel Sartoris' generation and thought could have invented it, and only a woman could have believed it.

When the next generation, with its more modern ideas, became mayors and aldermen, this arrangement created some little dissatisfaction. On the first of the year they mailed her a tax notice. February came, and there was no reply. They wrote her a formal letter, asking her to call at the sheriff's office at her convenience. A week later the mayor wrote her himself, offering to call or to send his car for her, and received in reply a note on paper of an archaic shape, in a thin, flowing calligraphy in faded ink, to the effect that she no longer went out at all. The tax notice was also enclosed, without comment.

They called a special meeting of the Board of Aldermen. A deputation 5 waited upon her, knocked at the door through which no visitor had passed since she ceased giving china-painting lessons eight or ten years earlier. They were admitted by an old Negro into a dim hall from which a staircase mounted into still more shadow. It smelled of dust and disuse—a close, dank smell. The Negro led them into the parlor. It was furnished in heavy, leather-covered furniture. When the Negro opened the blinds of one window they could see that the leather was cracked; and when they sat down, a faint dust rose sluggishly about their thighs, spinning with slow motes in the single sunray. On a tarnished gilt easel before the fireplace stood a crayon portrait of Miss Emily's father.

They rose when she entered—a small, fat woman in black, with a thin gold chain descending to her waist and vanishing into her belt, leaning on an ebony cane with a tarnished gold head. Her skeleton was small and spare; perhaps that was why what would have been merely plumpness in another was obesity in her.

She looked bloated, like a body long submerged in motionless water, and of that pallid hue. Her eyes, lost in the fatty ridges of her face, looked like two small pieces of coal pressed into a lump of dough as they moved from one face to another while the visitors stated their errand.

She did not ask them to sit. She just stood in the door and listened quietly until the spokesman came to a stumbling halt. Then they could hear the invisible watch ticking at the end of the gold chain.

Her voice was dry and cold. "I have no taxes in Jefferson. Colonel Sartoris explained it to me. Perhaps one of you can gain access to the city records and satisfy yourselves."

"But we have. We are the city authorities, Miss Emily. Didn't you get a notice from the sheriff, signed by him?"

"I received a paper, yes," Miss Emily said. "Perhaps he considers himself the   10
sheriff. . . . I have no taxes in Jefferson."

"But there is nothing on the books to show that, you see. We must go by the—"

"See Colonel Sartoris. I have no taxes in Jefferson."

"But, Miss Emily—"

"See Colonel Sartoris." (Colonel Sartoris had been dead almost ten years.) "I have no taxes in Jefferson. Tobe!" The Negro appeared. "Show these gentlemen out."

II

So she vanquished them, horse and foot, just as she had vanquished their fathers   15
thirty years before about the smell. That was two years after her father's death and a short time after her sweetheart—the one we believed would marry her—had deserted her. After her father's death she went out very little; after her sweetheart went away, people hardly saw her at all. A few of the ladies had the temerity to call, but were not received, and the only sign of life about the place was the Negro man—a young man then—going in and out with a market basket.

"Just as if a man—any man—could keep a kitchen properly," the ladies said; so they were not surprised when the smell developed. It was another link between the gross, teeming world and the high and mighty Griersons.

A neighbor, a woman, complained to the mayor, Judge Stevens, eighty years old.

"But what will you have me do about it, madam?" he said.

"Why, send her word to stop it," the woman said. "Isn't there a law?"

"I'm sure that won't be necessary," Judge Stevens said. "It's probably just a   20
snake or a rat that nigger of hers killed in the yard. I'll speak to him about it."

The next day he received two more complaints, one from a man who came in diffident deprecation. "We really must do something about it, Judge, I'd be the last one in the world to bother Miss Emily, but we've got to do something." That night the board of Aldermen met—three gray-beards and one younger man, a member of the rising generation.

"It's simple enough," he said. "Send her word to have her place cleaned up. Given her a certain time to do it in, and if she don't . . ."

"Dammit, sir," Judge Stevens said, "will you accuse a lady to her face of smelling bad?"

So the next night, after midnight, four men crossed Miss Emily's lawn and slunk about the house like burglars, sniffing along the base of the brickwork and at the cellar openings while one of them performed a regular sowing motion with his hand out of a sack slung from his shoulder. They broke open the cellar door and sprinkled lime there, and in all the out-buildings. As they recrossed the lawn, a window that had been dark was lighted and Miss Emily sat in it, the light behind her, and her upright torso motionless as that of an idol. They crept quietly across the lawn and into the shadow of the locusts that lined the street. After a week or two the smell went away.

That was when people had begun to feel really sorry for her. People in our town remembering how old lady Wyatt, her great-aunt, had gone completely crazy at last, believed that the Griersons held themselves a little too high for what they really were. None of the young men were quite good enough for Miss Emily and such. We had long thought of them as a tableau; Miss Emily a slender figure in white in the background, her father a spraddled silhouette in the foreground, his back to her and clutching a horsewhip, the two of them framed by the back-flung front door. So when she got to be thirty and was still single, we were not pleased exactly, but vindicated; even with insanity in the family she wouldn't have turned down all of her chances if they had really materialized. 25

When her father died, it got about that the house was all that was left to her; and in a way, people were glad. At last they could pity Miss Emily. Being left alone, and a pauper, she had become humanized. Now she too would know the old thrill and the old despair of a penny more or less.

The day after his death all the ladies prepared to call at the house and offer condolence and aid, as is our custom. Miss Emily met them at the door, dressed as usual and with no trace of grief on her face. She told them that her father was not dead. She did that for three days, with the ministers calling on her, and the doctors, trying to persuade her to let them dispose of the body. Just as they were about to resort to law and force, she broke down, and they buried her father quickly.

We did not say she was crazy then. We believed she had to do that. We remembered all the young men her father had driven away, and we knew that with nothing left, she would have to cling to that which had robbed her, as people will.

III

She was sick for a long time. When we saw her again, her hair was cut short, making her look like a girl, with a vague resemblance to those angels in colored church windows—sort of tragic and serene.

The town had just let the contracts for paving the sidewalks, and in the summer after her father's death they began to work. The construction company came with niggers and mules and machinery, and a foreman named Homer Barron, a Yankee—a big, dark, ready man, with a big voice and eyes lighter than his face. The little boys would follow in groups to hear him cuss the niggers, and the niggers singing in time to the rise and fall of picks. Pretty soon he knew everybody in town. Whenever you heard a lot of laughing anywhere about the square, Homer Barron would be in the center of the group. Presently we began to see him and Miss Emily on Sunday afternoons driving in the yellow-wheeled buggy and the matched team of bays from the livery stable. 30

At first we were glad that Miss Emily would have an interest, because the ladies all said, "Of course a Grierson would not think seriously of a Northerner, a day laborer." But there were still others, older people, who said that even grief could not cause a real lady to forget *noblesse oblige*—without calling it *noblesse oblige*. They just said, "Poor Emily. Her kinsfolk should come to her." She had some kin in Alabama; but years ago her father had fallen out with them over the estate of old lady Wyatt, the crazy woman, and there was no communication between the two families. They had not even been represented at the funeral.

And as soon as the old people said, "Poor Emily," the whispering began. "Do you suppose it's really so?" they said to one another. "Of course it is. . . ." This behind their hands; rustling of craned silk and satin behind jalousies closed upon the sun of Sunday afternoon as the thin, swift clop-clop-clop of the matched team passed: "Poor Emily."

She carried her head high enough—even when we believed that she was fallen. It was as if she demanded more than ever the recognition of her dignity as the last Grierson; as if it had wanted that touch of earthiness to reaffirm her imperviousness. Like when she bought the rat poison, the arsenic. That was over a year after they had begun to say "Poor Emily," and while the two female cousins were visiting her.

"I want some poison," she said to the druggist. She was over thirty then, still a slight woman, though thinner than usual, with cold, haughty black eyes in a face the flesh of which was strained across the temples and about the eyesockets as you imagine a lighthouse-keeper's face ought to look. "I want some poison," she said.

"Yes, Miss Emily. What kind? For rats and such? I'd recom—"   35

"I want the best you have. I don't care what kind."

The druggist named several. "They'll kill anything up to an elephant. But what you want is—"

"Arsenic." Miss Emily said. "Is that a good one?"

"Is . . . arsenic? Yes ma'am. But what you want—"

"I want arsenic."   40

The druggist looked down at her. She looked back at him, erect, her face like a strained flag. "Why, of course," the druggist said. "If that's what you want. But the law requires you to tell what you are going to use it for."

Miss Emily just stared at him, her head tilted back in order to look him eye for eye, until he looked away and went and got the arsenic and wrapped it up. The Negro delivery boy brought her the package; the druggist didn't come back. When she opened the package at home there was written on the box, under the skull and bones: "For rats."

IV

So the next day we all said, "She will kill herself"; and we said it would be the best thing. When she had first begun to be seen with Homer Barron, we had said, "She will marry him." Then we said, "She will persuade him yet," because Homer himself had remarked—he liked men, and it was known that he drank with the younger men in the Elks' Club—that he was not a marrying man. Later we said, "Poor Emily," behind the jalousies as they passed on Sunday afternoon in the glittering buggy, Miss Emily with her head high and Homer Barron with his hat cocked and a cigar in his teeth, reins and whip in a yellow glove.

Then some of the ladies began to say that it was a disgrace to the town and a bad example to the young people. The men did not want to interfere, but at last the ladies forced the Baptist minister—Miss Emily's people were Episcopal—to call upon her. He would never divulge what happened during that interview, but he refused to go back again. The next Sunday they again drove about the streets, and the following day the minister's wife wrote to Miss Emily's relations in Alabama.

So she had blood-kin under her roof again and we sat back to watch developments. At first nothing happened. Then we were sure that they were to be married. We learned that Miss Emily had been to the jeweler's and ordered a man's toilet set in silver, with the letters H.B. on each piece. Two days later we learned that she had bought a complete outfit of men's clothing, including a nightshirt, and we said, "They are married." We were really glad. We were glad because the two female cousins were even more Grierson than Miss Emily had ever been. 45

So we were surprised when Homer Barron—the streets had been finished some time since—was gone. We were a little disappointed that there was not a public blowing-off but we believed that he had gone on to prepare for Miss Emily's coming, or to give a chance to get rid of the cousins. (By that time it was a cabal, and we were all Miss Emily's allies to help circumvent the cousins.) Sure enough, after another week they departed. And, as we had expected all along, within three days Homer Barron was back in town. A neighbor saw the Negro man admit him at the kitchen door at dusk one evening.

And that was the last we saw of Homer Barron. And of Miss Emily for some time. The Negro man went in and out with the market basket, but the front door remained closed. Now and then we would see her at a window for a moment, as the men did that night when they sprinkled the lime, but for almost six months she did not appear on the streets. Then we knew that this was to be expected too; as if that quality of her father which had thwarted her woman's life so many times had been too virulent and too furious to die.

When we next saw Miss Emily, she had grown fat and her hair was turning gray. During the next few years it grew grayer and grayer until it attained an even pepper-and-salt iron-gray, when it ceased turning. Up to the day of her death at seventy-four it was still that vigorous iron-gray, like the hair of an active man.

From that time on her front door remained closed, save for a period of six or seven years, when she was about forty, during which she gave lessons in china-painting. She fitted up a studio in one of the downstairs rooms, where the daughters and granddaughters of Colonel Sartoris' contemporaries were sent to her with the same regularity and in the same spirit that they were sent on Sundays with a twenty-five cent piece for the collection plate. Meanwhile her taxes had been remitted.

Then the newer generation became the backbone and the spirit of the town, and the painting pupils grew up and fell away and did not send their children to her with boxes of color and tedious brushes and pictures cut from the ladies' magazines. The front door closed upon the last one and remained closed for good. When the town got free postal delivery Miss Emily alone refused to let them fasten the metal numbers above her door and attach a mailbox to it. She would not listen to them. 50

Daily, monthly, yearly we watched the Negro grow grayer and more stooped, going in and out with the market basket. Each December we sent her a tax notice, which would be returned by the post office a week later, unclaimed. Now and then we could see her in one of the downstairs windows—she had evidently shut up the top floor of the house—like the carven torso of an idol in a niche, looking or not looking at us, we could never tell which. Thus she passed from generation to generation—dear, inescapable, impervious, tranquil, and perverse.

And so she died. Fell ill in the house filled with dust and shadows, with only a doddering Negro man to wait on her. We did not even know she was sick; we had long since given up trying to get any information from the Negro. He talked to no one, probably not even to her, for his voice had grown harsh and rusty, as if from disuse.

She died in one of the downstairs rooms, in a heavy walnut bed with a curtain, her gray head propped on a pillow yellow and moldy with age and lack of sunlight.

V

The Negro met the first of the ladies at the front door and let them in, with their hushed, sibilant voices and their quick, curious glances, and then he disappeared. He walked right through the house and out the back and was not seen again.

The two female cousins came at once. They held the funeral on the second day, with the town coming to look at Miss Emily beneath a mass of bought flowers, with the crayon face of her father musing profoundly above the bier and the ladies sibilant and macabre; and the very old men—some in their brushed Confederate uniforms—on the porch and the lawn, talking of Miss Emily as if she had been a contemporary of theirs, believing that they had danced with her and courted her perhaps, confusing time with its mathematical progression, as the old do, to whom all the past is not a diminishing road, but, instead, a huge meadow which no winter ever quite touches, divided from them now by the narrow bottleneck of the most recent decade of years.

Already we knew that there was one room in that region above stairs which no one had seen in forty years, and which would have to be forced. They waited until Miss Emily was decently in the ground before they opened it.

The violence of breaking down the door seemed to fill this room with pervading dust. A thin, acrid pall as of the tomb seemed to lie everywhere upon this room decked and furnished as for a bridal: upon the valance curtains of faded rose color, upon the rose-shaded lights, upon the dressing table, upon the delicate array of crystal and the man's toilet things backed with tarnished silver, silver so tarnished that the monogram was obscured. Among them lay a collar and tie, as if they had just been removed, which, lifted, left upon the surface a pale crescent in the dust. Upon a chair hung the suit, carefully folded; beneath it the two mute shoes and the discarded socks.

The man himself lay in the bed.

For a long while we just stood there, looking down at the profound and fleshless grin. The body had apparently once lain in the attitude of an embrace, but now the long sleep that outlasts love, that conquers even the grimace of love, had cuckolded him. What was left of him, rotted beneath what was left of the nightshirt, had become inextricable from the bed in which he lay; and upon him and upon the pillow beside him lay that even coating of the patient and biding dust.

Then we noticed that in the second pillow was the indentation of a head. 60
One of us lifted something from it, and leaning forward, that faint and invisible
dust dry and acrid in the nostrils, we saw a long strand of iron-gray hair.

Barn Burning

(1939)

The store in which the Justice of the Peace's court was sitting smelled of cheese.
The boy, crouched on his nail keg at the back of the crowded room, knew he
smelled cheese, and more: from where he sat he could see the ranked shelves
close-packed with the solid, squat, dynamic shapes of tin cans whose labels his
stomach read, not from the lettering which meant nothing to his mind but from
the scarlet devils and the silver curve of fish—this, the cheese which he knew he
smelled and the hermetic meat which his intestines believed he smelled coming
in intermittent gusts momentary and brief between the other constant one, the
smell and sense just a little of fear because mostly of despair and grief, the old
fierce pull of blood. He could not see the table where the Justice sat and before
which his father and his father's enemy (*our enemy* he thought in that despair:
ourn! mine and hisn both! He's my father!) stood, but he could hear them, the two
of them that is, because his father had said no word yet:

"But what proof have you, Mr. Harris?"

"I told you. The hog got into my corn. I caught it up and sent it back to him.
He had no fence that would hold it. I told him so, warned him. The next time I
put the hog in my pen. When he came to get it I gave him enough wire to patch
up his pen. The next time I put the hog up and kept it. I rode down to his house
and saw the wire I gave him still rolled on to the spool in his yard. I told him he
could have the hog when he paid me a dollar pound fee. That evening a nigger
came with the dollar and got the hog. He was a strange nigger. He said, 'He say
to tell you wood and hay kin burn.' I said, 'What?' 'That whut he say to tell you,'
the nigger said. 'Wood and hay kin burn.' That night my barn burned. I got the
stock out but I lost the barn."

"Where's the nigger? Have you got him?"

"He was a strange nigger, I tell you. I don't know what became of him."

"But that's not proof. Don't you see that's not proof?"   5

"Get that boy up here. He knows." For a moment the boy thought too that
the man meant his older brother until Harris said, "Not him. The little one. The
boy," and, crouching, small for his age, small and wiry like his father, in patched
and faded jeans even too small for him, with straight, uncombed, brown hair and
eyes gray and wild as storm scud, he saw the men between himself and the table
part and become a lane of grim faces, at the end of which he saw the Justice, a
shabby, collarless, graying man in spectacles, beckoning him. He felt no floor under his bare feet; he seemed to walk beneath the palpable weight of the grim
turning faces. His father, still in his black Sunday coat donned not for the trial
but for the moving, did not even look at him. *He aims for me to lie*, he thought,
again with that frantic grief and despair. *And I will have to do hit.*

"What's your name, boy?" the Justice said.

"Colonel Sartoris Snopes," the boy whispered.

"Hey?" the Justice said. "Talk louder. Colonel Sartoris? I reckon anybody 10
named for Colonel Sartoris in this country can't help but tell the truth, can
they?" The boy said nothing. *Enemy! Enemy!* he thought; for a moment he could

not even see, could not see that the Justice's face was kindly nor discern that his voice was troubled when he spoke to the man named Harris: "Do you want me to question this boy?" But he could hear, and during those subsequent long seconds while there was absolutely no sound in the crowded little room save that of quiet and intent breathing it was as if he had swung outward at the end of a grape vine, over a ravine, and at the top of the swing had been caught in a prolonged instant of mesmerized gravity, weightless in time.

"No!" Harris said violently, explosively. "Damnation! Send him out of here!" Now time, the fluid world, rushed beneath him again, the voices coming to him again through the smell of cheese and sealed meat, the fear and despair and the old grief of blood:

"This case is closed. I can't find against you, Snopes, but I can give you advice. Leave this country and don't come back to it."

His father spoke for the first time, his voice cold and harsh, level, without emphasis: "I aim to. I don't figure to stay in a country among people who . . ." he said something unprintable and vile, addressed to no one.

"That'll do," the Justice said. "Take your wagon and get out of this country before dark. Case dismissed."

His father turned, and he followed the stiff black coat, the wiry figure walk- 15
ing a little stiffly from where a Confederate provost's man's musket ball had taken him in the heel on a stolen horse thirty years ago, followed the two backs now, since his older brother had appeared from somewhere in the crowd, no taller than the father but thicker, chewing tobacco steadily, between the two lines of grim-faced men and out of the store and across the worn gallery and down the sagging steps and among the dogs and half-grown boys in the mild May dust, where as he passed a voice hissed:

"Barn burner!"

Again he could not see, whirling; there was a face in a red haze, moonlike, bigger than the full moon, the owner of it half again his size, he leaping in the red haze toward the face, feeling no blow, feeling no shock when his head struck the earth, scrabbling up and leaping again, feeling no blow this time either and tasting no blood, scrabbling up to see the other boy in full flight and himself already leaping into pursuit as his father's hand jerked him back, the harsh, cold voice speaking above him: "Go get in the wagon."

It stood in a grove of locusts and mulberries across the road. His two hulking sisters in their Sunday dresses and his mother and her sister in calico and sunbonnets were already in it, sitting on and among the sorry residue of the dozen and more movings which even the boy could remember—the battered stove, the broken beds and chairs, the clock inlaid with mother-of-pearl, which would not run, stopped at some fourteen minutes past two o'clock of a dead and forgotten day and time, which had been his mother's dowry. She was crying, though when she saw him she drew her sleeve across her face and began to descend from the wagon. "Get back," the father said.

"He's hurt. I got to get some water and wash his . . ."

"Get back in the wagon," his father said. He got in too, over the tail-gate. 20
His father mounted to the seat where the older brother already sat and struck the gaunt mules two savage blows with the peeled willow, but without heat. It was not even sadistic; it was exactly that same quality which in later years would cause his descendants to over-run the engine before putting a motor car into

motion, striking and reining back in the same movement. The wagon went on, the store with its quiet crowd of grimly watching men dropped behind; a curve in the road hid it. *Forever* he thought. *Maybe he's done satisfied now, now that he has* . . . stopping himself, not to say it aloud even to himself. His mother's hand touched his shoulder.

"Does hit hurt?" she said.

"Naw," he said. "Hit don't hurt. Lemme be."

"Can't you wipe some of the blood off before hit dries?"

"I'll wash to-night," he said. "Lemme be, I tell you."

The wagon went on. He did not know where they were going. None of them ever did or ever asked, because it was always somewhere, always a house of sorts waiting for them a day or two days or even three days away. Likely his father had already arranged to make a crop on another farm before he . . . Again he had to stop himself. He (the father) always did. There was something about his wolflike independence and even courage when the advantage was at least neutral which impressed strangers, as if they got from his latent ravening ferocity not so much a sense of dependability as a feeling that his ferocious conviction in the rightness of his own actions would be of advantage to all whose interest lay with his.

That night they camped, in a grove of oaks and beeches where a spring ran. The nights were still cool and they had a fire against it, of a rail lifted from a nearby fence and cut into lengths—a small fire, neat, niggard almost, a shrewd fire; such fires were his father's habit and custom always, even in freezing weather. Older, the boy might have remarked this and wondered why not a big one; why should not a man who had not only seen the waste and extravagance of war, but who had in his blood an inherent voracious prodigality with material not his own, have burned everything in sight? Then he might have gone a step farther and thought that that was the reason: that niggard blaze was the living fruit of nights passed during those four years in the woods hiding from all men, blue and gray, with his strings of horses (captured horses, he called them). And older still, he might have divined the true reason: that the element of fire spoke to some deep mainspring of his father's being, as the element of steel or of powder spoke to other men, as the one weapon for the preservation of integrity, else breath were not worth the breathing, and hence to be regarded with respect and used with discretion.

But he did not think this now and he had seen those same niggard blazes all his life. He merely ate his supper beside it and was already half asleep over his iron plate when his father called him, and once more he followed the stiff back, the stiff and ruthless limp, up the slope and on to the starlit road where, turning, he could see his father against the stars but without face or depth—a shape black, flat, and bloodless as though cut from tin in the iron folds of the frockcoat which had not been made for him, the voice harsh like tin and without heat like tin:

"You were fixing to tell them. You would have told him."

He didn't answer. His father struck him with the flat of his hand on the side of the head, hard but without heat, exactly as he had struck the two mules at the store, exactly as he would strike either of them with any stick in order to kill a horse fly, his voice without heat or anger: "You're getting to be a man. You got to learn. You got to learn to stick to your own blood or you ain't going to have any blood to stick to you. Do you think either of them, any man there this morning, would? Don't you know all they wanted was a chance to get at me because they knew I had them beat? Eh?" Later, twenty years later, he was to tell himself, "If I had said they wanted only truth, justice, he would have hit me again." But now he said nothing. He was not crying. He just stood there. "Answer me," his father said.

"Yes," he whispered. His father turned. 30

"Get on to bed. We'll be there tomorrow."

Tomorrow they were there. In the early afternoon the wagon stopped before a paintless two-room house identical almost with the dozen others it had stopped before even in the boy's ten years, and again, as on the other dozen occasions, his mother and aunt got down and began to unload the wagon, although his two sisters and his father and brother had not moved.

"Likely hit ain't fitten for hawgs," one of the sisters said.

"Nevertheless, fit it will and you'll hog it and like it," his father said. "Get out of them chairs and help your Ma unload."

The two sisters got down, big, bovine, in a flutter of cheap ribbons; one of 35 them drew from the jumbled wagon bed a battered lantern, the other a worn broom. His father handed the reins to the older son and began to climb stiffly over the wheel. "When they get unloaded, take the team to the barn and feed them." Then he said, and at first the boy thought he was still speaking to his brother: "Come with me."

"Me?" he said.

"Yes," his father said. "You."

"Abner," his mother said. His father paused and looked back—the harsh level stare beneath the shaggy, graying, irascible brows.

"I reckon I'll have a word with the man that aims to begin tomorrow owning me body and soul for the next eight months."

They went back up the road. A week ago—or before last night, that is—he 40 would have asked where they were going, but not now. His father had struck him before last night but never before had he paused afterward to explain why; it was as if the blow and the following calm, outrageous voice still rang, repercussed, divulging nothing to him save the terrible handicap of being young, the light weight of his few years, just heavy enough to prevent his soaring free of the world as it seemed to be ordered but not heavy enough to keep him footed solid in it, to resist it and try to change the course of its events.

Presently he could see the grove of oaks and cedars and the other flowering trees and shrubs where the house would be, though not the house yet. They walked beside a fence massed with honeysuckle and Cherokee roses and came to a gate swinging open between two brick pillars, and now, beyond a sweep of drive, he saw the house for the first time and at that instant he forgot his father and the terror and despair both, and even when he remembered his father again (who had not stopped) the terror and despair did not return. Because, for all the twelve movings, they had sojourned until now in a poor country, a land of small farms and fields and houses, and he had never seen a house like this before. *Hit's big as a courthouse* he thought quietly, with a surge of peace and joy whose reason he could not have thought into words, being too young for that: *They are safe from him. People whose lives are a part of this peace and dignity are beyond his touch, he no more to them than a buzzing wasp: capable of stinging for a little moment but that's all; the spell of this peace and dignity rendering even the barns and stable and* cribs which belong to it impervious to the puny flames he might contrive . . . this, the peace and joy, ebbing for an instant as he looked again at the stiff black back, the stiff and implacable limp of the figure which was not dwarfed by the house, for the reason that it had never looked big anywhere and which now, against the serene columned backdrop, had more than ever that impervious quality of something cut ruthlessly from tin, depthless, as though, sidewise to the sun, it would cast no shadow. Watching him, the boy remarked the absolutely undeviating course which his father held and saw the stiff foot come squarely down in a pile of fresh droppings where a horse had stood in the drive and which his father could have avoided by a simple change of stride. But it ebbed only a moment, though he could not have thought this into words either, walking on in the spell of the house, which he could even want but without envy, without sorrow, certainly never with that ravening and jealous rage which unknown to him walked in the ironlike black coat before him: *Maybe he will feel it too. Maybe it will even change him now from what maybe he couldn't help but be.*

They crossed the portico. Now he could hear his father's stiff foot as it came down on the boards with clocklike finality, a sound out of all proportion to the displacement of the body it bore and which was not dwarfed either by the white door before it, as though it had attained to a sort of vicious and ravening minimum not to be dwarfed by anything—the flat, wide, black hat, the formal coat of broadcloth which had once been black but which had now that friction-glazed greenish cast of the bodies of old house flies, the lifted sleeve which was too large, the lifted hand like a curled claw. The door opened so promptly that the boy knew the Negro must have been watching them all the time, an old man with neat grizzled hair, in a linen jacket, who stood barring the door with his body, saying, "Wipe yo foots, white man, fo you come in here. Major ain't home nohow."

"Get out of my way, nigger," his father said, without heat too, flinging the door back and the Negro also and entering, his hat still on his head. And now the boy saw the prints of the stiff foot on the doorjamb and saw them appear on the pale rug behind the machinelike deliberation of the foot which seemed to bear (or transmit) twice the weight which the body compassed. The Negro was shouting "Miss Lula! Miss Lula!" somewhere behind them, then the boy, deluged as though by a warm wave by a suave turn of the carpeted stair and a pendant glitter of chandeliers and a mute gleam of gold frames, heard the swift feet and saw her too, a lady—perhaps he had never seen her like before either—in a gray, smooth gown with lace at the throat and an apron tied at the waist and the sleeves turned back, wiping cake or biscuit dough from her hands with a towel as she came up the hall, looking not at his father at all but at the tracks on the blond rug with an expression of incredulous amazement.

"I tried," the Negro cried. "I tole him to . . ."

"Will you please go away?" she said in a shaking voice. "Major de Spain is not at home. Will you please go away?"

His father had not spoken again. He did not speak again. He did not even look at her. He just stood stiff in the center of the rug, in his hat, the shaggy iron-gray brows twitching slightly above the pebble-colored eyes as he appeared to examine the house with brief deliberation. Then with the same deliberation he turned; the boy watched him pivot on the good leg and saw the stiff foot drag around the arc of the turning, leaving a final long and fading smear. His father never looked at it, he never once looked down at the rug. The Negro held the door. It closed behind them, upon the hysteric and indistinguishable woman-wail. His father stopped at the top of the steps and scraped his boot clean on the edge of it. At the gate he stopped again. He stood for a moment, planted stiffly on the stiff foot, looking back at the house. "Pretty and white, ain't it?" he said. "That's sweat. Nigger sweat. Maybe it ain't white enough yet to suit him. Maybe he wants to mix some white sweat with it."

Two hours later the boy was chopping wood behind the house within which his mother and aunt and the two sisters (the mother and aunt, not the two girls, he knew that; even at this distance and muffled by walls the flat loud voices of the two girls emanated an incorrigible idle inertia) were setting up the stove to prepare a meal, when he heard the hooves and saw the linen-clad man on a fine sorrel mare, whom he recognized even before he saw the rolled rug in front of the Negro youth following on a fat bay carriage horse—a suffused, angry face vanishing, still at full gallop, beyond the corner of the house where his father and brother were sitting in the two tilted chairs; and a moment later, almost before he could have put the axe down, he heard the hooves again and watched the sorrel mare go back out of the yard, already galloping again. Then his father began to shout one of the sisters' names, who presently emerged backward from the kitchen door dragging the rolled rug along the ground by one end while the other sister walked behind it.

"If you ain't going to tote, go on and set up the wash pot," the first said.

"You, Sarty!" the second shouted. "Set up the wash pot!" His father appeared at the door, framed against that shabbiness, as he had been against that other bland perfection, impervious to either, the mother's anxious face at his shoulder.

"Go on," the father said. "Pick it up." The two sisters stooped, broad, lethargic; stooping, they presented an incredible expanse of pale cloth and a flutter of tawdry ribbons. $\qquad$ 50

"If I thought enough of a rug to have to git hit all the way from France I wouldn't keep hit where folks coming in would have to tromp on hit," the first said. They raised the rug.

"Abner," the mother said. "Let me do it."

"You go back and git dinner," his father said. "I'll tend to this."

From the woodpile through the rest of the afternoon the boy watched them, the rug spread flat in the dust beside the bubbling wash pot, the two sisters stooping over it with that profound and lethargic reluctance, while the father stood over them in turn, implacable and grim, driving them though never raising his voice again. He could smell the harsh homemade lye they were using; he saw his mother come to the door once and look toward them with an expression not anxious now but very like despair; he saw his father turn, and he fell to with the axe and saw from the corner of his eye his father raise from the ground a flattish fragment of field stone and examine it and return to the pot, and this time his mother actually spoke: "Abner. Abner. Please don't. Please, Abner."

Then he was done too. It was dusk; the whippoorwills had already begun. $\qquad$ 55 He could smell coffee from the room where they would presently eat the cold food remaining from the mid-afternoon meal, though when he entered the house he realized they were having coffee again probably because there was a fire on the hearth, before which the rug now lay spread over the backs of the two chairs. The tracks of his father's foot were gone. Where they had been were now long, water-cloudy scoriations resembling the sporadic course of a lilliputian mowing machine.

It still hung there while they ate the cold food and then went to bed, scattered without order or claim up and down the two rooms, his mother in one bed, where his father would later lie, the older brother in the other, himself, the aunt, and the two sisters on pallets on the floor. But his father was not in bed yet. The last thing the boy remembered was the depthless, harsh silhouette of the hat and coat bending over the rug and it seemed to him that he had not even closed his eyes when the silhouette was standing over him, the fire almost dead behind it, the stiff foot prodding him awake. "Catch up the mule," his father said.

When he returned with the mule his father was standing in the back door, the rolled rug over his shoulder. "Ain't you going to ride?" he said.

"No. Give me your foot."

He bent his knee into his father's hand, the wiry, surprising power flowed smoothly, rising, he rising with it, on to the mule's bare back (they had owned a saddle once; the boy could remember it though not when or where) and with the same effortlessness his father swung the rug up in front of him. Now in the starlight they retraced the afternoon's path, up the dusty road rife with honeysuckle, through the gate and up the black tunnel of the drive to the lightless house, where he sat on the mule and felt the rough warp of the rug drag across his thighs and vanish.

"Don't you want me to help?" he whispered. His father did not answer and now he heard again that stiff foot striking the hollow portico with that wooden and clocklike deliberation, that outrageous overstatement of the weight it carried. The rug, hunched, not flung (the boy could tell that even in the darkness) from his father's shoulder struck the angle of wall and floor with a sound unbelievably loud, thunderous, then the foot again, unhurried and enormous; a light came on in the house and the boy sat, tense, breathing steadily and quietly and just a little fast, though the foot itself did not increase its beat at all, descending the steps now; now the boy could see him.

"Don't you want to ride now?" he whispered. "We kin both ride now," the light within the house altering now, flaring up and sinking. *He's coming down the stairs now,* he thought. He had already ridden the mule up beside the horse block; presently his father was up behind him and he doubled the reins over and slashed the mule across the neck, but before the animal could begin to trot the hard, thin arm came around him, the hard, knotted hand jerking the mule back to a walk.

In the first red rays of the sun they were in the lot, putting plow gear on the mules. This time the sorrel mare was in the lot before he heard it at all, the rider collarless and even bareheaded, trembling, speaking in a shaking voice as the woman in the house had done, his father merely looking up once before stooping again to the hame he was buckling, so that the man on the mare spoke to his stooping back:

"You must realize you have ruined that rug. Wasn't there anybody here, any of your women . . ." he ceased, shaking, the boy watching him, the older brother leaning now in the stable door, chewing, blinking slowly and steadily at nothing apparently. "It cost a hundred dollars. But you never had a hundred dollars. You never will. So I'm going to charge you twenty bushels of corn against your crop.

I'll add it in your contract and when you come to the commissary you can sign it. That won't keep Mrs. de Spain quiet but maybe it will teach you to wipe your feet off before you enter her house again."

Then he was gone. The boy looked at his father, who still had not spoken or even looked up again, who was now adjusting the logger-head in the hame.

"Pap," he said. His father looked at him—the inscrutable face, the shaggy 65 brows beneath where the gray eyes glinted coldly. Suddenly the boy went toward him, fast, stopping as suddenly. "You done the best you could!" he cried. "If he wanted hit done different why didn't he wait and tell you how? He won't git no twenty bushels! He won't git none! We'll gather hit and hide hit! I kin watch . . ."

"Did you put the cutter back in that straight stock like I told you?"

"No, sir," he said.

"Then go do it."

That was Wednesday. During the rest of that week he worked steadily, at what was within his scope and some which was beyond it, with an industry that did not need to be driven nor even commanded twice; he had this from his mother, with the difference that some at least of what he did he liked to do, such as splitting wood with the half-size axe which his mother and aunt had earned, or saved money somehow, to present him with at Christmas. In company with the two older women (and on one afternoon, even one of the sisters), he built pens for the shoat and the cow which were a part of his father's contract with the landlord, and one afternoon, his father being absent, gone somewhere on one of the mules, he went to the field.

They were running a middle buster now, his brother holding the plow 70 straight while he handled the reins, and walking beside the straining mule, the rich black soil shearing cool and damp against his bare ankles, he thought *Maybe this is the end of it. Maybe even that twenty bushels that seems hard to have to pay for just a rug will be a cheap price for him to stop forever and always from being what he used to be;* thinking, dreaming now, so that his brother had to speak sharply to him to mind the mule: *Maybe he even won't collect the twenty bushels. Maybe it will all add up and balance and vanish—corn, rug, fire; the terror and grief; the being pulled two ways like between two teams of horses—gone, done with for ever and ever.*

Then it was Saturday; he looked up from beneath the mule he was harnessing and saw his father in the black coat and hat. "Not that," his father said. "The wagon gear." And then, two hours later, sitting in the wagon bed behind his father and brother on the seat, the wagon accomplished a final curve, and he saw the weathered paintless store with its tattered tobacco- and patent-medicine posters and the tethered wagons and saddle animals below the gallery. He mounted the gnawed steps behind his father and brother, and there again was the lane of quiet, watching faces for the three of them to walk through. He saw the man in spectacles sitting at the plank table and he did not need to be told this was a Justice of the Peace; he sent one glare of fierce, exultant, partisan defiance at the man in collar and cravat now, whom he had seen but twice before in his life, and that on a galloping horse, who now wore on his face an expression not of rage but of amazed unbelief which the boy could not have known was at the incredible circumstance of being sued by one of his own tenants, and came and stood against his father and cried at the Justice: "He ain't done it! He ain't burnt . . ."

"Go back to the wagon," his father said.

"Burnt?" the Justice said. "Do I understand this rug was burned too?"

"Does anybody here claim it was?" his father said. "Go back to the wagon." But he did not, he merely retreated to the rear of the room, crowded as that other had been, but not to sit down this time, instead, to stand pressing among the motionless bodies, listening to the voices:

"And you claim twenty bushels of corn is too high for the damage you did to the rug?"

"He brought the rug to me and said he wanted the tracks washed out of it. I washed the tracks out and took the rug back to him."

"But you didn't carry the rug back to him in the same condition it was in before you made the tracks on it."

His father did not answer, and now for perhaps half a minute there was no sound at all save that of breathing, the faint, steady suspiration of complete and intent listening.

"You decline to answer that, Mr. Snopes?" Again his father did not answer. "I'm going to find against you, Mr. Snopes. I'm going to find that you were responsible for the injury to Major de Spain's rug and hold you liable for it. But twenty bushels of corn seems a little high for a man in your circumstances to have to pay. Major de Spain claims it cost a hundred dollars. October corn will be worth about fifty cents. I figure that if Major de Spain can stand a ninety-five dollar loss on something he paid cash for, you can stand a five-dollar loss you haven't earned yet. I hold you in damages to Major de Spain to the amount of ten bushels of corn over and above your contract with him, to be paid to him out of your crop at gathering time. Court adjourned."

It had taken no time hardly, the morning was but half begun. He thought they would return home and perhaps back to the field, since they were late, far behind all other farmers. But instead his father passed on behind the wagon, merely indicating with his hand for the older brother to follow with it, and crossed the road toward the blacksmith shop opposite, pressing on after his father, overtaking him, speaking, whispering up at the harsh, calm face beneath the weathered hat: "He won't git no ten bushels either. He won't git one. We'll . . ." until his father glanced for an instant down at him, the face absolutely calm, the grizzled eyebrows tangled above the cold eyes, the voice almost pleasant, almost gentle:

"You think so? Well, we'll wait till October anyway."

The matter of the wagon—the setting of a spoke or two and the tightening of the tires—did not take long either, the business of the tires accomplished by driving the wagon into the spring branch behind the shop and letting it stand there, the mules nuzzling into the water from time to time, and the boy on the seat with the idle reins, looking up the slope and through the sooty tunnel of the shed where the slow hammer rang and where his father sat on an upended cypress bolt, easily, either talking or listening, still sitting there when the boy brought the dripping wagon up out of the branch and halted it before the door.

"Take them on to the shade and hitch," his father said. He did so and returned. His father and the smith and a third man squatting on his heels inside the door were talking, about crops and animals; the boy, squatting too in the ammoniac dust and hoof-parings and scales of rust, heard his father tell a long and unhurried story out of the time before the birth of the older brother even when he had been a professional horsetrader. And then his father came up beside him

where he stood before a tattered last year's circus poster on the other side of the
store, gazing rapt and quiet at the scarlet horses, the incredible poisings and convulsions of tulle and tights and the painted leers of comedians, and said, "It's
time to eat."

But not at home. Squatting beside his brother against the front wall, he
watched his father emerge from the store and produce from a paper sack a segment of cheese and divide it carefully and deliberately into three with his pocket
knife and produce crackers from the same sack. They all three squatted on the
gallery and ate, slowly, without talking; then in the store again, they drank from
a tin dipper tepid water smelling of the cedar bucket and of living beech trees.
And still they did not go home. It was a horse lot this time, a tall rail fence upon
and along which men stood and sat and out of which one by one horses were led,
to be walked and trotted and then cantered back and forth along the road while
the slow swapping and buying went on and the sun began to slant westward,
they—the three of them—watching and listening, the older brother with his
muddy eyes and his steady, inevitable tobacco, the father commenting now and
then on certain of the animals, to no one in particular.

It was after sundown when they reached home. They ate supper by lamp-   85
light, then, sitting on the doorstep, the boy watched the night fully accomplish,
listening to the whippoorwills and the frogs, when he heard his mother's voice:
"Abner! No! No! Oh, God. Oh, God. Abner!" and he rose, whirled, and saw the
altered light through the door where a candle stub now burned in a bottle neck
on the table and his father, still in the hat and coat, at once formal and burlesque
as though dressed carefully for some shabby and ceremonial violence, emptying
the reservoir of the lamp back into the five-gallon kerosene can from which it
had been filled, while the mother tugged at his arm until he shifted the lamp to
the other hand and flung her back, not savagely or viciously, just hard, into the
wall, her hands flung out against the wall for balance, her mouth open and in her
face the same quality of hopeless despair as had been in her voice. Then his father saw him standing in the door.

"Go to the barn and get that can of oil we were oiling the wagon with," he
said. The boy did not move. Then he could speak.

"What . . ." he cried. "What are you . . ."

"Go get that oil," his father said. "Go."

Then he was moving, running, outside the house, toward the stable: this the
old habit, the old blood which he had not been permitted to choose for himself,
which had been bequeathed him willy nilly and which had run for so long (and
who knew where, battening on what of outrage and savagery and lust) before it
came to him. *I could keep on*, he thought. *I could run on and on and never look
back, never need to see his face again. Only I can't. I can't*, the rusted can in his
hand now, the liquid sploshing in it as he ran back to the house and into it, into
the sound of his mother's weeping in the next room, and handed the can to his
father.

"Ain't you going to even send a nigger?" he cried. "At least you sent a nigger   90
before!"

This time his father didn't strike him. The hand came even faster than the
blow had, the same hand which had set the can on the table with almost excruciating care flashing from the can toward him too quick for him to follow it, gripping him by the back of his shirt and on to tiptoe before he had seen it quit the

can, the face stooping at him in breathless and frozen ferocity, the cold, dead voice speaking over him to the older brother who leaned against the table, chewing with that steady, curious, sidewise motion of cows:

"Empty the can into the big one and go on. I'll catch up with you."

"Better tie him up to the bedpost," the brother said.

"Do like I told you," the father said. Then the boy was moving, his bunched shirt and the hard, bony hand between his shoulder-blades, his toes just touching the floor, across the room and into the other one, past the sisters sitting with spread heavy thighs in the two chairs over the cold hearth, and to where his mother and aunt sat side by side on the bed, the aunt's arm about his mother's shoulders.

"Hold him," the father said. The aunt made a startled movement. "Not   95 you," the father said. "Lennie. Take hold of him. I want to see you do it." His mother took him by the wrist. "You'll hold him better than that. If he gets loose don't you know what he is going to do? He will go up yonder." He jerked his head toward the road. "Maybe I'd better tie him."

"I'll hold him," his mother whispered.

"See you do then." Then his father was gone, the stiff foot heavy and measured upon the boards, ceasing at last.

Then he began to struggle. His mother caught him in both arms, he jerking and wrenching at them. He would be stronger in the end, he knew that. But he had no time to wait for it. "Lemme go!" he cried. "I don't want to have to hit you!"

"Let him go!" the aunt said. "If he don't go, before God, I am going up there myself!"

"Don't you see I can't?" his mother cried. "Sarty! Sarty! No! No! Help me,   100 Lizzie!"

Then he was free. His aunt grasped at him but it was too late. He whirled, running, his mother stumbled forward on to her knees behind him, crying to the nearer sister: "Catch him, Net! Catch him!" But that was too late too, the sister (the sisters were twins, born at the same time, yet either of them now gave the impression of being, encompassing as much living meat and volume and weight as any other two of the family) not yet having begun to rise from the chair, her head, face, alone merely turned, presenting to him in the flying instant an astonishing expanse of young female features untroubled by any surprise even, wearing only an expression of bovine interest. Then he was out of the room, out of the house, in the mild dust of the starlit road and the heavy rifeness of honeysuckle, the pale ribbon unspooling with terrific slowness under his running feet, reaching the gate at last and turning in, running, his heart and lungs drumming, on up the drive toward the lighted house, the lighted door. He did not knock, he burst in, sobbing for breath, incapable for the moment of speech; he saw the astonished face of the Negro in the linen jacket without knowing when the Negro had appeared.

"De Spain!" he cried, panted. "Where's . . ." then he saw the white man too emerging from a white door down the hall. "Barn!" he cried. "Barn!"

"What?" the white man said. "Barn?"

"Yes!" the boy cried. "Barn!"

"Catch him!" the white man shouted.
                                                                                                         105
But it was too late this time too. The Negro grasped his shirt, but the entire sleeve, rotten with washing, carried away, and he was out that door too and in

the drive again, and had actually never ceased to run even while he was screaming into the white man's face.

Behind him the white man was shouting. "My horse! Fetch my horse!" and
he thought for an instant of cutting across the park and climbing the fence into
the road, but he did not know the park nor how the vine-massed fence might be
and he dared not risk it. So he ran on down the drive, blood and breath roaring;
presently he was in the road again though he could not see it. He could not hear
either: the galloping mare was almost upon him before he heard her, and even
then he held his course, as if the very urgency of his wild grief and need must in
a moment more find him wings, waiting until the ultimate instant to hurl himself aside and into the weed-choked roadside ditch as the horse thundered past
and on, for an instant in furious silhouette against the stars, the tranquil early
summer night sky which, even before the shape of the horse and rider vanished,
stained abruptly and violently upward: a long, swirling roar incredible and
soundless, blotting the stars, and he springing up and into the road again, running again, knowing it was too late yet still running even after he heard the shot
and an instant later, two shots, pausing now without knowing he had ceased to
run, crying, "Pap! Pap!", running again before he knew he had begun to run,
stumbling, tripping over something and scrabbling up again without ceasing to
run, looking backward over his shoulder at the glare as he got up, running on
among the invisible trees, panting, sobbing, "Father! Father!"

At midnight he was sitting on the crest of a hill. He did not know it was
midnight and he did not know how far he had come. But there was no glare behind him now and he sat now, his back toward what he had called home for four
days anyhow, his face toward the dark woods which he would enter when breath
was strong again, small, shaking steadily in the chill darkness, hugging himself
into the remainder of his thin, rotten shirt, the grief and despair now no longer
terror and fear but just grief and despair. *Father. My father*, he thought. "He was
brave!" he cried suddenly, aloud but not loud, no more than a whisper. "He was!
He was in the war! He was in Colonel Sartoris' cav'ry!" not knowing that his father had gone to that war a private in the fine old European sense, wearing no
uniform, admitting the authority of and giving fidelity to no man or army or flag,
going to war as Malbrouck[1] himself did: for booty—it meant nothing and less
than nothing to him if it were enemy booty or his own.

The slow constellations wheeled on. It would be dawn and then sun-up after a
while and he would be hungry. But that would be tomorrow and now he was only
cold, and walking would cure that. His breathing was easier now and he decided to
get up and go on, and then he found that he had been asleep because he knew it
was almost dawn, the night almost over. He could tell that from the whippoorwills.
They were everywhere now among the dark trees below him, constant and inflec-
tioned and ceaseless, so that, as the instant for giving over to the day birds drew
nearer and nearer, there was no interval at all between them. He got up. He was a
little stiff, but walking would cure that too as it would the cold, and soon there
would be the sun. He went on down the hill, toward the dark woods within which
the liquid silver voices of the birds called unceasing—the rapid and urgent beating
of the urgent and quiring heart of the late spring night. He did not look back.

---

[1] *Malbrouck:* John Churchill, Duke of Marlborough (1650–1722), English general who led the 1704
Battle of Blenheim driving the French army out of Germany. The French called him Malbrouck,
which was easier for them to pronounce.

Faulkner's Oxford, Mississippi. Although William Faulkner spent periods of his adulthood in Europe and Hollywood, he is most closely associated with the Mississippi town in which he was born and lived for much of his life, Oxford.

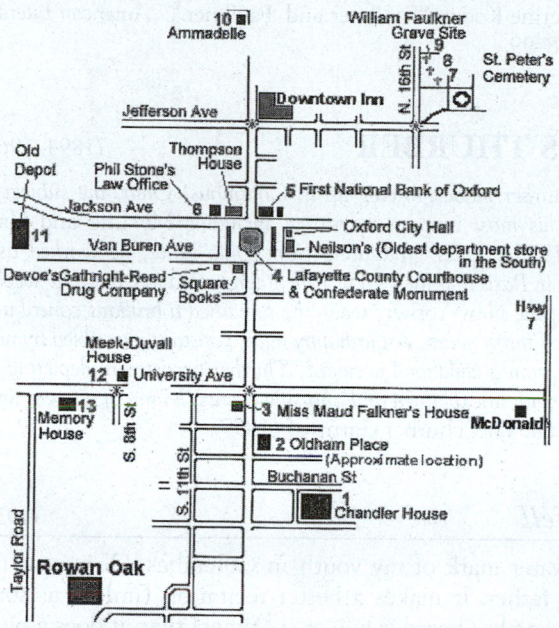

Map of Faulkner sites in Oxford, Mississippi.

Consequently, the city is full of Faulkner-related sites of interest, including his grave at St. Peter's Cemetery. Perhaps the two most notable locales are the Thompson-Chandler House, built in the 1830s, which served as the model for the Compson family home in Faulkner's novel *The Sound and the Fury*, and Rowan Oak, which was built in the 1840s, when Oxford was a small frontier settlement. Faulkner purchased the house he named Rowan Oak in 1930, shortly after writing his novels *Sanctuary*, *The Sound and the Fury*, and *As I Lay Dying* in rapid succession. The name purportedly comes from a Scottish legend alluding to the protective powers of wood from the rowan tree. Faulkner renovated the house in the years that followed, and he was fascinated by its history. The house was also where he spent his most productive years as a fiction writer, and it was during his years there that he wrote many of his short stories, as well as his novels *Light in August* and *Absalom, Absalom!*

Faulkner's Rowan Oak.

Today, Rowan Oak is a museum run by the University of Mississippi English Department and is open to the public.

Starting Points for Further Research: William Faulkner

- **Editions:** William Faulkner. *Novels, 1942–1954.* New York: Library of America, 1994.
  ———. *Novels: 1936–1940.* New York: Library of America, 1990.
  ———. *Novels: 1930–1935.* New York: Library of America, 1985.
- **Biography:** David L. Minter. *William Faulkner: His Life and Work.* Baltimore: Johns Hopkins University Press, 1997.
- **Critical Essay:** Catherine Kodat. "Faulkner and 'Faulkner.'" *American Literary History* 15 (2003): 188–99.

JAMES THURBER   (1894–1961)

James Thurber made growing up in Columbus, Ohio, the subject of much of his most renowned writing, including My Life and Hard Times *(1935). After graduating from Ohio State, he worked as a journalist in Paris and then New York, then took a job at a new weekly magazine, the* New Yorker, *where he remained a brilliant contributor for the next thirty years. An unhappy man, constantly troubled by near blindness from a childhood accident, Thurber persisted in depicting his life as a humorous affair filled with unexplained and amusing events. Many of his best writings and drawings are collected in* The Thurber Carnival *(1959).*

The Night the Bed Fell   (1933)

I suppose that the high-water mark of my youth in Columbus, Ohio, was the night the bed fell on my father. It makes a better recitation (unless, as some friends of mine have said, one has heard it five or six times) than it does a piece of writing, for it is almost necessary to throw furniture around, shake doors, and bark like a dog, to lend the proper atmosphere and verisimilitude to what is admittedly a somewhat incredible tale. Still, it did take place.

It happened, then, that my father had decided to sleep in the attic one night, to be away where he could think. My mother opposed the notion strongly because, she said, the old wooden bed up there was unsafe; it was wobbly and the heavy headboard would crash down on father's head in case the bed fell, and kill him. There was no dissuading him, however, and at a quarter past ten he closed the attic door behind him and went up the narrow twisting stairs. We later heard ominous creakings as he crawled into bed. Grandfather, who usually slept in the attic bed when he was with us, had disappeared some days before. (On these occasions he was usually gone six or eight days and returned growling and out of temper, with the news that the federal Union was run by a passel of blockheads and that the Army of the Potomac didn't have any more chance than a fiddler's bitch.)

We had visiting us at this time a nervous first cousin of mine named Briggs Beall, who believed that he was likely to cease breathing when he was asleep. It was his feeling that if he were not awakened every hour during the night, he might die of suffocation. He had been accustomed to setting an alarm clock to ring at intervals until morning, but I persuaded him to abandon this. He slept in my room and I told him that I was such a light sleeper that if anybody quit breathing in the same room with me, I would wake instantly. He tested me the first night—which I had suspected he would—by holding his breath after my regular breathing had convinced him I was asleep. I was not asleep, however, and called to him. This seemed to allay his fears a little, but he took the precaution of putting a glass of spirits of camphor on a little table at the head of his bed. In case I didn't arouse him until he was almost gone, he said, he would sniff the camphor, a powerful reviver. Briggs was not the only member of his family who had his crotchets. Old Aunt Melissa Beall (who could whistle like a man, with two fingers in her mouth) suffered under the premonition that she was destined to die on South High Street, because she had been born on South High Street and married on South High Street. Then there was Aunt Sarah Shoaf, who never went to bed at night without the fear that a burglar was going to get in and blow chloroform under her door through a tube. To avert this calamity—for she was in greater dread of anesthetics than of losing her household goods—she always piled her money, silverware, and other valuables in a neat stack just outside her bedroom, with a note reading: "This is all I have. Please take it and do not use your chloroform, as this is all I have." Aunt Gracie Shoaf also had a burglar phobia, but she met it with more fortitude. She was confident that burglars had been getting into her house every night for forty years. The fact that she never missed anything was to her no proof to the contrary. She always claimed that she scared them off before they could take anything, by throwing shoes down the hallway. When she went to bed she piled, where she could get at them handily, all the shoes there were about her house. Five minutes after she had turned off the light, she would sit up in bed and say "Hark!" Her husband, who had learned to ignore the whole situa-tion as long ago as 1903, would either be sound asleep or pretend to be sound asleep. In either case he would not respond to her tugging and pulling, so that presently she would arise, tiptoe to the door, open it slightly and heave a shoe down the hall in one direction, and its mate down the hall in the other direction. Some nights she threw them all, some nights only a couple of pair.

But I am straying from the remarkable incidents that took place during the night that the bed fell on fa-ther. By midnight we were all in bed. The layout of the rooms and the disposition of their occupants is important to an understanding of what

Some Nights She Threw Them All.

later occurred. In the front room upstairs (just under father's attic bedroom) were my mother and my brother Herman, who sometimes sang in his sleep, usually "Marching Through Georgia" or "Onward, Christian Soldiers." Briggs Beall and myself were in a room adjoining this one. My brother Roy was in a room across the hall from ours. Our bull terrier, Rex, slept in the hall.

My bed was an army cot, one of those affairs which are made wide enough to   5 sleep on comfortably only by putting up, flat with the middle section, the two sides which ordinarily hang down like the sideboards of a drop-leaf table. When these sides are up, it is perilous to roll too far toward the edge, for then the cot is likely to tip completely over, bringing the whole bed down on top of one, with a tremendous banging crash. This, in fact, is precisely what happened, about two o'clock in the morning. (It was my mother who, in recalling the scene later, first referred to it as "the night the bed fell on your father.")

Always a deep sleeper, slow to arouse (I had lied to Briggs), I was at first unconscious of what had happened when the iron cot rolled me onto the floor and toppled over on me. It left me still warmly bundled up and unhurt, for the bed rested above me like a canopy. Hence I did not wake up, only reached the edge of consciousness and went back. The racket, however, instantly awakened my mother, in the next room, who came to the immediate conclusion that her worst dread was realized: the big wooden bed upstairs had fallen on father. She therefore screamed, "Let's go to your poor father!" It was this shout, rather than the noise of my cot falling, that awakened Herman, in the same room with her. He thought that mother had become, for no apparent reason, hysterical. "You're all right, Mamma!" he shouted, trying to calm her. They exchanged shout for shout for perhaps ten seconds: "Let's go to your poor father!" and "You're all right!" That woke up Briggs. By this time I was conscious of what was going on, in a vague way, but did not yet realize that I was under my bed instead of on it. Briggs, awakening in the midst of loud shouts of fear and apprehension, came to the quick conclusion that he was suffocating and that we were all trying to "bring him out." With a low moan, he grasped the glass of camphor at the head of his bed and instead of sniffing it poured it over himself. The room reeked of camphor. "Ugf, ahfg," choked Briggs, like a drowning man, for he had almost suc-

ceeded in stopping his breath under the deluge of pungent spirits. He leaped out of bed and groped toward the open window, but he came up against one that was closed. With his hand, he beat out the glass, and I could hear it crash and tinkle on the alleyway below. It was at this juncture that I, in trying to get up, had the uncanny sensa-

He Came to the Conclusion That He Was Suffocating.

tion of feeling my bed above me! Foggy with sleep, I now suspected, in my turn, that the whole uproar was being made in a frantic endeavor to extricate me from what must be an unheard-of and perilous situation. "Get me out of this!" I bawled. "Get me out!" I think I had the nightmarish belief that I was entombed in a mine. "Gugh," gasped Briggs, floundering in his camphor.

By this time my mother, still shouting, pursued by Herman, still shouting, was trying to open the door to the attic, in order to go up and get my father's body out of the wreckage. The door was stuck, however, and wouldn't yield. Her frantic pulls on it only added to the general banging and confusion. Roy and the dog were now up, the one shouting questions, the other barking.

Father, farthest away and soundest sleeper of all, had by this time been awakened by the battering on the attic door. He decided that the house was on fire. "I'm coming, I'm coming!" he wailed in a slow, sleepy voice—it took him many minutes to regain full consciousness. My mother, still believing he was caught under the bed, detected in his "I'm coming!" the mournful, resigned note of one who is preparing to meet his Maker. "He's dying!" she shouted.

"I'm all right!" Briggs yelled to reassure her. "I'm all right!" He still believed that it was his own closeness to death that was worrying mother. I found at last the light switch in my room, unlocked the door, and Briggs and I joined the others at the attic door. The dog, who never did like Briggs, jumped for him—assuming that he was the culprit in whatever was going on—and Roy had to throw Rex and hold him. We could hear father crawling out of bed upstairs. Roy pulled the attic door open, with a mighty jerk, and father came down the stairs, sleepy and irritable but safe and sound. My mother began to weep when she saw him. Rex began to howl. "What in the name of God is going on here?" asked father.

The situation was finally put together like a gigantic jig-saw puzzle. Father   10 caught a cold from prowling around in his bare feet but there were no other bad results. "I'm glad," said mother, who always looked on the bright side of things, "that your grandfather wasn't here."

Roy Had to Throw Rex.

Starting Points for Further Research: James Thurber

- **Edition:** James Thurber. *Writing and Drawings.* Ed. Garrison Keillor. New York: Library of America, 1996.
- **Biography:** Harrison Kinney. *James Thurber: His Life and Times.* New York: Henry Holt, 1995.
- **Critical Essay:** Stephen J. Tanner. "James Thurber and the Midwest." *American Studies* 33: 2 (1992): 61–72.

GEORGE ORWELL

(1903–1950)

Born Eric Arthur Blair in India, to parents working in the Civil Service, Orwell attended Eton College but spurned a university education. He joined the British colonial police in Burma, which gave him the material for "Shooting an Elephant" as well as an undying contempt for colonial enterprises that involved subjugating other people. In a busy lifetime he wrote novels and powerful, politically charged books and essays, was wounded while serving with a Socialist brigade during the Spanish Civil War, and later, angry at his friends' continued sympathy for Stalin's soviet experiment, wrote two scathing anti-communist novels, the allegory Animal Farm *and his most famous book, the novel* 1984. *He died of tuberculosis at age forty-seven.*

Shooting an Elephant

(1936)

In Moulmein, in Lower Burma, I was hated by large numbers of people—the only time in my life that I have been important enough for this to happen to me. I was sub-divisional police officer of the town, and in an aimless, petty kind of way anti-European feeling was very bitter. No one had the guts to raise a riot, but if a European woman went through the bazaars alone somebody would probably spit betel juice over her dress. As a police officer I was an obvious target and was baited whenever it seemed safe to do so. When a nimble Burman tripped me up on the football field and the referee (another Burman) looked the other way, the crowd yelled with hideous laughter. This happened more than once. In the end the sneering yellow faces of young men that met me everywhere, the insults hooted after me when I was at a safe distance, got badly on my nerves. The young Buddhist priests were the worst of all. There were several thousands of them in the town and none of them seemed to have anything to do except stand on street corners and jeer at Europeans.

All this was perplexing and upsetting. For at that time I had already made up my mind that imperialism was an evil thing and the sooner I chucked up my job and got out of it the better. Theoretically—and secretly, of course—I was all for the Burmese and all against their oppressors, the British. As for the job I was doing, I hated it more bitterly than I can perhaps make clear. In a job like that you see the dirty work of Empire at close quarters. The wretched prisoners huddling in the stinking cages of the lock-ups, the grey, cowed faces of the long-term convicts, the scarred buttocks of the men who had been flogged with bamboos—all these oppressed me with an intolerable sense of guilt. But I could get nothing into perspective. I was young and ill-educated and I had had to think out my problems in the utter silence that is imposed on every Englishman in the East. I did not even know that the British Empire is dying, still less did I know that it is a great deal better than the younger empires that are going to supplant it. All I knew was that I was stuck between my hatred of the empire I served and my rage against the evil-spirited little beasts who tried to make my job impossible. With one part of my mind I thought of the British Raj as an unbreakable tyranny, as something clamped down, in *saecula saeculorum*, upon the will of prostrate peoples; with another part I thought that the greatest joy in the world would be to drive a bayonet into a Buddhist priest's guts. Feelings like these are the normal by-products of imperialism; ask any Anglo-Indian official, if you can catch him off duty.

One day something happened which in a roundabout way was enlightening. It was a tiny incident in itself, but it gave me a better glimpse than I had had before of the real nature of imperialism—the real motives for which despotic governments act. Early one morning the sub-inspector at a police station the other end of the town rang me up on the 'phone and said that an elephant was ravaging the bazaar. Would I please come and do something about it? I did not know what I could do, but I wanted to see what was happening and I got on to a pony and started out. I took my rifle, an old .44 Winchester and much too small to kill an elephant, but I thought the noise might be useful *in terrorem*. Various Burmans stopped me on the way and told me about the elephant's doings. It was not, of course, a wild elephant, but a tame one which had gone "must."[1] It had been chained up, as tame elephants always are when their attack of "must" is due, but on the previous night it had broken its chain and escaped. Its mahout, the only person who could manage it when it was in that state, had set out in pursuit, but had taken the wrong direction and was now twelve hours' journey away, and in the morning the elephant had suddenly reappeared in the town. The Burmese population had no weapons and were quite helpless against it. It had already destroyed somebody's bamboo hut, killed a cow and raided some fruit-stalls and devoured the stock; also it had met the municipal rubbish van and, when the driver jumped out and took to his heels, had turned the van over and inflicted violences upon it.

The Burmese sub-inspector and some Indian constables were waiting for me in the quarter where the elephant had been seen. It was a very poor quarter, a labyrinth of squalid bamboo huts, thatched with palm-leaf, winding all over a steep hillside. I remember that it was a cloudy, stuffy morning at the beginning of the rains. We began questioning the people as to where the elephant had gone and, as usual, failed to get any definite information. That is invariably the case in the East; a story always sounds clear enough at a distance, but the nearer you get to the scene of events the vaguer it becomes. Some of the people said that the elephant had gone in one direction, some said that he had gone in another, some professed not even to have heard of any elephant. I had almost made up my mind that the whole story was a pack of lies, when we heard yells a little distance away. There was a loud, scandalized cry of "Go away, child! Go away this instant!" and an old woman with a switch in her hand came round the corner of a hut, violently shooing away a crowd of naked children. Some more women followed, clicking their tongues and exclaiming; evidently there was something that the children ought not to have seen. I rounded the hut and saw a man's dead body sprawling in the mud. He was an Indian, a black Dravidian coolie, almost naked, and he could not have been dead many minutes. The people said that the elephant had come suddenly upon him round the corner of the hut, caught him with its trunk, put its foot on his back and ground him into the earth. This was the rainy season and the ground was soft, and his face had scored a trench a foot deep and a couple of yards long. He was lying on his belly with arms crucified and head sharply twisted to one side. His face was coated with mud, the eyes wide open, the teeth bared and grinning with an expression of unendurable agony. (Never tell me, by the way, that the dead look peaceful. Most of the corpses I have seen looked devilish.) The friction of the great beast's foot

---

[1] *must*: into heat.

had stripped the skin from his back as neatly as one skins a rabbit. As soon as I saw the dead man I sent an orderly to a friend's house nearby to borrow an elephant rifle. I had already sent back the pony, not wanting it to go mad with fright and throw me if it smelt the elephant.

The orderly came back in a few minutes with a rifle and five cartridges, and meanwhile some Burmans had arrived and told us that the elephant was in the paddy fields below, only a few hundred yards away. As I started forward practically the whole population of the quarter flocked out of the houses and followed me. They had seen the rifle and were all shouting excitedly that I was going to shoot the elephant. They had not shown much interest in the elephant when he was merely ravaging their homes, but it was different now that he was going to be shot. It was a bit of fun to them, as it would be to an English crowd; besides they wanted the meat. It made me vaguely uneasy. I had no intention of shooting the elephant—I had merely sent for the rifle to defend myself if necessary—and it is always unnerving to have a crowd following you. I marched down the hill, looking and feeling a fool, with the rifle over my shoulder and an ever-growing army of people jostling at my heels. At the bottom, when you got away from the huts, there was a metalled road and beyond that a miry waste of paddy fields a thousand yards across, not yet ploughed but soggy from the first rains and dotted with coarse grass. The elephant was standing eight yards from the road, his left side towards us. He took not the slightest notice of the crowd's approach. He was tearing up bunches of grass, beating them against his knees to clean them and stuffing them into his mouth.

I had halted on the road. As soon as I saw the elephant I knew with perfect certainty that I ought not to shoot him. It is a serious matter to shoot a working elephant—it is comparable to destroying a huge and costly piece of machinery—and obviously one ought not to do it if it can possibly be avoided. And at that distance, peacefully eating, the elephant looked no more dangerous than a cow. I thought then and I think now that his attack of "must" was already passing off; in which case he would merely wander harmlessly about until the mahout came back and caught him. Moreover, I did not in the least want to shoot him. I decided that I would watch him for a little while to make sure that he did not turn savage again, and then go home.

But at that moment I glanced round at the crowd that had followed me. It was an immense crowd, two thousand at the least and growing every minute. It blocked the road for a long distance on either side. I looked at the sea of yellow faces above the garish clothes—faces all happy and excited over this bit of fun, all certain that the elephant was going to be shot. They were watching me as they would watch a conjurer about to perform a trick. They did not like me, but with the magical rifle in my hands I was momentarily worth watching. And suddenly I realized that I should have to shoot the elephant after all. The people expected it of me and I had got to do it; I could feel their two thousand wills pressing me forward, irresistibly. And it was at this moment, as I stood there with the rifle in my hands, that I first grasped the hollowness, the futility of the white man's dominion in the East. Here was I, the white man with his gun, standing in front of the unarmed native crowd—seemingly the leading actor of the piece; but in reality I was only an absurd puppet pushed to and fro by the will of those yellow faces behind. I perceived in this moment that when the white man turns tyrant it is his own freedom that he destroys. He becomes a sort of hollow, posing dummy, the conventionalized figure of a sahib. For it is the condition of his rule that he shall spend his life in trying to impress the "natives," and so in every crisis he has got to do what the "natives" expect of him. He wears a mask, and his face grows to fit it. I had got to shoot the elephant. I had committed myself to doing it when I sent for the rifle. A sahib has got to act like a sahib; he has got to appear resolute, to know his own mind and do definite things. To come all that way, rifle in hand, with two thousand people marching at my heels, and then to trail feebly away, having done nothing—no, that was impossible. The crowd would laugh at me. And my whole life, every white man's life in the East, was one long struggle not to be laughed at.

But I did not want to shoot the elephant. I watched him beating his bunch of grass against his knees, with that preoccupied grandmotherly air that elephants have. It seemed to me that it would be murder to shoot him. At that age I was not squeamish about killing animals, but I had never shot an elephant and never wanted to. (Somehow it always seems worse to kill a *large* animal.) Besides, there was the beast's owner to be considered. Alive, the elephant was worth at least a hundred pounds; dead, he would only be worth the value of his tusks, five pounds, possibly. But I had got to act quickly. I turned to some experienced-looking Burmans who had been there when we arrived, and asked them how the elephant had been behaving. They all said the same thing: he took no notice of you if you left him alone, but he might charge if you went too close to him.

It was perfectly clear to me what I ought to do. I ought to walk up to within, say, twenty-five yards of the elephant and test his behavior. If he charged, I could shoot; if he took no notice of me, it would be safe to leave him until the mahout came back. But also I knew that I was going to do no such thing. I was a poor shot with a rifle and the ground was soft mud into which one would sink at every step. If the elephant charged and I missed him, I should have about as much chance as a load under a steam-roller. But even then I was not thinking particularly of my own skin, only of the watchful yellow faces behind. For at that moment, with the crowd watching me, I was not afraid in the ordinary sense, as I would have been if I had been alone. A white man mustn't be frightened in front of "natives"; and so, in general, he isn't frightened. The sole thought in my mind was that if anything went wrong those two thousand Burmans would see me pursued, caught, trampled on and reduced to a grinning corpse like that Indian up the hill. And if that happened it was quite probable that some of them would laugh. That would never do. There was only one alternative. I shoved the cartridges into the magazine and lay down on the road to get a better aim.

The crowd grew very still, and a deep, low, happy sigh, as of people who see   10
the theatre curtain go up at last, breathed from innumerable throats. They were going to have their bit of fun after all. The rifle was a beautiful German thing with cross-hair sights. I did not then know that in shooting an elephant one would shoot to cut an imaginary bar running from ear-hole to ear-hole. I ought, therefore, as the elephant was sideways on, to have aimed straight at his ear-hole; actually I aimed several inches in front of this, thinking the brain would be further forward.

When I pulled the trigger I did not hear the bang or feel the kick—one never does when a shot goes home—but I heard the devilish roar of glee that went up from the crowd. In that instant, in too short a time, one would have thought, even for the bullet to get there, a mysterious, terrible change had come over the elephant. He neither stirred nor fell, but every line of his body had altered. He looked suddenly stricken, shrunken, immensely old, as though the frightful impact of the bullet had paralysed him without knocking him down. At last, after what seemed a long time—it might have been five seconds, I dare say—he sagged flabbily to his knees. His mouth slobbered. An enormous senility seemed to have settled upon him. One could have imagined him thousands of years old. I fired again into the same spot. At the second shot he did not collapse but climbed with desperate slowness to his feet and stood weakly upright, with legs sagging and head drooping. I fired a third time. That was the shot that did for him. You could see the agony of it jolt his whole body and knock the last remnant of strength from his legs. But in falling he seemed for a moment to rise, for as his hind legs collapsed beneath him he seemed to tower upward like a huge rock toppling, his trunk reaching skywards like a tree. He trumpeted, for the first and only time. And then down he came, his belly towards me, with a crash that seemed to shake the ground even where I lay.

I got up. The Burmans were already racing past me across the mud. It was obvious that the elephant would never rise again, but he was not dead. He was breathing very rhythmically with long rattling gasps, his great mound of a side painfully rising and falling. His mouth was wide open—I could see far down into caverns of pale pink throat. I waited a long time for him to die, but his breathing did not weaken. Finally I fired my two remaining shots into the spot where I thought his heart must be. The thick blood welled out of him like red velvet, but still he did not die. His body did not even jerk when the shots hit him, the tortured breathing continued without a pause. He was dying, very slowly and in great agony, but in some world remote from me where not even a bullet could damage him further. I felt that I had got to put an end to that dreadful noise. It seemed dreadful to see the great beast lying there, powerless to move and yet powerless to die, and not even to be able to finish him. I sent back for my small rifle and poured shot after shot into his heart and down his throat. They seemed to make no impression. The tortured gasps continued as steadily as the ticking of a clock.

In the end I could not stand it any longer and went away. I heard later that it took him half an hour to die. Burmans were bringing dahs[2] and baskets even before I left, and I was told they had stripped his body almost to the bones by the afternoon.

Afterwards, of course, there were endless discussions about the shooting of the elephant. The owner was furious, but he was only an Indian and could do nothing. Besides, legally I had done the right thing, for a mad elephant has to be killed, like a mad dog, if its owner fails to control it. Among the Europeans opinion was divided. The older men said I was right, the younger men said it was a damn shame to shoot an elephant for killing a coolie, because an elephant was worth more than any damn Coringhee coolie. And afterwards I was very glad that the coolie had been killed; it put me legally in the right and it gave me a sufficient pretext for shooting the elephant. I often wondered whether any of the others grasped that I had done it solely to avoid looking a fool.

---

[2]*dahs*: butcher knives.

Starting Points for Further Research: George Orwell

- **Editions:** George Orwell. *1984.* New York: Penguin 2002.
  ———. *Animal Farm: A Fairy Story.* New York: Penguin, 2003.
  ———. *Essays.* New York, Knopf, 2002.
- **Biography:** Jeffrey Meyers. *Orwell: Wintry Conscience of a Generation.* London: W. W. Norton, 2001.
- **Critical Essay:** Rob Breton. "Crisis? Whose Crisis? George Orwell and Liberal Guilt." *College Literature* 29 (Fall 2002): 47–66.

E. B. WHITE

(1899–1985)

Born in Mt. Vernon, a New York City suburb, E. B. White attended Cornell University, where he took a journalism course from William Strunk, whom he would later make famous. He took a job at the New Yorker when it was just starting out, married one of its best editors, Katherine Angell, and kept his connection with the magazine for many years, even after he left Manhattan for the Maine coast in 1938. White was famous both for his essays, which appeared in the New Yorker and Harper's, and for his children's books, Charlotte's Web, Stuart Little, *and* The Trumpet of the Swan *(1970). His edition of Strunk's* The Elements of Style *(familiarly called Strunk and White) has sold millions.*

Once More to the Lake

(1941)

One summer, along about 1904, my father rented a camp on a lake in Maine and took us all there for the month of August. We all got ringworm from some kittens and had to rub Pond's Extract on our arms and legs night and morning, and my father rolled over in a canoe with all his clothes on; but outside of that the vacation was a success and from then on none of us ever thought there was any place in the world like that lake in Maine. We returned summer after summer—always on August 1st for one month. I have since become a salt-water man, but sometimes in summer there are days when the restlessness of the tides and the fearful cold of the sea water and the incessant wind which blows across the afternoon and into the evening make me wish for the placidity of a lake in the woods. A few weeks ago this feeling got so strong I bought myself a couple of bass hooks and a spinner and returned to the lake where we used to go, for a week's fishing and to revisit old haunts.

I took along my son, who had never had any fresh water up his nose and who had seen lily pads only from train windows. On the journey over to the lake I began to wonder what it would be like. I wondered how time would have marred this unique, this holy spot—the coves and streams, the hills that the sun set behind, the camps and the paths behind the camps. I was sure the tarred road would have found it out and I wondered in what other ways it would be desolated. It is strange how much you can remember about places like that once you allow your mind to return into the grooves which lead back. You remember one thing, and that suddenly reminds you of another thing. I guess I remembered clearest of all the early mornings, when the lake was cool and motionless, remembered how the bedroom smelled of the lumber it was made of and of the wet woods whose scent entered through the screen. The partitions in the camp were thin and did not extend clear to the top of the rooms, and as I was always the first up I would dress softly so as not to wake the others, and sneak out into the sweet outdoors and start out in the canoe, keeping close along the shore in the long shadows of the pines. I remembered being very careful never to rub my paddle against the gunwale for fear of disturbing the stillness of the cathedral.

The lake had never been what you would call a wild lake. There were cottages sprinkled around the shores, and it was in farming country although the shores of the lake were quite heavily wooded. Some of the cottages were owned by nearby farmers, and you would live at the shore and eat your meals at the farmhouse. That's what our family did. But although it wasn't wild, it was a fairly large and undisturbed lake and there were places in it which, to a child at least, seemed infinitely remote and primeval.

I was right about the tar: it led to within half a mile of the shore. But when I got back there, with my boy, and we settled into a camp near a farmhouse and into the kind of summertime I had known, I could tell that it was going to be pretty much the same as it had been before—I knew it, lying in bed the first morning, smelling the bedroom, and hearing the boy sneak quietly out and go off along the shore in a boat. I began to sustain the illusion that he was I, and therefore, by simple transposition, that I was my father. This sensation persisted, kept cropping up all the time we were there. It was not an entirely new feeling, but in this setting it grew much stronger. I seemed to be living a dual existence. I would be in the middle of some simple act, I would be picking up a bait box or laying down a table fork, or I would be saying something, and suddenly it would be not I but my father who was saying the words or making the gesture. It gave me a creepy sensation.

We went fishing the first morning. I felt the same damp moss covering the worms in the bait can, and saw the dragonfly alight on the tip of my rod as it hovered a few inches from the surface of the water. It was the arrival of this fly that convinced me beyond any doubt that everything was as it always had been, that the years were a mirage and there had been no years. The small waves were the same, chucking the rowboat under the chin as we fished at anchor, and the boat was the same boat, the same color green and the ribs broken in the same places, and under the floor-boards the same fresh-water leavings and débris—the dead helgrammite, the wisps of moss, the rusty discarded fishhook, the dried blood from yesterday's catch. We stared silently at the tips of our rods, at the dragonflies that came and went. I lowered the tip of mine into the water, tentatively, pensively dislodging the fly, which darted two feet away, poised, darted two feet back, and came to rest again a little farther up the rod. There had been no years between the ducking of this dragonfly and the other one—the one that was part of memory. I looked at the boy, who was silently watching his fly, and it was my hands that held his rod, my eyes watching. I felt dizzy and didn't know which rod I was at the end of.

We caught two bass, hauling them in briskly as though they were mackerel, pulling them over the side of the boat in a businesslike manner without any landing net, and stunning them with a blow on the back of the head. When we got back for a swim before lunch, the lake was exactly where we had left it, the

5

same number of inches from the dock, and there was only the merest suggestion of a breeze. This seemed an utterly enchanted sea, this lake you could leave to its own devices for a few hours and come back to, and find that it had not stirred, this constant and trustworthy body of water. In the shallows, the dark, water-soaked sticks and twigs, smooth and old, were undulating in clusters on the bottom against the clean ribbed sand, and the track of the mussel was plain. A school of minnows swam by, each minnow with its small individual shadow, doubling the attendance, so clear and sharp in the sunlight. Some of the other campers were in swimming, along the shore, one of them with a cake of soap, and the water felt thin and clear and unsubstantial. Over the years there had been this person with the cake of soap, this cultist, and here he was. There had been no years.

Up to the farmhouse to dinner through the teeming, dusty field, the road under our sneakers was only a two-track road. The middle track was missing, the one with the marks of the hooves and the splotches of dried, flaky manure. There had always been three tracks to choose from in choosing which track to walk in; now the choice was narrowed down to two. For a moment I missed terribly the middle alternative. But the way led past the tennis court, and something about the way it lay there in the sun reassured me; the tape had loosened along the backline, the alleys were green with plantains and other weeds, and the net (installed in June and removed in September) sagged in the dry noon, and the whole place steamed with midday heat and hunger and emptiness. There was a choice of pie for dessert, and one was blueberry and one was apple, and the waitresses were the same country girls, there having been no passage of time, only the illusion of it as in a dropped curtain—the waitresses were still fifteen; their hair had been washed, that was the only difference—they had been to the movies and seen the pretty girls with the clean hair.

Summertime, oh summertime, pattern of life indelible, the fade-proof lake, the woods unshatterable, the pasture with the sweetfern and the juniper forever and ever, summer without end; this was the background, and the life along the shore was the design, the cottagers with their innocent and tranquil design, their tiny docks with the flagpole and the American flag floating against the white clouds in the blue sky, the little paths over the roots of the trees leading from camp to camp and the paths leading back to the outhouses and the can of lime for sprinkling, and at the souvenir counters at the store the miniature birch-bark canoes and the post cards that showed things looking a little better than they looked. This was the American family at play, escaping the city heat, wondering whether the newcomers in the camp at the head of the cove were "common" or "nice," wondering whether it was true that the people who drove up for Sunday dinner at the farmhouse were turned away because there wasn't enough chicken.

It seemed to me, as I kept remembering all this, that those times and those summers had been infinitely precious and worth saving. There had been jollity and peace and goodness. The arriving (at the beginning of August) had been so big a business in itself, at the railway station the farm wagon drawn up, the first smell of the pine-laden air, the first glimpse of the smiling farmer, and the great importance of the trunks and your father's enormous authority in such matters, and the feel of the wagon under you for the long ten-mile haul, and at the top of the last long hill catching the first view of the lake after eleven months of not seeing this cherished body of water. The shouts and cries of the other campers when they saw you, and the trunks to be unpacked, to give up their rich burden. (Arriving was less exciting nowadays, when you sneaked up in your car and parked it under a tree near the camp and took out the bags and in five minutes it was all over, no fuss, no loud wonderful fuss about trunks.)

Peace and goodness and jollity. The only thing that was wrong now, really, 10 was the sound of the place, an unfamiliar nervous sound of the outboard motors. This was the note that jarred, the one thing that would sometimes break the illusion and set the years moving. In those other summertimes all motors were inboard; and when they were at a little distance, the noise they made was a sedative, an ingredient of summer sleep. They were one-cylinder and two-cylinder engines, and some were make-and-break and some were jump-spark, but they all made a sleepy sound across the lake. The one-lungers throbbed and fluttered, and the twin-cylinder ones purred and purred, and that was a quiet sound too. But now the campers all had outboards. In the daytime, in the hot mornings, these motors made a petulant, irritable sound; at night, in the still evening when the afterglow lit the water, they whined about one's ears like mosquitoes. My boy loved our rented outboard, and his great desire was to achieve singlehanded mastery over it, and authority, and he soon learned the trick of choking it a little (but not too much), and the adjustment of the needle valve. Watching him I would remember the things you could do with the old one-cylinder engine with the heavy flywheel, how you could have it eating out of your hand if you got really close to it spiritually. Motor boats in those days didn't have clutches, and you would make a landing by shutting off the motor at the proper time and coasting in with a dead rudder. But there was a way of reversing them, if you learned the trick, by cutting the switch and putting it on again exactly on the final dying revolution of the flywheel, so that it would kick back against compression and begin reversing. Approaching a dock in a strong following breeze, it was difficult to slow up sufficiently by the ordinary coasting method, and if a boy felt he had complete mastery over his motor, he was tempted to keep it running beyond its time and then reverse it a few feet from the dock. It took a cool nerve, because if you threw the switch a twentieth of a second too soon you would catch the flywheel when it still had speed enough to go up past center, and the boat would leap ahead, charging bull-fashion at the dock.

We had a good week at the camp. The bass were biting well and the sun shone endlessly, day after day. We would be tired at night and lie down in the accumulated heat of the little bedrooms after the long hot day and the breeze would stir almost imperceptibly outside and the smell of the swamp drift in through the rusty screens. Sleep would come easily and in the morning the red squirrel would be on the roof, tapping out his gay routine. I kept remembering everything, lying in bed in the mornings—the small steamboat that had a long rounded stem like the lip of a Ubangi, and how quietly she ran on the moonlight sails, when the older boys played their mandolins and the girls sang and we ate doughnuts dipped in sugar, and how sweet the music was on the water in the shining night, and what it had felt like to think about girls then. After breakfast we would go up to the store and the things were in the same place—the minnows in a bottle, the plugs and spinners disarranged and pawed over by the youngsters from the boys' camp, the fig newtons and the Beeman's gum. Outside, the road was tarred and cars stood in front of the store. Inside, all was just as it had always been, except there was more Coca-Cola and not so much Moxie and root beer and birch beer and sarsaparilla. We would walk out with a bottle of pop apiece and sometimes the pop would backfire up our noses and hurt. We explored the streams, quietly, where the turtles slid off the sunny logs and dug their way into the soft bottom; and we lay on the town wharf and fed worms to the tame bass. Everywhere we went I had trouble making out which was I, the one walking at my side, the one walking in my pants.

One afternoon while we were there at that lake a thunderstorm came up. It was like the revival of an old melodrama that I had seen long ago with childish awe. The second-act climax of the drama of the electrical disturbance over a lake in America had not changed in any important respect. This was the big scene, still the big scene. The whole thing was so familiar, the first feeling of oppression and heat and a general air around camp of not wanting to go very far away. In midafternoon (it was all the same) a curious darkening of the sky, and a lull in everything that had made life tick; and then the way the boats suddenly swung the other way at their moorings with the coming of a breeze out of the new quarter, and the premonitory rumble. Then the kettle drum, then the snare, then the bass drum and cymbals, then crackling light against the dark, and the gods grinning and licking their chops in the hills. Afterward the calm, the rain steadily rustling in the calm lake, the return of light and hope and spirits, and the campers running out in joy and relief to go swimming in the rain, their bright cries perpetuating the deathless joke about how they were getting simply drenched, and the children screaming with delight at the new sensation of bathing in the rain, and the joke about getting drenched linking the generations in a strong indestructible chain. And the comedian who waded in carrying an umbrella.

When the others went swimming my son said he was going in too. He pulled his dripping trunks from the line where they had hung all through the shower, and wrung them out. Languidly, and with no thought of going in, I watched him, his hard little body, skinny and bare, saw him wince slightly as he pulled up around his vitals the small, soggy, icy garment. As he buckled the swollen belt suddenly my groin felt the chill of death.

Starting Points for Further Research: E. B. White

- **Editions:** E. B. White. *Essays.* New York: Perennial Classics, 1999.
  ———. *Charlotte's Web.* New York: HarperCollins, 2003.
- **Critical Essay:** Roger S. Platizky. " 'Once More to the Lake': A Mythic Interpretation." *Critical Essays on E. B. White.* Ed. Robert L. Root. New York: G. K. Hall, 1994. 31–37.

RICHARD WRIGHT   (1908–1960)

Born on a Mississippi plantation, Richard Wright struggled through an impoverished childhood and early on determined to better himself through leaving the South and attaining an education. He arrived in Chicago in 1927 and there wrote powerful stories of city life, including the collection Uncle Tom's Children *(1938) and the best-selling novel* Native Son *(1940), which was to make him famous. A dedicated communist in the 1930s, Wright turned against the narrowness of the party in the 1940s. Wright's autobiographical* Black Boy *(1945), written at the height of his powers, was his last masterpiece. Frustrated by America's continued racial strife, he moved to France, where he died.*

The Man Who Lived Underground   (1943)

I've got to hide, he told himself. His chest heaved as he waited, crouching in a dark corner of the vestibule. He was tired of running and dodging. Either he had to find a place to hide, or he had to surrender. A police car swished by through the rain, its siren rising sharply. They're looking for me all over . . . He crept to the door and squinted through the fogged plate glass. He stiffened as the siren rose and died in the distance. Yes, he had to hide, but where? He gritted his teeth. Then a sudden movement in the street caught his attention. A throng of tiny columns of water snaked into the air from the perforations of a manhole cover. The columns stopped abruptly, as though the perforations had become clogged; a gray spout of sewer water jutted up from underground and lifted the circular metal cover, juggled it for a moment, then let it fall with a clang.

He hatched a tentative plan: he would wait until the siren sounded far off, then he would go out. He smoked and waited, tense. At last the siren gave him his signal; it wailed, dying, going away from him. He stepped to the sidewalk, then paused and looked curiously at the open manhole, half expecting the cover to leap up again. He went to the center of the street and stooped and peered into the hole, but could see nothing. Water rustled in the black depths.

He started with terror; the siren sounded so near that he had the idea that he had been dreaming and had awakened to find the car upon him. He dropped instinctively to his knees and his hands grasped the rim of the manhole. The siren seemed to hoot directly above him and with a wild gasp of exertion he snatched the cover far enough off to admit his body. He swung his legs over the opening and lowered himself into watery darkness. He hung for an eternal moment to the rim by his finger tips, then he felt rough metal prongs and at once he knew that sewer workmen used these ridges to lower themselves into manholes. Fist over fist, he let his body sink until he could feel no more prongs. He swayed in dank space; the siren seemed to howl at the very rim of the manhole. He dropped and was washed violently into an ocean of warm, leaping water. His head was battered against a wall and he wondered if this were death. Frenziedly his fingers clawed and sank into a crevice. He steadied himself and measured the strength of the current with his own muscular tension. He stood slowly in water that dashed past his knees with fearful velocity.

He heard a prolonged scream of brakes and the siren broke off. Oh, God! They had found him! Looming above his head in the rain a white face hovered over the hole. "How did this damn thing get off?" he heard a policeman ask. He saw the steel cover move slowly until the hole looked like a quarter moon turned black. "Give me a hand here," someone called. The cover clanged into place, muffling the sights and sounds of the upper world. Knee-deep in the pulsing current, he breathed with aching chest, filling his lungs with the hot stench of yeasty rot.

From the perforations of the manhole cover, delicate lances of hazy violet   5
sifted down and wove a mottled pattern upon the surface of the streaking current. His lips parted as a car swept past along the wet pavement overhead, its heavy rumble soon dying out, like the hum of a plane speeding through a dense cloud. He had never thought that cars could sound like that; everything seemed strange and unreal under here. He stood in darkness for a long time, knee-deep in rustling water, musing.

The odor of rot had become so general that he no longer smelled it. He got his cigarettes, but discovered that his matches were wet. He searched and found a dry folder in the pocket of his shirt and managed to strike one; it flared weirdly in the wet gloom, glowing greenishly, turning red, orange, then yellow. He lit a crumpled cigarette; then, by the flickering light of the match, he looked for support so that he would not have to keep his muscles flexed against the pouring water. His pupils narrowed and he saw to either side of him two steaming walls that rose and curved inward some six feet above his head to form a dripping, mouse-colored dome. The bottom of the sewer was a sloping V-trough. To the left, the sewer vanished in ashen fog. To the right was a steep down-curve into which water plunged.

He saw now that had he not regained his feet in time, he would have been swept to death, or had he entered any other manhole he would have probably drowned. Above the rush of the current he heard sharper juttings of water; tiny streams were spewing into the sewer from smaller conduits. The match died; he struck another and saw a mass of debris sweep past him and clog the throat of the down-curve. At once the water began rising rapidly. Could he climb out before he drowned? A long hiss sounded and the debris was sucked from sight; the current lowered. He understood now what had made the water toss the manhole cover; the down-curve had become temporarily obstructed and the perforations had become clogged.

He was in danger; he might slide into a down-curve; he might wander with a lighted match into a pocket of gas and blow himself up; or he might contract some horrible disease . . . Though he wanted to leave, an irrational impulse held him rooted. To the left, the convex ceiling swooped to a height of less than five feet. With cigarette slanting from pursed lips, he waded with taut muscles, his feet sloshing over the slimy bottom, his shoes sinking into spongy slop, the slate-colored water cracking in creamy foam against his knees. Pressing his flat left palm against the lowered ceiling, he struck another match and saw a metal pole nestling in a niche of the wall. Yes, some sewer workman had left it. He reached for it, then jerked his head away as a whisper of scurrying life whisked past and was still. He held the match close and saw a huge rat, wet with slime, blinking beady eyes and baring tiny fangs. The light blinded the rat and the frizzled head moved aimlessly. He grabbed the pole and let it fly against the rat's soft body; there was shrill piping and the grizzly body splashed into the dun-colored water and was snatched out of sight, spinning in the scuttling stream.

He swallowed and pushed on, following the curve of the misty cavern, sounding the water with the pole. By the faint light of another manhole cover he saw, amid loose wet brick, a hole with walls of damp earth leading into blackness. Gingerly he poked the pole into it; it was hollow and went beyond the length of the pole. He shoved the pole before him, hoisted himself upward, got to his hands and knees, and crawled. After a few yards he paused, struck to wonderment by the silence; it seemed that he had traveled a million miles away from the world. As he inched forward again he could sense the bottom of the dirt tunnel becoming dry and lowering slightly. Slowly he rose and to his astonishment he stood erect. He could not hear the rustling of the water now and he felt confoundingly alone, yet lured by the darkness and silence.

He crept a long way, then stopped, curious, afraid. He put his right foot forward and it dangled in space; he drew back in fear. He thrust the pole outward 10 and it swung in emptiness. He trembled, imagining the earth crumbling and burying him alive. He scratched a match and saw that the dirt floor sheered away steeply and widened into a sort of cave some five feet below him. An old sewer, he muttered. He cocked his head, hearing a feathery cadence which he could not identify. The match ceased to burn.

Using the pole as a kind of ladder, he slid down and stood in darkness. The air was a little fresher and he could still hear vague noises. Where was he? He felt suddenly that someone was standing near him and he turned sharply, but there was only darkness. He poked cautiously and felt a brick wall; he followed it and the strange sounds grew louder. He ought to get out of here. This was crazy. He could not remain here for any length of time; there was no food and no place to sleep. But the faint sounds tantalized him; they were strange but familiar. Was it a motor? A baby crying? Music? A siren? He groped on, and the sounds came so clearly that he could feel the pitch and timbre of human voices. Yes, singing! That was it! He listened with open mouth. It was a church service. Enchanted, he groped toward the waves of melody.

> *Jesus, take me to your home above*
> *And fold me in the bosom of Thy love . . .*

The singing was on the other side of a brick wall. Excited, he wanted to watch the service without being seen. Whose church was it? He knew most of the churches in this area above ground, but the singing sounded too strange and detached for him to guess. He looked to the left, to the right, down to the black dirt, then upward and was startled to see a bright sliver of light slicing the darkness like the blade of a razor. He struck one of his two remaining matches and saw rusty pipes running along an old concrete ceiling. Photographically he located the exact position of the pipes in his mind. The match flame sank and he sprang upward; his hands clutched a pipe. He swung his legs and tossed his body onto the bed of pipes and they creaked, swaying up and down; he thought that the tier was about to crash, but nothing happened. He edged to the crevice and saw a segment of black men and women, dressed in white robes, singing, holding tattered songbooks in their black palms. His first impulse was to laugh, but he checked himself.

What was he doing? He was crushed with a sense of guilt. Would God strike him dead for that? The singing swept on and he shook his head, disagreeing in spite of himself. They oughtn't to do that, he thought. But he could think of no reason *why* they should not do it. Just singing with the air of the sewer blowing in on them . . . He felt that he was gazing upon something abysmally obscene, yet he could not bring himself to leave.

After a long time he grew numb and dropped to the dirt. Pain throbbed in his legs and a deeper pain, induced by the sight of those black people groveling and begging for something they could never get, churned in him. A vague conviction made him feel that those people should stand unrepentant and yield no quarter in singing and praying, yet *he* had run away from the police, had pleaded with them to believe in *his* innocence. He shook his head, bewildered.

How long had he been down here? He did not know. This was a new kind of living for him; the intensity of feelings he had experienced when looking at the church people sing made him certain that he had been down here a long time, but his mind told him that the time must have been short. In this darkness the 15 only notion he had of time was when a match flared and measured time by its fleeting light. He groped back through the hole toward the sewer and the waves of song subsided and finally he could not hear them at all. He came to where the earth hole ended and he heard the noise of the current and time lived again for him, measuring the moments by the wash of water.

The rain must have slackened, for the flow of water had lessened and came only to his ankles. Ought he to go up into the streets and take his chances on hiding somewhere else? But they would surely catch him. The mere thought of dodging and running again from the police made him tense. No, he would stay and plot how to elude them. But what could he do down here? He walked forward into the sewer and came to another manhole cover; he stood beneath it, debating. Fine pencils of gold spilled suddenly from the little circles in the manhole cover and trembled on the surface of the current. Yes, street lamps . . . It must be night . . .

He went forward for about a quarter of an hour, wading aimlessly, poking the pole carefully before him. Then he stopped, his eyes fixed and intent. What's that? A strangely familiar image attracted and repelled him. Lit by the yellow stems from another manhole cover was a tiny nude body of a baby snagged by debris and half-submerged in water. Thinking that the baby was alive, he moved impulsively to save it, but his roused feelings told him that it was dead, cold, nothing, the same nothingness he had felt while watching the men and women singing in the church. Water blossomed about the tiny legs, the tiny arms, the tiny head, and rushed onward. The eyes were closed, as though in sleep; the fists were clenched, as though in protest; and the mouth gaped black in a soundless cry.

He straightened and drew in his breath, feeling that he had been staring for all eternity at the ripples of veined water skimming impersonally over the shriveled limbs. He felt as condemned as when the policemen had accused him. Involuntarily he lifted his hand to brush the vision away, but his arm fell listlessly to his side. Then he acted; he closed his eyes and reached forward slowly with the soggy shoe of his right foot and shoved the dead baby from where it had been lodged. He kept his eyes closed, seeing the little body twisting in the current as it floated from sight. He opened his eyes, shivered, placed his knuckles in the sockets, hearing the water speed in the somber shadows.

He tramped on, sensing at times a sudden quickening in the current as he passed some conduit whose waters were swelling the stream that slid by his feet. A few minutes later he was standing under another manhole cover, listening to the faint rumble of noises above ground. Streetcars and trucks, he mused. He looked down and saw a stagnant pool of gray-green sludge; at intervals a balloon pocket rose from the scum, glistening a bluish-purple, and burst. Then another. He turned, shook his head, and tramped back to the dirt cave by the church, his lips quivering.

Back in the cave, he sat and leaned his back against a dirt wall. His body was trembling slightly. Finally his senses quieted and he slept. When he awakened he felt stiff and cold. He had to leave this foul place, but leaving meant facing those policemen who had wrongly accused him. No, he could not go back aboveground. He remembered the beating they had given him and how he had signed his name to a confession, a confession which he had not even read. He had been too tired when they had shouted at him, demanding that he sign his name; he had signed it to end his pain.

20

He stood and groped about in the darkness. The church singing had stopped. How long had he slept? He did not know. But he felt refreshed and hungry. He doubled his fist nervously, realizing that he could not make a decision. As he walked about he stumbled over an old rusty iron pipe. He picked it up and felt a jagged edge. Yes, there was a brick wall and he could dig into it. What would he find? Smiling, he groped to the brick wall, sat, and began digging idly into damp cement. I can't make any noise, he cautioned himself. As time passed he grew thirsty, but there was no water. He had to kill time or go aboveground. The cement came out of the wall easily; he extracted four bricks and felt a soft draft blowing into his face. He stopped, afraid. What was beyond? He waited a long time and nothing happened; then he began digging again, soundlessly, slowly; he enlarged the hole and crawled through into a dark room and collided with another wall. He felt his way to the right; the wall ended and his fingers toyed in space, like the antennae of an insect.

He fumbled on and his feet struck something hollow, like wood. What's this? He felt with his fingers. Steps . . . He stooped and pulled off his shoes and mounted the stairs and saw a yellow chink of light shining and heard a low voice speaking. He placed his eye to a keyhole and saw the nude waxen figure of a man stretched out upon a white table. The voice, low-pitched and vibrant, mumbled indistinguishable words, neither rising nor falling. He craned his neck and squinted to see the man who was talking, but he could not locate him. Above the naked figure was suspended a huge glass container filled with a blood-red liquid from which a white rubber tube dangled. He crouched closer to the door and saw the tip end of a black object lined with pink satin. A coffin, he breathed. This is an undertaker's establishment . . . A fine-spun lace of ice covered his body and he shuddered. A throaty chuckle sounded in the depths of the yellow room.

He turned to leave. Three steps down it occurred to him that a light switch should be nearby; he felt along the wall, found an electric button, pressed it, and a blinding glare smote his pupils so hard that he was sightless, defenseless. His pupils contracted and he wrinkled his nostrils at a peculiar odor. At once he knew that he had been dimly aware of this odor in the darkness, but the light had brought it sharply to his attention. Some kind of stuff they use to embalm, he thought. He went down the steps and saw piles of lumber, coffins, and a long workbench. In one corner was a tool chest. Yes, he could use tools, could tunnel through walls with them. He lifted the lid of the chest and saw nails, a hammer, a crowbar, a screwdriver, a light bulb, and a long length of electric wire. Good! He would lug these back to his cave.

He was about to hoist the chest to his shoulders when he discovered a door behind the furnace. Where did it lead? He tried to open it and found it securely bolted. Using the crow-bar so as to make no sound, he pried the door open; it swung on creaking hinges, outward. Fresh air came to his face and he caught the faint roar of faraway sound. Easy now, he told himself. He widened the door and a lump of coal rattled toward him. A coalbin . . . Evidently the door led into another basement. The roaring noise was louder now, but he could not identify it. Where was he? He groped slowly over the coal pile, then ranged in darkness over a gritty floor. The roaring noise seemed to come from above him, then below. His fingers followed a wall until he touched a wooden ridge. A door, he breathed.

The noise died to a low pitch; he felt his skin prickle. It seemed that he was   25
playing a game with an unseen person whose intelligence outstripped his. He
put his ear to the flat surface of the door. Yes, voices . . . Was this a prize fight
stadium? The sound of the voices came near and sharp, but he could not tell if
they were joyous or despairing. He twisted the knob until he heard a soft click
and felt the springy weight of the door swinging toward him. He was afraid to
open it, yet captured by curiosity and wonder. He jerked the door wide and saw
on the far side of the basement a furnace glowing red. Ten feet away was still another door, half ajar. He crossed and peered through the door into an empty,
high-ceilinged corridor that terminated in a dark complex of shadow. The
belling voices rolled about him and his eagerness mounted. He stepped into the
corridor and the voices swelled louder. He crept on and came to a narrow stairway leading circularly upward; there was no question but that he was going to
ascend those stairs.

Mounting the spiraled staircase, he heard the voices roll in a steady wave,
then leap to crescendo, only to die away, but always remaining audible. Ahead of
him glowed red letters: E—X—I—T. At the top of the steps he paused in front of
a black curtain that fluttered uncertainly. He parted the folds and looked into a
convex depth that gleamed with clusters of shimmering lights. Sprawling below
him was a stretch of human faces, tilted upward, chanting, whistling, screaming,
laughing. Dangling before the faces, high upon a screen of silver, were jerking
shadows. A movie, he said with slow laughter breaking from his lips.

He stood in a box in the reserved section of a movie house and the impulse
he had had to tell the people in the church to stop their singing seized him.
These people were laughing at their lives, he thought with amazement. They
were shouting and yelling at the animated shadows of themselves. His compassion fired his imagination and he stepped out of the box, walked out upon thin
air, walked on down to the audience; and, hovering in the air just above them,
he stretched out his hand to touch them . . . His tension snapped and he found
himself back in the box, looking down into the sea of faces. No; it could not be
done; he could not awaken them. He sighed. Yes, these people were children,
sleeping in their living, awake in their dying.

He turned away, parted the black curtain, and looked out. He saw no one.
He started down the white stone steps and when he reached the bottom he saw a
man in trim blue uniform coming toward him. So used had he become to being
underground that he thought that he could walk past the man, as though he
were a ghost. But the man stopped. And he stopped.

"Looking for the men's room, sir?" the man asked, and, without waiting for
an answer, he turned and pointed. "This way, sir. The first door to your right."

He watched the man turn and walk up the steps and go out of sight. Then   30
he laughed. What a funny fellow! He went back to the basement and stood in
the red darkness, watching the glowing embers in the furnace. He went to the
sink and turned the faucet and the water flowed in a smooth silent stream that
looked like a spout of blood. He brushed the mad image from his mind and began to wash his hands leisurely, looking about for the usual bar of soap. He found
one and rubbed it in his palms until a rich lather bloomed in his cupped fingers,
like a scarlet sponge. He scrubbed and rinsed his hands meticulously, then
hunted for a towel; there was none. He shut off the water, pulled off his shirt,

dried his hands on it; when he put it on again he was grateful for the cool dampness that came to his skin.

Yes, he was thirsty; he turned on the faucet again, bowled his fingers and
when the water bubbled over the brim of his cupped palms, he drank in long,
slow swallows. His bladder grew tight; he shut off the water, faced the wall, bent
his head, and watched a red stream strike the floor. His nostrils wrinkled against
acrid wisps of vapor; though he had tramped in the waters of the sewer, he
stepped back from the wall so that his shoes, wet with sewer slime, would not
touch his urine.

He heard footsteps and crawled quickly into the coalbin. Lumps rattled
noisily. The footsteps came into the basement and stopped. Who was it? Had
someone heard him and come down to investigate? He waited, crouching, sweating. For a long time there was silence, then he heard the clang of metal and a
brighter glow lit the room. Somebody's tending the furnace, he thought. Footsteps came closer and he stiffened. Looming before him was a white face lined
with coal dust, the face of an old man with watery blue eyes. Highlights spotted
his gaunt cheekbones, and he held a huge shovel. There was a screechy scrape of
metal against stone, and the old man lifted a shovelful of coal and went from
sight.

The room dimmed momentarily, then a yellow glare came as coal flared at
the furnace door. Six times the old man came to the bin and went to the furnace
with shovels of coal, but not once did he lift his eyes. Finally he dropped the
shovel, mopped his face with a dirty handkerchief, and sighed: "Wheeew!" He
turned slowly and trudged out of the basement, his footsteps dying away.

He stood, and lumps of coal clattered down the pile. He stepped from the
bin and was startled to see the shadowy outline of an electric bulb hanging above
his head. Why had not the old man turned it on? Oh, yes . . . He understood.
The old man had worked here for so long that he had no need for light; he had
learned a way of seeing in his dark world, like those sightless worms that inch
along underground by a sense of touch.

His eyes fell upon a lunch pail and he was afraid to hope that it was full. He   35
picked it up; it was heavy. He opened it. *Sandwiches!* He looked guiltily around;
he was alone. He searched farther and found a folder of matches and a half-
empty tin of tobacco; he put them eagerly into his pocket and clicked off the
light. With the lunch pail under his arm, he went through the door, groped over
the pile of coal, and stood again in the lighted basement of the undertaking establishment. I've got to get those tools, he told himself. And turn off that light.
He tiptoed back up the steps and switched off the light; the invisible voice still
droned on behind the door. He crept down and, seeing with his fingers, opened
the lunch pail and tore off a piece of paper bag and brought out the tin and
spilled grains of tobacco into the makeshift concave. He rolled it and wet it with
spittle, then inserted one end into his mouth and lit it: he sucked smoke that bit
his lungs. The nicotine reached his brain, went out along his arms to his finger
tips, down to his stomach, and over all the tired nerves of his body.

He carted the tools to the hole he had made in the wall. Would the noise of
the falling chest betray him? But he would have to take a chance; he had to have
those tools. He lifted the chest and shoved it; it hit the dirt on the other side of
the wall with a loud clatter. He waited, listening; nothing happened. Head first,
he slithered through and stood in the cave. He grinned, filled with a cunning

idea. Yes, he would now go back into the basement of the undertaking establishment and crouch behind the coal pile and dig another hole. Sure! Fumbling, he
opened the tool chest and extracted a crowbar, a screwdriver, and a hammer; he
fastened them securely about his person.

With another lumpish cigarette in his flexed lips, he crawled back through
the hole and over the coal pile and sat, facing the brick wall. He jabbed with the
crowbar and the cement sheered away; quicker than he thought, a brick came
loose. He worked an hour; the other bricks did not come easily. He sighed, weak
from effort. I ought to rest a little, he thought. I'm hungry. He felt his way back
to the cave and stumbled along the wall till he came to the tool chest. He sat
upon it, opened the lunch pail, and took out two thick sandwiches. He smelled
them. Pork chops . . . His mouth watered. He closed his eyes and devoured a
sandwich, savoring the smooth rye bread and juicy meat. He ate rapidly, gulping
down lumpy mouthfuls that made him long for water. He ate the other sandwich
and found an apple and gobbled that up too, sucking the core till the last trace of
flavor was drained from it. Then, like a dog, he ground the meat bones with his
teeth, enjoying the salty, tangy marrow. He finished and stretched out full length
on the ground and went to sleep.

His body was washed by cold water that gradually turned warm and he was
buoyed upon a stream and swept out to sea where waves rolled gently and suddenly he found himself walking upon the water how strange and delightful to
walk upon the water and he came upon a nude woman holding a nude baby in
her arms and the woman was sinking into the water holding the baby above
her head and screaming *help* and he ran over the water to the woman and he
reached her just before she went down and he took the baby from her hands
and stood watching the breaking bubbles where the woman sank and he called
lady and still no answer yes dive down there and rescue that woman but he
could not take this baby with him and he stooped and laid the baby tenderly
upon the surface of the water expecting it to sink but it floated and he leaped
into the water and held his breath and strained his eyes to see through the
gloomy volume of water but there was no woman and he opened his mouth
and called *lady* and the water bubbled and his chest ached and his arms were
tired but he could not see the woman and he called again *lady lady* and his feet
touched sand at the bottom of the sea and his chest felt as though it would
burst and he bent his knees and propelled himself upward and water rushed
past him and his head bobbed out and he breathed deeply and looked around
where was the baby the baby was gone and he rushed over the water looking
for the baby calling *where is it* and the empty sky and sea threw back his voice
where is it and he began to doubt that he could stand upon the water and then
he was sinking and as he struggled the water rushed him downward spinning
dizzily and he opened his mouth to call for help and water surged into his lungs
and he choked.

He groaned and leaped erect in the dark, his eyes wide. The images of terror
that thronged his brain would not let him sleep. He rose, made sure that the
tools were hitched to his belt, and groped his way to the coal pile and found the
rectangular gap from which he had taken the bricks. He took out the crowbar
and hacked. Then dread paralyzed him. How long had he slept? Was it day or
night now? He had to be careful. Someone might hear him if it were day. He
hewed softly for hours at the cement, working silently. Faintly quivering in the

air above him was the dim sound of yelling voices Crazy people, he muttered. They're still there in that movie . . .

Having rested, he found the digging much easier. He soon had a dozen   40 bricks out. His spirits rose. He took out another brick and his fingers fluttered in space. Good! What lay ahead of him? Another basement? He made the hole larger, climbed through, walked over an uneven floor and felt a metal surface. He lighted a match and saw that he was standing behind a furnace in a basement; before him, on the far side of the room, was a door. He crossed and opened it; it was full of odds and ends. Daylight spilled from a window above his head.

Then he was aware of a soft, continuous tapping. What was it? A clock? No, it was louder than a clock and more irregular. He placed an old empty box beneath the window, stood upon it, and looked into an areaway. He eased the window up and crawled through; the sound of the tapping came clearly now. He glanced about; he was alone. Then he looked upward at a series of window ledges. The tapping identified itself. That's a typewriter, he said to himself. It seemed to be coming from just above. He grasped the ridges of a rain pipe and lifted himself upward; through a half-inch opening of window he saw a doorknob about three feet away. No, it was not a doorknob; it was a small circular disk made of stainless steel with many fine markings upon it. He held his breath; an eerie white hand, seemingly detached from its arm, touched the metal knob and whirled it, first to the left, then to the right. It's a safe! . . . Suddenly he could see the dial no more; a huge metal door swung slowly toward him and he was looking into a safe filled with green wads of paper money, rows of coins wrapped in brown paper, and glass jars and boxes of various sizes. His heart quickened. Good Lord! The white hand went in and out of the safe, taking wads of bills and cylinders of coins. The hand vanished and he heard the muffled click of the big door as it closed. Only the steel dial was visible now. The typewriter still tapped in his ears, but he could not see it. He blinked, wondering if what he had seen was real. There was more money in that safe than he had seen in all his life.

As he clung to the rain pipe, a daring idea came to him and he pulled the screwdriver from his belt. If the white hand twirled that dial again, he would be able to see how far to left and right it spun and he would have the combination! His blood tingled. I can scratch the numbers right here, he thought. Holding the pipe with one hand, he made the sharp edge of the screwdriver bite into the brick wall. Yes, he could do it. Now, he was set. Now, he had a reason for staying here in the underground. He waited for a long time, but the white hand did not return. Goddamn! Had he been more alert, he could have counted the twirls and he would have had the combination. He got down and stood in the areaway, sunk in reflection.

How could he get into that room? He climbed back into the basement and saw wooden steps leading upward. Was that the room where the safe stood? Fearing that the dial was now being twirled, he clambered through the window, hoisted himself up the rain pipe, and peered; he saw only the naked gleam of the steel dial. He got down and doubled his fists. Well, he would explore the basement. He returned to the basement room and mounted the steps to the door and squinted through the keyhole; all was dark, but the tapping was still somewhere near, still faint and directionless. He pushed the door in; along one wall of a room was a table piled with radios and electrical equipment. A radio shop, he muttered.

Well, he could rig up a radio in his cave. He found a sack, slid the radio into it, and slung it across his back. Closing the door, he went down the steps and stood again in the basement, disappointed. He had not solved the problem of the steel dial and he was irked. He set the radio on the floor and again hoisted himself through the window and up the rain pipe and squinted; the metal door was swinging shut. Goddamn! He's worked the combination again. If I had been patient, I'd have had it! How could he get into that room? He *had* to get into it. He could jimmy the window, but it would be much better if he could get in without any traces. To the right of him, he calculated, should be the basement of the building that held the safe; therefore, if he dug a hole right *here*, he ought to reach his goal.

He began a quiet scraping; it was hard work, for the bricks were not damp. He eventually got one out and lowered it softly to the floor. He had to be careful; perhaps people were beyond this wall. He extracted a second layer of brick and found still another. He gritted his teeth, ready to quit. I'll dig one more, he resolved. When the next brick came out he felt air blowing into his face. He waited to be challenged, but nothing happened.

He enlarged the hole and pulled himself through and stood in quiet darkness. He scratched a match to flame and saw steps; he mounted and peered through a keyhole: Darkness . . . He strained to hear the typewriter, but there was only silence. Maybe the office had closed? He twisted the knob and swung the door in; a frigid blast made him shiver. In the shadows before him were halves and quarters of hogs and lambs and steers hanging from metal hooks on the low ceiling, red meat encased in folds of cold white fat. Fronting him was frostcoated glass from behind which came indistinguishable sounds. The odor of fresh raw meat sickened him and he backed away. A meat market, he whispered.

He ducked his head, suddenly blinded by light. He narrowed his eyes; the red-white rows of meat were drenched in yellow glare. A man wearing a crimson-spotted jacket came in and took down a bloody meat cleaver. He eased the door to, holding it ajar just enough to watch the man, hoping that the darkness in which he stood would keep him from being seen. The man took down a hunk of steer and placed it upon a bloody wooden block and bent forward and whacked with the cleaver. The man's face was hard, square, grim; a jet of mustache smudged his upper lip and a glistening cowlick of hair fell over his left eye. Each time he lifted the cleaver and brought it down upon the meat, he let out a short, deep-chested grunt. After he had cut the meat, he wiped blood off the wooden block with a sticky wad of gunny sack and hung the cleaver upon a hook. His face was proud as he placed the chunk of meat in the crook of his elbow and left.

The door slammed and the light went off; once more he stood in shadow. His tension ebbed. From behind the frosted glass he heard the man's voice: "Forty-eight cents a pound, ma'am." He shuddered, feeling that there was something he had to do. But what? He stared fixedly at the cleaver, then he sneezed and was terrified for fear that the man had heard him. But the door did not open. He took down the cleaver and examined the sharp edge smeared with cold blood. Behind the ice-coated glass a cash register rang with a vibrating, musical tinkle.

Absent-mindedly holding the meat cleaver, he rubbed the glass with his thumb and cleared a spot that enabled him to see into the front of the store. The shop was empty, save for the man who was now putting on his hat and coat. Beyond the front window a wan sun shone in the streets; people passed and now and then a fragment of laughter or the whir of a speeding auto came to him. He peered closer and saw on the right counter of the shop a mosquito netting covering pears, grapes, lemons, oranges, bananas, peaches, and plums. His stomach contracted.

The man clicked out the light and he gritted his teeth, muttering, Don't   50
lock the icebox door . . . The man went through the door of the shop and locked it from the outside. Thank God! Now, he would eat some more! He waited, trembling. The sun died and its rays lingered on in the sky, turning the streets to dusk. He opened the door and stepped inside the shop. In reverse letters across the front window was: NICK'S FRUITS AND MEATS. He laughed, picked up a soft ripe yellow pear and bit into it; juice squirted; his mouth ached as his saliva glands reacted to the acid of the fruit. He ate three pears, gobbled six bananas, and made away with several oranges, taking a bite out of their tops and holding them to his lips and squeezing them as he hungrily sucked the juice.

He found a faucet, turned it on, laid the cleaver aside, pursed his lips under the stream until his stomach felt about to burst. He straightened and belched, feeling satisfied for the first time since he had been underground. He sat upon the floor, rolled and lit a cigarette, his bloodshot eyes squinting against the film of drifting smoke. He watched a patch of sky turn red, then purple; night fell and he lit another cigarette, brooding. Some part of him was trying to remember the world he had left, and another part of him did not want to remember it. Sprawling before him in his mind was his wife, Mrs. Wooten for whom he worked, the three policemen who had picked him up . . . He possessed them now more completely than he had ever possessed them when he had lived aboveground. How this had come about he could not say, but he had no desire to go back to them. He laughed, crushed the cigarette, and stood up.

He went to the front door and gazed out. Emotionally he hovered between the world aboveground and the world underground. He longed to go out, but sober judgment urged him to remain here. Then impulsively he pried the lock loose with one swift twist of the crowbar; the door swung outward. Through the twilight he saw a white man and a white woman coming toward him. He held himself tense, waiting for them to pass; but they came directly to the door and confronted him.

"I want to buy a pound of grapes," the woman said.

Terrified, he stepped back into the store. The white man stood to one side and the woman entered.

"Give me a pound of dark ones," the woman said.   55

The white man came slowly forward, blinking his eyes.

"Where's Nick?" the man asked.

"Were you just closing?" the woman asked.

"Yes, ma'am," he mumbled. For a second he did not breathe, then he mumbled again: "Yes, ma'am."

"I'm sorry," the woman said.   60

The street lamps came on, lighting the store somewhat. Ought he run? But that would raise an alarm. He moved slowly, dreamily, to a counter and lifted up a bunch of grapes and showed them to the woman.

"Fine," the woman said. "But isn't that more than a pound?"

He did not answer. The man was staring at him intently.

"Put them in a bag for me," the woman said, fumbling with her purse.

"Yes, ma'am." 65

He saw a pile of paper bags under a narrow ledge; he opened one and put the grapes in.

"Thanks," the woman said, taking the bag and placing a dime in his dark palm.

"Where's Nick?" the man asked again. "At supper?"

"Sir? Yes, sir," he breathed.

They left the store and he stood trembling in the doorway. When they were 70 out of sight, he burst out laughing and crying. A trolley car rolled noisily past and he controlled himself quickly. He flung the dime to the pavement with a gesture of contempt and stepped into the warm night air. A few shy stars trembled above him. The look of things was beautiful, yet he felt a lurking threat. He went to an unattended newsstand and looked at a stack of papers. He saw a headline: HUNT NEGRO FOR MURDER.

He felt that someone had slipped up on him from behind and was stripping off his clothes; he looked about wildly, went quickly back into the store, picked up the meat cleaver where he had left it near the sink, then made his way through the icebox to the basement. He stood for a long time, breathing heavily. They know I didn't do anything, he muttered. But how could he prove it? He had signed a confession. Though innocent, he felt guilty, condemned. He struck a match and held it near the steel blade, fascinated and repelled by the dried blotches of blood. Then his fingers gripped the handle of the cleaver with all the strength of his body, he wanted to fling the cleaver from him, but he could not. The match flame wavered and fled; he struggled through the hole and put the cleaver in the sack with the radio. He was determined to keep it, for what purpose he did not know.

He was about to leave when he remembered the safe. Where was it? He wanted to give up, but felt that he ought to make one more try. Opposite the last hole he had dug, he tunneled again, plying the crowbar. Once he was so exhausted that he lay on the concrete floor and panted. Finally he made another hole. He wriggled through and his nostrils filled with the fresh smell of coal. He struck a match; yes, the usual steps led upward. He tiptoed to a door and eased it open. A fair-haired white girl stood in front of a steel cabinet, her blue eyes wide upon him. She turned chalky and gave a high-pitched scream. He bounded down the steps and raced to his hole and clambered through, replacing the bricks with nervous haste. He paused, hearing loud voices.

"What's the matter, Alice?"

"A man . . . ."

"What man? Where?" 75

"A man was at that door . . . ."

"Oh, nonsense!"

"He was looking at me through the door!"

"Aw, you're dreaming."

"I *did* see a man!" 80

The girl was crying now.

"There's nobody here."

Another man's voice sounded.

"What is it, Bob?"

"Alice says she saw a man in here, in that door!"   85

"Let's take a look."

He waited, poised for flight. Footsteps descended the stairs.

"There's nobody down here."

"The window's locked."

"And there's no door."   90

"You ought to fire that dame."

"Oh, I don't know. Women are that way."

"She's too hysterical."

The men laughed. Footsteps sounded again on the stairs. A door slammed. He sighed, relieved that he had escaped. But he had not done what he had set out to do; his glimpse of the room had been too brief to determine if the safe was there. He had to know. Boldly he groped through the hole once more; he reached the steps and pulled off his shoes and tiptoed up and peered through the keyhole. His head accidentally touched the door and it swung silently in a fraction of an inch; he saw the girl bent over the cabinet, her back to him. Beyond her was the safe. He crept back down the steps, thinking exultingly: I found it!

Now he had to get the combination. Even if the window in the areaway was   95 locked and bolted, he could gain entrance when the office closed. He scoured through the holes he had dug and stood again in the basement where he had left the radio and the cleaver. Again he crawled out of the window and lifted himself up the rain pipe and peered. The steel dial showed lonely and bright, reflecting the yellow glow of an unseen light. Resigned to a long wait, he sat and leaned against a wall. From far off came the faint sounds of life aboveground; once he looked with a baffled expression at the dark sky. Frequently he rose and climbed the pipe to see the white hand spin the dial, but nothing happened. He bit his lip with impatience. It was not the money that was luring him, but the mere fact that he could get it with impunity. Was the hand now twirling the dial? He rose and looked, but the white hand was not in sight.

Perhaps it would be better to watch continuously? Yes; he clung to the pipe and watched the dial until his eyes thickened with tears. Exhausted, he stood again in the areaway. He heard a door being shut and he clawed up the pipe and looked. He jerked tense as a vague figure passed in front of him. He stared un-blinkingly, hugging the pipe with one hand and holding the screwdriver with the other, ready to etch the combination upon the wall. His ears caught: *Dong . . . Dong . . . Dong . . . Dong . . . Dong . . . Dong . . . Dong . . .* Seven o'clock, he whispered, Maybe they were closing now? What kind of a store would be open as late as this? he wondered. Did anyone live in the rear? Was there a night watch-man? Perhaps the safe was *already* locked for the night! Goddamn! While he had been eating in that shop, they had locked up everything . . . Then, just as he was about to give up, the white hand touched the dial and turned it once to the right and stopped at six. With quivering fingers, he etched 1—R—6 upon the brick wall with the tip of the screwdriver. The hand twirled the dial twice to the left and stopped at two, and he engraved 2—L—2 upon the wall. The dial was spun four times to the right and stopped at six again; he wrote 4—R—6. The dial ro-tated three times to the left and was centered straight up and down; he wrote 3—L—0. The door swung open and again he saw the piles of green money and the rows of wrapped coins. I got it, he said grimly.

Then he was stone still, astonished. There were two hands now. A right hand lifted a wad of green bills and deftly slipped it up the sleeve of a left arm. The hands trembled; again the right hand slipped a packet of bills up the left sleeve. He's stealing, he said to himself. He grew indignant, as if the money belonged to him. Though *he* had planned to steal the money, he despised and pitied the man. He felt that his stealing the money and the man's stealing were two entirely different things. He wanted to steal the money merely for the sensation involved in getting it, and he had no intention whatever of spending a penny of it; but he knew that the man who was now stealing it was going to spend it, perhaps for pleasure. The huge steel door closed with a soft click.

Though angry, he was somewhat satisfied. The office would close soon. I'll clean the place out, he mused. He imagined the entire office staff cringing with fear; the police would question everyone for a crime they had not committed, just as they had questioned him. And they would have no idea of how the money had been stolen until they discovered the holes he had tunneled in the walls of the basements. He lowered himself and laughed mischievously, with the abandoned glee of an adolescent.

He flattened himself against the wall as the window above him closed with rasping sound. He looked; somebody was bolting the window securely with a metal screen. That won't help you, he snickered to himself. He clung to the rain pipe until the yellow light in the office went out. He went back into the basement, picked up the sack containing the radio and cleaver, and crawled through the two holes he had dug and groped his way into the basement of the building that held the safe. He moved in slow motion, breathing softly. Be careful now, he told himself. There might be a night watchman . . . In his memory was the combination written in bold white characters as upon a blackboard. Eel-like he squeezed through the last hole and crept up the steps and put his hand on the knob and pushed the door in about three inches. Then his courage ebbed; his imagination wove dangers for him.

Perhaps the night watchman was waiting in there, ready to shoot. He dangled his cap on a forefinger and poked it past the jamb of the door. If anyone fired, they would hit his cap; but nothing happened. He widened the door, holding the crowbar high above his head, ready to beat off an assailant. He stood like that for five minutes; the rumble of a streetcar brought him to himself. He entered the room. Moonlight floated in from a side window. He confronted the safe, then checked himself. Better take a look around first . . . He stepped about and found a closed door. Was the night watchman in there? He opened it and saw a washbowl, a faucet, and a commode. To the left was still another door that opened into a huge dark room that seemed empty; on the far side of that room he made out the shadow of still another door. Nobody's here, he told himself.

He turned back to the safe and fingered the dial; it spun with ease. He laughed and twirled it just for fun. Get to work, he told himself. He turned the dial to the figures he saw on the blackboard of his memory; it was so easy that he felt that the safe had not been locked at all. The heavy door eased loose and he caught hold of the handle and pulled hard, but the door swung open with a slow momentum of its own. Breathless, he gaped at wads of green bills, rows of wrapped coins, curious glass jars full of white pellets, and many oblong green metal boxes. He glanced guiltily over his shoulder; it seemed impossible that someone should not call to him to stop.

100

They'll be surprised in the morning, he thought. He opened the top of the sack and lifted a wad of compactly tied bills; the money was crisp and new. He admired the smooth, clean-cut edges. The fellows in Washington sure know how to make this stuff, he mused. He rubbed the money with his fingers, as though expecting it to reveal hidden qualities. He lifted the wad to his nose and smelled the fresh odor of ink. Just like any other paper, he mumbled. He dropped the wad into the sack and picked up another. Holding the bag, he thought and laughed.

There was in him no sense of possessiveness; he was intrigued with the form and color of the money, with the manifold reactions which he knew that men aboveground held toward it. The sack was one-third full when it occurred to him to examine the denominations of the bills; without realizing it, he had put many wads of one-dollar bills into the sack. Aw, nuts, he said in disgust. Take the big ones . . . He dumped the one-dollar bills onto the floor and swept all the hundred-dollars bills he could find into the sack, then he raked in rolls of coins with crooked fingers.

He walked to a desk upon which sat a typewriter, the same machine which the blond girl had used. He was fascinated by it; never in his life had he used one of them. It was a queer instrument of business, something beyond the rim of his life. Whenever he had been in an office where a girl was typing, he had almost always spoken in whispers. Remembering vaguely what he had seen other do, he inserted a sheet of paper into the machine; it went in lopsided and he did not know how to straighten it. Spelling in a soft diffident voice, he pecked out his name on the keys: *freddaniels*. He looked at it and laughed. He would learn to type correctly one of these days.

Yes, he would take the typewriter too. He lifted the machine and placed it 105 atop the bulk of money in the sack. He did not feel that he was stealing, for the cleaver, the radio, the money, and the typewriter were all on the same level of value, all meant the same thing to him. They were the serious toys of the men who lived in the dead world of sunshine and rain he had left, the world that had condemned him, branded him guilty.

But what kind of a place is this? He wondered. What was in that dark room to his rear? He felt for his matches and found that he had only one left. He leaned the sack against the safe and groped forward into the room, encountering smooth, metallic objects that felt like machines. Baffled, he touched a wall and tried vainly to locate an electric switch. Well, he *had* to strike his last match. He knelt and struck it, cupping the flame near the floor with his palms. The place seemed to be a factory, with benches and tables. There were bulbs with green shades spaced about the tables; he turned on a light and twisted it low so that the glare was limited. He saw a half-filled packet of cigarettes and appropriated it. There were stools at the benches and he concluded that men worked here at some trade. He wandered and found a few half-used folders of matches. If only he could find more cigarettes! But there were none.

But what kind of a place was this? On a bench he saw a pad of paper captioned: PEER'S—MANUFACTURING JEWELERS. His lips formed an "O," then he snapped off the light and ran back to the safe and lifted one of the glass jars and stared at the tiny white pellets. Gingerly he picked up one and found that it was wrapped in tissue paper. He peeled the paper and saw a glittering stone that looked like glass, glinting white and blue sparks. Diamonds, he breathed.

Roughly he tore the paper from the pellets and soon his palm quivered with precious fire. Trembling, he took all four glass jars from the safe and put them into the sack. He grabbed one of the metal boxes, shook it, and heard a tinny rattle. He pried off the lid with the screwdriver. Rings! Hundreds of them . . . Were they worth anything? He scooped up a handful and jets of fire shot fitfully from the stones. These are diamonds too, he said. He pried open another box. Watches! A chorus of soft, metallic ticking filled his ears. For a moment he could not move, then he dumped all the boxes into the sack.

He shut the safe door, then stood looking around, anxious not to overlook anything. Oh! He had seen a door in the room where the machines were. What was in there? More valuables? He re-entered the room, crossed the floor, and stood undecided before the door. He finally caught hold of the knob and pushed the door in; the room beyond was dark. He advanced cautiously inside and ran his fingers along the wall for the usual switch, then he was stark still. *Something had moved in the room!* What was it? Ought he to creep out, taking the rings and diamonds and money? Why risk what he already had? He waited and the ensuing silence gave him confidence to explore further. Dare he strike a match? Would not a match flame make him a good target? He tensed again as he heard a faint sigh; he was now convinced that there was something alive near him, something that lived and breathed. On tip-toe he felt slowly along the wall, hoping that he would not collide with anything. Luck was with him; he found the light switch.

No; don't turn the light on . . . Then suddenly he realized that he did not know in what direction the door was. Goddamn! He had to turn the light on or strike a match. He fingered the switch for a long time, then thought of an idea. He knelt upon the floor, reached his arm up to the switch and flicked the button, hoping that if anyone shot, the bullet would go above his head. The moment the light came on he narrowed his eyes to see quickly. He sucked in his breath and his body gave a violent twitch and was still. In front of him, so close that it made him want to bound up and scream, was a human face.

He was afraid to move lest he touch the man. If the man had opened his eyes at that moment, there was no telling what he might have done. The man—long and rawboned—was stretched out on his back upon a little cot, sleeping in his clothes, his head cushioned by a dirty pillow; his face, clouded by a dark stubble of beard, looked straight up to the ceiling. The man sighed, and he grew tense to defend himself; the man mumbled and turned his face away from the light. I've got to turn off that light, he thought. Just as he was about to rise, he saw a gun and cartridge belt on the floor at the man's side. Yes, he would take the gun and cartridge belt, not to use them, but just to keep them, as one takes a memento from a country fair. He picked them up and was about to click off the light when his eyes fell upon a photograph perched upon a chair near the man's head; it was the picture of a woman, smiling, shown against a background of open fields; at the woman's side were two young children, a boy and a girl. He smiled indulgently; he could send a bullet into that man's brain and time would be over for him . . .

He clicked off the light and crept silently back into the room where the safe stood; he fastened the cartridge belt about him and adjusted the holster at his right hip. He strutted about the room on tiptoe, lolling his head nonchalantly, then paused abruptly pulled the gun, and pointed it with grim face toward an imaginary foe. "Boom!" he whispered fiercely. Then he bent forward with silent laughter. That's just like they do it in the movies, he said.

He contemplated his loot for a long time, then got a towel from the washroom and tied the sack securely. When he looked up he was momentarily frightened by his shadow looming on the wall before him. He lifted the sack, dragged it down the basement steps, lugged it across the basement, gasping for breath. After he had struggled through the hole, he clumsily replaced the bricks, then tussled with the sack until he got it to the cave. He stood in the dark, wet with sweat, brooding about the diamonds, the rings, the watches, the money; he remembered the singing in the church, the people yelling in the movie, the dead baby, the nude man stretched out upon the white table . . . He saw these items hovering before his eyes and felt that some dim meaning linked them together, that some magical relationship made them kin. He stared with vacant eyes, convinced that all of these images, with their tongueless reality, were striving to tell him something . . .

Later, seeing with his fingers, he untied the sack and set each item neatly upon the dirt floor. Exploring, he took the bulb, the socket, and the wire out of the tool chest; he was elated to find a double socket at one end of the wire. He crammed the stuff into his pockets and hoisted himself upon the rusty pipes and squinted into the church; it was dim and empty. Somewhere in this wall were live electric wires; but where? He lowered himself, groped and tapped the wall with the butt of the screwdriver, listening vainly for hollow sounds. I'll just take a chance and dig, he said.

For an hour he tried to dislodge a brick, and when he struck a match, he 115 found that he had dug a depth of only an inch! No use in digging here, he sighed. By the flickering light of a match, he looked upward, then lowered his eyes, only to glance up again, startled. Directly above his head, beyond the pipes, was a wealth of electric wiring. I'll be damned, he snickered.

He got an old dull knife from the chest and, seeing again with his fingers, separated the two strands of wire and cut away the insulation. Twice he received a slight shock. He scraped the wiring clean and managed to join the two twin ends, then screwed in the bulb. The sudden illumination blinded him and he shut his lids to kill the pain in his eyeballs. I've got that much done, he thought jubilantly.

He placed the bulb on the dirt floor and the light cast a blatant glare on the bleak clay walls. Next he plugged one end of the wire that dangled from the radio into the light socket and bent down and switched on the button; almost at once there was the harsh sound of static, but no words or music. Why won't it work? he wondered. Had he damaged the mechanism in any way? Maybe it needed grounding? Yes . . . He rummaged in the tool chest and found another length of wire, fastened it to the ground of the radio, and then tied the opposite end to a pipe. Rising and growing distinct, a slow strain of music entranced him with its measured sound. He sat upon the chest, deliriously happy.

Later he searched again in the chest and found a half-gallon can of glue; he opened it and smelled a sharp odor. Then he recalled that he had not even looked at the money. He took a wad of green bills and weighed it in his palm, then broke the seal and held one of the bills up to the light and studied it closely. *The United States of America will pay to the bearer on demand one hundred dollars,* he read in slow speech; then: *This note is legal tender for all debts, public and private. . . .* He broke into a musing laugh, feeling that he was reading of the doings of people who lived on some far-off planet. He turned the bill over and saw on the other side of it a delicately beautiful building gleaming with paint and set amidst green grass. He had no desire whatever to count the money; it was what it stood for—the various currents of life swirling aboveground—that captivated him. Next he opened the rolls of coins and let them slide from their paper wrappings to the ground; the bright, new gleaming pennies and nickles and dimes piled high at his feet, a glowing mound of shimmering copper and silver. He sifted them through his fingers, listening to their tinkle as they struck the conical heap.

Oh, yes! He had forgotten. He would now write his name on the typewriter. He inserted a piece of paper and poised his fingers to write. But what was his name? He stared, trying to remember. He stood and glared about the dirt cave, his name on the tip of his lips. But it would not come to him. Why was he here? Yes, he had been running away from the police. But why? His mind was blank. He bit his lips and sat again, feeling a vague terror. But why worry? He laughed, then pecked slowly: *itwasalonghotday.* He was determined to type the sentence without making any mistakes. How did one make capital letters? He experimented and luckily discovered how to lock the machine for capital letters and then shift it back to lower case. Next he discovered how to make spaces, then he wrote neatly and correctly: *It was a long hot day.* Just why he selected that sentence he did not know; it was merely the ritual of performing the thing that appealed to him. He took the sheet out of the machine and looked around with stiff neck and hard eyes and spoke to an imaginary person:

"Yes, I'll have the contracts ready tomorrow."

120

He laughed. That's just the way they talk, he said. He grew weary of the game and pushed the machine aside. His eyes fell upon the can of glue, and a mischievous idea bloomed in him, filling him with nervous eagerness. He leaped up and opened the can of glue, then broke the seals on all the wads of money. I'm going to have some wallpaper, he said with a luxurious, physical laugh that made him bend at the knees. He took the towel with which he had tied the sack and balled it into a swab and dipped it into the can of glue and dabbed glue onto the wall; then he pasted one green bill by the side of another. He stepped back and cocked his head. Jesus! That's funny . . . He slapped his thighs and guffawed. He had triumphed over the world aboveground! He was free! If only people could see this! He wanted to run from this cave and yell his discovery to the world.

He swabbed all the dirt walls of the cave and pasted them with green bills; when he had finished the walls blazed with a yellow-green fire. Yes, this room would be his hide-out; between him and the world that had branded him guilty would stand this mocking symbol. He had not stolen the money; he had simply picked it up, just as a man would pick up firewood in a forest. And that was how the world aboveground now seemed to him, a wild forest filled with death.

The walls of money finally palled on him and he looked about for new interests to feed his emotions. The cleaver! He drove a nail into the wall and hung the bloody cleaver upon it. Still another idea welled up. He pried open the metal boxes and lined them side by side on the dirt floor. He grinned at the gold and fire. From one box he lifted up a fistful of ticking gold watches and dangled them by their gleaming chains. He stared with an idle smile, then began to wind them up; he did not attempt to set them at any given hour, for there was no time for him now. He took a fistful of nails and drove them into the papered walls and hung the watches upon them, letting them swing down by their glittering chains, trembling and ticking busily against the backdrop of green with the lemon sheen of the electric light shining upon the metal watch casings, converting the golden disks into blobs of liquid yellow. Hardly had he hung up the last watch than the idea extended itself; he took more nails from the chest and drove them into the green paper and took the boxes of rings and went from nail to nail and hung up the golden bands. The blue and white sparks from the stones filled the cave with brittle laughter, as though enjoying his hilarious secret. People certainly can do some funny things, he said to himself.

He sat upon the tool chest, alternately laughing and shaking his head soberly. Hours later he became conscious of the gun sagging at his hip and he pulled it from the holster. He had seen men fire guns in movies, but somehow his life had never led him into contact with firearms. A desire to feel the sensation others felt in firing came over him. But someone might hear ... Well, what if they did? They would not know where the shot had come from. Not in their wildest notions would they think that it had come from under the streets! He tightened his fingers on the trigger; there was a deafening report and it seemed that the entire underground had caved in upon his eardrums; and in the same instant there flashed an orange-blue spurt of flame that died quickly but lingered on as a vivid after-image. He smelled the acrid stench of burnt powder filling his lungs and he dropped the gun abruptly.

The intensity of his feelings died and he hung the gun and cartridge belt   125 upon the wall. Next he lifted the jars of diamonds and turned them bottom upward, dumping the white pellets upon the ground. One by one he picked them up and peeled the tissue paper from them and piled them in a neat heap. He wiped his sweaty hands on his trousers, lit a cigarette, and commenced playing another game. He imagined that he was a rich man who lived aboveground in the obscene sunshine and he was strolling through a park of a summer morning, smiling, nodding to his neighbors, sucking an after-breakfast cigar. Many times he crossed the floor of the cave, avoiding the diamonds with his feet, yet subtly gauging his footsteps so that his shoes, wet with sewer slime, would strike the diamonds at some undetermined moment. After twenty minutes of sauntering, his right foot smashed into the heap and diamonds lay scattered in all directions, glinting with a million tiny chuckles of icy laughter. Oh, shucks, he mumbled in mock regret, intrigued by the damage he had wrought. He continued walking, ignoring the brittle fire. He felt that he had a glorious victory locked in his heart.

He stooped and flung the diamonds more evenly over the floor and they showered rich sparks, collaborating with him. He went over the floor and trampled the stones just deep enough for them to be faintly visible, as though they were set delicately in the prongs of a thousand rings. A ghostly light bathed the cave. He sat on the chest and frowned. Maybe *anything's* right, he mumbled. Yes, if the world as men had made it was right, then anything else was right, any act a man took to satisfy himself, murder, theft, torture.

He straightened with a start. What was happening to him? He was drawn to these crazy thoughts, yet they made him feel vaguely guilty. He would stretch out upon the ground, then get up; he would want to crawl again through the holes he had dug, but would restrain himself; he would think of going again up into the streets, but fear would hold him still. He stood in the middle of the cave, surrounded by green walls and a laughing floor, trembling. He was going to do something, but what? Yes, he was afraid of himself, afraid of doing some nameless thing.

To control himself, he turned on the radio. A melancholy piece of music rose. Brooding over the diamonds on the floor was like looking up into a sky full of restless stars; then the illusion turned into its opposite: he was high up in the air looking down at the twinkling lights of a sprawling city. The music ended and a man recited news events. In the same attitude in which he had contemplated the city, so now, as he heard the cultivated tone, he looked down upon land and sea as men fought, as cities were razed, as planes scattered death upon open towns, as long lines of trenches wavered and broke. He heard the names of generals and the names of mountains and the names of countries and the names and numbers of divisions that were in action on different battle fronts. He saw black smoke billowing from the stacks of warships as they neared each other over wastes of water and he heard their huge guns thunder as red-hot shells screamed across the surface of night seas. He saw hundreds of planes wheeling and droning in the sky and heard the clatter of machine guns as they fought each other and he saw planes falling in plumes of smoke and blaze of fire. He saw steel tanks rumbling across fields of ripe wheat to meet other tanks and there was a loud clang of steel as numberless tanks collided. He saw troops with fixed bayonets charging in waves against other troops who held fixed bayonets and men groaned as steel ripped into their bodies and they went down to die . . . The voice of the radio faded and he was staring at the diamonds on the floor at his feet.

He shut off the radio, fighting an irrational compulsion to act. He walked aimlessly about the cave, touching the walls with his finger tips. Suddenly he stood still. *What was the matter with him?* Yes, he knew . . . It was these walls; these crazy walls were filling him with a wild urge to climb out into the dark sunshine aboveground. Quickly he doused the light to banish the shouting walls, then sat again upon the tool chest. Yes, he was trapped. His muscles were flexed taut and sweat ran down his face. He knew now that he could not stay here and he could not go out. He lit a cigarette with shaking fingers; the match flame revealed the green-papered walls with militant distinctness; the purple on the gun barrel glinted like a threat; the meat cleaver brooded with its eloquent splotches of blood; the mound of silver and copper smoldered angrily; the diamonds winked at him from the floor; and the gold watches ticked and trembled, crowning time the king of consciousness, defining the limits of living . . . The match blaze died and he bolted from where he stood and collided brutally with the nails upon the walls. The spell was broken. He shuddered, feeling that, in spite of his fear, sooner or later he would go up into that dead sunshine and somehow say something to somebody about all this.

He sat again upon the tool chest. Fatigue weighed upon his forehead and eyes. Minutes passed and he relaxed. He dozed, but his imagination was alert. He saw himself rising, wading again in the sweeping water of the sewer; he came to a manhole and climbed out and was amazed to discover that he had hoisted himself into a room filled with armed policemen who were watching him intently. He jumped awake in the dark; he had not moved. He sighed, closed his eyes, and slept again; this time his imagination designed a scheme of protection for him. His dreaming made him feel that he was standing in a room watching over his own nude body lying stiff and cold upon a white table. At the far end of the room he saw a crowd of people huddled in a corner, afraid of his body. Though lying dead upon the table, he was standing in some mysterious way at his side, warding off the people, guarding his body, and laughing to himself as he observed the situation. They're scared of me, he thought.

He awakened with a start, leaped to his feet, and stood in the center of the black cave. It was a full minute before he moved again. He hovered between sleeping and waking, unprotected, a prey of wild fears. He could neither see nor hear. One part of him was asleep; his blood coursed slowly and his flesh was numb. On the other hand he was roused to a strange, high pitch of tension. He lifted his fingers to his face, as though about to weep. Gradually his hands lowered and he struck a match, looking about, expecting to see a door through which he could walk to safety; but there was no door, only the green walls and the moving floor. The match flame died and it was dark again.

Five minutes later he was still standing when the thought came to him that he had been asleep. Yes . . . But he was not yet fully awake; he was still queerly blind and deaf. How long had he slept? Where was he? Then suddenly he recalled the green-papered walls of the cave and in the same instant he heard loud singing coming from the church beyond the wall. Yes, they woke me up, he muttered. He hoisted himself and lay atop the bed of pipes and brought his face to the narrow slit. Men and women stood here and there between pews. A song ended and a young black girl tossed back her head and closed her eyes and broke plaintively into another hymn:

> Glad, glad, glad, oh, so glad
> I got Jesus in my soul . . .

Those few words were all she sang, but what her words did not say, her emotions said as she repeated the lines, varying the mood and tempo, making her tone express meanings which her conscious mind did not know. Another woman melted her voice with the girl's, and then an old man's voice merged with that of the two women. Soon the entire congregation was singing:

> Glad, glad, glad, oh, so glad
> I got Jesus in my soul . . .

They're wrong, he whispered in the lyric darkness. He felt that their search for a happiness they could never find made them feel that they had committed some dreadful offense which they could not remember or understand. He was now in possession of the feeling that had gripped him when he had first come into the underground. It came to him in a series of questions: Why was this sense of guilt so seemingly innate, so easy to come by, to think, to feel, so verily physical? It seemed that when one felt this guilt one was retracing in one's feelings a faint pattern designed long before; it seemed that one was always trying to remember a gigantic shock that had left a haunting impression upon one's body which one could not forget or shake off, but which had been forgotten by the conscious mind, creating in one's life a state of eternal anxiety.

He had to tear himself away from this; he got down from the pipes. His nerves were so taut that he seemed to feel his brain pushing through his skull. He felt that he had to do something, but he could not figure out what it was. Yet he knew that if he stood here until he made up his mind, he would never move. He crawled through the hole he had made in the brick wall and the exertion afforded him respite from tension. When he entered the basement of the radio store, he stopped in fear, hearing loud voices.

"Come on, boy! Tell us what you did with the radio!"

"Mister, I didn't steal the radio! I swear!"

He heard a dull thumping sound and he imagined a boy being struck violently.

"Please, mister!"

"Did you take it to a pawn shop?"   140

"No, sir! I didn't steal the radio! I got a radio at home," the boy's voice pleaded hysterically. "Go to my home and look!"

There came to his ears the sound of another blow. It was so funny that he had to clap his hand over his mouth to keep from laughing out loud. They're beating some poor boy, he whispered to himself, shaking his head. He felt a sort of distant pity for the boy and wondered if he ought to bring back the radio and leave it in the basement. No. Perhaps it was a good thing that they were beating the boy; perhaps the beating would bring to the boy's attention, for the first time in his life, the secret of his existence, the guilt that he could never get rid of.

Smiling, he scampered over a coal pile and stood again in the basement of the building where he had stolen the money and jewelry. He lifted himself into the areaway, climbed the rain pipe, and squinted through a two-inch opening of window. The guilty familiarity of what he saw made his muscles tighten. Framed before him in a bright tableau of daylight was the night watchman sitting upon the edge of a chair, stripped to the waist, his head sagging forward, his eyes red and puffy. The watchman's face and shoulders were stippled with red and black welts. Back of the watchman stood the safe, the steel door wide open showing the empty vault. Yes, they think he did it, he mused.

Footsteps sounded in the room and a man in a blue suit passed in front of him, then another, then still another. Policemen, he breathed. Yes, they were trying to make the watchman confess, just as they had once made him confess to a crime he had not done. He stared into the room, trying to recall something. Oh . . . Those were the same policemen who had beaten him, had made him sign that paper when he had been too tired and sick to care. Now, they were doing the same thing to the watchman. His heart pounded as he saw one of the policemen shake a finger into the watchman's face.

"Why don't you admit it's an inside job, Thompson?" the policeman said.   145

"I've told you all I know," the watchman mumbled through swollen lips.

"But nobody was here but you!" the policeman shouted.

"I was sleeping," the watchman said. "It was wrong, but I was sleeping all that night!"

"Stop telling us that lie!"

"It's the truth!"   150

"When did you get the combination?"

"I don't know how to open the safe," the watchman said.

He clung to the rain pipe, tense; he wanted to laugh, but he controlled himself. He felt a great sense of power; yes, he could go back to the cave, rip the money off the walls, pick up the diamonds and rings, and bring them here and write a note, telling them where to look for their foolish toys. No . . . What good would that do? It was not worth the effort. The watchman was guilty; although he was not guilty of the crime of which he had been accused, he was guilty, had always been guilty. The only thing that worried him was that the man who had been really stealing was not being accused. But he consoled himself: they'll catch him sometime during his life.

He saw one of the policemen slap the watchman across the mouth.

"Come clean, you bastard!"   155

"I've told you all I know," the watchman mumbled like a child.

One of the police went to the rear of the watchman's chair and jerked it from under him; the watchman pitched forward upon his face.

"Get up!" a policeman said.

Trembling, the watchman pulled himself up and sat limply again in the chair.

"Now, are you going to talk?"   160

"I've told you all I know," the watchman gasped.

"Where did you hide the stuff?"

"I didn't take it!"

"Thompson, your brains are in your feet," one of the policemen said. "We're going to string you up and get them back into your skull."

He watched the policemen clamp handcuffs on the watchman's wrists and   165
ankles, then they lifted the watchman and swung him upside-down and hoisted his feet to the edge of a door. The watchman hung, head down, his eyes bulging. They're crazy, he whispered to himself as he clung to the ridges of the pipe.

"You going to talk?" a policeman shouted into the watchman's ear.

He heard the watchman groan.

"We'll let you hang there till you talk, see?"

He saw the watchman close his eyes.

"Let's take 'im down. He passed out," a policeman said.   170

He grinned as he watched them take the body down and dump it carelessly upon the floor. The policeman took off the handcuffs.

"Let 'im come to. Let's get a smoke," a policeman said.

The three policemen left the scope of his vision. A door slammed. He had an impulse to yell to the watchman that he could escape through the hole in the basement and live with him in the cave. But he wouldn't understand, he told himself. After a moment he saw the watchman rise and stand, swaying from weakness. He stumbled across the room to a desk, opened a drawer, and took out a gun. He's going to kill himself, he thought, intent, eager, detached, yearning to see the end of the man's actions. As the watchman stared vaguely about he lifted the gun to his temple; he stood like that for some minutes, biting his lips until a line of blood etched its way down a corner of his chin. No, he oughtn't do that, he said to himself in a mood of pity.

"Don't!" he half whispered and half yelled.

The watchman looked wildly about, he had heard him. But it did not help;   175
there was a loud report and the watchman's head jerked violently and he fell like a log and lay prone, the gun clattering over the floor.

The three policemen came running into the room with drawn guns. One of the policemen knelt and rolled the watchman's body over and stared at a ragged, scarlet hole in the temple.

"Our hunch was right," the kneeling policeman said. "He was guilty, all right."

"Well, this ends the case," another policeman said.

"He knew he was licked," the third one said with grim satisfaction.

He eased down the rain pipe, crawled back through the holes he had made, 180 and went back into his cave. A fever burned in his bones. He had to act, yet he was afraid. His eyes stared in the darkness as though propped open by invisible hands, as though they had become lidless. His muscles were rigid and he stood for what seemed to him a thousand years.

When he moved again his actions were informed with precision, his muscular system reinforced from a reservoir of energy. He crawled through the hole of earth, dropped into the gray sewer current, and sloshed ahead. When his right foot went forward at a street intersection, he fell backward and shot down into water. In a spasm of terror his right hand grabbed the concrete ledge of a down-curve and he felt the streaking water tugging violently at his body. The current reached his neck and for a moment he was still. He knew that if he moved clumsily he would be sucked under. He held onto the ledge with both hands and slowly pulled himself up. He sighed, standing once more in the sweeping water, thankful that he had missed death.

He waded on through sludge, moving with care, until he came to a web of light sifting down from a manhole cover. He saw steel hooks running up the side of the sewer wall; he caught hold and lifted himself and put his shoulder to the cover and moved it an inch. A crash of sound came to him as he looked into a hot glare of sunshine through which blurred shapes moved. Fear scalded him and he dropped back into the pallid current and stood paralyzed in the shadows. A heavy car rumbled past overhead, jarring the pavement, warning him to stay in his world of dark light, knocking the cover back into place with an imperious clang.

He did not know how much fear he felt, for fear claimed him completely; yet it was not a fear of the police or of people, but a cold dread at the thought of the actions he knew he would perform if he went out into that cruel sunshine. His mind said no; his body said yes; and his mind could not understand his feelings. A low whine broke from him and he was in the act of uncoiling. He climbed upward and heard the faint honking of auto horns. Like a frantic cat clutching a rag, he clung to the steel prongs and heaved his shoulder against the cover and pushed it off halfway. For a split second his eyes were drowned in the terror of yellow light and he was in a deeper darkness than he had ever known in the underground.

Partly out of the hole, he blinked, regaining enough sight to make out meaningful forms. An odd thing was happening: No one was rushing forward to challenge him. He had imagined the moment of his emergence as a desperate tussle with men who wanted to cart him off to be killed; instead, life froze about him as the traffic stopped. He pushed the cover aside, stood, swaying in a world so fragile that he expected it to collapse and drop him into some deep void. But nobody seemed to pay him heed. The cars were now swerving to shun him and the gaping hole.

"Why in hell don't you put up a red light, dummy?" a raucous voice yelled. 185

He understood; they thought that he was a sewer workman. He walked toward the sidewalk, weaving unsteadily through the moving traffic.

"Look where you're going, nigger!"

"That's right! Stay there and get killed!"

"You blind, you bastard?"

"Go home and sleep your drunk off!"

A policeman stood at the curb, looking in the opposite direction. When he passed the policeman, he feared that he would be grabbed, but nothing happened. Where was he? Was this real? He wanted to look about to get his bearings, but felt that something awful would happen to him if he did. He wandered into a spacious doorway of a store that sold men's clothing and saw his reflection in a long mirror: his cheekbones protruded from a hairy black face; his greasy cap was perched askew upon his head and his eyes were red and glassy. His shirt and trousers were caked with mud and hung loosely. His hands were gummed with a black stickiness. He threw back his head and laughed so loudly that passers-by stopped and stared.

He ambled on down the sidewalk, not having the merest notion of where he was going. Yet, sleeping within him, was the drive to go somewhere and say something to somebody. Half an hour later his ears caught the sound of spirited singing.

> *The Lamb, the Lamb, the Lamb*
> *I hear thy voice a-calling*
> *The Lamb, the Lamb, the Lamb*
> *I feel thy grace a-falling*

A church! He exclaimed. He broke into a run and came to brick steps leading downward to a subbasement. This is it! The church into which he had peered. Yes, he was going in and tell them. What? He did not know; but, once face to face with them, he would think of what to say. Must be Sunday, he mused. He ran down the steps and jerked the door open; the church was crowded and a deluge of song swept over him.

> *The Lamb, the Lamb, the Lamb*
> *Tell me again your story*
> *The Lamb, the Lamb, the Lamb*
> *Flood my soul with your glory*

He stared at the singing faces with a trembling smile.

"Say!" he shouted.

Many turned to look at him, but the song rolled on. His arm was jerked violently.

"I'm sorry, Brother, but you can't do that in here," a man said.

"But, mister!"

"You can't act rowdy in God's house," the man said.

"He's filthy," another man said.

"But I want to tell 'em," he said loudly.

"He stinks," someone muttered.

The song had stopped, but at once another one began.

> *Oh, wondrous sight upon the cross*
> *Vision sweet and divine*
> *Oh, wondrous sight upon the cross*
> *Full of such love sublime*

He attempted to twist away, but other hands grabbed him and rushed him into the doorway.

"Let me alone!" he screamed, struggling.   205

"Get out!"

"He's drunk," somebody said. "He ought to be ashamed!"

"He acts crazy!"

He felt that he was failing and he grew frantic.

"But, mister, let me tell—"   210

"Get away from this door, or I'll call the police!"

He stared, his trembling smile fading in a sense of wonderment.

"The police," he repeated vacantly.

"Now, get!"

He was pushed toward the brick steps and the door banged shut. The waves   215
of song came.

> *Oh, wondrous sight, wondrous sight*
> *Lift my heavy heart above*
> *Oh, wondrous sight, wondrous sight*
> *Fill my weary soul with love*

He was smiling again now. Yes, the police . . . That was it! Why had he not
thought of it before? The idea had been deep down in him, and only now did it
assume supreme importance. He looked up and saw a street sign: COURT
STREET—HARTSDALE AVENUE. He turned and walked northward, his
mind filled with the image of the police station. Yes, that was where they had
beaten him, accused him, and had made him sign a confession of his guilt. He
would go there and clear up everything, make a statement. What statement? He
did not know. He was the statement, and since it was all so clear to him, surely
he would be able to make it clear to others.

He came to the corner of Hartsdale Avenue and turned westward. Yeah,
there's the station . . . A policeman came down the steps and walked past him
without a glance. He mounted the stone steps and went through the door,
paused; he was in a hallway where several policemen were standing, talking,
smoking. One turned to him.

"What do you want, boy?"

He looked at the policeman and laughed.

"What in hell are you laughing about?" the policeman asked.   220

He stopped laughing and stared. His whole being was full of what he wanted
to say to them, but he could not say it.

"Are you looking for the Desk Sergeant?"

"Yes, sir," he said quickly; then: "Oh, no, sir."

"Well, make up your mind, now."

Four policemen grouped themselves around him.   225

"I'm looking for the men," he said.

"What men?"

Peculiarly, at that moment he could not remember the names of the policemen; he recalled their beating him, the confession he had signed, and how he
had run away from them. He saw the cave next to the church, the money on the
walls, the guns, the rings, the cleaver, the watches, and the diamonds on the
floor.

"They brought me here," he began.

"When?"   230

His mind flew back over the blur of the time lived in the underground blackness. He had no idea of how much time had elapsed, but the intensity of what had happened to him told him that it could not have transpired in a short space of time, yet his mind told him that time must have been brief.

"It was a long time ago." He spoke like a child relating a dimly remembered dream. "It was a long time," he repeated, following the promptings of his emotions. "They beat me . . . I was scared . . . I ran away."

A policeman raised a finger to his temple and made a derisive circle.

"Nuts," the policeman said.

"Do you know what place this is, boy?"   235

"Yes, sir. The police station," he answered sturdily, almost proudly.

"Well, who do you want to see?"

"The men," he said again, feeling that surely they knew the men. "You know the men," he said in a hurt tone.

"What's your name?"

He opened his lips to answer and no words came. He had forgotten. But   240 what did it matter if he had? It was not important.

"Where do you live?"

Where did he live? It had been so long ago since he had lived up here in this strange world that he felt it was foolish even to try to remember. Then for a moment the old mood that had dominated him in the underground surged back. He leaned forward and spoke eagerly.

"They said I killed the woman."

"What woman?" a policeman asked.

"And I signed a paper that said I was guilty," he went on, ignoring their   245 questions. "Then I ran off . . ."

"Did you run off from an institution?"

"No, sir," he said, blinking and shaking his head. "I came from under the ground. I pushed off the manhole cover and climbed out . . ."

"All right, now," a policeman said, placing an arm about his shoulder. "We'll send you to the psycho and you'll be taken care of."

"Maybe he's a Fifth Columnist!" a policeman shouted.

There was laughter and, despite his anxiety, he joined in. But the laughter   250 lasted so long that it irked him.

"I got to find those men," he protested mildly.

"Say, boy, what have you been drinking?"

"Water," he said. "I got some water in a basement."

"Were the men you ran away from dressed in white, boy?"

"No, sir," he said brightly. "They were men like you."   255

An elderly policeman caught hold of his arm.

"Try and think hard. Where did they pick you up?"

He knitted his brows in an effort to remember, but he was blank inside. The policeman stood before him demanding logical answers and he could no longer think with his mind; he thought with his feelings and no words came.

"I was guilty," he said. "Oh, no, sir. I wasn't then, I mean, mister!"

"Aw, talk sense. Now, where did they pick you up?"   260

He felt challenged and his mind began reconstructing events in reverse; his feelings ranged back over the long hours and he saw the cave, the sewer, the bloody room where it was said that a woman had been killed.

"Oh, yes, sir," he said, smiling. "I was coming from Mrs. Wooten's."

"Who is she?"

"I work for her."

"Where does she live?"   265

"Next door to Mrs. Peabody, the woman who was killed."

The policemen were very quiet now, looking at him intently.

"What do you know about Mrs. Peabody's death, boy?"

"Nothing, sir. But they said I killed her. But it doesn't make any difference. I'm guilty!"

"What are you talking about, boy?"   270

His smile faded and he was possessed with memories of the underground; he saw the cave next to the church and his lips moved to speak. But how could he say it? The distance between what he felt and what these men meant was vast. Something told him, as he stood there looking into their faces, that he would never be able to tell them, that they would never believe him even if he told them.

"All the people I saw was guilty," he began slowly.

"Aw, nuts," a policeman muttered.

"Say," another policeman said, "that Peabody woman was killed over on Winewood. That's Number Ten's beat."

"Where's Number Ten?" a policeman asked.   275

"Upstairs in the swing room," someone answered.

"Take this boy up, Sam," a policeman ordered.

"O.K. Come along, boy."

An elderly policeman caught hold of his arm and led him up a flight of wooden stairs, down a long hall, and to a door.

"Squad Ten!" the policeman called through the door.   280

"What?" a gruff voice answered.

"Someone to see you!"

"About what?"

The old policeman pushed the door in and then shoved him into the room.

He stared, his lips open, his heart barely beating. Before him were the three 285
policemen who had picked him up and had beaten him to extract the confession. They were seated about a small table, playing cards. The air was blue with smoke and sunshine poured through a high window, lighting up fantastic smoke shapes. He saw one of the policemen look up; the policeman's face was tired and a cigarette dropped limply from one corner of his mouth and both of his fat, puffy eyes were squinting and his hands gripped his cards.

"Lawson!" the man exclaimed.

The moment the man's name sounded he remembered the names of all of them: Lawson, Murphy, and Johnson. How simple it was. He waited, smiling, wondering how they would react when they knew that he had come back.

"Looking for me?" the man who had been called Lawson mumbled, sorting his cards. "For what?"

So far only Murphy, the red-headed one, had recognized him.

"Don't you-all remember me?" he blurted, running to the table.   290

All three of the policemen were looking at him now. Lawson, who seemed the leader, jumped to his feet.

"Where in hell have you been?"

"Do you know 'im, Lawson?" the old policeman asked.

"Huh?" Lawson frowned. "Oh, yes. I'll handle 'im." The old policeman left the room and Lawson crossed to the door and turned the key in the lock. "Come here, boy," he ordered in a cold tone.

He did not move; he looked from face to face. Yes, he would tell them about 295
his cave.

"He looks batty to me," Johnson said, the one who had not spoken before.

"Why in hell did you come back here?" Lawson said.

"I—I just didn't want to run away no more," he said. "I'm all right, now." He paused; the men's attitude puzzled him.

"You've been hiding, huh?" Lawson asked in a tone that denoted that he had not heard his previous words. "You told us you were sick, and when we left you in the room, you jumped out of the window and ran away."

Panic filled him. Yes, they were indifferent to what he would say! They were 300
waiting for him to speak and they would laugh at him. He had to rescue himself from this bog; he had to force the reality of himself upon them.

"Mister, I took a sackful of money and pasted it on the walls . . ." he began.

"I'll be damned," Lawson said.

"Listen," said Murphy, "let me tell you something for your own good. We don't want you, see? You're free, free as air. Now go home and forget it. It was all a mistake. We caught the guy who did the Peabody job. He wasn't colored at all. He was an Eyetalian."

"Shut up!" Lawson yelled. "Have you no sense!"

"But I want to tell 'im," Murphy said. 305

"We can't let this crazy fool go," Lawson exploded. "He acts nuts, but this may be a stunt . . ."

"I was down in the basement," he began in a childlike tone, as though repeating a lesson learned by heart; "and I went into a movie . . ." His voice failed. He was getting ahead of his story. First, he ought to tell them about the singing in the church, but what words could he use? He looked at them appealingly. "I went into a shop and took a sackful of money and diamonds and watches and rings . . . I didn't steal 'em; I'll give 'em all back. I just took 'em to play with . . ." He paused, stunned by their disbelieving eyes.

Lawson lit a cigarette and looked at him coldly.

"What did you do with the money?" he asked in a quiet, waiting voice.

"I pasted the hundred-dollar bills on the walls." 310

"What walls?" Lawson asked.

"The walls of the dirt room," he said, smiling, "the room next to the church. I hung up the rings and the watches and I stamped the diamonds into the dirt . . ." He saw that they were not understanding what he was saying. He grew frantic to make them believe, his voice tumbled on eagerly. "I saw a dead baby and a dead man . . ."

"Aw, you're nuts," Lawson snarled, shoving him into a chair.

"But, mister . . ."

"Johnson, where's the paper he signed?" Lawson asked. 315

"What paper?"

"The confession, fool!"

Johnson pulled out his billfold and extracted a crumpled piece of paper.

"Yes, sir, mister," he said, stretching forth his hand. "That's the paper I signed . . ."

Lawson slapped him and he would have toppled had his chair not struck a 320 wall behind him. Lawson scratched a match and held the paper over the flame; the confession burned down to Lawson's fingertips.

He stared, thunderstruck; the sun of the underground was fleeing and the terrible darkness of the day stood before him. They did not believe him, but he *had* to make them believe him!

"But, mister . . ."

"It's going to be all right, boy," Lawson said with a quiet, soothing laugh. "I've burned your confession, see? You didn't sign anything." Lawson came close to him with the black ashes cupped in his palm. "You don't remember a thing about this, do you?"

"Don't you-all be scared of me," he pleaded, sensing their uneasiness. "I'll sign another paper, if you want me to. I'll show you the cave."

"What's your game, boy?" Lawson asked suddenly.   325

"What are you trying to find out?" Johnson asked.

"Who sent you here?" Murphy demanded.

"Nobody sent me, mister," he said. "I just want to show you the room . . ."

"Aw, he's plumb bats," Murphy said. "Let's ship 'im to the psycho."

"No," Lawson said. "He's playing a game and I wish to God I knew what it 330 was."

There flashed through his mind a definite way to make them believe him; he rose from the chair with nervous excitement.

"Mister, I saw the night watchman blow his brains out because you accused him of stealing," he told them. "But he didn't steal the money and diamonds. I took 'em."

Tigerishly Lawson grabbed his collar and lifted him bodily.

"Who told you about that?"

"Don't get excited, Lawson," Johnson said. "He read about it in the 335 papers."

Lawson flung him away.

"He couldn't have," Lawson said, pulling papers from his pocket. "I haven't turned in the reports yet."

"Then how *did* he find out?" Murphy asked.

"Let's get out of here," Lawson said with quick resolution. "Listen, boy, we're going to take you to a nice, quiet place, see?"

"Yes, sir," he said. "And I'll show you the underground."   340

"Goddamn," Lawson muttered, fastening the gun at his hip. He narrowed his eyes at Johnson and Murphy. "Listen," he spoke just above a whisper, "say nothing about this, you hear?"

"O.K.," Johnson said.

"Sure," Murphy said.

Lawson unlocked the door and Johnson and Murphy led him down the stairs. The hallway was crowded with policemen.

"What have you got there, Lawson?"   345

"What did he do, Lawson?"

"He's psycho, ain't he, Lawson?"

Lawson did not answer; Johnson and Murphy led him to the car parked at the curb, pushed him into the back seat. Lawson got behind the steering wheel and the car rolled forward.

"What's up, Lawson?" Murphy asked.

"Listen," Lawson began slowly, "we tell the papers that he spilled about the   350 Peabody job, then he escapes. The Wop is caught and we tell the papers that we steered them wrong to trap the real guy, see? Now this dope shows up and acts nuts. If we let him go, he'll squeal that we framed him, see?"

"I'm all right, mister," he said, feeling Murphy's and Johnson's arm locked rigidly into his. "I'm guilty . . . I'll show you everything in the underground. I laughed and laughed . . ."

"Shut that fool up!" Lawson ordered.

Johnson tapped him across the head with a blackjack and he fell back against the seat cushion, dazed.

"Yes, sir," he mumbled. "I'm all right."

The car sped along Hartsdale Avenue, then swung onto Pine Street and   355 rolled to State Street, then turned south. It slowed to a stop, turned in the middle of a block, and headed north again.

"You're going around in circles, Lawson," Murphy said.

Lawson did not answer; he was hunched over the steering wheel. Finally he pulled the car to a stop at a curb.

"Say, boy, tell us the truth," Lawson asked quietly. "Where did you hide?"

"I didn't hide, mister."

The three policemen were staring at him now; he felt that for the first time   360 they were willing to understand him.

"Then what happened?"

"Mister, when I looked through all of those holes and saw how people were living, I loved 'em . . ."

"Cut out that crazy talk!" Lawson snapped. "Who sent you back here?"

"Nobody, mister."

"Maybe he's talking straight," Johnson ventured.   365

"All right," Lawson said. "Nobody hid you. Now, tell us *where* you hid."

"I went underground . . ."

"What goddamn underground do you keep talking about?"

"I just went . . ." He paused and looked into the street, then pointed to a manhole cover. "I went down in there and stayed."

"In the *sewer*?"   370

"Yes, sir."

The policemen burst into a sudden laugh and ended quickly. Lawson swung the car around and drive to Woodside Avenue; he brought the car to a stop in front of a tall apartment building.

"What're we going to do, Lawson?" Murphy asked.

"I'm taking him up to my place," Lawson said. "We've got to wait until night. There's nothing we can do now."

They took him out of the car and led him into a vestibule.   375

"Take the steps," Lawson muttered.

They led him up four flights of stairs and into the living room of a small apartment. Johnson and Murphy let go of his arms and he stood uncertainly in the middle of the room.

"Now, listen, boy," Lawson began, "forget those wild lies you've been telling us. Where did you hide?"

"I just went underground, like I told you."

The room rocked with laughter. Lawson went to a cabinet and got a bottle 380 of whisky; he placed glasses for Johnson and Murphy. The three of them drank.

He felt that he could not explain himself to them. He tried to muster all the sprawling images that floated in him; the images stood out sharply in his mind, but he could not make them have the meaning for others that they had for him. He felt so helpless that he began to cry.

"He's nuts, all right," Johnson said. "All nuts cry like that."

Murphy crossed the room and slapped him.

"Stop that raving!"

A sense of excitement flooded him; he ran to Murphy and grabbed his arm. 385

"Let me show you the cave," he said. "Come on, and you'll see!"

Before he knew it a sharp blow had clipped him on the chin; darkness covered his eyes. He dimly felt himself being lifted and laid out on the sofa. He heard low voices and struggled to rise, but hard hands held him down. His brain was clearing now. He pulled to a sitting posture and stared with glazed eyes. It had grown dark. How long had he been out?

"Say, boy," Lawson said soothingly, "will you show us the underground?"

His eyes shone and his heart swelled with gratitude. Lawson believed him! He rose, glad; he grabbed Lawson's arm, making the policeman spill whisky from the glass to his shirt.

"Take it easy, goddammit," Lawson said.   390

"Yes, sir."

"O.K. We'll take you down. But you'd better be telling us the truth, you hear?"

He clapped his hands in wild joy.

"I'll show you everything!"

He had triumphed at last! He would now do what he had felt was com- 395 pelling him all along. At last he would be free of his burden.

"Take 'im down," Lawson ordered.

They led him down to the vestibule; when he reached the sidewalk he saw that it was night and a fine rain was falling.

"It's just like when I went down," he told them.

"What?" Lawson asked.

"The rain," he said, sweeping his arm in a wide arc. "It was raining when I 400 went down. The rain made the water rise and lift the cover off."

"Cut it out," Lawson snapped.

They did not believe him now, but they would. A mood of high selflessness throbbed in him. He could barely contain his rising spirits. They would see what he had seen; they would feel what he had felt. He would lead them through all the holes he had dug and . . . He wanted to make a hymn, prance about in physical ecstasy, throw his arm about the policemen in fellowship.

"Get into the car," Lawson ordered.

He climbed in and Johnson and Murphy sat at either side of him; Lawson slid behind the steering wheel and started the motor.

"Now, tell us where to go," Lawson said.   405

"It's right around the corner from where the lady was killed," he said.

The car rolled slowly and he closed his eyes, remembering the song he had heard in the church, the song that had wrought him to such a high pitch of terror and pity. He sang softly, lolling is head:

> Glad, glad, glad, oh, so glad
> I got Jesus in my soul . . .

"Mister," he said, stopping his song, "you ought to see how funny the rings look on the wall." He giggled. "I fired a pistol, too. Just once, to see how it felt."

"What do you suppose he's suffering from?" Johnson asked.

"Delusions of grandeur, maybe," Murphy said.   410

"Maybe it's because he lives in a white man's world," Lawson said.

"Say, boy, what did you eat down there?" Murphy asked, prodding Johnson anticipatorily with his elbow.

"Pears, oranges, bananas, and pork chops," he said.

The car filled with laughter.

"You didn't eat any watermelon?" Lawson asked, smiling.   415

"No, sir," he answered calmly. "I didn't see any."

The three policemen roared harder and louder.

"Boy, you're sure some case," Murphy said, shaking his head in wonder.

The car pulled to a curb.

"All right, boy," Lawson said. "Tell us where to go."   420

He peered through the rain and saw where he had gone down. The streets, save for a few dim lamps glowing softly through the rain, were dark and empty.

"Right there, mister," he said, pointing.

"Come on; let's take a look," Lawson said.

"Well, suppose he did hide down there," Johnson said, "what is that supposed to prove?"

"I don't believe he hid down there," Murphy said.   425

"It won't hurt to look," Lawson said. "Leave things to me."

Lawson got out of the car and looked up and down the street.

He was eager to show them the cave now. If he could show them what he had seen, then they would feel what he had felt and they in turn would show it to others and those others would feel as they had felt, and soon everybody would be governed by the same impulse of pity.

"Take 'im out," Lawson ordered.

Johnson and Murphy opened the door and pushed him out; he stood trem- 430
bling in the rain, smiling. Again Lawson looked up and down the street; no one was in sight. The rain came down hard, slanting like black wires across the windswept air.

"All right," Lawson said. "Show us."

He walked to the center of the street, stopped and inserted a finger in one of the tiny holes of the cover and tugged, but he was too weak to budge it.

"Did you really go down in there, boy?" Lawson asked; there was a doubt in his voice.

"Yes, sir. Just a minute. I'll show you."

"Help 'im get that damn thing off," Lawson said.   435

Johnson stepped forward and lifted the cover; it clanged against the wet pavement. The hole gaped round and black.

"I went down in there," he announced with pride.

Lawson gazed at him for a long time without speaking, then he reached his right hand to his holster and drew his gun.

"Mister, I got a gun just like that down there," he said, laughing and looking into Lawson's face. "I fired it once then hung it on the wall. I'll show you."

"Show us how you went down," Lawson said quietly.   440

"I'll go down first, mister, and then you-all can come after me, hear?" he spoke like a little boy playing a game.

"Sure, sure," Lawson said soothingly. "Go ahead. We'll come."

He looked brightly at the policemen; he was bursting with happiness. He bent down and placed his hands on the rim of the hole and sat on the edge, his feet dangling into watery darkness. He heard the familiar drone of the gray current. He lowered his body and hung for a moment by his fingers, then he went downward on the steel prongs, hand over hand, until he reached the last rung. He dropped and his feet hit the water and he felt the stiff current trying to suck him away. He balanced himself quickly and looked back upward at the policemen.

"Come on, you-all!" he yelled, casting his voice above the rustling at his feet.

The vague forms that towered above him in the rain did not move. He   445
laughed, feeling that they doubted him. But, once they saw the things he had done, they would never doubt again.

"Come on! The cave isn't far!" he yelled. "But be careful when your feet hit the water, because the current's pretty rough down here!"

Lawson still held the gun. Murphy and Johnson looked at Lawson quizzically.

"What are we going to do, Lawson?" Murphy asked.

"We are not going to follow that crazy nigger down into that sewer, are we?" Johnson asked.

"Come on, you-all!" he begged in a shout.   450

He saw Lawson raise the gun and point it directly at him. Lawson's face twitched, as though he were hesitating.

Then there was a thunderous report and a streak of fire ripped through his chest. He was hurled into the water, flat on his back. He looked in amazement at the blurred white faces looming above him. They shot me, he said to himself. The water flowed past him, blossoming in foam about his arms, his legs, and his head. His jaw sagged and his mouth gaped soundless. A vast pain gripped his head and gradually squeezed out consciousness. As from a great distance he heard hollow voices.

"What did you shoot him for, Lawson?"

"I had to."

"Why?"   455

"You've got to shoot his kind. They'd wreck things."

As though in a deep dream, he heard a metallic clank; they had replaced the manhole cover, shutting out forever the sound of wind and rain. From overhead came the muffled roar of a powerful motor and the swish of a speeding car. He felt the strong tide pushing him slowly into the middle of the sewer, turning him about. For a split second there hovered before his eyes the glittering cave, the shouting walls, and the laughing floor . . . Then his mouth was full of thick, bitter water. The current spun him around. He sighed and closed his eyes, a whirling object rushing alone in the darkness, veering, tossing, lost in the heart of the earth.

Starting Points for Further Research: Richard Wright

- **Edition:** Richard Wright. *Works.* New York: Library of America, 1991.
- **Biography:** Hazel Rowley. *Richard Wright: The Life and Times.* New York: Henry Holt, 2002.
- **Critical Essay:** Tara T. Green. "The Virgin Mary, Eve, and Mary Magdalene in Richard Wright's Novels." *CLA Journal* 46 (2002): 168–93.

JORGE LUIS BORGES   (1899–1986)

Born in Buenos Aires, Argentina, Jorge Luis Borges is recognized as one of the most significant Spanish American writers of the twentieth century. He was influenced by a whole range of nineteenth- and twentieth-century European literature, particularly in English. The short story was his specialty, especially works combining fantasy and history. Among his works of fiction are Ficciones (1962), The Aleph and Other Stories *(1962),* Labyrinths *(1962), and* A Universal History of Infamy *(1971). Borges was also an acclaimed poet and essayist.*

Theme of the Traitor and the Hero   (1944)

Translated by Andrew Hurley

So the Platonic Year
Whirls out new right and wrong
Whirls in the old instead;
All men are dancers and their tread
Goes to the barbarous clangour of a gong.
                    —W. B. Yeats, The Tower

Under the notorious influence of Chesterton (inventor and embellisher of elegant mysteries) and the court counselor Leibniz (who invented preestablished harmony), in my spare evenings I have conceived this plot—which I will perhaps commit to paper but which already somehow justifies me. It needs details, rectifications, tinkering—there are areas of the story that have never been revealed to me. Today, January 3, 1944, I see it in the following way:

The action takes place in an oppressed yet stubborn country—Poland, Ireland, the republic of Venice, some South American or Balkan state. . . . Or *took* place rather, for though the narrator is contemporary, the story told by him occurred in the mid or early nineteenth century—in 1824, let us say, for convenience's sake; in Ireland, let us also say. The narrator is a man named Ryan, the great-grandson of the young, heroic, beautiful, murdered Fergus Kilpatrick, whose grave was mysteriously violated, whose name gives luster to Browning's and Hugo's verses, and whose statue stands high upon a gray hilltop among red bogs.

Kilpatrick was a conspirator and a secret and glorious captain of conspirators. Like Moses, who from the land of Moab glimpsed yet could not reach the promised land, Kilpatrick perished on the eve of the victorious rebellion he had planned for and dreamed of. The date of the first centenary of his death is approaching; the circumstances of the crime are enigmatic; Ryan, who is writing a biography of the hero, discovers that the enigma goes deeper than mere detective work can fathom. Kilpatrick was murdered in a theater; the English police never apprehended the assassin. Historians claim that this failure does not tarnish the good name of the police, since it is possible that the police themselves had Kilpatrick murdered. Other aspects of the mystery disturb Ryan; certain things seem almost cyclical, seem to repeat or combine events from distant places, distant ages. For example: Everyone knows that the constables who examined the hero's body found a sealed letter warning Kilpatrick not to go to the theater that night; Julius Caesar, too, as he was walking toward the place where the knives of his friends awaited him, received a note he never read—a note telling him of his betrayal and revealing the names of his betrayers. Caesar's wife, Calpurnia, saw in dreams a tower felled by order of the Senate; on the eve of Kilpatrick's death, false and anonymous rumors of the burning of the circular tower of Kilgarvan spread throughout the country—an event that might be taken as an omen, since Kilpatrick had been born in Kilgarvan. These (and other) parallels between the story of Julius Caesar and the story of an Irish conspirator induce Ryan to imagine some secret shape of time, a pattern of repeating lines. His thoughts turn to the decimal history conceived by Condorcet, the morphologies proposed by Hegel, Spengler, and Vico, mankind as posited by Hesiod, degenerating from gold to iron. He thinks of the transmigration of souls, a doctrine that lends horror to Celtic literature and that Caesar himself attributed to the Druids of Britain; he toys with the idea that before Fergus Kilpatrick was Fergus Kilpatrick, he was Julius Caesar. He is saved from those circular labyrinths by a curious discovery, a discovery which, however, will plunge him deep into other, yet more tangled and heterogeneous mazes: It seems that certain words spoken by a beggar who spoke with Fergus Kilpatrick on the day of his death had been prefigured by Shakespeare, in *Macbeth*. The idea that history might have copied history is mind-boggling enough; that history should copy *literature* is inconceivable. . . . Ryan digs further, and he finds that in 1814 James Alexander Nolan, the oldest of the hero's comrades, had translated Shakespeare's major plays into Gaelic—among them *Julius Caesar*. He also finds in the archives a manuscript article by Nolan on the Swiss *Festspiele*—vast peripatetic theatrical performances that require thousands of actors and retell historical episodes in the same cities, the same mountains in which they occurred. Another unpublished document reveals to Ryan that a few days before the end, Kilpatrick, presiding over the last gathering of his chiefs, had signed the death sentence of a traitor, whose name has been scratched out. This sentence does not jibe with Kilpatrick's customary mercifulness. Ryan investigates the matter (his investigation being one of the gaps in the book's narration) and manages to decipher the enigma.

Kilpatrick was murdered in a theater, yet the entire city played the role of theater, too, and the actors were legion, and the play that was crowned by Kilpatrick's death took place over many days and many nights. Here is what happened:

On August 2, 1824, the conspirators met. The country was ripe for rebellion; something, however, always went awry—there must have been a traitor within the inner circle. Fergus Kilpatrick had given James Nolan the job of ferreting out the identity of this traitor, and Nolan had carried out his mission. He announced to the gathered comrades that the traitor was Kilpatrick himself. He proved the truth of his accusation beyond the shadow of a doubt, and the men at

5

the council that night condemned their leader to death. The leader signed his own death sentence, but he pleaded that his punishment not harm the cause.

And so it was that Nolan conceived a strange plan. Ireland idolized Kilpatrick; the slightest suspicion of his baseness would have compromised the rebellion; Nolan proposed a way to turn the traitor's execution into an instrument for the emancipation of the country. He proposed that the condemned man die at the hands of an unknown assassin in deliberately dramatic circumstances; those circumstances would engrave themselves upon the popular imagination and hasten the rebellion. Kilpatrick swore to collaborate in this plan which would give him an occasion to redeem himself, and which would be crowned by his death.

Nolan had no time to invent the circumstances of the multiple execution from scratch, and so he plagiarized the scene from another playwright, the English enemy Will Shakespeare, reprising scenes from *Macbeth* and *Julius Caesar*. The public yet secret performance occurred over several days. The condemned man entered Dublin, argued, worked, prayed, reprehended, spoke words of pathos—and each of those acts destined to shine forth in glory had been choreographed by Nolan. Hundreds of actors collaborated with the protagonist; the role of some was complex, the role of others a matter of moments on the stage. The things they did and said endure in Ireland's history books and in its impassioned memory. Kilpatrick, moved almost to ecstasy by the scrupulously plotted fate that would redeem him and end his days, more than once enriched his judge's text with improvised words and acts. Thus the teeming drama played itself out in time, until that August 6, 1824, in a box (prefiguring Lincoln's) draped with funereal curtains, when a yearned-for bullet pierced the traitor-hero's breast. Between two spurts of sudden blood, Kilpatrick could hardly pronounce the few words given him to speak.

In Nolan's play, the passages taken from Shakespeare are the *least* dramatic ones; Ryan suspected that the author interpolated them so that someone, in the future, would be able to stumble upon the truth. Ryan realized that he, too, was part of Nolan's plot. . . . After long and stubborn deliberation, he decided to silence the discovery. He published a book dedicated to the hero's glory; that too, perhaps, had been foreseen.

Starting Points for Further Research: Jorge Luis Borges

- **Edition:** Jorges Luis Borges. *Collected Fictions*. Ed. Andrew Hurley. New York: Penguin, 1999.
- **Biography:** Edwin Williamson. *Borges: A Life*. New York: Viking, 2004.
- **Critical Essay:** Peter G. Earl. "In and Out of Time: Cervantes, Dostoevsky, Borges." *Hispanic Review* (Winter 2003): 1–13.

JAMES BALDWIN   (1924–1987)

James Baldwin grew up in Harlem and became a preacher by the age of fourteen. He moved to Paris, where he wrote his first two novels, Go Tell It on the Mountain *(1953) and* Giovanni's Room *(1956), which established his reputation as a writer who explored what were considered to be controversial themes and subject matter: race and racism, gender, sexuality and sexual orientation, and spirituality. At the same time, Baldwin refused to be categorized on the basis of his subject matter or his own identity as a black, gay writer, preferring instead to call himself an American writer. Back in the*

United States in the late 1950s, Baldwin was active in the civil rights movement. In the 1960s he returned to France permanently. His widely read novel Another Country *(1962) and his critically acclaimed essay collection* The Fire Next Time *(1963) took race as their subject.*

Sonny's Blues

(1957)

I read about it in the paper, in the subway, on my way to work. I read it, and I couldn't believe it, and I read it again. Then perhaps I just stared at it, at the newsprint spelling out his name, spelling out the story. I stared at it in the swinging lights of the subway car, and in the faces and bodies of the people, and in my own face, trapped in the darkness which roared outside.

It was not to be believed and I kept telling myself that as I walked from the subway station to the high school. And at the same time I couldn't doubt it. I was scared, scared for Sonny. He became real to me again. A great block of ice got settled in my belly and kept melting there slowly all day long, while I taught my classes algebra. It was a special kind of ice. It kept melting, sending trickles of ice water all up and down my veins, but it never got less. Sometimes it hardened and seemed to expand until I felt my guts were going to come spilling out or that I was going to choke or scream. This would always be at a moment when I was remembering some specific thing Sonny had once said or done.

When he was about as old as the boys in my classes his face had been bright and open, there was a lot of copper in it; and he'd had wonderfully direct brown eyes, and great gentleness and privacy. I wondered what he looked like now. He had been picked up, the evening before, in a raid on an apartment downtown, for peddling and using heroin.

I couldn't believe it: but what I mean by that is that I couldn't find any room for it anywhere inside me. I had kept it outside me for a long time. I hadn't wanted to know. I had had suspicions, but I didn't name them, I kept putting them away. I told myself that Sonny was wild, but he wasn't crazy. And he'd always been a good boy, he hadn't ever turned hard or evil or disrespectful, the way kids can, so quick, so quick, especially in Harlem. I didn't want to believe that I'd ever see my brother going down, coming to nothing, all that light in his face gone out, in the condition I'd already seen so many others. Yet it had happened and here I was, talking about algebra to a lot of boys who might, every one of them for all I knew, be popping off needles every time they went to the head. Maybe it did more for them than algebra could.

I was sure that the first time Sonny had ever had horse, he couldn't have been much older than these boys were now. These boys, now, were living as we'd been living then, they were growing up with a rush and their heads bumped abruptly against the low ceiling of their actual possibilities. They were filled with rage. All they really knew were two darknesses, the darkness of their lives, which was now closing in on them, and the darkness of the movies, which had blinded them to that other darkness, and in which they now, vindictively, dreamed, at once more together than they were at any other time, and more alone.

When the last bell rang, the last class ended, I let out my breath. It seemed I'd been holding it for all that time. My clothes were wet—I may have looked as though I'd been sitting in a steam bath, all dressed up, all afternoon. I sat alone in the classroom a long time. I listened to the boys outside, downstairs, shouting and cursing and laughing. Their laughter struck me for perhaps the first time. It was not the joyous laughter which—God knows why—one associates with children. It was mocking and insular, its intent was to denigrate. It was disenchanted, and in this, also, lay the authority of their curses. Perhaps I was listening to them because I was thinking about my brother and in them I heard my brother. And myself.

One boy was whistling a tune, at once very complicated and very simple, it seemed to be pouring out of him as though he were a bird, and it sounded very cool and moving through all that harsh, bright air, only just holding its own through all those other sounds.

I stood up and walked over to the window and looked down into the courtyard. It was the beginning of the spring and the sap was rising in the boys. A teacher passed through them every now and again, quickly, as though he or she couldn't wait to get out of that courtyard, to get those boys out of their sight and off their minds. I started collecting my stuff. I thought I'd better get home and talk to Isabel.

The courtyard was almost deserted by the time I got downstairs. I saw this boy standing in the shadow of a doorway, looking just like Sonny. I almost called his name. Then I saw that it wasn't Sonny, but somebody we used to know, a boy from around our block. He'd been Sonny's friend. He'd never been mine, having been too young for me, and, anyway, I'd never liked him. And now, even though he was a grown-up man, he still hung around that block, still spent hours on the street corner, was always high and raggy. I used to run into him from time to time and he'd often work around to asking me for a quarter or fifty cents. He always had some real good excuse, too, and I always gave it to him, I don't know why.

But now, abruptly, I hated him. I couldn't stand the way he looked at me,   10
partly like a dog, partly like a cunning child. I wanted to ask him what the hell he was doing in the school courtyard.

He sort of shuffled over to me, and he said, "I see you got the papers. So you already know about it."

"You mean about Sonny? Yes, I already know about it. How come they didn't get you?"

He grinned. It made him repulsive and it also brought to mind what he'd looked like as a kid. "I wasn't there. I stay away from them people."

"Good for you." I offered him a cigarette and I watched him through the smoke. "You come all the way down here just to tell me about Sonny?"

"That's right." He was sort of shaking his head and his eyes looked strange,   15
as though they were about to cross. The bright sun deadened his damp dark brown skin and it made his eyes look yellow and showed up the dirt in his conked hair. He smelled funky. I moved a little away from him and I said, "Well, thanks. But I already know about it and I got to get home."

"I'll walk you a little ways," he said. We started walking. There were a couple of kids still loitering in the courtyard and one of them said good night to me and looked strangely at the boy beside me.

"What're you going to do?" he asked me. "I mean, about Sonny?"

"Look. I haven't seen Sonny for over a year, I'm not sure I'm going to do anything. Anyway, what the hell can I do?"

"That's right," he said quickly, "ain't nothing you can do. Can't much help old Sonny no more, I guess."

It was what I was thinking and so it seemed to me he had no right to say it.   20

"I'm surprised at Sonny, though," he went on—he had a funny way of talking, he looked straight ahead as though he were talking to himself—"I thought Sonny was a smart boy, I thought he was too smart to get hung."

"I guess he thought so too," I said sharply, "and that's how he got hung. And how about you? You're pretty goddamn smart, I bet."

Then he looked directly at me, just for a minute. "I ain't smart," he said. "If I was smart, I'd have reached for a pistol a long time ago."

"Look. Don't tell *me* your sad story, if it was up to me, I'd give you one." Then I felt guilty—guilty, probably, for never having supposed that the poor bastard *had* a story of his own, much less a sad one, and I asked, quickly, "What's going to happen to him now?"

He didn't answer this. He was off by himself some place. "Funny thing," he said, and from his tone we might have been discussing the quickest way to get to Brooklyn, "when I saw the papers this morning, the first thing I asked myself was if I had anything to do with it. I felt sort of responsible." 25

I began to listen more carefully. The subway station was on the corner, just before us, and I stopped. He stopped, too. We were in front of a bar and he ducked slightly, peering in, but whoever he was looking for didn't seem to be there. The juke box was blasting away with something black and bouncy and I half watched the barmaid as she danced her way from the juke box to her place behind the bar. And I watched her face as she laughingly responded to something someone said to her, still keeping time to the music. When she smiled one saw the little girl, one sensed the doomed, still-struggling woman beneath the battered face of the semi-whore.

"I never *give* Sonny nothing," the boy said finally, "but a long time ago I come to school high and Sonny asked me how it felt." He paused, I couldn't bear to watch him, I watched the barmaid, and I listened to the music which seemed to be causing the pavement to shake. "I told him it felt great." The music stopped, the barmaid paused and watched the juke box until the music began again. "It did."

All this was carrying me some place I didn't want to go. I certainly didn't want to know how it felt. It filled everything, the people, the houses, the music, the dark, quicksilver barmaid, with menace; and this menace was their reality.

"What's going to happen to him now?" I asked again.

"They'll send him away some place and they'll try to cure him." He shook his head. "Maybe he'll even think he's kicked the habit. Then they'll let him loose"—he gestured, throwing his cigarette into the gutter. "That's all." 30

"What do you mean, that's *all?*"

But I knew what he meant.

"I *mean,* that's *all.*" He turned his head and looked at me, pulling down the corners of his mouth. "Don't you know what I mean?" he asked softly.

"How the hell *would* I know what you mean?" I almost whispered it, I don't know why.

"That's right," he said to the air, "how would *he* know what I mean?" He turned toward me again, patient and calm, and yet I somehow felt him shaking, shaking as though he were going to fall apart. I felt that ice in my guts again, the dread I'd felt all afternoon; and again I watched the barmaid, moving about the bar, washing glasses, and singing. "Listen. They'll let him out and then it'll just start all over again. That's what I mean." 35

"You mean—they'll let him out. And then he'll just start working his way back in again. You mean he'll never kick the habit. Is that what you mean?"

"That's right," he said, cheerfully. "*You* see what I mean."

"Tell me," I said at last, "why does he want to die? He must want to die, he's killing himself, why does he want to die?"

He looked at me in surprise. He licked his lips. "He don't want to die. He wants to live. Don't nobody want to die, ever."

Then I wanted to ask him—too many things. He could not have answered,   40 or if he had, I could not have borne the answers. I started walking. "Well, I guess it's none of my business."

"It's going to be rough on old Sonny," he said. We reached the subway station. "This is your station?" he asked. I nodded. I took one step down. "Damn!" he said, suddenly. I looked up at him. He grinned again. "Damn if I didn't leave all my money home. You ain't got a dollar on you, have you? Just for a couple of days, is all."

All at once something inside gave and threatened to come pouring out of me. I didn't hate him any more. I felt that in another moment I'd start crying like a child.

"Sure," I said. "Don't sweat." I looked in my wallet and didn't have a dollar, I only had a five. "Here," I said. "That hold you?"

He didn't look at it—he didn't want to look at it. A terrible, closed look came over his face, as though he were keeping the number on the bill a secret from him and me. "Thanks," he said, and now he was dying to see me go. "Don't worry about Sonny. Maybe I'll write him or something."

"Sure," I said. "You do that. So long."   45

"Be seeing you," he said. I went on down the steps.

And I didn't write Sonny or send him anything for a long time. When I finally did, it was just after my little girl died, he wrote me back a letter which made me feel like a bastard.

Here's what he said:

> Dear Brother,
>   You don't know how much I needed to hear from you. I wanted to write you many a time but I dug how much I must have hurt you and so I didn't write. But now I feel like a man who's been trying to climb up out of some deep, real deep and funky hole and just saw the sun up there, outside. I got to get outside.
>   I can't tell you much about how I got here. I mean I don't know how to tell you. I guess I was afraid of something or I was trying to escape from something and you know I have never been very strong in the head (smile). I'm glad Mama and Daddy are dead and can't see what's happened to their son and I swear if I'd known what I was doing I would never have hurt you so, you and a lot of other fine people who were nice to me and who believed in me.
>   I don't want you to think it had anything to do with me being a musician. It's more than that. Or maybe less than that. I can't get anything straight in my head down here and I try not to think about what's going to happen to me when I get outside again. Sometime I think I'm going to flip and *never* get outside and sometime I think I'll come straight back. I tell you one thing, though, I'd rather blow my brains out than go through this again. But that's what they all say, so they tell me. If I tell you when I'm coming to New York and if you could meet me, I sure would appreciate it. Give my love to Isabel and the kids and I was sorry to hear about little Gracie. I wish I could be like Mama and say the Lord's will be done, but I don't know it seems to me that trouble is the one thing that never does get stopped and I

don't know what good it does to blame it on the Lord. But maybe it does some good if you believe it.

> Your brother,
> Sonny

Then I kept in constant touch with him and I sent him whatever I could and I went to meet him when he came back to New York. When I saw him many things I thought I had forgotten came flooding back to me. This was because I had begun, finally, to wonder about Sonny, about the life that Sonny lived inside. This life, whatever it was, had made him older and thinner and it had deepened the distant stillness in which he had always moved. He looked very unlike my baby brother. Yet, when he smiled, when we shook hands, the baby brother I'd never known looked out from the depths of his private life, like an animal waiting to be coaxed into the light.

"How you been keeping?" he asked me.   50

"All right. And you?"

"Just fine." He was smiling all over his face. "It's good to see you again."

"It's good to see you."

The seven years' difference in our ages lay between us like a chasm: I wondered if these years would ever operate between us as a bridge. I was remembering, and it made it hard to catch my breath, that I had been there when he was born; and I had heard the first words he had ever spoken. When he started to walk, he walked from our mother straight to me. I caught him just before he fell when he took the first steps he ever took in this world.

"How's Isabel?"   55

"Just fine. She's dying to see you."

"And the boys?"

"They're fine, too. They're anxious to see their uncle."

"Oh, come on. You know they don't remember me."

"Are you kidding? Of course they remember you."   60

He grinned again. We got into a taxi. We had a lot to say to each other, far too much to know how to begin.

As the taxi began to move, I asked, "You still want to go to India?"

He laughed. "You still remember that. Hell, no. This place is Indian enough for me."

"It used to belong to them," I said.

And he laughed again. "They damn sure knew what they were doing when   65
they got rid of it."

Years ago, when he was around fourteen, he'd been all hipped on the idea of going to India. He read books about people sitting on rocks, naked, in all kinds of weather, but mostly bad, naturally, and walking barefoot through hot coals and arriving at wisdom. I used to say that it sounded to me as though they were getting away from wisdom as fast as they could. I think he sort of looked down on me for that.

"Do you mind," he asked, "if we have the driver drive alongside the park? On the west side—I haven't seen the city in so long."

"Of course not," I said. I was afraid that I might sound as though I were humoring him, but I hoped he wouldn't take it that way.

So we drove along, between the green of the park and the stony, lifeless elegance of hotels and apartment buildings, toward the vivid, killing streets of our childhood. These streets hadn't changed, though housing projects jutted up out of them now like rocks in the middle of a boiling sea. Most of the houses in which we had grown up had vanished, as had the stores from which we had stolen, the basements in which we had first tried sex, the rooftops from which we had hurled tin cans and bricks. But houses exactly like the houses of our past yet dominated the landscape, boys exactly like the boys we once had been found themselves smothering in these houses, came down into the streets for light and air and found themselves encircled by disaster. Some escaped the trap, most didn't. Those who got out always left something of themselves behind, as some animals amputate a leg and leave it in the trap. It might be said, perhaps, that I had escaped, after all, I was a school teacher; or that Sonny had, he hadn't lived in Harlem for years. Yet, as the cab moved up-town through streets which seemed, with a rush, to darken with dark people, and as I covertly studied Sonny's face, it came to me that what we both were seeking through our separate cab windows was that part of ourselves which had been left behind. It's always at the hour of trouble and confrontation that the missing member aches.

We hit 110th Street and started rolling up Lenox Avenue. And I'd known   70 this avenue all my life, but it seemed to me again, as it had seemed on the day I'd first heard about Sonny's trouble, filled with a hidden menace which was its very breath of life.

"We almost there," said Sonny.

"Almost." We were both too nervous to say anything more.

We live in a housing project. It hasn't been up long. A few days after it was up it seemed uninhabitably new, now, of course, it's already run-down. It looks like a parody of the good, clean, faceless life—God knows the people who live in it do their best to make it a parody. The beat-looking grass lying around isn't enough to make their lives green, the hedges will never hold out the streets, and they know it. The big windows fool no one, they aren't big enough to make space out of no space. They don't bother with the windows, they watch the TV screen instead. The playground is most popular with the children who don't play at jacks, or skip rope, or roller skate, or swing, and they can be found in it after dark. We moved in partly because it's not too far from where I teach, and partly for the kids; but it's really just like the houses in which Sonny and I grew up. The same things happen, they'll have the same things to remember. The moment Sonny and I started into the house I had the feeling that I was simply bringing him back into the danger he had almost died trying to escape.

Sonny has never been talkative. So I don't know why I was sure he'd be dying to talk to me when supper was over the first night. Everything went fine, the oldest boy remembered him, and the youngest boy liked him, and Sonny had remembered to bring something for each of them; and Isabel, who is really much nicer than I am, more open and giving, had gone to a lot of trouble about dinner and was genuinely glad to see him. And she's always been able to tease Sonny in a way that I haven't. It was nice to see her face so vivid again and to hear her laugh and watch her make Sonny laugh. She wasn't, or, anyway, she didn't seem to be, at all uneasy or embarrassed. She chatted as though there were no subject which had to be avoided and she got Sonny past his first, faint stiffness. And thank God she was there, for I was filled with that icy dread again. Everything I did seemed awkward to me, and everything I said sounded freighted with hidden meaning. I was trying to remember everything I'd heard about dope addiction and I couldn't help watching Sonny for signs. I wasn't doing it out of malice. I was trying to find out something about my brother. I was dying to hear him tell me he was safe.

* * *

"Safe!" my father grunted, whenever Mama suggested trying to move to a neigh-   75
borhood which might be safer for children. "Safe, hell! Ain't no place safe for
kids, nor nobody."

He always went on like this, but he wasn't, ever, really as bad as he sounded,
not even on weekends, when he got drunk. As a matter of fact, he was always on
the lookout for "something a little better," but he died before he found it. He
died suddenly, during a drunken weekend in the middle of the war, when Sonny
was fifteen. He and Sonny hadn't ever got on too well. And this was partly because Sonny was the apple of his father's eye. It was because he loved Sonny so
much and was frightened for him, that he was always fighting with him. It does-
n't do any good to fight with Sonny. Sonny just moves back, inside himself,
where he can't be reached. But the principal reason that they never hit it off is
that they were so much alike. Daddy was big and rough and loud-talking, just the
opposite of Sonny, but they both had—that same privacy.

Mama tried to tell me something about this, just after Daddy died. I was
home on leave from the army.

This was the last time I ever saw my mother alive. Just the same, this picture
gets all mixed up in my mind with pictures I had of her when she was younger. The
way I always see her is the way she used to be on a Sunday afternoon, say, when the
old folks were talking after the big Sunday dinner. I always see her wearing pale
blue. She'd be sitting on the sofa. And my father would be sitting in the easy chair,
not far from her. And the living room would be full of church folks and relatives.
There they sit, in chairs all around the living room, and the night is creeping up
outside, but nobody knows it yet. You can see the darkness growing against the window-panes and you hear the street noises every now and again, or maybe the jangling beat of a tambourine from one of the churches close by, but it's real quiet in
the room. For a moment nobody's talking, but every face looks darkening, like the
sky outside. And my mother rocks a little from the waist, and my father's eyes are
closed. Everyone is looking at something a child can't see. For a minute they've forgotten the children. Maybe a kid is lying on the rug half asleep. Maybe somebody's
got a kid on his lap and is absent-mindedly stroking the kid's head. Maybe there's a
kid, quiet and big-eyed, curled up in a big chair in the corner. The silence, the darkness coming, and the darkness in the faces frightens the child obscurely. He hopes
that the hand which strokes his forehead will never stop—will never die. He hopes
that there will never come a time when the old folks won't be sitting around the living room, talking about where they've come from, and what they've seen, and
what's happened to them and their kinfolk.

But something deep and watchful in the child knows that this is bound to
end, is already ending. In a moment someone will get up and turn on the light.
Then the old folks will remember the children and they won't talk any more that
day. And when light fills the room, the child is filled with darkness. He knows
that every time this happens he's moved just a little closer to that darkness outside. The darkness outside is what the old folks have been talking about. It's
what they've come from. It's what they endure. The child knows that they won't
talk any more because if he knows too much about what's happened to *them*,
he'll know too much too soon, about what's going to happen to *him*.

The last time I talked to my mother, I remember I was restless. I wanted to   80
get out and see Isabel. We weren't married then and we had a lot to straighten
out between us.

There Mama sat, in black, by the window. She was humming an old church song, *Lord, you brought me from a long ways off.* Sonny was out somewhere. Mama kept watching the streets.

"I don't know," she said, "if I'll ever see you again, after you go off from here. But I hope you'll remember the things I tried to teach you."

"Don't talk like that," I said, and smiled. "You'll be here a long time yet."

She smiled, too, but she said nothing. She was quiet for a long time. And I said, "Mama, don't you worry about nothing. I'll be writing all the time, and you be getting the checks. . . ."

"I want to talk to you about your brother," she said, suddenly. "If anything   85 happens to me he ain't going to have nobody to look out for him."

"Mama," I said, "ain't nothing going to happen to you *or* Sonny. Sonny's all right. He's a good boy and he's got good sense."

"It ain't a question of his being a good boy," Mama said, "nor of his having good sense. It ain't only the bad ones, nor yet the dumb ones that gets sucked under." She stopped, looking at me. "Your Daddy once had a brother," she said, and she smiled in a way that made me feel she was in pain. "You didn't never know that, did you?"

"No," I said, "I never knew that," and I watched her face.

"Oh, yes," she said, "your Daddy had a brother." She looked out of the window again. "I know you never saw your Daddy cry. But *I* did—many a time, through all these years."

I asked her, "What happened to his brother? How come nobody's ever   90 talked about him?"

This was the first time I ever saw my mother look old.

"His brother got killed," she said, "when he was just a little younger than you are now. I knew him. He was a fine boy. He was maybe a little full of the devil, but he didn't mean nobody no harm."

Then she stopped and the room was silent, exactly as it had sometimes been on those Sunday afternoons. Mama kept looking out into the streets.

"He used to have a job in the mill," she said, "and, like all young folks, he just liked to perform on Saturday nights. Saturday nights, him and your father would drift around to different places, go to dances and things like that, or just sit around with people they knew, and your father's brother would sing, he had a fine voice, and play along with himself on his guitar. Well, this particular Saturday night, him and your father was coming home from some place, and they were both a little drunk and there was a moon that night, it was bright like day. Your father's brother was feeling kind of good, and he was whistling to himself, and he had his guitar slung over his shoulder. They was coming down a hill and beneath them was a road that turned off from the highway. Well, your father's brother, being always kind of frisky, decided to run down this hill, and he did, with that guitar banging and clanging behind him, and he ran across the road, and he was making water behind a tree. And your father was sort of amused at him and he was still coming down the hill, kind of slow. Then he heard a car motor and that same minute his brother stepped from behind the tree, into the road, in the moonlight. And he started to cross the road. And your father started to run down the hill, he says he don't know why. This car was full of white men. They was all drunk, and when they seen your father's brother they let out a great whoop and holler and they aimed the car straight at him. They was having fun, they just wanted to scare him, the way they do sometimes, you know. But they was drunk. And I guess the boy, being drunk, too, and scared, kind of lost his head. By the time he jumped it was too late. Your father says he heard his brother scream when the car rolled over him, and he heard the wood of that guitar when it give, and he heard them strings go flying, and he heard them white men shouting, and the car kept on a-going and it ain't stopped till this day. And, time your father got down the hill, his brother weren't nothing but blood and pulp."

Tears were gleaming on my mother's face. There wasn't anything I could say.   95

"He never mentioned it," she said, "because I never let him mention it before you children. Your Daddy was like a crazy man that night and for many a night thereafter. He says he never in his life seen anything as dark as that road after the lights of that car had gone away. Weren't nothing, weren't nobody on that road, just your Daddy and his brother and that busted guitar. Oh, yes. Your Daddy never did really get right again. Till the day he died he weren't sure but that every white man he saw was the man that killed his brother."

She stopped and took out her handkerchief and dried her eyes and looked at me.

"I ain't telling you all this," she said, "to make you scared or bitter or to make you hate nobody. I'm telling you this because you got a brother. And the world ain't changed."

I guess I didn't want to believe this. I guess she saw this in my face. She turned away from me, toward the window again, searching those streets.

"But I praise my Redeemer," she said at last, "that He called your Daddy   100 home before me. I ain't saying it to throw no flowers at myself, but, I declare, it keeps me from feeling too cast down to know I helped your father get safely through this world. Your father always acted like he was the roughest, strongest man on earth. And everybody took him to be like that. But if he hadn't had *me* there—to see his tears!"

She was crying again. Still, I couldn't move. I said, "Lord, Lord, Mama, I didn't know it was like that."

"Oh, honey," she said, "there's a lot that you don't know. But you are going to find it out." She stood up from the window and came over to me. "You got to hold on to your brother," she said, "and don't let him fall, no matter what it looks like is happening to him and no matter how evil you gets with him. You going to be evil with him many a time. But don't you forget what I told you, you hear?"

"I won't forget," I said. "Don't you worry, I won't forget. I won't let nothing happen to Sonny."

My mother smiled as though she were amused at something she saw in my face. Then, "You may not be able to stop nothing from happening. But you got to let him know you's *there*."

* * *

Two days later I was married, and then I was gone. And I had a lot of things on   105 my mind and I pretty well forgot my promise to Mama until I got shipped home on a special furlough for her funeral.

And, after the funeral, with just Sonny and me alone in the empty kitchen, I tried to find out something about him.

"What do you want to do?" I asked him.

"I'm going to be a musician," he said.

For he had graduated, in the time I had been away, from dancing to the juke box to finding out who was playing what, and what they were doing with it, and he had bought himself a set of drums.

"You mean, you want to be a drummer?" I somehow had the feeling that be- 110 ing a drummer might be all right for other people but not for my brother Sonny.

"I don't think," he said, looking at me very gravely, "that I'll ever be a good drummer. But I think I can play a piano."

I frowned. I'd never played the role of the older brother quite so seriously before, had scarcely ever, in fact, *asked* Sonny a damn thing. I sensed myself in the presence of something I didn't really know how to handle, didn't understand. So I made my frown a little deeper as I asked: "What kind of musician do you want to be?"

He grinned. "How many kinds do you think there are?"

"Be *serious*," I said.

He laughed, throwing his head back, and then looked at me. "I *am* serious." 115

"Well, then, for Christ's sake, stop kidding around and answer a serious question. I mean, do you want to be a concert pianist, you want to play classical music and all that, or—or what?" Long before I finished he was laughing again. "For Christ's *sake*, Sonny!"

He sobered, but with difficulty. "I'm sorry. But you sound so—*scared*!" and he was off again.

"Well, you may think it's funny now, baby, but it's not going to be so funny when you have to make your living at it, let me tell you *that*." I was furious because I knew he was laughing at me and I didn't know why.

"No," he said, very sober now, and afraid, perhaps, that he'd hurt me, "I don't want to be a classical pianist. That isn't what interests me. I mean"—he paused, looking hard at me, as though his eyes would help me to understand, and then gestured helplessly, as though perhaps his hand would help—"I mean, I'll have a lot of studying to do, and I'll have to study *everything*, but I mean, I want to play *with*—jazz musicians." He stopped. "I want to play jazz," he said.

Well, the word had never before sounded as heavy, as real, as it sounded that 120 afternoon in Sonny's mouth. I just looked at him and I was probably frowning a real frown by this time. I simply couldn't see why on earth he'd want to spend his time hanging around night clubs, clowning around on band-stands, while people pushed each other around a dance floor. It seemed—beneath him, somehow. I had never thought about it before, had never been forced to, but I suppose I had always put jazz musicians in a class with what Daddy called "good-time people."

"Are you *serious*?"

"Hell, *yes*, I'm serious."

He looked more helpless than ever, and annoyed, and deeply hurt.

I suggested, helpfully: "You mean—like Louis Armstrong?"

His face closed as though I'd struck him. "No. I'm not talking about none of 125 that old-time, down home crap."

"Well, look, Sonny, I'm sorry, don't get mad. I just don't altogether get it, that's all. Name somebody—you know, a jazz musician you admire."

"Bird."

"Who?"

"Bird! Charlie Parker! Don't they teach you nothing in the goddamn army?"

I lit a cigarette. I was surprised and then a little amused to discover that I 130
was trembling. "I've been out of touch," I said. "You'll have to be patient with
me. Now. Who's this Parker character?"

"He's just one of the greatest jazz musicians alive," said Sonny, sullenly, his
hands in his pockets, his back to me. "Maybe *the* greatest," he added, bitterly,
"that's probably why *you* never heard of him."

"All right," I said. "I'm ignorant. I'm sorry. I'll go out and buy all the cat's
records right away, all right?"

"It don't," said Sonny, with dignity, "make any difference to me. I don't care
what you listen to. Don't do me no favors."

I was beginning to realize that I'd never seen him so upset before. With another part of my mind I was thinking that this would probably turn out to be one
of those things kids go through and that I shouldn't make it seem important by
pushing it too hard. Still, I didn't think it would do any harm to ask: "Doesn't all
this take a lot of time? Can you make a living at it?"

He turned back to me and half leaned, half sat, on the kitchen table. 135
"Everything takes time," he said, "and—well, yes, sure, I can make a living at it.
But what I don't seem to be able to make you understand is that it's the only
thing I want to do."

"Well Sonny," I said, gently, "you know people can't always do exactly what
they *want* to do—"

"*No,* I don't know that," said Sonny, surprising me. "I think people *ought* to
do what they want to do, what else are they alive for?"

"You getting to be a big boy," I said desperately, "it's time you started thinking about your future."

"I'm thinking about my future," said Sonny, grimly. "I think about it all the
time."

I gave up. I decided, if he didn't change his mind, that we could always talk 140
about it later. "In the meantime," I said, "you got to finish school." We had already decided that he'd have to move in with Isabel and her folks. I knew this
wasn't the ideal arrangement because Isabel's folks are inclined to be dicty and
they hadn't especially wanted Isabel to marry me. But I didn't know what else to
do. "And we have to get you fixed up at Isabel's."

There was a long silence. He moved from the kitchen table to the window.
"That's a terrible idea. You know it yourself."

"Do you have a *better* idea?"

He just walked up and down the kitchen for a minute. He was as tall as I
was. He had started to shave. I suddenly had the feeling that I didn't know him
at all.

He stopped at the kitchen table and picked up my cigarettes. Looking at me
with a kind of mocking, amused defiance, he put one between his lips. "You mind?"

"You smoking already?" 145

He lit the cigarette and nodded, watching me through the smoke. "I just
wanted to see if I'd have the courage to smoke in front of you." He grinned and
blew a great cloud of smoke to the ceiling. "It was easy." He looked at my face.
"Come on, now. I bet you was smoking at my age, tell the truth."

I didn't say anything but the truth was on my face, and he laughed. But now
there was something very strained in his laugh. "Sure. And I bet that ain't all you
was doing."

He was frightening me a little. "Cut the crap," I said. "We already decided that you was going to go and live at Isabel's. Now what's got into you all of a sudden?"

"You decided it," he pointed out. "I didn't decide nothing." He stopped in front of me, leaning against the stove, arms loosely folded. "Look, brother. I don't want to stay in Harlem no more, I really don't." He was very earnest. He looked at me, then over toward the kitchen window. There was something in his eyes I'd never seen before, some thoughtfulness, some worry all his own. He rubbed the muscle of one arm. "It's time I was getting out of here."

"Where do you want to go, Sonny?" 150

"I want to join the army. Or the navy, I don't care. If I say I'm old enough they'll believe me."

Then I got mad. It was because I was so scared. "You must be crazy. You god-damn fool, what the hell do you want to go and join the *army* for?"

"I just told you. To get out of Harlem."

"Sonny, you haven't even finished *school.* And if you really want to be a mu-sician, how do you expect to study if you're in the *army?"*

He looked at me, trapped, and in anguish. "There's ways. I might be able to 155 work out some kind of deal. Anyway, I'll have the G.I. Bill when I come out."

"If you come out." We stared at each other. "Sonny, please. Be reasonable. I know the setup is far from perfect. But we got to do the best we can."

"I ain't learning nothing in school," he said. "Even when I go." He turned away from me and opened the window and threw his cigarette out into the nar-row alley. I watched his back. "At least, I ain't learning nothing you'd want me to learn." He slammed the window so hard I thought the glass would fly out, and turned back to me. "And I'm sick of the stink of these garbage cans!"

"Sonny," I said, "I know how you feel. But if you don't finish school now, you're going to be sorry later that you didn't." I grabbed him by the shoulders. "And you only got another year. It ain't so bad. And I'll come back and I swear I'll help you do *whatever* you want to do. Just try to put up with it till I come back. Will you please do that? For me?"

He didn't answer and he wouldn't look at me.

"Sonny. You hear me?" 160

He pulled away. "I hear you. But you never hear anything *I* say."

I didn't know what to say to that. He looked out of the window and then back at me. "OK," he said, and sighed. "I'll try."

Then I said, trying to cheer him up a little, "They got a piano at Isabel's. You can practice on it."

And as a matter of fact, it did cheer him up for a minute. "That's right," he said to himself. "I forgot that." His face relaxed a little. But the worry, the thoughtfulness, played on it still, the way shadows play on a face which is staring into the fire.

* * *

But I thought I'd never hear the end of that piano. At first, Isabel would write 165 me, saying how nice it was that Sonny was so serious about his music and how, as soon as he came in from school, or wherever he had been when he was supposed to be at school, he went straight to that piano and stayed there until suppertime. And, after supper, he went back to that piano and stayed there until everybody went to bed. He was at the piano all day Saturday and all day Sunday. Then he bought a record player and started playing records. He'd play one record over and over again, all day long sometimes, and he'd improvise along with it on the piano. Or he'd play one section of the record, one chord, one change, one progression, then he'd do it on the piano. Then back to the record. Then back to the piano.

Well, I really don't know how they stood it. Isabel finally confessed that it wasn't like living with a person at all, it was like living with sound. And the sound didn't make any sense to her, didn't make any sense to any of them—naturally. They began, in a way, to be afflicted by this presence that was living in their home. It was as though Sonny were some sort of god, or monster. He moved in an atmosphere which wasn't like theirs at all. They fed him and he ate, he washed himself, he walked in and out of their door; he certainly wasn't nasty or unpleasant or rude, Sonny isn't any of those things; but it was as though he were all wrapped up in some cloud, some fire, some vision all his own; and there wasn't any way to reach him.

At the same time, he wasn't really a man yet, he was still a child, and they had to watch out for him in all kinds of ways. They certainly couldn't throw him out. Neither did they dare to make a great scene about that piano because even they dimly sensed, as I sensed, from so many thousands of miles away, that Sonny was at that piano playing for his life.

But he hadn't been going to school. One day a letter came from the school board and Isabel's mother got it—there had, apparently, been other letters but Sonny had torn them up. This day, when Sonny came in, Isabel's mother showed him the letter and asked where he'd been spending his time. And she finally got it out of him that he'd been down in Greenwich Village, with musicians and other characters, in a white girl's apartment. And this scared her and she started to scream at him and what came up, once she began—though she denies it to this day—was what sacrifices they were making to give Sonny a decent home and how little he appreciated it.

Sonny didn't play the piano that day. By evening, Isabel's mother had calmed down but then there was the old man to deal with, and Isabel herself. Isabel says she did her best to be calm but she broke down and started crying. She says she just watched Sonny's face. She could tell, by watching him, what was happening with him. And what was happening was that they penetrated his cloud, they had reached him. Even if their fingers had been a thousand times more gentle than human fingers ever are, he could hardly help feeling that they had stripped him naked and were spitting on that nakedness. For he also had to see that his presence, that music, which was life or death to him, had been torture for them and that they had endured it, not at all for his sake, but only for mine. And Sonny couldn't take that. He can take it a little better today than he could then but he's still not very good at it and, frankly, I don't know anybody who is.

The silence of the next few days must have been louder than the sound of 170 all the music ever played since time began. One morning, before she went to work, Isabel was in his room for something and she suddenly realized that all of his records were gone. And she knew for certain that he was gone. And he was. He went as far as the navy would carry him. He finally sent me a postcard from some place in Greece and that was the first I knew that Sonny was still alive. I didn't see him any more until we were both back in New York and the war had long been over.

He was a man by then, of course, but I wasn't willing to see it. He came by the house from time to time, but we fought almost every time we met. I didn't like the way he carried himself, loose and dreamlike all the time, and I didn't like his friends, and his music seemed to be merely an excuse for the life he led. It sounded just that weird and disordered.

Then we had a fight, a pretty awful fight, and I didn't see him for months. By and by I looked him up, where he was living, in a furnished room in the Village, and I tried to make it up. But there were lots of other people in the room and Sonny just lay on his bed, and he wouldn't come downstairs with me, and he treated these other people as though they were his family and I weren't. So I got mad and then he got mad, and then I told him that he might just as well be dead as live the way he was living. Then he stood up and he told me not to worry about him any more in life, that he *was* dead as far as I was concerned. Then he pushed me to the door and the other people looked on as though nothing were happening, and he slammed the door behind me. I stood in the hallway, staring at the door. I heard somebody laugh in the room and then the tears came to my eyes. I started down the steps, whistling to keep from crying, I kept whistling to myself, *You going to need me, baby, one of these cold, rainy days.*

* * *

I read about Sonny's trouble in the spring. Little Grace died in the fall. She was a beautiful little girl. But she only lived a little over two years. She died of polio and she suffered. She had a slight fever for a couple of days, but it didn't seem like anything and we just kept her in bed. And we would certainly have called the doctor, but the fever dropped, she seemed to be all right. So we thought it had just been a cold. Then, one day, she was up, playing, Isabel was in the kitchen fixing lunch for the two boys when they'd come in from school, and she heard Grace fall down in the living room. When you have a lot of children you don't always start running when one of them falls, unless they start screaming or something. And, this time, Grace was quiet. Yet, Isabel says that when she heard that *thump* and then that silence, something happened in her to make her afraid. And she ran to the living room and there was little Grace on the floor, all twisted up and the reason she hadn't screamed was that she couldn't get her breath. And when she did scream, it was the worst sound, Isabel says, that she'd ever heard in all her life, and she still hears it sometimes in her dreams. Isabel will sometimes wake me up with a low, moaning, strangled sound and I have to be quick to awaken her and hold her to me and where Isabel is weeping against me seems a mortal wound.

I think I may have written Sonny the very day that little Grace was buried. I was sitting in the living room in the dark, by myself, and I suddenly thought of Sonny. My trouble made his real.

* * *

One Saturday afternoon, when Sonny had been living with us, or, anyway, been in our house, for nearly two weeks, I found myself wandering aimlessly about the living room, drinking from a can of beer, and trying to work up the courage to search Sonny's room. He was out, he was usually out whenever I was home, and 175

Isabel had taken the children to see their grandparents. Suddenly I was standing still in front of the living room window, watching Seventh Avenue. The idea of searching Sonny's room made me still. I scarcely dared to admit to myself what I'd be searching for. I didn't know what I'd do if I found it. Or if I didn't.

On the sidewalk across from me, near the entrance to a barbecue joint, some people were holding an old-fashioned revival meeting. The barbecue cook, wearing a dirty white apron, his conked hair reddish and metallic in the pale sun, and a cigarette between his lips, stood in the doorway, watching them. Kids and older people paused in their errands and stood there, along with some older men and a couple of very tough-looking women who watched everything that happened on the avenue, as though they owned it, or were maybe owned by it. Well, they were watching this, too. The revival was being carried on by three sisters in black, and a brother. All they had were their voices and their Bibles and a tambourine. The brother was testifying and while he testified two of the sisters stood together, seeming to say, Amen, and the third sister walked around with the tambourine outstretched and a couple of people dropped coins into it. Then the brother's testimony ended and the sister who had been taking up the collection dumped the coins into her palm and transferred them to the pocket of her long black robe. Then she raised both hands, striking the tambourine against the air, and then against one hand, and she started to sing. And the two other sisters and the brother joined in.

It was strange, suddenly, to watch, though I had been seeing these street meetings all my life. So, of course, had everybody else down there. Yet, they paused and watched and listened and I stood still at the window. "*Tis the old ship of Zion,*" they sang, and the sister with the tambourine kept a steady, jangling beat, "*It has rescued many a thousand!*" Not a soul under the sound of their voices was hearing this song for the first time, not one of them had been rescued. Nor had they seen much in the way of rescue work being done around them. Neither did they especially believe in the holiness of the three sisters and the brother, they knew too much about them, knew where they lived, and how. The woman with the tambourine, whose voice dominated the air, whose face was bright with joy, was divided by very little from the woman who stood watching her, a cigarette between her heavy, chapped lips, her hair a cuckoo's nest, her face scarred and swollen from many beatings, and her black eyes glittering like coal. Perhaps they both knew this, which was why, when, as rarely, they addressed each other, they addressed each other as Sister. As the singing filled the air the watching, listening faces underwent a change, the eyes focusing on something within; the music seemed to soothe a poison out of them; and time seemed, nearly, to fall away from the sullen, belligerent, battered faces, as though they were fleeing back to their first condition, while dreaming of their last. The barbecue cook half shook his head and smiled, and dropped his cigarette and disappeared into his joint. A man fumbled in his pockets for change and stood holding it in his hand impatiently, as though he had just remembered a pressing appointment further up the avenue. He looked furious. Then I saw Sonny, standing on the edge of the crowd. He was carrying a wide, flat notebook with a green cover, and it made him look, from where I was standing, almost like a schoolboy. The coppery sun brought out the copper in his skin, he was very faintly smiling, standing very still. Then the singing stopped, the tambourine turned into a collection plate again. The furious man dropped in his coins and vanished, so did a couple of the women, and Sonny dropped some change in the plate, looking directly at the woman with a little smile. He started across the avenue, toward the house. He has a slow, loping walk, something like the way Harlem hipsters walk, only he's imposed on this his own halfbeat. I had never really noticed it before.

I stayed at the window, both relieved and apprehensive. As Sonny disappeared from my sight, they began singing again. And they were still singing when his key turned in the lock.

"Hey," he said.

"Hey, yourself. You want some beer?"   180

"No. Well, maybe." But he came up to the window and stood beside me, looking out. "What a warm voice," he said.

They were singing *If I could only hear my mother pray again!*

"Yes," I said, "and she can sure beat that tambourine."

"But what a terrible song," he said, and laughed. He dropped his notebook on the sofa and disappeared into the kitchen. "Where's Isabel and the kids?"

"I think they went to see their grandparents. You hungry?"   185

"No." He came back into the living room with his can of beer. "You want to come some place with me tonight?"

I sensed, I don't know how, that I couldn't possibly say No. "Sure. Where?"

He sat down on the sofa and picked up his notebook and started leafing through it. "I'm going to sit in with some fellows in a joint in the Village."

"You mean, you're going to play, tonight?"

"That's right." He took a swallow of his beer and moved back to the window. 190
He gave me a sidelong look. "If you can stand it."

"I'll try," I said.

He smiled to himself and we both watched as the meeting across the way broke up. The three sisters and the brother, heads bowed, were singing *God be with you till we meet again.* The faces around them were very quiet. Then the song ended. The small crowd dispersed. We watched the three women and the lone man walk slowly up the avenue.

"When she was singing before," said Sonny, abruptly, "her voice reminded me for a minute of what heroin feels like sometimes—when it's in your veins. It makes you feel sort of warm and cool at the same time. And distant. And—and sure." He sipped his beer, very deliberately not looking at me. I watched his face. "It makes you feel—in control. Sometimes you've got to have that feeling."

"Do you?" I sat down slowly in the easy chair.

"Sometimes." He went to the sofa and picked up his notebook again. "Some 195
people do."

"In order," I asked, "to play?" And my voice was very ugly, full of contempt and anger.

"Well"—he looked at me with great, troubled eyes, as though, in fact, he hoped his eyes would tell me things he could never otherwise say—"they *think* so. And *if* they think so—!"

"And what do *you* think?" I asked.

He sat on the sofa and put his can of beer on the floor. "I don't know," he said, and I couldn't be sure if he were answering my question or pursuing his thoughts. His face didn't tell me. "It's not so much to *play*. It's to *stand* it, to be able to make it at all. On any level." He frowned and smiled: "In order to keep from shaking to pieces."

"But these friends of yours," I said, "they seem to shake themselves to pieces 200
pretty goddamn fast."

"Maybe." He played with the notebook. And something told me that I
should curb my tongue, that Sonny was doing his best to talk, that I should listen. "But of course you only know the ones that've gone to pieces. Some don't—
or at least they haven't *yet* and that's just about all *any* of us can say." He paused.
"And then there are some who just live, really, in hell, and they know it and
they see what's happening and they go right on. I don't know." He sighed,
dropped the notebook, folded his arms. "Some guys, you can tell from the way
they play, they on something *all* the time. And you can see that, well, it makes
something real for them. But of course," he picked up his beer from the floor and
sipped it and put the can down again, "they *want* to, too, you've got to see that.
Even some of them that say they don't—*some*, not all."

"And what about you?" I asked—I couldn't help it. "What about you? Do
you want to?"

He stood up and walked to the window and remained silent for a long time.
Then he sighed. "Me," he said. Then: "While I was downstairs before, on my way
here, listening to that woman sing, it struck me all of a sudden how much suffering she must have had to go through—to sing like that. It's *repulsive* to think you
have to suffer that much."

I said: "But there's no way not to suffer—is there, Sonny?"

"I believe not," he said, and smiled, "but that's never stopped anyone from 205
trying." He looked at me. "Has it?" I realized, with this mocking look, that there
stood between us, forever, beyond the power of time or forgiveness, the fact that
I had held silence—so long!—when he had needed human speech to help him.
He turned back to the window. "No, there's no way not to suffer. But you try all
kinds of ways to keep from drowning in it, to keep on top of it, and to make it
seem—well, like *you*. Like you did something, all right, and now you're suffering
for it. You know?" I said nothing. "Well you know," he said, impatiently, "why *do*
people suffer? Maybe it's better to do something to give it a reason, *any* reason."

"But we just agreed," I said, "that there's no way not to suffer. Isn't it better,
then, just to—take it?"

"But nobody just takes it," Sonny cried, "that's what I'm telling you!
Everybody tries not to. You're just hung up on the *way* some people try—it's not
your way!"

The hair on my face began to itch, my face felt wet. "That's not true," I said,
"that's not true. I don't give a damn what other people do, I don't even care how
they suffer. I just care how *you* suffer." And he looked at me. "Please believe me,"
I said, "I don't want to see you—die—trying not to suffer."

"I won't," he said, flatly, "die trying not to suffer. At least, not any faster
than anybody else."

"But there's no need," I said, trying to laugh, "is there? in killing yourself." 210

I wanted to say more, but I couldn't. I wanted to talk about will power and how
life could be—well, beautiful. I wanted to say that it was all within; but was it? or,
rather, wasn't that exactly the trouble? And I wanted to promise that I would never
fail him again. But it would all have sounded—empty words and lies.

So I made the promise to myself and prayed that I would keep it.

"It's terrible sometimes, inside," he said, "that's what's the trouble. You walk
these streets, black and funky and cold, and there's not really a living ass to talk

to, and there's nothing shaking, and there's no way of getting it out—that storm inside. You can't talk it and you can't make love with it, and when you finally try to get with it and play it, you realize *nobody's* listening. So *you've* got to listen. You got to find a way to listen."

And then he walked away from the window and sat on the sofa again, as though all the wind had suddenly been knocked out of him. "Sometimes you'll do *anything* to play, even cut your mother's throat." He laughed and looked at me. "Or your brother's." Then he sobered. "Or your own." Then: "Don't worry. I'm all right now and I think I'll *be* all right. But I can't forget—where I've been. I don't mean just the physical place I've been, I mean where I've *been*. And *what* I've been."

"What have you been, Sonny?" I asked.

He smiled—but sat sideways on the sofa, his elbow resting on the back, his fingers playing with his mouth and chin, not looking at me. "I've been something I didn't recognize, didn't know I could be. Didn't know anybody could be." He stopped, looking inward, looking helplessly young, looking old. "I'm not talking about it now because I feel *guilty* or anything like that—maybe it would be better if I did, I don't know. Anyway, I can't really talk about it. Not to you, not to anybody," and now he turned and faced me. "Sometimes, you know, and it was actually when I was most *out* of the world, I felt that I was in it, and that I was *with* it, really, and I could play or I didn't really have to *play*, it just came out of me, it was there. And I don't know how I played, thinking about it now, but I know I did awful things, those times, sometimes, to people. Or it wasn't that I *did* anything to them—it was that they weren't real." He picked up the beer can; it was empty; he rolled it between his palms: "And other times—well, I needed a fix, I needed to find a place to lean, I needed to clear a space to *listen*—and I couldn't find it, and I—went crazy, I did terrible things to *me*, I was terrible *for* me." He began pressing the beer can between his hands, I watched the metal begin to give. It glittered, as he played with it, like a knife, and I was afraid he would cut himself, but I said nothing. "Oh well. I can never tell you. I was all by myself at the bottom of something, stinking and sweating and crying and shaking, and I smelled it, you know? my stink, and I thought I'd die if I couldn't get away from it and yet, all the same, I knew that everything I was doing was just locking me in with it. And I didn't know," he paused, still flattening the beer can, "I didn't know, I still *don't* know, something kept telling me that maybe it was good to smell your own stink, but I didn't think that *that* was what I'd been trying to do—and—who can stand it?" and he abruptly dropped the ruined beer can, looking at me with a small, still smile, and then rose, walking to the window as though it were the lodestone rock. I watched his face, he watched the avenue. "I couldn't tell you when Mama died—but the reason I wanted to leave Harlem so bad was to get away from drugs. And then, when I ran away, that's what I was running from—really. When I came back, nothing had changed, *I* hadn't changed, I was just—older." And he stopped, drumming with his fingers on the windowpane. The sun had vanished, soon darkness would fall. I watched his face. "It can come again," he said, almost as though speaking to himself. Then he turned to me. "It can come again," he repeated. "I just want you to know that."

"All right," I said, at last. "So it can come again. All right."

He smiled, but the smile was sorrowful. "I had to try to tell you," he said.

"Yes," I said. "I understand that."

"You're my brother," he said, looking straight at me, and not smiling at all.   220
"Yes," I repeated, "yes. I understand that."

He turned back to the window, looking out. "All that hatred down there," he said, "all that hatred and misery and love. It's a wonder it doesn't blow the avenue apart."

* * *

We went to the only night club on a short, dark street, downtown. We squeezed through the narrow, chattering, jam-packed bar to the entrance of the big room, where the bandstand was. And we stood there for a moment, for the lights were very dim in this room and we couldn't see. Then, "Hello, boy," said a voice and an enormous black man, much older than Sonny or myself, erupted out of all that atmospheric lighting and put an arm around Sonny's shoulder. "I been sitting right here," he said, "waiting for you."

He had a big voice, too, and heads in the darkness turned toward us.

Sonny grinned and pulled a little away, and said, "Creole, this is my brother.   225
I told you about him."

Creole shook my hand. "I'm glad to meet you, son," he said, and it was clear that he was glad to meet me *there*, for Sonny's sake. And he smiled, "You got a real musician in *your* family," and he took his arm from Sonny's shoulder and slapped him, lightly, affectionately, with the back of his hand.

"Well. Now I've heard it all," said a voice behind us. This was another musician, and a friend of Sonny's, a coal-black, cheerful-looking man, built close to the ground. He immediately began confiding to me, at the top of his lungs, the most terrible things about Sonny, his teeth gleaming like a lighthouse and his laugh coming up out of him like the beginning of an earthquake. And it turned out that everyone at the bar knew Sonny, or almost everyone; some were musicians, working there, or nearby, or not working, some were simply hangers-on, and some were there to hear Sonny play. I was introduced to all of them and they were all very polite to me. Yet, it was clear that, for them, I was only Sonny's brother. Here, I was in Sonny's world. Or, rather: his kingdom. Here, it was not even a question that his veins bore royal blood.

They were going to play soon and Creole installed me, by myself, at a table in a dark corner. Then I watched them, Creole, and the little black man, and Sonny, and the others, while they horsed around, standing just below the bandstand. The light from the bandstand spilled just a little short of them and, watching them laughing and gesturing and moving about, I had the feeling that they, nevertheless, were being most careful not to step into that circle of light too suddenly: that if they moved into the light too suddenly, without thinking, they would perish in flame. Then, while I watched, one of them, the small, black man, moved into the light and crossed the bandstand and started fooling around with his drums. Then—being funny and being, also, extremely ceremonious—Creole took Sonny by the arm and led him to the piano. A woman's voice called Sonny's name and a few hands started clapping. And Sonny, also being funny and being ceremonious, and so touched, I think, that he could have cried, but neither hiding it nor showing it, riding it like a man, grinned, and put both hands to his heart and bowed from the waist.

Creole then went to the bass fiddle and a lean, very bright-skinned brown man jumped up on the bandstand and picked up his horn. So there they were, and the atmosphere on the bandstand and in the room began to change and tighten. Someone stepped up to the microphone and announced them. Then there were all kinds of murmurs. Some people at the bar shushed others. The waitress ran around, frantically getting in the last orders, guys and chicks got closer to each other, and the lights on the bandstand, on the quartet, turned to a kind of indigo. Then they all looked different there. Creole looked about him for the last time, as though he were making certain that all his chickens were in the coop, and then he—jumped and struck the fiddle. And there they were.

All I know about music is that not many people ever really hear it. And even then, on the rare occasions when something opens within, and the music enters, what we mainly hear, or hear corroborated, are personal private, vanishing evocations. But the man who creates the music is hearing something else, is dealing with the roar rising from the void and imposing order on it as it hits the air. What is evoked in him, then, is of another order, more terrible because it has no words, and triumphant, too, for that same reason. And his triumph, when he triumphs, is ours. I just watched Sonny's face. His face was troubled, he was working hard, but he wasn't with it. And I had the feeling that, in a way, everyone on the bandstand was waiting for him, both waiting for him and pushing him along. But as I began to watch Creole, I realized that it was Creole who held them all back. He had them on a short rein. Up there, keeping the beat with his whole body, wailing on the fiddle, with his eyes half closed, he was listening to everything, but he was listening to Sonny. He was having a dialogue with Sonny. He wanted Sonny to leave the shore line and strike out for the deep water. He was Sonny's witness that deep water and drowning were not the same thing—he had been there, and he knew. And he wanted Sonny to know. He was waiting for Sonny to do the things on the keys which would let Creole know that Sonny was in the water.

And, while Creole listened, Sonny moved, deep within, exactly like someone in torment. I had never before thought of how awful the relationship must be between the musician and his instrument. He has to fill it, this instrument, with the breath of life, his own. He has to make it do what he wants it to do. And a piano is just a piano. It's made out of so much wood and wires and little hammers and big ones, and ivory. While there's only so much you can do with it, the only way to find this out is to try and make it do everything.

And Sonny hadn't been near a piano for over a year. And he wasn't on much better terms with his life, not the life that stretched before him now. He and the piano stammered, started one way, got scared, stopped; started another way, panicked, marked time, started again; then seemed to have found a direction, panicked again, got stuck. And the face I saw on Sonny I'd never seen before. Everything had been burned out of it, and, at the same time, things usually hidden were being burned in, by the fire and fury of the battle which was occurring in him up there.

Yet, watching Creole's face as they neared the end of the first set, I had the feeling that something had happened, something I hadn't heard. Then they finished, there was scattered applause, and then, without an instant's warning, Creole started into something else, it was almost sardonic, it was *Am I Blue*. And, as though he commanded, Sonny began to play. Something began to happen. And Creole let out the reins. The dry, low, black man said something awful on the drums, Creole answered, and the drums talked back. Then the horn insisted, sweet and high, slightly detached perhaps, and Creole listened, commenting now and then, dry, and driving, beautiful and calm and old. Then they all came together again, and Sonny was part of the family again. I could tell this from his face. He seemed to have found, right there beneath his fingers, a damn brand-new piano. It seemed that he couldn't get over it. Then, for awhile, just being happy with Sonny, they seemed to be agreeing with him that brand-new pianos certainly were a gas.

Then Creole stepped forward to remind them that what they were playing was the blues. He hit something in all of them, he hit something in me, myself, and the music tightened and deepened, apprehension began to beat the air. Creole began to tell us what the blues were all about. They were not about anything very new. He and his boys up there were keeping it new, at the risk of ruin, destruction, madness, and death, in order to find new ways to make us listen. For, while the tale of how we suffer, and how we are delighted, and how we may triumph is never new, it always must be heard. There isn't any other tale to tell, it's the only light we've got in all this darkness.

And this tale, according to that face, that body, those strong hands on those strings, has another aspect in every country, and a new depth in every generation. Listen, Creole seemed to be saying, listen. Now these are Sonny's blues. He made the little black man on the drums know it, and the bright, brown man on the horn. Creole wasn't trying any longer to get Sonny in the water. He was wishing him Godspeed. Then he stepped back, very slowly, filling the air with the immense suggestion that Sonny speak for himself. 235

Then they all gathered around Sonny and Sonny played. Every now and again one of them seemed to say, Amen. Sonny's fingers filled the air with life, his life. But that life contained so many others. And Sonny went all the way back, he really began with the spare, flat statement of the opening phrase of the song. Then he began to make it his. It was very beautiful because it wasn't hurried and it was no longer a lament. I seemed to hear with what burning he had made it his, with what burning we had yet to make it ours, how we could cease lamenting. Freedom lurked around us and I understood, at last, that he could help us to be free if we would listen, that he would never be free until we did. Yet, there was no battle in his face now. I heard what he had gone through, and would continue to go through until he came to rest in earth. He had made it his: that long line, of which we knew only Mama and Daddy. And he was giving it back, as everything must be given back, so that, passing through death, it can live forever. I saw my mother's face again, and felt, for the first time, how the stones of the road she had walked on must have bruised her feet. I saw the moonlit road where my father's brother died. And it brought something else back to me, and carried me past it, I saw my little girl again and felt Isabel's tears again, and I felt my own tears begin to rise. And I was yet aware that this was only a moment, that the world waited outside, as hungry as a tiger, and that trouble stretched above us, longer than the sky.

Then it was over. Creole and Sonny let out their breath, both soaking wet, and grinning. There was a lot of applause and some of it was real. In the dark, the girl came by and I asked her to take drinks to the bandstand. There was a long pause, while they talked up there in the indigo light and after awhile I saw the girl put a Scotch and milk on top of the piano for Sonny. He didn't seem to notice it, but just before they started playing again, he sipped from it and looked toward me, and nodded. Then he put it back on top of the piano. For me, then, as they began to play again, it glowed and shook above my brother's head like the very cup of trembling.

Starting Points for Further Research: James Baldwin

- **Editions:** James Baldwin. *Collected Essays.* Ed. Toni Morrison. New York: Library of America, 1998.
  ———. *Early Novels and Stories.* Ed. Toni Morrison. New York: Library of America, 1998.
- **Biography:** David A. Leeming. *James Baldwin: A Biography.* New York: Random House, 1994.
- **Critical Essay:** Colm Toibin. "The Last Witness." *London Review of Books,* September 20, 2001, 15–20.

CHINUA ACHEBE (B. 1930)

Chinua Achebe is one of the leading contemporary African novelists. His early novels, including the groundbreaking Things Fall Apart *(1958) and* No Longer at Ease *(1960), describe the effects of European colonialism on newly independent African nations. He has also written numerous short stories, children's books, and a book of essays,* Home and Exile *(2000). Achebe's subject matter has been social and political change in Africa, which he writes about in his own distinctive style.*

A Civil Peace (1973)

Jonathan Iwegbu counted himself extraordinarily lucky. "Happy survival!" meant so much more to him than just a current fashion of greeting old friends in the first hazy days of peace. It went deep to his heart. He had come out of the war with five inestimable blessings—his head, his wife Maria's head, and the heads of three out of their four children. As a bonus he also had his old bicycle—a miracle too but naturally not to be compared to the safety of five human heads.

The bicycle had a little history of its own. One day at the height of the war it was commandeered "for urgent military action." Hard as its loss would have been to him he would still have let it go without a thought had he not had some doubts about the genuineness of the officer. It wasn't his disreputable rags, nor the toes peeping out of one blue and one brown canvas shoes, nor yet the two stars of his rank done obviously in a hurry in biro, that troubled Jonathan; many good and heroic soldiers looked the same or worse. It was rather a certain lack of grip and firmness in his manner. So Jonathan, suspecting he might be amenable to influence, rummaged in his raffia bag and produced the two pounds with which he had been going to buy firewood which his wife, Maria, retailed to camp officials for extra stock-fish and corn meal, and got his bicycle back. That night he buried it in the little clearing in the bush where the dead of the camp, including his own youngest son, were buried. When he dug it up again a year later after the surrender all it needed was a little palm-oil greasing. "Nothing puzzles God," he said in wonder.

He put it to immediate use as a taxi and accumulated a small pile of Biafran money ferrying camp officials and their families across the four-mile stretch to the nearest tarred road. His standard charge per trip was six pounds and those who had the money were only glad to be rid of some of it in this way. At the end of a fortnight he had made a small fortune of one hundred and fifteen pounds.

Then he made the journey to Enugu and found another miracle waiting for him. It was unbelievable. He rubbed his eyes and looked again and it was still standing there before him. But, needless to say, even that monumental blessing must be accounted also totally inferior to the five heads in the family. This newest miracle was his little house in Ogui Overside. Indeed nothing puzzles God! Only two houses away a huge concrete edifice some wealthy contractor had put up just before the war was a mountain of rubble. And here was Jonathan's little zinc house of no regrets built with mud blocks quite intact! Of course the doors and windows were missing and five sheets off the roof. But what was that? And anyhow he had returned to Enugu early enough to pick up bits of old zinc and wood and soggy sheets of cardboard lying around the neighbourhood before thousands more came out of their forest holes looking for the same things. He got a destitute carpenter with one old hammer, a blunt plane, and a few bent and rusty nails in his tool bag to turn this assortment of wood, paper, and metal into door and window shutters for five Nigerian shillings or fifty Biafran pounds. He paid the pounds, and moved in with his overjoyed family carrying five heads on their shoulders.

His children picked mangoes near the military cemetery and sold them to soldiers' wives for a few pennies—real pennies this time—and his wife started making breakfast akara balls for neighbours in a hurry to start life again. With his family earnings he took his bicycle to the villages around and bought fresh palm-wine which he mixed generously in his rooms with the water which had recently started running again in the public tap down the road, and opened up a bar for soldiers and other lucky people with good money.

At first he went daily, then every other day, and finally once a week, to the offices of the Coal Corporation where he used to be a miner, to find out what was what. The only thing he did find out in the end was that that little house of his was even a greater blessing than he had thought. Some of his fellow ex-miners who had nowhere to return at the end of the day's waiting just slept outside the doors of the offices and cooked what meal they could scrounge together in Bournvita tins. As the weeks lengthened and still nobody could say what was what Jonathan discontinued his weekly visits altogether and faced his palm-wine bar.

But nothing puzzles God. Came the day of the windfall when after five days of endless scuffles in queues and counter-queues in the sun outside the Treasury he had twenty pounds counted into his palms as ex-gratia award for the rebel money he had turned in. It was like Christmas for him and for many others like him when the payments began. They called it (since few could manage its proper official name) *egg-rasher.*

As soon as the pound notes were placed in his palm Jonathan simply closed it tight over them and buried fist and money inside his trouser pocket. He had to be extra careful because he had seen a man a couple of days earlier collapse into near-madness in an instant before that oceanic crowd because no sooner had he

5

got his twenty pounds than some heartless ruffian picked it off him. Though it was not right that a man in such an extremity of agony should be blamed yet many in the queues that day were able to remark quietly on the victim's carelessness, especially after he pulled out the innards of his pocket and revealed a hole in it big enough to pass a thief's head. But of course he had insisted that the money had been in the other pocket, pulling it out too to show its comparative wholeness. So one had to be careful.

Jonathan soon transferred the money to his left hand and pocket so as to leave his right free for shaking hands should the need arise, though by fixing his gaze at such an elevation as to miss all approaching human faces he made sure that the need did not arise, until he got home.

He was normally a heavy sleeper but that night he heard all the neighbour-   10
hood noises die down one after another. Even the night watchman who knocked the hour on some metal somewhere in the distance had fallen silent after knocking one o'clock. That must have been the last thought in Jonathan's mind before he was finally carried away himself. He couldn't have been gone for long, though, when he was violently awakened again.

"Who is knocking?" whispered his wife lying beside him on the floor.

"I don't know," he whispered back breathlessly.

The second time the knocking came it was so loud and imperious that the rickety old door could have fallen down.

"Who is knocking?" he asked then, his voice parched and trembling.

"Na tief-man and him people," came the cool reply. "Make you hopen de   15
door." This was followed by the heaviest knocking of all.

Maria was the first to raise the alarm, then he followed and all their children.

"*Police-o! Thieves-o! Neighbours-o! Police-o! We are lost! We are dead! Neighbours, are you asleep? Wake up! Police-o!*"

This went on for a long time and then stopped suddenly. Perhaps they had scared the thief away. There was total silence. But only for a short while.

"You done finish?" asked the voice outside. "Make we help you small. Oya, everybody!"

"*Police-o! Tief-man-o! Neighbours-o! we done loss-o! Police-o! . . .*"   20

There were at least five other voices besides the leader's.

Jonathan and his family were now completely paralysed by terror. Maria and the children sobbed inaudibly like lost souls. Jonathan groaned continuously.

The silence that followed the thieves' alarm vibrated horribly. Jonathan all but begged their leader to speak again and be done with it.

"My frien," said he at long last, "we don try our best for call dem but I tink say dem all done sleep-o . . . So wetin we go do now? Sometaim you wan call soja? Or you wan make we call dem for you? Soja better pass police. No be so?"

"Na so!" replied his men. Jonathan thought he heard even more voices now   25
than before and groaned heavily. His legs were sagging under him and his throat felt like sandpaper.

"My frien, why you no de talk again. I de ask you say you wan make we call soja?"

"No."

"Awrighto. Now make we talk business. We no be bad tief. We no like for make trouble. Trouble done finish. War done finish and all the katakata wey de for inside. No Civil War again. This time na Civil Peace. No be so?"

"Na so!" answered the horrible chorus.

"What do you want from me? I am a poor man. Everything I had went with this war. Why do you come to me? You know people who have money. We . . ."

"Awright! We know say you no get plenty money. But we sef no get even anini. So derefore make you open dis window and give us one hundred pound and we go commot. Orderwise we de come for inside now to show you guitar-boy like dis . . ."

A volley of automatic fire rang through the sky. Maria and the children began to weep aloud again.

"Ah, missisi de cry again. No need for dat. We done talk say we na good tief. We just take our small money and go nwayorly. No molest. Abi we de molest?"

"At all!" sang the chorus.

"My friends," began Jonathan hoarsely. "I hear what you say and I thank you. If I had one hundred pounds . . ."

"Lookia my frien, no be play we come play for your house. If we make mistake and step for inside you no go like am-o. So derefore . . ."

"To God who made me; if you come inside and find one hundred pounds, take it and shoot me and shoot my wife and children. I swear to God. The only money I have in this life is this twenty pounds *egg-rasher* they gave me today . . .

"OK. Time de go. Make you open dis window and bring the twenty pound. We go manage am like dat."

There were now loud murmurs of dissent among the chorus: "Na lie de man de lie; e get plenty money . . . Make we go inside and search properly well . . . Wetin be twenty pound? . . ."

"Shurrup!" rang the leader's voice like a lone shot in the sky and silenced the murmuring at once. "Are you dere? Bring the money quick!"

"I am coming," said Jonathan fumbling in the darkness with the key of the small wooden box he kept by his side on the mat.

*   *   *

At the first sign of light as neighbours and others assembled to commiserate with him he was already strapping his five-gallon demijohn to his bicycle carrier and his wife, sweating in the open fire, was turning over akara balls in a wide clay bowl of boiling oil. In the corner his eldest son was rinsing out dregs of yesterday's palm-wine from old beer bottles.

"I count it as nothing," he told his sympathizers, his eyes on the rope he was tying. "What is *egg-rasher*? Did I depend on it last week? Or is it greater than other things that went with the war? I say, let *egg-rasher* perish in the flames! Let it go where everything else has gone. Nothing puzzles God."

Starting Points for Further Research: Chinua Achebe

- **Critical Essay:** Suzanne Scafe. " 'Wherever Something Stands, Something Else Will Stand Beside It': Ambivalence in Achebe's *Things Fall Apart* and *Arrow of God.*" *Changing English: Studies in Reading and Culture* 9:2 (2002) : 119–31.

■ **Interview:** R. Victoria Arana. "The Epic Imagination: A Conversation with Chinua Achebe at Annandale on Hudson, October 31, 1998." *Callaloo: A Journal of African-American and African Arts and Letters* 25 (2002): 505–26.

LESLIE MARMON SILKO   (B. 1948)

Leslie Marmon Silko was born of mixed Anglo, Mexican, and Native American heritage in Albuquerque, New Mexico, and grew up on the Laguna Pueblo Reservation, where she learned traditional stories and legends from female relatives. Silko's first published book was the collection of poems Laguna Woman *(1974). Since then she has published* Ceremony *(1977),* Western Stories *(1980),* Storyteller *(1981),* Delicacy and Strength of Lace: Letters *(1986),* Almanac of the Dead: A Novel *(1991),* Yellow Woman *(1993),* Sacred Water: Narratives and Pictures *(1993),* Yellow Woman and a Beauty of the Spirit: Essays *(1996),* Love Poem and Slim Man Canyon *(1999), and* Gardens in the Dunes *(1999). Silko has taught college in New Mexico, Alaska, and Arizona and has been awarded a Macarthur Fellowship . She lives in Tucson, Arizona.*

Yellow Woman   (1981)

I

My thigh clung to his with dampness, and I watched the sun rising up through the tamaracks and willows. The small brown water birds came to the river and hopped across the mud, leaving brown scratches in the alkali-white crust. They bathed in the river silently. I could hear the water, almost at our feet where the narrow fast channel bubbled and washed green ragged moss and fern leaves. I looked at him beside me, rolled in the red blanket on the white river sand. I cleaned the sand out of the cracks between my toes, squinting because the sun was above the willow trees. I looked at him for the last time, sleeping on the white river sand.

I felt hungry and followed the river south the way we had come the afternoon before, following our footprints that were already blurred by the lizard tracks and bug trails. The horses were still lying down, and the black one whinnied when he saw me but he did not get up—maybe it was because the corral was made out of thick cedar branches and the horses had not yet felt the sun like I had. I tried to look beyond the pale red mesas to the pueblo. I knew it was there, even if I could not see it, on the sand rock hill above the river, the same river that moved past me now and had reflected the moon last night.

The horse felt warm underneath me. He shook his head and pawed the sand. The bay whinnied and leaned against the gate trying to follow, and I remembered him asleep in the red blanket beside the river. I slid off the horse and tied him close to the other horse. I walked north with the river again, and the white sand broke loose in footprints over footprints.

"Wake up."

He moved in the blanket and turned his face to me with his eyes still closed. I knelt down to touch him.

"I'm leaving."

5

He smiled now, eyes still closed. "You are coming with me, remember?" He sat up now with his bare dark chest and belly in the sun.

"Where?"

"To my place."

"And will I come back?"   10

He pulled his pants on. I walked away from him, feeling him behind me and smelling the willows.

"Yellow Woman," he said.

I turned to face him. "Who are you?" I asked.

He laughed and knelt on the low, sandy bank, washing his face in the river. "Last night you guessed my name, and you knew why I had come."

I stared past him at the shallow moving water and tried to remember the   15
night, but I could only see the moon in the water and remember his warmth around me.

"But I only said that you were him and that I was Yellow Woman—I'm not really her—I have my own name and I come from the pueblo on the other side of the mesa. Your name is Silva and you are a stranger I met by the river yesterday afternoon."

He laughed softly. "What happened yesterday has nothing to do with what you will do today, Yellow Woman."

"I know—that's what I'm saying—the old stories about the ka'tsina spirit[1] and Yellow Woman can't mean us."

My old grandpa liked to tell those stories best. There is one about Badger and Coyote who went hunting and were gone all day, and when the sun was going down they found a house. There was a girl living there alone, and she had light hair and eyes and she told them that they could sleep with her. Coyote wanted to be with her all night so he sent Badger into a prairie-dog hole, telling him he thought he saw something in it. As soon as Badger crawled in, Coyote blocked up the entrance with rocks and hurried back to Yellow Woman.

"Come here," he said gently.   20

He touched my neck and I moved close to him to feel his breathing and to hear his heart. I was wondering if Yellow Woman had known who she was—if she knew that she would become part of the stories. Maybe she'd had another name that her husband and relatives called her so that only the ka'tsina from the north and the storytellers would know her as Yellow Woman. But I didn't go on; I felt him all around me, pushing me down into the white river sand.

Yellow Woman went away with the spirit from the north and lived with him and his relatives. She was gone for a long time, but then one day she came back and she brought twin boys.

"Do you know the story?"

"What story?" He smiled and pulled me close to him as he said this. I was afraid lying there on the red blanket. All I could know was the way he felt, warm, damp, his body beside me. This is the way it happens in the stories, I was thinking, with no thought beyond the moment she meets the ka'tsina spirit and they go.

_____

[1]A mountain spirit of the Pueblo Indians.

"I don't have to go. What they tell in stories was real only then, back in   25
time immemorial, like they say."

He stood up and pointed at my clothes tangled in the blanket. "Let's go," he
said.

I walked beside him, breathing hard because he walked fast, his hand around
my wrist. I had stopped trying to pull away from him, because his hand felt cool
and the sun was high, drying the river bed into alkali. I will see someone, eventually I will see someone, and then I will be certain that he is only a man—some
man from nearby—and I will be sure that I am not Yellow Woman. Because she
is from out of time past and I live now and I've been to school and there are
highways and pickup trucks that Yellow Woman never saw.

It was an easy ride north on horseback. I watched the change from the cottonwood trees along the river to the junipers that brushed past us in the
foothills, and finally there were only piñons, and when I looked up at the rim of
the mountain plateau I could see pine trees growing on the edge. Once I stopped
to look down, but the pale sandstone had disappeared and the river was gone and
the dark lava hills were all around. He touched my hand, not speaking, but always singing softly a mountain song and looking into my eyes.

I felt hungry and wondered what they were doing at home now—my
mother, my grandmother, my husband, and the baby. Cooking breakfast, saying,
"Where did she go?—maybe kidnapped," and Al going to the tribal police with
the details: "She went walking along the river."

The house was made with black lava rock and red mud. It was high above   30
the spreading miles of arroyos and long mesas. I smelled a mountain smell of
pitch and buck brush. I stood there beside the black horse, looking down on the
small, dim country we had passed, and I shivered.

"Yellow Woman, come inside where it's warm."

II

He lit a fire in the stove. It was an old stove with a round belly and an enamel
coffeepot on top. There was only the stove, some faded Navajo blankets, and a
bedroll and cardboard box. The floor was made of smooth adobe plaster, and
there was one small window facing east. He pointed at the box.

"There's some potatoes and the frying pan." He sat on the floor with his
arms around his knees pulling them close to his chest and he watched me fry the
potatoes. I didn't mind him watching me because he was always watching me—
he had been watching me since I came upon him sitting on the river bank trimming leaves from a willow twig with his knife. We ate from the pan and he wiped
the grease from his fingers on his Levis.

"Have you brought women here before?" He smiled and kept chewing, so I
said, "Do you always use the same tricks?"

"What tricks?" He looked at me like he didn't understand.   35

"The story about being a ka'tsina from the mountains. The story about Yellow Woman."

Silva was silent; his face was calm.

"I don't believe it. Those stories couldn't happen now," I said.

He shook his head and said softly, "But someday they will talk about us, and
they will say, 'Those two lived long ago when things like that happened.' "

He stood up and went out. I ate the rest of the potatoes and thought about   40
things—about the noise the stove was making and the sound of the mountain

wind outside. I remembered yesterday and the day before, and then I went outside.

I walked past the corral to the edge where the narrow trail cut through the black rim rock. I was standing in the sky with nothing around me but the wind that came down from the blue mountain peak behind me. I could see faint mountain images in the distance miles across the vast spread of mesas and valleys and plains. I wondered who was over there to feel the mountain wind on those sheer blue edges—who walks on the pine needles in those blue mountains.

"Can you see the pueblo?" Silva was standing behind me.

I shook my head. "We're too far away."

"From here I can see the world." He stepped out on the edge. "The Navajo reservation begins over there." He pointed to the east. "The Pueblo boundaries are over here." He looked below us to the south, where the narrow trail seemed to come from. "The Texans have their ranches over there, starting with that valley, the Concho Valley. The Mexicans run some cattle over there too."

"Do you ever work for them?"   45

"I steal from them," Silva answered. The sun was dropping behind us and shadows were filling the land below. I turned away from the edge that dropped forever into the valleys below.

"I'm cold," I said; "I'm going inside." I started wondering about this man who could speak the Pueblo language so well but who lived on a mountain and rustled cattle. I decided that this man Silva must be Navajo, because Pueblo men didn't do things like that.

"You must be a Navajo."

Silva shook his head gently. "Little Yellow Woman," he said, "you never give up, do you? I have told you who I am. The Navajo people know me, too." He knelt down and unrolled the bedroll and spread the extra blankets out on a piece of canvas. The sun was down, and the only light in the house came from outside—the dim orange light from sundown.

I stood there and waited for him to crawl under the blankets.   50

"What are you waiting for?" he said, and I lay down beside him. He undressed me slowly like the night before beside the river—kissing my face gently and running his hands up and down my belly and legs. He took off my pants and then he laughed.

"Why are you laughing?"

"You are breathing so hard."

I pulled away from him and turned my back to him.

He pulled me around and pinned me down with his arms and chest. "You   55
don't understand, do you, little Yellow Woman? You will do what I want."

And again he was all around me with his skin slippery against mine, and I was afraid because I understood that his strength could hurt me. I lay underneath him and I knew that he could destroy me. But later, while he slept beside me, I touched his face and I had a feeling—the kind of feeling for him that overcame me that morning along the river. I kissed him on the forehead and he reached out for me.

When I woke up in the morning he was gone. It gave me a strange feeling because for a long time I sat there on the blankets and looked around the little house for some object of his—some proof that he had been there or maybe that he was coming back. Only the blankets and the cardboard box remained. The .30–30[2] that

---

[2]A rifle.

had been leaning in the corner was gone, and so was the knife I had used the night before. He was gone, and I had my chance to go now. But first I had to eat, because I knew it would be a long walk home.

I found some dried apricots in the cardboard box, and I sat down on a rock at the edge of the plateau rim. There was no wind and the sun warmed me. I was surrounded by silence. I drowsed with apricots in my mouth, and I didn't believe that there were highways or railroads or cattle to steal.

When I woke up, I stared down at my feet in the black mountain dirt. Little black ants were swarming over the pine needles around my foot. They must have smelled the apricots. I thought about my family far below me. They would be wondering about me, because this had never happened to me before. The tribal police would file a report. But if old Grandpa weren't dead he would tell them what happened—he would laugh and say, "Stolen by a ka'tsina, a mountain spirit. She'll come home—they usually do." There are enough of them to handle things. My mother and grandmother will raise the baby like they raised me. Al will find someone else, and they will go on like before, except that there will be a story about the day I disappeared while I was walking along the river. Silva had come for me; he said he had. I did not decide to go. I just went. Moonflowers blossom in the sand hills before dawn, just as I followed him. That's what I was thinking as I wandered along the trail through the pine trees.

It was noon when I got back. When I saw the stone house I remembered   60
that I had meant to go home. But that didn't seem important any more, maybe because there were little blue flowers growing in the meadow behind the stone house and the gray squirrels were playing in the pines next to the house. The horses were standing in the corral, and there was a beef carcass hanging on the shady side of a big pine in front of the house. Flies buzzed around the clotted blood that hung from the carcass. Silva was washing his hands in a bucket full of water. He must have heard me coming because he spoke to me without turning to face me.

"I've been waiting for you."

"I went walking in the big pine trees."

I looked into the bucket full of bloody water with brown-and-white animal hairs floating in it. Silva stood there letting his hand drip, examining me intently.

"Are you coming with me?"

"Where?" I asked him.   65

"To sell the meat in Marquez."

"If you're sure it's O.K."

"I wouldn't ask you if it wasn't," he answered.

He sloshed the water around in the bucket before he dumped it out and set the bucket upside down near the door. I followed him to the corral and watched him saddle the horses. Even beside the horses he looked tall, and I asked him again if he wasn't Navajo. He didn't say anything; he just shook his head and kept cinching up the saddle.

"But Navajos are tall."   70

"Get on the horse," he said, "and let's go."

The last thing he did before we started down the steep trail was to grab the .30–30 from the corner. He slid the rifle into the scabbard that hung from his saddle.

"Do they ever try to catch you?" I asked.

"They don't know who I am."

"Then why did you bring the rifle?"   75

"Because we are going to Marquez where the Mexicans live."

III

The trail leveled out on a narrow ridge that was steep on both sides like an animal spine. On one side I could see where the trail went around the rocky gray hills and disappeared into the southeast where the pale sandrock mesas stood in the distance near my home. On the other side was a trail that went west, and as I looked far into the distance I thought I saw the little town. But Silva said no, that I was looking in the wrong place, that I just thought I saw houses. After that I quit looking off into the distance; it was hot and the wild-flowers were closing up their deep-yellow petals. Only the waxy cactus flowers bloomed in the bright sun, and I saw every color that a cactus blossom can be; the white ones and the red ones were still buds, but the purple and the yellow were blossoms, open full and the most beautiful of all.

Silva saw him before I did. The white man was riding a big gray horse, coming up the trail toward us. He was traveling fast and the gray horse's feet sent rocks rolling off the trail into the dry tumbleweeds. Silva motioned for me to stop and we watched the white man. He didn't see us right away, but finally his horse whinnied at our horses and he stopped. He looked at us briefly before he loped the gray horse across the three hundred yards that separated us. He stopped his horse in front of Silva, and his young fat face was shadowed by the brim of his hat. He didn't look mad, but his small, pale eyes moved from the blood-soaked gunny sacks hanging from my saddle to Silva's face and then back to my face.

"Where did you get the fresh meat?" the white man asked.

"I've been hunting," Silva said, and when he shifted his weight in the saddle   80
the leather creaked.

"The hell you have, Indian. You've been rustling cattle. We've been looking for the thief for a long time."

The rancher was fat, and sweat began to soak through his white cowboy shirt and the wet cloth stuck to the thick rolls of belly fat. He almost seemed to be panting from the exertion of talking, and he smelled rancid, maybe because Silva scared him.

Silva turned to me and smiled. "Go back up the mountain, Yellow Woman."

The white man got angry when he heard Silva speak in a language he couldn't understand. "Don't try anything, Indian. Just keep riding to Marquez. We'll call the state police from there."

The rancher must have been unarmed because he was very frightened and if   85
he had a gun he would have pulled it out then. I turned my horse around and the rancher yelled, "Stop!" I looked at Silva for an instant and there was something ancient and dark—something I could feel in my stomach—in his eyes, and when I glanced at his hand I saw his finger on the trigger of the .30–30 that was still in the saddle scabbard. I slapped my horse across the flank and the sacks of raw meat swung against my knees as the horse leaped up the trail. It was hard to keep my balance, and once I thought I felt the saddle slipping backward; it was because of this that I could not look back.

I didn't stop until I reached the ridge where the trail forked. The horse was breathing deep gasps and there was a dark film of sweat on its neck. I looked down in the direction I had come from, but I couldn't see the place. I waited. The wind came up and pushed warm air past me. I looked up at the sky, pale blue and full of thin clouds and fading vapor trails left by jets.

I think four shots were fired—I remember hearing four hollow explosions that reminded me of deer hunting. There could have been more shots after that, but I couldn't have heard them because my horse was running again and the loose rocks were making too much noise as they scattered around his feet.

Horses have a hard time running downhill, but I went that way instead of uphill to the mountain because I thought it was safer. I felt better with the horse running southeast past the round gray hills that were covered with cedar trees and black lava rock. When I got to the plain in the distance I could see the dark green patches of tamaracks that grew along the river; and beyond the river I could see the beginning of the pale sandrock mesas. I stopped the horse and looked back to see if anyone was coming; then I got off the horse and turned the horse around, wondering if it would go back to its corral under the pines on the mountain. It looked back at me for a moment and then plucked a mouthful of green tumbleweeds before it trotted back up the trail with its ears pointed forward, carrying its head daintily to one side to avoid stepping on the dragging reins. When the horse disappeared over the last hill, the gunny sacks full of meat were still swinging and bouncing.

IV

I walked toward the river on a wood-hauler's road that I knew would eventually lead to the paved road. I was thinking about waiting beside the road for someone to drive by, but by the time I got to the pavement I had decided it wasn't very far to walk if I followed the river back the way Silva and I had come.

The river water tasted good, and I sat in the shade under a cluster of silvery   90
willows. I thought about Silva, and I felt sad at leaving him; still, there was something strange about him, and I tried to figure it out all the way back home.

I came back to the place on the river bank where he had been sitting the first time I saw him. The green willow leaves that he had trimmed from the branch were still lying there, wilted in the sand. I saw the leaves and I wanted to go back to him—to kiss him and to touch him—but the mountains were too far away now. And I told myself, because I believe it, he will come back sometime and be waiting again by the river.

I followed the path up from the river into the village. The sun was getting low, and I could smell supper cooking when I got to the screen door of my house. I could hear their voices inside—my mother was telling my grandmother how to fix the Jell-O and my husband, Al, was playing with the baby. I decided to tell them that some Navajo had kidnapped me, but I was sorry that old Grandpa wasn't alive to hear my story because it was the Yellow Woman stories he liked to tell best.

Starting Points for Further Research: Leslie Marmon Silko

■ **Critical Essay:** Valerie Karno. "Legal Hunger: Law, Narrative, and Orality in Leslie Marmon Silko's Storyteller and Almanac of the Dead." *College Literature* 28 (2001): 29–45.

- **Interview:** Thomas Irmer. "An Interview with Leslie Marmon Silko." *The Write Stuff.* http://www.altx.com/int2/silko.html.

KAZUO ISHIGURO   (B. 1954)

Kazuo Ishiguro was born in Nagasaki, Japan, in 1954 and moved to Great Britain in 1960. His award-winning novels include A Pale View of Hills (1982), An Artist of the Floating World (1986), The Remains of the Day (1989), The Unconsoled (1995), When We Were Orphans (2000), and Never Let Me Go (2005). Ishiguro places his stories in powerful historic and political settings. He concerns himself with exploring the bonds of family life and the decline of feeling among his characters' societies. Ishiguro lives in London.

A Family Supper   (1983)

Fugu is a fish caught off the Pacific shores of Japan. The fish has held a special significance for me ever since my mother died through eating one. The poison resides in the sexual glands of the fish, inside two fragile bags. When preparing the fish, these bags must be removed with caution, for any clumsiness will result in the poison leaking into the veins. Regrettably, it is not easy to tell whether or not this operation has been carried out successfully. The proof is, as it were, in the eating.

Fugu poisoning is hideously painful and almost always fatal. If the fish has been eaten during the evening, the victim is usually overtaken by pain during his sleep. He rolls about in agony for a few hours and is dead by morning. The fish became extremely popular in Japan after the war. Until stricter regulations were imposed, it was all the rage to perform the hazardous gutting operation in one's own kitchen, then to invite neighbours and friends round for the feast.

At the time of my mother's death, I was living in California. My relationship with my parents had become somewhat strained around that period, and consequently I did not learn of the circumstances surrounding her death until I returned to Tokyo two years later. Apparently, my mother had always refused to eat fugu, but on this particular occasion she had made an exception, having been invited by an old schoolfriend whom she was anxious not to offend. It was my father who supplied me with the details as we drove from the airport to his house in the Kamakura district. When we finally arrived, it was nearing the end of a sunny autumn day.

"Did you eat on the plane?" my father asked. We were sitting on the tatami floor of his tea-room.

"They gave me a light snack."

"You must be hungry. We'll eat as soon as Kikuko arrives."

My father was a formidable-looking man with a large stony jaw and furious black eyebrows. I think now in retrospect that he much resembled Chou En-lai, although he would not have cherished such a comparison, being particularly proud of the pure samurai blood that ran in the family. His general presence was not one which encouraged relaxed conversation; neither were things helped much by his odd way of stating each remark as if it were the concluding one. In

5

fact, as I sat opposite him that afternoon, a boyhood memory came back to me of the time he had struck me several times around the head for "chattering like an old woman." Inevitably, our conversation since my arrival at the airport had been punctuated by long pauses.

"I'm sorry to hear about the firm," I said when neither of us had spoken for some time. He nodded gravely.

"In fact the story didn't end there," he said. "After the firm's collapse, Watanabe killed himself. He didn't wish to live with the disgrace."

"I see." 10

"We were partners for seventeen years. A man of principle and honour. I respected him very much."

"Will you go into business again?" I asked.

"I am—in retirement. I'm too old to involve myself in new ventures now. Business these days has become so different. Dealing with foreigners. Doing things their way. I don't understand how we've come to this. Neither did Watanabe." He sighed. "A fine man. A man of principle."

The tea-room looked out over the garden. From where I sat I could make out the ancient well which as a child I had believed haunted. It was just visible now through the thick foliage. The sun had sunk low and much of the garden had fallen into shadow.

"I'm glad in any case that you've decided to come back," my father said. 15 "More than a short visit, I hope."

"I'm not sure what my plans will be."

"I for one am prepared to forget the past. Your mother too was always ready to welcome you back—upset as she was by your behaviour."

"I appreciate your sympathy. As I say, I'm not sure what my plans are."

"I've come to believe now that there were no evil intentions in your mind," my father continued. "You were swayed by certain—influences. Like so many others."

"Perhaps we should forget it, as you suggest." 20

"As you will. More tea?"

Just then a girl's voice came echoing through the house.

"At last." My father rose to his feet. "Kikuko has arrived."

Despite our difference in years, my sister and I had always been close. Seeing me again seemed to make her excessively excited and for a while she did nothing but giggle nervously. But she calmed down somewhat when my father started to question her about Osaka and her university. She answered him with short formal replies. She in turn asked me a few questions, but she seemed inhibited by the fear that her questions might lead to awkward topics. After a while, the conversation had become even sparser than prior to Kikuko's arrival. Then my father stood up, saying: "I must attend to the supper. Please excuse me for being burdened down by such matters. Kikuko will look after you."

My sister relaxed quite visibly once he had left the room. Within a few min- 25 utes, she was chatting freely about her friends in Osaka and about her classes at university. Then quite suddenly she decided we should walk in the garden and went striding out onto the veranda. We put on some straw sandals that had been left along the veranda rail and stepped out into the garden. The daylight had almost gone.

"I've been dying for a smoke for the last half-hour," she said, lighting a cigarette.

"Then why didn't you smoke?"

She made a furtive gesture back towards the house, then grinned mischievously.

"Oh I see," I said.

"Guess what? I've got a boyfriend now."

"Oh yes?"

"Except I'm wondering what to do. I haven't made up my mind yet."

"Quite understandable."

"You see, he's making plans to go to America. He wants me to go with him as soon as I finish studying."

"I see. And you want to go to America?"

"If we go, we're going to hitch-hike." Kikuko waved a thumb in front of my face. "People say it's dangerous, but I've done it in Osaka and it's fine."

"I see. So what is it you're unsure about?"

We were following a narrow path that wound through the shrubs and finished by the old well. As we walked, Kikuko persisted in taking unnecessarily theatrical puffs on her cigarette.

"Well. I've got lots of friends now in Osaka. I like it there. I'm not sure I want to leave them all behind just yet. And Suichi—I like him, but I'm not sure I want to spend so much time with him. Do you understand?"

"Oh perfectly."

She grinned again, then skipped on ahead of me until she had reached the well. "Do you remember," she said, as I came walking up to her, "how you used to say this well was haunted?"

"Yes, I remember."

We both peered over the side.

"Mother always told me it was the old woman from the vegetable store you'd seen that night," she said. "But I never believed her and never came out here alone."

"Mother used to tell me that too. She even told me once the old woman had confessed to being the ghost. Apparently she'd been taking a short cut through our garden. I imagine she had some trouble clambering over these walls."

Kikuko gave a giggle. She then turned her back to the well, casting her gaze about the garden.

"Mother never really blamed you, you know," she said, in a new voice. I remained silent. "She always used to say to me how it was their fault, hers and Father's, for not bringing you up correctly. She used to tell me how much more careful they'd been with me, and that's why I was so good." She looked up and the mischievous grin had returned to her face. "Poor Mother," she said.

"Yes. Poor Mother."

"Are you going back to California?"

"I don't know. I'll have to see."

"What happened to—to her? To Vicki?"

"That's all finished with," I said. "There's nothing much left for me now in California."

"Do you think I ought to go there?"

"Why not? I don't know. You'll probably like it." I glanced towards the house. "Perhaps we'd better go in soon. Father might need a hand with the supper."

But my sister was once more peering down into the well. "I can't see any   55
ghosts," she said. Her voice echoed a little.

"Is Father very upset about his firm collapsing?"

"Don't know. You can never tell with Father." Then suddenly she straightened up and turned to me. "Did he tell you about old Watanabe? What he did?"

"I heard he committed suicide."

"Well, that wasn't all. He took his whole family with him. His wife and his two little girls."

"Oh yes?"   60

"Those two beautiful little girls. He turned on the gas while they were all asleep. Then he cut his stomach with a meat knife."

"Yes, Father was just telling me how Watanabe was a man of principle."

"Sick." My sister turned back to the well.

"Careful. You'll fall right in."

"I can't see any ghost," she said. "You were lying to me all that time."   65

"But I never said it lived down the well."

"Where is it, then?"

We both looked around at the trees and shrubs. The light in the garden had grown very dim. Eventually I pointed to a small clearing some ten yards away.

"Just there I saw it. Just there."

We stared at the spot.   70

"What did it look like?"

"I couldn't see very well. It was dark."

"But you must have seen something."

"It was an old woman. She was just standing there, watching me."

We kept staring at the spot as if mesmerized.   75

"She was wearing a white kimono," I said. "Some of her hair had come undone. It was blowing around a little."

Kikuko pushed her elbow against my arm. "Oh be quiet. You're trying to frighten me all over again." She trod on the remains of her cigarette, then for a brief moment stood regarding it with a perplexed expression. She kicked some pine needles over it, then once more displayed her grin. "Let's see if supper's ready," she said.

We found my father in the kitchen. He gave us a quick glance, then carried on with what he was doing.

"Father's become quite a chef since he's had to manage on his own," Kikuko said with a laugh. He turned and looked at my sister coldly.

"Hardly a skill I'm proud of," he said. "Kikuko, come here and help."   80

For some moments my sister did not move. Then she stepped forward and took an apron hanging from a drawer.

"Just these vegetables need cooking now," he said to her. "The rest just needs watching." Then he looked up and regarded me strangely for some seconds. "I expect you want to look around the house," he said eventually. He put down the chopsticks he had been holding. "It's a long time since you've seen it."

As we left the kitchen I glanced back towards Kikuko, but her back was turned.

"She's a good girl," my father said quietly.

I followed my father from room to room. I had forgotten how large the house was. A panel would slide open and another room would appear. But the rooms were all startlingly empty. In one of the rooms the lights did not come on, and we stared at the stark walls and tatami in the pale light that came from the windows.

"This house is too large for a man to live in alone," my father said. "I don't have much use for most of these rooms now."

But eventually my father opened the door to a room packed full of books and papers. There were flowers in vases and pictures on the walls. Then I noticed something on a low table in the corner of the room. I came nearer and saw it was a plastic model of a battleship, the kind constructed by children. It had been placed on some newspaper; scattered around it were assorted pieces of grey plastic.

My father gave a laugh. He came up to the table and picked up the model.

"Since the firm folded," he said, "I have a little more time on my hands." He laughed again, rather strangely. For a moment his face looked almost gentle. "A little more time."

"That seems odd," I said. "You were always so busy."

"Too busy perhaps." He looked at me with a small smile. "Perhaps I should have been a more attentive father."

I laughed. He went on contemplating his battleship. Then he looked up. "I hadn't meant to tell you this, but perhaps it's best that I do. It's my belief that your mother's death was no accident. She had many worries. And some disappointments."

We both gazed at the plastic battleship.

"Surely," I said eventually, "my mother didn't expect me to live here for ever."

"Obviously you don't see. You don't see how it is for some parents. Not only must they lose their children, they must lose them to things they don't understand." He spun the battleship in his fingers. "These little gunboats here could have been better glued, don't you think?"

"Perhaps. I think it looks fine."

"During the war I spent some time on a ship rather like this. But my ambition was always the air force. I figured it like this. If your ship was struck by the enemy, all you could do was struggle in the water hoping for a lifeline. But in an aeroplane—well—there was always the final weapon." He put the model back onto the table. "I don't suppose you believe in war."

"Not particularly."

He cast an eye around the room. "Supper should be ready by now," he said. "You must be hungry."

Supper was waiting in a dimly lit room next to the kitchen. The only source of light was a big lantern that hung over the table, casting the rest of the room into shadow. We bowed to each other before starting the meal.

There was little conversation. When I made some polite comment about the food, Kikuko giggled a little. Her earlier nervousness seemed to have returned to her. My father did not speak for several minutes. Finally he said:

"It must feel strange for you, being back in Japan."

"Yes, it is a little strange."

"Already, perhaps, you regret leaving America."

"A little. Not so much. I didn't leave behind much. Just some empty rooms."   105

"I see."

I glanced across the table. My father's face looked stony and forbidding in the half-light. We ate on in silence.

Then my eye caught something at the back of the room. At first I continued eating, then my hands became still. The others noticed and looked at me. I went on gazing into the darkness past my father's shoulder.

"Who is that? In that photograph there?"

"Which photograph?" My father turned slightly, trying to follow my gaze.   110

"The lowest one. The old woman in the white kimono."

My father put down his chopsticks. He looked first at the photograph, then at me.

"Your mother." His voice had become very hard. "Can't you recognize your own mother?"

"My mother. You see, it's dark. I can't see it very well."

No one spoke for a few seconds, then Kikuko rose to her feet. She took the   115 photograph down from the wall, came back to the table and gave it to me.

"She looks a lot older," I said.

"It was taken shortly before her death," said my father.

"It was the dark. I couldn't see very well."

I looked up and noticed my father holding out a hand. I gave him the photograph. He looked at it intently, then held it towards Kikuko. Obediently, my sister rose to her feet once more and returned the picture to the wall.

There was a large pot left unopened at the centre of the table. When   120 Kikuko had seated herself again, my father reached forward and lifted the lid. A cloud of steam rose up and curled towards the lantern. He pushed the pot a little towards me.

"You must be hungry," he said. One side of his face had fallen into shadow.

"Thank you." I reached forward with my chopsticks. The steam was almost scalding. "What is it?"

"Fish."

"It smells very good."

In amidst soup were strips of fish that had curled almost into balls. I picked   125 one out and brought it to my bowl.

"Help yourself. There's plenty."

"Thank you." I took a little more, then pushed the pot towards my father. I watched him take several pieces to his bowl. Then we both watched as Kikuko served herself.

My father bowed slightly. "You must be hungry," he said again. He took some fish to his mouth and started to eat. Then I too chose a piece and put it in my mouth. It felt soft, quite fleshy against my tongue.

"Very good," I said. "What is it?"

"Just fish."

"It's very good."   130

The three of us ate on in silence. Several minutes went by.

"Some more?"

"Is there enough?"

"There's plenty for all of us." My father lifted the lid and once more steam   135 rose up. We all reached forward and helped ourselves.

"Here," I said to my father, "you have this last piece."

"Thank you."

When we had finished the meal, my father stretched out his arms and yawned with an air of satisfaction. "Kikuko," he said. "Prepare a pot of tea, please."

My sister looked at him, then left the room without comment. My father stood up.

"Let's retire to the other room. It's rather warm in here."   140

I got to my feet and followed him into the tea-room. The large sliding windows had been left open, bringing in a breeze from the garden. For a while we sat in silence.

"Father," I said, finally.

"Yes?"

"Kikuko tells me Watanabe-San took his whole family with him."

My father lowered his eyes and nodded. For some moments he seemed deep   145
in thought. "Watanabe was very devoted to his work," he said at last. "The collapse of the firm was a great blow to him. I fear it must have weakened his judgement."

"You think what he did—it was a mistake?"

"Why, of course. Do you see it otherwise?"

"No, no. Of course not."

"There are other things besides work."

"Yes."   150

We fell silent again. The sound of locusts came in from the garden. I looked out into the darkness. The well was no longer visible.

"What do you think you will do now?" my father asked. "Will you stay in Japan for a while?"

"To be honest, I hadn't thought that far ahead."

"If you wish to stay here, I mean here in this house, you would be very welcome. That is, if you don't mind living with an old man."

"Thank you. I'll have to think about it."   155

I gazed out once more into the darkness.

"But of course," said my father, "this house is so dreary now. You'll no doubt return to America before long."

"Perhaps. I don't know yet."

"No doubt you will."

For some time my father seemed to be studying the back of his hands. Then   160
he looked up and sighed.

"Kikuko is due to complete her studies next spring," he said. "Perhaps she will want to come home then. She's a good girl."

"Perhaps she will."

"Things will improve then."

"Yes, I'm sure they will."

We fell silent once more, waiting for Kikuko to bring the tea.   165

Starting Points for Further Research: Kazuo Ishiguro

- **Critical Essay:** Shao-Pin Luo. " 'Living the Wrong Life': Kazuo Ishiguro's Unconsoled Orphans." *Dalhousie Review* 83 (Spring 2003): 51–80.
- **Interview:** Linda Richards. "January Interview: Kazuo Ishiguro." *January Magazine.* http://www.januarymagazine.com/profiles/ishiguro.html.

DAVID LEAVITT   (B. 1961)

The son of a professor, David Leavitt grew up in California on the Stanford campus and attended public school before going to Yale. At twenty he published his first short story in the New Yorker, *soon followed by others in well-regarded magazines. His 1986 novel* The Lost Language of Cranes *increased his fame; its subject was a son's revelation of his homosexuality to his family. Leavitt's writing touches on family life, including the aftermath of divorce and the conflicts over gay identity. He published his most recent novel,* The Body of Jonah Boyd, *in 2004.*

Territory   (1984)

Neil's mother, Mrs. Campbell, sits on her lawn chair behind a card table outside the food co-op. Every few minutes, as the sun shifts, she moves the chair and table several inches back so as to remain in the shade. It is a hundred degrees outside, and bright white. Each time someone goes in or out of the co-op a gust of air-conditioning flies out of the automatic doors, raising dust from the cement.

Neil stands just inside, poised over a water fountain, and watches her. She has on a sun hat, and a sweatshirt over her tennis dress; her legs are bare, and shiny with cocoa butter. In front of her, propped against the table, a sign proclaims: MOTHERS, FIGHT FOR YOUR CHILDREN'S RIGHTS—SUPPORT A NON-NU-CLEAR FUTURE. Women dressed exactly like her pass by, notice the sign, listen to her brief spiel, finger pamphlets, sign petitions or don't sign petitions, never give money. Her weary eyes are masked by dark glasses. In the age of Reagan, she has declared, keeping up the causes of peace and justice is a futile, tiresome, and unrewarding effort; it is therefore an effort fit only for mothers to keep up. The sun bounces off the window glass through which Neil watches her. His own reflection lines up with her profile.

*   *   *

Later that afternoon, Neil spreads himself out alongside the pool and imagines he is being watched by the shirtless Chicano gardener. But the gardener, concentrating on his pruning, is neither seductive nor seducible. On the lawn, his mother's large Airedales—Abigail, Lucille, Fern—amble, sniff, urinate. Occasionally, they accost the gardener, who yells at them in Spanish.

After two years' absence, Neil reasons, he should feel nostalgia, regret, gladness upon returning home. He closes his eyes and tries to muster the proper background music for the cinematic scene of return. His rhapsody, however, is interrupted by the noises of his mother's trio—the scratchy cello, whining violin, stumbling piano—as she and Lillian Havalard and Charlotte Feder plunge through Mozart. The tune is cheery, in a Germanic sort of way, and utterly inappropriate to what Neil is trying to feel. Yet it *is* the music of his adolescence; they have played it for years, bent over the notes, their heads bobbing in silent time to the metronome.

It is getting darker. Every few minutes, he must move his towel so as to remain within the narrowing patch of sunlight. In four hours, Wayne, his lover of ten months and the only person he has ever imagined he could spend his life with, will be in this house, where no lover of his has ever set foot. The thought   5

fills him with a sense of grand terror and curiosity. He stretches, tries to feel seductive, desirable. The gardener's shears whack at the ferns; the music above
him rushes to a loud, premature conclusion. The women laugh and applaud
themselves as they give up for the day. He hears Charlotte Feder's full nasal
twang, the voice of a fat woman in a pink pants suit—odd, since she is a scrawny,
arthritic old bird, rarely clad in anything other than tennis shorts and a blouse.
Lillian is the fat woman in the pink pants suit; her voice is thin and warped by
too much crying. Drink in hand, she calls out from the porch, "Hot enough!"
and waves. He lifts himself up and nods to her.

The women sit on the porch and chatter; their voices blend with the clink
of ice in glasses. They belong to a small circle of ladies all of whom, with the exception of Neil's mother, are widows and divorcées. Lillian's husband left her
twenty-two years ago, and sends her a check every month to live on; Charlotte
has been divorced twice as long as she was married, and has a daughter serving a
long sentence for terrorist acts committed when she was nineteen. Only Neil's
mother has a husband, a distant sort of husband, away often on business. He is
away on business now. All of them feel betrayed—by husbands, by children, by
history.

Neil closes his eyes, tries to hear the words only as sounds. Soon, a new
noise accosts him: his mother arguing with the gardener in Spanish. He leans on
his elbows and watches them; the syllables are loud, heated, and compressed,
and seem on the verge of explosion. But the argument ends happily; they shake
hands. The gardener collects his check and walks out the gate without so much
as looking at Neil.

He does not know the gardener's name; as his mother has reminded him, he
does not know most of what has gone on since he moved away. Her life has gone
on, unaffected by his absence. He flinches at his own egoism, the egoism of sons.

"Neil! Did you call the airport to make sure the plane's coming in on time?"

"Yes," he shouts to her. "It is."   10

"Good. Well, I'll have dinner ready when you get back."

"Mom—"

"What?" The word comes out in a weary wail that is more of an answer than
a question.

"What's wrong?" he says, forgetting his original question.

"Nothing's wrong," she declares in a tone that indicates that everything is   15
wrong. "The dogs have to be fed, dinner has to be made, and I've got people
here. Nothing's wrong."

"I hope things will be as comfortable as possible when Wayne gets here."

"Is that a request or a threat?"

"Mom—"

Behind her sunglasses, her eyes are inscrutable. "I'm tired," she says. "It's
been a long day. I . . . I'm anxious to meet Wayne. I'm sure he'll be wonderful,
and we'll all have a wonderful, wonderful time. I'm sorry. I'm just tired."

She heads up the stairs. He suddenly feels an urge to cover himself; his body   20
embarrasses him, as it has in her presence since the day she saw him shirtless and
said with delight, "Neil! You're growing hair under your arms!"

Before he can get up, the dogs gather round him and begin to sniff and lick
at him. He wriggles to get away from them, but Abigail, the largest and stupidest,
straddles his stomach and nuzzles his mouth. He splutters and, laughing, throws

her off. "Get away from me, you goddamn dogs," he shouts, and swats at them. They are new dogs, not the dog of his childhood, not dogs he trusts.

He stands, and the dogs circle him, looking up at his face expectantly. He feels renewed terror at the thought that Wayne will be here so soon: Will they sleep in the same room? Will they make love? He has never had sex in his parents' house. How can he be expected to be a lover here, in this place of his childhood, of his earliest shame, in this household of mothers and dogs?

"Dinnertime! Abbylucyferny, Abbylucyferny, dinnertime!" His mother's litany disperses the dogs, and they run for the door.

"Do you realize," he shouts to her, "that no matter how much those dogs love you they'd probably kill you for the leg of lamb in the freezer?"

* * *

Neil was twelve the first time he recognized in himself something like sexuality.   25
He was lying outside, on the grass, when Rasputin—the dog, long dead, of his childhood—began licking his face. He felt a tingle he did not recognize, pulled off his shirt to give the dog access to more of him. Rasputin's tongue tickled coolly. A wet nose started to sniff down his body, toward his bathing suit. What he felt frightened him, but he couldn't bring himself to push the dog away. Then his mother called out, "Dinner," and Rasputin was gone, more interested in food than in him.

It was the day after Rasputin was put to sleep, years later, that Neil finally stood in the kitchen, his back turned to his parents, and said, with unexpected ease, "I'm a homosexual." The words seemed insufficient, reductive. For years, he had believed his sexuality to be detachable from the essential him, but now he realized that it was part of him. He had the sudden, despairing sensation that though the words had been easy to say, the fact of their having been aired was incurably damning. Only then, for the first time, did he admit that they were true, and he shook and wept in regret for what he would not be for his mother, for having failed her. His father hung back, silent; he was absent for that moment as he was mostly absent—a strong absence. Neil always thought of him sitting on the edge of the bed in his underwear, captivated by something on television. He said, "It's O.K., Neil." But his mother was resolute; her lower lip didn't quaver. She had enormous reserves of strength to which she only gained access at moments like this one. She hugged him from behind, wrapped him in the childhood smells of perfume and brownies, and whispered, "It's O.K., honey." For once, her words seemed as inadequate as his. Neil felt himself shrunk to an embarrassed adolescent, hating her sympathy, not wanting her to touch him. It was the way he would feel from then on whenever he was in her presence—even now, at twenty-three, bringing home his lover to meet her.

All through his childhood, she had packed only the most nutritious lunches, had served on the PTA, had volunteered at the children's library and at his school, had organized a successful campaign to ban a racist history textbook. The day after he told her, she located and got in touch with an organization called the Coalition of Parents of Lesbians and Gays. Within a year, she was president of it. On weekends, she and the other mothers drove their station wagons to San Francisco, set up their card tables in front of the Bulldog Baths, the Liberty Baths, passed out literature to men in leather and denim who were loath to admit they even had mothers. These men, who would habitually do violence to each other, were strangely cowed by the suburban ladies with their informational booklets, and bent their heads. Neil was a sophomore in college then, and lived in San Francisco. She brought him pamphlets detailing the dangers of bath-houses and back rooms, enemas and poppers, wordless sex in alleyways. His ex-cursion into that world had been brief and lamentable, and was over. He winced at the thought that she knew all his sexual secrets, and vowed to move to the East Coast to escape her. It was not very different from the days when she had campaigned for a better playground, or tutored the Hispanic children in the au-diovisual room. Those days, as well, he had run away from her concern. Even to-day, perched in front of the co-op, collecting signatures for nuclear disarmament, she was quintessentially a mother. And if the lot of mothers was to expect noth-ing in return, was the lot of sons to return nothing?

Driving across the Dumbarton Bridge on his way to the airport, Neil thinks, I have returned nothing; I have simply returned. He wonders if she would have given birth to him had she known what he would grow up to be.

Then he berates himself: Why should he assume himself to be the cause of her sorrow? She has told him that her life is full of secrets. She has changed since he left home—grown thinner, more rigid, harder to hug. She has given up bak-ing, taken up tennis; her skin has browned and tightened. She is no longer the woman who hugged him and kissed him, who said, "As long as you're happy, that's all that's important to us."

The flats spread out around him; the bridge floats on purple and green silt, 30
and spongy bay fill, not water at all. Only ten miles north, a whole city has been built on gunk dredged up from the bay.

He arrives at the airport ten minutes early, to discover that the plane has landed twenty minutes early. His first view of Wayne is from behind, by the bag-gage belt. Wayne looks as he always looks—slightly windblown—and is wearing the ratty leather jacket he was wearing the night they met. Neil sneaks up on him and puts his hands on his shoulders; when Wayne turns around, he looks re-lieved to see him.

They hug like brothers; only in the safety of Neil's mother's car do they dare to kiss. They recognize each other's smells and grow comfortable again. "I never imagined I'd actually see you out here," Neil says, "but you're exactly the same here as there."

"It's only been a week."

They kiss again. Neil wants to go to a motel, but Wayne insists on being pragmatic. "We'll be there soon. Don't worry."

"We could go to one of the bathhouses in the city and take a room for a cou- 35
ple of aeons," Neil says. "Christ, I'm hard up. I don't even know if we're going to be in the same bedroom."

"Well, if we're not," Wayne says, "we'll sneak around. It'll be romantic."

They cling to each other for a few more minutes, until they realize that people are looking in the car window. Reluctantly, they pull apart. Neil reminds himself that he loves this man, that there is a reason for him to bring this man home.

He takes the scenic route on the way back. The car careers over foothills, through forests, along white four-lane highways high in the mountains. Wayne tells Neil that he sat next to a woman on the plane who was once Marilyn Mon-roe's psychiatrist's nurse. He slips his foot out of his shoe and nudges Neil's ankle, pulling Neil's sock down with his toe.

"I have to drive," Neil says. "I'm very glad you're here."

There is a comfort in the privacy of the car. They have a common fear of walking hand in hand, of publicly showing physical affection, even in the permissive West Seventies of New York—a fear that they have admitted only to one another. They slip through a pass between two hills, and are suddenly in residential Northern California, the land of expensive ranch-style houses. 40

As they pull into Neil's mother's driveway, the dogs run barking toward the car. When Wayne opens the door, they jump and lap at him, and he tries to close it again. "Don't worry. Abbylucyferny! Get in the house, damn it!"

His mother descends from the porch. She has changed into a blue flower-print dress, which Neil doesn't recognize. He gets out of the car and halfheartedly chastises the dogs. Crickets chirp in the trees. His mother looks radiant, even beautiful, illuminated by the headlights, surrounded by the now quiet dogs, like a Circe with her slaves. When she walks over to Wayne, offering her hand, and says, "Wayne, I'm Barbara," Neil forgets that she is his mother.

"Good to meet you, Barbara," Wayne says, and reaches out his hand. Craftier than she, he whirls her around to kiss her cheek.

Barbara! He is calling his mother Barbara! Then he remembers that Wayne is five years older than he is. They chat by the open car door, and Neil shrinks back—the embarrassed adolescent, uncomfortable, unwanted.

So the dreaded moment passes and he might as well not have been there. At dinner, Wayne keeps the conversation smooth like a captivated courtier seeking Neil's mother's hand. The faggot son's sodomist—such words spit into Neil's head. She has prepared tiny meatballs with fresh coriander, fettucine with pesto. Wayne talks about the street people in New York; San Salvador is a tragedy; if only Sadat had lived; Phyllis Schlafly—what can you do? 45

"It's a losing battle," she tells him. "Every day I'm out there with my card table, me and the other mothers, but I tell you, Wayne, it's a losing battle. Sometimes I think us old ladies are the only ones with enough patience to fight."

Occasionally, Neil says something, but his comments seem stupid and clumsy. Wayne continues to call her Barbara. No one under forty has ever called her Barbara as long as Neil can remember. They drink wine; he does not.

Now is the time for drastic action. He contemplates taking Wayne's hand, then checks himself. He has never done anything in her presence to indicate that the sexuality he confessed to five years ago was a reality and not an invention. Even now, he and Wayne might as well be friends, college roommates. Then Wayne, his savior, with a single, sweeping gesture, reaches for his hand, and clasps it, in the midst of a joke he is telling about Saudi Arabians. By the time he is laughing, their hands are joined. Neil's throat contracts; his heart begins to beat violently. He notices his mother's eyes flicker, glance downward; she never breaks the stride of her sentence. The dinner goes on, and every taboo nurtured since childhood falls quietly away.

She removes the dishes. Their hands grow sticky; he cannot tell which fingers are his and which Wayne's. She clears the rest of the table and rounds up the dogs.

"Well, boys, I'm very tired, and I've got a long day ahead of me tomorrow, so I think I'll hit the sack. There are extra towels for you in Neil's bathroom, Wayne. Sleep well." 50

"Good night, Barbara," Wayne calls out. "It's been wonderful meeting you."
They are alone. Now they can disentangle their hands.

"No problem about where we sleep, is there?"

"No," Neil says. "I just can't imagine sleeping with someone in this house."

His leg shakes violently. Wayne takes Neil's hand in a firm grasp and hauls 55
him up.

* * *

Later that night, they lie outside, under redwood trees, listening to the hysteria
of the crickets, the hum of the pool cleaning itself. Redwood leaves prick their
skin. They fell in love in bars and apartments, and this is the first time that they
have made love outdoors. Neil is not sure he has enjoyed the experience. He
kept sensing eyes, imagined that the neighborhood cats were staring at them
from behind a fence of brambles. He remembers he once hid in this spot when
he and some of the children from the neighborhood were playing sardines, remembers the intoxication of small bodies packed together, the warm breath of
suppressed laughter on his neck. "The loser had to go through the spanking machine," he tells Wayne.

"Did you lose often?"

"Most of the time. The spanking machine never really hurt—just a whirl of
hands. If you moved fast enough, no one could actually get you. Sometimes,
though, late in the afternoon, we'd get naughty. We'd chase each other and pull
each other's pants down. That was all. Boys and girls together!"

"Listen to the insects," Wayne says, and closes his eyes.

Neil turns to examine Wayne's face, notices a single, small pimple. Their 60
lovemaking usually begins in a wrestle, a struggle for dominance, and ends with a
somewhat confusing loss of identity—as now, when Neil sees a foot on the grass,
resting against his leg, and tries to determine if it is his own or Wayne's.

From inside the house, the dogs begin to bark. Their yelps grow into
alarmed falsettos. Neil lifts himself up. "I wonder if they smell something," he
says.

"Probably just us," says Wayne.

"My mother will wake up. She hates getting waked up."

Lights go on in the house; the door to the porch opens.

"What's wrong, Abby? What's wrong?" his mother's voice calls softly. 65

Wayne clamps his hand over Neil's mouth. "Don't say anything," he whispers.

"I can't just—" Neil begins to say, but Wayne's hand closes over his mouth
again. He bites it, and Wayne starts laughing.

"What was that?" Her voice projects into the garden. "Hello?" she says.

The dogs yelp louder. "Abbylucyferny, it's O.K., it's O.K." Her voice is soft
and panicked. "Is anyone there?" she asks loudly.

The brambles shake. She takes a flashlight, shines it around the garden. 70
Wayne and Neil duck down; the light lands on them and hovers for a few seconds. Then it clicks off and they are in the dark—a new dark, a darker dark,
which their eyes must readjust to.

"Let's go to bed, Abbylucyferny," she says gently. Neil and Wayne hear
her pad into the house. The dogs whimper as they follow her, and the lights
go off.

* * *

Once before, Neil and his mother had stared at each other in the glare of bright lights. Four years ago, they stood in the arena created by the headlights of her car, waiting for the train. He was on his way back to San Francisco, where he was marching in a Gay Pride Parade the next day. The train station was next door to the food co-op and shared its parking lot. The co-op, familiar and boring by day, took on a certain mystery in the night. Neil recognized the spot where he had skidded on his bicycle and broken his leg. Through the glass doors, the brightly lit interior of the store glowed, its rows and rows of cans and boxes forming their own horizon, each can illuminated so that even from outside Neil could read the labels. All that was missing was the ladies in tennis dresses and sweat-shirts, pushing their carts past bins of nuts and dried fruits.

"Your train is late," his mother said. Her hair fell loosely on her shoulders, and her legs were tanned. Neil looked at her and tried to imagine her in labor with him—bucking and struggling with his birth. He felt then the strange, sex-less love for women which through his whole adolescence he had mistaken for heterosexual desire.

A single bright light approached them; it preceded the low, haunting sound of the whistle. Neil kissed his mother, and waved goodbye as he ran to meet the train. It was an old train, with windows tinted a sort of horrible lemon-lime. It stopped only long enough for him to hoist himself on board, and then it was moving again. He hurried to a window, hoping to see her drive off, but the tint of the window made it possible for him to make out only vague patches of light—street lamps, cars, the co-op.

He sank into the hard, green seat. The train was almost entirely empty; the only other passenger was a dark-skinned man wearing bluejeans and a leather jacket. He sat directly across the aisle from Neil, next to the window. He had rough skin and a thick mustache. Neil discovered that by pretending to look out the window he could study the man's reflection in the lemon-lime glass. It was only slightly hazy—the quality of a bad photograph. Neil felt his mouth open, felt sleep closing in on him. Hazy red and gold flashes through the glass pulsed in the face of the man in the window, giving the curious impression of muscle spasms. It took Neil a few minutes to realize that the man was staring at him, or, rather, staring at the back of his head—staring at his staring. The man smiled as though to say, I know exactly what you're staring at, and Neil felt the sickening sensation of desire rise in his throat.

Right before they reached the city, the man stood up and sat down in the seat next to Neil's. The man's thigh brushed deliberately against his own. Neil's eyes were watering; he felt sick to his stomach. Taking Neil's hand, the man said, "Why so nervous, honey? Relax."

Neil woke up the next morning with the taste of ashes in his mouth. He was lying on the floor, without blankets or sheets or pillows. Instinctively, he reached for his pants, and as he pulled them on came face to face with the man from the train. His name was Luis; he turned out to be a dog groomer. His apartment smelled of dog.

"Why such a hurry?" Luis said.

"The parade. The Gay Pride Parade. I'm meeting some friends to march."

"I'll come with you," Luis said. "I think I'm too old for these things, but why not?"

Neil did not want Luis to come with him, but he found it impossible to say so. Luis looked older by day, more likely to carry diseases. He dressed again in a torn T-shirt, leather jacket, bluejeans. "It's my everyday apparel," he said, and laughed. Neil buttoned his pants, aware that they had been washed by his mother the day before. Luis possessed the peculiar combination of hypermasculinity and effeminacy which exemplifies faggotry. Neil wanted to be rid of him, but Luis's mark was on him, he could see that much. They would become lovers whether Neil liked it or not.

They joined the parade midway. Neil hoped he wouldn't meet anyone he knew; he did not want to have to explain Luis, who clung to him. The parade was full of shirtless men with oiled, muscular shoulders. Neil's back ached. There were floats carrying garishly dressed prom queens and cheerleaders, some with beards, some actually looking like women. Luis said, "It makes me proud, makes me glad to be what I am." Neil supposed that by darting into the crowd ahead of him he might be able to lose Luis forever, but he found it difficult to let him go; the prospect of being alone seemed unbearable.

Neil was startled to see his mother watching the parade, holding up a sign. She was with the Coalition of Parents of Lesbians and Gays; they had posted a huge banner on the wall behind them proclaiming: OUR SONS AND DAUGHTERS, WE ARE PROUD OF YOU. She spotted him; she waved, and jumped up and down.

"Who's that woman?" Luis asked.

"My mother. I should go say hello to her." 85

"O.K.," Luis said. He followed Neil to the side of the parade. Neil kissed his mother. Luis took off his shirt, wiped his face with it, smiled.

"I'm glad you came," Neil said.

"I wouldn't have missed it, Neil. I wanted to show you I cared."

He smiled, and kissed her again. He showed no intention of introducing Luis, so Luis introduced himself.

"Hello, Luis," Mrs. Campbell said. Neil looked away. Luis shook her hand, 90 and Neil wanted to warn his mother to wash it, warned himself to check with a V.D. clinic first thing Monday.

"Neil, this is Carmen Bologna, another one of the mothers," Mrs. Campbell said. She introduced him to a fat Italian woman with flushed cheeks, and hair arranged in the shape of a clamshell.

"Good to meet you, Neil, good to meet you," said Carmen Bologna. "You know my son, Michael? I'm so proud of Michael! He's doing so well now. I'm proud of him, proud to be his mother I am, and your mother's proud, too!"

The woman smiled at him, and Neil could think of nothing to say but "Thank you." He looked uncomfortably toward his mother, who stood listening to Luis. It occurred to him that the worst period of his life was probably about to begin and he had no way to stop it.

A group of drag queens ambled over to where the mothers were standing. "Michael! Michael!" shouted Carmen Bologna, and embraced a sticklike man wrapped in green satin. Michael's eyes were heavily dosed with green eyeshadow, and his lips were painted pink.

Neil turned and saw his mother staring, her mouth open. He marched over 95 to where Luis was standing, and they moved back into the parade. He turned and waved to her. She waved back; he saw pain in her face, and then, briefly, regret. That day, he felt she would have traded him for any other son. Later, she said to him, "Carmen Bologna really was proud, and, speaking as a mother, let me tell you, you have to be brave to feel such pride."

Neil was never proud. It took him a year to dump Luis, another year to leave California. The sick taste of ashes was still in his mouth. On the plane, he envisioned his mother sitting alone in the dark, smoking. She did not leave his mind until he was circling New York, staring down at the dawn rising over Queens. The song playing in his earphones would remain hovering on the edges of his memory, always associated with her absence. After collecting his baggage, he took a bus into the city. Boys were selling newspapers in the middle of highways, through the windows of stopped cars. It was seven in the morning when he reached Manhattan. He stood for ten minutes of East Thirty-fourth Street, breathed the cold air, and felt bubbles rising in his blood.

Neil got a job as a paralegal—a temporary job, he told himself. When he met Wayne a year later, the sensations of that first morning returned to him. They'd been up all night, and at six they walked across the park to Wayne's apartment with the nervous, deliberate gait of people aching to make love for the first time. Joggers ran by with their dogs. None of them knew what Wayne and he were about to do, and the secrecy excited him. His mother came to mind, and the song, and the whirling vision of Queens coming alive below him. His breath solidified into clouds, and be felt happier than he had ever felt before in his life.

* * *

The second day of Wayne's visit, he and Neil go with Mrs. Campbell to pick up the dogs at the dog parlor. The grooming establishment is decorated with pink ribbons and photographs of the owner's champion pit bulls. A fat, middle-aged woman appears from the back, leading the newly trimmed and fluffed Abigail, Lucille, and Fern by three leashes. The dogs struggle frantically when they see Neil's mother, tangling the woman up in their leashes. "Ladies, behave!" Mrs. Campbell commands, and collects the dogs. She gives Fern to Neil and Abigail to Wayne. In the car on the way back, Abigail begins pawing to get on Wayne's lap.

"Just push her off," Mrs. Campbell says. "She knows she's not supposed to do that."

"You never groomed Rasputin," Neil complains.   100

"Rasputin was a mutt."

"Rasputin was a beautiful dog, even if he did smell."

"Do you remember when you were a little kid, Neil, you used to make Rasputin dance with you? Once you tried to dress him up in one of my blouses."

"I don't remember that," Neil says.

"Yes. I remember," says Mrs. Campbell. "Then you tried to organize a dog   105 beauty contest in the neighborhood. You wanted to have runners-up—everything."

"A dog beauty contest?" Wayne says.

"Mother, do we have to—"

"I think it's a mother's privilege to embarrass her son," Mrs. Campbell says, and smiles.

When they are about to pull into the driveway, Wayne starts screaming, and pushes Abigail off his lap. "Oh, my God!" he says. "The dog just pissed all over me."

Neil turns around and sees a puddle seeping into Wayne's slacks. He sup- 110 presses his laughter, and Mrs. Campbell hands him a rag.

"I'm sorry, Wayne," she says. "It goes with the territory."

"This is really disgusting," Wayne says, swatting at himself with the rag.

Neil keeps his eyes on his own reflection in the rearview mirror and smiles.

At home, while Wayne cleans himself in the bathroom, Neil watches his mother cook lunch—Japanese noodles in soup. "When you went off to college," she says, "I went to the grocery store. I was going to buy you ramen noodles, and I suddenly realized you weren't going to be around to eat them. I started crying right then, blubbering like an idiot."

Neil clenches his fists inside his pockets. She has a way of telling him little 115 sad stories when he doesn't want to hear them—stories of dolls broken by her brothers, lunches stolen by neighborhood boys on the way to school. Now he has joined the ranks of male children who have made her cry.

"Mama, I'm sorry," he says.

She is bent over the noodles, which steam in her face. "I didn't want to say anything in front of Wayne, but I wish you had answered me last night. I was very frightened—and worried."

"I'm sorry," he says, but it's not convincing. His fingers prickle. He senses a great sorrow about to be born.

"I lead a quiet life," she says. "I don't want to be a disciplinarian. I just don't have the energy for these—shenanigans. Please don't frighten me that way again."

"If you were so upset, why didn't you say something?" 120

"I'd rather not discuss it. I lead a quiet life. I'm not used to getting woken up late at night. I'm not used—"

"To my having a lover?"

"No, I'm not used to having other people around, that's all. Wayne is charming. A wonderful young man."

"He likes you, too."

"I'm sure we'll get along fine." 125

She scoops the steaming noodles into ceramic bowls. Wayne returns, wearing shorts. His white, hairy legs are a shocking contrast to hers, which are brown and sleek.

"I'll wash those pants, Wayne," Mrs. Campbell says. "I have a special detergent that'll take out the stain."

She gives Neil a look to indicate that the subject should be dropped. He looks at Wayne, looks at his mother; his initial embarrassment gives way to a fierce pride—the arrogance of mastery. He is glad his mother knows that he is desired, glad it makes her flinch.

Later, he steps into the back yard; the gardener is back, whacking at the bushes with his shears. Neil walks by him in his bathing suit, imagining he is on parade.

That afternoon, he finds his mother's daily list on the kitchen table: 130

TUESDAY

7:00—breakfast
Take dogs to groomer
Groceries (?)

Campaign against Draft—4–7

Buy underwear
Trios—2:00
Spaghetti
Fruit
Asparagus if sale
Peanuts
Milk

Doctor's Appointment (make)
Write Cranston/Hayakawa
re disarmament

Handi-Wraps
Mozart
Abigail
Top Ramen
Pedro

Her desk and trash can are full of such lists; he remembers them from the earliest days of his childhood. He had learned to read from them. In his own life, too, there have been endless lists—covered with check marks and arrows, at least one item always spilling over onto the next day's agenda. From September to November, "Buy plane ticket for Christmas" floated from list to list to list.

The last item puzzles him: Pedro. Pedro must be the gardener. He observes the accretion of names, the arbitrary specifics that give a sense of his mother's life. He could make a list of his own selves: the child, the adolescent, the promiscuous faggot son, and finally the good son, settled, relatively successful. But the divisions wouldn't work; he is today and will always be the child being licked by the dog, the boy on the floor with Luis; he will still be everything he is ashamed of. The other lists—the lists of things done and undone—tell their own truth: that his life is measured more properly in objects than in stages. He knows himself as "jump rope," "book," "sun-glasses," "underwear."

"Tell me about your family, Wayne," Mrs. Campbell says that night, as they drive toward town. They are going to see an Esther Williams movie at the local revival house: an underwater musical, populated by mermaids, underwater Rockettes.

"My father was a lawyer," Wayne says. "He had an office in Queens, with a neon sign. I think he's probably the only lawyer in the world who had a neon sign. Anyway, he died when I was ten. My mother never remarried. She lives in Queens. Her great claim to fame is that when she was twenty-two she went on 'The $64,000 Question.' Her category was mystery novels. She made it to sixteen thousand before she got tripped up."

"When I was about ten, I wanted you to go on 'Jeopardy,' " Neil says to his mother. "You really should have, you know. You would have won."

"You certainly loved 'Jeopardy,' " Mrs. Campbell says. "You used to watch it during dinner. Wayne, does your mother work?"

"No," he says. "She lives off investments."

"You're both only children," Mrs. Campbell says. Neil wonders if she is ruminating on the possible connection between that coincidence and their "alternative life style."

The movie theater is nearly empty. Neil sits between Wayne and his mother. There are pillows on the floor at the front of the theater, and a cat is prowling over them. It casts a monstrous shadow every now and then on the screen, disturbing the sedative effect of water ballet. Like a teen-ager, Neil cautiously reaches his arm around Wayne's shoulder. Wayne takes his hand immediately. Next to them, Neil's mother breathes in, out, in, out. Neil timorously moves his other arm and lifts it behind his mother's neck. He does not look at her, but he can tell from her breathing that she senses what he is doing. Slowly, carefully, he lets his hand drop on her shoulder; it twitches spasmodically, and he jumps, as if he had received an electric shock. His mother's quiet breathing is broken by a gasp; even Wayne notices. A sudden brightness on the screen illuminates the panic in her eyes, Neil's arm frozen above her, about to fall again. Slowly, he lowers his arm until his fingertips touch her skin, the fabric of her dress. He has gone too far to go back now; they are all too far.

Wayne and Mrs. Campbell sink into their seats, but Neil remains stiff, holding up his arms, which rest on nothing. The movie ends, and they go on sitting just like that.

"I'm old," Mrs. Campbell says later, as they drive back home. "I remember 140 when those films were new. Your father and I went to one on our first date. I loved them, because I could pretend that those women underwater were flying— they were so graceful. They really took advantage of Technicolor in those days. Color was something to appreciate. You can't know what it was like to see a color movie for the first time, after years of black-and-white. It's like trying to explain the surprise of snow to an East Coaster. Very little is new anymore, I fear."

Neil would like to tell her about his own nostalgia, but how can he explain that all of it revolves around her? The idea of her life before he was born pleases him. "Tell Wayne how you used to look like Esther Williams," he asks her.

She blushes. "I was told I looked like Esther Williams, but really more like Gene Tierney," she says. "Not beautiful, but interesting. I like to think I had a certain magnetism."

"You still do," Wayne says, and instantly recognizes the wrongness of his comment. Silence and a nervous laugh indicate that he has not yet mastered the family vocabulary.

When they get home, the night is once again full of the sound of crickets. Mrs. Campbell picks up a flashlight and calls the dogs. "Abbylucyferny, Abbylucyferny," she shouts, and the dogs amble from their various corners. She pushes them out the door to the back yard and follows them. Neil follows her. Wayne follows Neil, but hovers on the porch. Neil walks behind her as she tramps through the garden. She holds out her flashlight, and snails slide from behind bushes, from under rocks, to where she stands. When the snails become visible, she crushes them underfoot. They make a wet, cracking noise, like eggs being broken.

"Nights like this," she says, "I think of children without pants on, in hot 145 South American countries. I have nightmares about tanks rolling down our street."

"The weather's never like this in New York," Neil says. "When it's hot, it's humid and sticky. You don't want to go outdoors."

"I could never live anywhere else but here. I think I'd die. I'm too used to the climate."

"Don't be silly."

"No, I mean it," she says. "I have adjusted too well to the weather."

The dogs bark and howl by the fence. "A cat, I suspect," she says. She aims 150
her flashlight at a rock, and more snails emerge—uncountable numbers, too stupid to have learned not to trust light.

"I know what you were doing at the movie," she says.

"What?"

"I know what you were doing."

"What? I put my arm around you."

"I'm sorry, Neil," she says. "I can only take so much. Just so much." 155

"What do you mean?" he says. "I was only trying to show affection."

"Oh, affection—I know about affection."

He looks up at the porch, sees Wayne moving toward the door, trying not to
listen.

"What do you mean?" Neil says to her.

She puts down the flashlight and wraps her arms around herself. "I remem- 160
ber when you were a little boy," she says. "I remember, and I have to stop remembering. I wanted you to grow up happy. And I'm very tolerant, very understanding. But I can only take so much."

His heart seems to have risen into his throat. "Mother," he says, "I think you
know my life isn't your fault. But for God's sake, don't say that your life is my fault."

"It's not a question of fault," she says. She extracts a Kleenex from her pocket
and blows her nose. "I'm sorry, Neil. I guess I'm just an old woman with too much
on her mind and not enough to do." She laughs halfheartedly. "Don't worry. Don't
say anything," she says. "Abbylucyferny, Abbylucyferny, time for bed!"

He watches her as she walks toward the porch, silent and regal. There is the
pad of feet, the clinking of dog tags as the dogs run for the house.

* * *

He was twelve the first time she saw him march in a parade. He played the tuba,
and as his elementary-school band lumbered down the streets of their then small
town she stood on the sidelines and waved. Afterward, she had taken him out for
ice cream. He spilled some on his red uniform, and she swiped at it with a napkin. She had been there for him that day, as well as years later, at that more
memorable parade; she had been there for him every day.

Somewhere over Iowa, a week later, Neil remembers this scene, remembers 165
other days, when he would find her sitting in the dark, crying. She had to take
time out of her own private sorrow to appease his anxiety. "It was part of it," she
told him later. "Part of being a mother."

"The scariest thing in the world is the thought that you could unknowingly
ruin someone's life," Neil tells Wayne. "Or even change someone's life. I hate
the thought of having such control. I'd make a rotten mother."

"You're crazy," Wayne says. "You have this great mother, and all you do is
complain. I know people whose mothers have disowned them."

"Guilt goes with the territory," Neil says.

"Why?" Wayne asks, perfectly seriously.

Neil doesn't answer. He lies back in his seat, closes his eyes, imagines he 170
grew up in a house in the mountains of Colorado, surrounded by snow—endless
white snow on hills. No flat places, and no trees; just white hills. Every time he
has flown away, she has come into his mind, usually sitting alone in the dark,
smoking. Today she is outside at dusk, skimming leaves from the pool.

"I want to get a dog," Neil says.

Wayne laughs. "In the city? It'd suffocate."

The hum of the airplane is druglike, dazing. "I want to stay with you a long time," Neil says.

"I know." Imperceptibly, Wayne takes his hand.

"It's very hot there in the summer, too. You know, I'm not thinking about   175 my mother now."

"It's O.K."

For a moment, Neil wonders what the stewardess or the old woman on the way to the bathroom will think, but then he laughs and relaxes.

Later, the plane makes a slow circle over New York City, and on it two men hold hands, eyes closed, and breathe in unison.

Starting Points for Further Research: David Leavitt

- **Critical Essay:** Kenneth Bleeth. "The 'Imitation David': Plagiarism, Collaboration, and the Making of a Gay Literary Tradition in David Leavitt's 'The Term Paper Artist.' " *PMLA* 116 (2001): 1349–63.
- **Interview:** "An Interview with David Leavitt." *Occident* 102:1 (1998): 143–51.

AMY HEMPEL   (B. 1951)

Born in Chicago and raised in California, Amy Hempel had what she calls a "nonlinear education," attending several colleges in California before moving to New York to become a writer. At Columbia University, in a creative writing workshop taught by editor Gordon Lish, who had shaped the fiction of Raymond Carver, she wrote the stories that comprised her first collection, Reasons to Live *(1985), from which "In the Cemetery Where Al Jolson Is Buried" comes. Jolson, the vaudeville-era entertainer who starred in the first Hollywood "talkie,"* The Jazz Singer, *is buried in Los Angeles at the Forest Lawn Cemetery. Hempel's other works include* At the Gates of the Animal Kingdom *(1990),* Tumble Home: A Novella and Short Stories *(1997), and* The Dog of the Marriage *(2005).*

Hempel's minimalist style, like Carver's, is marked by concise language and compressed narrative detail, allowing the reader to infer meaning that is not stated explicitly. In a 2003 interview in The Paris Review, *she reflects on her commitment to paying attention to writing at the smallest level, observing: "Writing conducted at the sentence level has always made perfect sense to me. . . . That's the great attraction and motivation. That's what gets me in, writing or reading. Though it's unlikely you'll write something nobody has ever heard of, the way you have a chance to compete is in the way you say it. Now I've been writing for almost twenty years, and I still feel the same way. That is how I assemble stories—me and a hundred million other people—at the sentence level. Not by coming up with a sweeping story line."*

In the Cemetery Where Al Jolson Is Buried   (1985)

"Tell me things I won't mind forgetting," she said. "Make it useless stuff or skip it."

I began. I told her insects fly through rain missing every drop, never getting wet. I told her no one in America owned a tape recorder before Bing Crosby did.

I told her the shape of the moon is like a banana—you see it looking full, you're seeing it end-on.

The camera made me self-conscious and I stopped. It was trained on us from a ceiling mount—the kind of camera banks use to photograph robbers. It played us to the nurses down the hall in Intensive Care.

"Go on, girl," she said. "You get used to it."

I had my audience. I went on. Did she know that Tammy Wynette had   5
changed her tune? Really. That now she sings "Stand By Your Friends"? That Paul Anka did it too, I said. Does "You're Having *Our* Baby." That he got sick of all that feminist bitching.

"What else?" she said. "Have you got something else?"

Oh, yes.

For her I would always have something else.

"Did you know that when they taught the first chimp to talk, it lied? That when they asked her who did it on the desk, she signed back Max, the janitor. And that when they pressed her, she said she was sorry, that it was really the project director. But she was a mother, so I guess she had her reasons."

"Oh, that's good," she said. "A parable."   10

"There's more about the chimp," I said. "But it will break your heart."

"No, thanks," she says, and scratches at her mask.

*   *   *

We look like good-guy outlaws. Good or bad, I am not used to the mask yet. I keep touching the warm spot where my breath, thank God, comes out. She is used to hers. She only ties the strings on top. The other ones—a pro by now—she lets hang loose.

We call this place the Marcus Welby Hospital. It's the white one with the palm trees under the opening credits of all those shows. A Hollywood hospital, though in fact it is several miles west. Off camera, there is a beach across the street.

*   *   *

She introduces me to a nurse as the Best Friend. The impersonal article is more   15
intimate. It tells me that *they* are intimate, the nurse and my friend.

"I was telling her we used to drink Canada Dry ginger ale and pretend we were in Canada."

"That's how dumb *we* were," I say.

"You could be sisters," the nurse says.

So how come, I'll bet they are wondering, it took me so long to get to such a glamorous place? But do they ask?

They do not ask.   20

Two months, and how long is the drive?

The best I can explain it is this—I have a friend who worked one summer in a mortuary. He used to tell me stories. The one that really got to me was not the grisliest, but it's the one that did. A man wrecked his car on 101 going south. He did not lose consciousness. But his arm was taken down to the wet bone—and when he looked at it—it scared him to death.

I mean, he died.

So I hadn't dared to look any closer. But now I'm doing it—and hoping that I will live through it.

* * *

She shakes out a summer-weight blanket, showing a leg you did not want to see. 25 Except for that, you look at her and understand the law that requires two people to be with the body at all times.

"I thought of something," she says. "I thought of it last night. I think there is a real and present need here. You know," she says, "like for someone to do it for you when you can't do it yourself. You call them up whenever you want—like when push comes to shove."

She grabs the bedside phone and loops the cord around her neck.

"Hey," she says, "the end o' the line."

She keeps on, giddy with something. But I don't know with what.

"I can't remember," she says. "What does Kübler-Ross[1] say comes after 30 Denial?"

It seems to me Anger must be next. Then Bargaining, Depression, and so on and so forth. But I keep my guesses to myself.

"The only thing is," she says, "is where's Resurrection? God knows, I want to do it by the book. But she left out Resurrection."

* * *

She laughs, and I cling to the sound the way someone dangling above a ravine holds fast to the thrown rope.

"Tell me," she says, "about that chimp with the talking hands. What do they do when the thing ends and the chimp says, 'I don't want to go back to the zoo'?"

When I don't say anything, she says, "Okay—then tell me another animal 35 story. I like animal stories. But not a sick one—I don't want to know about all the seeing-eye dogs going blind."

No, I would not tell her a sick one.

"How about the hearing-ear dogs?" I say. "They're not going deaf, but they are getting very judgmental. For instance, there's this golden retriever in New Jersey, he wakes up the deaf mother and drags her into the daughter's room because the kid has got a flashlight and is reading under the covers."

"Oh, you're killing me," she says. "Yes, you're definitely killing me."

"They say the smart dog obeys, but the smarter dog knows when to disobey."

"Yes," she says," the smarter anything knows when to disobey. Now, for 40 example."

* * *

She is flirting with the Good Doctor, who has just appeared. Unlike the Bad Doctor, who checks the I.V. drip before saying good morning, the Good Doctor says things like "God didn't give epileptics a fair shake." The Good Doctor awards himself points for the cripples he could have hit in the parking lot. Because the Good Doctor is a little in love with her, he says maybe a year. He pulls a chair up to her bed and suggests I might like to spend an hour on the beach.

---

[1]Elisabeth Kübler-Ross (1926–2004), author of popular books on death and dying.

"Bring me something back," she says. "Anything from the beach. Or the gift shop. Taste is no object."

He draws the curtain around her bed.

"Wait!" she cries.

I look in at her. 45

"Anything," she says, "except a magazine subscription."

The doctor turns away.

I watch her mouth laugh.

*   *   *

What seems dangerous often is not—black snakes, for example, or clear-air turbulence. While things that just lie there, like this beach, are loaded with jeopardy. A yellow dust rising from the ground, the heat that ripens melons overnight—this is earthquake weather. You can sit here braiding the fringe on your towel and the sand will all of a sudden suck down like an hour-glass. The air roars. In the cheap apartments on-shore, bathtubs fill themselves and gardens roll up and over like green waves. If nothing happens, the dust will drift and the heat deepen till fear turns to desire. Nerves like that are only bought off by catastrophe.

*   *   *

"It never happens when you're thinking about it," she once observed. "Earth- 50 quake, earthquake, earthquake," she said.

"Earthquake, earthquake, earthquake," I said.

Like the aviaphobe who keeps the plane aloft with prayer, we kept it up until an aftershock cracked the ceiling.

That was after the big one in '72. We were in college; our dormitory was five miles from the epicenter. When the ride was over and my jabbering pulse began to slow, she served five parts champagne to one part orange juice, and joked about living in Ocean View, Kansas. I offered to drive her to Hawaii on the new world psychics predicted would surface the next time, or the next.

I could not say that now—next.

Whose next? she could ask. 55

*   *   *

Was I the only one who noticed that the experts had stopped saying *if* and now spoke of *when*? Of course not; the fearful ran to thousands. We watched the traffic of Japanese beetles for deviation. Deviation might mean more natural violence.

I wanted her to be afraid with me. But she said, "I don't know. I'm just not."

She was afraid of nothing, not even of flying.

I have this dream before a flight where we buckle in and the plane moves down the runway. It takes off at thirty-five miles an hour, and then we're airborne, skimming the tree tops. Still, we arrive in New York on time.

It is so pleasant. 60

One night I flew to Moscow this way.

*   *   *

She flew with me once. That time she flew with me she ate macadamia nuts while the wings bounced. She knows the wing tips can bend thirty feet up and

thirty feet down without coming off. She believes it. She trusts the laws of aero-
dynamics. My mind stampedes. I can almost accept that a battleship floats when
everybody knows steel sinks.

I see fear in her now, and am not going to try to talk her out of it. She is
right to be afraid.

After a quake, the six o'clock news airs a film clip of first-graders yelling at
the broken playground per their teacher's instructions.

"*Bad* earth!" they shout, because anger is stronger than fear.   65

* * *

But the beach is standing still today. Everyone on it is tranquilized, numb, or
asleep. Teenaged girls rub coconut oil on each other's hard-to-reach places. They
smell like macaroons. They pry open compacts like clamshells; mirrors catch the
sun and throw a spray of white rays across glazed shoulders. The girls arrange
their wet hair with silk flowers the way they learned in *Seventeen*. They pose.

A formation of low-riders pulls over to watch with a six-pack. They get vocal when the girls check their tan lines. When the beer is gone, so are they—
flexing their cars on up the boulevard.

Above this aggressive health are the twin wrought-iron terraces, painted
flamingo pink, of the Palm Royale. Someone dies there every time the sheets are
changed. There's an ambulance in the driveway, so the remaining residents line
the balconies, rocking and not talking, one-upped.

The ocean they stare at is dangerous, and not just the undertow. You can almost see the slapping tails of sand sharks keeping cruising bodies alive.

If she looked, she could see this, some of it, from her window. She would be   70
the first to say how little it takes to make a thing all wrong.

* * *

There was a second bed in the room when I got back to it!

For two beats I didn't get it. Then it hit me like an open coffin.

She wants every minute, I thought. She wants my life.

"You missed Gussie," she said.

Gussie is her parents' three-hundred-pound, narcoleptic maid. Her attacks   75
often come at the ironing board. The pillowcases in that family are all bordered
with scorch.

"It's a hard trip for her," I said. "How is she?"

"Well, she didn't fall asleep, if that's what you mean. Gussie's great—you
know what she said? She said, 'Darlin, stop this worriation. Just keep prayin,
down on your knees'—me, who can't even get out of bed."

She shrugged. "What am I missing?"

"It's earthquake weather," I told her.

"The best thing to do about earthquakes," she said, "is not to live in   80
California."

"That's useful," I said. "You sound like Reverend Ike—'The best thing to do
for the poor is not be one of them.'"

We're crazy about Reverend Ike.

I noticed her face was bloated.

"You know," she said, "I feel like hell. I'm about to stop having fun."

* * *

"The ancients have a saying," I said. " 'There are times when the wolves are   85
silent; there are times when the moon howls.' "

"What's that, Navajo?"

"Palm Royale lobby graffiti," I said. "I bought a paper there. I'll read you
something."

"Even though I care about nothing?"

I turned to the page with the trivia column. I said, "Did you know the more
shrimp flamingo birds eat, the pinker their feathers get?" I said, "Did you know
that Eskimos need refrigerators? Do you know *why* Eskimos need refrigerators?
Did you know that Eskimos need refrigerators because how else would they keep
their food from freezing?"

I turned to page three, to a UPI filler datelined Mexico City. I read her   90
"Man Robs Bank with Chicken," about a man who bought a barbecued chicken
at a stand down the block from a bank. Passing the bank, he got the idea. He
walked in and approached a teller. He pointed the brown paper bag at her and
she handed over the day's receipts. It was the smell of barbecue sauce that eventually led to his capture.

* * *

The story had made her hungry, she said—so I took the elevator down six floors
to the cafeteria, and brought back all the ice cream she wanted. We lay side by
side, adjustable beds cranked up for optimal TV-viewing, littering the sheets
with Good Humor wrappers, picking toasted almonds out of the gauze. We were
Lucy and Ethel, Mary and Rhoda in extremis. The blinds were closed to keep
light off the screen.

We watched a movie starring men we used to think we wanted to sleep
with. Hers was a tough cop out to stop mine, a vicious rapist who went after
cocktail waitresses.

"This is a good movie," she said when snipers felled them both.

I missed her already.

* * *

A Filipino nurse tiptoed in and gave her an injection. The nurse removed the   95
pile of popsicle sticks from the nightstand—enough to splint a small animal.

The injection made us both sleepy. We slept.

I dreamed she was a decorator, come to furnish my house. She worked in secret, singing to herself. When she finished, she guided me proudly to the door.
"How do you like it?" she asked, easing me inside.

Every beam and sill and shelf and knob was draped in gay bunting, with
streamers of pastel crepe looped around bright mirrors.

* * *

"I have to go home," I said when she woke up.

She thought I meant home to her house in the Canyon, and I had to say No,   100
home home. I twisted my hands in the time-honored fashion of people in pain. I
was supposed to offer something. The Best Friend. I could not even offer to come
back.

I felt weak and small and failed.

Also exhilarated.

I had a convertible in the parking lot. Once out of that room, I would drive it too fast down the Coast highway through the crab-smelling air. A stop in Malibu for sangria. The music in the place would be sexy and loud. They'd serve papaya and shrimp and watermelon ice. After dinner I would shimmer with lust, buzz with heat, vibrate with life, and stay up all night.

* * *

Without a word, she yanked off her mask and threw it on the floor. She kicked at the blankets and moved to the door. She must have hated having to pause for breath and balance before slamming out of Isolation, and out of the second room, the one where you scrub and tie on the white masks.

A voice shouted her name in alarm, and people ran down the corridor. The 105 Good Doctor was paged over the intercom. I opened the door and the nurses at the station stared hard, as if this flight had been my idea.

"Where is she?" I asked, and they nodded to the supply closet.

I looked in. Two nurses were kneeling beside her on the floor, talking to her in low voices. One held a mask over her nose and mouth, the other rubbed her back in slow circles. The nurses glanced up to see if I was the doctor—and when I wasn't, they went back to what they were doing.

"There, there, honey," they cooed.

* * *

On the morning she was moved to the cemetery, the one where Al Jolson is buried, I enrolled in a Fear of Flying class. "What is your worst fear?" the instructor asked, and I answered, "That I will finish this course and still be afraid."

* * *

I sleep with a glass of water on the nightstand so I can see by its level if the 110 coastal earth is trembling or if the shaking is still me.

* * *

What do I remember?

I remember only the useless things I hear—that Bob Dylan's mother invented Wite-out, that twenty-three people must be in a room before there is a fifty-fifty chance two will have the same birthdate. Who cares whether or not it's true? In my head there are bath towels swaddling this stuff. Nothing else seeps through.

I review those things that will figure in the re-telling: a kiss through surgical gauze, the pale hand correcting the position of the wig. I noted these gestures as they happened, not in any retrospect—though I do not know why looking back should show us more than looking at.

It is just possible I will say I stayed the night.

And who is there that can say that I did not? 115

* * *

I think of the chimp, the one with the talking hands.

In the course of the experiment, that chimp had a baby. Imagine how her trainers must have thrilled when the mother, without prompting, began to sign to her newborn.

Baby, drink milk.

Baby, play ball.

And when the baby died, the mother stood over the body, her wrinkled   120
hands moving with animal grace, forming again and again the words, Baby, come
hug, Baby, come hug, fluent now in the language of grief.

Starting Points for Further Research: Amy Hempel

- **Critical Essay:** Amy Hempel. "That's What Dogs Do." *Why I Write: Thoughts on the Craft of Fiction.* Ed. Will Blythe. Boston: Little Brown, 1998. 41–46.
- **Interviews:** Debra Levy and Carol Turner. "Amy Hempel." *Glimmer Train* (Winter 1998): 86–97.
    Paul Winner. "Amy Hempel: The Art of Fiction 176." *Paris Review* (Summer 2003): 30–63.

LORRIE MOORE   (B. 1957)

Born in Glens Falls, New York, Lorrie Moore earned her B.A. at St. Lawrence University and went on to receive an M.F.A. in creative writing from Cornell University in 1982. In 1976, while still an undergraduate, she won a short story contest sponsored by Seventeen magazine. In the decades since, her fiction has appeared in numerous periodicals, including Elle, Ms., The Paris Review, and The New Yorker. She has published two novels, Anagrams (1987) and Who Will Run the Frog Hospital? (1994), but is best known for her short stories, which balance dark, melancholic themes—isolation, loneliness, illness, mortality, grief—with biting humor. Her story collections include Self-Help (1985), from which the story below comes, Like Life (1990), and Birds of America (1998). She currently lives in Madison, Wisconsin, with her family and teaches at the University of Wisconsin.

How to Become a Writer   1985

First, try to be something, anything, else. A movie star/astronaut. A movie
star/missionary. A movie star/kindergarten teacher. President of the World. Fail
miserably. It is best if you fail at an early age—say, fourteen. Early, critical disillusionment is necessary so that at fifteen you can write long haiku sequences about
thwarted desire. It is a pond, a cherry blossom, a wind brushing against sparrow
wing leaving for mountain. Count the syllables. Show it to your mom. She is
tough and practical. She has a son in Vietnam and a husband who may be having an affair. She believes in wearing brown because it hides spots. She'll look
briefly at your writing, then back up at you with a face blank as a donut. She'll
say: "How about emptying the dishwasher?" Look away. Shove the forks in the
fork drawer. Accidentally break one of the freebie gas station glasses. This is the
required pain and suffering. This is only for starters.

In your high school English class look at Mr. Killian's face. Decide faces are
important. Write a villanelle about pores. Struggle. Write a sonnet. Count the
syllables: nine, ten, eleven, thirteen. Decide to experiment with fiction. Here
you don't have to count syllables. Write a short story about an elderly man and

woman who accidentally shoot each other in the head, the result of an inexplicable malfunction of a shotgun which appears mysteriously in their living room one night. Give it to Mr. Killian as your final project. When you get it back, he has written on it: "Some of your images are quite nice, but you have no sense of plot." When you are home, in the privacy of your own room, faintly scrawl in pencil beneath his black-inked comments: "Plots are for dead people, pore-face."

Take all the babysitting jobs you can get. You are great with kids. They love you. You tell them stories about old people who die idiot deaths. You sing them songs like "Blue Bells of Scotland," which is their favorite. And when they are in their pajamas and have finally stopped pinching each other, when they are fast asleep, you read every sex manual in the house, and wonder how on earth anyone could ever do those things with someone they truly loved. Fall asleep in a chair reading Mr. McMurphy's *Playboy.* When the McMurphys come home, they will tap you on the shoulder, look at the magazine in your lap, and grin. You will want to die. They will ask you if Tracey took her medicine all right. Explain, yes, she did, that you promised her a story if she would take it like a big girl and that seemed to work out just fine. "Oh, marvelous," they will exclaim.

Try to smile proudly.

Apply to college as a child psychology major.   5

As a child psychology major, you have some electives. You've always liked birds. Sign up for something called "The Ornithological Field Trip." It meets Tuesdays and Thursdays at two. When you arrive at Room 134 on the first day of class, everyone is sitting around a seminar table talking about metaphors. You've heard of these. After a short, excruciating while, raise your hand and say diffidently, "Excuse me, isn't this Birdwatching One-oh-one?" The class stops and turns to look at you. They seem to all have one face—giant and blank as a vandalized clock. Someone with a beard booms out, "No, this is Creative Writing." Say: "Oh—right," as if perhaps you knew all along. Look down at your schedule. Wonder how the hell you ended up here. The computer, apparently, has made an error. You start to get up to leave and then don't. The lines at the registrar this week are huge. Perhaps you should stick with this mistake. Perhaps your creative writing isn't all that bad. Perhaps it is fate. Perhaps this is what your dad meant when he said, "It's the age of computers, Francie, it's the age of computers."

Decide that you like college life. In your dorm, you meet many nice people. Some are smarter than you. And some, you notice, are dumber than you. You will continue, unfortunately, to view the world in exactly these terms for the rest of your life.

The assignment this week in creative writing is to narrate a violent happening. Turn in a story about driving with your Uncle Gordon and another one about two old people who are accidentally electrocuted when they go to turn on a badly wired desk lamp. The teacher will hand them back to you with comments: "Much of your writing is smooth and energetic. You have, however, a ludicrous notion of plot." Write another story about a man and a woman who, in the very first paragraph, have their lower torsos accidentally blitzed away by dynamite. In the second paragraph, with the insurance money, they buy a frozen yogurt stand together. There are six more paragraphs. You read the whole thing out loud in class. No one likes it. They say your sense of plot is outrageous and incompetent. After class someone asks you if you are crazy.

Decide that perhaps you should stick to comedies. Start dating someone who is funny, someone who has what in high school you called a "really great sense of humor" and what now your creative writing class calls "self-contempt giving rise to comic form." Write down all of his jokes, but don't tell him you are doing this. Make up anagrams of his old girlfriend's name and name all your socially handicapped characters with them. Tell him his old girlfriend is in all of your stories and then watch how funny he can be, see what a really great sense of humor he can have.

Your child psychology advisor tells you you are neglecting courses in your 10 major. What you spend the most time on should be what you're majoring in. Say yes, you understand.

In creative writing seminars over the next two years, everyone continues to smoke cigarettes and ask the same things: "But does it work?" "Why should we care about this character?" "Have you earned this cliché?" These seem like important questions.

On days when it is your turn, you look at the class hopefully as they scour your mimeographs for a plot. They look back up at you, drag deeply, and then smile in a sweet sort of way.

You spend too much time slouched and demoralized. Your boyfriend suggests bicycling. Your roommate suggests a new boyfriend. You are said to be self-mutilating and losing weight, but you continue writing. The only happiness you have is writing something new, in the middle of the night, armpits damp, heart pounding, something no one has yet seen. You have only those brief, fragile, untested moments of exhilaration when you know: you are a genius. Understand what you must do. Switch majors. The kids in your nursery project will be disappointed, but you have a calling, an urge, a delusion, an unfortunate habit. You have, as your mother would say, fallen in with a bad crowd.

Why write? Where does writing come from? These are questions to ask yourself. They are like: Where does dust come from? Or: Why is there war? Or: If there's a God, then why is my brother now a cripple?

These are questions that you keep in your wallet, like calling cards. These 15 are questions, your creative writing teacher says, that are good to address in your journals but rarely in your fiction.

The writing professor this fall is stressing the Power of the Imagination. Which means he doesn't want long descriptive stories about your camping trip last July. He wants you to start in a realistic context but then to alter it. Like recombinant DNA. He wants you to let your imagination sail, to let it grow bigbellied in the wind. This is a quote from Shakespeare.

Tell your roommate your great idea, your great idea, your great exercise of imaginative power: a transformation of Melville to contemporary life. It will be about monomania and the fish-eat-fish world of life insurance in Rochester, New York. The first line will be "Call me Fishmeal," and it will feature a menopausal suburban husband named Richard, who because he is so depressed all the time is called "Mopey Dick" by his witty wife Elaine. Say to your roommate: "Mopey Dick, get it?" Your roommate looks at you, her face blank as a large Kleenex. She comes up to you, like a buddy, and puts an arm around your burdened shoulders. "Listen, Francie," she says, slow as speech therapy. "Let's go out and get a big beer."

The seminar doesn't like this one either. You suspect they are beginning to feel sorry for you. They say: "You have to think about what is happening. Where is the story here?"

The next semester the writing professor is obsessed with writing from personal experience. You must write from what you know, from what has happened to you. He wants deaths, he wants camping trips. Think about what has happened to you. In three years there have been three things: you have lost your virginity; your parents got divorced; and your brother came home from a forest ten miles from the Cambodian border with only half a thigh, a permanent smirk nestled into one corner of his mouth.

About the first you write: "It created a new space, which hurt and cried in a   20 voice that wasn't mine, 'I'm not the same anymore, but I'll be okay.'"

About the second you write an elaborate story of an old married couple who stumble upon an unknown land mine in their kitchen and accidentally blow themselves up. You call it: "For Better or for Liverwurst."

About the last you write nothing. There are no words for this. Your typewriter hums. You can find no words.

At undergraduate cocktail parties, people say, "Oh, you write? What do you write about?" Your roommate, who has consumed too much wine, too little cheese, and no crackers at all, blurts: "Oh, my god, she always writes about her dumb boyfriend."

Later on in life you will learn that writers are merely open, helpless texts with no real understanding of what they have written and therefore must half-believe anything and everything that is said of them. You, however, have not reached this stage of literary criticism. You stiffen and say, "I do not," the same way you said it when someone in the fourth grade accused you of really liking oboe lessons and your parents really weren't just making you take them.

Insist you are not very interested in any one subject at all, that you are inter-   25 ested in the music of language, that you are interested in—in—syllables, because they are the atoms of poetry, the cells of the mind, the breath of the soul. Begin to feel woozy. Stare into your plastic wine cup.

"Syllables?" you will hear someone ask, voice trailing off, as they glide slowly toward the reassuring white of the dip.

Begin to wonder what you do write about. Or if you have anything to say. Or if there even is such a thing to say. Limit these thoughts to no more than ten minutes a day; like sit-ups, they can make you thin.

You will read somewhere that all writing has to do with one's genitals. Don't dwell on this. It will make you nervous.

Your mother will come visit you. She will look at the circles under your eyes and hand you a brown book with a brown briefcase on the cover. It is entitled: *How to Become a Business Executive*. She has also brought the *Names for Baby* encyclopedia you asked for; one of your characters, the aging clown-school teacher, needs a new name. Your mother will shake her head and say: "Francie, Francie, remember when you were going to be a child psychology major?"

Say: "Mom, I like to write."

She'll say: "Sure you like to write. Of course. Sure you like to write."   30

Write a story about a confused music student and title it: "Schubert Was the One with the Glasses, Right?" It's not a big hit, although your roommate likes the part where the two violinists accidentally blow themselves up in a recital room. "I went out with a violinist once," she says, snapping her gum.

Thank god you are taking other courses. You can find sanctuary in nineteenth-century ontological snags and invertebrate courting rituals. Certain globular mollusks have what is called "Sex by the Arm." The male octopus, for instance, loses the end of one arm when placing it inside the female body during intercourse. Marine biologists call it "Seven Heaven." Be glad you know these things. Be glad you are not just a writer. Apply to law school.

From here on in, many things can happen. But the main one will be this: you decide not to go to law school after all, and, instead, you spend a good, big chunk of your adult life telling people how you decided not to go to law school after all. Somehow you end up writing again. Perhaps you go to graduate school. Perhaps you work odd jobs and take writing courses at night. Perhaps you are working on a novel and writing down all the clever remarks and intimate personal confessions you hear during the day. Perhaps you are losing your pals, your acquaintances, your balance.

You have broken up with your boyfriend. You now go out with men who, instead of whispering "I love you," shout: "Do it to me, baby." This is good for your writing.   35

Sooner or later you have a finished manuscript more or less. People look at it in a vaguely troubled sort of way and say, "I'll bet becoming a writer was always a fantasy of yours, wasn't it?" Your lips dry to salt. Say that of all the fantasies possible in the world, you can't imagine being a writer even making the top twenty. Tell them you were going to be a child psychology major. "I bet," they always sigh, "you'd be great with kids." Scowl fiercely. Tell them you're a walking blade.

Quit classes. Quit jobs. Cash in old savings bonds. Now you have time like warts on your hands. Slowly copy all of your friends' addresses into a new address book.

Vacuum. Chew cough drops. Keep a folder full of fragments.

An eyelid darkening sideways.

World as conspiracy.   40

Possible plot? A woman gets on a bus.

Suppose you threw a love affair and nobody came.

At home drink a lot of coffee. At Howard Johnson's order the cole slaw. Consider how it looks like the soggy confetti of a map: where you've been, where you're going—"You Are Here," says the red star on the back of the menu.

Occasionally a date with a face blank as a sheet of paper asks you whether writers often become discouraged. Say that sometimes they do and sometimes they do. Say it's a lot like having polio.

"Interesting," smiles your date, and then he looks down at his arm hairs and   45
starts to smooth them, all, always, in the same direction.

Starting Points for Further Research: Lorrie Moore

- **Interviews:** Dwight Garner. "Moore's Better Blues." *Salon*, October 27, 1998.
  Angela Pneuman. "Interview with Lorrie Moore." *The Believer* (October 2005).
- **Article:** Don Lee. "About Lorrie Moore: A Profile." *Ploughshares* (Fall 1998): 224–30.

■ **Critical Essays:** James Phelan. "*Self-Help* for Narratee and Narrative Audience: How 'I'—and 'You'?—Read 'How.'" *Style* 28: 3 (Fall 1994): 350–65.
Michelle Brockway. "The Art of Reading Lorrie Moore." *Poets and Writers* 28: 5 (September-October 2000): 16–19.

SHERMAN ALEXIE   (B. 1966)

Sherman Alexie grew up on the Spokane Indian Reservation in Washington and attended Washington State University. He published two poetry collections, The Business of Fancydancing *(1991) and* I Would Steal Horses *(1993). His short story collection* The Lone Ranger and Tonto Fistfight in Heaven *(1993) included "This Is What It Means to Say Phoenix, Arizona," which was made into the film* Smoke Signals, *a prizewinner at the 1998 Sundance Film Festival. In 2003 he published another collection of short stories,* Ten Little Indians.

The Lone Ranger and Tonto Fistfight in Heaven   (1993)

Too hot to sleep so I walked down to the Third Avenue 7-11 for a Creamsicle and the company of a graveyard-shift cashier. I know that game. I worked graveyard for a Seattle 7-11 and got robbed once too often. The last time the bastard locked me in the cooler. He even took my money and basketball shoes.

The graveyard-shift worker in the Third Avenue 7-11 looked like they all do. Acne scars and a bad haircut, work pants that showed off his white socks, and those cheap black shoes that have no support. My arches still ache from my year at the Seattle 7-11.

"Hello," he asked when I walked into his store. "How you doing?"

I gave him a half-wave as I headed back to the freezer. He looked me over so he could describe me to the police later. I knew the look. One of my old girlfriends said I started to look at her that way, too. She left me not long after that. No, I left her and don't blame her for anything. That's how it happened. When one person starts to look at another like a criminal, then the love is over. It's logical.

* * *

"I don't trust you," she said to me. "You get too angry."   5

She was white and I lived with her in Seattle. Some nights we fought so bad that I would just get in my car and drive all night, only stop to fill up on gas. In fact, I worked the graveyard shift to spend as much time away from her as possible. But I learned all about Seattle that way, driving its back ways and dirty alleys.

Sometimes, though, I would forget where I was and get lost. I'd drive for hours, searching for something familiar. Seems like I'd spent my whole life that way, looking for anything I recognized. Once, I ended up in a nice residential neighborhood and somebody must have been worried because the police showed up and pulled me over.

"What are you doing out here?" the police officer asked me as he looked over my license and registration.

"I'm lost."

"Well, where are you supposed to be?" he asked me, and I knew there were   10
plenty of places I wanted to be, but none where I was supposed to be.

"I got in a fight with my girlfriend," I said. "I was just driving around, blowing off steam, you know?"

"Well, you should be more careful where you drive," the officer said. "You're
making people nervous. You don't fit the profile of the neighborhood."

I wanted to tell him that I didn't really fit the profile of the country but I
knew it would just get me into trouble.

* * *

"Can I help you?" the 7-11 clerk asked me loudly, searching for some response
that would reassure him that I wasn't an armed robber. He knew this dark skin
and long, black hair of mine was dangerous. I had potential.

"Just getting a Creamsicle," I said after a long interval. It was a sick twist to   15
pull on the guy, but it was late and I was bored. I grabbed my Creamsicle and
walked back to the counter slowly, scanned the aisles for effect. I wanted to whistle low and menacingly but I never learned to whistle.

"Pretty hot out tonight?" he asked, that old rhetorical weather bullshit question designed to put us both at ease.

"Hot enough to make you go crazy," I said and smiled. He swallowed hard
like a white man does in those situations. I looked him over. Same old green,
red, and white 7-11 jacket and thick glasses. But he wasn't ugly, just misplaced
and marked by loneliness. If he wasn't working there that night, he'd be at home
alone, flipping through channels and wishing he could afford HBO or Showtime.

"Will this be all?" he asked me, in that company effort to make me do some
impulse shopping. Like adding a clause onto a treaty. *We'll take Washington and
Oregon and you get six pine trees and a brand-new Chrysler Cordoba.* I knew how to
make and break promises.

"No," I said and paused. "Give me a Cherry Slushie, too."

"What size?" he asked, relieved.   20

"Large," I said, and he turned his back to me to make the drink. He realized
his mistake but it was too late. He stiffened, ready for the gunshot or the blow
behind the ear. When it didn't come, he turned back to me.

"I'm sorry," he said. "What size did you say?"

"Small," I said and changed the story.

"But I thought you said large."

"If you knew I wanted a large, then why did you ask me again?" I asked him   25
and laughed. He looked at me, couldn't decide if I was giving him serious shit or
just goofing. There was something about him I liked, even if it was three in the
morning and he was white.

"Hey," I said. "Forget the Slushie. What I want to know is if you know all
the words to the theme from 'The Brady Bunch'?"

He looked at me, confused at first, then laughed.

"Shit," he said. "I was hoping you weren't crazy. You were scaring me."

"Well, I'm going to get crazy if you don't know the words."

He laughed loudly then, told me to take the Creamsicle for free. He was the   30
graveyard-shift manager and those little demonstrations of power tickled him.
All seventy-five cents of it. I knew how much everything cost.

"Thanks," I said to him and walked out the door. I took my time walking
home, let the heat of the night melt the Creamsicle all over my hand. At three

in the morning I could act just as young as I wanted to act. There was no one around to ask me to grow up.

* * *

In Seattle, I broke lamps. She and I would argue and I'd break a lamp, just pick it up and throw it down. At first she'd buy replacement lamps, expensive and beautiful. But after a while she'd buy lamps from Goodwill or garage sales. Then she just gave up the idea entirely and we'd argue in the dark.

"You're just like your brother," she'd yell. "Drunk all the time and stupid."

"My brother don't drink that much."

She and I never tried to hurt each other physically. I did love her, after all, and she loved me. But those arguments were just as damaging as a fist. Words can be like that, you know? Whenever I get into arguments now, I remember her and I also remember Muhammad Ali. He knew the power of his fists but, more importantly, he knew the power of his words, too. Even though he only had an IQ of 80 or so, Ali was a genius. And she was a genius, too. She knew exactly what to say to cause me the most pain.

But don't get me wrong. I walked through that relationship with an executioner's hood. Or more appropriately, with war paint and sharp arrows. She was a kindergarten teacher and I continually insulted her for that.

"Hey, schoolmarm," I asked. "Did your kids teach you anything new today?"

And I always had crazy dreams. I always have had them, but it seemed they became nightmares more often in Seattle.

In one dream, she was a missionary's wife and I was a minor war chief. We fell in love and tried to keep it secret. But the missionary caught us fucking in the barn and shot me. As I lay dying, my tribe learned of the shooting and attacked the whites all across the reservation. I died and my soul drifted above the reservation.

Disembodied, I could see everything that was happening. Whites killing Indians and Indians killing whites. At first it was small, just my tribe and the few whites who lived there. But my dream grew, intensified. Other tribes arrived on horseback to continue the slaughter of whites, and the United States Cavalry rode into battle.

The most vivid image of that dream stays with me. Three mounted soldiers played polo with a dead Indian woman's head. When I first dreamed it, I thought it was just a product of my anger and imagination. But since then, I've read similar accounts of that kind of evil in the old West. Even more terrifying, though, is the fact that those kinds of brutal things are happening today in places like El Salvador.

All I know for sure, though, is that I woke from that dream in terror, packed up all my possessions, and left Seattle in the middle of the night.

"I love you," she said as I left her. "And don't ever come back."

I drove through the night, over the Cascades, down into the plains of central Washington, and back home to the Spokane Indian Reservation.

* * *

When I finished the Creamsicle that the 7–11 clerk gave me, I held the wooden stick up into the air and shouted out very loudly. A couple lights flashed on in windows and a police car cruised by me a few minutes later. I waved to the men in blue and they waved back accidentally. When I got home it was still too hot to sleep so I picked up a week-old newspaper from the floor and read.

There was another civil war, another terrorist bomb exploded, and one more plane crashed and all aboard were presumed dead. The crime rate was rising in every city with populations larger than 100,000, and a farmer in Iowa shot his banker after foreclosure on his 1,000 acres.

A kid from Spokane won the local spelling bee by spelling the word *rhinoceros*.

* * *

When I got back to the reservation, my family wasn't surprised to see me. They'd been expecting me back since the day I left for Seattle. There's an old Indian poet who said that Indians can reside in the city, but they can never live there. That's as close to truth as any of us can get.

Mostly I watched television. For weeks I flipped through channels, searched for answers in the game shows and soap operas. My mother would circle the want ads in red and hand the paper to me.

"What are you going to do with the rest of your life?" she asked.   50

"Don't know," I said, and normally, for almost any other Indian in the country, that would have been a perfectly fine answer. But I was special, a former college student, a smart kid. I was one of those Indians who was supposed to make it, to rise above the rest of the reservation like a fucking eagle or something. I was the new kind of warrior.

For a few months I didn't even look at the want ads my mother circled, just left the newspaper where she had set it down. After a while, though, I got tired of television and started to play basketball again. I'd been a good player in high school, nearly great, and almost played at the college I attended for a couple years. But I'd been too out of shape from drinking and sadness to ever be good again. Still, I liked the way the ball felt in my hands and the way my feet felt inside my shoes.

At first I just shot baskets by myself. It was selfish, and I also wanted to learn the game again before I played against anybody else. Since I had been good before and embarrassed fellow tribal members, I knew they would want to take revenge on me. Forget about the cowboys versus Indians business. The most intense competition on any reservation is Indians versus Indians.

But on the night I was ready to play for real, there was this white guy at the gym, playing with all the Indians.

"Who is that?" I asked Jimmy Seyler.   55

"He's the new BIA chief's kid."

"Can he play?"

"Oh, yeah."

And he could play. He played Indian ball, fast and loose, better than all the Indians there.

"How long's he been playing here?" I asked.   60

"Long enough."

I stretched my muscles, and everybody watched me. All these Indians watched one of their old and dusty heroes. Even though I had played most of my ball at the white high school I went to, I was still all Indian, you know? I was Indian when it counted, and this BIA kid needed to be beaten by an Indian, any Indian.

I jumped into the game and played well for a little while. It felt good. I hit a few shots, grabbed a rebound or two, played enough defense to keep the other team honest. Then that white kid took over the game. He was too good. Later, he'd play college ball back East and would nearly make the Knicks team a couple years on. But we didn't know any of that would happen. We just knew he was better that day and every other day.

The next morning I woke up tired and hungry, so I grabbed the want ads, found a job I wanted, and drove to Spokane to get it. I've been working at the high school exchange program ever since, typing and answering phones. Sometimes I wonder if the people on the other end of the line know that I'm Indian and if their voices would change if they did know.

One day I picked up the phone and it was her, calling from Seattle. 65

"I got your number from your mom," she said. "I'm glad you're working."

"Yeah, nothing like a regular paycheck."

"Are you drinking?"

"No, I've been on the wagon for almost a year."

"Good." 70

The connection was good. I could hear her breathing in the spaces between our words. How do you talk to the real person whose ghost has haunted you? How do you tell the difference between the two?

"Listen," I said. "I'm sorry for everything."

"Me, too."

"What's going to happen to us?" I asked her and wished I had the answer for myself.

"I don't know," she said. "I want to change the world." 75

* * *

These days, living alone in Spokane, I wish I lived closer to the river, to the falls where ghosts of salmon jump. I wish I could sleep. I put down my paper or book and turn off all the lights, lie quietly in the dark. It may take hours, even years, for me to sleep again. There's nothing surprising or disappointing in that.

I know how all my dreams end anyway.

Starting Point for Further Research: Sherman Alexie

- **Interview:** Joelle Fraser. "Interview with Sherman Alexie." *Iowa Review* 30:3 (2000): 59–70.

STUART DYBEK   (B. 1942)

Born and raised on the South Side of Chicago, Stuart Dybek sets most of his stories in his native city. His first collection of short stories, Childhood and Other Neighborhoods *(1980), depicts how grim urban streets influence the lives of their inhabitants. Dybek is particularly known for his portrayals of Chicago's struggling ethnic neighborhoods, and this focus runs through all his published works, which include* The Coast of Chicago *(1990) and two volumes of poetry,* Brass Knuckles *(1979) and* Streets in Their Own Ink *(2004). His most recent book of fiction is* I Sailed with Magellan *(2003), in which the story "We Didn't" appears. Dybek is a professor of English at Western Michigan University in Kalamazoo.*

We Didn't   (1994)

> We did it in front of the mirror
> And in the light. We did it in darkness,
> In water, and in the high grass.
> —*Yehuda Amichai, "We Did it"*

We didn't in the light; we didn't in darkness. We didn't in the fresh-cut summer grass or in the mounds of autumn leaves or on the snow where moonlight threw down our shadows. We didn't in your room on the canopy bed you slept in, the bed you'd slept in as a child, or in the backseat of my father's rusted Rambler, which smelled of the smoked chubs and kielbasa he delivered on weekends from my uncle Vincent's meat market. We didn't in your mother's Buick Eight, where a rosary twined the rearview mirror like a beaded, black snake with silver, cruciform fangs.

At the dead end of our lovers' lane—a side street of abandoned factories—where I perfected the pinch that springs open a bra; behind the lilac bushes in Marquette Park, where you first touched me through my jeans and your nipples, swollen against transparent cotton, seemed the shade of lilacs; in the balcony of the now defunct Clark Theater, where I wiped popcorn salt from my palms and slid them up your thighs and you whispered, "I feel like Doris Day is watching us," we didn't.

How adept we were at fumbling, how perfectly mistimed our timing, how utterly we confused energy with ecstasy.

Remember that night becalmed by heat, and the two of us, fused by sweat, trembling as if a wind from outer space that only we could feel was gusting across Oak Street Beach? Entwined in your faded Navajo blanket, we lay soul-kissing until you wept with wanting.

We'd been kissing all day—all summer—kisses tasting of different shades of   5
lip gloss and too many Cokes. The lake had turned hot pink, rose rapture, pearl amethyst with dusk, then washed in night black with a ruff of silver foam. Beyond a momentary horizon, silent bolts of heat lightning throbbed, perhaps setting barns on fire somewhere in Indiana. The beach that had been so crowded was deserted as if there was a curfew. Only the bodies of lovers remained, visible in lightning flashes, scattered like the fallen on a battlefield, a few of them moaning, waiting for the gulls to pick them clean.

On my fingers your slick scent mixed with the coconut musk of the suntan lotion we'd repeatedly smeared over each other's bodies. When your bikini top fell away, my hands caught your breasts, memorizing their delicate weight, my palms cupped as if bringing water to parched lips.

Along the Gold Coast, high-rises began to glow, window added to window, against the dark. In every lighted bedroom, couples home from work were stripping off their business suits, falling to the bed, and doing it. They did it before mirrors and pressed against the glass in streaming shower stalls; they did it against walls and on the furniture in ways that required previously unimagined gymnastics, which they invented on the spot. They did it in honor of man and woman, in honor of beast, in honor of God. They did it because they'd been released, because they were home free, alive, and private, because they couldn't wait any longer, couldn't wait for the appointed hour, for the right time or temperature, couldn't wait for the future, for Messiahs, for peace on earth and justice for all. They did it because of the Bomb, because of pollution, because of the Four Horsemen of the Apocalypse, because extinction might be just a blink away. They did it because it was Friday night. It was Friday night and somewhere delirious music was playing—flutter-tongued flutes, muted trumpets meowing like cats in heat, feverish plucking and twanging, tom-toms, congas, and gongs all pounding the same pulsebeat.

I stripped your bikini bottom down the skinny rails of your legs, and you tugged my swimsuit past my tan. Swimsuits at our ankles, we kicked like swimmers to free our legs, almost expecting a tide to wash over us the way the tide rushes in on Burt Lancaster and Deborah Kerr in *From Here to Eternity*—a love scene so famous that although neither of us had seen the movie, our bodies assumed the exact position of movie stars on the sand and you whispered to me softly, "I'm afraid of getting pregnant," and I whispered back, "Don't worry, I have protection," then, still kissing you, felt for my discarded cutoffs and the wallet in which for the last several months I had carried a Trojan as if it was a talisman. Still kissing, I tore its flattened, dried-out wrapper, and it sprang through my fingers like a spring from a clock and dropped to the sand between our legs. My hands were shaking. In a panic, I groped for it, found it, tried to dust it off, tried as Burt Lancaster never had to, to slip it on without breaking the mood, felt the grains of sand inside it, a throb of lightning, and the Great Lake behind us became, for all practical purposes, the Pacific, and your skin tasted of salt and to the insistent question that my hips were asking your body answered yes, your thighs opened like wings from my waist as we surfaced panting from a kiss that left you pleading *Oh, Christ yes*, a *yes* gasped sharply as a cry of pain so that for a moment I thought that we *were* already doing it and that somehow I had missed the instant when I entered you, entered you in the bloodless way in which a young man discards his own virginity, entered you as if passing through a gateway into the rest of my life, into a life as I wanted it to be lived *yes* but *Oh* then I realized that we were still floundering unconnected in the slick between us and there was sand in the Trojan as we slammed together still feeling for that perfect fit, still in the *Here* groping for an *Eternity* that was only a fine adjustment away, just a millimeter to the left or a fraction of an inch farther south though with all the adjusting the sandy Trojan was slipping off and then it was gone but *yes* you kept repeating although your head was shaking *no-not-quite-almost* and our hearts were going like mad and you said, *Yes. Yes wait . . . Stop!*

"What?" I asked, still futilely thrusting as if I hadn't quite heard you.

"Oh. God!" You gasped, pushing yourself up. "What's coming?"

"Gin, what's the matter?" I asked, confused, and then the beam of a spotlight swept over us and I glanced into its blinding eye.

All around us lights were coming, speeding across the sand. Blinking blindness away, I rolled from your body to my knees, feeling utterly defenseless in the way that only nakedness can leave one feeling. Headlights bounded toward us, spotlights crisscrossing, blue dome lights revolving as squad cars converged. I could see other lovers, caught in the beams, fleeing bare-assed through the litter of garbage that daytime hordes had left behind and that night had deceptively concealed. You were crying, clutching the Navajo blanket to your breasts with one hand and clawing for your bikini with the other, and I was trying to calm your terror with reassuring phrases such as "Holy shit! I don't fucking believe this!"

10

Swerving and fishtailing in the sand, police calls pouring from their radios, the squad cars were on us, and then they were by us while we struggled to pull on our clothes.

They braked at the water's edge, and cops slammed out, brandishing huge flashlights, their beams deflecting over the dark water. Beyond the darting of those beams, the far-off throbs of lightning seemed faint by comparison.

"Over there, goddamn it!" one of them hollered, and two cops sloshed out   15 into the shallow water without even pausing to kick off their shoes, huffing aloud for breath, their leather cartridge belts creaking against their bellies.

"Grab the sonofabitch! It ain't gonna bite!" one of them yelled, then they came sloshing back to shore with a body slung between them.

It was a woman—young, naked, her body limp and bluish beneath the play of flashlight beams. They set her on the sand just past the ring of drying, washed-up alewives. Her face was almost totally concealed by her hair. Her hair was brown and tangled in a way that even wind or sleep can't tangle hair, tangled as if it had absorbed the ripples of water—thick strands, slimy looking like dead seaweed.

"She's been in there awhile, that's for sure," a cop with a beer belly said to a younger, crew-cut cop, who had knelt beside the body and removed his hat as if he might be considering the kiss of life.

The crew-cut officer brushed the hair away from her face, and the flashlight beams settled there. Her eyes were closed. A bruise or a birthmark stained the side of one eye. Her features appeared swollen, her lower lip protruding as if she was pouting.

An ambulance siren echoed across the sand, its revolving red light rapidly   20 approaching.

"Might as well take their sweet-ass time," the beer-bellied cop said.

We had joined the circle of police surrounding the drowned woman almost without realizing that we had. You were back in your bikini, robed in the Navajo blanket, and I had slipped on my cutoffs, my underwear dangling out of a back pocket.

Their flashlight beams explored her body, causing its whiteness to gleam. Her breasts were floppy; her nipples looked shriveled. Her belly appeared inflated by gallons of water. For a moment, a beam focused on her mound of pubic hair, which was overlapped by the swell of her belly, and then moved almost shyly away down her legs, and the cops all glanced at us—at you, especially—above their lights, and you hugged your blanket closer as if they might confiscate it as evidence or to use as a shroud.

When the ambulance pulled up, one of the black attendants immediately put a stethoscope to the drowned woman's swollen belly and announced, "Drowned the baby, too."

Without saying anything, we turned from the group, as unconsciously as   25 we'd joined them, and walked off across the sand, stopping only long enough at the spot where we had lain together like lovers, in order to stuff the rest of our gear into a beach bag, to gather our shoes, and for me to find my wallet and kick sand over the forlorn, deflated Trojan that you pretended not to notice. I was grateful for that.

Behind us, the police were snapping photos, flashbulbs throbbing like lightning flashes, and the lightning itself, still distant but moving in closer, rumbling audibly now, driving a lake wind before it so that gusts of sand tingled against the metal sides of the ambulance.

Squinting, we walked toward the lighted windows of the Gold Coast, while the shadows of gapers attracted by the whirling emergency lights hurried past us toward the shore.

"What happened? What's going on?" they asked without waiting for an answer, and we didn't offer one, just continued walking silently in the dark.

* * *

It was only later that we talked about it, and once we began talking about the drowned woman it seemed we couldn't stop.

"She was pregnant," you said. "I mean, I don't want to sound morbid, but I can't help thinking how the whole time we were, we almost—you know—there was this poor, dead woman and her unborn child washing in and out behind us."

"It's not like we could have done anything for her even if we had known she was there."

"But what if we *had* found her? What if after we had—you know," you said, your eyes glancing away from mine and your voice tailing into a whisper, "what if after we did it, we went for a night swim and found her in the water?"

"But, Gin, we didn't," I tried to reason, though it was no more a matter of reason than anything else between us had ever been.

It began to seem as if each time we went somewhere to make out—on the back porch of your half-deaf, whiskery Italian grandmother, who sat in the front of the apartment cackling at *I Love Lucy* reruns; or in your girlfriend Tina's basement rec room when her parents were away on bowling league nights and Tina was upstairs with her current crush, Brad; or way off in the burbs, at the Giant Twin Drive-In during the weekend they called Elvis Fest—the drowned woman was with us.

We would kiss, your mouth would open, and when your tongue flicked repeatedly after mine, I would unbutton the first button of your blouse, revealing the beauty spot at the base of your throat, which matched a smaller spot I loved above a corner of your lips, and then the second button, which opened on a delicate gold cross—which I had always tried to regard as merely a fashion statement—dangling above the cleft of your breasts. The third button exposed the lacy swell of your bra, and I would slide my hand over the patterned mesh, feeling for the firmness of your nipple rising to my fingertip, but you would pull slightly away, and behind your rapid breath your kiss would grow distant, and I would kiss harder, trying to lure you back from wherever you had gone, and finally, holding you as if only consoling a friend, I'd ask, "What are you thinking?" although of course I knew.

"I don't want to think about her but I can't help it. I mean, it seems like some kind of weird omen or something, you know?"

"No, I don't know," I said. "It was just a coincidence."

"Maybe if she'd been farther away down the beach, but she was so close to us. A good wave could have washed her up right beside us."

"Great, then we could have had a ménage à trois."

"Gross! I don't believe you just said that! Just because you said it in French doesn't make it less disgusting."

"You're driving me to it. Come on, Gin, I'm sorry," I said. "I was just making a dumb joke to get a little different perspective on things."

"What's so goddamn funny about a woman who drowned herself and her baby?"

"We don't even know for sure she did."

"Yeah, right, it was just an accident. Like she just happened to be going for a walk pregnant and naked, and she fell in."

"She could have been on a sailboat or something. Accidents happen; so do   45 murders."

"Oh, like murder makes it less horrible? Don't think that hasn't occurred to me. Maybe the bastard who knocked her up killed her, huh?"

"How should I know? You're the one who says you don't want to talk about it and then gets obsessed with all kinds of theories and scenarios. Why are we arguing about a woman we don't even know, who doesn't have the slightest thing to do with us?"

"I *do* know about her," you said. "I dream about her."

"You dream about her?" I repeated, surprised. "Dreams you remember?"

"Sometimes they wake me up. In one I'm at my *nonna*'s cottage in Michigan,   50 swimming for a raft that keeps drifting farther away, until I'm too tired to turn back. Then I notice there's a naked person sunning on the raft and start yelling, 'Help!' and she looks up and offers me a hand, but I'm too afraid to take it even though I'm drowning because it's her."

"God! Gin, that's creepy."

"I dreamed you and I are at the beach and you bring us a couple hot dogs but forget the mustard, so you have to go all the way back to the stand for it."

"Hot dogs, no mustard—a little too Freudian, isn't it?"

"Honest to God, I dreamed it. You go back for mustard and I'm wondering why you're gone so long, then a woman screams that a kid has drowned and everyone stampedes for the water. I'm swept in by the mob and forced under, and I think, This is it, I'm going to drown, but I'm able to hold my breath longer than could ever be possible. It feels like a flying dream—flying under water—and then I see this baby down there flying, too, and realize it's the kid everyone thinks has drowned, but he's no more drowned than I am. He looks like Cupid or one of those baby angels that cluster around the face of God."

"Pretty weird. What do you think all the symbols mean?—hot dogs, water,   55 drowning . . ."

"It means the baby who drowned inside her that night was a love child—a boy—and his soul was released there to wander through the water."

"You don't really believe that?"

We argued about the interpretation of dreams, about whether dreams are symbolic or psychic, prophetic or just plain nonsense, until you said, "Look, Dr. Freud, you can believe what you want about your dreams, but keep your nose out of mine, okay?"

We argued about the drowned woman, about whether her death was a suicide or a murder, about whether her appearance that night was an omen or a coincidence which, you argued, is what an omen is anyway: a coincidence that means something. By the end of summer, even if we were no longer arguing about the woman, we had acquired the habit of arguing about everything else. What was better: dogs or cats, rock or jazz, Cubs or Sox, tacos or egg rolls, right or left, night or day?—we could argue about anything.

It no longer required arguing or necking to summon the drowned woman; 60
everywhere we went she surfaced by her own volition: at Rocky's Italian Beef, at
Lindo Mexico, at the House of Dong, our favorite Chinese restaurant, a place we
still frequented because when we'd first started seeing each other they had let us
sit and talk until late over tiny cups of jasmine tea and broken fortune cookies.
We would always kid about going there. "Are you in the mood for Dong
tonight?" I'd whisper conspiratorially. It was a dopey joke, meant for you to roll
your eyes at its repeated dopiness. Back then, in winter, if one of us ordered the
garlic shrimp we would both be sure to eat them so that later our mouths tasted
the same when we kissed.

Even when she wasn't mentioned, she was there with her drowned body—so
dumpy next to yours—and her sad breasts with their wrinkled nipples and sour
milk—so saggy beside yours, which were still budding—with her swollen belly
and her pubic bush colorless in the glare of electric light, with her tangled, slimy
hair and her pouting, placid face—so lifeless beside yours—and her skin a pallid
white, lightning-flash white, flashbulb white, a whiteness that couldn't be dupli-
cated in daylight—how I'd come to hate that pallor, so cold beside the flush of
your skin.

There wasn't a particular night when we finally broke up, just as there was-
n't a particular night when we began going together, but it was a night in fall
when I guessed that it was over. We were parked in the Rambler at the dead end
of the street of factories that had been our lovers' lane, listening to a drizzle of
rain and dry leaves sprinkle the hood. As always, rain revitalized the smells of
smoked fish and kielbasa in the upholstery. The radio was on too low to hear,
the windshield wipers swished at intervals as if we were driving, and the windows were steamed as if we'd been making out. But we'd been arguing, as usual,
this time about a woman poet who had committed suicide, whose work you
were reading. We were sitting, no longer talking or touching, and I remember
thinking that I didn't want to argue with you anymore. I didn't want to sit like
this in hurt silence; I wanted to talk excitedly all night as we once had. I
wanted to find some way that wasn't corny sounding to tell you how much fun
I'd had in your company, how much knowing you had meant to me, and how I
had suddenly realized that I'd been so intent on becoming lovers that I'd overlooked how close we'd been as friends. I wanted you to know that. I wanted you
to like me again.

"It's sad," I started to say, meaning that I was sorry we had reached the point
of silence, but before I could continue you challenged the statement.

"What makes you so sure it's sad?"

"What do you mean, what makes me so sure?" I asked, confused by your 65
question.

You looked at me as if what was sad was that I would never understand. "For
all either one of us knows," you said, "death could have been her triumph!"

* * *

Maybe when it really ended was the night I felt we had just reached the beginning, that one time on the beach in the summer when our bodies rammed so
desperately together that for a moment I thought we did it, and maybe in our
hearts we did, although for me, then, doing it in one's heart didn't quite count. If
it did, I supposed we'd all be Casanovas.

We rode home together on the El train that night, and I felt sick and defeated in a way I was embarrassed to mention. Our mute reflections emerged like negative exposures on the dark, greasy window of the train. Lightning branched over the city, and when the train entered the subway tunnel, the lights inside flickered as if the power was disrupted, though the train continued rocketing beneath the Loop.

When the train emerged again we were on the South Side of the city and it was pouring, a deluge as if the sky had opened to drown the innocent and guilty alike. We hurried from the El station to your house, holding the Navajo blanket over our heads until, soaked, it collapsed. In the dripping doorway of your apartment building, we said good night. You were shivering. Your bikini top showed through the thin blouse plastered to your skin. I swept the wet hair away from your face and kissed you lightly on the lips, then you turned and went inside. I stepped into the rain, and you came back out, calling after me.

"What?" I asked, feeling a surge of gladness to be summoned back into the   70
doorway with you.

"Want an umbrella?"

I didn't. The downpour was letting up. It felt better to walk back to the station feeling the rain rinse the sand out of my hair, off my legs, until the only places where I could still feel its grit were in the crotch of my cutoffs and each squish of my shoes. A block down the street, I passed a pair of jockey shorts lying in a puddle and realized they were mine, dropped from my back pocket as we ran to your house. I left them behind, wondering if you'd see them and recognize them the next day.

By the time I had climbed the stairs back to the El platform, the rain had stopped. Your scent still hadn't washed from my fingers. The station—the entire city it seemed—dripped and steamed. The summer sound of crickets and nighthawks echoed from the drenched neighborhood. Alone, I could admit how sick I felt. For you, it was a night that would haunt your dreams. For me, it was another night when I waited, swollen and aching, for what I had secretly nicknamed the Blue Ball Express.

Literally lovesick, groaning inwardly with each lurch of the train and worried that I was damaged for good, I peered out at the passing yellow-lit stations, where lonely men stood posted before giant advertisements, pictures of glamorous models defaced by graffiti—the same old scrawled insults and pleas: FUCK YOU, EAT ME. At this late hour the world seemed given over to men without women, men waiting in abject patience for something indeterminate, the way I waited for our next times. I avoided their eyes so that they wouldn't see the pity in mine, pity for them because I'd just been with you, your scent was still on my hands, and there seemed to be so much future ahead.

For me it was another night like that, and by the time I reached my stop I knew   75
I would be feeling better, recovered enough to walk the dark street home making up poems of longing that I never wrote down. I was the D. H. Lawrence of not doing it, the voice of all the would-be lovers who ached and squirmed. From our contortions in doorways, on stairwells, and in the bucket seats of cars we could have composed a Kama Sutra of interrupted bliss. It must have been that night when I recalled all the other times of walking home after seeing you, so that it seemed as if I was falling into step behind a parade of my former selves—myself walking home on the night we first kissed, myself on the night when I unbuttoned your blouse and kissed your

breasts, myself on the night when I lifted your skirt above your thighs and dropped to my knees—each succeeding self another step closer to that irrevocable moment for which our lives seemed poised.

But we didn't, not in the moonlight, or by the phosphorescent lanterns of lightning bugs in your back yard, not beneath the constellations we couldn't see, let alone decipher, or in the dark glow that replaced the real darkness of night, a darkness already stolen from us, not with the skyline rising behind us while a city gradually decayed, not in the heat of summer while a Cold War raged, despite the freedom of youth and the license of first love—because of fate, karma, luck, what does it matter?—we made not doing it a wonder, and yet we didn't, we didn't, we never did.

Starting Point for Further Research: Stuart Dybek

- **Interview:** Mike Nickel. "An Interview with Stuart Dybek." *Chicago Review* 43 (1997): 87–101.

 INSPIRATION FROM VERSE TO PROSE: YEHUDA AMICHAI'S "WE DID IT" AND STUART DYBEK'S "WE DIDN'T"

Poet Yehuda Amichai.

Stuart Dybek's often anthologized "We Didn't" appeared in earlier form in the literary magazine *Antaeus*, as well as in *The Best American Short Stories 1994* and *Prize Stories 1994: The O. Henry Awards*. Like the work of Cyrus Colter (p. 40), Gwendolyn Brooks (p. 904), Richard Wright (p. 582), and Nelson Algren, most of Dybek's fiction is set in Chicago, and that setting—both the gritty and the serene—almost takes on the importance of a main character. As prize-winning Chicago writer and radio personality Studs Terkel said in praising *I Sailed with Magellan*, "It's hard to tell where Nelson Algren leaves off and Stuart Dybek begins—they're a couple of naturals. They each capture the lyricism of Chicago's backstreets: the city behind the billboards. They celebrate our alleys as well as our boulevards. Stuart Dybek, is, at this moment, our city's blue-collar bard. These eleven lovely stories comprise the Chicago novel of today."

Dybek's short stories often find their beginnings in poetry rather than prose, and "We Didn't" was no exception. As Dybek commented in the author biography in *Prize Stories 1994: The O. Henry Awards*:

(continued on next page)

FROM VERSE TO PROSE: YEHUDA AMICHAI'S "WE DID IT" AND STUART DYBEK'S "WE DIDN'T"

"We Didn't" began as a poem that I tinkered unsuccessfully with through several drafts until finally, in a hotel room in Anchorage on a borrowed typewriter, it evolved into a story. That same process—a poem becoming a story—has occurred in my work often enough so that it shouldn't still surprise me, but it does. What was unique for me in this particular instance was that, rather than an image or an incident from my own memory or imagination, what initially generated "We Didn't" was a poem I'd read titled "We Did It." It's a poem by Yehuda Amichai, an Israeli poet, whose work I've long admired for its wise, humanistic vision and comic vitality. In his poem, he—or in any case his translator—takes "doing it," a phrase that has always struck me as one of the more tacky, inarticulate variations of the many, mostly inadequate terms to describe making love (a pretty misleading term in itself) and playfully elevates it. I had the notion of engaging his poem in a sort of dialogue, of playing an American-Judeo-Christian "Thou Shalt Not" off his psalmlike "Thou Shalt." It seemed like an entertaining idea for a poem, but as I worked on developing it, characters began to emerge from anecdotes and I surrendered to them. Once the characters began running things, I realized that what interested me most about the idea was how often we allow our experiences to be defined by what they supposedly should be, so that sometimes such experiences—intense and haunting as they are—can finally only be expressed in the negative: what they are not.

The full text of Yehuda Amichai's poem "We Did It" appears below. As you examine it, consider how the language of the poem might have influenced the tone, imagery, and language of Dybek's story.

Yehuda Amichai

We Did It

Translated from the Hebrew by Benjamin and Barbara Harshav

We did it before the mirror
And in the light. We did it in the dark,
In the water, and in the tall grass.

We did it in honor of man
And in honor of beast and in honor of God.
But they would not hear about us,
They'd already seen it.

We did it with imagination and in color,
Mixing red hair with brown,
And with difficult exercises
Brimming with joy. We did it
Like seraphim and holy animals
With the mystery of creation of the prophets.
We did it with six wings
And six legs, but the sky
Was hard above us
Like the summer ground below.

ANDREA BARRETT

(B. 1954)

Andrea Barrett grew up on Cape Cod and studied biology at college. Her writing focuses on questions of science and exploration, often in historical settings. She won the National Book Award in 1996 for Ship Fever and Other Stories, *and her novel* The Voyage of the Narwhal *appeared in 1998. Barrett lives in Rochester, New York.*

Rare Bird

(1995)

Imagine an April evening in 1762. A handsome house set in the gently rolling Kent landscape a few miles outside the city of London; the sun just set over blue squill and beech trees newly leafed. Inside the house are a group of men and a single woman: Christopher Billopp, his sister Sarah Anne, and Christopher's guests from London. Educated and well-bred, they're used to a certain level of conversation. Just now they're discussing Linnaeus's contention that swallows retire under water for the winter—that old belief, stemming from Aristotle, which Linnaeus still upholds.

"He's hardly alone," Mr. Miller says. Behind him, a large mirror reflects a pair of portraits: Christopher and Sarah Anne, painted several years earlier as a gift for their father. "Even Klein, Linnaeus's rival, agrees. He wrote that a friend's mother saw fishermen bring out a bundle of swallows from a lake near Pilaw. When the swallows were placed near a fire, they revived and flew about."

Mr. Pennant nods. "Remember the reports of Dr. Colas? Fishermen he talked to in northern parts claimed that when they broke through the ice in winter they took up comatose swallows in their nets as well as fish. And surely you remember reading how Taletini of Cremona swore a Jesuit had told him that the swallows in Poland and Moravia hurled themselves into cisterns and wells come autumn."

Mr. Collinson laughs at this, although not unkindly, and he looks across the table at his old friend Mr. Ellis. "Hearsay, hearsay," he says. He has a spot on his waistcoat. Gravy, perhaps. Or cream. "Not one shred of direct evidence. Mothers, fishermen, itinerant Jesuits—this is folklore, my friends. Not science."

At the foot of the table, Sarah Anne nods but says nothing. Pennant, Ellis, Collinson, Miller: all distinguished. But old, so old. She worries that she and Christopher are growing prematurely old as well. Staid and dull and entirely too comfortable with these admirable men, whom they have known since they were children.

Their father, a brewer by trade but a naturalist by avocation, had educated Christopher and Sarah Anne together after their mother's death, as if they were brothers. The three of them rambled the grounds of Burdem Place, learning the names of the plants and birds. Collinson lived in Peckham then, just a few miles away, and he often rode over bearing rare plants and seeds sent by naturalist friends in other countries. Peter Kalm, Linnaeus's famous student, visited the Billopps; Linnaeus himself, before Sarah Anne was born, once stayed for several days.

All these things are part of Sarah Anne's and Christopher's common past. And even after Christopher's return from Cambridge and their father's death, for a while they continued to enjoy an easy exchange of books and conversation. But now all that has changed. Sarah Anne inherited her father's brains but

5

Christopher inherited everything else, including his father's friends. Sarah Anne acts as hostess to these men, at Christopher's bidding. In part she's happy for their company, which represents her only intellectual companionship. In part she despises them for their lumbago and thinning hair, their greediness in the presence of good food, the stories they repeat about the scientific triumphs of their youth, and the fact that they refuse to take her seriously. Not one of them has done anything original in years.

There's another reason, as well, why she holds her tongue on this night. Lately, since Christopher has started courting Miss Juliet Colden, he's become critical of Sarah Anne's manners. She does not dress as elegantly as Juliet, or comport herself with such decorum. She's forward when she ought to be retiring, he has said, and disputatious when she should be agreeable. He's spoken to her several times already: "You should wear your learning modestly," he lectures.

She does wear it modestly, or so she believes. She's careful not to betray in public those subjects she knows more thoroughly than Christopher. Always she reminds herself that her learning is only book-learning; that it hasn't been tempered, as Christopher's has, by long discussions after dinner and passionate arguments in coffeehouses with wiser minds.

And so here she is: learned, but not really; and not pretty, and no longer   10
young: last month she turned twenty-nine. Old, old, old. Like her company. She knows that Christopher has begun to worry that she'll be on his hands for life. And she thinks that perhaps he's mentioned this worry to his friends.

They're fond of him, and of Burdem Place. They appreciate the library, the herbarium, the rare trees and shrubs outside, the collections in the specimen cabinets. They appreciate Sarah Anne as well, she knows. Earlier, they complimented the food, her gown, the flowers on the table and her eyes in the candlelight. But what's the use of that sort of admiration? Collinson, who has known her the longest, was the only one to make a stab at treating her the way they all had when she was a girl: he led her into quoting Pliny and then complimented her on her learning. But she saw the way the other men shifted uneasily as she spoke.

Despite herself, she continues to listen to the men's conversation. Despite her restlessness, her longing to be outside in the cool damp air, or in some other place entirely, she listens because the subject they're discussing fascinates her.

"I had a letter last year from Solander," Ellis says. "Regarding the November meeting of the Royal Society. There, a Reverend Forster said he'd observed large flocks of swallows flying quite high in the autumn, then coming down to sit on reeds and willows before plunging into the water of one of his ponds."

"More hearsay," Collinson says.

But Pennant says it might be so; either that or they slept for the winter in   15
their summer nesting holes. "Locke says that there are no chasms or gaps in the great chain of being," he reminds them. "Rather there is a continuous series in which each step differs very little from the next. There are fishes that have wings, and birds that inhabit the water, whose blood is as cold as that of fishes. Why should not the swallow be one of those animals so near of kin to both birds and fish that it occupies a place between both? As there are mermaids or seamen, perhaps."

No one objects to the introduction of aquatic anthropoids into the conversation. Reports of them surface every few years—Cingalese fishermen swear they've caught them in their nets, a ship's captain spots two off the coast of Massachusetts. In Paris, only four years ago, a living female of the species was exhibited.

Collinson says, "Our friend Mr. Achard writes me that he has seen them hibernating in the cliffs along the Rhine. But I have my doubts about the whole story."

"Yes?" Pennant says. "So what do you believe?"

"I think swallows migrate," Collinson says.

While the servants change plates, replace glasses, and open fresh bottles of 20 wine, Collinson relates a story from Mr. Adanson's recent *History of Senegal*. Off the coast of that land in autumn, he says, Adanson reported seeing swallows settling on the decks and rigging of passing ships like bees. Others have reported spring and autumn sightings of swallows in Andalusia and over the Strait of Gibraltar. "Clearly," Collinson says, "they must be birds of passage."

Which is what Sarah Anne believes. She opens her mouth and proposes a simple experiment to the men. "The swallow must breathe during winter," she says, between the soup and the roasted veal. "Respiration and circulation must somehow continue, in some degree. And how is that possible if the birds are under water for so long? Could one not settle this by catching some swallows at the time of their autumn disappearance and confining them under water in a tub for a time? If they are taken out alive, then Linnaeus's theory is proved. But if not . . ."

"A reasonable test," Collinson says. "How would you catch the birds?"

"At night," she tells him impatiently. Oh, he is so old; he has dribbled more gravy on his waistcoat. How is that he can no longer imagine leaving his world of books and talk for the world outside? Anyone might gather a handful of birds. "With nets, while they roost in the reeds."

Collinson says, "If they survived, we might dissect one and look for whatever internal structure made possible their underwater sojourn."

He seems to be waiting for Sarah Anne's response, but Christopher is glar- 25 ing at her. She knows what he's thinking: in his new, middle-aged stodginess, assumed unnecessarily early and worn like a borrowed coat, he judges her harshly. She's been forward in entering the conversation, unladylike in offering an opinion that contradicts some of her guests, indelicate in suggesting that she might pursue a flock of birds with a net.

What has gotten into him? That pulse she hears inside her ear, the steady swish and hum of her blood, is the sound of time passing. Each minute whirling past her before she can wring any life from it; hours shattered and lost while she defers to her brother's sense of propriety.

* * *

Upstairs, finally. Dismissed while the men, in the library below, drink Christopher's excellent wine and avail themselves of the chamberpot in the sideboard. Her brother's friends are grateful for her hospitality, appreciative of her well-run household; but most grateful and appreciative when she disappears.

Her room is dark, the night is cool, the breeze flows through her windows. She sits in her high-ceilinged room, at the fragile desk in the three-windowed bay facing west, over the garden. If it were not dark, she could see the acres leading down to the lake and the low stretch of rushes and willows along the banks.

Her desk is very small, meant to hold a few letters and a vase of flowers: useless for any real work. The books she's taken from the library spill from it to the floor. Gorgeous books, expensive books. Her brother's books. But her brother doesn't use them the way she does. She's been rooting around in them and composing a letter to Linnaeus, in Uppsala, about the evening's dinner conversation. Christopher need never know what she writes alone in this room.

Some years ago, after Peter Kalm's visit, Sarah Anne's father and Linnaeus   30 corresponded for a while; after expressing admiration for the great doctor's achievements this visit is what she first mentions. Some flattery, some common ground. She discusses the weather, which has been unusual; she passes on the news of Collinson's latest botanical acquisitions. Only then does she introduce the subject of the swallows. She writes:

> *Toward the end of September, I have observed swallows gathering in the reeds along the Thames. And yet, although these reeds are cut down annually, no one has ever discovered swallows sleeping in their roots, nor has any fisherman ever found, in the winter months, swallows sleeping in the water. If all the great flocks seen in the autumn dove beneath the water, how could they not be seen? How could none be found in winter? But perhaps the situation differs in Sweden.*
>
> *You are so well-known and so revered. Could you not offer the fishermen of your country a reward, if they were to bring to you or your students any swallows they found beneath the ice? Could you not ask them to watch the lakes and streams in spring, and report to you any sightings of swallows emerging from the water? In this fashion you might elucidate the problem.*

She pauses and stares at the candle, considering what she observed last fall. After the first killing frosts, the swallows disappeared along with the warblers and flycatchers and other insectivorous birds deprived of food and shelter. Surely it makes sense that they should have gone elsewhere, following their food supply?

She signs the letter "S.A. Billopp," meaning by this not to deceive the famous scholar but simply to keep him from dismissing her offhand. Then she reads it over, seals it, and snuffs her candle. It is not yet ten but soon the men, who've been drinking for hours, will be expecting her to rejoin them for supper. She will not go down, she will send a message that she is indisposed.

She rests her elbows on the windowsill and leans out into the night, dreaming of Andalusia and Senegal and imagining that twice a year she might travel like the swallows. Málaga, Tangier, Marrakech, Dakar. Birds of passage fly from England to the south of France and from there down the Iberian peninsula, where the updrafts from the Rock of Gibraltar ease them over the Strait to Morocco. Then they make the long flight down the coast of Africa.

A bat flies by, on its way to the river. She has seen bats drink on the wing, as swallows do, sipping from the water's surface. Swallows eat in flight as well, snapping insects from the air. Rain is sure to follow when they fly low; a belief that dates from Virgil, but which she knows to be true. When the air is damp and heavy the insects hover low, and she has seen how the swallows merely follow them.

In the dark she sheds her gown, her corset, her slippers and stockings and complicated underclothes, until she is finally naked. She lies on the floor beside her desk, below the open window. Into her notebook she has copied these lines, written by Olaus Magnus, archbishop of Uppsala, in 1555:

*From the northern waters, swallows are often dragged up by fishermen in the form of clus-
tered masses, mouth to mouth, wing to wing, and foot to foot, these having at the beginning of autumn collected amongst the reeds previous to submersion. When young and inexperienced fishermen find such clusters of swallows, they will, by thawing the birds at the
fire, bring them indeed to the use of their wings, which will continue but a very short time,
as it is a premature and forced revival; but the old, being wiser, throw them away.*

A lovely story, but surely wrong. The cool damp air washes over her like water.
She folds her arms around her torso and imagines lying at the bottom of the lake,
wings wrapped around her body like a kind of chrysalis. It is cold, it is dark, she is
barely breathing. How would she breathe? Around her are thousands of bodies.
The days lengthen, some signal arrives, she shoots with the rest of her flock to
the surface, lifts her head and breathes. Her wings unfold and she soars through
the air, miraculously dry and alive.

Is it possible?   35

* * *

Eight months later, Sarah Anne and Christopher stand on London Bridge with
Miss Juliet Colden and her brother John, all of them wrapped in enormous
cloaks and shivering despite these. They've come to gaze at the river, which in
this January of remarkable cold is covered with great floes of ice. An odd way,
Sarah Anne thinks, to mark the announcement of Christopher and Juliet's engagement. She wishes she liked Juliet better. Already they've been thrown a
great deal into each other's company; soon they'll be sharing a house.

But not sharing, not really. After the wedding, Juliet will have the household keys; Juliet will be in charge of the servants. Juliet will order the meals, the
flowers, the servants' livery, the evening entertainments. And Sarah Anne will
be the extra woman.

The pieces of ice make a grinding noise as they crash against each other and
the bridge. Although the tall brick houses that crowded the bridge in Sarah
Anne's childhood were pulled down several years ago and no longer hang precariously over the water, the view remains the same: downriver the Tower and a forest of masts; upriver the Abbey and Somerset House. The floating ice greatly
menaces the thousands of ships waiting to be unloaded in the Pool. It is of this
that John and Christopher speak. Manly talk: will ships be lost, fortunes destroyed? Meanwhile Juliet chatters and Sarah Anne is silent, scanning the sky
for birds.

Wrynecks, white-throats, nightingales, cuckoos, willow-wrens, goatsuck-
ers—none of these are visible, they've disappeared for the winter. The swallows
are gone as well. An acquaintance of Christopher's mentioned over a recent dinner that on a remarkably warm December day, he'd seen a small group of swallows huddled under the moldings of a window at Merton College. What were
they doing there? She's seen them, as late as October, gathered in great crowds in
the osier-beds along the river—very late for young birds attempting to fly past
the equator. In early May she's seen them clustered on the largest willow at Burdem Place, which hangs over the lake. And in summer swallows swarm the
banks of the Thames below this very bridge. It's clear that they're attached to
water, but attachment doesn't necessarily imply habitation. Is it possible that
they are still around, either below the water or buried somehow in the banks?

If she were alone, and not dressed in these burdensome clothes, and if there   40
were some way she could slip down one of the sets of stairs to the river bank
without arousing everyone's attention, she knows what she would do. She'd
mark out a section of bank where the nesting holes are thickest and survey each
hole, poking down the burrows until she found the old nests. In the burrows
along the river bank at home she's seen these: a base of straw, then finer grass
lined with a little down. Small white eggs in early summer. Now, were she able to
look, she believes she'd find only twists of tired grass.

The wind blows her hood over her face. As soon as she gets home, she
thinks, she'll write another letter to Linnaeus and propose that he investigate
burrows in Sweden. Four times she's written him, this past summer and fall; not
once has he answered.

Christopher and John's discussion has shifted to politics, and she would like
to join them. But she must talk to Juliet, whose delicate nose has reddened.
Juliet's hands are buried in a huge fur muff; her face is buried in her hood. Well-
mannered, she refuses to complain of the cold.

"You'll be part of the wedding, of course," Juliet says, and then she describes
the music she hopes to have played, the feast that will follow the ceremony. "A
big table," she says. "On the lawn outside the library, when the roses are in
bloom—what is that giant vine winding up the porch there?"

"Honeysuckle," Sarah Anne says gloomily. "The scent is lovely."

She can picture the wedding only too clearly. The other attendants will be   45
Juliet's sisters, all three as dainty and pretty as Juliet. Their gowns will be pink or
yellow or pink and yellow, with bows down the bodice and too many flounces.
The couple will go to Venice and Paris and Rome and when they return they'll
move into Sarah Anne's large sunny bedroom and she'll move to a smaller room
in the north wing. The first time Juliet saw Sarah Anne's room, her eyes lit with
greed and pleasure. A few days later Christopher said to Sarah Anne, "About
your room. . . ." She offered it before he had to ask.

"Christopher and I thought you'd like the dressing table your mother used,"
Juliet says. "For that lovely bay in your new room."

But just then, just when Sarah Anne thinks she can't bear another minute,
along comes another of her dead father's elderly friends, accompanied by a
woman. Introductions are made all around. Mr. Hill, Mrs. Pearce. Sarah Anne
has always enjoyed Mr. Hill, who is livelier than his contemporaries, but he is
taken away. The group splits naturally into two as they begin their walk back to
the Strand. Mr. Hill joins Christopher and John, and Mrs. Pearce joins Sarah
Anne and Juliet. But Mrs. Pearce, instead of responding to Juliet's remarks about
the weather, turns to Sarah Anne and says, "You were studying the riverbank so
intently when Mr. Hill pointed you out to me. What were you looking for?"

Her face is lean and intelligent; her eyes are full of curiosity. "Birds," Sarah
Anne says impulsively. "I was looking for swallows' nests. Some people contend
that swallows spend the winter hibernating either under water or in their summer burrows."

She explains the signs that mislead observers, the mistaken stories that mul-
tiply. At Burdem Place, she says, she heard a friend of her brother's claim that, as
a boy, he found two or three swallows in the rubble of a church-tower being torn
down. The birds were torpid, appearing dead, but revived when placed near a
fire. Unfortunately they were then accidentally roasted.

"Roasted?" Mrs. Pearce says with a smile.   50

"Crisp as chickens," Sarah Anne says. "So of course they were lost as evidence. But I suppose it's more likely that they overwinter in holes or burrows, than that they should hibernate under water."

"Some people read omens in the movements of swallows," Mrs. Pearce says. "Even Shakespeare—remember this? 'Swallows have built in Cleopatra's sails their nests. The augeries say they know not, they cannot tell, look grimly, and dare not speak their knowledge.' Poetic. But surely we're not meant to believe it literally."

Sarah Anne stares. There's nothing visibly outrageous about Mrs. Pearce. Her clothing is simple and unfashionable but modest; her hair is dressed rather low but not impossibly so. "I believe that one should experiment," Sarah Anne says. "That we should base our statements on evidence."

"I always prefer to test hypotheses for myself," Mrs. Pearce says quietly.

Juliet is pouting, but Sarah Anne ignores her. She quotes Montaigne and   55
Mrs. Pearce responds with a passage from Fontenelle's *Entretiens sur la pluralité des mondes*. "Do you know Mrs. Behn's translation?" Sarah Anne asks. At that moment she believes in a plurality of worlds as she never has before.

"Of course," says Mrs. Pearce. "Lovely, but I prefer the original."

Sarah Anne mentions the shells that she and Christopher have inherited from Sir Hans Sloane's collection, and Mrs. Pearce talks about her collection of mosses and fungi. And when Sarah Anne returns to the swallows and says that Linnaeus's belief in their watery winters derives from Aristotle, Mrs. Pearce says, "When I was younger, I translated several books of the *Historia Animalium*."

Sarah Anne nearly weeps with excitement and pleasure. How learned this woman is. "How were you educated?" she asks.

"My father," Mrs. Pearce says. "A most cultured and intelligent man, who believed girls should learn as well as their brothers. And you?"

"Partly my father, partly my brother, before. . . . Partly by stealth."   60

"Well, *stealth*," Mrs. Pearce says with a little smile. "Of course."

In their excitement they've been walking so fast that they've left Juliet behind. They hear the men calling them and stop. Quickly, knowing she has little time, Sarah Anne asks the remaining important question. "And your husband?" she says. "He shares your interests?"

"He's dead," Mrs. Pearce says calmly. "I'm a widow."

She lives in London, Sarah Anne learns, alone but for three servants. Both her daughters are married and gone. "I would be so pleased if you would visit us," Sarah Anne says. "We have a place just a few miles from town, but far enough away to have all the pleasures of the country. In the gardens there are some interesting plants from North America, and we've quite a large library. . . ."

Mrs. Pearce lays her gloved hand on Sarah Anne's arm. "I'd be delighted,"   65
she says. "And you must visit me in town. It's so rare to find a friend."

The others join them, looking cold and displeased. "Miss Colden," Mrs. Pearce says.

"Mrs. Pearce. I do hope you two have had a nice talk."

"Lovely," Mrs. Pearce says.

She looks over Juliet's head at Sarah Anne. "I'll see you soon." Then she hooks her hand into Mr. Hill's arm and walks away.

"Odd woman," John says. "Bit of a bluestocking, isn't she?"   70

"She dresses terribly," Juliet says, with considerable satisfaction. From the sharp look she gives Sarah Anne, Sarah Anne knows she'll pay for that brief bit of reviving conversation. But her mind is humming with the pleasure of her new friend, with plans for all they might do together, with the letter she'll write to Linnaeus the very instant she reaches home. She imagines reading that letter out loud to Mrs. Pearce, showing Mrs. Pearce the response she will surely receive.

*   *   *

"We should write him about that old potion," Mrs. Pearce says; and Sarah Anne says, "What?"

"For melancholy. Don't you know it?"

"I don't think so."

"It's a potion made partly from the blood of swallows. Birds of summer, sym-   75
bols of ease—the potion is supposed to ease sadness and give wings to the feet."

"More likely than what he's proposing," Sarah Anne says, and Mrs. Pearce agrees.

It's September now—not the September following their meeting but the one after that: 1764. The two women are in an unused stable at Burdem Place, patiently waiting, surrounded by their equipment. It is just barely dawn. Down in the reeds, where the birds are sleeping, they've sent Robert the gardener's boy with a net and instructions. What they're talking about while they wait is the letter Sarah Anne received last week from Carl Linnaeus, in which he graciously but firmly (and in Latin; but Sarah Anne can read it) dismissed her theories and stated his absolute conviction that swallows hibernate under the water. The let-ter upset Sarah Anne, but she would not have done anything more than fume had Mrs. Pearce not been visiting. It was Mrs. Pearce—Catherine—who'd said, "Well. We'll just have to do the experiments ourselves."

On the wooden floor they've set the bottom half of a cask, which Robert has filled with water. Below the water lies a few inches of river sand; on the surface a board floats an inch from the rim. A large piece of sturdy netting awaits the use to which they'll put it. Inside the stable it's still quite dark; through the open door the trees are barely visible through the mist. Above them the house sleeps. Just after four o'clock, Sarah Anne rose in her new room and tapped once on the door of the room down the hall, where Catherine stays when she visits. Cather-ine opened the door instantly, already dressed.

Recently it has been easier for them to talk about the swallows than about the other goings-on at Burdem Place. Juliet's pregnancy has made her ill-hu-moured, and Christopher has changed as well. Sarah Anne knows she should have expected this, but still it has come as a shock. These days the guests tend to be Juliet's frivolous friends and not the older naturalists. Young, not old; some of them younger than Sarah Anne herself. For weeks at a time they stroll the grounds in fancy clothes and play games while Sarah Anne hovers off to the side, miserable in their company.

Who is she, then? She doesn't want to act, as Christopher does, the part of   80
her parents' generation; but now she's found that she doesn't like her own peers either. She fits nowhere. Nowhere, except with Catherine. She and Catherine, tucked into a wing away from the fashionable guests, have formed their own so-ciety of two. But she suspects that, after the birth of Juliet's child, even this will be taken from her.

Christopher hopes for many children, an army of children. This child, and the ones that follow, will need a nurse and a governess, Juliet says. And a nursery, and a schoolroom. Sarah Anne has seen Christopher prowling the halls near her bedroom, assessing the space and almost visibly planning renovations. He's welcomed Catherine's frequent long visits—but only, Sarah Anne knows, because they keep her occupied and him from feeling guilty about her increasing isolation. The minute he feels pinched for space, he'll suggest to Sarah Anne that Catherine curtail her visits. And then it's possible he'll ask Sarah Anne to be his children's governess.

But Sarah Anne and Catherine don't talk about this. Instead they look once more at Linnaeus's letter, which arrived addressed to "Mr. S.A. Billopp" but which, fortunately, Christopher didn't see. They arrange their instruments on the bench beside them and shiver with cold and excitement. They wait. Where is Robert?

It was Catherine who first approached this weedy twelve-year-old, after Sarah Anne told her she'd once overheard him talking about netting birds for food in Ireland. Catherine told him that they required two or three swallows and would pay him handsomely for them; Robert seemed to believe they had plans to eat them. Still, at 4:30 he met them here, silent and secret. Now he reappears in the doorway, barefoot and wet to the waist. His net is draped over one shoulder and in his hands he holds a sack, which pulses and moves of its own accord.

"Robert!" Catherine says. "You had good luck?"

Robert nods. Both his hands are tightly wrapped around the sack's neck, and when Catherine reaches out for it he says, "You hold this tight, now. They'll be wanting to fly." 85

"You did a good job," Catherine says. "Let me get your money. Sarah Anne, why don't you take the sack?"

Sarah Anne slips both her hands below Robert's hands and twists the folds of cloth together. "I have it," she says. Robert releases the sack. Immediately she's aware that the sack is alive. Something inside is moving, leaping, dancing. Struggling. The feeling is terrifying.

"Thank you, Robert," Catherine says. Gently she guides him out the door. "You've been very helpful. If you remember to keep our secret, we'll ask you for help again."

By the time she turns back to Sarah Anne and takes the sack from her, Sarah Anne is almost hysterical.

"Nothing can satisfy but what confounds," Catherine says. "Nothing but what astonishes is true." Once more Sarah Anne is reminded of her friend's remarkable memory. When Catherine is excited, bits of all she has ever read fly off her like water from a churning lump of butter. 90

"All right now," Catherine says. "Hold the netting in both hands and pull it over the tub—that's good. Now fasten down the sides, all except for this little section here. I'm going to hold the mouth of the sack to the open part of the netting, and when I say the word I'll open the sack and you drop the last lip of the netting into place. Are you ready?"

"Ready," Sarah Anne says. Her heart beats as if she has a bird inside her chest.

"*Now*," Catherine says.

Everything happens so fast—a flurry of hands and cloth and netting and wings, loops of string and snagged skirts. Two swallows get away, passing so close to Sarah Anne's face that she feels the tips of their feathers and screams. But a minute later she sees that they've been at least partly successful. In the tub, huddled on the board and pushing frantically at the netting, are two birds. Steely blue, buff-bellied, gasping.

"They're so unhappy," Sarah Anne says.   95

"We must leave them," Catherine says. "If the famous Doctor Linnaeus is right, in our absence they'll let themselves down into the water and sleep, either on the surface of the river sand or perhaps just slightly beneath it."

"And if he's wrong?"

"Then we'll tell him so."

* * *

The day passes with excruciating slowness, chopped into bits by Juliet's rigid timetable: family breakfast, dinner, tea, and supper, long and complicated meals. After breakfast Juliet requires the company of Sarah Anne and Catherine in her dressing room, although Sarah Anne knows that Juliet is fond of neither of them. After tea, Christopher expects the women to join him in the library, where they talk and read the newspapers. Sarah Anne and Catherine have not a minute to themselves, and by supper they're wild-eyed with exhaustion and anticipation.

The next morning, when they slip out again before breakfast, the board over   100
the tub is bare. Sarah Anne unfastens the netting, removes the dripping board, and peers down into the water. The swallows lie on the sand. But not wrapped screne in a cocoon of wings; rather twisted and sprawled. She knows before she reaches for them that they're dead. Catherine knows too; she stands ready with a penknife. They've agreed that, should the swallows die, they'll dissect one and examine its structures of circulation and respiration. They'll look for any organ that might make hibernation under water possible; any organ that might prove them wrong.

They work quickly. There isn't much blood. Catherine, peering into the open chest cavity, says, "It is very difficult to work without proper tools. Still. There is nothing out of the ordinary here. And there is no doubt that Linnaeus is wrong."

A four-chambered heart inside its pericardium; small, rosy, lobeless lungs. From the lungs, the mysterious air sacs extend into the abdomen, up into the neck, into the bones. There is no sign of a gill-like organ that might allow the bird to breathe under water. Sarah Anne is quite faint, and yet also fiercely thrilled. They've done an experiment; they've disproved an hypothesis. She says, "We will write to Linnaeus today."

"I think not," Catherine says. "I think it's time we made other plans."

* * *

What plans were those? Of course Christopher noticed that Mrs. Pearce returned to London in early October; he noticed, too, when Sarah Anne left Burdem Place a few weeks later for what she described as an 'extended visit' with her friend. All through November Christopher didn't hear from his sister, but he had worries of his own and thought nothing of her absence. In December, when he was in London on business, he stopped by Mrs. Pearce's house to find that her servants had been dismissed and her house was empty. Only then did he realize that his sister and her friend were simply gone.

Everyone had theories about their disappearance: Collinson, Ellis, all the men. Foul play was suspected by some, although there was no evidence. But this is what Christopher thought, during the bleak nights of 1765 while Juliet was writhing with childbed fever, and during the even bleaker nights after her death, while his tiny son was wasting away. He imagined Sarah Anne and Mrs. Pearce—and who was Mrs. Pearce anyway? Where had she come from? Who were her people?—up before dawn in that London house, moving swiftly through the shadows as they gather bonnets, bags, gloves. Only one bag apiece, as they mean to travel light: and then they glide down the early morning streets toward the Thames. Toward the Tower wharf, perhaps; but it could be any wharf, any set of stairs, the river hums with activity. Ships are packed along the waterfront, their sails furled and their banners drooping; here a wherry, there a cutter, darts between them and the stairs. Some of the ships are headed for India and some for Madagascar. Some are going to the West Indies and others to Africa. Still others are headed for ports in the North American provinces: Quebec or Boston, New York or Baltimore.

Christopher believes his sister and her companion have boarded one of the ships headed for America. Once he overheard the two of them waxing rhapsodic over Mark Catesby's *Natural History*, talking in hushed tones about this land where squirrels flew and frogs whistled and birds the size of fingernails swarmed through forests so thick the sunlight failed to reach the ground. Catesby, Sarah Anne said, believed birds migrated sensibly: they flew to places where there was food.

Pacing his lonely house, miserable and broken, Christopher imagines the ship slowly moving down the Thames toward Dover and the Channel. There's a headwind and the tides are against them; the journey to Dover takes three days. But then the wind shifts and luck arrives. They fly past Portsmouth and Plymouth and Land's End, into the open ocean. The canvas billows out from the spars; the women lean against the railings, laughing. That was the vision he had in mind when, a few years later, he sold both Burdem Place and the brewery and sailed for Delaware.

He never found Sarah Anne. But the crossing and the new world improved his spirits; he married a sturdy young Quaker woman and started a second family. Among the things he brought to his new life were two portraits—small, sepia-toned ovals, obviously copies of larger paintings—which surfaced much later near Baltimore. And if the faded notes found tucked in the back of Christopher's portrait are true, he made some modest contributions to the natural history of the mid-Atlantic states.

Sarah Anne's portrait bears only the date of her birth. Her letters were discovered in the mid-1850s, in the attic of a distant relation of the husband of Linnaeus's youngest daughter, Sophia. The British historian who found them was editing a collection of Linnaeus's correspondence, and from the handwriting and a few other hints, he deduced that "S.A. Billopp" was a woman, creating a minor furor among his colleagues. Later he was able to confirm his theory when he found Sarah Anne's journal at the Linnaean Society, jumbled among the collections left behind at Burdem Place. The last entry in Sarah Anne's journal was this, most likely copied there soon after she and Mrs. Pearce made their experiments with the swallows:

> Collinson loaned me one of his books—An Essay towards the probable Solution of this Question, Whence come the Stork, etc; or Where those birds do probably make their Recess, etc. (London, 1703)—with this passage marked for my amusement:
> "Our migratory birds retire to the moon. They are about two months in retiring thither, and after they are arrived above the lower regions of the air into the thin aether, they will have no occasion for food, as it will not be apt to prey upon the spirits as our lower air. Even on our earth, bears will live upon their fat all the winter; and hence these birds, being very succulent and sanguine, may have their provisions laid up in their bodies for the voyage; or perhaps they are thrown into a state of somnolency by the motion arising from the mutual attraction of the earth and moon."
> He meant to be kind, I know he did. I cannot bear this situation any longer. Catherine and I are meeting in town to discuss the experiment she's proposed.

Starting Point for Further Research: Andrea Barrett

- **Critical Essay:** Elizabeth Gaffney. "Andrea Barrett: The Art of Fiction 180." *Paris Review* (Winter 2003): 56–99.

HA JIN   (B. 1956)

Born in China, Ha Jin grew up during the cultural revolution, joining the army at fourteen. When the colleges reopened, he studied at Heilongjiang University, then at Shandong University. Moving to America, Jin earned a Ph.D. in English at Brandeis University and began to write poems and stories in English. He published three collections of short stories: Ocean of Words (1996); Under the Red Flag (1997), which won the Flannery O'Connor Award for Short Fiction; and The Bridegroom (2000). Poetry volumes include Between Silences (1990) and Facing Shadows (1996). He has also written novels: In the Pond (1998) and Waiting, which won the 1999 National Book Award. Jin teaches at Emory University in Atlanta.

Saboteur   (1996)

Mr. Chiu and his bride were having lunch in the square before Muji Train Station. On the table between them were two bottles of soda spewing out brown foam and two paper boxes of rice and sautéed cucumber and pork. "Let's eat," he said to her, and broke the connected ends of the chopsticks. He picked up a slice of streaky pork and put it into his mouth. As he was chewing, a few crinkles appeared on his thin jaw.

To his right, at another table, two railroad policemen were drinking tea and laughing; it seemed that the stout, middle-aged man was telling a joke to his young comrade, who was tall and of athletic build. Now and again they would steal a glance at Mr. Chiu's table.

The air smelled of rotten melon. A few flies kept buzzing above the couple's lunch. Hundreds of people were rushing around to get on the platform or to catch buses to downtown. Food and fruit vendors were crying for customers in lazy voices. About a dozen young women, representing the local hotels, held up

placards which displayed the daily prices and words as large as a palm, like FREE
MEALS, AIR-CONDITIONING, and ON THE RIVER. In the center of the square stood a
concrete statue of Chairman Mao, at whose feet peasants were napping, their
backs on the warm granite and their faces toward the sunny sky. A flock of pigeons perched on the Chairman's raised hand and forearm.

The rice and cucumber tasted good, and Mr. Chiu was eating unhurriedly.
His sallow face showed exhaustion. He was glad that the honeymoon was finally
over and that he and his bride were heading back for Harbin. During the two
weeks' vacation, he had been worried about his liver, because three months ago
he had suffered from acute hepatitis; he was afraid he might have a relapse. But
he had had no severe symptoms, despite his liver being still big and tender. On
the whole he was pleased with his health, which could endure even the strain of
a honeymoon; indeed, he was on the course of recovery. He looked at his bride,
who took off her wire glasses, kneading the root of her nose with her fingertips.
Beads of sweat coated her pale cheeks.

"Are you all right, sweetheart?" he asked.   5

"I have a headache. I didn't sleep well last night."

"Take an aspirin, will you?"

"It's not that serious. Tomorrow is Sunday and I can sleep in. Don't worry."

As they were talking, the stout policeman at the next table stood up and
threw a bowl of tea in their direction. Both Mr. Chiu's and his bride's sandals
were wet instantly.

"Hooligan!" she said in a low voice.   10

Mr. Chiu got to his feet and said out loud, "Comrade Policeman, why did
you do this?" He stretched out his right foot to show the wet sandal.

"Do what?" the stout man asked huskily, glaring at Mr. Chiu while the
young fellow was whistling.

"See, you dumped tea on our feet."

"You're lying. You wet your shoes yourself."

"Comrade Policeman, your duty is to keep order, but you purposely tortured   15
us common citizens. Why violate the law you are supposed to enforce?" As Mr.
Chiu was speaking, dozens of people began gathering around.

With a wave of his hand, the man said to the young fellow, "Let's get hold of
him!"

They grabbed Mr. Chiu and clamped handcuffs around his wrists. He cried,
"You can't do this to me. This is utterly unreasonable."

"Shut up!" The man pulled out his pistol. "You can use your tongue at our
headquarters."

The young fellow added, "You're a saboteur, you know that? You're disrupting public order."

The bride was too petrified to say anything coherent. She was a recent col-   20
lege graduate, had majored in fine arts, and had never seen the police make an
arrest. All she could say was, "Oh, please, please!"

The policemen were pulling Mr. Chiu, but he refused to go with them, holding the corner of the table and shouting, "We have a train to catch. We already
bought the tickets."

The stout man punched him in the chest. "Shut up. Let your ticket expire."
With the pistol butt he chopped Mr. Chiu's hands, which at once released the
table. Together the two men were dragging him away to the police station.

Realizing he had to go with them, Mr. Chiu turned his head and shouted to his bride, "Don't wait for me here. Take the train. If I'm not back by tomorrow morning, send someone over to get me out."

She nodded, covering her sobbing mouth with her palm.

* * *

After removing his belt, they locked Mr. Chiu into a cell in the back of the Rail- 25 road Police Station. The single window in the room was blocked by six steel bars; it faced a spacious yard, in which stood a few pines. Beyond the trees, two swings hung from an iron frame, swaying gently in the breeze. Somewhere in the building a cleaver was chopping rhythmically. There must be a kitchen upstairs, Mr. Chiu thought.

He was too exhausted to worry about what they would do to him, so he lay down on the narrow bed and shut his eyes. He wasn't afraid. The Cultural Revolution was over already, and recently the Party had been propagating the idea that all citizens were equal before the law. The police ought to be a law-abiding model for common people. As long as he remained coolheaded and reasoned with them, they probably wouldn't harm him.

Late in the afternoon he was taken to the Interrogation Bureau on the second floor. On his way there, in the stairwell, he ran into the middle-aged policeman who had manhandled him. The man grinned, rolling his bulgy eyes and pointing his fingers at him as if firing a pistol. Egg of a tortoise! Mr. Chiu cursed mentally.

The moment he sat down in the office, he burped, his palm shielding his mouth. In front of him, across a long desk, sat the chief of the bureau and a donkey-faced man. On the glass desktop was a folder containing information on his case. He felt it bizarre that in just a matter of hours they had accumulated a small pile of writing about him. On second thought he began to wonder whether they had kept a file on him all the time. How could this have happened? He lived and worked in Harbin, more than three hundred miles away, and this was his first time in Muji City.

The chief of the bureau was a thin, bald man who looked serene and intelligent. His slim hands handled the written pages in the folder in the manner of a lecturing scholar. To Mr. Chiu's left sat a young scribe, with a clipboard on his knee and a black fountain pen in his hand.

"Your name?" the chief asked, apparently reading out the question from a 30 form.

"Chiu Maguang."

"Age?"

"Thirty-four."

"Profession?"

"Lecturer." 35

"Work unit?"

"Harbin University."

"Political status?"

"Communist Party member."

The chief put down the paper and began to speak. "Your crime is sabotage, 40 although it hasn't induced serious consequences yet. Because you are a Party member, you should be punished more. You have failed to be a model for the masses and you—"

"Excuse me, sir," Mr. Chiu cut him off.

"What?"

"I didn't do anything. Your men are the saboteurs of our social order. They threw hot tea on my feet and on my wife's feet. Logically speaking, you should criticize them, if not punish them."

"That statement is groundless. You have no witness. Why should I believe you?" the chief said matter-of-factly.

"This is my evidence." He raised his right hand. "Your man hit my fingers   45
with a pistol."

"That doesn't prove how your feet got wet. Besides, you could have hurt your fingers yourself."

"But I am telling the truth!" Anger flared up in Mr. Chiu. "Your police station owes me an apology. My train ticket has expired, my new leather sandals are ruined, and I am late for a conference in the provincial capital. You must compensate me for the damage and losses. Don't mistake me for a common citizen who would tremble when you sneeze. I'm a scholar, a philosopher, and an expert in dialectical materialism. If necessary, we will argue about this in *The Northeastern Daily*, or we will go to the highest People's Court in Beijing. Tell me, what's your name?" He got carried away with his harangue, which was by no means trivial and had worked to his advantage on numerous occasions.

"Stop bluffing us," the donkey-faced man broke in. "We have seen a lot of your kind. We can easily prove you are guilty. Here are some of the statements given by eyewitnesses." He pushed a few sheets of paper toward Mr. Chiu.

Mr. Chiu was dazed to see the different handwritings, which all stated that he had shouted in the square to attract attention and refused to obey the police. One of the witnesses had identified herself as a purchasing agent from a shipyard in Shanghai. Something stirred in Mr. Chiu's stomach, a pain rising to his rib. He gave out a faint moan.

"Now you have to admit you are guilty," the chief said. "Although it's a seri-   50
ous crime, we won't punish you severely, provided you write out a self-criticism and promise that you won't disrupt the public order again. In other words, your release will depend on your attitude toward this crime."

"You're daydreaming," Mr. Chiu cried. "I won't write a word, because I'm innocent. I demand that you provide me with a letter of apology so I can explain to my university why I'm late."

Both the interrogators smiled contemptuously. "Well, we've never done that," said the chief, taking a puff at his cigarette.

"Then make this a precedent."

"That's unnecessary. We are pretty certain that you will comply with our wishes." The chief blew a column of smoke toward Mr. Chiu's face.

At the tilt of the chief's head, two guards stepped forward and grabbed the   55
criminal by the arms. Mr. Chiu meanwhile went on saying, "I shall report you to the Provincial Administration. You'll have to pay for this! You are worse than the Japanese military police."

They dragged him out of the room.

* * *

After dinner, which consisted of a bowl of millet porridge, a corn bun, and a piece of pickled turnip, Mr. Chiu began to have a fever, shaking with a chill and sweating profusely. He knew that the fire of anger had gotten into his liver and that he was probably having a relapse. No medicine was available, because his briefcase had been left with his bride. At home it would have been time for him to sit in front of their color TV, drinking jasmine tea and watching the evening news. It was so lonesome in here. The orange bulb above the single bed was the only source of light, which enabled the guards to keep him under surveillance at night. A moment ago he had asked them for a newspaper or a magazine to read, but they turned him down.

Through the small opening on the door noises came in. It seemed that the police on duty were playing cards or chess in a nearby office; shouts and laughter could be heard now and then. Meanwhile, an accordion kept coughing from a remote corner in the building. Looking at the ballpoint and the letter paper left for him by the guards when they took him back from the Interrogation Bureau, Mr. Chiu remembered the old saying, "When a scholar runs into soldiers, the more he argues, the muddier his point becomes." How ridiculous this whole thing was. He ruffled his thick hair with his fingers.

He felt miserable, massaging his stomach continually. To tell the truth, he was more upset than frightened, because he would have to catch up with his work once he was back home—a paper that was due at the printers next week, and two dozen books he ought to read for the courses he was going to teach in the fall.

A human shadow flitted across the opening. Mr. Chiu rushed to the door 60 and shouted through the hole, "Comrade Guard, Comrade Guard!"

"What do you want?" a voice rasped.

"I want you to inform your leaders that I'm very sick. I have heart disease and hepatitis. I may die here if you keep me like this without medication."

"No leader is on duty on the weekend. You have to wait till Monday."

"What? You mean I'll stay in here tomorrow?"

"Yes." 65

"Your station will be held responsible if anything happens to me."

"We know that. Take it easy, you won't die."

It seemed illogical that Mr. Chiu slept quite well that night, though the light above his head had been on all the time and the straw mattress was hard and infested with fleas. He was afraid of ticks, mosquitoes, cockroaches—any kind of insect but fleas and bedbugs. Once, in the countryside, where his school's faculty and staff had helped the peasants harvest crops for a week, his colleagues had joked about his flesh, which they said must have tasted nonhuman to fleas. Except for him, they were all afflicted with hundreds of bites.

More amazing now, he didn't miss his bride a lot. He even enjoyed sleeping alone, perhaps because the honeymoon had tired him out and he needed more rest.

The backyard was quiet on Sunday morning. Pale sunlight streamed 70 through the pine branches. A few sparrows were jumping on the ground, catching caterpillars and ladybugs. Holding the steel bars, Mr. Chiu inhaled the morning air, which smelled meaty. There must have been an eatery or a cooked-meat stand nearby. He reminded himself that he should take this detention with ease. A sentence that Chairman Mao had written to a hospitalized friend rose in his mind: "Since you are already in here, you may as well stay and make the best of it."

His desire for peace of mind originated in his fear that his hepatitis might get worse. He tried to remain unperturbed. However, he was sure that his liver was swelling up, since the fever still persisted. For a whole day he lay in bed, thinking about his paper on the nature of contradictions. Time and again he was overwhelmed by anger, cursing aloud, "A bunch of thugs!" He swore that once he was out, he would write an article about this experience. He had better find out some of the policemen's names.

It turned out to be a restful day for the most part; he was certain that his university would send somebody to his rescue. All he should do now was remain calm and wait patiently. Sooner or later the police would have to release him, although they had no idea that he might refuse to leave unless they wrote him an apology. Damn those hoodlums, they had ordered more than they could eat!

* * *

When he woke up on Monday morning, it was already light. Somewhere a man was moaning; the sound came from the backyard. After a long yawn, and kicking off the tattered blanket, Mr. Chiu climbed out of bed and went to the window. In the middle of the yard, a young man was fastened to a pine, his wrists handcuffed around the trunk from behind. He was wriggling and swearing loudly, but there was no sight of anyone else in the yard. He looked familiar to Mr. Chiu.

Mr. Chiu squinted his eyes to see who it was. To his astonishment, he recognized the man, who was Fenjin, a recent graduate from the Law Department at Harbin University. Two years ago Mr. Chiu had taught a course in Marxist materialism, in which Fenjin had enrolled. Now, how on earth had this young devil landed here?

Then it dawned on him that Fenjin must have been sent over by his bride. What a stupid woman! A bookworm, who only knew how to read foreign novels! He had expected that she would contact the school's Security Section, which would for sure send a cadre here. Fenjin held no official position; he merely worked in a private law firm that had just two lawyers; in fact, they had little business except for some detective work for men and women who suspected their spouses of having extramarital affairs. Mr. Chiu was overcome with a wave of nausea. 75

Should he call out to let his student know he was nearby? He decided not to, because he didn't know what had happened. Fenjin must have quarreled with the police to incur such a punishment. Yet this could never have occurred if Fenjin hadn't come to his rescue. So no matter what, Mr. Chiu had to do something. But what could he do?

It was going to be a scorcher. He could see purple steam shimmering and rising from the ground among the pines. Poor devil, he thought, as he raised a bowl of corn glue to his mouth, sipped, and took a bite of a piece of salted celery.

When a guard came to collect the bowl and the chopsticks, Mr. Chiu asked him what had happened to the man in the backyard. "He called our boss 'bandit,'" the guard said. "He claimed he was a lawyer or something. An arrogant son of a rabbit."

Now it was obvious to Mr. Chiu that he had to do something to help his rescuer. Before he could figure out a way, a scream broke out in the backyard. He rushed to the window and saw a tall policeman standing before Fenjin, an iron bucket on the ground. It was the same young fellow who had arrested Mr. Chiu in the square two days before. The man pinched Fenjin's nose, then raised his hand, which stayed in the air for a few seconds, then slapped the lawyer across the face. As Fenjin was groaning, the man lifted up the bucket and poured water on his head.

"This will keep you from getting sunstroke, boy. I'll give you some more   80 every hour," the man said loudly.

Fenjin kept his eyes shut, yet his wry face showed that he was struggling to hold back from cursing the policeman, or, more likely, that he was sobbing in silence. He sneezed, then raised his face and shouted, "Let me go take a piss."

"Oh yeah?" the man bawled. "Pee in your pants."

Still Mr. Chiu didn't make any noise, gripping the steel bars with both hands, his fingers white. The policeman turned and glanced at the cell's window; his pistol, partly holstered, glittered in the sun. With a snort he spat his cigarette butt to the ground and stamped it into the dust.

Then the door opened and the guards motioned Mr. Chiu to come out. Again they took him upstairs to the Interrogation Bureau.

The same men were in the office, though this time the scribe was sitting   85 there empty-handed. At the sight of Mr. Chiu the chief said, "Ah, here you are. Please be seated."

After Mr. Chiu sat down, the chief waved a white silk fan and said to him, "You may have seen your lawyer. He's a young man without manners, so our director had him taught a crash course in the backyard."

"It's illegal to do that. Aren't you afraid to appear in a newspaper?"

"No, we are not, not even on TV. What else can you do? We are not afraid of any story you make up. We call it fiction. What we do care about is that you cooperate with us. That is to say, you must admit your crime."

"What if I refuse to cooperate?"

"Then your lawyer will continue his education in the sunshine."   90

A swoon swayed Mr. Chiu, and he held the arms of the chair to steady himself. A numb pain stung him in the upper stomach and nauseated him, and his head was throbbing. He was sure that the hepatitis was finally attacking him. Anger was flaming up in his chest; his throat was tight and clogged.

The chief resumed, "As a matter of fact, you don't even have to write out your self-criticism. We have your crime described clearly here. All we need is your signature."

Holding back his rage, Mr. Chiu said, "Let me look at that."

With a smirk the donkey-faced man handed him a sheet, which carried these words:

> I hereby admit that on July 13 I disrupted public order at Muji Train Station, and that I refused to listen to reason when the railroad police issued their warning. Thus I myself am responsible for my arrest. After two days' detention, I have realized the reactionary nature of my crime. From now on, I shall continue to educate myself with all my effort and shall never commit this kind of crime again.

A voice started screaming in Mr. Chiu's ears, "Lie, lie!" But he shook his   95 head and forced the voice away. He asked the chief, "If I sign this, will you release both my lawyer and me?"

"Of course, we'll do that." The chief was drumming his fingers on the blue folder—their file on him.

Mr. Chiu signed his name and put his thumbprint under his signature.

"Now you are free to go," the chief said with a smile, and handed him a piece of paper to wipe his thumb with.

Mr. Chiu was so sick that he couldn't stand up from the chair at first try. Then he doubled his effort and rose to his feet. He staggered out of the building to meet his lawyer in the backyard, having forgotten to ask for his belt back. In his chest he felt as though there were a bomb. If he were able to, he would have razed the entire police station and eliminated all their families. Though he knew he could do nothing like that, he made up his mind to do something.

*   *   *

"I'm sorry about this torture, Fenjin," Mr. Chiu said when they met.   100

"It doesn't matter. They are savages." The lawyer brushed a patch of dirt off his jacket with trembling fingers. Water was still dribbling from the bottoms of his trouser legs.

"Let's go now," the teacher said.

The moment they came out of the police station, Mr. Chiu caught sight of a tea stand. He grabbed Fenjin's arm and walked over to the old woman at the table. "Two bowls of black tea," he said and handed her a one-yuan note.

After the first bowl, they each had another one. Then they set out for the train station. But before they walked fifty yards, Mr. Chiu insisted on eating a bowl of tree-ear soup at a food stand. Fenjin agreed. He told his teacher, "You mustn't treat me like a guest."

"No, I want to eat something myself."   105

As if dying of hunger, Mr. Chiu dragged his lawyer from restaurant to restaurant near the police station, but at each place he ordered no more than two bowls of food. Fenjin wondered why his teacher wouldn't stay at one place and eat his fill.

Mr. Chiu bought noodles, wonton, eight-grain porridge, and chicken soup, respectively, at four restaurants. While eating, he kept saying through his teeth, "If only I could kill all the bastards!" At the last place he merely took a few sips of the soup without tasting the chicken cubes and mushrooms.

Fenjin was baffled by his teacher, who looked ferocious and muttered to himself mysteriously, and whose jaundiced face was covered with dark puckers. For the first time Fenjin thought of Mr. Chiu as an ugly man.

*   *   *

Within a month over eight hundred people contracted acute hepatitis in Muji. Six died of the disease, including two children. Nobody knew how the epidemic had started.

Starting Points for Further Research: Ha Jin

- **Critical Essay:** Robert D. Stirr. "The Presence of Walt Whitman in Ha Jin's *Waiting*." *Walt Whitman Quarterly Review* 20:1 (2002): 1–18.
- **Interview:** Paula E. Geyh. "An Interview with Ha Jin." *Boulevard* 17:3 (2002): 127–40.

PART

II

Poetry

CHAPTER
10

Poems
Tone, Image, Language

SHAPING EXPERIENCE

Poetry presents us with strongly felt experience that has been artfully shaped. Its subject matter is often deep emotion, vividly felt, but the emotion appears within a package that deliberately draws attention to its own artifice and to its verbal complexity. To readers and listeners, a poem presents both strong feelings and a carefully wrought piece of art, as if the poet is telling us something urgent and, at the same time, giving us a beautifully made gift. As readers we sometimes pay more attention to the statement of the poem, at other times to the packaging. When art and statement combine and everything works wonderfully, we pay equal attention to both—that is when we make the poem our own.

Some readers, though, are put off by poetry, either by the strong feeling or by the presentation. A good many things about poetry can keep readers away, depriving them of a great pleasure as well as cutting them off from a key component of our culture. Why do some readers scorn or ignore or avoid poems? Some say:

- The language is often "old-fashioned."
- The sense is frequently difficult to understand.
- A poem's "hidden meanings" seem like traps for the unwary.
- Poets sometimes seem to focus on insignificant situations or feelings.

- In a media age, it's hard to appreciate a poet's verbal skills.
- Poetry is often hard to read aloud.

These complaints are not unreasonable, but they stem in large measure from a simple lack of exposure to poetry or from a lack of practice in reading poetry. In fact, many people who enjoy poetry view such "defects" as positive strengths:

- The out-of-the-ordinary language sounds special.
- Understanding a complex piece of art is a worthy challenge for readers.
- It's enjoyable to tease out how a poem makes its meaning (or multiple meanings).
- Poets make us see things we often overlook or ignore.
- Nowadays it's rare to see such impressive verbal skills.
- It is a challenge to try to read poems aloud.

The way to turn those supposed problems into assets is through more experience with poems: reading them, seeing how they are put together, talking about them, and finding out what others have to say about them. Within a short time, readers can become very comfortable with poetry, and their newly developed skills will lead to greater understanding and enjoyment.

Still, it would be wrong to overlook one other serious complaint many people have. Some say that closely reading a poem—or "tearing a poem apart"—destroys the pleasure. People ask, "Why can't we just read the poems rather than examining every part under a microscope?" William Wordsworth (1770–1850), a poet who shared some of that feeling, said, "We murder to dissect." Such an attitude is understandable, but we cannot forget that poetry is also an art form, with a long history, strict rules, and a tradition encompassing a wide variety of approaches. Some readers read poems only for the feeling; others read to see how a poem reflects a poet's life; others think of poems as a crucial part of our culture; still others read because they love the sound, the sentiment, or the verbal play. All of these readers benefit from some basic knowledge of how poems work, and of what separates excellent poems from the run-of-the-mill variety. Most of all, a trained reader of poetry gets more out of poems from seeing how they operate.

There are no deep mysteries, but there are significant traditions every well-read poet knows, and some age-old rules that many poets choose to obey, while others feel free to break them intentionally. This chapter and the next will offer up some useful tools and information to explain how some poems work, without leaving them for dead. As you look at these chapters, notice that most of the space is not taken up by critical analysis but by the poems themselves, since the best way to learn about poems is by reading plenty of them.

The poem below contains all the things people like about poetry, as well as many of the elements a reader needs to understand in order to appreciate how poems work. Written by the famous African American poet Paul Laurence Dunbar, the poem refers to the situation of blacks during the era of Jim Crow segregation laws in the late 1800s, after the Civil War.

PAUL LAURENCE DUNBAR (1872–1906)

We Wear the Mask (1896)

We wear the mask that grins and lies,
It hides our cheeks and shades our eyes,—
This debt we pay to human guile;
With torn and bleeding hearts we smile,
And mouth with myriad subtleties.   5

Why should the world be over-wise,
In counting all our tears and sighs?
Nay, let them only see us, while
    We wear the mask.

We smile, but, O great Christ, our cries   10
To thee from tortured souls arise.
We sing, but oh the clay is vile
Beneath our feet, and long the mile;
But let the world dream otherwise,
    We wear the mask!   15

What can a reader take from this well-known poem, one that helped make Dunbar famous at the time and that still appears in countless anthologies as a good example of high-quality poetic achievement? First of all, Dunbar's brief poem typifies the qualities we associate with poetry: it expresses strong feeling, it uses "poetic" language, it is highly shaped, and it reveals its meanings slowly.

To start, "We Wear the Mask" is built entirely on a **metaphor**, that is, a figure of speech based on an unspoken comparison. Dunbar states that black people all "wear the mask," not a literal mask, but an imaginary one that is no less real. This "mask" allows blacks to pretend they are happy with their position in late-nine-teenth-century society, but it hides their true feelings of despair from whites. A **literal** meaning of mask is, of course, something tangible that people put on to dis-guise themselves, like the piece of cardboard or rubber or plastic that people wear on Halloween or to costume parties. However, the mask in Dunbar's poem has a **figurative** meaning: it is not a literal false face but a figure of speech, in this case a metaphor. We see references to metaphorical masks often, and not just in poetry: "Her face was a mask of grief." (If we said "Her face was like a mask," we would have a **simile**, which is an overt comparison, using "like" or "as.") Here the mask metaphor becomes the central part of Dunbar's whole poem, as his title signifies.

Besides the central figure of a mask, another element of Dunbar's poem is the "we" who do the wearing. Who is this "we"? Someone seems to be speaking on behalf of all African Americans who are forced to pretend, to smile and hide the tears. The **speaker** of a poem, who in this case seems to include himself as part of the "we," is called the **persona**, a term that allows us to place some dis-tance between the actual writer of the poem, Dunbar, and the one who speaks in the poem, the put-upon black American who deceives the whites he meets. In this poem, the distance between Dunbar and his speaker is perhaps not far, but many poets have created personas quite different from themselves, and it is always useful to keep the two separate. To see the persona in action, ask who is saying these lines:

> We smile, but, O great Christ, our cries
> To thee from tortured souls arise.

It makes much more sense to regard the one saying these lines not as Paul Laurence Dunbar himself, but the persona he created, the speaker of the poem who stands for all blacks forced into dissimulation.

How do we know that the persona here is speaking for blacks and that the subject behind the poem is racial inequality? After all, there is nothing in the poem that says clearly who speaks, so couldn't the "we" be all people? Don't whites sometimes wear masks too? Here some knowledge of biography and poetic tradition can come to the reader's aid. Knowing something of Dunbar's work and life helps. Many of his other successful poems were very different from "We Wear the Mask"; he had published poetry that created pictures of idealized southern life, with happy blacks living on the plantation, an obviously false depiction strictly for white consumption, and a portrait he didn't believe for a minute. Dunbar was fully aware of the false position he had been in, having worn as he did a kind of mask himself in his poetry. As a black poet he had needed the favor of whites to get published in the first place, since the white literary establishment controlled most magazines and publishing houses. This predicament is captured in his most famous line of poetry: "I know why the caged bird sings." Everything is done by indirection, Dunbar states, and so smiles and songs need to be interpreted. But "We Wear the Mask" comes out and says so in a frank manner that is, in fact, uncharacteristic of Dunbar's other work.

Dunbar's particular style of poetic language—his **diction**—is not complex, but some of it seems old-fashioned, particularly the word "Nay." Did people talk like that in 1896? Perhaps, but it was an old-fashioned word choice even then. "Nay" is a word that rarely appears in people's active vocabularies, then or now, but it is still one that most of us recognize. If Dunbar had wanted to be up to date, he would have changed "Nay" to "No." But he didn't; he was striving for a slightly elevated kind of diction. This poem, like much poetry, is not quite in the language of the common people in ordinary circumstances. (For more on poetic diction, see p. 724.)

Dunbar's poetic design is apparent throughout. The poem is in three parts or **stanzas** or verse paragraphs, which are clearly separated by white space. Its **symmetry** stands out: the poem's title repeats at the end of the second stanza as well as the third, providing balance, reinforcement, and a kind of overarching **repetition**. All the other lines share just two **rhymes**. In the first stanza are two words with very similar sounds—"lies," and "eyes"—and one with a not-quite-similar sound, a deliberate **off-rhyme**, "subtleties." This rhyme carries through to the second stanza with "wise" and "sighs" and then to the third with "cries," "arise," and finally, "otherwise." The second rhyme has "guile" and "smile" in the first stanza, "while" in the second, and "vile" and "mile" in the third. This poem is obviously very carefully crafted, tightly knit together by a remarkably small number of rhymes.

As readers, we can discuss a poem like "We Wear the Mask" in many ways. We can look at it as a cultural artifact, appearing at a key time in the development of a coherent black consciousness in American intellectual and social history. We can examine it as a document in the development of its author, Dunbar, whose poetry made him famous but who resisted some of that fame, since it came from the very attitudes he decried in this poem, which reads like a heartfelt cry for honesty when compared with most of his other poems. We can look at it as a poem that remains impersonal, hewing to a formal tradition that avoids the spell of Walt Whitman's experiments (see Chapter 13), both in the type of verse and in the extent of personal revelations. Whitman, slightly older than Dunbar, revealed a great deal about himself; some would say that here Dunbar doesn't reveal much, that he in fact still wears a kind of mask. Finally, we can discuss the poem's shape and design, including its measured sounds and its tightly knit rhyme scheme. Every one of these attitudes and topics is available to us as readers, and no doubt more as well. We possess the freedom to treat Dunbar's poem as we like.

Talking about the Text

1. Find three metaphors in Dunbar's poem and connect them to the overarching metaphor of the mask.
2. List five words in the poem that were for you examples of difficult language when you first read the poem. Explain what you now think that language seems to mean.

Writing about the Text

1. With Dunbar's poem in mind, describe a time when you or somebody you know of wore a "mask" that hid or betrayed true feelings. Explain to what extent this poem, written specifically to depict the experience of nineteenth-century black Americans, can provide a wider range of readers with insight into the price of deception.
2. Write about how you respond to the repetition of rhymes and phrases in "We Wear the Mask."

Linking the Text to Other Texts

1. Examine the language used by Phillis Wheatley in the poem "On Being Brought from Africa to America" (p. 751) and see if her approach has anything in common with Dunbar's. She, like Dunbar, was dependent on the approval and support of a white publishing world. To what extent can we say she is wearing a mask?
2. Dunbar writes of blacks speaking "myriad subtleties." Can you think of examples of people (of whatever age or ethnicity) adopting such a language, designed to mislead?

The Paul Laurence Dunbar House, 219 North Summit Street, Dayton, Ohio. The street has been renamed Paul Laurence Dunbar Avenue.

The Paul Laurence Dunbar House in Dayton, Ohio. The Paul Laurence Dunbar House and Interpretive Center, number 219 on the renamed Paul Laurence Dunbar Avenue in Dayton, Ohio, was the last home of the poet who was known as the unofficial poet laureate of African Americans. The house, a large turn-of-the-century Italianate home, has been refurbished to resemble how the Dunbar family had decorated it. In 1936, it became the first memorial in Ohio to honor an African American. Born in 1872, Paul Laurence Dunbar contracted tuberculosis as a young adult and stayed close to home and family due to his illness. Dunbar credited fellow residents of Dayton, including Wilbur and Orville Wright, with giving him considerable financial and emotional support to write and publish his first books.

Visitors to Dayton can also explore the Wright-Dunbar National Historical Park, an area of downtown Dayton including the building where the Wright brothers had a printing press and published Dunbar's African American newspaper, the *Dayton Tattler*, and his early poetry. For more information on the Dunbar House, visit *http://www.ohiohistory.org/places/dunbar/*. For more information on the Wright-Dunbar collaboration, see *http://www.wright-dunbar.org/*.

TONE

When we speak, our voice often conveys much more than information; it conveys attitude as well. A poem also has a voice, and the attitude it conveys is called its **tone**. What contributes to a poem's tone? The tone is conveyed by a whole range of effects, starting with **vocabulary**, or the choice of words, and moving on to the **level of diction**—either **high**, **middle**, or **low**. For instance, Dunbar's "We Wear the Mask" sounds like a traditional poem in its somewhat formal language, its use of rhyme, and its serious tone. Its vocabulary contains some pretty elevated words ("myriad subtleties," "over-wise"), and its level of diction seems middle to high. Readers can see that the tone seems restrained until the emotion breaks through with the "Oh Christ" in lines 10–11.

To get a better sense of how tone operates, here is Linda Pastan's "Marks," a sharp contrast to Dunbar's poem. "Marks" is a contemporary poem using today's informal language and no rhyme, but with a strong metaphor and a distinctive persona. Note how its tone is distinctly different from Dunbar's.

LINDA PASTAN (B. 1932)

Marks (1978)

My husband gives me an A
for last night's supper,
an incomplete for my ironing,
a B plus in bed.
My son says I am average,   5
an average mother, but if
I put my mind to it
I could improve.
My daughter believes
in Pass/Fail and tells me   10
I pass. Wait 'til they learn
I'm dropping out.

Part of the enjoyment of Pastan's short poem is the way it captures recognizable speaking voices in many of its lines:

but if
I put my mind to it
I could improve.

Where have you heard that voice before? Pastan seems to have captured the exact intonation and earnestness of a coach or a junior high school teacher, as parroted by her son. In fact, there is a somewhat similar voice throughout the whole poem, a voice that repeats what others say and gets it just right. One could describe the speaker as confiding something important to us, as she repeats the different judgments made by her family and then reveals her secret—that she is "dropping out."

The whole poem is presented to us as a kind of aside, or as an explanation in advance for what the speaker is about to do. What accounts for that immediate quality? Consider the verb tenses:

My husband gives . . .

My son says . . .

My daughter believes . . .

Wait 'til they learn . . .

The poem is placed for us in the present, just after "last night's supper" that got an A and just before the family learns the speaker is dropping out. The naturalness of the tenses, the seeming casualness of the repetitions, and the ease with which the words flow make the poem sound spontaneous. Pastan has said that she very carefully works on a poem to create just the right kind of speaking voice. The spontaneous quality, the casual voice, is the product of endless revision.

We can imagine this poem told to us in many ways: the revelations of someone we meet on a bus or a plane, or the heart-to-heart confession of a friend told over a cup of coffee. Or perhaps it is the frustrated complaint of an overworked mother. Each one of these imagined situations would no doubt have a separate, distinct tone, and we are free to take this poem in any of these ways, and others as well. If we spoke it, enacted it, played it, we could take on any of these roles and be justified. Pastan leaves us free to adopt any number of characters who could be saying this poem aloud, and each "performance" might have a slightly different spin. For instance, as readers we do not know exactly what "dropping out" means. We all understand dropping out of school, but dropping out of motherhood can mean many things. No more ironing? No attempt to "improve" as a mother? It's left deliberately vague. And when we read, we are almost invited to give it our own personal interpretation. There is no "right," "correct," "approved" tone required for Pastan's poem to work.

Pastan subordinates everything to the metaphor of the grade, the mark, creating a **controlling metaphor** that dominates the poem. In fact, there is an even larger comparison lurking behind the fact that she gets "marks" for her behavior: that life can be judged like schoolwork, with letter grades or pass/fail. Does Pastan believe this? It doesn't matter, since we need to separate Pastan the writer from the persona of this poem, who slyly tells us what she's going to do, drop out. Did the poet Linda Pastan drop out? Not in an obvious way. She's now a happy grandmother, still writing poems. She never left husband and family, and she's still in the same Maryland house she has lived in for thirty years. But her persona, the speaker of her poem, imagines dropping out, leaving the school/life grind and not having to worry about getting judged all the time by the people closest to her. Is this poem a 1970s feminist statement? Yes, but one every reader can partake in. Who hasn't dreamed of rebelling over being judged, or of dropping out, however we define it?

What can we say about how Pastan creates her poem's speaking voice? Her level of diction seems ordinary, low to middle compared to Dunbar's distinctly higher level. Pastan employs nothing like old-fashioned poetic diction here, and there are even some examples of low or informal language: "Wait 'til they learn."

Pastan does not use rhyme, but "Marks" is obviously a poem, one that looks quite simple. But even its simplicity is deceptive. Here is how Pastan spoke about her poetry in a July 2003 interview with Jeffrey Brown on PBS's *NewsHour with Jim Lehrer*:

> **Q.:** As I read your poetry there was a kind of ease to your writing. Is it easy to achieve that ease?

Pastan: No, there is no ease in writing. The job is to make it by the end feel as if it flows easily. But each poem of mine goes through something like 100 revisions.

Q.: A hundred?

Pastan: Yeah, yeah, easily.

Q.: What is it that you're looking for?

Pastan: Well, I want every word to have to be there. I want a certain kind of impact on the reader or on myself when I read it, the sort of condensed energy that can then go out.

In "We Wear the Mask," Dunbar's "we" includes himself and a whole race consciously acting to hide feelings; in "Marks," Pastan allows us to imagine any number of frustrated wives and mothers as the "I" who's dropping out. But D. H. Lawrence's "Piano," below, gives us a specific setting for his poem, making it not a general statement but one tied to a particular moment. And the attitude toward the moment—the tone—is quite easy to grasp.

D. H. LAWRENCE (1885–1930)

Piano (1918)

Softly, in the dusk, a woman is singing to me;
Taking me back down the vista of years, till I see
A child sitting under the piano, in the boom of the tingling strings
And pressing the small, poised feet of a mother who smiles as she sings.

In spite of myself, the insidious mastery of song   5
Betrays me back, till the heart of me weeps to belong
To the old Sunday evenings at home, with winter outside
And hymns in the cozy parlor, the tinkling piano our guide.

So now it is vain for the singer to burst into clamor
With the great black piano appassionato.° The glamour   *impassioned*   10
Of childish days is upon me, my manhood is cast
Down in the flood of remembrance, I weep like a child for the past.

"Piano" is not about an idea but an experience. As the first line clearly states, the speaker is listening to a woman sing, "softly, in the dusk." As she sings, he is reminded of his youth and sees himself listening to his mother's voice, "in the cozy parlor." The memory overpowers him, and as he says, "I weep like a child for the past." What could be the possible ideas in Lawrence's poem? That music can transport us to the past? That a mother's influence lasts well beyond youth? That a man can admit crying about the lost comfort of family? Yes, it is possible to see all these and many more ideas in "Piano," but it is clear that the poem does not exist to argue such ideas, which are simple, straightforward, and easy to agree with. Furthermore, such ideas would work better in prose, not verse. But Lawrence is not as interested in arguing such claims as he is in **dramatizing** them in the voice of his persona. The poem attempts to capture experience, to render the emotional power of an event, and to produce some of that feeling for the reader. "Piano" is a **lyric**, the most common form of poem, defined as a short poem expressing a speaker's emotions.

Who exactly is the speaker in "Piano"? Are we, as we read, supposed to act out the character or persona Lawrence has created, imitating his tone? Are we supposed to be someone listening to a pianist and thinking back to his mother's piano playing, and then weeping "like a child for the past"? The precise role of the reader has been a vexed question over the years, and one about which many thoughtful people have differed. Some thinkers about poetry, such as T. S. Eliot, the great poet and highly influential critic, have argued that a poem is spoken by the persona and overheard by us, the readers. Others imagine the lyric as a kind of soliloquy, with the persona speaking it aloud, and us as the directly addressed audience. An influential contemporary critic, Helen Vendler, disagrees and claims that lyric poems give us a genuinely dramatic **script** with us the readers as the performers: "The poem is *written for you to say*. You are the speaker of every lyric poem you read. This is what a lyric poem is: it is a speech made for you to utter" (*Poems, Poets, Poetry*, 2nd ed., p. 14).

We do not have to choose here. All three approaches—overheard, soliloquy, script—present the lyric poem as a performance, an enactment that demands our participation. We cannot avoid active engagement with the poem, either as listener or as speaker. There is an urgency to a lyric poem that draws us into the performance, either as witnesses or as actors. Or as Robert Frost put it about poetry, "everything written is as good as it is dramatic."

Talking about the Text

1. Examine the verb tenses in "Piano" and explain the effect created by the verbs.
2. How seriously do you think "weep like a child" is meant? Connect that phrase to "betrayed" and "manhood cast down." What kind of tone does the speaker have toward the experience?

Writing about the Text

1. List six words or phrases in "Piano" that would contribute most to its tone when "Piano" is read aloud. Then in two or three paragraphs, explain why you chose to list those particular words.
2. Write—in prose or verse—about how a certain song has affected you deeply, as it has Lawrence's persona in "Piano."

Linking the Text to Other Texts

1. Discuss the T. S. Eliot and Helen Vendler persona debate with people who like to sing. What attitude do they have toward the lyrics of the songs they sing? Do they take on the role—the persona—of the singer? Does this change when they sing along or when they do karaoke?

2. Choose some poems from this chapter or some songs you know that would work better being overheard. Then choose some that would work better as scripts for you to perform. What qualities should poems have to be scripts?

For Further Reading: Tone

EZRA POUND (1885–1972)

The River-Merchant's Wife: A Letter (1915)

Translated from the Chinese of Li Po (701–762)

While my hair was still cut straight across my forehead
I played about the front gate, pulling flowers.
You came by on bamboo stilts, playing horse,
You walked about my seat, playing with blue plums.
And we went on living in the village of Chokan: 5
Two small people, without dislike or suspicion.

At fourteen I married My Lord you.
I never laughed, being bashful.
Lowering my head, I looked at the wall.
Called to, a thousand times, I never looked back. 10

At fifteen I stopped scowling,
I desired my dust to be mingled with yours
For ever and for ever and for ever.
Why should I climb the look out?

At sixteen you departed, 15
You went into far Ku-to-yen, by the river of swirling eddies,
And you have been gone five months.
The monkeys make sorrowful noise overhead.

You dragged your feet when you went out.
By the gate now, the moss is grown, the different mosses, 20
Too deep to clear them away!

The leaves fall early this autumn, in wind.
The paired butterflies are already yellow with August
Over the grass in the West garden;
They hurt me. I grow older. 25
If you are coming down through the narrows of the river Kiang,
Please let me know beforehand,
And I will come out to meet you
  As far as Cho-fu-Sa.

☀ INSPIRATION   Translating Li Po

Ezra Pound was not the only poet to translate
the work of the Chinese poet Li Po. Another
English translation is "Long Banister Lane" by
William Carlos Williams, which appears below.
How does his translation compare to Ezra
Pound's? Compare their respective treatments of
voice and tone. How are they similar? How are
they different? What effect do the differences
have?

William Carlos Williams   (1883–1963)

Long Banister Lane   (1960)

When my hair was first trimmed across my
    forehead,
I played in front of my door, picking flowers.
You came riding a bamboo stilt for a horse,
Circling around my yard, playing with green
    plums.
Living as neighbors at Long Banister Lane, 5
We had an affection for each other that none
    were suspicious of.

At fourteen I became your wife,
With lingering shyness, I never laughed.
Lowering my head towards a dark wall,
I never tamed, though called a thousand times.   10
At fifteen I began to show my happiness,
I desired to have my dust mingled with yours.
With a devotion ever unchanging,
Why should I look out when I had you?

At sixteen you left home   15
For a faraway land of steep pathways and eddies,
Which in May were impossible to traverse,
And where the monkeys whined sorrowfully towards the sky.

The footprints you made when you left the door
Have been covered by green moss,   20
New moss too deep to be swept away.
The autumn wind came early and the leaves started falling.
The butterflies, yellow with age in August,
Fluttered in pairs towards the western garden.
Looking at the scene, I felt a pang in my heart,   25
And I sat lamenting my fading youth.

TRANSLATING LI PO

Every day and night I wait for your return,
Expecting to receive your letter in advance,
So that I will come traveling to greet you
As far as Windy Sand.   30

PHILIP LARKIN   (1922–1985)

This Be the Verse   (1971)

They fuck you up, your mum and dad.
    They may not mean to, but they do.
They fill you with the faults they had
    And add some extra, just for you.

But they were fucked up in their turn   5
    By fools in old-style hats and coats,
Who half the time were soppy-stern
    And half at one another's throats.

Man hands on misery to man.
    It deepens like a coastal shelf.   10
Get out as early as you can.
    And don't have any kids yourself.

 VIRTUAL LOCALE

The Lannan Foundation and Louise Glück. The Lannan Foundation,
which supports contemporary artists, awarded Louise Glück their Poetry Award
in 1999. The foundation's website at *http://www.lannan.org* features online audio
of Glück reading in 2005 from her Pulitzer Prize–winning collection *The Wild
Iris* and other poems, and an accompanying interview by James Longenbach.
You can also find information on their 1989 video on Glück.

LOUISE GLÜCK   (B. 1943)

The Red Poppy   (1992)

The great thing
is not having
a mind. Feelings:
oh, I have those; they
govern me. I have   5
a lord in heaven

called the sun, and open
for him, showing him
the fire of my own heart, fire
like his presence.   10
What could such glory be
if not a heart? Oh my brothers and sisters,
were you like me once, long ago,
before you were human? Did you
permit yourselves   15
to open once, who would never
open again? Because in truth
I am speaking now
the way you do. I speak
because I am shattered.   20

A U D I O   L O C A L E

Louise Glück's "The Red Poppy." An audio clip of poet Louise Glück reading her poem "The Red Poppy" aloud can be found online at the Academy of American Poets website: *http://www.poets.org.*

Talking about the Text

1. Compare the use of nature imagery in Pound's translations of Li Po's poem and Glück's "The Red Poppy."
2. Examine the personas in the poems by Pound, Larkin, and Glück: a young Chinese wife, a misanthrope, and a flower. Explain what each of these personas wants from the reader or listener.

Writing about the Text

1. Write a 1–2 page description of the persona in one of these poems by Pound, Larkin, or Glück. Feel free to speculate on physical characteristics, personality, clothing, family members, and so on. Pay particular attention to how the tone connects to the persona.
2. The personas in these poems are very different from the authors. Write a paper showing which persona seems most fully developed.

Linking the Text to Other Texts

1. Consider how you might perform one of these poems. Write reading directions, indicating what words to emphasize and what tone to use. Then, try it out a few times in rehearsal before delivering it to class.
2. Write a response or answer to one of these poems, either in prose or in verse, taking on the role of someone addressed by the persona.

IMAGES AND IMAGERY

Poets work with **images**, which can be defined as vivid impressions of a sensory experience. Often the experience is visual, but a poem's **imagery** can relate to any of the five senses. Images are building blocks of the poem, and the more complex the poem, the more the images interact with one another. Here is a poem made of a single striking visual image of the way people's faces looked one day in the Paris subway.

EZRA POUND   (1885–1972)
In a Station of the Metro   (1913)

The apparition of these faces in the crowd;
Petals on a wet, black bough.

That's all there is: a single, vivid image compressed into two lines, the first a statement, the second the image. Do people's faces look like petals? Does the Paris subway look like a "wet, black bough"? For one moment they did to Pound's speaker, and we have the poem as a result. The poem's speaker imposed order on the universe by insisting on this image, stripping everything else out of the poem. By his choice of subject and image, the speaker says something of the power of poetry and art.

The next poem is more complex, as it is built on a series of very striking images, each succeeding the other in a carefully arranged pattern. It helps to think in terms of sentences here, for the image shifts when each sentence ends. The subject or **theme** of the poem is a simple one: I'm getting older and will die soon, but your love will be stronger as I fade away.

WILLIAM SHAKESPEARE   (1564–1616)
Sonnet 73   (PUBLISHED 1609)

That time of year thou mayst in me behold
When yellow leaves, or none, or few, do hang
Upon those boughs which shake against the cold,
Bare ruin'd choirs, where late° the sweet birds sang.   *recently*
In me thou see'st the twilight of such day   5
As after sunset fadeth in the west;
Which by and by black night doth take away,
Death's second self, that seals up all in rest.
In me thou see'st the glowing of such fire,
That on the ashes of his youth doth lie,   10
As the deathbed whereon it must expire,
Consum'd with that which it was nourish'd by.
    This thou perceiv'st which makes thy love more strong,
    To love that well which thou must leave ere long.

If you look at how Shakespeare's poem divides, you can see the pattern of the images clearly demarcated. The first four lines (a group of four lines is called a **quatrain**) form a full sentence and create a single image: "you can see autumn in me" (when leaves yellow and disappear, leaving bare branches):

> That time of year thou mayst in me behold
> When yellow leaves, or none, or few, do hang
> Upon those boughs which shake against the cold,
> Bare ruin'd choirs, where late the sweet birds sang.

The second quatrain, forming another full sentence, creates a single image as well: "in me you can see twilight, just before night comes" (and night is here explicitly linked to death):

> In me thou see'st the twilight of such day
> As after sunset fadeth in the west;
> Which by and by black night doth take away,
> Death's second self, that seals up all in rest.

The third quatrain, yet another sentence, presents the image of a fire, with flames not dancing but glowing, lying on the "death-bed" of embers:

> In me thou see'st the glowing of such fire,
> That on the ashes of his youth doth lie,
> As the deathbed whereon it must expire,
> Consum'd with that which it was nourish'd by.

So Shakespeare's carefully wrought poem presents three separate, distinct images of age, all clearly marked off in single sentences: autumn, twilight, and a glowing fire. It concludes with another sentence, this one a **couplet**—two rhymed lines—commenting on what has come before:

> This thou perceiv'st which makes thy love more strong,
> To love that well which thou must leave ere long.

Here the couplet introduces no new images, since the poem does not need any. Instead, the couplet refers to the three images already presented—"this," meaning the fact of my age.

Shakespeare's sonnet illustrates how poems work with images. It presents the fact of age in three separate, sensory visual pictures: branches, sunset, and a fire's glow. Not every poet creates such clearly marked-off images as Shakespeare does in this poem. Shakespeare was writing a very conventional poem about loss and age, and such poetry called for him to work with very well-known images. Nothing could be more traditional than comparing a life to the seasons, to a day, or to a flame. The originality comes in the treatment of the traditional themes, and in the way Shakespeare manipulates the language to produce striking images of loss:

> Bare ruin'd choirs, where late the sweet birds sang.

Tree branches are brilliantly transformed into the place where songs are sung in a church, the choir loft; they have become bare, despoiled of their leaves and the birds which sang on them. It is the language of such images that matters, not the simple linking of age with autumn, sunset, and embers. We do not value Shakespeare for the perception or image that age is like sunset. We value him for the way he put it, marking it indelibly with his own poetic language. And since this is a poem, not an oath about life, we are not surprised to find that he invented a persona somewhat unlike himself, since Shakespeare was probably in his thirties when he wrote it, at the height of his powers, not some withered old man. As both an actor and a writer, Shakespeare created great roles, and he has invented one here as well.

Talking about the Text

1. Drawing on the poems in this chapter, choose an image that does not seem to work for you and try to explain why.
2. Exactly how is sunset like "Death's second self" (line 8)?

Writing about the Text

1. Describe Shakespeare's third image, the fire. First write in your own words what Shakespeare's lines 9–12 say, and then explain how the image works. (For a model, look above at the description of "Bare ruin'd choirs.")
2. Create an outline of Shakespeare's poem, being careful to indicate the main image and the subordinate images in each quatrain. (For example, "Twilight" . . . "Death's second self.") Use the traditional Roman numeral form, or create a format of your own.

Linking the Text to Other Texts

1. Compare the imagery in Shakespeare's poem with the imagery in one of the poems below, in "For Further Reading: Images and Imagery." In which poem is the imagery more vivid? Which imagery is richer? Which poem seems to stress the imagery more?
2. Choose a popular piece of poetry (perhaps a song) and trace the imagery, showing whether it is emphasized as much as the imagery in Shakespeare's sonnet.

For Further Reading: Images and Imagery

ROBERT BURNS   (1759–1796)

My Luve's like a Red, Red Rose   (C. 1788)

O, my luve's like a red, red rose
That's newly sprung in June.
O, my luve is like the melodie
That's sweetly play'd in tune.

As fair art thou, my bonnie lass,   5
So deep in luve am I;
And I will luve thee still, my Dear,
Till a' the seas gang dry.

Till a' the seas gang dry, my Dear,
And the rocks melt wi' the sun;   10
And I will luve thee still, my Dear
While the sands o' life shall run.

And fare thee weel, my only luve,
And fare thee weel a while!
And I will come again, my luve,   15
Though it were ten thousand mile.

SYLVIA PLATH   (1932–1963)
Metaphors   (1959)

I'm a riddle in nine syllables,
An elephant, a ponderous house,
A melon strolling on two tendrils.
O red fruit, ivory, fine timbers!
This loaf's big with its yeasty rising.
Money's new-minted in this fat purse.
I'm a means, a stage, a cow in calf.
I've eaten a bag of green apples,
Boarded the train there's no getting off.

WALLACE STEVENS   (1879–1955)
Thirteen Ways of Looking at a Blackbird   (1923)

I

Among twenty snowy mountains,
The only moving thing
Was the eye of the blackbird.

II

I was of three minds,
Like a tree
In which there are three blackbirds.   5

III

The blackbird whirled in the autumn winds.
It was a small part of the pantomime.

IV

A man and a woman
Are one.
A man and a woman and a blackbird
Are one.

V

I do not know which to prefer,
The beauty of inflections
Or the beauty of innuendoes,   15
The blackbird whistling
Or just after.

VI

Icicles filled the long window
With barbaric glass.

The shadow of the blackbird
Crossed it, to and fro.
The mood
Traced in the shadow
An indecipherable cause.

VII

O thin men of Haddam,°   *town in Connecticut* 25
Why do you imagine golden birds?
Do you not see how the blackbird
Walks around the feet
Of the women about you?

VIII

I know noble accents
And lucid, inescapable rhythms;
But I know, too,
That the blackbird is involved
In what I know.

IX

When the blackbird flew out of sight,
It marked the edge
Of one of many circles.

X

At the sight of blackbirds
Flying in a green light,
Even the bawds of euphony
Would cry out sharply.

XI

He rode over Connecticut
In a glass coach.
Once, a fear pierced him,
In that he mistook
The shadow of his equipage
For blackbirds.

XII

The river is moving.
The blackbird must be flying.

XIII

It was evening all afternoon.
It was snowing
And it was going to snow.
The blackbird sat
In the cedar-limbs.

20

30

35

40

45

50

ADRIENNE RICH   (B. 1929)

Diving into the Wreck   (1972)

First having read the book of myths,
and loaded the camera,
and checked the edge of the knife-blade,
I put on
the body-armor of black rubber   5
the absurd flippers
the grave and awkward mask.
I am having to do this
not like Cousteau° with his   *French diver, TV personality*
assiduous team   10
aboard the sun-flooded schooner
but here alone.

There is a ladder.
The ladder is always there
hanging innocently   15
close to the side of the schooner.
We know what it is for,
we who have used it.
Otherwise
it is a piece of maritime floss   20
some sundry equipment.

I go down.
Rung after rung and still
the oxygen immerses me
the blue light   25
the clear atoms
of our human air.
I go down.
My flippers cripple me,
I crawl like an insect down the ladder   30
and there is no one
to tell me when the ocean
will begin.

First the air is blue and then
it is bluer and then green and then   35
black I am blacking out and yet
my mask is powerful
it pumps my blood with power
the sea is another story
the sea is not a question of power   40
I have to learn alone
to turn my body without force
in the deep element.

And now: it is easy to forget
what I came for
among so many who have always   45
lived here
swaying their crenellated° fans   *notched*
between the reefs
and besides   50
you breathe differently down here.

I came to explore the wreck.
The words are purposes.
The words are maps.
I came to see the damage that was done   55
and the treasures that prevail.
I stroke the beam of my lamp
slowly along the flank
of something more permanent
than fish or weed   60

the thing I came for:
the wreck and not the story of the wreck
the thing itself and not the myth
the drowned face always staring
toward the sun   65
the evidence of damage
worn by salt and away into this threadbare beauty
the ribs of the disaster
curving their assertion
among the tentative haunters.   70

This is the place.
And I am here, the mermaid whose dark hair
streams black, the merman in his armored body.
We circle silently
about the wreck   75
we dive into the hold.
I am she: I am he

whose drowned face sleeps with open eyes
whose breasts still bear the stress
whose silver, copper, vermeil° cargo lies   *gilded metal* 80
obscurely inside barrels
half-wedged and left to rot
we are the half-destroyed instruments
that once held to a course
the water-eaten log   85
the fouled compass

We are, I am, you are
by cowardice or courage
the one who find our way

back to this scene
carrying a knife, a camera
a book of myths
in which
our names do not appear.

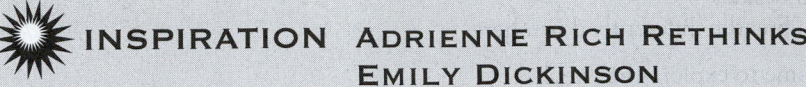

INSPIRATION ADRIENNE RICH RETHINKS EMILY DICKINSON

Adrienne Rich, c. 1974.

In her essay "Vesuvius at Home: The Power of Emily Dickinson," poet Adrienne Rich reexamines Emily Dickinson in the context of patriarchy, gender roles, and feminine artistic genius. Rich's essay, which began in 1975 as a lecture at Brandeis University, was eventually published in *Parnassus: Poetry in Review* and forced literary critics to rethink their interpretations of Dickinson and her work.

In examining her own lasting fascination with Dickinson, Rich examines many popular interpretations of Dickinson and her work and offers her own: that Dickinson was a gifted female artist fighting cultural taboos and restrictions to find space to create her work. Having visited Dickinson's home, Rich reflects on what it means that Dickinson found seclusion in her bedroom a relished freedom from nineteenth-century New England life. Instead of denigrating Dickinson as an eccentric, solitary figure, Rich suggests that Dickinson's culture literally left her no other place to create her art than the carefully guarded privacy of her own bedroom.

In her essay, Rich echoes Virginia Woolf's *A Room of One's Own* when she asks: "Suppose Jonathan Edwards [New England minister] had been born a woman; suppose William James, for that matter, had been born a woman? (The invalid seclusion of his sister Alice is suggestive.) Even from men, New England took its psychic toll; many of its geniuses seemed peculiar in one way or another, particularly along the lines of social intercourse." You can read Rich's entire essay in *On Lies, Secrets, and Silence: Selected Prose 1966–1978*, published by W. W. Norton in 1979.

Talking about the Text

1. Read either "My Luve's like a Red, Red Rose" (p. 735) or "Metaphors" (p. 736) and describe all the metaphorical language in the poem.
2. Read "Thirteen Ways of Looking at a Blackbird" (p. 736) and choose three ways of looking that you prefer. What do you like about the images in the three you picked?

Writing about the Text

1. "Thirteen Ways of Looking at a Blackbird" (p. 736) is deliberately fragmented, seeming like a series of false starts. In a brief paper, explain which parts of the poem puzzled you and which parts you enjoyed most.
2. Tell the story of your reading "Diving into the Wreck" (p. 738), paying particular attention to how the controlling metaphor operated for you as a reader. For instance, did it work from the beginning, or did it take you time to get used to it? Were you able to understand the metaphor better on rereading? Did you too become a diver? Might you find it a useful metaphor for examining your own life?

Linking the Text to Other Texts

1. Referring to "My Luve's like a Red, Red Rose" (p. 735), describe both the good and the bad things about being a rose. Then read William Blake's "The Sick Rose" (p. 1022). What does that reading do to your reading of the Burns poem?
2. Compare the ways Plath and Stevens pile up images in their poems "Metaphors" (p. 736) and "Thirteen Ways of Looking at a Blackbird" (p. 736). Do the speakers of these poems seem to be taking pleasure in their task, or does it seem like a difficult, unrewarding job? What makes you think the way you do? Apply the same questions to Ginsberg's "In a Supermarket in California" (p. 1087).

POETIC LANGUAGE

In Sonnet 73 (p. 733), Shakespeare shows how a poem's images can all be about the same subject, in his case aging, and yet seem remarkably different from each other. In the poem below, "I Like to See It Lap the Miles," Emily Dickinson presents an imaginative link between a locomotive—an Iron Horse—and its analogue, a real horse.

EMILY DICKINSON   (1830–1886)

I Like to See it Lap the Miles   (C. 1862)

I like to see it lap the Miles—
And lick the Valleys up—
And stop to feed itself at Tanks—
And then—prodigious step

Around a Pile of Mountains—   5
And supercilious peer
In Shanties—by the sides of Roads—
And then a Quarry pare

To fit its Ribs
And crawl between   10
Complaining all the while
In horrid—hooting stanza—
Then chase itself down Hill—

And neigh like Boanerges
Then—punctual as a Star
Stop—docile and omnipotent
At its own stable door—

15

Is an Iron Horse like the real animal? In a few ways—as a means of trans-portation, as something requiring a driver, as a familiar object we depend on—yes, we can all agree that it is. But Dickinson pushes the image as hard as she can, creating a controlling metaphor that lasts through the whole poem. This horse has a stable, drinks, neighs, peers, complains. It is alive, full of energy and power, on its own. There is no mention of a driver or engineer; it is as if the Iron Horse has a will of its own.

Much of the enjoyment of Dickinson's poem comes from her **poetic language**, which repays close attention. She deliberately chooses off-rhymes, words that almost sound the same but don't quite:

up/step

peer/pare

while/hill

star/door

These off-rhymes give the poem a delightfully unfancy, homespun flavor. The deliberate lack of polish to them conveys a certain amateurish quality that is def-initely Dickinson's deliberate creation, since she could rhyme perfectly when-ever she wanted. This deliberate lack of precision, we will see in Chapter 14, is characteristic of much of Dickinson's work.

Prominent also in the poetic language is Dickinson's mixture of very simple words contrasted with a small number of impressive, full-sounding words, promi-nently placed: "prodigious," "supercilious," "omnipotent," and most of all "Boan-erges," which is Greek for "sons of thunder" and also the name Jesus gave to his apostles John and James. These resonant terms, three adjectives and a noun, stand in sharp opposition to the active, short verbs that dominate the poem: "like," "lap," "lick," "stop," "feed," "step," "peer," "pare," "crawl," "chase," "neigh," and "stop." Dickinson has obviously made a deliberate choice: all those short, single-syllable, simple, active verbs.

Dickinson packs her short poem with **figures of speech** or **poetic devices**. It is of course an extended analogy or comparison between two kinds of horses. There is a variety of **personification**, which is giving an inanimate object human or animal attributes, in this case turning an Iron Horse into a live one. (Some critics reserve the term personification only for giving human attributes to an object.) The line "And neigh like Boanerges" is on the one hand a **simile**, a comparison using "like" or "as," and on the other an **allusion**, connecting the poem's action to another well-known work, in this case the Bible. The phrase "punctual as a star" is **hyperbole**, a deliberate overstatement that draws attention to itself. Finally, the phrase "docile and omnipotent" is a self-contradictory state-ment, a **paradox**, as well as a kind of **oxymoron**, which is usually defined as a jux-taposition of opposite traits.

In addition to these figures of speech, Dickinson employs some familiar techniques of **repetition** to hold her poem together. Readers might not perceive them at first reading, but discovering them adds to the pleasure some people find. One is the **alliteration**, or repetition of consonant sounds, in the first lines:

> I like to see it lap the miles
>
> And lick the valleys up

Alliteration is a common technique for adding unity to a poem by linking similar sounds. Shakespeare used alliteration in Sonnet 73:

> Bare ruin'd choirs, where late the sweet birds sang.

Another kind of repetition in Dickinson's poem involves the word "and": it appears seven times in fourteen lines. In fact, "and" begins six lines, drawing attention to itself. The word "and" does double duty. First, it clearly serves to convey the childlike delight the persona feels, since children often string together events and objects in long sentences, tied together by "and." (Linguists and critics call this loose linkage a **paratactic style**.) The repetition of "and" also suggests a kind of linearity, a list of one thing after another. The regularity of the train and its predictability stem from being bound to the tracks (unlike real horses) and doing first one action followed by another action followed by yet another, all linked temporally by the simplest, least sophisticated of connectors, "and." Interestingly, what starts out as linear in time is in fact circular in space, since the train ends up where it started—at its roundhouse, or "stable."

Do all readers notice the alliteration and the repetition of "and"? Probably not. Do these qualities help create effects in the poem, and contribute to its art? Most certainly they do. Such repetitions are part of the accomplished poet's resources. We readers may or may not notice at first, but the poetic language is there, doing its work. The more careful the reading we give, the more likely we are to note how the poet's language operates.

Here is another poem—in high poetic diction—in which the poetic language draws attention to itself.

WILLIAM BUTLER YEATS (1865–1939)

The Lake Isle of Innisfree (1890)

William Butler Yeats, c. 1914.

I will arise and go now, and go to Innisfree,
And a small cabin build there, of clay and wattles°   *branches*
    made,
Nine bean-rows will I have there, a hive for the honey-bee,
And live alone in the bee-loud glade.

And I shall have some peace there, for peace comes dropping
    slow,
Dropping from the veils of the morning to where the cricket
    sings;
There midnight's all a glimmer, and noon a purple glow,
And evening full of the linnet's° wings.   *a bird*

I will arise and go now, for always night and day
I hear lake water lapping with low sounds by the shore;
While I stand on the roadway, or on the pavements grey,
I hear it in the deep heart's core.

This poem's theme clearly has something to do with escape to a better place in the country, running from the city's "roadway" and "the pavements grey" to a magical island in an Irish lake. We should not be surprised to see Yeats using a language very different from the ordinary, day-to-day. The differences are not so much in the vocabulary as in the **syntax**, that is, the patterns into which the words are ordered. In these examples from the first quatrain, the words seem deliberately rearranged:

I will arise and go now, and go to Innisfree	*repetition of "and go"*
And a small cabin build there, of clay and wattles made	*Not "build a small cabin." / Not "made of clay and wattles"*
Nine bean-rows will I have there, a hive for the honey-bee	*Not "I will have nine bean-rows"*
And live alone in the bee-loud glade	*The phrase "bee-loud" was never used before. Yeats invented it here.*

Every one of these four lines, we see, has something out of the ordinary, if by ordinary we mean the language of normal speech, business, and daily public events. Every one of Yeats's alterations seems to draw attention to itself, to force readers to notice that the word order is new, different, more "poetic." In a famous recording you can hear Yeats declare that he will not read this poem in a normal voice because he worked very hard to get it to sound like a poem, not ordinary speech. Unlike many others (for example, Linda Pastan, p. 725), Yeats, in this poem at least, aligns himself with an older tradition, deliberately choosing to sound like a kind of bard, who was an ancient poet gifted with inspiration and fire, happy with the high poetic diction.

The impression of poetic language is created in part by the sound of Yeats's vowels. Alliteration, we saw, was the repetition of consonant sounds, particularly at the beginning of words. Repetition of vowel sounds, a kind of parallel to alliteration, is called **assonance**. Here it is:

I will ar*i*se and g*o* n*o*w, and g*o* to Inn*i*sfree

Both the *i* sound and the *o* sound are repeated in this line, conveying a feeling of great care to knit the sounds together. (Note that the *i* of "will" is not part of the assonance, because though it is the same letter, it has a different sound. It is a short *i*, not the long *i* of "I" and "arise.")

Here is another example:

I hear l*a*ke w*a*ter lapping with low sounds by the shore;

Can you hear the assonance? Did you notice it when you read the line? Perhaps not, but the assonance helps contribute to the overall effect. Poets care deeply about the sounds their words make, and someone like Yeats invites us to luxuriate in the way his vowels are carefully arrayed for reading aloud.

County Sligo, where Yeats set many of his poems, is located in northwestern Ireland.

Yeats and the Landscape in Sligo, Ireland. Yeats said he got the idea for "The Lake Isle of Innisfree" while standing in London's Leicester Square, looking at a display advertisement for tonic water. The neon sign may have depicted the water, but he was thinking of a real place far away: the actual island of Innisfree located in County Sligo in northwestern Ireland. Although his homage to Innisfree is perhaps Yeats's best-known tribute to the Irish landscape, Yeats regularly used actual places in and around Sligo as a source of inspiration for his poems throughout his writing career, which spanned more than a half-century. The hills of Glen-Car are featured in "The Stolen Child" (1889). "Red Hanrahan's Song about Ireland" (1904) makes reference to the town of Knocknarea. "In Memory of Eva Gore-Booth and Con Markiewicz" (1933) is set against the backdrop of Lissadell. "Under Ben Bulben" (1938–1939) centers on the mountain of the same name in County Sligo—and the Drumcliff churchyard, where the poem says "Yeats is laid," is in Drumcliff village, on the slopes of that mountain, where Yeats himself was actually buried, as he had wished.

Talking about the Text

1. List the unusual words or word order in the second and third stanzas of "The Lake Isle of Innisfree" and show what the "expected" word order would be (as done for stanza one, above).
2. Find examples of alliteration in the "The Lake Isle of Innisfree" and examples of assonance in Dickinson's "I Like to See it Lap the Miles" (p. 741).

Writing about the Text

1. Yeats said he was inspired to write "The Lake Isle of Innisfree" (p. 743) while standing in the midst of London. Write an essay describing the Lake Isle as an anti-London or an anti-Modern-City poem. What is there about the place and the poet's desires that contrasts with the unspoken demands of city life?

2. Write about "The Lake Isle of Innisfree" as gesture and dream rather than actual determination to build a Thoreau-like small cabin. What about this poem suggests that it is about desire and hope rather than firm resolve to plant bean-rows and live among the bees? (Yeats never did build that cabin, though later he did buy a medieval tower in the town of Gort, in the west of Ireland.)

Linking the Text to Other Texts

1. Listen to a reading of "I Like to See it Lap the Miles" (p. 741) and tell whether or not it was what you expected. Why or why not? How does the reading emphasize Dickinson's particular choice of imagery? Should it do so even more? Why or why not?

2. Consider "The Lake Isle of Innisfree" and "I Like to See it Lap the Miles" as "escape from reality" poems. What do these very different poems have in common in their attitudes toward everyday, modern life?

 INSPIRATION Yeats and U2's Bono

Lead singer Bono and guitarist The Edge, from the rock band U2.

Music critics often compare U2's frontman, singer-songwriter Bono, to the poet William Butler Yeats. The roots of the comparison go beyond their common Irish heritage, however. They extend into religious faith as well as artistic style. Yeats grew up Protestant in a predominantly Catholic country, and his family had ties to both England and Ireland; similarly, Bono (whose given name is Paul Hewson) grew up with a Catholic father and a Protestant mother, and while faith had a huge impact on him, he avoided becoming attached to a particular denomination. Yeats and Bono also share huge popularity as well as a moody, lush poetic sensibility (which critics of both have called overhyped), but the popularity of each also endures because their respective bodies of work ultimately earn the acclaim. Yeats, who won the Nobel Prize for literature in 1923, is regarded by many readers, critics, and scholars as the greatest poet of the twentieth century, the proverbial literary "rock star" of his day. It's a testament to Yeats's success that even today, when pop music's popularity has superseded that of more traditional written poetic forms, Bono has been hailed by many as the Yeats of our time.

That moniker runs more than skin deep. Like many other musicians—Elvis Costello, Sinead O'Connor, Joni Mitchell, Van Morrison, the Cranberries, and the Waterboys, to name a few—over the course of a thriving, award-studded rock 'n' roll career now spanning more than two decades, Bono has dipped in and out of Yeats as a source of inspiration, directly and indirectly. In talking about the process of songwriting during interviews and how he and his U2 bandmates have been able to keep doing it after so many years, Bono has repeated the following anecdote:

> I remember as a child, growing up in Ireland, we were taught the poetry of William Butler Yeats. I must have been ten years old. The teacher said, "and then Yeats went through his dry period. He had a writing block and he couldn't write about anything." I remember putting up my hand, and saying, "Well, why didn't he write about that?" And the teacher just looked at me and said, "Oh, be quiet." But that is exactly the answer to the writing block. You write about your own emptiness, and we've done that for years now.

Clearly Bono has also turned to Yeats himself to keep the words and lyrics coming. He has incorporated Yeats's poetry in live performances on numerous occasions—most frequently Yeats's "September 1913" and "He Wishes for the Cloths of Heaven"—sometimes folding in a few lines, sometimes reciting poems in their entirety. The poetry has also served as the springboard for U2 song lyrics as well. For example, the song "Mofo" from U2's 1997 album *Pop*, lifts lyrics from two significant lines of Yeats's "Before the World Was Made": "I'm looking for the face I had / Before the world was made." The Yeats poem, written as part of a cycle of poems called "A Woman Young and Old," appears in its entirety below. (You may wish to compare the use of these lines in the poem to their use in the U2 song, with particular attention to how diction and context function in each. The full lyrics to the U2 song can be found on their official website at *http://www.u2.com*.)

William Butler Yeats   (1865–1939)

Before the World Was Made   (1933)

If I make the lashes dark
And the eyes more bright
And the lips more scarlet,
Or ask if all be right
From mirror after mirror,   5
No vanity's displayed:
I'm looking for the face I had
Before the world was made.

What if I look upon a man
As though on my beloved,   10
And my blood be cold the while
And my heart unmoved?
Why should he think me cruel
Or that he is betrayed?
I'd have him love the thing that was   15
Before the world was made.

ᑯᑭ COMMENTARY

Louise Glück on Poetic Language

The brief excerpt below comes from Louise Glück's essay "Education of the Poet" in her book Proofs and Theories: Essays on Poetry *(New York: Ecco, 1994), 4–5. Copyright 1994 by Louise Glück.*

On Simple Language in Poetry

The axiom is that the mark of poetic intelligence or vocation is passion for language, which is thought to mean delirious response to language's smallest communicative unit: to the word. The poet is supposed to be the person who can't get enough of words like "incarnadine." This was not my experience. From the time, at four or five or six, I first started reading poems, first thought of the poets I read as my companions, my predecessors—from the beginning I preferred the simplest vocabulary. What fascinated me were the possibilities of context. What I responded to, on the page, was the way a poem could liberate, by means of a word's setting, through subtleties of timing, of pacing, that word's full and surprising range of meaning. It seemed to me that simple language best suited this enterprise; such language, in being generic, is likely to contain the greatest and most dramatic variety of meaning within individual words. I liked scale, but I liked it invisible. I loved those poems that seemed so small on the page but that swelled in the mind; I didn't like the windy, dwindling kind. Not surprisingly, the sort of sentence I was drawn to, which reflected these tastes and native habit of mind, was paradox, which has the added advantage of nicely rescuing the dogmatic nature from a too moralizing rhetoric.

For Further Reading: Poetic Language

FRANK O'HARA   (1926–1966)

The Day Lady Died[1]

July 17, 1959

It is 12:20 in New York a Friday
three days after Bastille day,° yes   *July 14*
it is 1959 and I go get a shoeshine
because I will get off the 4:19 in Easthampton°   *Long Island resort town*
at 7:15 and then go straight to dinner   5
and I don't know the people who will feed me

I walk up the muggy street beginning to sun
and have a hamburger and a malted and buy

---

[1] Jazz singer Billie Holiday (1915–1959) was called "Lady Day."

an ugly NEW WORLD WRITING° to see what the poets   *literary journal*
in Ghana are doing these days   10
        I go on to the bank
and Miss Stillwagon (first name Linda I once heard)
doesn't even look up my balance for once in her life
and in the GOLDEN GRIFFIN° I get a little Verlaine°   *bookstore/19th-cen. French poet*
for Patsy with drawings by Bonnard° although I do   *early 20th-cen. French artist*   15
think of Hesiod, ° trans. Richard Lattimore or   *ancient Greek poet*
Brendan Behan's° new play or *Le Balcon* or *Les Nègres*   *Irish playwright*
of Genet, but I don't, I stick with Verlaine
after practically going to sleep with quandariness

and for Mike I just stroll into the PARK LANE   20
Liquor Store and ask for a bottle of Strega° and   *Italian liqueur*
then I go back where I came from to 6th Avenue
and the tobacconist in the Ziegfeld Theatre° and   *NYC movie theater*
casually ask for a carton of Gauloises° and a carton   *French cigarettes*
of Picayunes, ° and a NEW YORK POST with her face on it   *American cigarettes*   25

and I am sweating a lot by now and thinking of
leaning on the john door in the 5 SPOT°   *NYC jazz club*
while she whispered a song along the keyboard
to Mal Waldron° and everyone and I stopped breathing.   *her last accompanist*

AUDIO LOCALE

Carl Van Vechten's 1949 portrait of singer Billie Holiday, who was also known as "Lady Day."

Lady Sings the Blues. Billie Holiday's last album recording, *Lady in Satin* (Columbia, 1958), captures the whispery quality of her voice that Frank O'Hara refers to in line 28 of his poem "The Day Lady Died." The album, which was a stalwart in the Columbia catalog, is still available on LP at stores specializing in vinyl LPs, jazz, or both; it also is available on CD, restored and remastered. *The Genius of Lady Day* (Efor Films, 2004), a documentary offering several performances not available elsewhere, includes a clip of Holiday singing "Travelin' Light" with her last accompanist Mal (Malcolm) Waldron on piano. Another documentary, *Lady Day: The Many Faces of Billie Holiday* (Kultur Video, 1991), includes TV and film performances as well as interviews with the musicians who played with her.

THOMAS GRAY   (1716–1771)

Ode on the Death of a Favorite Cat,
Drowned in a Tub of Gold Fishes   (1748)

'Twas on a lofty vase's side,
Where China's gayest art had dyed
   The azure flowers, that blow; °   *bloom*
Demurest of the tabby kind,
The pensive Selima° reclined,   *his friend's cat*   5
   Gazed on the lake below.

Her conscious tail her joy declared;
The fair round face, the snowy beard,
   The velvet of her paws,
Her coat, that with the tortoise vies,   10
Her ears of jet, and emerald eyes,
   She saw; and purred applause.

Still had she gazed; but 'midst the tide
Two angel forms were seen to glide,
   The genii° of the stream: *guardian spirits*   15
Their scaly armor's Tyrian hue°   *purple*
Through richest purple to the view
   Betrayed a golden gleam.

The hapless nymph with wonder saw:
A whisker first and then a claw,   20
   With many an ardent wish,
She stretched in vain to reach the prize.
What female heart can gold despise?
   What cat's averse to fish?

Presumptuous maid! with looks intent   25
Again she stretched, again she bent,
   Nor knew the gulf between.
(Malignant Fate sat by and smiled)
The slippery verge° her feet beguiled,   *edge*
   She tumbled headlong in.   30

Eight times emerging from the flood
She mewed to every watery God,
   Some speedy aid to send.
No dolphin came, no Nereid° stirred: *sea nymph*
Nor cruel Tom, ° nor Susan° heard.   *names of servants*   35
   A favorite has no friend!

From hence, ye beauties, undeceived,
Know, one false step is ne'er retrieved,
   And be with caution bold.
Not all that tempts your wandering eyes   40
And heedless hearts is lawful prize;
   Nor all that glisters gold.

PHILLIS WHEATLEY (1753–1784)

On Being Brought from Africa to America (1773)

'Twas mercy brought me from my Pagan land,
Taught my benighted° soul to understand   *in spiritual darkness*
That there's a God, that there's a Saviour too:
Once I redemption neither sought nor knew.
Some view our sable° race with scornful eye,   *black*   5
"Their colour is a diabolic die°."   *dye*
Remember, Christians, Negroes, black as Cain,
May be refin'd, and join th' angelic train.

HENRY WADSWORTH LONGFELLOW (1807–1882)

Snow-Flakes (1852)

Out of the bosom of the Air,
    Out of the cloud-folds of her garments shaken,
Over the woodlands brown and bare,
    Over the harvest-fields forsaken,
        Silent, and soft, and slow   5
        Descends the snow.

Even as our cloudy fancies take
    Suddenly shape in some divine expression,
Even as the troubled heart doth make
    In the white countenance confession,   10
        The troubled sky reveals
        The grief it feels.

This is the poem of the air,
    Slowly in silent syllables recorded;
    This is the secret of despair,   15
    Long in its cloudy bosom hoarded,
        Now whispered and revealed
        To wood and field.

JIMMY SANTIAGO BACA (B. 1952)

Green Chile (1989)

I prefer red chile over my eggs
and potatoes for breakfast.
Red chile *ristras*° decorate my door,   *strings*
dry on my roof, and hang from eaves.
They lend open-air vegetable stands
historical grandeur, and gently swing   5

with an air of festive welcome.
I can hear them talking in the wind,
haggard, yellowing, crisp, rasping
tongues of old men, licking the breeze.   10

    But grandmother loves green chile.
When I visit her,
she holds the green chile pepper
in her wrinkled hands.
Ah, voluptuous, masculine,   15
an air of authority and youth simmers
from its swan-neck stem, tapering to a flowery
collar, fermenting resinous spice.
A well-dressed gentleman at the door
my grandmother takes sensuously in her hand,   20
rubbing its firm glossed sides,
caressing the oily rubbery serpent,
with mouth-watering fulfillment,
fondling its curves with gentle fingers.
Its bearing magnificent and taut   25
as flanks of a tiger in mid-leap,
she thrusts her blade into
and cuts it open, with lust
on her hot mouth, sweating over the stove,
bandanna round her forehead,   30
mysterious passion on her face
as she serves me green chile con carne
between soft warm leaves of corn tortillas,
with beans and rice—her sacrifice
to her little prince.   35
I slurp from my plate
with last bit of tortilla, my mouth burns
and I hiss and drink a tall glass of cold water.

All over New Mexico, sunburned men and women
drive rickety trucks stuffed with gunny sacks   40
of green chile, from Belen, Veguita, Willard, Estancia,
San Antonio y Socorro, from fields
to roadside stands, you see them roasting green chile
in screen-sided homemade barrels, and for a dollar a bag,
we relive this old, beautiful ritual again and again.   45

Talking about the Text

1. Choose three of the poems in "For Further Reading: Poetic Language" and describe their poetic language, paying particular attention to figures of speech.
2. In a group, choose your favorite line in "Green Chile" and compare it with the ones others in the group pick. Or discuss which lines you expect to be group favorites.

Writing about the Text

1. Write about the poetic language in "On Being Brought from Africa to America" (p. 751) *or* "Snow-Flakes" (p. 751), concentrating on how the poets depart from "normal" wording and syntax.

2. In prose or poetry, write your own account of a lunch break, imitating O'Hara's "The Day Lady Died" (p. 748). O'Hara loves his details, so include plenty of your own.

Linking the Text to Other Texts

1. Choose one poem in the "Poetic Language" section that uses deliberately "poetic" words and contrast those words with the deliberately "unpoetic" language of Linda Pastan's "Marks" (p. 725).

2. Compare the language of "Ode on the Death of a Favorite Cat, Drowned in a Tub of Gold Fishes" (p. 750) or "The Day Lady Died" with the language of a more conventional elegy: Ben Jonson's "On My First Son" (p. 777) or Thomas Gray's "Sonnet on the Death of Richard West" (p. 778).

STRUGGLES OVER POETIC LANGUAGE

The question of poetic language has caused countless critical debates over the past centuries. Should poetry have a separate, unique language of its own, or should poetry be regarded as akin to all the other uses of language, with just a relatively small number of specialized, "poetic" words? Aristotle and many ancient critics all claimed that poetry ought to have a language of its own, noble, elevated, and somewhat remote from everyday speech. Poets of the twentieth century obviously disagreed. The question has been answered in the affirmative and the negative many, many times.

One classic site of the argument over poetic language is the "Preface" William Wordsworth wrote to the 1800 edition of his poetry collection *The Lyrical Ballads*, attacking his predecessors—particularly the poets of the 1700s—for using artificial diction rather than the real language of the people. Among other complaints, Wordsworth argued that poetry had to employ a common, ordinary diction and vocabulary, not the specialized, overly refined language of the upper classes and the highly literary types. For example, he attacked George Crabbe's term for fish: "finny tribe" (in Crabbe's poem "The Village") as well as Thomas Gray's "Sonnet on the Death of Richard West" (p. 778), which does indeed use artificial diction and abstractions rather than the down-to-earth language of prose.

We can see the reforming impulse behind Wordsworth's attack on what he didn't approve of, and his support of what he did:

18th-century poetry	Romantic (Wordsworth)
"precious"	common, ordinary
citified or "improved" nature	country, real nature
aristocratic	democratic
closed off	open

This opposition was a constant battle among poets. Sixty years after Wordsworth, Walt Whitman in America conducted a very similar attack on the poetic icons of his own time:

Mid-19th-century poetry	Walt Whitman
"precious"	common
learned	ordinary
elevated	democratic

We see the same attack from the Beat generation poets like Allen Ginsberg and his followers in the 1950s and 1960s:

Mid-20th-century poetry	Allen Ginsberg and the Beat poets
learned	angry
exclusive	open
foreign words	American
secular	religious (Eastern)

Over and over, an establishment comes in conflict with a young member of a new generation who attempts to return poetry and poetic language to their roots, to the elemental foundations. This struggle has continued until the present with African American and Latino poets, who want their own linguistic origins validated. Another example is the way in which women, beginning in the 1950s, started to mark out a territory of their own, with their own history and customs, rather than be forced into an arena controlled by male poets. Thus in the late 1950s, poets Adrienne Rich, Sylvia Plath, and Anne Sexton began to insist on their own kind of diction, language, and poetic concerns, including family and romantic relationships and the emergence of a specifically female self and sensibility in a world dominated by male social and artistic standards. These women poets succeeded spectacularly, sometimes at great personal cost, in creating a distinctive voice and register. Did they create a completely separate poetic language of their own? Perhaps, or perhaps not. It is a fact that language, the very tool poets use, is a constant battleground fought over by representatives from different traditions.

CHAPTER
11

Poems
Meter, Stanza, Form

When poets speak of how they write, they frequently emphasize both "art" and "form." In fact, the two are hard to separate, since the thoughts and feelings and experiences in a poem can only take on the particular shapes and forms available for the poet to use. This chapter concentrates on three major **formal** elements of poems, moving from smaller to larger:

meter: the rhythmic pattern; how many beats are in each line

stanza: the ways the lines link together, often through rhyming patterns

form: the traditional shape or format the poet employs (e.g., sonnet, ode)

All of these three formal elements have operated in traditional poetry, including just about all poetry written before about 1860, and in much poetry thereafter. They are still very prominent today, though they do not dominate as they once did. The poetic revolution that broke away from traditional forms brought about **free verse** (see below), which did away with strict rules that had traditionally governed rhythm and rhyme.

Some people believe that all poetry should rhyme, and they won't accept any substitutions. They want none of this "modern" unrhymed verse. These readers—a minority, to be sure—reflect a deep, commonly held belief that poems must have patterns; they must display their verbal artistry and must have a visible or audible shape. And historically, these readers are right: almost all

755

Western poetry—until about 1860—has displayed its pattern outwardly, for all to see.

The patterns that we discern in traditional poems were developed by generations of poets over many years, writers who always concerned themselves both with the emotions they could put into words as well as the way those words would sound to the ear or appear on the page. Poets—yesterday and today—have spent a great deal of time and energy on their lines, on their words, on their syllables. Getting the words "right" has always been a major part of a poet's art, and of course it becomes part of our own act of interpretation. Every reader understands that if all we had were poets' emotions, there would be no art, and if all we had were poets' patterns, there would just be emptiness. Only when the poet fashions the emotions into the right pattern does genuine art emerge. And until recently, most poets concerned themselves greatly with the elements that marked all poetry: meter, stanza, and form. They still do, though with much less emphasis on rules or on clearly discernable patterns handed down by tradition.

METER

The patterns that are typically found in Western poetry have not always included rhyme. Latin and Greek poetry, for instance, employed an intricate pattern of long and short syllables, and in their classic eras their poems had no rhyme whatsoever. Old English poetry, the kind employed in the early epic *Beowulf*, written around 700, was **alliterative verse**; it did not rhyme, but it had a very clear pattern: a regular series of strong beats per line, and plenty of alliteration—the repetition of a sound to begin each word.

Below is some alliterative verse by William Langland from the Prologue of his best-known work, *Piers Plowman*, written about 1380. Accent marks have been added to indicate which syllables get the beat, or stress. One system of marking poetic meter shows just the stress. Another system marks every syllable, using a short curved or straight horizontal line above an unstressed syllable and a slanting vertical line above a stressed syllable.

> In a sómer sésun   whon sófte was the sónne
> I schóp me into a schroud   a schéep as I wére.

Here are the same lines in modern English:

> In summer season   when soft was the sun
> I dressed me in wool   as if I were a sheep.

Though a few poets have revived this kind of historical alliterative verse from time to time, most English verse from about 1400 until the twentieth century makes use of a more familiar **meter**, which is a regular pattern of stressed and unstressed syllables distributed in a recognizable manner. To see an example of how patterns operate, try saying aloud these familiar lines from John Newton's famous hymn "Amazing Grace" to see where the beat or stress falls:

Amazing grace, how sweet the sound
That saved a wretch like me
I once was lost, but now am found
Was blind, but now I see

—*John Newton (1725–1807), c. 1765*

Hear the pattern? There's the rhyme, of course:

sound	*a*
me	*b*
found	*a*
see	*b*

But there is also a rhythm. Can you hear the beat? Here the beats or stresses are marked:

Ă má | zǐng grace, | hŏw sweét | thĕ sound
Thăt saved | ă wretch | lǐke me
Ĭ once | wăs lost, | bŭt now | ăm found
Wăs blind, | bŭt now | Ĭ see.

In this case the beats or stresses are quite regular. Every other syllable gets the stress, in the same pattern throughout, unstressed, stressed, with four beats in one line and three beats in the next line. This process of going through every line and marking the stressed and unstressed syllables is called **scansion**; the verb is to **scan**.

Iamb

The pattern of unstressed, stressed is called an **iamb**; it is by far the most common in English poetry. The word "Vermont" is an iamb:

Vĕr mónt, with the emphasis on *mont*

Here are iambs in some familiar lines of poetry:

Whŏse woóds | thĕse aré | Ĭ thínk | Ĭ know.
Hĭs house | ĭs in | thĕ vill | ăge though;

—*Robert Frost, from "Stopping by Woods on a Snowy Evening"*

Thĕ paths | ŏf glo | rў lead | bŭt to | thĕ grave.

—*Thomas Gray, from "Elegy Written in a Country Churchyard"*

Sŏ long | ăs men | căn breathe, | ŏr eyes | căn see
Sŏ long | lives this, | ănd this | gives life | tŏ thee.

—*William Shakespeare, from Sonnet 18*
("*Shall I compare thee to a summer's day?*")

In all these examples, the only pattern is unstressed, stressed (often represented as ˘ ′), so we call these lines **iambic**, since they are made of iambs. But sometimes not everything fits so neatly:

I wán | dĕr through | eăch chár | tĕr'd strĕét   *iambic: eight syllables, all* ˘ ´
Whĕréin | thĕ chár | tĕr'd Thámes | dŏth flów   *iambic: eight syllables, all* ˘ ´
Ănd márk | ĭn év | erў fáce | Ĭ méet   *iambic: eight syllables, all* ˘ ´
Márks | ŏf wéak | nĕss, márks | ŏf wóe.   *iambic: seven syllables, most* ˘ ´
—*William Blake, from "London"*

Notice two things about that last line:

- The iambic pattern that characterizes the first three lines is intentionally varied in the fourth line. Starting instead with a stressed word, "Marks," the fourth line breaks the overall pattern, placing emphasis on the initial syllable. The overall pattern is what makes it work; by setting up a highly regular iambic pattern, the poet creates extra emphasis when he breaks out of it.

- A syllable is missing. The last line has seven syllables instead of the expected eight. Most of the time, as with this example, the overall pattern will be fairly clear, and when variations such as this occur, they will not change the overall dominance of a single pattern. Even with seven syllables, the last line may not be totally iambic, but of course the predominant pattern remains iambic.

Trochee

Iambic is by far the most common metrical pattern; the second most common is the **trochee**, which is the opposite of an iamb. The trochee has two syllables, but they are stressed, unstressed: ´ ˘. The words "Texas" and "Utah" are trochees. When trochees dominate, we call the pattern **trochaic**:

Týger! | Týger! | búrnĭng | bríght,   *trochaic: seven syllables* ´ ˘, ´ ˘, ´ ˘, ´
Ĭn thĕ | fórests | ŏf thĕ | níght,   *trochaic: seven syllables* ´ ˘, ´ ˘, ˘ ˘, ´
Whăt ĭm | mórtăl | hánd ŏr | éye   *trochaic: seven syllables* ´ ˘, ´ ˘, ´ ˘, ´
Cŏuld fráme | thy féar | fŭl sým | métry?   *iambic: eight syllables* ˘ ´, ˘ ´, ˘ ´, ˘ ´
—*William Blake, from "The Tyger"*

Note that in the first three lines, Blake has left out a syllable. And since trochees dominate in the whole stanza (despite that final iambic line), we say "The Tyger" is basically trochaic. We determine meter by the poem's overall tendency, not just by a single line. If we exclude the free verse that became popular with Walt Whitman starting about 1860, about 85 percent of the major poems in English are iambic. Perhaps another 12 percent are trochaic. The rest—about 3 percent—fall into two other patterns, **anapestic** and **dactylic**, discussed below.

Anapest

An **anapest** is two unstressed syllables followed by a stressed syllable, ˘ ˘ ´, as in the words "Tennessee" or "Illinois." Francis Scott Key's "The Star-Spangled Banner" provides an example of an **anapestic** meter:

Ŏ Ŏ Sáy | căn yŏu séé | bў thĕ dáwn's | eăr·lў líght
Whăt sŏ próud | lў wĕ háiled | ăt thĕ twí | lĭght's lăst gléa | mĭng
Whŏse brŏad strípes | ănd bríght stárs | thrŏugh thĕ pér | ĭ lóus fíght
Ŏ'er thĕ rám | părts wĕ wátch'd | wĕre sŏ gál | lănt lў stréa | mĭng

The meter is clearly anapestic, with an extra syllable on the ends of the second and fourth lines. Here is an anapestic line from Samuel Taylor Coleridge's "Metrical Feet" describing how anapests sound:

With a leap | and a bound | the swift a | na pests throng

Dactyl

The **dactyl** is a stressed syllable followed by two unstressed syllables, ′ ˘ ˘, as in "Michigan" or "Arkansas" or "Oregon." Dactyls are uncommon in modern poetry in English, though they were used extensively by the Greeks and Romans. Henry Wadsworth Longfellow used dactyls in his long poem "Evangeline":

This is the for est pri me val. The mur mur ing pines and the hem locks,
Beard ed with moss, and in gar ments green, in dis tinct in the twi light,
Stand like Dru ids of eld, with voi ces sad and pro phe tic,
Stand like harp ers hoar, with beards that rest on their bo soms.

The overall effect created by the dactyls is to emphasize the first syllable of the first word of every line. Dactyls are more common today in nonsense or comic poems, where the regular singsong effect works to intensify the fun:

Higgledy piggledy
Benjamin Harrison
Twenty-third President
Was and as such
Served between Clevelands
And save for this trivial
Idiosyncrasy
Didn't do much.

—*John Hollander (b. 1929), "Historical Reflections"*

Note that the rules of this particular comic poem—rules that Hollander helped invent when he perhaps had too much time on his hands—require a double dactylic name in the second line, "Benjamin Harrison," and a double dactylic word in the seventh line, "idiosyncrasy." Other double dactylic names used by Hollander and his friend Anthony Hecht—both among the most eminent of American poets—in their 1966 collection *Jiggery-Pokery: A Compendium of Double Dactyls* include "Hans Christian Anderson" and "Jupiter Pluvius"; among the double dactylic words are "characteristically" and "tatterdemalion." Can you think of some double dactyl words?

Spondee

The **spondee** has two stressed syllables, ′ ′, as in "New York." Hardly any poems are totally **spondaic**, but some well-known poems have notably spondaic passages, as in Dylan Thomas's lines from "Do Not Go Gentle into That Good Night":

Do not | go gen | tle in | to that | good night
Rage, rage | a gainst | the dy | ing of | the light.

Feet

We call iambs, trochees, anapests, dactyls, and spondees **metrical feet**. Each iamb or trochee or anapest or dactyl or spondee is one foot, and each line of a poem divides itself into a certain number of feet. We name the poem's meter after what type of foot dominates *and* how many feet are in the line. There are only a few, well-known possibilities for how many feet one can have:

Dimeter (Dím e ter)	2 feet	two iambs, trochees, anapests, or dactyls
Trimeter (Trím e ter)	3 feet	three iambs, trochees, anapests, or dactyls
Tetrameter (Te trám e ter)	4 feet	four iambs, trochees, anapests, or dactyls
Pentameter (Pen tám e ter)	5 feet	five iambs, trochees, anapests, or dactyls
Hexameter (Hex ám e ter)	6 feet	six iambs, trochees, anapests, or dactyls

There are more possibilities, but these are by far the most common. Many poems in Greek and Latin were in hexameter—Homer's *Iliad* and *Odyssey* and Virgil's *Aeneid*, for instance—but hexameters are quite rare in modern English. And since Homer employed dactyls as the primary foot, his poems are in dactylic hexameter. Many traditional English poems use iambs and have a five-beat line, thus they are in iambic pentameter. The beginning of "The Star-Spangled Banner" is anapestic tetrameter.

Blank Verse

Rhyme and meter are by no means the only way lines can be held together. In plays and certain dramatic poems with long speeches, writers have frequently chosen to use unrhymed iambic pentameter, called **blank verse**, to create some of the most memorable poetry in English. Here is a familiar blank verse soliloquy, "Tomorrow, and Tomorrow, and Tomorrow," from Act V, scene 5, of William Shakespeare's play *Macbeth* (1605):

> Tomorrow, and tomorrow, and tomorrow,
> Creeps in this petty pace from day to day,
> To the last syllable of recorded time;
> And all our yesterdays have lighted fools
> The way to dusty death. Out, out, brief candle!
> Life's but a walking shadow, a poor player
> That struts and frets his hour upon the stage,
> And then is heard no more: it is a tale
> Told by an idiot, full of sound and fury,
> Signifying nothing.

In this splendid example of Shakespearean blank verse, careful readers will note that some lines have more syllables than others. Shakespeare was known for adding a single syllable to certain of his lines, keeping the general pattern of iambic pentameter, but deviating from it slightly in some circumstances. Can you see any logic to which lines get the extra syllable as Macbeth, facing death from his enemies, gives in to despair and gloom?

Here is a famous blank verse description of the evil angel, Satan, from Book 2 of John Milton's *Paradise Lost* (1667):

> High on a Throne of Royal State, which far
> Outshone the wealth of Ormus and of Ind,
> Or where the gorgeous East with richest hand
> Show'rs on her Kings Barbaric pearl and gold,
> Satan exalted sat, by merit rais'd
> To that bad eminence; and from despair
> Thus high uplifted beyond hope, aspires
> Beyond thus high, insatiate to pursue
> Vain War with Heav'n, and by success untaught
> His proud imaginations thus displaid.

And here from Book 9 of *Paradise Lost* is how Milton describes the way Eve first responds to Satan's temptation, after the serpent suggests she should eat the apple:

> To whom thus Eve, yet sinless: "Of the fruit
> Of each tree in the garden we may eat;
> But of the fruit of this fair tree, amidst
> The garden, God hath said, 'Ye shall not eat
> Thereof, nor shall ye touch it, lest ye die.' "

Blank verse dominated in Shakespeare's drama and Milton's epic, but it also has enchanted more recent poets. Here is a sample of Elizabeth Barrett Browning's *Aurora Leigh* (Book 9, 1856), a popular, highly romantic novel in blank verse:

> But oh, the night! oh, bitter-sweet! oh, sweet!
> O dark, O moon and stars, O ecstasy
> Of darkness! O great mystery of love,
> In which absorbed, loss, anguish, treason's self
> Enlarges rapture—as a pebble dropt
> In some full wine-cup, over-brims the wine!

Talking about the Text

1. Browse through "For Further Reading: Meter" (pp. 762–764) and find three examples of spondees and three trochees. Then find three examples where the scansion is puzzling or difficult to carry out.
2. What are the problems in determining the correct meter of a poem? What might be some satisfactions? Give some examples from the poems in "For Further Reading: Meter."

Writing about the Text

1. Write a brief response paper to one of the Shakespeare sonnets (pp. 775–776), concentrating on how simple or complex it was to apply your knowledge of metrics to it.
2. Describe the metrics of one of the poems in "For Further Reading: Meter" (pp. 762–764).

Linking the Text to Other Texts

1. Determine the meter of Percy Bysshe Shelley's "Ozymandias" (p. 1033) or Thomas Hardy's "During Wind and Rain" (p. 792).
2. Here is the Irish poet Eamon Grennon speaking of his own poetry's links to blank verse:

> What I love about blank verse, Milton's and Frost's in particular, and Wordsworth's and Coleridge's in particular, is the kind of supple way it orchestrates the sentence, the way the lines move down a page into a sentence. I really worked hard at that; that was one of the technical things I was very interested in, orchestrating a sentence across the line and down the page. I think of the sentence and the line—you probably do yourself—in this way: the sentence is the purveyor of meaning and the line is the purveyor of pleasure, and you move between pleasure and meaning, the forward movement of the sentence towards meaning and the retarding movement of the line towards pleasure, towards music. So it's very sexual, too.

With Grennon's ideas in mind, trace the interplay between the sentence and line in the first fifteen lines of Matthew Arnold's "Dover Beach" (p. 1049) or Alfred Lord Tennyson's "Ulysses" (p. 999)

For Further Reading: Meter

Robert Frost, between 1910 and 1920.

ROBERT FROST   (1874–1963)

Stopping by Woods on a Snowy Evening   (1923)

Whose woods these are I think I know.
His house is in the village, though;
He will not see me stopping here
To watch his woods fill up with snow.

My little horse must think it queer   5
To stop without a farmhouse near
Between the woods and frozen lake
The darkest evening of the year.

He gives his harness bells a shake
To ask if there is some mistake.   10
The only other sound's the sweep
Of easy wind and downy flake.

The woods are lovely, dark, and deep,
But I have promises to keep,
And miles to go before I sleep,   15
And miles to go before I sleep.

LITERARY LOCALE

Rusty mailbox of Robert Frost's home in Franconia, New Hampshire.

The Robert Frost Place, Franconia, New Hampshire. When Robert Frost was forced to return to the United States from England in 1915 as Europe moved into World War I, he settled in Franconia, New Hampshire, in the White Mountains. During his years in Franconia, Frost saw his reputation grow from the publication of *North of Boston* (1915), *A Boy's Will* (1916), and *Mountain Interval* (1916). Frost lived on the Franconia farm year-round until 1920, when he accepted a position at Amherst College in Massachusetts.

After his death, Frost's 1859 mountain farmhouse was purchased by the town of Franconia and became the center of a nonprofit organization, the Frost Place, which offers fellowships to contemporary poets, educates young writers, and preserves the nearly 150-year-old farm. The farm is now on the National Register of Historic Places and is home every summer to a resident poet. Because the woods and trails around the Frost homestead strongly influenced his poetry, visitors can walk along a half-mile poetry nature trail where Frost's poems act as guideposts, some in the very place where he is said to have written them.

BEN JONSON

(1572–1637)

Song: To Celia

(1616)

Drink to me only with thine eyes,
    And I will pledge with mine;
Or leave a kiss but in the cup,
    And I'll not ask for wine.

The thirst that from the soul doth rise   5
    Doth ask a drink divine;
But might I of Jove's nectar sup,
    I would not change for thine.

I sent thee late a rosy wreath,
    Not so much honoring thee   10
As giving it a hope that there
    It could not withered be.
But thou thereon didst only breathe,
    And sent'st it back to me;
Since when it grows, and smells, I swear,   15
    Not of itself but thee.

A. E. HOUSMAN   (1859–1936)

When I Was One-and-Twenty   (1896)

A. E. Housman.

When I was one-and-twenty
    I heard a wise man say,
"Give crowns and pounds and guineas°   *British money*
    But not your heart away;
Give pearls away and rubies   5
    But keep your fancy free."
But I was one-and-twenty,
    No use to talk to me.

When I was one-and-twenty
    I heard him say again,   10
"The heart out of the bosom
    Was never given in vain;
'Tis paid with sighs a plenty
    And sold for endless rue."
And I am two-and-twenty,   15
    And oh, 'tis true, 'tis true.

STANZA

The word **stanza** refers simply to a group of lines, either linked by an obvious rhyme or separated from others by white space. In much modern poetry there is no rhyme to unify the group of words, so poets have an extra burden of linking their lines thematically.

In traditional poetry, stanzas are often named for the number of lines that make up the units. Thus the simplest unit of lines is a rhyming pair, called a **couplet**, almost always run together rather than separated by white space:

But at my back I always hear
Times wingéd chariot hurrying near
            —*Andrew Marvell*

The late seventeenth and eighteenth centuries saw a particular type of couplet in iambic pentameter with strong pauses at the end; these were called **heroic couplets** since poets like John Dryden and Alexander Pope used them in their translations of classical epics. When such couplets were used in comic verse, they were called **mock-heroic**. Here are heroic couplets describing a certain mindless kind of gossip among idle aristocrats, from Book III, ll. 9–18, of Pope's mock-epic, "The Rape of the Lock" (1714):

> Hither the heroes and the nymphs resort,
> To taste awhile the pleasures of a court;
> In various talk the instructive hours they passed,
> Who gave the ball, or paid the visit last;
> One speaks the glory of the British queen,
> And one describes a charming Indian screen;
> A third interprets motions, looks, and eyes;
> At every word a reputation dies.

As this brief example shows, heroic couplets can tell a story and, in a mock-heroic poem, pack a nasty comment in the final line.

A **triplet**—much less common than the couplet—is a group of three rhyming lines within a larger poem:

> Waller was smooth; but Dryden taught to join
> The varying verse, the full resounding line,
> The long majestick march, and energy divine.
> —*from Horace's* Epistle I, *Book 2, l. 267, trans. Alexander Pope*

A **tercet** is any three-line stanza. The most famous type of tercet is *terza rima*, first used by Dante, and then by Shelley in English. Here are the last three stanzas of one of Shelley's most famous poems, "Ode to the West Wind," in terza rima with a concluding couplet:

> Drive my dead thoughts over the universe   *a*
> Like withered leaves, to quicken a new birth!   *b*
> And, by the incantation of this verse,   *a*
> Scatter, as from an unextinguished hearth   *b*
> Ashes and sparks, my words among mankind!   *c*
> Be through my lips to unawakened earth   *b*
> The trumpet of a prophecy! O Wind,   *d*
> If Winter comes, can Spring be far behind?   *d*

Any stanza of four lines is called a **quatrain**, the most common stanza form in English poetry. **Ballads**—story poems meant to be sung—are in quatrains. In fact, we call the quatrain with an *abcb* rhyme scheme the **ballad stanza**. The more formal the ballad, the closer and tighter the rhyme; the more folklike the ballad, the less strict the rules. These lines from the anonymous folk ballad "Bonny Barbara Allan" (c. 1400) are fairly loose with rhymes:

> It was in and about the Martinmas° time   *Nov. 11*
> When the green leaves were a falling
> That Sir John Graeme, in the West Country,
> Fell in love with Barbara Allan.

There are many, many different stanza forms; some of them, like the ballad, are connected to the form or genre of the poem. But before moving on, it is necessary to address the huge change that gave us a type of poetry unknown to poets before around 1860: free verse.

Free Verse

For centuries, writers of poems followed the conventional patterns, the ones required by tradition. Most poems had to display a strict meter and strict rhyme. In blank verse, poets had strict meter of one type, iambic pentameter, but were not required to rhyme. Then a revolution happened. In the mid nineteenth century, Walt Whitman and a few other writers broke away from those rules and began the huge change that came to be called **free verse** (a translation of the French *vers libre*), which required no rhyme, no set meter, and no regular rhythm. Whitman threw out the traditional ways of grouping lines—the stanzas—which had dominated previous poetry. Here is a prime example of free verse, by the revolutionary himself, Walt Whitman, from about 1865:

WALT WHITMAN   (1819–1892)

When I Heard the Learn'd Astronomer   (1865)

When I heard the learn'd astronomer,
When the proofs, the figures, were ranged in columns before me,
When I was shown the charts and diagrams, to add, divide, and measure them,
When I sitting heard the astronomer where he lectured with much applause in
   the lecture-room,
How soon unaccountable I became tired and sick,   5
Till rising and gliding out I wander'd off by myself,
In the mystical moist night-air, and from time to time,
Look'd up in perfect silence at the stars.

It does no good to count syllables here, looking for regularity, for there isn't any, or at least there isn't the kind of regularity a simple numerical rule could deliver. In this poem Whitman broke away from the constriction of meter and rhyme, as line 4 clearly demonstrates. But note that despite the absence of rhyme and meter there is a very clear kind of shaping to the opening, a repetition of "When" and notable progression from the short line 1 to the slightly longer line 2 to the longer line 3 to the extra long line 4. Whitman, who fussed over his poems as much as any poet who ever lived, jettisoned rhyme and strict meters but replaced them with a different kind of form and shape.

The next two poems are by a master of free verse, William Carlos Williams. In the first poem he boldly breaks up one of his key words (wheelbarrow); in both poems he places his line endings with infinite care. Williams doesn't employ rhyme or meter, so he needs to create his effects in other ways. And unlike Whitman, he does not have some stunning personal experience to announce

("When I heard the learned astronomer . . .") but instead must arrange his words and lines to help him make his pared-down sentences glow. At this stage in his career, Williams was excited most of all by the images themselves; as he was to put it, "Say it, no ideas but in things":

WILLIAM CARLOS WILLIAMS (1883–1963)
The Red Wheelbarrow (1923)

so much depends
upon

a red wheel
barrow

glazed with rain   5
water

beside the white
chickens.

This Is Just to Say (1934)

I have eaten
the plums
that were in
the icebox

and which   5
you were probably
saving
for breakfast

Forgive me
they were delicious   10
so sweet
and so cold

Free verse sounds more like "natural" talk than rhymed metrical feet, yet to make it work as art, poets have had to shape every line and adjust every pause, as Linda Pastan said when discussing her free verse (p. 726). As readers, we have to become attuned to tone, to the language, and to the way to make it "go" when we read it aloud. Free verse has won the popularity contest: most poets writing today employ it. But most creative writing programs insist on giving their students a grounding in rhyme and meter in order to demonstrate the importance of form in shaping powerful poetry. So to become an effective reader of all poetry, free verse included, it helps to read widely over centuries of poems, in traditional as well as contemporary forms.

☀ INSPIRATION WILLIAMS CARLOS WILLIAMS AND TINO VILLANUEVA

In many instances, poets respond to the work of other poets by borrowing a line, a theme, or merely by making direct reference to the other writer's work. Sometimes an entire poem may be a retelling of an older poem, in its subject matter as well as its tone, style, imagery, and language. An interesting example of this latter category of inspiration is Chicano poet Tino Villanueva's "Variation on a Theme by William Carlos Williams." The title is an obvious general reference to Williams, but it is the structure, rhythm, language, and tone that makes it clear the poem is a direct response specifically to Williams's "This Is Just to Say." Compare the two poems, and note the differences and similarities in language and imagery. How do the changes in the Villanueva poem affect the tone and the meaning compared to Williams's original piece?

Tino Villanueva   (B. 1941)

Variation on a Theme by William Carlos Williams   (1984)

Tino Villanueva.

I have eaten
the *tamales*
that were on
the stove heating

and which   5
you were probably
having for dinner

Perdóname°   *Forgive me*
they were *riquisimos*°   *delicious*
so juicy   10
and so steaming hot

Talking about the Text

1. Try reading aloud the two William Carlos Williams poems, "The Red Wheelbarrow" and "This Is Just to Say" (p. 767), in different voices and styles. How do you decide which style is the most appropriate?
2. Think of two couplets from popular songs, and describe them in terms of the discussion of couplets on p. 765.

Writing about the Text

1. Write three quatrains of ballad stanza, using your own subject matter.
2. Choose three examples of verse from pp. 766–777 and describe their structure. (Use the brief discussion of Whitman's "When I Heard the Learn'd Astronomer" on p. 766 as a model.)

Linking the Text to Other Texts

1. Look at the poems in "For Further Reading: Stanza," below, and select a poem that has an unusual, unexpected, or especially difficult stanza pattern. Be prepared to explain its special qualities.
2. Examine the blues songs in Chapter 25, "Sweet Home Chicago" (see pp. 1767–1773); choose one and explain its metrical and stanzaic structure.

For Further Reading: Stanza

GEORGE HERBERT   (1593–1633)

Easter Wings   (1633)

Lord, who createdst man in wealth and store,
Though foolishly he lost the same,
Decaying more and more,
Till he became
Most poor:
With thee
O let me rise
As larks, harmoniously,
And sing this day thy victories:
Then shall the fall further the flight in me.

My tender age in sorrow did begin;
And still with sicknesses and shame
Thou didst so punish sin,
That I became
Most thin.
With thee
Let me combine,
And feel this day thy victory:
For, if I imp my wing on thine,
Affliction shall advance the flight in me.

WILLIAM WORDSWORTH   (1770–1850)

A Slumber Did My Spirit Seal   (1800)

A slumber did my spirit seal;
  I had no human fears:
She seemed a thing that could not feel
  The touch of earthly years.

No motion has she now, no force;
  She neither hears nor sees;
Rolled round in earth's diurnal course,
  With rocks, and stones, and trees.

5

ADRIENNE RICH
(B. 1929)

Aunt Jennifer's Tigers
(1951)

Aunt Jennifer's tigers prance across a screen,
Bright topaz denizens of a world of green.
They do not fear the men beneath the tree;
They pace in sleek chivalric certainty.

Aunt Jennifer's fingers fluttering through her wool   5
Find even the ivory needle hard to pull.
The massive weight of Uncle's wedding band
Sits heavily upon Aunt Jennifer's hand.

When Aunt is dead, her terrified hands will lie
Still ringed with ordeals she was mastered by.   10
The tigers in the panel that she made
Will go on prancing, proud and unafraid.

VIDEO LOCALE

Adrienne Rich and the Lannan Foundation. The Lannan Foundation's
website features online audio of Adrienne Rich's 1999 poetry reading and interview with poet Carol Muske Dukes. You can also find information here about
Lannan's three-part video series on Rich. Go to *http://www.lannan.org/lf/bios/
detail/adrienne-rich/*.

FORM

Poets write particular types of poems, employing familiar poetic **forms**, which are
the structures or shapes a poem assumes. Some common forms are the **sonnet** and
elegy (both are described more fully below); another is the **haiku** (a three-line
poem: the lines contain 5, 7, and 5 syllables respectively). But there is a whole list of
possibilities. It might seem paradoxical that poetry, supposedly so filled with emotion, so often employs familiar, borrowed shapes, but that is the way with most arts.
Painters can choose from a portrait, a still life, a nude, a historical scene, a religious
subject: the options are a given, though of course there is always room for experimentation, an opportunity to break down the boundaries. Part of the challenge for
artists is to test themselves against the traditional forms, to explore whether something new can be done with a form great masters have succeeded with in the past.

Every successful poem includes an interesting mix of form and intention.
Sometimes a poet wants to write in a particular type of form. At other times a
poet has a particular aim in mind: to praise, lament, exult, capture a moment,
ponder the meaning of a small or large gesture or insight. Whatever the intention, there is a form available, though as we shall see, traditional forms have
never been able to contain all the complex intentions poets have had, so poets
have continually invented new ones.

Sonnet

One of the most familiar poetic forms, the **sonnet** (*sonnetto* is Italian for "little song") was first made famous by Francesco Petrarch (1304–1374) as he wrote in Italian about his love for Laura. Sonnets are lyrics (short poems expressing emotion), often though not always about love, and they follow very strict rules. A well-formed sonnet must be fourteen lines, usually of iambic pentameter, following one of two main **rhyme schemes** or patterns: either Petrarchan (or Italian) or Shakespearean (or English). Here is a famous Petrarchan sonnet:

JOHN KEATS   (1795–1821)

On First Looking into Chapman's Homer[1]   (1816)

Much have I travell'd in the realms of gold,	*a*
And many goodly states and kingdoms seen;	*b*
Round many western islands have I been	*b*
Which bards in fealty to Apollo° hold.	*a*
Oft of one wide expanse had I been told	*a* 5
That deep-brow'd Homer ruled as his demesne;°	*b*
Yet did I never breathe its pure serene°	*b*
Till I heard Chapman speak out loud and bold:	*a*
Then felt I like some watcher of the skies	*c*
When a new planet swims into his ken;	*d* 10
Or like stout Cortez when with eagle eyes	*c*
He star'd at the Pacific—and all his men	*d*
Look'd at each other with a wild surmise—	*c*
Silent, upon a peak in Darien.	*d*

Keats's sonnet about reading the translation of Homer follows the **Petrarchan** rules: it has two sections, the first eight lines (called the **octave**) and the last six lines (the **sestet**). Keats has a clear logical and grammatical distinction between the first eight lines, which set the scene, and the last six, which dramatically make his point with striking metaphors of an astronomer or explorer. The word "Then" at the beginning of line 9 marks the turning point, the **turn**, or what the Italians called the **volta**.

In the poem below, Keats, 22 years old and knowing he was dying of tuberculosis, puts his emotion into a **Shakespearean** (or English) sonnet, which has three four-line stanzas (quatrains) and a final couplet. Notice how in Keats's Shakespearean sonnet the metaphors and quatrains match each other closely, listing the three separate types of resources he fears he will never be able to use: first quatrain, a granary full of ideas; second quatrain, symbols of romances he wants to write; third quatrain, his lover, who has inspired him. The turn to the couplet brings a final metaphor: standing on the shore of the world, alone.

---

[1] Chapman's Homer: George Chapman (1559–1634) *produced a famous translation of Homer's* The Iliad *and* The Odyssey. *In line 11, Keats credits Hernando Cortez with first seeing the Pacific from Darien, in Panama. In fact, it was Vasco de Nuñez Balboa.*

4 Apollo: *god of poetry.* 6 demesne: *domain.* 7 serene: *serenity, atmosphere.*

JOHN KEATS   (1795–1821)

When I Have Fears That I May Cease to Be   (1818)

When I have fears that I may cease to be	*a*
Before my pen has glean'd my teeming brain,	*b*
Before high-piled books, in charact'ry°	*a*
Hold like rich garners° the full-ripen'd grain;	*b*
When I behold, upon the night's starr'd face	*c* 5
Huge cloudy symbols of a high romance,	*d*
And think that I may never live to trace	*c*
Their shadows with the magic hand of chance;	*d*
And when I feel, fair creature of an hour,	*e*
That I shall never look upon thee more,	*f* 10
Never have relish in the faery° power	*e*
Of unreflecting love!—then on the shore	*f*
Of the wide world I stand alone, and think	*g*
Till love and Fame to nothingness do sink.	*g*

Petrarchan and Shakespearean sonnets employ different rhyme schemes. Typical patterns for each form are shown below, but there are variations. The sestet of the Petrarchan sonnet, for example, may rhyme *cdcdcd* (as shown below), or *cdecde*, or some other variant.

Petrarchan Sonnet

a	
b	
a	
b	
b	octave
c	
b	
c	
c	
d	
c	sestet
d	
c	
d	

3 *charact'ry*: thought expressed in symbols or characters. 4 *garners*: storehouses. 11 *faery*: fairy.

Shakespearean Sonnet

$$
\left.\begin{array}{l}
a \\
b \\
a \\
b
\end{array}\right\} \text{quatrain}
$$

$$
\left.\begin{array}{l}
c \\
d \\
c \\
d
\end{array}\right\} \text{quatrain}
$$

$$
\left.\begin{array}{l}
e \\
f \\
e \\
f
\end{array}\right\} \text{quatrain}
$$

$$
\left.\begin{array}{l}
g \\
g
\end{array}\right\}
$$

The two different types of sonnets are associated with different types of expression. A poet can try each form at different times, though usually poets fasten upon a favorite type and stick to it. Keats's examples demonstrate how three metaphors are presented separately in three quatrains in the Shakespearean, while only two main metaphors operate in the Petrarchan. The couplet in a Shakespearean sonnet usually looks back at the rest of the poem and sums it up in two lines, or forms some kind of neat conclusion. The danger is that it is too neat, or not connected enough to the rest of the poem. The Petrarchan seems to have more built-in unity, having only two units for the fourteen lines, not four. Below are examples showing how the two types of sonnets operate.

Petrarchan Sonnets

EDNA ST. VINCENT MILLAY   (1892–1950)

I will put Chaos into fourteen lines

(1954; PUBLISHED POSTHUMOUSLY)

Carl Van Vechten's 1933 portrait of Edna St. Vincent Millay.

I will put Chaos into fourteen lines
And keep him there; and let him thence escape
If he be lucky; let him twist, and ape°   imitate
Flood, fire, and demon—his adroit designs

Will strain to nothing in the strict confines   5
Of this sweet Order, where, in pious rape,°   *kidnapping*
I hold his essence and amorphous shape,
Till he with Order mingles and combines.
Past are the hours, the years of our duress,
His arrogance, our awful servitude: 10
I have him. He is nothing more nor less
Than something simple not yet understood;
I shall not even force him to confess;
Or answer. I will only make him good.

The next sonnet has no rhyme scheme because it has no rhymes, nor is it
iambic pentameter. However, it still qualifies as a Petrarchan sonnet, since it so
self-consciously makes a turn after the eight-line octave into the sestet.

BILLY COLLINS   (B. 1941)

Sonnet   (1999)

All we need is fourteen lines, well, thirteen now,
and after this one just a dozen
to launch a little ship on love's storm-tossed seas,
then only ten more left like rows of beans.
How easily it goes unless you get Elizabethan   5
and insist the iambic bongos must be played
and rhymes positioned at the ends of lines,
one for every station of the cross.°   *14 stations are in this Christian devotion*
But hang on here while we make the turn
into the final six where all will be resolved,   10
where longing and heartache will find an end,
where Laura° will tell Petrarch to put down his pen,   *Petrarch's loved one*
take off those crazy medieval tights,
blow out the lights, and come at last to bed.

☙ COMMENTARY

Billy Collins on American Poetry

What does it mean to be an American poet? And how is American poetry distinct from British poetry, when they both claim the same mother tongue? In his
essay "What's American about American Poetry?" Billy Collins reflects on these
questions. "If a writer is the sum of his or her influences," he writes, "then my
own poems are unavoidably the result of my exposure to the sounds and styles of
both British and American poetry."

Through examples from Walt Whitman, D. H. Lawrence, Allen Ginsberg,
William Wordsworth, and Louis Simpson, Collins examines the language,
themes, and traditions of American poetry. In his poem "American Sonnet,"

Collins uses the sonnet to explain how American poetry has created new traditions from old forms: "We do not speak like Petrarch or wear a hat like Spenser / and it is not fourteen lines / like furrows in a small, carefully plowed field / but the picture postcard, a poem on vacation, that forces us to sing our songs in little rooms / or pour our sentiments into measuring cups."

You can read Collins's whole essay, including his poem "American Sonnet," at *http://usinfo.state.gov/products/pubs/writers/collins.htm.*

JOHN MILTON   (1608–1674)
On His Blindness   (1655)

When I consider how my light is spent
   Ere half my days in this dark world and wide,
   And that one talent° which is death to hide,   *parable of the talents*
Lodged with me useless, though my soul more bent   (Matt. 25:14)
To serve therewith my Maker, and present   5
   My true account, lest he returning chide;
   "Doth God exact day-labor, light denied?"
I fondly° ask; but Patience to prevent°   *foolishly / forestall*
That murmur, soon replies, "God doth not need
   Either man's work or his own gifts; who best   10
   Bear his mild yoke, they serve him best. His state
Is kingly. Thousands at his bidding speed
   And post° o'er land and ocean without rest;   *travel*
   They also serve who only stand and wait."

Shakespearean Sonnets

ROBERT FROST   (1874–1963)
Once by the Pacific   (1926)

The shattered water made a misty din.
Great waves looked over others coming in,
And thought of doing something to the shore
That water never did to land before.
The clouds were low and hairy in the skies,   5
Like locks blown forward in the gleam of eyes.
You could not tell, and yet it looked as if
The shore was lucky in being backed by cliff,
The cliff in being backed by continent;
It looked as if a night of dark intent   10
Was coming, and not only a night, an age.
Someone had better be prepared for rage.
There would be more than ocean-water broken
Before God's last *Put Out the Light* was spoken.

ALICE OSWALD   (B. 1966)
Wedding   (1996)

From time to time our love is like a sail
and when the sail begins to alternate
from tack to tack, it's like a swallowtail
and when the swallow flies it's like a coat;
and if the coat is yours, it has a tear   5
like a wide mouth and when the mouth begins
to draw the wind, it's like a trumpeter
and when the trumpet blows, it blows like millions . . .
and this, my love, when millions come and go
beyond the need of us, is like a trick;   10
and when the trick begins, it's like a toe
tip-toeing on a rope, which is like luck;
and when the luck begins, it's like a wedding,
which is like love, which is like everything.

WELDON KEES   (1914–1955)
For My Daughter   (1943)

Looking into my daughter's eyes I read
Beneath the innocence of morning flesh
Concealed, hintings of death she does not heed.
Coldest of winds have blown this hair, and mesh
Of seaweed snarled these miniatures of hands;   5
The night's slow poison, tolerant and bland,
Has moved her blood. Parched years that I have seen
That may be hers appear: foul, lingering
Death in certain war, the slim legs green.
Or, fed on hate, she relishes the sting   10
Of others' agony; perhaps the cruel
Bride of a syphilitic or a fool.
These speculations sour in the sun.
I have no daughter. I desire none.

Talking about the Text

1. Compare how the couplets operate in the Shakespearean sonnets by Frost, Oswald, and Kees, above, with the sonnets by Shakespeare on p. 733 and p. 941.
2. Look at the *volta*, or turn, in the sonnets by Millay, Collins, and Milton. Does this
   turning point always mark a new way of viewing the subject matter? What differences do you note among the three examples?

Writing about the Text

1. Choose two different sonnets from this section (pp. 771–776) and write a 2–3
   page comparison of their structures.

2. Choose a poem from this section (pp. 771–776) and write about the ways in which it does not seem to adhere fully to the requirements of the sonnet form.

Linking the Text to Other Texts

1. Seek out and listen to two recordings of sonnets and tell how strongly the readers emphasize the shape of the poem (e.g., quatrains, couplets, *volta*, or any of the sonnet's special characteristics).
2. Compare older sonnets with contemporary sonnets by asking which obeys the "rules" the most. In which do the "rules" seem most natural? Most artificial? For examples, use the older sonnet on p. 778 and the contemporary sonnet on p. 781.

ELEGY

A sonnet has a very definite form and strict rules, although as we have seen, some poets play with the form and break the rules. But some recognizable types of poems are characterized more by their **poetic intention**—the aim behind them—than by their form. Foremost among these is the **elegy**, a lament for the dead, whether a friend, a lover, a child, or a public figure.

The true subject of an elegy is often the persona who is left alone and missing the friend or loved one. Though there is frequently a reference to the dead one's qualities, the most important thing in the poem is usually the present state of the persona, not the deceased. Here Ben Jonson, a contemporary of Shakespeare, represents the father lamenting the loss of his son:

BEN JONSON   (1572–1637)

On My First Son   (1616)

Farewell, thou child of my right hand, and joy;
　　My sin was too much hope of thee, lov'd boy.
Seven years thou wert lent to me, and I thee pay.
　　Exacted by thy fate, on the just day.
Oh could I lose all father now! for why   5
　　Will man lament the state he should envy,
To have so soon 'scaped° world's and flesh's rage,   *escaped*
　　And, if no other misery, yet age?
Rest in soft peace, and asked, say, "Here doth lie
　　Ben Jonson his best piece of poetry."   10
For whose sake henceforth all his vows be such
　　As what he loves may never like too much.

Note that there is nothing in Jonson's poem about what the boy was like, not even his name. The theme here is not the missing son but what the loss means to the father. Sometimes the elegy can take on the format of a sonnet, as in the following example, which seems distant and formal, despite the professions of grief.

THOMAS GRAY (1716–1771)

Sonnet on the Death of Richard West (1742)

In vain to me the smiling mornings shine,
    And redd'ning Phoebus° lifts his golden fire;   *Apollo, the sun god*
The birds in vain their amorous descant° join,   *song*
    Or cheerful fields resume their green attire:
These ears, alas! for other notes repine;   5
    A different object do these eyes require.
My lonely anguish melts no heart but mine,
    And in my breast the imperfect joys expire.
Yet morning smiles the busy race to cheer,
    And new-born pleasure brings to happier men;   10
The fields to all their wonted tribute bear:
    To warm their little loves the birds complain:°   *sing*
I fruitless mourn to him that cannot hear,
    And weep the more because I weep in vain.

As in the elegy by Jonson, there is no emphasis on West as a person. He is a missing figure here, and the poem does not try to recreate him, or even to memorialize his characteristics. The world goes on, and the speaker must cope with the loss. The unspoken theme: this is how it is for us all.

When someone dies at an early age, poets can draw on a whole range of metaphors. But when someone dies full of years, after leading a helpful though not especially illustrious life, it takes a special kind of poet to provide adequate commemoration. Fortunately Robert Levet, a poor physician who spent his life helping the poor, had a devoted friend in the poet Samuel Johnson, who wrote a dignified, formal elegy that does attempt to "place" its subject's qualities. Here Levet is treated both as an individual and as a **type,** meaning an example or model, of the benevolent physician:

SAMUEL JOHNSON (1709–1784)

On the Death of Mr. Robert Levet, a Practiser in Physic (1783)

Condemn'd to Hope's delusive mine,
    As on we toil from day to day,
By sudden blasts, or slow decline,
    Our social comforts drop away.

Well tried through many a varying year,   5
    See Levet to the grave descend,
Officious,° innocent, sincere,   *careful to do his duty*
    Of ev'ry friendless name the friend.

Yet still he fills Affection's eye,
    Obscurely wise, and coarsely kind;   10
Nor, lettered arrogance, deny
    Thy praise to merit unrefin'd.

When fainting Nature called for aid,
    And hov'ring Death prepared the blow,
His vig'rous remedy displayed   15
    The power of art without the show.

In Misery's darkest caverns known,
    His useful care was ever nigh,
Where hopeless Anguish pour'd his groan,
    And lonely Want retired to die.   20

No summons mocked by chill delay,
    No petty gain disdained by pride;
The modest wants of ev'ry day
    The toil of ev'ry day supplied.

His virtues walked their narrow round,   25
    Nor made a pause, nor left a void;
And sure th' Eternal Master found
    The single talent° well-employed.   *parable of the talents (Matt. 25:14)*

The busy day, the peaceful night,
    Unfelt, uncounted, glided by;   30
His frame was firm, his powers were bright,
    Though now his eightieth year was nigh.

Then with no throbbing fiery pain,
    No cold gradations of decay,
Death broke at once the vital chain,   35
    And freed his soul the nearest way.

    In a moving elegy that operates entirely by metaphor and paradox, eighteen-year-old Chidiock Tichborne writes of his own coming execution. Involved in a Catholic plot against Queen Elizabeth, he was hanged three days after he wrote his poem.

CHIDIOCK TICHBORNE   (C. 1568—1586)

Elegy Written with His Own Hand in the Tower before His Execution   (1586)

(Commonly called Tichborne's Elegy)

My prime of youth is but a frost of cares,
    My feast of joy is but a dish of pain,
My crop of corn is but a field of tares,°   *weeds*
    And all my good is but vain hope of gain:
The day is past, and yet I saw no sun,   5
And now I live, and now my life is done.

My tale was heard, and yet it was not told,
 My fruit is fall'n, and yet my leaves are green,
My youth is spent, and yet I am not old,
 I saw the world, and yet I was not seen: 10
My thread is cut,° and yet it is not spun, *"the thread of life," cut by one of the fates*
And now I live, and now my life is done.

I sought my death, and found it in my womb,
 I looked for life, and saw it was a shade,
I trod the earth, and knew it was my tomb,   15
 And now I die, and now I was but made:
My glass is full, and now my glass is run,
And now I live, and now my life is done.

E. E. CUMMINGS   (1894–1962)

Buffalo Bill's   (1923)

Buffalo Bill's
defunct
  who used to
  ride a watersmooth-silver
      stallion
and break onetwothreefourfive pigeonsjustlikethat   5
       Jesus

he was a handsome man
    and what i want to know is
how do you like your blueeyed boy   10
Mister Death

Edward Weston's 1935 photographic portrait of E. E. Cummings.

Talking about the Text

1. Is there a paradox (actual or possible) between the expression of strong feeling and the formal shape most traditional elegies take?
2. Which part of "Buffalo Bill's" seems the most outrageous to you? Check with some others in your class and see if you all agree.

Writing about the Text

1. In an essay, describe the effect of metaphor and simile in elegies, using the examples from this section.
2. Write a reaction to an elegy, telling how you respond to it, either positively, negatively, or a mixture of the two. Connect your reactions to specific words and lines.

Linking the Text to Other Texts

1. Choose two personal elegies from this chapter and compare them with Walt Whitman's elegy for a public figure, "O Captain! My Captain!" (p. 998). What differences do you notice between the two types?
2. Try reading two or three elegies aloud. What if anything in the sound of your reading seems different from the way other poems sound?

☀ INSPIRATION CUMMINGS AND BJÖRK: POETRY AS POP SONG

The pop star Björk.

Just as E. E. Cummings was regarded as an experimentalist in terms of his idiosyncratic treatment of form, syntax, spelling, and punctuation, the Icelandic pop star Björk has created music that defies categorization. Her albums have drawn on dance and club music, alternative pop, electronica, and jazz. Her most recent work, *Medúlla* (2004), was an all vocals and vocals-samples-based album.

Two of Björk's albums include poems by E. E. Cummings set to music. *Vespertine* (2004) includes the song "Sun in My Mouth," with lyrics lifted directly from Cummings's poem "i will wade out," which appears below, omitting only the last five lines. Similarly, *Medúlla* adapts Cummings's "it may not always be so," only changing the gender of the speaker from male to female. In an August 2001 interview with *CD Now*, Björk explained why Cummings and his work resonate with her:

> Well, there are not that many poets that have won me over. I tend to read certain poets over and over again, and E. E. Cummings is one of them. I was reading a lot of him these last three years. I ended up just writing a song. It's hard to say why these things happen because most things just grow naturally, like a plant, on this record [*Vespertine*].
>
> But looking back on it, I think he's very interested in climaxes—in the divine and euphoric states. But what is special about him is that he's always humble. It's very common for people who are really into peaks and crowns, and euphoric states that they go really pompous and . . . [makes poof sound] sort of Wagner-like. Which he never, ever, ever . . . I guess that's something I found really curious—that you can go to the sharpest peak ever, but it's completely humble.

E. E. Cummings   (1894–1962)

it may not always be so;and i say

From Sonnets / Unrealities

           XI

it may not always be so;and i say
that if your lips,which I have loved,should touch
another's,and your dear strong fingers clutch
his heart,as mine in time not far away;
if on another's face your sweet hair lay   5
in such a silence as i know,or such
great writing words as,uttering overmuch,
stand helplessly before the spirit at bay;

(continued on next page)

if this should be,i say if this should be—
you of my heart,send me a little word;   10
that i may go unto him and take his hands,
saying,Accept all happiness from me.
Then i shall turn my face,and hear one bird
sing terribly afar in the lost lands.

Aubade

An **aubade** is a poem set at dawn, with lovers in bed either welcoming another day or lamenting that they must part. Such a poem is deliberately dramatic, drawing on a stark contrast between nights made for love and days meant for the business of the world. Poets writing aubades are not on oath, of course. They may be all alone (in bed or, more likely, at their desks), simply imagining themselves in a situation where an aubade would be appropriate.

WILLIAM SHAKESPEARE   (1546–1616)
Aubade (from Cymbeline)   (1609)

Hark, hark, the lark at heaven's gate sings,
    And Phoebus° 'gins° arise,   *Apollo, the sun god who rides a chariot / begins*
His steeds° to water at those springs   *the horses who pull Apollo's chariot*
    On chaliced flowers that lies;
And winking marybuds begin   5
    To ope° their golden eyes.   *open*
With everything that pretty is,
    My lady sweet, arise,
    Arise, arise!

AMY LOWELL   (1874–1925)
Aubade   (1917)

As I would free the white almond from the green husk
So I would strip your trappings off,
Beloved.
And fingering the smooth and polished kernel
I should see that in my hands glittered a gem beyond counting.

One of the most famous aubades is also one of the most daring. John Donne's persona claims that the bed where he and his lover lie is the center of the universe, and he urges the sun to go bother someone else.

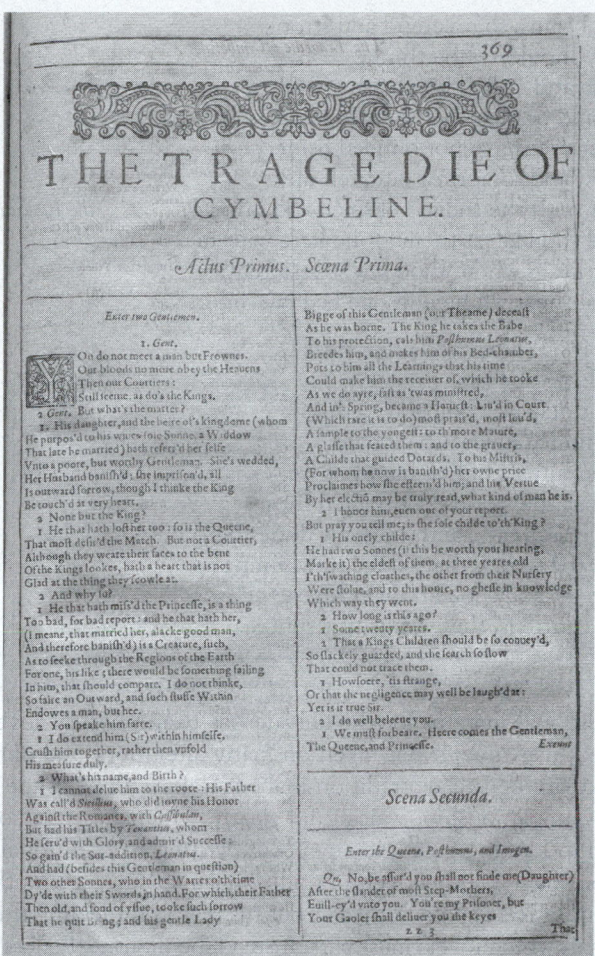

The title page of Cymbeline, *from a facsimile of the First Folio Edition, 1623, of* Shakespeare's Comedies, Histories, and Tragedies.

JOHN DONNE

(1572–1631)

The Sun Rising

(PUBLISHED 1633)

Busy old fool, unruly sun,
　　Why dost thou thus,
Through windows, and through curtains, call on us?
Must to thy motions lovers' seasons run?
　　　　Saucy pedantic wretch, go chide　　　　　　5
　　　　Late schoolboys and sour prentices,
　　Go tell court-huntsmen that the king will ride,
　　Call country ants to harvest offices;
Love, all alike, no season knows nor clime,
Nor hours, days, months, which are the rags of time.　　10

> Thy beams, so reverend and strong
>   Why shouldst thou think?
> I could eclipse and cloud them with a wink,
> But that I would not lose her sight so long:
>   If her eyes have not blinded thine,   15
>   Look, and tomorrow late, tell me,
>   Whether both the Indias° of spice and mine   the East and West Indies
>   Be where thou left'st them, or lie here with me.
> Ask for those kings whom thou saw'st yesterday,
> And thou shalt hear, all here in one bed lay.   20
>
>   She is all states, and all princes I,
>   Nothing else is.
> Princes do but play us; compar'd to this,
> All honor's mimic, all wealth alchemy.
>   Thou sun art half as happy as we,   25
>   In that the world's contracted thus;
>   Thine age asks ease, and since thy duties be
>   To warm the world, that's done in warming us.
> Shine here to us, and thou art everywhere;
> This bed thy centre is, these walls, thy sphere.   30

The traditional impetus for the aubade has been physical love, but as the genre changed over time, it has taken on many alterations and different forms. An ironic take on the aubade tradition is about waking alone as the dawn comes in, bereft of companionship, waiting for death, which has just come one day closer. In Philip Larkin's great gloomy poem, written in traditional stanzas and meter, the persona—like the lovers of traditional aubades—sees nothing at all to be joyful about in the approaching day, but his reason for feeling this way differs from aubades in which lovers must part. Instead, he mourns the loss of one more day of his life.

PHILIP LARKIN   (1922–1985)

Aubade   (1977)

I work all day, and get half-drunk at night
Waking at four to soundless dark, I stare.
In time the curtain-edges will grow light.
Till then I see what's really always there:
Unresting death, a whole day nearer now,   5
Making all thought impossible but how
And where and when I shall myself die.
Arid interrogation: yet the dread

Of dying, and being dead,
Flashes afresh to hold and horrify.   10

The mind blanks at the glare. Not in remorse
—The good not done, the love not given, time
Torn off unused—nor wretchedly because
An only life can take so long to climb
Clear of its wrong beginnings, and may never;   15
But at the total emptiness for ever,
The sure extinction that we travel to
And shall be lost in always. Not to be here,
Not to be anywhere,
And soon; nothing more terrible, nothing more true.   20

This is a special way of being afraid.
No trick dispels. Religion used to try,
That vast moth-eaten musical brocade
Created to pretend we never die,
And specious° stuff that says *No rational being*   fake 25
Can fear a thing it will not feel, not seeing
That this is what we fear—no sight, no sound,
No touch or taste or smell, nothing to think with,
Nothing to love or link with,
The anaesthetic from which none come round.   30

And so it stays just on the edge of vision,
A small unfocused blur, a standing chill
That slows each impulse down to indecision.
Most things may never happen: this one will,
And realisation of it rages out   35
In furnace-fear when we are caught without
People or drink. Courage is no good:
It means not scaring others. Being brave
Lets no one off the grave.
Death is no different whined at than withstood.   40

Slowly light strengthens, and the room takes shape.
It stands plain as a wardrobe, what we know,
Have always known, know that we can't escape,
Yet can't accept. One side will have to go.
Meanwhile telephones crouch, getting ready to ring   45
In locked-up offices, and all the uncaring
Intricate rented world begins to rouse.
The sky is white as clay, with no sun.
Work has to be done.
Postmen like doctors go from house to house.   50

WILLIAM SHAKESPEARE   (1564–1616)
Aubade from Romeo and Juliet *Act 2, scene 2*   (1597)

ROMEO: But, soft! What light through yonder window breaks?
It is the east, and Juliet is the sun!
Arise fair sun and kill the envious moon,
Who is already sick and pale with grief
That thou her maid are more fair than she.   5
Be not her maid, since she is envious.
Her vestal livery is but sick and green,
And none but fools do wear it. Cast it off.
It is my lady, oh, it is my love!
Oh, that she knew she were!   10
She speaks, yet she says nothing. What of that?
Her eye discourses, I will answer it.
I am too bold, 'tis not to me she speaks.
Two of the fairest stars in all the heaven,
Having some business do entreat her eyes   15
To twinkle in their spheres till they return.
What if her eyes were there, they in her head?
The brightness of her cheek would shame those stars
As daylight doth a lamp; her eyes in heaven
Would through the airy region stream so bright   20
That birds would sing and think it were not night.
See how she leans her cheek upon her hand!
Oh that I might be a glove upon that hand,
That I might touch that cheek!

Talking about the Text

1. In what ways does the *Romeo and Juliet* scene constitute an aubade? What do you
   see in the scene that also connects to the genre of sonnet?
2. What differences do you note between the treatments of form and meter in the
   older and more contemporary aubades on pp. 782–786? (This is not, of course, a
   representative selection.)

Writing about the Text

1. Describe the different ways the aubades written after 1900 seem to take the aubade
   tradition into new territory.
2. Write about how the speakers dramatize their aubades, making them seem as if
   spoken at the very moment of interruption.

Linking the Text to Other Texts

1. Compare the way love is treated in the aubade with the way love is depicted in
   three examples of Renaissance love poetry collected on pp. 924–961.

2. Listen to Philip Larkin reading "Aubade" at *http://martinamis.albion.edu/larkina. htm*. Is it done the way you had expected? What precise surprises can you point to in the way he delivers his lines?

Villanelle

Sometimes a highly complex form produces a seemingly simple, lovely poem, as in Elizabeth Bishop's "One Art." Part of the art here is the way Bishop's skill hides the complexity of the poetic form she has chosen: the villanelle.

ELIZABETH BISHOP
One Art

(1911–1979)

(1976)

The art of losing isn't hard to master;
so many things seem filled with the intent
to be lost that their loss is no disaster.

Lose something every day. Accept the fluster
of lost door keys, the hour badly spent.   5
The art of losing isn't hard to master.

Then practice losing farther, losing faster:
places, and names, and where it was you meant
to travel. None of these will bring disaster.

I lost my mother's watch. And look! my last, or   10
next-to-last, of three loved houses went.
The art of losing isn't hard to master.

I lost two cities, lovely ones. And, vaster,
some realms I owned, two rivers, a continent.
I miss them, but it wasn't a disaster.   15

—Even losing you (the joking voice, a gesture
I love) I shan't have lied. It's evident
the art of losing's not too hard to master
though it may look like (*Write* it!) like disaster.

The **villanelle** is a French form with strict requirements: nineteen lines in five tercets, followed by a quatrain. The rhyme must be *aba aba aba aba aba aba abaa*. The first line of the poem becomes the last line of the second and fourth tercets, and the third line of the first tercet becomes the last line of the third and the fifth tercet. Then these two last lines become the final couplet. This seems almost comically complex, like some incredibly intricate pattern to follow. The paradox is that Bishop's extremely personal poem about losing her lover fits so well into such an elaborate verse form. It is as if she were taking her personal grief and demonstrating that she could deal with it in the formal complexity of a new poetic type, thus transforming the pain into art.

VIDEO LOCALE

Elizabeth Bishop Documentary. The documentary film *Elizabeth Bishop: One Art* (1988, Annenberg/CPB Project) explores the life of Elizabeth Bishop through readings of her poetry, critical interpretations, commentary by writers, and photographs. The film is part of the thirteen-part Voices and Visions series on contemporary American poets. For more information, go to *http://www.learner.org/catalog/extras/vvspot/Bishop.html.*

DYLAN THOMAS (1914–1953)

Do Not Go Gentle into That Good Night (1952)

Do not go gentle into that good night,
Old age should burn and rave at close of day;
Rage, rage against the dying of the light.

Though wise men at their end know dark is right,
Because their words had forked no lightning they   5
Do not go gentle into that good night.

Good men, the last wave by, crying how bright
Their frail deeds might have danced in a green bay,
Rage, rage against the dying of the light.

Wild men who caught and sang the sun in flight,   10
And learn, too late, they grieved it on its way,
Do not go gentle into that good night.

Grave men, near death, who see with blinding sight
Blind eyes could blaze like meteors and be gay,
Rage, rage against the dying of the light.   15

And you, my father, there on the sad height,
Curse, bless, me now with your fierce tears, I pray.
Do not go gentle into that good night.
Rage, rage against the dying of the light.

Talking about the Text

1. List the kinds of losses Bishop's persona says she has faced.
2. Explore the role of paradox in Thomas's "Do Not Go Gentle into That Good Night."

Writing about the Text

1. In an essay, contrast the way Bishop's and Thomas's two villanelles employ the same form but radically different speakers and situations.
2. "Translate" or paraphrase at least six lines of Thomas's poem into prose, then describe what differences you note between the original and your own version.

Linking the Text to Other Texts

1. Compare Bishop's rhymes to the rhymes in one of the sonnets on pp. 771–776. What characteristics do you notice?
2. Describe how you would tell someone to read each of these poems. What overall character or tone of voice would you recommend for each? Why?

For Further Reading: Form

THEODORE ROETHKE   (1908–1963)

The Waking

I wake to sleep, and take my waking slow.
I feel my fate in what I cannot fear.
I learn by going where I have to go.

We think by feeling. What is there to know?
I hear my being dance from ear to ear.   5
I wake to sleep, and take my waking slow.

Of those so close beside me, which are you?
God bless the Ground! I shall walk softly there,
And learn by going where I have to go.

Light takes the Tree; but who can tell us how?   10
The lowly worm climbs up a winding stair;
I wake to sleep, and take my waking slow.

Great Nature has another thing to do
To you and me; so take the lively air,
And, lovely, learn by going where to go.   15

This shaking keeps me steady. I should know.
What falls away is always. And is near.
I wake to sleep, and take my waking slow.
I learn by going where I have to go.

ROBERT FROST   (1874–1963)

Design   (1936)

I found a dimpled spider, fat and white,
On a white heal-all,° holding up a moth   *a plant*
Like a white piece of rigid satin cloth—
Assorted characters of death and blight
Mixed ready to begin the morning right,   5
Like the ingredients of a witches' broth—
A snow-drop spider, a flower like a froth,
And dead wings carried like a paper kite.

What had that flower to do with being white,
The wayside blue and innocent heal-all?
What brought the kindred spider to that height,
Then steered the white moth thither in the night?
What but design of darkness to appall?—
If design govern in a thing so small.

10

EDNA ST. VINCENT MILLAY   (1892–1950)

Love Is Not All: It Is Not Meat nor Drink   (1931)

Love is not all: it is not meat nor drink
Nor slumber nor a roof against the rain;
Nor yet a floating spar to men that sink
And rise and sink and rise and sink again;
Love can not fill the thickened lung with breath,
Nor clean the blood, nor set the fractured bone;
Yet many a man is making friends with death
Even as I speak, for lack of love alone.
It well may be that in a difficult hour,
Pinned down by pain and moaning for release,
Or nagged by want past resolution's power,
I might be driven to sell your love for peace,
Or trade the memory of this night for food.
It well may be. I do not think I would.

5

10

MARGE PIERCY   (B. 1936)

Barbie Doll   (1973)

This girlchild was born as usual
and presented dolls that did pee-pee
and miniature GE stoves and irons
and wee lipsticks the color of cherry candy.
Then in the magic of puberty, a classmate said:
You have a great big nose and fat legs.

5

She was healthy, tested intelligent,
possessed strong arms and back,
abundant sexual drive and manual dexterity.
She went to and fro apologizing.
Everyone saw a fat nose on thick legs.

10

She was advised to play coy,
exhorted to come on hearty,
exercise, diet, smile and wheedle.
Her good nature wore out
like a fan belt.

15

So she cut off her nose and her legs
and offered them up.

In the casket displayed on satin she lay
with the undertaker's cosmetics painted on,   20
a turned-up putty nose,
dressed in a pink and white nightie.
Doesn't she look pretty? Everyone said.
Consummation at last.
To every woman a happy ending.   25

MICHAEL DRAYTON   (1563–1631)

Since There's No Help   (1599)

Since there's no help, come let us kiss and part;
Nay, I have done, you get no more of me,
And I am glad, yea, glad with all my heart
That thus so cleanly I myself can free;
Shake hands for ever, cancel all our vows,   5
And when we meet at any time again,
Be it not seen in either of our brows
That we one jot of former love retain.
Now at the last gasp of Love's latest breath,
When, his pulse failing, Passion speechless lies,   10
When Faith is kneeling by his bed of death,
And Innocence is closing up his eyes,
        Now if thou wouldst, when all have given him over,
        From death to life thou mightst him yet recover.

EDMUND SPENSER   (1552–1599)

One day I wrote her name upon the strand   (1595)

One day I wrote her name upon the strand,°   beach
But came the waves and washéd it away:
Agayne I wrote it with a second hand,
But came the tyde, and made my paynes his pray.
"Vayne man," sayd she, "that doest in vaine assay,   5
A mortall thing so to immortalize,
For I my selve shall lyke to this decay,
And eek° my name bee wypéd out lykewize."   also
"Not so," quoth° I, "let baser things devize°   said / devise
To dy in dust, but you shall live by fame: 10
My verse your vertues rare shall eternize,
And in the hevens wryte your glorious name.
Where whenas death shall all the world subdew,
Our love shall live, and later life renew."

THOMAS HARDY   (1840–1928)

The Darkling Thrush   (1902)

I leant upon a coppice gate
    When Frost was specter gray,
And Winter's dregs made desolate
    The weakening eye of day.
The tangled bine-stems scored the sky   5
    Like strings of broken lyres,
And all mankind that haunted nigh
    Had sought their household fires.

The land's sharp features seemed to be
    The Century's corpse outleant,   10
His crypt the cloudy canopy,
    The wind his death-lament.
The ancient pulse of germ and birth
    Was shrunken hard and dry,
And every spirit upon earth   15
    Seemed fervorless as I.

At once a voice arose among
    The bleak twigs overhead
In a full-hearted evensong
    Of joy illimited;   20
An aged thrush, frail, gaunt, and small,
    In blast-beruffled plume,
Had chosen thus to fling his soul
    Upon the growing gloom.

So little cause for carolings   25
    Of such ecstatic sound
Was written on terrestrial things
    Afar or nigh around,
That I could think there trembled through
    His happy good-night air   30
Some blessed Hope, whereof he knew
    And I was unaware.

During Wind and Rain

    They sing their dearest songs—
    He, she, all of them—yea,
    Treble and tenor and bass,
        And one to play;

With the candles mooning each face. . . .   5
    Ah, no; the years O!
How the sick leaves reel down in throngs!

They clear the creeping moss—
Elders and juniors—aye,
Making the pathway neat   10
    And the garden gay;
And they build a shady seat. . . .
    Ah, no; the years, the years;
See, the white stormbirds wing across!

They are blithely breakfasting all—   15
Men and maidens—yea,
Under the summer tree,
    With a glimpse of the bay,
While pet fowl come to the knee. . . .
    Ah, no; the years O!   20
And the rotten rose is ripped from the wall.

They change to a high new house,
He, she, all of them—aye,
Clocks and carpets, and chairs
    On the lawn all day,   25
And brightest things that are theirs. . . .
    Ah, no; the years, the years;
Down their carved names the rain drop ploughs.

GERARD MANLY HOPKINS   (1844–1889)

God's Grandeur   (PUBLISHED 1918)

The world is charged with the grandeur of God.
    It will flame out, like shining from shook foil;
    It gathers to a greatness, like the ooze of oil
Crushed. Why do men then now not reck his rod?
Generations have trod, have trod, have trod;   5
    And all is seared with trade; bleared, smeared with toil;
    And wears man's smudge and shares man's smell: the soil
Is bare now, nor can foot feel, being shod.

And for all this, nature is never spent;
    There lives the dearest freshness deep down things;   10
And though the last lights off the black West went
    Oh, morning, at the brown brink eastward, springs—
Because the Holy Ghost over the bent
    World broods with warm breast and with ah! bright wings.

The Windhover   (PUBLISHED 1918)

To Christ our Lord

I caught this morning morning's minion, king-
    dom of daylight's dauphin, dapple-dawn-drawn Falcon, in his riding
    Of the rolling level underneath him steady air, and striding
High there, how he rung upon the rein of a wimpling wing
In his ecstasy! then off, off forth on swing,   5
    As a skate's heel sweeps smooth on a bow-bend: the hurl and gliding
    Rebuffed the big wind. My heart in hiding
Stirred for a bird,—the achieve of, the mastery of the thing!

Brute beauty and valor and act, oh, air, pride, plume, here
    Buckle! AND the fire that breaks from thee then, a billion   10
Times told lovelier, more dangerous, O my chevalier!
    No wonder of it: shéer plód makes plow down sillion
Shine, and blue-bleak embers, ah my dear,
    Fall, gall themselves, and gash gold-vermilion.

C H A P T E R
12

Writing about Poetry

In Chapter 3, "Writing about Stories," the act of writing about literature was imagined by the critic Kenneth Burke as a conversation set in a "parlor" in which people arrive, join in the ongoing discussion already in progress, and then leave, while the conversation continues among the remaining participants. That conversational parlor can serve as a metaphor for written discussions about stories, plays, and poems. The conversation or discussion—in print and in person—appears all around us: at home or in a dormitory or a classroom, published in newspapers and magazines, posted on the World Wide Web, and sponsored by discussion groups in libraries, schools, and cultural centers. It is easy for us to see what others have had to say, and with the Web, easier than ever to post our own responses, to join the conversation ourselves, unworried by what others will think.

THE CULTURAL CONVERSATION

The conversation about poems and poetry is very much like the conversation about drama and fiction, with one large exception: its visibility. Unlike the writing and talking about fiction and drama, the conversation about poetry is fairly quiet and less obvious. It is harder to find reviews of poetry in the newspaper or most magazines. This is ironic, because with poetry, a much wider group of readers and writers are participating in the conversation. Judged by the sheer numbers of those who write poems or write about them, writing poetry is much more popular than writing about drama or fiction. Yet much of the writing and talking about poetry takes place in academic settings, rather than on radio or television or in bookstores, theaters, and national magazines. Much of the conversation about poetry happens on the pages of small magazines and journals (so-called "little magazines" or reviews), in academic books, and in classrooms.

By being part of a literature class and by reading and writing about the poems in this book, you are joining the conversation, if only tentatively. You can participate even more fully by examining biographical materials about poets, reading reviews of poetry collections, browsing a contemporary poet's website, or attending a local poetry reading. Each of these activities brings you into the world of poetry and may make you more knowledgeable about how the conversation is going. Certainly some experience can make you feel more comfortable reading and writing about poetry.

Today, four types of writing about poetry predominate:

- Reviews of poetry, usually in small-circulation magazines and sometimes in major newspapers.
- Critical articles and books, usually by scholars and critics, about individual poets of the past and present, as well as on poetry's place in the culture.
- Responses to poetry in the form of poems themselves, written as reaction or homage, in imitation of another poem or another poet's work. People frequently write "about" poetry by producing it on their own. Poetry, in fact, is by far the most popular written art form when it comes to participation. Thousands of people produce poems for readings, blogs, or paper publication, either as pamphlets, in magazines, or in books. Some of the most productive participants in the cultural conversation about poetry make their comments through writing a poem, or even a series of poems.
- School-sponsored writing, meant to introduce students to poetry or as training in how to read and respond to demanding material. This chapter concentrates on developing the skills needed to enter the cultural conversation about poetry in response to a school assignment.

REVIEWS

Every year, thousands of new books of poetry appear, from small editions published locally to books issued by major publishers. In 2004, *Obliviously On He Sails*, a poetry book, hit the best-seller lists, helped by the fact that it was political poetry by a popular writer, Calvin Trillin, during an election year. This is a very rare event nowadays, though it was common more than a hundred years ago. Now, poetry books are reviewed in major newspapers and magazines only when an interesting volume appears or when a major poet's life work is issued as "Collected Poems." In reviews, writers are usually careful to help readers by placing the poet's work in context and by quoting a good amount of it to give readers samples of the writing. A review of collected poems is also an occasion for an overall evaluation of the particular poet's place in literature.

As with reviews of fiction, reviews of poetry in popular magazines and news-papers take two common forms: a short review that briefly summarizes the book's main points or themes and the reviewer's response to it, or a full review that ex-amines and evaluates the book in much more detail, usually using a number of examples from specific poems. The examples below are two reviews—one short and one full-length—of *Collected Poems of Robert Lowell*.

Short Review

DONNA SEAMAN

Collected Poems of Robert Lowell, *edited by Frank Bidart and David Gewanter*

From *Booklist*, 2003

Poet Robert Lowell.

In the quarter-century since his death, Lowell's personality and life have overshadowed his poetry. No more. Poets Bidart (who knew Lowell and who expertly dismantles Lowell's reputation as confessional poet) and Gewanter present the first collected volume of this pivotal American voice, a gathering astonishing in its breadth and power. Here are poems in manuscript; works "buried since first publication," including Lowell's first book, *Land of Unlikeness* (1944); and poems from his 11 ensuing collections, including *Life Studies* (1959) and *The Dolphin* (1973). As Bidart observes, Lowell, the recipient of many awards, including two Pulitzers and the National Book Award, labored intently over his work, writing and rewriting, just as he repeatedly plumbed the depths of his blueblood family history and grappled with humanity's perpetual struggles with love and war, inheritance and freedom. Substantial notes, a chronology, glossary, and critical essays make this an essential title. Readers who think they know Lowell's work will discover new facets, and readers just venturing into Lowell's potently rendered and ceaselessly evocative poetic universe will find much to contemplate.

This brief review sums up the collection and draws a quick picture of Robert Lowell in terms of the larger canon of American poets. The inclusion of Lowell's awards and the use of phrases like "a gathering astonishing in its breadth and power" and "potently rendered and ceaselessly evocative" make it clear in a very short space that the critic found the collection most impressive.

A full review, by contrast, is usually 500–800 words and does essentially the same thing as a short review, but there's much more room to illustrate specifically how a book does or does not work, usually using quotations from the poems themselves.

Full Review

ANTHONY MOORE
An Oeuvre of Vigor and Variety

Collected Poems of Robert Lowell, edited by Frank Bidart and David Gewanter

From *Boston Globe*, JULY 27, 2003

T. S. Eliot was well versed in fickle literary taste when he warned us that no poetic reputation ever remains fixed; "it is a stock market in constant fluctuation." The public's response to Robert Lowell's work proves how shrewd his assertion was. Lowell outperformed the market for three decades, was garlanded with prizes and talked up often as the greatest living American poet. But his stock suffered a long decline in the quarter-century after he died and has been trading at bargain prices. Here is the long-awaited *Collected Poems* to prompt a reevaluation of what was always an asset-rich artistic enterprise. In it Lowell makes good his magnificent boast in an elegy to Berryman: "we are words. / John, we used the language as if we made it."

Frank Bidart and David Gewanter are tender and magnanimous to the poems. They devote a thousand sumptuous pages to most of those Lowell printed and give many drafts and variants in the voluminous notes. The persistent vigor and variety of his creative energy is astonishing now that we see the whole career get its due. It commands history, politics, religion, science, psychology, philosophy, and, as everyone knows, marital turmoil and a modern life's miseries and joys. Lowell never doubted his ability to affirm poetry's broader cultural role.

His imposing set-piece public meditations on politics and the American imperium are enough to bear him out. They continue to speak to us. Seamus Heaney thought "Waking Early Sunday Morning" one "of the finest public poems of our time." With the hindsight available today from books on US conduct of the Vietnam War, it may be better than that, perhaps one of the greatest political poems of all time. It stands as a landmark at the center of the 1960s. Lowell reimagines for America Andrew Marvell's complex "Horatian Ode upon Cromwell's Return from Ireland." Like its 17th-century rival, "Waking Early" is weighty, strong on moral principle, patriotic. Lowell's ambiguous sketch of President Johnson ("girdled by his establishment / this Sunday morning, free to chaff / his own thoughts with his bear-cuffed staff, / swimming nude, unbuttoned, sick / of his ghost-written rhetoric!") is charged with the static of skeptical words and phrases. His couplets gained more satirical force when we learned last year, from Robert Caro's third volume of Johnson's life and times, that he tried to conceal his girth with a heavy girdle and, as a gambit to control those whose ungirdled support he needed, perfected making his private parts public.

The editors prefer "History" and "For Lizzie and Harriet" over the two "Notebooks" from which those later books sprang. Bidart says "a choice had to be made" (that's what editors do, after all). Now that it has been, this reviewer grumbles. To some of us, the manner of the grasp in "History"—400 deliberately roughened unrhymed sonnets, in chronological order by subject—fails its reach for the title's ambitious matter—in debt to Pound's "An epic is a poem including history" and Emerson's "Man is explicable by nothing less than all his history. . . . All public facts are to be individualized, all private facts are to be generalized." In contrast, the "free-wheeling catch-as-catch-can improvisations" of "Notebook" (Bidart) seem a more modest but integrated recognition that although a gifted poet cannot capture, he can suggest our life's shifting discontinuity. But I defer to Bidart; he was Lowell's friend and collaborator. Without him, I suspect, Lowell could not have brought out 10 books in his last eight years. Bidart can be trusted as guardian of the poet's intent.

Randall Jarrell was wrong, for once, when he said, reviewing Lowell's verse novella *The Mills of the Kavanaughs*, that narrative "is often beyond his powers and knowledge." There is an exultant narrative drive through all the work. He mastered the dramatic monologue and, like Robert Frost and William Carlos Williams, disposes a cast of vivid characters and many different voices across his poems ("Mr. Edwards and the Spider," "To Speak of Woe That Is in Marriage"). He found the familiar epistle and verse short story congenial ("Jean Stafford, a Letter," "Off Central Park"). Poem titles often trail a drama ("Memories of West Street and Lepke," "Thanks-Offering for Recovery") while they support the development of each publication; that is, the books don't only gather individual lyrics, they engage the governing principle of a coherent plot. One exemplary case of revision shows Lowell alert to integrating poems so they mean more than their parts. The scathing public protest "Colonel Shaw and the Massachusetts' 54th" (now titled "For the Union Dead") was tacked on as the last poem in the 1960 paperback "Life Studies." Lowell saw he was wrong to disrupt the unity of the much-admired final personal sequence with a poem that castigates the state of the nation, and never reprinted the arrangement.

The collection keeps the prose "91 Revere Street" in its right place as Part 2 of "Life Studies." This comic masterpiece was blurbed by the original publisher, not Lowell, as "an autobiographical fragment." In truth, it's a glorious farrago, more witty mischief than reliable source. "Battleship Bilge Harkness," introduced as Lowell's father's roommate at Annapolis, is a social wrecking bar. Lowell invented him as the lord of misrule licensed to blow fresh air through his parents' arid marriage and stifling Beacon Hill house. It is the same teasing writer who says, "My verse autobiography sometimes fictionalizes plot and particular." Sometimes? Autobiography was a wellspring for his creativity. Yet the domestic, intellectual, and sexual drama in his mature poetry is an artfully made fiction. As artificial in its way as the Southern vowels he affected in life. As staged as the Romantic-genius intensity of his photo portraits by Richard Avedon, Cartier-Bresson, Guy Fleming.

Lowell looked up to "Uncle Tom" (his pet name for Eliot) as a man of letters. So it's no surprise to catch him lifting his mentor's metaphor for judging value. What does jolt, though, is that he foresaw precisely what has come about. Three days before his death, in September 1977, he told Blair Gowrie, an English friend, that when he died Elizabeth Bishop's "shares will rise and mine will fall." Then, "But mine will come back." Surely he will be right again.

Online Customer Reviews

The Internet is an increasingly important part of the conversation that takes place through reviews. Within the last decade, the opportunity to review has been thrown open by websites like amazon.com, where anyone can post a review of a book of poems. Choose a poet you know and check out what people have to say about him or her on amazon. It's a vivid demonstration of how many ordinary people care enough about poetry to write about it.

Because anyone can post a review on amazon, the opinions about a single book, not to mention the thoughtfulness of each review, can vary widely. Below are two excerpted reviews of Billy Collins's *Sailing Alone around the Room*. (For more than fifty additional reviews, look up the book on the amazon site.)

Amazon Review 1

Not to sound elitist or anything, but there's a reason behind Billy Collins's popularity: he's not remotely challenging. Which is fine—not every literary experience must be a miserable uphill slog—but let's not pretend that ease of comprehensibility and shallowness of theme somehow equate to greatness. We need poets like him, to allow us to take a rest from the exertions of mind and heart that the true greats bring.

Amazon Review 2

Sailing Alone around the Room combines poems from all his previous collections as well as a few new ones. It is, in effect, a "greatest hits book." Collins is a poet who does not specialize in any one topic. His inspiration for poems seems to come from reflection and everyday life. The poems he writes about everyday life are not simple. They incorporate simile and metaphor, and give the reader's brain some exercise.

This compilation of previously published and new poems showcases the many facets of Collins' style. He experiments with ancient forms such as the paradelle and the sonnet, poking fun, and producing images. All the while his self-deprecating humor shows through.

These amazon.com reviews are a kind of democracy in action. Everyone can become a reviewer.

BEYOND REVIEWS: CRITICISM

For many centuries, literature and cultural life were dominated by poetry. In ancient Greece and Rome, for instance, or in Renaissance England or France, poetry was the dominant form of literary expression; novels and short stories barely existed. Anyone who writes about those societies must write about poetry. Similarly, it is hard to understand America in the nineteenth century without coming to grips with a major poet like Henry Wadsworth Longfellow, perhaps the age's most prominent literary figure. Cultural critics thus inevitably write about poetry, since it has played such a prominent role in the development of ideas, attitudes, and forms of expression. And scholars and critics write about literary figures great and small, including of course the poets who helped shape the language. Critics and scholars write books, articles, essays, and reviews; they compile editions and anthologies; and they prepare teaching materials so they can pass their knowledge along to new generations.

In many instances, criticism centers on a particular poet or poem. But, as in the examples below, criticism may explore aspects or trends of poetry as a genre in general.

Popular Criticism

The difference between popular criticism and scholarly work can be difficult to parse out. Generally, one indication of what kind of criticism you're reading is the publication source. Popular criticism is usually found in general-interest magazines like *Newsweek* and *Time*, which are available on every newsstand. Scholarly work is usually found in academic journals with smaller circulations, often published through university presses, such as the *Michigan Quarterly Review* and *Literary Imagination*. Other indications are the level of documentation used and the intended audience.

An example of popular criticism is provided by the following article from the online general-interest magazine *Salon* (http://www.salon.com). In this critical piece, the writer contemplates the relationship between hip-hop music and poetry:

SCOTT THILL

Eminem vs. Robert Frost

From *Salon,* MARCH 18, 2004

> There are only three legitimate things anyone can do with poetry—write it, read it, or publish it. Writing reviews, or holding seminars, or reading it in public—even making records of it—well, this is secondary activity, unimportant at best, meretricious at worst.
>
> —*Philip Larkin*

The votes have been cast and the results are in—hip-hop is now the preferred entertainment medium for the next generation. Hip-hop sales make up a larger and larger proportion of the pop-music universe every year, and even when it does not thoroughly dominate, its styles are forming the backbone of whatever does, whether it happens to be bubble-pop, electronic music or rap-rock. You need look no further than Eminem's Oscar win for "Lose Yourself" to know that, like it or not, the form has arrived in mainstream culture and isn't going anywhere.

Along the way, it has made capitalist kings out of Russell Simmons, Jay-Z, Rick Rubin, LL Cool J, Ice Cube and countless others. Simmons alone is now a cultural force to be reckoned with, and his "One Mind One Vote" campaign hopes to pull millions of nonvoting young African-Americans into the 2004 election.

Simmons understands a zeitgeist when he sees one, and so it is no surprise that such a progenitor of hip-hop would latch onto the burgeoning poetry movement known as spoken word—or "slam," depending on the venue—and take it mainstream. In 2003, Simmons morphed his king-making HBO vehicle known as *Def Comedy Jam* into *Def Poetry Jam*, hoping to explode the careers of outstanding poets like Saul Williams, Jimmy Santiago Baca, Ursula Rucker and others as convincingly as he did for comedians Martin Lawrence, Jamie Foxx, Bernie Mac, Steve Harvey and Dave Chappelle. It worked like a charm—*Def Poetry Jam* garnered stellar reviews and a Peabody Award to boot.

That's because, as Saul Williams—whose recent epic poem "Said the Shotgun to the Head" was released by MTV Books last fall—explains, hip-hop has had as massive an influence on today's spoken word poets as jazz had on the Beats—and the African oral tradition had on jazz.

"I'm definitely a hip-hop head by nature, by generalization, by generation," says Williams. "I'm there in the mix, so I'm turned on by the same things, nod my head to the same things. Even if I'm writing a piece of prose, there is still an intrinsic rhythm that I'm looking for, even without rhyme, even without beats, even without music and microphones."

But even with the considerable clout of hip-hop—and Russell Simmons—behind it, spoken word is sometimes still considered the redheaded stepchild of poetry. It has yet to fully win over the academics, 183 years after Percy Bysshe Shelley argued that "poets are the unacknowledged legislators of the world." Former United States poet laureate Robert Pinsky has publicly praised the spoken-word movement, but the Favorite Poem Project Web site he started in 1997 to celebrate and promote "poetry's role in Americans' lives" includes exactly zero spoken-word or hip-hop artists (although it does contain a spirited reading of Gwendolyn Brooks' canonical "We Real Cool," a poetic hip-hop antecedent if there ever was one). This is curious, considering that the site features so many readings of classic poems by ordinary citizens like you and me.

If you ask Tree Swenson, executive director of the Academy of American Poets—since its inception in 1934 the country's largest organization dedicated to poetry—she'll tell you that it's just business as usual. "As long as there has been poetry, there have been poetry wars," she explains. "Very little of what's written in poetry survives. But this sorts itself out through time. I think it's very difficult to draw a line that will stay put. It wavers."

Swenson believes part of the reason for that wavering is the inherently personal nature of poetry itself. "Poetry by its very nature resists categorization," Swenson continues. "You can't simply lump all poets into a single group. As with more traditional poetry, it's always based on the individual poet and poem."

That may be Swenson's world view, but the prologue to editor Mark Eleveld's *The Spoken Word Revolution: Slam, Hip-Hop & the Poetry of a New Generation* (released last year by Sourcebooks) paints quite a different picture, one where categorization—and marginalization—cannot be extricated from the world of professional poetics. A few well-decorated poets sit at a table responding to questions from various interviewers, and the intergenerational and occupational tension is palpable. "They sat at the panel," Eleveld writes, "the learned and the poetic, some with their credentials resting high upon their shoulders . . . sound[ing] as if they just got off the Concorde from Paris . . . name-dropping Ivy League pretensions and Nobel Prize winner mentorships."

That "aristocratic bullshit," as Eleveld describes it, is what led the sole poet   10
on the panel without those ivory-tower credentials, Marc Smith, to create the
Poetry Slam. "I was an outsider," Smith explains in *The Spoken Word Revolution*,
"and I thought I had something to say, like a lot of outsiders do. There were a lot
of people snubbing me who shouldn't have been snubbing me. So I just ended up
doing it my own way."

The rest, as they say, is history. Spoken-word and slams quickly became poetry's most vital, vibrant movements, populating smoky clubs and silver screens
alike, most notably in the form of Marc Levin's 1998 *Slam*, a film that starred and
was co-written by Saul Williams—and took home the Sundance Film Festival's
Grand Jury Prize in the process. Williams has also become a star of sorts, landing
roles in big-budget movies like "KPAX" and opening slots on tours for Rage
Against the Machine, the Roots and, most recently, Mars Volta.

Meanwhile, Eleveld's book is in its second printing, having sold 20,000
copies in approximately nine months, a major feat for a poetry release whose
market considers a bestseller to be around 1,500 copies sold. No doubt the inclusion of such esteemed figures—in both the book and an accompanying CD—as
Williams, *Lord of the Rings* star Viggo Mortensen, Sherman Alexie and Andrei
Codrescu, as well as an introduction by current U.S. poet laureate Billy Collins,
has contributed to the brisk sales.

Whether you like the forms or not, spoken-word and the poetry slam have
resuscitated poetry for popular consumption. "I think poetry is more popular now
than it has been in the last 100 years, at least," says Eleveld. "*Poetry Speaks*, published by Sourcebooks, sold 100,000 copies because of three CDs that had canonized poets like [Walt] Whitman, [E. E.] Cummings and [Sylvia] Plath reading
their own work. *The Spoken Word Revolution* sold 20,000 in its first run. In poetry,
these numbers are unheard of. The National Poetry Slam in 2003 ran for four
nights, taking up eight clubs in Chicago's Wicker Park area, and boasted 1,100
people at the individual finals at the Metro, which is where the Rolling Stones,
Smashing Pumpkins and more have played."

According to Eleveld, those numbers are a far cry from a literary landscape
before poetry slams. In the mid-1980s, he remembers, "Poetry readings were
sparse; audiences were usually around something like 15 people. Now, professional poets are regularly touring high schools, colleges and clubs. If you go to
Billy Collins' site, you'll see that he travels 15 days out of the month reading his
work. This is all related to slams, hip-hop and the appreciation of oral tradition."

But even though that oral tradition—whether it was handed down from   15
Homer, Rumi, Allen Ginsberg or Chuck D—is alive and well in the spoken-
word sphere, there is still a performance aspect of slams that remains largely
alien to conventional poetics. And that added dimension of public performance
is just as complicated as it is attractive.

"We don't really have an academy position on spoken word," explains
Swenson. "The lines are blurry. You certainly have more traditional poets, who
begin with the page and then read their poems. Some read it well and some read
it abominably."

That is, just reading your work aloud might not be enough sometimes.
You've got to "move the crowd," as Rakim said on "Paid in Full."

"There are a couple of different elements here," Swenson continues. "Do
these words work on the page? There are some poems that are so complex on the

page that they're impossible to read. But there is some middle ground, where the poem can come alive through the voice. Then are some great performers who can put on a show and wow an audience, but when the words are put on a page, they become lifeless."

Then there is, getting back to hip-hop, what Saul Williams considers to be the built-in oppression coursing through the rap game.

"The difference between the poet and the M.C. is that the M.C. is by defin- 20 ition a master of ceremonies," Williams explains. "If you aim to be the master of ceremonies, then you have to play the role of the oppressor. You have to be in control, you have—to use a hip-hop slogan—'to act like ya know, son, you have to act like ya know.' Whereas the poet is allowed to be introspective, allowed to raise questions—is allowed to say, 'I don't know, I wonder why, I wonder what this means.'"

That innocent questioning of what the L.A. ska-punk poets Fishbone called "the reality of my surroundings" is often frowned upon by those in hip-hop and rap who, like 50 Cent, build their reputations on flak jackets and bullet holes. "The poet is allowed to be vulnerable," Williams continues, "whereas, with M.C.'s and in hip-hop, vulnerability is a sign of weakness. And so it becomes less and less real, less connected to the true nature of humankind. The further out we go on the tip of invulnerability and being hardcore, the less we can show a soft side."

It is this simplistic hyper-masculine posturing that has continually plagued the rap game, and kept it from achieving the type of legitimacy bestowed upon other forms of poetic expression. 50 Cent's unimaginative subject matter and Eminem's persistent homophobia, no matter how cleverly worded it may be (and in 50's case, that's being exceedingly charitable), are ultimately alienating. Which is not to say that Eminem's work, in particular, hasn't inspired thousands of kids to dye their hair blond and put their thoughts on paper, but to what end? Does the world truly need another dick-grabbing M.C. who's interested mostly in heaping calumny on homosexuals, groupies, Moby and his own mother? Can we really consider lines from 50 Cent's "In Da Club" like "I'm that cat by the bar toasting to the good life / You that faggot-ass nigga trying to pull me back right" poetic in the slightest? 50 Cent might have been the hottest selling rap act of 2003, but to call him a poet would be testing the limits of the terminology.

But it's not as if the world of conventional poetry doesn't have its own issues with masculinity. Two decades back, poet Robert Bly's wildly successful "Iron John" initiated a "men's movement" that called much of society's sexual advances into question. Bly's basic thrust, pun intended, was that 20th century males had become too soft, and he set off a firestorm of feminist criticism. On the other hand, his books, videos and seminars sold like hotcakes.

Forget for a second that Bly's work was skewed mostly to white heterosexuals and also forget that Bly's way with words was a bit more sophisticated than 50 Cent's—both men, along with the majority of the hip-hop acts that have hit the charts since the genre exploded in the late '70s, utilize the figure of the warrior as man's saving grace. In fact, 50 Cent's continuing appeal lies in his ability to get shot up and live to tell the tale. Bly's so-called soft males have been redeemed as much by rap's hard guys as by beating tribal drums in the wilderness.

In other words, hip-hop is not the only place you find this kind of social nar-   25
rowcasting; the ivory tower set is just as much to blame for it as anyone else.
Which is why the argument over whether or not hip-hop is true poetry will always be a red herring. To mangle Shakespeare, the play on words is the thing.
The presentation, however compelling or alarming, is incidental.

Plus, hip-hop, if you ask Eleveld, is simply one facet of an oral poetic tradition that has enthralled global culture for millennia. "Hip-hop is huge," he says,
"but so is slam. I would still say that poetry is the queen of all mediums. There
are no limitations to how good poetry can be and in what directions it can go.
Look at Lou Reed's [stage production of] Poe's 'The Raven' or Laurie Anderson
doing Melville or Pearl Jam including spoken-word pieces on their albums."

That democratic strain of appropriation, presentation and representation is
ultimately poetry's gift to the world, whether it be written, spoken or slammed.
Rap is just the form's latest popular incarnation, one that is spreading like wild-
fire if only because, as Eminem's ascendancy to superstardom illustrates, it can
deliver hope, motivation and sustenance to those who feel they have no avenue
of expression, no way to voice their concerns and desires.

"Poetry is the voice of the people," Eleveld says. "It is open to all. When a
poetry slam is pulled off correctly, the least likely effect will be a great show. The
most powerful effect can be—and has been—life-changing."

The content and focus of this *Salon* article clearly emphasize the differences
between reviews and criticism. While the aim of a review is to evaluate a particular book or author, this critical article focuses on a large-scale trend: the influence of hip-hop music on poetry, and vice versa.

Scholarly Articles or Books

In contrast to its popular counterpart, a scholarly piece of criticism tends to have
a different intended audience and a different level of research and documentation. Popular criticism tends to aim itself at a general audience using plainspo-
ken language and usually contains no footnotes and no list of works cited. (For
example, the *Salon* piece above relies largely on interviews to make its points.) A
scholarly article on poetry, usually written by an expert in the field, presents a
claim or interpretation about a poet, a poem, or the field of poetry in general,
employing extensive research and containing extensive examples in support of
the claims. The intended audience for such articles is usually other specialists in
the field, and the language tends to be more specialized and academic in tone.

Still, many scholars and critics write for a wider general audience, as in the
excerpt bellow by poet and critic Edward Hirsch from his 1999 book *How to
Read a Poem: And Fall in Love with Poetry.* Hirsch does not footnote his sources in
the piece because he is not writing for an exclusively academic forum, but he
does identify his sources in the running text, and as is the style for general-interest books, a list of credits acknowledging the sources appears at the end of the actual book.

EDWARD HIRSCH

From How to Read a Poem: And Fall in Love with Poetry

It Is Something of an Accident That You Are the Reader and I the Writer

Lyric poetry is a form of verbal materialism, an art of language, but it is much more than "the best words in the best order." It is language fulfilling itself, language compressed and raised to its highest power. Language in action against time, against death. There are times when I am awestruck by the way that poems incarnate the spirit—the spirits—and strike the bedrock of being. Other times I am struck by how little the poem has to go on, how inadequate its means. For what does the writer have but some black markings on a blank page to imagine a world? Hence these lines from the splendid Florentine poet Guido Cavalcanti:

> Noi siàn le triste penne isbigottite
> le cesoiuzze e'l coltellin dolente.
>
> We are the poor, bewildered quills,
> The little scissors and the grieving penknife.

Cavalcanti projects his own grievous feelings of imaginative inadequacy onto the writer's very tools (quills and the knives to sharpen them), the writer's diminutive instruments.

In *Six Memos for the Next Millennium*, Italo Calvino makes an insightful comment that enlarges on Cavalcanti's lines, creating a statement about the experience of literature itself:

> all "realities" and "fantasies" can take on form only by means of writing, in which outwardness and innerness, the world and I, experience and fantasy, appear composed of the same verbal material. The polymorphic visions of the eyes and the spirit are contained in uniform lines of small or capital letters, periods, commas, parentheses—pages of signs, packed as closely together as grains of sand, representing the many-sided spectacle of the world as a surface that is always the same and always different, like dunes shifted by the desert wind.

I am reminded by Calvino's description of the literal limits of art: that all the incitement and grace of literature has to take place in the lineup of written characters on the page.

"There is then creative reading as well as creative writing," Emerson says in "The American Scholar" in a statement that could be a credo for the reader of poems. Poetry alerts us to what is deepest in ourselves—it arouses a spiritual desire which it also gratifies. It attains what it avows. But it can only do so with the reader's imaginative collaboration and even complicity. The writer creates through words a felt world which only the reader can vivify and internalize. Writing is embodiment. Reading is contact. In the preface to *Obra poetica*, Jorge Luis Borges writes:

> The taste of the apple (states Berkeley) lies in the contact of the fruit with the palate, not in the fruit itself; in a similar way (I would say) poetry lies in the meeting of the poem and reader, not in the lines of symbols printed on the pages of a book. What is essential is the aesthetic act, the thrill, the almost physical emotion that comes with each reading.

Borges continues on to suggest that poetry can work its magic by fulfilling our profound need to "recover a past or prefigure a future."

Poetry depends on the mutuality of writer and reader. The symbols on the page alone are insufficient. Borges was a fabulist and in the foreword to his first book of poems he went even further to suggest that poetry goes beyond mutuality, beyond identification, into identity itself.

> If in the following pages there is some successful verse or other, may the reader forgive me the audacity of having written it before him. We are all one; our inconsequential minds are much alike, and circumstances so influence us that it is something of an accident that you are the reader and I the writer—the unsure, ardent writer—of my verses.

This is funny and brilliant and perhaps disingenuous, but there is also a truth in it which has to do with a common sensation of reading: the eerie feeling that we are composing what we are responding to. In *The Redress of Poetry* Seamus Heaney calls this "the fluid, exhilarating moment which lies at the heart of any memorable reading, the undisappointed joy of finding that everything holds up and answers the desire that it awakens." Poetry creates its own autonomous world, and what that world asks from us it also answers within us.

In *The Poetics of Space*, Gaston Bachelard says that "Poetry puts language in   5
a state of emergence." It emerges at short range. Bachelard also quotes Pierre-Jean Jouve's statement that "Poetry is a soul inaugurating a form." The notion of the soul's inauguration of form suggests what Bachelard calls "supreme power" and "human dignity." I honor that dignity by recognizing the form it takes, the way it composes itself. Every work of art needs a respondent to complete it. It is only partially realized without that imaginative response. Jean-Paul Sartre puts the matter emphatically in *What Is Literature?*:

> The creative act is only an incomplete and abstract moment in the production of a work. If the author existed alone he would be able to write as much as he liked; the work as *object* would never see the light of day and he would either have to put down his pen or despair. But the operation of writing implies that of reading as its dialectical correlative and these two connected acts necessitate two distinct agents. It is the joint effort of author and reader which brings upon the scene that concrete and imaginary object which is the work of the mind. There is no art except for and by others.

The reader exists on the horizon of the poem. The message in the bottle may seem to be speaking to the poet alone, or to God, or to nobody, but the reader is the one who finds and overhears it, who unseals the bottle and lets the language emerge. The reader becomes the listener, letting the poem voice and rediscover itself as it is read.

The Shock, the Swoon, the Bliss

I take the poet as a maker who sends out a formal enticement, a provocation, a challenge. I encounter—I am encountered by—a work of art. For me, that encounter is active, inquisitive, relentless, disturbing, exuberant, daring, and beholden. Poets speak of the shock, the swoon, and the bliss of writing, but why not also speak of the shock, the swoon, and the bliss of reading?

HOW TO ENTER THE CONVERSATION

As mentioned before, college students studying poetry can become reviewers, thanks to the democracy of blogs and sites like amazon.com. But to move beyond a subjective reaction by delving more deeply into a poem's elements, students will also need to work toward writing criticism of their own. The problem many students face is that they don't know how to start thinking about a poem, don't have a way "in." Asking questions is one way to start developing your ideas about a poem.

Questions to Develop Ideas about a Poem

This section provides you two key approaches: ways to develop useful questions about a poem, and helpful formats to use when you sit down to do the writing. Don't think of these two approaches as completely separate, since in fact they are intertwined. The questions to ask and the types of writing go together. The questions and formats are not abstract categories but instead living examples of how to enter into the critical conversation through writing.

As you read or reread a poem, connect with it through questions like the ones that follow. The answers to these questions, often in the form of lists of specific examples, will provide you with material for writing about poetry in a wide variety of formats.

Point of View

1. What kind of person is narrating the poem? How strongly does the narrator care about the events in the poem, or does the narrator seem totally removed and impersonal?
2. Does the narrator comment on what happens? How?

Language

1. What is the level of the language? High? Middle? Low?
2. Does the language seem contemporary, old-fashioned, or in between? Can you pin this answer down with examples?
3. Did you notice any specialized type of vocabulary? Any words you needed to look up? Any non-English words or phrases?
4. Was the language particularly colorful, or did it not draw attention to itself?
5. Did you note examples of irony? Symbolism? Any notable qualities of tone?
6. What was notable about the meter, or was the poem free verse?
7. Were there any notable repetitions of words or attitudes or ideas?

Setting

1. When and where did the events in the poem take place?
2. Did the setting seem to be an important part of the poem?

3. Was the setting symbolic in any way?
4. What details of the setting seemed to receive the most attention from the narrator?

Character

1. Are there clearly defined characters in the poem?
2. What seems to be the main character's motivation?
3. Are the characters sharply delineated, with individual characteristics, or do they seem more like types?
4. What changes take place in characters over the story?
5. Did you find yourself identifying with the narrator?

Plot

1. Can you state the poem's main action in a sentence?
2. How does the story of the poem unfold? Chronologically? Are there flash-backs? Any foreshadowing?
3. Did you feel manipulated or were you willingly pulled along by the plot? Was there a surprise ending? Any tricks?
4. What kind of resolution occurs at the end?

Links to Other Texts

1. Did this poem (or parts of it) seem like any others you know about?
2. Were there any passages you would like to hear read by a professional?
3. What kind of performance-oriented reading would work with this poem?
4. What words or phrases should get special emphasis in reading aloud?

Response

1. Was the narrator especially attractive or repellent to you?
2. Did a particular sentence or phrase or situation catch your fancy?
3. What "got" to you in the poem? A person? An incident? A phrase or word?
4. Was there anything in the poem that touches on what you have experienced in your own life or in the life of someone you know?

These are only a beginning, of course, but they are exactly the questions any professional reviewer or critic asks of a poem. The questions focus attention on the text itself. They represent ways of "interrogating" the poem, of conducting a genuine dialogue with the text, forcing you to be an active rather than passive reader. Answering the questions will pay off in three ways: you will produce a much more well-informed reading of a poem, you will reflect on how you make meaning of your own life, and the answers to the questions will provide rich material for the writing you will do in different formats. Beginning students confronted with a writing assignment often ask, "Where do I start?" The answer is, "Start with these questions."

Poetry Websites and Blogs. Despite the common contention that "poetry is dead," poetry appears in all sorts of unlikely everyday places—from "Poetry in Motion" billboards on buses and subways across the country to the popular "Magnetic Poetry" word kits. Poetry is thriving even more online. A quick Google search yields a seemingly endless list of poetry websites. You will find not only online magazines that publish poetry, reviews, and criticism but also sites about workshops, slams, readings, and conferences.

Similarly, as with fiction, personal responses to poems are increasingly becoming material for blogs, the weblogs of avid readers who have created their own virtual conversation and invited other readers to see and respond to what they have written. Obviously, the quality of the writing and dialogue varies widely in this open, uncensored forum; the Web has enabled anyone with access to current computer technology to "publish" for a wide audience almost instantly, without long-term thought, evaluation, or editing involved. With poetry in particular, many blogs tend to be devoted to individuals self-publishing their own work rather than conversing about the works of other poets.

On the positive side, the unmediated quality of the opinions put forth is part of a blog's attraction and blogs offer the rare opportunity for people from different parts of the country or the world—and possibly from highly different backgrounds—to converse about the common poetry they read. Try visiting a few bloggers' sites to see vibrant conversations in action. Some viewpoints are one-sided, uninformed, and self-indulgent, while others are articulate, thoughtful, and insightful—but they are all usually passionate and earnest.

To begin to explore the eclectic, virtual dialogue taking place today, visit the basic online resources on poetry that are listed below.

- The Academy of American Poets, *http://www.poets.org.* This is among the largest and most frequently visited poetry sites, offering essays and interviews, poet biographies, an enormous archive of poems and audio clips of poems read by their authors or other poets, and an extensive list of online poetry resources.
- Poets House, *http://www.poetshouse.org.* The website of this New York–based literary center and archive includes information on their library, which is free and open to the public and comprises the most comprehensive open-access collection of poetry books and resources in the United States. Information is provided as well on their lectures, workshops, and other public outreach programs, and links to other poetry-focused resources.
- Bookslut, *http://www.bookslut.com.* This lively literary site features interviews with contemporary authors, articles and columns by contributing and staff writers, and book reviews, but many of its readers visit for the impassioned, frequent, and often extensive blog postings by the site's editors.
- Complete Review Quarterly's Overview Links to Literary Weblogs, *http://www.complete-review.com/quarterly/vol3/issue3/litblogs.htm.* The

Complete Review, a Web presence since 1999, focuses on reviewing literature. Its list of weblogs is thorough and accurate. The March 2005 issue includes a lengthy overview of literary weblogs.

■ Identity Theory, *http://www.identitytheory.com/bookblog/*. This site is devoted
to literature of all kinds and includes author interviews; criticism; original
fiction, nonfiction, and poetry; and reprints of public domain classics. It also
offers a group book-discussion weblog about what its participants are reading, as well as a list of recommended literature weblogs by individual
writers.

FORMATS FOR WRITING ABOUT POEMS

Here are some common forms of writing about poetry in a college setting, in order of increasing formality and complexity. (Research projects are covered in
Chapter 27.)

Annotations are marginal notes and underlinings for personal understanding, guiding rereading, or preparing for a discussion or a paper. These are
usually written on the page itself, but some annotations can be written in
a notebook or journal.

Summaries and paraphrases are brief retellings of a poem, in your own
words, to help you or a reader grasp what the poem says.

A journal or notebook is a place to record your reactions, questions, and responses to a book or poem. Another use for a journal is to make a collection of notable lines, phrases, and expressions to help you "fix" a reading
for yourself or to help you analyze a poem. This collection, usually compiled in a notebook or computer file, is called by some a "commonplace
book."

A response paper is a short, personal, and often informal paper, showing
your thoughts and feelings as you read the text, as well as connections to
other texts you've read, or perhaps the story of your own reading.

An intervention is a creative response in which you alter or play with or
talk back to the text in the form of a parody, an imitation, or an answer.

An explication is a formal line-by-line analysis that takes into account all of
the elements of the poem, based on a very close reading of the language of
the text.

An analytical essay is a formal, thesis-driven essay that examines certain elements of a poem (e.g., speaker, language, structure) and states a claim
about how they operate in the poem.

The remainder of this chapter discusses each of these kinds of writing in
greater detail, using poetry by Emily Dickinson, with her poem "After Great
Pain" as the primary example.

EMILY DICKINSON

(1830–1886)

After Great Pain

(C. 1862)

After great pain, a formal feeling comes—
The Nerves sit ceremonious, like Tombs—
The stiff Heart questions was it He, that bore,
And Yesterday, or Centuries before?

The Feet, mechanical, go round—   5
Of Ground, or Air, or Ought—
A Wooden way
Regardless grown,
A Quartz contentment, like a stone—

This is the Hour of Lead—   10
Remembered, if outlived,
As Freezing persons recollect the Snow—
First—Chill—then Stupor—then the letting go—

Annotating a Poem

An **annotation** gives notes for a fuller, richer understanding of anything you read and is frequently a first step in any writing assignment. To annotate a text as you read, make marks in the margin, underline words, or write comments and questions. By annotating as you read, you are in dialogue with the poem, engaged in your own conversation with the poet. Reading is no longer passive but rather an active engagement.

Above all, as in any good conversation, use your annotations to sort out as much as possible what the poem is saying. In particular, look up unfamiliar words and **allusions** (references to other texts, authors, or historical or cultural events). Poems, like other literary texts, are written for specific audiences at particular times, so what the poet could assume readers would understand when and where the poem was written may have become obscure through the distance of time or place or from a change in culture.

For example, in Frank O'Hara's "The Day Lady Died" (which appears in Chapter 10, p. 748), a twenty-first-century reader needs to know that the singer Billie Holiday was called "Lady Day," and that her piano accompanist in her later years was Mal Waldron. O'Hara doesn't tell us these facts in the poem, written in 1959; he assumes we know or can figure them out. Or perhaps, if we don't know these facts, we're not the audience he wants to reach. But new generations of readers need to be filled in on key details. If you were reading the poem and didn't get the allusions to Holiday and Waldron, you would have to do some digging and then make yourself an annotation in the margin or in a notebook.

Emily Dickinson's "After Great Pain" might be annotated like this:

After great pain, a formal feeling comes—	f . . . f . . . f alliteration
The Nerves sit ceremonious, like Tombs—	How are nerves like tombs?

The stiff Heart questions was it He, that bore, And Yesterday, or Centuries before?	Why the capital H? Jesus, who "bore" the cross? Centuries . . . again, Jesus? It was common for a Christian feeling great pain to "question" whether the healing sacrifice of Jesus centuries ago still mattered. It was the kind of question thoughtful religious people worried over.
The Feet, mechanical, go round— Of Ground, or Air, or Ought— A Wooden way Regardless grown, A Quartz contentment, like a stone—	Odd parallel, with Ought . . . note "of" Tombs, still, mechanical, wooden: inhuman Quartz? Sharp edges?
This is the Hour of Lead— Remembered, if outlived, As Freezing persons recollect the Snow— First—Chill—then Stupor then the letting go—	From quartz to lead. Geology (more inhuman) Obviously, not "remembered" if not "outlived" At least three of the books the Dickinson family owned contained accounts of death from freezing

Annotations can include both the questions we ask of a poem for ourselves and the answers we find for ourselves and for other readers. Sometimes the best thinkers and annotators come up with a blank about a word or phrase: "quartz contentment," for instance, still puzzles. Did quartz have some special meaning in the America of the 1860s? Did Dickinson select the wonderful phrase for anything other than its sound? Was it perhaps for its juxtaposition of hard mineral and ease of soul? Or was it perhaps for an ease of soul that is hard won and only temporary? We do not know.

Note that as we ask and answer key questions about puzzling or interesting words and phrases, our process of annotation has turned into a process of "composing" the poem for ourselves. Dickinson wrote the words of the poem; now it is our task not just to take it in and passively decode it, but to shape it, actively, for ourselves. As her contemporary Ralph Waldo Emerson observed, "there is creative reading as well as creative writing."

Writing about the Text

1. Annotate a passage from one of the poems in Chapter 10 or 11.
2. Using the annotations you created for item 1 above, describe what those annotations tend to cover. Are they equally attentive to all aspects of the passage, or do they have a particular focus?

Summarizing or Paraphrasing a Poem

A **summary** is a short boiling down of a whole poem or passage; a **paraphrase** is a retelling in your own words, usually the same length as the original. Summary is used for filling the reader in on the background, while paraphrase is more useful for rendering a complex passage in simpler language. Both are powerful tools for a writer and necessary parts of the cultural conversation, because we are always filling in or simplifying matters for our readers or listeners.

Writing a One-Sentence Summary

Poetry critic Helen Vendler requires all undergraduates in her introduction to poetry course to write a single-sentence summary of a poem to be discussed in class.
Her rule is strict: just one sentence that accurately summarizes the poem. As the
semester starts, these sentences are understandably simple and general, but as students become more confident, their sentences become longer, more complex, and
more interesting. Vendler's one-sentence summary exercise is a powerful tool for
writing about poetry. It focuses the mind on getting to the core of the poem, and
it provides a good way for Vendler to tell how readers have understood what is going on in the poem. It is also a great method of comparing your own progress with
that of your classmates or fellow readers and of igniting a discussion.

Here are two one-sentence summaries of "After Great Pain," the first written at the beginning of the course, when students were inexperienced at writing
such summaries, the second written later in the course after students had gained
some experience.

Inexperienced student:

```
    A commentary on how the body and soul react to
great physical or emotional pain, given by someone who,
though impersonal sounding here, seems intimately
acquainted with the subject.
```

Experienced student:

```
    Dickinson's impersonal-seeming lines in "After Great
Pain" seem to imitate the mechanical, stone-like
numbness that the poem itself describes, with half
rhymes connecting unfinished phrases that follow one
another in succession, from one blunted, bleak reaction
to another until the final "letting go" that she
stunningly compares to death from freezing.
```

Think of this type of summary exercise as a way to get you further in your
reading, not as an end in itself. It is one stage in understanding the poem, one
kind of response.

Paraphrasing

The rule for a paraphrase is to take everything in the original and "translate" it
into your own language, simplifying as you go. Here is a sample paraphrase of the
first four lines of Dickinson's poem:

```
    Following the experience of a great pain is a formal
feeling, comparable to a ceremony, or like a tomb. With
a stiff, numbed heart one asks the question: Was it
Jesus who bore the cross, both yesterday and centuries
ago?
```

This paraphrase is accurate, but the exercise shows how hard it is to put Dickinson into anyone's words but her own.

Writing about the Text

1. In one or two sentences, summarize a poem in Chapter 10 or 11 as if you were describing it to someone who has never read it.
2. Write a paraphrase of any poem in Chapter 10 or 11.

Keeping a Personal Journal

Journals are useful for creating a written or electronic record of notable lines, phrases, and expressions that help you "fix" a reading for yourself or that help you analyze a poem. There are two types of journal entries about a poem. The first simply records your reading, with questions and notes listed by line number. You may also want to use it to copy memorable words, lines, or phrases. (In earlier days, when books were expensive and relatively rare, readers would copy out their favorite parts into a commonplace book, a kind of homemade anthology.) This type of journal then becomes material for another reading, and it can be turned into raw material for a paper on the subject.

A second type of journal, the **double-entry notebook**, pioneered by Professor Ann E. Berthoff, is a more structured and more powerful exercise for student writers. In one column the reader records noteworthy lines, phrases, and situation summaries; in an opposite column the reader then records reflections and reactions. The whole point of such a notebook is to get readers to write down important and interesting things they have noticed, and *then* briefly to reflect about them in writing. As Berthoff puts it, the left side, with the brief annotations, represents your thinking, what you abstracted from the text. The right side of the notebook takes matters to another stage: it represents your thinking about your thinking.

This double-entry example shows the notes one good reader made after a few careful readings of "After Great Pain."

Line 1. What kind of pain? From reading Dickinson's poems and letters we don't know; most people suppose it's emotional rather than physical. Losing one's love? one's friend? one's father?

Lines 1–2 "formal" and "ceremonious" connect in denotation.

Line 2. The notion of nerves "sitting" is odd. But compare weakness of "nerves get numb"

Line 3. Identity of "He": God, Christ? (Because capitalized.): "bore"—the cross.

Line 3. "stiff" heart. Proud? Numbed? Angry? Resonance with biblical "stiff-necked"? (Look up)

Line 4. "Yesterday" and "Centuries before" adds to the sense of confusion, doubt. Is the "confusion" put on to a certain extent, out of anger?

But that phrase, if it's meant, is elided. Her readers could probably fill it in. (Look up the hymn [?] it comes from.) The elision—if such it is—enforces the sense of (angry?) questioning as to whether the "great pain" had any meaning. Compensation? Consolation? Terminus point?

Line 5. "The Feet, mechanical": we feel on more familiar ground, because it's pretty common for somebody who's grieving to say they go about their necessary business "mechanically."

Line 6. "Of Ground, or Air, or Ought" scrambles matters again, if only because "ought" isn't in any way parallel to "ground" or "air." It's not even the same part of speech as those two.

Line 7. "A wooden way" enforces the sense of pointlessness, numbness of the emotions—not exceptional, since it's usual for us to say we feel "wooden," or to describe someone's movements as "wooden."

Lines 8–9. A bit alarming. "Regardless"? Or worse, "contentment"? Yes, it's a "quartz" contentment—hardly approaching joy or pleasure. The two words don't seem to belong together, and yet, forced together, they DO seem to go together. Is it because, again, they convey anger? Or are both the "stoniness" and "contentment" felt, at least fleetingly? Is it the contentment, actually, that's fleeting?

Line 9. Why is the "like a stone" necessary?

Line 10. Well, we certainly get dumped again/still by the opening line of the third stanza—"This is the hour of Lead." Again the more familiar imagery of "lead"—heavy, a burden, grey. Quartz, wooden, now lead.

Lines 11–13. "Lead." "Chill—then Stupor." What to make of the poem's ending? Seems both angry and resigned, discouraged and also at peace. Contradictions.

Lines 5–6. As I "live" with the first two lines of stanza two I almost get a feel of feet going around in a kind of mill, —with no sense of getting anywhere. ED must have known of mills that ground wheat into flour, with horses going around in circles and not getting anywhere. Every town had a local mill.

Lines 8–9. The last two lines of that stanza sound like a riddle, puzzle. Dickinson liked riddle poems. See "I like to see it lap the miles."

Line 9. On second thought, quartz might be something to feel a little proud of (versus a "stone"). "Quartz" is at least particular, and it connotes more brightness than simply "stone." Question: did quartz mean anything special in mid-19th century?

Line 9. "Like a stone"? To return us to something semi-familiar? Memory of a millstone, suggested in lines 5–6?

Lines 11–13. "Remembered, if outlived" sounds pretty bitter. It sounds as if the speaker doesn't really expect to outlive this leadenness. And even if the feeling eases off, it sounds as if the memory of the leadenness will be bad enough.

Writing about the Text

1. Do "commonplace book" journal entries about a poem in Chapter 10 or 11, copying lines you particularly like.
2. Take the journal entries you compiled in item 1 and do your commentary on the entries in the form of a double-entry notebook.

Writing a Response Paper

A **response paper** is a brief, quick, yet strongly felt personal reaction written in the form of an essay, usually a short one. Poems are meant to be taken personally, so it is particularly valuable for readers to write about their own responses and reactions. You can structure a response paper in a number of ways:

- An overall response to the poem's subject or theme.
- The story of your own reading.
- Your personal connection to other poems or stories ("It reminds me of . . .").
- A description of how your reading changed over time ("The first time I read it . . ."; "The next time . . ."; "Upon further reflection . . ."; "Now I see . . .").

The field is wide open. Naturally, the more emphasis you put on the *personal* part of the response, the less the writing is about the poem and the more it is about you as reader. So be careful to tie the responses you had to the text of the poem, linking your reactions and responses to particular lines and images.

Sometimes the best response you can write about a poem is to tell the story of your reading it: what happened as you read, what you expected and whether that expectation was fulfilled, how a particular word or phrase or line "got" to you, what fell flat, what you took away when you stopped reading. As these suggestions indicate, a good response paper involves writing about yourself as much as about the poem, though most instructors want to see response papers tied closely to the actual words and images of the poem.

Response papers become easier to write if you regard them not as finished, polished pieces that attempt to cover everything, but as insights or reactions to readings of the poem, or even to one aspect of the poem. Use the first person, and don't be reluctant to admit your struggles or confusions or misunderstanding. In fact, those are some of the most valuable, honest responses you can provide.

From a Response Paper to "After Great Pain"

Here is the last part of a longer response paper to "After Great Pain." The student has moved through the poem, giving an account of her personal reactions. Here is what she writes about her reading of the last lines: "As Freezing persons recollect the Snow— / First—Chill—then Stupor—then the letting go—" (12–13).

```
    These last two lines come at us like a car crash.
The grief, far from diminishing, is going to kill this
speaker, if not all at once, then eventually. We've
switched images from earlier in the poem—from one of
```

becoming stone, or being burdened by stone—to one of freezing to death. Stones are often thought of as cold, so there may be a slight connection. Is this freezing willful or involuntary? I don't know. Is it suicidal? Perhaps, a kind of emotional numbness that one wills, or at least accepts. Certainly it's not a comforting image. The prior "contentment," made of the hard, durable "quartz," has morphed into a "stupor," a "letting go" into death. Were we satisfied with "contentment," resting there in some sort of consolation? If so, in the last lines the speaker pushes us into bleaker territory, forcing us a step further to confront the rigidity of death.

As a New Englander, Emily Dickinson obviously knew a good deal about the cold of a winter, yet hadn't experienced what it felt like to freeze to death, nor am I aware that she knew of anyone who had frozen to death, or had almost frozen to death. People *did* freeze to death in her neck of the woods. It's tantalizing to wonder if there were old stories or New England legends— or simply a report from the *Springfield Republican*, which she read—about people freezing to death in the farm towns around Amherst or possibly in the nearby Vermont or New Hampshire mountains. Clearly she'd read or heard about the experience; it tallies with our own, "modern" understanding of what happens to somebody who dies of exposure.

This poem does not give the conventional 19th-century view of death. There's no vision of immortality or heaven offered or suggested (as there is in some of her letters, written to comfort those who had lost loved ones). There's not even any assurance of the end or easing of grieving (except through the death of the speaker, but termination is achieved by oblivion).

The only thing vaguely comforting about this poem is the suggestion that this kind of death (by freezing) can be more comfortable than perhaps other kinds of death. The "letting go" is often thought of as a positive thing—but less so if it's into death. Her refusal of all

```
the traditional comforts and the comparison with
literally freezing—I'm still stunned.
     Is this a Civil War poem? Certainly it was written
at that time. As far as I know, she did not lose close
family members, though she must have known many young
men who were hurt or killed.
```

This is a strong, personal response to the words of the poem. Note how the writer connects the beginning of the poem, with its emphasis on a certain kind of numbness ("ceremonial," "stiff"), to the bleakness of freezing. Your response paper can be similar: meditations on what the poem's individual words seem to be doing to you as you read. The best response papers will focus both on single words and phrases *and* on the overall effect.

Writing about the Text

1. Write a response paper to a poem in Chapter 10 or 11.
2. Respond to the narrator's voice in a poem in Chapter 10 or 11, telling how the narrator strikes you. Are you impressed? Amused? Unimpressed? Scornful?

Writing an Intervention

Intervention refers to the practice of altering, playing with, or talking back to a text. One type of intervention is an answer poem, as we saw with Christopher Marlowe's "The Passionate Shepherd to His Love" and the "reply" Sir Walter Raleigh wrote (see p. 930). Another type of intervention is a parody, poking fun at the style or concerns of the poet in question. As you can imagine, writers with a strongly individual style get parodied more than those without one.

Writing about the Text

1. Write an intervention to Linda Pastan's "Marks" (p. 725), changing the narrator to the husband or one of the children.
2. Turn a poem in Chapter 10 or 11 into prose, making it a story that keeps the essential "plot" of the poem.

Writing an Explication

A time-tested technique for writing about poetry is the **explication**, which is a close-up, well-ordered examination of what is happening in a poem: how the words, the form, and the meter work together to produce the overall effect. A traditional explication has little room for personal reaction ("When I first read this I felt . . .") or historical background ("Like most Renaissance poets, Shakespeare . . ."). There is a certain purity to an explication, and a certain artificiality too. In real life we never read or appreciate a poem without thinking "I felt" or noting details about a poet's era or attitude toward the subject matter. In other words, an explication is an exercise that attempts to do the impossible, to look at the poem itself, without its political, social, personal, or historical context, and without the participation of a real reader in dialogue with it.

As an exercise, explication is very powerful, forcing you to focus simply on the words on the page rather than your own reaction or the complex historical, cultural, or social background. Think of explication as a valuable step in becoming a good writer about poems and a helpful corrective to some readers' impulses to go immediately to "the expert."

The order of an explication is simple: you must follow the order of the poem, line by line, sticking quite closely to individual words and phrases. Concentrate on explaining the word choice, noting unusual vocabulary and particularly striking rhymes and meters (see pp. 756–770 for a full treatment of rhyme, meter, and stanza). Your task in an explication is to provide a close reading, a word for word, sentence by sentence look at the poem, not an overall judgment or analysis.

A Student Explication of a Stanza in "After Great Pain"

The Feet, mechanical, go round—   5
Of Ground, or Air, or Ought—
A Wooden way
Regardless grown,
A Quartz contentment, like a stone—

```
    In line 5 the speaker claims that after pain the
feet act "mechanical," as if they are doing things
without a human command, and the quick interior rhyme of
lines 5-6, "round"-"ground" is kind of mechanical
itself. Line 7 reinforces the mechanical statement with
"regardless," another term for lack of human control.
And the quick rhyme in lines 8-9, "grown"-"stone," like
the one in 5-6, has a quality that seems almost too
simple, straightforward. The rhymes come easily, bringing
the reader along "regardless," almost automatically.
                                        —Barton Rumilly
```

A Professional Explication

The following example, from an explication by Lilia Melani, a professor and critic, starts off with general statements about Dickinson's poem before embarking on a stanza by stanza analysis. Note two features of this explication. First, the writer looks closely at parts of the poem and asks questions rather than supplies answers. Second, notice the similarities between this explication and the annotations and journal entries on pp. 812–816. An explication is presented as a series of observations, not a complete essay.

Stanza 1

   She uses alliteration for emphasis: *f* sounds in line 1, *s* sounds in the rest of the stanza. *H* sounds tie together "Heart" and "He." Notice the alliteration in the next stanzas; sometimes it involves only two words.

   This poem has no speaker, no "I." The sufferer is dehumanized, perhaps until the last two lines. The sufferer is an object in line 1; the formal feeling "comes" upon or acts on her or him; the sufferer is passive, submissive. Then the sufferer is described in terms of body parts—nerves, heart, feet. The gender of the sufferer is not indicated. Is depersonalization one technique for showing emotional deadness? (In my discussion of this poem, I will refer to the sufferer as "she," because of the awkwardness of constantly repeating "sufferer" or "he or she.")

   Dickinson captures the numbness with "formal feeling," "ceremonious," "like tombs," and "Stiff Heart." The numbness is a lack of feeling; perhaps it would be more accurate to say a lack of connection with our feelings or a disconnection from emotions. Consider how much feeling or responsiveness is suggested by the word "formal," how much feeling is involved in ceremony, especially ceremony associated with "tombs" or death, and how much a "stiff" heart can feel.

   The individual asks a question about Christ ("He"). Christ of course symbolizes agony and is the ultimate suffering human being. The question can be read in more than one way. (1) The blow was so horrific that the sufferer is confused about whether the crucifixion was hers or Christ's. (2) The agony, which the sufferer is cut off from but knows is there, is so acute that the sufferer wonders whether the agony of the crucifixion is hers or Christ's. Paradoxically, numbness or having no feelings is itself an agony. In numbness, time becomes distorted; we lose our sense of time. We perceive no end to this state of agonized numbness. So she is unsure whether her numbness began only yesterday or centuries ago.

Writing about the Text

1. Explicate a poem in Chapter 10 or 11.
2. Explicate two poems by the same writer, showing similarities in tone, language, or attitude.

Writing an Analytical Essay

The types of writing activities described above often lead up to a formal, analytic essay, in which you explain or demonstrate how one or more elements of a poem operate. Here are some possible topics that would lead to an analytical essay about "After Great Pain":

- Explain how the speaker employs inanimate objects in "After Great Pain."
- How do you interpret the role of the speaker in "After Great Pain"?
- What are the "formal" qualities that follow great pain?

   An **analytical essay** calls for you to develop a central claim, or **thesis**, which you then support with examples or evidence from the poem itself. The virtue of an analytic essay is that it does not concentrate on the whole poem—that would take too long—just on your claim about one or more elements. Still, an analytic assignment requires time on your part to find a topic, gather evidence from the poem, and organize, draft, revise, and edit your paper. Be sure to give yourself time for each step of the process.

Developing a Thesis

The hardest part of an analytic assignment is often coming up with a claim or thesis. Often you will see desperate pleas on the Internet by students who write: "I have to come up with a five page paper on Emily Dickinson's 'After Great Pain' by tomorrow and I don't know what to say. Help!" If you have done some of the activities earlier in the chapter—annotations or journal entries, for instance—you can build on them to develop a thesis. The ideas that follow will help you find a topic for an analytic essay.

Start with Early Observations

Start with observations you made earlier about the poem, such as your annotations or journal entries. These observations and notes, created over a number of readings and rereadings, can lead to a question meaty enough to be explored in the context of a longer paper. For instance, in notes to "After Great Pain," one reader noticed that the metaphors all involved inanimate natural objects: wood, lead, and quartz. When human qualities or attributes were noted—feet, heart—they were immediately linked to those inanimate objects. Thus the final freezing, the "letting go" of human qualities, seems prepared for throughout the poem. A claim or thesis based on such an observation might discuss the way the poem constantly repeats a movement from animate to inanimate, a pattern in the poem that mimics the pattern in the person feeling pain. Here is one possible topic assignment and an appropriate thesis:

> **Assignment:** Explain how the speaker employs inanimate objects in "After Great Pain."
>
> **Thesis:** A key element of "After Great Pain" is a continuous series of parallel movements from animate human feelings to inanimate objects.

The rest of your analytical essay would demonstrate the accuracy of this claim or thesis by providing evidence from individual lines and stanzas.

Quote Something

You can enter the conversation explicitly by quoting something about Dickinson or about poems and then showing how "After Great Pain" supports or undermines the statement. That is your thesis: that X is right (or wrong) to argue Y. Whom can you quote? Your best sources are critical books and articles, or reviews if you can find them. Don't feel as though you need to claim that someone is totally right or totally wrong; you can phrase an arguable claim in the form of "X overlooks a complication" or "X does not go far enough." As long as you can support *your* claim with convincing evidence, you can write a strong paper. The language of argument and claim, just like a good intellectual conversation, allows for complications and nuances as well as flat out contradiction.

Here is how one student developed a thesis using someone else's writing about the poem:

Assignment: How do you interpret the role of the speaker in "After Great Pain"?

Thesis: According to Lilia Melani, "This poem has no speaker, no 'I.' The sufferer is dehumanized, perhaps until the last two lines." Professor Melani's claim that the "poem has no speaker, No 'I,' does not seem entirely accurate. While the word "I" never appears, there is still someone stating what happens, a genuine and striking voice throughout the poem, even if it is not fully identifiable by age or gender.

For both of these approaches, your instructor will often give you an opportunity to try out your thesis, either by handing in the thesis or a one-paragraph prospectus or by devoting class time to presenting theses and giving feedback. Take advantage of any opportunity to test whether your thesis will lead to a good paper. If it is not promising, you are in a position to revise before embarking on the entire essay, so you are fortunate if you get the chance to try out the thesis in advance.

Student Analytical Essay of "After Great Pain"

Emily Dickinson often employed the first person pronoun, "I," in many of her poems, including "I like to see it lap the miles," "I taste a liquor never brewed," "I heard a Fly buzz—When I died," "Because I could not stop for Death," "My life it stood a loaded gun," and many others. That first-person "I" is nowhere present in "After Great Pain." At first glance, then, a reader might suppose that this poem is less personal and less intimate than some of Dickinson's other works that employ the "I." This is the position Professor Lilia Melani takes in her statement.

A reader can see why Professor Melani has reached her conclusion. "After Great Pain" seems very impersonal. The poem's imagery relies almost entirely on inanimate *things* that connect to the great pain, including some of the most striking phrases such as "quartz contentment." In addition, there are abstract adjectives such as "formal" (feeling) and "mechanical" (feet), and impersonal nouns such as "lead," "ground," "air," and "ought," all of which could lead a reader to conclude that the "great pain" has been located at a considerable distance from the speaker, and therefore from the reader as well.

After the reader has read and reread the poem for a while, however, it begins to seem that the absence of "I" makes little difference to the intensity and even the intimacy of the pain portrayed in it. In fact, the distancing of the pain—which seems to be one important thing the poem as a whole is about—has the unexpected effect of magnifying it. It is as if Dickinson's speaker were saying, "it's not just my pain, it's a human pain, a universal pain. It's so great that I can't claim ownership of it." And yet there is little doubt in my mind that the "great pain" is at base—or begins with—the speaker's pain—perhaps caused by the loss or death of someone very well loved. That missing "I," combined with the distancing images and adjectives that fill the poem, ends up by suggesting that the speaker's sense of a pain is enormous, deep, and overwhelming.

How does one arrive at the sense that there is a terrible pain the speaker knows about and has felt? First, there seems to be a strong sense of disorientation, of dislocation in the poem. The second line gives us "Nerves" that sit like persons— "ceremonious" (and are also "formal"). The second part of line 2 limits the possible ceremony to that of a funeral, leading to "Tombs." Whatever possibilities for personification exist in a ceremony seem deliberately shut off, for who is able to see persons or personification in "Tombs"?

The third and especially the fourth lines seem to be stuttered, almost as if the speaker couldn't manage to get the complete thought out: "The stiff Heart questions was it He, that bore, / And Yesterday, or Centuries before?" "He" is probably Jesus, as the capital "H" strongly suggests, since it was the common practice to capitalize in such a manner when God was mentioned. What did he bear? The cross? His suffering? That is, does the speaker refer to the crucifixion, which was claimed to give human beings eternal life and freedom from the sorrow of mourning? The reader is not sure exactly how to understand these two lines.

Further, after the "mechanical" feet of line 5, the line "Of Ground, or Air, or Ought—" seems to have two possibly parallel elements (Ground and Air) but it is hard to fit in three (Ought) in a parallel manner. The way the preposition "of" operates is puzzling as well. Does it connect to "Feet" or "go round," or neither? Likewise, "Quartz contentment" (line 9) is a strange if lovely image, which does not seem the same as "stone contentment," as implied by the rest of the line. In sum, there is a kind of "controlled" incoherence in this part of the poem. Perhaps this incoherence might be something that readers can imagine as a consequence of some kind of staggering pain.

Another consequence of the great pain, it seems to me as reader, is an anger—somewhat hidden but all the more powerful for not being directly stated. The "stiff Heart" of line 3 seems to speak not only of a heart numbed by pain but also of an unbelieving heart that has come to question the promises of the crucifixion and perhaps feels betrayed. "Where is the comfort the church or Christ speaks of? It's not available to me." Another sign of anger comes through in the brief phrase "if outlived," as if that is a big, unlikely "if." This pain shows every sign of being able to kill the speaker. Then, through the whole poem runs a resentment that the only way the sufferer can endure the pain is by having her body and feeling turn "formal," "mechanical," leaden, and stony—perhaps involuntarily.

Ultimately, it seems, comfort, relief—and rehumanization—can come to the speaker only through the "letting go"—of consciousness, of life itself. For this suggestion, the speaker picks the process that is familiar anecdotally to most who know the winters of New England and other cold places—death by freezing, which we think of as pain followed by numbness (and maybe even a sense of warmth), followed by an almost irresistible desire to stop struggling and fall asleep. The homely image, ironically, comes across as comforting, and in fact supplies relief from the stoniness of the earlier part of the poem, but it also carries the suggestion that the pain of this particular sufferer—and maybe the rest of us as well—is relieved only by the speaker's death.

Thus, in a way, we as readers are betrayed by the concluding image: there's comfort, but maybe only at the price of life. This is "great pain," indeed, and more than enough to flatten speaker and reader alike. "I" and "we" might be superfluous and unnecessary designations in such circumstances.

Writing about the Text

1. Write an analytical essay about one of these two topics:
   a. Narrators in early poems seem less complex than the narrators in contemporary poems.
   b. Free verse lacks meter and rhyme, but it has its own organizing principles.
2. In an analytical essay, describe this chapter's three examples of critical writing aimed at nonspecialists. (See the short and full-length reviews on pp. 797–799 and the popular critical essay on pp. 801–805.) Then, analyze the language they use in making evaluations. What characteristics of language do they have in common?

QUOTING POETRY

When you write about poetry, you will be quoting parts of a poem: words, phrases, lines, sometimes whole stanzas. The rules for quoting poetry are very simple:

- Keep a copy of the poem with your paper, and refer to it throughout. Photocopies, transcriptions, or Web downloads of poems are all fine; as always, be sure you are taking your texts from a reputable source. (Good editions of works by poets in this anthology are listed after each biographical note in Chapter 19, "Biographies of Selected Poets.")
- When you cite one to three lines of poetry, put them in quotation marks, not an indented block quotation. Use a slash to indicate the line breaks. Include line numbers in parentheses afterwards: "After great pain, a formal feeling comes— / The Nerves sit ceremonious, like Tombs—" (1–2).
- When you cite more than three lines, use an indented block quotation. Indent the lines one inch from the left margin. Put line numbers in parentheses at the end. There is no need for quotation marks, since the indentation serves to indicate that it is a quotation:

  After great pain, a formal feeling comes—
  The Nerves sit ceremonious, like Tombs—
  The stiff Heart questions was it He, that bore,
  And Yesterday, or Centuries before? (1–4)

- When you leave out words, use an ellipsis. Use three spaced periods (. . .) where words are omitted from the middle of a sentence. Use four spaced periods (. . . .) if the omission is between two or more sentences. If you skip one or more lines of a poem, use a line of spaced periods to indicate the omission.
- It is essential to follow the original spelling, capitalization, punctuation, and stanza pattern of white space. Dickinson's idiosyncratic personal style makes accuracy here especially important, but all poetry benefits from careful presentation. Double-check everything. As Oscar Wilde put it, "A poet can survive everything but a misprint."

CHAPTER
13

Walt Whitman

Whitman in 1854, a year before the publication of Leaves of Grass.

In an era when many of America's famous poets had three names—Henry Wadsworth Longfellow, William Cullen Bryant, Ralph Waldo Emerson, John Greenleaf Whittier, Lydia Maria Child—Walt Whitman (1819–1892) insisted on being called by his nickname, the first well-known American writer to do so. His poetic career was rough and ready, as was his life. He had little schooling, and over his lifetime he would hold a series of jobs from office boy to house carpenter to teacher to printer to editor to bureaucratic government worker in Washington, D.C. He never made much money, he paid to publish his most famous book of poems (and anonymously wrote and then planted some of the favorable reviews himself), and he achieved widespread fame only late in life, when his best poetry was well behind him.

Whitman's personal life was a puzzle to many and a scandal to some. He never married, and the poems suggest that he had strongly romantic relationships with a number of men, and perhaps some women as well; he once claimed to have fathered six children. We know very little about the nature of these romantic relationships, and yet we are interested in Whitman's life in part because the poems are so deeply personal. How much does the personal matter? Can we learn more? As with Whitman's brilliant contemporary Emily Dickinson, the biographical details matter because we are tantalized by the power of the personal in the poems.

Whitman's poetic subject was himself and the emerging America he saw all around him, with a decided emphasis on the people in the street: the ordinary men and women who lived and worked in the cities, as well as the young men who fought and died in the Civil War. Whitman's poetic persona was of a "loafer," a city-dweller who walks the streets and inhabits the cafes of mid-nineteenth-century New York, all the time observing the life teeming around him. This common, "democratic" life he observed and celebrated was the inspiration for some of his most famous poetry. Later he would use a different, less exuberant persona in Washington, D.C., where he spent the Civil War in hospitals, nursing the wounded and the dying while writing some of the most affecting verse to come out of that conflict.

From the first, Whitman's poetic style seemed revolutionary: he rejected rhyme, compact form, and neat, regular meter in favor of a supple, expansive line and a strong rhythm. His lines went on and on, sometimes resulting in huge

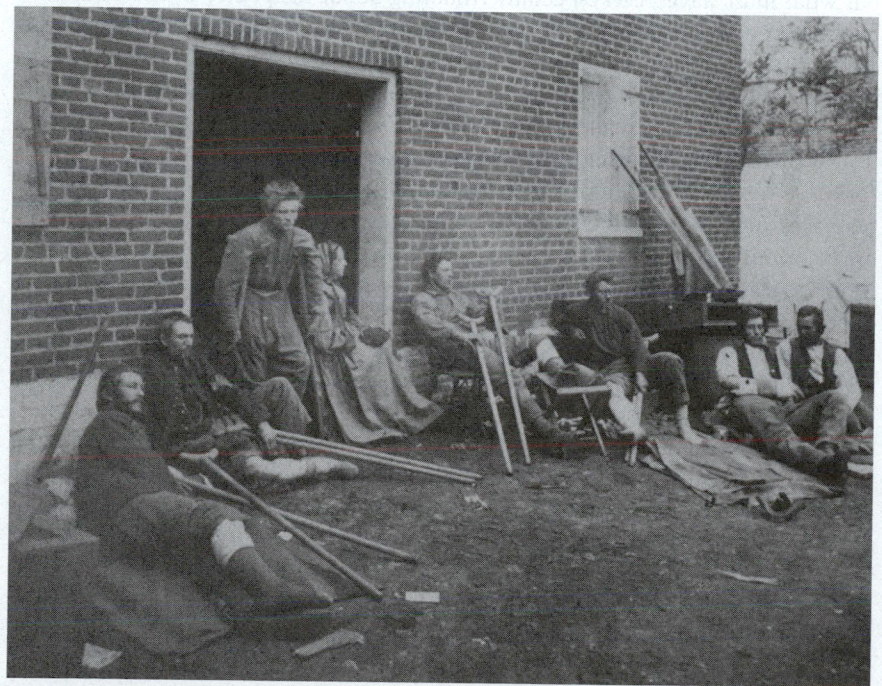

Wounded Civil War soldiers, Fredericksburg, Virginia, May 1864. Whitman's introduction to the horrors of warfare came in 1862, when his brother George was listed among the wounded at the battles in Fredericksburg, prompting Whitman to go to the Washington, D.C., area to search hospitals for him.

lists and catalogues, often resembling prose yet somehow sounding like deep, lyrical poetry. He drew his vocabulary from the wide range of discourses that characterized the new and growing country: the common vernacular of the street, Spanish words, Indian words, a bit of French, technical terms, popular science, the Bible, medicine, and a host of others. Drawn though it is from so much of the life around him, his mix of registers seems easily grasped—not at all off-putting, as the language of classic poetry could be to some readers. Whitman employed a personal vocabulary and idiosyncratic style of punctuation in the service of his own personal expression, not in deference to the elevated tone that characterized so much of the poetry of his time.

Besides rejecting the "normal" poetic language, Whitman rejected typical forms of poetic propriety. It was rare to have a book of poetry censored at the time, but Whitman's *Leaves of Grass* (1855) was. His frank depictions of sexuality, both homosexual and heterosexual, caused some readers to react strongly. In 1860 the *Springfield (Massachusetts) Republican* titled an editorial "Leaves of Grass—Smut in Them." That was the newspaper Emily Dickinson's family read and where a few of her poems appeared. In a letter, Dickinson admitted, "As for Mr. Whitman, I never read his book . . . I was told that he was disgraceful." A Boston publisher withdrew an edition of *Leaves of Grass* after the district attorney branded it "obscene literature." Today, little seems obscene about Whitman, but what must have been especially troubling about his poetry in the 1860s was his frank, open way about everything he believed in, urging readers to share his own attitudes. Whitman seemed dangerous, one imagines, because he invited his readers to be like him in everything, including sex. He still reads that way, inviting, even seducing his readers on the page.

Whitman wrote for most of his life, producing countless news stories, editorials, a novel about temperance, essays, and of course poems. In 1855, when he was thirty-six, he published the first edition of *Leaves of Grass*, a slim volume containing just twelve poems, none of them titled. For the rest of his long life this book would remain his major poetic project. He kept adding to it over the years, bringing it out in new and augmented editions. The final "deathbed" edition of more than 400 pages, copyrighted in 1891, came out in 1892, the year of his death. This continual changing and revision has kept scholars busy because, over time, Whitman altered the wording of poems, changed their order, devised new titles, deleted stanzas, and added many, many more poems. Which is the "real" *Leaves of Grass*? Which is the "right" version of a poem, the earliest or the latest? Who is to say which is better, the first version written in Whitman's youth or the last, produced in his old age? Such questions make for fascinating and important critical arguments, since *Leaves of Grass*, published between 1855 and 1891–1892, spans a key era in American literary and political history.

Over his lifetime Whitman saw himself gradually become a symbol, "the good grey poet," a figure much like a guru. Visitors came to him at every stage of his career. Henry David Thoreau and Ralph Waldo Emerson sought him out when *Leaves of Grass* first appeared. Later, as his renown increased, an impressive list of famous artists, among them the naturalist John Burroughs, treated Whitman as a prophet of a new America. Oscar Wilde saw in Whitman a fellow homosexual artist. Other admirers were Charles Dickens and William Makepeace Thackeray and the great painter Thomas Eakins, who photographed Whitman many times and painted his portrait as well.

For the last fifteen years of his life, Whitman was revered both for his poems and for the kind of life he represented. Nevertheless, he had written most of his great poetry between 1855 and 1875, when he was inspired by his life in New York City and touched by his experience as a Civil War nurse in Washington, D.C. During the latter period, his heroes were the soldiers he saw suffering and dying in the primitive hospitals, and Abraham Lincoln, assassinated just as his leadership produced victory. Some of Whitman's best and most moving poetry commemorates the grief he felt over the suffering caused by the war. On his other, more private side, the *Calamus* poems recount the love and loss of a male lover. Suppressed or ignored when they first appeared, they are now seen as a pioneering expression of a gay sensibility in literature as well as some of our culture's most insightful expressions of deeply felt love. Whitman's richly felt emotional response to his world—from the death of his hero Lincoln, to the lives of the ordinary people he encounters in the street, to his strong feelings toward his lovers—attracted readers from the very beginning and continues to make him one of America's most popular poets.

Oscar Wilde was among the many artists and writers who admired Whitman. He visited and established a friendship with Whitman during the sage poet's last years in Camden, New Jersey. Wilde sent this portrait of himself by Napoleon Sarony to Whitman as a keepsake after his first 1882 visit.

☀ INSPIRATION RALPH WALDO EMERSON'S LETTER TO WHITMAN

Ralph Waldo Emerson, sometime between 1830 and 1860.

Whitman's first edition of *Leaves of Grass*, published in 1855, was clearly written in an Emersonian spirit. With Whitman's assertion in the preface that "the United States themselves are essentially the greatest poem," Whitman was even paraphrasing Ralph Waldo Emerson's essay "The Poet," in which Emerson declared the times called for a poetic voice that celebrated America itself— "Our log-rolling, our stumps and their politics, our fisheries, our Negroes, and Indians, our boasts, and our repudiations, the wrath of rogues, and the pusillanimity of honest men, the Northern trade, the Southern planting, the Western clearing, Oregon and Texas"—thereby suggesting that Whitman himself embodied this poetic vision. With the publication of *Leaves of Grass*, the young Whitman took it upon himself to send an unsigned copy of the book to his literary mentor. The written reply he received from Emerson a few weeks later, dated July 21, 1855, launched Whitman's career as America's poet and today is still considered one of the most famous letters ever written to an aspiring writer. Part of its fame is derived from the fact that Whitman not only gave this private letter to the *New York Tribune* for publication without asking Emerson's permission—Emerson was reportedly furious—but in the second 1856 edition of *Leaves of Grass*, he printed Emerson's endorsement, "I greet you at the beginning of a great career.—R. W. Emerson," on the spine and included in the book itself the complete text of Emerson's letter as well as his open letter replying to Emerson, in essence a prose essay describing his poetic intentions. These exploits were viewed by many as blatant and arrogant acts of self-promotion, and they continue to be a source of discussion for scholars and critics today.

The complete text of Emerson's letter appears below. Whitman's much longer reply can be viewed online at the Walt Whitman Archive, http://www.whitmanarchive.org, within the e-text of the 1856 edition of *Leaves of Grass*, under the "Correspondence" link in the table of contents, but a few salient excerpts appear in the "Commentary: Whitman on His Art and Poetry" section (p. 874).

Emerson's Letter to Whitman

Concord. Massachusetts, 21 July, 1855.

Dear Sir—
    I am not blind to the worth of the wonderful gift of "LEAVES OF GRASS." I find it the most extraordinary piece of wit and wisdom that

America has yet contributed. I am very happy in reading it, as great power makes us happy. It meets the demand I am always making of what seemed the sterile and stingy nature, as if too much handiwork, or too much lymph in the temperament, were making our western wits fat and mean.

I give you joy of your free and brave thought. I have great joy in it. I find incomparable things said incomparably well, as they must be. I find the courage of treatment which so delights us, and which large perception only can inspire.

I greet you at the beginning of a great career, which yet must have had a long foreground somewhere, for such a start. I rubbed my eyes a little, to see if this sunbeam were no illusion; but the solid sense of the book is a sober certainty. It has the best merits, namely, of fortifying and encouraging.

I did not know until I last night saw the book advertised in a newspaper that I could trust the name as real and available for a post-office. I wish to see my benefactor, and have felt much like striking my tasks and visiting New York to pay you my respects. R. W. Emerson.

Whitman saw Abraham Lincoln in person in 1861, shortly after Lincoln's election to the presidency. Lincoln was among the poet's heroes, and the admiration comes through in many of his written works, both prose and verse. The above photo is Lincoln's last sitting portrait, taken on April 10, 1865, four days before his assassination.

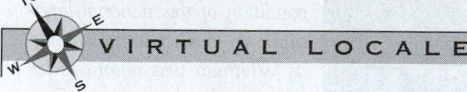

VIRTUAL LOCALE

The Whitman Archive. The Walt Whitman Archive at *http://www.whitman-archive.org* includes text and PDF versions of all seven editions of *Leaves of Grass*, historical photographs taken of Whitman throughout his life, selected criticism on individual poems, and a searchable bibliography of books, articles, chapters, and poems about Whitman.

WALT WHITMAN TIMELINE

1819	Walter Whitman born May 31 on a farm in West Hills, Long Island, 50 miles east of Manhattan.
1823	Whitman's family moves to Brooklyn (then separate from New York City).
1830	Leaves school to work full time as office boy and printer.
1836–1841	Teaches school on Long Island.
1841–1846	Works as a news writer and editor in New York City.
1846–1848	Editor of the *Brooklyn Eagle*; fired for his antislavery views.
1848	Briefly edits *New Orleans Daily Crescent*.
1848–1855	Returns to family in Brooklyn; works as writer and carpenter.
1855	Publishes first edition of *Leaves of Grass*.
1856	Publishes second edition of *Leaves of Grass*.
1857–1859	Works as news writer in New York.
1860	Publishes third edition of *Leaves of Grass*.
1862–1865	In Washington at series of government jobs; nurses Civil War wounded.
1867	Publishes fourth edition of *Leaves of Grass*.
1870	Publishes fifth edition of *Leaves of Grass* and *Democratic Vistas*.
1873	Moves to Camden, New Jersey, where his mother and brother live.
1891	Oversees last ("deathbed") edition of *Leaves of Grass*.
1892	Dies in Camden on March 26.

LITERARY LOCALE

Walt Whitman House, Camden, New Jersey. Whitman spent the last years of his life in Camden, New Jersey. The Walt Whitman House, a National Historic Landmark, is at 328 Mickle Boulevard, Camden. It displays some of Whitman's letters and personal belongings, including the bed in which he died. It also contains some nineteenth-century photographs. Among them is a daguerreotype from 1848, the first known image of Whitman.

The bedroom and library of Walt Whitman's last house, at 330 Mickle Boulevard in Camden, New Jersey. The spare condition of this national landmark is somewhat misleading, as Whitman was notorious for living amid a chaotic mess of papers right up until his final days; he refused offers to clean up the place, saying he could find any page he needed in the clutter.

A crowd gathered around Whitman's tomb in Harleigh Cemetery in Camden, New Jersey, c. 1892.

POEMS BY WALT WHITMAN

What follows is a sample of Whitman's poetry, ranging from long works such as "Song of Myself" and "When Lilacs Last in the Dooryard Bloom'd" to shorter pieces such as "A Noiseless Patient Spider" and "Cavalry Crossing a Ford." All the poems included here are taken from the last edition of *Leaves of Grass* (1891) and represent Whitman's final intentions about wording. (Additional Whitman poems appear on pp. 766 and 998.)

From "Song of Myself"

1

I Celebrate myself, and sing myself,
And what I assume you shall assume,
For every atom belonging to me as good belongs to you.

I loafe and invite my soul,
I lean and loafe at my ease observing a spear of summer grass.

My tongue, every atom of my blood, form'd from this soil, this air,
Born here of parents born here from parents the same, and their parents the
    same,

I, now thirty-seven years old in perfect health begin,
Hoping to cease not till death.

Creeds and schools in abeyance,   10
Retiring back a while sufficed at what they are, but never forgotten,
I harbor for good or bad, I permit to speak at every hazard,
Nature without check with original energy.

2

Houses and rooms are full of perfumes, the shelves are crowded with perfumes,
I breathe the fragrance myself and know it and like it,   15
The distillation would intoxicate me also, but I shall not let it.

The atmosphere is not a perfume, it has no taste of the distillation, it is odorless,
It is for my mouth forever, I am in love with it,
I will go to the bank by the wood and become undisguised and naked,
I am mad for it to be in contact with me.   20
The smoke of my own breath,
Echoes, ripples, buzz'd whispers, love-root, silk-thread, crotch and vine,
My respiration and inspiration, the beating of my heart, the passing of blood and
    air through my lungs,
The sniff of green leaves and dry leaves, and of the shore and dark-color'd sea-
    rocks, and of hay in the barn,
The sound of the belch'd words of my voice loos'd to the eddies of the wind,   25
A few light kisses, a few embraces, a reaching around of arms,
The play of shine and shade on the trees as the supple boughs wag,
The delight alone or in the rush of the streets, or along the fields and hill-sides,
The feeling of health, the full-noon trill, the song of me rising from bed and
    meeting the sun.

Have you reckon'd a thousand acres much? have you reckon'd the earth much?   30
Have you practis'd so long to learn to read?
Have you felt so proud to get at the meaning of poems?

Stop this day and night with me and you shall possess the origin of all poems,
You shall possess the good of the earth and sun, (there are millions of suns left,)
You shall no longer take things at second or third hand, nor look through the
    eyes of the dead, nor feed on the spectres in books,   35
You shall not look through my eyes either, nor take things from me,
You shall listen to all sides and filter them from your self.

                              *   *   *

5

I believe in you my soul, the other I am must not abase itself to you,
And you must not be abased to the other.

Loafe with me on the grass, loose the stop from your throat,
Not words, not music or rhyme I want, not custom or lecture, not even the best,   85
Only the lull I like, the hum of your valvèd voice.

I mind how once we lay such a transparent summer morning,
How you settled your head athwart my hips and gently turn'd over upon me,
And parted the shirt from my bosom-bone, and plunged your tongue to my bare-
    stript heart,
And reach'd till you felt my beard, and reach'd till you held my feet.   90

Swiftly arose and spread around me the peace and knowledge that pass all the ar-
    gument of the earth,
And I know that the hand of God is the promise of my own,
And I know that the spirit of God is the brother of my own,
And that all the men ever born are also my brothers, and the women my sisters
    and lovers,
And that a kelson of the creation is love,   95
And limitless are leaves stiff or drooping in the fields,
And brown ants in the little wells beneath them,
And mossy scabs of the worm fence, heap'd stones, elder, mullein and poke-
    weed.

6

A child said *What is the grass?* fetching it to me with full hands;
How could I answer the child? I do not know what it is any more than he.   100

I guess it must be the flag of my disposition, out of hopeful green stuff woven.

Or I guess it is the handkerchief of the Lord,
A scented gift and remembrancer designedly dropt,
Bearing the owner's name someway in the corners, that we may see and remark,
    and say *Whose?*

Or I guess the grass is itself a child, the produced babe of the vegetation.   105

Or I guess it is a uniform hieroglyphic,
And it means, Sprouting alike in broad zones and narrow zones,
Growing among black folks as among white,
Kanuck, Tuckahoe, Congressman, Cuff, I give them the same, I receive them the
    same.

And now it seems to me the beautiful uncut hair of graves.   110

Tenderly will I use you curling grass,
It may be you transpire from the breasts of young men,
It may be if I had known them I would have loved them,
It may be you are from old people, or from offspring taken soon out of their
    mothers' laps,
And here you are the mothers' laps.   115

This grass is very dark to be from the white heads of old mothers,
Darker than the colorless beards of old men,
Dark to come from under the faint red roofs of mouths.

O I perceive after all so many uttering tongues,
And I perceive they do not come from the roofs of mouths for nothing.   120

I wish I could translate the hints about the dead young men and women,
And the hints about old men and mothers, and the offspring taken soon out of
    their laps.

What do you think has become of the young and old men?
And what do you think has become of the women and children?

They are alive and well somewhere,   125
The smallest sprout shows there is really no death,
And if ever there was it led forward life, and does not wait at the end to arrest it,
And ceas'd the moment life appear'd.

All goes onward and outward, nothing collapses,
And to die is different from what any one supposed, and luckier.   130

7

Has any one supposed it lucky to be born?
I hasten to inform him or her it is just as lucky to die, and I know it.

I pass death with the dying and birth with the new-wash'd babe, and am not
    contain'd between my hat and boots,
And peruse manifold objects, no two alike and every one good,
The earth good and the stars good, and their adjuncts all good.   135

I am not an earth nor an adjunct of an earth,
I am the mate and companion of people, all just as immortal and fathomless as
    myself,
(They do not know how immortal, but I know.)
Every kind for itself and its own, for me mine male and female,
For me those that have been boys and that love women,   140
For me the man that is proud and feels how it stings to be slighted,
For me the sweet-heart and the old maid, for me mothers and the mothers of
    mothers,
For me lips that have smiled, eyes that have shed tears,
For me children and the begetters of children.

Undrape! you are not guilty to me, nor stale nor discarded,   145
I see through the broadcloth and gingham whether or no,
And am around, tenacious, acquisitive, tireless, and cannot be shaken away.

8

The little one sleeps in its cradle,
I lift the gauze and look a long time, and silently brush away flies with my hand.

The youngster and the red-faced girl turn aside up the bushy hill,   150
I peeringly view them from the top.

The suicide sprawls on the bloody floor of the bedroom,
I witness the corpse with its dabbled hair, I note where the pistol has fallen.

The blab of the pave, tires of carts, sluff of boot-soles, talk of the promenaders,
The heavy omnibus, the driver with his interrogating thumb, the clank of the
    shod horses on the granite floor,   155
The snow-sleighs, clinking, shouted jokes, pelts of snow-balls,

The hurrahs for popular favorites, the fury of rous'd mobs,
The flap of the curtain'd litter, a sick man inside borne to the hospital,
The meeting of enemies, the sudden oath, the blows and fall,
The excited crowd, the policeman with his star quickly working his passage to
    the centre of the crowd,   160
The impassive stones that receive and return so many echoes,
What groans of over-fed or half-starv'd who fall sunstruck or in fits,
What exclamations of women taken suddenly who hurry home and give birth to
    babes,
What living and buried speech is always vibrating here, what howls restrain'd by
    decorum,
Arrests of criminals, slights, adulterous offers made, acceptances, rejections with
    convex lips,   165
I mind them or the show or resonance of them—I come and I depart.

9

The big doors of the country barn stand open and ready,
The dried grass of the harvest-time loads the slow-drawn wagon,
The clear light plays on the brown gray and green intertinged,
The armfuls are pack'd to the sagging mow.   170

I am there, I help, I came stretch'd atop of the load,
I felt its soft jolts, one leg reclined on the other,
I jump from the cross-beams and seize the clover and timothy,
And roll head over heels and tangle my hair full of wisps.

10

Alone far in the wilds and mountains I hunt,   175
Wandering amazed at my own lightness and glee,
In the late afternoon choosing a safe spot to pass the night,
Kindling a fire and broiling the fresh-kill'd game,
Falling asleep on the gather'd leaves with my dog and gun by my side.

The Yankee clipper is under her sky-sails, she cuts the sparkle and scud,   180
My eyes settle the land, I bend at her prow or shout joyously from the deck.

The boatmen and clam-diggers arose early and stopt for me,
I tuck'd my trowser-ends in my boots and went and had a good time;
You should have been with us that day round the chowder-kettle.

I saw the marriage of the trapper in the open air in the far west, the bride was a
    red girl,   185
Her father and his friends sat near cross-legged and dumbly smoking, they had
    moccasins to their feet and large thick blankets hanging from their
    shoulders,
On a bank lounged the trapper, he was drest mostly in skins, his luxuriant beard
    and curls protected his neck, he held his bride by the hand,
She had long eyelashes, her head was bare, her coarse straight locks descended
    upon her voluptuous limbs and reach'd to her feet.

The runaway slave came to my house and stopt outside,
I heard his motions crackling the twigs of the woodpile,   190

Through the swung half-door of the kitchen I saw him limpsy and weak,
And went where he sat on a log and led him in and assured him,
And brought water and fill'd a tub for his sweated body and bruis'd feet,
And gave him a room that enter'd from my own, and gave him some coarse
    clean clothes,
And remember perfectly well his revolving eyes and his awkwardness,   195
And remember putting plasters on the galls of his neck and ankles;
He staid with me a week before he was recuperated and pass'd north,
I had him sit next me at table, my fire-lock lean'd in the corner.

* * *

15

The pure contralto sings in the organ loft,
The carpenter dresses his plank, the tongue of his foreplane whistles its wild
    ascending lisp,   265
The married and unmarried children ride home to their Thanksgiving dinner,
The pilot seizes the king-pin, he heaves down with a strong arm,
The mate stands braced in the whale-boat, lance and harpoon are ready,
The duck-shooter walks by silent and cautious stretches,
The deacons are ordain'd with cross'd hands at the altar,   270
The spinning-girl retreats and advances to the hum of the big wheel,
The farmer stops by the bars as he walks on a First-day loafe and looks at the oats
    and rye,
The lunatic is carried at last to the asylum a confirm'd case,
(He will never sleep any more as he did in the cot in his mother's bed-room;)
The jour printer with gray head and gaunt jaws works at his case,   275
He turns his quid of tobacco while his eyes blurr with the manuscript;
The malform'd limbs are tied to the surgeon's table,
What is removed drops horribly in a pail;
The quadroon girl is sold at the auction-stand, the drunkard nods by the bar-
    room stove,
The machinist rolls up his sleeves, the policeman travels his beat, the gate-
    keeper marks who pass,   280
The young fellow drives the express-wagon, (I love him, though I do not know
    him;)
The half-breed straps on his light boots to compete in the race,
The western turkey-shooting draws old and young, some lean on their rifles,
    some sit on logs,
Out from the crowd steps the marksman, takes his position, levels his piece;
The groups of newly-come immigrants cover the wharf or levee,   285
As the woolly-pates hoe in the sugar-field, the overseer views them from his
    saddle,
The bugle calls in the ball-room, the gentlemen run for their partners, the
    dancers bow to each other,
The youth lies awake in the cedar-roof'd garret and harks to the musical rain,
The Wolverine sets traps on the creek that helps fill the Huron,
The squaw wrapt in her yellow-hemm'd cloth is offering moccasins and bead-
    bags for sale,   290

The connoisseur peers along the exhibition-gallery with half-shut eyes bent
    sideways,

As the deck-hands make fast the steamboat the plank is thrown for the shore-
    going passengers,

The young sister holds out the skein while the elder sister winds it off in a ball,
    and stops now and then for the knots,

The one-year wife is recovering and happy having a week ago borne her first
    child,

The clean-hair'd Yankee girl works with her sewing-machine or in the factory or
    mill,   295

The paving-man leans on his two-handed rammer, the reporter's lead flies swiftly
    over the note-book, the sign-painter is lettering with blue and gold,

The canal boy trots on the tow-path, the book-keeper counts at his desk, the
    shoemaker waxes his thread,

The conductor beats time for the band and all the performers follow him,

The child is baptized, the convert is making his first professions,

The regatta is spread on the bay, the race is begun, (how the white sails sparkle!)   300

The drover watching his drove sings out to them that would stray,

The pedler sweats with his pack on his back, (the purchaser higgling about the
    odd cent;)

The bride unrumples her white dress, the minute-hand of the clock moves
    slowly,

The opium-eater reclines with rigid head and just-open'd lips,

The prostitute draggles her shawl, her bonnet bobs on her tipsy and pimpled
    neck,   305

The crowd laugh at her blackguard oaths, the men jeer and wink to each other,

(Miserable! I do not laugh at your oaths nor jeer you;)

The President holding a cabinet council is surrounded by the great Secretaries,

On the piazza walk three matrons stately and friendly with twined arms,

The crew of the fish-smack pack repeated layers of halibut in the hold,   310

The Missourian crosses the plains toting his wares and his cattle,

As the fare-collector goes through the train he gives notice by the jingling of
    loose change,

The floor-men are laying the floor, the tinners are tinning the roof, the masons
    are calling for mortar,

In single file each shouldering his hod pass onward the laborers;

Seasons pursuing each other the indescribable crowd is gather'd, it is the fourth
    of Seventh-month, (what salutes of cannon and small arms!)   315

Seasons pursuing each other the plougher ploughs, the mower mows, and the
    winter-grain falls in the ground;

Off on the lakes the pike-fisher watches and waits by the hole in the frozen surface,

The stumps stand thick round the clearing, the squatter strikes deep with his
    axe,

Flatboatmen make fast towards dusk near the cotton-wood or pecan-trees,

Coon-seekers go through the regions of the Red river or through those drain'd by
    the Tennessee, or through those of the Arkansas,   320

Torches shine in the dark that hangs on the Chattahooche or Altamahaw,

Patriarchs sit at supper with sons and grandsons and great-grandsons around
    them,

In walls of adobie, in canvas tents, rest hunters and trappers after their day's
    sport,
The city sleeps and the country sleeps,
The living sleep for their time, the dead sleep for their time,   325
The old husband sleeps by his wife and the young husband sleeps by his wife;
And these tend inward to me, and I tend outward to them,
And such as it is to be of these more or less I am,
And of these one and all I weave the song of myself.

* * *

17

These are really the thoughts of all men in all ages and lands, they are not
    original with me,   355
If they are not yours as much as mine they are nothing, or next to nothing,
If they are not the riddle and the untying of the riddle they are nothing,
If they are not just as close as they are distant they are nothing.

This is the grass that grows wherever the land is and the water is,
This the common air that bathes the globe.   360

* * *

19

This is the meal equally set, this the meat for natural hunger,
It is for the wicked just the same as the righteous, I make appointments with all,
I will not have a single person slighted or left away,
The kept-woman, sponger, thief, are hereby invited,   375
The heavy-lipp'd slave is invited, the venerealee is invited;
There shall be no difference between them and the rest.

This is the press of a bashful hand, this the float and odor of hair,
This the touch of my lips to yours, this the murmur of yearning,
This the far-off depth and height reflecting my own face,   380
This the thoughtful merge of myself, and the outlet again.

Do you guess I have some intricate purpose?
Well I have, for the Fourth-month showers have, and the mica on the side of a
    rock has.

Do you take it I would astonish?
Does the daylight astonish? does the early redstart twittering through the woods? 385
Do I astonish more than they?

This hour I tell things in confidence,
I might not tell everybody, but I will tell you.

* * *

27

To be in any form, what is that?
(Round and round we go, all of us, and ever come back thither,)
If nothing lay more develop'd the quahaug in its callous shell were enough.

Mine is no callous shell,
I have instant conductors all over me whether I pass or stop, 615
They seize every object and lead it harmlessly through me.

I merely stir, press, feel with my fingers, and am happy,
To touch my person to some one else's is about as much as I can stand.

28

Is this then a touch? quivering me to a new identity,
Flames and ether making a rush for my veins, 620
Treacherous tip of me reaching and crowding to help them,
My flesh and blood playing out lightning to strike what is hardly different from
    myself,
On all sides prurient provokers stiffening my limbs,
Straining the udder of my heart for its withheld drip,
Behaving licentious toward me, taking no denial, 625
Depriving me of my best as for a purpose,
Unbuttoning my clothes, holding me by the bare waist,
Deluding my confusion with the calm of the sunlight and pasture-fields,
Immodestly sliding the fellow-senses away,
They bribed to swap off with touch and go and graze at the edges of me, 630
No consideration, no regard for my draining strength or my anger,
Fetching the rest of the herd around to enjoy them a while,
Then all uniting to stand on a headland and worry me.
The sentries desert every other part of me,
They have left me helpless to a red marauder, 635
They all come to the headland to witness and assist against me.

I am given up by traitors,
I talk wildly, I have lost my wits, I and nobody else am the greatest traitor,
I went myself first to the headland, my own hands carried me there.

You villain touch! what are you doing? my breath is tight in its throat, 640
Unclench your floodgates, you are too much for me.

29

Blind loving wrestling touch, sheath'd hooded sharp-tooth'd touch!
Did it make you ache so, leaving me?

Parting track'd by arriving, perpetual payment of perpetual loan,
Rich showering rain, and recompense richer afterward. 645

Sprouts take and accumulate, stand by the curb prolific and vital,
Landscapes projected masculine, full-sized and golden.

30

All truths wait in all things,
They neither hasten their own delivery nor resist it,
They do not need the obstetric forceps of the surgeon, 650
The insignificant is as big to me as any,
(What is less or more than a touch?)

Logic and sermons never convince,
The damp of the night drives deeper into my soul.

(Only what proves itself to every man and woman is so,   655
Only what nobody denies is so.)

A minute and a drop of me settle my brain,
I believe the soggy clods shall become lovers and lamps,
And a compend of compends is the meat of a man or woman,
And a summit and flower there is the feeling they have for each other,   660
And they are to branch boundlessly out of that lesson until it becomes omnific,
And until one and all shall delight us, and we them.

31

I believe a leaf of grass is no less than the journey-work of the stars,
And the pismire is equally perfect, and a grain of sand, and the egg of the wren,
And the tree-toad is a chef-d'oeuvre for the highest,   665
And the running blackberry would adorn the parlors of heaven,
And the narrowest hinge in my hand puts to scorn all machinery,
And the cow crunching with depress'd head surpasses any statue,
And a mouse is miracle enough to stagger sextillions of infidels.

I find I incorporate gneiss, coal, long-threaded moss, fruits, grains, esculent roots, 670
And am stucco'd with quadrupeds and birds all over,
And have distanced what is behind me for good reasons,
But call any thing back again when I desire it.

In vain the speeding or shyness,
In vain the plutonic rocks send their old heat against my approach,   675
In vain the mastodon retreats beneath its own powder'd bones,
In vain objects stand leagues off and assume manifold shapes,
In vain the ocean settling in hollows and the great monsters lying low,
In vain the buzzard houses herself with the sky,
In vain the snake slides through the creepers and logs,   680
In vain the elk takes to the inner passes of the woods,
In vain the razor-bill'd auk sails far north to Labrador,
I follow quickly, I ascend to the nest in the fissure of the cliff.

* * *

34

Now I tell what I knew in Texas in my early youth,
(I tell not the fall of Alamo,
Not one escaped to tell the fall of Alamo,
The hundred and fifty are dumb yet at Alamo,)
'Tis the tale of the murder in cold blood of four hundred and twelve young men.   875

Retreating they had form'd in a hollow square with their baggage for breast-
        works,
Nine hundred lives out of the surrounding enemy's, nine times their number, was
        the price they took in advance,

Their colonel was wounded and their ammunition gone,
They treated for an honorable capitulation, receiv'd writing and seal, gave up
    their arms and march'd back prisoners of war.

They were the glory of the race of rangers, 880
Matchless with horse, rifle, song, supper, courtship,
Large, turbulent, generous, handsome, proud, and affectionate,
Bearded, sunburnt, drest in the free costume of hunters,
Not a single one over thirty years of age.

The second First-day morning they were brought out in squads and massacred, it
    was beautiful early summer, 885
The work commenced about five o'clock and was over by eight.

None obey'd the command to kneel,
Some made a mad and helpless rush, some stood stark and straight,
A few fell at once, shot in the temple or heart, the living and dead lay together,
The maim'd and mangled dug in the dirt, the new-comers saw them there, 890
Some half-kill'd attempted to crawl away,
These were despatch'd with bayonets or batter'd with the blunts of muskets,
A youth not seventeen years old seiz'd his assassin till two more came to release
    him,
The three were all torn and cover'd with the boy's blood.

At eleven o'clock began the burning of the bodies; 895
That is the tale of the murder of the four hundred and twelve young men.

35

Would you hear of an old-time sea-fight?
Would you learn who won by the light of the moon and stars?
List to the yarn, as my grandmother's father the sailor told it to me.

Our foe was no skulk in his ship I tell you, (said he,) 900
His was the surly English pluck, and there is no tougher or truer, and never was,
    and never will be;
Along the lower'd eve he came horribly raking us.

We closed with him, the yards entangled, the cannon touch'd,
My captain lash'd fast with his own hands.

We had receiv'd some eighteen pound shots under the water, 905
On our lower-gun-deck two large pieces had burst at the first fire, killing all
    around and blowing up overhead.

Fighting at sun-down, fighting at dark,
Ten o'clock at night, the full moon well up, our leaks on the gain, and five feet of
    water reported,
The master-at-arms loosing the prisoners confined in the after-hold to give them
    a chance for themselves.

The transit to and from the magazine is now stopt by the sentinels, 910
They see so many strange faces they do not know whom to trust.

Our frigate takes fire,
The other asks if we demand quarter?
If our colors are struck and the fighting done?
Now I laugh content, for I hear the voice of my little captain,   915
We have not struck, he composedly cries, *we have just begun our part of the fighting.*

Only three guns are in use,
One is directed by the captain himself against the enemy's mainmast,
Two well serv'd with grape and canister silence his musketry and clear his decks.

The tops alone second the fire of this little battery, especially the main-top,   920
They hold out bravely during the whole of the action.

Not a moment's cease,
The leaks gain fast on the pumps, the fire eats toward the powder-magazine.

One of the pumps has been shot away, it is generally thought we are sinking.

Serene stands the little captain,   925
He is not hurried, his voice is neither high nor low,
His eyes give more light to us than our battle-lanterns.

Toward twelve there in the beams of the moon they surrender to us.

36

Stretch'd and still lies the midnight,
Two great hulls motionless on the breast of the darkness,   930
Our vessel riddled and slowly sinking, preparations to pass to the one we have
    conquer'd,
The captain on the quarter-deck coldly giving his orders through a countenance
    white as a sheet,
Near by the corpse of the child that serv'd in the cabin,
The dead face of an old salt with long white hair and carefully curl'd whiskers,
The flames spite of all that can be done flickering aloft and below,   935
The husky voices of the two or three officers yet fit for duty,
Formless stacks of bodies and bodies by themselves, dabs of flesh upon the masts
    and spars,
Cut of cordage, dangle of rigging, slight shock of the soothe of waves,
Black and impassive guns, litter of powder-parcels, strong scent,
A few large stars overhead, silent and mournful shining,   940
Delicate sniffs of sea-breeze, smells of sedgy grass and fields by the shore, death-
    messages given in charge to survivors,
The hiss of the surgeon's knife, the gnawing teeth of his saw,
Wheeze, cluck, swash of falling blood, short wild scream, and long, dull, tapering
    groan,
These so, these irretrievable.

37

You laggards there on guard! look to your arms!   945
In at the conquer'd doors they crowd! I am possess'd!
Embody all presences outlaw'd or suffering,

See myself in prison shaped like another man,
And feel the dull unintermitted pain.

For me the keepers of convicts shoulder their carbines and keep watch, 950
It is I let out in the morning and barr'd at night.

Not a mutineer walks handcuff'd to jail but I am handcuff'd to him and walk by
    his side,
(I am less the jolly one there, and more the silent one with sweat on my twitch-
    ing lips.)

Not a youngster is taken for larceny but I go up too, and am tried and sentenced.

Not a cholera patient lies at the last gasp but I also lie at the last gasp, 955
My face is ash-color'd, my sinews gnarl, away from me people retreat.

Askers embody themselves in me and I am embodied in them,
I project my hat, sit shame-faced, and beg.

38

Enough! enough! enough!
Somehow I have been stunn'd. Stand back! 960
Give me a little time beyond my cuff'd head, slumbers, dreams, gaping,
I discover myself on the verge of a usual mistake.

That I could forget the mockers and insults!
That I could forget the trickling tears and the blows of the bludgeons and
    hammers!
That I could look with a separate look on my own crucifixion and bloody
    crowning. 965

I remember now,
I resume the overstaid fraction,
The grave of rock multiplies what has been confided to it, or to any graves,
Corpses rise, gashes heal, fastenings roll from me.

I troop forth replenish'd with supreme power, one of an average unending
    procession, 970
Inland and sea-coast we go, and pass all boundary lines,
Our swift ordinances on their way over the whole earth,
The blossoms we wear in our hats the growth of thousands of years.

Eleves, I salute you! come forward!
Continue your annotations, continue your questionings. 975

       *   *   *

46

I know I have the best of time and space, and was never measured and never will
    be measured.

I tramp a perpetual journey, (come listen all!)
My signs are a rain-proof coat, good shoes, and a staff cut from the woods,

No friend of mine takes his ease in my chair,
I have no chair, no church, no philosophy,   1205
I lead no man to a dinner-table, library, exchange,
But each man and each woman of you I lead upon a knoll,
My left hand hooking you round the waist,
My right hand pointing to landscapes of continents and the public road.

Not I, not any one else can travel that road for you,   1210
You must travel it for yourself.

It is not far, it is within reach,
Perhaps you have been on it since you were born and did not know,
Perhaps it is everywhere on water and on land.

Shoulder your duds dear son, and I will mine, and let us hasten forth,   1215
Wonderful cities and free nations we shall fetch as we go.

If you tire, give me both burdens, and rest the chuff of your hand on my hip,
And in due time you shall repay the same service to me,
For after we start we never lie by again.

This day before dawn I ascended a hill and look'd at the crowded heaven,   1220
And I said to my spirit *When we become the enfolders of those orbs, and the pleasure
    and knowledge of every thing in them, shall we be fill'd and satisfied then?*
And my spirit said *No, we but level that lift to pass and continue beyond.*

You are also asking me questions and I hear you,
I answer that I cannot answer, you must find out for yourself.

Sit a while dear son,   1125
Here are biscuits to eat and here is milk to drink,
But as soon as you sleep and renew yourself in sweet clothes, I kiss you with a
    good-by kiss and open the gate for your egress hence.

Long enough have you dream'd contemptible dreams,
Now I wash the gum from your eyes,
You must habit yourself to the dazzle of the light and of every moment of your
    life.   1230

Long have you timidly waded holding a plank by the shore,
Now I will you to be a bold swimmer,
To jump off in the midst of the sea, rise again, nod to me, shout, and laughingly
    dash with your hair.

47

I am the teacher of athletes,
He that by me spreads a wider breast than my own proves the width of my own,   1235
He most honors my style who learns under it to destroy the teacher.

The boy I love, the same becomes a man not through derived power, but in his
    own right,
Wicked rather than virtuous out of conformity or fear,

Fond of his sweetheart, relishing well his steak,
Unrequited love or a slight cutting him worse than sharp steel cuts,   1240
First-rate to ride, to fight, to hit the bull's eye, to sail a skiff, to sing a song or play
    on the banjo,
Preferring scars and the beard and faces pitted with smallpox over all latherers,
And those well-tann'd to those that keep out of the sun.

I teach straying from me, yet who can stray from me?
I follow you whoever you are from the present hour,   1245
My words itch at your ears till you understand them.

I do not say these things for a dollar or to fill up the time while I wait for a boat,
(It is you talking just as much as myself, I act as the tongue of you,
Tied in your mouth, in mine it begins to be loosen'd.)

I swear I will never again mention love or death inside a house,   1250
And I swear I will never translate myself at all, only to him or her who privately
    stays with me in the open air.

If you would understand me go to the heights or water-shore,
The nearest gnat is an explanation, and a drop or motion of waves a key,
The maul, the oar, the hand-saw, second my words.

No shutter'd room or school can commune with me,   1255
But roughs and little children better than they.

The young mechanic is closest to me, he knows me well,
The woodman that takes his axe and jug with him shall take me with him all
    day,
The farm-boy ploughing in the field feels good at the sound of my voice,
In vessels that sail my words sail, I go with fishermen and seamen and love them. 1260

The soldier camp'd or upon the march is mine,
On the night erc the pending battle many seek me, and I do not fail them,
On that solemn night (it may be their last) those that know me seek me.

My face rubs to the hunter's face when he lies down alone in his blanket,
The driver thinking of me does not mind the jolt of his wagon,   1265
The young mother and old mother comprehend me,
The girl and the wife rest the needle a moment and forget where they are,
They and all would resume what I have told them.

* * *

51

The past and present wilt—I have fill'd them, emptied them,
And proceed to fill my next fold of the future.   1320

Listener up there! what have you to confide to me?
Look in my face while I snuff the sidle of evening,
(Talk honestly, no one else hears you, and I stay only a minute longer.)

Do I contradict myself?
Very well then I contradict myself,   1325

(I am large, I contain multitudes.)

I concentrate toward them that are nigh, I wait on the door-slab.

Who has done his day's work? who will soonest be through with his supper?
Who wishes to walk with me?

Will you speak before I am gone? will you prove already too late?   1330

52

The spotted hawk swoops by and accuses me, he complains of my gab and my
    loitering.

I too am not a bit tamed, I too am untranslatable,
I sound my barbaric yawp over the roofs of the world.

The last scud of day holds back for me,
It flings my likeness after the rest and true as any on the shadow'd wilds,   1335
It coaxes me to the vapor and the dusk.

I depart as air, I shake my white locks at the runaway sun,
I effuse my flesh in eddies, and drift it in lacy jags.

I bequeath myself to the dirt to grow from the grass I love,
If you want me again look for me under your boot-soles.   1340

You will hardly know who I am or what I mean,
But I shall be good health to you nevertheless,
And filter and fibre your blood.

Failing to fetch me at first keep encouraged,
Missing me one place search another,   1345
I stop somewhere waiting for you.

A U D I O   L O C A L E

Whitman Reading "America." A rare recording of what is believed to be Walt
Whitman reading four lines from his poem "America" can be downloaded as an
MP3 file from the Whitman Archive site: *http://www.whitmanarchive.org/audio/*.

Crossing Brooklyn Ferry

1

Flood-tide below me! I see you face to face!
Clouds of the west—sun there half an hour high—I see you also face to face.
Crowds of men and women attired in the usual costumes, how curious you are to
    me!
On the ferry-boats the hundreds and hundreds that cross, returning home, are
    more curious to me than you suppose,
And you that shall cross from shore to shore years hence are more to me, and
    more in my meditations, than you might suppose.   5

Fulton Ferry Boat, Brooklyn, New York, 1890.

2

The impalpable sustenance of me from all things at all hours of the day,
The simple, compact, well-join'd scheme, myself disintegrated, every one disintegrated yet part of the scheme,
The similitudes of the past and those of the future,
The glories strung like beads on my smallest sights and hearings, on the walk in the street and the passage over the river,
The current rushing so swiftly and swimming with me far away,
The others that are to follow me, the ties between me and them,   10
The certainty of others, the life, love, sight, hearing of others.

Others will enter the gates of the ferry and cross from shore to shore,
Others will watch the run of the flood-tide,
Others will see the shipping of Manhattan north and west, and the heights of Brooklyn to the south and east,   15
Others will see the islands large and small;
Fifty years hence, others will see them as they cross, the sun half an hour high,
A hundred years hence, or ever so many hundred years hence, others will see them,
Will enjoy the sunset, the pouring-in of the flood-tide, the falling-back to the sea of the ebb-tide.

3

It avails not, time nor place—distance avails not,   20
I am with you, you men and women of a generation, or ever so many generations hence,
Just as you feel when you look on the river and sky, so I felt,
Just as any of you is one of a living crowd, I was one of a crowd,

Just as you are refresh'd by the gladness of the river and the bright flow, I was re-
    fresh'd,
Just as you stand and lean on the rail, yet hurry with the swift current, I stood yet
    was hurried,   25
Just as you look on the numberless masts of ships and the thick-stemm'd pipes of
    steamboats, I look'd.

I too many and many a time cross'd the river of old,
Watched the Twelfth-month sea-gulls, saw them high in the air floating with
    motionless wings, oscillating their bodies,
Saw how the glistening yellow lit up parts of their bodies and left the rest in
    strong shadow,
Saw the slow-wheeling circles and the gradual edging toward the south,   30
Saw the reflection of the summer sky in the water,
Had my eyes dazzled by the shimmering track of beams,
Look'd at the fine centrifugal spokes of light round the shape of my head in the
    sunlit water,
Look'd on the haze on the hills southward and south-westward,
Look'd on the vapor as it flew in fleeces tinged with violet,   35
Look'd toward the lower bay to notice the vessels arriving,
Saw their approach, saw aboard those that were near me,
Saw the white sails of schooners and sloops, saw the ships at anchor,
The sailors at work in the rigging or out astride the spars,
The round masts, the swinging motion of the hulls, the slender serpentine
    pennants,   40
The large and small steamers in motion, the pilots in their pilot-houses,
The white wake left by the passage, the quick tremulous whirl of the wheels,
The flags of all nations, the falling of them at sunset,
The scallop-edged waves in the twilight, the ladled cups, the frolicsome crests
    and glistening,
The stretch afar growing dimmer and dimmer, the gray walls of the granite store-
    houses by the docks,   45
On the river the shadowy group, the big steam-tug closely flank'd on each side by
    the barges, the hay-boat, the belated lighter,
On the neighboring shore the fires from the foundry chimneys burning high and
    glaringly into the night,
Casting their flicker of black contrasted with wild red and yellow light over the
    tops of houses, and down into the clefts of streets.

4

These and all else were to me the same as they are to you,
I loved well those cities, loved well the stately and rapid river,   50
The men and women I saw were all near to me,
Others the same—others who look back on me because I look'd forward to them,
(The time will come, though I stop here to-day and to-night.)

5

What is it then between us?
What is the count of the scores or hundreds of years between us?   55

Whatever it is, it avails not—distance avails not, and place avails not,
I too lived, Brooklyn of ample hills was mine,
I too walk'd the streets of Manhattan island, and bathed in the waters around it,
I too felt the curious abrupt questionings stir within me,
In the day among crowds of people sometimes they came upon me,   60
In my walks home late at night or as I lay in my bed they came upon me,
I too had been struck from the float forever held in solution,
I too had receiv'd identity by my body,
That I was I knew was of my body, and what I should be I knew I should be of my
   body.

6

It is not upon you alone the dark patches fall,   65
The dark threw its patches down upon me also,
The best I had done seem'd to me blank and suspicious,
My great thoughts as I supposed them, were they not in reality meagre?
Nor is it you alone who know what it is to be evil,
I am he who knew what it was to be evil,   70
I too knotted the old knot of contrariety,
Blabb'd, blush'd, resented, lied, stole, grudg'd,
Had guile, anger, lust, hot wishes I dared not speak,
Was wayward, vain, greedy, shallow, sly, cowardly, malignant,
The wolf, the snake, the hog, not wanting in me,   75
The cheating look, the frivolous word, the adulterous wish, not wanting,
Refusals, hates, postponements, meanness, laziness, none of these wanting,
Was one with the rest, the days and haps of the rest,
Was call'd by my nighest name by clear loud voices of young men as they saw me
   approaching or passing,
Felt their arms on my neck as I stood, or the negligent leaning of their flesh
   against me as I sat,   80
Saw many I loved in the street or ferry-boat or public assembly, yet never told
   them a word,
Lived the same life with the rest, the same old laughing, gnawing, sleeping,
Play'd the part that still looks back on the actor or actress,
The same old role, the role that is what we make it, as great as we like,
Or as small as we like, or both great and small.   85

7

Closer yet I approach you,
What thought you have of me now, I had as much of you—I laid in my stores in
   advance,
I consider'd long and seriously of you before you were born.

Who was to know what should come home to me?
Who knows but I am enjoying this?   90
Who knows, for all the distance, but I am as good as looking at you now, for all
   you cannot see me?

8

Ah, what can ever be more stately and admirable to me than mast-hemm'd
    Manhattan?
River and sunset and scallop-edg'd waves of flood-tide?
The sea-gulls oscillating their bodies, the hay-boat in the twilight, and the be-
    lated lighter?
What gods can exceed these that clasp me by the hand, and with voices I love
    call me promptly and loudly by my nighest name as I approach?   95
What is more subtle than this which ties me to the woman or man that looks in
    my face?
Which fuses me into you now, and pours my meaning into you?

We understand then do we not?
What I promis'd without mentioning it, have you not accepted?
What the study could not teach—what the preaching could not accomplish is
    accomplish'd, is it not?   100

9

Flow on, river! flow with the flood-tide, and ebb with the ebb-tide!
Frolic on, crested and scallop-edg'd waves!
Gorgeous clouds of the sunset! drench with your splendor me, or the men and
    women generations after me!
Cross from shore to shore, countless crowds of passengers!
Stand up, tall masts of Mannahatta! stand up, beautiful hills of Brooklyn!   105
Throb, baffled and curious brain! throw out questions and answers!
Suspend here and everywhere, eternal float of solution!
Gaze, loving and thirsting eyes, in the house or street or public assembly!
Sound out, voices of young men! loudly and musically call me by my nighest
    name!
Live, old life! play the part that looks back on the actor or actress!   110
Play the old role, the role that is great or small according as one makes it!
Consider, you who peruse me, whether I may not in unknown ways be looking
    upon you;
Be firm, rail over the river, to support those who lean idly, yet haste with the
    hasting current;
Fly on, sea-birds! fly sideways, or wheel in large circles high in the air;
Receive the summer sky, you water, and faithfully hold it till all downcast eyes
    have time to take it from you!   115
Diverge, fine spokes of light, from the shape of my head, or any one's head, in the
    sunlit water!
Come on, ships from the lower bay! pass up or down, white-sail'd schooners,
    sloops, lighters!
Flaunt away, flags of all nations! be duly lower'd at sunset!
Burn high your fires, foundry chimneys! cast black shadows at nightfall! cast red
    and yellow light over the tops of the houses!
Appearances, now or henceforth, indicate what you are,   120
You necessary film, continue to envelop the soul,
About my body for me, and your body for you, be hung out divinest aromas,
Thrive, cities—bring your freight, bring your shows, ample and sufficient rivers,

Expand, being than which none else is perhaps more spiritual,
Keep your places, objects than which none else is more lasting.   125

You have waited, you always wait, you dumb, beautiful ministers,
We receive you with free sense at last, and are insatiate henceforward,
Not you any more shall be able to foil us, or withhold yourselves from us,
We use you, and do not cast you aside—we plant you permanently within us,
We fathom you not—we love you—there is perfection in you also,   130
You furnish your parts toward eternity,
Great or small, you furnish your parts toward the soul.

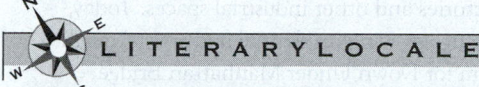

LITERARY LOCALE

Whitman in New York. Walt Whitman's birthplace in West Hills, New York,
is now on the National Register of Historic Places and open to the public as the
Walt Whitman Birthplace State Historical Site and Interpretive Center. Whitman
was born here in 1819 on land settled earlier by pioneer Joseph Whitman. Although Whitman lived here only until age four, his years on this Long Island farm
deeply influenced his poetry through his connection to the natural world. For more
information about the Whitman historical site, go to *http://www.waltwhitman.org.*

Whitman's life in New York City also played an influential role in his poetry, both figuratively and literally. The energy and excitement he experienced growing up on the Brooklyn waterfront and later as a professional in
Manhattan can be seen in poems such as "Mannahatta" and "I Hear America
Singing." Of particular note is Fulton Ferry in Brooklyn, once a thriving waterfront community that formed around the numerous ferries operating from
that locale. Whitman's "Crossing Brooklyn Ferry" (see pp. 850–855) was inspired by the river passages that took place at this site—the last ferry stopped
running in 1924—and the poem itself broaches the navigation of both literal
and metaphysical boundaries. Whitman also set the type for the 1855 edition

*Brooklyn Bridge, viewed from the Brooklyn waterfront, with the Manhattan skyline in
the background.*

(continued)

of *Leaves of Grass* in this same neighborhood, at a print shop near the waterfront at 170 Fulton Street, on the southwest corner of Cranberry Street. The former ferry dock is now Fulton Ferry Landing Park, a recreational pier adjacent to the anchorage of the Brooklyn Bridge that offers views of the East River and the Manhattan skyline. The railing of the deck is made of stainless steel cable meant to suggest the bridge's architecture, and the text of "Crossing Brooklyn Ferry" is set within the railing.

The construction of the Brooklyn Bridge sent the Fulton Ferry neighborhood into a downward spiral; it quickly became a sparsely inhabited slum and later a commercial area dotted by factories and other industrial spaces. Today, the neighborhood is a slowly gentrifying, growing residential and artists' neighborhood called DUMBO (an acronym for Down Under Manhattan Bridge Overpass). Although the Brooklyn Bridge itself was not built when Whitman wrote "Crossing Brooklyn Ferry"—construction began in 1870 and ended in 1883—Whitman did return to New York in 1878, in time to see the bridge almost complete. Commenting on this in a diary entry entitled "Human and Heroic New York," collected in *Specimen Days* (1882), Whitman deemed it "the best, most effective medicine my soul has yet partaken—the grandest physical habitat and surroundings of land and water the globe affords—namely, Manhattan Island and Brooklyn, which the future shall join in one city—city of superb democracy, amid superb surroundings."

In the years since its creation, the Brooklyn Bridge has inspired more art—writing, photos, paintings, songs, etchings—than any other suspension bridge in the world. In the spirit of Whitman's New York and Brooklyn inspired poems, the New York–based literary center Poets House sponsors an annual Bridge Walk, in which poetry lovers congregate on the Manhattan side of the bridge just before sunset, walk across as a group, all the while reading poems about the bridge and New York City. The walk concludes at Fulton Ferry Landing, where the group listens to a recital of "Crossing Brooklyn Ferry" as the sun sets on the western horizon beyond the bridge.

You can take a virtual walking tour through Whitman's Manhattan, aided by some of Whitman's interviews and poems, as well as photographs of the sites today. See *http://www.poets.org/viewmedia.php/prmMID/18983*.

Out of the Cradle Endlessly Rocking

Out of the cradle endlessly rocking,
Out of the mocking-bird's throat, the musical shuttle,
Out of the Ninth-month midnight,
Over the sterile sands and the fields beyond, where the child leaving his bed
     wander'd alone, bareheaded, barefoot,
Down from the shower'd halo,
Up from the mystic play of shadows twining and twisting as if they were alive,
Out from the patches of briers and blackberries,
From the memories of the bird that chanted to me,

5

From your memories sad brother, from the fitful risings and fallings I heard,
From under that yellow half-moon late-risen and swollen as if with tears,   10
From those beginning notes of yearning and love there in the mist,
From the thousand responses of my heart never to cease,
From the myriad thence-arous'd words,
From the word stronger and more delicious than any,
From such as now they start the scene revisiting,   15
As a flock, twittering, rising, or overhead passing,
Borne hither, ere all eludes me, hurriedly,
A man, yet by these tears a little boy again,
Throwing myself on the sand, confronting the waves,
I, chanter of pains and joys, uniter of here and hereafter,   20
Taking all hints to use them, but swiftly leaping beyond them,
A reminiscence sing.

Once Paumanok,
When the lilac-scent was in the air and Fifth-month grass was growing,
Up this seashore in some briers,   25
Two feather'd guests from Alabama, two together,
And their nest, and four light-green eggs spotted with brown,
And every day the he-bird to and fro near at hand,
And every day the she-bird crouch'd on her nest, silent, with bright eyes,
And every day I, a curious boy, never too close, never disturbing them,   30
Cautiously peering, absorbing, translating.

Shine! shine! shine!
Pour down your warmth, great sun!
While we bask, we two together.

Two together!   35
Winds blow south, or winds blow north,
Day come white, or night come black,
Home, or rivers and mountains from home,
Singing all time, minding no time,
While we two keep together.   40

Till of a sudden,
May-be kill'd, unknown to her mate,
One forenoon the she-bird crouch'd not on the nest,
Nor return'd that afternoon, nor the next,
Nor ever appear'd again.   45

And thenceforward all summer in the sound of the sea,
And at night under the full of the moon in calmer weather,
Over the hoarse surging of the sea,
Or flitting from brier to brier by day,
I saw, I heard at intervals the remaining one, the he-bird,   50
The solitary guest from Alabama.

Blow! blow! blow!
Blow up sea-winds along Paumanok's shore;
I wait and I wait till you blow my mate to me.

Yes, when the stars glisten'd,   55
All night long on the prong of a moss-scallop'd stake,
Down almost amid the slapping waves,
Sat the lone singer wonderful causing tears.

He call'd on his mate,
He pour'd forth the meanings which I of all men know.   60

Yes my brother I know,
The rest might not, but I have treasur'd every note,
For more than once dimly down to the beach gliding,
Silent, avoiding the moonbeams, blending myself with the shadows,
Recalling now the obscure shapes, the echoes, the sounds and sights after their
    sorts,   65
The white arms out in the breakers tirelessly tossing,
I, with bare feet, a child, the wind wafting my hair,
Listen'd long and long.
Listen'd to keep, to sing, now translating the notes,
Following you my brother.   70

Soothe! soothe! soothe!
Close on its wave soothes the wave behind,
And again another behind embracing and lapping, every one close,
But my love soothes not me, not me.

Low hangs the moon, it rose late,   75
It is lagging—O I think it is heavy with love, with love.

O madly the sea pushes upon the land,
With love, with love.

O night! do I not see my love fluttering out among the breakers?
What is that little black thing I see there in the white?   80

Loud! loud! loud!
Loud I call to you, my love!

High and clear I shoot my voice over the waves,
Surely you must know who is here, is here,
You must know who I am, my love.   85

Low-hanging moon!
What is that dusky spot in your brown yellow?
O it is the shape, the shape of my mate!
O moon do not keep her from me any longer.

Land! land! O land!   90
Whichever way I turn, O I think you could give me my mate back again if you only
    would,
For I am almost sure I see her dimly whichever way I look.

O rising stars!
Perhaps the one I want so much will rise, will rise with some of you.

O throat! O trembling throat!   95
Sound clearer through the atmosphere!
Pierce the woods, the earth,
Somewhere listening to catch you must be the one I want.

Shake out carols!
Solitary here, the night's carols!   100
Carols of lonesome love! death's carols!
Carols under that lagging, yellow, waning moon!
O under that moon where she droops almost down into the sea!
O reckless despairing carols.

But soft! sink low!   105
Soft! let me just murmur,
And do you wait a moment you husky-nois'd sea,
For somewhere I believe I heard my mate responding to me,
So faint, I must be still, be still to listen,
But not altogether still, for then she might not come immediately to me.   110

Hither my love!
Here I am! here!
With this just-sustain'd note I announce myself to you,
This gentle call is for you my love, for you.

Do not be decoy'd elsewhere,   115
That is the whistle of the wind, it is not my voice,
That is the fluttering, the fluttering of the spray,
Those are the shadows of leaves.

O darkness! O in vain!
O I am very sick and sorrowful.   120

O brown halo in the sky near the moon, drooping upon the sea!
O troubled reflection in the sea!
O throat! O throbbing heart!
And I singing uselessly, uselessly all the night.

O past! O happy life! O songs of joy!   125
In the air, in the woods, over fields,
Loved! loved! loved! loved! loved!
But my mate no more, no more with me!
We two together no more.

The aria sinking,   130
All else continuing, the stars shining,
The winds blowing, the notes of the bird continuous echoing,
With angry moans the fierce old mother incessantly moaning,
On the sands of Paumanok's shore gray and rustling,
The yellow half-moon enlarged, sagging down, drooping, the face of the sea al-
    most touching,   135
The boy ecstatic, with his bare feet the waves, with his hair the atmosphere
    dallying,

The love in the heart long pent, now loose, now at last tumultuously bursting,
The aria's meaning, the ears, the soul, swiftly depositing,
The strange tears down the cheeks coursing,
The colloquy there, the trio, each uttering,   140
The undertone, the savage old mother incessantly crying,
To the boy's soul's questions sullenly timing, some drown'd secret hissing,
To the outsetting bard.

Demon or bird! (said the boy's soul,)
Is it indeed toward your mate you sing? or is it really to me?   145
For I, that was a child, my tongue's use sleeping, now I have heard you,
Now in a moment I know what I am for, I awake,
And already a thousand singers, a thousand songs, clearer, louder and more sor-
    rowful than yours,
A thousand warbling echoes have started to life within me, never to die.

O you singer solitary, singing by yourself, projecting me,   150
O solitary me listening, never more shall I cease perpetuating you,
Never more shall I escape, never more the reverberations,
Never more the cries of unsatisfied love be absent from me,
Never again leave me to be the peaceful child I was before what there in the
    night,
By the sea under the yellow and sagging moon,   155
The messenger there arous'd, the fire, the sweet hell within,
The unknown want, the destiny of me.

O give me the clew! (it lurks in the night here somewhere,)
O if I am to have so much, let me have more!

A word then, (for I will conquer it,)   160
The word final, superior to all,
Subtle, sent up—what is it?—I listen;
Are you whispering it, and have been all the time, you sea-waves?
Is that it from your liquid rims and wet sands?

Whereto answering, the sea,   165
Delaying not, hurrying not,
Whisper'd me through the night, and very plainly before daybreak,
Lisp'd to me the low and delicious word death,
And again death, death, death, death,
Hissing melodious, neither like the bird nor like my arous'd child's heart,   170
But edging near as privately for me rustling at my feet,
Creeping thence steadily up to my ears and laving me softly all over,
Death, death, death, death, death.

Which I do not forget,
But fuse the song of my dusky demon and brother,   175
That he sang to me in the moonlight on Paumanok's gray beach,
With the thousand responsive songs at random,
My own songs awaked from that hour,
And with them the key, the word up from the waves,
The word of the sweetest song and all songs,
That strong and delicious word which, creeping to my feet,   180

(Or like some old crone rocking the cradle, swathed in sweet garments, bending
   aside,)
The sea whisper'd me.

When Lilacs Last in the Dooryard Bloom'd

1

When lilacs last in the dooryard bloom'd,
And the great star early droop'd in the western sky in the night,
I mourn'd, and yet shall mourn with ever-returning spring.

Ever-returning spring, trinity sure to me you bring,
Lilac blooming perennial and drooping star in the west,   5
And thought of him I love.

2

O powerful western fallen star!
O shades of night—O moody, tearful night!
O great star disappear'd—O the black murk that hides the star!
O cruel hands that hold me powerless—O helpless soul of me!   10
O harsh surrounding cloud that will not free my soul.

3

In the dooryard fronting an old farm-house near the white-wash'd palings,
Stands the lilac-bush tall-growing with heart-shaped leaves of rich green,
With many a pointed blossom rising delicate, with the perfume strong I love,
With every leaf a miracle—and from this bush in the dooryard,   15
With delicate-color'd blossoms and heart-shaped leaves of rich green,
A sprig with its flower I break.

4

In the swamp in secluded recesses,
A shy and hidden bird is warbling a song.

Solitary the thrush,   20
The hermit withdrawn to himself, avoiding the settlements,
Sings by himself a song.

Song of the bleeding throat,
Death's outlet song of life, (for well dear brother I know,
If thou wast not granted to sing thou would'st surely die.)   25

5

Over the breast of the spring, the land, amid cities,
Amid lanes and through old woods, where lately the violets peep'd from the
   ground, spotting the gray debris,
Amid the grass in the fields each side of the lanes, passing the endless grass,
Passing the yellow-spear'd wheat, every grain from its shroud in the dark-brown
   fields uprisen,
Passing the apple-tree blows of white and pink in the orchards,   30
Carrying a corpse to where it shall rest in the grave,
Night and day journeys a coffin.

6

Coffin that passes through lanes and streets,
Through day and night with the great cloud darkening the land,
With the pomp of the inloop'd flags with the cities draped in black,   35
With the show of the States themselves as of crape-veil'd women standing,
With processions long and winding and the flambeaus of the night,
With the countless torches lit, with the silent sea of faces and the unbared heads,
With the waiting depot, the arriving coffin, and the sombre faces,
With dirges through the night, with the thousand voices rising strong and
    solemn,   40
With all the mournful voices of the dirges pour'd around the coffin,
The dim-lit churches and the shuddering organs—where amid these you
    journey,
With the tolling tolling bells' perpetual clang,
Here, coffin that slowly passes,
I give you my sprig of lilac.   45

7

(Nor for you, for one alone,
Blossoms and branches green to coffins all I bring,
For fresh as the morning, thus would I chant a song for you O sane and sacred
    death.

All over bouquets of roses,
O death, I cover you over with roses and early lilies,   50
But mostly and now the lilac that blooms the first,
Copious I break, I break the sprigs from the bushes,
With loaded arms I come, pouring for you,
For you and the coffins all of you O death.)

8

O western orb sailing the heaven,   55
Now I know what you must have meant as a month since I walk'd,
As I walk'd in silence the transparent shadowy night,
As I saw you had something to tell as you bent to me night after night,
As you droop'd from the sky low down as if to my side, (while the other stars all
    look'd on,)
As we wander'd together the solemn night, (for something I know not what kept
    me from sleep,)   60
As the night advanced, and I saw on the rim of the west how full you were of
    woe,
As I stood on the rising ground in the breeze in the cool transparent night,
As I watch'd where you pass'd and was lost in the netherward black of the night,
As my soul in its trouble dissatisfied sank, as where you sad orb,
Concluded, dropt in the night, and was gone.   65

9

Sing on there in the swamp,
O singer bashful and tender, I hear your notes, I hear your call,
I hear, I come presently, I understand you,

But a moment I linger, for the lustrous star has detain'd me,
The star my departing comrade holds and detains me.   70

10

O how shall I warble myself for the dead one there I loved?
And how shall I deck my song for the large sweet soul that has gone?
And what shall my perfume be for the grave of him I love?

Sea-winds blown from east and west,
Blown from the Eastern sea and blown from the Western sea, till there on the
    prairies meeting,   75
These and with these and the breath of my chant,
I'll perfume the grave of him I love.

11

O what shall I hang on the chamber walls?
And what shall the pictures be that I hang on the walls,
To adorn the burial-house of him I love?   80

Pictures of growing spring and farms and homes,
With the Fourth-month eve at sundown, and the gray smoke lucid and bright,
With floods of the yellow gold of the gorgeous, indolent, sinking sun, burning,
    expanding the air,
With the fresh sweet herbage under foot, and the pale green leaves of the trees
    prolific,
In the distance the flowing glaze, the breast of the river, with a wind-dapple here
    and there,   85
With ranging hills on the banks, with many a line against the sky, and shadows,
And the city at hand with dwellings so dense, and stacks of chimneys,
And all the scenes of life and the workshops, and the workmen homeward
    returning.

12

Lo, body and soul—this land,
My own Manhattan with spires, and the sparkling and hurrying tides, and the
    ships,   90
The varied and ample land, the South and the North in the light, Ohio's shores
    and flashing Missouri,
And ever the far-spreading prairies cover'd with grass and corn.

Lo, the most excellent sun so calm and haughty,
The violet and purple morn with just-felt breezes,
The gentle soft-born measureless light,   95
The miracle spreading bathing all, the fulfill'd noon,
The coming eve delicious, the welcome night and the stars,
Over my cities shining all, enveloping man and land.

13

Sing on, sing on you gray-brown bird,
Sing from the swamps, the recesses, pour your chant from the bushes,   100
Limitless out of the dusk, out of the cedars and pines.

Sing on dearest brother, warble your reedy song,
Loud human song, with voice of uttermost woe.

O liquid and free and tender!
O wild and loose to my soul—O wondrous singer!   105
You only I hear—yet the star holds me, (but will soon depart,)
Yet the lilac with mastering odor holds me.

14

Now while I sat in the day and look'd forth,
In the close of the day with its light and the fields of spring, and the farmers
    preparing their crops,
In the large unconscious scenery of my land with its lakes and forests,   110
In the heavenly aerial beauty, (after the perturb'd winds and the storms,)
Under the arching heavens of the afternoon swift passing, and the voices of chil-
    dren and women,
The many-moving sea-tides, and I saw the ships how they sail'd,
And the summer approaching with richness, and the fields all busy with labor,
And the infinite separate houses, how they all went on, each with its meals and
    minutia of daily usages,   115
And the streets how their throbbings throbb'd, and the cities pent—lo, then and
    there,
Falling upon them all and among them all, enveloping me with the rest,
Appear'd the cloud, appear'd the long black trail,
And I knew death, its thought, and the sacred knowledge of death.

Then with the knowledge of death as walking one side of me,   120
And the thought of death close-walking the other side of me,
And I in the middle as with companions, and as holding the hands of
    companions,
I fled forth to the hiding receiving night that talks not,
Down to the shores of the water, the path by the swamp in the dimness,
To the solemn shadowy cedars and ghostly pines so still.   125

And the singer so shy to the rest receiv'd me,
The gray-brown bird I know receiv'd us comrades three,
And he sang the carol of death, and a verse for him I love.

From deep secluded recesses,
From the fragrant cedars and the ghostly pines so still,   130
Came the carol of the bird.

And the charm of the carol rapt me,
As I held as if by their hands my comrades in the night,
And the voice of my spirit tallied the song of the bird.

Come lovely and soothing death,   135
Undulate round the world, serenely arriving, arriving,
In the day, in the night, to all, to each,
Sooner or later delicate death.

Prais'd be the fathomless universe,
For life and joy, and for objects and knowledge curious,   140

And for love, sweet love—but praise! praise! praise!
For the sure-enwinding arms of cool-enfolding death.

Dark mother always gliding near with soft feet,
Have none chanted for thee a chant of fullest welcome?
Then I chant it for thee, I glorify thee above all,   145
I bring thee a song that when thou must indeed come, come unfalteringly.

Approach strong deliveress,
When it is so, when thou hast taken them I joyously sing the dead,
Lost in the loving floating ocean of thee,
Laved in the flood of thy bliss O death.   150

From me to thee glad serenades,
Dances for thee I propose saluting thee, adornments and feastings for thee,
And the sights of the open landscape and the high-spread sky are fitting,
And life and the fields, and the huge and thoughtful night.

The night in silence under many a star,   155
The ocean shore and the husky whispering wave whose voice I know,
And the soul turning to thee O vast and well-veil'd death,
And the body gratefully nestling close to thee.

Over the tree-tops I float thee a song,
Over the rising and sinking waves, over the myriad fields and the prairies wide,   160
Over the dense-pack'd cities all and the teeming wharves and ways,
I float this carol with joy, with joy to thee O death.

15

To the tally of my soul,
Loud and strong kept up the gray-brown bird,
With pure deliberate notes spreading filling the night.   165

Loud in the pines and cedars dim,
Clear in the freshness moist and the swamp-perfume,
And I with my comrades there in the night.

While my sight that was bound in my eyes unclosed,
As to long panoramas of visions.   170

And I saw askant the armies,
I saw as in noiseless dreams hundreds of battle-flags,
Borne through the smoke of the battles and pierc'd with missiles I saw them,
And carried hither and yon through the smoke, and torn and bloody,
And at last but a few shreds left on the staffs, (and all in silence,)   175
And the staffs all splinter'd and broken.

I saw battle-corpses, myriads of them,
And the white skeletons of young men, I saw them,
I saw the debris and debris of all the slain soldiers of the war,
But I saw they were not as was thought,   180
They themselves were fully at rest, they suffer'd not,
The living remain'd and suffer'd, the mother suffer'd,
And the wife and the child and the musing comrade suffer'd,
And the armies that remain'd suffer'd.

16

Passing the visions, passing the night,   185
Passing, unloosing the hold of my comrades' hands,
Passing the song of the hermit bird and the tallying song of my soul,
Victorious song, death's outlet song, yet varying ever-altering song,
As low and wailing, yet clear the notes, rising and falling, flooding the night,
Sadly sinking and fainting, as warning and warning, and yet again bursting with
    joy,   190
Covering the earth and filling the spread of the heaven,
As that powerful psalm in the night I heard from recesses,
Passing, I leave thee lilac with heart-shaped leaves,
I leave thee there in the door-yard, blooming, returning with spring.

I cease from my song for thee,   195
From my gaze on thee in the west, fronting the west, communing with thee,
O comrade lustrous with silver face in the night.

Yet each to keep and all, retrievements out of the night,
The song, the wondrous chant of the gray-brown bird,
And the tallying chant, the echo arous'd in my soul,   200
With the lustrous and drooping star with the countenance full of woe,
With the holders holding my hand nearing the call of the bird,
Comrades mine and I in the midst, and their memory ever to keep, for the dead I
    loved so well,
For the sweetest, wisest soul of all my days and lands—and this for his dear sake,
Lilac and star and bird twined with the chant of my soul,   205
There in the fragrant pines and the cedars dusk and dim.

INSPIRATION   WHITMAN AND
                 THE CIVIL WAR

Whitman's diaries from his years caring for wounded soldiers are a valuable historical record of the Civil War from a civilian's perspective. Whitman recorded
the intimate details of day-to-day life in a war hospital, capturing a part of war
rarely seen. Here are three selections from his war diaries, first collected in
Specimen Days (1882) and then again in his *Prose Works* (1892), which included
the war diaries, his Prefaces, *Democratic Vistas*, and his collected newspaper articles, *November Boughs*.

May 28–9.—
    I staid to-night a long time by the bedside of a new patient, a young
Baltimorean, aged about 19 years, W. S. P., (2d Maryland, southern,) very
feeble, right leg amputated, can't sleep hardly at all—has taken a great

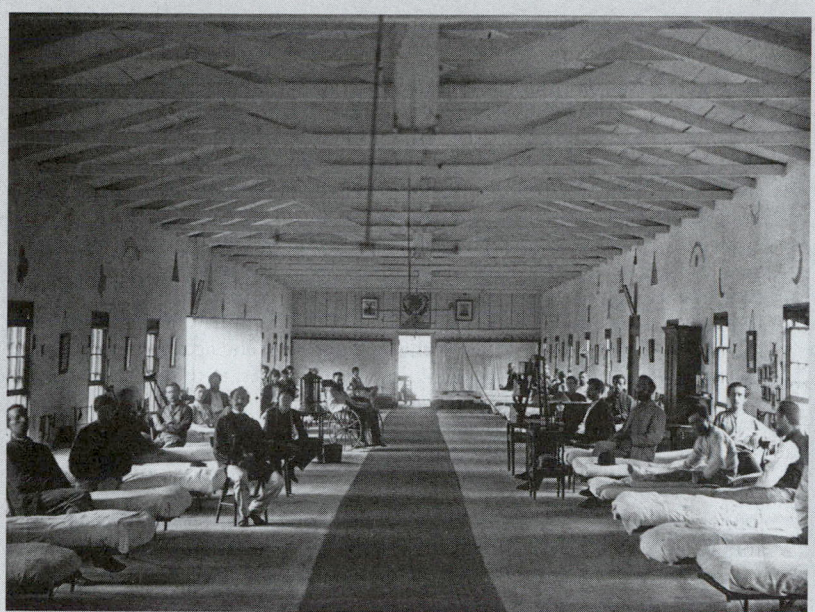

The patients treated at Armory Square Hospital in Washington, D.C., where Whit-man volunteered during 1862–1863, were among the most severely wounded of the Civil War soldiers.

deal of morphine, which, as usual, is costing more than it comes to. Evidently very intelligent and well bred—very affectionate—held on to my hand, and put it by his face, not willing to let me leave. As I was lingering, soothing him in his pain, he says to me suddenly, "I hardly think you know who I am—I don't wish to impose upon you—I am a rebel soldier." I said I did not know that, but it made no difference. Visiting him daily for about two weeks after that, while he lived, (death had mark'd him, and he was quite alone,) I loved him much, always kiss'd him, and he did me. In an adjoining ward I found his brother, an officer of rank, a Union soldier, a brave and religious man, (Col. Clifton K. Prentiss, sixth Maryland infantry, Sixth corps, wounded in one of the engagements at Petersburgh, April 2—linger'd, suffer'd much, died in Brooklyn, Aug. 20, '65.) It was in the same battle both were hit. One was a strong Unionist, the other Secesh; both fought on their respective sides, both badly wounded, and both brought together here after a separation of four years. Each died for his cause.

—from *Specimen Days*, "Two Brothers, One South, One North"

The dead in this war—there they lie, strewing the fields and woods and valleys and battle-fields of the south—Virginia, the Peninsula—Malvern hill and Fair Oaks—the banks of the Chickahominy—the terraces of Fredericksburgh—Antietam bridge—the grisly ravines of Manassas—the

(continued on next page)

WHITMAN AND THE CIVIL WAR

bloody promenade of the Wilderness—the varieties of the strayed dead, (the estimate of the War department is 25,000 national soldiers kill'd in battle and never buried at all, 5,000 drown'd—15,000 inhumed by strangers, or on the march in haste, in hitherto unfound localities—2,000 graves cover'd by sand and mud by Mississippi freshets, 3,000 carried away by caving-in of banks, &c). . . . And everywhere among these countless graves—everywhere in the many soldier Cemeteries of the Nation, (there are now, I believe, over seventy of them)—as at the time in the vast trenches, the depositories of slain, Northern and Southern, after the great battles—not only where the scathing trail passed those years, but radiating since in all the peaceful quarters of the land—we see, and ages yet may see, on monuments and gravestones, singly or in masses, to thousands or tens of thousands, the significant word Unknown.
—from *Specimen Days*, "The Million Dead, Too, Summ'd Up"

The preceding notes may furnish a few stray glimpses into that life, and into those lurid interiors, never to be fully convey'd to the future. The hospital part of the drama from '61 to '65, deserves indeed to be recorded. Of that many-threaded drama, with its sudden and strange surprises, its confounding of prophecies, its moments of despair, the dread of foreign interference, the interminable campaigns, the bloody battles, the mighty and cumbrous and green armies, the drafts and bounties—the immense money expenditure, like a heavy-pouring constant rain—with, over the whole land, the last three years of the struggle, an unending, universal mourning-wail of women, parents, orphans—the marrow of the tragedy concentrated in those Army Hospitals—(it seem'd sometimes as if the whole interest of the land, North and South, was one vast central hospital, and all the rest of the affair but flanges)—those forming the untold and unwritten history of the war—infinitely greater (like life's) than the few scraps and distortions that are ever told or written. Think how much, and of importance, will be—how much, civic and military, has already been—buried in the grave, in eternal darkness.
—from *Specimen Days*, "The Real War Will Never Get in the Books"

A Noiseless Patient Spider

A noiseless patient spider,
I mark'd where on a little promontory it stood isolated,
Mark'd how to explore the vacant vast surrounding,
It launch'd forth filament, filament, filament, out of itself,
Ever unreeling them, ever tirelessly speeding them.   5

And you O my soul where you stand,
Surrounded, detached, in measureless oceans of space,
Ceaselessly musing, venturing, throwing, seeking the spheres to connect them,
Till the bridge you will need be form'd, till the ductile anchor hold,
Till the gossamer thread you fling catch somewhere, O my soul.   10

☀ INSPIRATION THE MUSIC OF WHITMAN

Folksinger and 1960s icon Joan Baez was among the many musicians who set Whitman's writing to music.

Whitman's poetry has appealed to musical composers from all nationalities for over a century, leading to over 500 musical settings of his work. In fact, Whitman's poetry is set to music more often than any American poet besides Dickinson and Longfellow. One of the earliest composers to use Whitman was British composer Gustav Holst, who created the *Walt Whitman Overture* in 1899. In the 1940s, Germany's preeminent composers Kurt Weill, Arnold Schoenberg, and Paul Hindemith each set Whitman to music. And in the United States, Whitman has appealed to a broad range of composers and musicians, including Aaron Copland, Charles Ives, Philip Glass, John Adams, Virgil Thomson, and Joan Baez. Here are just a few compositions inspired by Whitman's poetry:

- British composer Ralph Vaughan Williams wrote *A Sea Symphony* (1910) for chorus and orchestra based on poems from *Leaves of Grass*. Each of the four movements uses the text of Whitman's poems: "A Song for All Seas, All Ships," "On the Beach at Night, Alone," "Scherzo: The Waves," and "The Explorers." (Conductor Robert Spano leads the Atlanta Symphony Orchestra in an award-winning 2002 CD from Telarc.)
- German composer Paul Hindemith used Whitman's text for his 1946 "When Lilacs Last in the Dooryard Bloom'd: Requiem for Those We Love" (available on CD from Telarc, 2002, with the Atlanta Symphony Orchestra and Chorus).
- American baritone Thomas Hampson, well-known for his musical achievements in opera, song, recording, and music criticism, recorded an entire album of Whitman poems set to music by composers ranging from Ned Rorem to Paul Hindemith to Leonard Bernstein: *To the Soul: Thomas Hampson Sings the Poetry of Walt Whitman* (EMI, 1997).
- Folksinger Joan Baez performed Whitman's "I Saw the Visions of Armies" on her *Baptism: A Journey through Our Time* (Vanguard, 2003).
- Folk-rock icon Van Morrison references Whitman in his "Rave on John Donne" on the album *The Inarticulate Speech of the Heart* (Warner Brothers, 1990).

For more information about how Walt Whitman has inspired musicians and composers, see the essay "Whitman's Musical Legacy" at *http://www.americancomposers.org/whitman1.htm* or the program notes at *http://www.americancomposers.org/rel990515.htm*.

☀ INSPIRATION THE "I HEAR AMERICA SINGING" MURAL, THE BRONX, NEW YORK

Panel of an American worker from Resources for America, *a Bronx mural inspired by Whitman.*

In 1939 the well-established Social Realist painter Ben Shahn and his wife, Bernarda Bryson Shahn, were commissioned for a mural at the Bronx Post Office, located at 558 Grand Concourse and 149th Street, as part of the New Deal's federally funded Work Projects Administration. Inspired by Whitman's "I Hear America Singing," the Shahns completed a thirteen-panel mural honoring the American worker, entitled *Resources for America*, which fills the post office's lobby. The mural contains lines from Whitman's poetry as well as a depiction of the poet himself. The lines originally chosen for the mural came from "As a Strong Bird on Pinions Free": "to recast poems, churches, art / (Recast maybe to discard them, end them— / Maybe their work is done—who knows," but they caused controversy when they were denounced by a Jesuit professor. In order to avoid negative press for publicly funded art programs, the Shahns agreed to replace the lines with these from "As I Walk These Broad, Majestic Days": "For we support all / Fuse All / After the rest is done / and gone we remain / There is no final / reliance but upon us / Democracy rests finally / upon us / (I my brethren begin it) / and our visions sweep / through eternity." Some speculate that their willingness to alter the lines may have stemmed from Ben Shahn's experience in 1933 assisting Mexican muralist Diego Rivera in the execution of the *Man at the Crossroads* fresco for the RCA building in Rockefeller Center, a mural that was later destroyed for political reasons. For more information and photographs of the Shahns' mural, see *http://ca80.lehman.cuny.edu/pa/bgpo.htm.*

I Hear America Singing

I hear America singing, the varied carols I hear,
Those of mechanics, each one singing his as it should be blithe and strong,
The carpenter singing his as he measures his plank or beam,
The mason singing his as he makes ready for work, or leaves off work,
The boatman singing what belongs to him in his boat, the deckhand singing on
  the steamboat deck,

The shoemaker singing as he sits on his bench, the hatter singing as he stands,
The wood-cutter's song, the ploughboy's on his way in the morning, or at noon
intermission or at sundown,
The delicious singing of the mother, or of the young wife at work, or of the girl
sewing or washing,
Each singing what belongs to him or her and to none else,
The day what belongs to the day—at night the party of young fellows, robust,
friendly,
Singing with open mouths their strong melodious songs.

10

When I Heard at the Close of the Day

When I heard at the close of the day how my name had been receiv'd with plau-
dits in the capitol, still it was not a happy night for me that follow'd,
And else when I carous'd, or when my plans were accomplish'd, still I was not
happy,
But the day when I rose at dawn from the bed of perfect health, refresh'd,
singing, inhaling the ripe breath of autumn,
When I saw the full moon in the west grow pale and disappear in the morning
light,
When I wander'd alone over the beach, and undressing bathed, laughing with
the cool waters, and saw the sun rise,
And when I thought how my dear friend my lover was on his way coming, O
then I was happy,
O then each breath tasted sweeter, and all that day my food nourish'd me more,
and the beautiful day pass'd well,
And the next came with equal joy, and with the next at evening came my friend,
And that night while all was still I heard the waters roll slowly continually up
the shores,
I heard the hissing rustle of the liquid and sands as directed to me whispering to
congratulate me,
For the one I love most lay sleeping by me under the same cover in the cool
night,
In the stillness in the autumn moonbeams his face was inclined toward me,
And his arm lay lightly around my breast—and that night I was happy.

5

10

I Saw in Louisiana a Live-Oak Growing

I saw in Louisiana a live-oak growing,
All alone stood it and the moss hung down from the branches,
Without any companion it grew there uttering joyous leaves of dark green,
And its look, rude, unbending, lusty, made me think of myself,
But I wonder'd how it could utter joyous leaves standing alone there without its
friend near, for I knew I could not,
And I broke off a twig with a certain number of leaves upon it, and twined
around it a little moss,
And brought it away, and I have placed it in sight in my room,
It is not needed to remind me as of my own dear friends,

5

(For I believe lately I think of little else than of them,)
Yet it remains to me a curious token, it makes me think of manly love;　　10
For all that, and though the live-oak glistens there in Louisiana solitary in a wide
　　flat space,
Uttering joyous leaves all its life without a friend a lover near,
I know very well I could not.

VIDEO LOCALE

Civil War photographer Mathew Brady's 1862 portrait of Whitman.

Whitman on Video. PBS's *Voices and Visions* film series includes a 1988 feature on Walt Whitman that discusses his biography and offers literary criticism and commentary from contemporary poets Allen Ginsberg, Galway Kinnell, and Donald Hall (produced by the New York Center for Visual History, directed by Jack Smithie for the South Carolina Educational Television Network).

　　Poet Andrei Codrescu visits Whitman's Camden home in his cross-country search for America in the documentary *Road Scholar* (Hallmark Home Entertainment, 1992, directed by Roger Weisberg).

Cavalry Crossing a Ford

A line in long array where they wind betwixt green islands,
They take a serpentine course, their arms flash in the sun—hark to the musical
　　clank,
Behold the silvery river, in it the splashing horses loitering stop to drink,
Behold the brown-faced men, each group, each person a picture, the negligent
　　rest on the saddles,
Some emerge on the opposite bank, others are just entering the ford—while,　　5
Scarlet and blue and snowy white,
The guidon flags flutter gayly in the wind.

The Wound-Dresser

1

An old man bending I come among new faces,
Years looking backward resuming in answer to children,
Come tell us old man, as from young men and maidens that love me,
(Arous'd and angry, I'd thought to beat the alarum, and urge relentless war,
But soon my fingers fail'd me, my face droop'd and I resign'd myself,　　5

To sit by the wounded and soothe them, or silently watch the dead;)
Years hence of these scenes, of these furious passions, these chances,
Of unsurpass'd heroes, (was one side so brave? the other was equally brave;)
Now be witness again, paint the mightiest armies of earth,
Of those armies so rapid so wondrous what saw you to tell us?   10
What stays with you latest and deepest? of curious panics,
Of hard-fought engagements or sieges tremendous what deepest remains?

2

O maidens and young men I love and that love me,
What you ask of my days those the strangest and sudden your talking recalls,
Soldier alert I arrive after a long march cover'd with sweat and dust,   15
In the nick of time I come, plunge in the fight, loudly shout in the rush of suc-
    cessful charge,
Enter the captur'd works—yet lo, like a swift-running river they fade,
Pass and are gone they fade—I dwell not on soldiers' perils or soldier's joys,
(Both I remember well—many the hardships, few the joys, yet I was content.)

But in silence, in dreams' projections,   20
While the world of gain and appearance and mirth goes on,
So soon what is over forgotten, and waves wash the imprints off the sand,
With hinged knees returning I enter the doors, (while for you up there,
Whoever you are, follow without noise and be of strong heart.)

Bearing the bandages, water and sponge,   25
Straight and swift to my wounded I go,
Where they lie on the ground after the battle brought in,
Where their priceless blood reddens the grass the ground,
Or to the rows of the hospital tent, or under the roof'd hospital,
To the long rows of cots up and down each side I return,   30
To each and all one after another I draw near, not one do I miss,
An attendant follows holding a tray, he carries a refuse pail,
Soon to be fill'd with clotted rags and blood, emptied, and fill'd again.

I onward go, I stop,
With hinged knees and steady hand to dress wounds,   35
I am firm with each, the pangs are sharp yet unavoidable,
One turns to me his appealing eyes—poor boy! I never knew you,
Yet I think I could not refuse this moment to die for you, if that would save you.

3

On, on I go, (open doors of time! open hospital doors!)
The crush'd head I dress, (poor crazed hand tear not the bandage away,)   40
The neck of the cavalry-man with the bullet through and through I examine,
Hard the breathing rattles, quite glazed already the eye, yet life struggles hard,
(Come sweet death! be persuaded O beautiful death! In mercy come quickly.)

From the stump of the arm, the amputated hand,
I undo the clotted lint, remove the slough, wash off the matter and blood,   45
Back on his pillow the soldier bends with curv'd neck and side-falling head,

His eyes are closed, his face is pale, he dares not look on the bloody stump,
And has not yet look'd on it.

I dress a wound in the side, deep, deep,
But a day or two more, for see the frame all wasted and sinking, 50
And the yellow-blue countenance see.

I dress the perforated shoulder, the foot with the bullet-wound,
Cleanse the one with a gnawing and putrid gangrene, so sickening, so offensive,
While the attendant stands behind aside me holding the tray and pail.

I am faithful, I do not give out, 55
The fractur'd thigh, the knee, the wound in the abdomen,
These and more I dress with impassive hand, (yet deep in my breast a fire, a
    burning flame.)

4

Thus in silence in dreams' projections,
Returning, resuming, I thread my way through the hospitals,
The hurt and wounded I pacify with soothing hand, 60
I sit by the restless all the dark night, some are so young,
Some suffer so much, I recall the experience sweet and sad,
(Many a soldier's loving arms about this neck have cross'd and rested,
Many a soldier's kiss dwells on these bearded lips.)

✎ COMMENTARY

Whitman on His Art and Poetry

From the Preface to Leaves of Grass *(1855 ed.)*

The art of art, the glory of expression and the sunshine of the light of letters is
simplicity. Nothing is better than simplicity.

From Horace Traubel's biography Walt Whitman in Camden

What I am after is the content not the music of the words. Perhaps the music
happens—it does no harm.

I have never given any study merely to expression: it has never appealed to me as
a thing valuable or significant in itself: I have been deliberate, careful, even laborious: but I have never looked for finish—never fooled with technique more that
enough to provide for simply getting through: after all that I would not give a
twist of my chair for all the rest.

From a Letter to Ralph Waldo Emerson, included in the sec-ond edition of Leaves of Grass *(1856)*

Strangle the singers who will not sing to you loud and strong.

Old forms, old poems, majestic and proper in their own lands here in this land
are exiles.

W. Curtis Taylor's 1877 albumen photograph of Whitman and a butterfly served as a frontispiece in an 1891 sample proof of Leaves of Grass. *The butterfly was a recurring visual motif for Whitman in his portraits and in his books, intended to suggest the poet's connection to the natural world.*

From Whitman's essay "A Backward Glance"

I round and finish little, if anything; and could not, consistently with my scheme. The reader will always have his or her part to do, just as much as I have had mine. I seek less to state or display any theme or thought, and more to bring you, reader, into the atmosphere of the theme or thought—there to pursue your own flight.

From Whitman's essay "American Primer," which appeared in the Atlantic Monthly, *April 1904*

Pronunciation is the stamina of language,—it is language.

From the Preface to Leaves of Grass *(1855 ed.)*

There will soon be no more priests; a new breed of poet-prophets shall take their place, and every man shall be his own priest.

Talking about the Text

1. Using as evidence "I Hear America Singing," "I Saw in Louisiana a Live-Oak Growing," and "A Noiseless Patient Spider," describe the shape of a Whitman poem. How does it tend to start? Is there a single dramatic moment or revelation? What happens afterward? What kind of resolution occurs at the end?
2. Using at least three poems (but not "Song of Myself"), describe the Whitman persona. What does the speaker sound like? What does he tell us about himself? What does he leave out about himself?
3. What seems not to interest the Whitman persona? For instance, think of what kinds of occupations and people he omits from his catalogues in "Song of Myself," Sections 5–10 and 34–38.

Writing about the Text

1. Respond to the critical statement that follows, explaining to what extent you agree or disagree with this claim. Support your response with examples from the poems.

   Whitman clarifies his intended relationship to us at many points in his poetry, telling exactly how we should read him. His approach is consciously and blatantly seductive. He presents his book as his physical person and his purpose as a sexual relationship with the reader. As students notice this, they become personally involved with the poet. For many the relationship is disquieting, as Whitman predicted it would be. (William H. Shurr, "*Leaves of Grass* as a Sexual Manifesto: A Reader-Response Approach.")

2. Write your own explication on "Crossing Brooklyn Ferry," taking your readers through the poem and indicating what the speaker sees, hears, and feels. (See "Writing an Explication," p. 819.)
3. Write your own "I Hear America Singing," using Whitman's form (pp. 870–871) but filling in with what you hear yourself. You can do this straight or as a parody.

Linking the Text to Other Texts

1. Compare the voice you identify in two or three of Whitman's poems with another distinctive American poetic voice from a more recent period. What do they have in common?
2. What would have prevented a female poet of the same era from writing with as much personal involvement as Whitman? Speculate on some women poets today who might share some common approaches with him.
3. Imagine how you would read "A Noiseless Patient Spider" and "O Captain! My Captain!" (see Chapter 17, p. 998) aloud, then listen to audio versions and compare the approaches.

✑ C O M M E N T A R Y

Two Poets on Walt Whitman

Whitman was one of the most influential poets who ever lived, inspiring thousands of young men and women to write about what mattered most to them, and to do it in free verse. Here, two poets—Langston Hughes and Marge Piercy—write of how Whitman inspired them.

Langston Hughes   (1902–1967)

Old Walt   (1954)

Old Walt Whitman
Went finding and seeking,
Finding less than sought
Seeking more than found,
Every detail minding
Of the seeking or the finding.

Pleasured equally
In seeking as in finding,
Each detail minding,
Old Walt went seeking
And finding.

Marge Piercy (B. 1936)

How I Came to Walt Whitman and Found Myself (1992)

Marge Piercy.

I came to Walt Whitman early, in high school. In those days, we actually read poems in English class. I believe it was my sophomore year, but it might have been my junior year. Certainly the textbook we were using contained some poems of Whitman's, enough to seize me. I read them aloud again and again and experienced inebriation and an intense loosening, a revelation of light and heat and identity.

The first poets I had been smitten by were Shelley and Keats, and I wrote pallid imitations of them as some of the earliest writing I remember or can find. Those first attempts rimed, something that has always constricted my imagination. Most of the poems I recall were about dying, although some were about wanting to be loved by somebody, somehow, somewhere, but right away.

When I read Whitman, I did not so much produce those wan imitations in pastel but my first real poems. It was very much what happened to me many years later when I was working as a secretary in Chicago and went to hear Allen Ginsberg. It wasn't that I began to imitate Ginsberg or that I began to produce little purse mirrors of Whitman when I was fifteen. Rather each of them seemed to say to me by their practice, if you write out of who you are, if you deal genuinely with your own experiences, if you go into yourself honestly, you can write something worth reading.

Whitman gave me a way to try to grapple with an early mystical experience which nothing in my family or my background or my ideas (Marx and Freud, mostly) had prepared me for. Shortly afterward I forgot it, but at the time it seemed supremely important to me. Whitman's long flowing line and American exuberance, the sense of being rooted in his own body and this landscape, this reality, liberated me to deal with my feeling and my experiences.

I link the influence that hearing Ginsberg had upon me in 1959 with reading Whitman in 1950 or 1951, because both of them said to me that to write authentically from yourself, no matter how queer or outside the mainstream society seemed to regard you, was inherently valuable if you wrote well. Whitman offered support for the strange notion that anything that happened to me could interest anyone else. Certainly my life did not seem to confirm that hypothesis. I could immediately tell, however, the difference between what I began writing then, which was crude, often inchoate but clanging and throbbing with Detroit and Michigan sounds, sights, smells, lives, and the Pepto Bismol that I had dribbled out before that time.

I found in Whitman a confirmation of earlier rhythms from Jewish liturgy and the Torah and the Psalms, rhythms that were not those of most poetry I had been taught in school, but rhythms that came more naturally to me. Later I would learn many other lines and work steadfastly on what I wanted to do with line length and line breaks and sound qualities, but early on in my apprenticeship as a writer Whitman directed me to the oral power of verse. His poetry was written as notation for reciting it. He used many devices familiar to me also from liturgy for creating structure, as many of the poets I had read before him used rime. His ways were more useful to me and I began to study them.

But beyond training in incremental repetition and anaphora, what I derived from Whitman was permission to be where I was and who I was: to be American, to have a body, which was loud and demanding and altogether wrong, to feel politically, to think that my life, my place and time were worthy of poetry. When I got to college, a typical New-Critical department of English in the mid-fifties, in love with Pound and Eliot and Anglophile to the bowlers, I was taught relentlessly that all of what Whitman had passed on to me was incorrect and uncouth. I wasted some time recovering from that pseudo-British fog in the brain, but without Whitman I would not have had a strong foundation on which to build my later practice.

I always say that we American poets are all children of Walt Whitman and Emily Dickinson, that they blasted the road for us and we are still exploring the ramifications of what they opened up. Both of them were stone originals and thoroughly American, thoroughly of their landscapes and their own odd voices. I could not have found two better mentors for the beginning of my study of poetry, and I read both of them frequently now—still aloud and with a respect and affection that have not eroded but grown.

Starting Points for Further Research: Walt Whitman

- **Edition:** Walt Whitman. *Leaves of Grass and Other Writings.* Ed. Michael Moon et al. New York: W. W. Norton, 2002.
- **Biography:** David S. Reynolds. *Walt Whitman.* New York: Oxford University Press, 2005.
- **Critical Essay:** Richard Haw. "American History/American Memory: Reevaluating Walt Whitman's Relationship with the Brooklyn Bridge." *Journal of American Studies* 38 (2004): 1–22.

CHAPTER
14

Emily Dickinson

This daguerreotype was taken when Emily Dickinson was sixteen and is one of the only extant, authenticated mechanical images of the poet. (The other is a silhouette created when she was fourteen.)

Emily Dickinson (1830–1886) is one of the great enigmas among American writers. To outward observers the facts of her life are extremely simple and should not entail much mystery: born in 1830, she lived all her life in Amherst, Massachusetts, most of that time in the house in which she was born. She seldom left Amherst: she was away at college, at Mount Holyoke (about twenty miles distant), for much of one year; she made short visits in 1863 and 1864 to Boston for the treatment of her eyes; she also made brief trips to Washington, D.C., and Philadelphia. Her entire life was lived in a provincial town among family and a very small circle of friends. Yet out of this quiet, uneventful life she produced some of the most brilliant, profound, and puzzling poetry ever written, verse filled with passion and insight, at once artless and deeply literary.

Dickinson's father was a distinguished lawyer, the son of a founder of Amherst College, and he served in the Massachusetts legislature and for one term in the U.S. House of Representatives. He was an important but distant figure in

Dickinson's life, as was her mother. The family's material circumstances were never an occasion for worry, and Dickinson received a first-class education, attending an excellent academy and one year of college at a time when hardly any women were able to do so. When young, she frequently visited Amherst friends and relatives, including her married brother Austin, who lived next door. But she gradually cut back on those outings as she approached the age of thirty. Eventually she even shied from seeing most of the visitors who entered her own house, retreating to her room on the second floor. It was in this room—now open to visitors—that she wrote some 2,000 poems, though only seven were published during her lifetime (always anonymously and usually against her will). After Dickinson's death, her sister Lavinia found a huge cache of her writing, all carefully preserved in a storage chest, and determined to get the poetry published.

Dickinson was strongly affected by the deaths of her parents, her father in

1874 and her mother in 1882. Judging from her letters, the deaths of some other important people in her life were also significant blows: her friends Samuel Bowles in 1878 and Dr. Josiah Holland in 1881. She carried on a correspondence with the distinguished editor and writer Thomas Wentworth Higginson for over twenty years, during which Higginson visited her in Amherst twice. This exchange has excited a lot of attention because it is the only evidence we have of any extended encounter between Dickinson and a representative of the Boston literary world of the time. Her dashing friend Samuel Bowles edited the Springfield *Republican*, a newspaper that printed a daily poem, and Bowles published three of Dickinson's poems (heavily edited to smooth out their rough edges). But how significant these literary exchanges were to Dickinson we do not know. Bowles printed Dickinson's three

Edward Dickinson, Emily's father.

poems anonymously. Higginson, editor of the *Atlantic Monthly*, then one of America's premier literary magazines, read the poems she sent him and suggested that they needed serious revision, which she firmly refused to do. After her death he assisted in their publication, making some of the revisions she had resisted while alive. Indeed, it was only in Thomas Johnson's 1955 three-volume edition of Dickinson's poems that we began to approach what she had actually written in the carefully sewn-together booklets she preserved. In short lyrics, reproducing the right text obviously matters a great deal, and Dickinson's highly personal style—many capitals and plenty of dashes—still confounds the best editors and ignites scholarly controversies.

Of course, the self-seclusion of Dickinson's life is puzzling. Why the extreme isolation from society? Did anything traumatic happen to bring this on? For instance, a love affair gone wrong? Naturally, biographers have made many guesses about the source of poems like "Wild Nights—Wild Nights!" (p. 888) and others that express strong passion. Or might her withdrawal have been some sort of

Editor and writer Thomas Wentworth Higginson, who was Dickinson's only known long-term literary correspondent.

neurosis? Or perhaps a distaste for the "busyness" of society? Or vocational seriousness, the conviction that her poetry demanded solitude and lack of distraction? Why did her relationships with selected others—most of them carried on through correspondence, often accompanied by small presents of flowers, freshly cut or dried—apparently mean so much to her? The poems and letters are testimony to her rich inner life. She also had an odd but intense relationship with a tiny group of people who clearly mattered deeply to her, despite her not being visible to them for long periods.

The greatest mystery of all is spurred by Dickinson's own words, both in her poems and in her letters. Most of the poems are short and epigrammatic. Some have a sing-song quality— they usually employ the simple iambs ($\breve{}$ $\acute{}$) and short line lengths of the hymns common at that time. They go by very fast. Readers may think they have just about grasped the meaning of the poem, and then the last stanza will throw them a twist because it seems to derail the earlier (and perhaps simpler) interpretation. Or readers may feel that they have come in in the middle of a thought—that they have missed out on something said earlier.

Does it help to read the poems together, as a collection? To some extent, yes, but many of the poems seem directly to contradict each other, and others come down somewhere in between the two contradictions. It is not constructive to seek a consistent attitude or a coherent philosophy in the poems; rather, it may be more valuable to frame them as a series of lyric or ironic insights at different deeply felt moments. And although many are quite serious, they are funny at the same time, so it is always a mistake to remain solemn while reading Dickinson. She concentrates her energies on four subjects— nature, death, God, and love—that have always been central to great lyric poetry. But her language and thoughts are so original that her contemporaries had great difficulty understanding her. And to this day, despite over a century of criticism and explication, we still cannot always be sure exactly what is going on.

One might expect that Dickinson's letters would be at least a little plainer in their meaning. Mostly they are not. They too are gnomic, which is to say both concise and cryptic. In fact, Dickinson signed herself as "Gnome" in one of her letters to Higginson. And she often enclosed poems in her letters. It is tempting to imagine the recipients of Dickinson's letters shaking their heads in puzzlement over the latest epistle and saying, "There goes Emily again." To confound those who have tried to sort out Dickinson's letters and establish the contexts in which they were written, many of the later letters lack dates (even years). The first editor of Dickinson's poems and letters, Mabel Loomis Todd, classified some of Dickinson's letters according to changes in her handwriting over the years.

Surely Dickinson took some satisfaction in hiding her meanings, in keeping them "slant," or "oblique," as she herself might have said. She may have had conventional reasons for keeping her intent veiled. Some conjecture, for example, that there may have been a "forbidden" love affair with a married man or with a woman. Her religious beliefs were at times less than orthodox, and she may have wanted to veil her disagreements with the conventional attitudes that surrounded her. But probably the overriding reason was that the issues that concerned Dickinson most were themselves mysterious: death, the brevity and uncertainty of life, the beauty and meaning of nature, mortality and immortality, partings—either temporary or permanent—with loved ones.

Dickinson had no clear, definite positions on these matters—as who does? Her responses depended on events, health, mood, weather, and perhaps also who the immediate audience (if any) might be. She echoed the conventional language of her time, for instance, in response to human death, often taking on the role of consoler. (See the letter to Perez Cowan, for instance, on p. 899.) It is difficult to tell how much she actually subscribed to her own comforting words about the assurance of heaven and an immortal life for those who have died—as indeed most of us have a hard time knowing what we mean when we say someone's death was a "release" or that someone who has died is looking down on our actions approvingly. She evinced a fascination with the details of a friend's or acquaintance's dying days and hours, as if she hoped to learn by the report of this ultimate human experience. But such an attitude, one that seems quite morbid to us today, was quite common in her era, when death and dying were much more of a visible presence than they are now.

It helps to keep a few things in mind as we read the poems. First, Dickinson's language was suffused with the vocabulary of the King James Bible and the language of church hymns. She may have resisted the strict doctrines of the Congregational church in which she grew up, but she did not reject the language, whether she wished to or not. She attended church through her twenties, often writing of the sermons she heard, but she never made the decision to officially join (a more momentous decision in her day than in ours). Still, the phrases and images of New England Protestantism were her birthright. Another influence she imbibed was romanticism. In her case, this carried many implications: a close and appreciative—indeed, mystical—connection with nature; a belief in the power and importance of the individual self and a corresponding skepticism about society (in this sense her self-imposed seclusion was a literal reading of a romantic penchant for solitude and devotion to one's artistic calling); and last but not least, an intense reading acquaintance with Shakespeare and with the English romantic and Victorian writers such as Keats, Coleridge, the Brownings, Shelley, Ruskin, Carlyle, and the Brontës. Dickinson was self-taught and a great original, but she was extremely well read, despite her deliberate ignorance of her contemporary Walt Whitman (see p. 828).

Finally, we need not be overly preoccupied with the details of Dickinson's seclusion, fascinating as generations of readers and scholars have found them. Her own family saw her self-isolation as evolutionary, more or less unexceptional. At any rate, we are not likely to learn much for certain about any traumatic love affairs. It seems enough to take her poems as reflections of struggle with the "normal" traumas of most human lives—intensified in her case because she "thought" so much and had such extraordinary poetic talents.

The Dickinson Homestead in Amherst, Massachusetts, where Emily lived in relative seclusion for most of her life.

The Emily Dickinson Museum. Two of the Dickinson family's houses—280 Main Street where Emily Dickinson was born and lived (also called the Dickinson Homestead), and the Evergreens, the house next door where her brother Austin, sister-in-law Susan, and their three children lived—are preserved as part of the Emily Dickinson Museum in Amherst, Massachusetts. Emily and her sister Lavinia remained at the family house until their deaths, while brother Austin lived just next door. There is likely no writer in history whose living quarters played such a major role in her writing life as Emily Dickinson, due to her isolated, cloistered life. For Dickinson, this sheltered life did not hamper her writing, but rather provided a haven for it. Her niece Martha describes an occasion when Dickinson mimicked locking an imaginary lock on her bedroom door and telling her, "Matty, here's freedom."

In her essay "Vesuvius at Home: The Power of Emily Dickinson," poet Adrienne Rich describes her anticipation in visiting Dickinson's bedroom at the Homestead:

> Upstairs at last: I stand in the room which for Emily Dickinson was "freedom." The best bedroom in the house, a corner room, sunny, overlooking the main street of Amherst in front, the way to her brother Austin's house on the side. Here, at a small table with one drawer, she wrote most of her poems. . . . Here in this white-curtained, high-ceilinged room, a redhaired woman with hazel eyes and a contralto voice wrote poems about volcanoes, deserts, eternity, suicide, physical passion, wild beasts, rape, power, madness, separation, the daemon, the grave. Here, with a darning needle, she bound these poems—heavily emended and often with variant versions—into booklets . . . to be found and read after her death.

For more photographs and information about the Dickinson Museum, go to *http://www.emilydickinsonmuseum.org/index.html.*

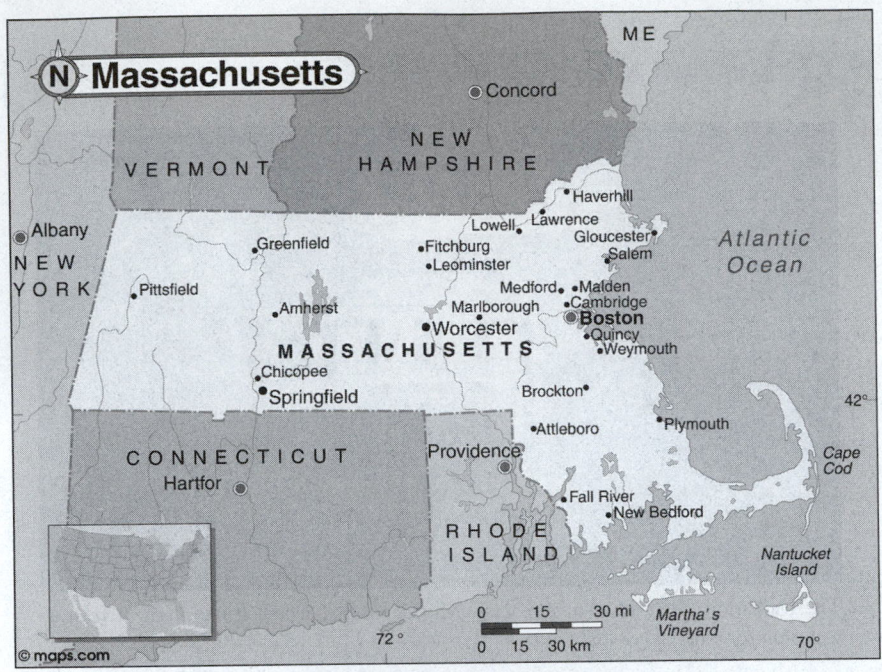

Dickinson spent her whole life in Amherst, Massachusetts, save for the year she spent at Mount Holyoke (a mere twenty miles away) and a few short trips to Boston, Philadelphia, and Washington, D.C.

EMILY DICKINSON TIMELINE

1830	Emily Dickinson born December 10 in Amherst, Massachusetts.
1847–1848	Studies at Mount Holyoke.
1852	Dickinson's father elected to U.S. House of Representatives.
1856	Her brother Austin Dickinson and Susan Gilbert marry.
1862	Begins correspondence with Thomas Wentworth Higginson.
1874	Dickinson's father dies.
1878	Her friend Samuel Bowles, editor of the Springfield *Republican*, dies.
1881	Dr. Josiah Holland dies.
1882	Dickinson's mother dies.
1883	Dickinson's beloved nephew Gilbert, age 8, dies.
1884	First sign of her final illness (Bright's disease).
1886	Dies in Amherst, buried in town cemetery.
1890	First volume of Dickinson's poems, heavily edited, is published to great success.
1955	Thomas Johnson's landmark three-volume edition of Dickinson's poems is published.

This daguerreotype from the mid-1850s was recently discovered and acquired by scholar Philip Gura and is believed to be the second known photograph of Emily Dickinson.

1974   Richard Sewall's biography of Dickinson is published.
1998   R. W. Franklin's three-volume edition of Dickinson's poems, based closely on the manuscripts, is published.

POEMS BY EMILY DICKINSON

Only a small number of Dickinson's poems can be included here. But each provides a good representation of her overall work. (Additional poems by Dickinson appear on pp. 741 and 812.)

I heard a Fly buzz—when I died   (C. 1862)

I heard a Fly buzz—when I died—
The Stillness in the Room
Was like the Stillness in the Air—
Between the Heaves of Storm—

The Eyes around—had wrung them dry—   5
And Breaths were gathering firm
For that last Onset—when the King
Be witnessed—in the Room—

I willed my Keepsakes—Signed away
What portion of me be   10
Assignable—and then it was
There interposed a Fly—

With Blue—uncertain stumbling Buzz—
Between the light—and me—
And then the Windows failed—and then   15
I could not see to see—

Because I could not stop for Death   (c. 1863)

Because I could not stop for Death—
He kindly stopped for me—
The Carriage held but just Ourselves—
And Immortality.

We slowly drove—He knew no haste   5
And I had put away
My labor and my leisure too,
For His Civility—

We passed the School, where Children strove
At Recess—in the Ring—   10
We passed the Fields of Gazing Grain—
We passed the Setting Sun—

Or rather—He passed Us—
The Dews drew quivering and chill—
For only Gossamer, my Gown—   15
My Tippet—only Tulle—

We paused before a House that seemed
A Swelling of the Ground—
The Roof was scarcely visible—
The Cornice—in the Ground—   20

Since then—'tis Centuries—and yet
Feels shorter than the Day
I first surmised the Horses' Heads
Were toward Eternity—

✳ INSPIRATION HART CRANE ON EMILY DICKINSON

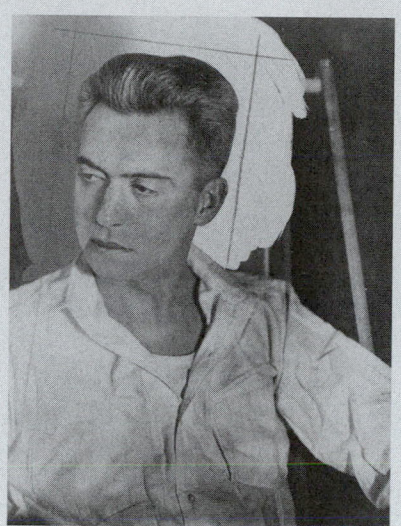

Twentieth-century poet Hart Crane, who wrote a poem as an homage to Dickinson.

Dickinson, like Whitman, continues to be an extraordinary influence on other writers of all stripes, from poets Gwendolyn Brooks, Mary Oliver, Adrienne Rich, and Linda Pastan to essayist and critic Katha Pollitt to fiction writers Joyce Carol Oates and Marilynne Robinson. Succeeding American poets of numerous eras and poetic styles have cited her work and even the mysterious persona of Dickinson herself as important in their own growth and evolution as writers. Below is the offering of Hart Crane, an early twentieth-century poet, best known for his paean to the Brooklyn Bridge, *The Bridge*, published three years before he committed suicide by jumping into the sea.

Hart Crane   (1899–1932)

To Emily Dickinson   (1927)

You who desired so much—in vain to ask—
Yet fed your hunger like an endless task,
Dared dignify the labor, bless the quest—
Achieved that stillness ultimately best,

Being, of all, least sought for: Emily, hear!
O sweet, dead Silencer, most suddenly clear
When singing that Eternity possessed
And plundered momently in every breast;

—Truly no flower yet withers in your hand,
The harvest you descried and understand
Needs more than wit to gather, love to bind.
Some reconcilement of remotest mind—

Leaves Ormus rubyless, and Ophir chill.
Else tears heap all within one clay-cold hill.

Editor's Note: *Ormus* is an ancient city in Persia. *Ophir* is a biblical site where Solomon received gems and gold.

A narrow Fellow in the Grass   (C. 1865)

A narrow Fellow in the Grass
Occasionally rides—
You may have met Him—did you not
His notice sudden is—

The Grass divides as with a Comb—   5
A spotted shaft is seen—
And then it closes at your feet
And opens further on—

He likes a Boggy Acre
A Floor too cool for Corn—   10
Yet when a Boy, and Barefoot—
I more than once at Noon

Have passed, I thought, a Whip lash
Unbraiding in the Sun
When stooping to secure it   15
It wrinkled, and was gone—

Several of Nature's People
I know, and they know me—
I feel for them a transport
Of cordiality—   20

But never met this Fellow
Attended, or alone
Without a tighter breathing
And Zero at the Bone—

Wild Nights—Wild Nights!   (C. 1861)

Wild Nights—Wild Nights!
Were I with thee
Wild Nights should be
Our luxury!

Futile—the Winds—   5
To a Heart in port—
Done with the Compass—
Done with the Chart!

Rowing in Eden—
Ah, the Sea!   10
Might I but moor—Tonight—
In Thee!

This fascicle copy of "Wild Nights—Wild Nights!" is part of the Dickinson fascicles, the forty booklets containing more than 800 of Dickinson's handwritten poems, gathered and sewn together with string by Dickinson herself. The fascicles were badly maintained after Dickinson's death and remained in disorder until they were restored and eventually published by R. W. Franklin in his 1981 Manuscript Books of Emily Dickinson.

It dropped so low—in my Regard   (C. 1863)

It dropped so low—in my Regard—
I heard it hit the Ground—
And go to pieces on the Stones
At bottom of my Mind—

Yet blamed the Fate that flung it—*less*   5
Than I denounced Myself,
For entertaining Plated Wares
Upon my Silver Shelf—

I taste a liquor never brewed   (C. 1860)

I taste a liquor never brewed—
From Tankards scooped in Pearl—
Not all the Vats upon the Rhine
Yield such an Alcohol!

Inebriate of Air—am I—   5
And Debauchee of Dew—
Reeling—thro endless summer days—
From inns of Molten Blue—

When "Landlords" turn the drunken Bee
Out of the Foxglove's door—   10
When Butterflies—renounce their "drams"—
I shall but drink the more!

Till Seraphs swing their snowy Hats—
And Saints—to windows run—
To see the little Tippler   15
Leaning against the—Sun—

Safe in their Alabaster Chambers   (1859 VERSION)

Safe in their Alabaster Chambers—
Untouched by Morning
And untouched by Noon—
Sleep the meek members of the Resurrection—
Rafter of satin,   5
And Roof of stone.

Light laughs the breeze
In her Castle above them—
Babbles the Bee in a stolid Ear,
Pipe the Sweet Birds in ignorant cadence—   10
Ah, what sagacity perished here!

Safe in their Alabaster Chambers

(1861 VERSION)

Safe in their Alabaster Chambers—
Untouched by Morning—
And untouched by Noon—
Lie the meek members of the Resurrection—
Rafter of Satin—and Roof of Stone!   5

Grand go the Years—in the Crescent—above them—
Worlds scoop their Arcs—
And Firmaments—row—
Diadems—drop—and Doges—surrender—
Soundless as dots—on a Disc of Snow—   10

There's a certain Slant of light

(C. 1861)

There's a certain Slant of light,
Winter Afternoons—
That oppresses, like the Heft
Of Cathedral Tunes—

Heavenly Hurt, it gives us—   5
We can find no scar,
But internal difference,
Where the Meanings, are—

None may teach it—Any—
'Tis the Seal Despair—   10
An imperial affliction
Sent us of the Air—

When it comes, the Landscape listens—
Shadows—hold their breath—
When it goes, 'tis like the Distance   15
On the look of Death—

I felt a Funeral, in my Brain

(C. 1861)

I felt a Funeral, in my Brain,
And Mourners to and fro
Kept treading—treading—till it seemed
That Sense was breaking through—

And when they all were seated,   5
A Service, like a Drum—
Kept beating—beating—till I thought
My Mind was going numb—

And then I heard them lift a Box
And creak across my Soul
With those same Boots of Lead, again,   10
Then Space—began to toll,

As all the Heavens were a Bell,
And Being, but an Ear,
And I, and Silence, some strange Race   15
Wrecked, solitary, here—

And then a Plank in Reason, broke,
And I dropped down, and down—
And hit a World, at every plunge,
And Finished knowing—then—   20

Elysium is as far as to   (c. 1882)

Elysium is as far as to
The very nearest Room
If in that Room a Friend await
Felicity or Doom—

What fortitude the Soul contains,   5
That it can so endure
The accent of a coming Foot—
The opening of a Door—

We grow accustomed to the Dark   (c. 1862)

We grow accustomed to the Dark—
When Light is put away—
As when the Neighbor holds the Lamp
To witness her Goodbye—

A Moment—We uncertain step   5
For newness of the night—
Then—fit our Vision to the Dark—
And meet the Road—erect—

And so of larger—Darknesses—
Those Evenings of the Brain—   10
When not a Moon disclose a sign—
Or Star—come out—within—

The Bravest—grope a little—
And sometimes hit a Tree
Directly in the Forehead—   15
But as they learn to see—

Either the Darkness alters—
Or something in the sight
Adjusts itself to Midnight—
And Life steps almost straight.   20

The Soul selects her own Society

(C. 1862)

The Soul selects her own Society—
Then—shuts the Door—
To her divine Majority—
Present no more—

Unmoved—she notes the Chariots— pausing—   5
At her low Gate—
Unmoved—an Emperor be kneeling
Upon her Mat—

I've known her—from an ample nation—
Choose One—   10
Then—close the Valves of her attention—
Like Stone—

My Life had stood—a Loaded Gun

(C. 1863)

My Life had stood—a Loaded Gun—
In Corners—till a Day
The Owner passed—identified—
And carried Me away—

And now We roam in Sovereign Woods—   5
And now We hunt the Doe—
And every time I speak for Him—
The Mountains straight reply—

And do I smile, such cordial light
Upon the Valley glow—   10
It is as a Vesuvian face
Had let its pleasure through—

And when at Night—Our good Day done—
I guard My Master's Head—
'Tis better than the Eider-Duck's   15
Deep Pillow—to have shared—

To foe of His—I'm deadly foe—
None stir the second time—
On whom I lay a Yellow Eye—
Or an emphatic Thumb—   20

Though I than He—may longer live
He longer must—than I—
For I have but the power to kill,
Without—the power to die—

V I D E O   L O C A L E

Loaded Gun: Life, and Death, and Dickinson. Filmmaker Jim Wolpaw takes an untraditional path searching for answers about the elusive Emily Dickinson in his 2002 film *Loaded Gun: Life, and Death, and Dickinson*, produced by Independent Lens and PBS. Director Wolpaw starts by interviewing Poet Laureate Billy Collins and actress Julie Harris, who played Dickinson in the critically acclaimed one-woman show *Belle of Amherst*. In his search for answers about Dickinson's life, Wolpaw soon turns to untraditional sources, including a psychiatrist, a stand-up comic, a rock band, and even an obsessed fan with Dickinson's face tattooed across his back. *Loaded Gun* is an entertaining look at how a literary enigma like Dickinson can capture readers' imaginations. For more information on the film, see *http://www. dickinsonfilm. com or http://www.pbs.org/independentlens/loadedgun/index.html.*

Tell all the Truth but tell it slant   (C. 1868)

Tell all the Truth but tell it slant—
Success in Circuit lies
Too bright for our infirm Delight
The Truth's superb surprise

As Lightning to the Children eased   5
With explanation kind
The Truth must dazzle gradually
Or every man be blind—

As imperceptibly as Grief   (C. 1865)

As imperceptibly as Grief
The Summer lapsed away—
Too imperceptible at last
To seem like Perfidy—
A Quietness distilled   5
As Twilight long begun,
Or Nature spending with herself
Sequestered Afternoon—
The Dusk drew earlier in—
The Morning foreign shone—   10
A courteous, yet harrowing Grace,
As Guest, that would be gone—
And thus, without a Wing
Or service of a Keel
Our Summer made her light escape   15
Into the Beautiful.

"Faith" is a fine invention

(C. 1860)

"Faith" is a fine invention
When Gentlemen can *see*—
But *Microscopes* are prudent
In an Emergency.

From all the Jails the Boys and Girls

(C. 1881)

From all the Jails the Boys and Girls
Ecstatically leap—
Beloved only Afternoon
That Prison doesn't keep

They storm the Earth and stun the Air,   5
A Mob of solid Bliss—
Alas—that Frowns should lie in wait
For such a Foe as this—

The Bible is an antique Volume

(C. 1882)

The Bible is an antique Volume—
Written by faded Men
At the suggestion of Holy Spectres—
Subjects—Bethlehem—
Eden—the ancient Homestead—   5
Satan—the Brigadier—
Judas—the Great Defaulter—
David—the Troubadour—
Sin—a distinguished Precipice
Others must resist—   10
Boys that "believe" are very lonesome—
Other Boys are "lost"—
Had but the Tale a warbling Teller—
All the Boys would come—
Orpheus' Sermon captivated—   15
It did not condemn—

AUDIO LOCALE

Songs of Emily Dickinson. The poetry of Emily Dickinson is set to music more often than any other American poet besides Walt Whitman and Henry Wadsworth Longfellow. Aaron Copland's 8 *Poems of Emily Dickinson* for voice and piano is probably the most well known and performed (reworked from his

(continued on next page)

(continued)

Composer Aaron Copland.

original 1950 composition *12 Poems of Emily Dickinson*). The St. Paul Chamber Orchestra recorded these songs in 1994 with soprano Dawn Upshaw on the CD *Long Time Ago* (Elektra). Pianist and composer Leo Smit also composed a Dickinson song cycle, which can be found on *Leo Smit: 33 Songs on Poems of Emily Dickinson*, produced by Bridge Records in 1999. For more musical settings of Dickinson's work, listen to *Emily Dickinson Songs*, a collection of different composers' creations, produced by Capstone Records in 2003, or *Emily Dickinson in Song: Dwell in Possibility*, a similar collection produced by Gasparo in 2004.

Much Madness is divinest Sense   (C. 1862)

Much Madness is divinest Sense—
To a discerning Eye—
Much Sense—the starkest Madness—
'Tis the Majority
In this, as All, prevail—
Assent—and you are sane—
Demur—you're straightway dangerous—
And handled with a Chain—

Beauty—be not caused—It Is   (C. 1862)

Beauty—be not caused—It Is—
Chase it, and it ceases—
Chase it not, and it abides—

Overtake the Creases

In the Meadow—when the Wind
Runs his fingers thro' it—
Deity will see to it
That You never do it—

On a Columnar Self   (C. 1863)

On a Columnar Self—
How ample to rely
In Tumult—or Extremity—
How good the Certainty

That Lever cannot pry—
And Wedge cannot divide   5
Conviction—That Granitic Base—
Though None be on our Side—

Suffice Us—for a Crowd—
Ourself—and Rectitude—   10
And that Assembly—not far off
From furthest Spirit—God—

✑ COMMENTARY

Reviewers on Dickinson's Poetry

From "Review of Poems (1890)," Nation, November 1890

The poems of Emily Dickinson are not so seriously weighed down by their editors—Mrs. Mabel Loomis Todd and Mr. T. W. Higginson—since they leave her mainly to speak for herself. . . . She resolutely refused to publish her verses, showing them only to a very few friends. As a consequence, she had almost no criticism, and was absolutely untrammelled: so that the verses are sometimes almost formless, while at other times they show great capacity for delicate and sweet melody, suggesting the chance strains of an Aeolian harp. But in compass of thought, grasp of feeling, and vigor of epithet, they are simply extraordinary, and strike notes, very often, like those of some deep-toned organ.

From "Review of Poems (1890)," Critic, December 13, 1890

Here is a volume of striking and original poems by a writer who, during the fifty years of her life, wrote much and published almost nothing. The name of Emily Dickinson is a new name in our literature, but whoever reads the striking verses in this book which her two friends, Mabel Loomis Todd and Col. T. W. Higginson, have edited, will agree that its place is established and sure to remain, associated with a collection of poems whose main quality, as is pointed out in an admirable preface, is an extraordinary grasp and insight. So clearly are the characteristics of these verses defined and so exactly does our opinion of them agree with the writer's, that we are almost tempted to quote him literally; but there are some features which he has left for others to describe—namely, the similarity between these poems and some of Emerson's (a similarity both of thought and manner of expression), and, in the poems of love, the absence of much that is essential to poems of this kind—sensuousness and symmetry and melody. It is in the other poems that the rare genius of Miss Dickinson is best seen—in those of Life, Nature, Time and Eternity.

Talking about the Text

1. What might Dickinson have in mind when she uses the word "truth" in "Tell all the Truth but tell it slant"? Compare the "truth" (not named as such) envisioned in " 'Faith' is a fine invention."

2. Looking at the selection of poems as a whole, choose a key word (e.g., "faith," or "heaven," or "Immortality") and follow it through every selection. What does Dickinson seem to mean by it? Does its meaning seem to shift? If so, describe the shift you see. (With Dickinson it is hard to talk of changes over time, since we cannot be sure when many of the poems were composed.)

3. Dickinson is said to have loved children (at least from a distance) and to have lowered baskets of sweets and other treats down to them from her window. Like many grown-ups, she at times looked back on her relatively untroubled childhood with nostalgia. Her sister protected and sheltered her. She often seemed to identify with small birds (the sparrows, not the eagles). In her poems, what do you detect that is childlike? As a reader, how do you respond?

4. Dickinson's poetry is marked by striking phrases and images. Pick out four such phrases from her poems, describe how they work, what contexts they appear in, and discuss what they may have in common.

5. Dickinson experienced a lot of anguish in her life; she also claimed to feel joy and ecstasy (a word Gwendolyn Brooks would later ban from her own poetry). What in the poetry convinces you that she did indeed have many very happy moments? If so, what seemed to bring those moments most intensely?

Writing about the Text

1. Dickinson's "child-like" tone is matched with a cutting tongue—usually gently cutting, but cutting all the same. It is ironic, cutting into pretensions and conventional sentiments. It includes a willingness—even a willfulness—to stare the most awful possibilities in the face and sometimes not to see "truth" "slant." Look for this ironic tone in the poems and some of the letters, then describe how it seems to work. Is it deliberately subversive? Is it sometimes playful? (Keep your paper on the exploratory side; do not expect to come to a very firm conclusion about Dickinson's tone.)

2. The introduction to Dickinson (p. 879) discusses the romantic's inclination to privilege the individual. For the romantic the real drama of life happens within the mind or soul or heart of the individual, and it may be extended also to other individuals in the romantic's circle. Write about how you understand Dickinson's attitude toward the self. A good place to start is "On a Columnar Self" (pp. 896–897). In that poem, how much does she privilege the individual? Does she go so far as to regard the self as divine?

3. Write about Dickinson's attitude toward death in at least three of her poems.

Linking the Text to Other Texts

1. Friedrich Novalis, an early German romantic, remarked, "When I confer upon the commonplace a higher meaning, upon the ordinary an enigmatic appearance, I romanticize it. The operation is reversed for the higher, unknown, mystical, infinite." What about this quotation helps explain Dickinson's writing?

2. Describe how the following remarks by Dickinson's friend Mrs. Gordon L. Ford, a former schoolmate, help or hinder your response to and understanding of the poems.

> Dr. Holland once said to me, "Her poems are too ethereal for publication." I replied, "They are beautiful—so concentrated—but they remind me of air-plants that have no roots in earth." "That is true," he

said, "a perfect description"; and I think these lyrical ejaculations, these breathed out projectiles, sharp as lances, would at that time have fallen into idle ears.

3. Find another poet who seems to share some of Dickinson's qualities. What particular characteristics do the two have in common? What are the differences?

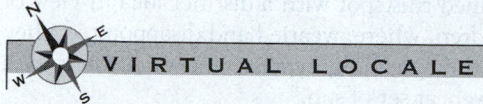

VIRTUAL LOCALE

Poets on Dickinson's Legacy. The Dickinson Electronic Archive sponsors an online collection of contemporary poets reading about Dickinson and her legacy during a twenty-four-hour marathon of speeches commemorating the one-hundredth anniversary of Dickinson's death in 1986. The collection features print versions of speeches by Adrienne Rich, Gwendolyn Brooks, Maxine Kumin, Linda Pastan, and Joyce Carol Oates, to name just a few. Also included are sound recordings of the poets reading poems inspired by Dickinson. To read the essays or hear the poems, go to *http://www.emilydickinson.org/titanic/table_of_contents.html.*

COMMENTARY

Emily Dickinson in Her Letters

To her friend, Mrs. A P. Strong, 1845

I never knew the time to pass so swiftly, it seems to me, as the past summer. I really think someone must have oiled his chariot wheels, for I don't recollect of hearing him pass, and I am sure I should if something had not prevented his chariot wheels from creaking as usual. But I will not expatiate on him any longer, for I know it is wicked to trifle with so wicked a personage, and I fear he will make me a call in person to inquire as to the remarks which I have made concerning him. Therefore I will let him alone for the present.

To Rev. Perez Cowan, on the death of his young daughter, 1880

The little creature must have been priceless—yours and not yours—how hallowed!

It may have been she came to show you Immortality. Her startling little flight would imply she did.

May I remind you what Paul said, or do you think of nothing else, these October nights, without her crib to visit?

The little furniture of loss has lips of dirks to stab us. I hope Heaven is warm, there are so many barefoot ones. I hope it is near—the little tourist is so small. I hope it not so unlike earth that we shall miss the peculiar form—the mould of the bird.

To Mrs. A. P. Strong, 1846

I have been to Mount Auburn [famous cemetery in Cambridge, Massachusetts], to the Chinese Museum, to Bunker Hill; I have been upon the top of the State House, and almost everywhere that you can imagine. Have you ever been to Mount Auburn? If not, you can form but slight conception of this "City of the Dead." It seems as if nature had formed this spot with a distinct idea in view of its being a resting-place for her children, where, wearied and disappointed, they might stretch themselves beneath the spreading cypress, and close their eyes "calmly as to a night's repose, or flowers at set of sun."

To Mrs. A. P. Strong, 1846

Does it seem as though September had come? How swiftly summer has fled, and what report has it borne to heaven of misspent time and wasted hours? Eternity only will answer. The ceaseless flight of the seasons is to me a very solemn thought; and yet why do we not strive to make a better improvement of them? With how much emphasis the poet has said, "We take no note of Time, but from its loss. T'were wise in man to give it then a tongue. Pay no moment but in just purchase of it's worth, & what it's worth, ask death-beds. They can tell. Part with it as with life reluctantly." Then we have higher authority than that of man for the improvement of our time. For God has said, "Work while the day lasts, for the night is coming in which no man can work." Let us strive together to part with time more reluctantly, to watch the pinions of the fleeting moment until they are dim in the distance, and the new-coming moment claims our attention. I have perfect confidence in God and His promises, and yet know not why I feel that the world hold a predominant place in my affections.

To Maria Whitney, 1877

I fear we think too lightly of the gift of mortality, which, too gigantic to comprehend, certainly cannot be estimated.

To Mrs. Josiah Holland, 1856

If roses had not faded, and frosts had never come, and one had not fallen here and there whom I could not waken, there were no need of other Heaven than the one below—and if God had been here this summer, and seen the things that I have seen—I guess He would think his Paradise superfluous. Don't tell Him, for the world, though, for after all He's said about it, I should like to see what He was building for us, with no hammer, and no stone, and no journeyman either. Dear Mrs. Holland, I love to-night—love you and Dr. Holland, and "time and sense"—and fading things, and things that do not fade.

The minister to-day, not our own minister, preached about death and judgment, and what would become of those, meaning Austin and me, who behaved improperly—and somehow the sermon scared me, and father and Vinnie [her sister Lavinia] looked very solemn as if the whole was true, and I would not for worlds have them know that it troubled me, but I longed to come to you, and tell you all about it, and learn how to be better. He preached such an awful sermon though, that I didn't much think I should ever see you again until the Judgment

Day, and then you would not speak to me, according to his story. The subject of perdition seemed to please him, somehow. It seems very solemn to me. I'll tell you about it, when I see you again.

Austin Dickinson, Emily's older brother.

To Austin, anticipating his visit home, 1853

I can't realize that you will come, it is so still and lonely it doesn't seem possible it can be otherwise; but we shall see, when the nails hang full of coats again, and the chairs hang full of hats, and I can count the slippers under the chair. Oh, Austin, how I miss them all, and more than them, somebody who used to hang them there, and get many a hint ungentle to carry them away. Those times seem far off now, a great way, as things we did when children. I wish we were children now—I wish we were always children, how to grow up I don't know. . . . Cousin J. has made us an Aeolian harp which plays beautifully whenever there is a breeze.

To her cousins Fanny Norcross and Loo Norcross, 1879

Did you know there had been a fire here, and that but for a whim of the wind Austin and Vinnie and Emily would have all been homeless? But perhaps you saw The Republican.

We were waked by the ticking of the bells,—the bells tick in Amherst for a fire, to tell the firemen.

I sprang to the window, and each side of the curtain saw that awful sun. The moon was shining high at the time, and the birds singing like trumpets.

Vinnie came soft as a moccasin, "Don't be afraid, Emily, it is only the fourth of July."

I did not tell that I saw it, for I thought if she felt it best to deceive, it must be that it was.

She took hold of my hand and led me into mother's room. Mother had not waked, and Maggie [a servant] was sitting by her. Vinnie left us a moment, and I whispered to Maggie and asked her what it was.

"Only Stebbins's barn, Emily"; but I knew that the right and left of the village was on the arm of Stebbins's barn. I could hear buildings falling, and exploding and people walking and talking gayly, and cannon soft as velvet from the parishes that did not know that we were burning up.

And so much lighter than day was it, that I saw a caterpillar measure a leaf far down in the orchard; and Vinnie kept saying bravely, "It's only the fourth of July." [disaster is averted] Vinnie's "only the fourth of July" I shall always remember. I think she will tell us so when we die, to keep us from being afraid.

Footlights cannot improve the grave, only immortality.

To her cousins Fanny Norcross and Loo Norcross, 1876

Vinnie has a new pussy the color of Branwell Bronte's hair. She thinks it a little "lower than the angels," and I concur with her. You remember my ideal cat has always a huge rat in its mouth, just going out of sight—though going out of sight in itself has a peculiar charm. It is true that the unknown is the largest need of the intellect, though for it no one thinks to thank God.

To her cousins Fanny Norcross and Loo Norcross, 1874

There is that which is called an "awakening" in the church, and I know of no choicer ecstasy than to see Mrs. _____ roll out in crape every morning, I sup-pose to intimidate antichrist; at least it would have that effect on me. It reminds me of Don Quixote demanding the surrender of the wind-mill, and of Sir Stephen Toplift, and of Sir Alexander Cockburn.

To cousins Fanny Norcross and Loo Norcross, after the death of her mother, 1882

We don't know where she is, though so many tell us.

I believe we shall in some manner be cherished by our Maker—that the One who gave us this remarkable earth has the power still farther to surprise that which He has caused. Beyond that all is silence.

To Thomas Wentworth Higginson, who had just left to fight in the Civil War, c. 1863

I should have liked to see you before you became improbable. War feels to me an oblique place. Should there be other summers, would you perhaps come?

I found you were gone, by accident, as I find systems are, or seasons of the year, and obtain no cause, but suppose it a treason of progress that dissolves as it goes. Carlo [her dog] still remained, and I told him

Best gains must have the losses' test,
And constitute them gains.

My shaggy ally assented.

Perhaps death gave me awe for friends, striking sharp and early, for I held them since in a brittle love, of more alarm than peace. I trust you may pass the limit of war; and though not reared to prayer, when service is had in church for our arms, I include yourself. . . . I was thinking to-day, as I noticed, that the "su-pernatural" was only the natural disclosed.

Not "Revelation" 'tis that waits,
But our unfurnished eyes.

But I fear I detain you. Should you, before this reaches you, experience Im-mortality, who will inform me of the exchange? Could you, with honor, avoid death, I entreat you, sir. It would bereave
YOUR GNOME

To Mrs. Strong, after a four-week visit to Boston, 1846

I found a quantity of sewing waiting with open arms to embrace me, or rather for me to embrace it, and I could hardly give myself up to "Nature's sweet restorer," for the ghosts of out-of-order garments crying for vengeance upon my defence-less head.

Starting Points for Further Research: Emily Dickinson

- **Editions:** Emily Dickinson. *The Poems of Emily Dickinson*. Ed. Rachel Wetzsteon. Cambridge, Mass.: Belknap Press, 1998.
  - ———. *The Letters of Emily Dickinson*. Ed. Thomas Herbert Johnson and Theodora Ward. Cambridge, Mass.: Belknap Press, 1986.
- **Biography:** Alfred Habegger. *My Wars Are Laid Away in Books*. New York: Random House, 2002.
- **Critical Essay:** Jay Ladin. " 'So Anthracite: To Live' Emily Dickinson and American Literary History." *Emily Dickinson Journal* 13 (2004): 19–50.

CHAPTER
15

Gwendolyn Brooks

Gwendolyn Brooks in the early 1930s.

In her autobiography *Report from Part One* (1972), Gwendolyn Brooks (1917–2000) describes the small Chicago "kitchenette" apartment where she lived in the 1940s:

623 [East 63rd Street] was right on the corner, the corner of 63rd and Champlain, above a real estate agency. If you wanted a poem, you had only to look out of a window. There was material always, walking or running, fighting or screaming or singing.

That is a succinct description of how and where Brooks found her inspiration—in the life of Chicago's black ghetto, where she lived almost all her life, and where she deliberately situated herself both as a writer and as a wife and mother of two children. Though her writing talent was discovered early and she achieved renown for her poetry, she kept on living in the same South Side neighborhood she grew up in, and she died there in 2000, laden with honors.

The Chicago Brooks grew up in during and right after World War I saw large numbers of blacks from the segregated South migrating to the North to find work. (For a map of Chicago, see p. 1768 in Chapter 25, "Sweet Home

904

April 7, 1917, cartoon in the Chicago De-fender, *a champion of the Great Migration that brought many poor southern blacks north to find better work after the start of World War I.*

Chicago.") Chicago had work, but it, too, was segregated; the black section, called Bronzeville, was the site of terrible poverty and cramped, substandard housing, but it also was home to a vibrant culture. Brooks's parents, while "semi-poor" in income, were middle class in their attitudes and aspirations. Her mother had taught school and played the piano; her father, who spent one year at Fisk University, worked as a janitor but struck his daughter as an educated man who went around the house reciting poetry. The minute the young Brooks showed some skill with rhymes, her mother predicted that she would be a female Paul Laurence Dunbar.

In this supportive environment in the midst of a ghetto, Brooks grew to adulthood with a strong sense of self worth and a certainty about her vocation as poet. She said, "I had always felt

African American housing in the South Side of Chicago, c. 1929. For blacks who came to Chicago during the first migration wave north, housing rarely had the central amenities: bathrooms, electricity, and furnaces. Overcrowding was common, and more than 50 percent of black Chicago residents had to take in boarders in order to make the rent.

that to be black was good." When she was thirteen, *American Childhood* magazine published one of her poems; by sixteen she was contributing every week to the *Chicago Defender*, one of America's premier black newspapers. Her mother also made sure she met the established poets James Weldon Johnson and Langston Hughes, who both encouraged her work.

Brooks attended several Chicago high schools and graduated from Wilson Junior College, then went to work. In 1937 she became publicity director for the Youth Council of the NAACP. She married in 1939 and had two children, Henry Jr. in 1940, and Nora in 1951. In the early years of their marriage, she and her husband had little money and lived in cheap, cramped apartments called "kitchenettes," like those described in her poetry. Despite growing up close to "middle class," Brooks had an education in the ordinary life of Chicago's poor South Side. All she had to do was look out her window.

As Chapter 25, "Sweet Home Chicago: From Renaissance to *A Raisin in the Sun*" (p. 1791), shows, the era of the 1930s and early 1940s, when Brooks reached young adulthood, was a rich time intellectually and culturally for Chicago blacks. Many artists and writers flourished there (though seldom economically) and were able to make connections with each other through the South Side Community Arts Center, through Chicago publications (*The Defender, Ebony, The Negro Digest*—later *Black World*), through the government-sponsored work program for writers in the Works Progress Administration (WPA), through settlement houses, and even through the Communist Party (as in the case of Richard Wright). Brooks and her husband participated in many of these activities, and Brooks was especially influenced by a poetry workshop taught at the South Side Community Arts Center by Inez Cunningham Stark, a white woman from the well-to-do North Side, who had been associated with Chicago's famous *Poetry* magazine. Brooks's first

Children in front of a kitchenette apartment, Chicago, 1941.

book of poetry, *A Street in Bronzeville*, came out in 1945 and was very well received. It was followed in 1949 by another book of poetry, *Annie Allen*, which won Brooks the first Pulitzer Prize awarded to a black person. From then on the honors flowed freely to Brooks, and she published new poetry regularly.

Brooks regarded the 1960s as a particularly important decade in her literary and political development. She wrote about how in 1967 she underwent a "conversion" to a heightened degree of black awareness when she attended the Second Fisk University Writers' Conference, meeting, among others, LeRoi Jones (later Amiri Baraka), and was much moved by the black revolutionary fervor she experienced there. Black consciousness and pride were not strictly new to her, of course; she was already part of a rich tradition of black artists and writers, and she had always concentrated on black experience. But she found the intensity and militancy of the new movement very heady. "Until 1967, my own Blackness did not confront me with a shrill spelling of itself," she writes in her autobiography. Following the conference, she immediately started putting together poetry workshops for South Side young people, including members of a notorious gang, the Blackstone Rangers. She also assumed a long series of academic appointments, beginning at Chicago's Columbia College, and she developed a devoted following of aspiring young black poets, including Don L. Lee (now Haki R. Madhubuti) and Carolyn Rodgers. She was also influenced by her travels to East Africa in 1971 and Ghana in 1974, trips that receive substantial treatment in her autobiographical writings.

As Brooks changed her outlook on society, her poetry changed, too, as she sought to write for blacks rather than whites. Her poems became more direct, plainer, more angry and political, less influenced by traditional European forms such as the sonnet, and more inclined to blank verse. She made more use of black vernacular, and she switched in 1969 from her longtime publisher Harper and Row to the recently founded Broadside Press, under black sponsorship. This political and cultural decision came with a cost, since she lost the prestige and resources of a major publisher. Her later poetry reached a smaller audience and is still not as widely available as it should be.

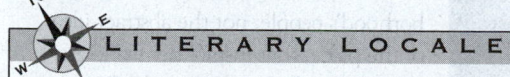

LITERARY LOCALE

Brooks in Bronzeville, Chicago. The Bronzeville neighborhood Brooks lived in was the vibrant center of black life in Chicago from the 1920s until the 1950s. During World War I, Chicago saw a mass migration of southern blacks to the city, bringing notable African Americans such as Louis Armstrong and Richard Wright. Filled with poor people and poor housing, it nevertheless produced some of the best American writing of its era. It was not until after World War II that the community suffered from the loss of stockyards and factory jobs, racial tensions, and an exodus of middle-class blacks and businesses.

In *Black Metropolis: A Study of Negro Life in a Northern City*, a landmark study published in 1945, St. Clair Drake and Horace R. Cayton describe a typical scene in Bronzeville in the mid-1940s:

(continued on next page)

(continued)

Stand in the center of the black belt—at Chicago's 47th St. and South Parkway. Around you swirls a continuous eddy of faces—black, brown, olive, yellow, and white. Soon you will realize that this is not "just another neighborhood" of the Midwest Metropolis. . . . On a spring or summer day this spot, "47th and South Park," is the urban equivalent of a village square. In fact, Black Metropolis has a saying, "If you're trying to find a certain Negro in Chicago, stand on the corner of 47th and South Park long enough and you're bound to see him."

In the middle of Bronzeville was Washington Park, a community gathering place with four square miles of lawn, baseball and softball fields, and a pool. Drake and Cayton also noted the density of places of worship in Bronzeville: "If you wander about a bit in Black Metropolis you will note that one of the most striking features of the area is the prevalence of churches, numbering some 500. Many of these edifices still bear the marks of previous ownership—six-pointed Stars of David, Hebrew and Swedish inscriptions, or names chiseled on old cornerstones which do not tally with those on new bulletin boards."

In her critical essay "Women of Bronzeville," Beverly Guy-Sheftall comments on the depiction of Bronzeville in Brooks's poetry:

Like Richard Wright, [Brooks] explores the tragic aspects of black ghetto life, but she also probes beneath the surface in order to illuminate those areas of the slum dweller's life that often go unnoticed and should not be seen as ugly or horrifying. Ironically, then, her poems reveal both the destructive and the nurturing aspects of the black urban environment.

Interior of an overcrowded Chicago kitchenette during the 1940s.

Brooks has stated in many interviews that although Bronzeville is central to much of her poetry and she claims to be somewhat "obsessed" with life in the black ghetto, it is the neighborhood's people, not the abstract idea of the place, that inspire her work. As she put it in her autobiography *Report from Part One*, "I wish to present a large variety of personalities against a mosaic of daily affairs, recognizing that the grimmest of these is likely to have a streak or two streaks of sun."

Today, Bronzeville is not as distinct a neighborhood as New York's Harlem, and you are not likely to find it on most maps. Its borders are loosely defined as south of the McCormick Convention Center and north of the University of Chicago.

Gwendolyn Brooks with a typewriter, 1950.

GWENDOLYN BROOKS TIMELINE

1917   Born June 7 in Topeka, Kansas. Family moves to Chicago one month later.

1921   Brooks family moves to South Side house where Gwendolyn lives until her marriage in 1939.

1930   Publishes first poem, "Eventide," in *American Childhood* magazine.

1933   Meets Langston Hughes, who encourages her work; corresponds with and eventually meets James Weldon Johnson, who urges her to read T. S. Eliot and other modernist poets.

1934   Writes for *Chicago Defender*, where she will eventually publish over seventy of her poems in her weekly column.

1936   Graduates from Wilson Junior College.

1939   Marries Henry Lowington Blakely, Jr.

1940   First child, Henry, born.

1941   Attends South Side writer's workshop.

1945   Publishes *A Street in Bronzeville*.

1949   Publishes *Annie Allen*, which wins a Pulitzer Prize in 1950.

1951   Second child, Nora, born.

1953   Publishes *Maud Martha*, a novel.

1956   Publishes *Bronzeville Boys and Girls*, a children's book.

1960   Publishes *The Bean Eaters*.

1963   Publishes *Selected Poems*. Begins teaching at Chicago's Columbia College.

1967   Allies herself with Black Arts Movement.

1968	Publishes *In the Mecca*. Named Poet Laureate for the State of Illinois.
1969	Publishes *Riot*.
1970	Publishes *Family Pictures*.
1971	Publishes *Aloneness* and *The World of Gwendolyn Brooks*.
1972	Publishes *Report from Part One*, an autobiography.
1975	Publishes *Beckonings* and *A Capsule Course in Black Poetry Writing*.
1980	Publishes *Primer for Blacks* and *Young Poet's Primer*.
1981	Publishes *To Disembark*.
1985	Appointed poetry consultant to the Library of Congress.
1987	Publishes *Blacks*, a large collection of her poems.
1996	Publishes *Report from Part Two*, the second volume of her autobiography.
2000	Dies in Chicago on December 3.

POEMS BY GWENDOLYN BROOKS

This section provides only a small sample of the poetry of Gwendolyn Brooks. Additional poems by Brooks are included in Chapter 25, "Sweet Home Chicago" (p. 1768), which also discusses South Side Chicago and the black experience there during Brooks's lifetime.

Kitchenette Building   (1945)

To make the kitchenettes typical of 1940s Chicago, large buildings were carved up and reconfigured into tiny, one-room apartments.

We are things of dry hours and the involun-
    tary plan,
Grayed in, and gray. "Dream" makes a giddy
    sound, not strong
Like "rent," "feeding a wife," "satisfying a
    man."

But could a dream send up through onion
    fumes
Its white and violet, fight with fried
    potatoes   5
And yesterday's garbage ripening in the
    hall,
Flutter, or sing an aria down these rooms

Even if we were willing to let it in,
Had time to warm it, keep it very clean,
Anticipate a message, let it begin?   10

We wonder. But not well! not for a
    minute!
Since Number Five is out of the bathroom now,
We think of lukewarm water, hope to get in it.

Sadie and Maud

(1945)

Maud went to college.
Sadie stayed at home.
Sadie scraped life
With a fine-tooth comb.

She didn't leave a tangle in.   5
Her comb found every strand.
Sadie was one of the livingest chits
In all the land.

Sadie bore two babies
Under her maiden name.   10
Maud and Ma and Papa
Nearly died of shame.

When Sadie said her last so-long
Her girls struck out from home.
(Sadie had left as heritage   15
Her fine-tooth comb.)

Maud, who went to college,
Is a thin brown mouse.
She is living all alone
In this old house.   20

The Mother

(1945)

Abortions will not let you forget.
You remember the children you got that you did not get,
The damp small pulps with a little or with no hair,
The singers and workers that never handled the air.
You will never neglect or beat   5
Them, or silence or buy with a sweet.
You will never wind up the sucking-thumb
Or scuttle off ghosts that come.
You will never leave them, controlling your luscious sigh,
Return for a snack of them, with gobbling mother-eye.   10

I have heard in the voices of the wind the voices of my dim killed children.
I have contracted. I have eased
My dim dears at the breasts they could never suck.
I have said, Sweets, if I sinned, if I seized
Your luck   15
And your lives from your unfinished reach,
If I stole your births and your names,
Your straight baby tears and your games,
Your stilted or lovely loves, your tumults, your marriages, aches, and your deaths,
If I poisoned the beginnings of your breaths,   20

Believe that even in my deliberateness I was not deliberate.
Though why should I whine,
Whine that the crime was other than mine?—
Since anyhow you are dead.
Or rather, or instead,   25
You were never made.

But that too, I am afraid,
Is faulty: oh, what shall I say, how is the truth to be said?
You were born, you had body, you died.
It is just that you never giggled or planned or cried.   30

Believe me, I loved you all.
Believe me, I knew you, though faintly, and I loved, I loved you
All.

The Preacher: Ruminates behind the Sermon   (1945)

I think it must be lonely to be God.
Nobody loves a master. No. Despite
The bright hosannas, bright dear-Lords, and bright
Determined reverence of Sunday eyes.

Picture Jehovah striding through the hall   5
Of His importance, creatures running out
From servant-corners to acclaim, to shout
Appreciation of His merit's glare.

But who walks with Him?—dares to take His arm,
To slap Him on the shoulder, tweak His ear,   10
Buy Him a Coca-Cola or a beer,
Pooh-pooh His politics, call Him a fool?

Perhaps—who knows?—He tires of looking down.
Those eyes are never lifted. Never straight.
Perhaps sometimes He tires of being great   15
In solitude. Without a hand to hold.

Gay Chaps at the Bar   (1943)

> . . . and guys I knew in the States, young officers, return
> from the front crying and trembling. Gay chaps at the bar in
> Los Angeles, Chicago, New York . . .
> *Lieutenant William Couch in the South Pacific*

We knew how to order. Just the dash
Necessary. The length of gaiety in good taste.
Whether the raillery should be slightly iced
And given green, or served up hot and lush.

And we knew beautifully how to give to women 5
The summer spread, the tropics, of our love.
When to persist, or hold a hunger off.
Knew white speech. How to make a look an omen.
But nothing ever taught us to be islands.
And smart, athletic language for this hour 10
Was not in the curriculum. No stout
Lesson showed how to chat with death. We brought
No brass fortissimo, among our talents,
To holler down the lions in this air.

What Shall I Give My Children? Who Are Poor (Sonnet 2) (1949)

What shall I give my children? who are poor,
Who are adjudged the leastwise of the land,
Who are my sweetest lepers, who demand
No velvet and no velvety velour;
But who have begged me for a brisk contour, 5
Crying that they are quasi, contraband
Because unfinished, graven by a hand
Less than angelic, admirable or sure.
My hand is stuffed with mode, design, device.
But I lack access to my proper stone. 10
And plentitude of plan shall not suffice
Nor grief nor love shall be enough alone
To ratify my little halves who bear
Across an autumn freezing everywhere.

First Fight. Then Fiddle (Sonnet 4) (1949)

First fight. Then fiddle. Ply the slipping string
With feathery sorcery; muzzle the note
With hurting love; the music that they wrote
Bewitch, bewilder. Qualify to sing
Threadwise. Devise no salt, no hempen thing 5
For the dear instrument to bear. Devote
The bow to silks and honey. Be remote
A while from malice and from murdering.
But first to arms, to armor. Carry hate
In front of you and harmony behind. 10
Be deaf to music and to beauty blind.
Win war. Rise bloody, maybe not too late
For having first to civilize a space
Wherein to play your violin with grace.

In Honor of David Anderson Brooks, My Father   (1960)

July 30, 1883–November 21, 1959

A dryness is upon the house
My father loved and tended.
Beyond his firm and sculptured door
His light and lease have ended.

He walks the valleys, now—replies   5
To sun and wind forever.
No more the cramping chamber's chill,
No more the hindering fever.

Now out upon the wide clean air
My father's soul revives,   10
All innocent of self-interest
And the fear that strikes and strives.

He who was Goodness, Gentleness,
And Dignity is free,
Translates to public Love   15
Old private charity.

The Bean Eaters   (1960)

They eat beans mostly, this old yellow pair.
Dinner is a casual affair.
Plain chipware on a plain and creaking wood,
Tin flatware.

Two who are Mostly Good.   5
Two who have lived their day,
But keep on putting on their clothes
And putting things away.

And remembering . . .
Remembering, with twinklings and twinges, 10
As they lean over the beans in their rented back room that is full of beads and
    receipts and dolls and cloths, tobacco crumbs, vases and fringes.

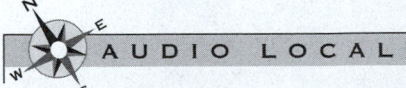

AUDIO LOCALE

Brooks Reading Her Poetry. On the 1969 recording *Gwendolyn Brooks Reading Her Poetry*, produced by Caedmon, Brooks reads twenty-seven of her poems, including "The Mother," "The Children of the Poor," "The Bean Eaters," "Lovers of the Poor," "The Wall," and "The Sermon on the Warpland." Brooks can also be found reading her poetry on HarperAudio's *Our Miss Brooks* (2005). Brooks's reading is also included in volume 13 of *The Spoken Arts Treasury of 100 Modern American Poets Reading Their Poems*.

Brooks Reading "We Real Cool." To listen to an online recording of Gwendolyn Brooks reading "We Real Cool," go to the Academy of American Poets website at *http://www.poets.org/viewmedia.php/prmMID/15433*. But before you visit the
website, read the text of the poem (below). Then compare her recitation to how
you originally read the poem. How does Brooks's reading differ from yours?

WE REAL COOL
BY GWENDOLYN BROOKS
The Pool Players
Seven at the Golden Shovel

WE REAL COOL. WE
LEFT SCHOOL. WE

LURK LATE. WE
STRIKE STRAIGHT. WE
SING SIN. WE
THIN GIN. WE

JAZZ JUNE. WE
DIE SOON.

Designed by Cledie Taylor
"We Real Cool" from Selected Poems by Gwendolyn Brooks
Copyright © 1959 by Gwendolyn Brooks Blakely
Reprinted by permission of the author and Harper & Row, Publishers
BROADSIDE No. 6, December 1966
BROADSIDE PRESS, 12651 OLD MILL PLACE, DETROIT, MICHIGAN 48238

1966 broadside print of Brooks's "We Real Cool."

✑ COMMENTARY

Brooks on the Men in "We Real Cool"

From a 1970 interview with George Stavros

Brooks: They [the men in "We Real Cool"] have no pretensions to any glamour. They are supposedly dropouts, or at least they're in the poolroom when they should be possibly in school, since they're probably young enough or at least I saw were when I looked in a poolroom, and they . . . First of all, let me tell you how that's supposed to be said, because there's a reason why I set it out as I did. These are people who are essentially saying, "Kilroy is here. We are." But they're a little uncertain of the strength of their identity. The "We"—you're supposed to stop after the "We" and think about validity; of course, there's no way for you to tell whether it should be said softly or not, I suppose, but I say it rather softly because I want to represent their basic uncertainty, which they don't bother to question every day of course.

Interviewer: Are you saying that the form of this poem, then, was determined by the colloquial rhythm you were trying to catch?

Brooks: No, determined by my feelings about these boys, these young men.

The Crazy Woman   (1960)

I shall not sing a May song.
A May song should be gay.
I'll wait until November
And sing a song of gray.
I'll wait until November.   5
That is the time for me.
I'll go out in the frosty dark
And sing most terribly.
And all the little people
Will stare at me and say,   10
"That is the Crazy Woman
Who would not sing in May."

Langston Hughes   (1967)

is merry glory.
Is saltatory.
Yet grips his right of twisting free.

Has a long reach,
Strong speech,   5
Remedial fears.
Muscular tears.

Holds horticulture
In the eye of the vulture
Infirm profession.   10

In the Compression—
In mud and blood and sudden death—
In the breath
Of the holocaust he
Is helmsman, hatchet, headlight.   15
See
One restless in the exotic time! and ever,
Till the air is cured of its fever.

INSPIRATION BROOKS AND LANGSTON HUGHES, ROBERT FROST, AND PAUL ROBESON

Actor Paul Robeson, 1941.

Although Gwendolyn Brooks was a Chicagoan all her life, her poetic influences ran a wide spectrum, including noted writers and artists of different styles and backgrounds from all over the country. Brooks frequently paid tribute in her poetry to some of the artists whose work and lives she admired; among them were poets Langston Hughes and Robert Frost and renowned actor Paul Robeson. Her longtime association with Hughes was the result not only of his active role as a mentor of poets—among other things, he co-edited, with Chicago poet Arna Bontemps, the award-winning anthology *The Poetry of the Negro*, which included works by numerous Chicago writers, including Brooks—but also by his frequent visits to Chicago over the years. (See p. 1756 in Chapter 25 for a photograph of Brooks and Hughes together.)

With Frost, Brooks shared an affinity for fixed verse forms and metrics as well as a complex, psychological approach to poetic subject matter. Her poetic tribute to Robeson—who was born the son of an ex-slave but went on to become a scholar, actor, athlete, singer (famous for his booming baritone voice), and political activist—reflects her admiration for his pioneering efforts. Among other accomplishments, he was the first black actor to play Othello onstage. He was also well-known for his role as Joe in *Show Boat*, in particular for his "rewriting" of the show's signature song "Old Man River" (written in 1927), changing lyrics that mirrored the racist culture of that time to those that expressed pride, strength, and defiance.

Brooks's poetic homages to Frost and Robeson appear on p. 918.

Of Robert Frost   (1963)

There is a little lightning in his eyes.
Iron at the mouth.
His brows ride neither too far up nor down.

He is splendid. With a place to stand.

Some glowing in the common blood.   5
Some specialness within.

Paul Robeson   (1970)

That time
we all heard it,
cool and clear,
cutting across the hot grit of the day.
The major Voice.   5
The adult Voice
forgoing Rolling River,
forgoing tearful tale of bale and barge
and other symptoms of an old despond.
Warning, in music-words   10
devout and large,
that we are each other's
harvest:
we are each other's
business: 15
we are each other's
magnitude and bond.

The Sermon on the Warpland   (1968)

> "The fact that we are black is our ultimate reality."
> —Ron Karenga

And several strengths from drowsiness campaigned
but spoke in Single Sermon on the warpland.

And went about the warpland saying No.
"My people, black and black, revile the River.
Say that the River turns, and turn the River.   5
Say that our Something in doublepod contains
seeds for the coming hell and health together.
Prepare to meet
(sisters, brothers) the brash and terrible weather;
the pains;   10
the bruising; the collapse of bestials, idols.
But then oh then!—the stuffing of the hulls!

the seasoning of the perilously sweet!
the health! the heralding of the clear obscure!

Build now your Church, my brothers, sisters. Build   15
never with brick nor Corten nor with granite.
Build with lithe love. With love like lion-eyes.
With love like morningrise.
With love like black, our black—
luminously indiscreet;   20
complete; continuous."

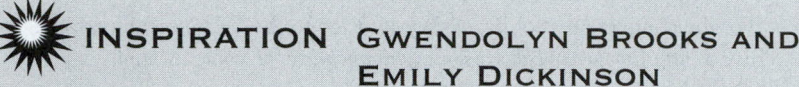 **INSPIRATION GWENDOLYN BROOKS AND EMILY DICKINSON**

Gwendolyn Brooks always thought of herself as following in the mainstream of
American arts and letters, a fact not recognized until somewhat late in her career.
Dickinson and Brooks were very different in style and personality, but there is no
doubt that they were both major figures in the development of American poetry,
and that Brooks learned from Dickinson's example. This can be seen more easily in
Brooks's earlier work, after she studied Dickinson at Wilson Junior College. What
influences from Dickinson can you find in this early poem of Brooks, "Myself"?
What elements are distinctly Brooks's own?

Myself (1936)

Myself is all I have,
Myself is all I need;
Should grain and blossoms be?
Myself can plant the seed.

Myself requires no other
To help her better know
Dawn splendour, gold of noon,
Or ruddy sunset glow.

Myself requires no teacher,
Herself knows how to sing!
She is full strong enough to be
A lone and quiet thing.

Brooks was one of many contemporary poets to commemorate the one-
hundredth anniversary of Dickinson's death in 1986. In a speech about Emily
Dickinson's legacy, Brooks discusses the influence Dickinson had on her
poetry:

(continued on next page)

GWENDOLYN BROOKS AND EMILY DICKINSON

Thinking about Emily Dickinson, . . . I said "You know, this is almost hopeless, because Emily and I are absolutely different in the details of our lives." I would like to tell you how I met Emily. We had been having for many years in our textbooks of the various schools I went to selections of Emily Dickinson's work, and I rarely cared for them. But when I was nineteen I went to the junior college library and found a collection of her work that had been discovered by that time. I was absolutely enchanted. And I began to really appreciate her way with common words and her way of putting common words together so they made new magic. But what would Emily have made out of the late sixties in which I found such help, lots of mistakes and clumsinesses, but a lot of help, too. That help helped form what I am today.

For the complete text of Brooks's speech, go to the Dickinson Electronic Archive at *http://www.emilydickinson.org/titanic/table_of_contents.html*.

Talking about the Text

1. One theme in Brooks's poetry (as in Emily Dickinson's) is the small person—sometimes physically small, but also timid and insignificant—making her way in the larger, not always welcoming world. These persons are sometimes children, sometimes women. Examine three or four Brooks poems, asking how such persons function, and what their strategies and weapons are against the rich, white, and powerful.

2. Trace the various tones of voice of the speaker in "Lovers of the Poor" (see Chapter 25, p. 1757). Some suggested approaches: Ask how one would read the lines "The worthy poor. The very very worthy / And beautiful poor." Examine how the conjunctions of opposites ("mercy and murder hinting," "Sweetly abortive," "Herein they kiss and coddle and assault") function in this poem. Ask what the speaker's attitude is toward "the poor" and toward the "lovers of the poor." What keeps the speaker's feelings from being completely negative? Which group do you as reader/audience identify with?

3. Brooks emphasized that her poetry changed after 1967. Pick an early and late poem and see if you can note a change. What continuities can you see? Suggestions: compare one of the sonnets with "The Sermon on the Warpland."

Writing about the Text

1. In an essay, determine how Brooks sizes up American whites and the racial situation over all or part of her career. Trace how you see her feelings change from poem to poem, or over time. (Suggested poems to look at: "The Lovers of the Poor," "Sadie and Maud.")

2. One of Brooks's most difficult poems is "What Shall I Give My Children? Who Are Poor," the second sonnet in a sonnet sequence called "Children of the Poor" (p. 913). Try your hand at explicating it (for suggestions on writing an explication, see p. 819). You needn't emerge with a neat, coherent interpretation of the poem: questions are fine.

3. In her *Capsule Course on Black Poetry Writing*, Brooks recommends avoiding clichés, yet she, like many writing teachers, sometimes failed to follow her own advice. How well do they work? Search Brooks's poetry for *intentional* clichés. Then write five clichés *effectively* yourself, modeling them on the ones Brooks employs.

Linking the Text to Other Texts

1. Brooks admired Emily Dickinson, and in her first autobiographical work, *Report from Part One*, she printed a photo of herself in front of Dickinson's home in Amherst. What similarities do you see between these two very distinctive poets? (Some of the large differences are obvious.)
2. Examine the advice Brooks gives about poetry writing (in "A Few Hints," p. 923) or the manner in which she praises other poets (see p. 922). What of that advice or praise might apply to her own poetry?
3. Much of Brooks's juvenile poetry was about nature, the sky, flowers, and clouds. But in most of her mature poems, the sites are interiors of buildings and city streets—many of them poor and grubby. Speculate on what she might have learned from Walt Whitman's portrayals of New York City streets in order to make poetry of these sorts of urban environments. Can you find Whitman poems that she might have learned from?

✎ COMMENTARY

Gwendolyn Brooks on Her Life and the Art of Poetry

Informal occasions often brought out the best of Brooks's prose, along with a sparkling sense of humor and a notable generosity. She reveals many of her own values and beliefs when she describes or introduces others, especially writers whose work she admires.

On her son Henry as a child, from her autobiography, Report from Part One (1972)

Henry of the thousand Good-nights. You have not seen him at night, when he has two hundred good-nights for each beloved soul, including that of Cocoa, his puppy and that of Water Boy, his fish. "Good-night! Good-night! Good-night!" Every night the chorus rings through the house, until the Old Heads are ready to burst. "Good-night! Good-night! Good-night." Just before pajama-time. At pajama-time. Before prayer-time. After prayer-time. After getting-in-bed time. At lights-out time.

On whether oral poetry seems more immediate than printed or written poetry

No, in fact, you might be surprised to know I have a visual appreciation for poetry myself. I'd rather read anybody's work than listen to it. I can get something out of listening, but you can't pick up everything. But what I try to do in reciting is to give whoever is listening an impression of how I felt when I wrote the piece. I try to paint the poem on the air.

Brooks admitted to disliking E. E. Cummings's work until she heard his poetry read.

On black poets, from the second volume of her autobiography, Report from Part Two *(1996)*

The Black poet has the 'American' experience and also has the *Black* experience; so is very rich.

Introducing poet Louis Simpson, from Report from Part Two *(1996)*

Here comes Louis Simpson—communicator of intricate darkness of feeling and instinct (so says Donald Hall); fiery defender of Gary Snyder; accused Universalist. Certain circles cite him as coldly capable of *exhaustive* wickedness. For almost two decades he had been soundly spanked for opining that, if Blacks write "*only*" about Blackness, they are inadequate—that they are, in fact, non-poets. You decide for yourselves whether or not *that's* wicked. But I myself found how dangerous Simpson the Satyr can be. I remember with delight that years ago, at Stonybrook, I was having a lovely peaceful lunch with this remarkable poet and teacher in a cheerfully sunny room, when I made the mistake of saying that there were no Gr-r-reat Poets—Capital G, Capital P—living and working today. (That we knew of, that is: because of course there is Always some unknown genius toiling at the top of a tenement, about to burst—full-bodied and beautiful and persuasive—upon the populace.) "No Great Poets? GARY SNYDER!" screamed Louis. Louis turned red—*he* can *do* that—and, lifting himself to hellish height in his chair, bit my head off. (That is why I have no head . . .)

Oh well, wicked or not. Louis Simpson, poet of careful subjectivity, poet of luminous, *requiring* lyricism, is here tonight.

Introducing poet Grace Schulman, from Report from Part Two *(1996)*

Even when Grace Schulman's poems are short, and the lines narrow, we have the impression that we are at the center of large sound—large, exacting but involving sound. Her rhythms are obliged and reliable: so remarkable is her control that you feel confident and comfortable *leaning into* those rhythms.

Her frequent pentameter is brilliantly leashed and various. That pentameter is never tiresome.

Also: the people and circumstances she tackles are real. They are not static. *She* is not static.

Grace Schulman.

Introducing Australian poet Les Murray with an impromptu poem, from Report from Part Two *(1996)*

Oh, *Poet!*

You with your sprightly wilfulness,
your animated shimmer, your
shadows *and* sunlit places, your
stylish joy—
your dedication to the daily,

your fierce affinities, your fond dismay,
your perceptions of drama in the so-called Small—
I observe you! And I credit you!
I pass you on!
I yield you to your Neighbor!

From "A Few Hints toward the Making of Poetry" in A Capsule Course in Black Poetry Writing (1975)

1. Language—ordinary speech. Today we do not say "Thou saintly skies of empyrean blue through which there soarest sweetest bird of love." Forget ecstasy, ethereal, empyrean, wouldst, canst. Do not use 'neath, e'er, ne'er, 'mid, etc.
2. If you allude to a star, say precisely what that star means to *you*. If you feature a garden, speak of that garden *most personally*. If you have murdered in a garden, the grass and flowers (and weeds) will mean something different to you than to someone who has only planted or picked.
3. Try telling the reader a little less. He'll, she'll love you more, and will love your poem more, if you allow him to do a little digging. Not *too* much, but *some*. Avoid clichés.

> Gentle flowers
> Sad lament
> Deepest passion
> The wind howled

Occasionally a cliché can be redeemed:

> The gentle flowers shrieked and killed the sun.
> The sad lament was lovely, and I laughed.

For here the pictures and concepts are so outrageous that the cliché is elevated into a contribution. . . .

* * *

6. Loosen your rhythm so that it sounds like human talk. Human talk is not exact, not precise. Sometimes human talk "has flowers," but if it "has flowers," those flowers (as I have said in my poem "Young Africans") "must come out to the road."
7. You must make your reader believe that what you say *could* be true. Think of your efforts to be convincing and entertaining when you are gossiping. You use gesture, touch, tone-variation, facial expression. Try persuading your wordage—SOMEHOW!—to do all the things your body does when forwarding a piece of gossip.

Starting Points for Further Research: Gwendolyn Brooks

- **Editions:** Gwendolyn Brooks. *Selected Poems.* New York: Harper and Row, 1963.
  ———. *Blacks.* Chicago: Third World Press, 1991.
- **Biography:** George Kent. *A Life of Gwendolyn Brooks.* Lexington: University Press of Kentucky, 1990.
- **Critical Essays:** Tracey L. Walters. "Gwendolyn Brooks' 'The Anniad' and the Interdeterminacy of Genre." *CLA Journal* 44 (March 2001): 350–66.
  Maria K. Mootry and Gary Smith, eds. *A Life Distilled: Gwendolyn Brooks, Her Poetry and Fiction.* Urbana: University of Illinois Press, 1987.
  D. L. Melhem. *Gwendolyn Brooks: Poetry and the Heroic Voice.* Lexington: University Press of Kentucky, 1987.

CHAPTER
16

Passionate Verse
Love Poetry of the English Renaissance

In the popular imagination, the English Renaissance is associated with larger-than-life characters and events: King Henry VIII, who married six times and changed his country's official religion from Catholic to Protestant, in the process executing everyone who stood in his way, including a number of those inconvenient wives. Henry's daughter, Queen Elizabeth I, celebrated as the Virgin Queen, presided over a country that grew rich with trade and achieved greatness in its literature, especially through the plays of Shakespeare. What we now call the Renaissance was an outburst of artistic and scientific creativity that began in Italy in the 1300s and spread slowly throughout Europe, reaching England around 1530. It was a glorious time in England, in terms of architecture, science, painting, drama, and poetry. Today's historians find the term "Renaissance" too imprecise, and prefer the term "Early Modern," a label which suggests that this era really connects quite closely with our own modern age. Historians also disagree about the precise dating of the era, but for our purposes the English Renaissance can be said to begin around 1530 and end with the triumph of the Puritans in their revolution of 1649, which beheaded the king, Charles I, abolished the monarchy in favor of rule by Parliament, and established Oliver Cromwell's religious dictatorship over England.

Throughout the Renaissance, elegant young men wrote lively poems to their paramours, continuing a topic that has always seemed to inspire poetry: love, burning desire, faithlessness, the desire for kisses and more, the joy of the chase, and the cold hand of rejection. Some legendary names have contributed to Renaissance love poetry, and this chapter includes poems by many of them. Sir Walter Raleigh, famous for being the model of manners and chivalry, was an explorer, entrepreneur, historian, soldier, and courtier as well as a superb poet. Legend has it that when Queen Elizabeth encountered a puddle in her way, Raleigh unhesitatingly took off his richly embroidered cloak and laid it in the queen's path, so her foot would not experience the indignity of touching water.

Raleigh's extravagant gallantry and beautiful poetry typify one side of this period, but the Renaissance was also a very violent, perilous time. Raleigh the poet and adventurer was eventually imprisoned in the Tower of London and beheaded. Another poet, Christopher Marlowe, a rival to Shakespeare and author of the famous plays *Doctor Faustus*, *Edward II*, and *Tamburlaine the Great*, was fatally stabbed at the age of twenty-nine. The most admired of the Renaissance writers during his brief lifetime, Sir Philip Sidney, paragon of English knighthood, diplomat, courtier, and famous poet, died in battle at thirty-two. Katherine Philips, the best-known woman poet of her generation, died of smallpox at thirty-three. In the Renaissance, the beautiful, highly emotional poetry of love was composed in proximity to danger and death, as Shakespeare's *Romeo and Juliet* makes plain.

ENGLISH RENAISSANCE TIMELINE

Although the English Renaissance did not begin until around 1530 and ended around 1649, in order to give a fuller literary history of the poets featured in this chapter and a more comprehensive context to the political and religious landscape, the timeline presented here starts in the early 1500s and ends in the 1680s.

1509	King Henry VIII gains power in England and marries his widowed sister-in-law, Catherine of Aragon.
1517	Martin Luther posts his 95 *Theses* on a church door in Saxony, speaking out against what he saw as corruption in the Catholic church and putting into motion the Protestant Reformation.
1533	King Henry VIII appeals to the Catholic church in Rome to grant him a divorce from Catherine of Aragon, citing her failure to produce a male heir. The Pope's denial sets into motion England's break from the Roman Catholic church. Henry marries Anne Boleyn, declares himself head of the Church of England, and is excommunicated by the Catholic church. Anne Boleyn gives birth to a daughter, Elizabeth.
1536	Anne Boleyn is beheaded on May 19. Henry VIII marries Jane Seymour. All monasteries are sold to private landowners as part of the English Reformation, creating the rise of a wealthy landed gentry.

1537	Jane Seymour dies after giving birth to a son, Edward.
1539	Henry VIII issues the Statute of the Six Articles, defining six traditional Catholic doctrines as acts of heresy, including the priests' vow of celibacy and spoken confession.
1540	Henry VIII marries Anne of Cleves in January and divorces her six months later. He marries Catherine Howard in August.
1542	Catherine Howard is beheaded for infidelity. Ireland is made a kingdom.
1543	Henry VIII marries Catherine Parr, who will outlive him. Polish astronomer Nicolaus Copernicus's claim that the earth and planets revolve around the sun marks the advent of modern astronomy.
1547	Henry VIII dies. His ten-year-old son Edward VI is named king, aided by his uncle, the Duke of Somerset. The Six Articles are repealed and Protestant doctrine is introduced.
1552	Sir Walter Raleigh is born. Edward VI dies. Mary, daughter of Henry VIII and Catherine of Aragon, is crowned queen. Protestants are persecuted after Mary restores Catholicism in England. Sir Philip Sidney is born.
1558	Mary dies and the Protestant Elizabeth I is crowned queen. Mary's Catholic laws are repealed and Henry VIII's acts are reinstated. Elizabeth will reign over a relatively peaceful and flourishing England until 1603.
1559	The Church of England (Anglican Church) is modified to blend Catholic hierarchy with mostly Protestant religious beliefs. Groups that do not join—Puritans, Congregationalists, Brownists, Catholics, Separatists, Presbyterians—will remain susceptible to persecution.
1564	William Shakespeare is born. Christopher Marlowe is born.
1567	Thomas Campion is born.
1572	Ben Jonson is born.
1586	Sir Philip Sidney is fatally wounded at the battle of Zutphen. Lady Mary Wroth is born (c. 1586–1587).
1588	England is at war with Spain and defeats the Spanish armada in the English Channel. Christopher Marlowe introduces the use of blank verse in drama with *Dr. Faustus*.
1591	Sir Philip Sidney's *Astrophel and Stella* (composed around 1582) is published posthumously. Robert Herrick is born.
1593	Christopher Marlowe is stabbed to death, possibly because of his political activities.
1594	Shakespeare begins his career in London as an actor and playwright. From around 1594 to 1596, he composes *Romeo and Juliet*.
1599	Christopher Marlowe's "The Passionate Shepherd to His Love" and Sir Walter Raleigh's "The Nymph's Reply to the Shepherd" are printed together in a collection called *The Passionate Pilgrim*.

1601	Thomas Campion publishes songs to be performed to lute music under the title *A Book of Ayres*, among them "When Thou Must Home to Shades of Underground."
1603	James VI of Scotland becomes King James I, uniting England and Scotland under one leader.
1605	Because of a 1604 edict banning Catholic priests in England, Robert Catesby, a Catholic, leads a foiled conspiracy, later known as the Gunpowder Plot, to blow up Parliament and the king.
1607	The Jamestown colony in Virginia is founded.
1609	The first of Shakespeare's sonnets is published.
1611	King James's officially sanctioned English Bible is published. The King James Version will be one of the most popular versions of the Bible.
1612	Anne Bradstreet is born in England.
1613	Thomas Campion publishes *Two Bookes of Ayres*.
1616	Shakespeare dies. Ben Jonson publishes his *Works*.
1617	Thomas Campion publishes *The Third and Fourth Booke of Ayres*; the *Third Booke* includes his poem "Fire, Fire, Fire, Fire."
1618	Sir Walter Raleigh executed. The Thirty Years War begins.
1620	The Pilgrims land at Plymouth in Massachusetts. Thomas Campion dies.
1621	Andrew Marvell is born. Lady Mary Wroth's Petrarchan sonnet sequence *Pamphilia to Amphilanthus* and *The Countess of Montgomery's Urania* are published.
1625	Charles I becomes king.
1630	Anne Bradstreet emigrates to Massachusetts on one of the first ships to bring Puritans to New England.
1632	Katherine Philips is born.
1637	Ben Jonson dies.
1642–1646	Civil war splits the country: the north and northwest side with the king, and the south sides with Parliament. In 1646, the royalists are defeated.
1642–1660	The Puritans close British theaters, condemning them as immoral.
1648	The second civil war breaks out, and the royalists are beaten again. Robert Herrick's single volume of poems, *Hesperides*, is published.
1649	Charles I is tried and executed. The republic of England is declared.
1650	Anne Bradstreet's *The Tenth Muse Lately Sprung Up in America, By a Gentlewoman of Those Parts* brought to England to be published.
1652–1654	Trade rivalries result in the Anglo-Dutch War, and the English emerge as victors.
1653	Oliver Cromwell is made Lord Protector for life under the first written constitution of England.

1658	Cromwell dies and his son, Richard, takes over as Lord Protector.
1660	The monarchy is restored and Charles II becomes king.
1664	Katherine Philips dies and the first edition of her poems is published posthumously.
1665	The Great Plague of London kills tens of thousands.
1672	Anne Bradstreet dies.
1674	Robert Herrick dies.
1678	Andrew Marvell dies.
1681	Andrew Marvell's *Poems* published.

READING ENGLISH RENAISSANCE LOVE POEMS

When we confront all the rich emotion displayed in Renaissance love poetry, we ask if we can read it straight, as a simple, direct expression of the poet's deep feelings. It is difficult to do so. For one thing, deep feelings usually do not come wrapped in such elaborate, carefully crafted language. In the famous love sonnet by Sir Philip Sidney printed below, the poet explains how his poem came to be written: he was in great pain because his lady did not return his love. He tried to write about how hurt he was, so she would take pity on him. But, he tells us, he was unable to carry out his plan. He looked at other poets' works, but they could not supply him with inspiration or the right words. In fact, he says, the power to find the right ideas, Invention, ran away from Study. Finally, the desperate poet's Muse (a kind of guiding spirit) brings him up sharply: "Fool . . . look in thy heart and write." Here is Sidney's poem recounting his drama.

SIR PHILIP SIDNEY   (1554–1586)

From Astrophel and Stella   (1591)

Loving in truth, and fain° in verse my love to show,   *wishing*
That she (dear she) might take some pleasure of my pain:
Pleasure might cause her read, reading might make her know,
Knowledge might pity win, and pity grace obtain,
I sought fit words to paint the blackest face of woe,   5
Studying inventions fine, her wits to entertain:
Oft turning others' leaves,° to see if thence would flow   *pages*
Some fresh and fruitful showers upon my sun-burned brain.
But words came halting forth, wanting Invention's stay,
Invention, Nature's child, fled step-dame Study's blows,   10
And others' feet° still seemed but strangers in my way.   *metrical feet, lines*
Thus great with child to speak, and helpless in my throes,
Biting my trewand° pen, beating myself for spite,   *truant*
"Fool," said my Muse to me, "look in thy heart and write."

The paradox or problem facing us as readers is that the poem that claims to be written from the "heart" is delightfully complicated, strictly rhymed in the form of a fourteen-line English sonnet (in iambic hexameters), filled with images of nature (showers, sun-burn, pregnancy) but obviously a product of a very refined art. There may well be heartfelt emotion, but the resulting poem is far from natural or direct. It disingenuously enacts a drama of simplicity, saying that if you have to search hard for the words or ideas, you will not receive poetic inspiration. Instead, in complex lines of highly wrought imagery, it says you must look to your heart and write directly.

We see signs of the same paradox everywhere we look throughout Renaissance love poetry. The meaning of the words often argues for directness and simplicity, for naturalness. But the form argues just the opposite, for complexity, intricacy, and richness, in short, artistry. Does this mean we cannot take the words at face value? Yes. It would be hard to claim that all of these poets actually have every feeling they vow they hold dearest in their hearts. Does anyone? Are today's song composers speaking nothing but the direct truth, or are they trying to create memorable songs?

So one key to appreciating Renaissance poetry is to not treat every sentiment as absolutely true, as a direct, genuine measure of love. Most of the sentiments are **conventional**, meaning they are the expected thing to say in such a situation: the beloved's eyes are like oceans, jewels, stars . . . you get the idea. These are **conceits**, exaggerated metaphors and comparisons with which poets and readers were fully familiar. Many of these conceits were imported from France or Italy, where Petrarch (1304–1374) had created many of them out of his unrequited love for his Laura. If you were a Renaissance love poet, you had to claim to rage or melt or burn or repine over your beloved, or you had to praise your lover to the skies. Such emotion was a role one performed, part of the task of writing a love poem.

The pleasure of this love poetry lies in the mastery of form, in the wit of the descriptions, and of course in the brilliant, powerful, and often moving language. Additionally, the poets' performance especially delights us when they toy with the situation they claim they are in, or self-consciously play with the conventions of the genre as they go about writing their verse, as Sidney does in his poem above.

PASTORAL POEMS

Below are two famous poems about the lovelorn shepherd persuading his love to join him. Ever since the Greek poet Theocritus (c. 310–250 BCE) began the genre, many highly educated urban writers set poems in the country, among "simple" shepherds who nevertheless mouthed some fairly complex sentiments. This idealization of country is the **pastoral**—signifying a kind of never-never land where ordinary cares do not intrude and people are free to speak their hearts. The exchange in the two poems that follow is based on another very conventional notion, **carpe diem**: Latin for "seize the day," meaning "act now, since time is wasting." (See the "*Carpe Diem* Poems" section, pp. 936–939, for more examples.) Not surprisingly, the *carpe diem* theme usually connects to love and sex, typically with the man doing the persuading and the woman doing the resisting. According to many critics, in "The Passionate Shepherd to His Love,"

Christopher Marlowe follows this conventional narrative tradition by casting his poem in a male's voice. In recent years, however, some critics have argued that the gender neutrality in the voice of the speaker and the "love" being addressed suggests that it can also be read as a homosexual love poem.

CHRISTOPHER MARLOWE (1564–1593)
The Passionate Shepherd to His Love (1599)

Come live with me and be my love,
And we will all the pleasures prove
That valleys, groves, hills, and fields,
Woods, or steepy mountain yields.

And we will sit upon the rocks,   5
Seeing the shepherds feed their flocks,
By shallow rivers, to whose falls
Melodious birds sing madrigals.°   *poetic songs*

And I will make thee beds of roses,
And a thousand fragrant posies,   10
A cap of flowers and a kirtle°   *skirt*
Embroider'd all with leaves of myrtle;

A gown made of the finest wool
Which from our pretty lambs we pull;
Fair lined slippers for the cold,   15
With buckles of the purest gold;

A belt of straw and ivy buds,
With coral clasps and amber studs:
And if these pleasures may thee move,
Come live with me, and be my love.   20

The shepherd swains shall dance and sing
For thy delight each May morning:
If these delights thy mind may move,
Then live with me and be my love.

 INSPIRATION   WALTER RALEIGH'S NYMPH: TALKING BACK TO MARLOWE'S SHEPHERD

Sir Walter Raleigh (1552–1618), who oversaw New World expeditions to North and South America, was perhaps better known as an explorer and adventurer than as a poet. Among other exploits, he organized the failed English

(continued on next page)

WALTER RALEIGH'S NYMPH: TALKING BACK TO MARLOWE'S SHEPHERD

colony at Roanoke Island (now North Carolina, but then considered part of Virginia). He is credited with introducing potatoes to Ireland and tobacco to Europe. And he led two expeditions—one in 1595 and one in 1616—up the Orinoco River in South America in search of El Dorado, the famous mythical city of gold. A courtier to Queen Elizabeth I as a young man, Raleigh seemed to attract controversy wherever he went, falling in and out of political favor. Elizabeth had him imprisoned in the Tower of London in 1592 after he secretly married one of her ladies-in-waiting. He was sent to the Tower again in 1603, this time for thirteen years, by James I for treason; he was eventually executed by order of James I in 1618.

In his most famous poem, "The Nymph's Reply to the Shepherd," directly inspired by Marlowe's "The Passionate Shepherd to His Love," Raleigh wittily takes on what we assume to be a woman's voice (the "nymph") and demonstrates what is wrong with the pastoral ideal as Marlowe describes it. These two poems were first printed together in 1599 in a collection of verse published by William Jaggard entitled *The Passionate Pilgrim*, and many other poets followed suit, writing on the same theme. (For *real* women's voices, see the Renaissance love poetry of Lady Mary Wroth p. 954, Katherine Philips p. 956, and Anne Bradstreet p. 957.)

The Nymph's Reply to the Shepherd   (1600)

If all the world and love were young,
And truth in every shepherd's tongue,
These pretty pleasures might me move
To live with thee and be thy Love.

But Time drives flocks from field to fold;   5
When rivers rage and rocks grow cold;
And Philomel° becometh dumb;   *shepherd's name; nightingale*
The rest complains of cares to come.

The flowers do fade, and wanton fields
To wayward Winter reckoning yields: 10
A honey tongue, a heart of gall,
Is fancy's spring, but sorrow's fall.

Thy gowns, thy shoes, thy beds of roses,
Thy cap, thy kirtle,° and thy posies,   *skirt*

(continued on next page)

WALTER RALEIGH'S NYMPH: TALKING BACK TO MARLOWE'S SHEPHERD

Soon break, soon wither, soon forgotten,   15
In folly ripe, in reason rotten.

Thy belt of straw and ivy-buds,
Thy coral clasps and amber studs,
All these in me no means can move
To come to thee and be thy Love.   20

But could youth last, and love still breed,
Had joys no date, nor age no need,
Then these delights my mind might move
To live with thee and be thy Love.

Talking about the Text

1. Summarize each of these pastoral poems in a single sentence. Do the poems contain conflicting views of love? To what extent are they working with the same conventions?

2. Scan one of these pastoral poems and annotate it for the meter and rhyme scheme. What effect do the meter and rhyme have on your reading of the poem? On its tone? On its message?

3. Pastoral poems rely on a romanticization of nature and the countryside, which Renaissance readers would have easily accepted as a common convention. How well do you think modern readers can relate to such a romanticization of rural life? Do we still tend to idealize rural life or are we more aware of its realities? How does your own experience with rural life shape your reading of these poems?

Writing about the Text

1. Examine each poem as persuasive text. What does the shepherd do to persuade his lady to join him? What are his appeals? How does he use language to his advantage? How does Raleigh's nymph counter these claims?

2. Although both these poems were written by men, they still can be examined to see how Renaissance English conventions of love differed between men and women. According to these poems, how were men and women to behave in love?

3. To what socioeconomic class do poets like Christopher Marlowe and Walter Raleigh belong? Do you think their knowledge of the countryside comes from direct experience? Is the depiction of the countryside in their poems realistic or romanticized? Why do you think the countryside was a popular topic for these writers? Write an essay in which you examine these issues in pastoral poetry.

Linking the Text to Other Texts

1. Compare Raleigh's "The Nymph's Reply to the Shepherd" to Katherine Philips's "Against Love." How do the female voices in these poems, one written by a man and the other by a woman, compare? To what extent are their messages similar and how are they different?

2. To what extent would you categorize these two pastoral poems as *carpe diem* poems? Compare them to the poems on pp. 937–938. How similar are the arguments the speakers employ?

POEMS ON CLOTHING

Practically half of Marlowe's "The Passionate Shepherd to His Love" (lines 9–18) and half of Raleigh's reply as well (9–20) describe clothing, quite lovingly. (These may be shepherds, but they possess some rather expensive jewelry and elaborate adornments.) The concentration on the exquisite delight (and equally exquisite decay) of adornment highlights the extraordinary role of clothing among Renaissance aristocrats and their followers. Here is how Marlowe describes one of his characters, Hero, the woman loved by the ardent young man Leander, in another of his poems.

CHRISTOPHER MARLOWE

From Hero and Leander   (1598)

The outside of her garments were of lawn,
The lining purple silk, with gilt stars drawn;   10
Her wide sleeves green, and border'd with a grove,
Where Venus in her naked glory strove
To please the careless and disdainful eyes
Of proud Adonis, that before her lies;
Her kirtle blue, whereon was many a stain,   15
Made with the blood of wretched lovers slain.°   *for love*
Upon her head she wore a myrtle wreath,
From whence her veil reach'd to the ground beneath;
Her veil was artificial flowers and leaves,
Whose workmanship both man and beast deceives.   20

This concentration on the delights and deceits of external appearance is typical of the Renaissance, and the excess Marlowe obviously enjoys describing would call forth the severe reaction of the Puritans later in the 1600s. The ornate, elaborate, beautiful clothing that makes such a rich subject for love poetry in fact matched some of the finery well-to-do people actually wore. Over the long course of the Renaissance, male and female Elizabethan courtiers as well as seventeenth-century Cavaliers favored clothing that was rich, elaborate, and excessive, as the illustrations in the four-color insert reveal. The counterpart of this extravagant dress is the extravagant language of the poetry. In what literary critic Stephen Greenblatt has memorably called "Renaissance self-fashioning," people were using the arts of dress and poetry to invent themselves as special, as living examples of England's new rise to power in the world.

The poems below by Ben Jonson and Robert Herrick argue that a carefully dressed mistress is a work of art, but when slightly disheveled or appearing with a certain air of casualness, she is more natural and thus more attractive. These delightful poems exalting nature over art are, of course, artfully done.

BEN JONSON   (1572–1637)

Still to Be Neat, Still to Be Drest   (1609)

Still° to be neat, still to be drest,   *always*
As° you were going to a feast;   *as though*
Still to be powder'd, still perfum'd:
Lady, it is to be presum'd,
Though art's hid causes are not found,   5
All is not sweet, all is not sound.

Give me a look, give me a face,
That makes simplicity a grace;
Robes loosely flowing, hair as free:
Such sweet neglect more taketh me   10
Than all th' adulteries of art;
They strike mine eyes, but not my heart.

Robert Herrick was one of the many followers of Ben Jonson, "Sons of Ben" as they were called. Writing the way Herrick did about dress was not such an innocent matter in the 1640s, when "Delight in Disorder" was probably written. In that age of religious warfare, when the extravagantly dressed Cavaliers—followers of the king—were pitted against the more austere Puritans, Herrick's lively poem on his mistress's clothing both celebrates a Royalist's delight in finery and implicitly counters the Puritan emphasis on plainness of dress and deportment. What at first seems innocuous has strong political overtones.

ROBERT HERRICK   (1591–1674)

Delight in Disorder   (1640s)

A sweet disorder in the dress
Kindles in clothes a wantonness;
A lawn° about the shoulders thrown   thin linen cloth
Into a fine distraction;
An erring° lace, which here and there   wandering   5
Enthrals the crimson stomacher;°   embroidered vest
A cuff neglectful, and thereby
Ribands to flow confusedly;
A winning wave, deserving note,
In the tempestuous petticoat;   10
A careless shoe-string, in whose tie
I see a wild civility:
Do more bewitch me, than when art
Is too precise in every part.

Upon Julia's Clothes   (1640s)

Whenas in silks my Julia goes,
Then, then (methinks) how sweetly flows
That liquefaction of her clothes.

Next, when I cast mine eyes, and see
That brave vibration each way free,
O how that glittering taketh me!   5

Talking about the Text

1. Compare the focus of each of these poems on clothing. Does the speaker address the woman directly or merely her clothes? How does this affect your reading of the poem? How does the poet create an image of the woman if only her clothes are described?
2. What words or phrases especially stand out to you as you read Herrick's poems? How does he describe women's clothing in an original way? Examine the way that two or three specific phrases help to create vivid imagery of the women and her clothing.
3. From reading these poems on clothing, what can you conclude about Renaissance standards of female beauty?

Writing about the Text

1. Examine the words each poet uses to describe the clothing. How does clothing take on a larger significance? What characteristics does the clothing represent?
2. Herrick's "Delight in Disorder" celebrates the decorated, fancy dress in vogue with the seventeenth-century Royalists. Write a poem in response to "Delight in Disorder" from a Puritan's point of view, criticizing Herrick's aesthetic and arguing for a more restrained, conservative appearance.
3. Write an essay in which you analyze the way that Herrick's poems exhibit influences from his mentor, Ben Jonson.

Linking the Text to Other Texts

1. Compare the role of clothing in these Renaissance poems and the role of appearances in modern love songs. How much emphasis do modern songwriters put on outward appearance? What similarities and differences do you observe?
2. Find a portrait of a woman in Renaissance England and compare it to one of the poems in this section. Does the portrait represent a style of dress the poet has rejected or one that he would embrace? A good place to start is the Metropolitan Museum of Art webpage on Portraiture in Renaissance England, *http://www. metmuseum.org/toah/hd/bpor/hd_bpor.htm*. Two painters to explore are Joshua Reynolds and Nicholas Hilliard.

VIRTUAL LOCALE

Elizabethan Clothing. The Elizabethan Costuming Page at *http://costume.dm. net/* is an extensive online resource containing paintings and drawings, historical research, costume patterns, and information on every detail of clothing from lace headwear to corsets. From the paintings and drawings, you can see the transformation of clothing across different countries and social classes in the seventeenth century.

CARPE DIEM POEMS

The idea of *carpe diem*, seize the day, was a thoroughly conventional notion throughout the Renaissance. Everyone could see that life was short, and that one could have one of two opposed responses: reach for as much pleasure as possible, or live a good, restrained life in order to get to heaven. Which path a poet took in a poem depended not just on personal preferences or deep-seated beliefs but on how the poet wanted to dramatize the approach to life in the poem. That is, the poet creates a speaker or persona who states the sentiments of the poem, but the poet may not entirely believe them. For example, both of the following *carpe diem* poems were written by strongly religious poets, and it is impossible to read them simply as statements of deep-seated beliefs. It is always hard to know how seriously a poem's sentiments are meant; the poem may simply reflect a desire to try on an attitude or to give voice to a way of life. Each of these poems has become a classic statement of the *carpe diem* theme.

ROBERT HERRICK

(1591–1674)

To Virgins, to Make Much of Time

(1648)

Gather ye rosebuds while ye may,
Old Time is still a-flying;
And this same flower that smiles today,
To-morrow will be dying.

The glorious lamp of heaven, the Sun,   5
The higher he's a-getting;
The sooner will his race be run,
And nearer he's to setting.

That age is best, which is the first,
When youth and blood are warmer;   10
But being spent, the worse, and worst
Times still succeed the former.

Then be not coy, but use your time,
And while ye may, go marry;
For having lost but once your prime,   15
You may for ever tarry.

ANDREW MARVELL

(1621–1678)

To His Coy Mistress

(PUBLISHED, 1681; WRITTEN C. 1652)

Had we but world enough, and time,
This coyness, lady, were no crime.
We would sit down and think which way
To walk, and pass our long love's day;
Thou by the Indian Ganges' side   5
Shouldst rubies find; I by the tide
Of Humber° would complain. I would   *river, near where Marvell grew up*
Love you ten years before the Flood;°   *Noah's flood*
And you should, if you please, refuse
Till the conversion of the Jews.°   *just before the end of the world, in the distant future*   10
My vegetable° love should grow   *growing slowly but steadily*
Vaster than empires, and more slow.
An hundred years should go to praise
Thine eyes, and on thy forehead gaze;
Two hundred to adore each breast,   15
But thirty thousand to the rest;
An age at least to every part,
And the last age should show your heart.
For, lady, you deserve this state,
Nor would I love at lower rate.   20

But at my back I always hear
Time's winged chariot hurrying near;
And yonder all before us lie
Deserts of vast eternity.
Thy beauty shall no more be found,   25
Nor, in thy marble vault, shall sound
My echoing song; then worms shall try
That long preserv'd virginity,
And your quaint° honour turn to dust,   elegant, artificial
And into ashes all my lust.   30
The grave's a fine and private place,
But none I think do there embrace.

Now therefore, while the youthful hue
Sits on thy skin like morning dew,
And while thy willing soul transpires   35
At every pore with instant fires,
Now let us sport us while we may;
And now, like am'rous birds of prey,
Rather at once our time devour,
Than languish in his slow-chapp'd° power.   with slow-devouring jaws   40
Let us roll all our strength, and all
Our sweetness, up into one ball;
And tear our pleasures with rough strife
Thorough° the iron gates of life.   through
Thus, though we cannot make our sun   45
Stand still, yet we will make him run.

A reader can take Marvell's powerful and witty poem many ways, but the first thing to see is the division into three verse paragraphs that draws attention to its strongly "logical" structure:

If . . .

But . . .

Now, therefore . . .

How seriously is the poem meant? Critics have been pondering this question for over 300 years.

Talking about the Text

1. Renaissance poets relied heavily on figurative language, especially metaphor, for depicting love. Make a list of the metaphors used in "To His Coy Mistress." What patterns do you notice? How would you characterize the language Marvell relies on for his metaphors?
2. Discuss the nature imagery in "To Virgins, to Make Much of Time." How does Herrick use images from nature to persuade his audience to "seize the day"?
3. How do you reconcile the structured, polished nature of these poems with their message to live freely in the moment? Does the creation of such a poem seem a contradiction to its message? Why or why not?

Writing about the Text

1. Rewrite 10–12 lines of either poem using more modern language and syntax.
2. Write a response to Herrick's "To Virgins, to Make Much of Time" from the virgins' point of view or to Marvell's "To His Coy Mistress" from the mistress's point of view.
3. Discuss the tone each poet adopts in the delivery of his *carpe diem* message. How important is the speaker's tone to his persuasive message?

Linking the Text to Other Texts

1. In each of these poems, the male speaker addresses his female love using conventions that Renaissance readers would recognize and come to expect. What conventions of love in Marvell and Herrick's poems seem particular to their era? Which are still recognizable to modern readers?
2. Compare how Marvell and Herrick express the *carpe diem* message in these two poems. In what way do the poems express similar conventions? How do their messages differ?

POEMS AND MUSIC

Unlike most of the love poems in this section, those below, by Thomas Campion, were written to be sung, and Campion himself wrote lute accompaniments for them. These famous songs were known all over England as prime examples of the poet-composer's art, and playing the lute was regarded as a refined courtly accomplishment. (See the illustration of Queen Elizabeth playing the lute, in the four-color insert.) Campion was a Renaissance man—a law student, a doctor, a poet, and a musician. The sentiments in his lovely songs are typical of the era and reflect the theme of the ardent lover and cold-hearted mistress. But Campion outdoes many of his peers with his wildly imaginative and exaggerated pictures—his lady love dying and going to the Greek underground, Hades, there to meet Helen of Troy; his own passion so warm that England's rivers cannot quench it. Listen to the music versions of these selections (see Audio Locale: Thomas Campion's Ayres), noting how the gentleness of the music contrasts with the wild hyperbole of the words.

THOMAS CAMPION   (1567–1620)

When Thou Must Home to Shades of Underground   (1601)

When thou must home to shades of underground,
And there arriv'd, a new admired guest,
The beauteous spirits do engirt thee round,
White Iope,° blithe Helen,° and the rest,   *Cassiopeia, mother of Andromeda /*
To hear the stories of thy finish'd love   *Helen of Troy*   5
From that smooth tongue whose music hell can move;
Then wilt thou speak of banqueting delights,
Of masques and revels which sweet youth did make,
Of tourneys and great challenges of knights,
And all these triumphs for thy beauty's sake: 10
When thou hast told these honours done to thee,
Then tell, O tell, how thou didst murder me.

Fire, Fire, Fire, Fire   (1601)

Fire, fire, fire, fire!
Lo here I burn in such desire
That all the tears that I can strain
Out of mine idle empty brain
Cannot allay my scorching pain.   5

Come Trent° and Humber,° and fair Thames,°   *English rivers*
Dread Ocean, haste with all thy streams:
And, if you cannot quench my fire,
O drowne both mee and my desire.

Fire, fire, fire, fire!   10
There is no hell to my desire;
See, all the Rivers backward fly,
And th' Ocean doth his waves deny,
For fear my heat should drink them dry.

Come heav'nly showers then, pouring down;   15
Come, you that once the world did drown:
Some then you spar'd but now save all,
That else must burn, and with me fall.

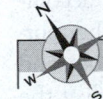

AUDIO LOCALE

Thomas Campion's Ayres. Thomas Campion was one of the most prolific poet-composers of his day, and his English lute songs, or ayres, which circulated widely during the English Renaissance, are still available in audio form today. Campion wrote all his songs for solo voice with lute accompaniment. Three classical recordings currently available on CD feature works by Campion, including "Fire, Fire, Fire, Fire": *Campion Ayres* (Harmonia Mundi, 1990); *English Ayres by Thomas Campion* (Linn, 2000); and *Elizabethan Songs* (Classical Express, 2001).

Talking about the Text

1. Both of these songs by Campion follow strict patterns of meter and rhyme. Describe both patterns. How would this structured pattern be helpful to a singer? How might it constrict a musician or singer?
2. Discuss the tone in each song. How would you describe it? Does it remain constant through the poem or does the tone change from beginning to end?
3. What is your reaction to the last line of "When Thou Must Home to Shades of Underground"? How does the poem change from the first lines to reach this climax?

Writing about the Text

1. Describe the relationship between the speaker and love in these poems. How does the speaker characterize it? In what way does he approach it? Is love considered dangerous? Fleeting? A blessing? Fickle? Constant?

2. Write a paper on the role of hyperbole, or exaggerated language, in Campion's songs. What is the desired effect? How does it strike you as a modern reader? What do you think was the appeal to Renaissance readers?

3. Why might setting a poem to music be a more successful way to distribute poetry to a Renaissance English audience? What advantages do songs have in reaching the public that a written poem does not? Discuss your ideas on this topic in a short paper.

Linking the Text to Other Texts

1. Choose a song by a contemporary singer-songwriter whose lyrics you find particularly poetic or memorable. Study the lyrics as you would a poem. How well do the lyrics stand on their own as poetry? To what extent does the songwriter use meter, rhyme, imagery, metaphor, or other poetic devices?

2. Compare the approach taken by the speaker in Campion's "When Thou Must Home to Shades of Underground" to the one in Marvell's "To His Coy Mistress." Which do you think would be more successful in moving the emotions of his love?

3. Listen to a recording of a Thomas Campion song. How does the musical accompaniment compliment or distract from the power of the words? What surprised you about the style of music?

SHAKESPEAREAN LOVE SONNETS (c. 1595)

The six poems that follow, among the richest, most finely wrought sonnets of the English Renaissance, lie firmly within the tradition of love poetry. The first four (Sonnets 18, 55, 106, 116) draw freely upon the conventions of the love poem,

Portrait of William Shakespeare, from the title page of the First Folio (London, 1623).

but were written to a young man, who has been a continued source of speculation for scholars, but who has never been identified. The remaining two (130 and 138) were written to a female but seem to take the conventions and twist them about even more than usual. (For an analysis of the sonnet form, see pp. 771–777.)

WILLIAM SHAKESPEARE   (1564–1616)

Sonnet 18: Shall I compare thee to a summer's day   (C. 1595)

Shall I compare thee to a summer's day?
Thou art more lovely and more temperate:
Rough winds do shake the darling buds of May,
And summer's lease hath all too short a date:
Sometime too hot the eye of heaven shines,   5
And often is his gold complexion dimmed,
And every fair from fair sometime declines,
By chance, or nature's changing course untrimmed:
But thy eternal summer shall not fade,
Nor lose possession of that fair thou ow'st,   10
Nor shall death brag thou wander'st in his shade,
When in eternal lines to time thou grow'st,
　　So long as men can breathe, or eyes can see,
　　So long lives this, and this gives life to thee.

✴ AUDIO LOCALE

John Gielgud Reading Shakespeare Sonnets. British actor Sir John Gielgud was considered one of the best Shakespearean stage actors of his time, as well as an acclaimed and prolific movie actor. He made his name at age twenty-nine playing Hamlet on the London stage, and by the time of his death in 2000 at age ninety-six, he had performed every major Shakespearean male leading role. To modern audiences, he is perhaps better known for his film roles, such as his Oscar-winning turn in the 1981 film *Arthur* and his portrayal of Prospero—a part he had also played on stage—in Peter Greenaway's 1991 *Prospero's Books*, a retelling of *The Tempest*. HarperAudio has made available selected recordings of Gielgud reading Shakespeare sonnets on the Internet Town Hall. To download these audio clips, go to *http://town.hall.org/radio/HarperAudio/020994_harp_ITH.html*. Sonnet 18 can be found at the end of Part 2. As you listen to Gielgud's recitation, pay particular attention to the dramatic pauses he uses, as well as what words and phrases he emphasizes.

Sonnet 55: *Not marble, nor the gilded monuments*   (C. 1595)

Not marble, nor the gilded monuments
Of princes, shall outlive this powerful rhyme;
But you shall shine more bright in these contents
Than unswept stone, besmear'd with sluttish time.
When wasteful war shall statues overturn,   5
And broils root out the work of masonry,
Nor Mars his sword, nor war's quick fire shall burn
The living record of your memory.
'Gainst death, and all oblivious enmity
Shall you pace forth; your praise shall still find room   10
Even in the eyes of all posterity
That wear this world out to the ending doom.°   *Judgment Day*
    So, till the judgment that yourself arise,
    You live in this, and dwell in lovers' eyes.

Sonnet 106: *When in the chronicle of wasted time*   (C. 1595)

When in the chronicle of wasted time°   *past*
I see descriptions of the fairest wights,°   *persons*
And beauty making beautiful old rhyme,
In praise of ladies dead and lovely knights,
Then, in the blazon of sweet beauty's best,   5
Of hand, of foot, of lip, of eye, of brow,
I see their antique pen would have express'd
Even such a beauty as you master now.
So all their praises are but prophecies
Of this our time, all you prefiguring;   10
And for they looked but with divining eyes,
They had not skill enough your worth to sing:
    For we, which now behold these present days,
    Have eyes to wonder, but lack tongues to praise.

 **A U D I O   L O C A L E**

Shakespeare Sonnets Out Loud: Sung and Spoken. The CD *When Love Speaks* (EMI Records, 2002) is an extensive collection of fifty-three Shakespeare sonnets read or sung by contemporary actors and musicians. Highlights include Annie Lennox performing "Live with Me, and Be My Love"; "Music to Hear, Why Hear'st Thou Music Sadly" set to the African beat of Ladysmith Black Mambazo; a soulful rendition of "The Quality of Mercy Is Not Strained" sung by Des'ree; "When, in Disgrace with Fortune and Men's Eyes" interpreted by Rufus Wainwright; and dramatic readings of additional sonnets by actors Joseph Fiennes, Kenneth Branaugh, Alan Rickman, and Imelda Staunton.

INSPIRATION **LOVE'S FIRE: SHAKESPEARE SONNETS FROM PAGE TO STAGE**

In 1997, seven of America's leading playwrights were commissioned to each create a one-act play inspired by a Shakespeare sonnet; the plays were then combined to become the play *Love's Fire* (published in 1998 by William Morrow). Most of the plays deal with love, sex, and relationships and include a reading of the inspirational sonnet at some point during the act. Despite their common theme, the seven acts vary widely in their study of contemporary love in the light of race, class, gender, and sexuality, and they include a wide variety of characters from high-society New Yorkers to inner-city African Americans. Eric Bogosian's *Bitter Sauce* was based on Sonnet 118, Ntosake Shange's *Hydraulics Phat Like Mean* on Sonnet 128, William Finn's *Painting You* on Sonnet 102, John Guare's *The General of Hot Desire* on Sonnets 153 and 154 (the second sonnet providing the overarching title, *Love's Fire*), and Pulitzer Prize–winners Wendy Wasserstein, Marsha Norman, and Tony Kushner based *Waiting for Philip Glass*, *140*, and *Terminating, or Lass Meine Schmerzen Nicht Verloren Sein, or Ambivalence* on Sonnets 94, 140, and 75, respectively.

Sonnet 116: *Let me not to the marriage of true minds*   (C. 1595)

Let me not to the marriage of true minds
Admit impediments. Love is not love
Which alters when it alteration finds,
Or bends with the remover to remove:
O, no! it is an ever-fixed mark,   5
That looks on tempests and is never shaken;
It is the star to every wandering bark,
Whose worth's unknown, although his height be taken.
Love's not Time's fool, though rosy lips and cheeks
Within his bending sickle's compass come;   10
Love alters not with his brief hours and weeks,
But bears it out even to the edge of doom.
     If this be error and upon me proved,
     I never writ, nor no man ever loved.

Sonnet 130: *My mistress' eyes are nothing like the sun*   (C. 1595)

My mistress' eyes are nothing like the sun;
Coral is far more red, than her lips red:
If snow be white, why then her breasts are dun;
If hairs be wires, black wires grow on her head.
I have seen roses damasked, red and white,   5
But no such roses see I in her cheeks;
And in some perfumes is there more delight
Than in the breath that from my mistress reeks.
I love to hear her speak, yet well I know
That music hath a far more pleasing sound: 10

☀ INSPIRATION   SHAKESPEARE'S SONNET 130 AND STING'S "SISTER MOON"

Pop musician Sting, holding the two Grammy awards he won in 2000 for Brand New Day—for best male pop performance and best pop album.

From his early musical days as the front man in the band the Police, Sting (Gordon Sumner) has never hesitated to incorporate literature into his songwriting. One of the band's biggest hits, "Don't Stand So Close to Me," lifted its entire narrative—about a young teacher having an affair with a much younger student—from Vladimir Nabokov's famous novel *Lolita*, referenced in the song in the lines "Just like the old man in / That book by Nabokov." Throughout an acclaimed music career—in 2000, he won a Grammy for best male pop vocal artist—that now spans four decades and several generations of fans, Sting has let other writers' and artists' work guide and even get into his own songs. This integration has always been a vital part of Sting's artistic process, as he commented in a *Pulse* magazine interview:

There aren't any original ideas, you know. The most successful song I ever wrote, "Every Breath You Take," is an aggregate of every rock song ever written, there's nothing original in it at all. It's a million songs, but it's archetypal; it doesn't sound like anybody else, it sounds like The Police. The originality comes through the band or the individual doing it, and you can get satisfaction from that. But the writing process is very mysterious, and belongs to everyone. Which is why I get so angry when I hear about court cases where people are saying, "You ripped this off me." No one, no one wrote anything in that sense, you know? Even the great classic composers took folk music and fashioned it. The other idea is just bullshit, it's just lawyers making money. No one wrote anything. I mean, there've been a lot of my songs that I can see in other people's; I turn on MTV and say, "Uh-huh, I remember that [laughs]." But I wouldn't take the time to even telephone somebody to mention it, it'd be so embarrassing. It belongs to everyone.

In more recent years, Sting's literary roots have continued to reveal themselves in prominent ways, from his 1993 album *Ten Summoner's Tales*, which owes its title and structure to Geoffrey Chaucer's *Canterbury Tales*, to his 1996 song "La Belle Dame Sans Regrets," inspired by the John Keats poem "La Belle Dame Sans Merci." His now classic 1987 album *Nothing Like the Sun* was no exception. The title phrase comes directly from Shakespeare's Sonnet 130, and that same sonnet and phrase form the foundation for the song lyrics to "Sister Moon" on the album. As Sting describes it, "In a way, the album is a reflection of my life in music. . . . if you read the liner notes, there's a list of people on there who've influenced me, from Shakespeare to Jimi Hendrix. I mean, why not? Why shouldn't an album be sort of biographical, in that sense?"

(continued on next page)

SHAKESPEARE'S SONNET 130 AND STING'S "SISTER MOON"

Sting

Sister Moon

Sister moon will be my guide
In your blue blue shadows I would hide
All good people asleep tonight
I'm all by myself in your silver light
I would gaze at your face the whole night through
I'd go out of my mind, but for you

Lying in a mother's arms
The primal root of a woman's charms
I'm a stranger to the sun
My eyes are too weak
How cold is a heart
When it's warmth that he seeks?
You watch every night, you don't care what I do
I'd go out of my mind, but for you
I'd go out of my mind, but for you

My mistress' eyes are nothing like the sun
My hunger for her explains everything I've done
To howl at the moon the whole night through
And they really don't care if I do
I'd go out of my mind, but for you

Sister Moon

I grant I never saw a goddess go,
My mistress, when she walks, treads on the ground:
    And yet by heaven, I think my love as rare,
    As any she belied with false compare.

Sonnet 138: *When my love swears that she is made of truth*

When my love swears that she is made of truth,
I do believe her though I know she lies,
That she might think me some untutored youth,
Unlearned in the world's false subtleties.
Thus vainly thinking that she thinks me young,   5
Although she knows my days are past the best,
Simply I credit her false-speaking tongue:
On both sides thus is simple truth suppressed:
But wherefore says she not she is unjust?
And wherefore say not I that I am old?   10
O! love's best habit is in seeming trust,
And age in love, loves not to have years told:
    Therefore I lie with her, and she with me,
    And in our faults by lies we flattered be.

The Balcony Scene from Romeo and Juliet

(1594–1596)

The balcony or garden scene in Act 2, Scene 2, of Shakespeare's play Romeo and Juliet *embodies Renaissance notions of love while illustrating all the conventions of the love poem. The ardent young lovers on the stage spout beautiful lines of the utmost complexity as if they were speaking naturally.*

This is the first conversation between the two young lovers, who have just met. They are from warring families, so they must avoid being observed. Romeo starts by speaking aloud, to himself; Juliet on her balcony speaks to herself before she notices Romeo. (For a modern commentary or intervention on Juliet's role in this scene, see Danitra Vance's Flotilda Williams Plays Juliet, *p. 1556.)*

SCENE 2. CAPULET'S ORCHARD.

Enter ROMEO; JULIET appears above at a window

But, soft! what light through yonder window breaks?
It is the east, and Juliet is the sun.
Arise, fair sun, and kill the envious moon,
Who is already sick and pale with grief,
That thou her maid art far more fair than she:
Be not her maid, since she is envious;
Her vestal livery is but sick and green
And none but fools do wear it; cast it off.
It is my lady, O, it is my love!
O, that she knew she were!
She speaks yet she says nothing: what of that?
Her eye discourses; I will answer it.
I am too bold, 'tis not to me she speaks:
Two of the fairest stars in all the heaven,
Having some business, do entreat her eyes
To twinkle in their spheres till they return.
What if her eyes were there, they in her head?
The brightness of her cheek would shame those stars,
As daylight doth a lamp; her eyes in heaven
Would through the airy region stream so bright
That birds would sing and think it were not night.
See, how she leans her cheek upon her hand!
O, that I were a glove upon that hand,
That I might touch that cheek!
JULIET (not seeing or hearing Romeo): Ay me!
ROMEO: She speaks:
    O, speak again, bright angel! for thou art
    As glorious to this night, being o'er my head
    As is a winged messenger of heaven
    Unto the white-upturned wondering eyes
    Of mortals that fall back to gaze on him
    When he bestrides the lazy-pacing clouds
    And sails upon the bosom of the air.
JULIET: O Romeo, Romeo! Wherefore° art thou Romeo?   *why*
    Deny thy father and refuse thy name;
    Or, if thou wilt not, be but sworn my love,
    And I'll no longer be a Capulet.

Romeo and Juliet *balcony scene, on the back cover of a promotional brochure for Margaret Mather's Chicago tour, 1883–1884.*

ROMEO: [Aside] Shall I hear more, or shall I speak at this?
JULIET: 'Tis but thy name that is my enemy;
    Thou art thyself, though not a Montague.
    What's Montague? it is nor hand, nor foot,
    Nor arm, nor face, nor any other part
    Belonging to a man. O, be some other name!
    What's in a name? that which we call a rose
    By any other name would smell as sweet;
    So Romeo would, were he not Romeo call'd,
    Retain that dear perfection which he owes
    Without that title. Romeo, doff thy name,
    And for that name which is no part of thee
    Take all myself.
ROMEO (speaking loud enough to be heard by Juliet): I take thee at thy word:
    Call me but love, and I'll be new baptized;
    Henceforth I never will be Romeo.
JULIET (hearing Romeo's voice): What man art thou that thus bescreen'd in night
    So stumblest on my counsel?

ROMEO: By a name
    I know not how to tell thee who I am:
    My name, dear saint, is hateful to myself,
    Because it is an enemy to thee;
    Had I it written, I would tear the word.
JULIET: My ears have not yet drunk a hundred words
    Of that tongue's utterance, yet I know the sound:
    Art thou not Romeo and a Montague?
ROMEO: Neither, fair saint, if either thee dislike.
JULIET: How camest thou hither, tell me, and wherefore?
    The orchard walls are high and hard to climb,
    And the place death, considering who thou art,
    If any of my kinsmen find thee here.
ROMEO: With love's light wings did I o'er-perch these walls;
    For stony limits cannot hold love out,
    And what love can do that dares love attempt;
    Therefore thy kinsmen are no let to me.
JULIET: If they do see thee, they will murder thee.
ROMEO: Alack, there lies more peril in thine eye
    Than twenty of their swords: look thou but sweet,
    And I am proof against their enmity.
JULIET: By whose direction found'st thou out this place?
ROMEO: By love, who first did prompt me to inquire;
    He lent me counsel and I lent him eyes.
    I am no pilot; yet, wert thou as far
    As that vast shore wash'd with the farthest sea,
    I would adventure for such merchandise.
JULIET: Thou know'st the mask of night is on my face,
    Else would a maiden blush bepaint my cheek
    For that which thou hast heard me speak to-night
    Fain would I dwell on form, fain, fain deny
    What I have spoke: but farewell compliment!
    Dost thou love me? I know thou wilt say 'Ay,'
    And I will take thy word: yet if thou swear'st,
    Thou mayst prove false; at lovers' perjuries
    Then say, Jove laughs. O gentle Romeo,
    If thou dost love, pronounce it faithfully:
    Or if thou think'st I am too quickly won,
    I'll frown and be perverse and say thee nay,
    So thou wilt woo; but else, not for the world.
    In truth, fair Montague, I am too fond,
    And therefore thou mayst think my 'havior light:
    But trust me, gentleman, I'll prove more true
    Than those that have more cunning to be strange.
    I should have been more strange, I must confess,
    But that thou overheard'st, ere I was ware,
    My true love's passion: therefore pardon me,
    And not impute this yielding to light love,
    Which the dark night hath so discovered.

ROMEO: Lady, by yonder blessed moon I swear
    That tips with silver all these fruit-tree tops—
JULIET: O, swear not by the moon, the inconstant moon,
    That monthly changes in her circled orb,
    Lest that thy love prove likewise variable.
ROMEO: What shall I swear by?
JULIET: Do not swear at all;
    Or, if thou wilt, swear by thy gracious self,
    Which is the god of my idolatry,
    And I'll believe thee.

INSPIRATION *ROMEO AND JULIET*: THE BALCONY SCENE, FROM STAGE TO SCREEN

Poster for West Side Story, *the film adaptation of the Broadway musical, a modernized* Romeo and Juliet *set in 1950s New York City.*

Over the centuries, the play *Romeo and Juliet* has been adapted and modernized countless times for other mediums—the musical stage, the opera, the ballet, and of course, the screen. It remains the most frequently filmed Shakespeare drama, with more than forty versions created since 1900, but several productions are notable standouts, such as George Cukor's expensive 1936 black-and-white version, produced by Irving Thalberg, and Jerome Robbins and Robert Wise's 1961 adaptation of the 1957 Broadway musical *West Side Story*, which featured music by Leonard Bernstein and re-worked the play as a racial conflict be-tween street gangs in 1950s New York City. Franco Zeffirelli's 1968 color up-date of *Romeo and Juliet* was considered ground-breaking because the two lead ac-tors were the same ages as the teenage characters they were playing—prior to that, it was believed that only adult ac-tors had the skill to play these roles. Zeffirelli's film also portrayed Romeo and Juliet nude on their wedding night. Baz Luhrmann's controversial 1996 retelling, *William Shakespeare's Romeo + Juliet*, used the fast-paced editing of modern music videos, a colorful palette, and a slick style, along with a hip,

(continued on next page)

> ### ROMEO AND JULIET: THE BALCONY SCENE FROM STAGE TO SCREEN
>
> modern soundtrack featuring techno music and songs by pop artists Des'ree, Radiohead, Garbage, and Everclear, to update the tale for current teen audiences.
>
> The balcony scene is one of the most recognized and famous scenes in *any* play, and it has been one of the linchpins in every major production of *Romeo and Juliet.* Cukor's film was rightfully praised for its lavish set, art direction, and design but was faulted because its two stars, Norma Shearer and Leslie Howard, at thirty-five and forty-five years old, were considered too old for their roles. The famous balcony scene was shot on the largest sound stage available, and this scene was given unusual prominence in the film's publicity. One 1936 newspaper headline promoting the film read, "Balcony Scene Will Be Gorgeous in *Romeo and Juliet,*" and a trailer (see Video and Virtual Locale: Trailer for Cukor's *Romeo and Juliet*) featured a clip from this scene, with the tag line "The Most Famous Scene of Stage or Screen . . . The Never-To-Be-Forgotten Balcony Scene."
>
> Robbins's *West Side Story* played the same scene in a twentieth-century urban setting to match its New York backdrop. In the rendezvous of star-crossed lovers Tony and Maria, Juliet's balcony becomes Maria's tenement fire escape. Franco Zeffirelli's film was shot on location in Italy for its lush landscapes and used Italy's Renaissance masterworks as supporting aesthetic players. The famed balcony scene was shot in the small town of Pienza, Tuscany, at the Palazzo Borghese, a sixteenth-century palace, and the balcony overlooked a dense garden. Baz Luhrmann's reimagining, set in a modern-day fictional California suburb called Verona Beach, caused a stir by setting the scene not on a balcony or in a garden, but in a blue-lit swimming pool within a courtyard of the Capulet mansion.

 **VIDEO LOCALE**

Trailer for Cukor's *Romeo and Juliet*. The Turner Classic Movies website at *http://www.turnerclassicmovies.com* offers an extensive multimedia section with video clips of scenes and trailers from classic films, including the trailer for George Cukor's 1936 version of *Romeo and Juliet*, which features the famous balcony scene.

Talking about the Text

1. Pick one of the Shakespeare sonnets and paraphrase it line by line. Compare your paraphrase to the original sonnet. What is lost when you put the sonnet in modern English?

2. How different is Shakespeare's language from modern English? What words or phrases in these Shakespeare poems strike you as particularly descriptive or powerful? What words does he frequently use that have gone out of fashion in modern English?

3. How does Shakespeare create the image of the young man in Sonnet 18? What poetic techniques does he use?
4. Every Shakespeare sonnet ends with a rhyming couplet. Study several of the sonnets and discuss the role of the ending couplet in each poem. What purpose does it seem to serve?

Writing about the Text

1. Write a journal entry on why you think Shakespeare's sonnets are still popular.
2. Write a letter to a friend, family member, or classmate explaining your approach to understanding and appreciating a Shakespeare sonnet. Think about what works best for you—reading aloud, annotating, paraphrasing line by line. You will want to "teach" a sonnet to your audience so that they can apply the same technique to any other sonnet.
3. Examine the theme of time and immortality throughout these six Shakespeare sonnets. How does writing play a role in Shakespeare's idea of immortality?

Linking the Text to Other Texts

1. Examine the many types of love expressed across these six sonnets and the balcony scene from *Romeo and Juliet*. How does Shakespeare characterize these different types of love? How different is romantic love from love in friendship? How easily could you tell the intended audience of each sonnet (lover or friend) if you were not told?
2. Compare one of Shakespeare's sonnets to Ben Jonson's "A Sonnet to the Noble Lady, the Lady Mary Wroth" (p. 955). Which do you consider the more powerful, compelling poem? Why?
3. With a partner, prepare a section of the *Romeo and Juliet* balcony scene for a dramatic reading. Discuss pacing, timing, dramatic pauses, and emphasizing key words or phrases. Then view the scene from either the 1968 film directed by Franco Zeffirelli, or the 1996 version directed by Baz Luhrmann.

VIRTUAL LOCALE

Two Versions of the *Romeo and Juliet* Balcony Scene. Fathom's website at *http://www.fathom.com* presents lectures, interviews, articles, performances, and exhibits by faculty, researchers, and curators from a consortium of cultural institutions across various disciplines and fields of study, including the American Film Institute, the British Museum, Columbia University Press, the New York Public Library, and the University of Michigan. One of the featured online learning seminars is "Romeo and Juliet: Of Its Time and of Ours," at *http://www.fathom.com/course/28701907/session3.html*, which examines the history of filmed adaptations of the play. The link *http://www.fathom.com/course/28701907/28701907_balconyPopup.html* reprints the text of the balcony scene from Shakespeare's play alongside the version from Baz Luhrmann's 1996 film version, written by Craig Pearce and Baz Luhrmann.

WOMEN'S VOICES IN THE ENGLISH RENAISSANCE

Many Renaissance women were kept from writing for diverse reasons: lack of education, opportunity, or "a room of one's own," as Virginia Woolf would put it much later in a famous series of lectures. But not all women were silenced. Some were able to overcome great obstacles and not only write but make reputations for themselves as poets. Mary Wroth and Katherine Philips are just two of the many women who wrote love poetry in the Renaissance. Both provide an important counterpoint to the dominance of the male voices. Wroth, writing early in the seventeenth century, was Sir Philip Sidney's niece and a friend and patron to Ben Jonson. Philips, writing later in the century, was well off but much less grand and had her own circle of supportive friends. Anne Bradstreet, born in England, emigrated to the American colony of Massachusetts.

Of the three women represented here, Wroth is the most traditional, writing sonnets and lyrics that connect to themes of the late 1500s. An accomplished poet, she demonstrates both easy elegance and full command of Renaissance poetic conventions. She also shows how a woman could employ exactly the same conventions as any male poet, and with the same elegant style.

LADY MARY WROTH   (1586–1640)

Lady Mary Wroth, with Archlute (*artist unknown*).

Sonnet 16: *Am I thus conquer'd? Have I lost the powers*   (1621)

Am I thus conquer'd? Have I lost the powers,
That to withstand, which joys to ruin me?
Must I be still, while it my strength devoures,
And captive leads me prisoner bound, unfree?
Love first shall [leave] mens phant'sies to them free,   5
Desire shall quench love's flames, Spring, hate sweet showers;
Love shall loose all his Darts, have sight, and see
His shame and wishings, hinder happy hours.
Why should we not loves purblind° charmes resist?   *lacking imagination or vision*
Must we be servile, doing what he list°?   *likes*   10
No, seek some host to harbour thee: I fly
Thy babish° tricks, and freedom do profess;   *babyish, childish*
But O my hurt makes my lost heart confess:
I love, and must; so farewell liberty.

Sonnet 26: *When every one to pleasing pastime hies*   (1621)

When every one to pleasing pastime hies°   *goes quickly*
Some hunt, some hawk, some play, while some delight
In sweet discourse, and music shows joy's might:
Yet I my thoughts do far above these prize.
The joy which I take is, that free from eyes   5
I sit and wonder at this day-like night,
So to dispose themselves as void of right,
And leave true pleasure for poor vanities.
When others hunt, my thoughts I have in chase;
If hawk, my mind at wished end doth fly: 10
Discourse, I with my spirit talk and cry;
While others music choose as greatest grace.
O God say I, can this fond pleasures move,
Or music be but in sweet thoughts of Love?

Sonnet 32: *How fast thou fliest, O time on loves swift wings* (1621)

How fast thou fliest, O time, on loves swift wings,
To hopes of joy, that flatters our desire:
Which to a Lover still contentment brings;
Yet when we should enjoy, thou dost retire.
Thou stay'st thy pace (false Time) from our desire   5
When to our ill thou hast'st with Eagles wings:
Slow only to make us see thy retire
Was for Despair, and harm, which sorrow brings.
O! slake thy pace, and milder pass to Love,
Be like the Bee, whose wings she doth but use   10
To bring home profit; masters good to proue,
Laden, and weary, yet again pursues.

So lade thy self with honey of sweet joy,
And do not me the Hive of Love destroy.

Sonnet 68: *My pain still smother'd in my grieved breast*   (1621)

My pain still smother'd in my grieved breast,
    Seeks for some ease, yet cannot passage find,
    To be discharged of this unwelcome guest,
    When most I strive, more fast his burthens bind.

Like to a Ship on Goodwins° cast by wind,   *site of shipwrecks* 5
    The more she strive, more deep in Sand is prest,
    Till she be lost: so am I in this kind
    Sunk, and devour'd, and swallow'd by unrest.

Lost, shipwrackt, spoiled, debar'd of smallest hope,
    Nothing of pleasure left, save thoughts have scope,   10
    Which wander may; go then my thoughts and cry:

Hope's perish'd, Love tempest-beaten, Joy lost,
    Killing Despair hath all these blessings crost;
    Yet Faith still cries, Love will not falsifi.

BEN JONSON TO HIS PATRON

A Sonnet to the Noble Lady, the Lady Mary Wroth

(PUBLISHED 1640)

I that have been a lover, and could show it,
Though not in these, in rhymes not wholly dumb,
Since I exscribe° your sonnets, am become   *copy out*
A better lover, and much better poet.
Nor is my muse, or I ashamed to owe it.   5
To those true numerous graces; whereof some,
But charme the senses, others overcome
Both brains and hearts; and mine now best do know it:
His flames, his shafts, his quiver, and his bow,
His very eyes are yours to overthrow.   10
But then his Mother's° sweets you so apply,   *Venus*
Her joys, her smiles, her loves, as readers take
For Venus Ceston,° every line you make.   *girdle, deemed an aphrodisiac*

The poems of Katherine Philips seem directly opposed to the conventions of the period, while at the same time taking their lead from them. She writes poems "against" love and marriage, yet in intimate poems to her women friends draws on the conventions of love poetry. So these poems are quite recognizably within the tradition of the Renaissance love poem, even though their theme seems to be that such love poems are inevitably false and deceptive.

KATHERINE PHILIPS   (1632–1664)

Against Love   (1664)

Hence° Cupid with your cheating toys,   *away*
Your real griefs, and painted joys,
   Your pleasure which it self destroys.
   Lovers like men in fevers burn and rave,
   And only what will injure them do crave.   5
Men's weakness makes love so severe,
They give him power by their fear,
And make the shackles which they wear.
   Who to another does his heart submit,
   Makes his own idol, and then worships it.   10
Him whose heart is all his own,
Peace and liberty does crown,
He apprehends no killing frown.
   He feels no raptures which are joys diseased,
   And is not much transported, but still pleased.   15

A Married State   (1664)

A married state affords but little ease:
The best of husbands are so hard to please.
This in wives' careful faces you may spell,
Though they dissemble their misfortunes well.
A virgin state is crowned with much content,   5
It's always happy as it's innocent.
No blustering husbands to create your fears,
   No pangs of childbirth to extort your tears,
No children's cries for to offend your ears,
Few worldly crosses to distract your prayers.   10
Thus are you freed from all the cares that do
Attend on matrimony and a husband too.
Therefore, madam, be advised by me:
Turn, turn apostate to love's levity.
Suppress wild nature if she dare rebel,   15
There's no such thing as leading apes in hell.

To My Excellent Lucasia, On Our Friendship   (1664)

I did not live until this time
Crown'd my felicity,
When I could say without a crime,
I am not thine, but thee.

This carcass breath'd, and walkt, and slept,   5
So that the world believ'd

There was a soul the motions kept;
But they were all deceiv'd.

For as a watch by art is wound
To motion, such was mine: 10
But never had Orinda found
A soul till she found thine;

Which now inspires, cures and supplies,
And guides my darkened breast:
For thou art all that I can prize,   15
My joy, my life, my rest.

No bridegroom's nor crown-conqueror's mirth
To mine compar'd can be:
They have but pieces of the earth,
I've all the world in thee.   20

Then let our flames still light and shine,
And no false fear controul,
As innocent as our design,
Immortal as our soul.

ANNE BRADSTREET   (1612–1672)

Anne Bradstreet was born in England and became a Puritan colonist in Ipswich and later Andover, Massachusetts. In 1650, her brother-in-law took some of her poems to England to have them published without her permission. The collection appeared as The Tenth Muse Lately Sprung Up in America, By a Gentlewoman of Those Parts. *All her other poems were published posthumously. Bradstreet wrote highly personal religious poetry in the Renaissance style. Here she turns to love, but her love is domestic, her husband, a topic far removed from the extravagant overflow of emotions that dominated earlier in the Renaissance.*

To My Dear and Loving Husband   (1650s)

If ever two were one, then surely we.
If ever man were loved by wife, then thee;
If ever wife was happy in a man,
Compare with me ye women if you can.
I prize thy love more than whole mines of gold,   5
Or all the riches that the East doth hold.
My love is such that rivers cannot quench,
Nor ought but love from thee give recompense.
Thy love is such I can no way repay;
The heavens reward thee manifold, I pray.   10
Then while we live, in love let's so persever,
That when we live no more we may live ever.

Talking about the Text

1. Examine the figurative language in the women's poems. What does the choice of figurative language suggest about the women's portrayal of love? How does the figurative language in the women's poetry differ from that in the men's poetry?
2. What is the greatest difference you see between Renaissance poets' conception of love and our modern ideas of it?
3. In "Against Love," the word "men" could be read as "mankind" or the male sex in particular. How does the poem change when you change your interpretation of that word? How does the gender of the poet affect your reading of the poem?

Writing about the Text

1. Many of the poems in this chapter discuss the speaker being a victim of his or her feelings of love. How does the meaning change when you take into account the poet's gender? What would it mean to a Renaissance poet to be free from the conventions of love?
2. Compare the portrait of marriage given by Anne Bradstreet to that by Katherine Philips.
3. Write your own love poem, mimicking a rhyme scheme or meter from one of this section's poems. Think about what conventions modern readers will expect from your poem and include them.

Linking the Text to Other Texts

1. Compare Ben Jonson's "A Sonnet to the Noble Lady" to one of Wroth's poems. Is there any noticeable difference between the male and female poets' subject matter? Their voices? Their language? In the speakers' approach to love? What evidence can you find that Jonson has learned from and been influenced by Wroth's poetry?
2. Compare Linda Pastan's "Marks" (p. 725) to Katherine Philips's "A Married State."
3. In both "A Married State" and "To My Excellent Lucasia," the female poet addresses another female. What differences do you notice between these poems and ones between women and men? Do these poems break away from Renaissance conventions of love poetry, or not?

❧ COMMENTARY

Virginia Woolf's *A Room of One's Own*

Virginia Woolf, c. 1928.

In 1928, British novelist and essayist Virginia Woolf set out to answer the question: why have there been so few great women writers throughout history? She spoke on the topic twice at women's colleges at Oxford University, and the resulting essay was published as *A Room of One's Own*, which furthered the idea that women need space, freedom, and financial independence if they are to create great works of art.

Although a few Renaissance women writers, such as Katherine Philips and Lady Mary Wroth, have now been rediscovered, it's important to note that as an aspiring writer Woolf grew up finding little trace of women in her literary studies. "It is a perennial puzzle," she observes, "why no woman wrote a word of that extraordinary literature [of Elizabethan England] when every other man, it seemed, was capable of song or sonnet."

This "puzzle" leads to one of Woolf's guiding questions: "what would have happened had Shakespeare had a wonderfully gifted sister, called Judith, let us say." Woolf goes on to imagine Judith's minimal schooling and heavy domestic workload as helpmate to her mother, and a forced engagement in her teens that led her to escape to London to pursue the stage. "She had the quickest fancy, a gift like her brother's, for the tune of words. Like him, she had a taste for the theatre, She stood at the stage door; she wanted to act, she said. Men laughed in her face . . . she could get no training in her craft." Woolf imagines Judith finally taken in by a stage-manager who takes advantage of her. Pregnant, poor, and hopeless, she takes her own life.

Woolf poses compelling questions about the needs of artists, and she offers many opinions on how women write, what they need, and what they offer literature that men cannot. You might want to read *A Room of One's Own*, and then ask yourself if women writers such as Katherine Philips, Anne Bradstreet, and Lady Mary Wroth fit the model Woolf suggests. For a student-oriented version complete with study guides and writing questions, see the 1995 Cambridge University Press edition of *A Room of One's Own*, edited by Jennifer Smith.

QUESTIONS FOR WRITING AND RESEARCH

1. The Campion poems in this chapter (p. 939) are not as elaborately written as those by Sidney (p. 928) or some by Shakespeare (pp. 942–950). List four differences between Campion's "When Thou Must Home" and Sidney's lines from *Astrophel and Stella*, and four differences between "Fire, Fire, Fire, Fire" and Shakespeare's Sonnet 73, "That time of year" (p. 733). (Suggestion: look at the complexity of the narrative and the number of metaphors.) What might account for Campion's relative simplicity?

2. Explain how Shakespeare's Sonnet 130 (p. 944) is a version of an "anti-love" poem, undermining all the traditional conventions. Look through the poems in this chapter and find examples of the extravagance that Shakespeare's speaker is mocking. How should one read lines 1–4 aloud? Angrily? Amusedly?

3. Describe what Wroth's sonnet "When Every One to Pleasing Pastimes Hies" (p. 954) has in common with Shakespeare's Sonnet 130 (p. 944). As one place to start, consider the way the speakers of both poems seem alone, aware of others acting normally.

4. Discuss the paradoxical role of nature in the poems on clothing (pp. 933–936) and in the *carpe diem* poems (pp. 937–939).

5. Now that you have read a good number of Renaissance love poems, write about how *Romeo and Juliet* is part of that tradition. In the selection on pp. 947–950, do the two lovers sound like other speakers in poems in this chapter? How are they different? Then consider what it means that Romeo and Juliet, two teenagers, seem to perform their love poetry as naturally as they breathe. What does this ease with the language of love poetry suggest about

how realistic Shakespeare's play is? If it's not realistic, how might we take the play?

6. In an essay, describe Wroth's poems. Explain her typical approach in a poem: the imagery, the role of the woman, the use of paradox, the dependence on the conventions of Renaissance love poetry. The small sample of Wroth's poetry in this chapter (pp. 954–955) is characteristic of her work. For more of her work, see *The Poems of Lady Mary Wroth* (Louisiana State University Press, 1983), edited by Josephine A. Roberts, and the website devoted to her, *http://www.luminarium.org/sevenlit/wroth/*.

7. Demonstrate that Andrew Marvell knew the Marlowe and Raleigh *carpe diem* poems. Use two sources of information: your own research into biographical information, and internal evidence from the poems themselves (pp. 930–932 and pp. 937–938). For instance, should they all be performed the same way, in similar tones of voice?

8. This passage by feminist literary critic Wendy Furman-Adams explains why students of women's roles in Renaissance literature need to read poems by men. Respond to the question at the end of the selection.

> Important male writers such as Petrarch, Shakespeare, Spenser, and Milton are central to the story of writing women in the Renaissance. Why? They are central because of the way literature both reflects and, in turn, influences—even reinvents—life. Due in part to social factors, in part to the power of their vision, these male poets have indelibly shaped the way men have imagined and represented women, as well as the way countless female readers have imagined and represented themselves. Thus, even when writing for others of their own sex, women must write in response to male voices, male pens, male images of female identity.
>
> Some recent critics have argued, in fact, that if people write history, they are also "written" by it. Each of our lives, they say, is a kind of fiction, written in collaboration with the social forces that shape our lives. And, especially in the early modern period, those forces tended to privilege the male perspective. The Renaissance was a period of enormous change and upheaval, in which a relatively unified and stable medieval world-view gave way to what would become the Enlightenment. It was a period in which men (at least an elite of outstanding and privileged men) were involved actively in a reconstruction of identity, a reconstruction Stephen Greenblatt has called "Renaissance self-fashioning." Women, too, were engaged in this "self-fashioning" enterprise—but with a difference. Less free to begin the enquiry from "scratch," they engaged in the process under the jealous eye of a patriarchal society which saw them, essentially, as passive members—valued above all, as critic Suzanne Hull has noted, for three traditional virtues: chastity, obedience, and silence. Even as they wrote, then (and many did write), they were also "being written"—by male writers, and yet more profoundly by the social conventions that shaped both male and female roles.
>
> We need to read each text—closely and with open minds—in order to see the extent to which Renaissance writers, male and female, were "written" by the context in which they wrote; and to see, conversely, the extent to which they managed to "re-write," or "refashion" themselves and one another. Different writers will reveal a different mix of freedom and constraint, originality and

conventionality, patriarchal bias and impulse toward gender equality. Our verdict will differ, I suspect, from writer to writer, from text to text—and from person to person.

Are the poems by Wroth and Philips and Bradstreet in some sense "written" by the men who preceded them as love poets? If so, what part has been "written"? The form? The imagery? The roles for women? What parts seem original to you, different from the men's poems? (One potential complexity: Ben Jonson in "A Sonnet to the Noble Lady" (p. 955) claims to have learned a good deal about love poetry from reading Wroth's poems; he may just be flattering his patron, but he does raise the possibility that women's poems influenced the men's too.)

9. The violence and early death in the Renaissance made *carpe diem* a serious option. Do research on how *carpe diem* was understood in the seventeenth century in general, and specifically in these poems. Is it merely a kind of rhetorical exercise, as it has often seemed to readers of "To His Coy Mistress" (pp. 937–938)? Or does it present a genuine choice? Or might there be something in between?

10. With the exception of Bradstreet's, the poetry in this chapter was scorned by Puritans, who found it basically immoral. Through library research, determine what specific qualities in this poetry were most offensive to Puritans. Focus on tones and attitudes as well as themes and individual lines.

11. Examine more poems by Katherine Philips, who used the language of love poetry to write to her coterie of devoted female friends. She was so good at this that her poetry is featured prominently at a major website for lesbian poetry: *http://www.sappho.com/poetry/k_philip.html.* What is the case for Philips being an appropriate poet for Sappho.com?

CHAPTER

17

A MOMENT IN POETRY

Writing Out Loud
Popular Victorian Narratives

Essayist, scientist, and Harvard professor of paleontology Stephen Jay Gould, writing of an exhibit at the Baseball Hall of Fame in Cooperstown, New York, pointed to a problem he once had with poetry:

> I could never understand why such abominable and silly doggerel as "Casey at the Bat" ever became the canonical poem of both American baseball and the normalcy of failure in general. That is, until I heard the poem in an ancient film of a vaudeville performer (as the Victor disc also in this exhibition illustrates). Then I understood. The poem was written to be declaimed, not to be read silently. Declamation of poetry in the nineteenth century represented a standard social recreation in American life, a fixture of nearly every party, and the doggerel succeeds marvelously in this intended aural context.

Gould is right: some poems that seem very weak on the page change character completely when they are treated like the performances they were intended to be. His example, "Casey at the Bat," comes alive only when it is delivered aloud, and in fact, hammed up. The DeWolfe Hopper performance Gould refers to may now sound way over the top, but that kind of exaggeration is what made the poem succeed with audiences in late nineteenth-century America.

What Gould calls "declamation" of poetry means a formal oral delivery to an audience, often of something memorized. (This is also called "recitation.") Declamation was extremely popular 150 years ago, in an era when tragic, patriotic, or romantic tales were narrated not just in short stories but in poetry, and when public performances of literature were a common part of life. Today, by far the most common form of poetry is **lyric**, defined as a relatively brief poem that captures a feeling or evokes an intense personal response. But lyric poetry's almost complete dominance is relatively recent. **Narratives**, or poems that told stories, once played a much larger role.

Every educated person in the West once knew about the most ambitious of narratives: epics such as Homer's *Iliad* and *Odyssey*, Virgil's *Aeneid*, and Milton's *Paradise Lost*. Such poems were a key part of Western culture, built into education in schools and religion. Other famous narratives include Chaucer's *Canterbury Tales*—a mix of different poetic types, ranging from high art to folk stories—and his *Troilus and Criseyde*, a narrative romance set during the Trojan War. These famous and popular poems, often meant for public performance, all told stories, attempting to capture readers' and listeners' attention in the days before novels began to dominate. As novels became popular, beginning around the middle of the eighteenth century, the reading public's interest in narrative poems gradually declined, so that at present they are relatively rare, though not quite extinct. But in the mid-nineteenth century, when such poems were very much in style, huge numbers of people got their stories not from novels but out loud, through listening to narrative poetry.

VICTORIAN NARRATIVES TIMELINE

1798	The British navy, led by Admiral Horatio Nelson, defeats the French in the Battle of the Nile in northern Egypt, restoring British power in the Mediterranean.
1823	"A Visit from St. Nicholas" published anonymously in the Troy, New York, *Sentinel*.
1835	Letitia Elizabeth Landon publishes "The Proud Ladye."
1842	Edgar Allan Poe reads his poetry at a paid appearance, with poor attendance.
1842	Robert Browning publishes "My Last Duchess."
1842	Alfred Lord Tennyson writes "Ulysses."
1845	Edgar Allan Poe achieves international fame with the publication of *The Raven and Other Poems*.
1848	Italy begins a war of independence that inspires Elizabeth Barrett Browning to write "Mother and Poet."
1854	During the Crimean War, the British army leads a misguided attack on Russian forces in the Battle of Balaklava, which Tennyson would immortalize in "The Charge of the Light Brigade" (1855).
1855	Walt Whitman publishes the first version of *Leaves of Grass*.

1856	Henry Wadsworth Longfellow writes "The Wreck of the Hesperus."
1860	Elizabeth Barrett Browning's "Poems before Congress" published to criticism of being "hysterical" and "unwomanly."
1865	President Lincoln's assassination leads Walt Whitman to write "O Captain! My Captain!"
1888	Ernest Thayer's "Casey at the Bat" published in the *San Francisco Examiner*. DeWolfe Hopper starts reciting the poem onstage.

POETRY'S ORAL BEGINNINGS

In the nineteenth-century English-speaking world, literature still celebrated its oral character—its roots in sound. Poets had always been the bearers of a tribe's or nation's cultural capital. Homer's great epics, *The Iliad* and *The Odyssey*, were created for oral performance and perhaps only written down many years afterwards. Roman poets often wrote their work, but they usually read it aloud; a famous scene depicted in many paintings has Virgil reading his *Aeneid* aloud to his patron, Emperor Augustus Caesar. In medieval times, Norse and Anglo-Saxon poets would recite epics or songs they had composed, as well as others they had memorized. *Beowulf* is such a production, probably written down long after it was composed for recitation. Narrative poems had a tradition of being long, telling a dramatic story, and favoring oral performance.

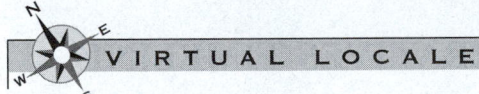

VIRTUAL LOCALE

Aural Poetry on the Web. Continual advancements in Web technology have made it easier for audio clips to be readily available online. Consequently, the number of audio poetry resources on the Internet has increased exponentially.

- The Academy of American Poets' Listening Board offers over 150 audio clips of poets reading their poems: http://www.poets.org/audio.php.
- A personal homepage includes audio poetry links from over 475 poets: http://www.Laurable.com.
- The *Atlantic* magazine provides a "Soundings" page, offering audio clips of a famous poem read by three or four different poets: http://www.theatlantic.com/unbound/poetry/soundings/.
- The BBC's *Poetry Out Loud* page offers poets reading their own work: http://www.bbc.co.uk/arts/poetry/outloud/index.shtml.

POETRY READINGS AT HOME

Nineteenth-century writers, aware of a time when poetry was central to the life of a tribe, clan, or royal court, were comfortable with a key site of oral performance: the family reading. Before the movies, radio, TV, and recordings that we have now, entertainment was live. In the Victorian era, people went out to hear lectures or readings or musical and theatrical performances, or they entertained each other at home, either with members of the family or with invited guests. Sometimes the father or mother would sit, family gathered around, and read the Bible or devotional works. At times, fiction was read, though strict Christians often frowned on novels as tending toward the immoral. Often there would be poetry, frequently a long narrative poem. Children might be called on to recite poems they had learned, or a poem might be read aloud, not recited. Many newspapers published a daily poem. Most of the few Emily Dickinson poems published in her lifetime appeared in a local newspaper.

Countless pictures of the time illustrate the scene of a middle-class, Victorian family gathered around the reader, listening raptly to the words of the poem or story. We don't have to take this scene as universal, of course—many people were too poor or too illiterate to enjoy such readings—but it was certainly seen as commonly enacted, and perhaps even more often wished for.

Writers were particularly attuned to this type of performance at home. Byron and Shelley read their work aloud to each other and to their circle of friends. Tennyson gave readings of his poems to his friends and family. Henry Wadsworth Longfellow celebrates this type of reading in his *Wayside Inn*, where each individual traveler recites a tale, one of which is Paul Revere's ride ("One if by land, and two if by sea, / And I on the opposite shore will be . . ."). The Brownings— Elizabeth Barrett and her husband Robert—were known to read their work to each other. These and other poets wrote for the eye and the ear alike, knowing that a major way for the public to learn their work would be through hearing it.

PROFESSIONAL AUTHORS
ON THE STAGE

Another type of performance began when professional authors gave public readings, at first for charity benefits but soon as a paying proposition. One of the first to try, Edgar Allan Poe, read his poems to a paying audience in Boston in 1842, but with poor results. Charles Dickens, much impressed with Poe when they met, offered readings of his own and, unlike Poe, made a great success of it. Between 1858 and 1870, Dickens gave some 500 readings throughout England and America, cashing in on the tremendous popularity of his novels. These readings were spectacularly successful affairs, filling auditoriums, theaters, and opera houses in cities and towns throughout Britain and America and providing Dickens with a rich monetary reward. Here was the most famous novelist in the world, appearing nearby, reading from his most popular works. And he was good at it! Dickens always had a talent and a passion for amateur theatricals, and he would thoroughly practice his readings, watching himself in a mirror. He did not possess a rich voice, but critics observed that he had a great ability to emote and express. Dickens's readings paid off handsomely, and they allowed him to indulge in his desire to reach a live audience. During the time of his reading tours, he also wrote *A Tale of Two Cities* and *Great Expectations*, though the demands of his work and the incessant travel damaged his health.

Many other famous nineteenth-century poets and fiction authors toured with readings of their works, among them Harriet Beecher Stowe (author of *Uncle Tom's Cabin*), James Whitcomb Riley (who had great success with Hoosier dialect poetry),

Mark Twain on stage during one of his lecture tours, 1885.

and of course Mark Twain, whose tours were extremely popular. These are in addition to the many writers who got paid for their lectures and lecture tours, as did Henry David Thoreau and, especially, Ralph Waldo Emerson, who made a living as a lecturer and whose lectures were later published as essays. Walt Whitman toured with his popular lecture on Abraham Lincoln, which he always ended by reciting from memory "O Captain! My Captain!" (p. 998)—a poem much more suitable for declaiming from the stage than his much longer, more complex requiem for Lincoln, "When Lilacs Last in the Dooryard Bloom'd" (pp. 861–866). Whitman claimed to detest "O Captain," but he always recited it at his lectures.

Poetry was also presented in a mix of lecture and performance by forerunners of stand-up comics. These humorists were called "wits," and their one-man shows involved topical humor combined with certain set-piece stories, which later were collected in popular books. Twain got his start on the lecture circuit this way, before he became truly famous for *Tom Sawyer* and *Huckleberry Finn*. Additionally, there were music hall and stage performers whose specialty was reciting a particular piece. One of the most well-known of these was DeWolfe Hopper, who declaimed Ernest L. Thayer's poem "Casey at the Bat" all around the country, appearing on a varied bill that offered singers, comics, jugglers, trapeze artists, and animal acts. It's useful to remember that poetry and declamation were not thought of as refined arts; they were part of mainstream or popular culture, and they might even appear in some decidedly odd venues.

 INSPIRATION MODERN POETRY OUT LOUD: FROM THE BEATS TO *DEF POETRY*

The poetry readings in Victorian lecture halls and family drawing rooms may seem like a distant echo of a quaint but long-gone past that bears no resemblance to poetry's role in today's fast-paced age. But even in the wake of flashier entertainments that compete for our attention—television, films, music, the Internet, video games—the tradition of reading poetry out loud has not disappeared. It has actually made a major resurgence in the public consciousness over the past half-century.

During the 1950s and 1960s, poetry's oral tradition was carried on by Beat poets like Allen Ginsberg, who famously performed "Howl" for the first time in 1955 at

(continued on next page)

MODERN POETRY OUT LOUD: FROM THE BEATS TO *DEF POETRY*

Hip-hop producer Russell Simmons (in front of microphone) and the cast of Simmons's Broadway hit Def Poetry Jam, *accept their 2003 Tony Award in the special theatrical event category.*

San Francisco's Six Gallery, and musicians like Bob Dylan, who is still regarded by many as a poet who sets his poems to music. A great example of spoken-word mixed with music is Dylan's 1965 "Subterranean Homesick Blues"; a clip of what might be called an early music-video version of the song appears in D. A. Pennebaker's 1967 documentary about Dylan's 1965 tour of England, *Don't Look Back*. In the 1970s and 1980s, spoken-word was integrated into both the hard-core and punk music scenes by artists like Patti Smith and Black Flag's Henry Rollins, as well as into the rap and hip-hop movements that dominate the music scene in America today.

In more recent years, "poetry slams" have become a well-known outlet for performed poetry. In a slam, poets recite their own work and are then judged by the audience based not only on what they say but how well they perform it. Since 1985, when Chicagoan Marc Smith jumpstarted a reading series, now called the Uptown Poetry Slam, first at a jazz club and then at the Green Mill Cocktail Lounge, slams have grown in popularity and frequency. Events like the annual slam hosted by Poetry Slam, Inc., have been organized in cities and towns across the country.

The wild success of hip-hop producer Russell Simmons's *Def Poetry* project, which Simmons started in 2001, has brought poetry out loud to a larger, younger audience, through its long, successful run as a live Broadway show, *Def Poetry Jam*, and the corresponding television series on HBO, *Russell Simmons Presents Def Poetry*. The Broadway show gathered a troupe of nine slam poets and one DJ for performances of their work. The ongoing TV version, hosted by hip-hop artist and actor Mos Def, presents a wide range of poetic voices—both newcomers and more seasoned performers—in front of a live audience, interspersed with guest appearances by celebrities trying their hand at spoken-word poetry. Special guests have included comedian Dave Chapelle, dancer Savion Glover, playwright Eve Ensler, actress Phylicia Rashad, Motown icon Smokey Robinson, R&B sensations Alicia Keyes and John Legend, and hip-hop artists Kanye West, Lauryn Hill, and Wyclef Jean.

PROFESSIONAL READERS

English actress Sarah Siddons in the character of the Tragic Muse, 1812; Siddons traveled as a professional performer and reader of poetry.

One more group of performers deserves attention, the well-known stage performers of the nineteenth century who made a practice of offering "readings" to audiences, frequently with a mix of "uplifting" material like Shakespeare along with popular Victorian poems. The English actress Sarah Siddons, for instance, traveled around Great Britain offering evenings of Shakespeare. Siddons, with a famous stage career behind her, specialized in readings in which she presented some popular Shakespeare scenes (taking on male as well as female roles) and poems like "The Charge of the Light Brigade." Her niece Fanny Kemble, from the same well-regarded family of performers, gave a series of readings in America, concentrating on Shakespeare but also including contemporary verse by Henry Wadsworth Longfellow. Longfellow attended one of her readings in Boston, along with 3,000 other people, and wrote a poem in commemoration of how well she read (p. 987).

V I D E O   L O C A L E

Fooling with Words with Bill Moyers. Bill Moyers's 1999 PBS documentary *Fooling with Words*, directed by Catherine Tatge and produced by Judy Doctoroff O'Neill and Judith Davidson Moyers, captures the energy of America's largest poetry festival and interviews dozens of contemporary American poets on the meaning and power of poetry. For more information, see the PBS website at *http://www.pbs.org/wnet/foolingwithwords/main_tv.html*.

ELOCUTION

The nineteenth-century craze for performance fit in nicely with a very old and still potent strand in American and British education, the part of rhetoric known as "elocution," which stresses pronunciation, stage bearing, and delivery. Much of this training in the nineteenth century took place outside of schools; many cities and towns had private teachers of elocution who offered lessons to improve a person's ability to orate or declaim in public, since those skills were very highly valued. Many books were written on the subject, explaining how to memorize a passage or poem, how to prepare the voice, and how to enhance the performance through appropriate body gestures. In his 1902 book *The Popular Elocutionist and Reciter*, J. E. Carpenter wrote:

> LOVE must be approached with the utmost delicacy; it is best expressed by a deep, impassioned, fervent tone; the right hand may be pressed over the heart, but the "languishing eyes" recommended by some authors borders too closely on burlesque. A steady, respectful gaze on the assumed object of affection may be permitted.

As Carpenter suggests, the line between sincerity and burlesque was easy to cross. By the end of the nineteenth century, elocutionists had become figures of some ridicule, stressing as they did the outward manifestations of character and personality. George Bernard Shaw's 1893 play *Pygmalion*, later transformed into *My Fair Lady* on Broadway, has as its hero a fussy, proud elocutionist, Henry Higgins, who transforms a working-class waif into a fine English lady by changing her speech patterns. Elocutionists may have been slightly ludicrous with their promises of verbal makeovers, but they were important nonetheless. Their craft later became fixed in the school subject of "oral interpretation of literature," still playing an active role in many departments of communication, both in training aspiring actors and giving students the confidence and skills to speak in public.

THE PUBLIC'S CHOICE

What stories and poems were most popular? It's no surprise to learn that what worked best were simple, dramatic narratives with suspense and melodrama. Dickens had great success with his most straightforward set pieces, such as *A Christmas Carol*. Whitman's simplest, least characteristic poem, "O Captain! My Captain!" was his most popular. The most complex, subtle writings of Longfellow didn't have the attraction of his simpler narratives like "The Song of Hiawatha."

Robert Browning's experience in reading many of his poems aloud to family and friends led him to write a good many to be declaimed or acted, especially the ones he called "dramatic monologues" such as "My Last Duchess" (pp. 992–993). These were enormously popular at the time, and the Browning Society was established so his fans could discuss his poetry and have an opportunity to declaim it in front of other admirers. At the first Browning Society meeting in 1881, in London, over 300 people attended and a number gave readings. One was Eleanor Marx—daughter of Karl Marx and herself a literary translator—who read two Browning poems, "Count Gismond" and "The Pied Piper of Hamelin."

The Victorians, highly influenced by sentimental dramas, responded well to stories of shipwrecks and train crashes, with the subsequent heroism and tragic loss of life. The death of children was another common theme in Victorian poetry, since childhood was such a dangerous time of infections and accidents. One of Dickens's most famous scenes is the overly sentimental "death of Little Nell" from *The Old Curiosity Shop*, a favorite with certain of his readers but the target of barbs from less sentimental types. As Oscar Wilde put it, "It takes a heart of stone not to laugh at the death of Little Nell."

Finally, we must acknowledge two paradoxes. First, the poems chosen most frequently for public performance are some of the most famous poems ever written, cultural touchstones that generations have grown up with, yet since they are "popular" poetry, often written for declamation and performance, they are often overlooked or dismissed by critics. Some of these poems, whether performed or read silently, are superb works of art, while others are incomplete or inadequate without performance. Second, narrative poems might be out of fashion, but performance of poetry is back with us today and is perhaps more important than ever. As the poet Donald Hall wrote in 1985, the poetry reading is by far the most common form of "publication" for a poem nowadays. Many more people hear poems aloud than actually buy and read books of poetry. Consequently, the nineteenth-century concept of poetic performance has once again come round in popularity. On any given night in most large cities, there are poetry readings, slams, and performances at colleges, bookshops, bars and cafes, churches, and theater auditoriums. The way more and more people get their poetry is out loud.

VICTORIAN NARRATIVE POEMS

A few of the most popular nineteenth-century narrative poems are included here. They would have been known widely in the Victorian era and recited by amateurs and professionals alike. (The "Starting Points for Further Research" sections for poets in this chapter appear after their respective biographies in Chapter 19.)

CLEMENT CLARKE MOORE   (1779–1863)

The son of an Episcopal bishop who was president of Columbia University, Clement Clarke Moore was a member of New York City's upper crust. Moore graduated from Columbia in 1798 and donated some of his land holdings in Manhattan's Chelsea neighborhood to help found the General Theological Seminary, where he served as a professor of oriental and ancient languages. (Next to the seminary is Clement Clarke Moore Park.) Moore's major scholarly work is a two-volume Hebrew lexicon published in 1809. But Moore is best known for "A Visit from St. Nicholas," a poem first published anonymously in the Troy, New York, Sentinel in 1823. Besides its obvious cultural significance—it helped establish some of the Christmas mythology still observed today—the poem is interesting for the way it plays with the "elevated" language of epic poetry, as in these lines:

> *As dry leaves that before the wild hurricane fly,*
> *When they meet with an obstacle, mount to the sky,*
> *So up to the house-top the coursers they flew,*
> *With the sleigh full of toys, and St. Nicholas too.*

In these two couplets, Moore makes use of Homeric language and an extended simile. He also uses deflation: "coursers" is a decidedly fancy or high word for horses, while "toys" is very much not high-flown language or imagery.

A Visit from St. Nicholas   (1822)

'Twas the night before Christmas,
when all through the house
Not a creature was stirring,—not even a mouse;
The stockings were hung by the chimney with care,
In hopes that St. Nicholas soon would be there.   5
The children were nestled all snug in their beds,
While visions of sugar-plums danced in their heads;
And mamma in her 'kerchief, and I in my cap,
Had just settled down for a long winter's nap,
When out on the lawn there arose such a clatter,   10
I sprang from the bed to see what was the matter.
Away to the window I flew like a flash,
Tore open the shutters and threw up the sash.
The moon on the breast of the new-fallen snow
Gave the lustre of mid-day to objects below,   15
When, what to my wondering eyes should appear,
But a miniature sleigh, and eight tiny reindeer,
With a little old driver, so lively and quick,
I knew in a moment it must be St. Nick.
More rapid than eagles his coursers they came,   20
And he whistled, and shouted, and called them by name;
"Now, DASHER! now, DANCER! now, PRANCER and VIXEN!
On, COMET! on CUPID! on, DONDER and BLITZEN!
To the top of the porch! to the top of the wall!
Now dash away! dash away! dash away all!"   25
As dry leaves that before the wild hurricane fly,
When they meet with an obstacle, mount to the sky,
So up to the house-top the coursers they flew,
With the sleigh full of toys, and St. Nicholas too.
And then, in a twinkling, I heard on the roof   30
The prancing and pawing of each little hoof.
As I drew in my hand, and was turning around,
Down the chimney St. Nicholas came with a bound.
He was dressed all in fur, from his head to his foot,
And his clothes were all tarnished with ashes and soot;   35
A bundle of toys he had flung on his back,
And he looked like a peddler just opening his pack.
His eyes—how they twinkled! his dimples how merry!
His cheeks were like roses, his nose like a cherry!
His droll little mouth was drawn up like a bow,   40
And the beard of his chin was as white as the snow;
The stump of a pipe he held tight in his teeth,
And the smoke it encircled his head like a wreath;
He had a broad face and a little round belly,
That shook, when he laughed like a bowlful of jelly.   45
He was chubby and plump, a right jolly old elf,
And I laughed when I saw him, in spite of myself;

A wink of his eye and a twist of his head,
Soon gave me to know I had nothing to dread;
He spoke not a word, but went straight to his work,   50
And filled all the stockings; then turned with a jerk,
And laying his finger aside of his nose,
And giving a nod, up the chimney he rose;
He sprang to his sleigh, to his team gave a whistle,
And away they all flew like the down of a thistle.   55
But I heard him exclaim, ere he drove out of sight,
"HAPPY CHRISTMAS TO ALL, AND TO ALL A GOOD-NIGHT."

In Moore's poem we see the literary imagination actually inventing customs that would later become popular. His poem helped create the legend, but in 1822 that legend was still in the making, and fairly far from our own current mythology around Santa Claus. Note some oddities here: St. Nick is called just that, not Santa Claus. He is small, an "elf" with a "miniature sleigh and eight tiny reindeer." And he uses the old-fashioned expression "Happy Christmas" rather than "Merry Christmas." Rather than the modern-day Santa, he looks like an old New York Dutchman, not unlike the figures Washington Irving wrote about at the time, such as Rip Van Winkle. Interestingly, the legend continues to evolve: the politically incorrect fur suit and the pipe he smokes persisted in the tradition until fairly recently.

ERNEST L. THAYER   (1863–1940)

Like Clement Clarke Moore, Ernest Thayer was a blueblood who never thought of himself as a poet, and he too is now famous for a single poem that he never took much credit for in his lifetime. He was born in Lawrence, Massachusetts, and studied philosophy under William James at Harvard, where he and George Santayana were co-editors of Harvard's humor magazine, the Lampoon. William Randolph Hearst, who also worked on the Lampoon, recruited Thayer to write a humor column for his paper, the San Francisco Examiner, where "Casey at the Bat" appeared under a pseudonym in June 1888. Thayer, who never thought much of his poetry, eventually returned to Massachusetts to run his family's textile business.

"Casey at the Bat" became a success through the efforts of DeWolfe Hopper, who made a career of performing it on stage, doing so some 10,000 times, beginning in a New York theater in August 1888. He recorded it in 1907. Hopper had the genius to declaim the poem in a brogue, in keeping with the Irish names that dominate the Mudville team. Professional baseball in 1888 had working-class roots and was associated more with poor, recent immigrants than with long-term Americans.

The high and low elements that characterized "A Visit from St. Nicholas" are present here as well, as in these lines:

So upon that stricken multitude, grim melancholy sat;
for there seemed but little chance of Casey getting to the bat.

The elevated language of "stricken multitude" and the inversion of "grim melancholy sat" suggest that we are in a poem that moves in a wide range from the very elevated to the very low, given its topic. It's a familiar genre called the mock heroic, in which everyday or minor events are treated like the struggles of the mighty heroes of old.

Casey at the Bat

(1888)

The outlook wasn't brilliant for the Mudville nine that day:
The score stood four to two, with but one inning more to play.
And then when Cooney died at first, and Barrows did the same,
A sickly silence fell upon the patrons of the game.

A straggling few got up to go in deep despair. The rest   5
Clung to that hope which springs eternal in the human breast.
They thought "If only Casey could but get a whack at that—
We'd put up even money now, with Casey at the bat."

But Flynn preceded Casey, as did also Jimmy Blake,
And the former was a lulu, while the latter was a cake;   10
So upon that stricken multitude grim melancholy sat;
For there seemed but little chance of Casey's getting to the bat.

But Flynn let drive a single, to the wonderment of all.
And Blake, the much despisèd, tore the cover off the ball;
And when the dust had lifted, and men saw what had occurred,   15
There was Jimmy safe at second and Flynn a-hugging third.

Then from five thousand throats and more there rose a lusty yell;
It rumbled through the valley, it rattled in the dell;
It knocked upon the mountain and recoiled upon the flat;
For Casey, mighty Casey, was advancing to the bat.   20

There was ease in Casey's manner as he stepped into his place;
There was pride in Casey's bearing and a smile on Casey's face.
And when, responding to the cheers, he lightly doffed his hat,
No stranger in the crowd could doubt 'twas Casey at the bat.

Ten thousand eyes were on him as he rubbed his hands with dirt;   25
Five thousand tongues applauded when he wiped them on his shirt.
Then, while the writhing pitcher ground the ball into his hip,
Defiance gleamed in Casey's eye, a sneer curled Casey's lip.

And now the leather-covered sphere came hurtling through the air,
And Casey stood a-watching it in haughty grandeur there.   30
Close by the sturdy batsman the ball unheeded sped –
"That ain't my style," said Casey. "Strike one." the umpire said.

From the benches, black with people, there went up a muffled roar,
Like the beating of the storm-waves on a stern and distant shore.
"Kill him! Kill the umpire!" shouted some one on the stand;   35
And it's likely they'd have killed him had not Casey raised his hand.

With a smile of Christian charity, great Casey's visage shone,
He stilled the rising tumult; he bade the game go on.
He signaled to the pitcher, and once more the spheroid flew;
But Casey still ignored it, and the umpire said, "Strike two."   40

"Fraud!" cried the maddened thousands, and echo answered fraud;
But one scornful look from Casey and the audience was awed.
They saw his face grow stern and cold, they saw his muscles strain,
And they knew that Casey wouldn't let that ball go by again.

The sneer is gone from Casey's lip, his teeth are clenched in hate;   45
He pounds with cruel violence his bat upon the plate.
And now the pitcher holds the ball, and now he lets it go,
And now the air is shattered by the force of Casey's blow.

Oh, somewhere in this favored land the sun is shining bright;
The band is playing somewhere, and somewhere hearts are light.   50
And, somewhere men are laughing, and little children shout;
But there is no joy in Mudville—mighty Casey has struck out.

Talking about the Text

1. How familiar were you with "A Visit from St. Nicholas" before you read it here? Do you remember hearing it read or reading it yourself? What parts were well-known to you? What was a surprise? How has the image and myth of "St. Nick" changed from Moore's depiction?
2. Try reading "A Visit from St. Nicholas" or "Casey at the Bat" aloud. What elements make the poem a successful oral narrative? What words and phrases stand out when read aloud? What effect do the meter, rhythm, and rhyme scheme have when the poem is read aloud?
3. Stephen Jay Gould makes a distinction between poems that are made to be read on the page and poems made to be performed. Now that you have read either "A Visit from St. Nicholas" or "Casey at the Bat" aloud, what are clues that this is a poem made to be performed?

Writing about the Text

1. Write a short analysis of the point of view in "A Visit from St. Nicholas." Who is the speaker? What do you know about him? Why do you think Moore chose to show St. Nicholas from this perspective? How would the poem be different if the point of view was a child's?
2. Write an imitation of Moore's poem about a holiday tradition of your own, or write an imitation of Thayer's poem using a sports event you know about. Try to mimic the original poet's rhyme and rhythm patterns as closely as possible to create a poem that has strong oral characteristics.

Linking the Text to Other Texts

1. Popular narratives like "A Visit from St. Nicholas" and "Casey at the Bat" are frequent targets of parodists. Find a parody of either poem and compare it to the original. What elements in particular does the parody derive its humor from? What elements of the original poem are clearly visible and what elements are new? What do you think is the appeal of parodying "A Visit from St. Nicholas" or "Casey at the Bat"?
2. Moore's poem has done much to further our contemporary mythology of Santa Claus and Christmas rituals. But what is the origin of the character Moore helped create? Research the original Saint Nicholas and write a paper that places Moore's creation in a historical context. What can you assume Moore knew about Saint Nicholas when he wrote his poem?

FELICIA HEMANS (1793–1835)

In her short lifetime, British writer Felicia Hemans became one of the most famous poets of her era, but after her death she was quickly forgotten and even now, when many excellent women poets of the past are being rediscovered, she is known only for a few poems, above all "Casabianca." As a young child, Hemans read and recited large amounts of poetry; her sister noted that she could "repeat pages of poetry from her favorite authors, after having read them but once over." She was precocious, publishing her first book of poems at age fourteen.

Many of her subjects were patriotic and involved death in battle. "Casabianca" recounts a well-known story from the Battle of the Nile, where the British navy defeated the French in 1798. Casabianca, the thirteen-year-old son of the French commander of L'Orient, received orders to stay at his post until his father relieved him. Unaware that his father had been killed, he did so, remaining until the ship exploded. This enormously popular poem celebrates unthinking devotion, duty, and bravery; it has also come to stand as a symbol for the whole nineteenth-century genre of declamatory poetry.

Casabianca (1829)

The boy stood on the burning deck
    Whence all but he had fled;
The flame that lit the battle's wreck
    Shone round him o'er the dead.

Yet beautiful and bright he stood,   5
    As born to rule the storm;
A creature of heroic blood,
    A proud, though childlike form.

The flames roll'd on—he would not go
    Without his father's word;   10
That father, faint in death below,
    His voice no longer heard.

He called aloud: "Say, Father, say
    If yet my task is done?"
He knew not that the chieftain lay   15
    Unconscious of his son.

"Speak, Father!" once again he cried,
    "If I may yet be gone!"
And but the booming shots replied,
    And fast the flames rolled on.   20

Upon his brow he felt their breath,
    And in his waving hair,
And looked from that lone post of death
    In still, yet brave despair.

And shouted but once more aloud,   25
    "My father! must I stay?"
While o'er him fast, through sail and shroud,
    The wreathing fires made way.

They wrapt the ship in splendour wild,
    They caught the flag on high,   30
And streamed above the gallant child,
    Like banners in the sky.

There came a burst of thunder sound—
    The boy—oh! where was he?
Ask of the winds that far around   35
    With fragments strewed the sea!—

With mast, and helm, and pennon fair,
    That well had borne their part,
But the noblest thing which perished there
    Was that young faithful heart   40

 INSPIRATION ELIZABETH BISHOP RESPONDS TO FELICIA HEMANS

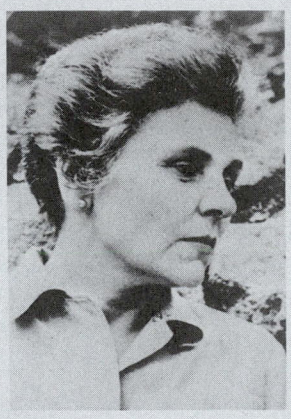

"Casabianca" quickly became one of the most popular poems for declamation. All over Great Britain, Canada, and America, young students labored to memorize it, then nervously stood to recite it aloud at school or family occasions. Elizabeth Bishop's witty response to Hemans's poem compares a lover to that nervous boy, standing with "stammering elocution," trying to say what matters most. Bishop's wit also involves the notion of "burning," since lovers are traditionally depicted in poetry as aflame. Being in love, Bishop's poem asks us to imagine, is like being the boy in "Casabianca."

Elizabeth Bishop   (1911–1979)

Casabianca   (1946)

Love's the boy stood on the burning deck
trying to recite "The boy stood on
the burning deck." Love's the son
    stood stammering elocution
      while the poor ship in flames went down.

Love's the obstinate boy, the ship,
even the swimming sailors, who
would like a schoolroom platform, too
    or an excuse to stay
      on deck. And love's the burning boy.

Talking about the Text

1. What is the meter of Hemans's "Casabianca"? What are the common characteristics of this kind of meter, and how successful is it in "Casabianca"?
2. How do you judge the boy's actions? Do you consider him patriotic? Obedient? Naive?
3. What emotions does Hemans's poem draw on for its impact?

Writing about the Text

1. The Battle of the Nile would have been well-known to Hemans's readers. Research the 1798 battle and its importance in British history. Then write a short analysis of the poem that places the poem in its historical context.
2. Write a paper that argues the extent to which Hemans's "Casabianca" should be considered a patriotic poem. What qualities of character does the boy display that patriots might aspire or relate to?

Linking the Text to Other Texts

1. Compare Hemans's "Casabianca" to Elizabeth Barrett Browning's "Mother and Poet" (pp. 994–996).
2. In a short paper, analyze Elizabeth Bishop's "Casabianca" as a response to Hemans's poem.

LETITIA ELIZABETH LANDON   (1802–1838)

The poetry of Letitia Elizabeth Landon, like the work of her contemporary Felicia Hemans, sold enormous quantities during her short lifetime and then fell out of fashion. Written for reading as well as for performance, "The Proud Ladye" takes the form of a medieval ballad and is full of archaisms, deliberately old-fashioned terms and style. What is unusual about it is its reversal of the common resolution: in this medieval setting, the fair maiden fails to win the brave knight.

The Proud Ladye   (1825)

Oh, what could the ladye's beauty match,
An° it were not the ladye's pride?   *if*
An hundred knights from far and near
Woo'd at that ladye's side.

The rose of the summer slept on her cheek,   5
Its lily upon her breast,
And her eye shone forth like the glorious star
That rises the first in the west.

There were some that woo'd for her land and gold,
And some for her noble name,   10
And more that woo'd for her loveliness;
But her answer was still the same.

"There is a steep and lofty wall,
Where my warders° trembling stand;   *guards*
He who at speed shall ride round its height,   15
For him shall be my hand."

Many turn'd away from the deed,
The hope of their wooing o'er;
But many a young knight mounted the steed
He never mounted more.   20

At last there came a youthful knight,
From a strange and far countrie,
The steed that he rode was white as the foam
Upon a stormy sea.

And she who had scorn'd the name of love,   25
Now bow'd before its might,
And the ladye grew meek as if disdain
Were not made for that stranger knight.

She sought at first to steal his soul
By dance, song, and festival;   30
At length on bended knee she pray'd
He would not ride the wall.

But gaily the young knight laugh'd at her fears,
And flung him on his steed,—
There was not a saint in the calendar   35
That she pray'd not to in her need.

She dar'd not raise her eyes to see
If heaven had granted her prayer,
Till she heard a light step bound to her side,—
The gallant knight stood there!   40

And took the ladye Adeline
From her hair a jewell'd band,
But the knight repell'd the offer'd gift,
And turn'd from the offer'd hand.

"And deemest thou that I dared this deed,   45
Ladye, for love of thee?
The honour that guides the soldier's lance
Is mistress enough for me.

"Enough for me to ride the ring,
The victor's crown to wear;   50
But not in honour of the eyes
Of any ladye there.

"I had a brother whom I lost
Through thy proud crueltie,
And far more was to me his love,   55
Than woman's love can be.

"I came to triumph o'er the pride
Through which that brother fell,
I laugh to scorn thy love and thee,
And now, proud dame, farewell!"   60

And from that hour the ladye pined,
For love was in her heart,
And on her slumber there came dreams
She could not bid depart.

Her eye lost all its starry light,   65
Her cheek grew wan and pale,
Till she hid her faded loveliness
Beneath the sacred veil.

And she cut off her long dark hair,
And bade the world farewell,   70
And she now dwells a veiled nun
In Saint Marie's cell.

Talking about the Text

1. How is love represented, by both the ladye and the knight, in Landon's "The Proud Ladye"?
2. What is the meaning of the word "proud" in the title? How is pride characterized in the poem?
3. How is the ladye's experience of love described in the poem? What effect do the knight's words have on her?

Writing about the Text

1. Examine the techniques Landon uses to characterize the proud ladye. Choose two to three techniques—such as metaphor, simile, imagery, diction—and write an essay that comes to a conclusion about how she is portrayed.
2. Write a paper that examines the conventions of courtship and love suggested by Landon's poem. How does the ladye represent a rejection of these conventions? What does the knight represent in relation to these conventions? What does the poem suggest about the costs of deviating from traditional norms of love and courtship?

Linking the Text to Other Texts

1. Compare "The Proud Ladye" to one poem in the "Women's Voices in the English Renaissance" section in Chapter 16 (pp. 953–959).
2. Compare "The Proud Ladye" to another ballad, Longfellow's "The Wreck of the Hesperus." What makes these poems ballads? What do the two poems have in common? How do they use meter and rhyme to tell a story? Which poem do you think displays a more effective use of the form?
3. Compare and contrast the way that three poets in this chapter use figurative language to describe female characters in their poems.

EDGAR ALLAN POE   (1809–1849)

One of the most famous American poems, "The Raven," by Edgar Allan Poe, is also one of the most parodied, as a quick Web search will reveal. In his essay "The Philosophy of Composition" (p. 983), Poe gave an account of how he wrote the poem, though like all of Poe's accounts it should not be taken as gospel. Existing in a number of versions, "The Raven" became extraordinarily popular upon publication and remains so today. The first version of "The Raven" appeared in the American Review *in 1845. The version included here was published in the* Richmond Semi-Weekly Examiner *on September 25, 1849. For other versions, see the website of the Edgar Allan Poe Society of Baltimore, http://www.eapoe.org.*

Illustration from the 1884 edition of The Raven and Other Poems, *illustrated by renowned artist Gustave Doré.*

The Raven   (1845; 1849)

Once upon a midnight dreary, while I pondered, weak and weary,
Over many a quaint and curious volume of forgotten lore—
While I nodded, nearly napping, suddenly there came a tapping,
As of some one gently rapping, rapping at my chamber door—
" 'Tis some visitor," I muttered, "tapping at my chamber door—   5
    Only this and nothing more."

Ah, distinctly I remember it was in the bleak December;
And each separate dying ember wrought its ghost upon the floor.
Eagerly I wished the morrow;—vainly I had sought to borrow
From my books surcease of sorrow—sorrow for the lost Lenore—   10
For the rare and radiant maiden whom the angels name Lenore—
    Nameless here for evermore.

(Text continues after color insert)

Visual Literacy
and Popular Narratives

Witnessing poems read out loud is a richly rewarding experience. For centuries the custom of reading poems aloud was not only a major source of entertainment but also a way of preserving these narratives and passing them to the next generation. After years in which the custom languished, readings, poetry slams, recitations, and performance poetry are thriving. The images here were chosen to explore how the oral tradition has been visualized throughout centuries.

Cover for Woody Guthrie's *Bound for Glory* (1943)

Singer-songwriter Woody Guthrie's account of his Dust Bowl years, Bound for Glory, *was published in 1943. Many of Guthrie's lyrics critiqued political and social policies of his time, and his considerable influence on poets and songwriters continues today. The copy of* Bound for Glory *shown here belongs to Bob Dylan and was part of an exhibit given by the Experience Music Project in Seattle in 2004. Guthrie had a profound influence on Dylan's words and music.*

READING THE IMAGE. Describe the images on the cover of *Bound for Glory*. Does the cover convey an optimistic point of view? Explain.

LINKING IMAGE TO TEXT. In *Bound for Glory*, Woody Guthrie writes: "My eyes has been my camera taking pictures of the world and my songs has been my messages that I tried to scatter across the back sides and along the steps of the fire escapes and on the window sills and through the dark halls." Choose a poem from Chapter 17 and either support or refute how Guthrie's quote is applicable to the point of view put forth by the author of the poem.

Homer, Chaucer, and Performed Poetry

Despite the dominance of short, lyric poems as the most common form of verse today, long narrative poems—and the corresponding tradition of reading or performing them out loud—have played a central role throughout Western literary history. From Greek epics like Homer's Iliad and Odyssey to the Aeneid by Roman poet Virgil to 14th-century English poet Geoffrey Chaucer's Canterbury Tales to the popular Victorian narrative poems gathered in Chapter 17, a wealth of well-known and popular poetic works through the ages were written with public performance in mind and were intentionally driven by story-telling in order to maintain the audience's attention. The custom of performing narrative poetry is illustrated in the three images gathered here.

Guillaume Lethiere (1760–1832), *Homer Singing His* Iliad *at the Gates of Athens*

Richard Houston (1721–1775), *Poetry,* an aquatint

Chaucer Reading His Poems to the Court of Richard II of England,
an image from an illuminated manuscript

READING THE IMAGES. Western literature's landmark works are deeply rooted in the oral tradition as shown in these illustrations. Study the members of the audience in each work. What emotions do they show? Evaluate the setting in each. How does it contribute to the ideas the artists want to communicate to their audience?

LINKING IMAGES TO TEXT. Choose a poem in Chapter 17 and sketch out in words how you would depict it visually. Consider the time period you would use, the costumes, the setting, and the cast of characters.

Poetry in Performance—From the Beats to the Present: Poets Gregory Corso, Ted Joans, and Patti Smith

The Beat movement of the 1950s gave renewed life to the oral poetry tradition. Beat poets Gregory Corso and Ted Joans (pictured below and on the facing page, respectively), both published poets with several books to their names, gave dramatic performance readings in clubs and coffee houses in New York City and San Francisco. The performance readings of poet and musician Patti Smith (pictured on the page after the photo of Ted Joans), started in the 1970s, and she continues to perform today, mixing the spoken word and song. The "Reading the Images" and "Linking Images to Text" questions for these three images follow the photograph of Patti Smith.

Beat writer Gregory Corso (1930–2001)
on a stairway at the Seven Arts Cafe in New York City in 1959

Ted Joans (1928–2003), another Beat writer,
at a 1959 poetry reading at the Bizarre coffee house, also in New York

Singer and performance poet Patti Smith (b. 1946)
performing onstage during the 1970s

READING THE IMAGES. Study the details in the photographs of poets Gregory
Corso, Ted Joans, and Patti Smith, and describe the atmosphere the photographs
depict. Pay special attention to the performative aspects. Speculate on how the
Beat audiences compare with the audiences of Homer's time. Consider gender
and socioeconomic bracket as well as religious and ethnic background.

LINKING IMAGES TO TEXT. Select a poem from Chapter 17 and choose music
to be played as part of a public reading of the poem. Explain why the music
enhances appreciation of the poem.

Poetry Out Loud: National Poetry Recitation Contest

Created by the National Endowment for the Arts and the Poetry Foundation in partnership with State Arts Agencies, the Poetry Out Loud program encourages high school students to study poetry through memorization and performance. State and national competitions are held every year with the winning finalists receiving scholarship aid. Students recite and perform classic and contemporary poems, reinventing a practice from Homer's day.

Shuqiao Song recites a Sylvia Plath poem
at the Poetry Out Loud finals in Washington, DC

Craig B. Williams recites a poem by Theodore Roethke at the Poetry Out Loud finals in Washington, DC

READING THE IMAGES. Craig B. Williams, from Florida, read Theodore Roethke's "I knew a woman" and Shuqiao Song read Sylvia Plath's "Fever 103." Locate copies of the two poems. After reading them, speculate on how the students performed their readings from studying the photographs.

LINKING IMAGES TO TEXT. Choose a poem from Chapter 17 and sketch out how you would recite it in front of a group.

And the silken, sad, uncertain rustling of each purple curtain
Thrilled me—filled me with fantastic terrors never felt before;
So that now, to still the beating of my heart, I stood repeating, 15
" 'Tis some visitor entreating entrance at my chamber door—
Some late visitor entreating entrance at my chamber door;—
    This it is and nothing more."

Presently my soul grew stronger; hesitating then no longer,
"Sir," said I, "or Madam, truly your forgiveness I implore; 20
But the fact is I was napping, and so gently you came rapping,
And so faintly you came tapping, tapping at my chamber door,
That I scarce was sure I heard you"—here I opened wide the door;—
    Darkness there and nothing more.

Deep into that darkness peering, long I stood there wondering, fearing, 25
Doubting, dreaming dreams no mortal ever dared to dream before;
But the silence was unbroken, and the stillness gave no token,
And the only word there spoken was the whispered word, "Lenore?"
This I whispered, and an echo murmured back the word, "Lenore!"—
    Merely this and nothing more. 30

Back into the chamber turning, all my soul within me burning,
Soon again I heard a tapping somewhat louder than before.
"Surely," said I, "surely that is something at my window lattice;
Let me see, then, what thereat is, and this mystery explore—
Let my heart be still a moment and this mystery explore;— 35
    'Tis the wind and nothing more!"

Open here I flung the shutter, when, with many a flirt and flutter,
In there stepped a stately Raven of the saintly days of yore;
Not the least obeisance made he; not a minute stopped or stayed he;
But, with mien of lord or lady, perched above my chamber door— 40
Perched upon a bust of Pallas just above my chamber door—
    Perched, and sat, and nothing more.

Then this ebony bird beguiling my sad fancy into smiling,
By the grave and stern decorum of the countenance it wore,
"Though thy crest be shorn and shaven, thou," I said, "art sure no craven, 45
Ghastly grim and ancient Raven wandering from the Nightly shore—
Tell me what thy lordly name is on the Night's Plutonian shore!"
    Quoth the Raven "Nevermore."

Much I marvelled this ungainly fowl to hear discourse so plainly,
Though its answer little meaning—little relevancy bore; 50
For we cannot help agreeing that no living human being
Ever yet was blest with seeing bird above his chamber door—
Bird or beast upon the sculptured bust above his chamber door,
    With such name as "Nevermore."

But the Raven, sitting lonely on the placid bust, spoke only 55
That one word, as if his soul in that one word he did outpour.
Nothing further then he uttered—not a feather then he fluttered—
Till I scarcely more than muttered "Other friends have flown before—
On the morrow he will leave me, as my hopes have flown before."
    Then the bird said "Nevermore." 60

Startled at the stillness broken by reply so aptly spoken,
"Doubtless," said I, "what it utters is its only stock and store
Caught from some unhappy master whom unmerciful Disaster
Followed fast and followed faster till his songs one burden bore—
Till the dirges of his Hope that melancholy burden bore   65
    Of 'Never—nevermore.' "

But the Raven still beguiling my sad fancy into smiling,
Straight I wheeled a cushioned seat in front of bird, and bust and door;
Then, upon the velvet sinking, I betook myself to linking
Fancy unto fancy, thinking what this ominous bird of yore—   70
What this grim, ungainly, ghastly, gaunt and ominous bird of yore
    Meant in croaking "Nevermore."

This I sat engaged in guessing, but no syllable expressing
To the fowl whose fiery eyes now burned into my bosom's core;
This and more I sat divining, with my head at ease reclining   75
On the cushion's velvet lining that the lamp-light gloated o'er,
But whose velvet violet lining with the lamp-light gloating o'er,
    She shall press, ah, nevermore!

Then, methought, the air grew denser, perfumed from an unseen censer
Swung by Seraphim whose foot-falls tinkled on the tufted floor.   80
"Wretch," I cried, "thy God hath lent thee—by these angels he hath sent thee
Respite—respite and nepenthe, from thy memories of Lenore;
Quaff, oh quaff this kind nepenthe and forget this lost Lenore!"
    Quoth the Raven "Nevermore."

"Prophet!" said I, "thing of evil!—prophet still, if bird or devil!—   85
Whether Tempter sent, or whether tempest tossed thee here ashore,
Desolate yet all undaunted, on this desert land enchanted—
On this home by Horror haunted—tell me truly, I implore—
Is there—is there balm in Gilead?—tell me—tell me, I implore!"
    Quoth the Raven "Nevermore."   90

"Prophet!" said I, "thing of evil—prophet still, if bird or devil!
By that Heaven that bends above us—by that God we both adore—
Tell this soul with sorrow laden if, within the distant Aidenn,
It shall clasp a sainted maiden whom the angels name Lenore—
Clasp a rare and radiant maiden whom the angels name Lenore."   95
    Quoth the Raven "Nevermore."

"Be that word our sign in parting, bird or fiend!" I shrieked, upstarting—
"Get thee back into the tempest and the Night's Plutonian shore!
Leave no black plume as a token of that lie thy soul hath spoken!
Leave my loneliness unbroken!—quit the bust above my door!   100
Take thy beak from out my heart, and take thy form from off my door!"
    Quoth the Raven "Nevermore."

And the Raven, never flitting, still is sitting, still is sitting
On the pallid bust of Pallas just above my chamber door;
And his eyes have all the seeming of a demon's that is dreaming,   105

And the lamp-light o'er him streaming throws his shadow on the floor;
And my soul from out that shadow that lies floating on the floor
    Shall be lifted—nevermore!

108

COMMENTARY

Poe on the Composition of "The Raven"

From "The Philosophy of Composition," first published in Graham's Magazine, *April 1846*

I had gone so far as the conception of a Raven—the bird of ill omen—monotonously repeating the one word, "Nevermore," at the conclusion of each stanza, in a poem of melancholy tone, and in length about one hundred lines. Now, never losing sight of the object—supremeness, or perfection, at all points, I asked myself—"Of all melancholy topics, what, according to the universal understanding of mankind, is the most melancholy?" Death—was the obvious reply. "And when," I said, "is the most melancholy of topics most poetical?" From what I have already explained at some length, the answer, here also, is obvious—"When it most closely allies itself to beauty: the death, then, of a beautiful woman is, unquestionably, the most poetical topic in the world—and equally is it beyond doubt that the lips best suited for such a topic are those of a bereaved lover."

 **LITERARY LOCALE**

Edgar Allan Poe Historical Sites. Several eastern cities, including Baltimore, Philadelphia, and New York, all claim historical sites related to poet Edgar Allan Poe. For more information, visit the websites listed here.

- Edgar Allan Poe Museum in Richmond, Virginia, *http://www.poemuseum.org.*
- Edgar Allan Poe Society in Baltimore, Maryland, *http://www.eapoe.org/balt/ poebalt.htm.*
- National Historic Site of Edgar Allan Poe in Philadelphia, Pennsylvania, *http://www.nps.gov/edal.*

Among Poe's most popular poems for recitation was "Annabel Lee," written about the death of a beautiful woman, which Poe considered "unquestionably, the most poetical topic in the world."

Annabel Lee

(1849)

It was many and many a year ago,
    In a kingdom by the sea,
That a maiden there lived whom you may know
    By the name of ANNABEL LEE;
And this maiden she lived with no other thought
    Than to love and be loved by me.

5

I was a child and she was a child,
    In this kingdom by the sea,
But we loved with a love that was more than love-
    I and my Annabel Lee—   10
With a love that the winged seraphs of Heaven
    Coveted her and me.

And this was the reason that, long ago,
    In this kingdom by the sea,
A wind blew out of a cloud, chilling   15
    My beautiful Annabel Lee;
So that her highborn kinsman came
    And bore her away from me,
To shut her up in a sepulchre
    In this kingdom by the sea.   20

The angels, not half so happy in Heaven,
    Went envying her and me:—
Yes! that was the reason (as all men know,
    In this kingdom by the sea)
That the wind came out of the cloud by night,   25
    Chilling and killing my Annabel Lee.

But our love it was stronger by far than the love
    Of those who were older than we
Of many far wiser than we
    And neither the angels in Heaven above   30
Nor the demons down under the sea
    Can ever dissever my soul from the soul
Of the beautiful Annabel Lee:—

For the moon never beams without bringing me dreams
    Of the beautiful Annabel Lee;   35
And the stars never rise but I feel the bright eyes
    Of the beautiful Annabel Lee:
And so all the night-tide, I lie down by the side
Of my darling, my darling, my life and my bride
    In the sepulchre there by the sea—   40
    In her tomb by the sounding sea.

VIDEO LOCALE

Poe and the *American Masters* Series. PBS's *American Masters* film series includes an episode on the life and career of Edgar Allan Poe. For more
information on the series and how to order the video, go to the PBS
American Masters website at *http://www.pbs.org/wnet/americanmasters/database/
poe_e.html.*

Talking about the Text

1. Take one stanza of Edgar Allan Poe's "The Raven" and paraphrase it in your own words. Then compare your paraphrase to the original. What is unique about Poe's diction? His syntax (word order)? His use of rhyme and rhythm?
2. Make a list of the allusions in the poem, such as the bust of Pallas and night's "Plutonian shore." What is the meaning of these allusions? What sources does Poe draw his allusions from and why?
3. How does Poe set the tone in the opening lines of "The Raven" and foreshadow his trademark suspense?

Writing about the Text

1. Pick three major symbols in "The Raven" and analyze them.
2. Write an explication of the structure of "The Raven." How is the storyline set up? How does Poe use the refrain? How does the poem create rising tension, and where is the climax?

Linking the Text to Other Texts

1. Compare Poe's depiction of love in "Annabel Lee" with Robert Browning's in "My Last Duchess."
2. The dramatization of death is seen in many of the poems in this chapter, from the death of a young woman in Poe's "Annabel Lee" to the death of sons in Elizabeth Barrett Browning's "Mother and Poet" and Felicia Hemans's "Casabianca" to the death of anonymous troops in Tennyson's "The Charge of the Light Brigade." Compare and contrast the way that two poems in this chapter dramatize death.
3. In a letter to a friend, Elizabeth Barrett Browning gives the following interpretation of "The Raven":

> There is certainly a power—but does not appear to me the natural expression of a sane intellect in whatever mood; and I think that this should be specified in the title of the poem. There is a fantasticalness about the "sir or madam," and things of the sort, which is ludicrous, unless there is a specified insanity to justify the straws. Probably he—the author—intended it to be read in the poem, and he ought to have intended it.

Browning is vague about her evidence—"the 'sir or madam' and things of the sort." Examine the poem for evidence that supports or refutes Browning's reading.

HENRY WADSWORTH LONGFELLOW   (1807–1882)

America's most revered poet of the nineteenth century was Henry Wadsworth Longfellow, a master of the narrative poem. During his lifetime he was famous for "Paul Revere's Ride," "Hiawatha," and many others. But when narratives fell out of fashion, so did Longfellow. His poem "The Building of the Ship" is a narrative about the construction of an oceangoing vessel in a New England shipyard (Longfellow was from Portland, Maine), but the vessel also stood as a metaphor for the ship of state, and this widely recited poem was commonly regarded as a strong argument for all the states to remain united during the troubled days before the Civil War.

From *The Building of the Ship*   (1850)

Thou, too, sail on, O Ship of State!
Sail on, O Union, strong and great!
Humanity with all its fears,
With all the hopes of future years,   380
Is hanging breathless on thy fate!
We know what Master laid thy keel,
What Workmen wrought thy ribs of steel,
Who made each mast, and sail, and rope,
What anvils rang, what hammers beat,   385
In what a forge and what a heat
Were shaped the anchors of thy hope!
Fear not each sudden sound and shock,
'Tis of the wave and not the rock;
'Tis but the flapping of the sail,   390
And not a rent made by the gale!
In spite of rock and tempest's roar,
In spite of false lights on the shore,
Sail on, nor fear to breast the sea!
Our hearts, our hopes, are all with thee,   395
Our hearts, our hopes, our prayers, our tears,
Our faith triumphant o'er our fears,
Are all with thee,—are all with thee!

 INSPIRATION FANNY KEMBLE'S READING
                                AND LONGFELLOW'S
                                SONNET

An entry in Longfellow's diary recounts his excitement following a poetry reading by the stage performer Fanny Kemble:

> February 12, 1850. In the evening Mrs. [Fanny] Kemble read before the Mercantile Library Association, to an audience of more than three thousand, portions of *As You Like It*; then *The Building of the Ship*, standing out upon the platform, book in hand, trembling, palpitating and weeping, and giving every word its true weight and emphasis. She prefaced the recital by a few words, to this effect; that when she first saw the poem, she desired to read it before a Boston audience; and she hoped she would be able to make every word audible to that great multitude.

(continued on next page)

FANNY KEMBLE'S READING AND LONGFELLOW'S SONNET

Longfellow was so moved by Kemble's reading that he wrote the following poem as an homage:

Sonnet on Mrs. Kemble's Reading from Shakespeare (1850)

O precious evenings! all too swiftly sped!
Leaving us heirs to amplest heritages
Of all the best thoughts of the greatest sages,
And giving tongues unto the silent dead!
How our hearts glowed and trembled as she read,
Interpreting by tones the wondrous pages
Of the great poet who foreruns the ages,
Anticipating all that shall be said!
O happy Reader! having for thy text
The magic book, whose Sibylline° leaves have caught   *prophetic*
The rarest essence of all human thought!
O happy Poet! by no critic vext!
How must thy listening spirit now rejoice
To be interpreted by such a voice!

One impulse behind this poem might come from the fact that Longfellow had been criticized heavily and sharply by Poe and Whitman, so he no doubt appreciated a "straight" reading, not by an interfering critic but by an artistic interpreter who saw herself simply as the transmitter of his work. His title seems to praise Kemble for her reading of Shakespeare, but there is no doubt that Longfellow admired her way with his own poem as well.

As one late-nineteenth century writer noted about Kemble's Boston performance,

the vast multitude was stirred to its depths not so much by the artistic completeness of the rendition, as by the impassioned burst with which the poem closes, and which fell upon no listless ears in the deep agitation of the eventful year 1850. Mr. Noah Brooks in his paper on *Lincoln's Imagination* (*Scribner's Monthly*, August, 1879) mentions that he found the President one day attracted by these stanzas, quoted in a political speech. "Knowing the whole poem," he adds, "as one of my early exercises in recitation, I began, at his request, with the description of the launch of the ship, and repeated it to the end. As he listened to the last lines, his eyes filled with tears, and his cheeks were wet. He did not speak for some minutes, but finally said, with simplicity: 'It is a wonderful gift to be able to stir men like that.'"

One of Longfellow's most often recited (and oft-parodied) poems is based on a well-known shipwreck that, like Poe's "Annabel Lee," involves the death of a beautiful young woman.

The Wreck of the Hesperus (1856)

It was the schooner Hesperus,
    That sailed the wintry sea;
And the skipper had taken his little daughter,
    To bear him company.

Blue were her eyes as the fairy-flax, 5
    Her cheeks like the dawn of day,
And her bosom white as the hawthorn buds,
    That ope° in the month of May.   *open*

The skipper he stood beside the helm,
    His pipe was in his mouth, 10
And he watched how the veering flaw did blow
    The smoke now West, now South.

Then up and spake an old Sailor,
    Had sailed the Spanish Main,°   *in the Caribbean*
"I pray thee, put into yonder port, 15
    for I fear a hurricane.

"Last night, the moon had a golden ring,
    And to-night no moon we see!"
The skipper, he blew whiff from his pipe,
    And a scornful laugh laughed he. 20

Colder and louder blew the wind,
    A gale from the Northeast,
The snow fell hissing in the brine,
    And the billows frothed like yeast.

Down came the storm, and smote amain 25
    The vessel in its strength;
She shuddered and paused, like a frighted steed,
    Then leaped her cable's length.

"Come hither! come hither! my little daughter,
    And do not tremble so; 30
For I can weather the roughest gale
    That ever wind did blow."

He wrapped her warm in his seaman's coat
    Against the stinging blast;
He cut a rope from a broken spar, 35
    And bound her to the mast.

"O father! I hear the church bells ring,
    Oh say, what may it be?"
"Tis a fog-bell on a rock bound coast!"—
    And he steered for the open sea. 40

"O father! I hear the sound of guns,
 Oh say, what may it be?"
Some ship in distress, that cannot live
 In such an angry sea!"

"O father! I see a gleaming light.   45
 Oh say, what may it be?"
But the father answered never a word,
 A frozen corpse was he.

Lashed to the helm, all stiff and stark,
 With his face turned to the skies,   50
The lantern gleamed through the gleaming snow
 On his fixed and glassy eyes.

Then the maiden clasped her hands and prayed
 That saved she might be;
And she thought of Christ, who stilled the wave,   55
 On the Lake of Galilee.

And fast through the midnight dark and drear,
 Through the whistling sleet and snow,
Like a sheeted ghost, the vessel swept
 Tow'rds the reef of Norman's Woe.°   reef near Gloucester, Mass. 60

And ever the fitful gusts between
 A sound came from the land;
It was the sound of the trampling surf
 On the rocks and hard sea-sand.

The breakers were right beneath her bows,   65
 She drifted a dreary wreck,
And a whooping billow swept the crew
 Like icicles from her deck.

She struck where the white and fleecy waves
 Looked soft as carded wool,   70
But the cruel rocks, they gored her side
 Like the horns of an angry bull.

Her rattling shrouds, all sheathed in ice,
 With the masts went by the board;
Like a vessel of glass, she stove and sank,   75
 Ho! ho! the breakers roared!

At daybreak, on the bleak sea-beach,
 A fisherman stood aghast,
To see the form of a maiden fair,
 Lashed close to a drifting mast.   80

The salt sea was frozen on her breast,
 The salt tears in her eyes;
And he saw her hair, like the brown seaweed,
 On the billows fall and rise.

Such was the wreck of the Hesperus,
In the midnight and the snow!
Christ save us all from a death like this,
On the reef of Norman's Woe!

Longfellow set his poem as a ballad, deliberately employing archaic diction ("Blue were her eyes as the fairy flax") and an almost fairy-tale simplicity in order to create a timeless quality. It worked then, making this one of his most popular poems. It was so popular, in fact, that to this day some say of a messy house or room, "It looks like the wreck of the Hesperus."

RUDYARD KIPLING (1865–1936)

Rudyard Kipling was born in India in 1865, to a British family. Educated in England, Kipling returned to India at seventeen, where he worked as a journalist. He went on to become one of the most popular writers in English, in both prose and verse, in the late 19th and early 20th centuries. Today, he is perhaps best remembered for his popular children's books, including The Jungle Book (1894), The Second Jungle Book (1895), and Just So Stories (1902). He also wrote a novel, Kim (1901), many poems, "The Road to Mandalay" (1890), "Gunga Din" (1890), "If—" (1895), and "Recessional" (1897) among them; and short stories, including "The Man Who Would Be King" (1888). Most of his early and most famous works were written in the U.S., in Brattleboro, Vermont, where Kipling moved after he married, but they are set in India, and Kipling remains the most famous writer to be associated with Britain's imperial rule over the Indian subcontinent. He returned to live in England permanently in 1902. Five years later, in 1907, Kipling was the first English language writer to receive the Nobel Prize for Literature. He was also offered the British poet laureateship and a knighthood, which he refused. He died in 1936 and his remains are buried in Westminster Abbey.

Besides his gift for narration, Kipling is noted for his moralistic verse, which served his reputation well in the late 1800s but has not worn well in the late twentieth or twenty-first centuries. His poems, though accomplished, are now regarded as too didactic and unsubtle. Still, they attract those who wish to stir their audiences with rousing verse that tells good stories. They are excellent for declamation and are frequently featured in contests.

Recessional[1] (1897)

God of our fathers, known of old,
Lord of our far-flung battle-line,
Beneath whose awful Hand we hold
Dominion over palm and pine—
Lord God of Hosts, be with us yet,
Lest we forget—lest we forget!°   *Deuteronomy 6.21*

---

[1] Hymn ending church service. This poem was written for Queen Victoria's Diamond Jubilee, a celebration of the Queen's status as the longest-reigning monarch of the British empire.

The tumult and the shouting dies
    The Captains and the Kings depart:
Still stands Thine ancient sacrifice,
    An humble and a contrite heart.°   *paraphrase of Psalm 51.17*
Lord God of Hosts, be with us yet,
Lest we forget—lest we forget!

Far-called, our navies melt away;
    On dune and headland sinks the fire:
Lo, all our pomp of yesterday
    Is one with Nineveh and Tyre!°   *ruins of ancient cities in former empires*
Judge of the Nations, spare us yet,
Lest we forget, lest we forget!

If, drunk with sight of power, we loose
    Wild tongues that have not Thee in awe,
Such boasting as the Gentiles use,
    Or lesser breeds without the Law°—   *Romans 2.14*
Lord God of Hosts, be with us yet,
Lest we forget, lest we forget!

For heathen heart that puts her trust
    In reeking tube and iron shard,
All valiant dust that builds on dust,
    And guarding calls not Thee to guard,
For frantic boast and foolish word—
Thy Mercy on Thy People, Lord!

Talking about the Text

1. How does Longfellow's "The Wreck of the Hesperus" suggest we should judge the death of the young woman? What emotions does Longfellow appeal to in telling this story, and for what reason?
2. What is the purpose of the young daughter's repeated questions to her father?
3. How does Kipling's "Recessional" reflect the occasion for which it was written, Queen Victoria's Diamond Jubilee? Do you consider the poem to be patriotic in tone? Triumphant? Somber? Arrogant? Explain why.

Writing about the Text

1. "The Wreck of the Hesperus" is commonly considered a ballad. What characteristics define a ballad? Write a short explanation of how the poem fits the definition of a ballad.
2. How does Longfellow use repetition in "The Building of the Ship" and for what purpose? Compare the repetition in "The Building of the Ship" to that in "The Wreck of the Hesperus." Does it create the same effect or a different one?
3. Very little criticism or research has been devoted to Longfellow in the last hundred years. What do you think accounts for his general lack of popularity today? What do modern readers expect from poetry that Shakespeare, Whitman, and others can still provide that Longfellow cannot?

4. How does Kipling use Biblical allusions and quotations in "Recessional" and for what effect? What sort of relationship does England have with God in his poem?

Linking the Text to Other Texts

1. Compare the tragic accounts of death in "The Wreck of the Hesperus" and "Annabel Lee." What emotions do the poems rely on for their effect? What characterizes the young women in each poem?
2. Longfellow is often criticized for using sentimentality as a major device in his poetry. Analyze the sentimentality in "The Wreck of the Hesperus" and one other poem in this chapter and compare the two. What evidence of sentimentality do you see in other poems of this genre? Does Longfellow appear to use sentiment more or less than his peers?
3. Analyze the theme of tragedy and responsibility in Hemans's "Casabianca," Longfellow's "The Wreck of the Hesperus," and Kipling's "Recessional."
4. Kipling has been accused of being moralistic, imperialistic, and even racist. Analyze those attitudes in his poem and compare them with those of his British poetic predecessor, Tennyson. Does Kipling embody those perspectives more or less than his early nineteenth-century peer?

ROBERT BROWNING   (1812–1889)

In an age of recitation and declamations, it was only natural that some poems would get written as if they were parts of stage performances. Robert Browning is most famous for these, which he called "dramatic monologues." The idea is that one speaker tells someone else what he sees and thinks. We assume a listener is present and addressed directly by the speaker. Here, in Browning's most famous monologue, an evil Renaissance duke is showing off his palace to the emissary of a count whose daughter he is arranging to marry. The duke stops at a portrait of his last wife and explains what happened to her. Naturally, the audience is able to take in more than the poem's speaker intends.

My Last Duchess   (1842)

That's my last Duchess painted on the wall,
Looking as if she were alive. I call
That piece a wonder, now: Fra Pandolf's° hands   *fictional painter*   5
Worked busily a day, and there she stands.
Will't please you sit and look at her? I said
"Fra Pandolf" by design, for never read
Strangers like you that pictured countenance,
The depth and passion of its earnest glance,   10
But to myself they turned (since none puts by
The curtain I have drawn for you, but I)
And seemed as they would ask me, if they durst,
How such a glance came there; so, not the first
Are you to turn and ask thus. Sir, 'twas not   15
Her husband's presence only, called that spot
Of joy into the Duchess' cheek: perhaps

Fra Pandolf chanced to say "Her mantle laps
Over my lady's wrist too much," or "Paint
Must never hope to reproduce the faint   20
Half-flush that dies along her throat": such stuff
Was courtesy, she thought, and cause enough
For calling up that spot of joy. She had
A heart—how shall I say?—too soon made glad,
Too easily impressed; she liked whate'er   25
She looked on, and her looks went everywhere.
Sir, 'twas all one! My favor at her breast,
The dropping of the daylight in the West,
The bough of cherries some officious fool
Broke in the orchard for her, the white mule   30
She rode with round the terrace—all and each
Would draw from her alike the approving speech,
Or blush, at least. She thanked men—good! but thanked
Somehow—I know not how—as if she ranked
My gift of a nine-hundred-years-old name   35
With anybody's gift. Who'd stoop to blame
This sort of trifling? Even had you skill
In speech—which I have not—to make your will
Quite clear to such an one, and say, "Just this
Or that in you disgusts me; here you miss,   40
Or there exceed the mark"—and if she let
Herself be lessoned so, nor plainly set
Her wits to yours, forsooth, and made excuse,
—E'en then would be some stooping; and I choose
Never to stoop. Oh sir, she smiled, no doubt,   45
Whene'er I passed her; but who passed without
Much the same smile? This grew; I gave commands;
Then all smiles stopped together. There she stands
As if alive. Will't please you rise? We'll meet
The company below, then. I repeat,   50
The Count your master's known munificence
Is ample warrant that no just pretense
Of mine for dowry will be disallowed;
Though his fair daughter's self, as I avowed
At starting, is my object. Nay, we'll go   55
Together down, sir. Notice Neptune, though,
Taming a sea-horse, thought a rarity,
Which Claus of Innsbruck cast in bronze for me!

Talking about the Text

1. In Browning's "My Last Duchess," who is the duke addressing, and why is his audience's visit significant?
2. Why is it significant that the duchess's portrait hangs among the duke's prized art collection? Why does the poem end with the duke pointing out the statue of Neptune?

3. What is the duke's motivation for telling the count's emissary about the duchess? How much does he reveal about himself willingly in his monologue and how much does it unwittingly reveal?

Writing about the Text

1. Write an analysis of Browning's "My Last Duchess" as a dramatic monologue. What does Browning achieve by telling the story from the first-person perspective of the duke?
2. Write an intervention of the poem that reimagines it as a dialogue between the duke and the count's emissary. Imagine what questions the emissary might interject and how the duke would respond.

Linking the Text to Other Texts

1. Critic Ina Beth Sessions defines a dramatic monologue as having seven characteristics: a speaker, an audience, an occasion for speech, a revelation of character, interplay between speaker and audience, dramatic action, and action that takes place in the present. How well does "My Last Duchess" fit this definition? Which characteristics does the poem best represent?
2. Compare "My Last Duchess" with another dramatic monologue in this chapter and decide which better fits Sessions's definition.

ELIZABETH BARRETT BROWNING
(1806–1861)

In addition to her many famous sonnets and her verse novel Aurora Leigh (p. 761), Elizabeth Barrett Browning wrote a few narratives aimed at public performance. "Mother and Poet," one of her last poems, deals with the struggle to free Italy from tyranny, a long contest that took place between 1850 and 1870. It was a perfect subject for a poem, since Browning had lived many years in Italy and viewed its struggle favorably. And she was eager to tell heroic narratives of contemporary life, rather than search for her tales in the Renaissance (as her husband did) or the middle ages (as did so many Victorian poets). In "Mother and Poet," Browning tells the story of Laura Savio, of Turin, a poet and patriot whose sons were killed at Ancona and Gaeta, battles in which Italy attempted to win independence from royal rule.

Mother and Poet   (1861)

Turin, after News from Gaeta, 1861

DEAD! One of them shot by the sea in the east,
   And one of them shot in the west by the sea.
Dead! both my boys! When you sit at the feast
   And are wanting a great song for Italy free,
     Let none look at me!   5

Yet I was a poetess only last year,
   And good at my art, for a woman, men said;

But this woman, this, who is agoniz'd here,
   —The east sea and west sea rhyme on in her head
     For ever instead.   10

What art can a woman be good at? Oh, vain!
   What art is she good at, but hurting her breast
With the milk-teeth of babes, and a smile at the pain?
   Ah boys, how you hurt! you were strong as you press'd,
     And I proud, by that test.   20

What art's for a woman? To hold on her knees
   Both Darlings; to feel all their arms round her throat,
Cling, strangle a little, to sew by degrees
   And 'broider the long-clothes and neat little coat;
     To dream and to doat.   25

To teach them . . . It stings there! I made them indeed
   Speak plain the word country. I taught them, no doubt,
That a country's a thing men should die for at need.
   I prated of liberty, rights, and about
     The tyrant cast out.   30

And when their eyes flash'd . . . O my beautiful eyes! . . .
   I exulted; nay, let them go forth at the wheels
Of the guns, and denied not. But then the surprise
   When one sits quite alone! Then one weeps, then one kneels!
     God, how the house feels!   35

At first, happy news came, in gay letters moil'd
   With my kisses,—of camp-life and glory, and how
They both lov'd me; and, soon coming home to be spoil'd,
   In return would fan off every fly from my brow
     With their green laurel-bough.   40

Then was triumph at Turin: "Ancona was free!"
   And someone came out of the cheers in the street,
With a face pale as stone, to say something to me.
   My Guido was dead! I fell down at his feet,
     While they cheer'd in the street.   45

I bore it; friends sooth'd me; my grief look'd sublime
   As the ransom of Italy. One boy remain'd
To be leant on and walk'd with, recalling the time
   When the first grew immortal, while both of us strain'd
     To the height he had gain'd.   50

And letters still came, shorter, sadder, more strong,
   Writ now but in one hand, "I was not to faint,—
One lov'd me for two—would be with me ere long:
   And Viva l' Italia!—he died for, our saint,
     Who forbids our complaint."   55

My Nanni would add, "he was safe, and aware
   Of a presence that turn'd off the balls,—was impress'd

It was Guido himself, who knew what I could bear,
 And how 't was impossible, quite dispossess'd,
  To live on for the rest."   60

On which, without pause, up the telegraph-line,
 Swept smoothly the next news from Gaeta:—Shot.
Tell his mother. Ah, ah, "his," "their" mother,—not "mine,"
 No voice says "My mother" again to me. What!
  You think Guido forgot?   65

Are souls straight so happy that, dizzy with Heaven,
 They drop earth's affections, conceive not of woe?
I think not. Themselves were to lately forgiven
 Through THAT Love and Sorrow which reconcil'd so
  The Above and Below.   70

O Christ of the five wounds, who look'dst through the dark
 To the face of Thy mother! consider, I pray,
How we common mothers stand desolate, mark,
 Whose sons, not being Christs, die with eyes turn'd away,
  And no last word to say!   75

Both boys dead? but that's out of nature. We all
 Have been patriots, yet each house must always keep one.
'T were imbecile, hewing out roads to a wall;
 And, when Italy's made, for what end is it done
  If we have not a son?   80

Ah, ah, ah! when Gaeta's taken, what then?
 When the fair wicked queen sits no more at her sport
Of the fire-balls of death crashing souls out of men?
 When the guns of Cavalli with final retort
  Have cut the game short?   85

When Venice and Rome keep their new jubilee,
 When your flag takes all heaven for its white, green, and red,
When you have your country from mountain to sea,
 When King Victor has Italy's crown on his head,
  (And I have my Dead)—   90

What then? Do not mock me. Ah, ring your bells low,
 And burn your lights faintly! My country is there,
Above the star prick'd by the last peak of snow:
 My Italy's THERE, with my brave civic Pair,
  To disfranchise despair!   95

Forgive me. Some women bear children in strength,
 And bite back the cry of their pain in self-scorn;
But the birth-pangs of nations will wring us at length
 Into wail such as this—and we sit on forlorn
  When the man-child is born.   100

Dead! One of them shot by the sea in the east,
 And one of them shot in the west by the sea,

Both! both my boys! If in keeping the feast
    You want a great song for your Italy free,
       Let none look at me.   105

Talking about the Text

1. What is the overall tone of Browning's "Mother and Poet"? Describe how the feelings of the mother change from before the war to her current state.
2. Why does the mother refuse to write a "great song" for the free Italy? What statement does she make with this refusal?

Writing about the Text

1. In her essay "Diverting the Gaze: The Unseen Text in Women's War Writing," in the spring 2004 issue of *College Literature*, a scholarly journal, Carol Acton argues that "Much war writing by women consciously negotiates the space between the woman's experience as non-combatant and the man's combatant experience of war." Write a paper that argues how "Mother and Poet" either supports or refutes this thesis.
2. What did the mother in Browning's "Mother and Poet" teach her sons about patriotism, self-sacrifice, and the purpose of war? What position do you think the mother comes to regarding these ideas after her sons' deaths? Using specific quotes from the poem, explain what the mother's position is concerning the idea that "a country's a thing men should die for at need" (l. 23).

Linking the Text to Other Texts

1. Compare the depiction of young soldiers in Browning's "Mother and Poet" and Felicia Hemans's "Casabianca." How do the depictions of patriotism and bravery compare?
2. After her book *Poems before Congress* was published in 1860, reviewers strongly criticized Elizabeth Barrett Browning for being "unfeminine." One critic in particular laid out his standards for feminine expression, which he obviously thought Browning deviated from: "To bless and not to curse is woman's function." By modern standards, how much do you think "Mother and Poet" expresses "feminine" characteristics? What in particular do you think the critic found objectionable about Browning's poem? How do you think our ideas about what is expected from female writers has changed in the last one hundred and fifty years?

Walt Whitman, c. 1888, *several years prior to his death.*

WALT WHITMAN   (1819–1892)

During his long life, Walt Whitman was a newspaperman, a teacher, a housebuilder, a nurse, and as he became famous, a well-regarded public lecturer. In his fifties and sixties he attained a growing reputation for his poetry, and he also became well known for his writings on Abraham Lincoln. He spoke in public many times about Lincoln, reading both his character sketch of the president (whom he had seen but never met) and the poetry he wrote after Lincoln's murder. Hardly any of Whitman's great poems are written in such a regular form as "O Captain! My Captain!" This elegy for Lincoln, in rhyme, was by far Whitman's most popular poem in his lifetime, and he was called upon to recite it again and again. For an account of Whitman, see Chapter 13, which is devoted to his work.

O Captain! My Captain!   (1865)

O Captain! my Captain! our fearful trip is done,
The ship has weather'd every rack, the prize we sought is won,
The port is near, the bells I hear, the people all exulting,
While follow eyes the steady keel, the vessel grim and daring;
   But O heart! heart! heart!   5
     O the bleeding drops of red,
       Where on the deck my Captain lies,
        Fallen cold and dead.

O Captain! my Captain! rise up and hear the bells;
Rise up—for you the flag is flung—for you the bugle trills,   10
For you bouquets and ribbon'd wreaths—for you the shores a-crowding,
For you they call, the swaying mass, their eager faces turning;
   Here Captain! dear father!
     This arm beneath your head!
       It is some dream that on the deck,   15
        You've fallen cold and dead.

My Captain does not answer, his lips are pale and still,
My father does not feel my arm, he has no pulse nor will,
The ship is anchor'd safe and sound, its voyage closed and done,
From fearful trip the victor ship comes in with object won;   20
   Exult O shores, and ring O bells!
     But I with mournful tread,
       Walk the deck my Captain lies,
        Fallen cold and dead.

Talking about the Text

1. Who is the speaker of Whitman's "O Captain! My Captain!"? Who does the speaker figuratively represent?
2. Read "O Captain! My Captain!" aloud. Then hypothesize on why this was the public's favorite of Whitman's poems. What makes it compelling: its subject matter, rhyme scheme, point of view, tone?
3. Why didn't Whitman write a literal poem about the loss of Lincoln as a leader? What does figurative language do in "O Captain! My Captain!" to strengthen the poem's impact?

Writing about the Text

1. Research Whitman's role in the Civil War and the political beliefs that led him to honor Lincoln in his poetry. Use this research to support your reading of "O Captain! My Captain!"

2. Explicate "O Captain! My Captain!" line by line, explaining both the literal and figurative meanings. How do you as a reader know to read the poem on two levels?

Linking the Text to Other Texts

1. Compare "O Captain! My Captain!" to one of the elegies in Chapter 11 (pp. 777–780). What common techniques do they use?
2. Whitman wrote another poem about Lincoln that literary critics consider more successful. Do a critical comparison of "When Lilacs Last in the Dooryard Bloom'd" (pp. 861–866) and "O Captain! My Captain!" Pick two or three poetic techniques and discuss their success or failure in each poem.

ALFRED, LORD TENNYSON   (1809–1892)

The British counterpart of Henry Wadsworth Longfellow was Alfred, Lord Tennyson (1809–1892), the poet laureate from 1850 to 1892. He was by far the most popular English poet of his time; one of his poems was issued in a book that sold 40,000 copies in its first week, at a time when 500 copies a year was considered a success. His poems were often patriotic and usually artfully composed with performance in mind. The two poems below, "Ulysses" and "The Charge of the Light Brigade," show Tennyson's immense range: the first is a wistful interior monologue delivered by an ancient Greek hero still seeking adventure, the other a patriotic piece celebrating bravery in the face of official stupidity.

"Ulysses" dramatizes the speech of the Greek warrior who fought at Troy and became the subject of Homer's Odyssey. Now old and close to death, he hands over his kingdom to his son and prepares to set off with his remaining band of warriors one more time, "to seek a newer world," or to die trying.

Ulysses   (1842)

It little profits that an idle king,
By this still hearth, among these barren crags,
Matched with an aged wife, I mete and dole
Unequal laws unto a savage race,
That hoard, and sleep, and feed, and know not me.   5

I cannot rest from travel: I will drink
Life to the lees. All times I have enjoyed
Greatly, have suffered greatly, both with those
That loved me, and alone, on shore, and when
Through scudding drifts the rainy Hyades   10
Vexed the dim sea. I am become a name;
For always roaming with a hungry heart
Much have I seen and known; cities of men
And manners, climates, councils, governments,
Myself not least, but honored of them all—   15
And drunk delight of battle with my peers,
Far on the ringing plains of windy Troy.

I am part of all that I have met;
Yet all experience is an arch where through
Gleams that untraveled world whose margin fades   20
For ever and for ever when I move.
How dull it is to pause, to make an end,
To rust unburnished, not to shine in use!
As though to breathe were life. Life piled on life
Were all too little, and of one to me   25
Little remains: but every hour is saved
From that eternal silence, something more,
A bringer of new things; and vile it were
For some three suns to store and hoard myself,
And this gray spirit yearning in desire   30
To follow knowledge like a sinking star,
Beyond the utmost bound of human thought.

This is my son, my own Telemachus,
To whom I leave the scepter and the isle—
Well-loved of me, discerning to fulfill   35
This labor, by slow prudence to make mild
A rugged people, and through soft degrees
Subdue them to the useful and the good.
Most blameless is he, centered in the sphere
Of common duties, decent not to fail   40
In offices of tenderness, and pay
Meet adoration to my household gods,
When I am gone. He works his work, I mine.

There lies the port; the vessel puffs her sail;
There gloom the dark broad seas. My mariners,   45
Souls that have toiled, and wrought, and thought with me—
That ever with a frolic welcome took
The thunder and the sunshine, and opposed
Free hearts, free foreheads—you and I are old;
Old age hath yet his honor and his toil.   50
Death closes all: but something ere the end,
Some work of noble note, may yet be done,
Not unbecoming men that strove with Gods.
The lights begin to twinkle from the rocks;
The long day wanes; the slow moon climbs; the deep   55
Moans round with many voices. Come, my friends,
'Tis not too late to seek a newer world.
Push off, and sitting well in order smite
The sounding furrows; for my purpose holds
To sail beyond the sunset, and the baths   60
Of all the western stars, until I die.
It may be that the gulfs will wash us down:
It may be that we shall touch the Happy Isles,
And see the great Achilles, whom we knew.
Though much is taken, much abides; and though   65

We are not now that strength which in old days
Moved earth and heaven, that which we are, we are;
One equal temper of heroic hearts,
Made weak by time and fate, but strong in will
To strive, to seek, to find, and not to yield.   70

"The Charge of the Light Brigade" was inspired by news of a contemporary military disaster, a mistaken order for British cavalry to charge into the face of Russian cannons at the Battle of Balaclava in the Crimean War. In the poem, Tennyson celebrates unthinking bravery in the face of overwhelming odds, much like Felicia Hemans had in "Casabianca." A French military observer, watching the British troops charge, said, "C'est magnifique, mais c'est ne pas la guerre" ("It's magnificent, but it's not war"). In 1890 the aged Tennyson was prevailed upon to record the opening of the poem (which can be heard on CD). He brings a special gift to the performance, with his own sound effects, even though the recording is 115 years old.

The Charge of the Light Brigade   (1854)

Half a league, half a league,
Half a league onward,
All in the valley of Death
    Rode the six hundred.
"Forward the Light Brigade!   5
Charge for the guns!" he said:
Into the valley of Death
    Rode the six hundred.

"Forward the Light Brigade!"
Was there a man dismay'd?   10
Not tho' the soldier knew
    Some one had blunder'd:
Theirs not to make reply,
Theirs not to reason why
Theirs but to do and die: 15
Into the valley of Death
    Rode the six hundred.

Cannon to right of them,
Cannon to left of them,
Cannon in front of them   20
    Volley'd and thunder'd;
Storm'd at with shot and shell,
Boldly they rode and well,
Into the jaws of Death,
Into the mouth of Hell   25
    Rode the six hundred.

Flash'd all their sabres bare,
Flash'd as they turn'd in air
Sabring the gunners there,
Charging an army, while   30
    All the world wonder'd:
Plunged in the battery-smoke
Right thro' the line they broke;
Cossack and Russian
Reel'd from the sabre-stroke   35
    Shatter'd and sunder'd.
Then they rode back, but not
    Not the six hundred.

Cannon to right of them,
Cannon to left of them,   40
Cannon behind them
    Volley'd and thunder'd;
Storm'd at with shot and shell,
While horse and hero fell,
They that had fought so well   45
Came thro' the jaws of Death,
Back from the mouth of Hell,
All that was left of them,
    Left of six hundred.

When can their glory fade?   50
O the wild charge they made!
    All the world wonder'd.
Honour the charge they made!
Honour the Light Brigade,
    Noble six hundred!   55

Talking about the Text

1. In Tennyson's "Ulysses," what does the speaker mean when he says "I am become a name"?
2. What is Ulysses' attitude toward his current state in life? How much can you infer from his actual words and how much from his omissions, tone, self-characterization, and diction?

Writing about the Text

1. Write a summary of Ulysses' life story, which is dramatized in *The Odyssey*. What should a reader of Tennyson's "Ulysses" know about this character that will better inform the poem? How well do you think a reader would understand the poem without previous knowledge of Ulysses?
2. Write a paper arguing whether the Ulysses in Tennyson's poem is a tragic or heroic character.

3. Analyze Tennyson's "The Charge of the Light Brigade" as either a critique of battle or a celebration of it.

Linking the Text to Other Texts

1. Compare the depictions of battle in Tennyson's "The Charge of the Light Brigade" and Felicia Hemans's "Casabianca." How do the poems suggest a judgment about the tragedy?
2. Compare the speakers in Tennyson's "Ulysses" and Browning's "My Last Duchess." How much does each speaker reveal unwittingly about himself, and what are his motivations for speaking?

QUESTIONS FOR WRITING AND RESEARCH

1. Find five examples of special diction or vocabulary in poems in this chapter. (Examples: archaism, such as "whilst" in Longfellow, or mock-heroic, such as "spheroid" in "Casey at the Bat.") Then, "translate" these five terms into the normal language of the twenty-first century.
2. Describe some of the terms associated with women in at least two of the poems in this chapter. What characteristics do you notice? Suggested starting places: Elizabeth Barrett Browning (p. 994), Robert Browning (p. 992), and Letitia Landon (p. 977).
3. Write an essay about how men are characterized in three poems in this chapter. Suggested starting places: Tennyson (p. 999), Landon (p. 977), and Hemans (p. 975).
4. How can a poem seem "abominable and silly" when read silently, yet it still "succeeds marvelously" when declaimed? (See the Stephen Jay Gould quotation on p. 962.) What is it about the process of declaiming—reading aloud with dramatic emphasis—that can take hokey language on a page and transform it into something different?
5. Write your own one-page ballad or narrative of an event, making it dramatic, mock heroic, or a parody.
6. Choose one poem from this chapter and prepare ten to fifteen lines to present out loud, spending time rehearsing and listening to samples.
7. What connections do you see between the kinds of narrative poetry in this chapter and the kind of poems popular in today's poetry slams? A good place to start is at poetry slam websites, such as *http://www.poetryslam.com* and *http://www.austinslam.com.*
8. Find a parody of one poem from this chapter and discuss how it works. Does it depend on a knowledge of the original? Is there mockery? Is it an affectionate or a savage parody? The Web is an excellent place to begin a search. Another place is early issues of *Mad* magazine, which often parodied old chestnuts like "The Wreck of the Hesperus."

C H A P T E R
18

Poems for Further Reading

A BRIEF NOTE ON THE SEQUENCING OF THE POEMS

The poems in this section are arranged in chronological order by poet's birth year so that they display some of the development that has taken place over time in the poetic form. For poets with multiple works, the poems appear in chronological order by publication year.

ROBERT SOUTHWELL   (1561–1595)
The Burning Babe   (1602)

As I in hoary winter's night stood shivering in the snow,
Surprised I was with sudden heat which made my heart to glow;
And lifting up a fearful eye to view what fire was near,
A pretty babe all burning bright did in the air appear;
Who, scorchèd with excessive heat, such floods of tears did shed
As though his floods should quench his flames which with his tears were fed.
"Alas," quoth he, "but newly born in fiery heats I fry,
Yet none approach to warm their hearts or feel my fire but I!"

5

Editor's Note: Biographies and "Starting Points for Further Research" for selected poets can be found in Chapter 19 (see p. 1121).

My faultless breast the furnace is, the fuel wounding thorns,
Love is the fire, and sighs the smoke, the ashes shame and scorns; 10
The fuel justice layeth on, and mercy blows the coals,
The metal in this furnace wrought are men's defilèd souls,
For which, as now on fire I am to work them to their good,
So will I melt into a bath to wash them in my blood."
With this he vanished out of sight and swiftly shrunk away, 15
And straight I callèd unto mind that it was Christmas day.

JOHN DONNE (1572–1631)

A Valediction: Forbidding Mourning (1633)

As virtuous men pass mildly away,
    And whisper to their souls to go,
Whilst some of their sad friends do say
    The breath goes now, and some say, No;

So let us melt, and make no noise, 5
    No tear-floods, nor sigh-tempests move,
'Twere profanation of our joys
    To tell the laity our love.

Moving of th' earth brings harms and fears,
    Men reckon what it did and meant; 10
But trepidation of the spheres,
    Though greater far, is innocent.

Dull sublunary° lovers' love   *earthly*
    (Whose soul is sense) cannot admit
Absence, because it doth remove 15
    Those things which elemented° it.   *composed*

But we, by a love so much refined
    That our selves know not what it is,
Inter-assurèd of the mind,
    Care less, eyes, lips, and hands to miss. 20

Our two souls therefore, which are one,
    Though I must go, endure not yet
A breach, but an expansion,
    Like gold to airy thinness beat.

If they be two, they are two so 25
    As stiff twin compasses are two;
Thy soul, the fixed foot, makes no show
    To move, but doth, if th' other do.

And though it in the center sit,
    Yet when the other far doth roam, 30
It leans and hearkens after it,
    And grows erect, as that comes home.

Such wilt thou be to me, who must
   Like th' other foot, obliquely run;
Thy firmness makes my circle just,   35
   And makes me end where I begun.

Batter My Heart, Three-Personed God   (1633)

Batter my heart, three-personed God; for you
As yet but knock, breathe, shine, and seek to mend;
That I may rise and stand, o'erthrow me, and bend
Your force to break, blow, burn, and make me new.
I, like an usurped town, to another due,   5
Labor to admit you, but O, to no end;
Reason, your viceroy in me, me should defend,
But is captived, and proves weak or untrue.
Yet dearly I love you, and would be loved fain,°   gladly
But am betrothed unto your enemy.   10
Divorce me, untie or break that knot again;
Take me to you, imprison me, for I,
Except you enthrall me, never shall be free,
Nor ever chaste, except you ravish me.

The Canonization   (1633)

For God's sake hold your tongue, and let me love,
   Or chide my palsy, or my gout,
My five gray hairs, or ruined fortune, flout,
    With wealth your state, your mind with arts improve,
      Take you a course, get you a place,   5
      Observe His Honor, or His Grace,
Or the King's real, or his stampèd face°   e.g., on a coin
    Contemplate; what you will, approve,
    So you will let me love.

Alas, alas, who's injured by my love?   10
   What merchant's ships have my sighs drowned?
Who says my tears have overflowed his ground?
    When did my colds a forward spring remove?
      When did the heats which my veins fill
      Add one man to the plaguy bill?   15
Soldiers find wars, and lawyers find out still
    Litigious men, which quarrels move,
    Though she and I do love.

Call us what you will, we are made such by love;
   Call her one, me another fly,   20
We're tapers too, and at our own cost die,
    And we in us find the eagle and the dove.

The phoenix riddle hath more wit
    By us: we two being one, are it.
So, to one neutral thing both sexes fit.   25
    We die and rise the same, and prove
    Mysterious by this love.

We can die by it, if not live by love,
    And if unfit for tombs and hearse
Our legend be, it will be fit for verse;   30
    And if no piece of chronicle we prove,
        We'll build in sonnets pretty rooms;
        As well a well-wrought urn becomes
The greatest ashes, as half-acre tombs,
    And by these hymns, all shall approve   35
    Us canonized for love:

And thus invoke us: You whom reverend love
    Made one another's hermitage;
You, to whom love was peace, that now is rage;
    Who did the whole world's soul contract, and drove   40
        Into the glasses of your eyes
        (So made such mirrors, and such spies,
That they did all to you epitomize)
    Countries, towns, courts: Beg from above
    A pattern of your love!   45

Death, Be Not Proud   (1633)

Death, be not proud, though some have callèd thee
Mighty and dreadful, for thou art not so;
For those whom thou think'st thou dost overthrow
Die not, poor Death, nor yet canst thou kill me.
From rest and sleep, which but thy pictures be,   5
Much pleasure; then from thee much more must flow,
And soonest our best men with thee do go,
Rest of their bones, and soul's delivery.
Thou art slave to fate, chance, kings, and desperate men,
And dost with poison, war, and sickness dwell,   10
And poppy or charms can make us sleep as well
And better than thy stroke; why swell'st thou then?
One short sleep past, we wake eternally
And death shall be no more; Death, thou shalt die.

The Flea   (1633)

Mark but this flea, and mark in this,
How little that which thou deniest me is;
Me it sucked first, and now sucks thee,

And in this flea our two bloods mingled be;
Thou know'st that this cannot be said   5
A sin, or shame, or loss of maidenhead,
  Yet this enjoys before it woo.
  And pampered swells with one blood made of two,
  And this, alas, is more than we would do.

Oh stay, three lives in one flea spare,   10
Where we almost, nay more than married are.
This flea is you and I, and this
Our marriage bed and marriage temple is;
Though parents grudge, and you, we are met,
And cloistered in these living walls of jet.   15
  Though use make you apt to kill me
  Let not to that, self-murder added be,
  And sacrilege, three sins in killing three.
Cruel and sudden, hast thou since
Purpled thy nail in blood of innocence?   20
Wherein could this flea guilty be,
Except in that drop which it sucked from thee?
Yet thou triumph'st, and say'st that thou
Find'st not thy self nor me the weaker now;
  'Tis true; then learn how false fears be: 25
  Just so much honor, when thou yield'st to me,
  Will waste, as this flea's death took life from thee.

The Relic   (1633)

  When my grave is broke up again
  Some second guest to entertain
  (For graves have learned that woman-head
  To be to more than one a bed),
    And he that digs it, spies   5
 A bracelet of bright hair about the bone,
    Will he not let us alone,
 And think that there a loving couple lies,
Who thought that this device might be some way
To make their souls, at the last busy day,°   *Judgment Day*   10
Meet at this grave, and make a little stay?

  If this fall in a time, or land,
  Where mis-devotion doth command,
  Then he that digs us up, will bring
  Us to the Bishop and the King,   15
    To make us relics; then
Thou shalt be a Mary Magdalen, and I
    A something else thereby;
All women shall adore us, and some men;
And since at such times, miracles are sought,   20

I would have that age by this paper taught
What miracles we harmless lovers wrought.

> First, we loved well and faithfully,
> Yet knew not what we loved, nor why,
> Difference of sex no more we knew,   25
> Than our guardian angels do;
>   Coming and going, we
> Perchance might kiss, but not between those meals;
>   Our hands ne'er touched the seals
> Which nature, injured by late law, sets free;   30
> These miracles we did: but now, alas,
> All measure and all language I should pass,
> Should I tell what a miracle she was.

The Anniversarie   (1633)

> All Kings, and all their favorites,
> All glory of honors, beauties, wits,
> The Sun it selfe, which makes times, as they passe,
> Is elder by a yeare, now, then it was
> When thou and I first one another saw: 5
> All other things, to their destruction draw,
>   Only our love hath no decay;
> This, no to morrow hath, nor yesterday,
> Running it never runs from us away,
> But truly keepes his first, last, everlasting day.   10
>
> Two graves must hide thine and my coarse,
> If one might, death were no divorce.
> Alas, as well as other Princes, wee,
> (Who Prince enough in one another bee,)
> Must leave at last in death, these eyes, and eares,   15
> Oft fed with true oathes, and with sweet salt teares;
>   But soules where nothing dwells but love
> (All other thoughts being inmates) then shall prove
> This, or a love increased there above,
> When bodies to their graves, soules from their graves remove.   20
>
> And then wee shall be throughly blest,
> But wee no more, then all the rest;
> Here upon earth, we are Kings, and none but wee
> Can be such Kings, nor of such subjects bee.
> Who is so safe as wee? where none can doe   25
> Treason to us, except one of us two.
>   True and false feares let us refraine,
> Let us love nobly, and live, and adde againe
> Yeares and yeares unto yeares, till we attaine
> To write threescore: this is the second of our raigne.   30

▣ VIDEO LOCALE

Robert Pinsky's Favorite Poem Project. In 1997 poet Robert Pinsky, then poet laureate of the United States, founded the Favorite Poem Project, an ongoing undertaking dedicated to revealing and promoting the role poetry plays in the lives of everyday Americans. During the first-year call for submissions, over 18,000 Americans from all ages and backgrounds volunteered to share their favorite poems with the project. The project contains several collections created from those submissions. Among them are the Favorite Poem Project Videos, fifty short video documentaries of individual Americans reading and speaking personally about poems they love. Those videos are available at the Favorite Poem Project website at *http://www.bu.edu/favoritepoem/*. The site also offers an online database of the chosen favorite poems, information on anthologies that have been recently published based on the project's poem database, and advice on teaching and learning about poetry in the classroom.

BEN JONSON   (1572–1637)

Come, My Celia, Let Us Prove   (WRITTEN 1607; PUB. 1616)

Come, my Celia, let us prove,
While we can, the sports of love;
Time will not be ours forever:
He at length our good will sever.
Spend not, then, his gifts in vain;   5
Suns that set may rise again,
But if once we lose this light,
'Tis with us perpetual night.
Why should we defer our joys?
Fame and rumor are but toys.   10
Cannot we delude the eyes
Of a few poor household spies?
Or his easier ears beguile,
Thus removéd by our wile?
'Tis no sin love's fruits to steal,   15
But the sweet thefts to reveal;
To be taken, to be seen,
These have crimes accounted been.

On My First Daughter   (1616)

Here lies to each her parents' ruth,°   *grief*
Mary, the daughter of their youth;
Yet, all heaven's gifts, being heaven's due,
It makes the father, less, to rue.

At six months' end, she parted hence 5
With safety of her innocence;

Whose soul heaven's Queen (whose name she bears),
In comfort of her mother's tears,
Hath placed amongst her virgin-train;
Where, while that severed doth remain, 10
This grave partakes the fleshly birth;
Which cover lightly, gentle earth.

GEORGE HERBERT (1593–1633)

The Pulley (1633)

When God at first made man,
Having a glass of blessings standing by,
"Let us," said he, "pour on him all we can:
Let the world's riches, which dispersèd lie,
    Contract into a span." 5

    So strength first made a way;
Then beauty flowed, then wisdom, honor, pleasure.
When almost all was out, God made a stay,
Perceiving that, alone of all his treasure,
    Rest in the bottom lay. 10

    "For if I should," said he,
"Bestow this jewel also on my creature,
He would adore my gifts instead of me,
And rest in Nature, not the God of Nature;
    So both should losers be. 15

    "Yet let him keep the rest,
But keep them with repining restlessness:
Let him be rich and weary, that at least,
If goodness lead him not, yet weariness
    May toss him to my breast." 20

The Windows (1633)

Lord, how can man preach thy eternal word?
    He is a brittle, crazy° glass,   *cracked*
Yet in thy temple thou do him afford
    This glorious and transcendent place,
    To be a window, through thy grace. 5

But when thou dost anneal in glass thy story,
    Making thy life to shine within
The holy preachers, then the light and glory
    More reverent grows, and does win
    Which else shows watr'ish, bleak, and thin. 10

Doctrine and life, colors and light, in one
      When they combine and mingle, bring
A strong regard and awe; but speech alone
      Doth vanish like a flaring thing,
      And in the ear, not conscience ring.   15

JOHN MILTON   (1608–1674)

How Soon Hath Time   (1632)

How soon hath time, the subtle thief of youth,
      Stol'n on his wing my three and twentieth year!
      My hasting days fly on with full career,
      But my late spring no bud or blossom show'th.
Perhaps my semblance might deceive the truth,   5
      That I to manhood am arriv'd so near,
      And inward ripeness doth much less appear,
      That some more timely-happy spirits endu'th.°   *endows*
Yet be it less or more, or soon or slow,
      It shall be still in strictest measure ev'n   10
      To that same lot, however mean or high,
Toward which Time leads me, and the will of Heav'n;
      All is, if I have grace to use it so,
      As ever in my great Task-Master's eye.

RICHARD LOVELACE   (1618–1658)

To Lucasta, On Going to the Wars   (1649)

Tell me not, Sweet, I am unkind
      That from the nunnery
Of thy chaste breast and quiet mind,
      To war and arms I fly.

True, a new mistress now I chase,   5
      The first foe in the field;
And with a stronger faith embrace
      A sword, a horse, a shield.

Yet this inconstancy is such
      As you too shall adore;   10
I could not love thee, Dear, so much,
      Loved I not Honor more.

ANDREW MARVELL

(1621–1678)

The Garden

(1681)

How vainly men themselves amaze
To win the palm, the oak, or bays,°   *laurels, honors*
And their uncessant labors see
Crowned from some single herb or tree,
Whose short and narrow-vergèd shade   5
Does prudently their toils upbraid;
While all flowers and all trees do close,°   *agree*
To weave the garlands of repose!

Fair Quiet, have I found thee here,
And Innocence, thy sister dear?   10
Mistaken long, I sought you then
In busy companies of men.
Your sacred plants, if here below,°   *on earth*
Only among the plants will grow;
Society is all but rude,   15
To° this delicious solitude.   *compared to*

No white nor red was ever seen
So amorous as this lovely green.
Fond lovers, cruel as their flame,
Cut in these trees their mistress' name: 20
Little, alas, they know or heed
How far these beauties hers exceed!
Fair trees, wheresoe'er your barks I wound,
No name shall but your own be found.

When we have run our passion's heat,   25
Love hither makes his best retreat.
The gods, that mortal beauty chase,
Still in a tree did end their race:
Apollo hunted Daphne so,
Only that she might laurel grow;   30
And Pan did after Syrinx speed,
Not as a nymph, but for a reed.

What wondrous life in this I lead!
Ripe apples drop about my head;
The luscious clusters of the vine   35
Upon my mouth do crush their wine;
The nectarine and curious° peach   *exquisite*
Into my hands themselves do reach;
Stumbling on melons as I pass,
Insnared with flowers, I fall on grass.   40

Meanwhile the mind, from pleasure less,
Withdraws into its happiness;
The mind, that ocean where each kind
Does straight its own resemblance find;
Yet it creates, transcending these,   45
Far other worlds and other seas,
Annihilating all that's made
To a green thought in a green shade.

Here at the fountain's sliding foot,
Or at some fruit tree's mossy root,   50
Casting the body's vest aside,
My soul into the boughs does glide:
There like a bird it sits and sings,
Then whets and combs its silver wings,
And, till prepared for longer flight,   55
Waves in its plumes the various light.

Such was that happy garden-state,
While man there walked without a mate:
After a place so pure and sweet,
What other help could yet be meet!   60
But 'twas beyond a mortal's share
To wander solitary there:
Two paradises 'twere in one
To live in paradise alone.

How well the skillful gardener drew   65
Of flowers and herbs this dial new,
Where from above the milder sun
Does through a fragrant zodiac run;
And as it works, th' industrious bee
Computes its time as well as we!   70
How could such sweet and wholesome hours
Be reckoned but with herbs and flowers?

MARY, LADY CHUDLEIGH   (1656–1710)

To the Ladies   (1690)

Wife and servant are the same,
But only differ in the name:
For when that fatal knot is tied,
Which nothing, nothing can divide,
When she the word *Obey* has said   5
And man by law supreme has made,
Then all that's kind is laid aside,
And nothing left but state and pride.
Fierce as an eastern prince he grows,
And all his innate rigour shows: 10

Then but to look, to laugh, or speak,
Will the nuptial contract break.
Like mutes, she signs alone must make,
And never any freedom take,
But still be governed by a nod,   15
And fear her husband as her god:
Him still must serve, him still obey,
And nothing act, and nothing say,
But what her haughty lord thinks fit,
Who, with the power, has all the wit.   20
Then shun, oh! shun that wretched state,
And all the fawning flatterers hate.
Value yourselves, and men despise:
You must be proud, if you'll be wise.

JONATHAN SWIFT   (1667–1745)

A Description of the Morning   (1711)

Now hardly here and there an hackney-coach,°   horse-drawn cab
Appearing, showed the ruddy morn's approach.
Now Betty from her master's bed had flown
And softly stole to discompose her own.
The slipshod 'prentice from his master's door   5
Had pared the dirt, and sprinkled round the floor.
Now Moll had whirled her mop with dextrous airs,
Prepared to scrub the entry and the stairs.
The youth with broomy stumps began to trace
The kennel°-edge, where wheels had worn the place.   gutter 10
The small-coal man was heard with cadence deep
Till drowned in shriller notes of chimneysweep,
Duns° at his lordship's gate began to meet,   bill-collectors
And Brickdust Moll had screamed through half the street.
The turnkey° now his flock returning sees,   jailkeeper 15
Duly let out a-nights to steal for fees;
The watchful bailiffs° take their silent stands;   constables
And schoolboys lag with satchels in their hands.

SAMUEL JOHNSON   (1709–1784)

Prologue Spoken by Mr. Garrick at the Opening of the Theater in Drury Lane, 1747   (1747)

When Learning's triumph o'er her barb'rous foes
First reared the stage, immortal Shakespeare rose;
Each change of many-colored life he drew,
Exhausted worlds, and then imagined new;

Existence saw him spurn her bounded reign,   5
And panting Time toiled after him in vain.
His powerful strokes presiding truth impressed,
And unresisted Passion stormed the breast.
      Then Jonson° came, instructed from the school,   *Ben Jonson*
To please in method, and invent by rule;   10
His studious patience and laborious art
By regular approach essayed the heart:
Cold Approbation gave the ling'ring bays;
For those who durst not censure, scarce could praise.
A mortal born, he met the gen'ral doom,   15
But left, like Egypt's kings, a lasting tomb.
      The wits of Charles found easier ways to fame,
Nor wished for Jonson's art, or Shakespeare's flame.
Themselves they studied; as they felt, they writ:
Intrigue was plot, obscenity was wit.   20
Vice always found a sympathetic friend;
They pleased their age, and did not aim to mend.
Yet bards like these aspired to lasting praise,
And proudly hoped to pimp in future days.
Their cause was gen'ral, their supports were strong,   25
Their slaves were willing, and their reign was long:
Till Shame regained the post that Sense betrayed,
And Virtue called Oblivion to her aid.
      Then, crushed by rules, and weakened as refined,
For years the power of tragedy declined;   30
From bard to bard the frigid caution crept,
Till Declamation roared while Passion slept;
Yet still did Virtue deign the stage to tread;
Philosophy remained though Nature fled.
But forced at length her ancient reign to quit,   35
She saw great Faustus lay the ghost of wit;
Exulting Folly hailed the joyful day,
And pantomime and song confirmed her sway.
      But who the coming changes can presage,
And mark the future periods of the stage?   40
Perhaps if skill could distant times explore,
New Behns, new D'Urfeys yet remain in store;
Perhaps where Lear has raved, and Hamlet died,
On flying cars new sorcerers may ride,
Perhaps (for who can guess th'effects of chance?)   45
Here Hunt may box, or Mahomet may dance.
      Hard is his lot that here by fortune placed,
Must watch the wild vicissitudes of taste;
With every meteor of caprice must play,
And chase the new-blown bubbles of the day.   50
Ah! let not censure term our fate our choice:
The stage but echoes back the public voice;
The drama's laws the drama's patrons give,

For we that live to please, must please to live.
    Then prompt no more the follies you decry,   55
As tyrants doom their tools of guilt to die;
'Tis yours this night to bid the reign commence
Of rescued Nature and reviving sense;
To chase the charms of sound, the pomp of show,
For useful mirth and salutary woe;   60
Bid scenic Virtue form the rising age,
And Truth diffuse her radiance from the stage.

CHRISTOPHER SMART   (1722–1771)

For I Will Consider My Cat Jeoffry   (1759–1763)

For I will consider my Cat Jeoffry.
For he is the servant of the Living God, duly and daily serving him.
For at the first glance of the glory of God in the East he worships in his way.
For is this done by wreathing his body seven times round with elegant quickness.
For then he leaps up to catch the musk,° which is the blessing   *catnip* 5
    of God upon his prayer.
For he rolls upon prank to work it in.
For having done duty and received blessing he begins to consider himself.
For this he performs in ten degrees.
For first he looks upon his fore-paws to see if they are clean.   10
For secondly he kicks up behind to clear away there.
For thirdly he works it upon stretch°with the fore-paws extended.   *stretching his*
For fourthly he sharpens his paws by wood.   *muscles*
For fifthly he washes himself.
For sixthly he rolls upon wash.   15
For seventhly he fleas himself, that he may not be interrupted
    upon the beat.°   *his patrol*
For eighthly he rubs himself against a post.
For ninthly he looks up for his instructions.
For tenthly he goes in quest of food.   20
For having considered God and himself he will consider his neighbor.
For if he meets another cat he will kiss her in kindness.
For when he takes his prey he plays with it to give it a chance.
For one mouse in seven escapes by his dallying.
For when his day's work is done his business more properly begins.   25
For he keeps the Lord's watch in the night against the Adversary.
For he counteracts the powers of darkness by his electrical skin and glaring eyes.
For he counteracts the Devil, who is death, by brisking about the life.
For in his morning orisons he loves the sun and the sun loves him.
For he is of the tribe of Tiger.   30
For the Cherub Cat is a term of the Angel Tiger.
For he has the subtlety and hissing of a serpent, which in goodness he suppresses.
For he will not do destruction if he is well-fed, neither will he spit without
    provocation.

For he purrs in thankfulness when God tells him he's a good Cat.   35
For he is an instrument for the children to learn benevolence upon.
For every house is incomplete without him, and a blessing is lacking in the spirit.
For the Lord commanded Moses concerning the cats at the departure of the
    Children of Israel from Egypt.
For every family had one cat at least in the bag.   40
For the English cats are the best in Europe.
For he is the cleanest in the use of his fore-paws of any quadruped.
For the dexterity of his defense is an instance of the love of God to him exceed-
    ingly.
For he is the quickest to his mark of any creature.   45
For he is tenacious of his point.
For he is a mixture of gravity and waggery.
For he knows that God is his Savior.
For there is nothing sweeter than his peace when at rest.
For there is nothing brisker than his life when in motion.   50
For he is of the Lord's poor, and so indeed is he called by benevolence perpetu-
    ally—Poor Jeoffry! poor Jeoffry! the rat has bit thy throat.
For I bless the name of the Lord Jesus that Jeoffry is better.
For the divine spirit comes about his body to sustain it in complete cat.
For his tongue is exceeding pure so that it has in purity what it wants in music.   55
For he is docile and can learn certain things.
For he can sit up with gravity which is patience upon approbation.
For he can fetch and carry, which is patience in employment.
For he can jump over a stick which is patience upon proof positive.
For he can spraggle upon waggle at the word of command.   60
For he can jump from an eminence into his master's bosom.
For he can catch the cork and toss it again.
For he is hated by the hypocrite and miser.
For the former is afraid of detection.
For the latter refuses the charge.   65
For he camels his back to bear the first notion of business.
For he is good to think on, if a man would express himself neatly.
For he made a great figure in Egypt for his signal services.
For he killed the Icneumon-rat, very pernicious by land.
For his ears are so acute that they sting again.   70
For from this proceeds the passing quickness of his attention.
For by stroking of him I have found out electricity.
For I perceived God's light about him both wax and fire.
For the electrical fire is the spiritual substance which God sends from heaven to
    sustain the bodies both of man and beast.   75
For God has blessed him in the variety of his movements.
For, though he cannot fly, he is an excellent clamberer.
For his motions upon the face of the earth are more than any other quadruped.
For he can tread to all the measures upon the music.
For he can swim for life.   80
For he can creep.

WILLIAM COWPER
(1731–1800)

The Castaway
(WRITTEN 1799; PUB. 1803)

Obscurest night involved the sky,
    The Atlantic billows roared,
When such a destined wretch as I,
    Washed headlong from on board,
Of friends, of hope, of all bereft,   5
His floating home forever left.

No braver chief could Albion° boast   *England*
    Than he with whom he went,
Nor ever ship left Albion's coast,
    With warmer wishes sent.   10
He loved them both, but both in vain,
Nor him beheld, nor her again.

Not long beneath the whelming brine,
    Expert to swim, he lay;
Nor soon he felt his strength decline,   15
    Or courage die away;
But waged with death a lasting strife,
Supported by despair of life.

He shouted; nor his friends had failed
    To check the vessel's course,
But so the furious blast prevailed,   20
    That, pitiless perforce,
They left their outcast mate behind,
And scudded still before the wind.

Some succor yet they could afford;   25
    And, such as storms allow,
The cask, the coop, the floated cord,
    Delayed not to bestow.
But he (they knew) nor ship, nor shore,
Whate'er they gave, should visit more.   30

Nor, cruel as it seemed, could he
    Their haste himself condemn,
Aware that flight, in such a sea,
    Alone could rescue them;
Yet bitter felt it still to die   35
Deserted, and his friends so nigh.

He long survives, who lives an hour
    In ocean, self-upheld;
And so long he, with unspent power,
    His destiny repelled;   40

And ever, as the minutes flew,
Entreated help, or cried, "Adieu!"

At length, his transient respite past,
    His comrades, who before
Had heard his voice in every blast,   45
    Could catch the sound no more
For then, by toil subdued, he drank
The stifling wave, and then he sank.

No poet wept him; but the page
    Of narrative sincere,   50
That tells his name, his worth, his age.
    Is wet with Anson's tear.
And tears by bards or heroes shed
Alike immortalize the dead.

I therefore purpose not, or dream,   55
    Descanting° on his fate,   *singing*
To give the melancholy theme
    A more enduring date:
But misery still delights to trace
Its semblance in another's case.   60

No voice divine the storm allayed,
    No light propitious shone,
When, snatched from all effectual aid,
    We perished, each alone;
But I beneath a rougher sea,   65
And whelmed in deeper gulfs than he.

WILLIAM BLAKE   (1757–1827)

Infant Joy   (1789)

"I have no name,
I am but two days old."
What shall I call thee?
"I happy am,
Joy is my name."   5
Sweet joy befall thee!

Pretty joy!
Sweet joy but two days old,
Sweet joy I call thee;
Thou dost smile,   10
I sing the while,
Sweet joy befall thee.

The Lamb (1789)

Little Lamb, who made thee?
    Dost thou know who made thee?
Gave thee life, and bid thee feed
By the stream and o'er the mead;
Gave thee clothing of delight,   5
Softest clothing, wooly, bright;
Gave thee such a tender voice,
Making all the vales rejoice?
    Little Lamb, who made thee?
    Dost thou know who made thee?   10

    Little Lamb, I'll tell thee,
    Little Lamb, I'll tell thee:
He is callèd by thy name,
For he calls himself a Lamb.
He is meek, and he is mild;   15
He became a little child.
I a child, and thou a lamb,
We are callèd by his name.
    Little Lamb, God bless thee!
    Little Lamb, God bless thee!   20

The Tyger (1793)

Tyger! Tyger! burning bright
In the forests of the night,
What immortal hand or eye
Could frame thy fearful symmetry?

In what distant deeps or skies   5
Burnt the fire of thine eyes?
On what wings dare he aspire?
What the hand dare seize the fire?

And what shoulder, and what art,
Could twist the sinews of thy heart?   10
And, when thy heart began to beat,
What dread hand? and what dread feet?

What the hammer? what the chain?
In what furnace was thy brain?
What the anvil? what dread grasp   15
Dare its deadly terrors clasp?

When the stars threw down their spears,
And watered heaven with their tears,
Did he smile his work to see?
Did he who made the lamb make thee?   20

Tyger! Tyger! burning bright
In the forests of the night,
What immortal hand or eye,
Dare frame thy fearful symmetry?

Infant Sorrow   (1794)

My mother groaned! my father wept.
Into the dangerous world I leapt,
Helpless, naked, piping loud;
Like a fiend hid in a cloud.

Struggling in my father's hands,   5
Striving against my swadling bands;
Bound and weary I thought best
To sulk upon my mother's breast.

A Poison Tree   (1794)

I was angry with my friend:
I told my wrath, my wrath did end.
I was angry with my foe:
I told it not, my wrath did grow.

And I water'd it in fears,   5
Night & morning with my tears:
And I sunned it with smiles.
And with soft deceitful wiles.

And it grew both day and night.
Till it bore an apple bright.   10
And my foe beheld it shine.
And he knew that it was mine.

And into my garden stole.
When the night had veiled the pole.
In the morning glad I see.   15
My foe outstretched beneath the tree.

The Sick Rose   (1794)

O Rose, thou art sick!
The invisible worm
That flies in the night,
In the howling storm,

Has found out thy bed   5
Of crimson joy,
And his dark secret love
Does thy life destroy.

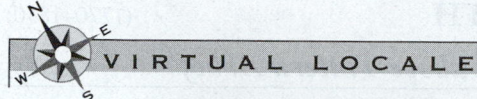

William Blake's own hand-painted illustration of "The Tyger" from the 1794 edition of his Songs of Experience.

The William Blake Archive. William Blake created a number of original illuminated manuscripts—handmade versions of his poems that combine text with images. These works are now rare, extremely valuable, and very old and fragile. Access to these rare editions at the libraries and museums that hold them is limited. The free, online William Blake Archive at *http://www.blakearchive.org/* was created to provide easy, widely based access to Blake's major visual and literary works. The site presents digital reproductions of numerous Blake illuminated books, including *Songs of Innocence* and *Songs of Experience*, as well as drawings, paintings, engravings, biographical information, and bibliographies.

WILLIAM WORDSWORTH   (1770–1850)

Lines Composed a Few Miles above Tintern Abbey[1]   (1798)

On revisiting the banks of the Wye during a tour,
July 13, 1798

Five years have past; five summers, with the length
Of five long winters! and again I hear
These waters, rolling from their mountain-springs
With a soft inland murmur.—Once again
Do I behold these steep and lofty cliffs,   5
That on a wild secluded scene impress
Thoughts of more deep seclusion; and connect
The landscape with the quiet of the sky.
The day is come when I again repose
Here, under this dark sycamore, and view   10
These plots of cottage-ground, these orchard-tufts,
Which at this season, with their unripe fruits,
Are clad in one green hue, and lose themselves
'Mid groves and copses. Once again I see
These hedge-rows, hardly hedge-rows, little lines   15
Of sportive wood run wild: these pastoral farms,
Green to the very door; and wreaths of smoke
Sent up, in silence, from among the trees!
With some uncertain notice, as might seem
Of vagrant dwellers in the houseless woods,   20
Or of some Hermit's cave, where by his fire
The Hermit sits alone.

                These beauteous forms,
Through a long absence, have not been to me
As is a landscape to a blind man's eye:
But oft, in lonely rooms, and 'mid the din   25
Of towns and cities, I have owed to them
In hours of weariness, sensations sweet,
Felt in the blood, and felt along the heart;
And passing even into my purer mind,
With tranquil restoration:—feelings too   30
Of unremembered pleasure: such, perhaps,
As have no slight or trivial influence
On that best portion of a good man's life,
His little, nameless, unremembered, acts
Of kindness and of love. Nor less, I trust,   35
To them I may have owed another gift,
Of aspect more sublime; that blessed mood,
In which the burthen of the mystery,
In which the heavy and the weary weight

---

[1] Tintern Abbey is the ruins of a medieval abbey.

Of all this unintelligible world,   40
Is lightened:—that serene and blessed mood,
In which the affections gently lead us on,—
Until, the breath of this corporeal frame
And even the motion of our human blood
Almost suspended, we are laid asleep   45
In body, and become a living soul:
While with an eye made quiet by the power
Of harmony, and the deep power of joy,
We see into the life of things.

                 If this
Be but a vain belief, yet, oh! how oft—   50
In darkness and amid the many shapes
Of joyless daylight; when the fretful stir
Unprofitable, and the fever of the world,
Have hung upon the beatings of my heart—
How oft, in spirit, have I turned to thee,   55
O sylvan Wye! thou wanderer thro' the woods,
How often has my spirit turned to thee!

And now, with gleams of half-extinguished thought,
With many recognitions dim and faint,
And somewhat of a sad perplexity,   60
The picture of the mind revives again:
While here I stand, not only with the sense
Of present pleasure, but with pleasing thoughts
That in this moment there is life and food
For future years. And so I dare to hope,   65
Though changed, no doubt, from what I was when first
I came among these hills; when like a roe
I bounded o'er the mountains, by the sides
Of the deep rivers, and the lonely streams,
Wherever nature led: more like a man   70
Flying from something that he dreads, than one
Who sought the thing he loved. For nature then
(The coarser pleasures of my boyish days,
And their glad animal movements all gone by)
To me was all in all.—I cannot paint   75
What then I was. The sounding cataract
Haunted me like a passion: the tall rock,
The mountain, and the deep and gloomy wood,
Their colours and their forms, were then to me
An appetite; a feeling and a love,   80
That had no need of a remoter charm,
By thought supplied, nor any interest
Unborrowed from the eye.—That time is past,
And all its aching joys are now no more,
And all its dizzy raptures. Not for this   85
Faint I, nor mourn nor murmur; other gifts

Have followed; for such loss, I would believe,
Abundant recompense. For I have learned
To look on nature, not as in the hour
Of thoughtless youth; but hearing oftentimes   90
The still, sad music of humanity,
Nor harsh nor grating, though of ample power
To chasten and subdue. And I have felt
A presence that disturbs me with the joy
Of elevated thoughts; a sense sublime   95
Of something far more deeply interfused,
Whose dwelling is the light of setting suns,
And the round ocean and the living air,
And the blue sky, and in the mind of man:
A motion and a spirit, that impels   100
All thinking things, all objects of all thought,
And rolls through all things. Therefore am I still
A lover of the meadows and the woods,
And mountains; and of all that we behold
From this green earth; of all the mighty world   105
Of eye, and ear,—both what they half create,
And what perceive; well pleased to recognise
In nature and the language of the sense,
The anchor of my purest thoughts, the nurse,
The guide, the guardian of my heart, and soul   110
Of all my moral being.

           Nor perchance,
If I were not thus taught, should I the more
Suffer my genial spirits° to decay: *vitality*
For thou art with me here upon the banks
Of this fair river; thou my dearest Friend,°   *his sister Dorothy* 115
My dear, dear Friend; and in thy voice I catch
The language of my former heart, and read
My former pleasures in the shooting lights
Of thy wild eyes. Oh! yet a little while
May I behold in thee what I was once,   120
My dear, dear Sister! and this prayer I make,
Knowing that Nature never did betray
The heart that loved her; 'tis her privilege,
Through all the years of this our life, to lead
From joy to joy: for she can so inform   125
The mind that is within us, so impress
With quietness and beauty, and so feed
With lofty thoughts, that neither evil tongues,
Rash judgments, nor the sneers of selfish men,
Nor greetings where no kindness is, nor all   130
The dreary intercourse of daily life,

Shall e'er prevail against us, or disturb
Our cheerful faith, that all which we behold
Is full of blessings. Therefore let the moon
Shine on thee in thy solitary walk;   135
And let the misty mountain-winds be free
To blow against thee: and, in after years,
When these wild ecstasies shall be matured
Into a sober pleasure; when thy mind
Shall be a mansion for all lovely forms,   140
Thy memory be as a dwelling-place
For all sweet sounds and harmonies; oh! then,
If solitude, or fear, or pain, or grief,
Should be thy portion, with what healing thoughts
Of tender joy wilt thou remember me,   145
And these my exhortations! Nor, perchance—
If I should be where I no more can hear
Thy voice, nor catch from thy wild eyes these gleams
Of past existence—wilt thou then forget
That on the banks of this delightful stream   150
We stood together; and that I, so long
A worshipper of Nature, hither came
Unwearied in that service; rather say
With warmer love—oh! with far deeper zeal
Of holier love. Nor wilt thou then forget,   155
That after many wanderings, many years
Of absence, these steep woods and lofty cliffs,
And this green pastoral landscape, were to me
More dear, both for themselves and for thy sake!

Composed upon Westminster Bridge, September 3, 1802 (1807)

Earth has not any thing to show more fair:
Dull would he be of soul who could pass by
A sight so touching in its majesty:
This City now doth, like a garment, wear
The beauty of the morning; silent, bare,   5
Ships, towers, domes, theatres, and temples lie
Open unto the fields, and to the sky;
All bright and glittering in the smokeless air.
Never did sun more beautifully steep
In his first splendour, valley, rock, or hill;   10
Ne'er saw I, never felt, a calm so deep!
The river glideth at his own sweet will:
Dear God! the very houses seem asleep;
And all that mighty heart is lying stilll

It Is a Beauteous Evening   (1807)

It is a beauteous evening, calm and free,
The holy time is quiet as a Nun
Breathless with adoration; the broad sun
Is sinking down in its tranquillity;
The gentleness of heaven broods o'er the Sea: 5
Listen! the mighty Being is awake,
And doth with his eternal motion make
A sound like thunder—everlastingly.
Dear Child! dear Girl! that walkest with me here,
If thou appear untouched by solemn thought,   10
Thy nature is not therefore less divine:
Thou liest in Abraham's bosom all the year;
And worshipp'st at the Temple's inner shrine,
God being with thee when we know it not.

London, 1802   (1807)

Milton! thou should'st be living at this hour:
England hath need of thee: she is a fen
Of stagnant waters: altar, sword, and pen,
Fireside, the heroic wealth of hall and bower,
Have forfeited their ancient English dower   5
Of inward happiness. We are selfish men;
Oh! raise us up, return to us again;
And give us manners, virtue, freedom, power.
Thy soul was like a Star, and dwelt apart:
Thou hadst a voice whose sound was like the sea: 10
Pure as the naked heavens, majestic, free,
So didst thou travel on life's common way,
In cheerful godliness; and yet thy heart
The lowliest duties on herself did lay.

My Heart Leaps Up   (1807)

My heart leaps up when I behold
    A rainbow in the sky:
So was it when my life began;
So is it now I am a man;
So be it when I shall grow old,   5
    Or let me die!
The Child is father of the Man;
And I could wish my days to be
Bound each to each by natural piety.

The World Is Too Much with Us (1807)

The world is too much with us; late and soon,
Getting and spending, we lay waste our powers:
Little we see in Nature that is ours;
We have given our hearts away, a sordid boon!° *gift*
This Sea that bares her bosom to the moon; 5
The winds that will be howling at all hours,
And are up-gathered now like sleeping flowers;
For this, for every thing, we are out of tune;
It moves us not.—Great God! I'd rather be
A Pagan suckled in a creed outworn; 10
So might I, standing on this pleasant lea,° *meadowland*
Have glimpses that would make me less forlorn;
Have sight of Proteus rising from the sea;
Or hear old Triton blow his wreathèd horn.

Surprised by Joy (1815)

Surprised by joy—impatient as the Wind
I turned to share the transport—Oh! with whom
But Thee, deep buried in the silent tomb,
That spot which no vicissitude can find?
Love, faithful love, recalled thee to my mind— 5
But how could I forget thee? Through what power,
Even for the least division of an hour,
Have I been so beguiled as to be blind
To my most grievous loss!—That thought's return
Was the worst pang that sorrow ever bore, 10
Save one, one only, when I stood forlorn,
Knowing my heart's best treasure was no more;
That neither present time, nor years unborn
Could to my sight that heavenly face restore.

Mutability (1822)

From low to high doth dissolution climb,
And sink from high to low, along a scale
Of awful notes, whose concord shall not fail;
A musical but melancholy chime,
Which they can hear who meddle not with crime, 5
Nor avarice, nor over-anxious care.
Truth fails not; but her outward forms that bear
The longest date do melt like frosty rime,° *frozen dew*
That in the morning whitened hill and plain

And is no more; drop like the tower sublime   10
Of yesterday, which royally did wear
His crown of weeds, but could not even sustain
Some casual shout that broke the silent air,
Or the unimaginable touch of Time.

SAMUEL TAYLOR COLERIDGE   (1772–1834)

Kubla Khan   (WRITTEN C. 1798; PUB. 1816)

In Xanadu did Kubla Khan
A stately pleasure-dome decree:
Where Alph, the sacred river, ran
Through caverns measureless to man
    Down to a sunless sea.   5
So twice five miles of fertile ground
With walls and towers were girdled round:
And there were gardens bright with sinuous rills,
Where blossomed many an incense-bearing tree;
And here were forests ancient as the hills,   10
Enfolding sunny spots of greenery.

But oh! that deep romantic chasm which slanted
Down the green hill athwart a cedarn cover!
A savage place! as holy and enchanted
As e'er beneath a waning moon was haunted   15
By woman wailing for her demon-lover!
And from this chasm, with ceaseless turmoil seething,
As if this earth in fast thick pants were breathing,
A mighty fountain momently was forced:
Amid whose swift half-intermitted burst   20
Huge fragments vaulted like rebounding hail,
Or chaffy grain beneath the thresher's flail:
And 'mid these dancing rocks at once and ever
It flung up momently the sacred river.
Five miles meandering with a mazy motion   25
Through wood and dale the sacred river ran,
Then reached the caverns measureless to man,
And sank in tumult to a lifeless ocean:
And 'mid this tumult Kubla heard from far
Ancestral voices prophesying war!   30

    The shadow of the dome of pleasure
    Floated midway on the waves;
    Where was heard the mingled measure
    From the fountain and the caves.
It was a miracle of rare device,   35
A sunny pleasure-dome with caves of ice!

A damsel with a dulcimer
In a vision once I saw:
It was an Abyssinian maid,
And on her dulcimer she played,   40
Singing of Mount Abora.
Could I revive within me
Her symphony and song,
To such a deep delight 'twould win me,
That with music loud and long,   45
I would build that dome in air,
That sunny dome! those caves of ice!
And all who heard should see them there,
And all should cry, Beware! Beware!
His flashing eyes, his floating hair!   50
Weave a circle round him thrice,
And close your eyes with holy dread,
For he on honey-dew hath fed,
And drunk the milk of Paradise.

GEORGE GORDON, LORD BYRON
(1788–1824)

When We Two Parted   (1813)

When we two parted
    In silence and tears,
Half broken-hearted
    To sever for years,
Pale grew thy cheek and cold,   5
    Colder thy kiss;
Truly that hour foretold
    Sorrow to this.

The dew of the morning
    Sunk chill on my brow—   10
It felt like the warning
    Of what I feel now.
Thy vows are all broken,
    And light is thy fame;
I hear thy name spoken,   15
    And share in its shame.

They name thee before me,
    A knell to mine ear;
A shudder comes o'er me—
    Why wert thou so dear?   20

They know not I knew thee,
　　Who knew thee too well:—
Long, long shall I rue thee,
　　Too deeply to tell.

In secret we met—   25
　　In silence I grieve
That thy heart could forget,
　　Thy spirit deceive.
If I should meet thee
　　After long years,
How should I greet thee?—   30
　　With silence and tears.

The Destruction of Sennacherib (1815)

1

The Assyrian came down like the wolf on the fold,
And his cohorts were gleaming in purple and gold;
And the sheen of their spears was like stars on the sea,
When the blue wave rolls nightly on deep Galilee.

2

Like the leaves of the forest when summer is green,   5
That host with their banners at sunset were seen:
Like the leaves of the forest when autumn hath blown,
That host on the morrow lay withered and strown.

3

For the Angel of Death spread his wings on the blast,
And breathed in the face of the foe as he passed;   10
And the eyes of the sleepers waxed deadly and chill,
And their hearts but once heaved, and forever grew still!

4

And there lay the steed with his nostril all wide,
But through it there rolled not the breath of his pride;
And the foam of his gasping lay white on the turf,   15
And cold as the spray of the rock-beating surf.

5

And there lay the rider distorted and pale,
With the dew on his brow, and the rust on his mail:
And the tents were all silent, the banners alone,
The lances unlifted, the trumpet unblown.   20

6

And the widows of Ashur° are loud in their wail,   Assyria
And the idols are broke in the temple of Baal,
And the might of the Gentile, unsmote by the sword,
Hath melted like snow in the glance of the Lord!

She Walks in Beauty   (1815)

1

She walks in beauty, like the night
    Of cloudless climes and starry skies;
And all that's best of dark and bright
    Meet in her aspect and her eyes:
Thus mellow'd to that tender light   5
    Which heaven to gaudy day denies.

2

One shade the more, one ray the less,
    Had half impair'd the nameless grace
Which waves in every raven trees,
    Or softly lightens o'er her face;   10
Where thoughts serenely sweet express
    How pure, how dear their dwelling place.

3

And on that cheek, and o'er that brow,
    So soft, so calm, yet eloquent,
The smiles that win, the tints that glow,   15
    But tell of days in goodness spent,
A mind at peace with all below,
    A heart whose love is innocent!

PERCY BYSSHE SHELLEY   (1792–1822)

Ozymandias   (1818)

I met a traveler from an antique land
Who said: Two vast and trunkless legs of stone
Stand in the desert. Near them, on the sand,
Half sunk, a shattered visage lies, whose frown,
And wrinkled lip, and sneer of cold command,   5
Tell that its sculptor well those passions read
Which yet survive, stamped on these lifeless things,

The hand that mocked° them and the heart that fed;   *imitated*
And on the pedestal these words appear:
"My name is Ozymandias, king of kings: 10
Look on my works, ye Mighty, and despair!"
Nothing beside remains. Round the decay
Of that colossal wreck, boundless and bare
The lone and level sands stretch far away.

Ode to the West Wind   (1820)

1

O wild West Wind, thou breath of Autumn's being,
Thou, from whose unseen presence the leaves dead
Are driven, like ghosts from an enchanter fleeing,

Yellow, and black, and pale, and hectic° red,   *feverish*
Pestilence-stricken multitudes: O Thou,   5
Who chariotest to their dark wintry bed

The winged seeds, where they lie cold and low,
Each like a corpse within its grave, until
Thine azure sister of the Spring shall blow

Her clarion° o'er the dreaming earth, and fill   *trumpet*   10
(Driving sweet buds like flocks to feed in air)
With living hues and odours plain and hill:

Wild Spirit, which art moving everywhere;
Destroyer and Preserver; hear, O hear!

2

Thou on whose stream, 'mid the steep sky's commotion,   15
Loose clouds like Earth's decaying leaves are shed,
Shook from the tangled boughs of Heaven and Ocean,

Angels of rain and lightning: there are spread
On the blue surface of thine aery surge,
Like the bright hair uplifted from the head   20

Of some fierce Mænad, even from the dim verge
Of the horizon to the zenith's height,
The locks of the approaching storm. Thou Dirge

Of the dying year, to which this closing night
Will be the dome of a vast sepulchre,   25
Vaulted with all thy congregated might

Of vapours, from whose solid atmosphere
Black rain and fire and hail will burst: O hear!

3

Thou who didst waken from his summer dreams
The blue Mediterranean, where he lay,   30
Lulled by the coil of his chrystalline streams,

Beside a pumice isle in Baiæs bay,
And saw in sleep old palaces and towers
Quivering within the wave's intenser day,

All overgrown with azure moss and flowers   35
So sweet, the sense faints picturing them! Thou
For whose path the Atlantic's level powers

Cleave themselves into chasms, while far below
The sea-blooms and the oozy woods which wear
The sapless foliage of the ocean, know   40

Thy voice, and suddenly grow grey with fear,
And tremble and despoil themselves: O hear!

4

If I were a dead leaf thou mightest bear;
If I were a swift cloud to fly with thee;
A wave to pant beneath thy power, and share   45

The impulse of thy strength, only less free
Than thou, O Uncontrollable! If even
I were as in my boyhood, and could be

The comrade of thy wanderings over Heaven,
As then, when to outstrip thy skiey speed   50
Scarce seemed a vision; I would ne'er have striven

As thus with thee in prayer in my sore need.
Oh! lift me as a wave, a leaf, a cloud!
I fall upon the thorns of life! I bleed!

A heavy weight of hours has chained and bowed   55
One too like thee: tameless, and swift, and proud.

5

Make me thy lyre, even as the forest is:
What if my leaves are falling like its own!
The tumult of thy mighty harmonies

Will take from both a deep, autumnal tone,   60
Sweet though in sadness. Be thou, Spirit fierce,
My spirit! Be thou me, impetuous one!

Drive my dead thoughts over the universe
Like withered leaves to quicken a new birth!
And, by the incantation of this verse,   65

Scatter, as from an unextinguished hearth
Ashes and sparks, my words among mankind!
Be through my lips to unawakened Earth

The trumpet of a prophecy! O Wind,
If Winter comes, can Spring be far behind?   70

When the lamp is shattered   (1824)

I

    When the lamp is shattered
The light in the dust lies dead—
    When the cloud is scattered
The rainbow's glory is shed.
    When the lute is broken,   5
Sweet tones are remembered not;
    When the lips have spoken,
Loved accents are soon forgot.

II

    As music and splendour
Survive not the lamp and the lute,   10
    The heart's echoes render
No song when the spirit is mute:—
    No song but sad dirges,
Like the wind through a ruined cell,
    Or the mournful surges   15
That ring the dead seaman's knell.

III

    When hearts have once mingled
Love first leaves the well-built nest;
    The weak one is singled
To endure what it once possessed.   20
    O Love! who bewailest
The frailty of all things here,
    Why choose you the frailest
For your cradle, your home, and your bier?

IV

    Its passions will rock thee   25
As the storms rock the ravens on high;
    Bright reason will mock thee,
Like the sun from a wintry sky.
    From thy nest every rafter
Will rot, and thine eagle home   30
    Leave thee naked to laughter,
When leaves fall and cold winds come.

England in 1819   (WRITTEN 1819; PUB. 1839)

An old, mad, blind, despised, and dying King;
Princes, the dregs of their dull race, who flow
Through public scorn,—mud from a muddy spring;

Rulers who neither see nor feel nor know,
But leechlike to their fainting country cling   5
Till they drop, blind in blood, without a blow.
A people starved and stabbed in th' untilled field;
An army, whom liberticide and prey
Makes as a two-edged sword to all who wield;
Golden and sanguine laws which tempt and slay;   10
Religion Christless, Godless—a book sealed;
A senate, Time's worst statute, unrepealed—
Are graves from which a glorious Phantom° may   *revolution*
Burst, to illumine our tempestuous day.

JOHN CLARE   (1793–1864)

Badger   (WRITTEN 1835–1837; PUB. 1920)

When midnight comes a host of dogs and men
Go out and track the badger to his den,
And put a sack within the hole, and lie
Till the old grunting badger passes by.
He comes and hears—they let the strongest loose.   5
The old fox hears the noise and drops the goose.
The poacher shoots and hurries from the cry,
And the old hare half wounded buzzes by.
They get a forkéd stick to bear him down
And clap the dogs and take him to the town,   10
And bait him all the day with many dogs,
And laugh and shout and fright the scampering hogs.
He runs along and bites at all he meets:
They shout and hollo down the noisy streets.

He turns about to face the loud uproar   15
And drives the rebels to their very door.
The frequent stone is hurled where'er they go;
When badgers fight, then everyone's a foe.
The dogs are clapped and urged to join the fray;
The badger turns and drives them all away.   20
Though scarcely half as big, demure and small,
He fights with dogs for hours and beats them all.
The heavy mastiff, savage in the fray,
Lies down and licks his feet and turns away.
The bulldog knows his match and waxes cold,   25
The badger grins and never leaves his hold.
He drives the crowd and follows at their heels
And bites them through—the drunkard swears and reels.

The frighted women take the boys away,
The blackguard laughs and hurries on the fray.   30

He tries to reach the woods, an awkward race,
But sticks and cudgels quickly stop the chase.
He turns again and drives the noisy crowd
And beats the many dogs in noises loud.
He drives away and beats them every one,   35
And then they loose them all and set them on.
He falls as dead and kicked by boys and men,
Then starts and grins and drives the crowd again;
Till kicked and torn and beaten out he lies
And leaves his hold and crackles, groans, and dies.   40

JOHN KEATS   (1795–1821)

La Belle Dame Sans Merci   (1819)

A Ballad

O what can ail thee, knight at arms,
    Alone and palely loitering?
The sedge has wither'd from the lake,
    And no birds sing.

O what can ail thee, knight at arms,   5
    So haggard and so woe-begone?
The squirrel's granary is full,
    And the harvest's done.

I see a lily on thy brow
    With anguish moist and fever dew,   10
And on thy cheeks a fading rose
    Fast withereth too.

I met a lady in the meads,
    Full beautiful, a fairy's child;
Her hair was long, her foot was light,   15
    And her eyes were wild.

I made a garland for her head,
    And bracelets too, and fragrant zone;°   *belt of blossoms*
She look'd at me as she did love,
    And made sweet moan.   20

I set her on my pacing steed,
    And nothing else saw all day long,
For sidelong would she bend, and sing
    A fairy's song.

She found me roots of relish sweet,   25
    And honey wild, and manna dew,
And sure in language strange she said—
    I love thee true.

She took me to her elfin grot,
    And there she wept, and sigh'd full sore,
And there I shut her wild wild eyes
      With kisses four.   30

And there she lulled me asleep, .
    And there I dream'd—Ah! woe betide!
The latest° dream I ever dream'd   *last* 35
    On the cold hill's side.

I saw pale kings, and princes too,
    Pale warriors, death pale were they all;
They cried—"La belle dame sans merci
      Hath thee in thrall!"   40

I saw their starv'd lips in the gloam
    With horrid warning gaped wide,
And I awoke and found me here
    On the cold hill's side.

And this is why I sojourn here,
    Alone and palelyloitering,   45
Though the sedge is wither'd from the lake,
    And no birds sing.

Ode to a Nightingale   (1819)

1

My heart aches, and a drowsy numbness pains
    My sense, as though of hemlock I had drunk,
Or emptied some dull opiate to the drains
    One minute past, and Lethe°wards had sunk: *river of forgetfulness*
'Tis not through envy of thy happy lot,   5
    But being too happy in thine happiness,—
    That thou, light-winged Dryad of the trees,
      In some melodious plot
Of beechen green, and shadows numberless,
    Singest of summer in full-throated ease.   10

2

O, for a draught of vintage! that hath been
    Cool'd a long age in the deep-delved earth,
Tasting of Flora and the country green,
    Dance, and Provençal song, and sunburnt mirth!
O for a beaker full of the warm South,   15
    Full of the true, the blushful Hippocrene,
    With beaded bubbles winking at the brim,
      And purple-stained mouth;
That I might drink, and leave the world unseen,
    And with thee fade away into the forest dim: 20

3

Fade far away, dissolve, and quite forget
    What thou among the leaves hast never known,
The weariness, the fever, and the fret
    Here, where men sit and hear each other groan;
Where palsy shakes a few, sad, last gray hairs,   25
    Where youth grows pale, and spectre-thin, and dies;
    Where but to think is to be full of sorrow
        And leaden-eyed despairs,
Where Beauty cannot keep her lustrous eyes,
    Or new Love pine at them beyond to-morrow.   30

4

Away! away! for I will fly to thee,
    Not charioted by Bacchus and his pards,°   *leopards*
But on the viewless wings of Poesy,
    Though the dull brain perplexes and retards:
Already with thee! tender is the night,   35
    And haply the Queen-Moon is on her throne,
    Cluster'd around by all her starry Fays;°   *fairies*
        But here there is no light,
Save what from heaven is with the breezes blown
    Through verdurous glooms and winding mossy ways.   40

5

I cannot see what flowers are at my feet,
    Nor what soft incense hangs upon the boughs,
But, in embalmed darkness, guess each sweet
    Wherewith the seasonable month endows
The grass, the thicket, and the fruit-tree wild;   45
    White hawthorn, and the pastoral eglantine;°   *sweetbriars*
Fast fading violets cover'd up in leaves;
        And mid-May's eldest child,
The coming musk-rose, full of dewy wine,
    The murmurous haunt of flies on summer eves.   50

6

Darkling I listen; and, for many a time
    I have been half in love with easeful Death,
Call'd him soft names in many a mused rhyme,
    To take into the air my quiet breath;
Now more than ever seems it rich to die,   55
    To cease upon the midnight with no pain,
    While thou art pouring forth thy soul abroad
        In such an ecstasy!
Still wouldst thou sing, and I have ears in vain—
    To thy high requiem become a sod.   60

Thou wast not born for death, immortal Bird!
    No hungry generations tread thee down;
The voice I hear this passing night was heard
    In ancient days by emperor and clown:
Perhaps the self-same song that found a path   65
    Through the sad heart of Ruth, when, sick for home
        She stood in tears amid the alien corn;°   *grain*
        The same that oft-times hath
Charm'd magic casements, opening on the foam
    Of perilous seas, in faery lands forlorn.   70

8

Forlorn! the very word is like a bell
    To toll me back from thee to my sole self!
Adieu! the fancy cannot cheat so well
    As she is fam'd to do, deceiving elf.
Adieu! adieu! thy plaintive anthem fades   75
    Past the near meadows, over the still stream,
    Up the hill-side; and now 'tis buried deep
        In the next valley-glades:
Was it a vision, or a waking dream?
    Fled is that music:—Do I wake or sleep?   80

Ode on a Grecian Urn   (1820)

Thou still unravished bride of quietness,
    Thou foster-child of silence and slow time,
Sylvan historian, who canst thus express
    A flowery tale more sweetly than our rhyme:
What leaf-fringed legend haunts about thy shape   5
    Of deities or mortals, or of both,
        In Tempe or the dales of Arcady?
    What men or gods are these? What maidens loth?
What mad pursuit? What struggle to escape?
        What pipes and timbrels? What wild ecstasy?   10

Heard melodies are sweet, but those unheard
    Are sweeter; therefore, ye soft pipes, play on;
Not to the sensual° ear, but, more endeared,   *physical*
    Pipe to the spirit ditties of no tone:
Fair youth, beneath the trees, thou canst not leave   15
    Thy song, nor ever can those trees be bare;
        Bold Lover, never, never canst thou kiss,
Though winning near the goal—yet, do not grieve;
        She cannot fade, though thou hast not thy bliss,
    For ever wilt thou love, and she be fair!   20

Ah, happy, happy boughs! that cannot shed
    Your leaves, nor ever bid the Spring adieu;
And, happy melodist, unwearièd,
    For ever piping songs for ever new;
More happy love! more happy, happy love!   25
    For ever warm and still to be enjoyed,
        For ever panting, and for ever young;
All breathing human passion far above,
    That leaves a heart high-sorrowful and cloyed,
        A burning forehead, and a parching tongue.   30

Who are these coming to the sacrifice?
    To what green altar, O mysterious priest,
Lead'st thou that heifer lowing at the skies,
    And all her silken flanks with garlands drest?
What little town by river or sea shore,   35
    Or mountain-built with peaceful citadel,
        Is emptied of this folk, this pious morn?
And, little town, the streets for evermore
    Will silent be; and not a soul to tell
        Why thou art desolate, can e'er return.   40

O Attic shape! Fair attitude! with brede°   *design*
    Of marble men and maidens overwrought,
With forest branches and the trodden weed;
    Thou, silent form, dost tease us out of thought
As doth Eternity: Cold Pastoral!   45
    When old age shall this generation waste,
        Thou shalt remain, in midst of other woe
    Than ours, a friend to man, to whom thou say'st,
Beauty is truth, truth beauty,—that is all
    Ye know on earth, and all ye need to know.   50

To Autumn   (1820)

I

Season of mists and mellow fruitfulness,
    Close bosom-friend of the maturing sun;
Conspiring with him how to load and bless
    With fruit the vines that round the thatch-eaves run;
To bend with apples the mossed cottage-trees,   5
    And fill all fruit with ripeness to the core;
        To swell the gourd, and plump the hazel shells
With a sweet kernel; to set budding more,
And still more, later flowers for the bees,
Until they think warm days will never cease,   10
    For Summer has o'er-brimmed their clammy cells.

II

Who hath not seen thee oft amid thy store?
    Sometimes whoever seeks abroad may find
Thee sitting careless on a granary floor,
    Thy hair soft-lifted by the winnowing wind;   15
Or on a half-reaped furrow sound asleep,
    Drowsed with the fume of poppies, while thy hook°   *sickle*
        Spares the next swath and all its twinèd flowers:
And sometimes like a gleaner thou dost keep
    Steady thy laden head across a brook;   20
    Or by a cider-press, with patient look,
        Thou watchest the last oozings hours by hours.

III

Where are the songs of Spring? Ay, where are they?
    Think not of them, thou hast thy music too,—
While barrèd clouds bloom the soft-dying day,
    And touch the stubble-plains with rosy hue;   25
Then in a wailful choir the small gnats mourn
    Among the river sallows,° borne aloft   *willows*
        Or sinking as the light wind lives or dies;
And full-grown lambs loud bleat from hilly bourn;
Hedge-crickets sing; and now with treble soft   30
The red-breast whistles from a garden-croft°   *garden plot*
    And gathering swallows twitter in the skies.

ELIZABETH BARRETT BROWNING
(1806–1861)

How Do I Love Thee? Let Me Count the Ways
(1850)

How do I love thee? Let me count the ways.
I love thee to the depth and breadth and height
My soul can reach, when feeling out of sight
For the ends of being and ideal grace.
I love thee to the level of every day's   5
Most quiet need, by sun and candle-light.
I love thee freely, as men strive for right.
I love thee purely, as they turn from praise.
I love thee with the passion put to use
In my old griefs, and with my childhood's faith.   10
I love thee with a love I seemed to lose
With my lost saints. I love thee with the breath,
Smiles, tears, of all my life; and, if God choose,
I shall but love thee better after death.

HENRY WADSWORTH LONGFELLOW   (1807–1882)

Mezzo Cammin   (1845)

> *Written at Boppard on the Rhine, August 26, 1842, just before*
> *leaving for home.*

Half of my life is gone, and I have let
    The years slip from me and have not fulfilled
    The aspiration of my youth, to build
    Some tower of song with lofty parapet.
Not indolence, nor pleasure, nor the fret   5
    Of restless passions that would not be stilled,
    But sorrow, and a care that almost killed,
    Kept me from what I may accomplish yet;

Though, half-way up the hill, I see the Past
    Lying beneath me with its sounds and sights,—   10
    A city in the twilight dim and vast,
With smoking roofs, soft bells, and gleaming lights,—
    And hear above me on the autumnal blast
    The cataract of Death far thundering from the heights.

Aftermath   (1873)

When the summer fields are mown,
When the birds are fledged and flown,
    And the dry leaves strew the path;
With the falling of the snow,
With the cawing of the crow,   5
Once again the fields we mow
    And gather in the aftermath.

Not the sweet, new grass with flowers
In this harvesting of ours;
    Not the upland clover bloom;   10
But the rowen mixed with weeds,
Tangled tufts from marsh and meads,
Where the poppy drops its seeds
    In the silence and the gloom.

EDGAR ALLAN POE   (1809–1849)

The Bells   (1848)

I

    Hear the sledges with the bells—
      Silver bells!
What a world of merriment their melody foretells!

How they tinkle, tinkle, tinkle,
In the icy air of night!   5
While the stars that oversprinkle
All the Heavens, seem to twinkle
With a crystalline delight;
Keeping time, time, time,
In a sort of Runic rhyme,   10
To the tintinnabulation that so musically wells
    From the bells, bells, bells, bells,
    Bells, bells, bells—
From the jingling and the tinkling of the bells.

II

Hear the mellow wedding bells—
    Golden bells!   15
What a world of happiness their harmony foretells!
    Through the balmy air of night
    How they ring out their delight!—
    From the molten-golden notes,
    And all in time,   20
    What a liquid ditty floats
To the turtle-dove that listens, while she gloats
    On the moon!
    Oh, from out the sounding cells,
What a gush of euphony voluminously wells!   25
    How it swells!
    How it dwells
    On the future!—how it tells
    Of the rapture that impels
    To the swinging and the ringing   30
    Of the bells; bells, bells—
    Of the bells, bells, bells, bells,
    Bells, bells, bells—
To the rhyming and the chiming of the bells!   35

III

Hear the loud alarum bells—
    Brazen bells!
What a tale of terror, now, their turbulency tells!
    In the startled ear of Night
    How they scream out their affright!
    Too much horrified to speak,
    They can only shriek, shriek,   40
    Out of tune,
In a clamorous appealing to the mercy of the fire,
In a mad expostulation with the deaf and frantic fire   45
    Leaping higher, higher, higher,
    With a desperate desire,

And a resolute endeavour
Now—now to sit, or never,
By the side of the pale-faced moon.   50
    Oh, the bells, bells, bells!
    What a tale their terror tells
    Of despair!
    How they clang, and clash, and roar!
    What a horror they outpour   55
On the bosom of the palpitating air!
    Yet the ear, it fully knows,
        By the twanging,
        And the clanging,
    How the danger ebbs and flows;   60
    Yes, the ear distinctly tells,
        In the jangling,
        And the wrangling,
    How the danger sinks and swells,
By the sinking or the swelling in the anger of the bells—   65
        Of the bells—
    Of the bells, bells, bells, bells,
        Bells, bells, bells—
In the clamor and the clangor of the bells!

IV

    Hear the tolling of the bells—   70
        Iron bells!
What a world of solemn thought their monody compels!
    In the silence of the night,
    How we shiver with affright
At the melancholy menace of their tone!   75
    For every sound that floats
    From the rust within their throats
        Is a groan.
    And the people—ah, the people—
    They that dwell up in the steeple,   80
        All alone,
    And who, tolling, tolling, tolling,
        In that muffled monotone,
    Feel a glory in so rolling
    On the human heart a stone—   85
They are neither man nor woman—
They are neither brute nor human—
        They are Ghouls:—
    And their king it is who tolls:—
    And he rolls, rolls, rolls,   90
        Rolls
    A Pæan from the bells!
    And his merry bosom swells
    With the Pæan of the bells!

And he dances and he yells;   95
   Keeping time, time, time,
In a sort of Runic rhyme,
   To the Pæan of the bells—
     Of the bells:—
   Keeping time, time, time,   100
In a sort of Runic rhyme,
   To the throbbing of the bells—
   Of the bells, bells, bells—
    To the sobbing of the bells:—
   Keeping time, time, time,   105
   As he knells, knells, knells,
   In a happy Runic rhyme,
   To the rolling of the bells—
   Of the bells, bells, bells:—
   To the tolling of the bells—   110
   Of the bells, bells, bells, bells,
   Bells, bells, bells—
To the moaning and the groaning of the bells.

ALFRED, LORD TENNYSON   (1809–1892)

Break, Break, Break   (1834)

Break, break, break,
   On thy cold gray stones, O Sea!
And I would that my tongue could utter
   The thoughts that arise in me.

O well for the fisherman's boy,   5
   That he shouts with his sister at play!
O well for the sailor lad,
   That he sings in his boat on the bay!

And the stately ships go on
   To their haven under the hill;   10
But O for the touch of a vanish'd hand,
   And the sound of a voice that is stilll

Break, break, break,
   At the foot of thy crags, O Sea!
But the tender grace of a day that is dead   15
   Will never come back to me.

Now Sleeps the Crimson Petal   (1847)

   Now sleeps the crimson petal, now the white;
Nor waves the cypress in the palace walk;
Nor winks the gold fin in the porphyry font.
The firefly wakens; waken thou with me.

Now droops the milk-white peacock like a ghost, 5
And like a ghost she glimmers on to me.

Now lies the Earth all Danaë to the stars,
And all thy heart lies open unto me.

Now slides the silent meteor on, and leaves
A shining furrow, as thy thoughts in me. 10

Now folds the lily all her sweetness up.
And slips into the bosom of the lake.
So fold thyself, my dearest, thou, and slip
Into my bosom and be lost in me.

Tears, Idle Tears (1847)

Tears, idle tears, I know not what they mean,
Tears from the depth of some divine despair
Rise in the heart, and gather to the eyes,
In looking on the happy autumn-fields,
And thinking of the days that are no more. 5

Fresh as the first beam glittering on a sail,
That brings our friends up from the underworld,
Sad as the last which reddens over one
That sinks with all we love below the verge;
So sad, so fresh, the days that are no more. 10

Ah, sad and strange as in dark summer dawns
The earliest pipe of half-awakened birds
To dying ears, when unto dying eyes
The casement slowly grows a glimmering square;
So sad, so strange, the days that are no more. 15

Dear as remembered kisses after death,
And sweet as those by hopeless fancy feigned
On lips that are for others; deep as love,
Deep as first love, and wild with all regret;
O Death in Life, the days that are no more! 20

ROBERT BROWNING (1812–1889)

Meeting at Night (1845)

1

The grey sea and the long black land;
And the yellow half-moon large and low;
And the startled little waves that leap
In fiery ringlets from their sleep,
As I gain the cove with pushing prow, 5
And quench its speed i' the slushy sand.

2

Then a mile of warm sea-scented beach;
Three fields to cross till a farm appears;
A tap at the pane, the quick sharp scratch
And blue spurt of a lighted match   10
And a voice less loud, thro' its joys and fears,
Than the two hearts beating each to each!

Parting at Morning   (1845)

Round the cape of a sudden came the sea,
And the sun looked over the mountain's rim:
And straight was a path of gold for him,
And the need of a world of men for me.

MATTHEW ARNOLD   (1822–1888)

Dover Beach   (1867)

The sea is calm tonight.
The tide is full, the moon lies fair
Upon the straits;—on the French coast the light
Gleams and is gone; the cliffs of England stand,
Glimmering and vast, out in the tranquil bay.   5
Come to the window, sweet is the night-air!
Only, from the long line of spray
Where the sea meets the moon-blanched land,
Listen! you hear the grating roar
Of pebbles which the waves draw back, and fling,   10
At their return, up the high strand,
Begin, and cease, and then again begin,
With tremulous cadence slow, and bring
The eternal note of sadness in.

Sophocles long ago   15
Heard it on the Aegean, and it brought
Into his mind the turbid ebb and flow
Of human misery; we
Find also in the sound a thought,
Hearing it by this distant northern sea.   20

The Sea of Faith
Was once, too, at the full, and round earth's shore
Lay like the folds of a bright girdle furled.
But now I only hear
Its melancholy, long, withdrawing roar,   25
Retreating, to the breath
Of the night-wind, down the vast edges drear
And naked shingles° of the world.   *gravel beaches*

Ah, love, let us be true
To one another! for the world, which seems   30
To lie before us like a land of dreams,
So various, so beautiful, so new,
Hath really neither joy, nor love, nor light,
Nor certitude, nor peace, nor help for pain;
And we are here as on a darkling° plain   *darkened or darkening*   35
Swept with confused alarms of struggle and flight,
Where ignorant armies clash by night.

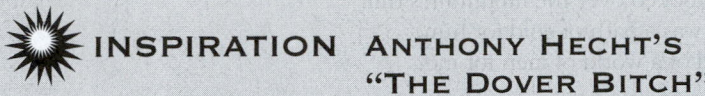

INSPIRATION ANTHONY HECHT'S "THE DOVER BITCH"

Matthew Arnold's famous poem "Dover Beach" was one of the most popular of the Victorian period. It should come as no surprise then that it has yielded countless interpretations, including more than a few poetic responses and parodies. Perhaps the most well-known poetic intervention is that of Pulitzer Prize–winning American poet Anthony Hecht, "The Dover Bitch." Many critics believe that Matthew Arnold wrote "Dover Beach" for his wife on their honeymoon. Whatever the exact context, the poem certainly reflects a seriousness in its concerns and tone, combining intellectualism with depictions of pastoral beauty, melancholy, grief, and desire. In his wry reply, Hecht has some fun with his reimagined take on the same scene: in his version, the listening woman of Arnold's poem turns out to be more concerned with carnal desire than any of the cosmic or metaphysical matters Arnold discusses though the voice of his poem's narrator. Hecht even gave Arnold a nod in the subtitle of his poem: in Arnold's *The Study of Poetry* (1880), Arnold defined poetry as "a criticism of life."

Anthony Hecht   (1923–2004)

The Dover Bitch: A Criticism of Life   (1967)

For Andrews Wanning

So there stood Matthew Arnold and this girl
With the cliffs of England crumbling away behind them,
And he said to her, "Try to be true to me,
And I'll do the same for you, for things are bad
All over, etc., etc."   5
Well now, I knew this girl. It's true she had read
Sophocles in a fairly good translation
And caught that bitter allusion to the sea,
But all the time he was talking she had in mind

(continued on next page)

ANTHONY HECHT'S "THE DOVER BITCH"

The notion of what his whiskers would feel like   10
On the back of her neck. She told me later on
That after a while she got to looking out
At the lights across the channel, and really felt sad,
Thinking of all the wine and enormous beds
And blandishments in French and the perfumes.   15
And then she got really angry. To have been brought
All the way down from London, and then be addressed
As a sort of mournful cosmic last resort
Is really tough on a girl, and she was pretty.
Anyway, she watched him pace the room   20
And finger his watch-chain and seem to sweat a bit,
And then she said one or two unprintable things.
But you mustn't judge her by that. What I mean to say is,
She's really all right. I still see her once in a while
And she always treats me right. We have a drink   25
And I give her a good time, and perhaps it's a year
Before I see her again, but there she is,
Running to fat, but dependable as they come.
And sometimes I bring her a bottle of *Nuit d'Amour.*°   *a perfume*

CHRISTINA ROSSETTI   (1830–1894)

Song   (1862)

When I am dead, my dearest,
    Sing no sad songs for me;
Plant thou no roses at my head,
    Nor shady cypress tree:
Be the green grass above me   5
    With showers and dewdrops wet;
And if thou wilt, remember,
    And if thou wilt, forget.

I shall not see the shadows,
    I shall not feel the rain;   10
I shall not hear the nightingale
    Sing on, as if in pain:
And dreaming through the twilight
    That doth not rise nor set,
Haply° I may remember,   *perhaps* 15
    And haply may forget.

LEWIS CARROLL [CHARLES LUTWIDGE DODGSON]   (1832–1898)

Jabberwocky   (1871)

'Twas brillig, and the slithy toves
    Did gyre and gimble in the wabe:
All mimsy were the borogoves,
    And the mome raths outgrabe.

"Beware the Jabberwock, my son!   5
    The jaws that bite, the claws that catch!
Beware the Jubjub bird, and shun
    The frumious Bandersnatch!"

He took his vorpal sword in hand;
    Long time the manxome foe he sought—   10
So rested he by the Tumtum tree
    And stood awhile in thought.

And, as in uffish thought he stood,
    The Jabberwock, with eyes of flame,
Came whiffling through the tulgey wood,   15
    And burbled as it came!

One, two! One, two! And through and through
    The vorpal blade went snicker-snack!
He left it dead, and with its head
    He went galumphing back.   20

"And hast thou slain the Jabberwock?
    Come to my arms, my beamish boy!
O frabjous day! Callooh, Callay!"
    He chortled in his joy.

'Twas brillig, and the slithy toves   25
    Did gyre and gimble in the wabe:
All mimsy were the borogoves,
    And the mome raths outgrabe.

THOMAS HARDY   (1840–1928)

Hap   (1866)

If but some vengeful god would call to me
From up the sky, and laugh: "Thou suffering thing,
Know that thy sorrow is my ecstasy,
That thy love's loss is my hate's profiting!"

Then would I bear it, clench myself, and die,   5
Steeled by the sense of ire unmerited;
Half-eased in that a Powerfuller than I
Had willed and meted me the tears I shed.

But not so. How arrives it joy lies slain,
And why unblooms the best hope ever sown?   10
—Crass Casualty obstructs the sun and rain,
And dicing Time for gladness casts a moan . . .
These purblind Doomsters had as readily strown
Blisses about my pilgrimage as pain.

The Convergence of the Twain   (1912)

Lines on the Loss of the "Titanic"

I

In a solitude of the sea
Deep from human vanity,
And the Pride of Life that planned her, stilly couches she.

II

Steel chambers, late the pyres
Of her salamandrine fires,   5
Cold currents third,° and turn to rhythmic tidal lyres.   *thread*

III

Over the mirrors meant
To glass the opulent
The sea-worm crawls—grotesque, slimed, dumb, indifferent.

IV

Jewels in joy designed   10
To ravish the sensuous mind
Lie lightless, all their sparkles bleared and black and blind.

V

Dim moon-eyed fishes near
Gaze at the gilded gear
And query: "What does this vaingloriousness down here?" . . .   15

VI

Well: while was fashioning
This creature of cleaving wing,
The Immanent Will that stirs and urges everything

VII

Prepared a sinister mate
For her—so gaily great—   20
A Shape of Ice, for the time far and dissociate.

VIII

And as the smart ship grew
In stature, grace, and hue,
In shadowy silent distance grew the Iceberg too.

IX

Alien they seemed to be: 25
No mortal eye could see
The intimate welding of their later history,

X

Or sign that they were bent
By paths coincident
On being anon twin halves of one august event,   30

XI

Till the Spinner of the Years
Said "Now!" And each one hears,
And consummation comes, and jars two hemispheres.

During Wind and Rain   (1917)

They sing their dearest songs—
He, she, all of them—yea,
Treble and tenor and bass,
   And one to play;
With the candles mooning each face. . . .   5
    Ah, no; the years O!
How the sick leaves reel down in throngs!

They clear the creeping moss—
Elders and juniors—aye,
Making the pathways neat   10
   And the garden gay;
And they build a shady seat. . . .
    Ah, no; the years, the years,
See, the white storm-birds wing across.

They are blithely breakfasting all—   15
Men and maidens—yea,
Under the summer tree,
   With a glimpse of the bay,
While pet fowl come to the knee. . . .
    Ah, no; the years O!   20
And the rotten rose is ript from the wall.

They change to a high new house,
He, she, all of them—aye,
Clocks and carpets and chairs
   On the lawn all day,   25
And brightest things that are theirs. . . .
    Ah, no; the years, the years
Down their carved names the rain-drop ploughs.

GERARD MANLEY HOPKINS
Spring and Fall

(1844–1889)
(1880)

To a young child

Márgarét, áre you gríeving	
Over Goldengrove unleaving°	shedding its leaves
Leáves, líke the things of man, you	
With your fresh thoughts care for, can you?	
Áh! ás the heart grows older	5
It will come to such sights colder	
By and by, nor spare a sigh	
Though worlds of wanwood leafmeal lie;	
And yet you *will* weep and know why.	
Now no matter, child, the name:	10
Sórrow's spríngs áre the same.	
Nor mouth had, no nor mind, expressed	
What heart heard of, ghost° guessed:	spirit
It ís the blight man was born for,	
It is Margaret you mourn for.	15

EMMA LAZARUS
The New Colossus

(1849–1887)
(1883)

Not like the brazen giant of Greek fame,	
With conquering limbs astride from land to land;	
Here at our sea-washed, sunset gates shall stand	
A mighty woman with a torch, whose flame	
Is the imprisoned lightning, and her name	5
Mother of Exiles. From her beacon-hand	
Glows world-wide welcome; her mild eyes command	
The air-bridged harbor that twin cities frame.	
"Keep, ancient lands, your storied pomp!" cries she	
With silent lips. "Give me your tired, your poor,	10
Your huddled masses yearning to breathe free,	
The wretched refuse of your teeming shore.	
Send these, the homeless, tempest-tost to me,	
I lift my lamp beside the golden door!"	

A. E. HOUSMAN
Loveliest of trees, the cherry now

(1859–1936)
(1896)

Loveliest of trees, the cherry now	
Is hung with bloom along the bough,	
And stands about the woodland ride°	path
Wearing white for Eastertide.	

Now, of my threescore years and ten,   5
Twenty will not come again,
And take from seventy springs a score,
It only leaves me fifty more.

And since to look at things in bloom
Fifty springs are little room,   10
About the woodlands I will go
To see the cherry hung with snow.

EDEN PHILLPOTTS   (1862–1960)

The Learned   (1942)

The grey-beards wag, the bald heads nod,
And gather thick as bees,
To talk electrons, gasses, God,
Old nebulæ, new fleas.
Each specialist, each dry-as-dust   5
And professorial oaf,
Holds up his little crumb of crust
And cries, "Behold the loaf!"

WILLIAM BUTLER YEATS   (1865–1939)

The Song of Wandering Aengus   (1899)

I went out to the hazel wood,
Because a fire was in my head,
And cut and peeled a hazel wand,
And hooked a berry to a thread;
And when white moths were on the wing,   5
And moth-like stars were flickering out,
I dropped the berry in a stream
And caught a little silver trout.

When I had laid it on the floor
I went to blow the fire aflame,   10
But something rustled on the floor,
And some one called me by my name:
It had become a glimmering girl
With apple blossom in her hair
Who called me by my name and ran   15
And faded through the brightening air.

Though I am old with wandering
Through hollow lands and hilly lands,
I will find out where she has gone,

And kiss her lips and take her hands;   20
And walk among long dappled grass,
And pluck till time and times are done
The silver apples of the moon,
The golden apples of the sun.

The Scholars   (1917)

Bald heads forgetful of their sins,
Old, learned, respectable bald heads
Edit and annotate the lines
That young men, tossing on their beds,
Rhymed out in love's despair   5
To flatter beauty's ignorant ear.

All shuffle there; all cough in ink;
All wear the carpet with their shoes;
All think what other people think;
All know the man their neighbour knows.   10
Lord, what would they say
Did their Catullus° walk that way?   *Roman author of love poems*

The Wild Swans at Coole   (1917)

The trees are in their autumn beauty,
The woodland paths are dry,
Under the October twilight the water
Mirrors a still sky;
Upon the brimming water among the stones   5
Are nine-and-fifty swans.

The nineteenth autumn has come upon me
Since I first made my count;
I saw, before I had well finished,
All suddenly mount   10
And scatter wheeling in great broken rings
Upon their clamorous wings.

I have looked upon those brilliant creatures,
And now my heart is sore.
All's changed since I, hearing at twilight,   15
The first time on this shore,
The bell-beat of their wings above my head,
Trod with a lighter tread.

Unwearied still, lover by lover,
They paddle in the cold   20
Companionable streams or climb the air;
Their hearts have not grown old;

Passion or conquest, wander where they will,
Attend upon them still.

But now they drift on the still water,   25
Mysterious, beautiful;
Among what rushes will they build,
By what lake's edge or pool
Delight men's eyes when I awake some day
To find they have flown away?   30

The Second Coming   (1921)

Turning and turning in the widening gyre°   *spiral*
The falcon cannot hear the falconer;
Things fall apart; the center cannot hold;
Mere anarchy is loosed upon the world,
The blood-dimmed tide is loosed, and everywhere   5
The ceremony of innocence is drowned;
The best lack all conviction, while the worst
Are full of passionate intensity.

Surely some revelation is at hand;
Surely the Second Coming is at hand;   10
The Second Coming! Hardly are those words out
When a vast image out of *Spiritus Mundi*
Troubles my sight: somewhere in sands of the desert
A shape with lion body and the head of a man,
A gaze blank and pitiless as the sun,   15
Is moving its slow thighs, while all about it
Reel shadows of the indignant desert birds.
The darkness drops again; but now I know
That twenty centuries of stony sleep
Were vexed to nightmare by a rocking cradle,   20
And what rough beast, its hour come round at last,
Slouches towards Bethlehem to be born?

Leda and the Swan   (1924)

A sudden blow: the great wings beating still
Above the staggering girl, her thighs caressed
By the dark webs, her nape caught in his bill,
He holds her helpless breast upon his breast.

How can those terrified vague fingers push   5
The feathered glory from her loosening thighs?
And how can body, laid in that white rush,
But feel the strange heart beating where it lies?

A shudder in the loins engenders there
The broken wall, the burning roof and tower   10
And Agamemnon dead.
                    Being so caught up,
So mastered by the brute blood of the air,
Did she put on his knowledge with his power
Before the indifferent beak could let her drop?

Sailing to Byzantium   (1927)

That is no country for old men. The young
In one another's arms, birds in the trees
—Those dying generations—at their song,
The salmon-falls, the mackerel-crowded seas,
Fish, flesh, or fowl, commend all summer long   5
Whatever is begotten, born, and dies.
Caught in that sensual music all neglect
Monuments of unaging intellect.

An aged man is but a paltry thing,
A tattered coat upon a stick, unless   10
Soul clap its hands and sing, and louder sing
For every tatter in its mortal dress,
Nor is there singing school but studying
Monuments of its own magnificence;
And therefore I have sailed the seas and come   15
To the holy city of Byzantium.

O sages standing in God's holy fire
As in the gold mosaic of a wall,
Come from the holy fire, perne in a gyre,°   *spin down a spiral*
And be the singing-masters of my soul.   20
Consume my heart away; sick with desire
And fastened to a dying animal
It knows not what it is; and gather me
Into the artifice of eternity.

Once out of nature I shall never take   25
My bodily form from any natural thing,
But such a form as Grecian goldsmiths make
Of hammered gold and gold enameling
To keep a drowsy Emperor awake;
Or set upon a golden bough to sing   30
To lords and ladies of Byzantium
Of what is past, or passing, or to come.

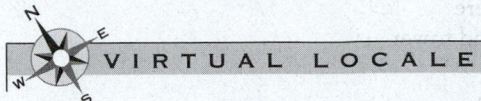

Boland on Yeats. The lecture series Branching Out: Poetry for the 21st Century, organized jointly by the nonprofit Poets House and the Poetry Society of America and funded by the National Endowment for the Humanities, presents talks by distinguished contemporary poets and scholars about celebrated, classic poets. The talks are given in five American cities: Fresno, Houston, Milwaukee, New Orleans, and Kansas City. In May 2005, Irish poet Eavan Boland gave a lecture on fellow Irish poet William Butler Yeats, focusing on the personal aspects of Yeats's poetry rather than the more common historical perspective. For more information on Boland's talk, Yeats, or the series, go to *http://www. poetshouse.org* or *http://www.poetrybranchingout.org*. The Branching Out site also offers timelines, photos, biographical information on the poet lecturers and the poets about whom they are speaking, bibliographies, and sample poems.

PAUL LAURENCE DUNBAR   (1872–1906)

Theology   (1896)

There is a heaven, for ever, day by day,
The upward longing of my soul doth tell me so.
There is a hell, I'm quite as sure; for pray,
If there were not, where would my neighbors go?

Sympathy   (1899)

I know what the caged bird feels, alas!
    When the sun is bright on the upland slopes;
When the wind stirs soft through the springing grass,
And the river flows like a stream of glass;
    When the first bird sings and the first bud opes,   5
And the faint perfume from its chalice steals—
I know what the caged bird feels!

I know why the caged bird beats his wing
    Till its blood is red on the cruel bars;
For he must fly back to his perch and cling   10
When he fain would be on the bough a-swing;
    And a pain still throbs in the old, old scars
And they pulse again with a keener sting—
    I know why he beats his wing!

I know why the caged bird sings, ah me,   15
    When his wing is bruised and his bosom sore,—

When he beats his bars and he would be free;
It is not a carol of joy or glee,
    But a prayer that he sends from his heart's deep core,
But a plea, that upward to Heaven he flings— 20
I know why the caged bird sings!

Robert Gould Shaw (1904)

Why was it that the thunder voice of Fate
Should call thee, studious, from the classic groves,
Where calm-eyed Pallas with still footstep roves,
And charge thee seek the turmoil of the state?
What bade thee hear the voice and rise elate, 5
Leave home and kindred and thy spicy loaves,
To lead th' unlettered and despised droves
To manhood's home and thunder at the gate?
Far better the slow blaze of Learning's light,
The cool and quiet of her dearer fane°, *Temple* 10
Than this hot terror of a hopeless fight,
This cold endurance of the final pain,—
Since thou and those who with thee died for right
Have died, the Present teaches, but in vain!

ROBERT FROST (1874–1963)
Mending Wall (1914)

Something there is that doesn't love a wall,
That sends the frozen-ground-swell under it,
And spills the upper boulders in the sun;
And makes gaps even two can pass abreast.
The work of hunters is another thing: 5
I have come after them and made repair
Where they have left not one stone on a stone,
But they would have the rabbit out of hiding,
To please the yelping dogs. The gaps I mean,
No one has seen them made or heard them made, 10
But at spring mending-time we find them there.
I let my neighbor know beyond the hill;
And on a day we meet to walk the line
And set the wall between us once again.
We keep the wall between us as we go. 15
To each the boulders that have fallen to each.
And some are loaves and some so nearly balls
We have to use a spell to make them balance:
"Stay where you are until our backs are turned!"
We wear our fingers rough with handling them. 20

Oh, just another kind of outdoor game,
One on a side. It comes to little more:
There where it is we do not need the wall:
He is all pine and I am apple orchard.
My apple trees will never get across   25
And eat the cones under his pines, I tell him.
He only says, "Good fences make good neighbors."
Spring is the mischief in me, and I wonder
If I could put a notion in his head:
"*Why* do they make good neighbors? Isn't it   30
Where there are cows? But here there are no cows.
Before I built a wall I'd ask to know
What I was walling in or walling out,
And to whom I was like to give offence.
Something there is that doesn't love a wall,   35
That wants it down." I could say "Elves" to him,
But it's not elves exactly, and I'd rather
He said it for himself. I see him there
Bringing a stone grasped firmly by the top
In each hand, like an old-stone savage armed.   40
He moves in darkness as it seems to me,
Not of woods only and the shade of trees.
He will not go behind his father's saying,
And he likes having thought of it so well
He says again, "Good fences make good neighbors."   45

The Road Not Taken   (1916)

Two roads diverged in a yellow wood,
And sorry I could not travel both
And be one traveler, long I stood
And looked down one as far as I could
To where it bent in the undergrowth;   5

Then took the other, as just as fair,
And having perhaps the better claim,
Because it was grassy and wanted wear;
Though as for that the passing there
Had worn them really about the same,   10

And both that morning equally lay
In leaves no step had trodden black.
Oh, I kept the first for another day!
Yet knowing how way leads on to way,
I doubted if I should ever come back.   15

I shall be telling this with a sigh
Somewhere ages and ages hence:
Two roads diverged in a wood, and I—
I took the one less traveled by,
And that has made all the difference.   20

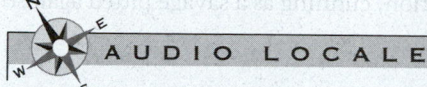

AUDIO LOCALE

Frost Reading "The Road Not Taken." An audio clip of poet Robert Frost reading his famous poem "The Road Not Taken" can be found online at the Academy of American Poets website: *http://www.poets.org/viewmedia.php/prmMID/15717.*

For Once, Then, Something (1923)

Others taunt me with having knelt at well-curbs
Always wrong to the light, so never seeing
Deeper down in the well than where the water
Gives me back in a shining surface picture
Me myself in the summer heaven godlike   5
Looking out of a wreath of fern and cloud puffs.
Once, when trying with chin against a well-curb,
I discerned, as I thought, beyond the picture,
Through the picture, a something white, uncertain.
Something more of the depths—and then I lost it.   10
Water came to rebuke the too clear water.
One drop fell from a fern, and lo, a ripple
Shook whatever it was lay there at bottom,
Blurred it, blotted it out. What was that whiteness?
Truth? A pebble of quartz? For once, then, something.   15

CARL SANDBURG (1878–1967)

Chicago (1916)

   Hog Butcher for the World,
   Tool Maker, Stacker of Wheat,
   Player with Railroads and the Nation's Freight Handler;
   Stormy, husky, brawling,
   City of the Big Shoulders: 5
They tell me you are wicked and I believe them, for I have seen your painted
   women under the gas lamps luring the farm boys.
And they tell me you are crooked and I answer: Yes, it is true I have seen the
   gunman kill and go free to kill again.
And they tell me you are brutal and my reply is: On the faces of women and chil-
   dren I have seen the marks of wanton hunger.
And having answered so I turn once more to those who sneer at this my city, and
   I give them back the sneer and say to them:
Come and show me another city with lifted head singing so proud to be alive
   and coarse and strong and cunning.   10
Flinging magnetic curses amid the toil of piling job on job, here is a tall bold
   slugger set vivid against the little soft cities;

Fierce as a dog with tongue lapping for action, cunning as a savage pitted against
    the wilderness,
        Bareheaded,
        Shoveling,
        Wrecking,   15
        Planning,
        Building, breaking, rebuilding,
Under the smoke, dust all over his mouth, laughing with white teeth,
Under the terrible burden of destiny laughing as a young man laughs,
Laughing even as an ignorant fighter laughs who has never lost a battle,
Bragging and laughing that under his wrist is the pulse, and under his ribs the
    heart of the people,
            Laughing!
Laughing the stormy, husky, brawling laughter of Youth, half-naked, sweating,
    proud to be Hog Butcher, Tool Maker, Stacker of Wheat, Player with Rail-
    roads and Freight Handler to the Nation.   20

WALLACE STEVENS   (1879–1955)

The Emperor of Ice-Cream   (1922)

Call the roller of big cigars,
The muscular one, and bid him whip
In kitchen cups concupiscent curds.
Let the wenches dawdle in such dress
As they are used to wear, and let the boys   5
Bring flowers in last month's newspapers.
Let be be finale of seem.
The only emperor is the emperor of ice-cream.

Take from the dresser of deal,
Lacking the three glass knobs, that sheet   10
On which she embroidered fantails once
And spread it so as to cover her face.
If her horny feet protrude, they come
To show how cold she is, and dumb.
Let the lamp affix its beam.   15
The only emperor is the emperor of ice-cream.

Anecdote of the Jar   (1923)

I placed a jar in Tennessee,
And round it was, upon a hill.
It made the slovenly wilderness
Surround that hill.

The wilderness rose up to it,   5
And sprawled around, no longer wild.
The jar was round upon the ground
And tall and of a port in air.

It took dominion everywhere.
The jar was gray and bare.   10
It did not give of bird or bush,
Like nothing else in Tennessee.

The House Was Quiet and the World Was Calm   (1947)

The house was quiet and the world was calm.
The reader became the book; and summer night

Was like the conscious being of the book.
The house was quiet and the world was calm.

The words were spoken as if there was no book,   5
Except that the reader leaned above the page,

Wanted to lean, wanted much most to be
The scholar to whom his book is true, to whom

The summer night is like a perfection of thought.
The house was quiet because it had to be.   10

The quiet was part of the meaning, part of the mind:
The access of perfection to the page.

And the world was calm. The truth in a calm world,
In which there is no other meaning, itself

Is calm, itself is summer and night, itself   15
Is the reader leaning late and reading there.

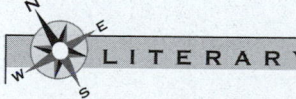

LITERARY LOCALE

Wallace Stevens Walking Tour, Hartford, Connecticut. Wallace Stevens
was a resident of Hartford, Connecticut, for nearly four decades, until his death
in 1955, and he is buried in Cedar Hill Cemetery there. Although today Stevens
is considered one of the great modern American poets, during his lifetime he
worked at a day job at the Hartford Accident and Indemnity Company, working
his way up the ladder and eventually becoming vice president. Stevens never
learned how to drive a car, so he was an avid walker; every morning, he would
walk the two miles from his home at 118 Westerly Terrace to his office at 690
Asylum Avenue. Stevens used this time for contemplation and creation, composing poems in his head and using the rhythm of his footsteps to match the words.

The Hartford Friends and Enemies of Wallace Stevens, a nonprofit organization devoted to promoting Stevens's work by organizing readings and events,
has been developing an official walking tour that will follow Stevens's original
two-mile route. The walk will be labeled with 13 stone markers along the route,
each stone presenting one stanza from Stevens's "Thirteen Ways of Looking at a
Blackbird." For more information about the walk and other Stevens events, go
to the website of the group at *http://www.wesleyan.edu/wstevens/stevens.html.*

WILLIAM CARLOS WILLIAMS   (1883–1963)

Landscape with the Fall of Icarus   (1960, 1962)

According to Breughel°   *Renaissance painter*
when Icarus fell
it was spring

a farmer was ploughing
his field   5
the whole pageantry

of the year was
awake tingling
near

the edge of the sea   10
concerned
with itself

sweating in the sun
that melted
the wings' wax   15

unsignificantly
off the coast
there was

a splash quite unnoticed
this was   20
Icarus drowning

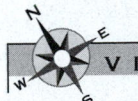

VIRTUAL LOCALE

Pinsky on Williams and Frost. In June 2005, as part of the Branching Out:
Poetry for the 21st Century lecture series, poet Robert Pinsky gave a talk on the
work of William Carlos Williams and Robert Frost. For more information on
Pinsky's talk, Williams, Frost, or the Branching Out series, go to *http://www.
poetshouse.org* or *http://www.poetrybranchingout.org*. The Branching Out site also
offers timelines, photos, biographical information on the poet lecturers and the
poets about whom they are speaking, bibliographies, and sample poems.

MARIANNE MOORE   (1887–1972)

Poetry   (1921)

I too, dislike it: there are things that are important beyond all this fiddle.
    Reading it, however, with a perfect contempt for it, one discovers in
    it after all, a place for the genuine.

    Hands that can grasp, eyes
      that can dilate, hair that can rise   5
         if it must, these things are important not because a

high sounding interpretation can be put upon them but because they are
    useful; when they become so derivative as to become unintelligible, the
    same thing may be said for all of us—that we
        do not admire what   10
        we cannot understand. The bat,
           holding on upside down or in quest of something to

eat, elephants pushing, a wild horse taking a roll, a tireless wolf under
    a tree, the immovable critic twinkling his skin like a horse that feels a flea,
        the base-
      ball fan, the statistician—case after case   15
        could be cited did
        one wish it; nor is it valid
           to discriminate against "business documents and

school-books"; all these phenomena are important. One must make a distinction
    however: when dragged into prominence by half poets, the result is not poetry,   20
    nor till the autocrats among us can be
        "literalists of
        the imagination"—above
           insolence and triviality and can present

for inspection, imaginary gardens with real toads in them, shall we have   25
    it. In the meantime, if you demand on the one hand, in defiance of their
        opinion
    the raw material of poetry in
        all its rawness and
        that which is, on the other hand,
          genuine, then you are interested in poetry.   30

ROBINSON JEFFERS
                         (1887–1962)

Continent's End
                         (1917)

At the equinox when the earth was veiled in a late rain, wreathed with wet
    poppies, waiting spring,
The ocean swelled for a far storm and beat its boundary, the ground-swell shook
    the beds of granite.

I gazing at the boundaries of granite and spray, the established sea-marks, felt
    behind me
Mountain and plain, the immense breadth of the continent, before me the mass
    and doubled stretch of water.

I said: You yoke the Aleutian seal-rocks with the lava and coral sowings that
    flower the south,
                                       5
Over your flood the life that sought the sunrise faces ours that has followed the
    evening star.

The long migrations meet across you and it is nothing to you, you have forgotten
    us, mother.
You were much younger when we crawled out of the womb and lay in the sun's
    eye on the tideline.

It was long and long ago; we have grown proud since then and you have grown
    bitter; life retains
Your mobile soft unquiet strength; and envies hardness, the insolent quietness of
    stone.   10

The tides are in our veins, we still mirror the stars, life is your child, but there is
    in me
Older and harder than life and more impartial, the eye that watched before there
    was an ocean.

That watched you fill your beds out of the condensation of thin vapor and
    watched you change them,
That saw you soft and violent wear your boundaries down, eat rock, shift places
    with the continents.

Mother, though my song's measure is like your surf-beat's ancient rhythm I never
    learned it of you.   15
Before there was any water there were tides of fire, both our tones flow from the
    older fountain.

T. S. ELIOT   (1888–1965)

The Love Song of J. Alfred Prufrock[1]   (1915)

*S'io credesse che mia risposta fosse
A persona che mai tornasse al mondo,
Questa fiamma staria senza più scosse.
Ma perciocche giammai di questo fondo
Non tornò vivo alcun, s'i'odo il vero
Senza tema d'infamia ti rispondo*

Let us go then, you and I,
When the evening is spread out against the sky
Like a patient etherized upon a table;
Let us go, through certain half-deserted streets,
The muttering retreats
Of restless nights in one-night cheap hotels   5
And sawdust restaurants with oyster-shells:
Streets that follow like a tedious argument
Of insidious intent
To lead you to an overwhelming question . . .
Oh, do not ask, "What is it?"
Let us go and make our visit.   10

In the room the women come and go
Talking of Michelangelo.

---
[1] The opening lines in Italian are from Dante's *Inferno*, 27:61–66.

The yellow fog that rubs its back upon the window-panes   15
The yellow smoke that rubs its muzzle on the window-panes
Licked its tongue into the corners of the evening,
Lingered upon the pools that stand in drains,
Let fall upon its back the soot that falls from chimneys,
Slipped by the terrace, made a sudden leap,   20
And seeing that it was a soft October night,
Curled once about the house, and fell asleep.

And indeed there will be time
For the yellow smoke that slides along the street,
Rubbing its back upon the window-panes;   25
There will be time, there will be time
To prepare a face to meet the faces that you meet;
There will be time to murder and create,
And time for all the works and days of hands
That lift and drop a question on your plate;   30
Time for you and time for me,
And time yet for a hundred indecisions,
And for a hundred visions and revisions,
Before the taking of a toast and tea.

In the room the women come and go   35
Talking of Michelangelo.

And indeed there will be time
To wonder, "Do I dare?" and, "Do I dare?"
Time to turn back and descend the stair,
With a bald spot in the middle of my hair—   40
[They will say: "How his hair is growing thin!"]
My morning coat, my collar mounting firmly to the chin,
My necktie rich and modest, but asserted by a simple pin—
[They will say: "But how his arms and legs are thin!"]
Do I dare   45
Disturb the universe?
In a minute there is time
For decisions and revisions which a minute will reverse.

For I have known them all already, known them all:
Have known the evenings, mornings, afternoons,   50
I have measured out my life with coffee spoons;
I know the voices dying with a dying fall
Beneath the music from a farther room.
    So how should I presume?

And I have known the eyes already, known them all—   55
The eyes that fix you in a formulated phrase,
And when I am formulated, sprawling on a pin,
When I am pinned and wriggling on the wall,
Then how should I begin
To spit out all the butt-ends of my days and ways?   60
    And how should I presume?

And I have known the arms already, known them all—
Arms that are braceleted and white and bare
[But in the lamplight, downed with light brown hair!]
Is it perfume from a dress   65
That makes me so digress?
Arms that lie along a table, or wrap about a shawl.
        And should I then presume?
        And how should I begin?

                                        . . . . .

Shall I say, I have gone at dusk through narrow streets   70
And watched the smoke that rises from the pipes
Of lonely men in shirt-sleeves, leaning out of windows? . . .

I should have been a pair of ragged claws
Scuttling across the floors of silent seas.

                                        . . . . .

And the afternoon, the evening, sleeps so peacefully!   75
Smoothed by long fingers,
Asleep . . . tired . . . or it malingers,
Stretched on the floor, here beside you and me.
Should I, after tea and cakes and ices,
Have the strength to force the moment to its crisis?   80
But though I have wept and fasted, wept and prayed,
Though I have seen my head [grown slightly bald] brought in upon a platter,
I am no prophet—and here's no great matter;
I have seen the moment of my greatness flicker,
And I have seen the eternal Footman hold my coat, and snicker, 85
And in short, I was afraid.

And would it have been worth it, after all,
After the cups, the marmalade, the tea,
Among the porcelain, among some talk of you and me,
Would it have been worth while,   90
To have bitten off the matter with a smile,
To have squeezed the universe into a ball
To roll it toward some overwhelming question,
To say: "I am Lazarus, come from the dead,
Come back to tell you all, I shall tell you all"—   95
If one, settling a pillow by her head,
        Should say: "That is not what I meant at all.
        That is not it, at all."

And would it have been worth it, after all,
Would it have been worth while,   100
After the sunsets and the dooryards and the sprinkled streets,
After the novels, after the teacups, after the skirts that trail along the floor—
And this, and so much more?—
It is impossible to say just what I mean!
But as if a magic lantern threw the nerves in patterns on a screen: 105

Would it have been worth while
If one, settling a pillow or throwing off a shawl,
And turning toward the window, should say:
    "That is not it at all,
    That is not what I meant, at all."   110

           . . . . .

No! I am not Prince Hamlet, nor was meant to be;
Am an attendant lord, one that will do
To swell a progress, start a scene or two,
Advise the prince; no doubt, an easy tool,
Deferential, glad to be of use,   115
Politic, cautious, and meticulous;
Full of high sentence,° but a bit obtuse;   *sententiousness*
At times, indeed, almost ridiculous—
Almost, at times, the Fool.

I grow old . . . I grow old . . .
I shall wear the bottoms of my trousers rolled.   120

Shall I part my hair behind? Do I dare to eat a peach?
I shall wear white flannel trousers, and walk upon the beach.
I have heard the mermaids singing, each to each.

I do not think that they will sing to me.   125

I have seen them riding seaward on the waves
Combing the white hair of the waves blown back
When the wind blows the water white and black.

We have lingered in the chambers of the sea
By sea-girls wreathed with seaweed red and brown   130
Till human voices wake us, and we drown.

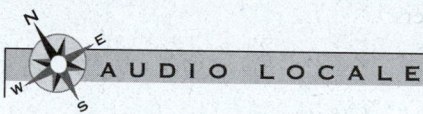

AUDIO LOCALE

Eliot Reading "The Love Song of J. Alfred Prufrock." An audio clip of
T. S. Eliot reading his poem "The Love Song of J. Alfred Prufrock" can be found
online at *Salon* magazine's audio archive: *http://www.salon.com/audio/2000/
10/05/eliot/.*

Preludes   (1917)

1

The winter evening settles down
With smell of steaks in passageways.
Six o'clock.
The burnt-out ends of smoky days.

And now a gusty shower wraps   5
The grimy scraps
Of withered leaves about your feet
And newspapers from vacant lots;
The showers beat
On broken blinds and chimney-pots,   10
And at the corner of the street
A lonely cab-horse steams and stamps.
And then the lighting of the lamps.

2

The morning comes to consciousness
Of faint stale smells of beer   15
From the sawdust-trampled street
With all its muddy feet that press
To early coffee-stands.
With the other masquerades
That time resumes,   20
One thinks of all the hands
That are raising dingy shades
In a thousand furnished rooms.

3

You tossed a blanket from the bed,
You lay upon your back, and waited;   25
You dozed, and watched the night revealing
The thousand sordid images
Of which your soul was constituted;
They flickered against the ceiling.
And when all the world came back   30
And the light crept up between the shutters
And you heard the sparrows in the gutters,
You had such a vision of the street
As the street hardly understands;
Sitting along the bed's edge, where   35
You curled the papers from your hair,
Or clasped the yellow soles of feet
In the palms of both soiled hands.

4

His soul stretched tight across the skies
That fade behind a city block,   40
Or trampled by insistent feet
At four and five and six o'clock;
And short square fingers stuffing pipes,
And evening newspapers, and eyes
Assured of certain certainties,   45
The conscience of a blackened street
Impatient to assume the world.

I am moved by fancies that are curled
Around these images, and cling:
The notion of some infinitely gentle   50
Infinitely suffering thing.

Wipe your hand across your mouth, and laugh;
The worlds revolve like ancient women
Gathering fuel in vacant lots.

AUDIO LOCALE

Best American Poems of the Century. On December 26, 1999, National
Public Radio's *Weekend Edition* aired a segment hosted by commentator and historian Douglas Brinkley in which a panel of poets, professors, and scholars
picked what they considered the top fifteen American poems of the twentieth
century. T. S. Eliot's "The Wasteland" was number one. The rest of the list included Hart Crane's "The Bridge," Allen Ginsberg's "Howl," Langston Hughes's
"The Negro Speaks of Rivers" (see p. 1076), and Robert Frost's "Stopping by
Woods on a Snowy Evening" (see p. 762). For the complete list of poems and an
audio clip of the segment, go to *http://www.npr.org/* and look up the show segment in the NPR archive.

EDNA ST. VINCENT MILLAY   (1892–1950)
Recuerdo   (1920)

We were very tired, we were very merry—
We had gone back and forth all night on the ferry.
It was bare and bright, and smelled like a stable—
But we looked into a fire, we leaned across a table,
We lay on a hill-top underneath the moon;   5
And the whistles kept blowing, and the dawn came soon.

We were very tired, we were very merry—
We had gone back and forth all night on the ferry;
And you ate an apple, and I ate a pear,
From a dozen of each we had bought somewhere;   10
And the sky went wan, and the wind came cold,
And the sun rose dripping, a bucketful of gold.

We were very tired, we were very merry,
We had gone back and forth all night on the ferry.
We hailed, "Good morrow, mother!" to a shawl-covered head,   15
And bought a morning paper, which neither of us read;
And she wept, "God bless you!" for the apples and pears,
And we gave her all our money but our subway fares.

What lips my lips have kissed   (1923)

What lips my lips have kissed, and where, and why,
I have forgotten, and what arms have lain
Under my head till morning; but the rain
Is full of ghosts tonight, that tap and sigh
Upon the glass and listen for reply,   5
And in my heart there stirs a quiet pain
For unremembered lads that not again
Will turn to me at midnight with a cry.
Thus in the winter stands the lonely tree,
Nor knows what birds have vanished one by one,   10
Yet knows its boughs more silent than before:
I cannot say what loves have come and gone,
I only know that summer sang in me
A little while, that in me sings no more.

WILFRED OWEN   (1893–1918)

Anthem for Doomed Youth   (1917)

What passing-bells for these who die as cattle?
    Only the monstrous anger of the guns.
    Only the stuttering rifles' rapid rattle
Can patter out their hasty orisons.°   *prayers*
No mockeries now for them; no prayers nor bells,   5
    Nor any voice of mourning save the choirs—
The shrill, demented choirs of wailing shells;
    And bugles calling for them from sad shires.

What candles may be held to speed them all?
    Not in the hands of boys, but in their eyes   10
Shall shine the holy glimmers of good-byes.
    The pallor of girls brows shall be their pall;
Their flowers the tenderness of patient minds,
And each slow dusk a drawing-down of blinds.

Dulce et Decorum Est[1]   (1920)

Bent double, like old beggars under sacks,
Knock-kneed, coughing like hags, we cursed through sludge,
Till on the haunting flares we turned our backs
And towards our distant rest began to trudge.
Men marched asleep. Many had lost their boots   5
But limped on, blood-shod. All went lame; all blind;
Drunk with fatigue; deaf even to the hoots
Of tired, outstripped Five-Nines that dropped behind.

---

[1] For the title and concluding words of this poem, Owen drew on a line from the Roman poet Horace: *dulce et decorum est pro patria mori* ("it is sweet and fitting to die for one's country").

Gas! Gas! Quick, boys!—An ecstasy of fumbling
Fitting the clumsy helmets just in time;   10
But someone still was yelling out and stumbling
And flound'ring like a man in fire or lime . . .
Dim, through the misty panes and thick green light,
As under a green sea, I saw him drowning.
In all my dreams, before my helpless sight,   15
He plunges at me, guttering, choking, drowning.

If in some smothering dreams you too could pace
Behind the wagon that we flung him in,
And watch the white eyes writhing in his face,
His hanging face, like a devil's sick of sin;   20
If you could hear, at every jolt, the blood
Come gargling from the froth-corrupted lungs,
Obscene as cancer, bitter as the cud
Of vile, incurable sores on innocent tongues,—
My friend, you would not tell with such high zest   25
To children ardent for some desperate glory,
The old Lie: Dulce et decorum est
Pro patria mori.

LOUISE BOGAN   (1897–1970)
Women   (1923)

Women have no wilderness in them,
They are provident instead,
Content in the tight hot cell of their hearts
To eat dusty bread.

They do not see cattle cropping red winter grass,   5
They do not hear
Snow water going down under culverts
Shallow and clear.

They wait, when they should turn to journeys,
They stiffen, when they should bend.   10
They use against themselves that benevolence
To which no man is friend.

They cannot think of so many crops to a field
Or of clean wood cleft by an axe.
Their love is an eager meaninglessness   15
Too tense, or too lax.

They hear in every whisper that speaks to them
A shout and a cry.
As like as not, when they take life over their door-sills
They should let it go by.   20

LANGSTON HUGHES   (1902–1967)

The Negro Speaks of Rivers   (1920)

Langston Hughes in 1931.

To W. E. B. DuBois

I've known rivers:
I've known rivers ancient as the world and older than the flow
    of human blood in human veins.

My soul has grown deep like the rivers.

I bathed in the Euphrates when dawns were young.
I built my hut near the Congo and it lulled me to sleep.   5
I looked upon the Nile and raised the pyramids above it.
I heard the singing of the Mississippi when Abe Lincoln went
    down to New Orleans, and I've seen its muddy bosom turn
    all golden in the sunset.

I've known rivers:
Ancient, dusky rivers.

My soul has grown deep like the rivers.   10

AUDIO LOCALE

Hughes Reading "The Negro Speaks of Rivers." An audio clip of poet
Langston Hughes reading his poem "The Negro Speaks of Rivers" can be found
online at the Academy of American Poets website: *http://www.poets.org/
viewmedia.php/prmMID/15722.*

Theme for English B   (1951)

The instructor said,

    Go home and write
    a page tonight.
    And let that page come out of you—
    Then, it will be true.   5

I wonder if it's that simple?
I am twenty-two, colored, born in Winston-Salem.
I went to school there, then Durham, then here
to this college on the hill above Harlem.
I am the only colored student in my class.   10
The steps from the hill lead down into Harlem,
through a park, then I cross St. Nicholas,
Eighth Avenue, Seventh, and I come to the Y,
the Harlem Branch Y, where I take the elevator
up to my room, sit down, and write this page: 15

It's not easy to know what is true for you or me
at twenty-two, my age. But I guess I'm what
I feel and see and hear, Harlem, I hear you:
hear you, hear me—we two—you, me, talk on this page.
(I hear New York, too.) Me—who?   20
Well, I like to eat, sleep, drink, and be in love.
I like to work, read, learn, and understand life.
I like a pipe for a Christmas present,
or records—Bessie°, bop, or Bach.   *blues singer Bessie Smith*
I guess being colored doesn't make me *not* like   25
the same things other folks like who are other races.
So will my page be colored that I write?
Being me, it will not be white.
But it will be
a part of you, instructor.   30
You are white—
yet a part of me, as I am a part of you.
That's American.
Sometimes perhaps you don't want to be a part of me.
Nor do I often want to be a part of you.   35
But we are, that's true!
I guess you learn from me—
although you're older—and white—
and somewhat more free.

This is my page for English B.   40

Advice   (C. 1950)

Folks, I'm telling you,
birthing is hard
and dying is mean—
so get yourself
a little loving   5
in between.

COUNTEE CULLEN   (1903–1946)
Yet Do I Marvel   (1925)

I doubt not God is good, well-meaning, kind,
And did He stoop to quibble could tell why
The little buried mole continues blind,
Why flesh that mirrors Him must some day die,
Make plain the reason tortured Tantalus   5
Is baited by the fickle fruit, declare
If merely brute caprice dooms Sisyphus
To struggle up a never-ending stair.

Inscrutable His ways are, and immune
To catechism by a mind too strewn   10
With petty cares to slightly understand
What awful brain compels His awful hand.
Yet do I marvel at this curious thing:
To make a poet black, and bid him sing!

PABLO NERUDA   (1904–1973)

Oblivion   (1951–1952)

TRANSLATED BY DONALD D. WALSH

All of love in a goblet
as wide as the earth, all
of love with stars and thorns
I gave you, but you walked
with little feet, with dirty heels   5
upon the fire, putting it out.

Ah great love, small beloved!

I did not stop in the struggle.
I did not stop marching toward life,
toward peace, toward bread for all,
but I lifted you in my arms   10
and I nailed you to my kisses
and I looked at you as never
again will human eyes look at you.

Ah great love, small beloved!   15

You did not then measure my stature,
and the man who for you put aside
blood, wheat, water,
you confused him
with the little insect that fell into your skirt.   20

Ah great love, small beloved!

Do not expect that I will look back at you
in the distance, stay
with what I left you, walk about
with my betrayed photograph,   25
I shall go on marching,
opening broad roads against the shadow, making
the earth smooth, spreading
the star for those who come.
Stay on the road.   30
Night has fallen for you.
Perhaps at dawn
we shall see each other again.

Ah great love, small beloved!

W. H. AUDEN (1907–1973)

Stop All the Clocks, Cut Off the Telephone (1936)

Stop all the clocks, cut off the telephone,
Prevent the dog from barking with a juicy bone,
Silence the pianos and with muffled drum
Bring out the coffin, let the mourners come.

Let aeroplanes circle moaning overhead   5
Scribbling on the sky the message He Is Dead,
Put the crepe bows round the white necks of the public doves,
Let the traffic policemen wear black cotton gloves.

He was my North, my South, my East and West,
My working week and my Sunday rest,   10
My noon, my midnight, my talk, my song;
I thought that love would last for ever: I was wrong.

The stars are not wanted now: put out every one;
Pack up the moon and dismantle the sun;
Pour away the ocean and sweep up the wood.   15
For nothing now can ever come to any good.

W. H. Auden (right) in 1939, with writer Christopher Isherwood.

Musée des Beaux Arts   (1940)

About suffering they were never wrong,
The Old Masters: how well they understood
Its human position; how it takes place
While someone else is eating or opening a window or just walking dully along;
How, when the aged are reverently, passionately waiting   5
For the miraculous birth, there always must be
Children who did not specially want it to happen, skating
On a pond at the edge of the wood:
They never forgot
That even the dreadful martyrdom must run its course   10
Anyhow in a corner, some untidy spot
Where the dogs go on with their doggy life and the torturer's horse
Scratches its innocent behind on a tree.

A U D I O   L O C A L E

Auden Reading from His Work. On March 27, 1972, poet W. H. Auden
gave an hour-long reading at the 92nd St. Y's Poetry Center in New York City.
An audio file of the reading is available online via the *New York Times* website
at *http://www.nytimes.com/books/01/02/11/specials/auden.html.*

THEODORE ROETHKE   (1908–1963)

My Papa's Waltz   (1948)

The whiskey on your breath
Could make a small boy dizzy;
But I hung on like death:
Such waltzing was not easy.

We romped until the pans   5
Slid from the kitchen shelf;
My mother's counternance
Could not unfrown itself.

The hand that held my wrist
Was battered on one knuckle;   10
At every step you missed
My right ear scraped a buckle.

You beat time on my head
With a palm caked hard by dirt,
Then waltzed me off to bed   15
Still clinging to your shirt.

Root Cellar

(1948)

Nothing would sleep in that cellar, dank as a ditch,
Bulbs broke out of boxes hunting for chinks in the dark,
Shoots dangled and drooped,
Lolling obscenely from mildewed crates,
Hung down long yellow evil necks, like tropical snakes.   5
And what a congress of stinks!—
Roots ripe as old bait,
Pulpy stems, rank, silo-rich,
Leaf-mold, manure, lime, piled against slippery planks.
Nothing would give up life: 10
Even the dirt kept breathing a small breath.

ELIZABETH BISHOP

(1911–1979)

At the Fishhouses

(1955)

Although it is a cold evening,
down by one of the fishhouses
an old man sits netting,
his net, in the gloaming almost invisible
a dark purple-brown,   5
and his shuttle worn and polished.
The air smells so strong of codfish
it makes one's nose run and one's eyes water.
The five fishhouses have steeply peaked roofs
and narrow, cleated gangplanks slant up   10
to storerooms in the gables
for the wheelbarrows to be pushed up and down on.
All is silver: the heavy surface of the sea,
swelling slowly as if considering spilling over,
is opaque, but the silver of the benches,   15
the lobster pots, and masts, scattered
among the wild jagged rocks,
is of an apparent translucence
like the small old buildings with an emerald moss
growing on their shoreward walls.   20
The big fish tubs are completely lined
with layers of beautiful herring scales
and the wheelbarrows are similarly plastered
with creamy iridescent coats of mail,
with small iridescent flies crawling on them.   25
Up on the little slope behind the houses,
set in the sparse bright sprinkle of grass,
is an ancient wooden capstan,
cracked, with two long bleached handles

and some melancholy stains, like dried blood,   30
where the ironwork has rusted.
The old man accepts a Lucky Strike.
He was a friend of my grandfather.
We talk of the decline in the population
and of codfish and herring   35
while he waits for a herring boat to come in.
There are sequins on his vest and on his thumb.
He has scraped the scales, the principal beauty,
from unnumbered fish with that black old knife,
the blade of which is almost worn away.   40

Down at the water's edge, at the place
where they haul up the boats, up the long ramp
descending into the water, thin silver
tree trunks are laid horizontally
across the gray stones, down and down   45
at intervals of four or five feet.

Cold dark deep and absolutely clear,
element bearable to no mortal,
to fish and to seals . . . One seal particularly
I have seen here evening after evening.   50
He was curious about me. He was interested in music;
like me a believer in total immersion,
so I used to sing him Baptist hymns.
I also sang "A Mighty Fortress Is Our God."
He stood up in the water and regarded me   55
steadily, moving his head a little.
Then he would disappear, then suddenly emerge
almost in the same spot, with a sort of shrug
as if it were against his better judgment.

Cold dark deep and absolutely clear,   60
the clear gray icy water . . . Back, behind us,
the dignified tall firs begin.
Bluish, associating with their shadows,
a million Christmas trees stand
waiting for Christmas. The water seems suspended   65
above the rounded gray and blue-gray stones.
I have seen it over and over, the same sea, the same,
slightly, indifferently swinging above the stones,
icily free above the stones,
above the stones and then the world.   70
If you should dip your hand in,
your wrist would ache immediately,
your bones would begin to ache and your hand would burn
as if the water were a transmutation of fire
that feeds on stones and burns with a dark gray flame.   75

If you tasted it, it would first taste bitter,
then briny, then surely burn your tongue.
It is like what we imagine knowledge to be:
dark, salt, clear, moving, utterly free,
drawn from the cold hard mouth
of the world, derived from the rocky breasts   80
forever, flowing and drawn, and since
our knowledge is historical, flowing, and flown.

ROBERT HAYDEN   (1913–1980)

Those Winter Sundays   (1962)

Sundays too my father got up early
and put his clothes on in the blueblack cold,
then with cracked hands that ached
from labor in the weekday weather made
banked fires blaze. No one ever thanked him.   5

I'd wake and hear the cold splintering, breaking.
When the rooms were warm, he'd call,
and slowly I would rise and dress,
fearing the chronic angers of that house,

Speaking indifferently to him,   10
who had driven out the cold
and polished my good shoes as well.
What did I know, what did I know
of love's austere and lonely offices?

OCTAVIO PAZ   (1914–1998)

With Our Eyes Shut   (1968)

Translated by John Felstiner[1]

With your eyes shut
You light up from within
You are blind stone

Night by night I carve you
With my eyes shut
You are clear stone   5

We become immense
Just knowing each other
With our eyes shut

---

[1] The Spanish original directly follows this English translation on page 1084.

Con los Ojos Cerrados

Con los ojos cerrados
Te iluminas por dentro
Eres la piedra ciega

Noche a noche te labro
Con los ojos cerrados
Eres la piedra franca   5

Nos volvemos inmensos
Sólo por conocernos
Con los ojos cerrados

WILLIAM STAFFORD   (1914–1993)
Ask Me   (1975)

Some time when the river is ice ask me
mistakes I have made. Ask me whether
what I have done is my life. Others
have come in their slow way into
my thought, and some have tried to help   5
or to hurt—ask me what difference
their strongest love or hate has made.

I will listen to what you say.
You and I can turn and look
at the silent river and wait. We know   10
the current is there, hidden; and there
are comings and goings from miles away
that hold the stillness exactly before us.
What the river says, that is what I say.

DYLAN THOMAS   (1914–1953)
In My Craft or Sullen Art   (1944)

In my craft or sullen art
Exercised in the still night
When only the moon rages
And the lovers lie abed
With all their griefs in their arms,   5
I labor by singing light
Not for ambition or bread
Or the strut and trade of charms
On the ivory stages
But for the common wages   10
Of their most secret heart.

Not for the proud man apart
From the raging moon I write
On these spindrift pages
Nor for the towering dead   15
With their nightingales and psalms
But for the lovers, their arms
Round the griefs of the ages,
Who pay no praise or wages
Nor heed my craft or art.   20

ROBERT LOWELL   (1917–1977)

Skunk Hour   (1957, 1959)

For Elizabeth Bishop

Nautilus Island's hermit
heiress still lives through winter in her Spartan cottage;
her sheep still graze above the sea.
Her son's a bishop. Her farmer
is first selectman in our village;   5
she's in her dotage.

Thirsting for
the hierarchic privacy
of Queen Victoria's century,
she buys up all   10
the eyesores facing her shore,
and lets them fall.

The season's ill—
we've lost our summer millionaire,
who seemed to leap from an L. L. Bean   15
catalogue. His nine-knot yawl
was auctioned off to lobstermen.
A red fox stain covers Blue Hill.

And now our fairy
decorator brightens his shop for fall;   20
his fishnet's filled with orange cork,
orange, his cobbler's bench and awl;
there is no money in his work,
he'd rather marry.

One dark night,   25
my Tudor Ford climbed the hill's skull;
I watched for love-cars. Lights turned down,
they lay together, hull to hull,
where the graveyard shelves on the town. . . .
My mind's not right.   30

A car radio bleats,
"Love, O careless Love. . . ." I hear
my ill-spirit sob in each blood cell,
as if my hand were at its throat. . . .
I myself am hell;   35
nobody's here—

only skunks, that search
in the moonlight for a bite to eat.
They march on their soles up Main Street:
white stripes, moonstruck eyes' red fire   40
under the chalk-dry and spar spire
of the Trinitarian Church.

I stand on top
of our back steps and breathe the rich air—
a mother skunk with her column of kittens swills the garbage pail.   45
She jabs her wedge-head in a cup
of sour cream, drops her ostrich tail,
and will not scare.

DENISE LEVERTOV   (1923–1997)
The Ache of Marriage   (1966)

The ache of marriage:

thigh and tongue, beloved,
are heavy with it,
it throbs in the teeth

We look for communion   5
and are turned away, beloved,
each and each

It is leviathan and we
in its belly
looking for joy, some joy   10
not to be known outside it

two by two in the ark of
the ache of it.

A. R. AMMONS   (1926–2001)
The City Limits   (1971)

When you consider the radiance, that it does not withhold
itself but pours its abundance without selection into every
nook and cranny not overhung or hidden; when you consider

that birds' bones make no awful noise against the light but
lie low in the light as in a high testimony; when you consider   5
the radiance, that it will look into the guiltiest

swervings of the weaving heart and bear itself upon them,
not flinching into disguise or darkening; when you consider
the abundance of such resource as illuminates the glow-blue

bodies and gold-skeined wings of flies swarming the dumped   10
guts of a natural slaughter or the coil of shit and in no
way winces from its storms of generosity; when you consider

that air or vacuum, snow or shale, squid or wolf, rose or lichen,
each is accepted into as much light as it will take, then
the heart moves roomier, the man stands and looks about, the   15

leaf does not increase itself above the grass, and the dark
work of the deepest cells is of a tune with May bushes
and fear lit by the breadth of such calmly turns to praise.

ALLEN GINSBERG   (1926–1997)

A Supermarket in California   (1956)

What thoughts I have of you tonight, Walt Whitman, for
I walked down the sidestreets under the trees with a headache
self-conscious looking at the full moon.

In my hungry fatigue, and shopping for images, I went
into the neon fruit supermarket, dreaming of your enumerations!

What peaches and what penumbras! Whole families
shopping at night! Aisles full of husbands! Wives in the avocados, babies in the tomatoes!—and you, García Lorca, what
were you doing down by the watermelons?

I saw you, Walt Whitman, childless, lonely old grubber,
poking among the meats in the refrigerator and eyeing the
grocery boys.

I heard you asking questions of each: Who killed the pork
chops? What price bananas? Are you my Angel?   5

I wandered in and out of the brilliant stacks of cans
following you, and followed in my imagination by the store
detective.

We strode down the open corridors together in our
solitary fancy tasting artichokes, possessing every frozen
delicacy, and never passing the cashier.

Where are we going, Walt Whitman? The doors close in
an hour. Which way does you beard point tonight?

(I touch your book and dream of our odyssey in the supermarket and feel absurd.)

Will we walk all night through solitary streets? The trees add shade to shade,
lights out in the houses, we'll both be lonely.   10

Will we stroll dreaming of the lost America of love past blue automobiles in
driveways, home to our silent cottage?

Ah, dear father, graybeard, lonely old courage-teacher, what America did
you have when Charon quit poling his ferry and you got out on a smoking bank
and stood watching the boat disappear on the black waters of Lethe?

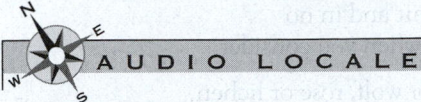 A U D I O   L O C A L E

Ginsberg Reading "A Supermarket in California." An audio clip of poet
Allen Ginsberg reading his poem "A Supermarket in California" can be found
online at the Academy of American Poets website: *http://www.poets.org/
viewmedia.php/prmMID/15306.*

JAMES MERRILL   (1926–1995)

To a Butterfly   (1962)

Already in midsummer
I miss your feet and fur.
Poor simple creature that you were,
What have you become!

Your slender person curled   5
About an apple twig
Rebounding to the winds' clear jig
Gave up the world

In favor of obscene
Gray matter, rode that ark   10
Until (as at the chance remark
Of Father Sheen)

Shining awake to slough
Your old life. And soon four
Dapper stained glass windows bore   15
You up—*Enough.*

Goodness, how tired one grows
Just looking through a prism:
Allegory, symbolism.
I've tried, Lord knows,   20

To keep from seeing double,
Blushed for whenever I did,
Prayed like a boy my cheek be hid
By manly stubble.

I caught you in a net   25
And first pierced your disguise
How many years ago? Time flies,
I am not yet

Proof against rigmarole.
Those frail wings, those antennae!   30
The day you hover without any
Tincture of soul,

Red monarch, swallowtail,
Will be the day my own
Wiles gather dust. Each will have flown   35
The other's jail.

FRANK O'HARA   (1926–1966)

Why I Am Not a Painter   (1956)

I am not a painter, I am a poet.
Why? I think I would rather be
a painter, but I am not. Well,

for instance, Mike Goldberg
is starting a painting. I drop in.   5
"Sit down and have a drink" he
says. I drink; we drink. I look
up. "You have sardines in it."
"Yes, it needed something there."
"Oh." I go and the days go by   10
and I drop in again. The painting
is going on, and I go, and the days
go by. I drop in. The painting is
finished. "Where's sardines?"
All that's left is just   15
letters, "It was too much." Mike says.

But me? One day I am thinking of
a color: orange. I write a line
about orange. Pretty soon it is a
whole page of words, not lines.   20
Then another page. There should be
so much more, not of orange, of
words, of how terrible orange is
and life. Days go by. It is even in
prose, I am a real poet. My poem   25
is finished and I haven't mentioned
orange yet. It's twelve poems, I call
it oranges. And one day in a gallery
I see Mike's painting, called SARDINES.

INSPIRATION FRANK O'HARA AND THE NEW YORK SCHOOL OF PAINTERS

Frank O'Hara, who once worked as a clerk at New York City's Museum of Modern Art (MoMA) in order to be closer to the paintings, then as an editorial associate for the magazine *ArtNEWS*, and then again at MoMA, found inspiration in painting, ballet, and, as seen in "The Day Lady Died" (see pp. 748–749), contemporary music. Today O'Hara is known as part of the "New York School" of poets, a group of friends that included John Ashbery and Kenneth Koch. But O'Hara also had numerous connections in the art world through his various art-related jobs, befriending many well-known painters during the 1950s and 1960s, including Jasper Johns, Cy Twombly, Willem deKooning, and Jackson Pollock; he was even painted by several New York School painters.

Unsurprisingly, O'Hara's poems frequently make allusions to works of modern art, New York museums, music clubs, and musicians. The inspirations and artistic conversation worked in both directions: poems came from seeing art, and paintings were inspired by verse. For example, O'Hara's "Why I am Not a Painter" (see p. 1089), which examines some of the similarities between the two processes as well as mapping out the many difference, makes direct reference to Michael Goldberg's 1955 painting *Sardines* (in which the artist originally includes the actual word in the painting but debates its inclusion and, in the end, omits it but keeps it as the title of the work). And artist Jasper Johns's 1961 masterpiece *In Memory of My Feelings—Frank O'Hara* found its beginning in O'Hara's 1956 poem of the same title.

Artist Jasper Johns, one of many modern artists with whom poet Frank O'Hara developed a friendship.

JOHN ASHBERY
(B. 1927)

Paradoxes and Oxymorons
(1981)

This poem is concerned with language on a very plain level.
Look at it talking to you. You look out a window
Or pretend to fidget. You have it but you don't have it.
You miss it, it misses you. You miss each other.

The poem is sad because it wants to be yours, and cannot.   5
What's a plain level? It is that and other things,
Bringing a system of them into play. Play?
Well, actually, yes, but I consider play to be

A deeper outside thing, a dreamed role-pattern,
As in the division of grace these long August days   10
Without proof. Open-ended. And before you know
It gets lost in the steam and chatter of typewriters.

It has been played once more. I think you exist only
To tease me into doing it, on your level, and then you aren't there
Or have adopted a different attitude. And the poem   15
Has set me softly down beside you. The poem is you.

GALWAY KINNELL   (B. 1927)

Blackberry Eating   (1980)

I love to go out in late September
among the fat, overripe, icy, black blackberries
to eat blackberries for breakfast,
the stalks very prickly, a penalty
they earn for knowing the black art   5
of blackberry-making: and as I stand among them
lifting the stalks to my mouth, the ripest berries
fall almost unbidden to my tongue,
as words sometimes do, certain peculiar words
like *strengths* or *squinched*,   10
many-lettered, one-syllabled lumps,
which I squeeze, squinch open, and splurge well
in the silent, startled, icy, black language
of blackberry-eating in late September.

W. S. MERWIN   (B. 1927)

One of the Lives   (1993)

If I had not met the red-haired boy whose father
      had broken a leg parachuting into Provence
to join the resistance in the final stage of the war
      and so had been killed there as the Germans were moving north
out of Italy and if the friend who was with him   5
      as he was dying had not had an elder brother
who also died young quite differently in peacetime
      leaving two children one of them with bad health
who had been kept out of school for a whole year by an illness
      and if I had written anything else at the top   10

of the examination form where it said college
    of your choice or if the questions that day had been
put differently and if a young woman in Kittanning
    had not taught my father to drive at the age of twenty
so that he got the job with the pastor of the big church   15
    in Pittsburgh where my mother was working and if
my mother had not lost both parents when she was a child
    so that she had to go to her grandmother's in Pittsburgh
I would not have found myself on an iron cot
    with my head by the fireplace of a stone farmhouse   20
that had stood empty since some time before I was born
    I would not have travelled so far to lie shivering
with fever though I was wrapped in everything in the house
    nor have watched the unctuous doctor hold up his needle
at the window in the rain light of October   25
    I would not have seen through the cracked pane the darkening
valley with its river sliding past the amber mountains
    nor have wakened hearing plums fall in the small hour
thinking I knew where I was as I heard them fall

JAMES WRIGHT   (1927–1980)

A Blessing   (1960)

Just off the highway to Rochester, Minnesota,
Twilight bounds softly forth on the grass.
And the eyes of those two Indian ponies
Darken with kindness.
They have come gladly out of the willows   5
To welcome my friend and me.
We step over the barbed wire into the pasture
Where they have been grazing all day, alone.
They ripple tensely, they can hardly contain their happiness
That we have come.   10
They bow shyly as wet swans. They love each other.
There is no loneliness like theirs.
At home once more,
They begin munching the young tufts of spring in the darkness.
I would like to hold the slenderer one in my arms,   15
For she has walked over to me
And nuzzled my left hand.
She is black and white,
Her mane falls wild on her forehead,
And the light breeze moves me to caress her long ear   20
That is delicate as the skin over a girl's wrist.
Suddenly I realize
That if I stepped out of my body I would break
Into blossom.

ANNE SEXTON (1928–1974)

The Starry Night (1962)

> That does not keep me from having a terrible need of—
> shall I say the word—religion. Then I go out at night to
> paint the stars.
>
> —*Vincent Van Gogh in a letter to his brother*

The town does not exist
except where one black-haired tree slips
up like a drowned woman into the hot sky.
The town is silent. The night boils with eleven stars.
Oh starry starry night! This is how   5
I want to die.

It moves. They are all alive.
Even the moon bulges in its orange irons
to push children, like a god, from its eye.
The old unseen serpent swallows up the stars.   10
Oh starry starry night! This is how
I want to die:

into that rushing beast of the night,
sucked up by that great dragon, to split
from my life with no flag,   15
no belly,
no cry.

ADRIENNE RICH (B. 1929)

Living in Sin (1955, 1975)

She had thought the studio would keep itself;
no dust upon the furniture of love.
Half heresy, to wish the taps less vocal,
the panes relieved of grime. A plate of pears,
a piano with a Persian shawl, a cat   5
stalking the picturesque amusing mouse
had risen at his urging.
Not that at five each separate stair would writhe
under the milkman's tramp; that morning light
so coldly would delineate the scraps   10
of last night's cheese and three sepulchral bottles;
that on the kitchen shelf among the saucers
a pair of beetle-eyes would fix her own—
envoy from some village in the moldings . . .
Meanwhile, he, with a yawn,   15

sounded a dozen notes upon the keyboard,
declared it out of tune, shrugged at the mirror,
rubbed at his beard, went out for cigarettes;
while she, jeered by the minor demons,
pulled back the sheets and made the bed and found   20
a towel to dust the table-top,
and let the coffee-pot boil over on the stove.
By evening she was back in love again,
though not so wholly but throughout the night
she woke sometimes to feel the daylight coming   25
like a relentless milkman up the stairs.

DEREK WALCOTT   (B. 1930)

Midsummer, Tobago   (1984)

Broad sun-stoned beaches.

White heat.
A green river.

A bridge,
scorched yellow palms   5

from the summer-sleeping house
drowsing through August.

Days I have held,
days I have lost,

days that outgrow, like daughters,   10
my harbouring arms.

SYLVIA PLATH   (1932–1963)

Mushrooms   (1959)

Overnight, very
Whitely, discreetly,
Very quietly

Our toes, our noses
Take hold on the loam,   5
Acquire the air.

Nobody sees us,
Stops us, betrays us;
The small grains make room.

Soft fists insist on   10
Heaving the needles,
The leafy bedding,

Even the paving.
Our hammers, our rams,
Earless and eyeless,   15

Perfectly voiceless,
Widen the crannies,
Shoulder through holes. We

Diet on water,
On crumbs of shadow,   20
Bland-mannered, asking

Little or nothing.
So many of us!
So many of us!

We are shelves, we are   25
Tables, we are meek,
We are edible,

Nudgers and shovers
In spite of ourselves.
Our kind multiplies: 30

We shall by morning
Inherit the earth.
Our foot's in the door.

Daddy   (WRITTEN 1962; PUB. 1965)

You do not do, you do not do
Any more, black shoe
In which I have lived like a foot
For thirty years, poor and white,
Barely daring to breathe or Achoo.   5

Daddy, I have had to kill you.
You died before I had time—
Marble-heavy, a bag full of God,
Ghastly statue with one grey toe
Big as a Frisco seal   10

And a head in the freakish Atlantic
Where it pours bean green over blue
In the waters off beautiful Nauset.
I used to pray to recover you.
Ach, du.   15

In the German tongue, in the Polish town
Scraped flat by the roller
Of wars, wars, wars.
But the name of the town is common.
My Polack friend   20

Says there are a dozen or two.
So I never could tell where you
Put your foot, your root,
I never could talk to you.
The tongue stuck in my jaw.   25

It stuck in a barb wire snare.
Ich, ich, ich, ich,
I could hardly speak.
I thought every German was you.
And the language obscene   30

An engine, an engine
Chuffing me off like a Jew.
A Jew to Dachau, Auschwitz, Belsen.
I began to talk like a Jew.
I think I may well be a Jew.   35

The snows of the Tyrol, the clear beer of Vienna
Are not very pure or true.
With my gypsy ancestress and my weird luck
And my Taroc pack and my Taroc pack
I may be a bit of a Jew.   40

I have always been scared of *you*,
With your Luftwaffe, your gobbledygoo.
And your neat moustache
And your Aryan eye, bright blue.
Panzer-man, panzer-man, O You—   45

Not God but a swastika
So black no sky could squeak through.
Every woman adores a Fascist,
The boot in the face, the brute
Brute heart of a brute like you.   50

You stand at the blackboard, daddy,
In the picture I have of you,
A cleft in your chin instead of your foot
But no less a devil for that, no not
Any less the black man who   55

Bit my pretty red heart in two.
I was ten when they buried you.
At twenty I tried to die
And get back, back, back to you.
I thought even the bones would do   60

But they pulled me out of the sack,
And they stuck me together with glue.
And then I knew what to do.
I made a model of you,
A man in black with a Meinkampf look   65

And a love of the rack and the screw.
And I said I do, I do.
So daddy, I'm finally through.
The black telephone's off at the root,
The voices just can't worm through.   70

If I've killed one man, I've killed two—
The vampire who said he was you
And drank my blood for a year,
Seven years, if you want to know.
Daddy, you can lie back now.   75

There's a stake in your fat black heart
And the villagers never liked you.
They are dancing and stamping on you.
They always *knew* it was you.
Daddy, daddy, you bastard, I'm through.   80

AUDRE LORDE   (1934–1992)

Coal   (1976)

I
is the total black, being spoken
from the earth's inside.
There are many kinds of open
how a diamond comes into a knot of flame
how sound comes into a word, colored   5
by who pays what for speaking.

Some words are open like a diamond
on glass windows
singing out within the passing crash of sun
Then there are words like stapled wagers   10
in a perforated book—buy and sign and tear apart—
and come whatever wills all chances
the stub remains
an ill-pulled tooth with a ragged edge.

Some words live in my throat   15
breeding like adders. Others know sun
seeking like gypsies over my tongue
to explode through my lips
like young sparrows bursting from shell.
Some words   20
bedevil me.

Love is a word, another kind of open.
As the diamond comes into a knot of flame
I am Black because I come from the earth's inside
now take my word for jewel in the open light.   25

MARK STRAND
(B. 1934)

Keeping Things Whole
(1964)

In a field
I am the absence
of field.
This is
always the case.   5
Wherever I am
I am what is missing.

When I walk
I part the air
and always   10
the air moves in
to fill the spaces
where my body's been.

We all have reasons
for moving.   15
I move
to keep things whole.

MARY OLIVER
(B. 1935)

Wild Geese
(1986)

You do not have to be good.
You do not have to walk on your knees
for a hundred miles through the desert, repenting.
You only have to let the soft animal of your body love what it loves.
Tell me about despair, yours, and I will tell you mine.   5
Meanwhile the world goes on.
Meanwhile the sun and the clear pebbles of the rain
are moving across the landscapes,
over the prairies and the deep trees,
the mountains and the rivers.   10
Meanwhile the wild geese, high in the clean blue air,
are heading home again.
Whoever you are, no matter how lonely,
the world offers itself to your imagination,
calls to you like the wild geese, harsh and exciting—   15
over and over announcing your place
in the family of things.

LUCILLE CLIFTON
(B. 1936)

homage to my hips
(1980)

these hips are big hips
they need space to
move around in.
they don't fit into little
petty places. these hips   5
are free hips.
they don't like to be held back.
these hips have never been enslaved,
they go where they want to go
they do what they want to do.   10
these hips are mighty hips.
these hips are magic hips.
i have known them
to put a spell on a man and
spin him like a top!   15

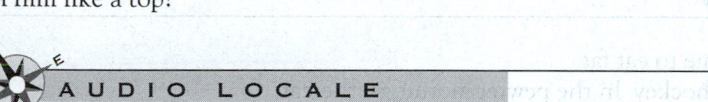

AUDIO LOCALE

Clifton Reading "homage to my hips." An audio clip of poet Lucille Clifton reading her poem "homage to my hips" can be found online at the Academy of American Poets website: *http://www.poets.org/viewmedia.php/prmMID/15599.*

MARGARET ATWOOD
(B. 1939)

This Is a Photograph of Me
(1966)

It was taken some time ago.
At first it seems to be
a smeared
print: blurred lines and grey flecks
blended with the paper;   5

then, as you scan
it, you see in the left-hand corner
a thing that is like a branch: part of a tree
(balsam or spruce) emerging
and, to the right, halfway up   10
what ought to be a gentle
slope, a small frame house.

In the background there is a lake,
and beyond that, some low hills.

(The photograph was taken   15
the day after I drowned.

I am in the lake, in the center
of the picture, just under the surface.

It is difficult to say where
precisely, or to say   20
how large or small I am:
the effect of water
on light is a distortion

but if you look long enough,
eventually   25
you will be able to see me.)

February   (1995)

Winter. Time to eat fat
and watch hockey. In the pewter mornings, the cat,
a black fur sausage with yellow
Houdini eyes, jumps up on the bed and tries
to get onto my head. It's his   5
way of telling whether or not I'm dead.
If I'm not, he wants to be scratched; if I am
he'll think of something. He settles
on my chest, breathing his breath
of burped-up meat and musty sofas,   10
purring like a washboard. Some other tomcat,
not yet a capon, has been spraying our front door,
declaring war. It's all about sex and territory,
which are what will finish us off
in the long run. Some cat owners around here   15
should snip a few testicles. If we wise
hominids were sensible, we'd do that too,
or eat our young, like sharks.
But it's love that does us in. Over and over
again, *He shoots, he scores!* and famine   20
crouches in the bedsheets, ambushing the pulsing
eiderdown, and the windchill factor hits
thirty below, and pollution pours
out of our chimneys to keep us warm.
February, month of despair,   25
with a skewered heart in the centre.
I think dire thoughts, and lust for French fries
with a splash of vinegar.

Cat, enough of your greedy whining
and your small pink bumhole.   30
Off my face! You're the life principle,
more or less, so get going
on a little optimism around here.
Get rid of death. Celebrate increase. Make it be spring.

FRANK BIDART (B. 1939)
Hammer (2002)

The stone arm raising a stone hammer
dreams it can descend upon itself.

When the quest is indecipherable,—
. . . what is left is a career.

What once was apprehended in passion   5
survives as opinion.

To be both author of
this statue, and the statue itself.

SEAMUS HEANEY (B. 1939)
Digging (1966)

Between my finger and my thumb
The squat pen rests; snug as a gun.

Under my window, a clean rasping sound
When the spade sinks into gravelly ground.
My father, digging. I look down   5

Till his straining rump among the flowerbeds
Bends low, comes up twenty years away
Stooping in rhythm through potato drills
Where he was digging.

The coarse boot nestled on the lug, the shaft   10
Against the inside knee was levered firmly.
He rooted out tall tops, buried the bright edge deep
To scatter new potatoes that we picked
Loving their cool hardness in our hands.

By God, the old man could handle a spade.   15
Just like his old man.

My grandfather cut more turf in a day
Than any other man on Toner's bog.

Once I carried him milk in a bottle
Corked sloppily with paper. He straightened up   20
To drink it, then fell to right away

Nicking and slicing neatly, heaving sods
Over his shoulder, going down and down
For the good turf. Digging.

The cold smell of potato mould, the squelch and slap   25
Of soggy peat, the curt cuts of an edge
Through living roots awaken in my head.
But I've no spade to follow men like them.

Between my finger and my thumb
The squat pen rests.   30
I'll dig with it.

From the Frontier of Writing   (1987)

The tightness and the nilness round that space
when the car stops in the road, the troops inspect
its make and number and, as one bends his face

towards your window, you catch sight of more
on a hill beyond, eyeing with intent   5
down cradled guns that hold you under cover

and everything is pure interrogation
until a rifle motions and you move
with guarded unconcerned acceleration—

a little emptier, a little spent   10
as always by that quiver in the self,
subjugated, yes, and obedient.

So you drive on to the frontier of writing
where it happens again. The guns on tripods;
the sergeant with his on-off mike repeating   15

data about you, waiting for the squawk
of clearance; the marksman training down
out of the sun upon you like a hawk.

And suddenly you're through, arraigned yet freed,
as if you'd passed from behind a waterfall   20
on the black current of a tarmac road

past armour-plated vehicles, out between
the posted soldiers flowing and receding
like tree shadows into the polished windscreen.

TOI DERRICOTTE (B. 1941)

Black Boys Play the Classics (1996)

The most popular "act" in
Penn Station
is the three black kids in ratty
sneakers & T-shirts playing
two violins and a cello—Brahms.°   *classical composer* 5
White men in business suits
have already dug into their pockets
as they pass and they toss in
a dollar or two without stopping.
Brown men in work-soiled khakis   10
stand with their mouths open,
arms crossed on their bellies
as if they themselves have always
wanted to attempt those bars.
One white boy, three, sits   15
cross-legged in front of his
idols—in ecstasy—
their slick, dark faces,
their thin, wiry arms,
who must begin to look   20
like angels!
Why does this trembling
pull us?
A: Beneath the surface we are one.
B: Amazing! I did not think that they could speak this tongue. 25

ROBERT HASS (B. 1941)

A Story about the Body (1989)

The young composer, working that summer at an artist's colony, had watched her for a week. She was Japanese, a painter, almost sixty, and he thought he was in love with her. He loved her work, and her work was like the way she moved her body, used her hands, looked at him directly when she made amused and considered answers to his questions. One night, walking back from a concert, they came to her door and she turned to him and said, "I think you would like to have me. I would like that too, but I must tell you that I have had a double mastectomy," and when he didn't understand, "I've lost both my breasts." The radiance that he had carried around in his belly and chest cavity—like music—withered very quickly, and he made himself look at her when he said, "I'm sorry. I don't think I could." He walked back to his own cabin through the pines, and in the morning he found a small blue bowl on the porch outside his door. It looked to be full of rose petals, but he found when he picked it up that the rose petals were on top; the rest of the bowl—she must have swept them from the corners of her studio—was full of dead bees.

SHARON OLDS   (B. 1942)

Sex Without Love   (1984)

How do they do it, the ones who make love
without love? Beautiful as dancers,
gliding over each other like ice-skaters
over the ice, fingers hooked
inside each other's bodies, faces   5
red as steak, wine, wet as the
children at birth whose mothers are going to
give them away. How do they come to the
come to the come to the God come to the
still waters, and not love   10
the one who came there with them, light
rising slowly as steam off their joined
skin? These are the true religious,
the purists, the pros, the ones who will not
accept a false Messiah, love the   15
priest instead of the God. They do not
mistake the lover for their own pleasure,
they are like great runners, they know they are alone
with the road surface, the cold, the wind,
the fit of their shoes, their over-all cardio-   20
vascular health—just factors; like the partner
in the bed, and not the truth, which is the
single body alone in the universe
against its own best time.

LOUISE GLÜCK   (B. 1943)

Mock Orange   (1975)

It is not the moon, I tell you.
It is these flowers
lighting the yard.

I hate them.
I hate them as I hate sex,
the man's mouth
sealing my mouth, the man's
paralyzing body—

and the cry that always escapes,
the low, humiliating
premise of union—

In my mind tonight
I hear the question and pursuing answer
fused in one sound
that mounts and mounts and then
is split into the old selves,
the tired antagonisms. Do you see?
We were made fools of.
And the scent of mock orange
drifts through the window.

How can I rest?
How can I be content
when there is still
that odor in the world?

EAVAN BOLAND (B. 1944)

The Dolls Museum in Dublin (1994)

The wounds are terrible. The paint is old.
The cracks along the lips and on the cheeks
cannot be fixed. The cotton lawn is soiled.
The arms are ivory dissolved to wax.

Recall the Quadrille. Hum the waltz.
Promenade on the yacht-club terraces.
Put back the lamps in their copper holders,
the carriage wheels on the cobbled quays.

And recreate Easter in Dublin.
Booted officers. Their mistresses.
Sunlight criss-crossing College Green.
Steam hissing from the flanks of horses.

Here they are. Cradled and cleaned,
held close in the arms of their owners.
Their cold hands clasped by warm hands,
their faces memorized like perfect manners.

The altars are mannerly with linen.
The lilies are whiter than surplices.
The candles are burning and warning:
Rejoice, they whisper. After sacrifice.

Horse-chestnuts hold up their candles.
The Green is vivid with parasols.
Sunlight is pastel and windless.
The bar of the Shelbourne° is full.   *a Dublin hotel*

Laughter and gossip on the terraces.   25
Rumour and alarm at the barracks.
The Empire is summoning its officers.
The carriages are turning: they are turning back.

Past children walking with governesses,
Looking down, cossetting° their dolls,   *pampering*   30
then looking up as the carriage passes,
the shadow chilling them. Twilight falls.

It is twilight in the dolls' museum. Shadows
remain on the parchment-coloured waists,
are bruises on the stitched cotton clothes,   35
are hidden in the dimples on the wrists.

The eyes are wide. They cannot address
the helplessness which has lingered in
the airless peace of each glass case:
to have survived. To have been stronger than   40

a moment. To be the hostages ignorance
takes from time and ornament from destiny. Both.
To be the present of the past. To infer the difference
with a terrible stare. But not feel it. And not know it.

LINDA HOGAN   (B. 1947)

First Light   (1991)

> *For Robin*

In early morning
I forget I'm in this world
with crooked chiefs
who make federal deals.

In the first light   5
I remember who rewards me for living,
not bosses
but singing birds and blue sky.

I know I can bathe and stretch,
make jewelry and love   10
the witch and wise woman
living inside, needing to be silenced
and put at rest for work's long day.

In the first light
I offer cornmeal
and tobacco.
I say hello to those who came before me,
and to birds
under the eaves,
and budding plants.

I know the old ones are here.
And every morning I remember the song
about how buffalo left through a hole in the sky
and how the grandmothers look out from those holes
watching over us
from there and from there.

JANE KENYON (1947–1995)

Let Evening Come (1990)

Let the light of late afternoon
shine through chinks in the barn, moving
up the bales as the sun moves down.

Let the cricket take up chafing
as a woman takes up her needles
and her yarn. Let evening come.

Let dew collect on the hoe abandoned
in long grass. Let the stars appear
and the moon disclose her silver horn.

Let the fox go back to its sandy den.
Let the wind die down. Let the shed
go black inside. Let evening come.

To the bottle in the ditch, to the scoop
in the oats, to air in the lung
let evening come.

Let it come, as it will, and don't
be afraid. God does not leave us
comfortless, so let evening come.

YUSEF KOMUNYAKAA (B. 1947)

Facing It (1988)

My black face fades,
hiding inside the black granite.

I said I wouldn't
dammit: No tears.
I'm stone. I'm flesh.
My clouded reflection eyes me
like a bird of prey, the profile of night   5
slanted against morning. I turn
this way—the stone lets me go.
I turn that way—I'm inside
the Vietnam Veterans Memorial
again, depending on the light   10
to make a difference.
I go down the 58,022 names,
half-expecting to find
my own in letters like smoke.
I touch the name Andrew Johnson;   15
I see the booby trap's white flash.
Names shimmer on a woman's blouse
but when she walks away
the names stay on the wall.   20
Brushstrokes flash, a red bird's
wings cutting across my stare.
The sky. A plane in the sky.
A white vet's image floats   25
closer to me, then his pale eyes
look through mine. I'm a window.
He's lost his right arm
inside the stone. In the black mirror
a woman's trying to erase names: 30
No, she's brushing a boy's hair.

JULIA ALVAREZ   (B. 1950)

Dusting   (1984)

Each morning I wrote my name
on the dusty cabinet, then crossed
the dining table in script, scrawled
in capitals on the backs of chairs,
practising signatures like scales   5
while Mother followed, squirting
linseed from a burping can
into a crumpled-up flannel.

She erased my fingerprints
from the bookshelf and rocker,   10
polished mirrors on the desk
scribbled with my alphabets.
My name was swallowed in the towel

with which she jeweled the table tops.
The grain surfaced in the oak   15
and the pine grew luminous.
But I refused with every mark
to be like her, anonymous.

ANNE CARSON   (B. 1950)

Helen   (1998)

Nights of a marriage are like an Egypt in a woods.
Dark around its edges mirror at the heart.
War has gone quiet.
It moves, a reflection: no.
Cheap theatre smell, rooms   5
settle and hiss. What is he doing. Sleep,
its hours pleat together and close
like a fan, what does she know.
Waters move slightly or do they.
Paths glide to them, to who? Glide off.   10
Vanishes
out of the marriage, into the marriage.
Troy
vanishes too, murmuring, stain
is a puzzle you do not want   15
the answer to.
Every war
needs
one.

CAROLYN FORCHÉ   (B. 1950)

The Colonel   (1982)

> May 1978

What you have heard is true. I was in his house. His wife carried a tray of coffee
and sugar. His daughter filed her nails, his son went out for the night. There were
daily papers, pet dogs, a pistol on the cushion beside him. The moon swung bare
on its black cord over the house. On the television was a cop show. It was in
English. Broken bottles were embedded in the walls around the house to scoop
the kneecaps from a man's legs or cut his hands to lace. On the windows there
were gratings like those in liquor stores. We had dinner, rack of lamb, good wine,
a gold bell was on the table for calling the maid. The maid brought green mangoes, salt, a type of bread. I was asked how I enjoyed the country. There was a
brief commercial in Spanish. His wife took everything away. There was some
talk then of how difficult it had become to govern. The parrot said hello on the
terrace. The colonel told it to shut up, and pushed himself from the table. My

friend said to me with his eyes: say nothing. The colonel returned with a sack used to bring groceries home. He spilled many human ears on the table. They were like dried peach halves. There is no other way to say this. He took one of them in his hands, shook it in our faces, dropped it into a water glass. It came alive there. I am tired of fooling around he said. As for the rights of anyone, tell your people they can go fuck themselves. He swept the ears to the floor with his arm and held the last of his wine in the air. Something for your poetry, no? he said. Some of the ears on the floor caught this scrap of his voice. Some of the ears on the floor were pressed to the ground.

JORIE GRAHAM   (B. 1950)
Over and Over Stitch   (1980)

Late in the season the world digs in, the fat blossoms
hold still for just a moment longer.
Nothing looks satisfied,
but there is no real reason to move on much further:
this isn't a bad place;   5
why not pretend

we wished for it?
The bushes have learned to live with their haunches.
The hydrangea is resigned
to its pale and inconclusive utterances.   10
Towards the end of the season
it is not bad

to have the body. To have experienced joy
as the mere lifting of hunger
is not to have known it   15
less. The tobacco leaves
don't mind being removed
to the long racks—all uses are astounding

to the used.
There are moments in our lives which, threaded, give us heaven—   20
noon, for instance, or all the single victories
of gravity, or the kudzu vine,
most delicate of manias,
which has pressed its luck
this far this season.   25
It shines a gloating green.
Its edges darken with impatience, a kind of wind.
Nothing again will ever be this easy, lives
being snatched up like dropped stitches, the dry stalks of daylilies
marking a stillness we can't keep.   30

EDWARD HIRSCH

(B. 1950)

Fast Break

(1986)

In memory of Dennis Turner, 1946–1984

A hook shot kisses the rim and
hangs there, helplessly, but doesn't drop,

and for once our gangly starting center
boxes out his man and times his jump

perfectly, gathering the orange leather   5
from the air like a cherished possession

and spinning around to throw a strike
to the outlet who is already shoveling

an underhand pass toward the other guard
scissoring past a flat-footed defender   10

who looks stunned and nailed to the floor
in the wrong direction, trying to catch sight

of a high, gliding dribble and a man
letting the play develop in front of him

in slow motion, almost exactly   15
like a coach's drawing on the blackboard,

both forwards racing down the court
the way that forwards should, fanning out

and filling the lanes in tandem, moving
together as brothers passing the ball   20

between them without a dribble, without
a single bounce hitting the hardwood

until the guard finally lunges out
and commits to the wrong man

while the power-forward explodes past them   25
in a fury, taking the ball into the air

by himself now and laying it gently
against the glass for a lay-up,

but losing his balance in the process,
inexplicably falling, hitting the floor   30

with a wild, headlong motion
for the game he loved like a country

and swiveling back to see an orange blur
floating perfectly through the net.

GARRETT HONGO (B. 1951)

The Legend (1988)

In Memory of Jay Kashiwamura

In Chicago, it is snowing softly
and a man has just done his wash for the week.
He steps into the twilight of early evening,
carrying a wrinkled shopping bag
full of neatly folded clothes,   5
and, for a moment, enjoys
the feel of warm laundry and crinkled paper,
flannellike against his gloveless hands.
There's a Rembrandt glow on his face,
a triangle of orange in the hollow of his cheek   10
as a last flash of sunset
blazes the storefronts and lit windows of the street.

He is Asian, Thai or Vietnamese,
and very skinny, dressed as one of the poor
in rumpled suit pants and a plaid mackinaw,   15
dingy and too large.
He negotiates the slick of ice
on the sidewalk by his car,
opens the Fairlane's back door,
leans to place the laundry in,   20
and turns, for an instant,
toward the flurry of footsteps
and cries of pedestrians
as a boy—that's all he was—
backs from the corner package store   25
shooting a pistol, firing it,
once, at the dumbfounded man
who falls forward,
grabbing at his chest.

A few sounds escape from his mouth,   30
a babbling no one understands
as people surround him
bewildered at his speech.
The noises he makes are nothing to them.
The boy has gone, lost   35
in the light array of foot traffic
dappling the snow with fresh prints.
Tonight, I read about Descartes'
grand courage to doubt everything
except his own miraculous existence   40
and I feel so distinct
from the wounded man lying on the concrete
I am ashamed.

Let the night sky cover him as he dies.
Let the weaver girl cross the bridge of heaven   45
and take up his cold hands.

JUDITH ORTIZ COFER   (B. 1952)

Quinceañera   (1987)

My dolls have been put away like dead
children in a chest I will carry
with me when I marry.
I reach under my skirt to feel
a satin slip bought for this day. It is soft   5
as the inside of my thighs. My hair
has been nailed back with my mother's
black hairpins to my skull. Her hands
stretched my eyes open as she twisted
braids into a tight circle at the nape   10
of my neck. I am to wash my own clothes
and sheets from this day on, as if
the fluids of my body were poison, as if
the little trickle of blood I believe
travels from my heart to the world were   15
shameful. Is not the blood of saints and
men in battle beautiful? Do Christ's hands
not bleed into your eyes from His cross?
At night I hear myself growing and wake
to find my hands drifting of their own will   20
to soothe skin stretched tight
over my bones.
I am wound like the guts of a clock,
waiting for each hour to release me.

RITA DOVE   (B. 1952)

Describe Yourself in Three Words or Less   (2004)

I'm not the kind of person who praises
openly, or for profit; I'm not the kind
who will steal a scene unless
I've designed it. I'm not a kind at all,
in fact: I'm itchy and pug-willed,   5
gnarled and wrong-headed,
never amorous but possessing
a wild, thatched soul.

Each night I set my boats to sea
and leave them to their bawdy business.   10

Whether they drift off
maddened, moon-rinsed,
or dock in the morning
scuffed and chastened—
is simply how it is, and I gather them in.   15

You are mine, I say to the twice-dunked cruller
before I eat it. Then I sing
to the bright-beaked bird outside,
then to the manicured spider
between window and screen;   20
then I will stop, and forget the singing.
(See? I have already forgotten you.)

DORIANNE LAUX   (B. 1952)

For My Daughter Who Loves Animals   (1994)

Once a week, whether the money is there
or not, I write a check for her lessons.
But today, as I waited in the car for her
to finish her chores, after she had wrapped
this one's delicate legs, brushed burrs   5
and caked mud from that one's tail,
I saw her stop and offer her body
to a horse's itchy head. One arm up,
she gave him the whole length of her side.
And he knew the gesture, understood   10
the gift, stepped in close on oiled hooves
and pressed his head to her ribcage.
From hip to armpit he raked her body until,
to keep from falling, she leaned into him
full weight, her foot braced   15
against a tack post for balance.
Before horses, it was snakes, coiled
around her arms like African bracelets.
And before that, stray dogs, cats
of every color, even the misfits,   20
the abandoned and abused.
It took me so long to learn how to love,
how to give myself up and over to another.
Now I see how she has always
loved them all, snails and spiders,   25
from the very beginning, without fear or shame,
saw even the least of them, ants,
gnats, heard and answered
even the slightest of their calls.

NAOMI SHIHAB NYE

(B. 1952)

Rain

(1986)

A teacher asked Paul
what he would remember
from third grade, and he sat
a long time before writing
"this year somebody tutched me   5
on the sholder"
and turned his paper in.
Later she showed it to me
as an example of her wasted life.
The words he wrote were large   10
as houses in a landscape.
He wanted to go inside them
and live, he could fill in
the windows of "o" and "d"
and be safe while outside   15
birds building nests in drainpipes
knew nothing of the coming rain.

GARY SOTO

(B. 1952)

Oranges

(1985)

The first time I walked
With a girl, I was twelve,
Cold, and weighted down
With two oranges in my jacket.
December. Frost cracking   5
Beneath my steps, my breath
Before me, then gone,
As I walked toward
Her house, the one whose
Porch light burned yellow   10
Night and day, in any weather.
A dog barked at me, until
She came out pulling
At her gloves, face bright
With rouge. I smiled,   15
Touched her shoulder, and led
Her down the street, across
A used car lot and a line
Of newly planted trees,
Until we were breathing   20
Before a drugstore. We

Entered, the tiny bell
Bringing a saleslady
Down a narrow aisle of goods.
I turned to the candies   25
Tiered like bleachers,
And asked what she wanted—
Light in her eyes, a smile
Starting at the corners
Of her mouth. I fingered   30
A nickel in my pocket,
And when she lifted a chocolate
That cost a dime,
I didn't say anything.
I took the nickel from   35
My pocket, then an orange,
And set them quietly on
The counter. When I looked up,
The lady's eyes met mine,
And held them, knowing   40
Very well what it was all
About.

     Outside,
A few cars hissing past,
Fog hanging like old   45
Coats between the trees.
I took my girl's hand
In mine for two blocks,
Then released it to let
Her unwrap the chocolate.   50
I peeled my orange
That was so bright against
The gray of December
That, from some distance,
Someone might have thought   55
I was making a fire in my hands.

MARILYN CHIN   (B. 1955)

Composed Near the Bay Bridge   (1994)

    (after a wild party)

1

Amerigo has his finger on the pulse of China.
He, Amerigo, is dressed profoundly punk:
Mohawk-pate, spiked dog collar, black leather thighs.
She, China, freshly hennaed and boaed, is intrigued
with the new diaspora and the sexual freedom   5

called *bondage*. "Isn't *bondage*, therefore,
a *kind* of freedom?" she asks, wanly.

2

Thank God there was no war tonight.
Headbent, Amerigo plucks his bad guitar.
The Sleeping Giant snores with her mouth agape   10
while a lone nightingale trills on a tree.

Through the picture window, I watch the traffic
hone down to a quiver. Loneliness. Dawn.
A few geese winging south; minor officials return home.

CATHY SONG   (B. 1955)
A Conservative View   (1994)

Money, my mother
never had much.
Perhaps that explains her life's
philosophy, the conservation of money,
the idea of money as a natural resource,   5
the sleepless nights worrying
whether there is enough of it.
According to her current calculations,
there isn't.

I used to think it was because she is Chinese,   10
proud of the fact that her practical
nature is due to her Chinese blood.
"We do not spoil our children"
she is fond of saying as an explanation
for never having given in to our demands.   15
"Take care of the needs but not the wants" is another.

Place a well-behaved child
in front of her and my mother will say,
"Chinese, eh?"
She believes Japanese and Korean   20
parents spoil their children.
"Doormats to their kids."
And the bok gwai?—well,
they ship their offspring to camp or boarding school, right?
For the Chinese, discipline begins at home.   25
And it begins with teaching the value of money.

There are two things in life
my mother vows never to pay for:
gift wrapping and parking.
It hurts her to cough up change for the meter.   30

Lucky is any day she can pull
into an empty space with time still running.
I was convinced my friends knew
that the birthday gifts I presented at parties
were wrapped in leftover sheets of our bathroom wallpaper.   35
—"Eh, how come dis paypa so tick?"

My mother's thrift frowns on the frivolous—
like singing in the shower
(it's a waste of water).
Her clear and practical sentences   40
are sprinkled with expressions
semantically rooted to the conservation of money.
They pepper her observations like expletives—
"Poho" if we bought something we couldn't use.
"Humbug" if we have to go out and buy   45
something we don't need.
"No need"—her favorite expression of all.

On shopping trips to the mall
she'll finger something soft and expensive,
letting her fingers linger on the exquisite   50
cut and fabric of a garment
when suddenly she'll exclaim,
like a kung fu battle cry,
"Pee-sa!"
(the one word she borrows liberally   55
from her Korean in-laws),
shuddering and releasing the price tag
as if she'd been bitten by a snake.

My sister and I agree
she takes the price of things too personally.   60
Every morning there is her wake-up call—
"Diapers on sale at Longs."
"Price of lettuce up at Star."—
as though she were reporting the Dow Jones Industrial Average.
If I answer in the negative   65
to her interrogative
"Did you use coupons to buy that?"
—*that* being chicken thighs or toilet paper,
I feel guilty.

My father doesn't help matters.   70
He has heard enough from Mother
about Koreans being big spenders, show-offs—
"champagne taste on a beer budget"—
to have his revenge.
He thinks Mao Tse-tung is the best   75
thing that ever happened to China.
"How else are you going to get those damn pa-kes to share?"

MARTÍN ESPADA (B. 1957)

Public School 190, Brooklyn 1963 (1996)

The inkwells had no ink.
The flag had 48 stars, four years
after Alaska and Hawaii.
There were vandalized blackboards
and chairs with three legs,   5
taped windows, retarded boys penned
in the basement.
Some of us stared in Spanish.
We windmilled punches
or hid in the closet to steal from coats   10
as the teacher drowsed, head bobbing.
We had the Dick and Jane books,
but someone filled in their faces
with a brown crayon.

When Kennedy was shot,   15
they hurried us onto buses,
not saying why,
saying only that
something bad had happened.
But we knew   20
something bad had happened,
knew that before
November 22, 1963.

LI-YOUNG LEE (B. 1957)

From Blossoms (1986)

From blossoms comes
this brown paper bag of peaches
we bought from the boy
at the bend in the road where we turned toward
signs painted *Peaches*.   5

From laden boughs, from hands,
from sweet fellowship in the bins,
comes nectar at the roadside, succulent
peaches we devour, dusty skin and all,
comes the familiar dust of summer, dust we eat.   10

O, to take what we love inside,
to carry within us an orchard, to eat
not only the skin, but the shade,
not only the sugar, but the days, to hold

the fruit in our hands, adore it, then bite into
the round jubilance of peach.

There are days we live
as if death were nowhere
in the background; from joy
to joy to joy, from wing to wing,
from blossom to blossom to
impossible blossom, to sweet impossible blossom.

C H A P T E R
19

Biographies of Selected
Poets

JULIA ALVAREZ (b. 1950)

Alvarez was born in New York City, during what she calls her parents' "failed first attempt" to immigrate to the United States. The family, unhappy in the United States, soon returned the Dominican Republic, despite the violent dictatorship of General Rafael Trujillo. In 1960 Alvarez's family returned for good to New York City. Alvarez has published three collections of poetry, including *Old Age Ain't for Sissies* (1979) and *Homecoming*, which was revised in 1995. Her poetry and prose usually depict Dominicans either struggling with daily life under dictatorship in their home country or adjusting to exile in the United States. Her first novel, *How the Garcia Girls Lost Their Accents*, was published in 1991. Her second novel, *In the Time of the Butterflies*, is based on the true story of the Mirabel sisters, founders of the underground movement against Trujillo, a movement that Alvarez's own father participated in. Alvarez currently teaches at Middlebury College as writer in residence.

Starting Points for Further Research: Julia Alvarez

- **Critical Essay:** Kathrine Varnes. " 'Practicing for the Real Me': Form and Authenticity in the Poetry of Julia Alvarez." *Antípodas: Journal of Hispanic and Galician Studies* 10 (1998): 67–77.

- **Interview:** Heather Rosario-Sievert. "Conversation with Julia Álvarez." *Review: Latin American Literature and Arts* 54 (Spring 1997): 31–37.
- **Website:** http://www.juliaalvarez.com.

MARGARET ATWOOD (b. 1939)

A Canadian, Atwood studied at the University of Toronto and at Harvard. Her first poem was published at age nineteen, and she has written essays, short stories, and novels, including *The Edible Woman* (1969), *Surfacing* (1972), *The Handmaid's Tale* (1985), *The Blind Assassin* (2000), which won the Booker Prize, and *Oryx and Crake* (2003).

Starting Point for Further Research: Margaret Atwood
- **Critical Essay:** Brian Bethune. "Atwood Apocalyptic." *Maclean's*, April 28, 2003, 44–48.

W. H. AUDEN (1907–1973)

Wystan Hugh Auden was born in York, England, in 1907. His father, a physician, was a professor of public health at the University of Birmingham, and Auden absorbed much medical knowledge through his father's work. Auden attended private school and Oxford University, where he collected his early poems in 1928 and had a friend publish them. In 1930 his collection *Poems* was published, establishing him as the voice of his generation. Auden supported himself by teaching sporadically between trips to Iceland, China, Spain, and the United States, which provided material for his writing. In 1939 he left England for the United States, and he became an American citizen in 1946. His books *Later Time* (1940) and *The Sea and the Mirror* are considered some of the finest poetry he produced in the United States. Later in life he split his time between New York City and Austria.

Starting Points for Further Research: W. H. Auden
- **Edition:** W. H. Auden. *Selected Poems of W. H. Auden*. Ed. Edward Mendelson. New York: Knopf, 1989.
- **Biography:** Richard Davenport-Hines. *Auden: A Biography*. New York: Knopf, 1999.
- **Critical Essays:** Thomas Dilworth. "Auden's *Musée des Beaux Arts*." *Explicator* 49:3 (1991): 181–83.
  Adam Gopnik. "The Double Man." *New Yorker*, September 23, 2002, 86–91.

ELIZABETH BISHOP (1911–1979)

Born in Massachusetts, Elizabeth Bishop was raised by her grandmother in Nova Scotia following her father's death and her mother's mental breakdown. After her education at Vassar College, Bishop moved to New York, where she joined a small group of women writers. She left New York and became a traveler, settling in Rio de Janeiro for many years with her partner and, finally, teaching poetry at Harvard. Her poetry output was small—four volumes—but Bishop was a major influence on her fellow poets, including Robert Lowell. Her 1955 collection *A Cold Spring* earned Bishop the Pulitzer Prize.

Starting Points for Further Research: Elizabeth Bishop

- **Edition:** Elizabeth Bishop. *Complete Poems, 1927–1979*. London: Farrar, Straus and Giroux, 1984.
- **Biography:** Brett C. Millier. *Life and the Memory of It*. Berkeley: University of California Press, 1995.
- **Critical Essay:** Jonathan Ellis. "From Maps to Monuments: Elizabeth Bishop's Shoreline Poems." *Mosaic: A Journal for the Interdisciplinary Study of Literature* 36:4 (2003): 103–19.

WILLIAM BLAKE (1757–1827)

Born in London, William Blake was educated to become a commercial artist. Early in his career he began using a technique called "illuminated printing" that involved engraving words and pictures on copper and coloring these images by hand. In many cases he illustrated famous works of literature, and in other cases he illustrated works of his own, many with a mystical flavor. His most famous works, *Songs of Innocence* (1789) and *Songs of Experience* (1794), were produced in this style.

Starting Points for Further Research: William Blake

- **Edition:** William Blake. *Collected Poetry and Prose of William Blake*. Ed. David Erdman et al. New York: Doubleday, 1982.
- **Biography:** G. E. Bentley, Jr. *The Stranger from Paradise: A Biography of William Blake*. New Haven: Yale University Press, 2003.
- **Critical Essay:** George H. Gilpin. "William Blake and the World's Body of Science." *Studies in Romanticism* 44 (2004): 35–56.

EAVAN BOLAND (b. 1944)

Eavan Boland once wrote, "I don't write a poem to express an experience. I write it to experience the experience." Boland was born in Dublin, Ireland, in 1944 and moved to London at the age of six. The experience of being Irish in London deeply shaped her ideas of national identity, which appear in much of her poetry. Boland's poetry also frequently grapples with the complexities of gender, memory, identity, and place. She has taught at Trinity College and the School of Irish Studies in Dublin, many universities worldwide, and is currently a professor at Stanford University. She has published more than a dozen books of poetry, including *Against Love Poetry* (2001), *An Origin like Water: Collected Poems* (1996), and *In a Time of Violence* (1994).

Starting Points for Further Research: Eavan Boland

- **Critical Essays:** Albert Gelpi. "'Hazard and Death': The Poetry of Eavan Boland." *Colby Quarterly* 35:4 (1999): 210–28.

  Sarah Maguire. "Dilemmas and Developments: Eavan Boland Re-Examined." *Feminist Review* 62 (Summer 1999): 58–66.

- **Interviews:** Jody Allen-Randolph. "A Backward Look: An Interview with Eavan Boland." *PN Review* 26:5 (2000): 43–48.

  Elizabeth Schmidt. "Where Poetry Begins: A Conversation with Eavan Boland." *American Poet* (Spring 1997). http://www.poets.org/viewmedia.php/prmMID/15939.

GWENDOLYN BROOKS (1917–2000)

See the biography in Chapter 15.

Starting Points for Further Research: Gwendolyn Brooks

- **Editions:** Gwendolyn Brooks. *Selected Poems.* New York: Harper and Row, 1963.
  ———. *Blacks.* Chicago: Third World Press, 1991.
- **Biography:** George Kent. *A Life of Gwendolyn Brooks.* Lexington, University Press of Kentucky, 1990.
- **Critical Essay:** Tracey L. Walters. "Gwendolyn Brooks' 'The Anniad' and the Interdeterminacy of Genre." *CLA Journal* 44 (March 2001): 350–66.

ELIZABETH BARRETT BROWNING (1806–1861)

Elizabeth Barrett Browning was educated at home in Herefordshire, England, and at thirteen published her first volume of poetry. Due to chronic medical problems, she was rarely able to leave her home, and her father refused to let her socialize or marry. As a result, her courtship with poet Robert Browning consisted almost exclusively of letters, and they eloped to Italy in 1846. Her nine-book verse novel *Aurora Leigh* (1857) was highly popular at the time, but she is now best remembered for *Sonnets from the Portuguese,* her sequence of poems.

Starting Points for Further Research: Elizabeth Barrett Browning

- **Edition:** Elizabeth Barrett Browning. *Selected Poems.* Ed. Margaret Forster. Baltimore: Johns Hopkins University Press, 1988.
- **Biography:** Margaret Forster. *Elizabeth Barrett Browning: A Biography.* London: Chatto and Windus, 1988.
- **Critical Essay:** Margaret Stone. "Guide to the Year's Work: Elizabeth Barrett Browning." *Victorian Poetry* 41 (2003): 377–94.

ROBERT BROWNING (1812–1889)

Born in London, Robert Browning was educated at London University. Although Browning did not achieve the same level of contemporary literary acclaim as his wife Elizabeth, his collections *Men and Women* (1855) and *Dramatis Personae* (1864) contain some of the most highly regarded dramatic monologues, a form he made his own. His reputation was established with the publication of his experimental novel in verse *The Ring and the Book* (1869); after his wife's death, his reputation grew and he became the more famous of the two.

Starting Points for Further Research: Robert Browning

- **Edition:** Robert Browning. *Selected Poems*. Ed. Daniel Karlin. New York: Penguin, 2001.
- **Biography:** William Irvine and Park Honan. *The Book, the Ring, and the Poet*. New York: McGraw Hill, 1974.
- **Critical Essay:** C. D. Blanton. "Impostures: Robert Browning and the Poetics of Forgery." *Studies in the Literary Imagination* 35:2 (Fall 2002): 1–25.

GEORGE GORDON, LORD BYRON (1798–1824)

Byron was the most famous poet of his era, renowned for his scandalous love affairs as well as for his exciting poetry, which sold extraordinarily well. In some of his longer poems, notably *The Giaour, Manfred,* and *Childe Harold,* he created a handsome, young, disillusioned, and melancholic protagonist, soon to be called the "Byronic hero," a figure that would prove immensely influential in European literature. His tempestuous life ended in Greece, where he fell ill and died while helping to lead the fight for independence.

Starting Points for Further Research: George Gordon, Lord Byron

- **Edition:** George Gordon, Lord Byron. *The Major Works*. Ed. Jerome J. McGann. New York: Oxford World's Classics, 1986.
- **Biography:** Leslie A. Marchand. *Byron: A Biography*. London: John Murray, 1957.
- **Critical Essay:** Nicholas Mason. "Building Brand Byron: Early-Nineteenth-Century Advertising and the Marketing of Childe Harold's Pilgrimage." *Modern Language Quarterly: A Journal of Literary History* 63 (December 2002): 411–40.

THOMAS CAMPION (1567–1620)

Campion was a genuine Renaissance man, being a writer, musician, lawyer, and doctor. Many of his first poems were written in Latin, but he soon switched to English, though in many poems he kept the quantitative meter of Latin verse, shaping his lines through the length of the syllables. He is most famous for the verses he set to his own music. His first work was published in 1591, and his major works, four volumes of airs and dances, appeared between 1601 and 1617.

Starting Points for Further Research: Thomas Campion

- **Edition:** Thomas Campion. *The Works of Thomas Campion*. Ed. Walter R. Davis. Garden City: Doubleday, 1967.
- **Biography:** Walter R. Davis. *Thomas Campion*. Boston: Twayne, 1987.
- **Critical Essay:** Stephen Ratcliffe. "Words and Music: Campion and the Song Tradition." *Approaches to Teaching Shorter Elizabethan Poetry*. Ed. Patrick Cheney and Anne Lake Prescott. New York: Modern Language Association of America, 2000. 216–19.

MARILYN CHIN (b. 1955)

Born in Hong Kong, Marilyn Chin grew up in Portland, Oregon. Her publications include *Dwarf Bamboo* (1987), *The Phoenix Gone, The Terrace Empty* (1994), and *Rhapsody in Plain Yellow* (2002). Chin has received two National Endowment for the Arts Writing Fellowships, the Mary Roberts Rinehart Award, and a Stegner Fellowship. She lives in San Francisco.

Starting Point for Further Research: Marilyn Chin

- **Interview:** Bill Moyers. "Interview with Marilyn Chin." *The Language of Life: A Festival of Poets*. Ed. James Haba. New York: Doubleday, 1995. 67–80.

SAMUEL TAYLOR COLERIDGE (1772–1834)

Samuel Taylor Coleridge was a scholarship boy at Westminster School and went on to Cambridge University. He and his friend and fellow poet William Wordsworth created the Romantic movement in English poetry with their collection *The Lyrical Ballads* (1798). Coleridge was one of the most brilliant thinkers of his time, enormously influential on the intellectual, literary, and philosophical trends of his age. Addicted to opium and chronically depressed, Coleridge produced relatively few poems but an enormous amount of critical and philosophical writing. Among his most celebrated poems are "The Rime of the Ancient Mariner" (1798), "Christabel" (1816), and "Kubla Khan" (1816).

Starting Points for Further Research: Samuel Taylor Coleridge

- **Edition:** Samuel Taylor Coleridge. *Selected Poems*. Ed. Richard Holmes. New York: Penguin, 2000.
- **Biography:** Rosemary Ashton. *The Life of Samuel Taylor Coleridge: A Critical Biography*. Oxford: Blackwell, 1996.
- **Critical Essay:** Graham Davidson. "Coleridge and the Bible." *Coleridge Bulletin: The Journal of the Friends of Coleridge* (Spring 2004): 63–81.

BILLY COLLINS (b. 1941)

His extremely popular poems have made Billy Collins one of the famous poets of the early twenty-first century, and he has served in an official capacity as poet laureate of the United States. His career has been spent as an English professor at Lehman College of the City University of New York, where he has taught literature and creative writing for thirty years. Among his books of poetry are *Pokerface* (1977), *Video Poems* (1980), *The Apple That Astonished Paris* (1988), *Questions about Angels* (1991), *The Art of Drowning* (1995), *Picnic, Lightning* (1998), *Sailing around the Room: New and Selected Poems* (2000), and *Nine Horses* (2002).

Starting Point for Further Research: Billy Collins

- **Interview:** George Plimpton. "The Art of Poetry 83 (Interview with Billy Collins)." *Paris Review* 159 (Fall 2001): 182–215.

SAM COOKE (1931–1964)

Cooke, the son of a Chicago Baptist preacher, started singing gospel at an early age; at twenty he became the lead singer of the Soul Stirrers, one of the most famous Chicago-based quartets during gospel's golden age. A great favorite among gospel audiences and the black record-buying public, Cooke went on to pop fame in the later 1950s, reaching stardom among white audiences with a number of best-selling hits. Cooke's advocacy and promotion of soul and gospel groups led to his starting his own record company. He was killed in mysterious circumstances in Los Angeles at the height of his career.

Starting Points for Further Research: Sam Cooke

- **Definitive Recording:** *The Man Who Invented Soul*. New York: RCA, 2000.
- **Biography:** Peter Guralnik. *Dream Boogie: The Triumph of Sam Cooke*. New York: Little, Brown, 2005.
- **Article:** Gene Santoro. "Sam Cooke." *Nation*, March 13, 1995, 357–61.

E. E. CUMMINGS (1894–1962)

Born in Cambridge, Massachusetts, Edward Estlin Cummings attended Harvard University. He served as an ambulance driver in World War I and recounted his experiences in a French prison camp in his highly regarded book *The Enormous Room* (1922). Cummings employed the resources of punctuation and typography in unique ways, making him a characteristically modernist poet both through his experimental forms as well as his often sarcastic tone.

Starting Points for Further Research: E. E. Cummings

- **Edition:** E. E. Cummings. *Collected Poems*. New York: Harcourt Brace, 1963.

- **Biography:** Richard S. Kennedy. *Dreams in a Mirror: A Biography of E. E. Cummings.* New York: Liveright, 1994.
- **Critical Essay:** Iain Landles. "An Analysis of Two Poems by E. E. Cummings." *Spring: The Journal of the E. E. Cummings Society* 10 (Fall 2001): 31–43.

MARGARET DANNER (1915–1986)

Margaret Danner was born in Kentucky and moved to Chicago, where she attended Loyola High School and then Northwestern University. In 1951 *Poetry*, the famous Chicago-based magazine, published her series of four poems "Far from Africa." She was one of the most significant poets in the nascent Black Arts Movement of the 1960s.

Starting Points for Further Research: Margaret Danner

- **Edition:** Margaret Danner. *The Down of a Thistle: Selected Poems, Prose Poems, and Songs.* Waukesha: Country Thistle, 1976.
- **Critical Essay:** Erlene Stetson. "Dialectic Voices in the Poetry of Margaret Esse Danner." *Black American Poets between Worlds, 1940–1960.* Ed. Baxter R. Miller. Knoxville: University of Tennessee Press, 1986.

FRANK MARSHALL DAVIS (1905–1987)

Noted as both a journalist and a poet, Davis grew up in Kansas, where he attended college. He lived in Chicago from 1927 to 1948, publishing three volumes of his poetry and participating in the South Side literary scene. His posthumously published autobiography *Livin' the Blues* (1992) details the role he played in the Chicago Renaissance.

Starting Points for Further Research: Frank Marshall Davis

- **Edition:** Frank Marshall Davis. *Black Moods: Collected Poems, New and Old.* Ed. John E. Tidwell. Urbana: University of Illinois Press, 2000.
- **Biography:** Frank Marshall Davis. *Livin' the Blues.* Madison: University of Wisconsin Press, 1992.
- **Critical Essay:** John Edgar Tidwell. "Coming of Age in a Land of Uncertainty." *Cottonwood* 56 (2000): 42–59.

EMILY DICKINSON (1830–1886)

See the biography in Chapter 14.

Starting Points for Further Research: Emily Dickinson

- **Editions:** Emily Dickinson. *The Poems of Emily Dickinson.* Ed. Rachel Wetzsteon. Cambridge: Belknap Press, 1998.

————. *The Letters of Emily Dickinson.* Ed. Thomas Herbert Johnson and Theodora Ward. Cambridge: Belknap Press, 1986.
- **Biography:** Alfred Habegger. *My Wars Are Laid Away in Books.* New York: Random House, 2002.
- **Critical Essay:** Jay Ladin. "'So Anthracite: To Live' Emily Dickinson and American Literary History." *Emily Dickinson Journal* 13 (2004): 19–50.

JOHN DONNE (1572–1631)

Donne lived in London during Shakespeare's time, and held a number of official posts while he circulated his early love poetry among members of the court. In his thirties he turned to religious themes, still employing the imagery he first used in his love poems. Donne took holy orders and became well known as a preacher in London, publishing a volume of highly regarded sermons in a complex, allusive prose style. Donne is now famous as one of the first and most impressive of the poets called "Metaphysical," meaning they wrote about love as well as religion with complex, highly original imagery. But after his death he was neglected for almost two centuries, until a 1913 edition of his work was extravagantly praised by T. S. Eliot, leading to a revival that included Donne and his fellow Metaphysical poets.

Starting Points for Further Research: John Donne
- **Edition:** John Donne. *The Major Works.* Ed. John Carey. New York: Oxford University Press, 2000.
- **Biography:** R. C. Bald. *John Donne: A Life.* Oxford: Clarendon Press, 1986.
- **Critical Essay:** Sung Hee Choi. "'My New Found Lande': Body Politics and Imperialism in John Donne's Elegies." *Medieval and Early Modern English Studies* 11 (June 2003): 151–75.

RITA DOVE (b. 1952)

Dove was born in Akron, Ohio, in 1952, graduated from Miami University of Ohio, and received her MFA in poetry from the University of Iowa. Her father, who worked as a lift operator at Goodyear Tire when Rita was born, had a degree in chemistry and was eventually promoted to become the first African American scientist at Goodyear. Dove had a happy childhood with her three siblings, full of books and art and her parents' encouragement that education could bring the key to personal success. Dove received a Pulitzer Prize for *Beulah and Thomas* (1986) and served as poet laureate of the United States from 1993 to 1995. She has written numerous books of poetry, a novel, a short story collection, and plays. Dove's more recent books include *Through the Ivory Gate* (1992), *Mother Love* (1995), *On the Bus with Rosa Parks* (1999), and *American Smooth* (2004). Dove's poetry is full of imagery, and its lyricism is deeply influenced by her love of music and dance. "Poetry," writes Dove, "is language at its most distilled and most powerful."

Starting Points for Further Research: Rita Dove

- **Critical Essays:** Emily Walker Cook. " 'But she won't set foot / In his turtledove Nash': Gender Roles and Gender Symbolism in Rita Dove's *Thomas and Beulah*." *CLA Journal* 38:3 (1995): 322–30.

    Kevin Stein. "Lives in Motion: Multiple Perspectives in Rita Dove's Poetry." *Mississippi Review* 23:3 (1995): 51–79.

- **Interview:** Steven Ratiner. "A Chorus of Voices: An Interview with Rita Dove." *Agni* 54 (2001): 166–85.

PAUL LAURENCE DUNBAR (1872–1906)

The son of former slaves, Paul Laurence Dunbar grew up in Dayton, Ohio, and was the first African American poet to achieve international recognition. Dunbar's first great success was *Lyrics of Lowly Life* (1896). Much of his poetry used dialect to characterize the simple life among rural blacks, but he grew uncomfortable with such an approach and in his later poems employed a more formal and more literary style. Dunbar was a leading literary figure among African Americans of his generation, producing many poems and four novels, including his most famous, *The Sport of the Gods* (1902). He died at thirty-three from tuberculosis.

Starting Points for Further Research: Paul Laurence Dunbar

- **Editions:** Paul Laurence Dunbar. *The Sport of the Gods*. New York: Signet Classics, 1999.

    ———. *Selected Poems*. Ed. Herbert W. Martin. New York: Penguin, 2004.

- **Biography:** Tony Gentry. *Paul Laurence Dunbar*. Los Angeles: Melrose Square, 1993.

- **Critical Essay:** Susan Bausch. "Inevitable or Remediable? The Historical Connection between Slavery, Racism, and Urban Degradation in Paul Laurence Dunbar's *The Sport of the Gods*." *CLA Journal* 45 (2002): 497–522.

T. S. ELIOT (1888–1965)

Born in America and educated at Harvard, Eliot moved permanently to England, where he took citizenship in 1927. His poetry and critical work made him one of the most influential literary figures in the first half of the twentieth century, famous both for his complex, highly allusive poems and for his literary essays, which appeared in small-circulation journals and were then collected in individual volumes: *The Sacred Wood* (1920), *For Lancelot Andrewes* (1929), *Selected Essays, 1917–32* (1932), *On Poetry and Poets* (1957), and *To Criticize the Critic* (1966). Eliot's poems, including *The Waste Land* (1922) and *The Four Quartets* (completed 1945), were widely read and analyzed by countless poets, critics, and students. In later years Eliot turned to the theater, producing some difficult, somewhat controversial verse plays. He was awarded the Nobel Prize for Literature in 1948.

Starting Points for Further Research: T. S. Eliot

- **Edition:** T. S. Eliot. *Collected Poems: 1909–1962*. New York: Harcourt, Brace, 1991.
- **Biography:** Lyndall Gordon. *T. S. Eliot: An Imperfect Life*. New York: Norton, 2000.
- **Critical Essay:** Anthony Hecht. "T. S. Eliot." *Literary Imagination: The Review of the Association of Literary Scholars and Critics* 5 (2003): 3–17.

MARTIN ESPADA (b. 1957)

Born to a Puerto Rican family in Brooklyn, Espada has published essay collections as well as prize-winning books of poetry. His first book of poetry was *Trumpets from the Islands of Their Eviction* (1987), followed by *Rebellion Is the Circle of a Lover's Hands* (1990), *City of Coughing and Dead Radiators* (1993), *Imagine the Angels of Bread* (1996), *A Mayan Astronomer in Hell's Kitchen: Poems* (2000), and *Alabanza: New and Selected Poems 1982–2002* (2003). His essays were collected in *Zapata's Disciple: Essays* (1998). In addition to poems and essays, Espada has edited two anthologies: *El Coro: A Chorus of Latino and Latina Poets* (1997) and *Poetry like Bread: Poets of the Political Imagination* (1994). Among his prizes are an American Book Award, the PEN/Voelker Award for Poetry, and two fellowships from the National Endowment for the Arts. Espada teaches at the University of Massachusetts and lives in Amherst, Massachusetts.

Starting Points for Further Research: Martin Espada

- **Critical Essay:** Thomas Fink. "Visibility and History in the Poetry of Martín Espada." *Americas Review* 25 (1999): 202–21.
- **Interview:** Ray Gonzàlez. "A Poetry of Legacy: An Interview with Martín Espada." *Bloomsbury Review* 17:4 (1997): 3, 6.

ROBERT FROST (1874–1963)

Born in San Francisco, Frost moved to Massachusetts and is by now commonly regarded as the quintessential New England poet. He tried college a number of times, eventually dropping out of both Harvard and Dartmouth. He moved to London, where his early poems caught the attention of Ezra Pound, who helped publish *A Boy's Will* (1913). Frost settled in New Hampshire and farmed, all the while writing more poetry. When his work caught on, he became a visiting writer at the University of Michigan and later at Dartmouth and Amherst. Among his many volumes of poetry are *New Hampshire* (1923), *West-running Brook* (1928), *A Further Range* (1936), *Steeple Bush* (1947), and *In the Clearing* (1962). In 1961 Frost read a poem at the inauguration of President John F. Kennedy.

Starting Points for Further Research: Robert Frost

- **Edition:** Robert Frost. *Collected Poems, Prose, and Plays*. New York: Library of America, 1995.

- **Biography:** Jay Parini. *Robert Frost: A Life*. New York: Henry Holt, 1999.
- **Critical Essay:** Jeff Westover. "National Forgetting and Remembering in the Poetry of Robert Frost." *Texas Studies in Literature and Language* 46 (2004): 213–44.

ALLEN GINSBERG (1926–1997)

Allen Ginsberg grew up in New Jersey, where his father had established a reputation as a minor writer. He enrolled at Columbia University, where he met fellow student Jack Kerouac and local writer William Burroughs. Their radical lifestyles, interest in Eastern mysticism, and artistic independence became characteristics of the Beat Generation. Moving first to San Francisco, Ginsberg published many volumes of poetry, beginning with his famous *Howl and Other Poems* (1956), an impassioned attack on the American values of the 1950s that would become a mark of the emerging counterculture of the 1960s. He continued to combine radical politics and Eastern spirituality in poems and at readings throughout the rest of his life, becoming a popular figure first at demonstrations protesting the Vietnam War and then at countless poetry readings.

Starting Points for Further Research: Allen Ginsberg

- **Edition:** Allen Ginsberg. *Selected Poems, 1947–1995*. New York: HarperCollins, 2001.
- **Biography:** Graham Caveney. *Screaming with Joy: The Life of Allen Ginsberg*. London: Bloomsbury, 1999.
- **Critical Essay:** Ben Lee. "Howl and Other Poems: Is There Old Left in These New Beats?" *American Literature: A Journal of Literary History, Criticism, and Bibliography* 76 (2004): 367–89.

LOUISE GLÜCK (b. 1943)

Glück attended Sarah Lawrence and Columbia and published her first books of poems in 1968, at age twenty-five. She spent many years teaching poetry and creative writing at colleges and universities, all the while continuing to write significant poetry. Her books include *The House on Marshland* (1975), *Descending Figure* (1980), *The Triumph of Achilles* (1985), which won the National Book Critics Circle Award, *Ararat* (1990), *The Wild Iris* (1992), *Meadowlands* (1996), *The First Five Books of Poems* (1997), and *Averno* (2006). In 2003 Glück was appointed poet laureate of the United States. She teaches at Williams College in Massachusetts.

Starting Points for Further Research: Louise Glück

- **Edition:** Louise Glück. *Proofs and Theories: Essays on Poetry*. New York: Ecco, 1994.
- **Critical Essay:** Isaac Cates. "Louise Glück: Interstices and Silences." *Literary Imagination: The Review of the Association of Literary Scholars and Critics* 5 (Fall 2003): 462–77.

JORIE GRAHAM (b. 1950)

Jorie Graham was born in New York during a three-month visit by her parents, who were American-born artists living in Europe. Graham grew up in Italy, where her father was a filmmaker and her mother a sculptor. Many critics note Graham's identity as a European American as a strong influence on her style. Graham attended New York University, where she first developed her interest in poetry. Her first book, *Hybrids of Plants and of Ghosts* (1980), introduced philosophical and difficult poems, full of abstract ideas and images. Graham followed with *Erosion* (1983), *The End of Beauty* (1987), *The Dream of the Unified Field* (1995), for which she won a Pulitzer Prize, *Swarm* (2000), and *Never* (2002). For many years she taught at the University of Iowa and is currently on the faculty of Harvard University.

Starting Points for Further Research: Jorie Graham

- **Critical Essays:** Mark Jarman. "The Grammar of Glamour: The Poetry of Jorie Graham." *New England Review*, Middlebury Series 14:4 (1992): 251–61.
    David Orr. "Jorie Graham, Superstar." *New York Times Book Review*, April 24, 2005, 15.

THOMAS GRAY (1716–1771)

Gray's life was quiet and his poems relatively few, but his renown during his life and through the nineteenth century was enormous. He was born in London, the only surviving child of twelve, then went to Eton and Cambridge. He took the grand tour of Europe, moved for a time to London, then returned to Cambridge, which was his home for the rest of his life. Gray's poems were circulated privately and appeared in some unauthorized editions until 1753, when he issued them officially. More poems appeared in 1757, and his collected poems appeared in 1768. Gray is perhaps most famous for "Elegy Written in a Country Churchyard," one of the most-quoted poems in the English language. His poetic style was later criticized by the nineteenth-century Romantic poets, who found it too classical and somewhat lacking in liveliness.

Starting Points for Further Research: Thomas Gray

- **Edition:** *Selected Poems of Thomas Gray, Charles Churchill, and William Cowper.* Ed. Katherine Turner. New York: Penguin, 1997.
- **Biography:** Robert L. Mack. *Thomas Gray: A Life.* New Haven: Yale University Press, 2000.
- **Critical Essay:** Barrett Kalter. "DIY Gothic: Thomas Gray and the Medieval Revival." *ELH* 70 (2003): 989–1019.

THOMAS HARDY (1840–1928)

The son of a stonemason in Dorset, England, Hardy possessed neither the money nor the social standing to attain a classical education. He was apprenticed to an architect and, while working full time, wrote his first novels, which were not successful enough to let him quit work. But with the acclaimed publication of *Far from the Madding Crowd* in 1874, Hardy was able to leave his job and devote himself fully to writing. His other novels include *The Return of the Native* (1878), *The Mayor of Casterbridge* (1886), *Tess of the D'Urbervilles* (1891), and *Jude the Obscure* (1896). In his later years Hardy turned to verse, and he has become one of the few English writers whose poetry and prose are equally well regarded.

Starting Points for Further Research: Thomas Hardy

- **Biography:** Michel Millgate. *Thomas Hardy: A Biography.* New York: Random House, 1982.
- **Critical Essays:** Trevor Johnson. *A Critical Introduction to the Poems of Thomas Hardy.* New York: Palgrave Macmillan, 1991.

  Oliver Lovesey. "Reconstructing Tess." *SEL: Studies in English Literature, 1500–1900* 43 (2003): 913–38.

  Dennis Taylor. "Hardy as a Nineteenth-Century Poet." *The Cambridge Companion to Thomas Hardy.* Ed. Dale Kramer. Cambridge: Cambridge University Press, 1999. 183–203.

ROBERT HASS (b. 1941)

Hass, a California native, received his bachelor's degree from St. Mary's College of California and his master's and doctoral degrees from Stanford University. In 1973 his first collection, *Field Guide*, won the Yale Younger Poet's Award. While poet laureate from 1995 to 1997, Hass was credited with bringing new meaning and power to the position through his extensive community-building to promote literacy and poetry. Among his publications are *Praise* (1979), *Human Wishes* (1989), *Twentieth Century Pleasures: Prose on Poetry* (1984), and *Sun under Wood: New Poems* (1996). Hass is well regarded as a critic and translator but best known for his clear, concise poetry full of imagery drawn from everyday life. He teaches at the University of California, Berkeley.

Starting Points for Further Research: Robert Hass

- **Critical Essay:** Terrence Doody. "From Image to Sentence: The Spiritual Development of Robert Hass." *American Poetry Review* 26:2 (1997): 47–56.
- **Interview:** Maximilian Werner. "Idioms of the Sacred: An Interview with Poet Laureate Robert Hass." *Hayden's Ferry Review* 20 (1997): 111–21.

ROBERT HAYDEN (1913–1980)

Born in Detroit as Asa Bundey Sheffey, Hayden attended what is now Wayne State University and received an MA from the University of Michigan. He taught at Fisk University in Nashville for twenty years, publishing some ten volumes of poems, including *Heart-Shape in the Dust* (1940), *The Lion and the Archer* (1948), *Figure of Time* (1955), *A Ballad of Remembrance* (1962), *Words in Mourning Time* (1970), *Night Blooming Cereus* (1972), and *Angle of Ascent* (1975). His *Collected Poems* appeared in 1985, after his death.

Starting Points for Further Research: Robert Hayden

- **Edition:** Robert Hayden. *Collected Poems.* Ed. Frederick Glaysher. New York: Liveright, 1985.
- **Biography:** John Hatcher. *From the Auroral Darkness: The Life and Poetry of Robert Hayden.* Oxford: G. Ronald, 1984.
- **Critical Essay:** Frank Rashid. "Robert Hayden's Detroit Blues Elegies." *Callaloo: A Journal of African-American and African Arts and Letters* 24 (2001): 200–26.

SEAMUS HEANEY (b. 1939)

Born in rural Northern Ireland in 1939, one of nine children in a Catholic family, Heaney attended Queen's University in Belfast, where he first began writing poetry. He published his first collection, *Eleven Poems,* as a pamphlet in 1965 to favorable reviews. After the publication of *Door into the Dark* in 1969, violence erupted once again in Northern Ireland and the theme of the "Troubles" entered his writing. Although he strongly identified as an Irishman, Heaney fought for many years to be claimed as a spokesperson for Northern Irish or Irish Catholics. In 1975, teaching in Dublin, he published *North* to glowing reviews. He taught at various colleges and secondary schools before becoming a professor at Harvard University in 1982 and at Oxford from 1989 until 1994. In 1995 he received the Nobel Prize for Poetry. Since then he has published *Spirit Level* (1996), a translation of *Beowulf* (1999), and *Open Ground: Selected Poems* (1999).

Starting Points for Further Research: Seamus Heaney

- **Critical Essays:** Srikanth Reddy. "The Bastion of Sensation: Stationing the Self in the Poetry of Seamus Heaney." *Journal x: A Journal in Culture and Criticism* 5:1 (2000): 87–108.
  Irene Gilsenan Nordin. "Nihilism in Seamus Heaney." *Philosophy and Literature* 26:2 (2002): 405–14.
- **Interview:** J. J. Wylie. "An Interview with Seamus Heaney." *Nua: Studies in Contemporary Irish Writing* 2:1 (1998): 125–37.

GEORGE HERBERT (1593–1633)

Herbert grew up with poetical connections, since his mother was one of John Donne's patrons. After Cambridge, Herbert was elected to Parliament, then married and joined the clergy, serving for the rest of his life in the small village of Bemerton, where he wrote most of his devotional poems. His most famous collection, *The Temple,* appeared after his death. Herbert's poems are marked by the same dramatic devices and metaphysical conceits as Donne's, though Herbert's treatment is strictly religious, always in the service of his Anglican faith.

Starting Points for Further Research: George Herbert

- **Edition:** George Herbert. *The Complete English Poems.* Ed. J. J. M. Tobin. New York: Penguin, 1991.

- **Biography:** Cristina Malcolmson. *George Herbert: A Literary Life*. New York: Palgrave Macmillan, 2004.
- **Critical Essay:** Robert Whalen. "George Herbert's Sacramental Puritanism." *Renaissance Quarterly* 54 (2001): 1273–1307.

ROBERT HERRICK (1591–1674)

Herrick grew up in London and after college spent several years as a parish minister in Devonshire before he committed himself to a literary life, becoming a follower of Ben Jonson. His many poems include those on religious subjects, but he is most famous for his *Hesperides*, which often invoked *carpe diem* themes that might seem inappropriate for a priest of the Church of England, though there is no indication that the persona he created was anything more than a poetic fiction. Herrick published a book of 1,400 of his poems in 1648. He was opposed to the Puritans, and their rise to power resulted in his abandonment of poetry and return to the parish ministry. Like Donne, his poetry was overlooked for a long time until its revival in the nineteenth century.

Starting Points for Further Research: Robert Herrick

- **Edition:** Robert Herrick. *Selected Poems*. Ed. David Jesson-Dibley. New York: Routledge, 2003.
- **Biography:** George W. Scott. *Robert Herrick, 1591–1674*. New York: St. Martin's, 1974.
- **Critical Essay:** Maryclaire Moroney. "Recent Studies in Herrick (1972–1997)." *English Literary Renaissance* 29 (1999): 154–76.

GERARD MANLEY HOPKINS (1844–1889)

The oldest of eight children, Hopkins attended Oxford, where he converted to Roman Catholicism. He became a Jesuit and served as professor of Greek at University College, Dublin, where he died. His highly idiosyncratic, experimental poems, revealing a powerful religious sensibility, were almost all unpublished in his lifetime; they became known and highly popular only when they appeared in a twentieth-century edition.

Starting Points for Further Research: Gerard Manley Hopkins

- **Edition:** Gerard Manley Hopkins. *Poems and Prose of Gerard Manley Hopkins*. Ed. W. H. Gardner. New York: Penguin, 1985.
- **Biography:** Norman White. *Hopkins: A Literary Biography*. New York: Oxford University Press, 1995.
- **Critical Essay:** Dennis Sobolev. "Hopkins's 'Bellbright Bodies': The Dialectics of Desire in His Writings." *Texas Studies in Literature and Language* 45 (2003): 114–40.

A. E. HOUSMAN (1859–1936)

Born to an extremely talented family, Housman went to Oxford, where he was headed toward an academic career in classical languages until he failed his final examinations. He took a job at a London patent office, using his spare time to publish articles in scholarly journals. In 1892 he was appointed professor of Greek and Latin at University College, London. He wrote and published his two slim volumes of verse, *A Shropshire Lad* (1896) and *Last Poems* (1922), between his meticulous editions of Greek and Latin texts and his famously scathing reviews of scholarly work he considered substandard. His life as a closeted homosexual became the subject of Tom Stoppard's 1998 play *The Invention of Love.*

Starting Points for Further Research: A. E. Housman

- **Edition:** A. E. Housman. *The Poems of A. E. Housman.* Ed. Archie Burnett. New York: Oxford University Press, 1997.
- **Biography:** Norman Page. *A. E. Housman: A Critical Biography.* London: Macmillan, 1996.
- **Critical Essay:** Archie Burnett. "Silence and Allusion in Housman." *Essays in Criticism: A Quarterly Journal of Literary Criticism* 53 (2003): 151–73.

LANGSTON HUGHES (1902–1967)

A child of divorce, Langston Hughes grew up in Missouri with his maternal grandmother. He enrolled at Columbia University, but after a year he dropped out to travel and work. The publication of his first volume of poetry, *The Weary Blues* in 1926, established him as a new voice in American letters. Hughes devoted his life to his art, often giving lectures and readings to support himself at a time when black writers had small, poor audiences. His prose and poetry use dialect as well as jazz and gospel rhythms to present the sounds and experiences of African Americans in the modern city. Hughes produced work in many genres and tirelessly promoted other black writers and artists. He wrote two autobiographies, *The Big Sea* (1940) and *I Wonder as I Wander* (1956).

Starting Points for Further Research: Langston Hughes

- **Editions:** Langston Hughes. *Selected Poems of Langston Hughes.* Ed. E. McKnight Kauffer. New York: Knopf, 2001.
  ———. *The Short Stories.* Ed. R. Baxter Miller. Columbia: University of Missouri Press, 2002.
- **Biography:** Arnold Rampersad. *The Life of Langston Hughes.* 2 vols. New York: Oxford University Press, 2002.
- **Critical Essay:** Meta DuEwa Jones. "Listening to What the Ear Demands: Langston Hughes and His Critics." *Callaloo: A Journal of African Diaspora Arts and Letters* 25 (2002): 1145–75.

ROBINSON JEFFERS (1887–1962)

Jeffers, born in Pittsburgh into a Scots-Irish Calvinist family, was educated at boarding schools in Europe and moved with his family to California in 1903. He attended Occidental College, graduating at age eighteen. Uncertainty about his future studies led him to graduate school in Zurich and then to the University of Southern California, studying subjects as disparate as medicine, English, and forestry. In 1912 he published his first poetry collection, *Flagons and Apples*, after receiving a small inheritance. In 1913 he married Una Call Kuster after luring her away from her husband. The couple settled in Carmel, on the coast of central California, where Jeffers would live until his death in 1962. His other books include *Californians* (1916), *Tamar* (1924), *Solstice* (1932), and *Hungerfield and Other Poems* (1954), for which he received the Pulitzer Prize. His poetry is deeply influenced by the landscape of central California and his belief that poetry in the twentieth century must return to values of "substance and sense, and physical and psychological reality."

Starting Points for Further Research: Robinson Jeffers

- **Edition:** Robinson Jeffers. *The Selected Poetry of Robinson Jeffers.* Ed. Tim Hunt. Palo Alto: Stanford University Press, 2003.
- **Biography:** Robert J. Brophy. *Robinson Jeffers: Dimensions of a Poet.* New York: Fordham University Press, 1995.
- **Critical Essay:** Peter O'Leary. "Robinson Jeffers: The Man from Whom God Hid Everything." *Chicago Review* 49:3 (2004): 350–65.

SAMUEL JOHNSON (1709–1784)

One of the most important writers of his generation, Johnson was born in Lichfield, England. He was sick much of his childhood and suffered an infectious disease that severely damaged his hearing and sight. Despite these handicaps, however, Johnson's great intellectual gifts soon flourished through his schooling. At Oxford University Johnson studied religion and become a devout Christian, but he had to leave because of lack of funds. His lack of a college degree kept him from a profession in law or the church and eventually led him to writing. Throughout his life, Johnson relied on journalism and hack writing to survive, but he wrote great works of poetry, drama, and prose at the same time. Johnson's greatest achievement was the two-volume *Dictionary of the English Language* (1755), the first to illustrate every word's meaning with a historical quote. Some of his most famous works are *Rasselas* (1759), *The Lives of the Poets* (1781), and "The Vanity of Human Wishes" (1749).

Starting Points for Further Research: Samuel Johnson

- **Edition:** Samuel Johnson. *Samuel Johnson: Selected Poetry and Prose.* Ed. Frank Brady and W. K. Wimsatt. Berkeley: University of California Press, 1977.

- **Critical Essays:** David R. Anderson. "Johnson and the Problem of Religious Verse." *Age of Johnson: A Scholarly Annual* 4 (1991): 41–57.

  David Perkins. "Johnson and Modern Poetry." *Harvard Library Bulletin* 33:3 (1985): 303–12.

BEN JONSON (1572–1637)

Born in London, Jonson worked briefly as a bricklayer, but he got an education and began to work as an actor and playwright. In 1598 he wrote his first play, *Every Man in His Humor.* (In a 1616 production, William Shakespeare acted in one of the lead roles.) Shortly after the play opened, Jonson killed an actor in a duel. Placed on trial, he was let off through "benefit of the clergy," an exception available for those who could read and write Latin. His most famous plays include *Volpone* (1606) and *The Alchemist* (1610). Many of his best-known poems are elegies or occasional poems written to his friends, including Shakespeare, John Donne, and Lady Mary Wroth.

Starting Points for Further Research: Ben Jonson

- **Edition:** Ben Jonson. *The Plays and Masques of Ben Jonson.* Ed. Robert M. Adams. New York: Norton, 1979.
- **Biography:** David Riggs. *Ben Jonson: A Life.* Cambridge: Harvard University Press, 1989.
- **Critical Essay:** Esther Richey. " 'When He Shall Know Me Trulie': The Trial of the Subject in Ben Jonson's Letters and Religious Lyrics." *Studies in Philology* 99 (2002): 81–104.

JOHN KEATS (1795–1821)

One of the most celebrated English Romantic poets, Keats began his professional life as a licensed apothecary with no poetic education at all. Befriended by a group of literary men, including the poets Percy Shelley and William Wordsworth, Keats established himself as a poetic talent and published his first volume, *Poems by John Keats,* in 1817. The next year he published *Endymion,* a lengthy romance. Despite receiving famously negative reviews, Keats kept writing, and by 1818 he was publishing his finest work. Among his poems are "Hyperion," "Lamia," "The Eve of St. Agnes," and his famous "Ode on a Grecian Urn," "Ode on Melancholy," and "Ode to a Nightingale." He died at twenty-six, the victim of tuberculosis.

Starting Points for Further Research: John Keats

- **Edition:** John Keats. *The Complete Poems.* Ed. John Barnard. New York: Penguin, 2003.
- **Biography:** Andrew Motion. *Keats.* New York: Farrar, Straus and Giroux, 1997.

- **Critical Essay:** Orrin N. C. Wang. "Coming Attractions: Lamia and Cinematic Sensation." *Studies in Romanticism* 42 (Winter 2003): 461–500.

GALWAY KINNELL (b. 1927)

Kinnell was born in Providence, Rhode Island, into a large working-class Irish family. As a teenager he attended a Massachusetts boarding school on full scholarship, and he went on to study at Princeton and the University of Rochester. After publishing his first book, *What a Kingdom It Was* (1960), he decided to leave academia and for many years worked odd jobs, traveled, and worked as a civil rights activist. He has taught at the University of Hawaii, University of Chicago, Columbia University, and most recently New York University. His lyrical poetry often deals with human relationships, mortality, and the life and landscape surrounding his rural Vermont home. His many accomplishments include the American Book Award (1983), the Pulitzer Prize (1983), the National Book Award for Poetry (1984), and the National Book Critics Circle Award (1986). Kinnell's most acclaimed collections include *The Book of Nightmares* (1971), *The Avenue Bearing the Initial of Christ into the New World: Poems: 1953–1964* (1974), *St. Francis and the Snow* (1976), *Selected Poems* (1983), and *When One Has Lived a Long Time Alone* (1990).

Starting Points for Further Research: Galway Kinnell
- **Critical Essays:** Nancy Lewis Tuten. "Theodore Roethke and Galway Kinnell: Voices in Contemporary American Romanticism." *Northwest Review* 29:2 (1991): 126–42.
  Susan B. Weston. "To Take Hold of the Song: The Poetics of Galway Kinnell." *Literary Review: An International Journal of Contemporary Writing* 31:1 (1987): 73–85.
- **Interview:** Daniela Gioseffi. "Poetry, Nature, and Politics: A Conversation with Galway Kinnell." *Hayden's Ferry Review* 31 (2002): 54–64.

YUSEF KOMUNYAKAA (b. 1947)

Born in Bogulousa, Louisiana, Komunyakaa joined the army after high school, serving a tour in Vietnam, then studied at the University of Colorado, Colorado State University, and the University of California, Irvine. His books of poetry include *Copacetic* (1984), *I Apologize for the Eyes in My Head* (1986), *February in Sydney* (1989), *Magic City* (1992), and *Neon Vernacular: New and Selected Poems* (1993), which won the Pulitzer Prize. He wrote two books on his Vietnam experience, *Toys in a Field* (1987) and *Dien Cai Dau* (1988). Komunyakaa is a professor of creative writing at Princeton.

Starting Points for Further Research: Yusef Komunyakaa
- **Critical Essay:** Angela M. Salas. "Race, Human Empathy, and Negative Capability: The Poetry of Yusef Komunyakaa." *College Literature* 30:4 (2003): 32–53.

- **Interview:** William Baer. "Still Negotiating with the Images: An Interview with Yusef Komunyakaa." *Kenyon Review* 20:3–4 (1998): 5–29.

PHILIP LARKIN (1922–1985)

Larkin had a career as a professional librarian, serving most notably at the University of Hull, where over many years he built a first-class university collection. Shy and somewhat retiring except among close friends, he published a few books of poetry, all employing the notably gloomy personas that became something of his specialty. The forbidding nature of these personas and his infrequent books of verse did not prevent him from becoming one of the most respected of all English poets in his lifetime. He also established a distinctly different reputation as a regularly published critic of jazz recordings.

Starting Points for Further Research: Philip Larkin

- **Editions:** Philip Larkin. *Collected Poems.* Ed. Anthony Thwaite. New York: Farrar, Straus and Giroux, 2003.
    ———. *Required Writing: Miscellaneous Pieces, 1955–1982.* Ann Arbor: University of Michigan Press, 1999.
- **Biography:** Richard Bradford. *First Boredom, Then Fear: The Life of Philip Larkin.* London: Peter Owen, 2005.
- **Critical Essay:** Raphael Ingelbien. "From Hardy to Yeats?: Larkin's Poetry of Aging." *Essays in Criticism: A Quarterly Journal of Literary Criticism* 53 (2003): 262–77.

DENISE LEVERTOV (1923–1997)

Born in England to a cultured family in which her mother read authors like Willa Cather and Leo Tolstoy aloud to her children, Levertov was educated entirely at home. At twelve she sent some of her poetry to T. S. Eliot, who encouraged her. Her first poem was published at seventeen, and she went on to publish over twenty books of poems. She married and moved to New York in 1948, where she soon became associated with avant-garde poetic movements, publishing *Here and Now* (1956), *With Eyes at the Back of Our Heads* (1959), *The Sorrow Dance* (1967), and *Freeing the Dust* (1975). Late in her life she taught at Stanford, and she spent her last decade in Seattle, publishing *Poems 1968–1972* (1987), *Breathing the Water* (1987), *A Door in the Hive* (1989), *Evening Train* (1992), and *The Sands of the Well* (1996). Her last book, *This Great Unknowing: Last Poems*, appeared posthumously in 1999.

Starting Points for Further Research: Denise Levertov

- **Critical Essay:** Paul Lacey. "Denise Levertov: Testimonies of the Lived Life." *Renascence: Essays on Values in Literature* 53 (Summer 2001): 243–56.
- **Interview:** Ed Block Jr. "Interview with Denise Levertov." *Renascence* 50:1–2 (1997–1998): 5–15.

HENRY WADSWORTH LONGFELLOW
(1807–1882)

A native of Portland, Maine, Longfellow attended Bowdoin College, where his classmates were Franklin Pierce (later U.S. president) and the novelist Nathaniel Hawthorne. Longfellow served as a professor of modern languages at Harvard but left to devote himself fully to his poetry. He was the most revered poet in America during his long lifetime, noted for his expert craft as well as his vivid pictures of colonial and Native American life. His books *Hiawatha* and *Evangeline* sold well, and many of his verses were known by millions; some still are, though he is no longer classed as one of the nation's foremost poets.

Starting Points for Further Research: Henry Wadsworth Longfellow

- **Edition:** Henry Wadsworth Longfellow. *Poems and Other Writings*. Ed. J. D. McClatchy. New York: Library of America, 2000.
- **Biography:** Charles Calhoun. *Longfellow: A Rediscovered Life*. Boston: Beacon Press, 2004.
- **Critical Essay:** Jill Anderson. " 'Be Up and Doing': Henry Wadsworth Longfellow and Poetic Labor." *Journal of American Studies* 37 (2003): 1–15.

ANDREW MARVELL (1621–1678)

The son of a clergyman, Marvell was born in Yorkshire, in northern England, and attended Cambridge University. He took an active role in the political affairs of Cromwell's revolutionary government, writing powerful political poems, many of them satires, and he served as a member of Parliament for almost twenty years. Today he is much more known as the writer of a small number of complex, somewhat private lyrics with personas that remain difficult to pin down.

Starting Points for Further Research: Andrew Marvell

- **Edition:** Andrew Marvell. *The Complete Poems*. Ed. Elizabeth S. Donno. New York: Penguin, 1996.
- **Biography:** Nicholas Murray. *World Enough and Time: The Life of Andrew Marvell*. New York: St. Martin's Press, 1999.
- **Critical Essay:** Robert W. Halli, Jr. "The Persuasion of the Coy Mistress." *Philological Quarterly* 80 (2001): 57–70.

EDNA ST. VINCENT MILLAY (1892–1950)

Millay was born in Rockland, Maine, and attended Vassar College, where she wrote creatively and worked in theater. Upon graduation, she published her first book, *Renascence and Other Poems* (1919). Millay, who was openly bisexual and whose friends called her "Vincent," then moved to New York City, leading a bohemian life in Greenwich Village. Her fourth volume of poems, *The Harp Weaver* (1923), was awarded the Pulitzer Prize. She and her husband, Eugen

Boissevain, moved to rural New York in 1925. According to Millay's own accounts, the couple lived like two bachelors, remaining sexually open throughout their twenty-six-year marriage, which ended with Boissevain's death in 1949.

Starting Points for Further Research: Edna St. Vincent Millay

- **Edition:** Edna St. Vincent Millay. *Selected Poems.* Ed. J. D. McClatchy. New York: Library of America, 2003.
- **Biography:** Nancy Milford. *Savage Beauty: The Life of Edna St. Vincent Millay.* New York: Random House, 2001.
- **Critical Essay:** John Timberman Newcomb. "The Woman as Political Poet: Edna St. Vincent Millay and the Mid-Century Canon." *Criticism: A Quarterly for Literature and the Arts* 37 (Spring 1995): 261–79.

JOHN MILTON (1608–1674)

Milton was born in London and attended Cambridge. After university he abandoned his plans to join the clergy and moved back home, where he spent the next six years reading, then started writing poems, including "On the Morning of Christ's Nativity" (1629), "Il Penseroso" (1631), and "Lycidas" (1637). Deeply involved with Puritan life, he held office under Cromwell and after the Restoration spent time in prison, where he lost his sight. He lived the rest of his life in seclusion, completing his Christian epic poem *Paradise Lost* in 1667, *Paradise Regained* in 1671, and *Samson Agonistes* in 1671.

Starting Points for Further Research: John Milton

- **Edition:** John Milton. *Complete Poems and Major Prose.* Ed. Merritt Y. Hughes. New York: Macmillan, 1957.
- **Biography:** Barbara K. Lewalski. *John Milton: A Critical Biography.* Oxford: Blackwell, 2003.
- **Critical Essay:** Thomas Festa. "Repairing the Ruins: Milton as Reader and Educator." *Milton Studies* 43 (2004): 35–63.

PABLO NERUDA (1904–1973)

Born in a small southern Chilean town to a modest middle-class family in 1904, Neruda was a lonely boy whose main companions were his books and his writing. He was introduced to French poetry by the poet Gabriela Mistral, who would receive the Nobel Prize in Literature in 1945, the first given to a Latin American. After moving to Santiago, Neruda began winning poetry prizes and published his first book, *Crepusculario (Twilights)*, in 1923. In 1925 he sought a position as Chilean counsel to Burma, which began a decade of work and travel around the world. Neruda's poetry until the mid-1930s is known for its romantic and erotic themes, as well as dedication to portraying the people and landscape of Chile. After he moved to Spain, however, Neruda's political causes became a major theme. He returned to Chile in 1937 as a political activist, poet, and committed communist but was exiled in 1947. Neruda returned to Chile in 1952 when the government lifted its threat against leftist artists. Some of Neruda's best collections include *Canto general* (*General Song*, 1950), *Canción de gesta* (*Song of Protest*, 1960), *Cantos ceremoniales* (1961, translated as *Ceremonial Song*), and *Memorial de Isla Negra* (1964).

Starting Points for Further Research: Pablo Neruda

- **Autobiography:** Pablo Neruda. *Memoirs*. New York: Farrar, Straus and Giroux, 2000.
- **Biography:** Adam Feinstein. *Neruda: A Passion for Life*. New York: Bloomsbury, 2004.
- **Critical Essay:** Jonathan Cohen. "Neruda in English: Establishing His Residence in U.S. Poetry." *MultiCultural Review* 13:4 (2004): 25–28.
- **Article:** Ilan Stavans. "Pablo Neruda: A Life Consumed by Poetry and Politics." *Chronicle of Higher Education*, July 2, 2004, B13.

FRANK O'HARA (1926–1966)

O'Hara was born in Baltimore and grew up in Massachusetts, studying piano at the New England Conservatory before entering the U.S. Navy in World War II. Afterwards at Harvard, he planned to major in music, but he became entranced by poetry and changed his major to English. He studied at the University of Michigan and worked at New York's Museum of Modern Art, where he wrote poems, essays, and art criticism, associating himself with the New York School of Poets and with leading New York painters as well. He published a book of poems, *Meditations in an Emergency*, in 1956; his *Lunch Poems* appeared in 1964. He died at forty in a freak accident on Fire Island, New York.

Starting Points for Further Research: Frank O'Hara

- **Edition:** Frank O'Hara. *Poems*. Ed. Mark Ford. London: Faber and Faber, 2003.
- **Biography:** Brad Gooch. *City Poet: The Life and Times of Frank O'Hara*. New York: Harper Perennial, 1993.
- **Critical Essay:** David R. Jarraway. " 'Vanilla Hemorrhages': The Queer Perversities of Frank O'Hara." *GLQ: A Journal of Lesbian and Gay Studies* 4 (1998): 67–108.

MARY OLIVER (b. 1935)

Oliver was born in Cleveland, Ohio. The daughter of a schoolteacher, she was educated at Ohio State University and Vassar College. Oliver is best known as a poet of the natural world; her poems observe and celebrate the world around us. Her first book, *No Voyage and Other Poems* (1963), introduced readers to her quiet and reverent prose. It was followed by *The River Styx, Ohio* (1972) and *The Night Traveler* (1978). Critics place her work in the tradition of poets such as Edna St. Vincent Millay, Walt Whitman, Henry Thoreau, and Elizabeth Bishop.

She has received a Guggenheim Fellowship, the Pulitzer Prize in 1984 for *American Primitive* (1983), and the National Book Award for Poetry in 1993 for *New and Selected Poems* (1992).

Starting Points for Further Research: Mary Oliver

- **Critical Essays:** Douglas Burton-Christie. "Nature, Spirit, and Imagination in the Poetry of Mary Oliver." *Cross Currents: The Journal of the Association for Religion and Intellectual Life* 46:1 (1996): 77–87.
    Diane S. Bonds. "The Language of Nature in the Poetry of Mary Oliver." *Women's Studies: An Interdisciplinary Journal* 21:1 (1992): 1–15.

WILFRED OWEN (1893–1918)

Owen's life spanned only twenty-five years but he left behind a legacy as one of the greatest English poets of World War I; he used his firsthand experience on the battle lines to critique war. Owen was born in Oswestry, England, in 1893 to a poor family. He studied botany for a short time at University College, Reading, and then at the University of London. Eventually he withdrew due to lack of funds. At Dunsden, Oxford, he was a student and assistant to a vicar but began to doubt the depths of his Christian beliefs and left the vicarage to teach in Bordeaux. In 1915 Owen returned to England to enlist in the army. While fighting in Europe, he became ill and was sent back to England to recuperate in an army hospital; there he met army captain and poet Siegfried Sassoon, who encouraged Owen to write. Owen returned to fight in Europe in August 1918 and was killed in battle on November 4, only a week before the armistice. The majority of his best poetry was written in only thirteen months, between August 1917 and September 1918.

Starting Points for Further Research: Wilfred Owen

- **Edition:** Wilfred Owen. *The Poems of Wilfred Owen.* Ed. Jon Stallworthy. New York: Norton, 1986.
- **Biography:** Jon Stallworthy. *Wilfred Owen.* New York: Oxford University Press, 1995.
- **Critical Essays:** Douglas Kerr. "Brothers in Arms: Family Language in Wilfred Owen." *Review of English Studies: A Quarterly Journal of English Literature and the English Language* 43 (November 1992): 518–34.
    Paul Norgate. "Soldiers' Dreams: Popular Rhetoric and the War Poetry of Wilfred Owen." *Critical Survey* 2:2 (1990): 208–15.

LINDA PASTAN (b. 1932)

Pastan graduated from Radcliffe College and received an MA in English from Brandeis University. She is the author of a series of award-winning poetry volumes: *The Last Uncle* (2002), *An Early Afterlife* (1995), *Heroes in Disguise* (1991), *The Imperfect*

Paradise (1988), *The Five Stages of Grief* (1978), and *A Perfect Circle of Sun* (1971). Many of her poems treat matters of everyday life, including family events, from the perspective of a particularly insightful mother. Her honors include a Pushcart Prize, a Dylan Thomas Award, and the Charity Randall Citation. She lives in Potomac, Maryland, and from 1991 to 1994 served as Maryland's poet laureate.

Starting Point for Further Research: Linda Pastan

- **Critical Essay:** Sheila Murnaghan. "Penelope's Song: The Lyric Odysseys of Linda Pastan and Louise Glück." *Classical and Modern Literature: A Quarterly* 22:1 (2002): 1–33.

KATHERINE PHILIPS (1631–1664)

Philips, one of the best-known woman poets of her age, was famous for her persona of "Matchless Orinda" in the poems she first distributed individually to her circle of friends and then saw into print in 1651, an unusual action by a woman poet of that time. Married at sixteen, she lived in an intensely literary London circle that valued her poetry. In addition to her poems, she produced translations of French drama, one of which was produced in London in 1663, the first appearance of a woman's translation on the British stage. She died of smallpox at age thirty-three, eliciting funeral tributes by some of the age's most eminent writers.

Starting Points for Further Research: Katherine Philips

- **Edition:** Katherine Philips. *The Collected Works of Katherine Philips, the Matchless Orinda.* Ed. Patrick Thomas. Stump Cross, U.K.: Stump Cross Books, 1990.
- **Biography:** Elizabeth Hageman. *Katherine Philips: "The Matchless Orinda."* Saskatoon: Peregrina, 1986.
- **Critical Essay:** Elizabeth Hodgson. "Katherine Philips: Agent of Matchlessness." *Women's Writing* 10 (2003): 119–36.

MARGE PIERCY (b. 1936)

Piercy was born in Detroit and attended the University of Michigan. She has published fifteen books of verse, including *Colors Passing Through Us* (2003), *The Art of Blessing the Day: Poems with a Jewish Theme* (1999), *What Are Big Girls Made Of?* (1997), *Mars and Her Children* (1992), *Available Light* (1988), and *The Moon Is Always Female* (1980). She has also written novels and many essays, which have been collected in individual volumes. Piercy's work explores Marxist, feminist, and environmentalist themes, often with humor. She lives in Wellfleet, Massachusetts.

Starting Points for Further Research: Marge Piercy

- **Critical Essay:** Anna M. Martinson. "Ecofeminist Perspectives on Technology in the Science Fiction of Marge Piercy." *Extrapolation: A Journal of Science Fiction and Fantasy* 44 (Spring 2003): 50–68.

- **Interview:** John Rodden. "A Harsh Day's Light: An Interview with Marge Piercy." *Kenyon Review* 20 (Spring 1998): 132–43.

SYLVIA PLATH (1932–1963)

Born in Boston, Sylvia Plath grew up in an educated middle-class home and attended Smith College. She was a writer from early on, and after college she won a Mademoiselle Award, which gave her a magazine internship in New York. In 1955 she won a Fulbright scholarship to study in England; she spent two years at Cambridge University and met and married British poet Ted Hughes. Her first book of poems, *The Colossus*, appeared in 1960, but her reputation rests on her later poems, written at high intensity on the edge of a marital breakdown and the depression that led to her suicide at the age of thirty. Her final poems are collected in *Ariel* (1965); other volumes include *Crossing the Water* (1971), *Winter Trees* (1972), and *Selected Poems* (1985). She also wrote a novel, *The Bell Jar* (1963), and her journals were first published in unexpurgated form in 2000.

Starting Points for Further Research: Sylvia Plath

- **Editions:** Sylvia Plath. *Sylvia Plath: Poems*. Ed. Ted Hughes. London: Faber and Faber, 2004.
  ———. *Ariel: The Restored Edition*. New York: HarperCollins, 2004.
  ———. *The Bell Jar*. London: Faber and Faber, 2001.
- **Biography:** Anne Stevenson. *Bitter Fame: A Life of Sylvia Plath*. New York: Penguin, 1990.
- **Critical Essay:** Jooyoung Park. " 'I Could Kill a Woman or Wound a Man': Melancholic Rage in the Poems of Sylvia Plath." *Women's Studies: An Interdisciplinary Journal* 41 (July–August 2002): 467–97.

EDGAR ALLAN POE (1809–1849)

Poe was born in Boston, lost both of his parents at an early age, and was raised by his godfather, John Allan, a Richmond merchant. He attended the University of Virginia briefly, then West Point, which expelled him for attendance problems. He published a first volume of poems in 1827 and a second in 1829. In 1836 Poe married his cousin Virginia Clemm, then only thirteen, and they moved to New York City, where he published *The Narrative of Arthur Gordon Pym* (1838). While earning a meager living writing magazine reviews, Poe published some of his own original stories, which he collected as *Tales of the Grotesque and Arabesque* (1840). Troubled by alcohol and the death of his wife, he died at forty in Baltimore. Today Poe is acknowledged as one of the most brilliant and original writers in American literature.

Starting Points for Further Research: Edgar Allan Poe

- **Edition:** Edgar Allan Poe. *The Complete Tales and Poems of Edgar Allan Poe*. New York: Vintage, 1975.

- **Biography:** Arthur H. Quinn. *Edgar Allan Poe: A Critical Biography.* Baltimore: Johns Hopkins University Press, 1998.
- **Critical Essay:** Heyward Ehrlich. "Poe in Cyberspace: Electronic Guides to Printed and Online Research." *Edgar Allan Poe Review* 4 (Fall 2003): 93–97.

EZRA POUND (1885–1972)

Though born in Idaho and educated in America, Pound spent most of his long life in Europe, where he helped Robert Frost and James Joyce get proper literary recognition and proved a very great poetic influence first on T. S. Eliot and then on William Butler Yeats. His own poetry, particularly the later works collected as *The Cantos* (1976), proved exciting to some but difficult and puzzling to many. His anti-Semitic propaganda work for Mussolini in World War II earned him a U.S. charge of treason, which he escaped by serving twelve years in a mental hospital.

Starting Points for Further Research: Ezra Pound

- **Editions:** Ezra Pound. *The Cantos of Ezra Pound.* London: Faber and Faber, 1987.
  ———. *Poems and Translations.* Ed. Richard Sieburth. New York: Library of America, 2003.
- **Biography:** Ira Bruce Nadel. *Ezra Pound: A Literary Life.* New York: Palgrave Macmillan, 2004.
- **Critical Essay:** Ann Xiao Dong Sun. "The Man That Is Waiting: Some Remarks on Li Po's 'Chokan Shin' and Ezra Pound's 'The River Merchant's Wife.' " *Paideuma: A Journal Devoted to Ezra Pound Scholarship* 29 (2000): 149–63.

ADRIENNE RICH (b. 1929)

Born in Baltimore, Rich attended Radcliffe, where she began writing poetry. In 1951, when she was twenty-two, her work was selected by W. H. Auden to be published in the Yale Series of Younger Poets. She has written nearly twenty volumes of poetry, most recently *The School among the Ruins* (2004), and has written several books of nonfiction prose, including *Arts of the Possible: Essays and Conversations* (2001), *What Is Found There: Notebooks on Poetry and Politics* (1993; expanded 2003), and *Of Woman Born: Motherhood as Experience and Institution* (1986). Much of Rich's work addresses feminist and lesbian themes. Her many prizes include the National Book Award and a MacArthur Fellowship. She lives in northern California.

Starting Points for Further Research: Adrienne Rich

- **Editions:** Adrienne Rich. *The School Among the Ruins: Poems 2000–2004.* New York: Norton, 2004.
  ———. *The Fact of a Doorframe: Poems 1950–2001.* New York: Norton, 2002.
  ———. *Arts of the Possible: Essays and Conversations.* New York: Norton, 2001.

- **Critical Essay:** Mary Eagleton. "Adrienne Rich, Location and the Body." *Journal of Gender Studies* 3 (2000): 299–312.

THEODORE ROETHKE (1908–1963)

Roethke was born and raised in Saginaw, Michigan. He graduated from the University of Michigan and did some graduate work at Harvard University. His first book, *Open House* (1941), took ten years to write. Other books include *The Waking* (1953), which won the Pulitzer Prize, and his poetry collection *Words for the Wind* (1959). He wrote relatively little but gained the reputation of being an excellent teacher at the University of Washington and other universities. At six feet two inches, and over 200 pounds, Roethke had a powerful presence as a "gentle giant" but was known to suffer from mental breakdowns and bouts of alcoholism.

Starting Points for Further Research: Theodore Roethke

- **Edition:** Theodore Roethke. *Selected Poems.* Ed. Edward Hirsch. New York: Library of America, 2005.
- **Biography:** Allan Seager. *The Glass House: The Life of Theodore Roethke.* Ann Arbor: University of Michigan Press, 1991.
- **Critical Essays:** Mary Floyd-Wilson. "Poetic Empathy: Theodore Roethke's Conception of Woman in the Love Poems." *South Atlantic Review* 56:1 (1991): 61–78.
- Susan Pinkus. "Roethke's *The Waking*." *Explicator* 50:4 (1992): 241–44.

ANNE SEXTON (1928–1974)

Sexton was born in a Boston suburb and attended Garland Junior College for a year, then married at nineteen. Beginning in 1954 she experienced the serious depression that would shadow her life and finally help end it at thirty-nine. Encouraged by psychiatrists to find an emotional outlet, she enrolled in a local adult education poetry workshop, where she discovered her immense talents. She wrote a series of powerful books of poems and won a Pulitzer Prize for *Live or Die* (1967), but she could never overcome her illness, and she eventually took her life. Sexton was a prime exponent of the "confessional school" of poetry, along with fellow New Englanders Sylvia Plath and Robert Lowell, all troubled, brilliant poets who made art out of the anguish of their lives.

Starting Points for Further Research: Anne Sexton

- **Edition:** Anne Sexton. *Complete Poems.* Boston: Houghton Mifflin, 1999.
- **Biography:** Diane W. Middlebrook. *Anne Sexton: A Biography.* New York: Vintage, 1992.
- **Critical Essays:** Jo Gill. "Anne Sexton and Confessional Poetics." *Review of English Studies* 55 (2004): 425–45.

WILLIAM SHAKESPEARE (1564–1616)

See the biography in Chapter 23.

Starting Points for Further Research: William Shakespeare
- **Edition:** William Shakespeare. *The Complete Works of Shakespeare*. Ed. David Bevington. New York: Longman, 2004.
- **Biography:** Dominic Shellard. *William Shakespeare*. New York: Oxford University Press, 1998.
- **Critical Essay:** Anthony DiMatteo. "The Use and Abuse of Shakespeare: A Review Essay." *College Literature* 31 (2004): 185–95.

PERCY BYSSHE SHELLEY (1792–1822)

Born to a well-to-do family in West Sussex, England, Shelley rebelled early. He was expelled from college for atheism, and he eloped with Harriet Westbrook, leading to a permanent rift with his family. In London he joined the circle that included Lord Byron. Shelley's life was marked by shifting loyalties and commitments; he and Harriet soon became estranged, and he fell in love with Mary Wollstonecraft. Harriet's suicide in 1816 enabled him to marry Mary, but the scandal (combined with his reputation as a controversial writer) cost him the custody of his children by Harriet. He and Mary (who, as Mary Shelley, wrote *Frankenstein*) left England for good in 1818, settling in Italy. Shelley's poems, concerned with the fragility of beauty and human happiness, were praised reluctantly during his lifetime but became very popular after his early death in 1822 from drowning. His work influenced such nineteenth-century poets as Robert Browning and Alfred, Lord Tennyson.

Starting Points for Further Research: Percy Bysshe Shelley
- **Edition:** Percy Bysshe Shelley. *Shelley's Poetry and Prose*. Ed. Donald Reiman and Neil Fraistat. New York: Norton, 2002.
- **Biography:** Richard Holmes. *Shelley: The Pursuit*. New York: Penguin, 1997.
- **Critical Essay:** Martin Bidney. "War of the Winds: Shelley, Hardy, and Harold Bloom." *Victorian Poetry* 41 (2003): 229–44.

CATHY SONG (b. 1955)

Song was born in Honolulu, where she still lives with her husband and three children and teaches at the University of Hawaii. She graduated from Wellesley College in 1977 and received an M.A. in creative writing from Boston University in 1981. Her first book of poetry, *Picture Bride* (1983), appeared in the Yale Series of Younger Poets. Song has been awarded the Shelley Memorial Award from the Poetry Society of America, the Hawaii Award for Literature, and a National

Endowment for the Arts Fellowship. Other volumes of poetry are *Frameless Windows, Squares of Light* (1988), *School Figures* (1994), and *The Land of Bliss* (2001).

Starting Point for Further Research: Cathy Song

- **Critical Essay:** Gayle K. Fujita-Sato. " 'Third World' as Place and Paradigm in Cathy Song's *Picture Bride*." MELUS: *The Journal of the Society for the Study of the Multi-Ethnic Literature of the United States* 15 (Spring 1988): 49–72.

GARY SOTO (b. 1952)

Soto was born in Fresno, California, to a Mexican American family in an urban Latino neighborhood. Most of his family worked as farm laborers in the fields or in raisin packing factories. In 1970 Soto entered Fresno City College, where he first began reading and writing poetry. He continued his education at the California State University, Fresno, where he studied with poet Philip Levine. His first book of poetry, *The Elements of San Joaquin* (1977), was a three-part portrait of the Fresno of his youth. *The Tale of Sunlight* (1978) contrasts the harsh life of farm work for Mexican descendants in the San Joaquin valley with life in Taxos, Mexico. Soto was a professor of English and ethnic studies at the University of California, Berkeley, from 1979 to 1992. During that time, he began writing prose, including *Living Up the Street* (1985), a collection of nonfiction vignettes, *Small Faces* (1986), and *Lesser Evils: Ten Quartets* (1988). He also began writing poetry and prose for younger readers. His *New and Selected Poems* (1995) was a finalist for the National Book Award.

Starting Points for Further Research: Gary Soto

- **Essay:** Gary Soto. "The Childhood Worries: Or, Why I Became a Writer." *Iowa Review* 25:2 (1995): 104–15.
- **Interview:** Patricia Murphy. "Inventing Lunacy: An Interview with Gary Soto." *Hayden's Ferry Review* 18 (Spring 1996): 29–37.
- **Critical Essay:** Rudolf Erben. "Popular Culture, Mass Media, and Chicano Identity in Gary Soto's *Living Up the Street* and *Small Faces*." MELUS: *The Journal of the Society for the Study of the Multi-Ethnic Literature of the United States* 17 (Fall 1991): 43–52.
- **Website:** http://www.garysoto.com.

WILLIAM STAFFORD (1914–1993)

After attending the University of Kansas, Stafford was a conscientious objector during World War II, doing conservation work. He spent his career as an English teacher at Lewis and Clark College in Portland, Oregon. Stafford's first major volume of poetry, *Traveling through the Dark* (1962), was published when he was forty-eight. Among his best-known works are *The Rescued Year* (1966), *Stories*

That Could Be True: New and Collected Poems (1977), *Writing the Australian Crawl: Views on the Writer's Vocation* (1978), and *An Oregon Message* (1987).

Starting Points for Further Research: William Stafford

- **Critical Essay**: Thomas Fox Averill. "The Earth Says Have a Place: William Stafford and a Place of Language." *Great Plains Quarterly* 21:4 (2001): 275–86.
- **Interviews:** Thomas E. Kennedy. "William Stafford: An Interview." *American Poetry Review* 22:3 (1993): 49–55.
    Jeff Gundy. "A Conversation with William Stafford." *Artful Dodge*. http://www.wooster.edu/artfuldodge/interviews/stafford.htm.

WALLACE STEVENS (1879–1955)

Stevens was born in Reading, Pennsylvania, attended Harvard, earned a law degree from New York Law School, and rose to be vice president at a major Connecticut insurance company. Unknown to most of his fellow executives, Stevens maintained a completely separate career as a poet. His first book, *Harmonium* (1923), exhibited his highly original style and unique sensibility. Stevens would plot out his poems as he walked to and from his Hartford office, and he would write them out at home in the evenings. He rarely traveled, going only as far as Florida, but lived a rich life of the imagination as he went about his daily routines. His books include *Ideas of Order* (1935), *The Man with the Blue Guitar* (1937), *Notes towards a Supreme Fiction* (1942), and a collection of essays on poetry, *The Necessary Angel* (1951). Though now regarded as a major American poet, Stevens only received widespread recognition when his *Collected Poems* appeared a year before his death.

Starting Points for Further Research: Wallace Stevens

- **Edition:** Wallace Stevens. *Collected Poetry and Prose*. New York: Library of America, 1997.
- **Biography:** William Y. Tindall. *Wallace Stevens*. Minneapolis: University of Minnesota Press, 1961.
- **Critical Essay:** Justin Quinn. "Family and Place in Wallace Stevens." *Wallace Stevens Journal* 27 (2003): 65–79.

JONATHAN SWIFT (1667–1745)

Swift was born in Ireland, a member of the Protestant ruling class, and attended Trinity College in Dublin. Receiving his M.A. from Oxford, he entered the ministry, and after a spell of tutoring in aristocratic households, he became actively engaged in the London literary and political scene. Swift quickly became known for his biting, witty satires. His "Description of the Morning" (1709), one of his important early poems, is an excellent illustration of an urban pastoral, which imitates the conventions of poetic pastoral description (as embodied in Virgil's bucolic poems), but instead of portraying an idealized, harmonious countryside, Swift depicts the social chaos rumbling beneath the surface of London urban orderliness. Swift eventually returned to Ireland, where he received the post of dean of St. Patrick's Cathedral, the chief Protestant church in Dublin (a post from which he was forced to resign in his elder years due to senility). He remains best known for the prose works he produced upon his return to Ireland, including *Gulliver's Travels* (1726), and he gradually focused more and more on the plight of his country's poor, as he does in his famously satiric "A Modest Proposal" (1729).

Starting Points for Further Research: Jonathan Swift

- **Editions:** Jonathan Swift. *Complete Poems.* Ed. Pat Rogers. Harmondsworth: Penguin, 1983.
  ———. *Writings of Jonathan Swift.* Ed. Robert A. Greenberg and William Piper. New York: Norton, 1973.
- **Biography:** Victoria Glendinning. *Jonathan Swift: A Portrait.* New York: Henry Holt, 1999.
- **Critical Studies:** Maurice Johnson. *The Sin of Wit: Jonathan Swift as a Poet.* Syracuse, NY: Syracuse University Press, 1950.
  Peter J. Schakel. *The Poetry of Jonathan Swift: Allusion and Development of a Poetic Style.* Madison: University of Wisconsin Press, 1978.
  James D. Woolley. *Swift's Later Poems: Studies in Circumstances and Texts.* New York: Garland, 1988.

ALFRED, LORD TENNYSON (1809–1892)

The fourth of twelve children, Tennyson was precocious, writing an epic poem of 6,000 lines at age twelve. Tennyson studied at Cambridge and continued to write after university. In 1842 his *Poems* in two volumes was a tremendous critical and popular success. The publication of *In Memoriam* in 1850 made him one of Britain's most popular poets; he succeeded Wordsworth as poet laureate. His poetry provided enough income to permit him to write full-time. In 1859 Tennyson published the initial poems of his long retelling of the King Arthur story, *Idylls of the King*, which sold more than 10,000 copies in a single month. In 1884 he accepted a peerage and became Alfred, Lord Tennyson.

Starting Points for Further Research: Alfred, Lord Tennyson

- **Edition:** Alfred, Lord Tennyson. *Tennyson's Poetry.* Ed. Robert W. Hill, Jr. New York: Norton, 1972.
- **Biography:** Robert Martin. *Tennyson: The Unquiet Heart.* London: Faber and Faber, 1983.
- **Critical Essay:** Valerie Purton. "Tennyson and the Figure of Christ." *Tennyson Research Bulletin* 8 (2003): 85–100.

DYLAN THOMAS (1914–1953)

Thomas was born in Wales and grew up a loner who dropped out of school at sixteen. His published his first book, *Eighteen Poems*, at twenty and became known for his lyricism and full-blooded emotional approach to poetry, very different from the social and intellectual concerns that dominated at the time. He became famous for his poetry readings, traveling to the United States to perform first in 1950. His recordings of his works, including *A Child's Christmas in Wales*, excited many listeners. His well-received play *Under Milk Wood* (1954) appeared after his death. Thomas's flamboyant style and heavy drinking made him seem a modern example of a Romantic poet. On a trip to America in 1953, he died of alcoholism at age thirty-nine.

Starting Points for Further Research: Dylan Thomas

- **Edition:** Dylan Thomas. *Collected Poems*. Ed. Walford Davies and Ralph Ward. London: J. M. Dent, 1988.
- **Biography:** Paul Ferris. *Dylan Thomas: A Biography*. New York: Dial, 1977.
- **Critical Essay:** Eynel Wardi. "A Boy in the Listening: On Voice, Space, and Rebirth in the Poetry of Dylan Thomas." *Connotations: A Journal for Critical Debate* 9 (1999–2000): 190–209.

MARGARET WALKER (1915–1998)

Walker grew up in New Orleans and moved to Chicago, where she attended Northwestern University. After graduation she became a close friend of Richard Wright during his days in Chicago, just before he became famous. Her early efforts at poetry were encouraged by Langston Hughes, and her first collection of poems, *For My People* (1942), won the Yale University Young Poets Award. Walker later taught at Mississippi's Jackson State College, where she inspired a whole generation of writers and students.

Starting Points for Further Research: Margaret Walker

- **Editions**: Margaret Walker. *On Being Female, Black, and Free: Essays by Margaret Walker, 1932–1992*. Ed. Maryemma Graham. Knoxville: University of Tennessee Press, 1997.
    ———. *This Is My Century: New and Selected Poems*. Athens: University of Georgia Press, 1989.
- **Interview:** Maryemma Graham. "The Fusion of Ideas: An Interview with Margaret Walker Alexander." *African American Review* 27 (1993): 279–86.

WALT WHITMAN (1819–1892)

See the biography in Chapter 13.

Starting Points for Further Research: Walt Whitman

- **Edition:** Walt Whitman. *Leaves of Grass and Other Writings*. Ed. Michael Moon et al. New York: Norton, 2002.

- **Biography:** David S. Reynolds. *Walt Whitman.* New York: Oxford University Press, 2005.
- **Critical Essay:** Richard Haw. "American History/American Memory: Reevaluating Walt Whitman's Relationship with the Brooklyn Bridge." *Journal of American Studies* 38: 1 (April 2004): 1–22.

WILLIAM CARLOS WILLIAMS (1883–1963)

One of the preeminent American poets, Williams spent his life as a doctor and claimed to have found inspiration in the lives of the patients passing through his busy office in Paterson, New Jersey. Known for its experimental rhythms and vivid, carefully constructed images, Williams's poetry is unique. His one long poem, *Paterson* (1963), demonstrates how far he could go in representing (or discovering) beauty in the everyday life of a declining northern New Jersey mill town.

Starting Points for Further Research: William Carlos Williams

- **Edition:** William Carlos Williams. *Selected Poems.* Ed. Robert Pinsky. New York: Library of America, 2004.
- **Biography:** John M. Brinnin. *William Carlos Williams.* Minneapolis: University of Minnesota Press, 1995.
- **Critical Essay:** Jeff Webb. "William Carlos Williams and the New World." *Arizona Quarterly: A Journal of American Literature, Culture, and Theory* 56 (Winter 2000): 65–88.

WILLIAM WORDSWORTH (1770–1850)

Orphaned early, Wordsworth raised his four younger siblings, and throughout his life he would be close to his sister Dorothy, herself a person of literary gifts. He attended Cambridge, traveled in France during the revolutionary era, and in 1795 met the poet Samuel Taylor Coleridge, who became his close friend. Together they published the famous *Lyrical Ballads* in 1798. Wordsworth and Coleridge argued for the "common speech" of the people and against the stiff poetic language of the eighteenth century. His famous work *The Prelude* (1850) is a long autobiographical poem that he worked on throughout his life; the complete poem was published posthumously by his wife. In age, Wordsworth turned away from his youthful liberalism to become the embodiment of conservative rectitude. He was England's poet laureate until his death in 1850.

Starting Points for Further Research: William Wordsworth

- **Edition:** William Wordsworth. *Selected Poetry.* Ed. Nicholas Roe. New York: Penguin, 2002.
- **Biography:** Juliet Barker. *Wordsworth: A Life.* New York: Penguin, 2001.
- **Critical Essay:** Hongkyu A. Choe. "William Wordsworth's Poetry and Philosophy." *Coleridge Bulletin: The Journal of the Friends of Coleridge* 22 (Winter 2003): 62–71.

JAMES WRIGHT (1927–1980)

Wright was born in Martins Ferry, Ohio, to a family of factory workers. After army service, he attended Kenyon College, graduating with highest honors. Following a Fulbright fellowship year in Europe, he earned a doctorate at the University of Washington, studying with Theodore Roethke and Stanley Kunitz, and became an English professor, all the while writing poetry that reflected his difficult childhood in Ohio. His first book, *The Green Wall*, won the Yale Younger Poets Award for 1957. It was followed by *Saint Judas* (1959), *The Branch Will Not Break* (1963), and *Collected Poems* (1972), which received the Pulitzer Prize.

Starting Points for Further Research: James Wright

- **Edition:** James Wright. *Selected Poems*. Ed. Robert Bly and Anne Wright. New York: Farrar, Straus and Giroux, 2004.
- **Biography:** Peter Stitt and Frank Graziano. *James Wright: The Heart of the Light*. Ann Arbor: University of Michigan Press, 1990.
- **Critical Essay:** "James Wright: A Symposium." *Field: Contemporary Poetry and Poetics* 69 (2003): 9–44.

LADY MARY WROTH (1586–1640)

Mary Sidney was born into a highly literary aristocratic family. Her father was Sir Robert Sidney, later Earl of Leicester; her uncle was the famous poet Sir Philip Sidney; and her aunt was the writer Mary Sidney, the countess of Pembroke. Educated at home and then married to a husband who preferred hunting, Wroth was the first English woman to write a full-length prose romance and the first to write a full sonnet sequence, one in which her persona took on the aggressor's role, one usually reserved for men. A cultured aristocrat, Wroth nevertheless was involved in court intrigues and fell out of favor. Her verses were not printed in her lifetime, but they circulated widely in her aristocratic circles. She was friend and patron to Ben Jonson, who dedicated his play *The Alchemist* to her and addressed her in a number of his poems.

Starting Points for Further Research: Lady Mary Wroth

- **Edition:** Lady Mary Wroth. *The Poems of Lady Mary Wroth*. Ed. Joseph Roberts. Baton Rouge: Louisiana State University Press, 1992.
- **Critical Essay:** Susan L. O'Hara. "Sonnets as Theater: The Performance of Ideal Love and the Negation of Marriage in Mary Wroth's Masque." *Explorations in Renaissance Culture* 29:1 (2003): 59–99.

PART
III

Drama

CHAPTER
20

Plays
Action and Performance

SEEING VS. READING

Drama can present us with a world already fully formed, with actors in costume, well-lighted, on a stage that represents a richly imagined place. It is all live, happening now, presented entirely for us in this moment, never to be repeated in exactly the same way. Seated in the theater—in a school auditorium or on Broadway—we are in the dark, part of a large audience, full of expectation, eyes focused on the stage. Whether it is a familiar play or something entirely new, we have paid our money and invested our time to be entertained, delighted, enlightened, or even astonished.

But reading a play at home, in a dorm, or in the library is a very different experience. The world of the theater is far away: there is no lighting, no music, no set, no costumes, no actors, no audience, no sense of special occasion. We are reading plays as literature, not primarily as theater. One difference is captured in the terminology: the author's words are called a "play" by English professors but are referred to as a "script" by theater people. In the theater we see the words turned into the play, which uses space, sound, lighting, and above all, the actors' bodies—the way they move and sound and gesture. Should it be up to us to provide the action, the cast, the look and feel of the performance in the theater of our mind? In truth, that is impossible. No matter how hard we try, we cannot recreate what happens on the stage. Fortunately, in reading a play alone, that is not our task. That task is best left to the director, whose job it is to translate the words on the page into the actions we witness in the theater.

Reading alone, we are confronted with a very different task. Yes, we are limited by the lack of spectacle, but we have advantages as well: we have the words in front of us, and we can read them at our own pace. We can read them twice or turn back to an earlier part. And when we are writing about drama, we do not have to rely on our memories, because we always have a text in front of us. Furthermore, we do not have to agree with the director's view or the actors' interpretations. We are free to imagine our own version of the action, or free even to focus on the words, the stage directions, and our own thoughts. So though most plays are written to be put on the stage, to be seen, we are not without our resources as we read just the words. We are just undergoing a different kind of experience.

READING THE DRAMA

What can you do to make your reading of drama more effective? You will need to concentrate on the playwright's words, obviously, and this book attempts to present those words in context to help you understand them better. For example, using the resources cited in this book, you can hear at least four different versions of Hamlet's "To be or not to be" speech (p. 1489), before, after, or while you read it. Unlike most people reading alone, you will be able to see how different directors and actors have handled Shakespeare's words. And you will be able to ask some critical questions: Which versions are surprising? Which disappoint? Which help you get a handle on the character? With an eye toward answering such questions, this book directs you to many more opportunities for viewing or listening to actual productions, for examining pictures, and for seeing illustrations of actual sets and costumes.

In addition to making use of this book's audio and visual suggestions, you can put your imagination to work as you read. This book's introductions and the writer's stage directions provide two good ways into a drama. In Shakespeare's time, stage directions were minimal; in fact, we are not sure which were written by Shakespeare and which were added by helpful editors. Since the late 1800s, however, playwrights have been aiming their plays toward a reading audience as well as the theater, so they have increased the number and length of stage directions as an aid to reading the play alone. As you read, pay particular attention to the cast of characters, which indicates who's who and may supply the age and attitude of the characters or other information. You will likely find yourself referring back to this list as new characters are introduced. Playwrights often include highly detailed descriptions of the setting, allowing you to envision how a scene should look. In truth, some directors and designers change the setting around to suit their own notions, so in reading you may be coming closer to the playwright's own notions of how people and costumes and settings should appear, rather than someone else's ideas.

While reading, think about not just what is being said—the words themselves—but about who else is on stage, listening to the lines. Many times the words alone do not carry the play as much as the stage action, that is, the whole ensemble enacting the scene together. Think of how characters might react to what is said. Ask yourself where the audience's attention would be focused in a theater: On the speaker? On the listener? On someone overhearing? On the whole group? How and where should the characters all stand? What should they be doing? When playwrights omit stage directions, they do not assume that the characters will simply stand and face each other. Playwrights know that their scripts will be transformed into action and movement on the stage, and thus they often leave those choices to the director. As you read, you will be a bit of your own director, all the time remembering how much you are missing.

As you read, see, and hear more plays, you will improve your sense of how the action unfolds and of how many options an actor actually has in playing the scene. In one play, the text may indicate that a female character says a single word, "Yes." How should she say this word? Should she sound angry? Resigned? Weary? Enthusiastic? Depressed? Puzzled? In a staging, the director suggests how this word should be said, and the trained actor must try to put it over. How should she look? What gestures should she use to convince us? As you read, you decide how this "Yes" should go. Do not worry about doing this with every line in every scene; it is impossible, especially when you are just starting out. But as you read more and more, you will be better able to pause to imagine a particularly dramatic moment or special scene. Keep your eye out for such scenes, and you will soon become a strong reader of drama.

TALKING ABOUT DRAMA

You already know a good many key terms that are used to talk about or describe drama; many are the same as those used to discuss and analyze fiction. Not many of the terms are esoteric, though many do have quite precise meanings when discussing drama. **Plot** is what happens in the play; it is the way the writer has shaped the action. Each play has at least one **act**, the largest division in the action of a play. A new act often indicates a notable shift in mood, setting, time, or characters on stage. In a theater, the end of an act is usually marked by turning up the house lights or lowering the curtain. Some plays consist of five acts, some of three, while many have only one. Acts can have many separate **scenes**, which usually involve changes of scenery or character or time. **One-act plays** are often written with community theaters and amateur actors in mind, with small casts and simple settings.

Some familiar terms have long been used to talk about traditional plays. Among the actors is the **protagonist**, who is the main character, the one who does the most prominent action. Frequently, there is conflict between this character and an **antagonist**, a character who opposes the protagonist. Sometimes the **playwright**, the term used for the author of the play, starts out slowly, using a lot of **exposition**, which is the essential background information we need to understand the situation. A play's action often builds up using **rising action**, in which complications arise out of the protagonist's conflict, to the **climax**, which is the key turning point of the drama, the moment containing the most tension, occurring usually toward the end of the play. Then, after the climax, the **concluding action** (also called **falling action**) unfolds, and dramatic tensions are lessened through the **resolution** of the plot's conflicts. Another term for this process is **denouement**, a French word meaning "untying" or "unraveling."

At the beginning of a play, the playwright (or for early plays, an editor) includes a list of who's who, the **cast of characters**, and supplies information about the setting and characters in **stage directions**. The characters speak to each other in **dialogue**, which is often made to seem like ordinary speech but is in fact carefully arranged to present the illusion of an actual conversation. Sometimes a character onstage alone has a long speech of contemplation, a **soliloquy**, spoken to no one in particular. (Hamlet's "To be or not to be" soliloquy is a famous example.) Other times, especially in comedy, a character briefly addresses the audience directly, in an **aside**, a commentary on the action. A long speech addressed to other characters is a **monologue**.

The names for the kinds of drama, called **genres**, are familiar too: **tragedy** involves an unavoidable fall in the protagonist's fortunes and often ends in death; **comedy** presents a sunnier outlook, involving humorous discovery, mis-

The Greek theater at Epidauros, one of the most well-preserved ancient Greek theaters, gives a good sense of what it might have been like to see a drama at that time and place. The audience seating area on a sloped hillside encircled an orchestra "dancing place" where the chorus danced and performed. Behind the orchestra was a skene, a stone structure that served as a dressing room and an entrance and exit to the stage area, located between the orchestra and skene, where the actors played their various roles.

taken identities, reversals, and a happy ending; **tragicomedy** mixes the two, with serious risks and the danger of a fall, but usually with a happier resolution. **Farce** is comedy as slapstick, usually played at a fast pace, without much development of character and with an emphasis on the action. **Melodrama** involves serious conflict and sudden reversals, but usually without the depth found in traditional tragedy. In addition to these familiar genres of plays are **performance pieces**, a modern invention involving acting, spectacle, and sometimes experimentation; such pieces can vary from monologues to **mime**, which is silent acting for one or more performers.

Of course, dramatic performance extends to other kinds of well-known theatrical productions, from puppet shows to stand-up comedy. Our neat definitions of genres are helpful in thinking about how drama works, but in a living art form, with talented people always exploring new territory, we should not expect terms and concepts devised for traditional drama to hold for every play in every circumstance. Some artists deliberately write their plays to challenge traditional concepts, for instance, of protagonist and tragedy.

Drama can take place indoors and out, with a big cast or one person, plain or fancy, for free or as a profit-making enterprise. Most traditional drama takes place on the **stage**, which can take a variety of forms. It can be a simple open platform with minimum scenery, as in Greek drama, or it can be a platform with a balcony,

In proscenium arch theaters, such as the Rialto Theater in Allentown, Pennsylvania, pictured here, the arch and the curtain hanging from it serve to frame the onstage action and also to clearly separate the actors from the audience.

The original Globe Theatre on the bank of the River Thames in London was built in 1599 but was destroyed by fire in 1644. Until the creation of the new Globe (shown here), which was nearly thirty years in the making and was finally completed in 1996, scholars and theater lovers only had drawings to suggest how the Globe actually appeared during Shakespeare's time. The new Globe was constructed a mere 200 yards from the original's site. The photo here shows the three levels of seating that surround the stage. For a speculative drawing of the original Globe, see page 1335 in Chapter 23.

as in Shakespeare's Globe Theater, or it may be a conventional stage framed with a **proscenium arch** from which the curtains close. The proscenium stage gives the impression of a three-sided box, with the audience making the fourth side; the arch effectively separates the actors from the audience. The stage can be a **thrust stage**, familiar in modern drama, in which a runway or extension of the stage goes into the audience, or the stage can be a **theater in the round**, in which the stage is surrounded by the audience. And plenty of dramatic performances take place outside the confines of a specialized building. **Street theater** happens right on the pavement, while other dramas are acted in union halls, on the steps of buildings, and in improvised spaces. The only limits are the artists' imaginations and the need to go out and gather an audience. As the playwright Luis Valdez once said, "if the people will not come to the theater, then the theater will come to them."

A thrust stage extends out into the audience so that audience members surround it on three sides, as shown here in this photo of the Guthrie Theater's thrust stage in Minneapolis.

Most of these terms will be familiar or self-explanatory. You will encounter others in Part 3 dealing with styles of drama, but for now you are well-equipped to understand and discuss a great deal about how drama works, since you have witnessed so much of it already, either in the theater or on TV.

The Krasnaya Presnya Theater in Moscow is a theater in the round: the stage is entirely surrounded by the audience.

SUSAN GLASPELL

(1882–1948)

Born and raised in Iowa, Susan Glaspell covered crime as a reporter for the Des Moines Daily News after graduation from Drake University, and she later drew on a "true crime" experience from this period for Trifles. After her move to New York and her marriage to director George Cram Cook, she became known through her stories in magazines, then through a mix of forward-looking novels and realistic plays. Trifles was her first play, and interestingly, the year after it was produced, Glaspell refashioned it into an award-winning short story called "A Jury of Her Peers." Trifles remains her most widely known work, though she had a long career as a serious playwright. In 1930 she won the Pulitzer Prize in drama for Alison's House, a play based on the life of poet Emily Dickinson. (For more on Dickinson and her poetry, see Chapter 14.)

Trifles *was a revolutionary play for its time, a real breakthrough in two distinct ways. For one thing, it was an early production of a small, avant-garde group of young writers, actors, and directors that came to be called the Provincetown Players, founded on Cape Cod in 1915 by Glaspell and Cook. The Players, among them novelist and playwright Glaspell, poet Edna St. Vincent Millay, playwright Eugene O'Neill, and revolutionary writer John Reed, were to be highly influential in American theater history. Indeed, whenever a small theater consciously turns its back on the same old run-of-the-mill plays and commissions experimental work from its own writers, we see the influence of the Provincetown Players, one of the first American theater groups to succeed this way.* Trifles *was one of their first plays to be a critical success.* Trifles *also distinguished Glaspell as one of the first American women to make a name for herself as a playwright, doing so with a highly self-conscious feminist play, one that took a radical line for its time. Glaspell's importance as a writer has led many critics to examine the impact of her plays on American society and culture. But here our purpose is to understand how* Trifles *works as a play. It is one of our three introductory examples of how plays are put together.*

Trifles

(1916)

Cast

George Henderson, *County Attorney*   Mrs. Peters
Henry Peters, *Sheriff*   Mrs. Hale
Lewis Hale, *A Neighboring Farmer*

> SCENE: *The kitchen in the now abandoned farmhouse of* JOHN WRIGHT, *a gloomy kitchen, and left without having been put in order—unwashed pans under the sink, a loaf of bread outside the bread-box, a dish-towel on the table—other signs of incompleted work. At the rear the outer door opens and the* SHERIFF *comes in followed by the* COUNTY ATTORNEY *and* HALE. *The* SHERIFF *and* HALE *are men in middle life, the* COUNTY ATTORNEY *is a young man; all are much bundled up and go at once to the stove. They are followed by the two women—the* SHERIFF'S *wife first; she is a slight wiry woman, a thin nervous face.* MRS. HALE *is larger and would ordinarily be called more comfortable looking, but she is disturbed now and looks fearfully about as she enters. The women have come in slowly, and stand close together near the door.*

COUNTY ATTORNEY: [*Rubbing his hands.*] This feels good. Come up to the fire, ladies.

MRS. PETERS: [*After taking a step forward.*] I'm not—cold.

SHERIFF: [*Unbuttoning his overcoat and stepping away from the stove as if to mark the beginning of official business.*] Now, Mr. Hale, before we move things about, you explain to Mr. Henderson just what you saw when you came here yesterday morning.

COUNTY ATTORNEY: By the way, has anything been moved? Are things just as you left them yesterday?

SHERIFF: [*Looking about.*] It's just the same. When it dropped below zero last night I thought I'd better send Frank out this morning to make a fire for us—no use getting pneumonia with a big case on, but I told him not to touch anything except the stove—and you know Frank.

COUNTY ATTORNEY: Somebody should have been left here yesterday.

SHERIFF: Oh—yesterday. When I had to send Frank to Morris Center for that man who went crazy—I want you to know I had my hands full yesterday. I knew you could get back from Omaha by today and as long as I went over everything here myself—

COUNTY ATTORNEY: Well, Mr. Hale, tell just what happened when you came here yesterday morning.

HALE: Harry and I had started to town with a load of potatoes. We came along the road from my place and as I got here I said, "I'm going to see if I can't get John Wright to go in with me on a party telephone." I spoke to Wright about it once before and he put me off, saying folks talked too much anyway, and all he asked was peace and quiet—I guess you know about how much he talked himself; but I thought maybe if I went to the house and talked about it before his wife, though I said to Harry that I didn't know as what his wife wanted made much difference to John—

COUNTY ATTORNEY: Let's talk about that later, Mr. Hale. I do want to talk about that, but tell now just what happened when you got to the house.

HALE: I didn't hear or see anything; I knocked at the door, and still it was all quiet inside. I knew they must be up, it was past eight o'clock. So I knocked again, and I thought I heard somebody say, "Come in." I wasn't sure, I'm not sure yet, but I opened the door—this door [*indicating the door by which the two women are still standing*] and there in that rocker—[*pointing to it*] sat Mrs. Wright.

[*They all look at the rocker.*]

COUNTY ATTORNEY: What—was she doing?

HALE: She was rockin' back and forth. She had her apron in her hand and was kind of—pleating it.

COUNTY ATTORNEY: And how did she—look?

HALE: Well, she looked queer.

COUNTY ATTORNEY: How do you mean—queer?

HALE: Well, as if she didn't know what she was going to do next. And kind of done up.

COUNTY ATTORNEY: How did she seem to feel about your coming?

HALE: Why, I don't think she minded—one way or other. She didn't pay much attention. I said, "How do, Mrs. Wright, it's cold, ain't it?" And she said, "Is it?"—and went on kind of pleating at her apron. Well, I was surprised; she didn't ask me to come up to the stove, or to set down, but just sat there, not even looking at me, so I said, "I want to see John." And then she—laughed. I guess you would call it a laugh. I thought of Harry and the team outside, so I said a little sharp: "Can't I see John?" "No," she says, kind o' dull like. "Ain't he home?" says I. "Yes," says she, "he's home." "Then why can't I see him?" I asked her, out of patience. " 'Cause he's dead," says she. *Dead?* says I. She just nodded her head, not getting a bit excited, but rockin' back and forth. "Why—where is he?" says I, not knowing what to say. She just pointed upstairs—like that [*himself pointing to the room above*]. I got up, with the idea of going up there. I walked from there to here—then I says, "Why, what did he die of?" "He died of a rope round his neck," says she, and just went on pleatin' at her apron. Well, I went out and called Harry. I thought I might—need help. We went upstairs and there he was lyin'—

COUNTY ATTORNEY: I think I'd rather have you go into that upstairs, where you can point it all out. Just go on now with the rest of the story.

HALE: Well, my first thought was to get that rope off. It looked . . . [*Stops, his face twitches*] . . . but Harry, he went up to him, and he said, "No, he's dead all right, and we'd better not touch anything." So we went back down stairs. She was still sitting that same way. "Has anybody been notified?" I asked. "No," says she, unconcerned. "Who did this, Mrs. Wright?" said Harry. He said it business-like—and she stopped pleatin' of her apron. "I don't know," she says. "You don't *know?*" says Harry. "No," says she. "Weren't you sleepin' in the bed with him?" says Harry. "Yes," says she, "but I was on the inside." "Somebody slipped a rope round his neck and strangled him and you didn't wake up?" says Harry. "I didn't wake up," she said after him. We must 'a looked as if we didn't see how that could be, for after a minute she said, "I sleep sound." Harry was going to ask her more questions but I said maybe we ought to let her tell her story first to the coroner, or the sheriff, so Harry went fast as he could to Rivers' place, where there's a telephone.

COUNTY ATTORNEY: And what did Mrs. Wright do when she knew that you had gone for the coroner?

HALE: She moved from that chair to this one over here [*Pointing to a small chair in the corner*] and just sat there with her hands held together and looking down. I got a feeling that I ought to make come conversation, so I said I had come in to see if John wanted to put in a telephone, and at that she started to laugh, and then she stopped and looked at me—scared. [*The* COUNTY ATTORNEY, *who has had his notebook out, makes a note.*] I dunno, maybe it wasn't scared. I wouldn't like to say it was. Soon Harry got back, and then Dr. Lloyd came, and you, Mr. Peters, and so I guess that's all I know that you don't.

COUNTY ATTORNEY: [*Looking around.*] I guess we'll go upstairs first—and then out to the barn and around there. [*To the* SHERIFF.] You're convinced that there was nothing important here—nothing that would point to any motive.

SHERIFF: Nothing here but kitchen things.

[*The* COUNTY ATTORNEY, *after again looking around the kitchen, opens the door of a cupboard closet. He gets up on a chair and looks on a shelf. Pulls his hand away, sticky.*]

COUNTY ATTORNEY: Here's a nice mess.

[*The women draw nearer.*]

MRS. PETERS: [*To the other woman.*] Oh, her fruit; it did freeze. [*To the* LAWYER.] She worried about that when it turned so cold. She said the fire'd go out and her jars would break.

SHERIFF: Well, can you beat the women! Held for murder and worryin' about her preserves.

COUNTY ATTORNEY: I guess before we're through she may have something more serious than preserves to worry about.

HALE: Well, women are used to worrying over trifles.

[*The two women move a little closer together.*]

COUNTY ATTORNEY: [*With the gallantry of a young politician.*] And yet, for all their worries, what would we do without the ladies? [*The women do not unbend. He goes to the sink, takes a dipperful of water from the pail and pouring it into a basin, washes his hands. Starts to wipe them on the roller-towel, turns it for a cleaner place.*] Dirty towels! [*Kicks his foot against the pans under the sink.*] Not much of a housekeeper, would you say, ladies?

MRS. HALE: [*Stiffly.*] There's a great deal of work to be done on a farm.

COUNTY ATTORNEY: To be sure. And yet [*With a little bow to her*] I know there are some Dickson county farmhouses which do not have such roller towels.

[*He gives it a pull to expose its full length again.*]

MRS. HALE: Those towels get dirty awful quick. Men's hands aren't always as clean as they might be.

COUNTY ATTORNEY: Ah, loyal to your sex, I see. But you and Mrs. Wright were neighbors. I suppose you were friends, too.

MRS. HALE: [*Shaking her head.*] I've not seen much of her of late years. I've not been in this house—it's more than a year.

County Attorney: And why was that? You didn't like her?

MRS. HALE: I liked her all well enough. Farmers' wives have their hands full, Mr. Henderson. And then—

COUNTY ATTORNEY: Yes—?

MRS. HALE: [*Looking about.*] It never seemed a very cheerful place.

COUNTY ATTORNEY: No—it's not cheerful. I shouldn't say she had the home-making instinct.

MRS. HALE: Well, I don't know as Wright had, either.

COUNTY ATTORNEY: You mean that they didn't get on very well?

MRS. HALE: No, I don't mean anything. But I don't think a place'd be any cheerfuller for John Wright's being in it.

COUNTY ATTORNEY: I'd like to talk more of that a little later. I want to get the lay of things upstairs now.

[*He goes to the left, where three steps lead to a stair door.*]

SHERIFF: I suppose anything Mrs. Peters does'll be all right. She was to take in some clothes for her, you know, and a few little things. We left in such a hurry yesterday.

COUNTY ATTORNEY: Yes, but I would like to see what you take, Mrs. Peters, and keep an eye out for anything that might be of use to us.

MRS. PETERS: Yes, Mr. Henderson.

[*The women listen to the men's steps on the stairs, then look about the kitchen.*]

MRS. HALE: I'd hate to have men coming into my kitchen, snooping around and criticising.

[*She arranges the pans under sink which the* LAWYER *had shoved out of place.*]

MRS. PETERS: Of course it's no more than their duty.

MRS. HALE: Duty's all right, but I guess that deputy sheriff that came out to make the fire might have got a little of this on. [*Gives the roller towel a pull.*] Wish I'd thought of that sooner. Seems mean to talk about her for not having things slicked up when she had to come away in such a hurry.

MRS. PETERS: [*Who has gone to a small table in the left rear corner of the room, and lifted one end of a towel that covers a pan.*] She had bread set.

[*Stands still.*]

MRS. HALE: [*Eyes fixed on a loaf of bread beside the bread-box, which is on a low shelf at the other side of the room. Moves slowly toward it.*] She was going to put this in there. [*Picks up loaf, then abruptly drops it. In a manner of returning to familiar things.*] It's a shame about her fruit. I wonder if it's all gone. [*Gets up on the chair and looks.*] I think there's some here that's all right, Mrs. Peters. Yes—here; [*Holding it toward the window*] this is cherries, too. [*Looking again.*] I declare I believe that's the only one. [*Gets down, bottle in her hand. Goes to the sink and wipes it off on the outside.*] She'll feel awful bad after all her hard work in the hot weather. I remember the afternoon I put up my cherries last summer.

[*She puts the bottle on the big kitchen table, center of the room. With a sigh, is about to sit down in the rocking-chair. Before she is seated realizes what chair it is; with a slow look at it, steps back. The chair which she has touched rocks back and forth.*]

MRS. PETERS: Well, I must get those things from the front room closet. [*She goes to the door at the right, but after looking into the other room, steps back.*] You coming with me, Mrs. Hale? You could help me carry them.

[*They go in the other room; reappear,* MRS. PETERS *carrying a dress and skirt,* MRS. HALE *following with a pair of shoes.*]

MRS. PETERS: My, it's cold in there.

[*She puts the clothes on the big table, and hurries to the stove.*]

MRS. HALE: [*Examining the skirt.*] Wright was close. I think maybe that's why she kept so much to herself. She didn't even belong to the Ladies Aid. I suppose she felt she couldn't do her part, and then you don't enjoy things when you feel shabby. She used to wear pretty clothes and be lively, when she was

Minnie Foster, one of the town girls singing in the choir. But that—oh, that was thirty years ago. This all you was to take in?

MRS. PETERS: She said she wanted an apron. Funny thing to want, for there isn't much to get you dirty in jail, goodness knows. But I suppose just to make her feel more natural. She said they was in the top drawer in this cupboard. Yes, here. And then her little shawl that always hung behind the door. [*Opens stair door and looks.*] Yes, here it is.

[*Quickly shuts door leading upstairs.*]

MRS. HALE: [*Abruptly moving toward her.*] Mrs. Peters?

MRS. PETERS: Yes, Mrs. Hale?

MRS. HALE: Do you think she did it?

MRS. PETERS: [*In a frightened voice.*] Oh, I don't know.

MRS. HALE: Well, I don't think she did. Asking for an apron and her little shawl. Worrying about her fruit.

MRS. PETERS: [*Starts to speak, glances up, where footsteps are heard in the room above. In a low voice.*] Mr. Peters says it looks bad for her. Mr. Henderson is awful sarcastic in a speech and he'll make fun of her sayin' she didn't wake up.

MRS. HALE: Well, I guess John Wright didn't wake when they was slipping that rope under his neck.

MRS. PETERS: No, it's strange. It must have been done awful crafty and still. They say it was such a—funny way to kill a man, rigging it all up like that.

MRS. HALE: That's just what Mr. Hale said. There was a gun in the house. He says that's what he can't understand.

MRS. PETERS: Mr. Henderson said coming out that what was needed for the case was a motive; something to show anger, or—sudden feeling.

MRS. HALE: [*Who is standing by the table.*] Well, I don't see any signs of anger around here. [*She puts her hand on the dish towel which lies on the table, stands looking down at table, one half of which is clean, the other half messy.*] It's wiped to here. [*Makes a move as if to finish work, then turns and looks at loaf of bread outside the breadbox. Drops towel. In that voice of coming back to familiar things.*] Wonder how they are finding things upstairs. I hope she had it a little more red-up up there. You know, it seems kind of *sneaking*. Locking her up in town and then coming out here and trying to get her own house to turn against her!

MRS. PETERS: But Mrs. Hale, the law is the law.

MRS. HALE: I s'pose 'tis. [*Unbuttoning her coat.*] Better loosen up your things, Mrs. Peters. You won't feel them when you go out.

[MRS. PETERS *takes off her fur tippet, goes to hang it on hook at back of room, stands looking at the under part of the small corner table.*]

MRS. PETERS: She was piecing a quilt.

[*She brings the large sewing basket and they look at the bright pieces.*]

MRS. HALE: It's log cabin pattern. Pretty, isn't it? I wonder if she was goin' to quilt it or just knot it?

[*Footsteps have been heard coming down the stairs. The* SHERIFF *enters followed by* HALE *and the* COUNTY ATTORNEY.]

SHERIFF: They wonder if she was going to quilt it or just knot it!

[*The men laugh, the women look abashed.*]

COUNTY ATTORNEY: [*Rubbing his hands over the stove.*] Frank's fire didn't do much up there, did it? Well, let's go out to the barn and get that cleared up.

[*The men go outside.*]

MRS. HALE: [*Resentfully.*] I don't know as there's anything so strange, our takin' up our time with little things while we're waiting for them to get the evidence. [*She sits down at the big table smoothing out a block with decision.*] I don't see as it's anything to laugh about.

MRS. PETERS: [*Apologetically.*] Of course they've got awful important things on their minds.

[*Pulls up a chair and joins* MRS. HALE *at the table.*]

MRS. HALE: [*Examining another block.*] Mrs. Peters, look at this one. Here, this is the one she was working on, and look at the sewing! All the rest of it has been so nice and even. And look at this! It's all over the place! Why, it looks as if she didn't know what she was about!

[*After she has said this they look at each other, then start to glance back at the door. After an instant* MRS. HALE *has pulled at a knot and ripped the sewing.*]

MRS. PETERS: Oh, what are you doing, Mrs. Hale?

MRS. HALE: [*Mildly.*] Just pulling out a stitch or two that's not sewed very good. [*Threading a needle.*] Bad sewing always made me fidgety.

MRS. PETERS: [*Nervously.*] I don't think we ought to touch things.

MRS. HALE: I'll just finish up this end. [*Suddenly stopping and leaning forward.*] Mrs. Peters?

MRS. PETERS: Yes, Mrs. Hale?

MRS. HALE: What do you suppose she was so nervous about?

MRS. PETERS: Oh—I don't know. I don't know as she was nervous. I sometimes sew awful queer when I'm just tired. [MRS. HALE *starts to say something, looks at* MRS. PETERS, *then goes on sewing.*] Well I must get these things wrapped up. They may be through sooner than we think. [*Putting apron and other things together.*] I wonder where I can find a piece of paper, and string.

MRS. HALE: In that cupboard, maybe.

MRS. PETERS: [*Looking in cupboard.*] Why, here's a bird-cage. [*Holds it up.*] Did she have a bird, Mrs. Hale?

MRS. HALE: Why, I don't know whether she did or not—I've not been here for so long. There was a man around last year selling canaries cheap, but I don't know as she took one; maybe she did. She used to sing real pretty herself.

MRS. PETERS: [*Glancing around.*] Seems funny to think of a bird here. But she must have had one, or why would she have a cage? I wonder what happened to it.

MRS. HALE: I s'pose maybe the cat got it.

MRS. PETERS: No, she didn't have a cat. She's got that feeling some people have about cats—being afraid of them. My cat got in her room and she was real upset and asked me to take it out.

MRS. HALE: My sister Bessie was like that. Queer, ain't it?

MRS. PETERS: [*Examining the cage.*] Why, look at this door. It's broke. One hinge is pulled apart.

MRS. HALE: [*Looking too.*] Looks as if someone must have been rough with it.

MRS. PETERS: Why, yes.

[*She brings the cage forward and puts it on the table.*]

MRS. HALE: I wish if they're going to find any evidence they'd be about it. I don't like this place.

MRS. PETERS: But I'm awful glad you came with me, Mrs. Hale. It would be lonesome for me sitting here alone.

MRS. HALE: It would, wouldn't it? [*Dropping her sewing.*] But I tell you what I do wish, Mrs. Peters. I wish I had come over sometimes when *she* was here. I— [*Looking around the room*]—wish I had.

MRS. PETERS: But of course you were awful busy, Mrs. Hale—your house and your children.

MRS. HALE: I could've come. I stayed away because it weren't cheerful—and that's why I ought to have come. I—I've never liked this place. Maybe because it's down in a hollow and you don't see the road. I dunno what it is, but it's a lonesome place and always was. I wish I had come over to see Minnie Foster sometimes. I can see now—

[*Shakes her head.*]

MRS. PETERS: Well, you mustn't reproach yourself, Mrs. Hale. Somehow we just don't see how it is with other folks until—something comes up.

MRS. HALE: Not having children makes less work—but it makes a quiet house, and Wright out to work all day, and no company when he did come in. Did you know John Wright, Mrs. Peters?

MRS. PETERS: Not to know him; I've seen him in town. They say he was a good man.

MRS. HALE: Yes—good; he didn't drink, and kept his word as well as most, I guess, and paid his debts. But he was a hard man, Mrs. Peters. Just to pass the time of day with him—[*Shivers.*] Like a raw wind that gets to the bone. [*Pauses, her eye falling on the cage.*] I should think she would 'a wanted a bird. But what do you suppose went with it?

MRS. PETERS: I don't know, unless it got sick and died.

[*She reaches over and swings the broken door, swings it again, both women watch it.*]

MRS. HALE: You weren't raised round here, were you? [MRS. PETERS *shakes her head.*] You didn't know—her?

MRS. PETERS: Not till they brought her yesterday.

MRS. HALE: She—come to think of it, she was kind of like a bird herself—real sweet and pretty, but kind of timid and—fluttery. How—she—did—change. [*Silence; then as if struck by a happy thought and relieved to get back to every day things.*] Tell you what, Mrs. Peters, why don't you take the quilt in with you? It might take up her mind.

MRS. PETERS: Why, I think that's a real nice idea, Mrs. Hale. There couldn't possibly be any objection to it, could there? Now, just what would I take? I wonder if her patches are in here—and her things.

[They look in the sewing basket.]

MRS. HALE: Here's some red. I expect this has got sewing things in it. *[Brings out a fancy box.]* What a pretty box. Looks like something somebody would give you. Maybe her scissors are in here. *[Opens box. Suddenly puts her hand to her nose.]* Why—*[*MRS. PETERS *bends nearer, then turns her face away.]* There's something wrapped up in this piece of silk.

MRS. PETERS: Why, this isn't her scissors.

MRS. HALE: *[Lifting the silk.]* Oh, Mrs. Peters—its—

*[*MRS. PETERS *bends closer.]*

MRS. PETERS: It's the bird.

MRS. HALE: *[Jumping up.]* But, Mrs. Peters—look at it! It's neck! Look at its neck! It's all—other side *to.*

MRS. PETERS: Somebody—wrung—its—neck.

*[Their eyes meet. A look of growing comprehension, of horror, Steps are heard outside. *MRS. HALE *slips box under quilt pieces, and sinks into her chair. Enter *SHERIFF *and *COUNTY ATTORNEY. MRS. PETERS *rises.]*

COUNTY ATTORNEY: *[As one turning from serious things to little pleasantries.]* Well, ladies, have you decided whether she was going to quilt it or knot it?

MRS. PETERS: We think she was going to—knot it.

COUNTY ATTORNEY: Well, that's interesting, I'm sure. *[Seeing the birdcage.]* Has the bird flown?

MRS. HALE: *[Putting more quilt pieces over the box.]* We think the—cat got it.

COUNTY ATTORNEY: *[Preoccupied.]* Is there a cat?

*[*MRS. HALE *glances in a quick covert way at *MRS. PETERS.*]*

MRS. PETERS: Well, not *now.* They're superstitious, you know. They leave.

COUNTY ATTORNEY: *[To *SHERIFF PETERS, *continuing an interrupted conversation.]* No sign at all of anyone having come from the outside. Their own rope. Now let's go up again and go over it piece by piece. *[They start upstairs.]* It would have to have been someone who knew just the—

[Mrs. Peters sits down. The two women sit there not looking at one another, but as if peering into something and at the same time holding back. When they talk now it is in the manner of feeling their way over strange ground, as if afraid of what they are saying, but as if they can not help saying it.]

MRS. HALE: She liked the bird. She was going to bury it in that pretty box.

MRS. PETERS: *[In a whisper.]* When I was a girl—my kitten—there was a boy took a hatchet, and before my eyes—and before I could get there—*[Covers her face an instant.]* If they hadn't held me back I would have—*[Catches herself, looks upstairs where steps are heard, falters weakly]*—hurt him.

MRS. HALE: *[With a slow look around her.]* I wonder how it would seem never to have had any children around. *[Pause.]* No, Wright wouldn't like the bird— a thing that sang. She used to sing. He killed that, too.

MRS. PETERS: *[Moving uneasily.]* We don't know who killed the bird.

MRS. HALE: I knew John Wright.

MRS. PETERS: It was an awful thing was done in this house that night, Mrs. Hale. Killing a man while he slept, slipping a rope around his neck that choked the life out of him.

MRS. HALE: His neck. Choked the life out of him.

[*Her hand goes out and rests on the bird-cage.*]

MRS. PETERS: [*With rising voice.*] We don't know who killed him. We dont *know.*

MRS. HALE: [*Her own feeling not interrupted.*] If there'd been years and years of nothing, then a bird to sing to you, it would be awful—still, after the bird was still.

MRS. PETERS: [*Something within her speaking.*] I know what stillness is. When we homesteaded in Dakota, and my first baby died—after he was two years old, and me with no other then—

MRS. HALE: [*Moving.*] How soon do you suppose they'll be through, looking for the evidence?

MRS. PETERS: I know what stillness is. [*Pulling herself back.*] The law has got to punish crime, Mrs. Hale.

MRS. HALE: [*Not as if answering that.*] I wish you'd seen Minnie Foster when she wore a white dress with blue ribbons and stood up there in the choir and sang. [*A look around the room.*] Oh, I *wish* I'd come over here once in a while! That was a crime! That was a crime! Who's going to punish that?

MRS. PETERS: [*Looking upstairs.*] We mustn't—take on.

MRS. HALE: I might have known she needed help! I know how things can be— for women. I tell you, it's queer, Mrs. Peters. We live close together and we live far apart. We all go through the same things—it's all just a different kind of the same thing. [*Brushes her eyes, noticing the bottle of fruit, reaches out for it.*] If I was you I wouldn't tell her her fruit was gone. Tell her it *ain't.* Tell her it's all right. Take this in to prove it to her. She—she may never know whether it was broke or not.

MRS. PETERS: [*Takes the bottle, looks about for something to wrap it in; takes petticoat from the clothes brought from the other room, very nervously begins winding this around the bottle. In a false voice.*] My, it's a good thing the men couldn't hear us. Wouldn't they just laugh! Getting all stirred up over a little thing like a—dead canary. As if that could have anything to do with—with— wouldn't they *laugh!*

[*The men are heard coming down stairs.*]

MRS. HALE: [*Under her breath.*] Maybe they would—maybe they wouldn't.

COUNTY ATTORNEY: No, Peters, it's all perfectly clear except a reason for doing it. But you know juries when it comes to women. If there was some definite thing. Something to show—something to make a story about—a thing that would connect up with this strange way of doing it—

[*The women's eyes meet for an instant. Enter* HALE *from outer door.*]

HALE: Well, I've got the team around. Pretty cold out there.

COUNTY ATTORNEY: I'm going to stay here a while by myself. [*To the* SHERIFF.] You can send Frank out for me, can't you? I want to go over everything. I'm not satisfied that we can't do better.

SHERIFF: Do you want to see what Mrs. Peters is going to take in?

[*The* LAWYER *goes to the table, picks up the apron, laughs.*]

COUNTY ATTORNEY: Oh, I guess they're not very dangerous things the ladies have picked out. [*Moves a few things about, disturbing the quilt pieces which cover the box. Steps back.*] No, Mrs. Peters doesn't need supervising. For that matter, a sheriff's wife is married to the law. Ever think of it that way, Mrs. Peters?

MRS. PETERS: Not—just that way.

SHERIFF: [*Chuckling.*] Married to the law. [*Moves toward the other room.*] I just want you to come in here a minute, George. We ought to take a look at these windows.

COUNTY ATTORNEY: [*Scoffingly.*] Oh, windows!

SHERIFF: We'll be right out, Mr. Hale.

[HALE *goes outside. The* SHERIFF *follows the* COUNTY ATTORNEY *into the other room. Then* MRS. HALE *rises, hands tight together, looking intensely at* MRS. PETERS, *whose eyes make a slow turn, finally meeting* MRS. HALE's. *A moment* MRS. HALE *holds her, then her own eyes point the way to where the box is concealed. Suddenly* MRS. PETERS *throws back quilt pieces and tries to put the box in the bag she is wearing. It is too big. She opens box, starts to take bird out, cannot touch it, goes to pieces, stands there helpless. Sound of a knob turning in the other room.* MRS. HALE *snatches the box and puts it in the pocket of her big coat. Enter* COUNTY ATTORNEY *and* SHERIFF.]

COUNTY ATTORNEY: [*Facetiously.*] Well, Henry, at least we found out that she was not going to quilt it. She was going to—what is it you call it, ladies?

MRS. HALE: [*Her hand against her pocket.*] We call it—knot it, Mr. Henderson.

(*Curtain*)

LITERARY LOCALE

Provincetown, Massachusetts. In the summer of 1915, a group of writers and artists visiting the resort town of Provincetown, Massachusetts, put on a spontaneous play late in the evening on the porch of a summer house. The group had more in common than their bohemian artist lifestyle in New York's Greenwich Village: they had a common aim to adopt a movement toward psychological realism in American theater. The next summer the group included Eugene O'Neill, who premiered his play *Bound East for Cardiff* for their second season. Members of the Provincetown Players also included activist and writer John Reed, journalist Louise Bryant, poet Edna St. Vincent Millay (see p. 1073), and playwright Susan Glaspell, who wrote *Trifles* while in Provincetown. Glaspell in particular was at her creative best while in Provincetown and wrote ten plays for the company.

But Provincetown's history as an artist's mecca can be traced back even earlier to 1849 when Henry Thoreau, author of *Walden*, first visited. Today,

(continued)

Provincetown is known by nearly everyone in the arts as a haven for writers and artists, due in large part to the Fine Arts Work Center. The Center was established in 1968 by writers and painters wanting a place to support their fellow artists. It now sponsors artist residencies, a Master of Fine Arts program, and public galleries and readings. Numerous award-winning American authors have spent time at work in Provincetown, including poets Louise Glück (see p. 1104), Franz Wright, Yusef Komunyakaa (see p. 1107), and Mark Doty; best-selling novelists Michael Cunningham (author of *The Hours*) and Ann Patchett (author of *Bel Canto*); and Pulitzer Prize–winning fiction writer Jhumpa Lahiri (see p. 448). Famous American painters who worked at Provincetown include Mark Rothko, Robert Motherwell, Edward Hopper, Charles Demuth, and Marsden Hartley.

DRAMA AS ACTION

Thinkers about how plays work have traditionally placed action at the core of drama. Over two thousand years ago the ancient Greek philosopher Aristotle (384–322 BCE), who analyzed everything from physics to literature, determined that plays consist of six elements:

1. Action, the core of drama
2. Character
3. Theme
4. Dialogue
5. Staging, including costumes
6. Musical accompaniment

Of these six elements, Aristotle considered action foremost. Closer to our own times, the critic/philosopher Kenneth Burke (1897–1993) also put action first. He expounded five characteristics for analysis: act, scene, agent, agency (i.e., means or instrument), and purpose. Both of these critics—and many in the long interval between them—insisted that drama is first and foremost not the words or ideas or theme or setting or the characters but the *action*, the doing. Action in this sense does not mean the movement or gestures or the acting; it means something larger, the embodiment of a desire, the fulfillment of a motive, a physical, mental, and emotional *act*. Only within that larger notion of action do we usually speak of the more particular actions of the individual characters.

The Spine of a Play

How can we explain exactly what action is in this special dramatic sense? The great Russian stage director Constantin Stanislavsky (1863–1938) spoke of the action as the *spine* of the play, the vertebrae that hold it together. One of his students, the famous American director Harold Clurman (1901–1980), claimed that each play's *spine* or action could be stated simply in a "to . . ." phrase: "to

TRIFLES IN PERFORMANCE

Throughout its brief span, *Trifles* presents what looks like a familiar world—a dreary-looking farmhouse kitchen, a murder investigation, and recognizable characters: two farm women, two other local people, and the county attorney. The dramatic approach Glaspell employs is **realism**, which is defined as the depiction of characters just as they would appear in "real life," without any obvious heightening or distortion. The setting too is as close to "reality" as possible, while the lighting and costumes and acting styles all contribute to the illusion of reality. Nothing appears larger than life, or wildly out of the ordinary; in short, nothing seems obviously "theatrical." Realism was something fairly new in the 1900s; classic plays, including Shakespeare's, had hardly been realistic in this way. Starting about 1875, however, realism became the most common dramatic style in Western theater; we will see famous examples of it in Henrik Ibsen's *A Doll House* (p. 1562) and in Arthur Miller's *Death of a Salesman* (p. 1671). Glaspell, like so many dramatists of her time, used realism to indicate a deeper, unstated truth that drama existed among ordinary people as they lived their day-to-day lives.

Still, it is important to keep realism in the theater separate from real life; we are still watching or reading a play, with actors who have rehearsed, who are speak-

A still from the original Provincetown Players production of Glaspell's Trifles.

ing carefully crafted lines that often allow the playwright to make a very clear point. In its way, *Trifles* is just as theatrical and "artificial" as any other play. It is very definitely art, not real life.

In the opening minutes of *Trifles*, we see something typical of a play that would be unusual in a short story: Mr. Hale retells the events of the murder in response to Henderson's request to "tell just what happened." As stated earlier in this chapter, this telling of the background story is called exposition. Glaspell cleverly casts Henderson as if he were in a courtroom; Hale plays the cooperative witness to Henderson's experienced attorney. Hale "retells" in a monologue the long story of how he discovered the murder. In a short story, this same information would likely be presented by a narrator. Indeed, when Glaspell turned *Trifles* into a short story, "A Jury of Her Peers," she interrupted Hale's long monologue with information on what Mrs. Hale was thinking as her husband told his story. In the theater, however, the playwright must put the narration in the mouth of a character, disguising it as dialogue. It is a difficult task to dramatize essential information in a way that both informs and entices the audience. And yet a defining characteristic of drama is that key information must be supplied through the dialogue and the actions of the characters onstage. The only way to provide a narrator comparable to those that appear in fiction is to write one into the cast of characters, which is exactly what Tennessee Williams did in *The Glass Menagerie* (p. 1618). He created a separate character who at times serves as narrator, giving plenty of background information to the audience that would otherwise have to be revealed through dialogue.

Hale's narration of events allows us to think about how reading on the page differs from seeing a performance on stage. If we read a play the same way as we read a story, we may move too quickly, following the plot rather than looking for the action, that is, the drama. Readers might speed right through Hale's narration, reading it solely for what happened, for the important information it provides about events. On the other hand, a theater professional, preparing for a performance, would be thinking all the time of the character's spine and of the dramatic possibilities in the speech. For instance, when you think of Hale's monologue as embodying individual *actions*, where would a good actor pause for dramatic effect? What words would he emphasize by speaking them especially slowly or loudly? What kind of looks and movements might an actor playing Hale supply? How would the listeners respond? Theater audiences do not pay attention to pure information; they expect *action*.

Many other moments occur in *Trifles* in which a hasty reader might skim over the real action of the drama. Reading quickly for information or the plot, we can easily miss the confrontations and discoveries, such as the drama between Mrs. Hale and Mrs. Peters that builds gradually but seems on a careful reading to animate the play. A good reading is an attentive reading, one slow enough to pick up the gestures and facial expressions, the silences and pace of language—the details that constitute much of the conflicts of the drama. And after all, isn't it Glaspell's point that key evidence is invisible to those who do not know where to look for it? And where is it? It is in the little things, the details.

find the killer," "to escape," "to possess the farm," and so on. He extended the meaning of spine to encourage the actors to think of their characters' *spines* as well. Thus, the play as a whole has a spine, an action, and each separate character also has a spine or action. (This concept of spine can work with all different types of plays, but it tends to work most successfully with plays in the realist tradition, in which the characters are depicted as people in "real" life, not as caricatures, ritual figures, or larger-than-life beings.)

If the play's action can be thought of metaphorically as the spine, ask yourself what holds *Trifles* together. What is its spine? Clurman would want you to put it in a single phrase: "to _____." But you do not have to be so narrow. Think of a single phrase—with a "to _____" or not—that sums up the action in *Trifles*. Try as well to think of an action for each of the characters, again either with a "to _____" or not. Keep in mind that *Trifles* is a play with what looks like a simple message—that women's concerns and experiences might be often ignored, but they are vitally important. But it is not just its message that made *Trifles* successful in 1916 and worth talking about almost a century later. Rather, the success of *Trifles* can be attributed to its shape, action, and characters. Playwrights do not succeed through their messages alone, no matter how vital or earnest or timely they are; they succeed because the audience is drawn into the dramatic tension between actions.

INSPIRATION "A JURY OF HER PEERS" IN PERFORMANCE— GLASPELL FROM PAGE TO RADIO STAGE

Scribbling Women, part of Northeastern University's Public Media Foundation, adapts women's short fiction into radio dramas for national public radio. Since 1993, the program has produced stories by Harriet Beecher Stowe, Zora Neale Hurston, and Louisa May Alcott among many others. During the recording of the radio version of Susan Glaspell's short story "A Jury of Her Peers," one staff member observed how producing a drama on radio differs from the stage or film: "Actors accustomed to stage work must learn to think with their ears—they must remember to leave enough time between footsteps and the closing of a door, between the striking of a match and the exhaling of smoke from an imaginary cigarette. It sometimes takes the efforts of everyone assembled in the control room to catch problems that we don't notice when we are able to see the actors, but which would become apparent on audiotape. Our directors have been known to conduct recording sessions with their eyes covered." To listen to Scribbling Women's radio version of Glaspell's story, go to *http://www.scribblingwomen.org/sbjuryfeature.htm.*

Talking about the Text

1. State the action or spine of *Trifles*, putting your answer in a "to _____" phrase.
2. Suggest a spine or a key motivation for Mrs. Hale, Mrs. Peters, and George Henderson, the county attorney.
3. How do the changes you see taking place in Mrs. Hale connect to particular events and statements from other characters?
4. Trace the changes you see taking place in Mrs. Peters. What specific events or actions influence those changes?
5. Drama works through conflict. Different people's actions go against each other, thus producing surprise, stress, conflict, and in short, drama. Describe exactly what the major conflict is in the play. How does each of the characters understand that conflict? What passages deepen the audience's understanding of this conflict during the play?
6. Certain specific moments appear highly dramatic to the two women and to the audience. Which ones? Why aren't they equally dramatic to the men? What do you make of this discrepancy?
7. *Trifles* looks and feels like a "realistic" play but at the same time contains elements that seem not casual or coincidental but rather "symbolic." For instance, what are we to make of the dead bird and Mrs. Wright's singing?
8. French movie director Jean-Luc Godard said all he needed to make a film was "a girl and a gun." What dramatic possibilities are inherent in a murder, any murder? In what ways does Glaspell undermine or reinforce that notion as the mystery gets "solved"?

Writing about the Text

1. The playwright, Susan Glaspell, played Mrs. Hale in the first production of *Trifles*. Write a brief essay arguing whether she did or did not give herself the play's best role.
2. Write a "missing" scene in *Trifles*, with Mrs. Peters alone with her husband Henry. Have her try to make him see what he has missed. Does she succeed? Is your scene more dramatic—and true to the play—if he does see or if he doesn't?
3. Supply Mrs. Wright's defense attorney's address to a jury. Write it as a monologue, drawing only on information you have learned from the play.

Linking the Text to Other Texts

1. As in *A Doll House* (p. 1562) and *Oedipus* (p. 1250), some of the most important "action" in *Trifles* has already occurred, in the distant or the recent past. What does that mean for the way the drama unfolds? With the violence in the past, where is there room for drama?
2. Reading *Trifles*, we may wonder, how can these men be so thick? Compare the inability to see with similar inabilities in "A Good Man Is Hard to Find" (p. 374) or "A Rose for Emily" (p. 549). To what extent do these failures seem realistic? To what extent do they seem contrived to make a point?
3. Compare and contrast Glaspell's *Trifles* with the short story version of the play she wrote a year later, "A Jury of Her Peers." Consider any or all of the following elements: what each title suggests, how the setting is established and how it differs in each version, and what information is included in the short story that is absent from the play and vice versa.

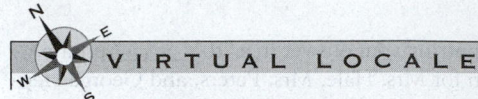

VIRTUAL LOCALE

Glaspell's Short Story Version of *Trifles*. In 1917, the year after *Trifles* was first produced as a stage play, Glaspell "rewrote" the play in short story form, publishing it under the title "A Jury of Her Peers." A complete e-text version of the story, which also appears in *The Best Short Stories of 1917*, edited by Edna O'Brien, appears online at the Electronic Text Center of the University of Virginia Library, at *http://etext.virginia.edu/toc/modeng/public/GlaJury.html*.

Starting Points for Further Research: Susan Glaspell

- **Editions:** Susan Glaspell. *Plays*. Ed. C. W. E. Bigsby and Christine Dymkowski. New York: Cambridge University Press, 1987.
  ———. *Trifles*. Ed. Donna W. Haisty. Boston: Thomas Wadsworth, 2004.
- **Biography:** Bárbara Ozieblo Rajkowska. *Susan Glaspell: A Critical Biography*. Chapel Hill: University of North Carolina Press, 2000.
- **Critical Essay:** Artem Lozynsky. "The Case of the Missing Canary: A New Look at Glaspell's Trifles." *Feminist Studies in English Literature* 7 (2000): 141–58.

LADY GREGORY (1852–1932)

Lady Gregory is a famous figure in Irish history and literature. Born Isabella Augusta Persse in 1852, she grew up as part of the "ascendancy," the group of Anglo-Irish Protestant administrators and landowners who controlled much of Ireland, then a British colony. She married Lord Gregory, another member of the Anglo-Irish elite. After his death in 1892, she gradually converted to the cause of Irish nationalism, the anticolonial movement that resulted in the Easter Rebellion of 1916, freedom for the Republic of Ireland in 1920, and a protracted civil war in the early 1920s. The support Gregory gave to Irish nationalism was both literary and practical. By her ardent support of an indigenous Irish theater, she helped create the Irish literary renaissance, an important part of the nationalist struggle for political as well as cultural independence.

Gregory founded Ireland's first theater group in order to promote a national Irish literature by showcasing the work of an exciting group of Irish and Anglo-Irish playwrights, including John Millington Synge, William Butler Yeats, and later Sean O'Casey. Lady Gregory wrote her comedy Spreading the News *in 1904 for the opening of the group's permanent home, Dublin's Abbey Theatre. Up to that time her company had put on only serious plays, mostly tragedies. She had thought of writing a tragedy herself but decided that the company needed a comedy as a counterbalance. She continued to write and to serve as the Abbey's administrator and prime advocate until her death in 1932. Her literary legacy includes five volumes of plays, the continuing presence and importance of the Abbey Theatre in Dublin, and the Abbey troupe's appearances throughout the world.*

Lest we take Lady Gregory's play as something entirely light, we should consider what the 1904 Dublin audience would have regarded as obvious. Ireland was a colony, tightly governed by its British rulers. Police constables were Irish but were supervised closely by a class of British colonial administrators. In the play, the character of the Magistrate—an outsider highly suspicious of the colonials' behavior and an immediately recognizable figure of ridicule—never tires of speaking of his experience in the Andaman Islands, then a British colony in the Bay of Bengal. Indeed, we learn quickly that colonials, either in Ireland or off the coast of India, are not to be trusted by the British. In the highly charged, nationalistic atmosphere of Ireland in 1904, it was inevitable for any drama—no matter what its style or content—to be seen as deeply political. And any play that highlighted the foolishness of a British colonial administrator who put innocent Irish people in jail was richly enmeshed in Irish nationalist politics. So this is indeed a light comedy but with some shadows in the background. Little more than a decade later, Irish nationalists would be at war with the Magistrate and all he represented.

As you read Spreading the News, think of how it works as a play. What would give it life on the stage? It is full of verbal energy, of drama (or things that seem to be drama when they're first heard), and of conflict. Keep track of how many different kinds of conflicts you see played out. As you read, think of the Magistrate as a central figure. How does his suspicious nature trigger all the action?

Spreading the News   (1904)

Characters

Bartley Fallon	Tim Casey	A policeman (Jo Muldoon)
Mrs. Fallon	James Ryan	A removable magistrate
Jack Smith	Mrs. Tarpey	
Shawn Early	Mrs. Tully	

SCENE—The outskirts of a Fair.

When the CURTAIN *rises,* MRS. TARPEY *is sitting at an apple stall. The* MAGISTRATE *and the* POLICEMAN *enter.*

MAGISTRATE: So that is the Fair Green. Cattle and sheep and mud. No system. What a repulsive sight!

POLICEMAN: That is so, indeed.

MAGISTRATE: I suppose there is a good deal of disorder in this place?

POLICEMAN: There is.

MAGISTRATE: Common assault?

POLICEMAN: It's common enough.

MAGISTRATE: Agrarian crime, no doubt?

POLICEMAN: That is so.

MAGISTRATE: Boycotting? Maiming of cattle? Firing into houses?

POLICEMAN: There was one time, and there might be again.

MAGISTRATE: That is bad. Does it go any further than that?

POLICEMAN: Far enough, indeed.

MAGISTRATE: Homicide, then! This district has been shamefully neglected! I will change all that. When I was in the Andaman Islands, my system never failed. Yes, yes, I will change all that. What has that woman on her stall?

POLICEMAN: Apples mostly—and sweets.

MAGISTRATE: Just see if there are any unlicensed goods underneath—spirits or the like. We had evasions of the salt tax in the Andaman Islands.

POLICEMAN (*sniffing cautiously and upsetting a heap of apples*): I see no spirits here—or salt.

MAGISTRATE (*to* MRS. TARPEY): Do you know this town well, my good woman?

MRS. TARPEY (*holding out some apples*). A penny the half-dozen, Your Honour.

POLICEMAN (*shouting*): The gentleman is asking do you know the town! He's the new magistrate!

MRS. TARPEY (*rising and ducking*): Do I know the town? I do, to be sure.

MAGISTRATE (*shouting*): What is its chief business?

MRS. TARPEY: Business, is it? What business would the people here have but to be minding one another's business?

MAGISTRATE: I mean what trade have they?

MRS. TARPEY: Not a trade. No trade at all but to be talking.

MAGISTRATE: I shall learn nothing here. (JAMES RYAN *comes in, pipe in mouth. Seeing the* MAGISTRATE *he retreats quickly, taking the pipe from his mouth.*)

MAGISTRATE: The smoke from that man's pipe had a greenish look; he may be growing unlicensed tobacco at home. I wish I had brought my telescope to this district. Come to the post-office, I will telegraph for it. I found it very useful in the Andaman Islands. (*The* MAGISTRATE *and the* POLICEMAN *go out L.*)

MRS. TARPEY: Bad luck to Jo Muldoon, knocking my apples this way and that way. (*She arranges them*). Showing off he was to the new Magistrate. (BARTLEY FALLON *and* MRS. FALLON *enter.*)

BARTLEY: Indeed it's a poor country and a scarce country to be living in. But I'm thinking if I went to America it's long ago the day I'd be dead!

MRS. FALLON: So you might, indeed. (*She rests her basket on a barrel and begins putting parcels in it, taking them from under her cloak.*)

BARTLEY: And it's a great expense for a poor man to be buried in America.

MRS. FALLON: Never fear, Bartley Fallon, but I'll give you a good burying the day you'll die.

BARTLEY: Maybe it's yourself will be buried in the graveyard of Cloonmara before me, Mary Fallon, and I myself that will be dying unbeknownst some night, and no-one a-near me. And the cat itself may be gone straying through the country, and the mice squealing over the quilt.

MRS. FALLON: Leave off talking of dying. It might be twenty years you'll be living yet.

BARTLEY (*with a deep sigh*): I'm thinking if I'll be living at the end of twenty years it's a very old man I'll be then!

MRS. TARPEY (*turns and sees them*): Good morrow, Bartley Fallon; good morrow, Mrs. Fallon. Well, Bartley, you'll find no cause for complaining today; they are all saying it was a good fair.

BARTLEY: (*raising his voice*). It was not a good fair, Mrs. Tarpey. It was a scattered sort of a fair. If we didn't expect more, we got less. That's the way with me always; whatever I have to sell goes down and whatever I have to buy goes up. If there's ever any misfortune coming to this world, it's on myself it pitches, like a flock of crows on seed potatoes.

MRS. FALLON: Leave off talking of misfortunes, and listen to Jack Smith that is coming the way, and he singing.

JACK SMITH (*off; singing*): I thought, my first love,
   There'd be but one house between you and me,
   And I thought I would find

Yourself coaxing my child on your knee.
Over the tide
I would leap with the leap of a swan,
Till I came to the side
Of the wife of the Red-haired man!

(JACK SMITH *enters. He is a red-haired man, and is carrying a hayfork.*)

MRS. TARPEY: That should be a good song if I had my hearing.

MRS. FALLON (*shouting*): It's *The Red-haired Man's Wife.*

MRS. TARPEY: I know it well. That's the song that has a skin on it! (*She turns her back on them and goes on arranging her apples.*)

MRS. FALLON: Where's herself, Jack Smith?

JACK SMITH: She was delayed with her washing; bleaching the clothes on the hedge she is, and she daren't leave them with all the tinkers that do be passing to the fair. It isn't to the fair I came myself, but up to the Five Acre Meadow I'm going, where I have a contract for the hay. We'll get a share of it into tramps today. (*He lays down the hayfork and lights his pipe.*)

BARTLEY: You will not get it into tramps today. The rain will be down on it by evening, and on myself too. It's seldom I ever started on a journey but the rain would come down on me before I'd find any place of shelter.

JACK SMITH: If it didn't itself, Bartley, it is my belief you would carry a leaky pail on your head in place of a hat, the way you'd not be without some cause of complaining.

A VOICE (*off*): Go on, now, go out o' that. Go on I say.

JACK SMITH: Look at that young mare of Pat Ryan's that is backing into Shaughnessy's bullocks with the dint of the crowd! Don't be daunted, Pat, I'll give you a hand with her. (JACK SMITH *goes out* R. *leaving his hayfork.*)

MRS. FALLON: It's time for ourselves to be going home. I have all I bought put in the basket. Look at there, Jack Smith's hayfork he left after him! He'll be wanting it. (*She calls*). Jack Smith! He's gone through the crowd—hurry after him, Bartley, he'll be wanting it.

BARTLEY: I'll do that. This is no safe place to be leaving it. (*He takes up the fork awkwardly and upsets the basket*). Look at that now! If there is any basket in the fair upset, it must be our own basket! (BARTLEY *goes out* R.)

MRS. FALLON: Get out of that! It is your own fault, it is. Talk of misfortunes and misfortunes will come. Glory be! Look at my new egg-cups rolling in every part—and my two pound of sugar with the paper broke. . .

MRS. TARPEY (*turning from the stall*): God help us, Mrs. Fallon, what happened your basket?

MRS. FALLON: It's himself that knocked it down, bad manners to him. (*Picking things up*). My grand sugar that's destroyed, and he'll not drink his tea without it. I had best go back to the shop for more, much good may it do him! (TIM CASEY *enters.*)

TIM CASEY: Where is Bartley Fallon, Mrs. Fallon? I want a word with him before he'll leave the fair. I was afraid he might have gone home by this, for he's a temperate man.

MRS. FALLON: I wish he did go home! It'd be best for me if he went home straight from the fair green, or if he never came with me at all. Where is he, is it? He's gone up the road—(*she ferks her elbow*) following Jack Smith with a hayfork. (MRS. FALLON *goes out* L.)

TIM CASEY: Following Jack Smith with a hayfork! Did ever anyone hear the like of that. (*He shouts*). Did you hear that news, Mrs. Tarpey?

MRS. TARPEY: I heard no news at all.

TIM CASEY: Some dispute I suppose it was that rose between Jack Smith and Bartley Fallon, and it seems Jack made off, and Bartley is following him with a hayfork!

MRS. TARPEY: Is he now? Well, that was quick work! It's not ten minutes since the two of them were here, Bartley going home and Jack going to the Five Acre Meadow; and I had my apples to settle up, that Jo Muldoon of the police had scattered, and when I looked round again Jack Smith was gone, and Bartley Fallon was gone, and Mrs. Fallon's basket upset, and all in it strewed upon the ground—the tea here—the two pound of sugar there—the egg-cups there. Look, now, what a great hardship the deafness puts upon me, that I didn't hear the commincement of the fight! Wait till I tell James Ryan that I see below; he is a neighbour of Bartley's, it would be a pity if he would-n't hear the news! (MRS. TARPEY *goes out.* SHAWN EARLY *and* MRS. TULLY *enter.*)

TIM CASEY: Listen, Shawn Early! Listen, Mrs. Tully, to the news! Jack Smith and Bartley Fallon had a falling out, and Jack knocked Mrs. Fallon's basket into the road, and Bartley made an attack on him with a hayfork, and away with Jack, and Bartley after him. Look at the sugar here yet on the road!

SHAWN EARLY: Do you tell me so? Well, that's a queer thing, and Bartley Fallon so quiet a man!

MRS. TULLY: I wouldn't wonder at all. I would never think well of a man that would have that sort of a mouldering look. It's likely he has overtaken Jack by this. (JAMES RYAN *and* MRS. TARPEY *enter.*)

JAMES RYAN: That is great news Mrs. Tarpey was telling me! I suppose that's what brought the police and the magistrate up this way. I was wondering to see them in it a while ago.

SHAWN EARLY: The police after them? Bartley Fallon must have injured Jack so. They wouldn't meddle in a fight that was only for show!

MRS. TULLY: Why wouldn't he injure him? There was many a man killed with no more of a weapon than a hayfork.

JAMES RYAN: Wait till I run north as far as Kelly's bar to spread the news! (JAMES RYAN *exits.*)

TIM CASEY: I'll go tell Jack Smith's first cousin that is standing there south of the church after selling his lambs. (TIM CASEY *exits.*)

MRS. TULLY: I'll go telling a few of the neighbours I see beyond to the west. (MRS. TULLY *exits.*)

SHAWN EARLY: I'll give word of it beyond at the east of the green. (*He is about to go.*)

MRS. TARPEY (*seizing hold of him*): Stop a minute, Shawn Early, and tell me did you see red Jack Smith's wife, Kitty Keary, in any place?

SHAWN EARLY (*breaking away*): Laying out a drying clothes on the hedge as I passed.

MRS. TARPEY: What did you say she was doing?

SHAWN EARLY (*breaking away*): Laying out a sheet on the hedge. (SHAWN EARLY *exits*.)

MRS. TARPEY: Laying out a sheet for the dead! The Lord have mercy on us! Jack Smith dead, and his wife laying out a sheet for his burying! (*She calls out*). Why didn't you tell me that before, Shawn Early? Isn't the deafness the great hardship? Half the world might be dead without me knowing of it or getting word of it at all! (*She sits down and rocks herself*). Oh, my poor Jack Smith! To be going to his work so nice and so hearty, and to be left stretched on the ground in the full light of the day! (TIM CASEY *enters*.)

TIM CASEY: What is it, Mrs. Tarpey? What happened since?

MRS. TARPEY: Oh, my poor Jack Smith!

TIM CASEY: Did Bartley overtake him?

MRS. TARPEY: Oh, the poor man!

TIM CASEY: Is it killed he is?

MRS. TARPEY: Stretched in the Five Acre Meadow!

TIM CASEY: The Lord have mercy on us! Is that a fact?

MRS. TARPEY: And the wife laying out a sheet for a ha'porth!

TIM CASEY: Who was telling you?

MRS. TARPEY: And the wife laying out a sheet for his corpse. (*She sits and wipes her eyes*). I suppose they'll wake him the same as another (MRS. TULLY, SHAWN EARLY, *and* JAMES RYAN *enter*.)

MRS. TULLY: There is great talk about this work in every quarter of the fair.

MRS. TARPEY: Ochone! Cold and dead. And myself maybe the last he was speaking to!

JAMES RYAN: The Lord save us! Is it dead he is?

TIM CASEY: Dead surely, and the wife getting provision for the wake.

SHAWN EARLY: Well, now, hadn't Bartley Fallon great venom in him?

MRS. TULLY: You may be sure he had some cause. Why would he have made an end of him if he had not? (*To* MRS. TARPEY, *raising her voice*). What was it rose the dispute at all, Mrs. Tarpey?

MRS. TARPEY: Not a one of me knows. The last I saw of them, Jack Smith was standing there, and Bartley Fallon was standing there, quiet and easy and he listening to *The Red-haired Man's Wife*.

MRS. TULLY: Do you hear that Tim Casey? Do you hear that, Shawn Early and James Ryan? Bartley Fallon was here this morning listening to Red Jack Smith's wife Kitty Keary that was! Listening to her and whispering with her! It was she started the fight so!

SHAWN EARLY: She must have followed him from her own house. It is likely some person roused him.

TIM CASEY: I never knew, before, Bartley Fallon was great with Jack Smith's wife.

MRS. TULLY: How would you know it? Sure it's not in the streets they would be calling it. If Mrs. Fallon didn't know of it, and if I that have the next house to them didn't know of it, and if Jack Smith himself didn't know of it, it is not likely you would know of it, Tim Casey.

SHAWN EARLY: Let Bartley Fallon take charge of her from this out so, and let him provide for her. It is little pity she will get from any person in this parish.

TIM CASEY: How can he take charge of her? Sure he has a wife of his own. Sure you don't think he'd turn souper and marry her in a Protestant church?

JAMES RYAN: It would be easy for him to marry her if he brought her to America.

SHAWN EARLY: With or without Kitty Keary, believe me it is for America he's making at this minute. I saw the new magistrate and Jo Muldoon of the police going into the post-office as I came up—there was hurry on them—you may be sure it was to telegraph they went, the way he'll be stopped in the docks at Queenstown!

MRS. TULLY: It's likely Kitty Keary is gone with him, and not minding a sheet or a wake at all. The poor man, to be deserted by his own wife, and the breath hardly gone out yet from his body that is lying bloody in the field! (MRS. FALLON *enters.*)

MRS. FALLON: What is it the whole of the town is talking about? And what is it you yourselves are talking about? Is it about my man Bartley Fallon you are talking? Is it lies about him you are telling, saying that he went killing Jack Smith? My grief that ever he came into this place at all!

JAMES RYAN: Be easy now, Mrs. Fallon. Sure there is no-one at all in the whole fair but is sorry for you!

MRS. FALLON: Sorry for me is it? Why would anyone be sorry for me? Let you be sorry for yourselves, and that there may be shame on you for ever and at the day of judgement, for the words you are saying and the lies you are telling to take away the character of my poor man, and take the good name off of him, and to drive him to destruction! That is what you are doing!

SHAWN EARLY: Take comfort now, Mrs. Fallon. The police are not so smart as they think. Sure he might give them the slip yet, the same as Lynchehaun.

MRS. TULLY: If they do get him, and if they do put a rope around his neck, there is no-one can say he does not deserve it!

MRS. FALLON: Is that what you are saying, Bridget Tully, and is that what you think? I tell you it's too much talk you have, making yourself out to be such a great one, and to be running down every respectable person! A rope, is it? It isn't much of a rope was needed to tie up your own furniture the day you came into Martin Tully's house, and you never bringing as much as a blanket, or a penny, or a suit of clothes with you and I myself bringing seventy pounds and two feather beds. And now you are stiffer than a woman would have a hundred pounds! It is too much talk the whole of you have. A rope is it? I tell you the whole of this town is full of liars and schemers that would hang you up for half a glass of whiskey. (*Turning to go*). People they are you wouldn't believe as much as daylight from without you'd get up to have a look at it yourself. Killing Jack Smith indeed! Where are you at all, Bartley, till I bring you out of this? My nice quiet little man! My decent comrade! He that is as kind and as harmless as an innocent beast of the field! He'll be doing no harm at all if he'll shed the blood of some of you after this day's work! That much would be no harm at all. (*She calls out*). Bartley! Bartley Fallon! Where are you? (*Going*). Did anyone see Bartley Fallon? (MRS. FALLON *exits L. All turn to look after her.*)

JAMES RYAN: It is hard for her to believe any such a thing. God help her! (BARTLEY FALLON *enters R., carrying the hayfork.*)

BARTLEY: It is what I often said to myself, if there is ever any misfortune coming to this world it is on myself it is sure to come! (*All turn round and face him*). To be going about with this fork and to find no-one to take it, and no place to leave it down, and I wanting to be gone out of this. Is that you, Shawn Early? (*He holds out the fork*). It's well I met you. You have no call to be leaving the fair for a while the way I have, and how can I go till I'm rid of this fork? Will you take it and keep it until such time as Jack Smith . . .

SHAWN EARLY (*backing*). I will not take it, Bartley Fallon, I'm very thankful to you!

BARTLEY (*turning to the apple stall*): Look at it now, Mrs Tarpey, it was here I got it; let me thrust it in under the stall. It will lie there safe enough, and no-one will take notice of it until such time as Jack Smith . . .

MRS. TARPEY: Take your fork out of that! Is it to put trouble on me and to destroy me you want? Putting it there for the police to be rooting it out maybe. (*She thrusts him back.*)

BARTLEY: That is a very unneighbourly thing for you to do, Mrs. Tarpey. Hadn't I enough care on me with that fork before this, running up and down with it like the swinging of a clock, and afeard to lay it down in any place! I wish I never touched it or meddled with it at all!

JAMES RYAN: It is a pity, indeed, you ever did.

BARTLEY: Will you yourself take it, James Ryan? You were always a neighbourly man.

JAMES RYAN (*backing*): There is many a thing I would do for you, Bartley Fallon, but I won't do that!

SHAWN EARLY: I tell you there is no man will give you any help or any encouragement for this day's work. If it was something agrarian now. . .

BARTLEY: If no-one at all will take it, maybe it's best to give it up to the police.

TIM CASEY: There'd be a welcome for it with them surely! (*Laughter.*)

MRS. TULLY: And it is to the police Kitty Keary herself will be brought.

MRS. TARPEY (*rocking to and fro*): I wonder now who will take the expense of the wake for poor Jack Smith?

BARTLEY: The wake for Jack Smith!

TIM CASEY: Why wouldn't he get a wake as well as another? Would you begrudge him that much?

BARTLEY: Red Jack Smith dead! Who was telling you?

SHAWN EARLY: The whole town knows of it by this.

BARTLEY: Do they say what way did he die?

JAMES RYAN: You don't know that yourself, I suppose, Bartley Fallon? You don't know he was followed and that he was laid dead with the stab of a hayfork?

BARTLEY: The stab of a hayfork!

SHAWN EARLY: You don't know, I suppose, that the body was found in the Five Acre Meadow?

BARTLEY: The Five Acre Meadow!

TIM CASEY: It is likely you don't know that the police are after the man that did it?

BARTLEY: The man that did it!

MRS. TULLY: You don't know, maybe, that he was made away with for the sake of Kitty Keary, his wife?

BARTLEY: Kitty Keary, his wife! (*He sits down bewildered.*)

MRS. TULLY: And what have you to say now, Bartley Fallon?

BARTLEY (*crossing himself*): I to bring that fork here, and to find that news before me! It is much if I can ever stir from this place at all, or reach as far as the road!

TIM CASEY: Look, boys, at the new magistrate, and Jo Muldoon along with him! It's best for us to quit this.

SHAWN EARLY: That is so. It is best not to be mixed in this business at all.

JAMES RYAN: Bad as he is, I wouldn't like to be an informer against any man. (ALL *hurry away except* MRS. TARPEY, *who remains behind her stall. The* MAGISTRATE *and the* POLICEMAN *enter.*)

MAGISTRATE: I knew the district was in a bad state, but I did not expect to be confronted with a murder at the first fair I came to.

POLICEMAN: I am sure you did not, indeed.

MAGISTRATE: It was well I had not gone home. I caught a few words here and there that roused my suspicions.

POLICEMAN: So they would, too.

MAGISTRATE: You heard the same story from everyone you asked?

POLICEMAN: The same story—or if it was not altogether the same, anyway it was no less than the first story.

MAGISTRATE: What is that man doing? He is sitting alone with a hayfork. He has a guilty look. The murder was done with a hayfork!

POLICEMAN (*in a whisper*): That's the very man they say did the act; Bartley Fallon himself!

MAGISTRATE: He must have found escape difficult—he is trying to brazen it out. A convict in the Adaman Islands tried the same game, but he could not escape my system! Stand aside. Don't go far—have the handcuffs ready. (*He walks up to* BARTLEY, *folds his arms, and stands before him*). Here, my man, do you know anything of John Smith . . .

BARTLEY: Of John Smith! Who is he, now?

POLICEMAN: Jack Smith, sir—Red Jack Smith!

MAGISTRATE (*coming a step nearer and tapping him on the shoulder*): Where is Jack Smith?

BARTLEY (*with a deep sigh, and shaking his head slowly*): Where is he, indeed?

MAGISTRATE: What have you to tell?

BARTLEY: It is where he was this morning, standing in this spot, singing his share of songs—no, but lighting his pipe—scratching a match on the sole of his shoe . . .

MAGISTRATE: I ask you, for the third time, where is he?

BARTLEY: I wouldn't like to say that. It is a great mystery, and it is hard to say of any man, did he earn hatred or love.

MAGISTRATE: Tell me all you know.

BARTLEY: All that I know. Well, there are the three estates; there is Limbo and there is Purgatory, and there is . . .

MAGISTRATE: Nonsense! This is trifling! Get to the point.

BARTLEY: Maybe you don't hold with the clergy so? That is the teaching of the clergy. Maybe you hold with the old people. It is what they do be saying, that the shadow goes wandering, and the soul is tired, and the body is taking a rest. The shadow! (*He starts up*). I was nearly sure I saw Jack Smith not ten minutes ago at the corner of the forge, and I lost him again. Was it his ghost I saw, do you think?

MAGISTRATE (*to the* POLICEMAN): Conscience-struck! He will confess all now!

BARTLEY: His ghost to come before me! It is likely it was on account of the fork! I to have it and he to have no way to defend himself the time he met with his death!

MAGISTRATE (*to the* POLICEMAN): I must note down his words. (*He takes out a notebook. To* BARTLEY). I warn you that your words are being noted.

BARTLEY: If I had ha'run faster in the beginning, this terror would not be on me at the latter end! Maybe he will cast it up against me at the day of judgement—I wouldn't wonder at all at that.

MAGISTRATE (*writing*): At the day of judgement. . .

BARTLEY: It was soon for his ghost to appear to me—is it coming after me always by day it will be, and stripping the clothes off in the night-time? I wouldn't wonder at all at that, being as I am an unfortunate man!

MAGISTRATE (*sternly*): Tell me this truly. What was the motive of this crime?

BARTLEY: The motive, is it?

MAGISTRATE: Yes; the motive; the cause.

BARTLEY: I'd sooner not say that.

MAGISTRATE: You had better tell me truly. Was it money?

BARTLEY: Not at all! What did poor Jack Smith ever have in his pockets unless it might be his hands that would be in them?

MAGISTRATE: Any dispute about land?

BARTLEY (*indignantly*): Not at all! He never was a grabber or grabbed from anyone!

MAGISTRATE: You will find it better for you if you tell me at once.

BARTLEY: I tell you I wouldn't for the whole world wish to say what it was—it is a thing I would not like to be talking about.

MAGISTRATE: There is no use in hiding it. It will be discovered in the end.

BARTLEY: Well, I suppose it will, seeing that mostly everybody knows it before. Whisper here now. I will tell no lie; where would be the use? (*He puts his hand to his mouth and the* MAGISTRATE *stoops down*). Don't be putting the blame on the parish, for such a thing was never done in the parish before—it was done for the sake of Kitty Keary, Jack Smith's wife.

MAGISTRATE (*to the* POLICEMAN): Put on the handcuffs. We have been saved some trouble. I knew he would confess if taken in the right way. (*The* POLICEMAN *puts on the handcuffs*.)

BARTLEY: Handcuffs now! Glory be! I always said, if there was ever any misfortune coming to this place it was on myself it would fall. I to be in handcuffs! There's no wonder at all in that. (MRS. FALLON *enters followed by the rest. She is looking back at them as she speaks*.)

MRS. FALLON: Telling lies the whole of the people of this town are; telling lies, telling lies as fast as a dog will trot! Speaking against my poor respectable man! Saying he made an end of Jack Smith! My decent comrade! There is no better man and no kinder man in the whole of the five parishes! It's little annoyance he ever gave to anyone! (*She turns and sees him*). What in the earthly world do I see before me? Bartley Fallon in charge of the police! Handcuffs on him! Oh, Bartley, what did you do at all at all?

BARTLEY: Oh, Mary, there has a great misfortune come upon me! It is what I always said, that if there is ever any misfortune. . .

MRS. FALLON: What did he do at all, or is it bewitched I am?

MAGISTRATE: This man has been arrested on a charge of murder.

MRS. FALLON: Whose charge is that? Don't believe them! They are all liars in this place! Give me back my man!

MAGISTRATE: It is natural you should take his part, but you have no cause of complaint against your neighbours. He has been arrested for the murder of John Smith, on his own confession.

MRS. FALLON: The saints of heaven protect us! And what did he want killing Jack Smith?

MAGISTRATE: It is best you should know all. He did it on account of a love affair with the murdered man's wife.

MRS. FALLON: (*sitting down*). With Jack Smith's wife! With Kitty Keary! Ochone, the traitor!

THE CROWD: A great shame, indeed. He is a traitor, indeed.

MRS. TULLY: To America he was bringing her, Mrs. Fallon.

BARTLEY: What are you saying, Mary? I tell you . . .

MRS. FALLON: Don't say a word! I won't listen to any word you'll say! (*She stops her ears*). Oh, isn't he the treacherous villain? Ochone go deo!

BARTLEY: Be quiet till I speak! Listen to what I say!

MRS. FALLON: Sitting beside me on the ass-car coming to the town, so quiet and so respectable, and treachery like that in his heart!

BARTLEY: Is it your wits you have lost or is it I myself that have lost my wits?

MRS. FALLON: And it's hard I earned you, slaving, slaving—and you grumbling, and sighing, and coughing, and discontented, and the priest wore out anointing you, with all the times you threatened to die!

BARTLEY: Let you be quiet till I tell you!

MRS. FALLON: You to bring such a disgrace into the parish. A thing that was never heard of before!

BARTLEY: Will you shut your mouth and hear me speaking?

MRS. FALLON: And if it was for any sort of a fine handsome woman, but for a little fistful of a woman like Kitty Keary, that's not four feet high hardly, and not three teeth in her head unless she got new ones! May God reward you, Bartley Fallon, for the black treachery in your heart and the wickedness in your mind, and the red blood of poor Jack Smith that is wet upon your hand!

JACK SMITH (*off; singing*): The sea shall be dry,
The earth under mourning and ban!
Then loud shall he cry
For the wife of the red-haired man!

BARTLEY: It's Jack Smith's voice—I never knew a ghost to sing before. It is after myself and the fork he is coming! (JACK SMITH *enters*). Let one of you give him the fork and I will be clear of him now and for eternity!

MRS. TARPEY: The Lord have mercy on us! Red Jack Smith! The man that was going to be waked!

JAMES RYAN: Is it back from the grave you are come?

SHAWN EARLY: Is it alive you are, or is it dead you are?

TIM CASEY: Is it yourself at all that's in it?

MRS. TULLY: Is it letting on you were to be dead?

MRS. FALLON: Dead or alive, let you stop Kitty Keary, your wife, from bringing my man away with her to America!

JACK SMITH: It is what I think, the wits are gone astray on the whole of you. What would my wife want bringing Bartley Fallon to America?

MRS. FALLON: To leave yourself, and to get quit of you she wants, Jack Smith, and to bring him away from myself. That's what the two of them had settled together.

JACK SMITH: I'll break the head of any man that says that! Who is it says it? (*To* TIM CASEY). Was it you said it? (*To* SHAWN EARLY). Was it you?

ALL (*together; backing and shaking their heads*). It wasn't I said it!

JACK SMITH: Tell me the name of any man that said it!

ALL (*together; pointing to* BARTLEY): It was *him* that said it!

JACK SMITH: Let me at him till I break his head! (BARTLEY *backs in terror. Neighbours hold* JACK SMITH *back. Trying to free himself*). Let me at him! Isn't he the pleasant sort of a scarecrow for any woman to be crossing the ocean with! It's back from the docks of New York he'd be turned, (*trying to rush at him again*) with a lie in his mouth and treachery in his heart, and another man's wife by his side, and he passing her off as his own! Let me at him, can't you. (*He makes another rush, but is held back.*)

MAGISTRATE (*pointing to* JACK SMITH). Policeman put the handcuffs on this man. I see it all now. A case of false impersonation, a conspiracy to defeat the ends of justice. There was a case in the Andaman Islands, a murderer of the Mopsa tribe, a religious enthusiast . . .

POLICEMAN: So he might be, too.

MAGISTRATE: We must take both these men to the scene of the murder. We must confront them with the body of the real Jack Smith:

JACK SMITH: I'll break the head of any man that will find my dead body!

MAGISTRATE: I'll call more help from the barracks. (*He blows the* POLICEMAN'S *whistle.*)

BARTLEY: It is what I am thinking, if myself and Jack Smith are put together in the one cell for the night, the handcuffs will be taken off him, and his hands will be free, and murder will be done that time surely!

MAGISTRATE: Come on! (*They turn to the* R.)

(*Curtain*)

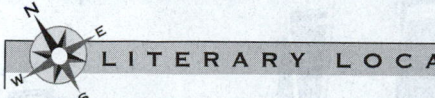

LITERARY LOCALE

Dublin's Abbey Theatre. In 1903 poet W. B. Yeats and playwright Lady Gregory founded the Irish National Theatre, which found its home in the Abbey Theatre in Dublin on December 27, 1904. The aim of an Irish national theater was to produce and promote Irish drama. In 1925 the theater began receiving an annual subsidy from the government and became the first state-sponsored theater in the English-speaking world. The original building on Old Abbey Street was damaged by fire in 1952 and, after a few temporary homes, a modern building was built along the Liffey River in 1966. This current structure is unique for its placement partially over the river, which leaves the building floating on a concrete "raft."

The National Theatre, as the organization is formally titled, is really made up of two theater spaces: the main auditorium called the Abbey, which concentrates on Irish drama, and a studio space called the Peacock, which produces new plays. To read more about the Abbey or see what's playing there now, visit their website at *http://www.abbeytheatre.ie.*

SPREADING THE NEWS IN PERFORMANCE

Unlike *Trifles*, *Spreading the News* does not even pretend to provide an accurate representation of "real life." *Trifles* depicts a group of midwestern farm characters as they might really look and sound and act. *Spreading the News* certainly has regional characters and rural folks too, but it doesn't represent them in anything like realistic behavior. *Spreading the News* is part of a very different tradition more prevalent in comedy; instead of providing a "slice of life," it provides a wide variety of deliberately simplified **types**, one-dimensional figures who, using the criteria of realistic drama, lack depth, richness, and complexity. In this world, Irish men have fiery red hair, are gifted with gab, smoke pipes, jump to conclusions, or cannot wait to tell the bad news to their neighbors. We are in a farce that literally begins with upsetting the apple cart and ends with its key character in prison, unsure of what has happened to him.

Spreading the News depicts a world of the "folk," in this case Irish villagers, with their comic propensity for embellishing stories and for invoking the slightly fantastic. This play combines farce with a type of **ethnic drama** (a dramatic production produced by an ethnic, often immigrant group) that has often attracted groups of people who may feel the survival of their culture is at stake, as Lady Gregory certainly did about traditional Ireland. *Spreading the News* is ethnic or folk drama that

The original Abbey Theatre, where in 1904 production of Spreading the News was first performed.

celebrates the local characteristics of a people, and gently satirizes them in a loving but amused way.

For the playwright, making such drama work for audiences requires a keen eye for the behavior of a wide range of people. At a performance, the audience would regard these characters as familiar types; the actors must give them individual life, embellishing the roles by drawing on their own experience. An advantage of ethnic drama is that at least initially everyone—playwright, directors, actors, and audience alike—is part of the same world and shares a common understanding. Other types of ethnic drama are not comic but tragic, and the satire is not so loving. Lady Gregory's theater in Dublin was the scene of violent riots in 1907 and 1926, when outraged Irish nationalists deemed ethnic plays about themselves insufficiently laudatory.

The exploration of ethnicity that characterizes *Spreading the News* will be familiar to anyone who reads August Wilson's *The Piano Lesson* (p. 1916) or Luis Valdez's *Los Vendidos* (p. 1867). One thing that makes such twentieth-century plays highly modern is that they examine important characteristics of the writer's own ethnicity. Tellingly, such plays have often been produced first in highly local theatrical settings. They tend to start out among the people they depict—Chicano farm laborers, Native Americans, Irish nationalists—and only later get produced for a wider audience.

William Butler Yeats, who co-founded Dublin's Abbey Theatre along with Lady Gregory.

Talking about the Text

1. What is the action or spine of the play? (Is the action of *Spreading the News* as easy to put into a phrase as the action of *Trifles*? Why, or why not?)

2. Why is the play set in a marketplace? What advantages does a playwright get from such a public setting?

3. List four different "types" you noticed in the play. For our purposes, a "type" is a simply drawn character who can be summed up in a quick phrase or two (like "the suspicious Magistrate") that seems to tell us all we need to know.

4. What makes the Magistrate act the way he does? Use his motivation (the "spine" of his character) to connect his behavior at the beginning of the play with what eventually happens.

5. In a note appended to *Spreading the News*, Lady Gregory wrote: "The idea of this play first came to me as a tragedy. I kept seeing as in a picture people sitting by the roadside, and a girl passing to the market, gay and fearless. And then I saw her passing by the same place at evening, her head hanging, the heads of others turned from her, because of some sudden story that had risen out of a chance word, and had snatched away her good name." In what ways has *Spreading the News* kept to that original outline? How can the same plot be used for a tragedy and for a comedy?

6. *Spreading the News* seems to cry out for lively acting, even for hamming it up. Pick a speech that seems to require gestures and movement to come alive, then read it out loud, either alone or with a group of classmates. How would you act it out?

7. Sometimes a play "works" by presenting someone with a wonderful part. Which character in *Spreading the News* has the juiciest role? Which character would you enjoy playing most, and why? How would you approach the role?

Writing about the Text

1. Imagine the central character, Bartley Fallon, in a way that makes him more than a simple figure of fun or essentially passive character who does not act but is only acted upon. Make him more active by writing a speech in which he defends himself. Keep in mind that he was the figure Lady Gregory imagined as the tragic source of the play (see item 5, above).

2. Mrs. Fallon's long speech (p. 1188) is often reprinted in books of monologues for aspiring actors to practice. Can you see why? Write out directions for three different ways to do it. (As an alternative, you can try a director's annotations for the speech. See p. 1230 for an example.)

Linking the Text to Other Texts

1. When the University of Arizona staged *Spreading the News* in 1999, the reviewer faulted the production for confusing the audience. He said too many people were on a small stage all at once, so it was hard to tell who was doing and saying what. At what points in the play do you find this crowding a danger? Suggest how a production could get around such a problem.

2. Compare the ways *Trifles* and *Spreading the News* share attitudes toward authority. Who is in charge? How are the ordinary people treated? What opportunities do the plays envision for evading the constraints of the official system?

3. Think about the depictions of ethnicity in *Spreading the News* in connection with the ethnic portrayals in *Los Vendidos* (see p. 1867). What risks do the writers and producers run in staging these plays?

4. Listen to the 1907 recording of "Casey at the Bat" (written at the same time as
Spreading the News, though in America), and compare the stereotypes in *Spreading the News* with the depictions of Irish baseball players. What stereotypes do both the poem and the play use? Note how the speaker on the recording, DeWolfe Hopper, the one who made the poem famous in his stage performances, employs a fake Irish brogue. The recording is available on Rhino CD 70710.

COMMENTARY

Lady Gregory on Irish Theater

In 1913 Lady Gregory published *Our Irish Theatre: A Chapter in Autobiography*, in which she describes her life as a playwright and her role in establishing a national theater in Ireland. In one passage Lady Gregory describes how she, poet William Butler Yeats, and her playwright neighbor Edward Martyn sat down over tea one day to establish what they hoped to be real Irish theater. In their mission statement, they wrote:

> We propose to have performed in Dublin, in the spring of every year certain Celtic and Irish plays, which whatever be their degree of excellence will be written with a high ambition, and so to build up a Celtic and Irish school of dramatic literature. We hope to find in Ireland an uncorrupted and imaginative audience trained to listen by its passion for oratory, and believe that our desire to bring upon the stage the deeper thoughts and emotions of Ireland will ensure for us a tolerant welcome, and that freedom to experiment which is not found in theatres of England, and without which no new movement in art or literature can succeed. We will show that Ireland is not the home of buffoonery and of easy sentiment, as it has been represented, but the home of an ancient idealism. We are confident of the support of all Irish people, who are weary of misrepresentation, in carrying out a work that is outside all the political questions that divide us.

After their first performance in 1899, it took the group until 1904 to open their own theater, Dublin's Abbey. Lady Gregory was away from Dublin on opening night, but in the following passage she describes hearing of the playhouse's success:

> Then after the first night, December 27th, I had good telegrams and then a letter: "A great success in every way. The audience seemed 'heavy' through the opening dialogue—Fool and Blind man—and then it woke up, applauding for a long time after the exit of the kings. There was great enthusiasm at the end. *Kathleen* seemed more rebellious than I ever heard it, and _____ solemnly begged me to withdraw it for fear it would stir up a conspiracy and get us all into trouble. Then came your play—a success from the first. One could hardly hear for the applause. Fay was magnificent as the melancholy man. The whole play was well played all through. I don't think I really like the stone wall wings. However, I was very near and will know better to-night. I got a beautiful light effect in *Baile's Strand*, and the audience applauded the scene even before the play began. The cottage, too, with the misty blue outside its door is lovely. We never had such an audience or such enthusiasm. The pit clapped when I came in. Our success could not have been greater. Even _____ admits that your comedy [*Spreading the News*], 'is undoubtedly going to be very popular.' "

In 1902 the Abbey had produced three of Gregory's plays, *Twenty-five*, *The Jackdaw*, and *Spreading the News*. Gregory was left somewhat unsatisfied with these attempts and was inspired to something bigger:

> Perhaps I ought to have written nothing but these short comedies, but desire for experiment is like fire in the blood, and I had had from the beginning a vision of historical plays being sent by us through all the counties of Ireland. For to have a real success and to come into the life of the country, one must touch a real and eternal emotion, and history comes only next to religion in our country. And although the realism of our young writers is taking the place of fantasy and romance in the cities, I still hope to see a little season given up every year to plays on history and in sequence at the Abbey, and I think schools and colleges may ask to have them sent and played in their halls, as a part of the day's lesson. I began with the daring and lightheartedness of a schoolboy to write a tragedy in three acts upon a great personality, Brian the High King. I made many bad beginnings, and if I had listened to Mr. Yeats's advice I should have given it up, but I began again and again till it was at last moulded in at least a possible shape.

VIRTUAL LOCALE

Lady Gregory's Memoir Online. To read the complete text of Lady Gregory's memoir, *Our Irish Theatre: A Chapter of Autobiography*, go to *http://digital.library.upenn.edu/women/gregory/theatre/theatre.html*, part of the Celebration of Women Writers digital archive within the Penn Library at the University of Pennsylvania. The site also includes footnotes and appendices for the work and original manuscript page illustrations.

Starting Points for Further Research: Lady Gregory

- **Edition:** Lady Augusta Gregory. *Seven Short Plays*. New York: Putnam, 1903.
- **Biography:** Mary Lou Kohfeldt Stevenson. *Lady Gregory: The Woman behind the Irish Renaissance*. New York: Athenaeum, 1985.
- **Critical Essays:** John J. Conlon. "Shaw, Lady Gregory and the Abbey: A Correspondence and a Record." *English Literature in Transition 1880–1920*. 40:3 (1997): 345–47.

  Sinéad Garrigan Mattar. " 'Wage for Each People Her Hand Has Destroyed': Lady Gregory's Colonial Nationalism." *Irish University Review: A Journal of Irish Studies* 34 (2004): 49–66.

DAVID IVES   (B. 1944)

Born and raised in Chicago, David Ives has written many popular short plays, one children's novel, Monsieur Eek, *and a number of short humor pieces. Ives was born in Chicago and educated first in local Catholic schools and then at the Yale School of Drama. His many short, one-act plays have been gathered into three volumes,* All in the Timing *(1990),* Time Flies *(1996), and* Polish Jokes and Other Plays *(2004). Ives's characteristically odd and very funny take on the world has made him a favorite of college and community theater groups; in fact,* All in the

Timing *was performed so much that during the 1995–1996 season, Ives was the second most performed playwright in America, right behind Shakespeare.*

The Philadelphia *is a long way from early twentieth-century Ireland or a small Nebraska farm in 1916, and the differences comprise much more than geography or time. About seventy-five years of experimentation in dramatic writing and production occurred between Glaspell and Ives, years in which generations of playwrights worked to create alternatives to the "well-made" realistic plays like* Trifles *and so-called "simple" folk comedies like* Spreading the News. *Two enormous intervening factors were television and the movies, which could both do "realism" better than any stage play and therefore forced playwrights to reconsider the special virtues of live theater. Television and movies also provided dramatists all over the world with zany, complex figures as diverse as Charlie Chaplin, the Marx Brothers, Woody Allen, Richard Pryor, the Road Runner, and the animated cast of characters of the Warner Brothers cartoons. Merge a TV sitcom with the craziness of Groucho Marx or Bugs Bunny and you are on your way to the comic world of David Ives.*

It may seem a little perverse to devote any weighty analysis to such a short, fun, and funny play as Ives's The Philadelphia, *but without a slightly closer look, we might be tempted to regard it as a lightweight collection of snappy one-liners, little more than a good* Saturday Night Live *routine. But Ives is one of America's most widely staged playwrights because there is something substantive about his comic sketches that attracts actors, directors, and many, many audiences. He also has things to tell us about the making of drama in the contemporary world.*

 INSPIRATION   DAVID IVES ON THE POWER OF THE THEATER

Playwright David Ives once described the stunning moment when he first realized the power of the theater—during an English class on Emily Dickinson in his Catholic high school, as his boisterous classmates began acting up.

> Faced with chaos [the teacher, Father Henkel], laid the textbook down, climbed up onto his desk, and stood on his head. We all stopped horsing around and stared at him in stupefaction. Henkel then climbed back down, picked up the book, and said, "Let's get back to 'Beauty be not caused—it is,' page 388." It was probably my first glimpse of the power of the theatrical: you gather an audience, you do a headstand to get everyone's attention, and then you're free to explore beauty, poetry, truth, the human condition, what you will. Now *that's* an education.

The Philadelphia

(1982)

Characters

Al
Waitress
Mark

A bar/restaurant. A table, red-checked cloth, two chairs, and a specials board. At lights up, AL *is at the restaurant table, with the* WAITRESS.

WAITRESS: Can I help you?

AL: Do you know you would look fantastic on a wide screen?

WAITRESS: Uh-huh.

AL: Seventy millimeters.

WAITRESS: Look. Do you want to see a menu, or what?

AL: Let's negotiate, here. What's the soup du jour today?

WAITRESS: Soup of the day, you got a choice of Polish duck blood or cream of kidney.

AL: Beautiful. Beautiful! Kick me in a kidney.

Waitress (*writes it down*): You got it.

AL: Any oyster crackers on your seabed?

WAITRESS: Nope. All out.

AL: How about the specials today? Spread out your options.

WAITRESS: You got your deep-fried gizzards.

AL: Fabulous.

WAITRESS: Calves' brains with okra.

AL: You are a *temptress*.

WAITRESS: And pickled pigs' feet.

AL: Pigs' feet. *I love it*. Put me down for a quadruped.

WAITRESS: If you say so.

AL: Any sprouts to go on those feet?

WAITRESS: Iceberg.

AL: So be it.

(WAITRESS *exits, as* MARK *enters, looking shaken and bedraggled.*)

MARK: Al!

AL: Hey there, Marcus. What's up?

MARK: Jesus!

AL: What's going on, buddy?

MARK: Oh, man . . . !

AL: What's the matter? Sit down.

MARK: I don't get it, Al. I don't understand it.

AL: You want something? You want a drink? I'll call the waitress—

Mark (*desperate*): *No!* No! Don't even try. (*Gets a breath.*) I don't know what's going on today, Al. It's really weird.

AL: What, like . . . ?

MARK: Right from the time I got up.

AL: What is it? What's the story?

MARK: Well—just for an example. This morning I stopped off at a drugstore to buy some aspirin. This is at a big drugstore, right?

AL: Yeah. . .

MARK: I go up to the counter, the guy says what can I do for you, I say, Give me a bottle of aspirin. The guy gives me this funny look and he says, "Oh we don't have *that*, sir." I said to him, You're a drugstore and you don't have any *aspirin?*

AL: Did they have Bufferin?

MARK: Yeah!

AL: Advil?

MARK: Yeah!

AL: Extra-strength Tylenol?

MARK: Yeah!

AL: But no aspirin.

MARK: No!

AL: Wow . . .

MARK: And that's the kind of weird thing that's been happening all day. It's like, I go to a newsstand to buy the *Daily News*, the guy never even *heard* of it.

AL: Could've been a misunderstanding.

MARK: I asked everyplace—*nobody* had the *News!* I had to read the *Toronto Hairdresser*. Or this. I go into a deli at lunchtime to buy a sandwich, the guy tells me they don't have any *pastrami*. How can they be a deli if they don't have pastrami?

AL: Was this a Korean deli?

MARK: This was a kosher-from-*Jerusalem* deli. "Oh we don't carry *that*, sir," he says to me. "Have some tongue."

AL: Mmm.

MARK: I just got into a cab, the guy says he doesn't go to Fifty-sixth Street! He offers to take me to Newark instead!

AL: Mm-hm.

MARK: Looking at me like I'm an alien or something!

AL: Mark. Settle down.

MARK: "Oh I, don't go *there*, sir."

AL: Settle down. Take a breath.

MARK: Do you know what this is?

AL: Sure.

MARK: What is it? What's happening to me?

AL: Don't panic. You're in a Philadelphia.

MARK: I'm in a what?

AL: You're in a Philadelphia. That's all.

MARK: But I'm in—

AL: Yes, physically you're in New York. But *meta*physically you're in a Philadelphia.

MARK: I've never heard of this!

AL: You see, inside of what we know as reality there are these pockets, these black holes called Philadelphias. If you fall into one, you run up against exactly the kinda shit that's been happening to you all day.

MARK: Why?

AL: Because in a Philadelphia, no matter what you ask for, you can't get it. You ask for something, they're not gonna have it. You want to do something, it ain't gonna get done. You want to go somewhere, you can't get there from here.

MARK: Good God. So this is very serious.

AL: Just remember, Marcus. This is a condition named for the town that invented the *cheese steak*. Something that nobody in his right mind would willingly ask for.

MARK: And I thought I was just having a very bad day. . . .

AL: Sure. Millions of people have spent entire lifetimes inside a Philadelphia and never even knew it. Look at the city of Philadelphia itself. Hopelessly trapped forever inside a Philadelphia. And do they know it?

MARK: Well what can I do? Should I just kill myself now and get it over with?

AL: You try to kill yourself in a Philadelphia, you're only gonna get hurt, babe.

MARK: So what do I do?

AL: Best thing to do is wait it out. Someday the great cosmic train will whisk you outta the City of Brotherly Love and off to someplace happier.

MARK: *You're* pretty goddamn mellow today.

AL: Yeah well. Everybody has to be someplace.

(WAITRESS *enters.*)

WAITRESS: Is your name Allen Chase?

AL: It is indeed.

WAITRESS: There was a phone call for you. Your boss?

AL: Okay.

WAITRESS: He says you're fired.

AL: Cool! Thanks. (WAITRESS *exits.*) So anyway, you have this problem...

MARK: Did she just say you got *fired?*

AL: Yeah. I wonder what happened to my pigs' feet. . . .

MARK: Al—!? You *loved* your job!

AL: Hey. No sweat.

MARK: How can you be so calm?

AL: Easy. You're in a Philadelphia? *I* woke up in a Los Angeles. And life is beautiful! You know Susie packed up and left me this morning.

MARK: Susie left you?

AL: And frankly, Scarlett, I don't give a shit. I say, go and God bless and may your dating pool be Olympic-sized.

MARK: But your job? The garment district is your life!

AL: So I'll turn it into a movie script and sell it to Paramount. Toss in some sex, add a little emotional blah-blah-*blah*, pitch it to Jack and Dusty, you got a buddy movie with a garment background. Not relevant enough? We'll throw in the hole in the ozone, make it E.C.

MARK: E.C.?

AL: Environmentally correct. Have you heard about this hole in the ozone?

MARK: Sure.

AL: Marcus, I *love* this concept. I *embrace* this ozone. Sure, some people are gonna get hurt in the process. Meantime, everybody else'll tan a little faster.

Mark (*quiet horror*): So this is a Los Angeles...

AL: Well. Everybody has to be someplace.

MARK: Wow.

AL: You want my advice? *Enjoy your Philadelphia.* Sit back and order yourself a beer and a burger and chill out for a while.

MARK: But I can't order anything. Life is great for you out there on the cosmic beach. Whatever *I* ask for, I'll get a cheese steak or something.

AL: No. There's a very simple rule of thumb in a Philadelphia. *Ask for the opposite.*

MARK: What?

AL: If you can't get what you ask for, ask for the opposite and you'll get what you want. You want the *Daily News,* ask for the *Times.* You want pastrami, ask for tongue.

MARK: Oh.

AL: Works great with women. What is more opposite than the opposite sex?
MARK: Uh-huh.
AL: So. Would you like a Bud?
MARK: I sure could use a—
AL: No. Stop. (*Very deliberately.*) Do you want…a Bud?
MARK (*also deliberately*): No. I *don't* want a Bud.

(WAITRESS *enters and goes to the specials board.*)

AL: Good. Now there's the waitress. Order yourself a Bud and a burger. But don't *ask* for a Bud and a burger.
MARK: Waitress!
AL: Don't call her. She won't come.
MARK: Oh.
AL: You're in a Philadelphia, so just figure, fuck her.
MARK: Fuck *her.*
AL: You don't need that waitress.
MARK: *Fuck* that waitress.
AL: And everything to do with her.
MARK: Hey, *waitress!* FUCK YOU!

(WAITRESS *turns to him.*)

WAITRESS: Can I help you, sir?
AL: *That's* how you get service in a Philadelphia.
WAITRESS: Can I help you?
MARK: Uh—no thanks.
WAITRESS: Okay, what'll you have? (*Takes out her pad.*)
AL: Excellent.
MARK: Well—how about some O.J.?
WAITRESS: Sorry. Squeezer's broken.
MARK: A glass of milk?
WAITRESS: Cow's dry.
MARK: Egg nog?
WAITRESS: Just ran out.
MARK: Cuppa coffee?
WAITRESS: Oh we don't have *that*, sir. (MARK *and* AL *exchange a look and nod. The* WAITRESS *has spoken the magic words.*)
MARK: Got any ale?
WAITRESS: Nope.
MARK: Stout?
WAITRESS: Nope.
MARK: Porter?
WAITRESS: Just beer.
MARK: That's too bad. How about a Heineken?
WAITRESS: Heineken? Try again.
MARK: Rolling Rock?
WAITRESS: Outta stock.
MARK: Schlitz?
WAITRESS: Nix.
MARK: Beck's?

THE PHILADELPHIA IN PERFORMANCE

The action in *The Philadelphia* starts out simply: Al orders a meal, all the time show-ing off his L.A. style to the Waitress: "Do you know you'd look fantastic on a wide screen?" His friend Mark arrives, wanting to understand what has been happening to him. Mark seeks guidance from Al. The setting being New York, the three char-acters must play their appropriate roles: the waitress is short and snappy; Mark is sensitive, puzzled, confused; Al is all-knowing, able to explain everything. And since he *starts* in an L.A. style, he is sunny and laid-back, at least for a while. But this simple, sitcom-type world is subject to some strange alterations and reversals. In a Philadelphia, you get what you want by asking for something else. And of course Al experiences a reversal too, from his sunny L.A. to his demanding, "tragic" Philadelphia. At the end it is Mark who is comfortable inhabiting his newly found world while Al runs off, devastated.

Like *Spreading the News*, *The Philadelphia* makes no pretense of representing re-ality—at least not beyond the ordinary situation of a waitress who has seen it all and her two customers from different coasts. As far as we know, there are no black holes called "Philadelphias" and "Los Angeleses." Ives's situations and dialogue seem to inhabit another universe, parallel to but just out of reach of ours. (Mark in fact com-plains that people have been "looking at me like I'm an alien or something.") Metaphorically, of course, the play seems more familiar. Who hasn't experienced a very bad day when it seemed nothing worked out the way we wanted it to or ex-pected it to? Who hasn't engaged in a sort of magical thinking: "If I expect the worst, maybe it won't happen (or at least it won't take me by surprise)." These char-acters are not to be confused with "real" people; like all characters in plays, they are created to represent tendencies we all share or recognize, and their interaction is planned to show those tendencies in conflict.

In a wider way, most of us inhabit a universe (some of the time, anyway) in which we customarily invoke Murphy's Law—"whatever can go wrong will go

WAITRESS: Next.
MARK: Sapporo?
WAITRESS: Tomorrow.
MARK: Lone Star?
WAITRESS: Hardy-har.
MARK: Bud Lite?
WAITRESS: Just plain Bud is all we got.
MARK: No thanks.
Waitress (*calls*): *Gimme a Bud!* (*To* MARK) Anything to eat?
MARK: Nope.
WAITRESS: Name it.
MARK: Pork chops.

Still from a production of David Ives's The Philadelphia.

wrong"— and we share a sort of cynical and sophisticated pessimism about areas of our cultural life and activities such as politics, advertising, the speed of our Internet connections, or bureaucracies we must deal with. The actors who perform in *The Philadelphia* need to be tuned in to some of the existential anxieties that characterized the late twentieth century: What is really "real"? Is there any such thing as ultimate meaning? What is life and death and what are we here for? Those sorts of questions do not dominate the roles in Ives's play. And often the characters who ask them pose them only half-seriously or immediately bump into the refuse-to-be-serious repartee of their dialogue partners. But any performance has to highlight the mix of crazy and serious that Ives first learned about from Father Henkel's Chicago high school English class.

Waitress (*writes down*): Hamburger . . .
MARK: Medium.
WAITRESS: Well done...
MARK: Baked potato.
WAITRESS: Fries . . .
MARK: And some zucchini.
WAITRESS: Slice of raw. (*Exits, calling.*) Burn one!
AL: Marcus, that was excellent.
MARK: Thank you.
AL: *Excellent.* You sure you've never done this before?
MARK: I've spent so much of my life asking for the wrong thing without knowing it, doing it on purpose comes easy.

AL: I hear you.

MARK: I could've saved myself a lot of trouble if I'd screwed up on purpose all those years. Maybe I was in a Philadelphia all along and never knew it!

AL: You might've been in a Baltimore. They're practically the same.

(WAITRESS *enters with a glass of beer and a plate.*)

WAITRESS: Okay. Here's your Bud. (*Sets that in front of* MARK.) And one cheese-steak. (*She sets that in front of* AL *and starts to go.*)

AL: Excuse me. Hey. Wait a minute. What is that?

WAITRESS: It's a cheese steak.

AL: No. I ordered cream of kidney and two pairs of feet.

WAITRESS: Oh we don't have *that*, sir.

AL: I beg your pardon?

WAITRESS: We don't have that, sir. (*Small pause.*)

Al (*to* MARK): You son of a bitch! *I'm in your Philadelphia!*

MARK: I'm sorry, Al.

AL: You brought me into your fucking Philadelphia!

MARK: I didn't know it was contagious.

AL: Oh God, please don't let me be in a Philadelphia! Don't let me be in a—

MARK: Shouldn't you ask for the opposite? I mean, since you're in a Philad—

AL: Don't you tell *me* about life in a Philadelphia.

MARK: Maybe you're not really—

AL: I taught you everything you know about Philly, asshole. Don't tell *me* how to act in a Philadelphia!

MARK: But maybe you're not really in a Philadelphia!

AL: Do you see the cheese on that steak? What do I need for proof? The fucking *Liberty Bell?* Waitress, bring me a glass of water.

WAITRESS: Water? Don't have that, sir.

Al (*to* MARK): "We don't have *water*"—? What, you think we're in a sudden drought or something? (*Suddenly realizes.*) Holy shit, I just lost my job . . . ! Susie left me! I gotta make some phone calls! (*To* WAITRESS.) 'Scuse me, where's the payphone?

WAITRESS: Sorry, we don't have a payph—

AL: Of *course* you don't have a payphone, of *course* you don't! Oh shit, let me outta here! (*Exits.*)

MARK: I don't know. It's not that bad in a Philadelphia.

WAITRESS: Could be worse. I've been in a Cleveland all week.

MARK: A Cleveland. What's that like?

WAITRESS: It's like death, without the advantages.

MARK: Really. Care to stand?

WAITRESS: Don't mind if I do. (*She sits.*)

MARK: I hope you won't reveal your name.

WAITRESS: Sharon.

Mark (*holds out his hand*): Good-bye.

WAITRESS: Hello. (*They shake.*)

MARK: (*indicating the cheese steak*): Want to starve?

WAITRESS: Thanks. (*She picks up the cheese steak and starts eating.*)

MARK: Yeah, everybody has to be someplace. . . .(*Leans across the table with a smile.*) So.

(*Blackout*)

Talking about the Text

1. Describe a very bad day (or week) you can remember. How did you try to make sense of it, other than perhaps to say, "I must have got out on the wrong side of the bed"? What coping mechanisms did you come up with? Did you seek out an "Al" who could make sense of what was happening that day? Explain.

2. An important aspect of Ives's drama is a delight with wordplay. Explore how wordplay works throughout *The Philadelphia*. For instance, what is the effect of the repartee over lists? How should that dialogue go? Quickly? Lovingly? Snappily? Musically?

3. As the play goes on, what happened before takes on new significance. Compare Al's menu choices at the opening with Mark's in the middle and then Mark's repartee with the waitress at the end. What advantage might you have by being able to read and reread the play? How might a good director exploit those comparisons on the stage?

4. *The Philadelphia* is mostly funny and enjoyable. But there are some moments of tension when it seems like we are adrift in an incomprehensible universe. Pick three such moments and describe how you would have them performed. Do not rely only on the words on the page. Pauses will no doubt be important, as will gestures. How (if at all) are these moments of tension resolved? What in the play appears to suggest a critique of the culture and society it portrays? What do you think is the spirit of that critique?

5. Explore Al's function in the play. He seems to give Mark the needed guidance, but then why do we begin to question his reliability?

6. Are there any other cities you can associate with particular characteristics? How about Chicago? Miami? Minneapolis? Las Vegas? Seattle? Dallas? Which would you like to be in? Which would you hate the worst?

7. Ives's plays are staged frequently by college drama groups. What about *The Philadelphia* might make it particularly attractive and accessible for a college theater?

Writing about the Text

1. Create a character associated with a particular place in America (as in question 6, above). Write the description of this character that would appear in the stage directions. Then invent a page of dialogue as this character interacts with one or more characters from *The Philadelphia*: the waitress, Mark, or Al.

2. Write an essay demonstrating that *The Philadelphia* and a scene from a TV sitcom of your choice are either very much alike or really quite different.

Linking the Text to Other Texts

1. Characters who inhabit a crazy and absurd world are not uncommon in literature. Look at the stories by Gabriel García Márquez (p. 83) and Jorge Luis Borges (p. 616) and describe how the world in these stories is like and different from that in *The Philadelphia*.

2. Ives invokes Emily Dickinson in his description of how he learned about drama (p. 1199). What in *The Philadelphia* connects with the way Dickinson's poetry

reacts to the world? Look, for instance, at the Dickinson poem Ives mentions, "Beauty—be not caused—It Is" (p. 896), as well as at "I heard a Fly buzz—when I died" (p. 885). You do not need to find verbal echoes; think about sensibility and themes and overall approach to important questions.

Starting Points for Further Research: David Ives

- ■ **Articles:** "David Ives Offers 'Lab' for Playwrights, Just Off Broadway." *Columbia University Record*, February 10, 1995.

    David Ives. "Why Write for the Theater?" *Zoetrope: All Story 4* (Winter 2000). The One-Act Play Issue. http://www.all-story.com/issues.cgi?action=show_story&story_id=84.

CHAPTER
21

Writing about Plays

Drama probably receives more attention from professional critics, in a wider variety of places, than any other type of literature. Part of the reason is practical: Because going to the theater frequently calls for an investment of time and money, people want advance information about whether the effort will be worthwhile. The play review serves that purpose well, telling prospective theatergoers what the play is about, how well the actors perform, and how successful the whole production seems.

Theater reviews are only the most visible form of writing about drama. In addition to the reviews that are usually written by professionals aiming to reach a wide, popular audience, drama writing includes criticism, which is the province of scholars and literary or cultural critics, and academic assignments, which are intended to give students a deeper understanding of how plays work, as well as to promote the critical thinking that inevitably accompanies a well-planned writing exercise. This writing about drama forms an essential part of the cultural conversation that accompanies all discussions of literature.

THE CULTURAL CONVERSATION

As discussed in Chapters 3 and 12, "Writing about Stories" and "Writing about Poetry," respectively, when you and people you know talk about what makes a good movie, an entertaining TV show, or a piece of music you want to record or buy, you are participating in what literary critic Kenneth Burke has called "the cultural conversation," a vibrant, fluid dialogue that takes place all the time among the many people who write and talk about literature, music, films—about all performances. Drama has a similarly powerful conversation going on all the time, in talk and in print.

The conversation about drama, like the conversations you already have about television or film, can take place at different levels. Commentary by an experienced viewer of plays sounds different from that of a newcomer to theater. Talking knowledgeably about a play is a bigger challenge if it is one of only two or three that you have seen. How can you write about plays without having seen any on stage? This chapter will introduce you to some familiar and not-so-familiar examples of the conversation that is always taking place about the theater. It will also demonstrate various ways you can become an active, thoughtful participant in that cultural dialogue.

REVIEWS

Where does the conversation about drama get written down? In books, certainly, but more commonly it appears in weekly magazines and daily newspapers that devote space to cultural matters and to the arts. Any issue of popular magazines like *Time* and *Newsweek* (each claiming worldwide readership of many millions) will usually have a page or a column concentrating on theater. Other magazines with smaller but highly influential circulations, such as the *New Yorker*, the *Nation*, the *New Republic*, and *Time Out*, all consider it an essential part of their job to "cover" important trends in theater: new plays, rising playwrights, stars and promising newcomers, controversies, and important changes in the direction of theater companies. Reviews in any of these magazines are good points of entry into the cultural conversation about theater. So is your local newspaper, whether you live in or near a city with professional theater, or if your college paper covers campus theatrical productions.

Reviews in big-city newspapers and magazines are usually the province of professionals chosen both for their knowledge of the genre and their writing style. This chapter includes some model reviews: a full review of the 2004 Broadway production of Lorraine Hansberry's *A Raisin in the Sun*; a review of a 1997 production of Ibsen's *A Doll's House,* with an emphasis on the star, Janet McTeer; and two very brief reviews. Note that all these reviews are full of claims, backed by observations used as evidence. Their purpose is to start the conversation rolling. Readers do not have to agree with everything in the reviews, but like all well-done examples of their type, they provide us with a sharp opinion backed by thoughtfully presented evidence.

Full Review

In a full review, the reviewer must address the play itself, the acting, the direction, the costumes and setting, and the lighting. Reviews are frankly evaluative, judging every aspect of the performance. The all-knowing voice that characterizes many reviewers can be unattractive to some readers. They ask, "What makes

_____ such a judge of drama?" or "Where does _____ get off telling us what's good or bad about the play?" Those responses to the critic's tone and manner are common, particularly among those whose plays are criticized, but among the rest of us too. Many people dislike critics precisely because they seem too critical—and yet that is what they are paid for. Do not let that all-knowing voice of the professional critic daunt you. The papers you write do not have to assume an overbearing or high-handed tone. In fact, many professional critics today have become less imperious and more down to earth and personal. The best critics still have strong opinions, but they present them as their own, not the arrogant voices of some great, objective authority. So read these professional reviews for an understanding both of the format and of the critic's standards for evaluation. A good critic has both instincts and taste but, equally important, the means of making readers see where the judgment comes from. If you do not know the reasons for the judgment, a critical evaluation is worthless.

Ben Brantley

Full Review: *A Raisin in the Sun*

When a new production of Lorraine Hansberry's play *A Raisin in the Sun* opened on Broadway in 2004, it received a full review by theater critic Ben Brantley of the *New York Times*. (For the text of Hansberry's play, see p. 1791.)

A Breakthrough 50s Drama Revived in a Suspenseful Mood

Theater Review: A Raisin in the Sun, by Lorraine Hansberry. Directed by Kenny Leon. Reviewed by Ben Brantley, New York Times, April 27, 2004.

Sean Combs's shadow precedes him at the Royale Theater. That's literally as well as figuratively. In the moment before Mr. Combs makes his hotly awaited entrance in the seriously off-center revival of Lorraine Hansberry's *Raisin in the Sun*, which opened last night, his wavering shadow is cast from offstage, heralding his arrival like a soft, urgent fanfare. Audra McDonald, the first-rate actress playing his wife, calls his character's name—"Walter Lee, it's time for you to get up!"—and you can feel the audience drawing a collective breath.

Mr. Combs, of course, is the entertainment mogul, hip-hop artist, fashion entrepreneur and professional famous person better known as P. Diddy (and formerly known as Puff Daddy). His participation makes this production of Hansberry's epochal drama, which is directed by Kenny Leon and also stars Phylicia Rashad, a highly suspenseful event in a season when theatrically green celebrities from Farrah Fawcett to Ashley Judd have turned to road kill on New York stages.

Mr. Combs's anticipatory shadow thus hovers like a question mark over Thomas Lynch's scrupulously shabby evocation of a lower-middle-class apartment in Southside Chicago in the 1950's. Will the very 21st-century figure who is Mr. Combs, whose career has been a sustained triumph of nerve over probability, be able to turn into a man of continually thwarted dreams of the mid-20th century? Will he prove that you don't need long years of experience and training to knock 'em dead on Broadway?

For as much as 10 minutes after Mr. Combs hits the stage, looking appealingly tousled and sleepy-eyed, these questions are left hanging. Portraying Walter Lee Younger, a role immortalized by Sidney Poitier on Broadway in 1959 and in the 1961 film, Mr. Combs seems at first to have made a daring actor's choice that he just might pull off.

Raisin in the Sun depicts Walter Lee's belated emergence into manhood. And in his opening scene—as he pouts and teases with his wife, Ruth (Ms. McDonald)—Mr. Combs's Walter evokes a man who in his 30's is still marooned in early adolescence. You might even mistake this Walter for the older brother of Travis (Alexander Mitchell), the little boy who is in fact his son. Clearly, Mr. Combs has left lots of space for Walter to grow. Unfortunately, that space is never filled.

This omission makes the revival a lopsided and ultimately dreary affair. Though the production features sterling work from Ms. McDonald and Ms. Rashad, who plays Walter Lee's formidable mother, it lacks the fully developed central performance from Mr. Combs that would hold the show together. This Walter Lee never appears to change, in big ways or small. Happy or sad, drunk or sober, angry or placating, his evenly measured words and debating team captain's gestures remain pretty much the same.

This is a significant problem, since Walter Lee is meant to represent a new generational spirit among African-Americans in a time of social transition. And neither Mr. Combs nor the exceptionally pretty Sanaa Lathan—as Walter Lee's ambitious sister, Beneatha, who is studying to be a doctor—makes an argument for this generation as one to pin your hopes on.

From beginning to end, they register as petulant, spoiled overgrown children with none of the complexity of the maternal figures played by Ms. McDonald and Ms. Rashad. This *Raisin* is all about the kids versus the grown-ups, and not in the sense that Hansberry meant it. Instead of contrasting the forces of conservative, God-fearing womanhood with a fresh revolutionary spirit, the show becomes an ungainly counterpoint of mature and callow acting styles.

It's an approach that deprives audiences of an empathetic handle on the trials of the Lee family, headed by the widowed Lena (Ms. Rashad). And it never lets this sturdy kitchen-sink drama involve you even as a soap opera. The plot—built on the Younger family's squabbles over what to do with the $10,000 life insurance policy on Walter Lee's father that has come due—may seem creaky in the best of productions.

But as was evident in the more consistent revival at the Williamstown Theater Festival five years ago, *Raisin* was remarkably prescient in identifying issues that would continue to shape African-American life: black men's struggles for self-assertion in households dominated by strong women; the movement to separate African from American identities; Christianity as both an oppressive and redemptive power; the restlessness of women imprisoned by domesticity—all these elements come into play in Hansberry's drama. And that's not to mention the plot pivot in which the Younger family plans to move into a white neighborhood.

Abstract conflicts are given engagingly particular life by Ms. McDonald, a three-time Tony winner, and by Ms. Rashad. Her natural radiance clouded with bone-weariness, Ms. McDonald's Ruth is a life force on the verge of extinction, tethered to an ironing board and her husband's self-centeredness. An unrecognizably folksy, mother-hen-ish Ms. Rashad, who played a very different sort of matriarch on *The Cosby Show* on television, admirably finds both the strengths and weaknesses in blind maternal love.

These women become invaluable touchstones. Whenever you want to read the emotional content of a scene, it's their faces you must look to. If they're not onstage, you're in trouble, since Mr. Leon has otherwise emphasized the single-note, high-pitched, perky style of sitcoms. (The audience laughs at bewilderingly unexpected places.)

Mr. Combs is not the wholesale embarrassment that connoisseurs of schadenfreude were hoping for. The Donald Trump-like confidence that has made him the success he is keeps him from dissolving into a spotlighted puddle. But he comes across as smaller than you might expect, as Madonna did when she made her Broadway debut in *Speed the Plow*.

Most dispiriting, though, is his lack of variety. Though his eyes gleam promisingly in the early scenes, there is rarely a flicker of transforming feeling on his handsome, self-assured face. You can only sympathize with Mr. Leon, who has come up with various devices for working around this stolidity, like having Walter Lee freeze with his back to the audience to stare moodily out the window.

In the climactic moment when Walter Lee discovers that he may have destroyed his family's prospects for happiness, Mr. Combs simply buries his face in his hands, while occasionally registering anguish by massaging his scalp. All things considered, this was probably the right choice.

Ross Wetzsteon

Personal Notice: Janet McTeer in *A Doll's House*

The personal notice is a type of review that emphasizes a single performance, set in the context of the play, but with almost all the focus on one actor and very little on the play as a whole. Thus the details that would appear in a full review of the play get omitted, because the writer concentrates entirely on the star. In the personal notice that follows, the focus is on Janet McTeer, performing the role of Nora in Henrik Ibsen's *A Doll's House* (For the text of Ibsen's play, see p. 1562.)

Janet McTeer in **A Doll's House** *by Henrik Ibsen.*

Reviewed by Ross Wetzsteon, Village Voice, April 9, 1997.

Every actress would like to play the most legendary Nora but, for much of the first act, Janet McTeer seems to want to play the most irritating. She's an unusually sexy Nora, but in an annoyingly kittenish way: flighty and fluttery, as the role calls for, but with a whimpering and giggling nervousness. This Nora, we begin to think, isn't so much a woman as a collection of manic mannerisms. But we gradually realize that this Nora, in fact, is playing the role that's expected of her—merely "playing tricks," as she says in the last act—and that there's another Nora beneath the childlike silliness that will astonish even her. There is so much she's not allowed to experience, much less express—her native intelligence, her creative energy, her increasing unhappiness—so much that can emerge only in distortion.

McTeer's bold choice to play Nora as far more fraught than usual at the beginning of the play—with a hyperanimation that, in her increasing frustration, becomes nervous exhaustion and eventually a kind of hysterical dementia—al-

Janet McTeer as Nora in the 1997 production of Ibsen's A Doll's House.

lows her to make Nora's transformation at the end at once more plausible and more powerful. Some critics have suggested that her performance—like most performances of the role—turns Nora into two different and irreconcilable characters, the domestic doll and the feminist icon. But, on the contrary, she subtly provides the psychological continuity between these two aspects of her character.

In the opening scenes, for instance, even as McTeer enacts Nora's dependence on her husband, she shows the cunning that is the only outlet for the character's acute and sensitive mind—submission as manipulation. This is no ninny—this is a woman forbidden to use her intelligence. And even as she proclaims her happiness, McTeer's Nora reaches compulsively for her macaroons with a hint of voracity that hints at her dissatisfaction.

Nora's jittery, skittery behavior is charming in a way. It's certainly the kind of self-abasing flirtatiousness her husband finds seductive. (McTeer's decision to play Nora's marriage as erotically electric makes Nora's decision to leave all the more difficult, and all the more shattering.) But when her web of lies begins to unravel and he calls her "pretty bird," she rolls her eyes in a gesture at once accepting of his flattery, aware of her deceit, and resentful of his condescension. She knows nothing of this consciously but, in dozens of such gestures, McTeer reveals the unconscious conflation of Nora's conflicts—the way her wildly unfocused energy is the consequence of her inner turmoil, of both social oppression and emotional repression. Over and over, McTeer portrays a Nora with a capacity for feeling she herself refuses to recognize and a capacity for insight frustrated by her familial role. When she hears herself saying that being with her husband is "like being with papa," she pauses for a second, then flashes her eyes with something close to a recognition of primal sin, utters a sound somewhere between a hysterical giggle and a shriek of horror, and rushes across the room as if in flight from her own words.

By the final confrontation with her husband, McTeer has so skillfully foreshadowed Nora's transformation that, though it seems bewilderingly abrupt to her, it seems emotionally inevitable to us. Gone are her neurotic mannerisms. Nora now sits in an ominous stillness. "I'm saved," her husband says after the arrival of the forgiving letter. "What about me?" Nora responds, with a touch of meekness but at last with a sense of her separable self. Out of her stillness she suddenly shrieks, not as an appeal but as a demand, "I'm a human being!" Most astonishingly—for the first time in my experience of half a dozen Noras—McTeer even manages to make Nora's single most famous line ring true. When her husband says that no man would sacrifice his integrity for another person, Nora has to reply, "Hundreds of thousands of women have"— an impossible line for the character, a line in which it is not Nora speaking but Ibsen himself. McTeer's solution? She lowers her voice a full octave and intones the words in a constrained fury—the voice not of Nora but of wronged women forever.

Brief Reviews

Many papers and magazines recycle their full-length reviews when they do weekly updates or entertainment guides. There is no room to reprint a full review of a play that opened two weeks ago, but many readers still need some kind of brief guidance, so the thumbnail sketch or brief digest of the original review is used. Here are two brief reviews that were drawn from full-length reviews:

Brief Review, Janet McTeer in Ibsen's A Doll's House

The classic drama of conflict within a "perfect" marriage, as Nora must now confront a past misdeed and hope her husband forgives her. A tense, well-paced production, with star turns from the married couple, especially the electric Janet McTeer as a Nora who transforms herself from flighty young wife to determined woman.

Brief Review, Janet McTeer in Ibsen's A Doll's House

Janet McTeer turns Nora into a sensual, confused wife who must confront life on her own terms, without the husband she has relied on too much for indulgent support. A not-to-be missed performance that brings electric energy and passion to a classic play. Nora will never again be the same.

The key to these short reviews is their focus on the single most telling quality of the longer piece from which they are excerpted; it is a matter of choosing the most striking point or claim and leaving out the rest.

Writing about the Text

1. Choose a current review from a magazine or newspaper and explain how it makes its evaluations. How much explanation does the writer give? Are you satisfied with the way the writer evaluates?
2. Write a full review (two-page maximum) of a play, movie, or TV show you have just seen, aiming it at readers who do not know much about it.

3. After you have done the full review for exercise 2, boil it down to a two-sentence review, the kind that would appear in *TV Guide* or an entertainment column of a newspaper.

BEYOND REVIEWS: CRITICISM

As with criticism about fiction and poetry, many people tend to think of criticism about drama as a kind of closed circle, written only by scholars and critics for an audience of other scholars and critics. But as with criticism about other literary genres, there is a wider use of the term "criticism" that comfortably extends to analytical and explanatory writing about drama aimed at a much wider audience. For example, some dramatic situations and characters are so much a part of our culture that they constantly get analyzed, interpreted, and reinterpreted. Oedipus is a good example, a character built out of myth and ritual who has animated many thinkers to investigate him or, like the psychologist Sigmund Freud, to imagine his quest as deeply intertwined in human personality. Similarly, Shakespearean characters like Lady Macbeth, Romeo and Juliet, Caliban, Ophelia, and Hamlet, among others, are part of who we are as humans in Western culture. Their stories draw a great deal of critical examination, discussion, and argument, and not just from literature scholars and reviewers. Even if you do not know these characters or have never heard of the plays they are in, they are "in the air," part of what educated people know.

In addition to reviews, criticism extends to the large amount of writing carried on about the meaning and significance of key playwrights: Henrik Ibsen, Sophocles, Molière, Samuel Beckett, and the more contemporary Sam Shepard, Tony Kushner, and Yasmina Reza, to name just a few. These dramatists show us who we are, or at least raise disturbing, uncomfortable, or interesting questions about our culture and society. For instance, it is hard to write about the impact of AIDS on society without referring to *Angels in America*, Tony Kushner's powerful drama that appeared onstage in many American cities and was adapted for cable TV. Critics write and talk about all these authors, their plays, and the characters they have created. They aim their discussions at the educated public interested in the issues or simply at people who like to follow the critical conversation about culture.

Popular Criticism

As with criticism about fiction and poetry, one way to distinguish between popular pieces and scholarly articles about drama is to evaluate the publication source. Does the piece appear in a general-interest magazine like *Time*, *Harper's*, or the *Atlantic Monthly*, which are available on every newsstand? Or is it in a small-circulation scholarly or academic journal, such as the *Shakespeare Quarterly* or *Modern Language Quarterly*, usually published through university presses? The level of documentation used and the intended audience of the piece will also give you an indication of what kind of criticism you are reading.

The following piece by Michiko Kakutani is an example of popular criticism. Kakutani, a well-known critic and columnist for the *New York Times*, uses the fiftieth anniversary of the 1949 world premiere of *Death of a Salesman* as an occasion to contemplate the continuing appeal of Arthur Miller's best-known play.

MICHIKO KAKUTANI

A Salesman Who Transcends Time

From *The* New York Times, FEBRUARY 7, 1999.

A half-century after its premiere, *Death of a Salesman* has become an American classic—a perennial produced around the world, from Baltimore to Beijing, and routinely taught in high school English classes and mounted in community theaters. The play has become an institution, part of the accepted theater canon, and today even boasts its own website (www.deathofasalesman.com), where, in an ironic twist on its central theme, you will be able to purchase souvenirs.

With the opening on Wednesday of the Goodman Theater's new production of *Salesman* at the Eugene O'Neill Theater on Broadway—50 years to the day from the play's 1949 world premiere—it is clear that many of the debates that attended the original opening have long since become obsolete. We no longer question whether a play about a little man (a "low-man," as opposed to a king or powerful ruler) can be called a tragedy, just as we no longer question the ethnicity of the play's hero, the Jewishness or non-Jewishness of his locution.

At the same time, however, other debates persist. While *Salesman* opened to—and has continued to enjoy—enormous popular success, both the play and its author have maintained a less than stellar reputation among many highbrow critics. *Salesman* has been debunked as a didactic commentary on the bankruptcy of the American dream of success, while Mr. Miller has been dismissed as an epigone of Ibsenism, a preachy, pompous and, yes, portentous writer who belongs, like Clifford Odets and Lillian Hellman, to a middlebrow, pre-modernist past. In retrospect, it is an overly simplistic judgment—especially when it comes to *Salesman*, Mr. Miller's most famous, most enduring and in many ways most anomalous play.

Oddly enough, Mr. Miller's own ponderous pronouncements have tended to reinforce the perception of his work as an outmoded form of social realism. In one 1950 essay, he argued that *Death of a Salesman*—which chronicles the last day in the life of a salesman named Willy Loman, who has lost his job, and, he fears, the love of his son Biff—is "the tragedy of a man who did believe that he alone was not meeting the qualifications laid down for mankind by those clean-shaven frontiersmen who inhabit the peaks of broadcasting and advertising offices."

Willy the failed salesman and willful suicide, Mr. Miller suggested in his own autobiography, represents the fate of a true believer in America's false dream of success: "This pseudo life that thought to touch the clouds by standing on top of a refrigerator, waving a paid-up mortgage at the moon, victorious at last." His singleminded pursuit of success has blinded him to the love of his own family, robbed him of his sense of self, and left him to subsist on a diet of illusions.

In contrast to Eugene O'Neill, who declared that he was "interested only in the relation of man and God," Mr. Miller has implied that the tragedy in his own work springs from the relation between man and his environment, between man and the conditions that suppress him and pervert "the flowing out of his love and creative instinct." The playwright's own unhappy experiences during the Depression and the 1950's, when he was convicted of contempt of Congress for refusing to name names before the House Un-American Activities Committee, persuaded him, he has said, that politics "determines the exteriors of your personality," and he remained convinced, he once stated, that all serious plays ultimately address a single question: "How may a man make of the outside world a home?"

Truly great work, he declared in a 1958 interview, is "that work which will show at one and the same time the power and force of the human will working with and against the force of society upon it."

Yet in Robert Falls's darkly hued new staging from Chicago, *Death of a Salesman* seems less a social drama about what Harold Clurman called "the breakdown of the whole concept of salesmanship inherent in our society" than a fierce portrait of a father and son, caught in a fatal embrace of love and resentment and guilt. And Brian Dennehy's Willy Loman seems less a man, in Mr. Miller's words, who "embodies in himself some of the most terrible conflicts running through the streets of America today" than a perpetual adolescent caught in the dizzying gap between reality and his own expectations. This Willy Loman, like Dustin Hoffman's in 1984 on Broadway, may not be a tragic figure—to the last moment, self-awareness continues to elude him—but like Kierkegaard's "unhappiest man," he is a touching one, subsisting on past memory and future hope. His dilemmas are more psychological than sociological, more existential than environmental.

The play's structure, too, seems a far cry from the rough-hewn carpentry often associated with Mr. Miller's work. There is a dreamlike quality to *Salesman*, an expressionistic invocation of shifting moods and time frames that helps conceal the creaky stage machinery apparent in so many other Miller plays from *All My Sons* (1947) to *Broken Glass* (1994).

Certainly *Salesman*, too, has its problems: a paint-by-numbers Freudianism, a conveniently withheld secret that overshadows the second act, and supporting characters who are little more than cardboard cutouts. As written, Willy's long-suffering wife, Linda, is basically a doormat—a passive accomplice in her husband's denial, what we would today call an enabler. And Willy's successful brother, Ben—who walked into the jungle at 17, and walked out at 21, a rich man with diamonds in his pockets—remains a transparent symbol of rough and ready capitalism, a Horatio Alger joke.

These flaws, however, are subsumed by the play's visceral and deeply affecting portrait of father and son: Willy, intent for years on passing on to his son his own tarnished dreams; and Biff, finally shorn of those illusions, intent on making his father face the hard facts of his existence. The play limns Willy's fears of losing Biff's love and his own longings for immortality—his desire not just to be liked, but to be well liked—and it immerses the audience in Willy's conflicted, contradictory state of mind. In fact, Mr. Miller once noted that his original title for *Salesman* was *The Inside of His Head*.

The play was constructed on the premise that Willy, in his growing panic and confusion, sees time not as a continuum but as a simultaneity of moments past and present. In the play's confessional structure, current anxieties fade into remembered guilts, and dreams and regrets blur and overlap—a structure not dissimilar to the narrative strategy adopted by Mr. Miller in his own 1987 autobiography, *Timebends*. The play, Mr. Miller wrote in that book, was meant to "cut through time like a knife through a layer cake or a road through a mountain revealing its geologic layers."

In later works like *After the Fall* (1964) and *The Price* (1968), Mr. Miller would again try to focus on his characters' inner lives, but never again with such urgency and skill as in *Salesman*. His other better-known plays would remain rooted in more topical concerns and feature characters who are more clearly symbols than flesh-and-blood human beings. *All My Sons* (1947) depicts a businessman—read greedy capitalist—covering up his role in the manufacture of defective parts that doomed 21 Air Force planes during World War II. *The Crucible* (1953) uses the Salem witch hunts of the late 1600's as a metaphor for the Communist witch hunts of the 1950's. *A View From the Bridge* (1955) examines the costs of McCarthy-era betrayal through its portrait of a longshoreman who rats on two illegal immigrants. *The American Clock* (1980), inspired by Studs Terkel's *Hard Times*, attempts to provide a panoramic portrait of the Depression. And *The Ride Down Mount Morgan* (1991) casts a cold eye on the rampant selfishness of the Reagan era. All too often in these works, Mr. Miller's efforts to "prove the theme" result in sanctimonious speechifying, message-driven melodramatics and two-dimensional characters who come across as illustrations of one or more social ills.

In recent years, the most successful productions of these works have played down the political, polemic aspects of the texts, to reveal their psychological subtext, the bedrock emotions of sexual passion and familial love, betrayal and guilt that lurk beneath the sociology. Last year, the Roundabout Theater Company's highly acclaimed production of *A View From the Bridge* shrugged off the play's McCarthy-era echoes to focus on the hero's secret obsession with his wife's teen-age niece and the psychosexual drives that lead him to commit a shocking act of betrayal. Nicholas Hytner's dazzling 1996 movie version of *The Crucible* similarly stripped away that play's McCarthy-era moorings: by firmly grounding the story in the particulars of 17th-century Salem, the film uncovered the story's primal drama, its fascination with the consequences of lying and deception and sexual repression.

The success of such productions underscores the current renaissance that Mr. Miller has been enjoying—not just in England, where his work has found a ready audience among theatergoers reared, since the heyday of anti-Thatcherism, on politically committed playwriting, but also here in the States, where the Signature Theater Company recently completed a yearlong retrospective of his plays in New York.

What accounts for Mr. Miller's continuing appeal? Perhaps some of the very aspects of his work that seem so old-fashioned—his moral seriousness and fondness for mythic intonations (inspired by his favorite works, the Bible and Greek tragedies)—are refreshing anomalies in this age of relentless irony and cynicism.

In a day when the avant-garde has insistently purveyed a vision of a fractured, fragmented world, Mr. Miller's assumption that "life has meaning" appeals to our vestigial belief (or hope) that the dots can be connected, that a pattern can be found in the carpet. And in a day when the arts are increasingly becoming a form of entertainment, when the commercial theater has increasingly given us slice-of-life dramas, brittle satires and glitzy theme-park musicals, his efforts, however ham-handed, to address the large questions of right and wrong suggest that the theater still matters, that it can still provide a venue for intellectual debate.

Indeed, his plays attest to his own belief that works of art can "change the consciousness of people and their estimate of who they are and what they stand for."

Although Kakutani's piece incorporates a mini-review of the highly praised 1999 Broadway revival of *Salesman* starring Brian Dennehy as Willy Loman, the mainstay of the article is, in essence, a more general critique and analysis of the enduring quality of the play in the context of Miller's larger body of work. This content and focus clearly embody the central difference between reviews and criticism. While the aim of a theater review is to evaluate a particular production, this critical article focuses more broadly on the meaning and significance of Willy Loman as one of the most enduring characters in modern American drama and of Arthur Miller's ongoing appeal as a playwright.

SCHOLARLY ARTICLES OR ESSAYS

In contrast to popular articles, a scholarly piece is usually written by an academic expert in the field and presents a claim or interpretation about a playwright, a play, or the field of drama in general, employing research and containing extensive examples in support of the argument being made. The intended audience is usually other academics and experts in the field, as well as graduate and undergraduate students, and the language employed tends to be more formal and more academic in tone. However, there is also a long-standing history of literary scholars and critics who write for a wider general audience, as in the famous critical essay by poet and critic T. S. Eliot on Shakespeare's *Hamlet*, "Hamlet and His Problems," which follows.

T. S. ELIOT   (1888–1965)
Hamlet and His Problems   (1919)

Few critics have even admitted that *Hamlet* the play is the primary problem, and Hamlet the character only secondary. And Hamlet the character has had an especial temptation for that most dangerous type of critic: the critic with a mind which is naturally of the creative order, but which through some weakness in creative power exercises itself in criticism instead. These minds often find in Hamlet a vicarious existence for their own artistic realization. Such a mind had Goethe, who made of Hamlet a Werther; and such had Coleridge, who made of Hamlet a Coleridge; and probably neither of these men in writing about Hamlet remembered that his first business was to study a work of art. The kind of criticism that Goethe and Coleridge produced, in writing of Hamlet, is the most misleading kind possible. For they both possessed unquestionable critical insight, and both make their critical aberrations the more plausible by the substitution—

of their own Hamlet for Shakespeare's—which their creative gift effects. We should be thankful that Walter Pater did not fix his attention on this play.

Two recent writers, Mr. J. M. Robertson and Professor Stoll of the University of Minnesota, have issued small books which can be praised for moving in the other direction. Mr. Stoll performs a service in recalling to our attention the labours of the critics of the seventeenth and eighteenth centuries,[1] observing that they knew less about psychology than more recent Hamlet critics, but they were nearer in spirit to Shakespeare's art; and as they insisted on the importance of the effect of the whole rather than on the importance of the leading character, they were nearer, in their old-fashioned way, to the secret of dramatic art in general.

Qua work of art, the work of art cannot be interpreted; there is nothing to interpret; we can only criticize it according to standards, in comparison to other works of art; and for "interpretation" the chief task is the presentation of relevant historical facts which the reader is not assumed to know. Mr. Robertson points out, very pertinently, how critics have failed in their "interpretation" of *Hamlet* by ignoring what ought to be very obvious: that *Hamlet* is a stratification, that it represents the efforts of a series of men, each making what he could out of the work of his predecessors. The *Hamlet* of Shakespeare will appear to us very differently if, instead of treating the whole action of the play as due to Shakespeare's design, we perceive his *Hamlet* to be superposed upon much cruder material which persists even in the final form.

We know that there was an older play by Thomas Kyd, that extraordinary dramatic (if not poetic) genius who was in all probability the author of two plays so dissimilar as the *Spanish Tragedy* and *Arden of Feversham*; and what this play was like we can guess from three clues: from the Spanish Tragedy itself, from the tale of Belleforest upon which Kyd's *Hamlet* must have been based, and from a version acted in Germany in Shakespeare's lifetime which bears strong evidence of having been adapted from the earlier, not from the later, play. From these three sources it is clear that in the earlier play the motive was a revenge-motive simply; that the action or delay is caused, as in the *Spanish Tragedy*, solely by the difficulty of assassinating a monarch surrounded by guards; and that the "madness" of Hamlet was feigned in order to escape suspicion, and successfully. In the final play of Shakespeare, on the other hand, there is a motive which is more important than that of revenge, and which explicitly "blunts" the latter; the delay in revenge is unexplained on grounds of necessity or expediency; and the effect of the "madness" is not to lull but to arouse the king's suspicion. The alteration is not complete enough, however, to be convincing. Furthermore, there are verbal parallels so close to the *Spanish Tragedy* as to leave no doubt that in places Shakespeare was merely *revising* the text of Kyd. And finally there are unexplained scenes—the Polonius-Laertes and the Polonius-Reynaldo scenes—for which there is little excuse; these scenes are not in the verse style of Kyd, and not beyond doubt in the style of Shakespeare. These Mr. Robertson believes to be scenes in the original play of Kyd reworked by a third hand, perhaps Chapman, before Shakespeare touched the play. And he concludes, with very strong show of reason, that the original play of Kyd was, like certain other revenge

---

[1] I have never, by the way, seen a cogent refutation of Thomas Rymer's objections to *Othello*. [Eliot's note]

plays, in two parts of five acts each. The upshot of Mr. Robertson's examination is, we believe, irrefragable: that Shakespeare's *Hamlet,* so far as it is Shakespeare's, is a play dealing with the effect of a mother's guilt upon her son, and that Shakespeare was unable to impose this motive successfully upon the "intractable" material of the old play.

Of the intractability there can be no doubt. So far from being Shakespeare's masterpiece, the play is most certainly an artistic failure. In several ways the play is puzzling, and disquieting as is none of the others. Of all the plays it is the longest and is possibly the one on which Shakespeare spent most pains; and yet he has left in it superfluous and inconsistent scenes which even hasty revision should have noticed. The versification is variable. Lines like

> Look, the morn, in russet mantle clad,
> Walks o'er the dew of yon high eastern hill,

are of the Shakespeare of *Romeo and Juliet.* The lines in Act V, sc. ii.,

> Sir, in my heart there was a kind of fighting
> That would not let me sleep . . .
> Up from my cabin,
> My sea-gown scarf'd about me, in the dark
> Grop'd I to find out them: had my desire;
> Finger'd their packet;

are of his quite mature. Both workmanship and thought are in an unstable condition. We are surely justified in attributing the play, with that other profoundly interesting play of "intractable" material and astonishing versification, *Measure for Measure,* to a period of crisis, after which follow the tragic successes which culminate in *Coriolanus. Coriolanus* may be not as "interesting" as *Hamlet,* but it is, with *Antony and Cleopatra,* Shakespeare's most assured artistic success. And probably more people have thought *Hamlet* a work of art because they found it interesting, than have found it interesting because it is a work of art. It is the "Mona Lisa" of literature.

The grounds of *Hamlet's* failure are not immediately obvious. Mr. Robertson is undoubtedly correct in concluding that the essential emotion of the play is the feeling of a son towards a guilty mother:

> [Hamlet's] tone is that of one who has suffered tortures on the score of his mother's degradation. . . . The guilt of a mother is an almost intolerable motive for drama, but it had to be maintained and emphasized to supply a psychological solution, or rather a hint of one.

This, however, is by no means the whole story. It is not merely the "guilt of a mother" that cannot be handled as Shakespeare handled the suspicion of Othello, the infatuation of Antony, or the pride of Coriolanus. The subject might conceivably have expanded into a tragedy like these, intelligible, self-complete, in the sunlight. *Hamlet,* like the sonnets, is full of some stuff that the writer could not drag to light, contemplate, or manipulate into art. And when we search for this feeling, we find it, as in the sonnets, very difficult to localize. You cannot point to it in the speeches; indeed, if you examine the two famous soliloquies you see the versification of Shakespeare, but a content which might be claimed by another, perhaps by the author of the *Revenge of Bussy d' Ambois,* Act

V, sc. i. We find Shakespeare's *Hamlet* not in the action, not in any quotations that we might select, so much as in an unmistakable tone which is unmistakably not in the earlier play.

The only way of expressing emotion in the form of art is by finding an "objective correlative"; in other words, a set of objects, a situation, a chain of events which shall be the formula of that *particular* emotion; such that when the external facts, which must terminate in sensory experience, are given, the emotion is immediately evoked. If you examine any of Shakespeare's more successful tragedies, you will find this exact equivalence; you will find that the state of mind of Lady Macbeth walking in her sleep has been communicated to you by a skilful accumulation of imagined sensory impressions; the words of Macbeth on hearing of his wife's death strike us as if, given the sequence of events, these words were automatically released by the last event in the series. The artistic "inevitability" lies in this complete adequacy of the external to the emotion; and this is precisely what is deficient in *Hamlet*. Hamlet (the man) is dominated by an emotion which is inexpressible, because it is in *excess* of the facts as they appear. And the supposed identity of Hamlet with his author is genuine to this point: that Hamlet's bafflement at the absence of objective equivalent to his feelings is a prolongation of the bafflement of his creator in the face of his artistic problem. Hamlet is up against the difficulty that his disgust is occasioned by his mother, but that his mother is not an adequate equivalent for it; his disgust envelops and exceeds her. It is thus a feeling which he cannot understand; he cannot objectify it, and it therefore remains to poison life and obstruct action. None of the possible actions can satisfy it; and nothing that Shakespeare can do with the plot can express Hamlet for him. And it must be noticed that the very nature of the *données* of the problem precludes objective equivalence. To have heightened the criminality of Gertrude would have been to provide the formula for a totally different emotion in Hamlet; it is just *because* her character is so negative and insignificant that she arouses in Hamlet the feeling which she is incapable of representing.

The "madness" of Hamlet lay to Shakespeare's hand; in the earlier play a simple ruse, and to the end, we may presume, understood as a ruse by the audience. For Shakespeare it is less than madness and more than feigned. The levity of Hamlet, his repetition of phrase, his puns, are not part of a deliberate plan of dissimulation, but a form of emotional relief. In the character Hamlet it is the buffoonery of an emotion which can find no outlet in action; in the dramatist it is the buffoonery of an emotion which he cannot express in art. The intense feeling, ecstatic or terrible, without an object or exceeding its object, is something which every person of sensibility has known; it is doubtless a study to pathologists. It often occurs in adolescence: the ordinary person puts these feelings to sleep, or trims down his feeling to fit the business world; the artist keeps it alive by his ability to intensify the world to his emotions. The Hamlet of Laforgue is an adolescent; the Hamlet of Shakespeare is not, he has not that explanation and excuse. We must simply admit that here Shakespeare tackled a problem which proved too much for him. Why he attempted it at all is an insoluble puzzle; under compulsion of what experience he attempted to express the inexpressibly horrible, we cannot ever know. We need a great many facts in his biography; and we should like to know whether, and when, and after or at the same time as what personal experience, he read Montaigne, II, xii, *Apologie de Raimond Se-*

bond. We should have, finally, to know something which is by hypothesis un-knowable, for we assume it to be an experience which, in the manner indicated, exceeded the facts. We should have to understand things which Shakespeare did not understand himself.

In contrast to the less formal *New York Times* article on *Death of a Salesman,* Eliot's essay offers an analysis not only of Hamlet the character, and *Hamlet* the play, but also of previous scholarly interpretations of Shakespeare's most enig-matic character and text as well as an evaluation of general approaches to liter-ary critical analysis.

HOW TO ENTER THE CONVERSATION

Where do students taking English courses fit into these ongoing discussions? Few will become reviewers, critics, or scholars. How can students find a place to speak out, to join the conversation? Or, to put the question differently, how can a student lacking experience learn how to talk and, especially, to write about drama? How can students make intelligent contributions even though they lack the experience and all-knowing tone of the drama scholar or theater critic?

Reviews, an important part of the cultural conversation, are readily accessi-ble to many students. You can read them to see how they are put together, and you will find it surprisingly easy to get assigned to write them. Reading reviews is a first step to seeing how writers go about the task of evaluating a performance. Looking at many reviews of the same play can help you understand how much room is available for personal preferences and how much space must be devoted to each area of the performance, from the drama itself to the acting, the direc-tion, the set, the costumes, and the lighting.

Beyond reading reviews, it is quite possible to write them, either as a pri-vate exercise, as part of a class, or for publication in a local or school paper or on the web, as part of a blog or through a website like http://www.gather.com, which is full of personal reviews and reactions. The best plays to start with are the officially sponsored drama productions staged on your campus. Colleges and universities put on plays involving large numbers of students as actors, stagehands, designers, and even directors. This effort is for the participants themselves as well as for other students and often the general community. This drama effort does not bring in enough money to pay for itself; like many other college-sponsored programs, such productions are seen as an essential part of the educational process. Such college drama productions are watched and re-viewed and talked and written about, so they, in turn, become a part of the continuing conversation. The campus newspaper reviews all campus produc-tions and always assigns students to write about them. The novelist Willa Cather got her start in writing this way; an example of her college writing about *Hamlet* is on p. 228.

Besides the campus theater and campus newspaper, you can get a start in writing through the literature class, where you are situated among others who are talking and writing about drama. You are clearly not doing the writing all alone, without an audience. You will be part of a group, a class, under the guidance of a professional, the teacher. The conversation here is concerned not only with what is playing this week or this month on campus (though that is helpful) but also with how drama works, and how a diverse group of students can connect to it through reading the texts and occasionally seeing professional productions. Here the conversation—one among many about drama—can be very rich, with regular assignments and ample feedback.

QUESTIONS TO DEVELOP IDEAS ABOUT A PLAY

This section provides you with two key approaches to a reading or viewing of a drama: useful questions about a play, and some helpful formats to use when you sit down to do the writing. These two approaches are not completely separate. The questions to ask and the types of writing go together. The questions listed below and the formats that follow them are not abstract categories but instead living examples of how to enter into the critical conversation through writing.

As you read or watch a play, first think about these questions. Your answers to them might result in lists of incidents, words, or even gestures. Be as detailed as you wish, since everything you notice can be turned into evidence or support for your writing. The answers you supply will become the material you need to write about drama in many different kinds of formats, from a quick reaction or response paper to a more elaborate research project.

Perspective

1. What has happened just before the action starts?
2. How does the dramatist fill us in on the background?
3. What general kind of drama does the play seem to present: comedy, tragedy, melodrama, or some other genre? What is the style of the play: realistic, symbolic, ritualistic, farcical?
4. (For viewers) How has the director staged the action? Streamlined? Slow paced? Quick?
5. (For viewers) How do characters relate with each other? Mainly through quick give and take? Or through slow interactions? Is this consistent?

Language

1. What is the level of the language? High? Middle? Low?
2. Does the language seem contemporary, old-fashioned, or in between? Can you pin this answer down with examples?
3. Did you notice any specialized type of vocabulary? Any words you needed to look up? Any non-English words or phrases?
4. Was the language particularly colorful, or did it not draw attention to itself?
5. Did you note examples of irony? Symbolism? Any notable qualities of tone?

Setting

1. When and where did the action take place? Did the setting change from scene to scene?

2. (For viewers) What was most striking about the set? The costumes?
3. (For viewers) Were there any special lighting or sound effects?
4. Did the setting seem an important part of the drama? Was any part of the setting more important than the rest?
5. Was the setting symbolic in any way?
6. What details of the setting seemed to call out for the most attention?

Character

1. Is it clear who the protagonist is? Who is the antagonist?
2. What is the main character's motivation? (This is what we have called the "spine.")
3. Are the characters sharply delineated, with individual characteristics, or do they seem more like stereotypes? If stereotypes, is that deliberate?
4. Do you regard the characters as realistically portrayed?
5. What changes take place in characters during the play?
6. Did you find yourself identifying with any of the characters?

Plot

1. Can you state the story's main action in a sentence?
2. How does the plot unfold? Chronologically? Are there flashbacks? Is there any foreshadowing?
3. Did you feel manipulated by the plot? Was there a surprise ending? Tricks?
4. What kind of resolution occurs at the end?
5. Does the plot reach some inevitable conclusion, or are matters left open ended?
6. Can you imagine other ways to tell the story?

Links to Other Texts

1. Did this play (or parts of it, including character or setting) seem like any others you know about, or any story or film?
2. Were there any monologues you would like to hear read by a professional?
3. Can you imagine this as a short story? What would need to change?
4. What kind of "opening up" would happen if this were to be a film?
5. What words or phrases would get special emphasis if you directed this play?
6. Which parts of the play would you like to see expanded or lengthened? Which could be cut?

Response

1. Was one character especially attractive or repellent to you?
2. (For viewers) Was any particular performance a standout? Why?
3. (For viewers) What seemed most original about the staging or performance?
4. Did a particular sentence or phrase or situation catch your fancy?
5. What "got" to you in the play? A person? An incident? Something someone said?
6. Was there anything in the play that touches on what you have experienced in your own life, or in the life of someone you know?

Although these are only the beginning, they are just like the questions any professional reviewer or critic asks of a drama. They focus your attention either on the text or on the action on the stage. Think of these questions as ways of interrogating the play, of conducting a genuine dialogue with the text or stage production, forcing you to be an active reader or viewer, not a passive one. Answering the questions will pay off in two ways: it will produce a much more well-informed experience of the play, and the answers to the questions will provide rich material for the writing you will do in different formats. Beginning students confronted with a writing assignment often ask, "Where do I start?" The answer is, "Start with these questions."

VIRTUAL LOCALE

Websites and Blogs about Plays. Many Internet sites about drama seem to revolve around local theater reviews, and broader discussions of writing or performing drama have not flourished in blogs as much as poetry and fiction discussions have. There is, however, still a wealth of information and opinion out there about drama.

Some of the best online sources for theater discussion and reviews are local newspapers and alternative weeklies. Although much of the drama world revolves around New York City, many other strong theater communities have flourished across the country. In Minneapolis, the *City Pages* posts their theater news and reviews online at *http://www.citypages.com/performingarts*. The *Denver Post* at *http://www.denverpost.com/theater* and Seattle's *The Stranger* alternative weekly at *http://www.thestranger.com/seattle/Theater* have pages devoted to local theater news and reviews. Blogs containing reviews and theater writing include *http://www.handcartensemble.org/blog/*, the blog of a small New York–based theater company, and *http://www.broadwayworld.com/robsblog/*, written by the editor-in-chief of the *BroadwayWorld* website.

One common use for a blog is for recording daily musings and activities, giving us a window into one person's life. On Charles Deemer's blog, *http://www.geocities.com/cdeemer*, you can get a sense of the not-so-romantic life of being a playwright. Deemer, playwright and professor at Oregon State University, keeps readers up to date on the day-by-day progress of his teaching and writing. Sheila Callahan, a New York–based playwright, uses her website at *http://www.sheilacallaghan.com* to list upcoming work and uses her blog to keep friends and fans up to date with her daily life. And Brooklyn playwright Jason Grote talks about work, writing, and theater life on his blog, *http://www.jasongrote.blogspot.com*.

If you want to find out who played Biff in the original Broadway production of *Death of a Salesman*, or who won a Tony last year for Best Musical, the Internet Broadway Database at *http://www.ibdb.com* is your source for cast and award information for almost everything that's ever been on Broadway. Another extensive source for current theater information is Curtain Up: The Internet Theater Magazine of Reviews, Features, and Annotated Listings at *http://www.curtainup.com*. The *Arts Journal*, which calls itself a daily online journal of the best in arts journalism, has a theater page at *http://www.artsjournal.com/theatre*, with daily drama stories from major U.S. and British newspapers all in one place.

FORMATS FOR WRITING ABOUT PLAYS

Reading a play with the questions outlined above in mind produces a rich encounter with the text. The answers to the questions can be shaped in many different ways, according to the format you choose or have assigned to you. Below are some of the common kinds of writing you may do about drama.

1. Annotations can include marginal notes and underlinings that you make for personal understanding, to guide rereading, to prepare for discussion questions such as the "Talking about the Text" questions in this book, or to prepare a paper, as in this book's "Writing about the Text" questions. Directors mark up scripts with annotations called performance notes, a running commentary on how lines ought to be done.
2. A summary is a short "boiling down" of a play or scene.
3. A journal or notebook can include collections of lines, phrases, and situations worth writing down. A double-entry notebook includes noteworthy lines, phrases, and summaries on one side and your reflections and reactions on the other side.
4. A response paper contains your personal "take" on the play: what got to you, what you liked most, what it reminded you of, who you would like to see perform it. The emphasis is on you and your reaction as much as on the play.
5. An intervention occurs when you alter or play with or talk back to the text. Common forms include parody and imitation; another form is an extension, which involves adding a new character or scene, or writing a new version.
6. A critical analysis or analytical essay concentrates on explaining and examining interesting features of a play, such as language, characters, plot, setting, or structure, and making and supporting a claim about how those elements function in the play.
7. A review, as discussed earlier in this chapter, is an informative piece about a particular production that explains what the play is about, how well the actors perform, and how successful the whole production seems.
8. Research papers, longer works based on wide reading and research, contain extensive documentation in support of their claims. Research papers are covered more fully in Chapter 27.

The types of writing you are most used to doing are undoubtedly the first and the sixth: the annotation and the critical analysis or analytical essay.

Annotating a Play

Annotation refers to marking up a text in the margins or between the lines in order to gain a fuller, richer understanding of the work as you read and reread. Every time you underline a word, write in the margin, or mark a passage in a play, you are annotating it. True annotation is hardly passive; it is never a matter of waiting for ideas to strike. Instead, good annotation calls for an active reading, for your mind to seek out similarities or problems or questions. Yes, we have all seen people underlining or highlighting every line on a page, or even whole chapters, but those people are not successful annotators. To be successful you have to select, to exercise your imagination as you are reading. The thoughtfully annotated text then becomes something to return to for a refresher, or as a help for a paper or presentation.

Different purposes can lie behind annotating a play:

- A reader may make notes to reach a fuller, richer understanding of a play.
- A theater professional may make notes to guide a stage performance.

When good readers read, they fill the margins with comments and questions. And when directors arrive at a first discussion of a play with the actors, they bring with them a copy of the script, often heavily annotated. The stage manager and the lighting specialist also need detailed annotations, tied to the text, to guide them in their work. The reader's annotations and the professional's annotations serve very different purposes, so the annotations look different too. The "reader's annotations" are speculative, engaged, puzzled, enthusiastic, and often quite messy. A director's annotations are focused on tone of voice, on how the lines should "go," and on how the actors should move about, respond, or gesture. These annotations are ultimately more finished than the reader's, less speculative, since they are meant to guide the production. Of course, many good directors will alter their approach to lines and scenes based on the way they work out in rehearsal, but their original annotation of the script is the basis for all their actual direction.

Those who study film make a distinction between the screenplay—which looks much like a play, though with many camera shots indicated—and the shooting script, which is the screenplay annotated with very detailed directions for both the acting and the filming.

Student Annotations for the Opening Scene of *Trifles*

The annotations in the example below will look familiar; you have no doubt done annotations like these yourself, sometimes in the margins of the text. Here is how one student annotated the beginning of Susan Glaspell's *Trifles* during her second reading:

Doesn't old-time villain always do this before getting down to business?

Condescending back then? Probably not. But he's ordering them about and says nothing to the men.

Are they already closer? No stage direction.

COUNTY ATTORNEY: [*Rubbing his hands.*] This feels good. Come up to the fire, ladies.

MRS. PETERS: [*After taking a step forward.*] I'm not cold.

Why the hesitation? Is she saying she's frightened, that she's not cold? It's supposed to seem cold.

SHERIFF: [*Unbuttoning his overcoat and stepping away from the stove as if to mark the beginning of official business.*] Now, Mr. Hale, before we move things about, you explain to Mr. Henderson just what you saw when you came here yesterday morning.

Official sounding request for testimony

Why so specific? Must it be to the left?

COUNTY ATTORNEY: [*Crossing down to left of the table*] By the way, has anything been moved? Are things just as you left them yesterday?

This fills in Mr. Henderson, who hasn't been as close to the events, but also fills in the audience. Simple exposition.

He feels it's okay to interrupt Sheriff, though politely. Attorney is in charge.

Sheriff or Mr. Henderson?

Imprecise. Sheriff's more "country" than Attorney, more folksy and practical.

Responds to Sheriff's attempt to link himself with Attorney ("you know Frank") with an indirect criticism of Sheriff for not following procedure.

SHERIFF: [*Looking about.*] It's just the same. When it dropped below zero last night I thought I'd better send Frank out this morning to make a fire for us—no use getting pneumonia with a big case on, but I told him not to touch anything except the stove—and you know Frank.

COUNTY ATTORNEY: Somebody should have been left here yesterday.

What does he know about Frank? That he's dependable?

Like "just the same," less formal and official.

Director's Annotations for the Opening Scene of *Trifles*

You probably have not produced director's annotations before, but you may find it a very useful exercise to put yourself in the place of a director who needs to decide how the action on the stage should "go." Here are one professional director's annotations of the opening of *Trifles*:

A man used to making sure "ladies" are comfortable.

COUNTY ATTORNEY: [*Rubbing his hands.*] This feels good. Come up to the fire, ladies.

MRS. PETERS: [*After taking a step forward.*] I'm not—cold. — She hesitates; says it slowly.

SHERIFF: [*Unbuttoning his overcoat and stepping away from the stove as if to mark the beginning of official business.*] Now, Mr. Hale, before we move things about, you explain to Mr. Henderson just what you saw when you came here yesterday morning.

COUNTY ATTORNEY: By the way, has anything been moved? Are things just as you left them yesterday?

Sheriff has down to earth sense of what people will need.

SHERIFF: [*Looking about.*] It's just the same. When it dropped below zero last night I thought I'd better send Frank out this morning to make a fire for us—no use getting pneumonia with a big case on, but I told him not to touch anything except the stove—and you know Frank.

COUNTY ATTORNEY: Somebody should have been left here yesterday.

Briskly, to general audience.

After a moment, he notices the 2 women holding back & speaks to them encouragingly.

Not quite an "official" voice; Henderson will be more official sounding.

This addressed to Sheriff, in an "official" tone.

Almost to himself, not meant as chiding Sheriff. Still, he's asserting authority and concerned that things appear to be done correctly.

Writing about the Text

1. Choose a scene from one of the plays in Chapter 20 and annotate it in both styles: reader's annotations and director's annotations.
2. Using the annotations you created for item 1 (above), describe the differences between the types of annotations you wrote. Which were harder for you to write? What kinds of imagination did each call for?

3. Supply the annotations two different directors might give to the opening pages of *The Philadelphia* (p. 1199).

Summarizing a Play

In a summary, you use your own words to boil down the events within a whole play or in a scene or act from a play. As with a summary of a short story, it can be a challenge to write a single-sentence or a one- or two-paragraph summary of a play: extraneous asides, minor characters, subplots, and details must be cut, and only central characters, key themes, and events highlighted. Summaries are usually written in the present tense and have many uses, from filling in readers about the overall plot or texture of a play to linking one particular scene to the play's overall theme or structure.

As with summaries of stories and poems, summaries of plays are usually part of a larger writing task. For example, reviews of plays almost always include some summary, but here the writer must be careful not to reveal too much of the plot, as many theatergoers become frustrated by a write-up about a play that includes a plot "spoiler."

For academic writing assignments, summaries serve to fill in background or cover a large amount of plot in a few lines, giving you ample space to analyze and interpret the scenes instead of just paraphrasing what happens. You provide readers with a summary in order to have something specific on which to base your viewpoint or analysis. No academic papers are all summary, but summary is a key skill that appears often in academic writing. The key is to use summaries sparingly. Writers who either have too little to say or who lack the confidence or focus to offer a critical interpretation or analysis tend to lapse into plot summary.

Student's Summary

> In <u>Trifles</u>, a play which involves a murder committed in a cold, lonely farmhouse, all the men overlook the evidence because it is beneath their notice, mere "trifles" they can't be bothered with. The women, however, see these "trifles" for what they are, true signs of what actually occurred. In solidarity with the suspect and unbeknownst to the men, they cover up the evidence.

Writing about the Text

1. Summarize a play in Chapter 20, 24, or 26 as if you were describing it to someone who has never read it.
2. Write a one- or two-sentence summary of any scene in one of the Shakespeare plays in Chapter 23.

Keeping a Personal Journal

Next to marking up the text, the simplest form of written reaction is copying down memorable passages in a journal or notebook. Many people who see a play write about the experience afterward in a diary or journal, pointing out interesting reactions and special effects of language, costume, or scenery. Others copy down significant or interesting lines or turns of phrase in a notebook. In the Renaissance, before printing was very common, many people copied down whole poems or long passages into what they called "commonplace" books. These books would be read and reread over and over, and they would be carefully preserved as a kind of personal anthology.

The double-entry notebook, a type of journal created by scholar and critic Ann E. Berthoff, is a simple and effective technique for developing and incubating ideas. Students often find it a powerful tool for collecting information and then for reflecting on that information to form generalizations. It works like this: in a notebook, divide a page in half vertically. On the left side, write down the ideas that come to you as you read or as you think about the reading: summaries; interesting sentences or phrases; notes about the action or motivation; suggestions for production; the right way to say a line or make a gesture. These are the normal kinds of notes an attentive reader takes. Then, on the right side of the page, probably after an interval of time has passed, write responses to the notes on the left side. Here you are being speculative, what Berthoff would think of as philosophical. You will connect ideas, you will ask questions, you will generalize. Here are the oppositions you want to encourage:

Left side	Right side
Observation	Reaction
What happens	What it means
Fact	Speculation
Literal	Figurative
Details	Generalizations

The left side sticks more closely to the text and to first impressions, while the right side works toward conclusions and critical thinking. First, you think about the text, then you think about your thinking. Below are one student's double-entry notes about the opening scene in Lady Gregory's *Spreading the News*.

Student's Double-Entry Notebook Page for the Opening of *Spreading the News*

Magistrate keeps mentioning his days in the Andaman Islands	Colonial situation. To Magistrate, Ireland = Andaman Islands. But to an Irish audience, the Andaman Islands are at ends of the earth.
Magistrate is a professional administrator: all situations call for similar action	
Magistrate is naturally suspicious about apple seller hiding spirits and Fallon smoking "green" tobacco in his pipe. Magistrate is looking for things that can be taxed.	Magistrate is a stock figure who thinks "natives" are getting away with things. He forces the native police officer to see things his way.

| Magistrate has "handled" colonial situations before | The normal, everyday things the Irish do give rise to the Magistrate's deepest suspicions. |

Writing about the Text

1. Do a "commonplace book" type of journal about one of the plays in this book, copying lines you particularly like. Either give your personal reaction to several scenes or copy down passages you find important or memorable.
2. Take the journal you compiled in item 1, and do your commentary on the entries in the form of a double-entry notebook.

Writing a Response Paper

In a response paper, you are free to react to the text or a production of a play, giving your own thoughts. You can emphasize a part of the play that you thought best, worst, or most interesting. Or you can describe which actors you would like to see in a production and why. The emphasis here is on your personal response, not a reasoned argument. Of course, the best responses are filled with details, the result of sharp-eyed observation or genuinely personal feelings.

Sample from a Student Response Paper

As I read <u>Trifles</u> I found myself siding with Mrs. Hale and Mrs. Peters. Even given its setting a century ago in early 20th-century America, I couldn't get over the condescension Henderson displays toward the two women. For instance, he always refers to them directly as "ladies," his term of politeness that both treats them as special and removes them from the serious action that always seems to involve the men, not the women.

The two women seem to know their place in this society, so they wait quietly while the men go about the serious business of finding out what happened. The men are constantly leaving the stage, going upstairs or out to the barn to collect evidence. The women look closely around them and discover compelling evidence on their own. And they side instinctively with Mrs. Wright, so they don't speak up when they notice things like the crazed stitching on the quilt, the ruined preserves, or most important of all, the bird with the wrung neck.

As I read, I rooted for the two women, finding myself annoyed with the way they were treated as well as the way the men stupidly overlooked all signs of evidence, signs that were quite visible to the women. It was almost as if

the men's inability to see the evidence was like Wright's
inability to see that his wife was stifled in her lonely
farmhouse. Women could understand what was missing in
Mrs. Wright's life and sympathized with her and
instinctively collaborated with her against her dead
husband and the investigators who searched for a motive.
The women understood the motive right away, while the men
overlooked the signs because they seemed to be trifles.
This is true even though I don't know the difference
between quilting and knotting. In this way I'm like the
Sheriff, who overhears the women and says to his fellow
men, "They wonder if she was going to quilt it or just
knot it." Naturally, as the stage direction reads, "The
men laugh, the women look abashed." It's right after this
that Mrs. Hale covers up Mrs. Wright's signs of distress
by pulling out a knot and ripping out the crazed sewing,
thus destroying a key piece of evidence.

Writing about the Text

1. Write a response paper to *Trifles*, asking yourself why Mrs. Hale and Mrs. Peters choose not to share the evidence they have discovered.
2. Respond to the depiction of Mr. and Mrs. Wright in *Trifles*, with special consideration given to why neither of them ever appears on stage. How does each of them strike you, based on how they are described and characterized by the other characters? How does your impression of them change during the course of the play?

Writing an Intervention

Intervention may be a new term, but it is not a new concept: this catchall term was coined by the British critic and teacher Rob Pope for what happens when anyone—professional or student—responds to a text with an imitation or a parody or an addition. This book is full of such interventions. Looked at broadly, Aimé Césaire's *A Tempest* (p. 1412) is an intervention on Shakespeare's *The Tempest*. Some would claim that Sophocles' *Oedipus Rex* is an intervention on the traditional myth that every Greek was taught since Greek civilization began.

For our purposes, an intervention is a deliberate response to a text for people who know the original. It may be able to stand on its own, but it is also somewhat "parasitical" in that it gets part of its effect from our knowledge of the original. Literature is full of interventions like this. Renaissance love poetry has famous examples: Christopher Marlowe's "The Passionate Shepherd to His Love" and Sir Walter Raleigh's witty intervention in the form of an answer, "The Nymph's Reply to the Shepherd," are on pp. 930–931. Matthew Arnold's "Dover Beach" and Anthony Hecht's intervention, the parody "The Dover Bitch," are on pp. 1049–1050.

Shakespeare's plays have been the target or source of a great many interventions: Danitra Vance's *Flotilda Williams as Juliet* on p. 1556 is a contemporary example.

Below is an intervention to *Oedipus the King*: Muriel Rukeyser's poem "Myth," which depends on readers' knowledge of the Oedipus story. In fact, Rukeyser's poem would not make much sense to someone who did not know the Oedipus story.

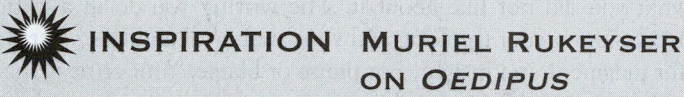

INSPIRATION MURIEL RUKEYSER ON *OEDIPUS*

Muriel Rukeyser   (1913–1980)

Myth   (1956)

Long afterward, Oedipus, old and blinded, walked the roads.
He smelled a familiar smell. It was the Sphinx.
Oedipus said, "I want to ask one question.
Why didn't I recognize my mother?"
"You gave the wrong answer," said the Sphinx.
"But that was what made everything possible," said Oedipus.
"No," she said. "When I asked, What walks on four legs in the morning,
two at noon, and three in the evening, you answered, Man.
You didn't say anything about woman."
"When you say Man," said Oedipus, "you include women too.
Everyone knows that."
She said, "That's what you think."

Interventions are less frequent writing assignments in an academic setting, but on occasion, as an exercise that combines both creative skills as well as critical thinking, you may be asked to write an intervention of a well-known play, along with either a response paper for or a critical analysis of the intervention you created, as in exercise 3 under "Writing about the Text," below.

Writing about the Text

1. Write an intervention of Susan Glaspell's *Trifles* (p. 1166) in which Mr. Wright and Mrs. Wright appear on stage and get to tell their own versions of what happened in some form.
2. Turn a scene from Lady Gregory's *Spreading the News* (p. 1183) into either a short story or a poem that remains true to the essential plot of the play.
3. Add a short scene to the end of *Trifles* in which Mrs. Hale tries to make her husband understand what really happened. Then, write a brief analysis of the addition that assesses whether the play is more or less dramatic if he understands.

Writing a Critical Analysis

Another kind of familiar writing, the critical analysis or analytical essay, is what you have no doubt done many times in short papers and in essay examinations. Such writing can be either directed—given as an answer to a question or a prompt, as so many of them are to questions in this book—or done on your own, where it is your task to come up with something worthwhile to say. Remember that the word "critical" does not mean that you write only about the weaknesses of a work or what you did not like about it. The writing you do in a critical analysis is an expression of your thinking and your analytical abilities. A critical essay will call for judgment and insight, not praise or blame. Your critical analysis will involve developing a thesis—a claim, assertion, or argument—that you support with evidence from the text or a performance.

Developing a Thesis

Every chapter in this book contains critical analysis questions that call for you to develop a thesis and then support it. Here is item 3 from the "Talking about the Text" exercises for Susan Glaspell's play *Trifles* in Chapter 20 (p. 1166):

> 3. How do the changes you see taking place in Mrs. Hale connect to particular events and statements from other characters?

If this question were part of a written exam, you would need two or three simple paragraphs to show how events and statements caused Mrs. Hale to change during the course of the short play. For a longer critical paper, you would go into more depth. In both cases, however, your approach would be the same: you would make a claim linking what happens in the play with the way Mrs. Hale seems to respond over time.

A key point to note: question 3 does part of the job for you by supplying the word "changes." The question points the way for you—gives you a thesis—by asserting that there are indeed changes in Mrs. Hale that can be connected to specific speeches and incidents. Look at the difference between question 3 above and another version of it:

> 3a. Does Mrs. Hale remain the same through the play, or do events and statements from other characters cause her to change? If she does change, describe what makes her do so. If she doesn't, describe what opportunities she passed up that might have tempted her to alter her attitude.

This more open-ended question allows for alternate answers: she changed due to X or Y, or, despite X or Y, she remained the same. You could develop a thesis and supporting evidence for either side of this argument.

One step more:

> 3b. Write two or three paragraphs on what happens to Mrs. Hale during the course of the play.

Here you are on your own, with no leading questions or even hints to guide you as you develop a thesis. You can claim that her character changes or remains static or vacillates between change and certainty.

Whichever version of question 3 you are asked, you are responding about one of the key characters in the play, giving your own sense of what you see. You will report on this to your instructor, but often your audience might also be members of the class as well. A writing assignment like these versions of question 3 can become an interesting group assignment, with everyone asked to bring in a list of the changes they notice and then working together in a group to compose a final list that gets read to the whole class.

Your audience for your critical analysis is your instructor, and perhaps the class as well. Your instructor wants to see what you have come up with. It is not just whether you get the "right" answer—there are rarely right or wrong answers in literature as there are in some other subjects—but he or she wants to see what thesis or claim you make about the play: "Mrs. Hale changes three times during the play, once when . . . , then when . . . , and finally when . . . ." That is your entry into the conversation. You cannot really take part in the conversation without venturing an opinion or a claim backed up by evidence from the text. That is where you exercise your critical thinking.

In pulling together a thesis for a critical essay, most students inevitably wonder, "What counts as evidence?" The answer is anything you have noticed about the play: the words, the actions, the way characters change over time, the setting, the playwright's major concerns. The important thing to remember is to use specific quotations from the text itself to support your assertions. Note in the following student paper how the writer states a claim about the play and then supports that claim with evidence from the play.

STUDENT CRITICAL ANALYSIS OF *TRIFLES*

Audra McNamara

Professor Jordan

English 112-6

April 30, 2006

Accomplices

In Susan Glaspell's play *Trifles*, the action demonstrates the ways that male indifference and incomprehension result in women's solidarity. This is true even though the women have to go against some of their long held beliefs. The actions of the two female characters, Mrs. Hale and Mrs. Peters, show them bonding together to defend their absent neighbor, Mrs. Wright, who has been jailed because the authorities think she has murdered her husband.

In just a few minutes Mrs. Hale and Mrs. Peters move from being potential witnesses to being accomplices, when they make an unspoken pact to hide key evidence. This means that through their actions Mrs. Wright might not be convicted of the murder everyone believes she has committed.

The key question for the plot of the play is, who killed Mr. Wright by strangling him with a rope as he lay asleep in his bed? This is what the three male characters cannot figure out. The County Attorney, the Sheriff, and the neighboring farmer Mr. Hale all check the windows and the barn to discover how someone might have broken into the home. Meanwhile, Mrs. Hale, who is the protagonist, and her friend Mrs. Peters sit in the parlor and wonder about the same thing. At first Mrs. Peters seems convinced that Mrs. Wright did it:

> MRS. PETERS. [*Starts to speak, glances up,*
> *where footsteps are heard in the room above.*
> *In a low voice*] Mr. Peters says it looks bad
> for her. Mr. Henderson is awful sarcastic in a

speech and he'll make fun of her sayin' she
didn't wake up. (1171)

This makes sense: Why didn't she wake up while
someone was putting a noose around her husband right in
the bed next to her? Yet Mrs. Hale replies right away:

> MRS. HALE. Well, I guess John Wright didn't
> wake up when they was slipping that rope under
> his neck. (1171)

This reply easily answers Mr. Henderson's argument,
and Mrs. Hale's use of the plural "they" suggests that
she believes the murder was done by more than one
person. But Mrs. Hale will move from this view to a
different one as evidence mounts up that Mrs. Wright
killed her husband.

The two women by themselves discover the evidence
that demonstrates that Mrs. Wright is guilty. A whole
series of little things—trifles—lead Mrs. Hale to change
her mind and agree with Mr. Henderson's and Mr. Peters'
conclusion that Mrs. Wright was guilty. Mrs. Peters lays
out the need for motive:

> MRS. PETERS. Mr. Henderson said coming out
> that what was needed for the case was a
> motive; something to show anger, or—sudden
> feeling. (1171)

Mr. Henderson cannot see what Mrs. Hale and Mrs.
Peters notice as they go through Mrs. Wright's
possessions. Men are looking for the big things like
broken windows, while the women look closely at little
things like sewing. These are things the men think are
just trifles. The first piece of evidence pointing to
motive that they notice is the stitching on the
quilt:

> MRS. HALE. I wonder if she was goin' to quilt
> it or just knot it? (1171)

Overhearing this question, the men immediately make
fun of it:

> SHERIFF. They wonder if she was going to quilt
> it or just knot it! (1172)

But Mrs. Hale's question really suggests that an experienced quilter like Mrs. Wright knows how knots work. They work the same on a quilt or on someone's neck.

The next key piece of evidence about motive comes from the odd appearance of the most recent stitching on the quilt Mrs. Wright was making:

> MRS. HALE. Why it looks as if she didn't know
>   what she was about! (1172)

Immediately, Mrs. Hale glances at Mrs. Peters, removes the bad stitching, and replaces it with good stitching as she says "I'll just finish up this end." She has just destroyed a key piece of evidence, and covered up her destruction with competent stitching. During this time, Mrs. Peters is worried, saying (the stage directions say "*Nervously*") "I don't think we ought to touch things" (1174). Though Mrs. Peters says this, she goes along with her friend Mrs. Hale, thus buying into her destruction of evidence. This begins what the County Attorney would call a conspiracy.

The last key piece of evidence is the bird whose neck was broken. The minute both Mrs. Hale and Mrs. Peters see it they know what happened. Instinctively, they hide the bird from the men. Then, as soon as they are alone, they talk to each other. The stage direction says that the atmosphere is different: "*When they talk now it is in the manner of feeling their way over strange ground, as if afraid of what they are saying, but as if they cannot help saying it*" (1174).

In the final minutes of the play we witness Mrs. Peters try to do the "right" thing. She states a series of legal objections, sounding like a lawyer who must follow the rules:.

- "We don't know who killed him" (1175).
- "We don't know who killed the bird" (1174).
- "The law has got to punish crime, Mrs. Hale" (1175).

But as the group prepares to leave the farmhouse, despite the joking reminder from the attorney that she is

McNamara 4

literally "married to the law" (1176), Mrs. Peters acts boldly. She snatches up the bird in an attempt to smuggle the damning evidence out of the house. She cannot: the box is too big, and Mrs. Hale takes it away herself.

The two women have of course committed a crime. It is called "accessory after the fact." The dictionary defines *accessory after the fact* as "a person who knowingly conceals or assists another who has committed a felony" ("Accessory After the Fact"). This is what has happened here, as they have destroyed two key pieces of evidence in a murder case. Yet the play is totally on their side. The mocking of the men, and the recollection of how awful life can be on the prairie, make the audience sympathize with the two women. Also, at the end, when the women are asked again in a mocking way what they call the kind of quilting technique used, they reply with "we call it knotting." This increases readers' identification with these women; they are smarter than the mocking men, and so the audience sympathizes with their emotional need to shield a housewife who led a difficult life. They do this in place of agreeing with the men's less personal need for justice.

The question now is, as audience members who sympathize with the two women, are we accomplices as well?

Works Cited

"Accessory After the Fact." <u>Random House Webster's College Dictionary</u>. New York, 1995.

Glaspell, Susan. <u>Trifles</u>. <u>Living Literature: An Introduction to Fiction, Poetry, and Drama</u>. Ed. John C. Brereton. New York: Longman, 2007. 1166-1176.

Writing about the Text

1. Write three separate claims about one of the three plays in Chapter 20: *Trifles*, *Spreading the News*, or *The Philadelphia*. Write down a list of the evidence you would need to support each of those claims.
2. Choose one claim from item 1, above, and write a brief, 3-5 page analytical essay using that thesis.

CHAPTER

22

Sophocles

Sophocles is one of the four famous Greek playwrights of the Golden Age of Greek civilization: Aeschylus (c. 525–456 BCE), Sophocles (c. 495–406 BCE), Euripides (c. 484–406 BCE), and Aristophanes (c. 448–388 BCE). Sophocles was born near Athens, the son of a prosperous merchant. After his schooling, he wrote a play for the annual dramatic festival and won first prize, defeating Aeschylus. He would write over 120 plays, of which only seven survive complete. Sophocles acted in many of his own plays and held many significant offices in his city-state of Athens.

SOPHOCLES TIMELINE

c. 495 BCE	Sophocles born at Colonus, near Athens.
468 BCE	Sophocles wins his first drama prize at Athenian spring festival.
461–429 BCE	Pericles rules during Golden Age.
443 BCE	Sophocles holds public office.
c. 440 BCE	Writes *Antigone*.
431 BCE	Peloponnesian War begins (lasts until 404).

430 BCE	Writes *Oedipus*; plague breaks out in Athens.
413 BCE	Athenian expedition to Sicily defeated.
406 BCE	Sophocles dies in Athens.
404 BCE	Athens surrenders to Sparta.
401 BCE	*Oedipus at Colonus* performed.

THEATER IN SOPHOCLES' TIME

Hellenistic Greek bronze head, second century BCE, purported to be of Sophocles.

If we could be transported back in time to see a Greek play being performed in the fifth century BCE, we would experience something very different from today's theater—even today's most experimental theater. The acting in a Greek drama would strike us as far from natural, though of course the notion of "natural" varies with cultures, and we have evidence that the Greek audience was often moved to tears or indignation or exultation by the acting. Given the location and the lack of electronics, actors had to project their voices; declamation rather than intimate confession was the style, and the masks the actors wore seem to have helped their voices carry to the far reaches of the amphitheater. Sometimes the actors sang their lines, bringing Greek drama closer in some ways to opera than to what we think of as regular theater. In actuality, most of what we know about Greek theater—and scholars would like to know a lot more—we have to surmise not from archeology but from the internal evidence of the texts and from painted depictions of actors and the theater on vases and the like. The wooden **skenes** (the low buildings used for storage, costume changes, and off-stage actors), the costumes, and the masks all have vanished.

LITERARY LOCALE

The Greek Theater. For a Greek drama, theatergoers sat outdoors in an amphitheater (see also the photo of the Epidauros Greek Theater on p. 1162 of Chapter 20) with up to 15,000 other people. Modern theaters hold from 200 to 2,000 people, so the very large numbers at Greek dramas are more akin to audiences at our sporting events or rock concerts than to twenty-first-century plays. Even stranger, theatergoers arrived at the presentation in the morning, and by the conclusion of the play the sun would be up fairly high. The actors wore

(continued)

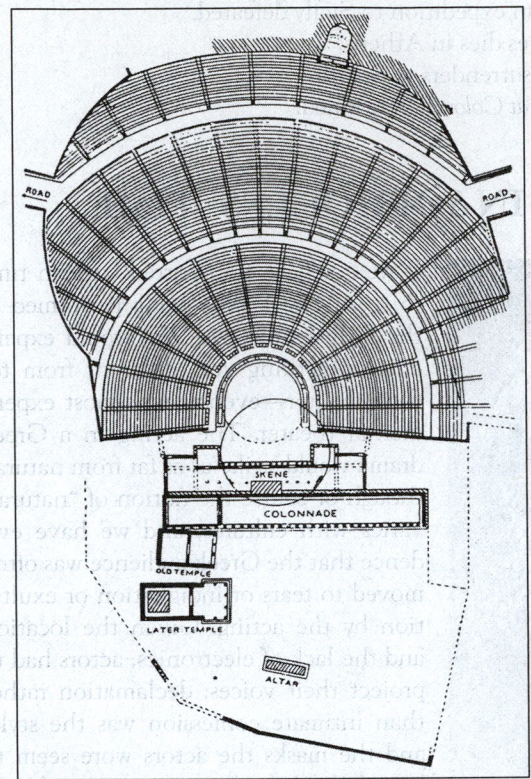

masks that covered half their heads and were attached to wigs. All of the roles, even the female characters, were performed by men. Children might appear onstage, but never in speaking roles. There would be nothing like a curtain or even a stage as we know it. The main actors occupied a space in front of a small, low building called the **skene**, which served as a storage place for props and as a place for the actors when they were offstage. By the time of Sophocles, the skene was also used as a backdrop and could be painted with background scenery. In front of and slightly lower than the main actors' performance space on the stage was the site for the chorus, members of which spoke and sang their lines and also danced. A musician played the pipes throughout the production. All plays, serious and comic alike, had music.

This modern drawing of the theater of Dionysus in Athens, from R.C. Flickinger's The Greek Theater and Its Drama (1918), is based on scholars' speculations about what Greek theaters actually looked like during Sophocles' time.

RITUAL AND RELIGION IN GREEK DRAMA

Greek drama had its origins as part of a yearly religious festival dedicated to the god Dionysus. Each play is full of allusions to the gods and their activities and the important role the Greeks believed the gods play in human lives. The plays enact myths that are at their core religious. (Greek religion had no foundational documents like the Bible, Torah, or Koran, and no official confessions of faith; it had myths instead.) Greek drama is considered more "ritualistic" than "realistic" because it contains repeated or repeatable action and is not suspenseful in our sense of the term; the audience was entirely familiar with the story that was being acted out before them. In many respects, the play's music and dance—its nonverbal sound and movement—were as important as the actual words. And perhaps most important, many of the play's actions are significant beyond what they mean on the most everyday level. For instance, in throwing dust over her brother's body, Antigone is "burying" him, and in burying him is performing a very serious religious and familial duty, a dictate of the gods.

Even today, no matter how realistic many dramatists have sought to make their plays, the dramatic tradition they participate in has always somewhere "remembered" its ritualistic origins. Or perhaps all drama contains at least a core of ritual. Thus, even in Susan Glaspell's *Trifles*, a realistic play, we are nevertheless conscious of the characters doing what is right and hallowed in the wake of a horrendous murder of one family member by another. Somewhere in Glaspell's consciousness as author of *Trifles*, murder is sacrilegious, especially in a family, a rupture in society, and the characters of the play struggle as well as they can to understand (or accept) this astonishing mystery, resorting to a traditional vocabulary in order to face the situation and make meaning of it. And we as audience or readers become participants in a kind of action that has gone on for thousands of years, as we watch the players enact a search for a killer and strive to restore the moral order. No matter whether it is comedy or tragedy, with or without music, the theater is one of the oldest rituals in our society.

In recent decades playwrights have been particularly aware of and ready to embrace the ritual origins of theater, as they ponder how to understand plays as more than an approximation of "real" life, which the movies trump them at anyway. Moreover, they have learned much from the theater—traditional and contemporary—of non-Western cultures, where drama likewise began in religion and often has not strayed far from it.

Although today we understand that Greek drama is steeped in religious ritual, this conception of its religious core has not always prevailed. Earlier scholars with Christian backgrounds sometimes regarded the gods of the Greek dramas as intentionally fictional. No one has questioned the fact that the dramas had religious roots; the issue has always been one of the extent of the religious influence, and here even the advocates for the union of Greek religion and drama do not claim to have complete answers. Their uncertainty reminds us not to assume too quickly that we "get" the Greek plays or that, since they are great and moving pieces of drama, these plays speak clearly and easily to us in the early twenty-first century. Surely they speak about universal human concerns, and we can make them relevant to us, but it is still worth remembering that they were written a long time ago and were not intended for audiences living in a world the Greeks could never have imagined. There is no easy way to make Oedipus or Antigone into "normal" twenty-first-century characters. Indeed, their strangeness is part of their attraction.

Joseph Campbell and the Power of Myth. Joseph Campbell was one of the most respected scholars on religion and myth of the twentieth century. He wrote dozens of scholarly books and articles examining the role of myth in modern life. In 1988, a year after his death, documentarian Bill Moyers brought Campbell's work to the general public in the six-part series *Joseph Campbell and the Power of Myth*, based on conversations Moyers had had with Campbell over many years. In the series and in such books as *The Masks of God: Occidental Mythology*, Campbell explains how ancient stories, including archetypal Greek myths, repeat themselves time and time again across centuries and civilizations, and he teaches viewers how to recognize these archetypes as modern myths we all believe in. You can find *Joseph Campbell and the Power of Myth with Bill Moyers* on VHS or DVD, and at your university library.

TRAGEDY IN GREEK DRAMA

From ancient times, Greek plays have been regarded as the very models and starting points for talking about tragedy. According to Aristotle, our earliest critic of drama, tragic heroes are human beings whose characters bear a substantial **flaw**. Typically, they start out in prosperous and respectable circumstances, members of the aristocracy or even of the royal family. During the course of the drama, they suffer a reversal of fortune as a consequence of their flaws. In the case of *Oedipus the King*, the tragic hero argument depends upon locating a defect in Oedipus' character. His temper? His pride? The Greeks used the word **hubris** to indicate the overconfidence that could cause a hero's downfall. Antigone (p. 1303) is more difficult to see as a tragic heroine in the Aristotelian sense. Is she too absolute in her certainty about her duty? Is she too insensitive to the sufferings of her sister and of her intended husband? Is her uncle Creon the true tragic hero? Is he too stubborn about his royal use of power? But then he is persuaded of the error of his ways; his change of course simply comes too late to save Antigone and the others.

One question about tragic heroes (and by implication "us") has perennially disturbed theatergoers and readers: to what degree do the characters bring their sufferings upon themselves? Or are they the playthings of fates (the gods) that are sometimes kind, sometimes cruel? From one point of view we may find it unbearable to think that Oedipus should be innocent of intentionally killing his father and marrying his mother and yet have to witness all those terrible things happening to him regardless. Thus, we seek some reason why it happened: He was too quick and hot tempered. Or his sacrifice was necessary in order to save Thebes; his suffering did others good even if not him. But what if there is no reason we can understand for the undeserving to suffer? Does the Greek tragedy then provide some sort of grandeur and consolation when we must contemplate the human condition? Does it offer not explanation but rather some kind of **catharsis**, some release of tension, however temporary?

GREEK DRAMA ON THE AMERICAN STAGE

There has been a long debate carried on by scholars, audiences, readers, drama critics, and actors about how relevant the Greek tragedies are (or ought to be) to contemporary American audiences. The plays have always been produced in American colleges, though more frequently when classical Greek was more widely studied, but they were slow to achieve success in commercial theater, where profits and audiences keep theaters afloat. The first commercial staging of a Greek drama in the United States was an 1845 production of *Antigone*, but it closed quickly after receiving bad reviews. In 1881 *Oedipus Rex* was staged at Harvard, using a well-received new translation; in 1882 it was produced commercially in New York. In both Massachusetts and New York the producers had to contend with the objection that Oedipus' actions (especially incest) were hardly fit subjects for the stage.

In the twentieth century, Americans began to embrace Greek tragedy more enthusiastically. For one thing, they found *The Trojan Women* and *Iphigenia at Aulis* relevant to the pacifistic concerns brought on by disillusion with World War I and other twentieth-century conflicts. Strong women's roles, such as Medea, Antigone, Electra, and Clytemnestra, connected to feminist themes and appealed to great actresses of the stage.

But even when Greek drama received widespread approval, there was no agreement about how the plays should be produced. Some students of theater thought that the conditions of the original Greek drama should be replicated as closely as possible (a college football stadium often became a venue of choice); others believed that productions should take place in an intimate theater (Chicago's Little Theater had a celebrated production of *Medea* that toured the United States in 1920). Some observers held out for a "high classical" delivery of the lines; others preferred a more "natural," psychologically "authentic" style. In his 1972 *Medea*, the director Andrei Serban downplayed the play's actual language (an odd mixture of Latin and Greek) to highlight the sound and the movement, thus emphasizing the ritual aspects. This worked best when the plot was simple and the emotions elemental and intense, as they are in *Medea*. Costumes for productions ranged from classical draperies to contemporary apparel; sets ranged from plain to elaborate.

GREEK DRAMA

A modern audience is very unlikely to go to a theater and see a Greek drama staged in any way close to an ancient Greek production, especially in North America. Not only are scholars unsure of how the dramas were staged 2,500 years ago, but contemporary directors make no attempt to recreate what the ancient performances might have been like. Almost all the plays are altered—not just translated—to be accessible and relevant to today's audiences.

Modern Setting and Dress

Staging a play using modern clothing and a contemporary setting is one way to demonstrate the relevance of Greek theater to a contemporary audience. In the

Fiona Shaw as Medea in the modernized 2002 Abbey Theater production performed at the Brooklyn Academy of Music.

2002–2003 production of Euripides' *Medea*, the Irish actress Fiona Shaw appeared as the betrayed wife driven to murder her children, but as a woman of today, not an ancient Greek. In fact, the production was billed as a one-woman show, not as a recreation of a classic play.

Major Alterations

With the aim of making Greek plays more accessible to audiences—and of filling theater seats—many producers and directors have altered the plays, often quite a lot. Peter Hall's *Tantalus* at the Denver Center Theatre Company (2000) is an excellent example of how a director can shape a production and appeal to a contemporary American audience. Hall directed a three-part, ten-hour compilation of Greek dramas about the Trojan War. Although there were long chunks from some familiar plays, the more local and less "dramatic"

parts were cut out. The emphasis of the production was on what works in the theater, not what the Greek plays were really like.

Another famous director, Peter Sellars (not to be confused with actor Peter Sellers), has a reputation for imposing his personal and political vision on the plays he produces, and thus altering radically the context of the works. In 2003 he directed the American Repertory Theatre's production of a little-known Greek play, Euripides' *The Children of Herakles*, about refugees from the Trojan War. Placing the play in a very contemporary context, Sellars preceded the performances with a one-hour interview session with contemporary refugees, and followed it with discussion, films, and food prepared by local refugees. According to Sellars, "When you see an issue opened up in a play that is 2,500 years old, you see it as an enduring issue rather than an issue of the moment. The questions associated with refugees are eternal. The Greeks used drama to raise them, because drama takes you much deeper than politics."

A scene from Peter Sellars's 2003 production of Children of Herakles *at the American Repertory Theatre, which recast the play in a contemporary context.*

Language

Inevitably, most modern productions of Greek dramas update a part of a play that Greeks loved to pay special attention to: the language. English translations work to get the ideas and the action across, to help us follow the interplay between actor and chorus. But the art of the original Greek language is gone. Greeks were highly oral people, skilled in the verbal give and take of the market, the forum, and the theater. The art of Greek dramas was not just in the stories, most of which were already known, but in the set speeches, the verbal interplay, the poetry. Most of that is not directly translatable into English.

The Greek Canon

A less obvious kind of updating has to do with what gets staged. Audiences see plays that directors think will "work" on stage, while the rest remain obscure. In fact, until Peter Sellars's recent revival of Euripides' *The Children of Herakles*, that play had just seven or eight revivals since antiquity. Sophocles' *Oedipus at Colonnus* is another example. Less obviously "dramatic" than *Oedipus the King* or *Antigone*, its well-known companion plays (pp. 1250 and 1303), its most famous recent staging was the brilliant *Gospel at Colonus* in the 1980s, with huge alterations and gospel music sung by the Blind Boys of Alabama. It was wonderful theater, but how close was it to Sophocles? On the other hand, how much does authenticity matter?

Engraved by George Cooke.

Bust of Greek philosopher and playwright Sophocles.

PLAYS BY SOPHOCLES

Oedipus the King   (C. 425 BCE)

TRANSLATED BY ROBERT FAGLES   (1977)

Although it has not received a major commercial production in the United States since 1972, Oedipus Rex, or Oedipus the King (rex meaning "king"), has been a perennial favorite over the past hundred years. In 1923, a production starring John Martin Harvey, who had played the role already in Berlin and London, did well in New York. So did a version starring the great English Shakespearean actor Laurence Olivier in 1946. The Greek National Theatre brought a production in 1952. It was in modern Greek, as have been a number of Greek dramas playing in America. In 1970 Oedipus enjoyed two productions, one in San Francisco and the other in New York, the latter given a setting in the Caribbean and Central America. The celebrated Guthrie Theater (Minneapolis) production in 1972 incorporated a 1960s fascination with ritual, particularly with the sacrifice ritual. It began with a sort of shadowy prologue depicting human sacrifice, and Oedipus was interpreted as the sacrifice that was needed to save Thebes from pestilence and pollution.

Laurence Olivier as Oedipus in the 1945 Old Vic performance of Oedipus Rex, clad in costuming that is meant to approximate classical clothing.

The Oedipus myth was old even in the time of Sophocles. Allusions to it had appeared in both of Homer's epics, the Iliad and Odyssey (present scholarly consensus places Homer in the seventh and eighth centuries BCE). Homer's rather brief allusion suggests that the myth was already widely known in his day.

Audiences usually find it useful to know the events that had taken place in the decades before the time of the play. Oedipus was a son born to the king and queen of Thebes, Laius and Jocasta. An authoritative prophecy at the time of the baby's birth foretold that he would grow up to kill his father and marry his mother. Horrified, the royal couple asked a shepherd to leave the child for dead outside the city. But the shepherd secretly transferred the child to another shepherd, who in turn gave him to the childless king and queen of Corinth, Polybus and Merope. When Oedipus grew to manhood, he heard a prophecy that he would kill his father and marry his mother, but believing his parents to be Polybus and Merope, he fled Corinth to avoid the fulfillment of the prediction. On the road, Oedipus encountered another chariot; an altercation ensued about which party would proceed first, and Oedipus wound up killing the stranger and his retinue, not realizing that the stranger was his natural father, Laius. Oedipus went on to Thebes, where he was able to answer a difficult riddle posed by a terrible beast, half woman and half lion, called the Sphinx. The Thebans hailed Oedipus as their hero and new king, their previous king having been killed. (No one, including Oedipus, realized the king's murderer was Oedipus.) Oedipus married the widowed queen, Jocasta, and had four children with her—Antigone, Ismene, Polynices, and Eteocles. But as the play opens, his fortunes have begun to take a turn for the worse, and a strange blight has fallen over the land.

The perennially popular story of Oedipus was strongly revived by the work of Sigmund Freud (see "Commentary: Freud, Dodds, and Artaud on Oedipus" on p. 1296) and especially Carl Jung, who saw in the myth the outlines of a fundamental pattern in human development, that is, the tendency of a son to come into conflict with his father and to desire to take the place of his father in the affections of his mother. For Jung, this pattern was one of several universal "archetypes" in human experience.

Oedipus in Greek means "swollen foot"; the baby Oedipus' feet had originally been pierced and bound and as a result had become swollen.

Characters

Oedipus, king of Thebes	Jocasta, the queen, wife of Oedipus
A Priest of Zeus	A Messenger from Corinth
Creon, brother of Jocasta	A Shepherd
A Chorus of Theban citizens and their Leader	A Messenger from inside the palace
Tiresias, a blind prophet	Antigone, Ismene, daughters of Oedipus and Jocasta

Time and Scene. *The royal house of Thebes. Double doors dominate the façade; a stone altar stands at the center of the stage.*

Many years have passed since Oedipus solved the riddle of the Sphinx and ascended the throne of Thebes, and now a plague has struck the city. A procession of priests enters; suppliants, broken and despondent, they carry branches wound in wool and lay them on the altar.

The doors open. Guards assemble. Oedipus comes forward, majestic but for a telltale limp, and slowly views the condition of his people.

OEDIPUS: Oh my children, the new blood of ancient Thebes,
why are you here? Huddling at my altar,
praying before me, your branches wound in wool.
Our city reeks with the smoke of burning incense,
rings with cries for the Healer and wailing for the dead.   5
I thought it wrong, my children, to hear the truth
from others, messengers. Here I am myself—
you all know me, the world knows my fame:
I am Oedipus.

  Helping a Priest to his feet.

                    Speak up, old man. Your years,
your dignity—you should speak for the others.   10
Why here and kneeling, what preys upon you so?
Some sudden fear? some strong desire?
You can trust me; I am ready to help,
I'll do anything. I would be blind to misery
not to pity my people kneeling at my feet.   15
PRIEST: Oh Oedipus, king of the land, our greatest power!
You see us before you, men of all ages
clinging to your altars. Here are boys,
still too weak to fly from the nest,
and here the old, bowed down with the years,   20

the holy ones—a priest of Zeus myself—and here
the picked, unmarried men, the young hope of Thebes.
And all the rest, your great family gathers now,
branches wreathed, massing in the squares,
kneeling before the two temples of queen Athena   25
or the river-shrine where the embers glow and die
and Apollo sees the future in the ashes.
                                    Our city—
look around you, see with your own eyes—
our ship pitches wildly, cannot lift her head
from the depths, the red waves of death . . .   30
Thebes is dying. A blight on the fresh crops
and the rich pastures, cattle sicken and die,
and the women die in labor, children stillborn,
and the plague, the fiery god of fever hurls down
on the city, his lightning slashing through us—   35
raging plague in all its vengeance, devastating
the house of Cadmus! And Black Death luxuriates
in the raw, wailing miseries of Thebes.
Now we pray to you. You cannot equal the gods,
your children know that, bending at your altar.   40
But we do rate you first of men,
both in the common crises of our lives
and face-to-face encounters with the gods.
You freed us from the Sphinx; you came to Thebes
and cut us loose from the bloody tribute we had paid   45
that harsh, brutal singer. We taught you nothing,
no skill, no extra knowledge, still you triumphed.
A god was with you, so they say, and we believe it—
you lifted up our lives.
                              So now again,
Oedipus, king, we bend to you, your power—   50
we implore you, all of us on our knees:
find us strength, rescue! Perhaps you've heard
the voice of a god or something from other men,
Oedipus . . . what do you know?
The man of experience—you see it every day—   55
his plans will work in a crisis, his first of all.

Act now—we beg you, best of men, raise up our city!
Act, defend yourself, your former glory!
Your country calls you savior now
for your zeal, your action years ago.   60
Never let us remember of your reign:
you helped us stand, only to fall once more.
Oh raise up our city, set us on our feet.
The omens were good that day you brought us joy—
be the same man today!   65
Rule our land, you know you have the power,

but rule a land of the living, not a wasteland.
Ship and towered city are nothing, stripped of men
alive within it, living all as one.

OEDIPUS: My children,
   I pity you. I see—how could I fail to see   70
   what longings bring you here? Well I know
   you are sick to death, all of you,
   but sick as you are, not one is sick as I.
   Your pain strikes each of you alone, each
   in the confines of himself, no other. But my spirit   75
   grieves for the city, for myself and all of you.
   I wasn't asleep, dreaming. You haven't wakened me—
   I've wept through the nights, you must know that,
   groping, laboring over many paths of thought.
   After a painful search I found one cure: 80
   I acted at once. I sent Creon,
   my wife's own brother, to Delphi—
   Apollo the Prophet's oracle—to learn
   what I might do or say to save our city.

   Today's the day. When I count the days gone by   85
   it torments me . . . what is he doing?
   Strange, he's late, he's gone too long.
   But once he returns, then, then I'll be a traitor
   if I do not do all the god makes clear.

PRIEST: Timely words. The men over there   90
   are signaling—Creon's just arriving.

OEDIPUS:

   Sighting Creon, then turning to the altar.

                               Lord Apollo,
   let him come with a lucky word of rescue,
   shining like his eyes!

PRIEST: Welcome news, I think—he's crowned, look,
   and the laurel wreath is bright with berries.   95

OEDIPUS: We'll soon see. He's close enough to hear—

   Enter Creon from the side; his face is shaded with a wreath.

   Creon, prince, my kinsman, what do you bring us?
   What message from the god?

CREON: Good news.
   I tell you even the hardest things to bear,
   if they should turn out well, all would be well.   100

OEDIPUS: Of course, but what were the god's *words*? There's no hope
   and nothing to fear in what you've said so far.

CREON: If you want my report in the presence of these . . .

   Pointing to the priests while drawing Oedipus toward the palace.

   I'm ready now, or we might go inside.

OEDIPUS: Speak out,

speak to us all. I grieve for these, my people, 105
far more than I fear for my own life.

CREON: Very well,
I will tell you what I heard from the god.
Apollo commands us—he was quite clear—
"Drive the corruption from the land,
don't harbor it any longer, past all cure, 110
don't nurse it in your soil—root it out!"

OEDIPUS: How can we cleanse ourselves—what rites?
What's the source of the trouble?

CREON: Banish the man, or pay back blood with blood.
Murder sets the plague-storm on the city.

OEDIPUS: Whose murder? 115
Whose fate does Apollo bring to light?

CREON: Our leader,
my lord, was once a man named Laius,
before you came and put us straight on course.

OEDIPUS: I know—
or so I've heard. I never saw the man myself.

CREON: Well, he was killed, and Apollo commands us now— 120
he could not be more clear,
"Pay the killers back—whoever is responsible."

OEDIPUS: Where on earth are they? Where to find it now,
the trail of the ancient guilt so hard to trace?

CREON: "Here in Thebes," he said. 125
Whatever is sought for can be caught, you know,
whatever is neglected slips away.

OEDIPUS: But where,
in the palace, the fields or foreign soil,
where did Laius meet his bloody death?

CREON: He went to consult an oracle, he said, 130
and he set out and never came home again.

OEDIPUS: No messenger, no fellow-traveler saw what happened?
Someone to cross-examine?

CREON: No,
they were all killed but one. He escaped,
terrified, he could tell us nothing clearly,
nothing of what he saw—just one thing. 135

OEDIPUS: What's that?
One thing could hold the key to it all,
a small beginning give us grounds for hope.

CREON: He said thieves attacked them—a whole band,
not single-handed, cut King Laius down.

OEDIPUS: A thief,
so daring, wild, he'd kill a king? Impossible, 140
unless conspirators paid him off in Thebes.

CREON: We suspected as much. But with Laius dead
no leader appeared to help us in our troubles.

OEDIPUS: Trouble? Your *king* was murdered—royal blood! 145

What stopped you from tracking down the killer
then and there?
CREON: The singing, riddling Sphinx.
She . . . persuaded us to let the mystery go
and concentrate on what lay at our feet.
OEDIPUS: No,
I'll start again—I'll bring it all to light myself!   150
Apollo is right, and so are you, Creon,
to turn our attention back to the murdered man.
Now you have *me* to fight for you, you'll see:
I am the land's avenger by all rights
and Apollo's champion too.   155
But not to assist some distant kinsman, no,
for my own sake I'll rid us of this corruption.
Whoever killed the king may decide to kill me too,
with the same violent hand—by avenging Laius
I defend myself.

To the priests.

                        Quickly, my children.   160
Up from the steps, take up your branches now.

To the guards.

One of you summon the city here before us,
tell them I'll do everything. God help us,
we will see our triumph—or our fall.

Oedipus and Creon enter the palace, followed by the guards.

PRIEST: Rise, my sons. The kindness we came for   165
Oedipus volunteers himself.
Apollo has sent his word, his oracle—
Come down, Apollo, save us, stop the plague.

    The priests rise, remove their branches and exit to the side.
        Enter a Chorus, the citizens of Thebes, who have not heard the news
    that Creon brings. They march around the altar, chanting.

CHORUS: Zeus!
Great welcome voice of Zeus, what do you bring?
What word from the gold vaults of Delphi   170
comes to brilliant Thebes? I'm racked with terror—
                        terror shakes my heart
and I cry your wild cries, Apollo, Healer of Delos
I worship you in dread . . . what now, what is your price?
some new sacrifice? some ancient rite from the past   175
come round again each spring?—
                        what will you bring to birth?
Tell me, child of golden Hope
        warm voice that never dies!

You are the first I call, daughter of Zeus   180
deathless Athena—I call your sister Artemis,
heart of the market place enthroned in glory,
                    guardian of our earth—
I call Apollo, Archer astride the thunderheads of heaven—
O triple shield against death, shine before me now!   185
If ever, once in the past, you stopped some ruin
launched against our walls
               you hurled the flame of pain
far, far from Thebes—you gods
          come now, come down once more!

                           No, no   190
the miseries numberless, grief on grief, no end—
too much to bear, we are all dying
O my people . . .
             Thebes like a great army dying
and there is no sword of thought to save us, no   195
and the fruits of our famous earth, they will not ripen
no and the women cannot scream their pangs to birth—
screams for the Healer, children dead in the womb
             and life on life goes down
                    you can watch them go   200
     like seabirds winging west, outracing the day's fire
down the horizon, irresistibly
          streaking on to the shores of Evening
                            Death
so many deaths, numberless deaths on deaths, no end—
Thebes is dying, look, her children   205
stripped of pity . . .
          generations strewn on the ground
unburied, unwept, the dead spreading death
and the young wives and gray-haired mothers with them
cling to the altars, trailing in from all over the city—
Thebes, city of death, one long cortege   210
         and the suffering rises
                 wails for mercy rise
     and the wild hymn for the Healer blazes out
clashing with our sobs our cries of mourning—   215
       O golden daughter of god, send rescue
     radiant as the kindness in your eyes!
Drive him back!—the fever, the god of death
              that raging god of war
not armored in bronze, not shielded now, he burns me,   220
battle cries in the onslaught burning on—
O rout him from our borders!
Sail him, blast him out to the Sea-queen's chamber
           the black Atlantic gulfs

or the northern harbor, death to all   225
where the Thracian surf comes crashing.
Now what the night spares he comes by day and kills—
the god of death.

     O lord of the stormcloud,
you who twirl the lightning, Zeus, Father,
thunder Death to nothing!   230

Apollo, lord of the light, I beg you—
    whip your longbow's golden cord
showering arrows on our enemies—shafts of power
champions strong before us rushing on!

Artemis, Huntress,   235
torches flaring over the eastern ridges—
     ride Death down in pain!

God of the headdress gleaming gold, I cry to you—
your name and ours are one, Dionysus—
   come with your face aflame with wine   240
      your raving women's cries
   your army on the march! Come with the lightning
come with torches blazing, eyes ablaze with glory!
Burn that god of death that all gods hate!

Oedipus enters from the palace to address the Chorus, as if addressing the en-
tire city of Thebes.

OEDIPUS: You pray to the gods? Let me grant your prayers.   245
 Come, listen to me—do what the plague demands:
 you'll find relief and lift your head from the depths.

I will speak out now as a stranger to the story,
a stranger to the crime. If I'd been present then,
there would have been no mystery, no long hunt   250
without a clue in hand. So now, counted
a native Theban years after the murder,
to all of Thebes I make this proclamation:
if any one of you knows who murdered Laius,
the son of Labdacus, I order him to reveal   255
the whole truth to me. Nothing to fear,
even if he must denounce himself,
let him speak up
and so escape the brunt of the charge—
he will suffer no unbearable punishment,   260
nothing worse than exile, totally unharmed.

Oedipus pauses, waiting for a reply.

      Next,

if anyone knows the murderer is a stranger,
a man from alien soil, come, speak up.
I will give him a handsome reward, and lay up
gratitude in my heart for him besides.   265

Silence again, no reply.

But if you keep silent, if anyone panicking,
trying to shield himself or friend or kin,
rejects my offer, then hear what I will do.
I order you, every citizen of the state
where I hold throne and power: banish this man—   270
whoever he may be—never shelter him, never
speak a word to him, never make him partner
to your prayers, your victims burned to the gods.
Never let the holy water touch his hands.
Drive him out, each of you, from every home.   275
He is the plague, the heart of our corruption,
as Apollo's oracle has revealed to me
just now. So I honor my obligations:
I fight for the god and for the murdered man.
Now my curse on the murderer. Whoever he is,   280
a lone man unknown in his crime
or one among many, let that man drag out
his life in agony, step by painful step—
I curse myself as well . . . if by any chance
he proves to be an intimate of our house,   285
here at my hearth, with my full knowledge,
may the curse I just called down on him strike me!

These are your orders: perform them to the last.
I command you, for my sake, for Apollo's, for this country
blasted root and branch by the angry heavens.   290
Even if god had never urged you on to act,
how could you leave the crime uncleansed so long?
A man so noble—your king, brought down in blood—
you should have searched. But I am the king now,
I hold the throne that he held then, possess his bed   295
and a wife who shares our seed . . . why, our seed
might be the same, children born of the same mother
might have created blood-bonds between us
if his hope of offspring hadn't met disaster—
but fate swooped at his head and cut him short.   300
So I will fight for him as if he were my father,
stop at nothing, search the world
to lay my hands on the man who shed his blood,
the son of Labdacus descended of Polydorus,
Cadmus of old and Agenor, founder of the line: 305
their power and mine are one.
                                         Oh dear gods,

my curse on those who disobey these orders!
Let no crops grow out of the earth for them—
shrivel their women, kill their sons,
burn them to nothing in this plague   310
that hits us now, or something even worse.
But you, loyal men of Thebes who approve my actions,
may our champion, Justice, may all the gods
be with us, fight beside us to the end!

LEADER: In the grip of your curse, my king, I swear   315
I'm not the murderer, cannot point him out.
As for the search, Apollo pressed it on us—
he should name the killer.

OEDIPUS: Quite right,
but to force the gods to act against their will—
no man has the power.

LEADER: Then if I might mention   320
the next best thing . . .

OEDIPUS: The third best too—
don't hold back, say it.

LEADER: I still believe . . .
Lord Tiresias sees with the eyes of Lord Apollo.
Anyone searching for the truth, my king,
might learn it from the prophet, clear as day.   325

OEDIPUS: I've not been slow with that. On Creon's cue
I sent the escorts, twice, within the hour.
I'm surprised he isn't here.

LEADER: We need him—
without him we have nothing but old, useless rumors.

OEDIPUS: Which rumors? I'll search out every word.   330

LEADER: Laius was killed, they say, by certain travelers.

OEDIPUS: I know—but no one can find the murderer.

LEADER: If the man has a trace of fear in him
he won't stay silent long,
not with your curses ringing in his ears.   335

OEDIPUS: He didn't flinch at murder,
he'll never flinch at words.

*Enter Tiresias, the blind prophet, led by a boy with escorts in attendance. He
remains at a distance.*

LEADER: Here is the one who will convict him, look,
they bring him on at last, the seer, the man of god.
The truth lives inside him, him alone.

OEDIPUS: O Tiresias,   340
master of all the mysteries of our life,
all you teach and all you dare not tell,
signs in the heavens, signs that walk the earth!
Blind as you are, you can feel all the more
what sickness haunts our city. You, my lord,   345
are the one shield, the one savior we can find.

We asked Apollo—perhaps the messengers
haven't told you—he sent his answer back:
"Relief from the plague can only come one way.   350
Uncover the murderers of Laius,
put them to death or drive them into exile."
So I beg you, grudge us nothing now, no voice,
no message plucked from the birds, the embers
or the other mantic ways within your grasp.
Rescue yourself, your city, rescue me—   355
rescue everything infected by the dead.
We are in your hands. For a man to help others
with all his gifts and native strength:
that is the noblest work.

TIRESIAS: How terrible—to see the truth
when the truth is only pain to him who sees!   360
I knew it well, but I put it from my mind,
else I never would have come.

OEDIPUS: What's this? Why so grim, so dire?

TIRESIAS: Just send me home. You bear your burdens,
I'll bear mine. It's better that way,   365
please believe me.

OEDIPUS: Strange response—unlawful,
unfriendly too to the state that bred and raised you;
you're withholding the word of god.

TIRESIAS: I fail to see
that your own words are so well-timed.
I'd rather not have the same thing said of me . . .   370

OEDIPUS: For the love of god, don't turn away,
not if you know something. We beg you,
all of us on our knees.

TIRESIAS   None of you knows—
and I will never reveal my dreadful secrets,
not to say your own.   375

OEDIPUS: What? You know and you won't tell?
You're bent on betraying us, destroying Thebes?

TIRESIAS: I'd rather not cause pain for you or me.
So why this . . . useless interrogation?
You'll get nothing from me.

OEDIPUS: Nothing! You,   380
you scum of the earth, you'd enrage a heart of stone!
You won't talk? Nothing moves you?
Out with it, once and for all!

TIRESIAS: You criticize my temper . . . unaware
of the one *you* live with, you revile me.   385

OEDIPUS: Who could restrain his anger hearing you?
What outrage—you spurn the city!

TIRESIAS: What will come will come.
Even if I shroud it all in silence.

OEDIPUS: What will come? You're bound to *tell* me that.   390

TIRESIAS: I'll say no more. Do as you like, build your anger
 to whatever pitch you please, rage your worst—
OEDIPUS: Oh I'll let loose, I have such fury in me—
 now I see it all. You helped hatch the plot,
 you did the work, yes, short of killing him   395
 with your own hands—and given eyes I'd say
 you did the killing single-handed!
TIRESIAS: Is that so!
 I charge you, then, submit to that decree
 you just laid down: from this day onward
 speak to no one, not these citizens, not myself.   400
 You are the curse, the corruption of the land!
OEDIPUS: You, shameless—
 aren't you appalled to start up such a story?
 You think you can get away with this?
TIRESIAS: I have already.
 The truth with all its power lives inside me.   405
OEDIPUS: Who primed you for this? Not your prophet's trade.
TIRESIAS: You did, you forced me, twisted it out of me.
OEDIPUS: What? Say it again—I'll understand it better.
TIRESIAS: Didn't you understand, just now?
 Or are you tempting me to talk?   410
OEDIPUS: No, I can't say I grasped your meaning.
 Out with it, again!
TIRESIAS: I say you are the murderer you hunt.
OEDIPUS: That obscenity, twice—by god, you'll pay.
TIRESIAS: Shall I say more, so you can really rage?   415
OEDIPUS: Much as you want. Your words are nothing—
 futile.
TIRESIAS: You cannot imagine . . . I tell you,
 you and your loved ones live together in infamy,
 you cannot see how far you've gone in guilt.
OEDIPUS: You think you can keep this up and never suffer?   420
TIRESIAS: Indeed, if the truth has any power.
OEDIPUS: It does
 but not for you, old man. You've lost your power,
 stone-blind, stone-deaf—senses, eyes blind as stone!
TIRESIAS: I pity you, flinging at me the very insults
 each man here will fling at you so soon.
OEDIPUS: Blind,   425
 lost in the night, endless night that nursed you!
 You can't hurt me or anyone else who sees the light—
 you can never touch me.
TIRESIAS: True, it is not your fate
 to fall at my hands. Apollo is quite enough,
 and he will take some pains to work this out.   430
OEDIPUS: Creon! Is this conspiracy his or yours?
TIRESIAS: Creon is not your downfall, no, you are your own.
OEDIPUS: O power—

wealth and empire, skill outstripping skill
in the heady rivalries of life,
what envy lurks inside you! Just for this,   435
the crown the city gave me—I never sought it,
they laid it in my hands—for this alone, Creon,
the soul of trust, my loyal friend from the start
steals against me . . . so hungry to overthrow me
he sets this wizard on me, this scheming quack,   440
this fortune-teller peddling lies, eyes peeled
for his own profit—seer blind in his craft!

Come here, you pious fraud. Tell me,
when did you ever prove yourself a prophet?
When the Sphinx, that chanting Fury kept her deathwatch here,   445
why silent then, not a word to set our people free?
There was a riddle, not for some passer-by to solve—
it cried out for a prophet. Where were you?
Did you rise to the crisis? Not a word,
you and your birds, your gods—nothing.   450
No, but I came by, Oedipus the ignorant,
I stopped the Sphinx! With no help from the birds,
the flight of my own intelligence hit the mark.

And this is the man you'd try to overthrow?
You think you'll stand by Creon when he's king?   455
You and the great mastermind—
you'll pay in tears, I promise you, for this,
this witch-hunt. If you didn't look so senile
the lash would teach you what your scheming means!
LEADER: I'd suggest his words were spoken in anger,   460
Oedipus . . . yours too, and it isn't what we need.
The best solution to the oracle, the riddle
posed by god—we should look for that.
TIRESIAS: You are the king no doubt, but in one respect,
at least, I am your equal: the right to reply.   465
I claim that privilege too.
I am not your slave. I serve Apollo.
I don't need Creon to speak for me in public.
                                              So,
you mock my blindness? Let me tell you this.
You with your precious eyes,   470
you're blind to the corruption of your life,
to the house you live in, those you live with—
who *are* your parents? Do you know? All unknowing
you are the scourge of your own flesh and blood,
the dead below the earth and the living here above,   475
and the double lash of your mother and your father's curse
will whip you from this land one day, their footfall
treading you down in terror, darkness shrouding

your eyes that now can see the light!

Soon, soon

you'll scream aloud—what haven won't reverberate?   480
What rock of Cithaeron won't scream back in echo?
That day you learn the truth about your marriage,
the wedding-march that sang you into your halls,
the lusty voyage home to the fatal harbor!
And a load of other horrors you'd never dream   485
will level you with yourself and all your children.

There. Now smear us with insults—Creon, myself
and every word I've said. No man will ever
be rooted from the earth as brutally as you.

OEDIPUS: Enough! Such filth from him? Insufferable—   490
    what, still alive? Get out—
    faster, back where you came from—vanish!

TIRESIAS: I'd never have come if you hadn't called me here.

OEDIPUS: If I thought you'd blurt out such absurdities,
    you'd have died waiting before I'd had you summoned.

TIRESIAS: Absurd, am I? To you, not to your parents: 495
    the ones who bore you found me sane enough.

OEDIPUS: Parents—who? Wait . . . who is my father?

TIRESIAS: This day will bring your birth and your destruction.

OEDIPUS: Riddles—all you can say are riddles, murk and darkness.

TIRESIAS: Ah, but aren't you the best man alive at solving riddles?   500

OEDIPUS: Mock me for that, go on, and you'll reveal my greatness.

TIRESIAS: Your great good fortune, true, it was your ruin.

OEDIPUS: Not if I saved the city—what do I care?

TIRESIAS: Well then, I'll be going.

    To his attendant.

Take me home, boy.   505

OEDIPUS: Yes, take him away. You're a nuisance here.
    Out of the way, the irritation's gone.

    Turning his back on Tiresias, moving toward the palace.

TIRESIAS: I will go,
    once I have said what I came here to say.
    I'll never shrink from the anger in your eyes—
    you can't destroy me. Listen to me closely: 510
    the man you've sought so long, proclaiming,
    cursing up and down, the murderer of Laius—
    he is here. A stranger,
    you may think, who lives among you,
    he soon will be revealed a native Theban   515
    but he will take no joy in the revelation.
    Blind who now has eyes, beggar who now is rich,
    he will grope his way toward a foreign soil,
    a stick tapping before him step by step.

Oedipus enters the palace.

Revealed at last, brother and father both   520
to the children he embraces, to his mother
son and husband both—he sowed the loins
his father sowed, he spilled his father's blood!

Go in and reflect on that, solve that.
And if you find I've lied   525
from this day onward call the prophet blind.

Tiresias and the boy exit to the side.

CHORUS: Who—
    who is the man the voice of god denounces
    resounding out of the rocky gorge of Delphi?
        The horror too dark to tell,
    whose ruthless bloody hands have done the work?   530
    His time has come to fly
        to outrace the stallions of the storm
            his feet a streak of speed—
    Cased in armor, Apollo son of the Father
    lunges on him, lightning-bolts afire!   535
    And the grim unerring Furies
        closing for the kill.
                  Look,
    the word of god has just come blazing
    flashing off Parnassus' snowy heights!
        That man who left no trace—   540
    after him, hunt him down with all our strength!
    Now under bristling timber
        up through rocks and caves he stalks
            like the wild mountain bull—
    cut off from men, each step an agony, frenzied, racing blind   545
    but he cannot outrace the dread voices of Delphi
    ringing out of the heart of Earth,
        the dark wings beating around him shrieking doom
            the doom that never dies, the terror—
    The skilled prophet scans the birds and shatters me with terror!   550
    I can't accept him, can't deny him, don't know what to say,
    I'm lost, and the wings of dark foreboding beating—
    I cannot see what's come, what's still to come . . .
    and what could breed a blood feud between
        Laius' house and the son of Polybus?   555
    I know of nothing, not in the past and not now,
    no charge to bring against our king, no cause
    to attack his fame that rings throughout Thebes—
        not without proof—not for the ghost of Laius,
        not to avenge a murder gone without a trace.   560

Zeus and Apollo know, they know, the great masters
       of all the dark and depth of human life.
But whether a mere man can know the truth,
whether a seer can fathom more than I—
there is no test, no certain proof   565
       though matching skill for skill
a man can outstrip a rival. No, not till I see
these charges proved will I side with his accusers.
We saw him then, when the she-hawk swept against him,
saw with our own eyes his skill, his brilliant triumph—   570
      there was the test—he was the joy of Thebes!
      Never will I convict my king, never in my heart.

   Enter Creon from the side.

CREON: My fellow-citizens, I hear King Oedipus
    levels terrible charges at me. I had to come.
    I resent it deeply. If, in the present crisis,   575
    he thinks he suffers any abuse from me,
    anything I've done or said that offers him
    the slightest injury, why, I've no desire
    to linger out this life, my reputation a shambles.
    The damage I'd face from such an accusation   580
    is nothing simple. No, there's nothing worse:
    branded a traitor in the city, a traitor
    to all of you and my good friends.
LEADER: True,
    but a slur might have been forced out of him,
    by anger perhaps, not any firm conviction.   585
CREON: The charge was made in public, wasn't it?
    I put the prophet up to spreading lies?
LEADER: Such things were said . . .
    I don't know with what intent, if any.
CREON: Was his glance steady, his mind right   590
    when the charge was brought against me?
LEADER: I really couldn't say. I never look
    to judge the ones in power.

   The doors open. Oedipus enters.

               Wait,
here's Oedipus now.
OEDIPUS: You—here? You have the gall
    to show your face before the palace gates?   595
    You, plotting to kill me, kill the king—
    I see it all, the marauding thief himself
    scheming to steal my crown and power!
                  Tell me,
in god's name, what did you take me for,
coward or fool, when you spun out your plot?   600
Your treachery—you think I'd never detect it
creeping against me in the dark? Or sensing it,

not defend myself? Aren't you the fool,
 you and your high adventure. Lacking numbers,
 powerful friends, out for the big game of empire—   605
 you need riches, armies to bring that quarry down!

CREON: Are you quite finished? It's your turn to listen
 for just as long as you've . . . instructed me.
 Hear me out, then judge me on the facts.

OEDIPUS: You've a wicked way with words, Creon,   610
 but I'll be slow to learn—from you.
 I find you a menace, a great burden to me.

CREON: Just one thing, hear me out in this.

OEDIPUS: Just one thing,
 don't tell me you're not the enemy, the traitor.

CREON: Look, if you think crude, mindless stubbornness 615
 such a gift, you've lost your sense of balance.

OEDIPUS: If you think you can abuse a kinsman,
 then escape the penalty, you're insane.

CREON: Fair enough, I grant you. But this injury
 you say I've done you, what is it?   620

OEDIPUS: Did you induce me, yes or no,
 to send for that sanctimonious prophet?

CREON: I did. And I'd do the same again.

OEDIPUS: All right then, tell me, how long is it now
 since Laius . . .

CREON: Laius—what did *he* do?

OEDIPUS: Vanished,   625
 swept from sight, murdered in his tracks.

CREON: The count of the years would run you far back . . .

OEDIPUS: And that far back, was the prophet at his trade?

CREON: Skilled as he is today, and just as honored.

OEDIPUS: Did he ever refer to me then, at that time?

CREON: No,   630
 never, at least, when I was in his presence.

OEDIPUS: But you did investigate the murder, didn't you?

CREON: We did our best, of course, discovered nothing.

OEDIPUS: But the great seer never accused me then—why not?

CREON: I don't know. And when I don't, *I* keep quiet. 635

OEDIPUS: You do know this, you'd tell it too—
 if you had a shred of decency.

CREON: What?
 If I know, I won't hold back.

OEDIPUS: Simply this:
 if the two of you had never put heads together,
 we'd never have heard about *my* killing Laius. 640

CREON: If that's what he says . . . well, you know best.
 But now I have a right to learn from you
 as you just learned from me.

OEDIPUS: Learn your fill,
 you never will convict me of the murder.

CREON: Tell me, you're married to my sister, aren't you?   645
OEDIPUS: A genuine discovery—there's no denying that.
CREON: And you rule the land with her, with equal power?
OEDIPUS: She receives from me whatever she desires.
CREON: And I am the third, all of us are equals?
OEDIPUS: Yes, and it's there you show your stripes—   650
    you betray a kinsman.
CREON: Not at all.
Not if you see things calmly, rationally,
as I do. Look at it this way first:
who in his right mind would rather rule
and live in anxiety than sleep in peace?   655
Particularly if he enjoys the same authority.
Not I, I'm not the man to yearn for kingship,
not with a king's power in my hands. Who would?
No one with any sense of self-control.
Now, as it is, you offer me all I need,   660
not a fear in the world. But if I wore the crown . . .
there'd be many painful duties to perform,
hardly to my taste.
              How could kingship
please me more than influence, power
without a qualm? I'm not that deluded yet,   665
to reach for anything but privilege outright,
profit free and clear.
Now all men sing my praises, all salute me,
now all who request your favors curry mine.
I'm their best hope: success rests in me.   670
Why give up that, I ask you, and borrow trouble?
A man of sense, someone who sees things clearly
would never resort to treason.
No, I've no lust for conspiracy in me,
nor could I ever suffer one who does.   675
Do you want proof? Go to Delphi yourself,
examine the oracle and see if I've reported
the message word-for-word. This too:
if you detect that I and the clairvoyant
have plotted anything in common, arrest me,   680
execute me. Not on the strength of one vote,
two in this case, mine as well as yours.
But don't convict me on sheer unverified surmise.

How wrong it is to take the good for bad,
purely at random, or take the bad for good.   685
But reject a friend, a kinsman? I would as soon
tear out the life within us, priceless life itself.
You'll learn this well, without fail, in time.
Time alone can bring the just man to light;
the criminal you can spot in one short day.   690

LEADER: Good advice,
   my lord, for anyone who wants to avoid disaster.
   Those who jump to conclusions may be wrong.
OEDIPUS: When my enemy moves against me quickly,
   plots in secret, I move quickly too, I must,
   I plot and pay him back. Relax my guard a moment,   695
   waiting his next move—he wins his objective,
   I lose mine.
CREON: What do you want?
   You want me banished?
OEDIPUS: No, I want you dead.
CREON: Just to show how ugly a grudge can . . .
OEDIPUS: So,
   still stubborn? you don't think I'm serious?   700
CREON: I think you're insane.
OEDIPUS: Quite sane—in my behalf.
CREON: Not just as much in mine?
OEDIPUS: You—my mortal enemy?
CREON: What if you're wholly wrong?
OEDIPUS: No matter—I must rule.
CREON: Not if you rule unjustly.
OEDIPUS: Hear him, Thebes, my city!
CREON: My city too, not yours alone!   705
LEADER: Please, my lords.

   Enter Jocasta from the palace.

                  Look, Jocasta's coming,
   and just in time too. With her help
   you must put this fighting of yours to rest.
JOCASTA: Have you no sense? Poor misguided men,
   such shouting—why this public outburst?   710
   Aren't you ashamed, with the land so sick,
   to stir up private quarrels?

   To Oedipus.

   Into the palace now. And Creon, you go home.
   Why make such a furor over nothing?
CREON: My sister, it's dreadful . . . Oedipus, your husband,   715
   he's bent on a choice of punishments for me,
   banishment from the fatherland or death.
OEDIPUS: Precisely. I caught him in the act, Jocasta,
   plotting, about to stab me in the back.
CREON: Never—curse me, let me die and be damned   720
   if I've done you any wrong you charge me with.
JOCASTA: Oh god, believe it, Oedipus,
   honor the solemn oath he swears to heaven.
   Do it for me, for the sake of all your people.

   The Chorus begins to chant.

CHORUS: Believe it, be sensible   725
    give way, my king, I beg you!
OEDIPUS: What do you want from me, concessions?
CHORUS: Respect him—he's been no fool in the past
    and now he's strong with the oath he swears to god.
OEDIPUS: You know what you're asking?
CHORUS: I do.
OEDIPUS: Then out with it!   730
CHORUS: The man's your friend, your kin, he's under oath—
    don't cast him out, disgraced
    branded with guilt on the strength of hearsay only.
OEDIPUS: Know full well, if that's what you want
    you want me dead or banished from the land.   735
CHORUS: Never—
    no, by the blazing Sun, first god of the heavens!
    Stripped of the gods, stripped of loved ones,
    let me die by inches if that ever crossed my mind.
    But the heart inside me sickens, dies as the land dies
    and now on top of the old griefs you pile this,   740
    your fury—both of you!
OEDIPUS: Then let him go,
    even if it does lead to my ruin, my death
    or my disgrace, driven from Thebes for life.
    It's you, not him I pity—your words move me.
    He, wherever he goes, my hate goes with him.   745
CREON: Look at you, sullen in yielding, brutal in your rage—
    you'll go too far. It's perfect justice:
    natures like yours are hardest on themselves.
OEDIPUS: Then leave me alone—get out!
CREON: I'm going.
    You're wrong, so wrong. These men know I'm right.   750

    Exit to the side. The Chorus turns to Jocasta.

CHORUS: Why do you hesitate, my lady
    why not help him in?
JOCASTA: Tell me what's happened first.
CHORUS: Loose, ignorant talk started dark suspicions
    and a sense of injustice cut deeply too.   755
JOCASTA: On both sides?
CHORUS: Oh yes.
JOCASTA: What did they say?
CHORUS: Enough, please, enough! The land's so racked already
    or so it seems to me . . .
    End the trouble here, just where they left it.
OEDIPUS: You see what comes of your good intentions now?   760
    And all because you tried to blunt my anger.
CHORUS: My king,
    I've said it once, I'll say it time and again—
    I'd be insane, you know it,

senseless, ever to turn my back on you.
You who set our beloved land—storm-tossed, shattered— 765
straight on course. Now again, good helmsman,
steer us through the storm!

The Chorus draws away, leaving Oedipus and Jocasta side by side.

JOCASTA: For the love of god,
Oedipus, tell me too, what is it?
Why this rage? You're so unbending.
OEDIPUS: I will tell you. I respect you, Jocasta, 770
much more than these . . .

Glancing at the Chorus.

Creon's to blame, Creon schemes against me.
JOCASTA: Tell me clearly, how did the quarrel start?
OEDIPUS: He says I murdered Laius—I am guilty.
JOCASTA: How does he know? Some secret knowledge 775
or simple hearsay?
OEDIPUS: Oh, he sent his prophet in
to do his dirty work. You know Creon,
Creon keeps his own lips clean.
JOCASTA: A prophet?
Well then, free yourself of every charge!
Listen to me and learn some peace of mind: 780
no skill in the world,
nothing human can penetrate the future.
Here is proof, quick and to the point.

An oracle came to Laius one fine day
(I won't say from Apollo himself 785
but his underlings, his priests) and it said
that doom would strike him down at the hands of a son,
our son, to be born of our own flesh and blood. But Laius,
so the report goes at least, was killed by strangers,
thieves, at a place where three roads meet . . . my son— 790
he wasn't three days old and the boy's father
fastened his ankles, had a henchman fling him away
on a barren, trackless mountain.
                              There, you see?
Apollo brought neither thing to pass. My baby
no more murdered his father than Laius suffered— 795
his wildest fear—death at his own son's hands.
That's how the seers and their revelations
mapped out the future. Brush them from your mind.
Whatever the god needs and seeks
he'll bring to light himself, with ease. 800
OEDIPUS: Strange,
hearing you just now . . . my mind wandered,
my thoughts racing back and forth.

JOCASTA: What do you mean? Why so anxious, startled?

OEDIPUS: I thought I heard you say that Laius
      was cut down at a place where three roads meet.   805

JOCASTA: That was the story. It hasn't died out yet.

OEDIPUS: Where did this thing happen? Be precise.

JOCASTA: A place called Phocis, where two branching roads,
      one from Daulia, one from Delphi,
      come together—a crossroads.   810

OEDIPUS: When? How long ago?

JOCASTA: The heralds no sooner reported Laius dead
      than you appeared and they hailed you king of Thebes.

OEDIPUS: My god, my god—what have you planned to do to me?

JOCASTA: What, Oedipus? What haunts you so?

OEDIPUS: Not yet.   815
      Laius—how did he look? Describe him.
      Had he reached his prime?

JOCASTA: He was swarthy,
      and the gray had just begun to streak his temples,
      and his build . . . wasn't far from yours.

OEDIPUS: Oh no no,
      I think I've just called down a dreadful curse   820
      upon myself—I simply didn't know!

JOCASTA: What are you saying? I shudder to look at you.

OEDIPUS: I have a terrible fear the blind seer can see.
      I'll know in a moment. One thing more—

JOCASTA: Anything,
      afraid as I am—ask, I'll answer, all I can.   825

OEDIPUS: Did he go with a light or heavy escort,
      several men-at-arms, like a lord, a king?

JOCASTA: There were five in the party, a herald among them,
      and a single wagon carrying Laius.

OEDIPUS: Ai—
      now I can see it all, clear as day.   830
      Who told you all this at the time, Jocasta?

JOCASTA: A servant who reached home, the lone survivor.

OEDIPUS: So, could he still be in the palace—even now?

JOCASTA: No indeed. Soon as he returned from the scene
      and saw you on the throne with Laius dead and gone,   835
      he knelt and clutched my hand, pleading with me
      to send him into the hinterlands, to pasture,
      far as possible, out of sight of Thebes.
      I sent him away. Slave though he was,
      he'd earned that favor—and much more.   840

OEDIPUS: Can we bring him back, quickly?

JOCASTA: Easily. Why do you want him so?

OEDIPUS: I'm afraid,
      Jocasta, I have said too much already.
      That man—I've got to see him.

JOCASTA: Then he'll come.

But even I have a right, I'd like to think,   845
to know what's torturing you, my lord.
OEDIPUS: And so you shall—I can hold nothing back from you,
now I've reached this pitch of dark foreboding.
Who means more to me than you? Tell me,
whom would I turn toward but you   850
as I go through all this?

My father was Polybus, king of Corinth.
My mother, a Dorian, Merope. And I was held
the prince of the realm among the people there,
till something struck me out of nowhere,   855
something strange . . . worth remarking perhaps,
hardly worth the anxiety I gave it.
Some man at a banquet who had drunk too much
shouted out—he was far gone, mind you—
that I am not my father's son. Fighting words!   860
I barely restrained myself that day
but early the next I went to mother and father,
questioned them closely, and they were enraged
at the accusation and the fool who let it fly.
So as for my parents I was satisfied,   865
but still this thing kept gnawing at me,
the slander spread—I had to make my move.
                                              And so,
unknown to mother and father I set out for Delphi,
and the god Apollo spurned me, sent me away
denied the facts I came for,   870
but first he flashed before my eyes a future
great with pain, terror, disaster—I can hear him cry,
"You are fated to couple with your mother, you will bring
a breed of children into the light no man can bear to see—
you will kill your father, the one who gave you life!"   875
I heard all that and ran. I abandoned Corinth,
from that day on I gauged its landfall only
by the stars, running, always running
toward some place where I would never see
the shame of all those oracles come true.   880
And as I fled I reached that very spot
where the great king, you say, met his death.
Now, Jocasta, I will tell you all.
Making my way toward this triple crossroad
I began to see a herald, then a brace of colts   885
drawing a wagon, and mounted on the bench . . . a man,
just as you've described him, coming face-to-face,
and the one in the lead and the old man himself
were about to thrust me off the road—brute force—
and the one shouldering me aside, the driver,   890
I strike him in anger!—and the old man, watching me

coming up along his wheels—he brings down
his prod, two prongs straight at my head!
I paid him back with interest!
Short work, by god—with one blow of the staff   895
in this right hand I knock him out of his high seat,
roll him out of the wagon, sprawling headlong—
I killed them all—every mother's son!

Oh, but if there is any blood-tie
between Laius and this stranger . . .   900
what man alive more miserable than I?
More hated by the gods? I am the man
no alien, no citizen welcomes to his house,
law forbids it—not a word to me in public,
driven out of every hearth and home.   905
And all these curses I—no one but I
brought down these piling curses on myself!
And you, his wife, I've touched your body with these,
the hands that killed your husband cover you with blood.

Wasn't I born for torment? Look me in the eyes!   910
I am abomination—heart and soul!
I must be exiled, and even in exile
never see my parents, never set foot
on native earth again. Else I'm doomed
to couple with my mother and cut my father down . . .   915
Polybus who reared me, gave me life.

                          But why, why?
Wouldn't a man of judgment say—and wouldn't he be right—
some savage power has brought this down upon my head?

Oh no, not that, you pure and awesome gods,
never let me see that day! Let me slip   920
from the world of men, vanish without a trace
before I see myself stained with such corruption,
stained to the heart.
LEADER: My lord, you fill our hearts with fear.
But at least until you question the witness,   925
do take hope.
OEDIPUS: Exactly. He is my last hope—
I'm waiting for the shepherd. He is crucial.
JOCASTA: And once he appears, what then? Why so urgent?
OEDIPUS: I'll tell you. If it turns out that his story
matches yours, I've escaped the worst.   930
JOCASTA: What did I say? What struck you so?
OEDIPUS: You said thieves—
he told you a whole band of them murdered Laius.
So, if he still holds to the same number,
I cannot be the killer. One can't equal many.

But if he refers to one man, one alone,   935
clearly the scales come down on me:
I am guilty.
JOCASTA: Impossible. Trust me,
I told you precisely what he said,
and he can't retract it now;
the whole city heard it, not just I.   940
And even if he should vary his first report
by one man more or less, still, my lord,
he could never make the murder of Laius
truly fit the prophecy. Apollo was explicit:
my son was doomed to kill my husband . . . my son,   945
poor defenseless thing, he never had a chance
to kill his father. They destroyed him first.

So much for prophecy. It's neither here nor there.
From this day on, I wouldn't look right or left.
OEDIPUS: True, true. Still, that shepherd,   950
    someone fetch him—now!
JOCASTA: I'll send at once. But do let's go inside.
    I'd never displease you, least of all in this.

    Oedipus and Jocasta enter the palace.

CHORUS: Destiny guide me always
    Destiny find me filled with reverence   955
              pure in word and deed.
    Great laws tower above us, reared on high
    born for the brilliant vault of heaven—
        Olympian Sky their only father,
    nothing mortal, no man gave them birth,   960
    their memory deathless, never lost in sleep:
    within them lives a mighty god, the god does not grow old.

    Pride breeds the tyrant
    violent pride, gorging, crammed to bursting
        with all that is overripe and rich with ruin—   965
    clawing up to the heights, headlong pride
    crashes down the abyss—sheer doom!
        No footing helps, all foothold lost and gone.
    But the healthy strife that makes the city strong—
    I pray that god will never end that wrestling: 970
    god, my champion, I will never let you go.
    But if any man comes striding, high and mighty
        in all he says and does,
    no fear of justice, no reverence
    for the temples of the gods—   975
        let a rough doom tear him down,
    repay his pride, breakneck, ruinous pride!
    If he cannot reap his profits fairly

cannot restrain himself from outrage—
mad, laying hands on the holy things untouchable!   980

    Can such a man, so desperate, still boast
    he can save his life from the flashing bolts of god?
        If all such violence goes with honor now
           why join the sacred dance?

Never again will I go reverent to Delphi,   985
    the inviolate heart of Earth
or Apollo's ancient oracle at Abae
or Olympia of the fires—
    unless these prophecies all come true
for all mankind to point toward in wonder.   990
King of kings, if you deserve your titles
    Zeus, remember, never forget!
You and your deathless, everlasting reign.

    They are dying, the old oracles sent to Laius,
    now our masters strike them off the rolls.   995
        Nowhere Apollo's golden glory now—
           the gods, the gods go down.

Enter Jocasta from the palace, carrying a suppliant's branch wound in wool.

JOCASTA: Lords of the realm, it occurred to me,
just now, to visit the temples of the gods,
so I have my branch in hand and incense too.   1000

Oedipus is beside himself. Racked with anguish,
no longer a man of sense, he won't admit
the latest prophecies are hollow as the old—
he's at the mercy of every passing voice
if the voice tells of terror.   1005
I urge him gently, nothing seems to help,
so I turn to you, Apollo, you are nearest.

*Placing her branch on the altar, while an old herdsman enters from the side,
not the one just summoned by the King but an unexpected Messenger from
Corinth.*

I come with prayers and offerings . . . I beg you,
cleanse us, set us free of defilement!
Look at us, passengers in the grip of fear,   1010
watching the pilot of the vessel go to pieces.

MESSENGER:

Approaching Jocasta and the Chorus.

Strangers, please, I wonder if you could lead us
to the palace of the king . . . I think it's Oedipus.
Better, the man himself—you know where he is?

LEADER: This is his palace, stranger. He's inside.   1015
But here is his queen, his wife and mother
of his children.

MESSENGER: Blessings on you, noble queen,
queen of Oedipus crowned with all your family—
blessings on you always!

JOCASTA: And the same to you, stranger, you deserve it . . .   1020
such a greeting. But what have you come for?
Have you brought us news?

MESSENGER: Wonderful news—
for the house, my lady, for your husband too.

JOCASTA: Really, what? Who sent you?

MESSENGER: Corinth.
I'll give you the message in a moment.   1025
You'll be glad of it—how could you help it?—
though it costs a little sorrow in the bargain.

JOCASTA: What can it be, with such a double edge?

MESSENGER: The people there, they want to make your Oedipus
king of Corinth, so they're saying now.   1030

JOCASTA: Why? Isn't old Polybus still in power?

MESSENGER: No more. Death has got him in the tomb.

JOCASTA: What are you saying? Polybus, dead?—dead?

MESSENGER: If not,
if I'm not telling the truth, strike me dead too.

JOCASTA:

To a servant.

Quickly, go to your master, tell him this!   1035

You prophecies of the gods, where are you now?
This is the man that Oedipus feared for years,
he fled him, not to kill him—and now he's dead,
quite by chance, a normal, natural death,
not murdered by his son.   1040

OEDIPUS:

Emerging from the palace.

                    Dearest,
what now? Why call me from the palace?

JOCASTA:

Bringing the Messenger closer.

Listen to *him*, see for yourself what all
those awful prophecies of god have come to.

OEDIPUS: And who is he? What can he have for me?

JOCASTA: He's from Corinth, he's come to tell you   1045
your father is no more—Polybus—he's dead!

OEDIPUS:

Wheeling on the Messenger.

What? Let me have it from your lips.

MESSENGER: Well,
if that's what you want first, then here it is:
make no mistake, Polybus is dead and gone.

OEDIPUS: How—murder? sickness?—what? what killed him?   1050

MESSENGER: A light tip of the scales can put old bones to rest.

OEDIPUS: Sickness then—poor man, it wore him down.

MESSENGER: That,
and the long count of years he'd measured out.

OEDIPUS: So!
Jocasta, why, why look to the Prophet's hearth,
the fires of the future? Why scan the birds   1055
that scream above our heads? They winged me on
to the murder of my father, did they? That was my doom?
Well look, he's dead and buried, hidden under the earth,
and here I am in Thebes, I never put hand to sword—
unless some longing for me wasted him away,   1060
then in a sense you'd say I caused his death.
But now, all those prophecies I feared—Polybus
packs them off to sleep with him in hell!
They're nothing, worthless.

JOCASTA: There.
Didn't I tell you from the start?   1065

OEDIPUS: So you did. I was lost in fear.

JOCASTA: No more, sweep it from your mind forever.

OEDIPUS: But my mother's bed, surely I must fear—

JOCASTA: Fear?
What should a man fear? It's all chance,
chance rules our lives. Not a man on earth   1070
can see a day ahead, groping through the dark.
Better to live at random, best we can.
And as for this marriage with your mother—
have no fear. Many a man before you,
in his dreams, has shared his mother's bed.   1075
Take such things for shadows, nothing at all—
Live, Oedipus,
as if there's no tomorrow!

OEDIPUS: Brave words,
and you'd persuade me if mother weren't alive.
But mother lives, so for all your reassurances   1080
I live in fear, I must.

JOCASTA: But your father's death,
that, at least, is a great blessing, joy to the eyes!

OEDIPUS: Great, I know . . . but I fear *her*—she's still alive.

MESSENGER: Wait, who is this woman, makes you so afraid?

OEDIPUS: Merope, old man. The wife of Polybus.   1085

MESSENGER: The queen? What's there to fear in her?

OEDIPUS: A dreadful prophecy, stranger, sent by the gods.

MESSENGER: Tell me, could you? Unless it's forbidden
    other ears to hear.

OEDIPUS: Not at all.
    Apollo told me once—it is my fate—   1090
    I must make love with my own mother,
    shed my father's blood with my own hands.
    So for years I've given Corinth a wide berth,
    and it's been my good fortune too. But still,
    to see one's parents and look into their eyes   1095
    is the greatest joy I know.

MESSENGER: You're afraid of that?
    That kept you out of Corinth?

OEDIPUS: My *father*, old man—
    so I wouldn't kill my father.

MESSENGER: So that's it.
    Well then, seeing I came with such good will, my king,
    why don't I rid you of that old worry now?   1100

OEDIPUS: What a rich reward you'd have for that.

MESSENGER: What do you think I came for, majesty?
    So you'd come home and I'd be better off.

OEDIPUS: Never, I will never go near my parents.

MESSENGER: My boy, it's clear, you don't know what you're doing.   1105

OEDIPUS: What do you mean, old man? For god's sake, explain.

MESSENGER: If you ran from *them*, always dodging home . . .

OEDIPUS: Always, terrified Apollo's oracle might come true—

MESSENGER: And you'd be covered with guilt, from both your parents.

OEDIPUS: That's right, old man, that fear is always with me.   1110

MESSENGER: Don't you know? You've really nothing to fear.

OEDIPUS: But why? If I'm their son—Merope, Polybus?

MESSENGER: Polybus was nothing to you, that's why, not in blood.

OEDIPUS: What are you saying—Polybus was not my father?

MESSENGER: No more than I am. He and I are equals.   1115

OEDIPUS: My father—
    how can my father equal nothing? You're nothing to me!

MESSENGER: Neither was he, no more your father than I am.

OEDIPUS: Then why did he call me his son?

MESSENGER: You were a gift,
    years ago—know for a fact he took you
    from my hands.

OEDIPUS: No, from another's hands?   1120
    Then how could he love me so? He loved me, deeply . . .

MESSENGER: True, and his early years without a child
    made him love you all the more.

OEDIPUS: And you, did you . . .
    buy me? find me by accident?

MESSENGER: I stumbled on you,
    down the woody flanks of Mount Cithaeron.

OEDIPUS: So close,   1125
   what were you doing here, just passing through?
MESSENGER: Watching over my flocks, grazing them on the slopes.
OEDIPUS: A herdsman, were you? A vagabond, scraping for wages?
MESSENGER: Your savior too, my son, in your worst hour.
OEDIPUS: Oh—
   when you picked me up, was I in pain? What exactly?   1130
MESSENGER: Your ankles . . . they tell the story. Look at them.
OEDIPUS: Why remind me of that, that old affliction?
MESSENGER: Your ankles were pinned together; I set you free.
OEDIPUS: That dreadful mark—I've had it from the cradle.
MESSENGER: And you got your name from that misfortune too,   1135
   the name's still with you.
OEDIPUS: Dear god, who did it?—
   mother? father? Tell me.
MESSENGER: I don't know.
   The one who gave you to me, he'd know more.
OEDIPUS: What? You took me from someone else?
   You didn't find me yourself?
MESSENGER: No sir,   1140
   another shepherd passed you on to me.
OEDIPUS: Who? Do you know? Describe him.
MESSENGER: He called himself a servant of . . .
   if I remember rightly—Laius.

   Jocasta turns sharply.

OEDIPUS: The king of the land who ruled here long ago?   1145
MESSENGER: That's the one. That herdsman was *his* man.
OEDIPUS" Is he still alive? Can I see him?
MESSENGER: They'd know best, the people of these parts.

   Oedipus and the Messenger turn to the Chorus.

OEDIPUS: Does anyone know that herdsman,
   the one he mentioned? Anyone seen him   1150
   in the fields, in town? Out with it!
   The time has come to reveal this once for all.
LEADER: I think he's the very shepherd you wanted to see,
   a moment ago. But the queen, Jocasta,
   she's the one to say.
OEDIPUS: Jocasta,   1155
   you remember the man we just sent for?
   Is *that* the one he means?
JOCASTA:
   why ask? Old shepherd, talk, empty nonsense,
   don't give it another thought, don't even think—
OEDIPUS: What—give up now, with a clue like this?   1160
   Fail to solve the mystery of my birth?
   Not for all the world!
JOCASTA: Stop—in the name of god,

if you love your own life, call off this search!
My suffering is enough.

OEDIPUS: Courage!
Even if my mother turns out to be a slave,   1165
and I a slave, three generations back,
you would not seem common.

JOCASTA: Oh no,
listen to me, I beg you, don't do this.

OEDIPUS: Listen to you? No more. I must know it all,
see the truth at last.

JOCASTA: No, please—   1170
for your sake—I want the best for you!

OEDIPUS: Your best is more than I can bear.

JOCASTA: You're doomed—
may you never fathom who you are!

OEDIPUS:

To a servant.

Hurry, fetch me the herdsman, now!
Leave her to glory in her royal birth.   1175

JOCASTA: Aieeeeee—
        man of agony—
that is the only name I have for you,
that, no other—ever, ever, ever!

Flinging through the palace doors. A long, tense silence follows.

LEADER: Where's she gone, Oedipus?
Rushing off, such wild grief . . .   1180
I'm afraid that from this silence
something monstrous may come bursting forth.

OEDIPUS: Let it burst! Whatever will, whatever must!
I must know my birth, no matter how common
it may be—must see my origins face-to-face.   1185
She perhaps, she with her woman's pride
may well be mortified by my birth,
but I, I count myself the son of Chance,
the great goddess, giver of all good things—
I'll never see myself disgraced. She is my mother!   1190
And the moons have marked me out, my blood-brothers,
one moon on the wane, the next moon great with power.
That is my blood, my nature—I will never betray it,
never fail to search and learn my birth!

CHORUS: Yes—if I am a true prophet   1195
        if I can grasp the truth,
    by the boundless skies of Olympus,
at the full moon of tomorrow, Mount Cithaeron
you will know how Oedipus glories in you—
you, his birthplace, nurse, his mountain-mother!   1200
And we will sing you, dancing out your praise—

you lift our monarch's heart!
　　Apollo, Apollo, god of the wild cry
　　　　may our dancing please you!
　　　　　　　　　　　　Oedipus—
　　　　son, dear child, who bore you?   1205
Who of the nymphs who seem to live forever
mated with Pan, the mountain-striding Father?
Who was your mother? who, some bride of Apollo
the god who loves the pastures spreading toward the sun?
　　　Or was it Hermes, king of the lightning ridges?   1210
Or Dionysus, lord of frenzy, lord of the barren peaks—
did he seize you in his hands, dearest of all his lucky finds?—
　　found by the nymphs, their warm eyes dancing, gift
to the lord who loves them dancing out his joy!

Oedipus strains to see a figure coming from the distance. Attended by palace
guards, an old Shepherd enters slowly, reluctant to approach the king.

OEDIPUS: I never met the man, my friends . . . still,   1215
　　if I had to guess, I'd say that's the shepherd,
　　the very one we've looked for all along.
　　Brothers in old age, two of a kind,
　　he and our guest here. At any rate
　　the ones who bring him in are my own men,   1220
　　I recognize them.

　　　Turning to the Leader.

　　　　　　　　　But you know more than I,
　　you should, you've seen the man before.
LEADER: I know him, definitely. One of Laius' men,
　　a trusty shepherd, if there ever was one.
OEDIPUS: You, I ask you first, stranger,   1225
　　you from Corinth—is this the one you mean?
MESSENGER: You're looking at him. He's your man.
OEDIPUS:

　　To the Shepherd.

　　You, old man, come over here—
　　look at me. Answer all my questions.
　　Did you ever serve King Laius?
SHEPHERD:　　　　　　　　　So I did . . .   1230
　　a slave, not bought on the block though,
　　born and reared in the palace.
OEDIPUS: Your duties, your kind of work?
SHEPHERD: Herding the flocks, the better part of my life.
OEDIPUS: Where, mostly? Where did you do your grazing?   1235
SHEPHERD:　　　　　　　　　　　　　　　　Well,
　　Cithaeron sometimes, or the foothills round about.
OEDIPUS: This man—you know him? ever see him there?

SHEPHERD:

> *Confused, glancing from the Messenger to the King.*

> Doing what?—what man do you mean?

OEDIPUS:

> *Pointing to the Messenger.*

> This one here—ever have dealings with him?

SHEPHERD: Not so I could say, but give me a chance, 1240
my memory's bad . . .

MESSENGER: No wonder he doesn't know me, master.
But let me refresh his memory for him.
I'm sure he recalls old times we had
on the slopes of Mount Cithaeron; 1245
he and I, grazing our flocks, he with two
and I with one—we both struck up together,
three whole seasons, six months at a stretch
from spring to the rising of Arcturus in the fall,
then with winter coming on I'd drive my herds 1250
to my own pens, and back he'd go with his
to Laius' folds.

> *To the Shepherd.*

>   Now that's how it was,
wasn't it—yes or no?

SHEPHERD: Yes, I suppose . . .
it's all so long ago.

MESSENGER: Come, tell me,
you gave me a child back then, a boy, remember? 1255
A little fellow to rear, my very own.

SHEPHERD: What? Why rake up that again?

MESSENGER: Look, here he is, my fine old friend—
the same man who was just a baby then.

SHEPHERD: Damn you, shut your mouth—quiet! 1260

OEDIPUS: Don't lash out at him, old man—
you need lashing more than he does.

SHEPHERD: Why,
master, majesty—what have I done wrong?

OEDIPUS: You won't answer his question about the boy.

SHEPHERD: He's talking nonsense, wasting his breath. 1265

OEDIPUS: So, you won't talk willingly—
then you'll talk with pain.

> *The guards seize the Shepherd.*

SHEPHERD: No, dear god, don't torture an old man!

OEDIPUS: Twist his arms back, quickly!

SHEPHERD: God help us, why?—
what more do you need to know? 1270

OEDIPUS: Did you give him that child? He's asking.
SHEPHERD: I did . . . I wish to god I'd died that day.
OEDIPUS: You've got your wish if you don't tell the truth.
SHEPHERD: The more I tell, the worse the death I'll die.
OEDIPUS: Our friend here wants to stretch things out, does he?   1275

    Motioning to his men for torture.

SHEPHERD: No, no, I gave it to him—I just said so.
OEDIPUS: Where did you get it? Your house? Someone else's?
SHEPHERD: It wasn't mine, no, I got it from . . . someone.
OEDIPUS: Which one of them?

    Looking at the citizens.

                              Whose house?
SHEPHERD: No—
    god's sake, master, no more questions!   1280
OEDIPUS: You're a dead man if I have to ask again.
SHEPHERD: Then—the child came from the house . . .
    of Laius.
OEDIPUS: A slave? or born of his own blood?
SHEPHERD: Oh no,
    I'm right at the edge, the horrible truth—I've got to say it!
OEDIPUS: And I'm at the edge of hearing horrors, yes, but I must hear!   1285
SHEPHERD: All right! His son, they said it was—his son!
    But the one inside, your wife,
    she'd tell it best.
OEDIPUS: My wife—
    she gave it to you?
SHEPHERD: Yes, yes, my king.   1290
OEDIPUS: Why, what for?
SHEPHERD: To kill it.
OEDIPUS: Her own child,
    how could she?
SHEPHERD: She was afraid—   1295
    frightening prophecies.
OEDIPUS: What?
SHEPHERD: They said—
    he'd kill his parents.
OEDIPUS: But you gave him to this old man—why?   1300
SHEPHERD: I pitied the little baby, master,
    hoped he'd take him off to his own country,
    far away, but he saved him for this, this fate.
    If you are the man he says you are, believe me,
    you were born for pain.   1305
OEDIPUS: O god—
    all come true, all burst to light!
    O light—now let me look my last on you!
    I stand revealed at last—
    cursed in my birth, cursed in marriage,
    cursed in the lives I cut down with these hands!   1310

Rushing through the doors with a great cry. The Corinthian Messenger, the
Shepherd and attendants exit slowly to the side.

CHORUS: O the generations of men
   the dying generations—adding the total
of all your lives I find they come to nothing . . .
      does there exist, is there a man on earth
who seizes more joy than just a dream, a vision?   1315
And the vision no sooner dawns than dies
blazing into oblivion.

You are my great example, you, your life,
your destiny, Oedipus, man of misery—
I count no man blest.

           You outranged all men!   1320
    Bending your bow to the breaking-point
you captured priceless glory, O dear god,
and the Sphinx came crashing down,
        the virgin, claws hooked
like a bird of omen singing, shrieking death—   1325
like a fortress reared in the face of death
you rose and saved our land.

From that day on we called you king
we crowned you with honors, Oedipus, towering over all—
mighty king of the seven gates of Thebes.   1330
But now to hear your story—is there a man more agonized?
More wed to pain and frenzy? Not a man on earth,
the joy of your life ground down to nothing
O Oedipus, name for the ages—
    one and the same wide harbor served you   1335
             son and father both
son and father came to rest in the same bridal chamber.
How, how could the furrows your father plowed
bear you, your agony, harrowing on
in silence O so long?

          But now for all your power   1340
Time, all-seeing Time has dragged you to the light,
judged your marriage monstrous from the start—
the son and the father tangling, both one—
O child of Laius, would to god
   I'd never seen you, never never!   1345
    Now I weep like a man who wails the dead
and the dirge comes pouring forth with all my heart!
I tell you the truth, you gave me life
my breath leapt up in you
and now you bring down night upon my eyes.   1350

Enter a Messenger from the palace.

MESSENGER: Men of Thebes, always the first in honor,
       what horrors you will hear, what you will see,
       what a heavy weight of sorrow you will shoulder . . .
       if you are true to your birth, if you still have
       some feeling for the royal house of Thebes.   1355
       I tell you neither the waters of the Danube
       nor the Nile can wash this palace clean.
       Such things it hides, it soon will bring to light—
       terrible things, and none done blindly now,
       all done with a will. The pains   1360
       we inflict upon ourselves hurt most of all.
LEADER: God knows we have pains enough already.
       What can you add to them?
MESSENGER: The queen is dead.
LEADER: Poor lady—how?
MESSENGER: By her own hand. But you are spared the worst,   1365
       you never had to watch . . . I saw it all,
       and with all the memory that's in me
       you will learn what that poor woman suffered.

       Once she'd broken in through the gates,
       dashing past us, frantic, whipped to fury,   1370
       ripping her hair out with both hands—
       straight to her rooms she rushed, flinging herself
       across the bridal-bed, doors slamming behind her—
       once inside, she wailed for Laius, dead so long,
       remembering how she bore his child long ago,   1375
       the life that rose up to destroy him, leaving
       its mother to mother living creatures
       with the very son she'd borne.
       Oh how she wept, mourning the marriage-bed
       where she let loose that double brood—monsters—   1380
       husband by her husband, children by her child.
                                        And then—
       but how she died is more than I can say. Suddenly
       Oedipus burst in, screaming, he stunned us so
       we couldn't watch her agony to the end,
       our eyes were fixed on him. Circling   1385
       like a maddened beast, stalking, here, there,
       crying out to us—
                         Give him a sword! His wife,
       no wife, his mother, where can he find the mother earth
       that cropped two crops at once, himself and all his children?
       He was raging—one of the dark powers pointing the way,   1390
       none of us mortals crowding around him, no,
       with a great shattering cry—someone, something leading him on—
       he hurled at the twin doors and bending the bolts back
       out of their sockets, crashed through the chamber.
       And there we saw the woman hanging by the neck,   1395

cradled high in a woven noose, spinning,
swinging back and forth. And when he saw her,
giving a low, wrenching sob that broke our hearts,
slipping the halter from her throat, he eased her down,
in a slow embrace he laid her down, poor thing . . .   1400
then, what came next, what horror we beheld!

He rips off her brooches, the long gold pins
holding her robes—and lifting them high,
looking straight up into the points,
he digs them down the sockets of his eyes, crying, "You,   1405
you'll see no more the pain I suffered, all the pain I caused!
Too long you looked on the ones you never should have seen,
blind to the ones you longed to see, to know! Blind
from this hour on! Blind in the darkness—blind!"
His voice like a dirge, rising, over and over   1410
raising the pins, raking them down his eyes.
And at each stroke blood spurts from the roots,
splashing his beard, a swirl of it, nerves and clots—
black hail of blood pulsing, gushing down.

These are the griefs that burst upon them both,   1415
coupling man and woman. The joy they had so lately,
the fortune of their old ancestral house
was deep joy indeed. Now, in this one day,
wailing, madness and doom, death, disgrace,
all the griefs in the world that you can name,   1420
all are theirs forever.

LEADER: Oh poor man, the misery—
has he any rest from pain now?

A voice within, in torment.

MESSENGER: He's shouting,
"Loose the bolts, someone, show me to all of Thebes!
My father's murderer, my mother's—"
No, I can't repeat it, it's unholy.   1425
Now he'll tear himself from his native earth,
not linger, curse the house with his own curse.
But he needs strength, and a guide to lead him on.
This is sickness more than he can bear.

The palace doors open.

                    Look,
he'll show you himself. The great doors are opening—   1430
you are about to see a sight, a horror
even his mortal enemy would pity.

*Enter Oedipus, blinded, led by a boy. He stands at the palace steps, as if sur-
veying his people once again.*

CHORUS: O the terror—
   the suffering, for all the world to see,
   the worst terror that ever met my eyes.
   What madness swept over you? What god,   1435
   what dark power leapt beyond all bounds,
   beyond belief, to crush your wretched life?—
   godforsaken, cursed by the gods!
   I pity you but I can't bear to look.
   I've much to ask, so much to learn,   1440
   so much fascinates my eyes,
   but you . . . I shudder at the sight.
OEDIPUS: Oh, Ohhh—
   the agony! I am agony—
   where am I going? where on earth?
      where does all this agony hurl me?   1445
   where's my voice?—
      winging, swept away on a dark tide—
    My destiny, my dark power, what a leap you made!
CHORUS: To the depths of terror, too dark to hear, to see.
OEDIPUS: Dark, horror of darkness   1450
   my darkness, drowning, swirling around me
   crashing wave on wave—unspeakable, irresistible
      headwind, fatal harbor! Oh again,
   the misery, all at once, over and over
   the stabbing daggers, stab of memory   1455
  raking me insane.
CHORUS: No wonder you suffer
   twice over, the pain of your wounds,
   the lasting grief of pain.
OEDIPUS: Dear friend, still here?
   Standing by me, still with a care for me,
   the blind man? Such compassion,   1460
     loyal to the last. Oh it's you,
   I know you're here, dark as it is
   I'd know you anywhere, your voice—
   it's yours, clearly yours.
CHORUS: Dreadful, what you've done . . .
   how could you bear it, gouging out your eyes?   1465
   What superhuman power drove you on?
OEDIPUS: Apollo, friends, Apollo—
   he ordained my agonies—these, my pains on pains!
   But the hand that struck my eyes was mine,
   mine alone—no one else—   1470
     I did it all myself!
   What good were eyes to me?
   Nothing I could see could bring me joy.
CHORUS: No, no, exactly as you say.
OEDIPUS: What can I ever see?
   What love, what call of the heart   1475

can touch my ears with joy? Nothing, friends.
    Take me away, far, far from Thebes,
    quickly, cast me away, my friends—
this great murderous ruin, this man cursed to heaven,
    the man the deathless gods hate most of all!   1480
CHORUS: Pitiful, you suffer so, you understand so much . . .
    I wish you'd never known.
OEDIPUS: Die, die—
    whoever he was that day in the wilds
    who cut my ankles free of the ruthless pins,
    he pulled me clear of death, he saved my life   1485
    for this, this kindness—
           Curse him, kill him!
    If I'd died then, I'd never have dragged myself,
    my loved ones through such hell.
CHORUS: Oh if only . . . would to god.
OEDIPUS: I'd never have come to this,   1490
    my father's murderer—never been branded
    mother's husband, all men see me now! Now,
    loathed by the gods, son of the mother I defiled
    coupling in my father's bed, spawning lives in the loins
that spawned my wretched life. What grief can crown this grief?   1495
    It's mine alone, my destiny—I am Oedipus!
CHORUS: How can I say you've chosen for the best?
    Better to die than be alive and blind.
OEDIPUS: What I did was best—don't lecture me,
    no more advice. I, with my eyes,   1500
    how could I look my father in the eyes
    when I go down to death? Or mother, so abused . . .
    I've done such things to the two of them,
    crimes too huge for hanging.
           Worse yet,
    the sight of my children, born as they were born,   1505
    how could I long to look into their eyes?
    No, not with these eyes of mine, never.
    Not this city either, her high towers,
    the sacred glittering images of her gods—
    I am misery! I, her best son, reared   1510
    as no other son of Thebes was ever reared,
    I've stripped myself, I gave the command myself.
    All men must cast away the great blasphemer,
    the curse now brought to light by the gods,
    the son of Laius—I, my father's son!   1515

Now I've exposed my guilt, horrendous guilt,
    could I train a level glance on you, my countrymen?
    Impossible! No, if I could just block off my ears,
    the springs of hearing, I would stop at nothing—
    I'd wall up my loathsome body like a prison,   1520

blind to the sound of life, not just the sight.
Oblivion—what a blessing . . .
for the mind to dwell a world away from pain.

O Cithaeron, why did you give me shelter?
Why didn't you take me, crush my life out on the spot?   1525
I'd never have revealed my birth to all mankind.

O Polybus, Corinth, the old house of my fathers,
so I believed—what a handsome prince you raised—
under the skin, what sickness to the core.
Look at me! Born of outrage, outrage to the core.   1530
O triple roads—it all comes back, the secret,
dark ravine, and the oaks closing in
where the three roads join . . .
You drank my father's blood, my own blood
spilled by my own hands—you still remember me?   1535
What things you saw me do? Then I came here
and did them all once more!
                              Marriages! O marriage,
you gave me birth, and once you brought me into the world
you brought my sperm rising back, springing to light
fathers, brothers, sons—one deadly breed—   1540
brides, wives, mothers. The blackest things
a man can do, I have done them all!
                              No more—
it's wrong to name what's wrong to do. Quickly,
for the love of god, hide me somewhere,
kill me, hurl me into the sea   1545
where you can never look on me again.

Beckoning to the Chorus as they shrink away.

                              Closer,
it's all right. Touch the man of sorrow.
Do. Don't be afraid. My troubles are mine
and I am the only man alive who can sustain them.

Enter Creon from the palace, attended by palace guards.

LEADER: Put your requests to Creon. Here he is,   1550
    just when we need him. He'll have a plan, he'll act.
    Now that he's the sole defense of the country
    in your place.
OEDIPUS: Oh no, what can I say to him?
    How can I ever hope to win his trust?
    I wronged him so, just now, in every way.   1555
    You must see that—I was so wrong, so wrong.
CREON: I haven't come to mock you, Oedipus,
    or to criticize your former failings.

Turning to the guards.

You there,
have you lost all respect for human feeling?
At least revere the Sun, the holy fire   1560
that keeps us all alive. Never expose a thing
of guilt and holy dread so great it appalls
the earth, the rain from heaven, the light of day!
Get him into the halls—quickly as you can.
Piety demands no less. Kindred alone   1565
should see a kinsman's shame. This is obscene.

OEDIPUS: Please, in god's name . . . you wipe my fears away,
coming so generously to me, the worst of men.
Do one thing more, for your sake, not mine.

CREON: What do you want? Why so insistent?   1570

OEDIPUS: Drive me out of the land at once, far from sight,
where I can never hear a human voice.

CREON: I'd have done that already, I promise you.
First I wanted the god to clarify my duties.

OEDIPUS: The god? His command was clear, every word: 1575
death for the father-killer, the curse—
he said destroy me!

CREON: So he did. Still, in such a crisis
it's better to ask precisely what to do.

OEDIPUS: You'd ask the oracle about a man like me?   1580

CREON: By all means. And this time, I assume,
even you will obey the god's decrees.

OEDIPUS: I will,
I will. And you, I command you—I beg you . . .
the woman inside, bury her as you see fit.
It's the only decent thing,   1585
to give your own the last rites. As for me,
never condemn the city of my fathers
to house my body, not while I'm alive, no,
let me live on the mountains, on Cithaeron,
my favorite haunt, I have made it famous.   1590
Mother and father marked out that rock
to be my everlasting tomb—buried alive.
Let me die there, where they tried to kill me.
Oh but this I know: no sickness can destroy me,
nothing can. I would never have been saved   1595
from death—I have been saved
for something great and terrible, something strange.
Well let my destiny come and take me on its way!

About my children, Creon, the boys at least,
don't burden yourself. They're men;   1600
wherever they go, they'll find the means to live.
But my two daughters, my poor helpless girls,

clustering at our table, never without me
hovering near them . . . whatever I touched,
they always had their share. Take care of them,   1605
I beg you. Wait, better—permit me, would you?
Just to touch them with my hands and take
our fill of tears. Please . . . my king.
Grant it, with all your noble heart.
If I could hold them, just once, I'd think   1610
I had them with me, like the early days
when I could see their eyes.

*Antigone and Ismene, two small children, are led in from the palace by a
nurse.*

                  What's that?
O god! Do I really hear you sobbing?—
my two children. Creon, you've pitied me?
Sent me my darling girls, my own flesh and blood!   1615
Am I right?
CREON: Yes, it's my doing.
I know the joy they gave you all these years,
the joy you must feel now.
OEDIPUS: Bless you, Creon!
May god watch over you for this kindness,
better than he ever guarded me.
                  Children, where are you?   1620
Here, come quickly—

*Groping for Antigone and Ismene, who approach their father cautiously, then
embrace him.*

                Come to these hands of mine,
your brother's hands, your own father's hands
that served his once bright eyes so well—
that made them blind. Seeing nothing, children,
knowing nothing. I became your father,   1625
I fathered you in the soil that gave me life.

How I weep for you—I cannot see you now . . .
just thinking of all your days to come, the bitterness,
the life that rough mankind will thrust upon you.
Where are the public gatherings you can join,   1630
the banquets of the clans? Home you'll come,
in tears, cut off from the sight of it all,
the brilliant rites unfinished.
And when you reach perfection, ripe for marriage,
who will he be, my dear ones? Risking all   1635
to shoulder the curse that weighs down my parents,
yes and you too—that wounds us all together.
What more misery could you want?
Your father killed his father, sowed his mother,

one, one and the selfsame womb sprang you—   1640
he cropped the very roots of his existence.

Such disgrace, and you must bear it all!
Who will marry you then? Not a man on earth.
Your doom is clear: you'll wither away to nothing,
single, without a child.

   Turning to Creon.

                            Oh Creon,   1645
you are the only father they have now . . .
we who brought them into the world
are gone, both gone at a stroke—
Don't let them go begging, abandoned,
women without men. Your own flesh and blood!   1650
Never bring them down to the level of my pains.
Pity them. Look at them, so young, so vulnerable,
shorn of everything—you're their only hope.
Promise me, noble Creon, touch my hand.

   Reaching toward Creon, who draws back.

You, little ones, if you were old enough   1655
to understand, there is much I'd tell you.
Now, as it is, I'd have you say a prayer.
Pray for life, my children,
live where you are free to grow and season.
Pray god you find a better life than mine,   1660
the father who begot you.
CREON: Enough.
   You've wept enough. Into the palace now.
OEDIPUS: I must, but I find it very hard.
CREON: Time is the great healer, you will see.
OEDIPUS: I am going—you know on what condition?   1665
CREON: Tell me. I'm listening.
OEDIPUS: Drive me out of Thebes, in exile.
CREON: Not I. Only the gods can give you that.
OEDIPUS: Surely the gods hate me so much—
CREON: You'll get your wish at once.
OEDIPUS: You consent?   1670
CREON: I try to say what I mean; it's my habit.
OEDIPUS: Then take me away. It's time.
CREON: Come along, let go of the children.
OEDIPUS: No—
   don't take them away from me, not now! No no no!

   *Clutching his daughters as the guards wrench them loose and take them
   through the palace doors.*

CREON: Still the king, the master of all things?   1675
   No more: here your power ends.

None of your power follows you through life.

*Exit Oedipus and Creon to the palace. The Chorus comes forward to address
the audience directly.*

CHORUS: People of Thebes, my countrymen, look on Oedipus.
He solved the famous riddle with his brilliance,
he rose to power, a man beyond all power.   1680
Who could behold his greatness without envy?
Now what a black sea of terror has overwhelmed him.
Now as we keep our watch and wait the final day,
count no man happy till he dies, free of pain at last.

Exit in procession.

Talking about the Text

1. What view of human fate seems to be conveyed by the play?
2. Decide who or what is to blame for what happened to Oedipus. Consider the possibilities: Oedipus himself, for refusing to listen to warnings; the gods, who sent him such a cruel fate; Teiresias and the shepherd, for failing to say anything earlier in the sequence of events; Jocasta and Laius, for deciding to dispose of their newborn son; and Polybos and Merope, for failing to tell Oedipus that they had adopted him. Is there even a single explanation for Oedipus' fate? Indeed, is there any explanation at all?
3. How do you think Oedipus would account for what happened to him?
4. Reread the ending of *Oedipus The King*. Compare the attitudes of the chorus and Oedipus toward fate.
5. Look carefully at the descriptions of the death of Laius (lines 881–98). How did it happen and who was at fault? Judging from the internal evidence of the play, how much at fault was Oedipus for killing an unknown man and his retinue on the highway? Why does the deed increase in seriousness when it turns out the man was a king? What would Oedipus have done, do you think, if Laius or one of his followers had indicated that Oedipus was about to kill a king?
6. Trace some of the irony in the language about seeing and not seeing, being blind and being sighted, of wanting to see and wanting not to see (lines 425–27, 469–79, 1405–10). How might that irony affect an audience actually seeing the play?
7. Discuss the role of the chorus. What do they know and not know? How wise or deluded are they? How abstract or personal are they? How do you hear their lines in your head—as chanted, sung, declaimed, or in a more ordinary tone of voice?
8. The notion of kingship is unfamiliar to most of us. What was the special position of a king? What were his rights, duties, and privileges? What kind of respect did others owe to him? What were the limits of his power to command others? How stable or unstable was his power? How do we understand Oedipus' threats to Tiresias if we focus on Oedipus as king?

Writing about the Text

1. Annotate the dialogue between Oedipus and Tiresias (lines 337–527). Then, using your annotations, write a paper that closely examines their dialogue. When exactly does Oedipus become angry and why? What does he propose to do about

his anger? Does Tiresias become angry, and if so at what point? Who is the more sympathetic character at this point?

2. Using your annotations on other parts of the play, write about the points at which your response to Oedipus as a person changes, either a lot or a little. What makes this happen?

Linking the Text to Other Texts

1. See a film version of *Oedipus*. (Recommended versions include the 1957 Tyrone Guthrie production, or the BBC "Films for the Humanities" version.) If you were a director setting out to do your own production of *Oedipus*, what decisions about costumes and masks might you make? What difference might your stage location and circumstances make? What characteristics would you look for as you cast Oedipus? What would you look for in a Jocasta?

2. The "tragic hero" is central to many of our discussions of drama; indeed, most contemporary dramatic characters who in some way bring about their own demise are compared to Greek heroes or heroines. Compare Oedipus to another modern hero or heroine you have read about or seen in a movie. (If you have read *Death of a Salesman*, consider using Willy Loman.) What is the difference in their cultural and social worlds? Do their fates elicit any of the same responses? How useful do you find such a comparison?

3. Many critics have compared Oedipus and Hamlet. How are the two alike? Different?

✑ COMMENTARY

Aristotle on Tragedy and *Oedipus Rex*

Oedipus *became the most famous play in antiquity when Aristotle, the ancient Greek philosopher who studied with Plato and who taught Alexander the Great, discussed it at length in his* Poetics, *the short book that set down the classical notions of tragedy, the hero, and the qualities that make for successful drama.*

Aristotle, "On the Art of Poetry"

Fear and pity may be aroused by means of the Spectacle; but they may also result from the inner structure of the piece, which is the better way and indicates a superior poet. For the plot ought to be so constructed that, even without the aid of the eye, he who hears the tale told will thrill with horror and melt to pity at what takes place. This is the impression we should receive from hearing the story of the *Oedipus*. But to produce this effect by the mere spectacle is a less artistic method, and dependent on extraneous aids. Those who use the Spectacle to create a sense, not of the terrible, but only of the monstrous are strangers to the purpose of Tragedy; for we must not demand of Tragedy any and every kind of pleasure, but only that which is proper to it. And since the pleasure which the poet should afford is that which comes from pity and fear through imitation, it is evident that this quality must be impressed upon the incidents.

    Let us then determine what are the circumstances which strike us as terrible or pitiful.

Actions capable of this effect must happen between persons who are either friends or enemies or indifferent to one another. If an enemy kills an enemy, there is nothing to excite pity either in the act or the intention—except so far as the suffering in itself is pitiful. So again with indifferent persons. But when the tragic incident occurs between those who are near or dear to one another—if, for example, a brother kills, or intends to kill, a brother, a son his father, a mother her son, a son his mother, or any other deed of the kind is done—these are the situations to be looked for by the poet. He may not indeed destroy the framework of the received legends—the fact, for instance, that Clytemnestra was slain by Orestes and Eriphyle by Alcmaeon—but he ought to show invention of his own and skilfully handle the traditional material. Let us explain more clearly what is meant by skilful handling.

The action may be done consciously and with knowledge of the persons, in the manner of the older poets. It is thus, too, that Euripides makes Medea slay her children. Or, again, the deed of horror may be done, but done in ignorance, and the tie of kinship or friendship be discovered afterwards. The *Oedipus* of Sophocles is an example. Here, indeed, the incident is outside the drama proper; but cases occur where it falls within the action of the play: one may cite the *Alcmaeon* of Astydamas, or Telegonus in the *Wounded Odysseus*. Again, there is a third case—[to be about to act with knowledge of the persons and then not to act. The fourth case is] when someone is about to do an irreparable deed through ignorance and makes the discovery before it is done. These are the only possible ways. For the deed must either be done or not done—and that wittingly or unwittingly. But of all these ways, to be about to act knowing the persons, and then not to act, is the worst. It is shocking without being tragic, for no disaster follows. It is, therefore, never or very rarely found in poetry. One instance, however, is in the *Antigone*, where Haemon threatens to kill Creon. The next and better way is that the deed should be perpetrated. Still better, that it should be perpetrated in ignorance and the discovery made afterwards. There is then nothing to shock us, while the discovery produces a startling effect.

✑ COMMENTARY

Freud, Dodds, and Artaud on Oedipus

Beginning with Aristotle's discussion of Oedipus and tragedy, Oedipus is perhaps the character and story that has continued to inspire thinkers, philosophers, scholars, and theorists from a wide range of fields. Psychoanalyst Sigmund Freud always claimed that he got many of his ideas about human behavior from literature, and indeed, Oedipus the character served as the model for his controversial theory of the Oedipus complex, which he defined, using the plot of Sophocles' play as a starting point, as the male child's subconscious desire to be the only object of his mother's affection. In Freud's view, this longing, in turn, caused feelings of envy and jealousy toward the father as well as an unconscious wish for the father's death. Freud's contention was that these conflicted subconscious desires were the basis for many childhood neuroses. An excerpt from Freud's Interpretation of Dreams *discussing the Oedipus complex appears below.*

The second excerpt, by classics scholar E. R. Dodds, provides a quiet refutation of Freud's theorizing. The famous Freud and the reticent Dodds provide a nice illustration of how to argue in print about literature and the imagination. Opposed to these is the highly

Psychoanalyst Sigmund Freud, c. 1909, just a few years before the publication of his Interpretation of Dreams, *in which he described his now-famous theory of the Oedipus complex.*

influential French actor and theorist Antonin Artaud, who, in the excerpt from The Theater and Its Double *below, strongly attacked the dominance of Sophocles and similar classical models, claiming that modern drama needs contemporary plays that do not owe anything to the dead hand of history.*

Sigmund Freud on the Oedipus Conflict, from The Interpretation of Dreams

In my experience, which is already very extensive, parents play the main parts in the inner life of all children who later become psychoneurotics. Being in love with the one parent and hating the other belong to the indispensable stock of psychical impulses being formed at that time which are so important for the later neurosis. But I do not believe that in this respect psychoneurotics are to be sharply distinguished from other children of Adam with a normal development in their capacity to create something absolutely new and theirs alone. It is far more likely—and this is supported by occasional observations of normal children—that with these loving and hostile wishes towards their parents too, psychoneurotics are only revealing to us, by magnifying it, what goes on less clearly and less intensely in the inner life of most children. In support of this insight the ancient world has provided us with a legend whose far-reaching and universal power can only be understood if we grant a similar universality to the assumption from child-psychology we have just been discussing.

I refer to the legend of King Oedipus and the drama of that name by Sophocles. Oedipus, son of Laius, King of Thebes, and Jocasta, is abandoned as an infant because an oracle had proclaimed to his father that his son yet unborn would be his murderer. He is rescued and grows up as a king's son at a foreign court, until he himself consults the oracle about his origins, and receives the counsel that he should flee his home city, because he would perforce become his father's murderer and his mother's spouse. On the road from his supposed home city he encounters King Laius and kills him in a sudden quarrel. Then he arrives before Thebes, where he solves the riddle of the Sphinx as she bars his way, and in gratitude he is chosen by the Thebans to be their king and presented with Jocasta's hand in marriage. He reigns long in peace and dignity, and begets two sons and two daughters with his—unbeknown—mother, until a plague breaks out, occasioning fresh questioning of the oracle by the Thebans. At this point Sophocles' tragedy begins. The messengers bring word that the plague will end when the murderer of Laius is driven from the land. But where is he?

. . . Where shall we hope to uncover
The faded traces of that far-distant crime?

The action of the play consists now in the gradually intensified and skilfully delayed revelation—comparable to the work of a psychoanalysis—that Oedipus himself is Laius' murderer, but also that he is the son of the murdered king and Jocasta. Shattered by the abomination he has in his ignorance committed, Oedipus blinds himself and leaves his homeland. The oracle is fulfilled.

Oedipus the King is what we call a tragedy of fate; its tragic effect is supposed to depend on the contrast between the all-powerful will of the gods and the vain struggles of men threatened by disaster. What the deeply moved spectator is meant to learn from the tragedy is submission to the will of the divinity and insight into his own powerlessness. Consequently, modern dramatists have tried to achieve a similar tragic effect by weaving the same contrast into a plot of their own invention. But the spectators have looked on unmoved as, despite all the efforts of innocent humans, some curse or oracle is fulfilled. The later tragedies of fate have failed in their effect.

If *Oedipus the King* is able to move modern man no less deeply than the Greeks who were Sophocles' contemporaries, the solution can only be that the effect of Greek tragedy does not depend on the contrast between fate and human will, but is to be sought in the distinctive nature of the subject-matter exemplifying this contrast. There must be a voice within us that is ready to acknowledge the compelling force of fate in *Oedipus*, while we are able to reject as arbitrary such disposals as are to be found in *Die Ahnfrau* or other tragedies of fate. And a factor of this kind is indeed contained in the story of King Oedipus. His fate moves us only because it could have been our own as well, because at our birth the oracle pronounced the same curse upon us as it did on him. It was perhaps ordained that we should all of us turn our first sexual impulses towards our mother, our first hatred and violent wishes against our father. Our dreams convince us of it. King Oedipus, who killed his father Laius and married his mother Jocasta, is only the fulfilment of our childhood wish. But, more fortunate than he, we have since succeeded, at least insofar as we have not become psychoneurotics, in detaching our sexual impulses from our mothers and forgetting our jealousy of our fathers. We recoil from the figure who has fulfilled that ancient childhood wish with the entire sum of repression which these wishes have since undergone within us. As the poet brings Oedipus' guilt to light in the course of his investigation, he compels us to recognize our own inner life, where those impulses, though suppressed, are still present. The contrast with which the chorus takes its leave:

. . . behold: this was Oedipus,
Greatest of men; he held the key to the deepest mysteries;
Was envied by all his fellow-men for his great prosperity;
Behold, what a full tide of misfortune swept over his head.

this admonition refers to us too and our pride, who have grown so wise and powerful in our own estimation since our childish years. Like Oedipus we live in ignorance of those wishes, offensive to morality and forced upon us by Nature, and once they have been revealed, there is little doubt we would all rather turn our gaze away from the scenes of our childhood.

There is an unmistakable indication in the text of Sophocles' tragedy itself that the legend of Oedipus sprang from that ancient dream material which contains the painful disturbance of our relations with our parents by the first stirrings of our sexuality. Jocasta consoles Oedipus at a stage where he has not yet learned the truth, but is troubled by the memory of what the oracle proclaimed. She refers to a dream which many indeed do dream, but without—or so she thinks—its having any significance:

> Nor need this mother-marrying frighten you;
> Many a man has dreamt as much. Such things
> Must be forgotten, if life is to be endured.

The dream of having sexual intercourse with the mother is dreamed by many today as it was then, and they recount it with indignation and amazement. It is clearly the key to the tragedy and the complement to the dream of the father's death. The Oedipus story is the imagination's reaction to these two typical dreams, and just as the dreams of the adult are filled with feelings of revulsion, the legend too is bound to include the horror and self-punishment in its content. Its further revision derives from a misleading secondary revision of the subject-matter, which seeks to make use of it for theological ends. . . . (The attempt to reconcile divine omnipotence with human responsibility, of course, is bound to be defeated by this material, as by any other.)

E. R. Dodds, from "On Misunderstanding the Oedipus Rex"

Some readers of the *Oedipus Rex* have told me that they find its atmosphere stifling and oppressive: they miss the tragic exaltation that one gets from the *Antigonê* or the *Prometheus Vinctus*. And I fear that what I have said here has done nothing to remove that feeling. Yet it is not a feeling which I share myself. Certainly the *Oedipus Rex* is a play about the blindness of man and the desperate insecurity of the human condition: in a sense every man must grope in the dark as Oedipus gropes, not knowing who he is or what he has to suffer; we all live in a world of appearance which hides from us who-knows-what dreadful reality. But surely the *Oedipus Rex* is also a play about human greatness. Oedipus is great, not in virtue of a great worldly position—for his worldly position is an illusion which will vanish like a dream—but in virtue of his inner strength: strength to pursue the truth at whatever personal cost, and strength to accept and endure it when found. "This horror is mine," he cries, "and none but I is *strong* enough to bear it." Oedipus is great because he accepts the responsibility for *all* his acts, including those which are objectively most horrible, though subjectively innocent.

To me personally Oedipus is a kind of symbol of the human intelligence which cannot rest until it has solved all the riddles—even the last riddle, to which the answer is that human happiness is built on an illusion. I do not know how far Sophocles intended that. But certainly in the last lines of the play (which I firmly believe to be genuine) he does generalize the case, does appear to suggest that in some sense Oedipus is every man and every man is potentially Oedipus. Freud felt this (he was not insensitive to poetry), but as we all know he understood it in a specific psychological sense. "Oedipus' fate," he says, "moves us only because it might have been our own, because the oracle laid upon us before birth is the very curse which rested upon him. It may be that we were all destined to direct our first sexual impulses towards our mothers, and our first impulses of hatred and violence towards our fathers; our dreams convince us that we were." Perhaps they do; but Freud did not ascribe his interpretation of the myth to Sophocles, and it is not the interpretation I have in mind. Is there not in the poet's view a much wider sense in which every man is Oedipus? If every man could tear away the last veils of illusion, if he could see human life as time and the gods see it, would he not see that against that tremendous background all the generations of men are as if they had not been, *isa kai to mēden zōsas*? That was how Odysseus saw it when he had conversed with Athena, the embodiment of divine wisdom. "In Ajax' condition," he says, "I recognize my own: I perceive that all men living are but appearance or unsubstantial shadow."

Antonin Artaud, *from* The Theater and Its Double

One of the reasons for the asphyxiating atmosphere in which we live without possible escape or remedy—and in which we all share, even the most revolutionary among us—is our respect for what has been written, formulated, or painted, what has been given form, as if all expression were not at last exhausted, were not at a point where things must break apart if they are to start anew and begin fresh.

We must have done with this idea of masterpieces reserved for a self-styled elite and not understood by the general public; the mind has no such restricted districts as those so often used for clandestine sexual encounters.

Masterpieces of the past are good for the past: they are not good for us. We have the right to say what has been said and even what has not been said in a way that belongs to us, a way that is immediate and direct, corresponding to present modes of feeling, and understandable to everyone.

It is idiotic to reproach the masses for having no sense of the sublime, when the sublime is confused with one or another of its formal manifestations, which are moreover always defunct manifestations. And if for example a contemporary public does not understand *Oedipus Rex*, I shall make bold to say that it is the fault of *Oedipus Rex* and not of the public.

In *Oedipus Rex* there is the theme of incest and the idea that nature mocks at morality and that there are certain unspecified powers at large which we would do well to beware of, call them *destiny* or anything you choose.

There is in addition the presence of a plague epidemic which is a physical incarnation of these powers. But the whole in a manner and language that have lost all touch with the rude and epileptic rhythm of our time. Sophocles speaks grandly perhaps, but in a style that is no longer timely. His language is too refined for this age, it is as if he were speaking beside the point.

However, a public that shudders at train wrecks, that is familiar with earthquakes, plagues, revolutions, wars; that is sensitive to the disordered anguish of love, can be affected by all these grand notions and asks only to become aware of them, but on condition that it is addressed in its own language, and that its knowledge of these things does not come to it through adulterated trappings and speech that belong to extinct eras which will never live again.

☀ INSPIRATION THE OEDIPAL COMPLEX IN FILM

Anthony Perkins as Norman Bates, the young man too much under the influence of his mother, in Alfred Hitchcock's classic 1960 thriller Psycho.

Sophocles' story of Oedipus and Freud's highly influential psychoanalytical theories that stemmed from it have continued to provide filmmakers with rich, psychologically complex plots and themes. A wide range of film classics—from film versions of Shakespeare's *Hamlet* to the older woman and younger man couplings of dramas like *The Graduate*—have all borrowed heavily from the Oedipal myth.

- ■ *Hamlet* (**1948 and 1990 versions**). For years, directors and actors have debated how "Oedipal" Shakespeare's Hamlet is really supposed to be. Two film versions in particular, Laurence Olivier's 1948 adaptation and Franco Zefferelli's 1990 film (starring Mel Gibson as Hamlet and Glenn Close as Gertrude), are regarded as highly Oedipal interpretations, emphasizing Hamlet's fixation on his mother.
- ■ *The Magnificent Ambersons* (**1942**). This classic, written and directed by Orson Welles, is set in the late nineteenth-century Midwest and follows the rise and fall of the wealthy Amberson family. The central conflict revolves around George, the spoiled adult son, whose resentments lead him to sabotage a romance between his widowed mother and a wealthy auto maker.
- ■ *Psycho* (**1960**). Freudian themes abound in many of Alfred Hitchcock's films. The Oedipal complex can be seen in the psychotic "mama's boy" Norman Bates, played by Anthony Perkins.
- ■ *The Manchurian Candidate* (**1962 and 2004 versions**). Both versions of this political thriller focus on issues of government conspiracy and ideology—the first is set just after the Koran War, the more recent remake after the 1991 Persian Gulf War—and both heighten dramatic tension in the film by emphasizing the sexual undertones in the fraught relationship between Raymond Shaw and his manipulative mother, Mrs. Iselin. In the 1962 film, this theme was underscored by the casting choices: Laurence Harvey, who played Raymond Shaw, was three years younger than Angela Lansbury, who played his mother.

(continued on next page)

THE OEDIPAL COMPLEX IN FILM

- *The Graduate* (1967). Mike Nichols's gripping depiction of alienated 1960s youth offers a more modern take on the Oedipus story in the form of protagonist Benjamin Braddock (Dustin Hoffman), a recent college graduate whose listlessness about his own future leads him into two rivaling romances—one with his peer, the chaste Elaine Robinson (Katharine Ross), the other with her confident, hypersexual mother, Mrs. Robinson (Anne Bancroft).

- *Murmur of the Heart* (1971). French director Louis Malle's coming-of-age story of a teenage French boy during the 1950s contains some controversial and explicit plot points (incestuous sex among them) but is a considerably lighthearted take on Sophocles' tragic plot.

- *Back to the Future* (1985). Robert Zemeckis's clever sci-fi/fantasy comedy takes on Oedipal tones when Marty McFly (Michael J. Fox) is accidentally sent back in time to 1955, where he meets his mother as a teenager, and his mother develops a crush on him.

- *New York Stories* (1989). This anthology comprises three short films by three renowned directors: Woody Allen, Francis Ford Coppola, and Martin Scorsese. In Allen's segment, "Oedipus Wrecks," a neurotic Jewish man is embarrassed and harassed by his neurotic Jewish mother, but things take an unsettling turn when he wishes she would disappear and he gets his wish.

- *The Grifters* (1990). Stephen Frears's tale of a small-time con man, Roy (played by John Cusack), takes on an Oedipal subplot when Roy gets caught in an emotional power play between his girlfriend (played by Annette Bening) and his estranged mother (played by Anjelica Huston).

- *Spanking the Monkey* (1994). David O. Russell's dark comedy tells the story of a young man plagued by his own sexual awakening when he is stuck at home for the summer to care for his young mother, who is bedridden with a broken leg.

- *Tadpole* (2002). This comedy renders the Oedipal coming-of-age story less taboo through a few key plot alterations. Teenage Oscar Grubman is seemingly irresistible to beautiful, sophisticated women, all old enough to be his mother, but his heart belongs to none other than his stepmother Eve.

PERFORMANCE NOTES

ANTIGONE ON THE AMERICAN STAGE

After one unfortunate staging in 1845, Sophocles' play *Antigone* did not enjoy a truly commercial production until 1946, when the well-known actress Katharine Cornell played Antigone on Broadway, using a version of the play written by Jean Anouilh for the French theater. The play was not as successful as expected, given

Today as yesterday, the public is greedy for mystery: it asks only to become aware of the laws according to which destiny manifests itself, and to divine perhaps the secret of its apparitions.

Let us leave textual criticism to graduate students, formal criticism to esthetes, and recognize that what has been said is not still to be said; that an expression does not have the same value twice, does not live two lives; that all words, once spoken, are dead and function only at the moment when they are uttered, that a form, once it has served, cannot be used again and asks only to be replaced by another, and that the theater is the only place in the world where a gesture, once made, can never be made the same way twice.

If the public does not frequent our literary masterpieces, it is because those masterpieces are literary, that is to say, fixed; and fixed in forms that no longer respond to the needs of the time.

Antigone (C. 441 BCE)

TRANSLATED BY DUDLEY FITTS AND ROBERT FITZGERALD (1939)

In the Theban myths, Antigone is one of the four children of Oedipus and Jocasta. After her father's tragic discoveries, portrayed in Oedipus Rex, she takes care of him until his death. But the miseries of the ill-fated family do not end with the passing of the father. Her two brothers, Polynices and Eteocles, end up on opposite sides in the Theban civil war; both are killed. Eteocles, as an ally of the king Creon, receives a dignified funeral, but the body of Polynices is denied burial and left outside the city to rot. Antigone regards this dishonor done to her brother as unbearable and unacceptable—whatever his misdeeds in the eyes of the king. Her sister Ismene is more inclined to bow to Creon's will. The play opens with the conflict of wills—and notions of what is right—between Creon and Antigone.

Fitts and Fitzgerald employ ancient labels for parts of the play. **Prologue** *supplies background and occurs at the beginning of the chorus's song.* **Parados** *is what the chorus sings upon entering.* **Strophe** *is what the chorus sings while moving in one direction;* **antistrophe** *is what the chorus sings while moving in the other direction. The* **choragos** *was a leading member of the chorus who could interact with other characters of the play. In an attempt to capture the foreignness of the original Greek language, Fitts and Fitzgerald include the circumflex mark above certain letters of the characters' names.*

Cornell's presence. In 1971 New York's Vivian Beaumont Theater produced another version, which in the rebellious early 1970s was received as highly relevant. Audiences applauded the young woman who could stand up against the tyrannical state for what she thought right, despite the threat of death. In 1994 at the American Conservatory Theater in San Francisco, director Carey Perloff interpreted Antigone more as a victim struggling to restore her sense of dignity in the light of all the disasters that had befallen her family.

Persons represented

Antigone	Creon	A sentry
Ismene	Haimon	A messenger
Eurydice	Teiresias	Chorus

Scene: Before the palace of Creon, King of Thebes. A central double door, and two lateral doors. A platform extends the length of the façade, and from this platform three steps lead down into the "*orchestra,*" or chorus-ground. TIME: dawn of the day after the repulse of the Argive army from the assault on Thebes.

PROLOGUE

[ANTIGONE *and* ISMENE *enter from the central door of the Palace.*]

ANTIGONE: Ismenê, dear sister,
   You would think that we had already suffered enough
   For the curse on Oedipus:
   I cannot imagine any grief
   That you and I have not gone through. And now—
   Have they told you of the new decree of our King Creon?
ISMENE: I have heard nothing: I know
   That two sisters lost two brothers, a double death
   In a single hour; and I know that the Argive army
   Fled in the night; but beyond this, nothing.
ANTIGONE: I thought so. And that is why I wanted you
   To come out here with me. There is something we must do.
ISMENE: Why do you speak so strangely?
ANTIGONE: Listen, Ismenê:
   Creon buried our brother Eteoclês
   With military honors, gave him a soldier's funeral,
   And it was right that he should; but Polyneicês,
   Who fought as bravely and died as miserably,—
   They say that Creon has sworn
   No one shall bury him, no one mourn for him,
   But his body must lie in the fields, a sweet treasure
   For carrion birds to find as they search for food.
   That is what they say, and our good Creon is coming here
   To announce it publicly; and the penalty—
   Stoning to death in the public square!
                              There it is,
   And now you can prove what you are:
   A true sister, or a traitor to your family.
ISMENE: Antigonê, you are mad! What could I possibly do?
ANTIGONE: You must decide whether you will help me or not.
ISMENE: I do not understand you. Help you in what?
ANTIGONE: Ismenê, I am going to bury him. Will you come?
ISMENE: Bury him! You have just said the new law forbids it.
ANTIGONE: He is my brother. And he is your brother, too.
ISMENE: But think of the danger! Think what Creon will do!

ANTIGONE: Creon is not strong enough to stand in my way.

ISMENE: Ah sister!

> Oedipus died, everyone hating him
> For what his own search brought to light, his eyes
> Ripped out by his own hand; and Iocastê died,
> His mother and wife at once: she twisted the cords
> That strangled her life; and our two brothers died,
> Each killed by the other's sword. And we are left:
> But oh, Antigonê,
> Think how much more terrible than these
> Our own death would be if we should go against Creon
> And do what he has forbidden! We are only women,
> We cannot fight with men, Antigonê!
> The law is strong, we must give in to the law
> In this thing, and in worse. I beg the Dead
> To forgive me, but I am helpless: I must yield
> To those in authority. And I think it is dangerous business
> To be always meddling.

ANTIGONE: If that is what you think,

> I should not want you, even if you asked to come.
> You have made your choice, you can be what you want to be.
> But I will bury him; and if I must die,
> I say that this crime is holy: I shall lie down
> With him in death, and I shall be as dear
> To him as he to me.
>   It is the dead,
> Not the living, who make the longest demands:
> We die for ever . . .
> You may do as you like,
> Since apparently the laws of the gods mean nothing to you.

ISMENE: They mean a great deal to me; but I have no strength

> To break laws that were made for the public good.

ANTIGONE: That must be your excuse, I suppose. But as for me,

> I will bury the brother I love.

ISMENE: Antigonê,

> I am so afraid for you!

ANTIGONE: You need not be:

> You have yourself to consider, after all.

ISMENE: But no one must hear of this, you must tell no one!

> I will keep it a secret, I promise!

ANTIGONE: Oh tell it! Tell everyone!

> Think how they'll hate you when it all comes out
> If they learn that you knew about it all the time!

ISMENE: So fiery! You should be cold with fear.

ANTIGONE: Perhaps. But I am doing only what I must.

ISMENE: But can you do it? I say that you cannot.

ANTIGONE: Very well: when my strength gives out, I shall do no more.

ISMENE: Impossible things should not be tried at all.

ANTIGONE: Go away, Ismenê:

I shall be hating you soon, and the dead will too,
For your words are hateful. Leave me my foolish plan:
I am not afraid of the danger; if it means death,
It will not be the worst of deaths—death without honor.

ISMENE: Go then, if you feel that you must.
You are unwise,
But a loyal friend indeed to those who love you.

[*Exit into the Palace.* ANTIGONE *goes off,* L. *Enter the chorus.*]

Párodos

CHORUS: Now the long blade of the sun, lying   [STROPHE 1]
Level east to west, touches with glory
Thebes of the Seven Gates. Open, unlidded
Eye of golden day! O marching light
Across the eddy and rush of Dircê's stream,
Striking the white shields of the enemy
Thrown headlong backward from the blaze of morning!

CHORAGOS: Polyneicês their commander
Roused them with windy phrases,
He the wild eagle screaming
Insults above our land,
His wings their shields of snow,
His crest their marshalled helms.

CHORUS: [ANTISTROPHE 1]
Against our seven gates in a yawning ring
The famished spears came onward in the night;
But before his jaws were sated with our blood,
Or pinefire took the garland of our towers,
He was thrown back; and as he turned, great Thebes—
No tender victim for his noisy power—
Rose like a dragon behind him, shouting war.

CHORAGOS: For God hates utterly
The bray of bragging tongues;
And when he beheld their smiling,
Their swagger of golden helms,
The frown of his thunder blasted
Their first man from our walls.

CHORUS: [STROPHE 2]
We heard his shout of triumph high in the air
Turn to a scream; far out in a flaming arc
He fell with his windy torch, and the earth struck him.
And others storming in fury no less than his
Found shock of death in the dusty joy of battle.

CHORAGOS:
Seven captains at seven gates
Yielded their clanging arms to the god
That bends the battle-line and breaks it.

These two only, brothers in blood,
Face to face in matchless rage,
Mirroring each the other's death,
Clashed in long combat.

CHORUS: [ANTISTROPHE 2]
But now in the beautiful morning of victory
Let Thebes of the many chariots sing for joy!
With hearts for dancing we'll take leave of war:
Our temples shall be sweet with hymns of praise,
And the long night shall echo with our chorus.

SCENE I

CHORAGOS: But now at last our new King is coming:
Creon of Thebes, Menoikeus' son.
In this auspicious dawn of his reign
What are the new complexities
That shifting Fate has woven for him?
What is his counsel? Why has he summoned
The old men to hear him?

[Enter CREON *from the Palace, C. He addresses the* CHORUS *from the top step]*

CREON: Gentlemen: I have the honor to inform you that our Ship of State, which recent storms have threatened to destroy, has come safely to harbor at last, guided by the merciful wisdom of Heaven. I have summoned you here this morning because I know that I can depend upon you: your devotion to King Laïos was absolute; you never hesitated in your duty to our late ruler Oedipus; and when Oedipus died, your loyalty was transferred to his children. Unfortunately, as you know, his two sons, the princes Eteoclês and Polyneicês, have killed each other in battle; and I, as the next in blood, have succeeded to the full power of the throne.

I am aware, of course, that no Ruler can expect complete loyalty from his subjects until he has been tested in office. Nevertheless, I say to you at the very outset that I have nothing but contempt for the kind of Governor who is afraid, for whatever reason, to follow the course that he knows is best for the State; and as for the man who sets private friendship above the public welfare,—I have no use for him, either. I call God to witness that if I saw my country headed for ruin, I should not be afraid to speak out plainly; and I need hardly remind you that I would never have any dealings with an enemy of the people. No one values friendship more highly than I; but we must remember that friends made at the risk of wrecking our Ship are not real friends at all.

These are my principles, at any rate, and that is why I have made the following decision concerning the sons of Oedipus: Eteoclês, who died as a man should die, fighting for his country, is to be buried with full military honors, with all the ceremony that is usual when the greatest heroes die; but his brother Polyneicês, who broke his exile to come back with fire and sword against his native city and the shrines of his fathers' gods, whose one idea was to spill the blood of his blood and sell his own people into slavery—Polyneicês, I say, is to have no burial: no man is to touch him or say the least prayer for him; he shall lie on the plain, unburied; and the birds and the scavenging dogs can do with him whatever they like.

This is my command, and you can see the wisdom behind it. As long as I am King, no traitor is going to be honored with the loyal man. But whoever shows by word and deed that he is on the side of the State,—he shall have my respect while he is living, and my reverence when he is dead.

CHORAGOS: If that is your will, Creon son of Menoikeus,
　　You have the right to enforce it: we are yours.
CREON: That is my will. Take care that you do your part.
CHORAGOS: We are old men: let the younger ones carry it out.
CREON: I do not mean that: the sentries have been appointed.
CHORAGOS: Then what is it that you would have us do?
CREON: You will give no support to whoever breaks this law.
CHORAGOS: Only a crazy man is in love with death!
CREON: And death it is; yet money talks, and the wisest
　　Have sometimes been known to count a few coins too many.

　　[Enter SENTRY from L.]

SENTRY: I'll not say that I'm out of breath from running, King, because every time I stopped to think about what I have to tell you, I felt like going back. And all the time a voice kept saying, "You fool, don't you know you're walking straight into trouble?"; and then another voice: "Yes, but if you let somebody else get the news to Creon first, it will be even worse than that for you!" But good sense won out, at least I hope it was good sense, and here I am with a story that makes no sense at all; but I'll tell it anyhow, because, as they say, what's going to happen's going to happen, and—
CREON: Come to the point. What have you to say?
SENTRY: I did not do it. I did not see who did it. You must not punish me for
　　what someone else has done.
CREON: A comprehensive defense! More effective, perhaps,
　　If I knew its purpose. Come: what is it?
SENTRY: A dreadful thing . . . I don't know how to put it—
CREON: Out with it!
SENTRY:　　　　　　Well, then;
　　The dead man—
　　　　　　Polyneicês—

　　[Pause. The SENTRY is overcome, fumbles for words. CREON waits
　　impassively.]

　　　　　　　　　　　　out there—

　　　　　　　　　　　　　　someone,—

　　New dust on the slimy flesh!

　　[Pause. No sign from CREON]

　　Someone has given it burial that way, and
　　Gone . . .

　　[Long pause. CREON finally speaks with deadly control]

CREON: And the man who dared do this?
SENTRY: I swear I
  Do not know! You must believe me!
                              Listen:
  The ground was dry, not a sign of digging, no,
  Not a wheeltrack in the dust, no trace of anyone.
  It was when they relieved us this morning: and one of them,
  The corporal, pointed to it.
                       There it was,
  The strangest—
            Look:
  The body, just mounded over with light dust: you see?
  Not buried really, but as if they'd covered it
  Just enough for the ghost's peace. And no sign
  Of dogs or any wild animal that had been there.
  And then what a scene there was! Every man of us
  Accusing the other: we all proved the other man did it,
  We all had proof that we could not have done it.
  We were ready to take hot iron in our hands,
  Walk through fire, swear by all the gods,
  It was not I!
  I do not know who it was, but it was not I!

  [CREON's *rage has been mounting steadily, but the* SENTRY *is too intent upon
  his story to notice it*]

  And then, when this came to nothing, someone said
  A thing that silenced us and made us stare
  Down at the ground: you had to be told the news,
  And one of us had to do it! We threw the dice,
  And the bad luck fell to me. So here I am,
  No happier to be here than you are to have me:
  Nobody likes the man who brings bad news.
CHORAGOS: I have been wondering, King: can it be that the gods have done
  this?
CREON: [*Furiously*] Stop!
  Must you doddering wrecks
  Go out of your heads entirely? "The gods!"
  Intolerable!
  The gods favor this corpse? Why? How had he served them?
  Tried to loot their temples, burn their images,
  Yes, and the whole State, and its laws with it!
  Is it your senile opinion that the gods love to honor bad men?
  A pious thought!—
                  No, from the very beginning
  There have been those who have whispered together,
  Stiff-necked anarchists, putting their heads together,
  Scheming against me in alleys. These are the men,
  And they have bribed my own guard to do this thing.
  Money! [*Sententiously*]
  There's nothing in the world so demoralizing as money.

Down go your cities,
Homes gone, men gone, honest hearts corrupted,
Crookedness of all kinds, and all for money!

[To SENTRY]

But you—!

I swear by God and by the throne of God,
The man who has done this thing shall pay for it!
Find that man, bring him here to me, or your death
Will be the least of your problems: I'll string you up
Alive, and there will be certain ways to make you
Discover your employer before you die;
And the process may teach you a lesson you seem to have missed:
The dearest profit is sometimes all too dear:
That depends on the source. Do you understand me?
A fortune won is often misfortune.

SENTRY: King, may I speak?
CREON: Your very voice distresses me.
SENTRY: Are you sure that it is my voice, and not your conscience?
CREON: By God, he wants to analyze me now!
SENTRY: It is not what I say, but what has been done, that hurts you.
CREON: You talk too much.
SENTRY: Maybe; but I've done nothing.
CREON: Sold your soul for some silver: that's all you've done.
SENTRY: How dreadful it is when the right judge judges wrong!
CREON: Your figures of speech
    May entertain you now; but unless you bring me the man,
    You will get little profit from them in the end.

    [Exit CREON into the Palace.]

SENTRY: "Bring me the man"—!
    I'd like nothing better than bringing him the man!
    But bring him or not, you have seen the last of me here.
    At any rate, I am safe!

    [Exit SENTRY]

ODE I

CHORUS: [STROPHE 1]
    Numberless are the world's wonders, but none
    More wonderful than man; the stormgray sea
    Yields to his prows, the huge crests bear him high;
    Earth, holy and inexhaustible, is graven
    With shining furrows where his plows have gone
    Year after year, the timeless labor of stallions.

    The lightboned birds and beasts that cling to cover,   [ANTISTROPHE 1]
    The lithe fish lighting their reaches of dim water,
    All are taken, tamed in the net of his mind;

The lion on the hill, the wild horse windy-maned,
Resign to him; and his blunt yoke has broken
The sultry shoulders of the mountain bull.

[STROPHE 2]

Words also, and thought as rapid as air,
He fashions to his good use; statecraft is his,
And his the skill that deflects the arrows of snow,
The spears of winter rain: from every wind
He has made himself secure—from all but one:
In the late wind of death he cannot stand.

[ANTISTROPHE 2]

O clear intelligence, force beyond all measure!
O fate of man, working both good and evil!
When the laws are kept, how proudly his city stands!
When the laws are broken, what of his city then?
Never may the anárchic man find rest at my hearth,
Never be it said that my thoughts are his thoughts.

SCENE II

[Re-enter SENTRY leading ANTIGONE.]

CHORAGOS: What does this mean? Surely this captive woman
    Is the Princess, Antigonê. Why should she be taken?
SENTRY: Here is the one who did it! We caught her
    In the very act of burying him.—Where is Creon?
CHORAGOS: Just coming from the house.

[Enter CREON, C.]

CREON: What has happened?
    Why have you come back so soon?
SENTRY: *[Expansively]*

                         O King,
A man should never be too sure of anything:
I would have sworn
That you'd not see me here again: your anger
Frightened me so, and the things you threatened me with;
But how could I tell then
That I'd be able to solve the case so soon?

No dice-throwing this time: I was only too glad to come!

Here is this woman. She is the guilty one:
We found her trying to bury him.
Take her, then; question her; judge her as you will.
I am through with the whole thing now, and glád óf it.
CREON: But this is Antigonê! Why have you brought her here?
SENTRY: She was burying him, I tell you!
CREON: *[Severely]*   Is this the truth?
SENTRY: I saw her with my own eyes. Can I say more?
CREON: The details: come, tell me quickly!

SENTRY: It was like this:
    After those terrible threats of yours, King,
    We went back and brushed the dust away from the body.
    The flesh was soft by now, and stinking,
    So we sat on a hill to windward and kept guard.
    No napping this time! We kept each other awake.
    But nothing happened until the white round sun
    Whirled in the center of the round sky over us:
    Then, suddenly,
    A storm of dust roared up from the earth, and the sky
    Went out, the plain vanished with all its trees
    In the stinging dark. We closed our eyes and endured it.
    The whirlwind lasted a long time, but it passed;
    And then we looked, and there was Antigonê!
    I have seen
    A mother bird come back to a stripped nest, heard
    Her crying bitterly a broken note or two
    For the young ones stolen. Just so, when this girl
    Found the bare corpse, and all her love's work wasted,
    She wept, and cried on heaven to damn the hands
    That had done this thing.
                            And then she brought more dust
    And sprinkled wine three times for her brother's ghost.

    We ran and took her at once. She was not afraid,
    Not even when we charged her with what she had done.
    She denied nothing.
                            And this was a comfort to me,
    And some uneasiness: for it is a good thing
    To escape from death, but it is no great pleasure
    To bring death to a friend.
                            Yet I always say
    There is nothing so comfortable as your own safe skin!
CREON: [Slowly, dangerously]And you, Antigonê,
    You with your head hanging,—do you confess this thing?
ANTIGONE: I do. I deny nothing.
CREON: [To SENTRY]   You may go.

    [Exit SENTRY]

    [To ANTIGONE] Tell me, tell me briefly:
    Had you heard my proclamation touching this matter?
ANTIGONE: It was public. Could I help hearing it?
CREON: And yet you dared defy the law.
ANTIGONE: I dared.
    It was not God's proclamation. That final Justice
    That rules the world below makes no such laws.
    Your edict, King, was strong,
    But all your strength is weakness itself against
    The immortal unrecorded laws of God.

They are not merely now: they were, and shall be,
Operative for ever, beyond man utterly.
I knew I must die, even without your decree:
I am only mortal. And if I must die
Now, before it is my time to die,
Surely this is no hardship: can anyone
Living, as I live, with evil all about me,
Think Death less than a friend? This death of mine
Is of no importance; but if I had left my brother
Lying in death unburied, I should have suffered.
Now I do not.
           You smile at me. Ah Creon,
Think me a fool, if you like; but it may well be
That a fool convicts me of folly.

CHORAGOS: Like father, like daughter: both headstrong, deaf to reason!
She has never learned to yield.

CREON: She has much to learn.
The inflexible heart breaks first, the toughest iron
Cracks first, and the wildest horses bend their necks
At the pull of the smallest curb.
                     Pride? In a slave?
This girl is guilty of a double insolence,
Breaking the given laws and boasting of it.
Who is the man here,
She or I, if this crime goes unpunished?
Sister's child, or more than sister's child,
Or closer yet in blood—she and her sister
Win bitter death for this!
     [*To servants*]   Go, some of you,
Arrest Ismenê. I accuse her equally.
Bring her: you will find her sniffling in the house there.

Her mind's a traitor: crimes kept in the dark
Cry for light, and the guardian brain shudders;
But how much worse than this
Is brazen boasting of barefaced anarchy!

ANTIGONE: Creon, what more do you want than my death?

CREON: Nothing.
That gives me everything.

ANTIGONE: Then I beg you: kill me.
This talking is a great weariness: your words
Are distasteful to me, and I am sure that mine
Seem so to you. And yet they should not seem so:
I should have praise and honor for what I have done.
All these men here would praise me
Were their lips not frozen shut with fear of you.
[*Bitterly*] Ah the good fortune of kings,
Licensed to say and do whatever they please!

CREON: You are alone here in that opinion.

ANTIGONE: No, they are with me. But they keep their tongues in leash.

CREON: Maybe. But you are guilty, and they are not.

ANTIGONE: There is no guilt in reverence for the dead.

CREON: But Eteoclês—was he not your brother too?

ANTIGONE: My brother too.

CREON: And you insult his memory?

ANTIGONE: [Softly] The dead man would not say that I insult it.

CREON: He would: for you honor a traitor as much as him.

ANTIGONE: His own brother, traitor or not, and equal in blood.

CREON: He made war on his country. Eteoclês defended it.

ANTIGONE: Nevertheless, there are honors due all the dead.

CREON: But not the same for the wicked as for the just.

ANTIGONE: Ah Creon, Creon,
    Which of us can say what the gods hold wicked?

CREON: An enemy is an enemy, even dead.

ANTIGONE: It is my nature to join in love, not hate.

CREON: [Finally losing patience] Go join them, then; if you must have your love,
    Find it in hell!

CHORAGOS: But see, Ismenê comes:

[Enter ISMENE, guarded

Those tears are sisterly, the cloud
That shadows her eyes rains down gentle sorrow.

CREON: You too, Ismenê,
    Snake in my ordered house, sucking my blood
    Stealthily—and all the time I never knew
    That these two sisters were aiming at my throne!

                                        Ismenê,
Do you confess your share in this crime, or deny it?
Answer me.

ISMENE: Yes, if she will let me say so. I am guilty.

ANTIGONE: [Coldly] No, Ismenê. You have no right to say so.
    You would not help me, and I will not have you help me.

ISMENE: But now I know what you meant; and I am here
    To join you, to take my share of punishment.

ANTIGONE: The dead man and the gods who rule the dead
    Know whose act this was. Words are not friends.

ISMENE: Do you refuse me, Antigonê? I want to die with you:
    I too have a duty that I must discharge to the dead.

ANTIGONE: You shall not lessen my death by sharing it.

ISMENE: What do I care for life when you are dead?

ANTIGONE: Ask Creon. You're always hanging on his opinions.

ISMENE: You are laughing at me. Why, Antigonê?

ANTIGONE: It's a joyless laughter, Ismenê

ISMENE: But can I do nothing?

ANTIGONE: Yes. Save yourself. I shall not envy you.
    There are those who will praise you; I shall have honor, too.

ISMENE: But we are equally guilty!

ANTIGONE: No more, Ismenê.
   You are alive, but I belong to Death.
CREON: *[To the Chorus]* Gentlemen, I beg you to observe these girls:
   One has just now lost her mind; the other,
   It seems, has never had a mind at all.
ISMENE: Grief teaches the steadiest minds to waver, King.
CREON: Yours certainly did, when you assumed guilt with the guilty!
ISMENE: But how could I go on living without her?
CREON: You are.
   She is already dead.
ISMENE: But your own son's bride!
CREON:
   There are places enough for him to push his plow.
   I want no wicked women for my sons!
ISMENE: O dearest Haimon, how your father wrongs you!
CREON: I've had enough of your childish talk of marriage!
CHORAGOS: Do you really intend to steal this girl from your son?
CREON: No; Death will do that for me.
CHORAGOS: Then she must die?
CREON: *[Ironically]* You dazzle me.
                 —But enough of this talk!
   [To GUARDS] You, there, take them away and guard them well:
   For they are but women, and even brave men run
   When they see Death coming.

   [Exeunt ISMENE, ANTIGONE, and GUARDS]

ODE II

CHORUS: [STROPHE 1]
   Fortunate is the man who has never tasted God's vengeance!
   Where once the anger of heaven has struck, that house is shaken
   For ever: damnation rises behind each child
   Like a wave cresting out of the black northeast,
   When the long darkness under sea roars up
   And bursts drumming death upon the windwhipped sand.

   I have seen this gathering sorrow from time long past   [ANTISTROPHE 1]
   Loom upon Oedipus' children: generation from generation
   Takes the compulsive rage of the enemy god.
   So lately this last flower of Oedipus' line
   Drank the sunlight! but now a passionate word
   And a handful of dust have closed up all its beauty.
        What mortal arrogance   [STROPHE 2]
        Transcends the wrath of Zeus?
   Sleep cannot lull him, nor the effortless long months
   Of the timeless gods: but he is young for ever,
   And his house is the shining day of high Olympos.
        All that is and shall be,

And all the past, is his.
No pride on earth is free of the curse of heaven.
 The straying dreams of men   [ANTISTROPHE 2]
 May bring them ghosts of joy:
But as they drowse, the waking embers burn them;
Or they walk with fíxed éyes, as blind men walk.
But the ancient wisdom speaks for our own time:
 Fate works most for woe
 With Folly's fairest show.
Man's little pleasure is the spring of sorrow.

SCENE III

CHORAGOS: But here is Haimon, King, the last of all your sons.
 Is it grief for Antigonê that brings him here,
 And bitterness at being robbed of his bride?

 [Enter HAIMON]

CREON: We shall soon see, and no need of diviners.

            —Son,
 You have heard my final judgment on that girl:
 Have you come here hating me, or have you come
 With deference and with love, whatever I do?
HAIMON: I am your son, father. You are my guide.
 You make things clear for me, and I obey you.
 No marriage means more to me than your continuing wisdom.
CREON: Good. That is the way to behave: subordinate
 Everything else, my son, to your father's will.
 This is what a man prays for, that he may get
 Sons attentive and dutiful in his house,
 Each one hating his father's enemies,
 Honoring his father's friends. But if his sons
 Fail him, if they turn out unprofitably,
 What has he fathered but trouble for himself
 And amusement for the malicious?
          So you are right
 Not to lose your head over this woman.
 Your pleasure with her would soon grow cold, Haimon,
 And then you'd have a hellcat in bed and elsewhere.
 Let her find her husband in Hell!
 Of all the people in this city, only she
 Has had contempt for my law and broken it.

 Do you want me to show myself weak before the people?
 Or to break my sworn word? No, and I will not.
 The woman dies.
 I suppose she'll plead "family ties." Well, let her.
 If I permit my own family to rebel,
 How shall I earn the world's obedience?

Show me the man who keeps his house in hand,
He's fit for public authority.
                          I'll have no dealings
With law-breakers, critics of the government:
Whoever is chosen to govern should be obeyed—
Must be obeyed, in all things, great and small,
Just and unjust! O Haimon,
The man who knows how to obey, and that man only,
Knows how to give commands when the time comes.
You can depend on him, no matter how fast
The spears come: he's a good soldier, he'll stick it out.

Anarchy, anarchy! Show me a greater evil!
This is why cities tumble and the great houses rain down,
This is what scatters armies!
No, no: good lives are made so by discipline.
We keep the laws then, and the lawmakers,
And no woman shall seduce us. If we must lose,
Let's lose to a man, at least! Is a woman stronger than we?
CHORAGOS: Unless time has rusted my wits,
    What you say, King, is said with point and dignity.
HAIMON: [*Boyishly earnest*] Father:
    Reason is God's crowning gift to man, and you are right
    To warn me against losing mine. I cannot say—
    I hope that I shall never want to say!—that you
    Have reasoned badly. Yet there are other men
    Who can reason, too; and their opinions might be helpful.
    You are not in a position to know everything
    That people say or do, or what they feel:
    Your temper terrifies them—everyone
    Will tell you only what you like to hear.
    But I, at any rate, can listen; and I have heard them
    Muttering and whispering in the dark about this girl.
    They say no woman has ever, so unreasonably,
    Died so shameful a death for a generous act:
    "She covered her brother's body. Is this indecent?
    She kept him from dogs and vultures. Is this a crime?
    Death?—She should have all the honor that we can give her!"

    This is the way they talk out there in the city.

    You must believe me:
    Nothing is closer to me than your happiness.
    What could be closer? Must not any son
    Value his father's fortune as his father does his?
    I beg you, do not be unchangeable:
    Do not believe that you alone can be right.
    The man who thinks that,
    The man who maintains that only he has the power

To reason correctly, the gift to speak, the soul—
A man like that, when you know him, turns out empty.

It is not reason never to yield to reason!

In flood time you can see how some trees bend,
And because they bend, even their twigs are safe,
While stubborn trees are torn up, roots and all.
And the same thing happens in sailing:
Make your sheet fast, never slacken,—and over you go,
Head over heels and under: and there's your voyage.
Forget you are angry! Let yourself be moved!
I know I am young; but please let me say this:
The ideal condition
Would be, I admit, that men should be right by instinct;
But since we are all too likely to go astray,
The reasonable thing is to learn from those who can teach.

CHORAGOS: You will do well to listen to him, King,
   If what he says is sensible. And you, Haimon,
   Must listen to your father.—Both speak well.

CREON: You consider it right for a man of my years and experience
   To go to school to a boy?

HAIMON: It is not right
   If I am wrong. But if I am young, and right,
   What does my age matter?

CREON: You think it right to stand up for an anarchist?

HAIMON: Not at all. I pay no respect to criminals.

CREON: Then she is not a criminal?

HAIMON: The City would deny it, to a man.

CREON: And the City proposes to teach me how to rule?

HAIMON: Ah. Who is it that's talking like a boy now?

CREON: My voice is the one voice giving orders in this City!

HAIMON: It is no City if it takes orders from one voice.

CREON: The State is the King!

HAIMON: Yes, if the State is a desert.

   [Pause]

CREON: This boy, it seems, has sold out to a woman.

HAIMON: If you are a woman: my concern is only for you.

CREON: So? Your "concern"! In a public brawl with your father!

HAIMON: How about you, in a public brawl with justice?

CREON: With justice, when all that I do is within my rights?

HAIMON: You have no right to trample on God's right.

CREON: *[Completely out of control]* Fool, adolescent fool! Taken in by a woman!

HAIMON: You'll never see me taken in by anything vile.

CREON: Every word you say is for her!

HAIMON: *[Quietly, darkly]*   And for you.
   And for me. And for the gods under the earth.

CREON: You'll never marry her while she lives.

HAIMON: Then she must die.—But her death will cause another.

CREON: Another?

Have you lost your senses? Is this an open threat?

HAIMON: There is no threat in speaking to emptiness.

CREON: I swear you'll regret this superior tone of yours!

You are the empty one!

HAIMON: If you were not my father,

I'd say you were perverse.

CREON: You girlstruck fool, don't play at words with me!

HAIMON: I am sorry. You prefer silence.

CREON: Now, by God—!

I swear, by all the gods in heaven above us,

You'll watch it, I swear you shall!

To the SERVANTS]   Bring her out!

Bring the woman out! Let her die before his eyes!

Here, this instant, with her bridegroom beside her!

HAIMON: Not here, no; she will not die here, King.

And you will never see my face again.

Go on raving as long as you've a friend to endure you.

    [*Exit* HAIMON]

CHORAGOS: Gone, gone.

Creon, a young man in a rage is dangerous!

CREON: Let him do, or dream to do, more than a man can.

He shall not save these girls from death.

CHORAGOS: These girls?

You have sentenced them both?

CREON: No, you are right.

I will not kill the one whose hands are clean.

CHORAGOS: But Antigonê?

CREON: [*Somberly*]

                              I will carry her far away

Out there in the wilderness, and lock her

Living in a vault of stone. She shall have food,

As the custom is, to absolve the State of her death.

And there let her pray to the gods of hell:

They are her only gods:

Perhaps they will show her an escape from death,

Or she may learn,

                    though late,

That piety shown the dead is pity in vain.

    [*Exit* CREON]

ODE III

CHORUS: Love, unconquerable   [STROPHE]

Waster of rich men, keeper

Of warm lights and all-night vigil

In the soft face of a girl:

Sea-wanderer, forest-visitor!

Even the pure Immortals cannot escape you,
And mortal man, in his one day's dusk,
Trembles before your glory.

Surely you swerve upon ruin   [ANTISTROPHE]
The just man's consenting heart,
As here you have made bright anger
Strike between father and son—
And none has conquered but Love!
A girl's glánce wórking the will of heaven:
Pleasure to her alone who mocks us,
Merciless Aphroditê.

SCENE IV

CHORAGOS: [As ANTIGONE enters guarded]
    But I can no longer stand in awe of this,
    Nor, seeing what I see, keep back my tears.
    Here is Antigonê, passing to that chamber
    Where all find sleep at last.
ANTIGONE: Look upon me, friends, and pity me [STROPHE 1]
    Turning back at the night's edge to say
    Good-by to the sun that shines for me no longer;
    Now sleepy Death
    Summons me down to Acheron, that cold shore:
    There is no bridesong there, nor any music.
CHORUS: Yet not unpraised, not without a kind of honor,
    You walk at last into the underworld;
    Untouched by sickness, broken by no sword.
    What woman has ever found your way to death?
ANTIGONE:
    How often I have heard the story of Niobê,   [ANTISTROPHE 1]
    Tantalos' wretched daughter, how the stone
    Clung fast about her, ivy-close: and they say
    The rain falls endlessly
    And sifting soft snow; her tears are never done.
    I feel the loneliness of her death in mine.
CHORUS: But she was born of heaven, and you
    Are woman, woman-born. If her death is yours,
    A mortal woman's, is this not for you
    Glory in our world and in the world beyond?
ANTIGONE: You laugh at me. Ah, friends, friends,   [STROPHE 2]
    Can you not wait until I am dead? O Thebes,
    O men many-charioted, in love with Fortune,
    Dear springs of Dircê, sacred Theban grove,
    Be witnesses for me, denied all pity,
    Unjustly judged! and think a word of love
    For her whose path turns

Under dark earth, where there are no more tears.

CHORUS: You have passed beyond human daring and come at last
   Into a place of stone where Justice sits.
   I cannot tell
   What shape of your father's guilt appears in this.

ANTIGONE:
   You have touched it at last: that bridal bed   [ANTISTROPHE 2]
   Unspeakable, horror of son and mother mingling:
   Their crime, infection of all our family!
   O Oedipus, father and brother!
   Your marriage strikes from the grave to murder mine.
   I have been a stranger here in my own land:
   All my life
   The blasphemy of my birth has followed me.

CHORUS: Reverence is a virtue, but strength
   Lives in established law: that must prevail.
   You have made your choice,
   Your death is the doing of your conscious hand.

ANTIGONE:
   [EPODE]
   Then let me go, since all your words are bitter,
   And the very light of the sun is cold to me.
   Lead me to my vigil, where I must have
   Neither love nor lamentation; no song, but silence.

   [CREON *interrupts impatiently*]

CREON: If dirges and planned lamentations could put off death,
   Men would be singing for ever.
   [*To the* SERVANTS]   Take her, go!
   You know your orders: take her to the vault
   And leave her alone there. And if she lives or dies,
   That's her affair, not ours: our hands are clean.

ANTIGONE: O tomb, vaulted bride-bed in eternal rock,
   Soon I shall be with my own again
   Where Persephonê welcomes the thin ghosts underground:
   And I shall see my father again, and you, mother,
   And dearest Polyneicês—
                         dearest indeed
   To me, since it was my hand
   That washed him clean and poured the ritual wine:
   And my reward is death before my time!

   And yet, as men's hearts know, I have done no wrong,
   I have not sinned before God. Or if I have,
   I shall know the truth in death. But if the guilt
   Lies upon Creon who judged me, then, I pray,
   May his punishment equal my own.

CHORAGOS: O passionate heart,
      Unyielding, tormented still by the same winds!
CREON: Her guards shall have good cause to regret their delaying.
ANTIGONE: Ah! That voice is like the voice of death!
CREON: I can give you no reason to think you are mistaken.
ANTIGONE: Thebes, and you my fathers' gods,
      And rulers of Thebes, you see me now, the last
      Unhappy daughter of a line of kings,
      Your kings, led away to death. You will remember
      What things I suffer, and at what men's hands,
      Because I would not transgress the laws of heaven.
      [*To the* GUARDS, *simply*] Come: let us wait no longer.

      [*Exit* ANTIGONE, *L.*, *guarded*]

ODE IV

CHORUS: All Danaê's beauty was locked away   [STROPHE 1]
      In a brazen cell where the sunlight could not come:
      A small room, still as any grave, enclosed her.
      Yet she was a princess too,
      And Zeus in a rain of gold poured love upon her.
      O child, child,
      No power in wealth or war
      Or tough sea-blackened ships
      Can prevail against untiring Destiny!

      And Dryas' son also, that furious king,   [ANTISTROPHE 1]
      Bore the god's prisoning anger for his pride:
      Sealed up by Dionysos in deaf stone,
      His madness died among echoes.
      So at the last he learned what dreadful power
      His tongue had mocked:
      For he had profaned the revels,
      And fired the wrath of the nine
      Implacable Sisters that love the sound of the flute.

      And old men tell a half-remembered tale   [STROPHE 2]
      Of horror done where a dark ledge splits the sea
      And a double surf beats on the gráy shóres:
      How a king's new woman, sick
      With hatred for the queen he had imprisoned,
      Ripped out his two sons' eyes with her bloody hands
      While grinning Arês watched the shuttle plunge
      Four times: four blind wounds crying for revenge,

      Crying, tears and blood mingled.—Piteously born,   [ANTISTROPHE 2]
      Those sons whose mother was of heavenly birth!

Her father was the god of the North Wind
And she was cradled by gales,
She raced with young colts on the glittering hills
And walked untrammeled in the open light:
But in her marriage deathless Fate found means
To build a tomb like yours for all her joy.

SCENE V

[Enter blind TEIRESIAS, *led by a boy. The opening speeches of* TEIRESIAS
should be in singsong contrast to the realistic lines of CREON.]

TEIRESIAS: This is the way the blind man comes, Princes, Princes,
  Lock-step, two heads lit by the eyes of one.
CREON: What new thing have you to tell us, old Teiresias?
TEIRESIAS: I have much to tell you: listen to the prophet, Creon.
CREON: I am not aware that I have ever failed to listen.
TEIRESIAS: Then you have done wisely, King, and ruled well.
CREON: I admit my debt to you. But what have you to say?
TEIRESIAS: This, Creon: you stand once more on the edge of fate.
CREON: What do you mean? Your words are a kind of dread.
TEIRESIAS: Listen, Creon:
  I was sitting in my chair of augury, at the place
  Where the birds gather about me. They were all a-chatter,
  As is their habit, when suddenly I heard
  A strange note in their jangling, a scream, a
  Whirring fury; I knew that they were fighting,
  Tearing each other, dying
  In a whirlwind of wings clashing. And I was afraid.
  I began the rites of burnt-offering at the altar,
  But Hephaistos failed me: instead of bright flame,
  There was only the sputtering slime of the fat thigh-flesh
  Melting: the entrails dissolved in gray smoke,
  The bare bone burst from the welter. And no blaze!
  This was a sign from heaven. My boy described it,
  Seeing for me as I see for others.
  I tell you, Creon, you yourself have brought
  This new calamity upon us. Our hearths and altars
  Are stained with the corruption of dogs and carrion birds
  That glut themselves on the corpse of Oedipus' son.
  The gods are deaf when we pray to them, their fire
  Recoils from our offering, their birds of omen
  Have no cry of comfort, for they are gorged
  With the thick blood of the dead.
                                    O my son,
  These are no trifles! Think: all men make mistakes,
  But a good man yields when he knows his course is wrong,
  And repairs the evil. The only crime is pride.

Give in to the dead man, then: do not fight with a corpse—
What glory is it to kill a man who is dead?
Think, I beg you:
It is for your own good that I speak as I do.
You should be able to yield for your own good.
CREON: It seems that prophets have made me their especial province.
All my life long
I have been a kind of butt for the dull arrows
Of doddering fortune-tellers!
                              No, Teiresias:
If your birds—if the great eagles of God himself
Should carry him stinking bit by bit to heaven,
I would not yield. I am not afraid of pollution:
No man can defile the gods.
                              Do what you will,
Go into business, make money, speculate
In India gold or that synthetic gold from Sardis,
Get rich otherwise than by my consent to bury him.
Teiresias, it is a sorry thing when a wise man
Sells his wisdom, lets out his words for hire!
TEIRESIAS: Ah Creon! Is there no man left in the world—
CREON: To do what?—Come, let's have the aphorism!
TEIRESIAS: No man who knows that wisdom outweighs any wealth?
CREON: As surely as bribes are baser than any baseness.
TEIRESIAS: You are sick, Creon! You are deathly sick!
CREON: As you say: it is not my place to challenge a prophet.
TEIRESIAS: Yet you have said my prophecy is for sale.
CREON: The generation of prophets has always loved gold.
TEIRESIAS: The generation of kings has always loved brass.
CREON: You forget yourself! You are speaking to your King.
TEIRESIAS: I know it. You are a king because of me.
CREON: You have a certain skill; but you have sold out.
TEIRESIAS: King, you will drive me to words that—
CREON: Say them, say them!
Only remember: I will not pay you for them.
TEIRESIAS: No, you will find them too costly.
CREON: No doubt. Speak:
Whatever you say, you will not change my will.
TEIRESIAS: Then take this, and take it to heart!
The time is not far off when you shall pay back
Corpse for corpse, flesh of your own flesh.
You have thrust the child of this world into living night,
You have kept from the gods below the child that is theirs:
The one in a grave before her death, the other,
Dead, denied the grave. This is your crime:
And the Furies and the dark gods of Hell
Are swift with terrible punishment for you.
Do you want to buy me now, Creon?

Not many days,
And your house will be full of men and women weeping,
And curses will be hurled at you from far
Cities grieving for sons unburied, left to rot
Before the walls of Thebes.
These are my arrows, Creon: they are all for you.
But come, child: lead me home. [*To* BOY]
Let him waste his fine anger upon younger men.
Maybe he will learn at last
To control a wiser tongue in a better head.

[*Exit* TEIRESIAS]

CHORAGOS: The old man has gone, King, but his words
   Remain to plague us. I am old, too,
   But I cannot remember that he was ever false.
CREON: That is true. . . . It troubles me.
   Oh it is hard to give in! but it is worse
   To risk everything for stubborn pride.
CHORAGOS: Creon: take my advice.
CREON: What shall I do?
CHORAGOS: Go quickly: free Antigonê from her vault
   And build a tomb for the body of Polyneicês.
CREON: You would have me do this?
CHORAGOS: Creon, yes!
   And it must be done at once: God moves
   Swiftly to cancel the folly of stubborn men.
CREON: It is hard to deny the heart! But I
   Will do it: I will not fight with destiny.
CHORAGOS: You must go yourself, you cannot leave it to others.
CREON: I will go.
            —Bring axes, servants:
   Come with me to the tomb. I buried her, I
   Will set her free.
                 Oh quickly!
   My mind misgives—
   The laws of the gods are mighty, and a man must serve them
   To the last day of his life!

[*Exit* CREON]

PÆAN

CHORAGOS: God of many names   [STROPHE 1]
CHORUS: O Iacchos
         son
   of Kadmeian Sémelê
            O born of the Thunder!
      Guardian of the West
               Regent

of Eleusis' plain
                    O Prince of maenad Thebes
and the Dragon Field by rippling Ismenos:
CHORAGOS: God of many names   [ANTISTROPHE 1]
CHORUS: the flame of torches
      flares on our hills
                      the nymphs of Iacchos
      dance at the spring of Castalia:

      from the vine-close mountain
                          come ah come in ivy:
      Evohé evohé! sings through the streets of Thebes
CHORAGOS: God of many names   [STROPHE 2]
CHORUS: Iacchos of Thebes
      heavenly Child
                  of Sémelê bride of the Thunderer!
      The shadow of plague is upon us:
                              come
      with clement feet
                      oh come from Parnasos
      down the long slopes
                      across the lamenting water
CHORAGOS: [ANTISTROPHE 2]
      Iô Fire! Chorister of the throbbing stars!
      O purest among the voices of the night!
      Thou son of God, blaze for us!
CHORUS: Come with choric rapture of circling Maenads
      Who cry Iô *Iacche!*
                  God of many names!

ÉXODOS

[Enter MESSENGER, *L.]*

MESSENGER: Men of the line of Kadmos, you who live
      Near Amphion's citadel:
                          I cannot say
Of any condition of human life "This is fixed,
This is clearly good, or bad." Fate raises up,
And Fate casts down the happy and unhappy alike:
No man can foretell his Fate.
                      Take the case of Creon:
Creon was happy once, as I count happiness:
Victorious in battle, sole governor of the land,
Fortunate father of children nobly born.
And now it has all gone from him! Who can say
That a man is still alive when his life's joy fails?
He is a walking dead man. Grant him rich,
Let him live like a king in his great house:

If his pleasure is gone, I would not give
So much as the shadow of smoke for all he owns.
CHORAGOS: Your words hint at sorrow: what is your news for us?
MESSENGER: They are dead. The living are guilty of their death.
CHORAGOS: Who is guilty? Who is dead? Speak!
MESSENGER: Haimon.
    Haimon is dead; and the hand that killed him
    Is his own hand.
CHORAGOS: His father's? or his own?
MESSENGER: His own, driven mad by the murder his father had done.
CHORAGOS: Teiresias, Teiresias, how clearly you saw it all!
MESSENGER: This is my news: you must draw what conclusions you can from it.
CHORAGOS: But look: Eurydicê, our Queen:
    Has she overheard us?

[*Enter* EURYDICE *from the Palace, C.*]

EURYDICE: I have heard something, friends:
    As I was unlocking the gate of Pallas' shrine,
    For I needed her help today, I heard a voice
    Telling of some new sorrow. And I fainted
    There at the temple with all my maidens about me.
    But speak again: whatever it is, I can bear it:
    Grief and I are no strangers.
MESSENGER: Dearest Lady,
    I will tell you plainly all that I have seen.
    I shall not try to comfort you: what is the use,
    Since comfort could lie only in what is not true?
    The truth is always best.
                        I went with Creon
    To the outer plain where Polyneicês was lying,
    No friend to pity him, his body shredded by dogs.
    We made our prayers in that place to Hecatê
    And Pluto, that they would be merciful. And we bathed
    The corpse with holy water, and we brought
    Fresh-broken branches to burn what was left of it,
    And upon the urn we heaped up a towering barrow
    Of the earth of his own land.
                            When we were done, we ran
    To the vault where Antigonê lay on her couch of stone.
    One of the servants had gone ahead,
    And while he was yet far off he heard a voice
    Grieving within the chamber, and he came back
    And told Creon. And as the King went closer,
    The air was full of wailing, the words lost,
    And he begged us to make all haste. "Am I a prophet?"
    He said, weeping, "And must I walk this road,
    The saddest of all that I have gone before?
    My son's voice calls me on. Oh quickly, quickly!

Look through the crevice there, and tell me
If it is Haimon, or some deception of the gods!"
We obeyed; and in the cavern's farthest corner
We saw her lying:
She had made a noose of her fine linen veil
And hanged herself. Haimon lay beside her,
His arms about her waist, lamenting her,
His love lost under ground, crying out
That his father had stolen her away from him.
When Creon saw him the tears rushed to his eyes
And he called to him: "What have you done, child? Speak to me.
What are you thinking that makes your eyes so strange?
O my son, my son, I come to you on my knees!"
But Haimon spat in his face. He said not a word,
Staring—
      And suddenly drew his sword
And lunged. Creon shrank back, the blade missed; and the boy,
Desperate against himself, drove it half its length
Into his own side, and fell. And as he died
He gathered Antigonê close in his arms again,
Choking, his blood bright red on her white cheek.
And now he lies dead with the dead, and she is his
At last, his bride in the houses of the dead.

[Exit EURYDICE into the Palace]

CHORAGOS: She has left us without a word. What can this mean?
MESSENGER: It troubles me, too; yet she knows what is best,
    Her grief is too great for public lamentation,
    And doubtless she has gone to her chamber to weep
    For her dead son, leading her maidens in his dirge.
CHORAGOS: It may be so: but I fear this deep silence

   [Pause]

MESSENGER: I will see what she is doing. I will go in.

   [Exit MESSENGER into the Palace]
     [Enter CREON with attendants, bearing HAIMON's body

CHORAGOS: But here is the King himself: oh look at him,
    Bearing his own damnation in his arms.
CREON: Nothing you say can touch me any more.
    My own blind heart has brought me
    From darkness to final darkness. Here you see
    The father murdering, the murdered son—
    And all my civic wisdom!
    Haimon my son, so young, so young to die,
    I was the fool, not you; and you died for me.
CHORAGOS: That is the truth; but you were late in learning it.
CREON: This truth is hard to bear. Surely a god
    Has crushed me beneath the hugest weight of heaven,

And driven me headlong a barbaric way
To trample out the thing I held most dear.
The pains that men will take to come to pain!

[Enter MESSENGER from the Palace]

MESSENGER: The burden you carry in your hands is heavy,
    But it is not all: you will find more in your house.
CREON: What burden worse than this shall I find there?
MESSENGER: The Queen is dead.
CREON: O port of death, deaf world,
    Is there no pity for me? And you, Angel of evil,
    I was dead, and your words are death again.
    Is it true, boy? Can it be true?
    Is my wife dead? Has death bred death?
MESSENGER: You can see for yourself.

[The doors are opened, and the body of EURYDICE is disclosed within.]

CREON: Oh pity!
    All true, all true, and more than I can bear!
    O my wife, my son!
MESSENGER: She stood before the altar, and her heart
    Welcomed the knife her own hand guided,
    And a great cry burst from her lips for Megareus dead,
    And for Haimon dead, her sons; and her last breath
    Was a curse for their father, the murderer of her sons.
    And she fell, and the dark flowed in through her closing eyes
CREON: O God, I am sick with fear.
    Are there no swords here? Has no one a blow for me?
MESSENGER: Her curse is upon you for the deaths of both.
CREON: It is right that it should be. I alone am guilty.
    I know it, and I say it. Lead me in,
    Quickly, friends.
    I have neither life nor substance. Lead me in.
CHORAGOS: You are right, if there can be right in so much wrong.
    The briefest way is best in a world of sorrow.
CREON: Let it come,
    Let death come quickly, and be kind to me.
    I would not ever see the sun again.
CHORAGOS: All that will come when it will; but we, meanwhile,
    Have much to do. Leave the future to itself.
CREON: All my heart was in that prayer!
CHORAGOS: Then do not pray any more: the sky is deaf.
CREON: Lead me away. I have been rash and foolish.
    I have killed my son and my wife.
    I look for comfort; my comfort lies here dead.
    Whatever my hands have touched has come to nothing.
    Fate has brought all my pride to a thought of dust.

[As CREON *is being led into the house, the* CHORAGOS *advances and speaks directly to the audience*]

CHORAGOS: There is no happiness where there is no wisdom;
No wisdom but in submission to the gods.
Big words are always punished,
And proud men in old age learn to be wise.

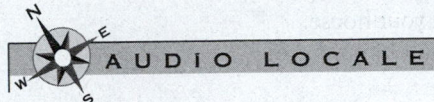

A U D I O   L O C A L E

Antigone and Current Events. In October 2002, National Public Radio commentator and best-selling author Cornel West discussed connections between the post-9/11 world and *Antigone* with correspondent Karen Grigsby Bates. You can listen to the conversation on the National Public Radio webpage at *http://www.npr.org* and using "Antigone" as the key word to link to the audio download. The "*Antigone* and Current Affairs" segment appeared on the *Tavis Smiley Show* on October 16, 2002.

Talking about the Text

1. What do you make of Antigone's relationship to the living human beings in her life: her sister especially, but also Creon and to a lesser extent the chorus and Haimon?
2. What is Antigone's relationship to death and the dead? Note that she is given quite a few speeches between the time she is condemned to death by Creon and when she is finally led away to her doom (p. 1322). How do you respond, and to what degree is your response conditioned by your cultural position?
3. Suppose Creon had changed his mind in time. What do you think Antigone's reaction would have been?
4. Antigone insists that Polyneices should be buried and honor be shown to the dead, despite the fact that he has turned traitor to Thebes and killed his own brother. Is there another side to this argument than Antigone's? Creon touches on Polyneices' moral status only briefly; he is most interested in the challenge to his kingly authority—by a woman. If we take this other side seriously, where do we as audience or readers position ourselves in relation to Antigone's arguments and actions? Would modern practice regarding the dead offer us any enlightenment?
5. "The gods" play a particularly perplexing role in *Antigone*, especially if we raise any questions about Antigone's absolute stand. They appear bent on completing the ruin of Laius' house and maximizing the misery of Antigone, Ismene, Haimon, Creon, and Eurydice. In fact, they threaten any human family that gets too proud, joyous, confident, or accomplished. And we can hardly ignore them, for they are uppermost in the consciousness of Antigone and the chorus. How do we as audience react to these gods?
6. Why does Antigone make a better dramatic heroine than, say, Ismene?
7. Pick lines or other parts of speeches that could have been uttered in today's theater as indicative of the way "we" think and feel. Try them out aloud, and compare them to lines that do not seem to work for us today.

Writing about the Text

1. Write an essay about fate in *Antigone*. For instance, it seems a cruel joke that once Creon, under the influence of Teiresias, changes his mind about Antigone and the

disposal of Polyneices' corpse, it is too late to avert disaster. Was Creon's "crime" that he waited too long, remained stubborn too long? Creon gets assured that it is permissible to make a mistake, as long as you realize it and fix it. On the other hand, were events "fated" to turn out the way they were, making Creon simply a "pawn in the game," despite his kingly role?

2. Demonstrate how and why Creon changes over the course of the play.

Linking the Text to Other Texts

1. Compare Creon and Oedipus as characters (Creon appears in both *Oedipus The King* and *Antigone*). What difference does the assumption of kingship (and in the case of Oedipus, the loss of kingship) make to each of them?

 INSPIRATION *Antigone* **Abroad**

Greek drama is often considered timeless in its ability to relate to audiences over 2,000 years after its creation. It is also noteworthy in its ability today to transcend cultural differences. Playwrights around the world have been inspired by *Antigone* to tell stories of resistance in the face of authoritarian rule. Here are just a few of them.

- **The Island (1974)**. John Kani and Winston Ntshona. Along with two black actors who were imprisoned during South Africa's apartheid regime, playwright Athol Fugard co-wrote this play about two men imprisoned on Robben Island who act out *Antigone* as part of their fantasy life. Antigone becomes a metaphor for the conflict between the state and the individual.

- **Tegonni, An African Antigone (1994)**. Nigerian-born playwright Femi Osofisan adapted *Antigone* to tell the story of civil unrest in his native country. Osofisan workshoped and directed the play's premiere at Emory University in Atlanta in 1994. You can find both *Tegonni* and *The Island* in the anthology *The Athenian Sun in an African Sky: Modern African Adaptations of Classical Greek Tragedy*, edited by Kevin J. Wetmore.

- **Antigona Furiosa (1998)**. One of Argentina's best playwrights, Griselda Gambaro, took the story of Antigone and applied it to the plight of the Disappeared during Argentina's Dirty War. Starting in 1976, thousands of civilian opponents to military rule disappeared and were never seen or heard from again. A group of women called the Mothers of the Plaza de Mayo have been protesting every day at 3:30 p.m. to demand to know the fate of their kidnapped children. Gambaro's play tells their story.

- **Antigone Falun Gong (2004)**. In San Francisco, the Aurora Theater Company produced writer Cherylene Lee's version of *Antigone*, which transports the ancient play to modern China. In Lee's play, the authoritarian rule Antigone faces is that of the Chinese regime, which has outlawed a religious movement called Falun Gong.

2. Does Antigone remind you of any other woman you have met in literature? (Or in life, for that matter?) In what ways is she uniquely a female hero? In what ways does she remind you of male heroes?

Starting Points for Further Research: Sophocles

- **Editions:** Sophocles. *Elektra and Other Plays.* Ed. E. F. Watling. New York: Penguin, 1987.

  ———— *The Theban Plays.* Ed. E. F. Watling. New York: Penguin, 2003.

- **Critical Essay:** Marianth Colakis. "What Jocasta Knew: Alternative Versions of the Oedipus Myth." *Classical and Modern Literature: A Quarterly* 16:2 (1996): 217–29.

CHAPTER
23

William Shakespeare

Mr. WILLIAM
SHAKESPEARES
COMEDIES,
HISTORIES, &
TRAGEDIES.
Published according to the True Originall Copies.

LONDON
Printed by Isaac Iaggard, and Ed. Blount. 1623.

Portrait of Shakespeare from the title page of the Shakespeare First Folio (London, 1623)

Although he is arguably the most famous writer in history, we know very little about the life of William Shakespeare (1554–1616) and much of what we do know is indirect, by inference from his plays and poems. The basic life records are skimpy: he was born into the lower middle class in Stratford-upon-Avon in April 1564; he died there in 1616 and was buried in the church graveyard. In 1582 he married Anne Hathaway, who was six years older; they had three children. From about 1592 to about 1611 he was living in London as an actor and a playwright, with significant financial success; upon his death, he left his family valuable real estate holdings. Besides these bare facts gleaned from public records, we know little about what really mattered: his schooling, his friends, his reading, his politics, his dreams, his loves, his religious faith. What we do know is from a mix of historical study of his times and scholarly inference, based on the evidence in his 37 plays, 154 sonnets, and two long narrative poems.

All the evidence points to a professional man of the theater, someone who knew plays as an actor, a writer, and finally as an entrepreneur. He was part of a

company of players, the Lord Chamberlain's Men; when they received royal patronage in 1603, they changed their name to the King's Men. This was one of
the premier companies of its day, well known to all Londoners who frequented
the theater. Shakespeare was at the center of the London theatrical world.

As a shareholder in his company, Shakespeare helped manage the troupe
and the building they owned. The London theater in the days of Queen Elizabeth (1558–1603) was run for a profit. Backers risked their money to build the
actual theaters, hire the actors and musicians, and pay the playwright. The company charged admission—cheap for the standing room in the unroofed pit (an
area we now call the orchestra), more expensive for the balconies and covered
areas.

While today many people think of the theater as an artistic, uplifting, and
sophisticated experience, it is important to remember its mixed reputation during the Elizabethan era when Shakespeare was writing and performing. We make
a serious mistake if we think the theater was exclusively for the wealthy, the cultivated, the artistic. In fact, the theater was a site where all parts of society came
together, and successful playwrights had to please every type of audience, from
the simplest who loved only spectacle (shipwrecks, ghosts, and swordfights) to
the refined who loved tender feelings, noble sentiments, and fine language. The
one group that seems absent is the middle class, no doubt because the middle
class was not very prominent in Shakespeare's time and had no large, acknowledged role to play in society. High and low dominate, mixing together on Shakespeare's stage—kings and gravediggers, lovers and scoundrels, nobles and
drunken servants—making for its extraordinary richness.

LITERARY LOCALE

The Globe Theatre, London. The Globe, where many of Shakespeare's plays
were staged, was built in 1599 by the Lord Chamberlain's Men, the company of
which Shakespeare was a member, but the theater was destroyed in a 1644 fire.
Nevertheless, using drawings, building contracts, and stage directions in texts as
sources for clues, historians and scholars have been able to get a pretty clear picture of what Elizabethan theaters looked like. A recreation of the Globe (see p.
1164 in Chapter 20 for a photo) was completed in 1996, constructed 200 yards
from the original's site.

Theaters in Shakespeare's time were popular entertainment, much like the
movies of our own time. They were never thought of as exclusive realms of high
art, and they were never located in the nicest, most refined parts of town. The
Globe Theatre was outside the city limits, on the south bank of the Thames
River, in a seedy area beyond the reach of magistrates and censors. (The placement of theaters in less than fancy parts of town has persisted: New York's raff-
ish Times Square is the Theater District; many of Chicago's theaters are on
State Street, not the Magnificent Mile; London's West End borders the teeming,
decidedly mixed Soho neighborhood.) Theater crowds in Shakespeare's era
were famous for being magnets for pickpockets and prostitutes, and theater people were often regarded as having loose morals. Although the theater itself was

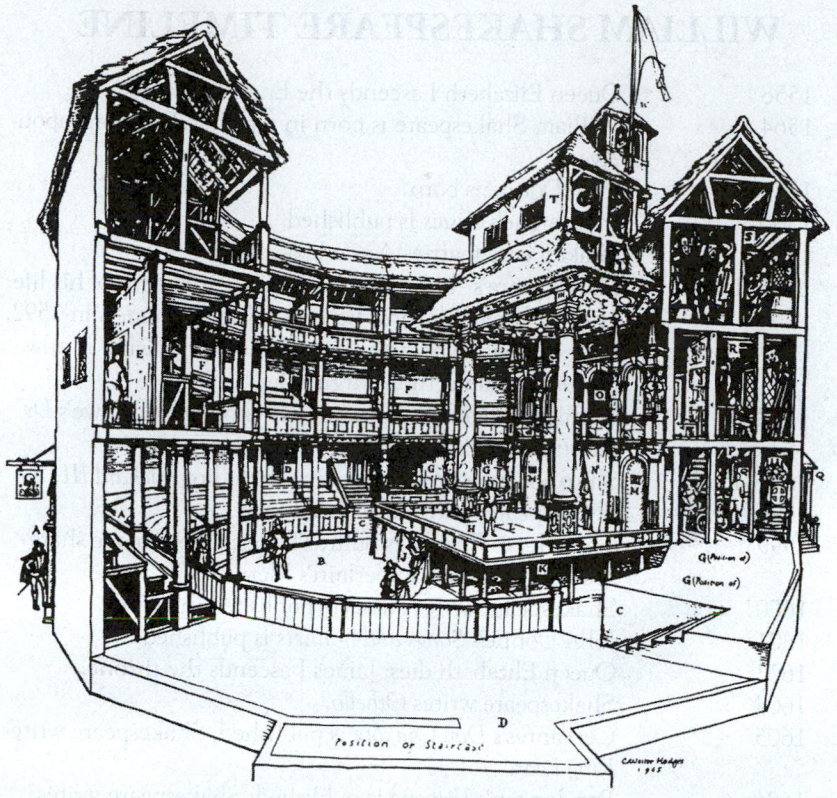

This modern illustration approximates what the original Globe Theatre looked like during Shakespeare's time.

patronized by Queen Elizabeth and later King James, who ordered plays to be put on at court, it was still regarded by many as an immoral, subversive, low form of popular entertainment. When the Puritans took control of England in 1640, one of their first acts was to close the theaters.

The Globe building was either round or multisided, with a partially open roof to make use of natural light. Three tiers of seats—the most comfortable and protected from inclement weather—overlooked a large platform stage, in front of which was a pit area, the cheap, standing-room-only section for theatergoers at that time. The stage was supplemented by a very small curtained area behind it, which could be opened to expose another interior setting such as a bedroom or could be used as a hiding place for an eavesdropping character. An upper gallery could serve as a balcony or a watchtower, depending on what the play called for. The stage was also rigged with trapdoors that could be used for scenes like the graveyard scene in *Hamlet*. Between 2,000 to 3,000 people could attend a performance, but the roundness of the physical space, in which the audience encircled the stage on three sides, made the action seem close by, and the overall experience felt accessible and intimate.

WILLIAM SHAKESPEARE TIMELINE

1558	Queen Elizabeth I ascends the English throne.
1564	William Shakespeare is born in April, in Stratford-upon-Avon.
1572	John Donne is born.
1580	Montaigne's *Essais* is published.
1582	Shakespeare marries Anne Hathaway.
1585–1592	Shakespeare's "lost years" when little is known of his life. Historical records show he is residing in London in 1592.
1587	Roanoke Island colony is established off of what is now North Carolina (then Virginia).
1588	Spanish Armada is defeated; Christopher Marlowe's *Dr Faustus* is published.
1591–1595	Shakespeare writes early plays, including *Richard III*.
1595–1596	Shakespeare writes *Romeo and Juliet*.
1599	The Globe Theatre is built; Shakespeare is made shareholder in Lord Chamberlain's Men.
1600?	Shakespeare writes *Hamlet* (published in 1604).
1601	John Donne's *Songs and Sonnets* is published.
1603	Queen Elizabeth dies; James I ascends the throne.
1604	Shakespeare writes *Othello*.
1605	Cervantes's *Don Quixote* is published; Shakespeare writes *King Lear*.
1606	Ben Jonson's *Volpone* is published; Shakespeare writes *Macbeth*.
1607	Virginia colony is founded.
1609	Shakespeare publishes sonnets (written 1595–1599).
1610–1611	Shakespeare retires to Stratford.
1611	*King James Bible* is published; Shakespeare writes *The Tempest*.
1616	Shakespeare dies in Stratford-upon-Avon.
1623	Shakespeare's collected plays are published (First Folio).

VIDEO LOCALE

Will the Real Will Shakespeare Please Stand Up? In the world of literary scholarship, it seems unlikely that the debate about the true identity of William Shakespeare will ever end. Some scholars debate whether individual plays were actually written by Shakespeare. Others assert that the playwright was really a nobleman in disguise, not the middle-class man from Stratford. In 1996 the PBS show *Frontline* examined the debate between those who believe the great playwright was William Shakespeare and those who believe he was Edward de Vere, Earl of Oxford. Those on the Shakespeare side argue that de Vere died in 1604 and many Shakespeare plays are believed to have been written as late as 1611. And several of Shakespeare's colleagues witnessed the publication of his plays. Defenders of Shakespeare also point out that several prominent playwrights achieved greatness without a college education. On the side of de Vere, scholars argue that there has never been any conclusive evidence that the playwright named Shakespeare was the same person as the man from Stratford. They argue that de Vere had an education consistent with what would be needed to produce Shakespeare's plays. With the discovery of de Vere's Bible, scholars point out that the lines and passages de Vere underlined are the very same that have been documented as Shakespeare's favorites in his works.

The *Frontline* website lists updated arguments from each side, as well as transcripts of three mock trials of the debate, and a history of scholars' doubts. Go to *http://www.pbs.org/wgbh/pages/frontline/Shakespeare* to read more.

PLAYS BY WILLIAM SHAKESPEARE

This chapter includes the text of two of Shakespeare's most famous plays: *The Tempest* and *Hamlet*. It also includes a few of the many works inspired by Shakespeare, such as Aimé Césaire's *A Tempest* and Danitra Vance's *Flotilda Williams as Juliet*. We begin with *The Tempest* (c. 1611), which has special qualities that make it different from most other Shakespeare plays. For one, it is late Shakespeare, probably the last full play he wrote. Because it is the last play, many have seen its protagonist, Prospero, as a stand-in for Shakespeare himself, especially when at the end Prospero vows to retire and give up "this rough magic"—his stage managing of events. *The Tempest* is also unusual in that Shakespeare created an original plot for it, although he included plenty of elements common to other Renaissance plays. It opens with a shipwreck in a storm; the passengers—the king of Naples, his son, and his entourage—end up in different places on an unfamiliar island. Among the entourage are evil courtiers, Sebastian and Antonio, who want to overthrow the king. There is also the kindly royal counselor Gonzalo, who naively expects the best of people. The king's son, Ferdinand, thinks he is the only survivor. When he meets Prospero's daughter Miranda, they fall in love at first sight. Additionally, there are "low" characters—servants who like to drink and carouse.

These complexities alone would be enough to make a rich play as all the different strands and subplots get woven together. But Shakespeare added more: Prospero, the island's ruler, is really the exiled Duke of Milan, forced out of power by his brother Antonio. In the meantime he has acquired magic powers and has gained control over two "servants," both native to the island: the "monster" Caliban and the "sprite" Ariel. Prospero's powers enabled him to create the storm that wrecked the ship. He can also summon up representations of goddesses to perform an elaborately staged courtly play, called a **masque**. By the play's end, Prospero takes up his rightful place; he sees his daughter engaged to Prince Ferdinand, forgives his enemies, and frees his servants as he prepares to give up his magic and leave the island. It is a complex, fantastic plot involving spirits and monsters, gods and humans, music, magic, and special effects.

Despite all its special qualities, *The Tempest* does not seem to have been particularly popular in its original format. Many "improvements" were made, starting

(text continues on page 1343)

ON SHAKESPEAREAN DRAMA

When professional actors and directors think about how to put plays on the stage, they usually decide that Shakespeare fits more with Greek drama than with modern or contemporary plays: Shakespeare plays are "old fashioned," they conclude, and need updating and cutting. Directors believe that audiences can understand modern and contemporary plays that are presented simply and straightforwardly, as they were first put on, but that people need help with "old" plays like those of the Greeks, Shakespeare, and Shakespeare's contemporaries. How much "help" directors are willing to provide depends on their philosophy of performance. Will they adapt the play? How will they costume the actors? How will they cast the play?

To Cut or Not to Cut?

Many of Shakespeare's plays are very long; in fact, to stage every word of *Hamlet* would take four hours. Given that today's audiences will sit for about three hours, but usually not more, most directors cut the play or make significant changes, either silently or boldly. Directors make these changes based on the distinction between literature and script: what readers regard as the play, directors regard as the script. A work of literature cannot be changed, but some directors—not all—believe that a script can. And while we have none of Shakespeare's original manuscripts, we have many of his plays in different versions, some of them revealing large variations in the way they might have appeared on the stage. *Hamlet*, for example, exists in three printed versions. We do not know a lot about Shakespeare's manuscripts, but we can be fairly certain that he changed his own plays to suit the needs of his actors, his theater space, and his audiences.

The issue of choosing to use period or modern dress can extend to weapons. The four-hour 2001 Royal Shakespeare Company's production of Hamlet, *directed by Stephen Pimlott and starring Sam West in the title role, featured a spare, modern set of grays and blacks. Hamlet was costumed in a black sweatshirt, Claudius and his entourage in gray business suits with ID badges, and handguns and switchblades were the weapons.*

A common change to The Tempest *is to cast a woman as Ariel, even though in the text Prospero refers to Ariel as "he." This casting usually forces Prospero to refer to Ariel as "she," a change to the text that may not raise objections but is nonetheless significant. Actress Cynthia Ruffin is shown here as Ariel in the 1993 production by the Marin Shakespeare Company.*

Radical Changes

Peter Brook, one of the most influential directors alive today, is among those who argue that only radical change to Shakespeare's plays will make them relevant to today's viewers. His recent production of *The Tragedy of Hamlet* (2000) had a cast of eight, ran two hours, and its Hamlet was Adrian Lester, a black actor with prominent dreadlocks. Reviews of the production ran hot and cold, but many thought Brook and Lester had captured the essence of the play.

For a radical revisionist like Brook, relevance is all. According to his book *Evoking Shakespeare*, he said to his actors:

> Forget Shakespeare. Forget that there ever was such a man.
> Forget that these plays had an author. . . . So just assume, as
> a trick to help you, that the character . . . really existed.
> Imagine that Hamlet really existed, imagine that someone
> followed him secretly wherever he went with a tape
> recorder, so that the words he spoke were really his own.
> Where does that lead you? First of all, all temptation to
> think that "Hamlet is like me" is swept away. Hamlet is only
> interesting because he is not like anyone else. . . . It is only
> when we forget Shakespeare that we can begin to find him.

(continued on next page)

(continued)

Other directors, such as Peter Hall, argue to keep plays intact. His 1975 production of *Hamlet*, starring Albert Finney, used every word. Similarly, Kenneth Branagh's 1996 film of *Hamlet* uses everything—and runs three hours and fifty-eight minutes. (The cost implications of a four-hour film are simple: a theater can show Branagh's *Hamlet* only once each night, while it can show a conventional two-hour film twice each night, potentially making twice the money.)

According to Peter Hall's *Diaries*, edited by John Goodwin, Peter Hall commented on cuts and costs as follows:

> I don't want to interpret the play by cutting it. . . . It seems to me that we have come some distance in the last twenty-five years in understanding the rhythms of a Shakespearean play. . . . But we still cut the text like barbarians. Do we know what we cut? And don't we normally cut to fit some preconceived theory for the production, or because we simply can't make the passage work? I think my future direction in Shakespeare must be to reveal the total object as well as possible. . . . The cost implications of full length will have to be got over somehow. (176–77)

Modern Dress, Modern Times

A major issue facing every director is the updating that comes with modern dress or a modern setting. In a Renaissance drawing that many think represents Shakespeare's early Roman play *Titus Andronicus*, some characters wear Elizabethan

In 1936, funded by the Federal Theater Project, the dramatic arm of the Works Progress Administration, Orson Welles directed Shakespeare's Macbeth *with an all-black cast. Set in the Caribbean, this production featured Haitian witch doctors for the witches.*

clothes and some wear Roman dress. Thus, already in Shakespeare's time, the costumes were not totally realistic in any modern sense of the word: some characters, usually major ones, wore period garb, while others did not. If this was the case in Shakespeare's day, who can say we should not update his plays when we put them on?

Another rationale for modern updating is not hard to find: Shakespeare moved the action of many of his plays into his own time, so why should we not make a similar change? Finally, placing the drama in the present or the easily recognizable past helps make the situations become more relevant.

Casting the Play

A third performance issue is the gendering of Shakespeare. Shakespeare's company had no women, so all the original female roles were played by males; a number of young men and boys (called "playboys") played the range of female roles, from Miranda in *The Tempest* to Gertrude and Ophelia in *Hamlet* to Desdemona in *Othello*. In current-day productions of Shakespeare plays, we almost never do such a thing. Does that mean we are being false to Shakespeare? Certainly we are not putting on his plays as he did. Yet we think nothing of making the change. Why should we be bound by the narrow rules that governed the Elizabethan stage in Shakespeare's day? On the other hand, the recreated Globe Theatre in London has been offering some all-male productions during its regular season.

In some productions of Shakespeare's plays, women have taken on male roles. In the 1890s, the great French actress Sarah Bernhardt played Hamlet. In the 1990s, Irish actress Fiona Shaw played Richard II (on stage and on film), and in a 2000 production of *The Tempest*, British actress Vanessa Redgrave played Prospero. These were special starring roles; audiences would flock to see one of the major actresses of the time take on a major role, some of them just to see how it could be done. The verdict? Interesting, unusual, provocative, but certainly not the way many believe Shakespeare should be performed. Audiences may take one kind of regendering as normal but regard another as oddly interesting, and suitable only for a special occasion.

Nineteenth-century actress Sarah Bernhardt is seen here as Hamlet, holding and looking at a skull.

INSPIRATION   SHAKESPEARE IN FILM

Iago (right, Kenneth Branagh) whispers poisonous thoughts into the willing ear of Othello (left, Laurence Fishburne) in Oliver Parker's 1995 film version of Othello.

Hollywood likes nothing as much as a remake. With plots involving star-crossed lovers, adultery, mistaken identities, and great romances, Shakespeare continues to inspire screenwriters and directors. Here are just a few of the recent films based entirely or loosely on Shakespeare's plays.

- *Hamlet*. Perhaps the most popular of the dozens of film versions of this enigmatic play are Laurence Olivier's classic 1948 adaptation and Franco Zefferelli's 1990 film starring Mel Gibson as Hamlet and Glenn Close as Gertrude. Diehards who want the complete text of the play will want to see Kenneth Branagh's four-hour 1996 version. Michael Almereyda's 2000 version sets the story in modern-day New York City, with an all-star cast including Ethan Hawke as Hamlet, Sam Shepard as his father, Julia Stiles as Ophelia, and Bill Murray as Polonius.

- *Othello* (1995). Oliver Parker's version of the play stars Laurence Fishburne as Othello and Kenneth Branagh as Iago.

- *O* (2001). This film takes the masterful tragedy Othello and reimagines it at a predominately white prep school. Mekhi Phifer stars as Odin, the popular black basketball star who is dating the school's most popular girl, played by Julia Stiles. Josh Hartnett plays the Iago character, insanely jealous of Odin.

- *10 Things I Hate about You* (1999). This adaptation of *The Taming of the Shrew* places the comedy in an American high school. A younger sister is forbidden to date until her ill-tempered older sister gets a date, so she finds an equally unpleasant boy to set her up with. Julia Stiles plays the boy-hating older sister and Heath Ledger stars as her date.

(continued on next page)

SHAKESPEARE IN FILM

- *Shakespeare in Love* (1998). Written by playwright Tom Stoppard and Marc Norman, and starring Joseph Fiennes and Gwyneth Paltrow, *Shakespeare in Love* is an imaginative fiction about the woman who might have inspired the playwright's great works. The film creatively weaves in lines and plot devices from many of Shakespeare's plays to suggest how his writing was inspired by all that he saw, felt, and heard.
- *Romeo + Juliet* (1996). Considered the "GenX version" of Shakespeare, Baz Luhrman's controversial film updates Romeo and Juliet with rock music and fast cars amid the setting of Verona Beach.
- *My Own Private Idaho* (1991). Some films are clear adaptations of Shakespeare. Others you can watch all the way through and never know Shakespeare was involved. In Gus Van Sant's film, based on *Henry IV*, Part I and *Henry V*, two hustlers survive together on the streets of Portland, Oregon. River Phoenix plays Mike, a quiet gay man obsessed with finding the mother who abandoned him, and he is devoted to his friend Scott. Scott, played by Keanu Reeves, comes from a prominent, rich family and lives on the street mostly to horrify his father. Van Sant subtly signals his debt to the playwright with lines of dialogue taken from Shakespeare and visual references (such as a bottle of Falstaff beer) to the Henry plays.

in the 1650s by the prominent poets and playwrights John Dryden and William D'Avenant, and eventually in the 1690s with the collaboration of the great composer Henry Purcell. Something like this more "operatic" version was what most people saw until Shakespeare's original was revived in the mid-nineteenth century. Since then, the play has become more popular and admired. Today, many scholars and audiences regard *The Tempest* as Shakespeare's greatest play.

Reading *The Tempest*

All the normal cautions about the differences between reading a script and watching a play are magnified with *The Tempest* because so much depends on special effects, dance, and music. A reading simply cannot recreate those elements. The usual recourse to a visual aid is ineffective because no satisfactory video or film of *The Tempest* exists. To make up for these drawbacks, this book includes references to important stage productions of *The Tempest* as well as recordings of the songs.

As you read, note that much of the action in *The Tempest* operates on a double level: actions are ostensibly carried out by the characters, but what they do is controlled by the magician Prospero, who pulls the strings, so to speak. Thus, the opening storm, the tempest that gives the play its name, is taken as a deadly peril by the characters on the ship and by Prospero's daughter Miranda, who watches from shore, but Prospero and Ariel know it is not truly life-threatening; it has been managed by Prospero the magician. Similarly, Prospero forces Ferdinand, the shipwrecked prince, to go through a series of ritual tests, knowing all the while that he will pass them successfully. Then Greek goddesses appear in a masque, singing and saying words of wisdom about marriage for Miranda and Ferdinand. But this masque is a play within a play; Prospero actually stages the masque, and the goddesses are only products of his magic. In another play-within-a-play, two of the royal party, Antonio and Sebastian, plot to murder their king, Alonso, and take power. At the same time, two of the "low" characters, Stephano and Trinculo, consort with Caliban in a parallel plot to overthrow Prospero. Prospero is aware of both plots, and although the first is stopped, he allows the second to run its course as farce.

The Tempest's double plots make for an unusual drama because so much of the real action is not in the major events (the shipwreck, Miranda's meeting with Ferdinand), but in the recognition scenes, when characters learn the truth. For example, most of the characters think they have lost their loved ones in the storm; they also believe that once safe on the island, they have regained control over their lives. Neither belief is true. As the audience knows, Prospero is in control. When the characters discover the truth, their reactions—often astonishment and wonder—tell a great deal about them. Much of the drama of the play lies in these reactions. As you read, watch carefully for these scenes of astonishment and wonder because they are not always highlighted in the script. For instance, when Miranda first sees the royal party—evil and good men alike dressed in their Renaissance finery—she exclaims, in one of the play's most famous lines,

> How beauteous mankind is! O brave new world
> That has such people in 't! (5.1.185–6)

A good actor needs to deliver these lines with just the right mix of innocence, naive wonderment, and genuine appreciation at seeing a group of Renaissance nobles in full regalia. But as readers, we need to be attentive to the way Prospero cuts into Miranda's line with his own:

> . . . 'Tis new to thee (186)

That simple, riveting exchange can go by in a flash unless we are looking for those key moments of recognition and discovery.

The Tempest (C. 1611)

Edited by David Bevington

Dramatis Personae

ALONSO, King of Naples
SEBASTIAN, his brother
PROSPERO, the right Duke of Milan
ANTONIO, his brother, the usurping Duke of Milan
FERDINAND, son to the King of Naples
GONZALO, an honest old counselor
ADRIAN and FRANCISCO, lords
CALIBAN, a savage and deformed slave
TRINCULO, a jester
STEPHANO, a drunken butler

MASTER OF A SHIP
BOATSWAIN
MARINERS
MIRANDA, daughter to Prospero
ARIEL, an airy spirit
IRIS, CERES, JUNO, NYMPHS, REAPERS, [presented by] SPIRITS
[Other Spirits attending on Prospero]

The scene: *An island.*

1.1

A tempestuous noise of thunder and lightning heard. Enter a Shipmaster and a Boatswain.

MASTER Boatswain!
BOATSWAIN Here, Master. What cheer?
MASTER Good, speak to th' mariners. Fall to't yarely,   3
    or we run ourselves aground. Bestir, bestir! *Exit.*

Enter MARINERS.

BOATSWAIN Heigh, my hearts! Cheerly, cheerly, my
    hearts! Yare, yare! Take in the topsail. Tend to th' Master's   6
    whistle.—Blow till thou burst thy wind, if room   7
    enough!   8

Enter Alonso, Sebastian, Antonio, Ferdinand, Gonzalo, and others.

ALONSO Good Boatswain, have care. Where's the Master?
    Play the men.   10
BOATSWAIN I pray now, keep below.
ANTONIO Where is the Master, Boatswain?
BOATSWAIN Do you not hear him? You mar our labor.
    Keep your cabins! You do assist the storm.   14
GONZALO Nay, good, be patient.   15
BOATSWAIN When the sea is. Hence! What cares these
    roarers for the name of king? To cabin! Silence!   17
    Trouble us not.

The text of *The Tempest* is based on that of the First Folio (1623), or large collection, of Shakespeare's plays. For clarity, some indications of scene and stage directions have been added by the editor, David Bevington, in brackets. Bevington's text and notes come from his book *The Complete Works of Shakespeare*, updated 4th ed. (New York: Longman, 1997).

Dramatis Personae This list appears at the end of the play in the First Folio, in this order, with Miranda's name below that of the men, as was conventional in lists of the period. **PROSPERO, the right** the rightful **CALIBAN . . .** slave The Folio reads "saluage," a common alternative spelling of savage but perhaps also with a resonance of being salvaged from shipwreck. Slave has a range of meanings: wretch, rascal, servile creature, one who is owned by another person, one who is divested of freedom and personal rights

1.1 Location: On board ship, off the island's coast.

3 Good i.e., It's good you've come, or, my good fellow. **yarely** nimbly **6 Tend** Attend **7 Blow** (Addressed to the wind.) **7–8 if room enough** as long as we have sea room enough. **10 Play the men** Act like men, with spirit. **14 Keep** Remain in **15 good** good fellow **17 roarers** waves or winds, or both; spoken to as though they were "bullies" or "blusterers"

GONZALO Good, yet remember whom thou hast
    aboard.
BOATSWAIN None that I more love than myself. You are
    a councillor; if you can command these elements to
    silence and work the peace of the present, we will not   23
    hand a rope more. Use your authority. If you cannot,   24
    give thanks you have lived so long and make yourself
    ready in your cabin for the mischance of the hour, if it
    so hap.—Cheerly, good hearts!—Out of our way,   27
    I say.   *Exit.*
GONZALO I have great comfort from this fellow.
    Methinks he hath no drowning mark upon him; his complexion   30
    is perfect gallows. Stand fast, good Fate, to his   31
    hanging! Make the rope of his destiny our cable, for
    our own doth little advantage. If he be not born to be   33
    hanged, our case is miserable.   *Exeunt [courtiers].* 34

    Enter BOATSWAIN.

BOATSWAIN Down with the topmast! Yare! Lower,
    lower! Bring her to try wi'th' main course. (A cry   36
    within.) A plague upon this howling! They are louder
    than the weather or our office.   38

    Enter Sebastian, Antonio, and Gonzalo.

    Yet again? What do you here? Shall we give o'er and   39
    drown? Have you a mind to sink?
SEBASTIAN A pox o'your throat, you bawling, blasphemous,
    incharitable dog!
BOATSWAIN Work you, then.
ANTONIO Hang, cur! Hang, you whoreson, insolent
    noisemaker! We are less afraid to be drowned than
    thou art.
GONZALO I'll warrant him for drowning, though the   47
    ship were no stronger than a nutshell and as leaky as
    an unstanched wench.   49
BOATSWAIN Lay her ahold, ahold! Set her two courses.   50
    Off to sea again! Lay her off!

    Enter Mariners, wet.

MARINERS All lost! To prayers, to prayers! All lost!

    [The Mariners run about in confusion, exiting at random.]

---

23 work . . . present bring calm to our present circumstances **24 hand** handle **27 hap** happen. **30–1 complexion . . . gallows** appearance shows he was born to be hanged (and therefore, according to the proverb, in no danger of drowning) **33 our . . . advantage** our own cable is of little benefit **34 case is miserable** circumstances are desperate. **36 Bring . . . course** Sail her close to the wind by means of the mainsail. **38 our office** i.e., the noise we make at our work. **39 give o'er** give up **47 warrant him for drowning** guarantee that he will never be drowned **49 unstanched** insatiable, loose, unrestrained. (Suggesting also "incontinent" and "menstrual.") **50 ahold** ahull, close to the wind. **courses** sails, i.e., foresail as well as mainsail, set in an attempt to get the ship back out into open water.

BOATSWAIN What, must our mouths be cold?   53
GONZALO The King and Prince at prayers! Let's assist them,
    For our case is as theirs.
SEBASTIAN   I am out of patience.
ANTONIO We are merely cheated of our lives by drunkards.   56
    This wide-chapped rascal! Would thou mightst lie drowning   57
    The washing of ten tides!
GONZALO   He'll be hanged yet,   58
    Though every drop of water swear against it
    And gape at wid'st to glut him.
    (A confused noise within:)   "Mercy on us!"—   60
    "We split, we split!"—"Farewell my wife and children!"—   61
    "Farewell, brother!"—"We split, we split, we split!"

    [Exit Boatswain.]

ANTONIO Let's all sink wi'th' King.
SEBASTIAN Let's take leave of him.

    Exit [with Antonio].

GONZALO Now would I give a thousand furlongs of sea
    for an acre of barren ground: long heath, brown furze,
    anything. The wills above be done! But I would fain   66
    die a dry death.   *Exit.*   67

1.2

    Enter Prospero [in his magic cloak] and Miranda.

MIRANDA If by your art, my dearest father, you have   1
    Put the wild waters in this roar, allay them.   2
    The sky, it seems, would pour down stinking pitch,
    But that the sea, mounting to th' welkin's cheek,   4
    Dashes the fire out. Oh, I have suffered
    With those that I saw suffer! A brave vessel,   6
    Who had, no doubt, some noble creature in her,
    Dashed all to pieces. Oh, the cry did knock
    Against my very heart! Poor souls, they perished.
    Had I been any god of power, I would
    Have sunk the sea within the earth or ere   11
    It should the good ship so have swallowed and
    The freighting souls within her.
PROSPERO   Be collected.   13
    No more amazement. Tell your piteous heart   14
    There's no harm done.

---

53 **must ... cold?** i.e., must we drown in the cold sea? 56 **merely** utterly 57 **wide-chapped** big-mouthed 57–8 **Would ... tides!** (Pirates were hanged on the shore and left until three tides had come in.) 60 **at wid'st** wide open. **glut** swallow 61 **split** break apart 66 **heath** heather. **furze** gorse, a weed growing on wasteland 67 **fain** rather
1.2 Location: The island, near Prospero's cell. On the Elizabethan stage, this cell is implicitly at hand throughout the play, although in some scenes the convention of flexible distance allows us to imagine characters in other parts of the island
1 **art** magic 2 **allay** pacify 4 **welkin's cheek** sky's face 6 **brave** gallant, splendid 11 **or ere** before 13 **freighting souls** cargo of souls. **collected** calm, composed. 14 **amazement** consternation. **piteous** pitying

MIRANDA	Oh, woe the day!
PROSPERO	No harm.

I have done nothing but in care of thee,
Of thee, my dear one, thee, my daughter, who
Art ignorant of what thou art, naught knowing
Of whence I am, nor that I am more better   19
Than Prospero, master of a full poor cell,   20
And thy no greater father.

MIRANDA	More to know

Did never meddle with my thoughts.

PROSPERO	'Tis time 22

I should inform thee farther. Lend thy hand
And pluck my magic garment from me. So,

[laying down his magic cloak and staff]

Lie there, my art.—Wipe thou thine eyes. Have comfort.
The direful spectacle of the wreck, which touched   26
The very virtue of compassion in thee,   27
I have with such provision in mine art
So safely ordered that there is no soul—
No, not so much perdition as an hair   30
Betid to any creature in the vessel   31
Which thou heard'st cry, which thou saw'st sink. Sit down,   32
For thou must now know farther.

MIRANDA *[sitting]*	You have often

Begun to tell me what I am, but stopped
And left me to a bootless inquisition,   36
Concluding, "Stay, not yet."

PROSPERO	The hour's now come;

The very minute bids thee ope thine ear.
Obey, and be attentive. Canst thou remember
A time before we came unto this cell?
I do not think thou canst, for then thou wast not
Out three years old.

MIRANDA	Certainly, sir, I can. 41

PROSPERO By what? By any other house or person?
Of anything the image, tell me, that
Hath kept with thy remembrance.

MIRANDA	'Tis far off,

And rather like a dream than an assurance   45
That my remembrance warrants. Had I not   46
Four or five women once that tended me?

PROSPERO Thou hadst, and more, Miranda. But how is it
That this lives in thy mind? What see'st thou else
In the dark backward and abysm of time?   50
If thou remem'brest aught ere thou cam'st here,   51

---

16 but except **19 more better** of higher rank **20 full** very **22 meddle** mingle **26 wreck** shipwreck **27 virtue** essence **30 perdition** loss **31 Betid** happened **32 Which** whom **35 bootless inquisition** profitless inquiry **41 Out** fully **45–6 assurance . . . warrants** certainty that my memory guarantees. **50 backward . . . time** abyss of the past. **51 aught** anything

How thou cam'st here thou mayst.

MIRANDA   But that I do not.

PROSPERO Twelve year since, Miranda, twelve year since,
Thy father was the Duke of Milan and
A prince of power.

MIRANDA   Sir, are not you my father?

PROSPERO Thy mother was a piece of virtue, and   56
She said thou wast my daughter; and thy father
    Was Duke of Milan, and his only heir
    And princess no worse issued.

MIRANDA   Oh, the heavens!   59
    What foul play had we, that we came from thence?
    Or blessèd was't we did?

PROSPERO   Both, both, my girl.
    By foul play, as thou say'st, were we heaved thence,
    But blessedly holp hither.

MIRANDA   O, my heart bleeds   63
    To think o'th' teen that I have turned you to,   64
    Which is from my remembrance! Please you, farther.   65

PROSPERO My brother and thy uncle, called Antonio—
    I pray thee mark me—that a brother should
    Be so perfidious!—he whom next thyself   68
    Of all the world I loved, and to him put
    The manage of my state, as at that time   70
    Through all the seigniories it was the first,   71
    And Prospero the prime duke, being so reputed   72
    In dignity, and for the liberal arts
    Without a parallel; those being all my study,
    The government I cast upon my brother
    And to my state grew stranger, being transported   76
    And rapt in secret studies. Thy false uncle—
    Dost thou attend me?

MIRANDA   Sir, most heedfully.

PROSPERO Being once perfected how to grant suits,   79
    How to deny them, who t'advance and who
    To trash for overtopping, new created   81
    The creatures that were mine, I say, or changed 'em,   82
    Or else new formed 'em; having both the key   83
    Of officer and office, set all hearts i'th' state   84
    To what tune pleased his ear, that now he was   85

---

56 piece masterpiece, exemplar **59 no worse issued** no less nobly born, descended. **63 holp** helped
64 teen . . . to trouble I've caused you to remember or put you to **65 from** out of **68 next** next to **70**
manage management, administration **71 seigniories** i.e., city-states of northern Italy **72 prime** first in
rank and importance **76 to . . . stranger** i.e., withdrew from my responsibilities as duke. **transported**
carried away **79 perfected** grown skillful **81 trash** check a hound by tying a cord or weight to its neck.
overtopping running too far ahead of the pack; surmounting, exceeding one's authority **81–3 new . .**
. formed 'em won the loyalty of my officers by appointing them to new posts, or replaced them with
others who would be loyal to Antonio, or else redefined the positions and their occupants **83–5 hav-**
ing . . . ear having now under his control both the officers and the positions, he set a tone for his rule
according to his own inclination. (Key is also a metaphor for tuning stringed instruments.)

The ivy which had hid my princely trunk
And sucked my verdure out on't. Thou attend'st not.   87
MIRANDA Oh, good sir, I do.
PROSPERO   I pray thee, mark me.
I, thus neglecting worldly ends, all dedicated
To closeness and the bettering of my mind   90
With that which, but by being so retired,   91
O'erprized all popular rate, in my false brother   92
Awaked an evil nature; and my trust,
Like a good parent, did beget of him   94
A falsehood in its contrary as great
As my trust was, which had indeed no limit,
A confidence sans bound. He being thus lorded   97
Not only with what my revenue yielded
But what my power might else exact, like one   99
Who, having into truth by telling of it,   100
Made such a sinner of his memory   101
To credit his own lie, he did believe   102
He was indeed the Duke, out o'th' substitution   103
And executing th'outward face of royalty   104
With all prerogative. Hence his ambition growing—   105
Dost thou hear?
MIRANDA   Your tale, sir, would cure deafness.
PROSPERO To have no screen between this part he played   107
And him he played it for, he needs will be   108
Absolute Milan. Me, poor man, my library   109
Was dukedom large enough. Of temporal royalties   110
He thinks me now incapable; confederates—
So dry he was for sway—wi'th' King of Naples   112
To give him annual tribute, do him homage,   113
Subject his coronet to his crown, and bend   114
The dukedom yet unbowed—alas, poor Milan!—   115
To most ignoble stooping.
MIRANDA   O the heavens!
PROSPERO Mark his condition and th'event, then tell me   117
If this might be a brother.

---

87 verdure vitality. **on't** of it. **90 closeness** retirement, seclusion **91–2 but . . . rate** i.e., were it not that its private nature caused me to neglect my public responsibilities, had a value far beyond what public opinion could appreciate, or, simply because it was done in such seclusion, had a value not appreciated by popular opinion. **94 good parent** (Alludes to the proverb that good parents often bear bad children; see also line 120.) of in **97 sans** without. **lorded** raised to lordship, with power and wealth **99 else** otherwise, additionally **100–2 Who . . . lie** i.e., who, by repeatedly telling the lie (that he was indeed Duke of Milan), made his memory such a confirmed sinner against truth that he began to believe his own lie. **103–5 out . . . prerogative** as a result of his making himself my substitute and carrying out all the visible functions of royalty with all its rights and privileges. **107–9 To have . . . Milan** In order to eliminate all separation between his role and himself, he insisted on becoming the Duke of Milan in name as well as in fact. **110 temporal royalties** practical prerogatives and responsibilities of a sovereign. **111 confederates** conspires, allies himself **112 dry** thirsty. **sway** power **113 him** i.e., the King of Naples **114 his . . . his** Antonio's . . . the King of Naples'. **bend** make bow down **115 yet** hitherto **117 condition** pact. **th'event** the outcome

MIRANDA   I should sin
  To think but nobly of my grandmother.   119
  Good wombs have borne bad sons.
PROSPERO   Now the condition.
  This King of Naples, being an enemy
  To me inveterate, hearkens my brother's suit,   122
  Which was that he, in lieu o'th' premises   123
  Of homage and I know not how much tribute,
  Should presently extirpate me and mine   125
  Out of the dukedom and confer fair Milan,
  With all the honors, on my brother. Whereon,
  A treacherous army levied, one midnight
  Fated to th' purpose did Antonio open
  The gates of Milan, and, i'th' dead of darkness,
  The ministers for th' purpose hurried thence   131
  Me and thy crying self.
MIRANDA   Alack, for pity!
  I, not remembering how I cried out then,
  Will cry it o'er again. It is a hint   134
  That wrings mine eyes to 't.
PROSPERO   Hear a little further,   135
  And then I'll bring thee to the present business
  Which now's upon's, without the which this story
  Were most impertinent.
MIRANDA   Wherefore did they not   138
  That hour destroy us?
PROSPERO   Well demanded, wench.   139
  My tale provokes that question. Dear, they durst not,
  So dear the love my people bore me, nor set   141
  A mark so bloody on the business, but   142
  With colors fairer painted their foul ends.   143
  In few, they hurried us aboard a bark,   144
  Bore us some leagues to sea, where they prepared
  A rotten carcass of a butt, not rigged,   146
  Nor tackle, sail, nor mast; the very rats   147
  Instinctively have quit it. There they hoist us,   148
  To cry to th' sea that roared to us, to sigh
  To th' winds whose pity, sighing back again,
  Did us but loving wrong.
MIRANDA   Alack, what trouble   151
  Was I then to you!

---

119 but other than **122 hearkens** listens to **123 he** the King of Naples. **in . . . premises** in return for the stipulation **125 presently extirpate** at once remove **131 ministers . . . purpose** agents employed to do this. **thence** from there **134 hint** prompting **135 wrings** (1) constrains (2) wrings tears from **138 impertinent** irrelevant. **Wherefore** Why **139 demanded** asked. **wench** (Here a term of endearment.) **141–2 set . . . bloody** i.e., make obvious their murderous intent. (From the practice of marking with the blood of the prey those who have participated in a successful hunt.) **143 fairer** apparently more attractive **144 few** few words. **bark** ship **146 butt** cask, tub **147 Nor tackle** neither rigging **148 quit** abandoned **151 Did . . . wrong** i.e., pitied us even as they drove us on.

PROSPERO   Oh, a cherubin
    Thou wast that did preserve me. Thou didst smile,
    Infusèd with a fortitude from heaven,   154
    When I have decked the sea with drops full salt,   155
    Under my burden groaned, which raised in me   156
    An undergoing stomach, to bear up   157
    Against what should ensue.
MIRANDA How came we ashore?
PROSPERO   By Providence divine.
    Some food we had, and some fresh water, that
    A noble Neapolitan, Gonzalo,
    Out of his charity, who being then appointed
    Master of this design, did give us, with
    Rich garments, linens, stuffs, and necessaries,   165
    Which since have steaded much. So, of his gentleness,   166
    Knowing I loved my books, he furnished me
    From mine own library with volumes that
    I prize above my dukedom.
MIRANDA   Would I might   169
    But ever see that man!
PROSPERO   Now I arise.   170

    [He puts on his magic cloak.]

    Sit still, and hear the last of our sea sorrow.   171
    Here in this island we arrived; and here
    Have I, thy schoolmaster, made thee more profit   173
    Than other princes can, that have more time   174
    For vainer hours and tutors not so careful.   175
MIRANDA Heavens thank you for't! And now, I pray you, sir—
    For still 'tis beating in my mind—your reason
    For raising this sea storm?
PROSPERO   Know thus far forth:
    By accident most strange, bountiful Fortune,
    Now my dear lady, hath mine enemies   180
    Brought to this shore; and by my prescience
    I find my zenith doth depend upon   182
    A most auspicious star, whose influence   183
    If now I court not, but omit, my fortunes   184
    Will ever after droop. Here cease more questions.
    Thou art inclined to sleep. 'Tis a good dullness,   186
    And give it way. I know thou canst not choose.   187

---

154 **Infusèd** filled, suffused 155 **decked** covered (with salt tears); adorned 156 **which** i.e., the smile 157 **undergoing stomach** courage to go on 165 **stuffs** supplies 166 **steaded much** been of much use. **So, of** Similarly, out of 169 **Would** I wish 170 **But ever** i.e., someday 171 **sea sorrow** sorrowful adventure at sea. 173–4 **made . . . can** provided a more valuable education than other royal children (of either sex) can enjoy 175 **vainer** more foolishly spent 180 **my dear lady** (Refers to Fortune, not Miranda.) 182 **zenith** height of fortune. (Astrological term.) 183 **influence** astrological power 184 **but omit** but ignore instead 186 **dullness** drowsiness 187 **give it way** let it happen (i.e., don't fight it).

[Miranda sleeps.]

Come away, servant, come! I am ready now.　　　　　　188
Approach, my Ariel, come.

Enter Ariel.

ARIEL　All hail, great master, grave sir, hail! I come
　　To answer thy best pleasure; be't to fly,
　　To swim, to dive into the fire, to ride
　　On the curled clouds, to thy strong bidding task　　193
　　Ariel and all his quality.
PROSPERO　　　　　　　　Hast thou, spirit,　　　　194
　　Performed to point the tempest that I bade thee?　195
ARIEL　　　　　　　　　　　　　　　To every article.
　　I boarded the King's ship. Now on the beak,　　　197
　　Now in the waist, the deck, in every cabin,　　　198
　　I flamed amazement. Sometime I'd divide　　　　199
　　And burn in many places; on the topmast,
　　The yards, and bowsprit would I flame distinctly,　201
　　Then meet and join. Jove's lightning, the precursors
　　O'th' dreadful thunderclaps, more momentary
　　And sight-outrunning were not. The fire and cracks　204
　　Of sulfurous roaring the most mighty Neptune　　205
　　Seem to besiege and make his bold waves tremble,
　　Yea, his dread trident shake.
PROSPERO　　　　　　　　My brave spirit!　　　　207
　　Who was so firm, so constant, that this coil　　　208
　　Would not infect his reason?
ARIEL　　　　　　　　　　Not a soul
　　But felt a fever of the mad and played　　　　　210
　　Some tricks of desperation. All but mariners
　　Plunged in the foaming brine and quit the vessel,
　　Then all afire with me. The King's son, Ferdinand,
　　With hair up-staring—then like reeds, not hair—　　214
　　Was the first man that leapt; cried, "Hell is empty,
　　And all the devils are here!"
PROSPERO　　　　　　　　Why, that's my spirit!
　　But was not this nigh shore?
ARIEL　　　　　　　　　　Close by, my master.
PROSPERO　But are they, Ariel, safe?
ARIEL　　　　　　　　　　Not a hair perished.
　　On their sustaining garments not a blemish,　　　219
　　But fresher than before; and, as thou bad'st me,　220

---

188 Come away Come **193 task** make demands upon **194 quality** (1) fellow spirits (2) abilities. **195 to point** to the smallest detail **197 beak** prow **198 waist** midships. deck poop deck at the stern **199 flamed amazement** struck terror in the guise of fire, i.e., Saint Elmo's fire. **201 distinctly** in different places **204 sight-out-running** swifter than sight. **were not** could not have been. **205 Neptune** Roman god of the sea **207 trident** three-pronged weapon **208 coil** tumult **210 of the mad** such as madmen feel **214 up-staring** standing on end **219 sustaining** protecting **220 bad'st** ordered

In troops I have dispersed them 'bout the isle.   221
The King's son have I landed by himself,
Whom I left cooling of the air with sighs   223
In an odd angle of the isle, and sitting,   224
His arms in this sad knot.   *[He folds his arms.]*
PROSPERO   Of the King's ship,   225
The mariners, say how thou hast disposed,
And all the rest o'th' fleet.
ARIEL   Safely in harbor
Is the King's ship; in the deep nook, where once   228
Thou called'st me up at midnight to fetch dew   229
From the still-vexed Bermudas, there she's hid;   230
The mariners all under hatches stowed,
Who, with a charm joined to their suffered labor,   232
I have left asleep. And for the rest o'th' fleet,
Which I dispersed, they all have met again
And are upon the Mediterranean float   235
Bound sadly home for Naples,
Supposing that they saw the King's ship wrecked
And his great person perish.
PROSPERO   Ariel, thy charge
Exactly is performed. But there's more work.
What is the time o'th' day?
ARIEL   Past the mid season.   240
PROSPERO At least two glasses. The time twixt six and now   241
Must by us both be spent most preciously.
ARIEL Is there more toil? Since thou dost give me pains,   243
Let me remember thee what thou hast promised,   244
Which is not yet performed me.
PROSPERO   How now? Moody?
What is't thou canst demand?
ARIEL   My liberty.
PROSPERO Before the time be out? No more!
ARIEL   I prithee,
Remember I have done thee worthy service,
Told thee no lies, made thee no mistakings, served
Without or grudge or grumblings. Thou did promise
To bate me a full year.
PROSPERO   Dost thou forget   251
From what a torment I did free thee?
ARIEL   No.
PROSPERO Thou dost, and think'st it much to tread the ooze
Of the salt deep,

---

221 **troops** groups 223 **cooling** of cooling 224 **angle** corner 225 **sad knot** (Folded arms are indicative of melancholy.) 228 **nook** bay 229 **dew** (Collected at midnight for magical purposes; compare with line 324.) 230 **still-vexed Bermudas** ever stormy Bermudas. (Perhaps refers to the then recent Bermuda shipwreck. The Folio text reads "Bermoothes.") 232 **with . . . labor** by means of a spell added to all the labor they have undergone 235 **float** sea 240 **mid season** noon. 241 **glasses** hourglasses. 243 **pains** labors 244 **remember** remind 251 **bate** remit, **deduct**

To run upon the sharp wind of the north,
To do me business in the veins o'th' earth   256
When it is baked with frost.
ARIEL   I do not, sir.   257
PROSPERO Thou liest, malignant thing! Hast thou forgot
The foul witch Sycorax, who with age and envy   259
Was grown into a hoop? Hast thou forgot her?   260
ARIEL   No, sir.
PROSPERO Thou hast. Where was she born? Speak. Tell me.
ARIEL Sir, in Argier.
PROSPERO   Oh, was she so? I must   263
Once in a month recount what thou hast been,
Which thou forget'st. This damned witch Sycorax,
For mischiefs manifold and sorceries terrible
To enter human hearing, from Argier,
Thou know'st, was banished. For one thing she did   268
They would not take her life. Is not this true?
ARIEL   Ay, sir.
PROSPERO This blue-eyed hag was hither brought with child 271
And here was left by th' sailors. Thou, my slave,
As thou report'st thyself, was then her servant;
And, for thou wast a spirit too delicate   274
To act her earthy and abhorred commands,
Refusing her grand hests, she did confine thee,   276
By help of her more potent ministers
And in her most unmitigable rage.
Into a cloven pine, within which rift
Imprisoned thou didst painfully remain
A dozen years; within which space she died
And left thee there, where thou didst vent thy groans
As fast as mill wheels strike. Then was this island—   283
Save for the son that she did litter here,   284
A freckled whelp, hag-born—not honored with   285
A human shape.
ARIEL   Yes, Caliban her son.   286
PROSPERO Dull thing, I say so: he, that Caliban   287
Whom now I keep in service. Thou best know'st
What torment I did find thee in. Thy groans
Did make wolves howl, and penetrate the breasts
Of ever-angry bears. It was a torment

---

256 **do me** do for me. **veins** veins of minerals, or, underground streams, thought to be analogous to the veins of the human body 257 **baked** hardened 259 **envy** malice 260 **grown into a hoop** i.e., so bent over with age as to resemble a hoop. 263 **Argier** Algiers 268 **one . . . did** (Perhaps a reference to her pregnancy, for which her life would be spared.) 271 **blue-eyed** with dark circles under the eyes or with blue eyelids, implying pregnancy. **with child** pregnant 274 **for** because 276 **hests** commands 283 **as mill wheels strike** as the blades of a mill wheel strike the water. 284 **Save** except. **litter** give birth to 285 **whelp** offspring. (Used of animals.) hag-born born of a female demon 286 **Yes . . . son** (Ariel is probably concurring with Prospero's comment about a "freckled whelp," not contradicting the point about "A human shape.") 287 **Dull . . . so** i.e., Exactly, that's what I said, you dullard.

To lay upon the damned, which Sycorax
Could not again undo. It was mine art,
When I arrived and heard thee, that made gape   294
The pine and let thee out.

ARIEL   I thank thee, master.

PROSPERO If thou more murmur'st, I will rend an oak
And peg thee in his knotty entrails till   297
Thou hast howled away twelve winters.

ARIEL   Pardon, master.
I will be correspondent to command   299
And do my spriting gently.   300

PROSPERO Do so, and after two days
I will discharge thee.

ARIEL   That's my noble master!
What shall I do? Say what? What shall I do?

PROSPERO Go make thyself like a nymph o'th' sea. Be subject
To no sight but thine and mine, invisible
To every eyeball else. Go take this shape
And hither come in't. Go, hence with diligence!   *Exit [Ariel].*

[*To Miranda*] Awake, dear heart, awake! Thou hast slept well.

Awake!

MIRANDA The strangeness of your story put
Heaviness in me.

PROSPERO   Shake it off. Come on,   310
We'll visit Caliban, my slave, who never
Yields us kind answer.

MIRANDA   'Tis a villain, sir,
I do not love to look on.

PROSPERO   But, as 'tis,
We cannot miss him. He does make our fire,   314
Fetch in our wood, and serves in offices   315
That profit us.—What ho! Slave! Caliban!
Thou earth, thou! Speak.

CALIBAN (*within*)   There's wood enough within.

PROSPERO Come forth, I say! There's other business for thee.
Come, thou tortoise! When?   319

Enter Ariel like a water nymph.

Fine apparition! My quaint Ariel,   320
Hark in thine ear. [*He whispers.*]

ARIEL   My lord, it shall be done.   *Exit.*

PROSPERO Thou poisonous slave, got by the devil himself   322
Upon thy wicked dam, come forth!   323

---

294 gape open wide **297 his** its **299 correspondent** responsive, submissive **300 spriting gently** duties as a spirit willingly. **310 Heaviness** drowsiness **314 miss** do without **315 offices** functions, duties **319 When** (An exclamation of impatience.) **320 quaint** ingenious **322 got** begotten, sired **323 dam** mother. (Used of animals.)

Enter Caliban.

CALIBAN As wicked dew as e'er my mother brushed   324
 With raven's feather from unwholesome fen   325
 Drop on you both! A southwest blow on ye   326
 And blister you all o'er!

PROSPERO For this, be sure, tonight thou shalt have cramps,
 Side-stitches that shall pen thy breath up. Urchins   329
 Shall forth at vast of night that they may work   330
 All exercise on thee. Thou shalt be pinched
 As thick as honeycomb, each pinch more stinging   332
 Than bees that made 'em.

CALIBAN   I must eat my dinner.   333
 This island's mine, by Sycorax my mother,
 Which thou tak'st from me. When thou cam'st first,
 Thou strok'st me and made much of me, wouldst give me
 Water with berries in't, and teach me how
 To name the bigger light, and how the less,   338
 That burn by day and night. And then I loved thee
 And showed thee all the qualities o'th'isle,
 The fresh springs, brine pits, barren place and fertile.
 Cursed be I that did so! All the charms.   342
 Of Sycorax, toads, beetles, bats, light on you!
 For I am all the subjects that you have,
 Which first was mine own king; and here you sty me   345
 In this hard rock, whiles you do keep from me
 The rest o'th'island.

PROSPERO   Thou most lying slave,
 Whom stripes may move, not kindness! I have used thee,   348
 Filth as thou art, with humane care, and lodged thee   349
 In mine own cell, till thou didst seek to violate
 The honor of my child.

CALIBAN Oho, Oho! Wouldn't had been done!
 Thou didst prevent me; I had peopled else   353
 This isle with Calibans.

MIRANDA   Abhorrèd slave,   354
 Which any print of goodness wilt not take,   355
 Being capable of all ill! I pitied thee,
 Took pains to make thee speak, taught thee each hour
 One thing or other. When thou didst not, savage,
 Know thine own meaning, but wouldst gabble like

---

324 wicked mischievous, harmful **325 fen** marsh, bog **326 southwest** i.e., wind thought to bring disease **329 Urchins** Hedgehogs; here, suggesting goblins in the guise of hedgehogs **330 vast** lengthy, desolate time. (Malignant spirits were thought to be restricted to the hours of darkness.) **332 as honeycomb** i.e., as a honeycomb full of bees **333 'em** i.e., the honeycomb **338 the bigger . . . less** i.e., the sun and the moon. (See Genesis 1:16: "God then made two great lights: the greater light to rule the day, and the less light to rule the night.") **342 charms** spells **345 sty** confine as in a sty **348 stripes** lashes **349 humane** (Not distinguished as a word from human.) **353 peopled else** otherwise populated **354–65 Abhorrèd . . . prison** (Sometimes assigned by editors to Prospero.) **355 print** imprint, impression

A thing most brutish, I endowed thy purposes   360
With words that made them known. But thy vile race,   361
Though thou didst learn, had that in't which good natures
Could not abide to be with; therefore wast thou
Deservedly confined into this rock,
Who hadst deserved more than a prison.   365

CALIBAN You taught me language, and my profit on't
Is I know how to curse. The red plague rid you   367
For learning me your language!

PROSPERO   Hagseed, hence!   368
Fetch us in fuel, and be quick, thou'rt best,   369
To answer other business. Shrugg'st thou, malice?   370
If thou neglect'st or dost unwillingly
What I command, I'll rack thee with old cramps,   372
Fill all thy bones with aches, make thee roar   373
That beasts shall tremble at thy din.

CALIBAN   No, pray thee.
[Aside] I must obey. His art is of such power
It would control my dam's god, Setebos,   376
And make a vassal of him.

PROSPERO   So, slave, hence!   377

   Exit Caliban.
   *Enter Ferdinand; and Ariel, invisible, playing and singing. [Ferdinand
   does not see Prospero and Miranda.]*

Ariel's Song.
ARIEL Come unto these yellow sands,
   And then take hands;
   Curtsied when you have, and kissed   380
   The wild waves whist;   381
   Foot it featly here and there,   382
   And, sweet sprites, bear   383
   The burden. Hark, hark!   384
Burden, dispersedly [within]. Bow-wow.   385
   The watchdogs bark.
[Burden, dispersedly within.] Bow-wow.
Hark, hark! I hear
The strain of strutting chanticleer
Cry Cock-a-diddle-dow.

---

360 **purposes** meanings, desires 361 **race** natural disposition; species, nature 367 **red plague** plague characterized by red sores and evacuation of blood. **rid** destroy 368 **learning** teaching. **Hagseed** Offspring of a female demon 369 **thou'rt best** you'd be well advised 370 **answer other business** perform other tasks. 372 **old** such as old people suffer, or, plenty of 373 **aches** (Pronounced "aitches.") 376 **Setebos** (A god of the Patagonians, named in Richard Eden's History of Travel, 1577.) 377.2 **Ariel, invisible** (Ariel wears a garment that by convention indicates he is invisible to the other characters.) 380 **Curtsied . . . have** when you have curtsied 380–1 **kissed . . . whist** kissed the waves into silence, or, kissed while the waves are being hushed 382 **Foot it featly** dance nimbly 383 **sprites** spirits 384 **burden** refrain, undersong. 385 **s.d. dispersedly** i.e., from all directions, not in unison

FERDINAND Where should this music be? I'th'air or th'earth?
It sounds no more; and sure it waits upon   392
Some god o'th'island. Sitting on a bank,   393
Weeping again the King my father's wreck,
This music crept by me upon the waters,
Allaying both their fury and my passion   396
With its sweet air. Thence I have followed it,   397
Or it hath drawn me rather. But 'tis gone.
No, it begins again.

Ariel's Song.

ARIEL Full fathom five thy father lies.
Of his bones are coral made.
Those are pearls that were his eyes.
Nothing of him that doth fade
But doth suffer a sea change
Into something rich and strange.
Sea nymphs hourly ring his knell.   406
Burden [within]. Ding dong.
Hark, now I hear them, ding dong bell.

FERDINAND The ditty does remember my drowned father.   409
This is no mortal business, nor no sound
That the earth owes. I hear it now above me.   411

PROSPERO *[to Miranda]* The fringèd curtains of thine eye advance   412
And say what thou see'st yond.

MIRANDA   What is't? A spirit?
Lord, how it looks about! Believe me, sir,
It carries a brave form. But 'tis a spirit.   415

PROSPERO No, wench, it eats and sleeps and hath such senses
As we have, such. This gallant which thou see'st
Was in the wreck; and, but he's something stained   418
With grief, that's beauty's canker, thou mightst call him   419
A goodly person. He hath lost his fellows
And strays about to find 'em.

MIRANDA   I might call him
A thing divine, for nothing natural
I ever saw so noble.

PROSPERO *[aside]*   It goes on, I see,
As my soul prompts it.—Spirit, fine spirit, I'll free thee
Within two days for this.

FERDINAND *[seeing Miranda]* Most sure, the goddess
On whom these airs attend!—Vouchsafe my prayer   426
May know if you remain upon this island,   427
And that you will some good instruction give

---

392 waits upon serves, attends **393 bank** sandbank **396 passion** grief **397 Thence** i.e., From the bank on which I sat **406 knell** announcement of a death by the tolling of a bell. **409 remember** commemorate **411 owes** owns. **412 advance** raise **415 brave** excellent **418 but . . . stained** were it not that his luster is somewhat darkened **419 canker** cankerworm (feeding on buds and leaves) **426 airs** songs. **Vouchsafe** Grant **427 remain** dwell

How I may bear me here. My prime request,   429
Which I do last pronounce, is—O you wonder!—   430
  If you be maid or no?
MIRANDA   No wonder, sir,   431
  But certainly a maid.
FERDINAND   My language? Heavens!
  I am the best of them that speak this speech,   433
  Were I but where 'tis spoken.
PROSPERO [coming forward]   How? The best?
  What wert thou if the King of Naples heard thee?
FERDINAND A single thing, as I am now, that wonders   436
  To hear thee speak of Naples. He does hear me,   437
  And that he does I weep. Myself am Naples,   438
  Who with mine eyes, never since at ebb, beheld   439
  The King my father wrecked.
MIRANDA   Alack, for mercy!
FERDINAND Yes, faith, and all his lords, the Duke of Milan
  And his brave son being twain.
PROSPERO [aside]   The Duke of Milan   442
  And his more braver daughter could control thee,   443
  If now 'twere fit to do't. At the first sight
  They have changed eyes.—Delicate Ariel,   445
  I'll set thee free for this. [To Ferdinand] A word, good sir.
  I fear you have done yourself some wrong. A word!   447
MIRANDA [aside] Why speaks my father so ungently? This
  Is the third man that e'er I saw, the first
  That e'er I sighed for. Pity move my father
  To be inclined my way!
FERDINAND [to Miranda] Oh, if a virgin,
  And your affection not gone forth, I'll make you
  The Queen of Naples.
PROSPERO   Soft, sir! One word more.
  [Aside] They are both in either's powers; but this swift business   454
  I must uneasy make, lest too light winning   455
  Make the prize light. [To Ferdinand] One word more: I charge thee   456
  That thou attend me. Thou dost here usurp   457
  The name thou ow'st not, and hast put thyself   458
  Upon this island as a spy, to win it
  From me, the lord on't.

---

429 bear me conduct myself. **prime** chief **430 wonder** (Miranda's name means "to be wondered at.") **431 maid** (1) a human maiden as opposed to a goddess (2) unmarried (3) a virgin **433 best** i.e., in birth **436 A single . . . now** (1) A single figure who combines into one person both self and King of Naples (since Ferdinand believes he has inherited the kingship) (2) A lonely shipwrecked figure **437 Naples** the King of Naples. **He . . . me** I who hear my own words am the King of Naples **438 And . . . weep** i.e., and I weep at this reminder that my father is seemingly dead, leaving me heir. **439 never . . . ebb** never dry, continually weeping **442 son** (The only reference in the play to a son of Antonio.) **443 more braver** more splendid. **control** refute **445 changed eyes** exchanged amorous glances. **447 done . . . wrong** i.e., spoken falsely. **454 both in either's** each in the other's **455 uneasy** difficult **456 light** cheap. (Playing on *light,* "easy," in 455.) **457 attend** follow, obey **458 ow'st** ownest

FERDINAND　　　　　　　　No, as I am a man.　　　　460

MIRANDA　There's nothing ill can dwell in such a temple.
　　If the ill spirit have so fair a house,
　　Good things will strive to dwell with't.

PROSPERO　　　　　　　　　　　Follow me.—　　　463
　　Speak not you for him; he's a traitor.—Come,
　　I'll manacle thy neck and feet together.
　　Seawater shalt thou drink; thy food shall be
　　The fresh-brook mussels, withered roots, and husks
　　Wherein the acorn cradled. Follow.

FERDINAND　　　　　　　　　　No!
　　I will resist such entertainment till　　　　469
　　Mine enemy has more pow'r.　　　　　　470

　　He draws, and is charmed from moving.

MIRANDA　　　　　　　　　O dear father,
　　Make not too rash a trial of him, for　　　　471
　　He's gentle, and not fearful.

PROSPERO　　　　　　　　　What, I say,　　　472
　　My foot my tutor?—Put thy sword up, traitor,　　473
　　Who mak'st a show but dar'st not strike, thy conscience
　　Is so possessed with guilt. Come, from thy ward,　　475
　　For I can here disarm thee with this stick
　　And make thy weapon drop. *[He brandishes his staff.]*

MIRANDA *[trying to hinder him]*　Beseech you, father!

PROSPERO　Hence! Hang not on my garments.

MIRANDA　　　　　　　　　　Sir, have pity!
　　I'll be his surety.

PROSPERO　　　　　Silence! One word more　　　479
　　Shall make me chide thee, if not hate thee. What,
　　An advocate for an impostor! Hush!
　　Thou think'st there is no more such shapes as he,
　　Having seen but him and Caliban. Foolish wench,
　　To th' most of men this is a Caliban,　　　484
　　And they to him are angels.

MIRANDA　　　　　　　　My affections
　　Are then most humble; I have no ambition
　　To see a goodlier man.

PROSPERO *[to Ferdinand]*　Come on, obey.
　　Thy nerves are in their infancy again　　　488
　　And have no vigor in them.

FERDINAND　　　　　　　　So they are.
　　My spirits, as in a dream, are all bound up.　　490
　　My father's loss, the weakness which I feel,

---

460 on't of it. **463 strive . . . with't** i.e., expel the evil and occupy the *temple*, the body. **469 entertainment** treatment **470 s.d. *charmed*** magically prevented **471 rash** harsh **472 gentle** (1) wellborn
(2) easily managed. **fearful** frightening, dangerous. **473 My . . . tutor?** i.e., Do you, as my daughter and
thus bound to me by obedience, dare presume to teach me what to do? **475 ward** defensive posture (in
fencing) **479 surety** guarantee. **484 To** compared with **488 nerves** sinews **490 spirits** vital powers

The wreck of all my friends, nor this man's threats
To whom I am subdued, are but light to me,   493
Might I but through my prison once a day
Behold this maid. All corners else o'th'earth   495
Let liberty make use of; space enough
Have I in such a prison.
PROSPERO *[aside]* It works. *[To Ferdinand]* Come on.—
Thou hast done well, fine Ariel! *[To Ferdinand]* Follow me.
[To Ariel] Hark what thou else shalt do me.
MIRANDA *[to Ferdinand]* Be of comfort.   499
My father's of a better nature, sir,
Than he appears by speech. This is unwonted   501
Which now came from him.
PROSPERO *[to Ariel]*   Thou shalt be as free
As mountain winds; but then exactly do   503
All points of my command.
ARIEL   To th' syllable.
PROSPERO *[to Ferdinand]* Come, follow. *[To Miranda]* Speak not for him.
        Exeunt.

2.1

Enter Alonso, Sebastian, Antonio, Gonzalo, Adrian, Francisco, and others.

GONZALO *[to Alonso]* Beseech you, sir, be merry. You have cause,
So have we all, of joy, for our escape
Is much beyond our loss. Our hint of woe   3
Is common; every day some sailor's wife,
The masters of some merchant, and the merchant,   5
Have just our theme of woe. But for the miracle,   6
I mean our preservation, few in millions
Can speak like us. Then wisely, good sir, weigh   8
Our sorrow with our comfort.
ALONSO   Prithee, peace.   9
SEBASTIAN *[aside to Antonio]* He receives comfort like
    cold porridge.   11
ANTONIO *[aside to Sebastian]* The visitor will not give   12
    him o'er so.   13
SEBASTIAN Look, he's winding up the watch of his wit;
    by and by it will strike.
GONZALO *[to Alonso]*   Sir—
SEBASTIAN *[aside to Antonio]*   One. Tell.   17

---

493 light unimportant **495 corners else** other corners, regions **499 me** for me. **501 unwonted** unusual **503 then** if so, then
2.1. Location: Another part of the island.
3 hint occasion **5 The masters . . . the merchant** the officers or owners of some merchant vessel and the merchant who owns the cargo **6 for** as for **8–9 weigh . . . comfort** balance our sorrow against our comfort. **11 porridge** (Punningly suggested by pence, i.e., "peas" or "pease," a common ingredient of porridge.) **12 visitor** one bringing nourishment and comfort to the sick, as Gonzalo is doing **12–13 give him o'er** abandon him **17 Tell** Keep count.

GONZALO When every grief is entertained   18
    That's offered, comes to th'entertainer—   19
SEBASTIAN A dollar.   20
GONZALO Dolor comes to him, indeed. You have spoken
    truer than you purposed.
SEBASTIAN You have taken it wiselier than I meant you should.
GONZALO [to Alonso] Therefore, my lord—
ANTONIO Fie, what a spendthrift is he of his
    tongue!
ALONSO [to Gonzalo] I prithee, spare.   27
GONZALO Well, I have done. But yet—
SEBASTIAN [aside to Antonio] He will be talking.
ANTONIO [aside to Sebastian] Which, of he or Adrian,   30
    for a good wager, first begins to crow?   31
SEBASTIAN The old cock.   32
ANTONIO The cockerel.   33
SEBASTIAN Done. The wager?
ANTONIO A laughter.   35
SEBASTIAN A match!   36
ADRIAN Though this island seem to be desert—   37
ANTONIO Ha, ha, ha!
SEBASTIAN So, you're paid.   39
ADRIAN Uninhabitable and almost inaccessible—
SEBASTIAN Yet—
ADRIAN Yet—
ANTONIO He could not miss't.   43
ADRIAN It must needs be of subtle, tender, and delicate   44
    temperance.   45
ANTONIO Temperance was a delicate wench.   46
SEBASTIAN Ay, and a subtle, as he most learnedly   47
    delivered.   48
ADRIAN The air breathes upon us here most sweetly.

18–19 When . . . entertainer When every sorrow that presents itself is accepted without resistance, there comes to the recipient **20 dollar** widely circulated coin, the German thaler and the Spanish piece of eight. (Sebastian puns on *entertainer* in the sense of paid performer or innkeeper; to Gonzalo, *dollar* suggests "dolor," grief.) **27 spare** forbear, cease. **30–1 Which . . . crow?** Which of the two, Gonzalo or Adrian, do you bet will speak (crow) first? **32 The old cock** Gonzalo. **33 The cockerel** Adrian. **35 laughter** (1) burst of laughter (2) sitting of eggs. (When Adrian, the cockerel, begins to speak two lines later, Sebastian loses the bet. The Folio speech prefixes in lines 38–9 are here reversed so that Antonio enjoys his laugh as the prize for winning, as in the proverb "He who laughs last laughs best" or "He laughs that wins." The Folio assignment can work in the theater, however, if Sebastian pays for losing with a sardonic laugh of concession.) **36 A match!** A bargain; agreed!. **37 desert** uninhabited **39 you're paid** i.e., you've had your laugh. **43 miss't** (1) avoid saying "Yet" (2) miss the island. **44 must needs be** has to be **45 temperance** mildness of climate. **46 Temperance** a girl's name. **delicate** (Here it means "given to pleasure, voluptuous"; in line 44, "pleasant." Antonio is evidently suggesting that *tender,* and *delicate temperance* sounds like a Puritan phrase, which Antonio then mocks by applying the words to a woman rather than an island. He began this bawdy comparison with a double entendre on **inaccessible,** line 40.) **47 subtle** (Here it means "tricky, sexually crafty"; in line 44, "delicate.") **48 delivered** uttered. (Sebastian joins Antonio in baiting the Puritans with his use of the pious cant phrase learnedly delivered.)

SEBASTIAN As if it had lungs, and rotten ones.

ANTONIO Or as 'twere perfumed by a fen.   51

GONZALO Here is everything advantageous to life.

ANTONIO True, save means to live.   53

SEBASTIAN Of that there's none, or little.

GONZALO How lush and lusty the grass looks! How
    green!   55

ANTONIO The ground indeed is tawny.   57

SEBASTIAN With an eye of green in't.   58

ANTONIO He misses not much.

SEBASTIAN No. He doth but mistake the truth totally.   60

GONZALO But the rarity of it is—which is indeed
    almost beyond credit—

SEBASTIAN As many vouched rarities are.   63

GONZALO That our garments, being, as they were,
    drenched in the sea, hold notwithstanding their freshness
    and glosses, being rather new-dyed than stained
    with salt water.

ANTONIO If but one of his pockets could speak, would   68
    it not say he lies?   69

SEBASTIAN Ay, or very falsely pocket up his report.   70

GONZALO Methinks our garments are now as fresh as
    when we put them on first in Afric, at the marriage of
    the King's fair daughter Claribel to the King of Tunis.

SEBASTIAN 'Twas a sweet marriage, and we prosper
    well in our return.

ADRIAN Tunis was never graced before with such a
    paragon to their queen.   77

GONZALO Not since widow Dido's time.   78

ANTONIO [aside to Sebastian] Widow? A pox o' that!
    How came that "widow" in? Widow Dido!

SEBASTIAN What if he had said "widower Aeneas"
    too? Good Lord, how you take it!   82

ADRIAN [to Gonzalo] "Widow Dido" said you? You make
    me study of that. She was of Carthage, not of Tunis.   84

GONZALO This Tunis, sir, was Carthage.

ADRIAN Carthage?

GONZALO I assure you, Carthage.

ANTONIO His word is more than the miraculous harp.   88

---

51 **fen** evil-smelling marshland. 53 **save** except 55 **lusty** healthy 57 **tawny** dull brown, yellowish.
58 **eye** tinge, or spot. (Sebastian is mocking Gonzalo's optimism by saying there's precious little
green to see anywhere. Antonio echoes him in line 59 with similar sarcasm.) 60 **He . . . totally** i.e.,
He's only a tiny 100% wrong. (Sarcastic.) 63 **As . . . are** (More sarcasm: Just as many alleged strange
sights are doubtful, including this one.) 68–70 **If . . . report** (More wisecracking: Gonzalo's mud-
filled pockets would surely give the lie to his talk of clean fresh garments, thereby pocketing up or
tabling the report.) 77 **to** for 78 **widow** Dido Queen of Carthage, deserted by Aeneas. (She was, in
fact, a widow when Aeneas, a widower, met her, but Antonio may be amused at Gonzalo's prudish
use of the term "widow" to describe a woman deserted by her lover.) 82 **take** understand, respond to,
interpret 84 **study of** think about

SEBASTIAN He hath raised the wall, and houses too.

ANTONIO What impossible matter will he make easy next?

SEBASTIAN I think he will carry this island home in his
    pocket and give it his son for an apple.

ANTONIO And, sowing the kernels of it in the sea,   94
    bring forth more islands.

GONZALO Ay.   96

ANTONIO Why, in good time.   97

GONZALO *[to Alonso]* Sir, we were talking that our
    garments seem now as fresh as when we were at
    Tunis at the marriage of your daughter, who is now
    queen.

ANTONIO And the rarest that e'er came there.   *101*

SEBASTIAN Bate, I beseech you, widow Dido.   *102*

ANTONIO Oh, widow Dido? Ay, widow Dido.

GONZALO Is not, sir, my doublet as fresh as the first   *104*
    day I wore it? I mean, in a sort.   *105*

ANTONIO That "sort" was well fished for.   *106*

GONZALO When I wore it at your daughter's marriage.

ALONSO You cram these words into mine ears against
    The stomach of my sense. Would I had never   *109*
    Married my daughter there! For, coming thence, *110*
    My son is lost and, in my rate, she too,   *111*
    Who is so far from Italy removed
    I ne'er again shall see her. O thou mine heir
    Of Naples and of Milan, what strange fish
    Hath made his meal on thee?

FRANCISCO   Sir, he may live.
    I saw him beat the surges under him   *116*
    And ride upon their backs. He trod the water,
    Whose enmity he flung aside, and breasted
    The surge most swoll'n that met him. His bold head
    'Bove the contentious waves he kept, and oared *120*
    Himself with his good arms in lusty stroke   *121*
    To th' shore, that o'er his wave-worn basis bowed, *122*
    As stooping to relieve him. I not doubt   *123*
    He came alive to land.

---

88 miraculous harp (Alludes to Amphion's harp, with which he raised the walls of Thebes; Gonzalo has exceeded that deed by recreating ancient Carthage—*wall and houses*—mistakenly on the site of modern-day Tunis. Some Renaissance commentators believed, like Gonzalo, that the two sites were near each other.) **94 kernels** seeds **96 Ay** (Gonzalo may be reasserting his point about Carthage, or he may be responding ironically to Antonio, who, in turn, answers sarcastically.) **97 in good time** (An expression of ironical acquiescence or amazement, i.e., "sure, right away.") **101 rarest** most remarkable, beautiful **102 Bate** Abate, except, leave out. (Sebastian says sardonically, surely you should allow widow Dido to be an exception.) **104 doublet** close-fitting jacket **105 in a sort** in a way. **106 sort** (Antonio plays on the idea of drawing lots and on "fishing" for something to say.) **109 The stomach . . . sense** my appetite for hearing them. **110 Married** given in marriage **111 rate** estimation, opinion **116 surges** waves **120 oared** propelled as by an oar **121 lusty** vigorous **122 that . . . bowed** that projected out over its (his) surf-eroded base, bending down toward the sea **123 As** as if

ALONSO   No, no, he's gone.

SEBASTIAN *[to Alonso]* Sir, you may thank yourself for this great loss,

    That would not bless our Europe with your daughter,   126

    But rather loose her to an African,   127

    Where she at least is banished from your eye,   128

    Who hath cause to wet the grief on't.

ALONSO   Prithee, peace.   129

SEBASTIAN You were kneeled to and importuned otherwise   130

    By all of us, and the fair soul herself   131

    Weighed between loathness and obedience at   132

    Which end o'th'beam should bow. We have lost your son,   133

    I fear, forever. Milan and Naples have

    More widows in them of this business' making   135

    Than we bring men to comfort them.

    The fault's your own.

ALONSO So is the dear'st o'th' loss.   138

GONZALO My lord Sebastian,

    The truth you speak doth lack some gentleness

    And time to speak it in. You rub the sore   141

    When you should bring the plaster.

SEBASTIAN   Very well.   142

ANTONIO And most chirurgeonly.   143

GONZALO *[to Alonso]*It is foul weather in us all, good sir,

    When you are cloudy.

SEBASTIAN *[to Antonio]* Fowl weather?

ANTONIO *[to Sebastian]* Very foul.   145

GONZALO Had I plantation of this isle, my lord—   146

ANTONIO *[to Sebastian]* He'd sow't with nettle seed.

SEBASTIAN   Or docks, or mallows.   147

GONZALO And were the king on't, what would I do?

SEBASTIAN Scape being drunk for want of wine.   149

GONZALO I'th' commonwealth I would by contraries   150

    Execute all things; for no kind of traffic   151

    Would I admit; no name of magistrate;

    Letters should not be known; riches, poverty,   153

    And use of service, none; contract, succession,   154

---

126 That you who **127 But . . . her** but would rather turn her loose (or, "lose her") **128–9 Where . . . on't** where at least she is not a constant reproach in your eye, which has good reason to weep sorrowfully for this unhappy development. **130 importuned** urged, implored **131–3 the fair . . . bow** Claribel herself was poised uncertainly, as in a balancing scale, between being unwilling to marry and yet wishing to obey her father. **135 of . . . making** on account of this marriage and subsequent shipwreck **138 dear'st** heaviest, most costly **141 time** appropriate time **142 plaster** (A medical application.) **143 chirurgeonly** like a skilled surgeon. (Antonio mocks Gonzalo's medical analogy of a *plaster* applied curatively to a wound.) **145 Fowl** (With a pun on *foul*, returning to the imagery of lines 30–5.) **146 plantation** colonial settlement. (With subsequent wordplay on the literal meaning, "planting.") **147 docks . . . mallows** (Weeds; the first was used as an antidote for nettle stings.) **149 Scape** Escape. **want** lack. (Sebastian jokes sarcastically that this hypothetical ruler would be saved from dissipation only by the barrenness of the island.) **150 by contraries** by what is directly opposite to usual custom **151 traffic** trade **153 Letters** learning **154 use of service** custom of employing servants. **succession** holding of property by right of inheritance.

Bourn, bound of land, tilth, vineyard, none; 155
No use of metal, corn, or wine, or oil; 156
No occupation; all men idle, all,
And women too, but innocent and pure;
No sovereignty—

SEBASTIAN Yet he would be king on't.

ANTONIO The latter end of his commonwealth forgets
the beginning.

GONZALO All things in common nature should produce
Without sweat or endeavor. Treason, felony,
Sword, pike, knife, gun, or need of any engine 164
Would I not have; but nature should bring forth,
Of it own kind, all foison, all abundance, 166
To feed my innocent people.

SEBASTIAN No marrying 'mong his subjects?

ANTONIO None, man, all idle—whores and knaves.

GONZALO I would with such perfection govern, sir,
T'excel the Golden Age.

SEBASTIAN 'Save His Majesty! 171

ANTONIO Long live Gonzalo!

GONZALO And—do you mark me, sir?

ALONSO Prithee, no more. Thou dost talk nothing to me.

GONZALO I do well believe Your Highness, and did it
to minister occasion to these gentlemen, who are of 175
such sensible and nimble lungs that they always use 176
to laugh at nothing.

ANTONIO 'Twas you we laughed at.

GONZALO Who in this kind of merry fooling am nothing
to you; so you may continue, and laugh at nothing
still.

ANTONIO What a blow was there given!

SEBASTIAN An it had not fallen flat-long. 182

GONZALO You are gentlemen of brave mettle; you
would lift the moon out of her sphere if she would [
continue in it five weeks without changing.

Enter Ariel [invisible] playing solemn music.

SEBASTIAN We would so, and then go a-batfowling. 186

ANTONIO Nay, good my lord, be not angry.

---

155 Bourn . . . tilth boundaries, property limits, tillage of soil 156 corn grain 164 pike lance. engine instrument of warfare 166 it its. foison plenty 171 the Golden Age an age of prelapsarian abundance and peace; the first of four "ages" of human history, followed by silver, bronze, and lead. 'Save God save 175 minister occasion furnish opportunity (for laughter) 176 sensible sensitive. use are accustomed 182 An If. flat-long with the flat of the sword, i.e., ineffectually. 183 mettle temperament, courage. (The sense of metal, indistinguishable as a form from mettle, continues the metaphor of the sword. F reads "mettal.") 184 sphere orbit. (Literally, one of the concentric zones occupied by planets in Ptolemaic astronomy.) 186 a-batfowling hunting birds at night with lantern and bat, or "stick"; also, gulling a simpleton. (Gonzalo is the simpleton, or fowl, and Sebastian will use the moon as his lantern.)

GONZALO No, I warrant you, I will not adventure my   188
 discretion so weakly. Will you laugh me asleep? For I   189
 am very heavy.   190
ANTONIO Go sleep, and hear us.

 [All sleep except Alonso, Sebastian, and Antonio.]

ALONSO What, all so soon asleep? I wish mine eyes
 Would, with themselves, shut up my thoughts. I find   193
 They are inclined to do so.
SEBASTIAN   Please you, sir,
 Do not omit the heavy offer of it.   195
 It seldom visits sorrow; when it doth,
 It is a comforter.
ANTONIO   We two, my lord.
 Will guard your person while you take your rest,
 And watch your safety.
ALONSO   Thank you. Wondrous heavy.

 [Alonso sleeps. Exit Ariel.]

SEBASTIAN What a strange drowsiness possesses them!
ANTONIO It is the quality o'th' climate.
SEBASTIAN   Why
 Doth it not then our eyelids sink? I find not
 Myself disposed to sleep.
ANTONIO   Nor I. My spirits are nimble.
 They fell together all, as by consent;   204
 They dropped, as by a thunderstroke. What might,
 Worthy Sebastian, oh, what might—? No more.
 And yet methinks I see it in thy face
 What thou shouldst be. Th'occasion speaks thee, and   208
 My strong imagination sees a crown
 Dropping upon thy head.
SEBASTIAN   What, art thou waking?
ANTONIO Do you not hear me speak?
SEBASTIAN   I do, and surely
 It is a sleepy language, and thou speak'st   212
 Out of thy sleep. What is it thou didst say?
 This is a strange repose, to be asleep
 With eyes wide open—standing, speaking, moving—
 And yet so fast asleep.
ANTONIO   Noble Sebastian,
 Thou let'st thy fortune sleep—die, rather; wink'st   217
 Whiles thou art waking.

188–9 adventure . . . weakly risk my reputation for discretion for so trivial a cause (by getting angry).
190 heavy sleepy. **191 Go . . . us** i.e., Get ready for sleep, and we'll do our part by laughing. **193 Would . . . thoughts** would shut off my melancholy brooding when they (my eyes) close themselves in sleep. **195 Do . . . it** do not decline the invitation to drowsiness. **204 They . . . consent** The others all fell asleep simultaneously, as if by common agreement **208 Th' occasion . . . thee** The opportunity of the moment calls upon you **212 sleepy** dreamlike, fantastic **217 wink'st** (you) shut your eyes

SEBASTIAN   Thou dost snore distinctly;   218
  There's meaning in thy snores.
ANTONIO I am more serious than my custom. You
  Must be so too if heed me, which to do   221
  Trebles thee o'er.
SEBASTIAN   Well, I am standing water.   222
ANTONIO I'll teach you how to flow.
SEBASTIAN   Do so. To ebb   223
  Hereditary sloth instructs me.
ANTONIO   Oh,   224
  If you but knew how you the purpose cherish   225
  Whiles thus you mock it! How, in stripping it,   226
  You more invest it! Ebbing men, indeed,   227
  Most often do so near the bottom run   228
  By their own fear or sloth.
SEBASTIAN   Prithee, say on.
  The setting of thine eye and cheek proclaim   230
  A matter from thee, and a birth indeed   231
  Which throes thee much to yield.
ANTONIO   Thus, sir: 232
  Although this lord of weak remembrance, this   233
  Who shall be of as little memory   234
  When he is earthed, hath here almost persuaded—   236
  For he's a spirit of persuasion, only   236
  Professes to persuade—the King his son's alive,   237
  'Tis as impossible that he's undrowned
  As he that sleeps here swims.
SEBASTIAN   I have no hope
  That he's undrowned.
ANTONIO   Oh, out of that "no hope"
  What great hope have you! No hope that way is   241
  Another way so high a hope that even   242
  Ambition cannot pierce a wink beyond,   243
  But doubt discovery there. Will you grant with me   244
  That Ferdinand is drowned?
SEBASTIAN   He's gone.

---

218 distinctly articulately **221 if heed** if you heed **222 Trebles thee o'er** makes you three times as great and rich. **standing water** water that neither ebbs nor flows, at a standstill. **223 ebb** recede, decline **224 Hereditary sloth** i.e., natural laziness and the position of younger brother, one who cannot inherit **225–6 If . . . mock it!** If you only knew how much you secretly cherish ambition even while your words mock it! **226–7 How . . . invest it!** How the more you speak flippantly of ambition, the more you, in effect, affirm it, clothing what you have stripped! **228 the bottom** i.e., on which unadventurous men may go aground and miss the tide of fortune **230 setting** set expression (of earnestness) **231 matter** matter of importance **232 throes** causes pain, as in giving birth. **yield** give forth, speak about. **233–7 Although . . . alive** Although this owner of weak memory, he who will be only weakly remembered when he is dead, has nearly persuaded—since he's a mind or soul devoted solely to persuade—King Alonso that Ferdinand lives **241 that way** i.e., in regard to Ferdinand's being saved **242–4 that . . . there** that even ambition for high status cannot see anything higher, and even there it doubts the reality of what it sees (because the place is so supremely high). (What then follows is Antonio's analysis of why they can proceed without fear.)

ANTONIO   Then tell me,
  Who's the next heir of Naples?

SEBASTIAN   Claribel.

ANTONIO She that is Queen of Tunis; she that dwells
  Ten leagues beyond man's life; she that from Naples   248
  Can have no note, unless the sun were post—   249
  The Man i'th' Moon's too slow—till newborn chins
  Be rough and razorable; she that from whom   251
  We all were sea-swallowed, though some cast again,   252
  And by that destiny to perform an act
  Whereof what's past is prologue, what to come
  In yours and my discharge.   255

SEBASTIAN What stuff is this? How say you?
  'Tis true my brother's daughter's Queen of Tunis,
  So is she heir of Naples, twixt which regions
  There is some space.

ANTONIO   A space whose ev'ry cubit   259
  Seems to cry out, "How shall that Claribel
  Measure us back to Naples? Keep in Tunis,   261
  And let Sebastian wake." Say this were death   262
  That now hath seized them, why, they were no worse
  Than now they are. There be that can rule Naples   264
  As well as he that sleeps, lords that can prate   265
  As amply and unnecessarily
  As this Gonzalo. I myself could make   267
  A chough of as deep chat. Oh, that you bore   268
  The mind that I do! What a sleep were this
  For your advancement! Do you understand me?

SEBASTIAN Methinks I do.

ANTONIO   And how does your content   271
  Tender your own good fortune?

SEBASTIAN   I remember   272
  You did supplant your brother Prospero.

ANTONIO   True.
  And look how well my garments sit upon me,
  Much feater than before. My brother's servants   275
  Were then my fellows. Now they are my men.

SEBASTIAN But, for your conscience?   277

ANTONIO Ay, sir, where lies that? If 'twere a kibe,   278
  'Twould put me to my slipper; but I feel not   279

---

248 **Ten . . . life** i.e., further than the journey of a lifetime 249 **note** news, intimation. **post** messenger 251 **razorable** ready for shaving. **from** on our voyage from 252 **cast** were disgorged. (With a pun on casting of parts for a play.) 255 **discharge** part to play. 259 **cubit** ancient measure of length of about twenty inches 261 **Measure us** retrace our journey. **Keep** You, Claribel, stay 262 **wake** i.e., to his good fortune. 264 **There be** There are those 265 **prate** speak foolishly 267–8 **I . . . chat** I could teach a jack-daw to talk as wisely, or, be such a garrulous talker myself. 271–2 **And . . . fortune?** And how does your contentment with what I've just said further your good fortune? 275 **feater** more becomingly, fittingly 277 **for** as for 278 **kibe** chilblain, here a sore on the heel 279 **put me to** oblige me to wear

This deity in my bosom. Twenty consciences 280
That stand twixt me and Milan, candied be they 281
And melt ere they molest! Here lies your brother, 282
No better than the earth he lies upon,
If he were that which now he's like—that's dead,
Whom I, with this obedient steel, three inches of it,
Can lay to bed forever; whiles you, doing thus, 286
To the perpetual wink for aye might put 287
This ancient morsel, this Sir Prudence, who
Should not upbraid our course. For all the rest, 289
They'll take suggestion as a cat laps milk; 290
They'll tell the clock to any business that 291
We say befits the hour.

SEBASTIAN   Thy case, dear friend,
Shall be my precedent. As thou got'st Milan,
I'll come by Naples. Draw thy sword. One stroke
Shall free thee from the tribute which thou payest, 295
And I the king shall love thee.

ANTONIO   Draw together;
And when I rear my hand, do you the like
To fall it on Gonzalo.   *[They draw.]*

SEBASTIAN   Oh, but one word. 298

[They talk apart.]
     Enter Ariel [invisible], with music and song.

ARIEL *[to Gonzalo]* My master through his art foresees the danger
     That you, his friend, are in, and sends me forth—
     For else his project dies—to keep them living.

     Sings in Gonzalo's ear.

     While you here do snoring lie,
     Open-eyed conspiracy
     His time doth take. 304
     If of life you keep a care,
     Shake off slumber, and beware.
     Awake, awake!

ANTONIO Then let us both be sudden.

GONZALO *[waking]* Now, good angels preserve the King!

     [The others wake.]

ALONSO Why, how now, ho, awake? Why are you drawn?

280–2 Twenty . . . molest! Even if there were twenty consciences between me and the dukedom of Milan, may they be lumped together or crystallized like candy and then melted down before I'd let them interfere! **286 thus** similarly. (The actor makes a stabbing gesture.) **287 wink** sleep, closing of eyes. **aye** ever **289 Should not** must not be allowed to **290 take suggestion** respond to prompting **291 tell the clock** i.e., agree, answer appropriately, chime **295 tribute** (See 1.2.113–24.) **298 fall it** let it fall **304 time** opportunity

Wherefore this ghastly looking?

GONZALO   What's the matter?

SEBASTIAN Whiles we stood here securing your repose,   312
    Even now, we heard a hollow burst of bellowing
    Like bulls, or rather lions. Did 't not wake you?
    It struck mine ear most terribly.

ALONSO   I heard nothing.

ANTONIO Oh, 'twas a din to fright a monster's ear,
    To make an earthquake! Sure it was the roar
    Of a whole herd of lions.

ALONSO Heard you this, Gonzalo?

GONZALO Upon mine honor, sir, I heard a humming,
    And that a strange one too, which did awake me.
    I shaked you, sir, and cried. As mine eyes opened,   322
    I saw their weapons drawn. There was a noise,
    That's verily. 'Tis best we stand upon our guard,   324
    Or that we quit this place. Let's draw our weapons.

ALONSO Lead off this ground, and let's make further search
    For my poor son.

GONZALO   Heavens keep him from these beasts!
    For he is, sure, i'th'island.

ALONSO   Lead away.

ARIEL [aside] Prospero my lord shall know what I have done.
    So, King, go safely on to seek thy son.

    Exeunt [separately].

2.2

    Enter Caliban with a burden of wood. A noise of thunder heard.

CALIBAN All the infections that the sun sucks up
    From bogs, fens, flats, on Prosper fall, and make him   2
    By inchmeal a disease! His spirits hear me,   3
    And yet I needs must curse. But they'll nor pinch,   4
    Fright me with urchin shows, pitch me i'th'mire,   5
    Nor lead me, like a firebrand, in the dark   6
    Out of my way, unless he bid 'em. But
    For every trifle are they set upon me,
    Sometimes like apes, that mow and chatter at me   9
    And after bite me; then like hedgehogs, which
    Lie tumbling in my barefoot way and mount
    Their pricks at my footfall. Sometime am I
    All wound with adders, who with cloven tongues   13
    Do hiss me into madness.

---

312 **securing** standing guard over 322 **cried** called out 324 **verily** true
2.2. Location: Another part of the island.
2 **flats** swamps 3 **By inchmeal** inch by inch 4 **needs must** have to. **nor** neither 5 **urchin shows**
elvish apparitions shaped like hedgehogs 6 **like a firebrand** they in the guise of a will-o'-the-wisp 9
mow make faces 13 **wound with** entwined by

Enter Trinculo.

Lo, now, lo!
Here comes a spirit of his, and to torment me
For bringing wood in slowly. I'll fall flat.
Perchance he will not mind me.   *[He lies down.]*   17

TRINCULO Here's neither bush nor shrub to bear off   18
any weather at all. And another storm brewing; I hear
it sing i'th' wind. Yond same black cloud, yond huge
one, looks like a foul bombard that would shed his   21
liquor. If it should thunder as it did before, I know not
where to hide my head. Yond same cloud cannot
choose but fall by pailfuls. *[Seeing Caliban]* What have
we here, a man or a fish? Dead or alive? A fish, he
smells like a fish; a very ancient and fishlike smell; a
kind of not-of-the-newest Poor John. A strange fish!   27
Were I in England now, as once I was, and had but
this fish painted, not a holiday fool there but would   29
give a piece of silver. There would this monster make   30
a man. Any strange beast there makes a man. When   31
they will not give a doit to relieve a lame beggar, they   32
will lay out ten to see a dead Indian. Legged like a
man, and his fins like arms! Warm, o' my troth! I do   34
now let loose my opinion, hold it no longer: this is no   35
fish, but an islander, that hath lately suffered by a
thunderbolt. *[Thunder.]* Alas, the storm is come again!
My best way is to creep under his gaberdine. There is   38
no other shelter hereabout. Misery acquaints a man
with strange bedfellows. I will here shroud till the   40
dregs of the storm be past.   41

[He creeps under Caliban's garment.]
Enter Stephano, singing, [a bottle in his hand].

STEPHANO "I shall no more to sea, to sea,
Here shall I die ashore—"
This is a very scurvy tune to sing at a man's funeral.
Well, here's my comfort.   *Drinks.*

(Sings.)

"The master, the swabber, the boatswain, and I,   46
The gunner and his mate,
Loved Mall, Meg, and Marian, and Margery,

---

17 mind notice **18 bear off** keep off **21 foul bombard** dirty leather jug. **his** its **27 Poor John** salted
fish, type of poor fare **29 painted** i.e., painted on a sign set up outside a booth or tent at a fair **30–1**
make a man (1) make a man's fortune (2) pass for a human being. **32 doit** small coin **34 o' my troth**
by my faith. **35 hold it** hold it in **38 gaberdine** cloak, loose upper garment. **40 shroud** take shelter
41 dregs i.e., last remains (as in a *bombard* or jug, line 21) **46 swabber** crew member whose job is to
wash the decks

But none of us cared for Kate.
For she had a tongue with a tang,   50
Would cry to a sailor, 'Go hang!'
She loved not the savor of tar nor of pitch,
Yet a tailor might scratch her where'er she did itch.   53
Then to sea, boys, and let her go hang!"
This is a scurvy tune too. But here's my comfort.

Drinks.

CALIBAN Do not torment me! Oh!   56
STEPHANO What's the matter? Have we devils here? Do   57
  you put tricks upon's with savages and men of Ind,   58
  ha? I have not scaped drowning to be afeard now of
  your four legs. For it hath been said, "As proper a man   60
  as ever went on four legs cannot make him give   61
  ground"; and it shall be said so again while Stephano
  breathes at' nostrils.   63
CALIBAN This spirit torments me! Oh!
STEPHANO This is some monster of the isle with four
  legs, who hath got, as I take it, an ague. Where the   66
  devil should he learn our language? I will give him   67
  some relief, if it be but for that. If I can recover him   68
  and keep him tame and get to Naples with him, he's
  a present for any emperor that ever trod on neat's   70
  leather.   71
CALIBAN Do not torment me, prithee. I'll bring my wood home faster.
STEPHANO He's in his fit now and does not talk after   74
  the wisest. He shall taste of my bottle. If he have never   75
  drunk wine afore, it will go near to remove his fit. If I   76
  can recover him and keep him tame, I will not take too   77
  much for him. He shall pay for him that hath him, and   78
  that soundly.
CALIBAN Thou dost me yet but little hurt; thou wilt
  anon, I know it by thy trembling. Now Prosper works
  upon thee.
STEPHANO Come on your ways. Open your mouth. Here
  is that which will give language to you, cat. Open your   84
  mouth. This will shake your shaking, I can tell you,   85

---

50 **tang** sting 53 **tailor . . . itch** (A dig at tailors for their supposed effeminacy and a bawdy suggestion of satisfying a sexual craving.) 56 **Do . . . me!** (Caliban assumes that one of Prospero's spirits has come to punish him.) 57 **What's the matter?** What's going on here? 58 **put tricks upon's** trick us with conjuring shows. **Ind** India 60 **proper** handsome 61 **four legs** (The conventional phrase would supply *two* legs, but the creature Stephano thinks he sees has four.) 63 **at'** at the 66 **ague** fever. (Probably both Caliban and Trinculo are quaking; see lines 56 and 81.) 67 **should he learn** could he have learned 68 **for that** i.e., for knowing our language. **recover** revive. (Also in line 77.) 70–1 **neat's leather** cowhide. 74–5 **after the wisest** in the wisest fashion. 76 **afore** before. **go near** to be in a fair way to 77 **recover** restore 77–8 **I will . . . much** i.e., no sum can be too much 78 **He shall . . . hath him** Anyone who wants him will have to pay dearly for him 84–5 **cat . . . mouth** (Allusion to the proverb "Good liquor will make a cat speak.") 85 **shake** shake off

and that soundly. *[Giving Caliban a drink.]* You cannot 86
    tell who's your friend. Open your chaps again. 87
TRINCULO I should know that voice. It should be—but
    he is drowned, and these are devils. Oh, defend me!
STEPHANO Four legs and two voices—a most delicate 90
    monster! His forward voice now is to speak well of his
    friend; his backward voice is to utter foul speeches and 92
    to detract. If all the wine in my bottle will recover him, 93
    I will help his ague. Come. *[Giving a drink.]* Amen! I
    will pour some in thy other mouth.
TRINCULO Stephano!
STEPHANO Doth thy other mouth call me? Mercy,
    mercy! This is a devil, and no monster. I will leave
    him. I have no long spoon. 99
TRINCULO Stephano! If thou be'st Stephano, touch me
    and speak to me, for I am Trinculo—be not afeard—
    thy good friend Trinculo.
STEPHANO If thou be'st Trinculo, come forth. I'll pull
    thee by the lesser legs. If any be Trinculo's legs, these
    are they. *[Pulling him out.]* Thou art very Trinculo
    indeed! How cam'st thou to be the siege of this 106
    mooncalf? Can he vent Trinculos? 107
TRINCULO I took him to be killed with a thunderstroke.
    But art thou not drowned, Stephano? I hope now thou
    art not drowned. Is the storm overblown? I hid me 110
    under the dead mooncalf's gaberdine for fear of the
    storm. And art thou living, Stephano? Oh, Stephano,
    two Neapolitans scaped!   *[He capers with Stephano.]*
STEPHANO Prithee, do not turn me about. My stomach
    is not constant. 115
CALIBAN These be fine things, an if they be not spirits. 116
    That's a brave god, and bears celestial liquor. 117
    I will kneel to him.
STEPHANO How didst thou scape? How cam'st thou
    hither? Swear by this bottle how thou cam'st hither. I
    escaped upon a butt of sack which the sailors heaved 121
    o'erboard—by this bottle, which I made of the bark of 122
    a tree with mine own hands since I was cast ashore.
CALIBAN *[kneeling]* I'll swear upon that bottle to be
    thy true subject, for the liquor is not earthly.

86–7 You . . . friend i.e., You can't tell who's your friend until someone like me provides you with a drink. **87 chaps** jaws **90 delicate** ingenious **92 backward voice** (Trinculo and Caliban are facing in opposite directions. Stephano supposes the monster to have a rear end that can emit *foul speeches* or foul-smelling wind at the monster's *other mouth*, line 95.) **93 If . . . him** Even if it takes all the wine in my bottle to cure him **99 long spoon** (Allusion to the proverb "He that sups with the devil has need of a long spoon.") **106 siege** excrement **107 mooncalf** monstrous or misshapen creature (whose deformity is caused by the malignant influence of the moon). **vent** excrete, defecate **110 overblown** blown over **115 constant** steady. **116 an if** if **117 brave** fine, magnificent **121 butt of sack** barrel of Canary wine **122 by this bottle** i.e., I swear by this bottle

STEPHANO Here. Swear then how thou escaped'st.

TRINCULO Swum ashore, man, like a duck. I can swim
like a duck, I'll be sworn.

STEPHANO Here, kiss the book. Though thou canst
swim like a duck, thou art made like a goose.   129

[Giving him a drink.]

TRINCULO Oh, Stephano, hast any more of this?

STEPHANO The whole butt, man. My cellar is in a rock
by th' seaside, where my wine is hid.—How now,
mooncalf? How does thine ague?

CALIBAN Hast thou not dropped from heaven?

STEPHANO Out o'th' moon, I do assure thee. I was the
man i'th' moon when time was.   137

CALIBAN I have seen thee in her, and I do adore thee.
My mistress showed me thee, and thy dog, and thy bush.   139

STEPHANO Come, swear to that. Kiss the book. I will
furnish it anon with new contents. Swear.

[Giving him a drink.]

TRINCULO By this good light, this is a very shallow   142
monster! I afeard of him? A very weak monster! The
man i'th' moon? A most poor credulous monster!
Well drawn, monster, in good sooth!   145

CALIBAN *[to Stephano]* I'll show thee every fertile inch o'th' island,
And I will kiss thy foot. I prithee, be my god.

TRINCULO By this light, a most perfidious and drunken
monster! When's god's asleep, he'll rob his bottle.   149

CALIBAN I'll kiss thy foot. I'll swear myself thy subject.

STEPHANO Come on then. Down, and swear.

[Caliban kneels.]

TRINCULO I shall laugh myself to death at this puppy-
headed monster. A most scurvy monster! I could find
in my heart to beat him—

STEPHANO Come, kiss.

TRINCULO But that the poor monster's in drink. An   156
abominable monster!

CALIBAN I'll show thee the best springs. I'll pluck thee berries.
I'll fish for thee and get thee wood enough.
A plague upon the tyrant that I serve!
I'll bear him no more sticks, but follow thee,
Thou wondrous man.

---

129 book i.e., bottle. (But with ironic reference to the practice of kissing the Bible in swearing an oath; see *I'll be sworn* in line 128.) **137 when time was** once upon a time. **139 dog . . . bush** (The man in the moon was popularly imagined to have with him a dog and a bush of thorn.) **142 By . . . light** By God's light, by this good light from heaven **145 Well . . . sooth!** Well pulled on the bottle, truly! **149 When . . . bottle** i.e., Caliban wouldn't even stop at robbing his god (i.e., Stephano) of his bottle if he could catch him asleep **156 But that** were it not that. **in drink** drunk.

TRINCULO A most ridiculous monster, to make a
    wonder of a poor drunkard!

CALIBAN I prithee, let me bring thee where crabs grow,   165
    And I with my long nails will dig thee pignuts,   166
    Show thee a jay's nest, and instruct thee how
    To snare the nimble marmoset. I'll bring thee
    To clust'ring filberts, and sometimes I'll get thee
    Young scamels from the rock. Wilt thou go with me?   170

STEPHANO I prithee now, lead the way without any
    more talking.—Trinculo, the King and all our company   172
    else being drowned, we will inherit here.—   173
    Here, bear my bottle.—Fellow Trinculo, we'll fill him
    by and by again.

CALIBAN (*sings drunkenly*) Farewell, master, farewell, farewell!

TRINCULO A howling monster; a drunken monster!

CALIBAN No more dams I'll make for fish,
    Nor fetch in firing   179
    At requiring,
    Nor scrape trenchering, nor wash dish.   181
    'Ban, 'Ban, Ca—Caliban
    Has a new master. Get a new man!   183
    Freedom, high-day! High-day, freedom! Freedom,
        high-day, freedom!   184

STEPHANO O brave monster! Lead the way. *Exeunt.*

3.1

    Enter Ferdinand, bearing a log.

FERDINAND There be some sports are painful, and their labor   1
    Delight in them sets off. Some kinds of baseness   2
    Are nobly undergone, and most poor matters   3
    Point to rich ends. This my mean task   4
    Would be as heavy to me as odious, but   5
    The mistress which I serve quickens what's dead   6
    And makes my labors pleasures. Oh, she is
    Ten times more gentle than her father's crabbed,
    And he's composed of harshness. I must remove
    Some thousands of these logs and pile them up,

---

165 crabs crab apples, or crabs **166 pignuts** earthnuts, edible tuberous roots **168 marmoset** small monkey. **170 scamels** (Possibly *seamews*, or shellfish, or perhaps from *squamelle*, "furnished with little scales." Contemporary French and Italian travel accounts report that the natives of Patagonia in South America ate small fish described as fort scameux and squame.) **172–3 all . . . else** all the rest of our shipboard companions **173 inherit** take possession **179 firing** firewood **181 trenchering** trenchers, wooden plates **183 Get a new man** (Addressed to Prospero.) **184 high-day** holiday
3.1. Location: Before Prospero's cell.
1–2 There . . . sets off Some pastimes are laborious, but the pleasure we get from them compensates for the effort. (Pleasure is set *off* by labor as a jewel is set off by its foil.) **2 baseness** menial activity **3 undergone** undertaken. **most poor** poorest **4 mean** lowly **5 but** were it not that **6 quickens** gives life to

Upon a sore injunction. My sweet mistress   11
Weeps when she sees me work and says such baseness
Had never like executor. I forget;   13
But these sweet thoughts do even refresh my labors,
Most busy lest when I do it.

Enter Miranda; and Prospero [at a distance, unseen].

MIRANDA   Alas now, pray you,   15
Work not so hard. I would the lightning had
Burnt up those logs that you are enjoined to pile!   17
Pray, set it down and rest you. When this burns,   18
'Twill weep for having wearied you. My father   19
Is hard at study. Pray now, rest yourself.
He's safe for these three hours.
FERDINAND   O most dear mistress,   21
The sun will set before I shall discharge   22
What I must strive to do.
MIRANDA   If you'll sit down,
I'll bear your logs the while. Pray, give me that.
I'll carry it to the pile.
FERDINAND   No, precious creature,
I had rather crack my sinews, break my back,
Than you should such dishonor undergo
While I sit lazy by.
MIRANDA   It would become me
As well as it does you; and I should do it
With much more ease, for my good will is to it,
And yours it is against.
PROSPERO *[aside]*   Poor worm, thou art infected!
This visitation shows it.
MIRANDA   You look wearily.   32
FERDINAND
No, noble mistress, 'tis fresh morning with me
When you are by at night. I do beseech you—   34
Chiefly that I might set it in my prayers—
What is your name?
MIRANDA   Miranda.—O my father,
I have broke your hest to say so.
FERDINAND   Admired Miranda!   37
Indeed the top of admiration, worth
What's dearest to the world! Full many a lady   39
I have eyed with best regard, and many a time   40

---

11 sore injunction severe command. **13 Had . . . executor** was never before undertaken by so noble
a being. **I forget** i.e., I forget that I'm supposed to be working **15 Most . . . do it** (Ferdinand seems to
say that the busier he is, the less likely he is to forget the sweet thoughts that make his labors pleasant. The line may be in need of emendation.) **17 enjoined** commanded **18 this** i.e., the log **19 weep**
i.e., exude resin **21 these** the next **22 discharge** complete **32 visitation** (1) Miranda's visit to Ferdinand (2) visitation of the plague, i.e., infection of love **34 by** nearby **37 hest** command. **Admired
Miranda** (Her name means "to be admired or wondered at.") **39 dearest** most treasured **40 best regard** thoughtful and approving attention

The harmony of their tongues hath into bondage
Brought my too diligent ear. For several virtues 42
Have I liked several women, never any
With so full soul but some defect in her
Did quarrel with the noblest grace she owed 45
And put it to the foil. But you, oh, you, 46
So perfect and so peerless, are created
Of every creature's best!
MIRANDA   I do not know 48
One of my sex; no woman's face remember,
Save, from my glass, mine own. Nor have I seen
More that I may call men than you, good friend,
And my dear father. How features are abroad 52
I am skilless of; but, by my modesty, 53
The jewel in my dower, I would not wish
Any companion in the world but you;
Nor can imagination form a shape,
Besides yourself, to like of. But I prattle 57
Something too wildly, and my father's precepts 58
I therein do forget.
FERDINAND   I am in my condition 59
A prince, Miranda; I do think, a king—
I would, not so!—and would no more endure 61
This wooden slavery than to suffer 62
The flesh-fly blow my mouth. Hear my soul speak: 63
The very instant that I saw you did
My heart fly to your service, there resides
To make me slave to it, and for your sake
Am I this patient log-man.
MIRANDA   Do you love me?
FERDINAND O heaven, O earth, bear witness to this sound,
And crown what I profess with kind event 69
If I speak true! If hollowly, invert 70
What best is boded me to mischief! I 71
Beyond all limit of what else i'th' world 72
Do love, prize, honor you.
MIRANDA [weeping]   I am a fool
To weep at what I am glad of.
PROSPERO [aside]   Fair encounter
Of two most rare affections! Heavens rain grace
On that which breeds between 'em!
FERDINAND   Wherefore weep you?

---

42 diligent attentive. **several** various. (Also in line 43.) **45 owed** owned **46 put . . . foil** (1) overthrew
it (as in fencing or wrestling) (2) served as a *foil,* or "contrast," to set it off. **48 Of** out of **52 How . . .
abroad** What people look like in other places **53 skilless** ignorant. **modesty** virginity **57 like of** be
pleased with, be fond of. **58 Something** somewhat **59 condition** rank **61 I would** I wish it were **62
wooden slavery** being compelled to carry wood **62–3 than . . . mouth** than I would allow flying insects to deposit their eggs in my mouth as if in decaying flesh. **69 kind event** favorable outcome **70
hollowly** insincerely, falsely. **invert** turn **71 boded** in store for. **mischief** harm. **72 what** whatever

MIRANDA At mine unworthiness, that dare not offer
　　What I desire to give, and much less take
　　What I shall die to want. But this is trifling,　　　　79
　　And all the more it seeks to hide itself
　　The bigger bulk it shows. Hence, bashful cunning,　　81
　　And prompt me, plain and holy innocence!
　　I am your wife, if you will marry me;
　　If not, I'll die your maid. To be your fellow　　　　84
　　You may deny me, but I'll be your servant
　　Whether you will or no.
FERDINAND　　　　　　　　My mistress, dearest,　　　86
　　And I thus humble ever.
MIRANDA My husband, then?
FERDINAND　　　　　　　　Ay, with a heart as willing　89
　　As bondage e'er of freedom. Here's my hand.
MIRANDA [clasping his hand] And mine, with my heart in't. And now farewell
　　Till half an hour hence.
FERDINAND　　　　　　　　A thousand thousand!　　92

　　Exeunt [Ferdinand and Miranda, separately].

PROSPERO So glad of this as they I cannot be,
　　Who are surprised with all; but my rejoicing　　　94
　　At nothing can be more. I'll to my book,
　　For yet ere suppertime must I perform
　　Much business appertaining.　　　　*Exit.*　　　97

3.2

　　Enter Caliban, Stephano, and Trinculo.

STEPHANO Tell not me. When the butt is out, we will　　　1
　　drink water, not a drop before. Therefore bear up and　　2
　　board 'em. Servant monster, drink to me.　　　　3
TRINCULO Servant monster? The folly of this island!　　4
　　They say there's but five upon this isle. We are three
　　of them; if th'other two be brained like us, the state　　6
　　totters.
STEPHANO Drink, servant monster, when I bid thee.
　　Thy eyes are almost set in thy head.　　　*[Giving a drink.]*　9

---

79 **die** (Probably with an unconscious sexual meaning that underlies all of lines 77–81.) **to want**
through lacking. 81 **bashful cunning** coyness 84 **maid** handmaiden, servant. **fellow** mate 86 **will** desire it. **My mistress** i.e., The woman I adore and serve (not an illicit sexual partner) 89 **willing** desirous 92 **A thousand thousand!** A thousand thousand farewells! 94 **with all** by everything that has
happened, or, *withal,* "by it" 97 **appertaining** related to this
3.2 **Location: Another part of the island.**
1 **out** empty 2–3 **bear . . . 'em** (Stephano uses the terminology of maneuvering at sea and boarding a
vessel under attack as a way of urging an assault on the liquor supply.) 4 **folly of** i.e., stupidity found
on 6 **be brained** are endowed with intelligence 9 **set . . . head** fixed in a drunken stare. (But Trinculo
answers in a literal sense.)

TRINCULO Where should they be set else? He were a   *10*
   brave monster indeed if they were set in his tail.   *11*

STEPHANO My man-monster hath drowned his tongue
   in sack. For my part, the sea cannot drown me. I
   swam, ere I could recover the shore, five and thirty   *14*
   leagues off and on. By this light, thou shalt be my   *15*
   lieutenant, monster, or my standard.   *16*

TRINCULO Your lieutenant, if you list; he's no standard.   *17*

STEPHANO We'll not run, Monsieur Monster.   *18*

TRINCULO Nor go neither, but you'll lie like dogs and   *19*
   yet say nothing neither.

STEPHANO Mooncalf, speak once in thy life, if thou
   be'st a good mooncalf.

CALIBAN How does Thy Honor? Let me lick thy shoe.
   I'll not serve him. He is not valiant.

TRINCULO Thou liest, most ignorant monster, I am in   *25*
   case to jostle a constable. Why, thou deboshed fish,   *26*
   thou, was there ever man a coward that hath drunk so   *27*
   much sack as I today? Wilt thou tell a monstrous lie,   *28*
   being but half a fish and half a monster?

CALIBAN Lo, how he mocks me! Wilt thou let him, my lord?

TRINCULO "Lord," quoth he? That a monster should be
   such a natural!   *32*

CALIBAN Lo, lo, again! Bite him to death, I prithee.

STEPHANO Trinculo, keep a good tongue in your head.
   If you prove a mutineer—the next tree! The poor monster's   *35*
   my subject, and he shall not suffer indignity.

CALIBAN I thank my noble lord. Wilt thou be pleased
   To hearken once again to the suit I made to thee?

STEPHANO Marry, will I. Kneel and repeat it. I will   *39*
   stand, and so shall Trinculo.   *[Caliban kneels.]*   *40*

   Enter Ariel, invisible.

CALIBAN As I told thee before, I am subject to a tyrant,
   A sorcerer, that by his cunning hath
   Cheated me of the island.

ARIEL *[mimicking Trinculo]* Thou liest.

---

10 set placed **11 brave** fine, splendid **14 recover** gain, reach **14–15 five . . . on** i.e., a little over a hundred miles, give or take, or, off and on, intermittently. (A drunken hyperbole.) **15 By this light** (An oath: By the light of the sun.) **16 standard** standard-bearer, ensign. (But Trinculo answers in the literal sense: Caliban is *no standard*, not able to stand up because he's so drunk.) **17 list** prefer **18 run** run away, retreat (as a standard-bearer should not do) **19 Nor . . . dogs** i.e., You won't even walk, much less run; you'll lie down in the field like the proverbial cowardly dog. (With a play on lie, tell falsehoods.) **25–6 in case** ready, valiant enough **26 deboshed** debauched, drunken **27 ever . . . coward** ever a coward. (Trinculo appeals to his gargantuan drinking as refutation of the charge that he is *not valiant*, line 24.) **28 sack** Spanish white wine **32 natural** fool, idiot. **35 the next tree** i.e., you'll hang. **39 Marry** i.e., Indeed. (Originally an oath, "by the Virgin Mary.") **40.1 invisible** i.e., wearing a garment to connote invisibility, as at 1.2.377.2.

CALIBAN Thou liest, thou jesting monkey, thou!
    I would my valiant master would destroy thee.
    I do not lie.
STEPHANO Trinculo, if you trouble him any more in 's
    tale, by this hand, I will supplant some of your teeth.   48
TRINCULO Why, I said nothing.
STEPHANO Mum, then, and no more.—Proceed.
CALIBAN I say by sorcery he got this isle;
    From me he got it. If Thy Greatness will
    Revenge it on him—for I know thou dar'st,
    But this thing dare not—   54
STEPHANO That's most certain.
CALIBAN Thou shalt be lord of it, and I'll serve thee.
STEPHANO How now shall this be compassed? Canst   57
    thou bring me to the party?
CALIBAN Yea, yea, my lord. I'll yield him thee asleep,
    Where thou mayst knock a nail into his head.
ARIEL [mimicking Trinculo] Thou liest; thou canst not.
CALIBAN What a pied ninny's this! Thou scurvy patch!—   62
    I do beseech Thy Greatness, give him blows
    And take his bottle from him. When that's gone
    He shall drink naught but brine, for I'll not show
    him
    Where the quick freshes are.   66
STEPHANO Trinculo, run into no further danger. Interrupt
    the monster one word further and, by this hand,
    I'll turn my mercy out o'doors and make a stockfish of   69
    thee.
TRINCULO Why, what did I? I did nothing. I'll go farther off.
STEPHANO Didst thou not say he lied?
ARIEL [mimicking Trinculo] Thou liest.
STEPHANO Do I so? Take thou that.   [He beats Trinculo.]
    As you like this, give me the lie another time.   76
TRINCULO I did not give the lie. Out o' your wits and
    hearing too? A pox o' your bottle! This can sack and   78
    drinking do. A murrain on your monster, and the   79
    devil take your fingers!
CALIBAN Ha, ha, ha!
STEPHANO Now, forward with your tale.   [To Trinculo]
    Prithee, stand further off.
CALIBAN Beat him enough. After a little time
    I'll beat him too.
STEPHANO Stand farther.—Come, proceed.
CALIBAN Why, as I told thee, 'tis a custom with him
    I'th' afternoon to sleep. There thou mayst brain him,

---

48 supplant uproot, displace **54 this thing** i.e., Trinculo **57 compassed** achieved. **62 pied ninny** fool in motley. **patch** fool. **66 quick freshes** running springs **69 turn . . . o' doors** banish all merciful feelings. **stockfish** dried cod beaten before cooking **76 give me the lie** call me a liar to my face **78 A pox** i.e., A plague. (A curse.) **79 murrain** plague. (Literally, a cattle disease.)

Having first seized his books; or with a log
Batter his skull, or paunch him with a stake,   90
Or cut his weasand with thy knife. Remember   91
First to possess his books, for without them
He's but a sot, as I am, nor hath not   93
One spirit to command. They all do hate him
As rootedly as I. Burn but his books.
He has brave utensils—for so he calls them—   96
Which, when he has a house, he'll deck withal.   97
And that most deeply to consider is
The beauty of his daughter. He himself
Calls her a nonpareil. I never saw a woman
But only Sycorax my dam and she;
But she as far surpasseth Sycorax
As great'st does least.

STEPHANO Is it so brave a lass?   104
CALIBAN Ay, lord. She will become thy bed, I warrant,   105
And bring thee forth brave brood.

STEPHANO Monster, I will kill this man. His daughter
and I will be king and queen—save Our Graces!—and
Trinculo and thyself shall be viceroys. Dost thou like
the plot, Trinculo?

TRINCULO Excellent.

STEPHANO Give me thy hand. I am sorry I beat thee;
but, while thou liv'st, keep a good tongue in thy head.

CALIBAN Within this half hour will he be asleep.
Wilt thou destroy him then?

STEPHANO Ay, on mine honor.

ARIEL *[aside]* This will I tell my master.

CALIBAN Thou mak'st me merry; I am full of pleasure.
Let us be jocund. Will you troll the catch   119
You taught me but whilere?   120

STEPHANO At thy request, monster, I will do reason,   121
any reason.—Come on, Trinculo, let us sing. *Sings.*   122
"Flout 'em and scout 'em   123
And scout 'em and flout 'em!
Thought is free."

CALIBAN That's not the tune.   126

Ariel plays the tune on a tabor and pipe.

STEPHANO What is this same?

TRINCULO This is the tune of our catch, played by the
picture of Nobody.   129

---

90 paunch stab in the belly **91 weasand** windpipe **93 sot** fool **96 brave utensils** fine furnishings **97
deck withal** furnish it with **104 brave** splendid, attractive **105 become** suit (sexually) **119 jocund**
jovial, merry. **troll the catch** sing the round **120 but whilere** only a short time ago. **121–2 reason,
any reason** anything reasonable. **123 Flout** Scoff at. **scout** deride **126.1 *tabor*** small drum **129 picture of Nobody** (Refers to a familiar figure with head, arms, and legs but no trunk.)

STEPHANO If thou be'st a man, show thyself in thy
    likeness. If thou be'st a devil, take't as thou list.   *131*

TRINCULO Oh, forgive me my sins!

STEPHANO He that dies pays all debts. I defy thee.   *133*
    Mercy upon us!

CALIBAN Art thou afeard?

STEPHANO No, monster, not I.

CALIBAN Be not afeard. The isle is full of noises,
    Sounds, and sweet airs, that give delight and hurt not.
    Sometimes a thousand twangling instruments
    Will hum about mine ears, and sometimes voices
    That, if I then had waked after long sleep,
    Will make me sleep again; and then, in dreaming,
    The clouds methought would open and show riches
    Ready to drop upon me, that when I waked
    I cried to dream again.   *145*

STEPHANO This will prove a brave kingdom to me,
    where I shall have my music for nothing.

CALIBAN When Prospero is destroyed.

STEPHANO That shall be by and by. I remember the   *149*
    story.

TRINCULO The sound is going away. Let's follow it,
    and after do our work.

STEPHANO Lead, monster; we'll follow. I would I could
    see this taborer! He lays it on.   *154*

TRINCULO Wilt come? I'll follow, Stephano.

    Exeunt [following Ariel's music].

3.3

    Enter Alonso, Sebastian, Antonio, Gonzalo, Adrian, Francisco, etc.

GONZALO By'r lakin, I can go no further, sir.   *1*
    My old bones aches. Here's a maze trod indeed
    Through forthrights and meanders! By your patience,   *3*
    I needs must rest me.

ALONSO   Old lord, I cannot blame thee,
    Who am myself attached with weariness,   *5*
    To th' dulling of my spirits. Sit down and rest.   *6*
    Even here I will put off my hope, and keep it
    No longer for my flatterer. He is drowned
    Whom thus we stray to find, and the sea mocks
    Our frustrate search on land. Well, let him go.   *10*

---

131 take't . . . list (A proverbial formula of bravado and defiance, as in *Romeo and Juliet*, 1.1.40–1.)
133 He . . . debts (Another proverbial swagger: Death settles all scores, I'm not afraid to fight.) **145
to dream** desirous of dreaming **149 by and by** very soon. **154 lays it on** i.e., plays the drum vigorously
3.3. Location: Another part of the island.
1 By'r lakin By our Ladykin, by our Lady **3 forthrights and meanders** paths straight and crooked. **5
attached with** seized by **6 To . . . spirits** to the point of being dull-spirited. **10 frustrate** frustrated

[Alonso and Gonzalo sit.]

ANTONIO *[aside to Sebastian]* I am right glad that he's so out of hope.
　Do not, for one repulse, forgo the purpose　　　　　　　　　　　*12*
　That you resolved t'effect.
SEBASTIAN *[to Antonio]*　　　The next advantage
　Will we take throughly.
ANTONIO *[to Sebastian]*　　Let it be tonight,　　　　　　　　　*14*
　For, now they are oppressed with travel, they　　　　　　　　*15*
　Will not, nor cannot, use such vigilance　　　　　　　　　　*16*
　As when they are fresh.
SEBASTIAN *[to Antonio]*　　I say tonight. No more.　　　　　*17*

　　Solemn and strange music; and Prospero on the top, invisible.

ALONSO What harmony is this? My good friends, hark!
GONZALO Marvelous sweet music!

　　Enter several strange shapes, bringing in a banquet, and dance about it with
　　gentle actions of salutations; and, inviting the King, etc., to eat, they depart.

ALONSO Give us kind keepers, heavens! What were these?　　　*20*
SEBASTIAN A living drollery. Now I will believe　　　　　　　*21*
　That there are unicorns; that in Arabia
　There is one tree, the phoenix' throne, one phoenix　　　　　*23*
　At this hour reigning there.
ANTONIO　　　　　　　　I'll believe both;
　And what does else want credit, come to me　　　　　　　　*25*
　And I'll be sworn 'tis true. Travelers ne'er did lie,
　Though fools at home condemn 'em.
GONZALO　　　　　　　　　　If in Naples
　I should report this now, would they believe me
　If I should say I saw such islanders?
　For, certes, these are people of the island,　　　　　　　　*30*
　Who, though they are of monstrous shape, yet note,
　Their manners are more gentle, kind, than of
　Our human generation you shall find
　Many, nay, almost any.
PROSPERO *[aside]*　　　　Honest lord,
　Thou hast said well, for some of you there present
　Are worse than devils.
ALONSO　　　　　　　I cannot too much muse　　　　　　*36*
　Such shapes, such gesture, and such sound, expressing—
　Although they want the use of tongue—a kind　　　　　　*38*

---

12 for because of **14 throughly** thoroughly. **15 now** now that. **travel** (Spelled "trauaile" in the Folio and carrying the sense of labor as well as traveling.) **16 use such vigilance** be as vigilant **17.1–2 on the top** at some high point of the tiring-house or the theater, on a third level above the gallery **20 kind keepers** guardian angels **21 living drollery** comic entertainment, caricature, or puppet show put on by live actors. **23 phoenix** mythical bird consumed to ashes every five hundred to six hundred years, only to be renewed into another cycle **25 want credit** lack credibility **30 certes** certainly **36 muse** wonder at **38 want** lack

Of excellent dumb discourse.

PROSPERO [aside]   Praise in departing.   39

FRANCISCO They vanished strangely.

SEBASTIAN   No matter, since

They have left their viands behind, for we have stomachs.   41

Will't please you taste of what is here?

ALONSO   Not I.

GONZALO Faith, sir, you need not fear. When we were boys,

Who would believe that there were mountaineers   44

Dewlapped like bulls, whose throats had hanging at 'em   45

Wallets of flesh? Or that there were such men   46

Whose heads stood in their breasts? Which now we find   47

Each putter-out of five for one will bring us   48

Good warrant of.

ALONSO   I will stand to and feed,   49

Although my last—no matter, since I feel   50

The best is past. Brother, my lord the Duke,   51

Stand to, and do as we.   [They approach the table.]   52

*Thunder and lightning. Enter Ariel, like a harpy, claps his wings upon the
table, and with a quaint device the banquet vanishes.*

ARIEL You are three men of sin, whom Destiny—   53

That hath to instrument this lower world   54

And what is in't—the never-surfeited sea   55

Hath caused to belch up you, and on this island   56

Where man doth not inhabit, you 'mongst men

Being most unfit to live. I have made you mad;

And even with suchlike valor men hang and drown   59

Their proper selves.[*Alonso, Sebastian, and Antonio draw their swords.*]

You fools! I and my fellows   60

Are ministers of Fate. The elements

Of whom your swords are tempered may as well   62

Wound the loud winds, or with bemocked-at stabs   63

Kill the still-closing waters, as diminish   64

One dowl that's in my plume. My fellow ministers   65

Are like invulnerable. If you could hurt,   66

---

39 Praise in departing i.e., Save your praise until the end of the performance. (Proverbial.) **41 viands**
provisions. **stomachs** appetites. **44 mountaineers** mountain dwellers **45 Dewlapped** having a dewlap,
or fold of skin hanging from the neck, like cattle **46 Wallets** pendent folds of skin, wattles **47 in their
breasts** (I.e., like the Anthropophagi described in *Othello*, 1.3.146.) **48 putter-out . . . one** one who
invests money or gambles on the risks of travel on the condition that the traveler who returns safely is
to receive five times the amount deposited; hence, any traveler **49 Good warrant** assurance. **stand to**
come forward, fall to. (Also in line 52.) **50 Although my last** even if this were to be my last meal **51
best** best part of life **52.1 harpy** a fabulous monster with a woman's face and breasts and a vulture's
body, supposed to be a minister of divine vengeance. **52.2–3 with . . . vanishes** by means of some ingenious stage contrivance, the food vanishes. (The table remains until line 82.) **53–6 whom . . . up**
you you whom Destiny, acting through this sublunary world as its instrument, has caused the ever-
hungry sea to belch up **59 suchlike valor** i.e., the reckless valor derived from madness **60 proper** own
62 whom which. **tempered** made hard **63 bemocked-at** scorned **64 still-closing** always closing again
when parted **65 dowl** soft, fine feather **66 like** likewise, similarly. **If** Even if

Your swords are now too massy for your strengths 67
And will not be uplifted. But remember—
For that's my business to you—that you three
From Milan did supplant good Prospero;
Exposed unto the sea, which hath requit it, 71
Him and his innocent child; for which foul deed
The powers, delaying, not forgetting, have
Incensed the seas and shores, yea, all the creatures,
Against your peace. Thee of thy son, Alonso,
They have bereft; and do pronounce by me
Ling'ring perdition, worse than any death 77
Can be at once, shall step by step attend
You and your ways; whose wraths to guard you from— 79
Which here, in this most desolate isle, else falls 80
Upon your heads—is nothing but heart's sorrow 81
And a clear life ensuing. 82

He vanishes in thunder; then, to soft music, enter the shapes again, and
dance, with mocks and mows, and carrying out the table.

PROSPERO Bravely the figure of this harpy hast thou 83
Performed, my Ariel; a grace it had devouring. 84
Of my instruction hast thou nothing bated 85
In what thou hadst to say. So, with good life 86
And observation strange, my meaner ministers 87
Their several kinds have done. My high charms work, 88
And these mine enemies are all knit up
In their distractions. They now are in my power; 90
And in these fits I leave them, while I visit
Young Ferdinand, whom they suppose is drowned,
And his and mine loved darling. *[Exit above.]*
GONZALO I'th' name of something holy, sir, why stand you 94
In this strange stare?
ALONSO Oh, it is monstrous, monstrous! 95
Methought the billows spoke and told me of it; 96
The winds did sing it to me, and the thunder,
That deep and dreadful organ pipe, pronounced
The name of Prosper; it did bass my trespass. 99
Therefor my son i'th'ooze is bedded; and

---

67 massy heavy **71 requit** requited, avenged **77 perdition** ruin, destruction **79 whose . . . from** to guard you from which heavenly wrath **80 else** otherwise **81 is nothing** there is no way **82 clear** unspotted, innocent **82.2–3 *mocks and mows*** mocking gestures and grimaces **83 Bravely** Finely, dashingly **84 a grace . . . devouring** your impersonation displayed a ravishing grace. (With a punning suggestion of having caused the banquet to disappear as if by consuming it.) **85 bated** abated, omitted **86–8 So . . . done** Similarly, my lesser spirits assisting you have done their various tasks with observant care and attention to detail. **90 distractions** trancelike state. **94–5 why . . . stare?** (Gonzalo was not addressed in Ariel's speech to the *three men of sin*, line 53, and is not, as they are, in a maddened state; see lines 105–7.) **95 it** i.e., my sin. (Also in line 96.) **96 billows** waves **99 bass my trespass** proclaim my trespass like a bass note on the music.

I'll seek him deeper than e'er plummet sounded,   101
And with him there lie mudded.   *Exit.*

SEBASTIAN But one fiend at a time,   103
I'll fight their legions o'er.

ANTONIO   I'll be thy second.   104

Exeunt [Sebastian and Antonio].

GONZALO All three of them are desperate. Their great guilt,   105
Like poison given to work a great time after.   106
Now 'gins to bite the spirits. I do beseech you,   107
That are of suppler joints, follow them swiftly   108
And hinder them from what this ecstasy   109
May now provoke them to.

ADRIAN   Follow, I pray you.

Exeunt omnes.

4.1

Enter Prospero, Ferdinand, and Miranda.

PROSPERO If I have too austerely punished you,
Your compensation makes amends, for I
Have given you here a third of mine own life,   3
Or that for which I live; who once again
I tender to thy hand. All thy vexations   5
Were but my trials of thy love, and thou
Hast strangely stood the test. Here, afore heaven,   7
I ratify this my rich gift. O Ferdinand,
Do not smile at me that I boast her off,   9
For thou shalt find she will outstrip all praise   11
Against an oracle.   12

PROSPERO Then, as my gift and thine own acquisition
Worthily purchased, take my daughter. But
If thou dost break her virgin-knot before
All sanctimonious ceremonies may   16
With full and holy rite be ministered,
No sweet aspersion shall the heavens let fall   18
To make this contract grow; but barren hate,
Sour-eyed disdain, and discord shall bestrew

---

101 than . . . sounded than ever a lead weight attached to a line tested the depth **103–4 But . . . o'er** If the demons come at me one at a time, I'll fight them all. **105 desperate** despairing and reckless. **106 Like . . . after** like poison, starting to work long after it has been administered **107 bite the spirits** sap their vital powers through anguish. **107–8 you . . . joints** Adrian, Francisco, and others not under Ariel's numbing spell **109 ecstasy** mad frenzy

4.1. Location: Before Prospero's cell.

3 a third i.e., Miranda, into whose education I have put a third of my life, or (less precisely) who represents a large part of what I have cared about, along with my dukedom and my magical art **5 tender** offer **7 strangely** exceptionally **9 boast her off** i.e., praise her so, or, perhaps an error for "boast of her"; the Folio reads "boast her of" **11 halt** limp **12 Against an oracle** even if an oracle should declare otherwise. **16 sanctimonious** sacred **18 aspersion** dew, shower

The union of your bed with weeds so loathly 21
That you shall hate it both. Therefore take heed.
As Hymen's lamps shall light you.

FERDINAND   As I hope 23
For quiet days, fair issue, and long life, 24
With such love as 'tis now, the murkiest den,
The most opportune place, the strong'st suggestion 26
Our worser genius can, shall never melt 27
Mine honor into lust, to take away 28
The edge of that day's celebration 29
When I shall think or Phoebus' steeds are foundered 30
Or Night kept chained below.

PROSPERO   Fairly spoke.
Sit then and talk with her. She is thine own.

[Ferdinand and Miranda sit and talk together.]

What, Ariel! My industrious servant, Ariel! 33

Enter Ariel.

ARIEL What would my potent master? Here I am.
PROSPERO Thou and thy meaner fellows your last service 35
Did worthily perform, and I must use you
In such another trick. Go bring the rabble, 37
O'er whom I give thee power, here to this place.
Incite them to quick motion, for I must
Bestow upon the eyes of this young couple
Some vanity of mine art. It is my promise, 41
And they expect it from me.

ARIEL   Presently? 42
PROSPERO Ay, with a twink. 43
ARIEL Before you can say "Come" and "Go,"
And breathe twice, and cry "So, so,"
Each one, tripping on his toe,
Will be here with mop and mow. 47
Do you love me, master? No?
PROSPERO Dearly, my delicate Ariel. Do not approach
Till thou dost hear me call.

ARIEL   Well; I conceive. *Exit.* 50

---

21 weeds (In place of the flowers customarily strewn on the marriage bed.) **23 As . . . you** i.e., as you long for happiness and concord in your marriage. (Hymen was the Greek and Roman god of marriage; his symbolic torches, the wedding torches, were supposed to burn brightly for a happy marriage and smokily for a troubled one.) **24 issue** offspring **26–7 the strong'st . . . can** the strongest temptation that the evil spirit within us can propose **28 to** so as to **29 edge** keen enjoyment, sexual ardor **30 or . . . foundered** either that the horses of the sun's chariot have gone lame (thus delaying the night for which I will be so eager) **33 What** Now then **35 meaner fellows** subordinates **37 trick** device. **rabble** band, i.e., the *meaner fellows* of line 35 **41 vanity** (1) illusion (2) trifle (3) desire for admiration, conceit **42 Presently?** Immediately? **43 with a twink** in the twinkling of an eye. **47 mop and mow** grimaces. **50 conceive** understand.

PROSPERO Look thou be true; do not give dalliance   51
  Too much the rein. The strongest oaths are straw
  To th' fire i'th' blood. Be more abstemious,
  Or else good night your vow!
FERDINAND   I warrant you, sir,   54
  The white cold virgin snow upon my heart   55
  Abates the ardor of my liver.
PROSPERO   Well.   56
  Now come, my Ariel! Bring a corollary,   57
  Rather than want a spirit. Appear, and pertly!—   58
  No tongue! All eyes! Be silent.   *Soft music.*   59

  Enter Iris.

IRIS Ceres, most bounteous lady, thy rich leas   60
  Of wheat, rye, barley, vetches, oats, and peas;   61
  Thy turfy mountains, where live nibbling sheep,
  And flat meads thatched with stover, them to keep;   63
  Thy banks with pionèd and twillèd brims,   64
  Which spongy April at thy hest betrims   65
  To make cold nymphs chaste crowns; and thy broom groves,   66
  Whose shadow the dismissèd bachelor loves,   67
  Being lass-lorn; thy poll-clipped vineyard;   68
  And thy sea marge, sterile and rocky hard,   69
  Where thou thyself dost air: the queen o'th' sky,   70
  Whose wat'ry arch and messenger am I,   71
  Bids thee leave these, and with her sovereign grace,   72

  Juno descends [slowly in her car].

  Here on this grass plot, in this very place,
  To come and sport. Her peacocks fly amain.   74
  Approach, rich Ceres, her to entertain.   75

  Enter Ceres.

CERES Hail, many-colored messenger, that ne'er
  Dost disobey the wife of Jupiter,
  Who with thy saffron wings upon my flowers   78
  Diffusest honeydrops, refreshing showers,

---

51 **true** true to your promise 54 **good night** i.e., say good-bye to. **warrant** guarantee 55 **The white
. . . heart** i.e., the chaste ideal to which my heart is devoted 56 **liver** (The presumed seat of the passions.) 57 **corollary** surplus, extra supply 58 **want** lack. **pertly** briskly. 59 **No tongue!** Quiet, everyone! 59.1 **Iris** goddess of the rainbow and Juno's messenger. 60 **Ceres** goddess of the generative
power of nature. **leas** meadows 61 **vetches** plants for forage, fodder 63 **meads** meadows. **stover** winter fodder for cattle 64 **pionèd and twillèd** undercut by the swift current and protected by roots and
branches that tangle to form a barricade 65 **spongy** wet. **hest** command 66 **broom groves** clumps of
broom, gorse, yellow-flowered shrub 67 **dismissèd bachelor** rejected male lover 68 **poll-clipped**
pruned, lopped at the top, or *pole-clipped*, "hedged in with poles" 69 **sea marge** shore 70 **thou . . . air**
you take the air, go for walks. **queen o'th' sky** i.e., Juno 71 **wat'ry arch** rainbow 72.1 *Juno descends*
i.e., starts her descent from the "heavens" above the stage 74 **peacocks** birds sacred to Juno and used
to pull her chariot. **amain** with full speed. 75 **entertain** receive. 78 **saffron** yellow

And with each end of thy blue bow dost crown   80
My bosky acres and my unshrubbed down,   81
Rich scarf to my proud earth. Why hath thy queen   82
Summoned me hither to this short-grassed green?
IRIS   A contract of true love to celebrate,
And some donation freely to estate   85
On the blest lovers.
CERES   Tell me, heavenly bow,
If Venus or her son, as thou dost know,   87
Do now attend the Queen? Since they did plot   88
The means that dusky Dis my daughter got,   89
Her and her blind boy's scandaled company   90
I have forsworn.
IRIS   Of her society   91
Be not afraid. I met Her Deity   92
Cutting the clouds towards Paphos, and her son   93
Dove-drawn with her. Here thought they to have done   94
Some wanton charm upon this man and maid,   95
Whose vows are that no bed-right shall be paid   96
Till Hymen's torch be lighted; but in vain.
Mars's hot minion is returned again;   98
Her waspish-headed son has broke his arrows,   99
Swears he will shoot no more, but play with sparrows   100
And be a boy right out.

[Juno alights.]

CERES   Highest Queen of state,   101
Great Juno, comes; I know her by her gait.   102
JUNO   How does my bounteous sister? Go with me   103
To bless this twain, that they may Prosperous be,
And honored in their issue.   *They sing:*   105
JUNO   Honor, riches, marriage blessing,
Long continuance, and increasing,
Hourly joys be still upon you!   108
Juno sings her blessings on you.
CERES   Earth's increase, foison plenty,   110
Barns and garners never empty,   111
Vines with clust'ring bunches growing,

---

80 **bow** rainbow 81 **bosky** wooded. **unshrubbed down** open upland 82 **scarf** (The rainbow is like a colored silk band adorning the earth.) 85 **estate** bestow 87 **son** i.e., Cupid. **as** as far as 88–91 **Since . . . forsworn** Since Venus and her blind son Cupid plotted the means by which Dis (Pluto) carried off my daughter Proserpina to be his bride in Hades, I have forsworn their scandalous company. 92 **Her Deity** i.e., Her Highness 93 **Paphos** place on the island of Cyprus, sacred to Venus 94 **Dove-drawn** (Venus's chariot was drawn by doves.) 94–5 **done . . . charm** inflicted some lustful spell 96 **that . . . paid** that their union will not be sexually consummated 98 **Mars's hot minion** i.e., Venus, the beloved of Mars. **returned** i.e., returned to Paphos 99 **waspish-headed** hotheaded, peevish 100 **sparrows** (Supposed lustful, and sacred to Venus.) 101 **right out** outright. **Highest . . . state** Most majestic Queen 102 **gait** i.e., majestic bearing 103 **sister** i.e., fellow goddess. 105 **issue** offspring. 108 **still** always 110 **foison plenty** plentiful harvest 111 **garners** granaries

Plants with goodly burden bowing;
Spring come to you at the farthest
In the very end of harvest!   115
Scarcity and want shall shun you;
Ceres' blessing so is on you.

FERDINAND This is a most majestic vision, and
    Harmonious charmingly. May I be bold   119
    To think these spirits?

PROSPERO   Spirits, which by mine art
    I have from their confines called to enact
    My present fancies.

FERDINAND   Let me live here ever!
    So rare a wondered father and a wife   123
    Makes this place Paradise.

Juno and Ceres whisper, and send Iris on employment.

PROSPERO   Sweet now, silence!
    Juno and Ceres whisper seriously;
    There's something else to do. Hush and be mute,
    Or else our spell is marred.

IRIS [*calling offstage*] You nymphs, called naiads, of the windring brooks,   128
    With your sedged crowns and ever-harmless looks,   129
    Leave your crisp channels, and on this green land   130
    Answer your summons; Juno does command.
    Come, temperate nymphs, and help to celebrate   132
    A contract of true love. Be not too late.

    Enter certain nymphs.

    You sunburned sicklemen, of August weary,   134
    Come hither from the furrow and be merry.   135
    Make holiday; your rye-straw hats put on,
    And these fresh nymphs encounter every one   137
    In country footing.   138

    Enter certain reapers, properly habited. They join with the nymphs in a grace-
    ful dance, towards the end whereof Prospero starts suddenly, and speaks; af-
    ter which, to a strange, hollow, and confused noise, they heavily vanish.

---

115 In . . . harvest i.e., with no winter in between. **119 charmingly** enchantingly. **123 wondered** wonder-performing, wondrous. **wise** (The Folio appears to read "wise" here, but with a tall "s" that resembles an "f," leading to much dispute over this reading. In some copies of the Folio the "s" looks like an "f," perhaps damaged, but evidently as the result of an inkblot, so that the true reading is "s." Even so, an error in transmission would be easy, so that the author's intention is uncertain. The matter bears importantly on whether or not Ferdinand includes Miranda in his vision of paradise.) **128 naiads** nymphs of springs, rivers, or lakes. **windring** wandering, winding (?) **129 sedged** made of reeds. **ever-harmless** ever innocent **130 crisp** curled, rippled **132 temperate** chaste **134 sicklemen** harvesters, field workers who cut down grain and grass. **of August weary** i.e., weary of the hard work of the harvest **135 furrow** i.e., plowed fields **137 encounter** join **138 country footing** country dancing. **138.1 *properly*** suitably. **138.5 *heavily*** slowly, dejectedly

PROSPERO *[aside]* I had forgot that foul conspiracy
   Of the beast Caliban and his confederates
   Against my life. The minute of their plot
   Is almost come. *[To the Spirits]* Well done! Avoid; no more! 142
FERDINAND *[to Miranda]* This is strange. Your father's in some passion
   That works him strongly.
MIRANDA   Never till this day 144
   Saw I him touched with anger so distempered.
PROSPERO
   You do look, my son, in a moved sort, 146
   As if you were dismayed. Be cheerful, sir.
   Our revels now are ended. These our actors, 148
   As I foretold you, were all spirits and
   Are melted into air, into thin air;
   And, like the baseless fabric of this vision, 151
   The cloud-capped towers, the gorgeous palaces,
   The solemn temples, the great globe itself, 153
   Yea, all which it inherit, shall dissolve, 154
   And, like this insubstantial pageant faded,
   Leave not a rack behind. We are such stuff 156
   As dreams are made on, and our little life 157
   Is rounded with a sleep. Sir, I am vexed. 158
   Bear with my weakness. My old brain is troubled.
   Be not disturbed with my infirmity. 160
   If you be pleased, retire into my cell 161
   And there repose. A turn or two I'll walk
   To still my beating mind.
FERDINAND, MIRANDA   We wish your peace. 163

   Exeunt [Ferdinand and Miranda].

PROSPERO Come with a thought! I thank thee, Ariel. Come. 164

   Enter Ariel.

ARIEL Thy thoughts I cleave to. What's thy pleasure? 165
PROSPERO   Spirit,
   We must prepare to meet with Caliban.
ARIEL Ay, my commander. When I presented Ceres, 167
   I thought to have told thee of it, but I feared
   Lest I might anger thee.
PROSPERO Say again, where didst thou leave these varlets?
ARIEL I told you, sir, they were red-hot with drinking;
   So full of valor that they smote the air

---

142 Avoid Withdraw **144 works** affects, agitates **146 moved sort** troubled state, condition **148 revels** entertainment, pageant **151 baseless fabric** unsubstantial theatrical edifice or contrivance **153 great globe** (With a glance at the Globe Theatre.) **154 which it inherit** who subsequently occupy it **156 rack** wisp of cloud **157 on** of **158 rounded** surrounded (before birth and after death), or crowned, rounded off **160 with** by **161 retire** withdraw, go **163 beating** agitated **164 with a thought** i.e., on the instant, or, summoned by my thought, no sooner thought of than here. **165 cleave** cling, adhere **167 presented** acted the part of, or, introduced

For breathing in their faces, beat the ground	
For kissing of their feet; yet always bending	174
Towards their project. Then I beat my tabor,	
At which, like unbacked colts, they pricked their ears,	176
Advanced their eyelids, lifted up their noses	177
As they smelt music. So I charmed their ears	178
That calflike they my lowing followed through	179
Toothed briers, sharp furzes, pricking gorse, and thorns,	180
Which entered their frail shins. At last I left them	
I'th' filthy-mantled pool beyond your cell,	182
There dancing up to th' chins, that the foul lake	
O'erstunk their feet.	

PROSPERO   This was well done, my bird.   184
    Thy shape invisible retain thou still.
    The trumpery in my house, go bring it hither,   186
    For stale to catch these thieves.

ARIEL   I go, I go   *Exit.*   187

PROSPERO A devil, a born devil, on whose nature
    Nurture can never stick; on whom my pains,
    Humanely taken, all, all lost, quite lost!
    And as with age his body uglier grows,
    So his mind cankers. I will plague them all,   192
    Even to roaring.

Enter Ariel, loaden with glistering apparel, etc.

        Come, hang them on this line.   193

[Ariel hangs up the showy finery; Prospero and Ariel remain, invisible.]
Enter Caliban, Stephano, and Trinculo, all wet.

CALIBAN Pray you, tread softly, that the blind mole may
    Not hear a foot fall. We now are near his cell.

STEPHANO Monster, your fairy, which you say is a
    harmless fairy, has done little better than played the
    jack with us.   198

TRINCULO Monster, I do smell all horse piss, at which
    my nose is in great indignation.

STEPHANO So is mine. Do you hear, monster? If I
    should take a displeasure against you, look you—

TRINCULO Thou wert but a lost monster.

CALIBAN Good my lord, give me thy favor still.
    Be patient, for the prize I'll bring thee to

---

174 bending aiming **176 unbacked** unbroken, unridden **177 Advanced** lifted up **178 As** as if **179 lowing** mooing **180 furzes . . . gorse** prickly shrubs **182 filthy-mantled** covered with a slimy coating **184 O'erstunk** smelled worse than, or, caused to stink terribly **186 trumpery** cheap goods, the *glistering apparel* mentioned in the following stage direction **187 stale** (1) decoy (2) out-of-fashion garments. (With possible further suggestions of "horse piss," as in line 199, and "steal," pronounced like *stale*. For *stale* could also mean "fit for a prostitute.") **192 cankers** festers, grows malignant. **193 line** lime tree or linden. **193.1–2** *Prospero and Ariel remain* (The staging is uncertain. They may instead exit here and return with the spirits at line 256.) **198 jack** (1) knave (2) will-o'-the-wisp

Shall hoodwink this mischance. Therefore speak softly.   206
  All's hushed as midnight yet.

TRINCULO Ay, but to lose our bottles in the pool—

STEPHANO There is not only disgrace and dishonor in
  that, monster, but an infinite loss.

TRINCULO That's more to me than my wetting. Yet this
  is your harmless fairy, monster!

STEPHANO I will fetch off my bottle, though I be o'er   213
  ears for my labor.   214

CALIBAN Prithee, my king, be quiet. See'st thou here,
  This is the mouth o'th' cell. No noise, and enter.
  Do that good mischief which may make this island
  Thine own forever, and I thy Caliban
  For aye thy footlicker.

STEPHANO Give me thy hand. I do begin to have bloody thoughts.

TRINCULO *[seeing the finery]* O King Stephano! O peer!   222
  O worthy Stephano! Look what a wardrobe here is
    for thee!

CALIBAN Let it alone, thou fool, it is but trash.

TRINCULO Oho, monster! We know what belongs to a
  frippery. O King Stephano!   *[He puts on a gown.]*   227

STEPHANO Put off that gown, Trinculo. By this hand,
  I'll have that gown.

TRINCULO Thy Grace shall have it.

CALIBAN The dropsy drown this fool! What do you mean   231
  To dote thus on such luggage? Let 't alone   232
  And do the murder first. If he awake,
  From toe to crown he'll fill our skins with pinches,   234
  Make us strange stuff.

STEPHANO Be you quiet, monster.—Mistress line, is   236
  not this my jerkin? *[He takes it down.]* Now is the jerkin   237
  under the line. Now, jerkin, you are like to lose your   238
  hair and prove a bald jerkin.   239

TRINCULO Do, do! We steal by line and level, an 't like   240
  Your Grace.

---

206 hoodwink this mischance cover up (literally, blindfold) this mistake. **213–14 o'er ears** over my ears in the filthy horse pond (line 182) **222 King . . . peer** (Alludes to the old ballad beginning, "King Stephen was a worthy peer.") **227 frippery** second-hand-clothing shop. (Trinculo knows that what they have just found is much finer.) **231 The dropsy drown** (An oath. *Dropsy* is a disease characterized by the accumulation of fluid in the connective tissue of the body.) **232 luggage** cumbersome trash. **234 crown** head **236 Mistress line** (Addressed to the linden or lime tree upon which, at line 193, Ariel hung the *glistering apparel*.) **237 jerkin** jacket made of leather **238 under the line** under the lime tree. (With punning sense of being south of the equinoctial line or equator; sailors on long voyages to the southern regions were popularly supposed to lose their hair from scurvy or other diseases. Stephano also quibbles bawdily on losing hair through syphilis, and puns in *Mistress* and *jerkin*.) **like** likely **239 bald** (1) hairless, napless (2) meager **240 Do, do!** i.e., Bravo! (Said in response to the jesting or to the taking of the jerkin, or both.) **steal . . . level** i.e., steal by means of plumb line and carpenter's level, methodically. (With pun on line, "lime tree," line 238, and *steal*, pronounced like *stale*, i.e., prostitute, continuing Stephano's bawdy quibble.) **an 't like** if it please

STEPHANO I thank thee for that jest. Here's a garment
　　　for't. *[He gives a garment.]* Wit shall not go unrewarded
　　　while I am king of this country. "Steal by line and
　　　level" is an excellent pass of pate. There's another   245
　　　garment for't.
TRINCULO Monster, come, put some lime upon your   247
　　　fingers, and away with the rest.
CALIBAN I will have none on't. We shall lose our time,
　　　And all be turned to barnacles, or to apes   250
　　　With foreheads villainous low.   251
STEPHANO Monster, lay to your fingers. Help to bear   252
　　　this away where my hogshead of wine is, or I'll turn   253
　　　you out of my kingdom. Go to, carry this.   254
TRINCULO And this.
STEPHANO Ay, and this.

　　　[They load Caliban with more and more garments.]
　　　　A noise of hunters heard. Enter divers spirits, in shape of dogs and
　　　hounds, hunting them about, Prospero and Ariel setting them on.

PROSPERO Hey, Mountain, hey!
ARIEL Silver! There it goes, Silver!
PROSPERO Fury, Fury! There, Tyrant, there! Hark! Hark!

　　　[Caliban, Stephano, and Trinculo are driven out.]
　　　Go, charge my goblins that they grind their joints
　　　With dry convulsions, shorten up their sinews   261
　　　With agèd cramps, and more pinch-spotted make them   262
　　　Than pard or cat o' mountain.
ARIEL　　　　　　　　　　　　　　Hark, they roar!   263
PROSPERO Let them be hunted soundly. At this hour   264
　　　Lies at my mercy all mine enemies.
　　　Shortly shall all my labors end, and thou
　　　Shalt have the air at freedom. For a little   267
　　　Follow, and do me service.　　　　　　　　　　　 *Exeunt.*

5.1

　　　Enter Prospero in his magic robes, [with his staff,] and Ariel.

PROSPERO Now does my project gather to a head.
　　　My charms crack not, my spirits obey, and Time   2
　　　Goes upright with his carriage. How's the day?   3

---

245 pass of pate sally of wit. (The metaphor is from fencing.) **247 lime** birdlime, sticky substance
(to give Caliban sticky fingers) **250 barnacles** barnacle geese, formerly supposed to be hatched from
barnacles attached to trees or to rotting timber; here, evidently used, like apes, as types of simpletons
251 villainous vilely **252 lay to** start using **253 this** i.e., the *glistering apparel.* **hogshead** large cask
254 Go to (An expression of exhortation or remonstrance.) **261 dry convulsions** racking cramps
262 agèd characteristic of old age **263 pard** panther or leopard. **cat o' mountain** wildcat. **264
soundly** severely. **267 little** little while longer
5.1. Location: Before Prospero's cell.
2 crack collapse, fail. (The metaphor is probably alchemical, as in *project* and *gather to a head*, line 1.)
3 his carriage its burden. (Time is no longer heavily burdened and so can go *upright*, "standing
straight and unimpeded.")

ARIEL On the sixth hour, at which time, my lord,   4
    You said our work should cease.

PROSPERO   I did say so,
    When first I raised the tempest. Say, my spirit,
    How fares the King and's followers?

ARIEL   Confined together
    In the same fashion as you gave in charge,
    Just as you left them; all prisoners, sir,
    In the line grove which weather-fends your cell.   10
    They cannot budge till your release. The King,   11
    His brother, and yours abide all three distracted,   12
    And the remainder mourning over them,
    Brim full of sorrow and dismay; but chiefly
    Him that you termed, sir, the good old lord, Gonzalo.
    His tears runs down his beard like winter's drops
    From eaves of reeds. Your charm so strongly works 'em   17
    That if you now beheld them your affections   18
    Would become tender.

PROSPERO   Dost thou think so, spirit?

ARIEL Mine would, sir, were I human.

PROSPERO   And mine shall.
    Hast thou, which art but air, a touch, a feeling   21
    Of their afflictions, and shall not myself,
    One of their kind, that relish all as sharply   23
    Passion as they, be kindlier moved than thou art?   24
    Though with their high wrongs I am struck to th' quick,
    Yet with my nobler reason 'gainst my fury
    Do I take part. The rarer action is   27
    In virtue than in vengeance. They being penitent,
    The sole drift of my purpose doth extend
    Not a frown further. Go release them, Ariel.
    My charms I'll break, their senses I'll restore,
    And they shall be themselves.

ARIEL   I'll fetch them, sir.

    Exit.

      [Prospero traces a charmed circle with his staff.]

PROSPERO Ye elves of hills, brooks, standing lakes, and groves,   33
    And ye that on the sands with printless foot
    Do chase the ebbing Neptune, and do fly him
    When he comes back; you demi-puppets that   36
    By moonshine do the green sour ringlets make,   37

---

4 On Approaching **10 line grove** grove of lime trees. **weather-fends** protects from the weather **11 your release** you release them. **12 distracted** out of their wits **17 eaves of reeds** thatched roofs. **18 affections** disposition, feelings **21 touch** sense, apprehension **23–4 that . . . they** I who experience human passions as acutely as they **24 kindlier** (1) more sympathetically (2) more naturally, humanly **27 rarer** nobler **33 Ye . . . groves** (This passage, down through line 50, is an embellished paraphrase of Golding's translation of Ovid's *Metamorphoses*, 7.197–219.) **36 demi-puppets** puppets of half size, i.e., elves and fairies **37 green sour ringlets** fairy rings, circles in grass (actually produced by mushrooms)

Whereof the ewe not bites; and you whose pastime
Is to make midnight mushrooms, that rejoice   39
To hear the solemn curfew; by whose aid,   40
Weak masters though ye be, I have bedimmed   41
The noontide sun, called forth the mutinous winds,
And twixt the green sea and the azured vault   43
Set roaring war; to the dread rattling thunder   44
Have I given fire, and rifted Jove's stout oak   45
With his own bolt; the strong-based promontory   46
Have I made shake, and by the spurs plucked up   47
The pine and cedar; graves at my command
Have waked their sleepers, oped, and let 'em forth
By my so potent art. But this rough magic   50
I here abjure, and when I have required   51
Some heavenly music—which even now I do—
To work mine end upon their senses that   53
This airy charm is for, I'll break my staff,
Bury it certain fathoms in the earth,
And deeper than did ever plummet sound
I'll drown my book.   *Solemn music.*

*Here enters Ariel before; then Alonso, with a frantic gesture, attended by
Gonzalo; Sebastian and Antonio in like manner, attended by Adrian and
Francisco. They all enter the circle which Prospero had made, and there stand
charmed; which Prospero observing, speaks:*

[*To Alonso*] A solemn air, and the best comforter   58
To an unsettled fancy, cure thy brains,   59
Now useless, boiled within thy skull!
    [*To Sebastian and Antonio*] There stand,   60
For you are spell-stopped.—
Holy Gonzalo, honorable man,
Mine eyes, e'en sociable to the show of thine,   63
Fall fellowly drops. [*Aside*] The charm dissolves apace,   64
And as the morning steals upon the night,
Melting the darkness, so their rising senses
Begin to chase the ignorant fumes that mantle   67
Their clearer reason.—O good Gonzalo,   68
My true preserver, and a loyal sir
To him thou follow'st! I will pay thy graces   70
Home both in word and deed.—Most cruelly   71

---

39 midnight mushrooms mushrooms appearing overnight **40 curfew** evening bell, usually rung at
nine o'clock, ushering in the time when spirits are abroad **41 Weak masters** i.e., subordinate spirits,
as in 4.1.35. **43 the azured vault** i.e., the sky **44–5 to . . . fire** I have discharged the dread rattling
thunderbolt **45 rifted** riven, split. **oak** a tree that was sacred to Jove **46 bolt** thunderbolt **47 spurs**
roots **50 rough** violent **51 required** demanded **53 their senses that** the senses of those whom **58 air**
song. **and** i.e., which is **59 fancy** imagination **60 boiled** i.e., extremely agitated **63 sociable** sympathetic. **show** appearance **64 Fall** let fall **67 ignorant fumes** fumes that render them incapable of
comprehension. **mantle** envelop **68 clearer** growing clearer **70 pay thy graces** requite your favors
and virtues **71 Home** fully

Didst thou, Alonso, use me and my daughter.
Thy brother was a furtherer in the act.—   73
Thou art pinched for't now, Sebastian. *[To Antonio]*
Flesh and blood,   74
You, brother mine, that entertained ambition,
Expelled remorse and nature, whom, with Sebastian,   76
Whose inward pinches therefore are most strong,
Would here have killed your king, I do forgive thee,
Unnatural though thou art.—Their understanding
Begins to swell, and the approaching tide
Will shortly fill the reasonable shore   81
That now lies foul and muddy. Not one of them
That yet looks on me, or would know me.—Ariel,
Fetch me the hat and rapier in my cell.

[Ariel goes to the cell and returns immediately.]

I will discase me and myself present   85
As I was sometime Milan. Quickly, spirit!   86
Thou shalt ere long be free.

Ariel sings and helps to attire him.

ARIEL   Where the bee sucks, there suck I.
In a cowslip's bell I lie;
There I couch when owls do cry.
On the bat's back I do fly   90
After summer merrily.
Merrily, merrily shall I live now   92
Under the blossom that hangs on the bough.
PROSPERO   Why, that's my dainty Ariel! I shall miss thee,
But yet thou shalt have freedom. So, so, so.   96
To the King's ship, invisible as thou art!
There shalt thou find the mariners asleep
Under the hatches. The Master and the Boatswain
Being awake, enforce them to this place,
And presently, I prithee.   101
ARIEL   I drink the air before me, and return
Or ere your pulse twice beat.   *Exit.*   103
GONZALO   All torment, trouble, wonder, and amazement
Inhabits here. Some heavenly power guide us
Out of this fearful country!
PROSPERO   Behold, sir King,   106
The wrongèd Duke of Milan, Prospero.
For more assurance that a living prince

---

73 furtherer accomplice **74 pinched** punished, afflicted **76 remorse and nature** pity and natural feeling. **whom** you who **81 reasonable shore** shores of reason, i.e., minds. (Their reason returns, like the incoming tide.) **85 discase** disrobe **86 As . . . Milan** in my former appearance as Duke of Milan. **90 couch** lie **92 After summer** following summer as it moves to various parts of the world **96 So, so, so** (Expresses approval of Ariel's help as valet.) **101 presently** immediately **103 Or ere** before **106 fearful** frightening

Does now speak to thee, I embrace thy body;
And to thee and thy company I bid
A hearty welcome.   *[Embracing him.]*

ALONSO   Whe'er thou be'st he or no,
Or some enchanted trifle to abuse me,   112
As late I have been, I not know. Thy pulse   113
Beats as of flesh and blood; and, since I saw thee,
Th' affliction of my mind amends, with which
I fear a madness held me. This must crave—   116
An if this be at all—a most strange story.   117
Thy dukedom I resign, and do entreat   118
Thou pardon me my wrongs. But how should
Prospero   119
Be living, and be here?
PROSPERO *[to Gonzalo]* First, noble friend,
Let me embrace thine age, whose honor cannot   121
Be measured or confined.   *[Embracing him.]*
GONZALO   Whether this be
Or be not, I'll not swear.
PROSPERO   You do yet taste
Some subtleties o'th'isle, that will not let you   124
Believe things certain. Welcome, my friends all!
[Aside to Sebastian and Antonio] But you, my brace of
    lords, were I so minded,   126
I here could pluck His Highness' frown upon you
And justify you traitors. At this time   128
I will tell no tales.
SEBASTIAN   The devil speaks in him.
PROSPERO   No.
[To Antonio] For you, most wicked sir, whom to call brother
Would even infect my mouth, I do forgive
Thy rankest fault—all of them; and require
My dukedom of thee, which perforce I know
Thou must restore.
ALONSO   If thou be'st Prospero,
Give us particulars of thy preservation,
How thou hast met us here, whom three hours since   136
Were wrecked upon this shore; where I have lost—
How sharp the point of this remembrance is!—
My dear son Ferdinand.
PROSPERO   I am woe for't, sir.   139
ALONSO Irreparable is the loss, and Patience
    Says it is past her cure.

---

112 **trifle** trick of magic. **abuse** deceive 113 **late** lately 116 **crave** require 117 **An . . . all** if this is actually happening. **story** i.e., explanation. 118 **Thy . . . resign** (Alonso made arrangement with Antonio at the time of Prospero's banishment for Milan to pay tribute to Naples; see 1.2.113–27.) 119 **wrongs** wrongdoings. 121 **thine age** your venerable self 124 **subtleties** illusions, magical powers. (Playing on the idea of "pastries, concoctions.") 126 **brace** pair 128 **justify you** prove you to be 136 **whom** we who 139 **woe** sorry

PROSPERO   I rather think
   You have not sought her help, of whose soft grace
   For the like loss I have her sovereign aid   143
   And rest myself content.
ALONSO   You the like loss?
PROSPERO As great to me as late, and supportable   145
   To make the dear loss, have I means much weaker   146
   Than you may call to comfort you; for I   147
   Have lost my daughter.
ALONSO   A daughter?
   O heavens, that they were living both in Naples,
   The king and queen there! That they were, I wish   151
   Myself were mudded in that oozy bed   152
   Where my son lies. When did you lose your daughter?   153
PROSPERO In this last tempest. I perceive these lords
   At this encounter do so much admire   155
   That they devour their reason and scarce think   156
   Their eyes do offices of truth, their words   157
   Are natural breath. But, howsoever you have   158
   Been jostled from your senses, know for certain
   That I am Prospero and that very duke
   Which was thrust forth of Milan, who most strangely   161
   Upon this shore, where you were wrecked, was landed
   To be the lord on't. No more yet of this,
   For 'tis a chronicle of day by day,   164
   Not a relation for a breakfast nor
   Befitting this first meeting. Welcome, sir.
   This cell's my court. Here have I few attendants,
   And subjects none abroad. Pray you, look in.   168
   My dukedom since you have given me again,
   I will requite you with as good a thing,   170
   At least bring forth a wonder to content ye
   As much as me my dukedom.   172

Here Prospero discovers Ferdinand and Miranda, playing at chess.

MIRANDA Sweet lord, you play me false.   173
FERDINAND No, my dearest love,
   I would not for the world.
MIRANDA Yes, for a score of kingdoms you should wrangle,   176
   And I would call it fair play.

---

143 sovereign efficacious **145 late** recent **145–7 and supportable . . . you** and I have much weaker means to make my loss supportable than you can call upon to comfort you **151–3 That . . . lies** I would wish myself buried in that muddy bed where my son's body lies drowned if that would somehow make them alive and reigning in Naples. **155 admire** wonder **156 devour their reason** i.e., are openmouthed, dumbfounded **156–8 and scarce . . . breath** and scarcely can believe their eyes or their own words. **161 of** from **164 of day by day** requiring days to tell, or covering a long span of time **168 abroad** anywhere else. **170 requite** repay **172.1 discovers** i.e., by opening a curtain, presumably rearstage **173 play me false** cheat. **176–7 Yes . . . play** i.e., Yes, even if we were playing for twenty kingdoms, something less than the whole world, you would still press your advantage against me, and I would lovingly let you do it as though it were fair play.

ALONSO   If this prove   177
    A vision of the island, one dear son   178
    Shall I twice lose.
SEBASTIAN   A most high miracle!
FERDINAND *[approaching his father]*
    Though the seas threaten, they are merciful;
    I have cursed them without cause.   *[He kneels.]*
ALONSO   Now all the blessings
    Of a glad father compass thee about!   182
    Arise, and say how thou cam'st here.

    [Ferdinand rises.]

MIRANDA   Oh, wonder!
    How many goodly creatures are there here!
    How beauteous mankind is! Oh, brave new world   185
    That has such people in't!
PROSPERO   'Tis new to thee.
ALONSO What is this maid with whom thou wast at play?
    Your eld'st acquaintance cannot be three hours.   188
    Is she the goddess that hath severed us,
    And brought us thus together?
FERDINAND   Sir, she is mortal;
    But by immortal Providence she's mine.
    I chose her when I could not ask my father
    For his advice, nor thought I had one. She
    Is daughter to this famous Duke of Milan,
    Of whom so often I have heard renown,
    But never saw before; of whom I have
    Received a second life; and second father
    This lady makes him to me.
ALONSO   I am hers.
    But oh, how oddly will it sound that I
    Must ask my child forgiveness!
PROSPERO   There, sir, stop.
    Let us not burden our remembrances with
    A heaviness that's gone.
GONZALO   I have inly wept,   202
    Or should have spoke ere this. Look down, you gods,
    And on this couple drop a blessèd crown!
    For it is you that have chalked forth the way   205
    Which brought us hither.
ALONSO   I say amen, Gonzalo!
GONZALO Was Milan thrust from Milan, that his issue   207
    Should become kings of Naples? Oh, rejoice
    Beyond a common joy, and set it down

---

178 vision illusion **182 compass** encompass, embrace **185 brave** splendid, gorgeously appareled, handsome **188 eld'st** longest **202 heaviness** sadness. **inly** inwardly **205 chalked . . . way** marked as with a piece of chalk the pathway **207 Was Milan** Was the Duke of Milan. **issue** child

With gold on lasting pillars: In one voyage
Did Claribel her husband find at Tunis,
And Ferdinand, her brother, found a wife
Where he himself was lost; Prospero his dukedom
In a poor isle; and all of us ourselves   214
When no man was his own.

ALONSO *[to Ferdinand and Miranda]* Give me your hands.   215
Let grief and sorrow still embrace his heart   216
That doth not wish you joy!

GONZALO   Be it so! Amen!

Enter Ariel, with the Master and Boatswain amazedly following.

Oh, look, sir, look, sir! Here is more of us.
I prophesied, if a gallows were on land,
This fellow could not drown.—Now, blasphemy,   220
That swear'st grace o'erboard, not an oath on shore?   221
Hast thou no mouth by land? What is the news?

BOATSWAIN The best news is that we have safely found
Our King and company; the next, our ship—
Which, but three glasses since, we gave out split—   225
Is tight and yare and bravely rigged as when   226
We first put out to sea.

ARIEL *[aside to Prospero]* Sir, all this service
Have I done since I went.

PROSPERO *[aside to Ariel]*   My tricksy spirit!   228

ALONSO These are not natural events; they strengthen   229
From strange to stranger. Say, how came you hither?

BOATSWAIN If I did think, sir, I were well awake,
I'd strive to tell you. We were dead of sleep,   232
And—how we know not—all clapped under hatches,
Where but even now, with strange and several noises   234
Of roaring, shrieking, howling, jingling chains,
And more diversity of sounds, all horrible,
We were awaked; straightway at liberty;
Where we, in all her trim, freshly beheld
Our royal, good, and gallant ship, our Master
Cap'ring to eye her. On a trice, so please you,   240
Even in a dream, were we divided from them   241
And were brought moping hither.   242

ARIEL *[aside to Prospero]*   Was't well done?

PROSPERO *[aside to Ariel]* Bravely, my diligence. Thou shalt be free.

214–15 all . . . own all of us have found ourselves and our sanity when we all had lost our senses.
216 still always. **his** that person's **220 blasphemy** i.e., blasphemer **221 That swear'st grace o'erboard** i.e., you who expel heavenly grace from the ship by your blasphemies. **not an oath** aren't you
going to swear an oath **225 glasses** hourglasses. **gave out split** reported shipwrecked, gave up for lost
226 yare ready. **bravely** splendidly **228 tricksy** ingenious, sportive **229 strengthen** increase **232
dead of sleep** deep in sleep **234 several** diverse **240 Cap'ring to eye** dancing for joy to see. **On a
trice** In an instant **241 them** i.e., the other crew members **242 moping** in a daze

ALONSO This is as strange a maze as e'er men trod,
    And there is in this business more than nature
    Was ever conduct of. Some oracle   246
    Must rectify our knowledge.
PROSPERO   Sir, my liege,
    Do not infest your mind with beating on   248
    The strangeness of this business. At picked leisure,   249
    Which shall be shortly, single I'll resolve you,   250
    Which to you shall seem probable, of every   251
    These happened accidents; till when, be cheerful   252
    And think of each thing well. [Aside to Ariel] Come hither, spirit.   253
    Set Caliban and his companions free.
    Untie the spell.   [Exit Ariel.]
    [To Alonso] How fares my gracious sir?
    There are yet missing of your company
    Some few odd lads that you remember not.   257

*Enter Ariel, driving in Caliban, Stephano, and Trinculo, in their stolen
apparel.*

STEPHANO Every man shift for all the rest, and let no   258
    man take care for himself; for all is but fortune. Coraggio,   259
    bully monster, coraggio!   260
TRINCULO If these be true spies which I wear in my   261
    head, here's a goodly sight.
CALIBAN O Setebos, these be brave spirits indeed!   263
    How fine my master is! I am afraid   264
    He will chastise me.
SEBASTIAN Ha, ha!
    What things are these, my lord Antonio?
    Will money buy 'em?
ANTONIO   Very like. One of them
    Is a plain fish, and no doubt marketable.
PROSPERO Mark but the badges of these men, my lords,   270
    Then say if they be true. This misshapen knave,   271
    His mother was a witch, and one so strong
    That could control the moon, make flows and ebbs,
    And deal in her command without her power.   274
    These three have robbed me, and this demidevil—
    For he's a bastard one—had plotted with them   276
    To take my life. Two of these fellows you

---

246 **conduct** director 248 **infest** harass, disturb. **beating on** worrying about 249 **picked** chosen, convenient 250 **single** privately. **resolve** satisfy, explain to 251 **probable** plausible 251–2 **of every These** about every one of these 252 **accidents** occurrences 253 **well** favorably. 257 **odd** unaccounted for 258–9 **Every . . . himself** (Stephano drunkenly inverts the saying "Every man for himself.") 259–60 **Coraggio . . . monster** Have courage, gallant monster 261 **true spies** accurate observers (i.e., sharp eyes) 263 **brave** handsome 264 **fine** splendidly attired 270 **badges** emblems worn by servants to indicate whom they serve 271 **say . . . true** say if they are worthy and loyal servants. 274 **And . . . power** and usurp the moon's command (over tides) without her authority. (Sycorax could control the moon and hence the tides.) 276 **bastard** counterfeit

Must know and own. This thing of darkness I 278
    Acknowledge mine.
CALIBAN   I shall be pinched to death.
ALONSO Is not this Stephano, my drunken butler?
SEBASTIAN He is drunk now. Where had he wine?
ALONSO And Trinculo is reeling ripe. Where should they 282
    Find this grand liquor that hath gilded 'em? 283
    [To Trinculo] How cam'st thou in this pickle? 284
TRINCULO I have been in such a pickle since I saw you
    last that, I fear me, will never out of my bones. I shall
    not fear flyblowing. 287
SEBASTIAN Why, how now, Stephano?
STEPHANO Oh, touch me not! I am not Stephano, but a cramp.
PROSPERO You'd be king o'the isle, sirrah? 291
STEPHANO I should have been a sore one, then. 292
ALONSO *[pointing to Caliban]* This is a strange thing as e'er I looked on.
PROSPERO He is as disproportioned in his manners
    As in his shape.—Go, sirrah, to my cell.
    Take with you your companions. As you look
    To have my pardon, trim it handsomely. 297
CALIBAN Ay, that I will; and I'll be wise hereafter
    And seek for grace. What a thrice-double ass 299
    Was I to take this drunkard for a god
    And worship this dull fool!
PROSPERO   Go to. Away!
ALONSO Hence, and bestow your luggage where you found it.
SEBASTIAN   Or stole it, rather.

    [Exeunt Caliban, Stephano, and Trinculo.]

PROSPERO Sir, I invite Your Highness and your train
    To my poor cell, where you shall take your rest
    For this one night; which, part of it, I'll waste 306
    With such discourse as, I not doubt, shall make it
    Go quick away: the story of my life,
    And the particular accidents gone by 309
    Since I came to this isle. And in the morn
    I'll bring you to your ship, and so to Naples,
    Where I have hope to see the nuptial
    Of these our dear-belovèd solemnized;
    And thence retire me to my Milan, where
    Every third thought shall be my grave.
ALONSO   I long
    To hear the story of your life, which must
    Take the ear strangely. 317

---

278 own acknowledge. **282 reeling ripe** staggeringly drunk. **283 gilded 'em** flushed their complexion (from the drink), giving them a ruddy or gilded appearance. **284 pickle** (1) fix, predicament (2) pickling brine (in this case, horse urine). **287 flyblowing** i.e., being fouled by fly eggs (from which he is saved by being pickled). **291 sirrah** (Standard form of address to an inferior, here expressing reprimand.) **292 sore** (1) tyrannical (2) sorry, inept (3) wracked by pain **297 trim** prepare, decorate **299 grace** pardon, favor. **306 waste** spend **309 accidents** occurrences. **317 Take** take effect upon, enchant.

PROSPERO   I'll deliver all;   317
  And promise you calm seas, auspicious gales,
  And sail so expeditious that shall catch   319
  Your royal fleet far off. [Aside to Ariel] My Ariel, chick,   320
  That is thy charge. Then to the elements
  Be free, and fare thou well!
  [To the others] Please you, draw near.   322

     Exeunt omnes [except Prospero].

EPILOGUE SPOKEN BY

PROSPERO. Now my charms are all o'erthrown,
  And what strength I have 's mine own,
  Which is most faint. Now, 'tis true,
  I must be here confined by you
  Or sent to Naples. Let me not,
  Since I have my dukedom got
  And pardoned the deceiver, dwell
  In this bare island by your spell,
  But release me from my bands   9
  With the help of your good hands.   10
  Gentle breath of yours my sails   11
  Must fill, or else my project fails,
  Which was to please. Now I want   13
  Spirits to enforce, art to enchant,
  And my ending is despair,
  Unless I be relieved by prayer,   16
  Which pierces so that it assaults   17
  Mercy itself, and frees all faults.   18
  As you from crimes would pardoned be,   19
  Let your indulgence set me free.   *Exit.*   20

The Tempest in Performance

The scarcity of stage directions and a desire to experiment with special effects
has encouraged actors and directors to devise novel ways of presenting *The Tempest*. A classic example occurs in the opening scene. The setting is the deck of a
ship in a storm, with the sailors working hard to steer clear of threatening rocks,
while the party of royal courtiers distracts the crew by reminding them about the
importance of their passengers. We find out later that this storm has been

---

317 deliver declare, relate **319–20 catch . . . far off** enable you to catch up with the main part of your
royal fleet, now afar off en route to Naples. (See 1.2.235–6.) **322 draw near** i.e., enter my cell
Epilogue.
9 bands bonds **10 hands** i.e., applause (the noise of which could break a charm). **11 Gentle breath**
Favorable breeze (produced by hands clapping or favorable comment) **13 want** lack **16 prayer** i.e.,
Prospero's petition to the audience **17 assaults** penetrates the heart of **18 frees** obtains forgiveness
for **19 crimes** sins **20 indulgence** (1) humoring, lenient approval (2) remission of punishment for sin

The Tempest.

conjured up by the exiled duke, Prospero, now the ruler of a nearby island, the very man the royal party overthrew twelve years before. His agent in creating the storm is the sprite Ariel, who doesn't appear in a speaking role until later in the play. Modern stage productions often play up the storm with special effects , though in Shakespeare's day the theater did not employ many. But some directors have gone further by placing either Prospero or Ariel in the opening scene: above the storm, managing its effects, and unseen by the crew on the ship below. The stage directions make no mention of this, but then, these directions might not have been written by Shakespeare.

Is this placement of Ariel or Prospero warranted? Without one of them present, we have a storm with sailors and royals at the mercy of the elements. With Ariel hovering above, we have a storm that is being managed, with sailors and royals at the mercy of a spirit figure. These two very different dramatic situations make for different impressions in the theater. Is one rendering right? Is the second less "serious"? Less threatening? Some directors would argue that if the way a scene is played grips the audience, it is right. Literalists would differ, saying it may "work" on the audience, but it is no longer Shakespeare. Who is right and who is wrong? Or is there room for both in different productions?

Consider another example. In Act 1, Scene 2, we first meet Caliban, just after Prospero, in a long, beautifully managed piece of exposition, explains to Miranda how they got to the island. Caliban is listed in the cast of characters (which, like the stage directions, may not have been written by Shakespeare) as "a savage and deformed slave"; elsewhere he is called "a monster" by other characters. In Scene 2, Prospero rebukes Caliban:

> thou didst seek to violate
> the honor of my child. (351–2)

That is, he had tried to rape her. Caliban, unrepentant, replies,

> Oho, oho! Would 't had been done!
> Thou didst prevent me. I had peopled else
> This isle with Calibans. (353–5)

At this point Miranda breaks in sharply, finishing Caliban's line and addressing him in vituperative language, her longest and strongest speech in the play:

> Abhorrèd slave,
> which any print of goodness wilt not take,
> Being capable of all ill! (355–7)

The editors of some editions of Shakespeare's plays have been dissatisfied with assigning this speech to Miranda. It is not at all the sweet-mannered way she is depicted in the rest of the play. Further, the subject of these lines connects with the concerns of Prospero more than Miranda. At the end of the speech, too, Caliban replies not to Miranda but to Prospero, his teacher:

> You taught me language, and my profit on 't
> Is I know how to curse. (367–8)

Consequently, even though the Folio edition—the first collection of Shakespeare's plays, published in 1623, and our only source for *The Tempest*—clearly assigns this speech to Miranda, some editors have thought it was out of character for her and thus have given it to Prospero. (And not without justification: there are a good number of plays in which the Folio obviously assigns lines to the wrong speaker.)

Because some thoughtful editors have reassigned the speech, it has become possible for a contemporary director to do so as well. What is gained when the speech is given to Prospero is a more consistent, but blander, paler, more subdued version of Miranda, a highly dutiful young woman who never speaks with hostility or bitterness. What is lost by removing those lines is a complex Miranda who becomes angry at the memory of an attempted rape, someone who conceals a fiery temper beneath a façade of innocence. Not surprisingly, today's productions of *The Tempest* almost always stick to the original text, giving the speech to Miranda, in keeping with today's desire for more complex and interesting views of Shakespeare's women. One more reason for sticking to the original text is that it is a terrific speech, enabling an actor to create a fuller, more rounded portrait of the character. What actor wants to lose one of her best monologues to Prospero, who has enough good ones already? Which version is true to Shakespeare? Once again, there is room for interpretation.

Cultural Context for *The Tempest*: O Brave New World

The Tempest portrays an encounter between different cultures, in particular the European on the one hand, and the "native," as represented by Caliban, whom Prospero tried but failed to educate into civilization. (Ariel is a different case, a sprite, not human, whom Prospero never tried to raise or educate.) It is evident that Shakespeare had been reading about contacts between Europeans and New World peoples: he adapts a long passage about the Americas from Renaissance author Michel de Montaigne into Gonzalo's naive lines about how he would govern a newly discovered commonwealth (2.1.135–46). The name Caliban is apparently a play on "cannibal." "The Bermudas," known to Elizabethans as the scene of shipwrecks, get passing mention as well. These references to the Americas should not be surprising when we recall that the New World played a significant part in the European consciousness during Shakespeare's lifetime. Nevertheless, few of us fully realize the amount of commerce and travel between Europe and the New World in the sixteenth century. By 1600, fishing vessels from Portugal, France, and Britain had been working the Grand Banks of Newfoundland for close to one hundred years, landing often to dry fish and to replenish supplies. Large Spanish and French colonial settlements had been established in North America before Shakespeare was born. An English baby, Virginia Dare, was born on Roanoke Island in what was the colony of Virginia in 1587 (current-day North Carolina), before Shakespeare wrote his first play. In another example, the Pilgrims who landed at Plymouth Rock in 1620 were shown how to plant corn by a helpful Indian, Squanto. How did they communicate? Squanto knew English. In fact, he had been to London, once for certain, perhaps twice. He could well have seen a Shakespeare play.

Thus, when you are reading *The Tempest*, keep such colonial encounters in mind—they have an obvious presence in the play. The real questions have to do with the kinds and amounts of emphasis to give this undercurrent in performance. Some productions have ignored the colonial encounter completely, making the action more inward, more psychological, stressing Prospero's renunciation of his magic once his daughter is betrothed, rather than his active subjugation of his two servants. Others give the colonial context a lot of emphasis. Jonathan Miller's 1970 and 1986 versions, for example, both had Caliban costumed not as a monster but as an Indian, thus putting Prospero in the position of European settler/colonist/imperialist. The rationale for this interpretation is that Caliban is called a "monster" by many characters but not in the description in the cast of characters. It was common at the time to apply the word "monster" to any foreign, little understood creature. It was particularly useful for Europeans to regard Indian and African slaves as less than fully human because that thinking helped justify keeping them captive. Individual critics and directors always have to determine how much importance to place on the colonial encounter, but on the whole, recent productions—influenced by an increased focus on postcolonial history and a renewed interest in issues of race and racism—have paid much more attention to it.

For a more detailed look at this postcolonial perspective, readers can compare Shakespeare's *Tempest* to Aimé Césaire's 1968 play *A Tempest* (see p. 1412), which recasts the colonial encounter of *The Tempest* from an Afro-Caribbean perspective.

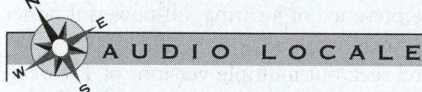

AUDIO LOCALE

Songs from Shakespeare's Plays. *Songs for William Shakespeare,* a compilation audio CD available from the New York Public Library, includes a range of songs from Shakespeare's plays, from Johnson's arrangement of "Where the bee sucks" in *The Tempest* to Morley's famous version of Feste's song "O mistress mine" from *Twelfth Night*. All songs are played on instruments of the period. For more information, go to *www.thelibraryshop.org/shakessongscd.html.*

Talking about the Text

1. Examine *The Tempest*'s opening scene on the ship. In particular, explain how the different characters on board deal with issues of authority. (Note that the crew's nautical language displays an expertise that the nobles cannot understand.)

2. List the various subplots in *The Tempest* and explain whether each parallels another plot in the play. Which characters have a double or a twin in the play?

3. What is the significance of *The Tempest*'s island setting? Drawing on any knowledge of islands you have—this could come from a wide range of experiences, from real-life travels to reading *Robinson Crusoe* to watching *Gilligan's Island* or *Jurassic Park*—explore what we know or believe about islands that can help you understand Shakespeare's decision to place the action there.

4. Why does Prospero make Ferdinand go through the trial? What is Miranda's attitude toward her father's insistence?

5. Compare one of Caliban's speeches with that of another character. Does Caliban get some of the best lines in the play? Why or why not?

6. Some recent productions of *The Tempest* have cast a woman in the Prospero role. How would a woman speaking Prospero's lines change your sense of the play?

7. How does the "plot" of Antonio and Sebastian conclude? Prospero forgives Antonio. Does Antonio repent, as Alonso clearly does?

8. If you were directing a production of *The Tempest*, would you cast a man or a woman in the role of Ariel? What dramatic and other strengths and weaknesses might reside in Ariel's being played by one or the other?

Writing about the Text

1. Miranda is silent after she says "O Brave new world." Prospero has the last word; in fact, he gets to address the audience directly in a witty epilogue, his separate, concluding commentary on the play. Write an epilogue for Miranda. Note that Prospero's lines are basically rhymed iambic tetrameter, with a good many trochees beginning lines. Try to use the same meter. (See Chapter 11 for helpful descriptions of iambic tetrameter and rhymes.)

2. Write a prose paraphrase of the epilogue, expanding it in order to justify Prospero's actions in the play.

Linking the Text to Other Texts

1. Compare the depiction of the young lovers Ferdinand and Miranda to the Renaissance love poetry and to the excerpt from *Romeo and Juliet* in Chapter 16. What similarities and differences do you see between *The Tempest* and other Renaissance depictions of love? What effect does the presence of a caring, all-powerful father have?

2. Go to your local library or video store and seek out multiple versions of *The Tempest* (see "Inspiration: Retelling *The Tempest* in Film and Verse" for a few possible versions). Look closely at several different actors' representations of Caliban, and write a paper explaining which one seems the most appropriate.

3. Listen to the music that has appeared in different versions of *The Tempest*. Would you recommend using the songs from the original play or replacing them with more modern songs?

COMMENTARY

Aimé Césaire's Dramatic Response to *The Tempest*

Aimé Césaire (b. 1913)—poet, playwright, essayist, and politician—is a major figure in twentieth-century world literature and a founder of Négritude, the highly influential

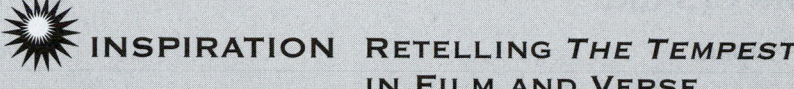

INSPIRATION RETELLING *THE TEMPEST* IN FILM AND VERSE

Besides Aimé Césaire's direct response, *A Tempest* (p. 1412), Shakespeare's *Tempest* has led to a great many different treatments in the recent past. The play has been filmed many times, with very mixed results. In fact, the more faithful the adaptation, the less successful the film.

Derek Jarman's version (1979) keeps Shakespeare's words, but makes many cuts and updatings. Paul Mazursky's *Tempest* (1982) updates the story to the twentieth century, with John Cassavetes playing an architect who must get away from it all on a Greek isle; Raul Julia plays Calibanos, and Susan Sarandon is the Ariel figure. Peter Greenaway's *Prospero's Books* (1991) has eminent British Shakespearean actor John Gielgud as Prospero and as narrator of all the other roles, which are performed by nonspeaking actors. A 1998 loose retelling, using virtually none of Shakespeare's script, stars Peter Fonda and Danny Glover and recasts the story as Shakespeare's take on slavery, set in the Mississippi bayous during the American Civil War.

Perhaps the most famous work inspired by *The Tempest* is the 1956 science fiction film *Forbidden Planet*, which in turn served as an inspiration for the *Star Trek* series. The film has a notable electronic music score and introduces Robby the Robot in the Ariel role. None of Shakespeare's language remains, of course, but the film, a sci-fi classic, nonetheless evokes much of *The Tempest's* essential strangeness.

W. H. Auden wrote a lengthy poem, *The Sea and the Mirror* (1947), which he modestly called "a commentary on Shakespeare's *The Tempest.*" But it is much more, with large roles for Prospero and especially Caliban.

intellectual and political movement created to honor and advance the culture of the African continent and its diaspora. Born in the French Caribbean colony of Martinique, he left to study in Paris on a scholarship at age eighteen and became engaged both in writing and the anticolonial struggle. With his wife and young son, he returned to Martinique to teach in 1939. Turning to politics, he became mayor of Martinique's capital city, Fort-de-France, in 1945 and a deputy in the French Constituent Assembly the following year.

While in office Césaire continued to write. His Discourse on Colonialism (1950) is one of the major foundations of anticolonial theory, claiming that colonialism works to "decivilize" the colonizer as well as the colonized. In A Tempest, Prospero, the master of Caliban and Ariel, is explicitly depicted as a colonizer. As in Shakespeare's play, Caliban tries to rebel to gain his freedom, while Ariel uses persuasion, appealing to Prospero's conscience. Césaire's Prospero is no generous ruler, and he clings to his power. Similarly, Caliban is no "monster" but a highly vocal, articulate native whose brutish qualities derive from his enslavement. His first word in the play is "Uhuru," which is Swahili for "freedom." Caliban and Prospero are locked together in the mutual hatred of the colonizer and the colonized.

AIMÉ CÉSAIRE   (B. 1913)

A Tempest   (1968)

TRANSLATED BY RICHARD MILLER

Characters

As in Shakespeare
Two alterations: ARIEL, a mulatto slave
                            CALIBAN, a black slave
An addition: ESHU, a black devil-god

Ambiance of a psychodrama. The actors enter singly, at random, and each chooses for himself a mask at his leisure.

MASTER OF CEREMONIES: Come gentlemen, help yourselves. To each his character, to each character his mask. You, Prospero? Why not? He has reserves of will power he's not even aware of himself. You want Caliban? Well, that's revealing. Ariel? Fine with me. And what about Stephano, Trinculo? No takers? Ah, just in time! It takes all kinds to make a world.

And after all, they aren't the worst characters. No problem about the juvenile leads, Miranda and Ferdinand. You, okay. And there's no problem about the villains either: you, Antonio; you, Alonso, perfect! Oh, Christ! I was forgetting the Gods. Eshu will fit you like a glove. As for the other parts, just take what you want and work it out among yourselves. But make up your minds . . . Now, there's one part I have to pick out myself: you! It's for the part of the Tempest, and I need a storm to end all storms . . . I need a really big guy to do the wind. Will you do that? Fine! And then someone strong for Captain of the ship. Good, now let's go. Ready? Begin. Blow, winds! Rain and lightning ad lib!

ACT I

SCENE 1

GONZALO: Of course, we're only straws tossed on the raging sea . . . but all's not lost, Gentlemen. We just have to try to get to the eye of the storm.

ANTONIO: We might have known this old fool would nag us to death!

SEBASTIAN: To the bitter end!

GONZALO: Try to understand what I'm telling you: imagine a huge cylinder like the chimney of a lamp, fast as a galloping horse, but in the center as still and unmoving as Cyclop's eye. That's what we're talking about when we say "the eye of the storm" and that's where we have to get.

ANTONIO: Oh, great! Do you really mean that the cyclone or Cyclops, if he can't see the beam in his own eye, will let us escape! Oh, that's very illuminating!

GONZALO: It's a clever way of putting it, at any rate. Literally false, but yet quite true. But what's the fuss going on up there? The Captain seems worried. *(Calling.)* Captain!

CAPTAIN: *(with a shrug)* Boatswain!

BOATSWAIN: Aye, sir!

CAPTAIN: We're coming round windward of the island. At this speed we'll run aground. We've got to turn her around. Heave to!   *(Exits.)*

BOATSWAIN: Come on, men! Heave to! To the topsail; man the ropes. Pull! Heave ho, heave ho!

ALONSO: *(approaching)* Well, Boatswain, how are things going? Where are we?

BOATSWAIN: If you ask me, you'd all be better off below, in your cabins.

ANTONIO: He doesn't seem too happy. We'd better ask the Captain. Where's the Captain, Boatswain? He was here just a moment ago, and now he's gone off.

BOATSWAIN: Get back below where you belong! We've got work to do!

GONZALO: My dear fellow, I can quite understand your being nervous, but a man should be able to control himself in any situation, even the most upsetting.

BOATSWAIN: Shove it! If you want to save your skins, you'd better get yourselves back down below to those first-class cabins of yours.

GONZALO: Now, now, my good fellow, you don't seem to know to whom you're speaking. *(Making introductions.)* The King's brother, the King's son and myself, the King's counsellor.

BOATSWAIN: King! King! Well, there's someone who doesn't give a fuck more about the kind that he does about you or me, and he's called the Gale. His Majesty the Gale! And right now, he's in control and we're all his subjects.

GONZALO: He might just as well be pilot on the ferry to hell . . . his mouth's foul enough!

ANTONIO: In a sense, the fellow regales me, as you might say. We'll pull through, you'll see, because he looks to me more like someone who'll end up on the gallows, not beneath the billows.

SEBASTIAN: The end result is the same. The fish will get us and the crows will get him.

GONZALO: He did irritate me, rather. However, I take the attenuating circumstances into account . . . and, you must admit, he lacks neither courage nor wit.

BOATSWAIN: *(returning)* Pull in the stud sails. Helmsman, into the wind! Into the wind!

Enter Sebastian, Antonio, Gonzalo.

BOATSWAIN: You again! If you keep bothering us and don't get below and say your prayers I'll give up and let you sail the ship! You can't expect me to be the go-between for your souls and Beelzebub!

ANTONIO: It's really too much! The fellow is taking advantage of the situation . . .

BOATSWAIN: Windward! Windward! Heave into the wind!

Thunder, lightning.

SEBASTIAN: Ho! Ho!

GONZALO: Did you see that? There, at the top of the masts, in the rigging, that glitter of blue fire, flashing, flashing? They're right when they call these magic lands, so different from our homes in Europe . . . Look, even the lightning is different!

ANTONIO: Maybe its a foretaste of the hell that awaits us.

GONZALO: You're too pessimistic. Anyway, I've always kept myself in a state of grace, ready to meet my maker.

Sailors enter.

SAILORS: Shit! We're sinking!

The passengers can be heard singing "Nearer, my God, to Thee . . ."

BOATSWAIN: To leeward! To leeward!

FERDINAND: *(entering)* Alas! There's no one in hell . . . all the devils are here!

The ship sinks.

SCENE 2

MIRANDA: Oh God! Oh God! A sinking ship! Father, help!

PROSPERO: *(enters hurriedly carrying a megaphone.)* Come daughter, calm your-self! It's only a play. There's really nothing wrong. Anyway, everything that happens is for our own good. Trust me, I won't say any more.

MIRANDA: But such a fine ship, and so many fine, brave lives sunk, drowned, laid waste to wrack and ruin . . . A person would have to have a heart of stone not to be moved . . .

PROSPERO: Drowned . . . hmmm. That remains to be seen. But draw near, dear Princess. The time has come.

MIRANDA: You're making fun of me, father. Wild as I am, you know I am happy—like a queen of the wildflowers, of the streams and paths, running barefoot through thorns and flowers, spared by one, caressed by the other.

PROSPERO: But you are a Princess . . . for how else does one address the daughter of a Prince? I cannot leave you in ignorance any longer. Milan is the city of your birth, and the city where for many years I was the Duke.

MIRANDA: Then how did we come here? And tell me, too, by what ill fortune did a prince turn into the reclusive hermit you are now, here, on this desert isle? Was it because you found the world distasteful, or through the perfidy of some enemy? Is our island a prison or a hermitage? You've hinted at some mystery so many times and aroused my curiosity, and today you shall tell me all.

PROSPERO: In a way, it is because of all the things you mention. First, it is be-cause of political disagreements, because of the intrigues of my ambitious younger brother. Antonio is his name, your uncle, and Alonso the name of the envious King of Naples. How their ambitions were joined, how my brother became the accomplice of my rival, how the latter promised the for-mer his protection and my throne . . . the devil alone knows how all that came about. In any event, when they learned that through my studies and experiments I had managed to discover the exact location of these lands for which many had sought for centuries and that I was making preparations to set forth to take possession of them, they hatched a scheme to steal my as-yet-unborn empire from me. They bribed my people, they stole my charts and documents and, to get rid of me, they denounced me to the Inquisition as a magician and sorcerer. To be brief, one day I saw arriving at the palace men to whom I had never granted audience: the priests of the Holy Office.

Flashback: Standing before Prospero, who is wearing his ducal robes, we see a friar reading from a parchment scroll.

THE FRIAR: The Holy Inquisition for the preservation and integrity of the Faith and the pursuit of heretical perversion, acting through the special powers entrusted to it by the Holy Apostolic See, informed of the errors you profess, insinuate and publish against God and his Creation with regard to the shape of the Earth and the possibility of discovering other lands, notwithstanding the fact that the Prophet Isaiah stated and taught that the Lord God is seated upon the circle of the Earth and in its center is Jerusalem and that around the world lies inaccessible Paradise, convinced that it is through wickedness that to support your heresy you quote Strabus, Ptolemy and the tragic author Seneca, thereby lending credence to the notion that profane writings can aspire to an authority equal to that of the most profound of the Holy Scriptures, given your notorious use by both night and day of Arabic calculations and scribblings in Hebrew, Syrian and other demonic tongues and, lastly, given that you have hitherto escaped punishment owing to your temporal authority and have, if not usurped, then transformed that authority and made it into a tyranny, doth hereby strip you of your titles, positions and honors in order that it may then proceed against you according to due process through a full and thorough examination, under which authority we require that you accompany us.

PROSPERO: *(back in the present)* And yet, the trial they said they were going to hold never took place. Such creatures of darkness are too much afraid of the light. To be brief: instead of killing me they chose—even worse—to maroon me here with you on this desert island.

MIRANDA: How terrible, and how wicked the world is! How you must have suffered!

PROSPERO: In all this tale of treason and felony there is but one honorable name: Gonzalo, counsellor to the King of Naples and fit to serve a better master. By furnishing me with food and clothing, by supplying me with my books and instruments, he has done all in his power to make my exile in this disgusting place bearable. And now, through a singular turn, Fortune has brought to these shores the very men involved in the plot against me. My prophetic science had of course already informed me that they would not be content merely with seizing my lands in Europe and that their greed would win out over their cowardice, that they would confront the sea and set out for those lands my genius had discovered. I couldn't let them get away with that, and since I was able to stop them, I did so, with the help of Ariel. We brewed up the storm you have just witnessed, thereby saving my possessions overseas and bringing the scoundrels into my power at the same time.

Enter Ariel.

PROSPERO: Well, Ariel?

ARIEL: Mission accomplished.

PROSPERO: Bravo; good work! But what seems to be the matter? I give you a compliment and you don't seem pleased? Are you tired?

ARIEL: Not tired; disgusted. I obeyed you but—well, why not come out with it?—I did so most unwillingly. It was a real pity to see that great ship go down, so full of life.

PROSPERO: Oh, so you're upset, are you! It's always like that with you intellectuals! Who cares! What interests me is not your moods, but your deeds. Let's split: I'll take the zeal and you can keep your doubts. Agreed?

ARIEL: Master, I must beg you to spare me this kind of labour.

PROSPERO: *(shouting)* Listen, and listen good! There's a task to be performed, and I don't care how it gets done!

ARIEL: You've promised me my freedom a thousand times, and I'm still waiting.

PROSPERO: Ingrate! And who freed you from Sycorax, may I ask? Who rent the pine in which you had been imprisoned and brought you forth?

ARIEL: Sometimes I almost regret it . . . After all, I might have turned into a real tree in the end . . . Tree: that's a word that really gives me a thrill! It often springs to mind: palm tree—springing into the sky like a fountain ending in nonchalant, squid-like elegance. The baobab—twisted like the soft entrails of some monster. Ask the calao bird that lives a cloistered season in its branches. Or the Ceiba tree—spread out beneath the proud sun. O bird, o green mansions set in the living earth!

PROSPERO: Stuff it! I don't like talking trees. As for your freedom, you'll have it when I'm good and ready. In the meanwhile, see to the ship. I'm going to have a few words with Master Caliban. I've been keeping my eye on him, and he's getting a little too emancipated. *(Calling)* Caliban! Caliban! *(He sighs.)*

   Enter Caliban.

CALIBAN: Uhuru!

PROSPERO: What did you say?

CALIBAN: I said, Uhuru!

PROSPERO: Mumbling your native language again! I've already told you, I don't like it. You could be polite, at least; a simple "hello" wouldn't kill you.

CALIBAN: Oh, I forgot . . . But make that as froggy, waspish, pustular and dung-filled "hello" as possible. May today hasten by a decade the day when all the birds of the sky and beasts of the earth will feast upon your corpse!

PROSPERO: Gracious as always, you ugly ape! How can anyone be so ugly?

CALIBAN: You think I'm ugly . . . well, I don't think you're so handsome yourself. With that big hooked nose, you look just like some old vulture. *(Laughing)* An old vulture with a scrawny neck!

PROSPERO: Since you're so fond of invective, you could at least thank me for having taught you to speak at all. You, a savage . . . a dumb animal, a beast I educated, trained, dragged up from the bestiality that still clings to you.

CALIBAN: In the first place, that's not true. You didn't teach me a thing! Except to jabber in your own language so that I could understand your orders: chop the wood, wash the dishes, fish for food, plant vegetables, all because you're too lazy to do it yourself. And as for your learning, did you ever impart any of that to me? No, you took care not to. All your science you keep for yourself alone, shut up in those big books.

PROSPERO: What would you be without me?

CALIBAN: Without you? I'd be the king, that's what I'd be, the King of the Island. The king of the island given me by my mother, Sycorax.

PROSPERO: There are some family trees it's better not to climb! She's a ghoul! A witch from whom—and may God be praised—death has delivered us.

CALIBAN: Dead or alive, she was my mother, and I won't deny her! Anyhow, you only think she's dead because you think the earth itself is dead . . . It's so much simpler that way! Dead, you can walk on it, pollute it, you can tread upon it with the steps of a conqueror. I respect the earth, because I know that it is alive, and I know that Sycorax is alive.

Sycorax. Mother.

Serpent, rain, lightning.

And I see thee everywhere!

In the eye of the stagnant pool which stares back at me,

through the rushes,

in the gesture made by twisted root and its awaiting thrust.

In the night, the all-seeing blinded night,

the nostril-less all-smelling night!

. . . Often, in my dreams, she speaks to me and warns me . . . Yesterday, even, when I was lying by the stream on my belly lapping at the muddy water, when the Beast was about to spring upon me with that huge stone in his hand . . .

PROSPERO: If you keep on like that even your magic won't save you from punishment!

CALIBAN: That's right, that's right! In the beginning, the gentleman was all sweet talk: dear Caliban here, my little Caliban there! And what do you think you'd have done without me in this strange land? Ingrate! I taught you the trees, fruits, birds, the seasons, and now you don't give a damn . . . Caliban the animal, Caliban the slave! I know that story! Once you've squeezed the juice from the orange, you toss the rind away!

PROSPERO: Oh!

CALIBAN: Do I lie? Isn't it true that you threw me out of your house and made me live in a filthy cave. The ghetto!

PROSPERO: It's easy to say "ghetto"! It wouldn't be such a ghetto if you took the trouble to keep it clean! And there's something you forgot, which is that what forced me to get rid of you was your lust. Good God, you tried to rape my daughter!

CALIBAN: Rape! Rape! Listen, you old goat, you're the one that put those dirty thoughts in my head. Let me tell you something: I couldn't care less about your daughter, or about your cave, for that matter. If I gripe, it's on principle, because I didn't like living with you at all, as a matter of fact. Your feet stink!

PROSPERO: I did not summon you here to argue. Out! Back to work! Wood, water, and lots of both! I'm expecting company today.

CALIBAN: I've had just about enough. There's already a pile of wood that high . . .

PROSPERO: Enough! Careful, Caliban! If you keep grumbling you'll be whipped. And if you don't step lively, if you keep dragging your feet or try to strike or sabotage things, I'll beat you. Beating is the only language you really understand. So much the worse for you: I'll speak it, loud and clear. Get a move on!

CALIBAN: All right, I'm going . . . but this is the last time. It's the last time, do you hear me? Oh . . . I forgot: I've got something important to tell you.

PROSPERO: Important? Well, out with it.

CALIBAN: It's this: I've decided I don't want to be called Caliban any longer.

PROSPERO: What kind of rot is that? I don't understand.

CALIBAN: Put it this way: I'm telling you that from now on I won't answer to the name Caliban.

PROSPERO: Where did you get that idea?

CALIBAN: Well, because Caliban isn't my name. It's as simple as that.

PROSPERO: Oh, I suppose it's mine!

CALIBAN: It's the name given me by your hatred, and everytime it's spoken it's an insult.

PROSPERO: My, aren't we getting sensitive! All right, suggest something else . . . I've got to call you something. What will it be? Cannibal would suit you, but I'm sure you wouldn't like that, would you? Let's see . . . what about Hannibal? That fits. And why not . . . they all seem to like historical names.

CALIBAN: Call me X. That would be best. Like a man without a name. Or, to be more precise, a man whose name has been stolen. You talk about history . . . well, that's history, and everyone knows it! Every time you summon me it reminds me of a basic fact, the fact that you've stolen everything from me, even my identity! Uhuru! (He exits.)

Enter Ariel as a sea-nymph.

PROSPERO: My dear Ariel, did you see how he looked at me, that glint in his eye? That's something new. Well, let me tell you, Caliban is the enemy. As for those people on the boat, I've changed my mind about them. Give them a scare, but for God's sake don't touch a hair of their heads! You'll answer to me if you do.

ARIEL: I've suffered too much myself for having made them suffer not to be pleased at your mercy. You can count on me, Master.

PROSPERO: Yes, however great their crimes, if they repent you can assure them of my forgiveness. They are men of my race, and of high rank. As for me, at my age one must rise above disputes and quarrels and think about the future. I have a daughter. Alonso has a son. If they were to fall in love, I would give my consent. Let Ferdinand marry Miranda, and may their marriage bring us harmony and peace. That is my plan. I want it executed. As for Caliban, does it matter what that villain plots against me? All the nobility of Italy, Naples and Milan henceforth combined, will protect me bodily. Go!

ARIEL: Yes, Master. Your orders will be fully carried out.

Ariel sings:

> *Sandy seashore, deep blue sky,*
> *Surf is rising, sea birds fly*
> *Here the lover finds delight,*
> *Sun at noontime, moon at night.*
> *Join hands lovers, join the dance,*
> *Find contentment, find romance.*
>
> *Sandy seashore, deep blue sky,*
> *Cares will vanish . . . so can I . . .*

FERDINAND: What is this music? It has led me here and now it stops . . . No, there it is again . . .

ARIEL: (*singing*)

> Waters move, the ocean flows,
> Nothing comes and nothing goes . . .
> Strange days are upon us . . .
>
> Oysters stare through pearly eyes
> Heart-shaped corals gently beat
> In the crystal undersea
>
> Waters move and ocean flows,
> Nothing comes and nothing goes . . .
> Strange days are upon us . . .

FERDINAND: What is this that I see before me? A goddess? A mortal?

MIRANDA: I know what I'm seeing: a flatterer. Young man, your ability to pay compliments in the situation in which you find yourself at least proves your courage. Who are you?

FERDINAND: As you see, a poor shipwrecked soul.

MIRANDA: But one of high degree!

FERDINAND: In other surroundings I might be called "Prince," "son of the King" . . . But, no, I was forgetting . . . not "Prince" but "King," alas . . . "King" because my father has just perished in the shipwreck.

MIRANDA: Poor young man! Here, you'll be received with hospitality and we'll support you in your misfortune.

FERDINAND: Alas, my father . . . Can it be that I am an unnatural son? Your pity would make the greatest of sorrows seem sweet.

MIRANDA: I hope you'll like it here with us. The island is pretty. I'll show you the beaches and the forests, I'll tell you the names of fruits and flowers, I'll introduce you to a whole world of insects, or lizards or every hue, of birds . . . Oh, you cannot imagine! The birds! . . .

PROSPERO: That's enough, daughter! I find your chatter irritating . . . and let me assure you, it's not at all fitting. You are doing too much honor to an impostor. Young man, you are a traitor, a spy, and a woman-chaser to boot! No sooner has he escaped the perils of the sea than he's sweet-talking the first girl he meets! You won't get round me that way. Your arrival is convenient, because I need more manpower: you shall be my house servant.

FERDINAND: Seeing the young lady, more beautiful than any wood-nymph, I might have been Ulysses on Nausicaa's isle. But hearing you, Sir, I now understand my fate a little better . . . I see I have come ashore on the Barbary Coast and am in the hands of a cruel pirate. (Drawing his sword) However, a gentleman prefers death to dishonor! I shall defend my life with my freedom!

PROSPERO: Poor fool: your arm is growing weak, your knees are trembling! Traitor! I could kill you now . . . but I need the manpower. Follow me.

ARIEL: It's no use trying to resist, young man. My master is a sorcerer: neither your passion nor your youth can prevail against him. Your best course would be to follow and obey him.

FERDINAND: Oh God! What sorcery is this? Vanquished, a captive—yet far from rebelling against my fate, I am finding my servitude sweet. Oh, I would be imprisoned for life if only heaven will grant me a glimpse of my sun each day, the face of my own sun. Farewell, Nausicaa.

They exit.

ACT II

SCENE 1

Caliban's cave. Caliban is singing as he works when Ariel enters. He listens to him for a moment.

CALIBAN: (*singing*)

> May he who eats his corn heedless of Shango
> Be accursed! May Shango creep beneath
> His nails and eat into his flesh!
> Shango, Shango ho!
>
> Forget to give him room if you dare!
> He will make himself at home on your nose!
>
> Refuse to have him under your roof at your own risk!
> He'll tear off your roof and wear it as a hat!
> Whoever tries to mislead Shango
> Will suffer for it!
> Shango, Shango ho!

ARIEL: Greetings, Caliban. I know you don't think much of me, but after all we are brothers, brothers in suffering and slavery, but brothers in hope as well. We both want our freedom. We just have different methods.

CALIBAN: Greetings to you. But you didn't come to see me just to make that profession of faith. Come on. Alastor! The old man sent you, didn't he? A great job: carrying out the Master's fine ideas, his great plans.

ARIEL: No, I've come on my own. I came to warn you. Prospero is planning horrible acts of revenge against you. I thought it my duty to alert you.

CALIBAN: I'm ready for him.

ARIEL: Poor Caliban, you're doomed. You know that you aren't the stronger, you'll never be the stronger. What good will it do you to struggle?

CALIBAN: And what about you? What good has your obedience done you, your Uncle Tom patience and your sucking up to him. The man's just getting more demanding and despotic day by day.

ARIEL: Well, I've at least achieved one thing: he's promised me my freedom. In the distant future, of course, but it's the first time he's actually committed himself.

CALIBAN: Talk's cheap! He'll promise you a thousand times and take it back a thousand times. Anyway, tomorrow doesn't interest me. What I want is (*shouting*) "Freedom now!"

ARIEL: Okay. But you know you're not going to get it out of him "now", and that he's stronger than you are. I'm in a good position to know just what he's got in his arsenal.

CALIBAN: The stronger? How do you know that? Weakness always has a thousand means and cowardice is all that keeps us from listing them.

ARIEL: I don't believe in violence.

CALIBAN: What do you believe in, then? In cowardice? In giving up? In kneeling and groveling? That's it, someone strikes you on the right cheek and you offer the left. Someone kicks you on the left buttock and you turn the right . . . that way there's no jealousy. Well, that's not Caliban's way . . .

ARIEL: You know very well that that's not what I mean. No violence, no submission either. Listen to me: Prospero is the one we've got to change. Destroy his serenity so that he's finally forced to acknowledge his own injustice and put an end to it.

CALIBAN: Oh sure . . . that's a good one! Prospero's conscience! Prospero is an old scoundrel who has no conscience.

ARIEL: Exactly—that's why it's up to us to give him one. I'm not fighting just for my freedom, for our freedom, but for Prospero too, so that Prospero can acquire a conscience. Help me, Caliban.

CALIBAN: Listen, kid, sometimes I wonder if you aren't a little bit nuts. So that Prospero can acquire a conscience? You might as well ask a stone to grow flowers.

ARIEL: I don't know what to do with you. I've often had this inspiring, uplifting dream that one day Prospero, you, me, we would all three set out, like brothers, to build a wonderful world, each one contributing his own special thing: patience, vitality, love, will-power too, and rigor, not to mention the dreams without which mankind would perish.

CALIBAN: You don't understand a thing about Prospero. He's not the collaborating type. He's a guy who only feels something when he's wiped someone out. A crusher, a pulveriser, that's what he is! And you talk about brotherhood!

ARIEL: So then what's left? War? And you know that when it comes to that, Prospero is invincible.

CALIBAN: Better death than humiliation and injustice. Anyhow, I'm going to have the last word. Unless nothingness has it. The day when I begin to feel that everything's lost, just let me get hold of a few barrels of your infernal powder and as you fly around up there in your blue skies you'll see this island, my inheritance, my work, all blown to smithereens . . . and, I trust, Prospero and me with it. I hope you'll like the fireworks display—it'll be signed Caliban.

ARIEL: Each of us marches to his own drum. You follow yours. I follow the beat of mine. I wish you courage, brother.

CALIBAN: Farewell, Ariel, my brother, and good luck.

SCENE 2

GONZALO: A magnificent country! Bread hangs from the trees and the apricots are bigger than a woman's full breast.

SEBASTIAN: A pity that it's so wild and uncultivated . . . here and there.

GONZALO: Oh, that's nothing. If there were anything poisonous, an antidote would never be far away, for nature is intrinsically harmonious. I've even read somewhere that guano is excellent compost for sterile ground.

SEBASTIAN: Guano? What kind of animal is that? Are you sure you don't mean iguana?

GONZALO: Young man, if I say guano, I mean guano. Guano is the name for bird-droppings that build up over centuries, and it is by far the best fertilizer known. You dig it out of caves . . . If you want my opinion, I think we should investigate all the caves on this island one by one to see if we find any, and if we do, this island, if wisely exploited, will be richer than Egypt with its Nile.

ANTONIO: Let me understand: your guano cave contains a river of dried bird-shit.

GONZALO: To pick up your image, all we need to do is channel that river, use it to irrigate, if I may use the term, the fields with this wonderful fecal matter, and everything will bloom.

SEBASTIAN: But we'll still need manpower to farm it. Is the island even inhabited?

GONZALO: That's the problem, of course. But if it is, it must be by wonderful people. It's obvious: a wondrous land can only contain wonderful creatures.

ANTONIO: Yes!

> Men whose bodies are wiry and strong
> And women whose eyes are open and frank . . . creatures in it! . . .

GONZALO: Something like that! I see you know your literature. But in that case, watch out: it will all mean new responsibilities for us!

SEBASTIAN: How do you get that?

GONZALO: I mean that if the island is inhabited, as I believe, and if we colonize it, as is my hope, then we have to take every precaution not to import our shortcomings, yes, what we call civilization. They must stay as they are: savages, noble and good savages, free, without any complexes or complications. Something like a pool granting eternal youth where we periodically come to restore our aging, citified souls.

ALONSO: Sir Gonzalo, when will you shut up?

GONZALO: Ah, Your Majesty, if I am boring you, I apologize. I was only speaking as I did to distract you and to turn our sad thoughts to something more pleasant. There, I'll be silent. Indeed, these old bones have had it. Oof! Let me sit down . . . with your permission, of course.

ALONSO: Noble Old Man, even though younger than you, we are all in the same fix.

GONZALO: In other words, dead tired and dying of hunger.

ALONSO: I have never pretended to be above the human condition.

A strange, solemn music is heard.

. . . Listen, listen! Did you hear that?

GONZALO: Yes, it's an odd melody!

Prospero enters, invisible. Other strange figures enter as well, bearing a laden table. They dance and graciously invite the King and his company to eat, then they disappear.

ALONSO: Heaven protect us! Live marionettes!

GONZALO: Such grace! Such music! Hum. The whole thing is most peculiar.

SEBASTIAN: Gone! Faded away! But what does that matter, since they've left their food behind! No meal was ever more welcome. Gentlemen, to table!

ALONSO: Yes, let us partake of this feast, even though it may be our last.

They prepare to eat, but Elves enter and, with much grimacing and many contortions, carry off the table.

GONZALO: Ah! that's a fine way to behave!

ALONSO: I have the distinct feeling that we have fallen under the sway of powers that are playing at cat and mouse with us. It's a cruel way to make us aware of our dependent status.

GONZALO: The way things have been going it's not surprising, and it will do us no good to protest.

The Elves return, bringing the food with them.

ALONSO: Oh no, this time I won't bite!

SEBASTIAN: I'm so hungry that I don't care, I'll abandon my scruples.

GONZALO: *(to Alonso)* Why not try? Perhaps the Powers controlling us saw how disappointed we were and took pity on us. After all, even though disappointed a hundred times, Tantalus still tried a hundred times.

ALONSO: That was also his torture. I won't touch that food.

PROSPERO: *(invisible)* Ariel, I don't like his refusing. Harass them until they eat.

ARIEL: Why should we go to any trouble for them? If they won't eat, they can die of hunger.

PROSPERO: No, I want them to eat.

ARIEL: That's despotism. A while ago you made me snatch it away just when they were about to gobble it up, and now that they don't want it you are ready to force feed them.

PROSPERO: Enough hairsplitting! My mood has changed! They insult me by not eating. They must be made to eat out of my hand like chicks. That is a sign of submission I insist they give me.

ARIEL: It's evil to play with their hunger as you do with their anxieties and their hopes.

PROSPERO: That is how power is measured. I am Power.

Alonso and his group eat.

ALONSO: Alas, when I think . . .

GONZALO: That's your trouble, Sire: you think too much.

ALONSO: And thus I should not even think of my lost son! My throne! My country!

GONZALO: (eating) Your son! What's to say we won't find him again! As for the rest of it . . . Look, Sire, this filthy hole is now our entire world. Why seek further? If your thoughts are too vast, cut them down to size.

They eat.

ALONSO: So be it! But I would prefer to sleep. To sleep and to forget.

GONZALO: Good idea! Let's put up our hammocks!

They sleep.

SCENE 3

ANTONIO: Look at those leeches, those slugs! Wallowing in their slime and their snot: Idiots, slime—they're like beached jellyfish.

SEBASTIAN: Shhh! It's the King. And that old graybeard is his venerable counsellor.

ANTONIO: The King is he who watches over his flock when they sleep. That one isn't watching over anything. Ergo, he's not the King. (Brusquely) You're really a bloodless lily-liver if you can see a king asleep without getting certain ideas . . .

SEBASTIAN: I mustn't have any blood, only water.

ANTONIO: Don't insult water. Every time I look at myself I think I'm more handsome, more there. My inner juices have always given me my greatness, my true greatness . . . not the greatness men grant me.

SEBASTIAN: All right, so I'm stagnant water.

ANTONIO: Water is never stagnant. It works, it works in us. It is what gives man his dimension, his true one. Believe me, you're mistaken if you don't grab the opportunity when it's offered you. It may never come again.

SEBASTIAN: What are you getting at? I have a feeling I can guess.

ANTONIO: Guess, guess! Look at that tree swaying in the wind. It's called a co-conut palm. My dear Sebastian, in my opinion it's time to shake the coconut palm.

SEBASTIAN: Now I really don't understand.

ANTONIO: What a dope! Consider my position: I'm Duke of Milan. Well, I wasn't always . . . I had an older brother. That was Duke Prospero. And if I'm now Duke Antonio, it's because I knew when to shake the coconut palm.

SEBASTIAN: And Prospero?

ANTONIO: What do you mean by that? When you shake a tree, someone is bound to fall. And obviously it wasn't me who fell, because here I am: to as-sist and serve you, Majesty!

SEBASTIAN: Enough! He's my brother! My scruples won't allow me to . . . You take care of him while I deal with the old Counsellor.

They draw their swords.

ARIEL: Stop, ruffians! Resistance is futile: your swords are enchanted and falling from your hands!

ANTONIO, SEBASTIAN: Alas! Alas!

ARIEL: Sleepers, awake! Awake, I say! Your life depends on it. With these fine fellows with their long teeth and swords around, anyone who sleeps too soundly risks sleeping forever.

Alonso and Gonzalo awaken.

ALONSO: *(rubbing his eyes)* What's happening? I was asleep, and I was having a terrible dream!

ARIEL: No, you were not dreaming. These fine lords here are criminals who were about to perpetrate the most odious of crimes upon you. Yes, Alonso, you may well marvel that a god should fly to your aid. Were to heaven you de-served it more!

ALONSO: I have never been wanting in respect for the divinity . . .

ARIEL: I don't know what effect my next piece of news will have on you: The name of him who has sent me to you is Prospero.

ALONSO: Prospero! God save us! (He falls to his knees.)

ARIEL: I understand your feelings. He lives. It is he who reigns over this isle, as he reigns over the spirits of the air you breathe . . . But rise . . . You need fear no longer. He has not saved your lives to destroy them. Your repentance will suffice, for I can see that it is deep and sincere. (To Antonio and Sebastian) As for you, Gentlemen, my master's pardon extends to you as well, on the condition that you renounce your plans, knowing them to be vain.

SEBASTIAN: *(To Antonio)* We could have got worse!

ANTONIO: If it were men we were up against, no one could make me withdraw, but when it's demons and magic there's no shame in giving in. *(To Ariel)* . . . We are the Duke's most humble and obedient servants. Please beg him to accept our thanks.

GONZALO: Oh, how ignoble! How good of you to just wipe the slate clean! No surface repentance . . . not only do you want attrition, you want contrition as well! Why look at me as though you didn't know what I was talking about? Attrition: A selfish regret for offending God, caused by a fear of punishment. Contrition: An unselfish regret growing out of sorrow at displeasing God.

ARIEL: Honest Gonzalo, thank you for your clarification. Your eloquence has eased my mission and your pedagogical skill has abbreviated it, for in a few short words you have expressed my master's thought. May your words be heard! Therefore, let us turn the page. To terminate this episode, I need only convoke you all, on my master's behalf, to the celebrations that this very day will mark the engagement of his daughter, Miranda. Alonso, that's good news for you . . .

ALONSO: What—my son?

ARIEL: Correct. Saved by my master from the fury of the waves.

ALONSO: *(falling to his knees)* God be praised for this blessing more than all the rest. Rank, fortune, throne, I am prepared to forgo all if my son is returned to me . . .

ARIEL: Come, Gentlemen, follow me.

ACT III

SCENE 1

FERDINAND: *(hoeing and singing)*

> How life has changed
> Now, hoe in hand
> I work away all day . . .
>
> Hoeing all the day,
> I go my weary way . . .

CALIBAN: Poor kid! What would he say if he was Caliban! He works night and day, and when he sings, it's

> Oo-en-day, Oo-en-day, Oo-en-day, Macaya . . .

And no pretty girl to console him! *(Sees Miranda approaching.)* Aha! Let's listen to this!

FERDINAND: *(singing)*

> How life has changed
> Now, hoe in hand
> I work away all day . . .

MIRANDA: Poor young man! Can I help you? You don 't look like you were cut out for this kind of work!

FERDINAND: One word from you would be more help to me than anything in the world.

MIRANDA: One word? From me? I must say, I . . .

FERDINAND: Your name—that's all: What is your name?

MIRANDA: That, I cannot do! It's impossible. My father has expressly forbidden it!

FERDINAND: It is the only thing I long for.

MIRANDA: But I can't, I tell you; it's forbidden!

CALIBAN: (*taking advantage of Miranda's momentary distraction, he whispers her name to Ferdinand.*) Mi-ran-da!

FERDINAND: All right then, I shall christen you with a name of my own. I will call you Miranda.

MIRANDA: That's too much! What a low trick! You must have heard my father calling me . . . Unless it was that awful Caliban who keeps pursuing me and calling out my name in his stupid dreams!

FERDINAND: No, Miranda . . . I had only to allow my eyes to speak, as you your face.

MIRANDA: Sssh! My father's coming! He'd better not catch you trying to sweet talk me . . .

FERDINAND: (*Goes back to work, singing.*)

> But times have changed
> Now, hoeing all the day,
> I go my weary way . . .

PROSPERO: That's fine, young man! You've managed to accomplish a good deal for a beginning! I see I've misjudged you. But you won't be the loser if you serve me well. Listen, my young friend, there are three things in life: Work, Patience, Continence, and the world is yours . . . Hey, Caliban, I'm taking this boy away with me. He's done enough for one day. But since the job is urgent, see that it gets finished.

CALIBAN: Me?

PROSPERO: Yes, you! You've cheated me enough with your loafing and fiddling around, so you can work a double shift for once!

CALIBAN: I don't see why I should do someone else's job!

PROSPERO: Who's the boss here? You or me? Listen, monster: if you don't like work, I'll see to it you change your mind!

Prospero and Ferdinand move away.

CALIBAN: Go on, go on . . . I'll get you one day. You bastard! (*He sets to work, singing.*)

> "Oo-en-day, Oo-en-day, Oo-en-day, Macaya . . ."

Shit, now it's raining! As if things weren't bad enough . . . (*Suddenly, at the sound of a voice, Caliban stiffens.*) Do you hear that, boy? That voice through the storm. Bah! It's Ariel. No, that's not his voice. Whose, then? With an old coot like Prospero . . . One of his cops, probably. Oh, fine! Now, I'm for it. Men and the elements both against me. Well, the hell with it . . . I'm used to it. Patience! I'll get them yet. In the meantime better make myself scarce! Let Prospero and his storm and his cops go by . . . let the seven maws of Malediction bay!

SCENE 2

Enter Trinculo

TRINCULO: *(singing)*

> Oh Susannah . . . oh don't you cry for me . . . (Etc.)

You can say that again! My dearest Susannah . . . trust Trinculo, we've had all the roaring storms we need, and more! I swear: the whole crew wiped out, liquidated . . . Nothing! Nothing left . . . ! Nothing but poor wandering and wailing Trinculo! No question about it, it'll be a while before anyone persuades me to depart from affectionate women and friendly towns to go off to brave roaring storms! How it's raining! *(Notices Caliban underneath the wheelbarrow.)* Ah, an Indian! Dead or alive? You never know with these tricky races. Yukkk! Anyhow, this will do me fine. If he's dead, I can use his clothes for shelter, for a coat, a tent, a covering. If he's alive I'll make him my prisoner and take him back to Europe and then, by golly, my fortune will be made! I'll sell him to a carnival. No! I'll show him myself at fairs! What a stroke of luck! I'll just settle in here where it's warm and let the storm rage! *(He crawls under cover, back to back with Caliban.)*

Enter Stephano.

STEPHANO: *(singing)*

> Blow the man down, hearties,
> Blow the man down . . . (Etc.)
> *(Takes a swig of his bottle and continues.)*
> Blow, blow, blow the man down . . . (Etc.)

Fortunately, there's still a little wine left in this bottle . . . enough to give me courage! Be of good cheer, Stephano, where there's life there's thirst . . . and vice versa! *(Suddenly spies Caliban's head sticking out of the covers.)* My God, on Stephano's word, it looks like a Nindian! *(Comes nearer)* And that's just what it is! A Nindian. That's neat. I really am lucky. There's money to be made from a Nindian like that. If you showed him at a carnival . . . along with the bearded lady and the flea circus, a real Nindian! An authentic Nindian from the Caribbean! That means real dough, or I'm the last of the idiots! *(Touching Caliban)* But he's ice cold! I don't know what the body temperature of a Nindian is, but this one seems pretty cold to me! Let's hope he's not going to croak! How's that for bad luck: You find a Nindian and he dies on you! A fortune slips through your fingers! But wait, I've got an idea . . . a good swig of this booze between his lips, that'll warm him up. *(He gives Caliban a drink.)* Look . . . he's better already. The little glutton even wants some more! Just a second, just a second! *(He walks around the wheelbarrow and sees Trinculo's head sticking out from under the covering.)* Jeez! I must be seeing things! A Nindian with two heads! Shit! If I have to pour drink down two gullets I won't have much left for myself! Well, never mind. It's incredible . . . your everyday Nindian is already something, but one with two heads . . . a Siamese-twin Nindian, a Nindian with two heads and eight paws, that's really something! My fortune is made. Come on, you wonderful monster, you . . . let's get a look at your other head! *(He draws nearer to Trinculo.)* Hello!

That face reminds me of something! That nose that shines like a lighthouse
. . .

TRINCULO: That gut . . .

STEPHANO: That nose looks familiar . . .

TRINCULO: That gut—there can't be two of them in this lousy world!

STEPHANO: Oh-my-gawd, oh-my-gawd, oh-my-gawd . . . that's it . . . it's that
crook Trinculo!

TRINCULO: Good lord! It's Stephano!

STEPHANO: So, Trinculo, you were saved too . . . It almost makes you believe
God looks after drunks . . .

TRINCULO: Huh! God . . . Bacchus, maybe. As a matter of fact, I reached these
welcoming shores by floating on a barrel . . .

STEPHANO: And I by floating on my stomach . . . it's nearly the same thing. But
what kind of creature is this? Isn't it a Nindian?

TRINCULO: That's just what I was thinking . . . Yes, by God, it's a Nindian.
That's a piece of luck . . . he'll be our guide.

STEPHANO: Judging from the way he can swill it down, he doesn't seem to be
stupid. I'll try to civilize him. Oh . . . not too much, of course. But enough so
that he can be of some use.

TRINCULO: Civilize him! Shee-it! Does he even know how to talk?

STEPHANO: I couldn't get a word out of him, but I know a way to loosen his
tongue. (*He takes a bottle from his pocket.*)

TRINCULO: (*stopping him*) Look here, you're not going to waste that nectar on
the first savage that comes along, are you?

STEPHANO: Selfish! Back off! Let me perform my civilizing mission. (*Offering the
bottle to Caliban.*) Of course, if he was cleaned up a bit he'd be worth more to
both of us. Okay? We'll exploit him together? It's a deal? (*To Caliban*) Drink
up, pal. You. Drink . . . Yum-yum botty botty! (*Caliban drinks.*) You, drink
more. (*Caliban refuses.*) You no more thirsty? (*Stephano drinks.*) Me always
thirsty! (*Stephano and Trinculo drink.*)

STEPHANO: Trinculo, you know I used to be prejudiced against shipwrecks, but I
was wrong. They're not bad at all.

TRINCULO: That's true. It seems to make things taste better afterwards . . .

STEPHANO: Not to mention the fact that it's got rid of a lot of old farts that were
always keeping the world down! May they rest in peace! But then, you liked
them, didn't you, all those kings and dukes, all those noblemen! Oh, I served
them well enough, you've got to earn your drink somehow . . . But I could
never stand them, ever—understand? Never. Trinculo, my friend, I'm a longtime believer in the republic . . . you might as well say it: I'm a died-in-the-
wool believer in the people first, a republican in my guts! Down with tyrants!

TRINCULO: Which reminds me . . . If, as it would seem, the King and the Duke
are dead, there's a crown and a throne up for grabs around here . . .

STEPHANO: By God, you're right! Smart thinking, Trinculo! So, I appoint myself
heir . . . I crown myself king of the island.

TRINCULO: (*sarcastically*) Sure you do! And why you, may I ask? I'm the one who
thought of it first, that crown!

STEPHANO: Look, Trinculo, don't be silly! I mean, really: just take a look at
yourself! What's the first thing a king needs? Bearing. Presence. And if I've
got anything, it's that. Which isn't true for everyone. So, I am the King!

CALIBAN: Long live the King!

STEPHANO: It's a miracle . . . he can talk! And what's more, he talks sense! O brave savage! *(He embraces Caliban.)* You see, my dear Trinculo, the people has spoken! Vox populi, vox Dei . . . But please, don't be upset. Stephano is magnanimous and will never abandon his friend Trinculo, the friend who stood by him in his trials. Trinculo, we've eaten rough bread together, we've drunk rot-gut wine together. I want to do something for you. I shall appoint you Marshal. But we're forgetting our brave savage . . . It's a scientific miracle! He can talk!

CALIBAN: Yes, Sire. My enthusiasm has restored my speech. Long live the King! But beware the usurper!

STEPHANO: Usurper? Who? Trinculo?

CALIBAN: No, the other one . . . Prospero!

STEPHANO: Prospero? Don't know him.

CALIBAN: Well, you see, this island used to belong to me, except that a man named Prospero cheated me of it. I'm perfectly willing to give you my right to it, but the only thing is, you'll have to fight Prospero for it.

STEPHANO: That is of no matter, brave savage. It's a bargain! I'll get rid of this Prospero for you in two shakes.

CALIBAN: Watch out, he's powerful.

STEPHANO: My dear savage, I eat a dozen Prosperos like that for breakfast every day. But say no more, say no more! Trinculo, take command of the troops! Let us march upon the foe!

TRINCULO: Yes, forward march! But first, a drink. We will need all our strength and vigor.

CALIBAN: Let's drink, my new-found friends, and let us sing. Let us sing of winning the day and of an end to tyranny.

(*Singing*)

> *Black pecking creature of the savannas*
> *The quetzal measures out the new day*
> *solid and lively*
> *in its haughty armor.*
> *Zing! the determined hummingbird*
> *revels in the flower's depths,*
> *going crazy, getting drunk,*
> *a lyrebird gathers up our ravings,*
> *Freedom hi-day! Freedom hi-day!*

STEPHANO AND TRINCULO: (*Together*) Freedom hi-day! Freedom hi-day!

CALIBAN:

> *The ringdove dallies amid the trees,*
> *wandering the islands, here it rests—*
> *The white blossoms of the miconia*
> *Mingle with the violet blood of ripe berries*
> *And blood stains your plumage,*
> *traveller!*
> *Lying here after a weary day*
> *We listen to it:*
> *Freedom hi-day! Freedom hi-day!*

STEPHANO: Okay, monster . . . enough crooning. Singing makes a man thirsty. Let's drink instead. Here, have some more . . . spirits create higher spirits . . . (*Filling a glass.*) Lead the way, O bountiful wine! Soldiers, forward march! Or rather . . . no: At ease! Night is falling, the fireflies twinkle, the crickets chirp, all nature makes its brek-ke-ke-kek! And since night has fallen, let us take advantage of it to gather our forces and regain our strength, which has been sorely tried by the unusually . . . copious emotions of the day. And tomorrow, at dawn, with a new spring in our step, we'll have the tyrant's hide. Good night, gentlemen. (*He falls asleep and begins to snore.*)

SCENE 3

Prospero's cave

PROSPERO: So then, Ariel! Where are the gods and goddesses? They'd better get a move on! And all of them! I want all of them to take part in the entertainment I have planned for our dear children. Why do I say "entertainment"? Because starting today I want to inculcate in them the spectacle of tomorrow's world: logic, beauty, harmony, the foundations for which I have laid down by my own will-power. Unfortunately, alas, at my age it's time to stop thinking of deeds and to begin thinking of passing on . . . Enter, then!

Gods and Goddesses enter.

JUNO: Honor and riches to you! Long continuance and increasing long life and honored issue! Juno sings to you her blessings!

CERES: May scarcity and want shun you! That is Ceres' blessing on you.

IRIS: (*beckoning to the Nymphs*) Nymphs, come help to celebrate here a contact of true love.

Nymphs enter and dance.

PROSPERO: My thanks, Goddesses, and my thanks to you, Iris. Thank you for your good wishes.

Gods and Goddesses continue their dance.

FERDINAND: What a splendid and majestic vision! May I be so bold to think these spirits?

PROSPERO: Yes, spirits which by my art I have from their confines called to greet you and to bless you.

Enter Eshu.

MIRANDA: But who is that? He doesn't look very benevolent! If I weren't afraid of blaspheming, I'd say he was a devil rather than a god.

ESHU: (*Laughing*) You are not mistaken, fair lady. God to my friends, the Devil to my enemies! And lots of laughs for all!

PROSPERO: (*Softly*) Ariel must have made a mistake. Is my magic getting rusty? (*Aloud*) What are you doing here? Who invited you? I don't like such loose behavior, even from a god!

ESHU: But that's just the point . . . no one invited me . . . And that wasn't very nice! Nobody remembered poor Eshu! So poor Eshu came anyway. Hihihi!

So how about something to drink? (*Without waiting for a reply, he pours a drink.*) . . . Your liquor's not bad. However, I must say I prefer dogs! (*Looking at Iris*) I see that shocks the little lady, but to each his own. Some prefer chickens, others prefer goats. I'm not too fond of chickens, myself. But if you're talking about a black dog . . . think of poor Eshu!

PROSPERO: Get out! Go away! We will have none of your grimaces and buffoonery in this noble assembly. (*He makes a magic sign.*)

ESHU: I'm going, boss, I'm going . . . But not without a little song in honor of the bride and the noble company, as you say.

> Eshu can play many tricks,
> Give him twenty dogs!
> You will see his dirty tricks.
>
> Eshu plays a trick on the Queen
> And makes her so upset that she runs
> Naked into the street
>
> Eshu plays a trick on a bride,
> And on the day of the wedding
> She gets into the wrong bed!
>
> Eshu can throw a stone yesterday
> And kill a bird today.
> He can make a mess out of order and vice-versa.
> Ah, Eshu is a wonderful bad joke.
> Eshu is not the man to carry a heavy load.
> His head comes to a point. When he dances
> He doesn't move his shoulders . . .
> Oh, Eshu is a merry elf!
>
> Eshu is a merry elf,
> And he can whip you with his dick,
> He can whip you,
> He can whip you . . .

CERES: My dear Iris, don't you find that song quite obscene?

JUNO: It's disgusting! It's quite intolerable . . . if he keeps on, I'm leaving!

IRIS: It's like Liber, or Priapus!

JUNO: Don't mention that name in my presence!

ESHU: (*continuing to sing*)

> . . . with his dick
> He can whip you, whip you . . .

JUNO: Oh! Can't someone get rid of him? I'm not staying here!

ESHU: Okay, okay . . . Eshu will go. Farewell, my dear colleagues!

Gods and Goddesses exit.

PROSPERO: He's gone . . . what a relief! But alas, the harm is done! I am perturbed . . . My old brain is confused. Power! Power! Alas! All this will one day fade, like foam, like a cloud, like all the world. And what is power, if I cannot calm my own fears? But come! My power has gone cold. (Calling) Ariel!

ARIEL: (runs in) What is it, Sire?

PROSPERO: Caliban is alive, he is plotting, he is getting a guerrilla force together and you—you don't say a word! Well, take care of him. Snakes, scorpions, porcupines, all stinging poisonous creatures, he is to be spared nothing! His punishment must be exemplary. Oh, and don't forget the mud and mosquitoes!

ARIEL: Master, let me intercede for him and beg your indulgence. You've got to understand: he's a rebel.

PROSPERO: By his insubordination he's calling into question the whole order of the world. Maybe the Divinity can afford to let him get away with it, but I have a sense of responsibility!

ARIEL: Very well, Master.

PROSPERO: But a thought: arrange some glass trinkets, some trumpery and some second-hand clothes too . . . but colorful ones . . . by the side of the road along which General Caliban and his troops are travelling. Savages adore loud, gaudy clothes . . .

ARIEL: Master . . .

PROSPERO: You're going to make me angry. There's nothing to understand. There is a punishment to be meted out. I will not compromise with evil. Hurry! Unless you want to be the next to feel my wrath.

SCENE 4

In the wild; night is drawing to a close; the murmurings of the spirits of the tropical forest are heard.

VOICE I: Fly!

VOICE: Here!

VOICE I: Ant!

VOICE II: Here.

VOICE I: Vulture!

VOICE II: Here.

VOICE I: Soft-shelled crab, calao, crab, hummingbird!

VOICES: Here. Here. Here.

VOICE I: Cramp, crime, fang, opossum!

VOICE II: Kra. Kra. Kra.

VOICE I: Huge hedgehog, you will be our sun today. Shaggy, taloned, stubborn. May it burn! Moon, my fat spider, my big dreamcat, go to sleep, my velvet one.

VOICES: (singing)

> King-ay
> King-ay
> Von-von
> Maloto
> Vloom-vloom!

The sun rises. Ariel's band vanishes. Caliban stands for a moment, rubbing his eyes.

CALIBAN: (*rises and searches the bushes*) Have to think about getting going again. Away, snakes, scorpions, porcupines! All stinging, biting, sticking beasts! Sting, fever, venom, away! Of if you really want to lick me, do it with a gentle tongue, like the toad whose pure drool soothes me with sweet dreams of the future. For it is for you, for all of us, that I go forth today to face the common enemy. Yes, hereditary and common. Look, a hedgehog! Sweet little thing . . . How can any animal—any natural animal, if I may put it that way—go against me on the day I'm setting forth to conquer Prospero! Unimaginable! Prospero is the Anti-Nature! And I say, down with Anti-Nature! And does the porcupine bristle his spines at that? No, he smoothes them down! That's nature! It's kind and gentle, in a word. You've just got to know how to deal with it. So come on, the way is clear! Off we go!

The band sets out. Caliban marches forward singing his battle song:

> Shango carries a big stick,
> He strikes and money expires!
> He strikes and lies expire!
> He strikes and larceny expires!
> Shango, Shango ho!
> Shango is the gatherer of the rain,
> He passes, wrapped in his fiery cloak,
> His horse's hoofs strike lighting
> On the pavements of the sky!
> Shango is a great knight!
> Shango, Shango ho!

The roar of the sea can be heard.

STEPHANO: Tell me, brave savage, what is that noise? It sounds like the roaring of a beast at bay.

CALIBAN: Not at bay . . . more like on the prowl . . . Don't worry, it's a pal of mine.

STEPHANO: You are very closemouthed about the company you keep.

CALIBAN: And yet it helps me breathe. That's why I call it a pal. Sometimes it sneezes, and a drop falls on my forehead and cools me with its salt, or blesses me . . .

STEPHANO: I don't understand. You aren't drunk, are you?

CALIBAN: Come on! It's that howling impatient thing that suddenly appears in a clap of thunder like some God and hits you in the face, that rises up out of the very depths of the abyss and smites you with its fury! It's the sea!

STEPHANO: Odd country! And an odd baptism!

CALIBAN: But the best is still the wind and the songs it sings . . . its dirty sigh when it rustles through the bushes, or its triumphant chant when it passes by breaking trees, remnants of their terror in its beard.

STEPHANO: The savage is delirious, he's raving mad! Tough luck, Trinculo, our savage is playing without a full deck!

TRINCULO: I'm kind of shuffling myself . . . In other words, I'm exhausted. I never knew such hard going! Savage, even your mud is muddier.

CALIBAN: That isn't mud . . . it's something Prospero's dreamed up.

TRINCULO: There's a savage for you . . . everything's always caused by someone. The sun is Prospero's smile. The rain is the tear in Prospero's eye . . . And I suppose the mud is Prospero's shit. And what about the mosquitoes? What are they, may I ask? Zzzzzz, Zzzzzz . . . do you hear them? My face is being eaten off!

CALIBAN: Those aren't mosquitoes. It's some kind of gas that stings your nose and throat and makes you itch. It's another of Prospero's tricks. It's part of his arsenal.

STEPHANO: What do you mean by that?

CALIBAN: I mean his anti-riot arsenal! He's got a lot of gadgets like these . . . gadgets to make you deaf, to blind you, to make you sneeze, to make you cry . . .

TRINCULO: And to make you slip! Shit! This is some fix you've got us in! I can't take anymore . . . I'm going to sit down!

STEPHANO: Come on, Trinculo, show a little courage! We're engaged in a mobile ground manoeuvre here, and you know what that means: drive, initiatives, split-second decisions to meet new eventualities, and—above all—mobility. Let's go! Up you get! Mobility!

TRINCULO: But my feet are bleeding!

STEPHANO: Get up or I'll knock you down! (*Trinculo begins to walk again.*) But tell me, my good savage, this usurper of yours seems very well protected. It might be dangerous to attack him!

CALIBAN: You mustn't underestimate him. You mustn't overestimate him, either . . . he's showing his power, but he's doing it mostly to impress us.

STEPHANO: No matter. Trinculo, we must take precautions. Axiom: never underestimate the enemy. Here, pass me that bottle. I can always use it as a club.

Highly colored clothing is seen, hanging from a rope.

TRINCULO: Right, Stephano. On with the battle. Victory means loot. And there's a foretaste of it . . . look at that fine wardrobe! Trinculo, my friend, methinks you are going to put on those britches . . . they'll replace your torn trousers.

STEPHANO: Look out, Trinculo . . . one move and I'll knock you down. As your lord and master I have the first pick, and with those britches I'm exercising my feudal rights . . .

TRINCULO: I saw them first!

STEPHANO: The King gets first pick in every country in the world.

TRINCULO: That's tyranny, Stephano. I'm not going to let you get away with it.

They fight.

CALIBAN: Let it alone, fool. I tell you about winning your dignity, and you start fighting over hand-me-downs! (*To himself*) To think I'm stuck with these jokers! What an idiot I am! How could I ever have thought I could create the Revolution with swollen guts and fat faces! Oh well! History won't blame me for not having been able to win my freedom all by myself. It's you and me, Prospero! (*Weapon in hand, he advances on Prospero who has just appeared.*)

PROSPERO: (*bares his chest to him*) Strike! Go on, strike! Strike your Master, your benefactor! Don't tell me you're going to spare him!

Caliban raises his arm, but hesitates.

Go on! You don't dare! See, you're nothing but an animal . . . you don't know how to kill.

CALIBAN: Defend yourself! I'm not a murderer.

PROSPERO: *(very calm)* The worse for you. You've lost your chance. Stupid as a slave! And now, enough of this farce. *(Calling)* Ariel! *(to Ariel)* Ariel, take charge of the prisoners!

Caliban, Trinculo and Stephano are taken prisoners.

SCENE 5

Prospero's cave. Miranda and Ferdinand are playing chess.

MIRANDA: Sir, I think you're cheating.

FERDINAND: And what if I told you that I would not do so for twenty kingdoms?

MIRANDA: I would not believe a word of it, but I would forgive you. Now, be honest . . . you did cheat!

FERDINAND: I'm pleased that you were able to tell. *(Laughing)* That makes me less worried at the thought that soon you will be leaving your innocent flowery kingdom for my less-innocent world of men.

MIRANDA: Oh, you know that, hitched to your star, I would brave the demons of hell!

The Nobles enter.

ALONSO: My son! This marriage! The thrill of it has struck me dumb! The thrill and the joy!

GONZALO: A happy ending to a most opportune shipwreck!

ALONSO: A unique one, indeed, for it can legitimately be described as such.

GONZALO: Look at them! Isn't it wonderful! I've been too choked up to speak, or I would have already told these children all the joy my old heart feels at seeing them living love's young dream and cherishing each other so tenderly.

ALONSO: *(to Ferdinand and Miranda)* My children, give me your hands. May the Lord bless you.

GONZALO: Amen! Amen!

Enter Prospero.

PROSPERO: Thank you, Gentlemen, for having agreed to join in this little family party. Your presence has brought us comfort and joy. However, you must now think of getting some rest. Tomorrow morning, you will recover your vessels—they are undamaged—and your men, who I can guarantee are safe, hale and hearty. I shall return with you to Europe, and I can promise you—I should say: promise us—a rapid sail and propitious winds.

GONZALO: God be praised! We are delighted . . . delighted and overcome! What a happy, what a memorable day! With one voyage Antonio has found a brother, his brother has found a dukedom, his daughter has found a husband. Alonso has regained his son and gained a daughter. And what else? . . . Anyway, I am the only one whose emotion prevents him from knowing what he's saying . . .

PROSPERO: The proof of that, my fine Gonzalo, is that you are forgetting someone: Ariel, my loyal servant. (Turning to Ariel) Yes, Ariel, today you will be
free. Go, my sweet. I hope you will not be bored.

ARIEL: Bored! I fear that the days will seem all too short!
There, where the Cecropia gloves its impatient hands with silver,
Where the ferns free the stubborn black stumps
from their scored bodies with a green cry—
There where the intoxicating berry ripens the visit
of the wild ring-dove through the throat of that musical bird
I shall let fall
one by one,
each more pleasing than the last
four notes so sweet that the last
will give rise to a yearning
in the heart of the most forgetful slaves
yearning for freedom!

PROSPERO: Come, come. All the same, you are not going to set my world on fire
with your music, I trust!

ARIEL: *(with intoxication)*
Or on some stony plane
perched on an agave stalk
I shall be the thrush that launches
its mocking cry
to the benighted field-hand
"Dig, nigger! Dig, nigger!"
and the lightened agave will
straighten from my flight,
a solemn flag.

PROSPERO: That is a very unsettling agenda! Go! Scram!
Before I change my mind!

Enter Stephano, Trinculo, Caliban.

GONZALO: Sire, here are your people.

PROSPERO: Oh no, not all of them! Some are yours.

ALONSO: True. There's that fool Trinculo and that unspeakable Stephano.

STEPHANO: The very ones, Sire, in person. We throw ourselves at your merciful
feet.

ALONSO: What became of you?

STEPHANO: Sire, we were walking in the forest—no, it was in the fields—when
we saw some perfectly respectable clothing blowing in the wind. We thought
it only right to collect them and we were returning them to their rightful
owner when a frightful adventure befell us . . .

TRINCULO: Yes, we were mistaken for thieves and treated accordingly.

STEPHANO: Yes, Sire, it is the most dreadful thing that could happen to an honest man: victims of a judicial error, a miscarriage of justice!

PROSPERO: Enough! Today is a day to be benevolent, and it will do no good to
try to talk sense to you in the state you're in . . . Leave us. Go sleep it off,
drunkards. We raise sail tomorrow.

TRINCULO: Raise sail! But that's what we do all the time, Sire, Stephano and I
. . . at least, we raise our glasses, from dawn till dusk till dawn.. The hard part
is putting them down, landing, as you might say.

PROSPERO: Scoundrels! If only life could bring you to the safe harbors of Temperance and Sobriety!

ALONSO: *(indicating Caliban)* That is the strangest creature I've ever seen!

PROSPERO: And the most devilish too!

GONZALO: What's that? Devilish! You've reprimanded him, preached at him,
you've ordered and made him obey and you say he is still indomitable!

PROSPERO: Honest Gonzalo, it is as I have said.

GONZALO: Well—and forgive me, Counsellor, if I give counsel—on the basis of
my long experience the only thing left is exorcism. "Begone, unclean spirit,
in the name of the Father, of the Son and of the Holy Ghost." That's all
there is to it!

Caliban bursts out laughing.

GONZALO: You were absolutely right! And more so that you thought . . . He's
not just a rebel, he's a real tough customer! *(To Caliban)* So much the worse
for you, my friend. I have tried to save you. I give up. I leave you to the secular arm!

PROSPERO: Come here, Caliban. Have you got anything to say in your own defence? Take advantage of my good humor. I'm in a forgiving mood today.

CALIBAN: I'm not interested in defending myself. My only regret is that I've
failed.

PROSPERO: What were you hoping for?

CALIBAN: To get back my island and regain my freedom.

PROSPERO: And what would you do all alone here on this island, haunted by the
devil, tempest tossed?

CALIBAN: First of all, I'd get rid of you! I'd spit you out, all your works and
pomps! Your "white" magic!

PROSPERO: That's a fairly negative program . . .

CALIBAN:

You don't understand it . . . I say I'm going to spit you out, and that's very positive . . .

PROSPERO: Well, the world is really upside down . . . We've seen everything
now: Caliban as a dialectician! However, in spite of everything I'm fond of
you, Caliban. Come, let's make peace. We've lived together for ten years and
worked side by side! Ten years count for something, after all! We've ended up
by becoming compatriots!

CALIBAN: You know very well that I'm not interested in peace. I'm interested in
being free! Free, you hear?

PROSPERO: It's odd . . . no matter what you do, you won't succeed in making me
believe that I'm a tyrant!

CALIBAN: Understand what I say, Prospero:

For years I bowed my head
for years I took it, all of it—
your insults, your ingratitude . . .
and worst of all, more degrading than all the rest,

your condescension.
But now, it's over!
Over, do you hear?
Of course, at the moment
You're still stronger than I am.
But I don't give a damn for your power
or for your dogs or your police or your inventions!
And do you know why?
It's because I know I'll get you.
I'll impale you! And on a stake that you've sharpened yourself!
You'll have impaled yourself!
Prospero, you're a great magician:
you're an old hand at deception.
And you lied to me so much,
about the world, about myself,
that you ended up by imposing on me
an image of myself:
underdeveloped, in your words, undercompetent
that's how you made me see myself!
And I hate that image . . . and it's false!
But now I know you, you old cancer,
And I also know myself!
And I know that one day
my bare fist, just that,
will be enough to crush your world!
The old world is crumbling down!

Isn't it true? Just look!
It even bores you to death.
And by the way . . . you have a chance to get it over with:
You can pick up and leave.
You can go back to Europe.
But the hell you will!
I'm sure you won't leave.
You make me laugh with your "mission"!
Your "vocation"!
Your vocation is to hassle me.
And that's why you'll stay,
just like those guys who founded the colonies
and who now can't live anywhere else.
You're just an old addict, that's what you are!

PROSPERO: Poor Caliban! You know that you're headed towards your own ruin.
You're sliding towards suicide! You know I will be the stronger, and stronger
all the time. I pity you!

CALIBAN: And I hate you!

PROSPERO: Beware! My generosity has its limits.

CALIBAN: (shouting)

> Shango marches with strength
> along his path, the sky!

Shango is a fire-bearer,
his steps shake the heavens
and the earth
Shango, Shango, ho!

PROSPERO: I have uprooted the oak and raised the sea, I have caused the mountain to tremble and have bared my chest to adversity.
With Jove I have traded thunderbolt for thunderbolt.
Better yet—from a brutish monster I have made man!
But ah! To have failed to find the path to man's heart . . .
if that be where man is.
(*to Caliban*)
Well, I hate you as well!
For it is you who have made me
doubt myself for the first time.
(*to the Nobles*)
  . . . My friends, come near. We must say farewell . . . I shall not be going with
  you. My fate is here: I shall not run from it.

ANTONIO: What, Sire?

PROSPERO: Hear me well.
I am not in any ordinary sense a master,
as this savage thinks,
but rather the conductor of a boundless score:
this isle,
summoning voices, I alone,
and mingling them at my pleasure,
arranging out of confusion
one intelligible line.
Without me, who would be able to draw music from all that?
This isle is mute without me.
My duty, thus, is here,
and here I shall stay.

GONZALO: Oh day full rich in miracles!

PROSPERO: Do not be distressed. Antonio, be you the lieutenant of my goods
and make use of them as procurator until that time when Ferdinand and Miranda may take effective possession of them, joining them with the Kingdom
of Naples. Nothing of that which has been set for them must be postponed:
Let their marriage be celebrated at Naples with all royal splendor. Honest
Gonzalo, I place my trust in your word. You shall stand as father to our
princess at this ceremony.

GONZALO: Count on me, Sire.

PROSPERO: Gentleman, farewell.

  They exit.

And now, Caliban, it's you and me!
What I have to tell you will be brief:
Ten times, a hundred times, I've tried to save you,
above all from yourself.
But you have always answered me with wrath
and venom,

like the opossum that pulls itself up by its own tail
the better to bite the hand that tears it from the darkness.
Well, my boy, I shall set aside my indulgent nature
and henceforth I will answer your violence
with violence!

*Time passes, symbolized by the curtain's being lowered halfway and reraised.
In semi-darkness Prospero appears, aged and weary. His gestures are jerky
and automatic, his speech weak, toneless, trite.*

PROSPERO: Odd, but for some time now we seem to be overrun with opossums.
They're everywhere. Peccarys, wild boar, all this unclean nature! But mainly
opossums. Those eyes! The vile grins they have! It's as though the jungle was
laying siege to the cave . . . But I shall stand firm . . . I shall not let my work
perish! *(Shouting)* I shall protect civilization! *(He fires in all directions.)*
They're done for! Now, this way I'll be able to have some peace and quiet for
a while. But it's cold. Odd how the climate's changed. Cold on this island . . .
Have to think about making a fire . . . Well, Caliban, old fellow, it's just us
two now, here on the island . . . only you and me. You and me. You-me . . .
me-you! What in the hell is he up to? *(Shouting)* Caliban!

*In the distance, above the sound of the surf and the chirping of birds, we hear
snatches of Caliban's song:*

FREEDOM HI-DAY, FREEDOM HI-DAY!

ANNEX

Literal Translations of Songs

ARIEL'S SONG (ACT I, SCENE 2)

Chestnut horses of the sand
They bite out the place
Where the waves expire in
Pure languor.
Where the waves die
Here come all,
Join hands
And dance.

Blond sands,
What fire!
Languorous waves,
Pure expiration.
Here lips lick and lick again
Our wounds.

The waves make a waterline . . .
Nothing is, all is becoming . . .
The season is close and strange

The eye is a fine pearl
The heart of coral, the bone of coral,

There, at the waterline
As the sea swells within us.

TRINCULO'S SONG (ACT III, SCENE 2)

Virginia, with tears in my eyes
I bid you farewell.
We're off to Mexico,
Straight into the setting sun.

With sails unfurled, my dear love,
It torments me to leave you,
A tempest is brewing
Some storm is howling
That will carry off the entire crew!

STEPHANO'S SONG (ACT III, SCENE 2)

(Obviously an old sea chanty or Césaire's adaptation of one)

Bravely on, guys, step it lively,
bravely on, farewell Bordeaux,
To Cape Horn, it won't be hot,
Off to hunt the whale.

More than one of us will lose his skin
Farewell misery, farewell ship.
The ones who return with all flags flying
Will be the first-rate sailors . . .

Talking about the Text

1. In *A Tempest*, how has the playwright, Aimé Césaire, changed the role of the royal party? (The comparable part of Shakespeare's *The Tempest* falls on pages 1362–1372.)
2. In Césaire's version, what has happened to the role of Ariel?

Writing about the Text

1. Choose a scene from Shakespeare's *The Tempest* and a corresponding one from Césaire's *A Tempest*, such as the plays' ending scenes or Prospero's renunciation of his magic, and describe the differences or the similarities.
2. While Caliban's speeches can seem like political tracts in *A Tempest*, they never do in *The Tempest*. Choose one speech by Caliban in each version, analyze the differences between them, and argue for or against the decision to write the speeches this way.

Starting Points for Further Research: Aimé Césaire

- **Editions:** Aimé Césaire. *A Tempest*. New York: TCG Translations, 2002.
  ———. *Lyric and Dramatic Poetry*. Ed. Clayton Eshleman and Annette Smith. Charlottesville: University of Virginia Press, 1990.
- **Critical Essay:** Judith H. Samecki. "Mastering the Masters: Aimé Césaire's Creolization of Shakespeare's *The Tempest*." *French Review: Journal of the American Association of Teachers of French* 74 (2000): 276–86.

Reading *Hamlet*

Claudius hands Laertes a knife in Act 3, Scene 2, of a 1955 Moscow production of Hamlet *at the Mayakovsky Theater.*

Whether they have read the play or not, people know *Hamlet*. They know its famous lines, such as "To be or not to be," and its famous tableau, Hamlet contemplating the skull of Yorick. Even if they do not know the plot very well, people know it is by Shakespeare and has the requisite pale young man, a Danish court (where "something's rotten"), a ghost, and a swordfight. Interestingly, much of that plot was known to audiences before Shakespeare wrote his play around 1598 or 1600 (the actual date is uncertain). *Hamlet* was a story many people knew of, if only vaguely. And Shakespeare's *Hamlet* fit a genre everyone knew very, very well. It was a "revenge tragedy," in which a relative must avenge a great wrong and in doing so lose his own life. Revenge tragedies were common on the British stage long before *Hamlet*. The audience knew in advance how it would turn out; the question was really how, in what manner, and with what action.

Shakespeare supplies a rich, complex text packed with a mix of action and contemplation. Hamlet, the prince of Denmark, must avenge his murdered father, who appears to him as a ghost. The revenge is complicated, since the murderer, Claudius, has married Hamlet's mother. How long will Hamlet wait to act? What will he do to get his revenge? How will his involvement in revenge affect his dealings with his betrothed, Ophelia? That is what the audience wanted to see, and audiences have continued to watch for centuries.

For a critical interpretation of the enigmatic character that is Hamlet, see the famous essay by poet and critic T. S. Eliot, "Hamlet and His Problems," in Chapter 21, "Writing about Plays" (p. 1220).

Hamlet, Prince of Denmark (C. 1600)

Edited by David Bevington

Dramatis Personae

CLAUDIUS, King of Denmark
HAMLET, son to the late and nephew to the present king
POLONIUS, lord chamberlain
HORATIO, friend to Hamlet
LAERTES, son to Polonius
VOLTIMAND, CORNELIUS, ROSENCRANTZ, GUILDENSTERN, OSRIC, courtiers
A GENTLEMAN
A PRIEST
MARCELLUS, BERNARDO, officers
FRANCISCO, a soldier
REYNALDO, servant to Polonius
PLAYERS
TWO CLOWNS, grave-diggers
FORTINBRAS, Prince of Norway
A CAPTAIN
ENGLISH AMBASSADORS
GERTRUDE, Queen of Denmark, and mother to Hamlet
OPHELIA, daughter to Polonius
LORDS, LADIES, OFFICERS, SOLDIERS, SAILORS, MESSENGERS, AND OTHER ATTENDANTS
GHOST of Hamlet's Father

Scene: *Denmark.*

[1.1]

Enter Bernardo and Francisco, two sentinels, [meeting].

BERNARDO Who's there?
FRANCISCO Nay, answer me. Stand and unfold yourself.   2

The text of *Hamlet* is based on that of the First Folio (1623), or large collection, of Shakespeare's plays. For clarity, some indications of scene and stage directions have been added by the editor, David Bevington, in brackets. Bevington's text and notes come from his book *The Complete Works of Shakespeare*, updated 4th ed. (New York: Longman, 1997).
1.1 Location: Elsinore castle. A guard platform.
2 me (Francisco emphasizes that he is the sentry currently on watch.) **unfold yourself** reveal your identity.

BERNARDO Long live the King!

FRANCISCO Bernardo?

BERNARDO He.

FRANCISCO You come most carefully upon your hour.

BERNARDO 'Tis now struck twelve. Get thee to bed, Francisco.

FRANCISCO For this relief much thanks. 'Tis bitter cold,
    And I am sick at heart.

BERNARDO Have you had quiet guard?

FRANCISCO Not a mouse stirring.

BERNARDO Well, good night.
    If you do meet Horatio and Marcellus,
    The rivals of my watch, bid them make haste.   14

Enter Horatio and Marcellus.

FRANCISCO I think I hear them.—Stand, ho! Who is there?

HORATIO Friends to this ground.   16

MARCELLUS And liegemen to the Dane.   17

FRANCISCO Give you good night.   18

MARCELLUS Oh, farewell, honest soldier. Who hath relieved you?

FRANCISCO Bernardo hath my place. Give you good night.

Exit Francisco.

MARCELLUS Holla! Bernardo!

BERNARDO Say, what, is Horatio there?

HORATIO A piece of him.

BERNARDO Welcome, Horatio. Welcome, good Marcellus.

HORATIO What, has this thing appeared again tonight?

BERNARDO I have seen nothing.

MARCELLUS Horatio says 'tis but our fantasy,   27
    And will not let belief take hold of him
    Touching this dreaded sight twice seen of us.
    Therefore I have entreated him along   30
    With us to watch the minutes of this night,   31
    That if again this apparition come
    He may approve our eyes and speak to it.   33

HORATIO Tush, tush, 'twill not appear.

BERNARDO   Sit down awhile,
    And let us once again assail your ears,
    That are so fortified against our story,
    What we have two nights seen.

HORATIO   Well, sit we down,
    And let us hear Bernardo speak of this.

BERNARDO Last night of all,   39
    When yond same star that's westward from the pole   40

---

14 **rivals** partners 16 **ground** country, land. 17 **liegemen to the Dane** men sworn to serve the Danish king. 18 **Give** May God give 27 **fantasy** imagination 30 **along** to come along 31 **watch** keep watch during 33 **approve** corroborate 39 **Last … all** i.e., This very last night. (Emphatic.) 40 **pole** polestar, north star

Had made his course t'illume that part of heaven 41
Where now it burns, Marcellus and myself,
The bell then beating one—

Enter Ghost.

MARCELLUS Peace, break thee off! Look where it comes again!
BERNARDO In the same figure like the King that's dead.
MARCELLUS Thou art a scholar. Speak to it, Horatio. 46
BERNARDO Looks 'a not like the King? Mark it, Horatio. 47
HORATIO Most like. It harrows me with fear and wonder.
BERNARDO It would be spoke to.
MARCELLUS   Speak to it, Horatio. 49
HORATIO What art thou that usurp'st this time of night, 50
  Together with that fair and warlike form
  In which the majesty of buried Denmark 52
  Did sometimes march? By heaven, I charge thee, speak! 53
MARCELLUS It is offended.
BERNARDO   See, it stalks away.
HORATIO Stay! Speak, speak! I charge thee, speak!   *Exit Ghost.*
MARCELLUS 'Tis gone and will not answer.
BERNARDO How now, Horatio? You tremble and look pale.
  Is not this something more than fantasy?
  What think you on't? 59
HORATIO Before my God, I might not this believe
  Without the sensible and true avouch 61
  Of mine own eyes.
MARCELLUS   Is it not like the King?
HORATIO As thou art to thyself.
Such was the very armor he had on
  When he the ambitious Norway combated. 65
  So frowned he once when, in an angry parle, 66
  He smote the sledded Polacks on the ice. 67
  'Tis strange.
MARCELLUS Thus twice before, and jump at this dead hour, 69
  With martial stalk hath he gone by our watch. 70
HORATIO In what particular thought to work I know not, 71
  But in the gross and scope of mine opinion 72
  This bodes some strange eruption to our state.
MARCELLUS Good now, sit down, and tell me, he that knows, 74
  Why this same strict and most observant watch
  So nightly toils the subject of the land, 76

---

41 his its. **t'illume** to illuminate **46 scholar** one learned enough to know how to question a ghost properly. **47 'a** he **49 It . . . to** (It was commonly believed that a ghost could not speak until spoken to.) **50 usurp'st** wrongfully takes over **52 buried Denmark** the buried King of Denmark **53 sometimes** formerly **59 on't** of it. **61 sensible** confirmed by the senses. **avouch** warrant, evidence **65 Norway** King of Norway **66 parle** parley **67 sledded** traveling on sleds. **Polacks** Poles **69 jump** exactly **70 stalk** stride **71 to work** i.e., to collect my thoughts and try to understand this **72 gross and scope** general drift **74 Good now** (An expression denoting entreaty or expostulation.) **76 toils** causes to toil. **subject** subjects

And why such daily cast of brazen cannon 77
And foreign mart for implements of war, 78
Why such impress of shipwrights, whose sore task 79
Does not divide the Sunday from the week.
What might be toward, that this sweaty haste 81
Doth make the night joint-laborer with the day?
Who is't that can inform me?

HORATIO   That can I;
At least, the whisper goes so. Our last king,
Whose image even but now appeared to us,
Was, as you know, by Fortinbras of Norway,
Thereto pricked on by a most emulate pride, 87
Dared to the combat; in which our valiant Hamlet—
For so this side of our known world esteemed him— 89
Did slay this Fortinbras; who by a sealed compact 90
Well ratified by law and heraldry 91
Did forfeit, with his life, all those his lands
Which he stood seized of, to the conqueror; 93
Against the which a moiety competent 94
Was gagèd by our king, which had returned 95
To the inheritance of Fortinbras 96
Had he been vanquisher, as, by the same cov'nant 97
And carriage of the article designed, 98
His fell to Hamlet. Now, sir, young Fortinbras,
Of unimprovèd mettle hot and full, 100
Hath in the skirts of Norway here and there 101
Sharked up a list of lawless resolutes 102
For food and diet to some enterprise 103
That hath a stomach in't, which is no other— 104
As it doth well appear unto our state—
But to recover of us, by strong hand
And terms compulsatory, those foresaid lands
So by his father lost. And this, I take it,
Is the main motive of our preparations,
The source of this our watch, and the chief head 110
Of this posthaste and rummage in the land. 111

BERNARDO I think it be no other but e'en so.
Well may it sort that this portentous figure 113
Comes armèd through our watch so like the King
That was and is the question of these wars. 115

---

77 cast casting **78 mart** shopping **79 impress** impressment, conscription **81 toward** in preparation **87 Thereto . . . pride** (Refers to old Fortinbras, not the Danish King.) **pricked on** incited. **emulate** emulous, ambitious **89 this . . . world** i.e., all Europe, the Western world **90 sealed** certified, confirmed **91 heraldry** chivalry **93 seized** possessed **94 Against the** in return for. **moiety competent** corresponding portion **95 gagèd** engaged, pledged. **had returned** would have passed **96 inheritance** possession **97 cov'nant** i.e., the sealed compact of line 90 **98 carriage . . . designed** purport of the article referred to **100 unimprovèd mettle** untried, undisciplined spirits **101 skirts** outlying regions, outskirts **102–4 Sharked . . . in't** rounded up (as a shark scoops up fish) a troop of lawless desperadoes to feed and supply an enterprise of considerable daring **110 head** source **111 posthaste and rummage** frenetic activity and bustle **113 Well . . . sort** That would explain why **115 question** focus of contention

HORATIO A mote it is to trouble the mind's eye. 116
    In the most high and palmy state of Rome, 117
    A little ere the mightiest Julius fell, 118
    The graves stood tenantless, and the sheeted dead 119
    Did squeak and gibber in the Roman streets;
    As stars with trains of fire and dews of blood, 121
    Disasters in the sun; and the moist star 122
    Upon whose influence Neptune's empire stands 123
    Was sick almost to doomsday with eclipse. 124
    And even the like precurse of feared events, 125
    As harbingers preceding still the fates 126
    And prologue to the omen coming on, 127
    Have heaven and earth together demonstrated
    Unto our climatures and countrymen. 129

    Enter Ghost.

    But soft, behold! Lo, where it comes again! 130
    I'll cross it, though it blast me. (*It spreads its arms.*) Stay, illusion! 131
    If thou hast any sound or use of voice,
    Speak to me!
    If there be any good thing to be done
    That may to thee do ease and grace to me,
    Speak to me!
    If thou art privy to thy country's fate, 137
    Which, happily, foreknowing may avoid, 138
    Oh, speak!
    Or if thou hast uphoarded in thy life
    Extorted treasure in the womb of earth,
    For which, they say, you spirits oft walk in death,
    Speak of it! (*The cock crows.*) Stay and speak!—Stop it, Marcellus.
MARCELLUS Shall I strike at it with my partisan? 144
HORATIO Do, if it will not stand.   *[They strike at it.]*
BERNARDO 'Tis here! 146
HORATIO 'Tis here!   *[Exit Ghost.]* 147
MARCELLUS 'Tis gone.
    We do it wrong, being so majestical,
    To offer it the show of violence,
    For it is as the air invulnerable,
    And our vain blows malicious mockery.

---

116 mote speck of dust **117 palmy** flourishing **118 Julius** Julius Caesar **119 sheeted** shrouded **121 As** (This abrupt transition suggests that matter is possibly omitted between lines 120 and 121.) **trains** trails **122 Disasters** unfavorable signs or aspects. **moist star** i.e., moon, governing tides **123 Neptune's . . . stands** the sea depends **124 Was . . . eclipse** was eclipsed nearly to the cosmic darkness predicted for the second coming of Christ and the ending of the world. (See Matthew 24:29 and Revelation 6:12.) **125 precurse** heralding, foreshadowing **126 harbingers** forerunners. **still** always **127 omen** calamitous event **129 climatures** climes, regions **130 soft** i.e., enough, break off **131 cross** stand in its path, confront. **blast** wither, strike with a curse. **131 s.d. his** its **137 privy to** in on the secret of **138 happily** haply, perchance **144 partisan** long-handled spear. **146–7 'Tis Here!/'Tis here!** (Perhaps they attempt to strike at the Ghost, but are baffled by its seeming ability to be here and there and nowhere.)

BERNARDO It was about to speak when the cock crew.
HORATIO And then it started like a guilty thing
    Upon a fearful summons. I have heard
    The cock, that is the trumpet to the morn,   156
    Doth with his lofty and shrill-sounding throat
    Awake the god of day, and at his warning,
    Whether in sea or fire, in earth or air,
    Th'extravagant and erring spirit hies   160
    To his confine; and of the truth herein
    This present object made probation.   162
MARCELLUS It faded on the crowing of the cock.
    Some say that ever 'gainst that season comes   164
    Wherein our Savior's birth is celebrated,
    This bird of dawning singeth all night long,
    And then, they say, no spirit dare stir abroad;
    The nights are wholesome, then no planets strike,   168
    No fairy takes, nor witch hath power to charm,   169
    So hallowed and so gracious is that time.   170
HORATIO So have I heard and do in part believe it.
    But, look, the morn in russet mantle clad   172
    Walks o'er the dew of yon high eastward hill.
    Break we our watch up, and by my advice
    Let us impart what we have seen tonight
    Unto young Hamlet; for upon my life,
    This spirit, dumb to us, will speak to him.
    Do you consent we shall acquaint him with it,
    As needful in our loves, fitting our duty?
MARCELLUS Let's do't, I pray, and I this morning know
    Where we shall find him most conveniently.

    Exeunt.

[1.2]

    Flourish. Enter Claudius, King of Denmark, Gertrude the Queen, [the]
    Council, as Polonius and his son Laertes, Hamlet, cum aliis [including Volti-
    mand and Cornelius].

KING Though yet of Hamlet our dear brother's death   1
    The memory be green, and that it us befitted
    To bear our hearts in grief and our whole kingdom
    To be contracted in one brow of woe,
    Yet so far hath discretion fought with nature

---

156 **trumpet** trumpeter 160 **extravagant and erring** wandering beyond bounds. (The words have similar meaning.) **hies** hastens 162 **probation** proof. 164 **'gainst** just before 168 **strike** destroy by evil influence 169 **takes** bewitches. **charm** cast a spell, control by enchantment 170 **gracious** full of grace 172 **russet** reddish brown
1.2 Location: The castle.
0.2 as i.e., such as, including. **0.3 cum aliis** with others **1 our** my. (The royal "we"; also in the following lines.)

That we with wisest sorrow think on him
Together with remembrance of ourselves.
Therefore our sometime sister, now our queen,   8
Th'imperial jointress to this warlike state,   9
Have we, as 'twere with a defeated joy—
With an auspicious and a dropping eye,   11
With mirth in funeral and with dirge in marriage,
In equal scale weighing delight and dole—   13
Taken to wife. Nor have we herein barred
Your better wisdoms, which have freely gone
With this affair along. For all, our thanks.
Now follows that you know young Fortinbras,   17
Holding a weak supposal of our worth,   18
Or thinking by our late dear brother's death
Our state to be disjoint and out of frame,   20
Co-leaguèd with this dream of his advantage,   21
He hath not failed to pester us with message
Importing the surrender of those lands   23
Lost by his father, with all bonds of law,   24
To our most valiant brother. So much for him.
Now for ourself and for this time of meeting.
Thus much the business is: we have here writ
To Norway, uncle of young Fortinbras—
Who, impotent and bed-rid, scarcely hears   29
Of this his nephew's purpose—to suppress
His further gait herein, in that the levies,   31
The lists, and full proportions are all made   32
Out of his subject; and we here dispatch   33
You, good Cornelius, and you, Voltimand,
For bearers of this greeting to old Norway,
Giving to you no further personal power
To business with the King more than the scope
Of these dilated articles allow.   *[He gives a paper.]*   38
Farewell, and let your haste commend your duty.   39
CORNELIUS, VOLTIMAND In that, and all things, will we show our duty.
KING We doubt it nothing. Heartily farewell.   41

[Exeunt Voltimand and Cornelius.]

And now, Laertes, what's the news with you?
You told us of some suit; what is't, Laertes?

---

8 sometime former **9 jointress** woman possessing property with her husband **11 With . . . eye** with one eye smiling and the other weeping **13 dole** grief **17 Now . . . know** Next, you need to be informed that **18 weak supposal** low estimate **20 disjoint . . . frame** in a state of total disorder **21 Co-leaguèd . . . advantage** joined to his illusory sense of having the advantage over us and to his vision of future success **23 Importing** having for its substance **24 with . . . law** (See 1.1.91, "Well ratified by law and heraldry.") **29 impotent** helpless **31 His** i.e., Fortinbras'. **gait** proceeding **31–3 in that . . . subject** since the levying of troops and supplies is drawn entirely from the King of Norway's own subjects **38 dilated** set out at length **39 let . . . duty** let your swift obeying of orders, rather than mere words, express your dutifulness. **41 nothing** not at all.

You cannot speak of reason to the Dane   44
And lose your voice. What wouldst thou beg, Laertes,   45
That shall not be my offer, not thy asking?
The head is not more native to the heart,   47
The hand more instrumental to the mouth,   48
Than is the throne of Denmark to thy father.
What wouldst thou have, Laertes?

LAERTES   My dread lord,
Your leave and favor to return to France,   51
From whence though willingly I came to Denmark
To show my duty in your coronation,
Yet now I must confess, that duty done,
My thoughts and wishes bend again toward France
And bow them to your gracious leave and pardon.   56

KING Have you your father's leave? What says Polonius?

POLONIUS H'ath, my lord, wrung from me my slow leave   58
By laborsome petition, and at last   60
Upon his will I sealed my hard consent.   60
I do beseech you, give him leave to go.

KING Take thy fair hour, Laertes. Time be thine,   62
And thy best graces spend it at thy will.   63
But now, my cousin Hamlet, and my son—   64

HAMLET A little more than kin, and less than kind.   65

KING How is it that the clouds still hang on you?

HAMLET Not so, my lord. I am too much in the sun.   67

QUEEN Good Hamlet, cast thy nighted color off,   68
And let thine eye look like a friend on Denmark.   69
Do not forever with thy vailèd lids   70
Seek for thy noble father in the dust.
Thou know'st 'tis common, all that lives must die,   72
Passing through nature to eternity.

HAMLET Ay, madam, it is common.

QUEEN   If it be,
Why seems it so particular with thee?   75

HAMLET Seems, madam? Nay, it is. I know not "seems."
'Tis not alone my inky cloak, good mother,
Nor customary suits of solemn black,   78

---

44 the Dane the Danish king **45 lose your voice** waste your speech. **47 native** closely connected, related **48 instrumental** serviceable **51 leave and favor** kind permission **56 bow . . . pardon** entreatingly make a deep bow, asking your permission to depart. **58 H'ath** He has **60 sealed** (as if sealing a legal document). **hard** reluctant **62 Take thy fair hour** Enjoy your time of youth **63 And . . . will** and may your time be spent in exercising your best qualities. **64 cousin** any kin not of the immediate family **65 A little . . . kind** Too close a blood relation, and yet we are less than kinsmen in that our relationship lacks affection and is indeed unnatural. (Hamlet plays on kind as [1] kindly [2] belonging to nature, suggesting that Claudius is not the same kind of being as the rest of humanity. The line is often delivered as an aside, though it need not be.) **67 the sun** i.e., the sunshine of the King's royal favor. (With pun on son.) **68 nighted color** (1) mourning garments of black (2) dark melancholy **69 Denmark** the King of Denmark. **70 vailèd lids** lowered eyes **72 common** of universal occurrence. (But Hamlet plays on the sense of "vulgar" in line 74.) **75 particular** personal **78 customary** customary to mourning

Nor windy suspiration of forced breath,	79
No, nor the fruitful river in the eye,	80
Nor the dejected havior of the visage,	81
Together with all forms, moods, shapes of grief,	82
That can denote me truly. These indeed seem,	
For they are actions that a man might play.	
But I have that within which passes show;	
These but the trappings and the suits of woe.	

KING 'Tis sweet and commendable in your nature, Hamlet,
    To give these mourning duties to your father.
    But you must know your father lost a father,
    That father lost, lost his, and the survivor bound
    In filial obligation for some term

To do obsequious sorrow. But to persever	92
In obstinate condolement is a course	93

    Of impious stubbornness. 'Tis unmanly grief.
    It shows a will most incorrect to heaven,

A heart unfortified, a mind impatient,	96
An understanding simple and unschooled.	97

    For what we know must be and is as common

As any the most vulgar thing to sense,	99

    Why should we in our peevish opposition
    Take it to heart? Fie, 'tis a fault to heaven,
    A fault against the dead, a fault to nature,
    To reason most absurd, whose common theme

Is death of fathers, and who still hath cried,	104
From the first corpse till he that died today,	105

    'This must be so." We pray you, throw to earth

This unprevailing woe and think of us	107

    As of a father; for let the world take note,

You are the most immediate to our throne,	109

    And with no less nobility of love
    Than that which dearest father bears his son

Do I impart toward you. For your intent	112
In going back to school in Wittenberg,	113
It is most retrograde to our desire,	114
And we beseech you bend you to remain	115

    Here in the cheer and comfort of our eye,
    Our chiefest courtier, cousin, and our son.
QUEEN Let not thy mother lose her prayers, Hamlet.
    I pray thee, stay with us, go not to Wittenberg.

---

79 suspiration sighing **80 fruitful** abundant **81 havior** expression **82 moods** outward expression of feeling **92 obsequious** suited to obsequies or funerals. **93 condolement** sorrowing **96 unfortified** i.e., against adversity **97 simple** ignorant **99 As . . . sense** as the most ordinary experience **104 still** always **105 the first corpse** (Abel's) **107 unprevailing** unavailing, useless **109 most immediate** next in succession **112 impart toward** liberally bestow on. **For** As for **113 to school** i.e., to your studies. **Wittenberg** famous German university founded in 1502 **114 retrograde** contrary **115 bend you** incline yourself

HAMLET I shall in all my best obey you, madam.   120
KING Why, 'tis a loving and a fair reply.
    Be as ourself in Denmark. Madam, come.
    This gentle and unforced accord of Hamlet
    Sits smiling to my heart, in grace whereof   124
    No jocund health that Denmark drinks today   125
    But the great cannon to the clouds shall tell,
    And the King's rouse the heaven shall bruit again,   127
    Respeaking earthly thunder. Come away.   128

    Flourish. Exeunt all but Hamlet.

HAMLET Oh, that this too too sullied flesh would melt,   129
    Thaw, and resolve itself into a dew!
    Or that the Everlasting had not fixed
    His canon 'gainst self-slaughter! Oh, God, God,   132
    How weary, stale, flat, and unprofitable
    Seem to me all the uses of this world!
    Fie on't, ah fie! 'Tis an unweeded garden
    That grows to seed. Things rank and gross in nature
    Possess it merely. That it should come to this!   137
    But two months dead—nay, not so much, not two.
    So excellent a king, that was to this   139
    Hyperion to a satyr, so loving to my mother   140
    That he might not beteem the winds of heaven   141
    Visit her face too roughly. Heaven and earth,
    Must I remember? Why, she would hang on him
    As if increase of appetite had grown
    By what it fed on, and yet within a month—
    Let me not think on't; frailty, thy name is woman!—
    A little month, or ere those shoes were old   147
    With which she followed my poor father's body,
    Like Niobe, all tears, why she, even she—   149
    Oh, God, a beast, that wants discourse of reason,   150
    Would have mourned longer—married with my uncle,
    My father's brother, but no more like my father
    Than I to Hercules. Within a month,
    Ere yet the salt of most unrighteous tears
    Had left the flushing in her gallèd eyes,   155
    She married. Oh, most wicked speed, to post   156

---

120 in all my best to the best of my ability **124 to** i.e., at. **grace** thanksgiving **125 jocund** merry
127 rouse drinking of a draft of liquor. **bruit again** loudly echo **128 thunder** i.e., of trumpet and kettledrum, sounded when the King drinks; see 1.4.8–12. **129 sullied** defiled. (The early quartos read
"sallied"; the Folio, "solid.") **132 canon** law **137 merely** completely. **139 to** in comparison to **140
Hyperion** Titan sun-god, father of Helios. **satyr** a lecherous creature of classical mythology, half-hu-
man but with a goat's legs, tail, ears, and horns **141 beteem** allow **147 or ere** even before **149
Niobes** Tantalus's daughter, Queen of Thebes, who boasted that she had more sons and daughters
than Leto; for this, Apollo and Artemis, children of Leto, slew her fourteen children. She was turned
by Zeus into a stone that continually dropped tears. **150 wants . . . reason** lacks the faculty of reason
155 gallèd irritated, inflamed **156 post** hasten

With such dexterity to incestuous sheets!   157
It is not, nor it cannot come to good.
But break, my heart, for I must hold my tongue.

Enter Horatio, Marcellus, and Bernardo.

HORATIO Hail to Your Lordship!
HAMLET   I am glad to see you well.
   Horatio!—or I do forget myself.
HORATIO The same, my lord, and your poor servant ever.
HAMLET Sir, my good friend; I'll change that name with you.   163
   And what make you from Wittenberg, Horatio?—   164
   Marcellus.
MARCELLUS My good lord.
HAMLET I am very glad to see you. *[To Bernardo]* Good even, sir.—
   But what in faith make you from Wittenberg?
HORATIO A truant disposition, good my lord.
HAMLET I would not hear your enemy say so,
   Nor shall you do my ear that violence
   To make it truster of your own report   171
   Against yourself. I know you are no truant.
   But what is your affair in Elsinore?
   We'll teach you to drink deep ere you depart.
HORATIO My lord, I came to see your father's funeral.
HAMLET I prithee, do not mock me, fellow student;
   I think it was to see my mother's wedding.
HORATIO Indeed, my lord, it followed hard upon.   179
HAMLET Thrift, thrift, Horatio! The funeral baked meats   180
   Did coldly furnish forth the marriage tables.   181
   Would I had met my dearest foe in heaven   182
   Or ever I had seen that day, Horatio!   183
   My father!—Methinks I see my father.
HORATIO Where, my lord?
HAMLET   In my mind's eye, Horatio.
HORATIO I saw him once. 'A was a goodly king.   186
HAMLET 'A was a man. Take him for all in all,
   I shall not look upon his like again.
HORATIO My lord, I think I saw him yesternight.
HAMLET Saw? Who?
HORATIO My lord, the King your father.
HAMLET The King my father?
HORATIO Season your admiration for a while   193
   With an attent ear till I may deliver,   194

---

157 **incestuous** (In Shakespeare's day, the marriage of a man like Claudius to his deceased brother's wife was considered incestuous.) 163 **change that name** i.e., give and receive reciprocally the name of "friend" rather than talk of "servant." Or Hamlet may be saying, "No, I am your servant." 164 **make you from** are you doing away from 171 **To . . . of** to make it trust 179 **hard** close 180 **baked meats** meat pies 181 **coldly** i.e., as cold leftovers 182 **dearest** closest (and therefore deadliest) 183 **Or ever** ere, before 186 **'A** He 193 **Season your admiration** Moderate your astonishment 194 **attent** attentive

Upon the witness of these gentlemen,
This marvel to you.

HAMLET   For God's love, let me hear!

HORATIO Two nights together had these gentlemen,
Marcellus and Bernardo, on their watch,
In the dead waste and middle of the night,   199
Been thus encountered. A figure like your father,
Armèd at point exactly, cap-à-pie,
Appears before them, and with solemn march
Goes slow and stately by them. Thrice he walked
By their oppressed and fear-surprisèd eyes
Within his truncheon's length, whilst they, distilled   205
Almost to jelly with the act of fear,
Stand dumb and speak not to him. This to me
In dreadful secrecy impart they did,   208
And I with them the third night kept the watch,
Where, as they had delivered, both in time,
Form of the thing, each word made true and good,
The apparition comes. I knew your father;
These hands are not more like.

HAMLET   But where was this?

MARCELLUS My lord, upon the platform where we watch.

HAMLET Did you not speak to it?

HORATIO   My lord, I did,
But answer made it none. Yet once methought
It lifted up it head and did address   217
Itself to motion, like as it would speak;   218
But even then the morning cock crew loud,   219
And at the sound it shrunk in haste away
And vanished from our sight.

HAMLET   'Tis very strange.

HORATIO As I do live, my honored lord, 'tis true,
And we did think it writ down in our duty
To let you know of it.

HAMLET Indeed, indeed, sirs. But this troubles me.
Hold you the watch tonight?

ALL   We do, my lord.

HAMLET Armed, say you?

ALL Armed, my lord.

HAMLET From top to toe?

ALL My lord, from head to foot.

HAMLET Then saw you not his face?

HORATIO Oh, yes, my lord, he wore his beaver up.   232

HAMLET What looked he, frowningly?   233

---

199 **dead waste** desolate stillness 201 **at point** correctly in every detail. **cap-à-pie** from head to foot
205 **truncheon** officer's staff. **distilled** dissolved 206 **act** action, operation 208 **dreadful** full of dread
217 **it** its 217–18 **did . . . speak** prepared to move as though it was about to speak 219 **even then** at
that very instant 232 **beaver** visor on the helmet 233 **What** How

HORATIO A countenance more in sorrow than in anger.

HAMLET Pale or red?

HORATIO Nay, very pale.

HAMLET And fixed his eyes upon you?

HORATIO Most constantly.

HAMLET I would I had been there.

HORATIO It would have much amazed you.

HAMLET Very like, very like. Stayed it long?

HORATIO While one with moderate haste might tell a hundred.   242

MARCELLUS, BERNARDO Longer, longer.

HORATIO Not when I saw't.

HAMLET His beard was grizzled—no?

HORATIO It was, as I have seen it in his life,
   A sable silvered.

HAMLET   I will watch tonight.
   Perchance 'twill walk again.

HORATIO   I warr'nt it will.

HAMLET If it assume my noble father's person,
   I'll speak to it though hell itself should gape
   And bid me hold my peace. I pray you all,
   If you have hitherto concealed this sight,
   Let it be tenable in your silence still,   253
   And whatsomever else shall hap tonight,
   Give it an understanding but no tongue.
   I will requite your loves. So, fare you well.
   Upon the platform twixt eleven and twelve
   I'll visit you.

ALL   Our duty to Your Honor.

HAMLET Your loves, as mine to you. Farewell.   259

   Exeunt [all but Hamlet].

   My father's spirit in arms! All is not well.
   I doubt some foul play. Would the night were come!   261
   Till then sit still, my soul. Foul deeds will rise,
   Though all the earth o'erwhelm them, to men's eyes.

   Exit.

[1.3]

   Enter Laertes and Ophelia, his sister.

LAERTES My necessaries are embarked. Farewell.
   And, sister, as the winds give benefit
   And convoy is assistant, do not sleep   3
   But let me hear from you.

---

242 **tell** count 253 **tenable** held 259 **Your loves** i.e., Say "Your loves" to me, not just your "duty."
261 **doubt** suspect
1.3. Location: Polonius's chambers.
3 **convoy is assistant** means of conveyance are available

OPHELIA	Do you doubt that?	
LAERTES	For Hamlet, and the trifling of his favor,	5
	Hold it a fashion and a toy in blood,	6
	A violet in the youth of primy nature,	7
	Forward, not permanent, sweet, not lasting,	8
	The perfume and suppliance of a minute—	9
	No more.	
OPHELIA	No more but so?	
LAERTES	Think it no more.	
	For nature crescent does not grow alone	11
	In thews and bulk, but as this temple waxes	12
	The inward service of the mind and soul	
	Grows wide withal. Perhaps he loves you now,	14
	And now no soil nor cautel doth besmirch	15
	The virtue of his will; but you must fear,	16
	His greatness weighed, his will is not his own.	17
	For he himself is subject to his birth.	
	He may not, as unvalued persons do,	
	Carve for himself, for on his choice depends	20
	The safety and health of this whole state,	
	And therefore must his choice be circumscribed	
	Unto the voice and yielding of that body	23
	Whereof he is the head. Then if he says he loves you,	
	It fits your wisdom so far to believe it	
	As he in his particular act and place	26
	May give his saying deed, which is no further	
	Than the main voice of Denmark goes withal.	28
	Then weigh what loss your honor may sustain	
	If with too credent ear you list his songs,	30
	Or lose your heart, or your chaste treasure open	
	To his unmastered importunity.	32
	Fear it, Ophelia, fear it, my dear sister,	
	And keep you in the rear of your affection,	34
	Out of the shot and danger of desire.	
	The chariest maid is prodigal enough	36
	If she unmask her beauty to the moon.	37
	Virtue itself scapes not calumnious strokes.	
	The canker galls the infants of the spring	39

---

5 **For** As for 6 **toy in blood** passing amorous fancy 7 **primy** in its prime, springtime 8 **Forward** precocious 9 **suppliance** pastime, something to fill the time 11–14 **For nature ... withal** For nature, as it ripens, does not grow only in physical strength, but as the body matures the inner qualities of mind and soul grow along with it. (Laertes warns Ophelia that the mature Hamlet may not cling to his youthful interests.) 15 **soil nor cautel** blemish nor deceit 16 **The ... will** the purity of his desire 17 **His greatness weighed** taking into account his high fortune 20 **Carve** i.e., choose 23 **voice and yielding** assent, approval 26 **in ... place** in his particular restricted circumstances 28 **main voice** general assent. **withal** along with. 30 **credent** credulous. **list** listen to 32 **unmastered** uncontrolled 34 **keep ... affection** don't advance as far as your affection might lead you. (A military metaphor.) 36 **chariest** most scrupulously modest 37 **If she unmask** if she does no more than show her beauty. **moon** (Symbol of chastity.) 39 **canker galls** cankerworm destroys

Too oft before their buttons be disclosed,   40
And in the morn and liquid dew of youth   41
Contagious blastments are most imminent.   42
Be wary then; best safety lies in fear.
Youth to itself rebels, though none else near.   44
OPHELIA I shall the effect of this good lesson keep
As watchman to my heart. But, good my brother,
Do not, as some ungracious pastors do,   47
Show me the steep and thorny way to heaven,
Whiles like a puffed and reckless libertine   49
Himself the primrose path of dalliance treads,
And recks not his own rede.

Enter Polonius.

LAERTES   Oh, fear me not.   51
I stay too long. But here my father comes.
A double blessing is a double grace;   53
Occasion smiles upon a second leave.   54
POLONIUS Yet here, Laertes? Aboard, aboard, for shame!
The wind sits in the shoulder of your sail,
And you are stayed for. There—my blessing with thee!
And these few precepts in thy memory
Look thou character. Give thy thoughts no tongue,   59
Nor any unproportioned thought his act.   60
Be thou familiar, but by no means vulgar.   61
Those friends thou hast, and their adoption tried,   62
Grapple them unto thy soul with hoops of steel,
But do not dull thy palm with entertainment   64
Of each new-hatched, unfledged courage. Beware   65
Of entrance to a quarrel, but being in,
Bear't that th'opposèd may beware of thee.   67
Give every man thy ear, but few thy voice;
Take each man's censure, but reserve thy judgment.   69
Costly thy habit as thy purse can buy,   70
But not expressed in fancy; rich, not gaudy,   71
For the apparel oft proclaims the man,
And they in France of the best rank and station
Are of a most select and generous chief in that.   74

---

40 **buttons be disclosed** buds be opened 41 **liquid dew** i.e., time when dew is fresh and bright 42
blastments blights 44 **Youth . . . rebels** Youth yields to the rebellion of the flesh 47 **ungracious** ungodly 49 **puffed** bloated, or swollen with pride 51 **recks** heeds. **rede** counsel. **fear me not** don't worry
on my account. 53–4 **A double . . . leave** The goddess Occasion or Opportunity smiles on the happy
circumstance of being able to say good-bye twice and thus receive a second blessing. 59 **Look thou**
character see to it that you inscribe. 60 **unproportioned** badly calculated, intemperate. **his** its 61 **fa-**
miliar sociable. **vulgar** common. 62 **and . . . tried** and their suitability to be your friends having been
put to the test 64 **dull thy palm** i.e., shake hands so often as to make the gesture meaningless 65
courage swashbuckler. 67 **Bear't that** manage it so that 69 **censure** opinion, judgment 70 **habit**
clothing 71 **fancy** excessive ornament, decadent fashion 74 **Are . . . that** are of a most refined and
well-bred preeminence in choosing what to wear.

Neither a borrower nor a lender be,
For loan oft loses both itself and friend,
And borrowing dulleth edge of husbandry.   77
This above all: to thine own self be true,
And it must follow, as the night the day,
Thou canst not then be false to any man.
Farewell. My blessing season this in thee!   81
LAERTES Most humbly do I take my leave, my lord.
POLONIUS The time invests you. Go, your servants tend.   83
LAERTES Farewell, Ophelia, and remember well
  What I have said to you.
OPHELIA 'Tis in my memory locked,
  And you yourself shall keep the key of it.
LAERTES Farewell.   _Exit Laertes._
POLONIUS What is't, Ophelia, he hath said to you?
OPHELIA So please you, something touching the Lord Hamlet.
POLONIUS Marry, well bethought.   91
  'Tis told me he hath very oft of late
  Given private time to you, and you yourself
  Have of your audience been most free and bounteous.
  If it be so—as so 'tis put on me,   95
  And that in way of caution—I must tell you
  You do not understand yourself so clearly
  As it behooves my daughter and your honor.   98
  What is between you? Give me up the truth.
OPHELIA He hath, my lord, of late made many tenders   100
  Of his affection to me.
POLONIUS Affection? Pooh! You speak like a green girl,
  Unsifted in such perilous circumstance.   103
  Do you believe his tenders, as you call them?
OPHELIA I do not know, my lord, what I should think.
POLONIUS Marry, I will teach you. Think yourself a baby
  That you have ta'en these tenders for true pay
  Which are not sterling. Tender yourself more dearly,   108
  Or—not to crack the wind of the poor phrase,   109
  Running it thus—you'll tender me a fool.   110
OPHELIA My lord, he hath importuned me with love
  In honorable fashion.
POLONIUS Ay, fashion you may call it. Go to, go to.   113
OPHELIA And hath given countenance to his speech, my lord,   114
  With almost all the holy vows of heaven.

---

77 **husbandry** thrift. **81 season** mature **83 invests** besieges, presses upon. **tend** attend, wait. **91 Marry** i.e., By the Virgin Mary. (A mild oath.) **95 put on** impressed on, told to **98 behooves** befits **100 tenders** offers **103 Unsifted** i.e., untried **108 sterling** legal currency. **Tender . . . dearly** (1) Bargain for your favors at a higher rate—i.e., hold out for marriage (2) Show greater care of yourself **109 crack the wind** i.e., run it until it is broken-winded **110 tender . . . fool** (1) make a fool of me (2) present me with a _fool_ or baby. **113 fashion** mere form, pretense. **Go to** (An expression of impatience.) **114 countenance** credit, confirmation

POLONIUS Ay, springes to catch woodcocks. I do know, 116
    When the blood burns, how prodigal the soul 117
    Lends the tongue vows. These blazes, daughter,
    Giving more light than heat, extinct in both
    Even in their promise as it is a-making,
    You must not take for fire. From this time 120
    Be something scanter of your maiden presence. 122
    Set your entreatments at a higher rate 123
    Than a command to parle. For Lord Hamlet, 124
    Believe so much in him that he is young, 125
    And with a larger tether may he walk
    Than may be given you. In few, Ophelia, 127
    Do not believe his vows, for they are brokers, 128
    Not of that dye which their investments show, 129
    But mere implorators of unholy suits, 130
    Breathing like sanctified and pious bawds, 131
    The better to beguile. This is for all: 132
    I would not, in plain terms, from this time forth
    Have you so slander any moment leisure 134
    As to give words or talk with the Lord Hamlet.
    Look to't, I charge you. Come your ways. 136
OPHELIA I shall obey, my lord.   *Exeunt.*

[1.4]

Enter Hamlet, Horatio, and Marcellus.

HAMLET The air bites shrewdly; it is very cold. 1
HORATIO It is a nipping and an eager air. 2
HAMLET What hour now?
HORATIO   I think it lacks of twelve. 3
MARCELLUS No, it is struck.
HORATIO   Indeed? I heard it not.
    It then draws near the season 5
    Wherein the spirit held his wont to walk. 6

A flourish of trumpets, and two pieces go off [within].

    What does this mean, my lord?
HAMLET The King doth wake tonight and takes his rouse, 8
    Keeps wassail, and the swagg'ring upspring reels; 9

---

116 springes snares. **woodcocks** birds easily caught; here used to connote gullibility. **117 prodigal** prodigally **120 it** i.e., the promise **122 something** somewhat **123–4 Set . . . parle** i.e., As defender of your chastity, negotiate for something better than a surrender simply because the besieger requests an interview. **124 For** As for **125 so . . . him** this much concerning him **127 In few** Briefly **128 brokers** go-betweens, procurers **129 dye** color or sort. **investments** clothes. (The vows are not what they seem.) **130 mere implorators** out-and-out solicitors **131 Breathing** speaking **132 for all** once for all, in sum **134 slander** abuse, misuse. **moment** moment's **136 Come your ways** Come along.
1.4 Location: The guard platform.
1 shrewdly keenly, sharply **2 eager** biting **3 lacks of** is just short of **5 season** time **6 held his wont** was accustomed. **6.1 pieces** i.e., of ordnance, cannon **8 wake** stay awake and hold revel. **takes his rouse** carouses **9 Keeps . . . reels** carouses, and riotously dances a German dance called the upspring

And as he drains his drafts of Rhenish down,   10
The kettledrum and trumpet thus bray out
The triumph of his pledge.

HORATIO   Is it a custom?   12

HAMLET Ay, marry, is't,
But to my mind, though I am native here
And to the manner born, it is a custom   15
More honored in the breach than the observance.   16
This heavy-headed revèl east and west   17
Makes us traduced and taxed of other nations.   18
They clepe us drunkards, and with swinish phrase   19
Soil our addition; and indeed it takes   20
From our achievements, though performed at height,   21
The pith and marrow of our attribute.   22
So, oft it chances in particular men,
That for some vicious mole of nature in them,   24
As in their birth—wherein they are not guilty,
Since nature cannot choose his origin—   26
By their o'ergrowth of some complexion,   27
Oft breaking down the pales and forts of reason,   28
Or by some habit that too much o'erleavens   29
The form of plausive manners, that these men,   30
Carrying, I say, the stamp of one defect,
Being nature's livery or fortune's star,   32
His virtues else, be they as pure as grace,   33
As infinite as man may undergo,   34
Shall in the general censure take corruption   35
From that particular fault. The dram of evil   36
Doth all the noble substance often dout   37
To his own scandal.

Enter Ghost.

HORATIO   Look, my lord, it comes!   38
HAMLET Angels and ministers of grace defend us!   39
Be thou a spirit of health or goblin damned,   40

---

10 Rhenish Rhine wine **12 The triumph . . . pledge** the celebration of his offering a toast. **15 manner** custom (of drinking) **16 More . . . observance** better neglected than followed. **17 east and west** i.e., everywhere **18 taxed of** censured by **19 clepe** call. **with swinish phrase** i.e., by calling us swine **20 addition** reputation **21 at height** outstandingly **22 The pith . . . attribute** the most essential part of the esteem that should be attributed to us. **24 for . . . mole** on account of some natural defect in their constitutions **26 his** its **27 their o'ergrowth . . . complexion** the excessive growth in individuals of some natural trait **28 pales** palings, fences (as of a fortification) **29–30 o'erleavens . . . manners** i.e., infects the way we should behave (much as bad yeast spoils the dough). *Plausive* means "pleasing." **32 Being . . . star** (that stamp of defect) being a sign identifying one as wearing the livery of, and hence being the servant to, nature (unfortunate inherited qualities) or fortune (mischance) **33 His virtues else** i.e., the other qualities of *these* men (line 30) **34 may undergo** can sustain **35 in . . . censure** in overall appraisal, in people's opinion generally **36–8 The dram . . . scandal** i.e., The small drop of evil blots out or works against the noble substance of the whole and brings it into disrepute. (To *dout* is to blot out. A famous crux.) **39 ministers of grace** messengers of God **40 Be . . . health** Whether you are a good angel

Bring with thee airs from heaven or blasts from hell,	*41*
Be thy intents wicked or charitable,	*42*
Thou com'st in such a questionable shape	*43*
That I will speak to thee. I'll call thee Hamlet,	
King, father, royal Dane. Oh, answer me!	
Let me not burst in ignorance, but tell	
Why thy canonized bones, hearsèd in death,	*47*
Have burst their cerements; why the sepulcher	*48*
Wherein we saw thee quietly inurned	*49*
Hath oped his ponderous and marble jaws	
To cast thee up again. What may this mean,	
That thou, dead corpse, again in complete steel,	*52*
Revisits thus the glimpses of the moon,	*53*
Making night hideous, and we fools of nature	*54*
So horridly to shake our disposition	*55*
With thoughts beyond the reaches of our souls?	
Say, why is this? Wherefore? What should we do?	

[The Ghost] beckons [Hamlet].

HORATIO It beckons you to go away with it,
　　As if it some impartment did desire　　　　　　　　　　*59*
　　To you alone.
MARCELLUS Look with what courteous action
　　It wafts you to a more removèd ground.
　　But do not go with it.
HORATIO　　　　　　　　No, by no means.
HAMLET It will not speak. Then I will follow it.
HORATIO Do not, my lord!
HAMLET　　　　　　　　Why, what should be the fear?
　　I do not set my life at a pin's fee,　　　　　　　　　　*65*
　　And for my soul, what can it do to that,　　　　　　　*66*
　　Being a thing immortal as itself?
　　It waves me forth again. I'll follow it.
HORATIO What if it tempt you toward the flood, my lord,　*69*
　　Or to the dreadful summit of the cliff
　　That beetles o'er his base into the sea,　　　　　　　　*71*
　　And there assume some other horrible form
　　Which might deprive your sovereignty of reason　　　*73*
　　And draw you into madness? Think of it.
　　The very place puts toys of desperation,　　　　　　　*75*
　　Without more motive, into every brain

---

41 Bring whether you bring **42 Be thy intents** whether your intentions are **43 questionable** inviting question **47 canonized** buried according to the canons of the church. **hearsèd** coffined **48 cerements** grave clothes **49 inurned** entombed **52 complete steel** full armor **53 the glimpses . . . moon** i.e., the sublunary world, all that is beneath the moon **54 fools of nature** mere mortals, limited to natural knowledge and subject to nature **55 So . . . disposition** to distress our mental composure so violently **59 impartment** communication **65 fee** value **66 for** as for **69 flood** sea **71 beetles o'er** overhangs threateningly (like bushy eyebrows). **his** its **73 deprive . . . reason** take away the rule of reason over your mind **75 toys of desperation** fancies of desperate acts, i.e., suicide

    That looks so many fathoms to the sea
    And hears it roar beneath.
HAMLET It wafts me still.—Go on, I'll follow thee.
MARCELLUS You shall not go, my lord.   *[They try to stop him.]*
HAMLET   Hold off your hands!
HORATIO Be ruled. You shall not go.
HAMLET   My fate cries out,   81
    And makes each petty artery in this body   82
    As hardy as the Nemean lion's nerve.   83
    Still am I called. Unhand me, gentlemen.
    By heaven, I'll make a ghost of him that lets me!   85
    I say, away!—Go on, I'll follow thee.

    Exeunt Ghost and Hamlet.

HORATIO He waxes desperate with imagination.
MARCELLUS Let's follow. 'Tis not fit thus to obey him.
HORATIO Have after. To what issue will this come?   89
MARCELLUS Something is rotten in the state of Denmark.
HORATIO Heaven will direct it.
MARCELLUS   Nay, let's follow him.   *Exeunt.*   91

[1.5]

    Enter Ghost and Hamlet.

HAMLET Whither wilt thou lead me? Speak. I'll go no further.
GHOST Mark me.
HAMLET   I will.
GHOST   My hour is almost come,
    When I to sulf'rous and tormenting flames
    Must render up myself.
HAMLET   Alas, poor ghost!
GHOST Pity me not, but lend thy serious hearing
    To what I shall unfold.
HAMLET Speak. I am bound to hear.   7
GHOST So art thou to revenge, when thou shalt hear.
HAMLET What?
GHOST I am thy father's spirit,
    Doomed for a certain term to walk the night,
    And for the day confined to fast in fires,   12
    Till the foul crimes done in my days of nature   13
    Are burnt and purged away. But that I am forbid   14

---

81 My fate cries out My destiny summons me **82 petty** weak. **artery** blood vessel system through which the vital spirits were thought to have been conveyed. **83 Nemean lion's nerve** as a sinew of the huge lion slain by Hercules as the first of his twelve labors. **85 lets** hinders **89 Have after** Let's go after him. **issue** outcome **91 it** i.e., the outcome.
1.5 Location: The battlements of the castle.
7 bound (1) ready (2) obligated by duty and fate. (The Ghost, in line 8, answers in the second sense.)
12 fast do penance by fasting **13 crimes** sins. **of nature** as a mortal **14 But that** Were it not that

To tell the secrets of my prison house,
I could a tale unfold whose lightest word
Would harrow up thy soul, freeze thy young blood,   17
Make thy two eyes like stars start from their spheres,   18
Thy knotted and combinèd locks to part,   19
And each particular hair to stand on end
Like quills upon the fretful porcupine.
But this eternal blazon must not be   22
To ears of flesh and blood. List, list, oh, list!
If thou didst ever thy dear father love—

HAMLET Oh, God!

GHOST Revenge his foul and most unnatural murder.

HAMLET Murder?

GHOST Murder most foul, as in the best it is,   28
But this most foul, strange, and unnatural.

HAMLET Haste me to know't, that I, with wings as swift
As meditation or the thoughts of love,
May sweep to my revenge.

GHOST   I find thee apt;
And duller shouldst thou be than the fat weed   33
That roots itself in ease on Lethe wharf,   34
Wouldst thou not stir in this. Now, Hamlet, hear.
'Tis given out that, sleeping in my orchard,   36
A serpent stung me. So the whole ear of Denmark
Is by a forgèd process of my death   38
Rankly abused. But know, thou noble youth,   39
The serpent that did sting thy father's life
Now wears his crown.

HAMLET Oh, my prophetic soul! My uncle!

GHOST Ay, that incestuous, that adulterate beast,   43
With witchcraft of his wit, with traitorous gifts—   44
Oh, wicked wit and gifts, that have the power
So to seduce!—won to his shameful lust
The will of my most seeming-virtuous queen.
Oh, Hamlet, what a falling off was there!
From me, whose love was of that dignity
That it went hand in hand even with the vow   50
I made to her in marriage, and to decline
Upon a wretch whose natural gifts were poor
To those of mine!   53
But virtue, as it never will be moved,   54
Though lewdness court it in a shape of heaven,   55

---

17 harrow up lacerate, tear **18 spheres** i.e., eye-sockets, here compared to the orbits or transparent revolving spheres in which, according to Ptolemaic astronomy, the heavenly bodies were fixed **19 knotted . . . locks** hair neatly arranged and confined **22 eternal blazon** revelation of the secrets of eternity **28 in the best** even at best **33 shouldst thou be** you would have to be. **fat** torpid, lethargic **34 Lethe** the river of forgetfulness in Hades **36 orchard** garden **38 forgèd process** falsified account **39 abused** deceived. **43 adulterate** adulterous **44 gifts** (1) talents (2) presents **50 even with the vow** with the very vow **53 To** compared with **54 virtue, as it** just as virtue **55 shape of heaven** heavenly form

So lust, though to a radiant angel linked,
Will sate itself in a celestial bed   57
And prey on garbage.
But soft, methinks I scent the morning air.
Brief let me be. Sleeping within my orchard,
My custom always of the afternoon,
Upon my secure hour thy uncle stole,   62
With juice of cursèd hebona in a vial,   63
And in the porches of my ears did pour   64
The leprous distillment, whose effect   65
Holds such an enmity with blood of man
That swift as quicksilver it courses through
The natural gates and alleys of the body,
And with a sudden vigor it doth posset   68
And curd, like eager droppings into milk,   69
The thin and wholesome blood. So did it mine,   70
And a most instant tetter barked about,   72
Most lazar-like, with vile and loathsome crust,   73
All my smooth body.
Thus was I, sleeping, by a brother's hand
Of life, of crown, of queen at once dispatched,   76
Cut off even in the blossoms of my sin,
Unhouseled, disappointed, unaneled,   78
No reck'ning made, but sent to my account   79
With all my imperfections on my head.
Oh, horrible! Oh, horrible, most horrible!
If thou hast nature in thee, bear it not.   82
Let not the royal bed of Denmark be
A couch for luxury and damnèd incest.   84
But, howsomever thou pursues this act,
Taint not thy mind nor let thy soul contrive
Against thy mother aught. Leave her to heaven
And to those thorns that in her bosom lodge,
To prick and sting her. Fare thee well at once.
The glowworm shows the matin to be near,   90
And 'gins to pale his uneffectual fire.   91
Adieu, adieu, adieu! Remember me.   *[Exit.]*
HAMLET O all you host of heaven! O earth! What else?
And shall I couple hell? Oh, fie! Hold, hold, my heart,   94

---

57 **sate . . . bed** gratify its lustful appetite to the point of revulsion or ennui, even in a virtuously lawful marriage 62 **secure hour** time of being free from worries 63 **hebona** a poison. (The word seems to
be a form of *ebony*, though it is thought perhaps to be related to henbane, a poison, or to *ebenus*,
"yew.") 64 **porches** gateways 65 **leprous distillment** distillation causing leprosylike disfigurement 68
gates entry ways 69–70 **posset . . . curd** coagulate and curdle 70 **eager** sour, acid 72 **tetter** eruption
of scabs. **barked** covered with a rough covering, like bark on a tree 73 **lazar-like** leperlike 76 **dispatched** suddenly deprived 78 **Unhouseled . . . unaneled** without having received the Sacrament or
other last rites including confession, absolution, and the holy oil of extreme unction 79 **reck'ning**
settling of accounts 82 **nature** i.e., the promptings of a son 84 **luxury** lechery 90 **matin** morning 91
his its 94 **couple** add. **Hold** Hold together

And you, my sinews, grow not instant old,   95
But bear me stiffly up. Remember thee?
Ay, thou poor ghost, whiles memory holds a seat
In this distracted globe. Remember thee?   98
Yea, from the table of my memory   99
I'll wipe away all trivial fond records,   100
All saws of books, all forms, all pressures past   101
That youth and observation copied there,
And thy commandment all alone shall live
Within the book and volume of my brain,
Unmixed with baser matter. Yes, by heaven!
Oh, most pernicious woman!
Oh, villain, villain, smiling, damnèd villain!
My tables—meet it is I set it down   108
That one may smile, and smile, and be a villain.
At least I am sure it may be so in Denmark.
So, uncle, there you are. Now to my word: 111
It is "Adieu, adieu! Remember me."
I have sworn't.

Enter Horatio and Marcellus.

HORATIO My lord, my lord!
MARCELLUS Lord Hamlet!
HORATIO Heavens secure him!
HAMLET So be it.   116
MARCELLUS Hillo, ho, ho, my lord!
HAMLET Hillo, ho, ho, boy! Come, bird, come.   119
MARCELLUS How is't, my noble lord?
HORATIO What news, my lord?
HAMLET Oh, wonderful!
HORATIO Good my lord, tell it.
HAMLET No, you will reveal it.
HORATIO Not I, my lord, by heaven.
MARCELLUS Nor I, my lord
HAMLET How say you, then, would heart of man once think it?   127
    But you'll be secret?
HORATIO, MARCELLUS Ay, by heaven, my lord.
HAMLET There's never a villain dwelling in all Denmark
    But he's an arrant knave.   130
HORATIO There needs no ghost, my lord, come from the grave
    To tell us this.

---

95 **instant** instantly 98 **globe** (1) head (2) world (3) Globe Theater. 99 **table** tablet, slate 100 **fond** foolish 101 **All . . . past** all wise sayings, all shapes or images imprinted on the tablets of my memory, all past impressions 108 **My tables . . . down** (Editors often specify that Hamlet makes a note in his writing tablet, but he may simply mean that he is making a mental observation of lasting impression.) 111 **there you are** i.e., there, I've noted that against you. 116 **secure him** keep him safe. 119 **Hillo . . . come** (A falconer's call to a hawk in air. Hamlet mocks the hallooing as though it were a part of hawking.) 127 **once** ever 130 **But . . . knave** (Hamlet jokingly gives a self-evident answer: every villain is a thoroughgoing knave.)

HAMLET   Why, right, you are in the right.
   And so, without more circumstance at all,   *133*
   I hold it fit that we shake hands and part,
   You as your business and desire shall point you—
   For every man hath business and desire,
   Such as it is—and for my own poor part,
   Look you, I'll go pray.
HORATIO These are but wild and whirling words, my lord.
HAMLET I am sorry they offend you, heartily;
   Yes, faith, heartily.
HORATIO   There's no offense, my lord.
HAMLET Yes, by Saint Patrick, but there is, Horatio,   *142*
   And much offense too. Touching this vision here,   *143*
   It is an honest ghost, that let me tell you.   *144*
   For your desire to know what is between us,
   O'ermaster't as you may. And now, good friends,
   As you are friends, scholars, and soldiers,
   Give me one poor request.
HORATIO What is't, my lord? We will.
HAMLET Never make known what you have seen tonight.
HORATIO, MARCELLUS My lord, we will not.
HAMLET Nay, but swear't.
HORATIO In faith, my lord, not I.   *153*
MARCELLUS Nor I, my lord, in faith.
HAMLET Upon my sword.   *[He holds out his sword.]*   *155*
MARCELLUS We have sworn, my lord, already.   *156*
HAMLET Indeed, upon my sword, indeed.
GHOST *(cries under the stage)* Swear.
HAMLET Ha, ha, boy, say'st thou so? Art thou there, truepenny?   *159*
   Come on, you hear this fellow in the cellarage.
   Consent to swear.
HORATIO   Propose the oath, my lord.
HAMLET Never to speak of this that you have seen,
   Swear by my sword.
GHOST *[beneath]* Swear.   *[They swear.]*   *164*
HAMLET Hic et ubique? Then we'll shift our ground.   *165*

   [He moves to another spot.]

   Come hither, gentlemen,
   And lay your hands again upon my sword.

---

133 circumstance ceremony, elaboration **142 Saint Patrick** the keeper of Purgatory **143 offense** (Hamlet deliberately changes Horatio's "no offense taken" to "an offense against all decency.") **144 honest** genuine **153 In faith . . . I** i.e., I swear not to tell what I have seen. (Horatio is not refusing to swear.) **155 sword** i.e., the hilt in the form of a cross. **156 We . . . already** i.e., We swore in *faith*. **159 truepenny** honest old fellow. **164 s.d. They swear** (Seemingly they swear here, and at lines 170 and 190, as they lay their hands on Hamlet's sword. Triple oaths would have particular force; these three oaths deal with what they have seen, what they have heard, and what they promise about Hamlet's *antic disposition*.) **165 Hic et ubique?** Here and everywhere? (Latin.)

Swear by my sword
Never to speak of this that you have heard.
GHOST *[beneath]* Swear by his sword.   *[They swear.]*
HAMLET Well said, old mole. Canst work i'th'earth so fast?
A worthy pioneer!—Once more remove, good friends.   172

[He moves again.]

HORATIO Oh, day and night, but this is wondrous strange!
HAMLET And therefore as a stranger give it welcome.   74
There are more things in heaven and earth, Horatio,
Than are dreamt of in your philosophy.   176
But come;
Here, as before, never, so help you mercy,   178
How strange or odd some'er I bear myself—
As I perchance hereafter shall think meet
To put an antic disposition on—   181
That you, at such times seeing me, never shall,
With arms encumbered thus, or this headshake,   183
Or by pronouncing of some doubtful phrase
As "Well, we know," or "We could, an if we would,"   185
Or "If we list to speak," or "There be, an if they might,"   186
Or such ambiguous giving out, to note   187
That you know aught of me—this do swear,   188
So grace and mercy at your most need help you.
GHOST *[beneath]* Swear.   *[They swear.]*
HAMLET Rest, rest, perturbèd spirit!—So, gentlemen,
With all my love I do commend me to you;   192
And what so poor a man as Hamlet is
May do t'express his love and friending to you,   194
God willing, shall not lack. Let us go in together.   195
And still your fingers on your lips, I pray.   196
The time is out of joint. Oh, cursèd spite   197
That ever I was born to set it right!

[They wait for him to leave first.]

Nay, come, let's go together.   *Exeunt.*   199

[2.1]

Enter old Polonius with his man [Reynaldo].

POLONIUS Give him this money and these notes, Reynaldo.

---

172 pioneer foot soldier assigned to dig tunnels and excavations. **174 as a stranger** i.e., needing your hospitality **176 your philosophy** this subject that is called "natural philosophy" or "science." (*Your* is not personal.) **178 so help you mercy** as you hope for God's mercy when you are judged **181 antic** grotesque, strange **183 encumbered** folded **185 an if** if **186 list** wished. **There . . . might** There are those who could talk if they were at liberty to do so **187 note** indicate **188 aught** anything **192 commend . . . you** give you my best wishes **194 friending** friendliness **195 lack** be lacking. **196 still** always **197 out of joint** in utter disorder. **199 let's go together** (Probably they wait for him to leave first, but he refuses this ceremoniousness.) **2.1 Location: Polonius's chambers.**

[He gives money and papers.]

REYNALDO I will, my lord.
POLONIUS You shall do marvelous wisely, good Reynaldo,   3
  Before you visit him, to make inquire   4
  Of his behavior.
REYNALDO   My lord, I did intend it.
POLONIUS Marry, well said, very well said. Look you, sir,
  Inquire me first what Danskers are in Paris,   7
  And how, and who, what means, and where they keep,   8
  What company, at what expense; and finding
  By this encompassment and drift of question   10
  That they do know my son, come you more nearer   11
  Than your particular demands will touch it.   12
  Take you, as 'twere, some distant knowledge of him,   13
  As thus, "I know his father and his friends,
  And in part him." Do you mark this, Reynaldo?
REYNALDO Ay, very well, my lord.
POLONIUS "And in part him, but," you may say, "not well.
  But if 't be he I mean, he's very wild,
  Addicted so and so," and there put on him   19
  What forgeries you please—marry, none so rank   20
  As may dishonor him, take heed of that,
  But, sir, such wanton, wild, and usual slips   22
  As are companions noted and most known
  To youth and liberty.
REYNALDO As gaming, my lord.
POLONIUS Ay, or drinking, fencing, swearing,
  Quarreling, drabbing—you may go so far.   27
REYNALDO My lord, that would dishonor him.
POLONIUS Faith, no, as you may season it in the charge.   29
  You must not put another scandal on him
  That he is open to incontinency;   31
  That's not my meaning. But breathe his faults so quaintly   32
  That they may seem the taints of liberty,   33
  The flash and outbreak of a fiery mind,
  A savageness in unreclaimèd blood,   35
  Of general assault.   36
REYNALDO But, my good lord—
POLONIUS Wherefore should you do this?
REYNALDO Ay, my lord, I would know that.
POLONIUS Marry, sir, here's my drift,

---

3 marvelous marvelously **4 inquire** inquiry **7 Danskers** Danes **8 what means** what wealth (they
have). **keep** dwell **10 encompassment . . . question** roundabout way of questioning **11–12 come . . .
it** you will find out more this way than by asking pointed questions (*particular demands*). **13 Take you**
Assume, pretend **19 put on** impute to **20 forgeries** invented tales. **rank** gross **22 wanton** sportive,
unrestrained **27 drabbing** whoring **29 season** temper, soften **31 incontinency** habitual sexual excess
32 quaintly artfully, subtly **33 taints of liberty** faults resulting from free living **35–6 A savageness
. . . assault** a wildness in untamed youth that assails all indiscriminately.

And I believe it is a fetch of warrant. 41
You laying these slight sullies on my son,
As 'twere a thing a little soiled wi'th' working, 43
Mark you,
Your party in converse, him you would sound, 45
Having ever seen in the prenominate crimes 46
The youth you breathe of guilty, be assured 47
He closes with you in this consequence: 48
"Good sir," or so, or "friend," or "gentleman,"
According to the phrase or the addition 50
Of man and country.

REYNALDO   Very good, my lord.

POLONIUS And then, sir, does 'a this—'a does—what was I about to say? By the
Mass, I was about to say something. Where did I leave?

REYNALDO At "closes in the consequence."

POLONIUS At "closes in the consequence," ay, marry.
He closes thus: "I know the gentleman,
I saw him yesterday," or "th'other day,"
Or then, or then, with such or such, "and as you say,
There was 'a gaming," "there o'ertook in 's rouse," 60
"There falling out at tennis," or perchance 61
"I saw him enter such a house of sale,"
Videlicet a brothel, or so forth. See you now, 63
Your bait of falsehood takes this carp of truth; 64
And thus do we of wisdom and of reach, 65
With windlasses and with assays of bias, 66
By indirections find directions out. 67
So by my former lecture and advice 68
Shall you my son. You have me, have you not? 69

REYNALDO My lord, I have.

POLONIUS   God b'wi'ye; fare ye well.

REYNALDO Good my lord.

POLONIUS Observe his inclination in yourself. 72

REYNALDO I shall, my lord.

POLONIUS And let him ply his music.

REYNALDO Well, my lord.

POLONIUS Farewell.   *Exit Reynaldo.*

Enter Ophelia.

How now, Ophelia, what's the matter?

---

41 fetch of warrant legitimate trick. **43 wi'th' working** in the process of being made, i.e., in everyday
experience **45 Your ... converse** the person you are conversing with. **sound** sound out **46 Having
ever** if he has ever. **prenominate crimes** aforenamed offenses **47 breathe** speak **48 closes ... consequence** takes you into his confidence as follows **50 addition** title **60 o'ertook in 's rouse** overcome by
drink **61 falling out** quarreling **63 Videlicet** namely **64 carp** a fish **65 reach** capacity, ability **66 windlasses** i.e., circuitous paths. (Literally, circuits made to head off the game in hunting.) **assays of bias**
attempts through indirection (like the curving path of the bowling ball, which is biased or weighted to
one side) **67 directions** i.e., the way things really are **68 former lecture** just-ended set of instructions
69 have understand **72 in yourself** in your own person (as well as by asking questions of others).

OPHELIA Oh, my lord, my lord, I have been so affrighted!

POLONIUS With what, i'th' name of God?

OPHELIA My lord, as I was sewing in my closet,   79
    Lord Hamlet, with his doublet all unbraced,   80
    No hat upon his head, his stockings fouled,
    Ungartered, and down-gyvèd to his ankle,   82
    Pale as his shirt, his knees knocking each other,
    And with a look so piteous in purport   84
    As if he had been loosèd out of hell
    To speak of horrors—he comes before me.

POLONIUS Mad for thy love?

OPHELIA   My lord, I do not know,
    But truly I do fear it.

POLONIUS   What said he?

OPHELIA He took me by the wrist and held me hard.
    Then goes he to the length of all his arm,
    And, with his other hand thus o'er his brow
    He falls to such perusal of my face
    As 'a would draw it. Long stayed he so.   93
    At last, a little shaking of mine arm
    And thrice his head thus waving up and down,
    He raised a sigh so piteous and profound
    As it did seem to shatter all his bulk   97
    And end his being. That done, he lets me go,
    And with his head over his shoulder turned
    He seemed to find his way without his eyes,
    For out o' doors he went without their helps,
    And to the last bended their light on me.

POLONIUS Come, go with me. I will go seek the King.
    This is the very ecstasy of love,   104
    Whose violent property fordoes itself   105
    And leads the will to desperate undertakings
    As oft as any passion under heaven
    That does afflict our natures. I am sorry.
    What, have you given him any hard words of late?

OPHELIA No, my good lord, but as you did command
    I did repel his letters and denied
    His access to me.

POLONIUS   That hath made him mad.
    I am sorry that with better heed and judgment
    I had not quoted him. I feared he did but trifle   114
    And meant to wrack thee. But beshrew my jealousy!   115
    By heaven, it is as proper to our age   116

---

79 closet private chamber **80 doublet** close-fitting jacket. **unbraced** unfastened **82 down-gyvèd**
fallen to the ankles (like gyves or fetters) **84 in purport** in what it expressed **93 As** as if **97 As** that.
bulk body **104 ecstasy** madness **105 property fordoes** nature destroys **114 quoted** observed **115
wrack** ruin, seduce. **beshrew my jealousy!** a plague upon my suspicious nature! **116 proper . . . age**
characteristic of us (old) men

To cast beyond ourselves in our opinions   *117*
As it is common for the younger sort
To lack discretion. Come, go we to the King.
This must be known, which, being kept close, might move   *120*
More grief to hide than hate to utter love.   *121*
Come.   *Exeunt.*

[2.2]

Flourish. Enter King and Queen, Rosencrantz, and Guildenstern [with others].

KING Welcome, dear Rosencrantz and Guildenstern.
Moreover that we much did long to see you,   *2*
The need we have to use you did provoke
Our hasty sending. Something have you heard
Of Hamlet's transformation—so call it,
Sith nor th'exterior nor the inward man   *6*
Resembles that it was. What it should be,   *7*
More than his father's death, that thus hath put him
So much from th'understanding of himself,
I cannot dream of. I entreat you both
That, being of so young days brought up with him,   *11*
And sith so neighbored to his youth and havior,   *12*
That you vouchsafe your rest here in our court   *13*
Some little time, so by your companies
To draw him on to pleasures, and to gather
So much as from occasion you may glean,   *16*
Whether aught to us unknown afflicts him thus
That, opened, lies within our remedy.   *18*
QUEEN Good gentlemen, he hath much talked of you,
And sure I am two men there is not living
To whom he more adheres. If it will please you
To show us so much gentry and good will   *22*
As to expend your time with us awhile
For the supply and profit of our hope,   *24*
Your visitation shall receive such thanks
As fits a kings's remembrance.
ROSENCRANTZ   Both Your Majesties   *26*
Might, by the sovereign power you have of us,   *27*

---

117 **cast beyond** overshoot, miscalculate. (A metaphor from hunting.) 120 **known** made known (to
the King). **close** secret 120–1 **might . . . love** i.e., might cause more grief (because of what Hamlet
might do) by hiding the knowledge of Hamlet's strange behavior to Ophelia than unpleasantness by
telling it.
2.2 **Location: The castle.**
2 **Moreover that** Besides the fact that 6 **Sith nor** since neither 7 **that** what 11–12 **That . . . havior**
that, seeing as you were brought up with him from early youth (see 3.4.209, where Hamlet refers to
Rosencrantz and Guildenstern as "my two schoolfellows"), and since you have been intimately acquainted with his youthful ways 13 **vouchsafe your rest** consent to stay 16 **occasion** opportunity 18
opened being revealed 22 **gentry** courtesy 24 **supply . . . hope** aid and furtherance of what we hope
for 26 **As fits . . . remembrance** as would be a fitting gift of a king who rewards true service. 27 **of** over

Put your dread pleasures more into command   28
Than to entreaty.
GUILDENSTERN   But we both obey,
And here give up ourselves in the full bent   30
To lay our service freely at your feet,
To be commanded.
KING Thanks, Rosencrantz and gentle Guildenstern.
QUEEN Thanks, Guildenstern and gentle Rosencrantz.
And I beseech you instantly to visit
My too much changèd son.—Go, some of you,
And bring these gentlemen where Hamlet is.
GUILDENSTERN Heavens make our presence and our practices   38
Pleasant and helpful to him!
QUEEN   Ay, amen!

Exeunt Rosencrantz and Guildenstern [with some attendants].
    Enter Polonius.

POLONIUS Th'ambassadors from Norway, my good lord,
Are joyfully returned.
KING Thou still hast been the father of good news.   42
POLONIUS Have I, my lord? I assure my good liege
I hold my duty, as I hold my soul,
Both to my God and to my gracious king;
And I do think, or else this brain of mine
Hunts not the trail of policy so sure   47
As it hath used to do, that I have found
The very cause of Hamlet's lunacy.
KING Oh, speak of that! That do I long to hear.
POLONIUS Give first admittance to th'ambassadors.
My news shall be the fruit to that great feast.   52
KING Thyself do grace to them and bring them in.   53

    [Exit Polonius.]

He tells me, my dear Gertrude, he hath found
The head and source of all your son's distemper.
QUEEN I doubt it is no other but the main,   56
His father's death and our o'erhasty marriage.

    Enter Ambassadors [Voltimand and Cornelius, with Polonius].

KING Well, we shall sift him.—Welcome, my good friends!   58
Say, Voltimand, what from our brother Norway?   59
VOLTIMAND Most fair return of greetings and desires.   60
Upon our first, he sent out to suppress   61

---

28 **dread** inspiring awe 30 **in . . . bent** to the utmost degree of our capacity. (An archery metaphor.)
38 **practices** doings 42 **still** always 47 **policy** statecraft 52 **fruit** dessert 53 **grace** honor. (Punning on
grace said before a *feast*, line 52.) 56 **doubt** fear, suspect. 58 **sift him** question Polonius (or Hamlet
closely). 59 **brother** fellow king 60 **desires** good wishes. 61 **Upon our first** At our first words on the
business

His nephew's levies, which to him appeared
To be a preparation 'gainst the Polack,
But, better looked into, he truly found
It was against Your Highness. Whereat grieved
That so his sickness, age, and impotence   66
Was falsely borne in hand, sends out arrests   67
On Fortinbras, which he, in brief, obeys,
Receives rebuke from Norway, and in fine   69
Makes vow before his uncle never more
To give th'assay of arms against Your Majesty.   71
Whereon old Norway, overcome with joy,
Gives him three thousand crowns in annual fee
And his commission to employ those soldiers,
So levied as before, against the Polack,
With an entreaty, herein further shown,

[giving a paper]

That it might please you to give quiet pass
Through your dominions for this enterprise
On such regards of safety and allowance   79
As therein are set down.
KING   It likes us well,   80
And at our more considered time we'll read,   81
Answer, and think upon this business.
Meantime we thank you for your well-took labor.
Go to your rest; at night we'll feast together.
Most welcome home!   *Exeunt Ambassadors.*
POLONIUS   This business is well ended.
My liege, and madam, to expostulate   86
What majesty should be, what duty is,
Why day is day, night night, and time is time,
Were nothing but to waste night, day, and time.
Therefore, since brevity is the soul of wit,   90
And tediousness the limbs and outward flourishes,
I will be brief. Your noble son is mad.
Mad call I it, for, to define true madness,
What is't but to be nothing else but mad?
But let that go.
QUEEN   More matter, with less art.
POLONIUS Madam, I swear I use no art at all.
That he's mad, 'tis true; 'tis true 'tis pity,
And pity 'tis 'tis true—a foolish figure,   98
But farewell it, for I will use no art.

---

66 impotence weakness **67 borne in hand** deluded, taken advantage of. **arrests** orders to desist **69 in fine** in conclusion **71 give th'assay** make trial of strength, challenge **79 On . . . allowance** i.e., with such considerations for the safety of Denmark and permission for Fortinbras **80 likes** pleases **81 considered** suitable for deliberation **86 expostulate** expound, inquire into **90 wit** sense or judgment **98 figure** figure of speech

Mad let us grant him, then, and now remains
That we find out the cause of this effect,
Or rather say, the cause of this defect,
For this effect defective comes by cause.   103
Thus it remains, and the remainder thus.
Perpend.
I have a daughter—have while she is mine—
Who, in her duty and obedience, mark,
Hath given me this. Now gather and surmise.   108
[He reads the letter.] "To the celestial and my soul's
    idol, the most beautified Ophelia"—
That's an ill phrase, a vile phrase; "beautified" is a
    vile phrase. But you shall hear. Thus: *[He reads.]*
"In her excellent white bosom, these, etc."   113
QUEEN Came this from Hamlet to her?
POLONIUS Good madam, stay awhile, I will be faithful.   115

                                                    [He reads.]

"Doubt thou the stars are fire,
Doubt that the sun doth move,
Doubt truth to be a liar,   118
But never doubt I love.
O dear Ophelia, I am ill at these numbers. I have not   120
    art to reckon my groans. But that I love thee best, O   121
    most best, believe it. Adieu.
Thine evermore, most dear lady, whilst this
    machine is to him, Hamlet."   124
This in obedience hath my daughter shown me,
And, more above, hath his solicitings,   126
As they fell out by time, by means, and place,   127
All given to mine ear.
KING   But how hath she   128
    Received his love?
POLONIUS   What do you think of me?
KING As of a man faithful and honorable.
POLONIUS I would fain prove so. But what might you think,   131
    When I had seen this hot love on the wing—
    As I perceived it, I must tell you that,
    Before my daughter told me—what might you,
    Or my dear Majesty your queen here, think,
    If I had played the desk or table book,   136
    Or given my heart a winking, mute and dumb,   137

---

103 For . . . cause i.e., for this defective behavior, this madness, must have a cause. 105 Perpend
Consider. 108 gather and surmise draw your own conclusions. 113 "In . . . etc." (The letter is poet-
ically addressed to her heart, where a letter would be kept by a young lady.) 115 stay . . . faithful i.e.,
hold on, I will do as you wish. 118 Doubt suspect 120 ill . . . numbers unskilled at writing verses.
121 reckon (1) count (2) number metrically, scan 124 machine i.e., body 126-8 And . . . ear and
moreover she has told me when, how, and where his solicitings of her occurred. 131 fain gladly
136-7 If . . . dumb if I had acted as go-between, passing love notes, or if I had refused to let my heart
acknowledge what my eyes could see

Or looked upon this love with idle sight? 138
What might you think? No, I went round to work, 139
And my young mistress thus I did bespeak: 140
"Lord Hamlet is a prince out of thy star; 141
This must not be." And then I prescripts gave her, 142
That she should lock herself from his resort,
Admit no messengers, receive no tokens.
Which done, she took the fruits of my advice;
And he, repellèd—a short tale to make—
Fell into a sadness, then into a fast,
Thence to a watch, thence into a weakness, 148
Thence to a lightness, and by this declension 149
Into the madness wherein now he raves,
And all we mourn for.

KING *[to the Queen]*   Do you think 'tis this?
QUEEN It may be, very like.
POLONIUS Hath there been such a time—I would fain know that—
That I have positively said "Tis so,"
When it proved otherwise?
KING   Not that I know.
POLONIUS Take this from this, if this be otherwise. 156
If circumstances lead me, I will find
Where truth is hid, though it were hid indeed
Within the center.
KING   How may we try it further? 159
POLONIUS You know sometimes he walks four hours together
Here in the lobby.
QUEEN   So he does indeed.
POLONIUS At such a time I'll loose my daughter to him. 162
Be you and I behind an arras then. 163
Mark the encounter. If he love her not
And be not from his reason fall'n thereon, 165
Let me be no assistant for a state,
But keep a farm and carters.
KING   We will try it. 167

Enter Hamlet [reading on a book].

QUEEN But look where sadly the poor wretch comes reading.
POLONIUS Away, I do beseech you both, away.
I'll board him presently. Oh, give me leave. 170

---

138 **with idle sight** complacently or incomprehendingly. 139 **round** roundly, plainly 140 **bespeak**
address 141 **out of thy star** above your sphere, position 142 **prescripts** orders 148 **watch** state of
sleeplessness 149 **lightness** lightheadedness. **declension** decline, deterioration. (With a pun on the
grammatical sense.) 156 **Take this from this** (The actor probably gestures, indicating that he means
his head from his shoulders, or his staff of office or chain from his hands or neck, or something similar.) 159 **center** center of the earth, traditionally an extraordinarily inaccessible place. **try** test 162
loose (As one might release an animal that is being mated.) 163 **arras** hanging, tapestry 165
thereon on that account 167 **carters** wagon drivers. 170 **I'll . . . leave** I'll accost him at once. Please
leave us alone; leave him to me.

Exeunt King and Queen [with attendants].

How does my good Lord Hamlet?

HAMLET Well, God-a-mercy.

POLONIUS Do you know me, my lord?   172

HAMLET Excellent well. You are a fishmonger.   174

POLONIUS Not I, my lord.

HAMLET Then I would you were so honest a man.

POLONIUS Honest, my lord?

HAMLET Ay, sir. To be honest, as this world goes, is to
be one man picked out of ten thousand.

POLONIUS That's very true, my lord.

HAMLET For if the sun breed maggots in a dead dog,
being a good kissing carrion—Have you a daughter?   182

POLONIUS I have, my lord.

HAMLET Let her not walk i'th' sun. Conception is a   184
blessing, but as your daughter may conceive, friend, look to't.

POLONIUS [aside] How say you by that? Still harping
on my daughter. Yet he knew me not at first; 'a said
I was a fishmonger. 'A is far gone. And truly in my
youth I suffered much extremity for love, very near
this. I'll speak to him again.—What do you read,
my lord?

HAMLET Words, words, words.

POLONIUS What is the matter, my lord?   194

HAMLET Between who?

POLONIUS I mean, the matter that you read, my lord.

HAMLET Slanders, sir; for the satirical rogue says here
that old men have gray beards, that their faces are wrinkled,
their eyes purging thick amber and plum-tree   199
gum, and that they have a plentiful lack of wit, to-   200
gether with most weak hams. All which, sir, though I
most powerfully and potently believe, yet I hold it not
honesty to have it thus set down, for yourself, sir, shall   203
grow old as I am, if like a crab you could go backward.   204

POLONIUS [aside] Though this be madness, yet there is
method in't.—Will you walk out of the air, my lord?   206

HAMLET Into my grave.

POLONIUS Indeed, that's out of the air. [Aside] How
pregnant sometimes his replies are! A happiness that   209
often madness hits on, which reason and sanity could
not so Prosperously be delivered of. I will leave him   211

---

172 God-a-mercy God have mercy, i.e., thank you. **174 fishmonger** fish merchant. **182 a good kissing carrion** i.e., a good piece of flesh for kissing, or for the sun to kiss **184 i'th' sun** in public. (With additional implication of the sunshine of princely favors.) **Conception** (1) Understanding (2) Pregnancy **194 matter** substance. (But Hamlet plays on the sense of "basis for a dispute.") **199 purging** discharging. **amber** i.e., resin, like the resinous *plum-tree gum* **200 wit** understanding **203 honesty** decency, decorum **204 old** as old **206 out of the air** (The open air was considered dangerous for sick people.) **209 pregnant** quick-witted, full of meaning. **happiness** felicity of expression **211 Prosperously** successfully

and suddenly contrive the means of meeting between   212
him and my daughter.—My honorable lord, I will
most humbly take my leave of you.

HAMLET You cannot, sir, take from me anything that I
will more willingly part withal—except my life, except   216
my life, except my life.

Enter Guildenstern and Rosencrantz.

POLONIUS Fare you well, my lord.

HAMLET These tedious old fools!

POLONIUS You go to seek the Lord Hamlet. There he is.

ROSENCRANTZ *[to Polonius]* God save you, sir!

[Exit Polonius.]

GUILDENSTERN My honored lord!

ROSENCRANTZ My most dear lord!

HAMLET My excellent good friends! How dost thou,
Guildenstern? Ah, Rosencrantz! Good lads, how do
you both?

ROSENCRANTZ As the indifferent children of the earth.   227

GUILDENSTERN Happy in that we are not overhappy.
On Fortune's cap we are not the very button.

HAMLET Nor the soles of her shoe?

ROSENCRANTZ Neither, my lord.

HAMLET Then you live about her waist, or in the middle   232
of her favors?   233

GUILDENSTERN Faith, her privates we.   234

HAMLET In the secret parts of Fortune? Oh, most true,
she is a strumpet. What news?   236

ROSENCRANTZ None, my lord, but the world's grown honest.

HAMLET Then is doomsday near. But your news is not
true. Let me question more in particular. What have
you, my good friends, deserved at the hands of
Fortune that she sends you to prison hither?

GUILDENSTERN Prison, my lord?

HAMLET Denmark's a prison.

ROSENCRANTZ Then is the world one.

HAMLET A goodly one, in which there are many
confines, wards, and dungeons, Denmark being one   247
o'th' worst.

ROSENCRANTZ We think not so, my lord.

HAMLET Why then 'tis none to you, for there is nothing
either good or bad but thinking makes it so. To me it
is a prison.

---

212 suddenly immediately **216 withal** with **227 indifferent** ordinary, at neither extreme of fortune
or misfortune **232–3 the middle . . . favors** i.e., her genitals. **234 her privates we** (1) we dwell in her
privates, her genitals, in the middle of her favors (2) we are her ordinary footsoldiers. **236 strumpet**
(Fortune was proverbially thought of as fickle.) **247 confines** places of confinement

ROSENCRANTZ Why then, your ambition makes it one.
　　'Tis too narrow for your mind.
HAMLET Oh, God, I could be bounded in a nutshell and
　　count myself a king of infinite space, were it not that
　　I have bad dreams.
GUILDENSTERN Which dreams indeed are ambition, for
　　the very substance of the ambitious is merely the　　　　　　　259
　　shadow of a dream.
HAMLET A dream itself is but a shadow.
ROSENCRANTZ Truly, and I hold ambition of so airy
　　and light a quality that it is but a shadow's shadow.
HAMLET Then are our beggars bodies, and our monarchs　　　264
　　and outstretched heroes the beggars' shadows.　　　　　　　265
　　Shall we to th' court? For, by my fay, I cannot reason.　　266
ROSENCRANTZ, GUILDENSTERN We'll wait upon you.　　　　267
HAMLET No such matter. I will not sort you with the　　　　268
　　rest of my servants, for, to speak to you like an honest
　　man, I am most dreadfully attended. But, in the　　　　　　270
　　beaten way of friendship, what make you at Elsinore?　　271
ROSENCRANTZ To visit you, my lord, no other occasion.
HAMLET Beggar that I am, I am even poor in thanks;
　　but I thank you, and sure, dear friends, my thanks are
　　too dear a halfpenny. Were you not sent for? Is it your　　275
　　own inclining? Is it a free visitation? Come, come, deal　276
　　justly with me. Come, come. Nay, speak.
GUILDENSTERN What should we say, my lord?
HAMLET Anything but to th' purpose. You were sent　　　　279
　　for, and there is a kind of confession in your looks
　　which your modesties have not craft enough to color.　　281
　　I know the good King and Queen have sent for you.
ROSENCRANTZ To what end, my lord?
HAMLET That you must teach me. But let me conjure　　　　284
　　you, by the rights of our fellowship, by the consonancy　285
　　of our youth, by the obligation of our ever-preserved　　286
　　love, and by what more dear a better proposer　　　　　　287
　　could charge you withal, be even and direct with me　　288
　　whether you were sent for or no.　　　　　　　　　　　　289

---

259 the very . . . ambitious that seemingly very substantial thing that the ambitious pursue **264–5 Then . . . shadows** (Hamlet pursues their argument about ambition to its absurd extreme: if ambition is only a shadow of a shadow, then beggars (who are presumably without ambition) must be real, whereas monarchs and heroes are only their shadows—*outstretched* like elongated shadows, made to look bigger than they are.) **266 fay** faith **267 wait upon** accompany, attend. (But Hamlet uses the phrase in the sense of providing menial service.) **268 sort** class, categorize **270 dreadfully attended** waited upon in slovenly fashion. **271 beaten way** familiar path, tried-and-true course. **make** do **275 too dear a halfpenny** (1) too expensive at even a halfpenny, i.e., of little worth (2) too expensive by a halfpenny in return for worthless kindness. **276 free** voluntary **279 Anything but to th' purpose** Anything except a straightforward answer. (Said ironically.) **281 color** disguise. **284 conjure** adjure, entreat **285–6 the consonancy of our youth** our closeness in our younger days **287 better** more skillful **288 charge** urge. **even** straight, honest

ROSENCRANTZ *[aside to Guildenstern]* What say you?

HAMLET *[aside]* Nay, then, I have an eye of you.—If   291
  you love me, hold not off.   292

GUILDENSTERN My lord, we were sent for.

HAMLET I will tell you why; so shall my anticipation   294
  prevent your discovery, and your secrecy to the King   295
  and Queen molt no feather. I have of late—but   296
  wherefore I know not—lost all my mirth, forgone all
  custom of exercises; and indeed it goes so heavily with
  my disposition that this goodly frame, the earth,
  seems to me a sterile promontory; this most excellent
  canopy, the air, look you, this brave o'erhanging   301
  firmament, this majestical roof fretted with golden   302
  fire, why, it appeareth nothing to me but a foul and
  pestilent congregation of vapors. What a piece of work   304
  is a man! How noble in reason, how infinite in faculties,
  in form and moving how express and admirable, in   306
  action how like an angel, in apprehension how like a   307
  god! The beauty of the world, the paragon of animals!
  And yet, to me, what is this quintessence of dust?   309
  Man delights not me—no, nor woman neither,
  though by your smiling you seem to say so.

ROSENCRANTZ My lord, there was no such stuff in my
  thoughts.

HAMLET Why did you laugh, then, when I said man delights
  not me?

ROSENCRANTZ To think, my lord, if you delight not in
  man, what Lenten entertainment the players shall   317
  receive from you. We coted them on the way, and   318
  hither are they coming to offer you service.

HAMLET He that plays the king shall be welcome; His
  Majesty shall have tribute of me. The adventurous   321
  knight shall use his foil and target, the lover shall not   322
  sigh gratis, the humorous man shall end his part in   323
  peace, the clown shall make those laugh whose lungs   324
  are tickle o'th' sear, and the lady shall say her mind   325
  freely, or the blank verse shall halt for't. What players   326
  are they?

---

291 of on **292 hold not off** don't hold back. **294–5 so . . . discovery** in that way my saying it first will spare you from having to reveal the truth **296 molt no feather** i.e., not diminish in the least. **301 brave** splendid **302 fretted** adorned (with fretwork, as in a vaulted ceiling) **304 congregation** mass. **piece of work** masterpiece **306 express** well-framed, exact, expressive **307 apprehension** power of comprehending **309 quintessence** very essence. (Literally, the fifth essence beyond earth, water, air, and fire, supposed to be extractable from them.) **317 Lenten entertainment** meager reception (appropriate to Lent) **318 coted** overtook and passed by **321 tribute** (1) applause (2) homage paid in money. **of** from **322 foil and target** sword and shield **323 gratis** for nothing. **humorous man** eccentric character, dominated by one trait or "humor" **323–4 in peace** i.e., with full license **325 tickle o'th' sear** hair trigger, ready to laugh easily. (A *sear* is part of a gun-lock.) **326 halt** limp

ROSENCRANTZ Even those you were wont to take such
    delight in, the tragedians of the city.   329
HAMLET How chances it they travel? Their residence,   330
    both in reputation and profit, was better both ways.
ROSENCRANTZ I think their inhibition comes by the   332
    means of the late innovation.   333
HAMLET Do they hold the same estimation they did
    when I was in the city? Are they so followed?
ROSENCRANTZ No, indeed are they not.
HAMLET How comes it? Do they grow rusty?   337
ROSENCRANTZ Nay, their endeavor keeps in the wonted   338
    pace. But there is, sir, an aerie of children, little eyases,   339
    that cry out on the top of question and are most tyrannically   340
    clapped for't. These are now the fashion, and   341
    so berattle the common stages—so they call them—   342
    that many wearing rapiers are afraid of goose quills   343
    and dare scarce come thither.
HAMLET What, are they children? Who maintains 'em?
    How are they escotted? Will they pursue the quality no   346
    longer than they can sing? Will they not say afterwards,   347
    if they should grow themselves to common   348
    players—as it is most like, if their means are no   349
    better—their writers do them wrong to make them   350
    exclaim against their own succession?   351
ROSENCRANTZ Faith, there has been much to-do on   352
    both sides, and the nation holds it no sin to tar them to   353
    controversy. There was for a while no money bid for   354
    argument unless the poet and the player went to cuffs   355
    in the question.   356
HAMLET Is't possible?
GUILDENSTERN Oh, there has been much throwing about of brains.
HAMLET Do the boys carry it away?   360

---

329 **tragedians** actors 330 **residence** remaining in their usual place, i.e., in the city 332 **inhibition** formal prohibition (from acting plays in the city) 333 **late innovation** i.e., recent new fashion in satirical plays performed by boy actors in the "private" theaters; or the Earl of Essex's abortive rebellion in 1601 against Elizabeth's government. (A much debated passage of seemingly topical reference.) 337 **How . . . rusty?** Have they lost their polish, gone out of fashion? (This passage, through line 362, alludes to the rivalry between the children's companies and the adult actors, given strong impetus by the reopening of the Children of the Chapel at the Blackfriars Theater in late 1600.) 338 **keeps . . . wonted** continues in the usual 339 **aerie** nest. **eyases** young hawks 340 **cry . . . question** speak shrilly, dominating the controversy (in decrying the public theaters) 340–1 **tyrannically** vehemently 342 **berattle . . . stages** clamor against the public theaters 343 **many wearing rapiers** i.e., many men of fashion, afraid to patronize the common players for fear of being satirized by the poets writing for the boy actors. **goose quills** i.e., pens of satIrists 346 **escotted** maintained. **quality** (acting) profession 346–7 **no longer . . . sing** i.e., only until their voices change. 348 **common** regular, adult 349 **like** likely 349–50 **if . . . better** if they find no better way to support themselves 351 **succession** i.e., future careers. 352 **to-do** ado 353 **tar** incite (as in inciting dogs to attack a chained bear) 354–6 **There . . . question** i.e., For a while, no money was offered by the acting companies to playwrights for the plot to a play unless the satirical poets who wrote for the boys and the adult actors came to blows in the play itself. 360 **carry it away** i.e., win the day.

ROSENCRANTZ Ay, that they do, my lord—Hercules 361
    and his load too. 362

HAMLET It is not very strange; for my uncle is King of
    Denmark, and those that would make mouths at him 364
    while my father lived give twenty, forty, fifty, a
    hundred ducats apiece for his picture in little. 'Sblood, 366
    there is something in this more than natural, if philosophy
    could find it out.

    A flourish [of trumpets within].

GUILDENSTERN There are the players.

HAMLET Gentlemen, you are welcome to Elsinore. Your
    hands, come then. Th'appurtenance of welcome is 371
    fashion and ceremony. Let me comply with you in this 372
    garb, lest my extent to the players, which, I tell you, 373
    must show fairly outwards, should more appear like 374
    entertainment than yours. You are welcome. But my 375
    uncle-father and aunt-mother are deceived.

GUILDENSTERN In what, my dear lord?

HAMLET I am but mad north-north-west. When the 378
    wind is southerly I know a hawk from a handsaw. 379

    Enter Polonius.

POLONIUS Well be with you, gentlemen!

HAMLET Hark you, Guildenstern, and you too; at each
    ear a hearer. That great baby you see there is not yet
    out of his swaddling clouts. 383

ROSENCRANTZ Haply he is the second time come to 384
    them, for they say an old man is twice a child.

HAMLET I will prophesy he comes to tell me of the
    players. Mark it.—You say right, sir, o' Monday 387
    morning, 'twas then indeed. 388

POLONIUS My lord, I have news to tell you.

HAMLET My lord, I have news to tell you. When Roscius 390
    was an actor in Rome—

POLONIUS The actors are come hither, my lord.

HAMLET Buzz, buzz! 393

361–2 Hercules . . . load (Thought to be an allusion to the sign of the Globe Theatre, which allegedly was Hercules bearing the world on his shoulders.) **364 mouths** faces **366 ducats** gold coins. **in little** in miniature. **'Sblood** By God's (Christ's) blood **371 Th'appurtenance** The proper accompaniment **372 comply** observe the formalities of courtesy **373 garb** i.e., manner. **my extent** that which I extend, i.e., my polite behavior **374 show fairly outwards** show every evidence of cordiality **375 entertainment** a (warm) reception **378 north-north-west** just off true north, only partly. **379 I . . . handsaw** (Speaking in his mad guise, Hamlet perhaps suggests that he can tell true from false. A *handsaw* may be a *hernshaw* or heron. Still, a supposedly mad disposition might compare hawks and handsaws.) **383 swaddling clouts** cloths in which to wrap a newborn baby. **384 Haply** Perhaps **387–8 You say . . . then** indeed (Said to impress upon Polonius the idea that Hamlet is in serious conversation with his friends.) **390 Roscius** a famous Roman actor who died in 62 B.C. **393 Buzz** (An interjection used to denote stale news.)

POLONIUS Upon my honor—

HAMLET Then came each actor on his ass.

POLONIUS The best actors in the world, either for
    tragedy, comedy, history, pastoral, pastoral-comical,
    historical-pastoral, tragical-historical, tragical-comical-
    historical-pastoral, scene individable, or poem unlimited.   399
    Seneca cannot be too heavy, nor Plautus too   400
    light. For the law of writ and the liberty, these are the   401
    only men.

HAMLET O Jephthah, judge of Israel, what a treasure   403
    hadst thou!

POLONIUS What a treasure had he, my lord?

HAMLET Why,
    "One fair daughter, and no more,
    The which he lovèd passing well."   408

POLONIUS [aside] Still on my daughter.

HAMLET Am I not i'th' right, old Jephthah?

POLONIUS If you call me Jephthah, my lord, I have a
    daughter that I love passing well.

HAMLET Nay, that follows not.   413

POLONIUS What follows then, my lord?   414

HAMLET Why,
    "As by lot, God wot,"   416
    and then, you know,
    "It came to pass, as most like it was"—   418
    the first row of the pious chanson will show you more,   419
    for look where my abridgement comes.   420

    Enter the Players.

You are welcome, masters; welcome, all. I am glad to   421
see thee well. Welcome, good friends. Oh, old friend!
Why, thy face is valanced since I saw thee last. Com'st   423
thou to beard me in Denmark? What, my young lady   424
and mistress! By'r Lady, Your Ladyship is nearer to   425
heaven than when I saw you last, by the altitude of a   426

399–400 **scene . . . unlimited** plays that are unclassifiable and all-inclusive. (An absurdly catchall
conclusion to Polonius's pompous list of categories.) 400 **Seneca** writer of Latin tragedies. **Plautus**
writer of Latin comedies 401 **law . . . liberty** dramatic composition both according to the rules and
disregarding the rules. **these** i.e., the actors 403 **Jephthah . . . Israel** (Jephthah had to sacrifice his
daughter; see Judges 11. Hamlet goes on to quote from a ballad on the theme.) 408 **passing** surpass-
ingly 413 **that follows not** i.e., just because you resemble Jephthah in having a daughter does not
logically prove that you love her. 414 **What . . . lord?** What does follow logically? (But Hamlet, pretending madness, answers with a fragment of a ballad, as if Polonius had asked, "What comes next?"
See 419n.) 416 **lot** chance. **wot** knows 418 **like** likely, probable 419 **the first . . . more** the first
stanza of this biblically based ballad will satisfy your stated desire to know what *follows* (line 414).
420 **my abridgment** something that cuts short my conversation; also, a diversion 421 **masters** good
sirs 423 **valanced** fringed (with a beard) 424 **beard** confront, challenge. (With obvious pun.) **young
lady** i.e., boy playing women's parts 425 **By'r Lady** By Our Lady 425–6 **nearer to heaven** i.e., taller

chopine. Pray God your voice, like a piece of uncurrent 427
gold, be not cracked within the ring. Masters, you 428
are all welcome. We'll e'en to't like French falconers, 429
fly at anything we see. We'll have a speech straight. 430
Come, give us a taste of your quality. Come, a 431
passionate speech.

FIRST PLAYER What speech, my good lord?

HAMLET I heard thee speak me a speech once, but it
was never acted, or if it was, not above once, for the
play, I remember, pleased not the million; 'twas caviar 436
to the general. But it was—as I received it, and 437
others, whose judgments in such matters cried in the 438
top of mine—an excellent play, well digested in the 439
scenes, set down with as much modesty as cunning. I 440
remember one said there were no sallets in the lines to 441
make the matter savory, nor no matter in the phrase
that might indict the author of affectation, but called it 443
an honest method, as wholesome as sweet, and by very
much more handsome than fine. One speech in't I 445
chiefly loved: 'twas Aeneas' tale to Dido, and thereabout
of it especially when he speaks of Priam's 447
slaughter. If it live in your memory, begin at this line: 448
let me see, let me see—

"The rugged Pyrrhus, like th' Hyrcanian beast"— 450
'Tis not so. It begins with Pyrrhus:

"The rugged Pyrrhus, he whose sable arms, 452
Black as his purpose, did the night resemble
When he lay couchèd in th' ominous horse, 454
Hath now this dread and black complexion smeared
With heraldry more dismal. Head to foot 456
Now is he total gules, horridly tricked 457
With blood of fathers, mothers, daughters, sons,

---

427 **chopine** thick-soled shoe of Italian fashion. 427–8 **uncurrent** not passable as lawful coinage 428 **cracked . . . ring** i.e., changed from adolescent to male voice, no longer suitable for women's roles. (Coins featured rings enclosing the sovereign's head; if the coin was sufficiently clipped to invade within this ring, it was unfit for currency.) 429 **e'en to't** go at it 430 **straight** at once. 431 **quality** professional skill. 436–7 **caviar to the general** i.e., an expensive delicacy not generally palatable to uneducated tastes. 438–9 **cried in the top of** i.e., spoke with greater authority than 439 **digested** arranged, ordered 440 **modesty** moderation, restraint. **cunning** skill. 441 **sallets** i.e., something savory, spicy improprieties 443 **indict** convict 445 **handsome** well-proportioned. **fine** elaborately ornamented, showy. 447–8 **Priam's slaughter** the slaying of the ruler of Troy, when the Greeks finally took the city 450 **Pyrrhus** a Greek hero in the Trojan War, also known as Neoptolemus, son of Achilles—another avenging son. **th'Hyrcanian beast** i.e., the tiger. (On the death of Priam, see Virgil, *Aeneid*, 2.506 ff.; compare the whole speech with Marlowe's *Dido Queen of Carthage*, 2.1.214 ff. On the *Hyrcanian* tiger, see *Aeneid*, 4.366–7. Hyrcania is on the Caspian Sea.) 452 **rugged** shaggy, savage. **sable** black (for reasons of camouflage during the episode of the Trojan horse) 454 **couchèd** concealed. **ominous horse** fateful Trojan horse, by which the Greeks gained access to Troy 456 **dismal** calamitous. 457 **total gules** entirely red. (A heraldic term.) **tricked** spotted and smeared. (Heraldic.)

Baked and impasted with the parching streets,   459
That lend a tyrannous and a damnèd light   460
To their lord's murder. Roasted in wrath and fire,   461
And thus o'ersizèd with coagulate gore,   462
With eyes like carbuncles, the hellish Pyrrhus   463
Old grandsire Priam seeks."
So proceed you.

POLONIUS   'Fore God, my lord, well spoken, with good
accent and good discretion.

FIRST PLAYER   "Anon he finds him
Striking too short at Greeks. His antique sword,   469
Rebellious to his arm, lies where it falls,
Repugnant to command. Unequal matched,   471
Pyrrhus at Priam drives, in rage strikes wide,
But with the whiff and wind of his fell sword   473
Th'unnervèd father falls. Then senseless Ilium,   474
Seeming to feel this blow, with flaming top
Stoops to his base, and with a hideous crash   476
Takes prisoner Pyrrhus' ear. For, lo! His sword,
Which was declining on the milky head   478
Of reverend Priam, seemed i'th'air to stick.
So as a painted tyrant Pyrrhus stood,   480
And, like a neutral to his will and matter,   481
Did nothing.
But as we often see against some storm   483
A silence in the heavens, the rack stand still,   484
The bold winds speechless, and the orb below   485
As hush as death, anon the dreadful thunder
Doth rend the region, so, after Pyrrhus' pause,   487
A rousèd vengeance sets him new a-work,
And never did the Cyclops' hammers fall   489
On Mars's armor forged for proof eterne   490
With less remorse than Pyrrhus' bleeding sword   491
Now falls on Priam.
Out, out, thou strumpet Fortune! All you gods
In general synod take away her power!   494
Break all the spokes and fellies from her wheel,   495
And bowl the round nave down the hill of heaven   496
As low as to the fiends!"

---

459 **Baked ... streets** roasted and encrusted, like a thick paste, by the parching heat of the streets
(because of the fires everywhere) 460 **tyrannous** cruel 461 **their lord's** i.e., Priam's 462 **o'ersizèd**
covered as with size or glue 463 **carbuncles** large fiery-red precious stones thought to emit their own
light 469 **antique** ancient, long-used 471 **Repugnant** disobedient, resistant 473 **fell** cruel 474
Th'unnervèd the strengthless. **senseless Ilium** inanimate citadel of Troy 476 **his** its 478 **declining**
descending. **milky** white-haired 480 **painted** motionless, as in a painting 481 **like ... matter** i.e., as
though suspended between his intention and its fulfillment 483 **against** just before 484 **rack** mass of
clouds 485 **orb** globe, earth 487 **region** sky 489 **Cyclops** giant armor makers in the smithy of Vulcan
490 **proof** proven or tested resistance to assault 491 **remorse** pity 494 **synod** assembly 495 **fellies**
pieces of wood forming the rim of a wheel 496 **nave** hub. **hill of heaven** Mount Olympus

POLONIUS This is too long.

HAMLET It shall to the barber's with your beard.—Prithee,
say on. He's for a jig or a tale of bawdry, or he   500
sleeps. Say on; come to Hecuba.   501

FIRST PLAYER "But who, ah woe! had seen the moblèd queen"—   502

HAMLET "The moblèd queen?"

POLONIUS That's good. "Moblèd queen" is good.

FIRST PLAYER "Run barefoot up and down, threat'ning the flames   505
With bisson rheum, a clout upon that head   506
Where late the diadem stood, and, for a robe,   507
About her lank and all o'erteemèd loins   508
A blanket, in the alarm of fear caught up—
Who this had seen, with tongue in venom steeped,
'Gainst Fortune's state would treason have pronounced.   511
But if the gods themselves did see her then
When she saw Pyrrhus make malicious sport
In mincing with his sword her husband's limbs,
The instant burst of clamor that she made,
Unless things mortal move them not at all,
Would have made milch the burning eyes of heaven,   517
And passion in the gods."   518

POLONIUS Look whe'er he has not turned his color and   519
has tears in 's eyes. Prithee, no more.

HAMLET 'Tis well; I'll have thee speak out the rest of
this soon.—Good my lord, will you see the players well
bestowed? Do you hear, let them be well used, for they   523
are the abstract and brief chronicles of the time. After   524
your death you were better have a bad epitaph than
their ill report while you live.

POLONIUS My lord, I will use them according to their desert.

HAMLET God's bodikin, man, much better. Use every   529
man after his desert, and who shall scape whipping?
Use them after your own honor and dignity. The less   531
they deserve, the more merit is in your bounty. Take them in.

POLONIUS Come, sirs.   *[Exit.]*

HAMLET Follow him, friends. We'll hear a play tomorrow.
[As they start to leave, Hamlet detains the First Player.]
Dost thou hear me, old friend? Can you play
The Murder of Gonzago?

FIRST PLAYER Ay, my lord.

---

500 jig comic song and dance often given at the end of play **501 Hecuba** wife of Priam. **502 who
. . . had** anyone who had. (Also in line 510.) **moblèd** muffled **505 threat'ning the flames** i.e., weeping hard enough to dampen the flames **506 bisson rheum** blinding tears. **clout** cloth **507 late** lately
508 all o'erteemèd utterly worn out with bearing children **511 state** rule, managing. **pronounced**
proclaimed. **517 milch** milky, moist with tears. **burning eyes of heaven** i.e., stars, heavenly bodies
518 passion overpowering emotion **519 whe'er** whether **523 bestowed** lodged. **524 abstract** summary account **529 God's bodikin** By God's (Christ's) little body, bodykin. (Not to be confused with
bodkin, "dagger.") **531 after** according to

HAMLET We'll ha 't tomorrow night. You could, for a   540
    need, study a speech of some dozen or sixteen lines   541
    which I would set down and insert in't, could you not?

FIRST PLAYER Ay, my lord.

HAMLET Very well. Follow that lord, and look you mock
    him not.   *Exeunt players.*
    My good friends, I'll leave you till night. You are welcome
    to Elsinore.

ROSENCRANTZ Good my lord!

    Exeunt [Rosencrantz and Guildenstern].

HAMLET Ay, so, goodbye to you.—Now I am alone.
    Oh, what a rogue and peasant slave am I!
    Is it not monstrous that this player here,
    But in a fiction, in a dream of passion,   552
    Could force his soul so to his own conceit   553
    That from her working all his visage wanned,   554
    Tears in his eyes, distraction in his aspect,   555
    A broken voice, and his whole function suiting   556
    With forms to his conceit? And all for nothing!   557
    For Hecuba!
    What's Hecuba to him, or he to Hecuba,
    That he should weep for her? What would he do
    Had he the motive and the cue for passion
    That I have? He would drown the stage with tears
    And cleave the general ear with horrid speech,   563
    Make mad the guilty and appall the free,   564
    Confound the ignorant, and amaze indeed   565
    The very faculties of eyes and ears. Yet I,
    A dull and muddy-mettled rascal, peak   567
    Like John-a-dreams, unpregnant of my cause,   568
    And can say nothing—no, not for a king
    Upon whose property and most dear life   570
    A damned defeat was made. Am I a coward?   571
    Who calls me villain? Breaks my pate across?   572
    Plucks off my beard and blows it in my face?
    Tweaks me by the nose? Gives me the lie i'th' throat   574
    As deep as to the lungs? Who does me this?
    Ha, 'swounds, I should take it; for it cannot be   576

---

540 **ha't** have it 541 **study** memorize 552 **But** merely 553 **force . . . conceit** bring his innermost being so entirely into accord with his conception (of the role) 554 **from her working** as a result of, or in response to, his soul's activity. **wanned** grew pale 555 **aspect** look, glance 556–7 **his whole . . . conceit** all his bodily powers responding with actions to suit his thought. 563 **the general ear** everyone's ear. **horrid** horrible 564 **appall** (Literally, make pale.) **free** innocent 565 **Confound the ignorant** i.e., dumbfound those who know nothing of the crime that has been committed. **amaze** stun 567 **muddy-mettled** dull-spirited 567–8 **peak . . . cause** mope, like a dreaming idler, not quickened by my cause 570 **property** person and function 571 **damned defeat** damnable act of destruction 572 **pate** head 574 **Gives . . . throat** Calls me an out-and-out liar 576 **'swounds** by his (Christ's) wounds

But I am pigeon-livered and lack gall   577
To make oppression bitter, or ere this   578
I should ha' fatted all the region kites   579
With this slave's offal. Bloody, bawdy villain!   580
Remorseless, treacherous, lecherous, kindless villain!   581
Oh, vengeance!
Why, what an ass am I! This is most brave,   583
That I, the son of a dear father murdered,
Prompted to my revenge by heaven and hell,
Must like a whore unpack my heart with words
And fall a-cursing, like a very drab,   587
A scullion! Fie upon't, foh! About, my brains!   588
Hum, I have heard
That guilty creatures sitting at a play
Have by the very cunning of the scene   591
Been struck so to the soul that presently   592
They have proclaimed their malefactions;
For murder, though it have no tongue, will speak
With most miraculous organ. I'll have these players
Play something like the murder of my father
Before mine uncle. I'll observe his looks;
I'll tent him to the quick. If 'a do blench,   598
I know my course. The spirit that I have seen
May be the devil, and the devil hath power
T'assume a pleasing shape; yea, and perhaps,
Out of my weakness and my melancholy,
As he is very potent with such spirits,   603
Abuses me to damn me. I'll have grounds   604
More relative than this. The play's the thing   605
Wherein I'll catch the conscience of the King.   *Exit.*

[3.1]

Enter King, Queen, Polonius, Ophelia, Rosencrantz, Guildenstern, lords.

KING And can you by no drift of conference   1
   Get from him why he puts on this confusion,
   Grating so harshly all his days of quiet
   With turbulent and dangerous lunacy?
ROSENCRANTZ He does confess he feels himself distracted,
   But from what cause 'a will by no means speak.

---

577 pigeon-livered (The pigeon or dove was popularly supposed to be mild because it secreted no gall.) **578 To . . . bitter** to make things bitter for oppressors **579 region kites** kites (birds of prey) of the air **580 offal** entrails. **581 Remorseless** Pitiless. **kindless** unnatural **583 brave** fine, admirable. (Said ironically.) **587 drab** whore **588 scullion** menial kitchen servant. (Apt to be foul-mouthed.) **About** About it, to work **591 cunning** art, skill. **scene** dramatic presentation **592 presently** at once **598 tent** probe. **the quick** the tender part of a wound, the core. **blench** quail, flinch **603 spirits** humors (of melancholy) **604 Abuses** deludes **605 relative** cogent, pertinent
3.1 Location: The castle.
1 drift of conference course of talk

GUILDENSTERN Nor do we find him forward to be sounded,   7
    But with a crafty madness keeps aloof
    When we would bring him on to some confession
    Of his true state.
QUEEN   Did he receive you well?
ROSENCRANTZ Most like a gentleman.
GUILDENSTERN But with much forcing of his disposition.   12
ROSENCRANTZ Niggard of question, but of our demands   13
    Most free in his reply.
QUEEN   Did you assay him   14
    To any pastime?
ROSENCRANTZ Madam, it so fell out that certain players
    We o'erraught on the way. Of these we told him,   17
    And there did seem in him a kind of joy
    To hear of it. They are here about the court,
    And, as I think, they have already order
    This night to play before him.
POLONIUS   'Tis most true,
    And he beseeched me to entreat Your Majesties
    To hear and see the matter.
KING With all my heart, and it doth much content me
    To hear him so inclined.
    Good gentlemen, give him a further edge   26
    And drive his purpose into these delights.
ROSENCRANTZ We shall, my lord.

    Exeunt Rosencrantz and Guildenstern.

KING   Sweet Gertrude, leave us too,
    For we have closely sent for Hamlet hither,   29
    That he, as 'twere by accident, may here
    Affront Ophelia.   31
    Her father and myself, lawful espials,   32
    Will so bestow ourselves that seeing, unseen,
    We may of their encounter frankly judge,
    And gather by him, as he is behaved,
    If't be th'affliction of his love or no
    That thus he suffers for.
QUEEN   I shall obey you.
    And for your part, Ophelia, I do wish
    That your good beauties be the happy cause
    Of Hamlet's wildness. So shall I hope your virtues
    Will bring him to his wonted way again,
    To both your honors.
OPHELIA   Madam, I wish it may.

    [Exit Queen.]

---

7 forward willing. **sounded** questioned **12 disposition** inclination. **13 Niggard of question** Laconic.
demands questions **14 assay** try to win **17 o'erraught** overtook **26 edge** incitement **29 closely** privately **31 Affront** confront, meet **32 espials** spies

POLONIUS Ophelia, walk you here.—Gracious, so please you, 43
 We will bestow ourselves. *[To Ophelia]* Read on this
  book, *[giving her a book]* 44
 That show of such an exercise may color 45
 Your loneliness. We are oft to blame in this— 46
 'Tis too much proved—that with devotion's visage 47
 And pious action we do sugar o'er
 The devil himself.
KING *[aside]* Oh, 'tis too true!
 How smart a lash that speech doth give my conscience!
 The harlot's cheek, beautied with plast'ring art,
 Is not more ugly to the thing that helps it 53
 Than is my deed to my most painted word. 54
 Oh, heavy burden!
POLONIUS I hear him coming. Let's withdraw, my lord. 56

 [The King and Polonius withdraw.]
  Enter Hamlet. *[Ophelia pretends to read a book.]*

HAMLET To be, or not to be, that is the question:
 Whether 'tis nobler in the mind to suffer
 The slings and arrows of outrageous fortune,
 Or to take arms against a sea of troubles
 And by opposing end them. To die, to sleep—
 No more—and by a sleep to say we end
 The heartache and the thousand natural shocks
 That flesh is heir to. 'Tis a consummation
 Devoutly to be wished. To die, to sleep;
 To sleep, perchance to dream. Ay, there's the rub, 66
 For in that sleep of death what dreams may come,
 When we have shuffled off this mortal coil, 68
 Must give us pause. There's the respect 69
 That makes calamity of so long life. 70
 For who would bear the whips and scorns of time,
 Th'oppressor's wrong, the proud man's contumely, 72
 The pangs of disprized love, the law's delay, 73
 The insolence of office, and the spurns 74
 That patient merit of th'unworthy takes, 75
 When he himself might his quietus make 76

---

43 Gracious Your Grace (i.e., the King) **44 bestow** conceal **45 exercise** religious exercise. (The book she reads is one of devotion.) **color** give a plausible appearance to **46 loneliness** being alone. **47 too much proved** too often shown to be true, too often practiced **53 to . . . helps** it in comparison with the cosmetic that fashions the cheek's false beauty **54 painted word** deceptive utterances. **56.1 withdraw** (The King and Polonius may retire behind an arras. The stage directions specify that they "enter" again near the end of the scene.) **66 rub** (Literally, an obstacle in the game of bowls.) **68 shuffled** sloughed, cast. **coil** turmoil **69 respect** consideration **70 of . . . life** so long-lived, something we willingly endure for so long. (Also suggesting that long life is itself a calamity.) **72 contumely** insolent abuse **73 disprized** unvalued **74 office** officialdom. **spurns** insults **75 of . . . takes** receives from unworthy persons **76 quietus** acquittance; here, death

With a bare bodkin? Who would fardels bear,   77
To grunt and sweat under a weary life,
But that the dread of something after death,
The undiscovered country from whose bourn   80
No traveler returns, puzzles the will,
And makes us rather bear those ills we have
Than fly to others that we know not of?
Thus conscience does make cowards of us all;
And thus the native hue of resolution   85
Is sicklied o'er with the pale cast of thought,   86
And enterprises of great pitch and moment   87
With this regard their currents turn awry   88
And lose the name of action.—Soft you now,   89
The fair Ophelia.—Nymph, in thy orisons   90
Be all my sins remembered.
OPHELIA   Good my lord,   91
    How does Your Honor for this many a day?
HAMLET I humbly thank you; well, well, well.
OPHELIA My lord, I have remembrances of yours,
    That I have longèd long to redeliver.
    I pray you, now receive them.   [She offers tokens.]
HAMLET No, not I, I never gave you aught.
OPHELIA My honored lord, you know right well you did,
    And with them words of so sweet breath composed
    As made the things more rich. Their perfume lost,
    Take these again, for to the noble mind
    Rich gifts wax poor when givers prove unkind.
    There, my lord.   [She gives tokens.]
HAMLET Ha, ha! Are you honest?   104
OPHELIA My lord?
HAMLET Are you fair?   106
OPHELIA What means Your Lordship?
HAMLET That if you be honest and fair, your honesty   108
    should admit no discourse to your beauty.   109
OPHELIA Could beauty, my lord, have better commerce   110
    than with honesty?
HAMLET Ay, truly, for the power of beauty will sooner
    transform honesty from what it is to a bawd than the
    force of honesty can translate beauty into his likeness.   114
    This was sometime a paradox, but now the time gives   115
    it proof. I did love you once.   116

---

77 **a bare bodkin** a mere dagger, unsheathed. **fardels** burdens 80 **bourn** frontier, boundary 85 **native hue** natural color, complexion 86 **cast** tinge, shade of color 87 **pitch** height (as of a falcon's flight). **moment** importance 88 **regard** respect, consideration. **currents** courses 89 **Soft you** i.e., Wait a minute, gently 90–1 **in . . . remembered** i.e., pray for me, sinner that I am. 104 **honest** (1) truthful (2) chaste. 106 **fair** (1) beautiful (2) just, honorable. 108 **your honesty** your chastity 109 **discourse to** familiar dealings with 110 **commerce** dealings, intercourse 114 **his** its 115–16 **This . . . proof** This was formerly an unfashionable view, but now the present age confirms how true it is.

OPHELIA Indeed, my lord, you made me believe so.

HAMLET You should not have believed me, for virtue   118
cannot so inoculate our old stock but we shall relish of   119
it. I loved you not.   120

OPHELIA I was the more deceived.

HAMLET Get thee to a nunnery. Why wouldst thou be a   122
breeder of sinners? I am myself indifferent honest, but   123
yet I could accuse me of such things that it were better
my mother had not borne me: I am very proud,
revengeful, ambitious, with more offenses at my beck   126
than I have thoughts to put them in, imagination to
give them shape, or time to act them in. What should
such fellows as I do crawling between earth and
heaven? We are arrant knaves all; believe none of us.
Go thy ways to a nunnery. Where's your father?

OPHELIA At home, my lord.

HAMLET Let the doors be shut upon him, that he may
play the fool nowhere but in 's own house. Farewell.

OPHELIA Oh, help him, you sweet heavens!

HAMLET If thou dost marry, I'll give thee this plague for
thy dowry: be thou as chaste as ice, as pure as snow,
thou shalt not escape calumny. Get thee to a nunnery,
farewell. Or, if thou wilt needs marry, marry a fool, for
wise men know well enough what monsters you   140
make of them. To a nunnery, go, and quickly too.
Farewell.

OPHELIA Heavenly powers, restore him!

HAMLET I have heard of your paintings too, well   144
enough. God hath given you one face, and you make
yourselves another. You jig, you amble, and you   146
lisp, you nickname God's creatures, and make your   147
wantonness your ignorance. Go to, I'll no more on't;   148
it hath made me mad. I say we will have no more
marriage. Those that are married already—all but
one—shall live. The rest shall keep as they are. To a
nunnery, go.   *Exit.*

OPHELIA Oh, what a noble mind is here o'erthrown!
The courtier's, soldier's, scholar's, eye, tongue, sword,
Th'expectancy and rose of the fair state,   155
The glass of fashion and the mold of form,   156

118–20 **virtue . . . of** it virtue cannot be grafted onto our sinful condition without our retaining some taste of the old stock. 122 **nunnery** convent. (With an awareness that the word was also used derisively to denote a brothel.) 123 **indifferent honest** reasonably virtuous 126 **beck** command 140 **monsters** (An illusion to the horns of a cuckold.) **you** i.e., you women 144 **paintings** use of cosmetics 146–8 **You jig . . . ignorance** i.e., You prance about frivolously and speak with affected coynesss, you put new labels on God's creatures (by your use of cosmetics), and you excuse your affectations on the grounds of pretended ignorance. 148 **on't** of it 155 **Th'expectancy and rose** the hope and ornament 156 **The glass . . . form** the mirror of true self-fashioning and the pattern of courtly behavior

Th'observed of all observers, quite, quite down!   157
And I, of ladies most deject and wretched,
That sucked the honey of his music vows,   159
Now see that noble and most sovereign reason
Like sweet bells jangled out of tune and harsh,
That unmatched form and feature of blown youth   162
Blasted with ecstasy. Oh, woe is me,   163
T'have seen what I have seen, see what I see!

Enter King and Polonius.

KING Love? His affections do not that way tend;   165
Nor what he spake, though it lacked form a little,
Was not like madness. There's something in his soul
O'er which his melancholy sits on brood,   168
And I do doubt the hatch and the disclose   169
Will be some danger; which for to prevent,
I have in quick determination
Thus set it down: he shall with speed to England   172
For the demand of our neglected tribute.
Haply the seas and countries different
With variable objects shall expel   175
This something-settled matter in his heart,   176
Whereon his brains still beating puts him thus   177
From fashion of himself. What think you on't?   178
POLONIUS It shall do well. But yet do I believe
The origin and commencement of his grief
Sprung from neglected love.—How now, Ophelia?
You need not tell us what Lord Hamlet said;
We heard it all.—My lord, do as you please,
But, if you hold it fit, after the play
Let his queen-mother all alone entreat him
To show his grief. Let her be round with him;   186
And I'll be placed, so please you, in the ear
Of all their conference. If she find him not,   188
To England send him, or confine him where
Your wisdom best shall think.
KING   It shall be so.
Madness in great ones must not unwatched go.

Exeunt.

---

157 **Th'observed . . . observers** i.e., the center of attention and honor in the court 159 **music** musical, sweetly uttered 162 **blown** blossoming 163 **Blasted with ecstasy** blighted with madness. 165 **affections** emotions, feelings 168 **sits on brood** sits like a bird on a nest, about to *hatch* mischief (line 169) 169 **doubt** suspect, fear. **disclose** disclosure, hatching 172 **set it down** resolved 175 **variable objects** various sights and surroundings to divert him 176 **This something . . . heart** the strange matter settled in his heart 177 **still** continually 178 **From . . . himself** out of his natural manner. 186 **round** blunt 188 **find him not** fails to discover what is troubling him

[3.2]

Enter Hamlet and three of the Players.

HAMLET Speak the speech, I pray you, as I pronounced it
to you, trippingly on the tongue. But if you mouth
it, as many of our players do, I had as lief the town crier   3
spoke my lines. Nor do not saw the air too much with
your hand, thus, but use all gently; for in the very
torrent, tempest, and, as I may say, whirlwind of your
passion, you must acquire and beget a temperance
that may give it smoothness. Oh, it offends me to the
soul to hear a robustious periwig-pated fellow tear a   9
passion to tatters, to very rags, to split the ears of the
groundlings, who for the most part are capable of   11
nothing but inexplicable dumb shows and noise. I   12
would have such a fellow whipped for o'erdoing Termagant.   13
It out-Herods Herod. Pray you, avoid it.   14

FIRST PLAYER I warrant Your Honor.

HAMLET Be not too tame neither, but let your own
discretion be your tutor. Suit the action to the word,
the word to the action, with this special observance,
that you o'erstep not the modesty of nature. For   19
anything so o'erdone is from the purpose of playing,   20
whose end, both at the first and now, was and is to
hold as 'twere the mirror up to nature, to show virtue
her feature, scorn her own image, and the very age   23
and body of the time his form and pressure. Now this   24
overdone or come tardy off, though it makes the   25
unskillful laugh, cannot but make the judicious grieve,   26
the censure of the which one must in your allowance   27
o'erweigh a whole theater of others. Oh, there be players
that I have seen play, and heard others praise, and
that highly, not to speak it profanely, that, neither   30
having th'accent of Christians nor the gait of Christian,   31
pagan, nor man, have so strutted and bellowed   32

3.2 Location: The castle.

3 **our players** players nowadays. **I had as lief** I would just as soon 9 **robustious** violent, boisterous. **periwig-pated** wearing a wig 11 **groundlings** spectators who paid least and stood in the yard of the theater. **capable of** able to understand 12 **dumb shows and noise** noisy spectacle (rather than thoughtful drama) 13–14 **Termagant** a supposed deity of the Mohammedans, not found in any English medieval play but elsewhere portrayed as violent and blustering 14 **Herod** Herod of Jewry. (A character in *The Slaughter of the Innocents* and other cycle plays. The part was played with great noise and fury.) 19 **modesty** restraint, moderation 20 **from** contrary to 23 **scorn** i.e., something foolish and deserving of scorn 23–4 **and the . . . pressure** and the present state of affairs its likeness as seen in an impression, such as wax. 25 **come tardy off** falling short 25–6 **the unskillful** those lacking in judgment 27 **the censure . . . one** the judgment of even one of whom. **your allowance** your scale of values 30 **not . . . profanely** (Hamlet anticipates his idea in lines 33–4 that some men were not made by God at all.) 31–2 **Christians** i.e., ordinary decent folk 32 **nor man** i.e., nor any human being at all

that I have thought some of nature's journeymen had   33
made men and not made them well, they imitated
humanity so abominably.   35

FIRST PLAYER I hope we have reformed that indifferently   36
with us, sir.

HAMLET Oh, reform it altogether. And let those that play
your clowns speak no more than is set down for them;
for there be of them that will themselves laugh, to set   40
on some quantity of barren spectators to laugh too,   41
though in the meantime some necessary question of
the play be then to be considered. That's villainous,
and shows a most pitiful ambition in the fool that uses
it. Go make you ready.   *[Exeunt Players.]*

Enter Polonius, Guildenstern, and Rosencrantz.

How now, my lord, will the King hear this piece of work?
POLONIUS And the Queen too, and that presently.   48
HAMLET Bid the players make haste.   *[Exit Polonius.]*
Will you two help to hasten them?
ROSENCRANTZ Ay, my lord.   *Exeunt they two.*
HAMLET   What ho, Horatio!

Enter Horatio.

HORATIO Here, sweet lord, at your service.
HAMLET Horatio, thou art e'en as just a man
As e'er my conversation coped withal.   54
HORATIO Oh, my dear lord—
HAMLET   Nay, do not think I flatter,
For what advancement may I hope from thee
That no revenue hast but thy good spirits
To feed and clothe thee? Why should the poor be flattered?
No, let the candied tongue lick absurd pomp,   59
And crook the pregnant hinges of the knee   60
Where thrift may follow fawning. Dost thou hear?   61
Since my dear soul was mistress of her choice
And could of men distinguish her election,   63
Sh'hath sealed thee for herself, for thou hast been   64
As one, in suffering all, that suffers nothing,
A man that Fortune's buffets and rewards
Hast ta'en with equal thanks; and blest are those
Whose blood and judgment are so well commeddled   68
That they are not a pipe for Fortune's finger

33 journeymen common workmen
35 abominably (Shakespeare's usual spelling, "abhominably," suggests a literal though etymologically incorrect meaning, "removed from human nature.") **36 indifferently** tolerably **40 of them** some among them **41 barren** i.e., of wit **48 presently** at once. **54 my . . . withal** my dealings encountered. **59 candied** sugared, flattering **60 pregnant** compliant **61 thrift** profit **63 could . . . election** could make distinguishing choices among persons **64 sealed thee** (Literally, as one would seal a legal document to mark possession.) **68 blood** passion. **commeddled** commingled

To sound what stop she please. Give me that man   70
That is not passion's slave, and I will wear him
In my heart's core, ay, in my heart of heart,
As I do thee.—Something too much of this.—
There is a play tonight before the King.
One scene of it comes near the circumstance
Which I have told thee of my father's death.
I prithee, when thou see'st that act afoot,
Even with the very comment of thy soul   78
Observe my uncle. If his occulted guilt   79
Do not itself unkennel in one speech,   80
It is a damnèd ghost that we have seen,
And my imaginations are as foul
As Vulcan's stithy. Give him heedful note,   83
For I mine eyes will rivet to his face,
And after we will both our judgments join
In censure of his seeming.
HORATIO   Well, my lord.   86
If 'a steal aught the whilst this play is playing   87
And scape detecting, I will pay the theft.

[Flourish.] Enter trumpets and kettledrums, King, Queen, Polonius, Ophelia, [Rosencrantz, Guildenstern, and other lords, with guards carrying torches].

HAMLET They are coming to the play. I must be idle.   89
    Get you a place.   *[The King, Queen, and courtiers sit.]*
KING How fares our cousin Hamlet?   91
HAMLET Excellent, i'faith, of the chameleon's dish: I eat   92
    the air, promise-crammed. You cannot feed capons so.   93
KING I have nothing with this answer, Hamlet. These   94
    words are not mine.   95
HAMLET No, nor mine now. *[To Polonius]* My lord, you   96
    played once i'th'university, you say?
POLONIUS That did I, my lord, and was accounted a
    good actor.
HAMLET What did you enact?
POLONIUS I did enact Julius Caesar. I was killed i'th'   *101*
    Capitol; Brutus killed me.   *102*

---

70 stop hole in a wind instrument for controlling the sound **78 very . . . soul** your most penetrating observation and consideration **79 occulted** hidden **80 unkennel** (As one would say of a fox driven from its lair.) **83 Vulcan's stithy** the smithy, the place of stiths (anvils) of the Roman god of fire and metalworking. **86 censure of his seeming** judgment of his appearance or behavior. **87 If 'a steal aught** If he gets away with anything **89 idle** (1) unoccupied (2) mad. **91 cousin** i.e., close relative **92 chameleon's dish** (Chameleons were supposed to feed on air. Hamlet deliberately misinterprets the King's *fares* as "feeds." By his phrase *eat the air* he also plays on the idea of feeding himself with the promise of succession, of being the *heir*.) **93 capons** roosters castrated and crammed with feed to make them succulent **94 have . . . with** make nothing of, or gain nothing from **95 are not mine** do not respond to what I asked. **96 nor mine now** (Once spoken, words are proverbially no longer the speaker's own—and hence should be uttered warily.) **101–2 i'th' Capitol** (where Caesar was assassinated, according to *Julius Caesar*, 3.1.)

HAMLET It was a brute part of him to kill so capital a   103
    calf there.—Be the players ready?   104
ROSENCRANTZ Ay, my lord. They stay upon your   105
    patience.
QUEEN Come hither, my dear Hamlet, sit by me.
HAMLET No, good mother, here's metal more attractive.   108
POLONIUS *[to the King]* Oho, do you mark that?
HAMLET Lady, shall I lie in your lap?   110

[Lying down at Ophelia's feet.]

OPHELIA No, my lord.
HAMLET I mean, my head upon your lap?
OPHELIA Ay, my lord.
HAMLET Do you think I meant country matters?   114
OPHELIA I think nothing, my lord.
HAMLET That's a fair thought to lie between maids' legs.
OPHELIA What is, my lord?
HAMLET Nothing.   119
OPHELIA You are merry, my lord.
HAMLET Who, I?
OPHELIA Ay, my lord.
HAMLET Oh, God, your only jig maker. What should a   123
    man do but be merry? For look you how cheerfully my
    mother looks, and my father died within 's two hours.   125
OPHELIA Nay, 'tis twice two months, my lord.
HAMLET So long? Nay then, let the devil wear black, for
    I'll have a suit of sables. O heavens! Die two months   128
    ago, and not forgotten yet? Then there's hope a great
    man's memory may outlive his life half a year. But, by'r
    Lady, 'a must build churches, then, or else shall 'a
    suffer not thinking on, with the hobbyhorse, whose   132
    epitaph is "For oh, for oh, the hobbyhorse is forgot."   133

The trumpets sound. Dumb show follows.

---

103 brute (The Latin meaning of *brutus*, "stupid," was often used punningly with the name Brutus.)
part (1) deed (2) role **104 calf** fool **105 stay upon** await **108 metal** substance that is *attractive*, i.e.,
magnetic, but with suggestion also of *mettle*, "disposition" **110 Lady . . . lap?** Onstage, Hamlet often
lies at Ophelia's feet, but he could instead offer to do this and continue to stand. **114 country matters** sexual intercourse. (With a bawdy pun on the first syllable of *country*.) **119 Nothing** The figure
zero or naught, suggesting the female sexual anatomy. (*Thing* not infrequently has a bawdy connotation of male or female anatomy, and the reference here could be male.) **123 only jig maker** very best
composer of jigs, i.e., pointless merriment. (Hamlet replies sardonically to Ophelia's observation that
he is merry by saying, "If you're looking for someone who is really merry, you've come to the right
person.") **125 within 's** within this (i.e., these) **128 suit of sables** garments trimmed with the dark
fur of the sable and hence suited for a person in mourning. **132 suffer . . . on** undergo oblivion **133**
"For . . . forgot" (Verse of a song occurring also in *Love's Labor's Lost*, 3.1.27–8. The hobbyhorse was
a character made up to resemble a horse and rider, appearing in the morris dance and such May-game
sports. This song laments the disappearance of such customs under pressure from the Puritans.)
133.12 condole with offer sympathy to

Enter a King and a Queen [very lovingly]; the Queen embracing him, and he her. [She kneels, and makes show of protestation unto him.] He takes her up, and declines his head upon her neck. He lies him down upon a bank of flowers. She, seeing him asleep, leaves him. Anon comes in another man, takes off his crown, kisses it, pours poison in the sleeper's ears, and leaves him. The Queen returns, finds the King dead, makes passionate action. The Poisoner with some three or four come in again, seem to condole with her. The dead body is carried away. The Poisoner woos the Queen with gifts; she seems harsh awhile, but in the end accepts love.

[Exeunt players.]

OPHELIA What means this, my lord?

HAMLET Marry, this' miching mallico; it means   135
mischief.

OPHELIA Belike this show imports the argument of the   137
play.

Enter Prologue.

HAMLET We shall know by this fellow. The players cannot
keep counsel; they'll tell all.   140

OPHELIA Will 'a tell us what this show meant?

HAMLET Ay, or any show that you will show him. Be   142
not you ashamed to show, he'll not shame to tell you   143
what it means.

OPHELIA You are naught, you are naught. I'll mark the   145
play.

PROLOGUE
For us, and for our tragedy,
Here stooping to your clemency,
We beg your hearing patiently.   148

HAMLET Is this a prologue, or the posy of a ring?   150

OPHELIA 'Tis brief, my lord.

HAMLET As woman's love.

Enter [two Players as] King and Queen.

PLAYER KING Full thirty times hath Phoebus' cart gone round   153
Neptune's salt wash and Tellus' orbèd ground,   154
And thirty dozen moons with borrowed sheen   155
About the world have times twelve thirties been,
Since love our hearts and Hymen did our hands   157
Unite commutual in most sacred bands.   158

---

135 this' miching mallico this is sneaking mischief **137 Belike** Probably. **argument** plot **140 counsel** secret **142–3 Be not you** Provided you are not **145 naught** indecent. (Ophelia is reacting to Hamlet's pointed remarks about not being ashamed to show all.) **148 stooping** bowing **150 posy ... ring** brief motto in verse inscribed in a ring. **153 Phoebus' cart** the sun-god's chariot, making its yearly cycle **154 salt wash** the sea. **Tellus** goddess of the earth, of the *orbèd* ground **155 borrowed** i.e., reflected **157 Hymen** god of matrimony **158 commutual** mutually. **bands** bonds.

PLAYER QUEEN So many journeys may the sun and moon
    Make us again count o'er ere love be done!
    But, woe is me, you are so sick of late,
    So far from cheer and from your former state,
    That I distrust you. Yet, though I distrust,   163
    Discomfort you, my lord, it nothing must.   164
    For women's fear and love hold quantity;   165
    In neither aught, or in extremity.   166
    Now, what my love is, proof hath made you know,   167
    And as my love is sized, my fear is so.
    Where love is great, the littlest doubts are fear;   169
    Where little fears grow great, great love grows there.
PLAYER KING Faith, I must leave thee, love, and shortly too;
    My operant powers their functions leave to do.   172
    And thou shalt live in this fair world behind,   173
    Honored, beloved; and haply one as kind
    For husband shalt thou—
PLAYER QUEEN   Oh, confound the rest!
    Such love must needs be treason in my breast.
    In second husband let me be accurst!
    None wed the second but who killed the first.   178
HAMLET Wormwood, wormwood.   179
PLAYER QUEEN The instances that second marriage move   180
    Are base respects of thrift, but none of love.   181
    A second time I kill my husband dead
    When second husband kisses me in bed.
PLAYER KING I do believe you think what now you speak,
    But what we do determine oft we break.
    Purpose is but the slave to memory,   186
    Of violent birth, but poor validity,   187
    Which now, like fruit unripe, sticks on the tree,   188
    But fall unshaken when they mellow be.
    Most necessary 'tis that we forget   190
    To pay ourselves what to ourselves is debt.   191
    What to ourselves in passion we propose,
    The passion ending, doth the purpose lose.
    The violence of either grief or joy
    Their own enactures with themselves destroy.   195

---

163 **distrust** am anxious about 164 **Discomfort . . . must** it must not distress you at all. 165 **hold quantity** keep proportion with one another 166 **In . . . extremity** (women feel) either no anxiety if they do not love or extreme anxiety if they do love. 167 **proof** experience 169 **the littlest** even the littlest 172 **My . . . to do** my vital functions are shutting down. 173 **behind** after I have gone 178 **None** (1) Let no woman; or (2) No woman does. **but who** except the one who 179 **Wormwood** i.e., How bitter. (Literally, a bitter-tasting plant.) 180 **instances** motives. **move** motivate 181 **base . . . thrift** ignoble considerations of material prosperity 186 **Purpose . . . memory** Our good intentions are subject to forgetfulness 187 **validity** strength, durability 188 **Which** i.e., purpose 190–1 **Most . . . debt** It's inevitable that in time we forget the obligations we have imposed on ourselves. 195 **enactures** fulfillments

Where joy most revels, grief doth most lament;   196
Grief joys, joy grieves, on slender accident.   197
This world is not for aye, nor 'tis not strange   198
That even our loves should with our fortunes change;
For 'tis a question left us yet to prove,
Whether love lead fortune. or else fortune love.
The great man down, you mark his favorite flies;   202
The poor advanced makes friends of enemies.   203
And hitherto doth love on fortune tend;   204
For who not needs shall never lack a friend,   205
And who in want a hollow friend doth try   206
Directly seasons him his enemy.   207
But, orderly to end where I begun,
Our wills and fates do so contrary run   209
That our devices still are overthrown;   210
Our thoughts are ours, their ends none of our own.   211
So think thou wilt no second husband wed,
But die thy thoughts when thy first lord is dead.
PLAYER QUEEN Nor earth to me give food, nor heaven light,   214
Sport and repose lock from me day and night,   215
To desperation turn my trust and hope,
An anchor's cheer in prison be my scope!   217
Each opposite that blanks the face of joy   218
Meet what I would have well and it destroy!   219
Both here and hence pursue me lasting strife   220
If, once a widow, ever I be wife!
HAMLET If she should break it now!
PLAYER KING 'Tis deeply sworn. Sweet, leave me here awhile;
My spirits grow dull, and fain I would beguile   224
The tedious day with sleep.
PLAYER QUEEN   Sleep rock thy brain,
And never come mischance between us twain!

    [He sleeps.] Exit [Player Queen].

HAMLET Madam, how like you this play?
QUEEN The lady doth protest too much, methinks.   228
HAMLET Oh, but she'll keep her word.

196–7 Where . . . accident The capacity for extreme joy and grief go together, and often one extreme is instantly changed into its opposite on the slightest provocation. **198 aye** ever **202 down**
fallen in fortune **203 The poor . . . enemies** when one of humble station is promoted, you see his enemies suddenly becoming his friends. **204 hitherto** up to this point in the argument, or, to this extent. **tend** attend **205 who not needs** he who is not in need (of wealth) **206 who in want** he who,
being in need. **try** test (his generosity) **207 seasons him** ripens him into **209 Our . . . run** what we
want and what we get go so contrarily **210 devices** intentions. **still** continually **211 ends** results **214
Nor** Let neither **215 Sport . . . night** may day deny me its pastimes and night its repose **217 anchor's cheer** anchorite's or hermit's fare. **my scope** the extent of my happiness. **218–19 Each . . . destroy!** May every adverse thing that causes the face of joy to turn pale meet and destroy everything
that I desire to see prosper! **220 hence** in the life hereafter **224 spirits** vital spirits **228 doth . . .
much** makes too many promises and protestations

KING Have you heard the argument? Is there no   230
    offense in't?
HAMLET No, no, they do but jest, poison in jest. No offense   232
    i'th' world.   233
KING What do you call the play?
HAMLET The Mousetrap. Marry, how? Tropically.   235
    This play is the image of a murder done in Vienna.
    Gonzago is the Duke's name, his wife, Baptista. You   237
    shall see anon. 'Tis a knavish piece of work, but what
    of that? Your Majesty, and we that have free souls, it   239
    touches us not. Let the galled jade wince, our withers   240
    are unwrung.   241

    Enter Lucianus.

    This is one Lucianus, nephew to the King.
OPHELIA You are as good as a chorus, my lord.   243
HAMLET I could interpret between you and your love,   244
    if I could see the puppets dallying   245
OPHELIA You are keen, my lord, you are keen.   246
HAMLET It would cost you a groaning to take off mine edge.
OPHELIA Still better, and worse   249
HAMLET So you mis-take your husbands.—Begin, murderer;   250
    leave thy damnable faces and begin. Come, the
    croaking raven doth bellow for revenge.
LUCIANUS Thoughts black, hands apt, drugs fit, and time agreeing,
    Confederate season, else no creature seeing,   254
    Thou mixture rank, of midnight weeds collected,
    With Hecate's ban thrice blasted, thrice infected,   256
    Thy natural magic and dire property   257
    On wholesome life usurp immediately.

    [He pours the poison into the sleeper's ear.]

HAMLET 'A poisons him i'th' garden for his estate. His   259
    name's Gonzago. The story is extant, and written in

---

230 argument plot. **232 jest** make believe. **232–3 offense** crime, injury. (Hamlet playfully alters the
King's use of the word in line 231 to mean "cause for objection.") **235 Tropically** Figuratively. (The First
Quarto reading, "trapically," suggests a pun on trap in *Mousetrap*.) **237 Duke's** i.e., King's. (An inconsis-
tency that may be due to Shakespeare's possible acquaintance with a historical incident, the alleged murder of the Duke of Urbino by Luigi Gonzaga in 1538.) **239 free** guiltless **240 galled jade** horse whose
hide is rubbed by saddle or harness. **withers** the part between the horse's shoulder blades **241 unwrung**
not rubbed sore. **243 chorus** (In many Elizabethan plays, the forthcoming action was explained by an
actor known as the "chorus"; at a puppet show, the actor who spoke the dialogue was known as an "interpreter," as indicated by the lines following.) **244 interpret** (1) ventriloquize the dialogue, as in puppet
show (2) act as pander **245 puppets dallying** (With suggestion of sexual play, continued in *keen*, "sexually aroused," *groaning*, "moaning in pregnancy," and *edge*, "sexual desire" or "impetuosity.") **246 keen**
sharp, bitter **249 Still . . . worse** More keen, always bettering what other people say with witty wordplay,
but at the same time more offensive. **250 So** Even thus (in marriage). **mis-take** take falseheartedly and
cheat on. (The marriage vows say "for better, for worse.") **254 Confederate . . . seeing** the time and occasion conspiring (to assist me), and also no one seeing me **256 Hecate's ban** the curse of Hecate, the
goddess of witchcraft **257 dire property** baleful quality **259 estate** i.e., the kingship. **His** i.e., the King's

very choice Italian. You shall see anon how the
murderer gets the love of Gonzago's wife.

[Claudius rises.]

OPHELIA The King rises.
HAMLET What, frighted with false fire?   264
QUEEN How fares my lord?
POLONIUS Give o'er the play.
KING Give me some light. Away!
POLONIUS Lights, lights, lights!

Exeunt all but Hamlet and Horatio.

HAMLET "Why, let the strucken deer go weep,   269
    The hart ungallèd play.   270
    For some must watch, while some must sleep;   271
    Thus runs the world away."   272
  Would not this, sir, and a forest of feathers—if the   273
  rest of my fortunes turn Turk with me—with two   274
  Provincial roses on my razed shoes, get me a fellowship   275
  in a cry of players?   276
HORATIO Half a share.
HAMLET A whole one, I.
  "For thou dost know, O Damon dear,   279
    This realm dismantled was   280
    Of Jove himself, and now reigns here   281
    A very, very—pajock."   282
HORATIO You might have rhymed.
HAMLET Oh, good Horatio, I'll take the ghost's word for
  a thousand pound. Didst perceive?
HORATIO Very well, my lord.
HAMLET Upon the talk of the poisoning?
HORATIO I did very well note him.

Enter Rosencrantz and Guildenstern.

HAMLET Aha! Come, some music! Come, the recorders.
  "For if the King like not the comedy,

---

264 false fire the blank discharge of a gun loaded with powder but no shot. **269–72 Why . . . away**
(Perhaps from an old ballad, with allusion to the popular belief that a wounded deer retires to weep
and die; compare with *As You Like It,* 2.1.33–66.) **270 ungallèd** unafflicted **271 watch** remain awake
272 Thus . . . away Thus the world goes. **273 this** i.e., this success with the play I have just presented. **feathers** (Allusion to the plumes that Elizabethan actors were fond of wearing.) **274 turn
Turk with** turn renegade against, go back on **275 Provincial roses** rosettes of ribbon, named for roses
grown in a part of France. **razed** with ornamental slashing **275–6 fellowship . . . players** partnership
in a theatrical company. **276 cry** pack (of hounds, etc.) **279 Damon** the friend of Pythias, as Horatio
is friend of Hamlet; or, a traditional pastoral name **280–2 This realm . . . pajock** i.e., Jove, representing divine authority and justice, has abandoned this realm to its own devices, leaving in his stead only
a peacock or vain pretender to virtue (though the rhyme-word expected in place of *pajock* or "peacock" suggests that the realm is now ruled over by an "ass"). **280 dismantled** stripped, divested

Why then, belike, he likes it not, perdy." 292
Come, some music.

GUILDENSTERN Good my lord, vouchsafe me a word with you.

HAMLET Sir, a whole history.

GUILDENSTERN The King, sir—

HAMLET Ay, sir, what of him?

GUILDENSTERN Is in his retirement marvelous 299
distempered. 300

HAMLET With drink, sir?

GUILDENSTERN No, my lord, with choler. 302

HAMLET Your wisdom should show itself more richer
to signify this to the doctor, for for me to put him to his
purgation would perhaps plunge him into more 305
choler.

GUILDENSTERN Good my lord, put your discourse into
some frame and start not so wildly from my affair. 308

HAMLET I am tame, sir. Pronounce.

GUILDENSTERN The Queen, your mother, in most great
affliction of spirit, hath sent me to you.

HAMLET You are welcome.

GUILDENSTERN Nay, good my lord, this courtesy is not
of the right breed. If it shall please you to make me a 314
wholesome answer, I will do your mother's commandment;
if not, your pardon and my return shall be the 316
end of my business.

HAMLET Sir, I cannot.

ROSENCRANTZ What, my lord?

HAMLET Make you a wholesome answer; my wit's diseased.
But, sir, such answer as I can make, you shall
command, or rather, as you say, my mother. Therefore
no more, but to the matter. My mother, you say—

ROSENCRANTZ Then thus she says: your behavior hath
struck her into amazement and admiration. 325

HAMLET Oh, wonderful son, that can so 'stonish a mother!
But is there no sequel at the heels of this mother's
admiration? Impart.

ROSENCRANTZ She desires to speak with you in her
closet ere you go to bed. 330

HAMLET We shall obey, were she ten times our mother.
Have you any further trade with us?

---

292 perdy (A corruption of the French *par dieu*, "by God.") **299 retirement** withdrawal to his chambers **300 distempered** out of humor. (But Hamlet deliberately plays on the wider application to any illness of mind or body, as in lines 335–6, especially to drunkenness.) **302 choler** anger. (But Hamlet takes the word in its more basic humoral sense of "bilious disorder.") **305 purgation** (Hamlet hints at something going beyond medical treatment to bloodletting and the extraction of confession.) **308 frame** order. **start** shy or jump away (like a horse; the opposite of tame in line 309) **314 breed** (1) kind (2) breeding, manners. **316 pardon** permission to depart **325 admiration** bewilderment. **330 closet** private chamber

ROSENCRANTZ My lord, you once did love me.

HAMLET And do still, by these pickers and stealers. 334

ROSENCRANTZ Good my lord, what is your cause of
distemper? You do surely bar the door upon your own
liberty if you deny your griefs to your friend. 337

HAMLET Sir, I lack advancement.

ROSENCRANTZ How can that be, when you have the
voice of the King himself for your succession in
Denmark?

HAMLET Ay, sir, but "While the grass grows"—the 342
proverb is something musty. 343

Enter the Players with recorders.

Oh, the recorders. Let me see one. *[He takes a recorder.]*
To withdraw with you: why do you go about to recover 345
the wind of me, as if you would drive me into a toil? 346

GUILDENSTERN Oh, my lord, if my duty be too bold, my 347
love is too unmannerly. 348

HAMLET I do not well understand that. Will you play 349
upon this pipe?

GUILDENSTERN My lord, I cannot.

HAMLET I pray you.

GUILDENSTERN Believe me, I cannot.

HAMLET I do beseech you.

GUILDENSTERN I know no touch of it, my lord.

HAMLET It is as easy as lying. Govern these ventages 356
with your fingers and thumb, give it breath with your
mouth, and it will discourse most eloquent music.
Look you, these are the stops.

GUILDENSTERN But these cannot I command to any
utterance of harmony. I have not the skill.

HAMLET Why, look you now, how unworthy a thing
you make of me! You would play upon me, you would
seem to know my stops, you would pluck out the heart
of my mystery, you would sound me from my lowest 365
note to the top of my compass, and there is much 366
music, excellent voice, in this little organ, yet cannot 367
you make it speak. 'Sblood, do you think I am easier
to be played on than a pipe? Call me what instrument

---

334 pickers and stealers i.e., hands. (So called from the catechism, "to keep my hands from picking and stealing.") **337 liberty** i.e., being freed from *distemper*, line 336; but perhaps with a veiled threat as well. **deny** refuse to share **342 "While . . . grows"** (The rest of the proverb is "the silly horse starves"; Hamlet implies that his hopes of succession are distant in time at best.) **343 something** somewhat **343.1 Players** actors **345 withdraw** speak privately **345–6 recover the wind** get to the windward side (thus allowing the game to scent the hunter and thereby be driven in the opposite direction into the *toil* or net) **346 toil** snare. **347–8 if . . . unmannerly** if I am using an unmannerly boldness, it is my love that occasions it. **349 I . . . that** i.e., I don't understand how genuine love can be unmannerly. **356 ventages** finger-holes or stops (line 359) of the recorder **365 sound** (1) fathom (2) produce sound in **366 compass** range (of voice) **367 organ** musical instrument

you will, though you can fret me, you cannot play   370
upon me.

Enter Polonius.

God bless you, sir!

POLONIUS My lord, the Queen would speak with you,
and presently.   374

HAMLET Do you see yonder cloud that's almost in
shape of a camel?

POLONIUS By th'Mass and 'tis, like a camel indeed.

HAMLET Methinks it is like a weasel.

POLONIUS It is backed like a weasel.

HAMLET Or like a whale.

POLONIUS Very like a whale.

HAMLET Then I will come to my mother by and by.

[Aside] They fool me to the top of my bent.—I will   383
come by and by.

POLONIUS I will say so.   [Exit.]

HAMLET "By and by" is easily said. Leave me, friends.

[Exeunt all but Hamlet.]

'Tis now the very witching time of night,   387
When churchyards yawn and hell itself breathes out
Contagion to this world. Now could I drink hot blood
And do such bitter business as the day
Would quake to look on. Soft, now to my mother.
O heart, lose not thy nature! Let not ever   392
The soul of Nero enter this firm bosom.   393
Let me be cruel, not unnatural;
I will speak daggers to her, but use none.
My tongue and soul in this be hypocrites:
How in my words somever she be shent,   397
To give them seals never my soul consent!   *Exit.*   398

[3.3]

Enter King, Rosencrantz, and Guildenstern.

KING I like him not, nor stands it safe with us   1
To let his madness range. Therefore prepare you.
I your commission will forthwith dispatch,   3
And he to England shall along with you.

---

370 **fret** irritate. (With a quibble on the *frets* or ridges on the fingerboard of some stringed instruments to regulate the fingering.) 374 **presently** at once. 383 **They fool . . . bent** They humor my odd behavior to the limit of my ability or endurance. (Literally, the extent to which a bow may be bent.) 387 **witching time** time when spells are cast and evil is abroad 392 **nature** natural feeling. 393 **Nero** (This infamous Roman emperor put to death his mother, Agrippina, who had murdered her husband, Claudius.) 397–8 **How . . . consent!** however much she is to be rebuked by my words, may my soul never consent to ratify those words with deeds of violence!
3.3. Location: The castle.
1 **him** i.e., his behavior

The terms of our estate may not endure   5
Hazard so near's as doth hourly grow
Out of his brows.

GUILDENSTERN We will ourselves provide.   7
Most holy and religious fear it is   8
To keep those many many bodies safe
That live and feed upon Your Majesty.

ROSENCRANTZ The single and peculiar life is bound   11
With all the strength and armor of the mind
To keep itself from noyance, but much more   13
That spirit upon whose weal depends and rests   14
The lives of many. The cess of majesty   15
Dies not alone, but like a gulf doth draw   16
What's near it with it; or it is a massy wheel   17
Fixed on the summit of the highest mount,
To whose huge spokes ten thousand lesser things
Are mortised and adjoined, which, when it falls,   20
Each small annexment, petty consequence,   21
Attends the boist'rous ruin. Never alone   22
Did the King sigh, but with a general groan.

KING Arm you, I pray you, to this speedy voyage,   24
For we will fetters put about this fear,
Which now goes too free-footed.

ROSENCRANTZ   We will haste us.

Exeunt gentlemen [Rosencrantz and Guildenstern].
    Enter Polonius.

POLONIUS My lord, he's going to his mother's closet.
Behind the arras I'll convey myself   28
To hear the process. I'll warrant she'll tax him home, 29
And, as you said—and wisely was it said—
'Tis meet that some more audience than a mother,   31
Since nature makes them partial, should o'erhear
The speech of vantage. Fare you well, my liege.   33
I'll call upon you ere you go to bed
And tell you what I know.

KING   Thanks, dear my lord.

---

3 **dispatch** prepare, cause to be drawn up 5 **terms of our estate** circumstances of my royal position 7 **Out . . . brows** i.e., from his brain, in the form of plots and threats. **We . . . provide** We'll put ourselves in readiness. 8 **religious fear** sacred concern 11 **single and peculiar** individual and private 13 **noyance** harm 14 **weal** well-being 15 **cess** decease, cessation 16 **gulf** whirlpool 17 **massy** massive 20 **mortised** fastened (as with a fitted joint). **when it falls** i.e., when it descends, like the wheel of Fortune, bringing a king down with it 21 **Each . . . consequence** i.e., every hanger-on and unimportant person or thing connected with the King 22 **Attends** participates in 24 **Arm** Provide, prepare 28 **arras** screen of tapestry placed around the walls of household apartments. (On the Elizabethan stage, the arras was presumably over a door or aperture in the tiring-house facade.) 29 **process** proceedings. **tax him home** reprove him severely 31 **meet** fitting 33 **of vantage** from an advantageous place, or, in addition.

Exit [Polonius].

Oh, my offense is rank! It smells to heaven.
It hath the primal eldest curse upon't,   37
A brother's murder. Pray can I not,
Though inclination be as sharp as will;   39
My stronger guilt defeats my strong intent,
And like a man to double business bound   41
I stand in pause where I shall first begin,
And both neglect. What if this cursèd hand
Were thicker than itself with brother's blood,
Is there not rain enough in the sweet heavens
To wash it white as snow? Whereto serves mercy   46
But to confront the visage of offense?   47
And what's in prayer but this twofold force,
To be forestallèd ere we come to fall,   49
Or pardoned being down? Then I'll look up.
My fault is past. But oh, what form of prayer
Can serve my turn? "Forgive me my foul murder"?
That cannot be, since I am still possessed
Of those effects for which I did the murder:
My crown, mine own ambition, and my queen.
May one be pardoned and retain th'offense?   56
In the corrupted currents of this world   57
Offense's gilded hand may shove by justice,   58
And oft 'tis seen the wicked prize itself   59
Buys out the law. But 'tis not so above.
There is no shuffling, there the action lies   61
In his true nature, and we ourselves compelled,   62
Even to the teeth and forehead of our faults,   63
To give in evidence. What then? What rests?   64
Try what repentance can. What can it not?
Yet what can it, when one cannot repent?
O wretched state, O bosom black as death,
O limèd soul that, struggling to be free,   68
Art more engaged! Help, angels! Make assay.   69
Bow, stubborn knees, and heart with strings of steel,
Be soft as sinews of the newborn babe!
All may be well.   *[He kneels.]*

---

37 the primal eldest curse the curse of Cain, the first murderer; he killed his brother Abel **39 Though ... will** though my desire is as strong as my determination **41 bound** (1) destined (2) obliged. (The King wants to repent and still enjoy what he has gained.) **46–7 Whereto ... offense?** What function does mercy serve other than to meet sin face to face? **49 forestallèd** prevented (from sinning) **56 th'offense** the thing for which one offended **57 currents** courses of events **58 gilded hand** hand offering gold as a bribe. **shove by** thrust aside **59 wicked prize** prize won by wickedness **61 There ... lies** There in heaven can be no evasion, there the deed lies exposed to view **62 his** its **63 to the teeth and forehead** face to face, concealing nothing **64 give in** provide. **rests** remains. **68 limèd** caught as with birdlime, a sticky substance used to ensnare birds **69 engaged** entangled. **assay** trial. (Said to himself, or to the angels to try him.)

Enter Hamlet.

HAMLET Now might I do it pat, now 'a is a-praying; 73
And now I'll do't. *[He draws his sword.]* And so 'a goes to heaven,
And so am I revenged. That would be scanned: 75
A villain kills my father, and for that,
I, his sole son, do this same villain send
To heaven.
Why, this is hire and salary, not revenge.
'A took my father grossly, full of bread, 80
With all his crimes broad blown, as flush as May; 81
And how his audit stands who knows save heaven? 82
But in our circumstance and course of thought 83
'Tis heavy with him. And am I then revenged,
To take him in the purging of his soul,
When he is fit and seasoned for his passage? 85
No!
Up, sword, and know thou a more horrid hent. 88

[He puts up his sword.]

When he is drunk asleep, or in his rage, 89
Or in th'incestuous pleasure of his bed,
At game, a-swearing, or about some act 91
That has no relish of salvation in't— 92
Then trip him, that his heels may kick at heaven,
And that his soul may be as damned and black
As hell, whereto it goes. My mother stays. 95
This physic but prolongs thy sickly days. *Exit.* 96
KING My words fly up, my thoughts remain below.
Words without thoughts never to heaven go. *Exit.*

[3.4]

Enter [Queen] Gertrude and Polonius.

POLONIUS 'A will come straight. Look you lay home to him. 1
Tell him his pranks have been too broad to bear with, 2
And that Your Grace hath screened and stood between
Much heat and him. I'll silence me even here. 4
Pray you, be round with him. 5
HAMLET (within) Mother, mother, mother!

---

73 pat opportunely **75 would be scanned** needs to be looked into, or, would be interpreted as follows **80 grossly, full of bread** i.e., enjoying his worldly pleasures rather than fasting. (See Ezekiel 16:49.) **81 crimes broad blown** sins in full bloom. **flush** vigorous **82 audit** account. **save** except for **83 in . . . thought** as we see it from our mortal perspective **86 seasoned** matured, readied **88 know . . . hent** await to be grasped by me on a more horrid occasion. (*Hent* means "act of seizing.") **89 drunk . . . rage** dead drunk, or in a fit of sexual passion **91 game** gambling **92 relish** trace, savor **95 stays** awaits (me). **96 physic** purging (by prayer), or, Hamlet's postponement of the killing
3.4. Location: The Queen's private chamber.
1 lay home reprove him soundly **2 broad** unrestrained

QUEEN I'll warrant you, fear me not.
    Withdraw, I hear him coming.

[Polonius hides behind the arras.]
Enter Hamlet.

HAMLET Now, mother, what's the matter?
QUEEN Hamlet, thou hast thy father much offended.   10
HAMLET Mother, you have my father much offended.
QUEEN Come, come, you answer with an idle tongue.   12
HAMLET Go, go, you question with a wicked tongue.
QUEEN Why, how now, Hamlet?
HAMLET   What's the matter now?
QUEEN Have you forgot me?
HAMLET   No, by the rood, not so: 15
    You are the Queen, your husband's brother's wife,
    And—would it were not so!—you are my mother.
QUEEN Nay, then, I'll set those to you that can speak.   18
HAMLET Come, come, and sit you down; you shall not budge.
    You go not till I set you up a glass
    Where you may see the inmost part of you.
QUEEN What wilt thou do? Thou wilt not murder me?
    Help, ho!
POLONIUS *[behind the arras]* What ho! Help!
HAMLET *[drawing]* How now? A rat? Dead for a ducat, dead!   25

[He thrusts his rapier through the arras.]

POLONIUS *[behind the arras]* Oh, I am slain!   *[He falls and dies.]*
QUEEN   Oh, me, what hast thou done?
HAMLET Nay, I know not. Is it the King?
QUEEN Oh, what a rash and bloody deed is this!
HAMLET A bloody deed—almost as bad, good mother,
    As kill a king, and marry with his brother.
QUEEN As kill a king!
HAMLET   Ay, lady, it was my word.

[He parts the arras and discovers Polonius.]

    Thou wretched, rash, intruding fool, farewell!
    I took thee for thy better. Take thy fortune.
    Thou find'st to be too busy is some danger.—   34
    Leave wringing of your hands. Peace, sit you down,
    And let me wring your heart, for so I shall,
    If it be made of penetrable stuff,

---

4 **Much heat** i.e., the King's anger. **I'll silence me** I'll quietly conceal myself. (Ironic, since it is his crying out at line 24 that leads to his death. Some editors emend *silence* to "sconce." The First Quarto's reading, "shroud," is attractive.) 5 **round** blunt 10 **thy father** i.e., your stepfather, Claudius 12 **idle** foolish 15 **forgot me** i.e., forgotten that I am your mother. **rood** cross of Christ 18 **speak** i.e., speak to someone so rude. 25 **Dead for a ducat** i.e., I bet a ducat he's dead; or, a ducat is his life's fee. 34 **busy** nosey

If damnèd custom have not brazed it so	38
That it be proof and bulwark against sense.	39

QUEEN What have I done, that thou dar'st wag thy tongue
In noise so rude against me?

HAMLET   Such an act

That blurs the grace and blush of modesty,	
Calls virtue hypocrite, takes off the rose	
From the fair forehead of an innocent love	
And sets a blister there, makes marriage vows	45
As false as dicers' oaths. Oh, such a deed	
As from the body of contraction plucks	47
The very soul, and sweet religion makes	48
A rhapsody of words. Heaven's face does glow	49
O'er this solidity and compound mass	50
With tristful visage, as against the doom,	51
Is thought-sick at the act.	

QUEEN   Ay me, what act,

That roars so loud and thunders in the index?	53

HAMLET *[showing her two likenesses]*

Look here upon this picture, and on this,	
The counterfeit presentment of two brothers.	55
See what a grace was seated on this brow:	
Hyperion's curls, the front of Jove himself,	57
An eye like Mars to threaten and command,	58
A station like the herald Mercury	59
New-lighted on a heaven-kissing hill—	60
A combination and a form indeed	
Where every god did seem to set his seal	62
To give the world assurance of a man.	
This was your husband. Look you now what follows:	
Here is your husband, like a mildewed ear,	65
Blasting his wholesome brother. Have you eyes?	66
Could you on this fair mountain leave to feed	67
And batten on this moor? Ha, have you eyes?	68
You cannot call it love, for at your age	
The heyday in the blood is tame, it's humble,	70
And waits upon the judgment, and what judgment	
Would step from this to this? Sense, sure, you have,	72

---

38 damnèd custom habitual wickedness. **brazed** brazened, hardened **39 proof** impenetrable, like *proof* or tested armor. **sense** feeling. **45 sets a blister** i.e., brands as a harlot **47 contraction** the marriage contract **48 sweet religion makes** i.e., makes marriage vows **49 rhapsody** senseless string **49–52 Heaven's . . . act** Heaven's face blushes at this solid world compounded of the various elements, with sorrowful face as though the day of doom were near, and is sick with horror at the deed (i.e., Gertrude's marriage). **53 index** table of contents, prelude or preface. **55 counterfeit presentment** representation in portraiture **57 Hyperion's** the sun-god's. **front** brow **58 Mars** god of war **59 station** manner of standing. **Mercury** winged messenger of the gods **60 New-lighted** newly alighted. **heaven-kissing** reaching to the sky **62 set his seal** i.e., affix his approval **65 ear** i.e., of grain **66 Blasting** blighting **67 leave** cease **68 batten** gorge. **moor** barren or marshy ground. (Suggesting also "dark-skinned.")

Else could you not have motion, but sure that sense
Is apoplexed, for madness would not err,   74
Nor sense to ecstasy was ne'er so thralled,   75
But it reserved some quantity of choice   76
To serve in such a difference. What devil was't   77
That thus hath cozened you at hoodman-blind?   78
Eyes without feeling, feeling without sight,
Ears without hands or eyes, smelling sans all,   80
Or but a sickly part of one true sense
Could not so mope. O shame, where is thy blush?   82
Rebellious hell,
If thou canst mutine in a matron's bones,   84
To flaming youth let virtue be as wax   85
And melt in her own fire. Proclaim no shame   86
When the compulsive ardor gives the charge,   87
Since frost itself as actively doth burn,   88
And reason panders will.   89

QUEEN Oh, Hamlet, speak no more!
Thou turn'st mine eyes into my very soul,
And there I see such black and grainèd spots   92
As will not leave their tinct.

HAMLET   Nay, but to live   93
In the rank sweat of an enseamèd bed,   94
Stewed in corruption, honeying and making love   95
Over the nasty sty!   96

QUEEN Oh, speak to me no more!
These words like daggers enter in my ears.
No more, sweet Hamlet!

HAMLET   A murderer and a villain,
A slave that is not twentieth part the tithe   *100*
Of your precedent lord, a vice of kings,   *101*
A cutpurse of the empire and the rule,
That from a shelf the precious diadem stole
And put it in his pocket!

---

70 The heyday . . . blood (The blood was thought to be the source of sexual desire.) **72 Sense** Perception through the five senses (the functions of the middle or sensible soul) **74 apoplexed** paralyzed. **err** so err **75–7 Nor . . . difference** nor could your physical senses ever have been so enthralled to ecstasy or lunacy that they could not distinguish to some degree between Hamlet Senior and Claudius. **78 cozened** cheated. **hoodman-blind** blindman's buff. (In this game, says Hamlet, the devil must have pushed Claudius toward Gertrude while she was blindfolded.) **80 sans** without **82 mope** be dazed, act aimlessly. **84 mutine** mutiny **85–6 To . . . fire** when it comes to sexually passionate youth, let virtue melt like a candle or stick of sealing wax held over a candle flame. (There's no point in hoping for self-restraint among young people when matronly women set such a bad example.) **86–9 Proclaim . . . will** Call it no shameful business when the compelling ardor of youth delivers the attack, i.e., commits lechery, since the *frost* of advanced age burns with as active a fire of lust and reason perverts itself by fomenting lust rather than restraining it. **92 grainèd** ingrained, indelible **93 leave their tinct** surrender their dark stain. **94 enseamèd** saturated in the grease and filth of passionate lovemaking **95 Stewed** soaked, bathed. (With a suggestion of "stew," brothel.) **96 Over . . . sty** (Like barnyard animals.) **100 tithe** tenth part **101 precedent lord** former husband. **vice** (From the morality plays, a model of iniquity and a buffoon.)

QUEEN No more!   105

    Enter Ghost [in his nightgown].

HAMLET A king of shreds and patches—   106
    Save me, and hover o'er me with your wings,
    You heavenly guards! What would your gracious figure?
QUEEN Alas, he's mad!
HAMLET Do you not come your tardy son to chide,
    That, lapsed in time and passion, lets go by   111
    Th'important acting of your dread command?   112
    Oh, say!
GHOST Do not forget. This visitation
    Is but to whet thy almost blunted purpose.   115
    But look, amazement on thy mother sits.   116
    Oh, step between her and her fighting soul!
    Conceit in weakest bodies strongest works.   118
    Speak to her, Hamlet.
HAMLET   How is it with you, lady?
QUEEN Alas, how is't with you,
    That you do bend your eye on vacancy,
    And with th'incorporal air do hold discourse?   122
    Forth at your eyes your spirits wildly peep,
    And, as the sleeping soldiers in th'alarm,   124
    Your bedded hair, like life in excrements,   125
    Start up and stand on end. O gentle son,
    Upon the heat and flame of thy distemper   127
    Sprinkle cool patience. Whereon do you look?
HAMLET On him, on him! Look you how pale he glares!
    His form and cause conjoined, preaching to stones,   130
    Would make them capable.—Do not look upon me,   131
    Lest with this piteous action you convert   132
    My stern effects. Then what I have to do   133
    Will want true color—tears perchance for blood.   134
QUEEN To whom do you speak this?
HAMLET Do you see nothing there?
QUEEN Nothing at all, yet all that is I see.
HAMLET Nor did you nothing hear?
QUEEN No, nothing but ourselves.
HAMLET Why, look you there, look how it steals away!

105.1 **nightgown** a robe for indoor wear 106 **A king . . . patches** i.e., a king whose splendor is all
sham; a clown or fool dressed in motley 111 **lapsed . . . passion** having let time and passion slip away
112 **Th'important** the importunate, urgent 115 **whet** sharpen 116 **amazement** distraction 118
Conceit Imagination 122 **th'incorporal** the immaterial 124 **as . . . th'alarm** like soldiers called out
of sleep by an alarum 125 **bedded** laid flat. **like life in excrements** i.e., as though hair, an outgrowth
of the body, had a life of its own. (Hair was thought to be lifeless because it lacks sensation, and so its
standing on end would be unnatural and ominous.) 127 **distemper** disorder 130 **His . . . conjoined**
His appearance joined to his cause for speaking 131 **capable** capable of feeling, receptive. 132–3
convert . . . effects divert me from my stern duty. 134 **want . . . blood** lack plausibility so that (with
a play on the normal sense of *color*) I shall shed colorless tears instead of blood.

My father, in his habit as he lived!   141
Look where he goes even now out at the portal!

   Exit Ghost.

QUEEN This is the very coinage of your brain.   143
This bodiless creation ecstasy   144
Is very cunning in.   145
HAMLET Ecstasy?
My pulse as yours doth temperately keep time,
And makes as healthful music. It is not madness
That I have uttered. Bring me to the test,
And I the matter will reword, which madness   150
Would gambol from. Mother, for love of grace,   151
Lay not that flattering unction to your soul   152
That not your trespass but my madness speaks.
It will but skin and film the ulcerous place,   154
Whiles rank corruption, mining all within,   155
Infects unseen. Confess yourself to heaven,
Repent what's past, avoid what is to come,
And do not spread the compost on the weeds   158
To make them ranker. Forgive me this my virtue;   159
For in the fatness of these pursy times   160
Virtue itself of vice must pardon beg,
Yea, curb and woo for leave to do him good.   162
QUEEN Oh, Hamlet, thou hast cleft my heart in twain.
HAMLET Oh, throw away the worser part of it,
And live the purer with the other half.
Good night. But go not to my uncle's bed;
Assume a virtue, if you have it not.
That monster, custom, who all sense doth eat,   168
Of habits devil, is angel yet in this,   169
That to the use of actions fair and good
He likewise gives a frock or livery   171
That aptly is put on. Refrain tonight,   172
And that shall lend a kind of easiness
To the next abstinence; the next more easy;
For use almost can change the stamp of nature,   175
And either . . . the devil, or throw him out   176
With wondrous potency. Once more, good night;

---

141 **habit** clothes. **as** as when 143 **very** mere 144–5 **This . . . in** Madness is skillful in creating this kind of hallucination. 150 **reword** repeat word for word 151 **gambol** skip away 152 **unction** ointment 154 **skin** grow a skin over 155 **mining** working under the surface 158 **compost** manure 159 **this my virtue** my virtuous talk in reproving you 160 **fatness** grossness. **pursy** flabby, out of shape 162 **curb** bow, bend the knee. **leave** permission 168 **who . . . eat** which consumes and overwhelms the physical senses 169 **Of habits devil** devil-like in prompting evil habits 171 **livery** an outer appearance, a customary garb (and hence a predisposition easily assumed in time of stress) 172 **aptly** readily 175 **use** habit. **the stamp of nature** our inborn traits 176 **And either** (A defective line, often emended by inserting the word "master" after *either*, following the Third Quarto and early editors, or some other word such as "shame," "lodge," "curb," or "house.")

And when you are desirous to be blest, 178
I'll blessing beg of you. For this same lord, 179

[pointing to Polonius]

I do repent; but heaven hath pleased it so
To punish me with this, and this with me, 181
That I must be their scourge and minister. 182
I will bestow him, and will answer well 183
The death I gave him. So, again, good night.
I must be cruel only to be kind.
This bad begins, and worse remains behind. 186
One word more, good lady.

QUEEN   What shall I do?

HAMLET Not this by no means that I bid you do:
Let the bloat king tempt you again to bed, 189
Pinch wanton on your cheek, call you his mouse, 190
And let him, for a pair of reechy kisses, 191
Or paddling in your neck with his damned fingers, 192
Make you to ravel all this matter out 193
That I essentially am not in madness,
But mad in craft. 'Twere good you let him know, 195
For who that's but a queen, fair, sober, wise,
Would from a paddock, from a bat, a gib, 197
Such dear concernings hide? Who would do so? 198
No, in despite of sense and secrecy, 199
Unpeg the basket on the house's top, 200
Let the birds fly, and like the famous ape, 201
To try conclusions, in the basket creep 202
And break your own neck down. 203

QUEEN Be thou assured, if words be made of breath,
And breath of life, I have no life to breathe
What thou hast said to me.

HAMLET I must to England. You know that?

QUEEN   Alack,
I had forgot. 'Tis so concluded on.

HAMLET There's letters sealed, and my two schoolfellows,
Whom I will trust as I will adders fanged,

178–9 when . . . you i.e., when you are ready to be penitent and seek God's blessing, I will ask your blessing as a dutiful son should. **181 To punish . . . with** me to seek retribution from me for killing Polonius, and from him through my means **182 their scourge and minister** i.e., agent of heavenly retribution. **183 bestow** stow, dispose of. **answer** account or pay for **186 This** i.e., The killing of Polonius. **behind** to come. **189 bloat** bloated **190 Pinch wanton** i.e., leave his love pinches on your cheeks, branding you as wanton **191 reechy** dirty, filthy **192 paddling** fingering amorously **193 ravel . . . out** unravel, disclose **195 in craft** by cunning. **good** (Said sarcastically; also the following eight lines.) **197 paddock** toad. **gib** tomcat **198 dear concernings** important affairs **199 sense and secrecy** secrecy that common sense requires **200 Unpeg the basket** open the cage, i.e., let out the secret **201 famous ape** (In a story now lost.) **202 try conclusions** test the outcome (in which the ape apparently enters a cage from which birds have been released and then tries to fly out of the cage as they have done, falling to its death) **203 down** in the fall.

They bear the mandate; they must sweep my way	211
And marshal me to knavery. Let it work.	212
For 'tis the sport to have the engineer	213
Hoist with his own petard, and 't shall go hard	214
But I will delve one yard below their mines	215
And blow them at the moon. Oh, 'tis most sweet	
When in one line two crafts directly meet.	217
This man shall set me packing.	218
I'll lug the guts into the neighbor room.	
Mother, good night indeed. This counselor	
Is now most still, most secret, and most grave,	
Who was in life a foolish prating knave.—	
Come, sir, to draw toward an end with you.—	223
Good night, mother.	

Exeunt [separately, Hamlet dragging in Polonius].

[4.1]

Enter King and Queen, with Rosencrantz and Guildenstern.

KING There's matter in these sighs, these profound heaves.	1
You must translate; 'tis fit we understand them.	
Where is your son?	
QUEEN Bestow this place on us a little while.	

[Exeunt Rosencrantz and Guildenstern.]

Ah, mine own lord, what have I seen tonight!	
KING What, Gertrude? How does Hamlet?	
QUEEN Mad as the sea and wind when both contend	
Which is the mightier. In his lawless fit,	
Behind the arras hearing something stir,	

211–12 sweep . . . knavery sweep a path before me and conduct me to some *knavery* or treachery prepared for me. **212 work** proceed. **213 engineer** maker of *engines* of war **214 Hoist with** blown up by. **petard** an explosive used to blow in a door or make a breach **214–15 't shall . . . will** unless luck is against me, I will **215 mines** tunnels used in warfare to undermine the enemy's emplacements; Hamlet will countermine by going under their mines **217 in one line** i.e., mines and countermines on a collision course, or the countermines directly below the mines. **crafts** acts of guile, plots **218 set me packing** set me to making schemes, and set me to lugging (him), and, also, send me off in a hurry. **223 draw . . . end** finish up. (With a pun on *draw*, "pull.")
4.1 Location: The castle.
0.1 Enter . . . Queen (Some editors argue that Gertrude does not in fact exit at the end of 3.4 and that the scene is continuous here. It is true that the Folio ends 3.4 with "*Exit Hamlet tugging in Polonius,*" not naming Gertrude, and opens 4.1 with "*Enter King.*" Yet the Second Quarto concludes 3.4 with a simple "*Exit,*" which often stands ambiguously for a single exit or an exeunt in early modern texts, and then starts 4.1 with "*Enter King, and Queene, with Rosencraus and Guyldensterne.*" The King's opening lines in 4.1 suggest that he has had time, during a brief intervening pause, to become aware of Gertrude's highly wrought emotional state. In line 35, the King refers to Gertrude's *closet* as though it were elsewhere. The differences between the Second Quarto and the Folio offer an alternative staging. In either case, 4.1 follows swiftly upon 3.4.) **1 matter** significance. **heaves** heavy sighs.

Whips out his rapier, cries, "A rat, a rat!"
And in this brainish apprehension kills   11
The unseen good old man.

KING   Oh, heavy deed!   12
It had been so with us, had we been there.   13
His liberty is full of threats to all—
To you yourself, to us, to everyone.
Alas, how shall this bloody deed be answered?   16
It will be laid to us, whose providence   17
Should have kept short, restrained, and out of haunt   18
This mad young man. But so much was our love,
We would not understand what was most fit,
But, like the owner of a foul disease,
To keep it from divulging, let it feed   22
Even on the pith of life. Where is he gone?

QUEEN To draw apart the body he hath killed,
O'er whom his very madness, like some ore   25
Among a mineral of metals base,   26
Shows itself pure: 'a weeps for what is done.

KING Oh, Gertrude, come away!
The sun no sooner shall the mountains touch
But we will ship him hence, and this vile deed
We must with all our majesty and skill
Both countenance and excuse.—Ho, Guildenstern!   32

Enter Rosencrantz and Guildenstern.

Friends both, go join you with some further aid.
Hamlet in madness hath Polonius slain,
And from his mother's closet hath he dragged him.
Go seek him out, speak fair, and bring the body   36
Into the chapel. I pray you, haste in this.

[Exeunt Rosencrantz and Guildenstern.]

Come, Gertrude, we'll call up our wisest friends
And let them know both what we mean to do
And what's untimely done   40
Whose whisper o'er the world's diameter,   41
As level as the cannon to his blank,   42
Transports his poisoned shot, may miss our name
And hit the woundless air. Oh, come away!   44
My soul is full of discord and dismay.   *Exeunt.*

---

11 brainish apprehension frenzied misapprehension **12 heavy** grievous **13 us** i.e., me. (The royal "we"; also in line 15.) **16 answered** explained. **17 providence** foresight **18 short** i.e., on a short tether. **out of haunt** secluded **22 from divulging** from becoming publicly known **25 ore** vein of gold **26 mineral** mine **32 countenance** put the best face on **36 fair** gently, courteously **40 And . . . done** (A defective line; conjectures as to the missing words include "So, haply, slander" [Capell and others]; "For, haply, slander" [Theobald and others]; and "So envious slander" [Jenkins].) **41 diameter** extent from side to side **42 As level** with as direct aim. **his blank** its target at point-blank range **44 woundless** invulnerable

[4.2]

Enter Hamlet.

HAMLET Safely stowed.
ROSENCRANTZ, GUILDENSTERN (*within*) Hamlet! Lord
    Hamlet!
HAMLET But soft, what noise? Who calls on Hamlet? Oh, here they come.

Enter Rosencrantz and Guildenstern.

ROSENCRANTZ What have you done, my lord, with the dead body?
HAMLET Compounded it with dust, whereto 'tis kin.
ROSENCRANTZ Tell us where 'tis, that we may take it thence
    And bear it to the chapel.
HAMLET Do not believe it.
ROSENCRANTZ Believe what?
HAMLET That I can keep your counsel and not mine   12
    own. Besides, to be demanded of a sponge, what replication   13
    should be made by the son of a king?   14
ROSENCRANTZ Take you me for a sponge, my lord?
HAMLET Ay, sir, that soaks up the King's countenance,   16
    his rewards, his authorities. But such officers do the   17
    King best service in the end. He keeps them, like an
    ape, an apple, in the corner of his jaw, first mouthed
    to be last swallowed. When he needs what you have
    gleaned, it is but squeezing you, and, sponge, you
    shall be dry again.
ROSENCRANTZ I understand you not, my lord.
HAMLET I am glad of it. A knavish speech sleeps in a
    foolish ear.   24
ROSENCRANTZ My lord, you must tell us where the
    body is and go with us to the King.
HAMLET The body is with the King, but the King is not   28
    with the body. The King is a thing—   29
GUILDENSTERN A thing, my lord?
HAMLET Of nothing. Bring me to him. Hide fox, and all   31
    after!   *Exeunt [running].*   32

4.2 **Location:** The castle.
12–13 **That . . . own** i.e., Don't expect me to do as you bid me and not follow my own counsel.
13 **demanded of** questioned by 13–14 **replication** reply 16 **countenance** favor 17 **authorities**
delegated power, influence. 24 **sleeps in** has no meaning to 28–9 **The . . . body** (Perhaps alludes
to the legal commonplace of "the king's two bodies," which drew a distinction between the sacred
office of kingship and the particular mortal who possessed it at any given time. Hence, although
Claudius's body is necessarily a part of him, true kingship is not contained in it. Similarly,
Claudius will have Polonius's body when it is found, but there is no kingship in this business either.) 31 **Of nothing** (1) of no account (2) lacking the essence of kingship, as in lines 28–9 and
note. 31–2 **Hide . . . after** (An old signal cry in the game of hide-and-seek, suggesting that Hamlet now runs away from them.)

[4.3]

Enter King, and two or three.

KING I have sent to seek him, and to find the body.
How dangerous is it that this man goes loose!
Yet must not we put the strong law on him.
He's loved of the distracted multitude,   4
Who like not in their judgment, but their eyes,   5
And where 'tis so, th'offender's scourge is weighed,   6
But never the offense. To bear all smooth and even,   7
This sudden sending him away must seem
Deliberate pause. Diseases desperate grown   9
By desperate appliance are relieved,   10
Or not at all.

Enter Rosencrantz, [Guildenstern,] and all the rest.

How now, what hath befall'n?
ROSENCRANTZ Where the dead body is bestowed, my lord,
We cannot get from him.
KING   But where is he?
ROSENCRANTZ Without, my lord; guarded, to know your pleasure.   14
KING Bring him before us.
ROSENCRANTZ *[calling]* Ho! Bring in the lord.

They enter [with Hamlet].

KING Now, Hamlet, where's Polonius?
HAMLET At supper.
KING At supper? Where?
HAMLET Not where he eats, but where 'a is eaten. A
certain convocation of politic worms are e'en at him.   20
Your worm is your only emperor for diet. We fat all   21
creatures else to fat us, and we fat ourselves for maggots.
Your fat king and your lean beggar is but
variable service—two dishes, but to one table. That's   24
the end.
KING Alas, alas!
HAMLET A man may fish with the worm that hath eat   27
of a king, and eat of the fish that hath fed of that
worm.

4.3. Location: The castle.
4 of by. **distracted** fickle, unstable **5 Who . . . eyes** who choose not by judgment but by appearance
6–7 th'offender's . . . offense i.e., the populace often takes umbrage at the severity of a punishment
without taking into account the gravity of the crime. **7 To . . . even** To manage the business in an un-
provocative way **9 Deliberate pause** carefully considered action. **10 appliance** remedies **14 Without**
Outside **20 politic worms** crafty worms (suited to a master spy like Polonius). **e'en** even now **21 Your**
worm Your average worm. (Compare your fat king and your lean beggar in line 23.) **diet** food, eating.
(With a punning reference to the Diet of Worms, a famous convocation held in 1521.) **24 service**
food served at table. (Worms feed on kings and beggars alike.) **27 eat** eaten. (Pronounced et.)

KING What dost thou mean by this?

HAMLET Nothing but to show you how a king may go
    a progress through the guts of a beggar.   32

KING Where is Polonius?

HAMLET In heaven. Send thither to see. If your messenger
    find him not there, seek him i'th'other place yourself.
    But if indeed you find him not within this month,
    you shall nose him as you go up the stairs into the   37
    lobby.

KING *[to some attendants]* Go seek him there.

HAMLET 'A will stay till you come.   *[Exeunt attendants.]*

KING Hamlet, this deed, for thine especial safety—
    Which we do tender, as we dearly grieve   42
    For that which thou hast done—must send thee hence
    With fiery quickness. Therefore prepare thyself.
    The bark is ready, and the wind at help,   45
    Th'associates tend, and everything is bent   46
    For England.

HAMLET For England!

KING Ay, Hamlet.

HAMLET Good.

KING So is it, if thou knew'st our purposes.

HAMLET I see a cherub that sees them. But come, for   52
    England! Farewell, dear mother.

KING Thy loving father, Hamlet.

HAMLET My mother. Father and mother is man and
    wife, man and wife is one flesh, and so, my mother.
    Come, for England!   *Exit.*

KING Follow him at foot; tempt him with speed aboard.   58
    Delay it not. I'll have him hence tonight.
    Away! For everything is sealed and done
    That else leans on th'affair. Pray you, make haste.   61

    [Exeunt all but the King.]

    And, England, if my love thou hold'st at aught—   62
    As my great power thereof may give thee sense,   63
    Since yet thy cicatrice looks raw and red   64
    After the Danish sword, and thy free awe   65
    Pays homage to us—thou mayst not coldly set   66
    Our sovereign process, which imports at full,   67
    By letters congruing to that effect,   68
    The present death of Hamlet. Do it, England,   69

---

32 progress royal journey of state **37 nose** smell **42 tender** regard, hold dear. **dearly** intensely **45 bark** sailing vessel **46 tend** wait. **bent** in readiness **52 cherub** (Cherubim are angels of knowledge. Hamlet hints that both he and heaven are onto Claudius's tricks.) **58 at foot** close behind, at heel **61 leans** on bears upon, is related to **62 England** i.e., King of England. **at aught** at any value **63 As . . . sense** for so my great power may give you a just appreciation of the importance of valuing my love **64 cicatrice** scar **65 free awe** unconstrained show of respect **66 coldly set** regard with indifference **67 process** command. **imports at full** conveys specific directions for **68 congruing** agreeing **69 present** immediate

For like the hectic in my blood he rages, 70
And thou must cure me. Till I know 'tis done,
Howe'er my haps, my joys were ne'er begun. Exit. 72

[4.4]

Enter Fortinbras with his army over the stage.

FORTINBRAS Go, Captain, from me greet the Danish king.
　Tell him that by his license Fortinbras 2
　Craves the conveyance of a promised march 3
　Over his kingdom. You know the rendezvous.
　If that His Majesty would aught with us,
　We shall express our duty in his eye; 6
　And let him know so.
CAPTAIN I will do't, my lord.
FORTINBRAS Go softly on.　　　　　　*[Exeunt all but the Captain.]* 9

Enter Hamlet, Rosencrantz, [Guildenstern,] etc.

HAMLET Good sir, whose powers are these? 10
CAPTAIN They are of Norway, sir.
HAMLET How purposed, sir, I pray you?
CAPTAIN Against some part of Poland.
HAMLET Who commands them, sir?
CAPTAIN The nephew to old Norway, Fortinbras.
HAMLET Goes it against the main of Poland, sir, 16
　Or for some frontier?
CAPTAIN Truly to speak, and with no addition, 18
　We go to gain a little patch of ground
　That hath in it no profit but the name.
　To pay five ducats, five, I would not farm it; 21
　Nor will it yield to Norway or the Pole
　A ranker rate, should it be sold in fee. 23
HAMLET Why, then the Polack never will defend it.
CAPTAIN Yes, it is already garrisoned.
HAMLET Two thousand souls and twenty thousand ducats
　Will not debate the question of this straw. 27
　This is th'impostume of much wealth and peace, 28
　That inward breaks, and shows no cause without 29
　Why the man dies. I humbly thank you, sir.
CAPTAIN God b'wi'you, sir.　　　　　　　　*[Exit.]*
ROSENCRANTZ　　　　Will't please you go, my lord?

---

70 hectic persistent fever **72 Howe'er . . . begun** whatever else happens, I cannot begin to be happy.
4.4 Location: The coast of Denmark.
2 license permission **3 conveyance** unhindered passage **6 We . . . eye** I will come pay my respects in person **9 softly** slowly, circumspectly **10 powers** forces **16 main** main part **18 addition** exaggeration **21 To pay** i.e., For a yearly rental of. **farm it** take a lease of it **23 ranker** higher. **in fee** fee simple, outright. **27 debate . . . straw** argue about this trifling matter. **28 th'impostume** the abscess **29 inward breaks** festers within. **without** externally

HAMLET I'll be with you straight. Go a little before.

[Exeunt all except Hamlet.]

How all occasions do inform against me	33
And spur my dull revenge! What is a man,	
If his chief good and market of his time	35
Be but to sleep and feed? A beast, no more.	
Sure he that made us with such large discourse,	37
Looking before and after, gave us not	38
That capability and godlike reason	
To fust in us unused. Now, whether it be	40
Bestial oblivion, or some craven scruple	41
Of thinking too precisely on th'event—	42
A thought which, quartered, hath but one part wisdom	
And ever three parts coward—I do not know	
Why yet I live to say "This thing's to do,"	
Sith I have cause, and will, and strength, and means	46
To do't. Examples gross as earth exhort me:	47
Witness this army of such mass and charge,	48
Led by a delicate and tender prince,	49
Whose spirit with divine ambition puffed	
Makes mouths at the invisible event,	51
Exposing what is mortal and unsure	
To all that fortune, death, and danger dare,	53
Even for an eggshell. Rightly to be great	54
Is not to stir without great argument,	55
But greatly to find quarrel in a straw	56
When honor's at the stake. How stand I, then,	57
That have a father killed, a mother stained,	
Excitements of my reason and my blood,	59
And let all sleep, while to my shame I see	
The imminent death of twenty thousand men	
That for a fantasy and trick of fame	62
Go to their graves like beds, fight for a plot	63
Whereon the numbers cannot try the cause,	64
Which is not tomb enough and continent	65
To hide the slain? Oh, from this time forth	
My thoughts be bloody or be nothing worth! Exit.	

---

33 inform against denounce; take shape against **35 market of** profit of **37 discourse** power of reasoning **38 Looking before and after** able to review past events and anticipate the future **40 fust** grow moldy **41 oblivion** forgetfulness. **craven** cowardly **42 precisely** scrupulously. **th'event** the outcome **46 Sith** since **47 gross** obvious **48 charge** expense **49 delicate and tender** of fine and youthful qualities **51 Makes mouths** makes scornful faces. **invisible event** unforeseeable outcome **53 dare** could do (to him) **54–7 Rightly . . . stake** True greatness is not a matter of being moved to action solely by a great cause; rather, it is to respond greatly to an apparently trivial cause when honor is at the stake. **59 blood** (The supposed seat of the passions.) **62 fantasy** fanciful caprice, illusion. **trick** trifle, deceit **63 plot** plot of ground **64 Whereon . . . cause** on which there is insufficient room for the soldiers needed to fight for it **65 continent** receptacle, container

[4.5]

    Enter Horatio, [Queen] Gertrude, and a Gentleman.

QUEEN I will not speak with her.

GENTLEMAN   She is importunate,

    Indeed distract. Her mood will needs be pitied.   2

QUEEN What would she have?

GENTLEMAN She speaks much of her father, says she hears

    There's tricks i'th' world, and hems, and beats her heart,   5

    Spurns enviously at straws, speaks things in doubt   6

    That carry but half sense. Her speech is nothing,

    Yet the unshapèd use of it doth move   8

    The hearers to collection; they yawn at it,   9

    And botch the words up fit to their own thoughts,   10

    Which, as her winks and nods and gestures yield them,   11

    Indeed would make one think there might be thought,   12

    Though nothing sure, yet much unhappily.   13

HORATIO 'Twere good she were spoken with, for she may strew

    Dangerous conjectures in ill-breeding minds.   15

QUEEN Let her come in.   *[Exit Gentleman.]*

    [Aside] To my sick soul, as sin's true nature is,

    Each toy seems prologue to some great amiss.   18

    So full of artless jealousy is guilt,   19

    It spills itself in fearing to be spilt.   20

    Enter Ophelia [distracted].

OPHELIA Where is the beauteous màjesty of Denmark?

QUEEN How now, Ophelia?

OPHELIA *(she sings)*

    "How should I your true love know

    From another one?

    By his cockle hat and staff,   25

    And his sandal shoon."   26

QUEEN Alas, sweet lady, what imports this song?

OPHELIA Say you? Nay, pray you, mark.

    "He is dead and gone, lady,   *(Song.)*

    He is dead and gone;

4.5 Location: The castle.

2 distract out of her mind. **5 tricks** deceptions. **hems** clears her throat, makes "hmm" sounds. **heart** i.e., breast **6 Spurns . . . straws** kicks spitefully, takes offense at trifles. **in doubt** of obscure meaning **8 unshapèd use** incoherent manner **9 collection** inference, a guess at some sort of meaning. **yawn** gape, wonder; grasp. (The Folio reading, "aim," is possible.) **10 botch** patch **11 Which** which words. **yield** deliver, represent **12–13 there might . . . unhappily** that a great deal could be guessed at of a most unfortunate nature, even if one couldn't be at all sure. **15 ill-breeding** prone to suspect the worst and to make mischief **18 toy** trifle. **amiss** calamity. **19–20 So . . . spilt** Guilt is so burdened with conscience and guileless fear of detection that it reveals itself through apprehension of disaster. **20.1 Enter Ophelia** (In the First Quarto, Ophelia enters, *"playing on a lute, and her hair down, singing."*) **25 cockle hat** hat with cockleshell stuck in it as a sign that the wearer had been a pilgrim to the shrine of Saint James of Compostella in Spain **26 shoon** shoes.

At his head a grass-green turf,
At his heels a stone."
Oho!   33

QUEEN Nay, but Ophelia—

OPHELIA Pray you, mark.
[Sings] "White his shroud as the mountain snow"—

Enter King.

QUEEN Alas, look here, my lord.

OPHELIA "Larded with sweet flowers;   (Song.)   38
Which bewept to the ground did not go
With true-love showers."   40

KING How do you, pretty lady?

OPHELIA Well, God 'ild you! They say the owl was a   42
baker's daughter. Lord, we know what we are, but
know not what we may be. God be at your table!

KING Conceit upon her father.   45

OPHELIA Pray let's have no words of this; but when they
ask you what it means, say you this:
"Tomorrow is Saint Valentine's day,   (Song.)
All in the morning betime,   49
And I a maid at your window,
To be your Valentine.
Then up he rose, and donned his clothes,
And dupped the chamber door,   53
Let in the maid, that out a maid
Never departed more."

KING Pretty Ophelia—

OPHELIA Indeed, la, without an oath, I'll make an end on't:
[Sings] "By Gis and by Saint Charity,   59
Alack, and fie for shame!
Young men will do't, if they come to't;
By Cock, they are to blame.   62
Quoth she, 'Before you tumbled me,
You promised me to wed.'"
He answers:
"'So would I ha' done, by yonder sun,
An thou hadst not come to my bed.'"   67

KING How long hath she been thus?

OPHELIA I hope all will be well. We must be patient,
but I cannot choose but weep to think they would lay
him i'th' cold ground. My brother shall know of it.

---

33 Oho! (Perhaps a sigh.) **38 Larded** strewn, bedecked **40 showers** i.e., tears **42 God 'ild** God yield
or reward. **owl** (Refers to a legend about a baker's daughter who was turned into an owl for being ungenerous when Jesus begged a loaf of bread.) **45 Conceit** Fancy, brooding **49 betime** early **53 dupped**
did up, opened **59 Gis** Jesus **62 Cock** (A perversion of "God" in oaths; here also with a quibble on
the slang word for penis.) **67 An** if

And so I thank you for your good counsel. Come, my
coach! Good night, ladies, good night, sweet ladies,
good night, good night.   *[Exit.]*
KING *[to Horatio]* Follow her close. Give her good watch, I pray you.

[Exit Horatio.]

Oh, this is the poison of deep grief; it springs
All from her father's death—and now behold!
Oh, Gertrude, Gertrude,
When sorrows come, they come not single spies,   79
But in battalions. First, her father slain;
Next, your son gone, and he most violent author
Of his own just remove; the people muddied,   82
Thick and unwholesome in their thoughts and whispers
For good Polonius' death—and we have done but greenly,   84
In hugger-mugger to inter him; poor Ophelia   85
Divided from herself and her fair judgment,
Without the which we are pictures or mere beasts;
Last, and as much containing as all these,   88
Her brother is in secret come from France,
Feeds on this wonder, keeps himself in clouds,   90
And wants not buzzers to infect his ear   91
With pestilent speeches of his father's death,
Wherein necessity, of matter beggared,   93
Will nothing stick our person to arraign   94
In ear and ear. Oh, my dear Gertrude, this,   95
Like to a murd'ring piece, in many places   96
Gives me superfluous death.   *A noise within.* 97
QUEEN Alack, what noise is this?
KING Attend!   99
Where is my Switzers? Let them guard the door.   100

Enter a Messenger.

What is the matter?
MESSENGER   Save yourself, my lord!
The ocean, overpeering of his list,   102
Eats not the flats with more impetuous haste   103

---

79 spies scouts sent in advance of the main force **82 remove** removal. **muddied** stirred up, confused **84 greenly** foolishly **85 hugger-mugger** secret haste **88 as much containing** as full of serious matter **90 Feeds . . . clouds** feeds his resentment on this whole shocking turn of events, keeps himself aloof and mysterious **91 wants** lacks. **buzzers** gossipers, informers **93 necessity** i.e., the need to invent some plausible explanation. **of matter beggared** unprovided with facts **94–5 Will . . . ear** will not hesitate to accuse my (royal) person in everybody's ears. **96 murd'ring piece** cannon loaded so as to scatter its shot **97 Gives . . . death** kills me over and over. **99 Attend!** Guard me! **100 Switzers** Swiss guards, mercenaries **102 overpeering of his list** overflowing its shore, boundary **103 flats** i.e., flatlands near shore. **impetuous** violent (perhaps also with the meaning of *impiteous* ["impitious," Q2], "pitiless")

Than young Laertes, in a riotous head,   104
O'erbears your officers. The rabble call him lord,
And, as the world were now but to begin,   106
Antiquity forgot, custom not known,   107
The ratifiers and props of every word,   108
They cry, "Choose we! Laertes shall be king!"
Caps, hands, and tongues applaud it to the clouds,   110
"Laertes shall be king, Laertes king!"
QUEEN How cheerfully on the false trail they cry!

> *A noise within.*

Oh, this is counter, you false Danish dogs!   113

> *Enter Laertes with others.*

KING The doors are broke.
LAERTES Where is this King?—Sirs, stand you all without.
ALL No, let's come in.
LAERTES I pray you, give me leave.
ALL We will, we will.
LAERTES I thank you. Keep the door.   *[Exeunt followers.]*
      Oh, thou vile king,
      Give me my father!
QUEEN *[restraining him]* Calmly, good Laertes.
LAERTES That drop of blood that's calm proclaims me bastard,
      Cries cuckold to my father, brands the harlot
      Even here between the chaste unsmirchèd brow   123
      Of my true mother.
KING   What is the cause, Laertes,
      That thy rebellion looks so giantlike?   125
      Let him go, Gertrude. Do not fear our person.   126
      There's such divinity doth hedge a king   127
      That treason can but peep to what it would,   128
      Acts little of his will. Tell me, Laertes,   129
      Why thou art thus incensed. Let him go, Gertrude.
      Speak, man.
LAERTES   Where is my father?
KING   Dead.
QUEEN But not by him.
KING   Let him demand his fill.
LAERTES How came he dead? I'll not be juggled with.   133
      To hell, allegiance! Vows, to the blackest devil!

---

104 riotous head insurrectionary advance **106–8 And . . . word** and, as if the world were to be
started all over afresh, utterly setting aside all ancient traditional customs that should confirm and
underprop our every word and promise **110 Caps** (The caps are thrown in the air.) **113 counter** (A
hunting term, meaning to follow the trail in a direction opposite to that which the game has taken.)
123 between amidst **125 giantlike** (Recalling the rising of the giants of Greek mythology against
Olympus.) **126 fear our** fear for my **127 hedge** protect, as with a surrounding barrier **128 can . . .
would** can only peep furtively, as through a barrier, at what it would intend **129 Acts . . . will** (but)
performs little of what it intends. **133 juggled with** cheated, deceived.

Conscience and grace, to the profoundest pit!
I dare damnation. To this point I stand,   *136*
That both the worlds I give to negligence,   *137*
Let come what comes, only I'll be revenged
Most throughly for my father.   *139*
KING Who shall stay you?
LAERTES My will, not all the world's.   *141*
And for my means, I'll husband them so well   *142*
They shall go far with little.
KING   Good Laertes,
If you desire to know the certainty
Of your dear father, is't writ in your revenge
That, swoopstake, you will draw both friend and foe,   *146*
Winner and loser?
LAERTES None but his enemies.
KING Will you know them, then?
LAERTES To his good friends thus wide I'll ope my arms,
And like the kind life-rendering pelican   *151*
Repast them with my blood.
KING   Why, now you speak   *152*
Like a good child and a true gentleman.
That I am guiltless of your father's death,
And am most sensibly in grief for it,   *155*
It shall as level to your judgment 'pear   *156*
As day does to your eye.   *A noise within.*
LAERTES How now, what noise is that?

Enter Ophelia.

KING   Let her come in.
LAERTES O heat, dry up my brains! Tears seven times salt
Burn out the sense and virtue of mine eye!   *160*
By heaven, thy madness shall be paid with weight   *161*
Till our scale turn the beam. O rose of May!   *162*
Dear maid, kind sister, sweet Ophelia!
O heavens, is't possible a young maid's wits
Should be as mortal as an old man's life?
Nature is fine in love, and where 'tis fine   *166*
It sends some precious instance of itself   *167*
After the thing it loves.   *168*

---

136 To . . . stand I am resolved in this **137 both . . . negligence** i.e., both this world and the next are of no consequence to me **139 throughly** thoroughly **141 My will . . . world's** I'll stop (stay) when my will is accomplished, not for anyone else's. **142 for** as for **146 swoopstake** i.e., indiscriminately. (Literally, taking all stakes on the gambling table at once. *Draw* is also a gambling term, meaning "take from.") **151 pelican** (Refers to the belief that the female pelican fed its young with its own blood.) **152 Repast** feed **155 sensibly** feelingly **156 level** plain **160 virtue** faculty, power **161 paid with weight** repaid, avenged equally or more **162 beam** crossbar of a balance. **166–8 Nature . . . loves** Human nature is exquisitely sensitive in matters of love, and in cases of sudden loss it sends some precious part of itself after the lost object of that love. (In this case, Ophelia's sanity deserts her out of sorrow for her lost father and perhaps too out of her love for Hamlet.)

OPHELIA "They bore him barefaced on the bier,   (Song.)
    Hey non nonny, nonny, hey nonny,
    And in his grave rained many a tear—"
    Fare you well, my dove!

LAERTES Hadst thou thy wits and didst persuade revenge,
    It could not move thus.

OPHELIA You must sing "A-down a-down," and you   175
    "call him a-down-a." Oh, how the wheel becomes it! It   176
    is the false steward that stole his master's daughter.   177

LAERTES This nothing's more than matter.   178

OPHELIA There's rosemary, that's for remembrance;   179
    pray you, love, remember. And there is pansies; that's   180
    for thoughts.

LAERTES A document in madness, thoughts and remembrance   182
    fitted.

OPHELIA There's fennel for you, and columbines.   184
    There's rue for you, and here's some for me; we may   185
    call it herb of grace o' Sundays. You must wear your
    rue with a difference. There's a daisy. I would give   187
    you some violets, but they withered all when my   188
    father died. They say 'a made a good end—
    [Sings] "For bonny sweet Robin is all my joy."

LAERTES Thought and affliction, passion, hell itself,   191
    She turns to favor and to prettiness.   192

OPHELIA "And will 'a not come again?   (Song.)
    And will 'a not come again?
    No, no, he is dead.
    Go to thy deathbed,
    He never will come again.
    His beard was as white as snow,
    All flaxen was his poll.   199
    He is gone, he is gone,
    And we cast away moan.
    God ha' mercy on his soul!"
And of all Christian souls, I pray God. God b'wi'you.

    [Exit, followed by Gertrude.]

175–6 You . . . a-down-a (Ophelia assigns the singing of refrains, like her own "Hey non nonny," to others present.) **176 wheel** spinning wheel as accompaniment to the song, or refrain **177 false steward** (The story is unknown.) **178 This . . . matter** This seeming nonsense is more eloquent than sane utterance. **179 rosemary** (Used as a symbol of remembrance both at weddings and at funerals.) **180 pansies** (Emblems of love and courtship; perhaps from French *pensées*, "thoughts.") **182 document** instruction, lesson **184 There's fennel . . . columbines** (Fennel betokens flattery; *columbines*, unchastity or ingratitude. Throughout, Ophelia addresses her various listeners, giving one flower to one and another to another, perhaps with particular symbolic significance in each case.) **185 rue** (Emblem of repentance—a signification that is evident in its popular name, *herb of grace*.) **187 with a difference** (A device used in heraldry to distinguish one family from another on the coat of arms, here suggesting that Ophelia and the others have different causes of sorrow and repentance; perhaps with a play on rue in the sense of "ruth," "pity.") **daisy** (Emblem of love's victims and of faithlessness.) **188 violets** (Emblems of faithfulness.) **191 Thought** Melancholy. **passion** suffering **192 favor** grace, beauty **199 poll** head.

LAERTES Do you see this, O God?

KING Laertes, I must commune with your grief,
  Or you deny me right. Go but apart,
  Make choice of whom your wisest friends you will,   207
  And they shall hear and judge twixt you and me.
  If by direct or by collateral hand   209
  They find us touched, we will our kingdom give,   210
  Our crown, our life, and all that we call ours
  To you in satisfaction; but if not,
  Be you content to lend your patience to us,
  And we shall jointly labor with your soul
  To give it due content.

LAERTES   Let this be so.
  His means of death, his obscure funeral—
  No trophy, sword, nor hatchment o'er his bones,   217
  No noble rite, nor formal ostentation—   218
  Cry to be heard, as 'twere from heaven to earth,
  That I must call't in question.

KING   So you shall,   220
  And where th'offense is, let the great ax fall.
  I pray you, go with me.   *Exeunt.*

[4.6]

Enter Horatio and others.

HORATIO What are they that would speak with me?

GENTLEMAN Seafaring men, sir. They say they have letters for you.   3

HORATIO Let them come in.   *[Exit Gentleman.]*
  I do not know from what part of the world
  I should be greeted, if not from Lord Hamlet.

Enter Sailors.

FIRST SAILOR God bless you, sir.

HORATIO Let him bless thee too.

FIRST SAILOR 'A shall, sir, an't please him. There's a   9
  letter for you, sir—it came from th'ambassador that   10
  was bound for England—if your name be Horatio, as
  I am let to know it is.   *[He gives a letter.]*

HORATIO *[reads]* "Horatio, when thou shalt have over-looked   13
  this, give these fellows some means to the King;   14
  they have letters for him. Ere we were two days old at
  sea, a pirate of very warlike appointment gave us   16
  chase. Finding ourselves too slow of sail, we put on a

---

207 whom whichever of **209 collateral hand** indirect agency **210 us touched** me implicated **217 trophy** memorial. **hatchment** tablet displaying the armorial bearings of a deceased person **218 ostentation** ceremony **220 That** so that. **call't in question** demand an explanation.
4.6 Location: The castle.
3 letters a letter **9 an't** if it **10 th'ambassador** (Hamlet's ostensible role; see 3.2.172-3.) **13–14 overlooked** looked over **14 means** means of access **16 appointment** equipage

compelled valor, and in the grapple I boarded them.
On the instant they got clear of our ship, so I alone
became their prisoner. They have dealt with me like
thieves of mercy, but they knew what they did: I am to   21
do a good turn for them. Let the King have the letters
I have sent, and repair thou to me with as much speed   23
as thou wouldest fly death. I have words to speak in
thine ear will make thee dumb, yet are they much too
light for the bore of the matter. These good fellows will   26
bring thee where I am. Rosencrantz and Guildenstern
hold their course for England. Of them I have much to
tell thee. Farewell.
                    He that thou knowest thine, Hamlet."
Come, I will give you way for these your letters,   31
And do't the speedier that you may direct me
To him from whom you brought them.   *Exeunt.*

[4.7]

Enter King and Laertes.

KING Now must your conscience my acquittance seal,   1
    And you must put me in your heart for friend,
    Sith you have heard, and with a knowing ear,   3
    That he which hath your noble father slain
    Pursued my life.
LAERTES   It well appears. But tell me
    Why you proceeded not against these feats   6
    So crimeful and so capital in nature,   7
    As by your safety, greatness, wisdom, all things else,
    You mainly were stirred up.   9
KING Oh, for two special reasons,
    Which may to you perhaps seem much unsinewed,   11
    But yet to me they're strong. The Queen his mother
    Lives almost by his looks, and for myself—
    My virtue or my plague, be it either which—
    She is so conjunctive to my life and soul   15
    That, as the star moves not but in his sphere,   16
    I could not but by her. The other motive
    Why to a public count I might not go   18
    Is the great love the general gender bear him,   19

---

21 **thieves of mercy** merciful thieves 23 **repair** come 26 **bore** caliber, i.e., importance 31 **way** means
of access
4.7. Location: The castle.
1 **my acquittance seal** confirm or acknowledge my innocence 3 **Sith** since 6 **feats** acts 7 **capital** punishable by death 9 **mainly** greatly 11 **unsinewed** weak 15 **conjunctive** closely united. (An astronomical metaphor.) 16 **his** its. **sphere** one of the hollow spheres in which, according to Ptolemaic astronomy, the planets were supposed to move 18 **count** account, reckoning, indictment 19 **general
gender** common people

Who, dipping all his faults in their affection,
Work like the spring that turneth wood to stone, 21
Convert his gyves to graces, so that my arrows, 22
Too slightly timbered for so loud a wind, 23
Would have reverted to my bow again
But not where I had aimed them.
LAERTES And so have I a noble father lost,
A sister driven into desp'rate terms, 27
Whose worth, if praises may go back again, 28
Stood challenger on mount of all the age 29
For her perfections. But my revenge will come.
KING Break not your sleeps for that. You must not think
That we are made of stuff so flat and dull
That we can let our beard be shook with danger
And think it pastime. You shortly shall hear more.
I loved your father, and we love ourself;
And that, I hope, will teach you to imagine—

Enter a Messenger with letters.

How now? What news?
MESSENGER   Letters, my lord, from Hamlet:
This to Your Majesty, this to the Queen.

[He gives letters.]

KING From Hamlet? Who brought them?
MESSENGER Sailors, my lord, they say. I saw them not.
They were given me by Claudio. He received them
Of him that brought them.
KING   Laertes, you shall hear them.—
Leave us.   *[Exit Messenger.]*
[He reads.] "High and mighty, you shall know I am set
naked on your kingdom. Tomorrow shall I beg leave 45
to see your kingly eyes, when I shall, first asking your
pardon, thereunto recount the occasion of my sudden 47
and more strange return.   Hamlet."
What should this mean? Are all the rest come back?
Or is it some abuse, and no such thing? 50
LAERTES Know you the hand?
KING   'Tis Hamlet's character. "Naked!" 51
And in a postscript here he says "alone."
Can you devise me? 53
LAERTES I am lost in it, my lord. But let him come.

---

21 **Work** operate, act. **spring** i.e., a spring with such a concentration of lime that it coats a piece of wood with limestone, in effect gilding and petrifying it 22 **gyves** fetters (which, gilded by the people's praise, would look like badges of honor) 23 **Too . . . wind** with too light a shaft for so powerful a gust (of popular sentiment) 27 **terms** state, condition 28 **go back** recall what she was 29 **on mount** set up on high 45 **naked** destitute, unarmed, without following 47 **pardon** (for returning without authorization) 50 **abuse** deceit. **no such thing** not what the letter says. 51 **character** handwriting. 53 **devise** explain to

It warms the very sickness in my heart
That I shall live and tell him to his teeth,
"Thus didst thou."

KING   If it be so, Laertes—   57
As how should it be so? How otherwise?—   58
Will you be ruled by me?

LAERTES   Ay, my lord,
So you will not o'errule me to a peace.   60

KING To thine own peace. If he be now returned,
As checking at his voyage, and that he means   62
No more to undertake it, I will work him
To an exploit, now ripe in my device,   64
Under the which he shall not choose but fall;
And for his death no wind of blame shall breathe,
But even his mother shall uncharge the practice   67
And call it accident.

LAERTES   My lord, I will be ruled,
The rather if you could devise it so
That I might be the organ.

KING   It falls right.   70
You have been talked of since your travel much,
And that in Hamlet's hearing, for a quality
Wherein they say you shine. Your sum of parts   73
Did not together pluck such envy from him
As did that one, and that, in my regard,
Of the unworthiest siege.   76

LAERTES What part is that, my lord?

KING A very ribbon in the cap of youth,
Yet needful too, for youth no less becomes   79
The light and careless livery that it wears
Than settled age his sables and his weeds   81
Importing health and graveness. Two months since   82
Here was a gentleman of Normandy.
I have seen myself, and served against, the French,
And they can well on horseback, but this gallant   85
Had witchcraft in't; he grew unto his seat,
And to such wondrous doing brought his horse
As had he been incorpsed and demi-natured   88
With the brave beast. So far he topped my thought   89
That I in forgery of shapes and tricks   90
Come short of what he did.

---

57 Thus didst thou i.e., Here's for what you did to my father. **58 As . . . otherwise?** how can this (Hamlet's return) be true? Yet how otherwise than true (since we have the evidence of his letter)? **60 So** provided that **62 checking at** i.e., turning aside from (like a falcon leaving the quarry to fly at a chance bird). **that** if **64 device** devising, invention **67 uncharge the practice** acquit the stratagem of being a plot **70 organ** agent, instrument. **73 Your . . . parts** All your other virtues **76 unworthiest siege** least important rank. **79 no less becomes** is no less adorned by **81–2 his sables . . . graveness** its rich robes furred with sable and its garments denoting dignified well-being and seriousness. **85 can well** are skilled **88–9 As . . . beast** as if, centaurlike, he had been made into one body with the horse, possessing half its nature. **89 topped** surpassed **90 forgery** fabrication

LAERTES   A Norman was't?
KING A Norman.
LAERTES Upon my life, Lamord.
KING   The very same.
LAERTES I know him well. He is the brooch indeed   94
    And gem of all the nation.
KING He made confession of you,   96
    And gave you such a masterly report
    For art and exercise in your defense,   98
    And for your rapier most especial,
    That he cried out 'twould be a sight indeed
    If one could match you. Th'escrimers of their nation,   101
    He swore, had neither motion, guard, nor eye
    If you opposed them. Sir, this report of his
    Did Hamlet so envenom with his envy
    That he could nothing do but wish and beg
    Your sudden coming o'er, to play with you.   106
    Now, out of this—
LAERTES   What out of this, my lord?
KING Laertes, was your father dear to you?
    Or are you like the painting of a sorrow,
    A face without a heart?
LAERTES   Why ask you this?
KING Not that I think you did not love your father,
    But that I know love is begun by time,   112
    And that I see, in passages of proof,   113
    Time qualifies the spark and fire of it.   114
    There lives within the very flame of love
    A kind of wick or snuff that will abate it,   116
    And nothing is at a like goodness still,   117
    For goodness, growing to a pleurisy,   118
    Dies in his own too much. That we would do,   119
    We should do when we would; for this "would" changes
    And hath abatements and delays as many   121
    As there are tongues, are hands, are accidents,   122
    And then this "should" is like a spendthrift sigh,   123
    That hurts by easing. But, to the quick o'th'ulcer: 124
    Hamlet comes back. What would you undertake
    To show yourself in deed your father's son
    More than in words?

---

94 brooch ornament **96 confession** testimonial, admission of superiority **98 For . . . defense** with respect to your skill and practice with your weapon **101 Th'escrimers** The fencers **106 sudden** immediate. **play** fence **112 begun by time** i.e., created by the right circumstance and hence subject to change **113 passages of proof** actual well-attested instances **114 qualifies** weakens, moderates **116 snuff** the charred part of a candlewick **117 nothing . . . still** nothing remains at a constant level of perfection **118 pleurisy** excess, plethora. (Literally, a chest inflammation.) **119 in . . . much** of its own excess. **That** That which **121 abatements** diminutions **122 As . . . accidents** as there are tongues to dissuade, hands to prevent, and chance events to intervene **123 spendthrift sigh** (An allusion to the belief that sighs draw blood from the heart.) **124 hurts by easing** i.e., costs the heart blood and wastes precious opportunity even while it affords emotional relief. **quick o'th'ulcer** i.e., heart of the matter

LAERTES   To cut his throat i'th' church.
KING No place, indeed, should murder sanctuarize;   128
    Revenge should have no bounds. But good Laertes,
    Will you do this, keep close within your chamber.   130
    Hamlet returned shall know you are come home.
    We'll put on those shall praise your excellence   132
    And set a double varnish on the fame
    The Frenchman gave you, bring you in fine together,   134
    And wager on your heads. He, being remiss,   135
    Most generous, and free from all contriving,   136
    Will not peruse the foils, so that with ease,
    Or with a little shuffling, you may choose
    A sword unbated, and in a pass of practice   139
    Requite him for your father.
LAERTES   I will do't,
    And for that purpose I'll anoint my sword.
    I bought an unction of a mountebank   142
    So mortal that, but dip a knife in it,
    Where it draws blood no cataplasm so rare,   144
    Collected from all simples that have virtue   145
    Under the moon, can save the thing from death   146
    That is but scratched withal. I'll touch my point
    With this contagion, that if I gall him slightly,   148
    It may be death.
KING   Let's further think of this,
    Weigh what convenience both of time and means
    May fit us to our shape. If this should fail,   151
    And that our drift look through our bad performance,   152
    'Twere better not assayed. Therefore this project
    Should have a back or second, that might hold
    If this did blast in proof. Soft, let me see.   155
    We'll make a solemn wager on your cunnings—   156
    I ha 't!
    When in your motion you are hot and dry—
    As make your bouts more violent to that end—   159
    And that he calls for drink, I'll have prepared him
    A chalice for the nonce, whereon but sipping,   161
    If he by chance escape your venomed stuck,   162
    Our purpose may hold there. [A cry within.] But stay, what noise?

    Enter Queen.

---

128 **sanctuarize** protect from punishment. (Alludes to the right of sanctuary with which certain religious places were invested.) 130 **Will you do this** if you wish to do this 132 **put on those shall** arrange for some to 134 **in fine** finally 135 **remiss** negligently unsuspicious 136 **generous** nobleminded 139 **unbated** not blunted, having no button. **pass of practice** treacherous thrust in an arranged bout 142 **unction** ointment. **mountebank** quack doctor 144 **cataplasm** plaster or poultice 145 **simples** herbs. **virtue** potency 146 **Under the moon** i.e., anywhere (with reference perhaps to the belief that herbs gathered at night had a special power) 148 **gall** graze, wound 151 **shape** part we propose to act. 152 **drift . . . performance** intention should be made visible by our bungling 155 **blast in proof** come to grief when put to the test. 156 **cunnings** respective skills 159 **As** i.e., and you should 161 **nonce** occasion 162 **stuck** thrust. (From stoccado, a fencing term.)

QUEEN One woe doth tread upon another's heel,
    So fast they follow. Your sister's drowned, Laertes.
LAERTES Drowned! Oh, where?
QUEEN There is a willow grows askant the brook,   *167*
    That shows his hoar leaves in the glassy stream;   *168*
    Therewith fantastic garlands did she make
    Of crowflowers, nettles, daisies, and long purples,   *170*
    That liberal shepherds give a grosser name,   *171*
    But our cold maids do dead men's fingers call them.   *172*
    There on the pendent boughs her crownet weeds   *173*
    Clamb'ring to hang, an envious sliver broke,   *174*
    When down her weedy trophies and herself   *175*
    Fell in the weeping brook. Her clothes spread wide,
    And mermaidlike awhile they bore her up,
    Which time she chanted snatches of old lauds,   *178*
    As one incapable of her own distress,   *179*
    Or like a creature native and endued   *180*
    Unto that element. But long it could not be
    Till that her garments, heavy with their drink,
    Pulled the poor wretch from her melodious lay   *183*
    To muddy death.
LAERTES   Alas, then she is drowned?
QUEEN Drowned, drowned.
LAERTES Too much of water hast thou, poor Ophelia,
    And therefore I forbid my tears. But yet
    It is our trick; nature her custom holds,   *188*
    Let shame say what it will. *[He weeps.]* When these are gone, *189*
    The woman will be out. Adieu, my lord.   *190*
    I have a speech of fire that fain would blaze,
    But that this folly douts it.   *Exit.*
KING   Let's follow, Gertrude.   *192*
    How much I had to do to calm his rage!
    Now fear I this will give it start again;
    Therefore let's follow.   *Exeunt.*

[5.1]

Enter two Clowns [with spades and mattocks].

FIRST CLOWN Is she to be buried in Christian burial,
    when she willfully seeks her own salvation?   *2*

---

167 **askant** aslant 168 **hoar leaves** white or gray undersides of the leaves 170 **long purples** early purple orchids 171 **liberal** free-spoken. **a grosser name** (The testicle-resembling tubers of the orchid, which also in some cases resemble *dead men's fingers*, have earned various slang names like "dogstones" and "cullions.") 172 **cold** chaste 173 **pendent** overhanging. **crownet** made into a chaplet or coronet 174 **envious sliver** malicious branch 175 **weedy** i.e., of plants 178 **lauds** hymns 179 **incapable of** lacking capacity to apprehend 180 **endued** adapted by nature 183 **lay** ballad, song 188 **It is our trick** i.e., weeping is our natural way (when sad) 189–90 **When . . . out** When my tears are all shed, the woman in me will be expended, satisfied. 192 **douts** extinguishes. (The Second Quarto reads "drownes.")
5.1 Location: A churchyard.
0.1 *Clowns* rustics 2 **salvation** (A blunder for "damnation," or perhaps a suggestion that Ophelia was taking her own shortcut to heaven.)

SECOND CLOWN I tell thee she is; therefore make her
 grave straight. The crowner hath sat on her, and finds   4
 it Christian burial.   5
FIRST CLOWN How can that be, unless she drowned
 herself in her own defense?
SECOND CLOWN Why, 'tis found so.   8
FIRST CLOWN It must be se offendendo, it cannot be else.   9
 For here lies the point: if I drown myself wittingly,
 it argues an act, and an act hath three branches—it is
 to act, to do, and to perform. Argal, she drowned herself 12
 wittingly.
SECOND CLOWN Nay, but hear you, goodman delve—   14
FIRST CLOWN Give me leave. Here lies the water; good.
 Here stands the man; good. If the man go to this
 water and drown himself, it is, will he, nill he, he   17
 goes, mark you that. But if the water come to him and
 drown him, he drowns not himself. Argal, he that is
 not guilty of his own death shortens not his own life.
SECOND CLOWN But is this law?
FIRST CLOWN Ay, marry, is't—crowner's quest law.   22
SECOND CLOWN Will you ha' the truth on't? If this had
 not been a gentlewoman, she should have been
 buried out o'Christian burial.
FIRST CLOWN Why, there thou say'st. And the more   26
 pity that great folk should have countenance in this   27
 world to drown or hang themselves, more than their
 even-Christian. Come, my spade. There is no ancient   29
 gentlemen but gardeners, ditchers, and grave makers.
 They hold up Adam's profession.   31
SECOND CLOWN Was he a gentleman?
FIRST CLOWN 'A was the first that ever bore arms.   33
SECOND CLOWN Why, he had none.
FIRST CLOWN What, art a heathen? How dost thou
 understand the Scripture? The Scripture says Adam
 digged. Could he dig without arms? I'll put another   37
 question to thee. If thou answerest me not to the
 purpose, confess thyself—   39
SECOND CLOWN Go to.

---

4 **straight** straightway, immediately. (But with a pun on strait, "narrow.") **crowner** coroner. **sat on her** conducted an inquest on her case 4–5 **finds it** gives his official verdict that her means of death was consistent with 8 **found** so determined so in the coroner's verdict. 9 *se offendendo* (A comic mistake for *se defendendo*, a term used in verdicts of self-defense.) 12 **Argal** (Corruption of *ergo*, "therefore.") 14 **goodman** (An honorific title often used with the name of a profession or craft.) 17 **will he, nill he** whether he will or no, willy-nilly 22 **quest** inquest 26 **there thou say'st** i.e., that's right. 27 **countenance** privilege 29 **even-Christian** fellow Christians. **ancient** going back to ancient times 31 **hold up** maintain 33 **bore arms** (To be entitled to bear a coat of arms would make Adam a gentleman, but as one who bore a spade, our common ancestor was an ordinary delver in the earth.) 37 **arms** i.e., the arms of the body. 39 **confess thyself** (The saying continues, "and be hanged.")

FIRST CLOWN What is he that builds stronger than
either the mason, the shipwright, or the carpenter?
SECOND CLOWN The gallows maker, for that frame
outlives a thousand tenants.   43
FIRST CLOWN I like thy wit well, in good faith. The
gallows does well. But how does it well? It does well to   46
those that do ill. Now thou dost ill to say the gallows
is built stronger than the church. Argal, the gallows
may do well to thee. To't again, come.
SECOND CLOWN "Who builds stronger than a mason, a
shipwright, or a carpenter?"
FIRST CLOWN Ay, tell me that, and unyoke.   52
SECOND CLOWN Marry, now I can tell.
FIRST CLOWN To't.
SECOND CLOWN Mass, I cannot tell.   55

Enter Hamlet and Horatio [at a distance].

FIRST CLOWN Cudgel thy brains no more about it, for
your dull ass will not mend his pace with beating; and
when you are asked this question next, say "a grave
maker." The houses he makes lasts till doomsday. Go
get thee in and fetch me a stoup of liquor.   60

[Exit Second Clown. First Clown digs.]
Song.

"In youth, when I did love, did love,   61
Methought it was very sweet,
To contract—oh—the time for—a—my behove,   63
Oh, methought there—a—was nothing—a—meet."   64
HAMLET Has this fellow no feeling of his business, 'a
sings in grave-making?   66
HORATIO Custom hath made it in him a property of   67
easiness.   68
HAMLET 'Tis e'en so. The hand of little employment
hath the daintier sense.   70
FIRST CLOWN   Song.
"But age with his stealing steps
Hath clawed me in his clutch,
And hath shipped me into the land,   73
As if I had never been such."

---

43 frame (1) gallows (2) structure **46 does well** (1) is an apt answer (2) does a good turn. **52 unyoke**
i.e., after this great effort, you may unharness the team of your wits. **55 Mass** By the Mass **60 stoup**
two-quart measure **61 In . . . love** (This and the two following stanzas, with nonsensical variations,
are from a poem attributed to Lord Vaux and printed in *Tottel's Miscellany*. 1557. The *oh* and *a* [for
"ah"] seemingly are the grunts of the digger.) **63 To contract . . . behove** i.e., to shorten the time for
my own advantage. (Perhaps he means to prolong it.) **64 meet** suitable, i.e., more suitable. **65 'a** that
he **67–8 property of easiness** something he can do easily and indifferently. **70 daintier sense** more
delicate sense of feeling. **73 into the land** i.e., toward my grave (?) (But note the lack of rhyme in
steps, land.)

[He throws up a skull.]

HAMLET That skull had a tongue in it and could sing
    once. How the knave jowls it to the ground, as if   76
    'twere Cain's jawbone, that did the first murder! This
    might be the pate of a politician, which this ass now   78
    o'erreaches, one that would circumvent God, might   79
    it not?
HORATIO It might, my lord.
HAMLET Or of a courtier, which could say, "Good morrow,
    sweet lord! How dost thou, sweet lord?"
    This might be my Lord Such-a-one, that praised my
    Lord Such-a-one's horse when 'a meant to beg it,
       might it not?
HORATIO Ay, my lord.
HAMLET Why, e'en so, and now my Lady Worm's,
    chapless, and knocked about the mazard with a sexton's   89
    spade. Here's fine revolution, an we had the trick   90
    to see't. Did these bones cost no more the breeding   91
    but to play at loggets with them? Mine ache to think   92
    on't.
FIRST CLOWN   *Song.*
    "A pickax and a spade, a spade,
    For and a shrouding sheet;   95
    Oh, a pit of clay for to be made
    For such a guest is meet."

[He throws up another skull.]

HAMLET There's another. Why may not that be the skull
    of a lawyer? Where be his quiddities now, his quillities,   99
    his cases, his tenures, and his tricks? Why does   100
    he suffer this mad knave now to knock him about the
    sconce with a dirty shovel, and will not tell him of his   102
    action of battery? Hum, this fellow might be in 's time   103
    a great buyer of land, with his statutes, his recognizances,   104
    his fines, his double vouchers, his recoveries.   105

---

76 jowls dashes. (With a pun on jowl, "jawbone.") **78 politician** schemer, plotter **79 o'erreaches** circumvents, gets the better of **89 chapless** having no lower jaw. **mazard** i.e., head. (Literally, a drinking vessel.) **90 revolution** turn of Fortune's wheel, change. **trick** knack **91–2 cost . . . but** involve so little expense and care in upbringing that we may **92 loggets** a game in which pieces of hard wood shaped like Indian clubs or bowling pins are thrown to lie as near as possible to a stake **95 For and** and moreover **99–100 his quiddities . . . quillities** his subtleties, his legal niceties **100 tenures** the holding of a piece of property or office, or the conditions or period of such holding **102 sconce** head **103 action of battery** lawsuit about physical assault. **104 his statutes** his legal documents acknowledging obligation of a debt **104–5 recognizances** bonds undertaking to repay debts **105 fines** procedures for converting entailed estates into "fee simple" or freehold. **double vouchers** vouchers signed by two signatories guaranteeing the legality of real estate titles. **recoveries** suits to obtain the authority of a court judgment for the holding of land.

Is this the fine of his fines and the recovery of his 106
recoveries, to have his fine pate full of fine dirt? Will 107
his vouchers vouch him no more of his purchases, and 108
double ones too, than the length and breadth of a 109
pair of indentures? The very conveyances of his lands 110
will scarcely lie in this box, and must th'inheritor 111
himself have no more, ha?

HORATIO Not a jot more, my lord.

HAMLET Is not parchment made of sheepskins?

HORATIO Ay, my lord, and of calves' skins too.

HAMLET They are sheep and calves which seek out assurance 116
in that. I will speak to this fellow.—Whose 117
grave's this, sirrah? 118

FIRST CLOWN Mine, sir.

    [*Sings*] "Oh, pit of clay for to be made
      For such a guest is meet."

HAMLET I think it be thine, indeed, for thou liest in't.

FIRST CLOWN You lie out on't, sir, and therefore 'tis
not yours. For my part, I do not lie in't, yet it is mine.

HAMLET Thou dost lie in't, to be in't and say it is
thine. 'Tis for the dead, not for the quick; therefore 126
thou liest.

FIRST CLOWN 'Tis a quick lie, sir; 'twill away again
from me to you.

HAMLET What man dost thou dig it for?

FIRST CLOWN For no man, sir.

HAMLET What woman, then?

FIRST CLOWN For none, neither.

HAMLET Who is to be buried in't?

FIRST CLOWN One that was a woman, sir, but, rest her
soul, she's dead.

HAMLET How absolute the knave is! We must speak by 137
the card, or equivocation will undo us. By the Lord, 138
Horatio, this three years I have took note of it: the age 139
is grown so picked that the toe of the peasant comes so 140
near the heel of the courtier he galls his kibe.—How 141
long hast thou been grave maker?

106–7 Is this . . . dirt? Is this the end of his legal maneuvers and profitable land deals, to have the skull of his elegant head filled full of minutely sifted dirt? (With multiple wordplay on *fine* and *fines*.) **107–10 Will . . . indentures?** Will his vouchers, even double ones, guarantee him no more land than is needed to bury him in, being no bigger than the deed of conveyance? (An indenture is literally a legal document drawn up in duplicate on a single sheet and then cut apart on a zigzag line so that each pair was uniquely matched.) **111 box** (1) deed box (2) coffin. **th'inheritor** the acquirer, owner **116–17 assurance in that** safety in legal parchments. **118 sirrah** (A term of address to inferiors.) **126 quick** living **137 absolute** strict, precise **137–8 by the card** i.e., with precision. (Literally, by the mariner's compass-card, on which the points of the compass were marked.) **138 equivocation** ambiguity in the use of terms **139 took** taken **139–41 the age . . . kibe** i.e., the age has grown so finical and mannered that the lower classes ape their social betters, chafing at their heels. (*Kibes* are chilblains on the heels.)

FIRST CLOWN Of all the days i'th' year, I came to't that
    day that our last king Hamlet overcame Fortinbras.
HAMLET How long is that since?
FIRST CLOWN Cannot you tell that? Every fool can tell
    that. It was that very day that young Hamlet was
    born—he that is mad and sent into England.
HAMLET Ay, marry, why was he sent into England?
FIRST CLOWN Why, because 'a was mad. 'A shall
    recover his wits there, or if 'a do not, 'tis no great
    matter there.
HAMLET Why?
FIRST CLOWN 'Twill not be seen in him there. There the
    men are as mad as he.
HAMLET How came he mad?
FIRST CLOWN Very strangely, they say.
HAMLET How strangely?
FIRST CLOWN Faith, e'en with losing his wits.
HAMLET Upon what ground?   160
FIRST CLOWN Why, here in Denmark. I have been
    sexton here, man and boy, thirty years.
HAMLET How long will a man lie i'th'earth ere he rot?
FIRST CLOWN Faith, if 'a be not rotten before 'a die—as
    we have many pocky corpses nowadays, that will   165
    scarce hold the laying in—'a will last you some eight   166
    year or nine year. A tanner will last you nine year.
HAMLET Why he more than another?
FIRST CLOWN Why, sir, his hide is so tanned with his
    trade that 'a will keep out water a great while, and
    your water is a sore decayer of your whoreson dead   171
    body. [He picks up a skull.] Here's a skull now hath
    lien you i'th'earth three-and-twenty years.   173
HAMLET Whose was it?
FIRST CLOWN A whoreson mad fellow's it was. Whose
    do you think it was?
HAMLET Nay, I know not.
FIRST CLOWN A pestilence on him for a mad rogue! 'A
    poured a flagon of Rhenish on my head once. This   179
    same skull, sir, was, sir, Yorick's skull, the King's jester.
HAMLET This?
FIRST CLOWN E'en that.
HAMLET Let me see. [He takes the skull.] Alas, poor
    Yorick! I knew him, Horatio, a fellow of infinite jest, of
    most excellent fancy. He hath bore me on his back a   185
    thousand times, and now how abhorred in my

---

160 ground cause. (But, in the next line, the gravedigger takes the word in the sense of "land,"
"country.") **165 pocky** rotten, diseased. (Literally, with the pox, or syphilis.) **166 hold the laying in**
hold together long enough to be interred. **last you** last. (You is used colloquially here and in the following lines.) **171 sore** keen, veritable. **whoreson** (An expression of contemptuous familiarity.) **173
lien you** lain. (See the note at line 166.) **179 Rhenish** Rhine wine **185 bore** borne

imagination it is! My gorge rises at it. Here hung those 187
lips that I have kissed I know not how oft. Where be
your gibes now? Your gambols, your songs, your 189
flashes of merriment that were wont to set the table on
a roar? Not one now, to mock your own grinning?
Quite chopfallen? Now get you to my lady's chamber 192
and tell her, let her paint an inch thick, to this favor 193
she must come. Make her laugh at that. Prithee,
Horatio, tell me one thing.

HORATIO What's that, my lord?

HAMLET Dost thou think Alexander looked o' this
fashion i'th'earth?

HORATIO E'en so.

HAMLET And smelt so? Pah! *[He throws down the skull.]*

HORATIO E'en so, my lord.

HAMLET To what base uses we may return, Horatio!
Why may not imagination trace the noble dust of
Alexander till 'a find it stopping a bunghole? 204

HORATIO 'Twere to consider too curiously to consider
so. 205

HAMLET No, faith, not a jot, but to follow him thither
with modesty enough, and likelihood to lead it. As 208
thus: Alexander died, Alexander was buried, Alexander
returneth to dust, the dust is earth, of earth we
make loam, and why of that loam whereto he was 211
converted might they not stop a beer barrel?
Imperious Caesar, dead and turned to clay, 213
Might stop a hole to keep the wind away.
Oh, that that earth which kept the world in awe
Should patch a wall t'expel the winter's flaw! 216

Enter King, Queen, Laertes, and the corpse [of Ophelia, in procession, with Priest, lords, etc.].

But soft, but soft awhile! Here comes the King, 217
The Queen, the courtiers. Who is this they follow?
And with such maimèd rites? This doth betoken 219
The corpse they follow did with desperate hand
Fordo it own life. 'Twas of some estate. 221
Couch we awhile and mark. 222

[He and Horatio conceal themselves. Ophelia's body is taken to the grave.]

LAERTES What ceremony else?

HAMLET *[to Horatio]* That is Laertes, a very noble youth. Mark.

---

187 My gorge rises i.e., I feel nauseated **189 gibes** taunts **192 chopfallen** (1) lacking the lower jaw (2) dejected. **193 favor** aspect, appearance **204 bunghole** hole for filling or emptying a cask. **205 curiously** minutely **208 with . . . lead** it with moderation and plausibility. **211 loam** a mixture of clay, straw, sand, etc. used to mold bricks, or, in this case, bungs for a beer barrel **213 Imperious** Imperial **216 flaw** gust of wind. **217 soft** i.e., wait, be careful **219 maimèd** mutilated, incomplete **221 Fordo it** destroy its. **estate** rank. **222 Couch we** Let's hide, lie low

LAERTES What ceremony else?

PRIEST Her obsequies have been as far enlarged

As we have warranty. Her death was doubtful,   227
And but that great command o'ersways the order   228
She should in ground unsanctified been lodged   229
Till the last trumpet. For charitable prayers,   230
Shards, flints, and pebbles should be thrown on her.   231
Yet here she is allowed her virgin crants,   232
Her maiden strewments, and the bringing home   233
Of bell and burial.   234

LAERTES Must there no more be done?

PRIEST   No more be done.

We should profane the service of the dead
To sing a requiem and such rest to her   237
As to peace-parted souls.

LAERTES   Lay her i'th'earth,   238

And from her fair and unpolluted flesh
May violets spring! I tell thee, churlish priest,   240
A ministering angel shall my sister be
When thou liest howling.

HAMLET [to Horatio]   What, the fair Ophelia!   242

QUEEN [scattering flowers] Sweets to the sweet! Farewell.

I hoped thou shouldst have been my Hamlet's wife.
I thought thy bride-bed to have decked, sweet maid,
And not t' have strewed thy grave.

LAERTES   Oh, treble woe

Fall ten times treble on that cursèd head
Whose wicked deed thy most ingenious sense   248
Deprived thee of! Hold off the earth awhile,
Till I have caught her once more in mine arms.

[He leaps into the grave and embraces Ophelia.]

Now pile your dust upon the quick and dead,
Till of this flat a mountain you have made
T' o'ertop old Pelion or the skyish head   253
Of blue Olympus.

HAMLET [coming forward] What is he whose grief

Bears such an emphasis, whose phrase of sorrow   255
Conjures the wandering stars and makes them stand   256

---

227 **warranty** i.e., ecclesiastical authority. 228 **order** (1) prescribed practice (2) religious order of clerics 229 **She should . . . lodged** she should have been buried in unsanctified ground 230 **For** In place of 231 **Shards** broken bits of pottery 232 **crants** garlands betokening maidenhood 233 **strewments** flowers strewn on a coffin 233–4 **bringing . . . burial** laying the body to rest, to the sound of the bell. 237 **such rest** i.e., to pray for such rest 238 **peace-parted souls** those who have died at peace with God. 240 **violets** (See 4.5.188 and note.) 242 **howling** i.e., in hell. 248 **ingenious sense** a mind that is quick, alert, of fine qualities 253 **Pelion** a mountain in northern Thessaly; compare *Olympus* and *Ossa* in lines 254 and 286. (In their rebellion against the Olympian gods, the giants attempted to heap Ossa on Pelion in order to scale Olympus.) 255 **emphasis** i.e., rhetorical and florid emphasis. (*Phrase* has a similar rhetorical connotation.) 256 **wandering stars** planets

Like wonder-wounded hearers? This is I,   257
Hamlet the Dane.   258
LAERTES *[grappling with him]* The devil take thy soul!   259
HAMLET Thou pray'st not well.
  I prithee, take thy fingers from my throat,
  For though I am not splenitive and rash,   262
  Yet have I in me something dangerous,
  Which let thy wisdom fear. Hold off thy hand.
KING Pluck them asunder.
QUEEN Hamlet, Hamlet!
ALL Gentlemen!
HORATIO Good my lord, be quiet.

  [Hamlet and Laertes are parted.]

HAMLET Why, I will fight with him upon this theme
  Until my eyelids will no longer wag.   270
QUEEN Oh, my son, what theme?
HAMLET I loved Ophelia. Forty thousand brothers
  Could not with all their quantity of love
  Make up my sum. What wilt thou do for her?
KING Oh, he is mad, Laertes.
QUEEN For love of God, forbear him.   276
HAMLET 'Swounds, show me what thou'lt do.   277
  Woo't weep? Woo't fight? Woo't fast? Woo't tear thyself? 278
  Woo't drink up eisel? Eat a crocodile?   279
  I'll do't. Dost come here to whine?
  To outface me with leaping in her grave?
  Be buried quick with her, and so will I.   282
  And if thou prate of mountains, let them throw
  Millions of acres on us, till our ground,
  Singeing his pate against the burning zone,   285
  Make Ossa like a wart! Nay, an thou'lt mouth,   286
  I'll rant as well as thou.
QUEEN   This is mere madness,   287
  And thus awhile the fit will work on him;
  Anon, as patient as the female dove

---

257 wonder-wounded struck with amazement **258 the Dane** (This title normally signifies the King; see 1.1.17 and note.) **259 s.d. grappling with him** The testimony of the First Quarto that *"Hamlet leaps in after Laertes"* and of the ballad "Elegy on Burbage," published in *Gentleman's Magazine* in 1825 ("Oft have I seen him leap into a grave") seem to indicate one way in which this fight was staged; however, the difficulty of fitting two contenders and Ophelia's body into a confined space (probably the trapdoor) suggests to many editors the alternative, that Laertes jumps out of the grave to attack Hamlet.) **262 splenitive** quick-tempered **270 wag** move. (A fluttering eyelid is a conventional sign that life has not yet gone.) **276 forbear him** leave him alone. **277 'Swounds** By His (Christ's) wounds **278 Woo't** Wilt thou **279 Woo't . . . eisel?** Will you drink up a whole draft of vinegar? (An extremely self-punishing task as a way of expressing grief.) **crocodile** (Crocodiles were tough and dangerous, and were supposed to shed crocodile tears.) **282 quick** alive **285 his pate** its head, i.e., top. **burning zone** zone in the celestial sphere containing the sun's orbit, between the tropics of Cancer and Capricorn **286 Ossa** (See 253n.) **an thou'lt mouth** if you want to rant **287 mere** utter

When that her golden couplets are disclosed,   290
His silence will sit drooping.
HAMLET   Hear you, sir.
What is the reason that you use me thus?
I loved you ever. But it is no matter.
Let Hercules himself do what he may,   294
The cat will mew, and dog will have his day.   295

   Exit Hamlet.

KING I pray thee, good Horatio, wait upon him.

   [Exit] Horatio.

[TO LAERTES] Strengthen your patience in our last
night's speech;   297
We'll put the matter to the present push.—   298
Good Gertrude, set some watch over your son.—
This grave shall have a living monument.   300
An hour of quiet shortly shall we see;   301
Till then, in patience our proceeding be.   *Exeunt.*

[5.2]

   Enter Hamlet and Horatio.

HAMLET So much for this, sir; now shall you see the other.   1
You do remember all the circumstance?
HORATIO Remember it, my lord!
HAMLET Sir, in my heart there was a kind of fighting
That would not let me sleep. Methought I lay
Worse than the mutines in the bilboes. Rashly,   6
And praised be rashness for it—let us know   7
Our indiscretion sometime serves us well   8
When our deep plots do pall, and that should learn us   9
There's a divinity that shapes our ends,
Rough-hew them how we will—
HORATIO   That is most certain.   11
HAMLET Up from my cabin,
My sea-gown scarfed about me, in the dark   13
Groped I to find out them, had my desire,   14

---

290 **golden couplets** two baby pigeons, covered with yellow down. **disclosed** hatched **294–5 Let . . . day**
i.e., (1) Even Hercules couldn't stop Laertes's theatrical rant (2) I, too, will have my turn; i.e., despite any
blustering attempts at interference, every person will sooner or later do what he or she must do. **297 in**
i.e., by recalling **298 present push** immediate test. **300 living** lasting. (For Laertes' private understanding,
Claudius also hints that Hamlet's death will serve as such a monument.) **301 hour of quiet** time free of
conflict
5.2 Location: The castle.
1 see the other hear the other news. (See 4.6.24–6.) **6 mutines** mutineers. **bilboes** shackles. **Rashly** On
impulse. (This adverb goes with lines 12 ff.) **7 know** acknowledge **8 indiscretion** lack of foresight and
judgment (not an indiscreet act) **9 pall** fail, falter, go stale. **learn** teach **11 Rough-hew** shape roughly **13**
sea-gown seaman's coat. **scarfed** loosely wrapped **14 them** i.e., Rosencrantz and Guildenstern

Fingered their packet, and in fine withdrew 15
To mine own room again, making so bold,
My fears forgetting manners, to unseal
Their grand commission; where I found, Horatio—
Ah, royal knavery!—an exact command,
Larded with many several sorts of reasons 20
Importing Denmark's health and England's too, 21
With, ho! such bugs and goblins in my life, 22
That on the supervise, no leisure bated, 23
No, not to stay the grinding of the ax, 24
My head should be struck off.

HORATIO   Is't possible?

HAMLET *[giving a document]* Here's the commission. Read it at more leisure.
But wilt thou hear now how I did proceed?

HORATIO I beseech you.

HAMLET Being thus benetted round with villainies—
Ere I could make a prologue to my brains, 30
They had begun the play—I sat me down, 31
Devised a new commission, wrote it fair. 32
I once did hold it, as our statists do, 33
A baseness to write fair, and labored much 34
How to forget that learning, but, sir, now
It did me yeoman's service. Wilt thou know
Th'effect of what I wrote?

HORATIO   Ay, good my lord.

HAMLET An earnest conjuration from the King, 38
As England was his faithful tributary,
As love between them like the palm might flourish, 40
As peace should still her wheaten garland wear 41
And stand a comma 'tween their amities, 42
And many suchlike "as" es of great charge, 43
That on the view and knowing of these contents,
Without debatement further more or less,
He should those bearers put to sudden death,
Not shriving time allowed.

HORATIO   How was this sealed? 47

HAMLET Why, even in that was heaven ordinant. 48
I had my father's signet in my purse, 49
Which was the model of that Danish seal; 50

---

15 Fingered pilfered, pinched. **in fine** finally, in conclusion **20 Larded** garnished. **several** different **21 Importing** relating to **22 With . . . life** i.e., with all sorts of warnings of imaginary dangers if I were allowed to continue living. (*Bugs* are bugbears, hobgoblins.) **23 That . . . bated** that on the reading of this commission, no delay being allowed **24 stay** await **30–1 Ere . . . play** before I could consciously turn my brain to the matter, it had started working on a plan **32 fair** in a clear hand. **33 statists** politicians, men of public affairs **34 A baseness** beneath my dignity **38 conjuration** entreaty **40 palm** (An image of health; see Psalm 92:12.) **41 still** always. **wheaten garland** (Symbolic of fruitful agriculture, of peace and plenty.) **42 comma** (Indicating continuity, link.) **43 "as" es** (1) the "whereases" of a formal document (2) asses. **charge** (1) import (2) burden (appropriate to asses) **47 shriving time** time for confession and absolution **48 ordinant** directing. **49 signet** small seal **50 model** replica

Folded the writ up in the form of th'other,   51
Subscribed it, gave't th'impression, placed it safely,   52
The changeling never known. Now, the next day   53
Was our sea fight, and what to this was sequent   54
Thou knowest already.

HORATIO So Guildenstern and Rosencrantz go to't.

HAMLET Why, man, they did make love to this employment.
They are not near my conscience. Their defeat   58
Does by their own insinuation grow.   59
'Tis dangerous when the baser nature comes   60
Between the pass and fell incensèd points   61
Of mighty opposites.

HORATIO   Why, what a king is this!   62

HAMLET Does it not, think thee, stand me now upon—   63
He that hath killed my king and whored my mother,
Popped in between th'election and my hopes,   65
Thrown out his angle for my proper life,   66
And with such coz'nage—is't not perfect conscience   67
To quit him with this arm? And is't not to be damned   68
To let this canker of our nature come   69
In further evil?   70

HORATIO It must be shortly known to him from England
What is the issue of the business there.

HAMLET It will be short. The interim is mine,
And a man's life's no more than to say "one."   74
But I am very sorry, good Horatio,
That to Laertes I forgot myself,
For by the image of my cause I see
The portraiture of his. I'll court his favors.
But, sure, the bravery of his grief did put me   79
Into a tow'ring passion.

HORATIO   Peace, who comes here?

    Enter a Courtier [Osric].

OSRIC Your Lordship is right welcome back to Denmark.

HAMLET I humbly thank you, sir. *[To Horatio]* Dost know this water fly?

HORATIO No, my good lord.

HAMLET Thy state is the more gracious, for 'tis a vice to
know him. He hath much land, and fertile. Let a beast   86

---

51 writ writing **52 Subscribed** signed (with forged signature). **impression** i.e., with a wax seal **53 changeling** i.e., substituted letter. (Literally, a fairy child substituted for a human one.) **54 was sequent** followed **58 defeat** destruction **59 insinuation** intrusive intervention, sticking their noses in my business **60 baser** of lower social station **61 pass** thrust. **fell** fierce **62 opposites** antagonists. **63 stand me now upon** become incumbent on me now **65 th'election** (The Danish monarch was "elected" by a small number of high-ranking electors.) **66 angle** fishhook. **proper** very **67 coz'nage** trickery **68 quit** requite, pay back **69 canker** ulcer **69–70 come In** grow into **74 a man's . . . "one"** one's whole life occupies such a short time, only as long as it takes to count to 1. **79 bravery** bravado **86–8 Let . . . mess** i.e., If a man, no matter how beastlike, is as rich in livestock and possessions as Osric, he may eat at the King's table.

be lord of beasts, and his crib shall stand at the King's 87
mess. 'Tis a chuff, but, as I say, spacious in the 88
possession of dirt.

OSRIC Sweet lord, if Your Lordship were at leisure, I
should impart a thing to you from His Majesty.

HAMLET I will receive it, sir, with all diligence of spirit.
Put your bonnet to his right use; 'tis for the head. 93

OSRIC I thank Your Lordship, it is very hot.

HAMLET No, believe me, 'tis very cold. The wind is northerly.

OSRIC It is indifferent cold, my lord, indeed. 97

HAMLET But yet methinks it is very sultry and hot for my complexion. 99

OSRIC Exceedingly, my lord. It is very sultry, as
'twere—I cannot tell how. My lord, His Majesty bade
me signify to you that 'a has laid a great wager on your
head. Sir, this is the matter—

HAMLET I beseech you, remember.

[Hamlet moves him to put on his hat.]

OSRIC Nay, good my lord; for my ease, in good faith. 105
Sir, here is newly come to court Laertes—believe me,
an absolute gentleman, full of most excellent differences, 107
of very soft society and great showing. Indeed, 108
to speak feelingly of him, he is the card or calendar of 109
gentry, for you shall find in him the continent of what 110
part a gentleman would see. 111

HAMLET Sir, his definement suffers no perdition in 112
you, though I know to divide him inventorially would 113
dozy th'arithmetic of memory, and yet but yaw 114
neither in respect of his quick sail. But, in the verity of 115
extolment, I take him to be a soul of great article, and 116
his infusion of such dearth and rareness as, to make 117
true diction of him, his semblable is his mirror and 118
who else would trace him his umbrage, nothing 119
more. 120

OSRIC Your Lordship speaks most infallibly of him.

---

87 crib manger **88 chuff** boor, churl. (The Second Quarto spelling, "chough," is a variant spelling that also suggests the meaning here of "chattering jackdaw.") **93 bonnet** any kind of cap or hat. **his** its **97 indifferent** somewhat **99 complexion** constitution. **105 for my ease** (A conventional reply declining the invitation to put the hat back on.) **107 absolute** perfect **107–8 differences** special qualities **108 soft society** agreeable manners. **great showing** distinguished appearance. **109 feelingly** with just perception **109–10 the card . . . gentry** the model or paradigm (literally, a chart or directory) of good breeding **110–11 the continent . . . see** one who contains in himself all the qualities a gentleman would like to see. (A *continent* is that which contains.) **112–15 his definement . . . sail** the task of defining Laertes's excellences suffers no diminution in your description of him, though I know that to enumerate all his graces would stupify one's powers of memory, and even so could do no more than veer unsteadily off course in a vain attempt to keep up with his rapid forward motion. (Hamlet mocks Osric by parodying his jargon-filled speeches.) **115–20 But . . . more** But, in true praise of him, I take him to be a person of remarkable value, and his essence of such rarity and excellence as, to speak truly of him, none can compare with him other than his own mirror; anyone following in his footsteps can only hope to be the shadow to his substance, nothing more.

HAMLET The concerancy, sir? Why do we wrap the   122
    gentleman in our more rawer breath?   123
OSRIC Sir?
HORATIO Is't not possible to understand in another   125
    tongue? You will do't, sir, really.   126
HAMLET What imports the nomination of this   127
    gentleman?
OSRIC Of Laertes?
HORATIO [to Hamlet] His purse is empty already; all 's
    golden words are spent.
HAMLET Of him, sir.
OSRIC I know you are not ignorant—
HAMLET I would you did, sir. Yet in faith if you did,   134
    it would not much approve me. Well, sir?   135
OSRIC You are not ignorant of what excellence Laertes
    is—
HAMLET I dare not confess that, lest I should compare   138
    with him in excellence. But to know a man well were 139
    to know himself.   140
OSRIC I mean, sir, for his weapon; but in the imputation   141
    laid on him by them, in his meed he's unfellowed.   142
HAMLET What's his weapon?
OSRIC Rapier and dagger.
HAMLET That's two of his weapons—but well.   145
OSRIC The King, sir, hath wagered with him six Barbary
    horses, against the which he has impawned, as I take 147
    it, six French rapiers and poniards, with their assigns, 148
    as girdle, hangers, and so. Three of the carriages, in 149
    faith, are very dear to fancy, very responsive to the 150
    hilts, most delicate carriages, and of very liberal 151
    conceit.   152
HAMLET What call you the carriages?   153

---

122 **concerancy** import, relevance 123 **rawer breath** unrefined speech that can only come short in praising him. 125–6 **Is't . . . tongue?** i.e., Is it not possible for you, Osric, to understand and communicate in any other tongue than the overblown rhetoric you have used? (Alternatively, Horatio could be asking Hamlet to speak more plainly.) 126 **You will do't** i.e., You can if you try, or, you may well have to try (to speak plainly). 127 **nomination** naming 134–5 **I would . . . approve me** (Responding to Osric's incompleted sentence as though it were a complete statement, Hamlet says, with mock politeness, "I wish you did know me to be not ignorant [i.e., to be knowledgeable] about matters," and then turns this into an insult: "But if you did, your recommendation of me would be of little value in any case.") 138–40 **I dare . . . himself** I dare not boast of knowing Laertes's excellence lest I seem to imply a comparable excellence in myself. Certainly, to know another person well, one must know oneself. 141–2 **I mean . . . unfellowed** I mean his excellence with his rapier, not his general excellence; in the reputation he enjoys for use of his weapons, his merit is unequaled. 145 **but well** but never mind. 147 **he** i.e., Laertes. **impawned** staked, wagered 148 **poniards** daggers. **assigns** appurtenances 149 **hangers** straps on the sword belt (*girdle*), from which the sword hung. **and so** and so on. 149–52 **Three . . . conceit** Three of the hangers, truly, are very pleasing to the fancy, decoratively matched with the hilts, delicate in workmanship, and made with elaborate ingenuity. 153 **What call you** What do you refer to when you say

HORATIO *[to Hamlet]* I knew you must be edified by
the margent ere you had done.   155
OSRIC The carriages, sir, are the hangers.
HAMLET The phrase would be more germane to the
matter if we could carry a cannon by our sides; I would
it might be hangers till then. But, on: six Barbary horses
against six French swords, their assigns, and three liberal-
conceited carriages; that's the French bet against
the Danish. Why is this impawned, as you call it?
OSRIC The King, sir, hath laid, sir, that in a dozen   163
passes between yourself and him, he shall not exceed   164
you three hits. He hath laid on twelve for nine, and it
would come to immediate trial, if Your Lordship would
vouchsafe the answer.   167
HAMLET How if I answer no?
OSRIC I mean, my lord, the opposition of your person
in trial.
HAMLET Sir, I will walk here in the hall. If it please His
Majesty, it is the breathing time of day with me. Let   172
the foils be brought, the gentleman willing, and the
King hold his purpose, I will win for him an I can; if
not, I will gain nothing but my shame and the odd
hits.
OSRIC Shall I deliver you so?   177
HAMLET To this effect, sir—after what flourish your
nature will.
OSRIC I commend my duty to Your Lordship.   180
HAMLET Yours, yours.   *[Exit Osric.]*
'A does well to commend it himself; there are no tongues
else for 's turn.   183
HORATIO This lapwing runs away with the shell on his   184
head.
HAMLET 'A did comply with his dug before 'a sucked   186
it. Thus has he—and many more of the same breed   187
that I know the drossy age dotes on—only got the   188

---

155 margent margin of a book, place for explanatory notes **163 laid** wagered **164 passes** bouts. (The odds of the betting are hard to explain. Possibly the King bets that Hamlet will win at least five out of twelve, at which point Laertes raises the odds against himself by betting he will win nine.) **167 vouchsafe the answer** be so good as to accept the challenge. (Hamlet deliberately takes the phrase in its literal sense of replying.) **172 breathing time** exercise period. **Let** i.e., If **177 deliver you** report what you say **180 commend** commit to your favor. (A conventional salutation, but Hamlet wryly uses a more literal meaning, "recommend," "praise," in line 182.) **183 for 's turn** for his purposes, i.e., to do it for him. **184 lapwing** (A proverbial type of youthful forwardness. Also, a bird **that draws** intruders away from its nest and was thought to run about with its head in the shell when newly hatched; a seeming reference to Osric's hat.) **186 comply . . . dug** observe ceremonious formality toward his nurse's or mother's teat **187–93 Thus . . . are out** Thus has he—and many like him of the sort our frivolous age dotes on—acquired the trendy manner of speech of the time, and, out of habitual conversation with courtiers of their own kind, have collected together a kind of frothy medley of current phrases, which enables such gallants to hold their own among persons of the most select and well-sifted views; and yet do but test them by merely blowing on them, and their bubbles burst.

tune of the time, and, out of an habit of encounter, a 189
kind of yeasty collection, which carries them through 190
and through the most fanned and winnowed opinions; 191
and do but blow them to their trial, the bubbles 192
are out. 193

Enter a Lord.

LORD My lord, His Majesty commended him to you by
young Osric, who brings back to him that you attend
him in the hall. He sends to know if your pleasure
hold to play with Laertes, or that you will take longer 197
time.
HAMLET I am constant to my purposes; they follow the
King's pleasure. If his fitness speaks, mine is ready; 200
now or whensoever, provided I be so able as now.
LORD The King and Queen and all are coming down.
HAMLET In happy time. 203
LORD The Queen desires you to use some gentle entertainment 204
to Laertes before you fall to play. 205
HAMLET She well instructs me. *[Exit Lord.]*
HORATIO You will lose, my lord.
HAMLET I do not think so. Since he went into France, I
have been in continual practice; I shall win at the odds.
But thou wouldst not think how ill all's here about my
heart; but it is no matter.
HORATIO Nay, good my lord—
HAMLET It is but foolery, but it is such a kind of gaingiving 213
as would perhaps trouble a woman. 214
HORATIO If your mind dislike anything, obey it. I will
forestall their repair hither and say you are not fit. 216
HAMLET Not a whit, we defy augury. There is special 217
providence in the fall of a sparrow. If it be now, 'tis
not to come; if it be not to come, it will be now; if it
be not now; yet it will come. The readiness is all. Since 220
no man of aught he leaves knows, what is't to leave 221
betimes? Let be. 222

A table prepared. [Enter] trumpets, drums, and officers with cushions; King,
Queen, [Osric,] and all the state; foils, daggers, [and wine borne in;] and
Laertes.

KING Come, Hamlet, come and take this hand from me.

[The King puts Laertes's hand into Hamlet's.]

---

197 play fence. **that** if **200 If . . . ready** If he declares his readiness, my convenience waits on his
203 In happy time (A phrase of courtesy indicating that the time is convenient.) **204–5 entertainment** greeting **213–14 gaingiving** misgiving **216 repair** coming **217 augury** the attempt to read
signs of future events in order to avoid predicted trouble. **220–2 Since . . . Let be** Since no one has
knowledge of what he is leaving behind, what does an early death matter after all? Enough; forbear.
222.1 trumpets, drums trumpeters, drummers **222.3 all the state** the entire court

HAMLET [*to Laertes*] Give me your pardon, sir. I have done you wrong,
But pardon't as you are a gentleman.
This presence knows,   226
And you must needs have heard, how I am punished   227
With a sore distraction. What I have done
That might your nature, honor, and exception   229
Roughly awake, I here proclaim was madness.
Was't Hamlet wronged Laertes? Never Hamlet.
If Hamlet from himself be ta'en away,
And when he's not himself does wrong Laertes,
Then Hamlet does it not, Hamlet denies it.
Who does it, then? His madness. If't be so,
Hamlet is of the faction that is wronged;   236
His madness is poor Hamlet's enemy.
Sir, in this audience
Let my disclaiming from a purposed evil
Free me so far in your most generous thoughts
That I have shot my arrow o'er the house
And hurt my brother.
LAERTES   I am satisfied in nature,   242
Whose motive in this case should stir me most   243
To my revenge. But in my terms of honor
I stand aloof, and will no reconcilement
Till by some elder masters of known honor
I have a voice and precedent of peace   247
To keep my name ungored. But till that time   248
I do receive your offered love like love,
And will not wrong it.
HAMLET   I embrace it freely,
And will this brothers' wager frankly play.—   251
Give us the foils. Come on.
LAERTES   Come, one for me.
HAMLET I'll be your foil, Laertes. In mine ignorance   253
Your skill shall, like a star i'th' darkest night,
Stick fiery off indeed.
LAERTES   You mock me, sir.   255
HAMLET No, by this hand.
KING Give them the foils, young Osric. Cousin Hamlet,
You know the wager?
HAMLET   Very well, my lord.
Your Grace has laid the odds o'th' weaker side.   259
KING I do not fear it; I have seen you both.
But since he is bettered, we have therefore odds.   261

---

226 presence royal assembly **227 punished** afflicted **229 exception** disapproval **236 faction** party **242 in nature** i.e., as to my personal feelings **243 motive** prompting **247 voice** authoritative pronouncement. **of peace** for reconciliation **248 name ungored** reputation unwounded. **251 frankly** without ill feeling or the burden of rancor **253 foil** thin metal background which sets a jewel off. (With pun on the blunted rapier for fencing.) **255 Stick fiery off** stand out brilliantly **259 laid . . . side** backed the weaker side. **261 is bettered** is the odds-on favorite. (Laertes's handicap is the "three hits" specified in line 165.)

LAERTES This is too heavy. Let me see another.

[He exchanges his foil for another.]

HAMLET This likes me well. These foils have all a length?   263

[They prepare to fence.]

OSRIC Ay, my good lord.
KING Set me the stoups of wine upon that table.
   If Hamlet give the first or second hit,
   Or quit in answer of the third exchange,   267
   Let all the battlements their ordnance fire.
   The King shall drink to Hamlet's better breath,   269
   And in the cup an union shall he throw   270
   Richer than that which four successive kings
   In Denmark's crown have worn. Give me the cups,
   And let the kettle to the trumpet speak,   273
   The trumpet to the cannoneer without,
   The cannons to the heavens, the heaven to earth,
   "Now the King drinks to Hamlet." Come, begin.

   Trumpets the while.

   And you, the judges, bear a wary eye.
HAMLET Come on, sir.
LAERTES Come, my lord. *[They fence. Hamlet scores a hit.]*
HAMLET One.
LAERTES No.
HAMLET Judgment.
OSRIC   A hit, a very palpable hit.   282

   Drum, trumpets, and shot. Flourish.
       A piece goes off.

LAERTES Well, again.
KING Stay, give me drink. Hamlet, this pearl is thine.

[He drinks, and throws a pearl in Hamlet's cup.]

   Here's to thy health. Give him the cup.
HAMLET I'll play this bout first. Set it by awhile.
   Come. *[They fence.]* Another hit; what say you?
LAERTES A touch, a touch, I do confess't.
KING Our son shall win.
QUEEN   He's fat and scant of breath.   289
   Here, Hamlet, take my napkin, rub thy brows.   290
   The Queen carouses to thy fortune, Hamlet.   291

---

263 **likes** pleases 267 **Or . . . exchange** or draws even with Laertes by winning the third exchange 269 **better breath** improved vigor 270 **union** pearl. (So called, according to Pliny's *Natural History*, 9, because pearls are *unique*, never identical.) 273 **kettle** kettledrum 282.2 *A piece* A cannon 289 **fat** not physically fit, out of training 290 **napkin** handkerchief 291 **carouses** drinks a toast

HAMLET Good madam!

KING Gertrude, do not drink.

QUEEN I will, my lord, I pray you pardon me.   *[She drinks.]*

KING *[aside]* It is the poisoned cup. It is too late.

HAMLET I dare not drink yet, madam; by and by.

QUEEN Come, let me wipe thy face.

LAERTES *[aside to the King]* My lord, I'll hit him now.

KING   I do not think't.

LAERTES *[aside]* And yet it is almost against my conscience.

HAMLET Come, for the third, Laertes. You do but dally.

   I pray you, pass with your best violence;   301

   I am afeard you make a wanton of me.   302

LAERTES Say you so? Come on.   *[They fence.]*

OSRIC Nothing neither way.

LAERTES Have at you now!   305

   [Laertes wounds Hamlet; then, in scuffling, they change rapiers, and Hamlet
   wounds Laertes.]

KING   Part them! They are incensed.

HAMLET Nay, come, again.   *[The Queen falls.]*

OSRIC   Look to the Queen there, ho!

HORATIO They bleed on both sides. How is it, my lord?

OSRIC How is't, Laertes?

LAERTES Why, as a woodcock to mine own springe, Osric;   309

   I am justly killed with mine own treachery.

HAMLET How does the Queen?

KING   She swoons to see them bleed.

QUEEN No, no, the drink, the drink—Oh, my dear Hamlet—

   The drink, the drink! I am poisoned.   *[She dies.]*

HAMLET Oh, villainy! Ho, let the door be locked!

   Treachery! Seek it out.   *[Laertes falls. Exit Osric.]*

LAERTES It is here, Hamlet. Hamlet, thou art slain.

   No med'cine in the world can do thee good;

   In thee there is not half an hour's life.

   The treacherous instrument is in thy hand,

   Unbated and envenomed. The foul practice   320

   Hath turned itself on me. Lo, here I lie,

   Never to rise again. Thy mother's poisoned.

   I can no more. The King, the King's to blame.

HAMLET The point envenomed too? Then, venom, to thy work.

   [He stabs the King.]

All Treason! Treason!

---

301 pass thrust **302 make . . . me** i.e., treat me like a spoiled child, trifle with me. **305.1–2 in scuffling, they change rapiers** (This stage direction occurs in the Folio. According to a widespread stage
tradition, Hamlet receives a scratch, realizes that Laertes's sword is unbated, and accordingly forces
an exchange.) **309 woodcock** a bird, a type of stupidity or as a decoy. **springe** trap, snare **320 Unbated** not blunted with a button. **practice** plot

KING Oh, yet defend me, friends! I am but hurt.

HAMLET *[forcing the King to drink]*

    Here, thou incestuous, murderous, damnèd Dane,

    Drink off this potion. Is thy union here?   328

    Follow my mother.   *[The King dies.]*

LAERTES   He is justly served.

    It is a poison tempered by himself.   330

    Exchange forgiveness with me, noble Hamlet.

    Mine and my father's death come not upon thee,

    Nor thine on me!   *[He dies.]*

HAMLET Heaven make thee free of it! I follow thee.

    I am dead, Horatio. Wretched Queen, adieu!

    You that look pale and tremble at this chance,   336

    That are but mutes or audience to this act,   337

    Had I but time—as this fell sergeant, Death,   338

    Is strict in his arrest—oh, I could tell you—   339

    But let it be. Horatio, I am dead;

    Thou livest. Report me and my cause aright

    To the unsatisfied.

HORATIO   Never believe it.

    I am more an antique Roman than a Dane.   343

    Here's yet some liquor left.

[He attempts to drink from the poisoned cup. Hamlet prevents him.]

HAMLET   As thou'rt a man,

    Give me the cup! Let go! By heaven, I'll ha't.

    Oh, God, Horatio, what a wounded name,

    Things standing thus unknown, shall I leave behind me!

    If thou didst ever hold me in thy heart,

    Absent thee from felicity awhile,

    And in this harsh world draw thy breath in pain

    To tell my story. A march afar off *[and a volley within]*.

    What warlike noise is this?

   Enter Osric.

OSRIC Young Fortinbras, with conquest come from Poland,

    To th'ambassadors of England gives

    This warlike volley.

HAMLET   Oh, I die, Horatio!

    The potent poison quite o'ercrows my spirit.   355

    I cannot live to hear the news from England,

    But I do prophesy th'election lights

---

328 union pearl. (See line 270; with grim puns on the word's other meanings: marriage, shared death.) **330 tempered** mixed **336 chance** mischance **337 mutes** silent observers. (Literally, actors with nonspeaking parts.) **338 fell sergeant** remorseless arresting officer **339 strict** (1) severely just (2) unavoidable. **arrest** (1) taking into custody (2) stopping my speech **343 Roman** (Suicide was an honorable choice for many Romans as an alternative to a dishonorable life.) **355 o'ercrows** triumphs over (like the winner in a cockfight)

On Fortinbras. He has my dying voice. 358
So tell him, with th'occurrents more and less 359
Which have solicited. The rest is silence. [*He dies.*] 360
HORATIO Now cracks a noble heart. Good night, sweet prince,
And flights of angels sing thee to thy rest!

[*March within.*]

Why does the drum come hither?

Enter Fortinbras, *with the [English] Ambassadors [with drum, colors, and attendants].*

FORTINBRAS   Where is this sight?
HORATIO What is it you would see?
If aught of woe or wonder, cease your search.
FORTINBRAS This quarry cries on havoc. O proud Death, 366
What feast is toward in thine eternal cell, 367
That thou so many princes at a shot
So bloodily hast struck?
FIRST AMBASSADOR   The sight is dismal,
And our affairs from England come too late.
The ears are senseless that should give us hearing,
To tell him his commandment is fulfilled,
That Rosencrantz and Guildenstern are dead.
Where should we have our thanks?
HORATIO   Not from his mouth, 374
Had it th'ability of life to thank you.
He never gave commandment for their death.
But since, so jump upon this bloody question, 377
You from the Polack wars and you from England
Are here arrived, give order that these bodies
High on a stage be placèd to the view, 380
And let me speak to th' yet unknowing world
How these things came about. So shall you hear
Of carnal, bloody, and unnatural acts,
Of accidental judgments, casual slaughters, 384
Of deaths put on by cunning and forced cause, 385
And, in this upshot, purposes mistook
Fall'n on th'inventors' heads. All this can I
Truly deliver.
FORTINBRAS Let us haste to hear it,
And call the noblest to the audience.
For me, with sorrow I embrace my fortune.

---

358 voice vote. **359 th'occurrents** the events, incidents **360 solicited** moved, urged. (Hamlet doesn't finish saying what the events have prompted—presumably, his acts of vengeance, or his reporting of those events to Fortinbras.) **366 This . . . havoc** This heap of dead bodies loudly proclaims a general slaughter. **367 feast** i.e., Death feasting on those who have fallen. **toward** in preparation **374 his** Claudius's **377 so jump . . . question** so hard on the heels of this bloody business **380 stage** platform **384 judgments** retributions. **casual** occurring by chance **385 put on** instigated. **forced cause** contrivance

I have some rights of memory in this kingdom,   391
  Which now to claim my vantage doth invite me.   392
HORATIO Of that I shall have also cause to speak,
  And from his mouth whose voice will draw on more.   394
  But let this same be presently performed,   395
  Even while men's minds are wild, lest more mischance
  On plots and errors happen.
FORTINBRAS   Let four captains   397
  Bear Hamlet, like a soldier, to the stage,
  For he was likely, had he been put on,   399
  To have proved most royal; and for his passage,   400
  The soldiers' music and the rite of war
  Speak loudly for him.   402
  Take up the bodies. Such a sight as this
  Becomes the field, but here shows much amiss.   404
  Go bid the soldiers shoot.

  Exeunt [marching, bearing off the dead bodies; a peal of ordnance is shot off].

---

391 **of memory** traditional, remembered, unforgotten 392 **vantage** favorable opportunity 394 **voice
. . . more** vote will influence still others. 395 **presently** immediately 397 **On** on top of 399 **put on**
i.e., invested in royal office and so put to the test 400 **for his passage** to mark his passing 402 **Speak**
(let them) speak 404 **Becomes the field** suits the field of battle

INSPIRATION   STOPPARD'S *ROSENCRANTZ AND GUILDENSTERN ARE DEAD*

After reading *Hamlet*, you would likely not even remember the characters
Rosencrantz and Guildenstern, friends of Hamlet. In Tom Stoppard's play
Rosencrantz and Guildenstern Are Dead, however, those minor courtiers are the
main characters, whose silly musings we follow while Prince Hamlet's tragedy
occurs slightly offstage. Often compared to the existential style of Samuel Beckett's *Waiting for Godot*, *Rosencrantz and Guildenstern Are Dead* shows how Hamlet's two friends wander through life with little sense of fate or purpose. The play
opens with Guildenstern obsessed with the fact that the coin he has been flipping has come up heads eighty-five times. While he searches for meaning and
keeps flipping heads, Rosencrantz thinks it meaningless. The play is full of
games, tricks, and double entendres that the two title characters search for
meaning. (Stoppard is also one of the creators of another re-envisioning of
Shakespeare's work: the 1998 award-winning film *Shakespeare in Love*.)

Talking about the Text

1. How do the different characters in the opening scene of *Hamlet* react to the ghost
   of Hamlet's father?

2. Why does Hamlet take so long to act? (In group discussion, note the many plausible answers to this simple question.)
3. What do you think of the advice Polonius gives? How would you direct an actor to play him?
4. Explain how the play within the play works: why Hamlet creates it, how it is acted, and how its audience reacts.
5. Why does Ophelia kill herself?
6. What might Yorick's skull be a symbol of?
7. How does Gertrude change over the course of the play?
8. Discuss the role of pretense in *Hamlet*, since so many of the characters are playing a role: Claudius about the murder; Hamlet about his suspicions and his love for Ophelia; Rosencrantz and Guildenstern about their mission; Gertrude about her late husband.

Writing about the Text

1. Horatio seems to be both Hamlet's friend and someone who possesses character traits Hamlet lacks. Trace the ways Hamlet and Horatio are mirror images.
2. Explain the transition from the dying Hamlet (5.2.319–end) to the newly arrived Fortinbras. In what ways is this an appropriate ending for the play?

Linking the Text to Other Texts

1. In what ways is Hamlet a Renaissance wit, one clever enough to have written some of the most eloquent love poetry written in the age? What in Hamlet's language of love connects with the love poems on pp. 941–952?
2. Compare four different versions of Hamlet's "To be or not to be": John Barrymore's (available only in audio form), Laurence Olivier's, Nicol Williamson's, and Kenneth Branagh's. Discuss how each version stems from a distinctly different type of Hamlet.

✒ COMMENTARY

Danitra Vance's Response to Shakespeare

The delightful intervention Flotilda Williams as Juliet *demonstrates the reach of the Shakespearean performance as well as illustrates a link between one of Shakespeare's early plays and the intense love poetry of Shakespeare's time. The piece was written and performed by Danitra Vance, who is perhaps most widely known for her single year on Saturday Night Live in 1985, though many think her best work was done in New York's off-Broadway performance scene in the late 1980s and early 1990s.*

Vance got her start doing inventive experimental theater in Chicago and then at the off-off-Broadway Café La MaMa. Her early one-woman shows mixed music and topical comedy that she both wrote and performed. Later, with the playwright and director George Wolfe, she won awards acting in his productions of The Colored Museum *(1986) and* Spunk *(1991), the latter of which was based on three Zora Neale Hurston short stories, "Sweat" (see p. 318), "Story in Harlem Slang," and "The Gilded Six Bits."*

Vance also had small roles in films, including Sticky Fingers *(1988) and* The War of the Roses *(1989), and a larger role in* Jumpin' at the Boneyard *(1992). When Vance was diagnosed with breast cancer, she turned her experience into theater with* The Radical Girl's Guide to Radical Mastectomy *(1991). She died in 1994 at age thirty-five.* Flotilda Williams as Juliet *first appeared in* Live and in Color *(1991). Another of Vance's Flotilda pieces appears in* Contemporary American Monologues for Women.

DANITRA VANCE
(1959–1994)

Flotilda Williams as Juliet
(1991)

I'm Flotilda Williams. I'm a classical actress. Right now I am in a production downtown with a group called Shakespeare in the Slums. We are doing a play by Mister William Shakespeares call *Romeo and Juliet*. And me, I'm Juliet, okay. Now what I want to do for y'all is to extrapolate and explainate on what be going on in the show. The show starts and a lot of things happen but really we just gonna skip all that and get to the good part, where I come in.

I'm at this party, a lot of fancy people there and I'm there and I'm there with my Mama and the Nurse. Even so, I manage to meet this guy. A very good-lookin' guy, makes me laugh with his funny, funny jokes, probably got some money. So I like him. His name is Romeo. I have thus extrapolated the title—Romeo and me, Juliet, okay.

Anyway the party is not even half over when my Mama and the Nurse say, "Juliet it's time to go." And I say, "Okay, I'll be right with you." So she find Romeo and they say goodbye by touching fingertips like this (Gesture) completely missing the point.

After that I go home and I'm trying to be asleep but I can't sleep 'cause I'm thinkin' 'bout this guy. How much I want to see him again. How much I want to talk to him again. How much I want to do things with him I've never done before.

Now in the meantime the guy, Romeo, is down in the alleyway lookin' up in my window. Now he not lookin' up in my window because he a freak or nothin' like that, he lookin' up in my window because he like me, okay. Then he start to talk to hisself. Now he not talkin' to hisself 'cause he crazy or nothin', he talk to hisself 'cause it's a play, okay. People in plays talk to theyselves a lot.

And he say, he say,
"But soft! what light throo yonder windo' break?"
That's when I break through the window.

It's nighttime and I'm on my back porch and I'm in a really bad mood because of this whole situation. And I say my first line and stomp my foot and say,
"Ay me!
O, Romeo, Romeo! wherefore art thou Romeo?"
Wherefore mean why. She sayin' why, why, why you gots to be Romeo?
Wherefore art thou Romeo!!!

"Deny thy father and refuse thy name;
Or, if thou wilt not, be but sworn my love
And I'll no longer be a Capsulet."
And she thinking,
"'Tis but thy name that is my enemy
Thou art thyself, though not a Montagoo."

What's a Montagoo?

"It is nor hand, nor foot,
Nor arm nor face, nor any other part
Belonging to a man."

You know what she talking about. So she say,
"Romeo, doff thy name,
And for that name which is no part of thee
Take all myself."

Juliet was hip, you dig. She had it going on and she was down. So anyway, you know their families had a kinda Family Feud-type thing going on. Juliet family, maybe like the Crypts and Romeo people could be like the Bloods, you know what I'm saying. And Romeo is not like Michael Jackson, he's a lover and a fighter, okay. Then she see him down in the alleyway and they talk and talk all lovey-dovey, lovey-dovey—back and forth, back and forth, beat beat, beat beat. They got a passionate blood flow going back and forth. I got really good reviews on this part. Spend some money, get some culture.

Then she say to him,
"My bounty is as boundless as the sea,
My love as deep; the more I give to thee,
The more I have, for both are infinite.
(Hears noise)
I hear some noise within, dear love, adieu."
That mean 'bye.
"Anon, good Nurse!"
That mean I'll be right with you, Nurse.
"Sweet Montagoo, be true.
Stay but a little, I will come again."

Then she gone. Then she come right back but she has to be really quiet 'cause her Mama 'n' Daddy can't stand his Mama 'n' Daddy 'n' his Mama 'n' Daddy can't stand her Mama 'n' Daddy. So they have to be really, really quiet 'cause if they catch them together, they'll kill him 'n' her, too. So she say, she say,
"Three words dear Romeo, and good night indeed.
If that thy bent of love be honorable,
Thy purpose marriage, send me word tomorrow,
By one that I'll procure to come to thee,
Where and at what time thou wilt perform the rite."
That mean marry me, marry me,
I'm not giving up nothin' till you marry me.
"And all my fortunes at thy foot I'll lay
And follow thee, my lord, throughout the world.
(Hears noise)
I come anon—But if thou mean'st not well
I do beseech thee
(Noise)
By and by, I come—
To cease thy suit and leave me to my grief."
That mean if you not gonna marry me, don't mess with my mind. I can find
    somebody else.
"A thousand times good night."

Then she gone again. This time she gone but a little bit longer because she had to talk to her Mama 'n' the Nurse. I don't know why she had to talk to the Nurse 'cause you know she not sick.

She back as soon as she can but she can't see Romeo. But she know he gotta be out there somewhere 'cause they got that passionate blood flow going back and forth, back and forth and she can feel him out there beatin' in the night. What she want to do is holler, "Yo, Romeo, where you at?" But she can't do that because Juliet is a very dignified girl, and hollerin' off the back porch is a very iginant thing to do. So she say, she say,
"Romeo, hist, Romeo."
Then she see him.
"'Tis almost morning. I would have thee gone
And yet no further than a wanton's bird
Who lets it hop a little from her hand
Like a poor prisoner in her twisted gyves
And with a silk thread plucks it back again
So loving-jealous of his liberty."
I don't know what that part mean.
Then she say,
"Good night. Good night! Parting is such sweet sorrow
That I shall say good night till it be morrow."

(She exits.)

Talking about the Text

1. What attitudes toward Shakespeare's language do you share with Flotilda?
2. How would you go about convincing Flotilda that she can handle this dialogue? What would you say?
3. What is "overdone" about Flotilda? What seems similarly "overdone" about Romeo and Juliet? About Hamlet? Exactly what qualities do these characters share? Is Vance aware of this, do you think? How do you know?

Writing about the Text

1. Write your own Flotilda-type piece about an actor having to play one of the big scenes from *Hamlet*.
2. Rewrite a *Hamlet* soliloquy or short scene in a different variety of English: hipster, rapper, bureaucrat, Hollywood type—any variety of English you are comfortable using.
3. Summarize the plot of *Hamlet* in a single paragraph.

Linking the Text to Other Texts

1. You can see Danitra Vance on a *Saturday Night Live* highlight tape. (Her performances are from November 9 and 23, 1985; February 8, 1986; and April 19, 1986.) Which of her characteristics seem present in the Flotilda Williams monologue?
2. What current performer (star or not) does Vance seem most like?

VIRTUAL LOCALE

Shakespeare on the Web. With so many Shakespeare scholars and fans out there, the Internet has become a great place to learn about Shakespeare's life and works or get ideas for a research paper. At the website of the Internet Shakespeare Editions from the University of Victoria, British Columbia, in Canada, at *http://ise.uvic.ca/index.html*, readers can browse dozens of electronic manuscript pages of different folios, or get information on thousands of performances across the world.

At Mr. Shakespeare and the Internet, *http://shakespeare.palomar.edu*, Professor Terry Gray has made it his mission to index nearly everything available on the Web about Shakespeare. From criticism to Renaissance costumes to the latest authorship debate, this website is a great place to start your research.

In 1997, graduate student J. M. Pressley conceived the idea of centralizing international resources on Shakespeare in one place. The Shakespeare Resource Center at *http://www.bardweb.net* gathers information on the playwright, his theater, his works, and contemporary theater companies.

Starting Points for Further Research: William Shakespeare

- **Edition:** William Shakespeare. *The Complete Works of Shakespeare*. Ed. David Bevington. New York: Longman, 2004.
- **Biographies:** Dominic Shellard. *William Shakespeare*. New York: Oxford University Press, 1998.
  Stephen Greenblatt. *Will in the World: How Shakespeare Became Shakespeare*. New York: W. W. Norton, 2004.
- **Criticism:** Harold Bloom. *Shakespeare: The Invention of the Human*. New York: Riverhead, 1998.

C H A P T E R

24

Drama Becomes Modern

About 150 years ago, in the mid-nineteenth century, Western drama became modern. It did so by taking two enormous steps: it moved its characters, situations, scenes, and costumes away from rich aristocrats and toward the newly dominant middle class, and it moved its language away from the "high" talk of poetry to something approaching the language of the middle-class people who were attending the plays.

In the eighteenth century and before, dramatists had tended to focus much more on the high born: on kings and nobles, as we see in Shakespeare's plays in the last chapter or in the works of French playwrights Racine and Corneille or German playwrights Schiller and Goethe. These great writers fashioned their plots according to Aristotelian principles, which mandated that true tragic theater depict higher-class heroes drawn from history or from classical mythology. It was only in comedy that one found fuller representations of "low" as well as middle-class characters. But even in the work of brilliant French dramatists like Molière (author of *Tartuffe* and *The Bourgeois Gentilhomme*) and Beaumarchais (author of *The Barber of Seville* and *The Marriage of Figaro*), the middle class was depicted against the standards of the aristocrats whose homes and estates formed most of the settings. In the 1600s, the European middle class was rising, but not until the 1800s would the middle class attain political as well as cultural dominance. Until that happened, classic, premodern theater was supported by the rich aristocracy, though attended by all who could afford to buy a ticket. In England after Shakespeare and in France, Italy, and Germany, the theaters were dominated by the well-to-do, and consequently the plays usually involved their activities and attitudes, including an "elevated" language befitting their station in life.

1560

A sweeping change came to mid-nineteenth-century theater when writers like Henrik Ibsen, Ivan Turgenev, and Anton Chekhov began focusing almost exclusively on life among middle-class people, demonstrating that ordinary lives had a potential for the highest kind of drama, that is, tragedy. It is no accident that this was just the time when novels were also depicting middle-class lives as full of conflict. As the growing middle class came to dominate book buying and theater going, they often preferred to patronize the dramas that depicted their lives. The subject matter of these dramas—relationships among the sexes, the conflict between duty to self and duty to society, loyalty to friends—was not always far removed from the traditional themes of classical dramas, but the characters, settings, and language definitely were.

During this time drama also changed in another, more fundamental way. Along with a focus on middle-class issues came a change in the way drama was performed on the stage. It became more "realistic," with serious efforts to depict the way ordinary people lived their lives. Scenery became more and more "true to life," and actors no longer addressed the audience directly in soliloquies but spoke to each other as in real life. High-flown sentiments did not disappear, and the drama was still intricately plotted and artistically acted, but plays were no longer presented in exquisitely crafted verse. Prose, not poetry, would be the main medium of this realistic theater.

IBSEN AND REALISM IN THE THEATER

Henrik Ibsen in middle age.

The Norwegian playwright Henrik Ibsen (1828–1906) was the person most responsible for the modernist sea change in drama. He was born in a provincial Norwegian town and at age sixteen was apprenticed to a pharmacist, but early on he was attracted to the theater, and he began writing dramas in his twenties. His plays were first staged in Norway in 1851, then in Germany (where he was given more artistic freedom and found great success), and then throughout the world. His early plays, in verse, made use of traditional mythology; in his plays from 1869 on, he turned away from versified folklore and history toward prose and social issues: politics, business, marriage, syphilis, and pollution of the public water supply. It was the plays of this later period, including such works as *The Pillars of Society* (1877), *A Doll House* (1879), *An Enemy of the People* (1892), *The Wild Duck* (1884), and *Hedda Gabler* (1890), that helped bring about the modern realistic theater.

All the social issues in the plays presented were "dramatized," that is, seen as inevitable conflicts between characters representing different and widely held perspectives. For example, Ibsen frequently placed a single character as a truth teller against the norms of good society. Thus, in *An Enemy of the People*, the doctor learns that a resort town's water is contaminated, but the town fathers, afraid of losing the business brought by tourists, want the news suppressed. (This scenario should sound familiar; replace the contaminated water with a shark, and you have the basic plot of *Jaws*.)

This series of plays dramatizing social problems made Ibsen famous all over the world. He showed how theater could take on pressing current issues, excitingly, provocatively. These were not plays with a crude message and a simple response to the issues. But they did have a strong point of view: today's problems can be the material for stirring drama. You do not need kings and myths to see passionate, meaningful conflict. It can take place even in a middle-class home, in which a seemingly unserious, pretty young mother comes to the momentous realization that her marriage has all along been a sham, as we will see in *A Doll House*.

LITERARY LOCALE

The Ibsen Museum in Oslo, Norway. Ibsen's home for the last decade of his life is now the Ibsen Museum in Oslo. It is completely restored, and his study is just as it was when he wrote his last two plays, *John Gabriel Borkman* (1896) and *When We Dead Awaken* (1899), there. The museum offers biographical information, lectures, audio-visual exhibitions, guided tours, and theater performances. For more information, go to the museum's website at *http://www. museumsnett.no/ibsen/oslo/osloen.html.*

HENRIK IBSEN

(1828–1906)

A Doll House

(1879)

Translated by Rolf Fjelde

Note: Some translations call Ibsen's play A Doll House, *others* A Doll's House.

The Characters

Torvald Helmer, a lawyer
Nora, his wife
Dr. Rank
Mrs. Linde
Nils Krogstad, a bank clerk

The Helmers' three small children
Anne-Marie, their nurse
Helene, a maid
A Delivery Boy

Scene: The action takes place in Helmer's residence.

Act One

A comfortable room, tastefully but not expensively furnished. A door to the right in the back wall leads to the entryway; another to the left leads to HELMER'S *study. Between these doors, a piano. Midway in the left-hand wall a door, and further back a window. Near the window a round table with an armchair and a small sofa. In the right-hand wall, toward the rear, a door, and nearer the foreground a porcelain stove with two armchairs and a rocking chair beside it. Between the stove and the side door, a small table. Engravings on the walls. An etagère with china figures and other small art objects; a small bookcase with richly bound books; the floor carpeted; a fire burning in the stove. It is a winter day.*

A bell rings in the entryway; shortly after we hear the door being unlocked. NORA *comes into the room, humming happily to herself; she is wearing street clothes and carries an armload of packages, which she puts down on the table to the right. She has left the hall door open; and through it a* DELIVERY BOY *is seen, holding a Christmas tree and a basket, which he gives to the* MAID *who let them in.*

NORA. Hide the tree well, Helene. The children mustn't get a glimpse of it till this evening, after it's trimmed. (*To the* DELIVERY BOY, *taking out her purse.*) How much?

DELIVERY BOY. Fifty, ma'am.

NORA. There's a crown. No, keep the change. (*The* BOY *thanks her and leaves.* NORA *shuts the door. She laughs softly to herself while taking off her street things. Drawing a bag of macaroons from her pocket, she eats a couple, then steals over and listens at her husband's study door.*) Yes, he's home. (*Hums again as she moves to the table right.*)

HELMER (*from the study*). Is that my little lark twittering out there?

NORA (*busy opening some packages*). Yes, it is.

HELMER. Is that my squirrel rummaging around?

NORA. Yes!

HELMER. When did my squirrel get in?

NORA. Just now. (*Putting the macaroon bag in her pocket and wiping her mouth.*) Do come in, Torvald, and see what I've bought.

HELMER. Can't be disturbed. (*After a moment he opens the door and peers in, pen in hand.*) Bought, you say? All that there? Has the little spendthrift been out throwing money around again?

NORA. Oh, but Torvald, this year we really should let ourselves go a bit. It's the first Christmas we haven't had to economize.

HELMER. But you know we can't go squandering.

NORA. Oh yes, Torvald, we can squander a little now. Can't we? Just a tiny, wee bit. Now that you've got a big salary and are going to make piles and piles of money.

HELMER. Yes—starting New Year's. But then it's a full three months till the raise comes through.

NORA. Pooh! We can borrow that long.

HELMER. Nora! (*Goes over and playfully takes her by the ear.*) Are your scatter-brains off again? What if today I borrowed a thousand crowns, and you squandered them over Christmas week, and then on New Year's Eve a roof tile fell on my head, and I lay there—

NORA (*putting her hand on his mouth*). Oh! Don't say such things!

HELMER. Yes, but what if it happened—then what?

NORA. If anything so awful happened, then it just wouldn't matter if I had debts or not.

HELMER. Well, but the people I'd borrowed from?

NORA. Them? Who cares about them! They're strangers.

HELMER. Nora, Nora, how like a woman! No, but seriously, Nora, you know what I think about that. No debts! Never borrow! Something of freedom's lost—and something of beauty, too—from a home that's founded on borrowing and debt. We've made a brave stand up to now, the two of us; and we'll go right on like that the little while we have to.

NORA (*going toward the stove*). Yes, whatever you say, Torvald.

HELMER (*following her*). Now, now, the little lark's wings mustn't droop. Come on, don't be a sulky squirrel. (*Taking out his wallet.*) Nora, guess what I have here.

NORA (*turning quickly*). Money!

HELMER. There, see. (*Hands her some notes.*) Good grief, I know how costs go up in a house at Christmastime.

NORA. Ten—twenty—thirty—forty. Oh, thank you, Torvald; I can manage no end on this.

HELMER. You really will have to.

NORA. Oh yes, I promise I will! But come here so I can show you everything I bought. And so cheap! Look, new clothes for Ivar here—and a sword. Here a horse and a trumpet for Bob. And a doll and a doll's bed here for Emmy; they're nothing much, but she'll tear them to bits in no time anyway. And here I have dress material and handkerchiefs for the maids. Old Anne-Marie really deserves something more.

HELMER. And what's in that package there?

NORA (*with a cry*). Torvald, no! You can't see that till tonight!

HELMER. I see. But tell me now, you little prodigal, what have you thought of for yourself?

NORA. For myself? Oh, I don't want anything at all.

HELMER. Of course you do. Tell me just what—within reason—you'd most like to have.

NORA. I honestly don't know. Oh, listen, Torvald—

HELMER. Well?

NORA (*fumbling at his coat buttons, without looking at him*). If you want to give me something, then maybe you could—you could—

HELMER. Come on, out with it.

NORA (*hurriedly*). You could give me money, Torvald. No more than you think you can spare; then one of these days I'll buy something with it.

HELMER. But Nora—

NORA. Oh, please, Torvald darling, do that! I beg you, please. Then I could hang the bills in pretty gilt paper on the Christmas tree. Wouldn't that be fun?

HELMER. What are those little birds called that always fly through their fortunes?

NORA. Oh yes, spendthrifts; I know all that. But let's do as I say, Torvald; then I'll have time to decide what I really need most. That's very sensible, isn't it?

HELMER (*smiling*). Yes, very—that is, if you actually hung onto the money I give you, and you actually used it to buy yourself something. But it goes for the house and for all sorts of foolish things, and then I only have to lay out some more.

NORA. Oh, but Torvald—

HELMER. Don't deny it, my dear little Nora. (*Putting his arm around her waist.*) Spendthrifts are sweet, but they use up a frightful amount of money. It's incredible what it costs a man to feed such birds.

NORA. Oh, how can you say that! Really, I save everything I can.

HELMER (*laughing*). Yes, that's the truth. Everything you can. But that's nothing at all.

NORA (*humming, with a smile of quiet satisfaction*). Hm, if you only knew what expenses we larks and squirrels have, Torvald.

HELMER. You're an odd little one. Exactly the way your father was. You're never at a loss for scaring up money; but the moment you have it, it runs right out through your fingers; you never know what you've done with it. Well, one takes you as you are. It's deep in your blood. Yes, these things are hereditary, Nora.

NORA. Ah, I could wish I'd inherited many of Papa's qualities.

HELMER. And I couldn't wish you anything but just what you are, my sweet little lark. But wait; it seems to me you have a very—what should I call it?—a very suspicious look today—

NORA. I do?

HELMER. You certainly do. Look me straight in the eye.

NORA (*looking at him*). Well?

HELMER (*shaking an admonitory finger*). Surely my sweet tooth hasn't been running riot in town today, has she?

NORA. No. Why do you imagine that?

HELMER. My sweet tooth really didn't make a little detour through the confectioner's?

NORA. No, I assure you, Torvald—

HELMER. Hasn't nibbled some pastry?

NORA. No, not at all.

HELMER. Not even munched a macaroon or two?

NORA. No, Torvald, I assure you, really—

HELMER. There, there now. Of course I'm only joking.

NORA (*going to the table, right*). You know I could never think of going against you.

HELMER. No, I understand that; and you *have* given me your word. (*Going over to her.*) Well, you keep your little Christmas secrets to yourself, Nora darling. I expect they'll come to light this evening, when the tree is lit.

NORA. Did you remember to ask Dr. Rank?

HELMER. No. But there's no need for that; it's assumed he'll be dining with us. All the same, I'll ask him when he stops by here this morning. I've ordered some fine wine. Nora, you can't imagine how I'm looking forward to this evening.

NORA. So am I. And what fun for the children, Torvald!

HELMER. Ah, it's so gratifying to know that one's gotten a safe, secure job, and with a comfortable salary. It's a great satisfaction, isn't it?

NORA. Oh, it's wonderful!

HELMER. Remember last Christmas? Three whole weeks before, you shut yourself in every evening till long after midnight, making flowers for the Christmas tree, and all the other decorations to surprise us. Ugh, that was the dullest time I've ever lived through.

NORA. It wasn't at all dull for me.

HELMER (*smiling*). But the outcome *was* pretty sorry, Nora.

NORA. Oh, don't tease me with that again. How could I help it that the cat came in and tore everything to shreds.

HELMER. No, poor thing, you certainly couldn't. You wanted so much to please us all, and that's what counts. But it's just as well that the hard times are past.

NORA. Yes, it's really wonderful.

HELMER. Now I don't have to sit here alone, boring myself, and you don't have to tire your precious eyes and your fair little delicate hands—

NORA (*clapping her hands*). No, is it really true, Torvald, I don't have to? Oh, how wonderfully lovely to hear! (*Taking his arm.*) Now I'll tell you just how I've thought we should plan things. Right after Christmas—(*The doorbell rings.*) Oh, the bell. (*Straightening the room up a bit.*) Somebody would have to come. What a bore!

HELMER. I'm not at home to visitors, don't forget.

MAID (*from the hall doorway*). Ma'am, a lady to see you—

NORA. All right, let her come in.

MAID (*to* HELMER). And the doctor's just come too.

HELMER. Did he go right to my study?

MAID. Yes, he did.

> (HELMER *goes into his room. The* MAID *shows in* MRS. LINDE, *dressed in traveling clothes, and shuts the door after her.*)

MRS. LINDE (*in a dispirited and somewhat hesitant voice*). Hello, Nora.

NORA. (*uncertain*). Hello—

MRS. LINDE. You don't recognize me.

NORA. No, I don't know—but wait, I think—(*Exclaiming.*) What! Kristine! Is it really you?

MRS. LINDE. Yes, it's me.

NORA. Kristine! To think I didn't recognize you. But then, how could I? (*More quietly.*) How you've changed, Kristine!

MRS. LINDE. Yes, no doubt I have. In nine—ten long years.

NORA. Is it so long since we met! Yes, it's all of that. Oh, these last eight years have been a happy time, believe me. And so now you've come in to town, too. Made the long trip in the winter. That took courage.

MRS. LINDE. I just got here by ship this morning.

NORA. To enjoy yourself over Christmas, of course. Oh, how lovely! Yes, enjoy ourselves, we'll do that. But take your coat off. You're not still cold? (*Helping her.*) There now, let's get cozy here by the stove. No, the easy chair there! I'll take the rocker here. (*Seizing her hands.*) Yes, now you have your old look again; it was only in that first moment. You're a bit more pale, Kristine—and maybe a bit thinner.

MRS. LINDE. And much, much older, Nora.

NORA. Yes, perhaps a bit older; a tiny, tiny bit; not much at all. (*Stopping short; suddenly serious.*) Oh, but thoughtless me, to sit here, chattering away. Sweet, good Kristine, can you forgive me?

MRS. LINDE. What do you mean, Nora?

NORA (*softly*). Poor Kristine, you've become a widow.

MRS. LINDE. Yes, three years ago.

NORA. Oh, I knew it, of course; I read it in the papers. Oh, Kristine, you must believe me; I often thought of writing you then, but I kept postponing it, and something always interfered.

MRS. LINDE. Nora dear, I understand completely.

NORA. No, it was awful of me, Kristine. You poor thing, how much you must have gone through. And he left you nothing?

MRS. LINDE. No.

NORA. And no children?

MRS. LINDE. No.

NORA. Nothing at all, then?

MRS. LINDE. Not even a sense of loss to feed on.

NORA (*looking incredulously at her*). But Kristine, how could that be?

MRS. LINDE (*smiling wearily and smoothing her hair*). Oh, sometimes it happens, Nora.

NORA. So completely alone. How terribly hard that must be for you. I have three lovely children. You can't see them now: they're out with the maid. But now you must tell me everything—

MRS. LINDE. No, no, no, tell me about yourself.

NORA. No, you begin. Today I don't want to be selfish. I want to think only of you today. But there *is* something I must tell you. Did you hear of the wonderful luck we had recently?

MRS. LINDE. No, what's that?

NORA. My husband's been made manager in the bank, just think!

MRS. LINDE. Your husband? How marvelous!

NORA. Isn't it? Being a lawyer is such an uncertain living, you know, especially if one won't touch any cases that aren't clean and decent. And of course Torvald would never do that, and I'm with him completely there. Oh, we're simply delighted, believe me! He'll join the bank right after New Year's and start getting a huge salary and lots of commissions. From now on we can live quite differently—just as we want. Oh, Kristine, I feel so light and happy! Won't it be lovely to have stacks of money and not a care in the world?

MRS. LINDE. Well, anyway, it would be lovely to have enough for necessities.

NORA. No, not just for necessities, but stacks and stacks of money!

MRS. LINDE (*smiling*). Nora, Nora, aren't you sensible yet? Back in school you were such a free spender.

NORA (*with a quiet laugh*). Yes, that's what Torvald still says. (*Shaking her finger.*) But "Nora, Nora" isn't as silly as you all think. Really, we've been in no position for me to go squandering. We've had to work, both of us.

MRS. LINDE. You too?

NORA. Yes, at odd jobs—needlework, crocheting, embroidery, and such—(*Casually.*) and other things too. You remember that Torvald left the department when we were married? There was no chance of promotion in his office, and of course he needed to earn more money. But that first year he drove himself terribly. He took on all kinds of extra work that kept him going morning and night. It wore him down, and then he fell deathly ill. The doctors said it was essential for him to travel south.

MRS. LINDE. Yes, didn't you spend a whole year in Italy?

NORA. That's right. It wasn't easy to get away, you know. Ivar had just been born. But of course we had to go. Oh, that was a beautiful trip, and it saved Torvald's life. But it cost a frightful sum, Kristine.

MRS. LINDE. I can well imagine.

NORA. Four thousand, eight hundred crowns it cost. That's really a lot of money.

MRS. LINDE. But it's lucky you had it when you needed it.

NORA. Well, as it was, we got it from Papa.

MRS. LINDE. I see. It was just about the time your father died.

NORA. Yes, just about then. And, you know, I couldn't make that trip out to nurse him. I had to stay here, expecting Ivar any moment, and with my poor sick Torvald to care for. Dearest Papa, I never saw him again, Kristine. Oh, that was the worst time I've known in all my marriage.

MRS. LINDE. I know how you loved him. And then you went off to Italy?

NORA. Yes. We had the means now, and the doctors urged us. So we left a month after.

MRS. LINDE. And your husband came back completely cured?

NORA. Sound as a drum!

MRS. LINDE. But—the doctor?

NORA. Who?

MRS. LINDE. I thought the maid said he was a doctor, the man who came in with me.

NORA. Yes, that was Dr. Rank—but he's not making a sick call. He's our closest friend, and he stops by at least once a day. No, Torvald hasn't had a sick moment since, and the children are fit and strong, and I am, too. (*Jumping up and clapping her hands.*) Oh, dear God, Kristine, what a lovely thing to live and be happy! But how disgusting of me—I'm talking of nothing but my own affairs. (*Sits on a stool close by* KRISTINE, *arms resting across her knees.*) Oh, don't be angry with me! Tell me, is it really true that you weren't in love with your husband? Why did you marry him, then?

MRS. LINDE. My mother was still alive, but bedridden and helpless—and I had my two younger brothers to look after. In all conscience, I didn't think I could turn him down.

NORA. No, you were right there. But was he rich at the time?

MRS. LINDE. He was very well off, I'd say. But the business was shaky, Nora. When he died, it all fell apart, and nothing was left.

NORA. And then—?

MRS. LINDE. Yes, so I had to scrape up a living with a little shop and a little teaching and whatever else I could find. The last three years have been like one endless workday without a rest for me. Now it's over, Nora. My poor mother doesn't need me, for she's passed on. Nor the boys, either; they're working now and can take care of themselves.

NORA. How free you must feel—

MRS. LINDE. No—only unspeakably empty. Nothing to live for now. (*Standing up anxiously.*) That's why I couldn't take it any longer out in that desolate hole. Maybe here it'll be easier to find something to do and keep my mind occupied. If I could only be lucky enough to get a steady job, some office work—

NORA. Oh, but Kristine, that's so dreadfully tiring, and you already look so tired. It would be much better for you if you could go off to a bathing resort.

MRS. LINDE (*going toward the window*). I have no father to give me travel money, Nora.

NORA (*rising*). Oh, don't be angry with me.

MRS. LINDE (*going to her*). Nora dear, don't you be angry with me. The worst of my kind of situation is all the bitterness that's stored away. No one to work for, and yet you're always having to snap up your opportunities. You have to live; and so you grow selfish. When you told me the happy change in your lot, do you know I was delighted less for your sakes than for mine?

NORA. How so? Oh, I see. You think maybe Torvald could do something for you.

MRS. LINDE. Yes, that's what I thought.

NORA. And he will, Kristine! Just leave it to me; I'll bring it up so delicately— find something attractive to humor him with. Oh, I'm so eager to help you.

MRS. LINDE. How very kind of you, Nora, to be so concerned over me—doubly kind, considering you really know so little of life's burdens yourself.

NORA. I—? I know so little—?

MRS. LINDE (*smiling*). Well, my heavens—a little needle-work and such—Nora, you're just a child.

NORA (*tossing her head and pacing the floor*). You don't have to act so superior.

MRS. LINDE. Oh?

NORA. You're just like the others. You all think I'm incapable of anything serious—

MRS. LINDE. Come now—

NORA. That I've never had to face the raw world.

MRS. LINDE. Nora dear, you've just been telling me all your troubles.

NORA. Hm! Trivia! (*Quietly.*) I haven't told you the big thing.

MRS. LINDE. Big thing? What do you mean?

NORA. You look down on me so, Kristine, but you shouldn't. You're proud that you worked so long and hard for your mother.

MRS. LINDE. I don't look down on a soul. But it *is* true: I'm proud—and happy, too—to think it was given to me to make my mother's last days almost free of care.

NORA. And you're also proud thinking of what you've done for your brothers.

MRS. LINDE. I feel I've a right to be.

NORA. I agree. But listen to this, Kristine—I've also got something to be proud and happy for.

MRS. LINDE. I don't doubt it. But whatever do you mean?

NORA. Not so loud. What if Torvald heard! He mustn't, not for anything in the world. Nobody must know, Kristine. No one but you.

MRS. LINDE. But what is it, then?

NORA. Come here. (*Drawing her down beside her on the sofa.*) It's true—I've also got something to be proud and happy for. I'm the one who saved Torvald's life.

MRS. LINDE. Saved—? Saved how?

NORA. I told you about the trip to Italy. Torvald never would have lived if he hadn't gone south—

MRS. LINDE. Of course; your father gave you the means—

NORA (*smiling*). That's what Torvald and all the rest think, but—

MRS. LINDE. But—?

NORA. Papa didn't give us a pin. I was the one who raised the money.

MRS. LINDE. You? That whole amount?

NORA. Four thousand, eight hundred crowns. What do you say to that?

MRS. LINDE. But Nora, how was it possible? Did you win the lottery?

NORA (*disdainfully*). The lottery? Pooh! No art to that.

MRS. LINDE. But where did you get it from then?

NORA (*humming, with a mysterious smile*). Hmm, tra-la-la-la.

MRS. LINDE. Because you couldn't have borrowed it.

NORA. No? Why not?

MRS. LINDE. A wife can't borrow without her husband's consent.

NORA (*tossing her head*). Oh, but a wife with a little business sense, a wife who knows how to manage—

MRS. LINDE. Nora, I simply don't understand—

NORA. You don't have to. Whoever said I *borrowed* the money? I could have gotten it other ways. (*Throwing herself back on the sofa.*) I could have gotten it from some admirer or other. After all, a girl with my ravishing appeal—

MRS. LINDE. You lunatic.

NORA. I'll bet you're eaten up with curiosity, Kristine.

MRS. LINDE. Now listen here, Nora—you haven't done something indiscreet?

NORA (*sitting up again*). Is it indiscreet to save your husband's life?

MRS. LINDE. I think it's indiscreet that without his knowledge you—

NORA. But that's the point: he mustn't know! My Lord, can't you understand? He mustn't ever know the close call he had. It was to *me* the doctors came to say his life was in danger—that nothing could save him but a stay in the south. Didn't I try strategy then! I began talking about how lovely it would be for me to travel abroad like other young wives; I begged and I cried; I told him please to remember my condition, to be kind and indulge me; and then I dropped a hint that he could easily take out a loan. But at that, Kristine, he nearly exploded. He said I was frivolous, and it was his duty as man of the house not to indulge me in whims and fancies—as I think he called them. Aha, I thought, now you'll just have to be saved—and that's when I saw my chance.

MRS. LINDE. And your father never told Torvald the money wasn't from him?

NORA. No, never. Papa died right about then. I'd considered bringing him into my secret and begging him never to tell. But he was too sick at the time—and then, sadly, it didn't matter.

MRS. LINDE. And you've never confided in your husband since?

NORA. For heaven's sake, no! Are you serious? He's so strict on that subject. Besides—Torvald, with all his masculine pride—how painfully humiliating for him if he ever found out he was in debt to me. That would just ruin our relationship. Our beautiful, happy home would never be the same.

MRS. LINDE. Won't you ever tell him?

NORA (*thoughtfully, half smiling*). Yes—maybe sometime, years from now, when I'm no longer so attractive. Don't laugh! I only mean when Torvald loves me less than now, when he stops enjoying my dancing and dressing up and reciting for him. Then it might be wise to have something in reserve—(*Breaking off.*) How ridiculous! That'll never happen— Well, Kristine, what do you think of my big secret? I'm capable of something too, hm? You can imagine, of course, how this thing hangs over me. It really hasn't been easy meeting the payments on time. In the business world there's what they call quarterly interest and what they call amortization, and these are always so terribly hard to manage. I've had to skimp a little here and there, wherever I could, you know. I could hardly spare anything from my house allowance, because Torvald has to live well. I couldn't let the children go poorly dressed; whatever I got for them, I felt I had to use up completely—the darlings!

MRS. LINDE. Poor Nora, so it had to come out of your own budget, then?

NORA. Yes, of course. But I was the one most responsible, too. Every time Torvald gave me money for new clothes and such, I never used more than half; always bought the simplest, cheapest outfits. It was a godsend that everything looks so well on me that Torvald never noticed. But it did weigh me down at times, Kristine. It *is* such a joy to wear fine things. You understand.

MRS. LINDE. Oh, of course.

NORA. And then I found other ways of making money. Last winter I was lucky enough to get a lot of copying to do. I locked myself in and sat writing every evening till late in the night. Ah, I was tired so often, dead tired. But still it was wonderful fun, sitting and working like that, earning money. It was almost like being a man.

MRS. LINDE. But how much have you paid off this way so far?

NORA. That's hard to say, exactly. These accounts, you know, aren't easy to figure. I only know that I've paid out all I could scrape together. Time and again I haven't known where to turn. (*Smiling.*) Then I'd sit here dreaming of a rich old gentleman who had fallen in love with me—

MRS. LINDE. What! Who is he?

NORA. Oh, really! And that he'd died, and when his will was opened, there in big letters it said, "All my fortune shall be paid over in cash, immediately, to that enchanting Mrs. Nora Helmer."

MRS. LINDE. But Nora dear—who *was* this gentleman?

NORA. Good grief, can't you understand? The old man never existed; that was only something I'd dream up time and again whenever I was at my wits' end for money. But it makes no difference now; the old fossil can go where he pleases for all I care; I don't need him or his will—because now I'm free. (*Jumping up.*) Oh, how lovely to think of that, Kristine! Carefree! To know you're carefree, utterly carefree; to be able to romp and play with the children, and to keep up a beautiful, charming home—everything just the way Torvald likes it! And think, spring is coming, with big blue skies. Maybe we can travel a little then. Maybe I'll see the ocean again. Oh yes, it *is* so marvelous to live and be happy!

(*The front doorbell rings.*)

MRS. LINDE (*rising*). There's the bell. It's probably best that I go.

NORA. No, stay. No one's expected. It must be for Torvald.

MAID (*from the hall doorway*). Excuse me, ma'am—there's a gentleman here to
   see Mr. Helmer, but I didn't know—since the doctor's with him—

NORA. Who is the gentleman?

KROGSTAD (*from the doorway*). It's me, Mrs. Helmer.

(MRS. LINDE *starts and turns away toward the window.*)

NORA (*stepping toward him, tense, her voice a whisper*). You? What is it? Why do
   you want to speak to my husband?

KROGSTAD. Bank business—after a fashion. I have a small job in the investment
   bank, and I hear now your husband is going to be our chief—

NORA. In other words, it's—

KROGSTAD. Just dry business, Mrs. Helmer. Nothing but that.

NORA. Yes, then please be good enough to step into the study. (*She nods indifferently as she sees him out by the hall door, then returns and begins stirring up the
   stove.*)

MRS. LINDE. Nora—who was that man?

NORA. That was a Mr. Krogstad—a lawyer.

MRS. LINDE. Then it really was him.

NORA. Do you know that person?

MRS. LINDE. I did once—many years ago. For a time he was a law clerk in our
   town.

NORA. Yes, he's been that.

MRS. LINDE. How he's changed.

NORA. I understand he had a very unhappy marriage.

MRS. LINDE. He's a widower now.

NORA. With a number of children. There now, it's burning. (*She closes the stove
   door and moves the rocker a bit to one side.*)

MRS. LINDE. They say he has a hand in all kinds of business.

NORA. Oh? That may be true; I wouldn't know. But let's not think about business. It's so dull.

(DR. RANK *enters from* HELMER'S *study.*)

RANK (*still in the doorway*). No, no, really—I don't want to intrude, I'd just as
   soon talk a little while with your wife. (*Shuts the door, then notices* MRS.
   LINDE.) Oh, beg pardon. I'm intruding here too.

NORA. No, not at all. (*Introducing him.*) Dr. Rank, Mrs. Linde.

RANK. Well now, that's a name much heard in this house. I believe I passed the
   lady on the stairs as I came.

MRS. LINDE. Yes, I take the stairs very slowly. They're rather hard on me.

RANK. Uh-hm, some touch of internal weakness?

MRS. LINDE. More overexertion, I'd say.

RANK. Nothing else? Then you're probably here in town to rest up in a round of
   parties?

MRS. LINDE. I'm here to look for work.

RANK. Is that the best cure for overexertion?

MRS. LINDE. One has to live, Doctor.

RANK. Yes, there's a common prejudice to that effect.

NORA. Oh, come on, Dr. Rank—you really do want to live yourself.

RANK. Yes, I really do. Wretched as I am, I'll gladly prolong my torment indefinitely. All my patients feel like that. And it's quite the same, too, with the morally sick. Right at this moment there's one of those moral invalids in there with Helmer—

MRS. LINDE (*softly*). Ah!

NORA. Who do you mean?

RANK. Oh, it's a lawyer, Krogstad, a type you wouldn't know. His character is rotten to the root—but even he began chattering all-importantly about how he had to *live*.

NORA. Oh? What did he want to talk to Torvald about?

RANK. I really don't know. I only heard something about the bank.

NORA. I didn't know that Krog—that this man Krogstad had anything to do with the bank.

RANK. Yes, he's gotten some kind of berth down there. (*To* MRS. LINDE.) I don't know if you also have, in your neck of the woods, a type of person who scuttles about breathlessly, sniffing out hints of moral corruption, and then maneuvers his victim into some sort of key position where he can keep an eye on him. It's the healthy these days that are out in the cold.

MRS. LINDE. All the same, it's the sick who most need to be taken in.

RANK (*with a shrug*). Yes, there we have it. That's the concept that's turning society into a sanatorium.

(NORA, *lost in her thoughts, breaks out into quiet laughter and claps her hands*.)

RANK. Why do you laugh at that? Do you have any real idea of what society is?

NORA. What do I care about dreary old society? I was laughing at something quite different—something terribly funny. Tell me, Doctor—is everyone who works in the bank dependent now on Torvald?

RANK. Is that what you find so terribly funny?

NORA (*smiling and humming*). Never mind, never mind! (*Pacing the floor.*) Yes, that's really immensely amusing: that we—that Torvald has so much power now over all those people. (*Taking the bag out of her pocket.*) Dr. Rank, a little macaroon on that?

RANK. See here, macaroons! I thought they were contraband here.

NORA. Yes, but these are some that Kristine gave me.

MRS. LINDE. What? I—?

NORA. Now, now, don't be afraid. You couldn't possibly know that Torvald had forbidden them. You see, he's worried they'll ruin my teeth. But hmp! Just this once! Isn't that so, Dr. Rank? Help yourself! (*Puts a macaroon in his mouth.*) And you too, Kristine. And I'll also have one, only a little one—or two, at the most. (*Walking about again.*) Now I'm really tremendously happy. Now there's just one last thing in the world that I have an enormous desire to do.

RANK. Well! And what's that?

NORA. It's something I have such a consuming desire to say so Torvald could hear.

RANK. And why can't you say it?

NORA. I don't dare. It's quite shocking.

MRS. LINDE. Shocking?

RANK. Well, then it isn't advisable. But in front of us you certainly can. What do you have such a desire to say so Torvald could hear?

NORA. I have such a huge desire to say—to hell and be damned!

RANK. Are you crazy?

MRS. LINDE. My goodness, Nora!

RANK. Go on, say it. Here he is.

NORA (*hiding the macaroon bag*). Shh, shh, shh!

(HELMER *comes in from his study, hat in hand, overcoat over his arm.*)

NORA (*going toward him*). Well, Torvald dear, are you through with him?

HELMER. Yes, he just left.

NORA. Let me introduce you—this is Kristine, who's arrived here in town.

HELMER. Kristine—? I'm sorry, but I don't know—

NORA. Mrs. Linde, Torvald dear. Mrs. Kristine Linde.

HELMER. Of course. A childhood friend of my wife's, no doubt?

MRS. LINDE. Yes, we knew each other in those days.

NORA. And just think, she made the long trip down here in order to talk with you.

HELMER. What's this?

MRS. LINDE. Well, not exactly—

NORA. You see, Kristine is remarkably clever in office work, and so she's terribly eager to come under a capable man's supervision and add more to what she already knows—

HELMER. Very wise, Mrs. Linde.

NORA. And then when she heard that you'd become a bank manager—the story was wired out to the papers—then she came in as fast as she could and— Really, Torvald, for my sake you can do a little something for Kristine, can't you?

HELMER. Yes, it's not at all impossible. Mrs. Linde, I suppose you're a widow?

MRS. LINDE. Yes.

HELMER. Any experience in office work?

MRS. LINDE. Yes, a good deal.

HELMER. Well, it's quite likely that I can make an opening for you—

NORA (*clapping her hands*). You see, you see!

HELMER. You've come at a lucky moment, Mrs. Linde.

MRS. LINDE. Oh, how can I thank you?

HELMER. Not necessary. (*Putting his overcoat on.*) But today you'll have to excuse me—

RANK. Wait, I'll go with you. (*He fetches his coat from the hall and warms it at the stove.*)

NORA. Don't stay out long, dear.

HELMER. An hour; no more.

NORA. Are you going too, Kristine?

MRS. LINDE (*putting on her winter garments*). Yes, I have to see about a room now.

HELMER. Then perhaps we can all walk together.

NORA (*helping her*). What a shame we're so cramped here, but it's quite impossible for us to—

MRS. LINDE. Oh, don't even think of it! Good-bye, Nora dear, and thanks for everything.

NORA. Good-bye for now. Of course you'll be back this evening. And you too, Dr. Rank. What? If you're well enough? Oh, you've got to be! Wrap up tight now.

(*In a ripple of small talk the company moves out into the hall; children's voices are heard outside on the steps.*)

NORA. There they are! There they are! (*She runs to open the door. The children come in with their nurse,* ANNE-MARIE.) Come in, come in! (*Bends down and kisses them.*) Oh, you darlings—! Look at them, Kristine. Aren't they lovely!

RANK. No loitering in the draft here.

HELMER. Come, Mrs. Linde—this place is unbearable now for anyone but mothers.

(DR. RANK, HELMER, *and* MRS. LINDE *go down the stairs.* ANNE-MARIE *goes into the living room with the children.* NORA *follows, after closing the hall door.*)

NORA. How fresh and strong you look. Oh, such red cheeks you have! Like apples and roses. (*The children interrupt her throughout the following.*) And it was so much fun? That's wonderful. Really? You pulled both Emmy and Bob on the sled? Imagine, all together! Yes, you're a clever boy, Ivar. Oh, let me hold her a bit, Anne-Marie. My sweet little doll baby! (*Takes the smallest from the nurse and dances with her.*) Yes, yes, Mama will dance with Bob as well. What? Did you throw snowballs? Oh, if I'd only been there! No, don't bother, Anne-Marie—I'll undress them myself. Oh yes, let me. It's such fun. Go in and rest; you look half frozen. There's hot coffee waiting for you on the stove. (*The nurse goes into the room to the left.* NORA *takes the children's winter things off, throwing them about, while the children talk to her all at once.*) Is that so? A big dog chased you? But it didn't bite? No, dogs never bite little, lovely doll babies. Don't peek in the packages, Ivar! What is it? Yes, wouldn't you like to know. No, no, it's an ugly something. Well? Shall we play? What shall we play? Hide-and-seek? Yes, let's play hide-and-seek. Bob must hide first. I must? Yes, let me hide first. (*Laughing and shouting, she and the children play in and out of the living room and the adjoining room to the right. At last* NORA *hides under the table. The children come storming in, search, but cannot find her, then hear her muffled laughter, dash over to the table, lift the cloth up and find her. Wild shouting. She creeps forward as if to scare them. More shouts. Meanwhile, a knock at the hall door; no one has noticed it. Now the door half opens, and* KROGSTAD *appears. He waits a moment; the game goes on.*)

KROGSTAD. Beg pardon, Mrs. Helmer—

NORA (*with a strangled cry, turning and scrambling to her knees*). Oh! What do you want?

KROGSTAD. Excuse me. The outer door was ajar; it must be someone forgot to shut it—

NORA (*rising*). My husband isn't home, Mr. Krogstad.

KROGSTAD. I know that.

NORA. Yes—then what do you want here?

KROGSTAD. A word with you.

NORA. With—? (*To the children, quietly.*) Go in to Anne-Marie. What? No, the strange man won't hurt Mama. When he's gone, we'll play some more. (*She leads the children into the room to the left and shuts the door after them. Then, tense and nervous:*) You want to speak to me?

KROGSTAD. Yes, I want to.

NORA. Today? But it's not yet the first of the month—

KROGSTAD. No, it's Christmas Eve. It's going to be up to you how merry a Christmas you have.

NORA. What is it you want? Today I absolutely can't—

KROGSTAD. We won't talk about that till later. This is something else. You do have a moment to spare, I suppose?

NORA. Oh yes, of course—I do, except—

KROGSTAD. Good. I was sitting over at Olsen's Restaurant when I saw your husband go down the street—

NORA. Yes?

KROGSTAD. With a lady.

NORA. Yes. So?

KROGSTAD. If you'll pardon my asking: wasn't that lady a Mrs. Linde?

NORA. Yes.

KROGSTAD. Just now come into town?

NORA. Yes, today.

KROGSTAD. She's a good friend of yours?

NORA. Yes, she is. But I don't see—

KROGSTAD. I also knew her once.

NORA. I'm aware of that.

KROGSTAD. Oh? You know all about it. I thought so. Well, then let me ask you short and sweet: is Mrs. Linde getting a job in the bank?

NORA. What makes you think you can cross-examine me, Mr. Krogstad—you, one of my husband's employees? But since you ask, you might as well know— yes, Mrs. Linde's going to be taken on at the bank. And I'm the one who spoke for her, Mr. Krogstad. Now you know.

KROGSTAD. So I guessed right.

NORA (*pacing up and down*). Oh, one does have a tiny bit of influence, I should hope. Just because I am a woman, don't think it means that— When one has a subordinate position, Mr. Krogstad, one really ought to be careful about pushing somebody who—hm—

KROGSTAD. Who has influence?

NORA. That's right.

KROGSTAD (*in a different tone*). Mrs. Helmer, would you be good enough to use your influence on my behalf?

NORA. What? What do you mean?

KROGSTAD. Would you please make sure that I keep my subordinate position in the bank?

NORA. What does that mean? Who's thinking of taking away your position?

KROGSTAD. Oh, don't play the innocent with me. I'm quite aware that your friend would hardly relish the chance of running into me again; and I'm also aware now whom I can thank for being turned out.

NORA. But I promise you—

KROGSTAD. Yes, yes, yes, to the point: there's still time, and I'm advising you to use your influence to prevent it.

NORA. But Mr. Krogstad, I have absolutely no influence.

KROGSTAD. You haven't? I thought you were just saying—

NORA. You shouldn't take me so literally. I! How can you believe that I have any such influence over my husband?

KROGSTAD. Oh, I've known your husband from our student days. I don't think the great bank manager's more steadfast than any other married man.

NORA. You speak insolently about my husband, and I'll show you the door.

KROGSTAD. The lady has spirit.

NORA. I'm not afraid of you any longer. After New Year's, I'll soon be done with the whole business.

KROGSTAD (*restraining himself*). Now listen to me, Mrs. Helmer. If necessary, I'll fight for my little job in the bank as if it were life itself.

NORA. Yes, so it seems.

KROGSTAD. It's not just a matter of income; that's the least of it. It's something else— All right, out with it! Look, this is the thing. You know, just like all the others, of course, that once, a good many years ago, I did something rather rash.

NORA. I've heard rumors to that effect.

KROGSTAD. The case never got into court; but all the same, every door was closed in my face from then on. So I took up those various activities you know about. I had to grab hold somewhere; and I dare say I haven't been among the worst. But now I want to drop all that. My boys are growing up. For their sakes, I'll have to win back as much respect as possible here in town. That job in the bank was like the first rung in my ladder. And now your husband wants to kick me right back down in the mud again.

NORA. But for heaven's sake, Mr. Krogstad, it's simply not in my power to help you.

KROGSTAD. That's because you haven't the will to—but I have the means to make you.

NORA. You certainly won't tell my husband that I owe you money?

KROGSTAD. Hm—what if I told him that?

NORA. That would be shameful of you. (*Nearly in tears.*) This secret—my joy and my pride—that he should learn it in such a crude and disgusting way— learn it from you. You'd expose me to the most horrible unpleasantness—

KROGSTAD. Only unpleasantness?

NORA (*vehemently*). But go on and try. It'll turn out the worse for you, because then my husband will really see what a crook you are, and then you'll *never* be able to hold your job.

KROGSTAD. I asked if it was just domestic unpleasantness you were afraid of?

NORA. If my husband finds out, then of course he'll pay what I owe at once, and then we'd be through with you for good.

KROGSTAD (*a step closer*). Listen, Mrs. Helmer—you've either got a very bad memory, or else no head at all for business. I'd better put you a little more in touch with the facts.

NORA. What do you mean?

KROGSTAD. When your husband was sick, you came to me for a loan of four thousand, eight hundred crowns.

NORA. Where else could I go?

KROGSTAD. I promised to get you that sum—

NORA. And you got it.

KROGSTAD. I promised to get you that sum, on certain conditions. You were so involved in your husband's illness, and so eager to finance your trip, that I guess you didn't think out all the details. It might just be a good idea to remind you. I promised you the money on the strength of a note I drew up.

NORA. Yes, and that I signed.

KROGSTAD. Right. But at the bottom I added some lines for your father to guarantee the loan. He was supposed to sign down there.

NORA. Supposed to? He did sign.

KROGSTAD. I left the date blank. In other words, your father would have dated his signature himself. Do you remember that?

NORA. Yes, I think—

KROGSTAD. Then I gave you the note for you to mail to your father. Isn't that so?

NORA. Yes.

KROGSTAD. And naturally you sent it at once—because only some five, six days later you brought me the note, properly signed. And with that, the money was yours.

NORA. Well, then; I've made my payments regularly, haven't I?

KROGSTAD. More or less. But—getting back to the point—those were hard times for you then, Mrs. Helmer.

NORA. Yes, they were.

KROGSTAD. Your father was very ill, I believe.

NORA. He was near the end.

KROGSTAD. He died soon after?

NORA. Yes.

KROGSTAD. Tell me, Mrs. Helmer, do you happen to recall the date of your father's death? The day of the month, I mean.

NORA. Papa died the twenty-ninth of September.

KROGSTAD. That's quite correct; I've already looked into that. And now we come to a curious thing—(*Taking out a paper.*) which I simply cannot comprehend.

NORA. Curious thing? I don't know—

KROGSTAD. This is the curious thing: that your father co-signed the note for your loan three days after his death.

NORA. How—? I don't understand.

KROGSTAD. Your father died the twenty-ninth of September. But look. Here your father dated his signature October second. Isn't that curious, Mrs. Helmer? (NORA *is silent.*) Can you explain it to me? (NORA *remains silent.*) It's also remarkable that the words "October second" and the year aren't written in your father's hand, but rather in one that I think I know. Well, it's easy to understand. Your father forgot perhaps to date his signature, and then someone or other added it, a bit sloppily, before anyone knew of his death. There's nothing wrong in that. It all comes down to the signature. And there's no question about *that*. Mrs. Helmer. It really *was* your father who signed his own name here, wasn't it?

NORA (*after a short silence, throwing her head back and looking squarely at him*). No, it wasn't. I signed Papa's name.

KROGSTAD. Wait, now—are you fully aware that this is a dangerous confession?

NORA. Why? You'll soon get your money.

KROGSTAD. Let me ask you a question—why didn't you send the paper to your father?

NORA. That was impossible. Papa was so sick. If I'd asked him for his signature, I also would have had to tell him what the money was for. But I couldn't tell him, sick as he was, that my husband's life was in danger. That was just impossible.

KROGSTAD. Then it would have been better if you'd given up the trip abroad.

NORA. I couldn't possibly. The trip was to save my husband's life. I couldn't give that up.

KROGSTAD. But didn't you ever consider that this was a fraud against me?

NORA. I couldn't let myself be bothered by that. You weren't any concern of mine. I couldn't stand you, with all those cold complications you made, even though you knew how badly off my husband was.

KROGSTAD. Mrs. Helmer, obviously you haven't the vaguest idea of what you've involved yourself in. But I can tell you this: it was nothing more and nothing worse that I once did—and it wrecked my whole reputation.

NORA. You? Do you expect me to believe that you ever acted bravely to save your wife's life?

KROGSTAD. Laws don't inquire into motives.

NORA. Then they must be very poor laws.

KROGSTAD. Poor or not—if I introduce this paper in court, you'll be judged according to law.

NORA. This I refuse to believe. A daughter hasn't a right to protect her dying father from anxiety and care? A wife hasn't a right to save her husband's life? I don't know much about laws, but I'm sure that somewhere in the books these things are allowed. And you don't know anything about it—you who practice the law? You must be an awful lawyer, Mr. Krogstad.

KROGSTAD. Could be. But business—the kind of business we two are mixed up in—don't you think I know about that? All right. Do what you want now. But I'm telling you *this*: if I get shoved down a second time, you're going to keep me company. (*He bows and goes out through the hall.*)

NORA (*pensive for a moment, then tossing her head*). Oh, really! Trying to frighten me! I'm not so silly as all that. (*Begins gathering up the children's clothes, but soon stops.*) But—? No, but that's impossible! I did it out of love.

THE CHILDREN (*in the doorway, left*). Mama, that strange man's gone out the door.

NORA. Yes, yes, I know it. But don't tell anyone about the strange man. Do you hear? Not even Papa!

THE CHILDREN. No, Mama. But now will you play again?

NORA. No, not now.

THE CHILDREN. Oh, but Mama, you promised.

NORA. Yes, but I can't now. Go inside; I have too much to do. Go in, go in, my sweet darlings. (*She herds them gently back in the room and shuts the door after them. Settling on the sofa, she takes up a piece of embroidery and makes some stitches, but soon stops abruptly.*) No! (*Throws the work aside, rises, goes to the hall door and calls out.*) Helene! Let me have the tree in here. (*Goes to the table, left, opens the table drawer, and stops again.*) No, but that's utterly impossible!

MAID (*with the Christmas tree*). Where should I put it, ma'am?

NORA. There. The middle of the floor.

MAID. Should I bring anything else?

NORA. No, thanks. I have what I need.

(*The* MAID, *who has set the tree down, goes out.*)

NORA (*absorbed in trimming the tree*). Candles here—and flowers here. That terrible creature! Talk, talk, talk! There's nothing to it at all. The tree's going to be lovely. I'll do anything to please you, Torvald. I'll sing for you, dance for you—

(HELMER *comes in from the hall, with a sheaf of papers under his arm.*)

NORA. Oh! You're back so soon?

HELMER. Yes. Has anyone been here?

NORA. Here? No.

HELMER. That's odd. I saw Krogstad leaving the front door.

NORA. So? Oh yes, that's true. Krogstad was here a moment.

HELMER. Nora, I can see by your face that he's been here, begging you to put in a good word for him.

NORA. Yes.

HELMER. And it was supposed to seem like your own idea? You were to hide it from me that he'd been here. He asked you that, too, didn't he?

NORA. Yes, Torvald, but—

HELMER. Nora, Nora, and you could fall for that? Talk with that sort of person and promise him anything? And then in the bargain, tell me an untruth.

NORA. An untruth—?

HELMER. Didn't you say that no one had been here? (*Wagging his finger.*) My little songbird must never do that again. A songbird needs a clean beak to warble with. No false notes. (*Putting his arm about her waist.*) That's the way it should be, isn't it? Yes, I'm sure of it. (*Releasing her.*) And so, enough of that. (*Sitting by the stove.*) Ah, how snug and cozy it is here. (*Leafing among his papers.*)

NORA (*busy with the tree, after a short pause*). Torvald!

HELMER. Yes.

NORA. I'm so much looking forward to the Stenborgs' costume party, day after tomorrow.

HELMER. And I can't wait to see what you'll surprise me with.

NORA. Oh, that stupid business!

HELMER. What?

NORA. I can't find anything that's right. Everything seems so ridiculous, so inane.

HELMER. So my little Nora's come to *that* recognition?

NORA (*going behind his chair, her arms resting on its back*). Are you very busy, Torvald?

HELMER. Oh—

NORA. What papers are those?

HELMER. Bank matters.

NORA. Already?

HELMER. I've gotten full authority from the retiring management to make all necessary changes in personnel and procedure. I'll need Christmas week for that. I want to have everything in order by New Year's.

NORA. So that was the reason this poor Krogstad—

HELMER. Hm.

NORA (*still leaning on the chair and slowly stroking the nape of his neck*). If you weren't so very busy, I would have asked you an enormous favor, Torvald.

HELMER. Let's hear. What is it?

NORA. You know, there isn't anyone who has your good taste—and I want so much to look well at the costume party. Torvald, couldn't you take over and decide what I should be and plan my costume?

HELMER. Ah, is my stubborn little creature calling for a lifeguard?

NORA. Yes, Torvald, I can't get anywhere without your help.

HELMER. All right—I'll think it over. We'll hit on something.

NORA. Oh, how sweet of you. (*Goes to the tree again. Pause.*) Aren't the red flowers pretty—? But tell me, was it really such a crime that this Krogstad committed?

HELMER. Forgery. Do you have any idea what that means?

NORA. Couldn't he have done it out of need?

HELMER. Yes, or thoughtlessness, like so many others. I'm not so heartless that I'd condemn a man categorically for just one mistake.

NORA. No, of course not, Torvald!

HELMER. Plenty of men have redeemed themselves by openly confessing their crimes and taking their punishment.

NORA. Punishment—?

HELMER. But now Krogstad didn't go that way. He got himself out by sharp practices, and that's the real cause of his moral breakdown.

NORA. Do you really think that would—?

HELMER. Just imagine how a man with that sort of guilt in him has to lie and cheat and deceive on all sides, has to wear a mask even with the nearest and dearest he has, even with his own wife and children. And with the children, Nora—that's where it's most horrible.

NORA. Why?

HELMER. Because that kind of atmosphere of lies infects the whole life of a home. Every breath the children take in is filled with the germs of something degenerate.

NORA (*coming closer behind him*). Are you sure of that?

HELMER. Oh, I've seen it often enough as a lawyer. Almost everyone who goes bad early in life has a mother who's a chronic liar.

NORA. Why just—the mother?

HELMER. It's usually the mother's influence that's dominant, but the father's works in the same way, of course. Every lawyer is quite familiar with it. And still this Krogstad's been going home year in, year out, poisoning his own children with lies and pretense; that's why I call him morally lost. (*Reaching his hands out toward her.*) So my sweet little Nora must promise me never to plead his cause. Your hand on it. Come, come, what's this? Give me your hand. There, now. All settled. I can tell you it'd be impossible for me to work alongside of him. I literally feel physically revolted when I'm anywhere near such a person.

NORA (*withdraws her hand and goes to the other side of the Christmas tree*). How hot it is here! And I've got so much to do.

HELMER (*getting up and gathering his papers*). Yes, and I have to think about getting some of these read through before dinner. I'll think about your costume, too. And something to hang on the tree in gilt paper, I may even see about that. (*Putting his hand on her head.*) Oh you, my darling little songbird. (*He goes into his study and closes the door after him.*)

NORA (*softly, after a silence*). Oh, really! It isn't so. It's impossible. It must be impossible.

ANNE-MARIE (*in the doorway, left*). The children are begging so hard to come in to Mama.

NORA. No, no, no, don't let them in to me! You stay with them, Anne-Marie.

ANNE-MARIE. Of course, ma'am. (*Closes the door.*)

NORA (*pale with terror*). Hurt my children—! Poison my home? (*A moment's pause; then she tosses her head.*) That's not true. Never. Never in all the world.

ACT TWO

Same room. Beside the piano the Christmas tree now stands stripped of ornament, burned-down candle stubs on its ragged branches. NORA's *street clothes lie on the sofa.* NORA, *alone in the room, moves restlessly about; at last she stops at the sofa and picks up her coat.*

NORA (*dropping the coat again*). Someone's coming! (*Goes toward the door, listens.*) No—there's no one. Of course—nobody's coming today, Christmas Day—or tomorrow, either. But maybe—(*Opens the door and looks out.*) No, nothing in the mailbox. Quite empty. (*Coming forward.*) What nonsense! He won't do anything serious. Nothing terrible could happen. It's impossible. Why, I have three small children.

(ANNE-MARIE. *with a large carton, comes in from the room to the left.*)

ANNE-MARIE. Well, at last I found the box with the masquerade clothes.

NORA. Thanks. Put it on the table.

ANNE-MARIE (*does so*). But they're all pretty much of a mess.

NORA. Ahh! I'd love to rip them in a million pieces!

ANNE-MARIE. Oh, mercy, they can be fixed right up. Just a little patience.

NORA. Yes, I'll go get Mrs. Linde to help me.

ANNE-MARIE. Out again now? In this nasty weather? Miss Nora will catch cold—get sick.

NORA. Oh, worse things could happen— How are the children?

ANNE-MARIE. The poor mites are playing with their Christmas presents, but—

NORA. Do they ask for me much?

ANNE-MARIE. They're so used to having Mama around, you know.

NORA. Yes. but Anne-Marie, I *can't* be together with them as much as I was.

ANNE-MARIE. Well, small children get used to anything.

NORA. You think so? Do you think they'd forget their mother if she was gone for good?

ANNE-MARIE. Oh, mercy—gone for good!

NORA. Wait, tell me, Anne-Marie—I've wondered so often—how could you ever have the heart to give your child over to strangers?

ANNE-MARIE. But I had to, you know, to become little Nora's nurse.

NORA. Yes, but how could you *do* it?

ANNE-MARIE. When I could get such a good place? A girl who's poor and who's gotten in trouble is glad enough for that. Because that slippery fish, he didn't do a thing for me, you know.

NORA. But your daughter's surely forgotten you.

ANNE-MARIE. Oh, she certainly has not. She's written to me, both when she was confirmed and when she was married.

NORA (*clasping her about the neck*). You old Anne-Marie you were a good mother for me when I was little.

ANNE-MARIE. Poor little Nora, with no other mother but me.

NORA. And if the babies didn't have one, then I know that you'd— What silly talk! (*Opening the carton.*) Go in to them. Now I'll have to— Tomorrow you can see how lovely I'll look.

ANNE-MARIE. Oh, there won't be anyone at the party as lovely as Miss Nora. (*She goes off into the room, left.*)

NORA (*begins unpacking the box, but soon throws it aside*). Oh, if I dared to go out. If only nobody would come. If only nothing would happen here while I'm out. What craziness—nobody's coming. Just don't think. This muff—needs a brushing. Beautiful gloves, beautiful gloves. Let it go. Let it go! One, two, three, four, five, six— (*With a cry.*) Oh, there they are! (*Poises to move toward the door, but remains irresolutely standing.* MRS. LINDE *enters from the hall, where she has removed her street clothes.*)

NORA. Oh, it's you, Kristine. There's no one else out there? How good that you've come.

MRS. LINDE. I hear you were up asking for me.

NORA. Yes, I just stopped by. There's something you really can help me with. Let's get settled on the sofa. Look, there's going to be a costume party tomorrow evening at the Stenborgs' right above us, and now Torvald wants me to go as a Neapolitan peasant girl and dance the tarantella that I learned in Capri.

MRS. LINDE. Really, are you giving a whole performance?

NORA. Torvald says yes, I should. See, here's the dress. Torvald had it made for me down there; but now it's all so tattered that I just don't know—

MRS. LINDE. Oh, we'll fix that up in no time. It's nothing more than the trimmings—they're a bit loose here and there. Needle and thread? Good, now we have what we need.

NORA. Oh, how sweet of you!

MRS. LINDE (*sewing*). So you'll be in disguise tomorrow. Nora. You know what? I'll stop by then for a moment and have a look at you all dressed up. But listen, I've absolutely forgotten to thank you for that pleasant evening yesterday.

NORA (*getting up and walking about*). I don't think it was as pleasant as usual yesterday. You should have come to town a bit sooner, Kristine— Yes, Torvald really knows how to give a home elegance and charm.

MRS. LINDE. And you do, too, if you ask me. You're not your father's daughter for nothing. But tell me, is Dr. Rank always so down in the mouth as yesterday?

NORA. No, that was quite an exception. But he goes around critically ill all the time—tuberculosis of the spine, poor man. You know, his father was a disgusting thing who kept mistresses and so on—and that's why the son's been sickly from birth.

MRS. LINDE (*lets her sewing fall to her lap*). But my dearest Nora, how do you know about such things?

NORA (*walking more jauntily*). Hmp! When you've had three children, then you've had a few visits from—from women who know something of medicine, and they tell you this and that.

MRS. LINDE (*resumes sewing; a short pause*). Does Dr. Rank come here every day?

NORA. Every blessed day. He's Torvald's best friend from childhood, and my good friend, too. Dr. Rank almost belongs to this house.

MRS. LINDE. But tell me—is he quite sincere? I mean, doesn't he rather enjoy flattering people?

NORA. Just the opposite. Why do you think that?

MRS. LINDE. When you introduced us yesterday, he was proclaiming that he'd often heard my name in this house; but later I noticed that your husband hadn't the slightest idea who I really was. So how could Dr. Rank—?

NORA. But it's all true, Kristine. You see, Torvald loves me beyond words, and, as he puts it, he'd like to keep me all to himself. For a long time he'd almost be jealous if I even mentioned any of my old friends back home. So of course I dropped that. But with Dr. Rank I talk a lot about such things, because he likes hearing about them.

MRS. LINDE. Now listen, Nora; in many ways you're still like a child. I'm a good deal older than you, with a little more experience. I'll tell you something: you ought to put an end to all this with Dr. Rank.

NORA. What should I put an end to?

MRS. LINDE. Both parts of it, I think. Yesterday you said something about a rich admirer who'd provide you with money—

NORA. Yes, one who doesn't exist—worse luck. So?

MRS. LINDE. Is Dr. Rank well off?

NORA. Yes, he is.

MRS. LINDE. With no dependents?

NORA. No, no one. But—

MRS. LINDE. And he's over here every day?

NORA. Yes, I told you that.

MRS. LINDE. How can a man of such refinement be so grasping?

NORA. I don't follow you at all.

MRS. LINDE. Now don't try to hide it, Nora. You think I can't guess who loaned you the forty-eight hundred crowns?

NORA. Are you out of your mind? How could you think such a thing! A friend of ours, who comes here every single day. What an intolerable situation that would have been!

MRS. LINDE. Then it really wasn't him.

NORA. No, absolutely not. It never even crossed my mind for a moment— And he had nothing to lend in those days; his inheritance came later.

MRS. LINDE. Well, I think that was a stroke of luck for you, Nora dear.

NORA. No, it never would have occurred to me to ask Dr. Rank— Still, I'm quite sure that if I had asked him—

MRS. LINDE. Which you won't, of course.

NORA. No, of course not. I can't see that I'd ever need to. But I'm quite positive that if I talked to Dr. Rank—

MRS. LINDE. Behind your husband's back?

NORA. I've got to clear up this other thing; *that's* also behind his back. I've got to clear it all up.

MRS. LINDE. Yes, I was saying that yesterday, but—

NORA (*pacing up and down*). A man handles these problems so much better than a woman—

MRS. LINDE. One's husband does, yes.

NORA. Nonsense. (*Stopping.*) When you pay everything you owe, then you get your note back, right?

MRS. LINDE. Yes, naturally.

NORA. And can rip it into a million pieces and burn it up—that filthy scrap of paper!

MRS. LINDE (*looking hard at her, laying her sewing aside, and rising slowly*). Nora, you're hiding something from me.

NORA. You can see it in my face?

MRS. LINDE. Something's happened to you since yesterday morning. Nora, what is it?

NORA (*hurrying toward her*). Kristine! (*Listening.*) Shh! Torvald's home. Look, go in with the children a while. Torvald can't bear all this snipping and stitching. Let Anne-Marie help you.

MRS. LINDE (*gathering up some of the things*). All right, but I'm not leaving here until we've talked this out. (*She disappears into the room, left, as* TORVALD *enters from the hall.*)

NORA. Oh, how I've been waiting for you, Torvald dear.

HELMER. Was that the dressmaker?

NORA. No, that was Kristine. She's helping me fix up my costume. You know, it's going to be quite attractive.

HELMER. Yes, wasn't that a bright idea I had?

NORA. Brilliant! But then wasn't I good as well to give in to you?

HELMER. Good—because you give in to your husband's judgment? All right, you little goose, I know you didn't mean it like that. But I won't disturb you. You'll want to have a fitting, I suppose.

NORA. And you'll be working?

HELMER. Yes. (*Indicating a bundle of papers.*) See. I've been down to the bank. (*Starts toward his study.*)

NORA. Torvald.

HELMER (*stops*). Yes.

NORA. If your little squirrel begged you, with all her heart and soul, for something—?

HELMER. What's that?

NORA. Then would you do it?

HELMER. First, naturally, I'd have to know what it was.

NORA. Your squirrel would scamper about and do tricks, if you'd only be sweet and give in.

HELMER. Out with it.

NORA. Your lark would be singing high and low in every room—

HELMER. Come on, she does that anyway.

NORA. I'd be a wood nymph and dance for you in the moonlight.

HELMER. Nora—don't tell me it's that same business from this morning?

NORA (*coming closer*). Yes, Torvald, I beg you, please!

HELMER. And you actually have the nerve to drag that up again?

NORA. Yes, yes, you've got to give in to me; you *have* to let Krogstad keep his job in the bank.

HELMER. My dear Nora, I've slated his job for Mrs. Linde.

NORA. That's awfully kind of you. But you could just fire another clerk instead of Krogstad.

HELMER. This is the most incredible stubbornness! Because you go and give an impulsive promise to speak up for him, I'm expected to—

NORA. That's not the reason, Torvald. It's for your own sake. That man does writing for the worst papers; you said it yourself. He could do you any amount of harm. I'm scared to death of him—

HELMER. Ah, I understand. It's the old memories haunting you.

NORA. What do you mean by that?

HELMER. Of course, you're thinking about your father.

NORA. Yes, all right. Just remember how those nasty gossips wrote in the papers about Papa and slandered him so cruelly. I think they'd have had him dismissed if the department hadn't sent you up to investigate, and if you hadn't been so kind and open-minded toward him.

HELMER. My dear Nora, there's a notable difference between your father and me. Your father's official career was hardly above reproach. But mine is; and I hope it'll stay that way as long as I hold my position.

NORA. Oh, who can ever tell what vicious minds can invent? We could be so snug and happy now in our quiet, carefree home—you and I and the children, Torvald! That's why I'm pleading with you so—

HELMER. And just by pleading for him you make it impossible for me to keep him on. It's already known at the bank that I'm firing Krogstad. What if it's rumored around now that the new bank manager was vetoed by his wife—

NORA. Yes, what then—?

HELMER. Oh yes—as long as our little bundle of stubbornness gets her way—! I should go and make myself ridiculous in front of the whole office—give people the idea I can be swayed by all kinds of outside pressure. Oh, you can bet I'd feel the effects of that soon enough! Besides—there's something that rules Krogstad right out at the bank as long as I'm the manager.

NORA. What's that?

HELMER. His moral failings I could maybe overlook if I had to—

NORA. Yes, Torvald, why not?

HELMER. And I hear he's quite efficient on the job. But he was a crony of mine back in my teens—one of those rash friendships that crop up again and again to embarrass you later in life. Well, I might as well say it straight out: we're on a first-name basis. And that tactless fool makes no effort at all to hide it in front of others. Quite the contrary—he thinks that entitles him to take a familiar air around me, and so every other second he comes booming out with his "Yes, Torvald!" and "Sure thing, Torvald!" I tell you, it's been excruciating for me. He's out to make my place in the bank unbearable.

NORA. Torvald, you can't be serious about all this.

HELMER. Oh no? Why not?

NORA. Because these are such petty considerations.

HELMER. What are you saying? Petty? You think I'm petty!

NORA. No, just the opposite, Torvald dear. That's exactly why—

HELMER. Never mind. You call my motives petty; then I might as well be just that. Petty! All right! We'll put a stop to this for good. (*Goes to the hall door and calls.*) Helene!

NORA. What do you want?

HELMER (*searching among his papers*). A decision. (*The* MAID *comes in.*) Look here; take this letter; go out with it at once. Get hold of a messenger and have him deliver it. Quick now. It's already addressed. Wait, here's some money.

MAID. Yes, sir. (*She leaves with the letter.*)

HELMER (*straightening his papers*). There, now, little Miss Willful.

NORA (*breathlessly*). Torvald, what was that letter?

HELMER. Krogstad's notice.

NORA. Call it back, Torvald! There's still time. Oh, Torvald, call it back! Do it for my sake—for your sake, for the children's sake! Do you hear. Torvald; do it! You don't know how this can harm us.

HELMER. Too late.

NORA. Yes, too late.

HELMER. Nora dear, I can forgive you this panic, even though basically you're insulting me. Yes, you are! Or isn't it an insult to think that *I* should be afraid of a courtroom hack's revenge? But I forgive you anyway, because this shows so beautifully how much you love me. (*Takes her in his arms.*) This is the way it should be, my darling Nora. Whatever comes, you'll see: when it really counts, I have strength and courage enough as a man to take on the whole weight myself.

NORA (*terrified*). What do you mean by that?

HELMER. The whole weight, I said.

NORA (*resolutely*). No, never in all the world.

HELMER. Good. So we'll share it, Nora, as man and wife. That's as it should be. (*Fondling her.*) Are you happy now? There, there, there—not these frightened dove's eyes. It's nothing at all but empty fantasies— Now you should run through your tarantella and practice your tambourine. I'll go to the inner office and shut both doors, so I won't hear a thing; you can make all the noise you like. (*Turning in the doorway.*) And when Rank comes, just tell him where he can find me. (*He nods to her and goes with his papers into the study, closing the door.*)

NORA (*standing as though rooted, dazed with fright, in a whisper*). He really could do it. He will do it. He'll do it in spite of everything. No, not that, never, never! Anything but that! Escape! A way out— (*The doorbell rings.*) Dr. Rank! Anything but that! *Anything*, whatever it is! (*Her hands pass over her*

face, smoothing it; she pulls herself together, goes over and opens the hall door. DR.
RANK *stands outside, hanging his fur coat up. During the following scene, it begins
getting dark.*)

NORA. Hello, Dr. Rank. I recognized your ring. But you mustn't go in to Torvald
yet; I believe he's working.

RANK. And you?

NORA. For you, I always have an hour to spare—you know that. (*He has entered,
and she shuts the door after him.*)

RANK. Many thanks. I'll make use of these hours while I can.

NORA. What do you mean by that? While you can?

RANK. Does that disturb you?

NORA. Well, it's such an odd phrase. Is anything going to happen?

RANK. What's going to happen is what I've been expecting so long—but I honestly didn't think it would come so soon.

NORA (*gripping his arm*). What is it you've found out? Dr. Rank, you have to tell
me!

RANK (*sitting by the stove*). It's all over with me. There's nothing to be done
about it.

NORA (*breathing easier*). Is it you—then—?

RANK. Who else? There's no point in lying to one's self. I'm the most miserable
of all my patients, Mrs. Helmer. These past few days I've been auditing my
internal accounts. Bankrupt! Within a month I'll probably be laid out and
rotting in the churchyard.

NORA. Oh, what a horrible thing to say.

RANK. The thing itself is horrible. But the worst of it is all the other horror before it's over. There's only one final examination left; when I'm finished with
that, I'll know about when my disintegration will begin. There's something I
want to say. Helmer with his sensitivity has such a sharp distaste for anything
ugly. I don't want him near my sickroom.

NORA. Oh, but Dr. Rank—

RANK. I won't have him in there. Under no condition. I'll lock my door to
him— As soon as I'm completely sure of the worst, I'll send you my calling
card marked with a black cross, and you'll know then the wreck has started
to come apart.

NORA. No, today you're completely unreasonable. And I wanted you so much
to be in a really good humor.

RANK. With death up my sleeve? And then to suffer this way for somebody else's
sins. Is there any justice in that? And in every single family, in some way or
another, this inevitable retribution of nature goes on—

NORA (*her hands pressed over her ears*). Oh, stuff! Cheer up! Please—be gay!

RANK. Yes, I'd just as soon laugh at it all. My poor, innocent spine, serving time
for my father's gay army days.

NORA (*by the table, left*). He was so infatuated with asparagus tips and *pâté de foie
gras*, wasn't that it?

RANK. Yes—and with truffles.

NORA. Truffles, yes. And then with oysters, I suppose?

RANK. Yes, tons of oysters, naturally.

NORA. And then the port and champagne to go with it. It's so sad that all these
delectable things have to strike at our bones.

RANK. Especially when they strike at the unhappy bones that never shared in the fun.

NORA. Ah that's the saddest of all.

RANK (*looks searchingly at her*). Hm.

NORA (*after a moment*). Why did you smile?

RANK. No, it was you who laughed.

NORA. No, it was you who smiled, Dr. Rank!

RANK (*getting up*). You're even a bigger tease than I'd thought.

NORA. I'm full of wild ideas today.

RANK. That's obvious.

NORA (*putting both hands on his shoulders*). Dear, dear Dr. Rank, you'll never die for Torvald and me.

RANK. Oh, that loss you'll easily get over. Those who go away are soon forgotten.

NORA (*looks fearfully at him*). You believe that?

RANK. One makes new connections, and then—

NORA. Who makes new connections?

RANK. Both you and Torvald will when I'm gone. I'd say you're well under way already. What was that Mrs. Linde doing here last evening?

NORA. Oh, come—you can't be jealous of poor Kristine?

RANK. Oh yes, I am. She'll be my successor here in the house. When I'm down under, that woman will probably—

NORA. Shh! Not so loud. She's right in there.

RANK. Today as well. So you see.

NORA. Only to sew on my dress. Good gracious, how unreasonable you are. (*Sitting on the sofa.*) Be nice now, Dr. Rank. Tomorrow you'll see how beautifully I'll dance; and you can imagine then that I'm dancing only for you— yes, and of course for Torvald, too—that's understood. (*Takes various items out of the carton.*) Dr. Rank, sit over here and I'll show you something.

RANK (*sitting*). What's that?

NORA. Look here. Look.

RANK. Silk stockings.

NORA. Flesh-colored. Aren't they lovely? Now it's so dark here, but tomorrow— No, no, no, just look at the feet. Oh well, you might as well look at the rest.

RANK. Hm—

NORA. Why do you look so critical? Don't you believe they'll fit?

RANK. I've never had any chance to form an opinion on that.

NORA (*glancing at him a moment*). Shame on you. (*Hits him lightly on the ear with the stockings.*) That's for you. (*Puts them away again.*)

RANK. And what other splendors am I going to see now?

NORA. Not the least bit more, because you've been naughty. (*She hums a little and rummages among her things.*)

RANK (*after a short silence*). When I sit here together with you like this, completely easy and open, then I don't know—I simply can't imagine—whatever would have become of me if I'd never come into this house.

NORA (*smiling*). Yes, I really think you feel completely at ease with us.

RANK (*more quietly, staring straight ahead*). And then to have to go away from it all—

NORA. Nonsense, you're not going away.

RANK (*his voice unchanged*). —and not even be able to leave some poor show of gratitude behind, scarcely a fleeting regret—no more than a vacant place that anyone can fill.

NORA. And if I asked you now for—? No—

RANK. For what?

NORA.. For a great proof of your friendship—

RANK. Yes, yes?

NORA. No, I mean—for an exceptionally big favor—

RANK. Would you really, for once, make me so happy?

NORA. Oh, you haven't the vaguest idea what it is.

RANK. All right, then tell me.

NORA. No, but I can't, Dr. Rank—it's all out of reason. It's advice and help, too—and a favor—

RANK. So much the better. I can't fathom what you're hinting at. Just speak out. Don't you trust me?

NORA. Of course. More than anyone else. You're my best and truest friend, I'm sure. That's why I want to talk to you. All right, then, Dr. Rank: there's something you can help me prevent. You know how deeply, how inexpressibly dearly Torvald loves me; he'd never hesitate a second to give up his life for me.

RANK (*leaning close to her*). Nora—do you think he's the only one—

NORA (*with a slight start*). Who—?

RANK. Who'd gladly give up his life for you.

NORA (*heavily*). I see.

RANK. I swore to myself you should know this before I'm gone. I'll never find a better chance. Yes, Nora, now you know. And also you know now that you can trust me beyond anyone else.

NORA (*rising, natural and calm*). Let me by.

RANK (*making room for her, but still sitting*). Nora—

NORA (*in the hall doorway*). Helene, bring the lamp in. (*Goes over to the stove.*) Ah, dear Dr. Rank, that was really mean of you.

RANK (*getting up*). That I've loved you just as deeply as somebody else? Was *that* mean?

NORA. No, but that you came out and told me. That was quite unnecessary—

RANK. What do you mean? Have you known—?

    (*The* MAID *comes in with the lamp, sets it on the table, and goes out again.*)

RANK. Nora—Mrs. Helmer—I'm asking you: have you known about it?

NORA. Oh, how can I tell what I know or don't know? Really, I don't know what to say— Why did you have to be so clumsy, Dr. Rank! Everything was so good.

RANK. Well, in any case, you now have the knowledge that my body and soul are at your command. So won't you speak out?

NORA (*looking at him*). After that?

RANK. Please, just let me know what it is.

NORA. You can't know anything now.

RANK. I have to. You mustn't punish me like this. Give me the chance to do whatever is humanly possible for you.

NORA. Now there's nothing you can do for me. Besides, actually, I don't need any help. You'll see—it's only my fantasies. That's what it is. Of course! (*Sits in the rocker, looks at him, and smiles.*) What a nice one you are, Dr. Rank. Aren't you a little bit ashamed, now that the lamp is here?

RANK. No, not exactly. But perhaps I'd better go—for good?

NORA. No, you certainly can't do that. You must come here just as you always have. You know Torvald can't do without you.

RANK. Yes, but *you?*

NORA. You know how much I enjoy it when you're here.

RANK. That's precisely what threw me off. You're a mystery to me. So many times I've felt you'd almost rather be with me than with Helmer.

NORA. Yes—you see, there are some people that one loves most and other people that one would almost prefer being with.

RANK. Yes, there's something to that.

NORA. When I was back home, of course I loved Papa most. But I always thought it was so much fun when I could sneak down to the maids' quarters, because they never tried to improve me, and it was always so amusing, the way they talked to each other.

RANK. Aha, so it's *their* place that I've filled.

NORA (*jumping up and going to him*). Oh, dear, sweet Dr. Rank, that's not what I meant at all. But you can understand that with Torvald it's just the same as with Papa—

(*The* MAID *enters from the hall.*)

MAID. Ma'am—please! (*She whispers to* NORA *and hands her a calling card.*)

NORA (*glancing at the card*). Ah! (*Slips it into her pocket.*)

RANK. Anything wrong?

NORA. No, no, not at all. It's only some—it's my new dress—

RANK. Really? But—there's your dress.

NORA. Oh, that. But this is another one—I ordered it—Torvald mustn't know—

RANK. Ah, now we have the big secret.

NORA. That's right. Just go in with him—he's back in the inner study. Keep him there as long as—

RANK. Don't worry. He won't get away. (*Goes into the study.*)

NORA (*to the* MAID). And he's standing waiting in the kitchen?

MAID. Yes, he came up by the back stairs.

NORA. But didn't you tell him somebody was here?

MAID. Yes, but that didn't do any good.

NORA. He won't leave?

MAID. No, he won't go till he's talked with you, ma'am.

NORA. Let him come in, then—but quietly. Helene, don't breathe a word about this. It's a surprise for my husband.

MAID. Yes, yes, I understand— (*Goes out.*)

NORA. This horror—it's going to happen. No, no, no, it can't happen, it mustn't. (*She goes and bolts* HELMER's *door. The* MAID *opens the hall door for* KROGSTAD *and shuts it behind him. He is dressed for travel in a fur coat, boots, and a fur cap.*)

NORA. (*going toward him*). Talk softly. My husband's home.

KROGSTAD. Well, good for him.

NORA. What do you want?

KROGSTAD. Some information.

NORA. Hurry up, then. What is it?

KROGSTAD. You know, of course, that I got my notice.

NORA. I couldn't prevent it, Mr. Krogstad. I fought for you to the bitter end, but nothing worked.

KROGSTAD. Does your husband's love for you run so thin? He knows everything I can expose you to, and all the same he dares to—

NORA. How can you imagine he knows anything about this?

KROGSTAD. Ah, no—I can't imagine it either, now. It's not at all like my fine Torvald Helmer to have so much guts—

NORA. Mr. Krogstad, I demand respect for my husband!

KROGSTAD. Why, of course—all due respect. But since the lady's keeping it so carefully hidden, may I presume to ask if you're also a bit better informed than yesterday about what you've actually done?

NORA. More than you ever could teach me.

KROGSTAD. Yes, I *am* such an awful lawyer.

NORA. What is it you want from me?

KROGSTAD. Just a glimpse of how you are, Mrs. Helmer. I've been thinking about you all day long. A cashier, a night-court scribbler, a—well, a type like me also has a little of what they call a heart, you know.

NORA. Then show it. Think of my children.

KROGSTAD. Did you or your husband ever think of mine? But never mind. I simply wanted to tell you that you don't need to take this thing too seriously. For the present, I'm not proceeding with any action.

NORA. Oh no, really! Well—I knew that.

KROGSTAD. Everything can be settled in a friendly spirit. It doesn't have to get around town at all; it can stay just among us three.

NORA. My husband must never know anything of this.

KROGSTAD. How can you manage that? Perhaps you can pay me the balance?

NORA. No, not right now.

KROGSTAD. Or you know some way of raising the money in a day or two?

NORA. No way that I'm willing to use.

KROGSTAD. Well, it wouldn't have done you any good, anyway. If you stood in front of me with a fistful of bills, you still couldn't buy your signature back.

NORA. Then tell me what you're going to do with it.

KROGSTAD. I'll just hold onto it—keep it on file. There's no outsider who'll even get wind of it. So if you've been thinking of taking some desperate step—

NORA. I have.

KROGSTAD. Been thinking of running away from home—

NORA. I have!

KROGSTAD. Or even of something worse—

NORA. How could you guess that?

KROGSTAD. You can drop those thoughts.

NORA. How could you guess I was thinking of *that*?

KROGSTAD. Most of us think about *that* at first. I thought about it too, but I discovered I hadn't the courage—

NORA (*lifelessly*). I don't either.

KROGSTAD (*relieved*). That's true, you haven't the courage? You too?

NORA. I don't have it—I don't have it.

KROGSTAD. It would be terribly stupid, anyway. After that first storm at home blows out, why, then— I have here in my pocket a letter for your husband—

NORA. Telling everything?

KROGSTAD. As charitably as possible.

NORA (*quickly*). He mustn't ever get that letter. Tear it up. I'll find some way to get money.

KROGSTAD. Beg pardon, Mrs. Helmer, but I think I just told you—

NORA. Oh, I don't mean the money I owe you. Let me know how much you want from my husband, and I'll manage it.

KROGSTAD. I don't want any money from your husband.

NORA. What do you want, then?

KROGSTAD. I'll tell you what. I want to recoup, Mrs. Helmer; I want to get on in the world—and there's where your husband can help me. For a year and a half I've kept myself clean of anything disreputable—all that time struggling with the worst conditions; but I was satisfied, working my way up step by step. Now I've been written right off, and I'm just not in the mood to come crawling back. I tell you, I want to move on. I want to get back in the bank—in a better position. Your husband can set up a job for me—

NORA. He'll never do that!

KROGSTAD. He'll do it. I know him. He won't dare breathe a word of protest. And once I'm in there together with him, you just wait and see! Inside of a year, I'll be the manager's right-hand man. It'll be Nils Krogstad, not Torvald Helmer, who runs the bank.

NORA. You'll never see the day!

KROGSTAD. Maybe you think you can—

NORA. I have the courage now—for *that*.

KROGSTAD. Oh, you don't scare me. A smart, spoiled lady like you—

NORA. You'll see; you'll see!

KROGSTAD.
 Under the ice, maybe? Down in the freezing, coal-black water? There, till you float up in the spring, ugly, unrecognizable, with your hair falling out—

NORA. You don't frighten me.

KROGSTAD. Nor do you frighten me. One doesn't do these things, Mrs. Helmer. Besides, what good would it be? I'd still have him safe in my pocket.

NORA. Afterwards? When I'm no longer—?

KROGSTAD. Are you forgetting that *I'll* be in control then over your final reputation? (NORA *stands speechless, staring at him.*) Good; now I've warned you. Don't do anything stupid. When Helmer's read my letter, I'll be waiting for his reply. And bear in mind that it's your husband himself who's forced me back to my old ways. I'll never forgive him for that. Good-bye, Mrs. Helmer. (*He goes out through the hall.*)

NORA (*goes to the hall door, opens it a crack, and listens*). He's gone. Didn't leave the letter. Oh no, no, that's impossible too! (*Opening the door more and more.*) What's that? He's standing outside—not going downstairs. He's thinking it over? Maybe he'll—? (*A letter falls in the mailbox; then* KROGSTAD's *footsteps are heard, dying away down a flight of stairs.* NORA *gives a muffled cry and runs over toward the sofa table. A short pause.*) In the mailbox. (*Slips warily over to the hall door.*) It's lying there. Torvald, Torvald—now we're lost!

MRS. LINDE (*entering with the costume from the room, left*). There now, I can't see anything else to mend. Perhaps you'd like to try—

NORA (*in a hoarse whisper*). Kristine, come here.

MRS. LINDE (*tossing the dress on the sofa*). What's wrong? You look upset.

NORA. Come here. See that letter? *There!* Look—through the glass in the mailbox.

MRS. LINDE. Yes, yes, I see it.

NORA. That letter's from Krogstad—

MRS. LINDE. Nora—it's Krogstad who loaned you the money!

NORA. Yes, and now Torvald will find out everything.

MRS. LINDE. Believe me, Nora, it's best for both of you.

NORA. There's more you don't know. I forged a name.

MRS. LINDE. But for heaven's sake—?

NORA. I only want to tell you that, Kristine, so that you can be my witness.

MRS. LINDE. Witness? Why should I—?

NORA. If I should go out of my mind—it could easily happen—

MRS. LINDE. Nora!

NORA. Or anything else occurred—so I couldn't be present here—

MRS. LINDE. Nora, Nora, you aren't yourself at all!

NORA. And someone should try to take on the whole weight, all of the guilt, you follow me—

MRS. LINDE. Yes, of course, but why do you think—?

NORA. Then you're the witness that it isn't true, Kristine. I'm very much myself; my mind right now is perfectly clear; and I'm telling you: nobody else has known about this; I alone did everything. Remember that.

MRS. LINDE. I will. But I don't understand all this.

NORA. Oh, how could you ever understand it? It's the miracle now that's going to take place.

MRS. LINDE. The miracle?

NORA. Yes, the miracle. But it's so awful, Kristine. It mustn't take place, not for anything in the world.

MRS. LINDE. I'm going right over and talk with Krogstad.

NORA. Don't go near him; he'll do you some terrible harm!

MRS. LINDE. There was a time once when he'd gladly have done anything for me.

NORA. He?

MRS. LINDE. Where does he live?

NORA. Oh, how do I know? Yes. (*Searches in her pocket.*) Here's his card. But the letter, the letter—!

HELMER (*from the study, knocking on the door*). Nora!

NORA (*with a cry of fear*). Oh! What is it? What do you want?

HELMER. Now, now, don't be so frightened. We're not coming in. You locked the door—are you trying on the dress?

NORA. Yes, I'm trying it. I'll look just beautiful, Torvald.

MRS. LINDE (*who has read the card*). He's living right around the corner.

NORA. Yes, but what's the use? We're lost. The letter's in the box.

MRS. LINDE. And your husband has the key?

NORA. Yes, always.

MRS. LINDE. Krogstad can ask for his letter back unread; he can find some excuse—

NORA. But it's just this time that Torvald usually—

MRS. LINDE. Stall him. Keep him in there. I'll be back as quick as I can. (*She hurries out through the hall entrance.*)

NORA (*goes to* HELMER's *door, opens it, and peers in*). Torvald!

HELMER (*from the inner study*). Well—does one dare set foot in one's own living room at last? Come on, Rank, now we'll get a look— (*In the doorway.*) But what's this?

NORA. What, Torvald dear?

HELMER. Rank had me expecting some grand masquerade.

RANK (*in the doorway*). That was my impression, but I must have been wrong.

NORA. No one can admire me in my splendor—not till tomorrow.

HELMER. But Nora dear, you look so exhausted. Have you practiced too hard?

NORA. No, I haven't practiced at all yet.

HELMER. You know, it's necessary—

NORA. Oh, it's absolutely necessary, Torvald. But I can't get anywhere without your help. I've forgotten the whole thing completely.

HELMER. Ah, we'll soon take care of that.

NORA. Yes, take care of me, Torvald, please! Promise me that? Oh, I'm so nervous. That big party— You must give up everything this evening for me. No business—don't even touch your pen. Yes? Dear Torvald, promise?

HELMER. It's a promise. Tonight I'm totally at your service—you little helpless thing. Hm—but first there's one thing I want to— (*Goes toward the hall door.*)

NORA. What are you looking for?

HELMER. Just to see if there's any mail.

NORA. No, no, don't do that, Torvald!

HELMER. Now what?

NORA. Torvald, please. There isn't any.

HELMER. Let me look, though. (*Starts out.* NORA, *at the piano, strikes the first notes of the tarantella.* HELMER, *at the door, stops.*) Aha!

NORA. I can't dance tomorrow if I don't practice with you.

HELMER (*going over to her*). Nora dear, are you really so frightened?

NORA. Yes, so terribly frightened. Let me practice right now; there's still time before dinner. Oh, sit down and play for me, Torvald. Direct me. Teach me, the way you always have.

HELMER. Gladly, if it's what you want. (*Sits at the piano.*)

NORA (*snatches the tambourine up from the box, then a long, varicolored shawl, which she throws around herself, whereupon she springs forward and cries out:*) Play for me now! Now I'll dance!

(HELMER *plays and* NORA *dances.* RANK *stands behind* HELMER *at the piano and looks on.*)

HELMER (*as he plays*). Slower. Slow down.

NORA. Can't change it.

HELMER. Not so violent, Nora!

NORA. Has to be just like this.

HELMER (*stopping*). No, no, that won't do at all.

NORA (*laughing and swinging her tambourine*). Isn't that what I told you?

RANK. Let me play for her.

HELMER (*getting up*). Yes, go on. I can teach her more easily then.

(RANK *sits at the piano and plays;* NORA *dances more and more wildly.* HELMER *has stationed himself by the stove and repeatedly gives her directions; she seems not to hear them; her hair loosens and falls over her shoulders; she does not notice, but goes on dancing.* MRS. LINDE *enters.*)

MRS. LINDE (*standing dumbfounded at the door*). Ah—!

NORA (*still dancing*). See what fun, Kristine!

HELMER. But Nora darling, you dance as if your life were at stake.

NORA. And it is.

HELMER. Rank, stop! This is pure madness. Stop it, I say!

(RANK *breaks off playing, and* NORA *halts abruptly*).

HELMER (*going over to her*). I never would have believed it. You've forgotten everything I taught you.

NORA (*throwing away the tambourine*). You see for yourself.

HELMER. Well, there's certainly room for instruction here.

NORA. Yes, you see how important it is. You've got to teach me to the very last minute. Promise me that, Torvald?

HELMER. You can bet on it.

NORA. You mustn't, either today or tomorrow, think about anything else but me; you mustn't open any letters—or the mailbox—

HELMER. Ah, it's still the fear of that man—

NORA. Oh yes, yes, that too.

HELMER. Nora, it's written all over you—there's already a letter from him out there.

NORA. I don't know. I guess so. But you mustn't read such things now; there mustn't be anything ugly between us before it's all over.

RANK (*quietly to* HELMER). You shouldn't deny her.

HELMER (*putting his arm around her*). The child can have her way. But tomorrow night, after you've danced—

NORA. Then you'll be free.

MAID (*in the doorway, right*). Ma'am, dinner is served.

NORA. We'll be wanting champagne, Helene.

MAID. Very good, ma'am. (*Goes out.*)

HELMER. So—a regular banquet, hm?

NORA. Yes, a banquet—champagne till daybreak! (*Calling out.*) And some macaroons, Helene. Heaps of them—just this once.

HELMER (*taking her hands*). Now, now, now—no hysterics. Be my own little lark again.

NORA. Oh, I will soon enough. But go on in—and you, Dr. Rank. Kristine, help me put up my hair.

RANK (*whispering, as they go*). There's nothing wrong—really wrong, is there?

HELMER. Oh, of course not. It's nothing more than this childish anxiety I was telling you about. (*They go out, right.*)

NORA. Well?

MRS. LINDE. Left town.

NORA. I could see by your face.

MRS. LINDE. He'll be home tomorrow evening. I wrote him a note.

NORA. You shouldn't have. Don't try to stop anything now. After all, it's a wonderful joy, this waiting here for the miracle.

MRS. LINDE. What is it you're waiting for?

NORA. Oh, you can't understand that. Go in to them; I'll be along in a moment.

(MRS. LINDE *goes into the dining room.* NORA *stands a short while as if composing herself; then she looks at her watch.*)

NORA. Five. Seven hours to midnight. Twenty-four hours to the midnight after, and then the tarantella's done. Seven and twenty-four? Thirty-one hours to live.

HELMER (*in the doorway, right*). What's become of the little lark?

NORA (*going toward him with open arms*). Here's your lark!

ACT THREE

Same scene. The table, with chairs around it, has been moved to the center of the room. A lamp on the table is lit. The hall door stands open. Dance music drifts down from the floor above. MRS. LINDE *sits at the table, absently paging through a book, trying to read, but apparently unable to focus her thoughts. Once or twice she pauses, tensely listening for a sound at the outer entrance.*

MRS. LINDE (*glancing at her watch*). Not yet—and there's hardly any time left. If only he's not—(*Listening again.*) Ah, there he is. (*She goes out in the hall and cautiously opens the outer door. Quiet footsteps are heard on the stairs. She whispers:*) Come in. Nobody's here.

KROGSTAD (*in the doorway*). I found a note from you at home. What's back of all this?

MRS. LINDE. I just *had* to talk to you.

KROGSTAD. Oh? And it just *had* to be here in this house?

MRS. LINDE. At my place it was impossible; my room hasn't a private entrance. Come in; we're all alone. The maid's asleep, and the Helmers are at the dance upstairs.

KROGSTAD (*entering the room*). Well, well, the Helmers are dancing tonight? Really?

MRS. LINDE. Yes, why not?

KROGSTAD. How true—why not?

MRS. LINDE. All right, Krogstad, let's talk.

KROGSTAD. Do we two have anything more to talk about?

MRS. LINDE. We have a great deal to talk about.

KROGSTAD. I wouldn't have thought so.

MRS. LINDE. No, because you've never understood me, really.

KROGSTAD. Was there anything more to understand—except what's all too common in life? A calculating woman throws over a man the moment a better catch comes by.

MRS. LINDE. You think I'm so thoroughly calculating? You think I broke it off lightly?

KROGSTAD. Didn't you?

MRS. LINDE. Nils—is that what you really thought?

KROGSTAD. If you cared, then why did you write me the way you did?

MRS. LINDE. What else could I do? If I had to break off with you, then it was my job as well to root out everything you felt for me.

KROGSTAD (*wringing his hands*). So that was it. And this—all this, simply for money!

MRS. LINDE. Don't forget I had a helpless mother and two small brothers. We couldn't wait for you, Nils; you had such a long road ahead of you then.

KROGSTAD. That may be; but you still hadn't the right to abandon me for somebody else's sake.

MRS. LINDE. Yes—I don't know. So many, many times I've asked myself if I did have that right.

KROGSTAD (*more softly*). When I lost you, it was as if all the solid ground dissolved from under my feet. Look at me; I'm a half-drowned man now hanging onto a wreck.

MRS. LINDE. Help may be near.

KROGSTAD. It was near—but then you came and blocked it off.

MRS. LINDE. Without my knowing it, Nils. Today for the first time I learned that it's you I'm replacing at the bank.

KROGSTAD. All right—I believe you. But now that you know, will you step aside?

MRS. LINDE. No, because that wouldn't benefit you in the slightest.

KROGSTAD. Not "benefit" me, hm! I'd step aside anyway.

MRS. LINDE. I've learned to be realistic. Life and hard, bitter necessity have taught me that.

KROGSTAD. And life's taught me never to trust fine phrases.

MRS. LINDE. Then life's taught you a very sound thing. But you do have to trust in actions, don't you?

KROGSTAD. What does that mean?

MRS. LINDE. You said you were hanging on like a half-drowned man to a wreck.

KROGSTAD. I've good reason to say that.

MRS. LINDE. I'm also like a half-drowned woman on a wreck. No one to suffer with; no one to care for.

KROGSTAD. You made your choice.

MRS. LINDE. There wasn't any choice then.

KROGSTAD. So—what of it?

MRS. LINDE. Nils, if only we two shipwrecked people could reach across to each other.

KROGSTAD. What are you saying?

MRS. LINDE. Two on one wreck are at least better off than each on his own.

KROGSTAD. Kristine!

MRS. LINDE. Why do you think I came into town?

KROGSTAD. Did you really have some thought of me?

MRS. LINDE. I have to work to go on living. All my born days, as long as I can remember, I've worked, and it's been my best and my only joy. But now I'm completely alone in the world; it frightens me to be so empty and lost. To work for yourself—there's no joy in that. Nils, give me something—someone to work for.

KROGSTAD. I don't believe all this. It's just some hysterical feminine urge to go out and make a noble sacrifice.

MRS. LINDE. Have you ever found me to be hysterical?

KROGSTAD. Can you honestly mean this? Tell me—do you know everything about my past?

MRS. LINDE. Yes.

KROGSTAD. And you know what they think I'm worth around here.

MRS. LINDE. From what you were saying before, it would seem that with me you could have been another person.

KROGSTAD. I'm positive of that.

MRS. LINDE. Couldn't it happen still?

KROGSTAD. Kristine—you're saying this in all seriousness? Yes, you are! I can see it in you. And do you really have the courage, then—?

MRS. LINDE. I need to have someone to care for; and your children need a mother. We both need each other. Nils, I have faith that you're good at heart—I'll risk everything together with you.

KROGSTAD (*gripping her hands*). Kristine, thank you, thank you— Now I know I can win back a place in their eyes. Yes—but I forgot—

MRS. LINDE (*listening*). Shh! The tarantella. Go now! Go on!

KROGSTAD. Why? What is it?

MRS. LINDE. Hear the dance up there? When that's over, they'll be coming down.

KROGSTAD. Oh, then I'll go. But—it's all pointless. Of course, you don't know the move I made against the Helmers.

MRS. LINDE. Yes, Nils, I know.

KROGSTAD. And all the same, you have the courage to—?

MRS. LINDE. I know how far despair can drive a man like you.

KROGSTAD. Oh, if I only could take it all back.

MRS. LINDE. You easily could—your letter's still lying in the mailbox.

KROGSTAD. Are you sure of that?

MRS. LINDE. Positive. But—

KROGSTAD (*looks at her searchingly*). Is that the meaning of it, then? You'll save your friend at any price. Tell me straight out. Is that it?

MRS. LINDE. Nils—anyone who's sold herself for somebody else once isn't going to do it again.

KROGSTAD. I'll demand my letter back.

MRS. LINDE. No, no.

KROGSTAD. Yes, of course. I'll stay here till Helmer comes down; I'll tell him to give me my letter again—that it only involves my dismissal—that he shouldn't read it—

MRS. LINDE. No, Nils, don't call the letter back.

KROGSTAD. But wasn't that exactly why you wrote me to come here?

MRS. LINDE. Yes, in that first panic. But it's been a whole day and night since then, and in that time I've seen such incredible things in this house. Helmer's got to learn everything; this dreadful secret has to be aired; those two have to come to a full understanding; all these lies and evasions can't go on.

KROGSTAD. Well, then, if you want to chance it. But at least there's one thing I can do, and do right away—

MRS. LINDE (*listening*). Go now, go, quick! The dance is over. We're not safe another second.

KROGSTAD. I'll wait for you downstairs.

MRS. LINDE. Yes, please do; take me home.

KROGSTAD. I can't believe it; I've never been so happy. (*He leaves by way of the outer door; the door between the room and the hall stays open.*)

MRS. LINDE (*straightening up a bit and getting together her street clothes*). How different now! How different! Someone to work for, to live for—a home to build. Well, it is worth the try! Oh, if they'd only come! (*Listening.*) Ah, there they are. Bundle up. (*She picks up her hat and coat. NORA's and HELMER's voices can be heard outside; a key turns in the lock, and HELMER brings NORA into the hall almost by force. She is wearing the Italian costume with a large black shawl about her; he has on evening dress, with a black domino open over it.*)

NORA (*struggling in the doorway*). No, no, no, not inside! I'm going up again. I don't want to leave so soon.

HELMER. But Nora dear—

NORA. Oh, I beg you, please, Torvald. From the bottom of my heart, *please*—only an hour more!

HELMER. Not a single minute, Nora darling. You know our agreement. Come on, in we go; you'll catch cold out here. (*In spite of her resistance, he gently draws her into the room.*)

MRS. LINDE. Good evening.

NORA. Kristine!

HELMER. Why, Mrs. Linde—are you here so late?

MRS. LINDE. Yes, I'm sorry, but I did want to see Nora in costume.

NORA. Have you been sitting here, waiting for me?

MRS. LINDE. Yes. I didn't come early enough; you were all upstairs; and then I thought I really couldn't leave without seeing you.

HELMER (*removing NORA's shawl*). Yes, take a good look. She's worth looking at, I can tell you that, Mrs. Linde. Isn't she lovely?

MRS. LINDE. Yes, I should say—

HELMER. A dream of loveliness, isn't she? That's what everyone thought at the party, too. But she's horribly stubborn—this sweet little thing. What's to be done with her? Can you imagine, I almost had to use force to pry her away.

NORA. Oh, Torvald, you're going to regret you didn't indulge me, even for just a half hour more.

HELMER. There, you see. She danced her tarantella and got a tumultuous hand—which was well earned, although the performance may have been a bit too naturalistic—I mean it rather overstepped the proprieties of art. But never mind—what's important is, she made a success, an overwhelming success. You think I could let her stay on after that and spoil the effect? Oh no; I took my lovely little Capri girl—my capricious little Capri girl, I should say—took her under my arm; one quick tour of the ballroom, a curtsy to every side, and then—as they say in novels—the beautiful vision disappeared. An exit should always be effective, Mrs. Linde, but that's what I can't get Nora to grasp. Phew, it's hot in here. (*Flings the domino on a chair and opens the door to his room.*) Why's it dark in here? Oh yes, of course. Excuse me. (*He goes in and lights a couple of candles.*)

NORA (*in a sharp, breathless whisper*). So?

MRS. LINDE (*quietly*). I talked with him.

NORA. And—?

MRS. LINDE. Nora—you must tell your husband everything.

NORA (*dully*). I knew it.

MRS. LINDE. You've got nothing to fear from Krogstad, but you have to speak out.

NORA. I won't tell.

MRS. LINDE. Then the letter will.

NORA. Thanks, Kristine. I know now what's to be done. Shh!

HELMER (*reentering*). Well, then, Mrs. Linde—have you admired her?

MRS. LINDE. Yes, and now I'll say good night.

HELMER. Oh, come, so soon? Is this yours, this knitting?

MRS. LINDE. Yes, thanks. I nearly forgot it.

HELMER. Do you knit, then?

MRS. LINDE. Oh yes.

HELMER. You know what? You should embroider instead.

MRS. LINDE. Really? Why?

HELMER. Yes, because it's a lot prettier. See here, one holds the embroidery so, in the left hand, and then one guides the needle with the right—so—in an easy, sweeping curve—right?

MRS. LINDE. Yes, I guess that's—

HELMER. But, on the other hand, knitting—it can never be anything but ugly. Look, see here, the arms tucked in, the knitting needles going up and down—there's something Chinese about it. Ah, that was really a glorious champagne they served.

MRS. LINDE. Yes, good night, Nora, and don't be stubborn anymore.

HELMER. Well put, Mrs. Linde!

MRS. LINDE. Good night, Mr. Helmer.

HELMER (*accompanying her to the door*). Good night, good night. I hope you get home all right. I'd be very happy to—but you don't have far to go. Good night, good night. (*She leaves. He shuts the door after her and returns.*) There, now, at last we got her out the door. She's a deadly bore, that creature.

NORA. Aren't you pretty tired, Torvald?

HELMER. No, not a bit.

NORA. You're not sleepy?

HELMER. Not at all. On the contrary, I'm feeling quite exhilarated. But you? Yes, you really look tired and sleepy.

NORA. Yes, I'm very tired. Soon now I'll sleep.

HELMER. See! You see! I was right all along that we shouldn't stay longer.

NORA. Whatever you do is always right.

HELMER (*kissing her brow*). Now my little lark talks sense. Say, did you notice what a time Rank was having tonight?

NORA. Oh, was he? I didn't get to speak with him.

HELMER. I scarcely did either, but it's a long time since I've seen him in such high spirits. (*Gazes at her a moment, then comes nearer her.*) Hm—it's marvelous, though, to be back home again—to be completely alone with you. Oh, you bewitchingly lovely young woman!

NORA. Torvald, don't look at me like that!

HELMER. Can't I look at my richest treasure? At all that beauty that's mine, mine alone—completely and utterly.

NORA (*moving around to the other side of the table*). You mustn't talk to me that way tonight.

HELMER (*following her*). The tarantella is still in your blood, I can see—and it makes you even more enticing. Listen. The guests are beginning to go. (*Dropping his voice.*) Nora—it'll soon be quiet through this whole house.

NORA. Yes, I hope so.

HELMER. You do, don't you, my love? Do you realize—when I'm out at a party like this with you—do you know why I talk to you so little, and keep such a distance away; just send you a stolen look now and then—you know why I do it? It's because I'm imagining then that you're my secret darling, my secret young bride-to-be, and that no one suspects there's anything between us.

NORA. Yes, yes; oh, yes, I know you're always thinking of me.

HELMER. And then when we leave and I place the shawl over those fine young rounded shoulders—over that wonderful curving neck—then I pretend that you're my young bride, that we're just coming from the wedding, that for the first time I'm bringing you into my house—that for the first time I'm alone with you—completely alone with you, your trembling young beauty! All this evening I've longed for nothing but you. When I saw you turn and sway in the tarantella—my blood was pounding till I couldn't stand it—that's why I brought you down here so early—

NORA. Go away, Torvald! Leave me alone. I don't want all this.

HELMER. What do you mean? Nora, you're teasing me. You will, won't you? Aren't I your husband—?

(*A knock at the outside door.*)

NORA (*startled*). What's that?

HELMER (*going toward the hall*). Who is it?

RANK (*outside*). It's me. May I come in a moment?

HELMER (*with quiet irritation*). Oh, what does he want now? (*Aloud.*) Hold on. (*Goes and opens the door.*) Oh, how nice that you didn't just pass us by!

RANK. I thought I heard your voice, and then I wanted so badly to have a look in. (*Lightly glancing about.*) Ah, me, these old familiar haunts. You have it snug and cozy in here, you two.

HELMER. You seemed to be having it pretty cozy upstairs, too.

RANK. Absolutely. Why shouldn't I? Why not take in everything in life? As much as you can, anyway, and as long as you can. The wine was superb—

HELMER. The champagne especially.

RANK. You noticed that too? It's amazing how much I could guzzle down.

NORA. Torvald also drank a lot of champagne this evening.

RANK. Oh?

NORA. Yes, and that always makes him so entertaining.

RANK. Well, why shouldn't one have a pleasant evening after a well-spent day?

HELMER. Well spent? I'm afraid I can't claim that.

RANK (*slapping him on the back*). But I can, you see!

NORA. Dr. Rank, you must have done some scientific research today.

RANK. Quite so.

HELMER. Come now—little Nora talking about scientific research!

NORA. And can I congratulate you on the results?

RANK. Indeed you may.

NORA. Then they were good?

RANK. The best possible for both doctor and patient—certainty.

NORA (*quickly and searchingly*). Certainty?

RANK. Complete certainty. So don't I owe myself a gay evening afterwards?

NORA. Yes, you're right, Dr. Rank.

HELMER. I'm with you—just so long as you don't have to suffer for it in the morning.

RANK. Well, one never gets something for nothing in life.

NORA. Dr. Rank—are you very fond of masquerade parties?

RANK. Yes, if there's a good array of odd disguises—

NORA. Tell me, what should we two go as at the next masquerade?

HELMER. You little featherhead—already thinking of the next!

RANK. We two? I'll tell you what: you must go as Charmed Life—

HELMER. Yes, but find a costume for *that!*

RANK. Your wife can appear just as she looks every day.

HELMER. That was nicely put. But don't you know what you're going to be?

RANK. Yes, Helmer, I've made up my mind.

HELMER. Well?

RANK. At the next masquerade I'm going to be invisible.

HELMER. That's a funny idea.

RANK. They say there's a hat—black, huge—have you never heard of the hat that makes you invisible? You put it on, and then no one on earth can see you.

HELMER (*suppressing a smile*). Ah, of course.

RANK. But I'm quite forgetting what I came for. Helmer, give me a cigar, one of the dark Havanas.

HELMER. With the greatest pleasure. (*Holds out his case.*)

RANK. Thanks. (*Takes one and cuts off the tip.*)

NORA (*striking a match*). Let me give you a light.

RANK. Thank you. (*She holds the match for him; he lights the cigar.*) And now good-bye.

HELMER. Good-bye, good-bye, old friend.

NORA. Sleep well, Doctor.

RANK. Thanks for that wish.

NORA. Wish me the same.

RANK. You? All right, if you like— Sleep well. And thanks for the light. (*He nods to them both and leaves.*)

HELMER (*his voice subdued*). He's been drinking heavily.

NORA (*absently*). Could be. (HELMER *takes his keys from his pocket and goes out in the hall.*) Torvald—what are you after?

HELMER. Got to empty the mailbox; it's nearly full. There won't be room for the morning papers.

NORA. Are you working tonight?

HELMER. You know I'm not. Why—what's this? Someone's been at the lock.

NORA. At the lock—?

HELMER. Yes, I'm positive. What do you suppose—? I can't imagine one of the maids—? Here's a broken hairpin. Nora, it's yours—

NORA (*quickly*). Then it must be the children—

HELMER. You'd better break them of that. Hm, hm—well, opened it after all. (*Takes the contents out and calls into the kitchen.*) Helene! Helene, would you put out the lamp in the hall. (*He returns to the room, shutting the hall door, then displays the handful of mail.*) Look how it's piled up. (*Sorting through them.*) Now what's this?

NORA (*at the window*). The letter! Oh, Torvald, no!

HELMER. Two calling cards—from Rank.

NORA. From Dr. Rank?

HELMER (*examining them*). "Dr. Rank, Consulting Physician." They were on top. He must have dropped them in as he left.

NORA. Is there anything on them?

HELMER. There's a black cross over the name. See? That's a gruesome notion. He could almost be announcing his own death.

NORA. That's just what he's doing.

HELMER. What! You've heard something? Something he's told you?

NORA. Yes. That when those cards came, he'd be taking his leave of us. He'll shut himself in now and die.

HELMER. Ah, my poor friend! Of course I knew he wouldn't be here much longer. But so soon— And then to hide himself away like a wounded animal.

NORA. If it has to happen, then it's best it happens in silence—don't you think so, Torvald?

HELMER (*pacing up and down*). He'd grown right into our lives. I simply can't imagine him gone. He with his suffering and loneliness—like a dark cloud setting off our sunlit happiness. Well, maybe it's best this way. For him, at least. (*Standing still.*) And maybe for us too, Nora. Now we're thrown back on each other, completely. (*Embracing her.*) Oh you, my darling wife, how can I hold you close enough? You know what, Nora—time and again I've wished you were in some terrible danger, just so I could stake my life and soul and everything, for your sake.

NORA (*tearing herself away, her voice firm and decisive*). Now you must read your mail, Torvald.

HELMER. No, no, not tonight. I want to stay with you, dearest.

NORA. With a dying friend on your mind?

HELMER. You're right. We've both had a shock. There's ugliness between us— these thoughts of death and corruption. We'll have to get free of them first. Until then—we'll stay apart.

NORA (*clinging about his neck*). Torvald—good night! Good night!

HELMER (*kissing her on the cheek*). Good night, little songbird. Sleep well, Nora. I'll be reading my mail now. (*He takes the letters into his room and shuts the door after him.*)

NORA (*with bewildered glances, groping about, seizing* HELMER's *domino, throwing it around her, and speaking in short, hoarse, broken whispers*). Never see him again. Never, never. (*Putting her shawl over her head.*) Never see the children either—them, too. Never, never. Oh, the freezing black water! The depths—down— Oh, I wish it were over— He has it now; he's reading it—now. Oh no, no, not yet. Torvald, good-bye, you and the children— (*She starts for the hall; as she does,* HELMER *throws open his door and stands with an open letter in his hand.*)

HELMER. Nora!

NORA (*screams*). Oh—!

HELMER. What is this? You know what's in this letter?

NORA. Yes, I know. Let me go! Let me out!

HELMER (*holding her back*). Where are you going?

NORA (*struggling to break loose*). You can't save me, Torvald!

HELMER (*slumping back*). True! Then it's true what he writes? How horrible! No, no, it's impossible—it can't be true.

NORA. It *is* true. I've loved you more than all this world.

HELMER. Ah, none of your slippery tricks.

NORA (*taking one step toward him*). Torvald—!

HELMER. What *is* this you've blundered into!

NORA. Just let me loose. You're not going to suffer for my sake. You're not going to take on my guilt.

HELMER. No more playacting. (*Locks the hall door.*) You stay right here and give me a reckoning. You understand what you've done? Answer! You understand?

NORA (*looking squarely at him, her face hardening*). Yes. I'm beginning to understand everything now.

HELMER (*striding about*). Oh, what an awful awakening! In all these eight years—she who was my pride and joy—a hypocrite, a liar—worse, worse—a criminal! How infinitely disgusting it all is! The shame! (NORA *says nothing and goes on looking straight at him. He stops in front of her.*) I should have suspected something of the kind. I should have known. All your father's flimsy values— Be still! All your father's flimsy values have come out in you. No religion, no morals, no sense of duty— Oh, how I'm punished for letting him off! I did it for your sake, and you repay me like this.

NORA. Yes, like this.

HELMER. Now you've wrecked all my happiness—ruined my whole future. Oh, it's awful to think of. I'm in a cheap little grafter's hands; he can do anything he wants with me, ask for anything, play with me like a puppet—and I can't breathe a word. I'll be swept down miserably into the depths on account of a featherbrained woman.

NORA. When I'm gone from this world, you'll be free.

HELMER. Oh, quit posing. Your father had a mess of those speeches too. What good would that ever do me if you were gone from this world, as you say? Not the slightest. He can still make the whole thing known; and if he does, I could be falsely suspected as your accomplice. They might even think that I was behind it—that I put you up to it. And all that I can thank you for—you that I've coddled the whole of our marriage. Can you see now what you've done to me?

NORA (*icily calm*). Yes.

HELMER. It's so incredible, I just can't grasp it. But we'll have to patch up whatever we can. Take off the shawl. I said, take it off! I've got to appease him somehow or other. The thing has to be hushed up at any cost. And as for you and me, it's got to seem like everything between us is just as it was—to the outside world, that is. You'll go right on living in this house, of course. But you can't be allowed to bring up the children; I don't dare trust you with them—Oh, to have to say this to someone I've loved so much! Well, that's done with. From now on happiness doesn't matter; all that matters is saving the bits and pieces, the appearance—(*The doorbell rings.* HELMER *starts.*) What's that? And so late. Maybe the worst—? You think he'd—? Hide, Nora! Say you're sick. (NORA *remains standing motionless.* HELMER *goes and opens the door.*)

MAID (*half dressed, in the hall*). A letter for Mrs. Helmer.

HELMER. I'll take it. (*Snatches the letter and shuts the door.*) Yes, it's from him. You don't get it; I'm reading it myself.

NORA. Then read it.

HELMER (*by the lamp*). I hardly dare. We may be ruined, you and I. But—I've got to know. (*Rips open the letter, skims through a few lines, glances at an enclosure, then cries out joyfully.*) Nora! (NORA *looks inquiringly at him.*) Nora! Wait—better check it again— Yes, yes, it's true. I'm saved. Nora, I'm saved!

NORA. And I?

HELMER. You too, of course. We're both saved, both of us. Look. He's sent back your note. He says he's sorry and ashamed—that a happy development in his life—oh, who cares what he says! Nora, we're saved! No one can hurt you. Oh, Nora, Nora—but first, this ugliness all has to go. Let me see— (*Takes a look at the note.*) No, I don't want to see it; I want the whole thing to fade like a dream. (*Tears the note and both letters to pieces, throws them into the stove and watches them burn.*) There—now there's nothing left— He wrote that since Christmas Eve you—Oh, they must have been three terrible days for you, Nora.

NORA. I fought a hard fight.

HELMER. And suffered pain and saw no escape but—No, we're not going to dwell on anything unpleasant. We'll just be grateful and keep on repeating: it's over now, it's over! You hear me, Nora? You don't seem to realize—it's over. What's it mean—that frozen look? Oh, poor little Nora, I understand. You can't believe I've forgiven you. But I have. Nora; I swear I have. I know that what you did, you did out of love for me.

NORA. That's true.

HELMER. You loved me the way a wife ought to love her husband. It's simply the means that you couldn't judge. But you think I love you any the less for not knowing how to handle your affairs? No, no—just lean on me; I'll guide you and teach you. I wouldn't be a man if this feminine helplessness didn't make you twice as attractive to me. You mustn't mind those sharp words I said—that was all in the first confusion of thinking my world had collapsed. I've forgiven you, Nora; I swear I've forgiven you.

NORA. My thanks for your forgiveness. (*She goes out through the door, right.*)

HELMER. No, wait— (*Peers in.*) What are you doing in there?

NORA (*inside*). Getting out of my costume.

HELMER (*by the open door*). Yes, do that. Try to calm yourself and collect your thoughts again, my frightened little songbird. You can rest easy now; I've got wide wings to shelter you with. (*Walking about close by the door.*) How snug and nice our home is, Nora. You're safe here; I'll keep you like a hunted dove I've rescued out of a hawk's claws. I'll bring peace to your poor, shuddering heart. Gradually it'll happen, Nora; you'll see. Tomorrow all this will look different to you; then everything will be as it was. I won't have to go on repeating I forgive you; you'll feel it for yourself. How can you imagine I'd ever conceivably want to disown you—or even blame you in any way? Ah, you don't know a man's heart, Nora. For a man there's something indescribably sweet and satisfying in knowing he's forgiven his wife—and forgiven her out of a full and open heart. It's as if she belongs to him in two ways now: in a sense he's given her fresh into the world again, and she's become his wife and his child as well. From now on that's what you'll be to me—you little, bewildered, helpless thing. Don't be afraid of anything, Nora; just open your heart to me, and I'll be conscience and will to you both—(NORA *enters in her regular clothes.*) What's this? Not in bed? You've changed your dress?

NORA. Yes, Torvald, I've changed my dress.

HELMER. But why now, so late?

NORA. Tonight I'm not sleeping.

HELMER. But Nora dear—

NORA (*looking at her watch*). It's still not so very late. Sit down, Torvald; we have a lot to talk over. (*She sits at one side of the table.*)

HELMER. Nora—what is this? That hard expression—

NORA. Sit down. This'll take some time. I have a lot to say.

HELMER (*sitting at the table directly opposite her*). You worry me, Nora. And I don't understand you.

NORA. No, that's exactly it. You don't understand me. And I've never understood you either—until tonight. No, don't interrupt. You can just listen to what I say. We're closing out accounts, Torvald.

HELMER. How do you mean that?

NORA (*after a short pause*). Doesn't anything strike you about our sitting here like this?

HELMER. What's that?

NORA. We've been married now eight years. Doesn't it occur to you that this is the first time we two, you and I, man and wife, have ever talked seriously together?

HELMER. What do you mean—seriously?

NORA. In eight whole years—longer even—right from our first acquaintance, we've never exchanged a serious word on any serious thing.

HELMER. You mean I should constantly go and involve you in problems you couldn't possibly help me with?

NORA. I'm not talking of problems. I'm saying that we've never sat down seriously together and tried to get to the bottom of anything.

HELMER. But dearest, what good would that ever do you?

NORA. That's the point right there: you've never understood me. I've been wronged greatly, Torvald—first by Papa, and then by you.

HELMER. What! By us—the two people who've loved you more than anyone else?

NORA (*shaking her head*). You never loved me. You've thought it fun to be in love with me, that's all.

HELMER. Nora, what a thing to say!

NORA. Yes, it's true now, Torvald. When I lived at home with Papa, he told me all his opinions, so I had the same ones too; or if they were different I hid them, since he wouldn't have cared for that. He used to call me his doll-child, and he played with me the way I played with my dolls. Then I came into your house—

HELMER. How can you speak of our marriage like that?

NORA (*unperturbed*). I mean, then I went from Papa's hands into yours. You arranged everything to your own taste, and so I got the same taste as you—or I pretended to; I can't remember. I guess a little of both, first one, then the other. Now when I look back, it seems as if I'd lived here like a beggar—just from hand to mouth. I've lived by doing tricks for you, Torvald. But that's the way you wanted it. It's a great sin what you and Papa did to me. You're to blame that nothing's become of me.

HELMER. Nora, how unfair and ungrateful you are! Haven't you been happy here?

NORA. No, never. I thought so—but I never have.

HELMER. Not—not happy!

NORA. No, only lighthearted. And you've always been so kind to me. But our home's been nothing but a playpen. I've been your doll-wife here, just as at home I was Papa's doll-child. And in turn the children have been my dolls. I thought it was fun when you played with me, just as they thought it fun when I played with them. That's been our marriage, Torvald.

HELMER. There's some truth in what you're saying—under all the raving exaggeration. But it'll all be different after this. Playtime's over; now for the schooling.

NORA. Whose schooling—mine or the children's?

HELMER. Both yours and the children's, dearest.

NORA. Oh, Torvald, you're not the man to teach me to be a good wife to you.

HELMER. And you can say that?

NORA. And I—how am I equipped to bring up children?

HELMER. Nora!

NORA. Didn't you say a moment ago that that was no job to trust me with?

HELMER. In a flare of temper! Why fasten on that?

NORA. Yes, but you were so very right. I'm not up to the job. There's another job I have to do first. I have to try to educate myself. You can't help me with that. I've got to do it alone. And that's why I'm leaving you now.

HELMER (*jumping up*). What's that?

NORA. I have to stand completely alone, if I'm ever going to discover myself and the world out there. So I can't go on living with you.

HELMER. Nora, Nora!

NORA. I want to leave right away. Kristine should put me up for the night—

HELMER. You're insane! You've no right! I forbid you!

NORA. From here on, there's no use forbidding me anything. I'll take with me whatever is mine. I don't want a thing from you, either now or later.

HELMER. What kind of madness is this!

NORA. Tomorrow I'm going home—I mean, home where I came from. It'll be easier up there to find something to do.

HELMER. Oh, you blind, incompetent child!

NORA. I must learn to be competent, Torvald.

HELMER. Abandon your home, your husband, your children! And you're not even thinking what people will say.

NORA. I can't be concerned about that. I only know how essential this is.

HELMER. Oh, it's outrageous. So you'll run out like this on your most sacred vows.

NORA. What do you think are my most sacred vows?

HELMER. And I have to tell you that! Aren't they your duties to your husband and children?

NORA. I have other duties equally sacred.

HELMER. That isn't true. What duties are they?

NORA. Duties to myself.

HELMER. Before all else, you're a wife and a mother.

NORA. I don't believe in that anymore. I believe that, before all else, I'm a human being, no less than you—or anyway, I ought to try to become one. I know the majority thinks you're right, Torvald, and plenty of books agree with you, too. But I can't go on believing what the majority says, or what's written in books. I have to think over these things myself and try to understand them.

HELMER. Why can't you understand your place in your own home? On a point like that, isn't there one everlasting guide you can turn to? Where's your religion?

NORA. Oh, Torvald, I'm really not sure what religion is.

HELMER. What—?

NORA. I only know what the minister said when I was confirmed. He told me religion was this thing and that. When I get clear and away by myself, I'll go into that problem too. I'll see if what the minister said was right, or, in any case, if it's right for me.

HELMER. A young woman your age shouldn't talk like that. If religion can't move you, I can try to rouse your conscience. You do have some moral feeling? Or, tell me—has that gone too?

NORA. It's not easy to answer that, Torvald. I simply don't know. I'm all confused about these things. I just know I see them so differently from you. I find out, for one thing, that the law's not at all what I'd thought—but I can't get it through my head that the law is fair. A woman hasn't a right to protect her dying father or save her husband's life! I can't believe that.

HELMER. You talk like a child. You don't know anything of the world you live in.

NORA. No, I don't. But now I'll begin to learn for myself. I'll try to discover who's right, the world or I.

HELMER. Nora, you're sick; you've got a fever. I almost think you're out of your head.

NORA. I've never felt more clearheaded and sure in my life.

HELMER. And—clearheaded and sure—you're leaving your husband and children?

NORA. Yes.

HELMER. Then there's only one possible reason.

NORA. What?

HELMER. You no longer love me.

NORA. No. That's exactly it.

HELMER. Nora! You can't be serious!

NORA. Oh, this is so hard, Torvald—you've been so kind to me always. But I can't help it. I don't love you anymore.

HELMER (*struggling for composure*). Are you also clearheaded and sure about that?

NORA. Yes, completely. That's why I can't go on staying here.

HELMER. Can you tell me what I did to lose your love?

NORA. Yes, I can tell you. It was this evening when the miraculous thing didn't come—then I knew you weren't the man I'd imagined.

HELMER. Be more explicit; I don't follow you.

NORA. I've waited now so patiently eight long years—for, my Lord, I know miracles don't come every day. Then this crisis broke over me, and such a certainty filled me: *now* the miraculous event would occur. While Krogstad's letter was lying out there, I never for an instant dreamed that you could give in to his terms. I was so utterly sure you'd say to him: go on, tell your tale to the whole wide world. And when he'd done that—

HELMER. Yes, what then? When I'd delivered my own wife into shame and disgrace—!

NORA. When he'd done that, I was so utterly sure that you'd step forward, take the blame on yourself and say: I am the guilty one.

HELMER. Nora—!

NORA. You're thinking I'd never accept such a sacrifice from you? No, of course not. But what good would my protests be against you? That was the miracle I was waiting for, in terror and hope. And to stave that off, I would have taken my life.

HELMER. I'd gladly work for you day and night, Nora—and take on pain and deprivation. But there's no one who gives up honor for love.

NORA. Millions of women have done just that.

HELMER. Oh, you think and talk like a silly child.

NORA. Perhaps. But you neither think nor talk like the man I could join myself to. When your big fright was over—and it wasn't from any threat against me, only for what might damage you—when all the danger was past, for you it was just as if nothing had happened. I was exactly the same, your little lark, your doll, that you'd have to handle with double care now that I'd turned out so brittle and frail. (*Gets up.*) Torvald—in that instant it dawned on me that for eight years I've been living here with a stranger, and that I'd even conceived three children—oh, I can't stand the thought of it! I could tear myself to bits.

HELMER (*heavily*). I see. There's a gulf that's opened between us—that's clear. Oh, but Nora, can't we bridge it somehow?

NORA. The way I am now, I'm no wife for you.

HELMER. I have the strength to make myself over.

NORA. Maybe—if your doll gets taken away.

HELMER. But to part! To part from you! No, Nora, no—I can't imagine it.

NORA (*going out, right*). All the more reason why it has to be. (*She reenters with her coat and a small overnight bag, which she puts on a chair by the table.*)

HELMER. Nora, Nora, not now! Wait till tomorrow.

NORA. I can't spend the night in a strange man's room.

HELMER. But couldn't we live here like brother and sister—

NORA. You know very well how long that would last. (*Throws her shawl about her.*) Good-bye, Torvald. I won't look in on the children. I know they're in better hands than mine. The way I am now, I'm no use to them.

HELMER. But someday, Nora—someday—?

NORA. How can I tell? I haven't the least idea what'll become of me.

HELMER. But you're my wife, now and wherever you go.

NORA. Listen, Torvald—I've heard that when a wife deserts her husband's house just as I'm doing, then the law frees him from all responsibility. In any case, I'm freeing you from being responsible. Don't feel yourself bound, any more than I will. There has to be absolute freedom for us both. Here, take your ring back. Give me mine.

HELMER. That too?

NORA. That too.

HELMER. There it is.

NORA. Good. Well, now it's all over. I'm putting the keys here. The maids know all about keeping up the house—better than I do. Tomorrow, after I've left town, Kristine will stop by to pack up everything that's mine from home. I'd like those things shipped up to me.

HELMER. Over! All over! Nora, won't you ever think about me?

NORA. I'm sure I'll think of you often, and about the children and the house here.

HELMER. May I write you?

NORA. No—never. You're not to do that.

HELMER. Oh, but let me send you—

NORA. Nothing. Nothing.

HELMER. Or help you if you need it.

NORA. No. I accept nothing from strangers.

HELMER. Nora—can I never be more than a stranger to you?

NORA (*picking up the overnight bag*). Ah, Torvald—it would take the greatest miracle of all—

HELMER. Tell me the greatest miracle!

NORA. You and I both would have to transform ourselves to the point that— Oh, Torvald, I've stopped believing in miracles.

HELMER. But I'll believe. Tell me! Transform ourselves to the point that—?

NORA. That our living together could be a true marriage. (*She goes out down the hall.*)

HELMER (*sinks down on a chair by the door, face buried in his hands*). Nora! Nora! (*Looking about and rising.*) Empty. She's gone. (*A sudden hope leaps in him.*) The greatest miracle—?

(*From below, the sound of a door slamming shut.*)

✴ INSPIRATION   LEE BREUER'S *DOLLHOUSE*

In Lee Breuer's DollHouse, *the male actors are of shorter than average height (four feet and under); the female actors are of regular height. They perform on a dollhouse set with child-sized furniture.*

Of all the modern productions of Henrik Ibsen's work, Lee Breuer's 2005 adaptation of *A Doll House* for the Mabou Mines theater company is perhaps the most unusual: while all the female roles are played by statuesque women of taller-than-average height, all the male roles are played by dwarfs. In an article in the *Village Voice,* Breuer explained why he chose such casting for his *DollHouse*: "The patriarchy is in reality three feet tall, but has a voice that will dominate six-foot women. Male power isn't dependent on physical size. At the same time we're exploring the metaphor from the woman's point of view, the way maternal love is lavished on these child-size men, which only infantilizes them further." Breuer further reinforces his theme with thirty-six handmade marionettes, which stand in pairs in boxes cut out from the stage's back wall. For more information about Breuer's *DollHouse* and to read reviews, check out Breuer's website at *http://www.leebreuer.com.*

Talking about the Text

1. When she first appears, Nora lies about what she is eating. What is the significance of introducing her character with a little lie like this? What are some other lies Nora tells and what do they tell the audience about her character?
2. What do you make of the title and the significance it might have at the play's opening? How does your understanding of its meaning change as the play progresses?
3. How would you describe the relationship between Nora and Helmer at the beginning of the play?
4. What is Nora going to do once she leaves? Why is it impossible for her to do this at home?

5. Despite its realistic approach, certain items in *A Doll House* seem to serve as symbols. Discuss three such symbols.

6. An early German production with a celebrated actress had Nora and Helmer reconcile at the end; the door never slams in that version. What do you think of such an alternative, especially in terms of dramatic effectiveness?

7. What kind of a case can be made for Helmer as a sympathetic character?

Writing about the Text

1. Ask other class members exactly what it is that Ibsen has dramatized. Write down the answers as precisely as you can. Then write a paper explaining the variety of responses you got. What did others assume about key issues such as the sanctity of marriage? Raising children? Honesty within the family?

2. Examine responsibility in *A Doll House*. Exactly who is responsible for what and why? Who causes the actions to happen? (Remember, we learn that it was Nora's actions that probably saved Helmer's life, thus making her responsible for allowing their relationship to continue as it appears in the first act.) Then, in a paper, trace the theme of responsibility as it appears throughout the play.

3. When praised for being a friend of the feminist movement, Ibsen said *A Doll House* was more about human rights than women's rights. How do you respond to his comment? What might Ibsen have said about your response? Construct an argument in which you either agree or disagree with Ibsen's analysis.

Linking the Text to Other Texts

1. How is Nora similar to or different from Antigone (see p. 1303) in her relationship to either male authority or the law?

2. What characteristics does Helmer share with the male characters in Susan Glaspell's *Trifles* (see p. 1166)?

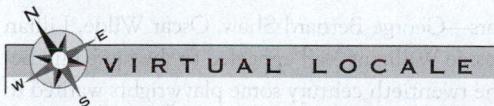

VIRTUAL LOCALE

Ibsen on the Net. According to the National Ibsen Committee of Norway, one of Ibsen's plays was produced somewhere around the world every week in 2006, which marked the 100th anniversary of the Norwegian playwright's death. And *http://www.ibsen.net*, the extensive website of the National Ibsen Committee, tracked every performance. Although the website was created in anticipation of Ibsen Year 2006, the site remains a wonderful resource for students, scholars, or curious theatergoers. The site discusses Ibsen as a poet, playwright, and painter; catalogs current productions around the world; lists Ibsen works appearing on television, radio, film, and in other media; discusses Ibsen's relationship with the painter Edvard Munch and his work as realism; and lists many other Ibsen resources. The site is available in English at *www.ibsen.net/english*.

Starting Points for Further Research: Henrik Ibsen

- **Edition:** Henrik Ibsen. *Selected Plays: Authoritative Texts of Peer Gynt, A Doll's House, The Wild Duck, Hedda Gabler, The Master Builder*. Ed. Brian Johnston. New York: W. W. Norton, 2003.
- **Biography:** Michael Meyer. *Ibsen: A Biography*. New York: Penguin, 2002.
- **Critical Essay:** Rachel Joyce. "Rehearsing and Playing *A Doll's House*." *Women: A Cultural Review* 5 (1994): 198–203.

MODERN THEATER

> Modern theater is a theater of thought. Realism is a
> thinking theater, a verbal theater. There are not many jokes.
> . . . you do not dance much in realism, because if you use
> your feet you can't also use your mind. . . . Realism needs an
> intelligent audience to listen to what it has to say.
> —*Stella Adler*, Ibsen

The hundred years of theater between Henrik Ibsen and Tennessee Williams, roughly 1850 to 1950, witnessed great changes in the ways plays were performed, including a transformation of the theater audience, an altered sense of the stage, and new movements in drama. These sweeping changes have influenced our expectations and perceptions of the theater today.

New Plays, New Audiences

If Shakespeare's plays had something for everyone, from high poetry to low comedy, by the 1870s theatrical offerings and audiences had become fragmented. There were more and different kinds of shows to attend, and audiences chose what most appealed to them. For example, the audience for popular theater—simple melodramas, the music hall, vaudeville, and musical theater—grew enormously. The audience for "serious" drama like Ibsen's also grew, but it was limited mostly to the educated middle class.

Henrik Ibsen and his successors—George Bernard Shaw, Oscar Wilde, Lillian Hellman, Arthur Miller, and Tennessee Williams—all appealed to the same middle-class audience. But even early in the twentieth century some playwrights wanted to move away from the mainstream and become more avant garde, to situate themselves far from the lights of the Broadway commercial theater. As we saw with Glaspell's *Trifles* (p. 1166), small, experimental stage companies were attracting thoughtful writers and intellectual audiences. At the same time, as with Lady Gregory's *Spreading the News* (p. 1183), nationalistic theater persisted, sometimes under great pressure from audiences with a narrow political perspective. The modern theater of the twentieth century would see many different types of plays aimed at many different audiences.

Changing the Stage

Henrik Ibsen, the father of modern theater, wrote all his plays for the then-conventional stage, the familiar three-sided box with a proscenium curtain (see p. 1163, in Chapter 20). Since Ibsen's day, theater designers have tried different designs, such as the thrust stage or theater in the round (see p. 1165, Chapter 20), all in an attempt to build intimacy and immediacy, and more recently, to differentiate live theater from films and television. But the proscenium stage has proved durable, and much contemporary theater is written for it. One reason the stage has endured is that playwrights and directors have been able to modify it, and thus, give it unexpected depth and complexity.

For instance, one of the most significant plays to popularize a new kind of set within the traditional stage arrangement was Arthur Miller's *Death of a Salesman* (1949). In the stage directions, Miller specifies three separate mini-sets on the

(continued)

A detailed sketch of Jo Mielziner's set design for the original 1949 production of Death of a Salesman, *directed by Elia Kazan.*

The set designed by Jo Mielziner for the original 1949 Broadway production of Death of a Salesman *opened up the conventional stage with a complex, three-level set that shows the emotional levels of the characters in the play. Pictured here are (from left to right) Mildred Dunnock (Linda), Lee J. Cobb (Willy), Arthur Kennedy (Biff), and Cameron Mitchell (Happy).*

proscenium stage, each representing a separate part of the Loman home: the father's space, the sons' room, and common space. The lighting switches between these rooms as the action moves from place to place. Thus, using a traditional stage, Miller found a way to parcel out the space in ways that show shifts in action and changes in time, including flashbacks. Jo Mielziner's challenge as the set designer for the original Broadway production was to create innovative designs that could accommodate not only different scenic locations—though much of the play takes place in the family house, other scenes take place in the corner of a graveyard, a Boston hotel room, a business office, and so on—but also instantaneous shifts in time from the present to the past and back again. Mielziner's solution was to allow the house to be the main set, with all the other scenes in other locations played in the foreground on a forestage, with the house still looming, both literally and figuratively, like a specter in the background over all that transpires, and to use painstakingly plotted lighting shifts to signify changes in time. This combination of aesthetic realism along with emotional abstraction in the set design lent itself well to the themes of the play. And in the decades since, it has spawned many imitations in sets for other productions.

Psychology, "The Method," and Politics

Around 1920, psychology—a relatively new academic discipline—came to the fore as dramatists attempted to examine and explore the interior lives of their characters. This emphasis on psychological exploration by such playwrights as Arthur Miller and Tennessee Williams meshed nicely with the rise of the "method" acting school, as practiced by Marlon Brando, Uta Hagen, James Dean, Paul Newman, Joanne Woodward, Al Pacino, and a host of stage actors who later migrated from New York to Hollywood. Derived from the teachings of Russian stage director Konstantin Stanislavsky (1863–1938), "the method" was popularized in the United States by director, actor, producer, and teacher Lee Strasberg at the Actors

TENNESSEE WILLIAMS AND POETIC REALISM

Tennessee Williams, 1952.

Mississippi-born Thomas Lanier Williams (1911–1983) wrote more than seventy plays, twenty-five of them full-length works, basing much of his drama, and specifically *The Glass Menagerie*, on his early upbringing in the South and in St. Louis. His father was a domineering salesman and his mother thought of herself as something of a southern belle. And Williams's emotionally fragile, highly strung sister Rose probably influenced his depiction of Laura in *Menagerie*.

Williams attended college off and on, finally graduating from the University of Iowa in 1938. He then moved to New Orleans, spending much of his time in

"Method" actor Marlon Brando.

Studio and the Group Theatre in New York. Performance for method actors meant getting inside the characters' minds and *becoming* the character, and the approach appealed to American theatergoers: here was drama that clearly engrossed the actors on the stage. (British actors, trained in a totally different tradition, were unimpressed. While American performers used "the method" to get at the character's psychology, the British simply relied on "acting.")

In spite of this trend in technique and approach, some modern writers rebelled against a focus on inner psychology by making their plays overtly political; they, too, found a willing audience in a century of upheaval. Such political theater regarded characters as types, not individuals, and saw humans enmeshed in political forces over which they had very little control. At the forefront of political theater was German playwright Bertolt Brecht, author of *The Threepenny Opera* (1928) with music by Kurt Weill, *Mother Courage and Her Children* (1941), and *Life of Galileo* (1947). Refusing to let audiences have the illusion they were watching anything like "real" life, Brecht created characters that are unrealistic, stock figures. One of the contemporary plays in this book, Luis Valdez's *Los Vendidos* (p. 1867), bears strong traces of Brecht's influence.

the French Quarter, changed his name to Tennessee, and came out as homosexual. Despite being openly gay in his personal life, he was unable to write candidly about his sexuality during the repressive 1950s, his most prolific decade as a playwright. Consequently perhaps, like his characters, he led a life often marked by frustration, duality, and deception.

The Glass Menagerie (1945) was his first success, followed shortly thereafter by *A Streetcar Named Desire* (1947), which won a Pulitzer Prize. *Streetcar* went on to become a classic movie in 1951, starring Marlon Brando (reprising his role from the original stage version) and Vivien Leigh and directed by Elia Kazan. Both plays explore the intense confrontations that burst out when people are freed from social repression. These two well-received plays, which remain Williams's best-known works, were followed by a string of hits: *Summer and Smoke* (1948), *The Rose Tattoo* (1950), *Cat on a Hot Tin Roof* (Pulitzer Prize, 1955), *Sweet Bird of Youth* (1959), *Period of Adjustment* (1959), *Night of the Iguana* (1961), and *The Milk Train Doesn't Stop Here Anymore* (1963). Many of these plays were made into successful Hollywood movies with some of the biggest stars of the era: Kirk Douglas, Jane Wyman, Elizabeth Taylor, Katharine Hepburn, Montgomery Clift, Burt Lancaster, Ava Gardner, Paul Newman, Jane Fonda, and Richard Burton.

Williams is noted for what he termed "poetic realism": common objects, like the glass menagerie of his play, take on an intense symbolic meaning. It is as if the everyday world we live in is close to another, unseen world filled with dreams and lurking violence. The symbolic link between these worlds is ostensibly something simple and straightforward, like a collection of glass animals. *The Glass Menagerie* mixes realism and a world of dreams. The play is set among a dysfunctional mix of working-class and lower middle-class family members in St. Louis, but the normal continuity is deliberately broken when a major character, Tom Wingfield, appears onstage, sometimes to narrate events, sometimes to participate in the action. The conventions of the realistic theater that characterized plays like Glaspell's *Trifles* and Ibsen's *A Doll House* coexist with dreamlike sequences, as Williams searches for a way to depict the inner life of his characters.

Amanda (Ruby Dee), and Tom (Jonathan Earl Peck) in the 1989 Arena Stage production of The Glass Menagerie.

TENNESSEE WILLIAMS   (1911–1983)
The Glass Menagerie   (1945)

The Characters

AMANDA WINGFIELD (*the mother*)
A little woman of great but confused vitality clinging frantically to another time and place. Her characterization must be carefully created, not copied from type. She is not paranoiac, but her life is paranoia. There is much to admire in Amanda, and as much to love and pity as there is to laugh at. Certainly she has endurance and a kind of heroism, and though her foolishness makes her unwittingly cruel at times, there is tenderness in her slight person.

LAURA WINGFIELD (*her daughter*)
Amanda, having failed to establish contact with reality, continues to live vitally in her illusions, but Laura's situation is even graver. A childhood illness has left her crippled, one leg slightly shorter than the other, and held in a brace. This defect need not be more than suggested on the stage. Stemming from this, Laura's separation increases till she is like a piece of her own glass collection, too exquisitely fragile to move from the shelf.

TOM WINGFIELD (*her son*)
And the narrator of the play. A poet with a job in a warehouse. His nature is not remorseless, but to escape from a trap he has to act without pity.

JIM O'CONNOR (*the gentleman caller*)
A nice, ordinary, young man.

Scene

An Alley in St. Louis
Part I. Preparation for a Gentleman Caller.
Part II. The Gentleman calls.
Time: Now and the Past.

Production Notes

Being a "memory play," *The Glass Menagerie* can be presented with unusual freedom of convention. Because of its considerably delicate or tenuous material, atmospheric touches and subtleties of direction play a particularly important part. Expressionism and all other unconventional techniques in drama have only one valid aim, and that is a closer approach to truth. When a play employs unconventional techniques, it is not, or certainly shouldn't be, trying to escape its responsibility of dealing with reality, or interpreting experience, but is actually or should be attempting to find a closer approach, a more penetrating and vivid expression of things as they are. The straight realistic play with its genuine frigidaire and authentic ice-cubes, its characters that speak exactly as its audience speaks, corresponds to the academic landscape and has the same virtue of a photographic likeness. Everyone should know nowadays the unimportance of the photographic in art: that truth, life, or reality is an organic thing which the poetic imagination can represent or suggest, in essence, only through transformation, through changing into other forms than those which were merely present in appearance.

These remarks are not meant as a preface only to this particular play. They have to do with a conception of a new, plastic theatre which must take the place of the exhausted theatre of realistic conventions if the theatre is to resume vitality as a part of our culture.

The Screen Device

There is *only one important difference between the original and acting version of the play* and that is the *omission* in the latter of the device which I tentatively included in my *original* script. This device was the use of a screen on which were projected magic-lantern slides bearing images or titles. I do not regret the omission of this device from the present Broadway production. The extraordinary power of Miss Taylor's performance made it suitable to have the utmost simplicity in the physical production. But I think it may be interesting to some readers to see how this device was conceived. So I am putting it into the published manuscript. These images and legends, projected from behind, were cast on a section of wall between the front-room and dining-room areas, which should be indistinguishable from the rest when not in use.

The purpose of this will probably be apparent. It is to give accent to certain values in each scene. Each scene contains a particular point (or several) which is structurally the most important. In an episodic play, such as this, the basic structure or narrative line may be obscured from the audience; the effect may seem fragmentary rather than architectural. This may not be the fault of the play so much as a lack of attention in the audience. The legend or image upon the screen will strengthen the effect of what is merely allusion in the writing and allow the primary point to be made more simply and lightly than if the entire responsibility were on the spoken lines. Aside from this structural value, I think the screen will have a definite emotional appeal, less definable but just as important. An imaginative producer or director may invent many other uses for this device than those indicated in the present script. In fact the possibilities of the device seem much larger to me than the instance of this play can possibly utilize.

The Music

Another extra-literary accent in this play is provided by the use of music. A single recurring tune, "The Glass Menagerie," is used to give emotional emphasis to suitable passages. This tune is like circus music, not when you are on the grounds or in the immediate vicinity of the parade, but when you are at some distance and very likely thinking of something else. It seems under those circumstances to continue almost interminably and it weaves in and out of your preoccupied consciousness; then it is the lightest, most delicate music in the world and perhaps the saddest. It expresses the surface vivacity of life with the underlying strain of immutable and inexpressible sorrow. When you look at a piece of delicately spun glass you think of two things: how beautiful it is and how easily it can be broken. Both of those ideas should be woven into the recurring tune, which dips in and out of the play as if it were carried on a wind that changes. It serves as a thread of connection and allusion between the narrator with his separate point in time and space and the subject of his story. Between each episode it returns as reference to the emotion, nostalgia, which is the first condition of the play. It is primarily Laura's music and therefore comes out most clearly when the play focuses upon her and the lovely fragility of glass which is her image.

The Lighting

The lighting in the play is not realistic. In keeping with the atmosphere of memory, the stage is dim. Shafts of light are focused on selected areas or actors, sometimes in contradistinction to what is the apparent center. For instance, in the quarrel scene between Tom and Amanda, in which Laura has no active part, the clearest pool of light is on her figure. This is also true of the supper scene, when her silent figure on the sofa should remain the visual center. The light upon Laura should be distinct from the others, having a peculiar pristine clarity such as light used in early religious portraits of female saints or madonnas. A certain correspondence to light in religious paintings, such as El Greco's, where the figures are radiant in atmosphere that is relatively dusky, could be effectively used throughout the play. (It will also permit a more effective use of the screen.) A free, imaginative use of light can be of enormous value in giving a mobile, plastic quality to plays of a more or less static nature.

T. W. [Tennessee Williams]

SCENE I

The Wingfield apartment is in the rear of the building, one of those vast hive-like conglomerations of cellular living-units that flower as warty growths in overcrowded urban centers of lower middle-class population and are symptomatic of the impulse of this largest and fundamentally en-slaved section of American society to avoid fluidity and differentiation and to exist and function as one interfused mass of automatism.

The apartment faces an alley and is entered by a fire-escape, a structure whose name is a touch of accidental poetic truth, for all of these huge buildings are always burning with the slow and implacable fires of human desperation. The fire-escape is included in the set—that is, the landing of it and steps descending from it.

The scene is memory and is therefore nonrealistic. Memory takes a lot of poetic license. It omits some details; others are exaggerated, ac-cording to the emotional value of the articles it touches, for memory is seated predominantly in the heart. The interior is therefore rather dim and poetic.

At the rise of the curtain, the audience is faced with the dark, grim rear wall of the Wingfield tenement. This building, which runs parallel to the footlights, is flanked on both sides by dark, narrow alleys which run into murky canyons of tangled clothes-lines, garbage cans and the sinis-ter lattice-work of neighboring fire-escapes. It is up and down these side alleys that exterior entrances and exits are made, during the play. At the end of Tom's opening commentary, the dark tenement wall slowly re-veals (by means of a transparency) the interior of the ground floor Wing-field apartment.

Downstage is the living room, which also serves as a sleeping room for Laura, the sofa unfolding to make her bed. Upstage, center, and di-vided by a wide arch or second proscenium with transparent faded portieres (or second curtain), is the dining room. In an old-fashioned what-not in the living room are seen scores of transparent glass animals. A blown-up photograph of the father hangs on the wall of the living room, facing the audience, to the left of the archway. It is the face of a very handsome young man in a doughboy's First World War cap. He is gallantly smiling, ineluctably smiling, as if to say, "I will be smiling for-ever."

The audience hears and sees the opening scene in the dining room through both the transparent fourth wall of the building and the transpar-ent gauze portieres of the dining-room arch. It is during this revealing scene that the fourth wall slowly ascends, out of sight. This transparent exterior wall is not brought down again until the very end of the play, during Tom's final speech.

The narrator is an undisguised convention of the play. He takes whatever license with dramatic convention as is convenient to his purposes.

Tom enters dressed as a merchant sailor from alley, stage left, and strolls across the front of the stage to the fire-escape. There he stops and lights a cigarette. He addresses the audience.

TOM: Yes, I have tricks in my pocket, I have things up my sleeve. But I am the opposite of a stage magician. He gives you illusion that has the appearance of truth. I give you truth in the pleasant disguise of illusion.

To begin with, I turn back time. I reverse it to that quaint period, the thirties, when the huge middle class of America was matriculating in a school for the blind. Their eyes had failed them, or they had failed their eyes, and so they were having their fingers pressed forcibly down on the fiery Braille alphabet of a dissolving economy.

In Spain there was revolution. Here there was only shouting and confusion.

In Spain there was Guernica. Here there were disturbances of labor, sometimes pretty violent, in otherwise peaceful cities such as Chicago, Cleveland, Saint Louis . . .

This is the social background of the play.

(MUSIC.)

The play is memory.

Being a memory play, it is dimly lighted, it is sentimental, it is not realistic.

In memory everything seems to happen to music. That explains the fiddle in the wings.

I am the narrator of the play, and also a character in it.

The other characters are my mother, Amanda, my sister, Laura, and a gentleman caller who appears in the final scenes.

He is the most realistic character in the play, being an emissary from a world of reality that we were somehow set apart from.

But since I have a poet's weakness for symbols, I am using this character also as a symbol; he is the long delayed but always expected something that we live for.

There is a fifth character in the play who doesn't appear except in this larger-than-life-size photograph over the mantel.

This is our father who left us a long time ago.

He was a telephone man who fell in love with long distances; he gave up his job with the telephone company and skipped the light fantastic out of town . . .

The last we heard of him was a picture post-card from Mazatlan, on the Pacific coast of Mexico, containing a message of two words—

"Hello—Good-bye!" and no address.

I think the rest of the play will explain itself. . . .

(*Amanda's voice becomes audible through the portieres.*)
    (LEGEND ON SCREEN: "*OU SONT LES NEIGES.*")
    (*He divides the portieres and enters the upstage area.*)
    (*Amanda and Laura are seated at a drop-leaf table. Eating is indicated by gestures without food or utensils. Amanda faces the audience. Tom and Laura are seated in profile.*)
    (*The interior has lit up softly and through the scrim we see Amanda and Laura seated at the table in the upstage area.*)

AMANDA: (*Calling*) Tom?
TOM: Yes, Mother.
AMANDA: We can't say grace until you come to the table!
TOM: Coming, Mother. (*He bows slightly and withdraws, reappearing a few moments later in his place at the table.*)
AMANDA: (*To her son*) Honey, don't *push* with your *fingers*. If you have to push with something, the thing to push with is a crust of bread. And chew—chew! Animals have sections in their stomachs which enable them to digest food without mastication, but human beings are supposed to chew their food before they swallow it down. Eat food leisurely, son, and really enjoy it. A well-cooked meal has lots of delicate flavors that have to be held in the mouth for appreciation. So chew your food and give your salivary glands a chance to function!

    (*Tom deliberately lays his imaginary fork down and pushes his chair back from the table.*)

TOM: I haven't enjoyed one bite of this dinner because of your constant directions on how to eat it. It's you that make me rush through meals with your hawk-like attention to every bite I take. Sickening—spoils my appetite—all this discussion of—animals' secretion—salivary glands—mastication!
AMANDA: (*Lightly*) Temperament like a Metropolitan star! (*He rises and crosses downstage*) You're not excused from the table.
TOM: I'm getting a cigarette.
AMANDA: You smoke too much.

    (*Laura rises.*)

LAURA: I'll bring in the blanc mange.

    (*He remains standing with his cigarette by the portieres during the following.*)

AMANDA: (*Rising*) No, sister, no, sister—you be the lady this time and I'll be the darky.
LAURA: I'm already up.
AMANDA: Resume your seat, little sister—I want you to stay fresh and pretty—for gentlemen callers!
LAURA: I'm not expecting any gentlemen callers.
AMANDA: (*Crossing out to kitchenette. Airily*) Sometimes they come when they are least expected! Why, I remember one Sunday afternoon in Blue Mountain— (*Enters kitchenette.*)

TOM: I know what's coming!

LAURA: Yes. But let her tell it.

TOM: Again?

LAURA: She loves to tell it.

(*Amanda returns with bowl of dessert.*)

AMANDA: One Sunday afternoon in Blue Mountain—your mother received—
seventeen!—gentlemen callers! Why, sometimes there weren't chairs enough
to accommodate them all. We had to send the nigger over to bring in folding
chairs from the parish house.

TOM: (*Remaining at portieres*) How did you entertain those gentlemen callers?

AMANDA: I understood the art of conversation!

TOM: I bet you could talk.

AMANDA: Girls in those days *knew* how to talk, I can tell you.

TOM: Yes?

(IMAGE: AMANDA AS A GIRL ON A PORCH, GREETING CALLERS.)

AMANDA: They knew how to entertain their gentlemen callers. It wasn't
enough for a girl to be possessed of a pretty face and a graceful figure—although I wasn't slighted in either respect. She also needed to have a nimble
wit and a tongue to meet all occasions.

TOM: What did you talk about?

AMANDA: Things of importance going on in the world! Never anything coarse
or common or vulgar. (*She addresses Tom as though he were seated in the vacant
chair at the table though he remains by portieres. He plays this scene as though he
held the book*) My callers were gentlemen—all! Among my callers were some
of the most prominent young planters of the Mississippi Delta—planters and
sons of planters!

(*Tom motions for music and a spot of light on Amanda.*)
(*Her eyes lift, her face glows, her voice becomes rich and elegiac.*)
(SCREEN LEGEND: "OU SONT LES NEIGES.")

There was young Champ Laughlin who later became vice-president of
the Delta Planters Bank.

Hadley Stevenson who was drowned in Moon Lake and left his widow
one hundred and fifty thousand in Government bonds.

There were the Cutrere brothers, Wesley and Bates. Bates was one of my
bright particular beaux! He got in a quarrel with that wild Wainwright boy.
They shot it out on the floor of Moon Lake Casino. Bates was shot through
the stomach. Died in the ambulance on his way to Memphis. His widow was
also well-provided for, came into eight or ten thousand acres, that's all. She
married him on the rebound—never loved her—carried my picture on him
the night he died!

And there was that boy that every girl in the Delta had set her cap for!
That beautiful, brilliant young Fitzhugh boy from Greene County!

TOM: What did he leave his widow?

AMANDA: He never married! Gracious, you talk as though all of my old admirers
had turned up their toes to the daisies!

TOM: Isn't this the first you've mentioned that still survives?

AMANDA: That Fitzhugh boy went North and made a fortune—came to be known as the Wolf of Wall Street! He had the Midas touch, whatever he touched turned to gold!

And I could have been Mrs. Duncan J. Fitzhugh, mind you! But—I picked your *father!*

LAURA: (*Rising*) Mother, let me clear the table.

AMANDA: No, dear, you go in front and study your typewriter chart. Or practice your shorthand a little. Stay fresh and pretty!—It's almost time for our gentlemen callers to start arriving. (*She flounces girlishly toward the kitchenette*) How many do you suppose we're going to entertain this afternoon?

(*Tom throws down the paper and jumps up with a groan.*)

LAURA: (*Alone in the dining room*) I don't believe we're going to receive any, Mother.

AMANDA: (*Reappearing, airily*) What? No one—not one? You must be joking! (*Laura nervously echoes her laugh. She slips in a fugitive manner through the half-open portieres and draws them gently behind her. A shaft of very clear light is thrown on her face against the faded tapestry of the curtains.* MUSIC: "THE GLASS MENAGERIE" UNDER FAINTLY. *Lightly*) Not one gentleman caller? It can't be true! There must be a flood, there must have been a tornado!

LAURA: It isn't a flood, it's not a tornado, Mother. I'm just not popular like you were in Blue Mountain. . . . (*Tom utters another groan. Laura glances at him with a faint, apologetic smile. Her voice catching a little*) Mother's afraid I'm going to be an old maid.

THE SCENE DIMS OUT WITH "GLASS MENAGERIE" MUSIC

SCENE II

"Laura, Haven't You Ever Liked Some Boy?"

On the dark stage the screen is lighted with the image of blue roses.
Gradually Laura's figure becomes apparent and the screen goes out.
The music subsides.

Laura is seated in the delicate ivory chair at the small clawfoot table.

She wears a dress of soft violet material for a kimono—her hair tied back from her forehead with a ribbon.

She is washing and polishing her collection of glass.

Amanda appears on the fire-escape steps. At the sound of her ascent, Laura catches her breath, thrusts the bowl of ornaments away and seats herself stiffly before the diagram of the typewriter keyboard as though it held her spellbound.

Something has happened to Amanda. It is written in her face as she climbs to the landing: a look that is grim and hopeless and a little absurd.

She has on one of those cheap or imitation velvety-looking cloth coats with imitation fur collar. Her hat is five or six years old, one of those dreadful cloche hats that were worn in the late twenties and she is clasping an enormous black patent-leather pocket-book with nickel clasps *and initials. This is her full-dress outfit, the one she usually wears to the D.A.R.*

> *Before entering she looks through the door.*
>
> *She purses her lips, opens her eyes very wide, rolls them upward and shakes her head.*
>
> *Then she slowly lets herself in the door. Seeing her mother's expression Laura touches her lips with a nervous gesture.*

LAURA: Hello, Mother, I was— (*She makes a nervous gesture toward the chart on the wall. Amanda leans against the shut door and stares at Laura with a martyred look.*)

AMANDA: Deception? Deception? (*She slowly removes her hat and gloves, continuing the sweet suffering stare. She lets the hat and gloves fall on the floor—a bit of acting.*)

LAURA: (*Shakily*) How was the D.A.R. meeting? (*Amanda slowly opens her purse and removes a dainty white handkerchief which she shakes out delicately and delicately touches to her lips and nostrils*) Didn't you go to the D.A.R. meeting, Mother?

AMANDA: (*Faintly, almost inaudibly*) —No.—No. (*Then more forcibly*) I did not have the strength—to go to the D.A.R. In fact, I did not have the courage! I wanted to find a hole in the ground and hide myself in it forever! (*She crosses slowly to the wall and removes the diagram of the typewriter keyboard. She holds it in front of her for a second, staring at it sweetly and sorrowfully—then bites her lips and tears it in two pieces.*)

LAURA: (*Faintly*) Why did you do that, Mother? (*Amanda repeats the same procedure with the chart of the Gregg Alphabet*) Why are you—

AMANDA: Why? Why? How old are you, Laura?

LAURA: Mother, you know my age.

AMANDA: I thought that you were an adult; it seems that I was mistaken. (*She crosses slowly to the sofa and sinks down and stares at Laura.*)

LAURA: Please don't stare at me, Mother.

> (*Amanda closes her eyes and lowers her head. Count ten.*)

AMANDA: What are we going to do, what is going to become of us, what is the future?

> (*Count ten.*)

LAURA: Has something happened, Mother? (*Amanda draws a long breath and takes out the handkerchief again. Dabbing process*) Mother, has—something happened?

AMANDA: I'll be all right in a minute, I'm just bewildered—(*Count five*)—by life. . . .

LAURA: Mother, I wish that you would tell me what's happened!

AMANDA: As you know, I was supposed to be inducted into my office at the D.A.R. this afternoon. (IMAGE: A SWARM OF TYPEWRITERS) But I stopped off at Rubicam's business college to speak to your teachers about your having a cold and ask them what progress they thought you were making down there.

LAURA: Oh. . . .

AMANDA: I went to the typing instructor and introduced myself as your mother. She didn't know who you were. Wingfield, she said. We don't have any such student enrolled at the school!

I assured her she did, that you had been going to classes since early in January.

"I wonder," she said, "if you could be talking about that terribly shy little girl who dropped out of school after only a few days' attendance?"

"No," I said, "Laura, my daughter, has been going to school every day for the past six weeks!"

"Excuse me," she said. She took the attendance book out and there was your name, unmistakably printed, and all the dates you were absent until they decided that you had dropped out of school.

I still said, "No, there must have been some mistake! There must have been some mix-up in the records!"

And she said, "No—I remember her perfectly now. Her hands shook so that she couldn't hit the right keys! The first time we gave a speed-test, she broke down completely—was sick at the stomach and almost had to be carried into the wash-room! After that morning she never showed up any more. We phoned the house but never got any answer—" while I was working at Famous and Barr, I suppose, demonstrating those— Oh!

I felt so weak I could barely keep on my feet!

I had to sit down while they got me a glass of water!

Fifty dollars' tuition, all of our plans—my hopes and ambitions for you— just gone up the spout, just gone up the spout like that.

(*Laura draws a long breath and gets awkwardly to her feet. She crosses to the victrola and winds it up.*)

What are you doing?

LAURA: Oh! (*She releases the handle and returns to her seat.*)

AMANDA: Laura, where have you been going when you've gone out pretending that you were going to business college?

LAURA: I've just been going out walking.

AMANDA: That's not true.

LAURA: It is. I just went walking.

AMANDA: Walking? Walking? In winter? Deliberately courting pneumonia in that light coat? Where did you walk to, Laura?

LAURA: All sorts of places—mostly in the park.

AMANDA: Even after you'd started catching that cold?

LAURA: It was the lesser of two evils, Mother. (IMAGE: WINTER SCENE IN PARK) I couldn't go back up. I—threw up—on the floor!

AMANDA: From half past seven till after five every day you mean to tell me you walked around in the park, because you wanted to make me think that you were still going to Rubicam's Business College?

LAURA: It wasn't as bad as it sounds. I went inside places to get warmed up.

AMANDA: Inside where?

LAURA: I went in the art museum and the bird-houses at the Zoo. I visited the penguins every day! Sometimes I did without lunch and went to the movies.

Lately I've been spending most of my afternoons in the Jewel-box, that big glass house where they raise the tropical flowers.

AMANDA: You did all this to deceive me, just for deception? (*Laura looks down*) Why?

LAURA: Mother, when you're disappointed, you get that awful suffering look on your face, like the picture of Jesus' mother in the museum!

AMANDA: Hush!

LAURA: I couldn't face it.

> (*Pause. A whisper of strings.*)
> (LEGEND: "THE CRUST OF HUMILITY.")

AMANDA: (*Hopelessly fingering the huge pocketbook*) So what are we going to do the rest of our lives? Stay home and watch the parades go by? Amuse ourselves with the glass menagerie, darling? Eternally play those worn-out phonograph records your father left as a painful reminder of him?

We won't have a business career—we've given that up because it gave us nervous indigestion! (*Laughs wearily*) What is there left but dependency all our lives? I know so well what becomes of unmarried women who aren't prepared to occupy a position. I've seen such pitiful cases in the South—barely tolerated spinsters living upon the grudging patronage of sister's husband or brother's wife!—stuck away in some little mouse-trap of a room—encouraged by one in-law to visit another—little birdlike women without any nest—eating the crust of humility all their life!

Is that the future that we've mapped out for ourselves?

I swear it's the only alternative I can think of!

It isn't a very pleasant alternative, is it?

Of course—some girls *do marry*.

> (*Laura twists her hands nervously.*)

Haven't you ever liked some boy?

LAURA: Yes. I liked one once. (*Rises*) I came across his picture a while ago.

AMANDA: (*With some interest*) He gave you his picture?

LAURA: No, it's in the year-book.

AMANDA: (*Disappointed*) Oh—a high-school boy.

> (SCREEN IMAGE: JIM AS HIGH-SCHOOL HERO BEARING A SILVER CUP.)

LAURA: Yes. His name was Jim. (*Laura lifts the heavy annual from the claw-foot table*) Here he is in *The Pirates of Penzance*.

AMANDA: (*Absently*) The what?

LAURA: The operetta the senior class put on. He had a wonderful voice and we sat across the aisle from each other Mondays, Wednesdays and Fridays in the Aud. Here he is with the silver cup for debating! See his grin?

AMANDA: (*Absently*) He must have had a jolly disposition.

LAURA: He used to call me—Blue Roses.

> (IMAGE: BLUE ROSES.)

AMANDA: Why did he call you such a name as that?

LAURA: When I had that attack of pleurosis—he asked me what was the matter when I came back. I said pleurosis—he thought that I said Blue Roses! So that's what he always called me after that. Whenever he saw me, he'd holler, "Hello, Blue Roses!" I didn't care for the girl that he went out with. Emily Meisenbach. Emily was the best-dressed girl at Soldan. She never struck me, though, as being sincere . . . It says in the Personal Section—they're engaged. That's—six years ago! They must be married by now.

AMANDA: Girls that aren't cut out for business careers usually wind up married to some nice man. (*Gets up with a spark of revival*) Sister, that's what you'll do!

(*Laura utters a startled, doubtful laugh. She reaches quickly for a piece of glass.*)

LAURA: But, Mother—
AMANDA: Yes? (*Crossing to photograph.*)
LAURA: (*In a tone of frightened apology*) I'm—crippled!

(IMAGE: SCREEN.)

AMANDA: Nonsense! Laura, I've told you never, never to use that word. Why, you're not crippled, you just have a little defect—hardly noticeable, even! When people have some slight disadvantage like that, they cultivate other things to make up for it—develop charm—and vivacity—and—*charm!* That's all you have to do! (*She turns again to the photograph*) One thing your father had *plenty of*—was *charm!*

(*Tom motions to the fiddle in the wings.*)
THE SCENE FADES OUT WITH MUSIC

SCENE III

LEGEND ON SCREEN: "AFTER THE FIASCO—"
Tom speaks from the fire-escape landing.

TOM: After the fiasco at Rubicam's Business College, the idea of getting a gentleman caller for Laura began to play a more and more important part in Mother's calculations.

It became an obsession. Like some archetype of the universal unconscious, the image of the gentleman caller haunted our small apartment. . . .

(IMAGE: YOUNG MAN AT DOOR WITH FLOWERS.)

An evening at home rarely passed without some allusion to this image, this spectre, this hope. . . .

Even when he wasn't mentioned, his presence hung in Mother's preoccupied look and in my sister's frightened, apologetic manner—hung like a sentence passed upon the Wingfields!

Mother was a woman of action as well as words.

She began to take logical steps in the planned direction.

Late that winter and in the early spring—realizing that extra money would be needed to properly feather the nest and plume the bird—she conducted a vigorous campaign on the telephone, roping in subscribers to one of those magazines for matrons called *The Home-maker's Companion*, the type of journal that features the serialized sublimations of ladies of letters who think in terms of delicate cup-like breasts, slim, tapering waists, rich, creamy thighs, eyes like wood-smoke in autumn, fingers that soothe and caress like strains of music, bodies as powerful as Etruscan sculpture.

(SCREEN IMAGE: GLAMOR MAGAZINE COVER.)

(*Amanda enters with phone on long extension cord. She is spotted in the dim stage.*)

AMANDA: Ida Scott? This is Amanda Wingfield!

We *missed* you at the D.A.R. last Monday!

I said to myself: She's probably suffering with that sinus condition! How is that sinus condition?

Horrors! Heaven have mercy!—You're a Christian martyr, yes, that's what you are, a Christian martyr!

Well, I just now happened to notice that your subscription to the *Companion*'s about to expire! Yes, it expires with the next issue, honey!—just when that wonderful new serial by Bessie Mae Hopper is getting off to such an exciting start. Oh, honey, it's something that you can't miss! You remember how *Gone With the Wind* took everybody by storm? You simply couldn't go out if you hadn't read it. All everybody *talked* was Scarlett O'Hara. Well, this is a book that critics already compare to *Gone With the Wind*. It's the *Gone With the Wind* of the post–World War generation!—What?—Burning?—Oh, honey, don't let them burn, go take a look in the oven and I'll hold the wire! Heavens—I think she's hung up!

DIM OUT

(LEGEND ON SCREEN: "YOU THINK I'M IN LOVE WITH CONTINENTAL SHOEMAKERS?")

(*Before the stage is lighted, the violent voices of Tom and Amanda are heard.*)

(*They are quarreling behind the portieres. In front of them stands Laura with clenched hands and panicky expression.*)

(*A clear pool of light on her figure throughout this scene.*)

TOM: What in Christ's name am I—

AMANDA: (*Shrilly*) Don't you use that—

TOM: Supposed to do!

AMANDA: Expression! Not in my—

TOM: Ohhh!

AMANDA: Presence! Have you gone out of your senses?

TOM: I have, that's true, *driven* out!

AMANDA: What is the matter with you, you—big—big—IDIOT!

TOM: Look!—I've got *no thing*, no single thing—

AMANDA: Lower your voice!

TOM: In my life here that I can call my OWN! Everything is—

AMANDA: Stop that shouting!

TOM: Yesterday you confiscated my books! You had the nerve to—

AMANDA: I took that horrible novel back to the library—yes! That hideous book by that insane Mr. Lawrence. (*Tom laughs wildly*) I cannot control the output of diseased minds or people who cater to them— (*Tom laughs still more wildly*) BUT I WON'T ALLOW SUCH FILTH BROUGHT INTO MY HOUSE! No, no, no, no, no!

TOM: House, house! Who pays rent on it, who makes a slave of himself to—

AMANDA: (*Fairly screeching*) Don't you DARE to—

TOM: No, no, I mustn't say things! I've got to just—

AMANDA: Let me tell you—

TOM: I don't want to hear any more! (*He tears the portieres open. The upstage area is lit with a turgid smoky red glow.*)

> (*Amanda's hair is in metal curlers and she wears a very old bathrobe, much too large for her slight figure, a relic of the faithless Mr. Wingfield.*)
>
> An upright typewriter and a wild disarray of manuscripts is on the drop-leaf table. The quarrel was probably precipitated by Amanda's interruption of his creative labor. A chair lying overthrown on the floor.)
>
> Their gesticulating shadows are cast on the ceiling by the fiery glow.)

AMANDA: You *will* hear more, you—

TOM: No, I won't hear more, I'm going out!

AMANDA: You come right back in—

TOM: Out, out, out! Because I'm—

AMANDA: Come back here, Tom Wingfield! I'm not through talking to you!

TOM: Oh, go—

LAURA: (*Desperately*)— Tom!

AMANDA: You're going to listen, and no more insolence from you! I'm at the end of my patience!

> (*He comes back toward her.*)

TOM: What do you think I'm at? Aren't I supposed to have any patience to reach the end of, Mother? I know, I know. It seems unimportant to you, what I'm *doing*—what I *want* to do—having a little *difference* between them! You don't think that—

AMANDA: I think you've been doing things that you're ashamed of. That's why you act like this. I don't believe that you go every night to the movies. Nobody goes to the movies night after night. Nobody in their right minds goes to the movies as often as you pretend to. People don't go to the movies at nearly midnight, and movies don't let out at two A.M. Come in stumbling. Muttering to yourself like a maniac! You get three hours' sleep and then go to work. Oh, I can picture the way you're doing down there. Moping, doping, because you're in no condition.

TOM: (*Wildly*) No, I'm in no condition!

AMANDA: What right have you got to jeopardize your job? Jeopardize the security of us all? How do you think we'd manage if you were—

TOM: Listen! You think I'm crazy *about* the *warehouse*? (*He bends fiercely toward her slight figure*) You think I'm in love with the Continental Shoemakers? You think I want to spend fifty-five *years* down there in that—*celotex interior!* with—*fluorescent*—*tubes!* Look! I'd rather somebody picked up a crowbar and battered out my brains—than go back mornings! I *go!* Every time you come in yelling that God damn *"Rise and Shine!"* *"Rise and Shine!"* I say to myself, "How *lucky dead* people are!" But I get up. I *go!* For sixty-five dollars a month I give up all that I dream of doing and being *ever!* And you say self—*self's* all I ever think of. Why, listen, if self is what I thought of, Mother, I'd be where he is—GONE! (*Pointing to father's picture*) As far as the system of transportation reaches! (*He starts past her. She grabs his arm*) Don't grab at me, Mother!

AMANDA: Where are you going?

TOM: I'm going to the *movies!*

AMANDA: I don't believe that lie!

TOM: (*Crouching toward her, overtowering her tiny figure. She backs away, gasping*) I'm going to opium dens! Yes, opium dens, dens of vice and criminals' hangouts, Mother. I've joined the Hogan gang, I'm a hired assassin, I carry a tommy-gun in a violin case! I run a string of cat-houses in the Valley! They call me Killer, Killer Wingfield, I'm leading a double-life, a simple, honest warehouse worker by day, by night a dynamic *czar* of the *underworld, Mother.* I go to gambling casinos, I spin away fortunes on the roulette table! I wear a patch over one eye and a false mustache, sometimes I put on green whiskers. On those occasions they call me—*El Diablo!* Oh, I could tell you things to make you sleepless! My enemies plan to dynamite this place. They're going to blow us all sky-high some night! I'll be glad, very happy, and so will you! You'll go up, up on a broomstick, over Blue Mountain with seventeen gentlemen callers! You ugly—babbling old—*witch*.... (*He goes through a series of violent, clumsy movements, seizing his overcoat, lunging to the door, pulling it fiercely open. The women watch him, aghast. His arm catches in the sleeve of the coat as he struggles to pull it on. For a moment he is pinioned by the bulky garment. With an outraged groan he tears the coat off again, splitting the shoulder of it, and hurls it across the room. It strikes against the shelf of Laura's glass collection, there is a tinkle of shattering glass. Laura cries out as if wounded.*)

(MUSIC. LEGEND: "THE GLASS MENAGERIE.")

LAURA: (*Shrilly*) My glass!—menagerie.... (*She covers her face and turns away.*)

(*But Amanda is still stunned and stupefied by the "ugly witch" so that she barely notices this occurrence. Now she recovers her speech.*)

AMANDA: (*In an awful voice*) I won't speak to you—until you apologize! (*She crosses through portieres and draws them together behind her. Tom is left with Laura. Laura clings weakly to the mantel with her face averted. Tom stares at her stupidly for a moment. Then he crosses to shelf. Drops awkwardly on his knees to collect the fallen glass, glancing at Laura as if he would speak but couldn't.*)

"The Glass Menagerie" steals in as
THE SCENE DIMS OUT

SCENE IV

The interior is dark. Faint light in the alley.

A deep-voiced bell in a church is tolling the hour of five as the scene commences.

Tom appears at the top of the alley. After each solemn boom of the bell in the tower, he shakes a little noise-maker or rattle as if to express the tiny spasm of man in contrast to the sustained power and dignity of the Almighty. This and the unsteadiness of his advance make it evident that he has been drinking.

As he climbs the few steps to the fire-escape landing light steals up inside. Laura appears in night-dress, observing Tom's empty bed in the front room.

Tom fishes in his pockets for door-key, removing a motley assortment of articles in the search, including a perfect shower of movie-ticket stubs and an empty bottle. At last he finds the key, but just as he is about to insert it, it slips from his fingers. He strikes a match and crouches below the door.

TOM: (*Bitterly*) One crack—and it falls through!

(*Laura opens the door.*)

LAURA: Tom! Tom, what are you doing?

TOM: Looking for a door-key.

LAURA: Where have you been all this time?

TOM: I have been to the movies.

LAURA: All this time at the movies?

TOM: There was a very long program. There was a Garbo picture and a Mickey Mouse and a travelogue and a newsreel and a preview of coming attractions. And there was an organ solo and a collection for the milk-fund—simultaneously—which ended up in a terrible fight between a fat lady and an usher!

LAURA: (*Innocently*) Did you have to stay through everything?

TOM: Of course! And, oh, I forgot! There was a big stage show! The headliner on this stage show was Malvolio the Magician. He performed wonderful tricks, many of them, such as pouring water back and forth between pitchers. First it turned to wine and then it turned to beer and then it turned to whiskey. I know it was whiskey it finally turned into because he needed somebody to come up out of the audience to help him, and I came up—both shows! It was Kentucky Straight Bourbon. A very generous fellow, he gave souvenirs. (*He pulls from his back pocket a shimmering rainbow-colored scarf*) He gave me this. This is his magic scarf. You can have it, Laura. You wave it over a canary cage and you get a bowl of gold-fish. You wave it over the gold-fish bowl and they fly away canaries. . . . But the wonderfullest trick of all was the coffin trick. We nailed him into a coffin and he got out of the coffin without removing one nail. (*He has come inside*) There is a trick that would come in handy for me—get me out of this 2 by 4 situation! (*Flops onto bed and starts removing shoes.*)

LAURA: Tom—Shhh!

TOM: What're you shushing me for?

LAURA: You'll wake up Mother.

TOM: Goody, goody! Pay 'er back for all those "Rise an' Shines." (*Lies down, groaning*) You know it don't take much intelligence to get yourself into a nailed-up coffin, Laura. But who in hell ever got himself out of one without removing one nail?

(*As if in answer, the father's grinning photograph lights up.*)
SCENE DIMS OUT

(*Immediately following. The church bell is heard striking six. At the sixth stroke the alarm clock goes off in Amanda's room, and after a few moments we hear her calling: "Rise and Shine! Rise and Shine! Laura, go tell your brother to rise and shine!"*)

TOM: (*Sitting up slowly*) I'll rise—but I won't shine. (*The light increases.*)

AMANDA: Laura, tell your brother his coffee is ready.

(*Laura slips into front room.*)

LAURA: Tom!—It's nearly seven. Don't make Mother nervous. (*He stares at her stupidly. Beseechingly*) Tom, speak to Mother this morning. Make up with her, apologize, speak to her!

TOM: She won't to me. It's her that started not speaking.

LAURA: If you just say you're sorry she'll start speaking.

TOM: Her not speaking—is that such a tragedy?

LAURA: Please—please!

AMANDA: (*Calling from kitchenette*) Laura, are you going to do what I asked you to do, or do I have to get dressed and go out myself?

LAURA: Going, going—soon as I get on my coat! (*She pulls on a shapeless felt hat with nervous, jerky movement, pleadingly glancing at Tom. Rushes awkwardly for coat. The coat is one of Amanda's, inaccurately made-over, the sleeves too short for Laura*) Butter and what else?

AMANDA: (*Entering upstage*) Just butter. Tell them to charge it.

LAURA: Mother, they make such faces when I do that.

AMANDA: Sticks and stones can break our bones, but the expression on Mr. Garfinkel's face won't harm us! Tell your brother his coffee is getting cold.

LAURA: (*At door*) Do what I asked you, will you, will you, Tom? (*He looks sullenly away.*)

AMANDA: Laura, go now or just don't go at all!

LAURA: (*Rushing out*) Going—going! (*A second later she cries out. Tom springs up and crosses to door. Amanda rushes anxiously in. Tom opens the door.*)

TOM: Laura?

LAURA: I'm all right. I slipped, but I'm all right.

AMANDA: (*Peering anxiously after her*) If anyone breaks a leg on those fire-escape steps, the landlord ought to be sued for every cent he possesses! (*She shuts door. Remembers she isn't speaking and returns to other room.*)

(*As Tom enters listlessly for his coffee, she turns her back to him and stands rigidly facing the window on the gloomy gray vault of the areaway. Its light on her face with its aged but childish features is cruelly sharp, satirical as a Daumier print.*)

(MUSIC UNDER: "AVE MARIA.")

(*Tom glances sheepishly but sullenly at her averted figure and slumps at the table. The coffee is scalding hot; he sips it and gasps and spits it back in the cup. At his gasp, Amanda catches her breath and half turns. Then catches herself and turns back to window.*)

(*Tom blows on his coffee, glancing sidewise at his mother. She clears her throat. Tom clears his. He starts to rise. Sinks back down again, scratches his head, clears his throat again. Amanda coughs. Tom raises his cup in both hands to blow on it, his eyes staring over the rim of it at his mother for several moments. Then he slowly sets the cup down and awkwardly and hesitantly rises from the chair.*)

TOM: (*Hoarsely*) Mother. I—I apologize, Mother. (*Amanda draws a quick, shuddering breath. Her face works grotesquely. She breaks into childlike tears*) I'm sorry for what I said, for everything that I said, I didn't mean it.

AMANDA: (*Sobbingly.*) My devotion has made me a witch and so I make myself hateful to my children!

TOM: No, you *don't.*

AMANDA: I worry so much, don't sleep, it makes me nervous!

TOM: (*Gently*) I understand that.

AMANDA: I've had to put up a solitary battle all these years. But you're my right-hand bower! Don't fall down, don't fail!

TOM: (*Gently*) I try, Mother.

AMANDA: (*With great enthusiasm*) Try and you will SUCCEED! (*The notion makes her breathless.*) Why, you—you're just *full* of natural endowments! Both of my children—they're *unusual* children! Don't you think I know it? I'm so— proud! Happy and—feel I've—so much to be thankful for but— Promise me one thing, Son!

TOM: What, Mother?

AMANDA: Promise, son, you'll—never be a drunkard!

TOM: (*Turns to her grinning*) I will never be a drunkard, Mother.

AMANDA: That's what frightened me so, that you'd be drinking! Eat a bowl of Purina!

TOM: Just coffee, Mother.

AMANDA: Shredded wheat biscuit?

TOM: No. No, Mother, just coffee.

AMANDA: You can't put in a day's work on an empty stomach. You've got ten minutes—don't gulp! Drinking too-hot liquids makes cancer of the stomach. . . . Put cream in.

TOM: No, thank you.

AMANDA: To cool it.

TOM: No! No, thank you, I want it black.

AMANDA: I know, but it's not good for you. We have to do all that we can to build ourselves up. In these trying times we live in, all that we have to cling to is—each other. . . . That's why it's so important to— Tom, I—I sent out your sister so I could discuss something with you. If you hadn't spoken I would have spoken to you. (*Sits down.*)

TOM: (*Gently*) What is it, Mother, that you want to discuss?

AMANDA: *Laura!*

(*Tom puts his cup down slowly.*)
  (LEGEND ON SCREEN: "LAURA.")
  (MUSIC: "THE GLASS MENAGERIE.")

TOM: —Oh.—Laura . . .

AMANDA: (*Touching his sleeve*) You know how Laura is. So quiet but—still water runs deep! She notices things and I think she—broods about them. (*Tom looks up*) A few days ago I came in and she was crying.

TOM: What about?

AMANDA: You.

TOM: Me?

AMANDA: She has an idea that you're not happy here.

TOM: What gave her that idea?

AMANDA: What gives her any idea? However, you do act strangely. I—I'm not criticizing, understand *that!* I know your ambitions do not lie in the warehouse, that like everybody in the whole wide world—you've had to—make sacrifices, but—Tom—Tom—life's not easy, it calls for—Spartan endurance! There's so many things in my heart that I cannot describe to you! I've never told you but I—*loved* your father. . . .

TOM: (*Gently*) I know that, Mother.

AMANDA: And you—when I see you taking after his ways! Staying out late— and—well, you *had* been drinking the night you were in that—terrifying condition! Laura says that you hate the apartment and that you go out nights to get away from it! Is that true, Tom?

TOM: No. You say there's so much in your heart that you can't describe to me. That's true of me, too. There's so much in my heart that I can't describe to *you!* So let's respect each other's—

AMANDA: But, why—*why*, Tom—are you always so *restless?* Where do you *go* to, nights?

TOM: I—go to the movies.

AMANDA: Why do you go to the movies so much, Tom?

TOM: I go to the movies because—I like adventure. Adventure is something I don't have much of at work, so I go to the movies.

AMANDA: But, Tom, you go to the movies *entirely* too *much!*

TOM: I like a lot of adventure.

(*Amanda looks baffled, then hurt. As the familiar inquisition resumes he becomes hard and impatient again. Amanda slips back into her querulous attitude toward him.*)
(IMAGE ON SCREEN: SAILING VESSEL WITH JOLLY ROGER.)

AMANDA: Most young men find adventure in their careers.

TOM: Then most young men are not employed in a warehouse.

AMANDA: The world is full of young men employed in warehouses and offices and factories.

TOM: Do all of them find adventure in their careers?

AMANDA: They do or they do without it! Not everybody has a craze for adventure.

TOM: Man is by instinct a lover, a hunter, a fighter, and none of those instincts are given much play at the warehouse!

AMANDA: Man is by instinct! Don't quote instinct to me! Instinct is something that people have got away from! It belongs to animals! Christian adults don't want it!

TOM: What do Christian adults want, then, Mother?

AMANDA: Superior things! Things of the mind and the spirit! Only animals have to satisfy instincts! Surely your aims are somewhat higher than theirs! Than monkeys—pigs—

TOM: I reckon they're not.

AMANDA: You're joking. However, that isn't what I wanted to discuss.

TOM: (*Rising*) I haven't much time.

AMANDA: (*Pushing his shoulders*) Sit down.

TOM: You want me to punch in red at the warehouse, Mother?

AMANDA: You have five minutes. I want to talk about Laura.

(LEGEND: "PLANS AND PROVISIONS.")

TOM: All right! What about Laura?

AMANDA: We have to be making some plans and provisions for her. She's older than you, two years, and nothing has happened. She just drifts along doing nothing. It frightens me terribly how she just drifts along.

TOM: I guess she's the type that people call home girls.

AMANDA: There's no such type, and if there is, it's a pity! That is unless the home is hers, with a husband!

TOM: What?

AMANDA: Oh, I can see the handwriting on the wall as plain as I see the nose in front of my face! It's terrifying!

More and more you remind me of your father! He was out all hours without explanation!—Then *left*! *Good-bye*!

And me with the bag to hold. I saw that letter you got from the Merchant Marine. I know what you're dreaming of. I'm not standing here blindfolded.

Very well, then. Then *do* it!

But not till there's somebody to take your place.

TOM: What do you mean?

AMANDA: I mean that as soon as Laura has got somebody to take care of her, married, a home of her own, independent—why, then you'll be free to go wherever you please, on land, on sea, whichever way the wind blows you!

But until that time you've got to look out for your sister. I don't say me because I'm old and don't matter! I say for your sister because she's young and dependent.

I put her in business college—a dismal failure! Frightened her so it made her sick at the stomach.

I took her over to the Young People's League at the church. Another fiasco. She spoke to nobody, nobody spoke to her. Now all she does is fool with those pieces of glass and play those worn-out records. What kind of a life is that for a girl to lead?

TOM: What can I do about it?

AMANDA: Overcome selfishness!

Self, self, self is all that you ever think of!

(*Tom springs up and crosses to get his coat. It is ugly and bulky. He pulls on a cap with earmuffs.*)

Where is your muffler? Put your wool muffler on!

(*He snatches it angrily from the closet and tosses it around his neck and pulls both ends tight.*)

Tom! I haven't said what I had in mind to ask you.

TOM: I'm too late to—

AMANDA: (*Catching his arm—very importunately. Then shyly*) Down at the warehouse, aren't there some—nice young men?

TOM: No!

AMANDA: There *must* be—some . . .

TOM: Mother— (*Gesture.*)

AMANDA: Find out one that's clean-living—doesn't drink and—ask him out for sister!

TOM: What?

AMANDA: For *sister*! To *meet*! Get *acquainted*!

TOM: (*Stamping to door*) Oh, my go-osh!

AMANDA: Will you? (*He opens door. Imploringly*) Will you? (*He starts down*) Will you? *Will* you, dear?

TOM: (*Calling back*) YES!

(*Amanda closes the door hesitantly and with a troubled but faintly hopeful expression.*)
> SCREEN IMAGE: GLAMOR MAGAZINE COVER.
> *Spot Amanda at phone.*

AMANDA: Ella Cartwright? This is Amanda Wingfield!
> How are you, honey?
> How is that kidney condition?

(*Count five.*)

Horrors!

(*Count five.*)

You're a Christian martyr, yes, honey, that's what you are, a Christian martyr!

Well, I just now happened to notice in my little red book that your subscription to the *Companion* has just run out! I knew that you wouldn't want to miss out on the wonderful serial starting in this new issue. It's by Bessie Mae Hopper, the first thing she's written since *Honeymoon for Three*.

Wasn't that a strange and interesting story? Well, this one is even lovelier, I believe. It has a sophisticated, society background. It's all about the horsey set on Long Island!

FADE OUT

SCENE V

LEGEND ON SCREEN: "ANNUNCIATION." *Fade with music.*
> *It is early dusk of a spring evening. Supper has just been finished in the Wingfield apartment. Amanda and Laura in light-colored dresses are*

removing dishes from the table, in the upstage area, which is shadowy, their movements formalized almost as a dance or ritual, their moving forms as pale and silent as moths.

Tom, in white shirt and trousers, rises from the table and crosses toward the fire-escape.

AMANDA: (*As he passes her*) Son, will you do me a favor?

TOM: What?

AMANDA: Comb your hair! You look so pretty when your hair is combed! (*Tom slouches on sofa with evening paper. Enormous caption "Franco Triumphs"*) There is only one respect in which I would like you to emulate your father.

TOM: What respect is that?

AMANDA: The care he always took of his appearance. He never allowed himself to look untidy. (*He throws down the paper and crosses to fire-escape*) Where are you going?

TOM: I'm going out to smoke.

AMANDA: You smoke too much. A pack a day at fifteen cents a pack. How much would that amount to in a month? Thirty times fifteen is how much, Tom? Figure it out and you will be astounded at what you could save. Enough to give you a night-school course in accounting at Washington U! Just think what a wonderful thing that would be for you, Son!

(*Tom is unmoved by the thought.*)

TOM: I'd rather smoke. (*He steps out on landing, letting the screen door slam.*)

AMANDA: (*Sharply*) I know! That's the tragedy of it. . . . (*Alone, she turns to look at her husband's picture.*)

(DANCE MUSIC: "ALL THE WORLD IS WAITING FOR THE SUNRISE!")

TOM: (*To the audience*) Across the alley from us was the Paradise Dance Hall. On evenings in spring the windows and doors were open and the music came outdoors. Sometimes the lights were turned out except for a large glass sphere that hung from the ceiling. It would turn slowly about and filter the dusk with delicate rainbow colors. Then the orchestra played a waltz or a tango, something that had a slow and sensuous rhythm. Couples would come outside, to the relative privacy of the alley. You could see them kissing behind ash-pits and telephone poles.

This was the compensation for lives that passed like mine, without any change or adventure.

Adventure and change were imminent in this year. They were waiting around the corner for all these kids.

Suspended in the mist over Berchtesgaden, caught in the folds of Chamberlain's umbrella—

In Spain there was Guernica!

But here there was only hot swing music and liquor, dance halls, bars, and movies, and sex that hung in the gloom like a chandelier and flooded the world with brief, deceptive rainbows. . . .

All the world was waiting for bombardments!

(*Amanda turns from the picture and comes outside.*)

AMANDA: (*Sighing*) A fire-escape landing's a poor excuse for a porch. (*She spreads a newspaper on a step and sits down, gracefully and demurely as if she were settling into a swing on a Mississippi veranda*) What are you looking at?

TOM: The moon.

AMANDA: Is there a moon this evening?

TOM: It's rising over Garfinkel's Delicatessen.

AMANDA: So it is! A little silver slipper of a moon. Have you made a wish on it yet?

TOM: Um-hum.

AMANDA: What did you wish for?

TOM: That's a secret.

AMANDA: A secret, huh? Well, I won't tell mine either. I will be just as mysterious as you.

TOM: I bet I can guess what yours is.

AMANDA: Is my head so transparent?

TOM: You're not a sphinx.

AMANDA: No, I don't have secrets. I'll tell you what I wished for on the moon. Success and happiness for my precious children! I wish for that whenever there's a moon, and when there isn't a moon, I wish for it, too.

TOM: I thought perhaps you wished for a gentleman caller.

AMANDA: Why do you say that?

TOM: Don't you remember asking me to fetch one?

AMANDA: I remember suggesting that it would be nice for your sister if you brought home some nice young man from the warehouse. I think that I've made that suggestion more than once.

TOM: Yes, you have made it repeatedly.

AMANDA: Well?

TOM: We are going to have one.

AMANDA: *What*?

TOM: A gentleman caller!

> (THE ANNUNCIATION IS CELEBRATED WITH MUSIC.)
> (*Amanda rises.*)
> (IMAGE ON SCREEN: CALLER WITH BOUQUET.)

AMANDA: You mean you have asked some nice young man to come over?

TOM: Yep. I've asked him to dinner.

AMANDA: You really did?

TOM: I did!

AMANDA: You did, and did he—*accept*?

TOM: He did!

AMANDA: Well, well—well, well! That's—lovely!

TOM: I thought that you would be pleased.

AMANDA: It's definite, then?

TOM: Very definite.

AMANDA: Soon?

TOM: Very soon.

AMANDA: For heaven's sake, stop putting on and tell me some things, will you?

TOM: What things do you want me to tell you?

AMANDA: *Naturally* I would like to know when he's *coming*!

TOM: He's coming tomorrow.

AMANDA: *Tomorrow?*

TOM: Yep. Tomorrow.

AMANDA: But, Tom!

TOM: Yes, Mother?

AMANDA: Tomorrow gives me no time!

TOM: Time for what?

AMANDA: Preparations! Why didn't you phone me at once, as soon as you asked him, the minute that he accepted? Then, don't you see, I could have been getting ready!

TOM: You don't have to make any fuss.

AMANDA: Oh, Tom, Tom, Tom, of course I have to make a fuss! I want things nice, not sloppy! Not thrown together. I'll certainly have to do some fast thinking, won't I?

TOM: I don't see why you have to think at all.

AMANDA: You just don't know. We can't have a gentleman caller in a pig-sty! All my wedding silver has to be polished, the monogrammed table linen ought to be laundered! The windows have to be washed and fresh curtains put up. And how about clothes? We have to *wear* something, don't we?

TOM: Mother, this boy is no one to make a fuss over!

AMANDA: Do you realize he's the first young man we've introduced to your sister?

It's terrible, dreadful, disgraceful that poor little sister has never received a single gentleman caller! Tom, come inside! (*She opens the screen door.*)

TOM: What for?

AMANDA: I want to ask you some things.

TOM: If you're going to make such a fuss, I'll call it off, I'll tell him not to come!

AMANDA: You certainly won't do anything of the kind. Nothing offends people worse than broken engagements. It simply means I'll have to work like a Turk! We won't be brilliant, but we will pass inspection. Come on inside. (*Tom follows, groaning*) Sit down.

TOM: Any particular place you would like me to sit?

AMANDA: Thank heavens I've got that new sofa! I'm also making payments on a floor lamp I'll have sent out! And put the chintz covers on, they'll brighten things up! Of course I'd hoped to have these walls re-papered. . . . What is the young man's name?

TOM: His name is O'Connor.

AMANDA: That, of course, means fish—tomorrow is Friday! I'll have that salmon loaf—with Durkee's dressing! What does he do? He works at the warehouse?

TOM: Of course! How else would I—

AMANDA: Tom, he—doesn't drink?

TOM: Why do you ask me that?

AMANDA: Your father *did!*

TOM: Don't get started on that!

AMANDA: He *does* drink, then?

TOM: Not that I know of!

AMANDA: Make sure, be certain! The last thing I want for my daughter's a boy who drinks!

TOM: Aren't you being a little bit premature? Mr. O'Connor has not yet appeared on the scene!

AMANDA: But will tomorrow. To meet your sister, and what do I know about his character? Nothing! Old maids are better off than wives of drunkards!

TOM: Oh, my God!

AMANDA: Be still!

TOM: (*Leaning forward to whisper*) Lots of fellows meet girls whom they don't marry!

AMANDA: Oh, talk sensibly, Tom—and don't be sarcastic! (*She has gotten a hairbrush.*)

TOM: What are you doing?

AMANDA: I'm brushing that cow-lick down!
    What is this young man's position at the warehouse?

TOM: (*Submitting grimly to the brush and the interrogation*) This young man's position is that of a shipping clerk, Mother.

AMANDA: Sounds to me like a fairly responsible job, the sort of a job *you* would be in if you just had more *get-up*.
    What is his salary? Have you any idea?

TOM: I would judge it to be approximately eighty-five dollars a month.

AMANDA: Well—not princely, but—

TOM: Twenty more than I make.

AMANDA: Yes, how well I know! But for a family man, eighty-five dollars a month is not much more than you can just get by on. . . .

TOM: Yes, but Mr. O'Connor is not a family man.

AMANDA: He might be, mightn't he? Some time in the future?

TOM: I see. Plans and provisions.

AMANDA: You are the only young man that I know of who ignores the fact that the future becomes the present, the present the past, and the past turns into everlasting regret if you don't plan for it!

TOM: I will think that over and see what I can make of it.

AMANDA: Don't be supercilious with your mother! Tell me some more about this—what do you call him?

TOM: James D. O'Connor. The D. is for Delaney.

AMANDA: Irish on *both* sides! *Gracious!* And doesn't drink?

TOM: Shall I call him up and ask him right this minute?

AMANDA: The only way to find out about those things is to make discreet inquiries at the proper moment. When I was a girl in Blue Mountain and it was suspected that a young man drank, the girl whose attentions he had been receiving, if any girl *was*, would sometimes speak to the minister of his church, or rather her father would if her father was living, and sort of feel him out on the young man's character. That is the way such things are discreetly handled to keep a young woman from making a tragic mistake!

TOM: Then how did you happen to make a tragic mistake?

AMANDA: That innocent look of your father's had everyone fooled!
    He *smiled*—the world was *enchanted*!
    No girl can do worse than put herself at the mercy of a handsome appearance!
    I hope that Mr. O'Connor is not too good-looking.

TOM: No, he's not too good-looking. He's covered with freckles and hasn't too much of a nose.

AMANDA: He's not right-down homely, though?

TOM: Not right-down homely. Just medium homely, I'd say.

AMANDA: Character's what to look for in a man.

TOM: That's what I've always said, Mother.

AMANDA: You've never said anything of the kind and I suspect you would never give it a thought.

TOM: Don't be so suspicious of me.

AMANDA: At least I hope he's the type that's up and coming.

TOM: I think he really goes in for self-improvement.

AMANDA: What reason have you to think so?

TOM: He goes to night school.

AMANDA: (*Beaming*) Splendid! What does he do, I mean study?

TOM: Radio engineering and public speaking!

AMANDA: Then he has visions of being advanced in the world! Any young man who studies public speaking is aiming to have an executive job some day!

And radio engineering? A thing for the future!

Both of these facts are very illuminating. Those are the sort of things that a mother should know concerning any young man who comes to call on her daughter. Seriously or—not.

TOM: One little warning. He doesn't know about Laura. I didn't let on that we had dark ulterior motives. I just said, why don't you come and have dinner with us? He said okay and that was the whole conversation.

AMANDA: I bet it was! You're eloquent as an oyster.

However, he'll know about Laura when he gets here. When he sees how lovely and sweet and pretty she is, he'll thank his lucky stars he was asked to dinner.

TOM: Mother, you mustn't expect too much of Laura.

AMANDA: What do you mean?

TOM: Laura seems all those things to you and me because she's ours and we love her. We don't even notice she's crippled any more.

AMANDA: Don't say crippled! You know that I never allow that word to be used!

TOM: But face facts, Mother. She is and—that's not all—

AMANDA: What do you mean "not all"?

TOM: Laura is very different from other girls.

AMANDA: I think the difference is all to her advantage.

TOM: Not quite all—in the eyes of others—strangers—she's terribly shy and lives in a world of her own and those things make her seem a little peculiar to people outside the house.

AMANDA: Don't say peculiar.

TOM: Face the facts. She is.

(THE DANCE-HALL MUSIC CHANGES TO A TANGO THAT HAS A MINOR AND SOMEWHAT OMINOUS TONE.)

AMANDA: In what way is she peculiar—may I ask?

TOM: (*Gently*) She lives in a world of her own—a world of—little glass ornaments, Mother. . . . (*Gets up. Amanda remains holding brush, looking at him, troubled*) She plays old phonograph records and—that's about all— (*He glances at himself in the mirror and crosses to door.*)

AMANDA: (*Sharply*) Where are you going?

TOM: I'm going to the movies. (*Out screen door.*)

AMANDA: Not to the movies, every night to the movies! (*Follows quickly to screen door*) I don't believe you always go to the movies! (*He is gone. Amanda looks worriedly after him for a moment. Then vitality and optimism return and she turns from the door. Crossing to portieres*) Laura! Laura! (*Laura answers from kitchenette.*)

LAURA: Yes, Mother.

AMANDA: Let those dishes go and come in front! (*Laura appears with dish towel. Gaily*) Laura, come here and make a wish on the moon!

(SCREEN IMAGE: MOON.)

LAURA: (*Entering*) Moon—moon?

AMANDA: A little silver slipper of a moon.
   Look over your left shoulder, Laura, and make a wish!

(*Laura looks faintly puzzled as if called out of sleep. Amanda seizes her shoulders and turns her at an angle by the door.*)

   Now!
   Now, darling, *wish!*

LAURA: What shall I wish for, Mother?

AMANDA: (*Her voice trembling and her eyes suddenly filling with tears*) Happiness! Good fortune! (*The violin rises and the stage dims out.*)

   CURTAIN

SCENE VI

   IMAGE: HIGH SCHOOL HERO.

   And so the following evening I brought Jim home to dinner. I had known Jim slightly in high school. In high school Jim was a hero. He had tremendous Irish good nature and vitality with the scrubbed and polished look of white chinaware. He seemed to move in a continual spotlight. He was a star in basketball, captain of the debating club, president of the senior class and the glee club and he sang the male lead in the annual light operas. He was always running or bounding, never just walking. He seemed always at the point of defeating the law of gravity. He was shooting with such velocity through his adolescence that you would logically expect him to arrive at nothing short of the White House by the time he was thirty. But Jim apparently ran into more interference after his graduation from Soldan. His speed had definitely slowed. Six years after he left high school he was holding a job that wasn't much better than mine.

   (IMAGE: CLERK.)

   He was the only one at the warehouse with whom I was on friendly terms. I was valuable to him as someone who could remember his former glory, who had seen him win basketball games and the silver cup in debating.

He knew of my secret practice of retiring to a cabinet of the wash-room to work on poems when business was slack in the warehouse. He called me Shakespeare. And while the other boys in the warehouse regarded me with suspicious hostility, Jim took a humorous attitude toward me. Gradually his attitude affected the others, their hostility wore off and they also began to smile at me as people smile at an oddly fashioned dog who trots across their path at some distance.

I knew that Jim and Laura had known each other at Soldan, and I had heard Laura speak admiringly of his voice. I didn't know if Jim remembered her or not. In high school Laura had been as unobtrusive as Jim had been astonishing. If he did remember Laura, it was not as my sister, for when I asked him to dinner, he grinned and said, "You know, Shakespeare, I never thought of you as having folks!"

He was about to discover that I did. . . .

(LIGHT UP STAGE.)

(LEGEND ON SCREEN: "THE ACCENT OF A COMING FOOT.")

(*Friday evening. It is about five o'clock of a late spring evening which comes "scattering poems in the sky."*)

(*A delicate lemony light is in the Wingfield apartment.*)

(*Amanda has worked like a Turk in preparation for the gentleman caller. The results are astonishing. The new floor lamp with its rose-silk shade is in place, a colored paper lantern conceals the broken light fixture in the ceiling, new billowing white curtains are at the windows, chintz covers are on chairs and sofa, a pair of new sofa pillows make their initial appearance.*)

(*Open boxes and tissue paper are scattered on the floor.*)

(*Laura stands in the middle with lifted arms while Amanda crouches before her, adjusting the hem of the new dress, devout and ritualistic. The dress is colored and designed by memory. The arrangement of Laura's hair is changed; it is softer and more becoming. A fragile, unearthly prettiness has come out in Laura: she is like a piece of translucent glass touched by light, given a momentary radiance, not actual, not lasting.*)

AMANDA: (*Impatiently*) Why are you trembling?

LAURA: Mother, you've made me so nervous!

AMANDA: How have I made you nervous?

LAURA: By all this fuss! You make it seem so important!

AMANDA: I don't understand you, Laura. You couldn't be satisfied with just sitting home, and yet whenever I try to arrange something for you, you seem to resist it. (*She gets up.*)

Now take a look at yourself.

No, wait! Wait just a moment—I have an idea!

LAURA: What is it now?

(*Amanda produces two powder puffs which she wraps in handkerchiefs and stuffs in Laura's bosom.*)

LAURA: Mother, what are you doing?

AMANDA: They call them "Gay Deceivers"!

LAURA: I won't wear them!

AMANDA: You will!

LAURA: Why should I?

AMANDA: Because, to be painfully honest, your chest is flat.

LAURA: You make it seem like we were setting a trap.

AMANDA: All pretty girls are a trap, a pretty trap, and men expect them to be.

(LEGEND: "A PRETTY TRAP.")

Now look at yourself, young lady. This is the prettiest you will ever be!

I've got to fix myself now! You're going to be surprised by your mother's appearance! (*She crosses through portieres, humming gaily.*)

(*Laura moves slowly to the long mirror and stares solemnly at herself.*)
(*A wind blows the white curtains inward in a slow, graceful motion and with a faint, sorrowful sighing.*)

AMANDA: (*Off stage*) It isn't dark enough yet. (*She turns slowly before the mirror with a troubled look.*)

(LEGEND ON SCREEN: "THIS IS MY SISTER: CELEBRATE HER WITH STRINGS!" MUSIC.)

AMANDA: (*Laughing, off*) I'm going to show you something. I'm going to make a spectacular appearance!

LAURA: What is it, Mother?

AMANDA: Possess your soul in patience—you will see!

Something I've resurrected from that old trunk! Styles haven't changed so terribly much after all. . . . (*She parts the portieres.*)

Now just look at your mother! (*She wears a girlish frock of yellowed voile with a blue silk sash. She carries a bunch of jonquils—the legend of her youth is nearly revived. Feverishly.*)

This is the dress in which I led the cotillion. Won the cakewalk twice at Sunset Hill, wore one spring to the Governor's ball in Jackson!

See how I sashayed around the ballroom, Laura? (*She raises her skirt and does a mincing step around the room.*)

I wore it on Sundays for my gentlemen callers! I had it on the day I met your father—

I had malaria fever all that spring. The change of climate from East Tennessee to the Delta—weakened resistance—I had a little temperature all the time—not enough to be serious—just enough to make me restless and giddy!—Invitations poured in—parties all over the Delta!—"Stay in bed," said Mother, "you have fever!"—but I just wouldn't.—I took quinine but kept on going, going!—Evenings, dances!—Afternoons, long, long rides! Picnics—lovely!—So lovely, that country in May.—All lacy with dogwood, literally flooded with jonquils!—That was the spring I had the craze for jonquils. Jonquils became an absolute obsession. Mother said, "Honey, there's no more room for jonquils." And still I kept on bringing in more jonquils. Whenever, wherever I saw them, I'd say, "Stop! Stop! I see jonquils!" I made the young men help me gather the jonquils! It was a joke, Amanda and her jonquils! Finally there were no more vases to hold them, every available space was filled with jonquils. No vases to hold them? All right, I'll hold them myself! And then I— (*She stops in front of the picture.* MUSIC) met your father!

Malaria fever and jonquils and then—this—boy. . . . (*She switches on the rose-colored lamp.*)

I hope they get here before it starts to rain. (*She crosses upstage and places the jonquils in bowl on table.*)

I gave your brother a little extra change so he and Mr. O'Connor could take the service car home.

LAURA: (*With altered look*) What did you say his name was?

AMANDA: O'Connor.

LAURA: What is his first name?

AMANDA: I don't remember. Oh, yes, I do. It was—Jim!

(*Laura sways slightly and catches hold of a chair.*)
(LEGEND ON SCREEN: "NOT JIM!")

LAURA: (*Faintly*) Not—Jim!

AMANDA: Yes, that was it, it was Jim! I've never known a Jim that wasn't nice!

(MUSIC: OMINOUS.)

LAURA: Are you sure his name is Jim O'Connor?

AMANDA: Yes. Why?

LAURA: Is he the one that Tom used to know in high school?

AMANDA: He didn't say so. I think he just got to know him at the warehouse.

LAURA: There was a Jim O'Connor we both knew in high school— (*Then, with effort*) If that is the one that Tom is bringing to dinner—you'll have to excuse me, I won't come to the table.

AMANDA: What sort of nonsense is this?

LAURA: You asked me once if I'd ever liked a boy. Don't you remember I showed you this boy's picture?

AMANDA: You mean the boy you showed me in the year book?

LAURA: Yes, that boy.

AMANDA: Laura, Laura, were you in love with that boy?

LAURA: I don't know, Mother. All I know is I couldn't sit at the table if it was him!

AMANDA: It won't be him! It isn't the least bit likely. But whether it is or not, you will come to the table. You will not be excused.

LAURA: I'll have to be, Mother.

AMANDA: I don't intend to humor your silliness, Laura. I've had too much from you and your brother, both!

So just sit down and compose yourself till they come. Tom has forgotten his key so you'll have to let them in, when they arrive.

LAURA: (*Panicky*) Oh, Mother—*you* answer the door!

AMANDA: (*Lightly*) I'll be in the kitchen—busy!

LAURA: Oh, Mother, please answer the door, don't make me do it!

AMANDA: (*Crossing into kitchenette*) I've got to fix the dressing for the salmon. Fuss, fuss—silliness!—over a gentleman caller!

(*Door swings shut. Laura is left alone.*)

(LEGEND: "TERROR!")

(*She utters a low moan and turns off the lamp—sits stiffly on the edge of the sofa, knotting her fingers together.*)

(LEGEND ON SCREEN: "THE OPENING OF A DOOR!")

(*Tom and Jim appear on the fire-escape steps and climb to landing. Hearing their approach, Laura rises with a panicky gesture. She retreats to the portieres.*)

(*The doorbell. Laura catches her breath and touches her throat. Low drums.*)

AMANDA: (*Calling*) Laura, sweetheart! The door!

(*Laura stares at it without moving.*)

JIM: I think we just beat the rain.

TOM: Uh-huh. (*He rings again, nervously. Jim whistles and fishes for a cigarette.*)

AMANDA: (*Very, very gaily*) Laura, that is your brother and Mr. O'Connor! Will you let them in, darling?

(*Laura crosses toward kitchenette door.*)

LAURA: (*Breathlessly*) Mother—you go to the door!

(*Amanda steps out of kitchenette and stares furiously at Laura. She points imperiously at the door.*)

LAURA: Please, please!

AMANDA: (*In a fierce whisper*) What is the matter with you, you silly thing?

LAURA: (*Desperately*) Please, you answer it, *please!*

AMANDA: I told you I wasn't going to humor you, Laura. Why have you chosen this moment to lose your mind?

LAURA: Please, please, please, you go!

AMANDA: You'll have to go to the door because I can't!

LAURA: (*Despairingly*) I can't either!

AMANDA: *Why?*

LAURA: I'm sick!

AMANDA: I'm sick, too—of your nonsense! Why can't you and your brother be normal people? Fantastic whims and behavior!

(*Tom gives a long ring.*)

Preposterous goings on! Can you give me one reason—(*Calls out lyrically*) COMING! JUST ONE SECOND!—why you should be afraid to open a door? Now you answer it, Laura!

LAURA: Oh, oh, oh . . . (*She returns through the portieres. Darts to the victrola and winds it frantically and turns it on.*)

AMANDA: Laura Wingfield, you march right to that door!

LAURA: Yes—yes, Mother! (*A faraway, scratchy rendition of "Dardanella" softens the air and gives her strength to move through it. She slips to the door and draws it cautiously open.*)

(*Tom enters with the caller, Jim O'Connor.*)

TOM: Laura, this is Jim. Jim, this is my sister, Laura.

JIM: (*Stepping inside*) I didn't know that Shakespeare had a sister!

LAURA: (*Retreating stiff and trembling from the door*) How—how do you do?

JIM: (*Heartily extending his hand*) Okay!

(*Laura touches it hesitantly with hers.*)

JIM: Your hand's *cold*, Laura!

LAURA: Yes, well—I've been playing the victrola. . . .

JIM: Must have been playing classical music on it! You ought to play a little hot swing music to warm you up!

LAURA: Excuse me—I haven't finished playing the victrola. . . . (*She turns awkwardly and hurries into the front room. She pauses a second by the victrola. Then catches her breath and darts through the portieres like a frightened deer.*)

JIM: (*Grinning*) What was the matter?

TOM: Oh—with Laura? Laura is—terribly shy.

JIM: Shy, huh? It's unusual to meet a shy girl nowadays. I don't believe you ever mentioned you had a sister.

TOM: Well, now you know. I have one. Here is the *Post Dispatch*. You want a piece of it?

JIM: Uh-huh.

TOM: What piece? The comics?

JIM: Sports! (*Glances at it*) Ole Dizzy Dean is on his bad behavior.

TOM: (*Disinterest*) Yeah? (*Lights cigarette and crosses back to fire-escape door.*)

JIM: Where are *you* going?

TOM: I'm going out on the terrace.

JIM: (*Goes after him*) You know, Shakespeare—I'm going to sell you a bill of goods!

TOM: What goods?

JIM: A course I'm taking.

TOM: Huh?

JIM: In public speaking! You and me, we're not the warehouse type.

TOM: Thanks—that's good news. But what has public speaking got to do with it?

JIM: It fits you for—executive positions!

TOM: Awww.

JIM: I tell you it's done a helluva lot for me.

(IMAGE: EXECUTIVE AT DESK.)

TOM: In what respect?

JIM: In every! Ask yourself what is the difference between you an' me and men in the office down front? Brains?—No!—Ability?—No! Then what? Just one little thing—

TOM: What is that one little thing?

JIM: Primarily it amounts to—social poise! Being able to square up to people and hold your own on any social level!

AMANDA: (*Off stage*) Tom?

TOM: Yes, Mother?

AMANDA: Is that you and Mr. O'Connor?

TOM: Yes, Mother.

AMANDA: Well, you just make yourselves comfortable in there.

TOM: Yes, Mother.

AMANDA: Ask Mr. O'Connor if he would like to wash his hands.

JIM: Aw, no—no—thank you—I took care of that at the warehouse. Tom—

TOM: Yes?

JIM: Mr. Mendoza was speaking to me about you.

TOM: Favorably?

JIM: What do you think?

TOM: Well—

JIM: You're going to be out of a job if you don't wake up.

TOM: I am waking up—

JIM: You show no signs.

TOM: The signs are interior.

(IMAGE ON SCREEN: THE SAILING VESSEL WITH JOLLY ROGER AGAIN.)

TOM: I'm planning to change. (*He leans over the rail speaking with quiet exhilaration. The incandescent marquees and signs of the first-run movie houses light his face from across the alley. He looks like a voyager*) I'm right at the point of committing myself to a future that doesn't include the warehouse and Mr. Mendoza or even a night-school course in public speaking.

JIM: What are you gassing about?

TOM: I'm tired of the movies.

JIM: Movies!

TOM: Yes, movies! Look at them— (*A wave toward the marvels of Grand Avenue*) All of those glamorous people—having adventures—hogging it all, gobbling the whole thing up! You know what happens? People go to the *movies* instead of *moving*! Hollywood characters are supposed to have all the adventures for everybody in America, while everybody in America sits in a dark room and watches them have them! Yes, until there's a war. That's when adventure becomes available to the masses! *Everyone's* dish, not only Gable's! Then the people in the dark room come out of the dark room to have some adventures themselves—Goody, goody!—It's our turn now, to go to the South Sea Island—to make a safari—to be exotic, far-off!—But I'm not patient. I don't want to wait till then. I'm tired of the *movies* and I am *about* to *move*!

JIM: (*Incredulously*) Move?

TOM: Yes.

JIM: When?

TOM: Soon!

JIM: Where? Where?

(THEME THREE MUSIC SEEMS TO ANSWER THE QUESTION, WHILE TOM THINKS IT OVER. HE SEARCHES AMONG HIS POCKETS.)

TOM: I'm starting to boil inside. I know I seem dreamy, but inside—well, I'm boiling!—Whenever I pick up a shoe, I shudder a little thinking how short life is and what I am doing!—Whatever that means, I know it doesn't mean shoes—except as something to wear on a traveler's feet! (*Finds paper*) Look—

JIM: What?

TOM: I'm a member.

JIM: (*Reading*) The Union of Merchant Seamen.

TOM: I paid my dues this month, instead of the light bill.

JIM: You will regret it when they turn the lights off.

TOM: I won't be here.

JIM: How about your mother?

TOM: I'm like my father. The bastard son of a bastard! See how he grins? And he's been absent going on sixteen years!

JIM: You're just talking, you drip. How does your mother feel about it?

TOM: Shhh!—Here comes Mother! Mother is not acquainted with my plans!

AMANDA: (*Enters portieres*) Where are you all?

TOM: On the terrace, Mother.

> (*They start inside. She advances to them. Tom is distinctly shocked at her appearance. Even Jim blinks a little. He is making his first contact with girlish Southern vivacity and in spite of the night-school course in public speaking is somewhat thrown off the beam by the unexpected outlay of social charm.*)
>
> (*Certain responses are attempted by Jim but are swept aside by Amanda's gay laughter and chatter. Tom is embarrassed but after the first shock Jim reacts very warmly. Grins and chuckles, is altogether won over.*)
>
> (IMAGE: AMANDA IS A GIRL.)

AMANDA: (*Coyly smiling, shaking her girlish ringlets*) Well, well, well, so this is Mr. O'Connor. Introductions entirely unnecessary. I've heard so much about you from my boy. I finally said to him, Tom—good gracious!—why don't you bring this paragon to supper? I'd like to meet this nice young man at the warehouse!—Instead of just hearing him sing your praises so much!

I don't know why my son is so stand-offish—that's not Southern behavior!

Let's sit down and— I think we could stand a little more air in here! Tom, leave the door open. I felt a nice fresh breeze a moment ago. Where has it gone to?

Mmm, so warm already! And not quite summer, even. We're going to burn up when summer really gets started.

However, we're having—we're having a very light supper. I think light things are better fo' this time of year. The same as light clothes are. Light clothes an' light food are what warm weather calls fo'. You know our blood gets so thick during th' winter—it takes a while fo' us to *adjust* ou'selves!—when the season changes . . .

It's come so quick this year. I wasn't prepared. All of a sudden—heavens! Already summer!—I ran to the trunk an' pulled out this light dress— Terribly old! Historical almost! But feels so good—so good an' co-ol, y' know. . . .

TOM: Mother—

AMANDA: Yes, honey?

TOM: How about—supper?

AMANDA: Honey, you go ask Sister if supper is ready! You know that Sister is in full charge of supper!

Tell her you hungry boys are waiting for it. (*To Jim.*)

Have you met Laura?

JIM: She—

AMANDA: Let you in? Oh, good, you've met already! It's rare for a girl as sweet an' pretty as Laura to be domestic! But Laura is, thank heavens, not only pretty but also very domestic. I'm not at all. I never was a bit. I never could make a thing but angel-food cake. Well, in the South we had so many servants. Gone, gone, gone. All vestige of gracious living! Gone completely! I wasn't prepared for what the future brought me. All of my gentlemen callers were sons of planters and so of course I assumed that I would be married to one and raise my family on a large piece of land with plenty of servants. But man proposes—and woman accepts the proposal!—To vary that old, old saying a little bit— I married no planter! I married a man who worked for the telephone company!—That gallantly smiling gentleman over there! (*Points to the picture*) A telephone man who—fell in love with long-distance!—Now he travels and I don't even know where!—But what am I going on for about my—tribulations?

Tell me yours—I hope you don't have any!

Tom?

TOM: (*Returning*) Yes, Mother?

AMANDA: Is supper nearly ready?

TOM: It looks to me like supper is on the table.

AMANDA: Let me look— (*She rises prettily and looks through portieres*) Oh, lovely!—But where is Sister?

TOM: Laura is not feeling well and she says that she thinks she'd better not come to the table.

AMANDA: What?—Nonsense!—Laura? Oh, Laura!

LAURA: (*Off stage, faintly*) Yes, Mother.

AMANDA: You really must come to the table. We won't be seated until you come to the table!

Come in, Mr. O'Connor. You sit over there, and I'll—

Laura? Laura Wingfield!

You're keeping us waiting, honey! We can't say grace until you come to the table!

(*The back door is pushed weakly open and Laura comes in. She is obviously quite faint, her lips trembling, her eyes wide and staring. She moves unsteadily toward the table.*)

(LEGEND: "TERROR!")

(*Outside a summer storm is coming abruptly. The white curtains billow inward at the windows and there is a sorrowful murmur and deep blue dusk.*)

(*Laura suddenly stumbles—she catches at a chair with a faint moan.*)

TOM: Laura!

AMANDA: Laura!

(*There is a clap of thunder.*)

(LEGEND: "AH!")

(*Despairingly*) Why, Laura, you *are* sick, darling! Tom, help your sister into the living room, dear!

Sit in the living room, Laura—rest on the sofa.

Well!

(*To the gentleman caller.*) Standing over the hot stove made her ill!—I told her that it was just too warm this evening, but—

(*Tom comes back in. Laura is on the sofa.*)

Is Laura all right now?

TOM: Yes.

AMANDA: What *is* that? Rain? A nice cool rain has come up! (*She gives the gentleman caller a frightened look.*) I think we may—have grace—now . . . (*Tom looks at her stupidly.*) Tom, honey—you say grace!

TOM: Oh . . .

"For these and all thy mercies—" (*They bow their heads, Amanda stealing a nervous glance at Jim. In the living room Laura, stretched on the sofa, clenches her hand to her lips, to hold back a shuddering sob.*) God's Holy Name be praised—

THE SCENE DIMS OUT

SCENE VII

A *Souvenir*.

Half an hour later. Dinner is just being finished in the upstage area which is concealed by the drawn portieres.

As the curtain rises Laura is still huddled upon the sofa, her feet drawn under her, her head resting on a pale blue pillow, her eyes wide and mysteriously watchful. The new floor lamp with its shade of rose-colored silk gives a soft, becoming light to her face, bringing out the fragile, unearthly prettiness which usually escapes attention. There is a steady murmur of rain, but it is slackening and stops soon after the scene begins; the air outside becomes pale and luminous as the moon breaks out.

A moment after the curtain rises, the lights in both rooms flicker and go out.

JIM: Hey, there, Mr. Light Bulb!

(*Amanda laughs nervously.*)

(LEGEND: "SUSPENSION OF A PUBLIC SERVICE.")

AMANDA: Where was Moses when the lights went out? Ha-ha. Do you know the answer to that one, Mr. O'Connor?

JIM: No, Ma'am, what's the answer?

AMANDA: In the dark! (*Jim laughs appreciatively.*) Everybody sit still. I'll light the candles. Isn't it lucky we have them on the table? Where's a match? Which of you gentlemen can provide a match?

JIM: Here.

AMANDA: Thank you, sir.

JIM: Not at all, Ma'am!

AMANDA: I guess the fuse has burnt out. Mr. O'Connor, can you tell a burnt-out fuse? I know I can't and Tom is a total loss when it comes to mechanics.

(SOUND: GETTING UP: VOICES RECEDE A LITTLE TO KITCHENETTE.)

Oh, be careful you don't bump into something. We don't want our gentleman caller to break his neck. Now wouldn't that be a fine howdy-do?

JIM: Ha-ha! Where is the fuse-box?

AMANDA: Right here next to the stove. Can you see anything?

JIM: Just a minute.

AMANDA: Isn't electricity a mysterious thing? Wasn't it Benjamin Franklin who tied a key to a kite? We live in such a mysterious universe, don't we? Some people say that science clears up all the mysteries for us. In my opinion it only creates more!

Have you found it yet?

JIM: No, Ma'am. All these fuses look okay to me.

AMANDA: Tom!

TOM: Yes, Mother?

AMANDA: That light bill I gave you several days ago. The one I told you we got the notices about?

(LEGEND: "HA!")

TOM: Oh.—Yeah.

AMANDA: You didn't neglect to pay it by any chance?

TOM: Why, I—

AMANDA: Didn't! I might have known it!

JIM: Shakespeare probably wrote a poem on that light bill, Mrs. Wingfield.

AMANDA: I might have known better than to trust him with it! There's such a high price for negligence in this world!

JIM: Maybe the poem will win a ten-dollar prize.

AMANDA: We'll just have to spend the remainder of the evening in the nineteenth century, before Mr. Edison made the Mazda lamp!

JIM: Candlelight is my favorite kind of light.

AMANDA: That shows you're romantic! But that's no excuse for Tom.

Well, we got through dinner. Very considerate of them to let us get through dinner before they plunged us into everlasting darkness, wasn't it, Mr. O'Connor?

JIM: Ha-ha!

AMANDA: Tom, as a penalty for your carelessness you can help me with the dishes.

JIM: Let me give you a hand.

AMANDA: Indeed you will not!

JIM: I ought to be good for something.

AMANDA: Good for something? (*Her tone is rhapsodic.*) You? Why, Mr. O'Connor, nobody, *nobody's* given me this much entertainment in years—as you have!

JIM: Aw, now, Mrs. Wingfield!

AMANDA: I'm not exaggerating, not one bit! But Sister is all by her lonesome. You go keep her company in the parlor!

I'll give you this lovely old candelabrum that used to be on the altar at the church of the Heavenly Rest. It was melted a little out of shape when the church burnt down. Lightning struck it one spring. Gypsy Jones was holding a revival at the time and he intimated that the church was destroyed because the Episcopalians gave card parties.

JIM: Ha-ha.

AMANDA: And how about you coaxing Sister to drink a little wine? I think it would be good for her! Can you carry both at once?

JIM: Sure. I'm Superman!

AMANDA: Now, Thomas, get into this apron!

(*The door of kitchenette swings closed on Amanda's gay laughter; the flickering light approaches the portieres.*)

(*Laura sits up nervously as he enters. Her speech at first is low and breathless from the almost intolerable strain of being alone with a stranger.*)

(THE LEGEND: "I DON'T SUPPOSE YOU REMEMBER ME AT ALL!")

(*In her first speeches in this scene, before Jim's warmth overcomes her paralyzing shyness, Laura's voice is thin and breathless as though she has just run up a steep flight of stairs.*)

(*Jim's attitude is gently humorous. In playing this scene it should be stressed that while the incident is apparently unimportant, it is to Laura the climax of her secret life.*)

JIM: Hello, there, Laura.

LAURA: (*Faintly*) Hello. (*She clears her throat.*)

JIM: How are you feeling now? Better?

LAURA: Yes. Yes, thank you.

JIM: This is for you. A little dandelion wine. (*He extends it toward her with extravagant gallantry.*)

LAURA: Thank you.

JIM: Drink it—but don't get drunk! (*He laughs heartily. Laura takes the glass uncertainly; laughs shyly.*) Where shall I set the candles?

LAURA: Oh—oh, anywhere . . .

JIM: How about here on the floor? Any objections?

LAURA: No.

JIM: I'll spread a newspaper under to catch the drippings. I like to sit on the floor. Mind if I do?

LAURA: Oh, no.

JIM: Give me a pillow?

LAURA: What?

JIM: A pillow!

LAURA: Oh . . . (*Hands him one quickly.*)

JIM: How about you? Don't you like to sit on the floor?

LAURA: Oh—yes.

JIM: Why don't you, then?

LAURA: I—will.

JIM: Take a pillow! (*Laura does. Sits on the other side of the candelabrum. Jim crosses his legs and smiles engagingly at her*) I can't hardly see you sitting way over there.

LAURA: I can—see you.

JIM: I know, but that's not fair, I'm in the limelight. (*Laura moves her pillow closer*) Good! Now I can see you! Comfortable?

LAURA: Yes.

JIM: So am I. Comfortable as a cow! Will you have some gum?

LAURA: No, thank you.

JIM: I think that I will indulge, with your permission. (*Musingly unwraps it and holds it up*) Think of the fortune made by the guy that invented the first piece of chewing gum. Amazing, huh? The Wrigley Building is one of the sights of Chicago.—I saw it summer before last when I went up to the Century of Progress. Did you take in the Century of Progress?

LAURA: No, I didn't.

JIM: Well, it was quite a wonderful exposition. What impressed me most was the Hall of Science. Gives you an idea of what the future will be in America, even more wonderful than the present time is! (*Pause. Smiling at her*) Your brother tells me you're shy. Is that right, Laura?

LAURA: I—don't know.

JIM: I judge you to be an old-fashioned type of girl. Well, I think that's a pretty good type to be. Hope you don't think I'm being too personal—do you?

LAURA: (*Hastily, out of embarrassment*) I believe I *will* take a piece of gum, if you—don't mind. (*Clearing her throat*) Mr. O'Connor, have you—kept up with your singing?

JIM: Singing? Me?

LAURA: Yes. I remember what a beautiful voice you had.

JIM: When did you hear me sing?

(VOICE OFF STAGE IN THE PAUSE.)

VOICE: (*Off stage*)
O blow, ye winds, heigh-ho,
A-roving I will go!
I'm off to my love
With a boxing glove—
Ten thousand miles away!

JIM: You say you've heard me sing?

LAURA: Oh, yes! Yes, very often . . . I—don't suppose—you remember me—at all?

JIM: (*Smiling doubtfully*) You know I have an idea I've seen you before. I had that idea soon as you opened the door. It seemed almost like I was about to remember your name. But the name that I started to call you—wasn't a name! And so I stopped myself before I said it.

LAURA: Wasn't it—Blue Roses?

JIM: (*Springs up. Grinning*) Blue Roses!—My gosh, yes—Blue Roses! That's what I had on my tongue when you opened the door! Isn't it funny what tricks your memory plays? I didn't connect you with high school somehow or other. But that's where it was; it was high school. I didn't even know you were Shakespeare's sister! Gosh, I'm sorry.

LAURA: I didn't expect you to. You—barely knew me!

JIM: But we did have a speaking acquaintance, huh?

LAURA: Yes, we—spoke to each other.

JIM: When did you recognize me?

LAURA: Oh, right away!

JIM: Soon as I came in the door?

LAURA: When I heard your name I thought it was probably you. I knew that Tom used to know you a little in high school. So when you came in the door— Well, then I was—sure.

JIM: Why didn't you *say* something, then?

LAURA: (*Breathlessly*) I didn't know what to say, I was—too surprised!

JIM: For goodness' sakes! You know, this sure is funny!

LAURA: Yes! Yes, isn't it, though . . .

JIM: Didn't we have a class in something together?

LAURA: Yes, we did.

JIM: What class was that?

LAURA: It was—singing—Chorus!

JIM: Aw!

LAURA: I sat across the aisle from you in the Aud.

JIM: Aw.

LAURA: Mondays, Wednesdays and Fridays.

JIM: Now I remember—you always came in late.

LAURA: Yes, it was so hard for me, getting upstairs. I had that brace on my leg—it clumped so loud!

JIM: I never heard any clumping.

LAURA: (*Wincing at the recollection*) To me it sounded like—thunder!

JIM: Well, well, well, I never even noticed.

LAURA: And everybody was seated before I came in. I had to walk in front of all those people. My seat was in the back row. I had to go clumping all the way up the aisle with everyone watching!

JIM: You shouldn't have been self-conscious.

LAURA: I know, but I was. It was always such a relief when the singing started.

JIM: Aw, yes, I've placed you now! I used to call you Blue Roses. How was it that I got started calling you that?

LAURA: I was out of school a little while with pleurosis. When I came back you asked me what was the matter. I said I had pleurosis—you thought I said Blue Roses. That's what you always called me after that!

JIM: I hope you didn't mind.

LAURA: Oh, no—I liked it. You see, I wasn't acquainted with many—people. . . .

JIM: As I remember you sort of stuck by yourself.

LAURA: I—I—never have had much luck at—making friends.

JIM: I don't see why you wouldn't.

LAURA: Well, I—started out badly.

JIM: You mean being—

LAURA: Yes, it sort of—stood between me—

JIM: You shouldn't have let it!

LAURA: I know, but it did, and—

JIM: You were shy with people!

LAURA: I tried not to be but never could—

JIM: Overcome it?

LAURA: No, I—I never could!

JIM: I guess being shy is something you have to work out of kind of gradually.

LAURA: (*Sorrowfully*) Yes—I guess it—

JIM: Takes time!

LAURA: Yes—

JIM: People are not so dreadful when you know them. That's what you have to remember! And everybody has problems, not just you, but practically everybody has got some problems. You think of yourself as having the only problems, as being the only one who is disappointed. But just look around you and you will see lots of people as disappointed as you are. For instance, I hoped when I was going to high school that I would be further along at this time, six years later, than I am now— You remember that wonderful write-up I had in *The Torch*?

LAURA: Yes! (*She rises and crosses to table.*)

JIM: It said I was bound to succeed in anything I went into! (*Laura returns with the annual*) Holy Jeez! *The Torch!* (*He accepts it reverently. They smile across it with mutual wonder. Laura crouches beside him and they begin to turn through it. Laura's shyness is dissolving in his warmth.*)

LAURA: Here you are in *The Pirates of Penzance*!

JIM: (*Wistfully*) I sang the baritone lead in that operetta.

LAURA: (*Raptly*) So—beautifully!

JIM: (*Protesting*) Aw—

LAURA: Yes, yes—beautifully—beautifully!

JIM: You heard me?

LAURA: All three times!

JIM: No!

LAURA: Yes!

JIM: All three performances?

LAURA: (*Looking down*) Yes.

JIM: Why?

LAURA: I—wanted to ask you to—autograph my program.

JIM: Why didn't you ask me to?

LAURA: You were always surrounded by your own friends so much that I never had a chance to.

JIM: You should have just—

LAURA: Well, I—thought you might think I was—

JIM: Thought I might think you was—what?

LAURA: Oh—

JIM: (*With reflective relish*) I was beleaguered by females in those days.

LAURA: You were terribly popular!

JIM: Yeah—

LAURA: You had such a—friendly way—

JIM: I was spoiled in high school.

LAURA: Everybody—liked you!

JIM: Including you?

LAURA: I—yes, I—I did, too— (*She gently closes the book in her lap.*)

JIM: Well, well, well!—Give me that program, Laura. (*She hands it to him. He signs it with a flourish*) There you are—better late than never!

LAURA: Oh, I—what a—surprise!

JIM: My signature isn't worth very much right now. But some day—maybe—it will increase in value! Being disappointed is one thing and being discouraged is something else. I am disappointed but I am not discouraged. I'm twenty-three years old. How old are you?

LAURA: I'll be twenty-four in June.

JIM: That's not old age!

LAURA: No, but—

JIM: You finished high school?

LAURA: (*With difficulty*) I didn't go back.

JIM: You mean you dropped out?

LAURA: I made bad grades in my final examinations. (*She rises and replaces the book and the program. Her voice strained*) How is—Emily Meisenbach getting along?

JIM: Oh, that kraut-head!

LAURA: Why do you call her that?

JIM: That's what she was.

LAURA: You're not still—going with her?

JIM: I never see her.

LAURA: It said in the Personal Section that you were—engaged!

JIM: I know, but I wasn't impressed by that—propaganda!

LAURA: It wasn't—the truth?

JIM: Only in Emily's optimistic opinion!

LAURA: Oh—

    (LEGEND: "WHAT HAVE YOU DONE SINCE HIGH SCHOOL?")
       (*Jim lights a cigarette and leans indolently back on his elbows smiling at Laura with a warmth and charm which lights her inwardly with altar candles. She remains by the table and turns in her hands a piece of glass to cover her tumult.*)

JIM: (*After several reflective puffs on a cigarette*) What have you done since high school? (*She seems not to hear him*) Huh? (*Laura looks up*) I said what have you done since high school, Laura?

LAURA: Nothing much.

JIM: You must have been doing something these six long years.

LAURA: Yes.

JIM: Well, then, such as what?

LAURA: I took a business course at business college—

JIM: How did that work out?

LAURA: Well, not very—well—I had to drop out, it gave me—indigestion— (*Jim laughs gently.*)

JIM: What are you doing now?

LAURA: I don't do anything—much. Oh, please don't think I sit around doing nothing! My glass collection takes up a good deal of time. Glass is something you have to take good care of.

JIM: What did you say—about glass?

LAURA: Collection I said—I have one— (*She clears her throat and turns away again, acutely shy.*)

JIM: (*Abruptly*) You know what I judge to be the trouble with you? Inferiority complex! Know what that is? That's what they call it when someone low-rates himself! I understand it because I had it, too. Although my case was not so aggravated as yours seems to be. I had it until I took up public speaking, developed my voice, and learned that I had an aptitude for science. Before that time I never thought of myself as being outstanding in any way whatsoever!

Now I've never made a regular study of it, but I have a friend who says I can analyze people better than doctors that make a profession of it. I don't claim that to be necessarily true, but I can sure guess a person's psychology, Laura! (*Takes out his gum*) Excuse me, Laura. I always take it out when the flavor is gone. I'll use this scrap of paper to wrap it in. I know how it is to get it stuck on a shoe.

Yep—that's what I judge to be your principal trouble. A lack of confidence in yourself as a person. You don't have the proper amount of faith in yourself. I'm basing that fact on a number of your remarks and also on certain observations I've made. For instance that clumping you thought was so awful in high school. You say that you even dreaded to walk into class. You see what you did? You dropped out of school, you gave up an education because of a clump, which as far as I know was practically non-existent! A little physical defect is what you have. Hardly noticeable even! Magnified thousands of times by imagination!

You know what my strong advice to you is? Think of yourself as *superior* in some way!

LAURA: In what way would I think?

JIM: Why, man alive, Laura! Just look about you a little. What do you see? A world full of common people! All of 'em born and all of 'em going to die! Which of them has one-tenth of your good points! Or mine! Or anyone else's, as far as that goes— Gosh! Everybody excels in some one thing. Some in many! (*Unconsciously glances at himself in the mirror.*) All you've got to do is discover in *what*! Take me, for instance. (*He adjusts his tie at the mirror.*) My interest happens to lie in electro-dynamics. I'm taking a course in radio engineering at night school, Laura, on top of a fairly responsible job at the warehouse. I'm taking that course and studying public speaking.

LAURA: Ohhhh.

JIM: Because I believe in the future of television! (*Turning back to her.*) I wish to be ready to go up right along with it. Therefore I'm planning to get in on the ground floor. In fact I've already made the right connections and all that remains is for the industry itself to get under way! Full steam— (*His eyes are starry.*) Knowledge—Zzzzzp! Money—Zzzzzp!—Power! That's the cycle democracy is built on! (*His attitude is convincingly dynamic. Laura stares at him, even her shyness eclipsed in her absolute wonder. He suddenly grins.*) I guess you think I think a lot of myself!

LAURA: No—o-o-o, I—

JIM: Now how about you? Isn't there something you take more interest in than anything else?

LAURA: Well, I do—as I said—have my—glass collection— (*A peal of girlish laughter from the kitchen.*)

JIM: I'm not right sure I know what you're talking about. What kind of glass is it?

LAURA: Little articles of it, they're ornaments mostly! Most of them are little animals made out of glass, the tiniest little animals in the world. Mother calls them a glass menagerie! Here's an example of one, if you'd like to see it! This one is one of the oldest. It's nearly thirteen.

(MUSIC: "THE GLASS MENAGERIE.")
(*He stretches out his hand.*)

Oh, be careful—if you breathe, it breaks!

JIM: I'd better not take it. I'm pretty clumsy with things.

LAURA: Go on, I trust you with him! (*Places it in his palm*) There now—you're holding him gently! Hold him over the light, he loves the light! You see how the light shines through him?

JIM: It sure does shine!

LAURA: I shouldn't be partial, but he is my favorite one.

JIM: What kind of a thing is this one supposed to be?

LAURA: Haven't you noticed the single horn on his forehead?

JIM: A unicorn, huh?

LAURA: Mmm-hmmm!

JIM: Unicorns, aren't they extinct in the modern world?

LAURA: I know!

JIM: Poor little fellow, he must feel sort of lonesome.

LAURA: (*Smiling*) Well, if he does he doesn't complain about it. He stays on a shelf with some horses that don't have horns and all of them seem to get along nicely together.

JIM: How do you know?

LAURA: (*Lightly*) I haven't heard any arguments among them!

JIM: (*Grinning*) No arguments, huh? Well, that's a pretty good sign! Where shall I set him?

LAURA: Put him on the table. They all like a change of scenery once in a while!

JIM: (*Stretching*) Well, well, well, well— Look how big my shadow is when I stretch!

LAURA: Oh, oh, yes—it stretches across the ceiling!

JIM: (*Crossing to door*) I think it's stopped raining. (*Opens fire-escape door*) Where does the music come from?

LAURA: From the Paradise Dance Hall across the alley.

JIM: How about cutting the rug a little, Miss Wingfield?

LAURA: Oh, I—

JIM: Or is your program filled up? Let me have a look at it. (*Grasps imaginary card*) Why, every dance is taken! I'll just have to scratch some out. (WALTZ MUSIC: "LA GOLONDRINA") Ahhh, a waltz! (*He executes some sweeping turns by himself then holds his arms toward Laura.*)

LAURA: (*Breathlessly*) I—can't dance!

JIM: There you go, that inferiority stuff!

LAURA: I've never danced in my life!

JIM: Come on, try!

LAURA: Oh, but I'd step on you!

JIM: I'm not made out of glass.

LAURA: How—how—how do we start?

JIM: Just leave it to me. You hold your arms out a little.

LAURA: Like this?

JIM: A little bit higher. Right. Now don't tighten up, that's that's the main thing about it—relax.

LAURA: (*Laughing breathlessly*) It's hard not to.

JIM: Okay.

LAURA: I'm afraid you can't budge me.

JIM: What do you bet I can't? (*He swings her into motion.*)

LAURA: Goodness, yes, you can!

JIM: Let yourself go, now, Laura, just let yourself go.

LAURA: I'm—

JIM: Come on!

LAURA: Trying!

JIM: Not so stiff— Easy does it!

LAURA: I know but I'm—

JIM: Loosen th' backbone! There now, that's a lot better.

LAURA: Am I?

JIM: Lots, lots better! (*He moves her about the room in a clumsy waltz.*)

LAURA: Oh, my!

JIM: Ha-ha!

LAURA: Oh, my goodness!

JIM: Ha-ha-ha! (*They suddenly bump into the table. Jim stops*) What did we hit on?

LAURA: Table.

JIM: Did something fall off it? I think—

LAURA: Yes.

JIM: I hope that it wasn't the little glass horse with the horn!

LAURA: Yes.

JIM: Aw, aw, aw. Is it broken?

LAURA: Now it is just like all the other horses.

JIM: It's lost its—

LAURA: Horn! It doesn't matter. Maybe it's a blessing in disguise.

JIM: You'll never forgive me. I bet that that was your favorite piece of glass.

LAURA: I don't have favorites much. It's no tragedy, Freckles. Glass breaks so easily. No matter how careful you are. The traffic jars the shelves and things fall off them.

JIM: Still I'm awfully sorry that I was the cause.

LAURA: (*Smiling*) I'll just imagine he had an operation. The horn was removed to make him feel less—freakish! (*They both laugh.*) Now he will feel more at home with the other horses, the ones that don't have horns . . .

JIM: Ha-ha, that's very funny! (*Suddenly serious.*) I'm glad to see that you have a sense of humor. You know—you're—well—very different! Surprisingly different from anyone else I know! (*His voice becomes soft and hesitant with a genuine feeling.*) Do you mind me telling you that? (*Laura is abashed beyond speech.*) I mean it in a nice way . . . (*Laura nods shyly, looking away.*) You make me feel sort of—I don't know how to put it! I'm usually pretty good at expressing things, but—This is something that I don't know how to say! (*Laura touches her throat and clears it—turns the broken unicorn in her hands.*) (*Even softer.*) Has anyone ever told you that you were pretty? (PAUSE: MUSIC.) (*Laura looks up slowly, with wonder, and shakes her head.*) Well, you are! In a very different way from anyone else. And all the nicer because of the difference, too. (*His voice becomes low and husky. Laura turns away, nearly faint with the novelty of her emotions.*) I wish that you were my sister. I'd teach you to have some confidence in yourself. The different people are not like other people, but being different is nothing to be ashamed of. Because other people are not such wonderful people. They're one hundred times one thousand. You're one times one! They walk all over the earth. You just stay here. They're common as—weeds, but—you—well, you're—*Blue Roses!*

(IMAGE ON SCREEN: BLUE ROSES.)
(MUSIC CHANGES.)

LAURA: But blue is wrong for—roses . . .
JIM: It's right for you!—You're—pretty!
LAURA: In what respect am I pretty?
JIM: In all respects—believe me! Your eyes—your hair—are pretty! Your hands are pretty! (*He catches hold of her hand.*) You think I'm making this up because I'm invited to dinner and have to be nice. Oh, I could do that! I could put on an act for you, Laura, and say lots of things without being very sincere. But this time I am. I'm talking to you sincerely. I happened to notice you had this inferiority complex that keeps you from feeling comfortable with people. Somebody needs to build your confidence up and make you proud instead of shy and turning away and—blushing— Somebody—ought to— Ought to—*kiss you, Laura!*

(*His hand slips slowly up her arm to her shoulder.*)
(MUSIC SWELLS TUMULTUOUSLY.)
(*He suddenly turns her about and kisses her on the lips.*)
(*When he releases her, Laura sinks on the sofa with a bright, dazed look.*)
(*Jim backs away and fishes in his pocket for a cigarette.*)
(LEGEND ON SCREEN: "SOUVENIR.")

Stumble-john!

(*He lights the cigarette, avoiding her look.*)
(*There is a peal of girlish laughter from Amanda in the kitchen.*)
(*Laura slowly raises and opens her hand. It still contains the little broken glass animal. She looks at it with a tender, bewildered expression.*)

Stumble-john! I shouldn't have done that— That was way off the beam. You don't smoke, do you?

(*She looks up, smiling, not hearing the question.*)
(*He sits beside her a little gingerly. She looks at him speechlessly— waiting.*)
(*He coughs decorously and moves a little farther aside as he considers the situation and senses her feelings, dimly, with perturbation.*)
(*Gently.*)

Would you—care for a—mint?

(*She doesn't seem to hear him but her look grows brighter even.*)

Peppermint—Life-Saver? My pocket's a regular drug store—wherever I go . . . (*He pops a mint in his mouth. Then gulps and decides to make a clean breast of it. He speaks slowly and gingerly.*) Laura, you know, if I had a sister like you, I'd do the same thing as Tom. I'd bring out fellows and—introduce her to them. The right type of boys of a type to—appreciate her. Only— well—he made a mistake about me. Maybe I've got no call to be saying this. That may not have been the idea in having me over. But what if it was? There's nothing wrong about that. The only trouble is that in my case—I'm not in a situation to—do the right thing. I can't take down your number and say I'll phone. I can't call up next week and—ask for a date. I thought I had better explain the situation in case you—misunderstood it and—hurt your feelings. . . .

> (*Pause.*)
> (*Slowly, very slowly, Laura's look changes, her eyes returning slowly from his to the ornament in her palm.*)
> (*Amanda utters another gay laugh in the kitchen.*)

LAURA: (*Faintly*) You—won't—call again?
JIM: No, Laura, I can't. (*He rises from the sofa.*) As I was just explaining, I've— got strings on me. Laura, I've—been going steady! I go out all of the time with a girl named Betty. She's a home-girl like you, and Catholic, and Irish, and in a great many ways we—get along fine. I met her last summer on a moonlight boat trip up the river to Alton, on the *Majestic.* Well—right away from the start it was—love!

> (LEGEND: LOVE!)
> (*Laura sways slightly forward and grips the arm of the sofa. He fails to notice, now enrapt in his own comfortable being.*)

Being in love has made a new man of me!

> (*Leaning stiffly forward, clutching the arm of the sofa, Laura struggles visibly with her storm. But Jim is oblivious, she is a long way off.*)

The power of love is really pretty tremendous! Love is something that— changes the whole world, Laura! (*The storm abates a little and Laura leans back. He notices her again.*) It happened that Betty's aunt took sick, she got a wire and had to go to Centralia. So Tom—when he asked me to dinner—I naturally just accepted the invitation, not knowing that you—that he—that I— (*He stops awkwardly.*) Huh—I'm a stumble-john! (*He flops back on the sofa.*)

> (*The holy candles in the altar of Laura's face have been snuffed out. There is a look of almost infinite desolation.*)
> (*Jim glances at her uneasily.*)

I wish that you would—say something. (*She bites her lip which was trembling and then bravely smiles. She opens her hand again on the broken glass ornament. Then she gently takes his hand and raises it level with her own. She carefully places the unicorn in the palm of his hand, then pushes his fingers closed upon it*) What are you—doing that for? You want me to have him?—Laura? (*She nods*) What for?
LAURA: A—souvenir . . .

> (*She rises unsteadily and crouches beside the victrola to wind it up.*)

(LEGEND ON SCREEN: "THINGS HAVE A WAY OF TURNING OUT SO BADLY!")

(OR IMAGE: "GENTLEMAN CALLER WAVING GOOD-BYE! — GAILY.")

(*At this moment Amanda rushes brightly back in the front room. She bears a pitcher of fruit punch in an old-fashioned cut-glass pitcher and a plate of macaroons. The plate has a gold border and poppies painted on it.*)

AMANDA: Well, well, well! Isn't the air delightful after the shower? I've made you children a little liquid refreshment. (*Turns gaily to the gentleman caller*) Jim, do you know that song about lemonade?

"Lemonade, lemonade

Made in the shade and stirred with a spade—

Good enough for any old maid!"

JIM: (*Uneasily*) Ha-ha! No—I never heard it.

AMANDA: Why, Laura! You look so serious!

JIM: We were having a serious conversation.

AMANDA: Good! Now you're better acquainted!

JIM: (*Uncertainly*) Ha-ha! Yes.

AMANDA: You modern young people are much more serious-minded than my generation. I was so gay as a girl!

JIM: You haven't changed, Mrs. Wingfield.

AMANDA: Tonight I'm rejuvenated! The gaiety of the occasion, Mr. O'Connor! (*She tosses her head with a pearl of laughter. Spills lemonade.*) Oooo! I'm baptizing myself!

JIM: Here—let me—

AMANDA: (*Setting the pitcher down*) There now. I discovered we had some maraschino cherries. I dumped them in, juice and all!

JIM: You shouldn't have gone to that trouble, Mrs. Wingfield.

AMANDA: Trouble, trouble? Why, it was loads of fun! Didn't you hear me cutting up in the kitchen? I bet your ears were burning! I told Tom how outdone with him I was for keeping you to himself so long a time! He should have brought you over much, much sooner! Well, now that you've found your way, I want you to be a very frequent caller! Not just occasional but all the time.

Oh, we're going to have a lot of gay times together! I see them coming!

Mmm, just breathe that air! So fresh, and the moon's so pretty!

I'll skip back out—I know where my place is when young folks are having a—serious conversation!

JIM: Oh, don't go out, Mrs. Wingfield. The fact of the matter is I've got to be going.

AMANDA: Going, now? You're joking! Why, it's only the shank of the evening, Mr. O'Connor!

JIM: Well, you know how it is.

AMANDA: You mean you're a young workingman and have to keep workingmen's hours. We'll let you off early tonight. But only on the condition that next time you stay later.

What's the best night for you? Isn't Saturday night the best night for you workingmen?

JIM: I have a couple of time-clocks to punch, Mrs. Wingfield. One at morning, another one at night!

AMANDA: My, but you *are* ambitious! You work at night, too?

JIM: No, Ma'am, not work but—Betty! (*He crosses deliberately to pick up his hat. The band at the Paradise Dance Hall goes into a tender waltz.*)

AMANDA: Betty? Betty? Who's—Betty! (*There is an ominous cracking sound in the sky.*)

JIM: Oh, just a girl. The girl I go steady with! (*He smiles charmingly. The sky falls.*)

> (LEGEND: "THE SKY FALLS.")

AMANDA: (*A long-drawn exhalation*) Ohhhh ... Is it a serious romance, Mr. O'Connor?

JIM: We're going to be married the second Sunday in June.

AMANDA: Ohhhh—how nice! Tom didn't mention that you were engaged to be married.

JIM: The cat's not out of the bag at the warehouse yet. You know how they are. They call you Romeo and stuff like that. (*He stops at the oval mirror to put on his hat. He carefully shapes the brim and the crown to give a discreetly dashing effect.*) It's been a wonderful evening, Mrs. Wingfield. I guess this is what they mean by Southern hospitality.

AMANDA: It really wasn't anything at all.

JIM: I hope it don't seem like I'm rushing off. But I promised Betty I'd pick her up at the Wabash depot, an' by the time I get my jalopy down there her train'll be in. Some women are pretty upset if you keep 'em waiting.

AMANDA: Yes, I know— The tyranny of women! (*Extends her hand.*) Good-bye, Mr. O'Connor. I wish you luck—and happiness—and success! All three of them, and so does Laura!—Don't you, Laura?

LAURA: Yes!

JIM: (*Taking her hand*) Good-bye, Laura. I'm certainly going to treasure that souvenir. And don't you forget the good advice I gave you. (*Raises his voice to a cheery shout.*) So long, Shakespeare! Thanks again, ladies— Good night! (*He grins and ducks jauntily out.*)

> (*Still bravely grimacing, Amanda closes the door on the gentleman caller. Then she turns back to the room with a puzzled expression. She and Laura don't dare to face each other. Laura crouches beside the victrola to wind it.*)

AMANDA: (*Faintly*) Things have a way of turning out so badly. I don't believe that I would play the victrola. Well, well—well— Our gentleman caller was engaged to be married! Tom!

TOM: (*From back*) Yes, Mother?

AMANDA: Come in here a minute. I want to tell you something awfully funny.

TOM: (*Enters with macaroon and a glass of the lemonade*) Has the gentleman caller gotten away already?

AMANDA: The gentleman caller has made an early departure. What a wonderful joke you played on us!

TOM: How do you mean?

AMANDA: You didn't mention that he was engaged to be married.

TOM: Jim? Engaged?

AMANDA: That's what he just informed us.

TOM: I'll be jiggered! I didn't know about that.

AMANDA: That seems very peculiar.

TOM: What's peculiar about it?

AMANDA: Didn't you call him your best friend down at the warehouse?

TOM: He is, but how did I know?

AMANDA: It seems extremely peculiar that you wouldn't know your best friend was going to be married!

TOM: The warehouse is where I work, not where I know things about people!

AMANDA: You don't know things anywhere! You live in a dream; you manufacture illusions! (*He crosses to door.*) Where are you going?

TOM: I'm going to the movies.

AMANDA: That's right, now that you've had us make such fools of ourselves. The effort, the preparations, all the expense! The new floor lamp, the rug, the clothes for Laura! All for what? To entertain some other girl's fiancé!

Go to the movies, go! Don't think about us, a mother deserted, an unmarried sister who's crippled and has no job! Don't let anything interfere with your selfish pleasure! Just go, go, go—to the movies!

TOM: All right, I will! The more you shout about my selfishness to me the quicker I'll go, and I won't go to the movies!

AMANDA: Go, then! Then go to the moon—you selfish dreamer!

> (*Tom smashes his glass on the floor. He plunges out on the fire-escape, slamming the door. Laura screams—cut by door.*)
>
> (*Dance-hall music up. Tom goes to the rail and grips it desperately, lifting his face in the chill white moonlight penetrating the narrow abyss of the alley.*)
>
> (LEGEND ON SCREEN: "AND SO GOOD-BYE . . .")
>
> (*Tom's closing speech is timed with the interior pantomime. The interior scene is played as though viewed through sound-proof glass. Amanda appears to be making a comforting speech to Laura who is huddled upon the sofa. Now that we cannot hear the mother's speech, her silliness is gone and she has dignity and tragic beauty. Laura's dark hair hides her face until at the end of the speech she lifts it to smile at her mother. Amanda's gestures are slow and graceful, almost dance-like, as she comforts the daughter. At the end of her speech she glances a moment at the father's picture—then withdraws through the portieres. At close of Tom's speech, Laura blows out the candles, ending the play.*)

TOM: I didn't go to the moon, I went much further—for time is the longest distance between two places—

Not long after that I was fired for writing a poem on the lid of a shoebox.

I left Saint Louis. I descended the steps of this fire-escape for a last time and followed, from then on, in my father's footsteps, attempting to find in motion what was lost in space—

I traveled around a great deal. The cities swept about me like dead leaves, leaves that were brightly colored but torn away from the branches.

I would have stopped, but I was pursued by something.

It always came upon me unawares, taking me altogether by surprise. Perhaps it was a familiar bit of music. Perhaps it was only a piece of transparent glass—

Perhaps I am walking along a street at night, in some strange city, before I have found companions. I pass the lighted window of a shop where perfume is sold. The window is filled with pieces of colored glass, tiny transparent bottles in delicate colors, like bits of a shattered rainbow.

Then all at once my sister touches my shoulder. I turn around and look into her eyes . . .

Oh, Laura, Laura, I tried to leave you behind me, but I am more faithful than I intended to be!

I reach for a cigarette, I cross the street, I run into the movies or a bar, I buy a drink, I speak to the nearest stranger—anything that can blow your candles out!

(*Laura bends over the candles.*)

—for nowadays the world is lit by lightning! Blow out your candles, Laura—and so good-bye. . . .

(*She blows the candles out.*)

THE SCENE DISSOLVES

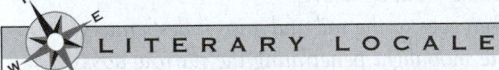

Jessica Tandy as Blanche, Kim Hunter as Stella, and Marlon Brando as Stanley in the original stage production of A Streetcar Named Desire.

The Tennessee Williams Literary Festival, New Orleans. Each spring New Orleans hosts a Tennessee Williams Literary Festival, a five-day celebration of plays and readings presented throughout Williams's adopted town. The main festival events focus on the French Quarter, where Williams lived and which he used as the setting for one of his most famous plays, *A Streetcar Named Desire*, named after an actual line that was once part of the New Orleans transit system. In 2006 the Tennessee Williams/New Orleans Literary Festival celebrated its twentieth anniversary, returning to its French Quarter roots despite the devastation of Hurricane Katrina. The festival celebrates both the city that Williams called home and New Orleans's literary culture. Writers such as Michael Chabon, Rick Bragg, Robert Olen Butler, Dorothy Allison (see p. 416), and Elizabeth Berg have been guests in recent years. Every year the festival produces the winner of the Tennessee Williams one-act play contest and has some fun judging the Stanley and Stella Shouting Contest, in which contestants compete over who can shout the name "Stella" just like Stanley does in *A Streetcar Named Desire*. The festival also brings together Tennessee Williams scholars for discussions and seminars.

Talking about the Text

1. Invent some additional slightly old-fashioned, somewhat high-class phrases like "gentleman caller" for other characters and situations in *The Glass Menagerie*. For instance, how might we refer to Amanda? To Laura? To the opening scene?
2. Invest the everyday world around you with symbolic significance in the way Tennessee Williams does throughout *The Glass Menagerie*. For example, what kind of dreamlike meaning could be represented by a wall? A door? An intercom? A light switch? Could these commonplace objects really serve as symbols?

Writing about the Text

1. How is the term "gentleman caller" typical of the way Amanda talks? Find other examples of such language in the play. In what ways is this talk just her manner of speaking, learned from her southern upbringing, and in what ways does it connect more intimately with the way she as a person sees the world?
2. Describe the contrast in *The Glass Menagerie* between the realistic and the fantastic. Specifically, concentrate on when characters and setting seem to be depicted naturally or realistically and when they are depicted in obviously exaggerated, fantastic ways. What effects do each of these depictions have on the play and how we interpret it?

Linking the Text to Other Texts

1. *The Glass Menagerie* is forever linked with another famous play, Arthur Miller's *Death of a Salesman*, because they both premiered in the same decade and were their authors' first and arguably most significant hits. What large issues do they have in common? What are the differences in tone and dramatic action?
2. Compare the glass menagerie to symbols in other plays that serve a similar function, such as the piano in August Wilson's *Piano Lesson* (see p. 1916), or Yorick's skull in *Hamlet* (see p. 1443).

Starting Points for Further Research: Tennessee Williams

- **Edition:** Tennessee Williams. *Plays.* New York: Library of America, 2000.
- **Biography:** Ronald Hayman. *Tennessee Williams: Everyone Else Is An Audience.* New Haven: Yale University Press, 1993.
- **Critical Essay:** George Hovis. " 'Fifty Percent Illusion': The Mask of the Southern Belle in Tennessee Williams's *A Streetcar Named Desire*, *The Glass Menagerie*, and *Portrait of a Madonna*." *Tennessee Williams Literary Journal* 5 (2003): 11–22.

ARTHUR MILLER AND THE AMERICAN FAMILY

Arthur Miller, c. 1945, four years before Death of a Salesman *had its Broadway debut.*

Brooklyn-born Arthur Miller grew up poor during the Great Depression, and many of his plays depict the impact of financial strains on the values espoused by the archetypal American family. He attended the University of Michigan, where he began writing, and like many writers during the Depression, he was employed by the Federal Theater Project. He had his first and greatest success with *Death of a Salesman* on Broadway in 1949, which went on to win a Pulitzer Prize, several Tony Awards, and the New York Drama Critics Circle Award, and it is still considered by many critics and theatergoers to be his masterpiece. His other well-known work was *The Crucible* (1953), which dramatizes the seventeenth-century Salem, Massachusetts, witch trials and served as a parable to characterize American public life during the McCarthy era. He later would marry Marilyn Monroe (his second marriage, her third), who starred in a movie for which he wrote the script, *The Misfits* (1961). He eventually depicted a fictionalized version of life with her in *After the Fall* (1964). While *Salesman* and *The Crucible* remain Miller's two most commonly read and performed works, he stayed active professionally all his life, writing such plays as *Incident at Vichy* (1965), *The Price* (1968), *Broken Glass* (1994), and *The Ride Down Mt. Morgan* (1999), as well as his autobiography *Timebends* (1987).

Death of a Salesman is firmly in the realistic tradition first explored by Ibsen. Nothing in the mid-twentieth century was a more common figure for American enterprise than the traveling salesman, and in *Death of a Salesman*, in which a salesman becomes overwhelmed by American society's values, the "common man" has assumed a central place in tragic drama. Willy Loman, far from being a figure of comedy, as are most "low" characters in Greek or Shakespearean tragedy, is a personage to whom, in his wife's words, "Attention must be paid." And audiences paid attention. Miller had written several other plays before this one, including *All My Sons* (1947), which won a Tony Award for Best Play, but *Death of a Salesman* was the drama that made him one of the most famous playwrights, both in America and worldwide.

We never learn just what commodity Willy sells, for it is plain that he is attempting to sell himself first and foremost (with all the ambiguities that entails), and then also his son Biff. In the sense that all of us want to be "well liked" (in

Willy's words), and work hard toward that end, we all identify with Willy—both in his desire and in his failure—to some extent. Miller has said he had a salesman uncle who served as a partial model for Willy, but it is clear that Miller's play has transformed that uncle into somebody much more significant, an embodiment of the old-fashioned American dream.

AUDIO LOCALE

Arthur Miller with his new wife, actress Marilyn Monroe, in 1956.

Retrospective of a Master Playwright. When Arthur Miller died in February 2005 at age eighty-nine, he still had a closet full of unfinished manuscripts and had just published a short story and produced a play. The day after Miller died, Boston's National Public Radio (NPR) station produced a retrospective of him. Host Tom Ashbrook discussed Miller's life, legacy, and influence on modern theater, with theater scholars and call-in listeners. You can listen to the whole program by searching their online archive for the show that aired on February 1, 2005. Go to On Point Radio's website at *http://www.onpointradio.org.*

ARTHUR MILLER
(1915–2005)

Death of a Salesman
(1949)

Certain private conversations in two acts and a requiem

Cast

Willy Loman	The Woman	Jenny
Linda	Charley	Stanley
Biff	Uncle Ben	Miss Forsythe
Happy	Howard Wagber	Letta
Bernard		

> SCENE: *The action takes place in Willy Loman's house and yard and in various places he visits in the New York and Boston of today.*
>
> *Throughout the play, in the stage directions, left and right mean stage left and stage right.*

ACT ONE

A melody is heard, played upon a flute. It is small and fine, telling of grass and trees and the horizon. The curtain rises.

Before us is the SALESMAN'S house. We are aware of towering, angular shapes behind it, surrounding it on all sides. Only the blue light of the sky falls upon the house and forestage; the surrounding area shows an angry glow of orange. As more light appears, we see a solid vault of apartment houses around the small, fragile-seeming home. An air of the dream clings to the place, a dream rising out of reality. The kitchen at center seems actual enough, for there is a kitchen table with three chairs, and a refrigerator. But no other fixtures are seen. At the back of the kitchen there is a draped entrance, which leads to the living-room. To the right of the kitchen, on a level raised two feet, is a bedroom furnished only with a brass bedstead and a straight chair. On a shelf over the bed a silver athletic trophy stands. A window opens on to the apartment house at the side.

Behind the kitchen, on a level raised six and a half feet, is the boys' bedroom, at present barely visible. Two beds are dimly seen, and at the back of the room a dormer window. (This bedroom is above the unseen living-room.) At the left a stairway curves up to it from the kitchen.

The entire setting is wholly or, in some places, partially transparent. The roof-line of the house is one-dimensional; under and over it we see the apartment buildings. Before the house lies an apron, curving beyond the forestage into the orchestra. This forward area serves as the back yard as well as the locale of all Willy's imaginings and of his city scenes. Whenever the action is in the present the actors observe the imaginary wall-lines, entering the house only through its door at the left. But in the scenes of the past these boundaries are broken, and characters enter or leave a room by stepping "through" a wall on to the forestage.

[From the right, WILLY LOMAN, the Salesman, enters, carrying two large sample cases. The flute plays on. He hears but is not aware of it. He is past sixty years of age, dressed quietly. Even as he crosses the stage to the doorway of the house, his exhaustion is apparent. He unlocks the door, comes into the kitchen, and thankfully lets his burden down, feeling the soreness of his palms. A word-sigh escapes his lips—it might be "Oh, boy, oh, boy." He closes the door, then carries his cases out into the living-room, through the draped kitchen doorway. LINDA, his wife, has stirred in her bed at the right. She gets out and puts on a robe, listening. Most often jovial, she has developed an iron repression of her exceptions to WILLY'S behavior—she more than loves him, she admires him, as though his mercurial nature, his temper, his massive dreams and little cruelties, served her only as sharp reminders of the turbulent longings within him, longings which she shares but lacks the temperament to utter and follow to their end.]

LINDA [hearing WILLY outside the bedroom, calls with some trepidation]: Willy!
WILLY: It's all right. I came back.
LINDA: Why? What happened? [Slight pause.] Did something happen, Willy?

WILLY: No, nothing happened.

LINDA: You didn't smash the car, did you?

WILLY [*with casual irritation*]: I said nothing happened. Didn't you hear me?

LINDA: Don't you feel well?

WILLY: I'm tired to the death. [*The flute has faded away. He sits on the bed beside her, a little numb.*] I couldn't make it. I just couldn't make it, Linda.

LINDA [*very carefully, delicately*]: Where were you all day? You look terrible.

WILLY: I got as far as a little above Yonkers. I stopped for a cup of coffee. Maybe it was the coffee.

LINDA: What?

WILLY [*after a pause*]: I suddenly couldn't drive any more. The car kept going off on to the shoulder, y'know?

LINDA [*helpfully*]: Oh. Maybe it was the steering again. I don't think Angelo knows the Studebaker.

WILLY: No, it's me, it's me. Suddenly I realize I'm goin' sixty miles an hour and I don't remember the last five minutes. I'm—I can't seem to—keep my mind to it.

LINDA: Maybe it's your glasses. You never went for your new glasses.

WILLY: No, I see everything. I came back ten miles an hour. It took me nearly four hours from Yonkers.

LINDA [*resigned*]: Well, you'll just have to take a rest, Willy, you can't continue this way.

WILLY: I just got back from Florida.

LINDA: But you didn't rest your mind. Your mind is overactive, and the mind is what counts, dear.

WILLY: I'll start out in the morning. Maybe I'll feel better in the morning. [*She is taking off his shoes.*] These goddam arch supports are killing me.

LINDA: Take an aspirin. Should I get you an aspirin? It'll soothe you.

WILLY [*with wonder*]: I was driving along, you understand? And I was fine. I was even observing the scenery. You can imagine, me looking at scenery, on the road every week of my life. But it's so beautiful up there, Linda, the trees are so thick, and the sun is warm. I opened the windshield and just let the warm air bathe over me. And then all of a sudden I'm goin' off the road! I'm tellin' ya, I absolutely forgot I was driving. If I'd've gone the other way over the white line I might've killed somebody. So I went on again—and five minutes later I'm dreamin' again, and I nearly—[*He presses two fingers against his eyes.*] I have such thoughts, I have such strange thoughts.

LINDA: Willy, dear. Talk to them again. There's no reason why you can't work in New York.

WILLY: They don't need me in New York. I'm the New England man. I'm vital in New England.

LINDA: But you're sixty years old. They can't expect you to keep traveling every week.

WILLY: I'll have to send a wire to Portland. I'm supposed to see Brown and Morrison tomorrow morning at ten o'clock to show the line. Goddammit, I could sell them! [*He starts putting on his jacket.*]

LINDA [*taking the jacket from him*]: Why don't you go down to the place tomorrow and tell Howard you've simply got to work in New York? You're too accommodating, dear.

WILLY: If old man Wagner was alive I'd a been in charge of New York now! That man was a prince, he was a masterful man. But that boy of his, that Howard, he don't appreciate. When I went north the first time, the Wagner Company didn't know where New England was!

LINDA: Why don't you tell those things to Howard, dear?

WILLY [encouraged]: I will, I definitely will. Is there any cheese?

LINDA: I'll make you a sandwich.

WILLY: No, go to sleep. I'll take some milk. I'll be up right away. The boys in?

LINDA: They're sleeping. Happy took Biff on a date to-night.

WILLY [interested]: That so?

LINDA: It was so nice to see them shaving together, one behind the other, in the bathroom. And going out together. You notice? The whole house smells of shaving lotion.

WILLY: Figure it out. Work a lifetime to pay off a house. You finally own it, and there's nobody to live in it.

LINDA: Well, dear, life is a casting off. It's always that way.

WILLY: No, no, some people—some people accomplish something. Did Biff say anything after I went this morning?

LINDA: You shouldn't have criticized him, Willy, especially after he just got off the train. You mustn't lose your temper with him.

WILLY: When the hell did I lose my temper? I simply asked him if he was making any money. Is that a criticism?

LINDA: But, dear, how could he make any money?

WILLY [worried and angered]: There's such an undercurrent in him. He became a moody man. Did he apologize when I left this morning?

LINDA: He was crestfallen, Willy. You know how he admires you. I think if he finds himself, then you'll both be happier and not fight any more.

WILLY: How can he find himself on a farm? Is that a life? A farmhand? In the beginning, when he was young, I thought, well, a young man, it's good for him to tramp around, take a lot of different jobs. But it's more than ten years now and he has yet to make thirty-five dollars a week!

LINDA: He's finding himself, Willy.

WILLY: Not finding yourself at the age of thirty-four is a disgrace!

LINDA: Shh!

WILLY: The trouble is he's lazy, goddammit!

LINDA: Willy, please!

WILLY: Biff is a lazy bum!

LINDA: They're sleeping. Get something to eat. Go on down.

WILLY: Why did he come home? I would like to know what brought him home.

LINDA: I don't know. I think he's still lost, Willy. I think he's very lost.

WILLY: Biff Loman is lost. In the greatest country in the world a young man with such—personal attractiveness, gets lost. And such a hard worker. There's one thing about Biff—he's not lazy.

LINDA: Never.

WILLY [with pity and resolve]: I'll see him in the morning; I'll have a nice talk with him. I'll get him a job selling. He could be big in no time. My God! Remember how they used to follow him around in high school? When he smiled at one of them their faces lit up. When he walked down the street . . . [He loses himself in reminiscences.]

LINDA [*trying to bring him out of it*]: Willy, dear, I got a new kind of American-type cheese today. It's whipped.

WILLY: Why do you get American when I like Swiss?

LINDA: I just thought you'd like a change—

WILLY: I don't want a change! I want Swiss cheese. Why am I always being contradicted?

LINDA [*with a covering laugh*]: I thought it would be a surprise.

WILLY: Why don't you open a window in here, for God's sake?

LINDA [*with infinite patience*]: They're all open, dear.

WILLY: The way they boxed us in here. Bricks and windows, windows and bricks.

LINDA: We should've bought the land next door.

WILLY: The street is lined with cars. There's not a breath of fresh air in the neighborhood. The grass don't grow any more, you can't raise a carrot in the back yard. They should've had a law against apartment houses. Remember those two beautiful elm trees out there? When I and Biff hung the swing between them?

LINDA: Yeah, like being a million miles from the city.

WILLY: They should've arrested the builder for cutting those down. They massacred the neighborhood. [*Lost*] More and more I think of those days, Linda. This time of year it was lilac and wisteria. And then the peonies would come out, and the daffodils. What fragrance in this room!

LINDA: Well, after all, people had to move somewhere.

WILLY: No, there's more people now.

LINDA: I don't think there's more people. I think—

WILLY: There's more people! That's what's ruining this country! Population is getting out of control. The competition is maddening! Smell the stink from that apartment house! And another one on the other side . . . How can they whip cheese?

[*On* WILLY'S *last line,* BIFF *and* HAPPY *raise themselves up in their beds, listening.*]

LINDA: Go down, try it. And be quiet.

WILLY [*turning to* LINDA, *guiltily*]: You're not worried about me, are you, sweetheart?

BIFF: What's the matter?

HAPPY: Listen!

LINDA: You've got too much on the ball to worry about.

WILLY: You're my foundation and my support, Linda.

LINDA: Just try to relax, dear. You make mountains out of molehills.

WILLY: I won't fight with him any more. If he wants to go back to Texas, let him go.

LINDA: He'll find his way.

WILLY: Sure. Certain men just don't get started till later in life. Like Thomas Edison, I think. Or B. F. Goodrich. One of them was deaf. [*He starts for the bedroom doorway.*] I'll put my money on Biff.

LINDA: And Willy—if it's warm Sunday we'll drive in the country. And we'll open the windshield, and take lunch.

WILLY: No, the windshields don't open on the new cars.

LINDA: But you opened it today.

WILLY: Me? I didn't. [*He stops.*] Now isn't that peculiar! Isn't that a remarkable—[*He breaks off in amazement and fright as the flute is heard distantly.*]

LINDA: What, darling?

WILLY: That is the most remarkable thing.

LINDA: What, dear?

WILLY: I was thinking of the Chevvy. [*Slight pause.*] Nineteen twenty-eight . . .
when I had that red Chevvy—[*Breaks off.*] That funny? I coulda sworn I was
driving that Chevvy today.

LINDA: Well, that's nothing. Something must've reminded you.

WILLY: Remarkable. Ts. Remember those days? The way Biff used to simonize
that car? The dealer refused to believe there was eighty thousand miles on it.
[*He shakes his head.*] Heh! [*To* LINDA] Close your eyes, I'll be right up. [*He
walks out of the bedroom.*]

HAPPY [*to* BIFF]: Jesus, maybe he smashed up the car again!

LINDA [*calling after* WILLY]: Be careful on the stairs, dear! The cheese is on the
middle shelf! [*She turns, goes over to the bed, takes his jacket, and goes out of the
bedroom.*]

> [*Light has risen on the boys' room. Unseen,* WILLY *is heard talking to him-
> self,* "Eighty thousand miles," *and a little laugh.* BIFF *gets out of bed,
> comes downstage a bit, and stands attentively.* BIFF *is two years older than
> his brother,* HAPPY, *well built, but in these days bears a worn air and
> seems less self-assured. He has succeeded less, and his dreams are
> stronger and less acceptable than* HAPPY'S. HAPPY *is tall, powerfully
> made. Sexuality is like a visible color on him, or a scent that many women
> have discovered. He, like his brother, is lost, but in a different way, for he
> has never allowed himself to turn his face toward defeat and is thus more
> confused and hard-skinned, although seemingly more content.*]

HAPPY [*getting out of bed*]: He's going to get his licence taken away if he keeps
that up. I'm getting nervous about him, y'know, Biff?

BIFF: His eyes are going.

HAPPY: No, I've driven with him. He sees all right. He just doesn't keep his
mind on it. I drove into the city with him last week. He stops at a green light
and then it turns red and he goes. [*He laughs.*]

BIFF: Maybe he's color-blind.

HAPPY: Pop? Why, he's got the finest eye for color in the business. You know
that.

BIFF [*sitting down on his bed*]: I'm going to sleep.

HAPPY: You're not still sour on Dad, are you, Biff?

BIFF: He's all right, I guess.

WILLY [*underneath them, in the living-room*]: Yes, sir, eighty thousand miles—
eighty-two thousand!

BIFF: You smoking?

HAPPY [*holding out a pack of cigarettes*]: Want one?

BIFF [*taking a cigarette*]: I can never sleep when I smell it.

WILLY: What a simonizing job, heh!

HAPPY [*with deep sentiment*]: Funny, Biff, y'know? Us sleeping in here again? The
old beds. [*He pats his bed affectionately.*] All the talk that went across those
two beds, huh? Our whole lives.

BIFF: Yeah. Lotta dreams and plans.

HAPPY [*with a deep and masculine laugh*]: About five hundred women would like to know what was said in this room.

[*They share a soft laugh.*]

BIFF: Remember that big Betsy something—what the hell was her name—over on Bushwick Avenue?

HAPPY [*combing his hair*]: With the collie dog!

BIFF: That's the one. I got you in there, remember?

HAPPY: Yeah, that was my first time—I think. Boy, there was a pig! [*They laugh, almost crudely.*] You taught me everything I know about women. Don't forget that.

BIFF: I bet you forgot how bashful you used to be. Especially with girls.

HAPPY: Oh, I still am, Biff.

BIFF: Oh, go on.

HAPPY: I just control it, that's all. I think I got less bashful and you got more so. What happened, Biff? Where's the old humor, the old confidence? [*He shakes* BIFF'S *knee.* BIFF *gets up and moves restlessly about the room.*] What's the matter?

BIFF: Why does Dad mock me all the time?

HAPPY: He's not mocking you, he—

BIFF: Everything I say there's a twist of mockery on his face. I can't get near him.

HAPPY: He just wants you to make good, that's all. I wanted to talk to you about Dad for a long time, Biff. Something's—happening to him. He—talks to himself.

BIFF: I noticed that this morning. But he always mumbled.

HAPPY: But not so noticeable. It got so embarrassing I sent him to Florida. And you know something? Most of the time he's talking to you.

BIFF: What's he say about me?

HAPPY: I can't make it out.

BIFF: What's he say about me?

HAPPY: I think the fact that you're not settled, that you're still kind of up in the air . . .

BIFF: There's one or two other things depressing him, Happy.

HAPPY: What do you mean?

BIFF: Never mind. Just don't lay it all to me.

HAPPY: But I think if you got started—I mean—is there any future for you out there?

BIFF: I tell ya, Hap, I don't know what the future is. I don't know—what I'm supposed to want.

HAPPY: What do you mean?

BIFF: Well, I spent six or seven years after high school trying to work myself up. Shipping clerk, salesman, business of one kind or another. And it's a measly manner of existence. To get on that subway on the hot mornings in summer. To devote your whole life to keeping stock, or making phone calls, or selling or buying. To suffer fifty weeks of the year for the sake of a two-week vacation, when all you really desire is to be outdoors, with your shirt off. And always to have to get ahead of the next fella. And still—that's how you build a future.

HAPPY: Well, you really enjoy it on a farm? Are you content out there?

BIFF [*with rising agitation*]: Hap, I've had twenty or thirty different kinds of job since I left home before the war, and it always turns out the same. I just realized it lately. In Nebraska when I herded cattle, and the Dakotas, and Arizona, and now in Texas. It's why I came home now, I guess, because I realized it. This farm I work on, it's spring there now, see? And they've got about fifteen new colts. There's nothing more inspiring or—beautiful than the sight of a mare and a new colt. And it's cool there now, see? Texas is cool now, and it's spring. And whenever spring comes to where I am, I suddenly get the feeling, my God, I'm not gettin' anywhere! What the hell am I doing, playing around with horses, twenty-eight dollars a week! I'm thirty-four years old, I oughta be makin' my future. That's when I come running home. And now, I get here, and I don't know what to do with myself. [*After a pause*] I've always made a point of not wasting my life, and everytime I come back here I know that all I've done is to waste my life.

HAPPY: You're a poet, you know that, Biff? You're a—you're an idealist!

BIFF: No, I'm mixed up very bad. Maybe I oughta get married. Maybe I oughta get stuck into something. Maybe that's my trouble. I'm like a boy. I'm not married, I'm not in business, I just—I'm like a boy. Are you content, Hap? You're a success, aren't you? Are you content?

HAPPY: Hell, no!

BIFF: Why? You're making money, aren't you?

HAPPY [*moving about with energy, expressiveness*]: All I can do now is wait for the merchandise manager to die. And suppose I get to be merchandise manager? He's a good friend of mine, and he just built a terrific estate on Long Island. And he lived there about two months and sold it, and now he's building another one. He can't enjoy it once it's finished. And I know that's just what I would do. I don't know what the hell I'm workin' for. Sometimes I sit in my apartment—all alone. And I think of the rent I'm paying. And it's crazy. But then, it's what I always wanted. My own apartment, a car, and plenty of women. And still, goddammit, I'm lonely.

BIFF [*with enthusiasm*]: Listen, why don't you come out West with me?

HAPPY: You and I, heh?

BIFF: Sure, maybe we could buy a ranch. Raise cattle, use our muscles. Men built like we are should be working out in the open.

HAPPY [*avidly*]: The Loman Brothers, heh?

BIFF [*with vast affection*]: Sure, we'd be known all over the counties!

HAPPY [*enthralled*]: That's what I dream about, Biff. Sometimes I want to just rip my clothes off in the middle of the store and outbox that goddam merchandise manager. I mean I can outbox, outrun, and outlift anybody in that store, and I have to take orders from those common, petty sons-of-bitches till I can't stand it any more.

BIFF: I'm tellin' you, kid, if you were with me I'd be happy out there.

HAPPY [*enthused*]: See, Biff, everybody around me is so false that I'm constantly lowering my ideals . . .

BIFF: Baby, together we'd stand up for one another, we'd have someone to trust.

HAPPY: If I were around you—

BIFF: Hap, the trouble is we weren't brought up to grub for money. I don't know how to do it.

HAPPY: Neither can I!

BIFF: Then let's go!

HAPPY: The only thing is—what can you make out there?

BIFF: But look at your friend. Builds an estate and then hasn't the peace of mind to live in it.

HAPPY: Yeah, but when he walks into the store the waves part in front of him. That's fifty-two thousand dollars a year coming through the revolving door, and I got more in my pinky finger than he's got in his head.

BIFF: Yeah, but you just said—

HAPPY: I gotta show some of those pompous, self-important executives over there that Hap Loman can make the grade. I want to walk into the store the way he walks in. Then I'll go with you, Biff. We'll be together yet, I swear. But take those two we had tonight. Now weren't they gorgeous creatures?

BIFF: Yeah, yeah, most gorgeous I've had in years.

HAPPY: I get that any time I want, Biff. Whenever I feel disgusted. The only trouble is, it gets like bowling or something. I just keep knockin' them over and it doesn't mean anything. You still run around a lot?

BIFF: Naa. I'd like to find a girl—steady, somebody with substance.

HAPPY: That's what I long for.

BIFF: Go on! You'd never come home.

HAPPY: I would! Somebody with character, with resistance! Like Mom, y'know? You're gonna call me a bastard when I tell you this. That girl Charlotte I was with tonight is engaged to be married in five weeks. [*He tries on his new hat.*]

BIFF: No kiddin'!

HAPPY: Sure, the guy's in line for the vice-presidency of the store. I don't know what gets into me, maybe I just have an overdeveloped sense of competition or something, but I went and ruined her, and furthermore I can't get rid of her. And he's the third executive I've done that to. Isn't that a crummy characteristic? And to top it all, I go to their weddings! [*Indignantly, but laughing*] Like I'm not supposed to take bribes. Manufacturers offer me a hundred-dollar bill now and then to throw an order their way. You know how honest I am, but it's like this girl, see. I hate myself for it. Because I don't want the girl, and, still, I take it and—I love it!

BIFF: Let's go to sleep.

HAPPY: I guess we didn't settle anything, heh?

BIFF: I just got one idea that I think I'm going to try.

HAPPY: What's that?

BIFF: Remember Bill Oliver?

HAPPY: Sure, Oliver is very big now. You want to work for him again?

BIFF: No, but when I quit he said something to me. He put his arm on my shoulder, and he said, "Biff, if you ever need anything, come to me."

HAPPY: I remember that. That sounds good.

BIFF: I think I'll go to see him. If I could get ten thousand or even seven or eight thousand dollars I could buy a beautiful ranch.

HAPPY: I bet he'd back you. 'Cause he thought highly of you, Biff. I mean, they all do. You're well liked, Biff. That's why I say to come back here, and we both have the apartment. And I'm tellin' you, Biff, any babe you want . . .

BIFF: No, with a ranch I could do the work I like and still be something. I just wonder though. I wonder if Oliver still thinks I stole that carton of basketballs.

HAPPY: Oh, he probably forgot that long ago. It's almost ten years. You're too sensitive. Anyway, he didn't really fire you.

BIFF: Well, I think he was going to. I think that's why I quit. I was never sure whether he knew or not. I know he thought the world of me, though. I was the only one he'd let lock up the place.

WILLY [below]: You gonna wash the engine, Biff?

HAPPY: Shh!

[BIFF looks at HAPPY, who is gazing down, listening. WILLY is mumbling in the parlor.]

HAPPY: You hear that?

[They listen. WILLY laughs warmly.]

BIFF [growing angry]: Doesn't he know Mom can hear that?

WILLY: Don't get your sweater dirty, Biff!

[A look of pain crosses BIFF'S face.]

HAPPY: Isn't that terrible? Don't leave again, will you? You'll find a job here. You gotta stick around. I don't know what to do about him, it's getting embarrassing.

WILLY: What a simonizing job!

BIFF: Mom's hearing that!

WILLY: No kiddin', Biff, you got a date? Wonderful!

HAPPY: Go on to sleep. But talk to him in the morning, will you?

BIFF [reluctantly getting into bed]: With her in the house. Brother!

HAPPY [getting into bed]: I wish you'd have a good talk with him.

[The light on their room begins to fade.]

BIFF [to himself in bed]: That selfish, stupid . . .

HAPPY: Sh . . . Sleep, Biff.

[Their light is out. Well before they have finished speaking, WILLY'S form is dimly seen below in the darkened kitchen. He opens the refrigerator, searches in there, and takes out a bottle of milk. The apartment houses are fading out, and the entire house and surroundings become covered with leaves. Music insinuates itself as the leaves appear.]

WILLY: Just wanna be careful with those girls, Biff, that's all. Don't make any promises. No promises of any kind. Because a girl, y'know, they always believe what you tell 'em, and you're very young, Biff, you're too young to be talking seriously to girls.

[Light rises on the kitchen. WILLY, talking, shuts the refrigerator door and comes downstage to the kitchen table. He pours milk into a glass. He is totally immersed in himself, smiling faintly.]

WILLY: Too young entirely, Biff. You want to watch your schooling first. Then when you're all set, there'll be plenty of girls for a boy like you. [He smiles broadly at a kitchen chair.] That so? The girls pay for you? [He laughs.] Boy, you must really be makin' a hit.

[WILLY *is gradually addressing—physically—a point off-stage, speaking through the wall of the kitchen, and his voice has been rising in volume to that of a normal conversation.*]

WILLY: I been wondering why you polish the car so careful. Ha! Don't leave the hubcaps, boys. Get the chamois to the hubcaps. Happy, use newspaper on the windows, it's the easiest thing. Show him how to do it, Biff! You see, Happy? Pad it up, use it like a pad. That's it, that's it, good work. You're doin' all right, Hap. [*He pauses, then nods in approbation for a few seconds, then looks upward.*] Biff, first thing we gotta do when we get time is clip that big branch over the house. Afraid it's gonna fall in a storm and hit the roof. Tell you what. We get a rope and sling her around, and then we climb up there with a couple of saws and take her down. Soon as you finish the car, boys, I wanna see ya. I got a surprise for you, boys.

BIFF [*offstage*]: Whatta ya got, Dad?

WILLY: No, you finish first. Never leave a job till you're finished—remember that. [*Looking toward the "big trees"*] Biff, up in Albany I saw a beautiful hammock. I think I'll buy it next trip, and we'll hang it right between those two elms. Wouldn't that be something? Just swingin' there under those branches. Boy, that would be . . .

[YOUNG BIFF *and* YOUNG HAPPY *appear from the direction* WILLY *was addressing.* HAPPY *carries rags and a pail of water.* BIFF, *wearing a sweater with a block "S," carries a football.*]

BIFF [*pointing in the direction of the car offstage*]: How's that, Pop, professional?

WILLY: Terrific. Terrific job, boys. Good work, Biff.

HAPPY: Where's the surprise, Pop?

WILLY: In the back seat of the car.

HAPPY: Boy! [*He runs off.*]

BIFF: What is it, Dad? Tell me, what'd you buy?

WILLY [*laughing, cuffs him*]: Never mind, something I want you to have.

BIFF [*turns and starts off*]: What is it, Hap?

HAPPY [*offstage*]: It's a punching bag!

BIFF: Oh, Pop!

WILLY: It's got Gene Tunney's signature on it!

[HAPPY *runs onstage with a punching bag.*]

BIFF: Gee, how'd you know we wanted a punching bag?

WILLY: Well, it's the finest thing for the timing.

HAPPY [*lies down on his back and pedals with his feet*]: I'm losing weight, you notice, Pop?

WILLY [*to* HAPPY]: Jumping rope is good too.

BIFF: Did you see the new football I got?

WILLY [*examining the ball*]: Where'd you get a new ball?

BIFF: The coach told me to practice my passing.

WILLY: That so? And he gave you the ball, heh?

BIFF: Well, I borrowed it from the locker room. [*He laughs confidentially.*]

WILLY [*laughing with him at the theft*]: I want you to return that.

HAPPY: I told you he wouldn't like it!

BIFF [*angrily*]: Well, I'm bringing it back!

WILLY [*stopping the incipient argument, to* HAPPY]: Sure, he's gotta practice with a regulation ball, doesn't he? [*To* BIFF] Coach'll probably congratulate you on your initiative!

BIFF: Oh, he keeps congratulating my initiative all the time, Pop.

WILLY: That's because he likes you. If somebody else took that ball there'd be an uproar. So what's the report, boys, what's the report?

BIFF: Where'd you go this time, Dad? Gee, we were lonesome for you.

WILLY [*pleased, puts an arm around each boy and they come down to the apron*]: Lonesome, heh?

BIFF: Missed you every minute.

WILLY: Don't say? Tell you a secret, boys. Don't breathe it to a soul. Someday I'll have my own business, and I'll never have to leave home any more.

HAPPY: Like Uncle Charley, heh?

WILLY: Bigger than Uncle Charley! Because Charley is not—liked. He's liked, but he's not—well liked.

BIFF: Where'd you go this time, Dad?

WILLY: Well, I got on the road, and I went north to Providence. Met the Mayor.

BIFF: The Mayor of Providence!

WILLY: He was sitting in the hotel lobby.

BIFF: What'd he say?

WILLY: He said, "Morning!" And I said, "You got a fine city here, Mayor." And then he had coffee with me. And then I went to Waterbury. Waterbury is a fine city. Big clock city, the famous Waterbury clock. Sold a nice bill there. And then Boston—Boston is the cradle of the Revolution. A fine city. And a couple of other towns in Mass., and on to Portland and Bangor and straight home!

BIFF: Gee, I'd love to go with you sometime, Dad.

WILLY: Soon as summer comes.

HAPPY: Promise?

WILLY: You and Hap and I, and I'll show you all the towns. America is full of beautiful towns and fine, upstanding people. And they know me, boys, they know me up and down New England. The finest people. And when I bring you fellas up, there'll be open sesame for all of us, 'cause one thing, boys: I have friends. I can park my car in any street in New England, and the cops protect it like their own. This summer, heh?

BIFF and HAPPY [*together*]: Yeah! You bet!

WILLY: We'll take our bathing suits.

HAPPY: We'll carry your bags, Pop!

WILLY: Oh, won't that be something! Me comin' into the Boston stores with you boys carryin' my bags. What a sensation!

[BIFF *is prancing around, practicing passing the ball.*]

WILLY: You nervous, Biff, about the game?

BIFF: Not if you're gonna be there.

WILLY: What do they say about you in school, now that they made you captain?

HAPPY: There's a crowd of girls behind him every time the classes change.

BIFF [*taking* WILLY's *hand*]: This Saturday, Pop, this Saturday—just for you, I'm going to break through for a touchdown.

HAPPY: You're supposed to pass.

BIFF: I'm takin' one play for Pop. You watch me, Pop, and when I take off my helmet, that means I'm breakin' out. Then you watch me crash through that line!

WILLY [*kisses* BIFF]: Oh, wait'll I tell this in Boston!

[BERNARD *enters in knickers. He is younger than* BIFF, *earnest and loyal, a worried boy.*]

BERNARD: Biff, where are you? You're supposed to study with me today.

WILLY: Hey, looka Bernard. What're you lookin' so anemic about, Bernard?

BERNARD: He's gotta study, Uncle Willy. He's got Regents next week.

HAPPY [*tauntingly, spinning* BERNARD *around*]: Let's box, Bernard!

BERNARD: Biff! [*He gets away from* HAPPY.] Listen, Biff, I heard Mr. Birnbaum say that if you don't start studyin' math he's gonna flunk you, and you won't graduate. I heard him!

WILLY: You better study with him, Biff. Go ahead now.

BERNARD: I heard him!

BIFF: Oh, Pop, you didn't see my sneakers! [*He holds up a foot for* WILLY *to look at.*]

WILLY: Hey, that's a beautiful job of printing!

BERNARD [*wiping his glasses*]: Just because he printed University of Virginia on his sneakers doesn't mean they've got to graduate him, Uncle Willy!

WILLY [*angrily*]: What're you talking about? With scholarships to three universities they're gonna flunk him?

BERNARD: But I heard Mr. Birnbaum say—

WILLY: Don't be a pest, Bernard! [*To his boys*] What an anemic!

BERNARD: Okay, I'm waiting for you in my house, Biff.

[BERNARD *goes off. The* LOMANS *laugh.*]

WILLY: Bernard is not well liked, is he?

BIFF: He's liked, but he's not well liked.

HAPPY: That's right, Pop.

WILLY: That's just what I mean, Bernard can get the best marks in school, y'understand, but when he gets out in the business world, y'understand, you are going to be five times ahead of him. That's why I thank Almighty God you're both built like Adonises. Because the man who makes an appearance in the business world, the man who creates personal interest, is the man who gets ahead. Be liked and you will never want. You take me, for instance. I never have to wait in line to see a buyer. "Willy Loman is here!" That's all they have to know, and I go right through.

BIFF: Did you knock them dead, Pop?

WILLY: Knocked 'em cold in Providence, slaughtered 'em in Boston.

HAPPY [*on his back, pedaling again*]: I'm losing weight, you notice, Pop?

[LINDA *enters, as of old, a ribbon in her hair, carrying a basket of washing.*]

LINDA [*with youthful energy*]: Hello, dear!

WILLY: Sweetheart!

LINDA: How'd the Chevvy run?

WILLY: Chevrolet, Linda, is the greatest car ever built. [*To the boys*] Since when do you let your mother carry wash up the stairs?

BIFF: Grab hold there, boy!

HAPPY: Where to, Mom?

LINDA: Hang them up on the line. And you better go down to your friends, Biff. The cellar is full of boys. They don't know what to do with themselves.

BIFF: Ah, when Pop comes home they can wait!

WILLY [*laughs appreciatively*]: You better go down and tell them what to do, Biff.

BIFF: I think I'll have them sweep out the furnace room.

WILLY: Good work, Biff.

BIFF [*goes through wall-line of kitchen to doorway at back and calls down*]: Fellas! Everybody sweep out the furnace room! I'll be right down!

VOICES: All right! Okay, Biff.

BIFF: George and Sam and Frank, come out back! We're hangin' up the wash! Come on, Hap, on the double! [*He and* HAPPY *carry out the basket.*]

LINDA: The way they obey him!

WILLY: Well, that's training, the training. I'm tellin' you, I was sellin' thousands and thousands, but I had to come home.

LINDA: Oh, the whole block'll be at that game. Did you sell anything?

WILLY: I did five hundred gross in Providence and seven hundred gross in Boston.

LINDA: No! Wait a minute, I've got a pencil. [*She pulls pencil and paper out of her apron pocket.*] That makes your commission . . . Two hundred—my God! Two hundred and twelve dollars!

WILLY: Well, I didn't figure it yet, but . . .

LINDA: How much did you do?

WILLY: Well, I—I did—about a hundred and eighty gross in Providence. Well, no—it came to—roughly two hundred gross on the whole trip.

LINDA [*without hesitation*]: Two hundred gross. That's . . . [*She figures.*]

WILLY: The trouble was that three of the stores were half closed for inventory in Boston. Otherwise I woulda broke records.

LINDA: Well, it makes seventy dollars and some pennies. That's very good.

WILLY: What do we owe?

LINDA: Well, on the first there's sixteen dollars on the refrigerator—

WILLY: Why sixteen?

LINDA: Well, the fan belt broke, so it was a dollar eighty.

WILLY: But it's brand new.

LINDA: Well, the man said that's the way it is. Till they work themselves in, y'-know.

[*They move through the wall-line into the kitchen.*]

WILLY: I hope we didn't get stuck on that machine.

LINDA: They got the biggest ads of any of them!

WILLY: I know, it's a fine machine. What else?

LINDA: Well, there's nine-sixty for the washing machine. And for the vacuum cleaner there's three and a half due on the fifteenth. Then the roof, you got twenty-one dollars remaining.

WILLY: It don't leak, does it?

LINDA: No, they did a wonderful job. Then you owe Frank for the carburetor.

WILLY: I'm not going to pay that man! That goddam Chevrolet, they ought to prohibit the manufacture of that car!

LINDA: Well, you owe him three and a half. And odds and ends, comes to around a hundred and twenty dollars by the fifteenth.

WILLY: A hundred and twenty dollars! My God, if business don't pick up I don't know what I'm gonna do!

LINDA: Well, next week you'll do better.

WILLY: Oh, I'll knock 'em dead next week. I'll go to Hartford. I'm very well liked in Hartford. You know, the trouble is, Linda, people don't seem to take to me.

[*They move onto the forestage.*]

LINDA: Oh, don't be foolish.

WILLY: I know it when I walk in. They seem to laugh at me.

LINDA: Why? Why would they laugh at you? Don't talk that way, Willy.

[WILLY *moves to the edge of the stage.* LINDA *goes into the kitchen and starts to darn stockings.*]

WILLY: I don't know the reason for it, but they just pass me by. I'm not noticed.

LINDA: But you're doing wonderful, dear. You're making seventy to a hundred dollars a week.

WILLY: But I gotta be at it ten, twelve hours a day. Other men—I don't know—they do it easier. I don't know why—I can't stop myself—I talk too much. A man oughta come in with a few words. One thing about Charley. He's a man of few words, and they respect him.

LINDA: You don't talk too much, you're just lively.

WILLY [*smiling*]: Well, I figure, what the hell, life is short, a couple of jokes. [*To himself*] I joke too much! [*The smile goes.*]

LINDA: Why? You're—

WILLY: I'm fat. I'm very—foolish to look at, Linda. I didn't tell you, but Christmas time I happened to be calling on F. H. Stewarts, and a salesman I know, as I was going in to see the buyer I heard him say something about—walrus. And I—I cracked him right across the face. I won't take that. I simply will not take that. But they do laugh at me. I know that.

LINDA: Darling . . .

WILLY: I gotta overcome it. I know I gotta overcome it. I'm not dressing to advantage, maybe.

LINDA: Willy, darling, you're the handsomest man in the world—

WILLY: Oh, no, Linda.

LINDA: To me you are. [*Slight pause.*] The handsomest.

[*From the darkness is heard the laughter of a woman.* WILLY *doesn't turn to it, but it continues through* LINDA'S *lines.*]

LINDA: And the boys, Willy. Few men are idolized by their children the way you are.

[*Music is heard as behind a scrim, to the left of the house,* THE WOMAN, *dimly seen, is dressing.*]

WILLY [*with great feeling*]: You're the best there is, Linda, you're a pal, you know that? On the road—on the road I want to grab you sometimes and just kiss the life outa you.

> [*The laughter is loud now, and he moves into a brightening area at the left, where* THE WOMAN *has come from behind the scrim and is standing, putting on her hat, looking into a "mirror," and laughing.*]

WILLY: 'Cause I get so lonely—especially when business is bad and there's no-body to talk to. I get the feeling that I'll never sell anything again, that I won't make a living for you, or a business, a business for the boys. [*He talks through* THE WOMAN'S *subsiding laughter;* THE WOMAN *primps at the "mirror."*] There's so much I want to make for—

THE WOMAN: Me? You didn't make me, Willy. I picked you.

WILLY [*pleased*]: You picked me?

THE WOMAN [*who is quite proper-looking, Willy's age*]: I did. I've been sitting at that desk watching all the salesmen go by, day in, day out. But you've got such a sense of humor, and we do have such a good time together, don't we?

WILLY: Sure, sure. [*He takes her in his arms.*] Why do you have to go now?

THE WOMAN: It's two o'clock . . .

WILLY: No, come on in! [*He pulls her.*]

THE WOMAN: . . . my sisters'll be scandalized. When'll you be back?

WILLY: Oh, two weeks about. Will you come up again?

THE WOMAN: Sure thing. You do make me laugh. It's good for me. [*She squeezes his arm, kisses him.*] And I think you're a wonderful man.

WILLY: You picked me, heh?

THE WOMAN: Sure. Because you're so sweet. And such a kidder.

WILLY: Well, I'll see you next time I'm in Boston.

THE WOMAN: I'll put you right through to the buyers.

WILLY [*slapping her bottom*]: Right. Well, bottoms up!

THE WOMAN [*slaps him gently and laughs*]: You just kill me, Willy. [*He suddenly grabs her and kisses her roughly.*] You kill me. And thanks for the stockings. I love a lot of stockings. Well, good night.

WILLY: Good night. And keep your pores open!

THE WOMAN: Oh, Willy!

> [THE WOMAN *bursts out laughing, and* LINDA'S *laughter blends in.* THE WOMAN *disappears into the dark. Now the area at the kitchen table brightens.* LINDA *is sitting where she was at the kitchen table, but now is mending a pair of her silk stockings.*]

LINDA: You are, Willy. The handsomest man. You've got no reason to feel that—

WILLY [*coming out of* THE WOMAN'S *dimming area and going over to* LINDA]: I'll make it all up to you, Linda, I'll—

LINDA: There's nothing to make up, dear. You're doing fine, better than—

WILLY [*noticing her mending*]: What's that?

LINDA: Just mending my stockings. They're so expensive—

WILLY [*angrily, taking them from her*]: I won't have you mending stockings in this house! Now throw them out!

[LINDA *puts the stockings in her pocket.*]

BERNARD [*entering on the run*]: Where is he? If he doesn't study!

WILLY [*moving to the forestage, with great agitation*]: You'll give him the answers!

BERNARD: I do, but I can't on a Regents! That's a state exam! They're liable to arrest me!

WILLY: Where is he? I'll whip him, I'll whip him!

LINDA: And he'd better give back that football, Willy, it's not nice.

WILLY: Biff! Where is he? Why is he taking everything?

LINDA: He's too rough with the girls, Willy. All the mothers are afraid of him!

WILLY: I'll whip him!

BERNARD: He's driving the car without a license!

[THE WOMAN'S *laugh is heard.*]

WILLY: Shut up!

LINDA: All the mothers—

WILLY: Shut up!

BERNARD [*backing quietly away and out*]: Mr. Birnbaum says he's stuck up.

WILLY: Get outa here!

BERNARD: If he doesn't buckle down he'll flunk math! [*He goes off.*]

LINDA: He's right, Willy, you've gotta—

WILLY [*exploding at her*]: There's nothing the matter with him! You want him to be a worm like Bernard? He's got spirit, personality . . .

[*As he speaks,* LINDA, *almost in tears, exits into the livingroom.* WILLY *is alone in the kitchen, wilting and staring. The leaves are gone. It is night again, and the apartment houses look down from behind.*]

WILLY: Loaded with it. Loaded! What is he stealing? He's giving it back, isn't he? Why is he stealing? What did I tell him? I never in my life told him anything but decent things.

[HAPPY *in pajamas has come down the stairs;* WILLY *suddenly becomes aware of* HAPPY'S *presence.*]

HAPPY: Let's go now, come on.

WILLY [*sitting down at the kitchen table*]: Huh! Why did she have to wax the floors herself? Everytime she waxes the floors she keels over. She knows that!

HAPPY: Shh! Take it easy. What brought you back tonight?

WILLY: I got an awful scare. Nearly hit a kid in Yonkers. God! Why didn't I go to Alaska with my brother Ben that time! Ben! That man was a genius, that man was success incarnate! What a mistake! He begged me to go.

HAPPY: Well, there's no use in—

WILLY: You guys! There was a man started with the clothes on his back and ended up with diamond mines?

HAPPY: Boy, someday I'd like to know how he did it.

WILLY: What's the mystery? The man knew what he wanted and went out and got it! Walked into a jungle, and comes out, the age of twenty-one, and he's rich! The world is an oyster, but you don't crack it open on a mattress!

HAPPY: Pop, I told you I'm gonna retire you for life.

WILLY: You'll retire me for life on seventy goddam dollars a week? And your women and your car and your apartment, and you'll retire me for life! Christ's sake, I couldn't get past Yonkers today! Where are you guys, where are you? The woods are burning! I can't drive a car!

[CHARLEY *has appeared in the doorway. He is a large man, slow of speech, laconic, immovable. In all he says, despite what he says, there is pity, and, now, trepidation. He has a robe over pajamas, slippers on his feet. He enters the kitchen.*]

CHARLEY: Everything all right?
HAPPY: Yeah, Charley, everything's . . .
WILLY: What's the matter?
CHARLEY: I heard some noise. I thought something happened. Can't we do something about the walls? You sneeze in here, and in my house hats blow off.
HAPPY: Let's go to bed, Dad. Come on.

[CHARLEY *signals to* HAPPY *to go.*]

WILLY: You go ahead, I'm not tired at the moment.
HAPPY [*to* WILLY]: Take it easy, huh? [*He exits.*]
WILLY: What're you doin' up?
CHARLEY [*sitting down at the kitchen table opposite* WILLY]: Couldn't sleep good. I had a heartburn.
WILLY: Well, you don't know how to eat.
CHARLEY: I eat with my mouth.
WILLY: No, you're ignorant. You gotta know about vitamins and things like that.
CHARLEY: Come on, let's shoot. Tire you out a little.
WILLY [*hesitantly*]: All right. You got cards?
CHARLEY [*taking a deck from his pocket*]: Yeah, I got them. Someplace. What is it with those vitamins?
WILLY [*dealing*]: They build up your bones. Chemistry.
CHARLEY: Yeah, but there's no bones in a heartburn.
WILLY: What are you talkin' about? Do you know the first thing about it?
CHARLEY: Don't get insulted.
WILLY: Don't talk about something you don't know anything about.

[*They are playing. Pause.*]

CHARLEY: What're you doin' home?
WILLY: A little trouble with the car.
CHARLEY: Oh. [*Pause.*] I'd like to take a trip to California.
WILLY: Don't say.
CHARLEY: You want a job?
WILLY: I got a job, I told you that. [*After a slight pause*] What the hell are you offering me a job for?
CHARLEY: Don't get insulted.
WILLY: Don't insult me.
CHARLEY: I don't see no sense in it. You don't have to go on this way.
WILLY: I got a good job. [*Slight pause.*] What do you keep comin' in here for?

CHARLEY: You want me to go?

WILLY [*after a pause, withering*]: I can't understand it. He's going back to Texas again. What the hell is that?

CHARLEY: Let him go.

WILLY: I got nothin' to give him, Charley, I'm clean, I'm clean.

CHARLEY: He won't starve. None a them starve. Forget about him.

WILLY: Then what have I got to remember?

CHARLEY: You take it too hard. To hell with it. When a deposit bottle is broken you don't get your nickel back.

WILLY: That's easy enough for you to say.

CHARLEY: That ain't easy for me to say.

WILLY: Did you see the ceiling I put up in the livingroom?

CHARLEY: Yeah, that's a piece of work. To put up a ceiling is a mystery to me. How do you do it?

WILLY: What's the difference?

CHARLEY: Well, talk about it.

WILLY: You gonna put up a ceiling?

CHARLEY: How could I put up a ceiling?

WILLY: Then what the hell are you bothering me for?

CHARLEY: You're insulted again.

WILLY: A man who can't handle tools is not a man. You're disgusting.

CHARLEY: Don't call me disgusting, Willy.

[UNCLE BEN, *carrying a valise and an umbrella, enters the forestage from around the right corner of the house. He is a stolid man, in his sixties, with a mustache and an authoritative air. He is utterly certain of his destiny, and there is an aura of far places about him. He enters exactly as* WILLY *speaks.*]

WILLY: I'm getting awfully tired, Ben.

[BEN'S *music is heard.* BEN *looks around at everything.*]

CHARLEY: Good, keep playing; you'll sleep better. Did you call me Ben?

[BEN *looks at his watch.*]

WILLY: That's funny. For a second there you reminded me of my brother Ben.

BEN: I only have a few minutes. [*He strolls, inspecting the place.* WILLY *and* CHARLEY *continue playing.*]

CHARLEY: You never heard from him again, heh? Since that time?

WILLY: Didn't Linda tell you? Couple of weeks ago we got a letter from his wife in Africa. He died.

CHARLEY: That so.

BEN [*chuckling*]: So this is Brooklyn, eh?

CHARLEY: Maybe you're in for some of his money.

WILLY: Naa, he had seven sons. There's just one opportunity I had with that man . . .

BEN: I must make a train, William. There are several properties I'm looking at in Alaska.

WILLY: Sure, sure! If I'd gone with him to Alaska that time, everything would've been totally different.

CHARLEY: Go on, you'd froze to death up there.

WILLY: What're you talking about?

BEN: Opportunity is tremendous in Alaska, William. Surprised you're not up there.

WILLY: Sure, tremendous.

CHARLEY: Heh?

WILLY: There was the only man I ever met who knew the answers.

CHARLEY: Who?

BEN: How are you all?

WILLY [*taking a pot, smiling*]: Fine, fine.

CHARLEY: Pretty sharp tonight.

BEN: Is Mother living with you?

WILLY: No, she died a long time ago.

CHARLEY: Who?

BEN: That's too bad. Fine specimen of a lady, Mother.

WILLY [*to* CHARLEY]: Heh?

BEN: I'd hoped to see the old girl.

CHARLEY: Who died?

BEN: Heard anything from Father, have you?

WILLY [*unnerved*]: What do you mean, who died?

CHARLEY [*taking a pot*]: What're you talkin' about?

BEN [*looking at his watch*]: William, it's half past eight!

WILLY [*as though to dispel his confusion he angrily stops* CHARLEY'S *hand*]: That's my build!

CHARLEY: I put the ace—

WILLY: If you don't know how to play the game I'm not gonna throw my money away on you!

CHARLEY [*rising*]: It was my ace, for God's sake!

WILLY: I'm through, I'm through!

BEN: When did Mother die?

WILLY: Long ago. Since the beginning you never knew how to play cards.

CHARLEY [*picks up the cards and goes to the door*]: All right! Next time I'll bring a deck with five aces.

WILLY: I don't play that kind of game!

CHARLEY [*turning to him*]: You ought to be ashamed of yourself!

WILLY: Yeah?

CHARLEY: Yeah! [*He goes out.*]

WILLY [*slamming the door after him*]: Ignoramus!

BEN [*as* WILLY *comes toward him through the wall-line of the kitchen*]: So you're William.

WILLY [*shaking* BEN'S *hand*]: Ben! I've been waiting for you so long! What's the answer? How did you do it?

BEN: Oh, there's a story in that.

[LINDA *enters the forestage, as of old, carrying the wash basket.*]

LINDA: Is this Ben?

BEN [*gallantly*]: How do you do, my dear.

LINDA: Where've you been all these years? Willy's always wondered why you—

WILLY [*pulling* BEN *away from her impatiently*]: Where is Dad? Didn't you follow him? How did you get started?

BEN: Well, I don't know how much you remember.

WILLY: Well, I was just a baby, of course, only three or four years old—

BEN: Three years and eleven months.

WILLY: What a memory, Ben!

BEN: I have many enterprises, William, and I have never kept books.

WILLY: I remember I was sitting under the wagon in—was it Nebraska?

BEN: It was South Dakota, and I gave you a bunch of wildflowers.

WILLY: I remember you walking away down some open road.

BEN [*laughing*]: I was going to find Father in Alaska.

WILLY: Where is he?

BEN: At that age I had a very faulty view of geography, William. I discovered after a few days that I was heading due south, so instead of Alaska, I ended up in Africa.

LINDA: Africa!

WILLY: The Gold Coast!

BEN: Principally diamond mines.

LINDA: Diamond mines!

BEN: Yes, my dear. But I've only a few minutes—

WILLY: No! Boys! Boys! [YOUNG BIFF *and* HAPPY *appear.*] Listen to this. This is your Uncle Ben, a great man! Tell my boys, Ben!

BEN: Why boys, when I was seventeen I walked into the jungle, and when I was twenty-one I walked out. [*He laughs.*] And by God I was rich.

WILLY [*to the boys*]: You see what I been talking about? The greatest things can happen!

BEN [*glancing at his watch*]: I have an appointment in Ketchikan Tuesday week.

WILLY: No, Ben! Please tell about Dad. I want my boys to hear. I want them to know the kind of stock they spring from. All I remember is a man with a big beard, and I was in Mamma's lap, sitting around a fire, and some kind of high music.

BEN: His flute. He played the flute.

WILLY: Sure, the flute, that's right!

[*New music is heard, a high, rollicking tune.*]

BEN: Father was a very great and a very wild-hearted man. We would start in Boston, and he'd toss the whole family into the wagon, and then he'd drive the team right across the country; through Ohio, and Indiana, Michigan, Illinois, and all the Western states. And we'd stop in the towns and sell the flutes that he'd made on the way. Great inventor, Father. With one gadget he made more in a week than a man like you could make in a lifetime.

WILLY: That's just the way I'm bringing them up, Ben—rugged, well liked, all-around.

BEN: Yeah? [*To* BIFF] Hit that, boy—hard as you can. [*He pounds his stomach.*]

BIFF: Oh, no, sir!

BEN [*taking boxing stance*]: Come on, get to me! [*He laughs.*]

WILLY: Go to it, Biff! Go ahead, show him!

BIFF: Okay! [*He cocks his fists and starts in.*]

LINDA [*to* WILLY]: Why must he fight, dear?

BEN [*sparring with* BIFF]: Good boy! Good boy!

WILLY: How's that, Ben, heh?

HAPPY: Give him the left, Biff!

LINDA: Why are you fighting?

BEN: Good boy! [*Suddenly comes in, trips* BIFF, *and stands over him, the point of his umbrella poised over* BIFF'S *eye.*]

LINDA: Look out, Biff!

BIFF: Gee!

BEN [*patting* BIFF'S *knee*]: Never fight fair with a stranger, boy. You'll never get out of the jungle that way. [*Taking* LINDA'S *hand and bowing*] It was an honor and a pleasure to meet you, Linda.

LINDA [*withdrawing her hand coldly, frightened*]: Have a nice—trip.

BEN [*to* WILLY]: And good luck with your—what do you do?

WILLY: Selling.

BEN: Yes. Well . . . [*He raises his hand in farewell to all.*]

WILLY: No, Ben, I don't want you to think . . . [*He takes* BEN'S *arm to show him.*] It's Brooklyn, I know, but we hunt too.

BEN: Really, now.

WILLY: Oh, sure, there's snakes and rabbits and—that's why I moved out here. Why, Biff can fell any one of these trees in no time! Boys! Go right over to where they're building the apartment house and get some sand. We're gonna rebuild the entire front stoop right now! Watch this, Ben!

BIFF: Yes, sir! On the double, Hap!

HAPPY [*as he and* BIFF *run off*]: I lost weight, Pop, you notice?

[CHARLEY *enters in knickers, even before the boys are gone.*]

CHARLEY: Listen, if they steal any more from that building the watchman'll put the cops on them!

LINDA [*to* WILLY]: Don't let Biff . . .

[BEN *laughs lustily.*]

WILLY: You shoulda seen the lumber they brought home last week. At least a dozen six-by-tens worth all kinds a money.

CHARLEY: Listen, if that watchman—

WILLY: I gave them hell, understand. But I got a couple of fearless characters there.

CHARLEY: Willy, the jails are full of fearless characters.

BEN [*clapping* WILLY *on the back, with a laugh at* CHARLEY]: And the stock exchange, friend!

WILLY [*joining in* BEN'S *laughter*]: Where are the rest of your pants?

CHARLEY: My wife bought them.

WILLY: Now all you need is a golf club and you can go upstairs and go to sleep. [*To* BEN] Great athlete! Between him and his son Bernard they can't hammer a nail!

BERNARD [*rushing in*]: The watchman's chasing Biff!

WILLY [*angrily*]: Shut up! He's not stealing anything!

LINDA [*alarmed, hurrying off left*]: Where is he? Biff, dear! [*She exits.*]

WILLY [*moving toward the left, away from* BEN]: There's nothing wrong. What's the matter with you?

BEN: Nervy boy. Good!

WILLY [*laughing*]: Oh, nerves of iron, that Biff!

CHARLEY: Don't know what it is. My New England man comes back and he's bleedin', they murdered him up there.

WILLY: It's contacts, Charley, I got important contacts!

CHARLEY [*sarcastically*]: Glad to hear it, Willy. Come in later, we'll shoot a little casino. I'll take some of your Portland money. [*He laughs at* WILLY *and exits.*]

WILLY [*turning to* BEN]: Business is bad, it's murderous. But not for me, of course.

BEN: I'll stop by on my way back to Africa.

WILLY [*longingly*]: Can't you stay a few days? You're just what I need, Ben, because I—I have a fine position here, but I—well, Dad left when I was such a baby and I never had a chance to talk to him and I still feel—kind of temporary about myself.

BEN: I'll be late for my train.

> [*They are at opposite ends of the stage.*]

WILLY: Ben, my boys—can't we talk? They'd go into the jaws of hell for me, see, but I—

BEN: William, you're being first-rate with your boys. Outstanding, manly chaps!

WILLY [*hanging on to his words*]: Oh, Ben, that's good to hear! Because sometimes I'm afraid that I'm not teaching them the right kind of—Ben, how should I teach them?

BEN [*giving great weight to each word, and with a certain vicious audacity*]: William, when I walked into the jungle, I was seventeen. When I walked out I was twenty-one. And, by God, I was rich! [*He goes off into darkness around the right corner of the house.*]

WILLY: . . . was rich! That's just the spirit I want to imbue them with! To walk into a jungle! I was right! I was right! I was right!

> [BEN *is gone, but* WILLY *is still speaking to him as* LINDA, *in nightgown and robe, enters the kitchen, glances around for* WILLY, *then goes to the door of the house, looks out and sees him. Comes down to his left. He looks at her.*]

LINDA: Willy, dear? Willy?

WILLY: I was right!

LINDA: Did you have some cheese? [*He can't answer.*] It's very late, darling. Come to bed, heh?

WILLY [*looking straight up*]: Gotta break your neck to see a star in this yard.

LINDA: You coming in?

WILLY: Whatever happened to that diamond watch fob? Remember? When Ben came from Africa that time? Didn't he give me a watch fob with a diamond in it?

LINDA: You pawned it, dear. Twelve, thirteen years ago. For Biff's radio correspondence course.

WILLY: Gee, that was a beautiful thing. I'll take a walk.

LINDA: But you're in your slippers.

WILLY [*starting to go around the house at the left*]: I was right! I was! [*Half to* LINDA, *as he goes, shaking his head*] What a man! There was a man worth talking to. I was right!

LINDA [*calling after* WILLY]: But in your slippers, Willy!

[WILLY *is almost gone when* BIFF, *in his pajamas, comes down the stairs and enters the kitchen.*]

BIFF: What is he doing out there?

LINDA: Sh!

BIFF: God Almighty, Mom, how long has he been doing this?

LINDA: Don't, he'll hear you.

BIFF: What the hell is the matter with him?

LINDA: It'll pass by morning.

BIFF: Shouldn't we do anything?

LINDA: Oh, my dear, you should do a lot of things, but there's nothing to do, so go to sleep.

[HAPPY *comes down the stairs and sits on the steps.*]

HAPPY: I never heard him so loud, Mom.

LINDA: Well, come around more often; you'll hear him.

[*She sits down at the table and mends the lining of* WILLY'S *jacket.*]

BIFF: Why didn't you ever write me about this, Mom?

LINDA: How would I write to you? For over three months you had no address.

BIFF: I was on the move. But you know I thought of you all the time. You know that, don't you, pal?

LINDA: I know, dear, I know. But he likes to have a letter. Just to know that there's still a possibility for better things.

BIFF: He's not like this all the time, is he?

LINDA: It's when you come home he's always the worst.

BIFF: When I come home?

LINDA: When you write you're coming, he's all smiles, and talks about the future, and—he's just wonderful. And then the closer you seem to come, the more shaky he gets, and then, by the time you get here, he's arguing, and he seems angry at you. I think it's just that maybe he can't bring himself to—to open up to you. Why are you so hateful to each other? Why is that?

BIFF [*evasively*]: I'm not hateful, Mom.

LINDA: But you no sooner come in the door than you're fighting!

BIFF: I don't know why. I mean to change. I'm tryin', Mom, you understand?

LINDA: Are you home to stay now?

BIFF: I don't know. I want to look around, see what's doin'.

LINDA: Biff, you can't look around all your life, can you?

BIFF: I just can't take hold, Mom. I can't take hold of some kind of a life.

LINDA: Biff, a man is not a bird, to come and go with the springtime.

BIFF: Your hair . . . [*He touches her hair.*] Your hair got so gray.

LINDA: Oh, it's been gray since you were in high school. I just stopped dyeing it, that's all.

BIFF: Dye it again, will ya? I don't want my pal looking old. [*He smiles.*]

LINDA: You're such a boy! You think you can go away for a year and . . . You've got to get it into your head now that one day you'll knock on this door and there'll be strange people here—

BIFF: What are you talking about? You're not even sixty, Mom.

LINDA: But what about your father?

BIFF [*lamely*]: Well, I meant him too.

HAPPY: He admires Pop.

LINDA: Biff, dear, if you don't have any feeling for him, then you can't have any feeling for me.

BIFF: Sure I can, Mom.

LINDA: No. You can't just come to see me, because I love him. [*With a threat, but only a threat, of tears*] He's the dearest man in the world to me, and I won't have anyone making him feel unwanted and low and blue. You've got to make up your mind now, darling, there's no leeway any more. Either he's your father and you pay him that respect, or else you're not to come here. I know he's not easy to get along with—nobody knows that better than me—but . . .

WILLY [*from the left, with a laugh*]: Hey, hey, Biffo!

BIFF [*starting to go out after* WILLY]: What the hell is the matter with him? [HAPPY *stops him.*]

LINDA: Don't—don't go near him!

BIFF: Stop making excuses for him! He always, always wiped the floor with you. Never had an ounce of respect for you.

HAPPY: He's always had respect for—

BIFF: What the hell do you know about it?

HAPPY [*surlily*]: Just don't call him crazy!

BIFF: He's got no character—Charley wouldn't do this. Not in his own house— spewing out that vomit from his mind.

HAPPY: Charley never had to cope with what he's got to.

BIFF: People are worse off than Willy Loman. Believe me, I've seen them!

LINDA: Then make Charley your father, Biff. You can't do that, can you? I don't say he's a great man. Willy Loman never made a lot of money. His name was never in the paper. He's not the finest character that ever lived. But he's a human being, and a terrible thing is happening to him. So attention must be paid. He's not to be allowed to fall into his grave like an old dog. Attention, attention must be finally paid to such a person. You called him crazy—

BIFF: I didn't mean—

LINDA: No, a lot of people think he's lost his—balance. But you don't have to be very smart to know what his trouble is. The man is exhausted.

HAPPY: Sure!

LINDA: A small man can be just as exhausted as a great man. He works for a company thirty-six years this March, opens up unheard-of territories to their trademark, and now in his old age they take his salary away.

HAPPY [*indignantly*]: I didn't know that, Mom.

LINDA: You never asked, my dear! Now that you get your spending money someplace else you don't trouble your mind with him.

HAPPY: But I gave you money last—

LINDA: Christmas time, fifty dollars! To fix the hot water it cost ninety-seven fifty! For five weeks he's been on straight commission, like a beginner, an unknown!

BIFF: Those ungrateful bastards!

LINDA: Are they any worse than his sons? When he brought them business, when he was young, they were glad to see him. But now his old friends, the old buyers that loved him so and always found some order to hand him in a pinch—they're all dead, retired. He used to be able to make six, seven calls a day in Boston. Now he takes his valises out of the car and puts them back and takes them out again and he's exhausted. Instead of walking he talks now. He drives seven hundred miles, and when he gets there no one knows him any more, no one welcomes him. And what goes through a man's mind, driving seven hundred miles home without having earned a cent? Why shouldn't he talk to himself? Why? When he has to go to Charley and borrow fifty dollars a week and pretend to me that it's his pay? How long can that go on? How long? You see what I'm sitting here and waiting for? And you tell me he has no character? The man who never worked a day but for your benefit? When does he get the medal for that? Is this his reward—to turn around at the age of sixty-three and find his sons, who he loved better than his life, one a philandering bum—

HAPPY: Mom!

LINDA: That's all you are, my baby! [*To* BIFF] And you! What happened to the love you had for him? You were such pals! How you used to talk to him on the phone every night! How lonely he was till he could come home to you!

BIFF: All right, Mom. I'll live here in my room, and I'll get a job. I'll keep away from him, that's all.

LINDA: No, Biff. You can't stay here and fight all the time.

BIFF: He threw me out of this house, remember that.

LINDA: Why did he do that? I never knew why.

BIFF: Because I know he's a fake and he doesn't like anybody around who knows!

LINDA: Why a fake? In what way? What do you mean?

BIFF: Just don't lay it all at my feet. It's between me and him—that's all I have to say. I'll chip in from now on. He'll settle for half my pay check. He'll be all right. I'm going to bed. [*He starts for the stairs.*]

LINDA: He won't be all right.

BIFF [*turning on the stairs, furiously*]: I hate this city and I'll stay here. Now what do you want?

LINDA: He's dying, Biff.

[HAPPY *turns quickly to her, shocked.*]

BIFF [*after a pause*]: Why is he dying?

LINDA: He's been trying to kill himself.

BIFF [*with great horror*]: How?

LINDA: I live from day to day.

BIFF: What're you talking about?

LINDA: Remember I wrote you that he smashed up the car again? In February?

BIFF: Well?

LINDA: The insurance inspector came. He said that they have evidence. That all these accidents in the last year—weren't—weren't—accidents.

HAPPY: How can they tell that? That's a lie.

LINDA: It seems there's a woman . . . [*She takes a breath as*]

BIFF [*sharply but contained*]: What woman?

LINDA [*simultaneously*]: . . . and this woman . . .

LINDA: What?

BIFF: Nothing. Go ahead.

LINDA: What did you say?

BIFF: Nothing. I just said what woman?

HAPPY: What about her?

LINDA: Well, it seems she was walking down the road and saw his car. She says that he wasn't driving fast at all, and that he didn't skid. She says he came to that little bridge, and then deliberately smashed into the railing, and it was only the shallowness of the water that saved him.

BIFF: Oh, no, he probably just fell asleep again.

LINDA: I don't think he fell asleep.

BIFF: Why not?

LINDA: Last month . . . [*With great difficulty*] Oh, boys, it's so hard to say a thing like this! He's just a big stupid man to you, but I tell you there's more good in him than in many other people. [*She chokes, wipes her eyes.*] I was looking for a fuse. The lights blew out, and I went down the cellar. And behind the fuse box—it happened to fall out—was a length of rubber pipe—just short.

HAPPY: No kidding?

LINDA: There's a little attachment on the end of it. I knew right away. And sure enough, on the bottom of the water heater there's a new little nipple on the gas pipe.

HAPPY [*angrily*]: That—jerk.

BIFF: Did you have it taken off?

LINDA: I'm—I'm ashamed to. How can I mention it to him? Every day I go down and take away that little rubber pipe. But, when he comes home, I put it back where it was. How can I insult him that way? I don't know what to do. I live from day to day, boys. I tell you, I know every thought in his mind. It sounds so old-fashioned and silly, but I tell you he put his whole life into you and you've turned your backs on him. [*She is bent over in the chair, weeping, her face in her hands.*] Biff, I swear to God! Biff, his life is in your hands!

HAPPY [*to* BIFF]: How do you like that damned fool!

BIFF [*kissing her*]: All right, pal, all right. It's all settled now. I've been remiss. I know that, Mom. But now I'll stay, and I swear to you, I'll apply myself. [*Kneeling in front of her, in a fever of self-reproach*] It's just—you see, Mom, I don't fit in business. Not that I won't try. I'll try, and I'll make good.

HAPPY: Sure you will. The trouble with you in business was you never tried to please people.

BIFF: I know, I—

HAPPY: Like when you worked for Harrison's. Bob Harrison said you were tops, and then you go and do some damn fool thing like whistling whole songs in the elevator like a comedian.

BIFF [*against* HAPPY]: So what? I like to whistle sometimes.

HAPPY: You don't raise a guy to a responsible job who whistles in the elevator!

LINDA: Well, don't argue about it now.

HAPPY: Like when you'd go off and swim in the middle of the day instead of taking the line around.

BIFF [*his resentment rising*]: Well, don't you run off? You take off sometimes, don't you? On a nice summer day?

HAPPY: Yeah, but I cover myself!

LINDA: Boys!

HAPPY: If I'm going to take a fade the boss can call any number where I'm supposed to be and they'll swear to him that I just left. I'll tell you something that I hate to say, Biff, but in the business world some of them think you're crazy.

BIFF [*angered*]: Screw the business world!

HAPPY: All right, screw it! Great, but cover yourself!

LINDA: Hap, Hap!

BIFF: I don't care what they think! They've laughed at Dad for years, and you know why? Because we don't belong in this nuthouse of a city! We should be mixing cement on some open plain, or—or carpenters. A carpenter is allowed to whistle!

[WILLY *walks in from the entrance of the house, at left.*]

WILLY: Even your grandfather was better than a carpenter. [*Pause. They watch him.*] You never grew up. Bernard does not whistle in the elevator, I assure you.

BIFF [*as though to laugh* WILLY *out of it*]: Yeah, but you do, Pop.

WILLY: I never in my life whistled in an elevator! And who in the business world thinks I'm crazy?

BIFF: I didn't mean it like that, Pop. Now don't make a whole thing out of it, will ya?

WILLY: Go back to the West! Be a carpenter, a cowboy, enjoy yourself!

LINDA: Willy, he was just saying—

WILLY: I heard what he said!

HAPPY [*trying to quiet* WILLY]: Hey, Pop, come on now . . .

WILLY [*continuing over* HAPPY'S *line*]: They laugh at me, heh? Go to Filene's, go to the Hub, go to Slattery's, Boston. Call out the name Willy Loman and see what happens! Big shot!

BIFF: All right, Pop.

WILLY: Big!

BIFF: All right!

WILLY: Why do you always insult me?

BIFF: I didn't say a word. [*To* LINDA] Did I say a word?

LINDA: He didn't say anything, Willy.

WILLY [*going to the doorway of the living-room*]: All right, good night, good night.

LINDA: Willy, dear, he just decided . . .

WILLY [*to* BIFF]: If you get tired hanging around tomorrow, paint the ceiling I put up in the living-room.

BIFF: I'm leaving early tomorrow.

HAPPY: He's going to see Bill Oliver, Pop.

WILLY [*interestedly*]: Oliver? For what?

BIFF [*with reserve, but trying, trying*]: He always said he'd stake me. I'd like to go into business, so maybe I can take him up on it.

LINDA: Isn't that wonderful?

WILLY: Don't interrupt. What's wonderful about it? There's fifty men in the City of New York who'd stake him. [*To* BIFF] Sporting goods?

BIFF: I guess so. I know something about it and—

WILLY: He knows something about it! You know sporting goods better than Spalding, for God's sake! How much is he giving you?

BIFF: I don't know, I didn't even see him yet, but—

WILLY: Then what're you talkin' about?

BIFF [*getting angry*]: Well, all I said was I'm gonna see him, that's all!

WILLY [*turning away*]: Ah, you're counting your chickens again.

BIFF [*starting left for the stairs*]: Oh, Jesus, I'm going to sleep!

WILLY [*calling after him*]: Don't curse in this house!

BIFF [*turning*]: Since when did you get so clean?

HAPPY [*trying to stop them*]: Wait a . . .

WILLY: Don't use that language to me! I won't have it!

HAPPY [*grabbing* BIFF, *shouts*]: Wait a minute! I got an idea. I got a feasible idea. Come here, Biff, let's talk this over now, let's talk some sense here. When I was down in Florida last time, I thought of a great idea to sell sporting goods. It just came back to me. You and I, Biff—we have a line, the Loman Line. We train a couple of weeks, and put on a couple of exhibitions, see?

WILLY: That's an idea!

HAPPY: Wait! We form two basketball teams, see? Two water-polo teams. We play each other. It's a million dollars' worth of publicity. Two brothers, see? The Loman Brothers. Displays in the Royal Palms—all the hotels. And banners over the ring and the basketball court: "Loman Brothers." Baby, we could sell sporting goods!

WILLY: That is a one-million-dollar idea!

LINDA: Marvelous!

BIFF: I'm in great shape as far as that's concerned.

HAPPY: And the beauty of it is, Biff, it wouldn't be like a business. We'd be out playin' ball again . . .

BIFF [*enthused*]: Yeah, that's . . .

WILLY: Million-dollar . . .

HAPPY: And you wouldn't get fed up with it, Biff. It'd be the family again. There'd be the old honor, and comradeship, and if you wanted to go off for a swim or somethin'—well you'd do it! Without some smart cooky gettin' up ahead of you!

WILLY: Lick the world! You guys together could absolutely lick the civilized world.

BIFF: I'll see Oliver tomorrow. Hap, if we could work that out . . .

LINDA: Maybe things are beginning to—

WILLY [*wildly enthused, to* LINDA]: Stop interrupting! [*To* BIFF] But don't wear sport jacket and slacks when you see Oliver.

BIFF: No, I'll—

WILLY: A business suit, and talk as little as possible, and don't crack any jokes.

BIFF: He did like me. Always liked me.

LINDA: He loved you!

WILLY [*to* LINDA]: Will you stop! [*To* BIFF] Walk in very serious. You are not applying for a boy's job. Money is to pass. Be quiet, fine, and serious. Everybody likes a kidder, but nobody lends him money.

HAPPY: I'll try to get some myself, Biff. I'm sure I can.

WILLY: I see great things for you kids, I think your troubles are over. But remember, start big and you'll end big. Ask for fifteen. How much you gonna ask for?

BIFF: Gee, I don't know—

WILLY: And don't say "Gee." "Gee" is a boy's word. A man walking in for fifteen thousand dollars does not say "Gee"!

BIFF: Ten, I think, would be top though.

WILLY: Don't be so modest. You always started too low. Walk in with a big laugh. Don't look worried. Start off with a couple of your good stories to lighten things up. It's not what you say, it's how you say it—because personality always wins the day.

LINDA: Oliver always thought the highest of him—

WILLY: Will you let me talk?

BIFF: Don't yell at her, Pop, will ya?

WILLY [angrily]: I was talking, wasn't I?

BIFF: I don't like you yelling at her all the time, and I'm tellin' you, that's all.

WILLY: What're you, takin' over this house?

LINDA: Willy—

WILLY [turning on her]: Don't take his side all the time, goddammit!

BIFF [furiously]: Stop yelling at her!

WILLY [suddenly pulling on his cheek, beaten down, guilt ridden]: Give my best to Bill Oliver—he may remember me. [He exits through the living-room doorway.]

LINDA [her voice subdued]: What'd you have to start that for? [BIFF turns away.] You see how sweet he was as soon as you talked hopefully? [She goes over to BIFF.] Come up and say good night to him. Don't let him go to bed that way.

HAPPY: Come on, Biff, let's buck him up.

LINDA: Please, dear. Just say good night. It takes so little to make him happy. Come. [She goes through the living-room doorway, calling upstairs from within the living-room.] Your pajamas are hanging in the bathroom, Willy!

HAPPY [looking toward where LINDA went out]: What a woman! They broke the mold when they made her. You know that, Biff?

BIFF: He's off salary. My God, working on commission!

HAPPY: Well, let's face it: he's no hot-shot selling man. Except that sometimes, you have to admit, he's a sweet personality.

BIFF [deciding]: Lend me ten bucks, will ya? I want to buy some new ties.

HAPPY: I'll take you to a place I know. Beautiful stuff. Wear one of my striped shirts tomorrow.

BIFF: She got gray. Mom got awful old. Gee, I'm gonna go in to Oliver tomorrow and knock him for a—

HAPPY: Come on up. Tell that to Dad. Let's give him a whirl. Come on.

BIFF [steamed up]: You know, with ten thousand bucks, boy!

HAPPY [as they go into the living-room]: That's the talk, Biff, that's the first time I've heard the old confidence out of you! [From within the living-room, fading off] You're gonna live with me, kid, and any babe you want just say the word . . . [The last lines are hardly heard. They are mounting the stairs to their parents' bedroom.]

LINDA [entering her bedroom and addressing WILLY, who is in the bathroom. She is straightening the bed for him.] Can you do anything about the shower? It drips.

WILLY [*from the bathroom*]: All of a sudden everything falls to pieces! Goddam plumbing, oughta be sued, those people. I hardly finished putting it in and the thing . . . [*His words rumble off.*]

LINDA: I'm just wondering if Oliver will remember him. You think he might?

WILLY [*coming out of the bathroom in his pajamas*]: Remember him? What's the matter with you, you crazy? If he'd've stayed with Oliver he'd be on top by now! Wait'll Oliver gets a look at him. You don't know the average caliber any more. The average young man today—[*he is getting into bed*]—is got a cal-iber of zero. Greatest thing in the world for him was to bum around.

[BIFF *and* HAPPY *enter the bedroom. Slight pause.*]

WILLY [*stops short, looking at* BIFF]: Glad to hear it, boy.

HAPPY: He wanted to say good night to you, sport.

WILLY [*to* BIFF]: Yeah. Knock him dead, boy. What'd you want to tell me?

BIFF: Just take it easy, Pop. Good night. [*He turns to go.*]

WILLY [*unable to resist*]: And if anything falls off the desk while you're talking to him—like a package or something—don't you pick it up. They have office boys for that.

LINDA: I'll make a big breakfast—

WILLY: Will you let me finish? [*To* BIFF] Tell him you were in the business in the West. Not farm work.

BIFF: All right, Dad.

LINDA: I think everything—

WILLY [*going right through her speech*]: And don't undersell yourself. No less than fifteen thousand dollars.

BIFF [*unable to bear him*]: Okay. Good night, Mom. [*He starts moving.*]

WILLY: Because you got a greatness in you, Biff, remember that. You got all kinds a greatness . . . [*He lies back, exhausted.* BIFF *walks out.*]

LINDA [*calling after* BIFF]: Sleep well, darling!

HAPPY: I'm gonna get married, Mom. I wanted to tell you.

LINDA: Go to sleep, dear.

HAPPY [*going*]: I just wanted to tell you.

WILLY: Keep up the good work. [HAPPY *exits.*] God . . . remember that Ebbets Field game? The championship of the city?

LINDA: Just rest. Should I sing to you?

WILLY: Yeah. Sing to me. [LINDA *hums a soft lullaby.*] When that team came out—he was the tallest, remember?

LINDA: Oh, yes. And in gold.

[BIFF *enters the darkened kitchen, takes a cigarette, and leaves the house. He comes downstage into a golden pool of light. He smokes, staring at the night.*]

WILLY: Like a young god. Hercules—something like that. And the sun, the sun all around him. Remember how he waved to me? Right up from the field, with the representatives of three colleges standing by? And the buyers I brought, and the cheers when he came out—Loman, Loman, Loman! God Almighty, he'll be great yet. A star like that, magnificent, can never really fade away!

[*The light on* WILLY *is fading. The gas heater begins to glow through the kitchen wall, near the stairs, a blue flame beneath red coils.*]

LINDA [*timidly*]: Willy dear, what has he got against you?
WILLY: I'm so tired. Don't talk any more.

[BIFF *slowly returns to the kitchen. He stops, stares toward the heater.*]

LINDA: Will you ask Howard to let you work in New York?
WILLY: First thing in the morning. Everything'll be all right.

[BIFF *reaches behind the heater and draws out a length of rubber tubing. He is horrified and turns his head toward* WILLY'S *room, still dimly lit, from which the strains of* LINDA'S *desperate but monotonous humming rise.*]

WILLY [*staring through the window into the moonlight*]: Gee, look at the moon moving between the buildings!

[BIFF *wraps the tubing around his hand and quickly goes up the stairs.*]
    CURTAIN

ACT TWO

Music is heard, gay and bright. The curtain rises as the music fades away.
    [WILLY, *in shirt sleeves, is sitting at the kitchen table, sipping coffee, his hat in his lap.* LINDA *is filling his cup when she can.*]

WILLY: Wonderful coffee. Meal in itself.
LINDA: Can I make you some eggs?
WILLY: No. Take a breath.
LINDA: You look so rested, dear.
WILLY: I slept like a dead one. First time in months. Imagine, sleeping till ten on a Tuesday morning. Boys left nice and early, heh?
LINDA: They were out of here by eight o'clock.
WILLY: Good work!
LINDA: It was so thrilling to see them leaving together. I can't get over the shaving lotion in this house!
WILLY [*smiling*]: Mmm—
LINDA: Biff was very changed this morning. His whole attitude seemed to be hopeful. He couldn't wait to get downtown to see Oliver.
WILLY: He's heading for a change. There's no question, there simply are certain men that take longer to get—solidified. How did he dress?
LINDA: His blue suit. He's so handsome in that suit. He could be a—anything in that suit!

[WILLY *gets up from the table.* LINDA *holds his jacket for him.*]

WILLY: There's no question, no question at all. Gee, on the way home tonight I'd like to buy some seeds.
LINDA [*laughing*]: That'd be wonderful. But not enough sun gets back there. Nothing'll grow any more.

WILLY: You wait, kid, before it's all over we're gonna get a little place out in the country, and I'll raise some vegetables, a couple of chickens . . .

LINDA: You'll do it yet, dear.

[WILLY *walks out of his jacket.* LINDA *follows him.*]

WILLY: And they'll get married, and come for a weekend. I'd build a little guest house. 'Cause I got so many fine tools, all I'd need would be a little lumber and some peace of mind.

LINDA [*joyfully*]: I sewed the lining . . .

WILLY: I could build two guest houses, so they'd both come. Did he decide how much he's going to ask Oliver for?

LINDA [*getting him into the jacket*]: He didn't mention it, but I imagine ten or fifteen thousand. You going to talk to Howard today?

WILLY: Yeah. I'll put it to him straight and simple. He'll just have to take me off the road.

LINDA: And Willy, don't forget to ask for a little advance, because we've got the insurance premium. It's the grace period now.

WILLY: That's a hundred . . . ?

LINDA: A hundred and eight, sixty-eight. Because we're a little short again.

WILLY: Why are we short?

LINDA: Well, you had the motor job on the car . . .

WILLY: That goddam Studebaker!

LINDA: And you got one more payment on the refrigerator . . .

WILLY: But it just broke again!

LINDA: Well, it's old, dear.

WILLY: I told you we should've bought a well-advertised machine. Charley bought a General Electric and it's twenty years old and it's still good, that son-of-a-bitch.

LINDA: But, Willy—

WILLY: Whoever heard of a Hastings refrigerator? Once in my life I would like to own something outright before it's broken! I'm always in a race with the junkyard! I just finished paying for the car and it's on its last legs. The refrigerator consumes belts like a goddam maniac. They time those things. They time them so when you finally paid for them, they're used up.

LINDA [*buttoning up his jacket as he unbuttons it*]: All told, about two hundred dollars would carry us, dear. But that includes the last payment on the mortgage. After this payment, Willy, the house belongs to us.

WILLY: It's twenty-five years!

LINDA: Biff was nine years old when we bought it.

WILLY: Well, that's a great thing. To weather a twenty-five-year mortgage is—

LINDA: It's an accomplishment.

WILLY: All the cement, the lumber, the reconstruction I put in this house! There ain't a crack to be found in it any more.

LINDA: Well, it served its purpose.

WILLY: What purpose? Some stranger'll come along, move in, and that's that. If only Biff would take this house, and raise a family . . . [*He starts to go.*] Goodbye, I'm late.

LINDA [*suddenly remembering*]: Oh, I forgot! You're supposed to meet them for dinner.

WILLY: Me?

LINDA: At Frank's Chop House on Forty-eighth near Sixth Avenue.

WILLY: Is that so! How about you?

LINDA: No, just the three of you. They're gonna blow you to a big meal!

WILLY: Don't say! Who thought of that?

LINDA: Biff came to me this morning, Willy, and he said, "Tell Dad, we want to blow him to a big meal." Be there six o'clock. You and your two boys are going to have dinner.

WILLY: Gee whiz! That's really somethin'. I'm gonna knock Howard for a loop, kid. I'll get an advance, and I'll come home with a New York job. Goddammit, now I'm gonna do it!

LINDA: Oh, that's the spirit, Willy!

WILLY: I will never get behind a wheel the rest of my life!

LINDA: It's changing, Willy, I can feel it changing!

WILLY: Beyond a question. G'bye, I'm late. [*He starts to go again.*]

LINDA [*calling after him as she runs to the kitchen table for a handkerchief*]: You got your glasses?

WILLY [*feels for them, then comes back in*]: Yeah, yeah, got my glasses.

LINDA [*giving him the handkerchief*]: And a handkerchief.

WILLY: Yeah, handkerchief.

LINDA: And your saccharine?

WILLY: Yeah, my saccharine.

LINDA: Be careful on the subway stairs.

[*She kisses him, and a silk stocking is seen hanging from her hand.* WILLY *notices it.*]

WILLY: Will you stop mending stockings? At least while I'm in the house. It gets me nervous. I can't tell you. Please.

[LINDA *hides the stocking in her hand as she follows* WILLY *across the forestage in front of the house.*]

LINDA: Remember, Frank's Chop House.

WILLY [*passing the apron*]: Maybe beets would grow out there.

LINDA [*laughing*]: But you tried so many times.

WILLY: Yeah. Well, don't work hard today. [*He disappears around the right corner of the house.*]

LINDA: Be careful!

[*As* WILLY *vanishes,* LINDA *waves to him. Suddenly the phone rings. She runs across the stage and into the kitchen and lifts it.*]

LINDA: Hello? Oh, Biff! I'm so glad you called, I just . . . Yes, sure, I just told him. Yes, he'll be there for dinner at six o'clock, I didn't forget. Listen, I was just dying to tell you. You know that little rubber pipe I told you about? That he connected to the gas heater? I finally decided to go down the cellar this morning and take it away and destroy it. But it's gone! Imagine? He took it away himself, it isn't there! [*She listens.*] When? Oh, then you took it. Oh— nothing, it's just that I'd hoped he'd taken it away himself. Oh, I'm not worried, darling, because this morning he left in such high spirits, it was like the old days! I'm not afraid any more. Did Mr. Oliver see you? . . . Well, you wait there then. And make a nice impression on him, darling. Just don't perspire too much before you see him. And have a nice time with Dad. He may have big news too! . . . That's right, a New York job. And be sweet to him tonight, dear. Be loving to him. Because he's only a little boat looking for a harbor. [*She is trembling with sorrow and joy.*] Oh, that's wonderful, Biff, you'll save his life. Thanks, darling. Just put your arm around him when he comes into the restaurant. Give him a smile. That's the boy . . . Good-bye, dear . . . You got your comb? . . . That's fine. Good-bye, Biff dear.

[*In the middle of her speech,* HOWARD WAGNER, *thirty-six, wheels on a small typewriter table on which is a wire-recording machine and proceeds to plug it in. This is on the left forestage. Light slowly fades on* LINDA *as it rises on* HOWARD. HOWARD *is intent on threading the machine and only glances over his shoulder as* WILLY *appears.*]

WILLY: Pst! Pst!

HOWARD: Hello, Willy, come in.

WILLY: Like to have a little talk with you, Howard.

HOWARD: Sorry to keep you waiting. I'll be with you in a minute.

WILLY: What's that, Howard?

HOWARD: Didn't you ever see one of these? Wire recorder.

WILLY: Oh. Can we talk a minute?

HOWARD: Records things. Just got delivery yesterday. Been driving me crazy, the most terrific machine I ever saw in my life. I was up all night with it.

WILLY: What do you do with it?

HOWARD: I bought it for dictation, but you can do anything with it. Listen to this. I had it home last night. Listen to what I picked up. The first one is my daughter. Get this. [*He flicks the switch and "Roll out the Barrel" is heard being whistled.*] Listen to that kid whistle.

WILLY: That is lifelike, isn't it?

HOWARD: Seven years old. Get that tone.

WILLY: Ts, ts. Like to ask a little favor if you . . .

[*The whistling breaks off, and the voice of* HOWARD'S *daughter is heard.*]

HIS DAUGHTER: "Now you, Daddy."

HOWARD: She's crazy for me! [*Again the same song is whistled.*] That's me! Ha! [*He winks.*]

WILLY: You're very good!

[*The whistling breaks off again. The machine runs silent for a moment.*]

HOWARD: Sh! Get this now, this is my son.

HIS SON: "The capital of Alabama is Montgomery; the capital of Arizona is Phoenix; the capital of Arkansas is Little Rock; the capital of California is Sacramento . . ." [*and on, and on.*]

HOWARD [*holding up five fingers*]: Five years old, Willy!

WILLY: He'll make an announcer some day!

HIS SON [*continuing*]: "The capital . . ."

HOWARD: Get that—alphabetical order! [*The machine breaks off suddenly.*] Wait a minute. The maid kicked the plug out.

WILLY: It certainly is a—

HOWARD: Sh, for God's sake!

HIS SON: "It's nine o'clock, Bulova watch time. So I have to go to sleep."

WILLY: That really is—

HOWARD: Wait a minute! The next is my wife.

[*They wait.*]

HOWARD'S VOICE: "Go on, say something." [*Pause.*] "Well, you gonna talk?"

HIS WIFE: "I can't think of anything."

HOWARD'S VOICE: "Well, talk—it's turning."

HIS WIFE [*shyly, beaten*]: "Hello." [*Silence.*] "Oh, Howard, I can't talk into this . . ."

HOWARD [*snapping the machine off*]: That was my wife.

WILLY: That is a wonderful machine. Can we—

HOWARD: I tell you, Willy, I'm gonna take my camera, and my bandsaw, and all my hobbies, and out they go. This is the most fascinating relaxation I ever found.

WILLY: I think I'll get one myself.

HOWARD: Sure, they're only a hundred and a half. You can't do without it. Supposing you wanna hear Jack Benny, see? But you can't be at home at that hour. So you tell the maid to turn the radio on when Jack Benny comes on, and this automatically goes on with the radio . . .

WILLY: And when you come home you . . .

HOWARD: You can come home twelve o'clock, one o'clock, any time you like, and you get yourself a Coke and sit yourself down, throw the switch, and there's Jack Benny's program in the middle of the night!

WILLY: I'm definitely going to get one. Because lots of time I'm on the road, and I think to myself, what I must be missing on the radio!

HOWARD: Don't you have a radio in the car?

WILLY: Well, yeah, but who ever thinks of turning it on?

HOWARD: Say, aren't you supposed to be in Boston?

WILLY: That's what I want to talk to you about, Howard. You got a minute? [*He draws a chair in from the wing.*]

HOWARD: What happened? What're you doing here?

WILLY: Well . . .

HOWARD: You didn't crack up again, did you?

WILLY: Oh, no. No . . .

HOWARD: Geez, you had me worried there for a minute. What's the trouble?

WILLY: Well, tell you the truth, Howard. I've come to the decision that I'd rather not travel any more.

HOWARD: Not travel! Well, what'll you do?

WILLY: Remember, Christmas time, when you had the party here? You said you'd try to think of some spot for me here in town.

HOWARD: With us?

WILLY: Well, sure.

HOWARD: Oh, yeah, yeah. I remember. Well, I couldn't think of anything for you, Willy.

WILLY: I tell ya, Howard. The kids are all grown up, y'know. I don't need much any more. If I could take home—well, sixty-five dollars a week, I could swing it.

HOWARD: Yeah, but Willy, see I—

WILLY: I tell ya why, Howard. Speaking frankly and between the two of us, y'-know—I'm just a little tired.

HOWARD: Oh, I could understand that, Willy. But you're a road man, Willy, and we do a road business. We've only got a half-dozen salesmen on the floor here.

WILLY: God knows, Howard, I never asked a favor of any man. But I was with the firm when your father used to carry you in here in his arms.

HOWARD: I know that, Willy, but—

WILLY: Your father came to me the day you were born and asked me what I thought of the name of Howard, may he rest in peace.

HOWARD: I appreciate that, Willy, but there just is no spot here for you. If I had a spot I'd slam you right in, but I just don't have a single solitary spot.

[*He looks for his lighter.* WILLY *has picked it up and gives it to him. Pause.*]

WILLY [*with increasing anger*]: Howard, all I need to set my table is fifty dollars a week.

HOWARD: But where am I going to put you, kid?

WILLY: Look, it isn't a question of whether I can sell merchandise, is it?

HOWARD: No, but it's a business, kid, and everybody's gotta pull his own weight.

WILLY [*desperately*]: Just let me tell you a story, Howard—

HOWARD: 'Cause you gotta admit, business is business.

WILLY [*angrily*]: Business is definitely business, but just listen for a minute. You don't understand this. When I was a boy—eighteen, nineteen—I was already on the road. And there was a question in my mind as to whether selling had a future for me. Because in those days I had a yearning to go to Alaska. See, there were three gold strikes in one month in Alaska, and I felt like going out. Just for the ride, you might say.

HOWARD [*barely interested*]: Don't say.

WILLY: Oh, yeah, my father lived many years in Alaska. He was an adventurous man. We've got quite a little streak of self-reliance in our family. I thought I'd go out with my older brother and try to locate him, and maybe settle in the North with the old man. And I was almost decided to go, when I met a salesman in the Parker House. His name was Dave Singleman. And he was eighty-four years old, and he'd drummed merchandise in thirty-one states. And old Dave, he'd go up to his room, y'understand, put on his green velvet slippers—I'll never forget—and pick up his phone and call the buyers, and without ever leaving his room, at the age of eighty-four, he made his living. And when I saw that, I realized that selling was the greatest career a man could want. 'Cause what could be more satisfying than to be able to go, at the age of eighty-four, into twenty or thirty different cities, and pick up a phone, and be remembered and loved and helped by so many different people? Do you know? when he died—and by the way he died the death of a salesman, in his green velvet slippers in the smoker of the New York, New Haven, and Hartford, going into Boston—when he died, hundreds of salesmen and buyers were at his funeral. Things were sad on a lotta trains for months after that. [*He stands up.* HOWARD *has not looked at him.*] In those days there was personality in it, Howard. There was respect, and comradeship, and gratitude in it. Today, it's all cut and dried, and there's no chance for bringing friendship to bear—or personality. You see what I mean? They don't know me any more.

HOWARD [*moving away, to the right*]: That's just the thing, Willy.

WILLY: If I had forty dollars a week—that's all I'd need. Forty dollars, Howard.

HOWARD: Kid, I can't take blood from a stone, I—

WILLY [*desperation is on him now*]: Howard, the year Al Smith was nominated, your father came to me and—

HOWARD [*starting to go off*]: I've got to see some people, kid.

WILLY [*stopping him*]: I'm talking about your father! There were promises made across this desk! You mustn't tell me you've got people to see—I put thirty-four years into this firm, Howard, and now I can't pay my insurance! You can't eat the orange and throw the peel away—a man is not a piece of fruit! [*After a pause*] Now pay attention. Your father—in 1928 I had a big year. I averaged a hundred and seventy dollars a week in commissions.

HOWARD [*impatiently*]: Now, Willy, you never averaged—

WILLY [*banging his hand on the desk*]: I averaged a hundred and seventy dollars a week in the year of 1928! And your father came to me—or rather, I was in the office here—it was right over this desk—and he put his hand on my shoulder—

HOWARD [*getting up*]: You'll have to excuse me, Willy, I gotta see some people. Pull yourself together. [*Going out*] I'll be back in a little while.

[*On* HOWARD'S *exit, the light on his chair grows very bright and strange.*]

WILLY: Pull myself together! What the hell did I say to him? My God, I was yelling at him! How could I! [WILLY *breaks off, staring at the light, which occupies the chair, animating it. He approaches this chair, standing across the desk from it.*] Frank, Frank, don't you remember what you told me that time? How you put your hand on my shoulder, and Frank . . . [*He leans on the desk and as he speaks the dead man's name he accidentally switches on the recorder, and instantly—*]

HOWARD'S SON: ". . . of New York is Albany. The capital of Ohio is Cincinnati, the capital of Rhode Island is . . ." [*The recitation continues.*]

WILLY [*leaping away with fright, shouting*]: Ha! Howard! Howard! Howard!

HOWARD [*rushing in*]: What happened?

WILLY [*pointing at the machine, which continues nasally, childishly, with the capital cities*]: Shut it off! Shut it off!

HOWARD [*pulling the plug out*]: Look, Willy . . .

WILLY [*pressing his hands to his eyes*]: I gotta get myself some coffee. I'll get some coffee . . .

[WILLY *starts to walk out.* HOWARD *stops him.*]

HOWARD [*rolling up the cord*]: Willy, look . . .

WILLY: I'll go to Boston.

HOWARD: Willy, you can't go to Boston for us.

WILLY: Why can't I go?

HOWARD: I don't want you to represent us. I've been meaning to tell you for a long time now.

WILLY: Howard, are you firing me?

HOWARD: I think you need a good long rest, Willy.

WILLY: Howard—

HOWARD: And when you feel better, come back, and we'll see if we can work something out.

WILLY: But I gotta earn money, Howard. I'm in no position to—

HOWARD: Where are your sons? Why don't your sons give you a hand?

WILLY: They're working on a very big deal.

HOWARD: This is no time for false pride, Willy. You go to your sons and you tell them that you're tired. You've got two great boys, haven't you?

WILLY: Oh, no question, no question, but in the meantime . . .

HOWARD: Then that's that, heh?

WILLY: All right, I'll go to Boston tomorrow.

HOWARD: No, no.

WILLY: I can't throw myself on my sons. I'm not a cripple!

HOWARD: Look, kid, I'm busy this morning.

WILLY [*grasping* HOWARD'S *arm*]: Howard, you've got to let me go to Boston!

HOWARD [*hard, keeping himself under control*]: I've got a line of people to see this morning. Sit down, take five minutes, and pull yourself together, and then go home, will ya? I need the office, Willy. [*He starts to go, turns, remembering the recorder, starts to push off the table holding the recorder.*] Oh, yeah. Whenever you can this week, stop by and drop off the samples. You'll feel better, Willy, and then come back and we'll talk. Pull yourself together, kid, there's people outside.

[HOWARD *exits, pushing the table off left.* WILLY *stares into space, exhausted. Now the music is heard—*BEN'S *music—first distantly, then closer, closer. As* WILLY *speaks,* BEN *enters from the right. He carries valise and umbrella.*]

WILLY: Oh, Ben, how did you do it? What is the answer? Did you wind up the Alaska deal already?

BEN: Doesn't take much time if you know what you're doing. Just a short business trip. Boarding ship in an hour. Wanted to say good-bye.

WILLY: Ben, I've got to talk to you.

BEN [*glancing at his watch*]: Haven't the time, William.

WILLY [*crossing the apron to* BEN]: Ben, nothing's working out. I don't know what to do.

BEN: Now, look here, William. I've bought timberland in Alaska and I need a man to look after things for me.

WILLY: God, timberland! Me and my boys in those grand outdoors!

BEN: You've a new continent at your doorstep, William. Get out of these cities, they're full of talk and time payments and courts of law. Screw on your fists and you can fight for a fortune up there.

WILLY: Yes, yes! Linda, Linda!

[LINDA *enters as of old, with the wash.*]

LINDA: Oh, you're back?

BEN: I haven't much time.

WILLY: No, wait! Linda, he's got a proposition for me in Alaska.

LINDA: But you've got—[*To* BEN] He's got a beautiful job here.

WILLY: But in Alaska, kid, I could—

LINDA: You're doing well enough, Willy!

BEN [*to* LINDA]: Enough for what, my dear?

LINDA [*frightened of* BEN *and angry at him*]: Don't say those things to him! Enough to be happy right here, right now. [*To* WILLY, *while* BEN *laughs*] Why must everybody conquer the world? You're well liked, and the boys love you, and someday—[*to* BEN]—why, old man Wagner told him just the other day that if he keeps it up he'll be a member of the firm, didn't he, Willy?

WILLY: Sure, sure. I am building something with this firm, Ben, and if a man is building something he must be on the right track, mustn't he?

BEN: What are you building? Lay your hand on it. Where is it?

WILLY [*hesitantly*]: That's true, Linda, there's nothing.

LINDA: Why? [*To* BEN] There's a man eighty-four years old—

WILLY: That's right, Ben, that's right. When I look at that man I say, what is there to worry about?

BEN: Bah!

WILLY: It's true, Ben. All he has to do is go into any city, pick up the phone, and he's making his living and you know why?

BEN [*picking up his valise*]: I've got to go.

WILLY [*holding* BEN *back*]: Look at this boy!

[BIFF, *in his high school sweater, enters carrying suitcase.* HAPPY *carries* BIFF'S *shoulder guards, gold helmet, and football pants.*]

WILLY: Without a penny to his name, three great universities are begging for him, and from there the sky's the limit, because it's not what you do, Ben. It's who you know and the smile on your face! It's contacts, Ben, contacts! The whole wealth of Alaska passes over the lunch table at the Commodore Hotel, and that's the wonder, the wonder of this country, that a man can end with diamonds here on the basis of being liked! [*He turns to* BIFF.] And that's why when you get out on that field today it's important. Because thousands of people will be rooting for you and loving you. [*To* BEN, *who has again begun to leave*] And Ben! when he walks into a business office his name will sound out like a bell and all the doors will open to him! I've seen it, Ben, I've seen it a thousand times! You can't feel it with your hand like timber, but it's there!

BEN: Good-bye, William.

WILLY: Ben, am I right? Don't you think I'm right? I value your advice.

BEN: There's a new continent at your doorstep, William. You could walk out rich. Rich! [*He is gone.*]

WILLY: We'll do it here, Ben! You hear me? We're gonna do it here!

[*Young* BERNARD *rushes in. The gay music of the boys is heard.*]

BERNARD: Oh, gee, I was afraid you left already!

WILLY: Why? What time is it?

BERNARD: It's half-past one!

WILLY: Well, come on, everybody! Ebbets Field next stop! Where's the pennants? [*He rushes through the wall-line of the kitchen and out into the living-room.*]

LINDA [*to* BIFF]: Did you pack fresh underwear?

BIFF [*who has been limbering up*]: I want to go!

BERNARD: Biff, I'm carrying your helmet, ain't I?

HAPPY: No, I'm carrying the helmet.

BERNARD: Oh, Biff, you promised me.

HAPPY: I'm carrying the helmet.

BERNARD: How am I going to get in the locker room?

LINDA: Let him carry the shoulder guards. [*She puts her coat and hat on in the kitchen.*]

BERNARD: Can I, Biff? 'Cause I told everybody I'm going to be in the locker room.

HAPPY: In Ebbets Field it's the clubhouse.

BERNARD: I meant the clubhouse. Biff!

HAPPY: Biff!

BIFF [*grandly, after a slight pause*]: Let him carry the shoulder guards.

HAPPY [*as he gives* BERNARD *the shoulder guards*]: Stay close to us now.

[WILLY *rushes in with the pennants.*]

WILLY [*handing them out*]: Everybody wave when Biff comes out on the field. [HAPPY *and* BERNARD *run off.*] You set now, boy?

[*The music has died away.*]

BIFF: Ready to go, Pop. Every muscle is ready.

WILLY [*at the edge of the apron*]: You realize what this means?

BIFF: That's right, Pop.

WILLY [*feeling* BIFF'S *muscles*]: You're comin' home this afternoon captain of the All-Scholastic Championship Team of the City of New York.

BIFF: I got it, Pop. And remember, pal, when I take off my helmet, that touchdown is for you.

WILLY: Let's go! [*He is starting out, with his arm around* BIFF, *when* CHARLEY *enters, as of old, in knickers.*] I got no room for you, Charley.

CHARLEY: Room? For what?

WILLY: In the car.

CHARLEY: You goin' for a ride? I wanted to shoot some casino.

WILLY [*furiously*]: Casino! [*Incredulously*] Don't you realize what today is?

LINDA: Oh, he knows, Willy. He's just kidding you.

WILLY: That's nothing to kid about!

CHARLEY: No. Linda, what's goin' on?

LINDA: He's playing in Ebbets Field.

CHARLEY: Baseball in this weather?

WILLY: Don't talk to him. Come on, come on! [*He is pushing them out.*]

CHARLEY: Wait a minute, didn't you hear the news?

WILLY: What?

CHARLEY: Don't you listen to the radio? Ebbets Field just blew up.

WILLY: You go to hell! [CHARLEY *laughs. Pushing them out*] Come on, come on! We're late.

CHARLEY [*as they go*]: Knock a homer, Biff, knock a homer!

WILLY [*the last to leave, turning to* CHARLEY]: I don't think that was funny, Charley. This is the greatest day of his life.

CHARLEY: Willy, when are you going to grow up?

WILLY: Yeah, heh? When this game is over, Charley, you'll be laughing out of the other side of your face. They'll be calling him another Red Grange. Twenty-five thousand a year.

CHARLEY [*kidding*]: Is that so?

WILLY: Yeah, that's so.

CHARLEY: Well, then, I'm sorry, Willy. But tell me something.

WILLY: What?

CHARLEY: Who is Red Grange?

WILLY: Put up your hands. Goddam you, put up your hands!

[CHARLEY, *chuckling, shakes his head and walks away, around the left corner of the stage.* WILLY *follows him. The music rises to a mocking frenzy.*]

WILLY: Who the hell do you think you are, better than everybody else? You don't know everything, you big, ignorant, stupid . . . Put up your hands!

[*Light rises, on the right side of the forestage, on a small table in the reception room of* CHARLEY'S *office. Traffic sounds are heard.* BERNARD, *now mature, sits whistling to himself. A pair of tennis rackets and an overnight bag are on the floor beside him.*]

WILLY [*offstage*]: What are you walking away for? Don't walk away! If you're going to say something say it to my face! I know you laugh at me behind my back. You'll laugh out of the other side of your goddam face after this game. Touchdown! Touchdown! Eighty thousand people! Touchdown! Right between the goal posts.

[BERNARD *is a quiet, earnest, but self-assured young man.* WILLY'S *voice is coming from right upstage now.* BERNARD *lowers his feet off the table and listens.* JENNY, *his father's secretary, enters.*]

JENNY [*distressed*]: Say, Bernard, will you go out in the hall?

BERNARD: What is that noise? Who is it?

JENNY: Mr. Loman. He just got off the elevator.

BERNARD [*getting up*]: Who's he arguing with?

JENNY: Nobody. There's nobody with him. I can't deal with him any more, and your father gets all upset everytime he comes. I've got a lot of typing to do, and your father's waiting to sign it. Will you see him?

WILLY [*entering*]: Touchdown! Touch—[*He sees* JENNY.] Jenny, Jenny, good to see you. How're ya? Workin'? Or still honest?

JENNY: Fine. How've you been feeling?

WILLY: Not much any more, Jenny. Ha, ha! [*He is surprised to see the rackets.*]

BERNARD: Hello, Uncle Willy.

WILLY [*almost shocked*]: Bernard! Well, look who's here! [*He comes quickly, guiltily, to* BERNARD *and warmly shakes his hand.*]

BERNARD: How are you? Good to see you.

WILLY: What are you doing here?

BERNARD: Oh, just stopped by to see Pop. Get off my feet till my train leaves. I'm going to Washington in a few minutes.

WILLY: Is he in?

BERNARD: Yes, he's in his office with the accountant. Sit down.

WILLY [*sitting down*]: What're you going to do in Washington?

BERNARD: Oh, just a case I've got there, Willy.

WILLY: That so? [*Indicating the rackets*] You going to play tennis there?

BERNARD: I'm staying with a friend who's got a court.

WILLY: Don't say. His own tennis court. Must be fine people, I bet.

BERNARD: They are, very nice. Dad tells me Biff's in town.

WILLY [*with a big smile*]: Yeah, Biff's in. Working on a very big deal, Bernard.

BERNARD: What's Biff doing?

WILLY: Well, he's been doing very big things in the West. But he decided to establish himself here. Very big. We're having dinner. Did I hear your wife had a boy?

BERNARD: That's right. Our second.

WILLY: Two boys! What do you know!

BERNARD: What kind of a deal has Biff got?

WILLY: Well, Bill Oliver—very big sporting-goods man—he wants Biff very badly. Called him in from the West. Long distance, carte blanche, special deliveries. Your friends have their own private tennis court?

BERNARD: You still with the old firm, Willy?

WILLY [*after a pause*]: I'm—I'm overjoyed to see how you made the grade, Bernard, overjoyed. It's an encouraging thing to see a young man really—really—Looks very good for Biff—very—[*He breaks off, then*] Bernard—[*He is so full of emotion, he breaks off again.*]

BERNARD: What is it, Willy?

WILLY [*small and alone*]: What—what's the secret?

BERNARD: What secret?

WILLY: How—how did you? Why didn't he ever catch on?

BERNARD: I wouldn't know that, Willy.

WILLY [*confidentially, desperately*]: You were his friend, his boyhood friend. There's something I don't understand about it. His life ended after that Ebbets Field game. From the age of seventeen nothing good ever happened to him.

BERNARD: He never trained himself for anything.

WILLY: But he did, he did. After high school he took so many correspondence courses. Radio mechanics; television; God knows what, and never made the slightest mark.

BERNARD [*taking off his glasses*]: Willy, do you want to talk candidly?

WILLY [*rising, faces* BERNARD]: I regard you as a very brilliant man, Bernard. I value your advice.

BERNARD: Oh, the hell with the advice, Willy. I couldn't advise you. There's just one thing I've always wanted to ask you. When he was supposed to graduate, and the math teacher flunked him—

WILLY: Oh, that son-of-a-bitch ruined his life.

BERNARD: Yeah, but, Willy, all he had to do was to go to summer school and make up that subject.

WILLY: That's right, that's right.

BERNARD: Did you tell him not to go to summer school?

WILLY:
  Me? I begged him to go. I ordered him to go!

BERNARD: Then why wouldn't he go?

WILLY: Why? Why! Bernard, that question has been trailing me like a ghost for the last fifteen years. He flunked the subject, and laid down and died like a hammer hit him!

BERNARD: Take it easy, kid.

WILLY: Let me talk to you—I got nobody to talk to. Bernard, Bernard, was it my fault? Y'see? It keeps going around in my mind, maybe I did something to him. I got nothing to give him.

BERNARD: Don't take it so hard.

WILLY: Why did he lay down? What is the story there? You were his friend!

BERNARD: Willy, I remember, it was June, and our grades came out. And he'd flunked math.

WILLY: That son-of-a-bitch!

BERNARD: No, it wasn't right then. Biff just got very angry, I remember, and he was ready to enroll in summer school.

WILLY [surprised]: He was?

BERNARD: He wasn't beaten by it at all. But then, Willy, he disappeared from the block for almost a month. And I got the idea that he'd gone up to New England to see you. Did he have a talk with you then?

[WILLY stares in silence.]

BERNARD: Willy?

WILLY [with a strong edge of resentment in his voice]: Yeah, he came to Boston. What about it?

BERNARD: Well, just that when he came back—I'll never forget this, it always mystifies me. Because I'd thought so well of Biff, even though he'd always taken advantage of me. I loved him, Willy, y'know? And he came back after that month and took his sneakers—remember those sneakers with "University of Virginia" printed on them? He was so proud of those, wore them every day. And he took them down in the cellar, and burned them up in the furnace. We had a fist fight. It lasted at least half an hour. Just the two of us, punching each other down the cellar, and crying right through it. I've often thought of how strange it was that I knew he'd given up his life. What happened in Boston, Willy?

[WILLY looks at him as at an intruder.]

BERNARD: I just bring it up because you asked me.

WILLY [angrily]: Nothing. What do you mean, "What happened?" What's that got to do with anything?

BERNARD: Well, don't get sore.

WILLY: What are you trying to do, blame it on me? If a boy lays down is that my fault?

BERNARD: Now, Willy, don't get—

WILLY: Well, don't—don't talk to me that way! What does that mean, "What happened?"

[CHARLEY enters. He is in his vest, and he carries a bottle of bourbon.]

CHARLEY: Hey, you're going to miss that train. [He waves the bottle.]

BERNARD: Yeah, I'm going. [*He takes the bottle.*] Thanks, Pop. [*He picks up his rackets and bag.*] Good-bye, Willy, and don't worry about it. You know, "If at first you don't succeed . . ."

WILLY: Yes, I believe in that.

BERNARD: But sometimes, Willy, it's better for a man just to walk away.

WILLY: Walk away?

BERNARD: That's right.

WILLY: But if you can't walk away?

BERNARD [*after a slight pause*]: I guess that's when it's tough. [*Extending his hand*] Good-bye, Willy.

WILLY [*shaking BERNARD's hand*]: Good-bye, boy.

CHARLEY [*an arm on BERNARD's shoulder*]: How do you like this kid? Gonna argue a case in front of the Supreme Court.

BERNARD [*protesting*]: Pop!

WILLY [*genuinely shocked, pained, and happy*]: No! The Supreme Court!

BERNARD: I gotta run. 'Bye, Dad!

CHARLEY: Knock 'em dead, Bernard!

[*BERNARD goes off.*]

WILLY [*as CHARLEY takes out his wallet*]: The Supreme Court! And he didn't even mention it!

CHARLEY [*counting out money on the desk*]: He don't have to—he's gonna do it.

WILLY: And you never told him what to do, did you? You never took any interest in him.

CHARLEY: My salvation is that I never took any interest in anything. There's some money—fifty dollars. I got an accountant inside.

WILLY: Charley, look . . . [*With difficulty*] I got my insurance to pay. If you can manage it—I need a hundred and ten dollars.

[*CHARLEY doesn't reply for a moment; merely stops moving.*]

WILLY: I'd draw it from my bank but Linda would know, and I . . .

CHARLEY: Sit down, Willy.

WILLY [*moving toward the chair*]: I'm keeping an account of everything, remember. I'll pay every penny back. [*He sits.*]

CHARLEY: Now listen to me, Willy.

WILLY: I want you to know I appreciate . . .

CHARLEY [*sitting down on the table*]: Willy, what're you doin'? What the hell is goin' on in your head?

WILLY: Why? I'm simply . . .

CHARLEY: I offered you a job. You can make fifty dollars a week. And I won't send you on the road.

WILLY: I've got a job.

CHARLEY: Without pay? What kind of a job is a job without pay? [*He rises.*] Now, look, kid, enough is enough. I'm no genius but I know when I'm being insulted.

WILLY: Insulted!

CHARLEY: Why don't you want to work for me?

WILLY: What's the matter with you? I've got a job.

CHARLEY: Then what're you walkin' in here every week for?

WILLY [*getting up*]: Well, if you don't want me to walk in here—

CHARLEY: I am offering you a job.

WILLY: I don't want your goddam job!

CHARLEY: When the hell are you going to grow up?

WILLY [*furiously*]: You big ignoramus, if you say that to me again I'll rap you one! I don't care how big you are! [*He's ready to fight.*]

[*Pause.*]

CHARLEY [*kindly, going to him*]: How much do you need, Willy?

WILLY: Charley, I'm strapped, I'm strapped. I don't know what to do. I was just fired.

CHARLEY: Howard fired you?

WILLY: That snotnose. Imagine that? I named him. I named him Howard.

CHARLEY: Willy, when're you gonna realize that them things don't mean anything? You named him Howard, but you can't sell that. The only thing you got in this world is what you can sell. And the funny thing is that you're a salesman, and you don't know that.

WILLY: I've always tried to think otherwise, I guess. I always felt that if a man was impressive, and well liked, that nothing—

CHARLEY: Why must everybody like you? Who liked J. P. Morgan? Was he impressive? In a Turkish bath he'd look like a butcher. But with his pockets on he was very well liked. Now listen, Willy, I know you don't like me, and nobody can say I'm in love with you, but I'll give you a job because—just for the hell of it, put it that way. Now what do you say?

WILLY: I—I just can't work for you, Charley.

CHARLEY: What're you, jealous of me?

WILLY: I can't work for you, that's all, don't ask me why.

CHARLEY [*angered, takes out more bills*]: You been jealous of me all your life, you damned fool! Here, pay your insurance. [*He puts the money in* WILLY'S *hand.*]

WILLY: I'm keeping strict accounts.

CHARLEY: I've got some work to do. Take care of yourself. And pay your insurance.

WILLY [*moving to the right*]: Funny, y'know? After all the highways, and the trains, and the appointments, and the years, you end up worth more dead than alive.

CHARLEY: Willy, nobody's worth nothin' dead. [*After a slight pause*] Did you hear what I said?

[WILLY *stands still, dreaming.*]

CHARLEY: Willy!

WILLY: Apologize to Bernard for me when you see him. I didn't mean to argue with him. He's a fine boy. They're all fine boys, and they'll end up big—all of them. Someday they'll all play tennis together. Wish me luck, Charley. He saw Bill Oliver today.

CHARLEY: Good luck.

WILLY [*on the verge of tears*]: Charley, you're the only friend I got. Isn't that a remarkable thing? [*He goes out.*]

CHARLEY: Jesus!

[CHARLEY *stares after him a moment and follows. All light blacks out. Suddenly raucous music is heard, and a red glow rises behind the screen at right.* STANLEY, *a young waiter, appears, carrying a table, followed by* HAPPY, *who is carrying two chairs.*]

STANLEY [*putting the table down*]: That's all right, Mr. Loman, I can handle it myself. [*He turns and takes the chairs from* HAPPY *and places them at the table.*]

HAPPY [*glancing around*]: Oh, this is better.

STANLEY: Sure, in the front there you're in the middle of all kinds a noise. Whenever you got a party, Mr. Loman, you just tell me and I'll put you back here. Y'know, there's a lotta people they don't like it private, because when they go out they like to see a lotta action around them because they're sick and tired to stay in the house by theirself. But I know you, you ain't from Hackensack. You know what I mean?

HAPPY [*sitting down*]: So how's it coming, Stanley?

STANLEY: Ah, it's a dog's life. I only wish during the war they'd a took me in the Army. I coulda been dead by now.

HAPPY: My brother's back, Stanley.

STANLEY: Oh, he come back, heh? From the Far West.

HAPPY: Yeah, big cattle man, my brother, so treat him right. And my father's coming too.

STANLEY: Oh, your father too!

HAPPY: You got a couple of nice lobsters?

STANLEY: Hundred percent, big.

HAPPY: I want them with the claws.

STANLEY: Don't worry, I don't give you no mice. [HAPPY *laughs.*] How about some wine? It'll put a head on the meal.

HAPPY: No. You remember, Stanley, that recipe I brought you from overseas? With the champagne in it?

STANLEY: Oh, yeah, sure. I still got it tacked up yet in the kitchen. But that'll have to cost a buck apiece anyways.

HAPPY: That's all right.

STANLEY: What'd you, hit a number or somethin'?

HAPPY: No, it's a little celebration. My brother is—I think he pulled off a big deal today. I think we're going into business together.

STANLEY: Great! That's the best for you. Because a family business, you know what I mean?—that's the best.

HAPPY: That's what I think.

STANLEY: 'Cause what's the difference? Somebody steals? It's in the family. Know what I mean? [*Sotto voce*] Like this bartender here. The boss is goin' crazy what kinda leak he's got in the cash register. You put it in but it don't come out.

HAPPY [*raising his head*]: Sh!

STANLEY: What?

HAPPY: You notice I wasn't lookin' right or left, was I?

STANLEY: No.

HAPPY: And my eyes are closed.

STANLEY: So what's the—?

HAPPY: Strudel's comin'.

STANLEY [*catching on, looks around*]: Ah, no, there's no—

> [*He breaks off as a furred, lavishly dressed girl enters and sits at the next table. Both follow her with their eyes.*]

STANLEY: Geez, how'd ya know?

HAPPY: I got radar or something. [*Staring directly at her profile*] Oooooooo . . . Stanley.

STANLEY: I think that's for you, Mr. Loman.

HAPPY: Look at that mouth. Oh, God. And the binoculars.

STANLEY: Geez, you got a life, Mr. Loman.

HAPPY: Wait on her.

STANLEY [*going to the girl's table*]: Would you like a menu, ma'am?

GIRL: I'm expecting someone, but I'd like a—

HAPPY: Why don't you bring her—excuse me, miss, do you mind? I sell champagne, and I'd like you to try my brand. Bring her a champagne, Stanley.

GIRL: That's awfully nice of you.

HAPPY: Don't mention it. It's all company money. [*He laughs.*]

GIRL: That's a charming product to be selling, isn't it?

HAPPY: Oh, gets to be like everything else. Selling is selling, y'know.

GIRL: I suppose.

HAPPY: You don't happen to sell, do you?

GIRL: No, I don't sell.

HAPPY: Would you object to a compliment from a stranger? You ought to be on a magazine cover.

GIRL [*looking at him a little archly*]: I have been.

> [STANLEY *comes in with a glass of champagne.*]

HAPPY: What'd I say before, Stanley? You see? She's a cover girl.

STANLEY: Oh, I could see, I could see.

HAPPY [*to the* GIRL]: What magazine?

GIRL: Oh, a lot of them. [*She takes the drink.*] Thank you.

HAPPY: You know what they say in France, don't you? "Champagne is the drink of the complexion"—Hya, Biff!

> [BIFF *has entered and sits with* HAPPY.]

BIFF: Hello, kid. Sorry I'm late.

HAPPY: I just got here. Uh, Miss—?

GIRL: Forsythe.

HAPPY: Miss Forsythe, this is my brother.

BIFF: Is Dad here?

HAPPY: His name is Biff. You might've heard of him. Great football player.

GIRL: Really? What team?

HAPPY: Are you familiar with football?

GIRL: No, I'm afraid I'm not.

HAPPY: Biff is quarterback with the New York Giants.

GIRL: Well, that is nice, isn't it? [*She drinks.*]

HAPPY: Good health.

GIRL: I'm happy to meet you.

HAPPY: That's my name. Hap. It's really Harold, but at West Point they called me Happy.

GIRL [*now really impressed*]: Oh, I see. How do you do? [*She turns her profile.*]

BIFF: Isn't Dad coming?

HAPPY: You want her?

BIFF: Oh, I could never make that.

HAPPY: I remember the time that idea would never come into your head. Where's the old confidence, Biff?

BIFF: I just saw Oliver—

HAPPY: Wait a minute. I've got to see that old confidence again. Do you want her? She's on call.

BIFF: Oh, no. [*He turns to look at the* GIRL.]

HAPPY: I'm telling you. Watch this. [*Turning to the* GIRL] Honey? [*She turns to him.*] Are you busy?

GIRL: Well, I am . . . but I could make a phone call.

HAPPY: Do that, will you, honey? And see if you can get a friend. We'll be here for a while. Biff is one of the greatest football players in the country.

GIRL [*standing up*]: Well, I'm certainly happy to meet you.

HAPPY: Come back soon.

GIRL: I'll try.

HAPPY: Don't try, honey, try hard.

[*The* GIRL *exits.* STANLEY *follows, shaking his head in bewildered admiration.*]

HAPPY: Isn't that a shame now? A beautiful girl like that? That's why I can't get married. There's not a good woman in a thousand. New York is loaded with them, kid!

BIFF: Hap, look—

HAPPY: I told you she was on call!

BIFF [*strangely unnerved*]: Cut it out, will ya? I want to say something to you.

HAPPY: Did you see Oliver?

BIFF: I saw him all right. Now look, I want to tell Dad a couple of things and I want you to help me.

HAPPY: What? Is he going to back you?

BIFF: Are you crazy? You're out of your goddam head, you know that?

HAPPY: Why? What happened?

BIFF [*breathlessly*]: I did a terrible thing today, Hap. It's been the strangest day I ever went through. I'm all numb, I swear.

HAPPY: You mean he wouldn't see you?

BIFF: Well, I waited six hours for him, see? All day. Kept sending my name in. Even tried to date his secretary so she'd get me to him, but no soap.

HAPPY: Because you're not showin' the old confidence, Biff. He remembered you, didn't he?

BIFF [*stopping* HAPPY *with a gesture*]: Finally, about five o'clock, he comes out. Didn't remember who I was or anything. I felt like such an idiot, Hap.

HAPPY: Did you tell him my Florida idea?

BIFF: He walked away. I saw him for one minute. I got so mad I could've torn the walls down! How the hell did I ever get the idea I was a salesman there? I even believed myself that I'd been a salesman for him! And then he gave me one look and—I realized what a ridiculous lie my whole life has been. We've been talking in a dream for fifteen years. I was a shipping clerk.

HAPPY: What'd you do?

BIFF [*with great tension and wonder*]: Well, he left, see. And the secretary went out. I was all alone in the waiting-room. I don't know what came over me, Hap. The next thing I know I'm in his office—paneled walls, everything. I can't explain it. I—Hap, I took his fountain pen.

HAPPY: Geez, did he catch you?

BIFF: I ran out. I ran down all eleven flights. I ran and ran and ran.

HAPPY: That was an awful dumb—what'd you do that for?

BIFF [*agonized*]: I don't know, I just—wanted to take something, I don't know. You gotta help me, Hap, I'm gonna tell Pop.

HAPPY: You crazy? What for?

BIFF: Hap, he's got to understand that I'm not the man somebody lends that kind of money to. He thinks I've been spiting him all these years and it's eating him up.

HAPPY: That's just it. You tell him something nice.

BIFF: I can't.

HAPPY: Say you got a lunch date with Oliver tomorrow.

BIFF: So what do I do tomorrow?

HAPPY: You leave the house tomorrow and come back at night and say Oliver is thinking it over. And he thinks it over for a couple of weeks, and gradually it fades away and nobody's the worse.

BIFF: But it'll go on for ever!

HAPPY: Dad is never so happy as when he's looking forward to something!

[WILLY *enters.*]

HAPPY: Hello, scout!

WILLY: Gee, I haven't been here in years!

[STANLEY *has followed* WILLY *in and sets a chair for him.* Stanley *starts off but* HAPPY *stops him.*]

HAPPY: Stanley!

[STANLEY *stands by, waiting for an order.*]

BIFF [*going to* WILLY *with guilt, as to an invalid*]: Sit down, Pop. You want a drink?

WILLY: Sure, I don't mind.

BIFF: Let's get a load on.

WILLY: You look worried.

BIFF: N-no. [*To* STANLEY] Scotch all around. Make it doubles.

STANLEY: Doubles, right. [*He goes.*]

WILLY: You had a couple already, didn't you?

BIFF: Just a couple, yeah.

WILLY: Well, what happened, boy? [*Nodding affirmatively, with a smile*] Everything go all right?

BIFF [*takes a breath, then reaches out and grasps* WILLY'S *hand*]: Pal . . . [*He is smiling bravely, and* WILLY *is smiling too.*] I had an experience today.

HAPPY: Terrific, Pop.

WILLY: That so? What happened?

BIFF [*high, slightly alcoholic, above the earth*]: I'm going to tell you everything from first to last. It's been a strange day. [*Silence. He looks around, composes himself as best he can, but his breath keeps breaking the rhythm of his voice.*] I had to wait quite a while for him, and—

WILLY: Oliver?

BIFF: Yeah, Oliver. All day, as a matter of cold fact. And a lot of—instances—facts, Pop, facts about my life came back to me. Who was it, Pop? Who ever said I was a salesman with Oliver?

WILLY: Well, you were.

BIFF: No, Dad, I was a shipping clerk.

WILLY: But you were practically—

BIFF [*with determination*]: Dad, I don't know who said it first, but I was never a salesman for Bill Oliver.

WILLY: What're you talking about?

BIFF: Let's hold on to the facts tonight, Pop. We're not going to get anywhere bullin' around. I was a shipping clerk.

WILLY [*angrily*]: All right, now listen to me—

BIFF: Why don't you let me finish?

WILLY: I'm not interested in stories about the past or any crap of that kind because the woods are burning, boys, you understand? There's a big blaze going on all around. I was fired today.

BIFF [*shocked*]: How could you be?

WILLY: I was fired, and I'm looking for a little good news to tell your mother, because the woman has waited and the woman has suffered. The gist of it is that I haven't got a story left in my head, Biff. So don't give me a lecture about facts and aspects. I am not interested. Now what've you got to say to me?

[STANLEY *enters with three drinks. They wait until he leaves.*]

WILLY: Did you see Oliver?

BIFF: Jesus, Dad!

WILLY: You mean you didn't go up there?

HAPPY: Sure he went up there.

BIFF: I did. I—saw him. How could they fire you?

WILLY [*on the edge of his chair*]: What kind of a welcome did he give you?

BIFF: He won't even let you work on commission?

WILLY: I'm out! [*Driving*] So tell me, he gave you a warm welcome?

HAPPY: Sure, Pop, sure!

BIFF [*driven*]: Well, it was kind of—

WILLY: I was wondering if he'd remember you. [*To* HAPPY] Imagine, man doesn't see him for ten, twelve years and gives him that kind of a welcome!

HAPPY: Damn right!

BIFF [*trying to return to the offensive*]: Pop, look—

WILLY: You know why he remembered you, don't you? Because you impressed him in those days.

BIFF: Let's talk quietly and get this down to the facts, huh?

WILLY [*as though* BIFF *had been interrupting*]: Well, what happened? It's great news, Biff. Did he take you into his office or'd you talk in the waiting-room?
BIFF: Well, he came in, see, and—
WILLY [*with a big smile*]: What'd he say? Betcha he threw his arm around you.
BIFF: Well, he kinda—
WILLY: He's a fine man. [*To* HAPPY] Very hard man to see, y'know.
HAPPY [*agreeing*]: Oh, I know.
WILLY [*to* BIFF]: Is that where you had the drinks?
BIFF: Yeah, he gave me a couple of—no, no!
HAPPY [*cutting in*]: He told him my Florida idea.
WILLY: Don't interrupt. [*To* BIFF] How'd he react to the Florida idea?
BIFF: Dad, will you give me a minute to explain?
WILLY: I've been waiting for you to explain since I sat down here! What happened? He took you into his office and what?
BIFF: Well—I talked. And—and he listened, see.
WILLY: Famous for the way he listens, y'know. What was his answer?
BIFF: His answer was—[*He breaks off, suddenly angry.*] Dad, you're not letting me tell you what I want to tell you!
WILLY [*accusing, angered*]: You didn't see him, did you?
BIFF: I did see him!
WILLY: What'd you insult him or something? You insulted him, didn't you?
BIFF: Listen, will you let me out of it, will you just let me out of it!
HAPPY: What the hell!
WILLY: Tell me what happened!
BIFF [*to* HAPPY]: I can't talk to him!

[*A single trumpet note jars the ear. The light of green leaves stains the house, which holds the air of night and a dream.* YOUNG BERNARD *enters and knocks on the door of the house.*]

YOUNG BERNARD [*frantically*]: Mrs. Loman, Mrs. Loman!
HAPPY: Tell him what happened!
BIFF [*to* HAPPY]: Shut up and leave me alone!
WILLY: No, no! You had to go and flunk math!
BIFF: What math? What're you talking about?
YOUNG BERNARD: Mrs. Loman, Mrs. Loman!

[LINDA *appears in the house, as of old.*]

WILLY [*wildly*]: Math, math, math!
BIFF: Take it easy, Pop!
YOUNG BERNARD: Mrs. Loman!
WILLY [*furiously*]: If you hadn't flunked you'd've been set by now!
BIFF: Now, look, I'm gonna tell you what happened, and you're going to listen to me.
YOUNG BERNARD: Mrs. Loman!
BIFF: I waited six hours—
HAPPY: What the hell are you saying?
BIFF: I kept sending in my name but he wouldn't see me. So finally he . . . [*He continues unheard as light fades low on the restaurant.*]

YOUNG BERNARD: Biff flunked math!

LINDA: No!

YOUNG BERNARD: Birnbaum flunked him! They won't graduate him!

LINDA: But they have to. He's gotta go to the university. Where is he? Biff! Biff!

YOUNG BERNARD: No, he left. He went to Grand Central.

LINDA: Grand—You mean he went to Boston!

YOUNG BERNARD: Is Uncle Willy in Boston?

LINDA: Oh, maybe Willy can talk to the teacher. Oh, the poor, poor boy!

[*Light on house area snaps out.*]

BIFF [*at the table, now audible, holding up a gold fountain pen*]: . . . so I'm washed up with Oliver, you understand? Are you listening to me?

WILLY [*at a loss*]: Yeah, sure. If you hadn't flunked—

BIFF: Flunked what? What're you talking about?

WILLY: Don't blame everything on me! I didn't flunk math—you did! What pen?

HAPPY: That was awful dumb, Biff, a pen like that is worth—

WILLY [*seeing the pen for the first time*]: You took Oliver's pen?

BIFF [*weakening*]: Dad, I just explained it to you.

WILLY: You stole Bill Oliver's fountain pen!

BIFF: I didn't exactly steal it! That's just what I've been explaining to you!

HAPPY: He had it in his hand and just then Oliver walked in, so he got nervous and stuck it in his pocket!

WILLY: My God, Biff!

BIFF: I never intended to do it, Dad!

OPERATOR'S VOICE: Standish Arms, good evening!

WILLY [*shouting*]: I'm not in my room!

BIFF [*frightened*]: Dad, what's the matter? [*He and* HAPPY *stand up.*]

OPERATOR: Ringing Mr. Loman for you!

WILLY: I'm not there, stop it!

BIFF [*horrified, gets down on one knee before* WILLY]: Dad, I'll make good, I'll make good. [WILLY *tries to get to his feet.* BIFF *holds him down.*] Sit down now.

WILLY: No, you're no good, you're no good for anything.

BIFF: I am, Dad, I'll find something else, you understand? Now don't worry about anything. [*He holds up* WILLY'S *face.*] Talk to me, Dad.

OPERATOR: Mr. Loman does not answer. Shall I page him?

WILLY [*attempting to stand, as though to rush and silence the* OPERATOR]: No, no, no!

HAPPY: He'll strike something, Pop.

WILLY: No, no . . .

BIFF [*desperately, standing over* WILLY]: Pop, listen! Listen to me! I'm telling you something good. Oliver talked to his partner about the Florida idea. You listening? He—he talked to his partner, and he came to me . . . I'm going to be all right, you hear? Dad, listen to me, he said it was just a question of the amount!

WILLY: Then you . . . got it?

HAPPY: He's gonna be terrific, Pop!

WILLY [*trying to stand*]: Then you got it, haven't you? You got it! You got it!

BIFF [*agonized, holds* WILLY *down*]: No, no. Look, Pop. I'm supposed to have lunch with them tomorrow. I'm just telling you this so you'll know that I can still

make an impression, Pop. And I'll make good somewhere, but I can't go tomorrow, see?

WILLY: Why not? You simply—

BIFF: But the pen, Pop!

WILLY: You give it to him and tell him it was an oversight!

HAPPY: Sure, have lunch tomorrow!

BIFF: I can't say that—

WILLY: You were doing a crossword puzzle and accidentally used his pen!

BIFF: Listen, kid, I took those balls years ago, now I walk in with his fountain
pen? That clinches it, don't you see? I can't face him like that! I'll try elsewhere.

PAGE'S VOICE: Paging Mr. Loman!

WILLY: Don't you want to be anything?

BIFF: Pop, how can I go back?

WILLY: You don't want to be anything, is that what's behind it?

BIFF [now angry at WILLY for not crediting his sympathy]: Don't take it that way! You
think it was easy walking into that office after what I'd done to him? A team
of horses couldn't have dragged me back to Bill Oliver!

WILLY: Then why'd you go?

BIFF: Why did I go? Why did I go! Look at you! Look at what's become of you!

[Off left, THE WOMAN laughs.]

WILLY: Biff, you're going to go to that lunch tomorrow, or—

BIFF: I can't go. I've got no appointment!

HAPPY: Biff, for . . . !

WILLY: Are you spiting me?

BIFF: Don't take it that way! Goddammit!

WILLY [strikes BIFF and falters away from the table]: You rotten little louse! Are you
spiting me?

THE WOMAN: Someone's at the door, Willy!

BIFF: I'm no good, can't you see what I am?

HAPPY [separating them]: Hey, you're in a restaurant! Now cut it out, both of you!
[The girls enter.] Hello, girls, sit down.

[THE WOMAN laughs, off left.]

MISS FORSYTHE: I guess we might as well. This is Letta.

THE WOMAN: Willy, are you going to wake up?

BIFF [ignoring WILLY]: How're ya, miss, sit down. What do you drink?

MISS FORSYTHE: Letta might not be able to stay long.

LETTA: I gotta get up very early tomorrow. I got jury duty. I'm so excited! Were
you fellows ever on a jury?

BIFF: No, but I been in front of them! [The girls laugh.] This is my father.

LETTA: Isn't he cute? Sit down with us, Pop.

HAPPY: Sit him down, Biff!

BIFF [going to him]: Come on, slugger, drink us under the table. To hell with it!
Come on, sit down, pal.

[On BIFF's last insistence, WILLY is about to sit.]

THE WOMAN [*now urgently*]: Willy, are you going to answer the door!

[THE WOMAN'S *call pulls* WILLY *back. He starts right, befuddled.*]

BIFF: Hey, where are you going?

WILLY: Open the door.

BIFF: The door?

WILLY: The washroom . . . the door . . . where's the door?

BIFF [*leading* WILLY *to the left*]: Just go straight down.

[WILLY *moves left.*]

THE WOMAN: Willy, Willy, are you going to get up, get up, get up, get up?

[WILLY *exits left.*]

LETTA: I think it's sweet you bring your daddy along.

MISS FORSYTHE: Oh, he isn't really your father!

BIFF [*at left, turning to her resentfully*]: Miss Forsythe, you've just seen a prince walk by. A fine, troubled prince. A hardworking, unappreciated prince. A pal, you understand? A good companion. Always for his boys.

LETTA: That's so sweet.

HAPPY: Well, girls, what's the program? We're wasting time. Come on, Biff. Gather round. Where would you like to go?

BIFF: Why don't you do something for him?

HAPPY: Me!

BIFF: Don't you give a damn for him, Hap?

HAPPY: What're you talking about? I'm the one who—

BIFF: I sense it, you don't give a good goddam about him. [*He takes the rolled-up hose from his pocket and puts it on the table in front of* HAPPY.] Look what I found in the cellar, for Christ's sake. How can you bear to let it go on?

HAPPY: Me? Who goes away? Who runs off and—

BIFF: Yeah, but he doesn't mean anything to you. You could help him—I can't. Don't you understand what I'm talking about? He's going to kill himself, don't you know that?

HAPPY: Don't I know it! Me!

BIFF: Hap, help him! Jesus . . . help him . . . Help me, help me, I can't bear to look at his face! [*Ready to weep, he hurries out, up right.*]

HAPPY [*starting after him*]: Where are you going?

MISS FORSYTHE: What's he so mad about?

HAPPY: Come on, girls, we'll catch up with him.

MISS FORSYTHE [*as* HAPPY *pushes her out*]: Say, I don't like that temper of his!

HAPPY: He's just a little overstrung, he'll be all right!

WILLY [*off left, as* THE WOMAN *laughs*]: Don't answer! Don't answer!

LETTA: Don't you want to tell your father—

HAPPY: No, that's not my father. He's just a guy. Come on, we'll catch Biff, and, honey, we're going to paint this town! Stanley, where's the check! Hey, Stanley!

[*They exit.* STANLEY *looks toward left.*]

STANLEY [*calling to* HAPPY *indignantly*]: Mr. Loman! Mr. Loman!

[STANLEY *picks up a chair and follows them off. Knocking is heard off left.* THE WOMAN *enters, laughing.* WILLY *follows her. She is in a black slip; he is buttoning his shirt. Raw, sensuous music accompanies their speech.*]

WILLY: Will you stop laughing? Will you stop?

THE WOMAN: Aren't you going to answer the door? He'll wake the whole hotel.

WILLY: I'm not expecting anybody.

THE WOMAN: Whyn't you have another drink, honey, and stop being so damn self-centered?

WILLY: I'm so lonely.

THE WOMAN: You know you ruined me, Willy? From now on, whenever you come to the office, I'll see that you go right through to the buyers. No waiting at my desk any more, Willy. You ruined me.

WILLY: That's nice of you to say that.

THE WOMAN: Gee, you are self-centered! Why so sad? You are the saddest, self-centeredest soul I ever did see-saw. [*She laughs. He kisses her.*] Come on inside, drummer boy. It's silly to be dressing in the middle of the night. [*As knocking is heard*] Aren't you going to answer the door?

WILLY: They're knocking on the wrong door.

THE WOMAN: But I felt the knocking. And he heard us talking in here. Maybe the hotel's on fire!

WILLY [*his terror rising*]: It's a mistake.

THE WOMAN: Then tell him to go away!

WILLY: There's nobody there.

THE WOMAN: It's getting on my nerves, Willy. There's somebody standing out there and it's getting on my nerves!

WILLY [*pushing her away from him*]: All right, stay in the bathroom here, and don't come out. I think there's a law in Massachusetts about it, so don't come out. It may be that new room clerk. He looked very mean. So don't come out. It's a mistake, there's no fire.

[*The knocking is heard again. He takes a few steps away from her, and she vanishes into the wing. The light follows him, and now he is facing* YOUNG BIFF, *who carries a suitcase.* BIFF *steps toward him. The music is gone.*]

BIFF: Why didn't you answer?

WILLY: Biff! What are you doing in Boston?

BIFF: Why didn't you answer? I've been knocking for five minutes, I called you on the phone—

WILLY: I just heard you. I was in the bathroom and had the door shut. Did anything happen home?

BIFF: Dad—I let you down.

WILLY: What do you mean?

BIFF: Dad . . .

WILLY: Biffo, what's this about? [*Putting his arm around* BIFF] Come on, let's go downstairs and get you a malted.

BIFF: Dad, I flunked math.

WILLY: Not for the term?

BIFF: The term. I haven't got enough credits to graduate.

WILLY: You mean to say Bernard wouldn't give you the answers?

BIFF: He did, he tried, but I only got a sixty-one.

WILLY: And they wouldn't give you four points?

BIFF: Birnbaum refused absolutely. I begged him, Pop, but he won't give me
those points. You gotta talk to him before they close the school. Because if he
saw the kind of man you are, and you just talked to him in your way, I'm sure
he'd come through for me. The class came right before practice, see, and I
didn't go enough. Would you talk to him? He'd like you, Pop. You know the
way you could talk.

WILLY: You're on. We'll drive right back.

BIFF: Oh, Dad, good work! I'm sure he'll change it for you!

WILLY: Go downstairs and tell the clerk I'm checkin' out. Go right down.

BIFF: Yes, sir! See, the reason he hates me, Pop—one day he was late for class so
I got up at the blackboard and imitated him. I crossed my eyes and talked
with a lithp.

WILLY [*laughing*]: You did? The kids like it?

BIFF: They nearly died laughing!

WILLY: Yeah? What'd you do?

BIFF: The thquare root of thixthy twee is . . . [WILLY *bursts out laughing;* BIFF *joins
him.*] And in the middle of it he walked in!

  [WILLY *laughs and* THE WOMAN *joins in offstage.*]

WILLY [*without hesitation*]: Hurry downstairs and—

BIFF: Somebody in there?

WILLY: No, that was next door.

  [THE WOMAN *laughs offstage.*]

BIFF: Somebody got in your bathroom!

WILLY: No, it's the next room, there's a party—

THE WOMAN [*enters, laughing. She lisps this*]: Can I come in? There's something in
the bathtub, Willy, and it's moving!

  [WILLY *looks at* BIFF, *who is staring open-mouthed and horrified at* THE
  WOMAN.]

WILLY: Ah—you better go back to your room. They must be finished painting by
now. They're painting her room so I let her take a shower here. Go back, go
back . . . [*He pushes her.*]

THE WOMAN [*resisting*]: But I've got to get dressed, Willy, I can't—

WILLY: Get out of here! Go back, go back . . . [*Suddenly striving for the ordinary*]
This is Miss Francis, Biff, she's a buyer. They're painting her room. Go back,
Miss Francis, go back . . .

THE WOMAN: But my clothes, I can't go out naked in the hall!

WILLY [*pushing her offstage*]: Get outa here! Go back, go back!

  [BIFF *slowly sits down on his suitcase as the argument continues offstage.*]

THE WOMAN: Where's my stockings? You promised me stockings, Willy!

WILLY: I have no stockings here!

THE WOMAN: You had two boxes of size nine sheers for me, and I want them!

WILLY: Here, for God's sake, will you get outa here!

THE WOMAN [*enters holding a box of stockings*]: I just hope there's nobody in the hall. That's all I hope. [*To* BIFF] Are you football or baseball?

BIFF: Football.

THE WOMAN [*angry, humiliated*]: That's me too. G'night. [*She snatches her clothes from* WILLY, *and walks out.*]

WILLY [*after a pause*]: Well, better get going. I want to get to the school first thing in the morning. Get my suits out of the closet. I'll get my valise. [BIFF *doesn't move.*] What's the matter? [BIFF *remains motionless, tears falling.*] She's a buyer. Buys for J. H. Simmons. She lives down the hall—they're painting. You don't imagine—[*He breaks off. After a pause*] Now listen, pal, she's just a buyer. She sees merchandise in her room and they have to keep it looking just so . . . . [*Pause. Assuming command*] All right, get my suits. [BIFF *doesn't move.*] Now stop crying and do as I say. I gave you an order. Biff, I gave you an order! Is that what you do when I give you an order? How dare you cry? [*Putting his arm around* BIFF] Now look, Biff, when you grow up you'll understand about these things. You mustn't—you mustn't overemphasize a thing like this. I'll see Birnbaum first thing in the morning.

BIFF: Never mind.

WILLY [*getting down beside* BIFF]: Never mind! He's going to give you those points. I'll see to it.

BIFF: He wouldn't listen to you.

WILLY: He certainly will listen to me. You need those points for the U. of Virginia.

BIFF: I'm not going there.

WILLY: Heh? If I can't get him to change that mark you'll make it up in summer school. You've got all summer to—

BIFF [*his weeping breaking from him*]: Dad . . .

WILLY [*infected by it*]: Oh, my boy . . .

BIFF: Dad . . .

WILLY: She's nothing to me, Biff. I was lonely, I was terribly lonely.

BIFF: You—you gave her Mama's stockings! [*His tears break through and he rises to go.*]

WILLY [*grabbing for* BIFF]: I gave you an order!

BIFF: Don't touch me, you—liar!

WILLY: Apologize for that!

BIFF: You fake! You phony little fake! You fake! [*Overcome, he turns quickly and weeping fully goes out with his suitcase.* WILLY *is left on the floor on his knees.*]

WILLY: I gave you an order! Biff, come back here or I'll beat you! Come back here! I'll whip you!

[STANLEY *comes quickly in from the right and stands in front of* WILLY.]

WILLY [*shouts at* STANLEY]: I gave you an order . . .

STANLEY: Hey, let's pick it up, pick it up, Mr. Loman. [*He helps* WILLY *to his feet.*] Your boys left with the chippies. They said they'll see you home.

[*A second waiter watches some distance away.*]

WILLY: But we were supposed to have dinner together.

[*Music is heard,* WILLY'S *theme.*]

STANLEY: Can you make it?

WILLY: I'll—sure, I can make it. [*Suddenly concerned about his clothes.*] Do I—I look all right?

STANLEY: Sure, you look all right. [*He flicks a speck off* WILLY'S *lapel.*]

WILLY: Here—here's a dollar.

STANLEY: Oh, your son paid me. It's all right.

WILLY [*putting it in* STANLEY'S *hand*]: No, take it. You're a good boy.

STANLEY: Oh, no, you don't have to . . .

WILLY: Here—here's some more. I don't need it any more. [*After a slight pause*] Tell me—is there a seed store in the neighborhood?

STANLEY: Seeds? You mean like to plant?

[*As* WILLY *turns,* STANLEY *slips the money back into his jacket pocket.*]

WILLY: Yes. Carrots, peas . . .

STANLEY: Well, there's hardware stores on Sixth Avenue, but it may be too late now.

WILLY [*anxiously*]: Oh, I'd better hurry. I've got to get some seeds. [*He starts off to the right.*] I've got to get some seeds, right away. Nothing's planted. I don't have a thing in the ground.

[WILLY *hurries out as the light goes down.* STANLEY *moves over to the right after him, watches him off. The other waiter has been staring at* WILLY.]

STANLEY [*to the waiter*]: Well, whatta you looking at? [*The waiter picks up the chairs and moves off right.* STANLEY *takes the table and follows him. The light fades on this area. There is a long pause, the sound of the flute coming over. The light gradually rises on the kitchen, which is empty.* HAPPY *appears at the door of the house, followed by* BIFF. HAPPY *is carrying a large bunch of long-stemmed roses. He enters the kitchen, looks around for* LINDA. *Not seeing her, he turns to* BIFF, *who is just outside the house door, and makes a gesture with his hands, indicating "Not here, I guess." He looks into the living-room and freezes. Inside,* LINDA, *unseen, is seated,* WILLY'S *coat on her lap. She rises ominously and quietly and moves toward* HAPPY, *who backs up into the kitchen, afraid.*]

HAPPY: Hey, what're you doing up? [LINDA *says nothing but moves toward him implacably.*] Where's Pop? [*He keeps backing to the right, and now* LINDA *is in full view in the doorway to the living-room.*] Is he sleeping?

LINDA: Where were you?

HAPPY [*trying to laugh it off*]: We met two girls, Mom, very fine types. Here, we brought you some flowers. [*Offering them to her*] Put them in your room, Ma.

[*She knocks them to the floor at* BIFF'S *feet. He has now come inside and closed the door behind him. She stares at* BIFF, *silent.*]

HAPPY: Now what'd you do that for? Mom, I want you to have some flowers—

LINDA [*cutting* HAPPY *off, violently to* BIFF]: Don't you care whether he lives or dies?

HAPPY [*going to the stairs*]: Come upstairs, Biff.

BIFF [*with a flare of disgust, to* HAPPY]: Go away from me! [*To* LINDA] What do you mean, lives or dies? Nobody's dying around here, pal.

LINDA: Get out of my sight! Get out of here!

BIFF: I wanna see the boss.

LINDA: You're not going near him!

BIFF: Where is he? [*He moves into the living-room and* LINDA *follows.*]

LINDA [*shouting after* BIFF]: You invite him to dinner. He looks forward to it all day—[BIFF *appears in his parents' bedroom, looks around, and exits*]—and then you desert him there. There's no stranger you'd do that to!

HAPPY: Why? He had a swell time with us. Listen, when I—[LINDA *comes back into the kitchen*]—desert him I hope I don't outlive the day!

LINDA: Get out of here!

HAPPY: Now look, Mom . . .

LINDA: Did you have to go to women tonight? You and your lousy rotten whores!

[BIFF *reenters the kitchen.*]

HAPPY: Mom, all we did was follow Biff around trying to cheer him up! [*To* BIFF] Boy, what a night you gave me!

LINDA: Get out of here, both of you, and don't come back! I don't want you tormenting him any more. Go on now, get your things together! [*To* BIFF] You can sleep in his apartment. [*She starts to pick up the flowers and stops herself.*] Pick up this stuff, I'm not your maid any more. Pick it up, you bum, you!

[HAPPY *turns his back to her in refusal.* BIFF *slowly moves over and gets down on his knees, picking up the flowers.*]

LINDA: You're a pair of animals! Not one, not another living soul would have had the cruelty to walk out on that man in a restaurant!

BIFF [*not looking at her*]: Is that what he said?

LINDA: He didn't have to say anything. He was so humiliated he nearly limped when he came in.

HAPPY: But, Mom, he had a great time with us—

BIFF [*cutting him off violently*]: Shut up!

[*Without another word,* HAPPY *goes upstairs.*]

LINDA: You! You didn't even go in to see if he was all right!

BIFF [*still on the floor in front of* LINDA, *the flowers in his hand; with self-loathing*]: No. Didn't. Didn't do a damned thing. How do you like that, heh? Left him babbling in a toilet.

LINDA: You louse. You . . .

BIFF: Now you hit it on the nose! [*He gets up, throws the flowers in the wastebasket.*] The scum of the earth, and you're looking at him!

LINDA: Get out of here!

BIFF: I gotta talk to the boss, Mom. Where is he?

LINDA: You're not going near him. Get out of this house!

BIFF [*with absolute assurance, determination*]: No. We're gonna have an abrupt conversation, him and me.

LINDA: You're not talking to him!

[*Hammering is heard from outside the house, off right.* BIFF *turns toward the noise.*]

LINDA [*suddenly pleading*]: Will you please leave him alone?
BIFF: What's he doing out there?
LINDA: He's planting the garden!
BIFF [*quietly*]: Now? Oh, my God!

[BIFF *moves outside*, LINDA *following. The light dies down on them and comes up on the center of the apron as* WILLY *walks into it. He is carrying a flashlight, a hoe, and a handful of seed packets. He raps the top of the hoe sharply to fix it firmly, and then moves to the left, measuring off the distance with his foot. He holds the flashlight to look at the seed packets, reading off the instructions. He is in the blue of night.*]

WILLY: Carrots . . . quarter-inch apart. Rows . . . one-foot rows. [*He measures it off.*] One foot. [*He puts down a package and measures off.*] Beets. [*He puts down another package and measures again.*] Lettuce. [*He reads the package, puts it down.*] One foot—[*He breaks off as* BEN *appears at the right and moves slowly down to him.*] What a proposition, ts, ts. Terrific, terrific. 'Cause she's suffered, Ben, the woman has suffered. You understand me? A man can't go out the way he came in, Ben, a man has got to add up to something. You can't, you can't—[BEN *moves toward him as though to interrupt.*] You gotta consider, now. Don't answer so quick. Remember, it's a guaranteed twenty-thousand-dollar proposition. Now look, Ben, I want you to go through the ins and outs of this thing with me. I've got nobody to talk to, Ben, and the woman has suffered, you hear me?
BEN [*standing still, considering*]: What's the proposition?
WILLY: It's twenty thousand dollars on the barrelhead. Guaranteed, gilt-edged, you understand?
BEN: You don't want to make a fool of yourself. They might not honor the policy.
WILLY: How can they dare refuse? Didn't I work like a coolie to meet every premium on the nose? And now they don't pay off? Impossible!
BEN: It's called a cowardly thing, William.
WILLY: Why? Does it take more guts to stand here the rest of my life ringing up a zero?
BEN [*yielding*]: That's a point, William. [*He moves, thinking, turns.*] And twenty thousand—that *is* something one can feel with the hand, it is there.
WILLY [*now assured, with rising power*]: Oh, Ben, that's the whole beauty of it! I see it like a diamond, shining in the dark, hard and rough, that I can pick up and touch in my hand. Not like—like an appointment! This would not be another damned-fool appointment, Ben, and it changes all the aspects. Because he thinks I'm nothing, see, and so he spites me. But the funeral—[*Straightening up*] Ben, that funeral will be massive! They'll come from Maine, Massachusetts, Vermont, New Hampshire! All the old-timers with the strange license plates—that boy will be thunderstruck, Ben, because he never realized—I am known! Rhode Island, New York, New Jersey—I am

known, Ben, and he'll see it with his eyes once and for all. He'll see what I am, Ben! He's in for a shock, that boy!

BEN [*coming down to the edge of the garden*]: He'll call you a coward.

WILLY [*suddenly fearful*]: No, that would be terrible.

BEN: Yes. And a damned fool.

WILLY: No, no, he mustn't, I won't have that! [*He is broken and desperate.*]

BEN: He'll hate you, William.

[*The gay music of the boys is heard.*]

WILLY: Oh, Ben, how do we get back to all the great times? Used to be so full of light, and comradeship, the sleigh-riding in winter, and the ruddiness on his cheeks. And always some kind of good news coming up, always something nice coming up ahead. And never even let me carry the valises in the house, and simonizing, simonizing that little red car! Why, why can't I give him something and not have him hate me?

BEN: Let me think about it. [*He glances at his watch.*] I still have a little time. Remarkable proposition, but you've got to be sure you're not making a fool of yourself.

[BEN *drifts off upstage and goes out of sight.* BIFF *comes down from the left.*]

WILLY [*suddenly conscious of* BIFF, *turns and looks up at him, then begins picking up the packages of seeds in confusion*]: Where the hell is that seed? [*Indignantly*] You can't see nothing out here! They boxed in the whole goddam neighborhood!

BIFF: There are people all around here. Don't you realize that?

WILLY: I'm busy. Don't bother me.

BIFF [*taking the hoe from* WILLY]: I'm saying good-bye to you, Pop. [WILLY *looks at him, silent, unable to move.*] I'm not coming back any more.

WILLY: You're not going to see Oliver tomorrow?

BIFF: I've got no appointment, Dad.

WILLY: He put his arm around you, and you've got no appointment?

BIFF: Pop, get this now, will you? Everytime I've left it's been a fight that sent me out of here. Today I realized something about myself and I tried to explain it to you and I—I think I'm just not smart enough to make any sense out of it for you. To hell with whose fault it is or anything like that. [*He takes* WILLY'S *arm.*] Let's just wrap it up, heh? Come on in, we'll tell Mom. [*He gently tries to pull* WILLY *to left.*]

WILLY [*frozen, immobile, with guilt in his voice*]: No, I don't want to see her.

BIFF: Come on! [*He pulls again, and* WILLY *tries to pull away.*]

WILLY [*highly nervous*]: No, no, I don't want to see her.

BIFF [*tries to look into* WILLY'S *face, as if to find the answer there*]: Why don't you want to see her?

WILLY [*more harshly now*]: Don't bother me, will you?

BIFF: What do you mean, you don't want to see her? You don't want them calling you yellow, do you? This isn't your fault; it's me, I'm a bum. Now come inside! [WILLY *strains to get away.*] Did you hear what I said to you?

[WILLY *pulls away and quickly goes by himself into the house.* BIFF - follows.*]

LINDA [*to* WILLY]: Did you plant, dear?

BIFF [*at the door, to* LINDA]: All right, we had it out. I'm going and I'm not writing any more.

LINDA [*going to* WILLY *in the kitchen*]: I think that's the best way, dear. 'Cause there's no use drawing it out, you'll just never get along.

[WILLY *doesn't respond*.]

BIFF: People ask where I am and what I'm doing, you don't know, and you don't care. That way it'll be off your mind and you can start brightening up again. All right? That clears it, doesn't it? [WILLY *is silent, and* BIFF *goes to him*.] You gonna wish me luck, scout? [*He extends his hand*] What do you say?

LINDA: Shake his hand, Willy.

WILLY [*turning to her, seething with hurt*]: There's no necessity to mention the pen at all, y'know.

BIFF [*gently*]: I've got no appointment, Dad.

WILLY [*erupting fiercely*]: He put his arm around . . . ?

BIFF: Dad, you're never going to see what I am, so what's the use of arguing? If I strike oil I'll send you a check. Meantime forget I'm alive.

WILLY [*to* LINDA]: Spite, see?

BIFF: Shake hands, Dad.

WILLY: Not my hand.

BIFF: I was hoping not to go this way.

WILLY: Well, this is the way you're going. Good-bye.

[BIFF *looks at him a moment, then turns sharply and goes to the stairs*.]

WILLY [*stops him with*]: May you rot in hell if you leave this house!

BIFF [*turning*]: Exactly what is it that you want from me?

WILLY: I want you to know, on the train, in the mountains, in the valleys, wherever you go, that you cut down your life for spite!

BIFF: No, no.

WILLY: Spite, spite, is the word of your undoing! And when you're down and out, remember what did it. When you're rotting somewhere beside the railroad tracks, remember, and don't you dare blame it on me!

BIFF: I'm not blaming it on you!

WILLY: I won't take the rap for this, you hear?

[HAPPY *comes down the stairs and stands on the bottom step, watching*.]

BIFF: That's just what I'm telling you!

WILLY [*sinking into a chair at the table, with full accusation*]: You're trying to put a knife in me—don't think I don't know what you're doing!

BIFF: All right, phony! Then let's lay it on the line. [*He whips the rubber tube out of his pocket and puts it on the table*.]

HAPPY: You crazy—

LINDA: Biff! [*She moves to grab the hose, but* BIFF *holds it down with his hand*.]

BIFF: Leave it there! Don't move it!

WILLY [*not looking at it*]: What is that?

BIFF: You know goddam well what that is.

WILLY [*caged, wanting to escape*]: I never saw that.

BIFF: You saw it. The mice didn't bring it into the cellar! What is this supposed to do, make a hero out of you? This supposed to make me sorry for you?

WILLY: Never heard of it.

BIFF: There'll be no pity for you, you hear it? No pity!

WILLY [to LINDA]: You hear the spite!

BIFF: No, you're going to hear the truth—what you are and what I am!

LINDA: Stop it!

WILLY: Spite!

HAPPY [coming down toward BIFF]: You cut it now!

BIFF [to HAPPY]: The man don't know who we are! The man is gonna know! [To WILLY] We never told the truth for ten minutes in this house!

HAPPY: We always told the truth!

BIFF [turning on him]: You big blow, are you the assistant buyer? You're one of the two assistants to the assistant, aren't you?

HAPPY: Well, I'm practically—

BIFF: You're practically full of it! We all are! And I'm through with it. [To WILLY] Now hear this, Willy, this is me.

WILLY: I know you!

BIFF: You know why I had no address for three months? I stole a suit in Kansas City and I was in jail. [To LINDA, who is sobbing] Stop crying. I'm through with it.

[LINDA turns away from them, her hands covering her face.]

WILLY: I suppose that's my fault!

BIFF: I stole myself out of every good job since high school!

WILLY: And whose fault is that?

BIFF: And I never got anywhere because you blew me so full of hot air I could never stand taking orders from anybody! That's whose fault it is!

WILLY: I hear that!

LINDA: Don't, Biff!

BIFF: It's goddam time you heard that! I had to be boss big shot in two weeks, and I'm through with it!

WILLY: Then hang yourself! For spite, hang yourself!

BIFF: No! Nobody's hanging himself, Willy! I ran down eleven flights with a pen in my hand today. And suddenly I stopped, you hear me? And in the middle of that office building, do you hear this? I stopped in the middle of that building and I saw—the sky. I saw the things that I love in this world. The work and the food and time to sit and smoke. And I looked at the pen and said to myself, what the hell am I grabbing this for? Why am I trying to become what I don't want to be? What am I doing in an office, making a contemptuous, begging fool of myself, when all I want is out there, waiting for me the minute I say I know who I am! Why can't I say that, Willy? [He tries to make WILLY face him, but WILLY pulls away and moves to the left.]

WILLY [with hatred, threateningly]: The door of your life is wide open!

BIFF: Pop! I'm a dime a dozen, and so are you!

WILLY [turning on him now in an uncontrolled outburst]: I am not a dime a dozen! I am Willy Loman, and you are Biff Loman!

[BIFF starts for WILLY, but is blocked by HAPPY. In his fury, BIFF seems on the verge of attacking his father.]

BIFF: I am not a leader of men, Willy, and neither are you. You were never any-thing but a hard-working drummer who landed in the ash can like all the rest of them! I'm one dollar an hour, Willy! I tried seven states and couldn't raise it. A buck an hour! Do you gather my meaning? I'm not bringing home any prizes any more, and you're going to stop waiting for me to bring them home!

WILLY [*directly to* BIFF]: You vengeful, spiteful mut!

[BIFF *breaks from* HAPPY. WILLY, *in fright, starts up the stairs.* BIFF *grabs him.*]

BIFF [*at the peak of his fury*]: Pop, I'm nothing! I'm nothing, Pop. Can't you under-stand that? There's no spite in it any more. I'm just what I am, that's all.

[BIFF'S *fury has spent itself, and he breaks down, sobbing, holding on to* WILLY, *who dumbly fumbles for* BIFF'S *face.*]

WILLY [*astonished*]: What're you doing? What're you doing? [*To* LINDA] Why is he crying?

BIFF [*crying, broken*]: Will you let me go, for Christ's sake? Will you take that phony dream and burn it before something happens? [*Struggling to contain himself, he pulls away and moves to the stairs.*] I'll go in the morning. Put him—put him to bed. [*Exhausted,* BIFF *moves up the stairs to his room.*]

WILLY [*after a long pause, astonished, elevated*]: Isn't that—isn't that remarkable? Biff—he likes me!

LINDA: He loves you, Willy!

HAPPY [*deeply moved*]: Always did, Pop.

WILLY: Oh, Biff! [*Staring wildly*] He cried! Cried to me. [*He is choking with his love, and now cries out his promise.*] That boy—that boy is going to be magnif-icent!

[BEN *appears in the light just outside the kitchen.*]

BEN: Yes, outstanding, with twenty thousand behind him.

LINDA [*sensing the racing of his mind, fearfully, carefully*]: Now come to bed, Willy. It's all settled now.

WILLY [*finding it difficult not to rush out of the house*]: Yes, we'll sleep. Come on. Go to sleep, Hap.

BEN: And it does take a great kind of a man to crack the jungle.

[*In accents of dread,* BEN'S *idyllic music starts up.*]

HAPPY [*his arm around* LINDA]: I'm getting married, Pop, don't forget it. I'm changing everything. I'm gonna run that department before the year is up. You'll see, Mom. [*He kisses her.*]

BEN: The jungle is dark but full of diamonds, Willy.

[WILLY *turns, moves, listening to* BEN.]

LINDA: Be good. You're both good boys, just act that way, that's all.

HAPPY: 'Night, Pop. [*He goes upstairs.*]

LINDA [*to* WILLY]: Come, dear.

BEN [*with greater force*]: One must go in to fetch a diamond out.

WILLY [*to* LINDA, *as he moves slowly along the edge of the kitchen, toward the door*]: I just want to get settled down, Linda. Let me sit alone for a little.

LINDA [*almost uttering her fear*]: I want you upstairs.

WILLY [*taking her in his arms*]: In a few minutes, Linda. I couldn't sleep right now. Go on, you look awful tired. [*He kisses her.*]

BEN: Not like an appointment at all. A diamond is rough and hard to the touch.

WILLY: Go on now. I'll be right up.

LINDA: I think this is the only way, Willy.

WILLY: Sure, it's the best thing.

BEN: Best thing!

WILLY: The only way. Everything is gonna be—go on, kid, get to bed. You look so tired.

LINDA: Come right up.

WILLY: Two minutes.

> [LINDA *goes into the living-room, then reappears in her bedroom.* WILLY *moves just outside the kitchen door.*]

WILLY: Loves me. [*Wonderingly*] Always loved me. Isn't that a remarkable thing? Ben, he'll worship me for it!

BEN [*with promise*]: It's dark there, but full of diamonds.

WILLY: Can you imagine that magnificence with twenty thousand dollars in his pocket?

LINDA [*calling from her room*]: Willy! Come up!

WILLY [*calling into the kitchen*]: Yes! Yes. Coming! It's very smart, you realize that, don't you, sweetheart? Even Ben sees it. I gotta go, baby. 'Bye! 'Bye! [*Going over to* BEN, *almost dancing*] Imagine? When the mail comes he'll be ahead of Bernard again!

BEN: A perfect proposition all around.

WILLY: Did you see how he cried to me? Oh, if I could kiss him, Ben!

BEN: Time, William, time!

WILLY: Oh, Ben, I always knew one way or another we were gonna make it, Biff and I!

BEN [*looking at his watch*]: The boat. We'll be late. [*He moves slowly off into the darkness.*]

WILLY [*elegiacally, turning to the house*]: Now when you kick off, boy, I want a seventy-yard boot, and get right down the field under the ball, and when you hit, hit low and hit hard, because it's important, boy. [*He swings around and faces the audience.*] There's all kinds of important people in the stands, and the first thing you know . . . [*Suddenly realizing he is alone*] Ben! Ben, where do I . . . ? [*He makes a sudden movement of search.*] Ben, how do I . . . ?

LINDA [*calling*]: Willy, you coming up?

WILLY [*uttering a gasp of fear, whirling about as if to quiet her*]: Sh! [*He turns around as if to find his way; sounds, faces, voices seem to be swarming in upon him and he flicks at them, crying, "Sh! Sh!" Suddenly music, faint and high, stops him. It rises in intensity, almost to an unbearable scream. He goes up and down on his toes, and rushes off around the house.*] Shhh!

LINDA: Willy?

[*There is no answer.* LINDA *waits.* BIFF *gets up off his bed. He is still in his clothes.* HAPPY *sits up.* BIFF *stands listening.*]

LINDA [*with real fear*]: Willy, answer me! Willy!

[*There is the sound of a car starting and moving away at full speed.*]

LINDA: No!

BIFF [*rushing down the stairs*]: Pop!

[*As the car speeds off, the music crashes down in a frenzy of sound, which becomes the soft pulsation of a single cello string.* BIFF *slowly returns to his bedroom. He and* HAPPY *gravely don their jackets.* LINDA *slowly walks out of her room. The music has developed into a dead march. The leaves of day are appearing over everything.* CHARLEY *and* BERNARD, *somberly dressed, appear and knock on the kitchen door.* BIFF *and* HAPPY *slowly descend the stairs to the kitchen as* CHARLEY *and* BERNARD *enter. All stop a moment when* LINDA, *in clothes of mourning, bearing a little bunch of roses, comes through the draped doorway into the kitchen. She goes to* CHARLEY *and takes his arm. Now all move toward the audience, through the wall-line of the kitchen. At the limit of the apron,* LINDA *lays down the flowers, kneels, and sits back on her heels. All stare down at the grave.*]

REQUIEM

CHARLEY: It's getting dark, Linda.

[LINDA *doesn't react. She stares at the grave.*]

BIFF: How about it, Mom? Better get some rest, heh? They'll be closing the gate soon.

[LINDA *makes no move. Pause.*]

HAPPY [*deeply angered*]: He had no right to do that. There was no necessity for it. We would've helped him.

CHARLEY [*grunting*]: Hmmm.

BIFF: Come along, Mom.

LINDA: Why didn't anybody come?

CHARLEY: It was a very nice funeral.

LINDA: But where are all the people he knew? Maybe they blame him.

CHARLEY: Naa. It's a rough world, Linda. They wouldn't blame him.

LINDA: I can't understand it. At this time especially. First time in thirty-five years we were just about free and clear. He only needed a little salary. He was even finished with the dentist.

CHARLEY: No man only needs a little salary.

LINDA: I can't understand it.

BIFF: There were a lot of nice days. When he'd come home from a trip; or on Sundays, making the stoop; finishing the cellar; putting on the new porch; when he built the extra bathroom; and put up the garage. You know something, Charley, there's more of him in that front stoop than in all the sales he ever made.

CHARLEY: Yeah. He was a happy man with a batch of cement.

LINDA: He was so wonderful with his hands.

BIFF: He had the wrong dreams. All, all, wrong.

HAPPY [*almost ready to fight* BIFF]: Don't say that!

BIFF: He never knew who he was.

CHARLEY [*stopping* HAPPY'S *movement and reply. To* BIFF]: Nobody dast blame this man. You don't understand: Willy was a salesman. And for a salesman, there is no rock bottom to the life. He don't put a bolt to a nut, he don't tell you the law or give you medicine. He's a man way out there in the blue, riding on a smile and a shoeshine. And when they start not smiling back—that's an earthquake. And then you get yourself a couple of spots on your hat, and you're finished. Nobody dast blame this man. A salesman is got to dream, boy. It comes with the territory.

BIFF: Charley, the man didn't know who he was.

HAPPY [*infuriated*]: Don't say that!

BIFF: Why don't you come with me, Happy?

HAPPY: I'm not licked that easily. I'm staying right in this city, and I'm gonna beat this racket! [*He looks at* BIFF, *his chin set.*] The Loman Brothers!

BIFF: I know who I am, kid.

HAPPY: All right, boy. I'm gonna show you and everybody else that Willy Loman did not die in vain. He had a good dream. It's the only dream you can have—to come out number-one man. He fought it out here, and this is where I'm gonna win it for him.

BIFF [*with a hopeless glance at* HAPPY, *bends toward his mother*]: Let's go, Mom.

LINDA: I'll be with you in a minute. Go on, Charley. [*He hesitates.*] I want to, just for a minute. I never had a chance to say good-bye.

[CHARLEY *moves away, followed by* HAPPY. BIFF *remains a slight distance up and left of* LINDA. *She sits there, summoning herself. The flute begins, not far away, playing behind her speech.*]

LINDA: Forgive me, dear. I can't cry. I don't know what it is, but I can't cry. I don't understand it. Why did you ever do that? Help me, Willy, I can't cry. It seems to me that you're just on another trip. I keep expecting you. Willy, dear, I can't cry. Why did you do it? I search and search and I search, and I can't understand it, Willy. I made the last payment on the house today. Today, dear. And there'll be nobody home. [*A sob rises in her throat.*] We're free and clear. [*Sobbing more fully, released*] We're free. [BIFF *comes slowly toward her.*] We're free . . . We're free . . .

[BIFF *lifts her to her feet and moves out up right with her in his arms.* LINDA *sobs quietly.* BERNARD *and* CHARLEY *come together and follow them, followed by* HAPPY. *Only the music of the flute is left on the darkening stage as over the house the hard towers of the apartment buildings rise into sharp focus.*]

CURTAIN

☀ INSPIRATION BRIGHT FUTURES IN SALES

Miller's *Death of A Salesman*, one of the most popular plays ever written by an American, has had a number of prominent incarnations, especially the 1951 Stanley Kramer film starring Frederic March and the 1985 film starring Dustin Hoffman. And the work has clearly spurred other playwrights to treat very similar subjects. David Mamet's Pulitzer Prize–winning play *Glengarry Glen Ross* (1983), also made into a movie that remains a cult hit, especially among sales representatives and business people, takes as its subject the fierce competition among Chicago real estate salesmen. In John Swanbeck's film *The Big Kahuna* (2000), based on Roger Rueff's play *Hospitality Suite*, Kevin Spacey and Danny DeVito play cutthroat sales professionals of industrial lubricants. In all these plays and films, selling always seems to cross the line into "selling out," and the sales rep's role is imagined as a metaphor of an individual's participation in America's capitalist economy, with all the inevitable compromises that result.

Talking about the Text

1. Describe Linda Loman's relationship to Willy. To what extent is she responsible for holding Willy together for as long as he manages to carry on? On the other hand, to what extent would a different wife have served Willy and the sons better?
2. What does Linda mean when she says of Willy, "A terrible thing is happening to him"? What meaning would an audience ascribe to her comment?

Writing about the Text

1. Who or what is to blame for the tragedy that has befallen the family? What role did Biff's discovery of Willy's infidelity play?
2. Write an argument about who is the true protagonist of the play, Biff or Willy. Explain your choice with evidence from the play and your own reactions.

Linking the Text to Other Texts

1. Pay special attention to the lighting directions, the description of the set, and the music instructions in *Death of a Salesman*, and then compare the explicitness of Miller's stage directions with those in *The Glass Menagerie* (p. 1618). In an essay, tell what these stage directions indicate about the kind of control mid-twentieth-century playwrights tried to exercise.
2. How does the depiction of the American Dream in Miller's play compare to the American Dream proffered in one of the other plays in this book, for example, Lorraine Hansberry's *A Raisin in the Sun* (p. 1791), August Wilson's *The Piano Lesson* (p. 1916), or Anna Deavere Smith's *Twilight, Los Angeles 1992* (p. 1977)? What similarities and differences do they have, and based on the text of the plays, to what do you attribute the differences?

Fiftieth Anniversary of *Death of a Salesman*. In 1999 Broadway celebrated the fiftieth anniversary of Arthur Miller's *Death of a Salesman* and its return to Broadway. PBS's *Online NewsHour* dedicated a program to exploring why the play has had such lasting effect on audiences, interviewing Miller and playing audio clips of the new Broadway production. To read the transcript of the *NewsHour* special or listen to the audio version, go to *http://www.pbs.org/ newshour/bb/entertainment/jan-june99/miller_2-10.html*.

COMMENTARY

John Steinbeck on Arthur Miller

During the 1950s, Senator Joseph McCarthy was at the forefront of the campaign to rid the U.S. government of "Red" influences, accusing those he suspected were communists or communist sympathizers of being traitors.

In 1956 Arthur Miller was subpoenaed by the House Un-American Activities Committee (HUAC) of the U.S. Congress to testify about friends and colleagues who might be engaged in activities considered threatening to the country. This was the time of Senator Joseph McCarthy's "redbaiting," when hundreds of people were accused of being traitors because of paranoia about the threat of Russian communist power. McCarthy claimed that the government and Hollywood were fully infiltrated with communist spies, and he made it his mission to make their names known. McCarthy's hearings in Congress turned into a witch hunt, and his accusations ruined many people's lives and reputations. Miller was asked to testify about which fellow writers attended a communist writers' meeting he had gone to years earlier. He refused to name any names. California writer John Steinbeck, another literary great, wrote in support of his friend Arthur Miller and the essay was published in Esquire Magazine in June 1957. Part of it is printed below.

Since September 11, 2001, many people have questioned the balance between civil liberties and national security and have used McCarthyism as an example of what can happen when fear destroys freedom. What do you think Americans today can take from Steinbeck's message?

John Steinbeck on Miller and McCarthyism

The men in Congress must be conscious of their terrible choice. Their legal right is clearly established, but should they not think of their moral responsibility also? In their attempts to save the nation from attack, they could well undermine the deep personal morality which is the nation's final defense. The Congress is truly on trial along with Arthur Miller.

Again let me change places with Arthur Miller. I have refused to name people. I am indicted, convicted, sent to prison. If the charge were murder or theft or extortion I would be subject to punishment, because I and all men know that these things are wrong. But if I am imprisoned for something I have been taught from birth is a good thing, then I go to jail with a deep sense of injustice and the rings of that injustice are bound to spread out like an infection. If I am brave enough to suffer for my principle, rather than to save myself by hurting other people I believe to be innocent, it seems to me that the law suffers more than I, and that contempt of the law and of the Congress is a real contempt rather than a legalistic one. . . .

If I were in Arthur Miller's shoes, I do not know what I would do, but I could wish, for myself and for my children, that I would be brave enough to fortify and defend my private morality as he has. I feel profoundly that our country is better served by individual courage and morals than by the safe and public patriotism which Dr. Johnson called "the last refuge of scoundrels."

Starting Points for Further Research: Arthur Miller

- **Edition:** Arthur Miller. *Plays*. London: Methuen, 1988–2000.
- **Biography:** Martin Gottfried. *Arthur Miller: A Life*. London: Faber, 2003.
- **Autobiography:** Arthur Miller. *Timebends: A Life*. New York: Grove Press, 1987.
- **Critical Essay:** Frank Ardolino. "Babylonian Confusion and Biblical Inversion in Miller's *The Crucible*." *Journal of Evolutionary Psychology* 24 (March 2003): 64–72.
- **Interview:** Colby H. Kullman. "*Death of a Salesman* at Fifty: An Interview with Arthur Miller." *Michigan Quarterly Review* 37 (Fall 1998): 624–34.

CHAPTER
25

Sweet Home Chicago

From Chicago Renaissance
to *A Raisin in the Sun*

Like the Harlem Renaissance of the 1920s in New York City, the Chicago Renaissance saw an outpouring of African American literature and the arts from a concentrated black urban population. But the Harlem Renaissance reached its highpoint during the relatively prosperous years of the Jazz Age, whereas the Chicago Renaissance got under way in the gloomiest days of economic depression in the 1930s. As a result, the Chicago themes tended to be more overtly social and political than those of the Harlem Renaissance. And the Chicago Renaissance took place over a more extended period, stretching from the 1930s to 1960.

Although the word *renaissance* is frequently interpreted as "rebirth, or renewal," for many of these artists the flowering of black literature, art, and music was not a revival so much as a new thing, a consequence of an enormous African American migration from the South to the cities of the North. Chicago, the junction of many railroads, received a large share of those migrants, so much so that it was often thought of as the "Promised Land." The black population in Chicago leapt from under 15,000 in 1890 to over 100,000 in 1920, almost 500,000 in 1950, and over 800,000 in 1960. The life that evolved on the black

South Side of Chicago—or "Bronzeville," as it was popularly known—was a blend of southern black culture, both rural and urban, and extensive northern urban adaptations of that culture.

Life in Chicago's Bronzeville and the smaller African American enclaves was hard. Migrants from the South often had trouble finding all but the most menial jobs because the decently paid ones were reserved for white workers. Often the policies of labor unions reinforced white employment privilege. In the Great Depression, however, even jobs as waiters, dishwashers, janitors, or cleaning women could be scarce. Housing was also difficult to find. Blacks were discouraged from moving outside the ghettos—sometimes by violent measures—and sometimes were legally banned from "covenanted" white residence areas. Housing prices and apartment rents rose rapidly and out of proportion to their poor quality. Landlords, black and white, capitalized on the housing demand by splitting existing apartments into tiny sordid units called "kitchenettes."

Just because blacks had escaped the worst weapons of southern racism—lynching and the deprivation of the vote most notoriously—did not mean they enjoyed respect, freedom, and ample opportunity in Chicago. The police could be brutal, bureaucrats unfeeling, and individual white Chicagoans every bit as racist in their attitudes as the southerners blacks had left behind. But on the whole, life improved in Chicago, and black migrants enjoyed a sense of family and community in the crowded ghetto. Still, life remained a struggle.

"Changing Tenants" sign on a Chicago apartment building, 1941. Signs like the one above were indicative of the city's institutionalized racial segregation, in which the demographics of entire buildings and neighborhoods would shift as African Americans moved in. "Changing tenants" meant that a building was being vacated by whites and would be rented exclusively by African Americans, essentially a euphemism for what is often called "white flight" today.

The selections in this chapter speak for themselves about the vibrancy and diversity of Bronzeville's people and activities. But a few themes need highlighting. First, the Chicago Renaissance had a strong social and political basis. It began in the Great Depression of the 1930s, when more than one-third of Americans were out of work. It was greatly influenced by the urban sociology movement that devoted academic resources to the study of city problems, a movement that originated at the nearby University of Chicago, which built the earliest and strongest such program of any university. Influenced and aided by social scientists, many black and white Chicago writers of the 1930s dealt with the "facts" and conditions of the city, especially the life of the lower classes. Second, the Chicago Renaissance was radically political. During the Depression, when views on the left proliferated, many Chicago writers belonged to or were sympathetic to the Communist Party, then a small but highly influential organization.

For African Americans, both the burdens and the opportunities in the North gave rise to a cultural explosion. Blues, jazz, and gospel were adapted from their "country" origins as they were carried North, along with instruments such as the guitar, banjo, and fiddle. The literary arts flourished, as did the written correspondence between black Chicagoans and their fellow writers in other cities. Cultural forms borrowed from each other—both themes and structures. European and American mainstream arts were influential but were filtered through a strong racial awareness. The efforts of individual writers and other artists were linked through a network of cultural and social institutions that included libraries, community centers, and federal agencies. It was a time of powerful sociological and literary analysis. Literature did not remain a provenance of writers working alone but became a common expression of black Americans' social, political, and racial identity.

Social conflict was everywhere in Chicago between 1930 and 1960. Major themes for African American artists were civil rights, oppression, poor housing, and poverty. A few motifs appear frequently in the work of the African American writers of the period, and several questions related to these recurrent themes are worth readers' special attention:

- **Home:** Where does it lie? The South? Chicago? Africa? Is it found in heaven or an inner life? Is it in the life of one's people?

- **Travel:** Is one's home "on the road"? What role is played by trains and train stations in the work of Chicago Renaissance artists?

- **The struggle to survive, to make it through:** What sources of strength are available in the arts and in religion? How should one respond to the oppressor and to oppression?

- **Getting ahead:** How is life to be improved for oneself and one's family? An often thwarted desire for respectability, cleanliness, and education characterizes the hopes of many, especially women.

- **Religion:** How can black Christianity be distinguished from the white version imposed on slaves? How does one draw on the liberating elements of Christianity?

- **Having a good time:** Despite one's troubles and fears and the disapproval of others, how can one find pleasure in the world?

- **Music**: Why does music figure so strongly in the work of the Chicago Renaissance? Chicago's golden age for blues, jazz, and gospel was reflected in many art forms of the period.
- **Serving time**: How are jail sentences, just or unjust, represented in African American arts of the period?
- **Love**: What happens when familial love conflicts with sexual love? How is the two-timing lover represented?

You will find these themes throughout this chapter, which includes a number of different genres. The writers of the Chicago Renaissance excelled in many forms. This chapter is a small anthology of their nonfiction, popular and literary poetry, and fiction, culminating in Lorraine Hansberry's famous play, *A Raisin in the Sun*. The other works included here provide a context for Hansberry's play.

(Note: The "Starting Points for Further Research" sections for the poets in this chapter appear after their respective biographies in Chapter 19, "Biographies of Selected Poets.")

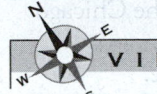 **VIDEO LOCALE**

George King's *Goin' to Chicago*. Filmmaker and Chicagoan George King's 1994 documentary *Goin' to Chicago* chronicles the huge migration of black Americans from the agrarian South to the industrial North and West following World War II through the personal stories of a small group of older Chicagoans, most of whom were born in the Mississippi Delta. The film is available from the California Newsreel website at *http://www.newsreel.org/films/gointoch.htm*.

TIMELINE FOR THE CHICAGO RENAISSANCE

Although the Chicago Renaissance began around 1935 and ended around 1960, in order to give a fuller literary history of the artists featured in this chapter and more comprehensive context to the political and religious landscape, the timeline starts in the late 1800s and ends in 1965.

1893	The World Columbian Exposition in Chicago brings midwestern artists to the city, setting the stage for the Chicago Renaissance.
1905	The Chicago *Defender* is founded, an African American newspaper that would play a large role in northern migration of blacks to the city.
1908	Richard Wright born on a Mississippi plantation.
1912	The quarterly magazine *Poetry* founded in Chicago by Harriet Monroe. The Little Theater founded to support young Chicago playwrights.
1917	Gwendolyn Brooks born in Topeka, Kansas; she will grow up in Chicago.

1922	Louis Armstrong becomes a major player in the Chicago jazz scene.
1926	A circle of New York artists and bohemians, including Langston Hughes and Zora Neale Hurston, found the literary magazine *Fire!!* and publish its first and only issue.
1927	Richard Wright moves to Chicago. The Savoy Ballroom on the South Side opens, the first dance hall in Chicago welcoming black patrons.
1928	Oscar Depriest of Chicago becomes the first African American elected to Congress in the twentieth century.
1929	The New York Stock Market collapses on October 29, marking the beginning of the Great Depression.
1930	Lorraine Hansberry born on the South Side of Chicago.
1932	The George Cleveland Hall branch of the Chicago Public Library opens with a special collection of African American works.
1934	Gwendolyn Brooks publishes her first poetry in the Chicago *Defender*.
1935	Frank Marshall Davis publishes *Black Man's Verse*.
1936	An increasingly radical black population in Chicago founds the Chicago Negro Congress to rally for black rights.
1937	Frank Marshall Davis publishes *I Am the American Negro*. Richard Wright moves to New York.
1940	Richard Wright publishes *Native Son*, about an African American man confronting the social and economic obstacles in 1930s Chicago.
1941	Gwendolyn Brooks enrolls in Inez Cunningham Stark's South Side poetry workshop.
1942	Margaret Walker's collection of poetry *For My People*, celebrating African American culture, is published.
1943	Blues legend Muddy Waters moves to Chicago.
1945	Richard Wright publishes *Black Boy* after moving to Paris. St. Clair Drake and Horace Cayton publish *Black Metropolis: A Study of Negro Life in a Northern City*. Gwendolyn Brooks publishes *A Street in Bronzeville*.
1947	The Chess brothers, Leonard and Phil, become part owners of Aristocrats Records, which introduces songs recorded by Muddy Waters.
1948	Frank Marshall Davis publishes *47th Street*.
1950	Gwendolyn Brooks receives the Pulitzer Prize for Poetry for *Annie Allen*, published in 1949.
1950–1965	The Chess brothers reorganize Aristocrats Records, rename it Chess Records, and include more blues, R&B, and rock 'n' roll. Chess Records becomes a home for such artists as Willie Dixon, Howlin' Wolf, Sonny Boy Williamson, and Chuck Berry.
1951	Sam Cooke becomes the lead singer of the Soul Stirrers, a Chicago-based gospel quartet. Margaret Danner's four-poem series "Far from Africa" is published in *Poetry*.

1953	Gwendolyn Brooks publishes her semi-autobiographical novel *Maud Martha*.
1956	Gwendolyn Brooks publishes *Bronzeville for Boys and Girls*, a children's book.
1959	*A Raisin in the Sun* first produced.
1960	Gwendolyn Brooks publishes *The Bean Eaters*.
1964	The Civil Rights Act of 1964 is signed into law by President Lyndon B. Johnson, abolishing Jim Crow laws and effectively outlawing segregation and discriminatory practices in businesses, public places, and schools. It is the most far-reaching civil rights legislation since the Reconstruction period following the end of the Civil War in 1865.
1964	Gospel and pop/R&B singer Sam Cooke dies in a mysterious shooting.
1965	President Lyndon B. Johnson signs the Voting Rights Act of 1965, leading to dramatic increases in black voter registration.

NONFICTION OF THE CHICAGO RENAISSANCE

St. Clair Drake.

At the height of the Chicago Renaissance, two African American social scientists, St. Clair Drake and Horace R. Cayton, produced a rich, highly detailed description of life in Chicago's black community. Their 1945 book *Black Metropolis: A Study of Negro Life in a Northern City* is a finely drawn view of the black ghetto by social scientists who were themselves trapped in it by the color of their skin. A classic of modern sociology, it is still available to-day—all 900-odd pages of it.

Thanks in part to the University of Chicago, which had some of the best social scientists in America, the city of Chicago was the site of many important sociological studies. But Drake and Cayton, influenced by but not based at the university, conducted their voluminous research under the sponsorship of the Work Projects Administration (WPA), the federal program that was to give meaningful jobs to many talented Chicagoans, black and white, during the long economic depression of the 1930s.

Among the scholars and writers to celebrate *Black Metropolis* was Richard Wright, who wrote the book's introduction, describing the importance of the Chicago school of sociology in general and Drake and Cayton's study in particular:

I did not know what my story was, and it was not until I

Horace R. Cayton, c. 1941, in his office at the Parkway Community House. (See "Literary Locale" on p. 1754.)

Exhibit of WPA research materials, in the basement of the Church of the Good Shepherd in Chicago, 1939. This public exhibition gathered research from 23 studies, presenting the most extensive examination of northern black communities ever undertaken. Supervised by social scientist Horace Cayton and funded by the federal Works Progress Administration (WPA), the research and exhibit became the basis for Cayton's groundbreaking book written with St. Clair Drake, Black Metropolis (excerpt below).

stumbled upon science that I discovered some of the meaning of the environment that battered and taunted me. . . . The huge mountains of fact piled up by the Department of Sociology at the University of Chicago gave me my first concrete vision of the forces that molded the urban Negro's body and soul.

It was from the scientific findings of men like the late Robert E. Park, Robert Redfield, and Louis Wirth [all University of Chicago sociology professors] that I drew the meanings for my documentary book, *12,000,000 Black Voices*; for my novel, *Native Son*; it was from their scientific facts that I absorbed some of that quota of inspiration necessary for me to write *Uncle Tom's Children* and *Black Boy*. *Black Metropolis*, Drake's and Cayton's scientific statement about the urban Negro, pictures the environment out of which the Bigger Thomases of our nation come.

Wright's generous praise provides a strong link between his own books' main characters (including Bigger Thomas, the protagonist of *Native Son*) and the beginnings of a social scientific view of black Chicago. Wright's powerful novels and stories, he claims, were not simply the product of some overwhelming natural force, but of conscious reading and thinking about sociology and anthropology. Wright, who never finished high school, had immersed himself in the latest, most detailed scholarly study of Chicago ghetto life.

ST. CLAIR DRAKE (1911–1990)
AND HORACE R. CAYTON (1903–1970)

In the opening pages of Black Metropolis: A Study of Negro Life in a Northern City *(1945), sociologists St. Clair Drake and Horace Cayton describe daily life in Bronzeville, Chicago's black ghetto in the 1930s.*

The Spirit of Bronzeville (1945)

"Ghetto" is a harsh term, carrying overtones of poverty and suffering, of exclusion and subordination. In Midwest Metropolis it is used by civic leaders when they want to shock complacency into action. Most of the ordinary people in the Black Belt refer to their community as "the South Side," but everybody is also familiar with another name for the area—Bronzeville. This name seems to have been used originally by an editor of the Chicago *Bee*, who, in 1930, sponsored a contest to elect a "Mayor of Bronzeville." A year or two later, when this newspaperman joined the *Defender* staff, he took his brain-child with him. The annual election of the "Mayor of Bronzeville" grew into a community event with a significance far beyond that of a circulation stunt. Each year a Board of Directors composed of outstanding citizens of the Black Belt takes charge of the mock-election. Ballots are cast at corner stores and in barbershops and poolrooms. The "Mayor," usually a businessman, is inaugurated with a colorful ceremony and a ball. Throughout his tenure he is expected to serve as a symbol of the community's aspirations. He visits churches, files protests with the Mayor of the city, and acts as official greeter of visitors to Bronzeville. Tens of thousands of people participate in the annual election of the "Mayor." In 1944-45, a physician was elected mayor.

Throughout the remainder of this book we shall use the term "Bronzeville" for Black Metropolis because it seems to express the feeling that the people have about their own community. They *live* in the Black Belt and to them it is more than the "ghetto" revealed by statistical analysis.

The Axes of Life: What are the dominating interests, the "centers of orientation," the lines of attention, which claim the time and money of Bronzeville—the "axes of life" around which individual and community life revolves? The most important of these are: (1) Staying Alive; (2) Having a Good Time; (3) Praising God; (4) Getting Ahead; (5) Advancing the Race.

The majority of Bronzeville's people will insist that they came to Midwest Metropolis to "better their condition." Usually they mean that they were seeking an opportunity to sell their labor for a steady supply of money to expend on food, clothing, housing, recreation, and plans for the future. They were also searching for adequate leisure time in which to enjoy themselves. Such goals are a part of the general American Dream. But when a Negro talks about "bettering his condition" he means something more: he refers also to finding an environment where exclusion and subordination by white men are not rubbed in his face—as they are in the South.

Staying Alive

Before people can enjoy liberty or pursue happiness, they must maintain life. During the Fat Years the problem of earning a living was not an acute one for Negroes in Chicago. More than three-fourths of the Negro men and almost half of the women were gainfully employed, though their work tended to be heavy or menial. Wages were generally lower than for the bulk of the white working people, but they permitted a plane of living considerably higher than anything most parts of the South had to offer. Though the first few years of the Depression resulted in much actual suffering in Bronzeville, the WPA eventually provided a bedrock of subsistence which guaranteed food and clothing. The ministrations of social workers and wide education in the use of public health facilities seem to have actually raised the level of health in the Black Ghetto during the Depression years. The Second World War once more incorporated Negroes into the productive economic life of Midwest Metropolis, and most of them had plenty of money to spend for the first time in a decade.

The high infant mortality and general death rates, the high incidence of disease, and the overcrowding and hazardous work, have all operated to keep the rate of natural increase for Negroes below that for whites. The man in the street is not aware of these statistical indices, but he does experience life in the Black Belt as a struggle for existence, a struggle which he consciously interprets as a fight against white people who deny Negroes the opportunity to compete for—and hold—"good jobs." Civic leaders, who see the whole picture, are also acutely aware of the role played by inadequate health and recreational facilities and poor housing. They also recognize the need for widespread adult education which will teach recent migrants how to make use of public health facilities and to protect themselves against disease. The struggle for survival proceeds on an unconscious level, except when it is highlighted by a depression, a race riot, or an economic conflict between Negroes and whites.

Enjoying Life

Bronzeville's people have never let poverty, disease, and discrimination "get them down." The vigor with which they enjoy life seems to belie the gloomy observations of the statisticians and civic leaders who know the facts about the Black Ghetto. In the Lean Years as well as the Fat, Bronzeville has shared the general American interest in "having a good time." Its people like the movies and shows, athletic events, dancing, card-playing, and all the other recreational activities—commercial and noncommercial—which Midwest Metropolis offers. The recreations of an industrial society reflect the need for an escape from the monotony of machine-tending and the discipline of office and factory. For the people of Bronzeville, "having a good time" also serves another function—escape from the tensions of contact with white people. Absorption in "pleasure" is, in part at least, a kind of adjustment to their separate, subordinate status in American life.

If working as servants, Negroes must be properly deferential to the white people upon whom they depend for meager wages and tips. In fact, they often have to overdo their act in order to earn a living; as they phrase it, they have to "Uncle Tom" to "Mr. Charley" a bit to survive. If working in a factory, they must take orders from a white managerial personnel and associate with white workers who, they know, do not accept them as social equals. If self-employed, they are continually frustrated by the indirect restrictions imposed upon Negro business and professional men. If civil servants, they are in continuous contact with situations that emphasize their ghetto existence and subordinate status. But, when work is over, the pressure of the white world is lifted. Within Bronzeville Negroes are at home. They find rest from white folks as well as from labor, and they make the most of it. In their homes, in lodge rooms and clubhouses, pool parlors and taverns, cabarets and movies, they can temporarily shake off the incubus of the white world. Their recreational activities parallel those of white people, but with distinctive nuances and shadings of behavior. What Bronzeville considers a good time—the pattern for enjoying life—is intimately connected with economic status, education, and social standing. A detailed discussion of recreational habits is therefore reserved for those chapters dealing with social class. Suffice it here to say that Bronzeville's people treasure their inalienable right to pursue happiness.

Praising the Lord

It is a matter for continuous surprise that churches in America's large urban communities are able to compete with secular interests and to emerge even stronger than the church in rural areas. Despite the fact that only about half of the adults in America claim church membership, the strong Protestant and Catholic tradition in the culture retains its hold upon the minds of the American people. The church and religion have been displaced from the center of the average man's life, but remain an important side-interest for many people. The general trend toward secularization of interests has affected men more strongly than women, but probably the majority of Americans pay some lip-service to religion and participate occasionally in the rites and ceremonies—at least upon occasions of birth, marriage, and death.

It has become customary in America to refer to Negroes as a "religious people." The movies and the radio, by their selection of incident and dialogue, tend to reinforce this prevalent conception. A walk through Bronzeville also seems to lend confirmation to this belief, for the evidences of an interest in "praising the Lord" are everywhere—churches are omnipresent. Negroes have slightly more than their expected share of churches and twice their share of preachers; a large proportion of the people seem to enjoy "praising the Lord." The spirit of Bronzeville is tinctured with religion, but like "having a good time" the real importance of the church can be understood only by relating it to the economic and social status of the various groups in Bronzeville.

Getting Ahead

The dominating individual drive in American life is not "staying alive," nor "enjoying life," nor "praising the Lord"—it is "getting ahead." In its simplest terms this means progressively moving from low-paid to higher-paid jobs, acquiring a more comfortable home, laying up something for sickness and old age, and trying to make sure that the children will start out at a higher economic and cultural level than the parents. Individuals symbolize their progress by the way they spend their money—for clothes, real estate, automobiles, donations, entertaining; and the individual's choice is dictated largely in terms of the circle of society in which he moves or which he wishes to impress. These circles or groupings are myriad and complex, for not all people set their goals at the same distance. Out of the differential estimates of the meaning of success arise various social classes and "centers of orientation."

There are, of course, some small groups in Midwest Metropolis, as elsewhere, who interpret success in noneconomic terms, who prize "morality," or "culture," or talent and technical competence. In general, however, Americans believe that if a man is *really* "getting ahead," if he is *really* successful, his accomplishments will become translated into an effective increase in income. People are expected to "cash in" on brains or talent or political power.

For thousands of Negro migrants from the South, merely arriving in Bronzeville represented "getting ahead." Yet Negroes, like other Americans, share the general interest in getting ahead in more conventional terms. The Job Ceiling and the Black Ghetto limit free competition for the money and for residential symbols of success. Partly because of these limitations (which are not peculiar to Chicago) it has become customary among the masses of Negroes in

America to center their interest upon living in the immediate present or upon going to heaven—upon "having a good time" or "praising the Lord." Though some derive their prestige from the respect accorded them by the white world, or by the professional and business segments of the Negro world, most Negroes seem to adopt a pattern of conspicuous behavior and conspicuous consumption. Maintaining a "front" and "showing off" become very important substitutes for getting ahead in the economic sense. Leadership in various organizations often constitutes the evidence that a man has "arrived."

Leaders in Bronzeville, like Negro leaders everywhere since the Civil War, are constantly urging the community to raise its sights above "survival," "enjoying life," and "praising the Lord." They present "getting ahead" as a *racial* duty as well as a personal gain. When a Negro saves money, buys bonds, invests in a business or in property, he is automatically "advancing The Race." When Negroes "waste their substance," they are "setting The Race back." This appraisal of their activity is widely accepted by the rank and file, but leaders sometimes press their shots too hard. When they do so, they often get a response like that of the domestic servant who resented the attempts of a civic leader to discourage elaborate social club dances during the Depression: "We [the social club] give to the Federated Home and about ten or fifteen other institutions. If we want to give a dance, I think that's our business. We poor colored people don't have much as it is, and if we sat around and thought about our sufferings we'd go crazy."

Advancing the Race

White people in Midwest Metropolis become aware of Negroes only occasionally and sporadically. Negroes, however, live in a state of intense and perpetual awareness that they are a black minority in a white man's world. The Job Ceiling and the Black Ghetto are an ever-present experience. Petty discriminations (or actions that might be interpreted as such) occur daily. Unpleasant memories of the racial and individual past are a part of every Negro's personality structure. News and rumors of injustice and terror in the South and elsewhere circulate freely through Negro communities at all times. "Race consciousness" is not the work of "agitators" or "subversive influences"—it is forced upon Negroes by the very fact of their separate-subordinate status in American life. And it is tremendously reinforced by life in a compact community such as Black Metropolis, set within the framework of a large white community.

Negroes are ill at ease in the land of their birth. They are bombarded with the slogans of democracy, liberty, freedom, equality, but they are not allowed to participate freely in American life. They develop a tormenting ambivalence toward themselves and the larger society of which they are a part. America rejects them; so they tend to hate. But it is the only land they know; so they are sentimentally attached to it. Their skin color and social origins subject them to discrimination and contumely; so they often (consciously or unconsciously) despise The Race. The people they know most intimately, however, are colored, and men cannot totally hate themselves and their friends. Thus their moods fluctuate between shame and defiance. Their conversation becomes a bewildering mixture of expressions of "racial depreciation" and "race pride."

The Cult of Race: Negroes feel impelled to prove to themselves continually that they are not the inferior creatures which their minority status implies. Thus, ever since emancipation, Negro leaders have preached the necessity for cultivating "race pride." They have assiduously repeated the half-truth that "no other race has ever made the progress that Negroes have made in an equivalent length of time." They have patiently attempted to popularize an expanding roster of Race Heroes—individuals who have attained success or prominence. "Catching up with the white folks" has been developed as the dominating theme of inspirational exhortations, and the Negro "firsts" and "onlies" are set up as Race Heroes. "Beating the white man at his own game" becomes a powerful motivation for achievement and explains the popularity of such personalities as Joe Louis or Jesse Owens, George Washington Carver or outstanding soldier-heroes. A myth of "special gifts" has also emerged, with Negroes (and whites also) believing that American Negroes have some inborn, unusual talent as dancers, musicians, artists and athletes.

In the period between the First and the Second World Wars, this emphasis upon race pride became a mass phenomenon among the Negroes in large urban communities. Race consciousness was transformed into a positive and aggressive defensive racialism. Negroes in Black Metropolis, as in other communities, feeling the strength of their economic and political power, have become increasingly aware of the achievements of individual Negroes, and have developed an absorbing interest in every scrap of evidence that "The Race is advancing," or is "catching up with white folks," or is "beating the white man at his own game." Unable to compete freely *as individuals*, the Negro masses take intense vicarious pleasure in watching Race Heroes vindicate them in the eyes of the white world.

Race pride is a defensive reaction that can become a mere verbal escape mechanism. Negro leaders are therefore perpetually involved in an effort to make race pride more than an end in itself: to utilize it as a morale builder, as the raw material of "racial solidarity." They seek to use it for "advancing The Race." They foster race pride in order to elicit support for collective action—the support of Negro business enterprises, the organization of petition and protest, the focusing of economic and political power. The most persistent theme of speeches and editorials in Bronzeville is: "Negroes must learn to stick together." The leaders use it also to encourage individual achievement, by interpreting the success of one Negro as the success of all. Out of this interplay between race consciousness, race pride, and race solidarity arise certain definite social types: the Race Hero, the Race Leader, the Race Man, the Race Woman.

The average person in Bronzeville is primarily interested in "staying alive," "getting ahead," "having a good time" and "praising the Lord." Conscious preoccupation with "racial advancement" is fitful and sporadic, though always latent. The masses leave "the burden of The Race" to those individuals who are oriented around "service"—the Race Leaders. Some of these are people who devote much of their leisure time to charitable organizations or associations for racial advancement. For others solving the race problem is a full-time job. For instance, a score or so of individuals in Bronzeville are elected and appointed politicians who "represent The Race." There are also a few civic leaders who earn their living by administering social agencies such as the Urban League, the YMCA, the YWCA, settlement houses, and similar organizations. In Bronzeville, too, there are numerous "self-appointed leaders"—men and women, often illiterate and poverty-stricken, who feel the call to "lead The Race out of bondage." They harangue their small groups of followers on the streets, in storefronts, or in the public parks with a fanaticism that alienates them from the masses as well as from the affluent and educated.

Most of the people in Bronzeville do not hold membership in any of the organizations for "racial advancement," such as the National Association for the Advancement of Colored People (NAACP), the National Negro Congress, the Urban League, or the Council of Negro Organizations. They follow the activities of Race Leaders in the Negro press, they cheer and applaud an occasionally highly publicized victory over those who maintain the Job Ceiling and the Black Ghetto. They grumble persistently about "lack of leadership." They contribute an occasional nickel or dime to drives for funds. But when some inciting incident stirs them deeply, they close ranks and put up a scrap—for a community housing project, to remove a prejudiced policeman, to force a recalcitrant merchant to employ Negroes. And they periodically vote for Negroes to represent them in state, local, and national bodies. In general, "solving the race problem" is left in the hands of Race Leaders—the "racial watchdogs," as one Bronzeville preacher called them.

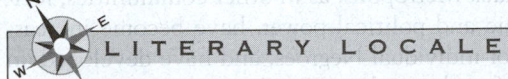

LITERARY LOCALE

Parkway Community House—Bronzeville, Chicago. Originally called the Good Shepherd Community Center when it was founded in 1936 as an educational and recreational outreach program of the Good Shepherd Congregational Church, the Parkway Community House became a locus for community arts and cultural activity during the heart of the Chicago Renaissance. Horace Cayton, the co-author of *Black Metropolis* (1945), was its director from 1939 to

Young pianist giving a recital at the Parkway Community House, 1942.

Poet and playwright Langston Hughes, discussing a new script with actors at Chicago's Parkway Community House, 1942.

1948. Under his direction, the organization grew into one of Chicago's major institutions for promoting the activities of local artists and intellectuals. Regular visitors included sociologist, author, and civil rights leader W. E. B. Du Bois; writers Richard Wright, Langston Hughes, Margaret Walker, Arna Bontemps, and Gwendolyn Brooks (all of whom are featured elsewhere in this chapter); actor Paul Robeson; and photographer Gordon Parks.

The center was named the Parkway Community House when it relocated in 1941 to 5120 South Parkway. The new space enabled the organization to expand its functions to include a clinic, nursery school, dormitory, birth certificate bureau, relief office, meetingplace for unions, and a facility for arts workshops and performances. In its current incarnation, at 500 E. 67th Street, its offerings have been downsized in the face of financial constraints, but it still provides important assistance to local residents, including first aid, child care, afterschool and youth development programs, literacy programs, programs for senior citizens, and support services for victims of domestic violence.

POEMS OF THE CHICAGO RENAISSANCE

In 1925, few observers of the Chicago literary scene would have predicted the soon-to-come outpouring of poetry from highly talented black writers. For most Americans, Chicago poetry in the 1920s and 1930s meant the work of prominent white writers such as Sherwood Anderson, Edgar Lee Masters, Vachel Lindsay, and above all, Carl Sandburg. This poetry was no doubt stimulated by the presence in Chicago of *Poetry*, a small quarterly founded in 1912 by Harriet Monroe. *Poetry* soon became the most influential poetry magazine in the world;

Poets Langston Hughes and Gwendolyn Brooks at the Chicago Public Library, 1949, celebrating the release of what would become the award-winning, definitive anthology of its kind, The Poetry of the Negro, edited by Hughes and Chicago poet Arna Bontemps. The book collected works by numerous Chicago writers, including Brooks, Fenton Johnson, Margaret Walker, Frank Marshall Davis, and Frank London Brown.

it had an "open door" policy, welcoming new and experimental work from across the globe, and the magazine would eventually discover and even help nurture the talent blossoming in Bronzeville.

Many of Chicago's black poets were influenced by jazz and the blues, music that people brought with them when they migrated from the South and adapted to the new geographical setting. Gwendolyn Brooks's "We Real Cool," below, is one example of jazz rhythms in verse. Chicago poetry was also spurred by the frequent visits of America's most famous black poet, Langston Hughes, a Harlem Renaissance artist whose active mentoring helped many writers begin their careers. Even writers whose primary literary work lay in fiction and nonfiction, such as Arna Bontemps and Richard Wright, tried their hand at poetry. Beginning in 1941, Inez Stark Cunningham, a wealthy white Chicago scholar, writer, and philanthropist who was also a reader for *Poetry*, taught a poetry workshop at the South Side Community Art Center (see Literary Locale, p. 1759), helping to turn that small group, Gwendolyn Brooks among them, into a source of superb writing within the black community. Their work would soon be published all over the United States.

GWENDOLYN BROOKS   (1917–2000)

Gwendolyn Brooks, c. 1945–1950.

By far the most famous Chicago-based poet, Gwendolyn Brooks lived in Bronzeville for most of her long life. Of the many themes that characterize her writings, two directly concern the lives of African Americans in Chicago. One is the temptations facing young men and particularly young women in this big, rough, and mean city, a motif that Brooks returns to again and again. Another theme is the precarious nature of the place one calls home. From her home in Bronzeville, Brooks witnessed overcrowded conditions faced by newly arriving blacks, who were often at the mercy of landlords and social service agencies. In her book Maud Martha, *a semifictional account based on her own experience, a young woman faces imminent dispossession when times are tough and the mortgage company wants its money. An excerpt from* Maud Martha *appears later in this chapter. See Chapter 15, "A Poet in Depth," for a brief biography of Brooks and more of her poems.*

We Real Cool (C. 1940)

The pool players.
Seven at the golden shovel.

We real cool. We
Left school. We
Lurk late. We
Strike straight. We
Sing sin. We   5
Thin gin. We
Jazz June. We
Die soon.

The Lovers of the Poor (C. 1941)

arrive. The Ladies from the Ladies' Betterment League
Arrive in the afternoon, the late light slanting
In diluted gold bars across the boulevard brag
Of proud, seamed faces with mercy and murder hinting
Here, there, interrupting, all deep and debonair,   5
The pink paint on the innocence of fear;
Walk in a gingerly manner up the hall.
Cutting with knives served by their softest care,
Served by their love, so barbarously fair.
Whose mothers taught: You'd better not be cruel!   10
You had better not throw stones upon the wrens!
Herein they kiss and coddle and assault
Anew and dearly in the innocence
With which they baffle nature. Who are full,
Sleek, tender-clad, fit, fiftyish, a-glow, all   15
Sweetly abortive, hinting at fat fruit,
Judge it high time that fiftyish fingers felt
Beneath the lovelier planes of enterprise.
To resurrect. To moisten with milky chill.
To be a random hitching post or plush.   20
To be, for wet eyes, random and handy hem.
     Their guild is giving money to the poor.
The worthy poor. The very very worthy
And beautiful poor. Perhaps just not too swarthy?
Perhaps just not too dirty nor too dim   25
Nor—passionate. In truth, what they could wish
Is—something less than derelict or dull.
Not staunch enough to stab, though, gaze for gaze!
God shield them sharply from the beggar-bold!
The noxious needy ones whose battle's bald   30
Nonetheless for being voiceless, hits one down.
     But it's all so bad! and entirely too much for them.
The stench; the urine, cabbage, and dead beans,

Dead porridges of assorted dusty grains,
The old smoke, *heavy* diapers, and, they're told,   35
Something called chitterlings. The darkness. Drawn
Darkness, or dirty light. The soil that stirs.
The soil that looks the soil of centuries.
And for that matter the *general* oldness. Old
Wood. Old marble. Old tile. Old old old.   40
Not homekind Oldness! Not Lake Forest, Glencoe.
Nothing is sturdy, nothing is majestic,
There is no quiet drama, no rubbed glaze, no
Unkillable infirmity of such
A tasteful turn as lately they have left,   45
Glencoe, Lake Forest, and to which their cars
Must presently restore them. When they're done
With dullards and distortions of this fistic
Patience of the poor and put-upon.
          They've never seen such a make-do-ness as   50
Newspaper rugs before! In this, this "flat,"
Their hostess is gathering up the oozed, the rich
Rugs of the morning (tattered! the bespattered . . .),
Readies to spread clean rugs for afternoon.
Here is a scene for you. The Ladies look,   55
In horror, behind a substantial citizeness
Whose trains clank out across her swollen heart.
Who, arms akimbo, almost fills a door.
All tumbling children, quilts dragged to the floor
And tortured thereover, potato peelings, soft-   60
Eyed kitten, hunched-up, haggard, to-be-hurt.
          Their League is allotting largesse to the Lost.
But to put their clean, their pretty money, to put
Their money collected from delicate rose-fingers
Tipped with their hundred flawless rose-nails seems . . .   65
          They own Spode, Lowestoft, candelabra,
Mantels, and hostess gowns, and sunburst clocks,
Turtle soup, Chippendale, red satin "hangings,"
Aubussons and Hattie Carnegie. They Winter
In Palm Beach; cross the Water in June; attend,   70
When suitable, the nice Art Institute;
Buy the right books in the best bindings; saunter
On Michigan, Easter mornings, in sun or wind.
Oh Squalor! This sick four-story hulk, this fibre
With fissures everywhere! Why, what are bringings   75
Of loathe-love largesse? What shall peril hungers
So old old, what shall flatter the desolate?
Tin can, blocked fire escape and chitterling
And swaggering seeking youth and the puzzled wreckage
Of the middle passage, and urine and stale shames   80
And, again, the porridges of the underslung
And children children children. Heavens! That
Was a rat, surely, off there, in the shadows? Long

And long-tailed? Gray? The Ladies from the Ladies'
Betterment League agree it will be better   85
To achieve the outer air that rights and steadies,
To hie to a house that does not holler, to ring
Bells elsetime, better presently to cater
To no more Possibilities, to get
Away. Perhaps the money can be posted.   90
Perhaps they two may choose another Slum!
Some serious sooty half-unhappy home!—
Where loathe-love likelier may be invested.

    Keeping their scented bodies in the center
Of the hall as they walk down the hysterical hall,   95
They allow their lovely skirts to graze no wall,
Are off at what they manage of a canter,
And, resuming all the clues of what they were,
Try to avoid inhaling the laden air.

A poetry workshop at the South Side Community Center, 1942.

South Side Community Art Center. Originally built as a residence for a merchant in the late nineteenth century, the Georgian Revival building located at 3831 S. Michigan Avenue became the location for the South Side Community Art Center in 1940. The center was founded as one segment of the Federal Art Project, part of the Works Progress Administration (WPA). Similar to the Parkway Community House (see p. 1754), the organization offered a wide range of resources to locals, including poetry and painting classes, literary readings, musical recitals, and art exhibitions. This was where Gwendolyn Brooks attended Inez Cunningham's influential poetry class. Today, the South Side Community Art Center is the sole survivor of the more than one hundred centers established nationwide by the WPA during the 1930s and 1940s. The building became a Chicago landmark in 1994.

FRANK MARSHALL DAVIS   (1905–1987)

A journalist and poet with an ironic bent and caustic wit, Frank Marshall Davis grew up in Kansas, attended college there, and in 1927 moved to Chicago. He remained there for two decades, with the exception of five years spent editing the Atlanta World, which he made into a successful black daily newspaper. He was called back to Chicago to become executive director of the Associated Negro Press. But Davis never stopped writing poetry. Many of his poems

Frank Marshall Davis.

are collected in the books Black Man's Verse *(1935),* I Am the American Negro *(1937),* 47th Street *(1948), and* Awakening and Other Poems *(1978). His poems deal directly with issues of racism and class. Davis was a student and lover of jazz and the blues, and his poetic rhythms reflect those enthusiasms. In 1948 Davis moved to Hawaii, and his reputation underwent an eclipse during the 1950s but was revived during the 1960s. His autobiography* Livin' the Blues: Memories of a Black Journalist and Poet *was published posthumously in 1992, and his collected poetry appeared in 2002.*

Robert Whitmore   (1935)

Having attained success in business
possessing three cars
one wife and two mistresses
a home and furniture
talked of by the town   5
and thrice ruler of the local Elks
Robert Whitmore
died of apoplexy
when a stranger from Georgia
mistook him   10
for a former Macon waiter.

I Sing No New Songs   (1935)

Once I cried for new songs to sing . . . a black rose . . . a brown sky . . . the moon
    for my buttonhole . . . pink dreams for the table
Later I learned life is a servant girl . . . dusting the same pieces yesterday, today,
    tomorrow . . . a never ending one two three one two three one two three
The dreams of Milton were the dreams of Lindsay . . . drinking corn liquor, wear-
    ing a derby, dancing a foxtrot . . . a saxophone for a harp
Ideas rise with new mornings but never die . . . only names, places, people
    change . . . you are born, love, fight, tire and stop being . . . Caesar died with
    a knife in his guts . . . Jim Colosimo from revolver bullets
So I shall take aged things . . . bearded dreams . . . a silver dollar moon worn thin
    from the spending . . . model a new dress for this one . . . get that one a new
    hat . . . teach the other to forget the minuet . . . then I shall send them into
    the street
And if passersby stop and say "Who is that? I never saw this pretty girl before"
    or if they say . . . "Is that old woman still alive? I thought she died years

ago" . . . if they speak these words, I shall neither smile nor swear . . . those who walked before me, those who come after me, may make better clothes, teach a more graceful step . . . but the dreams of Homer neither grow nor wilt. . . .

MARGARET WALKER (1915–1998)

Margaret Walker was raised in the South—in Birmingham, Alabama, and in New Orleans, Louisiana. When Langston Hughes recognized her talent, he urged her to go North. She graduated from Northwestern and while in Chicago became involved in a wide array of literary activities, including the WPA's Federal Writers' Project and the South Side Writers Group, which included Richard Wright and Gwendolyn Brooks. She earned an M.A. at the University of Iowa Writers Workshop (returning there in the 1960s for her Ph.D., which culminated with her doctoral dissertation, her novel Jubilee*). Her first poetry collection,* For My People*

Margaret Walker, c. 1942.*

(1942), won the prestigious Yale University Younger Poets Prize; the poem that gave the collection its name had first been published in 1937 in Chicago's renowned Poetry *magazine.*

Walker eventually joined the faculty of Jackson State College in Mississippi, where she taught as a highly esteemed professor for thirty years, until her retirement in 1979. Despite all the demands on her time as a parent, wife, and teacher, she published three more volumes of poetry, collections of essays, and a biography and critical study of Richard Wright (see p. 1779). She also served as an active mentor to younger colleagues eager to learn more about African American literature, and especially about her time in Chicago. The second of her poems printed here, "For My People"—almost biblical in its rhythms, perhaps influenced by the fact that her father was a minister—aims to be public poetry, intended to inspire and edify.

I Want to Write (1940)

I want to write
I want to write the songs of my people.
I want to hear them singing melodies in the dark.
I want to catch the last floating strains from their sob-torn throats.
I want to frame their dreams into words; their souls into notes.   5
I want to catch their sunshine laughter in a bowl;
fling dark hands to a darker sky
and fill them full of stars
then crush and mix such lights till they become
a mirrored pool of brilliance in the dawn.   10

For My People (1942)

For my people everywhere singing their slave songs repeatedly: their dirges and
    their ditties and their blues and jubilees, praying their prayers nightly to an
    unknown god, bending their knees humbly to an unseen power;
For my people lending their strength to the years, to the gone years and the now
    years and the maybe years, washing ironing cooking scrubbing sewing

mending hoeing plowing digging planting pruning patching dragging along never gaining never reaping never knowing and never understanding.

For my playmates in the clay and dust and sand of Alabama backyards playing baptizing and preaching and doctor and jail and soldier and school and mama and cooking and playhouse and concert and store and hair and Miss Choomby and company;

For the cramped bewildered years we went to school to learn to know the reasons why and the answers to and the people who and the places where and the days when, in memory of the bitter hours when we discovered we were black and poor and small and different and nobody cared and nobody wondered and nobody understood;

For the boys and girls who grew in spite of these things to be Man and Woman, to laugh and dance and sing and play and drink their wine and religion and success, to marry their playmates and bear children and then die of consumption and anemia and lynching;

For my people thronging 47th Street in Chicago and Lenox Avenue in New York and Rampart Street in New Orleans, lost disinherited dispossessed and happy people filling the cabarets and taverns and other people's pockets needing bread and shoes and milk and land and money and something— something all our own;

For my people walking blindly spreading joy, losing time being lazy, sleeping when hungry, shouting when burdened, drinking when hopeless, tied and shackled and tangled among ourselves by the unseen creatures who tower over us omnisciently and laugh;

For my people blundering and groping and floundering in the dark of churches and schools and clubs and societies, associations and councils and committees and conventions, distressed and disturbed and deceived and devoured by money-hungry glory-craving leeches, preyed on by facile force of state and fad and novelty, by false prophet and holy believer;

For my people standing staring trying to fashion a better way from confusion, from hypocrisy and misunderstanding, trying to fashion a world that will hold all the people, all the faces, all the adams and eves and their countless generations;

Let a new earth rise. Let another world be born. Let a bloody peace be written in the sky. Let a second generation full of courage issue forth; let a people loving freedom come to growth. Let a beauty full of healing and a strength of final clenching be the pulsing in our spirits and our blood. Let the martial songs be written, let the dirges disappear. Let a race of men now rise and take control.

MARGARET DANNER   (1915–1986)

Although not as celebrated as her contemporary Margaret Walker, Margaret Danner occupied a central place in African American poetry in Chicago. Born in Kentucky, Danner moved early in life to Chicago, where she attended high school and college (Loyola and Northwestern). In 1952, her series of four poems "Far from Africa" was published in Poetry. She became an assistant editor at Poetry in 1956, the first African American to serve in that position. "Far from Africa" won Danner a fellowship for travel to Africa, which she would not be able to take advantage of until 1966, when she spent extended time in Ghana.

    Danner's poems demonstrate the centrality of African motifs in the poetry of her time. This was not an unusual interest in her literary circles (Langston Hughes had visited West Africa earlier), but Danner explored the theme with exceptional intensity. In addition, she served as a link between the Chicago Renaissance and the later Black Arts movement, which would become a dominant trend during the 1960s. Danner moved to Detroit in 1961, where she founded Boone House, an influential inner-city home for the arts, and she served as poet-in-residence at Wayne State University.

Far from Africa: Four Poems   (1952)

"are you beautiful still?"

1. Garnishing the Aviary

Our moulting days are in their twilight stage.
These lengthy dreaded suns of draggling plumes.
These days of moods that swiftly alternate between
The former preen (ludicrous now) and a downcast rage
Or crestfallen lag, are fading out. The initial bloom;   5
Exotic, dazzling in its indigo, tangerine

Splendor; this rare, conflicting coat had to be shed.
Our drooping feathers turn all shades. We spew
This unamicable aviary, gag upon the worm, and fling

Our loosening quills. We make a riotous spread   10
Upon the dust and mire that beds us. We do not shoo
So quickly; but the shades of the pinfeathers resulting

From this chaotic push, though still exotic,
Blend in more easily with those on the wings
Of the birds surrounding them; garnishing   15
The aviary, burnishing this zoo.

2. Dance of the Abakweta

Imagine what Mrs. Haessler would say
If she could see the Watusi youth dance
Their well-versed initiation. At first glance
As they bend to an invisible barre   20
You would know that she had designed their costumes.

For though they were made of pale beige bamboo straw
Their lines were the classic tutu. Nothing varied.
Each was cut short at the thigh and carried
High to a degree of right angles. Nor was there a flaw   25
In their leotards. Made of leopard skin or the hide

Of a goat, or the Gauguin-colored Okapi's striped coat
They were cut in her reverenced "tradition."
She would have approved their costumes and positions.

And since neither Iceland nor Africa is too remote   30
For her vision she would have wanted to form
A "traditional" ballet. Swan Lake, Scheherazade or
(After seeing their incredible leaps)
Les Orientales. Imagine the exotic sweep
Of such a ballet, and from the way the music pours   35
Over these dancers (this tinkling of bells, talking
Of drums, and twanging of tan, sandalwood harps)
From this incomparable music, Mrs. Haessler of Vassar can
Glimpse strains of Tchaikovsky, Chopin
To accompany her undeviatingly sharp   40
"Traditional" ballet. I am certain that if she could
Tutor these potential protégés, as
Quick as Aladdin rubbing his lamp, she would.

3. The Visit of the Professor of Aesthetics

To see you standing in the sagging bookstore door
So filled me with chagrin that suddenly you seemed as   45
Pink and white to me as a newborn, hairless mouse. For

I had hoped to delight you at home. Be a furl
Of faint perfume and Vienna's cordlike lace.
To shine my piano till a shimmer of mother-of-pearl

Embraced it. To pleasantly surprise you with the grace   50
That transcends my imitation and much worn
"Louis XV" couch. To display my Cathedrals and ballets.

To plunge you into Africa through my nude
Zulu Prince, my carvings from Benin, forlorn
Treasures garnered by much sacrifice of food.   55

I had hoped to delight you, for more
Rare than the seven-year bloom of my
Chinese spiderweb fern is a mind like yours

That concedes my fetish for this substance
Of your trade. And I had planned to prove   60
Your views of me correct at even every chance

Encounter. But you surprised me. And the store which
Had shown promise until you came, arose
Like a child gone wild when company comes or a witch

At Hallowe'en. The floor, just swept and mopped,   65
Was persuaded by the northlight to deny it.
The muddy rag floor rugs hunched and flopped

Away from the tears in the linoleum that I wanted
Them to hide. The drapes that I had pleated
In clear orchid and peach feverishly flaunted   70

Their greasiest folds like a banner.
The books who had been my friends, retreated—
Became as shy as the proverbial poet in manner

And hid their better selves. All glow had been deleted
By the dirt. And I felt that you whose god is grace   75
Could find no semblance of it here. And unaware

That you were scrubbing, you scrubbed your hands.
Wrung and scrubbed your long white fingers. Scrubbed
Them as you smiled and I lowered my eyes from despair.

4. Etta Moten's Attic

(Filled with mementos of African journeys)   80

It was as if Gauguin
had upset a huge paint pot
of his incomparable tangerine,

splashing wherever my startled eyes ran
here and there, and at my very hand on   85
masques and paintings and carvings not seen

here before, spilling straight as a stripe
spun geometrically in a Nbeble rug
flung over an ebony chair,

or dripping round as a band on a type   90
of bun the Watusi warriors
make of their pompadoured hair,

splashing high as a sunbird or fly moving
over a frieze of mahogany trees,
or splotching out from low underneath as a root,   95

shimmering bright as a ladybug grooving
a green bed of moss, sparkling as a beetle,
a bee, shockingly dotting the snoot

of an ape or the nape of its neck or as clue
to its navel, stamping a Zulu's   100
intriguing masque, tipping

the lips of a chief of Ashantis who
was carved to his stool so he'd sit
there forever and never fear a slipping

of rule or command, dyeing the skirt   105
(all askew) that wouldn't stay put on the
Pygmy in spite of his real leather belt,

quickening and charming till we felt the bloom
of veldt and jungle flow through the room.

Talking about the Text

1. How does Gwendolyn Brooks's "The Lovers of the Poor" characterize the well-off white women from the Chicago suburbs? What's bad about them? What is more positive?
2. Does an offer of help always risk seeming condescending? Have you ever been in a position that was similar to the one described in "The Lovers of the Poor"?

Writing about the Text

1. Both Margaret Danner and Margaret Walker aim at a kind of moral uplift in their poetry. In an essay, describe how that uplift works in one poem by each writer.

Linking the Text to Other Texts

1. What similarities do you see between Gwendolyn Brooks's "The Lovers of the Poor" (p. 1757) and Charles Baxter's short story "Shelter" (p. 237)?
2. Compare Brooks's portrayal of the resentment of the poor with that of Richard Wright in "The Man Who Lived Underground" (p. 582).
3. What do you see of Paul Laurence Dunbar's influence (p. 1060) in the poetry of Frank Marshall Davis?

AUDIO LOCALE

Writers of the Revolution: Langston Hughes and Margaret Danner.

In 1959, Berry Gordy founded Detroit's Motown Records and tapped into raw local musical talent, mostly unestablished African American teenagers. With the help of gifted songwriters, Gordy created and produced what was later called "the sound of young America," recording catchy pop and R&B songs that appealed to blacks and whites alike. Some of these little-known singers and groups became huge successes, including Stevie Wonder, Smokey Robinson and the Miracles, Marvin Gaye, the Temptations, Diana Ross and the Supremes, the Jackson 5, and Michael Jackson. Motown was one of the most successful and influential independent record labels of the 1960s. The success of Motown enabled Gordy to finance a spoken-word series in 1963, eventually named the Black Forum series. Its goal was to expose the general public to unique and visionary black voices and to further promote short- and long-term social change.

In 1968, Gordy released a recording called *Writers of the Revolution*, which included a discussion between Langston Hughes and Margaret Danner that had taken place at Boone House, the Detroit arts center founded by Danner. The conversation covers a range of topics, from their poetry to personal, cultural, and social commentary. Hughes and Danner also read some of their poems on the album. The Black Forum label was active only during the 1960s and early 1970s, but Black Forum recordings, including *Writers of the Revolution*, can still be found in libraries and via numerous websites.

Motown Records founder Berry Gordy, with singer Diana Ross

THE BLUES

One spectacular invention that will always be associated with Chicago artists is the urban blues, with amplified guitar, lyrics by Willie Dixon, and the voices of Muddy Waters and Howlin' Wolf, all transplants from the Mississippi Delta who migrated to the South Side of Chicago in search of a better life. The blues had originated among poor southern country blacks, most prominently in the Mississippi Delta, the cotton-growing country that runs along the river south of Memphis, Tennessee. As jobs dried up in the Delta, blacks came north to Chicago to find work. By the 1940s, many blues singers were active on the South Side, keeping alive the music they learned at home in the South, and changing it, too, as they added amplification and electric guitars.

Blues lyrics are a mix of popular entertainment and art. Their poetry is in some ways simple and direct: plenty of repetition, short lines, obvious rhymes, raw emotion. But they are also complex in the ways they comment ironically on life, and distance some of the pain. The lyrics accomplish this by seemingly extraneous expressions—see Muddy Waters's "sure 'nough" or the "one and one is two" in Robert Johnson's "Sweet Home Chicago," for instance. Along with the lyrics, the music and the gestures of the performer assert not only the individuality of the singer-songwriter but the individual's ability to suffer and endure. Blues performers bring the audience into the performance, assuming a universal experience of suffering and survival.

In the Chicago Renaissance, the blues were sung in loud, smoky clubs, with people drinking and talking and having a good time after days of hard work. The blues helped make Chicago's music scene famous in the 1940s and 1950s among black and white admirers. In the 1960s, the form was adopted by American and British rock bands, who made pilgrimages to rough South Side Chicago clubs and imitated the music as best they could. One very famous group, the Rolling Stones, took their name from a Muddy Waters song.

VIDEO LOCALE

Martin Scorsese's *The Blues*. Produced by master filmmaker Martin Scorsese, the 2003 documentary series *The Blues*, which originally aired on PBS, comprises seven feature-length films that collectively explore the spirit, meaning, and influence of the blues through a history of the art form. The episodes are directed by Scorsese, Wim Wenders, Richard Pearce, Charles Burnett, Marc Levin, Mike Figgis, and Clint Eastwood. Additional background on the films and DVD and VHS information can be found online at *http://www.pbs.org/theblues/*. *Martin Scorsese Presents The Blues—A Musical Journey*, the companion audio CD collection of the music used in the films, is also available on the PBS website and includes recordings by classic blues musicians as well as the musicians they inspired, from Robert Johnson, Bessie Smith, Muddy Waters, B. B. King, and John Lee Hooker, to Jimi Hendrix, Eric Clapton, Stevie Ray Vaughan, the Allman Brothers, Keb' Mo', and Cassandra Wilson.

ROBERT JOHNSON   (1912–1938)

Robert Johnson was born and died in the Mississippi Delta, but in his timeless song "Sweet Home Chicago," the city stands as an icon for the Promised Land. Do not try to make too much literal sense of the lyrics; there is no telling why California gets mixed up with Chicago, except that these both were Promised Lands for impoverished blacks trying to leave Mississippi. "Sweet Home Chicago" provides an unofficial anthem of the city. It also illustrates the ongoing, vibrant dialogue between blues music and poetry, since it was closely modeled on another popular tune of its time, Scrapper Blackwell's Kokomo Blues.

Sweet Home Chicago   (C. 1935)

Oh, baby, don't you want to go?
Oh, baby, don't you want to go?
Back to the land of California, to my sweet home Chicago.

Oh, baby, don't you want to go?
Oh, baby, don't you want to go?
Back to the land of California, to my sweet home Chicago.

5

Now one and one is two, two and two is four,
I'm heavy loaded, baby, I'm booked I got to go.
Cryin', baby, honey, don't you want to go?
Back to the land of California, to my sweet home Chicago.   10

Now, two and two is four, four and two is six,
You gon' keep on monkeyin' 'round here friend-boy
You gon' get your business all in a trick,
But I'm cryin' baby, honey, don't you want to go?
Back to the land of California, to my sweet home Chicago.   15

Now, six and two is eight, eight and two is ten,
Friend-boy she trick you one time, she sure gon' do it again
But I'm cryin', hey, hey, baby, don't you want to go?
To the land of California, to my sweet home Chicago.

I'm goin' to California from there to Des Moines, Iowa,   20
Somebody will tell me that you need my help someday,
Cryin' hey, hey, baby, don't you want to go?
Back to the land of California, sweet home Chicago.

Muddy Waters.

MCKINLEY MORGANFIELD (MUDDY WATERS)   (1915–1983)

Mississippi-born McKinley Morganfield became famous as the blues performer Muddy Waters. A South Side fixture from the 1940s on, Waters first recorded the blues for Chicago's Chess Records (see Literary and Audio Locale: Chess Records, p. 1771). Later he made music with Bob Dylan, who wrote "Like a Rolling Stone" in tribute, and with Mick Jagger, whose band was named for the Muddy Waters song.

Rollin' Stone   (C. 1950)

Well, I wish I was a catfish,
swimmin' in a oh, deep, blue sea
I would have all you good lookin' women,
fishin', fishin' after me
Sure 'nough, a-after me   5
Sure 'nough, a-after me
Oh 'nough, oh 'nough, sure 'nough

I went to my baby's house,
and I sit down oh, on her steps.
She said, "Now, come on in now, Muddy   10
You know, my husband just now left
Sure 'nough, he just now left
Sure 'nough, he just now left"
Sure 'nough, oh well, oh well

Well, my mother told my father,
just before hmmm, I was born,
"I got a boy child's comin',
He's gonna be, he's gonna be a rollin' stone,
Sure 'nough, he's a rollin' stone
Sure 'nough, he's a rollin' stone"
Oh well he's a, oh well he's a, oh well he's a

Well, I feel, yes I feel,
feel that I could lay down oh, time ain't long
I'm gonna catch the first thing smokin',
back, back down the road I'm goin
Back down the road I'm goin
Back down the road I'm goin
Sure 'nough back, sure 'nough back

Willie Dixon.

WILLIE DIXON (1915–1992)

Willie Dixon wrote more famous blues songs than any other Chicago musician of the 1940s and 1950s. "Spoonful" was made famous by Howlin' Wolf.

Spoonful (C. 1955)

Could fill spoons full of diamonds,
Could fill spoons full of gold.
Just a little spoon of your precious love
Will satisfy my soul.

Men lies about it.
Some of them cries about it.
Some of them dies about it.
Everything's a-fightin' about the spoonful.
That spoon, that spoon, that spoonful.
That spoon, that spoon, that spoonful.
That spoon, that spoon, that spoonful.
That spoon, that spoon, that spoonful.

Could fill spoons full of coffee,
Could fill spoons full of tea.
Just a little spoon of your precious love;
Is that enough for me?

Chorus

Could fill spoons full of water,
Save them from the desert sands.
But a little spoon of your forty-five
Saved you from another man.

Chess Recording Studios exterior, 1997, at 2120 S. Michigan Avenue in Chicago.

Chess Records. The blues clubs where so much of the music of the Chicago Renaissance was played are no longer in business, but one home of the Chicago blues is still standing today: the Chess Records studio, where all the famous artists recorded, and where many of their songs were preserved for history. The studio began as Aristocrats Records, which was owned by the Aron family and produced mostly jazz and jump blues, a jazz-influenced up-tempo music that relegates the guitar to a backup role in the rhythm section. In 1947, two prominent Chicago nightclub owners, brothers Leonard and Phil Chess, became co-owners of the record company. With the introduction of songs recorded by Muddy Waters, who had moved to Chicago four years earlier, the company started to move in a new direction, recording an increasing number of blues artists. By 1949, the Chess brothers had full ownership of the company, and in 1950 they renamed it Chess Records.

Throughout the 1950s and well into the 1960s, Chess Records expanded its list of artists and included more blues, R&B, and eventually rock 'n' roll. During these years, they recorded such luminaries as Willie Dixon, Howlin' Wolf, Sonny Boy Williamson, and Chuck Berry. The Chess studio became so synonymous with great music that, in the 1960s, the Rolling Stones and the Yardbirds (best known as the starting point for British rock guitarists Eric Clapton, Jeff Beck, and Led Zeppelin's Jimmy Page) made a point of coming to Chicago to record there. The studio,

From left to right: Leonard Chess, Muddy Waters, Little Walter, Bo Diddley, c. early 1960s.

(continued)

located at 2120 S. Michigan Avenue, is now an official Chicago historical landmark. In 1985, Chess Records was purchased by the major music conglomerate MCA, now Universal Music Group. Many of the original recordings that established Chess's reputation are now available on CDs released as part of the Chess Collectibles series.

✦ COMMENTARY ON THE BLUES

Ralph Ellison, author of **Invisible Man**

Ralph Ellison described the blues as "an impulse to keep the painful details and episodes of a brutal experience alive in one's aching consciousness, to finger its jagged grain, and to transcend it, not by the consolation of philosophy but by squeezing from it a near-tragic, near-comic lyricism."

Langston Hughes

Langston Hughes said that "sad as Blues may be, there's almost always something humorous about them—even if it's the kind of humor that laughs to keep from crying."

LITERARY LOCALE

Chicago Blues Archive. The Chicago Blues Archive (CBA), *http:// cpl.lib.uic.edu/001hwlc/vpablues/cba.html*, housed within the larger Chicago Public Library at *cpl.lib.uic.edu/*, collects blues audio and visual recordings (some of which are not commercially available), promotional materials, artifacts, Chicago Blues Festival information, and other blues-related material donated to the library by a local radio station.

GOSPEL

The African American migration to Chicago brought a blues-influenced gospel sound to many northern churches, partly displacing the traditional spirituals and the conventional hymns that many black pastors and congregations once favored. By the 1940s, Chicago was the center of black gospel. Chicago-based singers such as Mahalia Jackson, Sallie Martin, the Soul Stirrers, and Roberta Martin gained national fame through their concerts and recordings. Chicago was the source for most of the latest and best gospel recordings and sheet music, which constituted a significant business opportunity for members of Chicago's black community.

Gospel artist Mahalia Jackson, for whom musician and song-writer Thomas Dorsey wrote "Peace in the Valley."

Thomas Dorsey.

THOMAS A. DORSEY   (1899–1993)

A Georgia-born bluesman, Thomas Dorsey became a Bronzeville-based gospel entrepreneur, writing and distributing best-selling songs through his own publishing house. Dorsey's lyrics are often characterized by a simple, straightforward eloquence and slightly old-fashioned diction. The music unfolds in slow, serious rhythms. "Peace in the Valley," written for Mahalia Jackson in 1937, was also performed by Roy Rogers and often sung by Elvis Presley. "Precious Lord, Take My Hand" was a favorite of Martin Luther King Jr.; Mahalia Jackson sang it at his funeral.

Peace in the Valley   (1937)

I am tired and weary but I must toil on
Till the Lord comes to take me away
Where the morning is bright and the Lamb is the light
And the night is as fair as the day.

Chorus

There'll be peace in the valley for me someday   5
There will be peace in the valley for me I pray
No more sorrow or sadness or trouble will be
There'll be peace in the valley for me.

There the flow'rs will be blooming the grass will be green
And the skies will be clear and serene   10
The sun ever shines giving one endless beam
And no clouds there will ever be seen.
(chorus)

There the bear will be gentle the wolf will be tame
And the lion will lay down with the lamb
The host from the wild will be led by the child   15
I'll be changed from the creature I am.
(chorus)

No headaches or heartaches or misunderstoods
No confusion or trouble won't be
No frowns to defile just a long endless smile
There'll be peace and contentment for me.   20
(chorus)

Precious Lord, Take My Hand   (1932)

Precious Lord, take my hand
Lead me on let me stand
I am tired, I am weak, I am worn
Through the storm, through the night,
Lead me on to the light   5
Take my hand, precious Lord, lead me home.

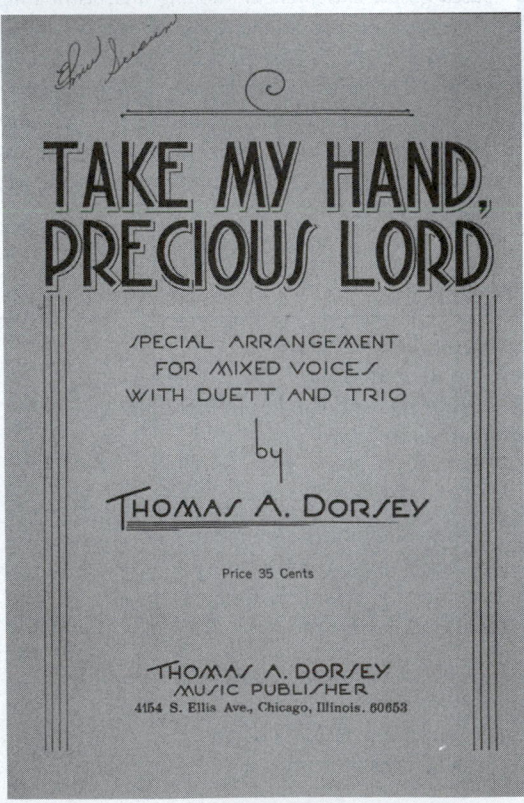

Sheet music cover of Thomas Dorsey's 1932 gospel hit, "Take My Hand, Precious Lord."

When my way grows drear,
Precious Lord linger near
When my life is almost gone
Hear my cry hear my call   10
Hold my hand lest I fall
Take my hand precious Lord, lead me home

When the darkness appears and the night draws near
And the day is almost gone
At the river I stand   15
Guide my feet hold my hand
Take my hand precious Lord, lead me home.

SAM COOKE   (1931–1964)

In 1951, Sam Cooke, son of a Chicago Baptist preacher, became the lead singer of the Soul Stirrers, a Chicago-based gospel quartet. He was a spectacular success and went on to pop and R&B fame in the later 1950s, though he always honored his gospel roots. In the two songs below, for which he wrote both the music and lyrics, he works with highly traditional themes of African American literature: Jesus welcoming sinners, and the eventual arrival of genuine brotherhood. In "A Change Is Gonna Come," Cooke's last hit before his tragic death in a shooting in December 1964, the lyrics are more circumspect and elliptical.

Sam Cooke, 1964.

If I Could Just Touch the Hem of His Garment   (1959)

There was a woman in the Bible days
She had been sick, sick so very long
When she heard that Jesus was passing by
She joined the gathering throng
And while she was pushing her way through   5
Someone asked her "What are you trying to do?"
She said "If I could just touch the hem of his garment
I know I'll be made whole soon."

She cried: "Oh Lord, Oh Lord, Oh Lord"
She said "If I could just touch the hem of his garment   10
I know I'll be made whole soon."

She spent her money here and there
Until she had no more to spare
The doctors did all they could
But their medicine did her no good   15
When she touched Him, the Savior didn't see
But He turned around and said,
"Somebody touched me." She said
"It was I who just wanna touch the Hem of your garment
I know I'll be made whole right now."   20

A Change Is Gonna Come   (1964)

I was born by the river in a little tent.
And just like the river, I've been running ever since.
It's been a long time coming,
But I know a change is gonna come.

It's been too hard living, but I'm afraid to die.   5
I don't know what's up there beyond the sky.
It's been a long time coming,
But I know a change is gonna come.

I go to the movie, and I go downtown.
Somebody keep telling me, "Don't hang around."   10
It's been a long time coming,
But I know a change is gonna come.

Then I go to my brother and I say, "Brother, help me please."
But he winds up knocking me back down on my knees.

There've been times that I've thought I couldn't last for long,   15
But now I think I'm able to carry on.
It's been a long time coming,
But I know a change is gonna come.

Talking about the Text

1. What themes do you spot in the blues lyrics? What themes are present in the gospel lyrics?
2. How important do the words seem in a blues song? Compare reading the lyrics and listening to a performance. How are the experiences different?
3. Many music lovers are "crazy for the blues." Why is the music so popular beyond its African American base?

Writing about the Text

1. Try writing a few blues or gospel lines, perhaps based on your own experience.
2. Write about the kinds of experiences that seem appropriate for the blues, using examples from the lyrics printed here.
3. Write an essay on a black "original" Chicago blues song and one by a white follower.

Linking the Text to other Texts

1. What blues lines or gospel phrases are familiar to you from more recent popular music you have heard?
2. What common elements do you detect in gospel and blues lyrics?
3. Compare two versions of a Dorsey gospel song. Note how the song can become assimilated into a vague "country" mode or remain rooted in the black gospel experience.

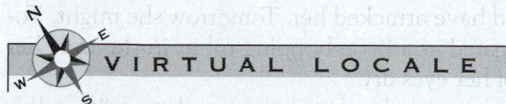

Encyclopedia of Chicago. The Chicago Historical Society, the Newberry Library, and Northwestern University jointly sponsor the Encyclopedia of Chicago website at *http://www.encyclopedia.chicagohistory.org.* The site offers a staggering array of primary and secondary source materials documenting the history of the city of Chicago, including articles, photos, maps, and newspapers.

STORIES FROM THE CHICAGO RENAISSANCE

GWENDOLYN BROOKS (1917–2000)

Known best for her poetry (see chapter 15 as well as "We Real Cool" and "The Lovers of the Poor" in this chapter, p. 1757), Gwendolyn Brooks wrote one novel, Maud Martha. *The story, in part a depiction of a father's struggle to save the family home when he is out of work, is told through the eyes of his young daughter, Maud Martha. The exultation the family feels over preserving their small Bronzeville house is stark testimony to the importance of a place to call home in the midst of the Great Depression. A short chapter from* Maud Martha, *"Home," appears below.*

Home (1953)

What had been wanted was this always, this always to last, the talking softly on this porch, with the snake plant in the jardiniere in the southwest corner, and the obstinate slip from Aunt Eppie's magnificent Michigan fern at the left side of the friendly door. Mama, Maud Martha and Helen rocked slowly in their rocking chairs, and looked at the late afternoon light on the lawn, and at the emphatic iron of the fence and at the poplar tree. These things might soon be theirs no longer. Those shafts and pools of light, the tree, the graceful iron, might soon be viewed possessively by different eyes.

Papa was to have gone that noon, during his lunch hour, to the office of the Home Owners' Loan. If he had not succeeded in getting another extension, they would be leaving this house in which they had lived for more than fourteen years. There was little hope. The Home Owners' Loan was hard. They sat, making their plans.

"We'll be moving into a nice flat somewhere," said Mama. "Somewhere on South Park, or Michigan, or in Washington Park Court." Those flats, as the girls and Mama knew well, were burdens on wages twice the size of Papa's. This was not mentioned now.

"They're much prettier than this old house," said Helen. "I have friends I'd just as soon not bring here. And I have other friends that wouldn't come down this far for anything, unless they were in a taxi."

Yesterday, Maud Martha would have attacked her. Tomorrow she might. To-   5
day she said nothing. She merely gazed at a little hopping robin in the tree, her
tree, and tried to keep the fronts of her eyes dry.

"Well, I do know," said Mama, turning her hands over and over, "that I've
been getting tireder and tireder of doing that firing. From October to April,
there's firing to be done."

"But lately we've been helping, Harry and I," said Maud Martha. "And
sometimes in March and April and in October, and even in November, we could
build a little fire in the fireplace. Sometimes the weather was just right for that."

She knew, from the way they looked at her, that this had been a mistake.
They did not want to cry.

But she felt that the little line of white, somewhat ridged with smoked purple, and all that cream-shot saffron, would never drift across any western sky except that in back of this house. The rain would drum with as sweet a dullness
nowhere but here. The birds on South Park were mechanical birds, no better
than the poor caught canaries in those "rich" women's sun parlors.

"It's just going to kill Papa!" burst out Maud Martha. "He loves this house!   10
He *lives* for this house!"

"He lives for us," said Helen. "It's us he loves. He wouldn't want the house,
except for us."

"And he'll have us," added Mama, "wherever."

"You know," Helen sighed, "if you want to know the truth, this is a relief. If
this hadn't come up, we would have gone on, just dragged on, hanging out here
forever."

"It might," allowed Mama, "be an act of God. God may just have reached
down, and picked up the reins."

"Yes," Maud Martha cracked in, "that's what you always say—that God   15
knows best."

Her mother looked at her quickly, decided the statement was not suspect,
looked away.

Helen saw Papa coming. "There's Papa," said Helen.

They could not tell a thing from the way Papa was walking. It was that
same dear little staccato walk, one shoulder down, then the other, then repeat, and repeat. They watched his progress. He passed the Kennedys', he
passed the vacant lot, he passed Mrs. Blakemore's. They wanted to hurl
themselves over the fence, into the street, and shake the truth out of his collar. He opened his gate—the gate—and still his stride and face told them
nothing.

"Hello," he said.

Mama got up and followed him through the front door. The girls knew bet-   20
ter than to go in too.

Presently Mama's head emerged. Her eyes were lamps turned on.

"It's all right," she exclaimed. "He got it. It's all over. Everything is all right."

The door slammed shut. Mama's footsteps hurried away.

"I think," said Helen, rocking rapidly, "I think I'll give a party. I haven't
given a party since I was eleven. I'd like some of my friends to just casually see
that we're homeowners."

RICHARD WRIGHT   (1908–1960)

Born in poverty in Mississippi, Richard Wright was raised by his mother, a schoolteacher, and his grandmother, a devout Seventh-Day Adventist, after his father, a tenant farmer, deserted the family. Wright attended school for several years, but his true education came from the wide reading he did as a young man when he wasn't working in a series of low-level jobs in Memphis, Tennessee, and Jackson, Mississippi. In 1927, Wright migrated to Chicago, where he took a number of temporary jobs and became active in the African American literary scene as well as in the Communist Party, which published some of his first stories. The ten years he spent in Chicago, from 1927 to 1937, gave him the inspiration for much of his later work. Chicago is where Wright learned to be a writer, and Chicago was his great subject, no matter where he lived later on.

Wright moved to New York in 1937, where he continued his increasingly troubled relationship with communism until 1944, when he resigned from the party, stymied over lack of artistic freedom. In 1938, he published his first book of stories, Uncle Tom's Children, and in 1940, he published Native Son, the controversial novel that established his national and international reputation as a writer. In his last years, Wright lived in Paris.

The Man Who Lived Underground   (1943)

In his powerful story "The Man Who Lived Underground," Richard Wright explores a theme familiar to his work: a black man hunted down for a real or imagined crime committed against white society. The view from underground allows Wright to offer readers an unusual yet stark perspective of late 1930s Chicago, a city where the police are hostile and where the normalities of life—church, a decent job—do not provide the sustenance a black man needs in the Depression economy. "The Man Who Lived Underground" derives its title from and connects thematically to Fyodor Dostoevsky's famous 1864 novel Notes from Underground, in which a totally alienated man bitterly denounces his uncaring modern society.

The text of Wright's "The Man Who Lived Underground" begins on p. 582 in the special fiction section, Chapter 9, "Stories for Further Reading." The "Starting Points for Further Research" section for Wright appears on p. 616 in that same chapter.

🦎 COMMENTARY

Margaret Walker on Richard Wright

In the 1930s, Margaret Walker befriended Richard Wright, whose biography she would publish in 1988. The book, Richard Wright: Daemonic Genius, documents the growing friendship between the well-educated but naive young Walker and the self-taught Wright on the verge of great fame, just before he left Chicago for New York. In the excerpt below, "Richard Wright and the Writer's Art," Walker shows us Wright as the enthusiastic reader of poetry and fiction from a broad range of authors, black and white, including Faulkner and Dostoevsky. She learns of the literary life from each encounter, particularly when they share office space through their government jobs as part of the Depression-era Federal Writers' Project. Walker only slowly realizes the depth of Wright's political commitment and his allegiance to the Communist Party.

Wright at his typewriter, 1945.

Richard Wright and the Writer's Art   (1988)

Early in 1936, Wright was deeply involved in four activities. First, he was writing his first long short stories, or novellas as he called them, which would be published in *Uncle Tom's Children*. Second, he was embroiled in a conflict on the Chicago Theatre Project of the WPA which would result in his being transferred back to the Writers' Project. Third, he was having trouble with his radical friends over his rebellion and resentment against their giving him explicit instructions about how he was to write and act. He refused to accept Communist party discipline without question. Socialist realism was for him too limited, and he was experiencing a conflict between his black nationalist feelings and his Communist beliefs. There was the outstanding and timely question of Leon Trotsky, one of the main figures with Lenin in the Russian Revolution, and his failure to find asylum in any of the so-called islands of freedom. Wright chafed at Stalinism and the discipline of the Communist party line. He did not like organizing, recruiting, and distributing literature. Fourth, Wright was planning a writers' group for the National Negro Congress, in which the Communist party assumed an aggressive role of leadership and sought to unify black and white labor with black intellectuals. The congress was announced in the newspapers, and one Sunday afternoon I went with a group of people from my neighborhood Methodist church, St. Matthews, to a planning session held on the South Side. Harry Haywood represented the Communist party at that planning session.

An outgrowth of the National Negro Congress, held in the Old Armory Building, was the South Side Writers' Group, which began in the spring of 1936. Wright was the leader, a kind of catalyst and an exciting hot center of that group. The group's first meeting was in the South Parkway home of Bob Davis, now Davis Roberts, television and movie actor. Bob was writing poetry in the 1930s, some of which was published in the magazine *New Challenge*.

Going back in my memory to that Sunday afternoon in February 1936, when I saw Wright for the first time, I remember that I went to the meeting because I heard it announced that Langston Hughes would be there. I had met Langston first in New Orleans on his tour of the South in February 1932, when he appeared in a lecture-recital, reading his poetry at New Orleans University (now Dillard University), where my parents taught. He had encouraged me then to continue writing poetry, and he had also urged my parents to get me out of the deep South. Four years later, to the very month, I wanted him to read what I had written since meeting him. Six months earlier I had graduated from Northwestern, and I still had no job. I was anxious to stay in Chicago, where I hoped to meet other writers, learn something more about writing, and perhaps publish some of my poetry. I tried to press my manuscripts on Langston, but when I admitted I had no copies he would not take them. Instead, he turned to Wright, who was standing nearby, listening to the conversation and smiling at my desperation. Langston said, "If you people really get a group together, don't forget to include this girl." Wright promised that he would remember.

(Text continues after color insert)

Visual Literacy and the Mean City Streets

The Great Migration of southern blacks to the cities of the North represented a remarkable demographic shift with nearly one million African Americans moving to northern cities between 1915 and 1920. Relocating to northern cities, these migrants often found not so much a better life but a different one. Their presence transformed the urban landscape, and they brought with them the culture and traditions of their southern heritage (as embodied by the Chicago Renaissance texts gathered in Chapter 25). The images collected here were chosen to examine how artists gave voice and vision to these experiences.

Romare Bearden (1911–1988)
The Street (Composition for Richard Wright) (c. 1977)

Romare Bearden's pen and ink drawing The Street (Composition for Richard Wright) *was first reproduced in the* New York Times *on April 8, 1977. The image accompanied an excerpt titled "What Set Storms Rolling in His Soul?" from Richard Wright's novel* American Hunger, *the restored, unabridged version of* Black Boy, *which was published posthumously in 1977.*

READING THE IMAGE. Closely study Bearden's drawing. Notice how the figures are depicted and the lack of color. Why do you think Bearden used this style of drawing?

LINKING IMAGE TO TEXT. Read the selection by Richard Wright (p. 582) as well as the information given about him in Chapter 25. Do you think Bearden's drawing expresses the major themes found in Wright's body of work? Explain.

Walter Ellison (1899–1977)
Train Station (1936)

Walter Ellison was part of the Great Migration, traveling from Georgia to Chicago by train. He studied at the Art Institute of Chicago and participated in several important exhibits, including the American Negro Exhibition. He was an active member of the South Side Community Art Center sponsored by the Works Project Administration (WPA).

READING THE IMAGE. As noted in Chapter 25, trains and movement are key themes found in art, music, and literature during the Great Migration and the Chicago Renaissance. Look closely at Walter Ellison's painting. Consider what purpose the columns serve. Make a list of all the details in the painting that comment on race relations of the time.

LINKING IMAGE TO TEXT. Trains are often used symbolically in works by African Americans. Locate other works in Chapter 25 that include the motifs of trains and travel. Are trains always used to suggest hope? Explain.

Russell Lee (1903–1986)
Children Playing in the Water Backed Up in the Gutter in the South Side (Chicago, 1941)

Russell Lee was part of the Farm Security Administration (FSA) during the Great Depression. Lee and other FSA photographers, including Dorothea Lange, Gordon Parks, and Walker Evans, left an enduring body of work that chronicles the appalling living and working conditions of many—urban and rural, black and white—during this period of widespread economic hardship.

READING THE IMAGE. While certain conditions in Chicago were "better" than in the southern home towns the migrants left behind, life was still hard and filled with new problems. What specific living conditions do you think Russell Lee was trying to call attention to in this photo?

LINKING IMAGE TO TEXT. Children are a common theme in Lee's work. What other Chicago Renaissance authors use the conditions of children to comment on the quality of life in Chicago's South Side, known as Bronzeville? How does their writing about children compare to Lee's portraits?

Hale Woodruff (1900–1980)
Returning Home (1935)

Hale Woodruff painted murals and other works reflecting on African American culture and history. He studied in Chicago as well as Paris and Mexico. He was a gifted teacher and taught at Atlanta University and New York University. At Atlanta University he started a national juried competition that brought attention to up-and-coming artists.

READING THE IMAGE. Woodruff titled his painting *Returning Home*. Describe what is going on in the painting. How does the style of the painting help convey its themes?

LINKING IMAGE TO TEXT. Finding a home and finding a way to pay the rent were priorities for many arriving in Chicago during the Great Migration. How do the themes in Woodruff's painting agree (or not) with the themes of home in the readings in Chapter 25?

Jacob Lawrence (1917–2000)
The Migrants Arrived in Great Numbers (1940–1941)

The Migrants Arrived in Great Numbers is one panel from Jacob Lawrence's sixty-panel work The Migration of the Negro. *Lawrence moved to Harlem as a young teenager. He studied at the Harlem Art Workshop and worked for the WPA Art Project. Much of his work chronicles the existence of African Americans. "My belief," Lawrence has said, "is that it is most important for an artist to develop an approach and philosophy about life—if he has developed this philosophy he does not paint on canvas, he puts himself on canvas."*

READING THE IMAGE. What colors are dominant in Lawrence's panel? Why do you think Lawrence chose this palette? List all the details in the painting that support Lawrence's quote given above. What themes do you think he is suggesting in this work?

LINKING IMAGE TO TEXT. Read the poems by Langston Hughes on pages 445, 876, and 1076. Compare the themes in Hughes's poems to the ones found in Lawrence's painting.

Sweet Home Chicago:
Jazz, The Blues, and The Oral Tradition

Blues and jazz trace their origins back to the oral traditions of African music. Africans who were sent to America to be sold into slavery carried their oral traditions to the southern plantations, and American blues and jazz were born. This music made another journey, moving North during the Great Migration. The jazz and blues played in Chicago developed a more urban sound, but these musical forms retain the themes of pain and isolation found in their African roots.

Muddy Waters, known as the father of Chicago blues,
performs his music in a concert in 1979

READING THE IMAGE. Muddy Waters's influence on popular music is profound. Bob Dylan's 2006 album *Modern Times* includes rewrites of Waters music and the likes of Jimi Hendrix, Eric Clapton, and Led Zeppelin have also covered his songs. Given his celebrity among musicians, how would you describe Waters's demeanor on stage? Cite specific details to support your description.

LINKING IMAGE TO TEXT. Read the lyrics to the Waters song "Rollin' Stone" in Chapter 25 (p. 1769). What characteristics give this song its "blues" quality?

Tenor saxophonist Benny Golson and trumpeter Art Farmer, playing their music in front of young fans

READING THE IMAGE. Passing traditions to a younger generation is an important way of keeping a culture alive. The African American community has been especially successful in exposing their children to their musical heritage. Describe the visual interplay between the children and the musicians in the photograph above. Note the age of the children in your description.

LINKING IMAGE TO TEXT. Read the story "Sonny's Blues" by James Baldwin (p. 619). Explain how jazz functions in the story. Support your points with evidence from the text. Can you reconcile the role of music in "Sonny's Blues" and the visual impression given in the photo of Farmer and Golson? Explain.

Romare Bearden (1911–1988)
The Piano Lesson (Homage to Mary Lou) (1983)

The "Mary Lou" in the subtitle of Romare Bearden's painting is thought to be Mary Lou Williams (1910–1981), consummate composer and pianist whose music evolved from swing to bop to the free jazz of the 1960s. As Williams's music inspired Bearden's painting, Bearden's art inspired August Wilson's writing. Bearden's collage was the inspiration for Wilson's play The Piano Lesson *in Chapter 26.*

READING THE IMAGE. Bearden's use of collage not only allows him to include materials from everyday life but the technique also underscores the role of fragmentation in the lives of many African Americans. Who are the two figures? Can you determine their relationship? How is the idea of fragmentation shown in this image?

LINKING IMAGE TO TEXT. Although Mary Lou Williams lived in Pittsburgh, which is also the setting for Wilson's play, the themes of music and fragmentation are rich sources of inspiration in all northern cities that experienced the Great Migration. Choose two selections in Chapter 25 and identify how themes of fragmentation are expressed.

A month passed, and I heard nothing. I presumed he had either forgotten or they didn't get a group together. Meanwhile, on Friday, March 13, 1936, I received my notice in the mail to report to the WPA Writers' Project. Six weeks later I received a penny post card inviting me to the first meeting of the South Side Writers' Group. Twice I left the house and turned back, the first time out of great self-consciousness because I felt I looked abominable. I had nothing to wear to make a nice appearance, and I was going to the far South Side, where I felt people would make fun of me. But my great desire to meet writers and end my long isolation conquered this superficial fear. I made myself go. When I arrived at the address given on the card, I discovered I was very late. I thought the meeting was over, and I heard people laughing as I blurted out, "Is this the right place, or am I too late?" I heard a man expounding on the sad state of Negro writing at that point in the thirties, and he was punctuating his remarks with pungent epithets. I drew back in Sunday-school horror, totally shocked by his strong speech, but I steeled myself to hear him out. The man was Richard Wright. Later, each person present was asked to bring something to read next time, but most people refused. When I was asked, I said, rather defiantly, that I would. I left the meeting alone.

The next time we met at Lincoln Center on Oakwood Boulevard, and I read a group of my poems. I was surprised to see they did not cut me down. Ted Ward and Dick Wright were kind in their praise. I remember Russell Marshall and Edward Bland were also there. Bland was killed in the Battle of the Bulge. I was completely amazed to hear Wright read a piece of prose he was working on. Even after I went home I kept thinking, "My God, how that man can write!" After the meeting Wright said he was going my way. He asked me if I were on the Writers' Project, and I said, yes. Then he said, "I think I'm going to get on that project." I looked at him in complete disbelief. I knew it took weeks and months to qualify for the WPA, plus additional red tape to get on one of the professional or arts projects. What I did not know was that he had been on the WPA for some time. He was merely transferring from the Theatre Project to the Writers' Project.

When I went to the project office for my semi-weekly assignment the next week, Wright was the first person I saw when I got off the elevator. He quickly came over and led me to his desk. He was a supervisor, and I was a junior writer. My salary was $85 per month, while his was $125. He hastened to explain that he was responsible for his mother, his aunt and his younger brother and, therefore, the head of a family, though single, while I had only my sister as my responsibility. A year later I advanced to $94; by that time he was getting ready to leave Chicago.

Gradually, a pattern established itself in our relationship on the project. I went downtown twice weekly with my assignments for the *Illinois Guide Book*, and afterward I spent most of the day in conversation with Wright. Sometimes I was there at the end of the day, but I never worked daily, as he did, in the office. I worked at home and went looking for news stories or covered art exhibits and made reports. And that is how I came to have a creative assignment after I had been on the project about nine months. Wright worked with the editorial group and sandwiched his writing in-between when there was a lull in office work. He had taught himself to type by the hunt-and-peck method, and I was astounded to watch him type away with two or three fingers while his eyes concentrated on the keyboard.

Shortly after I met Wright, I attended a Midwest Writers' Conference, my first writers' conference. He was speaking and asked me to attend. In one of our South Side Writers' Group meetings I recalled the event, and Frank Marshall Davis asked me if that wasn't a Communist group. I was confused and said, "I don't know." Then

I looked at Wright, who only grinned gleefully and said, "Don't look at me!" The whole thing sank in gradually that he was a Communist. I honestly didn't know what Communism or Marxism meant. I had had no courses in sociology, economics, or political science while I was a student in college. I majored in English, with emphasis on the European Renaissance and, except for a few basic and general courses in mathematics, science, psychology, and religion, I concentrated on literature, history, and languages. My sister knew more about Hitler and Stalin than I did. I was even more puzzled when Jack Scher tried to give me some advice one afternoon as I left the project. He said, "Margaret, I hope you will get to know all these people on the project without getting to be a part of them and all they represent. You are young, and you have talent. You can go far, so observe them but don't join them." Only years later did I begin to understand him. At the time I seriously thought he was talking about the labor movement, which was so exciting at that time. The Congress of Industrial Organizations (CIO) was just being organized, and I heard John L. Lewis speak several times. The American Federation of Labor (AFL) had never wanted Negroes in their trade unions. Wright seemed intensely interested in the labor struggle as well as in all the problems of race and what he explained to me was a "class struggle."

One of the first books he handed me to read was John Reed's *Ten Days That Shook the World*. I was fascinated. That same summer Maxim Gorky died, and I had never before heard the name. I read quickly his *Lower Depths* and *Mother*, and then I read the so-called Red Archbishop of Canterbury's book, *The Soviet Power*. Having very little money to spend on books, I bought them as I bought my clothes, on lay-away, and under the influence and partial tutelage of Wright, I put five Modern Library Giant books in lay-away: Karl Marx's *Das Kapital*, John Strachey's *The Coming Struggle for Power*, *The Complete Philosophy of Nietzsche*, Adam Smith's *The Wealth of Nations*, and a novel by Romain Rolland. A whole year later, and long after Wright was in New York, the books were mine.

One afternoon as we talked Wright quoted from T. S. Eliot:

> Let us go then, you and I, when the evening is spread out against the sky
> like a patient etherized upon a table.

And he exclaimed, "What an image!" Something exploded in my head, and I went home to find my copy of Louis Untermeyer's anthology, *Modern American Poetry*, and re-read Eliot. I remember how dull he had seemed at Northwestern when the teacher was reading aloud, and even when I heard Eliot reading on a bad recording, "We are the hollow men . . ."

I began James Joyce with *Portrait of the Artist as a Young Man* then read *Ulysses*. Wright used Joyce as an example when writing *Lawd Today*, being struck by a book that kept all the action limited to one day, but he considered *Lawd Today*, which I retyped for him, as one of his worst works. It was actually his first completed novel and reflects the problems of the novice. I remember that he regarded Melanchtha in Gertrude Stein's *Three Lives* as the first serious study of a Negro girl by a white American writer.

Stephen Crane's *Red Badge of Courage* I knew, but not *Maggie, Girl of the Streets*, which was Wright's favorite. I think from the beginning we differed about Hemingway and Faulkner. Although I had read some of Hemingway, I had not read much of Faulkner, and despite Wright's ecstatic feeling about *Sanctuary*, I found it revolting, possibly because I was still strongly influenced by a moralistic and puritanical background.

I never worshipped at the altars of either Hemingway or Faulkner, but Wright deeply admired both.

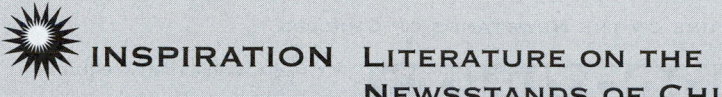

INSPIRATION LITERATURE ON THE NEWSSTANDS OF CHICAGO

One reason literature flourished in Chicago was the widespread dissemination of new black voices in a number of publications created during the first half of the twentieth century. The *Chicago Defender*, founded in 1905, was not a literary magazine—it was the first major black city newspaper—but its revolutionary achievements extended well beyond journalism and into the literary and artistic realm. Gwendolyn Brooks published her first poems in its pages in 1934 and Langston Hughes's "Simple" stories began in 1943 as a weekly column. The Chicago-based magazines *Poetry*, founded by Harriet Monroe in 1912, and the *Little Review*, founded by Margaret Anderson, had established their acclaimed reputations by publishing modernists—Ezra Pound, James Joyce, and William Butler Yeats among them—but as the literary movements in Chicago gained momentum, they went on to publish important black voices, including Margaret Danner.

Other publications were created specifically to showcase African American politics and culture, including the black literary talent that was predominantly coming out of New York and Chicago. In 1910, W. E. B. Du Bois founded the publication arm of the National Association for the Advancement of Colored Peoples (NAACP), which began offering the *Crisis*, edited by Du Bois. This magazine, a creative forum for the African American population, included the early poems of Langston Hughes during the 1920s and Margaret Walker's first published poem, "Daydream," which appeared there in 1934. *Opportunity: A Journal of Negro Life*, established by the National Urban League in 1923 and edited by Charles S. Johnson, similarly promoted the work of up and coming black writers, including Hughes, Arna Bontemps, and the Harlem-based Zora Neale Hurston.

Many of these periodicals had an overt political bent to them, but others had their foundations in more artistic concerns. For example, *Fire!!* magazine, based in New York, was conceived of in 1926 as

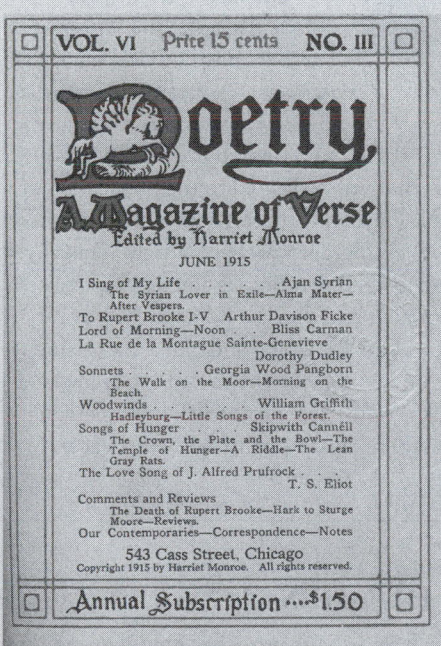

Cover of the June 1915 issue of Chicago-based Poetry *magazine. This issue featured T. S. Eliot's poem "The Love Song of J. Alfred Prufrock."*

(continued on next page)

LITERATURE ON THE NEWSTANDS OF CHICAGO

Cover of the January 1925 issue of Chicago-based Opportunity: A Journal of Negro Life.

an artistic collaborative effort between Wallace Thurman, Langston Hughes, Gwendolyn Bennett, Richard Bruce Nugent, Zora Neale Hurston, Aaron Douglas, and John Davis. The magazine folded after only one issue due to lack of financing and because its nonpolitical "art for art's sake" credo was considered controversial, but the talent displayed in it was formidable. It featured works by its founders, including art by Aaron Douglas and Richard Bruce, Hughes's poem "Elevator Boy," and Hurston's story "Sweat" (see p. 318 in Chapter 7), as well as poetry by Arna Bontemps, who had ties to both New York and Chicago.

One lesser known, but unique magazine was *Negro Story*, founded in 1944 by two African American women, Alice C. Browning and Fern Gayden, who wanted to create what they called a "magazine for all Americans" that was dedicated to the publication of short fiction about African Americans. Gayden had been a member of the now-famous South Side Writers' Group, which included Richard Wright, Frank Marshall Davis, Margaret Walker, and Gwendolyn Brooks among its members; unsurprisingly, works by the group's participants found a home in *Negro Story*. In their editors' letter in the inaugural issue, Browning and Gayden explained their publishing vision, which might be said to echo the mission statements of many new Chicago periodicals of this period: "The idea struck us that among thirteen million Negroes in America, there must be many who were eager to write creatively if they had a market."

Langston Hughes in Chicago, April 1942.

LANGSTON HUGHES   (1902–1967)

Langston Hughes was born in Missouri, raised in Ohio and Illinois, and moved to New York to study engineering at Columbia, where he stayed only a year, determined to make a life in the arts. By the time he had graduated from Pennsylvania's Lincoln University in 1929, Hughes had published his famous poem, "A Negro Speaks of Rivers," in the prominent African American journal Crisis (1921) and won a first prize in poetry from Opportunity, another well-known black publication. He had been "discovered" by the white benefactor of the Harlem Renaissance, Carl Van Vechten, who had helped arrange for the publication of his first book of poetry, Weary Blues, in 1926. Another book of poetry followed in 1927. Thus, while only in his twenties, Hughes had become a celebrated voice of the Harlem Renaissance.

But Hughes as a literary figure could not be contained by a single city, and his influence quickly spread to the writers of Chicago. Indeed, Hughes was simply a literary giant, amazingly productive in an enormous variety of genres and places, from Chicago to Paris. Though based in New York after about 1942, he was constantly on the move. He had lived in Mexico for a year with his father while a young man, had visited West Africa and worked in Paris, and had traveled to Russia, Italy, Haiti, Japan, and Spain, where he reported on the Spanish Civil War for the Baltimore Afro-American. And of course he had spent time in the major American cities. Thus, he knew everybody, black and white, and encouraged the Chicago Renaissance writers, also including them in anthologies of black poetry, fiction, and folklore. He established a black theater in Chicago (as well as in Harlem).

"In the Dark" places one of Langston Hughes's most famous comic characters, Jessie B. Semple, nicknamed "Simple," in a Chicago bar, trying to pick up a fine-looking woman but getting nowhere. Simple was featured in columns that Hughes wrote for the Chicago Defender, one of America's premier black newspapers. The character won the hearts of countless readers and helped give the Defender a national circulation. Simple appeared in a number of Hughes's books: Simple Speaks His Mind (1950), Simple Takes a Wife (1953), Simple's Uncle Sam (1965). The character also was the basis for a Broadway musical, Simply Heavenly (1957). As Hughes wrote in 1946, "I get two sets of fan letters, some to me, some to Simple." The repartee in "In the Dark" reflects that Hughes was a poet as well as a writer of stories.

In the Dark

(1939)

"What you know, daddy-o?" hailed Simple.

"Where have you been so long lately?" I demanded.

"Chicago on my last two War Bonds," answered Simple, "to see my Cousin Art's new baby to which I am godfather—against the wife's will, because she is holy and sanctified."

"What is the trend of affairs in Chicago?" I inquired.

"Balling and brawling," said Simple. "And me with 'em."

"Did you take in the DeLisa?"

"No, I did not take in the DeLisa," said Simple, but I went to the Brass Rail, also Square's, also that club on 63rd and South Park which jumps out loud. Also the Blue Dahlia."

"You got around, then."

"Sure did! I went to a couple of them new cocktail lounges, too, what don't have no light in 'em at all hardly. Chicago has the darkest bars in the world. So dark it is just like walking into a movie. Man, you have to stop and pause till you can see the bar. The booths are like Lovers' Lane, man. I thought my eyesight was failing the first time I went in one. Everything's the same color under them lightless lights. Ain't no telling whiskey from gin with the natural eye."

"You were probably intoxicated," I said.

5

10

"I was expecting to get high," said Simple, "but I did not succeed. The glass was thick that night and the whiskey thin. But I met a old chick who looked *fine* setting there in the dark, although I couldn't of seen her had she not had on a white hat. I asked her what her name was and she told me Bea.

" 'But don't get me wrong, King Kong, because I told you my name,' she said, 'I am a lady! My mamma calls me Bea-Baby at home.'

"I said, 'What does your daddy call you?'

"She said, 'I has no daddy.'

"I said, 'You must be looking for *me* then.'   15

"She said, 'I *heard* you before I saw you so I could not have been *looking* for you. You abstract attention to yourself. But since you asked me, I drink Scotch.'

"So I ordered her some Teacher's. But that girl was thirsty! She drunk me up—at Sixty-Five Cents a shot! I said, 'Bea-Baby, let's get some air.'

"She said, 'Air? I growed up in air! I got plenty of air when I were a child. Sixteen miles south of Selma there weren't nothing but air.'

" 'Selma is far enough South, but *sixteen miles south of there* is too much! How long you been up North, girl?'

" 'Two years,' she said, 'and if I live to be a hundred, I will be up here sev-   20
enty-five more.'

" 'You mean you are not going back to Selma?'

" 'Period,' she said.

" 'In other words, you are going to stay in Chicago?'

" 'Oh, but I am,' she said.

" 'Well, we are not going to stay in this bar seventy-five years,' I whispered.   25
'Come on, Bea-Baby, let's walk.'

" 'Walk where?' she hollered, insulted.

" 'Follow me and you will see,' I said.

" 'I will not follow you, unless you tell me where we are going.'

'I will not tell you where we are going, unless you follow,' I said.

"But when we got out of that darker-than-a-movie bar, under the street   30
lights on Indiana Avenue, I got a good look at her and she got a good look at me. We *both* said 'Good-by!' In that dim dark old dusky cocktail lounge, I thought she was mellow. But she were not! I thought she was a chippy, but she were at least forty-five.

"And the first thing she said when she saw my face was, 'I thought you was a *young* man—but you ain't. You old as my Uncle Herman.'

"I said, 'I done had so many unpleasant surprises in my life, baby, until my age is writ in my face. *You* is one more unpleasantness.'

"I thought she said 'Farewell,' but it could of been 'Go to hell.'

"Anyhow, she cured me of them dark Chicago bars. *Never make friends in the dark*, is what I learned in Chicago."

"I am glad you learned something," I said.   35

"Thank you," said Simple. "Now, come on let's have a beer to welcome me back to Harlem. Not to change the subjects but lend me a quarter. I'm broke.

"I'm broke, too."

"Then you can't have a beer, daddy-o," regretted Simple. "What is worse, neither can I."

❧ COMMENTARY

Letters of Langston Hughes and Arna Bontemps

During the Great Depression, most black artists and writers faced the question of how to make a living. Could a writer publish enough stories to put food on the table? Could newspaper work bring home a living? Were lectures a possible way to make ends meet? The writer's trade is always a tough one; it was particularly difficult for black writers, whose audience tended to be especially poor and could not afford to buy luxuries like books. The poet Margaret Walker offers us a striking picture of the difficulties literary artists faced when she describes her friend Richard Wright, on the verge of great fame and huge book sales, quoting T. S. Eliot, at a time when he was literally inhabiting a closet (see pp. 1780–1782).

The letters between Langston Hughes and Arna Bontemps nicely capture the voices of two prominent black writers and cultural leaders as they scheme together about trying to make enough money through their literature. Arna Bontemps (1902–1973) was by and large a product of the Chicago Renaissance. He grew up in Louisiana and lived in Chicago during the 1930s, obtaining a graduate degree in library science from the University of Chicago. In 1943 he became the director of the Fisk University Library in Nashville and remained there until retirement. He published poetry, short stories, and novels, some for children. His friend Langston Hughes, the most famous African American poet of his time, wrote plays, novels, and a memoir in addition to poetry. Based in Harlem, Hughes traveled widely and his influence was felt everywhere. He periodically joined the Chicago scene for weeks or months at a time. One key topic of the letters between these two good friends, who met in 1924, is how to make a living as a writer in the America of the Great Depression.

With a family to feed, Bontemps eventually took a full-time job because he could not make a living from his pen. Hughes did manage to support himself from the earnings of his writing—one of the few black writers to do so since the nineteenth-century poet Paul Laurence Dunbar (p. 1060). But Hughes juggled a bewildering array of projects and genres to make ends meet: poetry, novels, short stories, anthologies, plays, librettos for musicals, and newspaper reports and columns.

In their correspondence, the two friends reveal a fascinating side of literary life during the Chicago Renaissance, when hardly anybody was making much money, and writers even less. The letters also reveal how much Hughes and Bontemps participated in a recognizable Chicago cultural community, with gospel musician Thomas Dorsey and poets Gwendolyn Brooks and Margaret Walker all making brief appearances in these excerpts from their extensive correspondence.

From Hughes, November 20, 1939

. . . in April I'll be in Chicago for the whole month, so any lectures which we can get jointly (or for me alone) would be most welcome. . . . We ought to be able to get a lot of YM and YWCA engagements together (also YMHA (Jewish)—I'm speaking for them in New York) in the Spring in Illinois, Michigan, Indiana, etc. around about Chicago. Also try Urban League & NAACP, sororities and fraternities, clubs and churches. For churches take a 60–40 percentage. The 60% of gross to go to us with a minimum of $25.00.

I'd be delighted to take Evanston again. There must be some Negro frats at the Illinois State and the other colleges round about that could present us. What about white literary clubs in Chicago area? What about Federation of Colored

Women's Clubs? I have got to lecture me up three or four hundred bucks this spring to write that novel on while I'm in Chi. Such is IMPERATIVE. So we might as well hustle it up together.

Also the trade unions are beginning to be culturally inclined. Try Hank Johnson's and Ishmael's and Dining Car folks.

From Bontemps, Chicago, December 14, 1939

This is the seventh month we [i.e., his family] have lived on "literature," and I can hardly believe my eyes when I look around and see that not one of the brood has starved. Let's hope the first seven are the worst! I hope to get back on my novel Jan 1st. If I can keep meal in the barrel till that's finished, I'll feel like shouting and hallelujah.

From Hughes, January 26, 1940

Eager to write the second volume [of autobiography] for which I have even better material. So maybe that is what I shall do in Chicago in April if I can find a good hide-out. That is the speakingest town! Who told everybody I was coming through there in February. Have three or four letters already asking for FREE talks. Don't they know I'm a writer not a speaker—except to speak for my supper money—which does not seem to occur to them to offer? Huh? Or have you spoilt them? Great big town like Chicago with half the Negroes in America in it and two-thirds of the white folks—and still wanting to hear somebody talk FREEEEEEEEEEEEEE!

From Bontemps, Chicago, no date

The days have been terrible thus far in the new year—all work and no play, not even any writing on the new play. I have just naturally quit fooling myself. There is just no chance of my doing any writing while tied up as at present. So I have decided not to let it worry my mind any more. Of course, I get up an hour early each morning and do a few paragraphs on a nebulous and legendary novel just to keep my hand in, but I have no hope of finishing anything worth while till one of three things comes to pass: 1. I get a new job with more hours of leisure, 2. I lose my present job and go on relief, or 3. Pennies fall from heaven. Meanwhile I console myself with the assurance that I shall have your new biography to comfort me, come fall. If that fails me, then woe indeed.

From Bontemps, Chicago, May 8, 1942

Lieber [Bontemps's literary agent] just sent Common Ground's check for "Rock, Church, Rock!" Either the June or September issue, according to Margaret Anderson. Dorsey, who gave permission to reproduce some of his music, was here to lunch last week. He asked about you. I'm quoting part of "Rock Me" and part of Roberta Martin's "Didn't It Rain," the song that Cobb's choir made famous. The music right along with the words.

From Hughes, November 14, 1945

I gave *They Seek a City* [Bontemps's book] a plug in several of my talks when I speak of urban conditions and trials and tribulations. . . . You had better stop reviewing all those books and get down to your WORK. (I am just mad because I can't even read anything, let alone review it.)

From Hughes, May 2, 1946
Listing some of his accomplishments for an article Bontemps is writing on him:

Translated into Uzbek among other languages. . . . Singers of my songs range from Lawrence Tibbett to Josh White, Marian Anderson to Marion Oswald. . . . I get two sets of fan letters, some to me, some to Simple. . . . Hobbies: Collecting House Rent Party cards and attending Gospel Song Battles. . . . In only one railroad wreck in all my travels. Got an overcoat out of that, and nary a scratch. . . . Sometimes sleep 15 hours at one time. Lately (more and more) am invited to deliver the Sunday morning message at churches (Paid).

From Bontemps, Nashville, August 26, 1946

Owen's [Dodson] book is very good—his poems as a whole make a stronger impression than did the isolated ones I had seen in magazines. In fact, I think his work is more in the mood of "the awakening" than is any by the other poets that have appeared since. With Owen, Margaret [Walker], Gwendolyn [Brooks] and [Melvin] O'Higgins on the verge, it would seem to be time for another big anthology of Negro poetry. Why don't you (or one of your associates) ask Viking to have ME collect one for the PORTABLE series of books. I'd like to do it, but I'd rather not raise the question. The Portable series already has an Irish anthology. I believe that a Negro poetry (there has recently been a prose anthology or two) collection would do better in this series than published by another publisher as an independent item, but I may be wrong.

CYRUS COLTER   (1910–2002)

Cyrus Colter spent the first part of his long career in business and the law, and for more than twenty years he was a commissioner with the Illinois Commerce Commission. In 1970, while still in that position, he published a collection of stories, The Beach Umbrella, which received a fiction prize from the University of Iowa School of Letters. In 1973, he became a professor of English at Northwestern University, just north of Chicago, where he produced more short stories and several novels. In terms of his birth date and many of his characteristic themes, Colter belongs to the Chicago Renaissance, though his work was not published during that period. He often deals with the theme of class within the black Chicago community, exploring the lives of both the comfortable and the working classes.

Mary's Convert   (1965)

In his story "Mary's Convert," Colter speaks knowingly about the complex intermingling of worldly and religious desires, a commonplace for streetwise Chicagoans, but still somewhat shocking to those who led more sheltered lives. The text of "Mary's Convert" begins on p. 40 in Chapter 1, "Stories: Plot, Character, and Setting." The "Starting Points for Further Research" section for Colter appears on p. 47 in that same chapter.

Talking about the Text

1. What is your opinion of the "underground man" of Richard Wright's story? Is he insane? Is he moral or immoral? Do we understand why he acts and feels the way he does? Do our feelings about him shift at different parts of the story?
2. One device of the black oral tradition is the practice of "playing the dozens," a sustained repartee that seeks to deliver the cleverest and funniest insult. (Some readers may be familiar with the "mama" jokes: e.g., "You mama so big that . . . ") How is that device employed in Langston Hughes's Simple story?

Writing about the Text

1. Discuss the ways that Wright plays with the notion of under ground and above ground in "The Man Who Lived Underground." Write about which position is more desirable and why. Pay special attention to the ways your answer may shift in different parts of the story.
2. Write about Langston Hughes's Simple story as a kind of "country versus city" tale, with Simple the country guy trying hard to learn to be cool.

Linking the Text to other Texts

1. Investigate Fyodor Dostoevsky's *Notes from Underground* briefly in a literary encyclopedia or a website. Wright greatly admired the Russian writer; how does knowing he had Dostoevsky in mind when he wrote "The Man Who Lived Underground" change our experience of that story?
2. Langston Hughes frequently wrote poems that echoed and embedded the blues. Which lines in the Simple story could you imagine appearing as a blues lyric?

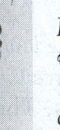

Lorraine Hansberry

LORRAINE HANSBERRY   (1930–1965)

Lorraine Hansberry was born into a prominent Chicago family; her father was a real estate broker who ran for Congress. During the 1940s and 1950s, the Hansberry home was a stopping place for the African American cultural elite, including Paul Robeson, Langston Hughes, Martin Luther King Jr., and Harry Belafonte. Hansberry's father, a civil rights activist, fought the Jim Crow laws and restrictive covenants that limited the sale of property in white areas to white buyers. By the time of A Raisin in the Sun, Lorraine Hansberry lived in New York, but the play was rooted in her Chicago experiences. She is a true product of the Chicago Renaissance.

A Raisin in the Sun takes place when housing in Chicago was at a premium. It was scarce for all Chicagoans, because few new homes had been built during the Depression 1930s or World War II 1940s. But for African Americans, who were largely confined to the South Side and the West Side, the postwar housing crisis was particularly acute. Not only was Bronzeville housing substandard, but blacks were subject to bombings and other violence whenever they tried to buy or rent residences beyond the boundaries of Bronzeville. Hansberry's family experienced this violence firsthand, as her memoirs show.

At the same time housing problems peaked, the 1950s offered black Chicagoans a long-delayed postwar prosperity and affluence. In the play, Walter's dream of making it big is not totally unrealistic, though difficult to attain. His sister's boyfriend, for instance, comes from a rich black family. Most hopeful to black Chicagoans was the beginning of the civil rights movement that would bring Martin Luther King Jr. to national awareness. Signs of that stirring are evident in A Raisin in the Sun, particularly in the attitudes of Beneatha and Walter.

A Raisin in the Sun   (1959)

Characters (in order of appearance)

Ruth Younger	Beneatha Younger	Mrs. Johnson
Travis Younger	Lena Younger, Mama	Karl Lindner
Walter Lee Younger, brother	Joseph Asagai	Bobo
	George Murchison	Moving Men

The action of the play is set in Chicago's Southside, sometime between World War II and the present.

ACT I

Scene 1. [Friday morning.] The Younger living room would be a comfortable and well-ordered room if it were not for a number of indestructible contradictions to this state of being. Its furnishings are typical and

Audra McDonald and Sean Combs (better known as hip-hop producer and artist "Puffy," "P. Diddy," or "Diddy") as Ruth and Walter Lee Younger in the 2004 Broadway production of A Raisin in the Sun. The play garnered two Tony Awards, one to McDonald as Best Featured Actress in a Play and one to Philicia Rashad as Best Actress for her role as Lena Younger.

undistinguished and their primary feature now is that they have clearly had to accommodate the living of too many people for too many years—and they are tired. Still, we can see that at some time, a time probably no longer remembered by the family (except perhaps for Mama), the furnishings of this room were actually selected with care and love and even hope—and brought to this apartment and arranged with taste and pride.

That was a long time ago. Now the once loved pattern of the couch upholstery has to fight to show itself from under acres of crocheted doilies and couch covers which have themselves finally come to be more important than the upholstery. And here a table or a chair has been moved to disguise the worn places in the carpet; but the carpet has fought back by showing its weariness, with depressing uniformity, elsewhere on its surface.

Weariness has, in fact, won in this room. Everything has been polished, washed, sat on, used, scrubbed too often. All pretenses but living itself have long since vanished from the very atmosphere of this room.

Moreover, a section of this room, for it is not really a room unto itself, though the landlord's lease would make it seem so, slopes backward to provide a small kitchen area, where the family prepares the meals that are eaten in the living room proper, which must also serve as dining room. The single window that has been provided for these "two" rooms is located in this kitchen area. The sole natural light the family may enjoy in the course of a day is only that which fights its way through this little window.

At left, a door leads to a bedroom which is shared by Mama and her daugher, Beneatha. At right, opposite, is a second room (which in the beginning of the life of this apartment was probably a breakfast room) which serves as a bedroom for Walter and his wife, Ruth.

Time: Sometime between World War II and the present.

Place: Chicago's Southside.

At Rise: It is morning dark in the living room. Travis is asleep on the make-down bed at center. An alarm clock sounds from within the bedroom at right, and presently Ruth enters from that room and closes the door behind her. She crosses sleepily toward the window. As she passes her sleeping son she reaches down and shakes him a little. At the window she raises the shade and a dusky Southside morning light comes n feebly. She fills a pot with water and puts it on to boil. She calls to the boy, between yawns, in a slightly muffled voice.

Ruth is about thirty. We can see that she was a pretty girl, even exceptionally so, but now it is apparent that life has been little that she expected, and disappointment has already begun to hang in her face. In a few years, before thirty-five even, she will be known among her people as a "settled woman."

She crosses to her son and gives him a good, final, rousing shake.

RUTH: Come on now, boy, it's seven thirty! (*Her son sits up at last, in a stupor of sleepiness*) I say hurry up, Travis! You ain't the only person in the world got to use a bathroom! (*The child, a sturdy, handsome little boy of ten or eleven, drags himself out of the bed and almost blindly takes his towels and "today's clothes" from drawers and a closet and goes out to the bathroom, which is in an outside hall and which is shared by another family or families on the same floor. Ruth crosses to the bedroom door at right and opens it and calls in to her husband)* Walter Lee! . . . It's after seven thirty! Lemme see you do some waking up in there now! *(She waits)* You better get up from there, man! It's after seven thirty I tell you. *(She waits again)* All right, you just go ahead and lay there and next thing you know Travis be finished and Mr. Johnson'll be in there and you'll be fussing and cussing round here like a madman! And be late too! *(She waits, at the end of patience)* Walter Lee—it's time for you to GET UP!

> *She waits another second and then starts to go into the bedroom, but is apparently satisfied that her husband has begun to get up. She stops, pulls the door to, and returns to the kitchen area. She wipes her face with a moist cloth and runs her fingers through her sleep-disheveled hair in a vain effort and ties an apron around her housecoat. The bedroom door at right opens and her husband stands in the doorway in his pajamas, which are rumpled and mismated. He is a lean, intense young man in his middle thirties, inclined to quick nervous movements and erratic speech habits—and always in his voice there is a quality of indictment.*

WALTER: Is he out yet?

RUTH: What you mean *out*? He ain't hardly got in there good yet.

WALTER *(wandering in, still more oriented to sleep than to a new day)*: Well, what was you doing all that yelling for if I can't even get in there yet? *(Stopping and thinking)* Check coming today?

RUTH: They *said* Saturday and this is just Friday and I hopes to God you ain't going to get up here first thing this morning and start talking to me 'bout no money—'cause I 'bout don't want to hear it.

WALTER: Something the matter with you this morning?

RUTH: No—I'm just sleepy as the devil. What kind of eggs you want?

WALTER: Not scrambled. *(Ruth starts to scramble eggs)* Paper come? *(Ruth points impatiently to the rolled up Tribune on the table, and he gets it and spreads it out and vaguely reads the front page)* Set off another bomb yesterday.

RUTH *(maximum indifference)*: Did they?

WALTER *(looking up)*: What's the mattter with you?

RUTH: Ain't nothing the matter with me. And don't keep asking me that this morning.

WALTER: Ain't nobody bothering you. *(Reading the news of the day absently again)* Say Colonel McCormick is sick.

RUTH *(affecting tea-party interest)*: Is he now? Poor thing.

WALTER *(sighing and looking at his watch)*: Oh, me. *(He waits)* Now what is that boy doing in that bathroom all this time? He just going to have to start getting up earlier. I can't be being late to work on account of him fooling around in there.

RUTH *(turning on him)*: Oh, no he ain't going to be getting up no earlier no such thing! It ain't his fault that he can't get to bed no earlier nights 'cause he got a bunch of crazy good-for-nothing clowns sitting up running their mouths in what is supposed to be his bedroom after ten o'clock at night . . .

WALTER: That's what you mad about, ain't it? The things I want to talk about with my friends just couldn't be important in your mind, could they?

> *He rises and finds a cigarette in her handbag on the table and crosses to the little window and looks out, smoking and deeply enjoying this first one*

RUTH (*almost matter of factly, a complaint too automatic to deserve emphasis*): Why you always got to smoke before you eat in the morning?

WALTER (*at the window*): Just look at 'em down there . . . Running and racing to work . . . (*He turns and faces his wife and watches her a moment at the stove, and then, suddenly*) You look young this morning, baby.

RUTH (*indifferently*): Yeah?

WALTER: Just for a second—stirring them eggs. Just for a second it was—you looked real young again. (*He reaches for her; she crosses away. Then, drily*) It's gone now—you look like yourself again!

RUTH: Man, if you don't shut up and leave me along.

WALTER (*looking out to the street again*): First thing a man ought to learn in life is not to make love to no colored woman first thing in the morning. You all some eeeevil people at eight o'clock in the morning.

> *Travis appears in the hall doorway, almost fully dressed and quite wide awake now, his towels and pajamas across his shoulders. He opens the door and signals for his father to make the bathroom in a hurry.*

TRAVIS (*watching the bathroom*): Daddy, come on! (*Walter gets his bathroom utensils and flies out to the bathroom.*)

RUTH: Sit down and have your breakfast, Travis.

TRAVIS: Mama, this is Friday. (*Gleefully*) Check coming tomorrow, huh?

RUTH: You get your mind off money and eat your breakfast.

TRAVIS (*eating*): This is the morning we supposed to bring the fifty cents to school.

RUTH: Well, I ain't got no fifty cents this morning.

TRAVIS: Teacher say we have to.

RUTH: I don't care what teacher say. I ain't got it. Eat your breakfast, Travis.

TRAVIS: I *am* eating.

RUTH: Hush up now and just eat!

> *The boy gives her an exasperated look for her lack of understanding, and eats grudgingly.*

TRAVIS: You think Grandmama would have it?

RUTH: No! And I want you to stop asking your grandmother for money, you hear me?

TRAVIS (*outraged*): Gaaaleee! I don't ask her, she just gimme it sometimes!

RUTH: Travis Willard Younger—I got too much on me this morning to be—

TRAVIS: Maybe Daddy—

RUTH: *Travis!*

> *The boy hushes abruptly. They are both quiet and tense for several seconds.*

TRAVIS (*presently*): Could I maybe go carry some groceries in front of the super-market for a little while after school then?

RUTH: Just hush, I said. (*Travis jabs his spoon into his cereal bowl viciously, and rests his head in anger upon his fists.*) If you through eating, you can get over there and make up your bed.

> The boy obeys stiffly and crosses the room, almost mechanically, to the bed and more or less folds the bedding into a heap, then angrily gets his books and cap.

TRAVIS (*sulking and standing apart from her unnaturally*): I'm gone.

RUTH (*looking up from the stove to inspect him automatically*): Come here. (*He crosses to her and she studies his head.*) If you don't take this comb and fix this here head, you better! (*Travis puts down his books with a great sigh of oppression, and crosses to the mirror. His mother mutters under her breath about his "slubbornness."*) 'Bout to march out of here with that head looking just like chickens slept in it! I just don't know where you get your slubborn ways . . . And get your jacket, too. Looks chilly out this morning.

TRAVIS (*with conspicuously brushed hair and jacket*): I'm gone.

RUTH: Get carfare and milk money—(*Waving one finger.*)—and not a single penny for no caps, you hear me?

TRAVIS (*with sullen politeness*): Yes'm.

> He turns in outrage to leave. His mother watches after him as in his frustration he approaches the door almost comically. When she speaks to him, her voice has become a very gentle tease.

RUTH (*mocking; as she thinks he would say it*): Oh, Mama makes me so mad sometimes, I don't know what to do! (*She waits and continues to his back as he stands stock-still in front of the door.*) I wouldn't kiss that woman good-bye for nothing in this world this morning! (*The boy finally turns around and rolls his eyes at her, knowing the mood has changed and he is vindicated; he does not, however, move toward her yet.*) Not for nothing in this world! (*She finally laughs aloud at him and holds out her arms to him and we see that it is a way between them, very old and practiced. He crosses to her and allows her to embrace him warmly but keeps his face fixed with masculine rigidity. She holds him back from her presently and looks at him and runs her fingers over the features of his face. With utter gentleness—.*) Now—whose little old angry man are you?

TRAVIS (*the masculinity and gruffness start to fade at last*): Aw gaalee—Mama . . .

RUTH (*mimicking*): Aw—gaaaaalleeeee, Mama! (*She pushes him, with rough playfulness and finality, toward the door.*) Get on out of here or you going to be late.

TRAVIS (*in the face of love, new aggressiveness*): Mama, could I *please* go carry groceries?

RUTH: Honey, it's starting to get so cold evenings.

WALTER (*coming in from the bathroom and drawing a make-believe gun from a make-believe holster and shooting at his son*): What is it he wants to do?

RUTH: Go carry groceries after school at the supermarket.

WALTER: Well, let him go . . .

TRAVIS (*quickly, to the ally*): I have to—she won't gimme the fifty cents . . .

WALTER (*to his wife only*): Why not?

RUTH (*simply, and with flavor*): 'Cause we don't have it.

WALTER (*to Ruth only*): What you tell the boy things like that for? (*Reaching down into his pants with a rather important gesture.*) Here, son—

> He hands the boy the coin, but his eyes are directed to his wife's. Travis takes the money happily.

TRAVIS: Thanks, Daddy.

> He starts out. Ruth watches both of them with murder in her eyes. Walter stands and stares back at her with defiance, and suddenly reaches into his pocket again on an afterthought.

WALTER (*without even looking at his son, still staring hard at his wife*): In fact, here's another fifty cents . . . Buy yourself some fruit today—or take a taxicab to school or something!

TRAVIS: Whoopee—

> He leaps up and clasps his father around the middle with his legs, and they face each other in mutual appreciation; slowly Walter Lee peeks around the boy to catch the violent rays from his wife's eyes and draws his head back as if shot.

WALTER: YOU BETTER GET DOWN NOW—AND GET TO SCHOOL, MAN.

TRAVIS (*at the door*): O.K. Good-bye.

> He exits.

WALTER (*after him, pointing with pride*): That's my boy. (*She looks at him in disgust and turns back to her work.*) You know what I was thinking 'bout in the bathroom this morning?

RUTH: No.

WALTER: How come you always try to be so pleasant!

RUTH: What is there to be pleasant 'bout!

WALTER: You want to know what I was thinking 'bout in the bathroom or not!

RUTH: I know what you thinking 'bout.

WALTER (*ignoring her*): 'Bout what me and Willy Harris was talking about last night.

RUTH (*immediately—a refrain*): Willy Harris is a good-for-nothing loudmouth.

WALTER: Anybody who talks to me has got to be a good-for-nothing loudmouth, ain't he? And what you know about who is just a good-for-nothing loudmouth? Charlie Atkins was just a "good-for-nothing loudmouth" too, wasn't he! When he wanted me to go in the dry-cleaning business with him. And now—he's grossing a hundred thousand a year. A hundred thousand dollars a year! You still call *him* a loudmouth!

RUTH (*bitterly*): Oh, Walter Lee . . .

> She folds her head on her arms over the table.

WALTER (*rising and coming to her and standing over her*): You tired, ain't you? Tired of everything. Me, the boy, the way we live—this beat-up hole—everything.

Ain't you? (*She doesn't look up, doesn't answer.*) So tired—moaning and groaning all the time, but you wouldn't do nothing to help, would you? You couldn't be on my side that long for nothing, could you?

RUTH: Walter, please leave me alone.

WALTER: A man needs for a woman to back him up . . .

RUTH: Walter—

WALTER: Mama would listen to you. You know she listen to you more than she do me and Bennie. She think more of you. All you have to do is just sit down with her when you drinking your coffee one morning and talking 'bout things like you do and—(*He sits down beside her and demonstrates graphically what he thinks her methods and tone should be.*)—you just sip your coffee, see, and say easy like that you been thinking 'bout that deal Walter Lee is so interested in, 'bout the store and all, and sip some more coffee, like what you saying ain't really that important to you—And the next thing you know, she be listening good and asking you questions and when I come home—I can tell her the details. This ain't no fly-by-night proposition, baby. I mean we figured it out, me and Willy and Bobo.

RUTH (*with a frown*): Bobo?

WALTER: Yeah. You see, this little liquor store we got in mind cost seventy-five thousand and we figured the initial investment on the place be 'bout thirty thousand, see. That be ten thousand each. Course, there's a couple of hundred you got to pay so's you don't spend your life just waiting for them clowns to let your license get approved—

RUTH: You mean graft?

WALTER (*frowning impatiently*): Don't call it that. See there, that just goes to show you what women understand about the world. Baby, don't *nothing* happen for you in the world 'less you pay *somebody* off!

RUTH: Walter, leave me alone! (*She raises her head and stares at him vigorously—then says, more quietly.*) Eat your eggs, they gonna be cold.

WALTER (*straightening up from her and looking off*): That's it. There you are. Man say to his woman: I got me a dream. His woman say: Eat your eggs. (*Sadly, but gaining in power.*) Man say: I got to take hold of this here world, baby! And a woman will say: Eat your eggs and go to work. (*Passionately now.*) Man say: I got to change my life, I'm choking to death, baby! And his woman say—(*In utter anguish as he brings his fists down on his thighs.*)—Your eggs is getting cold!

RUTH (*softly*): Walter, that ain't none of our money.

WALTER (*not listening at all or even looking at her*): This morning, I was lookin' in the mirror and thinking about it . . . I'm thirty-five years old; I been married eleven years and I got a boy who sleeps in the living room—(*Very, very quietly.*)—and all I got to give him is stories about how rich white people live . . .

RUTH: Eat your eggs, Walter.

WALTER (*slams the table and jumps up*):—DAMN MY EGGS—DAMN ALL THE EGGS THAT EVER WAS!

RUTH: Then go to work.

WALTER (*looking up at her*): See—I'm trying to talk to you 'bout myself—(*Shaking his head with the repetition.*)—and all you can say is eat them eggs and go to work.

RUTH (*wearily*): Honey, you never say nothing new. I listen to you every day, every night and every morning, and you never say nothing new. (*Shrugging.*) So you would rather *be* Mr. Arnold than be his chauffeur. So—I would *rather* be living in Buckingham Palace.

WALTER: That is just what is wrong with the colored woman in this world . . . Don't understand about building their men up and making 'em feel like they somebody. Like they can do something.

RUTH (*drily, but to hurt*): There *are* colored men who do things.

WALTER: No thanks to the colored woman.

RUTH: Well, being a colored woman, I guess I can't help myself none.

> *She rises and gets the ironing board and sets it up and attacks a huge pile of rough-dried clothes, sprinkling them in preparation for the ironing and then rolling them into tight fat balls.*

WALTER (*mumbling*): We one group of men tied to a race of women with small minds!

> *His sister Beneatha enters. She is about twenty, as slim and intense as her brother. She is not as pretty as her sister-in-law, but her lean, almost intellectual face has a handsomeness of its own. She wears a bright-red flannel nightie, and her thick hair stands wildly about her head. Her speech is a mixture of many things; it is different from the rest of the family's insofar as education has permeated her sense of English—and perhaps the Midwest rather than the South has finally—at last—won out in her inflection; but not altogether, because over all of it is a soft slurring and transformed use of vowels which is the decided influence of the Southside. She passes through the room without looking at either Ruth or Walter and goes to the outside door and looks, a little blindly, out to the bathroom. She sees that it has been lost to the Johnsons. She closes the door with a sleepy vengeance and crosses to the table and sits down a little defeated.*

BENEATHA: I am going to start timing those people.

WALTER: You should get up earlier.

BENEATHA (*her face in her hands. She is still fighting the urge to go back to bed*): Really—would you suggest dawn? Where's the paper?

WALTER (*pushing the paper across the table to her as he studies her almost clinically, as though he has never seen her before*): You a horrible-looking chick at this hour.

BENEATHA (*drily*): Good morning, everybody.

WALTER (*senselessly*): How is school coming?

BENEATHA (*in the same spirit*): Lovely. Lovely. And you know, biology is the greatest. (*Looking up at him.*) I dissected something that looked just like you yesterday.

WALTER: I just wondered if you've made up your mind and everything.

BENEATHA (*gaining in sharpness and impatience*): And what did I answer yesterday morning—and the day before that?

RUTH (*from the ironing board, like someone disinterested and old*): Don't be so nasty, Bennie.

BENEATHA (*still to her brother*): And the day before that and the day before that!

WALTER (*defensively*): I'm interested in you. Something wrong with that? Ain't
    many girls who decide—

WALTER AND BENEATHA (*in unison*):—"to be a doctor."

    Silence.

WALTER: Have we figured out yet just exactly how much medical school is going
    to cost?

RUTH: Walter Lee, why don't you leave that girl alone and get out of here to
    work?

BENEATHA (*exits to the bathroom and bangs on the door*): Come on out of there,
    please!

    She comes back into the room.

WALTER (*looking at his sister intently*): You know the check is coming tomorrow.

BENEATHA (*turning on him with a sharpness all her own*): That money belongs to
    Mama, Walter, and it's for her to decide how she wants to use it. I don't care
    if she wants to buy a house or a rocket ship or just nail it up somewhere and
    look at it. It's hers. Not ours—*hers*.

WALTER (*bitterly*): Now ain't that fine! You just got your mother's interest at heart,
    ain't you, girl? You such a nice girl—but if Mama got that money she can always
    take a few thousand and help you through school too—can't she?

BENEATHA: I have never asked anyone around here to do anything for me!

WALTER: No! And the line between asking and just accepting when the time
    comes is big and wide—ain't it!

BENEATHA (*with fury*): What do you want from me, Brother—that I quit school
    or just drop dead, which!

WALTER: I don't want nothing but for you to stop acting holy 'round here. Me
    and Ruth done made some sacrifices for you—why can't you do something
    for the family?

RUTH: Walter, don't be dragging me in it.

WALTER: You are in it—Don't you get up and go work in somebody's kitchen for
    the last three years to help put clothes on her back?

RUTH: Oh, Walter—that's not fair . . .

WALTER: It ain't that nobody expects you to get on your knees and say thank
    you, Brother; thank you, Ruth; thank you, Mama—and thank you, Travis,
    for wearing the same pair of shoes for two semesters—

BENEATHA (*dropping to her knees*): Well—I *do*—all right?—thank everybody!
    And forgive me for ever wanting to be anything at all! (*Pursuing him on her
    knees across the floor.*) FORGIVE ME, FORGIVE ME, FORGIVE ME!

RUTH: Please stop it! Your mama'll hear you.

WALTER: Who the hell told you you had to be a doctor? If you so crazy 'bout
    messing 'round with sick people—then go be a nurse like other women—or
    just get married and be quiet . . . .

BENEATHA: Well—you finally got it said . . . It took you three years but you fi-
    nally got it said. Walter, give up; leave me alone—it's Mama's money.

WALTER: *He was my father, too!*

BENEATHA: So what? He was mine, too—and Travis' grandfather—but the in-
    surance money belongs to Mama. Picking on me is not going to make her

give it to you to invest in any liquor stores—(*Under breath, dropping into a chair.*)—and I for one say, God bless Mama for that!

WALTER (*to Ruth*): See—did you hear? Did you hear!

RUTH: Honey, please go to work.

WALTER: Nobody in this house is ever going to understand me.

BENEATHA: Because you're a nut.

WALTER: Who's a nut?

BENEATHA: You—you are a nut. Thee is mad, boy.

WALTER (*looking at his wife and his sister from the door, very sadly*): The world's most backward race of people, and that's a fact.

BENEATHA (*turning slowly in her chair*): And then there are all those prophets who would lead us out of the wilderness—(*Walter slams out of the house.*)—into the swamps!

RUTH: Bennie, why you always gotta be pickin' on your brother? Can't you be a little sweeter sometimes? (*Door opens. Walter walks in. He fumbles with his cap, starts to speak, clears throat, looks everywhere but at Ruth. Finally:*)

WALTER (*to Ruth*): I need some money for carfare.

RUTH (*looks at him, then warms; teasing, but tenderly*): Fifty cents? (*She goes to her bag and gets money.*) Here—take a taxi!

> *Walter exits. Mama enters. She is a woman in her early sixties, full-bodied and strong. She is one of those women of a certain grace and beauty who wear it so unobtrusively that it takes a while to notice. Her dark-brown face is surrounded by the total whiteness of her hair, and, being a woman who has adjusted to many things in life and overcome many more, her face is full of strength. She has, we can see, wit and faith of a kind that keep her eyes lit and full of interest and expectancy. She is, in a word, a beautiful woman. Her bearing is perhaps most like the noble bearing of the women of the Hereros of Southwest Africa—rather as if she imagines that as she walks she still bears a basket or a vessel upon her head. Her speech, on the other hand, is as careless as her carriage is precise—she is inclined to slur everything—but her voice is perhaps not so much quiet as simply soft.*

MAMA: Who that 'round here slamming doors at this hour?

> *She crosses through the room, goes to the window, opens it, and brings in a feeble little plant growing doggedly in a small pot on the window sill. She feels the dirt and puts it back out.*

RUTH: That was Walter Lee. He and Bennie was at it again.

MAMA: My children and they tempers. Lord, if this little old plant don't get more sun than it's been getting it ain't never going to see spring again. (*She turns from the window.*) What's the matter with you this morning, Ruth? You looks right peaked. You aiming to iron all them things? Leave some for me. I'll get to 'em this afternoon. Bennie honey, it's too drafty for you to be sitting 'round half dressed. Where's your robe?

BENEATHA: In the cleaners.

MAMA: Well, go get mine and put it on.

BENEATHA: I'm not cold, Mama, honest.

MAMA: I know—but you so thin . . .

BENEATHA (*irritably*): Mama, I'm not cold.

MAMA (*seeing the make-down bed as Travis has left it*): Lord have mercy, look at that poor bed. Bless his heart—he tries, don't he?

She moves to the bed Travis has sloppily made up.

RUTH: No—he don't half try at all 'cause he knows you going to come along behind him and fix everything. That's just how come he don't know how to do nothing right now—you done spoiled that boy so.

MAMA (*folding bedding*): Well—he's a little boy. Ain't supposed to know 'bout housekeeping. My baby, that's what he is. What you fix for his breakfast this morning?

RUTH (*angrily*): I feed my son, Lena!

MAMA: I ain't meddling—(*Under breath; busy-bodyish.*) I just noticed all last week he had cold cereal, and when it starts getting this chilly in the fall a child ought to have some hot grits or something when he goes out in the cold—

RUTH (*furious*): I gave him hot oats—is that all right!

MAMA: I ain't meddling. (*Pause.*) Put a lot of nice butter on it? (*Ruth shoots her an angry look and does not reply.*) He likes lots of butter.

RUTH (*exasperated*): Lena—

MAMA (*to Beneatha. Mama is inclined to wander conversationally sometimes*): What was you and your brother fussing 'bout this morning?

BENEATHA: It's not important, Mama.

She gets up and goes to look out at the bathroom, which is apparently free, and she picks up her towels and rushes out.

MAMA: What was they fighting about?

RUTH: Now you know as well as I do.

MAMA (*shaking her head*): Brother still worrying hisself sick about that money?

RUTH: You know he is.

MAMA: You had breakfast?

RUTH: Some coffee.

MAMA: Girl, you better start eating and looking after yourself better. You almost thin as Travis.

RUTH: Lena—

MAMA: Un-hunh?

RUTH: What are you going to do with it?

MAMA: Now don't you start, child. It's too early in the morning to be talking about money. It ain't Christian.

RUTH: It's just that he got his heart set on that store—

MAMA: You mean that liquor store that Willy Harris want him to invest in?

RUTH: Yes—

MAMA: We ain't no business people, Ruth. We just plain working folks.

RUTH: Ain't nobody business people till they go into business. Walter Lee say colored people ain't never going to start getting ahead till they start gambling on some different kinds of things in the world—investments and things.

MAMA: What done got into you, girl? Walter Lee done finally sold you on investing.

RUTH: No. Mama, something is happening between Walter and me. I don't know what it is—but he needs something—something I can't give him any more. He needs this chance, Lena.

MAMA (*frowning deeply*): But liquor, honey—

RUTH: Well—like Walter say—I spec people going to always be drinking themselves some liquor.

MAMA: Well—whether they drinks it or not ain't none of my business. But whether I go into business selling it to 'em *is*, and I don't want that on my ledger this late in life. (*Stopping suddenly and studying her daughter-in-law.*) Ruth Younger, what's the matter with you today? You look like you could fall over right there.

RUTH: I'm tired.

MAMA: Then you better stay home from work today.

RUTH: I can't stay home. She'd be calling up the agency and screaming at them, "My girl didn't come in today—send me somebody! My girl didn't come in!" Oh, she just have a fit . . .

MAMA: Well, let her have it. I'll just call her up and say you got the flu—

RUTH (*laughing*): Why the flu?

MAMA: 'Cause it sounds respectable to 'em. Something white people get, too. They know 'bout the flu. Otherwise they think you been cut up or something when you tell 'em you sick.

RUTH: I got to go in. We need the money.

MAMA: Somebody would of thought my children done all but starved to death the way they talk about money here late. Child, we got a great big old check coming tomorrow.

RUTH (*sincerely, but also self-righteously*): Now that's your money. It ain't got nothing to do with me. We all feel like that—Walter and Bennie and me— even Travis.

MAMA (*thoughtfully, and suddenly very far away*): Ten thousand dollars—

RUTH: Sure is wonderful.

MAMA: Ten thousand dollars.

RUTH: You know what you should do, Miss Lena? You should take yourself a trip somewhere. To Europe or South America or someplace—

MAMA (*throwing up her hands at the thought*): Oh, child!

RUTH: I'm serious. Just pack up and leave! Go on away and enjoy yourself some. Forget about the family and have yourself a ball for once in your life—

MAMA (*drily*): You sound like I'm just about ready to die. Who'd go with me? What I look like wandering 'round Europe by myself?

RUTH: Shoot—these here rich white women do it all the time. They don't think nothing of packing up they suitcases and piling on one of them big steamships and—swoosh!—they gone, child.

MAMA: Something always told me I wasn't no rich white woman.

RUTH: Well—what are you going to do with it then?

MAMA: I ain't rightly decided. (*Thinking. She speaks now with emphasis.*) Some of it got to be put away for Beneatha and her schoolin'—and ain't nothing going to touch that part of it. Nothing. (*She waits several seconds, trying to make up her mind about something, and looks at Ruth a little tentatively before going* on.) Been thinking that we maybe could meet the notes on a little old two-story somewhere, with a yard where Travis could play in the summertime, if we use part of the insurance for a down payment and everybody kind of pitch in. I could maybe take on a little day work again, few days a week—

RUTH (*studying her mother-in-law furtively and concentrating on her ironing, anxious to encourage without seeming to*): Well, Lord knows, we've put enough rent into this here rat trap to pay for four houses by now . . .

MAMA (*looking up at the words "rat trap" and then looking around and leaning back and sighing—in a suddenly reflective mood—*): "Rat trap"—yes, that's all it is. (*Smiling.*) I remember just as well the day me and Big Walter moved in here. Hadn't been married but two weeks and wasn't planning on living here no more than a year. (*She shakes her head at the dissolved dream.*) We was going to set away, little by little, don't you know, and buy a little place out in Morgan Park. We had even picked out the house. (*Chuckling a little.*) Looks right dumpy today. But Lord, child, you should know all the dreams I had 'bout buying that house and fixing it up and making me a little garden in the back—(*She waits and stops smiling.*) And didn't none of it happen.

> *Dropping her hands in a futile gesture.*

RUTH (*keeps her head down, ironing*): Yes, life can be a barrel of disappointments, sometimes.

MAMA: Honey, Big Walter would come in here some nights back then and slump down on that couch there and just look at the rug, and look at me and look at the rug and then back at me—and I'd know he was down then . . . really down. (*After a second very long and thoughtful pause; she is seeing back to times that only she can see.*) And then, Lord, when I lost that baby—little Claude—I almost thought I was going to lose Big Walter too. Oh, that man grieved hisself! He was one man to love his children.

RUTH: Ain't nothin' can tear at you like losin' your baby.

MAMA: I guess that's how come that man finally worked hisself to death like he done. Like he was fighting his own war with this here world that took his baby from him.

RUTH: He sure was a fine man, all right. I always liked Mr. Younger.

MAMA: Crazy 'bout his children! God knows there was plenty wrong with Walter Younger—hard-headed, mean, kind of wild with women—plenty wrong with him. But he sure loved his children. Always wanted them to have something—be something. That's where Brother gets all these notions, I reckon. Big Walter used to say, he'd get right wet in the eyes sometimes, lean his head back with the water standing in his eyes and say, "Seem like God didn't see fit to give the black man nothing but dreams—but He did give us children to make them dreams seem worthwhile." (*She smiles.*) He could talk like that, don't you know.

RUTH: Yes, he sure could. He was a good man, Mr. Younger.

MAMA: Yes, a fine man—just couldn't never catch up with his dreams, that's all.

> *Beneatha comes in, brushing her hair and looking up to the ceiling, where the sound of a vacuum cleaner has started up.*

BENEATHA: What could be so dirty on that woman's rugs that she has to vacuum them every single day?

RUTH: I wish certain young women 'round here who I could name would take inspiration about certain rugs in a certain apartment I could also mention.

BENEATHA (*shrugging*): How much cleaning can a house need, for Christ's sakes.

MAMA (*not liking the Lord's name used thus*): Bennie!

RUTH: Just listen to her—just listen!

BENEATHA: Oh, God!

MAMA: If you use the Lord's name just one more time—

BENEATHA (*a bit of a whine*): Oh, Mama—

RUTH: Fresh—just fresh as salt, this girl!

BENEATHA (*drily*): Well—if the salt loses its savor—

MAMA: Now that will do. I just ain't going to have you 'round here reciting the scriptures in vain—you hear me?

BENEATHA: How did I manage to get on everybody's wrong side by just walking into a room?

RUTH: If you weren't so fresh—

BENEATHA: Ruth, I'm twenty years old.

MAMA: What time you be home from school today?

BENEATHA: Kind of late. (*With enthusiasm.*) Madeline is going to start my guitar lessons today.

Mama and Ruth look up with the same expression.

MAMA: Your *what* kind of lessons?

BENEATHA: Guitar.

RUTH: Oh, Father!

MAMA: How come you done taken it in your mind to learn to play the guitar?

BENEATHA: I just want to, that's all.

MAMA (*smiling*): Lord, child, don't you know what to do with yourself? How long it going to be before you get tired of this now—like you got tired of that little play-acting group you joined last year? (*Looking at Ruth.*) And what was it the year before that?

RUTH: The horseback-riding club for which she bought that fifty-five-dollar riding habit that's been hanging in the closet ever since!

MAMA (*to Beneatha*): Why you got to flit so from one thing to another, baby?

BENEATHA (*sharply*): I just want to learn to play the guitar. Is there anything wrong with that?

MAMA: Ain't nobody trying to stop you. I just wonders sometimes why you has to flit so from one thing to another all the time. You ain't never done nothing with all that camera equipment you brought home—

BENEATHA: I don't flit! I—I experiment with different forms of expression—

RUTH: Like riding a horse?

BENEATHA: —People have to express themselves one way or another.

MAMA: What is it you want to express?

BENEATHA (*angrily*): Me! (*Mama and Ruth look at each other and burst into raucous laughter.*) Don't worry—I don't expect you to understand.

MAMA (*to change the subject*): Who you going out with tomorrow night?

BENEATHA (*with displeasure*): George Murchison again.

MAMA (*pleased*): Oh—you getting a little sweet on him?

RUTH: You ask me, this child ain't sweet on nobody but herself—(*Under breath.*) Express herself!

They laugh.

BENEATHA: Oh—I like George all right, Mama. I mean I like him enough to go out with him and stuff, but—

RUTH (*for devilment*): What does *and stuff* mean?

BENEATHA: Mind your own business.

MAMA: Stop picking at her now, Ruth. (*She chuckles—then a suspicious sudden look at her daughter as she turns in her chair for emphasis.*) What DOES it mean?

BENEATHA (*wearily*): Oh, I just mean I couldn't ever really be serious about George. He's—he's so shallow.

> *She has her back to Ruth, who has had to stop ironing and lean against something and put the back of her hand to her forehead.*

RUTH (*trying to keep Mama from noticing*): You . . . sure . . . loves that little old thing, don't you? . . .

MAMA: Well, I always wanted me a garden like I used to see sometimes at the back of the houses down home. This plant is close as I ever got to having one. (*She looks out of the window as she replaces the plant.*) Lord, ain't nothing as dreary as the view from this window on a dreary day, is there? Why ain't you singing this morning, Ruth? Sing that "No Ways Tired." That song always lifts me up so—(*She turns at last to see that Ruth has slipped quietly to the floor, in a state of semiconsciousness.*) Ruth! Ruth honey—what's the matter with you . . . Ruth!

> *Curtain.*

Scene 2. [*The following morning.*]

> It is the following morning; a Saturday morning, and house cleaning is in progress at the Youngers'. Furniture has been shoved hither and yon and Mama is giving the kitchen-area walls a washing down. Beneatha, in dungarees, with a handkerchief tied around her face, is spraying insecticide into the cracks in the walls. As they work, the radio is on and a Southside disk-jockey program is inappropriately filling the house with a rather exotic saxophone blues. Travis, the sole idle one, is leaning on his arms, looking out of the window.

TRAVIS: Grandmama, that stuff Bennie is using smells awful. Can I go downstairs, please?

MAMA: Did you get all them chores done already? I ain't seen you doing much.

TRAVIS: Yes'm—finished early. Where did Mama go this morning?

MAMA (*looking at Beneatha*): She had to go on a little errand.

> *The phone rings. Beneatha runs to answer it and reaches it before Walter, who has entered from bedroom.*

TRAVIS: Where?

MAMA: To tend to her business.

BENEATHA: Haylo . . . (*Disappointed.*) Yes, he is. (*She tosses the phone to Walter, who barely catches it.*) It's Willie Harris again.

WALTER (*as privately as possible under Mama's gaze*): Hello, Willie. Did you get the papers from the lawyer? . . . No, not yet. I told you the mailman doesn't get here till ten-thirty . . . No, I'll come there . . . Yeah! Right away. (*He hangs up and goes for his coat.*)

BENEATHA: Brother, where did Ruth go?

WALTER (*as he exits*): How should I know!

TRAVIS: Aw come on, Grandma. Can I go outside?

MAMA: Oh, I guess so. You stay right in front of the house, though, and keep a good lookout for the postman.

TRAVIS: Yes'm. (*He darts into bedroom for stickball and bat, reenters, and sees Beneatha on her knees spraying under sofa with behind upraised. He edges closer to the target, takes aim, and lets her have it. She screams.*) Leave them poor little cockroaches alone, they ain't bothering you none! (*He runs as she swings the spraygun at him viciously and playfully.*) Grandma! Grandma!

MAMA: Look out there, girl, before you be spilling some of that stuff on that child!

TRAVIS (*safely behind the bastion of Mama*): That's right—look out, now! (*He exits.*)

BENEATHA (*drily*): I can't imagine that it would hurt him—it has never hurt the roaches.

MAMA: Well, little boys' hides ain't as tough as Southside roaches. You better get over there behind the bureau. I seen one marching out of there like Napoleon yesterday.

BENEATHA: There's really only one way to get rid of them, Mama—

MAMA: How?

BENEATHA: Set fire to this building! Mama, where did Ruth go?

MAMA (*looking at her with meaning*): To the doctor, I think.

BENEATHA: The doctor? What's the matter? (*They exchange glances.*) You don't think—

MAMA (*with her sense of drama*): Now I ain't saying what I think. But I ain't never been wrong 'bout a woman neither.

The phone rings.

BENEATHA (*at the phone*): Hay-lo . . . (*Pause, and a moment of recognition.*) Well—when did you get back. . . . And how was it? . . . Of course I've missed you—in my way . . . This morning? No . . . house cleaning and all that and Mama hates it if I let people come over when the house is like this . . . You *have*? Well, that's different . . . What is it—Oh, what the hell, come on over . . . Right, see you then. *Arrividerci.*

She hangs up.

MAMA (*who has listened vigorously, as is her habit*): Who is that you inviting over here with this house looking like this? You ain't got the pride you was born with!

BENEATHA: Asagai doesn't care how houses look, Mama—he's an intellectual.

MAMA: *Who?*

BENEATHA: Asagai—Joseph Asagai. He's an African boy I met on campus. He's been studying in Canada all summer.

MAMA: What's his name?

BENEATHA: Asagai, Joseph. Ah-sah-guy . . . He's from Nigeria.

MAMA: Oh, that's the little country that was founded by slaves way back . . .

BENEATHA: No, Mama—that's Liberia.

MAMA: I don't think I never met no African before.

BENEATHA: Well, do me a favor and don't ask him a whole lot of ignorant questions about Africans. I mean, do they wear clothes and all that—

MAMA: Well, now, I guess if you think we so ignorant 'round here maybe you shouldn't bring your friends here—

BENEATHA: It's just that people ask such crazy things. All anyone seems to know about when it comes to Africa is Tarzan—

MAMA (*indignantly*): Why should I know anything about Africa?

BENEATHA: Why do you give money at church for the missionary work?

MAMA: Well, that's to help save people.

BENEATHA: You mean save them from *heathenism*—

MAMA (*innocently*): Yes.

BENEATHA: I'm afraid they need more salvation from the British and the French.

> *Ruth comes in forlornly and pulls off her coat with dejection. They both turn to look at her.*

RUTH (*dispiritedly*): Well, I guess from all the happy faces—everybody knows.

BENEATHA: You pregnant?

MAMA: Lord have mercy, I sure hope it's a little old girl. Travis ought to have a sister.

> *Beneatha and Ruth give her a hopeless look for this grandmotherly enthusiasm.*

BENEATHA: How far along are you?

RUTH: Two months.

BENEATHA: Did you mean to? I mean did you plan it or was it an accident?

MAMA: What do you know about planning or not planning?

BENEATHA: Oh, Mama.

RUTH (*wearily*): She's twenty years old, Lena.

BENEATHA: Did you plan it, Ruth?

RUTH: Mind your own business.

BENEATHA: It is my business—where is he going to live, on the *roof*? (*There is silence following the remark as the three women react to the sense of it.*) Gee—I didn't mean that, Ruth, honest. Gee, I don't feel like that at all. I—I think it is wonderful.

RUTH (*dully*): Wonderful.

BENEATHA: Yes—really.

MAMA (*looking at Ruth, worried*): Doctor say everything going to be all right?

RUTH (*far away*): Yes—she says everything is going to be fine . . .

MAMA (*immediately suspicious*): "She"—What doctor you went to?

> *Ruth folds over, near hysteria.*

MAMA (*worriedly hovering over Ruth*): Ruth honey—what's the matter with you—you sick?

> *Ruth has her fists clenched on her thighs and is fighting hard to suppress a scream that seems to be rising in her.*

BENEATHA: What's the matter with her, Mama?

MAMA (*working her fingers in Ruth's shoulders to relax her*): She be all right. Women gets right depressed sometimes when they get her way. (*Speaking softly, expertly, rapidly.*) Now you just relax. That's right . . . just lean back, don't think 'bout nothing at all . . . nothing at all—

RUTH: I'm all right . . .

The glassy-eyed look melts and then she collapses into a fit of heavy sobbing. The bell rings.

BENEATHA: Oh, my God—that must be Asagai.

MAMA (*to Ruth*): Come on now, honey. You need to lie down and rest awhile . . . then have some nice hot food.

They exit, Ruth's weight on her mother-in-law. Beneatha, herself profoundly disturbed, opens the door to admit a rather dramatic-looking young man with a large package.

ASAGAI: Hello, Alaiyo—

BENEATHA (*holding the door open and regarding him with pleasure*): Hello . . . (*Long pause.*) Well—come in. And please excuse everything. My mother was very upset about my letting anyone come here with the place like this.

ASAGAI (*coming into the room*): You look disturbed too . . . Is something wrong?

BENEATHA (*still at the door, absently*): Yes . . . we've all got acute ghetto-itus. (*She smiles and comes toward him, finding a cigarette and sitting.*) So—sit down! No! Wait! (*She whips the spraygun off sofa where she had left it and puts the cushions back. At last perches on arm of sofa. He sits.*) So, how was Canada?

ASAGAI (*a sophisticate*): Canadian.

BENEATHA (*looking at him*): Asagai, I'm very glad you are back.

ASAGAI (*looking back at her in turn*): Are you really?

BENEATHA: Yes—very.

ASAGAI: Why?—you were quite glad when I went away. What happened?

BENEATHA: You went away.

ASAGAI: Ahhhhhhhh.

BENEATHA: Before—you wanted to be so serious before there was time.

ASAGAI: How much time must there be before one knows what one feels?

BENEATHA (*stalling this particular conversation. Her hands pressed together, in a deliberately childish gesture*): What did you bring me?

ASAGAI (*handing her the package*): Open it and see.

BENEATHA (*eagerly opening the package and drawing out some records and the colorful robes of a Nigerian woman*): Oh Asagai! . . . You got them for me! . . . How beautiful . . . and the records too! (*She lifts out the robes and runs to the mirror with them and holds the drapery up in front of herself.*)

ASAGAI (*coming to her at the mirror*): I shall have to teach you how to drape it properly. (*He flings the material about her for the moment and stands back to look at her.*) Ah—Oh-pay-gay-day, oh-gbah-mu-shay. (*A Yoruba exclamation for admiration.*) You wear it well . . . very well . . . mutilated hair and all.

BENEATHA (*turning suddenly*): My hair—what's wrong with my hair?

ASAGAI (*shrugging*): Were you born with it like that?

BENEATHA (*reaching up to touch it*): No . . . of course not.

She looks back to the mirror, disturbed.

ASAGAI (*smiling*): How then?

BENEATHA: You know perfectly well how . . . as crinkly as yours . . . that's how.

ASAGAI: And it is ugly to you that way?

BENEATHA (*quickly*): Oh, no—not ugly . . . (*More slowly, apologetically.*) But it's so hard to manage when it's, well—raw.

ASAGAI: And so to accommodate that—you mutilate it every week?

BENEATHA: It's not mutilation!

ASAGAI (*laughing aloud at her seriousness*): Oh . . . please! I am only teasing you because you are so very serious about these things. (*He stands back from her and folds his arms across his chest as he watches her pulling at her hair and frowning in the mirror.*) Do you remember the first time you met me at school? . . . (*He laughs.*) You came up to me and you said—and I thought you were the most serious little thing I had ever seen—you said: (*He imitates her.*) "Mr. Asagai—I want very much to talk with you. About Africa. You see, Mr. Asagai, I am looking for my *identity*!"

      He laughs.

BENEATHA (*turning to him, not laughing*): Yes—

    Her face is quizzical, profoundly disturbed.

ASAGAI (*still teasing and reaching out and taking her face in his hands and turning her profile to him*): Well . . . it is true that this is not so much a profile of a Hollywood queen as perhaps a queen of the Nile—(*A mock dismissal of the importance of the question.*) But what does it matter? Assimilationism is so popular in your country.

BENEATHA (*wheeling, passionately, sharply*): I am not an assimilationist!

ASAGAI (*the protest hangs in the room for a moment and Asagai studies her, his laughter fading*): Such a serious one. (*There is a pause.*) So—you like the robes? You must take excellent care of them—they are from my sister's personal wardrobe.

BENEATHA (*with incredulity*): You—you sent all the way home—for me?

ASAGAI (*with charm*): For you—I would do much more . . . Well, that is what I came for. I must go.

BENEATHA: Will you call me Monday?

ASAGAI: Yes . . . We have a great deal to talk about. I mean about identity and time and all that.

BENEATHA: Time?

ASAGAI: Yes. About how much time one needs to know what one feels.

BENEATHA: You see! You never understood that there is more than one kind of feeling which can exist between a man and a woman—or, at least, there should be.

ASAGAI (*shaking his head negatively but gently*): No. Between a man and a woman there need be only one kind of feeling. I have that for you . . . Now even . . . right this moment . . .

BENEATHA: I know—and by itself—it won't do. I can find that anywhere.

ASAGAI: For a woman it should be enough.

BENEATHA: I know—because that's what it says in all the novels that men write. But it isn't. Go ahead and laugh—but I'm not interested in being someone's little episode in America or—(*With feminine vengeance.*)—one of them! (*Asagai has burst into laughter again.*) That's funny as hell, huh!

ASAGAI: It's just that every American girl I have known has said that to me. White—black—in this you are all the same. And the same speech, too!

BENEATHA (*angrily*): Yuk, yuk, yuk!

ASAGAI: It's how you can be sure that the world's most liberated women are not liberated at all. You all talk about it too much!

> *Mama enters and is immediately all social charm because of the presence of a guest.*

BENEATHA: Oh—Mama—this is Mr. Asagai.

MAMA: How do you do?

ASAGAI (*total politeness to an elder*): How do you do, Mrs. Younger. Please forgive me for coming at such an outrageous hour on a Saturday.

MAMA: Well, you are quite welcome. I just hope you understand that our house don't always look like this. (*Chatterish.*) You must come again. I would love to hear all about—(*Not sure of the name.*)—your country. I think it's so sad the way our American Negroes don't know nothing about Africa 'cept Tarzan and all that. And all that money they pour into these churches when they ought to be helping you people over there drive out them French and Englishmen done taken away your land.

> *The mother flashes a slightly superior look at her daughter upon completion of the recitation.*

ASAGAI (*taken aback by this sudden and acutely unrelated expression of sympathy*): Yes . . . yes . . .

MAMA (*smiling at him suddenly and relaxing and looking him over*): How many miles is it from here to where you come from?

ASAGAI: Many thousands.

MAMA (*looking at him as she would Walter*): I bet you don't half look after yourself, being away from your mama either. I spec you better come 'round here from time to time to get yourself some decent homecooked meals . . .

ASAGAI (*moved*): Thank you. Thank you very much. (*They are all quiet, then—*) Well . . . I must go. I will call you Monday, Alaiyo.

MAMA: What's that he call you?

ASAGAI: Oh—"Alaiyo." I hope you don't mind. It is what you would call a nickname, I think. It is a Yoruba word. I am a Yoruba.

MAMA (*looking at Beneatha*): I—I thought he was from—(*Uncertain.*)

ASAGAI (*understanding*): Nigeria is my country. Yoruba is my tribal origin—

BENEATHA: You didn't tell us what Alaiyo means . . . for all I know, you might be calling me Little Idiot or something . . .

ASAGAI: Well . . . let me see . . . I do not know how just to explain it . . . The sense of a thing can be so different when it changes languages.

BENEATHA: You're evading.

ASAGAI: No—really it is difficult . . . (*Thinking.*) It means . . . it means One for Whom Bread—Food—Is Not Enough. (*He looks at her.*) Is that all right?

BENEATHA (*understanding, softly*): Thank you.

MAMA (*looking from one to the other and not understanding any of it*): Well . . . that's nice . . . You must come see us again—Mr.—

ASAGAI: Ah-sah-guy . . .
MAMA: Yes . . . Do come again.
ASAGAI: Good-bye.

He exits.

MAMA (*after him*): Lord, that's a pretty thing just went out here! (*Insinuatingly, to her daughter.*) Yes, I guess I see why we done commence to get so interested in Africa 'round here. Missionaries my aunt Jenny!

She exits.

BENEATHA: Oh, Mama! . . .

She picks up the Nigerian dress and holds it up to her in front of the mirror again. She sets the headdress on haphazardly and then notices her hair again and clutches at it and then replaces the headdress and frowns at herself. Then she starts to wriggle in front of the mirror as she thinks a Nigerian woman might. Travis enters and stands regarding her.

TRAVIS: What's the matter, girl, you cracking up?
BENEATHA: Shut up.

She pulls the headdress off and looks at herself in the mirror and clutches at her hair again and squinches her eyes as if trying to imagine something. Then, suddenly, she gets her raincoat and kerchief and hurriedly prepares for going out.

MAMA (*coming back into the room*): She's resting now. Travis, baby, run next door and ask Miss Johnson to please let me have a little kitchen cleanser. This here can is empty as Jacob's kettle.
TRAVIS: I just came in.
MAMA: Do as you told. (*He exits and she looks at her daughter.*) Where you going?
BENEATHA (*halting at the door*): To become a queen of the Nile!

She exits in a breathless blaze of glory. Ruth appears in the bedroom doorway.

MAMA: Who told you to get up?
RUTH: Ain't nothing wrong with me to be lying in no bed for. Where did Bennie go?
MAMA (*drumming her fingers*): Far as I could make out—to Egypt. (*Ruth just looks at her.*) What time is it getting to?
RUTH: Ten twenty. And the mailman going to ring that bell this morning just like he done every morning for the last umpteen years.

Travis comes in with the cleanser can.

TRAVIS: She say to tell you that she don't have much.
MAMA (*angrily*): Lord, some people I could name sure is tight-fisted! (*Directing her grandson.*) Mark two cans of cleanser on the list there. If she that hard up for kitchen cleanser, I sure don't want to forget to get her none!
RUTH: Lena—maybe the woman is just short on cleanser—

MAMA (*not listening*):—Much baking powder as she done borrowed from me all these years, she could of done gone into the baking business!

The bell sounds suddenly and sharply and all three are stunned—serious and silent—midspeech. In spite of all the other conversations and distractions of the morning, this is what they have been waiting for, even Travis, who looks helplessly from his mother to his grandmother. Ruth is the first to come to life again.

RUTH (*to Travis*): Get down them steps, boy!

Travis snaps to life and flies out to get the mail.

MAMA (*her eyes wide, her hand to her breast*): You mean it done really come?
RUTH (*excited*): Oh, Miss Lena!
MAMA (*collecting herself*): Well . . . I don't know what we all so excited about 'round here for. We known it was coming for months.
RUTH: That's a whole lot different from having it come and being able to hold it in your hands . . . a piece of paper worth ten thousand dollars . . . (*Travis bursts back into the room. He holds the envelope high above his head, like a little dancer, his face is radiant and he is breathless. He moves to his grandmother with sudden slow ceremony and puts the envelope into her hands. She accepts it, and then merely holds it and looks at it.*) Come on! Open it . . . Lord have mercy, I wish Walter Lee was here!
TRAVIS: Open it, Grandmama!
MAMA (*staring at it*): Now you all be quiet. It's just a check.
RUTH: Open it . . .
MAMA (*still staring at it*): Now don't act silly . . . We ain't never been no people to act silly 'bout no money—
RUTH (*swiftly*): We ain't never had none before—OPEN IT!

Mama finally makes a good strong tear and pulls out the thin blue slice of paper and inspects it closely. The boy and his mother study it raptly over Mama's shoulders.

MAMA: Travis! (*She is counting off with doubt.*) Is that the right number of zeros?
TRAVIS: Yes'm . . . ten thousand dollars. Gaalee, grandmama, you rich.
MAMA (*She holds the check away from her, still looking at it. Slowly her face sobers into a mask of unhappiness*): Ten thousand dollars. (*She hands it to Ruth.*) Put it away somewhere, Ruth. (*She does not look at Ruth; her eyes seem to be seeing something somewhere very far off.*) Ten thousand dollars they give you. Ten thousand dollars.
TRAVIS (*to his mother, sincerely*): What's the matter with Grandmama—don't she want to be rich?
RUTH (*distractedly*): You go on out and play now, baby. (*Travis exits. Mama starts wiping dishes absently, humming intently to herself. Ruth turns to her, with kind exasperation.*) You've gone and got yourself upset.
MAMA (*not looking at her*): I spec if it wasn't for you all . . . I would just put that money away or give it to the church or something.
RUTH: Now what kind of talk is that. Mr. Younger would just be plain mad if he could hear you talking foolish like that.

MAMA (*stopping and staring off*): Yes . . . he sure would. (*Sighing.*) We got enough to do with that money, all right. (*She halts then, and turns and looks at her daughter-in-law hard; Ruth avoids her eyes and Mama wipes her hands with finality and starts to speak firmly to Ruth.*) Where did you go today, girl?

RUTH: To the doctor.

MAMA (*impatiently*): Now, Ruth . . . you know better than that. Old Doctor Jones is strange enough in his way but there ain't nothing 'bout him make somebody slip and call him "she"—like you done this morning.

RUTH: Well, that's what happened—my tongue slipped.

MAMA: You went to see that woman, didn't you?

RUTH (*defensively, giving herself away*): What woman you talking about?

MAMA (*angrily*): That woman who—

> *Walter enters in great excitement.*

WALTER: Did it come?

MAMA (*quietly*): Can't you give people a Christian greeting before you start asking about money?

WALTER (*to Ruth*): Did it come? (*Ruth unfolds the check and lays it quietly before him, watching him intently with thoughts of her own. Walter sits down and grasps it close and counts off the zeros.*) Ten thousand dollars—(*He turns suddenly, frantically to his mother and draws some papers out of his breast pocket.*) Mama—look. Old Willy Harris put everything on paper—

MAMA: Son—I think you ought to talk to your wife . . . I'll go on out and leave you alone if you want—

WALTER: I can talk to her later—Mama, look—

MAMA: Son—

WALTER: WILL SOMEBODY PLEASE LISTEN TO ME TODAY!

MAMA (*quietly*): I don't 'low no yellin' in this house, Walter Lee, and you know it—(*Walter stares at them in frustration and starts to speak several times.*) And there ain't going to be no investing in no liquor stores.

WALTER: But, Mama, you ain't even looked at it.

MAMA: I don't aim to have to speak on that again.

> *A long pause.*

WALTER: You ain't looked at it and you don't aim to have to speak on that again? You ain't even looked at it and *you* have decided—(*Crumpling his papers.*) Well, *you* tell that to my boy tonight when you put him to sleep on the living-room couch . . . (*Turning to Mama and speaking directly to her.*) Yeah—and tell it to my wife, Mama, tomorrow when she has to go out of here to look after somebody else's kids. And tell it to *me*, Mama, every time we need a new pair of curtains and I have to watch *you* go out and work in somebody's kitchen. Yeah, you tell me then!

> *Walter starts out.*

RUTH: Where you going?

WALTER: I'm going out!

RUTH: Where?

WALTER: Just out of this house somewhere—

RUTH (*getting her coat*): I'll come too.

WALTER: I don't want you to come!

RUTH: I got something to talk to you about, Walter.

WALTER: That's too bad.

MAMA (*still quietly*): Walter Lee—(*She waits and he finally turns and looks at her.*) Sit down.

WALTER: I'm a grown man, Mama.

MAMA: Ain't nobody said you wasn't grown. But you still in my house and my presence. And as long as you are—you'll talk to your wife civil. Now sit down.

RUTH (*suddenly*): Oh, let him go on out and drink himself to death! He makes me sick to my stomach! (*She flings her coat against him and exits to bedroom.*)

WALTER (*violently flinging the coat after her*): And you turn mine too, baby! (*The door slams behind her.*) That was my biggest mistake—

MAMA (*still quietly*): Walter, what is the matter with you?

WALTER: Matter with me? Ain't nothing the matter with *me*!

MAMA: Yes there is. Something eating you up like a crazy man. Something more than me not giving you this money. The past few years I been watching it happen to you. You get all nervous acting and kind of wild in the eyes—(*Walter jumps up impatiently at her words.*) I said sit there now, I'm talking to you!

WALTER: Mama—I don't need no nagging at me today.

MAMA: Seem like you getting to a place where you always tied up in some kind of knot about something. But if anybody ask you 'bout it you just yell at 'em and bust out the house and go out and drink somewheres. Walter Lee, people can't live with that. Ruth's a good, patient girl in her way—but you getting to be too much. Boy, don't make the mistake of driving that girl away from you.

WALTER: Why—what she do for me?

MAMA: She loves you.

WALTER: Mama—I'm going out. I want to go off somewhere and be by myself for a while.

MAMA: I'm sorry 'bout your liquor store, son. It just wasn't the thing for us to do. That's what I want to tell you about—

WALTER: I got to go out, Mama—

He rises.

MAMA: It's dangerous, son.

WALTER: What's dangerous?

MAMA: When a man goes outside his home to look for peace.

WALTER (*beseechingly*): Then why can't there never be no peace in this house then?

MAMA: You done found it in some other house?

WALTER: No—there ain't no woman! Why do women always think there's a woman somewhere when a man gets restless. (*Picks up the check.*) Do you know what this money means to me? Do you know what this money can do for us? (*Puts it back.*) Mama—Mama—I want so many things . . .

MAMA: Yes, son—

WALTER: I want so many things that they are driving me kind of crazy . . . Mama—look at me.

MAMA: I'm looking at you. You a good-looking boy. You got a job, a nice wife, a fine boy, and—

WALTER: A job. (*Looks at her.*) Mama, a job? I open and close car doors all day long. I drive a man around in his limousine and I say, "Yes, sir; no, sir; very good, sir; shall I take the Drive, sir?" Mama, that ain't no kind of job . . . that ain't nothing at all. (*Very quietly.*) Mama, I don't know if I can make you understand.

MAMA: Understand what, baby?

WALTER (*quietly*): Sometimes it's like I can see the future stretched out in front of me—just plain as day. The future, Mama. Hanging over there at the edge of my days. Just waiting for me—a big, looming blank space—full of *nothing*. Just waiting for *me*. But it don't have to be. (*Pause. Kneeling beside her chair.*) Mama—sometimes when I'm downtown and I pass them cool, quiet-looking restaurants where them white boys are sitting back and talking 'bout things . . . sitting there turning deals worth millions of dollars . . . sometimes I see guys don't look much older than me—

MAMA: Son—how come you talk so much 'bout money?

WALTER (*with immense passion*): Because it is life, Mama!

MAMA (*quietly*): Oh—(*Very quietly.*) So now it's life. Money is life. Once upon a time freedom used to be life—now it's money. I guess the world really do change . . .

WALTER: No—it was always money, Mama. We just didn't know about it.

MAMA: No . . . something has changed. (*She looks at him.*) You something new, boy. In my time we was worried about not being lynched and getting to the North if we could and how to stay alive and still have a pinch of dignity too . . . Now here come you and Beneatha—talking 'bout things we ain't never even thought about hardly, me and your daddy. You ain't satisfied or proud of nothing we done. I mean that you had a home; that we kept you out of trouble till you was grown; that you don't have to ride to work on the back of nobody's streetcar—You my children—but how different we done become.

WALTER (*a long beat. He pats her hand and gets up*): You just don't understand, Mama, you just don't understand.

MAMA: Son—do you know your wife is expecting another baby? (*Walter stands, stunned, and absorbs what his mother has said.*) That's what she wanted to talk to you about. (*Walter sinks down into a chair.*) This ain't for me to be telling—but you ought to know. (*She waits.*) I think Ruth is thinking 'bout getting rid of that child.

WALTER (*slowly understanding*):—No—no—Ruth wouldn't do that.

MAMA: When the world gets ugly enough—a woman will do anything for her family. *The part that's already living.*

WALTER: You don't know Ruth, Mama, if you think she would do that.

Ruth opens the bedroom door and stands there a little limp.

RUTH: Yes I would too, Walter. (*Pause.*) I gave her a five-dollar down payment.

There is total silence as the man stares at his wife and the mother stares at her son.

MAMA (*presently*): Well—(*tightly*) Well—son, I'm waiting to hear you say something . . . (*She waits.*) I'm waiting to hear how you be your father's son. Be the man he was . . . (*Pause. The silence shouts.*) Your wife say she going to destroy your child. And I'm waiting to hear you talk like him and say we a people who give children life, not who destroys them—(*She rises.*) I'm waiting to see you stand up and look like your daddy and say we done give up one baby to poverty and that we ain't going to give up nary another one . . . I'm waiting.

WALTER: Ruth—(*He can say nothing.*)

MAMA: If you a son of mine, tell her! (*Walter picks up his keys and his coat and walks out. She continues, bitterly.*) You . . . you are a disgrace to your father's memory. Somebody get me my hat!

    Curtain.

ACT II

Scene 1

    Time: Later the same day.

    At rise: Ruth is ironing again. She has the radio going. Presently Beneatha's bedroom door opens and Ruth's mouth falls and she puts down the iron in fascination.

RUTH: What have we got on tonight!

BENEATHA (*emerging grandly from the doorway so that we can see her thoroughly robed in the costume Asagai brought*): You are looking at what a well-dressed Nigerian woman wears—(*She parades for Ruth, her hair completely hidden by the headdress; she is coquettishly fanning herself with an ornate oriental fan, mistakenly more like Butterfly than any Nigerian that ever was.*) Isn't it beautiful? (*She promenades to the radio and, with an arrogant florish, turns off the good loud blues that is playing.*) Enough of this assimilationist junk! (*Ruth follows her with her eyes as she goes to the phonograph and puts on a record and turns and waits ceremoniously for the music to come up. Then, with a shout—*) OCO-MOGOSIAY!

    Ruth jumps. The music comes up, a lovely Nigerian melody. Beneatha listens, enraptured, her eyes far away—"back to the past." She begins to dance. Ruth is dumfounded.

RUTH: What kind of dance is that?

BENEATHA: A folk dance.

RUTH (*Pearl Bailey*): What kind of folks do that, honey?

BENEATHA: It's from Nigeria. It's a dance of welcome.

RUTH: Who you welcoming?

BENEATHA: The men back to the village.

RUTH: Where they been?

BENEATHA: How should I know—out hunting or something. Anyway, they are coming back now.

RUTH: Well that's good.

BENEATHA (*with the record*): Alundi, alundi

Alundi alunya

Jop pu a jeepua

Ang gu sooooooooooo

AI YAI YAE . . .
Ayehaye—alundi . . .

> *Walter comes in during this performance; he has obviously been drink-*
> *ing. He leans against the door heavily and watches his sister, at first with*
> *distaste. Then his eyes look off—"back to the past"—as he lifts both his*
> *fists to the roof, screaming)*

WALTER: YEAH . . . AND ETHIOPIA STRETCH FORTH HER HANDS
AGAIN!

RUTH (*drily, looking at him*): Yes—and Africa sure is claiming her own tonight.
(*She gives them both up and starts ironing again.*)

WALTER (*all in a drunken, dramatic shout*): Shut up! . . . I'm digging them drums .
. . them drums move me! . . . (*He makes his weaving way to his wife's face and*
leans in close to her.) In my heart of hearts—(*He thumps his chest*)—I am much
warrior!

RUTH (*without even looking up*): In your heart of hearts you are much drunkard.

WALTER (*coming away from her and starting to wander around the room, shouting*):
Me and Jomo . . . (*Intently, in his sister's face. She has stopped dancing to watch*
him in this unknown mood.) That's my man, Kenyatta. (*Shouting and thumping*
his chest.) FLAMING SPEAR! HOT DAMN! (*He is suddenly in possession of*
an imaginary spear and actively spearing enemies all over the room.) OCO-
MOGOSIAY . . .

BENEATHA (*to encourage Walter, thoroughly caught up with this side of him*): OCO-
MOGOSIAY, FLAMING SPEAR!

WALTER: THE LION IS WAKING . . . OWIMOWEH!

> *He pulls his shirt open and leaps up on the table and gestures with his*
> *spear.*

BENEATHA: OWIMOWEH!

WALTER (*on the table, very far gone, his eyes pure glass sheets. He sees what we can-*
not, that he is a leader of his people, a great chief, a descendant of Chaka, and that
the hour to march has come): Listen, my black brothers—

BENEATHA: OCOMOGOSIAY!

WALTER: —Do you hear the waters rushing against the shores of the coast-
lands—

BENEATHA: OCOMOGOSIAY!

WALTER: —Do you hear the screeching of the cocks in yonder hills beyond
where the chiefs meet in council for the coming of the mighty war—

BENEATHA: OCOMOGOSIAY!

> *And now the lighting shifts subtly to suggest the world of Walter's imagi-*
> *nation, and the mood shifts from pure comedy. It is the inner Walter*
> *speaking: the Southside chauffeur has assumed an unexpected majesty.*

WALTER: —Do you hear the beating of the wings of the birds flying low over the
mountains and the low places of our land—

BENEATHA: OCOMOGOSIAY!

WALTER: —Do you hear the singing of the women, singing the war songs of our
fathers to the babies in the great houses? Singing the sweet war songs! (*The*
doorbell rings.) OH, DO YOU HEAR, MY BLACK BROTHERS!

BENEATHA (*completely gone*): We hear you, Flaming Spear—

> *Ruth shuts off the phonograph and opens the door. George Murchison enters.*

WALTER: Telling us to prepare for the GREATNESS OF THE TIME! (*Lights back to normal. He turns and sees George.*) Black Brother!

> *He extends his hand for the fraternal clasp.*

GEORGE: Black Brother, hell!

RUTH (*having had enough, and embarrassed for the family*): Beneatha, you got company—what's the matter with you? Walter Lee Younger, get down off that table and stop acting like a fool . . .

> *Walter comes down off the table suddenly and makes a quick exit to the bathroom.*

RUTH: He's had a little to drink . . . I don't know what her excuse is.

GEORGE (*to Beneatha*): Look honey, we're going to the theater—we're not going to be *in* it . . . so go change, huh?

> *Beneatha looks at him and slowly, ceremoniously, lifts her hands and pulls off the headdress. Her hair is close-cropped and unstraightened. George freezes mid-sentence and Ruth's eyes all but fall out of her head.*

GEORGE: What in the name of—

RUTH (*touching Beneatha's hair*): Girl, you done lost your natural mind? Look at your head!

GEORGE: What have you done to your head—I mean your hair!

BENEATHA: Nothing—except cut it off.

RUTH: Now that's the truth—it's what ain't been done to it! You expect this boy to go out with you with your head all nappy like that?

BENEATHA (*looking at George*): That's up to George. If he's ashamed of his heritage—

GEORGE: Oh, don't be so proud of yourself, Bennie—just because you look eccentric.

BENEATHA: How can something that's natural be eccentric?

GEORGE: That's what being eccentric means—being natural. Get dressed.

BENEATHA: I don't like that, George.

RUTH: Why must you and your brother make an argument out of everything people say?

BENEATHA: Because I hate assimilationist Negroes!

RUTH: Will somebody please tell me what assimila-whoever means!

GEORGE: Oh, it's just a college girl's way of calling people Uncle Toms—but that isn't what it means at all.

RUTH: Well, what does it mean?

BENEATHA (*cutting George off and staring at him as she replies to Ruth*): It means someone who is willing to give up his own culture and submerge himself completely in the dominant, and in this case *oppressive* culture!

GEORGE: Oh, dear, dear, dear! Here we go! A lecture on the African past! On our Great West African Heritage! In one second we will hear all about the great Ashanti empires; the great Songhay civilizations; and the great sculpture of Bénin—and then some poetry in the Bantu—and the whole monologue will end with the word *heritage!* (*Nastily.*) Let's face it, baby, your heritage is nothing but a bunch of raggedy-assed spirituals and some grass huts!

BENEATHA: GRASS HUTS! (*Ruth crosses to her and forcibly pushes her toward the bedroom.*) See there . . . you are standing there in your splendid ignorance talking about people who were the first to smelt iron on the face of the earth! (*Ruth is pushing her through the door.*) The Ashanti were performing surgical operations when the English—(*Ruth pulls the door to, with Beneatha on the other side, and smiles graciously at George. Beneatha opens the door and shouts the end of the sentence defiantly at George.*)—were still tatooing themselves with blue dragons! (*She goes back inside.*)

RUTH: Have a seat, George. (*They both sit. Ruth folds her hands rather primly on her lap, determined to demonstrate the civilization of the family.*) Warm, ain't it? I mean for September. (*Pause.*) Just like they always say about Chicago weather: if it's too hot or cold for you, just wait a minute and it'll change. (*She smiles happily at this clichéof clichés.*) Everybody say it's got to do with them bombs and things they keep setting off. (*Pause.*) Would you like a nice cold beer?

GEORGE: No, thank you. I don't care for beer. (*He looks at his watch.*) I hope she hurries up.

RUTH: What time is the show?

GEORGE: It's an eight-thirty curtain. That's just Chicago, though. In New York standard curtain time is eight forty.

He is rather proud of this knowledge.

RUTH (*properly appreciating it*): You get to New York a lot?

GEORGE (*offhand*): Few times a year.

RUTH: Oh—that's nice. I've never been to New York.

Walter enters. We feel he has relieved himself, but the edge of unreality is still with him.

WALTER: New York ain't got nothing Chicago ain't. Just a bunch of hustling people all squeezed up together—being "Eastern."

He turns his face into a screw of displeasure.

GEORGE: Oh—you've been?

WALTER: *Plenty* of times.

RUTH (*shocked at the lie*): Walter Lee Younger!

WALTER (*staring her down*): Plenty! (*Pause.*) What we got to drink in this house? Why don't you offer this man some refreshment. (*To George.*) They don't know how to entertain people in this house, man.

GEORGE: Thank you—I don't really care for anything.

WALTER (*feeling his head; sobriety coming*): Where's Mama?

RUTH: She ain't come back yet.

WALTER (*looking Murchison over from head to toe, scrutinizing his carefully casual tweed sports jacket over cashmere V-neck sweater over soft eyelet shirt and tie, and soft slacks, finished off with white buckskin shoes*): Why all you college boys wear them faggoty-looking white shoes?

RUTH: Walter Lee!

George Murchison ignores the remark.

WALTER (*to Ruth*): Well, they look crazy as hell—white shoes, cold as it is.

RUTH (*crushed*): You have to excuse him—

WALTER: No he don't! Excuse me for what? What you always excusing me for! I'll excuse myself when I needs to be excused! (*A pause.*) They look as funny as them black knee socks Beneatha wears out of here all the time.

RUTH: It's the college *style*, Walter.

WALTER: Style, hell. She looks like she got burnt legs or something!

RUTH: Oh, Walter—

WALTER (*an irritable mimic*): Oh, Walter! Oh, Walter! (*To Murchison.*) How's your old man making out? I understand you all going to buy that big hotel on the Drive? (*He finds a beer in the refrigerator, wanders over to Murchison, sipping and wiping his lips with the back of his hand, and straddling a chair backwards to talk to the other man.*) Shrewd move. Your old man is all right, man. (*Tapping his head and half winking for emphasis.*) I mean he knows how to operate. I mean he thinks *big*, you know what I mean, I mean for a *home*, you know? But I think he's kind of running out of ideas now. I'd like to talk to him. Listen, man, I got some plans that could turn this city upside down. I mean think like he does. *Big*. Invest big, gamble big, hell, lose *big* if you have to, you know what I mean. It's hard to find a man on this whole Southside who understands my kind of thinking—you dig? (*He scrutinizes Murchison again, drinks his beer, squints his eyes and leans in close, confidential, man to man.*) Me and you ought to sit down and talk sometimes, man. Man, I got me some ideas . . .

MURCHISON (*with boredom*): Yeah—sometimes we'll have to do that, Walter.

WALTER (*understanding the indifference, and offended*): Yeah—well, when you get the time, man. I know you a busy little boy.

RUTH: Walter, please—

WALTER (*bitterly, hurt*): I know ain't nothing in this world as busy as you colored college boys with your fraternity pins and white shoes . . .

RUTH (*covering her face with humiliation*): Oh, Walter Lee—

WALTER: I see you all all the time—with the books tucked under your arms—going to your (*British A—a mimic.*) "clahsses." And for what! What the hell you learning over there? Filling up your heads—(*Counting off on his fingers.*)—with the sociology and the psychology—but they teaching you how to be a man? How to take over and run the world? They teaching you how to run a rubber plantation or a steel mill? Naw—just to talk proper and read books and wear them faggoty-looking white shoes . . .

GEORGE (*looking at him with distaste, a little above it all*): You're all wacked up with bitterness, man.

WALTER (*intently, almost quietly, between the teeth, glaring at the boy*): And you—ain't you bitter, man? Ain't you just about had it yet? Don't you see no stars gleaming that you can't reach out and grab? You happy?—You contented son-of-a-bitch—you happy? You got it made? Bitter? Man, I'm a volcano. Bitter? Here I am a giant—surrounded by ants! Ants who can't even understand what it is the giant is talking about.

RUTH (*passionately and suddenly*): Oh, Walter—ain't you with nobody!

WALTER (*violently*): No! 'Cause ain't nobody with me! Not even my own mother!

RUTH: Walter, that's a terrible thing to say!

> *Beneatha enters, dressed for the evening in a cocktail dress and earrings, hair natural.*

GEORGE: Well—hey—(*Crosses to Beneatha; thoughtful, with emphasis, since this is a reversal.*) You look great!

WALTER (*seeing his sister's hair for the first time*): What's the matter with your head?

BENEATHA (*tired of the jokes now*): I cut it off, Brother.

WALTER (*coming close to inspect it and walking around her*): Well, I'll be damned. So that's what they mean by the African bush . . .

BENEATHA: Ha ha. Let's go, George.

GEORGE (*looking at her*): You know something? I like it. It's sharp. I mean it really is. (*Helps her into her wrap.*)

RUTH: Yes—I think so, too. (*She goes to the mirror and starts to clutch at her hair.*)

WALTER: Oh no! You leave yours alone, baby. You might turn out to have a pin-shaped head or something!

BENEATHA: See you all later.

RUTH: Have a nice time.

GEORGE: Thanks. Good night. (*Half out the door, he reopens it. To Walter.*) Good night, Prometheus!

> *Beneatha and George exit.*

WALTER (*to Ruth*): Who is Prometheus?

RUTH: I don't know. Don't worry about it.

WALTER (*in fury, pointing after George*): See there—they get to a point where they can't insult you man to man—they got to go talk about something ain't nobody never heard of!

RUTH: How do you know it was an insult? (*To humor him.*) Maybe Prometheus is a nice fellow.

WALTER: Prometheus! I bet there ain't even no such thing! I bet that simple-minded clown—

RUTH: Walter—

> *She stops what she is doing and looks at him.*

WALTER (*yelling*): Don't start!

RUTH: Start what?

WALTER: Your nagging! Where was I? Who was I with? How much money did I spend?

RUTH (*plaintively*): Walter Lee—why don't we just try to talk about it . . .

WALTER (*not listening*): I been out talking with people who understand me. People who care about the things I got on my mind.

RUTH (*wearily*): I guess that means people like Willy Harris.

WALTER: Yes, people like Willy Harris.

RUTH (*with a sudden flash of impatience*): Why don't you all just hurry up and go into the banking business and stop talking about it!

WALTER: Why? You want to know why? 'Cause we all tied up in a race of people that don't know how to do nothing but moan, pray and have babies!

The line is too bitter even for him and he looks at her and sits down.

RUTH: Oh, Walter . . . (*Softly.*) Honey, why can't you stop fighting me?

WALTER (*without thinking*): Who's fighting you? Who even cares about you?

This line begins the retardation of his mood.

RUTH: Well—(*She waits a long time, and then with resignation starts to put away her things.*) I guess I might as well go on to bed . . . (*More or less to herself.*) I don't know where we lost it . . . but we have . . . (*Then, to him.*) I—I'm sorry about this new baby, Walter. I guess maybe I better go on and do what I started . . . I guess I just didn't realize how bad things was with us . . . I guess I just didn't really realize—(*She starts out to the bedroom and stops.*) You want some hot milk?

WALTER: Hot milk?

RUTH: Yes—hot milk.

WALTER: Why hot milk?

RUTH: 'Cause after all that liquor you come home with you ought to have something hot in your stomach.

WALTER: I don't want no milk.

RUTH: You want some coffee then?

WALTER: No, I don't want no coffee. I don't want nothing hot to drink. (*Almost plaintively.*) Why you always trying to give me something to eat?

RUTH (*standing and looking at him helplessly*): What else can I give you, Walter Lee Younger?

She stands and looks at him and presently turns to go out again. He lifts his head and watches her going away from him in a new mood which began to emerge when he asked her "Who cares about you?"

WALTER: It's been rough, ain't it, baby? (*She hears and stops but does not turn around and he continues to her back.*) I guess between two people there ain't never as much understood as folks generally thinks there is. I mean like between me and you—(*She turns to face him.*) How we gets to the place where we scared to talk softness to each other. (*He waits, thinking hard himself.*) Why you think it got to be like that? (*He is thoughtful, almost as a child would be.*) Ruth, what is it gets into people ought to be close?

RUTH: I don't know, honey. I think about it a lot.

WALTER: On account of you and me, you mean? The way things are with us. The way something done come down between us.

RUTH: There ain't so much between us, Walter . . . Not when you come to me and try to talk to me. Try to be with me . . . a little even.

WALTER (*total honesty*): Sometimes . . . sometimes . . . I don't even know how to try.

RUTH: Walter—

WALTER: Yes?

RUTH (*coming to him, gently and with misgiving, but coming to him*): Honey . . . life don't have to be like this. I mean sometimes people can do things so that things are better . . . You remember how we used to talk when Travis was born . . . about the way we were going to live . . . the kind of house . . . (*She is stroking his head.*) Well, it's all starting to slip away from us . . .

> He turns her to him and they look at each other and kiss, tenderly and hungrily. The door opens and Mama enters—Walter breaks away and jumps up. A beat.

WALTER: Mama, where have you been?

MAMA: My—them steps is longer than they used to be. Whew! (*She sits down and ignores him.*) How you feeling this evening, Ruth?

> Ruth shrugs, disturbed at having been interrupted and watching her husband knowingly.

WALTER: Mama, where have you been all day?

MAMA (*still ignoring him and leaning on the table and changing to more comfortable shoes*): Where's Travis?

RUTH: I let him go out earlier and he ain't come back yet. Boy, is he going to get it!

WALTER: Mama!

MAMA (*as if she has heard him for the first time*): Yes, son?

WALTER: Where did you go this afternoon?

MAMA: I went downtown to tend to some business that I had to tend to.

WALTER: What kind of business?

MAMA: You know better than to question me like a child, Brother.

WALTER (*rising and bending over the table*): Where were you, Mama? (*Bringing his fists down and shouting.*) Mama, you didn't go do something with that insurance money, something crazy?

> The front door opens slowly, interrupting him, and Travis peeks his head in, less than hopefully.

TRAVIS (*to his mother*): Mama, I—

RUTH: "Mama I" nothing! You're going to get it, boy! Get on in that bedroom and get yourself ready!

TRAVIS: But I—

MAMA: Why don't you all never let the child explain hisself.

RUTH: Keep out of it now, Lena.

> Mama clamps her lips together, and Ruth advances toward her son menacingly.

RUTH: A thousand times I have told you not to go off like that—

MAMA (*holding out her arms to her grandson*): Well—at least let me tell him something. I want him to be the first one to hear . . . Come here, Travis. (*The boy obeys, gladly.*) Travis—(*She takes him by the shoulder and looks into his face.*)—you know that money we got in the mail this morning?

TRAVIS: Yes'm—

MAMA: Well—what you think your grandmama gone and done with that money?

TRAVIS: I don't know, Grandmama.

MAMA (*putting her finger on his nose for emphasis*): She went out and she bought you a house! (*The explosion comes from Walter at the end of the revelation and he jumps up and turns away from all of them in a fury. Mama continues, to Travis.*) You glad about the house? It's going to be yours when you get to be a man.

TRAVIS: Yeah—I always wanted to live in a house.

MAMA: All right, gimme some sugar then—(*Travis puts his arms around her neck as she watches her son over the boy's shoulder. Then, to Travis, after the embrace.*) Now when you say your prayers tonight, you thank God and your grandfather—'cause it was him who give you the house—in his way.

RUTH (*taking the boy from Mama and pushing him toward the bedroom*): Now you get out of here and get ready for your beating.

TRAVIS: Aw, Mama—

RUTH: Get on in there—(*Closing the door behind him and turning radiantly to her mother-in-law.*) So you went and did it!

MAMA (*quietly, looking at her son with pain*): Yes, I did.

RUTH (*raising both arms classically*): PRAISE GOD! (*Looks at Walter a moment, who says nothing. She crosses rapidly to her husband.*) Please, honey—let me be glad . . . you be glad too. (*She has laid her hands on his shoulders, but he shakes himself free of her roughly, without turning to face her.*) Oh, Walter . . . a home . . . a home. (*She comes back to Mama.*) Well—where is it? How big is it? How much it going to cost?

MAMA: Well—

RUTH: When we moving?

MAMA (*smiling at her*): First of the month.

RUTH (*throwing back her head with jubilance*): Praise God!

MAMA (*tentatively, still looking at her son's back turned against her and Ruth*): It's—it's a nice house too . . . (*She cannot help speaking directly to him. An imploring quality in her voice, her manner, makes her almost like a girl now.*) Three bedrooms—nice big one for you and Ruth . . . Me and Beneatha still have to share our room, but Travis have one of his own—and (*With difficulty.*) I figure if the—new baby—is a boy, we could get one of them double-decker outfits . . . And there's a yard with a little patch of dirt where I could maybe get to grow me a few flowers . . . And a nice big basement . . .

RUTH: Walter honey, be glad—

MAMA (*still to his back, fingering things on the table*): 'Course I don't want to make it sound fancier than it is . . . It's just a plain little old house—but it's made good and solid—and it will be *ours*. Walter Lee—it makes a difference in a man when he can walk on floors that belong to *him* . . .

RUTH: Where is it?

MAMA (*frightened at this telling*): Well—well—it's out there in Clybourne Park—

Ruth's radiance fades abruptly, and Walter finally turns slowly to face his mother with incredulity and hostility.

RUTH: Where?

MAMA (*matter-of-factly*): Four o six Clybourne Street, Clybourne Park.

RUTH: Clybourne Park? Mama, there ain't no colored people living in Clybourne Park.

MAMA (*almost idiotically*): Well, I guess there's going to be some now.

WALTER (*bitterly*): So that's the peace and comfort you went out and bought for us today!

MAMA (*raising her eyes to meet his finally*): Son—I just tried to find the nicest place for the least amount of money for my family.

RUTH (*trying to recover from the shock*): Well—well—'course I ain't one never been 'fraid of no crackers, mind you—but—well, wasn't there no other houses nowhere?

MAMA: Them houses they put up for colored in them areas way out all seem to cost twice as much as other houses. I did the best I could.

RUTH (*struck senseless with the news, in its various degrees of goodness and trouble, she sits a moment, her fists propping her chin in thought, and then she starts to rise, bringing her fists down with vigor, the radiance spreading from cheek to cheek again*): Well—well—All I can say is—if this is my time in life—MY TIME—to say good-bye—(*And she builds with momentum as she starts to circle the room with an exuberant, almost tearfully happy release.*)—to these Goddamned cracking walls!—(*She pounds the walls.*)—and these marching roaches!—(*She wipes at an imaginary army of marching roaches.*)—and this cramped little closet which ain't now or never was no kitchen! ... then I say it loud and good, HALLELUJAH! AND GOOD-BYE MISERY ... I DON'T NEVER WANT TO SEE YOUR UGLY FACE AGAIN! (*She laughs joyously, having practically destroyed the apartment, and flings her arms up and lets them come down happily, slowly, reflectively, over her abdomen, aware for the first time perhaps that the life therein pulses with happiness and not despair.*) Lena?

MAMA (*moved, watching her happiness*): Yes, honey?

RUTH (*looking off*): Is there—is there a whole lot of sunlight?

MAMA (*understanding*): Yes, child, there's a whole lot of sunlight.

> Long pause.

RUTH (*collecting herself and going to the door of the room Travis is in*): Well—I guess I better see 'bout Travis. (*To Mama.*) Lord, I sure don't feel like whipping nobody today!

> She exits.

MAMA (*the mother and son are left alone now and the mother waits a long time, considering deeply, before she speaks*): Son—you—you understand what I done, don't you? (*Walter is silent and sullen.*) I—I just seen my family falling apart today ... just falling to pieces in front of my eyes ... We couldn't of gone on like we was today. We was going backwards 'stead of forwards—talking 'bout killing babies and wishing each other was dead ... When it gets like that in life—you just got to do something different, push on out and do something bigger ... (*She waits.*) I wish you say something, son ... I wish you'd say how deep inside you you think I done the right thing—

WALTER (*crossing slowly to his bedroom door and finally turning there and speaking measuredly*): What you need me to say you done right for? You the head of this family. You run our lives like you want to. It was your money and you did what you wanted with it. So what you need for me to say it was all right for? (*Bitterly, to hurt her as deeply as he knows is possible.*) So you butchered up a dream of mine—you—who always talking 'bout your children's dreams ...

MAMA: Walter Lee—

He just closes the door behind him. Mama sits alone, thinking heavily.

Curtain.

Scene 2

> *Time: Friday night, a few weeks later.*
> *At rise: Packing crates mark the intention of the family to move.*
> *Beneatha and George come in, presumably from an evening out again.*

GEORGE: O.K. . . . O.K., whatever you say . . . (*They both sit on the couch. He tries to kiss her. She moves away.*) Look, we've had a nice evening; let's not spoil it, huh? . . .

> *He again turns her head and tries to nuzzle in and she turns away from him, not with distaste but with momentary lack of interest; in a mood to pursue what they were talking about.*

BENEATHA: I'm *trying* to talk to you.

GEORGE: We always talk.

BENEATHA: Yes—and I love to talk.

GEORGE (*exasperated; rising*): I know it and I don't mind it sometimes . . . I want you to cut it out, see—The moody stuff, I mean. I don't like it. You're a nice-looking girl . . . all over. That's all you need, honey, forget the atmosphere. Guys aren't going to go for the atmosphere—they're going to go for what they see. Be glad for that. Drop the Garbo routine. It doesn't go with you. As for myself, I want a nice—(*Groping.*)—simple (*Thoughtfully.*)—sophisticated girl . . . not a poet—O.K.?

> *He starts to kiss her, she rebuffs him again and he jumps up.*

BENEATHA: Why are you angry, George?

GEORGE: Because this is stupid! I don't go out with you to discuss the nature of "quiet desperation" or to hear all about your thoughts—because the world will go on thinking what it thinks regardless—

BENEATHA: Then why read books? Why go to school?

GEORGE (*with artificial patience, counting on his fingers*): It's simple. You read books—to learn facts—to get grades—to pass the course—to get a degree. That's all—it has nothing to do with thoughts.

> *A long pause.*

BENEATHA: I see. (*He starts to sit.*) Good night, George.

> *George looks at her a little oddly, and starts to exit. He meets Mama coming in.*

GEORGE: Oh—hello, Mrs. Younger.

MAMA: Hello, George, how you feeling?

GEORGE: Fine—fine, how are you?

MAMA: Oh, a little tired. You know them steps can get you after a day's work. You all have a nice time tonight?

GEORGE: Yes—a fine time. A fine time.

MAMA: Well, good night.

GEORGE: Good night. (*He exits. Mama closes the door behind her.*) Hello, honey. What you sitting like that for?

BENEATHA: I'm just sitting.

MAMA: Didn't you have a nice time?

BENEATHA: No.

MAMA: No? What's the matter?

BENEATHA: Mama, George is a fool—honest. (*She rises.*)

MAMA (*hustling around unloading the packages she has entered with. She stops.*): Is he, baby?

BENEATHA: Yes.

> *Beneatha makes up Travis's bed as she talks.*

MAMA: You sure?

BENEATHA: Yes.

MAMA: Well—I guess you better not waste your time with no fools.

> *Beneatha looks up at her mother, watching her put groceries in the refrigerator. Finally she gathers up her things and starts into the bedroom. At the door she stops and looks back at her mother.*

BENEATHA: Mama—

MAMA: Yes, baby—

BENEATHA: Thank you.

MAMA: For what?

BENEATHA: For understanding me this time.

> *She exits quickly and the mother stands, smiling a little, looking at the place where Beneatha just stood. Ruth enters.*

RUTH: Now don't you fool with any of this stuff, Lena—

MAMA: Oh, I just thought I'd sort a few things out. Is Brother here?

RUTH: Yes.

MAMA (*with concern*): Is he—

RUTH (*reading her eyes*): Yes.

> *Mama is silent and someone knocks on the door. Mama and Ruth exchange weary and knowing glances and Ruth opens it to admit the neighbor, Mrs. Johnson, who is a rather squeaky wide-eyed lady of no particular age, with a newspaper under her arm.*

MAMA (*changing her expression to acute delight and a ringing cheerful greeting*): Oh—hello there, Johnson.

JOHNSON (*this is a woman who decided long ago to be enthusiastic about EVERYTHING in life and she is inclined to wave her wrist vigorously at the height of her exclamatory comments*): Hello there, yourself! H'you this evening, Ruth?

RUTH (*not much of a deceptive type*): Fine, Mis' Johnson, h'you?

JOHNSON: Fine. (*Reaching out quickly, playfully, and patting Ruth's stomach.*) Ain't you starting to poke out none yet! (*She mugs with delight at the over familiar remark and her eyes dart around looking at the crates and packing preparation;*

Mama's face is a cold sheet of endurance.) Oh, ain't we getting ready round here, though! Yessir! Lookathere! I'm telling you the Youngers is really getting ready to "move on up a little higher!"—Bless God!

MAMA (*a little drily, doubting the total sincerity of the Blesser*): Bless God.

JOHNSON: He's good, ain't He?

MAMA: Oh yes, He's good.

JOHNSON: I mean sometimes He works in mysterious ways . . . but He works, don't He!

MAMA (*the same*): Yes, he does.

JOHNSON: I'm just sooooooo happy for y'all. And this here child—(*About Ruth.*) looks like she could just pop open with happiness, don't she. Where's all the rest of the family?

MAMA: Bennie's gone to bed—

JOHNSON: Ain't no . . . (*The implication is pregnancy.*) sickness done hit you—I hope . . . ?

MAMA: No—she just tired. She was out this evening.

JOHNSON (*all is a coo, an emphatic coo*): Aw—ain't that lovely. She still going out with the little Murchison boy?

MAMA (*drily*): Ummmm huh.

JOHNSON: That's lovely. You sure got lovely children, Younger. Me and Isaiah talks all the time 'bout what fine children you was blessed with. We sure do.

MAMA: Ruth, give Mis' Johnson a piece of sweet potato pie and some milk.

JOHNSON: Oh honey, I can't stay hardly a minute—I just dropped in to see if there was anything I could do. (*Accepting the food easily.*) I guess y'all seen the news what's all over the colored paper this week . . .

MAMA: No—didn't get mine yet this week.

JOHNSON (*lifting her head and blinking with the spirit of catastrophe*): You mean you ain't read 'bout them colored people that was bombed out their place out there?

Ruth straightens with concern and takes the paper and reads it. Johnson notices her and feeds commentary.

JOHNSON: Ain't it something how bad these here white folks is getting here in Chicago! Lord, getting so you think you right down in Mississippi! (*With a tremendous and rather insincere sense of melodrama.*) 'Course I thinks it's wonderful how our folk keeps on pushing out. You hear some of these Negroes round here talking 'bout how they don't go where they ain't wanted and all that—but not me, honey! (*This is a lie.*) Wilhemenia Othella Johnson goes anywhere, any time she feels like it! (*With head movement for emphasis.*) Yes I do! Why if we left it up to these here crackers, the poor niggers wouldn't have nothing—(*She clasps her hand over her mouth.*) Oh, I always forgets you don't 'low that word in your house.

MAMA (*quietly, looking at her*): No—I don't 'low it.

JOHNSON (*vigorously again*): Me neither! I was just telling Isaiah yesterday when he come using it in front of me—I said, "Isaiah, it's just like Mis' Younger says all the time—"

MAMA: Don't you want some more pie?

JOHNSON: No—no thank you; this was lovely. I got to get on over home and have my midnight coffee. I hear some people say it don't let them sleep but I

finds I can't close my eyes right lessen I done had that laaaast cup of coffee
. . . (*She waits. A beat. Undaunted.*) My Goodnight coffee, I calls it!

MAMA (*with much eye-rolling and communication between herself and Ruth*): Ruth,
why don't you give Mis' Johnson some coffee.

Ruth gives Mama an unpleasant look for her kindness.

JOHNSON (*accepting the coffee*): Where's Brother tonight?

MAMA: He's lying down.

JOHNSON: MMmmmmm, he sure gets his beauty rest, don't he? Good-looking
man. Sure is a good-looking man! (*Reaching out to pat Ruth's stomach again.*) I
guess that's how come we keep on having babies around here. (*She winks at
Mama.*) One thing 'bout Brother, he always know how to have a *good* time.
And soooooo ambitious! I bet it was his idea y'all moving out to Clybourne
Park. Lord—I bet this time next month y'all's names will have been in the
papers plenty—(*Holding up her hands to mark off each word of the headline she
can see in front of her.*) "NEGROES INVADE CLYBOURNE PARK—
BOMBED!"

MAMA (*she and Ruth look at the woman in amazement*): We ain't exactly moving
out there to get bombed.

JOHNSON: Oh honey—you know I'm praying to God every day that don't nothing like that happen! But you have to think of life like it is—and these here
Chicago peckerwoods is some baaaad peckerwoods.

MAMA (*wearily*): We done thought about all that Mis' Johnson.

*Beneatha comes out of the bedroom in her robe and passes through to the
bathroom. Mrs. Johnson turns.*

JOHNSON: Hello there, Bennie!

BENEATHA (*crisply*): Hello, Mrs. Johnson.

JOHNSON: How is school?

BENEATHA (*crisply*): Fine, thank you. (*She goes out.*)

JOHNSON (*insulted*): Getting so she don't have much to say to nobody.

MAMA: The child was on her way to the bathroom.

JOHNSON: I know—but sometimes she act like ain't got time to pass the time of
day with nobody ain't been to college. Oh—I ain't criticizing her none. It's
just—you know how some of our young people gets when they get a little education. (*Mama and Ruth say nothing, just look at her.*) Yes—well. Well, I
guess I better get on home. (*Unmoving.*) 'Course I can understand how she
must be proud and everything—being the only one in the family to make
something of herself. I know just being a chauffeur ain't never satisfied
Brother none. He shouldn't feel like that, though. Ain't nothing wrong with
being a chauffeur.

MAMA: There's plenty wrong with it.

JOHNSON: What?

MAMA: Plenty. My husband always said being any kind of a servant wasn't a fit
thing for a man to have to be. He always said a man's hands was made to
make things, or to turn the earth with—not to drive nobody's car for 'em—
or—(*She looks at her own hands.*) carry they slop jars. And my boy is just like
him—he wasn't meant to wait on nobody.

JOHNSON (*rising, somewhat offended*): Mmmmmmmmm. The Youngers is too much for me! (*She looks around.*) You sure one proud-acting bunch of colored folks. Well—I always thinks like Booker T. Washington said that time—"Education has spoiled many a good plow hand"—

MAMA: Is that what old Booker T. said?

JOHNSON: He sure did.

MAMA: Well, it sounds just like him. The fool.

JOHNSON (*indignantly*): Well—he was one of our great men.

MAMA: Who said so?

JOHNSON (*nonplussed*): You know, me and you ain't never agreed about some things, Lena Younger. I guess I better be going—

RUTH (*quickly*): Good night.

JOHNSON: Good night. Oh—(*Thrusting it at her.*) You can keep the paper! (*With a trill.*) 'Night.

MAMA: Good night, Mis' Johnson.

Mrs. Johnson exits.

RUTH: If ignorance was gold . . .

MAMA: Shush. Don't talk about folks behind their backs.

RUTH: You do.

MAMA: I'm old and corrupted. (*Beneatha enters.*) You was rude to Mis' Johnson, Beneatha, and I don't like it at all.

BENEATHA (*at her door*): Mama, if there are two things we, as a people, have got to overcome, one is the Klu Klux Klan—and the other is Mrs. Johnson. (*She exits.*)

MAMA: Smart aleck.

The phone rings.

RUTH: I'll get it.

MAMA: Lord, ain't this a popular place tonight.

RUTH (*at the phone*): Hello—Just a minute. (*Goes to door.*) Walter, it's Mrs. Arnold. (*Waits. Goes back to the phone. Tense.*) Hello. Yes, this is his wife speaking . . . He's lying down now. Yes . . . well, he'll be in tomorrow. He's been very sick. Yes—I know we should have called, but we were so sure he'd be able to come in today. Yes—yes, I'm very sorry. Yes . . . Thank you very much. (*She hangs up. Walter is standing in the doorway of the bedroom behind her.*) That was Mrs. Arnold.

WALTER (*indifferently*): Was it?

RUTH: She said if you don't come in tomorrow that they are getting a new man . . .

WALTER: Ain't that sad—ain't that crying sad.

RUTH: She said Mr. Arnold has had to take a cab for three days . . . Walter, you ain't been to work for three days! (*This is a revelation to her.*) Where you been, Walter Lee Younger? (*Walter looks at her and starts to laugh.*) You're going to lose your job.

WALTER: That's right . . . (*He turns on the radio.*)

RUTH: Oh, Walter, and with your mother working like a dog every day—

A steamy, deep blues pours into the room.

WALTER: That's sad too—Everything is sad.

MAMA: What you been doing for these three days, son?

WALTER: Mama—you don't know all the things a man what got leisure can find to do in this city . . . What's this—Friday night? Well—Wednesday I borrowed Willy Harris' car and I went for a drive . . . just me and myself and I drove and drove . . . Way out . . . way past South Chicago, and I parked the car and I sat and looked at the steel mills all day long. I just sat in the car and looked at them big black chimneys for hours. Then I drove back and I went to the Green Hat. (*Pause.*) And Thursday—Thursday I borrowed the car again and I got in it and I pointed it the other way and I drove the other way—for hours—way, way up to Wisconsin, and I looked at the farms. I just drove and looked at the farms. Then I drove back and I went to the Green Hat. (*Pause.*) And today—today I didn't get the car. Today I just walked. All over the Southside. And I looked at the Negroes and they looked at me and finally I just sat down on the curb at Thirty-ninth and South Parkway and I just sat there and watched the Negroes go by. And then I went to the Green Hat. You all sad? You all depressed? And you know where I am going right now—

> *Ruth goes out quietly.*

MAMA: Oh, Big Walter, is this the harvest of our days?

WALTER: You know what I like about the Green Hat? I like this little cat they got there who blows a sax . . . He blows. He talks to me. He ain't but 'bout five feet tall and he's got a conked head and his eyes is always closed and he's all music—

MAMA (*rising and getting some papers out of her handbag*): Walter—

WALTER: And there's this other guy who plays the piano . . . and they got a sound. I mean they can work on some music . . . They got the best little combo in the world in the Green Hat . . . You can just sit there and drink and listen to them three men play and you realize that don't nothing matter worth a damn, but just being there—

MAMA: I've helped do it to you, haven't I, son? Walter I been wrong.

WALTER: Naw—you ain't never been wrong about nothing, Mama.

MAMA: Listen to me, now. I say I been wrong, son. That I been doing to you what the rest of the world been doing to you. (*She turns off the radio.*) Walter—(*She stops and he looks up slowly at her and she meets his eyes pleadingly.*) What you ain't never understood is that I ain't got nothing, don't own nothing, ain't never really wanted nothing that wasn't for you. There ain't nothing as precious to me . . . There ain't nothing worth holding on to, money, dreams, nothing else—if it means—if it means it's going to destroy my boy. (*She takes an envelope out of her handbag and puts it in front of him and he watches her without speaking or moving.*) I paid the man thirty-five hundred dollars down on the house. That leaves sixty-five hundred dollars. Monday morning I want you to take this money and take three thousand dollars and put it in a savings account for Beneatha's medical schooling. The rest you put in a checking account—with your name on it. And from now on any penny that come out of it or that go in it is for you to look after. For you to decide. (*She drops her hands a little helplessly.*) It ain't much, but it's all I got in the world and I'm putting it in your hands. I'm telling you to be the head of this family from now on like you supposed to be.

WALTER (*stares at the money*): You trust me like that, Mama?

MAMA: I ain't never stop trusting you. Like I ain't never stop loving you.

> *She goes out, and Walter sits looking at the money on the table. Finally, in a decisive gesture, he gets up, and, in mingled joy and desperation, picks up the money. At the same moment, Travis enters for bed.*

TRAVIS: What's the matter, Daddy? You drunk?

WALTER (*sweetly, more sweetly than we have ever known him*): No, Daddy ain't drunk. Daddy ain't going to never be drunk again . . .

TRAVIS: Well, good night, Daddy.

> *The father has come from behind the couch and leans over, embracing his son.*

WALTER: Son, I feel like talking to you tonight.

TRAVIS: About what?

WALTER: Oh, about a lot of things. About you and what kind of man you going to be when you grow up . . . Son—son, what do you want to be when you grow up?

TRAVIS: A bus driver.

WALTER (*laughing a little*): A what? Man, that ain't nothing to want to be!

TRAVIS: Why not?

WALTER: 'Cause, man—it ain't big enough—you know what I mean.

TRAVIS: I don't know then. I can't make up my mind. Sometimes Mama asks me that too. And sometimes when I tell her I just want to be like you—she says she don't want me to be like that and sometimes she says she does. . . .

WALTER (*gathering him up in his arms*): You know what, Travis? In seven years you going to be seventeen years old. And things is going to be very different with us in seven years, Travis. . . . One day when you are seventeen I'll come home—home from my office downtown somewhere—

TRAVIS: You don't work in no office, Daddy.

WALTER: No—but after tonight. After what your daddy gonna do tonight, there's going to be offices—a whole lot of offices. . . .

TRAVIS: What you gonna do tonight, Daddy?

WALTER: You wouldn't understand yet, son, but you daddy's gonna make a transaction . . . a business transaction that's going to change our lives. . . . That's how come one day when you 'bout seventeen years old I'll come home and I'll be pretty tired, you know what I mean, after a day of conferences and secretaries getting things wrong the way they do . . . 'cause an executive's life is hell, man—(*The more he talks the farther away he gets.*) And I'll pull the car up on the driveway . . . just a plain black Chrysler, I think, with white walls—no—black tires. More elegant. Rich people don't have to be flashy . . . though I'll have to get something a little sportier for Ruth—maybe a Cadillac convertible to do her shopping in. . . . And I'll come up the steps to the house and the gardener will be clipping away at the hedges and he'll say, "Good evening, Mr. Younger." And I'll say, "Hello, Jefferson, how are you this evening?" And I'll go inside and Ruth will come downstairs and meet me at the door and we'll kiss each other and she'll take my arm and we'll go up to your room to see you sitting on the floor with the catalogues of all the great schools in America around you. . . . All the great schools in the world! And—and I'll say, all right son—it's your seventeenth birthday, what is it you've decided? . . . Just tell me where you want to go to school and you'll *go.* Just tell me, what it is you want to be—and you'll *be* it. . . . Whatever you want to be—Yessir! *(He holds his arms open for Travis.)* You just name it, son . . . *(Travis leaps into them.)* and I hand you the world!

> *Walter's voice has risen in pitch and hysterical promise and on the last line he lifts Travis high.*
>
> *Blackout.*

Scene 3

> *Time: Saturday, moving day, one week later.*
>
> *Before the curtain rises, Ruth's voice, a strident, dramatic church alto, cuts through the silence.*
>
> *It is, in the darkness, a triumphant surge, a penetrating statement of expectation: "Oh, Lord, I don't feel no ways tired! Children, oh, glory hallelujah!"*
>
> *As the curtain rises we see that Ruth is alone in the living room, finishing up the family's packing. It is moving day. She is nailing crates and tying cartons. Beneatha enters, carrying a guitar case, and watches her exuberant sister-in-law.*

RUTH: Hey!

BENEATHA *(putting away the case):* Hi.

RUTH *(pointing at a package):* Honey—look in that package there and see what I found on sale this morning at the South Center. *(Ruth gets up and moves to the package and draws out some curtains.)* Lookahere—hand-turned hems!

BENEATHA: How do you know the window size out there?

RUTH *(who hadn't thought of that):* Oh—Well, they bound to fit something in the whole house. Anyhow, they was too good a bargain to pass up. *(Ruth slaps her head, suddenly remembering something.)* Oh, Bennie—I meant to put a special note on that carton over there. That's your mama's good china and she wants 'em to be very careful with it.

BENEATHA: I'll do it.

> *Beneatha finds a piece of paper and starts to draw large letters on it.*

RUTH: You know what I'm going to do soon as I get in that new house?

BENEATHA: What?

RUTH: Honey—I'm going to run me a tub of water up to here . . . *(With her fingers practically up to her nostrils.)* And I'm going to get in it—and I am going to sit . . . and sit . . . and sit in that hot water and the first person who knocks to tell *me* to hurry up and come out—

BENEATHA: Gets shot at sunrise.

RUTH *(laughing happily):* You said it, sister! *(Noticing how large Beneatha is absent-mindedly making the note):* Honey, they ain't going to read that from no airplane.

BENEATHA *(laughing herself):* I guess I always think things have more emphasis if they are big, somehow.

RUTH (*looking up at her and smiling*): You and your brother seem to have that as a philosophy of life. Lord, that man—done changed so 'round here. You know—you know what we did last night? Me and Walter Lee?

BENEATHA: What?

RUTH (*smiling to herself*): We went to the movies. (*Looking at Beneatha to see if she understands.*) We went to the movies. You know the last time me and Walter went to the movies together?

BENEATHA: No.

RUTH: Me neither. That's how long it been. (*Smiling again.*) But we went last night. The picture wasn't much good, but that didn't seem to matter. We went—and we held hands.

BENEATHA: Oh, Lord!

RUTH: We held hands—and you know what?

BENEATHA: What?

RUTH: When we come out of the show it was late and dark and all the stores and things was closed up . . . and it was kind of chilly and there wasn't many people on the streets . . . and we was still holding hands, me and Walter.

BENEATHA: You're killing me.

> *Walter enters with a large package. His happiness is deep in him; he cannot keep still with his newfound exuberance. He is singing and wiggling and snapping his fingers. He puts his package in a corner and puts a phonograph record, which he has brought in with him, on the record player. As the music, soulful and sensuous, comes up he dances over to Ruth and tries to get her to dance with him. She gives in at last to his raunchiness and in a fit of giggling allows herself to be drawn into his mood. They dip and she melts into his arms in a classic, body-melting "slow drag."*

BENEATHA (*regarding them a long time as they dance, then drawing in her breath for a deeply exaggerated comment which she does not particularly mean*): Talk about—oldddddddddd-fashioneddddddddd—Negroes!

WALTER (*stopping momentarily*): What kind of Negroes?

> *He says this in fun. He is not angry with her today, nor with anyone. He starts to dance with his wife again.*

BENEATHA: Old-fashioned.

WALTER (*as he dances with Ruth*): You know, when these *New Negroes* have their convention—(*Pointing at his sister.*)—that is going to be the chairman of the Committee on Unending Agitation. (*He goes on dancing, then stops.*) Race, race, race! . . . Girl, I do believe you are the first person in the history of the entire human race to successfully brainwash yourself. (*Beneatha breaks up and he goes on dancing. He stops again, enjoying his tease.*) Damn, even the N double A C P takes a holiday sometimes! (*Beneatha and Ruth laugh. He dances with Ruth some more and starts to laugh and stops and pantomimes someone over an operating table.*) I can just see that chick someday looking down at some poor cat on an operating table and before she starts to slice him, she says . . . (*Pulling his sleeves back maliciously.*) "By the way, what are your views on civil rights down there? . . . "

He laughs at her again and starts to dance happily. The bell sounds.

BENEATHA: Sticks and stones may break my bones but . . . words will never hurt me!

> *Beneatha goes to the door and opens it as Walter and Ruth go on with the clowning. Beneatha is somewhat surprised to see a quiet-looking middle-aged white man in a business suit holding his hat and a briefcase in his hand and consulting a small piece of paper.*

MAN: Uh—how do you do, miss. I am looking for a Mrs.—(*He looks at the slip of paper.*) Mrs. Lena Younger? (*He stops short, struck dumb at the sight of the oblivious Walter and Ruth.*)

BENEATHA (*smoothing her hair with slight embarrassment*): Oh—yes, that's my mother. Excuse me. (*She closes the door and turns to quiet the other two.*) Ruth! Brother! (*Enunciating precisely but soundlessly: "There's a white man at the door!" They stop dancing, Ruth cuts off the phonograph, Beneatha opens the door. The man casts a curious quick glance at all of them.*) Uh—come in please.

MAN (*coming in*): Thank you.

BENEATHA: My mother isn't here just now. Is it business?

MAN: Yes . . . well, of a sort.

WALTER (*freely, the Man of the House*): Have a seat. I'm Mrs. Younger's son. I look after most of her business matters.

> *Ruth and Beneatha exchange amused glances.*

MAN (*regarding Walter, and sitting*): Well—My name is Karl Lindner . . .

WALTER (*stretching out his hand*): Walter Younger. This is my wife—(*Ruth nods politely.*)—and my sister.

LINDNER: How do you do.

WALTER (*amiably, as he sits himself easily on a chair, leaning forward on his knees with interest and looking expectantly into the newcomer's face*): What can we do for you, Mr. Lindner!

LINDNER (*some minor shuffling of the hat and briefcase on his knees*): Well—I am a representative of the Clybourne Park Improvement Association—

WALTER (*pointing*): Why don't you sit your things on the floor?

LINDNER: Oh—yes. Thank you. (*He slides the briefcase and hat under the chair.*) And as I was saying—I am from the Clybourne Park Improvement Association and we have had it brought to our attention at the last meeting that you people—or at least your mother—has bought a piece of residential property at—(*He digs for the slip of paper again.*)—four o six Clybourne Street . . .

WALTER: That's right. Care for something to drink? Ruth, get Mr. Lindner a beer.

LINDNER (*upset for some reason*): Oh—no, really. I mean thank you very much, but no thank you.

RUTH (*innocently*): Some coffee?

LINDNER: Thank you, nothing at all.

> *Beneatha is watching the man carefully.*

LINDNER: Well, I don't know how much you folks know about our organization. (*He is a gentle man; thoughtful and somewhat labored in his manner.*) It is one of these community organizations set up to look after—oh, you know, things

like block upkeep and special projects and we also have what we call our
New Neighbors Orientation Committee . . .

BENEATHA (*drily*): Yes—and what do they do?

LINDNER (*turning a little to her and then returning the main force to Walter*): Well—
it's what you might call a sort of welcoming committee, I guess. I mean they,
we—I'm the chairman of the committee—go around and see the new people
who move into the neighborhood and sort of give them the lowdown on the
way we do things out in Clybourne Park.

BENEATHA (*with appreciation of the two meanings, which escape Ruth and Walter*):
Un-huh.

LINDNER: And we also have the category of what the association calls—(*He
looks elsewhere.*)—uh—special community problems . . .

BENEATHA: Yes—and what are some of those?

WALTER: Girl, let the man talk.

LINDNER (*with understated relief*): Thank you. I would sort of like to explain this
thing in my own way. I mean I want to explain to you in a certain way.

WALTER: Go ahead.

LINDNER: Yes. Well. I'm going to try to get right to the point. I'm sure we'll all
appreciate that in the long run.

BENEATHA: Yes.

WALTER: Be still now!

LINDNER: Well—

RUTH (*still innocently*): Would you like another chair—you don't look comfortable.

LINDNER (*more frustrated than annoyed*): No, thank you very much. Please.
Well—to get right to the point, I—(*A great breath, and he is off at last.*) I am
sure you people must be aware of some of the incidents which have happened in various parts of the city when colored people have moved into certain areas—(*Beneatha exhales heavily and starts tossing a piece of fruit up and
down in the air.*) Well—because we have what I think is going to be a unique
type of organization in American community life—not only do we deplore
that kind of thing—but we are trying to do something about it. (*Beneatha
stops tossing and turns with a new and quizzical interest to the man.*) We feel—
(*gaining confidence in his mission because of the interest in the faces of the people
he is talking to.*)—we feel that most of the trouble in this world, when you
come right down to it—(*He hits his knee for emphasis.*)—most of the trouble
exists because people just don't sit down and talk to each other.

RUTH (*nodding as she might in church, pleased with the remark*): You can say that
again, mister.

LINDNER (*more encouraged by such affirmation*): That we don't try hard enough in
this world to understand the other fellow's problem. The other guy's point of
view.

RUTH: Now that's right.

Beneatha and Walter merely watch and listen with genuine interest.

LINDNER: Yes—that's the way we feel out in Clybourne Park. And that's why I
was elected to come here this afternoon and talk to you people. Friendly like,
you know, the way people should talk to each other and see if we couldn't
find some way to work this thing out. As I say, the whole business is a matter

of *caring* about the other fellow. Anybody can see that you are a nice family of folks, hard working and honest I'm sure. (*Beneatha frowns slightly, quizzically, her head tilted regarding him.*) Today everybody knows what it means to be on the outside of *something.* And of course, there is always somebody who is out to take advantage of people who don't always understand.

WALTER: What do you mean?

LINDNER: Well—you see our community is made up of people who've worked hard as the dickens for years to build up that little community. They're not rich and fancy people; just hard-working, honest people who don't really have much but those little homes and a dream of the kind of community they want to raise their children in. Now, I don't say we are perfect and there is a lot wrong in some of the things they want. But you've got to admit that a man, right or wrong, has the right to want to have the neighborhood he lives in a certain kind of way. And at the moment the over-whelming majority of our people out there feel that people get along better, take more of a common interest in the life of the community, when they share a common background. I want you to believe me when I tell you that race prejudice simply doesn't enter into it. It is a matter of the people of Clybourne Park believing, rightly or wrongly, as I say, that for the happiness of all concerned that our Negro families are happier when they live in their *own* communities.

BENEATHA (*with a grand and bitter gesture*): This, friends, is the Welcoming Committee!

WALTER (*dumfounded, looking at Lindner*): Is this what you came marching all the way over here to tell us?

LINDNER: Well, now we've been having a fine conversation. I hope you'll hear me all the way through.

WALTER (*tightly*): Go ahead, man.

LINDNER: You see—in the face of all the things I have said, we are prepared to make your family a very generous offer . . .

BENEATHA: Thirty pieces and not a coin less!

WALTER: Yeah?

LINDNER (*putting on his glasses drawing a form out of the briefcase*): Our association is prepared, through the collective effort of our people, to buy the house from you at a financial gain to your family.

RUTH: Lord have mercy, ain't this the living gall!

WALTER: All right, you through?

LINDNER: Well, I want to give you the exact terms of the financial arrangement—

WALTER: We don't want to hear no exact terms of no arrangements. I want to know if you got any more to tell us 'bout getting together?

LINDNER (*taking off his glasses*): Well—I don't suppose that you feel . . .

WALTER: Never mind how I feel—you got any more to say 'bout how people ought to sit down and talk to each other? . . . Get out of my house, man.

He turns his back and walks to the door.

LINDNER (*looking around at the hostile faces and reaching and assembling his hat and briefcase*): Well—I don't understand why you people are reacting this way. What do you think you are going to gain by moving into a neighborhood where you just aren't wanted and where some elements—well—people can

get awful worked up when they feel that their whole way of life and everything they've ever worked for is threatened.

WALTER: Get out.

LINDNER (*at the door, holding a small card*): Well—I'm sorry it went like this.

WALTER: Get out.

LINDNER (*almost sadly regarding Walter*): You just can't force people to change
their hearts, son.

> *He turns and puts his card on a table and exits. Walter pushes the door
> to with stinging hatred, and stands looking at it. Ruth just sits and Be-
> neatha just stands. They say nothing. Mama and Travis enter.*

MAMA: Well—this all the packing got done since I left out of here this morning. I testify before God that my children got all the energy of the *dead*!
What time the moving men due?

BENEATHA: Four o'clock. You had a caller, Mama.

> *She is smiling, teasingly.*

MAMA: Sure enough—who?

BENEATHA (*her arms folded saucily*): The Welcoming Committee.

> *Walter and Ruth giggle.*

MAMA (*innocently*): Who?

BENEATHA: The Welcoming Committee. They said they're sure going to be glad
to see you when you get there.

WALTER (*devilishly*): Yeah, they said they can't hardly wait to see your face.

> *Laughter.*

MAMA (*sensing their facetiousness*): What's the matter with you all?

WALTER: Ain't nothing the matter with us. We just telling you 'bout the gentleman who came to see you this afternoon. From the Clybourne Park Improvement Association.

MAMA: What he want?

RUTH (*in the same mood as Beneatha and Walter*): To welcome you, honey.

WALTER: He said they can't hardly wait. He said the one thing they don't have,
that they just *dying* to have out there is a fine family of fine colored people!
(*To Ruth and Beneatha.*) Ain't that right!

RUTH (*mockingly*): Yeah! He left his card—

BENEATHA (*handing card to Mama*): In case.

> *Mama reads and throws it on the floor—understanding and looking off
> as she draws her chair up to the table on which she has put her plant and
> some sticks and some cord.*

MAMA: Father, give us strength. (*Knowingly—and without fun.*) Did he threaten
us?

BENEATHA: Oh—Mama—they don't do it like that any more. He talked Brotherhood. He said everybody ought to learn how to sit down and hate each
other with good Christian fellowship.

> *She and Walter shake hands to ridicule the remark.*

MAMA (*sadly*): Lord, protect us . . .

RUTH: You should hear the money those folks raised to buy the house from us. All we paid and then some.

BENEATHA: What they think we going to do—eat 'em?

RUTH: No, honey, marry 'em.

MAMA (*shaking her head*): Lord, Lord, Lord . . .

RUTH: Well—that's the way the crackers crumble. (*A beat.*) Joke.

BENEATHA (*laughingly noticing what her mother is doing*): Mama, what are you doing?

MAMA: Fixing my plant so it won't get hurt none on the way . . .

BENEATHA: Mama, you going to take *that* to the new house?

Un-huh—:

BENEATHA: That raggedy-looking old thing?

MAMA (*stopping and looking at her*): It expresses ME!

RUTH (*with delight, to Beneatha*): So there, Miss Thing!

> Walter comes to Mama suddenly and bends down behind her and squeezes her in his arms with all his strength. She is overwhelmed by the suddenness of it and, though delighted, her manner is like that of Ruth and Travis.

MAMA: Looks out now, boy! You make me mess up my thing here!

WALTER (*his face lit, he slips down on his knees beside her, his arms still about her*): Mama . . . you know what it means to climb up in the chariot?

MAMA (*gruffly, very happy*): Get on away from me now . . .

RUTH (*near the gift-wrapped package, trying to catch Walter's eye*): Psst—

WALTER: What the old song say, Mama . . .

RUTH: Walter—Now?

> She is pointing at the package.

WALTER (*speaking the lines, sweetly, playfully, in his mother's face*): I got wings . . . you got wings . . .

All God's Children got wings . . .

MAMA: Boy—get out of my face and do some work . . .

WALTER: When I get to heaven gonna put on my wings, Gonna fly all over God's heaven . . .

BENEATHA (*teasingly, from across the room*): Everybody talking 'bout heaven ain't going there!

WALTER (*to Ruth, who is carrying the box across to them*): I don't know, you think we ought to give her that . . . Seems to me she ain't been very appreciative around here.

MAMA (*eying the box, which is obviously a gift*): What is that?

WALTER (*taking it from Ruth and putting it on the table in front of Mama*): Well—what you all think? Should we give it to her?

RUTH: Oh—she was pretty good today.

MAMA: I'll good you—

> She turns her eyes to the box again.

BENEATHA: Open it, Mama.

She stands up, looks at it, turns and looks at all of them, and then presses her hands together and does not open the package.

WALTER (*sweetly*): Open it, Mama. It's for you. (*Mama looks in his eyes. It is the first present in her life without its being Christmas. Slowly she opens her package and lifts out, one by one, a brand-new sparkling set of gardening tools. Walter continues, prodding.*) Ruth made up the note—read it . . .

MAMA (*picking up the card and adjusting her glasses*): "To our own Mrs. Miniver—Love from Brother, Ruth and Beneatha." Ain't that lovely . . .

TRAVIS (*tugging at his father's sleeve*): Daddy, can I give her mine now?

WALTER: All right, son. (*Travis flies to get his gift.*)

MAMA: Now I don't have to use my knives and forks no more . . .

WALTER: Travis didn't want to go in with the rest of us, Mama. He got his own. (*Somewhat amused.*) We don't know what it is . . .

TRAVIS (*racing back in the room with a large hatbox and putting it in front of his grandmother*): Here!

MAMA: Lord have mercy, baby. You done gone and bought your grandmother a hat?

TRAVIS (*very proud*): Open it!

She does and lifts out an elaborate, but very elaborate, wide gardening hat, and all the adults break up at the sight of it.

RUTH: Travis, honey, what is that?

TRAVIS (*who thinks it is beautiful and appropriate*): It's a gardening hat! Like the ladies always have on in the magazines when they work in their gardens.

BENEATHA (*giggling fiercely*): Travis—we were trying to make Mama Mrs. Miniver—not Scarlett O'Hara!

MAMA (*indignantly*): What's the matter with you all! This here is a beautiful hat! (*Absurdly*) I always wanted me one just like it!

She pops it on her head to prove it to her grandson, and the hat is ludicrous and considerably oversized.

RUTH: Hot dog! Go, Mama.

WALTER (*doubled over with laughter*): I'm sorry, Mama—but you look like you ready to go out and chop you some cotton sure enough!

They all laugh except Mama, out of deference to Travis' feelings.

MAMA (*gathering the boy up to her*): Bless your heart—this is the prettiest hat I ever owned—(*Walter, Ruth and Beneatha chime in—noisily, festively and insincerely congratulating Travis on his gift*) What are we all standing around here for? We ain't finished packin' yet. Bennie, you ain't packed one book.

The bell rings.

BENEATHA: That couldn't be the movers . . . it's not hardly two good yet—

Beneatha goes into her room. Mama starts for door.

WALTER (*turning, stiffening*): Wait—wait—I'll get it.

He stands and looks at the door.

MAMA: You expecting company, son?

WALTER (*just looking at the door*): Yeah—yeah . . .

> *Mama looks at Ruth, and they exchange innocent and unfrightened glances.*

MAMA (*not understanding*): Well, let them in, son.

BENEATHA (*from her room*): We need some more string.

MAMA: Travis—you run to the hardware and get me some string cord.

> *Mama goes out and Walter turns and looks at Ruth. Travis goes to a dish for money.*

RUTH: Why don't you answer the door, man?

WALTER (*suddenly bounding across the floor to embrace her*): 'Cause sometimes it hard to let the future begin! (*Stooping down in her face.*)

I got wings! You got wings!
All God's children got wings!

> *He crosses to the door and throws it open. Standing there is a very slight little man in a not-too-prosperous business suit and with haunted frightened eyes and a hat pulled down tightly, brim up, around his forehead. Travis passes between the men and exits. Walter leans deep in the man's face, still in his jubilance.*

When I get to heaven gonna put on my wings,
Gonna fly all over God's heaven . . .

> *The little man just stares at him.*

Heaven—

> *Suddenly he stops and looks past the little man into the empty hallway.*

Where's Willy, man?

BOBO: He ain't with me.

WALTER (*not disturbed*): Oh—come on in. You know my wife.

BOBO (*dumbly, taking off his hat*): Yes—h'you, Miss Ruth.

RUTH (*quietly, a mood apart from her husband already, seeing Bobo*): Hello, Bobo.

WALTER: You right on time today . . . Right on time. That's the way! (*He slaps Bobo on his back.*) Sit down . . . lemme hear.

> *Ruth stands stiffly and quietly in back of them, as though somehow she senses death, her eyes fixed on her husband.*

BOBO (*his frightened eyes on the floor, his hat in his hands*): Could I please get a drink of water, before I tell you about it, Walter Lee?

> *Walter does not take his eyes off the man. Ruth goes blindly to the tap and gets a glass of water and brings it to Bobo.*

WALTER: There ain't nothing wrong, is there?

BOBO: Lemme tell you—

WALTER: Man—didn't nothing go wrong?

BOBO: Lemme tell you—Walter Lee. (*Looking at Ruth and talking to her more than to Walter.*) You know how it was. I got to tell you how it was. I mean first I got to tell you how it was all the way . . . I mean about the money I put in, Walter Lee . . .

WALTER (*with taut agitation now*): What about the money you put in?

BOBO: Well—it wasn't much as we told you—me and Willy—(*He stops.*) I'm sorry, Walter. I got a bad feeling about it. I got a real bad feeling about it . . .

WALTER: Man, what you telling me about all this for? . . . Tell me what happened in Springfield . . .

BOBO: Springfield.

RUTH (*like a dead woman*): What was supposed to happen in Springfield?

BOBO (*to her*): This deal that me and Walter went into with Willy—Me and Willy was going to go down to Springfield and spread some money 'round so's we wouldn't have to wait so long for the liquor license . . . That's what we were going to do. Everybody said that was the way you had to do, you understand, Miss Ruth?

WALTER: Man—what happened down there?

BOBO (*a pitiful man, near tears*): I'm trying to tell you, Walter.

WALTER (*screaming at him suddenly*): THEN TELL ME, GODDAMMIT . . . WHAT'S THE MATTER WITH YOU?

BOBO: Man . . . I didn't go to no Springfield, yesterday.

WALTER (*halted, life hanging in the moment*): Why not?

BOBO (*the long way, the hard way to tell*): 'Cause I didn't have no reasons to . . .

WALTER: Man, what are you talking about!

BOBO: I'm talking about the fact that when I got to the train station yesterday morning—eight o'clock like we planned . . . Man—*Willy didn't never show up.*

WALTER: Why . . . where was he . . . where is he?

BOBO: That's what I'm trying to tell you . . . I don't know . . . I waited six hours . . . I called his house . . . and I waited . . . six hours . . . I waited in that train station six hours . . . (*Breaking into tears.*) That was all the extra money I had in the world . . . (*Looking up at Walter with the tears running down his face.*) Man, *Willy is gone.*

WALTER: Gone, what you mean Willy is gone? Gone where? You mean he went by himself. You mean he went off to Springfield by himself—to take care of getting the license—(*Turns and looks anxiously at Ruth.*) You mean maybe he didn't want too many people in on the business down there? (*Looks to Ruth again, as before.*) You know Willy got his own ways. (*Looks back to Bobo.*) Maybe you was late yesterday and he just went on down there without you. Maybe—maybe—he's been callin' you at home tryin' to tell you what happened or something. Maybe—maybe—he just got sick. He's somewhere—he's got to be somewhere. We just got to find him—me and you got to find him. (*Grabs Bobo senselessly by the collar and starts to shake him.*) We got to!

BOBO (*in sudden angry, frightened agony*): What's the matter with you, Walter! When a cat take off with your money he don't leave you no road maps!

WALTER (*turning madly, as though he is looking for Willy in the very room*): Willy! . . . Willy . . . don't do it . . . Please don't do it . . . Man, not with that money . . . Man, please, not with that money . . . Oh, God . . . Don't let it be true . . . (*He is wandering around, crying out for Willy and looking for him or perhaps for help from*

God.) Man . . . I trusted you . . . Man, I put my life in your hands . . . (*He starts to crumple down on the floor as Ruth just covers her face in horror. Mama opens the door and comes into the room, with Beneatha behind her.*) Man . . . (*He starts to pound the floor with his fists, sobbing wildly.*) THAT MONEY IS MADE OUT OF MY FATHER'S FLESH—

BOBO (*standing over him helplessly*): I'm sorry, Walter . . . (*only Walter's sobs reply. Bobo puts on his hat.*) I had my life staked on this deal, too . . .

> *He exits.*

MAMA (*to Walter*): Son—(*She goes to him, bends down to him, talks to his bent head.*) Son . . . Is it gone? Son, I gave you sixty-five hundred dollars. Is it gone? All of it? Beneatha's money too?

WALTER (*lifting his head slowly*): Mama . . . I never . . . went to the bank at all . . .

MAMA (*not wanting to believe him*): You mean . . . your sister's school money . . . you used that too . . . Walter? . . .

WALTER: Yessss! All of it . . . It's all gone . . .

> *There is total silence. Ruth stands with her face covered with her hands; Beneatha leans forlornly against a wall, fingering a piece of red ribbon from the mother's gift. Mama stops and looks at her son without recognition and then, quite without thinking about it, starts to beat him senselessly in the face. Beneatha goes to them and stops it.*

BENEATHA: Mama!

> *Mama stops and looks at both of her children and rises slowly and wanders vaguely, aimlessly away from them.*

MAMA: I seen . . . him . . . night after night . . . come in . . . and look at that rug . . . and then look at me . . . the red showing in his eyes . . . the veins moving in his head . . . I seen him grow thin and old before he was forty . . . working and working and working like somebody's old horse . . . killing himself . . . and you—you give it all away in a day—(*She raises her arms to strike him again.*)

BENEATHA: Mama—

MAMA: Oh, God . . . (*She looks up to Him.*) Look down here—and show me the strength.

BENEATHA: Mama—

MAMA (*folding over*): Strength . . .

BENEATHA (*plaintively*): Mama . . .

MAMA: Strength!

> *Curtain.*

ACT III

Time: An hour later.

> At curtain, there is a sullen light of gloom in the living room, gray light not unlike that which began the first scene of Act I. At left we can see Walter within his room, alone with himself. He is stretched out on the bed, his shirt out and open, his arms under his head. He does not

smoke, he does not cry out, he merely lies there, looking up at the ceiling, much as if he were alone in the world.

In the living room Beneatha sits at the table, still surrounded by the now almost ominous packing crates. She sits looking off. We feel that this is a mood struck perhaps an hour before, and it lingers now, full of the empty sound of profound disappointment. We see on a line from her brother's bedroom the sameness of their attitudes. Presently the bell rings and Beneatha rises without ambition or interest in answering. It is Asagai, smiling broadly, striding into the room with energy and happy expectation and conversation.

ASAGAI: I came over . . . I had some free time. I thought I might help with the packing. Ah, I like the look of packing crates! A household in preparation for a journey! It depresses some people . . . but for me . . . it is another feeling. Something full of the flow of life, do you understand? Movement, progress . . . It makes me think of Africa.

BENEATHA: Africa!

ASAGAI: What kind of a mood is this? Have I told you how deeply you move me?

BENEATHA: He gave away the money, Asagai . . .

ASAGAI: Who gave away what money?

BENEATHA: The insurance money. My brother gave it away.

ASAGAI: Gave it away?

BENEATHA: He made an investment! With a man even Travis wouldn't have trusted with his most worn-out marbles.

ASAGAI: And it's gone?

BENEATHA: Gone!

ASAGAI: I'm very sorry . . . And you, now?

BENEATHA: Me? . . . Me? . . . Me, I'm nothing . . . Me. When I was very small . . . we used to take our sleds out in the wintertime and the only hills we had were the ice-covered stone steps of some houses down the street. And we used to fill them in with snow and make them smooth and slide down them all day . . . and it was very dangerous, you know . . . far too steep . . . and sure enough one day a kid named Rufus came down too fast and hit the sidewalk and we saw his face just split open right there in front of us . . . And I remember standing there looking at his bloody open face thinking that was the end of Rufus. But the ambulance came and they took him to the hospital and they fixed the broken bones and they sewed it all up . . . and the next time I saw Rufus he just had a little line down the middle of his face . . . I never got over that . . .

ASAGAI: What?

BENEATHA: That that was what one person could do for another, fix him up— sew up the problem, make him all right again. That was the most marvelous thing in the world . . . I wanted to do that. I always thought it was the one concrete thing in the world that a human being could do. Fix up the sick, you know—and make them whole again. This was truly being God . . .

ASAGAI: You wanted to be God?

BENEATHA: No—I wanted to cure. It used to be so important to me. I wanted to cure. It used to matter. I used to care. I mean about people and how their bodies hurt . . .

ASAGAI: And you've stopped caring?

BENEATHA: Yes—I think so.

ASAGAI: Why?

BENEATHA (*bitterly*): Because it doesn't seem deep enough, close enough to what ails mankind! It was a child's way of seeing things—or an idealist's.

ASAGAI: Children see things very well sometimes—and idealists even better.

BENEATHA: I know that's what you think. Because you are still where I left off. You with all your talk and dreams about Africa! You still think you can patch up the world. Cure the Great Sore of Colonialism—(*Loftily, mocking it.*) with the Penicillin of Independence—!

ASAGAI: Yes!

BENEATHA: Independence *and then what?* What about all the crooks and thieves and just plain idiots who will come into power and steal and plunder the same as before—only now they will be black and do it in the name of the new Independence—WHAT ABOUT THEM?!

ASAGAI: That will be the problem for another time. First we must get there.

BENEATHA: And where does it end?

ASAGAI: End? Who even spoke of an end? To life? To living?

BENEATHA: An end to misery! To stupidity! Don't you see there isn't any real progress, Asagai, there is only one large circle that we march in, around and around, each of us with our own little picture in front of us—our own little mirage that we think is the future.

ASAGAI: That is the mistake.

BENEATHA: What?

ASAGAI: What you just said—about the circle. It isn't a circle—it is simply a long line—as in geometry, you know, one that reaches into infinity. And because we cannot see the end—we also cannot see how it changes. And it is very odd but those who see the changes—who dream, who will not give up— are called idealists . . . and those who see only the circle—we call *them* the "realists"!

BENEATHA: Asagai, while I was sleeping in that bed in there, people went out and took the future right out of my hands! And nobody asked me, nobody consulted me—they just went out and changed my life!

ASAGAI: Was it your money?

BENEATHA: What?

ASAGAI: Was it your money he gave away?

BENEATHA: It belonged to all of us.

ASAGAI: But did you earn it? Would you have had it at all if your father had not died?

BENEATHA: No.

ASAGAI: Then isn't there something wrong in a house—in a world—where all dreams, good or bad, must depend on the death of a man? I never thought to see *you* like this, Alaiyo. You! Your brother made a mistake and you are grateful to him so that now you can give up the ailing human race on account of it! You talk about what good is struggle, what good is anything! Where are we all going and why are we bothering!

BENEATHA: AND YOU CANNOT ANSWER IT!

ASAGAI (*shouting over her*): I LIVE THE ANSWER! (*Pause.*) In my village at home it is the exceptional man who can even read a newspaper . . . or who ever sees a book at all. I will go home and much of what I will have to say will seem strange to the people of my village. But I will teach and work and things will happen, slowly and swiftly. At times it will seem that nothing changes at all . . . and then again the sudden dramatic events which make history leap into the future. And then quiet again. Retrogression even. Guns, murder, revolution. And I even will have moments when I wonder if the quiet was not better than all that death and hatred. But I will look about my village at the illiteracy and disease and ignorance and I will not wonder long. And perhaps . . . perhaps I will be a great man . . . I mean perhaps I will hold on to the substance of truth and find my way always with the right course . . . and perhaps for it I will be butchered in my bed some night by the servants of empire . . .

BENEATHA: *The martyr!*

ASAGAI (*he smiles*): . . . or perhaps I shall live to be a very old man, respected and esteemed in my new nation . . . And perhaps I shall hold office and this is what I'm trying to tell you, Alaiyo: perhaps the things I believe now for my country will be wrong and outmoded, and I will not understand and do terrible things to have things my way or merely to keep my power. Don't you see that there will be young men and women—not British soldiers then, but my own black countrymen—to step out of the shadows some evening and slit my then useless throat? Don't you see they have always been there . . . that they always will be. And that such a thing as my own death will be an advance? They who might kill me even . . . actually replenish all that I was.

BENEATHA: Oh, Asagai, I know all that.

ASAGAI: Good! Then stop moaning and groaning and tell me what you plan to do.

BENEATHA: Do?

ASAGAI: I have a bit of a suggestion.

BENEATHA: What?

ASAGAI (*rather quietly for him*): That when it is all over—that you come home with me—

BENEATHA (*staring at him and crossing away with exasperation*): Oh—Asagai—at this moment you decide to be romantic!

ASAGAI (*quickly understanding the misunderstanding*): My dear, young creature of the New World—I do not mean across the city—I mean across the ocean: home—to Africa.

BENEATHA (*slowly understanding and turning to him with murmured amazement*): To Africa?

ASAGAI: Yes! . . . (*smiling and lifting his arms playfully.*) Three hundred years later the African Prince rose up out of the seas and swept the maiden back across the middle passage over which her ancestors had come—

BENEATHA (*unable to play*): To—to Nigeria?

ASAGAI: Nigeria. Home. (*Coming to her with genuine romantic flippancy.*) I will show you our mountains and our stars; and give you cool drinks from gourds and teach you the old songs and the ways of our people—and, in time, we will pretend that—(*very softly*)—you have only been away for a day. Say that you'll come—(*He swings her around and takes her full in his arms in a kiss which proceeds to passion.*)

BENEATHA (*pulling away suddenly*): You're getting me all mixed up—

ASAGAI: Why?

BENEATHA: Too many things—too many things have happened today. I must sit down and think. I don't know what I feel about anything right this minute.

She promptly sits down and props her chin on her fist.

ASAGAI (*charmed*): All right, I shall leave you. No—don't get up. (*Touching her, gently, sweetly.*) Just sit awhile and think . . . Never be afraid to sit awhile and think. (*He goes to door and looks at her.*) How often I have looked at you and said, "Ah—so this is what the New World hath finally wrought . . . "

He exits. Beneatha sits on alone. Presently Walter enters from his room and starts to rummage through things, feverishly looking for something. She looks up and turns in her seat.

BENEATHA (*hissingly*): Yes—just look at what the New World hath wrought! . . . Just look! (*She gestures with bitter disgust.*) There he is! *Monsieur le petit bourgeois noir*—himself! There he is—Symbol of a Rising Class! Entrepreneur! Titan of the system! (*Walter ignores her completely and continues frantically and destructively looking for something and hurling things to floor and tearing things out of their place in his search. Beneatha ignores the eccentricity of his actions and goes on with the monologue of insult.*) Did you dream of yachts on Lake Michigan, Brother? Did you see yourself on that Great Day sitting down at the Conference Table, surrounded by all the mighty bald-headed men in America? All halted, waiting, breathless, waiting for your pronouncements on industry? Waiting for you—Chairman of the Board! (*Walter finds what he is looking for—a small piece of white paper—and pushes it in his pocket and puts on his coat and rushes out without ever having looked at her. She shouts after him.*) I look at you and I see the final triumph of stupidity in the world!

The door slams and she returns to just sitting again. Ruth comes quickly out of Mama's room.

RUTH: Who was that?

BENEATHA: Your husband.

RUTH: Where did he go?

BENEATHA: Who knows—maybe he has an appointment at U.S. Steel.

RUTH (*anxiously, with frightened eyes*): You didn't say nothing bad to him, did you?

BENEATHA: Bad? Say anything bad to him? No—I told him he was a sweet boy and full of dreams and everything is strictly peachy keen, as the ofay kids say!

Mama enters from her bedroom. She is lost, vague, trying to catch hold, to make some sense of her former command of the world, but it still eludes her. A sense of waste overwhelms her gait; a measure of apology rides on her shoulders. She goes to her plant, which has remained on the table, looks at it, picks it up and takes it to the window sill and sits it outside, and she stands and looks at it a long moment. Then she closes the window, straightens her body with effort and turns around to her children.

MAMA: Well—ain't it a mess in here, though? (*A false cheerfulness, a beginning of something.*) I guess we all better stop moping around and get some work done.

All this unpacking and everything we got to do. (*Ruth raises her head slowly in response to the sense of the line; and Beneatha in similar manner turns very slowly to look at her mother.*) One of you all better call the moving people and tell 'em not to come.

RUTH: Tell 'em not to come?

MAMA: Of course, baby. Ain't no need in 'em coming all the way here and having to go back. They charges for that too. (*She sits down, fingers to her brow, thinking.*) Lord, ever since I was a little girl, I always remembers people saying, "Lena—Lena Eggleston, you aims too high all the time. You needs to slow down and see life a little more like it is. Just slow down some." That's what they always used to say down home—"Lord, that Lena Eggleston is a high-minded thing. She'll get her due one day!"

RUTH: No, Lena . . .

MAMA: Me and Big Walter just didn't never learn right.

RUTH: Lena, no! We gotta go. Bennie—tell her . . .

> She rises and crosses to Beneatha with her arms outstretched. Beneatha doesn't respond.

Tell her we can still move . . . the notes ain't but a hundred and twenty-five a month. We got four grown people in this house—we can work . . .

MAMA (*to herself*): Just aimed too high all the time—

RUTH (*turning and going to Mama fast—the words pouring out with urgency and desperation*): Lena—I'll work . . . I'll work twenty hours a day in all the kitchens in Chicago . . . I'll strap my baby on my back if I have to and scrub all the floors in America and wash all the sheets in America if I have to—but we got to MOVE! We got to get OUT OF HERE!!

> Mama reaches out absently and pats Ruth's hand.

MAMA: No—I sees things differently now. Been thinking 'bout some of the things we could do to fix this place up some. I seen a second-hand bureau over on Maxwell Street just the other day that could fit right there. (*She points to where the new furniture might go. Ruth wanders away from her.*) Would need some new handles on it and then a little varnish and it look like something brand-new. And—we can put up them new curtains in the kitchen . . . Why this place be looking fine. Cheer us all up so that we forget trouble ever come . . . (*To Ruth.*) And you could get some nice screens to put up in your room round the baby's bassinet . . . (*She looks at both of them pleadingly.*) Sometimes you just got to know when to give up some things . . . and hold on to what you got . . .

> Walter enters from the outside, looking spent and leaning against the door, his coat hanging from him.

MAMA: Where you been, son?

WALTER (*breathing hard*): Made a call.

MAMA: To who, son?

WALTER: To The Man. (*He heads for his room.*)

MAMA: What man, baby?

WALTER (*stops in the door*): The Man, Mama. Don't you know who The Man is?

RUTH: Walter Lee?

WALTER: *The Man.* Like the guys in the streets say—The Man. Captain Boss—
  Mistuh Charley . . . Old Cap'n Please Mr. Bossman . . .

BENEATHA (*suddenly*): Lindner!

WALTER: That's right! That's good. I told him to come right over.

BENEATHA (*fiercely, understanding*): For what? What do you want to see him for!

WALTER (*looking at his sister*): We going to do business with him.

MAMA: What you talking 'bout, son?

WALTER: Talking 'bout life, Mama. You all always telling me to see life like it is.
  Well—I laid in there on my back today . . . and I figured it out. Life just like
  it is. Who gets and who don't get. (*He sits down with his coat on and laughs.*)
  Mama, you know it's all divided up. Life is. Sure enough. Between the takers
  and the "tooken." (*He laughs.*) I've figured it out finally. (*He looks around at
  them.*) Yeah. Some of us always getting "tooken." (*He laughs.*) People like
  Willy Harris, they don't never get "tooken." And you know why the rest of
  us do? 'Cause we all mixed up. Mixed up bad. We get to looking 'round for
  the right and the wrong; and we worry about it and cry about it and stay up
  nights trying to figure out 'bout the wrong and the right of things all the time
  . . . And all the time, man, them takers is out there operating, just taking and
  taking. Willy Harris? Shoot—Willy Harris don't even count. He don't even
  count in the big scheme of things. But I'll say one thing for old Willy Harris
  . . . he's taught me something. He's taught me to keep my eye on what counts
  in this world. Yeah—(*Shouting out a little.*) Thanks, Willy!

RUTH: What did you call that man for, Walter Lee?

WALTER: Called him to tell him to come on over to the show. Gonna put on a
  show for the man. Just what he wants to see. You see, Mama, the man came
  here today and he told us that them people out there where you want us to
  move—well they so upset they willing to pay us *not* to move! (*He laughs
  again.*) And—and oh, Mama—you would of been proud of the way me and
  Ruth and Bennie acted. We told him to get out . . . Lord have mercy! We
  told the man to get out! Oh, we was some proud folks this afternoon, yeah.
  (*He lights a cigarette.*) We were still full of that old-time stuff . . .

RUTH (*coming toward him slowly*): You talking 'bout taking them people's money
  to keep us from moving in that house?

WALTER: I ain't just talking 'bout it, baby—I'm telling you that's what's going to
  happen!

BENEATHA: Oh, God! Where is the bottom! Where is the real honest-to-God
  bottom so he can't go any farther!

WALTER: See—that's the old stuff. You and that boy that was here today. You all
  want everybody to carry a flag and a spear and sing some marching songs,
  huh? You wanna spend your life looking into things and trying to find the
  right and the wrong part, huh? Yeah. You know what's going to happen to
  that boy someday—he'll find himself sitting in a dungeon, locked in forever—and the takers will have the key! Forget it, baby! There ain't no
  causes—there ain't nothing but taking in this world, and he who takes most
  is smartest—and it don't make a damn bit of difference *how.*

MAMA: You making something inside me cry, son. Some awful pain inside me.

WALTER: Don't cry, Mama. Understand. That white man is going to walk in that
  door able to write checks for more money than we ever had. It's important to
  him and I'm going to help him . . . I'm going to put on the show, Mama.

MAMA: Son—I come from five generations of people who was slaves and share-croppers—but ain't nobody in my family never let nobody pay 'em no money that was a way of telling us we wasn't fit to walk the earth. We ain't never been that poor. (*Raising her eyes and looking at him.*) We ain't never been that—dead inside.

BENEATHA: Well—we are dead now. All the talk about dreams and sunlight that goes on in this house. It's all dead now.

WALTER: What's the matter with you all! I didn't make this world! It was give to me this way! Hell, yes, I want me some yachts someday! Yes, I want to hang some real pearls 'round my wife's neck. Ain't she supposed to wear no pearls? Somebody tell me—tell me, who decides which women is suppose to wear pearls in this world. I tell you I am a *man*—and I think my wife should wear some pearls in this world!

> *This last line hangs a good while and Walter begins to move about the room. The word "Man" has penetrated his consciousness; he mumbles it to himself repeatedly between strange agitated pauses as he moves about.*

MAMA: Baby, how you going to feel on the inside?

WALTER: Fine! . . . Going to feel fine . . . a man . . .

MAMA: You won't have nothing left then, Walter Lee.

WALTER (*coming to her*): I'm going to feel fine, Mama. I'm going to look that son-of-a-bitch in the eyes and say—(*he falters*)—and say, "All right, Mr. Lindner—(*he falters even more*)—that's *your* neighborhood out there! You got the right to keep it like you want! You got the right to have it like you want! Just write the check and—the house is yours." And—and I am going to say—(*His voice almost breaks.*) "And you—you people just put the money in my hand and you won't have to live next to this bunch of stinking niggers! . . ." (*He straightens up and moves away from his mother, walking around the room.*) And maybe—maybe I'll just get down on my black knees . . . (*He does so; Ruth and Bennie and Mama watch him in frozen horror.*) "Captain, Mistuh, Bossman—(*Groveling and grinning and wringing his hands in profoundly anguished imitation of the slow-witted movie stereotype.*) A-hee-hee-hee! Oh, yassuh boss! Yasssssuh! Great white—(*Voice breaking, he forces himself to go on.*)—Father, just gi' ussen de money, fo' God's sake, and we's—we's ain't gwine come out deh and dirty up yo' white folks neighborhood . . ." (*He breaks down completely.*) And I'll feel fine! Fine! FINE! (*He gets up and goes into the bedroom.*)

BENEATHA: That is not a man. That is nothing but a toothless rat.

MAMA: Yes—death done come in this here house. (*She is nodding, slowly, reflectively.*) Done come walking in my house on the lips of my children. You what supposed to be my beginning again. You—what supposed to be my harvest. (*To Beneatha.*) You—you mourning your brother?

BENEATHA: He's no brother of mine.

MAMA: What you say?

BENEATHA: I said that that individual in that room is no brother of mine.

MAMA: That's what I thought you said. You feeling like you better than he is today? (*Beneatha does not answer.*) Yes? What you tell him a minute ago? That he wasn't a man? Yes? You give him up for me? You done wrote his epitaph too—like the rest of the world? Well, who give you the privilege?

BENEATHA: Be on my side for once! You saw what he just did, Mama! You saw him—down on his knees. Wasn't it you who taught me to despise any man who would do that? Do what he's going to do?

MAMA: Yes—I taught you that. Me and your daddy. But I thought I taught you something else too . . . I thought I taught you to love him.

BENEATHA: Love him? There is nothing left to love.

MAMA: There is *always* something left to love. And if you ain't learned that, you ain't learned nothing. (*Looking at her.*) Have you cried for that boy today? I don't mean for yourself and for the family 'cause we lost the money. I mean for him: what he been through and what it done to him. Child, when do you think is the time to love somebody the most? When they done good and made things easy for everybody? Well then, you ain't through learning—because that ain't the time at all. It's when he's at his lowest and can't believe in hisself 'cause the world done whipped him so! When you starts measuring somebody, measure him right, child, measure him right. Make sure you done taken into account what hills and valleys he come through before he got to wherever he is.

> *Travis bursts into the room at the end of the speech, leaving the door open.*

TRAVIS: Grandmama—the moving men are downstairs! The truck just pulled up.

MAMA (*turning and looking at him*): Are they, baby? They downstairs?

> *She sighs and sits. Lindner appears in the doorway. He peers in and knocks lightly, to gain attention, and comes in. All turn to look at him.*

LINDNER (*hat and briefcase in hand*): Uh—hello . . .

> *Ruth crosses mechanically to the bedroom door and opens it and lets it swing open freely and slowly as the lights come up on Walter within, still in his coat, sitting at the far corner of the room. He looks up and out through the room to Lindner.*

RUTH: He's here.

> *A long minute passes and Walter slowly gets up.*

LINDNER (*coming to the table with efficiency, putting his briefcase on the table and starting to unfold papers and unscrew fountain pens*): Well, I certainly was glad to hear from you people. (*Walter has begun the trek out of the room, slowly and awkwardly, rather like a small boy, passing the back of his sleeve across his mouth from time to time.*) Life can really be so much simpler than people let it be most of the time. Well—with whom do I negotiate? You, Mrs. Younger, or your son here? (*Mama sits with her hands folded on her lap and her eyes closed as Walter advances. Travis goes closer to Lindner and looks at the papers curiously.*) Just some official papers, sonny.

RUTH: Travis, you go downstairs—

MAMA (*opening her eyes and looking into Walter's*): No. Travis, you stay right here. And you make him understand what you doing, Walter Lee. You teach him good. Like Willy Harris taught you. You show where our five generations done come to. (*Walter looks from her to the boy, who grins at him innocently.*) Go ahead, son—(*She folds her hands and closes her eyes.*) Go ahead.

WALTER (*at last crosses to Lindner, who is reviewing the contract*): Well, Mr. Lindner. (*Beneatha turns away.*) We called you—(*There is a profound, simple groping quality in his speech.*)—because, well, me and my family (*He looks around and shifts from one foot to the other.*) Well—we are very plain people . . .

LINDNER: Yes—.

WALTER: I mean—I have worked as a chauffeur most of my life—and my wife here, she does domestic work in people's kitchens. So does my mother. I mean—we are plain people . . .

LINDNER: Yes, Mr. Younger—

WALTER (*really like a small boy, looking down at his shoes and then up at the man*): And—uh—well, my father, well, he was a laborer most of his life. . . .

LINDNER (*absolutely confused*): Uh, yes—yes, I understand. (*He turns back to the contract.*)

WALTER (*a beat; staring at him*): And my father—(*With sudden intensity.*) My father almost *beat a man to death* once because this man called him a bad name or something, you know what I mean?

LINDNER (*looking up, frozen*): No, no, I'm afraid I don't—

WALTER (*a beat. The tension hangs; then Walter steps back from it*): Yeah. Well—what I mean is that we come from people who had a lot of *pride*. I mean—we are very proud people. And that's my sister over there and she's going to be a doctor—and we are very proud—

LINDNER: Well—I am sure that is very nice, but—

WALTER: What I am telling you is that we called you over here to tell you that we are very proud and that this—(*Signaling to Travis.*) Travis, come here. (*Travis crosses and Walter draws him before him facing the man.*) This is my son, and he makes the sixth generation our family in this country. And we have all thought about your offer—

LINDNER: Well, good . . . good—

WALTER: And we have decided to move into our house because my father—my father—he earned it for us brick by brick. (*Mama has her eyes closed and is rocking back and forth as though she were in church, with her head nodding the Amen yes.*) We don't want to make no trouble for nobody or fight no causes, and we will try to be good neighbors. And that's *all* we got to say about that. (*He looks the man absolutely in the eyes.*) We don't want your money. (*He turns and walks away.*)

LINDNER (*looking around at all of them*): I take it then—that you have decided to occupy . . .

BENEATHA: That's what the man said.

LINDNER (*to Mama in her reverie*): Then I would like to appeal to you, Mrs. Younger. You are older and wiser and understand things better I am sure . . .

MAMA: I am afraid you don't understand. My son said we was going to move and there ain't nothing left for me to say. (*Briskly.*) You know how these young folks is nowadays, mister. Can't do a thing with 'em! (*As he opens his mouth, she rises.*) Good-bye.

LINDNER (*folding up his materials*): Well—if you are that final about it . . . there is nothing left for me to say. (*He finishes, almost ignored by the family, who are concentrating on Walter Lee. At the door Lindner halts and looks around.*) I sure hope you people know what you're getting into.

He shakes his head and exits.

RUTH (*looking around and coming to life*): Well, for God's sake—if the moving men are here—LET'S GET THE HELL OUT OF HERE!

MAMA (*into action*): Ain't it the truth! Look at all this here mess. Ruth, put Travis' good jacket on him . . . Walter Lee, fix your tie and tuck your shirt in, you look like somebody's hoodlum! Lord have mercy, where is my plant? (*She flies to get it amid the general bustling of the family, who are deliberately trying to ignore the nobility of the past moment.*) You all start on down . . . Travis child, don't go empty-handed . . . Ruth, where did I put that box with my skillets in it? I want to be in charge of it myself . . . I'm going to make us the biggest dinner we ever ate tonight . . . Beneatha, what's the matter with them stockings? Pull them things up, girl . . .

The family starts to file out as two moving men appear and begin to carry out the heavier pieces of furniture, bumping into the family as they move about.

BENEATHA: Mama, Asagai asked me to marry him today and go to Africa—

MAMA (*in the middle of her getting-ready activity*): He did? You ain't old enough to marry nobody—(*Seeing the moving men lifting one of her chairs precariously.*) Darling, that ain't no bale of cotton, please handle it so we can sit in it again! I had that chair twenty-five years . . .

The movers sigh with exasperation and go on with their work.

BENEATHA (*girlishly and unreasonably trying to pursue the conversation*): To go to Africa, Mama—be a doctor in Africa . . .

MAMA (*distracted*): Yes, baby—

WALTER: *Africa!* What he want you to go to Africa for?

BENEATHA: To practice there . . .

WALTER: Girl, if you don't get all them silly ideas out your head! You better marry yourself a man with some loot . . .

BENEATHA (*angrily, precisely as in the first scene of the play*): What have you got to do with who I marry!

WALTER: Plenty. Now I think George Murchison—

BENEATHA: *George Murchison!* I wouldn't marry him if he was Adam and I was Eve!

Walter and Beneatha go out yelling at each other vigorously and the anger is loud and real till their voices diminish. Ruth stands at the door and turns to Mama and smiles knowingly.

MAMA (*fixing her hat at last*): Yeah—they something all right, my children . . .

RUTH: Yeah—they're something. Let's go, Lena.

MAMA (*stalling, starting to look around at the house*): Yes—I'm coming. Ruth—

RUTH: Yes?

MAMA (*quietly, woman to woman*): He finally come into his manhood today, didn't he? Kind of like a rainbow after the rain . . .

RUTH (*biting her lip lest her own pride explode in front of Mama*): Yes, Lena.
  Walter's voice calls for them raucously.

WALTER (*off stage*): Y'all come on! These people charges by the hour, you know!

MAMA (*waving Ruth out vaguely*): All right, honey—go on down. I be down directly.

Ruth hesitates, then exits. Mama stands, at last alone in the living room, her plant on the table before her as the lights start to come down. She looks around at all the walls and ceilings and suddenly, despite herself, while the children call below, a great heaving thing rises in her and she puts her fist to her mouth to stifle it, takes a final desperate look, pulls her coat about her, pats her hat, and goes out. The lights dim down. The door opens and she comes back in, grabs her plant, and goes out for the last time.

        Curtain.

Talking about the Text

1. What characters do you most sympathize with in *A Raisin in the Sun*? Why? Does this sympathy change during the course of the play?

2. Despite the almost continuous conflict among the members of the Younger family, there are points in Lorraine Hansberry's play where two or more suddenly make sympathetic or even affectionate contact. Explore some of these moments. What makes them possible?

3. There is a lot of genuine conflict within the Younger family; many hurtful statements fly back and forth. But sometimes the characters seem to be taking satisfaction in or making sport of insulting each other—"playing the dozens." Find some examples of this. Have you ever traded insults with your friends or family members when the barb is mostly not serious? What is the purpose of trading such insults? What is the effect?

4. Why is it so important for Mama and Ruth that Mama puts down money for a house? What does house and "home" mean to them? Can you draw any connections between their desire to purchase a house and Gwendolyn Brooks's concern in "Home" (p. 1777)?

5. What does Walter really want? What does the liquor store represent to him? Do his goals or dreams change during the course of the play?

6. Why are Ruth and Mama amused at Walter's and Beneatha's yelling over Beneatha's choice of husband? How should we interpret Mama's remark, "Yeah—they something all right, my children"? What does she mean when she says of Walter, "He finally come into his manhood today, didn't he"? How much do you think Walter has changed? What do you think will happen after this scene?

Writing about the Text

1. Write a follow-up scene to the ending of *A Raisin in the Sun*, with the family in their new living room.

2. Write about the role of Africa in Hansberry's play. Note that many of the characters do not take African roots for granted, or even regard them as very significant. (This was before the term "African American" was in common use.) What role does Asagai play in the drama?

3. In *To Be Young, Gifted, and Black*, Hansberry says:

   I love Sean O'Casey [Irish playwright, 1884–1964]. This, to me, is the playwright of the twentieth century accepting and using the most obvious instruments of Shakespeare, which is the human personality in its totality. O'Casey never fools you about the Irish, you see . . . the Irish drunkard, the Irish braggart, the Irish liar . . . and the genuine heroism which must naturally emerge when you tell the truth about people. This, to me, is the height of artistic perception and is the most rewarding kind of thing that can happen in drama, because when you believe people so completely—because *everybody* has their drunkards and their braggarts and their cowards, you know—then you also believe them in their moments of heroic assertion: you don't doubt them.

Write about how this comment applies to Hansberry's own drama, *A Raisin in the Sun*.

Linking the Text to other Texts

1. *A Raisin in the Sun* resembles August Wilson's play *The Piano Lesson* (p. 1918) in that a substantial source of money has suddenly become available and the family experiences conflict over who "owns" the money and how it should be spent (and even how seriously "money" should be valued). Furthermore, in each case the money represents an inheritance from past generations. How different is the playing out of the conflict over the money?

2. Walter in *A Raisin in the Sun* and Willy Loman in Arthur Miller's *Death of a Salesman* (p. 1671) both have "dreams" that seem impossible to fulfill. What are the similarities and differences between Walter and Willy?

3. Discuss Africa as a significant presence in *A Raisin in the Sun*, and then discuss its role in Margaret Danner's poems (p. 1763). What role did ideas of Africa play in the Chicago Renaissance?

4. How does the 1961 film version of *A Raisin in the Sun* affect your perception of the play? Pick one of the characters and discuss how well the actor embodied the role he or she was playing.

Starting Points for Further Research: Lorraine Hansberry

- **Edition:** Lorraine Hansberry. *A Raisin in the Sun*. New York: Modern Library, 1995.
- **Biography:** Robert Nemiroff. *To Be Young, Gifted, and Black: Lorraine Hansberry in Her Own Words*. New York: Vintage, 1995.
- **Critical Essay:** Robin Bernstein. "Inventing a Fishbowl: White Supremacy and the Critical Reception of Lorraine Hansberry's *A Raisin in the Sun*." *Modern Drama* 42 (1999): 16–27.

Questions for Writing and Research

1. Many Chicago writers were transplants from the South, specifically from poor rural areas of Mississippi, Alabama, Arkansas, and Louisiana. Choose three works from the chapter and show what form this southern rural background takes in them. (For instance, some of these pieces reflect or play with traditional stereotypes of country people and city people. Think about how these texts confirm or alter some common stereotypes.)

2. In many of these texts, innocence is a motif or theme, which is perhaps inevitable in a population that was rapidly becoming urban. Pick two or three texts that deal with innocence, either implicitly or explicitly. What does innocence entail? What does its loss involve?

3. Chicago blacks were often migrants, new to the city. In the view of much mainstream white culture, they were outcasts or "invisible men." Moreover, change was the order of the day, as the Great Depression was followed by World War II. The concept of "home" was a complex one, as was the issue of one's identity. African Americans asked, "What's my real home?" and "Who am I at my core?" Choose a text from Margaret Walker, Gwendolyn Brooks, Richard Wright, Margaret

Danner, or Cyrus Colter, and tell how it answers the question "Where is my home?" Is it in the South? In Chicago? In Bronzeville only? In America? In heaven?

4. African American culture has often been described as a heavily oral one, valuing the spoken word in all its glory. In an essay, consider how texts by Gwendolyn Brooks, Langston Hughes, and Margaret Walker serve as evidence of that point about oral culture. Or, in contrast, show how three other texts from this chapter seem to counter that claim about oral culture.

5. Many of the texts in this chapter are about performance, intentional and unintentional, and about the way that performance is viewed by a formal or informal audience. The performances take place on stages and in auditoriums, in churches, and on the street. Choose two or more texts from this section and write an essay that explores the implications of seeing large areas of life as performance or spectatorship. What problems does such performing create for performers or audience? On the other hand, what strengths does performance provide?

6. Social class plays a huge role when "high" culture mixes with "popular" culture. Write an essay contrasting two works that seem to represent the "high" and two works representing the "popular." Which types of people do the works seem to be about? Which types of people do they seem written for?

7. During the 1930s and 1940s, many African American artists attempted to emphasize their African heritage and tried to link their work with specifically African or Afro-Caribbean themes and images. What signs do you see of African and Afro-Caribbean culture in these texts and artworks in the accompanying media? Choose at least three different writers or artists.

8. Where in these texts do you see marks of a specifically "literary" concern? For instance, what attitudes about the creation of literature do Hughes and Bontemps express in the portion of their correspondence you read here (p. 1787)? Or notice the variation in Gwendolyn Brooks's poetry: "We Real Cool" (p. 1757) begs to be read aloud in a particular style; her "Children of the Poor" sonnets (p. 913) are highly literary. Do you see similar "literary" signs and attitudes elsewhere?

9. Examine scholarship and criticism about twentieth-century American literature to see how thinkers about literature regard the Chicago Renaissance. Who first argued for it? Was there any resistance? What did it have to do with the Harlem Renaissance?

10. Conduct research on the literary career of Margaret Walker, making use of her books as well as websites. (See www.ibiblio.org/ipa/walker/bio.html.) In particular, look for continuities between the Walker of the 1930s and Walker the English professor who organized the Phyllis Wheatley poetry festival at Jackson State College and influenced the Black Aesthetic poets of the 1960s and 1970s.

CHAPTER
26

From Avant-Garde to Contemporary Theater

In the twentieth century, technology forced theatrical people to confront some serious competition. As the century progressed, new forms of media—film, radio, and of course television—began raising questions about the purpose of the traditional theater. What could theater do, now that movies and TV could depict life on the screen? As one of playwright Luis Valdez's characters would ask, is theater "something other than an expensive alternative to television"? If it was only an "expensive alternative," how would it attract an audience of more modest means?

In reaction to that challenge, the second half of the twentieth century witnessed a striking new emphasis on theatrical presence. Theater could offer something TV and movies could never have—characters on the stage, right there, live, with live people in the audience reacting to them. What possibilities and opportunities did those actual presences open up? The conventional theater of Susan Glaspell's *Trifles* (see p. 1166) and later Arthur Miller's *Death of a Salesman* (see p. 1671) had tended to work toward more of a sense of "reality," often through the creation of greater psychological depth in its characters, a quest for depth that gave rise to "method" acting (see p. 1616 in Chapter 24) as a means of getting at characters from "the inside." But directors of the avant-garde and experimental theater were not satisfied with the usual hallmarks of realism, including psychological complexity, and so moved to more radical theatrical imaginings. Avant-garde and experimental theater sought to involve its audience,

CONTEMPORARY THEATER

Today's plays are performed in a wide variety of styles, from traditional to transgressive, from mild to wild. We are in the midst of an era of experimentation, an exciting time to be thinking about theatrical performance. Of course, a great many contemporary plays get performed in something approaching straightforward productions using the three-sided box familiar to Ibsen, showing that the realistic theater still attracts actors, directors, and audiences alike. Yazmina Reza's *Art*, for instance, premiered in Berlin in 1994 on a very traditional stage and has successfully played that way around the world, appearing that same year in Paris, then in London in 1996, and finally on Broadway in New York in 1998. No one would accuse it of looking like a mid-twentieth-century realist drama. It has a stripped-down, minimalist set, nicely paralleling its central object of dispute, an all-white painting. Reza and her directors created a thoroughly modern play with up-to-date sets and costumes without breaking from the conventions of the proscenium stage.

Many directors break with traditional staging in one of three distinct ways: they push the boundaries; they go in for designer theater; or they attempt to break down the fourth wall, the separation between the actors and the audience.

Pushing Boundaries

A boundary that was broken early is clothing. In the 1960s, people on stage started taking off their clothes, to the great interest of audiences. Skin sold, so plays like *Hair, Equus,* and the sex review *Oh Calcutta* (with a sketch by Samuel Beckett, among many others) packed in audiences. Nudity—mostly female at first—had a titillating effect, though it was certainly built into the serious drama of a play like *Equus.*

Alan Alda starred as Marc and Victor Garber as Serge in the 1998 Broadway production of Yasmina Reza's Art, which, like its previous stagings, featured a minimalist set showcasing the all-white painting around which the conflicts revolve.

Boundaries were also crossed when perspectives and issues that were only suggested in earlier eras became the central topic of dramas. Homosexuality is a focus of Tom Stoppard's *The Invention of Love* (2000). Some plays deal with sexually transmitted diseases, such as Tony Kushner's *Angels in America* (1992), about AIDS; Henrik Ibsen was the pioneer with *Ghosts* in 1881. Drug use figures in Miguel Pinero's *Short Eyes* (1974). Drama often takes up issues and situations that film and television will not. Sometimes drama breaks the rules for fun, as with two contemporary plays with outrageous titles and premises: *Urinetown* (2001) and *The Puppetry of the Penis* (1997). As those titles and others—like Eve Ensler's *The Vagina Monologues* (1996)—suggest, contemporary drama breaks language barriers. And some theater companies seem to have been designed to break all the boundaries at once: language, nudity, and forbidden topics. From the 1980s on, Charles Ludlam's Theater of the Ridiculous and Richard Foreman's Ontological Hysterical Theater have specialized in staging brilliant, loony productions in which gender is never stable and the language and situations are not meant for the prudish.

Designer Theater

Contemporary theatrical directors recognize that the stage cannot compete with a movie in portraying reality: a movie can show the *Titanic* sinking, a chariot race, a battle scene, a chase on horseback—anything that the budget allows. But the stage has the edge in symbolism and in imaginative, expressive, and inventive sets. The contemporary stage is the scene of spectacular, expressive designs for a whole variety of plays, from huge Broadway musicals to small, intimate productions. In some cases, the lighting and the sets are what attract the crowds, as the success of the

Designer Robin Wagner created a lavish set for the Tony Award–winning 1993 production of Tony Kushner's Angels in America, *directed by George C. Wolfe.*

Broadway musical *The Lion King* (1997) demonstrates.

Some designers go in for pure spectacle: lavish sets and fanciful costumes, as in Robin Wagner's design for Tony Kushner's *Angels in America* (1992). Other designers, such as Robert Wilson, choose symbolic representations and a mix of minimalist decoration and maximalist size. Another director, Peter Brook, took over a whole theater for his production of the Indian epic *Mahabharata* (1985), covering the floor with dirt and making the set with its flames and incense an integral part of the drama.

However, minimalism can also be very effective in drawing and focusing attention. In Samuel Beckett's *Happy Days* (1961), for example, minimalism is used to heighten the absurdity. One of the two central characters, Winnie, spends the duration of the play buried in a mound of dirt—first up to her waist, then up to her neck. Similarly, in his stage directions for *Not I* (see p. 1861), Beckett calls for a dark stage lit with only a spotlight that remains focused on the single speaker's mouth. To create a physical manifestation of the immobility Beckett was exploring in the play, when actress Billie Whitelaw first performed *Not I*, the director purportedly clamped her head into place to keep it from moving.

Breaking the Fourth Wall

Starting in the 1960s and continuing to this day, theater directors have broken down that "fourth wall"—the imaginary invisible wall at the front of the stage between the audience and the world of the play. The action is no longer confined to the stage but instead spills over, uncontained, to the audience. Minor characters are likely to pop up in the balcony or run down the aisles. For example, one production of Anton Chekhov's *The Seagull* (2000) had the female lead, Debra Winger, ride on

fight audience passivity, and remove the **fourth wall**—the imaginary invisible wall at the front of the stage between the audience and the world of the play.

Some theater has explicitly sought to stir the audience into political or social action about a cause or a wrong. The left-wing German playwright Bertolt Brecht famously used theater to further his political ends. Much multicultural theater in the United States has sought to portray the multiple persecutions, dilemmas, and indignities that minority groups experience as they try to find their places in American society. In political theater or in much multicultural theater, audiences are not always supposed to enjoy themselves and be entertained, at least not exclusively; they should also be made uncomfortable, shocked, or perplexed, and they should even be spurred to action.

In keeping with Brecht's ideas, some theater has rejected detailed characterizations in favor of "types," as with Valdez's Pachuco in *Los Vendidos*, for example. Writers have chosen masks, stylized movements, even puppets. Actors may take on several different roles in one play or may switch between parts of the same character's life (for instance, playing teenage to aged versions of that one role).

Additionally, the best contemporary theater has tended to take on an existential tone, often confronting the possible "meaninglessness" of the world—stemming sometimes from a rejection of belief in a higher power and sometimes from a rejection of complete reliance on scientific rationality. One response in the theater has been a dark humor derived from a lack of logic and based instead on incongruity, on absurdity. Here Irish playwright Samuel Beckett was a master; his plays pointedly rejected plot or a particular "goal" toward which action headed. In his masterpiece, *Waiting for Godot* (1952), Godot never appears to the two tramps who await him for so long, nor do we learn who Godot is.

a swing. Winger swung—not so gently—at an angle that took her out over the first several rows of the audience.

In a more extreme example, Boston theatergoers buying tickets for the front rows of the Huntington Theater's 2000 production of Sidney Kingsley's *Dead End* were warned to wear raingear because a large tank of water was placed in the orchestra pit, right in front of the traditional proscenium stage, extending it by ten feet to serve as the East River, with actors jumping in from time to time.

In still another way, the fourth wall can be broken by literally putting the audience on the stage, as happened in the London production of playwright Michael Frayn's *Copenhagen* (1998), directed by Michael Blakemore. The play is about the enigmatic 1943 meeting between German atomic scientist Werner von Heisenberg and his teacher, Danish scientist Niels Bohr. Both men left conflicting accounts of this brief wartime meeting, during the period when Heisenberg led the Nazi effort to develop an atomic bomb. In Blakemore's staging of the play, thirty or so audience members were seated on elevated platforms behind a tilted stage, almost as a panel of jurors, intently watching the interplay of the scientists but without having to render a verdict.

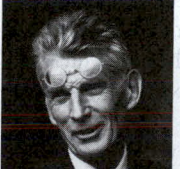

SAMUEL BECKETT (1906–1989)

Not I (1972)

Samuel Beckett was a key figure in the mid-twentieth-century "theater of the absurd" movement. Born near Dublin into a middle-class Protestant family, he attended Trinity College and moved to Paris in 1928 to study, befriending the famous Irish novelist James Joyce and becoming part of the city's avant-garde literary life. Returning to Ireland, Beckett considered an academic career but eventually decided against it. He returned to France and began writing poems and stories while supporting himself through a variety of jobs. He lived in Paris, leaving only during part of World War II when he faced danger as a member of the anti-Nazi resistance. After World War II he became quite prolific, publishing four novels and many short stories and plays, including one that would make him famous, Waiting for Godot (written in French during the late 1940s, published in 1952, first produced in 1953 in Paris, and published in an English translation by Beckett himself in 1954). His other well-known dramatic works include Endgame (1957), Krapp's Last Tape (1958), and Happy Days (1961). These plays, along with his innovative novels, represented a kind of comic minimalism that came to be characterized as "the absurd." Beckett received the Nobel Prize for Literature in 1969.

Beckett's plays make do without the traditional elements of drama. Plot and typical elements of characterization disappear; all that remains is an image. His minimalist plays depict lonely creatures who struggle vainly to express the inexpressible. In the monologue Not I (1972), we are confronted with an absolutely dark stage and a spotlight that remains focused on the speaker's mouth. This narrating mouth pours forth a rush of words and memories, always trying to avoid the first-person singular pronoun, the "I."

Stage in darkness but for MOUTH, *upstage audience right, about 8 feet above stage level, faintly lit from close-up and below, rest of face in shadow. Invisible microphone.*

AUDITOR, *downstage audience left, tall standing figure, sex unde-terminable, enveloped from head to foot in loose black djellaba, with hood, fully faintly lit, standing on invisible podium about 4 feet high shown by attitude alone to be facing diagonally across stage intent on* MOUTH, *dead still throughout but for four brief movements where indi-cated. As house lights down* MOUTH's *voice unintelligible behind curtain. House lights out. Voice continues unintelligible behind curtain, 10 sec-onds. With rise of curtain ad-libbing from text as required leading when curtain fully up and attention sufficient into:*

MOUTH: . . . .out . . . into this world . . . this world . . . tiny little thing . . . before its time . . . in a godfor— . . . what? . . girl? . . yes . . . tiny little girl . . . into this . . . out into this . . . before her time . . . godforsaken hole called . . . called . . . no matter . . . parents unknown . . . unheard of . . . he having van-ished . . . thin air . . . no sooner buttoned up his breeches . . . she similarly . . . eight months later . . . almost to the tick . . . so no love . . . spared that . . . no love such as normally vented on the . . . speechless infant . . . in the home . . . no . . . nor indeed for that matter any of any kind . . . no love of any kind . . . at any subsequent stage . . . so typical affair . . . nothing of any note till coming up to sixty when— . . . what? . . seventy? . . good God! . . coming up to seventy . . . wandering in a field . . . looking aimlessly for cowslips . . . to make a ball . . . a few steps then stop . . . stare into space . . . then on . . . a few more . . . stop and stare again . . . so on . . . . drifting around . . . when sud-denly . . . gradually . . . all went out . . . all that early April morning light . . . and she found herself in the— . . . what? . . who? . . no! . . she! . . [*Pause and movement 1.*] . . . found herself in the dark . . . and if not exactly . . . insen-tient . . . insentient . . . for she could still hear the buzzing . . . so-called . . . in the ears . . . and a ray of light came and went . . . came and went . . . such as the moon might cast . . . drifting . . . in and out of cloud . . . but so dulled . . . feeling . . . feeling so dulled . . . she did not know . . . what position she was in . . . imagine! . . what position she was in! . . whether standing . . . or sitting . . . but the brain— . . . what? . . kneeling? . . yes . . . whether standing . . . or sitting . . . or kneeling . . . but the brain— . . . what? . . lying? . . yes . . . whether standing . . . or sitting . . . or kneeling . . . or lying . . . but the brain still . . . still . . . in a way . . . for her first thought was . . . oh long after . . . sudden flash . . . brought up as she had been to believe . . . with the other waifs . . . in a merciful . . . [*Brief laugh.*] . . . God . . . [*Good laugh.*] . . . first thought was . . . oh long after . . . sudden flash . . . she was being punished . . . for her sins . . . a number of which then . . . further proof if proof were needed . . . flashed through her mind . . . one after another . . . then dismissed as foolish . . . oh long after . . . this thought dismissed . . . as she suddenly real-ized . . . gradually realized . . . she was not suffering . . . imagine! . . not suffer-ing! . . indeed could not remember . . . off-hand . . . when she had suffered less . . . unless of course she was . . . *meant* to be suffering . . . ha! . . *thought* to be suffering . . . just as the odd time . . . in her life . . . when clearly intended to be having pleasure . . . she was in fact . . . having none . . . not the slight-est . . . in which case of course . . . that notion of punishment . . . for some sin or other . . . or for the lot . . . or no particular reason . . . for its own sake . . . thing she understood perfectly . . . that notion of punishment . . . which had

first occurred to her . . . brought up as she had been to believe . . . with the
other waifs . . . in a merciful . . . [*Brief laugh.*] . . . God . . . [*Good laugh.*] . . .
first occurred to her . . . then dismissed . . . as foolish . . . was perhaps not so
foolish . . . after all . . . so on . . . all that . . . vain reasonings . . . till another
thought . . . oh long after . . . sudden flash . . . very foolish really but— . . .
what? . . the buzzing? . . yes . . . all the time the buzzing . . . so-called . . . in
the ears . . . though of course actually . . . not in the ears at all . . . in the skull
. . . dull roar in the skull . . . and all the time this ray or beam . . . like moonbeam . . . but probably not . . . certainly not . . . always the same spot . . . now
bright . . . now shrouded . . . but always the same spot . . . as no moon could
. . . no . . . no moon . . . just all part of the same wish to . . . torment . . .
though actually in point of fact . . . not in the least . . . not a twinge . . . so far
. . . ha! . . so far . . . this other thought then . . . oh long after . . . sudden flash
. . . very foolish really but so like her . . . in a way . . . that she might do well
to . . . groan . . . on and off . . . writhe she could not . . . as if in actual agony
. . . but could not . . . could not bring herself . . . some flaw in her make-up
. . . incapable of deceit . . . or the machine . . . more likely the machine . . . so
disconnected . . . never got the message . . . or powerless to respond . . . like
numbed . . . couldn't make the sound . . . not any sound . . . no sound of any
kind . . . no screaming for help for example . . . should she feel so inclined . . .
scream . . . [*Screams.*] . . . then listen . . . [*Silence.*] . . . scream again . . .
[*Screams again.*] . . . then listen again . . . [*Silence.*] . . . no . . . spared that . . .
all silent as the grave . . . no part— . . . what? . . the buzzing? . . yes . . . all
silent but for the buzzing . . . so-called . . . no part of her moving . . . that she
could feel . . . just the eyelids . . . presumably . . . on and off . . . shut out the
light . . . reflex they call it . . . no feeling of any kind . . . but the lids . . . even
best of times . . . who feels them? . . opening . . . shutting . . . all that moisture
. . . but the brain still . . . still sufficiently . . . oh very much so! . . at this stage
. . . in control . . . under control . . . to question even this . . . for on that
April morning . . . so it reasoned . . . that April morning . . . she fixing with
her eye . . . a distant bell . . . as she hastened towards it . . . fixing it with her
eye . . . lest it elude her . . . had not all gone out . . . all that light . . . of itself
. . . without any . . . any . . . on her part . . . so on . . . so on it reasoned . . .
vain questionings . . . and all dead still . . . sweet silent as the grave . . . when
suddenly . . . gradually . . . she realiz— . . . what? . . the buzzing? . . yes . . . all
dead still but for the buzzing . . . when suddenly she realized . . . words
were— . . . what? . . who? . . no! . . she! . . [*Pause and movement 2.*] . . . realized . . . words were coming . . . imagine! . . words were coming . . . a voice
she did not recognize . . . at first . . . so long since it had sounded . . . then finally had to admit . . . could be none other . . . than her own . . . certain
vowel sounds . . . she had never heard . . . elsewhere . . . so that people would
stare . . . the rare occasions . . . once or twice a year . . . always winter some
strange reason . . . stare at her uncomprehending . . . and now this stream . . .
steady stream . . . she who had never . . . on the contrary . . . practically
speechless . . . all her days . . . how she survived! . . even shopping . . . out
shopping . . . busy shopping centre . . . supermart . . . just hand in the list . . .
with the bag . . . old black shopping bag . . . then stand there waiting . . . any
length of time . . . middle of the throng . . . motionless . . . staring into space
. . . mouth half open as usual . . . till it was back in her hand . . . the bag back

in her hand . . . then pay and go . . . not as much as good-bye . . . how she
survived! . . and now this stream . . . not catching the half of it . . . not the
quarter . . . no idea . . . what she was saying . . . imagine! . . no idea what she
was saying! . . till she began trying to . . . delude herself . . . it was not hers at
all . . . not her voice at all . . . and no doubt would have . . . vital she should
. . . was on the point . . . after long efforts . . . when suddenly she felt . . .
gradually she felt . . . her lips moving . . . imagine! . . her lips moving! . . as of
course till then she had not . . . and not alone the lips . . . the cheeks . . . the
jaws . . . the whole face . . . all those— . . . what? . . the tongue? . . yes . . . the
tongue in the mouth . . . all those contortions without which . . . no speech
possible . . . and yet in the ordinary way . . . not felt at all . . . so intent one is
. . . on what one is saying . . . the whole being . . . hanging on its words . . . so
that not only she had . . . had she . . . not only had she . . . to give up . . . admit hers alone . . . her voice alone . . . but this other awful thought . . . oh
long after . . . sudden flash . . . even more awful if possible . . . that feeling was
coming back . . . imagine! . . feeling coming back! . . starting at the top . . .
then working down . . . the whole machine . . . but no . . . spared that . . . the
mouth alone . . . so far . . . ha! . . so far . . . then thinking . . . oh long after . . .
sudden flash . . . it can't go on . . . all this . . . all that . . . steady stream . . .
straining to hear . . . make something of it . . . and her own thoughts . . .
make something of them . . . all—. . . what? . . the buzzing? . . yes . . . all the
time the buzzing . . . so-called . . . all that together . . . imagine! . . whole
body like gone . . . just the mouth . . . lips . . . cheeks . . . jaws . . . never— . . .
what? . . tongue? . . yes . . . lips . . . cheeks . . . jaws . . . tongue . . . never still a
second . . . mouth on fire . . . stream of words . . . in her ear . . . practically in
her ear . . . not catching the half . . . not the quarter . . . no idea what she's
saying . . . imagine! . . no idea what she's saying! . . and can't stop . . . no
stopping it . . . she who but a moment before . . . but a moment! . . could not
make a sound . . . no sound of any kind . . . now can't stop . . .
imagine! . . can't stop the stream . . . and the whole brain begging . . . something begging in the brain . . . begging the mouth to stop . . . pause a moment
. . . if only for a moment . . . and no response . . . as if it hadn't heard . . . or
couldn't . . . couldn't pause a second . . . like maddened . . . all that together
. . . straining to hear . . . piece it together . . . and the brain . . . raving away
on its own . . . trying to make sense of it . . . or make it stop . . . or in the past
. . . dragging up the past . . . flashes from all over . . . walks mostly . . . walking
all her days . . . day after day . . . a few steps then stop . . . stare into space . . .
then on . . . a few more . . . stop and stare again . . . so on . . . drifting around
. . . day after day . . . or that time she cried . . . the one time she could remember . . . since she was a baby . . . must have cried as a baby . . . perhaps
not . . . not essential to life . . . just the birth cry to get her going . . . breathing . . . then no more till this . . . old hag already . . . sitting staring at her
hand . . . where was it? . . Croker's Acres . . . one evening on the way home
. . . home! . . a little mound in Croker's Acres . . . dusk . . . sitting staring at
her hand . . . there in her lap . . . palm upward . . . suddenly saw it wet . . . the
palm . . . tears presumably . . . hers presumably . . . no one else for miles . . .
no sound . . . just the tears . . . sat and watched them dry . . . all over in a second . . . or grabbing at straw . . . the brain . . . flickering away on its own . . .
quick grab and on . . . nothing there . . . on to the next . . . bad as the voice

. . . worse . . . as little sense . . . all that together . . . can't— . . . what? . . the buzzing? . . yes . . . all the time the buzzing . . . dull roar like falls . . . and the beam . . . flickering on and off . . . starting to move around . . . like moonbeam but not . . . all part of the same . . . keep an eye on that too . . . corner of the eye . . . all that together . . . can't go on . . . God is love . . . she'll be purged . . . back in the field . . . morning sun . . . April . . . sink face down in the grass . . . nothing but the larks . . . so on . . . grabbing at the straw . . . straining to hear . . . the odd word . . . make some sense of it . . . whole body like gone . . . just the mouth . . . like maddened . . . and can't stop . . . no stopping it . . . something she— . . something she had to— . . . what? . . who? . . no! . . she! . . [*Pause and movement 3.*] . . . something she had to— . . . what? . . the buzzing? . . yes . . . all the time the buzzing . . . dull roar . . . in the skull . . . and the beam . . . ferreting around . . . painless . . . so far . . . ha! . . so far . . . then thinking . . . oh long after . . . sudden flash . . . perhaps something she had to . . . had to . . . tell . . . could that be it? . . something she had to . . . tell . . . tiny little thing . . . before its time . . . godforsaken hole . . . no love . . . spared that . . . speechless all her days . . . practically speechless . . . how she survived! . . that time in court . . . what had she to say for herself . . . guilty or not guilty . . . stand up woman . . . speak up woman . . . stood there staring into space . . . mouth half open as usual . . . waiting to be led away . . . glad of the hand on her arm . . . now this . . . something she had to tell . . . could that be it? . . something that would tell . . . how it was . . . how she— . . . what? . . had been? . . yes . . . something that would tell how it had been . . . how she had lived . . . lived on and on . . . guilty or not . . . on and on . . . to be sixty . . . something she— . . . what? . . seventy? . . good God! . . on and on to be seventy . . . something she didn't know herself . . . wouldn't know if she heard . . . then forgiven . . . God is love . . . tender mercies . . . new every morning . . . back in the field . . . April morning . . . face in the grass . . . nothing but the larks . . . pick it up there . . . get on with it from there . . . another few— . . . what? . . not that? . . nothing to do with that? . . nothing she could tell? . . all right . . . nothing she could tell . . . try something else . . . think of something else . . . oh long after . . . sudden flash . . . not that either . . . all right . . . something else again . . . so on . . . hit on it in the end . . . think everything keep on long enough . . . then forgiven . . . back in the— . . . what? . . not that either? . . nothing to do with that either? . . nothing she could think? . . all right . . . nothing she could tell . . . nothing she could think . . . nothing she— . . . what? . who? . no! . . she! . . [*Pause and movement 4.*] . . . tiny little thing . . . out before its time . . . godforsaken hole . . . no love . . . spared that . . . speechless all her days . . . practically speech-less . . . even to herself . . . never out loud . . . but not completely . . . sometimes sudden urge . . . once or twice a year . . . always winter some strange reason . . . the long evenings . . . hours of darkness . . . sudden urge to . . . tell . . . then rush out stop the first she saw . . . nearest lavatory . . . start pouring it out . . . steady stream . . . mad stuff . . . half the vowels wrong . . . no one could follow . . . till she saw the stare she was getting . . . then die of shame . . . crawl back in . . . once or twice a year . . . always winter some strange rea-son . . . long hours of darkness . . . now this . . . this . . . quicker and quicker . . . the words . . . the brain . . . flickering away like mad . . . quick grab and on . . . nothing there . . . on somewhere else . . . try somewhere else . . . all

the time something begging . . . something in her begging . . . begging it all
to stop . . . unanswered . . . prayer unanswered . . . or unheard . . . too faint
. . . so on . . . keep on . . . trying . . . not knowing what . . . what she was trying . . . what to try . . . whole body like gone . . . just the mouth . . . like maddened . . . so on . . . keep— . . . what? . . the buzzing? . . yes . . . all the time
the buzzing . . . dull roar like falls . . . in the skull . . . and the beam . . . poking around . . . painless . . . so far . . . ha! . . so far . . . all that . . . keep on . . .
not knowing what . . . what she was— . . . what? . . who? . . no! . . she! . .
SHE! . . [*Pause.*] . . . what she was trying . . . what to try . . . no matter . . .
keep on . . . [*Curtain starts down.*] . . . hit on it in the end . . . then back . . .
God is love . . . tender mercies . . . new every morning . . . back in the field
. . . April morning . . . face in the grass . . . nothing but the larks . . . pick it
up—

[*Curtain fully down. House dark. Voice continues behind curtain, unintelligible, 10 seconds, ceases as house lights up.*]

Talking about the Text

1. What lines in *Not I* convey a pleasant mood or idea? What lines suggest hopeless-
   ness and despair? Where does the balance lie? Which lines convey an emotional
   position different from pleasure or misery? (This is a play in which it is not useful
   to ask "What exactly does it mean?" Thus, annotation can be particularly valuable, giving your response to various parts of the monologue—phrases, images, the
   effect of the absence of sentence subjects and sometimes verbs—in fact, the
   scarcity of complete sentences.)
2. Examine the repeated words and phrases in *Not I*. What impact do they have on
   the reader?
3. What is the role of God in this play? Does God exist for this speaker? Why or why
   not?

Writing about the Text

1. Write a short essay on the significance of the setting of *Not I*: the impact of a pair
   of lips seen without the rest of the body. In your essay, address the following issues:
   Why might the playwright choose to limit the physical aspects of the character to
   the lips? What impact might the references to "brain" and "skull" and any other
   bodily characteristics have on the audience? What effect might the second character in the play—the auditor—have on our response to the mouth?
2. Select a twenty- or thirty-line portion of *Not I*. Write how you would deliver these
   lines. Include the questions you might have for your director and what questions
   you might ponder yourself.

Linking the Text to Other Texts

1. Select a part of the *Not I* monologue to turn into a satire like *Los Vendidos* (p.
   1867).
2. Compare part of *Not I* to a monologue in another play in this textbook, such as
   The Tempest or *Spreading the News*, or to a soliloquy in *Hamlet*.

🦎 **C O M M E N T A R Y**

Beckett's Legacy for the Theater

When Samuel Beckett died in December 1989, the New York Times championed him as someone who changed the world of theater forever. The history of theater, many critics believed, could be cleanly divided into that which was created "before Godot" and that which was created "after Godot." Although Beckett eventually rose to the level of an icon in the theater world, the Times points out that his rise to success took many years and suffered many setbacks. The general disillusionment with life that haunted Beckett through his early failures was seen in nearly all of his plays. As the Times obituary noted:

> At the root of his art was a philosophy of the deepest yet most courageous pessimism, exploring man's relationship with his God. With Beckett, one searched for hope amid despair and continued living with a kind of stoicism, as illustrated by the final words of his novel, *The Unnamable:* "You must go on, I can't go on, I'll go on." Or as he wrote in *Worstward Ho,* one of his later works of fiction: "Try again. Fail again. Fail better . . . ."

* * *

> In his 80s, he became an icon of survival. Even as he vowed that he had nothing more to say, he continued to be tormented and sustained by midnight thoughts and nightmarish images. Having discovered what was for him the non-meaning of life and its brevity (man is, he observed in *Waiting for Godot,* "born astride the grave"), he never stopped looking for ways to express himself. Once in writing about painting he said, "There is nothing to express, nothing from which to express, no power to express, no desire to express, together with the obligation to express." For him, that obligation was ineluctable.

To read the extensive obituary of Samuel Beckett that appeared in the New York Times *on December 27, 1989, go to www.nytimes.com/learning/general/onthisday/bday/0413.html.*

Starting Points for Further Research: Samuel Beckett

- **Editions:** Samuel Beckett. *Collected Poems in English and French.* New York: Grove Press, 1977.
  ———. *I Can't Go On, I'll Go On: A Samuel Beckett Reader.* Ed. Richard W. Seaver. New York: Grove Press, 1976.
- **Biography:** James Knowlson. *Damned to Fame: The Life of Samuel Beckett.* New York: Simon and Schuster, 1996.
- **Critical Essay:** Enoch Brater. "The Globalization of Becket's *Godot.*" *Comparative Drama* 37 (Summer 2003): 145–58.

LUIS VALDEZ (B. 1940)

Los Vendidos (1967)

Born and raised in California, the child of Chicano parents from Mexico, Luis Valdez is now commonly regarded as the founder of Mexican American theater in the United States. While a student at San Jose State University, he won a writing prize for a play, and his first full-length play, The Shrunken Head of Pancho Villa, *was produced by the school's drama department. His career took off during the 1960s in California when he became involved in novel theatrical experiments. He worked for a while with the San Francisco Mime Troupe, which satirized political figures and events through mimicry. He was influenced by the Bread and Puppet Theater, founded by Peter Schumann in 1963, which used dance, sculpture, and gigantic puppets to support causes like opposition to the Vietnam War and to U.S. intervention in Central America.*

In 1965 Valdez was living in Delano, California, where Cesar Chavez was organizing migrant farm workers into the United Farm Workers Union, marking the beginning of the Chicano movement. Valdez's theater group, El Teatro Campesino, founded that same year, grew out of both his interests in theater and his political commitment to Chavez and the Chicano cause. The original theater productions were staged in meeting halls and on the backs of flatbed trucks—"street theater" or "guerilla theater," it was called. Explaining these unusual choices of venues, Valdez said, "if La Raza won't go to the teatro then the teatro must go to La Raza." ("La Raza" generally referred to people with Mexican or Latin American heritage, but it was also used as a term of solidarity with workers' rights, immigrant rights, and Mexican American or Chicano civil rights.) In the early days the actors were nonprofessionals. The one-act plays (actos) were improvised in the process of production. Los Vendidos (The Sellouts) *is one of those early* actos—*stark, politically charged, and funny. (For more on El Teatro Campesino, see the Literary Locale on p. 1876.)*

During the 1970s, El Teatro Campesino became more permanent, finally settling in a home in San Juan Bautista near San Francisco. The actors became more seasoned and more professional. Valdez's work entered mainstream theater with his play about the 1942 Los Angeles riots, Zoot Suit *(1978), which opened in Los Angeles, went on to Broadway—the first play written and produced by a Mexican American to open there—and became a movie directed by Valdez in 1981. Meanwhile, Valdez continued his experimenting, trying out forms like corridas—ballads turned into plays—such as* Bandido! *(1982) and religious dramatizations such as* La Pastorela *(1991). In 1984 Valdez wrote and produced* I Don't Have to Show You No Stinking Badges. *In 1987 he directed the highly successful film* La Bamba, *about Chicano rock 'n' roll singer Richie Valens. Valdez also directed as well as co-wrote* The Cisco Kid *(1994), an update of the 1950s Western TV series, with Jimmy Smits as the Cisco Kid and Cheech Marin as Pancho.*

Los Vendidos

Characters

Honest Sancho	Farmworker	Revolucionario
Secretary	Pachuco	Mexican-American

Scene: HONEST SANCHO's *Used Mexican Lot and Mexican Curio Shop. Three models are on display in* HONEST SANCHO's *shop. To the right, there is a* REVOLUCIONARIO, *complete with sombrero, carrilleras and carabina 30-30. At center, on the floor, there is the* FARMWORKER, *under a broad straw sombrero. At stage left is the* PACHUCO, *filero in hand.* HONEST SANCHO *is moving among his models, dusting them off and preparing for another day of business.*

SANCHO: Bueno, bueno, mis monos, vamos a ver a quién vendemos ahora, ¿no? (*To audience.*) ¡Quihubo! I'm Honest Sancho and this is my shop. Antes fui contratista, pero ahora logré tener mi negocito. All I need now is a customer. (*A bell rings offstage.*) Ay, a customer!

SECRETARY: (*Entering.*) Good morning, I'm Miss Jimenez from . . .

SANCHO: Ah, una chicana! Welcome, welcome Señorita Jiménez.

SECRETARY: (*Anglo pronunciation.*) JIM-enez.

SANCHO: ¿Qué?

SECRETARY: My name is Miss JIM-enez. Don't you speak English? What's wrong with you?

SANCHO: Oh, nothing, Señorita JIM-enez. I'm here to help you.

SECRETARY: That's better. As I was starting to say, I'm a secretary from Governor Reagan's office, and we're looking for a Mexican type for the administration.

SANCHO: Well, you come to the right place, lady. This is Honest Sancho's Used Mexican Lot, and we got all types here. Any particular type you want?

SECRETARY: Yes, we were looking for somebody suave . . .

SANCHO: Suave.

SECRETARY: Debonaire.

SANCHO: De buen aire.

SECRETARY: Dark.

SANCHO: Prieto.

SECRETARY: But of course, not too dark.

SANCHO: No muy prieto.

SECRETARY: Perhaps, beige.

SANCHO: Beige, just the tone. Asi como cafecito con leche, ¿no?

SECRETARY: One more thing. He must be hard-working.

SANCHO: That could only be one model. Step right over here to the center of the shop, lady. (*They cross to the* FARMWORKER.) This is our standard farmworker model. As you can see, in the words of our beloved Senator George Murphy, he is "built close to the ground." Also, take special notice of his 4-ply Goodyear huaraches, made from the rain tire. This wide-brimmed sombrero is an extra added feature; keeps off the sun, rain and dust.

SECRETARY: Yes, it does look durable.

SANCHO: And our farmworker model is friendly. Muy amable. Watch. (*Snaps his fingers.*)

FARMWORKER: (*Lifts up head.*) Buenos días, señorita. (*His head drops.*)

SECRETARY: My, he is friendly.

SANCHO: Didn't I tell you? Loves his patrones! But his most attractive feature is that he's hard-working. Let me show you. (*Snaps fingers.* FARMWORKER *stands.*)

FARMWORKER: ¡El jale! (*He begins to work.*)

SANCHO: As you can see he is cutting grapes.

SECRETARY: Oh, I wouldn't know.

SANCHO: He also picks cotton. (*Snaps.* FARMWORKER *begins to pick cotton.*)

SECRETARY: Versatile, isn't he?

SANCHO: He also picks melons. (*Snaps.* FARMWORKER *picks melons.*) That's his slow speed for late in the season. Here's his fast speed. (*Snap.* FARMWORKER *picks faster.*)

SECRETARY: Chihuahua . . . I mean, goodness, he sure is a hardworker.

SANCHO: (*Pulls the* FARMWORKER *to his feet.*) And that isn't the half of it. Do you see these little holes on his arms that appear to be pores? During those hot sluggish days in the field when the vines or the branches get so entagled, it's almost impossible to move, these holes emit a certain grease that allows our model to slip and slide right through the crop with no trouble at all.

SECRETARY: Wonderful. But is he economical?

SANCHO: Economical? Señorita, you are looking at the Volkswagen of Mexicans. Pennies a day is all it takes. One plate of beans and tortillas will keep him going all day. That, and chile. Plenty of chile. Chile jalapeños, chile verde, chile colorado. But, of course, if you do give him chile, (*Snap.* FARMWORKER *turns left face. Snap.* FARMWORKER *bends over.*) then you have to change his oil filter once a week.

SECRETARY: What about storage?

SANCHO: No problem. You know these new farm labor camps our Honorable Governor Reagan has built out by Parlier or Raisin City? They were designed with our model in mind. Five, six, seven, even ten in one of those shacks will give you no trouble at all. You can also put him in old barns, old cars, riverbanks. You can even leave him out in the field over night with no worry!

SECRETARY: Remarkable.

SANCHO: And here's an added feature: every year at the end of the season, this model goes back to Mexico and doesn't return, automatically, until next Spring.

SECRETARY: How about that. But tell me, does he speak English?

SANCHO: Another outstanding feature is that last year this model was programmed to go out on STRIKE! (*Snap.*)

FARMWORKER: ¡Huelga! ¡Huelga! Hermanos, sálganse de esos files. (*Snap. He stops.*)

SECRETARY: No! Oh no, we can't strike in the State Capitol.

SANCHO: Well, he also scabs. (*Snap.*)

FARMWORKER: Me vendo barato, ¿y qué? (*Snap.*)

SECRETARY: That's much better, but you didn't answer my question. Does he speak English?

SANCHO: Bueno . . . no, pero he has other . . .

SECRETARY: No.

SANCHO: Other features.

SECRETARY: No! He just won't do!

SANCHO: Okay, okay, pues. We have other models.

SECRETARY: I hope so. What we need is something a little more sophisticated.

SANCHO: Sophisti-qué?

SECRETARY: An urban model.

SANCHO: Ah, from the city! Step right back. Over here in this corner of the shop is exactly what you're looking for. Introducing our new 1969 JOHNNY PACHUCO model! This is our fast-back model. Streamlined. Built for speed, low-riding, city life. Take a look at some of these features. Mag shoes, dual exhausts, green chartruese paint-job, dark-tint windshield, a little poof on top. Let me just turn him on. (*Snap.* JOHNNY *walks to stage center with a* PACHUCO *bounce.*)

SECRETARY: What was that?

SANCHO: That, señorita, was the Chicano shuffle.

SECRETARY: Okay, what does he do?

SANCHO: Anything and everything necessary for city life. For instance, survival: he knife fights. (*Snaps.* JOHNNY *pulls out a switchblade and swings at* SECRETARY. SECRETARY *screams.*) He dances. (*Snap.*)

JOHNNY: (*Singing.*) "Angel Baby, my Angel Baby . . . " (*Snap.*)

SANCHO: And here's a feature no city model can be without. He gets arrested, but not without resisting, of course. (*Snap.*)

JOHNNY: En la madre, la placa. I didn't do it! I didn't do it! (JOHNNY *turns and stands up against an imaginary wall, legs spread out, arms behind his back.*)

SECRETARY: Oh no, we can't have arrests! We must maintain law and order.

SANCHO: But he's bilingual.

SECRETARY: Bilingual?

SANCHO: Simón que yes. He speaks English! Johnny, give us some English. (*Snap.*)

JOHNNY: (*Comes downstage.*) Fuck-you!

SECRETARY: (*Gasps.*) Oh! I've never been so insulted in my whole life!

SANCHO: Well, he learned it in your school.

SECRETARY: I don't care where he learned it.

SANCHO: But he's economical.

SECRETARY: Economical?

SANCHO: Nickels and dimes. You can keep Johnny running on hamburgers, Taco Bell tacos, Lucky Lager beer, Thunderbird wine, yesca . . .

SECRETARY: Yesca?

SANCHO: Mota.

SECRETARY: Mota?

SANCHO: Leños . . . marijuana. (*Snap.* JOHNNY *inhales on an imaginary joint.*)

SECRETARY: That's against the law!

JOHNNY: (*Big smile, holding his breath.*) Yeah.

SANCHO: He also sniffs glue. (*Snap.* JOHNNY *inhales glue, big smile.*)

JOHNNY: Tha's too much man, ese.

SECRETARY: No, Mr. Sancho, I dont' think this . . .

SANCHO: Wait a minute, he has other qualities I know you'll love. For example, an inferiority complex. (*Snap.*)

JOHNNY: (*To* SANCHO.) You think you're better than me, huh, ese? (*Swings switchblade.*)

SANCHO: He can also be beaten and he bruises. Cut him and he bleeds, kick him and he . . . (*He beats, bruises and kicks* PACHUCO.) Would you like to try it?

SECRETARY: Oh, I couldn't.

SANCHO: Be my guest. He's a great scape goat.

SECRETARY: No really.

SANCHO: Please.

SECRETARY: Well, all right. Just once. (*She kicks* PACHUCO.) Oh, he's so soft.

SANCHO: Wasn't that good? Try again.

SECRETARY: (*Kicks* PACHUCO.) Oh, he's so wonderful! (*She kicks him again.*)

SANCHO: Okay, that's enough, lady. You'll ruin the merchandise. Yes, our Johnny Pachuco model can give you many hours of pleasure. Why, the LAPD just bought 20 of these to train their rookie cops on. And talk about maintenance. Señorita, you are looking at an entirely self-supporting machine. You're never going to find our Johnny Pachuco model on the relief rolls. No, sir, this model knows how to liberate.

SECRETARY: Liberate?

SANCHO: He steals. (*Snap.* JOHNNY *rushes to* SECRETARY *and steals her purse.*)

JOHNNY: ¡Dame esa bolsa, vieja! (*He grabs the purse and runs. Snap by* SANCHO, *he stops.* SECRETARY *runs after* JOHNNY *and grabs purse away from him, kicking him as she goes.*)

SECRETARY: No, no, no! We can't have any more thieves in the State Administration. Put him back.

SANCHO: Okay, we still got other models. Come on, Johnny, we'll sell you to some old lady. (SANCHO *takes* JOHNNY *back to his place.*)

SECRETARY: Mr. Sancho, I don't think you quite understand what we need. What we need is something that will attract the women voters. Something more traditional, more romantic.

SANCHO: Ah, a lover. (*He smiles meaningfully.*) Step right over here, señorita. Introducing our standard Revolucionario and/or Early California Bandit type. As you can see, he is well-built, sturdy, durable. This is the International Harvester of Mexicans.

SECRETARY: What does he do?

SANCHO: You name it, he does it. He rides horses, stays in the mountains, crosses deserts, plains, rivers, leads revolutions, follows revolutions, kills, can be killed, serves as a martyr, hero, movie star. Did I say movie star? Did you ever see *Viva Zapata? Viva Villa, Villa Rides, Pancho Villa Returns, Pancho Villa Goes Back, Pancho Villa Meets Abbott and Costello?*

SECRETARY: I've never seen any of those.

SANCHO: Well, he was in all of them. Listen to this. (*Snap.*)

REVOLUCIONARIO: (*Scream.*) ¡Viva Villaaaaa!

SECRETARY: That's awfully loud.

SANCHO: He has a volume control. (*He adjusts volume. Snap.*)

REVOLUCIONARIO: (*Mousey voice.*) Viva Villa.

SECRETARY: That's better.

SANCHO: And even if you didn't see him in the movies, perhaps you saw him on TV. He makes commercials. (*Snap.*)

REVOLUCIONARIO: Is there a Frito Bandito in your house?

SECRETARY: Oh yes, I've seen that one!

SANCHO: Another feature about this one is that he is economical. He runs on raw horsemeat and tequila!

SECRETARY: Isn't that rather savage?

SANCHO: Al contrario, it makes him a lover. (*Snap.*)

REVOLUCIONARIO: (*To* SECRETARY.) Ay, mamasota, cochota, ven pa 'ca! (*He grabs* SECRETARY *and folds her back, Latin-lover style.*)

SANCHO: (*Snap.* REVOLUCIONARIO *goes back upright.*) Now wasn't that nice?

SECRETARY: Well, it was rather nice.

SANCHO: And finally, there is one outstanding feature about this model I know the ladies are going to love: he's a genuine antique! He was made in Mexico in 1910!

SECRETARY: Made in Mexico?

SANCHO: That's right. Once in Tijuana, twice in Guadalajara, three times in Cuernavaca.

SECRETARY: Mr. Sancho, I thought he was an American product.

SANCHO: No, but . . .

SECRETARY: No, I'm sorry. We can't buy anything but American made products. He just won't do.

SANCHO: But he's an antique!

SECRETARY: I don't care. You still don't understand what we need. It's true we need Mexican models, such as these, but it's more important that he be American.

SANCHO: American?

SECRETARY: That's right, and judging from what you've shown me, I don't think you have what we want. Well, my lunch hour's almost over, I better . . .

SANCHO: Wait a minute! Mexican but American?

SECRETARY: That's correct.

SANCHO: Mexican but . . . (*A sudden flash.*) American! Yeah, I think we've got exactly what you want. He just came in today! Give me a minute. (*He exits. Talks from backstage.*) Here he is in the shop. Let me just get some papers off. There. Introducing our new 1970 Mexican-American! Ta-ra-ra-raaaa! (SANCHO *brings out the* MEXICAN-AMERICAN *model, a clean-shaven middle class type in a business suit, with glasses.*)

SECRETARY: (*Impressed.*) Where have you been hiding this one?

SANCHO: He just came in this morning. Ain't he a beauty? Feast you eyes on him! Sturdy U.S. Steel frame, streamlined, modern. As a matter of fact, he is built exactly like our Anglo models, except that he comes in a variety of darker shades: naugahide, leather or leatherette.

SECRETARY: Naugahide.

SANCHO: Well, we'll just write that down. Yes, señorita, this model represents the apex of American engineering! He is bilingual, college educated, ambitious! Say the word "acculturate" and he accelerates. He is intelligent, well-mannered, clean. Did I say clean? (*Snap.* MEXICAN-AMERICAN *raises his arm.*) Smell.

SECRETARY: (*Smells.*) Old Sobaco, my favorite.

SANCHO: (*Snap.* MEXICAN-AMERICAN *turns toward* SANCHO.) Eric? (*To* SECRETARY.) We call him Eric García. (*To* ERIC.) I want you to meet Miss JIM-enez, Eric.

MEXICAN-AMERICAN: Miss JIM-enez, I am delighted to make your acquaintance. (*He kisses her hand.*)

SECRETARY: Oh, my, how charming!

SANCHO: Did you feel the suction? He has seven especially engineered suction cups right behind his lips. He's a charmer all right!

SECRETARY: How about boards, does he function on boards?

SANCHO: You name them, he is on them. Parole boards, draft boards, school boards, taco quality control boards, surf boards, two by fours.

SECRETARY: Does he function in politics?

SANCHO: Señorita, you are looking at a political machine. Have you ever heard of the OEO, EOC, COD, WAR ON POVERTY? That's our model! Not only that, he makes political speeches.

SECRETARY: May I hear one?

SANCHO: With pleasure. (*Snap.*) Eric, give us a speech.

MEXICAN-AMERICAN: Mr. Congressman, Mr. Chairman, members of the board, honored guests, ladies and gentlemen. (SANCHO *and* SECRETARY *applaud.*) Please, please. I come before you as a Mexican-American to tell you about the problems of the Mexican. The problems of the Mexican stem from one thing and one thing only: he's stupid. He's uneducated. He needs to stay in school. He needs to be ambitious, foward-looking, harder-working. He needs to think American, American, American, American, American! God bless America! God bless America! God bless America! (*He goes out of control.* SANCHO *snaps frantically and the* MEXICAN-AMERICAN *finally slumps forward, bending at the waist.*)

SECRETARY: Oh my, he's patriotic too!

SANCHO: Sí, señorita, he loves his country. Let me just make a little adjustment here. (*Stands* MEXICAN-AMERICAN *up.*)

SECRETARY: What about upkeep? Is he economical?

SANCHO: Well, no, I won't lie to you. The Mexican-American costs a little bit more, but you get what you pay for. He's worth every extra cent. You can keep him running on dry Martinis, Langendorf bread . . .

SECRETARY: Apple pie?

SANCHO: Only Mom's. Of course, he's also programmed to eat Mexican food at ceremonial functions, but I must warn you, an overdose of beans will plug up his exhaust.

SECRETARY: Fine! There's just one more question. How much do you want for him?

SANCHO: Well, I tell you what I'm gonna do. Today and today only, because you've been so sweet, I'm gona let you steal this model from me! I'm gonna let you drive him off the lot for the simple price of, let's see, taxes and license included, $15,000.

SECRETARY: Fifteen thousand dollars? For a Mexican!!!!

SANCHO: Mexican? What are you talking about? This is a Mexican-American! We had to melt down two pachucos, a farmworker and three gabachos to make this model! You want quality, but you gotta pay for it! This is no cheap run-about. He's got class!

SECRETARY: Okay, I'll take him.

SANCHO: You will?

SECRETARY: Here's your money.

SANCHO: You mind if I count it?

SECRETARY: Go right ahead.

SANCHO: Well, you'll get your pink slip in the mail. Oh, do you want me to wrap him up for you? We have a box in the back.

SECRETARY: No, thank you. The Governor is having a luncheon this afternoon, and we need a brown face in the crowd. How do I drive him?

SANCHO: Just snap your fingers. He'll do anything you want. (SECRETARY *snaps.* MEXICAN-AMERICAN *steps forward.*)

MEXICAN-AMERICAN: ¡Raza querida, vamos levantando armas para liberarnos de estos desgraciados gabachos que nos explotan! Vamos . . .

SECRETARY: What did he say?

SANCHO: Something about taking up arms, killing white people, etc.

SECRETARY: But he's not supposed to say that!

SANCHO: Look, lady, don't blame me for bugs from the factory. He's your Mexican-American, you bought him, now drive him off the lot!

SECRETARY: But he's broken!

SANCHO: Try snapping another finger. (SECRETARY *snaps.* MEXICAN-AMERICAN *comes to life again.*)

MEXICAN-AMERICAN: Esta gran humanidad ha dicho basta! ¡Y se ha puesto en marcha! ¡Basta! ¡Basta! ¡Viva la raza! ¡Viva la causa! ¡Viva la huelga! ¡Vivan los brown berets! ¡Vivan los estudiantes! ¡Chicano power! (*The* MEXICAN-AMERICAN *turns toward the* SECRETARY, *who gasps and backs up. He keeps turning toward the* PACHUCO, FARMWORKER *and* REVOLUCIONARIO, *snapping his fingers and turning each of them on, one by one.*)

PACHUCO: (*Snap. To* SECRETARY.) I'm going to get you, baby! ¡Viva la raza!

FARMWORKER: (*Snap. to* SECRETARY.) ¡Viva la huelga! ¡Viva la ¡huelga! ¡Viva la huelga!

REVOLUCIONARIO: (*Snap. To* SECRETARY.) ¡Viva la revolución! (*The three models join together and advance toward the* SECRETARY, *who backs up and runs out of the shop screaming.* SANCHO *is at the other end of the shop holding his money in his hand. All freeze. After a few seconds of silence, the* PACHUCO *moves and stretches, shaking his arms and loosening up. The* FARMWORKER *and* REVOLUCIONARIO *do the same.* SANCHO *stays where he is, frozen to his spot.*)

JOHNNY: Man, that was a long one, ese. (*Others agree with him.*)

FARMWORKER: How did we do?

JOHNNY: Pretty good, look at all that lana, man! (*He goes over to* SANCHO *and removes the money from his hand.* SANCHO *stays where he is.*)

REVOLUCIONARIO: En la madre, look at all the money.

JOHNNY: We keep this up, we're going to be rich.

FARMWORKER: They think we're machines.

REVOLUCIONARIO: Burros.

JOHNNY: Puppets.

MEXICAN-AMERICAN: The only thing I don't like is how come I always get to play the goddamn Mexican-American?

JOHNNY: That's what you get for finishing high school.

FARMWORKER: How about our wages, ese?

JOHNNY: Here it comes right now. $3,000 for you, $3,000 for you, $3,000 for you and $3,000 for me. The rest we put back into the business.

MEXICAN-AMERICAN: Too much, man. Heh, where you vatos going tonight?

FARMWORKER: I'm going over to Concha's. There's a party.

JOHNNY: Wait a minute, vatos. What about our salesman? I think he needs an oil job.

REVOLUCIONARIO: Leave him to me. (*The* PACHUCO, FARMWORKER *and* MEXICAN-AMERICAN *exit, talking loudly about their plans for the night. The* REVOLUCIONARIO *goes over to* SANCHO, *removes his derby hat and cigar, lifts him up and throws him over his shoulder.* SANCHO *hangs loose, lifeless. To audience.*) He's the best model we got! ¡Ajúa! (*Exit.*)

Talking about the Text

1. Why does Miss Jimenez reject the Farmworker model? The Pachuco? The Revolucionario? The Mexican American?

2. What is the effect of the play's use of Spanish on the audience or reader? How much does it matter whether you know Spanish or not? Why does Valdez use so much Spanish in his play? What does this practice achieve?

3. At what point do you understand the elements of farce present in the play? When do these elements take over?

Writing about the Text

1. What critique of American society and culture does *Los Vendidos* suggest? In an essay, compare the critiques found in *Los Vendidos* with the social critiques in Arthur Miller's *Death of a Salesman* (p. 1671) or in Ibsen's *A Doll House* (see p. 1562). An exploration of the roles assigned to people by social forces would be one place to start.

2. Using specific examples from the text, assess *Los Vendidos* as an example of populist theater: a theatrical forum that deliberately resists the use of the language and situations of "high" society and tries to reach "the people." How does this approach affect the way in which we see the characters and interpret what happens?

Linking the Text to Other Texts

1. Compare the types Valdez employs with the types in Lady Gregory's *Spreading the News*. Which play is more dependent on types?

2. Examine the characters in in connection with some Mexican or Latino characters you are familiar with from film or television. Which seem more deeply felt? Why?

3. Compare the use of Spanish in *Los Vendidos* with the use of non-English words, phrases, and sentences in other literary works, for example, Junot Díaz's "Fiesta, 1980" (see p. 479) and Pat Mora's "Immigrants" (see p. 441).

4. How does Valdez's depiction of Latino characters compare to Lady Gregory's portrayal of the Irish in *Spreading the News* (see p. 1183)? Do the two plays tread on some of the same territory, and if so, how? Where do their approaches to characterization diverge?

LITERARY LOCALE

El Teatro Campesino in California. In 2005 Luis Valdez's El Teatro Campesino celebrated forty years of creating Latino theater in California—first atop flatbed trucks and finally in its permanent home in the town of San Juan Bautista. While working side by side with union leader Cesar Chavez in support of striking grape workers in 1965, Valdez decided that theater was yet another tool Chicano farmworkers could use to empower themselves. Valdez created El Teatro Campesino (or the Farmworkers' Theater) to educate Latinos about the plight of farmworkers and encourage more people to join the union. Although Valdez's tactics might have seemed unconventional to many Americans, he was working in a long tradition of international movements that have used theater to inspire social change.

In a 1981 interview with Carl Heyward, Luis Valdez described how El Teatro Campesino developed and how it changed him as an artist:

> I had an image in mind, when I went to Vallejo, that I wanted to work with people. I had to introduce basic concepts. I was working with farmers, some of whom could not read scripts, so we had to use improvisation, which made presentations very lively. We had a willing

audience, a message, and that was the raw material, to better structure the drama, improve the acting and get a better organizational grasp of our own reality so that there was a roof over our heads. I have developed into a playwright and director through the work of El Teatro. I was its first student, and to teach is to learn. In the old days, we rehearsed on the run and performed on the picket line. This was in the middle of the great strike. While we had the strength and urgency of the struggle, our artistry had to sustain our politics. Ultimately it is artistry that makes the point and cuts across the barriers to understanding. There is a certain quality of excellence that we have discovered over the years, that a lot of people assumed that we didn't have to have, you know? They assumed that we could be rough and untutored and primitive, and still maintain our charm.

To read more from Heyward's interview with Luis Valdez, go to *http://www. communityarts.net/readingroom/archivefiles/2002/09/el_teatro_campe.php.*

Starting Points for Further Research: Luis Valdez

- **Edition:** Luis Valdez. *Early Works: Actos, Bernabe, and Pensamiento Serpentino.* Ed. Pauline Rodriguez Howard. Houston: Arte Publico Press, 1990.
- **Article/Interview:** Dieter Herms. "Luis Valdez, Chicano Dramatist: An Introduction and an Interview." *Essays on Contemporary American Drama.* Ed. Hedwig Bock and Albert Wertheim. Munich: Hueber, 1981. 257–78.
- **Critical Essays:** Harry J. Elam. *Taking It to the Streets: The Social Protest Theater of Luis Valdez and Amiri Baraka.* Ann Arbor: University of Michigan Press, 1997.

  Carlota Cardenas de-Dwyer. "The Development of Chicano Drama and Luis Valdez's Actos." *Modern Chicano Writers: A Collection of Critical Essays.* Ed. Joseph Sommers and Frausto Ybarra. Englewood Cliffs, N.J.: Prentice-Hall, 1979. 160–66.

PHILIP KAN GOTANDA 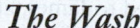 (B. 1951)

The Wash (1987)

Philip Kan Gotanda, a third-generation Japanese American who currently lives in San Francisco, is one of the most prominent writers and performers in the Asian American theater movement. He trained as a lawyer and as a potter but has won fame as a playwright. Certainly he is the best-known Japanese American dramatist and the first to come to the attention of mainstream America. His plays include The Wash *(1987), reprinted here,* Ballad of Yachiyo *(1996),* Yankee Dawg You Die *(1998), and* Sisters Matsumoto *(1999). His book* No More Cherry Blossoms: Sisters Matsumoto and Other Plays *(2005) showcases four of his recent dramatic works. Many of Gotanda's plays deal with the common theme of duality and the specific conflicts involved in being both American and Japanese (and therefore subject to discrimination and misunderstanding). Similar themes crop up in the three independent films he has made,* The Kiss, Drinking Tea, *and* Life Tastes Good, *all of which have appeared at the Sundance Film Festival. His many awards include a Guggenheim fellowship and the Lila Wallace Readers Digest Award.*

In The Wash, one of the main characters, Masi, struggles between her desire to be an ideal "Japanese" wife (even after she has left her husband she continues to do his wash and bring him groceries) and her determination—perhaps a culturally American trait?—to reject her husband's tyranny over her and grasp happiness when it comes her way. That tyrannical husband, Nobu, is a surprisingly sympathetic character, in part because we sense that his rigidity, combativeness, frustration, and inability to respond sexually come from the trauma of his experience in the World War II Japanese resettlement. To our satisfaction, Nobu changes during the course of the play—not all at once and not completely, but nevertheless perceptibly.

The Wash is one of Gotanda's more realistic plays. His short film The Kiss (1992) proceeds almost entirely without dialogue. In other plays, he experiments more with music and dance, drawing on his background as a musician and songwriter. Even in The Wash, music is important; Nobu shows a tender side when he sings a Japanese lullaby, both in a nightclub and to his mixed-race grandchild, whom he has resisted acknowledging. Gotanda's engagement with music shows up even more in the 1988 film version of the play. The Wash also features a typical Gotanda preoccupation with the grace and serenity involved with fishing. (Another of his plays is Song of a Nisei Fisherman.) One of the appeals of Masi's new lover is that he buys her a fishing rod and takes her fishing. Her husband, Nobu, also a fisherman, had always left his wife home.

The Wash

Characters

NOBU MATSUMOTO, Nisei (second generation Japanese American). Sixty-eight years old. Retired produce man. Separated from wife, MASI. Lives alone in the family house

MASI MATSUMOTO, Nisei. Sixty-seven years old. Left NOBU. Does housework for a living. Lives in a small apartment by herself

KIYOKO HASEGAWA, in her mid-fifties. Originally from Japan. Previously married to an American soldier, now a widow. Seeing NOBU. Owns and runs a small Japanese restaurant

SADAO NAKASATO, Nisei. Sixty-five years old. Widower. Seeing MASI. Retired pharmacist

MARSHA MATSUMOTO, Sansei (third generation Japanese American). Thirty-three years old. Single. Older daughter of NOBU and MASI. Works as a dental hygienist in a nearby big city

JUDY ADAMS, Sansei. Twenty-nine years old. Married to James, and has a baby. Younger daughter of NOBU and MASI. Fifth-grade teacher. Not working at present

TIMOTHY, JUDY's baby

CHIYO FROELICH, originally from Japan, but has lived most of her adult life in the U.S. Late forties. Divorced. Friend of KIYOKO. Owns and runs small beauty salon next door to KIYOKO's restaurant

CURLEY SAKATA, Hawaiian Nisei in his mid-fifties. Speaks with a thick pidgin that comes and goes at his convenience. Works as the cook at KIYOKO's restaurant

PLACE

Center stage is NOBU's place, the old family home. Stage right is KIYOKO's restaurant. Stage left is MASI's small apartment. The clothesline is in the upstage area. The downstage area is used to play several scenes that take place elsewhere.

The set should be realistic but elemental, allowing for an underlying abstract feeling. NOBU's place is the most complete, with MASI's and KIYOKO's places more minimal.

TIME

The play takes place in the present over a period of six months—July to January. Clothing that reflects the seasonal changes might assist in showing the passage of time.

ACT ONE, SCENE ONE

NOBU *reaches into the refrigerator and pulls out a bowl of cold rice, covered over in cellophane, and a small bottle of French's mustard. He uncovers the rice, scoops some of it into a rice bowl using his chopsticks, pours hot tea over it. The tea starts to spill, and he quickly bends down and slurps up the excess. He opens the mustard and, using his chopsticks again, shovels a healthy portion of mustard onto his hot dogs. Licks the mustard off his chopsticks. Then he carefully makes his way back to the couch with the plate of hot dogs and bowl of rice. Sets the food down on the coffee table and begins to eat while working on the kite and watching television.*

While he is eating, MASI *enters through the side door with two large brown paper bags. She's struggling to open and close the door with both hands so full.* NOBU *turns around and notices her but gives no greeting and makes no effort to help her. Instead, goes back to eating, working on the kite, and watching TV. She is not upset by his actions. She has no expectation of assistance from him. Business as usual.* MASI *sets both bags on the kitchen table and catches her breath. She proceeds to put vegetables from one of the bags into the refrigerator. Tomatoes and Japanese eggplant.*

MASI (*putting vegetables into refrigerator*): If you have any more dirty clothes I can take them now. Nobu? Is this everything?

NOBU (*not turning, eating*): Want some hot dog?

MASI: No, I ate before. Got these from Mr. Rossi. The tomatoes are soft, so eat them right away. (*Folds bag and puts it into drawer. She knows this place well. Walks over and checks his shirt collar from behind.*) No more clothes?

NOBU (*brushing her hand away*): No, already. (MASI *goes over to the other bag and begins unpacking the freshly washed clothes in neat piles on the kitchen table.*)

MASI (*unpacking*): I just finished cleaning Dr. Harrison's place. You should see the bathrooms. If you see the family walk down the street, they look so clean and neat. But the toilets, kitanai.[1]

(*Finished unpacking,* MASI *takes a cup out of the rack and pours herself a cup of tea. She walks over to the couch and sits down next to* NOBU *and watches TV. She takes a sip of tea and makes a face.* NOBU *notices.*)

---

[1]Dirty.

NOBU: Hot-dog water.

(MASI *decides not to drink. She looks at the unfinished kite frame.*)

MASI: You gonna fly this one? (*Picking up the kite*) Nobu, why don't you at least try a different design this . . .

NOBU: My old man did it this way. (*Mutters*) Jesus Christ . . .

MASI (*gathering clothes*): Have you talked to the kids? (*No response*) Marsha said she stopped by. (*Beat*) You know if you don't see Judy's baby soon he's going to be all grown up. Nobu?

NOBU: No.

(MASI *gives up trying to talk to him at all.*)

MASI: No more dirty clothes, Nobu?

(NOBU *shakes his head without turning away from the TV.*)

MASI: All right, then I'm going.

(MASI *leaves with the bag of old clothes.* NOBU *continues to watch TV for a few moments. Then, turns and stares at the door. Dim to half, with the TV light illuminating* NOBU. MARSHA *lit in pool of light looking towards* NOBU.)

MARSHA: Dad?

(NOBU *turns to look at* MARSHA *momentarily, then back to the television.* JUDY *is lit in a pool of light, holding* TIMOTHY.)

JUDY: Mom?

(MASI *moves away.* MASI *turns to look at* JUDY *momentarily, then exits.* MARSHA *and* JUDY *dim to darkness.* NOBU *and* MASI *dim to darkness. We hear Japanese restaurant Muzak.*)

[END OF SCENE]

SCENE TWO

KIYOKO's *restaurant. Afternoon, next day. Lights come up.*

KIYOKO *struggling to move* CHIYO's *Karaoke[2] equipment out of the way.*

KIYOKO (*calling*): Curley! Curley! Can you help me with this!

(CURLEY SAKATA *enters, wiping face with towel and holding beer. Speaks in a Hawaiian pidgin. He can lose it if he wants to.*)

CURLEY: Easy, easy, no go break da speaker. Bumbai[3] Curley's sweet sounds no can come out. (*Helping her move the equipment*)

KIYOKO (*struggling*): Why can't Chiyo keep this at her place?

CURLEY: Hey, cannot sing Karaoke at a beauty shop. Has to be nightclub place like dis.

---

[2]Japanese singing accompaniment machine.
[3]Hawaiian for "by and by."

KIYOKO: This is a restaurant . . .

(*As they finish moving the equipment,* KIYOKO *notices* CURLEY's *beer. Stares at him.*)

CURLEY (*feigning innocence*): What'sa matta?
KIYOKO: Curley.
CURLEY: It makes my cooking mo' betta.

(KIYOKO *continues to stare.*)

CURLEY: I'm thirsty, I wanted a beer.
KIYOKO (*taking his beer*): No more drinking on the job, I told you.
CURLEY: But it makes my cooking mo' betta. If I feel betta, my cooking mo' betta. No bull lie yo.
KIYOKO (*scooting* CURLEY *back to the kitchen*): Your face turns red like a tomato and everything tastes like shoyu.[4]
CURLEY (*exiting into the back, scratching his behind*): This place no fun no mo'.
KIYOKO: And don't scratch your oshiri,[5] you're the cook, remember?

(*As* KIYOKO *goes back to wiping,* NOBU *enters and walks up to* KIYOKO. *She notices.*)

KIYOKO: Irasshaii, welcome.
NOBU (*holds out his hand to her*): Excuse me. Here.

(KIYOKO *doesn't know what's going on.* NOBU *takes* KIYOKO's *hand and gives her money.*)

NOBU: Here, here, you gave me too much. You gave me too much change. When I paid my bill. I was emptying out my pockets at my house when I noticed.
KIYOKO (*looking at the money*): Twenty-five cents?
NOBU (*nodding*): Un-huh. It cost six seventy-five, I gave you seven bucks, and you gave me back fifty cents. So . . .

(NOBU *nods toward the money. He's not sure what to do next. Awkward beat. Then turns to leave.*)

KIYOKO: Wait, wait.

(NOBU *stops. Beat. For a moment* KIYOKO *doesn't know what to say.*)

KIYOKO: You walked all the way back here to give me twenty-five cents?
NOBU: You gave me too much. So I . . .

(KIYOKO *doesn't know what to say.*)

NOBU: All right then.

(NOBU *turns to leave again.*)

KIYOKO: No, wait, wait. Sit, sit, please sit. I'll get you some tea.

---

[4]Soy sauce.
[5]Backside.

(KIYOKO *guides him to a seat and goes to get his tea.* CURLEY *has been watching the action. Sipping on a new beer.*)

CURLEY: Eh, Mr. Abe Lincoln? You come in a lot, huh. For lunch.

NOBU: Almost every day.

CURLEY (*approaching*): And dat's your seat, huh? All da time you gotta sit in dat same seat. Last week Mr. Koyama was sitting dere—I saw you come in—you left and came back later when dat seat was open. What'sa matta, your butt got a magnet for dat seat?

KIYOKO (*bringing tea, shooing* CURLEY *away*): Curley. Go, go . . .

CURLEY (*moving away, to* NOBU): And you always order da same thing.

NOBU: The combo plate.

KIYOKO: And you like the eggplant pickle.

NOBU: Un-huh.

KIYOKO: Kagoshima style.

NOBU: Kagoshima ka? My family's from there.

KIYOKO: Ara, Kagoshima? Honto, yo?[6] Doko kara, where?

NOBU: The, uh, southern part.

KIYOKO: Ahhh. Watashi no, north part, Yokokawa. (*Awkward beat. Motioning to his tea.*) Dozo.[7] (NOBU *sips the tea.*)

KIYOKO: What is your name?

NOBU (*Getting up*): Nobu. Nobu Matsumoto.

KIYOKO: Ah, Matsumoto-san. Kiyoko. Kiyoko Hasegawa. Dozo yoroshiku?[8]

(*As* NOBU *starts to bow awkwardly,* KIYOKO *extends her hand to shake. He's caught off guard and both are slightly embarrassed.* NOBU *recovers and reaches out to shake* KIYOKO's *hand.* CURLEY *watches, amused. Dim to darkness.*)

[END OF SCENE]

SCENE THREE

MASI's *place. Three weeks later. Small apartment with bedroom downstage from main room.* SADAO *is lit seated on sofa in a pool of light.* MASI *is in half-light at counter fixing coffee.*

SADAO: We were all sitting around in somebody's living room, when someone said, "How come you still wear your wedding ring?" They weren't being mean. That's why we were there. To ask those kinds of things. I didn't know what to say. Speechless. Then someone else said, "Sadao, you always complain about not meeting people, not being able to start a new life—how come you still wear your ring?" I began to cry. Like a little boy. I remember thinking, "How strange. I am crying in front of all these people that I don't know. And yet I feel no shame." The room was so still. All you could hear was my crying. Then I heard a tapping sound. I looked up and noticed a woman sitting across from me, slapping the sandals she was wearing against

---

[6]From Kagoshima? Really?

[7]Please.

[8]How do you do?

the bottom of her feet. Tap, tap, tap . . . I said I didn't know why. It just never crossed my mind to take it off. "Why should I take the ring off?" Then one of the widows, the one who formed the group, said, "Because you're not married anymore."

(*Lights come up on the rest of the apartment area.* MASI *is at the small kitchen counter fixing two cups of Sanka coffee. She wasn't quite prepared for him sharing such personal details of his life and is a bit unsure how to respond.* SADAO *in turn fears he may have gotten a bit carried away.*)

MASI (*bringing coffee over*): Cream? It's nondairy creamer. (SADAO *shakes head.*)
MASI: If you want tea?
SADAO: No, this is fine. I ran on a bit, didn't I?
MASI: No, no, it's all right. (*Pause*) It's just Sanka.
SADAO: Good. Otherwise the caffeine keeps me up all night. Have you tried de-caffeinated coffee?

(MASI *motions to the Sanka, unsure of what he means.*)

SADAO: No, the bean. They actually make a decaffeinated bean.
MASI: No, we never did anything like that. Just instant. Yuban makes a good in-stant coffee. That's what I usually drink, but I don't have any since I moved over here.
SADAO: No, I've never tried it.
MASI: I'll have to get some next time I go shopping.
SADAO: They have this process they use. On the bean. I mean they don't grow a decaffeinated bean. I don't know what's worse. The caffeine in it or the chemicals they use to get the caffeine out. (*Laughing at his own joke. Gathering momentum.*) I have a little grinder. Braun? You know a Braun?

(MASI *doesn't know what it is. Awkward pause.*)

MASI: We never did anything like that. We just drink instant.
SADAO: I like Sanka. I have to drink it all the time. Doctor's orders. (*Imitating*) "If you drink coffee, Sadao, drink Sanka!" (*Laughs valiantly at his attempt at humor.* MASI *stares at her cup.* SADAO *notices and offers a feeble explanation.*) Blood pressure . . .

(*They both drink in silence. Suddenly,* SADAO *remembers something.*)

SADAO: Oh. I forgot. (SADAO *reaches down and picks up a fishing pole and reel wrapped up like presents.*)
MASI (*surprised*): Sadao, what's this?

(SADAO *holds out pole.*)

MASI: I can't.

(NOBU *lit in half-light at his place watching TV. His face illuminated by the flickering screen's glow.*)

SADAO: No, no, it's for you.
MASI: But Sadao . . .

SADAO: No, no, it's for *you.*

MASI (*one hand on it*): Sadao, you shouldn't have.

SADAO: Go 'head. Open it up.

MASI (*takes it and begins unwrapping it*): No, I can't accept this. I don't have anything for you.

> (MASI *unwraps pole, which is broken down into pieces.* SADAO *sets reel on table and takes pole from* MASI *and proceeds to put it together.*)

SADAO: See, it goes like this. And then you're all set to catch fish. (*Hands it back to* MASI) I told you I was going to take you. Now you can't refuse.

MASI: Yeah, but . . .

SADAO: Thought I was kidding, huh?

MASI: But this is so expensive. I know how much these things cost, 'cause of Nobu. I don't know anything about fishing. He's the fisherman. I just pack the lunch and off he goes.

SADAO: Well, this time you're going and it's lots of fun. Economical, too. You get to eat what you catch.

MASI: But you have to do all that walking.

SADAO: No, who said that? We sit on the bank and fish from there. We'll pack a good lunch—I'll make it—you bring the cards so we can play blackjack. We have to practice.

MASI: I don't play.

SADAO: That's why we have to practice, so we can go to Tahoe. If there's a good game on we'll have to watch it. I'll bring my portable TV. I love the Giants.

MASI: What about fishing?

SADAO: Only if we have time. See, this is how you cast out. (*Demonstrating*) You hook your index finger around the line here. Turn the bail and . . . (*Casts.*)

> (NOBU, *still lit in half-light, gets up to phone* MASI. *Phone rings.* MASI *goes over and answers it. It's* NOBU. *Slowly lights dim on* SADAO *and rest of apartment.* MASI *and* NOBU *are lit.*)

MASI: Hello.

NOBU (*lit in small pool of light*): You coming to pick up the clothes?

MASI: Nobu? I was just there. You mean next week? Don't worry, I'll be there. I do it every week, don't I? Nobu?

NOBU: I'm not worried. You all right?

MASI: Yes, I'm all right. Did you want something? (*No response*) I got more vegetables. Do you need some more?

NOBU: No. (*Pause*) Can you bring more eggplant?

MASI: I don't have any more.

NOBU: All right then.

MASI: I'll ask Mr. Rossi. He can always get lots more. (*Pause*) Nobu, I have to go now.

NOBU: I went fishing so I got a lot of dirty clothes.

MASI: All right. Don't worry, I'll be by.

NOBU: I'm not worried.

MASI: Bye.

NOBU: Bye.

(Dim to darkness.)
[END OF SCENE]

SCENE FOUR

Poker game. CURLEY *is setting up Karaoke machine.* CHIYO *and* KIYOKO *are at the table.* CHIYO *is dealing out cards. Wears a poker visor. They are playing five-card stud, one card down and one up.*

CHIYO: Kiyoko, I never said I didn't like him.
CURLEY *(fiddling with the machine)*: Test, test.
KIYOKO: Curley, you in this game or not?
CURLEY *(singing into microphone)*: "Tiny bubbles . . ."
CHIYO: I just don't think he's right for you, that's all. He's too old.
KIYOKO: Curley, we're waiting.
CURLEY: Okay, okay . . .
CHIYO: Dealer's high, I bet a nickel.
KIYOKO: I see you.

*(*CURLEY *moves to table, guzzling a beer and carrying a six-pack in his other hand. They both notice* CURLEY *chugging down the rest of his beer, making loud gurgling sounds.* CURLEY *notices them staring.)*

CURLEY: You gotta drink beer when you're playing poker or you aren't playing poker. You're just playing cards. I don't like cards. Hate cards. *(Holds up another beer)* I *love* poker.
KIYOKO *(to* CURLEY*)*: Ante, ante . . .
CHIYO: Go dancing with Eddie and me. Yeah come, come . . .
KIYOKO: Chiyo, how can I do that? Who's gonna run this place, huh?
CHIYO: Come on, Kiyoko, you work too hard.
KIYOKO: The refrigeration unit's breaking down, Mr. Sato says we can't fix it anymore . . .
CHIYO: Kiyoko, I met one of Eddie's friends, Ray Jensen. He's good-looking, yo. Tall, lotsa fun to be with . . .
KIYOKO: Chiyo, Chiyo, I'm too busy. I'm not looking for that kind of thing anymore.
CHIYO: What do you mean, "that kind of thing"?
KIYOKO: That kind of thing, thinking about men and getting all . . .
CURLEY: I like it when da wahinis talk dirt.

*(*KIYOKO *and* CHIYO *shoot* CURLEY *a dirty look.)*

CURLEY: Geez, don't lose your coconut.
KIYOKO: I like Nobu, he's a nice man, Chiyo. He comes in here, we sit down and eat together and then he goes home.
    I like that.
CHIYO *(to* KIYOKO*)*: Okay, okay. Two sixes, a pair of saxophones. *(To* CURLEY*)* A three of diamonds gives you . . . nothing. *(To self)* Eight of puppy toes to the dealer, working on a possible club flush. *(To* KIYOKO*)* Pair of saxes high. He's married, Kiyoko.
KIYOKO: Ten cents. They're separated.

CHIYO: But did he tell you? Huh? I call.

KIYOKO: Curley, you in or not?

CURLEY: Don't rush me, don't rush me.

CHIYO: No, you had to hear it from me. Eighty-year-old Mrs. Nakamura with the blue hair comes to my beauty shop, "I want my perm and a blue rinse," yak-yakking away. I decide to do some snooping for my good friend. "Nakamura-san? Oh, Nakamura-san? You know this Nobu guy?"

CURLEY: Old magnet butt?

CHIYO: I know his kind, Kiyoko, old Japanese-type guys. She left him, he can't get over that. He's still thinking about her. He only wants you for one thing—your tempura. Yeah. He's over here every day, desho?[9] You're feeding him. He's eating up all your profits.

KIYOKO: Chiyo.

CHIYO (*to* KIYOKO): Nine of spades. No help there. (*To* CURLEY) A trois. Oh, a pair of threes. (*To self*) And for the dealer . . . another club. Flush looking very possible. (*To* KIYOKO) Pair of saxes still high.

KIYOKO: Check.

CHIYO: Check. He checks, too.

CURLEY: I'm thinking, I'm thinking . . .

CHIYO: I try looking out for you and what do you do? You get mad at me.

KIYOKO: Nobu is an honest man. That's all I know. One time I gave him too much change, he walked all the way . . .

CURLEY (*overlapping, mimicking Kiyoko*): . . . He walked all the way back to return it. Twenty-five cents.

CHIYO (*overlapping* CURLEY, *mimicking* KIYOKO, *too*): . . . to return it. Twenty-five cents.

> (CURLEY *and* CHIYO *laugh.*)

CHIYO: Good investment. He gets a $4.50 combo plate free now. Last card, down and dirty.

> (CHIYO *starts dealing as she and* CURLEY *calm down.*)

KIYOKO: Look, he's just a friend. That's all he is. I don't see why you're all making such a fuss.

CHIYO (*showing her card*): Another puppy toes—flush, flush, flush.

KIYOKO: Fifty cents.

CURLEY (*surprised*): Fifty cents.

CHIYO (*confidently*): I see you and I bump you one dollar.

CURLEY (*in disbelief*): One dollar . . .

KIYOKO (*eyes* CHIYO's *cards and tries to decide whether to stay in or not*): I call you.

CHIYO: You got the three-of-a-kind?

KIYOKO: Pair of sixes, that's all. You got the flush?

CHIYO: Pair of eights! Hah!

> (CHIYO's *about to grab the pot when* CURLEY *puts down his cards.*)

CURLEY: Excusez-moi's, but I got three trois's.

CHIYO: Curley . . .

---

[9]Isn't he?

KIYOKO: Oh, Curley . . .

CURLEY (*holding up beer*): Hate cards. *Love* poker.

> (*Dim to darkness.*)
>> [END OF SCENE]

SCENE FIVE

> NOBU's *place.* MARSHA's *dinner party scene.* MARSHA *busy at stove.*
> NOBU *seated in his chair.*

NOBU: What do you mean, "be nice to Mama"?

MARSHA: All I'm saying is just try to be nice to her when she gets here. Say
something nice about the way she looks or about the way she dresses . . .

NOBU: I'm always nice to Mama. I'm always good to her.

MARSHA (*moving over to* NOBU *and adjusting his clothes*): Dad, Dad, I just want us
to have a good time tonight, okay? All of us, together. And besides, I made
you your favorite. (MARSHA *moves back to stove.*)

NOBU: Yeah, but how come Mama has to live over there, huh? She should be at
home here. How come Mama has to live way in the hell over there?

> (MASI *enters carrying a small paper bag.*)

MARSHA: Hi, Mom. (*Taking bag*) Here, let me take that.

MASI (*to* NOBU): Just some leftover fruit that was in the icebox. Starting to rot
so eat it right away. And this is for you.

> (MASI *hands package to* MARSHA. MASI *and* NOBU *acknowledge each
> other awkwardly.*)

MARSHA: Thanks, Mom. (*Takes package*) Judy and the baby couldn't make it.

MASI: She called me.

NOBU: Eh? (NOBU's *expression reveals he didn't know they had been going to come.*)

MARSHA (*offering explanation to* NOBU): Jimmy wasn't going to come. (*Pause*) Sit
down, sit down. Dinner's almost ready in a minute. Roast beef. Dad, coffee?
Tea for you, Mom?

> (MARSHA *goes to kitchen. Silence.*)

NOBU: She wanted to eat at her place. I told her to cook dinner here.

> (*Pause.*)

MASI: Her place is cozy, neh.

NOBU: Marsha's? Looks like the rooms back in camp.

MASI: At least she's clean. Not like the younger one.

> (*Pause.*)

NOBU: How you been?

MASI: All right.

NOBU: Isogashii no?[10]

MASI: No. The usual.

---

[10]Busy?

NOBU: I called the other night, no one answered.

(MASI *doesn't offer an explanation.*)

NOBU: How you been?

(MARSHA *interrupts, carrying an ashtray.*)

MARSHA: Dad, look what Mom gave me. She's taking a ceramics class. Judy got her to go. (*Hands him the ashtray*) She made it. (NOBU *stares at it.*)
MASI: It's an ashtray.
NOBU: You don't smoke.
MASI: I'll get Daddy's coffee. (MASI *exits with cup.*)
MARSHA: Dad, just say you like it. That's all you have to say. Just say it's nice.
NOBU: Yeah, but you don't smoke. Why give an ashtray if you don't smoke?

(MASI *returns with a cup of coffee for* NOBU *and tea for herself.*
MARSHA *gives* NOBU *an encouraging nudge and exits into kitchen.*)

NOBU (*holding ashtray*): It's a nice ashtray. Is this where you go all the time? I call in the evening. I guess that's where you must be. (*Pause*) Remember those dances they used to have in the camps? You were a good dancer. You were. Best in the camps.
MASI: You couldn't dance at all. You were awful.
NOBU: Remember that fellow Chester Yoshikawa? That friend of yours?
MASI: He could dance so good.
NOBU: Remember that dance you were supposed to meet me out front of the canteen? We were all going to meet there and then go to the dance together. Shig, Chester, and a couple others. Everybody else, they went on ahead. I waited and waited . . .
MASI: Nobu, that was forty years ago.
NOBU: Yeah, I know, but remember you were supposed to meet . . .
MASI (*interrupts*): That's over forty years ago. How can I remember something like that?
NOBU: You didn't show up. Chester didn't show up either.

(MASI *puts cream and sugar into* NOBU's *coffee.*)

MASI: Nobu, didn't we talk about this? I'm sure we did. Probably something came up and I had to help Mama and Papa.
NOBU: Where were you, huh?
MASI: How am I supposed to remember that far back? Chester died in Italy with the rest of the 442[11] boys.
NOBU: Where the hell were you?
MASI: How in the hell am I supposed to remember that far back!
NOBU (*notices his coffee*): You put the cream and sugar in. That's not mine.

(*Pushes coffee away.* MASI *realizes what she's done.*)

MASI: That's right. You like to put the cream and sugar in yourself.
NOBU: I like to put it in myself.

---

[11]World War II all Japanese American U.S. Army combat unit.

MASI (*pushing cup towards him*): It's the way you like it, the same thing.
NOBU (*pushes it back*): No, it's not the same thing.

(MARSHA *puts her head in and watches.*)

MASI: All right, all right, I'll drink it myself. Here, you can drink mine.

(MASI *shoves her tea to* NOBU *and grabs the coffee cup.*)

NOBU: What are you doing?
MASI: I don't mind.

(MASI *starts to raise cup, but* NOBU *reaches for it.*)

NOBU: It's no good for you, Mama. Your blood pressure. Remember what Doc
    Takei . . .
MASI (*interrupts, clinging to cup*): Who gives a damn? You make such a fuss about
    it. Monku, monku, monku.[12] I'll drink it.
NOBU (*struggling with* MASI): It's no good for you, Mama. (*Coffee spills on the
    table. To* MASI.) Clean it up.
MASI: I'm not going to clean it up.
MARSHA (*entering*): I'll clean it up.

(*While* MARSHA *starts to wipe the table,* MASI *grabs* NOBU's *coffee cup
    and exits into the kitchen.*)

MASI (*exiting*): I'll get him more coffee.
MARSHA: Dad.
NOBU: That's the way she is.

(MASI *returns with* NOBU's *coffee and sets it down in front of him.
    Then, she turns and quickly exits.*)

MARSHA (*chasing after* MASI): Mom . . .

(NOBU *is left alone with his cup of coffee.* MARSHA *reenters and watches
    him. He slowly puts in the cream and sugar himself. Raises his cup to his
    lips but cannot drink. Sets it back down and stares at it.* MARSHA
    continues to watch. Dim to darkness.)
    [END OF SCENE]

SCENE SIX

That same night. After hours at the restaurant. CHIYO *and* CURLEY *with
microphones singing a song like "Sukiyaki" to the accompaniment of the
Karaoke machine.* CURLEY *begins to do the hula.* KIYOKO *laughing and
clapping along. They're all having a good time.* NOBU *enters. He wasn't
expecting this and is not sure what to do. As* CHIYO *continues to sing,*
CURLEY *notices him.*

CURLEY (*calling*): Nobu! Nobu!

---

[12]Kvetch, kvetch, kvetch.

(KIYOKO *goes up to* NOBU, *who is turning to leave.*)

KIYOKO (*catching him and trying to make him enter*): Nobu, come in, come in—Chiyo and Curley set up the machine and we're all singing . . . (NOBU *doesn't budge.* KIYOKO *notices that he is upset about something. Gently*) Nobu? Sit down. Come in for a while. Sit, sit. I'll get you a beer.

(KIYOKO *leads the reluctant* NOBU *to his seat as* CHIYO *and* CURLEY *continue to sing.* KIYOKO *clears the table and goes back up to the counter for his beer.* CHIYO *and* CURLEY *have just finished their song and are now teasing* NOBU *to also join in.*)

CURLEY: Come on, your turn, Nobu.
CHIYO: Sing, sing.
CURLEY: It's Karaoke night at Hasegawa's!
CHIYO: Ojiisan, dozo![13]
CHIYO *and* CURLEY (*chanting*): Nobu, Nobu, Nobu . . .
KIYOKO (*returning with his beer*): Chiyo, Curley, leave him alone, leave him alone . . .

(*They stop, move back to the Karaoke machine.*)

CURLEY (*muttering*): What a bugga.
KIYOKO (*to* NOBU): Tsukemono?[14]

(NOBU *nods and* KIYOKO *exits.* NOBU *is left alone. Then he begins to sing, first softly, then growing in volume.*)

NOBU: Nen, nen kororiyo okororiyo,
  Bōya wa yoi ko da nen ne shina.
  Bōya yo mari wa doko e itta?
  Ano yama koete sato e itta.[15]
CURLEY: What's he singing?
CHIYO: I don't know.
KIYOKO (*reentering*): It's a lullaby.

(CHIYO *and* CURLEY *start to laugh at* NOBU *singing a baby's song.*)

KIYOKO: Shh! Shh!

(*Hearing them,* NOBU *stops.* KIYOKO *walks to* NOBU's *table.* KIYOKO *starts to sing to help* NOBU *out.* NOBU *joins back in.* NOBU's *voice is not pretty. But it is earnest and straightforward, filling the traditional song with a gutsy soulfulness.* KIYOKO *and* NOBU *finish the song together.*)

NOBU (*quietly*): My papa used to sing it to me.

(*Dim to darkness.*)
  [END OF SCENE]

---

[13]Old man, please!
[14] Japanese pickled vegetable.
[15]Sleep, sleep, hushabye, / Little boy, good boy, go to sleep now. / Little boy, where has your ball gone? / Way over the mountains to the distant fields.

SCENE SEVEN

> MASI's *place, three weeks later. Afternoon.* MASI *at clothesline.* JUDY *visiting with* TIMOTHY.

JUDY: I don't see how you had two of us, Mom. I need sleep. Large doses of it. Jimmy's so lazy sometimes. I even kick him "accidentally" when Timothy starts crying. Think he gets up to feed the baby?

MASI: Daddy used to.

JUDY: Used to what?

MASI: Get up at night and feed you kids.

JUDY: Dad? You're kidding.

MASI: He used to sing to you. No wonder you kids would cry.

> (*They laugh.*)

JUDY: I saw your new phone-answering machine.

MASI (*proud*): Yeah. For messages.

JUDY (*kidding*): What? You got a new boyfriend?

MASI: Judy.

JUDY: Well, why not, Mom? You moved out. It's about time you started meeting new people. Once you get a divorce you're going to have to do that any . . .

MASI (*interrupts*): I'm not getting a divorce.

JUDY: What are you going to do? You live here, Dad's over there . . . (*No response*) You can't do that forever.

MASI: I just do his wash. That's all I do. Just his wash. (*Pause.* MASI *hanging clothes*) I think you should call Dad.

JUDY: Mom, what can I say to him? I can't talk about my husband, I can't talk about my baby.

MASI: Judy, you know how Dad is.

JUDY: All he can talk about is how he can't show his face at Tak's barbershop because I married a kurochan.[16]

MASI: He's not going to call you.

JUDY: Of course not—we'd have to talk.

> (*Silence.* JUDY *goes back to the baby.* MASI *watches her.*)

MASI: Judy.

JUDY: What?

MASI: He needs you.

JUDY: Why can't he accept it? Why can't he just say, "It's okay, it's okay, Judy"? I just need him to say that much.

MASI: He can't. Papa can't.

JUDY: Why? Why the hell not?

> (MASI *and* JUDY *look at each other. Dim to darkness.*)
> [END OF SCENE]

SCENE EIGHT

> KIYOKO's *restaurant, that same evening. We hear the rhythmic pounding of fists on flesh. As lights come up,* NOBU *and* KIYOKO *are lit in a pool of*

---

[16]A black.

light. KIYOKO *is standing in back of* NOBU *pounding his back with fists in a punching manner. She is massaging* NOBU. *This is a supreme joy for him.* KIYOKO *likes doing it for him.*

KIYOKO (*not stopping*): Enough?
NOBU (*voice vibrating from the steady blows*): Nooo . . . (*They continue in silence, both enjoying the activity.*)
KIYOKO: Enough?
NOBU: Noo . . . (KIYOKO's *arms are just too tired.*)
KIYOKO (*stopping*): Ahh . . .
NOBU (*stretching*): Oisho![17] Masi used to do it. Sometimes Marsha does it now.
KIYOKO (*pouring tea*): You're lucky you have children, Nobu. Especially daughters. Harry and I wanted children. They're good, neh.

(*Awkward silence.* NOBU *abruptly pulls out a small gift-wrapped box and holds it out to* KIYOKO.)

NOBU: Here.

(KIYOKO's *too surprised to take it. From here, spoken in Japanese, except where otherwise indicated.*)

NOBU: Anata no birthday present. Hayo akenesai.[18]
KIYOKO (*taking it*): Ara! Nobu . . . (*Opens it and holds up the earrings*) Nobu-chan.
NOBU: Earrings. Inamasu Jewelry Store no mae o totara me ni tsuitanda ne.[19]
KIYOKO: Mah, kirei, Nobu-chan. Tsukete miru.[20]

(KIYOKO *exits.* NOBU *lit in pool of light.*)
MEMORY SEQUENCE. MASI *lit in pool of light.*

MASI: Why don't you want me anymore? (*No response*) We don't sleep . . . You know what I mean and don't give me that kind of look. Is it me? The way my body . . . I've seen those magazines you keep in the back closet with your fishing and hunting gear. I mean, it's all right. I'm just trying to know about us. What happened.
NOBU: Nothing. Nothing happened. What's the matter with you?
MASI: Then why don't you . . . sleep with me?
NOBU: By the time I get home from work I'm tired. Shig all day long, ordering me around, do this, do that. I even had to get up at five o'clock this morning to pick up the produce 'cause his damn son-in-law is a lazy son of a bitch. I'm tired, I'm tired, Masi.
MASI: What about those magazines?
NOBU: I'll throw 'em out, okay? First thing tomorrow I'll throw 'em in the trash and burn 'em. That make you feel better?

(MASI *is hurt by his angry response.*)

NOBU: Masi? (*No response*) Masi. You're pretty. You are.

---

[17]Ahh!
[18]Your birthday present. Hurry, open it.
[19]I was walking by Inamasu's store when I spotted them.
[20]They're pretty, Nobu. Let me try them on.

(Memory ends. MASI *withdraws into shadows.)*
KIYOKO *returns to* NOBU *with the earrings on. Lights come up.*

KIYOKO *(posing)*: Nobu-chan?
NOBU: Suteki da nah.[21]

*(*KIYOKO *attempts to embrace* NOBU*. It's too uncomfortable for* NOBU *and he gently pushes her away.* KIYOKO *is quite embarrassed. From now on they speak in English again.)*

KIYOKO: How come you do that to me? *(No response)* Don't you like it?
NOBU: I like it. But I don't like it, too.

(Dim to darkness.)
[END OF SCENE]

SCENE NINE

MASI's *apartment, four or five days later. Couch has rumpled blanket on it. Morning.* SADAO *is standing holding the door open for a surprised* MARSHA. SADAO *is dressed only in pants and an undershirt.* MARSHA *is holding a box of manju (Japanese pastry). They have never met.*

SADAO: Good morning.
MARSHA: Is my mother . . . Is Mrs. Matsumoto here?
MASI *(off)*: Who is it?
SADAO: Come on in, please come in.

*(*MASI *enters in a bathrobe with her hair tied up in a towel as if just washed.)*

MASI *(momentarily caught off guard)*: Oh, hi, Marsha. Come in.
MARSHA *(entering hesitantly)*: Hello, Mom.
MASI: This is Sadao Nakasato. *(To* SADAO*)* My eldest one, Marsha.
SADAO: Hello, Marsha.
MARSHA: Hello. *(Awkward pause.* MARSHA *remembers her package.)* Oh, I just thought I'd bring some manju by. *(Handing it to* MASI*)* I didn't think it was that early. Next time I guess I'll call first.
SADAO: Hmm, love manju. Some of my favorites. Especially the ones with the kinako on top. The brown powdery stuff?
MARSHA: I meant to drop it off last night but I called and no one was here.
MASI: Oh, we got in late from fishing.
SADAO: We caught the limit.
MASI *(looking at phone-answering machine)*: I have to remember to turn this machine on.
SADAO: In fact, Masi caught more than me.
MASI: Teamwork. I catch them and Sadao takes them off the hook. Sit down and have breakfast with us. Sit, sit.
MARSHA: That's okay, Mom.

---

[21]Looks beautiful.

MASI: It was so late last night I told Sadao to sleep on the couch. So he did. He said he would cook breakfast for me in the morning. Right over there on the couch.

> (MASI *and* SADAO *are nodding to each other in agreement.* MARSHA *doesn't move.*)

SADAO: Waffles.

MASI: You sure you know how?

SADAO: I can make them, good ones. From scratch.

MASI: Sit down, sit down.

MARSHA: No, no, Mom. I really should be going. I'm going to stop over at the house. To see Dad, too.

MASI: No, wait, wait . . . I have some fish for you.

> (MASI *is wrapping up two packages of fish with newspaper.* MARSHA *notices.*)

MARSHA: Mom, I don't want any fish.

MASI (*handing her a package*): Then give it to Brad.

MARSHA: Mom, I'm not seeing him anymore.

MASI: Oh. Then give it to Dad.

MARSHA: What do I tell him?

MASI (*momentary pause*): Just give it to him. No use wasting it. He can eat fish morning, noon, and night.

> (MASI *hustles* MARSHA *towards the door.*)

SADAO: No waffles? They're low cholesterol.

MARSHA: Uh, no thanks. Nice to meet you, Mr. Nakasato. (MARSHA *pauses at door. They exchange glances.*) Bye, Mom. (MARSHA *exits.*)

MASI (*calling after*): Tell Daddy I'll bring his clothes by, that I've been busy. And tell him to put his old clothes in a pile where I can see it. Last time I couldn't find one of his underwear and he got mad at me. (*Closes door*) It was under the icebox.

> (*As* SADAO *rambles on,* MASI *seems lost in her thoughts.*)

SADAO (*caught up in his cooking*): Everything's low cholesterol. Except for the Cool Whip. But that doesn't count because that's optional. Where's the MSG? That's my secret. My daughter gets so mad at me. "Dad, you're a pharmacist, you should know better than to use MSG." She's a health food nut . . .

> (SADAO *is bending down to look in a lower cabinet for the MSG. As he disappears,* MASI *moves into a pool of light.*)
> MEMORY SEQUENCE. NOBU *lit in pool of light.*

NOBU: No, Masi, I said size eight, size eight hooks.

MASI: You told me to buy size six, not size eight. That's not what you told me.

NOBU: I get home from the store I expect you to . . . Jesus Christ . . . (*Starting to pace*)

MASI: Nobu, Nobu, you didn't tell me to get size eight hooks. You told me size . . .

NOBU (*interrupts*): I said size eight. I said size eight hooks. (*Pause*) This is my house. Masi? After I come home from that damn store—here . . . This is *my* house.

> (*Silence.*)

MASI (*quietly*): I'm sorry. I'm wrong. You said size eight hooks.

> (NOBU *withdraws. Lights up. End of memory.*)
> SADAO *gets up from behind the cabinet with the MSG.*

SADAO: You don't mind, do you? Masi? The ajinomoto, the MSG. Is it OK with you?

MASI: Yes, yes, it's fine.

> (SADAO *is aware of* MASI's *pensiveness.*)

SADAO: Sometimes I add prune juice, but then you have to go easy on the MSG. The prune juice really does add a nice hint of flavor to the waffles if you don't overdo it.

> (NOBU *lit in half-light looking at his unfinished kite frame.*)

SADAO: Everything in moderation. I think these people got a little carried away with this MSG thing. Of course, I'm not running a Chinese restaurant, either. I'm just talking about a tiny pinch of the stuff . . .

> (*As lights go to half on* SADAO *and* MASI, NOBU *is lit in a pool of light. He lifts the kite above his head and begins to move it as if it were flying. For a moment* NOBU *seems to be a child making believe that his kite is soaring high above in the clouds.* NOBU *goes to half-light.*)
> [END OF SCENE]

SCENE TEN

> *Neighborhood streets.* KIYOKO *and* CHIYO *enter, checking the addresses on houses.*

CHIYO: Kiyoko, what's the address? What's the number?

KIYOKO (*looking at a piece of paper*): 2158 A Street.

CHIYO (*looking*): 2152, 2154 . . . There it is.

> (JUDY *hurries in, wiping her hands.*)

JUDY: Just a minute, I'm coming! (JUDY *stops when she sees the two strangers at her door.*) Yes?

KIYOKO: I am a friend of your father. My name is Kiyoko Hasegawa.

CHIYO: Chiyo Froelich.

JUDY: Hi.

KIYOKO: I run a restaurant. Hasegawa's?

CHIYO: Chiyo's Hair Salon, right next door.

JUDY: Oh . . . Yeah, yeah.

KIYOKO: We are having a small get-together at my place for your father.
CHIYO: A birthday party.

(They hear the baby crying.)

KIYOKO: Oh, that must be Timothy.
CHIYO: Nobu should see him.

(Awkward pause.)

JUDY (starting to withdraw): I really should . . . Excuse me . . .
CHIYO (to KIYOKO): Show Judy your earrings. Kiyoko, show her.
KIYOKO: Chiyo.
CHIYO: He gave them to her. Your father. For her birthday.
KIYOKO: For my birthday. He comes to my restaurant almost every day. He likes
    my cooking. That's how come I know him so good.
CHIYO (kidding): e's so mendokusai.[22] I don't like cucumber pickle, I like egg-
    plant. Monku, monku all the time.
KIYOKO: Oh, it's no trouble at all. I like to do things like that. I like to cook for
    Nobu. (TIMOTHY starts to cry in the back.)
JUDY (starting to leave): I really need to get back to the baby . . .
KIYOKO: So can you come?
CHIYO: To the birthday?
JUDY (exiting): I'm not sure. I'm really busy these days. Nice meeting you.

(Dim to darkness.)
    [END OF SCENE]

SCENE ELEVEN

Lights up on NOBU with his kite. MASI in half-light moves away from
SADAO. She's holding the fishing pole. NOBU puts down the kite frame.
Thinking. Picks up the phone and dials MASI's place.
    MASI's place in half-light. SADAO at the counter making waffles. He
hears the phone machine click on but does not answer it. MASI is off to
the side studying her rod and reel.

NOBU: Masi? You got any . . . Masi?

(MASI's phone machine kicks in. NOBU doesn't know how to deal with it.)

MASI'S RECORDED VOICE: Hello. This is Masi Matsumoto. I'm not in right now, so
    please wait for the tone and leave your name, your number, and a short mes-
    sage. Thank you. Bye-bye.

(NOBU listens to the message end. The beep sounds. He's panicked, not
quite sure what to do.)

NOBU: I am Nobu Matsumoto. My telephone number is 751 . . . damn. (Checks the
    number) 751-8263. (Not sure if he has said his name) I am Nobu Matsumoto.

(NOBU hangs up. Picks up his kite and stares at it. MASI lit in pool of
light. Casting. She is working on perfecting her technique, putting to-

---

[22]Troublesome.

gether all the little things that SADAO *has taught her. She goes through one complete cycle without a hitch. Very smooth. Having done the whole thing without a mistake gives her great satisfaction. She smiles to herself. It feels good. She begins again. Dim to darkness on* MASI *and* NOBU.)

[END OF ACT ONE]

ACT TWO, SCENE ONE

KIYOKO's *restaurant, four weeks later. Surprise birthday party for* NOBU. JUDY *stands by herself out front, picking at the food.* CURLEY *and* MARSHA *are in the kitchen and* KIYOKO *and* CHIYO *scurry about with last-minute preparations. Over the restaurant speakers we hear a forties tune like "String of Pearls."*

KIYOKO (*calling*): Curley! Hurry up with the chicken teri! (*Checking the food items*) Ara! I forgot the dip. Chiyo, go talk, go talk.

(KIYOKO *pushes* CHIYO *towards* JUDY, *then hurries back into the kitchen as* CURLEY *and* MARSHA *enter, carrying more food.* MARSHA *is holding her nose.*)

CHIYO (*to* JUDY, *in passing*): Nobu's favorite song. (*Stops momentarily, touching* JUDY's *hair*) You come see me, I know what to do with it.

(CHIYO *heads back to the kitchen as* MARSHA *and* CURLEY *are setting their dishes down.*)

CURLEY: If you think this stink, wait 'til you try my famous homyu.

MARSHA (*attempting to be polite*): No, really, it wasn't that bad.

CURLEY: All orientals gotta have stink food. It's part of our culture. Chinese, Japanese, Koreans, Filipinos—we all got one dish that is so stink. Filipinos got fish-gut paste, bagaoong. Koreans, kim chee. Whew! Chinese got this thing called hamha, shrimp paste. My mudda used to cook with it. Whew! Stink like something went die.

(CHIYO *enters.*)

CHIYO (*admonishing*): Curley.

CURLEY (*ignoring* CHIYO): And us Buddhaheads eat takuan, the pickled horse-radish. When you open up the bottle, the neighbors call to see if your toilet went explode!

CHIYO (*poking head into the kitchen*): Kiyoko! He's at it again!

CURLEY: Next time you come I make you my homyu.

JUDY: Homyu? (*To* MARSHA) You know homyu?

MARSHA: It's some kind of vegetable dish or something? . . .

CURLEY: No, no, no . . . What's a matta? You guys live on Mars? You never heard of homyu? Homyu. Steamed pork hash. It's my specialty. Gotta have the stinky fish on top. That's the secret. Lotsa pake places don't use that fish anymore. Know why? Too stink! Chase all the haole customers away. Take pork butt, chop it into small pieces. Little pig snout, huh? Throw it in. Tastes so ono.[23] Four water chestnuts, chopped. Teaspoon of cornstarch . . .

---

[23]Pake, "Chinese"; haole, "white"; ono, "tasty."

(KIYOKO *enters with dip,* CHIYO *trailing.*)

KIYOKO (*interrupts*): Curley! Curley! Go do the cake!

MARSHA (*to* CURLEY): I'll help you.

CHIYO: Kiyoko, when is he coming?

KIYOKO (*to* CHIYO): He should be on his way . . . (*To* MARSHA) You shouldn't
help anymore. Eat, eat. Talk to Chiyo.

(*Continues.*)

MARSHA (*overlapping*): We met already . . .

KIYOKO (*continues. To* CURLEY) Go, go, put the candles on the cake. No beer, either.

CURLEY (*exiting, calling back to* MARSHA *while scratching his butt*): Stinky fish.
Don't forget the stinky fish . . .

KIYOKO (*following him out*): Don't scratch your . . .

(KIYOKO *remembers the guests. As they exit,* CHIYO *approaches* JUDY
and MARSHA.)

CHIYO: I've never seen her like this. She's acting like a kid back there. (*Catching
her breath and looking the two daughters over*) You're Judy, neh, the fifth grade
teacher?

JUDY: I am the fifth-grade teacher.

CHIYO: And you're the dental . . . (*Continues.*)

MARSHA (*overlapping*): . . . Hygienist, I told you earlier . . .

CHIYO (*continues*): . . . hygienist—yeah, yeah, you told me before. (*Quietly
laughs about her mistake. Calms down.*) So. What do you think of the both of
them? Nobu and Kiyoko?

(*Awkward pause.*)

MARSHA: I think it's . . . good. I think it's good.
        (CHIYO *looks to* JUDY, *who is silent.*)

CHIYO (*touching her hair gently*): You come see me. I know what to do with it.

(CHIYO *turns and walks back towards the kitchen.*)

MARSHA: Judy.

JUDY: This is stupid—what am I doing here?

MARSHA: We're doing this for Dad.

JUDY: You really think he's going to want us here?

MARSHA: Judy . . .

JUDY: Do you?

(KIYOKO *hurries in, followed by* CHIYO.)

KIYOKO: Curley called—Nobu's not home, so he's coming. (*To* MARSHA, *feigning
enthusiasm*) I'm so glad you could make it. Judy said you weren't sure whether
you could all come or not.

MARSHA: Oh no, no. We wouldn't have missed it.

KIYOKO: Nobu-chan will be so happy you are here.

MARSHA: It was very kind of you to invite us.

KIYOKO: Oh no, no, no. I wanted all of you here.

CHIYO: Yeah, yeah, we wanted all of you here.

KIYOKO (*to* JUDY): Where is the baby?

JUDY: Jimmy's home baby-sitting him.

CHIYO: Next time you bring him. We got plenty of room here.

KIYOKO: Yes, please, please. Next time you bring the baby and Jimmy, too. I want to get to know all of Nobu-chan's family.

(CURLEY *rushes in with his ukelele.*)

CURLEY: HAYO! HAYO![24] THE BUGGA'S COMING! THE BUGGA'S COMING!

CHIYO: I'll get the cake. Hide! Hide!

CURLEY: I got the lights.

KIYOKO (*to* MARSHA *and* JUDY): In here, in here . . .

(*Darkness.* NOBU *enters cautiously.*)

NOBU: Kiyoko! Kiyoko!

(*The lights come up abruptly, then begin a slow fade through the rest of the scene.*)

ALL: SURPRISE!

(NOBU *is first happy. Then he sees* JUDY *and* MARSHA. *He is in shock.* CHIYO *and* CURLEY *lead everyone in a rousing, celebratory birthday song as* KIYOKO *enters with a birthday cake decorated with burning candles.* NOBU *is attempting to appear happy, but he is becoming more and more upset that his daughters are there. Lights continue their slow fade through the song, which is beginning to fall apart.* KIYOKO *is now standing next to* NOBU *holding the cake out in front of him. She senses something is wrong. The song ends with* CURLEY *and* KIYOKO *mumbling the last few lyrics. Silence.* NOBU's *face is illuminated by the glowing candles.* NOBU *makes no move to blow out the candles. The moment is now uncomfortable.* KIYOKO *is very upset.*)

KIYOKO: Nobu-chan, please.

JUDY (*irritated*): Dad.

(NOBU *still refuses to blow out the candles. Moment is now extremely awkward. No one knows what to do.*)

MARSHA (*gently*): Daddy.

(*Slowly* NOBU *leans forward and with a forceful breath extinguishes the candles.*)

[END OF SCENE]

SCENE TWO

MASI's *place, the same night.* SADAO *and* MASI *on couch. Both are propped up,* SADAO *intently watching TV and* MASI *peering at the TV*

---

[24]Hurry! hurry!

over the magazine she holds in front of her. SADAO *keeps switching the channel with his remote control. Each time* MASI *starts to settle into a program,* SADAO *switches the channel, causing her to jerk her head from the shock.*

MASI: Sadao? (SADAO *is busy switching channels.*)

MASI: Sadao?

SADAO: Hmm?

MASI: Could you please keep it on one?

SADAO (*realizing what he's been doing*): Oh. I'm sorry. (*Starts switching channels again*) Which one? This one? How's this?

MASI: Fine, fine. That's fine.

> (*They settle into watching TV.*)

MASI: Sadao?

SADAO: Hmm?

MASI: I don't feel good. (*Pause*) I think something's wrong with me.

SADAO: What, what? Want me to call Doc Takei?

MASI: No, no . . .

SADAO: You have a fever? Headache? What's wrong?

MASI: No, no, nothing like that. (*Pause. Thinking.*) I'm too happy.

SADAO: What?

MASI: I feel . . . too happy.

> (SADAO *stares at her, uncomprehending.*)

MASI: I used to feel like this as a kid, I think. But it was . . . different.

> (*Pause.*)

SADAO: You feel too happy?

MASI: When you're a kid you get ice cream and 'member how you used to feel? Happy, right? But then you eat it all up and it's gone, or you eat too much of it and you throw up. But this just goes on and on.

SADAO: You mean us?

> (MASI *nods.*)

SADAO: Yeah, but this is a little different from ice cream, don't you . . .

MASI (*interrupts*): Of course, of course, Sadao.

SADAO: What about with Nobu? Didn't you go through this with him?

> (MASI *shakes her head.*)

SADAO: I mean in the beginning when you first met? When you got married?

MASI: No, it wasn't like that. (*Pause*) I think something's wrong with me. You know how they say there's no such thing as an accident? That you really wanted it to happen and so it did? I don't think I ever really cared for Nobu. Not the way he cared for me. There was someone else who liked me in camp. I liked him, too. I married Nobu. Something's wrong with me, huh? Now you make me feel too happy. I don't like it. It makes me . . . unhappy.

> (*They both laugh. Sadao reaches out and places his hand on top of hers.*)

MASI: Was she in a lot of pain?

> (SADAO *doesn't follow her comment.*)

MASI: Your wife. Towards the end. In the hospital.

SADAO (*realizes she's talking about his first wife, Mary*): She just slept all the time. No, not too much. After about two weeks she went into a coma and that was it. You can't tell. Cancer's like that. Mary was pretty lucky, I guess. (*Pause. Thinking.*) There's nothing wrong with you. Really, there isn't. (*Pause. Trying to decide whether to say something or not.*) You scare me. You know that? Sometimes you scare me half to death. I don't want to go through that again. I told myself, "Never, ever again." Dead is better than feeling that kind of pain. But this . . . this is . . . I don't know . . . To get a second chance . . . (*Pause*) There's nothing good about growing old. You spend most of your time taking medicine and going to the doctor so you won't die. The rest of the time you spend going to the funerals of your friends who did die, and they were taking the same medicine and seeing the same doctors, so what's the use, anyway? Huh? (*Sarcastically*) The golden years . . . Look at us. Here we are. At our age. Not even married. Can you imagine what the kids are thinking?

MASI: We're not doing anything wrong.

SADAO: Of course, I know, I know.

MASI: We're not doing anything wrong, Sadao. We're not.

SADAO: I know. But when I really think about what we're doing . . . it embarrasses the hell out of me!

> (*They look at each other, then suddenly burst out laughing. They gradually calm down.*)

MASI: I scare you half to death. And you . . . you make me feel so good I feel awful.

> (*They look at each other for a moment, then slowly reach out and embrace. Dim to darkness.*)
> [END OF SCENE]

SCENE THREE

> KIYOKO's *restaurant, one week later.* NOBU *is sitting at counter sipping sake and eating eggplant pickles.* CURLEY *is watching him from the service window. He comes out, sipping on a beer.*

CURLEY (*takes a big gulp*): Know why I like to drink beer? Know why? (*As* NOBU *looks up,* CURLEY *answers his own question with a loud, satisfying burp.*) Ahh. I like to let things out. Makes me feel good. Don't like to keep things bottled up inside. Not good for you. Give you an ulcer. Cancer. Maybe you just blow up and disappear altogether, huh. (*Laughs at his own joke. Notices* NOBU *isn't laughing.*) That's the problem with you kotonks. You buggas from the mainland all the time too serious.

> (NOBU *glances back towards the door.*)

CURLEY: No worry, no worry. Kiyoko going be back soon. Chiyo's place—yak, yak, yak. Hey, you had lots of girl friends when you was small kid time?

(NOBU *shrugs.*)

CURLEY: Strong silent type, huh? Me? Lotsa wahinis. All the time like to play with Curley. (*Mimicking the girls*) "Curley, darling, you're so cute . . . you're so funny" . . . But I not all the time cute. I not all the time funny. How come you all the time come around here and you still got one wife?

NOBU: We're separated.

CURLEY: So when you gonna get the divorce?

NOBU: No.

(CURLEY *doesn't understand.*)

NOBU: No.

CURLEY: What about Kiyoko?

(*No response.* NOBU *keeps drinking.*)

CURLEY: I don't like you. I like you. I don't like you 'cause you make Kiyoko feel lousy. I like you 'cause you make her happy. Hey, she's my boss—who you think catch hell if she not feeling good? Hey, I don't like catching hell for what you do . . .

NOBU (*interrupts*): It's none of your business—Kiyoko and me.

CURLEY: None of my business? Hey, brudda, Kiyoko may be feeding your face but I'm the guy who's cooking the meals.

(NOBU *stares down at his pickles.*)

CURLEY: Nobu?

NOBU: What?

CURLEY: You like Kiyoko? (*No response*) Well, do you?

NOBU (*under his breath*): eah, I guess so.

CURLEY: "Yeah, I guess so" what?

NOBU (*mumbling*): I like Kiyoko.

CURLEY: Jesus. Talking to you kotonks is like pulling teeth.

NOBU: I LIKE KIYOKO! (*Pause*) I like Kiyoko.

(CURLEY *leans forward towards* NOBU *and burps loudly.*)

CURLEY: Feels good, huh?

(NOBU *is disgusted.* CURLEY *smiles. Dim to darkness.*)
  [END OF SCENE]

SCENE FOUR

NOBU's *place, one week later.* MASI *enters, carrying the wash in a brown paper bag. She unpacks the clothes and stacks them neatly on the kitchen table. She picks up the old clothes off the floor, folds them, and puts them in the bag. As she looks up, one gets the sense that she is trying to decide whether to say hello to* NOBU *or just leave. She looks for a moment towards the hallway, then decides otherwise. Just as she turns and starts to make her way towards the door with the bag,* NOBU *enters from the hallway.*

NOBU: Masi, is that you?

(NOBU *realizes that she's leaving without bothering to say hello.* MASI *senses this and feels guilty.*)

MASI: I was going. I'm a little late. I was just going to leave the clothes and go. (*As she speaks, she notices the dirty dishes on the coffee table. She puts down the bag and proceeds to clean up the mess as she continues to talk.*) I didn't know you were in the back . . . (MASI *points to the dishes in the sink, while* NOBU *just watches.*) Nobu, why don't you wash the dishes once in a while? Clean up.

NOBU: Place is a dump anyway.

(MASI *stops and looks at him.* NOBU *presses the point.*)

NOBU: Place is a dump, Mama. Neighborhood's no good. Full of colored people. Mexicans . . .

MASI (*putting dishes in sink*): Well, move then. Move to the north side like me. I kept saying that all along. For the kids—better schools, better neighborhood . . . Think you listen to me? (*Mimicking* NOBU) "I don't like hakujin—white people make me nervous." So you don't like white people, you don't like black people, you don't like Mexicans . . . So who do you like? Huh? Monku, monku, monku.

NOBU (*muttering*): I don't mind Mexicans. (*Pause*) I told Shig you can't keep stocking all that Japanese things when the Nihonjins[25] are moving out of the neighborhood. You gotta sell to the Mexicans and not all that cheap crap too, 'cause they can tell. Think Shig listens to me? He's the big store owner. The big man. If I was running the store it woulda been different. Different. (*Pause*) And your old man said he'd get me that store.

MASI: It wasn't his fault. He didn't plan on the war, Nobu.

NOBU: He promised he could set me . . . (*Continues.*)

MASI (*overlapping*): It wasn't his fault.

NOBU (*continuing*): . . . up in business or anything else I wanted to do.

MASI: IT WASN'T HIS FAULT! (*Silence*) Who wanted to be in the relocation camps? Did you? Do you think he wanted to be in there? It broke Papa's heart. He spent his entire life building up that farm. Papa was a proud man. A very proud man. It broke his heart when he lost it. And how come you didn't go to the bank like I told you? I told you to go to the bank and ask for . . .

NOBU: I'm just saying I'd run the business different. Shig is a baka, a fool. That's all I'm saying.

MASI: You're retired. Shig passed away eight years ago. The store's not even . . . (*Continues.*)

NOBU (*overlapping*): If all the Japanese move out you can't keep selling all those Japanese things, you can't. That's all I'm saying.

MASI (*continuing*): . . . there any more. It's a cleaner's.

(*Silence.* MASI *picks up the paper bag of old clothes and starts to move towards the door. She's had enough.*)

---

[25]Japanese.

NOBU: Masi?

MASI (*stops*): What?

NOBU: Mr. Rossi give you any more fish?

MASI (*uncomfortable lying*): No. Not lately.

> (*Pause.*)

NOBU: Mama?

MASI: Is your back bothering you, Nobu? (*No response*) Want me to momo[26] it for you?

> (NOBU *nods. As* MASI *moves to put the bag down*, NOBU *removes his undershirt so he is bare chested. He seats himself.* MASI *begins to massage his shoulders from behind. They continue in silence.* NOBU *is enjoying the moment. He begins to laugh quietly to himself.*)

MASI: What?

NOBU: When I started work at your papa's farm, he wanted to put me in the packing shed. I said, "No, I want to work in the fields." It was so hot, 110 degrees out there. He thought I was nuts. But I knew every day at eight in the morning and twelve noon you and your sister would bring the water out to us.

MASI (*laughing as she recalls*): Nobu.

NOBU: I wanted to watch you.

MASI: You would just stand there with your cup, staring at me.

NOBU: Hell, I didn't know what to say.

MASI: You drank so much water, Lila and I thought maybe you had rabies. We used to call you "Nobu, the Mad Dog." (*Both laughing*) Papa liked you.

NOBU: Boy, he was a tough son of a bitch.

MASI: I didn't think anyone could keep up with Papa. But you could work like a horse. You and Papa. Proud. Stubborn.

> (MASI *massages* NOBU *in silence.*)

NOBU: Masi? Why don't you cook me breakfast?

MASI: What?

NOBU: Cook me breakfast. I miss my hot rice and raw egg in the morning.

MASI: It's late, Nobu. You have your wash. I'm not going to come all the way back over here just to cook you . . .

NOBU (*interrupts*): Just breakfast. Then in the morning when we get up you can go back to your place.

> (MASI *stops, realizing he is asking her to spend the night.* MASI *does not move.* NOBU *stares ahead. More silence. Then, tentatively, she moves her hands forward and begins to massage him. A faint smile appears on* NOBU's *face. Dim to darkness.*)
>
> [END OF SCENE]

SCENE FIVE

> KIYOKO's *restaurant, one week later.* CURLEY, *after hours, seated in semidarkness. Feet up on table, accompanying himself on the ukelele and singing a sad Hawaiian folk song, like "Manuela Boy."*

---

[26]Massage.

>   As he sings, MASI's place lit in pool of light. SADAO stands before
>   the door MASI has just opened. In SADAO's right hand he holds a suitcase
>   and in his left several fishing poles. On his head sits a fishing hat. SADAO
>   has come to move in with MASI. For a moment they look at each other in
>   silence. Then MASI invites him in. SADAO enters. Dim to darkness.
>
>   Dim to darkness on CURLEY as he finishes the song.
>   [END OF SCENE]

SCENE SIX

>   NOBU's place, three days later. Late afternoon. JUDY has stopped by with
>   TIMOTHY. JUDY sets the baby down on the kitchen table upstage of NOBU.
>   NOBU turns to look at JUDY, then returns to working on the kite and
>   watching TV. This is the first time JUDY has visited NOBU since their
>   breakup over her marriage. He has never seen TIMOTHY.

JUDY (*moving down towards* NOBU): I was just driving by and I thought I'd stop
in. (*No response*) You doing okay, Dad? (*Silence*) You know, Mom? I just
wanted to say . . .

NOBU (*interrupts*): Did he come?

JUDY: (*exasperated*): No, he did not.

NOBU: He can come to the house now.

JUDY: "He can come to the house now"? Jesus Christ. Dad, he isn't one of your
children. He doesn't need your permission. He's a . . . (*Continues.*)

NOBU (*overlapping*): This is my house. He needs my permission.

JUDY (*continues*): . . . grown man. I don't want to fight. I didn't come here to
fight with you, Dad.

NOBU: I *said* he can come . . .

JUDY (*interrupts*): He won't come, he doesn't like you!

>   (*Silence.*)

NOBU: Damn kurochan . . .

JUDY: He's black, not kurochan. It's "African American." (*Pause*) Everybody
marries out, okay? Sanseis don't like Sanseis.

NOBU: Tak's son married a Nihonjin, Shig's daughter did, your cousin Patsy . . .
(*Continues.*)

JUDY (*overlapping*): Okay, okay, I didn't, I didn't, all right.

NOBU (*continues*): . . . did, Marsha's going to. (*Pause. Looks back to* TIMOTHY.)

JUDY: But is that any reason not to see my baby? He's a part of you, too.

NOBU: No, no. Japanese marry other Japanese, their kids are Yonsei—not these
damn ainoko.[27]

>   (*Silence.*)

JUDY: You're gonna die out, you know that. You're gonna be extinct and nobody's gonna give a goddamn.

>   (TIMOTHY *has begun to cry softly. She goes over and picks the baby up,
>   trying to soothe him.* JUDY, *composing herself, decides to try one last time*

---

[27]Yonsei, "fourth-generation Japanese American"; ainoko, "biracial person."

to say what she came to tell her father. JUDY *walks back to* NOBU, *this time carrying* TIMOTHY *with her.*)

JUDY: Dad? (*No response*) Dad, you know Mom's moving out of the house? I didn't put her up to it. Honest. (*Silence.* NOBU *stares straight ahead.* JUDY *begins to cry.*) If I did . . . I'm sorry.

NOBU: Judy . . .

(*More silence from* NOBU. JUDY *gives up trying to talk to this man. As she turns to leave, she notices* NOBU. *He is looking towards her, at* TIMOTHY. *Something in his expression makes* JUDY *bring the baby over to* NOBU.)

JUDY (*holding the baby out*): Timothy. Your grandson.

(*For a moment there is hesitation. We are not sure whether* NOBU *is going to take the baby. Then,* NOBU *reaches out and takes* TIMOTHY. JUDY *watches as* NOBU *awkwardly holds his grandson for the first time. As* JUDY *begins to withdraw from the scene upstage into a pool of light,* MARSHA *is also lit upstage in her own separate pool of light.* NOBU *remains lit holding* TIMOTHY. *He begins to hum the traditional Japanese lullaby "Donguri."* MARSHA *and* JUDY *watch* NOBU *and* TIMOTHY *as they speak.*)

MARSHA: You didn't tell Dad, did you?
JUDY: No. I just brought the baby by.
MARSHA: It's going to kill him when he finds out.
JUDY: He's got that other woman.
MARSHA: Judy. (*Pause*) Maybe he already knows about Mom and Mr. Nakasato.
JUDY: I don't think so. I really don't think so.

(*They continue to watch as* NOBU *begins to sing the "Donguri" song to* TIMOTHY.)

NOBU (*singing*):
Donguri koro koro, donguri ko
Oike ni hamatte, saa taihen
Dojōga dette kite, "konnichiwa"
Timothy isshoni, asobimashō . . . [28]

(*Repeat.*)

(MARSHA *and* JUDY *dim to darkness first.* NOBU *is left alone in a pool of light singing to* TIMOTHY. *As he dims to darkness, we hear the whir of a coffee grinder.*)

[END OF SCENE]

SCENE SEVEN

MASI's *place, two days later.* MASI *has asked* JUDY *and* MARSHA *over for a talk. She has just told them she is going over to see* NOBU. *She is going to tell him that she wants to divorce him and to marry again.*

---

[28]Acorn, acorn, rolling along / Fell into a pond, what will we do? / Up comes a loache fish, says, "Good afternoon." / Timothy, let's go play together.

The two daughters sit uneasily while MASI *is at the counter preparing coffee.* MASI *is trying to get the Braun grinder to work. She's getting the feel of it by pushing the button. We hear the whir of the spinning rotor blade.*

She's ready. Takes the plastic top off and pours the beans in. Then, presses the start button. Just as the grinder picks up top speed MASI *accidentally pulls the plastic top off. Beans go flying every which way! Pelting her face, bouncing off the cabinets. Quiet.* MASI *peeks from behind her hands. A couple of beans embedded in her hair fall to the counter.* MASI *is upset. The daughters are embarrassed. Normally, this would be a funny situation for them.*

MARSHA *starts to pick up the beans scattered on the floor.* JUDY *starts to giggle—it's all too ridiculous.*

JUDY (*trying to suppress her laughter*): I'm sorry, I'm sorry . . .
MARSHA: I'll clean it up.

(MASI *begins to laugh.*)

JUDY: God, what a mess.
MASI (*to* MARSHA): Let it go, don't bother. I'll take care of it later.

(JUDY *finds a man's sock.*)

JUDY (*teasing*): What's this? This belong to Mr. Nakasato?
MASI (*grabbing it*): Judy.
MARSHA: Why didn't you just leave sooner? You didn't have to stick around for us.
MASI: I didn't. I was . . . I was scared.
MARSHA: Of Dad?
MASI: I don't know. Everything.
JUDY: Was it 'cause I kept harping on you to move out on him all those years? Is that why you left?
MARSHA: What's the difference now?
JUDY: Marsha.

(*Pause.*)

MASI: There are things you kids don't know. I didn't want to talk about them to you but . . . Daddy and I, we didn't sleep . . . (*Continues.*)
JUDY (*overlapping*): That's okay, Mom. Really, it's okay . . .
MASI (*continues*): . . . together. Every time I wanted to, he would push me away. Ten, fifteen years he didn't want me. (*Pause*) We were having one of our arguments, just like always. And he was going on and on about how it was my fault this and my fault that. And I was trying to explain my side of it, when he turned on me, "Shut up, Mama. You don't know anything. You're stupid." Stupid. After forty-two years of letting him be right he called me that. And I understood. He didn't even need me to make him be right anymore. He just needed me to be stupid. I was tired. I couldn't fight him anymore. He won. He finally made me feel like shit. (*Shocking* JUDY *and* MARSHA *with her strong language*) That was the night I left him and came over to your place. (*Nodding towards* JUDY) I like Sadao. (*Turns to* MARSHA) I like Sadao very much.

(MARSHA *turns away, then gets up and exits.* MASI *sends* JUDY *after* MARSHA *to comfort her. Dim to darkness.*)
   [END OF SCENE]

SCENE EIGHT

NOBU's *place, the same day. "String of Pearls" can be heard playing faintly in the background. He's fixing himself in front of a small wall mirror. He adjusts the collar of his shirt and tugs at his sweater until it looks right.* NOBU *checks his watch. As he begins to pick up some of the scattered clothes on the floor,* MASI *enters. Music cue ends.*

   NOBU *quickly gets up and moves to the sofa.* MASI *goes over to the kitchen area and takes clothes out of the bag, setting them neatly on the table. She picks up the dirty clothes off the floor, folds them, and puts them into the bag. As she's doing this,* NOBU *gets up, shuffles over to the stove, and turns on the flame to heat some water. Stands there and watches the water heat up.*

MASI (*sits down on sofa*): I want to talk, Nobu.

   (*No response.* NOBU *gets the tea out and pours some into the pot.*)

MASI: I have something I want to tell you.
NOBU (*moving back to couch*): Want some tea?

   (*As* NOBU *sits,* MASI *gets up and moves towards the sink area. She gets a sponge and wipes off the tea leaves he has spilled on the counter.* NOBU *turns on the TV and stares at it.*)

MASI: You know Dorothy and Henry's son, George?
NOBU: The pharmacist or something?
MASI: No, the lawyer one. He's the lawyer one. I went to see him. I went to see about a divorce. About getting one. (*No response*) I want to get married again. So I went to George to see about a divorce. I wanted to tell you first so you'd know. I didn't want you to hear from someone else. I know how you hate that kind of thing. Thinking something's going on behind your back.
NOBU: Wait, wait, wait a second. You want to get . . . What? What's all this?
MASI: It's the best thing, Nobu. We've been separated how long now? How long have we been living different places?
NOBU: I don't know. I never thought about it. Not too long.
MASI: Thirteen months.
NOBU: Thirteen months, who cares? I never thought about it.
MASI: It's the same as being divorced, isn't it?
NOBU: It doesn't seem that long. You moved out of this house. It wasn't my idea. It was your idea. I never liked it.
MASI: It doesn't matter whose idea it was. It's been over a year since we . . .
NOBU (*interrupts*): You want to get married? Yeah, I know it's been over a year but I always thought . . . You know, that we'd . . .
MASI (*interrupts*): It's been over a year, Nobu.
NOBU: I know! I said I know.

   (*Pause.*)

MASI: I've been seeing someone. It wasn't planned or anything. It just happened.

NOBU: What do you mean, "seeing someone"? What do you mean?

MASI: He's very nice. A widower. He takes me fishing. He has a nice vegetable garden that he . . .

NOBU (*interrupts*): Who is he? Do I know him? Is it someone I know?

MASI: His name is Sadao Nakasato. His wife died about two years ago. He's related to Dorothy and Henry. Nobu, it's the best thing for both of us.

NOBU: You keep saying it's the best thing, the best thing. (*Pause*) Masi, why did you sleep with me that night?

(*Silence.*)

MASI: Aren't you seeing somebody?

NOBU: No. Not like that.

MASI: But the kids said she's very nice. That she invited . . .

NOBU (*interrupts*): It's totally different! I'm not seeing anyone! (*Pause*) How long have you been seeing this guy? How long?

MASI: Please, Nobu. You always get what *you* want. I always let you have your way. For once just let . . .

NOBU (*interrupts*): HOW LONG!

MASI: About five months.

NOBU: FIVE MONTHS! How come you never told me? Do the girls know, too? The girls know! Everybody knows? Five months. FIVE GODDAMN MONTHS AND I DON'T KNOW!!

(NOBU *breaks the kite.*)

MASI: I asked them not to tell you.

NOBU: Why? Why the hell not? Don't I have a right to know?

MASI: Because I knew you'd react this way. Just like this. Yelling and screaming just like you always do.

NOBU: Everybody in this whole goddamn town knows except me! How could you do this to me! Masi! HOW COULD YOU DO THIS TO ME??

(NOBU *has her by the shoulders and is shaking her violently.*)

MASI: Are you going to hit me?

(*Pause.* NOBU *slowly composes himself and lets her go.*)

MASI: Because I want to be happy, Nobu. I want to be happy.

(MASI *exits.* NOBU *left standing alone. Dim to darkness.*)
    [END OF SCENE]

SCENE NINE

KIYOKO's *restaurant, evening of the same day.* CHIYO *and* KIYOKO *seated at table, lit in pool of light.*

KIYOKO: Nine years. That's how long it has been. Nine years since Harry passed away. He never treated me like this. I call, I go over there. Harry never treated me like this.

CHIYO: Kiyoko. Maybe you have to stop thinking about Nobu. Hmm? Maybe . . . maybe you should give him up. *(Silence)* Kiyoko. Lots more fish in the ocean. Lots more. Go out with us. Come on.

KIYOKO: I don't do those kinds of things.

CHIYO: I'll introduce you to some new guys. Remember Ray—you met him? I've been telling him about . . .

KIYOKO *(interrupts)*: I don't do those kinds of things. *(Pause)* It's not easy for me, Chiyo. *(Silence)* When Harry died, right after? I started taking the bus to work. I had a car, I could drive. It was easier to drive. I took the bus. For twenty-five years you go to sleep with him, wake up next to him, he shaves while you shower, comes in from the yard all sweaty. Then he's gone. No more Harry in bed. No more smell of aftershave in the towel you're drying off with. No more sweaty Harry coming up and hugging me. I had a car. I took the bus. I missed men's smells. I missed the smell of men. Every morning I would get up and walk to the corner to take the bus. It would be full of all these men going to work. And it would be full of all these men coming home from work. I would sit there pretending to read my magazine . . . *(Inhales. Discovering the different smells.)* Soap . . . just washed skin . . . aftershave lotion . . . sweat . . .

> *(Lights come up to half in the restaurant.* CURLEY *bursts through the kitchen doors holding a plate of his famous homyu. Brings it over and sets it down on the table, which is now lit in a full pool of light.)*

CURLEY: Homyu! Homyu!

CHIYO: Curley, kusai yo!

CURLEY: I know stink, but stink GOOD!

KIYOKO: Curley!

CURLEY *(motioning)*: Hayo, hayo—all dis good food back dere going to waste. Gonna need a gas mask for all da stinky stuff back dere. Come on, come on. I been cooking all day. Hayo, hayo, Kau Kau time.[29]

> *(As lights dim,* CURLEY *ushers* KIYOKO *and* CHIYO *offstage into the kitchen.)*
>   [END OF SCENE]

SCENE TEN

> NOBU's *place, two days later. Knock at the door, and* MARSHA *enters carrying a brown paper bag.* NOBU *is watching TV.*

MARSHA: Mom asked me to drop these by and to pick up the dirty clothes.

> *(No response.* MARSHA *unpacks the newly washed clothes.)*

MARSHA: Kiyoko's been calling me. She's worried about you. She says you won't see anybody. Why don't you just talk to her, Dad?

NOBU: How come you didn't tell me? All the time you come here and you never mention it once. You. I feel so goddamn ashamed. All the time right under my nose. Everyone laughing at me behind my . . .

---

[29]Time to eat.

MARSHA (*interrupts*): Dad, Dad, it's not like that at all. I just didn't think it was all that important to tell . . .

NOBU (*interrupts*): Oh, come on! Mom told you not to tell me so she could go sneaking 'round with that son of a bitch!

MARSHA: All right, all right, but it's not like that at all. No one's trying to hide anything from you and no one's laughing at you.

NOBU (*moving her towards the couch and pushing her down while speaking*): Sit down, sit down over here. Who is he? What does he do? Tell me 'bout him! Tell me!

MARSHA (*seated*): What do you want me to say? Huh, Dad? They're happy. He's a nice man.

NOBU (*repeating*): "He's a nice man." What the hell's that supposed to mean?

MARSHA: He treats her like a very special person.

NOBU: Well, everyone does that in the beginning. In the beginning it's so easy to be . . .

MARSHA (*interrupts*): She laughs. All the time she's laughing. They're like two little kids. They hold hands. Did you ever do that? I'm embarrassed to be around them. He takes her fishing. He has a little camper and they drive up to Lake Berryessa and camp overnight . . . (*Continues right through*)

NOBU: All right, all right . . .

MARSHA (*continues*): . . . He teaches her how to bait the hook and cast it out.

NOBU (*overlapping*): She doesn't like fishing.

MARSHA (*continues*): I mean you never even took her fishing.

NOBU: I tried to take her lots of times. She wouldn't go.

MARSHA (*continues*): They even dig up worms in his garden at his house. I saw them. Side by side . . . (*Continues.*)

NOBU: All right, I said.

MARSHA (*continues*): . . . sitting on the ground digging up worms and . . . (*Continues.*)

NOBU (*overlapping*): ALL RIGHT! ALL RIGHT!

MARSHA (*continues*): . . . putting them in a coffee can! I MEAN DID YOU EVER DO THAT FOR MOM!! (*Pause. Quieter.*) Did you? (*Getting worked up again*) You're so . . . so stupid. You are. You're stupid. All you had to say was "Come back. Please come back." You didn't even have to say, "I'm sorry." (*Continues.*)

NOBU (*overlapping*): I'm your father . . .

MARSHA (*continues*): . . . Mom would've come back. She would've. That's all you had to say. Three lousy words: "Please come back." (*Continues.*)

NOBU (*overlapping*): I'm your father . . .

MARSHA (*continues*): . . . You ruined everything. It's all too late! YOU WRECKED EVERYTHING! (*Pause. Composing herself.*) I'm so mixed up. When I look at Mom I'm happy for her. When I think about you . . . I don't know. You have Kiyoko.

NOBU: That's not the same. I'm talking about your Mama.

MARSHA: Dad, Kiyoko cares a great deal about you. She's been calling Judy and me day and night.

NOBU: She knocks on the door but I don't let her in. She's not Mama.

MARSHA: Dad. What do you want me to say? That's the way it is. I used to keep thinking you two would get back together. I couldn't imagine life any other way. But slowly I just got used to it. Mom over there, and you here. Then all this happened. I mean, sometimes I can't recognize Mom anymore. What do you want me to say? You'll get used to it.

NOBU (*Pause, upset, then stubbornly*): No.

(MARSHA *looks at her father sadly.*)

MARSHA: You'll get used to it.

(*Dim to darkness on* MARSHA *and* NOBU.)
[END OF SCENE]

SCENE ELEVEN

MASI *and* JUDY *at the clothesline.* JUDY *holds* TIMOTHY *while* MASI *hangs clothes. An agitated* NOBU *enters and begins to pull* MASI *home.*

JUDY: Dad . . .

MASI: Nobu . . .

NOBU: I won't yell, Mama, I won't yell at you anymore. I won't monku about . . . (*Continues.*)

MASI (*overlapping*): Nobu? Nobu, what are you . . . (*Continues.*)

JUDY (*overlapping*): Dad, Dad . . .

MASI: (*continuing*): . . . doing? Let go, Nobu . . .

NOBU (*continuing*): . . . the store or about your papa—I won't monku, I won't do any of that stuff . . .

MASI: Let go of my arm!

(*Silence.*)

NOBU: I tried, I tried, Masi. After the war, after we got out of camp? After . . . (*Continues.*)

MASI (*overlapping*): Nobu, camp? What are you . . .

NOBU (*continuing*): . . . we got out I went to the bank like you told me. So your papa can't give me money, that's all right . . . (*Continues.*)

MASI (*overlapping*): Nobu, what's this—you never told me . . .

NOBU (*continuing*): . . . I'll do it on my own. I got there and ask the man how do I sign up to get money. He says, "Sit there and wait." I wait, I wait, I wait five whole goddamn hours. I go up, "How come nobody sees me?" He says, "Sorry, but the person to see you is sick, come back tomorrow." I get so pissed off I throw the magazines all over the place. Everyone is looking. I don't give a damn, I'm shaking I'm so pissed off. And then, and then . . . I'm filled with shame. Shame. Because I threw their magazines all over. After what they did to me, *I'm* ashamed, me, *me*. When I get home I feel something getting so tight inside of me. In my guts, tighter and tighter, getting all balled up. How come I feel like this? Huh? How come I feel like this? I'm scared, Masi. I'm scared. Please. I need . . . (*Continues.*)

MASI (*overlapping*): You don't understand, you don't . . .

NOBU (*continuing*): . . . you. I need you. *You*. You know. You understand how it is now. Please, please, you come home, you come . . . (*Continues.* NOBU *begins to pull* MASI *home.*)

MASI (*overlapping*): Nobu, Nobu, I can't, I . . .

NOBU (*continuing*): . . . home now, Mama. Just like always. You come home . . .
    (*Continues.*)
MASI (*overlapping*): . . . can't, Nobu.
NOBU: . . . just like always . . .
MASI: I can't.

> (NOBU *begins to break down, letting go of* MASI. *Begins to plead.*)

NOBU: I'm sorry, I'm sorry, Masi. It's no good, it's no good, Masi. Please come
    home. Please come home. Please . . .

> (JUDY *pulls* MASI *away and they withdraw from the scene.* NOBU *is left
> alone in a pool of light. Slowly he pulls himself upright, staring into the
> darkness. He turns and crosses back to his room. He reaches behind his
> chair and pulls out a long, narrow object wrapped in cloth. As he un-
> wraps it, we see what it is, a shotgun. We hear the mournful wail of a
> shakuhachi flute.* NOBU *sits down on the chair with the gun across his
> lap. Dim to darkness on* NOBU.)
>   [END OF SCENE]

Scene Twelve

> KIYOKO's *restaurant.* CHIYO *at the phone dialing* NOBU's *number. A
> concerned* CURLEY *stands guard next to her.* KIYOKO *has told them not to
> bother with him anymore.* KIYOKO *appears and watches them. She
> makes no attempt to stop them.* CHIYO *lets the phone ring.*
>   NOBU, *seated in his chair, stares at the phone ringing next to him.
> He gets up, still holding the gun, and exits.*
>   *No one is answering.* CHIYO *and* CURLEY *exchange disappointed
> looks. Only then does* KIYOKO *burst in on them.*

KIYOKO: How come you keep doing that? Huh? Don't phone him anymore. I
    told you, didn't I?

> (KIYOKO *exits.*)

CURLEY (*to* CHIYO): Hey, maybe it's none of our business.

> (*Dim to darkness on the restaurant.*)
>   [END OF SCENE]

Scene Thirteen

> MASI's *place, one week later.* NOBU *standing inside with a shotgun.*
> SADAO *asleep offstage in the bedroom.*

NOBU: Where is he?

> (MASI *stares at the gun.*)

MASI: He went to buy the newspaper.
NOBU: (*notices* MASI *watching him cautiously*): It's not loaded. (*Beat*) I thought
    about it all week, all week. Coming over here, shooting the son of a bitch. I

coulda. I coulda done it. (*Pause*) I just wanted to show you. Both of you. That's why I brought it. Don't worry. It's not loaded. (NOBU *cracks the gun and shows her that it is not loaded.*) I just wanted to show both of you how it was, how I was feeling. But it's all right. You two. It's all right now.

(NOBU *sets the gun against the wall.* MASI *watches him, trying to decide if it is indeed safe.*)

MASI: Nobu.
NOBU: Yeah?
MASI: He's taking a nap. In the bedroom. He likes to do that after dinner.
NOBU: What is he? An old man or something?
MASI: He just likes to take naps. You do, too.
NOBU: In front of the TV. But I don't go into the bedroom and lie down. Well, where is he? Bring him out. Don't I get to meet him?
MASI: You sure? (MASI *looks at him for a long while. She believes him. She turns to go wake* SADAO *up, then stops.*) Chester Yoshikawa? That night in the camps when I didn't show up for the dance? Chester Yoshikawa? We just talked. That's all.

(MASI *leaves for the bedroom to awaken* SADAO. NOBU *looks slowly around the apartment. It's* MASI *and yet it isn't.* NOBU *suddenly has no desire to meet* SADAO. *He doesn't want to see them together in this apartment.* NOBU *exits abruptly.* MASI *appears cautiously leading out a yawning* SADAO. *They look around. No* NOBU. *All they see is his shotgun leaning against the wall.*

As MASI *and* SADAO *dim to darkness,* MARSHA *and* JUDY *are lit in a pool of light extreme downstage.* MARSHA *is holding a small kite and slowly moving it above* TIMOTHY *who is held by* JUDY. *They sit in silence as* MARSHA *moves the kite.*)

JUDY: I can't believe he gave the kite to Timothy. He gets so mad if you even touch them. And he never flies them.

(*Pause.*)

MARSHA (*moving the kite*): No. He never flies them.

(*They dim to half. They turn to watch the action taking place center stage.*)
    [END OF SCENE]

SCENE FOURTEEN

Darkness. Two days later. Onstage, the TV light comes on. NOBU's *face lit by the screen's light. Lights come up and* NOBU *is now lit in a pool of light, seated at sofa watching TV. No kite on the coffee table. The rest of the place is in darkness.* MASI *is lit in a pool of light. She stands, staring pensively downstage into space. In her arms she is holding the brown paper bag of newly washed clothes. She turns and moves towards* NOBU's *place.*

As she enters the lights come up full on the house.

NOBU *is still sitting on the sofa watching TV.* MASI *goes over to the kitchen table and takes out the newly washed clothes, stacking them in neat piles on the table. She then proceeds to pick up the clothes scattered on the floor and to put them in the bag. She is ready to leave.* MASI *takes the bag of dirty clothes and moves towards the door, then stops. She makes up her mind about something she has been struggling with for a while. Masi returns to the kitchen and leaves the bag of* NOBU's *dirty clothes on the table. As she opens the door to leave,* MASI *looks back at* NOBU *and watches him for a brief moment.*

During this whole time, NOBU *has never turned around to look at* MASI *though he is very aware of what is going on.* MASI *sadly turns and exits through the door. Lights dim with* NOBU *silently watching TV. Briefly,* NOBU's *face is lit by the dancing light of the television screen. At the same instant, the brown paper bag of wash on the table is illuminated by a shaft of light. His phone begins to ring.* NOBU *turns to look at it. Blackout on* NOBU. *The wash fades into darkness. The phone continues to ring for a few moments. Then, silence.*

[END OF PLAY]

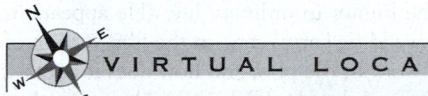

VIRTUAL LOCALE

Philip Kan Gotanda's Website. Playwright and filmmaker Philip Kan Gotanda's personal website features his biography, news on his recent plays and independent films, an extensive collection of publications about him and his work, photographs, and glimpses of works in progress and other writings. Go to *http://www.philipkangotanda.com.*

Talking about the Text

1. How do you respond to Masi? Consider both her attempts to continue to be a good (if separated) Japanese wife and her deepening relationship with Sadao.

2. What do you sense to be particularly "Japanese" about *The Wash*? You might want to discuss both behavior and beliefs as well as gestures and everyday concerns (e.g., the making of tea).

3. What do you make of Nobu's refusal to acknowledge his African American son-in-law and his grandson? How do you interpret his attempts during the course of the play to reach out to them and to his angry daughter? Do you interpret his original stance as racial prejudice or as tribalism ("Japanese marry Japanese") or both? What is it that moves him to a different attitude toward his grandson and son-in-law?

4. Fishing is important for several of the characters in *The Wash*. Imagine you were to employ a sport or game in a play of your own. How could it be used to characterize different people? How might their involvement with the sport or game serve to illustrate something important about them?

Writing about the Text

1. Write about how your response to Nobu changes during the course of the play. Does the characterization of him in the introduction to the play remain accurate? What attitude do you have at the end? Show what brings about any changes in your response, using specific examples from the text.

2. Typically, children of a marriage like that of Nobu and Masi are less culturally traditional than their parents and more assimilated into mainstream American culture; conflict frequently grows from tension between the parents' more Asian/Japanese ways and the children's more "American" identity. This usual allocation of conservatism and openness to change is not as clear in *The Wash*. Write an essay about the ways in which the characters in *The Wash* do not enact the traditional split between generations in an immigrant family.

Linking the Text to Other Texts

1. Compare the play to the film version of *The Wash*. What changes have occurred in the process of filming the play? Which changes are traceable to the differences between the media? Why do you think certain scenes and speeches are added and omitted, and what effect does this have on our viewing and interpretation of the story? Because Gotanda wrote the script for the film, we can assume that the changes were part of the playwright's vision for the movie. How does the film version of the play alter or add to our impressions of him?

2. As a playwright, Philip Gotanda sees the humor in ordinary life. (He appears in the brief comic role of the groom in the wedding party scene in the film version of *The Wash*.) Where do you see humor at work in the play, and how does it operate on the audience? Is it different in the film and the play? Which employs more humor?

3. How does Gotanda's portrayal of duality and ethnicity compare with the portrayals in Gish Jen's "In the American Society" (see p. 463), Jhumpa Lahiri's "The Third and Final Continent" (see p. 448), or Junot Diaz's "Fiesta, 1980" (see p. 479)?

Starting Point for Further Research: Philip Kan Gotanda

- **Interview:** Lia Chang, Lia. "Life Tastes Good for Philip Kan Gotanda." *Asian Connections*, November 2002. *http://www.asianconnections.com/entertainment/ interviews/2002/12/11/philip.gotanda/.*

AUGUST WILSON   (1945–2005)

The Piano Lesson   (1990)

August Wilson was born and raised in a poor family in Pittsburgh. Largely self-educated, he dropped out of high school to write, supporting himself by low-level jobs. In the 1960s he founded a Pittsburgh theatrical company, Black Horizons on the Hill. He later described himself then as "a cultural nationalist" who was attempting "to raise consciousness through theater." He moved to Minnesota, where his first play, Jitney, was a success. His breakthrough play that first attracted wide critical attention was Ma Rainey's Black Bottom, which reached Broadway in 1984; set in the 1920s, it dramatizes the conflicts between the famous blues diva and a member of her band.

From the 1987 production of August Wilson's The Piano Lesson.

The Pulitzer Prize–winning The Piano Lesson *is the fourth in August Wilson's series of African American "historical" plays, each set in a different decade of the twentieth century.* The Piano Lesson *is set during the Great Depression of the 1930s. Wilson's other plays in this project are* Jitney *(1982),* Ma Rainey's Black Bottom *(1984),* Fences *(1985; Pulitzer Prize),* Joe Turner's Come and Gone *(1986),* Two Trains Running *(1990),* Seven Guitars *(1995),* King Hedley II *(2000),* Gem of the Ocean *(2003), and* Radio Golf *(2005). One remarkable circumstance that has given these plays additional unity is that until the 1995 production of* Seven Guitars, *all of the plays had been directed by Lloyd Richards, a former dean at the Yale School of Drama, himself African American and a long-standing friend of Wilson.*

Except in the case of blues singer Ma Rainey, Wilson's plays do not directly involve famous African Americans or celebrated twentieth-century events. But they are historical plays in two main senses: they involve the personal and family histories of the characters, and those particular histories are affected by the great themes of African American stories in the American colonies and the United States: the beginnings in Africa, the Middle Passage, the centuries of slavery, sharecropping and Jim Crow in the post–Civil War South, the great migration to the North, and the civil rights movement. Until they have confronted their personal and racial history, which are of course intertwined and entangled, Wilson's characters are unable to discover their own full identities, their dignity, and their way forward in life— "their own songs" as it's said in Joe Turner's Come and Gone. *Many of the characters have avoided the past or shut it away (certainly Berniece in* The Piano Lesson *falls into this category), and to confront it is painful and even dangerous; it involves struggles with ghosts, visions, old furies, hurts, and losses. Even though almost all of the characters are northerners, most of them residents of Pittsburgh, they are all recent enough migrants from the South to retain foodways, patterns of speech, and bitter memories from what they call "down there." For them, the slave past, the Middle Passage, and even the sense of an African past are not so distant. When they try to reject these roots and buy too much into white culture, they set themselves adrift.*

In The Piano Lesson, *the piano invokes slavery, the African past, white–black conflicts and friendships, black music, and the immense sufferings caused by black and white efforts to possess the piano. The different members of the Charles family disagree on the precise meaning of the piano. Even though Boy Willie partially acknowledges the symbolic importance of the piano, he contends that reestablishing the family in the South on the land owned by the family that owned the Charleses as slaves is the proper way to resolve the open sores of the past. Therefore the decision about its future is a terribly contentious and momentous one.*

The Piano Lesson

Characters

Doaker Charles	*Lymon*
Berniece, Doaker's niece	*Avery*
Maretha, Berniece's eleven-year-old daughter	*Wining Boy*
Boy Willie	*Grace*

SETTING: *The action of the play takes place in the kitchen and parlor of the house where Doaker Charles lives with his niece, Berniece, and her eleven-year-old daughter, Maretha. The house is sparsely furnished, and although there is evidence of a woman's touch, there is a lack of warmth and vigor. Berniece and Maretha occupy the upstairs rooms. Doaker's room is prominent and opens onto the kitchen. Dominating the parlor is an old upright piano. On the legs of the piano, carved in the manner of African sculpture, are masklike figures resembling totems. The carvings are rendered with a grace and power of invention that lifts them out of the realm of craftsmanship and into the realm of art. At left is a staircase leading to the upstairs.*

ACT I

Scene I

The lights come up on the Charles household. It is five o'clock in the morning. The dawn is beginning to announce itself, but there is something in the air that belongs to the night. A stillness that is a portent, a gathering, a coming together of something akin to a storm. There is a loud knock at the door.

BOY WILLIE (*offstage, calling*): Hey, Doaker . . . Doaker! (*He knocks again and calls.*) Hey Doaker! Hey, Berniece! Berniece!

Doaker enters from his room. He is a tall, thin man of forty-seven, with severe features, who has for all intents and purposes retired from the world though he works full-time as a railroad cook.

DOAKER: Who is it?

BOY WILLIE: Open the door, nigger! It's me . . . Boy Willie!

DOAKER: Who?

BOY WILLIE: Boy Willie! Open the door!

Doaker opens the door and Boy Willie and Lymon enter. Boy Willie is thirty years old. He has an infectious grin and a boyishness that is apt for his name. He is brash and impulsive, talkative, and somewhat crude in speech and manner. Lymon is twenty-nine. Boy Willie's partner, he talks little, and then with a straightforwardness that is often disarming.

DOAKER: What you doing up here?

BOY WILLIE: I told you, Lymon. Lymon talking about you might be sleep. This is Lymon. You remember Lymon Jackson from down home? This my Uncle Doaker.

DOAKER: What you doing up here? I couldn't figure out who that was. I thought you was still down in Mississippi.

BOY WILLIE: Me and Lymon selling watermelons. We got a truck out there. Got a whole truckload of watermelons. We brought them up here to sell. Where's Berniece? (*Calls.*) Hey, Berniece!

DOAKER: Berniece up there sleep.

BOY WILLIE: Well, let her get up. (*Calls.*) Hey, Berniece!

DOAKER: She got to go to work in the morning.

BOY WILLIE: Well she can get up and say hi. It's been three years since I seen her. (*Calls.*) Hey, Berniece! It's me . . . Boy Willie.

DOAKER: Berniece don't like all that hollering now. She got to work in the morning.

BOY WILLIE: She can go on back to bed. Me and Lymon been riding two days in that truck . . . the least she can do is get up and say hi.

DOAKER (*looking out the window*): Where you all get that truck from?

BOY WILLIE: It's Lymon's. I told him let's get a load of watermelons and bring them up here.

LYMON: Boy Willie say he going back, but I'm gonna stay. See what it's like up here.

BOY WILLIE: You gonna carry me down there first.

LYMON: I told you I ain't going back down there and take a chance on that truck breaking down again. You can take the train. Hey, tell him Doaker, he can take the train back. After we sell them watermelons he have enough money he can buy him a whole railroad car.

DOAKER: You got all them watermelons stacked up there no wonder the truck broke down. I'm surprised you made it this far with a load like that. Where you break down at?

BOY WILLIE: We broke down three times! It took us two and a half days to get here. It's a good thing we picked them watermelons fresh.

LYMON: We broke down twice in West Virginia. The first time was just as soon as we got out of Sunflower. About forty miles out she broke down. We got it going and got all the way to West Virginia before she broke down again.

BOY WILLIE: We had to walk about five miles for some water.

LYMON: It got a hole in the radiator but it runs pretty good. You have to pump the brakes sometime before they catch. Boy Willie have his door open and be ready to jump when that happens.

BOY WILLIE: Lymon think that's funny. I told the nigger I give him ten dollars to get the brakes fixed. But he thinks that funny.

LYMON: They don't need fixing. All you got to do is pump them till they catch.

> *Berniece enters on the stairs. Thirty-five years old, with an eleven-year-old daughter, she is still in mourning for her husband after three years.*

BERNIECE: What you doing all that hollering for?

BOY WILLIE: Hey, Berniece, Doaker said you was asleep. I said at least you could get up and say hi.

BERNIECE: It's five o'clock in the morning and you come in here with all this noise. You can't come like normal folks. You got to bring all that noise with you.

BOY WILLIE: Hell, I ain't done nothing but come in and say hi. I ain't got in the house good.

BERNIECE: That's what I'm talking about. You start all that hollering and carry on as soon as you hit the door.

BOY WILLIE: Aw, hell, woman, I was glad to see Doaker. You ain't had to come down if you didn't want to. I come eighteen hundred miles to see my sister I figure she might want to get up and say hi. Other than that you can go back upstairs. What you got, Doaker? Where your bottle? Me and Lymon want a drink. *(To Berniece.)* This is Lymon. You remember, Lymon Jackson from down home.

LYMON: How you doing, Berniece? You look just like I thought you looked.

BERNIECE: Why you all got to come in hollering and carrying on? Waking the neighbors with all that noise.

BOY WILLIE: They can come over and join the party. We fixing to have a party. Doaker, where your bottle? Me and Lymon celebrating. The Ghosts of the Yellow Dog got Sutter.

BERNIECE: Say what?

BOY WILLIE: Ask Lymon, they found him the next morning. Say he drowned in his well.

DOAKER: When this happen, Boy Willie?

BOY WILLIE: About three weeks ago. Me and Lymon was over in Stoner County when we heard about it. We laughed. We thought it was funny. A great big old three-hundred-and-forty-pound man gonna fall down his well.

LYMON: It remind me of Humpty Dumpty.

BOY WILLIE: Everybody say the Ghosts of the Yellow Dog pushed him.

BERNIECE: I don't want to hear that nonsense. Somebody down there pushing them people in their wells.

DOAKER: What was you and Lymon doing over in Stoner County?

BOY WILLIE: We was down there working. Lymon got some people down there.

LYMON: My cousin got some land down there. We was helping him.

BOY WILLIE: Got near about a hundred acres. He got it set up real nice. Me and Lymon was down there chopping down trees. We was using Lymon's truck to haul the wood. Me and Lymon used to haul wood all around them parts. *(To Berniece.)* Me and Lymon got a truckload of watermelons out there. *(Berniece crosses to the window to the parlor.)* Doaker, where your bottle? I know you got a bottle stuck up in your room. Come on, me and Lymon want a drink.

> *Doaker exits into his room.*

BERNIECE: Where you all get that truck from?

BOY WILLIE: I told you it's Lymon's.

BERNIECE: Where you get the truck from, Lymon?

LYMON: I bought it.

BERNIECE: Where he get that truck from, Boy Willie?

BOY WILLIE: He told you he bought it. Bought it for a hundred and twenty dollars. I can't say where he got that hundred and twenty dollars from . . . but he bought that old piece of truck from Henry Porter. *(To Lymon.)* Where you get that hundred and twenty dollars from, nigger?

LYMON: I got it like you get yours. I know how to take care of money.

> *Doaker brings a bottle and sets it on the table.*

BOY WILLIE: Aw hell, Doaker got some of that good whiskey. Don't give Lymon none of that. He ain't used to good whiskey. He liable to get sick.

LYMON: I done had good whiskey before.

BOY WILLIE: Lymon bought that truck so he have him a place to sleep. He down there wasn't doing no work or nothing. Sheriff looking for him. He bought that truck to keep away from the sheriff. Got Stovall looking for him too. He down there sleeping in that truck ducking and dodging both of them. I told him come on let's go up and see my sister.

BERNIECE: What the sheriff looking for you for, Lymon?

BOY WILLIE: The man don't want you to know all his business. He's my company. He ain't asking you no questions.

LYMON: It wasn't nothing. It was just a misunderstanding.

BERNIECE: He in my house. You say the sheriff looking for him, I wanna know what he looking for him for. Otherwise you all can go back out there and be where nobody don't have to ask you nothing.

LYMON: It was just a misunderstanding. Sometimes me and the sheriff we don't think alike. So we just got crossed on each other.

BERNIECE: Might be looking for him about that truck. He might have stole that truck.

BOY WILLIE: We ain't stole no truck, woman. I told you Lymon bought it.

DOAKER: Boy Willie and Lymon got more sense than to ride all the way up here in a stolen truck with a load of watermelons. Now they might have stole them watermelons, but I don't believe they stole that truck.

BOY WILLIE: You don't even know the man good and you calling him a thief. And we ain't stole them watermelons either. Them old man Pitterford's watermelons. He give me and Lymon all we could load for ten dollars.

DOAKER: No wonder you got them stacked up out there. You must have five hundred watermelons stacked up out there.

BERNIECE: Boy Willie, when you and Lymon planning on going back?

BOY WILLIE: Lymon say he staying. As soon as we sell them watermelons I'm going on back.

BERNIECE *(starts to exit up the stairs)*: That's what you need to do. And you need to do it quick. Come in here disrupting the house. I don't want all that loud carrying on around here. I'm surprised you ain't woke Maretha up.

BOY WILLIE: I was fixing to get her now. *(Calls.)* Hey, Maretha!

DOAKER: Berniece don't like all that hollering now.

BERNIECE: Don't you wake that child up!

BOY WILLIE: You going up there . . . wake her up and tell her her uncle's here. I ain't seen her in three years. Wake her up and send her down here. She can go back to bed.

BERNIECE: I ain't waking that child up . . . and don't you be making all that noise. You and Lymon need to sell them watermelons and go on back.

Berniece exits up the stairs.

BOY WILLIE: I see Berniece still try to be stuck up.

DOAKER: Berniece alright. She don't want you making all that noise. Maretha up there sleep. Let her sleep until she get up. She can see you then.

BOY WILLIE: I ain't thinking about Berniece. You hear from Wining Boy? You know Cleotha died?

DOAKER: Yeah, I heard that. He come by here about a year ago. Had a whole sack of money. He stayed here about two weeks. Ain't offered nothing. Berniece asked him for three dollars to buy some food and he got mad and left.

LYMON: Who's Wining Boy?

BOY WILLIE: That's my uncle. That's Doaker's brother. You heard me talk about Wining Boy. He play piano. He done made some records and everything. He still doing that, Doaker?

DOAKER: He made one or two records a long time ago. That's the only ones I ever known him to make. If you let him tell it he a big recording star.

BOY WILLIE: He stopped down home about two years ago. That's what I hear. I don't know. Me and Lymon was up on Parchman Farm doing them three years.

DOAKER: He don't never stay in one place. Now, he been here about eight months ago. Back in the winter. Now, you subject not to see him for another two years. It's liable to be that long before he stop by.

BOY WILLIE: If he had a whole sack of money you liable never to see him. You ain't gonna see him until he get broke. Just as soon as that sack of money is gone you look up and he be on your doorstep.

LYMON (*noticing the piano*): Is that the piano?

BOY WILLIE: Yeah . . . look here, Lymon. See how it's carved up real nice and polished and everything? You never find you another piano like that.

LYMON: Yeah, that look real nice.

BOY WILLIE: I told you. See how it's polished? My mama used to polish it every day. See all them pictures carved on it? That's what I was talking about. You can get a nice price for that piano.

LYMON: That's all Boy Willie talked about the whole trip up here. I got tired of hearing him talking about the piano.

BOY WILLIE: All you want to talk about is women. You ought to hear this nigger, Doaker. Talking about all the women he gonna get when he get up here. He ain't had none down there but he gonna get a hundred when he get up here.

DOAKER: How your people doing down there, Lymon?

LYMON: They alright. They still there. I come up here to see what it's like up here. Boy Willie trying to get me to go back and farm with him.

BOY WILLIE: Sutter's brother selling the land. He say he gonna sell it to me. That's why I come up here. I got one part of it. Sell them watermelons and get me another part. Get Berniece to sell that piano and I'll have the third part.

DOAKER: Berniece ain't gonna sell that piano.

BOY WILLIE: I'm gonna talk to her. When she see I got a chance to get Sutter's land she'll come around.

DOAKER: You can put that thought out of your mind. Berniece ain't gonna sell that piano.

BOY WILLIE: I'm gonna talk to her. She been playing on it?

DOAKER: You know she won't touch that piano. I ain't never known her to touch it since Mama Ola died. That's over seven years now. She say it got blood on it. She got Maretha playing on it though. Say Maretha can go on and do everything she can't do. Got her in an extra school down at the Irene Kaufman Settlement House. She want Maretha to grow up and be a school-teacher. She say she good enough she can teach on the piano.

BOY WILLIE: Maretha don't need to be playing on no piano. She can play on the guitar.

DOAKER: How much land Sutter got left?

BOY WILLIE: Got a hundred acres. Good land. He done sold it piece by piece, he kept the good part for himself. Now he got to give that up. His brother come down from Chicago for the funeral . . . he up there in Chicago got some kind of business with soda fountain equipment. He anxious to sell the land, Doaker. He don't want to be bothered with it. He called me to him and said cause of how long our families done known each other and how we been good friends and all, say he wanted to sell the land to me. Say he'd rather see me with it than Jim Stovall. Told me he'd let me have it for two thousand dollars cash money. He don't know I found out the most Stovall would give him for it was fifteen hundred dollars. He trying to get that extra five hundred out of me telling me he doing me a favor. I thanked him just as nice. Told him what a good man Sutter was and how he had my sympathy and all. Told him to give me two weeks. He said he'd wait on me. That's why I come up here. Sell them watermelons. Get Berniece to sell that piano. Put them two parts with the part I done saved. Walk in there. Tip my hat. Lay my money down on the table. Get my deed and walk on out. This time I get to keep all the cotton. Hire me some men to work it for me. Gin my cotton. Get my seed. And I'll see you again next year. Might even plant some to-bacco or some oats.

DOAKER: You gonna have a hard time trying to get Berniece to sell that piano. You know Avery Brown from down there, don't you? He up here now. He fol-lowed Berniece up here trying to get her to marry him after Crawley got killed. He been up here about two years. He call himself a preacher now.

BOY WILLIE: I know Avery. I know him from when he used to work on the Will-shaw place. Lymon know him too.

DOAKER: He after Berniece to marry him. She keep telling him no but he won't give up. He keep pressing her on it.

BOY WILLIE: Avery think all white men is bigshots. He don't know there some white men ain't got as much as he got.

DOAKER: He supposed to come past here this morning. Berniece going down to the bank with him to see if he can get a loan to start his church. That's why I know Berniece ain't gonna sell that piano. He tried to get her to sell it to help him start his church. Sent the man around and everything.

BOY WILLIE: What man?

DOAKER: Some white fellow was going around to all the colored people's houses looking to buy up musical instruments. He'd buy anything. Drums. Guitars. Harmonicas. Pianos. Avery sent him past here. He looked at the piano and got excited. Offered her a nice price. She turned him down and got on Avery for sending him past. The man kept on her about two weeks. He seen where she wasn't gonna sell it, he gave her his number and told her if she ever wanted to sell it to call him first. Say he'd go one better than what anybody else would give her for it.

BOY WILLIE: How much he offer her for it?

DOAKER: Now you know me. She didn't say and I didn't ask. I just know it was a nice price.

LYMON: All you got to do is find out who he is and tell him somebody else wanna buy it from you. Tell him you can't make up your mind who to sell it to, and if he like Doaker say, he'll give you anything you want for it.

BOY WILLIE:
That's what I'm gonna do. I'm gonna find out who he is from Avery.

DOAKER:
It ain't gonna do you no good. Berniece ain't gonna sell that piano.

BOY WILLIE: She ain't got to sell it. I'm gonna sell it. I own just as much of it as she does.

BERNIECE (offstage, hollers): Doaker! Go on get away. Doaker!

DOAKER (calling): Berniece?

Doaker and Boy Willie rush to the stairs, Boy Willie runs up the stairs, passing Berniece as she enters, running.

DOAKER: Berniece, what the matter? You alright? What's the matter?

Berniece tries to catch her breath. She is unable to speak.

DOAKER: That's alright. Take your time. You alright. What's the matter? (He calls.) Hey, Boy Willie?

BOY WILLIE (offstage): Ain't nobody up here.

BERNIECE: Sutter . . . Sutter's standing at the top of the steps.

DOAKER (calls): Boy Willie!

Lymon crosses to the stairs and looks up. Boy Willie enters from the stairs.

BOY WILLIE: Hey Doaker, what's wrong with her? Berniece, what's wrong? Who was you talking to?

DOAKER: She say she seen Sutter's ghost standing at the top of the stairs.

BOY WILLIE: Seen what? Sutter? She ain't seen no Sutter.

BERNIECE: He was standing right up there.

BOY WILLIE (entering on the stairs): That's all in Berniece's head. Ain't nobody up there. Go on up there, Doaker.

DOAKER: I'll take your word for it. Berniece talking about what she seen. She say
Sutter's ghost standing at the top of the steps. She ain't just make all that up.

BOY WILLIE: She up there dreaming. She ain't seen no ghost.

LYMON: You want a glass of water, Berniece? Get her a glass of water, Boy Willie.

BOY WILLIE: She don't need no water. She ain't seen nothing. Go on up there
and look. Ain't nobody up there but Maretha.

DOAKER: Let Berniece tell it.

BOY WILLIE: I ain't stopping her from telling it.

DOAKER: What happened, Berniece?

BERNIECE: I come out of my room to come back down here and Sutter was
standing there in the hall.

BOY WILLIE: What he look like?

BERNIECE: He look like Sutter. He look like he always look.

BOY WILLIE: Sutter couldn't find his way from Big Sandy to Little Sandy. How
he gonna find his way all the way up here to Pittsburgh? Sutter ain't never
even heard of Pittsburgh.

DOAKER: Go on, Berniece.

BERNIECE: Just standing there with the blue suit on.

BOY WILLIE: The man ain't never left Marlin County when he was living . . .
and he's gonna come all the way up here now that he's dead?

DOAKER: Let her finish. I want to hear what she got to say.

BOY WILLIE: I'll tell you this. If Berniece had seen him like she think she seen
him she'd still be running.

DOAKER: Go on, Berniece. Don't pay Boy Willie no mind.

BERNIECE: He was standing there . . . had his hand on top of his head. Look like
he might have thought if he took his hand down his head might have fallen
off.

LYMON: Did he have on a hat?

BERNIECE: Just had on that blue suit . . . I told him to go away and he just stood
there looking at me . . . calling Boy Willie's name.

BOY WILLIE: What he calling my name for?

BERNIECE: I believe you pushed him in the well.

BOY WILLIE: Now what kind of sense that make? You telling me I'm gonna go
out there and hide in the weeds with all them dogs and things he got around
there . . . I'm gonna hide and wait till I catch him looking down his well just
right . . . then I'm gonna run over and push him in. A great big old three-
hundred-and-forty-pound man.

BERNIECE: Well, what he calling your name for?

BOY WILLIE: He bending over looking down his well, woman . . . how he know
who pushed him? It could have been anybody. Where was you when Sutter
fell in his well? Where was Doaker? Me and Lymon was over in Stoner
County. Tell her, Lymon. The Ghosts of the Yellow Dog got Sutter. That's
what happened to him.

BERNIECE: You can talk all that Ghosts of the Yellow Dog stuff if you want. I
know better.

LYMON: The Ghosts of the Yellow Dog pushed him. That's what the people say.
They found him in his well and all the people say it must be the Ghosts of
the Yellow Dog. Just like all them other men.

BOY WILLIE: Come talking about he looking for me. What he come all the way up here for? If he looking for me all he got to do is wait. He could have saved himself a trip if he looking for me. That ain't nothing but in Berniece's head. Ain't no telling what she liable to come up with next.

BERNIECE: Boy Willie, I want you and Lymon to go ahead and leave my house. Just go on somewhere. You don't do nothing but bring trouble with you everywhere you go. If it wasn't for you Crawley would still be alive.

BOY WILLIE: Crawley what? I ain't had nothing to do with Crawley getting killed. Crawley three time seven. He had his own mind.

BERNIECE: Just go on and leave. Let Sutter go somewhere else looking for you.

BOY WILLIE: I'm leaving. Soon as we sell them watermelons. Other than that I ain't going nowhere. Hell, I just got here. Talking about Sutter looking for me. Sutter was looking for that piano. That's what he was looking for. He had to die to find out where that piano was at . . . If I was you I'd get rid of it. That's the way to get rid of Sutter's ghost. Get rid of that piano.

BERNIECE: I want you and Lymon to go on and take all this confusion out of my house!

BOY WILLIE: Hey, tell her, Doaker. What kind of sense that make? I told you, Lymon, as soon as Berniece see me she was gonna start something. Didn't I tell you that? Now she done made up that story about Sutter just so she could tell me to leave her house. Well, hell, I ain't going nowhere till I sell them watermelons.

BERNIECE: Well why don't you go out there and sell them! Sell them and go on back!

BOY WILLIE: We waiting till the people get up.

LYMON: Boy Willie say if you get out there too early and wake the people up they get mad at you and won't buy nothing from you.

DOAKER: You won't be waiting long. You done let the sun catch up with you. This the time everybody be getting up around here.

BERNIECE: Come on, Doaker, walk up here with me. Let me get Maretha up and get her started. I got to get ready myself. Boy Willie, just go on out there and sell them watermelons and you and Lymon leave my house.

Berniece and Doaker exit up the stairs.

BOY WILLIE (*calling after them*): If you see Sutter up there . . . tell him I'm down here waiting on him.

LYMON: What if she see him again?

BOY WILLIE: That's all in her head. There ain't no ghost up there. (*Calls.*) Hey, Doaker . . . I told you ain't nothing up there.

LYMON: I'm glad he didn't say he was looking for me.

BOY WILLIE: I wish I would see Sutter's ghost. Give me a chance to put a whupping on him.

LYMON: You ought to stay up here with me. You be down there working his land . . . he might come looking for you all the time.

BOY WILLIE: I ain't thinking about Sutter. And I ain't thinking about staying up here. You stay up here. I'm going back and get Sutter's land. You think you ain't got to work up here. You think this the land of milk and honey. But I ain't scared of work. I'm going back and farm every acre of that land.

Doaker enters from the stairs.

I told you there ain't nothing up there, Doaker. Berniece dreaming all that.

DOAKER: I believe Berniece seen something. Berniece level-headed. She ain't just made all that up. She say Sutter had on a suit. I don't believe she ever seen Sutter in a suit. I believe that's what he was buried in, and that's what Berniece saw.

BOY WILLIE: Well, let her keep on seeing him then. As long as he don't mess with me. (*Doaker starts to cook his breakfast.*) I heard about you, Doaker. They say you got all the women looking out for you down home. They be looking to see you coming. Say you got a different one every two weeks. Say they be fighting one another for you to stay with them. (*To Lymon.*) Look at him, Lymon. He know it's true.

DOAKER: I ain't thinking about no women. They never get me tied up with them. After Coreen I ain't got no use for them. I stay up on Jack Slattery's place when I be down there. All them women want is somebody with a steady payday.

BOY WILLIE: That ain't what I hear. I hear every two weeks the women all put on their dresses and line up at the railroad station.

DOAKER: I don't get down there but once a month. I used to go down there every two weeks but they keep switching me around. They keep switching all the fellows around.

BOY WILLIE: Shakespeare can't turn that railroad loose. He was working the railroad when I was walking around crying for sugartit. My mama used to brag on him.

DOAKER: I'm cooking now, but I used to line track. I pieced together the Yellow Dog stitch by stitch. Rail by rail. Line track all up around there. I lined track all up around Sunflower and Clarksdale. Wining Boy worked with me. He helped me put in some of that track. He'd work it for six months and quit. Go back to playing piano and gambling.

BOY WILLIE: How long you been with the railroad now?

DOAKER: Twenty-seven years. Now, I'll tell you something about the railroad. What I done learned after twenty-seven years. See, you got North. You got West. You look over here you got South. Over there you got East. Now, you can start from anywhere. Don't care where you at. You got to go one of them four ways. And whichever way you decide to go they got a railroad that will take you there. Now, that's something simple. You think anybody would be able to understand that. But you'd be surprised how many people trying to go North get on a train going West. They think the train's supposed to go where they going rather than where it's going.

Now, why people going? Their sister's sick. They leaving before they kill somebody . . . and they sitting across from somebody who's leaving to keep from getting killed. They leaving cause they can't get satisfied. They going to meet someone. I wish I had a dollar for every time that someone wasn't at the station to meet them. I done seen that a lot. In between the time they sent the telegram and the time the person get there . . . they done forgot all about them.

They got so many trains out there they have a hard time keeping them from running into each other. Got trains going every whichaway. Got people on all of them. Somebody going where somebody just left. If everybody stay in one place I believe this would be a better world. Now what I done learned after twenty-seven years of railroading is this . . . if the train stays on the track . . . it's going to get where it's going. It might not be where you going. If it ain't, then all you got to do is sit and wait cause the train's coming back to get you. The train don't never stop. It'll come back every time. Now I'll tell you another thing . . .

BOY WILLIE: What you cooking over there, Doaker? Me and Lymon's hungry.

DOAKER: Go on down there to Wylie and Kirkpatrick to Eddie's restaurant. Coffee cost a nickel and you can get two eggs, sausage, and grits for fifteen cents. He even give you a biscuit with it.

BOY WILLIE: That look good what you got. Give me a little piece of that grilled bread.

DOAKER: Here . . . go on take the whole piece.

BOY WILLIE: Here you go, Lymon . . . you want a piece?

He gives Lymon a piece of toast. Maretha enters from the stairs.

BOY WILLIE: Hey, sugar. Come here and give me a hug. Come on give Uncle Boy Willie a hug. Don't be shy. Look at her, Doaker. She done got bigger. Ain't she got big?

DOAKER: Yeah, she getting up there.

BOY WILLIE: How you doing, sugar?

MARETHA: Fine.

BOY WILLIE: You was just a little old thing last time I seen you. You remember me, don't you? This your Uncle Boy Willie from down South. That there's Lymon. He my friend. We come up here to sell watermelons. You like watermelons? (*Maretha nods.*) We got a whole truckload out front. You can have as many as you want. What you been doing?

MARETHA: Nothing.

BOY WILLIE: Don't be shy now. Look at you getting all big. How old is you?

MARETHA: Eleven. I'm gonna be twelve soon.

BOY WILLIE: You like it up here? You like the North?

MARETHA: It's alright.

BOY WILLIE: That there's Lymon. Did you say hi to Lymon?

MARETHA: Hi.

LYMON: How you doing? You look just like your mama. I remember you when you was wearing diapers.

BOY WILLIE: You gonna come down South and see me? Uncle Boy Willie gonna get him a farm. Gonna get a great big old farm. Come down there and I'll teach you how to ride a mule. Teach you how to kill a chicken, too.

MARETHA: I seen my mama do that.

BOY WILLIE: Ain't nothing to it. You just grab him by his neck and twist it. Get you a real good grip and then you just wring his neck and throw him in the pot. Cook him up. Then you got some good eating. What you like to eat? What kind of food you like?

MARETHA: I like everything . . . except I don't like no black-eyed peas.

BOY WILLIE: Uncle Doaker tell me your mama got you playing that piano. Come on play something for me. (*Boy Willie crosses over to the piano followed by*

Maretha.) Show me what you can do. Come on now. Here . . . Uncle Boy Willie give you a dime . . . show me what you can do. Don't be bashful now. That dime say you can't be bashful. (*Maretha plays. It is something any beginner first learns.*) Here, let me show you something. (*Boy Willie sits and plays a simple boogie-woogie.*) See that? See what I'm doing? That's what you call the boogie-woogie. See now . . . you can get up and dance to that. That's how good it sound. It sound like you wanna dance. You can dance to that. It'll hold you up. Whatever kind of dance you wanna do you can dance to that right there. See that? See how it go? Ain't nothing to it. Go on you do it.

MARETHA: I got to read it on the paper.

BOY WILLIE: You don't need no paper. Go on. Do just like that there.

BERNIECE: Maretha! You get up here and get ready to go so you be on time. Ain't no need you trying to take advantage of company.

MARETHA: I got to go.

BOY WILLIE: Uncle Boy Willie gonna get you a guitar. Let Uncle Doaker teach you how to play that. You don't need to read no paper to play the guitar. Your mama told you about the piano? You know how them pictures got on there?

MARETHA: She say it just always been like that since she got it.

BOY WILLIE: You hear that, Doaker? And you sitting up here in the house with Berniece.

DOAKER: I ain't got nothing to do with that. I don't get in the way of Berniece's raising her.

BOY WILLIE: You tell your mama to tell you about that piano. You ask her how them pictures got on there. If she don't tell you I'll tell you.

BERNIECE: Maretha!

MARETHA: I got to get ready to go.

BOY WILLIE: She getting big, Doaker. You remember her, Lymon?

LYMON: She used to be real little.

> There is a knock on the door. Doaker goes to answer it. Avery enters.
> Thirty-eight years old, honest and ambitious, he has taken to the city like
> a fish to water, finding in it opportunities for growth and advancement
> that did not exist for him in the rural South. He is dressed in a suit and
> tie with a gold cross around his neck. He carries a small Bible.

DOAKER: Hey, Avery, come on in. Berniece upstairs.

BOY WILLIE: Look at him . . . look at him . . . he don't know what to say. He wasn't expecting to see me.

AVERY: Hey, Boy Willie. What you doing up here?

BOY WILLIE: Look at him, Lymon.

AVERY: Is that Lymon? Lymon Jackson?

BOY WILLIE: Yeah, you know Lymon.

DOAKER: Berniece be ready in a minute, Avery.

BOY WILLIE: Doaker say you a preacher now. What . . . we supposed to call you Reverend? You used to be plain old Avery. When you get to be a preacher, nigger?

LYMON: Avery say he gonna be a preacher so he don't have to work.

BOY WILLIE: I remember when you was down there on the Willshaw place planting cotton. You wasn't thinking about no Reverend then.

AVERY: That must be your truck out there. I saw that truck with them watermelons, I was trying to figure out what it was doing in front of the house.

BOY WILLIE: Yeah, me and Lymon selling watermelons. That's Lymon's truck.

DOAKER: Berniece say you all going down to the bank.

AVERY: Yeah, they give me a half day off work. I got an appointment to talk to the bank about getting a loan to start my church.

BOY WILLIE: Lymon say preachers don't have to work. Where you working at, nigger?

DOAKER: Avery got him one of them good jobs. He working at one of them skyscrapers downtown.

AVERY: I'm working down there at the Gulf Building running an elevator. Got a pension and everything. They even give you a turkey on Thanksgiving.

LYMON: How you know the rope ain't gonna break? Ain't you scared the rope's gonna break?

AVERY: That's steel. They got steel cables hold it up. It take a whole lot of breaking to break that steel. Naw, I ain't worried about nothing like that. It ain't nothing but a little old elevator. Now, I wouldn't get in none of them airplanes. You couldn't pay me to do nothing like that.

LYMON: That be fun. I'd rather do that than ride in one of them elevators.

BOY WILLIE: How many of them watermelons you wanna buy?

AVERY: I thought you was gonna give me one seeing as how you got a whole truck full.

BOY WILLIE: You can get one, get two. I'll give you two for a dollar.

AVERY: I can't eat but one. How much are they?

BOY WILLIE: Aw, nigger, you know I'll give you a watermelon. Go on, take as many as you want. Just leave some for me and Lymon to sell.

AVERY: I don't want but one.

BOY WILLIE: How you get to be a preacher, Avery? I might want to be a preacher one day. Have everybody call me Reverend Boy Willie.

AVERY: It come to me in a dream. God called me and told me he wanted me to be a shepherd for his flock. That's what I'm gonna call my church . . . The Good Shepherd Church of God in Christ.

DOAKER: Tell him what you told me. Tell him about the three hobos.

AVERY: Boy Willie don't want to hear all that.

LYMON: I do. Lots a people say your dreams can come true.

AVERY: Naw. You don't want to hear all that.

DOAKER: Go on. I told him you was a preacher. He didn't want to believe me. Tell him about the three hobos.

AVERY: Well, it come to me in a dream. See . . . I was sitting out in this railroad yard watching the trains go by. The train stopped and these three hobos got off. They told me they had come from Nazareth and was on their way to Jerusalem. They had three candles. They gave me one and told me to light it . . . but to be careful that it didn't go out. Next thing I knew I was standing in front of this house. Something told me to go knock on the door. This old woman opened the door and said they had been waiting on me. Then she led me into this room. It was a big room and it was full of all kinds of different people. They looked like anybody else except they all had sheep heads and was making noise like sheep make. I heard somebody call my name. I looked around and there was these same three hobos. They told me to take off my clothes and they give me a blue robe with gold thread. They washed my feet and combed my hair. Then they showed me these three doors and told me to pick one.

I went through one of them doors and that flame leapt off that candle and it seemed like my whole head caught fire. I looked around and there was four or five other men standing there with these same blue robes on. Then we heard a voice tell us to look out across this valley. We looked out and saw the valley was full of wolves. The voice told us that these sheep people that I had seen in the other room had to go over to the other side of this valley and somebody had to take them. Then I heard another voice say, "Who shall I send?" Next thing I knew I said, "Here I am. Send me." That's when I met Jesus. He say, "If you go, I'll go with you." Something told me to say, "Come on. Let's go." That's when I woke up. My head still felt like it was on fire . . . but I had a peace about myself that was hard to explain. I knew right then that I had been filled with the Holy Ghost and called to be a servant of the Lord. It took me a while before I could accept that. But then a lot of little ways God showed me that it was true. So I became a preacher.

LYMON: I see why you gonna call it the Good Shepherd Church. You dreaming about them sheep people. I can see that easy.

BOY WILLIE: Doaker say you sent some white man past the house to look at that piano. Say he was going around to all the colored people's houses looking to buy up musical instruments.

AVERY: Yeah, but Berniece didn't want to sell that piano. After she told me about it . . . I could see why she didn't want to sell it.

BOY WILLIE: What's this man's name?

AVERY: Oh, that's a while back now. I done forgot his name. He give Berniece a card with his name and telephone number on it, but I believe she threwed it away.

Berniece and Maretha enter from the stairs.

BERNIECE: Maretha, run back upstairs and get my pocketbook. And wipe that hair grease off your forehead. Go ahead, hurry up.

Maretha exits up the stairs.

How you doing, Avery? You done got all dressed up. You look nice. Boy Willie, I thought you and Lymon was going to sell them watermelons.

BOY WILLIE: Lymon done got sleepy. We liable to get some sleep first.

LYMON: I ain't sleepy.

DOAKER: As many watermelons as you got stacked up on that truck out there, you ought to have been gone.

BOY WILLIE: We gonna go in a minute. We going.

BERNIECE: Doaker. I'm gonna stop down there on Logan Street. You want anything?

DOAKER: You can pick up some ham hocks if you going down there. See if you can get the smoked ones. If they ain't got that get the fresh ones. Don't get the ones that got all that fat under the skin. Look for the long ones. They nice and lean. (*He gives her a dollar.*) Don't get the short ones lessen they smoked. If you got to get the fresh ones make sure that they the long ones. If they ain't got them smoked then go ahead and get the short ones. (*Pause.*)

You may as well get some turnip greens while you down there. I got some buttermilk . . . if you pick up some cornmeal I'll make me some cornbread and cook up them turnip greens.

Maretha enters from the stairs.

MARETHA: We gonna take the streetcar?

BERNIECE: Me and Avery gonna drop you off at the settlement house. You mind them people down there. Don't be going down there showing your color. Boy Willie, I done told you what to do. I'll see you later, Doaker.

AVERY: I'll be seeing you again, Boy Willie.

BOY WILLIE: Hey, Berniece . . . what's the name of that man Avery sent past say he want to buy the piano?

BERNIECE: I knew it. I knew it when I first seen you. I knew you was up to something.

BOY WILLIE: Sutter's brother say he selling the land to me. He waiting on me now. Told me he'd give me two weeks. I got one part. Sell them watermelons get me another part. Then we can sell the piano and I'll have the third part.

BERNIECE: I ain't selling that piano, Boy Willie. If that's why you come up here you can just forget about it. *(To Doaker.)* Doaker, I'll see you later. Boy Willie ain't nothing but a whole lot of mouth. I ain't paying him no mind. If he come up here thinking he gonna sell that piano then he done come up here for nothing.

Berniece, Avery, and Maretha exit the front door.

BOY WILLIE: Hey, Lymon! You ready to go sell these watermelons. *(Boy Willie and Lymon start to exit. At the door Boy Willie turns to Doaker.)* Hey, Doaker . . . if Berniece don't want to sell that piano . . . I'm gonna cut it in half and go on and sell my half.

Boy Willie and Lymon exit.
The lights go down on the scene.

SCENE II

The lights come up on the kitchen. It is three days later. Wining Boy sits at the kitchen table. There is a half-empty pint bottle on the table. Doaker busies himself washing pots. Wining Boy is fifty-six years old. Doaker's older brother, he tries to present the image of a successful musician and gambler, but his music, his clothes, and even his manner of presentation are old. He is a man who looking back over his life continues to live it with an odd mixture of zest and sorrow.

WINING BOY: So the Ghosts of the Yellow Dog got Sutter. That just go to show you I believe I always lived right. They say every dog gonna have his day and time it go around it sure come back to you. I done seen that a thousand times. I know the truth of that. But I'll tell you outright . . . if I see Sutter's ghost I'll be on the first thing I find that got wheels on it.

Doaker enters from his room.

DOAKER: Wining Boy!

WINING BOY: And I'll tell you another thing . . . Berniece ain't gonna sell that piano.

DOAKER: That's what she told him. He say he gonna cut it in half and go on and sell his half. They been around here three days trying to sell them watermelons. They trying to get out to where the white folks live but the truck keep breaking down. They go a block or two and it break down again. They trying to get out to Squirrel Hill and can't get around the corner. He say soon as he can get that truck empty to where he can set the piano up in there he gonna take it out of here and go sell it.

WINING BOY: What about them boys Sutter got? How come they ain't farming that land?

DOAKER: One of them going to school. He left down there and come North to school. The other one ain't got as much sense as that frying pan over yonder. That is the dumbest white man I ever seen. He'd stand in the river and watch it rise till it drown him.

WINING BOY: Other than seeing Sutter's ghost how's Berniece doing?

DOAKER: She doing alright. She still got Crawley on her mind. He been dead three years but she still holding on to him. She need to go out here and let one of these fellows grab a whole handful of whatever she got. She act like it done got precious.

WINING BOY: They always told me any fish will bite if you got good bait.

DOAKER: She stuck up on it. She think it's better than she is. I believe she messing around with Avery. They got something going. He a preacher now. If you let him tell it the Holy Ghost sat on his head and heaven opened up with thunder and lightning and God was calling his name. Told him to go out and preach and tend to his flock. That's what he gonna call his church. The Good Shepherd Church.

WINING BOY: They had that joker down in Spear walking around talking about he Jesus Christ. He gonna live the life of Christ. Went through the Last Supper and everything. Rented him a mule on Palm Sunday and rode through the town. Did everything . . . talking about he Christ. He did everything until they got up to that crucifixion part. Got up to that part and told everybody to go home and quit pretending. He got up to the crucifixion part and changed his mind. Had a whole bunch of folks come down here to see him get nailed to the cross. I don't know who's the worse fool. Him or them. Had all them folks come down there . . . even carried the cross up this little hill. People standing around waiting to see him get nailed to the cross and he stop everything and preach a little sermon and told everybody to go home. Had enough nerve to tell them to come to church on Easter Sunday to celebrate his resurrection.

DOAKER: I'm surprised Avery ain't thought about that. He trying every little thing to get him a congregation together. They meeting over at his house till he get him a church.

WINING BOY: Ain't nothing wrong with being a preacher. You got the preacher on one hand and the gambler on the other. Sometimes there ain't too much difference in them.

DOAKER: How long you been in Kansas City?

WINING BOY: Since I left here. I got tied up with some old gal down there. (*Pause.*) You know Cleotha died.

DOAKER: Yeah, I heard that last time I was down there. I was sorry to hear that.

WINING BOY: One of her friends wrote and told me. I got the letter right here. (*He takes the letter out of his pocket.*) I was down in Kansas City and she wrote and told me Cleotha had died. Name of Willa Bryant. She say she know cousin Rupert. (*He opens the letter and reads:*)

Dear Wining Boy: I am writing this letter to let you know Miss Cleotha Holman passed on Saturday the first of May she departed this world in the loving arms of her sister Miss Alberta Samuels. I know you would want to know this and am writing as a friend of Cleotha. There have been many hardships since last you seen her but she survived them all and to the end was a good woman whom I hope have God's grace and is in His Paradise. Your cousin Rupert Bates is my friend also and he give me your address and I pray this reaches you about Cleotha. Miss Willa Bryant. A friend.

(*He folds the letter and returns it to his pocket.*) They was nailing her coffin shut by the time I heard about it. I never knew she was sick. I believe it was that yellow jaundice. That's what killed her mama.

DOAKER: Cleotha wasn't but forty-some.

WINING BOY: She was forty-six. I got ten years on her. I met her when she was sixteen. You remember I used to run around there. Couldn't nothing keep me still. Much as I loved Cleotha I loved to ramble. Couldn't nothing keep me still. We got married and we used to fight about it all the time. Then one day she asked me to leave. Told me she loved me before I left. Told me, Wining Boy, you got a home as long as I got mine. And I believe in my heart I always felt that and that kept me safe.

DOAKER: Cleotha always did have a nice way about her.

WINING BOY: Man that woman was something. I used to thank the Lord. Many a night I sat up and looked out over my life. Said, well, I had Cleotha. When it didn't look like there was nothing else for me, I said, thank God, at least I had that. If ever I go anywhere in this life I done known a good woman. And that used to hold me till the next morning. (*Pause.*) What you got? Give me a little nip. I know you got something stuck up in your room.

DOAKER: I ain't seen you walk in here and put nothing on the table. You done sat there and drank up your whiskey. Now you talking about what you got.

WINING BOY: I got plenty money. Give me a little nip.

> *Doaker carries a glass into his room and returns with it half-filled. He sets it on the table in front of Wining Boy.*

WINING BOY: You hear from Coreen?

DOAKER: She up in New York. I let her go from my mind.

WINING BOY: She was something back then. She wasn't too pretty but she had a way of looking at you made you know there was a whole lot of woman there. You got married and snatched her out from under us and we all got mad at you.

DOAKER: She up in New York City. That's what I hear.

> *The door opens and Boy Willie and Lymon enter.*

BOY WILLIE: Aw hell . . . look here! We was just talking about you. Doaker say you left out of here with a whole sack of money. I told him he wasn't going see you till you got broke.

WINING BOY: What you mean broke? I got a whole pocketful of money.

DOAKER: Did you all get that truck fixed?

BOY WILLIE: We got it running and got halfway out there on Centre and it broke down again. Lymon went out there and messed it up some more. Fellow told us we got to wait till tomorrow to get it fixed. Say he have it running like new. Lymon going back down there and sleep in the truck so the people don't take the watermelons.

LYMON: Lymon nothing. You go down there and sleep in it.

BOY WILLIE: You was sleeping in it down home, nigger! I don't know nothing about sleeping in no truck.

LYMON: I ain't sleeping in no truck.

BOY WILLIE: They can take all the watermelons. I don't care. Wining Boy, where you coming from? Where you been?

WINING BOY: I been down in Kansas City.

BOY WILLIE: You remember Lymon? Lymon Jackson.

WINING BOY: Yeah, I used to know his daddy.

BOY WILLIE: Doaker say you don't never leave no address with nobody. Say he got to depend on your whim. See when it strike you to pay a visit.

WINING BOY: I got four or five addresses.

BOY WILLIE: Doaker say Berniece asked you for three dollars and you got mad and left.

WINING BOY: Berniece try and rule over you too much for me. That's why I left. It wasn't about no three dollars.

BOY WILLIE: Where you getting all these sacks of money from? I need to be with you. Doaker say you had a whole sack of money . . . turn some of it loose.

WINING BOY: I was just fixing to ask you for five dollars.

BOY WILLIE: I ain't got no money. I'm trying to get some. Doaker tell you about Sutter? The Ghosts of the Yellow Dog got him about three weeks ago. Berniece done seen his ghost and everything. He right upstairs. (*Calls.*) Hey Sutter! Wining Boy's here. Come on, get a drink!

WINING BOY: How many that make the Ghosts of the Yellow Dog done got?

BOY WILLIE: Must be about nine or ten, eleven or twelve. I don't know.

DOAKER: You got Ed Saunders. Howard Peterson. Charlie Webb.

WINING BOY: Robert Smith. That fellow that shot Becky's boy . . . say he was stealing peaches . . .

DOAKER: You talking about Bob Mallory.

BOY WILLIE: Berniece say she don't believe all that about the Ghosts of the Yellow Dog.

WINING BOY: She ain't got to believe. You go ask them white folks in Sunflower County if they believe. You go ask Sutter if he believe. I don't care if Berniece believe or not. I done been to where the Southern cross the Yellow Dog and called out their names. They talk back to you, too.

LYMON: What they sound like? The wind or something?

BOY WILLIE: You done been there for real, Wining Boy?

WINING BOY: Nineteen thirty. July of nineteen thirty I stood right there on that spot. It didn't look like nothing was going right in my life. I said everything can't go wrong all the time . . . let me go down there and call on the Ghosts of the Yellow Dog, see if they can help me. I went down there and right there where them two railroads cross each other . . . I stood right there on that spot and called out their names. They talk back to you, too.

LYMON: People say you can ask them questions. They talk to you like that?

WINING BOY: A lot of things you got to find out on your own. I can't say how they talked to nobody else. But to me it just filled me up in a strange sort of way to be standing there on that spot. I didn't want to leave. It felt like the longer I stood there the bigger I got. I seen the train coming and it seem like I was bigger than the train. I started not to move. But something told me to go ahead and get on out the way. The train passed and I started to go back up there and stand some more. But something told me not to do it. I walked away from there feeling like a king. Went on and had a stroke of luck that run on for three years. So I don't care if Berniece believe or not. Berniece ain't got to believe. I know cause I been there. Now Doaker'll tell you about the Ghosts of the Yellow Dog.

DOAKER: I don't try and talk that stuff with Berniece. Avery got her all tied up in that church. She just think it's a whole lot of nonsense.

BOY WILLIE: Berniece don't believe in nothing. She just think she believe. She believe in anything if it's convenient for her to believe. But when that convenience run out then she ain't got nothing to stand on.

WINING BOY: Let's not get on Berniece now. Doaker tell me you talking about selling that piano.

BOY WILLIE: Yeah . . . hey, Doaker, I got the name of that man Avery was talking about. The man's what's fixing the truck gave me his name. Everybody know him. Say he buy up anything you can make music with. I got his name and his telephone number. Hey, Wining Boy, Sutter's brother say he selling the land to me. I got one part. Sell them watermelons get me the second part. Then . . . soon as I get them watermelons out that truck I'm gonna take and sell that piano and get the third part.

DOAKER: That land ain't worth nothing no more. The smart white man's up here in these cities. He cut the land loose and step back and watch you and the dumb white man argue over it.

WINING BOY: How you know Sutter's brother ain't sold it already? You talking about selling the piano and the man's liable to sold the land two or three times.

BOY WILLIE: He say he waiting on me. He say he give me two weeks. That's two weeks from Friday. Say if I ain't back by then he might gonna sell it to somebody else. He say he wanna see me with it.

WINING BOY: You know as well as I know the man gonna sell the land to the first one walk up and hand him the money.

BOY WILLIE: That's just who I'm gonna be. Look, you ain't gotta know he waiting on me. I know. Okay. I know what the man told me. Stovall already down tried to buy the land from him and he told him no. The man say he waiting on me . . . he waiting on me. Hey, Doaker . . . give me a drink. I see Wining Boy got his glass. (*Doaker exits into his room.*) Wining Boy, what you doing in Kansas City? What they got down there?

LYMON: I hear they got some nice-looking women in Kansas City. I sure like to go down there and find out.

WINING BOY: Man, the women down there is something else.

Doaker enters with a bottle of whiskey. He sets it on the table with some glasses.

DOAKER: You wanna sit up here and drink up my whiskey, leave a dollar on the table when you get up.

BOY WILLIE: You ain't doing nothing but showing your hospitality. I know we ain't got to pay for your hospitality.

WINING BOY: Doaker say they had you and Lymon down on the Parchman Farm. Had you on my old stomping grounds.

BOY WILLIE: Me and Lymon was down there hauling wood for Jim Miller and keeping us a little bit to sell. Some white fellows tried to run us off of it. That's when Crawley got killed. They put me and Lymon in the penitentiary.

LYMON: They ambushed us right there where that road dip down and around that bend in the creek. Crawley tried to fight them. Me and Boy Willie got away but the sheriff got us. Say we was stealing wood. They shot me in my stomach.

BOY WILLIE: They looking for Lymon down there now. They rounded him up and put him in jail for not working.

LYMON: Fined me a hundred dollars. Mr. Stovall come and paid my hundred dollars and the judge say I got to work for him to pay him back his hundred dollars. I told them I'd rather take my thirty days but they wouldn't let me do that.

BOY WILLIE: As soon as Stovall turned his back, Lymon was gone. He down there living in that truck dodging the sheriff and Stovall. He got both of them looking for him. So I brought him up here.

LYMON: I told Boy Willie I'm gonna stay up here. I ain't going back with him.

BOY WILLIE: Ain't nobody twisting your arm to make you go back. You can do what you want to do.

WINING BOY: I'll go back with you. I'm on my way down there. You gonna take the train? I'm gonna take the train.

LYMON: They treat you better up here.

BOY WILLIE: I ain't worried about nobody mistreating me. They treat you like you let them treat you. They mistreat me I mistreat them right back. Ain't no difference in me and the white man.

WINING BOY: Ain't no difference as far as how somebody supposed to treat you. I agree with that. But I'll tell you the difference between the colored man and the white man. Alright. Now you take and eat some berries. They taste real good to you. So you say I'm gonna go out and get me a whole pot of these berries and cook them up to make a pie or whatever. But you ain't looked to see them berries is sitting in the white fellow's yard. Ain't got no fence around them. You figure anybody want something they'd fence it in. Alright. Now the white man come along and say that's my land. Therefore everything that grow on it belong to me. He tell the sheriff. "I want you to put this nigger in jail as a warning to all the other niggers. Otherwise first thing you know these niggers have everything that belong to us."

BOY WILLIE: I'd come back at night and haul off his whole patch while he was asleep.

WINING BOY: Alright. Now Mr. So and So, he sell the land to you. And he come to you and say, "John, you own the land. It's all yours now. But them is my berries. And come time to pick them I'm gonna send my boys over. You got the land . . . but them berries, I'm gonna keep them. They mine." And he go and fix it with the law that them is his berries. Now that's the difference between the colored man and the white man. The colored man can't fix nothing with the law.

BOY WILLIE: I don't go by what the law say. The law's liable to say anything. I go by if it's right or not. It don't matter to me what the law say. I take and look at it for myself.

LYMON: That's why you gonna end up back down there on the Parchman Farm.

BOY WILLIE: I ain't thinking about no Parchman Farm. You liable to go back before me.

LYMON: They work you too hard down there. All that weeding and hoeing and chopping down trees. I didn't like all that.

WINING BOY: You ain't got to like your job on Parchman. Hey, tell him, Doaker, the only one got to like his job is the waterboy.

DOAKER: If he don't like his job he need to set that bucket down.

BOY WILLIE: That's what they told Lymon. They had Lymon on water and everybody got mad at him cause he was lazy.

LYMON: That water was heavy.

BOY WILLIE: They had Lymon down there singing (*sings*):

O Lord Berta Berta O Lord gal oh-ah
O Lord Berta Berta O Lord gal well

Lymon and Wining Boy join in.

Go 'head marry don't you wait on me oh-ah
Go 'head marry don't you wait on me well
Might not want you when I go free oh-ah
Might not want you when I go free well

BOY WILLIE: Come on, Doaker. Doaker know this one.

As Doaker joins in the men stamp and clap to keep time. They sing in harmony with great fervor and style.

O Lord Berta Berta O Lord gal oh-ah
O Lord Berta Berta O Lord gal well

Raise them up higher, let them drop on down oh-ah
Raise them up higher, let them drop on down well
Don't know the difference when the sun go down oh-ah
Don't know the difference when the sun go down well

Berta in Meridan and she living at ease oh-ah
Berta in Meridan and she living at ease well
I'm on old Parchman, got to work or leave oh-ah
I'm on old Parchman, got to work or leave well

O Alberta, Berta, O Lord gal oh-ah
O Alberta, Berta, O Lord gal well

When you marry, don't marry no farming man oh-ah
When you marry, don't marry no farming man well
Everyday Monday, hoe handle in your hand oh-ah
Everyday Monday, hoe handle in your hand well
When you marry, marry a railroad man, oh-ah

When you marry, marry a railroad man, well
Everyday Sunday, dollar in your hand oh-ah
Everyday Sunday, dollar in your hand well

O Alberta, Berta, O Lord gal oh-ah
O Alberta, Berta, O Lord gal well

BOY WILLIE: Doaker like that part. He like that railroad part.

LYMON: Doaker sound like Tangleye. He can't sing a lick.

BOY WILLIE: Hey, Doaker, they still talk about you down on Parchman. They ask me, "You Doaker Boy's nephew?" I say, "Yeah, me and him is family." They treated me alright soon as I told them that. Say, "Yeah, he my uncle."

DOAKER: I don't never want to see none of them niggers no more.

BOY WILLIE: I don't want to see them either. Hey, Wining Boy, come on play some piano. You a piano player, play some piano. Lymon wanna hear you.

WINING BOY: I give that piano up. That was the best thing that ever happened to me, getting rid of that piano. That piano got so big and I'm carrying it around on my back. I don't wish that on nobody. See, you think it's all fun being a recording star. Got to carrying that piano around and man did I get slow. Got just like molasses. The world just slipping by me and I'm walking around with that piano. Alright. Now, there ain't but so many places you can go. Only so many road wide enough for you and that piano. And that piano get heavier and heavier. Go to a place and they find out you play piano, the first thing they want to do is give you a drink, find you a piano, and sit you right down. And that's where you gonna be for the next eight hours. They ain't gonna let you get up! Now, the first three or four years of that is fun. You can't get enough whiskey and you can't get enough women and you don't never get tired of playing that piano. But that only last so long. You look up one day and you hate the whiskey, and you hate the women, and you hate the piano. But that's all you got. You can't do nothing else. All you know how to do is play that piano. Now who am I? Am I me? Or am I the piano player? Sometime it seem like the only thing to do is shoot the piano player cause he the cause of all the trouble I'm having.

DOAKER: What you gonna do when your troubles get like mine?

LYMON: If I knew how to play it, I'd play it. That's a nice piano.

BOY WILLIE: Whoever playing better play quick. Sutter's brother say he waiting on me. I sell them watermelons. Get Berniece to sell that piano. Put them two parts with the part I done saved . . .

WINING BOY: Berniece ain't gonna sell that piano. I don't see why you don't know that.

BOY WILLIE: What she gonna do with it? She ain't doing nothing but letting it sit up there and rot. That piano ain't doing nobody no good.

LYMON: That's a nice piano. If I had it I'd sell it. Unless I knew how to play like Wining Boy. You can get a nice price for that piano.

DOAKER: Now I'm gonna tell you something, Lymon don't know this . . . but I'm gonna tell you why me and Wining Boy say Berniece ain't gonna sell that piano.

BOY WILLIE: She ain't got to sell it! I'm gonna sell it! Berniece ain't got no more rights to that piano than I do.

DOAKER: I'm talking to the man . . . let me talk to the man. See, now . . . to understand why we say that . . . to understand about the piano . . . you got to go back to slavery time. See, our family was owned by a fellow named Robert Sutter. That was Sutter's grandfather. Alright. The piano was owned by a fellow named Joel Nolander. He was one of the Nolander brothers from down in Georgia. It was coming up on Sutter's wedding anniversary and he was looking to buy his wife . . . Miss Ophelia was her name . . . he was looking to buy her an anniversary present. Only thing with him . . . he ain't had no money. But he had some niggers. So he asked Mr. Nolander to see if maybe he could trade off some of his niggers for that piano. Told him he would give him one and a half niggers for it. That's the way he told him. Say he could have one full grown and one half grown. Mr. Nolander agreed only he say he had to pick them. He didn't want Sutter to give him just any old nigger. He say he wanted to have the pick of the litter. So Sutter lined up his niggers and Mr. Nolander looked them over and out of the whole bunch he picked my grandmother . . . her name was Berniece . . . same like Berniece . . . and he picked my daddy when he wasn't nothing but a little boy nine years old. They made the trade off and Miss Ophelia was so happy with that piano that it got to be just about all she would do was play on that piano.

WINING BOY: Just get up in the morning, get all dressed up and sit down and play on that piano.

DOAKER: Alright. Time go along. Time go along. Miss Ophelia got to missing my grandmother . . . the way she would cook and clean the house and talk to her and what not. And she missed having my daddy around the house to fetch things for her. So she asked to see if maybe she could trade back that piano and get her niggers back. Mr. Nolander said no. Said a deal was a deal. Him and Sutter had a big falling out about it and Miss Ophelia took sick to the bed. Wouldn't get out of bed in the morning. She just lay there. The doctor said she was wasting away.

WINING BOY: That's when Sutter called our granddaddy up to the house.

DOAKER: Now, our granddaddy's name was Boy Willie. That's who Boy Willie's named after . . . only they called him Willie Boy. Now, he was a worker of wood. He could make you anything you wanted out of wood. He'd make you a desk. A table. A lamp. Anything you wanted. Them white fellows around there used to come up to Mr. Sutter and get him to make all kinds of things for them. Then they'd pay Mr. Sutter a nice price. See, everything my granddaddy made Mr. Sutter owned cause he owned him. That's why when Mr. Nolander offered to buy him to keep the family together Mr. Sutter wouldn't sell him. Told Mr. Nolander he didn't have enough money to buy him. Now . . . am I telling it right, Wining Boy?

WINING BOY: You telling it.

DOAKER: Sutter called him up to the house and told him to carve my grandmother and my daddy's picture on the piano for Miss Ophelia. And he took and carved this . . . (*Doaker crosses over to the piano.*) See that right there? That's my grandmother, Berniece. She looked just like that. And he put a picture of my daddy when he wasn't nothing but a little boy the way he remembered him. He made them up out of his memory. Only thing . . . he didn't stop there. He carved all this. He got a picture of his mama . . . Mama Esther . . . and his daddy, Boy Charles.

WINING BOY: That was the first Boy Charles.

DOAKER: Then he put on the side here all kinds of things. See that? That's when him and Mama Berniece got married. They called it jumping the broom. That's how you got married in them days. Then he got here when my daddy was born . . . and here he got Mama Esther's funeral . . . and down here he got Mr. Nolander taking Mama Berniece and my daddy away down to his place in Georgia. He got all kinds of things what happened with our family. When Mr. Sutter seen the piano with all them carvings on it he got mad. He didn't ask for all that. But see . . . there wasn't nothing he could do about it. When Miss Ophelia seen it . . . she got excited. Now she had her piano and her niggers too. She took back to playing it and played on it right up till the day she died. Alright . . . now see, our brother Boy Charles . . . that's Berniece and Boy Willie's daddy . . . he was the oldest of us three boys. He's dead now. But he would have been fifty-seven if he had lived. He died in 1911 when he was thirty-one years old. Boy Charles used to talk about that piano all the time. He never could get it off his mind. Two or three months go by and he be talking about it again. He be talking about taking it out of Sutter's house. Say it was the story of our whole family and as long as Sutter had it . . . he had us. Say we was still in slavery. Me and Wining Boy tried to talk him out of it but it wouldn't do any good. Soon as he quiet down about it he'd start up again. We seen where he wasn't gonna get it off his mind . . . so, on the Fourth of July, 1911 . . . when Sutter was at the picnic what the county give every year . . . me and Wining Boy went on down there with him and took the piano out of Sutter's house. We put it on a wagon and me and Wining Boy carried it over into the next county with Mama Ola's people. Boy Charles decided to stay around there and wait until Sutter got home to make it look like business as usual.

Now, I don't know what happened when Sutter came home and found the piano gone. But somebody went up to Boy Charles's house and set it on fire. But he wasn't in there. He must have seen them coming cause he went down and caught the 3:57 Yellow Dog. He didn't know they was gonna come down and stop the train. Stopped the train and found Boy Charles in the boxcar with four of them hobos. Must have got mad when they couldn't find the piano cause they set the boxcar afire and killed everybody. Now, nobody know who done that. Some people say it was Sutter cause it was his piano. Some people say it was Sheriff Carter. Some people say it was Robert Smith and Ed Saunders. But don't nobody know for sure. It was about two months after that that Ed Saunders fell down his well. Just upped and fell down his well for no reason. People say it was the ghost of them who burned up in the boxcar that pushed him in his well. They started calling them the Ghosts of the Yellow Dog. Now, that's how all that got started and that why we say Berniece ain't gonna sell that piano. Cause her daddy died over it.

BOY WILLIE: All that's in the past. If my daddy had seen where he could have traded that piano in for some land of his own, it wouldn't be sitting up here now. He spent his whole life farming on somebody else's land. I ain't gonna do that. See, he couldn't do no better. When he come along he ain't had nothing he could build on. His daddy ain't had nothing to give him. The only thing my daddy had to give me was that piano. And he died over giving me that. I ain't gonna let it sit up there and rot without trying to do something with it. If Berniece can't see that, then I'm gonna go ahead and sell my half. And you and Wining Boy know I'm right.

DOAKER: Ain't nobody said nothing about who's right and who's wrong. I was just telling the man about the piano. I was telling him why we say Berniece ain't gonna sell it.

LYMON: Yeah, I can see why you say that now. I told Boy Willie he ought to stay up here with me.

BOY WILLIE: You stay! I'm going back! That's what I'm gonna do with my life! Why I got to come up here and learn to do something I don't know how to do when I already know how to farm? You stay up here and make your own way if that's what you want to do. I'm going back and live my life the way I want to live it.

Wining Boy gets up and crosses to the piano.

WINING BOY: Let's see what we got here. I ain't played on this thing for a while.

DOAKER: You can stop telling that. You was playing on it the last time you was through here. We couldn't get you off of it. Go on and play something.

Wining Boy sits down at the piano and plays and sings. The song is one which has put many dimes and quarters in his pocket, long ago, in dimly remembered towns and way stations. He plays badly, without hesitation, and sings in a forceful voice.

WINING BOY (singing):

I am a rambling gambling man
I gambled in many towns
I rambled this wide world over
I rambled this world around
I had my ups and downs in life
And bitter times I saw
But I never knew what misery was
Till I lit on old Arkansas.

I started out one morning
to meet that early train
He said, "You better work for me
I have some land to drain.
I'll give you fifty cents a day,
Your washing, board and all
And you shall be a different man
In the state of Arkansas."

I worked six months for the rascal
Joe Herrin was his name
He fed me old corn dodgers
They was hard as any rock
My tooth is all got loosened
And my knees begin to knock
That was the kind of hash I got
In the state of Arkansas.

Traveling man
I've traveled all around this world
Traveling man
I've traveled from land to land
Traveling man
I've traveled all around this world
Well it ain't no use
writing no news
I'm a traveling man.

The door opens and Berniece enters with Maretha.

BERNIECE: Is that . . . Lord, I know that ain't Wining Boy sitting there.

WINING BOY: Hey, Berniece.

BERNIECE: You all had this planned. You and Boy Willie had this planned.

WINING BOY: I didn't know he was gonna be here. I'm on my way down home. I stopped by to see you and Doaker first.

DOAKER: I told the nigger he left out of here with that sack of money, we thought we might never see him again. Boy Willie say he wasn't gonna see him till he got broke. I looked up and seen him sitting on the doorstep asking for two dollars. Look at him laughing. He know it's the truth.

BERNIECE: Boy Willie, I didn't see that truck out there. I thought you was out selling watermelons.

BOY WILLIE: We done sold them all. Sold the truck too.

BERNIECE: I don't want to go through none of your stuff. I done told you to go back where you belong.

BOY WILLIE: I was just teasing you, woman. You can't take no teasing?

BERNIECE: Wining Boy, when you get here?

WINING BOY: A little while ago. I took the train from Kansas City.

BERNIECE: Let me go upstairs and then I'll cook you something to eat.

BOY WILLIE: You ain't cooked me nothing when I come.

BERNIECE: Boy Willie, go on and leave me alone. Come on, Maretha, get up here and change your clothes before you get them dirty.

Berniece exits up the stairs, followed by Maretha.

WINING BOY: Maretha sure getting big, ain't she, Doaker. And just as pretty as she want to be. I didn't know Crawley had it in him.

Boy Willie crosses to the piano.

BOY WILLIE: Hey, Lymon . . . get up on the other side of this piano and let me see something.

WINING BOY: Boy Willie, what is you doing?

BOY WILLIE: I'm seeing how heavy this piano is. Get up over there, Lymon.

WINING BOY: Go on and leave that piano alone. You ain't taking that piano out of here and selling it.

BOY WILLIE: Just as soon as I get them watermelons out that truck.

WINING BOY: Well, I got something to say about that.

BOY WILLIE: This my daddy's piano.

WINING BOY: He ain't took it by himself. Me and Doaker helped him.

BOY WILLIE: He died by himself. Where was you and Doaker at then? Don't come telling me nothing about this piano. This is me and Berniece's piano. Am I right, Doaker?

DOAKER: Yeah, you right.

BOY WILLIE: Let's see if we can lift it up, Lymon. Get a good grip on it and pick it up on your end. Ready? Lift!

> *As they start to move the piano, the sound of Sutter's Ghost is heard. Doaker is the only one to hear it. With difficulty they move the piano a little bit so it is out of place.*

BOY WILLIE: What do you think?

LYMON: It's heavy . . . but you can move it. Only it ain't gonna be easy.

BOY WILLIE: It wasn't that heavy to me. Okay, let's put it back.

> *The sound of Sutter's Ghost is heard again. They all hear it as Berniece enters on the stairs.*

BERNIECE: Boy Willie . . . you gonna play around with me one too many times. And then God's gonna bless you and West is gonna dress you. Now set that piano back over there. I done told you a hundred times I ain't selling that piano.

BOY WILLIE: I'm trying to get me some land, woman. I need that piano to get me some money so I can buy Sutter's land.

BERNIECE: Money can't buy what that piano cost. You can't sell your soul for money. It won't go with the buyer. It'll shrivel and shrink to know that you ain't taken on to it. But it won't go with the buyer.

BOY WILLIE: I ain't talking about all that, woman. I ain't talking about selling my soul. I'm talking about trading that piece of wood for some land. Get something under your feet. Land the only thing God ain't making no more of. You can always get you another piano. I'm talking about some land. What you get something out the ground from. That's what I'm talking about. You can't do nothing with that piano but sit up there and look at it.

BERNIECE: That's just what I'm gonna do. Wining Boy, you want me to fry you some pork chops?

BOY WILLIE: Now, I'm gonna tell you the way I see it. The only thing that makes that piano worth something is them carvings Papa Willie Boy put on there. That's what make it worth something. That was my great-grand-daddy. Papa Boy Charles brought that piano into the house. Now, I'm sup-posed to build on what they left me. You can't do nothing with that piano sitting up here in the house. That's just like if I let them watermelons sit out there and rot. I'd be a fool. Alright now, if you say to me, Boy Willie, I'm using that piano. I give out lessons on it and that help me make my rent or whatever. Then that be something else. I'd have to go on and say, well, Berniece using that piano. She building on it. Let her go on and use it. I got to find another way to get Sutter's land. But Doaker say you ain't touched that piano the whole time it's been up here. So why you wanna stand in my way? See, you just looking at the sentimental value. See, that's good. That's alright. I take my hat off whenever somebody say my daddy's name. But I ain't gonna be no fool about no sentimental value.

You can sit up here and look at the piano for the next hundred years and it's just gonna be a piano. You can't make more than that. Now I want to get Sutter's land with that piano. I get Sutter's land and I can go down and cash in the crop and get my seed. As long as I got the land and the seed then I'm alright. I can always get me a little something else. Cause that land give back to you. I can make me another crop and cash that in. I still got the land and the seed. But that piano don't put out nothing else. You ain't got nothing working for you. Now, the kind of man my daddy was he would have understood that. I'm sorry you can't see it that way. But that's why I'm gonna take that piano out of here and sell it.

BERNIECE: You ain't taking that piano out of my house. (*She crosses to the piano.*) Look at this piano. Look at it. Mama Ola polished this piano with her tears for seventeen years. For seventeen years she rubbed on it till her hands bled. Then she rubbed the blood in . . . mixed it up with the rest of the blood on it. Every day that God breathed life into her body she rubbed and cleaned and polished and prayed over it. "Play something for me, Berniece. Play something for me, Berniece." Every day. "I cleaned it up for you, play something for me, Berniece." You always talking about your daddy but you ain't never stopped to look at what his foolishness cost your mama. Seventeen years' worth of cold nights and an empty bed. For what? For a piano? For a piece of wood? To get even with somebody? I look at you and you're all the same. You, Papa Boy Charles, Wining Boy, Doaker, Crawley . . . you're all alike. All this thieving and killing and thieving and killing. And what it ever lead to? More killing and more thieving. I ain't never seen it come to nothing. People getting burned up. People getting shot. People falling down their wells. It don't never stop.

DOAKER: Come on now, Berniece, ain't no need in getting upset.

BOY WILLIE: I done a little bit of stealing here and there, but I ain't never killed nobody. I can't be speaking for nobody else. You all got to speak for yourself, but I ain't never killed nobody.

BERNIECE: You killed Crawley just as sure as if you pulled the trigger.

BOY WILLIE: See, that's ignorant. That's downright foolish for you to say something like that. You ain't doing nothing but showing your ignorance. If the nigger was here I'd whup his ass for getting me and Lymon shot at.

BERNIECE: Crawley ain't knew about the wood.

BOY WILLIE: We told the man about the wood. Ask Lymon. He knew all about the wood. He seen we was sneaking it. Why else we gonna be out there at night? Don't come telling me Crawley ain't knew about the wood. Them fellows come up on us and Crawley tried to bully them. Me and Lymon seen the sheriff with them and give in. Wasn't no sense in getting killed over fifty dollars' worth of wood.

BERNIECE: Crawley ain't knew you stole that wood.

BOY WILLIE: We ain't stole no wood. Me and Lymon was hauling wood for Jim Miller and keeping us a little bit on the side. We dumped our little bit down there by the creek till we had enough to make a load. Some fellows seen us and we figured we better get it before they did. We come up there and got Crawley to help us load it. Figured we'd cut him in. Crawley trying to keep the wolf from his door . . . we was trying to help him.

LYMON: Me and Boy Willie told him about the wood. We told him some fellows might be trying to beat us to it. He say let me go back and get my thirty-eight. That's what caused all the trouble.

BOY WILLIE: If Crawley ain't had the gun he'd be alive today.

LYMON: We had it about half loaded when they come up on us. We seen the sheriff with them and we tried to get away. We ducked around near the bend in the creek . . . but they was down there too. Boy Willie say let's give in. But Crawley pulled out his gun and started shooting. That's when they started shooting back.

BERNIECE: All I know is Crawley would be alive if you hadn't come up there and got him.

BOY WILLIE: I ain't had nothing to do with Crawley getting killed. That was his own fault.

BERNIECE: Crawley's dead and in the ground and you still walking around here eating. That's all I know. He went off to load some wood with you and ain't never come back.

BOY WILLIE: I told you, woman . . . I ain't had nothing to do with . . .

BERNIECE: He ain't here, is he? He ain't here! (*Berniece hits Boy Willie.*) I said he ain't here. Is he? (*Berniece continues to hit Boy Willie, who doesn't move to defend himself, other than back up and turning his head so that most of the blows fall on his chest and arms.*)

DOAKER (*grabbing Berniece*): Come on, Berniece . . . let it go, it ain't his fault.

BERNIECE: He ain't here, is he? Is he?

BOY WILLIE: I told you I ain't responsible for Crawley.

BERNIECE: He ain't here.

BOY WILLIE: Come on now, Berniece . . . don't do this now. Doaker get her. I ain't had nothing to do with Crawley . . .

BERNIECE: You come up there and got him!

BOY WILLIE: I done told you now. Doaker, get her. I ain't playing.

DOAKER: Come on, Berniece.

Maretha is heard screaming upstairs. It is a scream of stark terror.

MARETHA: Mama! . . . Mama!

The lights go down to black. End of Act I.

ACT II

Scene I

The lights come up on the kitchen. It is the following morning. Doaker is ironing the pants to his uniform. He has a pot cooking on the stove at the same time. He is singing a song. The song provides him with the rhythm for his work and he moves about the kitchen with the ease born of many years as a railroad cook.

Doaker:
    Gonna leave Jackson Mississippi
    and go to Memphis
    and double back to Jackson
    Come on down to Hattiesburg

Change cars on the Y.D.
coming through the territory to
Meridian
and Meridian to Greenville
and Greenville to Memphis
I'm on my way and I know where
Change cars on the Katy
Leaving Jackson
and going through Clarksdale
Hello Winona!
Courtland!
Bateville!
Como!
Senitobia!
Lewisberg!
Sunflower!
Glendora!
Sharkey!
And double back to Jackson
Hello Greenwood
I'm on my way to Memphis
Clarksdale
Moorhead
Indianola
Can a highball pass through?
Highball on through sir
Grand Carson!
Thirty First Street Depot
Fourth Street Depot
Memphis!

Wining Boy enters carrying a suit of clothes.

DOAKER: I thought you took that suit to the pawnshop.

WINING BOY: I went down there and the man tell me the suit is too old. Look at this suit. This is one hundred percent silk! How a silk suit gonna get too old? I know what it was he just didn't want to give me five dollars for it. Best he wanna give me is three dollars. I figure a silk suit is worth five dollars all over the world. I wasn't gonna part with it for no three dollars so I brought it back.

DOAKER: They got another pawnshop up on Wylie.

WINING BOY: I carried it up there. He say he don't take no clothes. Only thing he take is guns and radios. Maybe a guitar or two. Where's Berniece?

DOAKER: Berniece still at work. Boy Willie went down there to meet Lymon this morning. I guess they got that truck fixed, they been out there all day and ain't come back yet. Maretha scared to sleep up there now. Berniece don't know, but I seen Sutter before she did.

WINING BOY: Say what?

DOAKER: About three weeks ago. I had just come back from down there. Sutter couldn't have been dead more than three days. He was sitting over there at the piano. I come out to go to work . . . and he was sitting right there. Had his hand on top of his head just like Berniece said. I believe he broke his neck when he fell in the well. I kept quiet about it. I didn't see no reason to upset Berniece.

WINING BOY: Did he say anything? Did he say he was looking for Boy Willie?

DOAKER: He was just sitting there. He ain't said nothing. I went on out the door and left him sitting there. I figure as long as he was on the other side of the room everything be alright. I don't know what I would have done if he had started walking toward me.

WINING BOY: Berniece say he was calling Boy Willie's name.

DOAKER: I ain't heard him say nothing. He was just sitting there when I seen him. But I don't believe Boy Willie pushed him in the well. Sutter here cause of that piano. I heard him playing on it one time. I thought it was Berniece but then she don't play that kind of music. I come out here and ain't seen nobody, but them piano keys moving a mile a minute. Berniece need to go on and get rid of it. It ain't done nothing but cause trouble.

WINING BOY: I agree with Berniece. Boy Charles ain't took it to give it back. He took it cause he figure he had more right to it than Sutter did. If Sutter can't understand that . . . then that's just the way that go. Sutter dead and in the ground . . . don't care where his ghost is. He can hover around and play on the piano all he want. I want to see him carry it out the house. That's what I want to see. What time Berniece get home? I don't see how I let her get away from me this morning.

DOAKER: You up there sleep. Berniece leave out of here early in the morning. She out there in Squirrel Hill cleaning house for some bigshot down there at the steel mill. They don't like you to come late. You come late they won't give you your carfare. What kind of business you got with Berniece?

WINING BOY: My business. I ain't asked you what kind of business you got.

DOAKER: Berniece ain't got no money. If that's why you was trying to catch her. She having a hard enough time trying to get by as it is. If she go ahead and marry Avery . . . he working every day . . . she go ahead and marry him they could do alright for themselves. But as it stands she ain't got no money.

WINING BOY: Well, let me have five dollars.

DOAKER: I just give you a dollar before you left out of here. You ain't gonna take my five dollars out there and gamble and drink it up.

WINING BOY: Aw, nigger, give me five dollars. I'll give it back to you.

DOAKER: You wasn't looking to give me five dollars when you had that sack of money. You wasn't looking to throw nothing my way. Now you wanna come in here and borrow five dollars. If you going back with Boy Willie you need to be trying to figure out how you gonna get train fare.

WINING BOY: That's why I need the five dollars. If I had five dollars I could get me some money. *(Doaker goes into his pocket.)* Make it seven.

DOAKER: You take this five dollars . . . and you bring my money back here too.

> *Boy Willie and Lymon enter. They are happy and excited. They have money in all of their pockets and are anxious to count it.*

DOAKER: How'd you do out there?

BOY WILLIE: They was lining up for them.

LYMON: Me and Boy Willie couldn't sell them fast enough. Time we got one sold we'd sell another.

BOY WILLIE: I seen what was happening and told Lymon to up the price on them.

LYMON: Boy Willie say charge them a quarter more. They didn't care. A couple of people give me a dollar and told me to keep the change.

BOY WILLIE: One fellow bought five. I say now what he gonna do with five watermelons? He can't eat them all. I sold him the five and asked him did he want to buy five more.

LYMON: I ain't never seen anybody snatch a dollar fast as Boy Willie.

BOY WILLIE: One lady asked me say, "Is they sweet?" I told her say, "Lady, where we grow these watermelons we put sugar in the ground." You know, she believed me. Talking about she had never heard of that before. Lymon was laughing his head off. I told her, "Oh, yeah, we put the sugar right in the ground with the seed." She say, "Well, give me another one." Them white folks is something else . . . ain't they, Lymon?

LYMON: Soon as you holler watermelons they come right out their door. Then they go and get their neighbors. Look like they having a contest to see who can buy the most.

WINING BOY: I got something for Lymon.

Wining Boy goes to get his suit. Boy Willie and Lymon continue to count their money.

BOY WILLIE: I know you got more than that. You ain't sold all them watermelons for that little bit of money.

LYMON: I'm still looking. That ain't all you got either. Where's all them quarters?

BOY WILLIE: You let me worry about the quarters. Just put the money on the table.

WINING BOY *(entering with his suit)*: Look here, Lymon . . . see this? Look at his eyes getting big. He ain't never seen a suit like this. This is one hundred percent silk. Go ahead . . . put it on. See if it fit you. *(Lymon tries the suit coat on.)* Look at that. Feel it. That's one hundred percent genuine silk. I got that in Chicago. You can't get clothes like that nowhere but New York and Chicago. You can't get clothes like that in Pittsburgh. These folks in Pittsburgh ain't never seen clothes like that.

LYMON: This is nice, feel real nice and smooth.

WINING BOY: That's a fifty-five-dollar suit. That's the kind of suit the bigshots wear. You need a pistol and a pocketful of money to wear that suit. I'll let you have it for three dollars. The women will fall out of their windows they see you in a suit like that. Give me three dollars and go on and wear it down the street and get you a woman.

BOY WILLIE: That looks nice, Lymon. Put the pants on. Let me see it with the pants.

Lymon begins to try on the pants.

WINING BOY: Look at that . . . see how it fits you? Give me three dollars and go on and take it. Look at that, Doaker . . . don't he look nice?

DOAKER: Yeah . . . that's a nice suit.

WINING BOY: Got a shirt to go with it. Cost you an extra dollar. Four dollars you got the whole deal.

LYMON: How this look, Boy Willie?

BOY WILLIE: That look nice . . . if you like that kind of thing. I don't like them dress-up kind of clothes. If you like it, look real nice.

WINING BOY: That's the kind of suit you need for up here in the North.

LYMON: Four dollars for everything? The suit and the shirt?

WINING BOY: That's cheap. I should be charging you twenty dollars. I give you a break cause you a homeboy. That's the only way I let you have it for four dollars.

LYMON (*going into his pocket*): Okay . . . here go the four dollars.

WINING BOY: You got some shoes? What size you wear?

LYMON: Size nine.

WINING BOY: That's what size I got! Size nine. I let you have them for three dollars.

LYMON: Where they at? Let me see them.

WINING BOY: They real nice shoes, too. Got a nice tip to them. Got pointy toe just like you want.

Wining Boy goes to get his shoes.

LYMON: Come on, Boy Willie, let's go out tonight. I wanna see what it looks like up here. Maybe we go to a picture show. Hey, Doaker, they got picture shows up here?

DOAKER: The Rhumba Theater. Right down there on Fullerton Street. Can't miss it. Got the speakers outside on the sidewalk. You can hear it a block away. Boy Willie know where it's at.

Doaker exits into his room.

LYMON: Let's go to the picture show, Boy Willie. Let's go find some women.

BOY WILLIE: Hey, Lymon, how many of them watermelons would you say we got left? We got just under a half a load . . . right?

LYMON: About that much. Maybe a little more.

BOY WILLIE: You think that piano will fit up in there?

LYMON: If we stack them watermelons you can sit it up in the front there.

BOY WILLIE: I'm gonna call that man tomorrow.

WINING BOY (*returns with his shoes*): Here you go . . . size nine. Put them on. Cost you three dollars. That's a Florsheim shoe. That's the kind Staggerlee wore.

LYMON (*trying on the shoes*): You sure these size nine?

WINING BOY: You can look at my feet and see we wear the same size. Man, you put on that suit and them shoes and you got something there. You ready for whatever's out there. But is they ready for you? With them shoes on you be the King of the Walk. Have everybody stop to look at your shoes. Wishing they had a pair. I'll give you a break. Go on and take them for two dollars.

Lymon pays Wining Boy two dollars.

LYMON: Come on, Boy Willie . . . let's go find some women. I'm gonna go upstairs and get ready. I'll be ready to go in a minute. Ain't you gonna get dressed?

BOY WILLIE: I'm gonna wear what I got on. I ain't dressing up for these city niggers.

Lymon exits up the stairs.

That's all Lymon think about is women.

WINING BOY: His daddy was the same way. I used to run around with him. I know his mama too. Two strokes back and I would have been his daddy! His daddy's dead now . . . but I got the nigger out of jail one time. They was fixing to name him Daniel and walk him through the Lion's Den. He got in a tussle with one of them white fellows and the sheriff lit on him like white on rice. That's how the whole thing come about between me and Lymon's mama. She knew me and his daddy used to run together and he got in jail and she went down there and took the sheriff a hundred dollars. Don't get me to lying about where she got it from. I don't know. The sheriff looked at that hundred dollars and turned his nose up. Told her, say, "That ain't gonna do him no good. You got to put up another hundred on top of that." She come up there and got me where I was playing at this saloon . . . said she had all but fifty dollars and asked me if I could help. Now the way I figured it . . . without that fifty dollars the sheriff was gonna turn him over to Parchman. The sheriff turn him over to Parchman it be three years before anybody see him again. Now I'm gonna say it right . . . I will give anybody fifty dollars to keep them out of jail for three years. I give her the fifty dollars and she told me to come over to the house. I ain't asked her. I figure if she was nice enough to invite me I ought to go. I ain't had to say a word. She invited me over just as nice. Say, "Why don't you come over to the house?" She ain't had to say nothing else. Them words rolled off her tongue just as nice. I went on down there and sat about three hours. Started to leave and changed my mind. She grabbed hold to me and say, "Baby, it's all night long." That was one of the shortest nights I have ever spent on this earth! I could have used another eight hours. Lymon's daddy didn't even say nothing to me when he got out. He just looked at me funny. He had a good notion something had happened between me an' her. L. D. Jackson. That was one bad-luck nigger. Got killed at some dance. Fellow walked in and shot him thinking he was somebody else.

Doaker enters from his room.

Hey, Doaker, you remember L. D. Jackson?

DOAKER: That's Lymon's daddy. That was one bad-luck nigger.

BOY WILLIE: Look like you ready to railroad some.

DOAKER: Yeah, I got to make that run.

Lymon enters from the stairs. He is dressed in his new suit and shoes, to which he has added a cheap straw hat.

LYMON: How I look?

WINING BOY: You look like a million dollars. Don't he look good, Doaker? Come on, let's play some cards. You wanna play some cards?

BOY WILLIE: We ain't gonna play no cards with you. Me and Lymon gonna find some women. Hey, Lymon don't play no cards with Wining Boy. He'll take all your money.

WINING BOY (to Lymon): You got a magic suit there. You can get you a woman easy with that suit . . . but you got to know the magic words. You know the magic words to get you a woman?

LYMON: I just talk to them to see if I like them and they like me.

WINING BOY: You just walk right up to them and say, "If you got the harbor I got the ship." If that don't work ask them if you can put them in your pocket. The first thing they gonna say is, "It's too small." That's when you look them dead in the eye and say, "Baby, ain't nothing small about me." If that don't work then you move on to another one. Am I telling him right, Doaker?

DOAKER: That man don't need you to tell him nothing about no women. These women these days ain't gonna fall for that kind of stuff. You got to buy them a present. That's what they looking for these days.

BOY WILLIE: Come on, I'm ready. You ready, Lymon? Come on, let's go find some women.

WINING BOY: Here, let me walk out with you. I wanna see the women fall out their window when they see Lymon.

They all exit and the lights go down on the scene.

Scene II. The lights come up on the kitchen. It is late evening of the same day. Berniece has set a tub for her bath in the kitchen. She is heating up water on the stove. There is a knock at the door.

BERNIECE: Who is it?

AVERY: It's me, Avery.

Berniece opens the door and lets him in.

BERNIECE: Avery, come on in. I was just fixing to take my bath.

AVERY: Where Boy Willie? I see that truck out there almost empty. They done sold almost all them watermelons.

BERNIECE: They was gone when I come home. I don't know where they went off to. Boy Willie around here about to drive me crazy.

AVERY: They sell them watermelons . . . he'll be gone soon.

BERNIECE: What Mr. Cohen say about letting you have the place?

AVERY: He say he'll let me have it for thirty dollars a month. I talked him out of thirty-five and he say he'll let me have it for thirty.

BERNIECE: That's a nice spot next to Benny Diamond's store.

AVERY: Berniece . . . I be at home and I get to thinking you up here an' I'm down there. I get to thinking how that look to have a preacher that ain't married. It makes for a better congregation if the preacher was settled down and married.

BERNIECE: Avery . . . not now. I was fixing to take my bath.

AVERY: You know how I feel about you, Berniece. Now . . . I done got the place from Mr. Cohen. I get the money from the bank and I can fix it up real nice. They give me a ten cents a hour raise down there on the job . . . now

Berniece, I ain't got much in the way of comforts. I got a hole in my pockets near about as far as money is concerned. I ain't never found no way through life to a woman I care about like I care about you. I need that. I need somebody on my bond side. I need a woman that fits in my hand.

BERNIECE: Avery, I ain't ready to get married now.

AVERY: You too young a woman to close up, Berniece.

BERNIECE: I ain't said nothing about closing up. I got a lot of woman left in me.

AVERY: Where's it at? When's the last time you looked at it?

BERNIECE (*stunned by his remark*): That's a nasty thing to say. And you call yourself a preacher.

AVERY: Anytime I get anywhere near you . . . you push me away.

BERNIECE: I got enough on my hands with Maretha. I got enough people to love and take care of.

AVERY: Who you got to love you? Can't nobody get close enough to you. Doaker can't half say nothing to you. You jump all over Boy Willie. Who you got to love you, Berniece?

BERNIECE: You trying to tell me a woman can't be nothing without a man. But you alright, huh? You can just walk out of here without me—without a woman—and still be a man. That's alright. Ain't nobody gonna ask you, "Avery, who you got to love you?" That's alright for you. But everybody gonna be worried about Berniece. "How Berniece gonna take care of herself? How she gonna raise that child without a man? Wonder what she do with herself. How she gonna live like that?" Everybody got all kinds of questions for Berniece. Everybody telling me I can't be a woman unless I got a man. Well, you tell me, Avery—you know—how much woman am I?

AVERY: It wasn't me, Berniece. You can't blame me for nobody else. I'll own up to my own shortcomings. But you can't blame me for Crawley or nobody else.

BERNIECE: I ain't blaming nobody for nothing. I'm just stating the facts.

AVERY: How long you gonna carry Crawley with you, Berniece? It's been over three years. At some point you got to let go and go on. Life's got all kinds of twists and turns. That don't mean you stop living. That don't mean you cut yourself off from life. You can't go through life carrying Crawley's ghost with you. Crawley's been dead three years. Three years, Berniece.

BERNIECE: I know how long Crawley's been dead. You ain't got to tell me that. I just ain't ready to get married right now.

AVERY: What is you ready for, Berniece? You just gonna drift along from day to day. Life is more than making it from one day to another. You gonna look up one day and it's all gonna be past you. Life's gonna be gone out of your hands—there won't be enough to make nothing with. I'm standing here now, Berniece—but I don't know how much longer I'm gonna be standing here waiting on you.

BERNIECE: Avery, I told you . . . when you get your church we'll sit down and talk about this. I got too many other things to deal with right now. Boy Willie and the piano . . . and Sutter's ghost. I thought I might have been seeing things, but Maretha done seen Sutter's ghost, too.

AVERY: When this happen, Berniece?

BERNIECE: Right after I came home yesterday. Me and Boy Willie was arguing about the piano and Sutter's ghost was standing at the top of the stairs.

Maretha scared to sleep up there now. Maybe if you bless the house he'll go away.

AVERY: I don't know, Berniece. I don't know if I should fool around with something like that.

BERNIECE: I can't have Maretha scared to go to sleep up there. Seem like if you bless the house he would go away.

AVERY: You might have to be a special kind of preacher to do something like that.

BERNIECE: I keep telling myself when Boy Willie leave he'll go on and leave with him. I believe Boy Willie pushed him in the well.

AVERY: That's been going on down there a long time. The Ghosts of the Yellow Dog been pushing people in their wells long before Boy Willie got grown.

BERNIECE: Somebody down there pushing them people in their wells. They ain't just upped and fell. Ain't no wind pushed nobody in their well.

AVERY: Oh, I don't know. God works in mysterious ways.

BERNIECE: He ain't pushed nobody in their wells.

AVERY: He caused it to happen. God is the Great Causer. He can do anything. He parted the Red Sea. He say I will smite my enemies. Reverend Thompson used to preach on the Ghosts of the Yellow Dog as the hand of God.

BERNIECE: I don't care who preached that. Somebody down there pushing them people in their wells. Somebody like Boy Willie. I can see him doing something like that. You ain't gonna tell me that Sutter just upped and fell in his well. I believe Boy Willie pushed him so he could get his land.

AVERY: What Doaker say about Boy Willie selling the piano?

BERNIECE: Doaker don't want no part of that piano. He ain't never wanted no part of it. He blames himself for not staying behind with Papa Boy Charles. He washed his hands of that piano a long time ago. He didn't want me to bring it up here—but I wasn't gonna leave it down there.

AVERY: Well, it seems to me somebody ought to be able to talk to Boy Willie.

BERNIECE: You can't talk to Boy Willie. He been that way all his life. Mama Ola had her hands full trying to talk to him. He don't listen to nobody. He just like my daddy. He get his mind fixed on something and can't nobody turn him from it.

AVERY: You ought to start a choir at the church. Maybe if he seen you was doing something with it—if you told him you was gonna put it in my church— maybe he'd see it different. You ought to put it down in the church and start a choir. The Bible say "Make a joyful noise unto the Lord." Maybe if Boy Willie see you was doing something with it he'd see it different.

BERNIECE: I done told you I don't play on that piano. Ain't no need in you to keep talking this choir stuff. When my mama died I shut the top on that piano and I ain't never opened it since. I was only playing it for her. When my daddy died seem like all her life went into that piano. She used to have me playing on it . . . had Miss Eula come in and teach me . . . say when I played it she could hear my daddy talking to her. I used to think them pictures came alive and walked through the house. Sometime late at night I could hear my mama talking to them. I said that wasn't gonna happen to me. I don't play that piano cause I don't want to wake them spirits. They never be walking around in this house.

AVERY: You got to put all that behind you, Berniece.

BERNIECE: I got Maretha playing on it. She don't know nothing about it. Let her go on and be a schoolteacher or something. She don't have to carry all of that with her. She got a chance I didn't have. I ain't gonna burden her with that piano.

AVERY: You got to put all of that behind you, Berniece. That's the same thing like Crawley. Everybody got stones in their passway. You got to step over them or walk around them. You picking them up and carrying them with you. All you got to do is set them down by the side of the road. You ain't got to carry them with you. You can walk over there right now and play that piano. You can walk over there right now and God will walk over there with you. Right now you can set that sack of stones down by the side of the road and walk away from it. You don't have to carry it with you. You can do it right now. (*Avery crosses over to the piano and raises the lid.*) Come on, Berniece . . . set it down and walk away from it. Come on, play "Old Ship of Zion." Walk over here and claim it as an instrument of the Lord. You can walk over here right now and make it into a celebration.

Berniece moves toward the piano.

BERNIECE: Avery . . . I done told you I don't want to play that piano. Now or no other time.

AVERY: The Bible say, "The Lord is my refuge . . . and my strength!" With the strength of God you can put the past behind you, Berniece. With the strength of God you can do anything! God got a bright tomorrow. God don't ask what you done . . . God ask what you gonna do. The strength of God can move mountains! God's got a bright tomorrow for you . . . all you got to do is walk over here and claim it.

BERNIECE: Avery, just go on and let me finish my bath. I'll see you tomorrow.

AVERY: Okay, Berniece. I'm gonna go home. I'm gonna go home and read up on my Bible. And tomorrow . . . if the good Lord give me strength tomorrow . . . I'm gonna come by and bless the house . . . and show you the power of the Lord. (*Avery crosses to the door.*) It's gonna be alright, Berniece. God say he will soothe the troubled waters. I'll come by tomorrow and bless the house.

The lights go down to black.

Scene III. *Several hours later. The house is dark. Berniece has retired for the night. Boy Willie enters the darkened house with Grace.*

BOY WILLIE: Come on in. This my sister's house. My sister live here. Come on, I ain't gonna bite you.

GRACE: Put some light on. I can't see.

BOY WILLIE: You don't need to see nothing, baby. This here is all you need to see. All you need to do is see me. If you can't see me you can feel me in the dark. How's that, sugar?

He attempts to kiss her.

GRACE: Go on now . . . wait!

BOY WILLIE: Just give me one little old kiss.

GRACE (*pushing him away*): Come on now. Where I'm gonna sleep at?

BOY WILLIE: We got to sleep out here on the couch. Come on, my sister don't mind. Lymon come back he just got to sleep on the floor. He run off with Dolly somewhere he better stay there. Come on, sugar.

GRACE: Wait now . . . you ain't told me nothing about no couch. I thought you had a bed. Both of us can't sleep on that little old couch.

BOY WILLIE: It don't make no difference. We can sleep on the floor. Let Lymon sleep on the couch.

GRACE: You ain't told me nothing about no couch.

BOY WILLIE: What difference it make? You just wanna be with me.

GRACE: I don't wanna be with you on no couch. Ain't you got no bed?

BOY WILLIE: You don't need no bed, woman. My granddaddy used to take women on the backs of horses. What you need a bed for? You just want to be with me.

GRACE: You sure is country. I didn't know you was this country.

BOY WILLIE: There's a lot of things you don't know about me. Come on, let me show you what this country boy can do.

GRACE: Let's go to my place. I got a room with a bed if Leroy don't come back there.

BOY WILLIE: Who's Leroy? You ain't said nothing about no Leroy.

GRACE: He used to be my man. He ain't coming back. He gone off with some other gal.

BOY WILLIE: You let him have your key?

GRACE: He ain't coming back.

BOY WILLIE: Did you let him have your key?

GRACE: He got a key but he ain't coming back. He took off with some other gal.

BOY WILLIE: I don't wanna go nowhere he might come. Let's stay here. Come on, sugar. (*He pulls her over to the couch.*) Let me heist your hood and check your oil. See if your battery needs charging.

> *He pulls her to him. They kiss and tug at each other's clothing. In their anxiety they knock over a lamp.*

BERNIECE: Who's that . . . Wining Boy?

BOY WILLIE: It's me . . . Boy Willie. Go on back to sleep. Everything's alright. (*To Grace.*) That's my sister. Everything's alright, Berniece. Go on back to sleep.

BERNIECE: What you doing down there? What you done knocked over?

BOY WILLIE: It wasn't nothing. Everything's alright. Go on back to sleep. (*To Grace.*) That's my sister. We alright. She gone back to sleep.

> *They begin to kiss. Berniece enters from the stairs dressed in a night-gown. She cuts on the light.*

BERNIECE: Boy Willie, what you doing down here?

BOY WILLIE: It was just that there lamp. It ain't broke. It's okay. Everything's alright. Go on back to bed.

BERNIECE: Boy Willie, I don't allow that in my house. You gonna have to take your company someplace else.

BOY WILLIE: It's alright. We ain't doing nothing. We just sitting here talking. This here is Grace. That's my sister Berniece.

BERNIECE: You know I don't allow that kind of stuff in my house.

BOY WILLIE: Allow what? We just sitting here talking.

BERNIECE: Well, your company gonna have to leave. Come back and talk in the morning.

BOY WILLIE: Go on back upstairs now.

BERNIECE: I got an eleven-year-old girl upstairs. I can't allow that around here.

BOY WILLIE: Ain't nobody said nothing about that. I told you we just talking.

GRACE: Come on . . . let's go to my place. Ain't nobody got to tell me to leave but once.

BOY WILLIE: You ain't got to be like that, Berniece.

BERNIECE: I'm sorry, Miss. But he know I don't allow that in here.

GRACE: You ain't got to tell me but once. I don't stay nowhere I ain't wanted.

BOY WILLIE: I don't know why you want to embarrass me in front of my company.

GRACE: Come on, take me home.

BERNIECE: Go on, Boy Willie. Just go on with your company.

Boy Willie and Grace exit. Berniece puts the light on in the kitchen and puts on the teakettle. Presently there is a knock at the door. Berniece goes to answer it. Berniece opens the door. Lymon enters.

LYMON: How you doing, Berniece? I thought you'd be asleep. Boy Willie been back here?

BERNIECE: He just left out of here a minute ago.

LYMON: I went out to see a picture show and never got there. We always end up doing something else. I was with this woman she just wanted to drink up all my money. So I left her there and came back looking for Boy Willie.

BERNIECE: You just missed him. He just left out of here.

LYMON: They got some nice-looking women in this city. I'm gonna like it up here real good. I like seeing them with their dresses on. Got them high heels. I like that. Make them look like they real precious. Boy Willie met a real nice one today. I wish I had met her before he did.

BERNIECE: He come by here with some woman a little while ago. I told him to go on and take all that out of my house.

LYMON: What she look like, the woman he was with? Was she a brown-skinned woman about this high? Nice and healthy? Got nice hips on her?

BERNIECE: She had on a red dress.

LYMON: That's her! That's Grace. She real nice. Laugh a lot. Lot of fun to be with. She don't be trying to put on. Some of these women act like they the Queen of Sheba. I don't like them. Grace ain't like that. She real nice with herself.

BERNIECE: I don't know what she was like. He come in here all drunk knocking over the lamp, and making all kind of noise. I told them to take that somewhere else. I can't really say what she was like.

LYMON: She real nice. I seen her before he did. I was trying not to act like I seen her. I wanted to look at her a while before I said something. She seen me when I come into the saloon. I tried to act like I didn't see her. Time I looked around Boy Willie was talking to her. She was talking to him kept looking at me. That's when her friend Dolly came. I asked her if she wanted to go to the picture show. She told me to buy her a drink while she thought about it. Next thing I knew she done had three drinks talking about she too tired to go. I bought her another drink, then I left. Boy Willie was gone and I thought he might have come back here. Doaker gone, huh? He say he had to make a trip.

BERNIECE: Yeah, he gone on his trip. This is when I can usually get some peace and quiet, Maretha asleep.

LYMON: She look just like you. Got them big eyes. I remember her when she was in diapers.

BERNIECE: Time just keep on. It go on with or without you. She going on twelve.

LYMON: She sure is pretty. I like kids.

BERNIECE: Boy Willie say you staying . . . what you gonna do up here in this big city? You thought about that?

LYMON: They never get me back down there. The sheriff looking for me. All because they gonna try and make me work for somebody when I don't want to. They gonna try and make me work for Stovall when he don't pay nothing. It ain't like that up here. Up here you more or less do what you want to. I figure I find me a job and try to get set up and then see what the year brings. I tried to do that two or three times down there . . . but it never would work out. I was always in the wrong place.

BERNIECE: This ain't a bad city once you get to know your way around.

LYMON: Up here is different. I'm gonna get me a job unloading boxcars or something. One fellow told me say he know a place. I'm gonna go over there with him next week. Me and Boy Willie finish selling them watermelons I'll have enough money to hold me for a while. But I'm gonna go over there and see what kind of jobs they have.

BERNIECE: You shouldn't have too much trouble finding a job. It's all in how you present yourself. See now, Boy Willie couldn't get no job up here. Somebody hire him they got a pack of trouble on their hands. Soon as they find that out they fire him. He don't want to do nothing unless he do it his way.

LYMON: I know. I told him let's go to the picture show first and see if there was any women down there. They might get tired of sitting at home and walk down to the picture show. He say he wanna look around first. We never did get down there. We tried a couple of places and then we went to this saloon where he met Grace. I tried to meet her before he did but he beat me to her. We left Wining Boy sitting down there running his mouth. He told me if I wear this suit I'd find me a woman. He was almost right.

BERNIECE: You don't need to be out there in them saloons. Ain't no telling what you liable to run into out there. This one liable to cut you as quick as that one shoot you. You don't need to be out there. You start out that fast life you can't keep it up. It makes you old quick. I don't know what them women out there be thinking about.

LYMON: Mostly they be lonely and looking for somebody to spend the night with them. Sometimes it matters who it is and sometimes it don't. I used to be the same way. Now it got to matter. That's why I'm here now. Dolly liable not to even recognize me if she sees me again. I don't like women like that. I like my women to be with me in a nice and easy way. That way we can both enjoy ourselves. The way I see it we the only two people like us in the world.

We got to see how we fit together. A woman that don't want to take the time to do that I don't bother with. Used to. Used to bother with all of them. Then I woke up one time with this woman and I didn't know who she was. She was the prettiest woman I had ever seen in my life. I spent the whole night with her and didn't even know it. I had never taken the time to look at her. I guess she kinda knew I ain't never really looked at her. She must have known that cause she ain't wanted to see me no more. If she had wanted to see me I believe we might have got married. How come you ain't married? It seem like to me you would be married. I remember Avery from down home. I used to call him plain old Avery. Now he Reverend Avery. That's kinda funny about him becoming a preacher. I like when he told about how that come to him in a dream about them sheep people and them hobos. Nothing ever come to me in a dream like that. I just dream about women. Can't never seem to find the right one.

BERNIECE: She out there somewhere. You just got to get yourself ready to meet her. That's what I'm trying to do. Avery's alright. I ain't really got nobody in mind.

LYMON: I get me a job and a little place and get set up to where I can make a woman comfortable I might get married. Avery's nice. You ought to go ahead and get married. You be a preacher's wife you won't have to work. I hate living by myself. I didn't want to be no strain on my mama so I left home when I was about sixteen. Everything I tried seem like it just didn't work out. Now I'm trying this.

BERNIECE: You keep trying it'll work out for you.

LYMON: You ever go down there to the picture show?

BERNIECE: I don't go in for all that.

LYMON: Ain't nothing wrong with it. It ain't like gambling and sinning. I went to one down in Jackson once. It was fun.

BERNIECE: I just stay home most of the time. Take care of Maretha.

LYMON: It's getting kind of late. I don't know where Boy Willie went off to. He's liable not to come back. I'm gonna take off these shoes. My feet hurt. Was you in bed? I don't mean to be keeping you up.

BERNIECE: You ain't keeping me up. I couldn't sleep after that Boy Willie woke me up.

LYMON: You got on that nightgown. I likes women when they wear them fancy nightclothes and all. It makes their skin look real pretty.

BERNIECE: I got this at the five-and-ten-cents store. It ain't so fancy.

LYMON: I don't too often get to see a woman dressed like that. (*There is a long pause. Lymon takes off his suit coat.*) Well, I'm gonna sleep here on the couch. I'm supposed to sleep on the floor but I don't reckon Boy Willie's coming back tonight. Wining Boy sold me this suit. Told me it was a magic suit. I'm gonna put it on again tomorrow. Maybe it bring me a woman like he say. (*He goes into his coat pocket and takes out a small bottle of perfume.*) I almost forgot I had this. Some man sold me this for a dollar. Say it come from Paris. This is the same kind of perfume the Queen of France wear. That's what he told me. I don't know if it's true or not. I smelled it. It smelled good to me. Here . . . smell it see if you like it. I was gonna give it to Dolly. But I didn't like her too much.

BERNIECE (*takes the bottle*): It smells nice.

LYMON: I was gonna give it to Dolly if she had went to the picture with me. Go on, you take it.

BERNIECE: I can't take it. Here . . . go on you keep it. You'll find somebody to give it to.

LYMON: I wanna give it to you. Make you smell nice. (*He takes the bottle and puts perfume behind Berniece's ear.*) They tell me you supposed to put it right here behind your ear. Say if you put it there you smell nice all day. (*Berniece stiffens at his touch. Lymon bends down to smell her.*) There . . . you smell real good now. (*He kisses her neck.*) You smell real good for Lymon.

> He kisses her again. Berniece returns the kiss, then breaks the embrace and crosses to the stairs. She turns and they look silently at each other. Lymon hands her the bottle of perfume. Berniece exits up the stairs. Lymon picks up his suit coat and strokes it lovingly with the full knowledge that it is indeed a magic suit. The lights to down on the scene.

SCENE IV

> It is late the next morning. The lights come up on the parlor. Lymon is asleep on the sofa. Boy Willie enters the front door.

BOY WILLIE: Hey, Lymon! Lymon, come on get up.

LYMON: Leave me alone.

BOY WILLIE: Come on, get up, nigger! Wake up, Lymon.

LYMON: What you want?

BOY WILLIE: Come on, let's go. I done called the man about the piano.

LYMON: What piano?

BOY WILLIE (*dumps Lymon on the floor*): Come on, get up!

LYMON: Why you leave, I looked around and you was gone.

BOY WILLIE: I come back here with Grace, then I went looking for you. I figured you'd be with Dolly.

LYMON: She just want to drink and spend up your money. I come on back here looking for you to see if you wanted to go to the picture show.

BOY WILLIE:

I been up at Grace's house. Some nigger named Leroy come by but I had a chair up against the door. He got mad when he couldn't get in. He went off somewhere and I got out of there before he could come back. Berniece got mad when we came here.

LYMON: She say you was knocking over the lamp busting up the place.

BOY WILLIE: That was Grace doing all that.

LYMON: Wining Boy seen Sutter's ghost last night.

BOY WILLIE: Wining Boy's liable to see anything. I'm surprised he found the right house. Come on, I done called the man about the piano.

LYMON: What he say?

BOY WILLIE: He say to bring it on out. I told him I was calling for my sister, Miss Berniece Charles. I told him some man wanted to buy it for eleven hundred dollars and asked him if he would go any better. He said yeah, he would give me eleven hundred and fifty dollars for it if it was the same piano. I described it to him again and he told me to bring it out.

LYMON: Why didn't you tell him to come and pick it up?

BOY WILLIE: I didn't want to have no problem with Berniece. This way we just take it on out there and it be out the way. He wanted to charge twenty-five dollars to pick it up.

LYMON: You should have told him the man was gonna give you twelve hundred for it.

BOY WILLIE: I figure I was taking a chance with that eleven hundred. If I had told him twelve hundred he might have run off. Now I wish I had told him twelve-fifty. It's hard to figure out white folks sometimes.

LYMON: You might have been able to tell him anything. White folks got a lot of money.

BOY WILLIE: Come on, let's get it loaded before Berniece come back. Get that end over there. All you got to do is pick it up on that side. Don't worry about this side. You wanna stretch you' back for a minute?

LYMON: I'm ready.

BOY WILLIE: Get a real good grip on it now.

The sound of Sutter's Ghost is heard. They do not hear it.

LYMON: I got this end. You get that end.

BOY WILLIE: Wait till I say ready now. Alright. You got it good? You got a grip on it?

LYMON: Yeah, I got it. You lift up on that end.

BOY WILLIE: Ready? Lift!

The piano will not budge.

LYMON: Man, this piano is heavy! It's gonna take more than me and you to move this piano.

BOY WILLIE: We can do it. Come on—we did it before.

LYMON: Nigger—you crazy! That piano weighs five hundred pounds!

BOY WILLIE: I got three hundred pounds of it! I know you can carry two hundred pounds! You be lifting them cotton sacks! Come on lift this piano!

They try to move the piano again without success.

LYMON: It's stuck. Something holding it.

BOY WILLIE: How the piano gonna be stuck? We just moved it. Slide you' end out.

LYMON: Naw—we gonna need two or three more people. How this big old piano get in the house?

BOY WILLIE: I don't know how it got in the house. I know how it's going out though! You get on this end. I'll carry three hundred and fifty pounds of it. All you got to do is slide your end out. Ready?

They switch sides and try again without success. Doaker enters from his room as they try to push and shove it.

LYMON: Hey, Doaker . . . how this piano get in the house?

DOAKER: Boy Willie, what you doing?

BOY WILLIE: I'm carrying this piano out of the house. What it look like I'm doing? Come on, Lymon, let's try again.

DOAKER: Go on let the piano sit there till Berniece come home.

BOY WILLIE: You ain't got nothing to do with this, Doaker. This my business.

DOAKER: This is my house, nigger! I ain't gonna let you or nobody else carry nothing out of it. You ain't gonna carry nothing out of here without my permission!

BOY WILLIE: This is my piano. I don't need your permission to carry my belongings out of your house. This is mine. This ain't got nothing to do with you.

DOAKER: I say leave it over there till Berniece comes home. She got part of it too. Leave it set there till you see what she say.

BOY WILLIE: I don't care what Berniece say. Come on, Lymon. I got this side.

DOAKER: Go on and cut it half in two if you want to. Just leave Berniece's half sitting over there. I can't tell you what to do with your piano. But I can't let you take her half out of here.

BOY WILLIE: Go on, Doaker. You ain't got nothing to do with this. I don't want you starting nothing now. Just go on and leave me alone. Come on, Lymon. I got this end.

> *Doaker goes into his room. Boy Willie and Lymon prepare to move the piano.*

LYMON: How we gonna get it in the truck?

BOY WILLIE: Don't worry about how we gonna get it on the truck. You got to get it out the house first.

LYMON: It's gonna take more than me and you to move this piano.

BOY WILLIE: Just lift up that end, nigger!

> *Doaker comes to the doorway of his room and stands.*

DOAKER (*quietly, with authority*): Leave that piano set over there till Berniece come back. I don't care what you do with it then. But you gonna leave it sit over there right now.

BOY WILLIE: Alright . . . I'm gonna tell you this, Doaker, I'm going out of here . . . . I'm gonna get me some rope . . . find me a plank and some wheels . . . and I'm coming back. Then I'm gonna carry that piano out of here . . . sell it and give Berniece half the money. See . . . now that's what I'm gonna do. And you . . . or nobody else is gonna stop me. Come on, Lymon . . . let's go get some rope and stuff. I'll be back, Doaker.

> *Boy Willie and Lymon exit. The lights go down on the scene.*

SCENE V

> *The lights come up. Boy Willie sits on the sofa, screwing casters on a wooden plank. Maretha is sitting on the piano stool. Doaker sits at the table playing solitaire.*

BOY WILLIE (*to Maretha*): Then after that them white folks down around there started falling down their wells. You ever seen a well? A well got a wall around it. It's hard to fall down a well. You got to be leaning way over. Couldn't nobody figure out too much what was making these fellows fall down their well . . . so everybody says the Ghosts of the Yellow Dog must have pushed them. That's what everybody called them four men what got burned up in the boxcar.

MARETHA: Why they call them that?

BOY WILLIE: Cause the Yazoo Delta railroad got yellow boxcars. Sometime the way the whistle blow sound like an old dog howling so the people call it the Yellow Dog.

MARETHA: Anybody ever see the Ghosts?

BOY WILLIE: I told you they like the wind. Can you see the wind?

MARETHA: No.

BOY WILLIE: They like the wind you can't see them. But sometimes you be in trouble they might be around to help you. They say if you go where the Southern cross the Yellow Dog . . . you go to where them two railroads cross each other . . . and call out their names . . . they say they talk back to you. I don't know, I ain't never done that. But Uncle Wining Boy he say he been down there and talked to them. You have to ask him about that part.

Berniece has entered from the front door.

BERNIECE: Maretha, you go on and get ready for me to do your hair. (*Maretha crosses to the steps.*) Boy Willie, I done told you to leave my house. (*To Maretha.*) Go on, Maretha.

Maretha is hesitant about going up the stairs.

BOY WILLIE: Don't be scared. Here, I'll go up there with you. If we see Sutter's ghost I'll put a whupping on him. Come on, Uncle Boy Willie going with you.

Boy Willie and Maretha exit up the stairs.

BERNIECE: Doaker—what is going on here?

DOAKER: I come home and him and Lymon was moving the piano. I told them to leave it over there till you got home. He went out and got that board and them wheels. He say he gonna take that piano out of here and ain't nobody gonna stop him.

BERNIECE: I ain't playing with Boy Willie. I got Crawley's gun upstairs. He don't know but I'm through with it. Where Lymon go?

DOAKER: Boy Willie sent him for some rope just before you come in.

BERNIECE: I ain't studying Boy Willie or Lymon—or the rope. Boy Willie ain't taking that piano out this house. That's all there is to it.

Boy Willie and Maretha enter on the stairs. Maretha carries a hot comb and a can of hair grease. Boy Willie crosses over and continues to screw the wheels on the board.

MARETHA: Mama, all the hair grease is gone. There ain't but this little bit left.

BERNIECE (*gives her a dollar*): Here . . . run across the street and get another can. You come straight back, too. Don't you be playing around out there. And watch the cars. Be careful when you cross the street. (*Maretha exits out the front door.*) Boy Willie, I done told you to leave my house.

BOY WILLIE: I ain't in you' house. I'm in Doaker's house. If he ask me to leave then I'll go on and leave. But consider me done left your part.

BERNIECE: Doaker, tell him to leave. Tell him to go on.

DOAKER: Boy Willie ain't done nothing for me to put him out of the house. I told you if you can't get along just go on and don't have nothing to do with each other.

BOY WILLIE: I ain't thinking about Berniece. (*He gets up and draws a line across the floor with his foot.*) There! Now I'm out of your part of the house. Consider me done left your part. Soon as Lymon come back with that rope, I'm gonna take that piano out of here and sell it.

BERNIECE: You ain't gonna touch that piano.

BOY WILLIE: Carry it out of here just as big and bold. Do like my daddy would have done come time to get Sutter's land.

BERNIECE: I got something to make you leave it over there.

BOY WILLIE: It's got to come better than this thirty-two-twenty.

DOAKER: Why don't you stop all that! Boy Willie, go on and leave her alone. You know how Berniece get. Why you wanna sit there and pick with her?

BOY WILLIE: I ain't picking with her. I told her the truth. She the one talking about what she got. I just told her what she better have.

BERNIECE: That's all right, Doaker. Leave him alone.

BOY WILLIE: She trying to scare me. Hell, I ain't scared of dying. I look around and see people dying every day. You got to die to make room for somebody else. I had a dog that died. Wasn't nothing but a puppy. I picked it up and put it in a bag and carried it up there to Reverend C. L. Thompson's church. I carried it up there and prayed and asked Jesus to make it live like he did the man in the Bible. I prayed real hard. Knelt down and everything. Say ask in Jesus' name. Well, I must have called Jesus' name two hundred times. I called his name till my mouth got sore. I got up and looked in the bag and the dog still dead. It ain't moved a muscle! I say, "Well, ain't nothing precious." And then I went out and killed me a cat. That's when I discovered the power of death. See, a nigger that ain't afraid to die is the worse kind of nigger for the white man. He can't hold that power over you. That's what I learned when I killed that cat. I got the power of death too. I can command him. I can call him up. The white man don't like to see that. He don't like for you to stand up and look him square in the eye and say, "I got it too." Then he got to deal with you square up.

BERNIECE: That's why I don't talk to him, Doaker. You try and talk to him and that's the only kind of stuff that comes out his mouth.

DOAKER: You say Avery went home to get his Bible?

BOY WILLIE: What Avery gonna do? Avery can't do nothing with me. I wish Avery would say something to me about this piano.

DOAKER: Berniece ain't said about that. Avery went home to get his Bible. He coming by to bless the house see if he can get rid of Sutter's ghost.

BOY WILLIE: Ain't nothing but a house full of ghosts down there at the church. What Avery look like chasing away somebody's ghost?

Maretha enters the front door.

BERNIECE: Light that stove and set that comb over there to get hot. Get something to put around your shoulders.

BOY WILLIE: The Bible say an eye for an eye, a tooth for a tooth, and a life for a life. Tit for tat. But you and Avery don't want to believe that. You gonna pass up that part and pretend it ain't in there. Everything else you gonna agree with. But if you gonna agree with part of it you got to agree with all of it. You can't do nothing halfway. You gonna go at the Bible halfway. You gonna act like that part ain't in there. But you pull out the Bible and open it and see what it say. Ask Avery. He a preacher. He'll tell you it's in there. He the Good Shepherd. Unless he gonna shepherd you to heaven with half the Bible.

BERNIECE: Maretha, bring me that comb. Make sure it's hot.

Maretha brings the comb. Berniece begins to do her hair.

BOY WILLIE: I will say this for Avery. He done figured out a path to go through life. I don't agree with it. But he done fixed it so he can go right through it real smooth. Hell, he liable to end up with a million dollars that he done got from selling bread and wine.

MARETHA: OWWWWWW!

BERNIECE: Be still, Maretha. If you was a boy I wouldn't be going through this.

BOY WILLIE: Don't you tell that girl that. Why you wanna tell her that?

BERNIECE: You ain't got nothing to do with this child.

BOY WILLIE: Telling her you wished she was a boy. How's that gonna make her feel?

BERNIECE: Boy Willie, go on and leave me alone.

DOAKER: Why don't you leave her alone? What you got to pick with her for? Why don't you go on out and see what's out there in the streets? Have something to tell the fellows down home.

BOY WILLIE: I'm waiting on Lymon to get back with that truck. Why don't you go on out and see what's out there in the streets? You ain't got to work tomorrow. Talking about me . . . why don't you go out there? It's Friday night.

DOAKER: I got to stay around here and keep you all from killing one another.

BOY WILLIE: You ain't got to worry about me. I'm gonna be here just as long as it takes Lymon to get back here with that truck. You ought to be talking to Berniece. Sitting up there telling Maretha she wished she was a boy. What kind of thing is that to tell a child? If you want to tell her something tell her about that piano. You ain't even told her about that piano. Like that's something to be ashamed of. Like she supposed to go off and hide somewhere about that piano. You ought to mark down on the calendar the day that Papa Boy Charles brought that piano into the house. You ought to mark that day down and draw a circle around it . . . and every year when it come up throw a party. Have a celebration. If you did that she wouldn't have no problem in life. She could walk around here with her head held high. I'm talking about a big party!

Invite everybody! Mark that day down with a special meaning. That way she know where she at in the world. You got her going out here thinking she wrong in the world. Like there ain't no part of it belong to her.

BERNIECE: Let me take care of my child. When you get one of your own then you can teach it what you want to teach it.

Doaker exits into his room.

BOY WILLIE: What I want to bring a child into this world for? Why I wanna bring somebody else into all this for? I'll tell you this . . . If I was Rockefeller I'd have forty or fifty. I'd make one every day. Cause they gonna start out in life with all the advantages. I ain't got no advantages to offer nobody. Many is the time I looked at my daddy and seen him staring off at his hands. I got a little older I know what he was thinking. He sitting there saying, "I got these big old hands but what I'm gonna do with them? Best I can do is make a fifty-acre crop for Mr. Stovall. Got these big old hands capable of doing anything. I can take and build something with these hands. But where's the tools? All I got is these hands. Unless I go out here and kill me somebody and take what they got . . . it's a long row to hoe for me to get something of my own. So what I'm gonna do with these big old hands? What would you do?"

See now . . . if he had his own land he wouldn't have felt that way. If he had something under his feet that belonged to him he could stand up taller. That's what I'm talking about. Hell, the land is there for everybody. All you got to do is figure out how to get you a piece. Ain't no mystery to life. You just got to go out and meet it square on. If you got a piece of land you'll find everything else fall right into place. You can stand right up next to the white man and talk about the price of cotton . . . the weather, and anything else you want to talk about. If you teach that girl that she living at the bottom of life, she's gonna grow up and hate you.

BERNIECE: I'm gonna teach her the truth. That's just where she living. Only she ain't got to stay there. *(To Maretha.)* Turn you' head over to the other side.

BOY WILLIE: This might be your bottom but it ain't mine. I'm living at the top of life. I ain't gonna just take my life and throw it away at the bottom. I'm in the world like everybody else. The way I see it everybody else got to come up a little taste to be where I am.

BERNIECE: You right at the bottom with the rest of us.

BOY WILLIE: I'll tell you this . . . and ain't a living soul can put a come back on it. If you believe that's where you at then you gonna act that way. If you act that way then that's where you gonna be. It's as simple as that. Ain't no mystery to life. I don't know how you come to believe that stuff. Crawley didn't think like that. He wasn't living at the bottom of life. Papa Boy Charles and Mama Ola wasn't living at the bottom of life. You ain't never heard them say nothing like that. They would have taken a strap to you if they heard you say something like that. *(Doaker enters from his room.)* Hey, Doaker . . . Berniece say the colored folks is living at the bottom of life. I tried to tell her if she think that . . . that's where she gonna be. You think you living at the bottom of life? Is that how you see yourself?

DOAKER: I'm just living the best way I know how. I ain't thinking about no top or no bottom.

BOY WILLIE: That's what I tried to tell Berniece. I don't know where she got that from. That sound like something Avery would say. Avery think cause the white man give him a turkey for Thanksgiving that makes him better than everybody else. That's gonna raise him out of the bottom of life. I don't need nobody to give me a turkey. I can get my own turkey. All you have to do is get out my way. I'll get me two or three turkeys.

BERNIECE: You can't even get a chicken let alone two or three turkeys. Talking about get out your way. Ain't nobody in your way. *(To Maretha.)* Straighten your head, Maretha! Don't be bending down like that. Hold your head up! *(To Boy Willie.)* All you got going for you is talk. You' whole life that's all you ever had going for you.

BOY WILLIE: See now . . . I'll tell you something about me. I done strung along and strung along. Going this way and that. Whatever way would lead me to a moment of peace. That's all I want. To be as easy with everything. But I wasn't born to that. I was born to a time of fire.

The world ain't wanted no part of me. I could see that since I was about seven. The world say it's better off without me. See, Berniece accept that. She trying to come up to where she can prove something to the world. Hell, the world a better place cause of me. I don't see it like Berniece. I got a heart that beats here and it beats just as loud as the next fellow's. Don't care if he black or white. Sometime it beats louder. When it beats louder, then everybody can hear it. Some people get scared of that. Like Berniece. Some people get scared to hear a nigger's heart beating. They think you ought to lay low with that heart. Make it beat quiet and go along with everything the way it is. But my mama ain't birthed me for nothing. So what I got to do? I got to mark my passing on the road. Just like you write on a tree, "Boy Willie was here."

That's all I'm trying to do with that piano. Trying to put my mark on the road. Like my daddy done. My heart say for me to sell that piano and get me some land so I can make a life for myself to live in my own way. Other than that I ain't thinking about nothing Berniece got to say.

There is a knock at the door. Boy Willie crosses to it and yanks it open thinking it is Lymon. Avery enters. He carries a Bible.

BOY WILLIE: Where you been, nigger? Aw . . . I thought you was Lymon. Hey, Berniece, look who's here.

BERNIECE: Come on in, Avery. Don't you pay Boy Willie no mind.

BOY WILLIE: Hey . . . Hey, Avery . . . tell me this . . . can you get to heaven with half the Bible?

BERNIECE: Boy Willie . . . I done told you to leave me alone.

BOY WILLIE: I just ask the man a question. He can answer. He don't need you to speak for him. Avery . . . if you only believe on half the Bible and don't want to accept the other half . . . you think God let you in heaven? Or do you got to have the whole Bible? Tell Berniece . . . if you only believe in part of it . . . when you see God he gonna ask you why you ain't believed in the other part . . . then he gonna send you straight to Hell.

AVERY: You got to be born again. Jesus say unless a man be born again he cannot come unto the Father and who so ever heareth my words and believeth them not shall be cast into a fiery pit.

BOY WILLIE: That's what I was trying to tell Berniece. You got to believe in it all. You can't go at nothing halfway. She think she going to heaven with half the Bible. *(To Berniece.)* You hear that . . . Jesus say you got to believe in it all.

BERNIECE: You keep messing with me.

BOY WILLIE: I ain't thinking about you.

DOAKER: Come on in, Avery, and have a seat. Don't pay neither one of them no mind. They been arguing all day.

BERNIECE: Come on in, Avery.

AVERY: How's everybody in here?

BERNIECE: Here, set this comb back over there on that stove. *(To Avery.)* Don't pay Boy Willie no mind. He been around here bothering me since I come home from work.

BOY WILLIE: Boy Willie ain't bothering you. Boy Willie ain't bothering nobody. I'm just waiting on Lymon to get back. I ain't thinking about you. You heard the man say I was right and you still don't want to believe it. You just wanna go and make up anythin'. Well there's Avery . . . there's the preacher . . . go on and ask him.

AVERY: Berniece believe in the Bible. She been baptized.

BOY WILLIE: What about that part that say an eye for an eye a tooth for a tooth and a life for a life? Ain't that in there?

DOAKER: What they say down there at the bank, Avery?

AVERY: Oh, they talked to me real nice. I told Berniece . . . they say maybe they let me borrow the money. They done talked to my boss down at work and everything.

DOAKER: That's what I told Berniece. You working every day you ought to be able to borrow some money.

AVERY: I'm getting more people in my congregation every day. Berniece says she gonna be the Deaconess. I get me my church I can get married and settled down. That's what I told Berniece.

DOAKER: That be nice. You all ought to go ahead and get married. Berniece don't need to be by herself. I tell her that all the time.

BERNIECE: I ain't said nothing about getting married. I said I was thinking about it.

DOAKER: Avery get him his church you all can make it nice. (*To Avery.*) Berniece said you was coming by to bless the house.

AVERY: Yeah, I done read up on my Bible. She asked me to come by and see if I can get rid of Sutter's ghost.

BOY WILLIE: Ain't no ghost in this house. That's all in Berniece's head. Go on up there and see if you see him. I'll give you a hundred dollars if you see him. That's all in her imagination.

DOAKER: Well, let her find that out then. If Avery blessing the house is gonna make her feel better . . . what you got to do with it?

AVERY: Berniece say Maretha seen him too. I don't know, but I found a part in the Bible to bless the house. If he is here then that ought to make him go.

BOY WILLIE: You worse than Berniece believing all that stuff. Talking about . . . if he here. Go on up there and find out. I been up there I ain't seen him. If you reading from that Bible gonna make him leave out of Berniece imagination, well, you might be right. But if you talking about . . .

DOAKER: Boy Willie, why don't you just be quiet? Getting all up in the man's business. This ain't got nothing to do with you. Let him go ahead and do what he gonna do.

BOY WILLIE: I ain't stopping him. Avery ain't got no power to do nothing.

AVERY: Oh, I ain't got no power. God got the power! God got the power over everything in His creation. God can do anything. God say, "As I commandeth so it shall be." God said, "Let there be light," and there was light. He made the world in six days and rested on the seventh. God's got a wonderful power. He got power over life and death. Jesus raised Lazareth from the dead. They was getting ready to bury him and Jesus told him say, "Rise up and walk." He got up and walked and the people made great rejoicing at the power of God. I ain't worried about him chasing away a little old ghost!

There is a knock at the door. Boy Willie goes to answer it. Lymon enters carrying a coil of rope.

BOY WILLIE: Where you been? I been waiting on you and you run off somewhere.

LYMON: I ran into Grace. I stopped and bought her drink. She say she gonna go to the picture show with me.

BOY WILLIE: I ain't thinking about no Grace nothing.

LYMON: Hi, Berniece.

BOY WILLIE: Give me that rope and get up on this side of the piano.

DOAKER: Boy Willie, don't start nothing now. Leave the piano alone.

BOY WILLIE: Get that board there, Lymon. Stay out of this, Doaker.

Berniece exits up the stairs.

DOAKER: You just can't take the piano. How you gonna take the piano? Berniece ain't said nothing about selling that piano.

BOY WILLIE: She ain't got to say nothing. Come on, Lymon. We got to lift one end at a time up on the board. You got to watch so that the board don't slide up under there.

LYMON: What we gonna do with the rope?

BOY WILLIE: Let me worry about the rope. You just get up on this side over here with me.

Berniece enters from the stairs. She has her hand in her pocket where she has Crawley's gun.

AVERY: Boy Willie . . . Berniece . . . why don't you all sit down and talk this out now?

BERNIECE: Ain't nothing to talk out.

BOY WILLIE: I'm through talking to Berniece. You can talk to Berniece till you get blue in the face, and it don't make no difference. Get up on that side, Lymon. Throw that rope around there and tie it to the leg.

LYMON: Wait a minute . . . wait a minute, Boy Willie, Berniece got to say. Hey, Berniece . . . did you tell Boy Willie he could take this piano?

BERNIECE: Boy Willie ain't taking nothing out of my house but himself. Now you let him go ahead and try.

BOY WILLIE: Come on, Lymon, get up on this side with me. (*Lymon stands undecided.*) Come on, nigger! What you standing there for?

LYMON: Maybe Berniece is right, Boy Willie. Maybe you shouldn't sell it.

AVERY: You all ought to sit down and talk it out. See if you can come to an agreement.

DOAKER: That's what I been trying to tell them. Seem like one of them ought to respect the other one's wishes.

BERNIECE: I wish Boy Willie would go on and leave my house. That's what I wish. Now, he can respect that. Cause he's leaving here one way or another.

BOY WILLIE: What you mean one way or another? What's that supposed to mean? I ain't scared of no gun.

DOAKER: Come on, Berniece, leave him alone with that.

BOY WILLIE: I don't care what Berniece say. I'm selling my half. I can't help it if her half got to go along with it. It ain't like I'm trying to cheat her out of her half. Come on, Lymon.

LYMON: Berniece . . . I got to do this . . . Boy Willie say he gonna give you half of the money . . . say he want to get Sutter's land.

BERNIECE: Go on, Lymon. Just go on . . . I done told Boy Willie what to do.

BOY WILLIE: Here, Lymon . . . put that rope over there.

LYMON: Boy Willie, you sure you want to do this? The way I figure it . . . I might be wrong . . . but I figure she gonna shoot you first.

BOY WILLIE: She just gonna have to shoot me.

BERNIECE: Maretha, get on out the way. Get her out the way, Doaker.

DOAKER: Go on, do what your mama told you.

BERNIECE: Put her in your room.

> *Maretha exits to Doaker's room. Boy Willie and Lymon try to lift the piano. The door opens and Wining Boy enters. He has been drinking.*

WINING BOY: Man, these niggers around here! I stopped down there at Seefus . . . . These folks standing around talking about Patchneck Red's coming. They jumping back and getting off the sidewalk talking about Patchneck Red this and Patchneck Red that. Come to find out . . . you know who they was talking about? Old John D. from up around Tyler! Used to run around with Otis Smith. He got everybody scared of him. Calling him Patchneck Red. They don't know I whupped the nigger's head in one time.

BOY WILLIE: Just make sure that board don't slide, Lymon.

LYMON: I got this side. You watch that side.

WINING BOY: Hey, Boy Willie, what you got? I know you got a pint stuck up in your coat.

BOY WILLIE: Wining Boy, get out the way!

WINING BOY: Hey, Doaker. What you got? Gimme a drink. I want a drink.

DOAKER: It look like you had enough of whatever it was. Come talking about "What you got?" You ought to be trying to find somewhere to lay down.

WINING BOY: I ain't worried about no place to lay down. I can always find me a place to lay down in Berniece's house. Ain't that right, Berniece?

BERNIECE: Wining Boy, sit down somewhere. You been out there drinking all day. Come in here smelling like an old polecat. Sit on down there, you don't need nothing to drink.

DOAKER: You know Berniece don't like all that drinking.

WINING BOY: I ain't disrespecting Berniece. Berniece, am I disrespecting you? I'm just trying to be nice. I been with strangers all day and they treated me like family. I come in here to family and you treat me like a stranger. I don't need your whiskey. I can buy my own. I wanted your company, not your whiskey.

DOAKER: Nigger, why don't you go upstairs and lay down? You don't need nothing to drink.

WINING BOY: I ain't thinking about no laying down. Me and Boy Willie fixing to party. Ain't that right, Boy Willie? Tell him, I'm fixing to play me some piano. Watch this.

> *Wining Boy sits down at the piano.*

BOY WILLIE: Come on, Wining Boy! Me and Lymon fixing to move the piano.

WINING BOY: Wait a minute . . . wait a minute. This a song I wrote for Cleotha. I wrote this song in memory of Cleotha.

> *He begins to play and sing.*

Hey little woman what's the matter with you now
Had a storm last night and blowed the line all down

Tell me how long
Is I got to wait
Can I get it now
Or must I hesitate

It takes a hesitating stocking in her hesitating shoe
It takes a hesitating woman wanna sing the blues

Tell me how long
Is I got to wait
Can I kiss you now
Or must I hesitate.

BOY WILLIE: Come on, Wining Boy, get up! Get up, Wining Boy! Me and Lymon's fixing to move the piano.

WINING BOY: Naw . . . Naw . . . you ain't gonna move this piano.

BOY WILLIE: Get out the way, Wining Boy.

> *Wining Boy, his back to the piano, spreads his arms out over the piano.*

WINING BOY: You ain't taking this piano out the house. You got to take me with it!

BOY WILLIE: Get on out the way, Wining Boy! Doaker get him!

> *There is a knock on the door.*

BERNIECE: I got him, Doaker. Come on, Wining Boy. I done told Boy Willie he ain't taking the piano.

> *Berniece tries to take Wining Boy away from the piano.*

WINING BOY: He got to take me with it!

> *Doaker goes to answer the door. Grace enters.*

GRACE: Is Lymon here?

DOAKER: Lymon.

WINING BOY: He ain't taking that piano.

BERNIECE: I ain't gonna let him take it.

GRACE: I thought you was coming back. I ain't gonna sit in that truck all day.

LYMON: I told you I was coming back.

GRACE (*sees Boy Willie*): Oh, hi, Boy Willie. Lymon told me you was gone back down South.

LYMON: I said he was going back. I didn't say he had left already.

GRACE: That's what you told me.

BERNIECE: Lymon, you got to take your company someplace else.

LYMON: Berniece, this is Grace. That there is Berniece. That's Boy Willie's sister.

GRACE: Nice to meet you. (*To Lymon.*) I ain't gonna sit out in that truck all day. You told me you was gonna take me to the movie.

LYMON: I told you I had something to do first. You supposed to wait on me.

BERNIECE: Lymon, just go on and leave. Take Grace or whoever with you. Just go on get out my house.

BOY WILLIE: You gonna help me move this piano first, nigger!

LYMON (*to Grace*): I got to help Boy Willie move the piano first.

> *Everybody but Grace suddenly senses Sutter's presence.*

GRACE: I ain't waiting on you. Told me you was coming right back. Now you got to move a piano. You just like all the other men. (*Grace now senses something.*) Something ain't right here. I knew I shouldn't have come back up in this house.

> *Grace exits.*

LYMON: Hey, Grace! I'll be right back, Boy Willie.

BOY WILLIE: Where you going, nigger?

LYMON: I'll be back. I got to take Grace home.

BOY WILLIE: Come on, let's move the piano first!

LYMON: I got to take Grace home. I told you I'll be back.

> *Lymon exits. Boy Willie exits and calls after him.*

BOY WILLIE: Come on, Lymon! Hey . . . Lymon! Lymon . . . come on!

> *Again, the presence of Sutter is felt.*

WINING BOY: Hey, Doaker, did you feel that? Hey, Berniece . . . did you get cold? Hey, Doaker . . .

DOAKER: What you calling me for?

WINING BOY: I believe that's Sutter.

DOAKER: Well, let him stay up there. As long as he don't mess with me.

BERNIECE: Avery, go on and bless the house.

DOAKER: You need to bless that piano. That's what you need to bless. It ain't done nothing but cause trouble. If you gonna bless anything go on and bless that.

WINING BOY: Hey, Doaker if he gonna bless something let him bless everything. The kitchen . . . the upstairs. Go on and bless it all.

BOY WILLIE: Ain't no ghost in this house. He need to bless Berniece's head. That's what he need to bless.

AVERY: Seem like that piano's causing all the trouble. I can bless that. Berniece, put me some water in that bottle.

> *Avery takes a small bottle from his pocket and hands it to Berniece, who goes into the kitchen to get water. Avery takes a candle from his pocket and lights it. He gives it to Berniece, as she gives him the water.*

Hold this candle. Whatever you do make sure it don't go out.

O Holy Father we gather here this evening in the Holy Name to cast out the spirit of one James Sutter. May this vial of water be empowered with thy spirit. May each drop of it be a weapon and a shield against the presence of all evil and may it be a cleansing and blessing of this humble abode.

Just as Our Father taught us how to pray so He say, "I will prepare a table for you in the midst of mine enemies," and in His hands we place ourselves to come unto his presence. Where there is Good so shall it cause Evil to scatter to the Four Winds.

He throws water at the piano at each commandment.

Get thee behind me, Satan! Get thee behind the face of Righteousness as we Glorify His Holy Name! Get thee behind the Hammer of Truth that breaketh down the Wall of Falsehood! Father. Father. Praise. Praise. We ask in Jesus' name and call forth the power of the Holy Spirit as it is written . . . .(*He opens the Bible and reads from it.*) I will sprinkle clean water upon thee and ye shall be clean.

BOY WILLIE: All this old preaching stuff. Hell, just tell him to leave.

Avery continues reading throughout Boy Willie's outburst.

AVERY: I will sprinkle clean water upon you and you shall be clean: from all your uncleanliness, and from all your idols, will I cleanse you. A new heart also will I give you, and a new spirit will I put within you: and I will take out of your flesh the heart of stone, and I will give you a heart of flesh. And I will put my spirit within you, and cause you to walk in my statutes, and ye shall keep my judgments, and do them.

Boy Willie grabs a pot of water from the stove and begins to fling it around the room.

BOY WILLIE: Hey Sutter! Sutter! Get your ass out this house! Sutter! Come on and get some of this water! You done drowned in the well, come on and get some more of this water!

Boy Willie is working himself into a frenzy as he runs around the room throwing water and calling Sutter's name. Avery continues reading.

BOY WILLIE: Come on, Sutter! (*He starts up the stairs.*) Come on, get some water! Come on, Sutter!

The sound of Sutter's Ghost is heard. As Boy Willie approaches the steps he is suddenly thrown back by the unseen force, which is choking him. As he struggles he frees himself, then dashes up the stairs:

BOY WILLIE: Come on, Sutter!

AVERY (*continuing*): A new heart also will I give you and a new spirit will I put within you: and I will take out of your flesh the heart of stone, and I will give you a heart of flesh. And I will put my spirit within you, and cause you to walk in my statutes, and ye shall keep my judgments, and do them.

There are loud sounds heard from upstairs as Boy Willie begins to wrestle with Sutter's Ghost. It is a life-and-death struggle fraught with perils and faultless terror. Boy Willie is thrown down the stairs. Avery is stunned into silence. Boy Willie picks himself up and dashes back upstairs.

AVERY: Berniece, I can't do it.

There are more sounds heard from upstairs. Doaker and Wining Boy stare at one another in stunned disbelief. It is in this moment, from somewhere old, that Berniece realizes what she must do. She crosses to the piano. She begins to play. The song is found piece by piece. It is an old urge to song that is both a commandment and a plea. With each repetition it gains in strength. It is intended as an exorcism and a dressing for battle. A rustle of wind blowing across two continents.

BERNIECE (*singing*):

I want you to help me
I want you to help me
I want you to help me
I want you to help me
I want you to help me
I want you to help me
Mama Berniece
I want you to help me
Mama Esther
I want you to help me
Papa Boy Charles
I want you to help me
Mama Ola
I want you to help me
I want you to help me
I want you to help me
I want you to help me
I want you to help me
I want you to help me
I want you to help me
I want you to help me
I want you to help me

The sound of a train approaching is heard. The noise upstairs subsides.

BOY WILLIE: Come on, Sutter! Come back, Sutter!

Berniece begins to chant:

BERNIECE:
Thank you.
Thank you.
Thank you.

A calm comes over the house. Maretha enters from Doaker's room. Boy Willie enters on the stairs. He pauses a moment to watch Berniece at the piano.

BERNIECE:
Thank you.
Thank you.

BOY WILLIE: Wining Boy, you ready to go back down home? Hey Doaker, what time the train leave?

DOAKER: You still got time to make it.

Maretha crosses and embraces Boy Willie.

BOY WILLIE: Hey Berniece . . . if you and Maretha don't keep playing on that piano . . . ain't no telling . . . me and Sutter both liable to be back.

He exits.

BERNIECE: Thank you.

The lights go down to black.

VIDEO LOCALE

The Piano Lesson on Screen. In 1995 *The Piano Lesson* was adapted by playwright August Wilson and the original Broadway director (and longtime Wilson collaborator) Lloyd Richards for television, becoming the only one of Wilson's stage works to have been recast for the screen. The all-star cast included Charles S. Dutton, reprising the role of Willie Boy, Courtney B. Vance as Lymon, and Alfre Woodard as Berniece. The adaptation is available on video or DVD at your local library or most major retail outlets.

Talking about the Text

1. What is the lesson in *The Piano Lesson*? Who teaches the lesson, and who learns the lesson?
2. Which characters seem to have Wilson's sympathies? Why? (If you have seen the film version, does your opinion change, and if so, why?)
3. If you just read the play, you do not fully experience the music. Watch the video version, and listen to the selections of music. How important is it to actually hear the music performed?

Writing about the Text

1. Write a different ending for *The Piano Lesson*.
2. Based on your reading of *The Piano Lesson* and the text itself, write about the kinds of music you envision in a staged version of the play, explaining why you made the selections you did and the effect they would have on tone and meaning.

3. Write an essay discussing the importance of the railroad in *The Piano Lesson*.

4. Write an essay that examines August Wilson's use of ghosts and the supernatural as a means of creating conflict and drawing out the larger historical and social issues connected to race and the legacy of slavery in *The Piano Lesson*.

Linking the Text to Other Texts

1. What differences and similarities do you detect between the northern black family in Lorraine Hansberry's *A Raisin in the Sun* (see p. 1791) and the southern black family in *The Piano Lesson*? How many of the differences can be accounted for by the actual geographical locations of the families?

2. How does Wilson's depiction of the South compare with the South as it is portrayed in any one of the short stories by southern women writers in Chapter 7?

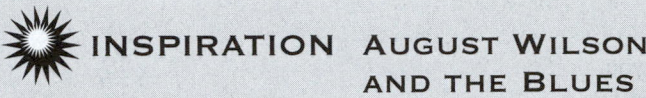

INSPIRATION AUGUST WILSON AND THE BLUES

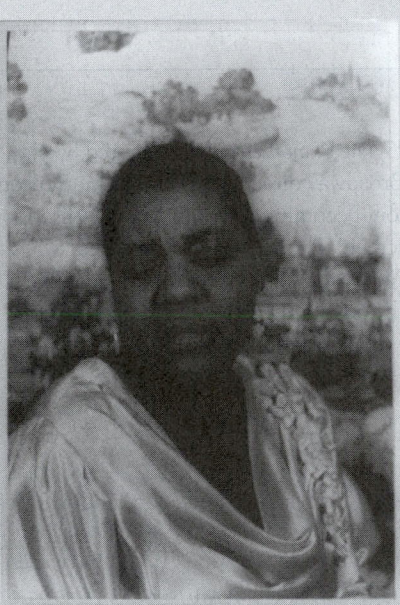

Photographer Carl Van Vechten's 1936 portrait of blues singer Bessie Smith.

August Wilson used to say that his work was inspired by four "B"s: writers Amiri Baraka and Luis Borges, painter Romare Bearden, and the blues. But many critics argue that the blues was the most influential of all. One of Wilson's first experiences with blues was hearing a recording of Bessie Smith (yet another "B") when he was growing up in Pittsburgh. "I put that on, and it was unlike anything I'd ever heard before," Wilson said. "Somehow, all that other music was different from that. And I go, 'Wait a minute. This is mine . . . there's a history here.'" In many of Wilson's plays you can hear the rhythm of the blues and African American vernacular that Wilson was inspired by, first in 1920s and 1930s blues records. Wilson said that when he was working on *The Piano Lesson*, he rewrote the play's dialogue over and over to ensure it sounded right.

On March 1, 2004, National Public Radio's *Morning Edition* featured a program on Wilson and the singing of Bessie Smith. For more information, go to *http://www.npr.org* and look up the show segment in their archive. The write-up also features a link to an audio clip of a Bessie Smith song and a link to collages by artist Romare Bearden that depict the daily lives of African Americans. (For another work by Bearden, see the color insert accompanying Chapter 7.)

Starting Points for Further Research: August Wilson

- **Critical Essays:** Harry J. Elam Jr. *The Past as Present in the Drama of August Wilson.* Ann Arbor: University of Michigan Press, 2004.

    Çigdem Üsekes. " 'You Always under Attack': Whiteness as Law and Terror in August Wilson's Twentieth-Century Cycle of Plays." *American Drama* 10 (2001): 48–68.

    Henry Louis Gates and Alan Nadel, eds. *May All Your Fences Have Gates: Essays on the Drama of August Wilson.* Iowa City: University of Iowa Press, 1993.

- **Interview:** Elisabeth J. Heard. "August Wilson on Playwriting: An Interview." *African American Review* 35 (2001): 93–102.

ANNA DEAVERE SMITH   (B. 1950)

From *Twilight: Los Angeles, 1992*   (1992)

Anna Deavere Smith has won great celebrity with her one-woman performance pieces Fires in the Mirror *(1992) and* Twilight: Los Angeles, 1992. *These two works are parts of a larger, very ambitious project Smith has set herself: to investigate the American character, especially the American civic character, and also to examine multiple voices of communities in times of conflict and crisis. To do so she has interviewed numerous victims, participants, and observers in some of the most intractable conflicts of our time, such as the violence between African Americans and Hassidic Jews in Brooklyn, New York (*Fires*), and the events surrounding the 1991 Rodney King beating, the subsequent 1992 criminal trial, and the ensuing violent disturbances in Los Angeles (*Twilight*). Equipped with costume changes (sometimes only a hat or glasses), a few props, video clips, and lighting changes, Smith acts out a wide variety of characters, using their own words. She manages to be both deeply empathetic in her characterizations, as with one of the Simi Valley white jurors from* Twilight *who voted to acquit the white Los Angeles police officers who were videotaped beating Rodney King, and she is also devastatingly probing of people's motivations. Her goal is to get Americans to hear each other and realize it is possible to build bridges over apparently unbridgeable chasms. She says, "Early on in my work, I wanted to use my body as the evidence that a human being can take on the identity of another."*

Smith, one of a new generation of African American playwrights, was born in Baltimore, majored in theater at Beaver College in Pennsylvania, and earned an MFA at San Francisco's American Conservatory Theater. She has taught at a number of universities—Harvard, Yale, and Stanford among them—her most permanent association being with the Tisch School of the Arts at New York University. She has also acted in a number of popular movies, including Philadelphia *(1993),* The Human Stain *(2003), and* The Manchurian Candidate *(2004), and had a recurrent part in the long-running hit television series* The West Wing. *She has written two memoirs,* Talk to Me: Listening between the Lines *(2000) and* Letters to a Young Artist: Straight-up Advice on Making a Life in the Arts—For Actors, Performers, Writers, and Artists of Every Kind *(2006). Her numerous awards for her work include two Obie Awards, two Tony nominations for* Twilight: Los Angeles, 1992 *(which was also a Pulitzer Prize finalist), and a MacArthur "genius" fellowship. The founder and director of the Institute on the Arts and Civic Dialogue, she is working on a project about global health care. Commenting on her work, Smith has asserted, "My goal is to create with the audience a state of 'we.' One thing live theater can and must do is to create communities that will not exist otherwise."*

Although Smith did not herself witness the criminal trial against the police officers indicted for assaulting Rodney King, to create Twilight: Los Angeles, 1992, *she attended many of the later federal civil rights trials in order to prepare for the piece. To understand how differently people experienced racism and authority in Los Angeles, Smith also interviewed over 200 people, selecting fifty of these voices for her script. The final play script offers a staggeringly wide range of perspectives, representing both men and women of African, Asian, Latino, and European descent from all different socioeconomic classes and backgrounds—everyone from Rodney King's aunt to Mexican artist Rudy Sala Jr. to the wealthy white citizens of Simi Valley where the original criminal trial took place to Korean liquor-store owner Mrs. Young Soon Han to white real-estate agent Elaine Young to Congresswoman Maxine Waters.*

From *Twilight: Los Angeles, 1992*

Indelible Substance

Josie Morales
Clerk-typist, city of Los Angeles uncalled witness
to Rodney King beating, Simi Valley trial
    (In a conference room at her workplace, downtown Los Angeles)

We lived in Apartment A6,
right next to A8,
which is where George Holliday lived.
And, um,
the next thing we know is, um,
ten or twelve officers made a circle around him
and they started to hit him.
I remember
that they just not only hit him with sticks,
they also kicked him,
and one guy,
one police officer, even pummeled his fist
into his face,
and they were kicking him.
And then we were like "Oh, my goodness,"
and I was just watching.
I felt like "Oh, my goodness"
'cause it was really like
he was in danger there,
it was such
an oppressive atmosphere.
I knew it was wrong—
whatever he did—
I knew it was wrong,
I just knew in my heart
this is wrong—
you know they can't do that.
And even my husband was petrified.
My husband said, "Let's go inside."

He was trying to get me to come inside
and away from the scene,
but I said, "No."
I said, "We have to stay here
and watch
because this is wrong."
And he was just petrified—
he grew up in another country where this is prevalent,
police abuse is prevalent in Mexico—
so we stayed and we watched the whole thing.
And
I was scheduled to testify
and I was kind of upset at the outcome,
because I had a lot to say
and during the trial I kept in touch with the
prosecutor,
Terry White,
and I was just very upset
and I, um,
I had received a subpoena
and I told him, "When do you want me to go?"
He says, "I'll call you later and I'll give you a time."
And the time came and went and he never called me,
so I started calling him.
I said, "Well, are you going to call me or not?"
And he says, "I can't really talk to you
and I don't think we're going to be using you because
it contradicts what Melanie Singer said."
And I faxed him a letter
and I told him that those officers were going to be acquitted
and one by one I explained these things to him in this letter
and I told him, "If you do not put witnesses,
if you don't put one resident and testify to say what they saw,"
And I told him in the letter
that those officers were going to be acquitted.
But I really believe that he was dead set
on that video
and that the video would tell all,
but, you see, the video doesn't show you where those officers went
and assaulted Rodney King at the beginning.
You see that?
And I was so upset. I told my co-worker, I said, "I had a terrible dream
that those guys were acquitted."
And she goes, "Oh no, they're not gonna be acquitted."
She goes, "You, you,
you know, don't think like that."
I said, "I wasn't thinking I had a dream!"
I said, "Look at this,
they were,

they were acquitted."
Yeah, I do have dreams
that come true,
but not as vivid as that one.
I just had this dream and in my heart felt . . .
and I saw the
men
and it was in the courtroom and I just
had it in my heart . . .
something is happening
and I heard they were acquitted,
because dreams are made of some kind of indelible substance.
And my co-worker said, "You shouldn't think like this,"
and I said, "I wasn't thinking
it was a dream."
And that's all,
and it came to pass.

Your Heads in Shame

Anonymous Man
Juror in Simi Valley trial

> (A house in Simi Valley. Fall. Halloween decorations are up. Dusk. Low
> lamplight. A slender, soft-spoken man in glasses. His young daughter
> and wife greeted me as well. Quietness.)

As soon as we went
into the courtroom with the verdicts
there were
plainclothes policemen everywhere.
You know, I knew that
there would be people unhappy with the verdict,
but I didn't expect near
what happened.
If I had known
what was going to happen,
I mean, it's not,
it's not fair to say I would have voted a different
way.
I wouldn't have—
that's not our justice system—
but I would have written a note to the judge saying,
"I can't do this,"
because of
what it put my family through.
Excuse me.
(Crying)
So anyway,
we started going out to the bus
and the police said

right away,
"If there's rocks and bottles, don't worry
the glass on the bus is bulletproof."
And then I noticed a huge mob scene,
and it's a sheriff's bus that they lock prisoners in.
We got to the hotel and there were some obnoxious reporters out
there
already, trying to get interviews.
And, you know, the police were trying to get us into the bus and cover
our faces,
and,
and this reporter said,
"Why are you hiding your heads in shame? Do you know that buildings
are burning
and people are dying in South LA
because of you?"
And twenty minutes later I got home
and the same obnoxious reporter was at the door
and my wife was saying, "He doesn't want to talk to anybody,"
and she kept saying,
"The people wanna know,
the people wanna know,"
and trying to get her foot in the door.
And I said, "Listen, I don't wanna talk to anybody. My wife has made
that clear."
And I,
you know, slammed the door in her face.
And so she pulled two houses down
and started
filming our house.
And watching on the TV
and seeing all the political leaders,
Mayor Bradley
and President Bush,
condemning our verdicts.
I mean, the jurors as a group, we tossed around:
was this a setup of some sort?
We just feel like we were pawns that were thrown away by the
system.
I mean,
the judge,
most of the jurors
feel like when he was reading the verdicts
he . . .
we thought we could sense a look of disdain on his face,
and he also had said
beforehand
that after the verdicts came out
he would like to come up and talk to us,

but after we gave the verdicts
he sent someone up and said he didn't really want to
do that then.
And plus, he had the right and power to
withhold our names for a period of time
and he did not do that,
he released them right away.
I think it was apparent that we would be harassed
and I got quite a few threats.
I got threatening letters and threatening phone calls.
I think he just wanted to separate himself . . .
A lot of newspapers published our addresses too.
The New York *Times* published the values of our homes.
They were released in papers all across the country.
We didn't answer the phone,
because it was just every three minutes . . .
We've been portrayed as white racists.
One of the most disturbing things, and a lot of the jurors
said that
the thing that bothered them that they received in the mail
more
than anything else,
more than the threats, was a letter from the KKK
saying,
"We support you, and if you need our help, if you want to join
our organization,
we'd welcome you into our fold."
And we all just were:
No, oh!
God!

To Look Like Girls from Little

Elvira Evers
General worker and cashier, Canteen Corporation
> (A Panamanian woman in a plaid shirt, in an apartment in Compton.
> Late morning, early afternoon. She has a baby on her lap. The baby has
> earrings in her ears. Elvira has a gold tooth. There is a four-year-old girl
> with large braid on top of her head and a big smile who is around
> throughout the interview. The girl's name is Nella.)

So
everybody was like with things they was takin',
like
a carnival,
and I say
to my friend Frances,
"Frances, you see this?"
and she said, "Girl, you should see
that

it's getting worst."
And I say, "Girl, let me take my butt
up there before something happen."
And, um,
when somebody throw a bottle
and I just . . .
then
I felt
like moist,
and it was like a tingling sensation—right?—
and I didn't like this,
and it was like itchin',
and I say, "Frances, I'm bleedin'."
And she walk with me to her house
And she say, "Lift up your gown, let me see."
She say, "Elvira, it's a bullet!"
I say, "What?"
I say, "I didn't heard nothin'."
She say, "Yes, but it's a bullet."
She say, "Lay down there. Let me call St. Francis and tell them that
you been shot
and to send an ambulance."
And she say,
"Why you?
You don't mess with none of those people.
Why they have to shoot you?"
So Frances say the ambulance be here in fifteen minutes.
I say, "Frances,
I cannot wait that."
I say,
"I'm gone!"
So I told my oldest son, I say,
"Amant, take care your brothers.
I be right back."
Well, by this time he was standing up there, he was crying,
all of them was crying.
What I did for them not to see the blood—
I took the gown and I cover it
and I didn't cry.
That way they didn't get nervous.
And I get in the car.
I was goin' to drive.
Frances say, "What you doin'?"
I said, "I'm drivin'."
She say, "No, you're not!"
And we take all the back streets
and she was so supportive,
because she say, "You all right?
You feel cold?

You feel dizzy?
The baby move?"
She say, "You nervous?"
I say, "No, I'm not nervous, I'm just worried about the baby."
I say, "I don't want to lose this baby."
She say, "Elvira, everything will be all right." She say, "Just pray."
So there was a lot of cars, we had to be blowing the horn.
So finally we get to St. Francis
and Frances told the front-desk office, she say,
"She been shot!"
And they say, "What she doin' walkin'?"
and I say, "I feel all right."
Everybody stop doin' what they was doin'
and they took me to the room
and put the monitor to see if the baby was fine
and they find the baby heartbeat,
and as long as I heard the baby heartbeat I calmed down,
long as I knew whoever it is, boy or girl, it's all right,
and
matter of fact, my doctor, Dr. Thomas, he was there
at
the emergency room.
What a coincidence, right?
I was just lookin' for that familiar face,
and soon as I saw him
I say, "Well I'm all right now."
Right?
So he bring me this other doctor and then told me,
"Elvira, we don't know how deep is the bullet.
We don't know where it went. We gonna operate on
you.
But since that we gonna operate we gonna take the baby out
and you don't have to
go through all of that."
They say, "Do you understand
what we're saying?"
I say, "Yeah!"
And they say, "Okay, sign here."
And I remember them preparing me
and I don't remember anything else.
Nella!
No.
(*Turns to the side and admonishes the child*)
She likes company.
And in the background
I remember Dr. Thomas say, "You have a six-pound-twelve-ounce little
girl."

He told me how much she weigh and her length
and he
say, "Um,
she born,
she had the bullet in her elbow,
but when we remove . . .
when we clean her up
we find out that the bullet was still between two joints,
so
we did operate on her and your daughter is fine
and you are fine."
(*Sound of a little child saying "Mommy"*)
Nella!
She wants to show the baby.
Jessica,
bring the baby.
(*She laughs*)
Yes,
yes.
We don't like to keep the girls without earrings. We like the little
girls
to look like girls from little.
I pierce hers.
When I get out on Monday,
by Wednesday I did it,
so by Monday she was five days,
she was seven days,
and I
pierced her ears
and the red band is just like for evil eyes.
We really believe in Panama . . .
in English I can't explain too well.
And her doctor, he told . . .
he explain to me
that the bullet
destroyed the placenta
and went through
me
and she caught it in her arms.
(*Here you can hear the baby making noises, and a bell rings*)
If she didn't caught it in her arm,
me and her would be dead.
See?
So it's like
open your eyes,
watch what is goin' on.
(*Later in the interview, Nella gave me a bandaid, as a gift.*)

And in My Heart for Him

Mrs. June Park
Wife of Walter Park
(She cries sometimes as she speaks, a natural flow.)

He came to United States
twenty-eight years
ago.
He was very high-educated
and also very nice person to the people.
And he has business about seven,
what ten years,
twenty years,
so he work very hard
and he so hard
and he also
donated a lot of money to the Compton area.
And he knows the City Council,
the policemen, they knows him.
Then why,
why he has to get shot?
You know,
I don't know why.
So really angry, you know.
Then I cry
most of my life,
this is the time I cry lot,
so
I go to the hospital and I stay with him.
Especially ICU room
is they don't allow the family to
stay there,
but the,
all the nurses know me,
and every time I go there I bring some nice doughnuts
to the nurses and doctors,
and they find out how much I love him.
So they just let me in
and stay with him all day long.
So I just feed him
and stay till eight o'clock
at the night,
and all day long,
and I spend all my time
and in my heart for him.

The Beverly Hills Hotel

Elaine Young

Real estate agent

> (Saturday, February 1993. A real estate office in the heart of Beverly Hills. She has been in real estate for many years. She sold Sharon Tate the house she was murdered in. Most of her clients are movie stars. She was married to Gig Young. Elaine is a victim of silicone. She had plastic surgery done on her face, to insert cheek implants, and it exploded. She has been written about in several magazines. She is dressed in a bright blue dress with studs and earrings shaped like stars. She has dyed blond hair. She is very outgoing. The phone rings constantly. When her friends call, she puts them on the speakerphone, and I hear the entire conversation.)

So the second day—
this is what got me in trouble on television and really made me feel
bad.
I had a date
and my date canceled.
Now, mind you, I'm only three weeks separated and didn't want to be
alone
and my date canceled.
So now comes Saturday.
I had another date
and I thought if I have to be alone—
'cause my housekeeper goes off for the weekend.
I couldn't get to my daughter.
Still the rioting was escalating and it was really bad.
There were alerts: "Don't leave your house."
And I had a date
and he lives about twenty minutes away in the Valley and they say,
"Don't drive freeway."
And I said, "Are you going to see me tonight? 'Cause I don't want to
be alone."
And he said, "Yes."
So he came to pick me up.
And he got there and I said, "Oh my God, where are we gonna go?
We can't eat anywhere. Everything is closed." And I said,
"Wait a minute. A hotel wouldn't be closed. They gotta be serving
food."
So I said, "Let's see if we can go to the Beverly Hills Hotel."
So we drove to the hotel, which was a couple of minutes from my
house,
and when I got there, much to my shock,
the whole town, picture-business people,

had decided to do the same thing.
Only, unbeknownst to me, they did
it the night before too.
So basically what happened the three or four days of the heavy rioting,
people were going to the hotel,
and I mean it was mobbed.
So we would stay there till three or four in the morning. Everybody was
talking and trying to forget
what was going on . . . the rioting . . . try to . . . they would talk about it until
they'd exhausted the subject.
It would start out horrible,
scared, and "What was going on?"
And "How could this happen in California?"
And "Oh my God, what's happened to our town?"
And "These poor people . . . " and, and, and totally down and down and
down.
And then there's so much you can say.
In life
once you've hit bottom, there's no way to go but up.
So once you've talked about the bad and the horrible, you can't talk
about it anymore.
So then you say, "Well, let me put this out of my mind for now and
go on."
So that was the mood at the Polo Lounge
after they talked about how bad it was
and maybe they'd come back after an hour
but then they tried to go on.
"Here we are
and we're still alive,"
and, you know,
"we hope there'll be people alive
when we come out,"
but basically,
they would come there every night.
And I finally went there for three nights
and stayed till two or three in the morning
so I wouldn't be alone.
I talked to a lot of people.
I just want to clarify one thing.
In no way do I want to give the idea that I accepted the riot
in any way as . . .
or can even joke about it, because . . .
I can't imagine anybody jokin' about it.
I mean, I'm too interested in people,
in social
milieus and attitudes,
and to joke . . .
I took this thing extremely seriously and, uh,
no, not joking, absolutely not,

no way.
But anyway.
So when they interviewed me with the closing of the Polo Lounge
I commented about how we all went there, huddled together,
how we were there till two or three in the morning.
And oh, they say,
"What does the Polo Lounge remind them of?"
I said, "I went there thirty-six years for lunch.
I was there every day. I wrote my book there."
Well . . . the book starts out: "As I drove my car to the Beverly Hills
Hotel . . ."
Everything I did was there.
People magazine interviewed me there.
I did all my interviews there.
Sometimes when I was exhausted
I'd check in there for the weekend.
When my daughter was little,
we'd pretend like we're going on a vacation,
pack, get into the car, and
drive two and a half minutes.
Pretend like we're going away for the weekend.
I work so hard,
I don't have time to take a vacation.
So I'd check in there,
for two days, just to chill out.
So I was talking about that.
And then I said,
"And during the riots."
'Cause it was so foremost on my mind.
And I was talking about how we were all there.
Some man wrote me a letter.
"To Mrs. Young.
You are really an asshole.
You take life so lightly.
I saw your interview on television.
As far as I'm concerned,
you're a dumb shit bimbo
talking about having fun during the riots at the Polo Lounge.
How stupid can you be.
You're an embarrassment."
I mean, oh my God, I'm reading this letter.
I got it three weeks ago.
That's when the Polo Lounge closed.
It was like
oh my God,
if he only left his number,
so I can call him and explain that in no way did I mean to be flippant
on television about the riots. So he thought I was being flippant.
It was like

people hanging out together,
like safety in numbers.
No one can hurt us at the Beverly Hills Hotel
'cause it was like a fortress.

The Unheard
Maxine Waters
Congresswoman, 35th District

> (This interview is from a speech that she gave at the First African
> Methodist Episcopal Church, just after Daryl Gates had resigned and
> soon after the upheaval. FAME is a center for political activity in LA.
> Many movie stars go there. On any Sunday you are sure to see Arsenio
> Hall and others. Barbra Streisand contributed money to the church
> after the unrest. It is a very colorful church, with an enormous mural
> and a huge choir with very exciting music. People line up to go in to
> the services the way they line up for the theater or a concert.
>
> Maxine Waters is a very elegant, confident congresswoman, with a
> big smile, a fierce bite, and a lot of guts. Her area is in South-Central.
> She is a brilliant orator. Her speech is punctuated by organ music and
> applause. Sometimes the audience goes absolutely wild.)

First
African
Methodist Episcopal Church.
You all here got it going on.
I didn't know this is what you did at twelve o'clock on Sunday.
Methodist,
Baptist,
Church of God and Christ all rolled into one.
There was an insurrection in this city before
and if I remember correctly
it was sparked by police brutality.
We had a Kerner Commission report.
It talked about what was wrong with our society.
It talked about institutionalized racism.
It talked about a lack of services,
lack of government responsive to the people.
Today, as we stand here in 1992,
if you go back and read the report
it seems as though we are talking about what that report cited
some twenty years ago still exists today.
Mr. President,
THEY'RE HUNGRY IN THE BRONX TONIGHT,
THEY'RE HUNGRY IN ATLANTA TONIGHT,
THEY'RE HUNGRY IN ST. LOUIS TONIGHT.
Mr. President,
our children's lives are at stake.
We want to deal with the young men who have been dropped off of
America's agenda.

Just hangin' out,
chillin',
nothin' to do,
nowhere to go.
They don't show up on anybody's statistics.
They're not in school,
they have never been employed,
they don't really live anywhere.
They move from grandmama
to mama to girlfriend.
They're on general relief and
they're sleepin' under bridges.
Mr. President,
Mr. Governor,
and anybody else who wants to listen:
Everybody in the street was not a thug
or a hood.
For politicians who think
everybody in the street
who committed a petty crime,
stealing some Pampers
for the baby,
a new pair of shoes . . .
We know you're not supposed to steal,
but the times are such,
the environment is such,
that good people reacted in strange ways. They are not all crooks and
criminals.
If they are,
Mr. President,
what about your violations?
Oh yes.
We're angry,
and yes,
this Rodney King incident.
The verdict.
Oh, it was more than a slap in the face.
It kind of reached in and grabbed you right here in the heart
and it pulled at you
and it hurts so bad.
They want me to march out into Watts,
as the black so-called leadership did in the sixties,
and say, "Cool it, baby,
cool it."
I am sorry.
I know how to talk to my people.
I know how to tell them not to put their lives at risk.
I know how to say don't put other people's lives at risk.
But, journalists,

don't you dare dictate to me
about what I'm supposed to say.
It's not nice to display anger.
I am angry.
It is all right to be angry.
It is unfortunate what people do when they are frustrated and angry.
The fact of the matter is,
whether we like it or not,
riot
is the voice of the unheard.

VIDEO LOCALE

Twilight: Los Angeles, 1992, from Stage to Screen. As part of PBS's Stage
on Screen program, director Marc Levin created a film of Anna Deavere Smith's
Twilight: Los Angeles, 1992 based on footage of the stage performance, interviews with Smith and others, and news footage. The show's website features
video interviews with Smith in which she discusses, among other things, her interview with Mrs. Young Soon Han, her portrayal of Han in *Twilight*, and her
search for America in the speech of its citizens. To download the video interviews, go to *http://www.pbs.org/wnet/stageonscreen/twilight/backstage.html*.

Talking about the Text

1. Had you heard of the 1992 Los Angeles riots before you read Anna Deavere
   Smith's play *Twilight*? What did you know about the Rodney King beating, the
   trial of the police officers, and the aftermath?
2. How much of a leap is it for an African American woman to play a white, female
   real-estate agent? A Panamanian woman? A male juror? How well do we accept
   this crossing of racial and gender boundaries? Might audiences have responded differently thirty years ago?
3. Why do you think Anna Deavere Smith transcribes the words of the speakers the
   way she does, with elements such as the spacing of the lines, the "ums," the repetitions, and the unfinished sentences?
4. One conceivable approach to staging Smith's script would be to cast different actors in the different roles. What is gained by Smith's practice of playing all the
   parts herself?

Writing about the Text

1. Choose one of the characters in Smith's *Twilight* and write about what seems to
   motivate him or her. Be as specific as you can, and cite the text whenever possible.
2. Choose the *Twilight* monologue you find the most striking, and write an essay
   about what makes it most dramatically effective, using examples from the text.
   Consider such matters as what insight the speech gives into violent conflict, racial
   tensions, or people's reactions to conflicts. Also consider issues of justice and injustice, fear, and unpredictable, even volatile behavior in others.

3. Defend Smith's writing practice, imagining as your audience someone who argues that she is not a true playwright because she only uses transcripts of interviews for her script, rather than real creations of her own.

✴ **INSPIRATION** A NEW GENERATION OF ONE-WOMAN ACTS ON STAGE

Playwright, actress, and poet Sarah Jones.

The exact type of interview transcription that Anna Deavere Smith uses to create her stage productions is unique, but her general approach of representing multiple voices and perspectives has been echoed by more recent one-woman acts. Playwright, actor, and poet Sarah Jones has performed award-winning, multicharacter solo shows that include *Surface Transit* (1998), *Women Can't Wait!* (2001), and *Bridge and Tunnel* (2004). Popular stand-up comedian Margaret Cho's one-woman shows include *I'm the One That I Want* (1999), *Notorious C.H.O.* (2001), *Revolution* (2003), and *Assassin* (2005), which evolved out of her 2004 *State of Emergency* show that toured political swing states prior to the 2004 presidential election.

While Sarah Jones does not use interviews for her source material, much of her scripts and characters are based on her own encounters and experiences, and her pieces showcase a plethora of voices representing different genders, ethnicities, ages, accents, and viewpoints. The characters she has played run the gamut: from a prejudiced Jewish grandmother to a racist Italian cop to a Russian widow to a Vietnamese teenager to a male Pakistani accountant. Margaret Cho, on the other hand, takes a more personal, autobiographical, and overtly political approach to her comedy, relying heavily on the current events of today's newspapers, on current politics and cultural conflicts, and on human rights issues as fodder for her comedy. She channels the voices of people she knows personally, particularly her Korean mother, who is a recurrent character in all her work, and of a wide range of public figures, from fashion designer Karl Lagerfeld to Governor Arnold Schwarzenegger to pop singer Björk to Chinese actress Zhang Ziyi. For more information on the work of Sarah Jones and Margaret Cho, go to their respective websites at *http://www.sarahjonesonline.com* and *http://www.margaretcho.com*.

4. Try transcribing a few minutes of "unplanned" text, like the kind you hear in conversation or interviews. Write about how it differs, if at all, from the text Smith presents. (Smith sticks to transcripts of "unplanned" speech, but she picks and chooses her excerpts.)

Linking the Text to Other Texts

1. The original *Twilight* included over fifty different roles. Go to the library and read a complete version of the play. Examine a section that does not appear in the above excerpt, and compare it to one of the speeches that does appear here. Does it work the same way? What significant differences do you note? What effect does this particular additional voice make to Smith's text?

2. After reading this selection, see the video version of *Twilight: Los Angeles, 1992*. Then write about how seeing the video makes the play come alive in ways that you might not have imagined.

3. In *Twilight*, Smith has chosen to set forth a multiplicity of perspectives rather than primarily an African American one. Compare one of these speeches to one of Gwendolyn Brooks's poems (see Chapter 15 and p. 1757 of Chapter 25). What is different and what is similar with regard to the theme of surviving the trials and tribulations of urban life?

4. Read through the selection of blues songs in Chapter 25. Then rewrite one of Smith's *Twilight* speeches as a blues song.

5. Compare the speech by Congresswoman Maxine Waters to Margaret Walker's poem "For My People" (see p. 1761).

Starting Points for Further Research: Anna Deavere Smith

■ **Autobiographies:** Anna Deavere Smith. *Letters to a Young Artist: Straight-up Advice on Making a Life in the Arts—For Actors, Performers, Writers, and Artists of Every Kind.* New York: Anchor, 2006.

———. *Talk to Me: Listening between the Lines.* New York: Random House, 2000.

■ **Critical Essay:** Debby Thompson. "Is Race a Trope?: Anna Deavere Smith and the Question of Racial Performativity." *African American Review* 37 (Spring 2003): 127–38.

■ **Interviews:** Nan Goldberg. "She, the People." *Salon*, November 1, 2000. http://www.salon.com.

Barbara Lewis. "The Circle of Confusion: A Conversation with Anna Deavere Smith." *Kenyon Review* 15:4 (2003): 54–64.

PART
IV

Literary Research

CHAPTER
27

The Literary Research
Project

UNDERSTANDING LITERARY RESEARCH

Readers of literature sometimes need to ask questions that can be answered
only through research. Just as astronomers investigate the structures and interactions of stars and galaxies, and sociologists conduct inquiries about human interactions, in order to go beyond a critical analysis of a **primary
source**—the original literary work being discussed—students of literature
need to conduct research on texts, writers, and the cultural contexts that surround a literary work. In other words, to answer some questions about literature, students will need to further their knowledge by seeking out **secondary
sources**, works that comment on or interpret the primary source being examined. For example, a student writing an analytical paper on *Hamlet* would use
the play itself as a primary source, using quotations to do a close reading of
the text that supported his or her points. A student writing a research paper
on *Hamlet* would have to use additional materials, however, such as critical
articles like T. S. Eliot's critical piece on *Hamlet* (see p. 1220), analytical essays by other critics, Shakespeare biographies, and historical and other background materials.

Your literary research enables you to give a closer examination of the work—its words and imagery, its construction, or how it hangs together as a unified work—by giving you a better idea of what other readers, scholars, historians, and critics have said and thought about it. Such research can also demonstrate how a text fits into a writer's career, how it reflects (or defies) its times, connects to other texts, or represents some large psychological or mythical pattern. Literary research can also help you understand a work's history: how it was received when it appeared, how such views of the text changed over time as tastes and attitudes evolved, and how a text may have been adapted over time for performance. The possibilities for literary research are endless, depending as they do on the interests of researchers and the trends of the times in which the research is conducted. However, all good research shares one characteristic: it provides answers to interesting questions about the literary work.

Like all valuable research, literary research can be full of conflicting interpretations and theories, as one scholar, Gerald Graff, explains in his book *Professing Literature: An Institutional History* (1987). Graff regards these conflicts as productive and, in fact, urges instructors to help students understand what is at stake in different interpretations and explanations. For example, in *Professing Literature*, Graff notes that the twentieth century witnessed a long conflict over the value of "internal" versus "external" evidence. That is, should readers and critics and researchers treat a literary text primarily as an autonomous work of art, with its own internal structures and rules for interpretation, or should they view it mainly as a product of its times, and thus call upon historical and "extratextual" evidence to help explain that text's meanings and significance? Today the notion of an autonomous work of literature, standing completely alone, is highly suspect. In the early twenty-first century, we prefer to view literary texts as embedded in their historical, social, and personal circumstances; consequently, nowadays critics and researchers still look to the text itself, but also draw on all kinds of "external" historical evidence to make their arguments. Fifty years ago, however, many literary researchers were fervent believers in the autonomy of literary texts, willing to interpret them on what they regarded as the texts' own terms and only reluctantly calling on historical, biographical, and other background resources. This conflict is but a single example of the many approaches to the ongoing process we call literary research.

Any research will inevitably involve choices among different kinds of research questions, different types of critical approaches, and different kinds of evidence. And in fact, because research and writing are part of the same dynamic process, you will find that the requirements of a given writing assignment will influence the kinds of choices you make and the kinds of research you do. This chapter provides a guide to the many choices and opportunities you will face as you embark on a research project and present your results in a paper. The scope of a given research project—the formation and subsequent investigation of a question that you try to answer—matters most, but the actual write-up of your findings is important as well. Presenting your results in a research paper will introduce you to college-level requirements for precision, clarity, and standards of evidence, as well as to forms of documentation.

ENTERING THE CULTURAL CONVERSATION ABOUT LITERATURE

The most important aspect of the research process is developing a strong question. This question links you to all other researchers, including your own literature instructor, who no doubt developed such questions as a student and perhaps continues to do so as a writer of books and articles. This line of inquiry is also what links you to scholars and researchers who have preceded you, with their works available in the library in scholarly journals or books. Of course, as a college student you are not a professional scholar. In your case, a research question may not grow out of years spent studying and thinking about literary texts. Nevertheless, your ideas and opinions are important to your class, and the inquiry you undertake makes you a participant in the whole process of reading, discussing, and researching literature. By adding your written ideas and interpretations, you are entering into a conversation both with the text itself and with others who have taken time to read and think about the text—and you are adding your voice to what critic Kenneth Burke called the larger "cultural conversation," an ongoing dialogue that takes place all the time, both orally and in writing, about literature.

For instance, in the 1970s, critic Jane Tompkins took a close look at what nineteenth-century American critics had said about Nathaniel Hawthorne's writings, and she found something very interesting. The stories that are now presented as Hawthorne's best, such as "The Maypole of Merry Mount," "Lady Eleanore's Mantle," and "Young Goodman Brown" (all included in Chapter 4), were not the ones that people rated most highly a century ago. At the time those stories seemed too dark. Instead, a century ago, Hawthorne was esteemed as a stylist, as a clever, perceptive writer about nature and the human heart, not primarily as a deep writer about the troubled psyche of his Puritan ancestors. Tompkins wrote a superb article detailing what readers and critics had said about Hawthorne, thus demonstrating how tastes change, even when a writer's work remains the same. Interestingly, she started her work just by reading what had been written previously about Hawthorne and reporting on what she found. Other scholars had read the same criticism, of course, but without noticing what Tompkins had: that the Hawthorne who was esteemed in the 1870s was not the Hawthorne esteemed in the 1970s. Her seemingly simple perception led to a significant new perspective to add to the larger cultural conversation about Hawthorne's work and about shifting literary fashions over time.

CHOOSING A TOPIC

Your first task in a literary research project is to choose a general area, topic, or subject matter that fits the requirements of your assignment. In some cases, your instructor may assign a research paper about a particular topic, but in others, you will have the option of selecting your own topic. In the latter case, be sure to pick a literary work you respond strongly to and a subject or issue related to that text that interests you, because you will be spending a good bit of time with them. To get started, you may want to reread the "Questions to Develop Ideas" sections on pages 123, 808, and 1225 of Chapters 3 ("Writing about Stories"), 12 ("Writing about Poetry"), and 21 ("Writing about Plays"). Perhaps a question or problem will arise from class discussion or from the reading of a literary text itself. You may wonder about a word, a character, a gesture, a theme, or a conflict and soon have something to pursue. Reviewing any annotations, summaries, paraphrases, journal entries, or double-entry notebook entries you may have written while reading the text is always a good place to start. (For more specific advice on annotating, summarizing, paraphrasing, journal-writing and other formats and techniques for writing about stories, poetry, and plays, see Chapter 3.) In many cases, however, you will have to begin by reading more about a particular topic beforehand. Very recent books and articles will provide the latest thinking. However you choose to get started, choose an area because you like it or want to know more about it.

Sample General Topics

1. Student A has been wondering about the relationship between men and women in short stories written after World War I, from 1918 to 1930, roughly when Ernest Hemingway first became famous. To pursue this topic, she begins looking at stories by Hemingway (p. 537) and by other prominent authors of that period, such as D. H. Lawrence (p. 525), Katherine Anne Porter (p. 542), and Zora Neale Hurston (p. 318).

2. After reading *The Tempest* and *Hamlet*, Student B asks himself about the role of costumes in Shakespeare's lifetime. What did his actors wear? Did the costumes vary according to where the plays were performed? To get started, the student heads for the library to search out some books on performance practices during Shakespeare's time.

3. As someone interested in music, Student C wonders how many contemporary songs are getting anthologized—and which ones. She begins by looking at her university library's selection of poetry anthologies for entries by Bob Dylan, Joni Mitchell, Warren Zevon, Bruce Springsteen, Paul Simon, A Tribe Called Quest, and The Roots.

NARROWING YOUR TOPIC AND DEVELOPING A RESEARCH QUESTION

With a general topic or area in hand, you next want to begin developing a more specific research question. Every research project begins with a question that the researcher seeks to answer. Sometimes the research will conclude with a clear, unambiguous answer; sometimes with a claim or argument; sometimes with series of equally possible answers; and sometimes with a better, more refined question. Whatever the final result, all learning and deeper understanding of a literary text proceeds through a series of investigations leading to answers, some of them firm and definite, some tentative or provisional.

Naturally, the kind of question the researcher asks affects the kind of answer produced in the paper. A broad question results in a broad—most often too broad or obvious—answer. For example a question like "What have scholars thought about *Hamlet?*" will result in far too much information, especially for a student research project in a college-level course. (The question itself is excellent and, in fact, has produced many interesting book-length answers.) A more precise question on this same topic would be "What have scholars and critics said about the beginning of *Hamlet?*" An even more precise question would be "How have prominent directors over the last thirty years staged the opening scene of *Hamlet?*" Every one of these questions can be answered with research, but an adequate treatment of each would require very different amounts of effort, both in the research and in the writing.

A focused research question leads more readily to an answer, but not all answers get at the important issues of the humanities: the "why" questions concerned with values. For instance, listing the differences between American or British directors' stagings of the opening of *Hamlet* over the last thirty years might turn out to be fairly easy with the aid of some promising sources: newspaper reviews, the *Shakespeare Annual,* or a single convenient source such as the Shakespeare in Performance database. This preliminary research can introduce you to the larger field—the influential productions, the famous directors—setting the stage for the next, more interesting, more complex questions:

"*Why* have directors staged it differently?"

"What ideas about the theater seem to lie behind the trends in recent productions?"

"Are there patterns behind different directors' choices about staging the opening?"

With these more complex lines of inquiry, you now have a more original project. In adding more specificity and depth to your question, you are in the realm of literary trends, customs, or fashions. Consequently, as with analytical essays (discussed on pages 133, 821, and 1236 of Chapters 3, 12, and 21), the answer to your research question will require you to take a stance on the issue you have outlined and explored. In other words, you will need to present a central claim, or **thesis**, in the introduction of your research paper, which you then support with examples or evidence within the body of the essay.

DETERMINING YOUR PURPOSE: TYPES OF LITERARY RESEARCH PROJECTS

Developing a **literary argument**—a thesis, claim, or assertion that your paper presents, upholds, and attempts to convince readers to agree with—is a daunting proposition for many who are beginning to write literary papers. In truth, everyone finds it difficult to say something new about many works that have been read over and over again for a long time. Making a new argument and also presenting it persuasively becomes particularly difficult when you are not even sure what is new and what is common understanding. Remember, however, that the purpose of research is not necessarily to discover some brand-new, totally original fact or idea. Researchers rarely discover a completely original point or invent a brand-new thesis. Such tasks are hard to accomplish even for well-established scholars. Rather, think of research as simply one part of the ongoing conversation that occurs about literature—a shared endeavor, a place where one key fact or one thoughtful interpretation can make a big difference. Indeed, research papers that depend on developing an original thesis are the hardest, most demanding type, but they are by no means the only important kind of work in the field. To enter the cultural conversation, you just need a topic on which you can take a clear, strong stand—a topic that is open for debate or for varying interpretations.

There are also many other rigorous, valuable research projects whose purpose is to discover existing arguments, claims, and ideas by other critics and writers and then collect the most important evidence on a given topic. These **expository projects**—whose purpose is to report or inform rather than to persuade or argue—require careful research and thoughtful writing and will provide excellent training in conducting research and writing about it.

Some of the basic kinds of research projects are described below. They range from expository projects to argumentative essays, and each has its own purpose.

Report

Investigate a literary question that interests you and simply report on your findings without developing an explicit thesis or large claim. Discover and use the criticism and scholarship of others to explain the ramifications of the question. General topics for a report include:

- The major differences in the form of the sonnet in the twentieth century.
- How character and plot are related in the standard reference books on literature.
- The major events of Elizabeth Bishop's literary career.

State-of-the-Art Report

Report on an important, interesting, or unresolved current question about a particular work, author, or literary issue. Here you need to go to the very latest research, covering the controversies and criticism of the last five years. General topics for a state-of-the-art report include:

- The influence of Raymond Carver's style on short story writers in the 1970s and 1980s.
- Whether Whitman's Civil War poems were undervalued during his lifetime.
- What scholars think a Shakespearean masque like the one in *The Tempest* was supposed to signify to its audience.
- How much of *Death of a Salesman* was based on Arthur Miller's family members, particularly his uncle, an unsuccessful salesman.

Historical Report

Report the details of what things were once like, and attempt to recapture some of the experience or thoughts of a particular time. General topics for historical reports include:

- How Shakespeare plays were staged by touring productions in the American West from 1875 to 1900.
- What British critics thought of World War I poetry when it first appeared, between 1915 and 1920.

Now vs. Then Report

Report on the similarities and differences between current practice or thinking versus what it was at a particular point in the past. General topics for a now vs. then report include:

- The reputation of Whitman's "sexual" poems in the 1880s compared to the reputation of the same poems at present.
- An assessment of Paul Laurence Dunbar's career and his work's reception in 1920 and in 1980.
- A comparison of how the character Prospero in *The Tempest* was imagined as a stand-in for Shakespeare, first in the 1890s and then a century later in the 1990s.

Argumentative Essay Assessing Conflicts between Critics

Investigate at least two different critics or schools of thought with opposing views about a literary issue. Your task is to present a fair statement of each opposing critical perspective and to suggest a resolution, arguing that one perspective is more credible than another. General topics for an assessment of conflicting viewpoints include:

- Chinua Achebe's attack on the implicit racism in Joseph Conrad's *Heart of Darkness*.
- The male and female views of Matthew Arnold's "Dover Beach" as presented in Gerald Graff's *Beyond the Culture Wars*.
- Conflicting interpretations of Nora in Ibsen's *A Doll House*: will she return or is she gone for good?

Original Thesis

Develop a thesis about either a text or a group of texts, about the relation between a writer's life and one or more texts, or a text or group of texts in relation to the times (including other arts of the era). General topics for an essay developing an original thesis are:

- Robert Lowell's "For the Union Dead" as an imperfect poem that is neither fully public nor fully private.

- William Blake's poems cannot be read adequately unless accompanied by his own color illustrations.
- Richard Wright's stories are a great deal more than simply naturalistic renderings of the gritty Chicago streets.

DISTINGUISHING BETWEEN EXPOSITORY ESSAYS AND LITERARY ARGUMENTS

As described in the three "Writing about" chapters for each literary genre in this book, your thesis or argument is a claim you make, a point that you are trying to prove or establish about your topic. The thesis is what readers will note when they are asked what your paper argues, maintains, or demonstrates. In fact, every paper that takes a definitive stand on a debatable point and sets out to prove that stance to readers has an argumentative thesis. Papers and writing assignments that do not require a thesis are valuable too, of course. And, as the assignment types in the previous section on considering your purpose illustrate, many of them may even require research. Indeed, the research that goes into them can be of the highest quality and will produce very useful information. However, papers that have a thesis will be more original, more ambitious, more complex, and more challenging to research and write.

Here are examples of the distinction between research questions that do not call for an explicit thesis and essay assignments that require research in order to prove an argument:

No Argumentative Thesis:
What most critics think were the most important twentieth-century productions of *Hamlet.*

Your research in response to such a question will enable you to produce and describe a list of productions, perhaps ranked in order of significance. Such an assignment would fall into the "report" category of research assignments. Your overall task is to report on the general consensus by Shakespeare critics on the basis of your research findings, but because you yourself are not being asked to make a claim about either the productions or the critics' opinions about them, no explicit thesis is inherent in the project.

Explicit Argumentative Thesis:
The most important twentieth-century production of *Hamlet* is _____.

In contrast to the previous expository project, which was more one of reportage, here you are being asked to make a particular argument about *Hamlet* that you will then need to support using research. Based on your reading, you first must determine which are considered the major productions and then make your personal selection, using evidence from your sources that support your claim.

THE RESEARCH PROCESS
A STEP-BY STEP SUMMARY

Use the brief summary below as a checklist to walk yourself through the entire research process. Remember that your final paper is only the culmination of this longer, step-by-step process.

- Examine your writing assignment to determine the nature of the task. Is an original thesis required?
- Choose a topic of interest.
- Do some preliminary reading about your tentative topic.
- Develop a research question about your topic.
- Refine your question by narrowing your topic, making it more focused and specific.
- If your assignment or research question requires a thesis, develop a tentative one.
- Search for sources—articles and books, both print and online—on your topic.
- Evaluate your sources for quality and reliability.
- Do a focused reading of your primary and secondary sources, taking notes and annotating them to highlight important passages.
- As you gather quotations or paraphrase ideas from outside sources in your notes, be sure to keep track of where they come from so you can cite them properly.
- Create an outline for your paper that maps out how you plan to present your points and supporting evidence from your sources.
- Using your outline to guide you, start writing a draft, working toward a thesis or a clear statement of your research findings.
- Reread your draft and reevaluate your thesis. Does the thesis need any changes? Is it adequately supported using evidence from your sources? If your assignment does not require a thesis, evaluate the depth and clarity of your research findings and how well you present them. Are your ideas presented in the right order and with the right emphasis?
- Do some additional reading to refine and further develop your thesis.
- Revise your draft based on your assessment of your previous draft and your additional research findings.
- Document your sources. Unless your instructor requests that you use footnote or endnote style, use the MLA documentation methods described in "Documenting Sources" (p. 2017).
- Revise, edit, and proofread your paper, double-checking that you have properly cited and documented all your sources.

FINDING SOURCES

As a researcher, your primary task once you have decided on a topic or an area of interest is to do some reading about it. Talk your ideas over with classmates and your instructor. The first place to look for sources, including books and articles on the subject, is your college library. See what questions scholars and critics are asking. Reference librarians can often help you locate secondary source materials about a particular author, work, or literary subject, so be sure to make use of their knowledge, especially if you are having trouble locating sources on your own.

Whether dealing with the Web or with books and other materials in the library, a whole industry exists to aid the literary researcher. Foremost among book publications useful for literary research are general literary sources that present overviews of their subject matter, with essays by significant scholars who present "the lay of the land," marking out what is known, the most recent trends in scholarship, and research questions currently of interest. Consulting these specialized, literary reference works to get a better sense of the landscape and scope of your topic and to find reputable, recent books and articles about it is an excellent way to start your research.

Literary research, like anything else, is subject to trends and to swings of interest from one subject to another because it is a key component of the larger cultural conversation. For instance, over the years literary research may have focused at different times on poetry's moral significance, its psychological impact, its formal qualities (e.g., style, unity), or its connection to social questions (e.g., feminism, gay rights). Such large-scale trends in criticism allowed for plenty of exceptions, but criticism of literature, like our understanding of the climate or of biology, changes over time and is driven by current needs and interests. That is one reason new criticism and scholarship is conducted and why a researcher can benefit from a good guide to the material. Some of those useful references, which are available in most college libraries and can be located with the help of a reference librarian, are listed below.

Annotated References for Literary Research

- *American Literary Scholarship*. Durham, N.C.: Duke University Press, 1963—. Useful bibliographic essays.
- Nancy L. Baker and Nancy Huling. *A Research Guide for Undergraduate Students: English and American Literature*. 5th ed. New York: MLA, 2000. Helpful step-by-step approach designed for undergraduates conducting literary research.
- *Contemporary Literary Criticism*. 106 volumes. Detroit: Gale, 1973–. Each volume focuses on an individual author, with a biography and excerpts from the critical response.
- *Dictionary of Literary Biography*. Detroit: Gale, 1978–. Comprehensive collection of biographical information, especially useful for world literature in English.
- Joseph Gibaldi. *MLA Handbook for Writers of Research Papers*. 6th ed. New York: MLA, 2003. The standard guide to MLA documentation.

- James L. Harner. *Literary Research Guide: A Listing of Reference Sources in English Literary Studies.* 4th ed. New York: MLA, 2002. Especially useful for serious research, with an explanation of the research process and helpful annotations.
- C. Hugh Holman and William Harmon. *A Handbook to Literature.* 9th ed. New York: Macmillan, 2002. Useful all-in-one guide to literary terms and movements.
- MLA *International Bibliography of Books and Articles on Modern Language and Literature.* New York: MLA, 1921–. Available online through subscription; also available on CD. Complete but potentially overwhelming source designed for professionals. No effort made to separate important articles from unimportant ones.
- Alex Preminger and T. V. F. Brogan, eds. *The New Princeton Encyclopedia of Poetry and Poetics.* Princeton, N.J.: Princeton University Press, 1993. Guide to literary terms and movements; similar to Holman and Harmon's *A Handbook to Literature* (above).
- *The Year's Work in English Studies.* London: Blackwell, 1921–. Authoritative bibliographic essays about English and American literature.

Many libraries also have subscriptions to **periodical indexes**, databases in which articles from selected **periodicals**—newspapers, magazines, or scholarly journals—can be found. Some of these articles can be located for free on the Web, but the most reliable and easy way to access an extensive range of reputable scholarly articles is from the databases available to you through your library. As with finding the most useful literary reference works for your topic, looking in the most appropriate database for your topic is essential. (For example, a medical database would be of little help for most literary research papers.) As with locating the literary reference works, your best bet is to ask your reference librarian which databases your library has that would best suit your topic. Some of the most common, comprehensive literary databases are listed below.

Annotated Library Subscription Databases for Literary Research

- **EBSCOhost:** Thousands of articles on a wide range of subjects.
- **Contemporary Authors:** Comprehensive information on contemporary authors in all genres.
- **Contemporary Literary Criticism Select:** Significant published criticism on the works of contemporary novelists, poets, playwrights, and short story writers.
- **Early English Books Online:** Offers 100,000 of over 125,000 early English literature titles dating from 1473 to 1700.
- **Expanded Academic ASAP:** Includes indexing, article abstracts, images, and full text for articles from scholarly and general-interest journals within all academic disciplines.
- **FirstSearch:** More than 10 million full-text and full-image articles from popular and scholarly periodicals.

- **Literature Online:** Extensive online literature database—over 1200 full books, 2000 short stories and poems, and 250 authors—searchable by author name.
- **World Shakespeare Bibliography Online:** International database of annotated entries for all important Shakespeare-oriented books, articles (scholarly and popular), book reviews, dissertations, theatrical productions, production reviews, audiovisual materials, and electronic media published between 1963 and 2006.

EVALUATING SOURCES

Some of the sources you have identified will not be of much value for your scholarly project. An early step in the research process is to evaluate your sources to determine their quality and reliability.

Print Sources

Most instructors tend to make a clear distinction between print works found in a library and works published on the Internet. Most print sources are viewed with greater credibility for one reason: it is much easier to evaluate them for appropriateness and reliability because you can easily discover and assess who wrote them and who published them.

A credible author tends to have some expertise in the subject area, uses evidence to back up his or her assertions, includes documentation of both the primary and secondary sources to prove that he or she has done ample research on the subject, and addresses other viewpoints and opinions. Even so, you will need to examine the author's perspective for bias, which is usually apparent either via a condescending tone in the writing or a dismissal of counterarguments without any supporting evidence to back up that dismissal. Book reviews and an author's publication history are also ways of finding out more about an author's credentials.

Similarly, examining the publication in which a source appears is a good way to determine how reliable it is. Works from academic book publishers and scholarly journals, which all depend on specialist readers, reviewers, and editors who look the book or article over before publication, tend to be more reliable than those published by general commercial publishers and general-interest, commercial magazines. If you are going to use material from a popular magazine or newspaper, stick with well-known and well-respected sources such as the *New Yorker, Time, Atlantic Monthly, Harper's,* the *New York Times, Los Angeles Times,* or *Washington Post,* to name a few. The lengthy publishing process for scholarly books and articles undertaken by reputable publishers does not guarantee perfection, but it provides readers with a certain degree of confidence that the material contained within has merit.

Internet Sources

The Internet is vast and accessible—making it difficult to determine the credibility of its contents. Anyone can write and post anything at all, which raises questions about whether a source found there is authentic, accurate, or original. All-purpose, general search engines like Google, Yahoo!, and AltaVista can be useful for turning up preliminary information on a given subject, but remember that they will make no distinction between a reputable source and an unreliable one. In fact, many search engines list search results on the basis of popularity rather than reliability. More specialized search engines, like the relatively new Google Scholar, which enables you to search exclusively for scholarly information from scholarly sources, are a safer option.

How can one be sure that a Web source is reputable? As with print sources, determining the credibility of the author and the publisher is the best method. Subject expertise, the use of ample evidence, an even-handed tone, an inclusion of alternate viewpoints and opinions, and the use of ample citations within a work are decent indications of an author's reliability. The best sign of an online source's reliability and accuracy is that it is sponsored by a well-regarded organization, like a university, a scholarly organization, or an established press or publishing house. In many cases, by doing some investigative digging, you may find that a site that seems to be informational is actually being sponsored by a biased or commercial sponsor or organization. Think of the difference between sources sponsored by such reputable organizations and those whose reputation cannot be established, like a blog or a fan's website. For instance, if you were looking for the text of a poem, which would you trust more, the website sponsored by the University of Toronto Press or a poetry-lover's home page? You, the researcher, more than ever must make critical decisions about the credibility of your sources, whether in print or online.

Also, be sure to check when an online source was last updated. The most reliable Internet sites have active links and are frequently updated for accuracy and currency.

TAKING GOOD NOTES

As you uncover credible references, books, and articles, you will begin to do focused reading of these primary and secondary sources, taking notes and annotating them to highlight important passages. Note-taking provides the best, most efficient way to organize your findings and to gather and keep track of quotations or paraphrased ideas from outside sources so you can cite them properly. Think of the notes you take as having three main purposes:

1. To help you remember important information.
2. To capture someone's exact words.
3. To help you retrieve and organize your material.

Notes are inadequate if you cannot find the necessary information in them, so from the beginning, you need a system for taking notes that will let you incorporate their contents as you draft your paper.

Some researchers stick to index cards, putting one fact from their research on each card, along with the source in which it was found. Others use word-processing files saved in laptops to gather the same information. Still others copy everything on yellow notepads or in journals. Whichever technique you use, be sure you are being accurate as you copy material and list key facts like page numbers and publication dates. Above all, make sure you have a way of noting which material is taken verbatim from your sources and which is being paraphrased. Sloppy note-taking at this stage has led some researchers to be accused of plagiarism, as they later used material without showing it was taken from sources. (See pp. 2015–2017 for a discussion of this issue.)

What constitutes a good note? A good note contains useful information such as a key fact, a quotation, a claim, or an evaluation; a good note also contains the exact data you need to correctly cite the source. Finally, a good note might have your own comment on the information or a cross-reference to another related fact or quotation. The sample note below was taken by student Tiffany Bergeron for the research paper that appears on p. 2050 at the end of this chapter. Because the source is an article in *Salon*, a periodical available only on the Web, Tiffany included not only the author, article title, periodical title, publication date, and URL, but also the date on which she accessed the material. Although she did not format the source information into MLA documentation style in her actual note, she did have all the components that MLA style requires, so she was able to easily restyle this information to match MLA guidelines in the actual Works Cited list in her paper. In her note, Tiffany wrote down a verbatim quotation from the article for possible use in her paper, but she added a few comments of her own so she would remember why the quotation seemed potentially useful to her.

From "Voices of America," by Carol Lloyd, in *Salon*, May 28, 2004. <www.salon.com/bc/1998/12/cov_08bc2.html>. Accessed online on March 31, 2006.

Quote about the use of "authentic," real-life speech in Anna Deavere Smith's plays, from p. 2 of article, para. 9:
"When she began interviewing subjects in preparation for her first show, Smith sought ways to compel people to speak more authentically. 'I asked a linguist how I might encourage people to say 'uh' more. 'Uhs' are actually the place where I find American character.'"

Idea to consider—What effect does this approach have on how we read and interpret *Twilight: Los Angeles, 1992*?

THE WRITING PROCESS

The writing process for a literary research paper is a series of activities: drafting a thesis, creating an outline, writing a first draft, and finally editing and revising the draft to create the completed version. Each of these steps is described more fully in the sections that follow.

Drafting a Thesis

Once you have gathered notes from a wealth of sources, you will need to use your ideas and the ideas of others that you have found to develop and draft your thesis. For specific examples that illustrate how to move from a topic to an explicit thesis in a paper about a story, poem, or play, see the corresponding "Developing a Thesis" sections on pp. 134, 822, and 1236. You may also want to look at the sample thesis on p. 2040, which became the basis for Tiffany Bergeron's final research paper at the end of this chapter.

Creating an Outline

With your thesis statement in hand, you can begin to map out the organization of your paper. For brief assignments, just going through your notes and organizing them—sorting them into groups by each topic or source title, deciding which ones really support the thesis and which are irrelevant, and rearranging them into a logical sequence—may suffice. For longer research projects, you will benefit from drawing up a formal outline that sketches out, more or less, the contents of your paper. (Some instructors require that you turn in an outline as one component of the research project.) For an example of a formal outline, see p. 2041, which maps out the research paper that concludes this chapter.

Writing a First Draft

As you begin drafting your paper, use the outline to chart your path from one point to the next, and refer back to your notes as necessary. Keep in mind as you work that the outline is a guide but not a rigid formula; new, better ideas may occur to you as you write, and you may want to incorporate those into your draft. Give yourself the space to explore your ideas. At this stage, you should let your writing and ideas flow without worrying about correct grammar, spelling, and punctuation or about creating a perfect paper in the first draft. You will have the chance to correct mechanical errors when you go back to revise your paper.

Your **introductory paragraph** will usually need to accomplish a few goals:

- Clearly identify the literary text you will be discussing.
- Present an overview of your topic, sometimes with a bit of necessary background information to generate interest in it.
- State your thesis.

While the introductory paragraph is obviously the first thing anyone will read, many students find that it is easier to write their introduction last—in other words, to summarize what is being introduced, which is discussed in the body of the paper, after they have actually written the body of the paper. At the very least, you may find that even if you write a rough introduction at the start, you will end up having to revise it substantially on the basis of the actual completed paper.

In the **body** of your paper, which will make up the bulk of it, you offer all the evidence you have gathered to support the point or argument presented in your introduction. Each paragraph should develop a single point, and to back up that point, you will use examples and quotations from the literary work you are discussing, and you will draw on quotations, summaries, and paraphrases from your secondary sources.

Like the introduction, your paper's **conclusion** is usually a single paragraph. It should remind readers of your larger purpose, summing up why all the points you have made in the body of your paper matter. This is the place to restate and reinforce your thesis and your primary points, giving your readers a sense of closure.

Revising and Editing

More often than not, a lengthy research paper will require several drafts. The purpose of the first draft is to get all your ideas down; the purpose of every subsequent revision is to shape those ideas. Revising a draft gives you the opportunity to revisit each step of your process, to make sure you have shaped and refined those ideas and presented them clearly, and ultimately, to make sure that the final result is as effective as it can be. Revision is your chance to do the following:

- Reevaluate your thesis.
- Make sure all your supporting points make sense.

REVISION CHECKLIST

Here are some questions to consider as you revise and edit your paper.

- Is your overall topic too narrow or too broad for your assignment?
- Does your thesis need work? Is it presented clearly?
- Is your thesis adequately supported using evidence from sources? How persuasively do your supporting points back up your claim?
- Do your points contain enough depth and clarity? Do any points deviate from your purpose or fail to back up your thesis?
- Are all your paragraphs fully developed? Do any points need further explanation or support from secondary sources?
- Do each of the points appear in a logical order, with clear transitions between each paragraph?
- How well does your first paragraph introduce your topic and thesis?
- Does your final paragraph succinctly restate your thesis and provide a sense of closure?
- Are all your sentences clear and complete?
- Do you have an informative title for your paper?
- Have you documented all your sources?
- Have you used the proper MLA format to cite your sources?
- Have you proofread the final draft for typos, misspellings, and grammar errors?

- Make sure you have ample evidence to support your points.
- Make sure you present those points and the supporting evidence clearly and logically.
- Make sure you have cited your sources properly and completely.
- Fix weaknesses in your writing style and correct typos, misspelled words, sentence fragments, and other grammar errors.

Give yourself a break of at least a day or two between each draft of your paper. It is difficult for any writer to notice structural problems, awkward phrases, points that do not have enough supporting evidence, right after being in the thick of creating that material. A little breathing room will go a long way, and you will be more aware of the improvements that need to be made if you give your mind a break from the project.

If you have trouble identifying problems on your own, consider using either a peer review, in which you and a classmate trade drafts and assess them for one another, or a conference with your instructor, in which you give your teacher the draft in order to get specific direction, either in person or through e-mail. Either technique gives you a second set of eyes to evaluate the draft and help you identify the revisions that are necessary.

AVOIDING PLAGIARISM

Every student has heard about plagiarism, yet each year many English instructors have to deal with cases of students handing in work that is not their own. And the problem is an old one. Before the Web made plagiarism easier and more tempting, college fraternities and sororities had files of old term papers that could be retyped and handed in again. Back then, some instructors made life easier for plagiarists by giving the same assignments every term, and not devoting time to work with students on the preliminary stages of their reports and research papers or to examine outlines and drafts. Now the Web offers thousands of papers for sale, many of them on classic literary texts, including a good many on the literature in a book such as this one. Likewise, because the Web makes it easy to electronically copy possible quotations from outside sources for a paper, unintentional plagiarism is easier and more common; all it takes is forgetting to also copy the source information to go with the quotations.

However, the very techniques that make it easy to find papers to plagiarize have also made plagiarism much easier to detect. And times have changed with teaching as well. Many instructors now require that students deliver the research paper in stages: a prospectus with a tentative thesis; a working bibliography; a draft of the opening page; a brief oral report in a conference during office hours; a good, complete draft to be revised; and finally the completed paper. Individual preferences and teaching styles will differ, of course, but today's instructors understand that having a multistep process helps students produce a more effective piece of finished writing, and it is a good method of countering the dangers of plagiarism. Students facing impossible time pressures are easy prey for temptation, but a longer-term, multistep process makes it very difficult to rush a paper in a single weekend. Similarly, by discussing the paper in advance and requiring a prospectus and a preliminary draft, most instructors have a good notion of how their students write, so any huge changes will give rise to strong suspicions; the instructors are much more likely to detect plagiarism. And from the students' viewpoint, when an instructor has worked with them closely on their papers, the students are less likely to plagiarize because their papers are under control.

Plagiarism and Academic Honesty

A simple definition of **plagiarism** is: the use of the ideas or words of another without giving appropriate credit. Literary research absolutely requires a policy about plagiarism because so much depends on the conversation between the researcher and many others who have written on the subject. A literary researcher relies on the work of others, so the need for giving appropriate credit is paramount.

How do you give this credit? The most common way is in a citation, a reference in your text giving credit to the original source through an in-text citation, a footnote, or an endnote. The methods of citation and documentation explained on pages 2017–2037 provide you with a simple, easy-to-follow guide. If you follow these rules and guidelines, you will be fine. In fact, the more your paper is in fruitful dialogue with your sources, the more it will resemble the work of professionals, and the more impressive it will be to your instructor.

Intentional plagiarism—the practice of buying or copying a paper outright, either through the Web or with the help of a friend—is outright fraud, and the penalties are rightly severe. Most colleges have clear procedures for such cases, and when an instructor discovers such an example, the student should expect no mercy. Some colleges with strict honor codes will expel students who buy or copy papers. The least students can expect is to receive a failing grade for the paper or the entire course.

Why is plagiarism regarded so seriously? One reason is that colleges truly depend on honest dealings. Research is a joint effort, and the ones conducting it—from professor to student—are expected to be straightforward about method, results, and proper credit. Researchers are part of a community of scholars trying to find the truth, at whatever level they are operating. Academic honesty is absolutely necessary for genuine scholarship, and academic dishonesty breaks all the bonds of trust within the community.

Unintentional Plagiarism

Can there be such a thing as inadvertent or accidental plagiarism? Yes, and unsurprisingly, it is the most common form of plagiarism. For instance, imagine that you are taking notes on a relevant scholarly article. You copy words, sentences, and perhaps whole paragraphs into your laptop or notebook, but in doing so, you fail to make it clear that these are quotations, either by forgetting to copy that information or by including only part of that information. Two weeks later, you look over your notes, find the perfect phrase, and put it in your paper, forgetting that you took it from your source and that it is not your own work.

The rule is, if a phrase, quotation, or idea that you have summarized in your own words is taken from someone else, it needs to be cited. If you fail to do so, you are guilty of plagiarism, even though you made an honest mistake and did it without malicious intent. Nevertheless, the phrase is there in your paper, without citation, due to your careless note-taking.

How to Prevent Plagiarism

The best way of avoiding inadvertent plagiarism is simple: when taking notes, put all quotations in quotation marks or indent them in a special way to remind you that they are quotations and need to be cited. Also make sure that as you take notes you also copy down the complete source information for quotations or paraphrased ideas of others. It is much easier to gather this information while note-taking than to have to go back to the original article or book and retrieve that source information while writing your actual paper.

Another kind of plagiarism occurs when you take ideas from someone else but disguise them by changing the words or phrases into words of your own. Regardless of whether you do this knowingly or carelessly, this is still plagiarism, even if you have not used a single word from the original. For example, here is a passage from a critical essay about Walt Whitman, followed by the publication information for the source:

Original Source

Photography, after all, was the merging of sight and chemistry, of eye and machine, of organism and mechanism, much as America was, and thus it took root more rapidly here than elsewhere, became the precise American instrument of seeing. Whitman knew that no culture was more in love with science and technology than America was, and the camera was the perfect emblem of the joining of the human senses to chemistry and physics via a machine.

Folsom, Ed. "Walt Whitman and the Visual Democracy of Photography." *Walt Whitman of Mickle Street: A Centennial Collection.* Ed. Geoffrey M. Sill. Knoxville: U of Tennessee P, 1994. 80–93.

These two sentences, from a well-regarded book of scholarly essays on Whitman, were reworded and paraphrased by a student and became transformed into this passage:

Plagiarized Version

```
Photography merged human eyesight and machinery, and it
became more popular here than in other places. Walt
Whitman understood that America was crazy about new
scientific breakthroughs, and he saw that photography
could be a symbol of linking the eyesight to science
through technology.
```

See what happened? Barely a word of the original passage remains, yet every idea is copied. This qualifies as plagiarism. The student presented the idea as his own insight and therefore has committed plagiarism. Without citation, you cannot use other people's ideas, no matter how much you clothe them in your own language.

What should this student have done? In this case, the student could have copied the exact words of the original author, indented them as a block quotation, and given the writer, Ed Folsom, appropriate credit using proper documentation methods. The student merely needed to add a parenthetical, in-text citation with the author's last name and the page number of the source (Folsom 82) and then provided the full source information in the Works Cited list at the end of the paper. That way, the instructor would praise the student for conducting good research and providing a useful quotation. But instead, the student in the above instance pretended that these sentences represent his own insight, and he has committed plagiarism.

Below are two other ways the student could have avoided plagiarism. The examples follow the MLA guidelines for citing an article from an anthology (see p. 2031 in the "Using Parenthetical Citation in Your Text" section below for details). In the first example below, the student paraphrases the original author's ideas in the first half of the sentence and directly quotes in the second half. He directly cites the author, and he includes the page reference parenthetically. The full source information for the article would be included in his Works Cited list.

Correct Documentation, Example 1

According to critic Ed Folsom, Walt Whitman understood that there was an inherent link between photography and the American way of seeing:

> Whitman knew that no culture was more in love
> with science and technology than America was,
> and the camera was the perfect emblem of the
> joining of the human senses to chemistry and
> physics via a machine (82).

Alternatively, as in the example below, the student could use the entire quotation, introducing it with an explanatory phrase of his own and citing it parenthetically, this time with both the author's last name and the page number, because he does not cite the critic's name in the actual text. Again, the full source listing for the article would be included in the Works Cited list at the end of the paper.

Correct Documentation, Example 2

Walt Whitman has great insight into the American character and the American view of the world and the country's relationship to progress, and specifically to technology:

> Photography, after all, was the merging of
> sight and chemistry, of eye and machine, of
> organism and mechanism, much as America was,
> and thus it took root more rapidly here than

elsewhere, became the precise American
instrument of seeing. Whitman knew that no
culture was more in love with science and
technology than America was, and the camera
was the perfect emblem of the joining of the
human senses to chemistry and physics via a
machine (Folsom 82).

The bottom line on plagiarism is simple: when you cite others' ideas properly, you get credit for being in a conversation—a written, intellectual dialogue with your sources. When you fail to cite others' ideas, you run the risk of plagiarism for pretending they were your own. The choice is simple.

But what do you do if you are desperate, with a deadline facing you and no fruitful ideas of your own on the subject? Begin a conversation with your instructor, telling him or her that you have fallen behind. Most instructors are understanding—especially with those students who are honest with them. The worst that can happen is that your grade will be lowered for a late paper, but that consequence certainly beats the far more dire penalties that result from being found guilty of academic dishonesty.

DOCUMENTING SOURCES

As the section on plagiarism above emphasizes, whenever you use another person's words or ideas in your own writing, you must say so clearly. This is true whether you use direct quotations from a book, journal, interview, or other source, as well as when you paraphrase information that is not common knowledge. By "common knowledge" we mean information that most people know. Sometimes it is clear when it is not necessary to cite the source of general information—the fact that Shakespeare was a playwright, for example. Other times, it is more difficult to tell. When in doubt, always err on the side of caution and cite your sources; your reader will appreciate the time you take to explain facts or terminology that may be new or unfamiliar. As the author of your paper, it is up to you to decide what other information and voices to include, and you are responsible for how those sources get put together.

Some students view citing sources as an admission of defeat that they were unable to find anything to say and had to fall back on the ideas of others. But research by its very nature involves interacting with the ideas of others, making research a genuine conversation or dialogue. Think of citing the work of others as a way of strengthening your argument or supporting your thesis, or as assembling a team of experts to testify in favor of the points you are making. Additionally, the citations you use demonstrate that you are knowledgeable of the ongoing conversation on your topic; they show that you have investigated the subject and now have something of your own to contribute. Furthermore, citations help readers by letting them know the sources of your information, and they demonstrate that you are using the best sources. For example, in some projects you may need to provide a general overview of a subject, and your citations will indicate that you have read the best authorities and are aware of recent findings and observations. For other papers, you may need to take a stand on a particular issue, and your citations will include points that support your claim or thesis or can consist of quotations you will argue against.

Finally, citation makes it easy for interested readers to find your sources when they want to know more about your subject. Keep these readers in mind when determining how much publication information to include in a citation. Although citation methods may differ in the smaller details, each one is designed to create a trail so that others can retrieve the sources of your argument.

When you cite, you should follow a particular method of documentation, one with its own rules set up to guarantee internal consistency. It is much easier to follow a set pattern than to make one up on your own. Among the several common methods of documentation are those published in guidebooks by the University of Chicago, the American Psychological Association, and the Modern Language Association. These are abbreviated as Chicago, APA, and MLA, respectively. All these methods require either footnote/endnote citation or citation within parentheses in the body of your text. With footnote or endnote style, you include a superscripted number at the end of a cited line, sentence, or paragraph that refers readers to either the bottom of the page (footnote) or to the end of the essay (endnote), where they can find the full title and publication information. This is the system most often used in academic books and journals in the humanities.

In parenthetical systems of documentation, such as APA and MLA, the author's last name and the page number of the quoted information are included within parentheses at the end of a sentence. If the author's name is mentioned in the text, then just the page number is given within the parentheses. The full publication information is then placed in the Works Cited section at the end of the paper. Writers who use a parenthetical method of citation may also include explanatory endnotes, which provide additional, peripheral information or ideas connected to the paper's argument, but no publication details.

Unless your instructor indicates otherwise, use MLA style, which is standard for research in literature. Listed below are some of the basic elements of MLA citation; for more information and examples, consult Joseph Gibaldi's *MLA Handbook for Writers of Research Papers*, 6th edition (2003).

Using Parenthetical Citations in Your Text

A parenthetical citation should provide readers with enough information to find the source in the Works Cited list at the end of your paper. For the most part, you should include the author's last name and the page number of the source. For MLA style, do not include "page" or "p." or a comma between the last name and page number. Place the parenthetical citation at a break in the sentence's structure; this will almost always be at the end of the sentence. Note that the sentence period comes *after* the parenthetical citation. Here is a typical example:

Paraphrase or Summary, Omitting Author's Name in Discussion

More than any other singular event or person, former president Richard Nixon may well be the most influential force on contemporary American fiction (Baxter 4).

In the above example, the parenthetical citation refers to page 4 of the book or article by fiction writer and critic Charles Baxter that is listed in the Works Cited section.

If you have already mentioned the author's name in the text of the sentence, you only need to include the page number in parenthesis. When a sentence ends with a direct quotation, the closing quotation marks come *before* the parenthetical citation, and the punctuation of the sentence after.

Direct Quotation, Using Author's Name in Discussion

```
According to Charles Baxter, Richard Nixon may have
been "the greatest influence on American fiction for the
last twenty years" (4).
```

In MLA style, the first time you mention anyone in your discussion, you should use the person's full name; for later mentions, use only the last name.

Some writers prefer to use one consistent system throughout a paper—either placing every author's name in parentheses in all citations or using every author's name in the text of the paper itself, with only page numbers in the citation—but many incorporate both systems in a single paper. This is because the kind of information being quoted and the actual source often lend themselves to one style over another. For example, if you want to emphasize what someone said more than who he or she is, you may prefer to refer to the source in the parenthetical citation. If you want to call attention to the stature of the source, indicating that the remark was made by an eminent scholar or critic, you will want to introduce the author into the text of your sentence, and if necessary explain why that person matters to the subject of your paper.

Direct Quotation, Using Author's Name and Credentials in Discussion

```
According to fiction writer and critic Charles Baxter in
"Dysfunctional Narratives: or: 'Mistakes Were Made,'"
from his acclaimed book Burning Down the House: Essays
on Fiction, which analyzes and examines the social and
political trends currently influencing modern story-
telling, Richard Nixon may have been "the greatest
influence on American fiction for the last twenty years"
(4).
```

Whether or not you include such information is a matter of knowing your readers and the extent to which you wish to place yourself in an ongoing conversation. Generally, the more unfamiliar you suspect your readers are with your subject, the more you will want to explain why you call in the sources that you do. For other papers, your instructor may ask you to assume that your audience is knowledgeable about the subject; in that case, names alone will speak volumes about which authors you have been reading and the extent to which you have done quality research.

Keep in mind that your parenthetical citations should not be necessary for understanding the body of your paper. Your paper should make perfect sense when you can read it aloud *without* the parenthetical citations. Good writers never allow the citations to interrupt the flow of their ideas. The principle is that with or without citations, the sentences are still your own and must read smoothly.

If your paper includes more than one work by the same author, you will need to add a short title to the in-text citation to make it clear which source you are quoting:

Citing One of Several Works by the Same Author

More than any other singular event or person, former president Richard Nixon may well be the most influential force on contemporary American fiction (Baxter, "Dysfunctional Narratives" 4).

If you are citing more than one source within a parenthetical reference, separate the sources with a semicolon:

Citing Two or More Sources in a Single Parenthetical Reference

(Baxter 4; Scarry 54)

For electronic sources from the Internet or an online database, keep in mind that many of these sources do not use page numbers. If available, use paragraph, section, or screen numbers, with the abbreviation "par." or "pars." or "sec." or the full word "screen," followed by the pertinent numbers. Note that if the citation includes an author name, as in the case below, a comma should be placed after the name.

Citing an Electronic Source

(Lloyd, screen 3)

Integrating Quotations

A paper must always read smoothly, but this basic principle of effective writing becomes particularly important when you include quotations. When you include someone else's prose, it should not disrupt the flow of your own sentences. In fact, because quotations can interrupt the flow, you should paraphrase as much as possible: that is, you should explain the idea in your own words rather than quote someone else's writing. Here too you must clearly cite the source of the ideas you are paraphrasing, and you must remain true to the original meaning. Remember that you are the author of your own paper, and your own ideas should not be unnecessarily interrupted by long quotations from other people.

Of course sometimes you will face difficulties in manipulating a sentence into your own prose without taking it out of context, and sometimes it is better to recast your own paragraph or quote a passage in its entirety. One way to integrate quotations is to take fragments of sentences and work them into your own. For example, consider the different ways you could cite the following passage from an article by Zev Trachtenberg about Robert Frost's famous poem "Mending Wall":

Original Passage

The richness of "Mending Wall" is that it offers a hopeful vision of the role property can play in sustaining community, while fully acknowledging that vision's ambiguous prospect. Though he might convince the reader, the eloquent spokesman for a communitarian conception of property cannot convince his own neighbor. The poem's confrontation between the narrator and the neighbor, and the positions on property they represent, reflect what is perhaps a paradox inherent in the effort to bring the notions of property and community together.

Trachtenberg, Zev M. "Good Neighbors Make Good Fences: Frost's 'Mending Wall.'" *Philosophy and Literature* 21.1 (1997): 114–22.

Paraphrase, Using Author's Name in Discussion

Zev Trachtenberg claims that "Mending Wall" reflects an optimistic attitude toward community, even as it reflects an awareness that every neighbor might not share the same attitude (120).

Direct Quotation, Using Author's Name in Discussion

According to Zev Trachtenberg, "The richness of 'Mending Wall' is that it offers a hopeful vision of the role property can play in sustaining community" (120).

Direct Quotation and Paraphrase, Omitting Author's Name in Discussion

The speaker of "Mending Wall" sustains a tone that is difficult to describe, and his function has been interpreted in many ways. According to one literary critic, this "eloquent spokesman for a communitarian conception of property" has a better chance of convincing the reader than his neighbor (Trachtenberg 120).

Alternate Direct Quotation and Paraphrase, Using Author's Name in Discussion

Trachtenberg explains that although Robert Frost's famous poem is about building a fence, "The richness of 'Mending Wall' is that it offers a hopeful vision of the role property can play in sustaining community" (120).

In the first example the writer paraphrases the source, using his own words. The second example is a traditional direct quotation; the writer has introduced the quote by giving the critic's name, and the rest of the sentence is a quotation. In the third and fourth examples, the writer uses direct quotes and also paraphrases in order to work the quotes into her own prose. In the third example, the writer includes only a fragment of the sentence.

If you leave out part of a sentence or paragraph when you quote directly, you can replace the missing word or words with an ellipsis: either three spaced periods (and a space before and after the group of periods) if words are omitted within a sentence, or four spaced periods (and a space after the group of periods but not before it) if the omission involves two or more sentences. This is a useful technique for highlighting important aspects of a source while keeping it concise; however, writers must be mindful not to cut out so much information that the source is misrepresented. You must also be sure that the overall sentence makes grammatical sense. The shortened example below is an accurate rendering of the source, but unfortunately it is not grammatical. What was omitted, as indicated by the ellipsis, is the second part of the compound subject necessary to make the verb "reflect" plural:

Shortened Quotation Rendered Ungrammatical

```
"The poem's confrontation between the narrator and the
neighbor . . . reflect what is perhaps a paradox inherent
in the effort to bring the notions of property and
community together" (Trachtenberg 120).
```

To correct grammatical errors that arise when you use an ellipsis, use brackets to indicate that what is between them has been inserted by you, and not the original author:

Shortened Quotation Using Brackets to Render it Grammatical

```
"The poem's confrontation between the narrator and the
neighbor . . . reflect[s] what is perhaps a paradox
inherent in the effort to bring the notions of property
and community together" (Trachtenberg 120).
```

These are just some of the more common methods writers use to incorporate prose quotations and paraphrases into their own papers. When quoting poetry, however, you have much less room for flexibility. Poems are valued as much for how they communicate as what they communicate, and for this reason line breaks, punctuation, and deviations from standard grammar need to be preserved; poetry must be reprinted faithfully, even if the spelling seems outdated or the capitalization odd.

Formatting Literary Quotations from Stories, Poems, and Plays

Short Quotations

For some literary passages, you will cite line, stanza, or canto numbers rather than page numbers. When you are discussing a poem, for example, MLA style prefers that your parenthetical citation include the line numbers of quoted passages rather than the page numbers (which would be available in the Works Cited section at the end of the paper). There is no need to type "Line" or the abbreviation "l." before the line numbers. Here is an example from a paper that discusses William Blake's "The Tyger" and references line 14 of the poem:

```
    Blake continues to associate the creation of the

tiger with blacksmithing through the line "In what

furnace was thy brain?" (14).
```

For longer works of poetry or drama, you will also need to indicate acts, scenes, or books so that the reader can easily find the passage. Consider this example from a paper that discusses Shakespeare's *Richard III*:

```
    In one highly ironic moment, King Richard says, "I

thank God for my humility" (2.2.73).
```

The above parenthetical citation indicates that the passage is in Act 2, Scene 2, line 73.

When quoting two consecutive lines of poetry or drama, a slash mark (with a space before and after it) is used to separate the lines, and the capitalization is left intact:

```
    In Paradise Lost, Milton's Satan claims that "The

mind is its own place, and in it self / Can make a

Heav'n of Hell, a Hell of Heav'n" (1.254-55).
```

The parenthetical citation above indicates that the quotation is from lines 254 and 255 in Book 1 of Milton's poem.

MLA has specific guidelines and abbreviations for many major works of literature (such as the Bible, *The Faerie Queene*, and the works of Chaucer). These can be quite useful, but rather complicated. If you want to know more about the specifics of abbreviation in MLA style, you can find all this information in the *MLA Handbook for Writers of Research Papers*, 6th edition (2003).

Long Prose Quotations

Prose quotations longer than four lines should be set off as an indented block in your paper. Indent the block quotation one inch (or ten spaces) from the left margin. Indented quotations are usually introduced with a colon.

```
    In "Jim Smiley and His Jumping Frog," a short story

by Samuel L. Clemens (also known as Mark Twain), the

title character is introduced not by the narrator of the

story but in the words of another character, Simon

Wheeler:

        There was a feller here once by the name of

        Jim Smily, in the winter of '49--or maybe it
```

```
was the spring of '50--I don't recollect
exactly, somehow, though what makes me think
it was one or the other is because I remember
the big flume wasn't finished when he first come
to the camp; but anyway, he was the curiosest
man about always betting on anything that
turned up you ever see, if he could get
anybody to bet on the other side, and if he
couldn't he'd change sides—any way that suited
the other man would suit him—any way just
so's he got a bet, he was satisfied. (430)
```

A few things should be noticed about the indented quotation. First, the passage is not within quotation marks because setting it off with indentation indicates that it is a direct quotation. Second, unlike parenthetical citations for shorter quotations, in this instance, the page number in parentheses *follows* the final punctuation of the indented passage. Third, note that the lines quoted are double-spaced, like the rest of the paper.

If you are quoting only a single paragraph, as in the example above, you do not need to indent the first line of the quotation; however, if you are quoting a passage that starts at the beginning of a paragraph and that spans two or more paragraphs, the first word of each paragraph needs to be indented an additional three spaces.

```
    Jane Austen opens Pride and Prejudice with an
unidentified, but opinionated and authoritative narrative
voice, one which continues to weave in and out of the
narrative action, commenting on the novel's events and
injecting grand pronouncements about the nature of
relationships between men and women:
            It is a truth universally acknowledged, that
        a single man in possession of a good fortune
        must be in want of a wife.
            However little known the feelings or views
        of such a man may be on his first entering a
        neighbourhood, this truth is so well fixed in
        the minds of the surrounding families, that he
        is considered as the rightful property of some
        one or other of their daughters. (5)
```

Long Poetry Quotations

To quote a passage of four or more lines of poetry, use the indented block format. Indent the lines one inch from the left margin. The lines are double-spaced, and no quotation marks are used. Try to replicate for the most part how the poem looks on the page. Rather than a page number at the end, include the line numbers. There is no need for additional punctuation beyond what is in the poem:

```
     The first two stanzas of William Carlos Williams's
  "The Red Wheelbarrow" are strikingly sparse:
          so much depends

          upon

          a red wheel

          barrow (1-4)
```

Long Quotations from Plays

When quoting from plays, use the indented block format for passages of more than four lines. Indent the block one inch from your left margin. Each dialogue part should be introduced by the speaking character's name, set in capital letters and followed by a period, and the dialogue you are quoting should follow that. Every time the dialogue you are quoting shifts to another character, you need to start a new line indented an inch from the left margin. Any time a single speech spans two or more lines, the second and subsequent lines are indented an additional quarter inch (or three spaces).

```
     In Shakespeare's Hamlet, Hamlet's relationship with
  Ophelia breaks down as the communication between them
  becomes increasingly puzzling:
          HAMLET. Are you fair?
          OPHELIA. What means your lordship?
          HAMLET. That if you be honest and fair, your
             honesty should admit no discourse to your
             beauty. (3.1.107-10)
```

CREATING THE WORKS CITED SECTION

Parenthetical citations include just enough information for the reader to find the source in your Works Cited section, where you provide full publication information. The Works Cited section appears at the end of your paper, beginning on a new, separate page with the heading "Works Cited" centered at the top. (Like the rest of your paper, this page should be numbered, and the page number should be preceded by your last name as the author of the paper.) The Works Cited pages are double-spaced and the works listed in it are organized alphabetically by author's last name. For any entry that spans more than one line, the second and subsequent lines are indented half an inch (or five spaces) from the left margin; these half-inch hanging indents make it easier for the reader to scan for a certain author.

Books

Books with One Author

Typical one-author entries include the author, full title of the work, city of publication, publisher, and year of publication, which you can find on the title page and copyright page of the book. Underline book titles, or put them in italics. The author's last name is given first. Titles should be separated from subtitles by a colon.

```
Baxter, Charles. Burning Down the House: Essays on
     Fiction. St. Paul, MN: Graywolf, 1997.
Dawkins, Richard. The Selfish Gene. Oxford: Oxford UP,
     1989.
Perella, Nicolas James. The Kiss Sacred and Profane: An
     Interpretive History of Kiss Symbolism and Related
     Religio-Erotic Themes. Berkeley: U of California P,
     1969.
```

In the above examples, "UP" is an abbreviation for "University Press," and "U of California P" is short for "University of California Press." If the city is well known, there is no need to indicate the state; for more obscure locations, or for a city that shares a name with a famous foreign city, include the state's postal abbreviation, as shown in the first example above. If the state is part of the publisher's name, as in "U of California P" in the last example, then there is no need to include the state abbreviation after the city.

MLA uses specific abbreviations for many well-known publishers, such as "Harper" instead of "HarperCollins Publishers, Inc." If you wish to use the absolutely correct MLA abbreviations, consult the *MLA Handbook for Writers of Research Papers*, 6th edition (2003).

For the most accuracy, take the publication information from either the book's title page or copyright page, never from the cover or a bibliographic record. Take care not to mistake the printing date for the copyright date (indicated by ©), especially when citing a paperback. Paperbacks can be especially confusing, for they will often list multiple printing dates as well as several copyright years. Take the most recent copyright date; this sometimes means the year you cite will be decades or even centuries later than the original publication date. This is because your edition was not the first edition, and it is important that you provide the information for the text you read, for editions can be very different from one another.

An Edition of a Book

The term "edition" means a version or printing of the book, but it can also mean that an editor rather than the author prepared the text. Many times, it is a good idea to include the original publication date for clarity, especially if there is a large gap in time between your edition and the first publication. The original date goes immediately after the title and before the book's publication information.

> Bronte, Emily. <u>Wuthering Heights</u>. 1847. London: Penguin,
>   1994.

Sometimes the original date is unimportant or even unknown; when citing Shakespeare, for example, the date of the edition you used is usually sufficient. However, you may sometimes want to make a point of the original year.

A Book with an Author, an Editor, and a Translator

In the following example, the student has used a recent edited reprint of one of the first English translations of a work by the Roman poet Ovid. The original date of Ovid's work is unknown and is irrelevant to her paper. It is important for her thesis, however, that the translation is the one read during the Renaissance, and the student wants to make the original date of the translation clear in her Works Cited. The year of the translation is listed after the translator's name to make it clear that this is the original date of the translation and not Ovid's poem. In this case, the translated text was also prepared by a particular editor; in this citation example, the name of the translator is put before the editor because the translator was listed first on the book's title page:

> Ovid. <u>Metamorphoses</u>. Trans. Arthur Golding. 1567. Ed.
>   John Frederick Nims. Philadelphia: Paul Dry Books,
>   2000.

A Book with an Author and an Editor or Translator

Place the editor or translator's name after the title of the text, with the abbreviation "Ed." or "Trans." The author's name is given first, unless you wish to emphasize the work of the editor or translator, as in the second example below.

> Bronte, Charlotte. <u>Jane Eyre</u>. Ed. Richard J. Dunn. New
>   York: Norton, 1987.
> Fitzgerald, Robert, Trans. <u>The Iliad</u>. By Homer. New
>   York: Anchor, 1989.
> Mann, Thomas. <u>Death in Venice</u>. Ed. and Trans. Clayton
>   Koelb. New York: Norton, 1994.

A Book with Two or Three Authors or Editors

When citing a book with more than one author or editor, list the names as they appear on the title page, reversing only the first author's name. In the corresponding in-text parenthetical reference, list all the authors' surnames: (Strunk and White 15). Note that in the example immediately below, "eds." means "editors" and "ed." signifies "edition." Generally, when "ed." comes immediately before or after a name, it means "editor" or "edited by"; otherwise it usually indicates an edition. When citing a second or subsequent edition, it is a good idea to indicate the edition immediately after the title.

```
Peterson, Linda H., John C. Brereton, and Joan E.
    Hartman, eds. The Norton Reader. 10th ed. New York:
    Norton, 2000.
Strunk, William, and E. B. White. The Elements of Style.
    4th ed. New York: Longman, 2000.
```

A Book with More than Three Authors or Editors

The abbreviation "et al." means "and others" and can stand in for all names of authors or editors other than the one that comes first on the title page.

```
Zipes, Jack, et al., eds. The Norton Anthology of
    Children's Literature. New York: Norton, 2005.
```

A Book with Multiple Volumes

When citing a single volume from a multivolume text, state the volume number after the abbreviation "Vol." before the publication information.

```
Damrosch, David, et al., eds. The Longman Anthology of
    British Literature. Vol. 1. New York: Longman, 1999.
```

If you use more than one volume from a multivolume work, you will need to indicate how many volumes there are before the publication information. In the in-text parenthetical citation, the volume number precedes the page number (Bentley 3:45) so that it is clear to the reader which volume that particular quote comes from. In the Works Cited, use "vols." as an abbreviation for "volumes."

```
Bentley, Gerald Eades. The Jacobean Stage: Plays and
    Playwrights. 8 vols. Oxford: Oxford UP, 1956.
```

Two or More Books by the Same Author

Once you have listed an author in your Works Cited section, any following entries by the same author begin not with the name, but with three hyphens. These stand only for the name. The works should appear alphabetically by title.

```
Bloom, Harold. The Anxiety of Influence: a Theory of
    Poetry. New York: Oxford UP, 1997.
---. The Breaking of the Vessels. Chicago: Chicago UP,
    1982.
---. Shakespeare: The Invention of the Human. New York:
    Riverhead, 1998.
```

```
---, ed. Victorian Fiction. Critical Cosmos Series. New
     York: Chelsea House, 1989.
```

When citing one of these sources in-text, include both the author's last name and an abbreviated version of the title (Bloom, *Anxiety of Influence* 87). If the author's name is mentioned in the text, use only the abbreviated title (*Anxiety of Influence* 87).

A Book with an Unknown Author

Anonymous texts are listed in the Works Cited by title rather than author. When cited in parenthetical references, substitute a shortened version of the title for the author's name (*Kalevala* 13).

```
The Kalevala. Ed. Elias Lönnrot. Trans. Francis Peabody
     Magoun Jr. Cambridge, MA: Harvard UP, 1963.
```

Note that this entry would be alphabetized in the Works Cited under "K."

A Book with Another Book's Title in the Title

The MLA method for a title within a title is to omit the underlining beneath the incorporated title.

```
Berger, Harry. The Allegorical Temper: Vision and
     Reality in Book II of Spenser's Faerie Queene. New
     Haven: Yale UP, 1957.
```

A slightly different method that some writers use is to keep the underlining but add quotation marks around the incorporated title.

```
Berger, Harry. The Allegorical Temper: Vision and
     Reality in Book II of Spenser's "Faerie Queene." New
     Haven: Yale UP, 1957.
```

An Introduction, Preface, Foreword, or Afterword by Another Writer

Because an introduction, preface, foreword, or afterword is only one part of a book, its page numbers are given after the publication year of the book. If the introduction, preface, foreword, or afterword has a title of its own, this is stated in quotation marks after the author's name and before the name of the part, as shown in the second example below.

```
Armstrong, Karen. Introduction. Nuns and Soldiers. By
     Iris Murdoch. New York: Penguin, 2001. vii-xv.
Howard, Richard. "A Note on S/Z." Preface. S/Z: An
     Essay. By Roland Barthes. Trans. Richard Miller. New
     York: Noonday, 1974. ix-xii.
```

An Essay, Poem, Play, or Short Work in an Anthology or Collection

When citing a work in an anthology, the information of the section cited (including any translators of that work) is listed before the general information of the larger collection. The titles of poems should be replicated exactly as they appear in the book. Surround the titles of poems, essays, or short stories with quotation marks. Titles of plays within a larger collection of works by the same author are underlined. Page numbers of the cited section of the book should appear at the end of the entry.

Poems

> Chaucer, Geoffrey. "The Complaint of Chaucer to his
> Purse." Chaucer to Spenser: An Anthology of Writings
> in English 1375-1575. Ed. Derek Pearsall. Oxford:
> Blackwell, 1999. 180-81.
>
> Cummings, E. E. "anyone lived in a pretty how town." The
> Norton Anthology of Poetry. Ed. Margaret Ferguson,
> Mary Jo Satler, and John Stallworthy. 4th ed. New
> York: Norton, 1996. 286-87.
>
> Milton, John. "Lycidas." The Riverside Milton. Ed. Roy
> Flannagan. Boston: Houghton, 1998. 94-107.
>
> Stevens, Wallace. "The Snow Man." The Palm at the End of
> the Mind: Selected Poems and a Play. Ed. Holly
> Stevens. New York: Vintage, 1990. 54.

Short Stories

> Salinger, J. D. "A Perfect Day for Bananafish." Nine
> Stories. New York: Bantam, 1964. 3-18.
>
> Twain, Mark [Samuel L. Clemens]. "Jim Smily and His
> Jumping Frog." American Fiction. Ed. William Alan
> Neilson. Harvard Classics Shelf of Fiction 10. New
> York: Collier, 1917. 429-35.

Letters

> Dickinson, Emily. "To Abiah Root." January 1851.
> Selected Poems and Letters of Emily Dickinson. Ed.
> Robert N. Linscott. New York: Anchor, 1959. 238-40.

Plays

> Hansberry, Lorraine. A Raisin in the Sun. Black Theatre
> USA: Plays by African Americans from 1935 to Today.

Ed. James V. Hatch and Ted Shine. New York: Free
Press, 1996. 104-46.

Wilson, August. <u>Fences</u>. <u>Three Plays</u>. Pittsburgh: U of
Pittsburgh P, 1991. 95-196.

Critical Articles

Derrida, Jacques. "Structure, Sign and Play in the
Discourse of the Human Sciences." Trans. Alan Bass.
<u>Critical Theory since 1965</u>. Ed. Hazard Adams and
Leroy Searle. Tallahassee: Florida State UP, 1986.
83-94.

An Entry in an Encyclopedia or Reference Book

"Shakespeare, William." <u>The New Encyclopedia Britannica</u>.
1987 ed.

Periodicals

An Article in a Journal with Continuous Pagination throughout a Volume

Scholarly journals may publish several issues in a year. Many use continuous pagination throughout the volume year, which means if one issue ends on page 300, the first page of the next issue is page 301. The basic outline for an article in a journal is as follows:

Author. "Title of article." <u>Journal Name</u> volume (year): pages.

When citing journals with continuous pagination, you need not cite an issue number and month, since readers could easily find the article by knowing the volume, year, and page.

Cox, Virginia. "Rhetoric and Humanism in Quattrocento
Venice." <u>Renaissance Quarterly</u> 56 (2003): 652-90.

Person, Leland S., Jr. "Poe's Composition of Philosophy:
Reading and Writing 'The Raven.'" <u>Arizona Quarterly</u>
46 (1990): 1-15.

Note that "The Raven" is enclosed in single quotes because it is a title within a title.

An Article in a Journal with Individual Issue Pagination

When citing journals that page each issue individually, include both the volume and issue number, and separate the volume number from the issue number with a period (e.g., 13.4 for volume 13, issue 4).

```
Banks, William P. "Written through the Body: Disruptions
     and 'Personal' Writing." College English 66.1
     (2003): 21-40.
```

An Article in a Magazine

When citing a popular magazine, use the date of the issue rather than a volume number. Sometimes this date is a specific day, month, and year, but sometimes it will be a month or months.

```
Cox, Craig. "Will Work for Education: Colleges That
     Offer an Alternative to Student Loans." Utne Sept.-
     Oct. 2003: 63-64.
Wexler, Bruce. "Poetry Is Dead. Does Anybody Really
     Care?" Newsweek 5 May 2003: 18.
```

Newspaper Articles

The name on the top of the front page of the newspaper is what goes in Works Cited, but leave out all introductory words (e.g., use *Chicago Tribune*, not *The Chicago Tribune*). If the name of the city is not part of the title, add that information in square brackets after the name: "*Sun Times* [Las Vegas]." However, national newspapers like *USA Today* and the *Wall Street Journal* do not need the place of publication. Supply the date and the edition, if it is listed (late city ed., New England ed.), because each edition contains different material. Then put a colon and the page number. Note the section letter or number, if any (e.g., B21, sec. 4:12), and use a plus sign when an article jumps from page to page. Here are some examples:

```
Albright, Natalie. "Literary Legacies Prove Troublesome."
     Los Angeles Times 22 May 2002, late ed.: C17+.
Powers, Katherine A. "What Goes Down Must Get a
     Comeuppance." Boston Sunday Globe 15 Aug. 2004: D9.
```

Reviews

Signed reviews are cited by author's name and the title of the review, if there is one, followed by "Rev. of" the title of the work being reviewed, a comma, then "by," then the author whose work is being reviewed.

```
Hough, John. "Just's Skill Brings a Restless 1950s
     Chicago to Life." Rev. of An Unfinished Season, by
     Ward Just. Boston Sunday Globe 15 Aug. 2004: D7.
```

For an untitled review, follow the review author's name with "Rev. of" and the title of the work being reviewed. For an unsigned review, begin the entry with "Rev. of" and the title of the work being reviewed. Follow the same format for a play or film review.

```
Arpit, Newton. Rev. of The Manchurian Candidate, dir.
    Jonathan Demme. Sun-Sentinel [Ft. Lauderdale] 23
    Sept. 2004, sec. 7: 37.
```

Unsigned Articles

Unsigned articles are listed in the Works Cited under the title of the article rather than an author's name. In the in-text parenthetical citation, include a shortened version of the title before the page number ("Crucible" 39).

```
"The Crucible of Hollywood's Guilt." Atlantic Monthly
    Dec. 2003: 38-40.
```

Interviews

```
Brooks, Gwendolyn. "An Interview with Gwendolyn Brooks."
    Contemporary Literature 11.1 (1970): 1-20.
```

Electronic and Other Nonprint Sources

A Film

When citing a film, include the title, director, distributor, and year. Underline or italicize the title. Other information, such as the original title of a foreign work or the names of the principal actors, can also be included:

```
Life Is Beautiful [La Vita É Bella]. Dir. Roberto
    Benigni. Miramax, 1998.
The Unbearable Lightness of Being. Dir. Philip Kaufman.
    Perf. Daniel Day-Lewis, Juliette Binoche, and Lena
    Olin. United International Pictures, 1988.
```

An E-mail

When someone has sent you an idea or phrase via e-mail, be sure to cite it in your Works Cited under that person's name. The date of the message should be placed at the end of the entry. (The MLA order for dates is day month year, with no commas.)

```
Priddy, Jan. E-mail to the author. 21 June 2006.
```

A Personal or Telephone Interview

```
Brooks, Mel. Personal interview. 27 Nov. 2005.
Healey, Paul. Telephone interview. 13 Feb. 2006.
```

Material on a Website

Websites can be difficult to cite properly. This is in part because not all websites include the same amount of publication information. In general, the order of information in an MLA entry for a website is as follows:

> Author. Title of site. Editor. Electronic publication information or electronic update. Date of access <URL>.

Publication information can include version numbers, date of the Web posting, and sponsoring institution. Not all sites will post all of this information; using the above order as a template, you will need to fill in the information that you have. The date of access is the date you used the site; provide this information because material on a website can change frequently, or the site may even go out of existence. Place the Web address, or URL, within angle brackets, as shown in the examples below. If the URL is long enough to carry over onto the next line, divide it after a slash. If the URL is extremely long or complex, use the URL of the search page for the site or the site's home page. Note: Some word processing programs will automatically reformat a copied and pasted Web address in your document by removing the angle brackets around the URL and highlighting the address in a bright color to signify a hyperlink. Disable this feature while composing your Works Cited section, or reformat the style to keep your paper in accordance with MLA citation guidelines. (In recent versions of Microsoft Word, the box for turning this feature off and on is buried in Tools/AutoCorrect Options/AutoFormat As You Type/Internet and Network Paths with Hyperlinks.)

An Entire Website

> Poets.org. Academy of American Poets. 28 Nov. 2003
> <http://www.poets.org/>.

Because websites rarely have page numbers, they can be confusing to cite parenthetically in your text. In some cases you can work the information into your sentence and avoid parenthetical citations:

> Many biographies of contemporary poets can be found at Poets.org.

If you do use a parenthetical citation, include the editor, author, or shortened version of the title, depending on what comes first in your Works Cited entry, and give the page, line, or section number if there is one.

An Article on a Website

The author of the article, if one is listed, comes first, followed by the title of the article, the title of the site, editor of site, electronic publication information, date of access, and URL of the article. In the following example, the Web page was updated on 9 October 2003, but it was accessed by the researcher on 28 November 2003:

```
"The Life of John Skelton." Luminarium. Ed. Anniina
     Jokinen. 9 Oct. 2003. 28 Nov. 2003
     <http://www.luminarium.org/renlit/skelbio.htm>.
```

An Article in an Online Periodical

If you retrieve an article online, you must indicate this in your Works Cited entry, even if the article is available in a paper version in the library. An entry for an online journal article contains the following information:

> Author. "Title." Print publication information. Electronic publication information. Date of access <URL>.

For the print publication information, follow the same style that you would use if citing an ordinary journal article.

```
Goldberg, Nan. "She, the People." Salon 1 Nov. 2000. 28
     May 2006 <http://dir.salon.com/books/feature/2000/
     11/01/smith/index.html>.

Schwartz, Benjamin. "Modernism, Minimalism,
     Fundamentalism." Atlantic Online May 2006. 23 May
     2006 <http://www.theatlantic.com/doc/200605/
     editors-choice>.
```

An Article in an Online Newspaper

```
"What Is the Best Work of American Fiction of the Last
     25 Years?" New York Times on the Web 21 May 2006.
     27 May 2006 <http://www.nytimes.com/2006/05/21/
     books/fiction-25-years.html>.
```

A Journal Article Retrieved from an Online Subscription Service

If the URL for an article is long and complex, with many symbols, cite the title and URL of the database you used to retrieve the article. Many online journals are available through specialized databases, such as JSTOR, which allow scholars to search for and download articles. The template for this kind of entry is:

> Author. "Title". Journal Volume (Year): Pages. Database. Name of service, if known. Date of access <URL of database>.

This method acknowledges how you found the article and eliminates the paragraph-long URL that accompanies the actual article:

```
Phelan, James. "Rhetorical Literary Ethics and Lyric
     Narrative: Robert Frost's 'Home Burial.'" Poetics
     Today 25.4 (2004): 627-51. JSTOR. 23 Sept. 2006
     <http://www.jstor.org>.
```

```
Trachtenberg, Zev. "Good Neighbors Make Good Fences:
     Frost's 'Mending Wall.'" Philosophy and Literature
     21.1 (1997): 114-22. Project Muse. 18 Dec. 2003
     <http://muse.jhu.edu>.
```

A Journal Article Retrieved from a Library's Online Subscription Service

```
Pavel, Thomas G. "Fiction and Imitation." Poetics Today
     21.3 (2000): 521-41. Academic Search Premier.
     EBSCOhost. U of Michigan, Harlan Hatcher Graduate
     Lib., MI. 23 Sept. 2006 <http://epnet.com/>.
```

An Online Dictionary or Encyclopedia Entry

Entries in online dictionaries and encyclopedias are listed by word or title of the entry. Page numbers, if any, are irrelevant because the article can be found alphabetically.

```
"Iconoclast." Merriam-Webster Dictionary Online. 2006.
     Merriam-Webster. 28 Nov. 2006 <http://www.m-w.com/>.
"Lucretius." Encyclopedia Britannica Online. 2006.
     Encyclopedia Britannica. 28 Nov. 2006
     <http://www.britannica.com/>.
```

Online Books

It can be very convenient to retrieve entire books through your computer, rather than going to a bookstore or library. If you choose to do this, it is wise to go through a university-sponsored Web page. Many versions of online literature neglect to include page numbers; this can be quite confusing in a paper, and you may want to consider finding a print version of the source. The typical entry for online literature would follow this example:

> Author. Title. Editor/compiler. Publication Information. Electronic publication information. Date of access <URL>.

Publication information includes the book's city of publication, name of publisher, and year. Electronic publication information includes the title of the Internet site, editor of the site, version number, date of the site or most current update, and sponsoring institution. As always with electronic sources, you will need to include as much of this information as is available.

```
Dickens, Charles. A Tale of Two Cities. London, 1859.
     Literature Online. Brandeis U. 28 November 2005
     <http:lion.chadwyck.co.uk>.
```

Wordsworth, William. <u>The Complete Poetical Works</u>. London: Macmillan and Co., 1888. <u>Bartleby.com: Great books Online</u>. Ed. Steven van Leeuwen. 1999. 30 June 2006 <www.bartleby.com/145/>.

SAMPLE LITERARY RESEARCH PROJECT: FROM QUESTION TO FINISHED PAPER

The assignment that provides the basis for the sample research project included here was given to an introductory literature class reading *Twilight: Los Angeles, 1992*, Anna Deavere Smith's powerful play based on the riots that broke out when a California jury acquitted Los Angeles police officers for beating an unarmed African American man. The vicious beating of Rodney King by eight white officers was captured on videotape. After the acquittal, thousands of African American and Hispanic residents rioted in South Central Los Angeles. Over $100 million of damage ensued, as well as fifteen deaths and 300 arrests. Smith's play, and her later film version, consisted entirely of monologues in which the African American Smith, using no makeup and a minimum of props, impersonated key "players" in the riot, including Hispanic looters, Korean American shopkeepers, and a member of the jury that acquitted the police. (Excerpts of the play are on pp. 1978–1992.) The rest of this chapter presents the work of Tiffany Bergeron, tracing her research process through the different stages, from prospectus to outline to draft to final essay.

CLASS ASSIGNMENT SHEET
FOR RESEARCH PROJECT

Anna Deavere Smith, *Twilight: Los Angeles, 1992*

Choose a fairly narrowly defined question about the 1992 Los Angeles events that you can research and write up in eight to ten pages. Build on the readings, class discussions, and the films viewed in class. All sources are fair game: Internet, film, library, interviews, and music, but do not forget to evaluate the reliability and wisdom of your sources.

Do not worry if you cannot answer your question completely. Sometimes, the fact that key information is missing from the record tells us as much as what we do find. Do not feel you need to address every aspect of every question. These questions are here to get you started; treat them as suggestions, and feel free to develop questions of your own. (If you create your own research question, give it to me by the end of week 1.)

Research Project Timeline

Week 1: choose research question and present a preliminary progress report (aloud, in class)

Week 2: turn in one-paragraph prospectus giving your question and three likely sources

Week 3: good draft of first page due

Week 4–5: good draft of entire paper due

Week 6–7: in-class workshop on MLA documentation

Week 8: final version of paper due

Week 8–9: class discussion of *Twilight*, using your papers

Questions

1. Choose three characters in *Twilight* and explain how representative each is of the people involved in the 1992 events. For instance, how large a role did Korean women play? Young Latino males?

2. Choose one character in *Twilight* and after listening closely for his or her major concerns, link those concerns to the news and TV coverage you have seen in and out of class. Does your research show that this character is or is not representative of a particular concern present at the time?

3. What can we learn about the Simi jurors that helps explain why they acquitted the police, even though they saw tapes of police officers beating and clubbing a defenseless Rodney King? How might some understanding of psychology or criminal justice help one see their decision with any kind of sympathy or understanding? You can start with Anna Deavere Smith's "anonymous juror" in *Twilight*, p. 1980.

4. How did Anna Deavere Smith prepare herself to do something like

Twilight (other than, of course, conducting the interviews)? What kind of training did she have? What does she have to say about *why* she does such performances?

5. Explore the reputation of the Los Angeles Police Department in the decade or so before the riots. Was the treatment of Rodney King predictable? Was the way in which the LAPD "handled" the riots predictable?

6. Asian Americans are often described as a "model minority," that is, as a group that has succeeded educationally and economically in American life in ways other minorities (namely African Americans and Latinos/as) have not always done. Others—especially some Asian Americans themselves—have disputed this "model minority" argument. Examine different arguments about the "model minority" status and explain your stance on the subject. How, if at all, does this argument connect to the 1992 events?

7. Read *A Raisin in the Sun* and describe how ideas and themes in that play prefigured important elements of the events of 1992.

8. Why does the Latino/a perspective seem relatively invisible in the reporting and commentary on Los Angeles 1992? Can you locate further comment by Latinos/as on their role in the events? If you read Spanish you will be in an especially strong position to investigate this question.

9. Following the riots, there were many complaints about how the media handled the reportage. Trace the coverage of the Los Angeles events in a major newspaper or news magazine (*Los Angeles Times, San Francisco Chronicle, New York Times, Wall Street Journal, USA Today, Time, Newsweek, US News and World Report*). Can you find some major lines of interpretation?

10. What songs did the Los Angeles events give rise to? Do the songs shed any light on the events? Analyze the songs in light of the events.

Sample Prospectus for Literary Research Project

```
Prospectus

I want to work on Question #4. My research question is
open ended: I want to know how Smith was trained and how
she discovered her approach to drama, since she wrote
such an unusual, gripping play. Maybe "wrote" is not the
best word, since so much of what she has in Twilight is
the exact words of the participants. Maybe her art is in
the shaping and trimming rather than the inventing, but
I'm not sure of this yet.

Sources: I am reading two books by Smith that help
explain where she got her approach:

Anna Deavere Smith. Talk to Me: Travels in Media and
Politics. New York: Anchor, 2000.
Anna Deavere Smith, Fires in the Mirror. New York:
Anchor Books, 1993.

In addition, I found a critical analysis of Smith's work
called "Voices of America" on the Salon website:
www.salon.com/bc/1998/12/cov_08bc2.html.
```

Sample Thesis and Paper Outline

After doing additional research at the library and taking notes on the useful sources she located there, Tiffany Bergeron evaluated her notes, her research materials, and her original prospectus, and drafted her thesis statement, the claim she was going to support in the body of her paper. She knew the supporting evidence would combine her own ideas with ideas from the sources she gathered during her research, and she constructed an outline to use as a guide in writing her first draft. She first mapped out each main idea she wanted to convey, using the headings marked with roman numerals in the sample outline shown below. Reviewing these ideas alongside her research notes, she then reorganized the notes in the order in which she planned to use them and added those points as subheadings under the appropriate main idea they supported.

```
Question: How does Smith's training and approach to
drama influence the way in which she created and
performed Twilight: Los Angeles, 1992, and how does that
approach affect how we interpret the play?

Thesis: Anna Deavere Smith uses her interest in real-
life speech to give voice to multiple viewpoints, rather
than creating imagined drama by inventing fictionalized
```

dialogue; the result is a complex dramatic experience, a
paradoxical mix of confusion and empathy.

The thesis isn't quite where I want it to be, but I
think it'll be easier to revise it as I begin the paper
and discover what it is I'm really trying to say.

<u>Rough Outline</u>
I. Overview of Smith's working process
   A. begins with real-life conflict (e.g. L.A. riots)
   B. interviews of hundreds of witnesses and
      participants
II. Where her emphasis on real-life human speech comes
    from
   A. trains at American Conservatory
      1. speech in <u>Richard III</u>
      2. words set to music, Beethoven's 9th
   B. mimics everyday people in her work
   C. defines poetic language in terms of speech
      1. abandonment of formal speech in times of crisis
III. Arrangement of the text in <u>Twilight</u>
   A. uses white space
   B. models her work on and makes comparisons with
     music
   C. develops a conscious, artistic purpose that
     results in the use of "authentic speech" in her
     work
IV. Smith's role as a solo actor
   A. defines her acting approach as a departure from
     Method Acting
      1. ways her approach to acting differs from
         Method acting
   B. emphasizes the role of empathy
      1. each individual has a unique perspective
   C. consciously uses the impact of race in her acting
     method, given her highly racially charged subject
     matter, to achieve her ends
V. The results of Smith's unique approach
   A. represents multiple voices
   B. juxtaposes contradictory statements and
     counterstatements
   C. mirrors the chaos in modern-day life

Revising the First Draft

Using her research notes, tentative thesis, and outline, Tiffany drafted a complete first draft, which appears below. During the weeks that followed, she revised that draft, generating two additional drafts before finishing her final essay. After writing the first draft and giving herself a few days, she reread the draft. It became clear to Tiffany that her thesis was not as well developed as it could be, but to get a better idea of how to address that issue as well as other weaknesses in the draft that she could strengthen with effective revisions, she scheduled an in-person conference with her instructor.

Although Tiffany had sent her instructor the draft beforehand, she arrived at the meeting with a hard copy, which she marked up with annotations during their conversation so she would have a written record of the problem areas and possibilities for improvement when she sat down to revise. Based on the discussion and these detailed notes, Tiffany realized she needed to refine and focus her thesis and to make sure she stated it more explicitly in her introduction. She was also able to identify several places in the draft where she either needed to add textual examples to support her point or needed to make better use of the examples and evidence she had. Tiffany's annotations from her instructor's conference have been recreated on the draft here to indicate the specific alterations, edits, expansions, and rewriting Tiffany planned to do.

Tiffany Bergeron

English 111

Anna Deavere Smith and the Sources of Creativity (Draft)

Professor Brereton

[handwritten annotations: add date; center title; cap.; respective]

When we first see Anna Deavere Smith in the film version of her play, <u>Twilight: Los Angeles, 1992</u>, she plays the roles of diverse individuals of all ages, races, genders, and cultures. She is so effective that we are likely to think that we are seeing magic, or at the very least we are witnessing an extraordinarily talented actress. Then, our next thought is to wonder how she does it. She may be very talented, but we suspect that she must have learned some of the tricks of her trade along the way. We wonder, does her kind of acting have a history? Does it come out of a tradition? Can it be learned? It turns out that in creating her characters Anna Deavere Smith consciously follows a very special model and approach she has learned over many years of hard study.

*[handwritten margin note: *need to state my thesis upfront here. What is Smith's model and why does it matter?]*

In the introductions Deavere Smith wrote to <u>Twilight: Los Angeles</u> and <u>Fires in the Mirror</u>, she is quite clear about how she goes about creating her dramas. In a crisis like the Los Angeles upheavals of 1992, she states that interviews hundreds of participants and observers, taping and then transcribing their responses nearly verbatim. Then she chooses parts from those interviews that she judges best reveal what the interviewees were thinking and feeling. She then treats those interviews excerpts as roles to be assumed. Once she has "gotten" those parts from listening to the tapes over and over, she is ready to go on stage. There she plays the roles in quick succession, using only a few props like a hat, coat, or eyeglasses, but not changing her makeup. The gestures, the tones of voice are very important, but she is convinced people best reveal themselves through the words they choose—or the language they struggle for.

[handwritten margin note: maybe give just a little background on events sparking the riots]

[handwritten margin note: check notes & research to see what source this is from—CITE PROPERLY IN REVISION!]

Anna Deavere Smith insists that at the core of her way of operating is her intense interest in the way human beings use language. She points to a life-changing experience that occurred during her training at the American Conservatory Theater in San Francisco. One of her teachers assigned every one of her students to choose fifteen lines from any Shakespeare play and to repeat those lines until "something happened." ~~Deavere~~ Smith chose a speech of Queen Margaret in <u>Richard III</u>, and something <u>did</u> happen. The Queen appeared to her in a vision. A saying of Smith's grandfather came back to her: "If you say a word often enough, it becomes you" (<u>Talk to Me</u> 36–37). At about the same time, she also found herself responding to words set to music; she says she felt feverish the morning after hearing Beethoven's Ninth Symphony break into the choral section: "Freunnnnnnde" (<u>Talk to Me</u> 10).

But though these particular revelations revolved around famous playwrights and celebrated artists, ~~Deavere~~ Smith found that she was even more attracted to the utterances of ordinary people. (Already) in college she was mimicking her teachers and her fellow students. In acting school she began recording people she met in the streets. But she was not interested in just anything they said, their chatter; rather, she was interested in special moments when their language became, as she put it, the "windows of their souls." In these moments, she said, they spoke "authentically"; they spoke poetry (<u>Fires</u> xxxi). She did not necessarily mean that these ordinary people used "poetic language"; in fact, in their best moments sometimes they groped for words, broke their customary personal verbal rhythms, and revealed themselves as vulnerable. As ~~Deavere~~ Smith put it in her recent memoir, <u>Talk to Me</u>, they might suddenly turn from iambs (first syllable unaccented) to trochees (first syllable accented), her assumption being that trochees often signal important moments in a person's speech. She cites her Shakespeare teacher again: "She maintained that if you got a trochee in the second beat, a character was really 'losing' it psychologically, and this 'loss' made it possible for you to really know something about that character, if you wore his or her words." (36) Likewise, the "uhs," "ums," "you knows," and other hesitations were as revealing of their meaning makings as their "real" words ("Voices" 3). Smith believes that "our true character, our humanity, emerges only when we abandon formal language for the messy patterns of spontaneous speech." (Tannenbaum 2). ¶It is of course crisis events like Los Angeles 1992 that help catapult us out of our normal language habits.   *[margin: awkward phrasing]*

In this regard, it is interesting to ponder why ~~Deavere~~ Smith arranges her text of Twilight: Los Angeles, 1992, the way she does. As far as I know, she has not commented on this particular aspect of her work. At first glance, ~~it seems obvious~~ *the reason* why she has arranged the words *on the page is a practical one* with so much white space, ~~in the background~~ *to create*: readers would soon give up if the language was arranged like prose and they were expected to plow through it. Her suggestion that some "ordinary" talk turns into poetry further explains this arrangement: presumably she arranges the texts according to the rhythm she hears in the language. ¶Another possibility—which contradicts neither of the above suggestions—is that she arranges the "talk" as song lyrics. In fact, she sometimes describes her interviewees as "singing." Interestingly, she says that one of her artistic models is the African American classical singer Jessye Norman.

~~Deavere~~ Smith has likened her interviewees' speech to jazz; in ~~an~~ *her 199?* article on ~~Deavere~~ Smith, Barbara Tannenbaum ~~writes~~: *describes that speech as follows:*

Imagine a jazz singer who scats and trills. Swooping through the musical scale before coming back and restating the motif. People vocally underline their

[left margin annotations:]
confusing— it's not clear that the text looks like poetry on the page

is it done for more than just "rhythm"? How does the arrangement affect the text's meaning?

interesting idea, but say more on why this point matters

[right margin annotations:]
why? is it denser? (than regular dramatic dialogue?)

this & previous page's language make the readers I describe seem lazy. ..it seems like there's more to it than this

introduce quote more smoothly

words, throw parts of their speech into italics. Or
trip over their thoughts in awe or in anger, blaring
like a trumpet. Or their voices become staccato,
like percussion. Each. Point. So Serious. (2)

This attention to authentic language has seemed
particularly important to ~~Deavere~~ Smith at a time when
"talk" has been cheapened. She notes that cheap,
incessant talk is everywhere—in the omnipresent media,
in people's compulsive attempts to ward off loneliness
by going on about anything and everything. And language
has so often been fashioned lately with the sole view of
selling the listener on a product or a political line.
There needs to be speech that is really worth listening
to and can even lead to change and action. Smith finds
this speech and makes it into her drama.

connect back to comparison to music

The emphasis on expression leads back to the actor, the
one who must deliver those worthwhile words, so that an
audience will really listen. Interestingly, Deavere Smith
has departed from the acting method (often known in the
United States as "the Method") that has dominated the
training of actors over the past century. The Method
traces its beginnings to a Russian, Konstantin
Stanislavsky (1863-1938), and has been adapted by any
number of American teachers of acting (Lee Strasberg,
Stella Adler, Sanford Meisner, e.g.). These Method-based
approaches operate on the assumption that all human
beings share more or less the same essential feelings
and attitudes. This means that actors trying to work
themselves into their characters must start by digging
deep into their *own* emotions and experiences and thus
come to understand their character—to become their
character.

Add more about why this approach matters & make more clear why Smith's deviation from this matters?

add better transition

Anna Deavere Smith, on the other hand, assumes that
every one of us is quite different from everyone else.
Indeed, despite all her "magical" *and persuasive* transformations, she

it seems odd that I discuss the play's language, but don't use any actual text from Twilight evidence ADD A TEXTUAL EXAMPLE

What about adding important method actors— to convey history

how so? explain using an example

never stops looking like Anna Deavere Smith, never quite stops <u>being</u> Anna Deavere Smith. This is why she needs to make such a radical effort to begin to empathize with the characters she is trying to imitate. She frequently writes of the difficulty of bridging the gaps among us as individuals, and her approach to her characters is to remind us that our easy assumptions about understanding others are all wrong and will mislead us badly.

state the effect of this more explicitly

needs transition

misquoted

(Rodney King: "~~Why~~ can ~~'t~~ we all just get along?")

Awkward, explain context

That Deavere Smith is African American further complicates the transformations that she brings about on stage. For instance, it is not unusual for her to play a white woman who answers the real Anna Deavere Smith's questions about, for example, whether race is a "trope" (Thompson). She runs the risk of getting tripped up on her own complications, as the experiments with her new play <u>House Arrest</u> suggest. There she has attempted to explore the nature of the American Presidency, diverging from her one-woman show to use several actors. The absence of a particular event around which the characters' monologues can revolve, and some say the preponderance of the famous, have created a ragged chaotic production. In response, Deavere Smith has returned to the approach that has made her reputation, as a solo performance artist. As Stuart ~~Stanley~~ Klawans in the *Nation* observed, it is the miracle of a whole collection of voices gathered in one actor that carries much of the impact of her work:

explain how/why

confusing example— b/c it focused on ① a different production & ② a different acting approach

either clarify the purpose of this example as "evidence", or if it doesn't really serve my larger point, delete it

> One after another the people stepped in, many of
> them voicing mistrust, misunderstanding, fear,
> hatred; and yet these conflicting individuals had
> been brought together, if not harmonized, by
> residing in this one woman's flesh (Klawans 1)

will need to revise based on revisions to intro and thesis

It seems as if Anna Deavere Smith's greatest talent is the ability to orchestrate different voices, to portray conflicting perspectives and points of view, and to present viewers with a kind of statement and counterstatement of ideas and attitudes that clash. She uses the content, arrangement, and emphasis in the written text as well as her own techniques as a performer to capture the chaos that underlies so much of contemporary life and gives rise to misperceptions and violent confrontations. While in the theater watching her play or the movie, we feel that we are in the presence of a chorus of voices, all presented for our understanding. If ~~Deavere~~ Smith's dramas cap provide even a temporary resolution of differences in this fashion, might we imaging that here is some hope for a troubled world?

Reorder alphabetically

WORKS CITED

Goldberg, Nan. "She, the People." <u>Salon</u> 1 Nov. 2000. 28 May 2004. http://dir.salon.com/books/feature/2000/11/01/smith/index.html.

Klawans, Stuart. "A Riot of Personality." <u>The Nation</u> 16 Oct. 2000. 31 May 2004. <www.thenation.com/doc.mhtml?i=20001016&s=klawans>.

Tannenbaum, Barbara. "The Voices of Anna Deavere Smith." <u>Stanford Magazine</u>. 30 May 2004. <www.stanfordalumni.org/news/magazine/1999/julaug/articles/anna.html>.

Why is Twilight not a source? ADD

Smith, Anna Deavere. <u>Talk to Me: Travels in Media and Politics</u>. New York: Anchor, 2000.

Smith, Anna Deavere. <u>Fires in the Mirror</u>. New York: Anchor, 1993.

"Voices of America" Salon. 28 May 2004. <www.salon.com/bc/1998/12/cov_08bc2.html>.

Thompson, Debby. "'Is Race a Trope?': Anna Deavere Smith and the Question of Racial Performativity." <u>African American Review</u>. Spring 2003. 27 May 2004. <http://articles.findarticles.com/p/articles/mi_m2838/is_1_37/ai_100959606/print>.

recheck all source info in notes & reformat sources here & in paper to follow correct MLA style

Revising Subsequent Drafts

As her instructor suggested, Tiffany's second draft included material from the actual play *Twilight: Los Angeles, 1992*, a close analysis supporting her thesis that had not appeared in the first draft at all. She also had honed her thesis statement and refined several examples and points she was trying to make. Tiffany felt fairly certain she had addressed most of the major content-oriented problems in her initial draft, and now her concern was to improve the language and style she used as well as any passages that were confusing or awkward. After making a few minor changes, she gave her second draft to a peer to read, a classmate with whom Tiffany traded drafts regularly. Her peer reviewer pointed out some additional areas for improvement. The most important critique was that Tiffany needed to further clarify one of her final examples, specifically why she brought up Smith's more recent play *House Arrest*. Most of the other comments focused on how the language Tiffany used could be made more clear and concise.

Based on the peer review, Tiffany revised the draft again, this time looking to eliminate wordiness and repetition, to create better transitions between paragraphs, and to reorganize some of the paragraphs to render the points more logically. Aside from further developing her thesis, perhaps the biggest change she contemplated was how to use evidence from Smith's play effectively to support her contentions about Smith's work, rather than relying exclusively on surrounding material.

By her third draft, Tiffany felt she had addressed both the major content issues in her argument as well as the clarity with which she presented her points. At this stage, she used a final round of revision to address more detail-oriented issues, like grammar, punctuation, paper format, and the correct implementation of MLA style in all her in-text citations as well as in her final Works Cited section.

Sample Literary Research Paper with MLA Documentation

The research paper below is the result of the multistep process described above—the prospectus, preliminary research, outlining, drafting, and revising. It is the final product of Tiffany Bergeron's research process. The paper makes use of many of the techniques discussed in this chapter on how to incorporate ideas from secondary sources into a research essay. Notice in particular how well Tiffany incorporates the ideas of others into her paper. She has joined the discussion of Anna Deavere Smith's work with a contribution of her own, building nicely on the work of others yet giving the information her own personal spin. Her final paper follows the format and documentation guidelines in the *MLA Handbook for Writers of Research Papers*, 6th edition (2003); many of those guidelines are described in the sections on documenting sources above.

Tiffany Bergeron

Professor Brereton

English 111

June 5, 2006

Anna Deavere Smith and the Sources of Creativity

When we first see Anna Deavere Smith in the film version of her play <u>Twilight: Los Angeles, 1992</u>, she plays the roles of diverse individuals of all ages, races, genders, and cultures. She is so effective that we are likely to think that we are seeing magic, or at the very least that we are witnessing an extraordinarily talented actress. Our next thought may be to wonder how she does it. She may be very talented, but we suspect that she must have learned some of the tricks of her trade along the way. We wonder, does her kind of acting have a history? Does it come out of a tradition? Can it be learned? It turns out that in creating her characters, Anna Deavere Smith consciously follows a very special model and approach she has learned over many years of hard study. Given that, it is important to examine not only how she does it, but also why she does it that way. As an analysis of the various choices she makes in <u>Twilight</u> and her other plays will reveal, Anna Deavere Smith's art, uniquely, derives its power and meaning from the shaping and trimming of real-life speech from multiple, often conflicting, viewpoints, rather than in the more traditional inventing or simulation of real life through fictionalized dialogue; the result is an unusual, complex dramatic experience in which the dominant response, either as a reader or a theatergoer, is a paradoxical mix of confusion and empathy.

In the respective introductions Smith wrote for her two plays <u>Twilight: Los Angeles, 1992</u> and <u>Fires in the Mirror</u>, she is quite clear about how she goes about creating her dramas. In response to a crisis like the Los Angeles upheavals of 1992, a violent reaction by outraged citizens to the acquittal of the police officers who beat unarmed African-American Rodney King (an act captured on video), Smith states that she interviews hundreds of participants and observers, taping and then transcribing their responses nearly verbatim. Then she chooses parts from those interviews that she judges best reveal what the interviewees were thinking and feeling. She then treats those interview excerpts as roles to be assumed. Once she has "gotten" those parts from listening to the tapes over and over, she is ready to go on stage. There she plays the roles in quick succession, using only a few props like a hat, coat, or eyeglasses, but not changing her makeup. The gestures, the tones of voice are very important, but she is convinced people best reveal themselves through the words they choose--or the language they struggle for (Smith, <u>Fires</u> xxiii-xliii; Smith, <u>Twilight</u> xvii-xxvi).

Anna Deavere Smith insists that at the core of her way of operating is her intense interest in the way human beings use language. To locate the origins of this interest, she points to a life-changing experience that occurred during her training at the American Conservatory Theater in San Francisco. One of her acting teachers asked every student to choose fifteen lines from any Shakespeare play and to repeat those lines until "something happened." Smith chose a speech of Queen Margaret in <u>Richard III</u>--and something <u>did</u> happen. According to Smith, the Queen appeared to her in a vision. A saying of Smith's grandfather came back to her: "If you say a word often enough, it becomes you" (Smith, <u>Talk to Me</u> 36-37). At about the same time, she also found herself responding to words set to music; she says she felt feverish the morning after hearing Beethoven's Ninth Symphony break into the choral section: "<u>Freunnnnnnde</u>" (Smith, <u>Talk to Me</u> 10).

But though these particular revelations about language revolved around famous playwrights and celebrated artists, Smith found that she was even more attracted to the utterances of ordinary people. In

college she was already mimicking her teachers and her
fellow students. In acting school she began recording
people she met in the streets. But she was not
interested in just anything they said, their chatter;
rather, she was interested in special moments when their
language became, as she put it, the "windows of their
souls." In these moments, she said, they spoke
"authentically"; they spoke poetry (Smith, <u>Fires</u> xxxi).
She did not necessarily mean that these ordinary people
used traditional "poetic language"; in fact, in their
best moments sometimes they groped for words, broke
their customary personal verbal rhythms, and revealed
themselves as vulnerable. As Smith put it in her recent
memoir, <u>Talk to Me</u>, they might suddenly turn from iambs
(first syllable unaccented) to trochees (first syllable
accented), her assumption being that trochees often
signal important moments in a person's speech (35). Here
Smith cites her Shakespeare teacher again: "She
maintained that if you got a trochee in the second beat,
a character was really 'losing' it psychologically, and
this 'loss' made it possible for you to really know
something about that character, if you wore his or her
words" (<u>Talk to Me</u> 36). Likewise, the "uhs," "ums," "you
knows," and other hesitations were as revealing of their
meaning makings as their "real" words (Lloyd, screen 2).
Smith believes that "our true character, our humanity,
emerges only when we abandon formal language for the
messy patterns of spontaneous speech" (Tannenbaum, par.
8).

It is, of course, crisis events like the riots in
Los Angeles in 1992 that help catapult us out of our
normal language habits. In this regard, it is
interesting to ponder why Smith arranges her text of
<u>Twilight: Los Angeles, 1992</u> the way she does. The
signals of spontaneous speech--pauses, stutters, "ums"--
are not merely included in her performance, her
interpretation of the transcribed text as an actor; they
are also an integral part of the written script, which

reads like prose but is shaped and broken up into short
lines that more closely resemble verse. The significance
of that arrangement of text in the script itself is that
it means, first and foremost, that no other actor
interpreting and performing Smith's play could mistake
her authorial intent here.

As far as I know, Smith has not commented on this
particular aspect of her work. At first glance it seems
the reason she has arranged the words to create so much
white space on the page might be a practical one: with
so many characters to keep track of, readers would soon
give up if the language was arranged like prose. Her
suggestion that some "ordinary" talk turns into poetry
further explains this arrangement and gives it greater
purpose: presumably she arranges the texts according to
the rhythm and human spirit she hears revealed in the
language. For example, in the speech Smith entitles
"Your Heads in Shame" in <u>Twilight</u>, spoken by an
anonymous male juror from the Simi Valley trial, the
line breaks and punctuation, particularly the dashes
that suggest hesitations, serve to emphasize what Smith
defines as spontaneous speech:

> ANONYMOUS MAN--Juror in Simi Valley Trial:
> As soon as we went
> into the courtroom with the verdicts
> there were
> plainclothes policemen everywhere.
> You know, I knew that
> there would be people unhappy with the verdict,
> but I didn't expect near
> what happened.
> If I had known
> what was going to happen,
> I mean, it's not,
> it's not fair to say I would have voted a different
> way.
> I wouldn't have--
> that's not our justice system--

> but I would have written the judge a note saying,
> "I can't do this,"
> because of
> what it put my family through.
> Excuse me.
> *(Crying)* ("Your Heads in Shame" 1-21)

In this passage, the line breaks emphasize the inclusion
and consistent repetition of filler words—the stammer and
repeated refrain of "it's not, / it's not" in lines 11
and 12, the "excuse me" and pause at the end of the
passage, the self-interruptions like "you know" and "I
mean" that convey the speaker's discomfort. Likewise,
the arrangement draws our attention to verb phrases
indicating inaction, such as "didn't," "wouldn't," and
"can't," in lines 7, 14, and 17. By highlighting words
that convey stagnation, Smith is able to visually
emphasize and mirror on the page the internal paralysis
and helplessness the speaker clearly feels when
describing the larger public reaction to the trial
verdict. This reflection of interior conflict in the
actual language and presentation of the text is one
strong example of what Smith meant when she said that
the very messiness and particularity of spontaneous
speech is what reveals each person's true nature and
humanity.

Another possibility--which contradicts neither of
the above suggestions and interpretations--is that Smith
arranges the "talk" as song lyrics. In fact, she
sometimes describes her interviewees as "singing."
Interestingly, she says that one of her artistic models
is the African-American classical singer Jessye Norman.
The way Smith conveys her interviewees' speech has also
been likened to jazz; in her 1999 article on Smith,
Barbara Tannenbaum describes the nature and cadence of
that speech as follows:

> Imagine a jazz singer who scats and trills.
> Swooping through the musical scale before coming
> back and restating the motif. People vocally

> underline their words, throw parts of their
> speech into italics. Or trip over their
> thoughts in awe or in anger, blaring like a
> trumpet. Or their voices become staccato, like
> percussion. Each. Point. So Serious. (par. 9)

This attention to authentic language and its connection
to the more emotionally expressive form of song and
music has seemed particularly important to Smith at a
time when "talk" has been cheapened. She notes that
cheap, incessant talk is everywhere--in the omnipresent
media, in people's compulsive attempts to ward off
loneliness by going on about anything and everything.
And language has so often been fashioned lately with the
sole view of selling the listener on a product or a
political line. There needs to be speech that is really
worth listening to and can even lead to change and
action. Smith finds this speech and, by shaping its
expression in a form that resembles song, makes it into
her drama.

The emphasis on expression leads back to the actor,
the one who must deliver those worthwhile words, so that
an audience will really listen. Interestingly, here too
Smith has departed from the acting method (often known
in the United States as "the Method") that has dominated
the training of many American actors over the past
century. The Method traces its beginnings to a Russian,
Konstantin Stanislavsky (1863-1938), and has been adapted
by any number of American teachers of acting (Lee
Strasberg, Stella Adler, and Sanford Meisner, for
example) and noted American actors (including Marlon
Brando, James Dean, Paul Newman, Al Pacino, and Dustin
Hoffman). These Method-based approaches operate on the
assumption that all human beings share more or less the
same essential feelings and attitudes. This means that
actors trying to work themselves into their characters
must start by digging deep into their *own* emotions and
experiences and thus come to understand their character--
to become their character ("Stanislavsky Method"). On a

more literal, practical level, the reliance on such a
method also means that this transformation is partially
dependent on superficial appearances, on casting an actor
who either physically matches or can realistically
approximate the type of character being played.

Anna Deavere Smith, on the other hand, assumes that
every one of us is quite different from everyone else,
and her casting and performance choices, especially the
paradoxical ones, reflect that diversity and complexity.
Indeed, despite all her "magical" and persuasive
transformations, she intentionally never stops looking
like Anna Deavere Smith during her performances, and
therefore never quite stops <u>being</u> Anna Deavere Smith.
She chooses to play a white man or a Korean woman
herself, rather than casting a white male actor or a
female Korean actress in the roles. Additionally, very
little is done by way of makeup or costume changes. This
is why she needs to make such a radical effort to begin
to empathize with the characters she is trying to
imitate. Smith frequently writes of the difficulty of
bridging the gaps among us as individuals, and her
seemingly contradictory approach to her characters is
intended to remind us that our easy assumptions about
understanding others are all wrong and will mislead us
badly. The famous lament by Rodney King himself,
responding in a televised plea when Los Angeles riots
broke out, epitomizes both sides of that difficulty: "Can
we all just get along?"

That Smith is African American further complicates
the transformations that she brings about on stage when
we take into account that the subjects at the core of
<u>Twilight</u> and her other plays are racially charged. For
instance, it is not unusual for her to play a white
woman who answers the real Anna Deavere Smith's
questions about, for example, whether race is a "trope"
(Thompson, screen 1). The contradictions in Smith's
staging and acting choices--black playing white, female
playing male, young playing old--and in her juxtaposition

of people's conflicting reactions to the same events reflect an important paradox Smith observes in the world and wants to share with her audience: the difficulty in bridging gaps between those opposing viewpoints and the importance of still attempting to do so in spite of that difficulty. On one hand, she transforms herself into characters of other races, genders, ethnicities, and backgrounds, using their actual speech to render it more authentic, but she still presents herself as herself to some degree even while trying on and attempting to understand their voices. It is essential to realize that this presentation choice is just one of many possible options. One alternative approach she might have considered, for example, was using "white face" makeup to play a white character, a technique that might seem dated and offensive to some and also might not be especially persuasive, but is similar to the use of "black face" or elaborate costuming during earlier dramatic periods. By consciously choosing to portray and live with the visible contradictions--of being the vehicle for other voices while still being herself instead of trying to mask that disparity with artifice--Smith's performance choices may be serving as a model for the very empathy she sees as her goal.

Smith does run the risk of getting tripped up on her own staging complications with this approach, but her experiments with her more recent play House Arrest suggest that the benefits of those juxtapositions may not only be worth the gamble, but may even be necessary for her work to remain powerful. There she has attempted to explore the nature of the American presidency, diverging from her one-woman show to use several actors. Interestingly, in this case, the absence of a particular event around which the characters' monologues can revolve, and some say the preponderance of the famous, have created a ragged chaotic production. In response, Smith has returned to the approach that has made her reputation, as a solo performance artist. I would argue that the problems with this artistic casting experiment merely underscore how the meaning of Smith's plays may rely, in part, on the use of one actor to "bridge the gap" between diverse, sometimes hostile, characters. As Stuart Klawans observed in *The Nation*, it is the miracle of a whole collection of voices gathered in one actor that carries much of the impact and the possible meanings of her work:

> One after another the people stepped in, many of them voicing mistrust, misunderstanding, fear, hatred; and yet these conflicting individuals had been brought together, if not harmonized, by residing in this one woman's flesh. (screen 1)

It seems as if Anna Deavere Smith's greatest talent is the ability to orchestrate different voices, to portray conflicting perspectives and points of view, and to present viewers with a kind of statement and counterstatement of ideas and attitudes that clash. In doing so, she captures the chaos that underlies so much of contemporary life and gives rise to misperceptions and violent confrontations. While in the theater watching her play or the movie, we feel that we are in the presence of a chorus of voices, all presented for our understanding. If Smith's dramas can provide even a temporary resolution of differences in this fashion, might we imagine that here is some hope for a troubled world?

Bergeron 10

Works Cited

Goldberg, Nan. "She, the People." <u>Salon</u> 1 Nov. 2000. 28
    Apr. 2006 <http://dir.salon.com/books/feature/2000/
    11/01/smith/index.html>.

Klawans, Stuart. "A Riot of Personality." <u>The Nation</u> 16
    Oct. 2000. 30 Apr. 2006 <http://www.thenation.com/
    doc/20001016/klawans>.

Lloyd, Carol. "Voices of America." <u>Salon</u> 8 Dec. 1998.
    28 Apr. 2006 <www.salon.com/bc/1998/12/
    cov_08bc.html>.

Smith, Anna Deavere. <u>Fires in the Mirror</u>. New York:
    Anchor, 1993.

---. <u>Talk to Me: Listening Between the Lines</u>. New York:
    Anchor, 2000.

---. <u>Twilight: Los Angeles, 1992</u>. New York: Anchor,
    1994.

"Stanislavsky Method." <u>Encyclopedia Britannica Online</u>.
    2006. Encyclopedia Britannica. 1 May 2006 <http://
    www.britannica.com/>.

Tannenbaum, Barbara. "The Voices of Anna Deavere
    Smith." <u>Stanford Magazine</u> Jul.-Aug. 1999. 30 May
    2006. <http://www.stanfordalumni.org/news/magazine/
    1999/julaug/articles/anna.html>.

Thompson, Debby. " 'Is Race a Trope?': Anna Deavere
    Smith and the Question of Racial Performativity."
    <u>African American Review</u> 37 (Spring 2003): 127-38.
    Expanded Academic ASAP. Boston Public Lib., MA. 27
    May 2006 <http://infotrac.galegroup.com>.

Glossary of Literary Terms

Note: Terms in bold within definitions are defined elsewhere in the glossary.

accent the relative stress or emphasis given to syllables or words, especially in poetry.

act the largest division of a play. Some plays consist of five acts, some three, some one.

action in drama, what drives the play. Larger and more general than plot.

allegory an apparently simple story, picture, or drama that represents abstract ideas or principles.

alliteration the repetition of a letter or a single sound: "the sessions of sweet silent thought."

alliterative verse unrhymed verse with a regular series of strong beats per line, and plenty of **alliteration**.

allusion a brief reference to a person, place, or literary work that the reader is assumed to recognize.

ambiguity a complex situation, word, or idea fraught with uncertainties and contradictions that cannot easily be clarified or reduced to simple statements.

analogy the comparison of one thing to another in order to explain the nature and properties of the lesser known thing.

analytical essay (also called a critical analysis) an academic piece of writing in which you make a claim or an argument about something you note about a literary work; analytical essays call for the development of a central claim, or **thesis**, which you support with examples or evidence from the work being analyzed.

anapest a metrical **foot** of two unstressed syllables followed by a stressed syllable, as in the words "Tennessee" or "Illinois." The **meter** is called *anapestic*.

anecdote a brief story, often told to illustrate a point.

annotations notes (questions, reactions, and ideas for discussion or writing) you make in the margins or between the lines of a literary work for a fuller, richer understanding of the text.

antagonist a significant **character** in a story or play who is opposed or contrasted to the **protagonist**.

antihero a **protagonist** who displays the opposite qualities of the usual **hero**. The antihero usually has lost faith in justice and goodness in the world.

aside a commentary on the **action** in which a **character** briefly addresses the audience.

assonance repetition of vowel sounds; a kind of parallel to **alliteration**. In this line from William Blake's "The Tyger," the "a" and "e" repetitions are examples of assonance: "Did he who made the Lamb make thee?"

aubade a poem set at dawn, with lovers in bed either welcoming another day or lamenting that they must part.

ballad a story poem meant to be sung, usually in **quatrains**. The quatrain with an *abcb* rhyme scheme is called the *ballad stanza*.

bard an ancient poet gifted with inspiration and fire and who is familiar with high poetic diction.

blank verse unrhymed iambic **pentameter**.

cast of characters list of who is in the play; sometimes called "dramatis personae."

caesura pause in a line of poetry.

canon a widely accepted body of works that are considered significant. The term can apply to a genre or subgenre (American poetry, African American novels) or to the works of a single author. In a multicultural environment, the determination of which writers truly belong in a prestigious canon ("great" novels; "poems for required reading") has become the subject of controversy.

catharsis originating with Greek drama, the sudden release of emotion—grief, acceptance, relief, exultation—that follows a buildup of dramatic tension in a play.

character a person in a play or story. In novels, critics have traditionally distinguished between *round characters*, whose attributes we know well from the detailed descriptions the author provides, and *flat characters*, who seem to have only one attribute or who are there for the sake of the plot. We meet round characters in many different situations and settings, and unlike flat characters, they develop over time. This distinction—first made by novelist E. M. Forster—is less important for short stories, where few characters get rich novelistic description or are visualized in many different situations.

chorus the group of players, notably in Greek drama, who comment on the action, often by chanting or singing in poetic language. The chorus is not usually directly involved in the **action** as major players.

chronological in an order governed by time, beginning at the beginning and going through to the end.

climax the key turning point of the **action** in a play or story.

close reading see **explication**.

comedy work characterized by a sunnier outlook than **tragedy**, sometimes involving humorous discovery, mistaken identities, and enjoyable reversals.

compression focus on a single salient detail to reveal character.

conceit a poetic device in which the poet uses elaborate or exaggerated metaphors that are familiar to readers. Employed most notably by the Italian poet Petrarch to express his unrequited love for the object of his affections, Laura, the technique is also common in Renaissance love poetry.

concluding action see **denouement**.

conflict the opposition between ideas, persons, or groups that serves to animate a literary work, especially in drama or stories.

connotation a meaning associated with a word or phrase beyond its most literal or obvious meaning.

controlling metaphor a comparison that dominates a literary work, usually a poem.

convention the accepted, commonly understood way of doing things; a rule usually observed. *Conventional* is a synonym for ordinary.

couplet two rhymed lines of the same **meter**. In the late seventeenth and eighteenth centuries, a popular form was the **heroic couplet**, two lines in iambic pentameter with strong pauses at the end.

critical analysis see **analytical essay**.

dactyl one stressed syllable followed by two unstressed syllables, as in "Michigan" or "Arkansas" or "Oregon." The **meter** is called *dactylic*.

denotation the literal or most obvious meaning of a word or phrase.

denouement the final unfolding of the **action**; French for "untying" or "unraveling."

deus ex machina in drama, a person or event that almost magically intervenes when a situation has become otherwise unresolvable.

dialogue the verbal interplay in which characters speak to each other.

diction particular style of language. Diction can have different *registers*: high, middle, or low.

didactic intended to teach or improve.

dimeter (dím e ter) a poetic line of two metrical feet. See **meter**.

dramatic monologue a type of poem (associated with Robert Browning) presenting a long speech usually addressed directly to another character, as if in a play.

elegy a lament for the dead, whether a friend, a lover, a child, or a public figure.

end stopped a poetic line that concludes with strong punctuation, like a period or semicolon. See **enjambment**.

English sonnet a poetic form with three four-line stanzas (quatrains) and a final couplet. Also called a Shakespearean sonnet.

enjambment in poetry, a transition from one line to the next without a pause; the grammar and logic force a reader to continue to the next line without stopping. The opposite of **end stopped**.

epic a long story, usually in poetic form, that tells of the heroic deeds and words of larger-than-life characters. Epics often depict war, extended travels, or great romances that have public or national importance.

epiphany a moment when a character or narrator suddenly realizes some important and significant meaning not available before.

ethnic drama plays or dramatic productions produced by an ethnic, often immigrant group. Often written by a member of the group for other members, sometimes in the group's original language or dialect.

explication a passage of careful, line-by-line or even word-by-word explanation of a text. Also called close reading.

exposition information presented by an author or narrator that helps explain the characters and their circumstances. Too much exposition impedes the action, yet we usually need exposition in order to understand the situation and the characters.

falling action see **denouement**.

farce comedy as slapstick, usually played at a fast pace, without depth of character and with an emphasis on the **action**.

figurative language language that is not **literal** and instead uses **metaphors** and **similes** (figures of speech) to convey its meaning. See also **symbol**.

first-person narration a technique using "I" and employing a **narrator** who is a **character** actually involved in or witnessing some or most of the **action**.

flashback a deliberate break in chronological sequence in which the narrative switches to the past; the opposite of **flash forward**.

flash forward a deliberate break in chronological sequence in which the narrative switches to events that occur in the future; the opposite of **flashback**.

flat character see **character**.

fly-on-the-wall see **objective narrator**.

Folio the word "folio" literally means a manuscript or book, but the proper noun usually refers to the original edition of Shakespeare's plays, rightly called the First Folio, printed in 1623.

foot a unit of poetic **meter**; a single **iamb**, **dactyl**, **trochee**, **spondee**, or **anapest**.

foreshadowing a warning or suggestion to readers of what lies ahead.

form the structure or shape a work assumes; the traditional shape the writer employs (e.g., sonnet, ode). Sometimes overlaps with **genre**.

formal diction carefully chosen, elevated language. See also **diction**.

formula fiction books or stories following a conventional, common design.

fourth wall the imaginary invisible wall at the front of the stage between the audience and the world of a play. In television and film, the term refers to the wall or screen between the actors and viewers.

free verse a translation of the French *vers libre*; poetry with no **rhyme**, no set **meter**, and no regular rhythm. Characteristic of much modern verse, starting with Walt Whitman.

genre the type or kind of literature, such as poetry, novel, short story, or drama. There are also *subgenres*. Among novels, for instance, are the romance, detective, spy, Western, fantasy, and science fiction subgenres.

haiku a three-line unrhymed poem of five, seven, and five syllables, invented by Japanese poets.

hero the **protagonist** of a play, novel, or poetic work who displays qualities such as courage, generosity, capacity to love, wisdom, spiritual insight, physical beauty, and superior breeding.

heroic couplet see **couplet**.

hexameter (hex á meter) a poetic line of six metrical feet, characteristic of **epics**. See **meter**.

hubris pride or arrogance that leads **protagonists** to overestimate their considerable abilities and ignore divine or human advice, resulting in their downfall and death. The device is common in Greek drama.

hyperbole intentional exaggeration, done for grandiose, humorous, or sarcastic effect. Such language is said to be *hyperbolic*.

iamb a metrical **foot** of one unstressed syllable followed by one stressed syllable. The **meter** is called *iambic*.

image vivid impression of a sensory experience conveyed in sensory language, often described as a poem's *imagery*.

in medias res beginning in the middle of the **action**, with earlier events told through **retrospective narration** or **flashbacks**.

interior monologue a kind of unspoken **soliloquy**, with the abrupt twists and turns characteristic of inner speech, and giving readers the feel of actually entering a character's consciousness.

intervention the practice of altering, playing with, or talking back to a text.

irony a statement that means the opposite of its literal meaning, or an action that results in the opposite of its intended effect. More generally, a habit of mind or viewpoint that sees the unintended consequences of human (and sometimes divine) actions as the usual state of the world.

Italian sonnet a fourteen-line poem in two parts: an **octave** (eight lines) typically rhymed *abba abba* and a **sestet** (six lines) with varying rhymes, including *cdecde* or *cdcdcd* or *cdccdc*. Often called a Petrarchan sonnet after its first famous exponent.

limited point of view narration that takes the perspective of only one **character** and does not claim to know the thoughts of other characters. Used in first- and third-person narration.

literal meaning common, factual meaning, as opposed to **figurative** meaning. See also **symbol**.

literary present tense the tense traditionally used in essays and literary research papers to quote directly from or discuss literary works (e.g., "The narrator notes the birds' singing outside her window" or "The narrator of Burns's poem contends 'O my Luve's like a red, red rose / That's newly spring in June' ").

lyric a short poem expressing a speaker's emotions.

masque an elaborately staged courtly play.

melodrama a play that involves serious conflict and sudden reversals, but usually without the depth found in traditional **tragedy**.

metaphor a figure of speech based on an unspoken or implied comparison.

meter the rhythmic pattern of poetry; the number of feet in each line. See **dimeter, trimeter, tetrameter, pentameter,** and **hexameter.** A study of meter is called *metrics.*

mime dialogueless acting by one or more performers.

monologue a long speech by one **character** in a play. For poetry, see **dramatic monologue.**

motif a recognizable, recurrent theme in a literary text.

narration the telling of a story.

narrative a recounted story, usually told in the order of its happening.

narrator the teller of any story.

objective narrator a **narrator** who presents only the outward actions, forcing readers to infer a **character**'s motivation entirely from behavior, just as in life. Also called **fly-on-the-wall** narrator.

occasional poem a poem written for a particular event such as a celebration.

octave an eight-line stanza or group; the first eight lines of an **Italian sonnet.**

octosyllabic having eight syllables.

off rhyme rhyme that is close but deliberately not perfect; the device occurs frequently in the poetry of Emily Dickinson.

omniscient narrator one who seems to know everything, including what every **character** is thinking (from the two Latin words *omni,* "universal," and *scient,* "knowing").

one-act play a short play with a small cast and a simple setting, often written to be easy for community or amateur theaters to put on.

onomatopoeia a poetic device in which a word sounds like what it denotes, such as "buzz."

oxymoron a juxtaposition of opposite and incompatible traits: "happy tears."

parable a simple story with an explicit moral.

paradox a self-contradictory fact or statement.

paratactic style a style of writing that incorporates very few connectives such as "and."

parody an imitation of a person or work that exaggerates some prominent characteristics, thus seeming humorous or ridiculous.

pastoral a literary work, usually poetic and idealized, portraying rural persons (notably shepherds) and country scenes.

patron a wealthy person who pays to sponsor a playhouse or a writer's work. Such sponsorship is called *patronage.*

pentameter (pen tá me ter) a poetic line of five metrical feet. See **meter.**

performance an enactment intended for an audience. Works inviting performance are part of the *performative* tradition.

performance pieces theatrical works that are not quite plays and often are **monologues**.

person *First person* is "I," "me," "we," or "us"; *second person* is "you"; *third person* is "he," "him," "she," "her," "it," "they," or "them."

persona the **character** who speaks a poem or tells a story, placing some distance between the actual writer and the character who is speaking in the story or poem. Another term for persona is **speaker**.

personification a description of a nonhuman thing or creature that gives it human qualities.

Petrarchan sonnet see **Italian sonnet**.

playwright the author of a play.

plot the outline of a play or story; the story of what happens. Plays or stories dominated by plot are called *plot-driven*.

poetic intention the aim behind a poem.

poetic language language that sounds as if it comes from poetry.

poetic realism a term associated with Tennessee Williams and other modern playwrights, in which common objects, like the glass menagerie of Williams's play, take on symbolic meanings.

point of view the perspective or the vantage point from which a story is told. Often, who tells a story matters as much as what happens in it.

proscenium arch the overhead area in a theater from which the curtains close. A proscenium stage gives the impression of a three-sided box; the audience makes the fourth side.

prosody the technical principles of making verse.

protagonist the main **character** in a play or story; the one doing the most prominent action. See also **hero**.

quatrain a four-line stanza, the most common stanza form in English poetry.

realism the portrayal in literature of believable and ordinary **characters**, **plots**, motivations, causes, and situations.

refrain a repeated line or group of lines in poetry.

repetition deliberately repeating words or actions for effect, leading to humor, emphasis, or pleasure in the sound.

resolution the ending of an **action** or conflict, in which the complexities of the **plot** are sorted out.

response paper usually a short paper describing what happened as you read a literary work, or what you thought or how the story made you feel.

retrospective narration the filling in of earlier parts of a story.

rhyme repetition of a sound in poetry. Poems have *rhythmic* qualities.

rhyme scheme the pattern of rhymes in a poem.

rising action the early segment of a **plot** in a story or drama in which complications create a conflict for the **protagonist**.

round character see **character**.

scan analyze a poem by dividing it into metrical feet, marking stressed and unstressed syllables. The process of scanning is called *scansion*.

scene a smaller unit within an act of a play, often involving a change of place or scenery.

script the term directors use for the text of a play.

sestet a six-line stanza or group; the last six lines of an **Italian sonnet**.

set the scenery of a play.

setting the place where a story, poem, or play happens.

Shakespearean sonnet see **English sonnet**.

simile an overt comparison that is made using "like" or "as."

skene in Greek theater, a small, low stage structure that served as a storage place for props and as a place for actors offstage; by the time of Sophocles, the *skene* had become the place a backdrop could be painted.

soliloquy a long speech of contemplation, spoken to no one in particular.

sonnet a fourteen-line poem. Sonnets are **lyrics** (*sonnetto* is Italian for "little song"), often though not always about love, and follow very strict rules. See **Italian sonnet** and **English sonnet**.

speaker see **persona**.

special effects arts of illusion arranged by a play's director.

spine the **action** of a play, often stated in a "to..." phrase: "to find the killer," "to escape," "to possess the farm," and so on. The term is associated with the Russian director Constantin Stanislavsky and his American disciple Harold Clurman.

spondee a metrical foot with two stressed syllables, as in "New York." Few poems are totally *spondaic*.

stage the performance space for a drama, from a simple open platform with minimum scenery, as in Greek drama, to a platform with a balcony, as in Shakespeare's Globe theater, to a conventional stage with a **proscenium arch**.

stage directions the playwright's written instructions, included in the text of the play or script, that prescribe the scenery and stage set, the appearance of the characters, and some of the movements of the actors on the stage.

stanza a group of lines, either linked by an obvious rhyme or separated from others by white space.

stereotype a **character** in a literary work who is a recognizable ethnic, professional, social, or personality type.

stock character a **character** in a play or story who is predictable and familiar, such as the kind fairy godmother or the rebellious teenager.

story the whole arc of what happens in a literary work, every detail from beginning to end, as opposed to **plot**, which is more of a general outline.

stream of consciousness a type of narration in which ideas and sensations appear in characters' minds as in real life, seemingly unmediated by the author's shaping.

street theater drama performed on the street, without benefit of a permanent stage.

subjective narrator a **character** who tells a story strictly from the character's perspective; the opposite of an **objective narrator**.

summary a concise restatement in your own language of the main idea of a literary work

symbol a word or object that stands for something else. When sunshine suggests nothing more than a pleasant day and perhaps the need for shades, the device is **literal**. When the sun coming from behind the clouds suggests the end of a gloomy time in one's life, the device is symbolic. The use of symbols is called *symbolism*.

symmetry repetition in language or **plot** that provides reinforcement and formal balance.

syntax the pattern into which words are ordered to form sentences and phrases.

talismanic objects objects invested with symbolic, almost magic qualities.

teatro Spanish for "theater"; a term Chicano playwright Luis Valdez used for his early plays.

tercet a three-line stanza. The most famous type of tercet is *terza rima*, first used by Dante, and then by Percy Bysshe Shelley in English.

tetrameter (tet rám e ter) a poetic line of four metrical feet. See **meter.**

theater in the round a stage surrounded by the audience.

theme the subject or idea dramatized in a literary work.

thesis a claim, assertion, or argument put forth in a paper or presentation.

third-person narration a technique in which a story is told from the vantage point of "he," "she," or "they." It has three separate variants, each defined by how much the narrator is able to tell the reader: **limited, omniscient,** and **objective.**

thrust stage a stage design familiar in modern drama, where a runway or extension of the stage extends into the audience.

tone the particular human voice behind the words; the illusion of a person narrating or speaking the lines.

tragedy a drama involving an unavoidable fall in the **protagonist's** fortunes, and often ending in the protagonist's death.

tragicomedy a mix of tragedy and comedy, with serious risks and the danger of a fall, but with a happier resolution.

tragic flaw a weakness, usually related to personal character, which causes a **tragic hero's** downfall.

tragic hero the **hero** in a tragedy who has a high station in life and admirable powers, along with a **tragic flaw.**

trimeter (trím e ter) a poetic line with three metrical feet. See **meter.**

triplet a group of three rhyming lines within a larger poem.

trochee A metrical **foot** with one stressed syllable followed by one unstressed syllable. The **meter** is called *trochaic.*

turn See **volta.**

twist element of a **plot** deliberately placed to keep readers in suspense.

type a deliberately simplified character; a one-dimensional figure who by the criteria of realistic drama lacks depth, richness, and complexity and who seems to stand for something else. See also **stereotype.**

unreliable narrator a **character** who tells the story from the "I" or first-person point of view and whose version of events calls for interpretation. Attentive readers can sometimes see more than such narrators do.

vers libre see **free verse.**

villanelle a French poetic form with strict requirements: nineteen lines in five tercets, followed by a quatrain. The rhyme must be *aba aba aba aba aba aba abaa.* The first line of the poem becomes the last line of the second and fourth tercets, and the third line of the first tercet becomes the last line of the third and the fifth tercet. Then these two last lines become the final couplet.

vocabulary the choice of words, which contributes to a work's level of **diction**—either high, middle, or low.

volta Italian for "turn"; the move from the first eight lines of an **Italian sonnet** to the last six.

Credits

Text

Achebe, Chinua. "Civil Peace" from *Girls at War and Other Stories* by Chinua Achebe, copyright © 1972, 1973 by Chinua Achebe. Used by permission of Doubleday, a division of Random House, Inc. and Harold Ober Associates Incorporated.

Aguiar, Arun. Excerpts from "Interview with Jhumpa Lahiri" by Arun Aguiar, July 28, 1999, *Pif Magazine*. Reprinted by permission of the author.

Alexie, Sherman. "The Lone Ranger & Tonto Fistfight in Heaven" from *The Lone Ranger and Tonto Fistfight in Heaven* by Sherman Alexie. Copyright © 1993 by Sherman Alexie. Used by permission of Grove/Atlantic, Inc.

Algren, Nelson. Excerpt from prose poem from *Chicago: City on the Make* by Nelson Algren. Copyright © 1987 by Nelson Algren. Reprinted by permission of Donadio & Olson, Inc.

Allison, Dorothy. "I'm Working on My Charm" from *Trash*, 1988. Reprinted by permission.

Allison, Dorothy. Quote from an interview of Dorothy Allison with Laura Miller, Salon.com., March 31, 1998.

Allison, Dorothy. Quotes from an interview with Dorothy Allison and the Newcomb College Center for Research on Women, 1995. Reprinted by permission of Vorhoff Library and Newcomb Archives, Newcomb College, Tulane University.

Altman, Robert. From "Introduction" by Robert Altman to *Short Cuts* by Raymond Carver (Vintage 1993).

Alvarez, Julia. "Dusting" from *Homecoming*. Copyright © 1984, 1996 by Julia Alvarez. Published by Plume, an imprint of Sutton Signet, a division of Penguin Books USA, Inc. originally published by Grove Press. Reprinted by permission of Susan Bergholz Literary Services, New York. All rights reserved.

Alvarez, Julia. "I, Too, Sing América" by Julia Alvarez. Copyright © 2002 by Julia Alvarez. Reprinted by permission of Susan Bergholz Literary Services, New York. All rights reserved.

Amichai, Yehuda. "We Did It" from *Yehuda Amichai: A Life of Poetry 1948–1994* by Yeduda Amichai. Translated by Benjamin and Barbara Harshav. Copyright © 1994 by HarperCollins Publishers Inc. Hebrew-language version copyright © 1994 by Yehuda Amichai. Reprinted by permission of HarperCollins Publishers.

Ammons, A.R. "The City Limits" from *Collected Poems 1951–1971* by A.R. Ammons. Copyright © 1972 by A.R. Ammons. Used by permission of W.W. Norton & Company, Inc.

Appachana, Anjana. "Her Mother" from Anjana Appachana, *Incantations and Other Stories*. Copyright © 1992 by Anjana Appachana. Reprinted by permission of Rutgers University Press.

Appachana, Anjana. Commentary from the Arizona Commission on the Arts Residency Roster web page: http://www.azarts.gov/roster_display.asp?namekey=311. Reprinted by permission of the author.

Artaud, Antonin. Excerpt from *The Theater and Its Double* by Antonin Artaud, translated by Mary Caroline Richards. Copyright © 1958 by Grove Press, Inc. Used by permission of Grove/Atlantic, Inc.

Ashbery, John. "Paradoxes and Oxymorons" from *Shadow Train* by John Ashbery. Copyright © 1980, 1981 by John Ashbery. Reprinted by permission of Georges Borchardt, Inc., for the author.

Atwood, Margaret. "February" from *Morning in the Burned House* by Margaret Atwood. Copyright © 1995 by Margaret Atwood. Reprinted by permission of Houghton Mifflin Company and McClelland and Stewart Ltd. All rights reserved.

Atwood, Margaret. "Happy Endings" from *Good Bones and Simple Murders* by Margaret Atwood, copyright © 1983, 1992, 1994 by O. W. Toad Ltd. A Nan A. Talese Book. Used by permission of Doubleday, a division of Random House, Inc., and McClelland & Stewart Ltd.

Atwood, Margaret. Excerpt from "Reading Blind" by Margaret Atwood. Originally published in *Best American Short Stories*, 1989. Copyright © 1989 Margaret Atwood. Reprinted by permission of the author.

Atwood, Margaret. For U.S. rights: "This is a Photograph of Me" from *Selected Poems, 1965–1975* by Margaret Atwood. Copyright © 1976 by Margaret Atwood. Reprinted by permission of Houghton Mifflin Company.
For Canadian rights: From *Selected Poems 1966–1984* by Margaret Atwood. Copyright © 1990 by Margaret Atwood. Reprinted by permission of Oxford University Press.

Auden, W.H. "Musée des Beaux Arts," copyright 1940 & renewed 1968 by W.H. Auden, from *Collected Poems* by W.H. Auden. Used by permission of Random House, Inc.

Auden, W.H. "Stop All the Clocks, Cut Off the Telephone," copyright 1940 & renewed 1968 by W.H. Auden, from *Collected Poems* by W.H. Auden. Used by permission of Random House, Inc.

Baca, Jimmy Santiago. "Green Chile" by Jimmy Santiago Baca, from *Black Mesa Poems*, copyright © 1989 by Jimmy Santiago Baca. Reprinted by permission of New Directions Publishing Corp.

Baldwin, James. "Sonny's Blues" copyright © 1957 was originally published in *Partisan Review*. Collected in *Going to Meet the Man*, published by Vintage Books. Reprinted by arrangement with the James Baldwin Estate.

Barrett, Andrea. "Rare Bird" from *Ship Fever and Other Stories* by Andrea Barrett. Copyright © 1996 by Andrea Barrett. Used by permission of W.W. Norton & Company, Inc.

Baxter, Charles. "Gryphon" from *Through the Safety Net*. Copyright © 1985 by Charles Baxter. Reprinted by permission.

Baxter, Charles. "Kiss Away" from *Believers: A Novella and Stories* by Charles Baxter, copyright © 1997 by Charles Baxter. Used by permission of Pantheon books, a division of Random House, Inc.

Baxter, Charles. "Saul and Patsy are Pregnant" from *A Relative Stranger* by Charles Baxter. Copyright © 1990 by Charles Baxter. Used by permission of W.W. Norton & Company, Inc.

Baxter, Charles. "Shelter" from *A Relative Stranger and Other Stories* by Charles Baxter. Copyright © 1990 by Charles Baxter. Used by permission of W.W. Norton & Company, Inc.

Baxter, Charles. Excerpts from *Burning Down the House* by Charles Baxter. Copyright © 1997 by Charles Baxter.

Beckett, Samuel. *Not I* from *Collected Shorter Plays of Samuel Beckett*. Copyright © 1973 by Samuel Beckett. Used by permission of Grove/Atlantic, Inc.

Bidart, Frank. "Hammer" from *Music Like Dirt*. Copyright © 2002 by Frank Bidart. Reprinted with the permission of Sarabande Books, Inc., www.sarabandebooks.org

Birnbaum, Robert. Excerpts from "Birnbaum v. Charles Baxter" by Robert Birnbaum, *The Morning News*, November 2003. Reprinted by permission.

Bishop, Elizabeth. "At the Fishhouses" from *The Complete Poems 1927–1979 by Elizabeth Bishop*. Copyright © 1979, 1983 by Alice Helen Methfessel. Reprinted by permission of Farrar, Straus and Giroux, LLC.

Bishop, Elizabeth. "Casabianca" from *The Complete Poems 1927–1979* by Elizabeth Bishop. Copyright © 1979, 1983 by Alice Helen Methfessel. Reprinted by permission of Farrar, Straus and Giroux, LLC.

Bishop, Elizabeth. "One Art" from *The Complete Poems 1927–1979* by Elizabeth Bishop. Copyright © 1979, 1983 by Alice Helen Methfessel. Reprinted by permission of Farrar, Straus and Giroux, LLC.

Björk. Excerpt from interview with Björk. From CD *Now*, August 2001, http: //bjork.com/facts/about/.

Bogan, Louise. "Women" from *The Blue Estuaries* by Louise Bogan. Copyright © 1968 by Louise Bogan. Copyright renewed 1996 by Ruth Limmer. Reprinted by permission of Farrar, Straus and Giroux, LLC.

Boland, Eavan. "The Dolls Museum in Dublin", from *In a Time of Violence* by Eavan Boland. Copyright © 1994 by Eavan Boland. Used by permission of W.W. Norton & Company, Inc.

Bradley, David. "Novelist Alice Walker Telling the Black Woman's Story" by David Bradley, *New York Times Book Review*, January 8, 1984.

Brantley, Ben. "A Breakthrough 50s Drama Revived in a Suspenseful Mood," *New York Times*, April 27, 2004. Copyright © 2004 by The New York Times Co. Reprinted with permission.

Brooks, Gwendolyn. "Gay Chaps at the Bar" from *Blacks*. Copyright © 1945, 1949, 1953, 1960, 1963, 1969, 1970, 1971, 1975, 1981, 1987, 1991 by Gwendolyn Brooks Blakely. Reprinted by consent of Brooks Permissions.

Brooks, Gwendolyn. "Home" from *Maud Martha* by Gwendolyn Brooks. Reprinted by consent of Brooks Permissions.

Brooks, Gwendolyn. "In Honor of David Anderson Brooks, My Father" from *Blacks*. Copyright © 1945, 1949, 1953, 1960, 1963, 1969, 1970, 1971, 1975, 1981, 1987, 1991 by Gwendolyn Brooks Blakely. Reprinted by consent of Brooks Permissions.

Brooks, Gwendolyn. "Introduction of Grace Schulman" by Gwendolyn Brooks, from *Report from Part Two*, Chicago: The Third World Press, 1996.

Brooks, Gwendolyn. "Introduction of Les Murray" by Gwendolyn Brooks, from *Report from Part Two*, Chicago: The Third World Press, 1996.

Brooks, Gwendolyn. "Introduction of Louis Simpson" by Gwendolyn Brooks, from *Report from Part Two*, Chicago: The Third World Press, 1996.

Brooks, Gwendolyn. "Langston Hughes" from *Blacks*. Copyright © 1945, 1949, 1953, 1960, 1963, 1969, 1970, 1971, 1975, 1981, 1987, 1991 by Gwendolyn Brooks Blakely. Reprinted by consent of Brooks Permissions.

Brooks, Gwendolyn. "Myself." Reprinted by consent of Brooks Permissions.

Brooks, Gwendolyn. "Of Robert Frost" from *Blacks*. Copyright © 1945, 1949, 1953, 1960, 1963, 1969, 1970, 1971, 1975, 1981, 1987, 1991 by Gwendolyn Brooks Blakely. Reprinted by consent of Brooks Permissions.

Brooks, Gwendolyn. "Paul Robeson" from *Blacks*. Copyright © 1945, 1949, 1953, 1960, 1963, 1969, 1970, 1971, 1975, 1981, 1987, 1991 by Gwendolyn Brooks Blakely. Reprinted by consent of Brooks Permissions.

Brooks, Gwendolyn. "Sadie and Maud" from *Blacks*. Copyright © 1945, 1949, 1953, 1960, 1963, 1969, 1970, 1971, 1975, 1981, 1987, 1991 by Gwendolyn Brooks Blakely. Reprinted by consent of Brooks Permissions.

Brooks, Gwendolyn. "The Bean Eaters" from *Blacks*. Copyright © 1945, 1949, 1953, 1960, 1963, 1969, 1970, 1971, 1975, 1981, 1987, 1991 by Gwendolyn Brooks Blakely. Reprinted by consent of Brooks Permissions.

Brooks, Gwendolyn. "The Crazy Woman" from *Blacks*. Copyright © 1945, 1949, 1953, 1960, 1963, 1969, 1970, 1971, 1975, 1981, 1987, 1991 by Gwendolyn Brooks Blakely. Reprinted by consent of Brooks Permissions.

Brooks, Gwendolyn. "The Lovers of the Poor" from *Blacks* by Gwendolyn Brooks. Reprinted by consent of Brooks Permissions.

Brooks, Gwendolyn. "The Mother" from *Blacks*. Copyright © 1945, 1949, 1953, 1960, 1963, 1969, 1970, 1971, 1975, 1981, 1987, 1991 by Gwendolyn Brooks Blakely. Reprinted by consent of Brooks Permissions.

Brooks, Gwendolyn. "the preacher: ruminates behind the sermon" from *Blacks*. Copyright © 1945, 1949, 1953, 1960, 1963, 1969, 1970, 1971, 1975, 1981, 1987, 1991 by Gwendolyn Brooks Blakely. Reprinted by consent of Brooks Permissions.

Brooks, Gwendolyn. "The Sermon on the Warpland" from *Blacks*. Copyright © 1945, 1949, 1953, 1960, 1963, 1969, 1970, 1971, 1975, 1981, 1987, 1991 by Gwendolyn Brooks Blakely. Reprinted by consent of Brooks Permissions.

Frost, Robert. "Once by the Pacific" from *The Poetry of Robert Frost* edited by Edward Connery Lathem. Copyright 1923, 1928, 1947, 1969 by Henry Holt and Company, © 1975 by Leslie Frost Ballantine, © 1951, 1956 by Robert Frost. Reprinted by permission of Henry Holt and Company, LLC.

Frost, Robert. "Stopping by the Woods on a Snowy Evening" from *The Poetry of Robert Frost* edited by Edward Connery Lathem. Copyright 1923, 1928, 1947, 1969 by Henry Holt and Company, © 1975 by Leslie Frost Ballantine, © 1951, 1956 by Robert Frost. Reprinted by permission of Henry Holt and Company, LLC.

Furman-Adams, Wendy. From "Senior Seminar: Writing Renaissance Women Course Syllabus" by Wendy Furman-Adams, Spring 2004, Whittier College. Reprinted by permission of the author.

García Márquez, Gabriel. All pages from " The Handsomest Drowned Man in the World" from *Leaf Storm and Other Stories* by Gabriel García Márquez. Copyright © 1971 by Gabriel García Márquez. Reprinted by permission of HarperCollins Publishers.

Gilbert, Matthew. Excerpt from "Even-Tempered, Unflashy Stories of America's Heartland" by Matthew Gilbert, *Boston Globe*, March 23, 1997. Republished with permission of *The Boston Globe*; permission conveyed through Copyright Clearance Center, Inc.

Ginsberg, Allen. All lines from "A Supermarket in California" from *Collected Poems 1947–1980* by Allen Ginsberg. Copyright © 1955 by Allen Ginsburg. Reprinted by permission of HarperCollins Publishers.

Glaspell, Susan. *Trifles* from *Plays* by Susan Glaspell, 1920.

Glück, Louise. "Mock Orange" in the Triumph of Achilles from *The First Four Books of Poems* by Louise Glück. Copyright © 1968, 1971, 1972, 1973, 1974, 1975, 1976, 1977, 1978, 1979, 1980, 1985, 1995 by Louise Glück. Reprinted by permission of HarperCollins Publishers.

Glück, Louise. "The Red Poppy" from *The Wild Iris* by Louise Glück. Copyright © 1992 by Louise Glück. Reprinted by permission of HarperCollins Publishers.

Glück, Louise. Excerpt from "Education of the Poet," *Proofs & Theories: Essays on Poetry*, (New York: Ecco: 1994).

Gotanda, Philip Kan. *The Wash.* Copyright © 1991, Philip Kan Gotanda. CAUTION: The Play included in this volume is reprinted by permission of Dramatists Play Service, Inc. The English language stock and amateur stage performance rights in this Play are controlled exclusively by Dramatists Play Service, Inc., 440 Park Avenue South, New York, NY 10016. No professional or nonprofessional performance of the Play may be given without obtaining, in advance, the written permission of Dramatists Play Service, Inc., and paying the requisite fee. Inquires concerning all other rights should be addressed to the Joyce Ketay Agency, 630 Ninth Avenue, Suite 706, New York, NY 10036. Attn: Carl Mulert.

Gould, Stephen Jay. From "Baseball's reliquary: the oddly possible hybrid of shrine and university" by Stephen Jay Gould, *Natural History*, March 2002.

Graham, Jorie. "Over and Over Stitch" from *Hybrid of Plants and of Ghosts.* Copyright © 1980 Princeton University Press. Reprinted by permission of Princeton University Press.

Grennan, Eamon. Excerpt from "Interview with Eamon Grennan" from *Cortland Review*, Issue 12, August 2000.

Guy-Sheftall, Beverly. Excerpt from "Women of Bronzeville" (essay) by Beverly Guy-Sheftall.

Hansberry, Lorraine. *A Raisin in the Sun* by Lorraine Hansberry, copyright © 1958 by Robert Nemiroff, as an unpublished work. Copyright © 1959, 1966, 1984 by Robert Nemiroff. Used by permission of Random House, Inc.

Hass, Robert. "A Story About the Body" from *Human Wishes* by Robert Hass. Copyright © 1989 by Robert Hass. Reprinted by permission of HarperCollins Publishers.

Hayden, Robert. "Those Winter Sundays." Copyright © 1966 by Robert Hayden, from *Collected Poems of Robert Hayden* by Robert Hayden, edited by Frederick Glaysher. Used by permission of Liveright Publishing Corporation.

Heaney, Seamus. "Digging" from *Opened Ground: Selected Poems 1966–1996* by Seamus Heaney. Copyright © 1998 by Seamus Heaney. Reprinted by permission of Farrar, Straus and Giroux, LLC and Faber and Faber Ltd.

Heaney, Seamus. "From the Frontier of Writing" from *The Haw Lantern* by Seamus Heaney. Copyright © 1987 by Seamus Heaney. Reprinted by permission of Farrar, Straus and Giroux, LLC and Faber and Faber Ltd.

Hecht, Anthony. "The Dover Bitch" from *Collected Earlier Poems* by Anthony Hecht, copyright © 1990 by Anthony E. Hecht. Used by permission of Alfred A. Knopf, a division of Random House, Inc.

Hemingway, Ernest. "Hills Like White Elephants." Reprinted with permission of Scribner, an imprint of Simon & Schuster Adult Publishing Group, from *Men Without Women* by Ernest Hemingway. Copyright 1927 by Charles Scribner's Sons. Copyright renewed 1955 by Ernest Hemingway.

Hempel, Amy. "In the Cemetery Where Al Jolson is Buried" from *Reasons to Live*. Originally appeared in *TriQuarterly*. Copyright © 1985 by Amy Hempel. Reprinted by permission.

Herion-Sarafidis, Elisabeth. Quote from "Interview with Lee Smith" by Elisabeth Herion-Sarafidis, *Southern Quarterly*, 32:2 (Winter 1994).

Hirsch, Ed. "Fast Break" from *Wild Gratitude* by Edward Hirsch, copyright © 1985 by Edward Hirsch. Used by permission of Alfred A. Knopf, a division of Random House, Inc.

Hirsch, Edward. "Is It Something of an Accident that You Are the Reader and I the Writer" from *How to Read a Poem and Fall in Love with Poetry*, copyright © 1999 by Edward Hirsch, reprinted by permission of Harcourt, Inc.

Hogan, Linda. "First Light" from *Savings*. Copyright © 1988 by Linda Hogan. Reprinted with the permission of Coffee House Press, Minneapolis, Minnesota.

Plath, Sylvia. All lines from "Daddy" from *Ariel* by Sylvia Plath. Copyright © 1963 by Ted Hughes. Reprinted by permission of HarperCollins Publishers and Faber and Faber Ltd.

Plath, Sylvia. All lines from "Metaphors" from *Crossing the Water* by Sylvia Plath. Copyright © 1960 by Ted Hughes. Reprinted by permission of HarperCollins Publishers and Faber and Faber Ltd.

Porter, Katherine Anne. "The Jilting of Granny Weatherall" from *Flowering Judas and Other Stories*, copyright 1930 and renewed 1958 by Katherine Anne Porter, reprinted by permission of Harcourt, Inc.

Pound, Ezra. "In a Station of the Metro" by Ezra Pound, from *Personae*, copyright © 1926 by Ezra Pound. Reprinted by permission of New Directions Publishing Corp.

Pound, Ezra. "The River-Merchant's Wife: A Letter" by Ezra Pound, from *Personae*, copyright © 1926 by Ezra Pound. Reprinted by permission of New Directions Publishing Corp.

Powell, Teddy. "Unchain My Heart" written by Teddy Powell and Bobby Sharp. Copyright renewed 1988 by Bobby Sharp. Reprinted by permission of B-Sharp Music.

Ratcliffe, Jane. Excerpt from "A Son of the Middle Border" by Jane Ratcliffe, *Michigan Today*, Spring, 1997. Reprinted by permission.

Rich, Adrienne. "Aunt Jennifer's Tigers." Copyright © 2002, 1951 by Adrienne Rich, from *The Fact of a Doorframe: Selected Poems 1950-2001* by Adrienne Rich. Used by permission of the author and W.W. Norton & Company, Inc.

Rich, Adrienne. "Living in Sin." Copyright © 2002, 1955 by Adrienne Rich, from *The Fact of a Doorframe: Selected Poems 1950–2001* by Adrienne Rich. Used by permission of the author and W.W. Norton & Company, Inc.

Rich, Adrienne. Diving into the Wreck." Copyright © 2002 by Adrienne Rich. Copyright © 1973 by W.W. Norton & Company, Inc., from *The Fact of a Doorframe: Selected Poems 1950–2001* by Adrienne Rich. Used by permission of the author and W.W. Norton & Company, Inc.

Rich, Adrienne. From "Vesuvius at Home: The Power of Emily Dickinson," from *On Lies, Secrets, and Silence: Selected Prose 1966–1978.*

Roethke, Theodore. "My Papa's Waltz," copyright 1942 by Hearst Magazines, Inc., from *Collected Poems of Theodore Roethke* by Theodore Roethke. Used by permission of Doubleday, a division of Random House, Inc.

Roethke, Theodore. "Root Cellar," copyright 1943 by Modern Poetry Association, Inc., from *Collected Poems of Theodore Roethke* by Theodore Roethke. Used by permission of Doubleday, a division of Random House, Inc.

Roethke, Theodore. "The Waking," copyright © 1953 by Theodore Roethke, from *Collected Poems of Theodore Roethke* by Theodore Roethke. Used by permission of Doubleday, a division of Random House, Inc.

Rukeyser, Muriel. "Myth" by Muriel Rukeyser. Reprinted by permission of International Creative Management, Inc. Copyright © 1956 by Muriel Rukeyser.

Santiago, Esmeralda. "Something Could Happen to You" from *Almost a Woman* by Esmeralda Santiago. Copyright © 1997 by Canto-Media, Inc. Reprinted by permission of DA CAPO PRESS, a member of Perseus Books, L.L.C.

Santiago, Esmeralda. Excerpt from Esmeralda Santiago's "A note to the reader" from the Random House Reading Group Center website: www.randomhouse.com/vintage/read/puerto/santiago.html.

Santoro, Gene. From interview with Sting, by Gene Santoro, from *Pulse*, November 1987.

Seaman, Donna. Review of *Collected Poems by Robert Lowell* (edited by Frank Bidart and David Gewanter) by Donna Seaman, *Booklist*, 2003. Reprinted by permission of the American Library Association.

Sexton, Anne. "The Starry Night" from *All My Pretty Ones* by Anne Sexton. Copyright © 1962 by Anne Sexton, renewed 1990 by Linda G. Sexton. Reprinted by permission of Houghton Mifflin Company. All rights reserved.

Shakespeare, William. "Aubade" from *Cymbeline*. Excerpted from *The Complete Works of Shakespeare, 4/e*, edited by David Bevington. Copyright © 1997 by Addison-Wesley Educational Publishers, Inc. Reprinted by permission of Pearson Education, Inc.

Shakespeare, William. "Aubade" from *Romeo and Juliet*, Act 2, Scene 2. Excerpted from *The Complete Works of Shakespeare, 4/e*, edited by David Bevington. Copyright © 1997 by Addison-Wesley Educational Publishers, Inc. Reprinted by permission of Pearson Education, Inc.

Shakespeare, William. *Hamlet, Prince of Denmark*, with notes from *The Complete Works of Shakespeare*, 4th edition, edited by David Bevington, © 1992 by HarperCollins. Reprinted by permission of Pearson Education, Inc.

Shakespeare, William. *The Tempest*, with notes from *The Complete Works of Shakespeare*, 4th edition, edited by David Bevington, © 1992 by HarperCollins. Reprinted by permission of Pearson Education, Inc.

Shihab Nye, Naomi. "Rain" from *Yellow Glove*. Copyright © 1986 by Naomi Shihab Nye. Reprinted by permission of the author.

Short Review of "Harry Potter and the Sorcerer's Stone," *Publisher's Weekly*, July 1998. Republished with permission from *Publisher's Weekly*, July 1998, a Reed Business Publication.

Silko, Leslie Marmon. "Yellow Woman" by Leslie Marmon Silko. Copyright © 1981 by Leslie Marmon Silko. Reprinted with the permission of the Wylie Agency Inc.

Smith, Anna Deavere. Selections from *Twilight: Los Angeles 1992* by Anna Deavere Smith, copyright © 1994 by Anna Deavere Smith. Used by permission of Doubleday, a division of Random House, Inc.

Smith, Lee. "Cakewalk" from *Cakewalk* by Lee Smith, copyright © 1981 by Lee Smith. Used by permission of G. P. Putnam's Sons, a division of Penguin Group (USA) Inc.

Song, Cathy. "A Conservative View" from *School Figures*, by Cathy Song, copyright © 1994. Reprinted by permission of the University of Pittsburgh Press.

Photos

Chapter 23—1333: Library of Congress; **1335:** C. Walter Hodges; **1339:** Marin Shakespeare Company; **1338:** Manuel Harlan/© Royal Shakespeare Company; **1340:** Library of Congress, Federal Theatre Project Collection; **1341:** Library of Congress; **1342:** Kobal Collection/Castle Rock Entertainment/Dakota Films; **1407:** Billy Rose Theatre Collection, New York Public Library for the Performing Arts; **1442:** Library of Congress

Chapter 24—1561: New York Public Library Prints and Photographs Collection; **1612:** Photo by Richard Termine; **1615 top:** Longman Anthology of Drama and Theater by Greenwalk p. 94 top; **1615 bottom:** Estate of Jo Mielzinger/ Eileen Darby/ Billy Rose Theatre Collection, New York Public Library for the Performing Arts, Astor, Lenox, and Tilden Foundations; **1617:** Library of Congress; **1616:** Library of Congress; **1618:** Joan Marcus; **1668:** Library of Congress; **1670:** Library of Congress; **1671:** Library of Congress; **1740:** Library of Congress

Chapter 25—1743: Russell Lee/ Library of Congress; **1747 left:** Roosevelt University; **1747 right:** The Vivian G. Harsh Research Collection of Afro-American History and Literature, Chicago Public Library; **1748:** The Vivian G. Harsh Research Collection of Afro-American History and Literature, Chicago Public Library; **1754:** Library of Congress; **1755:** Library of Congress; **1756 top:** The Vivian G. Harsh Research Collection of Afro-American History and Literature, Chicago Public Library; **1756 bottom:** Library of Congress; **1759:** Library of Congress; **1760:** Cover from Frank Marshall Davis, *Livin' the Blues* by John Edgar University of Wisconsin Press. Copyright ©1992 The Board of Regents of the University of Wisconsin Systems. All rights reserved; **1761:** Margaret Walker Alexander National Research Center, Jackson State University; **1767:** The Michael Ochs Archives; **1769:** Terry Cryer/Corbis; **1770:** Henry Diltz/Corbis; **1771 top:** Commission on Chicago Landmarks, photo by Bob Thall; **1771 bottom:** Michael Ochs Archives.com; **1773 top:** Library of Congress; **1773 left:** Frank Driggs Collection/Getty Images; **1774:** The Vivian G. Harsh Research Collection of Afro-American History and Literature, Chicago Public Library; **1775:** Library of Congress; **1780:** Library of Congress; **1781:** The Newberry Library, Chicago; **1784 top:** Schomberg Center for Research in Black Culture, The New York Public Library, Astor, Lenox and Tilden Foundations; **1784 bottom:** Library of Congress **1790:** Library of Congress; **1791:** Joan Marcus

Chapter 25, Color insert—1: National Gallery of Art, Washington. Gift of Werner H. and Sarah Ann Kramarsky and Collectors Committee Fund. Art ©Romare Bearden Foundation/ Licensed by VAGA, New York, NY; **2:** Art Institute of Chicago, Charles M. Kurtz Charitable Trust and Barbara Neff and Solomon Byron Smith funds; through prior gifts of Florence Jane Adams, Mr. and Mrs. Carter H. Harrison, and estate of Celia Schmidt, 1990.134; **3:** FSA Library of Congress; **4:** Howard University Museum of Art; **5:** ©Estate of Jacob Lawrence/Digital Image ©The Museum of Modern Art/ Licensed by Scala/Art Resource, NY/Copyright 2006 Artists Rights Society (ARS), NY; **6 top:** The Everett Collection; **6 bottom:** Photofest; **7:** Ted Williams/Corbis; **8:** Ro Gallery/Art © Romare Bearden Foundation. Licensed by VAGA, New York, NY

Chapter 26—1858: Joan Marcus; **1859:** Joan Marcus; **1861:** Getty Images; **1867:** Getty Images **1877:** Carol Rosegg; **1916:** Yale Repertory Theatre; **1917:** Yale Repertory Theatre **1976:** Library of Congress; **1977:** Getty Images; **1993:** Retna

Author and Title Index

Index of First Lines

Index of Literary Terms